D1202960

OFFICIAL
BASEBALL
GUIDE
for
1971

•

PUBLISHER
C. C. JOHNSON SPINK

EDITORS
PAUL MAC FARLANE

CHRIS ROEWE
LARRY WIGGE
LARRY VICKREY

•

PUBLISHED BY
The Sporting News
1212 North Lindbergh Boulevard
St. Louis, Missouri 63166

Government of Organized Baseball

⊖ ✕ ⊖

MAJOR LEAGUES

COMMISSIONER—Bowie K. Kuhn

SECRETARY-TREASURER—Alexander H. Hadden

HEADQUARTERS—680 Fifth Avenue,
New York, N. Y. 10019

Telephone—265-6200 (area code 212)

Teletype—212-640-4279

EXECUTIVE COUNCIL—Bowie K. Kuhn, Commissioner; Joseph E. Cronin, president of American League; Charles S. Feeney, president of National League; Robert O. Reynolds, representative of American League (alternate, Calvin Griffith), and Walter F. O'Malley, representative of National League (alternate, John J. McHale).

ADMINISTRATIVE OFFICER—John Johnson

DIRECTOR OF RADIO AND TELEVISION—Thomas Dawson

DIRECTOR OF PUBLIC RELATIONS—Joseph L. Reichler

DIRECTOR OF AMATEUR AND COLLEGE BASEBALL—James T. Gallagher

CO-ORDINATOR OF INTER-AMERICAN BASEBALL—Roberto Maduro

NATIONAL ASSOCIATION REPRESENTATIVES—Phillip Piton, President of the National Association, and members of National Association Executive Committee.

⊖ ✕ ⊖

NATIONAL ASSOCIATION
OF PROFESSIONAL BASEBALL LEAGUES

PRESIDENT-TREASURER—Phillip Piton

VICE-PRESIDENT—Sam C. Smith, Jr.

ASSISTANT TO PRESIDENT—Daniel F. O'Brien

SECRETARY TO PRESIDENT—Katheryn Oyer

FIELD REPRESENTATIVES—Robert L. Freitas, Warren LeTarte

HEADQUARTERS—720 East Broad Street, Columbus, O. 43215

Telephone—221-7591 (area code 614)

EXECUTIVE COMMITTEE — Sam C. Smith, Jr., chairman, president of Southern League; George H. Sisler, Jr., president of International League; Jim Doster, president of Midwest League.

TABLE OF CONTENTS

COVER PHOTOS: Top left, Johnny Bench, catcher, Cincinnati—THE SPORTING NEWS N. L. Player of the Year; top right, Sam McDowell, pitcher, Cleveland—THE SPORTING NEWS A. L. Pitcher of the Year; bottom left, Bob Gibson, pitcher, St. Louis—THE SPORTING NEWS N. L. Pitcher of the Year; bottom right, Harmon Killebrew, third baseman, Minnesota—THE SPORTING NEWS A. L. Player of the Year.

JOSEPH E. CRONIN
President of American League

AMERICAN LEAGUE

Including

Club Governments

Club Reviews of 1970 Season

Club Day-By-Day Scores

A. L. Team Pictures

1970 League Leaders

1970 Official A. L. Averages

All-Time A. L. Player Performance Tables

American League

Organized 1900

JOSEPH E. CRONIN
President-Secretary-Treasurer

WILLIAM HARRIDGE
Chairman of the Board

THOMAS A. YAWKEY
Vice-President

ROBERT F. HOLBROOK
Executive Assistant

DICK BUTLER
Supervisor of Umpires

JOHN J. SHEEHAN
Director of Publicity

Headquarters—520 Boylston Street, Boston, Mass. 02116

Telephones—COpley 7-2500, 7-2501, 7-2502 (area code 617)

Public Relations—COpley 7-2504, 7-2505 (area code 617)

Headquarters of Board Chairman—310 S. Michigan Blvd., Chicago, Ill. 60604

Telephone—HArrison 7-4262 (area code 312)

Directors, 1970: Baltimore, Detroit, Kansas City, Minnesota, Oakland, Washington.

Umpires—G. Merlyn Anthony, Lawrence Barnett, Nestor Chylak, Bill Deegan, Donald Denkinger, Louis DiMuro, John Flaherty, Arthur Frantz, Russell Goetz, William Haller, G. James Honochick, William Kunkel, Ronald Luciano, George Maloney, Larry Napp, Jerome Neudecker, James Odom, James O'Donnell, David Phillips, John Rice, Henry Soar, Martin Springstead, Robert Stewart, Frank Umont.

Official Statistician—Howe News Bureau, 105 W. Madison street, Chicago, Ill. 60602. Telephone: STate 2-4216 (area code 312).

Players cannot be transferred from one major league club to another after June 15 to the close of the championship season except through regular waiver channels.

Waiver price, $20,000. Interleague waivers, $20,000, except for selected players and draft-excluded players.

BALTIMORE ORIOLES

Chairman of the Board—Jerold C. Hoffberger
Chairman of Executive Committee and Treasurer—Zanvyl Krieger
Executive Vice-President—J. Frank Cashen
Vice-President-Director of Player Personnel—Harry I. Dalton
Vice-President for Business Affairs—Jack Dunn III
Vice-President-Controller-Secretary—Joseph P. Hamper, Jr.
Business Manager—Herbert E. Armstrong
Public Relations Director—Robert W. Brown
Traveling Secretary—Philip E. Itzoe

Promotions Director—Walter R. Freeman, Jr.
Ticket Manager—William P. Roberts
Assistant Ticket Manager—Joseph B. Codd
Director of Scouting—Walter G. Shannon
Director of Player Development—Don Pries
Administrative Assistant, Scouting Department—Jack Pastore
Minor League Business Coordinator—James M. McLaughlin
Special Assistant to Director of Player Personnel—James Russo
Assistant Public Relations Director—Frances M. Moulden
Sales Manager—William T. Anderson
Manager—Earl S. Weaver
Club Physician—Dr. Leonard Wallenstein
Executive offices—Memorial Stadium, Baltimore, Md. 21218
Telephone—CHesapeake 3-9800 (area code 301)

Scouts—Jack Baker, Dick Bowie, John (Jocko) Collins, Jerry Cunningham, Arthur Ehlers, Mark Esper, Jim Foster, Burleigh Grimes, George Henderson, Charles Hum, Al Kubski, Anthony Lipari, Jim Martz, Frank McGowan, Don McShane, Willie Moore, Bobby Morgan, Ken Parker, Damon Phillips, Ray Poitevint, German Rivera, Mike Rogan, Ray Scarborough, John Stokoe, Rip Tutor, Charles Wallgren, Bill Werle, E. E. Whitsett, Walter Youse.

Park location—Memorial Stadium, 33rd street, Ellerslie avenue, 36th street and Ednor road.

Seating capacity—52,137

Field dimensions—Home plate to left field at foul line, 309 feet; to center field, 410 feet; to right field at foul line, 309 feet.

BOSTON RED SOX

President—Thomas A. Yawkey
Executive Vice-President-General Manager—Richard H. O'Connell
Vice-President, Legal Affairs—John F. Donovan, Jr.
Vice-President, Player Personnel—Haywood C. Sullivan
Vice-President, Administration—John P. Alevizos
Treasurer—Joseph T. Cummiskey
Secretary—Joseph LaCour
Director, Player Procurement, Scouting—Neil T. Mahoney
Director, Minor League Clubs—Edward F. Kenney
Traveling Secretary—John J. Rogers
Director of Public Relations—William C. Crowley
Statistician-Assistant Director of Public Relations—Arthur J. Keefe
Community Relations, Speaking—Thomas B. Dowd
Manager—Edward M. Kasko
Club Physician—Dr. Thomas M. Tierney
Executive offices—24 Jersey street, Boston, Mass. 02215
Telephone—267-9440 (area code 617)

Scouts—Milton Bolling, Ray Boone, Mace Brown, Irving (Jack) Burns, Pete Cerrone, Maurice DeLoof, George Digby, Howard (Danny) Doyle, Frank Fahey, Earl Johnson, Stan Johnson, Charles Koney, Wilfred Lefebvre, Felix Maldonado, Frank Malzone, C. J. (Socko) McCarey, Bill McCarren, Sam Mele, Frank (Bots) Nekola, Willie Paffen, Meade Palmer, Dave Philley, Anthony Ravish, Roderick Rice, Edward Scott, Matt Sczesny, Marvin Stendel, Joseph Stephenson, Alphonse (Tommy) Thomas, Larry Thomas, Charlie Wagner, Glenn Wright.

Park location—Fenway Park, Jersey street, Lansdowne street and Ipswich street.

Seating capacity—33,379

Field dimensions—Home plate to left field at foul line, 315 feet; to center field, 420 feet; to right field at foul line, 302 feet; average right field distance, 382 feet.

CALIFORNIA ANGELS

BOARD OF DIRECTORS

Gene Autry, Chairman of the Board; Robert O. Reynolds, President; Clair L. Stout, Secretary; Forrest Shumway, J. D. Stetson Coleman, Joseph A. Thomas, alternate.

FRONT-OFFICE STAFF

President—Robert O. Reynolds
Executive Vice-President and General Manager—Dick Walsh
Assistant to General Manager—Dick Wiencek
Consultant—Fred Haney
Vice-President and Treasurer—Francis X. Leary
Secretary—Clair L. Stout
Minor League Director—Thomas W. Sommers
Director of Publicity and Speakers' Bureau—George Goodale
Director of Promotions and Public Relations—George Lederer
Traveling Secretary—Gerald (Jerry) Waring
Ticket Manager—Dick Foster
Stadium Operations Director—Ted Bowsfield
Assistant Ticket Manager—Carl Gordon
Group Sales—John Lindell
Manager—Harold (Lefty) Phillips
Club Physician—Dr. Jules Rasinski
Executive offices—Anaheim Stadium, 2000 State College Blvd., Anaheim, Calif. 92806
Telephone—633-2000, (area code 714)

Scouts—Carl Ackerman, Dolph Camilli, Rex Carr, Bob Clear, Ray Coley, Richard C. Hanlon, Fibber Hirayama, John H. Jackson, Nicholas Kamzic, Dave Kosher, Thomas (Pep) Lee, John (Jocko) Little, Ken Myers, Jack Paepke, Bob Reasonover, Pat Rogan, Harry E. Smith, John Streza, Larry Stubing, Gordon Windhorn.

Park location—Anaheim Stadium, 2000 State College Boulevard

Seating capacity—43,200

Field dimensions—Home plate to left field at foul line, 333 feet; to center field, 400 feet; to right field at foul line, 333 feet.

CHICAGO WHITE SOX

President—John W. Allyn
Vice-President and Business Manager—Leo Breen
Director of Player Personel—Roland Hemond
Executive Vice-President—Stuart K. Holcomb
Vice-President and Director of Park Operations—Ed Holstein
Publicity Director—Howard Roberts
Traveling Secretary and Club Statistician—Don Unferth
Farm Director—Glen C. Miller
Director of Player Development—C. V. Davis
Director of Speakers' Bureau—Paul (Dizzy) Trout
Ticket Director—Tom Maloney
Assistant Treasurer—Roy Milostan
Manager—Chuck Tanner
Club Physicians—Dr. William Allen and Dr. Gerald Loftus
Executive offices—35th Street and Dan Ryan, Chicago, Ill. 60616
Telephone—924-1000 (area code 312)

Scouts—Bruce Andrew, Pel Austin, Ken Blackman, Pat Gainey, Charles Gault, Sam Hairston, Bennie Huffman, Gary Johnson, Grover (Deacon) Jones, Jack Kelich, Bill Kimball, Bill Lentini, Dario Lodigiani, Bennie Meyer, Pete Milito, Hugh Mulcahy, Herb Newberry, George Noga, Mel Preibisch, Fred Shaffer, Steve Vrablik, Walt Widmayer, Hugh Wise.

Park location—Comiskey Park, 35th Street and Dan Ryan, Chicago, Ill. 60616.

Seating capacity—46,550

Field dimensions—Home plate to left field at foul line, 352 feet; to center field, 400 feet; to right field at foul line, 352 feet.

CLEVELAND INDIANS

Chairman of Board—Vernon Stouffer
President-Treasurer—Gabe Paul
Vice-President-Director of Player Personnel—Henry J. Peters
Vice-President—James Stouffer
Secretary—Louis S. Peirce
Assistant Secretary-Treasurer—Nicholas C. Seekely
Public Relations Director—Ed Uhas
Regional Public Relations Director—Dino Lucarelli
Traveling Secretary—Bob Hofman
Director of Stadium Operations—Daniel W. Zerbey
Ticket Manager—Joseph W. Whearty
Manager—Alvin Dark
Club Physician—Dr. Walter O. Lewin
Executive offices—Municipal Stadium, Cleveland, Ohio 44114
Telephone—861-1200 (area code 216)

Scouts—Spurgeon Chandler, Loyd Christopher, Henry J. Dotterer, Robert Goff, James Gruzdis, John Kall, Joseph Morlan, Paul O'Dea, Regie Otero.

Park location—Municipal Stadium, foot of West Third street

Seating capacity—76,977

Field dimensions—Home plate to left field at foul line, 320 feet; to center field, 400 feet; to right field at foul line, 320 feet.

DETROIT TIGERS

President—John E. Fetzer
Executive Vice-President-General Manager—James A. Campbell
Vice-President—Richard B. (Rick) Ferrell
Secretary-Treasurer—Harry M. Sisson
Director of Public Relations—Hal Middlesworth
Director of Player Development—Walter A. (Hoot) Evers
Director of Player Procurement—Edward G. Katalinas
Business Manager—Alex Callam
Traveling Secretary—Vince Desmond
Director of Stadium Operations—Ralph Snyder
Minor League Secretary—Dave Miller
Director of Ticket Sales—Norman P. Otto
Assistant Director of Public Relations—Bill A. Brown
Sales Promotions & Special Events—Lew Matlin
Television Network Operations, Sales Manager—Neal K. Fenkell
Assistant to Business Manager—Tom Keating
Manager—Billy Martin
Club Physician—Clarence Livingood, M. D.
Executive offices—Tiger Stadium, Detroit, Mich. 48216
Telephone—962-4000 (area code 313)

Scouts—Reno Bertoia, Wayne Blackburn, Charles (Buster) Chatham, Jim Command, Joe Cusick, Louis D'Annunzio, Ralph DeFranco, Mike de la Hoz, George (Pat) Dery, Jack Deutsch, Bernie deViveiros, George Ferrell, Denny Galehouse, Mercer Harris, Joseph Holden, Irving (Rabbit) Jacobson, Herman Kander, George Kell, John Klippstein, Bill Lajoie, Ray Meyers, Marvin Owen, William Pierre, George Popovich, Bob Prentice, Frank Sansosti, John Skurski, Bob Sullivan, Jack Tighe, Edwin (Cy) Williams, Rico Zuccaro.

Park location—Tiger Stadium, Michigan avenue, Cochrane avenue, Kaline drive and Trumbull avenue.

Seating capacity—54,220

Field dimensions—Home plate to left field at foul line, 340 feet; to center field, 440 feet; to right field at foul line, 325 feet.

KANSAS CITY ROYALS

President—Ewing Kauffman
Executive Vice-President—Cedric Tallis
Vice-President-Treasurer—Charles Truitt
Director of Minor League Operations and Scouting—James (Lou) Gorman
Stadium Operations Director—Jay Leishman
Controller-Assistant Business Manager—Doug Adams
Director of Public Relations—Bob Wirz
Traveling Secretary—Rick Current
Ticket Manager—Wayne Causey
Group Sales Manager—Tom Hall
Assistant Farm Director—John Schuerholz
Assistant Scouting Director—Spencer (Herk) Robinson
Assistant Public Relations Director—Gene Diefendorf
Coordinator of Instruction—Joe Gordon
Manager—Bob Lemon
Club Physician—Dr. Paul Meyer
Executive offices—Municipal Stadium
Mailing Address—P. O. Box 1969, Kansas City, Mo. 64141
Telephone—241-4101 (area code 816)

Scouts—Jimmie Adair, Herb Anderson, Gary Blaylock, Dan Carnevale, Tom Ferrick, Bill Fischer, Owen Friend, Jim Garland, Rosey Gilhousen, Dick Hager, Jay Hankins, John Jorgensen, Bill Kearns, Art Lilly, Bill McKeon, Dale McReynolds, Charlie Metro, John Metro, Larry (Bo) Osborne, Eddie Sawyer, Norm Siebern, Art Stewart, Joe Thomas, Bob Thurman.

Park location—Municipal Stadium, 22nd and Brooklyn

Seating capacity—35,057

Field dimensions—Home plate to left field at foul line, 369 feet; to center field, 421 feet; to right field at foul line, 338 feet.

MILWAUKEE BREWERS

President—Allan H. (Bud) Selig
Vice-President—Edmund B. Fitzgerald
Vice-President—Judge Robert E. Cannon
Vice-President-Director of Baseball Operations—Frank Lane
Secretary—Richard W. Cutler
Director of Scouting and Player Development—Bobby Mattick
Director of Minor League Operations—Bob Quinn
Administrative Assistant, Scouting and Farm Departments—Tony Siegle
Treasurer—Bob Schoenbachler
Traveling Secretary—Tom Ferguson
Director of Public Relations—Bill Curley
Director of Ticket Operations and Promotions—Dick Hackett
Director of Stadium Operations—Gabe Paul, Jr.
Manager—Dave Bristol

Executive offices, Milwaukee Brewers Baseball Club, Inc., Milwaukee County Stadium, S. 44th street off Bluemound road.

Scouts—Bennie Borgmann, Bill Clark, Felix Delgado, Bill Enos, Tom Giordano, James Gleeson, Gordon Goldsberry, Sanfrid Johnson, Bradley Kohler, Karl Kuehl, Roland LeBlanc, Ed Lewis, Bob Mavis, Jack Sanford, Earl Silverthorn.

Park Location—S. 44th street off Bluemound road.

Seating capacity—47,611

Field dimensions—Home plate to left field at foul line, 320 feet; to center field, 402 feet; to right field at foul line, 315 feet.

MINNESOTA TWINS

President—Calvin R. Griffith
Vice-President-Assistant Treasurer—Mrs. Thelma Griffith Haynes
Treasurer—Eugene V. Young
Secretary-Controller—Oswald L. Bluege
Director—Wheelock Whitney
Vice-President and Traveling Secretary—Howard T. Fox, Jr.
Vice-President—Clark Griffith
Vice-President—William S. Robertson
Vice-President—James K. Robertson
Vice-President-Farm Director—George Brophy
Assistant Farm Director—Jim Rantz
Director of Public Relations—Tom Mee
Assistant Public Relations Director—Tom Cronin
Ticket Manager—Charles Lavender
Group Promotions—Don Cassidy
Stadium Superintendent—Richard Ericson
Assistant Controller—Jack Alexander
Assistant Ticket Manager—Lou Ramackel
Manager—Bill Rigney
Club Physicians—Dr. Leonard J. Michienzi and Dr. Harvey O'Phelan

Executive offices—Metropolitan Stadium, 8001 Cedar avenue, Bloomington. Minn. 55420.

Telephone—884-4031 (area code 612)

Scouts—Peter Appleton, Floyd Baker, Zinn Beck, Ray Bellino, Otto Bluege, Bob Butler, Ellis Clary, Edward Dunn, Gerry Flathman, Jesse Flores, Jesse Flores, Jr., Frank Franchi, Angelo Giuliani, Ray Holton, Phil Howser, Lee Irwin, Pete Lesmeister, William Messmann, Jim Miller, Marvin Olson, Bob O'Regan, Carlos Pascual, Spencer (Red) Robbins, Stanley Rogers, Herb Stein, Edward Stevens, Walter Via, Mike Wallace, Early Wynn, Andy Young.

Park location—Metropolitan Stadium, 8001 Cedar avenue, Bloomington, Minn. 55420.

Seating capacity—45,921

Field dimensions—Home plate to left field at foul line, 346 feet; to center field, 425 feet; to right field at foul line, 330 feet.

NEW YORK YANKEES

Chairman of the Board and President—Michael Burke
Executive Vice-President and General Manager—Leland S. MacPhail, Jr.
Vice-President, Administration—Howard Berk
Vice-President, Public Relations—Robert O. Fishel
Field Director, Player Development—Clyde Kluttz
Business Manager, Player Development—George Pfister
Controller—John J. Collins
Ticket Director—James Gleason
Traveling Secretary—Bruce Henry
Season Box Director—Michael Rendine
Director of Accounting & Financial Analysis—Thomas McMinn
Executive Producer—Charles Milton
Manager, Special Projects—Fred Bachman
Manager, Speakers' Bureau—Jackie Farrell
Broadcast Coordinator and Statistician—William Kane
Assistant Director, Public Relations—Martin Appel
Manager, General Accounting—David Weidler
Manager—Ralph Houk
Club Physician—Dr. Sidney S. Gaynor
Executive Offices—Yankee Stadium, Bronx, N. Y. 10451
Telephone—293-4300 (Area Code 212)

Scouts—Luis Arroyo, Cloyd Boyer, George Case, Mark Christman, Patrick Colgan, Pete Coscarart, Harry Craft, Al Cuccinello, Arthur Dede, Atley Donald, Joseph Frisa, Tom Greenwade, Randy Gumpert, Don Gutteridge, Roy Hamey, Willis Hudlin, Gordon Jones, Donald Lee, Hector Lopez, Lou Maguolo, Buster

Mills, Bill Monbouquette, Tom Morgan, Lamar North, Frank O'Rourke, Jose Seda, George Selkirk, Steve Souchock. Eddie Taylor, Jack Warner, Gene Woodling.

Park location—Yankee Stadium, East 161st street and River avenue

Park Telephone—293-4300 (area code 212)

Seating capacity—65,010

Field dimensions—Home plate to left field at foul line, 301 feet; to center field, 461 feet; to right field at foul line, 296 feet.

OAKLAND A'S

President—Charles O. Finley
Secretary and Treasurer—Charles O. Finley, Jr.
Controller—Robert Boen
Director of Minor League Operations—Philip Seghi
Ticket Manager—Carl Finley
Director of Public Relations—Michael Haggerty
Director of Promotions—Tom Massey
Traveling Secretary and Public Relations—Tom Corwin
Group Sales and Advertising—Ron Mihelic
Administrative Assistant, Minor League—Norman Koselke
Club Physicians—Dr. Harry Walker and Dr. Charles Hudson
Manager—Dick Williams
Executive offices—Oakland-Alameda County Coliseum, Oakland, Calif. 94621
Telephone—635-4300 (area code 415)

Scouts—George Bradley, Fred Goodman, Eli Grba, Warren Hacker, Billy Herman, Al Hollingsworth, William Jackson, Dave Madison, Ambrose Palica, Phillip Pote, James Robinson, Legrant Scott, Michale Sgobba, Jack Vallely.

Park location—Oakland-Alameda County Coliseum, Nimitz freeway and Hegenberger road.

Seating capacity—50,000

Field dimensions—Home plate to left field at foul line, 330 feet; to center field, 400 feet; to right field at foul line, 330 feet.

WASHINGTON SENATORS

President—Robert E. Short
Vice-President-Manager—Ted Williams
Vice-President-Treasurer—Frank V. Fetzner
Vice-President—James H. Lemon
Vice-President-Administration—Joseph R. Burke
Secretary—William R. Busch
Assistant Treasurer—Charles Wangner
Press Relations Director-Traveling Secretary—Burton Hawkins
Farm Director—Hal Keller
Promotion, Advertising Director—Oscar Molomot
Special Assignments—Stanley R. (Bucky) Harris, Bill Jurges, John T. Sheehan, Dick Gernert, Edward S. Doherty
Ticket Office Director—John F. Morrissey
Club Physician—Dr. George A. Resta
Executive offices—Robert F. Kennedy Memorial Stadium, 22nd and East Capitol streets, Washington, D. C. 20003.
Telephone—546-2880 (area code 202)

Scouts—Harley Anderson, Lee Anthony, Joe Branzell, Hiram Brathwaite, Paddy Cottrell, Hillis Layne, Joseph W. Lewis, Joe Marchese, Neal Millard, Harry Strohm, Tommy Thompson, Al Zarilla.

Park location—Robert F. Kennedy Memorial Stadium, 22nd and East Capitol streets.

Seating capacity—45,016

Field dimensions—Home plate to left field at foul line, 335 feet; to center field, 410 feet; to right field at foul line, 335 feet.

DAVE McNALLY—Winning his 20th game, third time in row.

EAST DIVISION

Birds Spread-Eagle Field Again

By PHIL JACKMAN

During the last two years, there has been a two-game difference in the way the Baltimore Orioles played baseball.

Now two games doesn't sound like much when you stack 1970's overall record of 115-55 against 1969's log of 113-57. But, oh, what a difference.

It's the difference between a bunch of misty eyes at an airport and a bedlamic clubhouse scene . . . . between a check for $18,300 and $14,900 . . . . between a seemingly endless winter of "what happeneds?" and a short one of "nice goings."

In the last five years, the Orioles now have had it both ways and you can take Brooks Robinson's word for it when he says 1969 was, well, a drag.

It was so much of a drag losing the World Series to the Mets in five games after being the prohibitive favorite, Brooks, on the eve of the Birds' first trip last April, punched out one of those identification strips for his suitcase saying: "Brooks Robinson, Baltimore Orioles, 1970 World Champions."

Then, for six months, he went out and played like a madman to assure there would be no encores of the Orioles' less than inspiring performance in the Met Series.

He capped it with a show in this year's Series against Cincinnati they will be talking about for years to come. He batted .429, fielded 3.500, won himself a car as the hero of the dismantling of the Big Red Machine and, probably, a $100,000 contract for the 1971 season.

But while Brooks was the be-all and end-all of the World Series, Baltimore's charge to its second world championship in five years was a many-splendored thing.

The Orioles had everything:

Three 20-game winners in Mike Cuellar (24), Dave McNally (24) and Jim Palmer (20) . . . . the league's best defensive infield with Boog Powell at first, Dave Johnson at second, Mark Belanger at shortstop and Mr. Third Base at third base . . . . the league's best leadoff man in Don Buford . . . . a guy, Paul Blair, in center field Ted Williams says is the best he's ever seen at the position . . . and, of course, Frank Robinson, the driving force.

That was the first string. Behind this gang came a muscular bench, featuring the team's leading hitter, Merv Rettenmund . . . . a bullpen that, although slightly erratic, won 30 games and saved 30 others . . . . and a catching combine that accounted for 72 runs while slugging 17 homers.

At the controls was Earl Weaver, a man who has won 265 of 406 regular-season baseball games since taking over as the O's manager 2½ years ago. That's 124 games over .500 with a team that was six over (43-37) the morning he took over.

BALTIMORE ORIOLES, 1970

Front row—Phoebus, Buford, Frey, coach; Hunter, coach; Weaver, manager; Bamberger, coach; Staller, coach; McNally, Salmon. Second row—Reid, equipment manager; Etchebarren, Powell, Richert, Belanger, Leonhard, B. Robinson, Hendricks, Rettenmund, Johnson, Watt, Salvon, trainer. Back row—Lopez, Palmer, Drabowsky, F. Robinson, Cuellar, Hall, Grich, Motton, Crowley, Blair. Seated in front—Mazzone, batboy.

Boog Powell, the Baltimore Orioles' leading power man in '70 and the league's Most Valuable Player, shows a large measure of his determination as he drives another ball out of the park.

But you know all that, the personnel. The cast hasn't changed that much since the mid-Sixties and scarcely at all the last two years.

How the Orioles actually smeared the American League East, swept the Twins in the Championship Series for the second successive year and won the World Series went like this.

The Birds started out by winning five in a row, a club record. They ended up by winning 11 in a row, also a club record. In between, they spent all but eight days in first place, latching onto the top spot for good April 26 when Buford hit a three-run homer in the eighth to beat the Royals, 10-9.

This victory, incidentally, was one of a dozen Baltimore rung up against K. C. bringing to 23 the string of successes the O's have had in this some-what one-sided rivalry. This, of course, is an all-time mark.

The Tigers hung very close to the Orioles through the first month of the season before dropping back and surrendering the runner-up spot to the Yankees.

The Yanks hung a comfortable distance back until the end of May when the O's were guilty of their only stretch of nondescript baseball.

From May 29 when Cuellar flipped a two-hitter and Powell bashed a homer to beat Andy Messersmith and the Angels, 2-0, until the second game of July 19 when Tom Phoebus lost to Bob Miller and the White Sox, Baltimore played just .500 ball over a 46-game stretch.

What hurt was the fact that Blair got hit in the face with a Ken Tatum fast ball and was either in the hospital or on the disabled list for

Uproariously jubilant Earl Weaver, manager of the Orioles, who'd just learned they had won the East Division, helps douse Phil Jackman, Bird correspondent for THE SPORTING NEWS, who wore ''special'' gear.

three weeks. But also in slumps were a couple of the pitchers, starters McNally and Cuellar.

McNally went nearly a month without a victory before rolling into high gear July 26 with an 11-1 win over Jim Perry in Minnesota. The next time he was to get beat was September 2 in New York, a run of nine in a row.

At the same time, Cuellar was due to take off. From July 28 to September 13, he won 10 of 11 and both he and McNally entered the final month of the season with 20 wins to their credit already.

Fact is, during the month of August, McNally, Cuellar and Palmer made 23 starts, pitched 15 complete games and had an 18-2 record. This blitz and the month's record of 22-8 doubled the club's grip on first place from six to a dozen games and September was played strictly for fun and next year's contract.

Surprisingly, the Birds played August with reserves, for the most part, Bobby Grich, Chico Salmon and Curt Motton ducking in and out of the lineup frequently and Rettenmund all but becoming an outfield regular as he took turns spelling Buford, Blair and F. Robby.

If there was ever any question where the Orioles went wrong in 1969, it had to be in their actions after wrapping up the half-pennant in mid-September.

Earl Weaver began resting his regulars from that moment on and you got the feeling they never did get righted once put back together for the last week of the regular season.

Weaver says this is not so and he can cite three straight wins over the Twins and an opening victory in the World Series over Tom Seaver as proof. Still, in just one of those four games were the O's impressive.

This time, when Weaver put the juggernaut back together, it clicked as evidenced by its 11-game run of wins down the stretch. Last fall, the O's lost five of their last six regular-season jousts.

During the streak, the Birds played five extra-inning games and five one-runners. All this practice in tight ball games, indeed all their experience in winning a record 40 one-run games during the season, was to come in handy in post-season play.

Not against the Twins in the playoffs, because this series was a bomb run, the Birds winning, 10-6, 11-3 and 6-1. But, in the Series, it was a different story.

Starting out in Cincinnati, the O's fell behind the first day, 3-0, and the second day, 4-0. They had all they could do to climb back to post 4-3 and 6-5 victories. The two other Series wins were by 9-3 scores and, in between, the Reds' propensity for blowing leads rubbed off and Baltimore lost, 6-5.

But that's the team. As individuals, Powell had his second straight banner year, smashing 35 homers, plating 114 runs and capping it all by winning the Most Valuable Player trophy. For the second straight year, writers and broadcasters traveling with the team voted Boog the club MVP by a wide margin.

Dave Johnson, THE SPORTING NEWS A. L. All-Star fielder at second base in 1969, repeated his award in 1970, finishing the season with a fielding average of .990 and with an errorless game streak of 43. At the same time, Johnson raised his batting average a point to .281.

Belanger could have left his bats at home for all the good they did him until August, but he never let the sick stick affect his fielding. Mark did come around with the bat after the All-Star break, hitting about .250 over the last half to end up at .218.

You shouldn't even ask about the first half, please.

After four straight down years, Brooks Robinson began to wonder about his hitting. He erased all self-doubt by hanging between .280 and .290 all season and he knocked in 94 runs, his best production since plating an even century in 1966.

Buford's average took a tumble from .291 to .272, but maybe this was because he was upping his home-run output from 11 to 17 and driving in more runs. More important, he drew a club-record 109 walks and easily led the team in runs scored with 99.

Blair got only better with the glove, but had his problems at bat after being beaned. Over the last six weeks of the season, however. he jacked his batting average 30 points to .267.

Frank Robinson got off to his customary good start, but a series of run-ins with walls and a shoulder injury cut down his effectiveness in the second half. He finished off the season by going 6-for-11 to hike his average to .306.

Andy Etchebarren and Elrod Hendricks both expressed a desire to catch more during the season, but Weaver can point to the team's success under the alternating system to cut the legs from beneath their arguments.

Hendricks had his best year yet for home runs and RBIs, while improving as a catcher. Etchebarren had perhaps his steadiest campaign to date, all things considered.

While flipping in and out of the lineup at all of the outfield positions, Rettenmund hit .322 with 18 homers and 58 RBIs, which hardly sounds like a substitute's figures. They are not, Merv getting to bat 338 times as Weaver once again did a masterful job of keeping all hands happy.

Chico Salmon and Curt Motton didn't have good years, averagewise but their homer and RBI productions were up, and it was easy to see Weaver had more confidence in them defensively.

The only new man in the cast was Terry Crowley, who took Bobby Floyd's spot on the 25-man roster. Terry entered the last three weeks of the season hitting .291 with four game-winning hits when a slump set in. It shaded an otherwise banner rookie season and the kid says he's looking forward to playing more next season.

The big disappointment in the starting rotation came in Tom Phoebus and Jim Hardin's refusal to step forward and claim the No. 4 spot. They combined for just 11 wins in 40 starts, but McNally, Cuellar and Palmer were so strong you didn't notice.

With a total of 68 wins, the Birds' Big Three became baseball's winningest trio since World War II, beating by one the 67 victories registered by Bob Lemon, Early Wynn and Mike Garcia in 1952.

The best of the Oriole bullpenners in 1970 were Pete Richert, who led the team in ERA and saves, and Dick Hall, who won 10 games and who the last two years has won two playoff games.

Eddie Watt had an off year, but still picked up seven wins and a

dozen saves while Moe Drabowsky won four games after coming over in a trade in mid-June.

Marcelino Lopez was just 1-1 and Dave Leonhard had no record, but both pitched well in the second half after slow starts.

But nothing could possibly dim the brilliance of the Orioles' 1970 season—from start to finish.

SCORES OF BALTIMORE ORIOLES' 1970 GAMES

Date	Result		Winner	Loser
APRIL—				
7—At Cleve.	W	8-2	McNally	McDowell
8—At Cleve.	W	3-2	Cuellar	Moore
9—At Cleve.	W	13-1	Phoebus	Hand
10—Detroit	W	3-2‡	Hall	Lolich
11—Detroit	W	5-3	McNally	Wilson
12—Detroit	L	2-7	Niekro	Cuellar
16—Wash.	L	2-4	Coleman	Palmer
17—N. York	L	1-4§	McDaniel	Hall
18—N. York	W	5-4	McNally	Peterson
19—N. York	W	4-3	Cuellar	Burbach
19—N. York	L	5-8	Verbanic	Hardin
20—At Bos.	W	3-2*	Palmer	Culp
22—At Bos.	L	2-5	Romo	McNally
24—At K. C.	W	7-5	Hardin	Hedlund
25—At K. C.	W	9-3	Palmer	Butler
26—At K. C.	W	10-9	Hall	Fitzmorris
28—At Chi.	W	4-2	Cuellar	Janeski
29—At Chi.	W	18-2	Palmer	Sisk
30—At Chi.	L	3-6	John	Phoebus
MAY—				
1—Minn.	W	9-3	McNally	Boswell
2—Minn.	L	2-4	Perry	Cuellar
3—Minn.	L	3-4	Kaat	Palmer
5—Kan. C.	W	7-3	Phoebus	Drago
6—Kan. C.	W	3-1	McNally	Butler
7—Kan. C.	W	7-6	Watt	Drabowsky
8—Chicago	W	6-1	Palmer	Janeski
9—Chicago	W	4-3	Phoebus	John
10—Chicago	W	7-2	McNally	Arrigo
10—Chicago	W	4-2	Hall	Wood
12—At Minn.	W	5-4	Cuellar	Perry
13—At Minn.	L	4-5‡	Perranoski	Watt
15—At Wash.	W	4-3§	Richert	Knowles
16—At Wash.	W	4-3	McNally	Cox
18—At N. Y.	L	4-10	Peterson	Cuellar
19—At N. Y.	W	5-1	Palmer	Cumberland
20—At Det.	L	0-4	Lolich	Phoebus
21—At Det.	L	4-6	Cain	McNally
21—At Det.	W	3-1	Richert	Hiller
22—Boston	W	7-4	Hall	Peters
23—Boston	W	3-0	Palmer	Culp
24—Boston	W	2-1‡	Watt	Lyle
24—Boston	L	3-4	Siebert	Phoebus
25—Cleve.	W	6-2	McNally	Miller
26—Cleve.	W	7-0	Hardin	Chance
27—Cleve.	W	5-4	Hall	Paul
29—At Calif.	W	2-0	Cuellar	Messersmith
30—At Calif.	L	2-3	Murphy	Hall
31—At Calif.	L	1-6	Wright	McNally
JUNE—				
2—At Oak.	W	5-1	Palmer	Dobson
3—At Oak.	L	1-4	Grant	Cuellar
4—At Oak.	L	2-4	Hunter	Phoebus
5—At Milw.	W	3-2	McNally	Bolin
6—At Milw.	L	4-6	Brabender	Palmer
7—At Milw.	W	7-6	Cuellar	Pattin
9—Calif.	L	5-7§	Fisher	Hall
10—Calif.	W	2-1	Palmer	Wright
11—Calif.	W	9-1	Cuellar	May
12—Oakland	L	2-4§	Grant	Watt
13—Oakland	L	7-10	Hunter	McNally
14—Oakland	W	4-2‡	Palmer	Talbot
15—Milw.	L	6-9	Sanders	Watt
17—Milw.	L	1-5	Brabender	McNally
19—Wash.	W	12-10	Palmer	Bosman
19—Wash.	W	3-2y	Richert	Knowles
20—Wash.	W	5-4	Cuellar	Coleman
21—Wash.	W	4-2	McNally	Such
22—At Bos.	W	9-8	Hall	Lyle
JUNE—				
23—At Bos.	L	1-5	Culp	Palmer
24—At Bos.	L	5-6	Wagner	Watt
25—At Bos.	W	13-8z	Drabowsky	Santiago
26—At Wash.	W	12-2	McNally	Coleman
27—At Wash.	L	3-5	Hannan	Palmer
28—At Wash.	L	3-4x	Hannan	Watt
29—At Wash.	L	3-5	Shellenback	Lopez
30—Cleve.	W	4-2	McNally	Dunning
JULY—				
1—Cleve.	W	3-0	Palmer	Austin
2—Cleve.	L	9-10	Higgins	Drabowsky
3—Detroit	W	4-0	Cuellar	Lolich
4—Detroit	L	5-6	Hiller	Richert
5—Detroit	W	2-0	Palmer	McLain
7—N. York	W	6-2‡	Cuellar	McDaniel
8—N. York	W	9-8	Drabowsky	McDaniel
9—N. York	L	5-7††	Cumberland	Lopez
10—At Det.	W	2-1	Cain	Palmer
11—At Det.	W	6-5	Cuellar	Niekro
12—At Det.	L	3-7	Lolich	McNally
12—At Det.	W	13-3	Hall	McLain
16—Minn.	W	5-1	Cuellar	Hall
17—Minn.	L	5-6‡	Perranoski	Watt
18—Minn.	L	3-6	Perry	McNally
19—At Chi.	W	8-2	Palmer	Horlen
19—At Chi.	L	3-7	Miller	Phoebus
20—At Chi.	W	14-5	Cuellar	Janeski
21—At K. C.	W	2-1	Watt	Johnson
22—At K. C.	W	4-3y	Richert	Abernathy
23—At K. C.	W	5-4	Palmer	Drago
24—At Minn.	L	0-8	Kaat	Cuellar
25—At Minn.	W	6-5	R. Hall	T. Hall
26—At Minn.	W	11-1	McNally	Perry
27—At Minn.	L	2-5	Blyleven	Palmer
28—Chicago	W	4-2	Cuellar	Horlen
29—Chicago	L	1-2	Wood	Hardin
31—Kan. C.	W	3-1	McNally	Morehead
AUGUST—				
1—Kan. C.	W	9-1	Palmer	Drago
2—Kan. C.	W	10-8	Cuellar	Rooker
4—Boston	W	5-2	McNally	Culp
5—Boston	W	3-0	Palmer	Siebert
6—At Cleve.	L	0-4	Chance	Cuellar
6—At Cleve.	W	7-1	Hardin	Dunning
7—At Cleve.	L	4-10	Higgins	Hall
8—At N. Y.	W	4-2	McNally	Kekich
9—At N. Y.	L	4-6§	Aker	Hall
9—At N. Y.	W	12-9§	Watt	Klimkowski
11—At Calif.	W	7-0	Cuellar	Mes'rsmith
12—At Calif.	W	5-4	McNally	May
13—At Calif.	L	2-3	Queen	Drabowsky
14—At Oak.	L	0-4	Dobson	Hardin
15—At Oak.	W	7-1	Cuellar	Segui
16—At Oak.	W	2-1	McNally	Hunter
17—At Milw.	W	3-2	Palmer	Krausse
18—At Milw.	W	3-0	Hardin	Pattin
19—At Milw.	W	3-2	Cuellar	Lockwood
21—Calif.	W	5-0	McNally	Murphy
22—Calif.	L	2-3‡	Messersmith	Watt
22—Calif.	W	6-5	Cuellar	Queen
25—Oakland	W	5-1	McNally	Segui
26—Oakland	W	5-1	Palmer	Hunter
27—Oakland	W	6-4	Cuellar	Dobson
28—Milw.	L	1-2	Pattin	Hardin
28—Milw.	W	8-4	Richert	Brabender
29—Milw.	W	6-1	McNally	Bolin
30—Milw.	L	2-5	Lockwood	Palmer
31—At N. Y.	W	10-2	Cuellar	Bahnsen

NEW YORK YANKEES, 1970

Front row—Peterson, Cater, Clarke, White, Howser, coach; Houk, manager; Turner, coach; Hegan, coach; Mantle, coach; Blefary. Second row—Soares, trainer; Baker, Ward, Kenney, Aker, McCormick, Ellis, Gibbs, Lyttle, Munson, Michael, Henry, traveling secretary. Back row—Hansen, Bahnsen, Stottlemyre, McDaniel, Hamilton, Waslewski, Kline, Klimkowski, Woods. Seated in front—Slater, LaBoy, batboys.

SEPTEMBER—			Winner	Loser	SEPTEMBER—			Winner	Loser
1—At N. Y.	L	2-4	Peterson	Hardin	17—At Wash.	L	0-2	Bosman	Cuellar
2—At N. Y.	L	2-3	Kekich	McNally	18—Cleve.	W	4-3§	Richert	Lasher
3—At N. Y.	W	8-4	Palmer	Stottlemyre	19—Cleve.	L	2-4	Kittwage	McNally
4—At Bos.	W	8-6	Drabowsky	Hartenstein	20—Cleve.	W	7-0	Palmer	Paul
5—At Bos.	W	3-2	Hall	Culp	21—Detroit	W	4-3x	Hardin	Timmerman
6—At Bos.	L	8-9§	Lyle	Richert	22—Detroit	W	10-2	Phoebus	Reed
7—At Det.	L	2-5	Niekro	Palmer	24—Detroit	W	7-4	Cuellar	Hiller
8—At Det.	W	6-3	Lopez	Lolich	25—At Cleve.	W	9-7y	Richert	Hand
9—N. York	W	1-0	Cuellar	Kline	26—At Cleve.	W	7-4§	Watt	Lasher
10—N. York	W	2-1	McNally	Bahnsen	27—At Cleve.	W	4-3	Hall	McDowell
11—Boston	W	3-2y	Watt	Lyle	29—Wash.	W	3-2‡	Drabowsky	Coleman
12—Boston	W	5-1	Phoebus	Peters	29—Wash.	W	3-2§	Watt	Knowles
13—Boston	W	13-2	Cuellar	Brett	30—Wash.	W	6-2	McNally	Hannan
15—At Wash.	W	6-2	McNally	Cox	OCTOBER—				
16—At Wash.	L	0-2	Gogolewski	Palmer	1—Wash.	W	3-2	Hardin	Pina

* Game halted by rain in top of seventh. † Game halted by rain with one out in top of eighth. ‡ 10 innings. § 11 innings. x 12 innings. y 13 innings. z 14 innings.

Yankees Regain Pride With No. 2 Finish

By JIM OGLE

With a mini-champagne party to celebrate their best finish since the 1964 pennant, The American East runner-up Yankees look to the future with high hopes as the emergence of several rookie stars and the acquisition of Danny Cater lifted the club to a sparkling 93-69 record—fourth best in the majors.

Ralph Houk, American League Manager of the Year, turned in another of his scintillating pilot jobs as he overcame several disappointments to keep the club on the move. After an ordinary start, the Yankees enjoyed a 17-7 June (best in the majors for the month) to move within three games of the leader from Baltimore.

A general batting slump early in July killed any hopes of making a fight for the division title, but Houk rallied his forces and took over second place for keeps in August and beat off all challenges the rest of the way.

Thurman Munson, the best young player the Yanks have unveiled since Mickey Mantle in 1951, was a prime reason for the New Yorkers' return to respectability. Rookie first baseman John Ellis and rookie pitcher Steve Kline also showed enough to make the Yanks' future look brighter.

For the first time since 1961, the Yankees had two .300 hitters. Munson led the club with .302, while Cater finished over .300 for the first time in his career at .301. Munson had only one hit his first 30 at-bats, but came strong the second half of the season to establish himself as a future star.

Roy White just missed the .300 mark, but enjoyed the finest year of his career as he hit new highs in nearly every offensive department. Roy hit 22 homers, drove in 94 runs, scored 109, stole 24 bases and hit a sparkling .296.

While pitching ace Mel Stottlemyre ran into a 15-13 year in which nothing broke right for him, Fritz Peterson took over as the leader by joining the 20-victory club for the first time with a 20-11 record. Pete did it the hard way by winning his last three decisions, including his first victory ever at Fenway Park in the last game of the season.

Lindy McDaniel, the veteran reliever, was another vital cog in the second-place finish. McDaniel tied the club record for saves at 29, which Luis Arroyo had established in 1961. Lindy also picked up nine victories.

Jack Aker, despite some back trouble the second half, also contributed to the upsurge with 16 saves.

Seeking a fourth and fifth starter all year, Houk hopes he has found them in Mike Kekich and Kline, who moved into regular rotation the final six weeks and did some fine pitching.

All in all, it was the most satisfying Yankee season since the drought started in 1965. It was the fourth year of the Five-Year-Plan instituted by the triumvirate of President Mike Burke, General Manager Lee MacPhail and Houk when they joined hands for the start of the 1967 season.

To the surprise of many, Mickey Mantle returned to Yankee Stadium as a coach in the final six weeks of the campaign.

SCORES OF NEW YORK YANKEES' 1970 GAMES

Date	Result	Score	Winner	Loser
APRIL—				
7—Boston	L	3-4	Peters	Stottlemyre
9—Boston	W	4-3	Peterson	Culp
11—Cleve.	L	0-3	Chance	Bahnsen
12—Cleve.	L	1-2	McDowell	Stottlemyre
12—Cleve.	W	5-4	Aker	Higgins
14—At Bos.	L	3-8	Culp	Peterson
15—At Bos.	L	2-6	Lonborg	Burbach
16—At Bos.	L	5-8	Stange	Aker
17—At Balt.	W	4-1§	McDaniel	Hall
18—At Balt.	L	4-5	McNally	Peterson
19—At Balt.	L	3-4	Cuellar	Burbach
19—At Balt.	W	8-5	Verbanic	Hardin
20—At Wash.	W	11-2	Bahnsen	Brunet
21—At Wash.	L	5-7	Cox	Stottlemyre
22—At Wash.	L	1-2z	Grzenda	Klimkowski
23—At Wash.	W	11-6	Cumberland	Such
25—Oakland	L	0-3	Dobson	Bahnsen
26—Oakland	W	8-3	Stottlemyre	Odom
28—Calif.	W	7-5	Peterson	Wright
29—Calif.	L	2-3	Messersmith	Cumberland
30—Calif.	L	0-1	Bahnsen	May
MAY—				
1—Milw.	W	6-3	Stottlemyre	Brabender
2—Milw.	W	7-6	Hamilton	Gelnar
3—Milw.	W	8-7	Hamilton	Meyer
3—Milw.	W	4-2	McDaniel	Krausse
5—At Oak.	L	3-11	Hunter	Bahnsen
6—At Oak.	W	7-6	Stottlemyre	Downing
7—At Oak.	W	7-3	Peterson	Fingers
8—At Calif.	L	3-4	Wright	Klimkowski
9—At Calif.	L	3-11	Messersmith	Kekich
10—At Calif.	W	4-3	Aker	May
11—At Milw.	W	5-5	......	......
12—At Milw.	W	9-5†	Peterson	Krausse
13—At Milw.	L	1-3	Morris	Cumberland
15—Detroit	W	4-1	Bahnsen	Lolich
16—Detroit	W	7-4	Hamilton	Scherman
18—Balt.	W	10-4	Peterson	Cuellar
19—Balt.	L	1-5	Palmer	Cumberland
20—Wash.	L	0-2	Bosman	Bahnsen
21—Wash.	W	2-0	Stottlemyre	Such
22—At Cleve.	W	7-4	Peterson	Chance
23—At Cleve.	L	3-4y	Hennigan	Hamilton
24—At Cleve.	W	6-5	McDaniel	Lasher
24—At Cleve.	W	8-7§	McDaniel	Lasher
25—At Det.	L	3-4	Cain	Hamilton
26—At Det.	L	0-3	Wilson	Stottlemyre
27—At Det.	W	4-2	Peterson	Niekro
29—At Minn.	W	4-2	Kekich	Perry
30—At Minn.	L	6-10	Perranoski	Hamilton
31—At Minn.	L	6-7‡	Williams	McDaniel
JUNE—				
2—Kan. C.	W	3-2	Peterson	Johnson
3—Kan. C.	W	5-3	Kekich	Drago
4—Kan. C.	W	2-1x	McDaniel	Rooker
5—Chicago	W	10-1	Stottlemyre	Janeski
6—Chicago	W	3-1	Cumberland	Horlen
7—Chicago	L	3-4x	Wood	McDaniel
9—Minn.	W	5-2	Bahnsen	Kaat
10—Minn.	W	2-1	Stottlemyre	Blyleven
12—At K. C.	W	5-0	Peterson	Morehead
13—At K. C.	W	9-4x	McDaniel	Wright
JUNE—				
14—At K. C.	W	3-2	Hamilton	Burgmeier
16—At Chi.	W	6-2	Stottlemyre	John
17—At Chi.	L	3-6	Janeski	Peterson
18—At Bos.	W	3-2	Waslewski	Culp
19—At Bos.	L	4-7	Siebert	Bahnsen
20—At Bos.	W	8-3	Stottlemyre	Nagy
21—At Bos.	W	14-10§	McDaniel	Santiago
24—Cleve.	L	2-7	McDowell	Stottlemyre
24—Cleve.	W	5-4	Bahnsen	Lasher
25—Cleve.	W	3-1	Peterson	Dunning
27—Boston	L	0-4	Peters	Waslewski
28—Boston	L	3-5	Brett	Stottlemyre
28—Boston	W	8-2	Bahnsen	Culp
30—At Det.	L	3-5	Cain	Peterson
JULY—				
1—At Det.	L	5-6§	Timmerman	Klimkowski
2—At Det.	L	0-5	Niekro	Stottlemyre
3—Wash.	L	3-4	Brunet	Bahnsen
4—Wash.	W	4-2	Klimkowski	Cox
5—Wash.	L	3-7	Bosman	Peterson
5—Wash.	L	3-7	Shellenback	Waslewski
7—At Balt.	L	2-6‡	Cuellar	McDaniel
8—At Balt.	L	8-9	Drabowsky	McDaniel
9—At Balt.	W	7-5*	Cumberland	Lopez
10—At Wash.	L	1-2	Bosman	Kline
11—At Wash.	W	3-1	Hannan	Snellenback
12—At Wash.	L	3-7	Hannan	Stottlemyre
16—Oakland	L	2-8	Dobson	Peterson
16—Oakland	W	4-1	Bahnsen	Segui
17—Oakland	W	7-1	Stottlemyre	Hunter
18—Oakland	W	7-2	Kline	Roland
19—Calif.	L	2-5	May	Cumberland
19—Calif.	L	1-3	Murphy	Kekich
20—Calif.	W	6-1	Peterson	Messersmith
21—Milw.	W	4-2	Bahnsen	Lockwood
22—Milw.	L	1-4	Bolin	Stottlemyre
24—At Oak.	L	0-11	Dobson	Kline
25—At Oak.	L	0-1	Segui	Peterson
26—At Oak.	L	3-4	Hunter	Bahnsen
27—At Calif.	W	5-2‡	Stottlemyre	May
28—At Calif.	W	6-5	McCormick	Garrett
29—At Calif.	W	8-3	Klimkowski	Wright
31—At Milw.	W	7-3	Bahnsen	Bolin
31—At Milw.	W	5-3	Peterson	Brabender
AUGUST—				
1—At Milw.	W	4-1x	Klimkowski	Humphreys
2—At Milw.	L	5-9	Gelnar	Klimkowski
4—At Cleve.	L	1-6	Hargan	Kline
5—At Cleve.	W	7-3	Peterson	McDowell
6—Detroit	L	1-2	Kilkenny	Stottlemyre
6—Detroit	W	7-5	Klimkowski	Hiller
7—Detroit	W	5-1	Waslewski	Cain
8—Balt.	L	2-4	McNally	Kekich
9—Balt.	W	6-4§	Aker	Hall
9—Balt.	L	9-12§	Watt	Klimkowski
11—Chicago	W	7-1	Stottlemyre	Janeski
12—Chicago	L	1-5	Johnson	Bahnsen
13—Chicago	W	4-3	Aker	Weaver
14—Kan. C.	W	3-2‡	McDaniel	Drago
15—Kan. C.	W	5-4	Klimkowski	Burgmeier
16—Kan. C.	W	5-1	Bahnsen	Rooker
18—At Minn.	L	7-8	Hall	McDaniel

AUGUST—			Winner	Loser
19—At Minn.	L	0-3	Perry	Peterson
20—At Minn.	W	4-3	Stottlemyre	Zepp
21—At Chi.	W	4-2	Kline	Janeski
22—At Chi.	L	2-3	Johnson	Bahnsen
23—At Chi.	L	0-2	John	Peterson
23—At Chi.	W	7-5	Kekich	Miller
24—At K. C.	L	7-8	Burgmeier	Klimkowski
25—At K. C.	W	2-1	Peterson	Drago
26—At K. C.	W	3-0	Bahnsen	Bunker
28—Minn.	W	6-0	Peterson	Kaat
28—Minn.	W	2-1	Kekich	Perranoski
29—Minn.	L	1-3	Zepp	Stottlemyre
30—Minn.	W	5-2	Kline	Blyleven
31—Balt.	L	2-10	Cuellar	Bahnsen
SEPTEMBER—				
1—Balt.	W	4-2	Peterson	Hardin
2—Balt.	W	3-2	Kekich	McNally
3—Balt.	L	4-8	Palmer	Stottlemyre
4—Cleve.	W	3-2	Kline	Hand
5—Cleve.	W	3-1	Bahnsen	Dunning
6—Cleve.	W	4-1	Peterson	Paul
7—At Wash.	W	4-3	Kline	Bosman

SEPTEMBER—			Winner	Loser
8—At Wash.	W	7-3	Stottlemyre	Shellenback
9—At Balt.	L	0-1	Cuellar	Kline
10—At Balt.	L	1-2	McNally	Bahnsen
11—At Cleve.	L	2-3	Paul	Peterson
12—At Cleve.	L	3-4§	Chance	Klimkowski
13—At Cleve.	L	1-3	Hargan	Stottlemyre
15—Boston	W	8-6	Bahnsen	Culp
15—Boston	W	3-2	Kline	Nagy
16—Boston	L	1-3	Moret	Peterson
17—Boston	L	4-5‡	Bolin	Aker
18—At Det.	W	5-0	Klimkowski	Kilkenny
19—At Det.	W	7-6	McCormick	Timmerman
20—At Det.	W	5-1	Kline	Lolich
21—Wash.	W	5-2	Peterson	Gogolewski
22—Wash.	W	2-1	Stottlemyre	Bosman
23—Wash.	W	6-4	Gardner	Coleman
25—Detroit	L	1-3	Lolich	Kline
25—Detroit	W	8-3	McDaniel	Scherman
26—Detroit	W	2-1	Peterson	Reed
27—Detroit	W	4-2	Stottlemyre	Hiller
29—At Bos.	L	4-5	Bolin	Kline
30—At Bos.	W	4-3	Peterson	Nagy

* Game halted by rain with one out in last of eighth.   † Game halted by rain with two outs in last of ninth.   ‡ 10 innings.   § 11 innings.   x 12 innings.   y 13 innings.   z 18 innings.

Bosox Land in Bunker With Hill Woes

By LARRY CLAFLIN

For the first time in four years, the Red Sox were never in contention for the pennant in 1970, and a fairly sharp plunge in attendance resulted. Another result was a drastic revision in the team's makeup at the end of the year.

Eddie Kasko took over as manager from the popular (with the fans) Dick Williams, and Kasko did not fare very well. Neither did his ball club until it spurted somewhat in September and gained third place, 21 games behind Baltimore and six behind New York, in the American League's East Division.

The dismissal of Williams as manager after the 1969 season was supposed to bring new happiness and camaraderie to the ball club. Much was written in spring training about the Red Sox being happier without the stern and sarcastic Williams. Happiness, however, did not bring notable success to the club.

Early-season pitching woes quickly ended any designs the Red Sox might have had on the pennant. By the time the pitching improved, it was too late.

Gary Peters, a new acquisition, started terribly after a sensational spring training record. He wound up with 16 wins, however, with a fine second half.

Jim Lonborg started well with four victories, but he soon faded with a renewal of his arm miseries. He was pitching in the minors by the time the season ended. His major league future is doubtful.

Sonny Siebert also started poorly, but he came on strong and had a good year. Ray Culp was good all year and was voted the team's best pitcher by the Boston baseball writers for the second straight season. He was the club's top winner with 17 victories.

The bullpen disappointed, with Sparky Lyle failing to repeat his excellent work of 1969.

As usual, the Red Sox did plenty of hitting. Carl Yastrzemski lost his

BOSTON RED SOX, 1970

Front row—Menez, batboy; Rogers, traveling secretary; Camilli, coach; Popowski, coach; Kasko, manager; C. Wagner, coach; Lenhardt, coach; LeRoux, trainer; Justice, batboy. Second row—Orlando, visiting club equipment manager; Yastrzemski, Petrocelli, Andrews, Smith, Scott, W. Conigliaro, Moses, A. Conigliaro, Fitzpatrick, equipment manager. Third row—Schofield, Kennedy, Satriano, Thomas, Pavletich, Romo, Brett, Fiore, Hartenstein. Back row—Lyle, Koonce, Siebert, Culp, Peters, Lee, G. Wagner, Phillips, Nagy.

fourth batting title on the final day of the season, but ended up with a career-high batting average.

Rico Petrocelli had another good year, but not as good as '69. Tony Conigliaro hit a career high in homers, but he was traded, anyway.

Mike Andrews started miserably with the bat, finished strongly and was traded. Rookie Billy Conigliaro had a good year. Only a September fade marred his excellent season.

The Boston bench was a disappointment. The hitting simply wasn't there.

When the season ended with a loss of about 250,000 in attendance, the Red Sox made some drastic moves. For the first time in memory, they traded hitters for speed and defense. They took huge gambles at the World Series and at the winter meetings in Los Angeles.

Conigliaro went to the Angels in a six-player trade in October. In November, the Red Sox traded for Luis Aparicio of the White Sox. Even at age 36, Aparicio loomed large in Boston plans, mostly because of his defensive genius.

Manager Kasko and General Manager Dick O'Connell both said they made the trades to bolster the team's defense and put some speed into the top of the batting order in front of the heavy sluggers. Kasko admitted he was weary of waiting for home runs on the road, home runs which came with far less frequency than at home in little Fenway Park.

Kasko's rookie year as manager was not particularly comfortable. The fans stayed cool toward him and the press was at times slightly tough. But, Owner Tom Yawkey and O'Connell both backed him to the hilt, at least outwardly.

As a new season approached, it was obvious that Kasko was on the spot. He seemed well aware of that fact.

Boston fans, who have turned out to the tune of more than 7,000,000 in four years, were not keen on the big trades. The pressure is heavier on the Red Sox to win than it has been in many years.

SCORES OF BOSTON RED SOX' 1970 GAMES

APRIL—			Winner	Loser	MAY—			Winner	Loser
7—At N. Y.	W	4-3	Peters	Stottlemyre	11—At Calif.	L	1-2z	LaRoche	Brett
9—At N. Y.	L	3-4	Peterson	Culp	12—At Calif.	L	5-6	Garrett	Lyle
10—At Wash.	W	4-1	Lonborg	Coleman	13—At Calif.	L	3-5	Tatum	Stange
11—At Wash.	L	3-4	Bosman	Siebert	15—Cleve.	L	0-3	McDowell	Peters
12—At Wash.	L	5-6	Cox	Peters	16—Cleve.	W	6-2	Culp	Higgins
14—N. York	W	8-3	Culp	Peterson	19—Detroit	W	5-4	Lonborg	Lasher
15—N. York	W	6-2	Lonborg	Burbach	20—At Cleve.	L	2-7	McDowell	Siebert
16—N. York	W	8-5	Stange	Aker	21—At Cleve.	L	7-10	Miller	Lee
17—At Det.	L	2-3‡	Lasher	Brett	22—At Balt.	L	4-7	Hall	Peters
18—At Det.	L	1-5	Lolich	Lee	23—At Balt.	L	0-3	Palmer	Culp
20—Balt.	L	2-3*	Palmer	Culp	24—At Balt.	L	1-2†	Watt	Lyle
22—Balt.	W	5-2	Romo	McNally	24—At Balt.	W	4-3	Siebert	Phoebus
25—Milw.	L	4-10	Krausse	Stange	25—Wash.	W	5-3	Lee	Bosman
25—Milw.	W	3-0	Peters	Bolin	26—Wash.	L	5-7	Grzenda	Peters
26—Milw.	L	3-5	Brabender	Culp	27—Wash.	L	5-7	Knowles	Culp
27—Oakland	W	4-3	Romo	Hunter	29—Chicago	W	4-3	Lonborg	Wood
28—Oakland	W	2-1	Lee	Downing	30—Chicago	W	7-5	Romo	Crider
29—Oakland	W	5-3	Siebert	Dobson	31—Chicago	L	13-22	Weaver	Peters
30—Oakland	W	8-7	Peters	Roland	JUNE—				
MAY—					2—Minn.	W	5-1	Culp	Perry
1—Calif.	W	8-3	Culp	Murphy	4—Minn.	W	5-1	Siebert	Kaat
2—Calif.	L	4-8	Garrett	Jarvis	5—Kan. C.	W	4-2	Nagy	Butler
5—At Milw.	W	6-0	Siebert	Brabender	7—Kan. C.	W	7-4	Stange	Burgmeier
6—At Milw.	L	3-4	Bolin	Phillips	7—Kan. C.	W	5-2	Romo	Fitzmorris
7—At Milw.	L	1-5	Krausse	Culp	9—At Chi.	L	2-4	Janeski	Siebert
8—At Oak.	L	1-7	Dobson	Lonborg	10—At Chi.	W	7-6y	Romo	Wood
9—At Oak.	W	5-3	Siebert	Segui	12—At Minn.	L	2-5	Perry	Peters
10—At Oak.	L	4-7	Fingers	Peters	13—At Minn.	W	6-4	Culp	Kaat

DETROIT TIGERS, 1970

Front row—Wert, Wilson, Resinger, coach; Moses, coach; Smith, manager; Okrie, coach; Roarke, coach; Gutierrez, McAuliffe, Horton. Second row—Behm, trainer; Hand, equipment manager; Kaline, G. Brown, Szotkiewicz, McLain, Northrup, Maddox, Desmond, special events director. Third row—Freehan, Niekro, Timmerman, Price, Cash, Hiller, Cain, Stanley. Back row—Lolich, Jones, I. Brown, Scherman, Kilkenny, Patterson. Seated in front—Smith, DeSantis, batboys.

JUNE—			Winner	Loser
14—At Minn.	L	2-10	Blyleven	Siebert
15—At K. C.	L	6-7	Monteagudo	Koonce
16—At K. C.	W	7-5	Peters	Butler
17—At K. C.	W	3-1	Brett	Morehead
18—N. York	L	2-3	Waslewski	Culp
19—N. York	W	7-4	Siebert	Pahnsen
20—N. York	L	3-8	Stottlemyre	Nagy
21—N. York	L	10-14‡	McDaniel	Santiago
22—Balt.	L	8-9	Hall	Lyle
23—Balt.	W	5-1	Culp	Palmer
24—Balt.	W	6-5	Wagner	Watt
25—Balt.	L	8-13y	Drabowsky	Santiago
27—At N. Y.	W	4-0	Peters	Wasiewski
28—At N. Y.	W	5-3	Brett	Stottlemyre
28—At N. Y.	L	2-8	Bahnsen	Culp
30—Wash.	L	1-3	Bosman	Siebert
JULY—				
1—Wash.	W	6-5	Nagy	Coleman
2—Wash.	W	5-0	Peters	Such
3—Cleve.	W	2-1	Culp	Hennigan
3—Cleve.	W	5-4	Wagner	Ellsworth
4—Cleve.	W	5-1	Siebert	Dunning
5—Cleve.	W	8-4	Nagy	Austin
6—At Det.	L	3-6	Cain	Peters
7—At Det.	W	8-4	Culp	Wilson
7—At Det.	L	3-4†	Kilkenny	Koonce
8—At Det.	L	2-3	Lolich	Phillips
9—At Det.	L	3-7	Patterson	Wagner
10—At Cleve.	W	7-1	Peters	Hand
11—At Cleve.	L	1-3	McDowell	Brett
12—At Cleve.	W	6-2	Culp	Dunning
12—At Cleve.	W	8-2	Siebert	Lasher
16—Milw.	W	6-5†	Romo	Bolin
17—Milw.	W	8-2	Siebert	Brabender
18—Milw.	L	5-10	Krausse	Lyle
19—Oakland	W	9-4	Culp	Pingers
20—Oakland	L	2-3	Dobson	Brett
21—Calif.	L	6-10	Wright	Nagy
22—Calif.	W	7-4	Peters	Bradley
22—Calif.	W	8-3	Siebert	Queen
23—Calif.	L	1-4	Tatum	Brett
24—At Milw.	L	4-8	Krausse	Culp
25—At Milw.	L	2-6	Pattin	Nagy
26—At Milw.	W	12-5	Peters	Lockwood
28—At Oak.	L	4-6	Dobson	Romo
29—At Oak.	W	4-1	Culp	Segui
30—At Oak.	L	1-2	Hunter	Koonce
31—At Calif.	W	2-0	Siebert	Murphy
AUGUST—				
1—At Calif.	W	8-0	Peters	Garrett
2—At Calif.	L	3-8	Bradley	Romo
4—At Balt.	L	2-5	McNally	Culp
5—At Balt.	L	0-3	Palmer	Siebert
6—At Wash.	L	2-5	Cox	Peters
7—At Wash.	W	3-1	Koonce	Hannan

AUGUST—			Winner	Loser
8—Detroit	L	5-6	Patterson	Hartenstein
9—Detroit	W	7-4	Culp	Lolich
10—Detroit	W	11-10	Siebert	Niekro
12—Kan. C.	W	7-4	Peters	Rooker
12—Kan. C.	L	3-4	Abernathy	Brett
13—Kan. C.	L	3-11	Fitzmorris	Romo
14—Minn.	W	8-1	Culp	Zepp
15—Minn.	W	5-3	Siebert	Perry
15—Minn.	W	11-7	Wagner	Perranoski
16—Minn.	L	6-9	Blyleven	Peters
17—Chicago	W	7-2	Koonce	Johnson
18—Chicago	W	8-4	Brett	Miller
19—Chicago	L	5-13	Wood	Culp
21—At K. C.	L	1-2§	Abernathy	Brett
22—At K. C.	W	8-1	Peters	Rooker
23—At K. C.	L	3-4	Johnson	Lyle
25—At Minn.	W	1-0	Brett	Hall
26—At Minn.	L	0-7	Blyleven	Culp
27—At Minn.	L	2-5	Perry	Siebert
28—At Chi.	W	5-4	Peters	John
29—At Chi.	L	9-13	Miller	Hartenstein
30—At Chi.	W	21-11	Brett	Janeski
30—At Chi.	W	4-1	Nagy	Magnuson
31—Detroit	W	4-2	Culp	Lolich
SEPTEMBER—				
1—Detroit	L	9-10	Patterson	Siebert
2—Detroit	L	4-6	Patterson	Lyle
2—Detroit	W	10-1	Koonce	Cain
3—Detroit	W	5-2	Brett	Niekro
4—Balt.	L	6-8	Drabowsky	Hartenstein
5—Balt.	L	2-3	Hall	Culp
6—Balt.	W	9-8‡	Lyle	Richert
7—At Cleve.	W	4-3	Peters	McDowell
7—At Cleve.	L	2-8	Chance	Koonce
8—At Cleve.	W	4-3	Brett	Hargan
9—At Det.	W	4-1	Nagy	Kilkenny
10—At Det.	W	14-0	Culp	Cain
11—At Balt.	L	2-3x	Watt	Lyle
12—At Balt.	L	1-5	Phoebus	Peters
13—At Balt.	L	2-13	Cuellar	Brett
15—At N. Y.	W	6-8	Bahnsen	Culp
16—At N. Y.	W	2-3	Kline	Nagy
16—At N. Y.	W	3-1	Moret	Peterson
17—At N. Y.	W	5-4†	Bolin	Aker
19—Wash.	W	7-3	Brett	Coleman
19—Wash.	W	11-3	Nagy	Hannan
20—Wash.	W	3-1	Culp	Shellenback
21—Cleve.	W	2-1	Siebert	Hand
22—Cleve.	W	8-2	Peters	McDowell
23—Cleve.	L	2-5	Hargan	Brett
24—At Wash.	W	4-3	Romo	Hannan
25—At Wash.	W	5-1	Culp	Shellenback
26—At Wash.	W	6-3	Siebert	Gogolewski
27—At Wash.	W	10-1	Peters	Bosman
29—N. York	W	5-4	Bolin	Kline
30—N. York	L	3-4	Peterson	Nagy

* Game halted by rain in top of seventh.   † 10 innings.   ‡ 11 innings.   § 12 innings.   x 13 innings.   y 14 innings.   z 16 innings.

Absenteeism Big Factor in Poor Tiger Production

By WATSON SPOELSTRA

What goes up must come down and the Tigers nearly hit bottom in the disenchanting 1970 season.

Remember the world champion Tigers of 1968? They finished a dozen games in front of the Orioles.

The slide began for Detroit the following season, but in 1970 they drifted 29 games back of the Orioles.

The 79-83 record for fourth place in the American League East wasn't good enough. The day after the season ended, Manager Mayo Smith was replaced by Billy Martin, who signed for $60,000 a year for two seasons.

Obviously, it wasn't all Mayo's fault. Denny McLain, his best pitcher,

was suspended three times and wound up spending only 58 games in uniform. In 14 starts, Denny slithered to a 3-5 record with one complete game. Denny was dealt to Washington as a result of the turmoil he created.

Willie Horton tore up his left ankle pursuing a fly ball in late July and never did get back.

Bill Freehan underwent spinal surgery for a lingering back condition and was out the last month.

Just about every other Tiger had a bad year at the plate. The Tigers finished 12th and last in the American League with a .238 team average.

Detroit gathered only 1,282 hits for a lowly 22nd place in both major leagues.

The pitching went sour and Mickey Lolich was the top winner with 14 games. Mickey also dropped 19 decisions for a backpedaling performance not seen in Detroit for 18 years.

The staff earned-run average of 4.09 was the highest in Detroit in two decades.

The defense wasn't there most of the time and Manager Martin said he was giving top priority to shoring up the fielding.

There were a few individual plus factors. Al Kaline finished his 18th Detroit season and passed the 2,500 hit mark. Detroit had a day in Kaline's honor on August 2 that cutdid anything Tiger Stadium ever has seen.

When the season was over, Kaline had played in his 2,357th game, putting him second only to Ty Cobb in Detroit.

Unheralded Cesar Gutierrez achieved an American League first with a 7-for-7 batting performance against Cleveland in the 12-inning second game of the June 21 doubleheader.

Les Cain, young lefthander, won eight straight games early in the year for a pitching highlight. Later, Daryl Patterson took seven in a row as a relief pitcher.

The No. 1 happening of all was Tom Timmerman's bullpen work. The big righthander racked up 27 saves and won six games while making 61 appearances for the Detroit record.

SCORES OF DETROIT TIGERS' 1970 GAMES

APRIL—		Winner	Loser		MAY—		Winner	Loser
6—At Wash.	W 5-0	Lolich	Bosman		10—Kan. C.	L 7-9	Fitzmorris	Lasher
7—At Wash.	L 4-14	Cox	Wilson		11—Chicago	L 5-9	Crider	Niekro
8—At Wash.	W 3-0	Niekro	Brunet		12—Chicago	L 2-7	Janeski	Cain
10—At Balt.	L 2-3*	Hall	Lolich		15—At N. Y.	L 1-4	Bahnsen	Lolich
11—At Balt.	L 3-5	McNally	Wilson		16—At N. Y.	L 4-7	Hamilton	Scherman
12—At Balt.	W 7-2	Niekro	Cuellar		19—At Bos.	L 4-5	Lonborg	Lasher
14—Cleve.	W 12-4	Lolich	Hand		20—Balt.	W 4-0	Lolich	Phoebus
16—Cleve.	W 4-2	Wilson	Chance		21—Balt.	W 6-4	Cain	McNally
17—Boston	W 3-2†	Lasher	Brett		21—Balt.	L 1-3	Richert	Hiller
18—Boston	W 5-1	Lolich	Lee		22—Wash.	W 3-2	Niekro	Hannan
21—At Cleve.	W 5-3	Wilson	Hargan		23—Wash.	L 5-6	Shellenback	Patterson
22—At Cleve.	W 5-0	Lolich	McDowell		24—Wash.	L 4-6	Coleman	Lolich
24—At Minn.	W 8-6	Hiller	Hall		25—N. York	W 4-3	Cain	Hamilton
25—At Minn.	L 3-4	Williams	Timmerman		26—N. York	W 5-0	Wilson	Stottlemyre
26—At Minn.	L 0-6	Tiant	Lolich		27—N. York	L 2-3	Peterson	Niekro
28—At K. C.	W 8-3	Niekro	Bunker		29—At Milw.	W 5-4	Lolich	Lockwood
29—At K. C.	W 8-2	Kilkenny	Drago		30—At Milw.	L 7-9	Gelnar	Hiller
30—At K. C.	L 2-3*	Wright	Lasher		31—At Milw.	L 6-7	Baldwin	Saunders
MAY—					JUNE—			
1—At Chi.	L 6-13	Horlen	Cain		2—At Calif.	L 2-3*	Doyle	Niekro
2—At Chi.	L 2-3	Wood	Niekro		3—At Calif.	W 5-4†	Hiller	Fisher
3—At Chi.	W 6-5	Kilkenny	Wynne		4—At Calif.	W 4-2	Cain	Murphy
5—Minn.	L 5-8	Tiant	Lolich		5—At Oak.	L 2-4	Segui	Wilson
6—Minn.	W 5-2	Cain	Boswell		6—At Oak.	W 6-4	Niekro	Dobson
7—Minn.	L 2-6	Perry	Niekro		7—At Oak.	L 2-5	Lindblad	Lolich
8—Kan. C.	L 3-9	Johnson	Kilkenny		9—Milw.	W 8-3	Cain	Peters
9—Kan. C.	W 7-4	Hiller	Hedlund		10—Milw.	W 7-5	Saunders	Gelnar

			Winner	Loser					Winner	Loser
JUNE—						**AUGUST—**				
11—Milw.	W	6-2	Niekro	Brabender		6—At N. Y.	W	2-1	Kilkenny	Stottlemyre
12—Calif.	L	2-5	Messersmith	Hiller		6—At N. Y.	L	5-7	Klimkowski	Hiller
13—Calif.	W	6-5	Patterson	Tatum		7—At N. Y.	L	1-5	Waslewski	Cain
14—Calif.	W	8-4	Wilson	Wright		8—At Bos.	W	6-5	Patterson	Hartenstein
15—Oakland	L	7-12	Dobson	Niekro		9—At Bos.	L	4-7	Culp	Lolich
16—Oakland	W	5-1	Kilkenny	Fingers		10—At Bos.	L	10-11	Siebert	Niekro
17—Oakland	W	9-7	Scherman	Segui		11—At Milw.	W	2-1	Kilkenny	Downing
19—At Cleve.	L	2-4	McDowell	Lolich		12—At Milw.	L	5-6	Brabender	Timmerman
20—At Cleve.	L	1-2	Chance	Wilson		13—At Milw.	L	2-3	Pattin	McLain
21—At Cleve.	W	6-5	Niekro	Hand		14—At Calif.	L	3-7	Wright	Lolich
21—At Cleve.	W	9-8‡	Timmerman	Hennigan		15—At Calif.	W	5-1	Niekro	Allen
23—At Wash.	L	2-6	Brunet	Lolich		16—At Calif.	W	7-1	Cain	May
24—At Wash.	W	3-2*	Scherman	Knowles		17—At Oak.	W	5-3	Patterson	Grant
25—At Wash.	W	2-1	Cain	Bosman		18—At Oak.	W	3-1	Lolich	Dobson
26—Cleve.	W	7-1	Niekro	Hand		19—At Oak.	L	0-7	Segui	Kilkenny
27—Cleve.	L	0-3	Austin	Lolich		21—Milw.	W	6-4	Cain	Downing
28—Cleve.	L	2-8	McDowell	Wilson		22—Milw.	W	5-2	McLain	Krausse
28—Cleve.	W	5-1	Kilkenny	Paul		23—Milw.	W	1-0	Lolich	Pattin
30—N. York	W	5-3	Cain	Peterson		25—Calif.	L	4-6‡	Messersmith	Timmerman
JULY—						25—Calif.	L	6-10	Tatum	LaGrow
1—N. York	W	6-5†	Timmerman	Klimkowski		26—Calif.	L	3-6	Wright	McLain
2—N. York	W	5-0	Niekro	Stottlemyre		28—Oakland	L	2-5	Odom	Lolich
3—At Balt.	L	0-4	Cuellar	Lolich		29—Oakland	L	2-5	Segui	Cain
4—At Balt.	W	6-5	Hiller	Richert		30—Oakland	W	6-5	Timmerman	Locker
5—At Balt.	L	0-2	Palmer	McLain		31—At Bos.	L	2-4	Culp	Lolich
6—Boston	W	6-3	Cain	Peters		**SEPTEMBER—**				
7—Boston	W	4-8	Culp	Wilson		1—At Bos.	W	10-9	Patterson	Siebert
7—Boston	W	4-8*	Kilkenny	Koonce		2—At Bos.	W	6-4	Patterson	Lyle
8—Boston	W	3-2	Lolich	Phillips		2—At Bos.	L	1-10	Koonce	Cain
9—Boston	W	7-3	Patterson	Wagner		3—At Bos.	L	2-5	Brett	Niekro
10—Balt.	W	4-2	Cain	Palmer		4—At Wash.	W	6-3	Patterson	Knowles
11—Balt.	L	5-6	Cuellar	Niekro		5—At Wash.	L	2-3§	Pina	Reed
11—Balt.	W	7-3	Lolich	McNally		6—At Wash.	W	8-7‡	Scherman	Hannan
12—Balt.	L	3-13	Hall	McLain		7—Balt.	W	5-2	Niekro	Palmer
16—At Chi.	W	11-6	Scherman	Janeski		8—Balt.	L	3-6	Lopez	Lolich
17—At Chi.	W	4-3	Timmerman	Wood		9—Boston	L	1-4	Nagy	Kilkenny
17—At Chi.	W	5-4	Lolich	Magnuson		10—Boston	L	0-14	Culp	Cain
19—At K. C.	W	2-0	Niekro	Drago		11—Wash.	L	2-4	Gogolewski	Niekro
19—At K. C.	W	6-4	Reed	Abernathy		12—Wash.	W	6-4	Timmerman	Grzenda
20—At K. C.	L	0-2	Rooker	Cain		13—Wash.	L	0-10	Coleman	Kilkenny
21—At Minn.	W	5-2	McLain	Zepp		15—At Cleve.	L	3-4	Mingori	Reed
22—At Minn.	L	1-2	Perry	Lolich		16—At Cleve.	W	6-3	Lolich	Paul
23—At Minn.	L	1-2	Blyleven	Niekro		17—At Cleve.	L	2-6	McDowell	Niekro
24—Chicago	L	2-5	Stange	Timmerman		18—N. York	L	0-5	Klimkowski	Kilkenny
24—Chicago	W	5-4	Hiller	Wood		19—N. York	L	6-7	McCormick	Timmerman
25—Chicago	W	9-4	McLain	Crider		20—N. York	L	1-5	Kline	Lolich
26—Chicago	L	0-4	John	Lolich		21—At Balt.	L	3-4‡	Hardin	Timmerman
28—Kan. C.	L	6-7	Abernathy	Scherman		22—At Balt.	L	2-10	Phoebus	Reed
29—Kan. C.	W	10-3	Cain	Rooker		24—At Balt.	L	4-7	Cuellar	Hiller
30—Kan. C.	L	2-3*	Abernathy	Timmerman		25—At N. Y.	W	3-1	Lolich	Kline
31—Minn.	W	10-9	Timmerman	Hamm		25—At N. Y.	L	3-8	McDaniel	Scherman
AUGUST—						26—At N. Y.	L	1-2	Peterson	Reed
1—Minn.	L	4-12*	Perranoski	Scherman		27—At N. Y.	L	2-4	Stottlemyre	Hiller
2—Minn.	L	3-4	Zepp	Niekro		29—Cleve.	L	2-5	Hargan	Lolich
3—Wash.	L	0-4	Bosman	Kilkenny		30—Cleve.	W	4-3	Reed	Rittwage
4—Wash.	L	1-4	Brown	McLain		**OCTOBER—**				
5—Wash.	W	3-1	Lolich	Shellenback		1—Cleve.	W	1-0	Hiller	Paul

* 10 innings.   † 11 innings.   ‡ 12 innings.   § 14 innings.

Indians See Hope in Higher Totem Pole Finish

By RUSSELL SCHNEIDER

On the surface. the improvement of the Cleveland Indians in 1970 was just one place higher, from sixth to fifth, in the American League East.

But the season was much better than that for the Tribe, which finished only 10 notches or five victories below .500 (76-86), 32 games in back of champion Baltimore, three behind fourth-place Detroit, and six ahead of cellar-dwelling Washington.

In 1969, when the bottom dropped out and the roof caved in on the Indians, they were 37 lengths under .500 (62-99), sixth by 46½ games, and trailed fifth-place New York by 18.

CLEVELAND INDIANS, 1970

Front row—Pinson, Klimchock, Deal, coach; Farrell, coach; Dark, manager; Lipon, coach; Evers, coach; Brown, Rollins. Second row—Bock, trainer; Fosse, Heidemann, Fuller, Foster, Hennigan, Leon, Lasher, Sims, Nettles, Paul, Hawkins, traveling secretary. Back row—Hand, Hinton, Dunning, Austin, McDowell, Ellsworth, Higgins, Uhlaender, Chance, Horton. Seated in front—Buynak, equipment manager; Shafer, batboy.

Even more importantly. however, is that, unlike the previous year, when the curtain fell on 1970, there was genuine optimism and hope for the baseball future in Cleveland.

That's primarily because of the almost-total youth movement to which the Indians were committed—with gratifying results—at the beginning of the 1970 season.

By season's end, the following otherwise-anonymous players had established themselves as being ready for 1971: catcher Ray Fosse, second baseman Eddie Leon, shortstop Jack Heidemann, third baseman Graig Nettles, outfielders Roy Foster and Buddy Bradford, and pitchers Rich Hand, Mike Paul, Steve Dunning, Phil Hennigan, Rick Austin and Steve Mingori.

At the same time, Steve Hargan made it all the way back from a 1968 elbow operation that had jeopardized his pitching career. Sam McDowell became a 20-game winner for the first time. And a few other youngsters made initially impressive impressions in late-season opportunities—namely infielder John Lowenstein, outfielder Ted Ford and pitchers Jim Rittwage and Vince Colbert.

So 1970, despite what the final standing of the clubs would indicate at first glance, wasn't bad at all for the Indians.

There were some negative aspects, of course, beginning with a badly-fractured right leg suffered by Ken Harrelson early in spring training (March 19) that kept him out of action until late September.

And Tony Horton missed the final six weeks of the season as he was sent home because of extreme physical exhaustion.

But by and large, 1970 represented an upturn, although it didn't begin that way.

The Indians got off to another losing start and were only 7-11 for the month of April. May was no better, as their record was just 9-16, but then things improved markedly. The Tribe was 16-12 for June, and 17-15 for July.

Then, after climbing as close as they ever got to the .500 mark (55-57 and 56-58), the Indians regressed slightly for the month of August, when their record was 15-15, and they finished with just 12-17 in September after losing five of the last six games, and nine of 12.

From May 29 until the end, Cleveland's record was a respectable 62-60, and after the All-Star Game break it was 38-38.

Individually, the outstanding Tribesmen were McDowell, who won 20 and lost 12 with a 2.92 earned-run average and led the American League in strikeouts (304 in 305 innings) for the third straight year and fifth in the last six; Fosse, who hit .307, top figure on the club, with 18 homers and 61 RBIs, and whose injury (broken index finger, September 3) might have been the biggest reason for the team's late letdown; Vada Pinson, who hit .286 and a career high of 24 homers with 82 RBIs, and Foster, THE SPORTING NEWS A. L. Rookie Player of the Year, with a .268 average and 23 homers.

Other good performances were registered by Hargan, whose 11-3 record included 10-1 from July 18 after a 37-day exile in Wichita (American Association); Leon, at .248, whose 56 RBIs were ranked No. 2 among all the second basemen in the A. L.; Nettles, who overcame a horrible start to bat .235 and lead the club with 26 homers, and Chuck Hinton, the "spare

part" of the Indians, who became their ace pinch-hitter, batting .318 with nine homers and 29 RBIs in 195 at-bats.

So, everything considered, 1970 was a pretty good year for Cleveland baseball. At least, it provided promise for the future.

SCORES OF CLEVELAND INDIANS' 1970 GAMES

APRIL—			Winner	Loser
7—Balt.	L	2-8	McNally	McDowell
8—Balt.	L	2-3	Cuellar	Moore
9—Balt.	L	1-13	Phoebus	Hand
11—At N. Y.	W	3-0	Chance	Bahnsen
12—At N. Y.	W	2-1	McDowell	Stottlemyre
12—At N. Y.	L	4-5	Aker	Higgins
14—At Det.	L	4-12	Lolich	Hand
16—At Det.	L	2-4	Wilson	Chance
18—Wash.	W	9-4	McDowell	Bosman
21—Detroit	L	3-5	Wilson	Hargan
22—Detroit	L	0-5	Lolich	McDowell
24—Chicago	W	4-1	Moore	Arrigo
25—Chicago	W	6-5	Hargan	John
26—Chicago	L	0-2	Horlen	Chance
27—At Minn.	W	5-1	McDowell	Boswell
28—At Minn.	W	3-1	Moore	Perry
29—At Minn.	L	0-1	Kaat	Hand
30—At Minn.	L	1-4	Tiant	Hargan
MAY—				
1—At K. C.	W	7-5	Hennigan	Drabowsky
2—At K. C.	L	3-4x	Hedlund	Miller
3—At K. C.	W	6-3	Moore	Rooker
5—At Chi.	L	1-2	John	Chance
6—At Chi.	L	1-2	Horlen	McDowell
8—Minn.	L	6-7	Williams	Moore
9—Minn.	L	3-5	Perranoski	Higgins
10—Minn.	W	5-4	McDowell	Boswell
13—Kan. C.	L	0-1‡	Fitzmorris	Hennigan
15—At Bos.	W	2-0	McDowell	Peters
16—At Bos.	L	2-6	Culp	Higgins
18—At Wash.	L	3-7	Brunet	Hand
19—At Wash.	L	1-3	Coleman	Moore
20—Boston	W	7-2	McDowell	Siebert
21—Boston	W	10-7	Miller	Lee
22—N. York	L	4-7	Peterson	Chance
23—N. York	W	4-3§	Hennigan	Hamilton
24—N. York	L	5-6	McDaniel	Lasher
24—N. York	L	7-8†	McDaniel	Lasher
25—At Balt.	L	2-6	McNally	Miller
26—At Balt.	L	0-7	Hardin	Chance
27—At Balt.	L	4-5	Hall	Paul
29—At Oak.	W	2-1	McDowell	Odom
30—At Oak.	L	4-5	Fingers	Moore
31—At Oak.	W	3-2	Ellsworth	Hunter
JUNE—				
2—At Milw.	W	4-1	McDowell	Brabender
2—At Milw.	W	9-5	Hennigan	Lockwood
3—At Milw.	W	7-6	Miller	Pattin
4—At Milw.	W	8-4	Hennigan	Peters
5—At Calif.	L	1-2	Wright	Paul
6—At Calif.	L	1-2	May	McDowell
7—At Calif.	W	6-4	Hand	Mes'rsmith
9—Oakland	L	2-5	Hunter	Moore
10—Oakland	L	4-6	Lindblad	Paul
11—Oakland	W	6-5*	Ellsworth	Lindblad
12—Milw.	L	1-4	Pattin	Hand
13—Milw.	W	10-6	Chance	Krausse
14—Milw.	W	9-2	Dunning	Lockwood
15—Calif.	W	3-2†	Chance	Queen
16—Calif.	W	9-2	Hand	Mes'rsmith
18—Wash.	W	6-3	Lasher	Shellenback
19—Detroit	W	4-2	McDowell	Lolich
20—Detroit	W	2-1	Chance	Wilson
21—Detroit	L	2-7	Niekro	Hand
21—Detroit	L	8-9‡	Timmerman	Hennigan
24—At N. Y.	W	7-2	McDowell	Stottlemyre
24—At N. Y.	L	4-5	Bahnsen	Lasher
25—At N. Y.	L	1-3	Peterson	Dunning
25—At Det.	L	1-7	Niekro	Hand
26—At Det.	W	3-0	Austin	Lolich
27—At Det.	W	8-2	McDowell	Wilson
28—At Det.	L	1-5	Kilkenny	Paul
30—At Balt.	L	2-4	McNally	Dunning

JULY—			Winner	Loser
1—At Balt.	L	0-3	Palmer	Austin
2—At Balt.	W	10-9	Higgins	Drabowsky
3—At Bos.	L	1-2	Culp	Hennigan
3—At Bos.	L	4-5	Wagner	Ellsworth
4—At Bos.	L	1-5	Siebert	Dunning
5—At Bos.	L	4-8	Nagy	McDowell
6—Wash.	W	6-4	McDowell	Coleman
7—Wash.	W	7-3	Ellsworth	Hannan
7—Wash.	W	7-5	Hennigan	Such
8—Wash.	W	6-5	Hennigan	Knowles
9—Wash.	L	3-9	Cox	Austin
10—Boston	L	1-7	Peters	Hand
11—Boston	W	3-1	McDowell	Brett
12—Boston	L	2-6	Culp	Dunning
13—Boston	L	2-8	Siebert	Lasher
16—At K. C.	W	6-0	Hand	Rooker
17—At K. C.	W	6-0	Dunning	Johnson
18—At K. C.	W	4-1	Hargan	Butler
19—At Minn.	W	3-1	McDowell	Blyleven
20—At Minn.	L	2-4	Kaat	Austin
21—Chicago	L	3-5	John	Dunning
22—Chicago	W	6-2	Hargan	Magnuson
23—Chicago	W	5-2	McDowell	Horlen
24—Kan. C.	L	2-5	Rooker	Hand
25—Kan. C.	L	4-8	Burgmeier	Lasher
26—Kan. C.	W	6-5	Dunning	Wright
26—Kan. C.	W	3-0	Hargan	Morehead
28—Minn.	L	2-5	Kaat	McDowell
29—Minn.	W	9-8	Chance	Boswell
30—Minn.	W	3-2	Hargan	Perry
31—At Chi.	L	4-5	Murphy	Ellsworth
AUGUST—				
1—At Chi.	W	3-2	McDowell	Janeski
1—At Chi.	W	4-2	Hand	Crider
2—At Chi.	L	7-8	Wood	Ellsworth
4—N. York	W	6-1	Hargan	Kline
5—N. York	L	3-7	Peterson	McDowell
6—Balt.	W	4-0	Chance	Cuellar
6—Balt.	L	1-7	Hardin	Dunning
7—Balt.	W	10-4	Higgins	Hall
8—At Wash.	W	4-2	Colbert	Knowles
9—At Wash.	L	3-7	Coleman	McDowell
9—At Wash.	W	6-3	Higgins	Brown
11—At Oak.	L	5-6	Roland	Chance
12—At Oak.	L	4-11	Lachemann	Austin
13—At Oak.	W	4-3	McDowell	Lindblad
14—At Milw.	L	3-4†	Bolin	Chance
16—At Milw.	L	3-4	Sanders	Higgins
17—At Calif.	L	0-3	Murphy	McDowell
18—At Calif.	L	1-12	Wright	Chance
19—At Calif.	W	2-0	Hand	May
21—Oakland	W	6-3	McDowell	Hunter
22—Oakland	W	6-5*	Higgins	Lachemann
23—Oakland	W	8-6	Austin	Locker
25—Milw.	L	2-4*	Sanders	Higgins
26—Milw.	W	7-2	Hargan	Downing
27—Milw.	L	2-14	Krausse	Dunning
28—Calif.	L	2-3	Tatum	Higgins
29—Calif.	L	5-1	Hand	Murphy
29—Calif.	W	14-1	McDowell	Garrett
30—Calif.	L	9-10	Messersmith	Colbert
31—At Wash.	L	4-5	Cox	Dunning
SEPTEMBER—				
1—At Wash.	W	4-3	Paul	Brown
2—At Wash.	L	1-4	Bosman	McDowell
3—At Wash.	W	4-2	Hargan	Hannan
4—At N. Y.	L	2-3	Kline	Hand
5—At N. Y.	L	1-3	Bahnsen	Dunning
6—At N. Y.	L	1-4	Peterson	Paul
7—Boston	L	1-4	Peters	McDowell
7—Boston	W	8-2	Chance	Koonce
8—Boston	L	3-4	Brett	Hargan

SEPTEMBER—		Winner	Loser	SEPTEMBER—		Winner	Loser
9—Wash.	L 4-5	Coleman	Hand	21—At Bos.	L 1-2	Siebert	Hand
10—Wash.	W 13-4	Dunning	Cox	22—At Bos.	L 2-8	Peters	McDowell
11—N. York	W 3-2	Paul	Peterson	23—At Bos.	W 5-2	Hargan	Brett
12—N. York	W 4-3†	Chance	Klimkowski	25—Balt.	L 7-9§	Richert	Hand
13—N. York	W 3-1	Hargan	Stottlemyre	26—Balt.	L 4-7†	Watt	Lasher
15—Detroit	W 4-3	Mingori	Reed	27—Balt.	L 3-4	Hall	McDowell
16—Detroit	L 3-6	Lolich	Paul	29—At Det.	W 5-2	Hargan	Lolich
17—Detroit	W 6-2	McDowell	Niekro	30—At Det.	L 3-4	Reed	Rittwage
18—At Balt.	L 3-4†	Richert	Lasher				
19—At Balt.	W 4-2	Rittwage	McNally	OCTOBER—			
20—At Balt.	L 0-7	Palmer	Paul	1—At Det.	L 0-1	Hiller	Paul

* 10 innings.   † 11 innings.   ‡ 12 innings.   § 13 innings.   x 17 innings.

Washington—Last in Peace and Last in War

By MERRELL WHITTLESEY

Player reps, Marvin Miller, sportswriters and commentators complain about the season being too long and they offer varied reasons, some of them weak. For the Washington Senators, the 1970 season was too long and they have statistical proof.

They lost their last 14 games.

Ted Williams avoided the sophomore jinx 30 years ago. He hit .327 his first year with the Red Sox and .344 his second. But the sophomore jinx hit him in Ted's second year as manager.

The Senators finished in the cellar in the American League East and, according to Owner Bob Short, he lost $1 million. Attendance dropped off almost 100,000. The club fell on sorry times.

There was some consolation in Frank Howard's feat of capturing two-thirds of the Triple Crown with his 126 RBIs and 44 homers, but the season was long for Hondo, who had a poor September.

It was also a frustrating month for Dick Bosman, the ERA king of 1969, who at one time had his sights on giving the Senators their first 20-game winner since Bob Porterfield in 1953. Bosman finished with 16-12. Bosman had two defeats and a no-decision game in his last three outings. His 2-0 victory over the Orioles September 17 was the Senators' last victory of the season.

Williams frequently placed the blame for the Senators' letdown on the cleanup spot in the order, where Mike Epstein batted in only 56 runs while he was there, and those who alternated with him were no better, plus Joe Coleman's failure to develop as a 15-game winner. Coleman and Casey Cox dropped off from their 1969 victory pace, and Jim Hannan lost his last six games.

The Senators had the player with the craziest set of statistics in the league in reliever Darold Knowles, who saved 27 games for others, but on his own won 2 and lost 14. The Senators simply could not get a run for the lefty in a tie ball game and, as he admitted, his pitching was not as good as it should have been.

The Senators lost the Presidential opener for the eighth straight year, but made big news in April when they traded Ken McMullen to the Angels for Aurelio Rodriguez and Rick Reichardt. After patting themselves on the back all season for getting Rodriguez, Short traded him away to the Tigers in the 8-player World Series time swap co-featuring Denny McLain.

The Senators won season's series from only the White Sox and Brewers,

WASHINGTON SENATORS, 1970

Front row—Unser, Hudson, coach; Susce, coach; Camacho, coach; Williams, manager; Wilber, coach; Terwilliger, coach; Fox, coach; Cullen; F. Baxter, clubhouse manager. Second row—Zeigler, trainer; Howard, French, Stroud, Knowles, B. Allen, Grzenda, Dukes, Maye, Casanova, Shellenback, McMullen. Back row—Ramos, H. Allen, Hannan, Epstein, Such, Cox, Brunet, Pina, Coleman, Bosman, Brinkman. Seated in front—E. Baxter, Oppermann, batboys.

although Milwaukee dealt Williams' team an early-season setback by sweeping a May series of three one-run games. They tied the Tigers and, surprisingly, the Twins. They finished one under .500 at home, but on the road lost 21 more than they won.

The Senators were respectable against righthanders, but were down 14 to southpaws, although Ted maneuvered and platooned as much or more than any manager in the league, and stoutly defended his moves.

Short is impatient when it comes to development of the big bonus players. He finally insisted that Williams bring up Jeff Burroughs for a look, but later admitted that it probably was a mistake. The 19-year-old Californian simply was not ready, and not only wasted a couple of weeks with the Senators, but could not get going at Denver when he was sent back.

Tom Grieve spent the last half of the season in the majors in a platoon and pinch-hitting role, but showed only a .198 average in 116 at-bats.

Howard led the league in walks as well as homers and RBIs and his strikeouts were not bad at 125. Many of his homers, of course, were tape-measure jobs, with perhaps the longest at Anaheim where, for a split second, it appeared that one of Hondo's best belts was going to hit the Big A. The guess was 475 feet. The 15-minute clubhouse ban stuck for the Knights of the Keyboard, a ban that prompted Dick Young to ask in a column at the end of the season, "If it is supposed to be so helpful to the players, how come the Senators finished last?" Ted had a little spat with the Knights in midsummer over what he termed excessive second-guessing, but after a couple of grim days, Ted greeted the writers with a cheery, "Where have you all been?" and everybody made up.

Ted said the 14-game losing streak did not affect his thinking for 1971. His mind on what was needed had been made up by Labor Day. Bosman sounded off late in the season, claiming some of the players were letting the club down, but Ted did not think so. He said he would have reacted more sternly to the 14-game streak if it had come earlier. "What good would it do now?" he asked, before a final clubhouse meeting in which he told the Senators all but eight or 10 should do some soul-searching over the winter.

SCORES OF WASHINGTON SENATORS' 1970 GAMES

APRIL—		Winner	Loser	MAY—		Winner	Loser
6—Detroit	L 0-5	Lolich	Bosman	6—At Calif.	L 2-4	Fisher	Knowles
7—Detroit	W 14-4	Cox	Wilson	7—At Calif.	L 0-8	Murphy	Coleman
8—Detroit	L 0-3	Niekro	Brunet	9—At Milw.	L 2-3*	Gelnar	Grzenda
10—Boston	L 1-4	Lonborg	Coleman	10—At Milw.	L 5-6	Pattin	Knowles
11—Boston	W 4-3	Bosman	Siebert	11—At Milw.	L 6-7	O'Donoghue	Grzenda
12—Boston	W 6-5	Cox	Peters	12—At Oak.	L 3-5†	Segui	Brunet
16—At Balt.	W 4-2	Coleman	Palmer	13—At Oak.	L 1-8	Odom	Shellenback
18—At Cleve.	L 4-9	McDowell	Bosman	15—Balt.	L 3-4†	Richert	Knowles
20—N. York	L 2-11	Bahnsen	Brunet	16—Balt.	L 3-4	McNally	Cox
21—N. York	W 7-5	Cox	Stottlemyre	18—Cleve.	W 7-3	Brunet	Hand
22—N. York	W 2-1y	Grzenda	Klimkowski	19—Cleve.	W 3-1	Coleman	Moore
23—N. York	L 6-11	Cumberland	Such	20—At N. Y.	W 2-0	Bosman	Bahnsen
24—Calif.	W 5-3	Bosman	Mes'rsmith	21—At N. Y.	L 0-2	Stottlemyre	Such
25—Calif.	L 3-5	May	Brunet	22—At Det.	L 2-3	Niekro	Hannan
26—Calif.	L 2-3	Murphy	Cox	23—At Det.	W 6-5	Shellenback	Patterson
27—Milw.	W 6-5*	Pina	Locker	24—At Det.	W 6-4	Coleman	Lolich
28—Milw.	W 9-6	Such	Lauzerique	25—At Bos.	L 3-5	Lee	Bosman
29—Milw.	W 4-0	Bosman	Krausse	26—At Bos.	W 7-5	Grzenda	Peters
30—Milw.	W 12-2	Brunet	Bolin	27—At Bos.	W 7-5	Knowles	Culp
				29—Kan. C.	W 5-4‡	Shellenback	Bunker
MAY—				30—Kan. C.	W 3-2	Bosman	Butler
1—Oakland	L 5-12	Hunter	Cox	31—Kan. C.	L 5-6	Burgmeier	Knowles
2—Oakland	L 3-6	Downing	Coleman				
3—Oakland	L 1-3	Fingers	Bosman	JUNE—			
4—Oakland	W 6-4	Pina	Segui	2—Chicago	W 4-3	Pina	Wood
5—At Calif.	W 6-1	Brunet	Mes'rsmith	3—Chicago	W 5-4	Coleman	John

		Winner	Loser				Winner	Loser
JUNE—					**AUGUST—**			
4—Chicago	L 3-7	Crider	Bosman		3—At Det.	W 4-0	Bosman	Kilkenny
5—Minn.	L 1-2	Blyleven	Cox		4—At Det.	W 4-1	Brown	McLain
6—Minn.	L 2-4	Perry	Hannan		5—At Det.	L 1-3	Lolich	Shellenback
7—Minn.	L 9-10†	Zepp	Grzenda		6—Boston	W 5-2	Cox	Peters
9—At K. C.	L 1-8	Drago	Cox		7—Boston	L 1-3	Koonce	Hannan
10—At K. C.	W 8-1	Coleman	Rooker		8—Cleve.	L 2-4	Colbert	Knowles
12—At Chi.	L 0-6	John	Brunet		9—Cleve.	W 7-3	Coleman	McDowell
13—At Chi.	W 12-7	Hannan	Janeski		9—Cleve.	L 3-6	Higgins	Brown
14—At Chi.	W 8-4	Bosman	Horlen		11—Minn.	W 3-2†	Knowles	Blyleven
14—At Chi.	W 5-3	Cox	Crider		12—Minn.	W 5-3	Hannan	Tiant
15—At Minn.	L 3-5	Zepp	Coleman		13—Minn.	L 1-0	Bosman	Kaat
16—At Minn.	L 3-7	Perry	Grzenda		14—Chicago	W 6-5*	Grzenda	Wood
17—At Minn.	W 3-1	Brunet	Kaat		15—Chicago	W 4-2	Brown	Crider
18—At Cleve.	L 3-6	Lasher	Shellenback		16—Chicago	W 2-1	Cox	Janeski
19—At Balt.	L 10-12	Palmer	Bosman		17—Kan. C.	W 7-0	Hannan	Johnson
19—At Balt.	L 2-3§	Richert	Knowles		18—Kan. C.	L 8-12	Fitzmorris	Bosman
20—At Balt.	L 4-5	Cuellar	Coleman		19—Kan. C.	L 1-2	Drago	Coleman
21—At Balt.	L 2-4	McNally	Such		21—At Minn.	L 3-4	Williams	Cox
23—Detroit	W 6-2	Brunet	Lolich		22—At Minn.	W 5-4*	Pina	Hall
24—Detroit	L 2-3*	Scherman	Knowles		23—At Minn.	W 11-1	Bosman	Perry
25—Detroit	L 1-2	Cain	Bosman		25—At Chi.	L 3-4	Wood	Knowles
26—Balt.	L 2-12	McNally	Coleman		26—At Chi.	L 1-3	Janeski	Cox
27—Balt.	W 5-3	Hannan	Palmer		28—At K. C.	W 2-1	Bosman	Johnson
28—Balt.	W 4-3‡	Hannan	Watt		28—At K. C.	L 1-3	Rooker	Hannan
29—Balt.	W 5-3	Shellenback	Cuellar		29—At K. C.	W 11-4	Brunet	Fitzmorris
30—At Bos.	W 3-1	Bosman	Siebert		30—At K. C.	L 3-4	Burgmeier	Pina
JULY—					31—Cleve.	W 5-4	Cox	Dunning
1—At Bos.	L 5-6	Nagy	Coleman		**SEPTEMBER—**			
2—At Bos.	L 0-5	Peters	Such		1—Cleve.	L 3-4	Paul	Brown
3—At N. Y.	W 4-3	Brunet	Bahnsen		2—Cleve.	W 4-1	Bosman	McDowell
4—At N. Y.	L 2-4	Klimkowski	Cox		3—Cleve.	L 2-4	Hargan	Hannan
5—At N. Y.	W 7-3	Bosman	Peterson		4—Detroit	W 3-6	Patterson	Knowles
5—At N. Y.	W 7-3	Shellenback	Waslewski		5—Detroit	W 3-2x	Pina	Reed
6—At Cleve.	L 4-6	McDowell	Coleman		6—Detroit	L 7-8‡	Scherman	Hannan
7—At Cleve.	W 3-7	Ellsworth	Hannan		7—N. York	L 3-4	Kekich	Bosman
7—At Cleve.	L 5-7	Hennigan	Such		8—N. York	L 3-7	Stottlemyre	Shellenback
8—At Cleve.	L 5-6	Hennigan	Knowles		9—At Cleve.	W 5-4	Coleman	Hand
9—At Cleve.	W 9-3	Cox	Austin		10—At Cleve.	L 4-13	Dunning	Cox
10—N. York	W 2-1	Bosman	Kline		11—At Det.	W 4-2	Gogolewski	Niekro
11—N. York	L 1-3	Bahnsen	Shellenback		12—At Det.	L 4-6	Timmerman	Grzenda
12—N. York	W 7-3	Hannan	Stottlemyre		13—At Det.	W 10-0	Coleman	Kilkenny
16—Calif.	L 2-3	LaRoche	Grzenda		15—Balt.	L 2-6	McNally	Cox
17—Calif.	L 0-10	Wright	Cox		16—Balt.	W 2-0	Gogolewski	Palmer
18—Calif.	W 4-0	Brunet	Bradley		17—Balt.	W 2-0	Bosman	Cuellar
19—Milw.	W 4-3	Shellenback	Humphreys		18—At Bos.	L 3-7	Brett	Coleman
20—Milw.	W 2-0	Hannan	Downing		19—At Bos.	L 3-11	Nagy	Hannan
21—Oakland	L 0-4	Segui	Bosman		20—At Bos.	L 1-3	Culp	Shellenback
22—Oakland	L 3-4	Lachemann	Knowles		21—At N. Y.	L 2-5	Peterson	Gogolewski
24—At Calif.	W 9-8*	Hannan	Tatum		22—At N. Y.	L 1-2	Stottlemyre	Bosman
25—At Calif.	W 5-0	Shellenback	Wright		23—At N. Y.	L 4-6	Gardner	Coleman
26—At Calif.	L 10-11†	Garrett	Knowles		24—Boston	L 3-4	Romo	Hannan
28—At Milw.	L 1-5	Downing	Hannan		25—Boston	L 1-5	Culp	Shellenback
29—At Milw.	W 4-2	Bosman	Krausse		26—Boston	L 3-6	Siebert	Gogolewski
30—At Milw.	L 2-6	Pattin	Brunet		27—Boston	L 1-10	Peters	Bosman
31—At Oak.	L 4-5	Lindblad	Knowles		29—At Balt.	L 2-3*	Drabowsky	Coleman
AUGUST—					29—At Balt.	L 2-3†	Watt	Knowles
1—At Oak.	L 0-5	Dobson	Cox		30—At Balt.	L 2-6	McNally	Hannan
2—At Oak.	W 6-2	Hannan	Segui		**OCTOBER—**			
2—At Oak.	L 0-1	Grant	Pina		1—At Balt.	L 2-3	Hardin	Pina

* 10 innings.   † 11 innings.   ‡ 12 innings.   § 13 innings.   x 14 innings.   y 18 innings.

WEST DIVISION

Twins Win Again — Best in West

By BOB FOWLER

Although they were champions of the West Division in 1969, the Twins underwent an intensive model changeover for 1970.

There was Bill Rigney, the man who had managed California for eight-plus seasons, who succeeded fired Billy Martin as Minnesota's manager. There were new coaches Marv Grissom, Bob Rodgers and Frank Crosetti.

Pitchers Luis Tiant and Stan Williams and outfielder Brant Alyea were obtained. Gone were the likes of Dean Chance, Ted Uhlaender, Bob Miller, John Roseboro, Joe Grzenda and Graig Nettles.

Martin and President Calvin Griffith had had several disagreements, resulting in the leadership change. Changes in player personnel resulted from the Twins losing three straight playoff games to Baltimore and looking bad doing it.

In 1970, Minnesota's mission was to win another division title and gain revenge against the Orioles. The Twins successfully defended their billing as the best in the West, but the playoffs proved to be another disaster.

When the season began, Rigney said he realized many of the regulars who enjoyed their best years ever in 1969 wouldn't hit as well again. To compensate, he said he hoped the pitching would improve. It didn't.

There had been two 20-game winners under Martin, but only Jim Perry could top that figure for Rigney, winning 24 and the league's Cy Young Award. Dave Boswell, Martin's other 20-game winner, had a 3-7 record and was plagued with physical and emotional problems throughout the year, finally ending the season on the disabled list in early August.

Luis Tiant, once a 20-game winner at Cleveland, had a 7-3 mark, but was lost for much of the season with a cracked shoulder blade. Jim Kaat, once a 20-game winner, too, had a 14-10 mark, but was erratic most of the season.

Those four were to have formed Rigney's starting rotation, but due to injuries and ineffectiveness, substitutions were needed.

A 19-year-old rookie named Bert Blyleven was promoted from the minor leagues in early June and he posted a 10-9 record, although at 19 he was the youngest player in the major leagues.

Another rookie righthander, Bill Zepp, was promoted from the bullpen in midseason and posted a 9-4 mark.

Tommy Hall, a 150-pound southpaw, also was promoted from the bullpen and ended with an 11-6 record.

The loss of Zepp and Hall left the bullpen with two capable relievers, Ron Perranoski and Williams. They appeared in 67 and 68 games, respectively, Perranoski saving a league record 34 with seven wins and Williams posting a 10-1 record with 15 saves.

While the pitching may have been erratic, the hitting was inconsistent, too.

As Rigney expected, there were drops. Harmon Killebrew hit 41 homers with 113 RBIs, but had 49 and 140 in 1969. Rich Reese hit .322 for Martin, but only .261 for Rigney. Leo Cardenas hit .280 in 1969, .247 a year later.

There was an injury, too. Rod Carew, the defending league batting champion, was leading again with a .376 average when he was hit while pivoting on a double play June 22. He needed knee surgery and didn't return until late September, when he pinch-hit a few times.

Rookie second baseman Danny Thompson filled in adequately on defense but hit only .219.

There were some outstanding individual performances.

Tony Oliva had the best year of his career with a .325 average, 23 homers and 107 RBIs. Cesar Tovar hit .300 for the first time in his career. Alyea had 16 homers and 61 RBIs with a .291 average in only 258 at-bats.

MINNESOTA TWINS, 1970

Front row—Tovar, Killebrew, Thompson, Rodgers, manager; Grissom, coach; Robertson, coach; Morgan, coach; Quilici, Tischinski, Tiant. Second row—Benson, clubhouse attendant; Crump, equipment manager; Cardenas, Renick, Perranoski, Holt, Zepp, Ratliff, Mitterwald, Boswell, Hall, Lentz, trainer; Wiesner, visiting clubhouse attendant. Back row—Carew, Reese, Alyea, Blyleven, Perry, Woodson, Williams, Manuel, Kaat, Allison, Oliva, Hamm. Seated in front—Cisewski, Boberg, Fisher, batboys.

As you might suspect, the team encountered several peaks and valleys. It started the season by compiling the league's best record in the first month of play.

Then it struggled through the summer and finally hit its worst streak one week in August, losing nine straight.

But the Twins regained their winning ways the final month when they opposed all West Division teams and again won the title by nine games over Oakland. They won 98 games, too, one more than the 1969 edition.

Then came October and the Orioles. The Twins were optimistic because they had taken the regular-season series from Baltimore, 7-5, including winning four of six in Baltimore.

But the Orioles won three straight again and it was back to the drawing board for Griffith and Rigney.

"We need to improve our pitching in 1971," Rigney said. "And we must defend the game better, especially in center field."

The Twins also will need a new third baseman since Griffith revealed he wants to move Killebrew to first for the remainder of his career.

With these moves, the Twins might make it 3-for-3 in the West.

And, perhaps, they can win a playoff game, if not a playoff, against the league's eastern establishment.

SCORES OF MINNESOTA TWINS' 1970 GAMES

APRIL—			Winner	Loser	JUNE—			Winner	Loser
7—At Chi.	W	12-0	Perry	John	2—At Bos.	L	1-5	Culp	Perry
9—At Chi.	W	6-4	Williams	Horlen	4—At Bos.	L	1-5	Siebert	Kaat
11—Oakland	W	8-2	Kaat	Odom	5—At Wash.	W	2-1	Blyleven	Cox
15—At Calif.	W	8-2	Perry	Messersmith	6—At Wash.	W	4-2	Perry	Hannan
16—At Calif.	L	2-3	May	Boswell	7—At Wash.	W	10-9‡	Zepp	Grzenda
17—At Oak.	L	2-5	Hunter	Kaat	9—At N. Y.	L	2-5	Bahnsen	Kaat
18—At Oak.	W	11-5	Tiant	Downing	10—At N. Y.	L	1-2	Stottlemyre	Blyleven
19—At Oak.	W	6-3	Perry	Dobson	12—Boston	W	5-2	Perry	Peters
21—Chicago	W	4-3	Kaat	John	13—Boston	L	4-6	Culp	Kaat
22—Chicago	W	3-1*	Tiant	Horlen	14—Boston	W	10-2	Blyleven	Siebert
23—Chicago	L	5-7	Sisk	Perranoski	15—Wash.	W	5-3	Zepp	Coleman
24—Detroit	L	6-8	Hiller	Hall	16—Wash.	W	7-3	Perry	Grzenda
25—Detroit	W	4-3	Williams	Timmerman	17—Wash.	L	1-3	Brunet	Kaat
26—Detroit	W	6-0	Tiant	Lolich	19—At K. C.	L	1-5	Drago	Blyleven
27—Cleveland	L	1-5	McDowell	Boswell	20—At K. C.	L	3-5	Rooker	Boswell
28—Cleveland	L	1-3	Moore	Perry	21—At K. C.	W	11-2	Perry	Butler
29—Cleveland	W	1-0	Kaat	Hand	22—At Milw.	W	4-3	Kaat	Brabender
30—Cleveland	W	4-1	Tiant	Hargan	23—At Milw.	L	3-4	Baldwin	Hall
MAY—					24—At Milw.	W	3-2	Boswell	Pattin
1—At Balt.	L	3-9	McNally	Boswell	25—At Milw.	L	1-4	Krausse	Perry
2—At Balt.	W	4-2	Perry	Cuellar	26—At Chi.	L	2-4	Miller	Kaat
3—At Balt.	W	4-3	Kaat	Palmer	27—At Chi.	W	9-1	Blyleven	Janeski
5—At Det.	W	8-5	Tiant	Lolich	28—At Chi.	W	9-1	Hall	Horlen
6—At Det.	L	2-5	Cain	Boswell	28—At Chi.	L	10-11	Murphy	Woodson
7—At Det.	W	9-6	Perry	Niekro	29—Kan. C.	W	5-4	Perry	Drago
8—At Cleve.	W	7-6	Williams	Moore	30—Kan. C.	W	8-5	Woodson	Johnson
9—At Cleve.	W	5-3	Perranoski	Higgins	**JULY—**				
10—At Cleve.	L	4-5	McDowell	Boswell	1—Kan. C.	W	2-1†	Perranoski	Rooker
12—Balt.	L	4-5	Cuellar	Hall	2—Kan. C.	W	5-2	Hall	Fitzmorris
13—Balt.	W	5-4†	Perranoski	Watt	3—Chicago	W	8-2	Perry	Horlen
14—Kan. C.	W	5-2	Hall	Morehead	4—Chicago	L	3-5§	Wood	Woodson
16—At Milw.	W	11-7	Boswell	Brabender	5—Chicago	W	12-3	Kaat	Miller
17—At Milw.	W	6-1	Perry	Krausse	6—At Oak.	W	2-1	Zepp	Segui
18—At K. C.	W	7-5	Zepp	Hedlund	7—At Oak.	W	4-2	Williams	Dobson
19—At K. C.	W	5-4†	Perranoski	Burgmeier	8—At Oak.	W	8-6	Perry	Hunter
20—At K. C.	W	10-5	Boswell	Johnson	9—At Calif.	W	4-2	Hall	Fisher
22—Calif.	L	2-3	Wright	Perry	10—At Calif.	L	1-2	Messersmith	Kaat
23—Calif.	W	5-4	Williams	Tatum	11—At Calif.	W	5-2	Zepp	Wright
24—Calif.	L	5-6	Doyle	Perranoski	12—At Calif.	L	2-6	LaRoche	Perry
25—Milw.	W	6-5	Hall	Lockwood	16—At Balt.	L	1-5	Cuellar	Hall
26—Milw.	W	6-2	Kaat	Bolin	17—At Balt.	W	6-5†	Perranoski	Watt
28—Milw.	W	11-2	Tiant	Morris	18—At Balt.	W	6-3	Perry	McNally
29—N. York	W	2-4	Kekich	Perry	19—Cleveland	L	1-3	McDowell	Blyleven
30—N. York	W	10-6	Perranoski	Hamilton	20—Cleveland	W	4-2	Kaat	Austin
31—N. York	W	7-6†	Williams	McDaniel	21—Detroit	L	2-5	McLain	Zepp

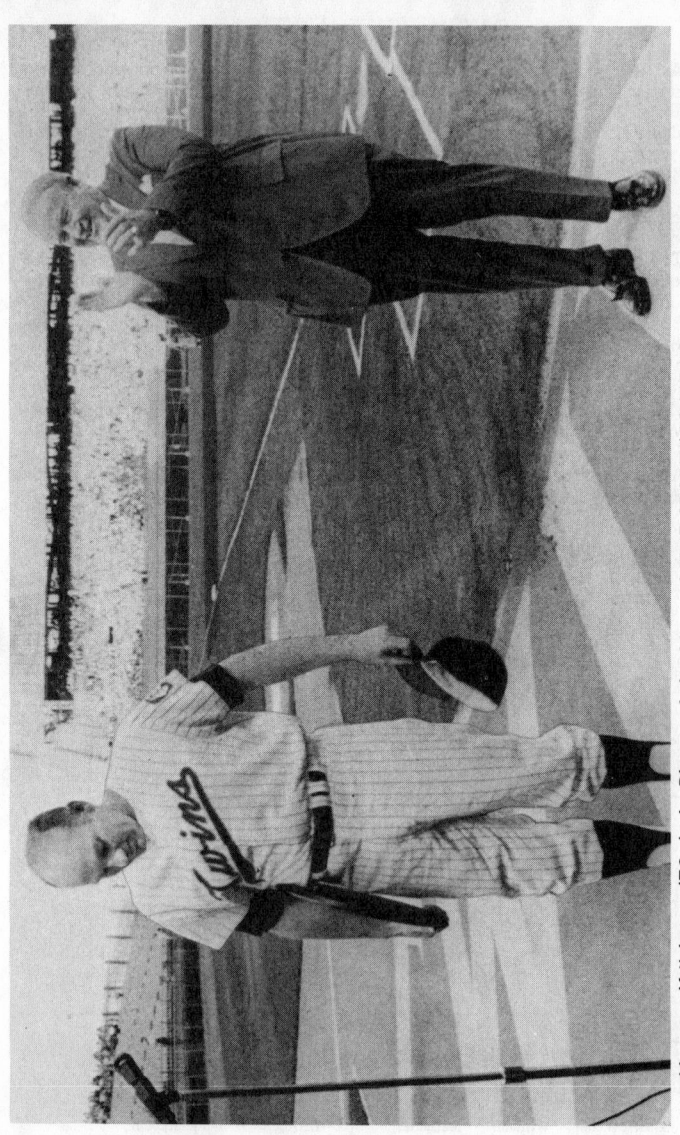

Harmon Killebrew, '70 A. L. Player of the Year of THE SPORTING NEWS, receives his 1969 MVP plaque from league head Joe Cronin.

Tony Oliva, who led Twin regulars in batting, crosses the plate after a 2-run homer against the A's. Danny Thompson (left), who was on base, and Rich Reese extend him five.

JULY—			Winner	Loser
22—Detroit	W	2-1	Perry	Lolich
23—Detroit	W	2-1	Blyleven	Niekro
24—Balt.	W	8-0	Kaat	Cuellar
25—Balt.	L	5-6	R. Hall	T. Hall
26—Balt.	L	1-11	McNally	Perry
27—Balt.	W	5-2	Blyleven	Palmer
28—At Cleve.	W	5-2	Kaat	McDowell
29—At Cleve.	L	8-9	Chance	Boswell
30—At Cleve.	L	2-3	Hargan	Perry
31—At Det.	L	9-10	Timmerman	Hamm
AUGUST—				
1—At Det.	W	12-4†	Perranoski	Scherman
2—At Det.	W	4-3	Zepp	Niekro
3—Milw.	W	2-1	Perry	Pattin
3—Milw.	L	2-4	Krausse	Tiant
4—Milw.	W	5-2	Blyleven	Bolin
5—Calif.	L	5-7	Queen	Perranoski
6—Calif.	W	2-1x	Williams	Doyle
7—Oakland	L	2-1†	Perry	Lachemann
8—Oakland	W	3-1	Tiant	Fingers
9—Oakland	L	0-3	Dobson	Blyleven
9—Oakland	L	3-6	Roland	Kaat
10—Oakland	L	3-7	Segui	Perranoski
11—At Wash.	L	2-3‡	Knowles	Blyleven
12—At Wash.	L	3-5	Hannan	Tiant
13—At Wash.	L	0-1	Bosman	Kaat
14—At Bos.	L	1-8	Culp	Zepp
15—At Bos.	L	3-5	Siebert	Perry
15—At Bos.	L	7-11	Wagner	Perranoski
16—At Bos.	W	9-6	Blyleven	Peters
18—N. York	W	8-7	Hall	McDaniel
19—N. York	W	3-0	Perry	Peterson
20—N. York	L	3-4	Stottlemyre	Zepp
21—Wash.	W	4-3	Williams	Cox
22—Wash.	L	4-5†	Pina	Hall
23—Wash.	L	1-11	Bosman	Perry
25—Boston	L	0-1	Brett	Hall
26—Boston	W	7-0	Blyleven	Culp
27—Boston	W	5-2	Perry	Siebert

AUGUST—			Winner	Loser
28—At N. Y.	L	0-6	Peterson	Kaat
28—At N. Y.	L	1-2	Kekich	Perranoski
29—At N. Y.	W	3-1	Zepp	Stottlemyre
30—At N. Y.	L	2-5	Kline	Blyleven
SEPTEMBER—				
1—At Milw.	W	4-0	Perry	Krausse
1—At Milw.	W	7-1‡	Kaat	Bolin
3—At Milw.	L	3-8	Pattin	Zepp
4—At Calif.	W	4-0	Blyleven	May
5—At Calif.	W	4-3	Perry	Murphy
6—At Calif.	W	3-1	Hall	Wright
7—Milw.	W	7-6	Williams	Krausse
7—Milw.	W	8-3	Haydel	Downing
8—Milw.	L	2-3	Pattin	Perranoski
9—Oakland	W	3-1	Perry	Dobson
10—Oakland	W	6-1	Hall	Hunter
10—Oakland	W	7-2	Kaat	Odom
11—Chicago	W	6-0	Zepp	Moore
12—Chicago	L	3-5	Johnson	Blyleven
13—Chicago	L	7-8	Crider	Williams
15—Calif.	W	7-5	Williams	Queen
15—Calif.	L	3-5	LaRoche	Perranoski
16—Calif.	L	1-5	Wright	Blyleven
17—Calif.	W	4-3	Perry	Murphy
18—At Chi.	W	5-4	Zepp	Johnson
19—At Chi.	W	5-3	Hall	John
20—At Chi.	W	8-1	Blyleven	Janeski
21—At Oak.	L	0-6	Blue	Perry
22—At Oak.	W	5-3	Kaat	Dobson
23—At Oak.	W	7-4	Hall	Hunter
25—At K. C.	W	1-0	Perry	Bunker
26—At K. C.	L	0-5	Johnson	Blyleven
27—At K. C.	L	3-4	Rooker	Tiant
28—Kan. C.	W	1-0	Hall	Drago
29—Kan. C.	L	13-14§	Abernathy	Hamm
30—Kan. C.	W	6-4	Haydel	York
OCTOBER—				
1—Kan. C.	W	4-0	Kaat	Johnson

* 5 innings. † 10 innings. ‡ 11 innings. § 12 innings. x 14 innings.

OAKLAND ATHLETICS, 1970

Front row—Donaldson, Odom, Posedel, coach; Hofman, coach; Hoscheit, coach; McNamara, manager; Lau, coach; Dahlgren, hitting instructor; Jackson, Hovley, Campaneris. Second row—Ciensczyk, equipment manager; Shishido, visiting clubhouse attendant; Tenace, Womack, Fernandez, Bando, Grant, Lindblad, Locker, Hunter, M. Lachemann, Rudi, LaRussa, Corwin, traveling secretary; Romo, trainer. Back row—Lewis, Mincher, Davis, Monday, Alou, Fingers, Duncan, Roland, Segui, Green, Dobson.

A's Hit Stone Wall, Jackson Hits Nothing

By RON BERGMAN

From start to finish, nothing seemed to work out as planned for the Athletics in 1970.

They stumbled out of the gate and quickly found themselves 7½ games behind and ten down in the loss column by the early date of May 21. The A's ranged from 11 games out on July 18 to 3½ on August 15, but by the time the season came to its acrimonious conclusion, they were in exactly the same position as the year before—second place in American League West, nine games back of the Twins.

The annual beheading of the manager took place one day after the A's posted an 89-73 record, their best since the old Philadelphia A's of 1932. Owner Charlie Finley dropped the blade on John McNamara's neck and, like a barber wearing a black hood, beckoned former Red Sox Skipper Dick Williams to be his 11th manager in 11 years.

Engendered by sagacious trades and the elevation of the popular McNamara from third base coach to manager, the A's began the season full of hope for a divisional flag. Much of the optimism stemmed from the 47-homer production by Reggie Jackson in 1969. But Jackson was a holdout for the first month of spring training and the lack of preparation contributed to a very slow start.

Jackson contended that subsequent sporadic benchings were on the personal orders of Finley, who at one point threatened to send the slugger to the minors. The two men traded charges throughout the season until the matter came to a head on September 5 in Oakland after Jackson pinch-hit a grand-slam homer.

As he crossed the plate, Jackson took off his cap, scowled up toward the owner's box and mouthed something. Finley reacted good-naturedly at first, but when the A's moved into the owner's home base of Chicago two days later, it was a different story.

Following a sweep of the Labor Day doubleheader from the White Sox for the eighth consecutive A's victory, Jackson was summoned to the manager's hotel suite where Finley also was present. A public apology attributed to Jackson emerged. Back in the starting lineup, Jackson had hit three homers in four games and gone 7-for-11. Now chastened, Jackson traveled with the team to the next series in Minnesota, dropped a crucial fly ball in the first game and went 0-for-9 with five strikeouts as the A's lost all three games and their last chance to challenge the Twins.

Jackson finished his often-interrupted season with 23 homers and 26 stolen bases, giving some indication of what might have been had harmony reigned. He wasn't the only disappointment by far. Second baseman Dick Green slumped to .190 and fielded poorly in the first half of the season. John (Blue Moon) Odom couldn't overcome arm troubles on his way to a so-so 9-8 record.

Without veteran reliever Mudcat Grant's 24 saves and six victories, the A's would've dropped out of sight completely. Grant became a fan favorite before he was dealt to the Pirates on September 13 for cash and a player later identified as minor league outfielder Angel Mangual.

Shortstop Campy Campaneris captured the stolen base title for the

fifth time in six years. His roommate and close friend, Diego Segui, was the league's earned-run leader at 2.56.

Despite not being able to win a game in August for the second straight year, Catfish Hunter finished 18-14, most victories by an A's pitcher since they moved from Philadelphia in 1955. Chuck Dobson shared the league shutout mark with five and once convincingly won eight starts in a row before elbow problems slowed him down.

Rookie lefthander Vida Blue gave some hope for the future with a no-hitter against the Twins on September 21 after being called up from the American Association for the last month. He hurled a one-hitter against the Royals on September 11.

First baseman Don Mincher led the team with a career-high 27 homers and outfielder Joe Rudi, never able to bat over .189 in three previous big league trials, hit .309 after the benchings of Jackson gave him a chance to play.

Judicious juggling of catchers Frank Fernandez, Dave Duncan and Gene Tenace produced 32 homers and 93 RBIs from that one position.

The A's drew 778,355 at home in 77 dates, an increase of 123 fans over the previous year. They played to 971,568 in 72 dates on the road.

SCORES OF OAKLAND ATHLETICS' 1970 GAMES

APRIL—		Winner	Loser	JUNE—		Winner	Loser
7—At K. C.	W 6-4	Odom	Bunker	2—Balt.	L 1-5	Palmer	Dobson
8—At K. C.	L 0-2	Drago	Hunter	3—Balt.	W 4-1	Grant	Cuellar
9—At K. C.	L 1-3	Ruder	Dobson	4—Balt.	W 4-2	Hunter	Phoebus
11—At Minn.	L 2-8	Kaat	Odom	5—Detroit	W 4-2	Segui	Wilsor.
13—Milw.	W 2-1	Hunter	Pattin	6—Detroit	L 4-6	Niekro	Dobson
14—Milw.	W 9-1	Downing	Brabender	7—Detroit	W 5-2	Lindblad	Lolich
15—Chicago	L 0-7	Janeski	Dobson	9—At Cleve.	W 5-2	Hunter	Moore
16—Chicago	W 5-1	Odom	John	10—At Cleve.	W 6-4	Lindblad	Paul
17—Minn.	W 5-2	Hunter	Kaat	11—At Cleve.	L 5-6*	Ellsworth	Lindblad
18—Minn.	L 5-11	Tiant	Downing	12—At Balt.	W 4-2†	Grant	Watt
19—Minn.	L 3-6	Perry	Dobson	13—At Balt.	W 10-7	Hunter	McNally
20—Kan. C.	L 2-4†	Hedlund	Segui	14—At Balt.	L 2-4*	Palmer	Talbot
21—Kan. C.	W 4-3	Hunter	Rooker	15—At Det.	W 12-7	Dobson	Niekro
22—Kan. C.	W 2-1	Downing	Bunker	16—At Det.	L 1-5	Kilkenny	Fingers
25—At N. Y.	W 3-0	Dobson	Bahnsen	17—At Det.	L 7-9	Scherman	Segui
26—At N. Y.	L 3-8	Stottlemyre	Odom	19—Chicago	L 2-4	Horlen	Odom
27—At Bos.	L 3-4	Romo	Hunter	20—Chicago	W 8-5	Grant	Moore
28—At Bos.	L 1-2	Lee	Downing	21—Chicago	W 6-3	Hunter	John
29—At Bos.	L 3-5	Siebert	Dobson	21—Chicago	W 5-4	Fingers	Miller
30—At Bos.	L 7-8	Peters	Roland	22—Kan. C.	W 2-1	Locker	Burgmeier
MAY—				23—Kan. C.	L 5-7	Drago	Dobson
1—At Wash.	W 12-5	Hunter	Cox	24—Kan. C.	W 5-1	Osteen	Rooker
2—At Wash.	W 6-3	Downing	Coleman	26—At Milw.	L 2-3§	Humphreys	Dobson
3—At Wash.	W 3-1	Fingers	Bosman	27—At Milw.	L 1-3	Brabender	Fingers
3—At Wash.	L 4-6	Pina	Segui	28—At Milw.	W 4-1	Segui	Bolin
5—N. York	W 11-3	Hunter	Bahnsen	28—At Milw.	W 4-1	Dobson	Downing
6—N. York	L 6-7	Stottlemyre	Downing	30—At Chi.	W 4-3	Hunter	John
7—N. York	L 5-7	Peterson	Fingers	JULY—			
8—Boston	W 7-1	Dobson	Lonborg	1—At Chi.	W 3-0	Fingers	Janeski
9—Boston	L 3-5	Siebert	Segui	2—At Chi.	W 10-6	Lachemann	Moore
10—Boston	W 7-4	Fingers	Peters	3—At Calif.	L 0-4	Wright	Dobson
12—Wash.	W 5-3†	Segui	Brunet	4—At Calif.	W 7-4	Hunter	May
13—Wash.	W 8-1	Odom	Shellenback	5—At Calif.	L 1-5	Messersmith	Fingers
15—Calif.	L 4-5	Tatum	Hunter	6—Minn.	L 1-2	Zepp	Segui
16—Calif.	W 11-3	Dobson	Murphy	7—Minn.	L 2-4	Williams	Dobson
16—Calif.	L 1-7	Wright	Odom	8—Minn.	L 6-8	Perry	Hunter
17—Calif.	W 6-5*	Roland	Garrett	10—Milw.	L 1-2	Bolin	Fingers
19—At Milw.	L 3-6	Morris	Hunter	11—Milw.	W 11-1	Segui	Brabender
20—At Milw.	L 7-8	Pattin	Fingers	12—Milw.	W 4-3	Grant	Pattin
22—At Chi.	W 9-8	Lindblad	Wood	12—Milw.	L 1-2	Krause	Hunter
23—At Chi.	W 12-2	Hunter	Horlen	16—At N. Y.	W 8-2	Dobson	Peterson
24—At Chi.	W 5-1	Dobson	John	16—At N. Y.	L 1-4	Bahnsen	Segui
24—At Chi.	W 5-2	Odom	Johnson	17—At N. Y.	L 1-7	Stottlemyre	Hunter
26—At Calif.	L 2-4	Murphy	Fingers	18—At N. Y.	L 2-7	Kline	Roland
27—At Calif.	W 4-3	Hunter	Wright	19—At Bos.	L 4-9	Culp	Fingers
28—At Calif.	W 2-0	Dobson	May	20—At Bos.	W 3-2	Dobson	Brett
29—Cleveland	L 1-2	McDowell	Odom	21—At Wash.	W 4-0	Segui	Bosman
30—Cleveland	W 5-4	Fingers	Moore	22—At Wash.	W 4-3	Lachemann	Knowles
31—Cleveland	L 2-3	Ellsworth	Hunter	24—N. York	W 11-0	Dobson	Kline

JULY—			Winner	Loser
25—N. York	W	1-0	Segui	Peterson
26—N. York	W	4-3	Hunter	Bahnsen
28—Boston	W	6-4	Dobson	Romo
29—Boston	L	1-4	Culp	Segui
30—Boston	W	2-1	Hunter	Koonce
31—Wash.	W	5-4	Lindblad	Knowles
AUGUST—				
1—Wash.	W	5-0	Dobson	Cox
2—Wash.	L	2-6	Hannan	Segui
3—Wash.	W	1-0	Grant	Pina
3—Calif.	L	0-5	May	Hunter
4—Calif.	W	4-3	Odom	Wright
5—At K. C.	W	4-1	Dobson	Drago
6—At K. C.	L	3-5	Fitzmorris	Locker
7—At Minn.	L	1-2†	Perry	Lachemann
8—At Minn.	L	1-3	Tiant	Fingers
9—At Minn.	W	3-0	Dobson	Blyleven
9—At Minn.	W	6-3	Roland	Kaat
10—At Minn.	W	7-3	Segui	Perranoski
11—Cleveland	W	6-5	Roland	Chance
12—Cleveland	W	11-4	Lachemann	Austin
13—Cleveland	L	3-4	McDowell	Lindblad
14—Balt.	W	4-0	Dobson	Hardin
15—Balt.	L	1-7	Cuellar	Segui
15—Balt.	L	1-2	McNally	Hunter
17—Detroit	L	3-5	Patterson	Grant
18—Detroit	L	1-3	Lolich	Dobson
19—Detroit	W	7-0	Segui	Kilkenny
21—At Cleve.	L	3-6	McDowell	Hunter
22—At Cleve.	L	5-6*	Higgins	Lachemann
23—At Cleve.	L	6-8	Austin	Locker
25—At Balt.	L	1-5	McNally	Segui
26—At Balt.	L	1-5	Palmer	Hunter
27—At Balt.	L	4-6	Cuellar	Dobson
28—At Det.	W	6-2	Odom	Lolich

AUGUST—			Winner	Loser
29—At Det.	W	5-2	Segui	Cain
30—At Det.	L	5-6	Timmerman	Locker
SEPTEMBER—				
1—Chicago	W	6-5	Lindblad	Wood
2—Chicago	W	2-1	Odom	Johnson
3—Chicago	W	4-3	Locker	Wood
4—Kan. C.	W	5-0	Hunter	Fitzmorris
5—Kan. C.	W	8-3	Lindblad	Drago
6—Kan. C.	W	7-1	Odom	Bunker
7—At Chi.	W	7-4	Fingers	John
7—At Chi.	L	3-7	Segui	Johnson
9—At Minn.	L	1-3	Perry	Dobson
10—At Minn.	L	1-6	Hall	Hunter
10—At Minn.	L	2-7	Kaat	Odom
11—At K. C.	W	3-0	Blue	Bunker
12—At K. C.	W	3-2	Grant	Johnson
13—At K. C.	L	7-8†	Blue	Grant
13—At K. C.	L	7-8‡	Abernathy	Lachemann
15—At Milw.	L	0-1	Lockwood	Odom
15—At Milw.	W	6-5	Locker	Sanders
16—At Milw.	W	4-1	Fingers	Krausse
18—Calif.	W	3-2	Dobson	Tatum
19—Calif.	W	2-1	Hunter	Garrett
20—Calif.	L	2-4	Wright	Roland
21—Minn.	W	6-0	Blue	Perry
22—Minn.	L	3-5	Kaat	Dobson
23—Minn.	L	4-7	Hall	Hunter
25—At Calif.	W	6-0	Odom	Wright
26—At Calif.	W	4-3	Lindblad	Fisher
27—At Calif.	L	4-9	Garrett	Dobson
29—Milw.	W	1-3	Hunter	Downing
30—Milw.	L	1-4	Lockwood	Odom
OCTOBER—				
1—Milw.	W	5-4	Lindblad	Sanders

* 10 innings.   † 11 innings.   ‡ 12 innings.   § 15 innings.

Angels Fly High With Alex' Bat

By ROSS NEWHAN

They won the first five games of 1970 and they won the last five. In between, it was as if the team from Anaheim was simply one more exhibit from Disneyland's Magic Kingdom.

A team that finished 20 games under .500 in 1969, the new year was a fantasy, a year in which the Angels maintained a shot at winning the West Division title until the final weeks of September.

The catalyst was a stoic outfielder who came in trade from Cincinnati, a man who brought to the Angels both talent and temperament, an offensive force that reawakened the attack of a team which had finished last in batting average during the previous summer.

Alex Johnson and Chico Ruiz were acquired from the Reds in exchange for Jim McGlothlin, Pedro Borbon and Vern Geishert. The Angels gave up pitching and received everything they anticipated, including problems in the person of Johnson.

A hitter of acknowledged ability and a complex personality who had resisted analysis in Philadelphia, St. Louis and Cincinnati, Johnson was the same in Anaheim.

Occasionally, he failed to hustle. Occasionally, there were problems with teammates. Occasionally, he was fined.

They were frustrating occasions, indeed, but above it all the moody, often-sullen outfielder was at all times an offensive threat, a swift sword in a heretofore dull attack.

Johnson became the first Angel to collect 200 hits in a season. He be-

CALIFORNIA ANGELS, 1970

Front row—Cowan, Alomar, Koenig, coach; Reiser, coach; Phillips, manager; Bridges, coach; Sherry, coach; Egan, Voss, Oyler, Bender, clubhouse attendant. Second row—Waring, traveling secretary; Doyle, Messersmith, K. Tatum, LaRoche, J. Tatum, Wright, May, Ruiz, Fregosi, Frederico, trainer; Hailey, equipment manager. Back row—Johnson, Murphy, Queen, Garrett, Fisher, Spencer, McMullen, Repoz, Reynolds, Johnstone. Seated in front —Anderson, Newman, Howells, Manazer, batboys.

came the first to collect two hits or more in 55 games. He became the first to win a batting championship.

It was in the final game of 1970 that Johnson went two-for-three to overtake Boston's Carl Yastrzemski and win the batting crown by .0003. Johnson's average rounded out to .329 and his presence rounded out the Angels.

Jim Fregosi, the man who batted in front of Johnson, enjoyed his finest offensive season, delivering 16 game-winning hits. Jim Spencer, the man who batted behind Johnson, matured quickly, hit .300 for a large portion of the season and finished at .274.

There was the firepower of Johnson and the cool patience of Manager Lefty Phillips and also 169 hits, 82 runs, 35 stolen bases and a 22-game hitting streak from the nomadic Sandy Alomar, who continued to build a home for himself as the Angels' leadoff man.

It added up to a team record for hits (1,391) and average (.251) in a season and the Angels were only three games behind Minnesota when they opened a three-game series against the Twins on September 4 at Anaheim Stadium.

Three days later the Angels were six back. Swept by the Twins, demoralized California lost nine in a row to erase the dream of a pennant and insure a third-place finish.

The record of 86-76 equaled the club mark for wins in a season and it might have been better except for a string of injuries during the second half, a frustrating siege that eroded continuity.

Trainer Freddie Frederico administered to Ken McMullen (rib and hamstring pull), Andy Messersmith (rib and shoulder), Jose Azcue (wrist), Greg Garrett (sore arm) and Jim Fregosi (back and shoulder). Frederico seemed to be occupied with ailing athletes the whole season long.

The most serious of the injuries was to Messersmith, the 16-game winner of 1969.

Messersmith strained the muscles on the left side of his rib cage in mid-May, kept the pain a secret, pitched inconsistently and finally revealed the injury to his exasperated manager in mid-August.

Sent to the bullpen, Messersmith responded brilliantly, saving game after game until he pulled the rotary muscle in his shoulder and was unavailable for the last half of September.

With Messersmith winning only 11 games, balm was provided by the remarkable comeback of Clyde Wright, who won only one game in 1969 and then won 22 in 1970.

Wright resurrected his pride pitching for Ponce in the Puerto Rican Winter League. During the summer that followed, the southpaw became the Angels' ace, hurled a no-hitter, pitched in the All-Star Game and set a club record for victories and starts (39) in a season.

Behind Wright, Tom Murphy won 16 games and there was encouraging work from youngsters Garrett, Tom Bradley and Lloyd Allen. In addition, the bullpen set a club record with 49 saves, including 17 by Ken Tatum, who since has been dealt to Boston, which sent Tony Conigliaro to the Angelenos.

After drawing only 758,388 to the Big A in 1969, the Angels attracted 1,077,741.

The anticipated return of a healthy Messersmith bodes well for 1971

when the performance of the team from Anaheim may be looked upon as more reality then fantasy.

SCORES OF CALIFORNIA ANGELS' 1970 GAMES

APRIL—

Date	Result	Winner	Loser
7—At Milw.	W 12-0	Messersmith	Krausse
8—At Milw.	W 6-1	Murphy	Pattin
10—At K. C.	W 11-7	Wright	Nelson
11—At K. C.	W 6-3	Messersmith	Bunker
12—At K. C.	W 7-5	Fisher	Drago
14—Chicago	L 1-3	Horlen	Wright
15—Minn.	L 2-8	Perry	Mes'rsmith
16—Minn.	W 3-2	May	Boswell
17—Kan. C.	L 5-7	Morehead	Murphy
18—Kan. C.	W 7-1	Wright	Bunker
19—Kan. C.	L 1-4x	Rooker	Queen
20—Milw.	W 5-4†	Doyle	Krausse
21—Milw.	W 3-1	Murphy	Pattin
22—Milw.	W 3-1	Wright	Lauzerique
24—At Wash.	L 3-5	Bosman	Mes'rsmith
25—At Wash.	W 5-3	May	Brunet
26—At Wash.	W 3-2	Murphy	Cox
28—At N. Y.	L 5-7	Peterson	Wright
29—At N. Y.	W 3-2	Messersmith	Cumberland
30—At N. Y.	L 0-1	Bahnsen	May

MAY—

Date	Result	Winner	Loser
1—At Bos.	L 3-8	Culp	Murphy
2—At Bos.	W 8-4	Garrett	Jarvis
5—Wash.	L 1-6	Brunet	Mes'rsmith
6—Wash.	W 4-2	Fisher	Knowles
7—Wash.	W 8-0	Murphy	Coleman
8—N. York	W 4-3	Wright	Klimkowski
9—N. York	W 11-3	Messersmith	Kekich
10—N. York	L 3-4	Aker	May
11—Boston	W 2-1z	LaRoche	Brett
12—Boston	W 6-5	Garrett	Lyle
13—Boston	W 5-3	Tatum	Stange
15—At Oak.	W 5-4	Tatum	Hunter
16—At Oak.	L 3-11	Dobson	Murphy
17—At Oak.	W 7-1	Wright	Odom
17—At Oak.	L 5-6†	Roland	Garrett
18—At Chi.	W 6-1	Messersmith	Wynne
19—At Chi.	W 3-0	May	Horlen
20—At Chi.	L 2-3	John	Murphy
22—At Minn.	W 3-2	Wright	Perry
23—At Minn.	L 4-5	Williams	Tatum
24—At Minn.	W 6-5	Doyle	Perranoski
26—Oakland	W 4-2	Murphy	Fingers
27—Oakland	L 3-4	Hunter	Wright
28—Oakland	L 0-2	Dobson	May
29—Balt.	L 0-2	Cuellar	Mes'rsmith
30—Balt.	W 3-2	Murphy	Hall
31—Balt.	W 6-1	Wright	McNally

JUNE—

Date	Result	Winner	Loser
2—Detroit	W 3-2†	Doyle	Niekro
3—Detroit	L 4-5‡	Hiller	Fisher
4—Detroit	L 2-4	Cain	Murphy
5—Cleve.	W 2-1	Wright	Paul
6—Cleve.	W 2-1	May	McDowell
7—Cleve.	L 4-6	Hand	Mes'rsmith
9—At Balt.	W 7-5‡	Fisher	Hall
10—At Balt.	L 1-2	Palmer	Wright
11—At Balt.	L 1-9	Cuellar	May
12—At Det.	W 5-2	Messersmith	Hiller
13—At Det.	L 5-6	Patterson	Tatum
14—At Det.	L 4-8	Wilson	Wright
15—At Cleve.	W 2-3§	Chance	Queen
15—At Cleve.	L 2-9	Hand	Mes'rsmith
19—Milw.	L 2-5	Pattin	Murphy
20—Milw.	W 4-0	Wright	Krausse
21—Milw.	W 6-5†	Tatum	Humphreys
23—Chicago	W 3-7	Janeski	Mes'rsmith
24—Chicago	W 3-1	Murphy	Horlen
24—Chicago	W 2-1	Queen	Moore
25—Chicago	W 7-3	Wright	John
26—At K. C.	W 5-4	Kealey	Butler
27—At K. C.	L 0-2	Burgmeier	Mes'rsmith
28—At K. C.	W 2-1	Murphy	Rooker
28—At K. C.	L 1-13	Fitzmorris	Garrett
29—At Milw.	W 10-3	Wright	Pattin

JUNE—

Date	Result	Winner	Loser
30—At Milw.	L 4-5	Krausse	May

JULY—

Date	Result	Winner	Loser
1—At Milw.	W 4-3	Garrett	Lockwood
2—At Milw.	W 10-7	Murphy	Prabender
3—Oakland	W 4-0	Wright	Dobson
4—Oakland	L 4-7	Hunter	May
5—Oakland	W 5-1	Messersmith	Fingers
6—Kan. C.	W 6-2	Murphy	Rooker
7—Kan. C.	L 3-4	Abernathy	Fisher
8—Kan. C.	W 3-2	Tatum	Abernathy
9—Minn.	L 2-4	Hall	I'isher
10—Minn.	W 2-1	Messersmith	Kaat
11—Minn.	L 2-5	Zepp	Wright
12—Minn.	W 6-2	LaRoche	Perry
16—At Wash.	W 3-2	LaRoche	Grzenda
17—At Wash.	W 10-0	Wright	Cox
18—At Wash.	L 0-4	Brunet	Bradley
19—At N. Y.	W 5-2	May	Cumberland
19—At N. Y.	W 3-1	Murphy	Kekich
20—At N. Y.	L 1-6	Peterson	Mes'rsmith
21—At Bos.	W 10-6	Wright	Nagy
22—At Bos.	L 4-7	Peters	Bradley
22—At Bos.	L 3-8	Siebert	Queen
23—At Bos.	W 4-1	Tatum	Brett
24—Wash.	L 3-9†	Hannan	Tatum
25—Wash.	L 0-5	Shellenback	Wright
26—Wash.	W 11-10‡	Garrett	Knowles
27—N. York	L 2-5†	Stottlemyre	May
28—N. York	L 5-6	McCormick	Garrett
29—N. York	L 3-8	Klimkowski	Wright
31—Boston	L 0-2	Siebert	Murphy

AUGUST—

Date	Result	Winner	Loser
1—Boston	L 0-8	Peters	Garrett
2—Boston	W 8-3	Bradley	Romo
3—At Oak.	W 5-0	May	Hunter
4—At Oak.	L 3-4	Odom	Wright
5—At Minn.	W 7-5	Queen	Perranoski
6—At Minn.	L 1-2y	Williams	Doyle
7—At Chi.	W 4-6	Fisher	Murphy
8—At Chi.	L 1-8	Miller	May
9—At Chi.	W 5-0	Wright	John
9—At Chi.	W 6-3	Murphy	Crider
11—Balt.	L 0-7	Cuellar	Mes'rsmith
12—Balt.	L 4-5	McNally	May
13—Balt.	W 2-2	Queen	Drabowsky
14—Detroit	W 7-3	Wright	Lolich
15—Detroit	L 1-5	Niekro	Allen
16—Detroit	L 1-7	Cain	May
17—Cleve.	W 3-0	Murphy	McDowell
18—Cleve.	W 12-1	Wright	Chance
19—Cleve.	L 0-2	Hand	May
21—At Balt.	L 0-5	McNally	Murphy
22—At Balt.	W 3-2†	Messersmith	Watt
23—At Balt.	L 5-6	Cuellar	Queen
25—At Det.	W 6-4§	Messersmith	Timmerman
25—At Det.	W 10-6	Tatum	LaGrow
26—At Det.	W 6-3	Wright	McLain
28—At Cleve.	W 3-2	Tatum	Higgins
28—At Cleve.	L 1-5	Hand	Murphy
29—At Cleve.	L 1-14	McDowell	Garrett
30—At Cleve.	W 10-9	Messersmith	Colbert

SEPTEMBER—

Date	Result	Winner	Loser
1—Kan. C.	L 0-4	Bunker	Murphy
2—Kan. C.	W 3-1	Wright	Johnson
3—Kan. C.	W 1-0	Bradley	Rooker
4—Minn.	L 0-4	Blyleven	May
5—Minn.	L 3-4	Perry	Murphy
6—Minn.	L 1-3	Hall	Wright
7—At K. C.	L 1-4	Johnson	Bradley
8—At K. C.	L 0-12	Rooker	May
9—At Chi.	L 4-11	Janeski	Murphy
9—At Chi.	L 1-3*	Wynne	Wright
11—Milw.	L 1-2	Krausse	Bradley
12—Milw.	L 2-3	Gelnar	LaRoche
13—Milw.	W 2-1	Murphy	Pattin

SEPTEMBER—			Winner	Loser	SEPTEMBER—			Winner	Loser
15—At Minn.	L	5-7	Williams	Queen	25—Oakland	L	0-6	Odom	Wright
15—At Minn.	W	5-3	LaRoche	Perranoski	26—Oakland	L	3-4	Lindblad	Fisher
16—At Minn.	W	5-1	Wright	Blyleven	27—Oakland	W	9-4	Garrett	Dobson
17—At Minn.	L	3-4	Perry	Murphy	28—Chicago	W	4-3	Murphy	Johnson
18—At Oak.	L	2-3	Dobson	Tatum	29—Chicago	W	9-2	Wright	Wynne
19—At Oak.	L	1-2	Hunter	Garrett	30—Chicago	W	5-1	Allen	John
20—At Oak.	W	4-2	Wright	Roland					
21—At Milw.	W	7-6	Murphy	Krausse	OCTOBER—				
22—At Milw.	L	2-4	Pattin	Queen					
24—At Milw.	L	3-7	Morris	Bradley	1—Chicago	W	5-4x	May	Magnuson

* 8 innings.   † 10 innings.   ‡ 11 innings.   § 12 innings.   x 13 innings.   y 14 innings.   z 16 innings.

Royals Treated Unkindly by Fates and Feuds

By JOE McGUFF

The 1969 season was a heady experience for the Royals. They surprised themselves and the rest of the American League by winning 69 games and came into 1970 riding an updraft of optimism. There was talk of a .500 season and rapid development into a contender.

It was a delightful dream, but one that failed to materialize.

The Royals got off to a slow start and suffered a substantial number of key injuries. By June, they had fired Manager Charlie Metro and replaced him with Bob Lemon. The managerial change produced no immediate improvement and it was not until September that the Royals began to play up to their pre-season expectations.

They finished the season in fourth place with a 65-97 record and discovered that expansion ball clubs do not necessarily improve in a straight line of progression.

The Royals' problems began in spring training when friction developed between Metro and his players. Metro had replaced Joe Gordon, who had resigned following the close of the 1969 season. The friction carried over into the regular season and reached something of a peak when Metro removed Pat Kelly and Bob Oliver from a game because of mental errors.

Metro was dismissed on June 9 following a disastrous eastern trip on which the Royals won only one game in nine starts.

Injuries played an important part in the Royals' failure to match their 1969 pace. The pitching staff was especially hard hit.

Wally Bunker, who was the club's leading pitcher in 1969 with a 12-11 record, developed shoulder trouble in spring training and lost six straight games at the outset of the season. He was put on the disabled list and did not pitch again until the closing stages of the season, when he demonstrated that he had recovered fully from his ailment.

Mike Hedlund, a promising young pitcher in 1969, developed a virus infection while pitching winter ball. He complained of extreme fatigue during spring training and was sent back to the minors. Roger Nelson, the Royals' No. 1 choice in the expansion draft, also had arm trouble.

Bill Butler, regarded as the most promising young pitcher on the staff, developed elbow trouble. In 1969, he had a 9-10 record. pitched four shutouts and was named to the major league rookie all-star team. In 1970, Butler slumped to a 4-12 record and spent the latter part of the season with Omaha (American Association).

In addition to their pitching losses, the Royals suffered a big loss when

KANSAS CITY ROYALS, 1970

Front row—Rodriguez, Oliver, Willhite, batting practice pitcher; Carnevale, coach; Schultz, coach; Lemon, manager; Dunlop, coach; Strickland, coach; Kirkpatrick, Drabowsky, Monteagudo. Second row—Sigloch, assistant equipment manager; Severson, Burgmeier, Hernandez, Keough, Rooker, Taylor, Morehead, Campanis, Schaal, Kelly, Zych, equipment manager. Back row—Jones, trainer; Matchick, Fitzmorris, Piniella, Nelson, Johnson, Butler, Wright, Drago, Otis, Sorrell, Current, traveling secretary. Seated in front—Guenther, batboy.

Joe Keough was injured on June 28 and was not able to play again. Keough suffered a broken leg and a dislocated ankle sliding into home plate. He was the Royals' leading hitter at the time with a .322 averge.

Although a great many things went wrong, the season was not without its redeeming features.

Bob Oliver proved to be one of the Royals' most pleasant surprises. Oliver batted .254 in 1969 with 13 homers and 43 RBIs. At one point he was sent back to the minors. He hit well from the start in 1970 and led the Royals in home runs with 27 and runs batted in with 99. He batted .260. Oliver started the season at third base, but finished the year at first, which is the position he prefers.

The Royals uncovered two young stars in Amos Otis and Bob Johnson, who were obtained from the Mets in the Joe Foy trade. Otis was an outstanding center fielder and batted .284. He hit 11 homers and drove in 58 runs. He stole 33 bases in 35 attempts.

Johnson started the season in the bullpen, but by June had become a member of the starting rotation. He had an 8-13 record and led the club in strikeouts with 206, breaking the all-time Kansas City record.

Lou Piniella, who was the American League Rookie of the Year in 1969, thumbed his nose at the Sophomore Jinx and came back to hit .301. He had 11 homers and 88 runs batted in.

Cookie Rojas, acquired from the Cardinals, took over at second base and helped to steady the infield. Paul Schaal was outstanding at third base through the closing stages of the season. The biggest gap was at shortstop, where the Royals tried several different players.

From the Royals' standpoint, 1970 will not go down as a vintage year, but if the pitching staff is sound in 1971, the Royals may well have laid the foundation for a better team.

SCORES OF KANSAS CITY ROYALS' 1970 GAMES

APRIL—		Winner	Loser	MAY—		Winner	Loser
7—Oakland	L 4-6	Odom	Bunker	17—At Chi.	W 3-2*	Fitzmorris	Wood
8—Oakland	W 2-0	Drago	Hunter	17—At Chi.	W 8-4†	Rooker	Wood
9—Oakland	W 3-1	Butler	Dobson	18—Minn.	L 5-7	Zepp	Hedlund
10—Calif.	L 7-11	Wright	Nelson	19—Minn.	L 4-5*	Perranoski	Burgmeier
11—Calif.	L 3-6	Messersmith	Bunker	20—Minn.	L 5-10	Boswell	Johnson
12—Calif.	L 5-7	Fisher	Drago	22—Milw.	W 6-3	Drago	Bolin
16—At Milw.	W 8-6	Butler	Krausse	23—Milw.	W 3-1	Rooker	Krausse
17—At Calif.	W 7-5	Morehead	Murphy	24—Milw.	W 6-5*	Drabowsky	Brabender
18—At Calif.	L 1-7	Wright	Bunker	25—Chicago	W 7-1	Morehead	Crider
19—At Calif.	W 4-1‡	Rooker	Queen	26—Chicago	L 1-3	Janeski	Johnson
20—At Oak.	W 4-2†	Hedlund	Segui	27—Chicago	W 4-3	Drago	Horlen
21—At Oak.	L 3-4	Hunter	Rooker	29—At Wash.	L 4-5‡	Shellenback	Bunker
22—At Oak.	L 1-2	Downing	Bunker	30—At Wash.	L 2-3	Bosman	Butler
24—Balt.	L 5-7	Hardin	Hedlund	31—At Wash.	W 6-5	Burgmeier	Knowles
25—Balt.	L 3-9	Palmer	Butler	JUNE—			
26—Balt.	L 9-10	Hall	Fitzmorris	2—At N. Y.	L 2-3	Peterson	Johnson
28—Detroit	L 3-8	Niekro	Bunker	3—At N. Y.	L 3-5	Kekich	Drago
29—Detroit	L 2-8	Kilkenny	Drago	4—At N. Y.	L 1-2‡	McDaniel	Rooker
30—Detroit	W 3-2*	Wright	Lasher	5—At Bos.	L 2-4	Nagy	Butler
MAY—				7—At Bos.	L 4-7	Stange	Burgmeier
1—Cleve.	L 5-7	Hennigan	Drabowsky	7—At Bos.	L 2-5	Romo	Fitzmorris
2—Cleve.	W 4-3x	Hedlund	Miller	9—Wash.	W 8-1	Drago	Cox
3—Cleve.	L 3-6	Moore	Rooker	10—Wash.	L 1-8	Coleman	Rooker
5—At Balt.	L 3-7	Phoebus	Butler	12—N. York	L 0-5	Peterson	Morehead
6—At Balt.	L 1-3	McNally	Butler	13—N. York	L 4-9‡	McDaniel	Wright
7—At Balt.	L 6-7	Watt	Drabowsky	14—N. York	L 2-3	Hamilton	Burgmeier
8—At Det.	W 9-3	Johnson	Kilkenny	15—Boston	W 7-6	Monteagudo	Koonce
9—At Det.	L 4-7	Hiller	Hedlund	16—Boston	L 5-7	Peters	Butler
10—At Det.	W 9-7	Fitzmorris	Lasher	17—Boston	L 1-3	Brett	Morehead
13—At Cleve.	W 1-0‡	Fitzmorris	Hennigan	19—Minn.	W 5-1	Drago	Blyleven
14—At Minn.	L 2-5	Hall	Morehead	20—Minn.	W 5-3	Rooker	Boswell
15—At Chi.	L 3-9	Horlen	Nelson	21—Minn.	L 2-11	Perry	Butler
16—At Chi.	L 1-6	John	Johnson	22—At Oak.	L 1-2	Locker	Burgmeier

JUNE—			Winner	Loser
23—At Oak.	W	7-5	Drago	Dobson
24—At Oak.	L	1-5	Osteen	Rooker
26—Calif.	L	4-5	Kealey	Butler
27—Calif.	W	2-0	Burgmeier	Mes'rsmith
28—Calif.	L	1-2	Murphy	Rooker
28—Calif.	W	13-1	Fitzmorris	Garrett
29—At Minn.	L	4-5	Perry	Drago
30—At Minn.	L	5-8	Woodson	Johnson

JULY—				
1—At Minn.	L	1-2*	Perranoski	Rooker
2—At Minn.	L	2-5	Hall	Fitzmorris
3—At Milw.	W	5-3*	Abernathy	Humphreys
3—At Milw.	W	4-3	Johnson	Downing
4—At Milw.	W	8-6	Abernathy	Baldwin
5—At Milw.	L	1-2	Lockwood	Butler
6—At Calif.	L	2-6	Murphy	Rooker
7—At Calif.	W	4-3	Abernathy	Fisher
8—At Calif.	L	2-3	Tatum	Abernathy
10—Chicago	W	8-6	Johnson	Janeski
10—Chicago	W	2-0	Rooker	Miller
11—Chicago	W	4-0	Butler	Horlen
12—Chicago	L	5-10	John	Drago
16—Cleve.	L	0-6	Hand	Rooker
17—Cleve.	L	0-6	Dunning	Johnson
18—Cleve.	L	1-4	Hargan	Butler
19—Detroit	L	0-2	Niekro	Drago
19—Detroit	L	4-6	Reed	Abernathy
20—Detroit	W	3-0	Rooker	Cain
21—Balt.	L	1-2	Watt	Johnson
22—Balt.	L	3-4§	Richert	Abernathy
23—Balt.	L	4-5	Palmer	Drago
24—At Cleve.	W	5-2	Rooker	Hand
25—At Cleve.	L	6-9	Chance	Bunker
25—At Cleve.	W	8-4	Burgmeier	Lasher
26—At Cleve.	L	5-6	Dunning	Wright
26—At Cleve.	L	0-3	Hargan	Morehead
28—At Det.	W	7-6	Abernathy	Scherman
29—At Det.	L	3-10	Cain	Rooker
30—At Det.	W	3-2*	Abernathy	Timmerman
31—At Balt.	L	1-3	McNally	Morehead

AUGUST—				
1—At Balt.	L	1-9	Palmer	Drago
2—At Balt.	L	8-10	Cuellar	Rooker
3—At Chi.	W	7-2	Johnson	Miller
4—At Chi.	L	1-2	John	Butler
5—Oakland	L	1-4	Dobson	Drago
6—Oakland	W	5-3	Fitzmorris	Locker
7—Milw.	W	4-0	Johnson	Lockwood
7—Milw.	W	10-2	Morehead	Krause
8—Milw.	L	3-5	Pattin	Butler
9—Milw.	L	2-4	Bolin	Drago

AUGUST—			Winner	Loser
12—At Bos.	L	4-7	Peters	Rooker
12—At Bos.	W	4-3	Abernathy	Brett
13—At Bos.	W	11-3	Fitzmorris	Romo
14—At N. Y.	L	2-3*	McDaniel	Drago
15—At N. Y.	L	4-5	Klimkowski	Burgmeier
16—At N. Y.	L	1-5	Bahnsen	Rooker
17—At Wash.	L	0-7	Hannan	Johnson
18—At Wash.	W	12-8	Fitzmorris	Bosman
19—At Wash.	W	2-1	Drago	Coleman
21—Boston	W	2-1‡	Abernathy	Brett
22—Boston	L	1-8	Peters	Rooker
23—Boston	W	4-3	Johnson	Lyle
24—N. York	W	8-7	Burgmeier	Klimkowski
25—N. York	L	1-2	Peterson	Drago
26—N. York	L	0-3	Bahnsen	Bunker
28—Wash.	L	1-2	Bosman	Johnson
28—Wash.	W	3-1	Rooker	Hannan
29—Wash.	L	4-11	Brunet	Fitzmorris
30—Wash.	W	4-3	Burgmeier	Pina

SEPTEMBER—				
1—At Calif.	W	4-0	Bunker	Murphy
2—At Calif.	L	1-3	Wright	Johnson
3—At Calif.	L	0-1	Bradley	Rooker
4—At Calif.	L	0-5	Hunter	Fitzmorris
5—At Oak.	L	3-8	Lindblad	Drago
6—At Oak.	L	1-7	Odom	Bunker
7—Calif.	W	4-1	Johnson	Bradley
8—Calif.	W	12-0	Rooker	May
10—Milw.	W	2-0	Butler	Lockwood
10—Milw.	W	10-2	Drago	Morris
11—Oakland	L	0-3	Blue	Bunker
12—Oakland	L	2-3	Grant	Johnson
13—Oakland	W	8-7†	Burgmeier	Grant
15—Oakland	W	8-7‡	Abernathy	Lachemann
17—At Milw.	L	3-4§	Sanders	Burgmeier
18—At Milw.	W	3-4	Downing	Butler
19—At Milw.	W	4-1	Bunker	Morris
20—At Milw.	L	3-4	Lockwood	Johnson
21—At Chi.	L	4-8y	Wood	Monteagudo
21—At Chi.	W	8-2y	York	Weaver
22—At Chi.	W	2-1	Drago	Wynne
22—At Chi.	W	6-2	Fitzmorris	Magnuson
23—At Chi.	L	0-6	Johnson	Splittorff
25—Minn.	L	0-1	Perry	Bunker
26—Minn.	W	5-0	Johnson	Tiant
27—Minn.	W	4-3	Rooker	Tiant
28—At Minn.	L	0-1	Hall	Drago
29—At Minn.	W	14-13‡	Abernathy	Hamm
30—At Minn.	L	4-6	Haydel	York

OCTOBER—				
1—At Minn.	L	0-4	Kaat	Johnson

* 10 innings. † 11 innings. ‡ 12 innings. § 13 innings. x 17 innings. y Games of September 15-16, at Kansas City, transferred to Chicago.

Brewers Hoist Suds Over Rewarding Record

By LARRY WHITESIDE

The second miracle of Milwaukee was not as impressive as the first, but the Brewers nonetheless left their impression on Wisconsinites and the baseball world in 1970.

General Manager Marvin Milkes called it a "great comeback for a team of orphans." He should know for he was the man who had to suffer through three ownerships and the transfer of the franchise from Seattle to Milwaukee only four days before the 1970 season began.

But the Brewers not only gained a degree of respectability on the field, finishing in a tie for fourth place with Kansas City, after placing last in the American League's West Division in 1969, but cheered the baseball world by nearly reaching their goal of 1,000,000 fans in the first year of operation. Milwaukee turned out 933,690 strong, a tribute to its history as a great baseball town.

The franchise went to Milwaukee only four days before the opening day of the 1970 season, but an amazing crowd of 37,237 fans poured into Milwaukee County Stadium, a facility originally built to house the Milwaukee Braves, who had fled to Atlanta.

Clearly it was not love at first sight, for Milwaukee fans were accustomed to quality baseball, something which the Brewers in the beginning lacked most of all.

But, by June 15, Milkes had given young, tough Manager Dave Bristol the nucleus of the club that would soon catch the local imagination. The faces were new and so was the spirit, but the Brewers became an overnight hit.

Gene Brabender, the 13-game winner of the first season for the expansion club, developed shoulder ailments and he was ineffectve for most of the season. Tommy Harper, who stole 73 bases in 1969, was found wanting as a second baseman and shifted to third. Mike Hegan, son of the former Cleveland catcher, Jim Hegan, now a Yankee coach, and Ted Kubiak, obtained from Oakland, were the only veterans who were assured of jobs, at first.

Milkes, through trades, beefed up the roster by acquiring such players as Ted Savage, Russ Snyder, Max Alvis, Dave May, Roberto Pena, Hank Allen and Bob Burda.

From the farm system he pulled up Ken Sanders (1.76 ERA, 50 games), and young Danny Walton, later to be hobbled by a knee injury, who did much to help the club to establish itself with Milwaukee fans. Walton hit over .300 the first two months of the season and, for a time, was the team's only legitimate home-run threat.

Harper took up the slack when bats failed and became one of the game's best hitters and most exciting players. He overnight developed a stroke that enabled him to become only the fifth man in major league history to hit over 30 home runs and steal over 30 bases in a season. He finished the year with 179 hits, including 31 home runs and 35 doubles.

Milwaukee developed its own special breed of fan, most prominent of which was the "Brew Crew," a young enthusiastic group who populated the left field bleachers. They came originally to cheer Walton and stayed to become Brewer backers.

On August 16, a Bat Day crowd of 44,387 watched the Brewers whip Cleveland, 4-3. And Bernie Brewer (69-year-old scoreboard-sitter Milt Mason) slid down a rope to humanity after having been perched atop the scoreboard since July 6, awaiting a 40,000 crowd before he'd descend from his lair.

"That was the day Milwaukeeans took us to their hearts," said Bristol, who was rewarded at season's end with a one-year extension of his contract, and that of his coaches.

SCORES OF MILWAUKEE BREWERS' 1970 GAMES

APRIL—			Winner	Loser	APRIL—			Winner	Loser
7—Calif.	L	0-12	Messersmith	Krausse	20—At Calif.	L	4-5†	Doyle	Krausse
8—Calif.	L	1-6	Murphy	Pattin	21—At Calif.	L	1-3	Murphy	Pattin
10—At Chi.	L	4-5	Janeski	Brabender	22—At Calif.	L	1-3	Wright	Lauzerique
11—At Chi.	W	8-4	O'Donoghue	Rounsaville	25—At Bos.	W	10-4	Krausse	Stange
12—At Chi.	W	5-2	Krausse	John	25—At Bos.	L	0-3	Peters	Bolin
12—At Chi.	W	16-2	Lauzerique	Arrigo	26—At Bos.	W	5-3	Brabender	Culp
13—At Oak.	L	1-2	Hunter	Pattin	27—At Wash.	L	5-6†	Pina	Locker
14—At Oak.	L	1-9	Downing	Brabender	28—At Wash.	L	6-9	Such	Lauzerique
16—Kan. C.	L	6-8	Butler	Krausse	29—At Wash.	L	0-4	Bosman	Krausse
18—Chicago	L	5-8	Wood	Gelnar	30—At Wash.	L	2-12	Brunet	Bolin

MILWAUKEE BREWERS, 1970

Front row—Doyle, visiting clubhouse assistant manager; McMillan, coach; Moore, coach; Bristol, manager; Stock, coach; Ermer, coach; Ferguson, traveling secretary; Rayer, trainer. Second row—Kiscinski, visiting clubhouse manager; Burda, Savage, Meyer, Bolin, Snyder, Baldwin, Pattin, Harper, Sullivan, equipment manager. Third row—Walton, Alvis, McNertney, Roof, Morris, Hegan, Francona, Lockwood, McBride, batboy. Back row—Gil, Kubiak, Krausse, Humphreys, Gelnar, Hershberger, Sanders, May, Pena. Kneeling in front—Bradshaw, Rinn and Napholz, ballboys; Street, batboy.

MAY—			Winner	Loser
1—At N. Y.	L	3-6	Stottlemyre	Brabender
2—At N. Y.	L	6-7	Hamilton	Gelnar
3—At N. Y.	L	7-8	Hamilton	Meyer
3—At N. Y.	L	2-4	McDaniel	Krausse
5—Boston	L	0-6	Siebert	Brabender
6—Boston	W	4-3	Bolin	Phillips
7—Boston	W	5-1	Krausse	Culp
9—Wash.	W	3-2†	Gelnar	Grzenda
10—Wash.	W	6-5	Pattin	Knowles
10—Wash.	W	7-6	O'Donoghue	Grzenda
11—N. York	T	5-5	......	......
12—N. York	L	5-9*	Peterson	Krausse
13—N. York	W	3-1	Morris	Cumberland
16—Minn.	L	1-11	Boswell	Brabender
17—Minn.	L	1-6	Perry	Krausse
19—Oakland	W	6-3	Morris	Hunter
20—Oakland	W	8-7	Pattin	Fingers
22—At K. C.	L	3-6	Drago	Bolin
23—At K. C.	L	1-3	Rooker	Krausse
24—At K. C.	L	5-6†	Drabowsky	Brabender
25—At Minn.	L	5-6	Hall	Lockwood
26—At Minn.	L	2-6	Kaat	Bolin
28—At Minn.	L	2-11	Tiant	Morris
29—Detroit	L	4-5	Lolich	Lockwood
30—Detroit	W	9-7	Gelnar	Hiller
31—Detroit	W	7-6	Baldwin	Saunders

JUNE—				
2—Cleve.	L	1-4	McDowell	Brabender
2—Cleve.	L	5-9	Hennigan	Lockwood
3—Cleve.	L	6-7	Miller	Pattin
4—Cleve.	L	4-8	Hennigan	Peters
5—Balt.	L	2-3	McNally	Bolin
6—Balt.	W	6-4	Brabender	Palmer
7—Balt.	L	6-7	Cuellar	Pattin
8—Chicago	W	5-3	Krausse	Johnson
9—At Det.	L	3-8	Cain	Peters
10—At Det.	L	5-7	Saunders	Gelnar
11—At Det.	L	2-6	Niekro	Brabender
12—At Cleve.	W	4-1	Pattin	Hand
13—At Cleve.	L	6-10	Chance	Krausse
14—At Cleve.	L	2-9	Dunning	Lockwood
15—At Balt.	W	9-6	Sanders	Watt
17—At Balt.	W	5-1	Brabender	McNally
19—At Calif.	W	5-2	Pattin	Murphy
20—At Calif.	L	0-4	Wright	Krausse
21—At Calif.	L	5-6†	Tatum	Humphreys
22—Minn.	L	3-4	Kaat	Brabender
23—Minn.	W	4-3	Baldwin	Hall
24—Minn.	L	2-3	Boswell	Pattin
25—Minn.	W	4-1	Krausse	Perry
26—Oakland	W	3-2y	Humphreys	Dobson
27—Oakland	W	3-1	Brabender	Fingers
28—Oakland	L	1-4	Segui	Bolin
28—Oakland	L	1-4	Dobson	Downing
29—Calif.	L	3-10	Wright	Pattin
30—Calif.	W	5-4	Krausse	May

JULY—				
1—Calif.	L	3-4	Garrett	Lockwood
2—Calif.	L	7-10	Murphy	Brabender
3—Kan. C.	L	3-5†	Abernathy	Humphreys
3—Kan. C.	L	3-4	Johnson	Downing
4—Kan. C.	L	6-8	Abernathy	Baldwin
5—Kan. C.	W	2-1	Lockwood	Butler
6—Chicago	W	3-1	Brabender	Janeski
7—Chicago	W	4-3§	Pattin	Wood
7—Chicago	W	1-0	Krausse	Horlen
8—Chicago	L	1-2	John	Downing
9—Chicago	L	5-6	Crider	Lockwood
10—At Oak.	W	2-1	Bolin	Fingers
11—At Oak.	L	1-11	Segui	Brabender
12—At Oak.	L	3-4	Grant	Pattin
12—At Oak.	W	2-1	Krausse	Hunter
16—At Bos.	L	5-6†	Romo	Bolin
17—At Bos.	L	2-8	Siebert	Brabender
18—At Bos.	W	10-5	Krausse	Lyle
19—At Wash.	L	3-4	Shellenback	Humphreys

JULY—			Winner	Loser
20—At Wash.	L	0-2	Hannan	Downing
21—At N. Y.	L	2-4	Bahnsen	Lockwood
22—At N. Y.	W	3-1	Bolin	Stottlemyre
24—Boston	W	8-4	Krausse	Culp
25—Boston	W	6-2	Pattin	Nagy
26—Boston	L	5-12	Peters	Lockwood
28—Wash.	W	5-1	Downing	Hannan
29—Wash.	L	2-4	Bosman	Krausse
30—Wash.	W	6-2	Pattin	Brunet
31—N. York	L	3-7	Bahnsen	Bolin
31—N. York	L	3-5	Peterson	Brabender

AUGUST—				
1—N. York	L	1-4§	Klimkowski	Humphreys
2—N. York	W	9-5	Gelnar	Klimkowski
3—At Minn.	L	1-2	Perry	Pattin
4—At Minn.	W	-2	Krausse	Tiant
4—At Minn.	L	2-5	Blyleven	Bolin
5—At Chi.	W	8-5	Magnuson	Brabender
6—At Chi.	L	3-7	Janeski	Downing
7—At K. C.	L	0-4	Johnson	Lockwood
7—At K. C.	L	2-10	Morehead	Krausse
8—At K. C.	W	5-3	Pattin	Butler
9—At K. C.	W	4-2	Bolin	Drago
11—Detroit	L	1-2	Kilkenny	Downing
12—Detroit	W	6-5	Brabender	Timmerman
13—Detroit	W	3-2	Pattin	McLain
14—Cleve.	W	4-3‡	Bolin	Chance
16—Cleve.	W	4-3	Sanders	Higgins
17—Balt.	L	2-3	Palmer	Krausse
18—Balt.	L	0-3	Hardin	Pattin
19—Balt.	L	2-3	Cuellar	Lockwood
21—At Det.	L	4-6	Cain	Downing
22—At Det.	L	2-5	McLain	Krausse
23—At Det.	L	0-1	Lolich	Pattin
25—At Cleve.	W	4-2†	Sanders	Higgins
26—At Cleve.	L	2-7	Hargan	Downing
27—At Cleve.	W	14-2	Krausse	Dunning
28—At Balt.	W	2-1	Pattin	Hardin
28—At Balt.	L	4-8	Richert	Brabender
29—At Balt.	L	4-9	McNally	Bolin
30—At Balt.	W	5-2	Lockwood	Palmer

SEPTEMBER—				
1—Minn.	L	0-4	Perry	Krausse
1—Minn.	L	1-7†	Kaat	Bolin
3—Minn.	W	8-3	Pattin	Zepp
4—Chicago	W	3-2†	Sanders	Murphy
7—At Minn.	L	6-7	Williams	Krausse
7—At Minn.	W	8-3	Haydel	Downing
8—At Minn.	W	3-2	Pattin	Perranoski
10—At K. C.	L	0-2	Butler	Lockwood
10—At K. C.	L	2-10	Drago	Morris
11—At Calif.	W	2-1	Krausse	Bradley
12—At Calif.	W	3-2	Gelnar	LaRoche
13—At Calif.	L	1-2	Murphy	Pattin
15—Oakland	W	1-0	Lockwood	Odom
16—Oakland	L	5-6	Locker	Sanders
16—Oakland	L	1-4	Fingers	Krausse
17—Kan. C.	W	4-3x	Sanders	Burgmeier
18—Kan. C.	W	4-3	Downing	Butler
19—Kan. C.	L	1-4	Bunker	Morris
20—Kan. C.	W	4-3	Lockwood	Johnson
21—Calif.	L	6-7	Murphy	Krausse
22—Calif.	W	4-2	Pattin	Queen
24—Calif.	W	7-3	Morris	Bradley
25—At Chi.	L	1-5	John	Lockwood
25—At Chi.	L	3-2	Humphreys	Janeski
26—At Chi.	W	9-5§	Morris	Murphy
27—At Chi.	W	0-3	Pattin	Horlen
29—At Oak.	L	3-4	Hunter	Downing
30—At Oak.	W	4-1	Lockwood	Odom

OCTOBER—				
1—At Oak.	L	4-5	Lindblad	Sanders

*Game halted by rain with two outs in last of ninth.   † 10 innings.   ‡ 11 innings.   § 12 innings.
x 13 innings.   y 15 innings.

CHICAGO WHITE SOX, 1970

Front row—Saad, trainer; Rosenbaum, batting practice pitcher; Aparicio, Moss, coach; Adair, coach; Gutteridge, manager; Appling, coach; Mulcahy, coach; Williams, Hopkins, Berry. Second row—Licklider, equipment manager; Wood, John, Sisk, Arrigo, Janeski, May, O'Brien, Rounsaville, Wynne, Knoop, Roberts, traveling secretary. Back row—Horlen, Heinsen, batting practice catcher; Herrmann, Melton, Secrist, Murphy, Christian, Morales, Matias, McCraw, Bradford, Josephson. Seated in front—Sakamoto, White, Reed, batboys.

White Sox' Severe Anemia Causes Head Shakes

By EDGAR MUNZEL

For the White Sox, 1970 was sheer disaster. It was a "lost" season in every sense of the word. There were record losses on the field as well as at the gate with the result that, in the end, it led to a drastic shakeup of the entire top echelon of the organization by Owner John Allyn.

The White Sox lost more games than any team in the club's 70-year history with a final record of 56-106. It was only the third time any White Sox aggregation had reached the century mark in defeats. The others were the forlorn seventh-place troupe of 1932 that dropped 102 and the sad sacks of 1948, who lost 101.

Attendance last season plunged to 495,355, down approximately 100,000 from the total of 589,546 of 1969, which had been aided by Milwaukee's contribution of 196,684 for the 11 games the White Sox had shifted there. But Brewtown had its own ball club last season and the White Sox had to fight it out on their own with Chicago's reluctant South Side fans.

Allyn, who had taken over the ball club only the preceding fall, when he bought out his older brother Arthur, went along with the situation until September and then decided to rip things apart at the top-management level.

First, he dropped a bomb on the front office at Comiskey Park. On September 2, he discharged Ed Short as vice-president and director of player personnel and replaced him with Roland Hemond, farm director of the Angels.

He also did some extensive re-shuffling. Stu Holcomb, who had been public relations director, was moved up to replace Leo Breen as executive vice-president. The latter was dropped out of the head position and made business manager and treasurer. Breen, however, retains his even more important post as president of the Artnell Corporation, the holding company of which the White Sox are just one division. In other office shuffling, traveling secretary Howard Roberts, who is nearing retirement, switched jobs with publicitor Don Unferth.

The next day, September 3, Allyn completed the big shakeup by the firing of Don Gutteridge as manager and the hiring of Charles (Chuck) Tanner, who had piloted Hawaii to a division title in the Pacific Coast League.

Although Gutteridge's dismissal was not to be effective until the end of the season, Don preferred to step out immediately. Coach Jimmy Adair filled in until Tanner completed the Pacific Coast League playoffs and joined the White Sox September 15.

Gutteridge had succeeded Al Lopez as manager May 3, 1969, after the senor, in his second managerial term with the White Sox, was forced into retirement by ill health. Short had served the White Sox for 20 years, first as publicitor, then traveling secretary and finally as general manager and personnel director.

Both Short and Gutteridge apparently were fall guys in a situation where a ball club had declined suddenly because of the deterioration of a pitching staff that once was one of the best in baseball.

With a "Big Three" of Gary Peters, Joe Horlen and Tommy John, the White Sox were first in the American League in pitching in 1966 with an

earned-run average of 2.68 and again in 1967 with a dazzling 2.45. They still were effective in 1968, finishing fourth with 2.75. But, in 1969, White Sox pitching soared to 4.21 and last season it shot even higher to 4.54, two runs per game more than three years ago.

Peters was traded away to Boston the previous winter and his two former sidekicks couldn't carry the load. John toiled more innings than ever before (269), but finished with 12-17. Horlen was 6-16 after being out from July 31 to September 7 for a knee cartilage operation. He was pitching well at the finish, even though he couldn't win. Jerry Janeski was 10-17 as a rookie with another freshman, Bart Johnson, looking promising in the final weeks.

Wilbur Wood again had an exhausting season in the bullpen. For the third straight year, he led the league in appearances with 77 and was 9-13 with 21 saves.

The White Sox defense undoubtedly contributed to the ineffectiveness of the pitching, though Luis Aparicio and Ken Berry were prominent exceptions. Oddly enough, Ken and Little Looey, both picked by major league managers and coaches to THE SPORTING NEWS All-Star glove team, were traded away for more youthful talent during the winter meetings.

Aparicio, despite his 36 years, had his greatest season. The shortstop magician hit .313 and, by playing game No. 2,219, broke Luke Appling's all-time major league record for most games played at shortstop. Berry, outstanding in center field, hit a personal high of .276.

Three other bright spots were Bill Melton, Ed Herrmann and Carlos May. Bill set a new White Sox club record for homers with 33 and also established a new high of 23 at Comiskey Park. Herrmann hit 19 homers and batted in 52 runs in 96 games.

May made a remarkable comeback after having the top of his right thumb blown off in a mortar firing accident at the Pendleton Marine base in August of 1969. He hit .285, walloped 12 homers and drove in 68 runs.

Amazingly, he threw very well despite having only a stump for a right thumb. In the closing weeks of the season, Tanner switched him from left field to first base, where he plans on starting him in 1971.

SCORES OF CHICAGO WHITE SOX' 1970 GAMES

APRIL—			Winner	Loser	MAY—			Winner	Loser
7—Minn.	L	0-12	Perry	John	6—Cleve.	W	2-1	Horlen	McDowell
9—Minn.	L	4-6	Williams	Horlen	8—At Balt.	L	1-6	Palmer	Janeski
10—Milw.	W	5-4	Janeski	Brabender	9—At Balt.	L	3-4	Phoebus	John
11—Milw.	L	4-8	O'Donoghue	Rounsaville	10—At Balt.	L	2-7	McNally	Arrigo
12—Milw.	L	2-5	Krausse	John	10—At Balt	L	2-4	Hall	Wood
12—Milw.	L	2-16	Lauzerique	Arrigo	11—At Det.	W	9-5	Crider	Niekro
14—At Calif.	W	3-1	Horlen	Wright	12—At Det.	W	7-2	Janeski	Cain
15—At Oak.	W	7-0	Janeski	Dobson	15—Kan. C.	W	9-3	Horlen	Nelson
16—At Oak.	L	1-5	Odom	John	16—Kan. C.	W	6-1	John	Johnson
18—At Milw.	W	8-5	Wood	Gelnar	17—Kan. C.	L	2-3‡	Fitzmorris	Wood
21—At Minn.	L	3-4	Kaat	John	17—Kan. C.	L	4-8§	Rooker	Wood
22—At Minn.	L	1-3*	Tiant	Horlen	18—Calif.	L	1-6	Messersmith	Wynne
23—At Minn.	W	7-5	Sisk	Perranoski	19—Calif.	L	0-3	May	Horlen
24—At Cleve.	L	1-4	Moore	Arrigo	20—Calif.	W	3-2	John	Murphy
25—At Cleve.	L	5-6	Hargan	John	22—Oakland	L	8-9	Lindblad	Wood
26—At Cleve.	W	2-0	Horlen	Chance	23—Oakland	L	2-12	Hunter	Horlen
28—Balt.	L	2-4	Cuellar	Janeski	24—Oakland	L	1-5	Dobson	John
29—Balt.	L	2-18	Palmer	Sisk	24—Oakland	L	2-5	Odom	Johnson
30—Balt.	W	6-3	John	Phoebus	25—At K. C.	L	1-7	Morehead	Crider
MAY—					26—At K. C.	W	3-1	Janeski	Johnson
1—Detroit	W	13-6	Horlen	Cain	27—At K. C.	L	3-4	Drago	Horlen
2—Detroit	W	3-2	Wood	Niekro	29—At Bos.	L	3-4	Lonborg	Wood
3—Detroit	L	5-6	Kilkenny	Wynne	30—At Bos.	L	5-7	Romo	Crider
5—Cleve.	W	2-1	John	Chance	31—At Bos.	W	22-13	Weaver	Peters

JUNE—			Winner	Loser
2—At Wash.	L	3-4	Pina	Wood
3—At Wash.	L	4-5	Coleman	John
4—At Wash.	W	7-3	Crider	Bosman
5—At N. Y.	L	1-10	Stottlemyre	Janeski
6—At N. Y.	L	1-3	Cumberland	Horlen
7—At N. Y.	W	4-3x	Wood	McDaniel
8—At Milw.	L	2-5	Krausse	Johnson
9—Boston	W	4-2	Janeski	Siebert
10—Boston	L	6-7z	Romo	Wood
12—Wash.	W	6-0	John	Brunet
13—Wash.	L	7-12	Hannan	Janeski
14—Wash.	L	4-8	Bosman	Horlen
14—Wash.	L	3-5	Cox	Crider
16—N. York	L	2-6	Stottlemyre	John
17—N. York	W	6-3	Janeski	Peterson
19—At Oak.	W	4-2	Horlen	Odom
20—At Oak.	L	5-8	Grant	Moore
21—At Oak.	L	3-6	Hunter	John
21—At Oak.	L	4-5	Fingers	Miller
23—At Calif.	W	7-3	Janeski	Mes'rsmith
24—At Calif.	L	1-3	Murphy	Horlen
24—At Calif.	L	1-2	Queen	Moore
25—At Calif.	L	3-7	Wright	John
26—Minn.	W	4-2	Miller	Kaat
27—Minn.	L	1-9	Blyleven	Janeski
28—Minn.	L	1-9	Hall	Horlen
28—Minn.	W	11-10	Murphy	Woodson
30—Oakland	L	3-4	Hunter	John
JULY—				
1—Oakland	L	0-3	Fingers	Janeski
2—Oakland	L	6-10	Lachemann	Moore
3—At Minn.	L	2-8	Perry	Horlen
3—At Minn.	W	5-3x	Wood	Woodson
5—At Minn.	L	3-12	Kaat	Miller
6—At Milw.	L	1-3	Brabender	Janeski
7—At Milw.	L	3-4x	Pattin	Wood
8—At Milw.	L	0-1	Krausse	Horlen
8—At Milw.	W	2-1	John	Downing
9—At Milw.	W	6-5	Crider	Lockwood
10—At K. C.	L	6-8	Johnson	Janeski
10—At K. C.	L	0-2	Rooker	Miller
11—At K. C.	L	0-4	Butler	Drago
12—At K. C.	W	10-5	John	Drago
16—Detroit	L	6-11	Scherman	Janeski
17—Detroit	L	3-4	Timmerman	Wood
18—Detroit	L	4-5	Lolich	Magnuson
19—Balt.	L	2-8	Palmer	Horlen
19—Balt.	W	7-3	Miller	Phoebus
20—Balt.	L	5-14	Cuellar	Janeski
21—At Cleve.	W	5-3	John	Dunning
22—At Cleve.	L	2-6	Hargan	Magnuson
23—At Cleve.	L	2-5	McDowell	Horlen
24—At Det.	W	5-2	Stange	Timmerman
24—At Det.	L	4-9	Hiller	Wood
24—At Det.	L	4-9	McLain	Crider
26—At Det.	W	4-0	John	Lolich
28—At Balt.	L	2-4	Cuellar	Horlen
29—At Balt.	W	2-1	Wood	Hardin
31—Cleve.	W	5-4	Murphy	Ellsworth

AUGUST—			Winner	Loser
1—Cleve.	L	2-3	McDowell	Janeski
2—Cleve.	L	2-4	Hand	Crider
2—Cleve.	W	8-7	Wood	Ellsworth
3—Kan. C.	L	2-7	Johnson	Miller
4—Kan. C.	W	2-1	John	Butler
5—Milw.	W	9-3	Magnuson	Brabender
6—Milw.	W	7-3	Janeski	Downing
7—Calif.	L	4-6	Fisher	Murphy
8—Calif.	W	8-1	Miller	May
9—Calif.	L	0-5	Wright	John
9—Calif.	L	3-6	Murphy	Crider
11—At N. Y.	L	1-7	Stottlemyre	Janeski
12—At N. Y.	L	1-5	Johnson	Rahnsen
13—At N. Y.	L	3-4	Aker	Weaver
14—At Wash.	L	5-6‡	Grzenda	Wood
15—At Wash.	L	2-4	Brown	Crider
16—At Wash.	L	1-2	Cox	Janeski
17—At Bos.	L	2-7	Koonce	Johnson
18—At Bos.	L	4-8	Brett	Miller
19—At Bos.	W	13-5	Wood	Culp
21—N. York	L	2-4	Kline	Janeski
22—N. York	W	3-2	Johnson	Bahnsen
23—N. York	L	2-0	John	Peterson
23—N. York	L	5-7	Kekich	Miller
25—Wash.	W	4-3	Wood	Knowles
27—Wash.	W	3-1	Janeski	Cox
28—Boston	L	4-5	Peters	John
29—Boston	W	13-9	Miller	Hartenstein
30—Boston	L	11-21	Brett	Janeski
30—Boston	L	1-4	Nagy	Magnuson
SEPTEMBER—				
1—At Oak.	L	5-6	Lindblad	Wood
3—At Oak.	L	1-2	Odom	Johnson
4—At Oak.	L	3-4	Locker	Wood
4—At Milw.	L	2-3‡	Sanders	Murphy
7—Oakland	L	4-7	Fingers	John
7—Oakland	L	5-7	Segui	Johnson
9—Calif.	W	11-4	Janeski	Murphy
9—Calif.	W	3-1†	Wynne	Wright
11—At Minn.	L	0-6	Zepp	Moore
12—At Minn.	W	5-3	Johnson	Blyleven
13—At Minn.	W	8-7	Crider	Williams
18—Minn.	L	4-5	Zepp	Johnson
19—Minn.	L	3-5	Hall	John
20—Minn.	L	1-8	Blyleven	Janeski
21—Kan. C.	W	8-4a	Wood	Monteagudo
21—Kan. C.	L	2-8a	York	Weaver
22—Kan. C.	L	1-2	Drago	Wynne
22—Kan. C.	L	2-3	Fitzmorris	Magnuson
23—Kan. C.	W	6-0	Johnson	Splittorff
25—Milw.	W	5-1	John	Lockwood
25—Milw.	L	2-3	Humphreys	Janeski
26—Milw.	L	5-9x	Morris	Murphy
27—Milw.	L	3-9	Pattin	Horlen
28—At Calif.	L	3-4	Murphy	Johnson
29—At Calif.	L	2-9	Wright	Wynne
30—At Calif.	L	1-5	Allen	John
OCTOBER—				
1—At Calif.	L	4-5y	May	Magnuson

* 5 innings.   † 8 innings.   ‡ 10 innings.   § 11 innings.   x 12 innings.   y 13 innings.   z 14 innings.   a Games of September 15-16, at Kansas City, transferred to Chicago.

American League Player Representatives

The American League player representatives for the 1971 season are as follows:

Steve Hamilton, Chicago White Sox, American League representative

Brooks Robinson—Baltimore Orioles	Dave Morehead—Kansas City Royals
Gary Peters—Boston Red Sox	Jim Perry—Minnesota Twins
Jim Fregosi—California Angels	Chuck Dobson—Oakland Athletics
Joel Horlen—Chicago White Sox	Jack Aker—New York Yankees
Sam McDowell—Cleveland Indians	Lew Krausse—Milwaukee Brewers
Jim Price—Detroit Tigers	Jim French—Washington Senators

(For Players Association and N. L. team representatives, see Page 159)

ALEX JOHNSON
• ANGELS •
BATTING CHAMPION
(.3289)

CARL YASTRZEMSKI
• RED SOX •
RUNS (125), TOTAL
BASES (335), SLUGGING
PERCENTAGE (.592)

FRANK HOWARD
• SENATORS •
HOME RUNS (44), RUNS
BATTED IN (126), BASES
ON BALLS (132)

1970 AMERICAN LEAGUE LEADERS

MIKE CUELLAR
• ORIOLES •
WINS (24-tied),
COMPLETE GAMES (21),
GAMES STARTED (40-tied),
WINNING PERCENTAGE (.750)

SAM McDOWELL
• INDIANS •
STRIKEOUTS (304),
INNINGS PITCHED
(305-tied)

JIM PALMER
• ORIOLES •
SHUTOUTS (5-tied),
INNINGS PITCHED
(305-tied)

American League Averages for 1970

CHAMPIONSHIP WINNERS IN PREVIOUS YEARS

1900—Chicago* .... .607	1923—New York .... .645	1947—New York .... .630
1901—Chicago .... .610	1924—Washington .... .597	1948—Cleveland† .... .626
1902—Philadelphia ...... .610	1925—Washington .... .636	1949—New York .... .630
1903—Boston .... .659	1926—New York .... .591	1950—New York .... .636
1904—Boston .... .617	1927—New York .... .714	1951—New York .... .636
1905—Philadelphia ...... .622	1928—New York .... .656	1952—New York .... .617
1906—Chicago .... .616	1929—Philadelphia ...... .693	1953—New York .... .656
1907—Detroit .... .613	1930—Philadelphia ...... .662	1954—Cleveland .... .721
1908—Detroit .... .588	1931—Philadelphia ...... .704	1955—New York .... .623
1909—Detroit .... .645	1932—New York .... .695	1956—New York .... .630
1910—Philadelphia ...... .680	1933—Washington .... .651	1957—New York .... .636
1911—Philadelphia ...... .669	1934—Detroit .... .656	1958—New York .... .597
1912—Boston .... .691	1935—Detroit .... .616	1959—Chicago .... .610
1913—Philadelphia ...... .627	1936—New York .... .667	1960—New York .... .630
1914—Philadelphia ...... .651	1937—New York .... .662	1961—New York .... .673
1915—Boston .... .669	1938—New York .... .651	1962—New York .... .593
1916—Boston .... .591	1939—New York .... .702	1963—New York .... .646
1917—Chicago .... .649	1940—Detroit .... .584	1964—New York .... .611
1918—Boston .... .595	1941—New York .... .656	1965—Minnesota .... .630
1919—Chicago .... .629	1942—New York .... .669	1966—Baltimore .... .606
1920—Cleveland .... .636	1943—New York .... .636	1967—Boston .... .568
1921—New York .... .641	1944—St. Louis .... .578	1968—Detroit .... .636
1922—New York .... .610	1945—Detroit .... .575	1969—Baltimore (East)‡ .. .673
	1946—Boston .... .675	

*Not recognized as major league in 1900. †Defeated Boston in one-game playoff for pennant. ‡Defeated Minnesota (West) in Championship Series.

STANDING OF CLUBS AT CLOSE OF SEASON

EAST DIVISION

Club	Balt.	N.Y.	Bos.	Det.	Clev.	Wash.	Minn.	Oak.	Cal.	K.C.	Mil.	Chi.	W.	L.	Pct.	G.B.
Baltimore	..	11	13	11	14	12	5	7	7	12	7	9	108	54	.667	....
New York	7	..	8	11	10	10	7	6	7	11	9	7	93	69	.574	15
Boston	5	10	..	9	12	12	7	7	5	7	5	8	87	75	.537	21
Detroit	7	7	9	..	11	9	4	6	6	6	8	6	79	83	.488	29
Cleveland	4	8	6	7	..	11	6	7	6	8	7	6	76	86	.469	32
Washington	6	8	6	9	7	..	6	2	5	6	7	8	70	92	.432	38

WEST DIVISION

Club	Minn.	Oak.	Cal.	K.C.	Mil.	Chi.	Balt.	N.Y.	Bos.	Det.	Clev.	Wash.	W.	L.	Pct.	G.B.
Minnesota	..	13	10	13	13	12	7	5	5	8	6	6	98	64	.605	....
Oakland	5	..	10	11	10	16	5	6	5	6	5	10	89	73	.549	9
California	8	8	..	10	12	12	5	5	7	6	6	7	86	76	.531	12
Kansas City	5	7	8	..	12	11	0	1	5	6	4	6	65	97	.401	33
Milwaukee	5	8	6	6	..	11	5	3	7	4	5	6	65	97	.401	33
Chicago	6	2	6	7	7	..	3	5	4	6	6	4	56	106	.346	42

TIE GAME—New York at Milwaukee, May 11 (5-5), nine innings.

CHAMPIONSHIP SERIES—Baltimore defeated Minnesota, three games to none.

RECORD AT HOME

EAST DIVISION

Club	Balt.	N.Y.	Bos.	Clev.	Det.	Wash.	Minn.	Oak.	Calif.	Mil.	K.C.	Chi.	W.	L.	Pct.
Baltimore	..-.	6-3	8-1	7-2	7-2	8-1	2-4	4-2	4-2	2-4	6-0	5-1	59	22	.728
New York	4-5	..-.	4-5	6-3	7-2	5-4	5-1	4-2	3-3	5-1	6-0	4-2	53	28	.654
Boston	4-5	5-4	..-.	7-2	6-3	6-3	5-1	5-1	3-3	3-3	4-2	4-2	52	29	.642
Cleveland	2-7	5-4	4-5	..-.	4-5	7-2	3-3	4-2	2-4	3-3	3-3	4-2	43	38	.531
Detroit	5-4	5-4	6-3	6-3	..-.	3-6	2-4	3-3	2-4	6-0	2-4	2-4	42	39	.519
Washington	5-4	4-5	3-6	5-4	3-6	..-.	3-3	1-5	2-4	6-0	3-3	5-1	40	41	.494

WEST DIVISION

Club	Minn.	Oak.	Cal.	Mil.	K.C.	Chi.	Balt.	N.Y.	Bos.	Clev.	Det.	Wash.	W.	L.	Pct.
Minnesota	..-.	6-3	4-5	7-2	8-1	5-4	3-3	4-2	4-2	3-3	4-2	3-3	51	30	.630
Oakland	2-7	..-.	5-4	6-3	7-2	7-2	3-3	4-2	4-2	3-3	3-3	5-1	49	32	.605
California	3-6	4-5	..-.	6-3	5-4	7-2	3-3	2-4	4-2	4-2	2-4	3-3	43	38	.531
Milwaukee	3-6	5-4	3-6	..-.	4-5	5-3	1-5	2-4	4-2	2-4	4-2	5-1	38	42	.475
Kansas City	4-5	5-4	4-5	7-2	..-.	5-2	0-6	1-5	3-3	1-5	2-4	3-3	35	44	.443
Chicago	2-7	0-9	4-5	4-6	5-6	..-.	2-4	3-3	2-4	4-2	2-4	3-3	31	53	.369

NOTE—Chicago at Milwaukee, September 6, postponed, played at Chicago, September 25; Chicago at Kansas City, September 15, 16, postponed, played at Chicago, September 21 (doubleheader).

RECORD ABROAD

EAST DIVISION

Club	Balt.	N.Y.	Det.	Bos.	Clev.	Wash.	Minn.	Cal.	Oak.	K.C.	Mil.	Chi.	W.	L.	Pct.
Baltimore	..-.	5-4	4-5	5-4	7-2	4-5	3-3	3-3	3-3	6-0	5-1	4-2	49	32	.605
New York	3-6	..-.	4-5	4-5	4-5	5-4	2-4	4-2	2-4	5-1	4-2	3-3	40	41	.494
Detroit	2-7	2-7	..-.	3-6	5-4	6-3	2-4	4-2	3-3	4-2	2-4	4-2	37	44	.457
Boston	1-8	5-4	3-6	..-.	5-4	6-3	2-4	2-4	2-4	3-3	2-4	4-2	35	46	.432
Cleveland	2-7	3-6	3-6	2-7	..-.	4-5	3-3	2-4	3-3	5-1	4-2	2-4	33	48	.407
Washington	1-8	4-5	6-3	3-6	2-7	..-.	3-3	3-3	1-5	3-3	1-5	3-3	30	51	.370

WEST DIVISION

Club	Minn.	Cal.	Oak.	K.C.	Mil.	Chi.	Balt.	N.Y.	Det.	Bos.	Clev.	Wash.	W.	L.	Pct.
Minnesota	..-.	6-3	7-2	5-4	6-3	7-2	4-2	1-5	4-2	1-5	3-3	3-3	47	34	.580
California	5-4	..-.	4-5	5-4	6-3	5-4	2-4	3-3	3-3	2-4	4-2	4-2	43	38	.531
Oakland	3-6	5-4	..-.	4-5	4-5	9-0	2-4	2-4	3-3	1-5	2-4	5-1	40	41	.494
Kansas City	1-8	4-5	2-7	..-.	5-4	6-5	0-6	0-6	4-2	2-4	3-3	3-3	30	53	.361
Milwaukee	2-7	3-6	3-6	2-7	..-.	6-4	4-2	1-5	0-6	3-3	3-3	0-6	27	55	.329
Chicago	4-5	2-7	2-7	2-5	3-5	..-.	1-5	2-4	4-2	2-4	2-4	1-5	25	53	.321

SHUTOUT GAMES

Club	Oak.	Balt.	Minn.	Bos.	Wash.	Clev.	Det.	K.C.	Chi.	Calif.	N.Y.	Mil.	W.	L.	Pct.
Oakland	...	1	2	0	3	0	1	2	1	2	3	0	15	5	.750
Baltimore	0	...	0	2	0	3	2	0	0	3	1	1	12	6	.667
Minnesota	0	1	...	1	0	1	1	3	2	1	1	1	12	6	.667
Boston	0	0	1	...	1	0	0	0	2	1	2	1	8	4	.667
Washington	0	2	1	0	...	0	2	1	0	2	1	1	11	10	.524
Cleveland	0	1	0	1	0	...	1	3	0	1	1	0	8	9	.471
Detroit	0	1	0	0	2	2	...	1	0	0	2	1	9	11	.450
Kansas City	1	0	1	0	0	1	1	...	2	3	0	2	11	14	.440
Chicago	1	0	0	0	1	1	1	1	...	0	1	0	6	8	.429
California	2	0	0	0	2	1	0	1	2	...	0	2	10	15	.400
New York	0	0	1	0	1	0	1	2	0	1	...	0	6	11	.353
Milwaukee	1	0	0	0	0	0	0	0	1	0	0	...	2	11	.154

OFFICIAL AMERICAN LEAGUE BATTING AVERAGES

Compiled by Howe News Bureau, Chicago, Ill.

CLUB BATTING

Club	G.	AB.	R.	OR.	H.	TB.	2B.	3B.	HR.	RBI.	SH.	SF.	SB.	CS.	Pct.
Minnesota	162	5483	744	605	1438	2209	230	41	153	694	79	38	57	52	.2622
Boston	162	5535	786	722	1450	2367	252	28	203	743	34	47	50	48	.2619
Baltimore	162	5545	792	574	1424	2224	213	25	179	748	64	46	84	39	.257
Chicago	162	5514	633	822	1394	1995	192	20	123	587	51	48	53	33	.253
California	162	5532	631	630	1391	2010	197	40	114	598	69	37	69	27	.251
New York	162	5492	680	612	1381	2004	208	41	111	627	60	46	105	61	.251
Cleveland	162	5463	649	675	1358	2150	197	23	183	617	76	45	25	36	.249
Oakland	162	5376	678	593	1338	2107	208	24	171	630	73	36	131	68	.249
Kansas City	162	5503	611	705	1341	1916	202	41	97	572	63	27	97	53	.244
Milwaukee	163	5395	613	751	1305	1933	202	24	126	571	115	32	91	73	.242
Washington	162	5460	626	689	1302	1956	184	28	138	588	43	44	38	72	.238
Detroit	162	5377	666	731	1282	2009	207	38	148	619	83	49	29	30	.238
Totals		65675	8109	8109	16404	24880	2492	373	1746	7589	811	489	863	562	.250

INDIVIDUAL BATTING

(Top Fifteen Qualifiers for Batting Championship—502 or More Plate Appearances)

*Bats lefthanded. †Switch-hitter.

Player and Club	G.	AB.	R.	H.	TB.	2B.	3B.	HR.	RBI.	SH.	SF.	SB.	CS.	Pct.
Johnson, Alexander, California	156	614	85	202	282	26	6	14	86	0	3	17	2	.3289
Yastrzemski, Carl, Boston*	161	566	125	186	335	29	0	40	102	0	2	23	13	.3286
Oliva, Pedro (Tony), Minnesota*	157	628	96	204	323	36	7	23	107	1	4	5	4	.325
Aparicio, Luis, Chicago	146	552	86	173	223	29	3	5	43	5	5	8	3	.313
Robinson, Frank, Baltimore	132	471	88	144	245	24	1	25	78	0	6	2	1	.306
Smith, C. Reginald, Boston†	147	580	109	176	288	32	7	22	74	0	5	10	7	.303
Munson, Thurman, New York	132	453	59	137	188	25	4	6	53	5	4	5	7	.302
Piniella, Louis, Kansas City	144	542	54	163	230	24	5	11	88	2	5	3	6	.301
Cater, Danny, New York	155	582	64	175	229	26	5	6	76	1	2	4	2	.301
Tovar, Cesar, Minnesota	161	650	120	195	287	36	13	10	54	10	6	30	15	.300
Powell, John, Baltimore*	154	526	82	156	289	28	0	35	114	0	8	1	1	.297
Harper, Tommy, Milwaukee	154	604	104	179	315	35	4	31	82	3	4	38	16	.296
Scott, George, Boston	127	480	50	142	224	24	5	16	63	0	4	4	11	.296
White, Roy, New York†	162	609	109	180	288	30	6	22	94	1	7	24	10	.296
Pinson, Vada, Cleveland*	148	574	74	164	276	28	6	24	82	0	6	7	6	.286

DEPARTMENTAL LEADERS: G—Alomar, White, 162; AB—Clarke, 686; R—Yastrzemski, 125; H—Oliva, 204; TB—Yastrzemski, 335; 2B—Oliva, Otis, Tovar, 36; 3B—Tovar, 13; HR—Howard, 44; RBI—Howard, 126; SH—Leon, 23; SF—Heidemann, Petrocelli, 10; SB—Campaneris, 42; CS—Jackson, 17.

EXPLANATION OF ABBREVIATION TERMS

G—Games Played. AB—At Bats. R—Runs. H—Hits. TB—Total Bases. 2B—Two-Base Hits. 3B—Three-Base Hits. HR—Home Runs. RBI—Runs Batted In. SH—Sacrifice Hits. SF—Sacrifice Flies. SB—Stolen Bases. CS—Caught Stealing. BB—Bases on Balls. IBB—Intentional Bases on Balls. HP—Hit by Pitcher. SO—Strikeouts. Pct.—Percentage. GIDP—Grounded into Double Plays. Slg.Pct.—Slugging Percentage. OR—Opponents' Runs. LOB—Left on Bases. PO—Putouts. A—Assists. E—Errors. TC—Total Chances. DP—Double Plays. TP—Triple Plays. PB—Passed Balls. G—Games Pitched. GS—Games Started. CG—Complete Games. GF—Games Finished in Relief. IG—Games Not Finished as Relief Pitcher. ShO—Shutouts. W—Games Won. L—Games Lost. IP—Innings Pitched. BFP—Total Batters Facing Pitcher. ER—Earned Runs. HB—Hit Batsmen. WP—Wild Pitches. Bk—Balks. ERA—Earned-Run Average. Sv—Saves.

(All Players in Ten or More Games—Listed Alphabetically)

Player and Club	G.	AB.	R.	H.	TB.	2B.	3B.	HR.	RBI.	SH.	SF.	SB.	CS.	Pct.
Abernathy, Ted, Kansas City	36	14	1	3	3	0	0	0	2	3	0	0	0	.214
Aker, Jack, New York	41	16	0	1	1	0	0	0	1	1	0	0	0	.063
Alcaraz, A. Luis, Kansas City	35	120	10	20	30	5	1	1	14	1	1	0	0	.167
Allen, Bernard, Washington*	104	261	31	61	94	7	1	8	29	1	0	0	2	.234
Allen, Harold, 22 Wash-28 Mil	50	99	7	22	28	6	0	0	8	0	1	0	1	.222
Allison, W. Robert, Minnesota	47	72	15	15	23	5	0	1	7	0	0	1	0	.208
Alomar, Santos, California†	162	672	82	169	197	18	2	2	36	11	2	35	12	.251
Alou, Felipe, Oakland	154	575	70	156	211	25	3	8	55	4	6	10	5	.271
Alvarado, Luis, Boston	59	183	19	41	55	11	0	1	10	2	2	1	2	.224
Alvis, R. Maxwell, Milwaukee	62	115	16	21	32	2	0	3	12	0	0	1	2	.183
Alyea, Garrabrant, Minnesota	94	258	34	75	137	12	1	16	61	0	1	3	3	.291
Andrews, Michael, Boston	151	589	91	149	230	28	1	17	65	4	4	2	1	.253
Aparicio, Luis, Chicago	146	552	86	173	223	29	3	5	43	5	5	8	3	.313
Austin, Rick, Cleveland	31	18	0	2	3	1	0	0	0	0	0	0	0	.111
Azcue, Jose, California	114	351	19	85	106	13	1	2	25	1	3	0	0	.242
Bahnsen, Stanley, New York	36	74	3	11	13	0	1	0	1	8	0	0	0	.149
Baker, Frank, New York*	35	117	6	27	33	4	1	0	11	0	0	1	2	.231
Baldwin, David, Milwaukee	28	2	0	1	1	0	0	0	0	0	0	0	0	.500
Bando, Salvatore, Oakland	155	502	93	132	216	20	2	20	75	7	3	6	10	.263
Barber, Steven, Minnesota	19	2	0	0	0	0	0	0	0	1	0	0	0	.000
Belanger, Mark, Baltimore	145	459	53	100	119	6	5	1	36	9	2	13	2	.218
Berry, A. Kent, Chicago	141	463	45	128	165	12	2	7	50	1	2	6	4	.276
Billings, Richard, Washington	11	24	3	6	11	2	0	1	1	0	0	0	0	.250
Blair, Paul, Baltimore	133	480	79	128	210	24	2	18	65	5	4	24	11	.267
Blanco, C. Oswaldo, Chicago	34	66	4	13	13	0	0	0	8	0	2	0	1	.197
Blefary, Curtis, New York*	99	269	34	57	90	6	0	9	37	0	3	1	3	.212
Blyleven, Rikalbert, Minnesota	27	50	2	7	7	0	0	0	1	7	0	0	0	.140
Bolin, Bobby, 32 Mil-6 Bos	38	37	3	7	10	0	0	1	2	6	0	0	0	.189
Bosman, Richard, Washington	36	80	4	11	11	0	0	0	2	6	0	0	0	.138
Boswell, David, Minnesota	20	25	0	4	5	1	0	0	0	0	0	0	0	.160
Brabender, Eugene, Milwaukee	29	41	1	4	6	2	0	0	2	3	0	0	1	.098
Bradford, Charles, 32Chi-75Cle	107	254	33	49	87	9	1	9	31	1	2	1	3	.193
Bradley, Thomas, California	17	18	0	3	4	1	0	0	1	3	0	0	0	.167
Brett, Kenneth, Boston*	41	41	8	13	22	3	0	2	3	1	0	0	0	.317
Brinkman, Edwin, Washington	158	625	63	164	188	17	2	1	40	1	4	8	9	.262
Brown, Isaac, Detroit	56	94	17	27	44	5	0	4	15	4	1	0	0	.287
Brown, Jackie, Washington	24	13	1	2	2	0	0	0	0	0	0	0	0	.154
Brown, Larry, Cleveland	72	155	17	40	49	5	2	0	15	3	2	1	0	.258
Brown, W. Gates, Detroit*	81	124	18	28	40	3	0	3	24	0	3	0	0	.226
Brunet, George, Washington	24	38	4	6	10	1	0	1	4	4	0	0	0	.158
Buford, Donald, Baltimore†	144	504	99	137	207	15	2	17	66	3	5	16	8	.272
Bunker, Wallace, Kansas City	24	31	3	2	2	0	0	0	1	1	0	0	0	.065
Burda, E. Robert, Milwaukee*	78	222	19	55	76	9	0	4	20	2	3	1	0	.248
Burgmeier, Thomas, Kansas City*	42	14	1	2	2	0	0	0	1	3	0	0	0	.143
Butler, William, Kansas City	25	44	0	2	2	0	0	0	2	1	0	0	0	.045
Cain, Leslie, Detroit*	29	68	2	11	15	1	0	1	9	3	0	0	0	.162
Camilli, Louis, Cleveland†	16	15	0	0	0	0	0	0	0	0	0	0	0	.000
Campaneris, Dagoberto, Oak	147	603	97	168	270	28	4	22	64	3	4	42	10	.279
Campanis, James, Kansas City	31	54	6	7	13	0	0	2	2	0	0	0	0	.130
Cardenas, Leonardo, Minnesota	160	588	67	145	220	34	4	11	65	13	2	2	5	.247
Carew, Rodney, Minnesota*	51	191	27	70	100	12	3	4	28	0	0	4	6	.366
Casanova, Paul, Washington	104	328	25	75	116	17	3	6	30	0	4	0	0	.229
Cash, Norman, Detroit*	130	370	58	96	163	18	2	15	53	0	5	0	1	.259
Cater, Danny, New York	155	582	64	175	229	26	5	6	76	1	2	4	2	.301
Chance, W. Dean, Cleveland	45	42	1	3	3	0	0	0	3	4	1	0	0	.071
Christian, Robert, Chicago	12	15	3	4	7	0	0	1	3	0	0	0	0	.267
Clarke, Horace, New York†	158	686	81	172	212	24	2	4	46	2	7	23	7	.251
Colbert, Vincent, Cleveland	23	2	0	0	0	0	0	0	0	0	0	0	0	.000
Coleman, Joseph, Washington	39	67	5	8	9	1	0	0	6	4	0	0	0	.119
Collins, Kevin, Detroit*	25	24	2	5	9	1	0	1	3	0	0	0	0	.208
Comer, H. Wayne, 13Mil-77Wash	90	146	22	31	35	4	0	0	9	1	1	4	1	.212
Conigliaro, Anthony, Boston	146	560	89	149	279	20	1	36	116	0	6	4	2	.266
Conigliaro, William, Boston	114	398	59	108	184	16	3	18	58	1	3	3	7	.271
Cowan, Billy, California	68	134	20	37	63	9	1	5	25	0	0	1	0	.276
Cox, J. Casey, Washington	37	58	1	7	7	0	0	0	2	7	0	0	0	.121

Player and Club	G.	AB.	R.	H.	TB.	2B.	3B.	HR.	RBI.	SH.	SF.	SB.	CS.	Pct.
Crider, Jerry, Chicago	32	24	2	2	3	1	0	0	0	2	0	0	0	.083
Crowley, Terrence, Baltimore*	83	152	25	39	59	5	0	5	20	2	1	2	0	.257
Cuellar, Miguel, Baltimore*	41	112	6	10	17	1	0	2	7	9	0	0	0	.089
Cullen, Timothy, Washington	123	262	22	56	73	10	2	1	18	2	3	3	2	.214
Culp, Raymond, Boston	33	97	3	12	13	1	0	0	4	5	0	0	0	.124
Cumberland, John, New York	15	17	0	1	1	0	0	0	2	3	0	0	0	.059
Dalrymple, Clayton, Baltimore*	13	32	4	7	11	1	0	1	3	0	1	0	0	.219
Davis, H. Thomas, Oakland	66	200	17	58	72	9	1	1	27	2	2	2	4	.290
Derrick, J. Michael, Boston*	24	33	3	7	8	1	0	0	5	0	1	0	1	.212
Dobson, Charles, Oakland	41	93	4	11	12	1	0	0	8	5	0	0	0	.118
Donaldson, John, Oakland*	41	89	4	22	29	2	1	1	11	0	0	1	0	.247
Downing, Alphonso, 10 Oak-17 Mil	27	35	0	4	4	0	0	0	2	8	0	0	0	.114
Doyle, Paul, California*	40	3	0	0	0	0	0	0	0	0	0	0	0	.000
Drabowsky, Myron, 24KC-21Balt	45	9	0	1	1	0	0	0	0	1	0	0	0	.111
Drago, Richard, Kansas City	35	76	2	4	4	0	0	0	1	9	0	0	0	.053
Driscoll, James, Oakland*	21	52	2	10	13	0	0	1	2	1	0	0	0	.192
Duncan, David, Oakland	86	232	21	60	97	7	0	10	29	2	2	0	0	.259
Dunning, Steven, Cleveland	19	31	0	5	5	0	0	0	1	3	0	0	0	.161
Egan, Thomas, California	79	210	14	50	68	6	0	4	20	1	2	0	0	.238
Ellis, John, New York	78	226	24	56	91	12	1	7	29	0	3	0	1	.248
Ellsworth, Richard, 29Cle-14Mil*	43	4	0	0	0	0	0	0	0	1	0	0	0	.000
Epstein, Michael, Washington*	140	430	55	110	191	15	3	20	56	0	6	2	3	.256
Etchebarren, Andrew, Baltimore	78	230	19	56	80	10	1	4	28	0	2	4	1	.243
Fanzone, Carmen, Boston	10	15	0	3	4	1	0	0	3	0	1	0	0	.200
Fernandez, Frank, Oakland	94	252	30	54	104	5	0	15	44	0	0	1	0	.214
Fingers, Roland, Oakland	45	39	1	4	7	0	0	1	1	4	0	0	0	.103
Fiore, Michael, 25 KC-41 Bos*	66	122	11	20	22	2	0	0	8	0	1	1	1	.164
Fisher, Eddie, California	67	11	1	1	1	0	0	0	0	3	0	0	0	.091
Fitzmorris, Alan, Kansas City†	45	31	5	9	13	4	0	0	5	0	0	0	0	.290
Floyd, Robert, 3 Balt-14 KC	17	45	5	14	18	4	0	0	1	1	0	1	1	.311
Ford, Theodore, Cleveland	26	46	5	8	12	1	0	1	1	0	0	0	0	.174
Fosse, Raymond, Cleveland	120	450	62	138	211	17	1	18	61	4	3	1	5	.307
Foster, Roy, Cleveland	139	477	66	128	223	26	0	23	60	1	1	3	3	.268
Francona, John, 32 Oak-52 Mil*	84	98	6	23	29	3	0	1	10	3	0	1	0	.235
Freehan, William, Detroit	117	395	44	95	166	17	3	16	52	3	4	0	3	.241
Fregosi, James, California	158	601	95	167	276	33	5	22	82	2	4	2	2	.278
French, R. James, Washington*	69	166	20	35	43	3	1	1	13	2	0	0	1	.211
Fuller, Vern, Cleveland	29	33	3	6	11	2	0	1	2	0	0	0	0	.182
Garrett, Gregory, California†	32	15	0	1	1	0	0	0	0	1	0	0	0	.067
Gelnar, John, Milwaukee	53	12	1	1	1	0	0	0	0	0	0	0	0	.083
Gibbs, Jerry, New York*	49	153	23	46	83	9	2	8	26	0	2	2	0	.301
Gil, T. Gustavo, Milwaukee	64	119	12	22	29	4	0	1	12	4	2	2	0	.185
Gonzalez, A. Antonio, Calif*	26	92	9	28	33	2	0	1	12	2	0	3	2	.304
Goossen, Gregory, 21Mil-21Wash	42	83	5	20	29	6	0	1	4	0	1	0	0	.241
Grant, James, Oakland	72	9	0	2	2	0	0	0	1	5	0	0	0	.222
Green, Richard, Oakland	135	384	34	73	92	7	0	4	29	5	2	3	0	.190
Grich, Robert, Baltimore	30	95	11	20	27	1	3	0	8	0	0	1	1	.211
Grieve, Thomas, Washington	47	116	12	23	39	5	1	3	10	0	0	0	0	.198
Griffin, Douglas, California	18	55	2	7	8	1	0	0	4	1	0	0	0	.127
Grzenda, Joseph, Washington	49	12	0	0	0	0	0	0	0	0	0	0	0	.000
Gutierrez, Cesar, Detroit	135	415	40	101	124	11	6	0	22	14	3	4	3	.243
Hall, Richard, Baltimore	32	12	2	1	1	0	0	0	1	0	0	0	0	.083
Hall, Tom, Minnesota*	53	44	4	8	8	0	0	0	1	6	0	0	0	.182
Hamilton, Steven, 35 NY-3 Chi*	38	6	0	0	0	0	0	0	0	0	0	0	0	.000
Hamm, Peter, Minnesota	10	1	0	0	0	0	0	0	0	0	0	0	0	.000
Hand, Richard, Cleveland	35	41	2	6	6	0	0	0	5	5	2	0	0	.146
Hannan, James, Washington	42	31	1	4	4	0	0	0	1	2	0	0	0	.129
Hansen, Ronald, New York	59	91	13	27	43	4	0	4	14	1	1	0	1	.297
Hardin, James, Baltimore	36	45	2	3	5	0	1	0	4	2	0	0	0	.067
Hargan, Steven, Cleveland	28	45	4	5	6	1	0	0	0	8	0	0	0	.111
Harper, Tommy, Milwaukee	154	604	104	179	315	35	4	31	82	3	4	38	16	.296
Harrelson, Kenneth, Cleveland	17	39	3	11	15	1	0	1	1	0	0	0	0	.282
Hartenstein, Charles, Boston	17	2	0	0	0	0	0	0	0	0	0	0	0	.000
Hegan, J. Michael, Milwaukee*	148	476	70	116	174	21	2	11	52	8	4	9	7	.244
Heidemann, Jack, Cleveland	133	445	44	94	130	14	2	6	37	4	10	2	4	.211
Hendricks, Elrod, Baltimore*	106	322	32	78	123	9	0	12	41	2	4	1	0	.242
Hennigan, Phillip, Cleveland	42	7	1	1	2	1	0	0	1	2	0	0	0	.143

Player and Club	G.	AB.	R.	H.	TB.	2B.	3B.	HR.	RBI.	SH.	SF.	SB.	CS.	Pct.
Hernandez, Jacinto, Kansas City	83	238	14	55	67	4	1	2	10	6	1	1	3	.231
Herrmann, Edward, Chicago*	96	297	42	84	150	9	0	19	52	2	0	0	1	.283
Hershberger, N. Michael, Mil	49	98	7	23	31	5	0	1	6	0	0	1	2	.235
Higgins, Dennis, Cleveland	58	12	1	3	3	0	0	0	1	1	0	0	0	.250
Hill, Herman, Minnesota*	27	22	8	2	2	0	0	0	0	1	0	0	0	.091
Hiller, John, Detroit	47	23	0	0	0	0	0	0	0	1	0	0	0	.000
Hinton, Charles, Cleveland	107	195	24	62	93	4	0	9	29	2	2	0	2	.318
Holt, James, Minnesota	142	319	37	85	109	9	3	3	40	1	4	3	1	.266
Hopkins, Gail, Chicago*	116	287	32	82	110	8	1	6	29	0	5	0	0	.286
Horlen, Joel, Chicago	28	52	2	6	7	1	0	0	1	5	0	0	0	.115
Horton, Anthony, Cleveland	115	413	48	111	187	19	3	17	59	0	5	3	2	.269
Horton, Willie, Detroit	96	371	53	113	186	18	2	17	69	0	3	0	1	.305
Hovley, Stephen, 40Mil-720ak*	112	235	25	57	67	10	0	0	17	0	0	8	1	.243
Howard, Frank, Washington	161	566	90	160	309	15	1	44	126	0	6	1	2	.283
Humphreys, Robert, 5Wash-23Mil	28	9	0	0	0	0	0	0	0	1	0	0	0	.000
Hunter, James, Oakland	43	90	10	18	27	4	1	1	6	6	1	0	0	.200
Jackson, Reginald, Oakland*	149	426	57	101	195	21	4	23	66	2	3	26	17	.237
Janeski, Gerard, Chicago	35	66	0	5	5	0	0	0	5	7	0	0	0	.076
Jarvis, Raymond, Boston	15	0	0	0	0	0	0	0	0	1	0	0	0	.000
John, Thomas, Chicago	38	84	4	17	18	1	0	0	0	5	0	0	0	.202
Johnson, Alexander, California	156	614	85	202	282	26	6	14	86	0	3	17	2	.3289
Johnson, C. Barth, Chicago	18	29	3	8	10	2	0	0	2	2	0	0	0	.276
Johnson, David, Baltimore	149	530	68	149	208	27	1	10	53	3	1	2	1	.281
Johnson, Robert D., Kansas City	40	57	2	6	7	1	0	0	3	8	0	0	1	.105
Johnson, Robert W., Oakland	30	46	6	8	12	1	0	1	2	0	1	2	1	.174
Johnstone, John, California*	119	320	34	76	129	10	5	11	39	3	3	1	0	.238
Jones, J. Dalton, Detroit*	89	191	29	42	67	7	0	6	21	1	3	1	1	.220
Josephson, Duane, Chicago	96	285	28	90	116	12	1	4	41	1	4	0	1	.316
Kaat, James, Minnesota*	56	76	17	15	19	1	0	1	8	4	1	0	0	.197
Kaline, Albert, Detroit	131	467	64	130	210	24	4	16	71	3	7	2	2	.278
Kealey, Steven, California	17	4	0	1	1	0	0	0	0	0	0	0	0	.250
Kekich, Michael, New York	26	32	2	3	3	0	0	0	2	2	0	0	0	.094
Kelly, H. Patrick, Kansas City*	136	452	56	106	142	16	1	6	38	0	1	34	16	.235
Kennedy, John, 25 Mil-43 Bos	68	184	23	47	76	9	1	6	23	3	1	0	1	.255
Kenney, Gerald, New York*	140	404	46	78	114	10	7	4	35	3	2	20	6	.193
Keough, Joseph, Kansas City*	57	183	28	59	81	6	2	4	21	3	1	1	1	.322
Kilkenny, Michael, Detroit	37	39	0	3	3	0	0	0	1	4	1	0	0	.077
Killebrew, Harmon, Minnesota	157	527	96	143	288	20	1	41	113	0	8	0	3	.271
Kirkpatrick, Edgar, Kan City*	134	424	59	97	172	17	2	18	62	1	0	4	4	.229
Klimchock, Louis, Cleveland*	41	56	5	9	12	0	0	1	2	0	1	0	0	.161
Klimkowski, Ronald, New York	45	19	0	1	1	0	0	0	0	4	0	0	0	.053
Kline, Steven, New York	16	28	3	5	5	0	0	0	2	4	0	0	0	.179
Knoop, Robert, Chicago	130	402	34	92	124	13	2	5	36	1	4	0	1	.229
Knowles, Darold, Washington*	71	20	0	1	1	0	0	0	1	2	0	0	0	.050
Koonce, Calvin, Boston	23	21	5	2	2	0	0	0	3	1	0	0	0	.095
Krausse, Lewis, Milwaukee	38	65	3	9	11	0	1	0	4	7	0	0	1	.138
Kubiak, Theodore, Milwaukee†	158	540	63	136	169	9	6	4	41	13	0	4	9	.252
Lachemann, Marcel, Oakland	41	8	0	0	0	0	0	0	0	0	0	0	0	.000
LaGrow, Lerrin, Detroit	10	1	0	0	0	0	0	0	0	0	0	0	0	.000
Lahoud, Joseph, Boston*	17	49	6	12	19	1	0	2	5	0	0	0	0	.245
Lamont, Gene, Detroit†	15	44	3	13	21	3	1	1	4	1	0	0	0	.295
LaRoche, David, California*	38	8	0	2	3	1	0	0	0	0	0	0	0	.250
LaRussa, Anthony, Oakland	52	106	6	21	27	4	1	0	6	0	1	0	0	.198
Lasher, Frederick, 12 Det-43 Clev	55	9	0	0	0	0	0	0	0	1	0	0	0	.000
Lauzerique, George, Milwaukee	11	10	2	2	5	0	0	1	4	3	0	0	0	.200
Lee, William, Boston*	11	11	0	0	0	0	0	0	0	0	0	0	0	.000
Leon, Eduardo, Cleveland	152	549	58	136	194	20	4	10	56	23	3	1	2	.248
Leonhard, David, Baltimore	25	1	0	0	0	0	0	0	0	0	0	0	0	.000
Lewis, Allan, Oakland†	25	8	8	2	5	0	0	1	1	0	0	7	1	.250
Lindblad, Paul, Oakland*	62	6	0	0	0	0	0	0	0	1	0	0	0	.000
Locker, Robert, 28 Mil-38 Oak†	66	7	0	1	1	0	0	0	0	0	0	0	0	.143
Lockwood, Claude, Milwaukee	27	53	2	12	16	1	0	1	2	12	1	0	0	.226
Lolich, Michael, Detroit†	42	82	4	11	11	0	0	3	7	0	1	0	0	.134
Lopez, Marcelino, Baltimore	25	13	0	1	1	0	0	0	0	0	0	0	0	.077
Lowenstein, John, Cleveland*	17	43	5	11	19	3	1	1	6	0	0	1	0	.256
Lyle, Albert, Boston*	63	13	2	0	0	0	0	0	1	0	0	0	0	.000
Lyttle, James, New York*	87	126	20	39	57	7	1	3	14	2	2	3	6	.310
Maddox, Elliott, Detroit	109	258	30	64	94	13	4	3	24	1	1	2	3	.248

Player and Club	G.	AB.	R.	H.	TB.	2B.	3B.	HR.	RBI.	SH.	SF.	SB.	CS.	Pct.
Magnuson, James, Chicago	13	11	1	0	0	0	0	0	0	1	0	0	0	.000
Manuel, Charles, Minnesota*	59	64	4	12	15	0	0	1	7	0	2	0	0	.188
Matchick, J. Thomas, 10 Boston-55 Kan City*	65	172	13	32	39	3	2	0	11	1	0	0	1	.186
Matias, John, Chicago*	58	117	7	22	30	2	0	2	6	0	0	1	0	.188
May, Carlos, Chicago*	150	555	83	158	230	28	4	12	68	0	6	12	5	.285
May, David, 25 Balt-101 Mil*	126	373	42	88	124	8	2	8	37	4	1	8	6	.236
May, Rudolph, California*	38	69	0	6	8	2	0	0	2	2	1	0	0	.087
Maye, A. Lee, 96 Wash-6 Chi*	102	261	28	68	103	12	1	7	31	0	0	4	2	.261
McAuliffe, Richard, Detroit*	146	530	73	124	183	21	1	12	50	3	2	5	6	.234
McCraw, Tommy, Chicago*	129	332	39	73	106	11	2	6	31	2	2	12	3	.220
McDaniel, Lyndall, New York	62	24	2	4	5	1	0	0	2	2	1	0	0	.167
McDowell, Samuel, Cleveland*	40	105	5	13	16	0	0	1	2	8	0	0	0	.124
McKinney, C. Richard, Chicago	43	119	12	20	37	5	0	4	17	0	1	3	2	.168
McLain, Dennis, Detroit	14	31	2	2	3	1	0	0	0	3	0	0	0	.065
McMullen, Kenneth, 15 Wash-124 Calif	139	481	55	110	169	11	3	14	64	1	3	1	0	.229
McNally, David, Baltimore	41	105	14	14	23	6	0	1	6	6	0	0	0	.133
McNertney, Gerald, Milwaukee	111	296	27	72	103	11	1	6	22	5	2	1	4	.243
McRae, Norman, Detroit	19	1	0	0	0	0	0	0	0	0	0	0	0	.000
Melton, William, Chicago	141	514	74	135	251	15	4	33	96	1	9	2	4	.263
Mendoza, C. Rigoberto, Minnesota	16	16	2	3	3	0	0	0	2	0	0	0	0	.188
Messersmith, John A., California	38	70	4	11	17	3	0	1	2	5	0	0	0	.157
Meyer, Robert, Milwaukee	10	3	0	1	1	0	0	0	0	0	2	0	0	.333
Michael, Eugene, New York†	134	435	42	93	111	10	1	2	38	4	4	3	1	.214
Miller, Robert, 15 Clev-16 Chi	31	28	0	5	5	0	0	0	2	2	0	0	0	.179
Mincher, Donald, Oakland*	140	463	62	114	213	18	0	27	74	4	7	5	4	.246
Mingori, Stephen, Cleveland*	21	1	0	0	0	0	0	0	0	0	0	0	2	.000
Mitchell, Robert, New York	10	22	1	5	7	2	0	0	4	0	0	0	2	.227
Mitterwald, George, Minnesota	117	369	36	82	143	12	2	15	46	4	3	5	2	.222
Monday, Robert, Oakland*	112	376	63	109	172	19	7	10	37	5	1	17	11	.290
Monteagudo, Aurelio, Kansas City	21	2	0	0	0	0	0	0	0	0	0	0	0	.000
Montgomery, Robert, Boston	22	78	8	14	19	2	0	1	4	0	1	0	0	.179
Moore, R. Barry, 13 Clev-24 Chi*	37	40	3	7	7	0	0	0	2	2	0	0	0	.175
Morales, Richard, Chicago	62	112	6	18	23	2	0	1	2	0	1	1	0	.161
Morehead, David, Kansas City	28	36	1	6	7	1	0	0	1	3	0	0	0	.167
Morris, John, Milwaukee	20	17	2	3	4	1	0	0	0	0	0	0	0	.176
Moses, Gerald, Boston	92	315	26	83	121	18	1	6	35	1	1	1	1	.263
Motton, Curtell, Baltimore	52	84	16	19	33	3	1	3	19	2	0	1	2	.226
Munson, Thurman, New York	132	453	59	137	188	25	4	6	53	5	4	5	7	.302
Murcer, Bobby, New York*	159	581	95	146	244	23	4	23	78	4	6	15	10	.251
Murphy, Daniel, Chicago*	51	6	3	2	5	0	0	1	1	0	0	0	0	.333
Murphy, Thomas, California	39	76	7	14	18	1	0	1	7	8	1	0	0	.184
Nagelson, Russell, 17Clev-28Det*	45	56	8	9	13	1	0	1	4	1	0	0	0	.161
Nagy, Michael, Boston	23	44	3	11	14	1	1	0	4	2	0	0	0	.250
Nelson, David, Washington	47	107	5	17	18	1	0	0	4	2	2	2	1	.159
Nettles, Graig, Cleveland*	157	549	81	129	222	13	1	26	62	0	0	3	1	.235
Nettles, James, Minnesota*	13	20	3	5	5	0	0	0	1	0	0	0	1	.250
Niekro, Joseph, Detroit	39	66	8	13	18	3	1	0	7	15	0	0	0	.197
Northrup, James, Detroit*	139	504	71	132	231	21	3	24	80	2	5	3	6	.262
O'Brien, Sydney, Chicago	121	441	48	109	150	13	2	8	44	0	2	3	3	.247
Odom, John, Oakland	37	54	8	13	24	2	0	3	7	1	0	1	0	.241
O'Donoghue, John, Milwaukee	25	2	0	0	0	0	0	0	0	0	0	0	0	.000
Oliva, Pedro (Tony), Minnesota*	157	628	96	204	323	36	7	23	107	1	4	5	4	.325
Oliver, Robert, Kansas City	160	612	83	159	276	24	6	27	99	2	3	3	3	.260
Ortiz, Jose, Chicago	15	24	4	8	9	1	0	0	1	1	0	1	0	.333
Otis, Amos, Kansas City	159	620	91	176	263	36	9	11	58	6	5	33	2	.284
Oyler, Raymond, California	24	24	2	2	2	0	0	0	1	2	0	0	0	.083
Palmer, James, Baltimore	44	113	13	17	20	0	0	1	9	7	0	0	0	.150
Patterson, Daryl, Detroit*	43	11	0	0	0	0	0	0	0	0	0	0	0	.000
Pattin, Martin, Milwaukee	43	70	4	9	10	1	0	0	3	7	1	0	0	.129
Paul, Michael, Cleveland*	30	26	2	4	4	0	0	0	0	1	0	0	0	.154
Pavletich, Donald, Boston	32	65	4	9	12	1	1	0	6	0	1	1	0	.138
Pena, Roberto, 19 Oak-121 Mil	140	474	40	114	145	20	1	3	45	7	4	4	6	.241
Perranoski, Ronald, Minnesota*	67	24	0	1	1	0	0	0	0	1	0	0	0	.042
Perry, James, Minnesota	41	97	9	24	31	4	0	1	6	10	1	0	0	.247
Peters, Gary, Boston*	37	82	12	20	28	3	1	1	11	2	0	0	0	.244
Peterson, Fred, New York†	39	90	7	20	29	3	0	2	7	7	1	0	0	.222

Player and Club	G.	AB.	R.	H.	TB.	2B.	3B.	HR.	RBI.	SH.	SF.	SB.	CS.	Pct.
Petrocelli, Americo, Boston	157	583	82	152	276	31	3	29	103	2	10	1	1	.261
Phillips, Norman E., Boston	18	3	0	0	0	0	0	0	0	0	0	0	0	.000
Phoebus, Thomas, Baltimore	27	43	2	7	8	1	0	0	3	3	0	0	0	.163
Pina, Horacio, Washington	61	3	0	0	0	0	0	0	0	0	0	0	0	.000
Piniella, Louis, Kansas City	144	542	54	163	230	24	5	11	88	2	5	3	6	.301
Pinson, Vada, Cleveland☆	148	574	74	164	276	28	6	24	82	0	6	7	6	.286
Powell, John, Baltimore☆	154	526	82	156	289	28	0	35	114	0	8	1	1	.297
Price, James, Detroit	52	132	12	24	43	4	0	5	15	1	2	0	0	.182
Queen, Melvin, California☆	37	16	1	4	4	0	0	0	1	0	0	0	0	.250
Quilici, Frank, Minnesota	111	141	19	32	41	3	0	2	12	2	2	0	2	.227
Ratliff, Paul, Minnesota☆	69	149	19	40	66	7	2	5	22	0	0	0	0	.268
Reed, Robert, Detroit	17	12	1	1	1	0	0	0	0	0	0	0	0	.083
Reese, Richard, Minnesota☆	153	501	63	131	186	15	5	10	56	4	4	5	4	.261
Reichardt, Frederic, 9 Calif-107 Wash	116	283	43	71	134	14	2	15	47	0	3	2	4	.251
Renick, Warren, Minnesota	81	179	20	41	70	8	0	7	25	2	0	0	2	.229
Repoz, Roger, California☆	137	407	50	97	180	17	6	18	47	6	2	4	2	.238
Rettenmund, Mervin, Balt	106	338	60	109	184	17	2	18	58	4	2	13	7	.322
Reynolds, Thomas, California	59	120	11	30	38	3	1	1	6	0	0	1	1	.250
Richert, Peter, Baltimore☆	50	4	0	0	0	0	0	0	0	0	0	0	0	.000
Rivers, John, California☆	17	25	6	8	10	2	0	0	3	1	0	1	0	.320
Robertson, Jerry, Detroit†	11	0	0	0	0	0	0	0	0	0	0	0	0	.000
Robinson, Brooks, Baltimore	158	608	84	168	261	31	4	18	94	1	7	1	1	.276
Robinson, Frank, Baltimore	132	471	88	144	245	24	1	25	78	0	6	2	1	.306
Rodriguez, Aurelio, 17 Calif-142 Wash	159	610	70	152	256	33	7	19	83	0	5	15	6	.249
Rodriguez, Eliseo, Kansas City	80	231	25	52	67	8	2	1	15	1	4	2	1	.225
Rojas, Octavio, Kansas City	98	384	36	100	125	13	3	2	28	4	1	3	7	.260
Roland, James, Oakland	28	6	0	0	0	0	0	0	0	0	0	0	0	.000
Rollins, Richard, 14 Mil-42 Clev	56	68	9	15	22	1	0	2	9	0	1	0	0	.221
Romo, Vicente, Boston	48	27	2	4	7	0	0	1	2	2	1	0	0	.148
Roof, Phillip, Milwaukee	110	321	39	73	121	7	1	13	37	3	1	3	2	.227
Rooker, James, Kansas City	41	70	12	14	21	4	0	1	13	2	1	0	0	.200
Roseboro, John, Washington☆	46	86	7	20	27	4	0	1	6	0	0	1	1	.233
Rudi, Joseph, Oakland	106	350	40	108	168	23	2	11	42	5	2	3	1	.309
Ruiz, Hiraldo, California†	68	107	10	26	31	3	1	0	12	4	1	3	0	.243
Salmon, Ruthford, Baltimore	63	172	19	43	68	4	0	7	22	3	0	2	2	.250
Sanders, Kenneth, Milwaukee	50	13	3	3	3	0	0	0	2	0	1	0	0	.231
Satriano, Thomas, Boston☆	59	165	21	39	59	9	1	3	14	0	0	0	0	.236
Savage, Theodore, Milwaukee	114	276	43	77	133	10	5	12	50	5	3	10	6	.279
Schaal, Paul, Kansas City	124	380	50	102	135	12	3	5	35	1	2	7	4	.268
Scherman, Frederick, Detroit☆	48	12	1	2	2	0	0	0	0	1	0	0	0	.167
Schofield, J. Richard, Boston†	76	139	16	26	34	1	2	1	14	0	2	0	1	.187
Scott, George, Boston	127	480	50	142	224	24	5	16	63	0	4	4	11	.296
Segui, Diego, Oakland	47	43	2	5	5	0	0	0	2	6	1	0	0	.116
Severson, Richard, Kansas City†	77	240	22	60	76	11	1	1	22	3	0	0	0	.250
Shellenback, James, Wash☆	40	30	3	2	3	1	0	0	2	4	0	0	0	.067
Siebert, Wilfred, Boston	33	77	5	10	13	3	0	0	4	4	0	0	0	.130
Silverio, Tomas, California☆	15	15	1	0	0	0	0	0	0	0	0	0	1	.000
Sims, Duane, Cleveland☆	110	345	46	91	172	12	0	23	56	1	0	0	4	.264
Sisk, Tommie, Chicago	17	4	0	1	1	0	0	0	0	0	0	0	0	.250
Smith, C. Bernard, Milwaukee	44	76	8	21	29	3	1	1	6	1	0	1	3	.276
Smith, C. Reginald, Boston†	147	580	109	176	288	32	7	22	74	0	5	10	7	.303
Snyder, Russell, Milwaukee☆	124	276	34	64	87	11	0	4	31	5	4	1	3	.232
Sorrell, Bill, Kansas City☆	57	135	12	36	50	2	0	4	14	0	0	1	0	.267
Spence, J. Robert, Chicago☆	46	130	11	29	47	4	1	4	15	1	2	0	0	.223
Spencer, James, California☆	146	511	61	140	204	20	4	12	68	6	5	0	2	.274
Spriggs, George, Kansas City☆	51	130	12	27	38	2	3	1	7	0	1	4	3	.208
Stange, A. Lee, 20 Bos-16 Chi	36	6	0	0	0	0	0	0	0	1	0	0	0	.000
Stanley, Mitchell, Detroit	142	568	83	143	225	21	11	13	47	7	3	10	1	.252
Stottlemyre, Melvin, New York	38	85	8	16	28	2	2	2	7	3	0	0	0	.188
Stroud, Edwin, Washington☆	129	433	69	115	151	11	5	5	32	2	1	29	8	.266
Such, Richard, Washington☆	22	13	1	3	4	1	0	0	1	0	0	0	0	.231
Szotkiewicz, Kenneth, Detroit☆	47	84	9	9	19	1	0	3	9	1	1	0	0	.107
Tartabull, Jose, Oakland☆	24	13	5	3	3	0	0	0	2	1	0	1	1	.231
Tatum, Jarvis, California	75	181	28	43	50	7	0	0	5	1	1	1	0	.238
Tatum, Kenneth, California	62	11	2	2	5	0	0	1	3	0	0	0	0	.182
Taylor, Robert, Kansas City	57	55	3	9	12	3	0	0	6	0	0	0	0	.164

Player and Club	G.	AB.	R.	H.	TB.	2B.	3B.	HR.	RBI.	SH.	SF.	SB.	CS.	Pct.
Tenace, F. Gene, Oakland	38	105	19	32	59	6	0	7	20	0	0	0	2	.305
Tepedino, Frank, New York*	16	19	2	6	8	2	0	0	2	0	0	0	1	.316
Thomas, George, Boston	38	99	13	34	48	8	0	2	13	0	0	0	0	.343
Thompson, Danny, Minnesota	96	302	25	66	75	9	0	0	22	6	3	0	0	.219
Tiant, Luis, Minnesota	18	32	7	13	17	4	0	0	4	3	0	1	0	.406
Timmerman, Thomas, Detroit	61	16	0	0	0	0	0	0	0	0	0	0	0	.000
Tischinski, Thomas, Minnesota	24	46	6	9	12	0	0	1	2	1	0	0	0	.196
Tovar, Cesar, Minnesota	161	650	120	195	287	36	13	10	54	10	6	30	15	.300
Uhlaender, Theodore, Cleve*	141	473	56	127	185	21	2	11	46	3	8	3	6	.268
Unser, Delbert, Washington*	119	322	37	83	105	5	1	5	30	4	2	1	1	.258
Voss, William, California*	80	181	21	44	63	4	3	3	30	1	5	2	1	.243
Wagner, Gary, Boston	38	6	0	1	1	0	0	0	0	0	0	0	0	.167
Walton, Daniel, Milwaukee	117	397	32	102	175	20	1	17	66	0	1	2	3	.257
Ward, Peter, New York*	66	77	5	20	29	2	2	1	18	0	1	0	0	.260
Waslewski, Gary, New York	26	10	0	1	1	0	0	0	1	1	0	0	0	.100
Watt, Edward, Baltimore	53	8	1	1	1	0	0	0	0	0	0	0	0	.125
Weaver, D. Floyd, Chicago	31	7	1	0	0	0	0	0	0	1	0	0	0	.000
Wert, Donald, Detroit	128	363	34	79	110	13	0	6	33	5	3	1	3	.218
White, Roy, New York†	162	609	109	180	288	30	6	22	94	1	7	24	10	.296
Wicker, Floyd, Milwaukee*	15	41	3	8	12	1	0	1	3	0	0	0	0	.195
Williams, Stanley, Minnesota	68	19	0	0	0	0	0	0	0	2	2	3	3	.251
Williams, Walter, Chicago	110	315	43	79	108	18	1	3	15	2	2	3	3	.251
Wilson, R. Earl, Detroit	18	31	2	6	10	1	0	1	3	2	1	0	0	.194
Wood, Wilbur, Chicago	77	18	2	2	3	1	0	0	3	2	0	0	0	.111
Woods, Ronald, New York	95	225	30	51	86	5	3	8	27	3	1	4	2	.227
Woodson, Richard, Minnesota	21	2	0	0	0	0	0	0	0	0	0	0	0	.000
Wright, Clyde, California	47	105	9	18	28	4	0	2	10	4	0	0	0	.171
Wright, Kenneth, Kansas City	47	4	0	0	0	0	0	0	0	0	0	0	0	.000
Wynne, Billy, Chicago*	12	13	0	1	1	0	0	0	0	0	0	0	0	.077
Yastrzemski, Carl, Boston*	161	566	125	186	335	29	0	40	102	0	2	23	13	.3286
Zepp, William, Minnesota	43	44	3	6	6	0	0	0	0	2	0	0	0	.136

(Fewer Than Ten Games)

Player and Club	G.	AB.	R.	H.	TB.	2B.	3B.	HR.	RBI.	SH.	SF.	SB.	CS.	Pct.
Adair, K. Jerry, Kansas City	7	27	0	4	4	0	0	0	1	1	0	0	1	.148
Allen, Lloyd, California	8	4	0	0	0	0	0	0	0	0	0	0	0	.000
Arrigo, Gerald, Chicago*	5	4	0	0	0	0	0	0	0	1	0	0	0	.000
Baylor, Donald, Baltimore	8	17	4	4	4	0	0	0	4	0	1	1	1	.235
Beene, Fred, Baltimore†	4	0	0	0	0	0	0	0	0	0	0	0	0	.000
Biittner, Larry, Washington*	2	2	0	0	0	0	0	0	0	0	0	0	0	.000
Blue, Vida, Oakland*	6	15	1	3	7	1	0	1	3	1	0	0	0	.200
Brinkman, Charles, Chicago	9	20	4	5	6	1	0	0	0	0	0	0	0	.250
Brooks, Robert, Oakland	7	18	2	6	13	1	0	2	5	0	0	0	1	.333
Brown, E. Randolph, California*	5	4	0	0	0	0	0	0	0	0	0	0	0	.000
Brubaker, Bruce, Milwaukee	1	0	0	0	0	0	0	0	0	0	0	0	0	.000
Brye, Stephen, Minnesota	9	11	1	2	3	1	0	0	2	0	0	0	0	.182
Burbach, William, New York	4	5	0	0	0	0	0	0	0	0	0	0	0	.000
Burroughs, Jeffrey, Washington	6	12	1	2	2	0	0	0	1	0	0	0	0	.167
Carlos, Francisco, Washington	5	0	0	0	0	0	0	0	0	0	0	0	0	.000
Colson, Loyd, New York	1	0	0	0	0	0	0	0	0	0	0	0	0	.000
Cox, Terry, California	3	0	0	0	0	0	0	0	0	0	0	0	0	.000
Curtis, John, Boston*	1	0	0	0	0	0	0	0	0	0	0	0	0	.000
Dempsey, J. Rikard, Minnesota	5	7	1	0	0	0	0	0	0	0	0	0	0	.000
Dukes, N. Jan, Washington*	5	1	0	0	0	0	0	0	0	0	0	0	0	.000
Eddy, Donald, Chicago	7	0	0	0	0	0	0	0	0	0	0	0	0	.000
Freed, Roger, Baltimore	4	13	0	2	2	0	0	0	1	0	1	0	0	.154
Gardner, Richard, New York	1	3	0	1	2	1	0	0	0	0	0	0	0	.333
Gogolewski, William, Wash*	8	7	0	0	0	0	0	0	0	2	0	0	0	.000
Haney, W. Larry, Oakland	2	2	2	0	0	0	0	0	0	0	0	0	0	.000
Haydel, J. Harold, Minnesota	4	3	2	2	6	1	0	1	0	0	0	0	0	.667
Hedlund, Michael, Kansas City†	9	4	0	0	0	0	0	0	0	1	0	0	0	.000
Hicks, James, California	4	4	0	1	1	0	0	0	0	0	0	0	0	.250
Hosley, Timothy, Detroit	7	12	1	2	5	0	0	1	2	0	1	0	0	.167
Jones, Gary, New York*	2	0	0	0	0	0	0	0	0	0	0	0	0	.000
Koegel, Peter, Milwaukee	7	8	2	2	5	0	0	1	0	0	0	0	0	.250
Kusnyer, Arthur, Chicago	4	10	0	1	1	0	0	0	0	0	0	0	0	.100

Player and Club	G.	AB.	R.	H.	TB.	2B.	3B.	HR.	RBI.	SH.	SF.	SB.	CS.	Pct.
Lonborg, James, Boston	9	9	2	4	8	1	0	1	1	0	0	0	0	.444
Martinez, John, Kansas City	6	9	1	1	1	0	0	0	0	0	0	0	0	.111
McCormick, Michael, New York※	9	5	1	1	1	0	0	0	0	0	0	0	0	.200
Mills, Richard, Boston	2	0	0	0	0	0	0	0	0	0	0	0	0	.000
Moloney, Richard, Chicago	1	0	0	0	0	0	0	0	0	0	0	0	0	.000
Moret, Rogelio, Boston†	3	3	0	0	0	0	0	0	0	0	0	0	0	.000
Nash, Charles, Minnesota	4	4	1	1	1	0	0	0	0	0	0	0	0	.250
Nelson, Roger, Kansas City	4	0	0	0	0	0	0	0	0	2	0	0	1	.000
Nen, Richard, Washington※	6	5	1	1	1	0	0	0	0	0	0	0	0	.200
Oates, Johnny, Baltimore※	5	18	2	5	7	0	1	0	2	0	1	0	0	.278
O'Riley, Donald, Kansas City	9	3	0	0	0	0	0	0	0	2	0	0	0	.000
Osteen, Darrell, Oakland	3	2	0	0	0	0	0	0	0	0	0	0	0	.000
O'Toole, Dennis, Chicago	3	0	0	0	0	0	0	0	0	0	0	0	0	.000
Perez, Martin, California	3	3	0	0	0	0	0	0	1	0	0	0	0	.000
Peters, Raymond, Milwaukee†	2	0	0	0	0	0	0	0	0	0	0	0	0	.000
Ramos, Pedro, Washington†	5	1	0	0	0	0	0	0	0	0	0	0	0	.000
Riddleberger, Dennis, Wash	8	0	0	0	0	0	0	0	0	0	0	0	0	.000
Rittwage, James, Cleveland	8	8	1	3	4	1	0	0	0	0	0	0	0	.375
Rodriquez, Roberto, Oak	6	1	0	0	0	0	0	0	0	0	0	0	0	.000
Rounsaville, Virle, Chicago	8	0	0	0	0	0	0	0	0	0	0	0	0	.000
Santiago, Jose, Boston	9	3	1	2	2	0	0	0	0	0	0	0	0	.667
Saunders, Dennis, Detroit†	8	5	0	0	0	0	0	0	0	0	0	0	0	.000
Secrist, Donald, Chicago※	9	0	0	0	0	0	0	0	0	0	0	0	0	.000
Shank, Harvey, California	1	0	0	0	0	0	0	0	0	0	0	0	0	.000
Splittorff, Paul, Kansas City※	2	2	0	1	1	0	0	0	0	0	0	0	0	.500
Stanley, Frederick, Milw†	6	0	1	0	0	0	0	0	0	0	0	0	0	.000
Talbot, Fred, Oakland	1	0	0	0	0	0	0	0	0	0	0	0	0	.000
Twitchell, Wayne, Milwaukee	2	0	0	0	0	0	0	0	0	0	0	0	0	.000
Valdespino, Hilario, Milwaukee※	8	9	0	0	0	0	0	0	0	0	0	0	0	.000
Verbanic, Joseph, New York	7	3	0	1	1	0	0	0	0	0	0	0	0	.333
Wolf, Walter, California	4	0	0	0	0	0	0	0	0	0	0	0	0	.000
Womack, Horace, Oakland※	2	0	0	0	0	0	0	0	0	0	0	0	0	.000
York, James, Kansas City	4	2	0	0	0	0	0	0	0	0	0	0	0	.000

AWARDED FIRST BASE ON INTERFERENCE: Hegan 2 (Etchebarren, Fosse), Alcaraz (Fosse), Fosse (Tischinski), McNertney (Fosse), Price (Satriano), J. Tatum (Casanova), Yastrzemski (Roof).

OBSTRUCTION: Roof on Matchick.

GRAND SLAM HOME RUNS: Baltimore 7—Buford, Hendricks, Powell, Rettenmund, B. Robinson, F. Robinson 2; Boston 5—Andrews, A. Conigliaro 2, Petrocelli 2; California 2—Johnstone, Voss; Chicago 2—Herrmann 2; Cleveland 4—Bradford, Fosse, Horton, Pinson; Detroit 4—Horton, McAuliffe, Northrup, Price; Kansas City 1—Kirkpatrick; Milwaukee 3—Kubiak, Pena, Snyder; Minnesota 6—Alyea 2, Cardenas, Reese, Renick 2; New York 1—White; Oakland 2—Fernandez, Jackson; Washington 2—Epstein, Reichardt. LEAGUE TOTAL 39.

HIT INTO TRIPLE PLAYS: Otis, A. Rodriguez.

PLAYERS USED DURING THE 1970 SEASON: 428.

PLAYERS WITH TWO OR MORE CLUBS DURING 1970 SEASON
(Alphabetically Arranged With Player's First Club on Top)

Player and Club	G.	AB.	R.	H.	TB.	2B.	3B.	HR.	RBI.	SH.	SF.	Tot.Int. BB.	BB.	HP.	SO.	SB.	CS.	GI DP.	Pct.
H. Allen, Washington	22	38	3	8	10	2	0	0	4	0	1	5	1	0	9	0	0	0	.211
H. Allen, Milwaukee	28	61	4	14	18	4	0	0	4	0	0	7	0	0	5	0	1	2	.230
Bolin, Milwaukee	32	36	3	7	10	0	0	1	2	6	0	2	0	1	17	0	0	0	.194
Bolin, Boston	6	1	0	0	0	0	0	0	0	0	0	0	0	0	0	0	0	0	.000
Bradford, Chicago	32	91	8	17	26	3	0	2	8	1	1	10	0	0	30	1	2	5	.187
Bradford, Cleveland	75	163	25	32	61	6	1	7	23	0	1	21	1	1	43	0	1	8	.196
Comer, Milwaukee	13	17	1	1	1	0	0	0	1	0	0	0	0	0	3	0	0	1	.059
Comer, Washington	77	129	21	30	34	4	0	0	8	1	1	22	0	1	16	4	1	2	.233
Downing, Oakland	10	11	0	2	2	0	0	0	1	1	0	0	0	0	5	0	0	0	.182
Downing, Milwaukee	17	24	0	2	2	0	0	0	1	7	0	0	0	0	12	0	0	0	.083

Player and Club	G.	AB.	R.	H.	TB.	2B.	3B.	HR.	RBI.	SH.	SF.	BB.	Tot.Int. BB.	HP.	SO.	SB.	CS.	GI. DP.	Pct.
Drabowsky, Kan City	24	4	0	1	1	0	0	0	0	0	0	0	0	0	2	0	0	0	.250
Drabowsky, Baltimore	21	5	0	0	0	0	0	0	0	1	0	0	0	0	3	0	0	0	.000
Ellsworth, Cleveland	29	4	0	0	0	0	0	0	0	0	0	0	0	0	2	0	0	0	.000
Ellsworth, Milw	14	0	0	0	0	0	0	0	0	1	0	0	0	0	0	0	0	0	.000
Fiore, Kansas City	25	72	6	13	15	2	0	0	4	0	0	13	0	0	24	1	1	1	.181
Fiore, Boston	41	50	5	7	7	0	0	0	4	0	1	8	1	0	4	0	0	1	.140
Floyd, Baltimore	3	2	0	0	0	0	0	0	0	1	0	0	0	0	2	0	0	0	.000
Floyd, Kansas City	14	43	5	14	18	4	0	0	9	0	1	4	0	0	9	0	1	0	.326
Francona, Oakland	32	33	2	8	11	0	0	1	6	1	0	6	1	1	6	0	0	4	.242
Francona, Milwaukee	52	65	4	15	18	3	0	0	4	2	0	6	1	0	15	1	0	0	.231
Goossen, Milwaukee	21	47	3	12	18	3	0	1	3	0	0	10	0	2	12	0	0	1	.255
Goossen, Washington	21	36	2	8	11	3	0	0	1	0	1	2	0	0	8	0	0	1	.222
Hamilton, New York	35	6	0	0	0	0	0	0	0	0	0	0	0	0	2	0	0	0	.000
Hamilton, Chicago	3	0	0	0	0	0	0	0	0	0	0	0	0	0	0	0	0	0	.000
Hovley, Milwaukee	40	135	17	38	47	9	0	0	16	0	0	17	1	1	11	5	1	4	.281
Hovley, Oakland	72	100	8	19	20	1	0	0	1	0	0	5	1	0	11	3	0	2	.190
Humphreys, Wash	5	0	0	0	0	0	0	0	0	0	0	0	0	0	0	0	0	0	.000
Humphreys, Milwaukee	23	9	0	0	0	0	0	0	0	1	0	1	0	0	4	0	0	0	.000
Kennedy, Milwaukee	25	55	8	14	22	2	0	2	6	2	0	5	0	0	9	0	1	2	.255
Kennedy, Boston	43	129	15	33	54	7	1	4	17	1	1	6	1	1	14	0	0	2	.256
Lasher, Detroit	12	1	0	0	0	0	0	0	0	0	0	0	0	0	1	0	0	0	.000
Lasher, Cleveland	43	8	0	0	0	0	0	0	0	1	0	0	0	0	4	0	0	0	.000
Locker, Milwaukee	28	1	0	0	0	0	0	0	0	0	0	0	0	0	0	0	0	0	.000
Locker, Oakland	38	6	0	1	1	0	0	0	0	0	0	0	0	0	4	0	0	0	.167
Matchick, Boston	10	14	2	1	1	0	0	0	0	0	0	2	0	0	2	0	1	0	.071
Matchick, Kansas City	55	158	11	31	38	3	2	0	11	1	0	5	2	1	23	0	0	8	.196
May, Baltimore	25	31	6	6	11	0	1	1	6	0	0	4	0	0	4	0	0	3	.194
May, Milwaukee	101	342	36	82	113	8	1	7	31	4	1	44	6	2	56	8	6	9	.240
Maye, Washington	96	255	28	67	102	12	1	7	30	0	0	21	1	1	32	4	2	3	.263
Maye, Chicago	6	6	0	1	1	0	0	0	1	0	0	0	0	0	1	0	0	0	.167
McMullen, Washington	15	59	5	12	14	2	0	0	3	0	0	5	0	0	10	0	0	2	.203
McMullen, California	124	422	50	98	155	9	3	14	61	1	3	59	10	3	81	1	0	13	.232
Miller, Cleveland	15	5	0	1	1	0	0	0	0	0	0	1	0	0	1	0	0	1	.200
Miller, Chicago	16	23	0	4	4	0	0	0	2	2	0	3	0	0	5	0	0	1	.174
Moore, Cleveland	13	21	1	2	2	0	0	0	1	0	0	0	0	0	2	0	0	1	.095
Moore, Chicago	24	19	2	5	5	0	0	0	2	1	0	1	0	0	4	0	0	0	.263
Nagelson, Cleveland	17	24	3	3	7	1	0	1	2	0	0	3	0	0	9	0	0	0	.125
Nagelson, Detroit	28	32	5	6	6	0	0	0	2	1	0	5	0	0	6	0	0	0	.188
Pena, Oakland	19	58	4	15	16	1	0	0	3	1	0	3	0	0	4	1	1	2	.259
Pena, Milwaukee	121	416	36	99	129	19	1	3	42	6	4	25	4	2	45	3	5	13	.238
Reichardt, California	9	6	1	1	1	0	0	0	1	0	1	3	1	0	0	0	0	0	.167
Reichardt, Washington	107	277	42	70	133	14	2	15	46	0	2	23	2	9	69	2	4	13	.253
Rodriguez, California	17	63	6	17	23	2	2	0	7	0	0	3	0	1	6	0	1	2	.270
Rodriguez, Washington	142	547	64	135	233	31	5	19	76	0	5	37	5	7	81	15	5	17	.247
Rollins, Milwaukee	14	25	3	5	6	1	0	0	5	0	1	3	0	0	4	0	0	0	.200
Rollins, Cleveland	42	43	6	10	16	0	0	2	4	0	0	3	0	0	5	0	0	0	.233
Stange, Boston	20	5	0	0	0	0	0	0	0	1	0	1	0	0	3	0	0	0	.000
Stange, Chicago	16	1	0	0	0	0	0	0	0	0	0	0	0	0	1	0	0	0	.000

MISCELLANEOUS AMERICAN LEAGUE BATTING RECORDS

CLUB MISCELLANEOUS RECORDS

Club	Tot. BB.	Int. BB.	HP.	SO.	ShO.	GI DP.	LOB	Slug Pct.
Boston	594	47	40	855	4	137	1149	.428
Minnesota	501	65	42	905	6	132	1103	.403
Baltimore	717	64	44	952	6	110	1262	.401
Cleveland	503	42	37	909	9	119	1111	.394
Oakland	584	55	36	977	5	121	1118	.392
Detroit	656	56	34	825	11	134	1187	.374
New York	588	48	25	808	11	115	1152	.365
California	447	56	29	922	15	118	1115	.363
Chicago	477	41	42	872	8	132	1145	.362
Washington	635	68	46	989	10	133	1196	.358
Milwaukee	592	54	36	985	11	130	1162	.358
Kansas City	514	42	21	958	14	126	1074	.348
Totals	6808	638	432	10957	110	1507	13774	.379

INDIVIDUAL MISCELLANEOUS RECORDS

(Top 15 Qualifiers for Slugging Championship)

Player and Club	G.	Tot. BB.	Int. BB.	HP.	SO.	GI DP.	Slug Pct.
Yastrzemski, Boston	161	128	12	1	66	12	.592
Powell, Baltimore	154	104	18	5	80	14	.549
Killebrew, Minnesota	157	128	23	2	84	28	.546
Howard, Washington	161	132	29	2	125	23	.546
Harper, Milwaukee	154	77	5	4	107	8	.522
F. Robinson, Baltimore	132	69	9	7	70	13	.520
Oliva, Minnesota	157	38	12	3	67	16	.514
A. Conigliaro, Boston	146	43	4	8	93	11	.498
Smith, Boston	147	51	1	4	60	13	.497
Melton, Chicago	141	56	2	9	107	7	.488
Pinson, Cleveland	148	28	7	3	69	12	.481
White, New York	162	95	11	0	66	13	.473
Petrocelli, Boston	157	67	6	2	82	16	.473
Foster, Cleveland	139	54	4	12	75	15	.468
Scott, Boston	127	44	5	2	95	13	.467

Departmental Leaders: TBB—Howard, 132; IBB—Howard, 29; HP—Foster, 12; SO—Jackson, 135; GIDP—Killebrew, 28.

(All Players in Ten or More Games—Listed Alphabetically)

Player and Club	G.	Tot. BB.	Int. BB.	HP.	SO.	GI DP.	Slug Pct.
Abernathy, Kansas City	36	0	0	0	5	0	.214
Aker, New York	41	0	0	0	6	1	.063
Alcaraz, Kansas City	35	4	0	0	13	2	.250
B. Allen, Washington	104	43	4	0	21	4	.360
H. Allen, Washington-Milwaukee	50	12	1	0	14	2	.283
Allison, Minnesota	47	14	0	1	20	2	.319
Alomar, California	162	49	2	1	65	7	.293
Alou, Oakland	154	32	6	1	31	13	.367
Alvarado, Boston	59	9	2	0	30	5	.301
Alvis, Milwaukee	62	5	1	0	20	5	.278
Alyea, Minnesota	94	28	0	3	51	12	.531
Andrews, Boston	151	81	0	3	63	10	.390
Aparicio, Chicago	146	53	1	1	34	11	.404
Austin, Cleveland	31	3	0	0	10	0	.167
Azcue, California	114	24	4	2	40	12	.302
Bahnsen, New York	36	2	0	0	34	0	.176
Baker, New York	35	14	0	2	26	1	.282
Baldwin, Milwaukee	28	0	0	0	0	0	.500
Bando, Oakland	155	118	5	6	88	12	.430
Barber, Minnesota	19	0	0	0	0	0	.000
Belanger, Baltimore	145	52	3	5	65	4	.259

Player and Club	G.	Tot. BB.	Int. BB.	HP.	SO.	GI DP.	Slug Pct.
Berry, Chicago	141	43	10	6	61	19	.356
Billings, Washington	11	2	0	0	3	1	.458
Blair, Baltimore	133	56	1	3	93	9	.438
Blanco, Chicago	34	3	0	0	14	1	.197
Blefary, New York	99	43	3	3	37	6	.335
Blyleven, Minnesota	27	1	0	0	25	0	.140
Bolin, Milwaukee-Boston	38	2	0	1	17	0	.270
Bosman, Washington	36	1	0	0	29	0	.138
Boswell, Minnesota	20	0	0	0	11	0	.200
Brabender, Milwaukee	29	0	0	0	27	1	.146
Bradford, Chicago-Cleveland	107	31	1	1	73	13	.343
Bradley, California	17	1	0	0	9	0	.222
Brett, Boston	41	2	0	1	7	1	.537
Brinkman, Washington	158	60	0	5	41	15	.301
I. Brown, Detroit	56	13	0	1	26	2	.468
Brown, Washington	24	0	0	0	5	0	.154
Brown, Cleveland	72	20	1	0	14	6	.316
W. G. Brown, Detroit	81	20	0	1	14	3	.323
Brunet, Washington	24	1	0	1	21	0	.263
Buford, Baltimore	144	109	8	8	55	1	.411
Bunker, Kansas City	24	7	0	0	13	0	.065
Burda, Milwaukee	78	16	1	3	17	5	.342
Burgmeier, Kansas City	42	1	0	0	5	0	.143
Butler, Kansas City	25	4	0	0	31	1	.045
Cain, Detroit	29	1	0	0	18	1	.221
Camilli, Cleveland	16	2	0	0	2	1	.000
Campaneris, Oakland	147	36	1	4	73	5	.448
Campanis, Kansas City	31	4	1	1	14	1	.241
Cardenas, Minnesota	160	42	2	4	101	11	.374
Carew, Minnesota	51	11	0	2	28	1	.524
Casanova, Washington	104	10	2	1	47	5	.354
Cash, Detroit	130	72	6	5	58	16	.441
Cater, New York	155	34	6	2	44	19	.393
Chance, Cleveland	45	2	0	0	32	0	.071
Christian, Chicago	12	1	0	0	4	0	.467
Clarke, New York	158	35	5	2	35	12	.309
Colbert, Cleveland	23	0	0	0	1	0	.000
Coleman, Washington	39	12	0	1	28	2	.134
Collins, Detroit	25	1	0	0	10	0	.375
Comer, Milwaukee-Washington	90	22	0	1	19	3	.240
A. Conigliaro, Boston	146	43	4	8	93	11	.498
W. Conigliaro, Boston	114	35	0	7	73	12	.462
Cowan, California	68	11	2	1	29	2	.470
Cox, Washington	37	1	0	0	30	0	.121
Crider, Chicago	32	0	0	0	5	1	.125
Crowley, Baltimore	83	35	3	0	26	5	.388
Cuellar, Baltimore	41	2	0	0	48	0	.152
Cullen, Washington	123	31	6	3	38	10	.279
Culp, Boston	33	3	0	0	39	2	.134
Cumberland, New York	15	0	0	0	12	0	.059
Dalrymple, Baltimore	13	7	2	0	4	0	.344
Davis, Oakland	66	8	1	1	18	4	.360
Derrick, Boston	24	0	0	0	11	1	.242
Dobson, Oakland	41	1	0	0	12	4	.129
Donaldson, Oakland	41	9	3	0	6	3	.326
Downing, Oakland-Milwaukee	27	0	0	0	17	0	.114
Doyle, California	40	0	0	0	3	0	.000
Drabowsky, Kansas City-Baltimore	45	0	0	0	5	0	.111
Drago, Kansas City	35	2	0	0	44	0	.053
Driscoll, Oakland	21	2	0	1	15	1	.250
Duncan, Oakland	86	22	2	0	38	5	.418
Dunning, Cleveland	19	1	0	0	14	0	.161
Egan, California	79	14	1	1	67	4	.324
Ellis, New York	78	18	0	2	47	5	.403
Ellsworth, Cleveland-Milwaukee	43	0	0	0	2	0	.000
Epstein, Washington	140	73	6	9	117	7	.444

Player and Club	G.	Tot. BB.	Int. BB.	HP.	SO.	GI DP.	Slug Pct.
Etchebarren, Baltimore	78	21	2	3	41	10	.348
Fanzone, Boston	10	2	0	1	2	1	.267
Fernandez, Oakland	94	40	4	2	76	6	.413
Fingers, Oakland	45	2	0	0	11	1	.179
Fiore, Kansas City-Boston	66	21	1	0	28	2	.180
Fisher, California	67	0	0	0	3	0	.091
Fitzmorris, Kansas City	45	3	0	0	9	0	.419
Floyd, Baltimore-Kansas City	17	4	0	0	11	0	.400
Ford, Cleveland	26	3	0	0	13	0	.261
Fosse, Cleveland	120	39	5	1	55	9	.469
Foster, Cleveland	139	54	4	12	75	15	.468
Francona, Oakland-Milwaukee	84	12	2	1	21	4	.296
Freehan, Detroit	117	52	5	4	48	11	.420
Fregosi, California	158	69	3	3	92	7	.459
French, Washington	69	38	2	0	23	5	.259
Fuller, Cleveland	29	3	0	0	9	0	.333
Garrett, California	32	1	0	0	9	0	.067
Gelnar, Milwaukee	53	1	0	0	6	0	.083
Gibbs, New York	49	7	1	1	14	4	.542
Gil, Milwaukee	64	21	4	0	12	3	.244
Gonzalez, California	26	2	0	1	11	3	.359
Goossen, Milwaukee-Washington	42	12	0	2	20	2	.349
Grant, Oakland	72	5	0	0	1	0	.222
Green, Oakland	135	38	5	3	73	13	.240
Grich, Baltimore	30	9	0	0	21	2	.284
Grieve, Washington	47	14	1	1	38	1	.336
Griffin, California	18	6	1	0	5	3	.145
Grzenda, Washington	49	0	0	0	11	0	.000
Gutierrez, Detroit	135	18	6	1	39	8	.299
Hall, Baltimore	32	0	0	0	3	1	.083
Hall, Minnesota	53	0	0	0	9	1	.182
Hamilton, New York-Chicago	38	0	0	0	2	0	.000
Hamm, Minnesota	10	0	0	0	0	0	.000
Hand, Cleveland	35	1	0	0	11	0	.146
Hannan, Washington	42	1	0	1	13	0	.129
Hansen, New York	59	19	0	1	9	1	.473
Hardin, Baltimore	36	4	0	0	21	1	.111
Hargan, Cleveland	28	1	0	0	15	0	.133
Harper, Milwaukee	154	77	5	4	107	8	.522
Harrelson, Cleveland	17	6	0	0	4	1	.385
Hartenstein, Boston	17	1	0	0	2	0	.000
Hegan, Milwaukee	148	67	3	1	116	9	.366
Heidemann, Cleveland	133	34	8	2	88	7	.292
Hendricks, Baltimore	106	33	4	4	44	4	.382
Hennigan, Cleveland	42	2	0	1	3	0	.286
Hernandez, Kansas City	83	15	0	2	50	5	.282
Herrmann, Chicago	96	31	3	3	41	5	.505
Hershberger, Milwaukee	49	10	0	0	8	4	.316
Higgins, Cleveland	58	2	0	0	4	1	.250
Hill, Minnesota	27	0	0	0	6	0	.091
Hiller, Detroit	47	1	0	0	9	0	.000
Hinton, Cleveland	107	25	1	0	34	3	.477
Holt, Minnesota	142	17	3	0	32	9	.342
Hopkins, Chicago	116	28	5	1	19	5	.383
Horlen, Chicago	28	2	0	0	14	2	.135
Horton, Cleveland	115	30	5	4	54	18	.453
Horton, Detroit	96	28	6	2	43	7	.501
Hovley, Milwaukee-Oakland	112	22	2	1	22	6	.285
Howard, Washington	161	132	29	2	125	23	.546
Humphreys, Washington-Milwaukee	28	1	0	0	4	0	.000
Hunter, Oakland	43	2	0	0	23	1	.300
Jackson, Oakland	149	75	11	8	135	10	.458
Janeski, Chicago	35	2	0	0	31	2	.076
Jarvis, Boston	15	0	0	0	0	0	.000
John, Chicago	38	2	0	1	17	3	.214
Johnson, California	156	35	9	7	68	25	.459

Player and Club	G.	Tot. BB.	Int. BB.	HP.	SO.	GI DP.	Slg. Pct.
Johnson, Chicago	18	1	0	0	6	0	.345
Johnson, Baltimore	149	66	8	0	68	11	.392
Johnson, Kansas City	40	6	0	0	34	0	.123
Johnson, Oakland	30	3	0	1	2	2	.261
Johnstone, California	119	24	6	1	53	7	.403
Jones, Detroit	89	33	4	1	33	3	.351
Josephson, Chicago	96	24	2	3	28	10	.407
Kaat, Minnesota	56	6	1	1	20	2	.250
Kaline, Detroit	131	77	5	1	49	20	.450
Kealey, California	17	0	0	0	3	0	.250
Kekich, New York	26	2	0	0	7	0	.094
Kelly, Kansas City	136	76	3	2	105	6	.314
Kennedy, Milwaukee-Boston	68	11	1	1	23	4	.413
Kenney, New York	140	52	2	0	44	11	.282
Keough, Kansas City	57	23	3	0	18	6	.443
Kilkenny, Detroit	37	0	0	0	19	0	.077
Killebrew, Minnesota	157	128	23	2	84	28	.546
Kirkpatrick, Kansas City	134	55	8	1	65	9	.406
Klimchock, Cleveland	41	3	1	1	9	1	.214
Klimkowski, New York	45	0	0	0	9	0	.053
Kline, New York	16	4	0	1	10	0	.179
Knoop, Chicago	130	34	4	2	79	7	.308
Knowles, Washington	71	0	0	1	9	0	.050
Koonce, Boston	23	4	0	0	8	0	.095
Krausse, Milwaukee	38	8	0	0	31	1	.169
Kubiak, Milwaukee	158	72	16	0	51	18	.313
Lachemann, Oakland	41	1	0	0	4	0	.000
LaGrow, Detroit	10	0	0	0	0	0	.000
Lahoud, Boston	17	7	1	0	6	1	.388
Lamont, Detroit	15	2	0	1	9	0	.477
LaRoche, California	38	1	0	0	0	1	.375
LaRussa, Oakland	52	15	1	1	19	0	.255
Lasher, Detroit-Cleveland	55	0	0	0	5	0	.000
Lauzerique, Milwaukee	11	0	0	0	1	0	.500
Lee, Boston	11	0	0	0	5	0	.000
Leon, Cleveland	152	47	2	2	89	11	.353
Leonhard, Baltimore	25	1	0	0	1	0	.000
Lewis, Oakland	25	0	0	0	0	0	.625
Lindblad, Oakland	62	0	0	0	4	0	.000
Locker, Milwaukee-Oakland	66	0	0	0	4	0	.143
Lockwood, Milwaukee	27	1	0	0	11	0	.302
Lolich, Detroit	42	12	0	0	29	3	.134
Lopez, Baltimore	25	3	0	0	11	0	.077
Lowenstein, Cleveland	17	1	0	0	9	1	.442
Lyle, Boston	63	1	0	0	2	0	.000
Lyttle, New York	87	10	1	0	26	2	.452
Maddox, Detroit	109	30	1	3	42	6	.364
Magnuson, Chicago	13	0	0	0	3	0	.000
Manuel, Minnesota	59	6	2	1	17	1	.234
Matchick, Boston-Kansas City	65	7	2	1	25	8	.227
Matias, Chicago	58	3	1	1	22	2	.256
May, Chicago	150	79	9	3	96	25	.414
May, Baltimore-Milwaukee	126	48	6	2	60	12	.332
May, California	38	4	0	0	31	1	.116
Maye, Washington-Chicago	102	21	1	1	33	3	.395
McAuliffe, Detroit	146	101	7	3	62	1	.345
McCraw, Chicago	129	21	3	4	50	1	.319
McDaniel, New York	62	0	0	0	7	0	.208
McDowell, Cleveland	40	2	0	0	42	0	.152
McKinney, Chicago	43	11	0	1	25	4	.311
McLain, Detroit	14	0	0	0	13	0	.097
McMullen, Washington-California	139	64	10	3	91	15	.351
McNally, Baltimore	41	15	0	0	53	3	.219
McNertney, Milwaukee	111	22	4	4	33	14	.348
McRae, Detroit	19	0	0	0	0	0	.000
Melton, Chicago	141	56	2	9	107	7	.488

Player and Club	G.	Tot. BB.	Int. BB.	HP.	SO.	GI DP.	Slg. Pct.
Mendoza, Minnesota	16	0	0	0	1	0	.188
Messersmith, California	38	0	0	0	28	0	.243
Meyer, Milwaukee	10	0	0	0	0	0	.333
Michael, New York	134	50	5	0	93	8	.255
Miller, Cleveland-Chicago	31	4	0	0	6	2	.179
Mincher, Oakland	140	56	11	3	71	9	.460
Mingori, Cleveland	21	0	0	0	0	0	.000
Mitchell, New York	10	2	0	1	3	0	.318
Mitterwald, Minnesota	117	34	6	2	84	11	.388
Monday, Oakland	112	58	0	2	99	8	.457
Monteagudo, Kansas City	21	0	0	0	1	0	.000
Montgomery, Boston	22	6	0	1	20	4	.244
Moore, Cleveland-Chicago	37	1	0	0	6	1	.175
Morales, Chicago	62	9	0	0	16	2	.205
Morehead, Kansas City	28	1	0	1	16	2	.205
Morris, Milwaukee	20	0	0	0	15	1	.194
Moses, Boston	92	21	9	2	45	6	.384
Motton, Baltimore	52	18	0	1	20	0	.393
Munson, New York	132	57	6	7	56	13	.415
Murcer, New York	159	87	5	2	100	7	.420
Murphy, Chicago	51	2	0	0	2	1	.833
Murphy, California	39	5	0	0	32	1	.237
Nagelson, Cleveland-Detroit	45	8	0	0	15	0	.232
Nagy, Boston	23	0	0	0	8	1	.318
Nelson, Washington	47	7	0	0	24	2	.168
Nettles, Cleveland	157	81	3	3	77	12	.404
Nettles, Minnesota	13	1	0	0	5	0	.250
Niekro, Detroit	39	7	0	0	17	0	.273
Northrup, Detroit	139	58	6	7	68	12	.458
O'Brien, Chicago	121	22	1	2	62	10	.340
Odom, Oakland	37	3	0	0	18	1	.444
O'Donoghue, Milwaukee	25	0	0	0	1	0	.000
Oliva, Minnesota	157	38	12	3	67	16	.514
Oliver, Kansas City	160	42	4	3	126	15	.451
Ortiz, Chicago	15	2	0	1	2	0	.375
Otis, Kansas City	159	68	3	1	67	8	.424
Oyler, California	24	3	0	0	6	0	.083
Palmer, Baltimore	44	2	0	0	48	0	.177
Patterson, Detroit	43	0	0	0	9	1	.000
Pattin, Milwaukee	43	1	0	0	28	0	.143
Paul, Cleveland	30	0	0	0	7	0	.154
Pavletich, Boston	32	10	0	0	15	2	.185
Pena, Oakland-Milwaukee	140	28	4	2	49	15	.306
Perranoski, Minnesota	67	0	0	0	15	0	.042
Perry, Minnesota	40	1	0	0	14	1	.320
Peters, Boston	37	8	0	0	11	3	.341
Peterson, New York	39	0	0	1	24	0	.322
Petrocelli, Boston	157	67	6	2	82	16	.473
Phillips, Boston	18	0	0	0	0	0	.000
Phoebus, Baltimore	27	0	0	0	16	0	.186
Pina, Washington	61	0	0	0	2	1	.000
Piniella, Kansas City	144	35	6	2	42	15	.424
Pinson, Cleveland	148	28	7	3	69	12	.481
Powell, Baltimore	154	104	18	5	80	14	.549
Price, Detroit	52	21	0	0	23	6	.326
Queen, California	37	0	0	0	2	0	.250
Quilici, Minnesota	111	15	3	0	16	6	.291
Ratliff, Minnesota	69	15	2	7	51	1	.443
Reed, Detroit	17	1	0	0	4	0	.083
Reese, Minnesota	153	48	5	7	70	7	.371
Reichardt, California-Washington	116	26	3	9	69	13	.473
Renick, Minnesota	81	22	0	0	29	6	.391
Repoz, California	137	45	6	3	90	2	.442
Rettenmund, Baltimore	106	38	1	3	59	8	.544
Reynolds, California	59	6	0	1	10	5	.317
Richert, Baltimore	50	1	0	0	3	0	.000

Player and Club	G.	Tot. BB.	Int. BB.	HP.	SO.	GI DP.	Slg. Pct.
Rivers, California	17	3	0	1	5	0	.400
Robertson, Detroit	11	0	0	0	0	0	.000
B. Robinson, Baltimore	158	53	5	4	53	18	.429
F. Robinson, Baltimore	132	69	9	7	70	13	.520
Rodriguez, California-Washington	159	40	5	8	87	19	.420
Rodriguez, Kansas City	80	27	2	4	35	11	.290
Rojas, Kansas City	98	20	0	0	29	8	.326
Roland, Oakland	28	1	0	0	4	0	.000
Rollins, Milwaukee-Cleveland	56	6	0	0	9	0	.324
Romo, Boston	48	0	0	1	4	0	.259
Roof, Milwaukee	110	32	1	5	72	10	.377
Rooker, Kansas City	41	2	0	1	35	3	.300
Roseboro, Washington	46	18	5	0	10	1	.314
Rudi, Oakland	106	16	1	2	61	11	.480
Ruiz, California	68	7	1	1	16	4	.290
Salmon, Baltimore	63	8	0	1	30	3	.395
Sanders, Milwaukee	50	2	0	1	7	0	.231
Satriano, Boston	59	21	3	1	23	7	.358
Savage, Milwaukee	114	57	1	2	44	6	.482
Schaal, Kansas City	124	43	1	1	39	10	.355
Scherman, Detroit	48	0	0	0	1	0	.167
Schofield, Boston	76	21	2	1	26	8	.245
Scott, Boston	127	44	5	2	95	13	.467
Segui, Oakland	47	0	0	0	18	1	.116
Severson, Kansas City	77	16	2	1	33	5	.317
Shellenback, Washington	40	1	0	0	8	0	.100
Siebert, Boston	33	1	0	2	17	2	.169
Silverio, California	15	2	1	0	4	0	.000
Sims, Cleveland	110	46	1	6	59	5	.499
Sisk, Chicago	17	0	0	0	2	0	.250
Smith, Milwaukee	44	11	1	2	12	1	.382
Smith, Boston	147	51	1	4	60	13	.497
Snyder, Milwaukee	124	16	1	0	40	6	.315
Sorrell, Kansas City	57	10	4	0	13	5	.370
Spence, Chicago	46	11	0	1	32	3	.362
Spencer, California	146	28	6	0	61	9	.399
Spriggs, Kansas City	51	14	0	0	32	0	.292
Stange, Boston-Chicago	36	1	0	0	4	0	.000
Stanley, Detroit	142	45	1	0	56	19	.396
Stottlemyre, New York	38	14	0	0	25	0	.329
Stroud, Washington	129	40	2	3	79	13	.349
Such, Washington	22	1	0	0	4	1	.308
Szotkiewicz, Detroit	47	12	2	0	29	1	.226
Tartabull, Oakland	24	0	0	0	2	0	.385
J. Tatum, California	75	17	1	0	35	5	.276
K. Tatum, California	62	0	0	0	5	0	.455
Taylor, Kansas City	57	6	2	1	16	1	.218
Tenace, Oakland	38	23	2	0	30	2	.562
Tepedino, New York	16	1	0	0	2	1	.421
Thomas, Boston	38	11	0	2	12	3	.485
Thompson, Minnesota	96	7	0	0	39	6	.248
Tiant, Minnesota	18	1	0	0	6	0	.531
Timmerman, Detroit	61	0	0	0	9	0	.000
Tischinski, Minnesota	24	9	1	0	6	1	.261
Tovar, Minnesota	161	52	5	8	47	9	.442
Uhlaender, Cleveland	141	39	3	1	44	6	.391
Unser, Washington	119	30	3	0	29	4	.326
Voss, California	80	23	2	2	18	3	.348
Wagner, Boston	38	0	0	0	4	0	.167
Walton, Milwaukee	117	51	4	6	126	6	.441
Ward, New York	66	9	0	0	17	1	.377
Waslewski, New York	26	0	0	0	9	0	.100
Watt, Baltimore	53	0	0	0	3	0	.125
Weaver, Chicago	31	0	0	0	2	0	.000
Wert, Detroit	128	44	7	4	56	13	.303
White, New York	162	95	11	0	66	13	.473

Player and Club	G.	Tot. BB.	Int. BB.	HP.	SO.	GI DP.	Slg. Pct.
Wicker, Milwaukee	15	1	0	0	8	2	.293
Williams, Minnesota	68	0	0	0	13	0	.000
Williams, Chicago	110	19	0	2	30	5	.343
Wilson, Detroit	18	2	0	0	16	1	.323
Wood, Chicago	77	0	0	0	11	0	.167
Woods, New York	95	33	3	0	35	10	.382
Woodson, Minnesota	21	0	0	0	0	0	.000
Wright, California	47	2	0	0	32	2	.267
Wright, Kansas City	47	0	0	0	2	0	.000
Wynne, Chicago	12	1	0	0	7	0	.077
Yastrzemski, Boston	161	128	12	1	66	12	.592
Zepp, Minnesota	43	1	0	0	31	0	.136

(Fewer Than Ten Games)

Player and Club	G.	Tot. BB.	Int. BB.	HP.	SO.	GI DP.	Slg. Pct.
Adair, Kansas City	7	5	1	0	3	1	.148
Allen, California	8	0	0	0	1	0	.000
Arrigo, Chicago	5	0	0	0	2	0	.000
Baylor, Baltimore	8	2	0	0	3	0	.235
Beene, Baltimore	4	0	0	0	0	0	.000
Biittner, Washington	2	0	0	0	0	0	.000
Blue, Oakland	6	1	0	0	7	1	.467
Brinkman, Chicago	9	3	0	0	3	0	.300
Brooks, Oakland	7	1	0	0	7	0	.722
Brown, California	5	0	0	0	0	0	.000
Brubaker, Milwaukee	1	0	0	0	0	0	.000
Brye, Minnesota	9	2	0	0	4	0	.273
Burbach, New York	4	0	0	0	4	0	.000
Burroughs, Washington	6	2	0	0	5	0	.167
Carlos, Washington	5	0	0	0	0	0	.000
Colson, New York	1	0	0	0	0	0	.000
Cox, California	3	0	0	0	0	0	.000
Curtis, Boston	1	0	0	0	0	0	.000
Dempsey, Minnesota	5	1	0	0	1	1	.000
Dukes, Washington	5	0	0	0	0	0	.000
Eddy, Chicago	7	0	0	0	0	0	.000
Freed, Baltimore	4	3	0	0	4	0	.154
Gardner, New York	1	0	0	0	1	0	.667
Gogolewski, Washington	8	1	0	0	4	0	.000
Haney, Oakland	2	2	0	0	1	0	.000
Haydel, Minnesota	4	0	0	0	1	0	2.000
Hedlund, Kansas City	9	0	0	0	4	0	.000
Hicks, California	4	0	0	0	2	0	.250
Hosley, Detroit	7	0	0	0	6	0	.417
Jones, New York	2	0	0	0	0	0	.000
Koegel, Milwaukee	7	1	0	0	3	0	.625
Kusnyer, Chicago	4	0	0	0	4	0	.100
Lonborg, Boston	9	0	0	0	2	0	.889
Martinez, Kansas City	6	2	0	0	1	1	.111
McCormick, New York	9	0	0	0	3	0	.200
Mills, Boston	2	0	0	0	0	0	.000
Moloney, Chicago	1	0	0	0	0	0	.000
Moret, Boston	3	0	0	0	1	0	.000
Nash, Minnesota	4	1	0	0	1	0	.250
Nelson, Kansas City	4	1	0	0	0	0	.000
Nen, Washington	6	0	0	0	0	0	.200
Oates, Baltimore	5	2	0	0	0	0	.389
O'Riley, Kansas City	9	0	0	0	0	0	.000
Osteen, Oakland	3	0	0	0	0	0	.000
O'Toole, Chicago	3	0	0	0	0	0	.000
Perez, California	3	0	0	0	0	0	.000
Peters, Milwaukee	2	0	0	0	0	0	.000
Ramos, Washington	5	1	0	0	0	0	.000
Riddleberger, Washington	8	0	0	0	0	0	.000
Rittwage, Cleveland	8	0	0	0	0	0	.500

Player and Club	G.	Tot. BB.	Int. BB.	HP.	SO.	GI DP.	Slg. Pct.
Rodriquez, Oakland	6	0	0	0	0	0	.000
Rounsaville, Chicago	8	0	0	0	0	0	.000
Santiago, Boston	9	0	0	0	0	0	.667
Saunders, Detroit	8	0	0	0	3	0	.000
Secrist, Chicago	9	0	0	0	0	0	.000
Shank, California	1	0	0	0	0	0	.000
Splittorff, Kansas City	2	0	0	0	0	0	.500
Stanley, Milwaukee	6	0	0	0	0	0	.000
Talbot, Oakland	1	0	0	0	0	0	.000
Twitchell, Milwaukee	2	0	0	0	0	0	.000
Valdespino, Milwaukee	8	0	0	0	4	1	.000
Verbanic, New York	7	0	0	0	1	0	.333
Wolf, California	4	0	0	0	0	0	.000
Womack, Oakland	2	0	0	0	0	0	.000
York, Kansas City	4	0	0	0	1	0	.000

AMERICAN LEAGUE FIELDING AVERAGES

CLUB FIELDING

Club	G.	PO.	A.	E.	TC.	DP.	TP.	PB.	Pct.
Washington	162	4373	1946	116	6435	173	0	12	.982
Baltimore	162	4436	1694	117	6247	148	0	12	.981
New York	163	4415	1932	130	6477	146	0	12	.980
California	162	4387	1775	127	6289	169	1	27	.980
Minnesota	162	4345	1636	123	6104	130	0	11	.980
Cleveland	162	4354	1743	133	6230	168	1	23	.979
Milwaukee	163	4340	1721	136	6197	142	0	9	.978
Detroit	162	4342	1645	133	6120	142	0	15	.978
Oakland	162	4328	1680	141	6149	152	0	12	.977
Kansas City	162	4391	1708	152	6251	162	0	16	.976
Chicago	162	4291	2062	165	6518	187	0	27	.975
Boston	162	4339	1602	156	6097	131	0	13	.974
Totals		52341	21144	1629	75114	1850	2	189	.978

INDIVIDUAL FIELDING
(Ten or More Games)
(Position Leader in Capitals)

*Throws lefthanded.

FIRST BASEMEN

Player and Club	G.	PO.	A.	E.	DP.	Pct.
Kirkpatrick, K C.	16	139	9	0	13	1.000
Francona, 6 Oak- 13 Mil*	19	100	10	0	13	1.000
Pavletich, Bos	16	80	8	0	10	1.000
Harrelson, Clev	13	80	7	0	15	1.000
Ward, N Y	13	83	3	0	7	1.000
Cowan, Cal	14	69	6	0	7	1.000
Jones, Det	10	43	4	0	4	1.000
SPENCER, Cal*	.142	1212	85	7	131	.995
Hegan, Mil*	.139	1097	113	7	104	.994
Horton, Clev	.112	898	73	6	106	.994
Spence, Chi	37	305	28	2	36	.994
Hinton, Clev	40	164	8	1	14	.994
Oliver, K C	.115	1020	65	8	100	.993
Blanco, Chi	22	144	8	1	9	.993
Powell, Balt	.145	1209	89	10	107	.992
Reese, Minn*	.146	1118	82	10	94	.992
Epstein, Wash*	.122	1100	70	10	104	.992
Cater, N Y	.131	981	70	8	79	.992
Ellis, N Y	53	449	37	4	35	.992

Player and Club	G.	PO.	A.	E.	DP.	Pct.
Repoz, Cal*	18	127	3	1	9	.992
Goossen, 15 Mil- 2 Wash	17	109	8	1	12	.992
Fiore, 20 K C- 17 Bos*	37	191	22	2	14	.991
Rudi, Oak	28	196	13	2	16	.991
Crowley, Balt*	23	102	6	1	9	.991
Mincher, Oak	.137	1109	91	12	107	.990
Yastrzemski, Bos.	94	696	61	8	62	.990
Scott, Bos	59	480	36	5	42	.990
Kaline, Det	52	374	31	4	39	.990
Cash, Det*	.114	868	70	10	76	.989
McNertney, Mil	13	74	7	1	3	.988
Hopkins, Chi	77	629	42	9	67	.987
Howard, Wash	48	429	25	6	37	.987
McCraw, Chi*	59	357	33	5	34	.987
Killebrew, Minn.	28	204	9	3	14	.986
Sims, Clev	29	180	18	3	15	.985
Matias, Chi*	18	118	10	2	13	.985
Keough, K C*	18	113	11	3	13	.976

Triple Plays—Cowan, Sims.

FIRST BASEMEN—Continued
(Fewer Than Ten Games)

Player and Club	G.	PO.	A.	E.	DP.	Pct.	Player and Club	G.	PO.	A.	E.	DP.	Pct.
Blefary, N Y	6	56	2	0	9	1.000	Savage, Mil	1	5	0	0	0	1.000
Fregosi, Cal	6	49	7	0	4	1.000	Johnson, Oak	1	4	0	0	0	1.000
Klimchock, Clev.	5	35	1	0	4	1.000	Nagelson, Det	1	4	0	0	0	1.000
H. Allen, Mil.	4	25	1	0	2	1.000	Alou, Oak	1	3	0	0	1	1.000
Burda, Mil.*	7	24	1	0	2	1.000	Piniella, K C	1	3	0	0	0	1.000
Pena, Mil	7	24	0	0	0	1.000	Kennedy, Mil	1	3	0	0	0	1.000
Freed, Balt	3	21	1	0	6	1.000	Salmon, Balt	2	3	0	0	0	1.000
Pinson, Clev*	7	19	1	0	2	1.000	Ruiz, Cal	2	2	0	0	1	1.000
Sorrell, K C	3	15	3	0	0	1.000	Fuller, Clev	1	0	1	0	0	1.000
Nash, Minn	2	11	0	0	2	1.000	Stanley, Det	9	67	6	1	10	.986
Tepedino, N Y*	1	10	0	0	0	1.000	May, Chi	7	73	11	2	6	.977
Silverio, Cal*	1	7	0	0	0	1.000	F. Robinson, Balt.	7	41	2	1	3	.977
Holt, Minn	2	7	0	0	0	1.000	Davis, Oak	8	59	3	2	9	.969
Collins, Det	1	5	1	0	0	1.000	Allison, Minn.	7	36	4	2	2	.952
Derrick, Bos	1	6	0	0	1	1.000	Taylor, K C	1	5	2	1	1	.875
Carew, Minn	1	6	0	0	0	1.000	McDowell, Clev*.	1	0	0	0	0	.000
Nen, Wash*	1	4	1	0	0	1.000	Roof, Mil	1	0	0	0	0	.000

SECOND BASEMEN

Player and Club	G.	PO.	A.	E.	DP.	Pct.	Player and Club	G.	PO.	A.	E.	DP.	Pct.
Matchick, 1 Bos- 10 K C	11	22	23	0	7	1.000	Alomar, Cal	153	375	460	18	119	.979
Lowenstein, Clev..	10	12	31	0	5	1.000	Green, Oak	127	259	332	13	66	.978
CULLEN, Wash ..	112	211	262	3	65	.994	Gil, In	38	70	61	3	13	.978
Alcaraz, K C	31	65	68	1	12	.993	McAuliffe, Det..	127	280	333	16	75	.975
Johnson, Balt	149	379	390	8	101	.990	Andrews, Bos	148	342	350	19	74	.973
Kubiak, Mil	91	233	238	5	63	.989	Severson, K C	25	44	55	3	11	.971
Quilici, Minn	73	107	121	3	25	.987	B. Allen, Wash	80	169	175	11	47	.969
Thompson, Minn..	81	144	204	5	35	.986	LaRussa, Oak	44	67	89	5	21	.969
Nelson, Wash	33	64	79	2	19	.986	Schofield, Bos	15	28	35	2	6	.969
Donaldson, Oak ..	21	24	48	1	7	.986	Griffin, Cal	11	21	33	2	9	.964
Jones, Det	35	59	70	2	18	.985	Harper, Mil	22	50	54	4	10	.963
Knoop, Chi	126	276	403	11	102	.984	Carew, Minn	45	73	122	8	26	.961
Leon, Clev	141	342	378	13	102	.982	O'Brien, Chi	43	96	127	10	31	.957
Rojas, K C	97	217	283	9	69	.982	I. Brown, Det	23	41	31	5	8	.935
Pena, Mil	15	26	29	1	4	.982	Salmon, Balt	12	19	22	3	2	.932
Brown, Clev	16	28	25	1	6	.981	Kennedy, 16 Mil- 2 Bos	18	29	37	5	8	.930
Morales, Chi	12	24	25	1	2	.980	Fuller, Clev	16	18	16	3	4	.919
Clarke, N Y	157	379	478	18	95	.979							

Triple Plays—Alomar, Leon.

(Fewer Than Ten Games)

Player and Club	G.	PO.	A.	E.	DP.	Pct.	Player and Club	G.	PO.	A.	E.	DP.	Pct.
Grich, Balt.	9	28	31	0	5	1.000	Hansen, N Y	1	0	2	0	0	1.000
Adair, K C	7	24	20	0	6	1.000	Floyd, Balt	1	2	0	0	0	1.000
Michael, N Y	3	11	9	0	1	1.000	Stanley, Mil	2	1	1	0	0	1.000
Allen, Mil	5	4	8	0	2	1.000	Hinton, Clev	3	0	1	0	0	1.000
Klimchock, Clev ..	5	4	8	0	2	1.000	Ruiz, Cal	3	1	0	0	0	1.000
Kenney, N Y	2	3	7	0	1	1.000	McDowell, Clev*.	1	1	0	0	0	1.000
Mendoza, Minn..	4	7	3	0	0	1.000	Schaal, K C	6	14	19	1	3	.971
Camilli, Clev	2	4	1	0	0	1.000	Driscoll, Oak	7	13	16	1	5	.967
Maddox, Det	1	2	1	0	1	1.000	Tovar, Minn	8	17	10	2	5	.931
Wert, Det	2	1	2	0	0	1.000	Buford, Balt	3	2	4	1	0	.857

THIRD BASEMEN

Player and Club	G.	PO.	A.	E.	DP.	Pct.	Player and Club	G.	PO.	A.	E.	DP.	Pct.
Gil, Mil	14	9	31	0	1	1.000	B. Robinson, Balt	156	157	321	17	30	.966
B. Allen, Wash	12	7	29	0	2	1.000	Rodriguez, 17 Cal- 136 Wash	153	118	377	18	41	.965
Hansen, N Y	11	5	16	0	1	1.000	Kennedy, 5 Mil- 33 Bos	38	34	68	4	6	.962
Thompson, Minn..	37	3	11	0	3	1.000	McMullen, 15 Wash-122 Cal.	137	154	306	19	39	.960
Renick, Minn	30	22	52	1	5	.987	Kenney, N Y	135	111	300	17	18	.960
Ruiz, Cal	27	21	43	1	4	.985							
Petrocelli, Bos	18	14	37	1	3	.981							
NETTLES, Clev	154	134	358	17	40	.967							

THIRD BASEMEN—Continued

Player and Club	G.	PO.	A.	E.	DP.	Pct.	Player and Club	G.	PO.	A.	E.	DP.	Pct.
Oliver, K C	46	57	80	6	11	.958	McAuliffe, Det....	12	3	24	2	5	.931
Bando, Oak	152	158	258	20	22	.954	Cater, N Y	42	24	83	8	10	.930
Wert, Det	117	94	191	14	20	.953	Alvarado, Bos	29	20	59	6	2	.929
Killebrew, Minn	138	108	203	17	14	.948	Melton, Chi	70	47	179	18	19	.926
Jones, Det	18	9	25	2	4	.944	Maddox, Det	40	41	83	11	8	.919
Harper, Mil	128	123	275	24	23	.943	Alvis, Mil	36	15	55	7	4	.909
Salmon, Balt	11	3	13	1	1	.941	Rollins, 7 Mil-						
Schaal, K. C.	97	69	159	15	12	.938	5 Clev	12	3	15	2	3	.900
O'Brien, Chi	68	59	137	13	18	.938	Schofield, Bos	15	9	25	4	2	.895
Scott, Bos	68	71	113	13	13	.934	Morales, Chi	20	11	21	4	4	.889
Brown, Clev	17	10	18	2	2	.933	Sorrell, K C	29	17	45	9	3	.873
McKinney, Chi	23	14	40	4	2	.931	Quilici, Minn	27	7	12	3	1	.864

Triple Plays—Ruiz, Nettles.

(Fewer Than Ten Games)

Player and Club	G.	PO.	A.	E.	DP.	Pct.	Player and Club	G.	PO.	A.	E.	DP.	Pct.
Floyd, K C	6	6	10	0	0	1.000	Cowan, Cal	2	1	0	0	0	1.000
Griffin, Cal	8	3	9	0	0	1.000	Johnson, Oak	6	4	16	1	1	.952
Fuller, Clev	4	0	6	0	0	1.000	Lowenstein, Clev.	2	1	6	2	1	.778
Green, Oak	5	2	4	0	1	1.000	Pena, Oak	5	3	7	3	3	.769
Donaldson, Oak.	1	0	3	0	1	1.000	Fanzone, Bos	5	4	8	4	1	.750
Oyler, Cal	2	1	2	0	0	1.000	Thomas, Bos	6	5	4	3	1	.750
Matchick, 2 Bos-							Ellis, N Y	5	0	3	1	0	.750
1 K C	3	1	2	0	0	1.000	Tovar, Minn	4	2	3	3	0	.625
Buford, Chi	3	1	2	0	0	1.000	I. Brown, Det	1	1	2	2	0	.600
Mendoza, Minn	5	1	2	0	0	1.000	Blair, Balt	1	0	0	1	0	.000
Reynolds, Cal	1	2	0	0	0	1.000	Comer, Wash	1	0	0	1	0	.000
Michael, N Y	4	0	2	0	0	1.000	Alomar, Cal	1	0	0	1	0	.000
Leon, Clev	1	0	1	0	0	1.000	Bradford, Clev	1	0	0	0	0	.000
Grich, Balt	1	0	1	0	0	1.000	Camilli, Clev	1	0	0	0	0	.000
Maye, Wash	1	0	1	0	0	1.000	Reichardt, Wash.	1	0	0	0	0	.000
Hinton, Clev	2	1	0	0	0	1.000	Rittwage, Clev	1	0	0	0	0	.000

SHORTSTOPS

Player and Club	G.	PO.	A.	E.	DP.	Pct.	Player and Club	G.	PO.	A.	E.	DP.	Pct.
Oyler, Cal	13	6	10	0	1	1.000	Morales, Chi	24	14	45	2	8	.967
Matchick, 1 Bos-							Severson, K C	50	83	147	9	34	.962
43 K C	44	64	130	3	32	.985	Heidemann, Clev.	132	216	354	23	79	.961
Hansen, N Y	15	20	39	1	6	.983	Michael, N Y	123	248	379	28	78	.957
Alvarado, Bos	27	25	75	2	15	.980	Gutierrez, Det	135	183	326	23	60	.957
PENA, 12 Oak-							Kubiak, Mil	73	128	174	14	35	.956
99 Mil	111	169	303	10	61	.979	Hernandez, K. C.	77	142	187	17	38	.951
Cardenas, Minn	160	280	487	17	91	.978	Brown, Clev	27	34	62	5	15	.950
Aparicio, Chi	146	251	483	18	99	.976	Alomar, Cal	10	16	21	2	5	.949
Brinkman, Wash	157	301	569	23	103	.974	Salmon, Balt	33	36	52	5	9	.946
Fregosi, Cal	150	264	468	20	99	.973	McAuliffe, Det	15	16	34	3	3	.943
Campaneris, Oak.	143	267	414	19	92	.973	Leon, Clev	23	26	40	5	10	.930
Baker, N Y	35	62	118	5	22	.973	Grich, Balt	20	28	47	7	4	.915
Szotkiewicz, Det.	44	32	101	4	20	.971	Schaal, K C	10	12	18	3	4	.909
Petrocelli, Bos.	141	262	393	20	77	.970	Maddox, Det	19	6	14	2	0	.909
Belanger, Balt.	143	212	412	19	78	.970	Floyd, 2 Balt.-						
McKinney, Chi	11	20	41	2	7	.968	8 K C	10	19	26	6	5	.882

(Fewer Than Ten Games)

Player and Club	G.	PO.	A.	E.	DP.	Pct.	Player and Club	G.	PO.	A.	E.	DP.	Pct.
Rodriguez, Wash.	7	9	21	0	1	1.000	Driscoll, Oak	7	17	13	5	3	.857
Donaldson, Oak.	6	7	15	0	1	1.000	O'Brien, Chi	5	3	7	2	1	.833
Kennedy, Mil	4	5	7	0	0	1.000	Perez, Cal	2	3	2	1	0	.833
Johnson, Balt	2	3	1	0	1	1.000	Ruiz, Cal	3	2	3	1	0	.833
Schofield, Bos.	3	0	4	0	0	1.000	Lowenstein, Clev.	1	0	0	0	0	.000
Cullen, Wash	6	1	3	0	0	1.000	Quilici, Minn	1	0	0	0	0	.000
Camilli, Clev	3	0	3	0	0	1.000	Renick, Minn	1	0	0	0	0	.000
Thompson, Minn.	6	9	14	1	1	.958							

OUTFIELDERS

Player and Club	G.	PO.	A.	E.	DP.	Pct.
STANLEY, Det ..	132	317	3	0	0	1.000
Melton, Chi	71	111	8	0	3	1.000
Maye, Wash	68	75	4	0	1	1.000
Allen, 17 Wash- 14 Mil	31	36	3	0	0	1.000
Motton, Balt ...	21	32	1	0	0	1.000
Ford, Clev	12	24	1	0	0	1.000
Kirkpatrick, K C..	19	24	0	0	0	1.000
Harper, Mil	13	19	1	0	0	1.000
Allison, Minn ...	17	18	0	0	0	1.000
Wicker, Mil	12	16	0	0	0	1.000
Hill, Minn	14	15	1	0	0	1.000
Nettles, Minn* ...	11	8	0	0	0	1.000
Manuel, Minn	11	7	0	0	0	1.000
Repoz, Cal*	110	203	6	1	2	.995
Holt, Minn	130	201	2	1	0	.995
White, N Y	161	315	6	2	0	.994
Northrup, Det ..	136	284	4	2	1	.993
Stroud, Wash ..	118	271	8	2	3	.993
Murcer, N Y ...	155	375	15	3	3	.992
Uhlaender, Clev..	134	225	5	2	1	.991
May, Chi	141	203	12	2	2	.991
Otis, K C	159	388	15	4	6	.990
Blair, Balt ...	128	368	10	4	3	.990
May, 9 Balt- 99 Mil	108	260	6	3	0	.989
Lyttle, N Y	70	84	2	1	0	.989
Berry, Chi	138	331	9	4	2	.988
Kaline, Det	91	156	3	2	1	.988
Buford, Balt ..	130	221	13	3	3	.987
F. Robinson, Bal..	120	221	9	3	3	.987
Burda, Mil*	64	71	3	1	1	.987
Reichardt, 1 Cal- 79 Wash	80	135	0	2	0	.985
Keough, K C* ...	34	63	2	1	0	.985
Piniella, K C ..	139	247	6	4	2	.984
Unser, Wash* ..	103	173	8	3	2	.984
Maddox, Det	37	55	2	1	1	.983
Pinson, Clev* ..	141	265	8	5	3	.982
Bradford, 27 Chi- 64 Clev	91	165	2	3	0	.982
Horton, Det	96	154	10	3	1	.982
Rudi, Oak	63	106	5	2	1	.982
J. Tatum, Cal..	58	108	2	2	0	.982
Monday, Oak* ...	109	257	3	5	2	.981
Johnstone, Cal ..	100	200	7	4	3	.981
Alyea, Minn	75	93	4	2	0	.980
Voss, Cal*	35	86	7	2	1	.979
Smith, Mil	39	46	0	1	0	.979
Tovar, Minn ...	151	370	12	9	1	.977
Smith, Bos	145	361	15	9	1	.977
Alou, Oak	145	287	11	7	3	.977
A. Conigliaro, Bos	146	252	7	6	1	.977
Hovley, 38 Mil- 42 Oak*	80	126	2	3	1	.977
Rettenmund, Bal..	93	201	6	5	1	.976
Hinton, Clev	35	36	4	1	0	.976
Woods, N Y	78	108	6	3	1	.974
Howard, Wash ..	120	172	6	5	4	.973
Crowley, Balt* ...	27	36	0	1	0	.973
Blefary, N Y	79	103	1	3	0	.972
Thomas, Bos	26	35	0	1	0	.972
Renick, Minn ...	25	30	2	1	0	.970
Reynolds, Cal ...	32	61	1	2	0	.969
Oliva, Minn	157	351	12	12	4	.968
W. Conigliaro, Bos	108	201	8	7	0	.968
Snyder, Mil	106	140	1	5	0	.966
Foster, Clev ...	131	188	6	7	0	.965
Walton, Mil	114	162	4	6	0	.965
Kelly, K C*	118	254	8	10	2	.963
Comer, 5 Mil- 58 Wash	63	75	2	3	0	.963
Davis, Oak	45	51	1	2	0	.963
Lahoud, Bos* ...	13	23	3	1	0	.963
Gonzalez, Cal ...	24	46	2	2	0	.960
Johnson, Cal ...	156	269	11	12	0	.959
Jackson, Oak* ..	142	251	8	12	0	.956
Yastrzemski, Bos..	69	120	3	6	0	.953
Savage, Mil	82	119	3	6	0	.953
Spriggs, K C ...	36	57	4	3	0	.953
G. Brown, Det...	26	37	1	2	0	.950
Williams, Chi ...	79	119	12	7	1	.949
McCraw, Chi* ...	49	70	2	4	0	.947
Hershberger, Mil..	35	34	1	2	0	.946
Sims, Clev	36	48	3	3	1	.944
Matias, Chi* ...	22	14	2	1	1	.941
Grieve, Wash ...	39	46	0	3	0	.939
Cowan, Cal	27	26	0	2	0	.929

(Fewer Than Ten Games)

Player and Club	G.	PO.	A.	E.	DP.	Pct.
Mitchell, N Y....	7	20	0	0	0	1.000
Baylor, Balt	6	15	0	0	0	1.000
Ortiz, Chi	8	10	3	0	0	1.000
Cater, N Y	7	11	0	0	0	1.000
Rivers, Cal*	5	10	0	0	0	1.000
Nagelson, 4 Clev- 4 Det	8	9	0	0	0	1.000
Hegan, Mil*	8	7	0	0	0	1.000
Derrick, Bos	2	5	0	0	0	1.000
Burroughs, Wash..	3	5	0	0	0	1.000
Sorrell, K C	4	5	0	0	0	1.000
Freed, Balt	1	4	0	0	0	1.000
Goossen, Wash ...	5	4	0	0	0	1.000
Brooks, Oak	5	4	0	0	0	1.000
Brye, Minn	6	4	0	0	0	1.000
Francona, Oak*...	1	3	0	0	0	1.000
Tartabull, Oak*...	6	3	0	0	0	1.000
Fernandez, Oak	1	2	0	0	0	1.000
Lowenstein, Clev..	2	2	0	0	0	1.000
Lewis, Oak	2	2	0	0	0	1.000
Christian, Chi....	4	2	0	0	0	1.000
Koegel, Mil	1	1	0	0	0	1.000
Campanis, K C ...	1	1	0	0	0	1.000
Nettles, Clev	3	1	0	0	0	1.000
Silverio, Cal* ...	5	1	0	0	0	1.000
I. Brown, Det ...	4	7	0	1	0	.875
Fiore, Bos.*	2	0	0	1	0	.000
Blanco, Chi	1	0	0	0	0	.000
French, Wash	1	0	0	0	0	.000
Moses, Bos	1	0	0	0	0	.000
Perry, Minn	1	0	0	0	0	.000
Rooker, K C* ...	1	0	0	0	0	.000
Tepedino, N Y*..	1	0	0	0	0	.000
Valdespino, Mil*..	1	0	0	0	0	.000

CATCHERS

Player and Club	G.	PO.	A.	E.	DP.	PB.	Pct.
Roseboro, Wash..	30	122	6	0	1	2	1.000
Lamont, Det	15	87	8	0	0	3	1.000
Dalrymple, Balt	11	78	4	0	1	1	1.000
Pavletich, Bos....	10	43	4	0	1	1	1.000
FREEHAN, Det..114		742	42	2	6	8	.997
Mitterwald, Min 117		740	62	3	8	8	.996
Fernandez, Oak..	76	405	25	3	6	7	.993
Sims, Clev	39	277	13	2	2	4	.993
Azcue, Cal 112		587	51	6	10	17	.991
Moses, Bos	88	578	45	6	3	6	.990
Tenace, Oak	30	180	18	2	7	1	.990
Tischinski, Minn	22	90	7	1	0	1	.990
Fosse, Clev ...120		854	70	10	7	17	.989
Munson, N Y ...125		631	80	8	11	10	.989
Roof, Mil 107		596	47	8	6	5	.988
Casanova, Wash 100		461	48	6	12	2	.988
Herrmann, Chi....	88	433	51	6	10	14	.988
Rodriguez, K C..	75	451	32	6	5	7	.988
Egan, Cal	79	367	31	5	4	10	.988
Gibbs, N Y	44	208	19	3	1	1	.987
Hendricks, Balt..	95	509	35	8	6	10	.986
Campanis, K C..	13	63	7	1	1	4	.986
Josephson, Chi..	84	353	38	6	7	11	.985
Satriano, Bos ...	51	318	19	5	5	3	.985
McNertney, Mil..	94	387	46	7	3	4	.984
Etchebarren, Bal	76	392	29	7	3	1	.984
Montgomery, Bo	22	143	13	3	3	3	.981
Ratliff, Minn...	53	183	11	4	4	2	.980
Price, Det	38	266	8	6	2	4	.979
Kirkpatrick, K C	89	463	61	12	12	5	.978
Duncan, Oak	73	373	28	9	9	4	.978
French, Wash ...	62	267	23	8	4	5	.973

(Fewer Than Ten Games)

Player and Club	G.	PO.	A.	E.	DP.	PB.	Pct.
Hinton, Clev	4	28	2	0	0	2	1.000
Billings, Wash..	8	25	3	0	0	3	1.000
Hosley, Det	4	22	3	0	0	0	1.000
Hopkins, Chi	8	16	0	0	0	1	1.000
Ellis, N Y.......	2	12	1	0	0	1	1.000
Taylor, K C	3	7	0	0	0	0	1.000
Haney, Oak	1	6	0	0	0	0	1.000
Brown, Cal	5	1	0	0	0	0	1.000
Brinkman, Chi ..	9	32	5	1	1	0	.974
Martinez, K C...	5	20	3	1	0	0	.958
Kusnyer, Chi ...	3	12	4	1	0	1	.941
Oates, Balt	4	30	1	2	1	0	.939
Dempsey, Minn..	3	12	0	1	0	0	.923
Green, Oak	1	0	0	0	0	0	.000
Ruiz, Cal	1	0	0	0	0	0	.000

PITCHERS

Player and Club	G.	PO.	A.	E.	DP.	Pct.
BOSMAN, Wash ..36		19	32	0	3	1.000
Coleman, Wash ..	39	16	30	0	3	1.000
Hargan, Clev	23	13	24	0	3	1.000
Wood, Chi*	77	7	27	0	3	1.000
Johnson, K C....	40	13	20	0	0	1.000
Kline, N Y	16	14	14	0	2	1.000
Grant, Oak	72	6	22	0	3	1.000
Miller, 15 Clev- 15 Chi	30	6	20	0	2	1.000
Hardin, Balt	36	9	14	0	1	1.000
Hennigan, Clev..	42	12	11	0	1	1.000
McLain, Det	14	7	14	0	1	1.000
Baldwin, Mil	28	6	14	0	1	1.000
Grzenda, Wash*..	49	3	16	0	1	1.000
Ellsworth, 29 Clev- 14 Mil*	43	4	14	0	1	1.000
Morris, Mil*	20	2	15	0	3	1.000
Austin, Clev*	31	4	13	0	1	1.000
Williams, Minn...	68	8	8	0	0	1.000
Johnson, Chi	18	4	11	0	2	1.000
Hiller, Det*	47	3	10	0	0	1.000
Roland, Oak*	28	3	9	0	0	1.000
Garrett, Cal*	32	0	12	0	0	1.000
Abernathy, K C..	36	3	9	0	0	1.000
LaRoche, Cal* ...	38	5	7	0	1	1.000
Watt, Balt	53	2	10	0	1	1.000
Lee, Bos*	11	1	10	0	1	1.000
Boswell, Minn ...	18	6	5	0	1	1.000
Humphreys, 5 Wash- 23 Mil	28	5	6	0	1	1.000
Doyle, Cal*	40	1	10	0	1	1.000
Drabowsky, 24 K C- 21 Balt	45	3	8	0	0	1.000
Lindblad, Oak*...	62	1	10	0	0	1.000
Magnuson, Chi.*..	13	3	6	0	0	1.000
Leonhard, Balt ..	23	0	9	0	1	1.000
Cumberland, N Y*	15	2	6	0	0	1.000
Such, Wash.	21	1	7	0	1	1.000
Richert, Balt*	50	0	8	0	0	1.000
Lyle, Bos*	63	1	7	0	0	1.000
Lauzerique, Mil...	11	3	3	0	0	1.000
Reed, Det	16	2	4	0	0	1.000
Brown, Wash	24	4	2	0	0	1.000
Hall, Balt	32	3	3	0	0	1.000
Queen, Cal	34	1	5	0	0	1.000
Barber, Minn	18	1	3	0	0	1.000
Meyer, Mil*	10	0	3	0	0	1.000
LaGrow, Det.....	10	1	1	0	0	1.000
Hamm, Minn	10	1	0	0	0	1.000
Hartenstein, Bos.	17	0	1	0	0	1.000
Phillips, Bos	18	0	1	0	0	1.000
Stottlemyre, N Y	37	22	51	1	3	.986
Horlen, Chi	28	22	42	1	1	.985
Pattin, Mil	37	18	40	1	3	.983
Perry, Minn	40	11	47	1	0	.983
Niekro, Det	38	17	35	1	1	.981
Krausse, Mil	37	21	27	1	0	.980
McNally, Balt*...	40	10	37	1	4	.979
Dobson, Oak	41	19	28	1	3	.979
Drago, K C	35	10	33	1	5	.977
Hunter, Oak	40	17	24	1	3	.976
Fisher, Cal	67	11	25	1	1	.973
Phoebus, Balt....	27	14	20	1	0	.971
Fitzmorris, K C	43	12	21	1	1	.971
Lockwood, Mil ...	27	14	18	1	1	.970
Hannan, Wash ...	42	7	25	1	0	.970
Palmer, Balt	39	21	42	2	4	.969
Koonce, Bos	23	10	19	1	2	.967
Lolich, Det*	40	9	46	2	1	.965
Nagy, Bos	23	12	15	1	1	.964
Kilkenny, Det* ...	36	6	20	1	1	.963
Gelnar, Mil	53	6	20	1	2	.963
Siebert, Bos	33	25	26	2	3	.962
Sanders, Mil	50	5	19	1	1	.960

Player and Club	G.	PO.	A.	E.	DP.	Pct.
Bolin, 32 Mil-6 Bos	38	5	18	1	0	.958
Klimkowski, N Y	45	5	18	1	0	.958
Cuellar, Balt*	40	9	34	2	1	.956
Peterson, N Y*..	39	12	52	3	7	.955
Blyleven, Minn	27	5	16	1	1	.955
Shellenback, Wash*	39	5	16	1	1	.955
Higgins, Clev	58	7	14	1	0	.955
Pina, Wash	61	5	15	1	0	.952
Moore, *13 Clev-24 Chi	37	11	28	2	1	.951
Rooker, K C*	38	6	32	2	4	.950
K. Tatum, Cal	62	4	15	1	0	.950
Cox, Wash	37	13	24	2	0	.949
Wilson, Det	18	5	13	1	1	.947
Wright, Cal*	39	18	33	3	1	.944
Tiant, Minn	18	3	14	1	2	.944
Brunet, Wash*	24	2	15	1	2	.944
Waslewski, N Y	26	7	10	1	0	.944
Timmerman, Det.	61	7	10	1	0	.944
Hand, Clev	35	11	22	2	2	.943
Fingers, Oak	45	7	26	2	3	.943
Knowles, Wash*..	71	8	25	2	2	.943
Cain, Det*	29	8	24	2	0	.941
Butler, K C*	25	3	13	1	1	.941
Lachemann, Oak..	41	1	15	1	1	.941
Segui, Oak	47	17	14	2	2	.939
Aker, N Y	41	4	11	1	0	.938
Scherman, Det*	48	8	7	1	2	.938
Perranoski, Minn*	67	0	15	1	0	.938
Kaat, Minn*	45	15	43	4	5	.935
Brett, Bos*	41	9	20	2	0	.935
Bahnsen, N Y	36	17	40	4	3	.934
Bradley, Cal	17	5	9	1	0	.933
Murphy, Chi	51	4	10	1	1	.933
Odom, Oak	29	22	30	4	2	.929
Downing, 10 Oak-17 Mil*	27	9	30	3	2	.929
Patterson, Det	43	5	8	1	0	.929
May, Cal*	38	5	33	3	1	.927
Zepp, Minn	43	8	17	2	1	.926
Dunning, Clev	19	7	17	2	2	.923
Wynne, Chi	12	1	11	1	1	.923
Burgmeier, K C*	41	3	20	2	0	.920
Chance, Clev.	45	3	20	2	2	.920
Peters, Bos*	34	7	27	3	3	.919
Hamilton, 35 N Y-3 Chi*	38	0	11	1	0	.917
Janeski, Chi	35	15	37	5	6	.912
Murphy, Cal	39	22	29	5	3	.911
John, Chi*	37	15	65	8	3	.909
Brabender, Mil..	29	13	17	3	1	.909
Crider, Chi	32	3	7	1	0	.909
McDowell, Clev*..	39	3	35	4	1	.905
Culp, Bos	33	22	24	5	4	.902
Romo, Bos	48	7	20	3	1	.900
Sisk, Chi	17	1	8	1	1	.900
O'Donoghue, Mil*	25	2	7	1	1	.900
Wright, K C	47	1	8	1	0	.900
Messersmith, Cal..	37	12	23	4	3	.897
McDaniel, N Y	62	7	19	3	2	.897
Morehead, K C....	28	7	10	2	0	.895
Colbert, Clev	23	2	6	1	0	.889
Paul, Clev*	30	2	6	1	1	.889
Wagner, Bos	38	5	3	1	0	.889
Kekich, N Y*....	26	5	10	2	0	.882
Bunker, K C	24	5	17	3	0	.880
Locker, 28 Mil-38 Oak	66	3	17	3	0	.870
Mingori, Clev*	21	3	3	1	0	.857
Stange, 20 Bos-16 Chi	36	4	7	2	0	.846
Hall, Minn*	52	2	9	2	1	.846
McRae, Det	19	3	2	1	0	.833
Weaver, Chi.	31	4	4	2	0	.800
Jarvis, Bos	15	1	3	1	0	.800
Woodson, Minn....	21	1	6	2	0	.778
Monteagudo, KC	21	1	2	1	0	.750
Lasher, 12 Det-43 Clev	55	1	8	4	0	.692
Lopez, Balt*	25	2	6	4	1	.667
Robertson, Det....	11	0	1	1	0	.500
Kealey, Cal	17	0	1	1	0	.500

(Fewer Than Ten Games)

Player and Club	G.	PO.	A.	E.	DP.	Pct.
Gogolewski, Wash	8	1	9	0	1	1.000
Verbanic, N Y	7	2	7	0	0	1.000
Blue, Oak*	6	1	7	0	0	1.000
Lonborg, Bos	9	2	5	0	1	1.000
Saunders, Det	8	2	5	0	0	1.000
Rittwage, Clev	8	2	4	0	1	1.000
Allen, Cal	8	2	2	0	1	1.000
Nelson, K C	4	0	3	0	0	1.000
Eddy, Chi*	7	2	1	0	0	1.000
O'Riley, K C	9	2	1	0	0	1.000
Curtis, Bos*	1	0	2	0	0	1.000
Dukes, Wash*	5	1	1	0	0	1.000
Carlos, Wash	5	1	1	0	0	1.000
Rodriguez, Oak	6	1	1	0	0	1.000
Santiago, Bos	8	2	0	0	0	1.000
Secrist, Chi*	9	0	2	0	0	1.000
McCormick, N Y *	9	1	1	0	0	1.000
Talbot, Oak	1	0	1	0	0	1.000
Gardner, N Y*....	1	0	1	0	0	1.000
Splittorff, K C*..	2	0	1	0	1	1.000
Peters. Mil........	2	0	1	0	0	1.000
Womack, Oak	2	0	1	0	0	1.000
Moret, Bos*	3	0	1	0	0	1.000
Ramos, Wash	4	0	1	0	0	1.000
Haydel, Minn	4	0	1	0	0	1.000
Arrigo, Chi*	5	0	1	0	0	1.000
Hedlund, K C	9	0	1	0	0	1.000
Burbach, N Y	4	0	2	1	0	.667
Mills, Bos	2	1	1	1	0	.500
Rounsaville, Chi..	8	0	1	1	0	.500
Riddleberger, W*	8	0	0	0	0	.000
Beene, Balt	4	0	0	0	0	.000
Wolf, Cal	4	0	0	0	0	.000
York, K C	4	0	0	0	0	.000
Cox, Cal	3	0	0	0	0	.000
Osteen, Oak	3	0	0	0	0	.000
O'Toole, Chi	3	0	0	0	0	.000
Jones, N Y	2	0	0	0	0	.000
Twitchell, Mil....	2	0	0	0	0	.000
Brubaker, Mil	1	0	0	0	0	.000
Colson, N Y	1	0	0	0	0	.000
Moloney, Chi	1	0	0	0	0	.000
Shank, Cal	1	0	0	0	0	.000

Note: Biittner and Hicks appeared only as pinch-hitters as shown in batting table and therefore are not listed in fielding records.

AMERICAN LEAGUE PITCHING AVERAGES

CLUB PITCHING

Club	G	CG	Sv.	IP	H	AB	R	ER	HR	SH.	SF.	Int. BB.	Tot. BB.	HB.	SO.	WP.	Bk.	ERA.
Baltimore	162	60	31	1478⅔	1317	5493	574	517	139	70	44	40	469	23	941	44	5	3.15
Minnesota	162	26	58	1448⅓	1329	5451	605	520	130	55	42	51	486	37	940	38	4	3.23
New York	163	36	49	1471⅓	1386	5566	612	530	130	62	38	54	451	26	777	32	2	3.24
Oakland	162	33	40	1442⅓	1253	5356	605	529	134	66	40	45	542	34	858	56	1	3.30
California	162	21	40	1462⅓	1280	5403	630	566	154	63	32	67	559	43	922	52	2	3.48
Kansas City	162	30	25	1457⅓	1346	5439	689	615	138	92	47	29	559	41	915	52	10	3.78
Washington	162	20	40	1446⅓	1375	5457	705	620	139	62	50	75	641	35	823	51	5	3.80
Boston	162	38	44	1446⅓	1391	5531	722	622	156	59	30	49	611	27	1003	70	5	3.87
Cleveland	162	34	35	1451⅓	1333	5389	670	625	163	74	36	62	594	44	1076	53	4	3.91
Detroit	162	33	29	1447⅓	1443	5555	731	658	153	57	46	31	689	40	1045	56	5	4.09
Milwaukee	163	31	27	1462⅔	1397	5478	751	676	146	80	44	68	623	35	895	46	3	4.21
Chicago	162	20	30	1430⅓	1554	5557	822	722	164	71	22	67	587	44	762	63	4	4.54
Totals		382	467	17447	16404	65675	8109	7200	1746	811	489	638	6808	432	10957	617	55	3.71

NOTE: Totals for earned runs for several clubs do not agree with the composite totals for all pitchers of each respective club due to instances in which provisions of Section 10.18 (f) of the Scoring Rules were applied. The following differences are to be noted: Boston club total, 622; individual pitchers' total, 626; Chicago, 722 and 725; New York, 530 and 531.

PITCHERS' RECORDS

(Fifteen Leading Qualifiers for Earned-Run Leadership—162 or More Innings)

*Throws lefthanded.

Pitcher and Club	G	GS	CG	W.	L.	Pct.	Sv.	IP.	H.	AB.	R.	ER.	HR.	SH.	SF.	Tot. BB.	Int. BB.	HB.	SO.	WP.	Bk.	ERA.
Segui, Diego, Oakland	47	19	3	10	10	.500	12	162	130	586	54	46	9	21	4	68	14	4	95	5	0	2.56
Palmer, James, Baltimore	39	39	17	20	10	.667	0	305	263	1139	130	92	21	14	7	110	3	6	199	10	3	2.71
Wright, Clyde, California*	39	39	22	22	12	.647	0	261	226	975	97	82	24	24	8	88	4	1	110	8	0	2.83
Peterson, Fred, New York*	39	37	8	20	11	.645	0	260	247	994	102	77	24	25	6	40	1	7	127	7	2	2.91
McDowell, Samuel, Cleveland*	39	39	19	20	12	.625	0	305	236	1107	107	99	25	8	4	131	6	10	304	17	1	2.92
Messersmith, John A., California*	37	26	6	11	10	.524	2	195	144	702	75	65	21	23	6	104	9	9	162	6	2	3.00
Perry, James, Minnesota	40	40	13	24	12	.667	0	279	258	1063	112	94	27	20	8	57	10	11	168	9	0	3.03
Culp, Raymond, Boston	33	33	15	17	14	.548	0	251	211	943	104	85	22	20	2	91	7	8	197	10	0	3.05
Johnson, Robert D., Kansas City	40	26	10	8	13	.381	1	214	178	782	82	73	18	18	12	82	8	11	206	6	1	3.07
Stottlemyre, Melvin, New York	37	37	14	15	13	.536	0	271	262	1028	110	93	28	12	9	84	6	6	126	10	0	3.09
Blyleven, Rikalbert, Minnesota	27	25	5	10	9	.526	0	164	143	616	66	58	17	17	5	47	8	2	135	2	3	3.18
McNally, David, Baltimore*	40	40	16	24	9	.727	0	296	277	1107	114	106	29	15	1	78	3	9	185	8	0	3.22
John, Thomas, Chicago*	37	37	14	12	17	.414	1	269	253	1009	117	101	19	14	3	101	16	7	138	17	2	3.28
Bahnsen, Stanley, New York	36	35	14	14	17	.560	0	233	227	885	100	86	23	11	4	75	3	9	116	3	0	3.32

Departmental Leaders: G—Wood, 77; L—Lolich, 19; Saves—Perranoski, 34; Pct.—Cuellar, 34; GS—Cuellar, Dobson, Hunter, McNally, Perry, 40; CG—Cuellar, 21; ShO—Dobson, Palmer, 5; W—Cuellar, McNally, Perry, 24; Pct.—Cuellar, .750; IP—McDowell, Palmer, 305; H—McNally, Palmer, 277; AB—Palmer, 1139; R—Krausse, 130; ER—Cuellar, 115; HR—Cuellar, 34; SH—McNally, Rooker, 15; SF—C. Cox, 12; BB—McDowell, 131; IBB—Knowles, 16; HB—Culp, R. Johnson, 11; SO—McDowell, 304; WP—John, 17; Balk—Blyleven, Garrett, Palmer, 3.

(All Pitchers—Listed Alphabetically)

*Throws lefthanded.

Pitcher and Club	G.	GS.	CG.	W.	L.	Sv.	Pct.	IP.	H.	AB.	R.	ER.	HR.	SH.	SF.	Tot.Int. BB.BB.	HB.	SO.	WP.	Bk.	ERA.
Abernathy, Ted, Kansas City	36	0	0	9	3	12	.750	56	41	196	23	16	3	9	0	38	0	49	1	0	2.57
Aker, Jack, New York	41	0	0	4	1	10	.667	70	57	252	19	17	3	6	2	20	1	36	1	0	2.06
Allen, Lloyd, California	8	2	0	1	1	0	.500	24	23	88	7	7	4	1	1	11	2	12	1	0	2.63
Arrigo, Gerald, Chicago*	5	0	0	0	2	0	.000	13	24	61	20	19	0	3	0	7	1	12	1	0	13.15
Austin, Rick, Cleveland*	31	8	1	2	7	0	.286	68	74	263	36	36	10	5	4	26	2	53	3	0	4.76
Bahnsen, Stanley, New York	36	35	6	14	11	0	.560	233	227	885	100	86	23	4	11	76	3	116	3	0	3.32
Baldwin, David, Milwaukee	28	0	0	2	0	1	.667	35	25	122	11	14	2	4	0	18	0	26	0	0	2.57
Barber, Steven, Minnesota	18	0	0	2	1	0	.667	27	26	99	14	14	1	3	0	14	1	14	0	0	4.67
Beene, Fred, Baltimore	4	0	0	0	0	0	.000	8	8	25	5	4	1	0	0	5	0	4	0	0	6.00
Blue, Vida, Oakland*	6	6	0	0	0	0	1.000	39	20	132	8	8	1	2	0	15	0	35	0	0	6.00
Blyleven, Rikalbert, Minnesota	27	25	5	10	9	0	.526	164	143	616	66	58	17	8	2	47	0	135	2	3	3.18
Bolin, Bobby, 32 Milwaukee-6 Boston	38	3	0	7	5	2	.583	81	77	537	84	72	20	6	6	72	5	89	5	3	4.63
Bosman, Richard, Washington	36	34	7	16	12	0	.571	231	231	865	81	77	16	7	8	72	2	134	4	0	3.00
Boswell, David, Minnesota	20	15	3	5	13	0	.389	69	80	274	55	49	12	2	7	44	3	45	6	0	6.39
Brabender, Eugene, Milwaukee	28	21	2	6	15	0	.300	129	127	499	94	86	18	2	7	44	1	76	6	0	6.00
Bradley, Thomas, California	17	11	1	5	6	0	.286	69	71	263	49	44	8	3	3	33	1	53	5	0	4.11
Brett, Kenneth, Boston*	41	14	1	8	9	5	.471	139	118	530	71	62	17	3	6	37	6	155	6	0	4.08
Brown, Jackie, Washington	24	5	0	5	5	0	.500	57	49	212	28	25	8	7	4	37	1	47	0	0	3.95
Brubaker, Bruce, Milwaukee	1	1	0	0	0	0	.000	2	2	8	2	2	0	0	0	1	0	0	0	0	9.00
Brunet, George, Washington*	20	20	2	8	10	0	.571	118	124	451	64	58	10	2	1	48	2	67	5	1	4.42
Bunker, Wallace, Kansas City	24	15	2	2	11	0	.154	122	109	458	63	57	16	5	0	50	5	59	5	0	4.20
Burbach, William, New York	4	4	0	0	3	0	.000	10	12	63	19	19	2	0	1	9	1	10	0	0	10.06
Burgmeier, Thomas, Kansas City*	41	1	0	6	6	2	.500	68	57	250	30	24	4	6	1	23	1	43	2	0	3.77
Butler, William, Kansas City*	25	12	2	4	12	0	.250	141	117	511	66	59	17	4	4	87	1	75	3	0	3.83
Cain, Leslie, Detroit*	29	5	0	12	7	0	.632	181	167	675	92	77	15	6	0	98	7	156	9	1	1.50
Carlos, Francisco, Washington	5	0	0	0	0	0	.529	6	6	20	6	3	1	1	0	5	0	6	0	0	4.24
Chance, W. Dean, Cleveland	45	19	5	9	8	1	.529	155	172	599	80	73	18	11	1	59	6	109	9	1	7.26
Colbert, Vincent, Cleveland	23	0	0	1	2	0	.500	31	37	124	25	18	4	0	2	11	0	25	4	0	3.58
Coleman, Joseph, Washington	39	29	6	8	12	0	.400	219	190	816	98	87	25	3	7	89	0	152	14	0	4.50
Colson, Loyd, New York	1	0	0	0	0	0	.000	2	4	12	4	0	0	0	0	4	0	3	0	0	4.45
Cox, J. Casey, Washington	37	30	0	8	12	0	.400	192	211	740	108	95	27	10	12	44	4	68	3	0	4.50
Cox, Terry, California	32	8	0	0	1	4	.000	10	10	49	10	10	1	0	0	4	0	2	1	0	4.45
Crider, Jerry, Chicago	40	8	0	4	7	0	.364	91	101	351	49	45	13	2	8	34	0	40	0	1	3.47
Cuellar, Miguel, Baltimore*	40	40	21	24	8	0	.750	298	273	1128	126	115	34	9	3	69	6	190	6	1	3.05
Culp, Raymond, Boston	33	33	15	17	14	0	.548	251	211	943	104	85	22	12	2	91	11	197	10	0	3.94
Cumberland, John, New York*	15	8	0	3	4	0	.429	64	62	246	31	28	9	10	3	15	1	38	0	1	13.50
Curtis, John, Boston*	2	0	0	0	2	0	.000	4	12	12	4	4	1	0	0	3	0	1	0	0	3.74
Dobson, Charles, Oakland	41	40	13	16	15	0	.516	267	230	1005	122	101	32	6	5	81	7	149	10	8	3.53
Downing, Alphonso, 10 Oak-17 Mil*	27	22	3	5	13	0	.278	135	135	496	66	53	13	8	4	79	4	79	4	2	5.14
Doyle, Paul, California*	40	0	0	3	1	4	.750	42	43	161	25	24	7	7	1	27	6	34	3	0	3.52
Drabowsky, Myron, 24 KC-21 Balt	45	0	0	5	6	3	.556	58	58	258	30	27	10	2	5	21	7	59	5	0	3.75
Drago, Richard, Kansas City	35	34	7	9	9	0	.500	239	239	899	110	100	20	6	1	72	1	127	4	1	2.57
Dukes, N. Jan, Washington*	5	0	0	0	0	0	.000	7	6	25	4	4	0	0	0	5	0	4	3	0	4.98
Dunning, Steven, Cleveland	19	17	0	9	9	0	.308	94	93	357	55	52	16	4	2	54	3	77	1	0	4.98

Pitcher and Club	G.	GS.	CG.	W.	L.	Sv.	Pct.	IP.	H.	AB.	R.	ER.	HR.	SH.	SF.	BB.	BB.	HB.	SO.	WP.	Bk.	ERA.
Eddy, Donald, Chicago*	7	0	0	0	3	0	.000	12	10	41	4	3	0	0	1	6	0	0	9	0	0	2.25
Ellsworth, Richard, 29 Clev-14 Mil*	43	1	0	3	3	3	.500	59	60	220	26	25	4	4	2	17	2	0	22	0	0	3.81
Fingers, Roland, Oakland	45	8	1	7	9	2	.438	148	137	549	65	60	13	5	4	48	5	2	79	6	0	3.65
Fisher, Eddie, California	67	0	0	4	4	8	.500	130	117	490	51	44	15	3	6	35	8	1	74	1	0	3.05
Fitzmorris, Alan, Kansas City	43	11	2	8	5	1	.615	118	112	441	60	58	14	6	2	52	2	1	47	12	0	4.42
Gardner, Richard, New York*	1	1	0	0	0	0	.000	7	6	29	4	4	0	0	0	6	0	0	6	0	0	5.14
Garrett, Gregory, California*	32	7	0	5	6	0	.455	75	48	253	23	22	4	5	1	44	4	1	53	3	0	2.64
Gelnar, John, Milwaukee	53	5	0	4	3	7	.571	92	98	354	46	43	7	7	5	25	5	1	48	3	0	4.21
Gogolewski, William, Washington	8	5	1	0	3	0	.000	83	104	322	47	44	18	3	4	30	0	3	54	1	0	4.76
Grant, James, Oakland	72	0	0	6	2	24	.750	123	84	443	26	25	8	8	0	30	8	0	19	3	0	1.83
Grzenda, Joseph, Washington*	49	0	0	1	2	2	.333	61	51	223	18	21	3	5	0	17	4	0	36	0	0	4.98
Hall, Richard, Baltimore	32	0	0	10	5	3	.667	75	61	262	28	26	7	2	1	7	1	0	43	1	0	3.10
Hall, Tom, Minnesota*	52	11	0	11	6	4	.647	155	101	544	44	44	14	8	1	66	5	1	184	3	1	2.55
Hamilton, Steven, 35 NY-3 Chi*	38	0	0	4	3	3	.571	48	40	174	18	16	3	11	2	17	5	3	36	0	0	3.00
Hamm, Peter, Minnesota	10	0	0	0	1	0	.000	16	20	65	10	10	3	1	6	7	0	0	3	0	0	5.63
Hand, Richard, Cleveland	35	25	3	6	13	0	.316	160	132	580	71	68	27	7	1	69	4	3	110	3	1	3.83
Hannan, James, Washington	42	19	3	9	11	0	.450	128	119	476	65	57	17	0	3	54	8	3	61	0	1	4.01
Hardin, James, Baltimore	36	19	3	6	5	0	.545	143	150	561	60	57	13	8	4	26	8	1	78	3	0	3.54
Hargan, Steven, Cleveland	26	19	8	11	3	0	.786	143	101	503	47	46	14	7	3	53	11	3	72	0	0	2.90
Hartenstein, Charles, Boston	17	0	0	1	0	0	1.000	7	18	31	13	6	2	5	0	4	0	0	5	1	0	8.05
Haydel, J. Harold, Minnesota	4	0	0	0	0	0	.000	15	9	60	5	5	1	0	1	7	1	0	4	0	0	3.00
Hedlund, Michael, Kansas City	9	0	0	1	0	0	1.000	18	18	60	13	12	2	1	2	4	2	0	5	0	1	7.20
Hennigan, Phillip, Cleveland	42	0	0	2	3	3	.400	69	69	262	34	31	7	5	7	43	4	4	82	1	0	4.00
Higgins, Dennis, Cleveland	58	0	0	4	6	3	.400	90	69	330	41	40	8	3	2	54	4	4	82	1	0	4.00
Hiller, John, Detroit*	47	0	0	6	6	3	.500	104	90	375	39	35	12	7	1	46	4	4	89	1	0	3.03
Horlen, Joel, Chicago	35	26	4	6	16	0	.273	172	198	690	99	93	18	12	8	41	3	4	77	3	0	4.87
Humphreys, Robert, 5 Wash23 Mil	28	0	0	2	2	0	.563	62	41	187	20	17	4	10	5	31	0	3	38	2	0	2.94
Hunter, James, Oakland	40	40	9	18	14	0	.563	262	253	1013	124	111	40	9	10	74	5	5	178	6	0	3.81
Janeski, Gerard, Chicago	35	35	4	10	17	0	.370	206	247	824	125	109	22	3	2	63	9	2	79	1	0	4.76
Jarvis, Raymond, Boston	15	0	0	0	0	0	.000	17	17	62	8	7	2	12	5	10	0	4	8	0	0	3.94
John, Thomas, Chicago*	37	37	10	12	17	0	.414	269	253	1009	117	98	17	7	7	46	16	0	138	17	0	3.28
Johnson, C. Barth, Chicago	15	15	4	2	8	0	.364	53	92	343	53	73	11	1	2	71	3	3	71	2	0	4.80
Johnson, Robert D., Kansas City	40	33	10	8	13	0	.381	214	192	782	82	73	18	9	0	82	11	3	206	6	0	3.07
Jones, Gary, New York*	17	0	0	0	0	0	.000	8	8	8	2	0	0	0	9	8	0	0	14	0	0	0.00
Kaat, James, Minnesota*	45	34	10	14	10	0	.583	230	244	895	110	91	26	7	2	58	2	3	120	1	0	3.56
Kealey, Steven, California	17	0	0	2	1	0	.667	22	14	73	14	14	2	2	1	14	1	0	14	0	0	4.09
Kekich, Michael, New York*	26	21	3	7	6	0	.538	129	103	386	74	69	11	9	5	55	3	0	105	3	0	4.82
Kilkenny, Michael, Detroit*	45	21	1	7	6	0	.538	141	141	505	77	81	10	5	2	70	7	7	63	2	0	5.16
Klimkowski, Ronald, New York	45	0	0	6	7	0	.462	99	98	359	38	29	7	1	1	24	3	3	40	0	0	2.66
Kline, Steven, New York	16	15	5	6	6	0	.500	100	99	389	42	38	6	8	5	29	8	0	37	0	0	3.42
Knowles, Darold, Washington*	71	0	0	2	14	27	.125	119	99	432	36	27	4	11	2	71	16	0	71	3	0	2.04
Koonce, Calvin, Boston	23	0	0	3	4	4	.429	76	64	277	32	30	7	4	6	27	6	2	37	0	0	3.55
Krausse, Lewis, Milwaukee	41	35	8	13	18	0	.419	216	235	855	130	114	33	12	5	67	15	4	130	1	0	4.75
Lachemann, Marcel, Oakland	37	0	0	4	3	4	.500	58	58	218	18	18	6	6	2	21	2	1	39	2	0	2.79
LaGrow, Lerrin, Detroit	10	0	0	1	1	0	.500	12	16	52	11	10	2	0	1	6	0	0	7	0	0	7.50
LaRoche, David, California*	38	0	0	4	1	4	.800	50	41	183	20	19	6	2	1	21	1	1	44	1	1	3.42

Pitcher and Club	G	GS	CG	W	L	Sv.	Pct.	IP	H	AB	R	ER	HR	SH	SF.	BB.	BB.	HB.	SO.	WP.	Bk.	ERA.
Lasher, Frederick, 12 Det-43 Clev	55	1	0	2	10	8	.167	57	67	252	40	31	6	4	6	42	2	1	52	2	1	4.16
Lauzerique, George, Milwaukee	11	5	0	1	2	0	.333	35	41	139	27	27	7	1	1	14	1	1	24	0	0	6.94
Lee, William, Boston	11	11	1	2	2	1	.500	37	48	150	20	19	3	2	0	14	1	0	19	4	0	4.62
Leonhard, David, Baltimore	23	5	0	2	2	0	.500	28	32	109	20	16	5	4	3	18	1	0	14	2	0	5.14
Lindblad, Paul, Oakland	62	0	0	8	2	2	.800	63	52	234	23	16	7	2	1	28	0	4	42	5	0	3.07
Locker, Robert, 28 Mil-38 Oak	66	0	0	4	1	3	.800	88	86	332	39	30	5	6	4	29	5	6	52	2	0	4.29
Lockwood, Claude, Milwaukee	27	26	3	5	12	0	.294	174	173	651	91	83	22	2	10	79	5	5	93	5	1	4.29
Lolich, Michael, Detroit	40	40	13	14	19	0	.424	273	272	1045	125	115	27	12	10	109	15	2	230	14	0	3.79
Lonborg, James, Boston	9	9	0	4	1	0	.800	34	33	127	12	12	4	0	2	9	0	0	21	0	0	3.18
Lopez, Marcelino, Baltimore	25	3	0	1	1	1	.500	51	47	217	15	12	5	4	3	37	1	2	49	0	0	2.07
Lyle, Albert, Boston	63	0	0	1	7	20	.125	67	62	254	37	29	7	7	5	36	12	1	51	1	0	3.90
Magnuson, James, Chicago	13	6	0	1	5	0	.167	45	45	171	24	24	5	4	1	17	1	1	20	8	0	4.80
May, Rudolph, California	38	34	0	7	13	0	.350	209	190	774	102	93	20	13	3	81	3	1	164	8	1	4.00
McCormick, Michael, New York	9	4	0	1	0	0	1.000	22	28	88	15	14	2	0	1	16	1	0	12	0	0	6.00
McDaniel, Lyndall, New York	62	0	0	9	5	29	.643	112	88	406	25	25	7	5	4	23	10	7	81	3	0	2.01
McDowell, Samuel, Cleveland	39	39	19	20	12	0	.625	305	236	1107	108	99	25	8	4	131	10	3	304	17	0	2.92
McLain, Dennis, Detroit	14	14	1	3	5	0	.375	91	100	366	51	47	9	0	4	28	1	3	52	0	0	4.65
McNally, David, Baltimore	40	40	16	24	9	0	.727	296	277	1107	114	106	29	15	11	78	2	7	185	1	0	3.22
McRae, Norman, Detroit	19	0	0	0	0	0	.000	31	24	115	13	10	2	1	0	25	0	1	16	0	0	2.90
Messersmith, John A., California	37	26	6	11	10	5	.524	195	144	702	75	65	13	7	0	78	12	6	162	6	0	3.00
Meyer, Robert, 15 Clev-15 Chi	30	14	0	3	4	0	.429	98	123	392	56	52	12	9	5	48	15	0	51	3	0	4.78
Miller, Robert, Boston	10	0	0	0	0	0	.000	20	17	75	8	6	0	2	0	12	0	1	18	0	0	2.70
Mills, Richard, Boston	2	0	0	0	0	0	.000	6	3	17	0	0	0	0	0	4	0	0	3	0	0	0.00
Mingori, Stephen, Cleveland	21	0	0	1	0	1	1.000	27	17	100	8	7	1	2	0	12	0	0	16	0	0	2.25
Moloney, Richard, Chicago	1	0	0	0	0	0	.000	4	6	18	4	3	0	0	0	5	0	0	3	0	0	6.50
Monteagudo, Aurelio, Kansas City	37	1	0	1	1	0	.500	50	55	198	30	24	4	5	8	22	4	2	40	4	0	3.61
Moore, R. Barry, 13 Chi-24 Chi	31	19	5	1	3	0	.250	141	155	548	90	83	20	5	8	80	3	1	69	9	0	5.30
Morehead, David, Kansas City	28	17	1	3	5	0	.375	122	121	464	64	49	16	6	3	62	4	0	69	9	0	3.38
Moret, Rogelio, Boston	3	3	0	1	0	0	1.000	18	18	31	8	3	3	0	0	4	0	0	16	0	0	3.95
Morris, John, Milwaukee	20	9	0	4	3	0	.571	73	70	277	33	32	4	8	3	22	4	1	40	1	0	5.67
Murphy, Daniel, Chicago	51	0	0	2	3	0	.400	81	81	300	51	51	11	4	3	81	8	4	42	6	0	4.24
Murphy, Thomas, Boston	39	38	11	16	13	0	.552	222	223	854	107	107	32	8	3	64	10	7	99	8	0	4.47
Nagy, Michael, Boston	23	20	4	6	5	0	.545	129	138	502	71	64	16	4	4	18	3	1	56	4	0	10.00
Nelson, Roger, Kansas City	4	2	0	0	2	1	.000	18	18	43	15	14	2	0	1	9	0	0	3	0	0	4.06
Niekro, Joseph, Detroit	38	34	6	12	13	0	.480	213	221	830	107	96	28	10	5	72	7	8	101	3	0	3.81
Odom, John, Oakland	29	20	6	9	8	0	.529	156	138	565	66	66	14	4	5	66	14	0	88	13	0	5.09
O'Donoghue, John, Milwaukee	25	0	0	1	0	1	1.000	23	29	97	15	13	2	3	1	9	0	0	13	0	0	5.48
O'Riley, Donald, Kansas City	9	3	0	0	2	0	.000	23	29	94	13	13	2	0	0	9	0	0	13	1	0	6.00
Osteen, Darrell, Oakland	3	0	0	1	0	1	1.000	6	5	26	4	1	1	0	1	2	0	0	3	0	0	3.00
O'Toole, Dennis, Chicago	3	0	0	0	0	0	.000	14	14	14	9	9	0	0	1	3	0	0	3	0	0	2.71
Palmer, James, Baltimore	39	39	17	20	10	0	.667	305	263	1139	98	92	21	14	3	100	3	5	199	3	0	4.85
Patterson, Daryl, Detroit	43	0	0	7	1	3	.875	78	78	301	47	42	4	9	1	39	5	0	55	6	0	3.40
Pattin, Martin, Milwaukee	37	29	11	14	12	0	.538	233	204	867	91	88	27	9	6	71	7	5	161	5	0	4.81
Paul, Michael, Cleveland	15	15	0	2	8	0	.200	88	108	336	47	47	13	3	4	47	9	0	70	9	0	2.43
Perranoski, Ronald, Minnesota	67	0	0	7	8	34	.467	111	108	417	38	30	13	7	4	42	7	1	55	0	0	3.03
Perry, James, Minnesota	40	40	13	24	12	0	.667	279	258	1063	112	94	20	8	10	57	10	3	168	3	0	3.03

Pitcher and Club	G.	GS.	CG.	W.	L.	Sv.	Pct.	IP.	H.	AB.	R.	ER.	HR.	SH.	SF.	BB.	BB.	HB.	SO.	WP.	Bk.	ERA.
Peters, Gary, Boston°	34	34	10	16	11	0	.593	222	221	859	114	100	20	4	7	83	2	7	155	16	4	4.05
Peters, Raymond, Milwaukee	2	2	0	0	1	0	.000	2		12		7			1	3			1	0	0	31.50
Peterson, Fred, New York°	39	37	8	20	11	0	.645	260	247	994	102	84	24	10	4	40	1	2	127	2	0	2.91
Phillips, Norman E., Boston°	18	0	0	5	2	0	.500	24	29	93	25	17	4	2	1	10	0	1	23	2	1	5.25
Phoebus, Thomas, Baltimore	27	21	3	5	5	0	.625	135	106	485	58	46	11	6	4	62	2	6	72	2	0	3.07
Pina, Horacio, Washington	61	0	0	3	6	6	.333	71	66	264	25	22	4	9	3	28	3	0	41	4	0	2.79
Queen, Melvin, California	34	0	0	2	4	0	.333	8	10	34	7	4	1	2	0	6	0	0	4	0	1	4.20
Ramos, Pedro, Washington	4	0	0	0	2	2	.000	46	50	185	25	28	5	1	0	14	3	0	10	1	0	7.88
Reed, Robert, Detroit	16	4	0	2	0	0	.778	55	36	186	14	12	5	1	4	24	0	0	26	4	1	4.89
Richert, Peter, Baltimore°	50	0	0	7	2	13	.500	32	18	32	12	11	5	1	1	21	0	0	66	0	0	1.96
Riddleberger, Dennis, Washington°	8	3	0	1	1	0	.000	26	19	93	8	10	1	0	1	5	1	1	16	0	0	1.00
Rittwage, James, Cleveland	11	0	0	0	1	0	.000	12	10	62	12	12	0	2	1	11	0	0	11	0	0	4.15
Robertson, Jerry, Detroit	6	0	0	0	0	0	.000	15	13	44	9	6	0	1	1	8	0	2	8	0	0	3.60
Rodriquez, Roberto, Oakland°	28	0	0	3	3	1	.500	43	28	155	18	13	2	2	1	23	0	1	26	2	0	3.00
Roland, James, Oakland°	48	10	6	7	5	6	.700	108	115	422	51	49	14	3	6	43	4	0	71	5	0	2.72
Romo, Vicente, Boston	38	0	0	3	4	0	.400	204	190	755	99	80	11	15	2	102	6	4	117	3	0	4.08
Rooker, James, Kansas City°	50	29	9	5	5	0	.714	92	64	318	8	7	13	1	0	25	2	0	64	0	0	3.53
Rounsaville, Virle, Chicago°	8	0	0	0	2	0	.000	3	16	28	18	18	0	1	0	8	0	0	0	0	0	10.50
Sanders, Kenneth, Milwaukee	8	0	0	2	1	1	.500	70	51	51	13	13	5	7	1	5	1	0	8	8	0	1.76
Santiago, Jose, Boston	48	0	0	4	4	1	.500	15	16	257	28	25	0	1	1	28	0	1	58	6	0	10.64
Saunders, Dennis, Detroit	9	0	0	0	0	2	.500	162	61	57	5	5	1	3	0	12	0	1	8	0	0	3.21
Scherman, Frederick, Detroit°	47	19	7	4	10	0	.500	130	19	586	54	46	9	3	2	68	3	0	95	0	0	3.21
Secrist, Donald, Chicago°	1	0	0	0	0	1	.462	117	107	11	57	48	0	0	6	4	0	1	10	0	0	5.40
Segui, Diego, Oakland	39	14	2	6	7	1	.652	223	207	435	98	85	6	11	4	51	2	2	57	9	5	2.56
Shank, Harvey, California	33	33	7	15	8	0	.500	27	37	835	28	20	29	0	2	60	5	5	142	0	0	0.00
Shellenback, James, Washington°	17	17	0	3	0	0	.000	50	62	134	27	7	7	0	1	13	0	5	16	6	0	3.69
Siebert, Wilfred, Boston	2	0	0	0	2	0	.536	271	262	41	110	93	10	2	3	84	6	1	28	0	0	5.45
Sisk, Tommie, Chicago	36	37	3	3	7	0	.167	50	48	208	37	30	23	1	0	8	2	0	10	1	0	7.00
Splittorff, Paul, Kansas City°	37	0	0	0	2	12	.636	7	2	1028	2	93	8	3	3	4	8	0	126	3	0	5.40
Stange, A. Lee, 20 Boston-16 Chicago	37	0	2	7	7	0	.000	89	8	186	7	42	10	12	6	45	6	3	41	0	0	3.09
Stottlemyre, Melvin, New York	21	5	14	7	8	17	.700	85	68	327	35	110	12	1	4	1	6	0	50	6	0	7.56
Such, Richard, Washington	62	0	0	0	1	0	.462	9	58	342	36	42	12	2	4	26	5	2	50	0	0	9.00
Talbot, Fred, Oakland	18	17	0	3	7	27	.000	16	90	330	44	35	9	3	8	41	9	2	50	6	0	2.93
Tatum, Kenneth, California	61	0	0	7	2	0	.750	85	20	62	21	39	2	0	2	34	11	0	49	0	0	3.39
Tiant, Luis, Minnesota	7	0	0	3	2	0	.500	36	2	9	8	2	0	0	0	12	1	0	5	0	0	4.13
Timmerman, Thomas, Detroit	38	0	0	0	7	7	.500	55	40	62	9	15	3	2	4	19	4	1	8	1	0	9.00
Twitchell, Wayne, Milwaukee	26	5	0	3	3	0	.333	44	36	155	21	19	4	4	0	21	5	4	20	2	0	4.50
Verbanic, Joseph, New York	53	3	0	3	2	12	.909	55	42	192	20	20	5	3	3	29	5	0	27	1	0	3.38
Wagner, Gary, Boston	31	0	0	0	7	15	.000	63	44	184	20	19	7	8	5	29	5	1	33	0	0	3.11
Waslewski, Gary, New York	68	0	0	10	6	0	.400	52	52	223	33	30	9	4	3	25	6	4	51	3	0	3.27
Watt, Edward, Baltimore	18	16	4	0	6	0	.000	62	85	408	34	25	15	6	4	32	2	0	76	4	0	4.35
Weaver, D. Floyd, Chicago	16	0	0	0	0	0	.000	96	87	365	53	47	10	0	1	32	0	0	74	2	0	1.99
Williams, Stanley, Minnesota	2	0	0	0	0	0	.000	5	3	17	5	3	1	1	0	4	0	0	5	0	0	4.41
Wilson, R. Earl, Detroit									4	13	5	5	2	0	0	1	0	0	3	0	0	5.40
Wolf, Walter, California																						15.00
Womack, Horace, Oakland																						

Pitcher and Club	G	GS	CG	Sv.	W.	L.	Pct.	IP.	H.	AB	R.	ER	HR.	SH.	SF.	BB.	BB.	HB.	SO	WP.	Bk.	IG.	ShO.	ERA.
Wood, Wilbur, Chicago*	77	0	0	21	9	13	.409	122	118	458	50	38	7	2	1	36		7	85	4	0	5	2	2.80
Woodson, Richard, Minnesota	21			1	2	2	.500	31	29	119	18	13	8	4	6	19		0	22	1	0	1	0	3.77
Wright, Clyde, California*	39		22	0	22	12	.647	261	226	975	97	82	24	10	3	88		4	110	8	1	4	0	2.83
Wright, Kenneth, Kansas City	39	9	0	1	1	2	.333	53	54	188	33	31	8	2	1	29		7	30	8	0	1	0	5.26
Wynne, Billy, Chicago	47	12	0	0	1	4	.200	44	54	181	30	26	8	5	3	22		2	29	2	0	2	0	5.32
York, James, Kansas City	12	0	0	0	0	1	.000	8	8	28	3	3	0	0	1	9		0	6	0	0		0	3.38
Zepp, William, Minnesota	43	20	9	0	9	4	.692	151	154	578	63	54	9	7	5	51		2	64	4	0	4	0	3.22

TIE GAMES—Bolin (Mil.) Hamilton (N.Y.) Klimkowski, Lauzerique, Locker (Mil.), Meyer, O'Donoghue, Stottlemyre, 1 each.

NO-HIT GAMES—Wright, California, defeated Oakland, 4 to 0, at California, July 3; Blue, Oakland, defeated Minnesota, 6 to 0, at Oakland, September 21.

PITCHERS WITH TWO OR MORE CLUBS DURING 1970 SEASON
(Alphabetically Arranged With the Pitcher's First Club on Top)

Pitcher and Club	G.	GS.	CG.	Sv.	W.	L.	Pct.	IP.	H.	AB	R.	ER	HR.	SH.	SF.	BB. (Tot.)	BB. (Int.)	HB.	SO	WP.	Bk.	ERA.	Fin.	ShO.
Bolin, Milwaukee	32	20	3	2	5	11	.313	132	131	512	84	72	20	6	6	67	7	4	81	1	0	4.91	17	0
Bolin, Boston	6			1	2	2	1.000		25							22	2		8			0.00	4	0
Downing, Oakland	10	6	1		1	1	.500	41	39	155	19	18	5	1	4	22	0	3	26	1	0	3.95	15	0
Downing, Milwaukee	17	16	1		1	5	.167	94⅓	79	341	35	35	8	8	3	59	2	0	53	8	0	3.34	15	1
Drabowsky, Kan City	24	0	0	2	2	4	.333	35⅔	28	129	13	13	3	3	3	12	3	2	38	1	0	3.28	14	0
Drabowsky, Baltimore	21	0	0	1	4	2	.667	33⅓	30	129	17	14	7	1	0	15	3	1	21	0	0	3.78	10	0
Ellsworth, Cleveland	29	1	0	0	3	3	.500	43⅔	49	164	23	22	4	4	1	14	2	1	13	1	0	4.54	11	1
Ellsworth, Milwaukee	14	0	0	0	0	3	.000	15⅔	11	56	3	3	0	0	0	4	0	0	9	1	0	1.72	4	0
Hamilton, New York	35	0	0	3	4	3	.571	45⅓	36	162	16	14	3	1	1	16	5	0	33	2	0	2.78	16	0
Hamilton, Chicago	5	0	0	0	0	2	.000	6⅔	4	12	2	2	1	0	1	5	0	1	6	0	0	6.00	3	0
Humphreys, Wash	5	0	0	0	0	1	.000	9	10	20	2	2	1	0	0	9	0	0	6	0	2	1.35	2	0
Humphreys, Mil	23	1	0	3	2	4	.333	57⅔	57	167	18	16	3	3	2	22	3	2	32	2	2	3.15	12	0
Lasher, Detroit	12	0	0	0	1	3	.250	31⅓	37	121	18	12	1	1	5	10	1	3	19	1	0	5.00	8	0
Lasher, Cleveland	43	1	0	5	1	7	.125	56⅓	49	211	21	18	1	1	0	19	3	5	33	4	4	4.06	13	0
Locker, Milwaukee	28	0	0	3	0	1	.000	28	35	113	14	13	1	4	1	10	2	0	19	1	1	3.41	16	0
Locker, Oakland	38	0	0	4	3	3	.500	70⅓	88	279	42	39	11	5	4	33	5	3	36	0	2	2.88	16	0
Miller, Cleveland	15	2	0	1	2	2	.500		70	267	34	33	8	3	2	46	3	1	35	2	0	4.18	6	1
Miller, Chicago	15	12	0	0	2	3	.400		85	281	56	50	12	8	6	34	3	8	34	5	0	5.01	12	1
Moore, Cleveland	13	12	3	0	3	5	.375	70⅓	70	267	34	33	8	8	2	46	3	1	35	2	0	4.22	12	1
Moore, Chicago	24	7	0	0	0	4	.000	70⅔	85	281	56	50	12	6	4	34	4	8	34	5	0	6.37	7	0
Stange, Boston	20			0	2	2	.500	27⅓	34	113	24	21	5	3	1	12	3	2	15	1	1	5.60	5	0
Stange, Chicago	16			2	1	0	1.000	22⅓	28	95	13	13	5	2	1	14	1	0	14	1	0	5.24	4	0

*Games not finished as relief pitcher.

ADDITIONAL CLUB PITCHING RECORDS

(Rated According to Highest Number of Complete Games Pitched)

Club	ShO.	OH.	1H.	2H.	3H.	4H.	GS&TO.	Fin.	*IG.	CG.
Baltimore	12	0	0	3	4	11	162	102	126	60
Boston	8	0	1	1	6	6	162	124	160	38
New York	6	0	0	0	5	6	163	127	112	36
Cleveland	8	0	1	5	6	6	162	128	187	34
Oakland	15	1	2	1	7	12	162	129	180	33
Detroit	9	0	1	2	3	8	162	129	159	33
Milwaukee	2	0	0	3	2	8	163	132	151	31
Kansas City	11	0	0	1	7	15	162	132	136	30
Minnesota	12	0	0	4	3	7	162	136	133	26
California	10	1	0	2	7	6	162	141	173	21
Chicago	6	0	0	1	3	6	162	142	138	20
Washington	11	0	2	1	4	7	162	142	174	20
Totals	110	2	7	24	57	98				382

Note: Club combination shutout and low-hit games included.

ADDITIONAL PITCHERS' RECORDS

(Rated According to Highest Number of Complete Games Pitched)

NOTE: Shutouts and Low Hit Records for Individual Pitchers Are for Complete Games Only.

(*) Games Not Finished as Relief Pitcher

Pitcher and Club	ShO.	OH.	1H.	2H.	3H.	4H.	GS.	TO.	Fin.	*IG.	CG.
Cuellar, Baltimore	4	0	0	1	1	4	40	19	0	0	21
McDowell, Cleveland	1	0	0	2	3	2	39	20	2	0	§19
Palmer, Baltimore	5	0	0	2	3	3	39	22	0	0	17
McNally, Baltimore	1	0	0	0	0	2	40	24	0	0	16
Culp, Boston	1	0	0	0	2	1	33	18	0	0	15
Stottlemyre, New York	0	0	0	0	0	2	37	23	0	0	14
Lolich, Detroit	3	0	0	0	1	0	39	26	0	1	13
Perry, Minnesota	4	0	0	1	0	1	40	27	0	0	13
Dobson, Oakland	5	0	1	0	3	5	40	27	1	0	13
Pattin, Milwaukee	0	0	0	0	0	1	29	18	2	6	11
Johnson, Kansas City	1	0	0	1	1	2	26	16	7	7	10
Peters, Boston	4	0	0	0	0	1	34	24	0	0	10
John, Chicago	3	0	0	1	1	2	37	27	0	0	10
Hunter, Oakland	1	0	0	0	0	0	40	31	0	0	9
Hargan, Cleveland	1	0	0	2	1	0	19	11	1	3	8
Krausse, Milwaukee	1	0	0	0	0	2	35	27	2	0	8
Peterson, New York	2	0	0	0	2	0	37	29	0	2	8
Siebert, Boston	2	0	1	1	1	0	33	26	0	0	7
Bosman, Washington	3	0	1	0	0	2	34	27	1	1	7
Drago, Kansas City	1	0	0	0	0	2	34	27	1	0	7
Wright, California	2	1	0	0	1	1	39	32	0	0	7
Messersmith, California	1	0	0	0	0	1	26	20	8	3	6
Rooker, Kansas City	3	0	0	0	1	1	29	23	5	4	6
Coleman, Washington	1	0	0	0	1	0	29	23	4	6	6
Niekro, Detroit	2	0	1	0	0	1	34	28	2	2	6
Bahnsen, New York	2	0	0	0	0	1	35	29	0	1	6
Kline, New York	0	0	0	0	1	0	15	10	0	1	5
Blyleven, Minnesota	1	0	0	1	1	2	25	20	1	1	5
Cain, Detroit	0	0	0	0	0	1	29	24	0	0	5
Murphy, California	2	0	0	0	1	1	38	33	0	1	5
Wilson, Detroit	1	0	0	0	0	2	16	12	0	2	4

Pitcher and Club	ShO.	OH.	1H.	2H.	3H.	4H.	GS.	TO.	Fin.	*IG.	CG.
Nagy, Boston	0	0	0	0	0	1	20	16	1	2	4
Horlen, Chicago	0	0	0	0	0	0	26	22	1	1	4
Odom, Oakland	1	0	0	1	0	1	29	25	0	0	4
Kaat, Minnesota	1	0	0	0	0	0	34	30	3	8	4
Janeski, Chicago	1	0	0	0	1	0	35	31	0	0	4
Segui, Oakland	2	0	0	0	1	1	19	16	14	14	3
Hardin, Baltimore	2	0	0	0	0	0	19	16	4	13	3
Bolin, Milwaukee-Boston	0	0	0	0	0	0	20	17	11	7	3
Kilkenny, Detroit	0	0	0	0	0	2	21	18	5	10	3
Phoebus, Baltimore	0	0	0	1	0	0	21	18	2	4	3
Hand, Cleveland	1	0	1	0	0	1	25	22	5	5	3
Lockwood, Milwaukee	1	0	0	1	0	1	26	23	0	1	3
Blue, Oakland	2	1	1	0	0	0	6	4	0	0	2
Morris, Milwaukee	0	0	0	0	1	0	9	7	4	7	2
Fitzmorris, Kansas City	0	0	0	0	0	0	11	9	14	18	2
Shellenback, Washington	1	0	0	1	0	0	14	12	6	19	2
Bunker, Kansas City	1	0	0	0	0	2	15	13	4	5	2
Johnson, Chicago	1	0	0	0	0	0	15	13	1	2	2
Tiant, Minnesota	1	0	0	0	1	1	17	15	1	0	2
Brunet, Washington	1	0	0	0	0	0	20	18	1	3	2
Brabender, Milwaukee	0	0	0	0	0	0	21	19	3	5	2
Downing, Oakland-Milwaukee	0	0	0	1	1	0	22	20	1	4	2
Butler, Kansas City	1	0	0	0	1	0	25	23	0	0	2
May, California	2	0	0	1	0	0	34	32	1	3	2
Klimkowski, New York	1	0	0	0	1	0	3	2	10	32	1
Rittwage, Cleveland	0	0	0	0	0	0	3	2	0	6	§1
Lauzerique, Milwaukee	0	0	0	0	0	0	4	3	1	6	1
Hiller, Detroit	1	0	0	1	0	0	5	4	18	24	1
Brown, Washington	0	0	0	0	0	1	5	4	6	13	1
Austin, Cleveland	1	0	0	0	0	0	8	7	7	16	1
Koonce, Boston	0	0	0	0	1	0	8	7	6	9	1
Cumberland, New York	0	0	0	0	0	0	8	7	5	2	1
Hall, Minnesota	0	0	0	0	0	0	11	10	13	28	1
Bradley, California	0	0	0	0	0	0	11	10	0	6	1
Brett, Boston	0	0	0	0	1	0	14	13	9	18	1
Kekich, New York	0	0	0	0	0	0	14	13	4	8	1
McLain, Detroit	0	0	0	0	0	0	14	13	0	0	1
Paul, Cleveland	0	0	0	0	0	0	15	14	3	12	1
Hannan, Washington	1	0	1	0	0	0	17	16	10	15	1
Morehead, Kansas City	0	0	0	0	0	0	17	16	2	9	1
Chance, Cleveland	1	0	0	0	0	1	19	18	14	12	1
Fingers, Oakland	0	0	0	0	0	0	19	18	9	17	1
Zepp, Minnesota	1	0	0	0	0	0	20	19	6	17	1
Cox, Washington	0	0	0	0	0	0	30	29	1	6	1

§Pitchers making two appearances in one game: McDowell, July 6 and September 2; Rittwage, September 25.

COMBINATION SHUTOUT GAMES (26)—Chance-Paul-Higgins, Cleveland vs. New York, April 11; Horlen-Wood, Chicago vs Cleveland, April 26; Kaat-Williams, Minnesota vs. Cleveland, April 29; Butler-Fitzmorris-Wright, Kansas City vs. Cleveland, May 13; Bosman-Knowles, Washington vs. New York, May 20; Stottlemyre-Hamilton, New York vs. Washington, May 21; Wright-K. Tatum, California vs. Milwaukee, June 20; Morehead-Burgmeier-Johnson, Kansas City vs. California, June 27; Fingers-Lindblad-Grant, Oakland vs. Chicago, July 1; Dunning-Hennigan, Cleveland vs. Kansas City, July 17; Niekro-Timmerman, Detroit vs. Kansas City, July 19 (first game); Hannan-Knowles, Washington vs. Milwaukee, July 20; Segui-Lindblad, Oakland vs. Washington, July 21; Fingers-Grant, Oakland vs. Washington, August 2 (second game); Bosman-Grzenda, Washington vs. Detroit, August 3; Johnson-Abernathy, Kansas City vs. Milwaukee, August 7 (first game); Wright-Queen, California vs. Chicago, August 9 (first game); Dobson-Grant, Oakland vs. Baltimore, August 14; Hand-Higgins, Cleveland vs California, August 19; Lolich-Timmerman, Detroit vs. Milwaukee, August 23; Romo-Brett-Wagner, Boston vs. Minnesota, August 25; Blyleven-Perranoski, Minnesota vs. California, September 4; Butler-Abernathy, Kansas City vs. Milwaukee, September 10 (first game); Gogolewski-Knowles, Washington vs. Baltimore, September 16; Hall-Perranoski, Minnesota vs. Kansas City, September 28; Kaat-Williams-Perranoski, Minnesota vs. Kansas City, October 1.

RECORDS OF PITCHERS WHO DID NOT PITCH A COMPLETE GAME
(Rated According to the Most Games Started and Taken Out)

Pitcher and Club	GS& TO.	Fin.	*IG.	Pitcher and Club	GS& TO.	Fin.	*IG.
Moore, Cleveland-Chicago	19	6	12	Scherman, Detroit	0	20	28
Dunning, Cleveland	17	1	1	Lindblad, Oakland	0	19	43
Boswell, Minnesota	15	1	2	Doyle, California	0	18	22
Miller, Cleveland-Chicago	14	7	9	Wagner, Boston	0	18	20
Romo, Boston	10	15	23	Burgmeier, Kansas City	0	17	24
Wynne, Chicago	9	1	2	Hall, Baltimore	0	17	15
Crider, Chicago	8	9	15	Hamilton, New York-Chicago	0	16	22
Garrett, California	7	11	14	Baldwin, Milwaukee	0	16	12
Magnuson, Chicago	6	3	4	Wright, Kansas City	0	14	33
Waslewski, New York	5	5	16	Patterson, Detroit	0	14	29
Such, Washington	5	3	13	Monteagudo, Kansas City	0	12	9
Lee, Boston	5	2	4	Lachemann, Oakland	0	11	30
Gogolewski, Washington	5	0	3	LaRoche, California	0	11	27
Reed, Detroit	4	4	8	Colbert, Cleveland	0	10	13
Lonborg, Boston	4	3	2	Barber, Minnesota	0	10	8
McCormick, New York	4	3	2	Phillips, Boston	0	10	8
Burbach, New York	4	0	0	Stange, Boston-Chicago	0	9	27
Grzenda, Washington	3	19	27	O'Donoghue, Milwaukee	0	9	16
Queen, California	3	17	14	Mingori, Cleveland	0	8	13
Weaver, Chicago	3	14	14	Woodson, Minnesota	0	8	13
Lopez, Baltimore	3	4	18	Robertson, Detroit	0	5	6
Arrigo, Chicago	3	1	1	Secrist, Chicago	0	5	4
Fisher, California	2	36	29	Riddleberger, Washington	0	5	3
Roland, Oakland	2	6	20	Leonard, Baltimore	0	4	19
O'Riley, Kansas City	2	5	2	McRae, Detroit	0	4	15
Allen, California	2	0	6	Hartenstein, Boston	0	4	13
Nelson, Kansas City	2	0	2	Saunders, Detroit	0	4	4
Peters, Milwaukee	2	0	0	Hamm, Minnesota	0	3	7
Lasher, Detroit-Cleveland	1	21	33	Hedlund, Kansas City	0	3	6
Hennigan, Cleveland	1	17	24	Eddy, Chicago	0	3	4
Ellsworth, Cleveland-Milwaukee	1	15	27	Verbanic, New York	0	3	4
Humphreys, Wash-Milwaukee	1	14	13	Carlos, Washington	0	3	2
Sisk, Chicago	1	2	14	Wolf, California	0	3	1
Moret, Boston	1	2	0	York, Kansas City	0	3	1
Osteen, Oakland	1	1	1	Jarvis, Boston	0	2	13
Splittorff, Kansas City	1	0	1	LaGrow, Detroit	0	2	8
Gardner, New York	1	0	0	Santiago, Boston	0	2	6
Wood, Chicago	0	62	15	Haydel, Minnesota	0	2	2
Perranoski, Minnesota	0	52	15	Cox, California	0	2	1
McDaniel, New York	0	51	11	O'Toole, Chicago	0	2	1
Grant, Oakland	0	49	23	Womack, Oakland	0	2	0
Knowles, Washington	0	49	22	Kealey, California	0	1	16
Timmerman, Detroit	0	43	18	Meyer, Milwaukee	0	1	9
Lyle, Boston	0	40	23	Rounsaville, Chicago	0	1	7
Williams, Minnesota	0	36	32	Dukes, Washington	0	1	4
Watt, Baltimore	0	35	18	Beene, Baltimore	0	1	3
K. Tatum, California	0	33	29	Ramos, Washington	0	1	3
Locker, Milwaukee-Oakland	0	32	34	Jones, New York	0	1	1
Abernathy, Kansas City	0	31	5	Mills, Boston	0	1	1
Pina, Washington	0	30	31	Brubaker, Milwaukee	0	1	0
Sanders, Milwaukee	0	30	20	Colson, New York	0	1	0
Higgins, Cleveland	0	29	29	Moloney, Chicago	0	1	0
Aker, New York	0	28	13	Talbot, Oakland	0	1	0
Murphy, Chicago	0	26	25	Rodriquez, Oakland	0	0	6
Richert, Baltimore	0	25	25	Twitchell, Milwaukee	0	0	2
Drabowsky, Kan City-Baltimore	0	24	21	Curtis, Boston	0	0	1
Gelnar, Milwaukee	0	23	30	Shank, California	0	0	1

*Games not finished as relief pitcher.

1970 A. L. Pitching Against Each Club

Pitcher	Bos. W—L	Cal. W—L	Chi. W—L	Clev. W—L	Det. W—L	K.C. W—L	Mil. W—L	Minn. W—L	N.Y. W—L	Oak. W—L	Wash. W—L	Totals W—L
Cuellar	0—0	4—0	3—0	1—1	3—1	1—0	2—0	2—2	4—1	2—1	1—2	24— 8
McNally	1—1	2—1	1—0	3—1	1—2	2—0	2—1	2—1	3—1	2—1	5—0	24— 9
Palmer	3—1	1—0	3—0	2—0	1—2	3—0	1—2	0—2	2—0	3—0	1—3	20—10
Hall	3—0	0—2	1—0	2—1	2—0	1—0	0—0	1—0	0—2	0—0	0—0	10— 5
Richert	0—1	0—0	0—0	2—0	1—1	1—0	1—0	0—0	0—0	0—0	2—0	7— 2
Watt	2—1	0—1	0—0	1—0	0—0	2—0	0—1	0—2	1—0	1—1	1—1	7— 7
Hardin	0—0	0—0	0—1	2—0	1—0	1—0	1—1	0—0	0—2	0—1	1—0	6— 5
Phoebus	1—1	0—0	1—2	1—0	1—1	1—0	0—0	0—0	0—0	0—0	0—0	5— 5
Drabowsky	2—0	0—1	0—0	0—1	0—0	0—0	0—0	0—0	1—0	0—0	1—0	4— 2
Lopez	0—0	0—0	0—0	0—0	0—0	0—0	0—0	0—0	0—1	0—0	0—0	1— 1
Totals	13—5	7—5	9—3	14—4	11—7	12—0	7—5	5—7	11—7	7—5	12—6	108—54

No Decisions—Beene, Leonhard.

Pitcher	Balt. W—L	Cal. W—L	Chi. W—L	Clev. W—L	Det. W—L	K.C. W—L	Mil. W—L	Minn. W—L	N.Y. W—L	Oak. W—L	Wash. W—L	Totals W—L
Culp	1—1	1—0	0—1	3—0	4—0	0—0	0—3	3—1	1—0	2—0	2—1	17—14
Peters	0—2	2—0	1—1	3—1	0—1	3—0	2—0	0—2	2—0	1—1	2—3	16—11
Siebert	1—1	2—0	0—1	3—1	1—1	0—0	2—0	2—2	1—0	2—0	1—2	15— 8
Brett	0—1	0—2	2—0	1—2	1—1	1—2	0—0	1—0	1—0	0—1	1—0	8— 9
Romo	1—0	0—1	2—0	0—0	0—0	1—1	1—0	0—0	0—0	1—1	1—0	7— 3
Nagy	0—0	0—1	1—0	1—0	1—0	1—0	0—1	0—0	0—3	0—0	2—0	6— 5
Lonborg	0—0	0—0	1—0	0—0	1—0	0—0	0—0	0—0	1—0	0—1	1—0	4— 1
Wagner	1—0	0—0	0—0	1—0	0—1	0—0	0—0	1—0	0—0	0—0	0—0	3— 1
Koonce	0—0	0—0	1—0	0—1	1—1	0—1	0—0	0—0	0—1	0—1	1—0	3— 4
Bolin	0—0	0—0	0—0	0—0	0—0	0—0	0—0	0—0	0—3	2—0	0—0	2— 0
Lee	0—0	0—0	0—0	0—1	0—1	0—0	0—0	0—0	0—0	1—0	1—0	2— 2
Stange	0—0	0—1	0—0	0—0	0—0	1—0	0—1	0—0	1—0	0—0	0—0	2— 2
Moret	0—0	0—0	0—0	0—0	0—0	0—0	0—0	0—0	1—0	0—0	0—0	1— 0
Lyle	1—3	0—1	0—0	0—0	0—1	0—1	0—1	0—0	0—0	0—0	0—0	1— 7
Jarvis	0—0	0—1	0—0	0—0	0—0	0—0	0—0	0—0	0—0	0—0	0—0	0— 1
Phillips	0—0	0—0	0—0	0—0	0—1	0—0	0—1	0—0	0—0	0—0	0—0	0— 2
Santiago	0—1	0—0	0—0	0—0	0—0	0—0	0—0	0—0	0—1	0—0	0—0	0— 2
Hartenstein	0—1	0—0	0—1	0—0	0—1	0—0	0—0	0—0	0—0	0—0	0—0	0— 3
Totals	5—13	5—7	8—4	12—6	9—9	7—5	5—7	7—5	10—8	7—5	12—6	87—75

No Decisions—Curtis, Mills.

Pitcher	Balt. W—L	Bos. W—L	Chi. W—L	Clev. W—L	Det. W—L	K.C. W—L	Mil. W—L	Minn. W—L	N.Y. W—L	Oak. W—L	Wash. W—L	Totals W—L
Wright	1—1	1—0	3—2	2—0	2—1	3—0	3—0	2—2	3—3	1—1	1—1	22—13
Murphy	1—1	0—2	3—2	1—1	0—1	2—2	5—1	0—2	1—0	1—1	2—0	16—13
Messersmith	1—2	0—0	1—1	1—2	2—0	1—1	1—0	1—1	2—1	1—0	0—2	11—10
K. Tatum	0—0	2—0	0—0	1—0	1—1	1—0	1—0	0—1	0—0	0—1	0—1	7— 4
May	0—2	0—0	2—1	1—1	0—1	0—1	0—1	1—1	1—3	2—1	1—0	7—13
Garrett	0—0	2—1	0—0	0—1	0—0	0—1	1—0	0—0	1—2	1—0	0—0	5— 6
LaRoche	0—0	1—0	0—0	0—0	0—0	0—0	0—1	2—0	0—0	0—0	1—0	4— 1
Fisher	1—0	0—0	1—0	0—0	0—1	1—1	0—0	0—1	0—0	0—1	1—0	4— 4
Doyle	0—0	0—0	0—0	0—0	1—0	0—0	1—0	1—1	0—0	0—0	0—0	3— 1
Queen	1—1	0—1	1—0	0—1	0—0	0—1	0—1	1—1	0—0	0—0	0—0	3— 6
Bradley	0—0	1—1	0—0	0—0	0—0	1—1	0—2	0—0	0—0	0—0	0—1	2— 5
Kealey	0—0	0—0	0—0	0—0	0—0	1—0	0—0	0—0	0—0	0—0	0—0	1— 0
Allen	0—0	0—0	1—0	0—0	0—0	0—0	0—0	0—0	0—0	0—0	0—0	1— 1
Totals	5—7	7—5	12—6	6—6	6—6	10—8	12—6	8—10	5—7	8—10	7—5	86—76

No Decisions—Cox, Shank, Wolf.

CHICAGO—56-106

Pitcher	Balt. W—L	Bos. W—L	Cal. W—L	Clev. W—L	Det. W—L	K.C. W—L	Mil. W—L	Minn. W—L	N.Y. W—L	Oak. W—L	Wash. W—L	Totals W—L
John	1—1	0—1	1—3	2—1	1—0	3—0	2—1	0—3	1—1	0—5	1—1	12—17
Janeski	0—3	1—1	2—0	0—1	1—1	1—1	2—2	0—2	1—3	1—1	1—2	10—17
Wood	1—1	1—2	0—0	1—0	1—2	1—2	1—1	1—0	1—0	0—3	1—2	9—13
Horlen	0—2	0—0	1—2	2—1	1—0	1—2	0—2	0—4	0—1	1—1	0—1	6—16
Miller	1—0	1—1	1—0	0—0	0—0	0—2	0—0	1—1	0—1	0—1	0—0	4—6
Crider	0—0	0—1	0—0	0—1	1—1	0—1	1—0	1—0	0—0	0—0	0—0	4—7
Johnson	0—0	0—1	0—1	0—0	0—0	1—0	0—1	1—1	2—0	0—3	0—0	4—7
Murphy	0—0	0—0	0—1	1—0	0—0	0—0	0—2	1—0	0—0	0—0	0—0	2—3
Stange	0—0	0—0	0—0	0—0	1—0	0—0	0—0	0—0	0—0	0—0	0—0	1—0
Sisk	0—1	0—0	0—0	0—0	0—0	0—0	1—0	0—0	0—0	0—0	0—0	1—1
Weaver	0—0	1—0	0—0	0—0	0—0	0—1	0—0	0—0	0—1	0—0	0—0	1—2
Wynne	0—0	0—0	1—2	0—0	0—1	1—0	1—0	0—0	0—0	0—0	0—0	1—4
Magnuson	0—0	0—1	0—1	1—0	1—0	0—1	1—0	0—0	0—0	0—0	0—0	1—5
Rounsaville	0—0	0—0	0—0	0—0	0—0	0—0	0—1	0—0	0—0	0—0	0—0	0—1
Arrigo	0—1	0—0	0—0	0—1	0—0	0—0	0—0	0—0	0—0	0—2	0—0	0—3
Moore	0—0	0—0	0—1	1—0	0—0	0—0	0—0	0—0	0—1	0—0	0—0	0—4
Totals	3—9	4—8	6—12	6—6	6—6	7—11	7—11	6—12	5—7	2—16	4—8	56—106

No Decisions—Eddy, Hamilton, Moloney, O'Toole, Secrist.

CLEVELAND—76-86

Pitcher	Balt. W—L	Bos. W—L	Cal. W—L	Chi. W—L	Det. W—L	K.C. W—L	Mil. W—L	Minn. W—L	N.Y. W—L	Oak. W—L	Wash. W—L	Totals W—L
McDowell	0—2	3—2	1—2	2—1	3—1	0—0	1—0	3—1	2—1	3—0	2—2	20—12
Hargan	0—0	1—1	0—0	2—0	1—1	2—0	1—0	1—1	2—0	0—0	1—0	11—3
Chance	1—1	0—1	1—1	0—2	1—1	1—0	1—1	1—0	2—1	0—1	0—0	9—8
Hennigan	0—0	0—1	0—0	0—0	0—1	1—1	2—0	0—0	1—0	0—0	2—0	6—3
Hand	0—2	0—2	4—0	1—0	0—3	1—1	0—1	0—1	0—1	0—0	0—2	6—13
Higgins	2—0	0—1	0—1	0—0	0—0	0—0	0—2	0—1	0—1	1—0	1—0	4—6
Dunning	0—2	0—2	0—0	0—1	0—0	2—0	1—1	0—0	0—2	0—0	1—1	4—9
Ellsworth	0—0	0—1	0—0	0—2	0—0	0—0	0—0	0—0	0—0	2—0	1—0	3—3
Moore	0—1	0—0	0—0	1—0	0—0	1—0	0—0	1—1	0—0	0—2	0—1	3—5
Miller	0—1	1—0	0—0	0—0	0—0	0—1	1—0	0—0	0—0	0—0	0—0	2—2
Austin	0—1	0—1	0—0	0—0	1—0	0—0	0—0	0—1	0—0	1—1	0—1	2—5
Paul	0—2	0—0	0—1	0—0	0—3	0—0	0—0	0—0	1—1	0—1	1—0	2—8
Mingori	0—0	0—0	0—0	0—0	1—0	0—0	0—0	0—0	0—0	0—0	0—0	1—0
Colbert	0—0	0—0	0—1	0—0	0—0	0—0	0—0	0—0	0—0	1—0	0—0	1—1
Rittwage	1—0	0—0	0—0	0—0	0—1	0—0	0—0	0—0	0—0	0—0	0—0	1—1
Lasher	0—2	0—1	0—0	0—0	0—0	0—1	0—0	0—0	0—3	0—0	1—0	1—7
Totals	4—14	6—12	6—6	6—6	7—11	8—4	7—5	6—6	8—10	7—5	11—7	76—86

No Decisions—None.

DETROIT—79-83

Pitcher	Balt. W—L	Bos. W—L	Cal. W—L	Chi. W—L	Clev. W—L	K.C. W—L	Mil. W—L	Minn. W—L	N.Y. W—L	Oak. W—L	Wash. W—L	Totals W—L
Lolich	2—3	2—2	0—1	1—1	3—3	0—0	2—0	0—3	1—2	1—2	2—2	14—19
Cain	2—0	1—2	2—0	0—2	0—0	1—1	2—0	1—0	2—1	0—1	1—0	12—7
Niekro	2—1	0—2	1—1	0—2	2—1	2—0	1—0	3—1	1—1	2—1	2—1	12—13
Patterson	0—0	4—0	1—0	0—0	0—0	0—0	0—0	0—0	0—0	1—0	1—1	7—1
Kilkenny	0—0	0—1	0—0	1—0	1—0	1—1	1—0	0—0	1—1	1—1	0—2	7—6
Hiller	1—2	0—0	1—1	1—0	1—0	1—0	0—1	1—0	0—2	0—0	0—0	6—6
Timmerman	0—1	0—0	0—0	1—1	1—0	0—0	0—1	1—1	1—1	1—0	1—0	6—7
Scherman	0—0	0—0	0—0	1—0	0—0	0—0	0—0	0—1	0—2	1—0	2—0	4—4
Wilson	0—1	0—1	1—0	0—0	2—2	0—0	0—0	0—0	1—0	0—1	0—1	4—6
McLain	0—2	0—0	0—1	1—0	0—0	0—0	1—1	1—0	0—0	0—0	0—0	3—5
Reed	0—1	0—0	0—0	0—0	1—1	1—0	0—0	0—1	0—0	0—0	0—1	2—4
Saunders	0—0	0—0	0—0	0—0	0—0	0—0	1—1	0—0	0—0	0—0	0—0	1—1
Lasher	0—0	1—1	0—0	0—0	0—0	0—0	0—2	0—0	0—0	0—0	0—0	1—3
LaGrow	0—0	0—0	0—1	0—0	0—0	0—0	0—0	0—0	0—0	0—0	0—0	0—1
Totals	7—11	9—9	6—6	6—6	11—7	6—6	8—4	4—8	7—11	6—6	9—9	79—83

No Decisions—McRae, Robertson.

KANSAS CITY—65-97

Pitcher	Balt. W—L	Bos. W—L	Cal. W—L	Chi. W—L	Clev. W—L	Det. W—L	Mil. W—L	Minn. W—L	N.Y. W—L	Oak. W—L	Wash. W—L	Totals W—L
Rooker	0—1	0—2	2—3	2—0	1—2	1—1	1—0	2—1	0—2	0—2	1—1	10—15
Abernathy	2—0	1—1	0—0	0—0	2—1	2—0	1—0	0—0	1—0	0—0	0—0	9— 3
Drago	0—3	0—0	0—1	2—1	0—0	0—2	2—1	1—2	0—3	2—2	2—0	9—15
Fitzmorris	0—1	1—1	1—0	2—0	1—0	1—0	0—0	0—0	0—0	1—1	1—1	8— 5
Johnson	0—1	1—0	1—1	2—2	0—1	1—0	2—1	1—3	0—1	0—1	0—2	8—13
Burgmeier	0—0	0—1	1—0	0—0	1—0	0—0	0—1	0—1	1—2	1—1	2—0	6— 6
Butler	0—2	0—2	0—1	1—1	0—1	0—0	2—3	0—1	0—0	1—0	0—1	4—12
Morehead	0—1	0—1	1—0	1—0	0—1	0—0	1—0	0—0	0—1	0—0	0—0	3— 5
Hedlund	0—1	0—0	0—0	0—0	1—0	0—1	0—0	0—0	0—0	1—0	0—0	2— 3
Bunker	0—0	0—0	1—2	0—0	0—1	0—1	1—0	0—1	0—1	0—4	0—1	2—11
Monteagudo	0—0	1—0	0—0	0—1	0—0	0—0	0—0	0—0	0—0	0—0	0—0	1— 1
York	0—0	0—0	0—0	1—0	0—0	0—0	0—0	0—1	0—0	0—0	0—0	1— 1
Drabowsky	0—1	0—0	0—0	0—0	0—1	0—0	1—0	0—0	0—0	0—0	0—0	1— 2
Wright	0—0	0—0	0—0	0—0	0—1	1—0	0—0	0—0	0—1	0—0	0—0	1— 2
Splittorff	0—0	0—0	0—0	0—1	0—0	0—0	0—0	0—0	0—0	0—0	0—0	0— 1
Nelson	0—0	0—0	0—1	0—1	0—0	0—0	0—0	0—0	0—0	0—0	0—0	0— 2
Totals	0—12	5—7	8—10	11—7	4—8	6—6	12—6	5—13	1—11	7—11	6—6	65—97

No Decisions—O'Riley.

MILWAUKEE—65-97

Pitcher	Balt. W—L	Bos. W—L	Cal. W—L	Chi. W—L	Clev. W—L	Det. W—L	K.C. W—L	Minn. W—L	N.Y. W—L	Oak. W—L	Wash. W—L	Totals W—L
Pattin	1—2	1—0	2—4	2—0	1—1	1—1	1—0	2—2	0—0	1—2	2—0	14—12
Krausse	0—1	4—0	2—4	3—0	1—1	0—1	0—3	2—3	0—2	1—1	0—2	13—18
Brabender	2—1	1—2	0—1	1—2	0—1	1—1	0—1	0—2	0—2	1—2	0—0	6—15
Sanders	1—0	0—0	0—0	1—0	2—0	0—0	1—0	0—0	0—0	0—2	0—0	5— 2
Bolin	0—2	1—2	0—0	0—0	1—0	0—0	1—1	0—3	1—1	1—1	0—1	5—11
Lockwood	1—1	0—1	0—1	0—2	0—2	0—1	2—2	0—1	2—0	0—0	0—1	5—12
Gelnar	0—0	0—0	1—0	0—1	0—0	1—1	0—0	0—0	1—1	0—0	1—0	4— 3
Morris	0—0	0—0	1—0	1—0	0—0	0—0	0—2	0—1	1—0	1—0	0—0	4— 3
O'Donoghue	0—0	0—0	0—0	1—0	0—0	0—0	0—0	0—0	0—0	1—0	0—0	2— 0
Baldwin	0—0	0—0	0—0	0—0	0—0	1—0	0—1	1—0	0—0	0—0	0—0	2— 1
Humphreys	0—0	0—0	0—1	1—0	0—0	0—0	0—0	0—0	0—1	1—0	0—1	2— 4
Downing	0—0	0—0	0—0	0—2	0—1	0—2	1—1	0—1	0—0	0—2	1—1	2—10
Lauzerique	0—0	0—0	0—1	1—0	0—0	0—0	0—0	0—0	0—0	0—0	0—1	1— 2
Locker	0—0	0—0	0—0	0—0	0—0	0—0	0—0	0—0	0—0	0—0	0—1	0— 1
Meyer	0—0	0—0	0—0	0—0	0—0	0—0	0—0	0—0	0—1	0—0	0—0	0— 1
Peters	0—0	0—0	0—0	0—0	0—0	0—1	0—0	0—0	0—0	0—0	0—0	0— 2
Totals	5—7	7—5	6—12	11—7	5—7	4—8	6—12	5—13	3—9	8—10	5—7	65—97

No Decisions—Brubaker, Ellsworth, Twitchell.

MINNESOTA—98-64

Pitcher	Balt. W—L	Bos. W—L	Cal. W—L	Chi. W—L	Clev. W—L	Det. W—L	K.C. W—L	Mil. W—L	N.Y. W—L	Oak. W—L	Wash. W—L	Totals W—L
Perry	2—2	2—2	3—2	2—0	0—2	2—0	3—0	3—1	1—1	4—1	2—1	24—12
Kaat	2—0	0—2	0—1	2—1	3—0	0—0	1—0	3—0	0—2	3—2	0—2	14—10
Hall	0—2	0—1	2—0	2—0	0—0	0—1	3—0	1—1	1—0	2—0	0—1	11— 6
Williams	0—0	0—0	3—0	1—1	1—0	1—0	0—0	1—0	1—0	1—0	1—0	10— 1
Blyleven	1—0	3—0	1—1	2—1	0—1	1—0	0—2	1—0	0—2	0—1	1—1	10— 9
Zepp	0—0	0—1	1—0	2—0	0—0	1—1	1—0	0—1	1—1	1—0	2—0	9— 4
Tiant	0—0	0—0	0—0	1—0	1—0	0—0	0—1	1—1	0—0	2—0	0—1	7— 3
Perranoski	2—0	0—1	0—3	0—1	1—0	1—0	2—0	0—1	1—1	0—1	0—0	7— 8
Boswell	0—1	0—0	0—1	0—0	0—3	0—1	1—1	2—0	0—0	0—0	0—0	3— 7
Haydel	0—0	0—0	0—0	0—0	0—9	0—0	1—0	1—0	0—0	0—0	0—0	2— 0
Woodson	0—0	0—0	0—0	0—2	0—0	0—0	1—0	0—0	0—0	0—0	0—0	1— 2
Hamm	0—0	0—0	0—0	0—0	0—0	0—1	0—1	0—0	0—0	0—0	0—0	0— 2
Totals	7—5	5—7	10—8	12—6	6—6	8—4	13—5	13—5	5—7	13—5	6—6	98—64

No Decisions—Barber.

NEW YORK—93-69

Pitcher	Balt. W—L	Bos. W—L	Cal. W—L	Chi. W—L	Clev. W—L	Det. W—L	K.C. W—L	Mil. W—L	Minn. W—L	Oak. W—L	Wash. W—L	Totals W—L
Peterson	2—1	2—2	2—0	0—2	4—1	2—1	3—0	2—0	1—1	1—2	1—1	20—11
Stottlemyre	0—1	1—2	1—0	3—0	0—3	1—3	0—0	1—1	2—1	3—0	3—2	15—13
Bahnsen	0—2	2—1	1—0	0—2	2—1	1—0	2—0	2—0	1—0	1—3	2—2	14—11
McDaniel	1—2	1—0	0—0	1—0	2—0	1—0	3—0	1—0	0—2	0—0	0—0	9— 5
Kekich	1—1	0—0	0—2	1—0	0—0	0—0	1—0	0—0	2—0	1—0	0—0	6— 3
Kline	0—1	1—1	0—0	1—0	1—1	1—1	0—0	1—1	0—0	0—0	1—0	6— 6
Klimkowski	0—1	0—0	1—1	0—0	0—0	2—1	1—1	1—1	0—0	0—0	0—1	6— 7
Aker	0—1	0—2	1—0	1—0	1—0	0—0	0—0	0—0	0—0	0—0	0—0	4— 2
Hamilton	0—0	0—0	0—0	0—0	0—1	1—1	1—0	2—0	0—1	0—0	0—0	4— 3
Cumberland	1—1	0—0	0—2	1—0	0—0	0—0	0—0	0—0	0—0	0—0	1—0	3— 4
McCormick	0—0	0—0	0—0	0—0	0—0	1—0	0—0	0—0	0—0	0—0	0—1	2— 2
Waslewski	0—0	1—1	0—0	0—0	0—0	1—0	0—0	0—0	0—0	0—0	0—0	1— 0
Gardner	0—0	0—0	0—0	0—0	0—0	0—0	0—0	0—0	0—0	0—0	0—0	1— 0
Verbanic	1—0	0—0	0—0	0—0	0—0	0—0	0—0	0—0	0—0	0—0	0—0	1— 0
Burbach	0—1	0—1	0—0	0—0	0—0	0—0	0—0	0—0	0—0	0—0	0—0	0— 2
Totals	7—11	8—10	7—5	7—5	10—8	11—7	11—1	9—3	7—5	6—6	10—8	93—69

No Decisions—Colson, Jones.

OAKLAND—89-73

Pitcher	Balt. W—L	Bos. W—L	Cal. W—L	Chi. W—L	Clev. W—L	Det. W—L	K.C. W—L	Mil. W—L	Minn. W—L	N.Y. W—L	Wash. W—L	Totals W—L
Hunter	2—2	1—1	3—2	3—0	1—2	0—0	2—1	2—2	1—3	2—1	1—0	18—14
Dobson	1—2	3—1	3—2	1—1	0—0	1—2	1—2	1—1	1—4	3—0	1—0	16—15
Segui	0—2	0—2	0—0	1—0	0—0	3—1	0—1	2—0	1—1	1—1	2—2	10—10
Odom	0—0	0—0	2—1	3—1	0—1	1—0	2—0	0—2	0—2	0—1	1—0	9— 8
Lindblad	0—0	0—0	1—0	2—0	1—2	0—0	1—0	1—0	1—0	0—0	0—0	8— 2
Fingers	0—0	1—1	0—2	3—0	1—0	0—1	0—0	1—3	0—1	0—1	1—0	7— 9
Grant	0—0	0—1	0—0	1—0	0—0	0—0	0—1	1—1	0—0	1—0	0—0	6— 2
Downing	0—0	0—1	0—0	0—0	0—0	0—0	1—0	1—0	0—1	0—1	1—0	3— 3
Lachemann	0—0	0—0	0—0	1—0	1—1	0—0	0—1	0—0	0—1	0—0	0—0	3— 3
Locker	0—0	0—0	0—0	1—0	0—1	0—1	1—1	1—0	0—0	0—0	0—0	3— 3
Roland	0—0	0—1	1—1	0—0	1—0	0—0	0—0	0—0	0—0	0—0	0—0	2— 0
Blue	0—0	0—0	0—0	0—0	0—0	0—0	0—0	1—0	1—0	0—0	0—0	2— 0
Osteen	0—0	0—0	0—0	0—0	0—0	0—0	1—0	0—0	0—0	0—0	0—0	1— 0
Talbot	0—1	0—0	0—0	0—0	0—0	0—0	0—0	0—0	0—0	0—0	0—0	0— 1
Totals	5—7	5—7	10—8	16—2	5—7	6—6	11—7	10—8	5—13	6—6	10—2	89—73

No Decisions—Rodriquez, Womack.

WASHINGTON—70-92

Pitcher	Balt. W—L	Bos. W—L	Cal. W—L	Chi. W—L	Clev. W—L	Det. W—L	K.C. W—L	Mil. W—L	Minn. W—L	N.Y. W—L	Oak. W—L	Totals W—L
Bosman	1—1	2—2	1—0	1—1	1—1	1—2	2—1	2—0	2—0	3—2	0—2	16—12
Hannan	2—1	0—3	1—0	1—0	0—2	0—2	1—1	1—1	1—1	1—0	1—0	9—11
Brunet	0—0	0—0	2—1	0—1	1—0	1—1	1—0	1—1	0—1	1—1	0—1	8— 6
Coleman	1—3	0—3	0—1	1—0	3—1	2—0	1—1	0—0	0—1	0—1	0—1	8—12
Cox	0—2	2—0	0—2	2—1	2—1	1—0	0—1	0—0	0—2	1—1	0—2	8—12
Shellenback	1—0	0—2	1—0	0—0	0—1	1—1	1—0	1—0	0—0	1—2	0—1	6— 7
Pina	0—1	0—0	0—0	1—0	0—0	1—0	0—0	1—0	1—0	0—0	1—1	5— 3
Grzenda	0—0	1—0	0—1	0—0	0—0	0—1	0—0	0—2	0—2	1—0	0—0	3— 6
Brown	0—0	0—0	0—0	1—0	0—2	1—0	0—0	0—0	0—0	0—0	0—0	2— 2
Gogolewski	1—0	0—1	0—0	0—0	0—0	1—0	0—0	0—0	0—0	0—1	0—0	2— 2
Knowles	0—3	1—0	0—2	0—1	0—2	0—2	0—1	0—1	1—0	0—0	0—2	2—14
Such	0—1	0—1	0—0	0—0	0—1	0—0	0—0	1—0	0—0	0—0	0—0	1— 5
Totals	6—12	6—12	5—7	8—4	7—11	9—9	6—6	7—5	6—6	8—10	2—10	70—92

No Decisions—Carlos, Dukes, Humphreys, Ramos, Riddleberger.

AMERICAN LEAGUE YEARLY FINISHES

Year	Balt.	Bos.	Calif.	Chi.	Cleve.	Det.	Minn.	N.Y.	Oak.	Wash.
1901	5	2	..	1	7	3	†6	..	†4	..
1902	8	3	..	4	5	7	†6	..	†1	..
1903	*6	1	..	7	3	5	†8	4	†2	..
1904	*6	1	..	3	4	7	†8	2	†5	..
1905	*8	4	..	2	5	5	†7	6	†1	..
1906	*5	8	..	1	3	6	†7	2	†4	..
1907	*6	7	..	3	4	1	†8	5	†2	..
1908	*4	5	..	3	2	1	†7	8	†6	..
1909	*7	3	..	4	6	1	†8	5	†2	..
1910	*8	4	..	6	5	3	†7	2	†1	..
1911	*8	5	..	4	3	2	†7	6	†1	..
1912	*7	1	..	4	5	6	†2	8	†3	..
1913	*8	4	..	5	3	6	†2	7	†1	..
1914	*5	2	..	x6	8	4	†3	x6	†1	..
1915	*6	1	..	3	7	2	†4	5	†8	..
1916	*5	1	..	2	6	3	†7	4	†8	..
1917	*7	2	..	1	3	4	†5	6	†8	..
1918	*5	1	..	6	2	7	†3	4	†8	..
1919	*5	6	..	1	2	4	†7	3	†8	..
1920	*4	5	..	2	1	7	†4	3	†8	..
1921	*3	5	..	7	2	6	†4	1	†8	..
1922	*2	8	..	5	4	3	†6	1	†7	..
1923	*5	8	..	7	3	2	†4	1	†6	..
1924	*4	7	..	8	6	3	†1	2	†5	..
1925	*3	8	..	5	6	4	†1	7	†2	..
1926	*7	8	..	5	2	6	†4	1	†3	..
1927	*7	8	..	5	6	4	†3	1	†2	..
1928	*3	8	..	5	7	6	†4	1	†2	..
1929	*4	8	..	7	3	6	†5	2	†1	..
1930	*6	8	..	7	4	5	†2	3	†1	..
1931	*5	6	..	8	4	7	†3	2	†1	..
1932	*6	8	..	7	4	5	†3	1	†2	..
1933	*8	7	..	6	4	5	†2	2	†3	..
1934	*6	4	..	5	3	1	†7	2	†5	..
1935	*7	4	..	5	3	1	†6	2	†8	..
1936	*7	6	..	3	5	2	†4	1	†8	..
1937	*8	5	..	3	4	2	†6	1	†7	..
1938	*7	2	..	6	3	4	†5	1	†8	..
1939	*8	2	..	4	3	5	†6	1	†7	..
1940	*6	x4	..	x4	2	1	†7	3	†8	..
1941	x*6	2	..	3	x4	x4	x†6	1	†8	..
1942	*3	2	..	6	4	5	†7	1	†8	..
1943	*6	7	..	4	3	5	†2	1	†8	..
1944	*1	4	..	7	x5	2	†8	3	x†5	..
1945	*3	7	..	6	5	1	†2	4	†8	..
1946	*7	1	..	5	6	2	†4	3	†8	..
1947	*8	3	..	6	4	2	†7	1	†5	..
1948	*6	2	..	8	1	5	†7	3	†4	..
1949	*7	2	..	6	3	4	†8	1	†5	..
1950	*7	3	..	6	4	2	†5	1	†8	..
1951	*8	3	..	4	2	5	†7	1	†6	..
1952	*7	6	..	3	2	8	†5	1	†4	..
1953	*8	4	..	3	2	6	†5	1	†7	..
1954	7	4	..	3	1	5	†6	2	†8	..
1955	7	4	..	3	2	5	†8	1	†6	..
1956	6	4	..	3	2	5	†7	1	†8	..
1957	5	3	..	2	6	4	†8	1	†7	..
1958	6	3	..	2	4	5	†8	1	†7	..
1959	6	5	..	1	2	4	†8	3	†7	..
1960	2	7	..	3	4	6	†5	1	†8	..
1961	3	6	§8	4	5	2	7	1	x†9	x9
1962	7	8	§3	5	6	4	2	1	†9	10
1963	4	7	§9	2	x5	x5	3	1	†8	10
1964	3	8	§5	2	x6	4	x6	1	†10	9
1965	3	9	§7	2	5	4	1	6	†10	8
1966	1	9	6	4	5	3	2	10	†7	8
1967	x6	1	5	4	8	x2	x2	9	†10	x6
1968	2	4	x8	x8	3	1	7	5	6	10

		EAST DIVISION						WEST DIVISION			
Year	Balt.	Bos.	Cleve.	Det.	N.Y.	Wash.	Calif.	Chi.	K.C.	Mil.	Minn.	Oak.
1969	1	3	6	2	5	4	3	5	4	y6	1	2
1970	1	3	5	4	2	6	3	6	x4	x4	1	2

*Record of predecessor St. Louis club. †Predecessor Philadelphia (1901-54), Kansas City (1955-67). §Known as Los Angeles Angels from 1961 to September 2, 1965. yPredecessor Seattle club.
xTied for position.
Note—In 1901, Milwaukee was eighth. In 1902, St. Louis was second.

AMERICAN LEAGUE PENNANT WINNERS

Year Club	Manager	W.	L.	Pct.	*G.A.
1901—Chicago	Clark Griffith	83	53	.610	4
1902—Philadelphia	Connie Mack	83	53	.610	5
1903—Boston	James Collins	91	47	.659	14½
1904—Boston	James Collins	95	59	.617	1½
1905—Philadelphia	Connie Mack	92	56	.622	2
1906—Chicago	Fielder Jones	93	58	.616	3
1907—Detroit	Hugh Jennings	92	58	.613	1½
1908—Detroit	Hugh Jennings	90	63	.588	½
1909—Detroit	Hugh Jennings	98	54	.645	3½
1910—Philadelphia	Connie Mack	102	48	.680	14½
1911—Philadelphia	Connie Mack	101	50	.669	13½
1912—Boston	Garland Stahl	105	47	.691	14
1913—Philadelphia	Connie Mack	96	57	.627	6½
1914—Philadelphia	Connie Mack	99	53	.651	8½
1915—Boston	William Carrigan	101	50	.669	2½
1916—Boston	William Carrigan	91	63	.591	2
1917—Chicago	Clarence Rowland	100	54	.649	9
1918—Boston	Edward Barrow	75	51	.595	2½
1919—Chicago	William Gleason	88	52	.629	3½
1920—Cleveland	Tristram Speaker	98	56	.636	2
1921—New York	Miller Huggins	98	55	.641	4½
1922—New York	Miller Huggins	94	60	.610	1
1923—New York	Miller Huggins	98	54	.645	16
1924—Washington	Stanley (Bucky) Harris	92	62	.597	2
1925—Washington	Stanley (Bucky) Harris	96	55	.636	8½
1926—New York	Miller Huggins	91	63	.591	3
1927—New York	Miller Huggins	110	44	.714	19
1928—New York	Miller Huggins	101	53	.656	2½
1929—Philadelphia	Connie Mack	104	46	.693	18
1930—Philadelphia	Connie Mack	102	52	.662	8
1931—Philadelphia	Connie Mack	107	45	.704	13½
1932—New York	Joseph McCarthy	107	47	.695	13
1933—Washington	Joseph Cronin	99	53	.651	7
1934—Detroit	Gordon (Mickey) Cochrane	101	53	.656	7
1935—Detroit	Gordon (Mickey) Cochrane	93	58	.616	3
1936—New York	Joseph McCarthy	102	51	.667	19½
1937—New York	Joseph McCarthy	102	52	.662	13
1938—New York	Joseph McCarthy	99	53	.651	9½
1939—New York	Joseph McCarthy	106	45	.702	17
1940—Detroit	Delmar Baker	90	64	.584	1
1941—New York	Joseph McCarthy	101	53	.656	17
1942—New York	Joseph McCarthy	103	51	.669	9
1943—New York	Joseph McCarthy	98	56	.636	13½
1944—St. Louis	J. Luther Sewell	89	65	.578	1
1945—Detroit	Stephen O'Neill	88	65	.575	1½
1946—Boston	Joseph Cronin	104	50	.675	12
1947—New York	Stanley (Bucky) Harris	97	57	.630	12
1948—Cleveland†	Louis Boudreau	97	58	.626	1
1949—New York	Charles (Casey) Stengel	97	57	.630	1
1950—New York	Charles (Casey) Stengel	98	56	.636	3
1951—New York	Charles (Casey) Stengel	98	56	.636	5
1952—New York	Charles (Casey) Stengel	95	59	.617	2
1953—New York	Charles (Casey) Stengel	99	52	.656	8½
1954—Cleveland	Alfonso Lopez	111	43	.721	8
1955—New York	Charles (Casey) Stengel	96	58	.623	3
1956—New York	Charles (Casey) Stengel	97	57	.630	9
1957—New York	Charles (Casey) Stengel	98	56	.636	8
1958—New York	Charles (Casey) Stengel	92	62	.597	10
1959—Chicago	Alfonso Lopez	94	60	.610	5
1960—New York	Charles (Casey) Stengel	97	57	.630	8
1961—New York	Ralph Houk	109	53	.673	8
1962—New York	Ralph Houk	96	66	.593	5
1963—New York	Ralph Houk	104	57	.646	10½
1964—New York	Lawrence (Yogi) Berra	99	63	.611	1
1965—Minnesota	Sabath (Sam) Mele	102	60	.630	7
1966—Baltimore	Henry A. Bauer	97	63	.606	9
1967—Boston	Richard H. Williams	92	70	.568	1
1968—Detroit	E. Mayo Smith	103	59	.636	12
1969—Baltimore (E)**	Earl S. Weaver	109	53	.673	19
1970—Baltimore (E)**	Earl S. Weaver	108	54	.677	15

*Games ahead of second-place club. †Defeated Boston in one-game playoff.
**Won Championship Series.

AMERICAN LEAGUE LEADING BATSMEN

Year—Player and Club	G.	AB.	R.	H.	TB.	2B.	3B.	HR.	RBI.	B.A.
1901—Napoleon Lajoie, Philadelphia ...131	543	145	229	342	48	13	13	..	.422
1902—Edward Delahanty, Washington ...123	474	103	178	279	41	15	10	..	.376
1903—Napoleon Lajoie, Cleveland 126	488	90	173	260	40	13	7	..	.355
1904—Napoleon Lajoie, Cleveland 140	554	92	211	304	50	14	5	..	.381
1905—Elmer Flick, Cleveland 131	496	71	152	231	29	19	4	..	.306
1906—George Stone, St. Louis 154	581	91	208	288	24	19	6	..	.358
1907—Tyrus Cobb, Detroit 150	605	97	212	286	29	15	5	116	.350
1908—Tyrus Cobb, Detroit 150	581	88	188	276	36	20	4	101	.324
1909—Tyrus Cobb, Detroit 156	573	116	216	296	33	10	9	115	.377
1910—Tyrus Cobb, Detroit 140	509	106	196	282	36	13	8	88	.385
1911—Tyrus Cobb, Detroit 146	591	147	248	367	47	24	8	144	.420
1912—Tyrus Cobb, Detroit 140	553	119	227	322	30	23	7	90	.410
1913—Tyrus Cobb, Detroit 122	428	70	167	229	18	16	4	65	.390
1914—Tyrus Cobb, Detroit 97	345	69	127	177	22	11	2	57	.368
1915—Tyrus Cobb, Detroit 156	563	114	208	274	31	13	3	95	.369
1916—Tristram Speaker, Cleveland 151	546	102	211	274	41	8	2	83	.386
1917—Tyrus Cobb, Detroit 152	588	107	225	336	44	23	7	108	.383
1918—Tyrus Cobb, Detroit 111	421	83	161	217	19	14	3	64	.382
1919—Tyrus Cobb, Detroit 124	497	92	191	256	36	13	1	69	.384
1920—George Sisler, St. Louis 154	631	137	257	399	49	18	19	122	.407
1921—Harry Heilmann, Detroit 149	602	114	237	365	43	14	19	139	.394
1922—George Sisler, St. Louis 142	586	134	246	348	42	18	8	105	.420
1923—Harry Heilmann, Detroit 144	524	121	211	331	44	11	18	115	.403
1924—George (Babe) Ruth, New York ...153	529	143	200	391	39	7	46	121	.378
1925—Harry Heilmann, Detroit 150	573	97	225	326	40	11	13	133	.393
1926—Henry Manush, Detroit 136	498	95	188	281	35	8	14	86	.378
1927—Harry Heilmann, Detroit 141	505	106	201	311	50	9	14	120	.398
1928—Leon (Goose) Goslin, Washington ..135	456	80	173	280	36	10	17	102	.379
1929—Lew Fonseca, Cleveland 148	566	97	209	301	44	15	6	103	.369
1930—Aloysius Simmons, Philadelphia ..138	554	152	211	392	41	16	36	165	.381
1931—Aloysius Simmons, Philadelphia ..128	513	105	200	329	37	13	22	128	.390
1932—Dale Alexander, Detroit-Boston ..124	392	58	144	201	27	3	8	60	.367
1933—James Foxx, Philadelphia 149	573	125	204	403	37	9	48	163	.356
1934—H. Louis Gehrig, New York 154	579	128	210	409	40	6	49	165	.363
1935—Chas. (Buddy) Myer, Washington ..151	616	115	215	288	36	11	5	100	.349
1936—Lucius Appling, Chicago 138	526	111	204	267	31	7	6	128	.388
1937—Charles Gehringer, Detroit 144	564	133	209	293	40	1	14	96	.371
1938—James Foxx, Boston 149	565	139	197	398	33	9	50	175	.349
1939—Joseph DiMaggio, New York 120	462	108	176	310	32	6	30	126	.381
1940—Joseph DiMaggio, New York 132	508	93	179	318	28	9	31	133	.352
1941—Theodore Williams, Boston 143	456	135	185	335	33	3	37	120	.406
1942—Theodore Williams, Boston 150	522	141	186	338	34	5	36	137	.356
1943—Lucius Appling, Chicago 155	585	63	192	238	33	2	3	80	.328
1944—Louis Boudreau, Cleveland 150	584	91	191	255	45	5	3	67	.327
1945—George Stirnweiss, New York 152	632	107	195	301	32	22	10	64	.309
1946—Jas. (Mickey) Vernon, Washington .148	587	88	207	298	51	8	8	85	.353
1947—Theodore Williams, Boston 156	528	125	181	335	40	9	32	114	.343
1948—Theodore Williams, Boston 137	509	124	188	313	44	3	25	127	.369
1949—George Kell, Detroit 134	522	97	179	244	38	9	3	59	.343
1950—William Goodman, Boston 110	424	91	150	193	25	3	4	68	.354
1951—Ferris Fain, Philadelphia 117	425	63	146	200	30	3	6	57	.344
1952—Ferris Fain, Philadelphia 145	538	82	176	231	43	3	2	59	.327
1953—Jas. (Mickey) Vernon, Washington .152	608	101	205	315	43	11	15	115	.337
1954—Roberto Avila, Cleveland 143	555	112	189	265	27	2	15	67	.341
1955—Albert Kaline, Detroit 152	588	121	200	321	24	8	27	102	.340
1956—Mickey Mantle, New York 150	533	132	188	376	22	5	52	130	.353
1957—Theodore Williams, Boston 132	420	96	163	307	28	1	38	87	.388
1958—Theodore Williams, Boston 129	411	81	135	240	23	2	26	85	.328
1959—Harvey Kuenn, Detroit 139	561	99	198	281	42	7	9	71	.353
1960—James (Pete) Runnels, Boston 143	528	80	169	208	29	2	2	35	.320
1961—Norman Cash, Detroit 159	535	119	193	354	22	8	41	132	.361
1962—James (Pete) Runnels, Boston 152	562	80	183	256	33	5	10	60	.326
1963—Carl Yastrzemski, Boston 151	570	91	183	271	40	3	14	68	.321
1964—Pedro (Tony) Oliva, Minnesota ...161	672	109	217	374	43	9	32	94	.323
1965—Pedro (Tony) Oliva, Minnesota ...149	576	107	185	283	40	5	16	98	.321
1966—Frank Robinson, Baltimore 155	576	122	182	367	34	2	49	122	.316
1967—Carl Yastrzemski, Boston 161	579	112	189	360	31	4	44	121	.326
1968—Carl Yastrzemski, Boston 157	539	90	162	267	32	2	23	74	.301
1969—Rodney Carew, Minnesota 123	458	79	152	214	30	4	8	56	.332
1970—Alexander Johnson, California 156	614	85	202	282	26	6	14	86	.329

LEADING PITCHERS—AMERICAN LEAGUE

(15 OR MORE VICTORIES)

Year Pitcher	Club	Won	Lost	Pct.
1901—Clark Griffith	Chicago	24	7	.774
1902—William Bernhard	Philadelphia-Cleveland	18	5	.783
1903—Earl Moore	Cleveland	22	7	.759
1904—John Chesbro	New York	41	12	.774
1905—Jess Tannehill	Boston	22	9	.710
1906—Edward Plank	Philadelphia	19	6	.760
1907—William Donovan	Detroit	25	4	.862
1908—Edward Walsh	Chicago	40	15	.727
1909—George Mullin	Detroit	29	8	.784
1910—Albert (Chief) Bender	Philadelphia	23	5	.821
1911—Albert (Chief) Bender	Philadelphia	17	5	.773
1912—Joseph Wood	Boston	34	5	.872
1913—Walter Johnson	Washington	36	7	.837
1914—Albert (Chief) Bender	Philadelphia	17	3	.850
1915—Ernest Shore	Boston	19	8	.704
George Foster	Boston	19	8	.704
1916—George (Babe) Ruth	Boston	23	12	.657
1917—Ewell (Reb) Russell	Chicago	15	5	.750
1918—Samuel Jones	Boston	16	5	.762
1919—Edward Cicotte	Chicago	29	7	.806
1920—James Bagby	Cleveland	31	12	.721
1921—Carl Mays	New York	27	9	.750
1922—Leslie (Joe) Bush	New York	26	7	.788
1923—Herbert Pennock	New York	19	6	.760
1924—Walter Johnson	Washington	23	7	.767
1925—Stanley Coveleski	Washington	20	5	.800
1926—George Uhle	Cleveland	27	11	.711
1927—Waite Hoyt	New York	22	7	.759
1928—Alvin Crowder	St. Louis	21	5	.808
1929—Robert Grove	Philadelphia	20	6	.769
1930—Robert Grove	Philadelphia	28	5	.848
1921—Carl Mays	Philadelphia	31	4	.886
1932—John Allen	New York	17	4	.810
1933—Robert Grove	Philadelphia	24	8	.750
1934—Vernon Gomez	New York	26	5	.839
1935—Elden Auker	Detroit	18	7	.720
1936—Monte Pearson	New York	19	7	.731
1937—John Allen	Cleveland	15	1	.938
1938—Charles (Red) Ruffing	New York	21	7	.750
1939—Robert Grove	Boston	15	4	.789
1940—Lynwood (Schoolboy) Rowe	Detroit	16	3	.842
1941—Vernon Gomez	New York	15	5	.750
1942—Ernest Bonham	New York	21	5	.808
1943—Spurgeon (Spud) Chandler	New York	20	4	.833
1944—Cecil (Tex) Hughson	Boston	18	5	.783
1945—Harold Newhouser	Detroit	25	9	.735
1946—David (Boo) Ferriss	Boston	25	6	.806
1947—Allie Reynolds	New York	19	8	.704
1948—John Kramer	Boston	18	5	.783
1949—Ellis Kinder	Boston	25	6	.806
1950—Victor Raschi	New York	21	8	.724
1951—Robert Feller	Cleveland	22	8	.733
1952—Robert Shantz	Philadelphia	24	7	.774
1953—Edmund Lopat	New York	16	4	.800
1954—Sandalio Consuegra	Chicago	16	3	.842
1955—Thomas Byrne	New York	16	5	.762
1956—Edward (Whitey) Ford	New York	19	6	.760
1957—Richard Donovan	Chicago	16	6	.727
Thomas Sturdivant	New York	16	6	.727
1958—Robert Turley	New York	21	7	.750
1959—Robert Shaw	Chicago	18	6	.750
1960—James Perry	Cleveland	18	10	.643
1961—Edward (Whitey) Ford	New York	25	4	.862
1962—Raymond Herbert	Chicago	20	9	.690
1963—Edward (Whitey) Ford	New York	24	7	.774
1964—Wallace Bunker	Baltimore	19	5	.792
1965—James (Mudcat) Grant	Minnesota	21	7	.750
1966—Wilfred (Sonny) Siebert	Cleveland	16	8	.667
1967—Joel Horlen	Chicago	19	7	.731
1968—Dennis McLain	Detroit	31	6	.838
1969—James Palmer	Baltimore	16	4	.800
1970—Miguel Cuellar	Baltimore	24	8	.750

CHARLES S. FEENEY
President of National League

NATIONAL LEAGUE

Including

Club Governments

Club Reviews of 1970 Season

Club Day-By-Day Scores

N. L. Team Pictures

1970 League Leaders

1970 Official N. L. Averages

All-Time N. L. Player Performance Tables

National League

Organized 1876

CHARLES S. FEENEY
President-Treasurer

JOHN J. McHALE
Vice-President

FRED G. FLEIG
Secretary

DAVE GROTE
Director of Public Relations

Headquarters—Mills Building, 220 Montgomery St., San Francisco, Calif. 94104

Telephone—986-1300 (area code 415)

Executive Committee, 1971—Judge Roy Hofheinz, M. Donald Grant, Peter O'Malley.

Umpires—Al Barlick, Kenneth Burkhart, Nick Colosi, Henry (Shag) Crawford, David Davidson, Frank Dezelan, August Donatelli, Robert Engel, Thomas Gorman, H. Douglas Harvey, John Kibler, Stanley Landes, Andy Olsen, Chris Pelekoudas, Paul Pryor, Mel Steiner, Dick Stello, Ed Sudol, Ed Vargo, Anthony Venzon, Harry Wendelstedt, Lee Weyer, William G. Williams.

Official Statistician—Elias Sports Bureau, Inc., 11 West 42nd street, New York, N.Y. 10036. Telephone—LOngacre 5-6362 (area code 212).

Players cannot be transferred from one major league club to another after June 15 to the close of the championship season except through regular waiver channels.

Waiver price, $20,000. Interleague waivers, $20,000, except for selected players and draft-excluded players.

ATLANTA BRAVES

Chairman and President—William C. Bartholomay
Chairman, Executive Committee—Thomas A. Reynolds
Vice-President, Baseball Operations—Paul R. Richards
Vice-President—Richard A. Cecil
Business Manager—Jack Carlin
Controller—Frank Summersell
Director of Advertising—Austin Brown
Ticket Sales Director—John Riddle
Minor League Administrator—Eddie Robinson
Administrative Assistant, Minor Leagues—Bill Lucas
Director of Public Relations and Promotions—Lee Walburn
Assistant Director of Public Relations and Promotions—Bob Hope
Public Relations and Promotions Assistant—Dave Witter
Director of Broadcasting—Otis Hubbard
Associate Director of Broadcasting—Ernie Johnson
Traveling Secretary—Donald Davidson
Manager—Luman Harris
Executive offices—Atlanta Stadium, Atlanta, Ga., 30312
Telephone—522-7630 (area code 404)

Scouts—Joe Bowman, John Groth, Jim Hercinger, Al LaMacchia, Robert MacKinney, John O'Neil, Nap Reyes, Jay Ritchie, Ed Roebuck, Connie Ryan, Bill Serena, Paul Snyder, Clyde Sukeforth, Bert Thiel, Al Unser, Randy Waddill, Bill Wight, Al Zachary, Bob Zuk.

Park location—Atlanta Stadium, Capitol avenue off South Expressway

Seating capacity—51,383

Park telephone—522-7630 (area code 404)

Field dimensions—Home plate to left field at foul line, 330 feet; to center field, 400 feet; to right field at foul line, 330 feet.

CHICAGO CUBS

President—Philip K. Wrigley
Vice-President—John Holland
Secretary-Treasurer—Bill Heymans
Assistant Secretary-Treasurer—E. R. Saltwell
Director of Player Procurement and Development—Gene Lawing
Player Development Supervisor—Carroll (Whitey) Lockman
Information and Services—Charles Shriver
Information and Services—Dave Lamont
Traveling Secretary—Blake Cullen
Assistant Traveling Secretary—Gus Settergren
Honorary Vice-President—Charles J. Grimm

Ticket Manager—Jack Maloney
Manager—Leo Durocher
Club Physician—Dr. Jacob Suker
Executive offices—Wrigley Field, N. Clark and Addison streets, Chicago, Ill. 60613. Telephone—281-5050 (area code 312).
Scouts—Billy Capps, Frank DeMoss, Ralph DiLullo, Albert Grosch, Gene Handley, Al Heist, John Hennessy, Roy Johnson, G. L. (Doc) Mathis, Lennie Merullo, John (Buck) O'Neill, William Prince, H. W. (Bud) Pritchard, Jose G. Santiago, Stephen Ray, Elvin Tappe, H. D. (Rube) Wilson, Mel Wright.
Park location—Wrigley Field, Addison street, N. Clark street, Waveland avenue and Sheffield avenue.
Seating capacity—36,645
Field dimensions—Home plate to left field at foul line, 355 feet; to center field, 400 feet; to right field at foul line, 353 feet.

CINCINNATI REDS

President—Francis L. Dale
Executive Vice-President-General Manager—Robert L. Howsam
Vice-President—A. E. Knowlton
Treasurer—William J. Williams
Secretary—Andrew Hopple
Assistant Secretary—Henry Hobson, Jr.
Assistant to Executive Vice-President—Dick Wagner
Director of Player Personnel—Sheldon (Chief) Bender
Director of Scouting—Joe Bowen
Special Assistant for Scouting—Rex Bowen
Director of Publicity—Roger Ruhl
Assistant Director of Publicity—Bob Rathgeber
Director of Broadcasting—John Soller
Traveling Secretary—Paul Campbell
Controller—D. L. Porco
Director Speakers' Bureau—Gordon Coleman
Director Ticket Services—Robert J. Farrell
Director Group Sales—Tom Cooper
Director Promotions and Sales—Sonny Tate
Director Stadium Operations—Terry Barthelmas
Director of Advertising—John Miller
Manager—George (Sparky) Anderson
Club Physician—Dr. George Ballou
Executive offices—100 Riverfront Stadium, Cincinnati, O. 45202
Telephone—421-4510 (area code 513)
Scouts—Cliff Alexander, Larry Barton, Porter Blinn, Wilfredo Calvino, Joseph Caputo, Bill Clark, Reno DeBenedetti, Larry Doughty, Elmer Gray, Bill Jamieson, Chester Montgomery, Tony Robello, Ray Shore, Neil Summers, Fred Uhlman, George Zuraw.
Park location—Riverfront Stadium, downtown Cincinnati, bounded by Second street to Ohio River & from Elm street to Broadway.
Seating capacity—51,744
Field dimensions—Home plate to left field at foul line, 330 feet; to center field, 404 feet; to right field at foul line, 330 feet.

HOUSTON ASTROS

President and Chairman of the Board—Judge Roy Hofheinz
Senior Vice-President, Astrodomain Corp.—John D. O'Connell
First Vice-President-General Counsel—Bill McDonald
Vice-President-General Manager—H. B. (Spec) Richardson
Vice-President-Director of Player Personnel—Tal Smith
Executive Assistant, Player Personnel—John Mullen
Vice-President—Earl Allen
Vice-President—John Beck
Vice-President—Grady Hatton
Vice-President-Conventions and Expositions—Don S. Vaughn
Treasurer—John Easter
Secretary—W. E. James
Assistant Secretary—Mary Frances Hofheinz
Publicity Director—Wayne Chandler
Director Stadium Operations—Owen Martinez
Traveling Secretary—Art Perkins

Director Radio-TV Network—Bob Boyne
Ticket Manager—Don Andrews
Director Marketing and Sales—Ed Howard
Season Sales—Bill Reeves
Manager—Harry Walker
Club Physicians—Dr. Joe W. King, Dr. Hatch Cummings, Dr. H. J. Brelsford
Executive Offices—Astrodome, Houston, Texas, 77001
Telephone—748-4500 (Area Code 713)
Scouts—Jim Baumer, Stan Benjamin, Homer Blackburn, Dick Bogard, Ed
Burke, Jerry Davison, Gustavo Escobar, Paul Florence, Pat Gillick, Earl Gilpin,
Epy Guerrero, Herb Hippauf, Stan Hollmig, John Jemison, Gordon Lakey, Walt
Matthews, John Miller, Bill Pleis, Cliff Polking, Leo Posada, Wharton Ralstin,
Earl Rapp, Billy Smith, Jim Walton, Jim Wilson.
Park location—Astrodome, Kirby Drive and Interstate Loop 610.
Seating capacity—44,500
Field dimensions—Home plate to left field at foul line, 340 feet; to center
field, 406 feet; to right field at foul line, 340 feet.

LOS ANGELES DODGERS
BOARD OF DIRECTORS
Walter F. O'Malley, Chairman of the Board; Peter O'Malley, President; James
A. Mulvey, Vice-President; Sylvan Oestreicher, Treasurer; Harry M. Bardt, H. C.
McClellan, Robert L. Gordon.
FRONT-OFFICE STAFF
President—Peter O'Malley
Vice-President, Public Relations and Promotions—Arthur E. Patterson
Vice-President, Player Personnel and Scouting—Al Campanis
Vice-President, Minor League Operations—William P. Schweppe
Secretary—E. John Burns
Controller and Assistant Treasurer—Ken Hasemann
Director, Advertising, Novelties and Souvenirs—Danny Goodman
Director, Dodgertown (PGA Pro. Dodgertown Golf Clubs)—Dick Bird
Director, Group Sales—Tom Seeberg
Director, Stadium Operations—Bob Smith
Director, Ticket Operations—Walter Nash
Director, Stadium Club and Transportation—Bob Schenz
Director, Publicity—Fred Claire
Director, Dodger Network—David Van de Walker
Director, Community Relations—Don Newcombe
Director, Speakers' Bureau—Tuck Stainback
Administrative Assistant—Ike Ikuhara
Executive Pilot—Captain Lewis Carlisle
Traveling Secretary—Lee Scott
Resident Engineer—Ira Hoyt
Auditor—Michael Strange
Manager—Walter E. Alston
Club Physicians—Dr. Frank Jobe, Dr. Robert Woods
Executive offices—Dodger Stadium, 1000 Elysian Park avenue, Los Angeles,
Calif. 90012.
Telephone—225-1411 (area code 213)
Scouts—Boyd Bartley, Bill Brenzel, Dick Calvert, John Carey, Luther
Harvel, Gail Henley, Goldie Holt, Tony John, Dale Jones, John Keenan, Ed
Liberatore, Dick McLaughlin, Lew Morton, Greg Mulleavy, Bob Nieman, Ray
Perry, Rudy Rufer, Corito Varona, Ben Wade, Guy Wellman, Bert Wells.
Park location—Dodger Stadium, 1000 Elysian Park avenue
Park telephone—225-1411 (area code 213)
Seating capacity—56,000
Field dimensions—Home plate to left field at foul line, 330 feet; to center
field, 400 feet; to right field at foul line, 330 feet.

MONTREAL EXPOS
BOARD OF DIRECTORS
Charles R. Bronfman, chairman; Paul Beaudry, vice-chairman; Lorne C.
Webster, vice-chairman; Charlemagne Beaudry, Hugh Hallward, John J. Mc-
Hale, Sydney Maislin.
FRONT-OFFICE STAFF
President—John J. McHale
General Manager—James Fanning

Team Manager—Gene Mauch
Director of Scouting—Mel Didier
Director of Minor League Operations—Danny Menendez
Assistant to the President—James M. Faszholz
Controller—Harry Renaud
Director of Public Relations—Larry Chiasson
Director & Producer, Broadcast Operations—Ray Blomquist
Traveling Secretary—Dick Rock
Director of Operations—Marc Cloutier
Manager, Group Sales—Roger Savard
Manager, Tickets—Lucien Geoffrion
Manager, Special Services—Jean Benoit
Stadium Business Manager—Gerry Trudeau
Assistant, Public Relations—Fernand Liboiron
Administrative Aide, Scouting & Minor League Departments—Rodger Brulotte
Club Physician—Dr. Robert Brodrick
Head Groundskeeper—Lubie Veal
Executive Offices—1010 Ste. Catherine street W., Montreal 110, Quebec
Telephone 875-2300 (area code 514)

Scouts—Ralph (Buzz) Boyle, Bill Earnhart, Carl Greene, Ray Hayworth, Ed Lopat, George McQuinn, Pat Mullin, John (Red) Murff, Bob Oldis, Floyd (Pat) Patterson, Andre Pratte, Al Ronning, John (Honey) Russell, Roy (Red) Smith, Bob Zuk.

Scouts (part-time):—Lee Angelich, Terry Boyle, Thomas (Tom) Bridges, Nelson Castellano, Clayton Colbert, Bob Guess, Wade H. Fatheree, R. C. Gaskill, John H. Gibson, Joe Garcia, Willie Harris, Tom Kane, Houston Kennedy, Allen Leeder, George Lial, Thomas (Tom) McCormack, Wayne Morgan, Ramon Naranjo, John Ramey, Claude St. Vincent, William Schudlich, Arnold Stroechker, James W. (Zack) Taylor, Ed Winceniak.

Park location—Jarry Park, 285 Faillon street West, Montreal 327, Quebec
Seating capacity—28,456

Field dimensions—Home plate to left field at foul line, 340 feet; to center field, 417 feet; to right field at foul line, 340 feet.

NEW YORK METS

Chairman of the Board—M. Donald Grant
President—Mrs. Joan W. Payson
Executive Vice-President-Treasurer—G. Herbert Walker, Jr.
Vice-President-General Manager—Robert B. Scheffing
Vice-President-Business Manager— James K. Thomson
Vice-President—Charles D. (Casey) Stengel
Secretary—Luke B. Lockwood
Directors—Mrs. Joan W. Payson, M. Donald Grant, G. Herbert Walker, Jr., Frederick K. Trask, Luke B. Lockwood, George M. Weiss
Director of Minor League Operations—Joe McDonald
Director of Player Development—Dorrel (Whitey) Herzog
Director of Scouting—Nelson Burbrink
Controller—William Murray
Ticket Manager—Bob Mandt
Director of Public Relations—Harold Weissman
Promotion Director—Arthur Richman
Road Secretary—Lou Niss
Manager—Gilbert Hodges
Club Physician—Dr. Peter LaMotte
Executive offices—William A. Shea Stadium, Roosevelt avenue and 126th street, Flushing, N. Y. 11368.
Telephone—NR 2-2000 (area code 212)

Scouts—Jack Cassini, Buck Elliott, Nino Escalera, Tom (Red) Fazio, Dee Fondy, Sterling Fowble, Charles Frey, Lloyd Gearhart, Pete Gebrian, Bill Herring, Jim Hughes, Clarence (Bubber) Jonnard, Bill Kelly, Hank Kelly, Hershel Martin, Walter Millies, Harry Minor, Julian Morgan, Roy Partee, Warren (Sheriff) Robinson, Marvin Scott, Russ Sehon, Walter Shannon, Jr., Barney Smith, Harry (Whitey) Stevens, George (Birdie) Tebbetts, Paul Tretiak, Flushing, N. Y. 11368.

Park location—William A. Shea Stadium, Roosevelt avenue and 126th street, Ollie Vanek, Len Zanke, Edward (Dutch) Zwilling.

Ticket Information—NR 2-3000 (area code 212)
Seating capacity—55,300
Field dimensions—Home plate to left field at foul line, 341 feet; to center field, 410 feet; to right field at foul line, 341 feet.

PHILADELPHIA PHILLIES

President—R. R. M. Carpenter, Jr.
Executive Vice-President-Treasurer—George F. H. Harrison
Vice-President & General Manager—John J. Quinn
Vice-President Business Operations—William Y. Giles
Director—R. Sturgis Ingersoll
Secretary-Assistant Treasurer—R. R. M. Carpenter III
Assistant to the President—Frank B. Powell
Director of Farm System—Paul Owens
Director of Stadium Personnel—Patrick Cassidy
Director of Publicity & Public Relations—Larry Shenk
Traveling Secretary—Edward G. Ferenz
Director of Ticket Sales—Thomas T. Hudson
Director of Promotions—Frank H. Sullivan
Controller—G. Theodore Harrison
Player Personnel Advisor—Eugene J. Martin
Assistant Director of Farm System—G. Dallas Green
Executive Secretary-Farm System—William V. Gargano
Ticket Manager—Raymond B. Krise
Park Superintendent—Andrew J. Clarke
Publicity Consultant—Albert T. Cartwright
Manager—Frank Lucchesi
Club Physician—Dr. James Walker
Executive offices—Philadelphia Veterans Stadium, Broad street and Pattison avenue, Philadelphia, Pa. 19148. Telephone—HO 3-6000 (area code 215)
Scouts—Hugh Alexander, Emil Belich, Edward Bockman, Lloyd Brown, Merrill Combs, Thomas Demark, Paul Duval, Warren Halversen, Bill Harper, Wilbur Johnson, Lou Kahn, Joseph Labate, Wes Livengood, Anthony Lucadello, Ben Marmo, Ray Mueller, John Ogden. Tom Oliver, Gus Poulos, Bob Riley, A. C. Swails, Dick Teed, Elmer Valo.
Park location—Broad street and Pattison avenue
Seating capacity—56,371
Field dimensions—Home plate to left field at foul line, 330 feet; to center field, 408 feet; to right field at foul line, 330 feet

PITTSBURGH PIRATES

Chairman of the Board—John W. Galbreath
President—Daniel M. Galbreath
Vice-President-Secretary—Thomas P. Johnson
Vice-President—Harry L. (Bing) Crosby
Director—Edwin Gott
Director—James M. Johnson
Director—Thomas P. Johnson, Jr.
Director—John A. Mayer
Director—James W. Phillips
Director—Willard F. Rockwell, Jr.
General Manager—Joe L. Brown
Assistant to General Manager—Joseph M. O'Toole
Special Assistant to the General Manager and Director of Public Relations—William Guilfoile
Director of Group Sales and Promotions—Jack Berger
Traveling Secretary—John Fitzpatrick
Ticket Manager—Charles Muse
Treasurer—Arthur C. Routzong
Manager—Daniel Murtaugh
Director of Scouting and Minor League Clubs—Harding Peterson
Assistant Director of Scouting—Merrill S. Hess
Assistant Directors of Minor League Clubs—William G. Turner, Murray Cook
Special Assignments—Bill Burwell, George Detore, Howie Haak, Harold (Pie) Traynor, Jerry Gardner, Jim Maxwell, George Sisler
Club Physician—Dr. Joseph Finegold
Executive offices—Three Rivers Stadium, 600 Stadium Circle, Pittsburgh, Pa. 15212.
Telephone—323-1000 (area code 412)

Scouts—Harding Peterson, director of scouting; Merrill S. Hess, assistant director of scouting; Gene Baker, Edward (Babe) Barberis, Ben Bassetti, Bud Baurle, Ken Beardslee, Antonio Bojos, Chet Brewer, Bill Bryan, Sid Cohen, Frank Coimbre, Cecil Cole, Dick Cole, Joe Consoli, Chuck Cottier, Dick Coury, Larry D'Amato, Al Daniels, Bill Darden, Vince DeBenedetto, Larry DeHaven, Morris (Dutch) Deutsch, Jack DiGrace, Ed Farnum, Gene Fears, Richard Foley, Joe Frisina, Ray Goodman, Jack Heimbuecher, Herb Hess, Peter Hodan, Robert Hughes, Bill Kennedy, Ron King, Bob Kring, Max Macon, Edsel Martz, Ray McGillicuddy, Steve Molaro, Andy Moynihan, Bill Nolan, Steve Oleschuk, George Owen, Pat Owens, Deni Pacini, Hank Pavlik, Medardo Perez, Dick Phillips, Clark Porter, George Pratt, Dick Probola, Herb Raybourn, Michael Roberts, Cucho Rodriguez, Otis Ruby, Bill Schmidt, George Schmidt, Les Stewart, Tom Venditelli, Bob Whalen, Karl E. Wilken, Lenny Yochim.

Park location—Three Rivers Stadium, 600 Stadium Circle

Seating capacity—50,235

Field dimensions—Home plate to left field at foul line, 340 feet; to center field, 410 feet; to right field at foul line, 340 feet.

ST. LOUIS CARDINALS

President—August A. Busch, Jr.
Executive Vice-President—Richard A. Meyer
Vice-President—John Pahlmann
Vice-President—August A. Busch III
Vice-President-General Manager—V. P. (Bing) Devine
Senior Vice-President—Stan Musial
Assistant to General Manager—James L. Toomey
Secretary and Treasurer—John L. Hayward
Assistant Treasurer—Harry F. Suellentrop
Controller—John L. Seifert
Business Manager—Joseph V. McShane
Director of Scouts—George Silvey
Director of Minor League Clubs—Bob Kennedy
Minor League and Scouting Administrative Assistants—Arthur Fetzner and John Claiborne
Chief Scout—Joe Monahan
Director of Public Relations—Robert E. Harlan
Assistant Director of Public Relations—Paul Fauks
Traveling Secretary—Leo Ward
Director of Sales and Promotions—James C. Bayens
Group Sales—Jerry Lovelace
Ticket Director—Michael Bertani
Director of Women's Affairs—Ruth Snow
Manager—Albert (Red) Schoendienst
Club Physician—Dr. Stan London
Executive offices—Busch Memorial Stadium, 250 Stadium Plaza, St. Louis, Mo. 63102.
Telephone—GArfield 1-3060 (area code 314)

Scouts—John Barkley, Dave Bartosch, James Belz, Dennis Boyle, Ed Collins, Piper Davis, Robert Diaz, Angel Figueroa, Lonnie Ford, Ray Garland, Jim Gillis, Robert Harrison, George Hasser, Fred Hawn, Harry Hayes, Byron Humphrey, James Johnston, Lucius (Jeff) Jones, Bob Keely, Robert Kucher, Carl Lais, W. H. (Buddy) Lewis, Eddie Lyons, Herb Mancini, C. A. (Runt) Marr, Tony Martinez, Joe Mathes, Fred McAlister, Jr., Jack McMahan, Joseph Moody, Maurice (Mo) Mozzali, Carlos Negron, Reinaldo Oliver, Gerald Oswald, Jim Powers, Charles (Chase) Riddle, Dominic (Mike) Ryba, William Sayles, Hal Smith, Charles Tarbox, John Tatum, Tommy Thomas, Charles (Tim) Thompson, Quincy Trouppe, Robert O. Walker, Harrison Wickel.

Park location—Busch Memorial Stadium, Broadway, Walnut street, Stadium Plaza and Spruce street.

Seating capacity—50,126

Field dimensions—Home plate to left field at foul line, 330 feet; to center field, 414 feet; to right field at foul line, 330 feet.

SAN DIEGO PADRES

BOARD OF DIRECTORS

C. S. Shannon, Chairman; C. Arnholt Smith, E. J. Bavasi, Dr. Robert K. Kerlan, Hugh Friedman, J. F. Mulvaney, Philip Toft.

FRONT-OFFICE STAFF

President—E. J. Bavasi
Vice-President and General Manager—Edwin W. Leishman
Vice-President and Director of Minor League Operations—Peter Bavasi
Vice-President—J. F. Mulvaney
Vice-President—Lewis Lipton
Treasurer—Philip Toft
Assistant Treasurer—Donald C. Heffner
Secretary—Hugh Friedman
Controller—Ronald J. Sutter
Assistant to the President—Joseph W. Ziegler
Director of Scouting—Robert Fontaine
Business Manager—Richard Thompson
Director of Public Relations—Frank Sims
Director of Promotions—Harold Parrott
Group Sales—Al Hogan
Ticket Manager—Joseph J. Sullivan
Traveling Secretary, Trainer—John Mattei
Manager—Preston Gomez
Assistant Trainer—Angelo Tunis
Team Physicians—H. Paul Bauer, M. D.; Paul L. Davidson, M. D.
Equipment Manager—Ray Peralta
Visiting Clubhouse Custodian—Herman Levy
Groundskeeper—Tom Gonzales
Stadium Superintendent—Jack Noyes
Executive offices—9449 Friars road, San Diego, Calif. 92120
Telephone—283-4494 (area code 714)
Scouts—Jack Bloomfield, Ken Bracey, Cliff Ditto, Leon Hamilton, Marty Keough, Gus Lombardo, Jim Marshall, Richard Schlenker, Don Williams.
Park location—San Diego Stadium, 9449 Friars road
Seating capacity—50,000
Field dimensions—Home plate to left field at foul line, 330 feet; to center field, 420 feet; to right field at foul line, 330 feet.

SAN FRANCISCO GIANTS

President—Horace C. Stoneham
Vice-President—Charles H. (Pete) Stoneham
Treasurer—Edgar P. Feeley
Secretary—Edward T. Brannick
Controller—Charles B. Rupert
Assistant to the President—Jerry Donovan
Director of Player Development—Carl Hubbell
Farm Director and Scouting Coordinator—Jack Schwarz
Public Relations Director—Garry Schumacher
Traveling Secretary—Frank Bergonzi
Ticket Manager—Peter M. Hoffmann
Publicity—Art Santo Domingo
Promotion Director—John Taddeucci
Speakers' Bureau—Walter Mails and Joe Orengo
Manager—Charles Fox
Club Physician—Dr. Eldor C. Sailor
Executive offices—Candlestick Park, San Francisco, Calif. 94124
Telephone—467-8000 (area code 415)
Scouts—John D. Anderson, Allen Andrews, Frank Burke, Francis A. Buscher, Armando Chacon, Walker Cress, Hugh East, Gil English, Jack Fulmer, Thomas Futch, Frank Genovese, George Genovese, Alphonse Gerard, Edward Hallauer, Herman Hannah, Robert Hartsfield, Cappy Harada, Joe Henderson, Thomas J. Hull, Carl Kentling, John Kerr, Richard Klaus, Harvey Koepf, Leo Labossiere, Jim Lyke, Sal Margaglione, Horacio Martinez, Edward F. Montague, Marty Philps, John Piurek, Evo M. Pusich, Hugh Poland, Alex Pompez, Ron Reynolds, Henry Sauer, Jack Shafer, Thomas C. Sheehan, Nick Shinkoff, Charles A. Stoneham, Herman Strutz, Gene Thompson, Dick Wilson, Pedro Zorrilla.

Park location—Candlestick Park, Bayshore
Seating capacity—42,500
Field dimensions—Home plate to left field at foul line, 335 feet; to center field, 410 feet; to right field at foul line, 335 feet.

EAST DIVISION

Patient Murtaugh Nursed Bucs to Flag

By CHARLEY FEENEY

It was a season of success mixed with frustration for the 1970 Pirates who found pitching help in the strangest places and who lost the National League playoffs (0-3) to the Reds because of inept hitting.

The Pirates, handled by Danny Murtaugh who was voted the Major League Manager of the Year in THE SPORTING NEWS poll, overcame many obstacles to become champions of the East Division.

Their super star, Roberto Clemente, who batted .352, missed 54 games and in four others he was used only as a pinch-hitter.

Their home-run slugger, Willie Stargell (31), failed to start 35 games.

Their pitching staff was riddled with injuries. At various times during the season, three of their starters—Bob Moose, Steve Blass and Dock Ellis—were sidelined for a month at a time.

A four-game lifetime winner going into the 1970 season, Luke Walker emerged as the club ace, winning 15 games.

Dave Giusti brought back the days of Roy Face in Pittsburgh. Giusti, acquired from the Cardinals in a deal shortly after the 1969 season, finished with a 9-3 record and 26 saves.

The 1970 season was a year of growing up for the Baby Bucs. Manny Sanguillen emerged as a solid catcher, finishing with a .325 average—third best in the league.

Al Oliver, forced to the outfield when Bob Robertson showed he could hit major league pitching, played left and right field in addition to first base and finished at .270 with 83 RBIs—second to Stargell's 85.

Robertson, a power-swinging righthanded first baseman, had fantastic figures for a part-time ballplayer.

He batted 390 times in 117 games and hit 27 homers with 82 RBIs and a .287 average.

Richie Hebner became a disappointment in the field, but he carried the same stick he did in his rookie season. Hebner finished at .290.

Murtaugh's maneuvering was a key to the club's ability to finish ahead of the Cubs and Mets in the East Division dogfight.

Murtaugh used two infields. Dave Cash, a rookie, and Bill Mazeroski, the sweet-fielding veteran, shared second base; Gene Alley and Freddie Patek, at 5-4 the smallest man in the majors, shared shortstop, and Jose Pagan played third along with Hebner.

The Pirates stumbled often early in the season. They were two games under .500 when rookie righty Jim Nelson shut out the Cardinals, 1-0, in the second game of a doubleheader on June 22.

It was the beginning of a seven-game winning streak which made the Bucs believe in themselves. Nelson, who started the streak and was back in the minors by August, won game No. 7 on June 28 at Forbes Field. It was the second half of a doubleheader against the Cubs and it marked the end of 61-year-old Forbes Field, which had opened its gates for baseball on June 30, 1909, with the Cubs shading the Honus Wagner-led Bucs, 3-2.

PITTSBURGH PIRATES, 1970

Front row—Pagan, Alou, Martinez, Virdon, coach; Oceak, coach; Murtaugh, manager; Osborn, coach; Leppert, coach; Oliver, Patek, Sanguillen. Second row—Dr. Finegold, team physician; Bartirome, trainer; Clemente, Garber, Hartenstein, Giusti, Hebner, Ricketts, coach; Robertson, Stargell, Alley, Blass, J. Hallahan, equipment manager; Fitzpatrick, traveling secretary. Back row—Mazeroski, Marone, Veale, Moose, Ellis, J. May, Jeter, Walker, Dal Canton, Gibbon. Seated in front—T. Hallahan, Patrisko, batboys.

This is The Whistler in his rocking chair, from which he calmly led the troubled Pirates to the East Division championship. Manager Danny Murtaugh also led the Bucs to a flag in 1960.

Three Rivers Stadium opened on July 16 with the Bucs losing to the Reds, 3-2.

The 1970 edition of the Pirates grew hot in early July. With their seven-game June win streak behind them, the Bucs kept moving, winning 10 of their next 14 games.

On July 11, they took first place. They lost it on July 31, regained it on August 2, and fell into a tie with the Mets on September 9, but regained it on September 11 when the Mets lost while the Bucs were idle.

The season was full of personal performances.

On June 12 in San Diego, Dock Ellis, in the first half of a twi-night doubleheader, pitched a no-hit, no-run game. Ellis walked eight, hit a batter, and his no-hitter was saved in the seventh inning when glove whiz Mazeroski made a diving, backhanded grab of pinch-hitter Ramon Webster's line drive.

On August 1 in Atlanta, Stargell had a bombing day. He slugged two home runs and three doubles for 14 total bases (tying an N. L. record) as the Bucs trampled the Braves, 20-10.

On August 22 and 23 in Los Angeles, Clemente banged out five hits in each game against the Dodgers.

Along the way, such pitchers as Alvin McBean, Orlando Pena, Dick Colpaert, Fred Cambria, Johnny Lamb, George Brunet and Mudcat Grant arrived to help.

Pena was a batting practice pitcher for the Kansas City Royals in June.

He pitched batting practice for the Royals prior to an exhibition game with the Pirates in Kansas City on June 8.

After the game, Pena was signed as a Buc reliever.

He helped, but by late August he was cut loose.

Grant, a veteran righty acquired from Oakland on September 14, was of tremendous help in the stretch drive.

Some things didn't change in 1970. Matty Alou picked up 201 hits. This was no surprise. His sub .300 average (.297) was. It was the first time since Alou became a Buc in 1966 that the vet center fielder dropped below .300.

Bob Veale, expected to be at least a .500 pitcher, was 10-15.

Walker, shuffled from the bullpen and starting rotation, became a steady performer in mid August.

Bruce Dal Canton (9-4) came out of the pen to succeed as a starter when Murtaugh's staff ran into a flood of injuries.

The Bucs overcame adversity in 1970. Few people expected them to hold off the challenge of the Cubs and Mets who appeared to have more pitching strength.

The Bucs proved they were the best in the East. They won the season series from the Cubs, 10-8, and they were 12-6 with the Mets, winning six of their last seven games against them in the September pressure days.

The year 1971 looks to be a good one for the Pirates. They have several good, young players who learned to win in 1970.

They overcame pitching problems and, in the end, it was the pitchers who were holding the club together.

SCORES OF PITTSBURGH PIRATES' 1970 GAMES

Date	Result	Winner	Loser	Date	Result	Winner	Loser
APRIL—				**MAY—**			
7—N. York	L 3-5†	Taylor	Hartenstein	20—Phila.	W 3-2§	Dal Canton	Selma
9—N. York	W 2-1	Ellis	Koosman	21—At Mon.	L 6-7	Dillman	Walker
10—At Phila.	L 0-2	Fryman	Veale	22—At Mon.	L 3-6	Stoneman	Moose
11—At Phila.	W 4-0	Walker	G. Jackson	23—At Mon.	W 8-4	Ellis	McGinn
12—At Phila.	W 3-1*	Blass	Bunning	24—At Mon.	W 3-0	Veale	Morton
14—At N. Y.	W 3-1*	Hartenstein	McGraw	26—At Chi.	L 3-6	Holtzman	Blass
16—At N. Y.	W 7-4	Dal Canton	Cardwell	27—At Chi.	W 4-0	Moose	Jenkins
17—St. Louis	L 2-5	Culver	Blass	28—At Chi.	L 7-8	Colborn	Garber
18—St. Louis	L 1-6	Carlton	Walker	29—S. Fran.	W 6-3	Veale	Robertson
20—Houston	W 3-1	Ellis	Bouton	30—S. Fran.	L 11-13	Bryant	Blass
21—Houston	W 9-8	Veale	Dierker	31—S. Fran.	W 7-3	Moose	Marichal
22—Houston	W 6-1	Blass	Lemaster	**JUNE—**			
23—Atlanta	W 8-6	Walker	Jarvis	1—S. Diego	W 5-1	Ellis	Coombs
24—Atlanta	L 0-9	Nash	Moose	2—S. Diego	L 8-14	Herbel	Veale
25—Atlanta	W 8-7	Giusti	Wilhelm	4—Los Ang.	L 0-5	Osteen	Blass
26—Atlanta	L 0-2	Niekro	Veale	5—Los Ang.	W 3-0	Moose	Moeller
27—Chicago	L 0-1	Decker	Blass	6—Los Ang.	W 7-6‡	Giusti	Pena
28—Chicago	W 6-1	Walker	Holtzman	7—Los Ang.	W 3-1	Veale	Foster
29—Chicago	L 5-10	Hands	Moose	9—At S. F.	W 5-1	Blass	Marichal
MAY—				10—At S. F.	L 2-4	Perry	Moose
1—At Cinn.	L 4-6	Simpson	Ellis	12—At S. D.	W 2-0	Ellis	Roberts
2—At Cinn.	L 2-7	McGlothlin	Veale	12—At S. D.	L 2-5	Coombs	Veale
3—At Cinn.	L 7-11	Merritt	Blass	13—At S. F.	W 7-2	Blass	Santorini
4—At Atl.	L 3-5	Nash	Walker	14—At S. D.	L 1-2	Kirby	Moose
5—At Atl.	L 6-12	Stone	Moose	15—At L. A.	W 5-2	Nelson	Moeller
6—At Atl.	L 0-3	Niekro	Ellis	16—At L. A.	L 0-1	Sutton	Giusti
7—At Hous.	W 9-5	Walker	Bouton	17—At L. A.	L 0-4	Osteen	Ellis
8—At Hous.	L 5-7	Ray	Blass	19—Montreal	W 8-4	Dal Canton	Dillman
9—At Hous.	W 6-3	Moose	Griffin	20—Montreal	W 4-2	Blass	Morton
10—At Hous.	L 2-9	Dierker	Ellis	21—Montreal	L 2-3	Nye	Veale
11—Cinn.	W 4-1	Veale	McGlothlin	22—St. Louis	L 1-6	Reuss	Ellis
12—Cinn.	L 3-5	Merritt	Blass	22—St. Louis	W 1-0*	Nelson	Linzy
13—At St. L.	W 5-1	Moose	Gibson	23—St. Louis	W 7-2	Moose	Taylor
14—At St. L.	L 7-11	Johnson	Garber	24—St. Louis	W 4-3†	Walker	McCool
15—Montreal	L 1-2	McGinn	Veale	25—St. Louis	W 3-2	Giusti	Carlton
16—Montreal	W 4-3	Walker	Raymond	27—Chicago	W 2-1	Ellis	Jenkins
17—Montreal	W 7-1	Strohmayer	Garber	28—Chicago	W 3-2	Giusti	Hands
18—Phila.	W 2-1	Moose	Bunning	28—Chicago	W 4-1	Nelson	Pappas
19—Phila.	L 0-2	Short	Ellis	29—At N. Y.	L 2-3	Seaver	Blass
				30—At N. Y.	L 6-7	Koosman	Veale

JULY—		Winner	Loser	AUGUST—		Winner	Loser
1—At N. Y.	W 4-3	Ellis	McAndrew	16—S. Diego	L 6-8	Herbel	Pena
3—At Chi.	W 16-14	Giusti	Regan	17—S. Fran.	L 4-5	Perry	Dal Canton
4—At Chi.	W 10-6	Blass	Holtzman	18—S. Fran.	W 6-2	Blass	Pitlock
4—At Chi.	L 2-7	Pappas	Veale	19—S. Fran.	W 4-7	Marichal	Walker
5—At Chi.	W 5-2	Ellis	Jenkins	21—At L. A.	L 1-2	Osteen	Veale
6—At Phila.	W 7-5	Nelson	Bunning	22—At L. A.	W 2-1x	Dal Canton	Mikkelsen
7—At Phila.	W 4-2	Veale	Short	23—At L. A.	W 11-0	Blass	Foster
8—At Phila.	L 0-2	Wise	Blass	25—At S. D.	L 3-4	Dukes	Walker
9—At St. L.	W 6-0	Ellis	Carlton	26—At S. D.	L 1-2	Dobson	Cambria
10—At St. L.	W 6-2	Giusti	Gibson	28—At S. F.	L 1-5	Marichal	Moose
11—At St. L.	W 8-7	Dal Canton	Taylor	29—At S. F.	L 9-10*	McMahon	Dal Canton
12—At St. L.	W 7-6*	Giusti	Hrabosky	30—At S. F.	L 3-7	Jerry J'nson	Walker
16—Cinn.	L 2-3	Carroll	Ellis	30—At S. F.	L 1-2	Bryant	Giusti
17—Cinn.	W 4-3	Giusti	Simpson	SEPTEMBER—			
18—Cinn.	L 1-3*	Merritt	Giusti	1—At Mon.	W 8-4	Veale	Stoneman
19—Cinn.	W 7-3	Walker	Gullett	2—At Mon.	L 7-10	Marshall	Gibbon
20—At Hous.	L 4-5‡	Cook	Dal Canton	4—Phila.	W 4-3y	Blass	Wise
21—At Hous.	L 1-3	Wilson	Nelson	5—Phila.	W 6-4	Cambria	Lersch
22—Atlanta	W 5-3	Dal Canton	Stone	6—Phila.	W 4-3*	Walker	Selma
23—Atlanta	W 6-5	Colpaert	McQueen	7—Chicago	W 8-3	Moose	Pappas
24—Houston	W 11-0	Ellis	Griffin	7—Chicago	L 2-9	Jenkins	Veale
25—Houston	L 4-8	Cook	Veale	8—Chicago	L 3-10	Hands	Blass
26—Houston	L 4-6*	Lemaster	Giusti	9—St. Louis	L 4-6	Bertaina	Cambria
28—At Cinn.	W 4-3	Dal Canton	McGlothlin	10—St. Louis	W 2-0	Walker	Briles
29—At Cinn.	L 3-4	Nolan	Ellis	12—At Chi.	W 5-4	Moose	Jenkins
30—At Cinn.	L 4-8	Cloninger	Veale	13—At Chi.	L 2-3	Hands	Blass
31—At Atl.	L 3-4	Jarvis	Nelson	15—At Phila.	W 8-3	Walker	Lersch
AUGUST—				16—At Phila.	W 5-3	Moose	Bunning
				17—At Phila.	L 2-3	Short	Lamb
1—At Atl.	W 20-10	Pena	Stone	19—At N. Y.	W 3-2	Blass	McAndrew
2—At Atl.	W 10-7	Ellis	Nash	20—At N. Y.	W 2-1	Walker	Gentry
3—At Mon.	L 0-8	McGinn	Moose	20—At N. Y.	L 1-4	Koosman	Moose
4—At Mon.	W 4-2	Veale	Marshall	20—At N. Y.	W 9-5*	Giusti	McGraw
5—Phila.	W 4-0	Walker	Wise	22—Montreal	L 0-1	Stoneman	Ellis
6—Phila.	W 4-0	Ellis	Bunning	22—Montreal	W 3-1z	Veale	Wegener
6—Phila.	W 8-3	Dal Canton	Champion	23—Montreal	L 2-3	Morton	Brunet
7—N. York	W 6-1	Moose	McAndrew	24—Montreal	W 8-0	Walker	Renko
8—N. York	L 9-12	Koosman	Veale	25—N. York	W 4-3	Grant	Chance
9—N. York	W 8-3	Walker	Ryan	26—N. York	W 4-3	Grant	Herbel
10—N. York	L 2-10	Seaver	Ellis	27—N. York	W 2-1	Ellis	McAndrew
11—Los Ang.	L 4-5	Osteen	Dal Canton	29—At S. L.	W 7-2	Dal Canton	Gibson
12—Los Ang.	L 4-11	Mikkelsen	Moose	30—At St. L.	L 3-4	Briles	Grant
14—S. Diego	W 2-1	Pena	Roberts	OCTOBER—			
14—S. Diego	W 10-1	Walker	Dobson	1—At St. L.	W 9-5	Brunet	Cleveland
15—S. Diego	W 9-3	Veale	Wilson				

* 10 innings.   † 11 innings.   ‡ 12 innings.   § 14 innings.   x 16 innings.   y Suspended game, completed September 5.   z Game of September 3, at Montreal, transferred to Pittsburgh.

Cubs Repeat Bridesmaid Role

By JEROME HOLTZMAN

The Chicago Cubs, for the second successive year, set much of the early pace in the National League East. They led, or were tied, for the divisional lead for 64 consecutive days, from April 22 through June 24, but were unable to catch fire in the September stretch. They finished with an 84-78 record, five games behind champion Pittsburgh.

Veteran outfielder Billy Williams was the team's individual star. Williams was among the league leaders in most offensive departments. He led in runs scored with 137, highest total in the majors in the last 22 years; he tied for the lead in hits with 205; second in homers with 42; tied for second in RBIs, with 129, and batted .322, fourth highest in the league.

Additionally, Williams became the first National Leaguer to play 1,000 consecutive games. He reached this milestone on April 30 and then continued to extend his league record, finally benching himself on September 3, after his streak had reached 1,117 games. Williams explained the streak had gone far enough and that he wanted to end the pressure and

CHICAGO CUBS, 1970

Reading from top to bottom, first row—Pepitone, Gura, Popovich, Colborn, Hiatt. Second row—Hickman, Hands, Amalfitano, coach; Smith. Third row—Williams, Santo, Walker, coach; Decker. Fourth row—Hundley, Durocher, manager; Lowrey, coach; Martin. Fifth row—Banks, Beckert, Becker, coach; Rodriquez. Sixth row—Kessinger, Holtzman, Franks, coach; James. Seventh row—Callison, Pappas, Jenkins, Regan, Spangler.

"get the monkey off my back." He returned to the lineup the next day and didn't sit out again.

While Williams was having his best season, Ernie Banks, his fellow slugger and the long-time Mr. Cub, appeared to be nearing the end of his career. It was Banks' least productive season. Bothered by a knee injury, Banks spent 29 days on the disabled list and much of the time on the bench. He appeared in 72 games, had only 222 official at-bats and had 12 homers and 44 RBIs, half his previous totals. A rare moment of gratification for Banks came on May 12 when he slammed his No. 500 career homer.

The Cubs, nonetheless, had a robust attack. They were second in the league in scoring with a five-run average, and hit 179 homers, second only to Cincy's Big Red Machine and only three shy of the Cubs' all-time season record. As a team, they batted a solid .259 with only one regular, catcher Randy Hundley, below the club average. Moreover, Hundley had an excuse. He was out for three months with a knee injury that required surgery.

Third baseman Ron Santo and outfielder-first baseman Jim Hickman followed Williams in the batting order, giving the Cubs a devastating 3-4-5 triumvirate. No other team, not even the powerful Reds or Giants, had three such sluggers, all of whom had 25 or more homers and 100 or more runs batted in.

It was an especially exhilarating year for Hickman, a nine-year major league veteran who in only one previous season had had enough at-bats to qualify for the league batting title. Playing every day and at 33 years of age, Hickman suddenly emerged as one of the league's big hitters, with a .315 average, 32 homers and 115 runs batted in. Santo was next with 26 homers and 114 RBIs.

Outfielders Johnny Callison and Joe Pepitone also added considerable fire power. Acquired in a winter deal with the Phillies, Callison had 19 homers and 68 RBIs. Pepitone also was in Chicago flannels for the first time. He came from Houston in a July 29 waiver transaction, immediately solved the Wrigleys' center field problem and drove in 31 runs in his first 31 games as a Cub. He finished with 26 homers, 12 as a Cub.

The starting pitching was also well above average. Ferguson Jenkins, recovering from an early 3-7 slump, again led the staff with a 22-16 record, his fourth successive 20-victory season. Bill Hands was 18-15 and Ken Holtzman 17-11. No other N. L. clubs could match the Cubs in big winners. Only Cincinnati and Los Angeles had two starters with 15 or more victories.

Milt Pappas, a veteran and knowledgeable righthander and who was to be the first of five midseason waiver pickups, gave the Cubs a strong No. 4 starter. He responded by winning 10 games, six of them complete-game triumphs. From July 4 to the season's end, only Jenkins exceeded Pappas' victory total.

But this excellence in starting pitching was offset by a weak bullpen. Frantic in his search for an effective reliever, Manager Leo Durocher hopped from one late-inning finisher to another and then, in desperation, virtually quit on his relievers entirely. In the last two months, when the pressure was greatest, Durocher went to his bullpen only as a last recourse, and usually when it was too late.

The result was that the Cubs led the league in complete games with 59 and that Jenkins, Hands and Holtzman were among the league's top eight pitchers in innings pitched. Conversely, the Cubs had only 25 saves for the entire season and Phil Regan, their No. 1 reliever and a two-time Fireman Trophy winner, ranked 23rd in the majors in Fireman points. Often ineffective, and later rusty from inactivity, Regan earned only three saves and won only two games in relief over the club's final 119 games.

Vice-President John Holland, the club's trade-maker, in a gallant effort, was constantly trying ta patch the bullpen and buying relief pitchers, including Juan Pizarro, Bob Miller and Hoyt Wilhelm, but none helped.

Yet, despite it all the Cubs were a season-long pennant factor and were not eliminated until their 158th game.

On the night of September 4, they were only .0004 points out and tied for the lead in the games-behind column.

A 6-4 defeat by the Expos September 20, was perhaps the most crucial and memorable of the entire season. The Wrigleys were ahead, 4-2, with one out in the eighth inning. Regan, working relief, got Rusty Staub to hit a potential, inning-ending double play grounder, but the ball glanced off the glove of first baseman Hickman for a hit. The Expos then rallied to win. Had the Cubs been able to hold this lead, they would have picked up a half-game on the Pirates who, on this same afternoon, split a doubleheader with the Mets. The Cubs clinched second on the final day of the season with a victory over the Mets.

Financially, the Cubs were again a whopping success. They had a home gate of 1,642,705, which was only 32,288 short of equaling their record attendance of 1969. A 40,000 crowd on September 6 for a Sunday game against the Mets was lost because of rain and the game had to be transferred to New York.

SCORES OF CHICAGO CUBS' 1970 GAMES

APRIL—		Winner	Loser	MAY—		Winner	Loser
7—At Phila.	L 0-2	Short	Jenkins	19—At Cinn.	L 1-3	Nolan	Decker
9—At Phila.	L 3-5	Wilson	Holtzman	22—At N. Y.	W 6-4	Colborn	Koosman
10—At Mon.	W 2-1	Aguirre	Sparma	23—At N. Y.	W 14-8	Jenkins	Gentry
12—At Mon.	L 0-2	Stoneman	Jenkins	24—At N. Y.	W 3-1	Hands	Seaver
14—Phila.	W 5-4	Holtzman	Short	24—At N. Y.	L 1-3	Ryan	Decker
15—Phila.	W 5-1	Hands	Wise	26—Pitts.	W 6-3	Holtzman	Blass
16—Phila.	W 6-5‡	Aguirre	Hoerner	27—Pitts.	L 0-4	Moose	Jenkins
17—Montreal	W 8-7	Regan	Raymond	28—Pitts.	W 8-7	Colborn	Garber
18—Montreal	W 8-1	Holtzman	Renko	30—S. Diego	L 4-11	Herbel	Dunegan
21—St. Louis	W 7-4	Hands	Gibson	30—S. Diego	W 8-7	Regan	Dukes
22—St. Louis	W 7-5	Jenkins	Torrez	31—S. Diego	W 7-4	Jenkins	Corkins
24—Houston	W 6-3	Holtzman	Griffin	JUNE—			
25—Houston	W 11-5	Hands	Bouton	1—Los Ang.	L 4-5†	Sutton	Hands
26—Houston	W 6-3	Jenkins	Dierker	3—Los Ang.	W 6-5§	Aguirre	Pena
27—At Pitts.	W 1-0	Decker	Blass	5—S. Fran.	W 12½-5	Jenkins	Marichal
28—At Pitts.	L 1-6	Walker	Holtzman	6—S. Fran.	L 3-5	Perry	Hands
29—At Pitts.	W 10-5	Hands	Moose	7—S. Fran.	W 8-4	Regan	Davison
30—At Atl.	L 2-9	Stone	Jenkins	9—At S. D.	W 7-3	Jenkins	Kirby
MAY—				10—At S. D.	L 8-11	Dobson	Dunegan
1—At Atl.	L 2-3	Niekro	Decker	11—At S. D.	W 7-1	Hands	Corkins
2—At Atl.	L 2-4	Jarvis	Holtzman	12—At L. A.	W 2-1	Holtzman	Foster
4—At Hous.	L 2-7	Bouton	Hands	13—At L. A.	W 7-1	Jenkins	Osteen
5—At Hous.	L 1-3	Dierker	Jenkins	14—At L. A.	L 4-5	Brewer	Regan
7—Cinn.	L 2-5	McGlothlin	Decker	16—At S. F.	L 2-3	Perry	Hands
8—Cinn.	W 10-7	Holtzman	Merritt	17—At S. F.	W 6-1	Holtzman	Pitlock
9—Cinn.	W 8-1	Hands	Nolan	18—At S. F.	W 6-0	Jenkins	Robertson
10—Cinn.	L 6-7	Carroll	Jenkins	19—St. Louis	L 3-5y	Hrabosky	Barber
11—Atlanta	L 6-7‡	Niekro	Reynolds	20—St. Louis	W 8-3	Hands	Torrez
12—Atlanta	W 4-3§	Regan	Priddy	21—St. Louis	L 0-3	Carlton	Holtzman
13—N. York	L 0-4	Gentry	Hands	21—St. Louis	L 2-3	Gibson	Regan
15—At St. L.	L 0-1	Torrez	Regan	22—N. York	L 5-9	Taylor	Jenkins
16—At St. L.	W 3-2	Holtzman	Carlton	23—N. York	L 10-12‡	Taylor	Regan
17—At St. L.	L 3-4	Campisi	Jenkins	24—N. York	L 5-9	Seaver	Hands
18—At Cinn.	W 12-5	Hands	Washburn	24—N. York	L 1-6	Ryan	Reynolds

JUNE—			Winner	Loser
25—N. York	L	3-8	Koosman	Holtzman
27—At Pitts.	L	1-2	Ellis	Jenkins
28—At Pitts.	L	2-3	Giusti	Hands
28—At Pitts.	L	1-4	Nelson	Pappas
29—At St. L.	L	6-8	Carlton	Regan
30—At St. L.	L	4-5	Gibson	Gura
JULY—				
1—At St. L.	W	5-0	Jenkins	Reuss
3—Pitts.	L	14-16	Giusti	Regan
4—Pitts.	L	6-10	Blass	Holtzman
4—Pitts.	W	7-2	Pappas	Veale
5—Pitts.	L	2-5	Ellis	Jenkins
6—Montreal	W	3-2	Hands	Morton
6—Montreal	W	14-2	Decker	Wegener
7—Montreal	W	10-7	Rodriquez	Reed
8—Montreal	W	5-1	Pappas	Renko
8—Montreal	L	4-5	McGinn	Holtzman
10—Phila.	W	2-0	Jenkins	G. Jackson
11—Phila.	L	4-10	Koerner	Rodriquez
12—Phila.	W	10-2	Holtzman	Short
16—At Hous.	L	1-2	Wilson	Holtzman
17—At Hous.	L	2-5	Dierker	Jenkins
18—At Hous.	W	7-3	Hands	Billingham
19—At Hous.	W	7-1	Pappas	Griffin
30—At Atl.	L	1-3	Niekro	Holtzman
20—At Atl.	L	0-5*	Cardwell	Decker
21—At Atl.	W	8-2	Jenkins	Jarvis
22—Cinn.	W	10-2	Hands	Merritt
23—Cinn.	W	1-0	Pappas	Carroll
24—Atlanta	W	11-1	Holtzman	Reed
25—Atlanta	L	0-9	Niekro	Jenkins
26—Atlanta	L	3-8	Jarvis	Hands
26—Atlanta	W	7-6	Colborn	Cardwell
28—Houston	L	4-10	Billingham	Pappas
29—Houston	W	9-2	Holtzman	Dierker
30—Houston	W	6-3	Jenkins	Griffin
31—At Cinn.	W	7-1	Hands	Simpson
31—At Cinn.	W	11-7	Rodriquez	Merritt
AUGUST—				
1—At Cinn.	L	4-6	Granger	Regan
2—At Cinn.	L	3-4§	Granger	Colborn
3—At N. Y.	W	8-1	Jenkins	Koosman
4—At N. Y.	L	0-4	Ryan	Decker
5—At Mon.	L	2-6	Wegener	Pappas
5—At Mon.	W	11-3	Gura	Renko
6—At Mon.	W	4-2	Holtzman	Morton
7—At Phila.	L	1-4	G. Jackson	Jenkins
8—At Phila.	L	3-6	Short	Hands
9—At Phila.	W	4-1	Pappas	Wise
9—At Phila.	L	1-6	Lersch	Gura

AUGUST—			Winner	Loser
11—S. Fran.	W	4-1	Jenkins	Reberger
12—S. Fran.	L	3-6	Carrithers	Hands
13—S. Fran.	W	6-3	Pappas	Perry
14—Los Ang.	L	9-13	Norman	Gura
15—Los Ang.	L	7-9	Mikkelsen	Jenkins
15—Los Ang.	W	13-2	Holtzman	Moeller
16—Los Ang.	W	5-2	Hands	Osteen
17—S. Diego	W	7-0	Pappas	Kirby
18—S. Diego	L	3-11	Dobson	Decker
19—S. Diego	W	12-2	Jenkins	Roberts
21—At S. F.	L	1-5	Reberger	Hands
22—At S. F.	W	15-0	Holtzman	Perry
23—At S. F.	L	3-4	Marichal	Pappas
24—At L. A.	W	4-2	Jenkins	Vance
25—At L. A.	L	1-4	Moeller	Hands
26—At L. A.	L	5-8	Osteen	Holtzman
27—At S. D.	W	5-1	Pappas	Wilson
28—At S. D.	W	8-4	Jenkins	Doyle
30—At S. D.	W	3-0	Hands	Roberts
SEPTEMBER—				
1—Phila.	L	2-3x	Fryman	Regan
2—Phila.	W	17-2	Pappas	G. Jackson
3—Phila.	W	7-2	Jenkins	Short
4—N. York	W	7-4	Rodriquez	Frisella
5—N. York	L	3-5	Koosman	Holtzman
7—At Pitts.	L	3-8	Moose	Pappas
7—At Pitts.	W	9-2	Jenkins	Veale
8—At Pitts.	W	10-3	Hands	Blass
9—Montreal	L	2-3	Marshall	Rodriquez
10—Montreal	W	9-3	Pappas	O'Don'hue
12—Pitts.	L	4-5	Moose	Jenkins
13—Pitts.	W	3-2	Hands	Blass
15—St. Louis	W	5-3	Holtzman	Carlton
16—St. Louis	L	1-8	Gibson	Pappas
17—St. Louis	L	2-9	Reuss	Hands
18—At Mon.	W	3-2	Jenkins	Stoneman
18—At Mon.	W	5-4‡	Regan	O'Don'hue
19—At Mon.	W	8-4	Holtzman	Morton
20—At Mon.	L	4-6	Reed	Regan
23—At St. L.	L	1-2	Gibson	Jenkins
23—At St. L.	L	1-2	Reuss	Hands
24—At St. L.	W	7-1	Holtzman	Torrez
25—At Phila.	L	3-5	Wise	Pappas
26—At Phila.	L	1-7	Lersch	Hands
27—At Phila.	W	5-3	Jenkins	Bunning
28—At N. Y.	L	3-6‡z	Frisella	Wilhelm
29—At N. Y.	L	1-5	Koosman	Pappas
30—At N. Y.	W	2-0	Hands	Ryan
OCTOBER—				
1—At N. Y.	W	4-1	Jenkins	McAndrew

* Game halted by rain with two outs in top of sixth. † Game halted by rain with two outs in top of seventh. ‡ 10 innings. § 11 innings. x 13 innings. y 17 innings. z Game of September 6, at Chicago, transferred to New York.

Mets Close, But Lose 'Amazing' Tag

By JACK LANG

It's a simple matter to pinpoint what went wrong with the defending world champion Mets in 1970. Their pitchers didn't pitch, their leading hitter didn't hit and their relief pitchers did not relieve.

It added up to a third-place finish for the Amazing Mets and about as disappointing a season as any they have endured thus far. Not even the 120 losses in 1962 were as bitter to swallow as the skid to third in 1970.

The reason was that the Mets very easily could have won it all again. The Pittsburgh Pirates, winning the East Division, did it with only 89 victories. The Mets "hung close" all year and, as Manager Gil Hodges frequently pointed out while refusing to give up hope, "All we need is a little winning streak to get going." The Mets never did get going.

The longest winning streak they enjoyed was seven games in early

NEW YORK METS, 1970

Front row—McKenna, trainer; Sacha, batboy; Berra, coach; Pignatano, coach; Yost, coach; Walker, coach; Curtin, batboy; Deer, trainer. Second row—Gentry, Weis, McGraw, Harrelson, Hodges, manager; Jones, Sadecki, Dyer, Foy, Grote. Third row—Agee, McAndrew, Marshall, Boswell, Garrett, Jorgensen, Frisella, Taylor, Folkers, Niss, traveling secretary. Back row—Torman, equipment manager; Singleton, Seaver, Swoboda, Koosman, Clendenon, Shamsky, Ryan, Neuer, clubhouse attendant.

July. That streak ended July 9. Two days later, the Mets dropped out of first place and the rest of the season was one of frustration.

Right up until the final weekend of the season, the Mets were alive. They had two excellent opportunities to overtake the Pirates. They faced the Bucs in a four-game series at Shea Stadium September 18-20 and lost three of the four as they stranded 29 runners in the three losing games. That week, they bounced back to win a pair from the Phillies while the Pirates were losing to Montreal and they went into Pittsburgh for the final showdown on September 25-27. This time, they lost all three games as the Bucs clinched the East crown. This time, they stranded 32 runners.

Clearly, the opportunities were there in both series, but the Mets could not get the big hit in any game. The only one of the seven they won, Jerry Koosman had to pitch a two-hitter.

The Mets' frustrations in those two final series with the Pirates were typical of the entire season. There was always something the Mets seemed to be lacking.

Take Tom Seaver, their pitching ace. He won his first six straight and was 14-5 at the All-Star break. And every one of those losses was a tough one which might have been reversed if the Mets had scored a run or two. Then, in the second half, Seaver, his arm weary, could do no right. He won only four of his last 16 starts and finished with a 18-12 record—quite a comedown from his 25 victories of the Year of The Miracle.

Seaver did lead the league pitchers in strikeouts and in the earned-run average department. One April 22, he became the first pitcher ever to strike out 19 batters in a day game. Seaver did it against San Diego and accomplished the record with a flourish, striking out the last 10 batters in order.

But Seaver was the only big winner the Mets had. Jerry Koosman was once again sidelined for nearly two months with elbow and shoulder trouble; Gary Gentry disappointed after a fine rookie season and also had arm trouble, and Jim McAndrew, after nursing a tender arm for the first half, did yeoman work in the second half, but seemed to be sharing the burden by himself.

A fine pick-up for the Mets and one who came in handy as the young-sters failed was veteran lefthander Ray Sadecki. He turned in an 8-4 log. Most disappointing was the bullpen of Tug McGraw and Ron Taylor. They were one of the strengths of the pennant team the year before, but they didn't quite measure up to those standards until McGraw flashed his old form again late in the season. Taylor managed to save 13 games, but was so inconsistent down the stretch, Gil Hodges did not even use him the final three weeks.

If the pitching was a disappointment, consider how the Mets felt when Cleon Jones, their .340 hitter of the previous year, failed to find his groove until mid-August. Ensnarled in the worst slump of his career, Cleon did not reach the .250 level until August 16. He finished strong with .277, but by then it was too late. A 23-game hitting streak late in the season, a club record, helped Jones finished with a respectable average.

While Jones had a miserable season for the most part, Donn Clendenon and Tommie Agee went quite the other way. Agee hit .286, walloped 24 homers and set a club record with 31 stolen bases. The only dampers on his otherwise brilliant season were his record 156 strikeouts and a bother-

some knee that sidelined him the last week and could be a problem this year.

Clendenon, used sparingly by Hodges early, a fact which later was cited by fans as a reason for the club's demise, had an outstanding year. The big first baseman batted .288, hit 22 homers aand set a club mark with 97 runs batted in.

Bud Harrelson at shortstop and Ken Boswell at second helped give the Mets a strong defensive infield. But listed among the many disappointments was Joe Foy, the third baseman obtained from Kansas City the previous winter. Joe was so bad the Mets sent him to the minors at the end of the year.

Despite all of their problems, the Mets managed to stay in the race all the way and this led to a box-office bonanza. Home attendance for 72 dates was 2,697,479, the second-ranked baseball attendance figure in history and the greatest ever for a New York sports team.

SCORES OF NEW YORK METS' 1970 GAMES

APRIL—			Winner	Loser	JUNE—			Winner	Loser
7—At Pitts.	W	5-3‡	Taylor	Hartenstein	8—At Hous.	W	2-0	McAndrew	Billingham
9—At Pitts.	L	1-2	Ellis	Koosman	9—At Hous.	W	2-1	Seaver	Griffin
10—At St. L.	L	3-7	Culver	McAndrew	10—At Hous.	L	3-5	Lemaster	Ryan
11—At St. L.	W	4-1	Gentry	Briles	12—Atlanta	W	8-1	Gentry	Niekro
12—At St. L.	W	6-4	Seaver	Carlton	13—Atlanta	W	4-1	Sadecki	McQueen
14—Pitts.	L	4-6†	Hartenstein	McGraw	14—Atlanta	W	7-5	Seaver	Jarvis
16—Pitts.	L	4-7	Dal Canton	Cardwell	16—Cinn.	W	8-1	McAndrew	Merritt
17—Phila.	W	6-0	Seaver	G. Jackson	17—Cinn.	L	4-7	Carroll	Taylor
18—Phila.	W	7-0	Ryan	Bunning	19—Phila.	W	13-3	Seaver	Bunning
19—Phila.	L	2-3†	Wise	Koosman	20—Phila.	L	1-2	Short	Koosman
19—Phila.	W	10-2	McAndrew	Short	22—At Chi.	W	9-5	Taylor	Jenkins
21—S. Diego	L	3-5	Herbel	Koonce	23—At Chi.	W	12-10†	Taylor	Regan
22—S. Diego	W	2-1	Seaver	Corkins	24—At Chi.	W	9-5	Seaver	Hands
24—At L. A.	L	0-1z	Lamb	Taylor	24—At Chi.	W	6-1	Ryan	Reynolds
25—At L. A.	L	0-1	Osteen	Ryan	25—At Chi.	W	8-3	Koosman	Holtzman
26—At L. A.	W	3-1	Seaver	Vance	26—At Mon.	L	5-6	Renko	McAndrew
28—At S. F.	W	5-2	Gentry	Perry	27—At Mon.	W	8-3	Gentry	McGinn
29—At S. F.	L	6-8	Linzy	Taylor	28—At Mon.	L	2-3	Morton	Sadecki
30—At S. F.	W	4-1	Ryan	McCormick	29—Pitts.	W	3-2	Seaver	Blass
					30—Pitts.	W	7-6	Koosman	Veale
MAY—									
1—At S. D.	W	2-1	Seaver	Santorini	**JULY—**				
2—At S. D.	L	4-5	Kirby	McAndrew	1—Pitts.	L	3-4	Ellis	McAndrew
3—At S. D.	L	3-4†	Roberts	Koonce	2—At Phila	L	1-6	Bunning	Gentry
3—At S. D.	W	3-2	Gentry	Dobson	3—At Phila.	L	2-3	Short	Cardwell
5—Los Ang.	L	0-4	Vance	Ryan	3—At Phila.	W	4-3	Sadecki	Wise
6—Los Ang.	W	5-4	Seaver	Sutton	4—At Phila.	W	7-2	Seaver	G. Jackson
7—Los Ang.	L	4-7†	Lamb	McAndrew	5—At Phila.	W	5-4	Koosman	Fryman
8—S. Fran.	L	1-7	Puente	Gentry	6—St. Louis	W	10-3	McAndrew	Reuss
9—S. Fran.	W	14-5	Koosman	Linzy	7—St. Louis	W	4-3	Frisella	Campisi
10—S. Fran.	L	7-11	Marichal	Ryan	8—St. Louis	W	7-5	Sadecki	Briles
11—Montreal	L	0-3	McGinn	Seaver	9—Montreal	W	7-1	Seaver	Nye
12—Montreal	W	8-4	Sadecki	Morton	10—Montreal	L	7-9	Morton	Koosman
13—At Chi.	W	4-0	Gentry	Hands	11—Montreal	L	2-6	Wegener	McAndrew
15—At Phila.	W	4-0	Seaver	Fryman	12—Montreal	L	3-5	Reed	Sadecki
16—At Phila.	W	6-0	Koosman	G. Jackson	16—At L. A.	L	1-3	Singer	McAndrew
18—At Mon.	L	4-8	Raymond	McGraw	17—At L. A.	L	0-1†	Sutton	McGraw
19—At Mon.	W	7-4	Sadecki	McGinn	18—At L. A.	W	4-3	Frisella	Brewer
20—At Mon.	L	0-2	Morton	Seaver	19—At S. F.	L	3-5	McMahon	Taylor
22—Chicago	L	4-6	Colborn	Koosman	19—At S. F.	W	7-6†	Taylor	McMahon
23—Chicago	L	8-14	Jenkins	Gentry	20—At S. F.	L	4-7	Davison	Folkers
24—Chicago	L	1-3	Hands	Seaver	21—At S. D.	W	3-0	McAndrew	Kirby
24—Chicago	W	3-1	Ryan	Decker	22—At S. D.	L	4-5†	Baldschun	Ryan
26—St. Louis	W	5-1	Sadecki	Torrez	24—Los Ang.	W	2-1†	McGraw	Brewer
27—St. Louis	W	3-0	Gentry	Carlton	25—Los Ang.	W	6-4	Frisella	Pena
28—St. Louis	L	2-9	Gibson	McAndrew	26—Los Ang.	L	3-5	Sutton	Gentry
29—Houston	L	0-5	Billingham	Seaver	27—S. Fran.	W	5-3	Seaver	Perry
30—Houston	W	4-3	Ryan	Dierker	28—S. Fran.	W	12-2	McAndrew	Robertson
31—Houston	W	14-4	Sadecki	Lemaster	29—S. Fran.	L	2-4	Pitlock	Folkers
31—Houston	W	4-3y	McGraw	Lemaster	31—S. Diego	W	6-5	Frisella	Herbel
JUNE—									
2—At Atl.	L	1-4	Niekro	Gentry	**AUGUST—**				
4—At Atl.	L	1-3	Jarvis	Seaver	1—S. Diego	W	4-2	Seaver	Wilson
5—At Cinn.	L	4-5*	McGlothlin	Ryan	2—S. Diego	L	0-3	Coombs	McAndrew
6—At Cinn.	L	1-5	Merritt	Sadecki	2—S. Diego	L	2-4	Willis	Frisella
7—At Cinn.	L	2-10	Simpson	Gentry	3—Chicago	L	1-6	Jenkins	Koosman
					4—Chicago	W	4-0	Ryan	Decker

AUGUST—		Winner	Loser	SEPTEMBER—		Winner	Loser
5—At St. L.	W 5-3	Frisella	Carlton	3—At St. L.	L 3-5	Carlton	Gentry
6—At St. L.	L 0-3	Briles	Seaver	4—At Chi.	L 4-7	Rodriquez	Frisella
7—At Pitts.	L 1-6	Moose	McAndrew	5—At Chi.	W 5-3	Koosman	Holtzman
8—At Pitts.	W 12-9	Koosman	Veale	7—Montreal	W 5-4	Frisella	Marshall
9—At Pitts.	L 3-8	Walker	Ryan	7—Montreal	W 5-1	McAndrew	McGinn
10—At Pitts.	W 10-2	Seaver	Ellis	8—Montreal	W 10-5	McGraw	Renko
11—At Cinn.	L 1-8	Nolan	McAndrew	9—Phila.	L 2-3	Lersch	Frisella
12—At Cinn.	W 2-1	Gentry	Cloninger	9—Phila.	W 3-1	Sadecki	G. Jackson
13—At Cinn.	L 1-6	Merritt	Sadecki	10—Phila.	W 3-2y	Herbel	Hoerner
14—At Atl.	L 2-10	Reed	Ryan	11—St. Louis	L 2-5	Gibson	Seaver
14—At Atl.	W 4-2	Koosman	Jarvis	12—St. Louis	W 3-0	McAndrew	Reuss
15—At Atl.	L 2-3	Wilhelm	Seaver	13—St. Louis	L 4-5x	Linzy	Herbel
16—At Atl.	W 2-1	McAndrew	Nash	14—At Mon.	W 9-5†	Frisella	Marshall
18—Houston	W 7-1	Gentry	Dierker	15—At Mon.	L 4-5†	O'Donoghue	Koosman
19—Houston	L 4-9	Blasingame	Seaver	16—At Mon.	L 2-4	Renko	Seaver
21—Cinn.	W 4-1	Koosman	Cloninger	18—Pitts.	L 2-3	Blass	McAndrew
22—Cinn.	L 2-3	Merritt	McGraw	19—Pitts.	L 1-2	Walker	Gentry
23—Cinn.	W 5-4	Taylor	Granger	20—Pitts.	W 4-1	Koosman	Moose
23—Cinn.	L 5-7	Gullett	Seaver	20—Pitts.	L 5-9†	Giusti	McGraw
25—Atlanta	L 6-7	Jarvis	Ryan	22—At Phila.	W 7-6	Ryan	Selma
26—Atlanta	L 7-9	Priddy	Gentry	23—At Phila.	W 5-4	McGraw	Selma
27—Atlanta	W 5-1	McAndrew	Niekro	25—At Pitts.	L 3-4	Grant	Chance
28—At Hous.	L 1-2	Blasingame	Seaver	26—At Pitts.	L 3-4	Grant	Herbel
29—At Hous.	L 8-9†	Culver	McGraw	27—At Pitts.	L 1-2	Ellis	McAndrew
30—At Hous.	L 5-9	Wilson	Ryan	28—Chicago	W 6-3†a	Frisella	Wilhelm
31—At St. L.	W 11-5	Koosman	Briles	29—Chicago	W 3-1	Koosman	Pappas
SEPTEMBER—				30—Chicago	L 0-2	Hands	Ryan
1—At St. L.	W 4-3§	Herbel	Gibson	OCTOBER—			
2—At St. L.	W 7-3	Seaver	Reuss	1—Chicago	L 1-4	Jenkins	McAndrew

* Game halted by rain with one out in bottom of eighth.   † 10 innings.   ‡ 11 innings.   § 12 innings.   x 13 innings.   y 14 innings.   z 15 innings.   a Game of September 6, at Chicago, transferred to New York.

Hill Problem in Mound City

By NEAL RUSSO

The top headline on a story from the Cardinals' spring training camp last February 22 read: "Cardinals' No. 1 Problem: Filling In Bullpen Roster." The man who was quoted that day, pitching coach Billy Muffett, wasn't telling a lie—but after all, it was Washington's Birthday.

About six months later, Muffett was gone, but the headline could have remained the same. By season's end, the bullpen had betrayed the club so often that its status looked even worse than it did before the season began.

"I knew we were going to have some trouble with our relievers, but I never dreamed it would be that bad," said Manager Red Schoendienst after his Redbirds finished a sorry fourth.

But wait a minute. The Cardinal starters must share the blame with the firemen as those chiefly responsible for the team's foldup. Picked to win by some experts and rated a top contender by quite a few others, the Redbirds sputtered after a sizzling 7-2 getaway, then absolutely collapsed in July.

Nobody could find a worse July in the history of the Cardinals, and it would have been even more of a debacle if they hadn't won four of their last five in that month. They finished the month with an 8-21 mark after seeing the July log sink to 4-20 with 17 losses in 19 games (two eight-game losing streaks).

That thud you heard July 25 in Cincinnati was the Redbirds turning into Deadbirds with a 5-3 loss to the rampaging Reds. That setback dropped the Cardinals to rock bottom in the East Division. Their record fell to 41-57 a night later as they skidded 13 lengths from the top.

ST. LOUIS CARDINALS, 1970

Front row—Davalillo, Ramirez, Reuss, Carl Taylor, Muffett, coach; Schoendienst, manager; Sisler, coach; Milliken, coach; Kissell, coach; Zeller, coach; McCool. Second row—Bauman, trainer; Hartenstein, Torre, Hrabosky, Chuck Taylor, Hague, Campisi, Linzy, Beauchamp, Carlton, Gieselmann, assistant trainer. Back row—Brock, Briles, Cardenal, Allen, Lee, Shannon, Maxvill, Javier, Gibson. Seated in front—Deason, Risch, batboys.

With the top clubs in the division floundering, the Cardinals managed to come back to life with a six-game winning streak, their longest of 1970, through August 4. Their hot spell consisted of eight victories in nine games. 11 in 13, 14 in 17 (through August 12). Now they were just eight games off the pace.

Then came six losses in the next eight games, all at home. But a 7-2 invasion of California enabled Schoendienst's men to march home only 5½ games from first place. The Birds had won 19 of 29 in August and 23 of 34 since their 2-17 swoon. Now it was August 30 and they were going home for four games with the Mets and three with the Expos.

Alas, the Mets won the first three and the Expos took the first two. The Cardinals never recovered from that 2-5 home stand, which was typical of their luck at Busch Stadium all season. They lost five of their last seven games in winding up 13 games from the division penthouse.

The Cardinals also closed in fourth place in 1969, and they were also mired 13 games back at the end of that year, too. However, the '69 Birds won 11 games more (87) than their '70 counterparts (76). The Cards' 76 wins were their fewest since the 154-game schedule days.

With Rich Allen leading the way on 34 home runs, 101 runs batted in and 12 game-winning RBIs, the Birds puffed up their offense. They scored 149 more runs than they collected the previous year. However. they yielded 207 more runs than in 1969 when the pitching staff's 2.94 ERA was the best in the National League and the second best in the majors.

The St. Louis pitching staff, victimized to some extent by the Astro-Turf installed at Busch Stadium, saw its ERA zoom to 4.05. Bob Gibson had his usual great year as he refused to let down, even though the club faltered most of the season. The Cy Young Award winner had a 23-7 record and a 3.12 ERA. If the rest of the staff had compiled only a mere .500 record (66-66), the Birds would have wound up with 89 victories.

That's how many victories the Pirates totaled in grabbing the East Division crown.

Gibby also had 23 complete games in 34 starts. The rest of the staff had just 28 route jobs. The entire staff amassed only 20 saves and quite a few pitchers in the major leagues topped that meager total.

Still, as G. M. Bing Devine pointed out, much of the collapse of the bullpen was a direct adjunct of the failures of the starting crew. Relievers had to be rushed into action much earlier than was advisable. Steve Carlton was the guiltiest member of the starting staff, falling from 17-11 to 10-19. His loss total was the biggest for a Cardinal since Jesse Haines was tagged for 20 setbacks in 1920.

One of the most killing problems was the inability to win with any consistency at home. The Cardinals had a 34-47 record at Busch Stadium where the home fan cheering obviously didn't do much good even though more than 1,600,000 turned out for the St. Louis games.

The Birds folded despite an exceptional year for Joe Torre and good seasons for Lou Brock, Jose Cardenal and Allen, plus Joe Hague, playing his first full season. Also despite a dazzling .300 average for the pinch-hitters, topped by Vic Davalillo's record-smashing performance. His 24 pinch-hits smashed the N. L. mark for one season by two and tied Dave Philley for the major league standard.

Besides reaching the 200-hit plateau for the third time and batting .304,

Brock set a major league record by stealing 50 or more bases for the sixth straight year.

SCORES OF ST. LOUIS CARDINALS' 1970 GAMES

Date	Result	Winner	Loser
APRIL—			
8—At Mon.	W 7-2	Gibson	Stoneman
9—At Mon.	W 7-3	Torrez	Renko
10—N. York	W 7-3	Culver	McAndrew
11—N. York	L 1-4	Gentry	Briles
12—N. York	L 4-6	Seaver	Carlton
14—Montreal	W 6-5*	Campisi	Reed
15—Montreal	W 10-0	Torrez	Sparma
17—At Pitts.	W 5-2	Culver	Blass
18—At Pitts.	W 6-1	Carlton	Walker
21—At Chi.	L 4-7	Hands	Gibson
22—At Chi.	L 5-7	Jenkins	Torrez
24—Cinn.	W 3-1	Culver	Simpson
25—Cinn.	L 2-3	Merritt	Carlton
26—Cinn.	W 4-1	Gibson	McGlothlin
28—Atlanta	L 2-3	Wilhelm	Torrez
29—Atlanta	L 6-10	Priddy	Taylor
MAY—			
1—Houston	L 3-9	Dierker	Carlton
2—Houston	L 3-5*	Gladding	Hilgendorf
3—Houston	W 7-4	Briles	Griffin
3—Houston	L 1-8	Lemaster	Culver
4—At Cinn.	L 3-7	Nolan	Torrez
5—At Cinn.	L 1-5	Simpson	Carlton
8—At Atl.	L 1-8	Priddy	Taylor
9—At Atl.	L 3-5	Nash	Culver
10—At Atl.	W 6-5	Jonnson	Priddy
11—Phila.	W 3-0	Carlton	Bunning
12—Phila.	W 9-5	Taylor	Palmer
13—Pitts.	L 1-5	Moose	Gibson
14—Pitts.	W 11-7	Johnson	Garber
15—Chicago	W 1-0	Torrez	Regan
16—Chicago	L 2-3	Holtzman	Carlton
17—Chicago	W 4-3	Campisi	Jenkins
18—At Hous.	L 0-6	Dierker	Gibson
19—At Hous.	W 12-3	Guzman	Spinks
20—At Hous.	W 3-2	Torrez	Griffin
21—At Phila.	L 3-4	Hoerner	Linzy
22—At Phila.	W 6-3	Linzy	M. Jackson
23—At Phila.	W 3-1	Gibson	Bunning
24—At Phila.	L 5-6*	M. Jackson	Taylor
26—At N. Y.	L 1-5	Sadecki	Torrez
27—At N. Y.	L 0-3	Gentry	Carlton
28—At N. Y.	W 9-2	Gibson	McAndrew
29—Los Ang.	L 6-8	Pena	McCool
30—Los Ang.	L 6-7	Osteen	Guzman
31—Los Ang.	L 6-8†	Pena	Culver
JUNE—			
2—S. Fran.	W 12-1	Carlton	Perry
3—S. Fran.	W 6-5	Gibson	Reberger
5—S. Diego	L 2-3	Dobson	Torrez
6—S. Diego	L 4-5	Herbel	Carlton
7—S. Diego	W 10-7	Gibson	Herbel
9—At L. A.	W 4-0	Taylor	Osteen
10—At L. A.	L 2-4	Moeller	Torrez
11—At L. A.	L 1-2‡	Brewer	Linzy
12—At S. F.	W 4-1	Gibson	Pitlock
13—At S. F.	L 5-6	McMahon	Campisi
14—At S. F.	L 4-7	Marichal	Taylor
15—At S. D.	W 5-4	Torrez	Dobson
16—At S. D.	L 0-4	Roberts	Carlton
17—At S. D.	W 8-0	Gibson	Coombs
19—At Chi.	W 5-3y	Hrabosky	Barber
20—At Chi.	L 3-8	Hands	Torrez
21—At Chi.	W 3-0	Carlton	Holtzman
21—At Chi.	W 3-2	Gibson	Regan
22—At Pitts.	W 6-1	Reuss	Ellis
22—At Pitts.	L 0-1*	Nelson	Linzy
23—At Pitts.	L 3-7	Moose	Taylor
24—At Pitts.	L 3-4†	Walker	McCool
25—At Pitts.	L 2-3	Giusti	Carlton
26—Phila.	W 7-0	Gibson	Wise
27—Phila.	W 9-8	Abernathy	Hoerner
28—Phila.	W 5-4	Torrez	Selma
28—Phila.	L 3-8*	Selma	McCool
29—Chicago	W 8-6	Carlton	Regan
30—Chicago	W 5-4	Gibson	Gura

Date	Result	Winner	Loser
JULY—			
1—Chicago	L 0-5	Jenkins	Reuss
2—At Mon.	L 10-13	Morton	Torrez
3—At Mon.	W 9-7	Taylor	Stoneman
4—At Mon.	L 0-8	Renko	Carlton
5—At Mon.	W 6-3	Gibson	Nye
6—At N. Y.	L 3-10	McAndrew	Reuss
7—At N. Y.	L 3-4	Frisella	Campisi
8—At N. Y.	L 5-7	Sadecki	Briles
9—Pitts.	L 0-6	Ellis	Carlton
10—Pitts.	L 2-6	Giusti	Gibson
11—Pitts.	L 7-8	Dal Canton	Taylor
12—Pitts.	L 6-7*	Giusti	Hrabosky
16—Atlanta	L 3-7	Jarvis	Carlton
17—Atlanta	W 11-6	Briles	Stone
18—Atlanta	L 7-8†	Wilhelm	Linzy
19—Atlanta	W 3-1	Torrez	Reed
20—Cinn.	L 0-4*	Nolan	Reuss
20—Cinn.	L 3-4	Granger	Chlupsa
21—Cinn.	L 5-6	Carroll	Carlton
22—Houston	L 9-13	Culver	Briles
23—Houston	L 2-3	Billingham	Gibson
24—At Cinn.	L 0-4	Nolan	Torrez
25—At Cinn.	L 3-5	Cloninger	Reuss
26—At Cinn.	L 5-12	Simpson	Carlton
27—At Cinn.	W 16-9	Taylor	Merritt
28—At Atl.	W 6-4	Gibson	Nash
29—At Atl.	L 7-9	Reed	Linzy
30—At Atl.	W 4-2	Reuss	Niekro
31—At Hous.	W 5-1	Carlton	Cook
AUGUST—			
1—At Hous.	W 14-7	Briles	Wilson
2—At Hous.	W 3-2	Gibson	Billingham
3—At Phila.	W 4-1	Torrez	G. Jackson
4—At Phila.	W 3-2	Reuss	Short
5—N. York	L 3-5	Frisella	Carlton
6—N. York	W 3-0	Briles	Seaver
7—Montreal	W 2-1	Gibson	McGinn
8—Montreal	W 11-10	Hrabosky	Raymond
9—Montreal	L 6-7	Wegener	Carlton
9—Montreal	W 4-0	Reuss	Stoneman
11—S. Diego	W 11-10	Parker	Herbel
12—S. Diego	W 5-4x	Gibson	Willis
13—S. Diego	L 7-9	Kirby	Cleveland
14—S. Fran.	W 2-1§	Taylor	McMahon
14—S. Fran.	L 4-5*	McMahon	Hilgendorf
15—S. Fran.	L 2-3	Carrithers	Briles
16—S. Fran.	L 2-5	Bryant	Cleveland
17—Los Ang.	W 11-8	Gibson	Sutton
18—Los Ang.	L 2-7	Vance	Reuss
19—Los Ang.	L 2-4	Brewer	Carlton
21—At S. D.	W 14-8	Briles	Wilson
22—At S. D.	W 7-0	Gibson	Coombs
23—At S. D.	W 8-7	Linzy	Dobson
25—At S. F.	L 2-4	Pitlock	Carlton
26—At S. F.	L 7-8	Davison	Hilgendorf
27—At S. F.	W 4-1	Gibson	Perry
28—At L. A.	W 1-0	Reuss	Sutton
29—At L. A.	W 3-2	Taylor	Brewer
30—At L. A.	W 2-1	Carlton	Vance
31—At L. A.	L 5-11	Koosman	Briles
SEPTEMBER—			
1—N. York	L 3-4‡	Herbel	Gibson
2—N. York	L 3-7	Seaver	Reuss
3—N. York	W 5-3	Carlton	Gentry
4—Montreal	L 7-9§	Raymond	Cleveland
5—Montreal	L 0-6	Stoneman	Bertaina
6—Montreal	W 7-2	Gibson	O'Donoghue
7—At Phila.	L 1-5	Short	Reuss
7—At Phila.	L 2-3§	Hoerner	Chlupsa
8—At Phila.	W 6-3	Carlton	Wise
9—At Pitts.	W 6-4	Bertaina	Cambria
10—At Pitts.	L 0-2	Walker	Briles
11—At N. Y.	W 5-2	Gibson	Seaver
12—At N. Y.	L 0-3	McAndrew	Reuss
13—At N. Y.	W 5-4§	Linzy	Herbel
15—At Chi.	L 3-5	Holtzman	Carlton

SEPTEMBER—			Winner	Loser	SEPTEMBER—			Winner	Loser
16—At Chi.	W	8-1	Gibson	Pappas	25—At Mon.	L	5-7	Reed	Taylor
17—At Chi.	W	9-2	Reuss	Hands	26—At Mon.	W	7-2	Carlton	McGinn
18—Phila.	L	7-9	G. Jackson	Briles	27—At Mon.	L	0-1†	Morton	Hilzendorf
19—Phila.	L	6-10	Wise	Bertaina	29—Pitts.	L	2-7	Dal Canton	Gibson
20—Phila.	L	4-7*	Selma	Parker	30—Pitts.	W	4-3	Briles	Grant
23—Chicago	W	2-1	Gibson	Jenkins					
23—Chicago	W	2-1	Reuss	Hands	OCTOBER—				
24—Chicago	L	1-7	Holtzman	Torrez	1—Pitts.	L	5-9	Brunet	Cleveland

* 10 innings.   † 11 innings.   ‡ 12 innings.   § 13 innings.   x 14 innings.   y 17 innings.

Phils Couldn't Ward Off Hospital Cases

By ALLEN LEWIS

For the second straight season, injuries ruined any hopes the Phillies had of pulling off a surprise in the National League's East Division.

The most serious injuries and the ones that damaged the Phillies' chances most severely happened in the same inning on May 2 at San Francisco when both the club's catchers, Tim McCarver and Mike Ryan, were injured.

Each suffered a broken bone in his hand, and the Phillies were forced to bring up two minor league catchers to carry the load. Later, Coach Doc Edwards had to be activated when injuries sidelined both Mike Compton and Del Bates, the two receivers promoted from the Quakers' top farm club at Eugene.

McCarver missed 111 games, not returning until September, while Ryan, who had been injured late in March and was hurt again in mid-August, missed a total of 86 games.

The Phillies sorely missed McCarver's bat and Ryan's defensive work.

The Quakers scored fewer runs than any team in the National League by a wide margin, and it wasn't until the final game of the season that they avoided finishing in the division cellar.

Catchers weren't the only players injured, but they were the most serious. Next in line was a mishap suffered by third baseman Don Money, who enjoyed a remarkable season in his sophomore year after being a rookie disappointment as a shortstop in 1969.

What appeared to be a routine ground ball took a freak hop and hit Money in the right eye May 21, very nearly causing him to lose his vision permanently.

Money was sidelined for more than a month, missing 27 games at a time when he was among the league leaders in batting with a .356 average.

Although Don slid gradually downward and, by collecting only one hit in his last 13 times at bat missed the .300 mark, his .295 average and his excellent play at third base marked the youngster as one of the game's comeback players of the year.

Manager Frank Lucchesi, finally receiving his big league chance after piloting in the minors for 19 seasons, didn't let the injuries—and almost every regular except first baseman Deron Johnson was sidelined at one time or another—impede his major task of getting the rebuilding program under way.

All around the league, Lucchesi was hailed for his competent work in the face of adversity, and particularly for his patience with young players.

The confidence he showed in Money after Don had batted only .229

PHILADELPHIA PHILLIES, 1970

Front row—Bowa, Gamble, Parrilla, Edwards, coach; Myatt, coach; Lucchesi; manager; DeMars, coach; Rippelmeyer, coach; Compton, Taylor, Doyle. Second row—Reynolds, McCarver, Laxton, G. Jackson, Money, Lis, Reid, Skrable, Briggs, Selma, Seger, trainer. Third row—Luzinski, Wilson, Stone, Hisle, Wise, Johnson, Browne, Joseph, Harmon, Hoerner, Palmer. Back row—Allen, Bunning, Bayless, Short, Champion, Wenz, James, M. Jackson, Fryman, Ryan.

as a rookie and wasn't certain if he could make the grade, was a case in point, but even more striking was his handling of rookie shortstop Larry Bowa.

Bowa, who ranked second among shortstops in fielding and committed only 13 errors in 143 games, was struggling at the plate so badly early in the season that most observers thought Lucchesi would have to bench him. As much as he was needed, some even envisioned him sent back to the minors.

Lucchesi refused to give up on Larry, however, and the determined youngster finally found his stride, and finished hitting .250 after going into June with a sub-.200 average. He also led the club with 24 stolen bases, and his 18-game hitting streak in September was the longest by a Phil in more than a decade.

Johnson, who enjoyed his second-best season in homers with 27 and in runs batted in with 93, was the Phillies' clutch hitter all season long.

Although his average was only .256, Johnson was easily the team leader in game-winning RBIs with 15.

Next in line was veteran infielder Tony Taylor, who enjoyed his top offensive season and batted .301 to lead the club.

Center fielder Larry Hisle, who hit only .205, and second baseman Denny Doyle, who batted just three points higher, were the major disappointments.

A shoulder injury that never completely healed hampered Doyle, who had only five hits in his last 73 times at bat.

Although the Phillies' pitching staff moved up from 10th place in the league in 1969 to seventh, the earned-run average was almost the same. And if it hadn't been for the excellence of the Phillies' top two relief pitchers, the Quakers might have had the loop's worst hurling.

Dick Selma was the workhorse, appearing in 73 games, saving 22 and compiling a 2.75 ERA to go with eight wins and nine losses. He led the staff in strikeouts with 153, 19 more than his total of innings pitched.

Joe Hoerner, like Selma a trade acquisition. had a 9-5 record and a 2.64 ERA and posted nine saves in 44 games.

Top winner on the staff for the second straight year was Rick Wise with 13 victories, but the righthander lost 14. Veteran Chris Short, with a 9-16 record, and Grant Jackson (5-15) were major disappointments. Jim Bunning pitched better than his 10-15 record indicates, while Barry Lersch (6-3), who didn't become a starter until August, was the most pleasant mound development among the younger hurlers.

The Phillies' youth movement drew almost 200,000 more fans than in 1969 to Connie Mack Stadium in its final season. The Phillies expect to double their 708,247 attendance total of 1970 next season in their new home—Philadelphia's 56,000-seat Veterans Stadium, due to open April 10.

SCORES OF PHILADELPHIA PHILLIES' 1970 GAMES

APRIL—			Winner	Loser	APRIL—			Winner	Loser
7—Chicago	W	2-0	Short	Jenkins	19—At N. Y.	W	3-2†	Wise	Koosman
9—Chicago	W	5-3	Wilson	Holtzman	19—At N. Y.	L	2-10	McAndrew	Short
10—Pitts.	W	2-0	Fryman	Veale	22—S. Fran.	W	6-1	Fryman	Robertson
11—Pitts.	L	0-4	Walker	G. Jackson	24—At S. D.	W	5-4	G. Jackson	Dobson
12—Pitts.	L	1-3†	Blass	Bunning	25—At S. D.	W	1-0	Bunning	Santorini
14—At Chi.	L	4-5	Holtzman	Short	26—At S. D.	W	3-2	Short	Roberts
15—At Chi.	L	1-5	Hands	Wise	27—At L. A.	W	4-3	Wise	Sutton
16—At Chi.	L	5-6†	Aguirre	Hoerner	28—At L. A.	W	3-2†	Selma	Foster
17—At N. Y.	L	0-6	Seaver	G. Jackson	29—At L. A.	L	1-6	Osteen	G. Jackson
18—At N. Y.	L	0-7	Ryan	Bunning					

MAY—

		Winner	Loser
1—At S. F.	L 1-3	Robertson	Bunning
1—At S. F.	L 1-7	Perry	Short
3—At S. F.	W 8-6x	Hoerner	Bryant
3—At S. F.	W 13-6	Palmer	Reberger
5—S. Diego	L 8-11	Roberts	Selma
6—S. Diego	W 4-3	Selma	Kirby
7—S. Diego	L 2-3	Dobson	Short
8—Los Ang.	L 4-8§	Pena	Hoerner
9—Los Ang.	L 0-9y	Norman	Selma
10—Los Ang.	L 0-7	Sutton	G. Jackson
11—At St. L.	L 0-3	Carlton	Bunning
12—At St. L.	L 5-9	Taylor	Palmer
13—Montreal	L 6-7	Raymond	Wise
15—N. York	L 0-4	Seaver	Fryman
16—N. York	L 0-6	Koosman	G. Jackson
18—At Pitts.	L 1-2	Moose	Bunning
19—At Pitts.	W 2-0	Short	Ellis
20—At Pitts.	L 2-3y	Dal Canton	Selma
21—St. Louis	W 4-3	Hoerner	Linzy
22—St. Louis	L 5-6	Linzy	M. Jackson
23—St. Louis	L 1-3	Gibson	Bunning
24—St. Louis	W 6-5‡	M. Jackson	Taylor
26—At Mon.	W 3-2	Wise	Stoneman
27—At Mon.	W 3-0	Fryman	McGinn
28—At Mon.	W 5-3‡	Hoerner	Dillman
29—At Atl.	L 2-5	Jarvis	Short
30—At Atl.	W 7-5	Bunning	Neibauer
31—At Atl.	L 1-9	Nash	Wise

JUNE—

		Winner	Loser
2—At Cinn.	L 2-7*	Simpson	Fryman
3—At Cinn.	W 11-4	Bunning	Borbon
5—At Hous.	L 7-8‡	Ray	Selma
6—At Hous.	W 7-3	Wise	Wilson
7—At Hous.	W 10-3	Fryman	Dierker
9—Atlanta	W 2-1	Bunning	Jarvis
10—Atlanta	L 1-5	Stone	Short
11—Atlanta	L 4-6	Nash	Wise
12—Cinn.	L 1-3	Simpson	Fryman
13—Cinn.	W 6-3	Bunning	Nolan
14—Cinn.	L 1-10	McGlothlin	Short
16—Houston	W 2-1x	Hoerner	Bouton
17—Houston	W 4-2	Fryman	Dierker
19—At N. Y.	L 3-13	Seaver	Bunning
20—At N. Y.	W 2-1	Short	Koosman
22—Montreal	W 6-0	Fryman	Stoneman
22—Montreal	W 3-2	Wise	Renko
23—Montreal	L 1-2	McGinn	Bunning
24—Montreal	L 0-8	Morton	Short
25—Montreal	W 3-2‡	Hoerner	Raymond
26—At St. L.	L 0-7	Gibson	Wise
27—At St. L.	L 8-9	Abernathy	Hoerner
28—At St. L.	L 4-5	Torrez	Selma
28—At St. L.	W 8-3†	Selma	McCool
30—At Mon.	L 1-8	Renko	Wise

JULY—

		Winner	Loser
1—At Mon.	L 1-11	Nye	Fryman
1—At Mon.	L 1-4	McGinn	G. Jackson
2—N. York	W 6-1	Bunning	Gentry
2—N. York	W 3-2	Short	Cardwell
3—N. York	L 3-4	Sadecki	Wise
4—N. York	L 2-7	Seaver	G. Jackson
5—N. York	L 4-5	Koosman	Fryman
6—Pitts.	L 5-7	Nelson	Bunning
8—Pitts.	L 2-4	Veale	Short
8—Pitts.	W 2-0	Wise	Blass
10—At Chi.	L 0-2	Jenkins	G. Jackson
11—At Chi.	W 10-4	Hoerner	Rodriquez
12—At Chi.	L 2-10	Holtzman	Short
16—At S. D.	W 10-7	Selma	Willis
17—At S. D.	W 8-3	Wise	Kirby
18—At S. D.	W 7-4	Bunning	Wilson
19—At L. A.	W 9-4	Wenz	Brewer
19—At L. A.	W 4-2	Lersch	Mikkelsen
20—At L. A.	L 3-9	Singer	Fryman

JULY—

		Winner	Loser
21—At S. F.	W 9-6	Wise	Marichal
22—At S. F.	W 5-2	Bunning	Perry
24—S. Diego	W 4-3	G. Jackson	Herbel
25—S. Diego	W 9-2	Lersch	Roberts
26—S. Diego	L 2-16	Dobson	Wise
27—Los Ang.	W 10-3	Fryman	Osteen
28—Los Ang.	L 2-6	Moeller	Bunning
31—S. Fran.	L 3-8	Marichal	G. Jackson
31—S. Fran.	L 2-7	Reberger	Short

AUGUST—

		Winner	Loser
1—S. Fran.	W 6-5‡	Selma	Jerry J'nson
1—S. Fran.	W 6-1	Wise	Carrithers
2—S. Fran.	W 7-6	Wenz	Davison
3—St. Louis	L 1-4	Torrez	G. Jackson
4—St. Louis	L 2-3	Reuss	Short
5—At Pitts.	L 0-4	Walker	Wise
6—At Pitts.	L 0-4	Ellis	Bunning
6—At Pitts.	L 3-8	Dal Canton	Champion
7—Chicago	W 4-1	G. Jackson	Jenkins
8—Chicago	W 6-3	Short	Hands
9—Chicago	L 1-4	Pappas	Wise
9—Chicago	W 6-1	Lersch	Gura
11—At Hous.	W 6-5	Bunning	Billingham
12—At Hous.	L 0-4	Dierker	G. Jackson
13—At Hous.	L 3-4	Ray	Selma
14—At Cinn.	W 5-4	Wise	Behney
15—At Cinn.	L 4-5y	Washburn	Champion
16—At Cinn.	L 2-4	Cloninger	Bunning
17—At Cinn.	L 3-9	Merritt	G. Jackson
18—At Atl.	L 2-3	Wilhelm	Short
19—At Atl.	L 2-3	Jarvis	Wise
20—At Atl.	L 2-6	Reed	Lersch
21—Houston	W 9-3	Bunning	Billingham
21—Houston	L 1-9	Wilson	G. Jackson
22—Houston	W 2-1	Hoerner	Gladding
23—Houston	W 4-0	Wise	Blasingame
25—Cinn.	W 3-2§	Selma	Granger
26—Cinn.	L 5-6	Merritt	Bunning
27—Cinn.	W 6-3	G. Jackson	McGlothlin
28—Atlanta	W 5-2	Short	Nash
29—Atlanta	W 10-9	Hoerner	Reed
30—Atlanta	W 4-2	Lersch	Jarvis

SEPTEMBER—

		Winner	Loser
1—At Chi.	W 3-2x	Fryman	Regan
2—At Chi.	L 2-17	Pappas	G. Jackson
3—At Chi.	L 2-7	Jenkins	Short
4—At Pitts.	L 3-4z	Blass	Wise
5—At Pitts.	L 4-6	Cambria	Lersch
6—At Pitts.	L 3-4†	Walker	Selma
7—St. Louis	W 5-1	Short	Reuss
7—St. Louis	W 3-2x	Hoerner	Chlupsa
8—St. Louis	L 3-6	Carlton	Wise
9—At N. Y.	W 3-2	Lersch	Frisella
9—At N. Y.	L 1-3	Sadecki	G. Jackson
10—At N. Y.	L 2-3y	Herbel	Hoerner
11—At Mon.	L 0-1	Morton	Short
12—At Mon.	L 3-4	Renko	Palmer
13—At Mon.	L 2-4	O'Donoghue	Hoerner
15—Pitts.	L 3-8	Walker	Lersch
16—Pitts.	L 3-5	Moose	Bunning
17—Pitts.	W 3-2	Short	Lamb
18—At St. L.	W 9-7	G. Jackson	Briles
19—At St. L.	W 10-6	Wise	Bertaina
20—At St. L.	W 7-4†	Selma	Parker
22—N. York	L 6-7	Ryan	Selma
23—N. York	L 4-5	McGraw	Selma
25—Chicago	W 5-3	Wise	Pappas
26—Chicago	W 7-1	Lersch	Hands
27—Chicago	L 3-5	Jenkins	Bunning
29—Montreal	W 3-10	Renko	Short
30—Montreal	L 4-5	Stoneman	Wise

OCTOBER—

		Winner	Loser
1—Montreal	W 2-1†	Selma	Reed

* Game halted by rain with one out in top of eighth.   † 10 innings.   ‡ 11 innings.   § 12 innings.
x 13 innings.   y 14 innings.   z Suspended game, completed September 5.

Mauch Ate Words With Relish

Gene Mauch, manager of the Expos, who is considered one of the top brains among baseball thinkers and strategists, sat himself on a stool, faced the corner and promised never again to make outlandish statements in public. It seems that Gene had stated rather off-the-cuffly at a local hot-stove dinner prior to the opening of the 1970 season that the Expos would "Win 70 in '70."

Newsmen hopped on that figure—70 victories—because a 52-110 season record the previous year had given no signs of a stepup in production. Mauch winced at the effect his chance remark had made on the local fans. The chant was picked up and the die was cast.

So, what did the Expos do? Sit back on their duffs and watch the embarrassment of their manager? No, they proceeded to win 73 games, a pickup of 21 victories over '69.

Carl Morton, who had an 0-3 record while appearing in eight games in 1969 with the Expos, broke the shackles that bind young hurlers and won 18 games, losing only 11, and had a respectable 3.60 earned-run average. Carl sparkled with a two-hitter against the Phils September 11 and threw a trio of three-hit games—against the Dodgers May 1, the Mets May 20 and the Phillies June 24. For this string of excellence, he was chosen by the National League players, coaches and managers as THE SPORTING NEWS Rookie Pitcher of the Year.

In all, the Expos' staff hurled seven three-hitters. The others were by Dan McGinn (2), Bill Stoneman and Steve Renko.

When it is considered that the Expos were last in team batting average and also in team ERA among all the National League clubs, the enormity of Montreal's improvement over its 1969 record can be better appreciated. Not a single Expo was among the top 15 qualifiers for the batting title, but chief architects of the rise included the overall production by Rusty Staub (.274, 94 RBIs and 30 home runs), the injured Ron Fairly in only 119 games (.288, 61 RBIs and 15 home runs), Bob Bailey (.287, 84 RBIs nad 28 home runs), hard-working John Bateman with 68 RBIs and 15 home runs and clutch-glove Bobby Wine, who contributed 51 runs batted in.

Nestled in the basement of the N. L. East Division most of the year, the Expos hopped into fifth place ahead of the Phils after the close of activity on September 30, the next-to-last day of the season. Bill Stoneman had earned the nod over the Phillies, 5-4, with relief help from Howie Reed and Mike Marshall. But, on the final day, Montreal lost a 2-1, 10-inning squeaker to Dick Selma in relief and dropped into the basement, losing out to the same Quakers by one-half game.

Montreal began the season as though winning was as bad as robbing. When Stoneman threw a 2-0 three-hitter against the Cubs April 12, it marked the only victory for the Expos until April 25, when they downed the Giants in San Francisco, 7-3. Ten losses had been accumulated in this period. However, they ran up two five-victory streaks, one of four-game duration and six times three wins in succession. Their longest losing span was 11 straight in May.

Montreal fans stormed Jarry Park throughout the season to cheer along their darlings. The club admitted that many times it could have pulled crowds of over 40,000, but tiny Jarry can't possibly hold that number. Two times the Expos had crowds that topped 30,000 and on nine dates

MONTREAL EXPOS, 1970

Front row—Wine, Fairey, Staub, Williams, coach; Zimmerman, coach; Mauch, manager; Bragan, coach; McLish, coach; Brand, Raymond, Fairly. Second row—Liscio, trainer; Day, Strohmayer, McGinn, Sutherland, Stoneman, Laboy, Staehle, Marshall, Hahn, Mashore, Stone, equipment manager; Kirby, traveling secretary. Back row—Piche, Gosger, O'Donoghue, Morton, Bateman, Reed, Renko, Nye, Phillips, Wegener, Jones, Bailey.

there were standing-room-only signs out. The park seats only 28,456 officially.

Not satisfied to come out ahead on his rash statement prior to the '70 season, Mauch already has supplied the cry of 1971 by predicting, "We'll win 81 in '71.' "

We'll see how it all comes out next year.

SCORES OF MONTREAL EXPOS' 1970 GAMES

APRIL—			Winner	Loser
6—At Cinn.	L	1-5	Merritt	Sparma
8—St. Louis	L	2-7	Gibson	Stoneman
9—St. Louis	L	3-7	Torrez	Renko
10—Chicago	L	1-2	Aguirre	Sparma
12—Chicago	W	2-0	Stoneman	Jenkins
14—At St. L.	L	5-6*	Campisi	Reed
15—At St. L.	L	0-10	Torrez	Sparma
17—At Chi.	L	7-8	Regan	Raymond
18—At Chi.	L	1-8	Holtzman	Renko
22—Los Ang.	L	2-9	Sutton	Stoneman
24—At S. F.	L	3-12	Perry	McGinn
25—At S. F.	W	7-3	McGinn	Bryant
26—At S. F.	L	1-11	McCormick	Stoneman
26—At S. F.	W	3-2	Morton	Robertson
28—At S. D.	W	4-2	Reed	Corkins
28—At S. D.	W	7-3	Renko	Coombs
29—At S. D.	L	0-10	Dobson	Sparma
30—At L. A.	L	1-2	Vance	Stoneman
MAY—				
1—At L. A.	W	3-1	Morton	Sutton
2—At L. A.	L	3-7	Moeller	Waslewski
3—At L. A.	L	1-15	Osteen	Renko
5—S. Fran.	L	1-4	Robertson	Stoneman
7—S. Fran.	W	15-8	Morton	Perry
8—S. Diego	L	1-11	Corkins	Waslewski
8—S. Diego	W	7-6†	Raymond	Ross
9—S. Diego	L	0-6	Coombs	Stoneman
10—S. Diego	L	4-5	Kirby	Reed
11—At N. Y.	W	3-0	McGinn	Seaver
12—At N. Y.	L	4-8	Sadecki	Morton
13—At Phila.	W	7-6	Raymond	Wise
15—At Pitts.	W	2-1	McGinn	Veale
16—At Pitts.	L	3-4	Walker	Raymond
17—At Pitts.	W	8-7	Strohmayer	Garber
18—N. York	W	8-4	Raymond	McGraw
19—N. York	L	4-7	Sadecki	McGinn
20—N. York	W	2-0	Morton	Seaver
21—Pitts.	W	7-6	Dillman	Walker
22—Pitts.	W	6-3	Stoneman	Moose
23—Pitts.	L	4-8	Ellis	McGinn
24—Pitts.	L	0-3	Veale	Morton
26—Phila.	L	2-3	Wise	Stoneman
27—Phila.	W	0-3	Fryman	McGinn
28—Phila.	L	2-5†	Hoerner	McGinn
29—At Cinn.	L	4-6	Carroll	Raymond
30—At Cinn.	L	4-5*	Granger	Dillman
31—At Cinn.	L	4-6	Merritt	Reed
JUNE—				
2—At Hous.	L	4-6	Ray	Morton
3—At Hous.	L	0-5	Billingham	Moore
4—At Hous.	L	0-8	Griffin	McGinn
5—At Atl.	W	3-2	Dillman	Wilhelm
6—At Atl.	W	12-4	Stoneman	Nash
7—At Atl.	W	10-1	Morton	Niekro
9—Cinn.	L	4-6	Nolan	Moore
10—Cinn.	L	0-7	McGlothlin	Wegener
11—Cinn.	W	8-4	Morton	Merritt
12—Houston	W	4-2	Reed	Marshall
13—Houston	W	2-5	Billingham	Stoneman
14—Houston	W	2-1	Renko	Lemaster
16—Atlanta	L	5-7	Pappas	Morton
17—Atlanta	L	5-6	Jaster	Raymond
18—Atlanta	W	10-7	Stoneman	Jaster
19—At Pitts.	L	4-8	Dal Canton	Dillman
20—At Pitts.	L	2-4	Blass	Morton
21—At Pitts.	W	3-2	Nye	Veale
22—At Phila.	L	0-6	Fryman	Stoneman
22—At Phila.	L	2-3	Wise	Renko
23—At Phila.	W	2-1	McGinn	Bunning
24—At Phila.	W	8-0	Morton	Short
25—At Phila.	L	2-3†	Hoerner	Raymond

JUNE—			Winner	Loser
26—N. York	W	6-5	Renko	McAndrew
27—N. York	L	3-8	Gentry	McGinn
28—N. York	W	3-2	Morton	Sadecki
30—Phila.	W	8-1	Renko	Wise
JULY—				
1—Phila.	W	11-1	Nye	Fryman
1—Phila.	W	4-1	McGinn	G. Jackson
2—St. Louis	W	13-10	Morton	Torrez
3—St. Louis	L	7-9	Taylor	Stoneman
5—St. Louis	W	8-0	Renko	Carlton
6—At Chi.	L	2-3	Hands	Morton
6—At Chi.	L	2-14	Decker	Wegener
7—At Chi.	L	7-10	Rodriquez	Reed
8—At Chi.	L	1-5	Pappas	Renko
8—At Chi.	W	5-4	McGinn	Holtzman
9—At N. Y.	L	4-5	Seaver	Nye
10—At N. Y.	W	9-7	Morton	Koosman
11—At N. Y.	W	6-2	Wegener	McAndrew
12—At N. Y.	W	5-3	Reed	Sadecki
17—At S. F.	W	7-3	Morton	Marichal
18—At S. F.	L	1-10	Perry	Wegener
19—At S. D.	L	5-6	Coombs	Renko
19—At S. D.	W	6-5	Strohmayer	Roberts
20—At S. D.	L	1-3	Dobson	Marshall
21—At L. A.	W	5-2	Morton	Sutton
22—At L. A.	L	10-12	Pena	Raymond
24—S. Fran.	L	7-8	Davison	Renko
25—S. Fran.	W	7-5	Reed	Pitlock
25—S. Fran.	W	10-5	Morton	Reberger
26—S. Fran.	L	2-6	Marichal	Marshall
28—S. Diego	W	5-4	Strohmayer	Coombs
29—S. Diego	W	4-3	Morton	Kirby
30—Los Ang.	L	3-7	Singer	McGinn
31—Los Ang.	L	5-8	Sutton	Marshall
AUGUST—				
1—Los Ang.	W	11-6	Nye	Foster
1—Los Ang.	W	6-5	Renko	Osteen
2—Los Ang.	L	3-6	Lamb	Strohmayer
3—Pitts.	W	8-0	McGinn	Moose
4—Pitts.	L	2-4	Veale	Marshall
5—Chicago	W	6-2	Wegener	Pappas
5—Chicago	L	3-11	Gura	Renko
6—Chicago	L	2-4	Holtzman	Morton
7—At St. L.	L	1-2	Gibson	McGinn
8—At St. L.	L	10-11	Hrabosky	Raymond
9—At St. L.	W	7-6	Wegener	Carlton
9—At St. L.	L	0-4	Reuss	Stoneman
11—At Atl.	L	0-1	Nash	Morton
12—At Atl.	L	7-8	Priddy	Stoneman
13—At Atl.	L	1-4	Stone	Wegener
14—At Hous.	W	10-2	Renko	Cook
15—At Hous.	L	3-7	Wilson	Morton
16—At Hous.	W	5-3	Raymond	Cook
18—At Cinn.	W	7-4	Renko	Behney
19—At Cinn.	W	8-6	Marshall	Nolan
21—Atlanta	W	6-4	Morton	Niekro
22—Atlanta	W	4-1	Renko	Nash
24—Atlanta	L	0-6	Stone	Stoneman
25—Houston	L	3-6‡	Cook	Marshall
26—Houston	L	4-5	Gladding	Renko
27—Houston	L	4-5	Dierker	Wegener
28—Cinn.	W	4-3*	Raymond	Granger
29—Cinn.	L	3-4†	Carroll	Morton
30—Cinn.	W	5-1	Renko	Merritt
SEPTEMBER—				
1—Pitts.	L	4-8	Veale	Stoneman
2—Pitts.	W	10-7	Marshall	Gibbon
4—At St. L.	W	9-7‡	Raymond	Cleveland
5—At St. L.	W	6-0	Stoneman	Bertaina
6—At St. L.	L	2-7	Gibson	O'Donoghue

CINCINNATI REDS, 1970

Front row—Bravo, Rose, Stewart, Carbo. Second row—Long, batboy; Gullett, McRae, Kluszewski, coach; Scherger, coach; Anderson, manager; Grammas, coach; Shepard, coach; Tolan, Chaney, Campbell, traveling secretary. Third row—Stowe, equipment manager; Corrales, McGlothlin, Washburn, Carroll, Cline, Helms, Concepcion, Woodward, Granger, Cooper, trainer. Back row—Cloninger, Nolan, May, Maloney, Simpson, Perez, Noriega, Merritt, Bench.

SEPTEMBER—			Winner	Loser	SEPTEMBER—			Winner	Loser
7—At N. Y.	L	4-5	Frisella	Marshall	19—Chicago	L	4-8	Holtzman	Morton
7—At N. Y.	L	1-5	McAndrew	McGinn	20—Chicago	W	6-4	Reed	Regan
8—At N. Y.	L	5-10	McGraw	Renko	22—At Pitts.	W	1-0§	Stoneman	Ellis
9—At Chi.	W	3-2	Marshall	Rodriquez	22—At Pitts.	L	1-3	Veale	Wegener
10—At Chi.	L	3-9	Pappas	O'Donoghue	23—At Pitts.	W	3-2	Morton	Brunet
11—Phila.	W	1-0	Morton	Short	24—At Pitts.	L	0-8	Walker	Renko
12—Phila.	W	4-3	Renko	Palmer	25—St. Louis	W	7-5	Reed	Taylor
13—Phila.	W	4-2	O'Donoghue	Hoerner	26—St. Louis	L	2-7	Carlton	McGinn
14—N. York	W	5-9*	Frisella	Marshall	27—St. Louis	W	1-0†	Morton	Hilgendorf
15—N. York	W	5-4*	O'Donoghue	Koosman	29—At Phila.	W	10-3	Renko	Short
16—N. York	W	4-2	Renko	Seaver	30—At Phila.	W	5-4	Stoneman	Wise
18—Chicago	L	2-3	Jenkins	Stoneman	OCTOBER—				
18—Chicago	L	4-5*	Regan	O'Donoghue	1—At Phila.	L	1-2*	Selma	Reed

* 10 innings.   † 11 innings.   ‡ 12 innings.   § Game of September 3, at Montreal, transferred to Pittsburgh.

WEST DIVISION

Big Red Machine Won—Many Repairs

By JIM FERGUSON

The season was only 10 days old when it happened. Jim Maloney, ace of the Cincinnati pitching staff, slapped a grounder toward short and broke out of the batter's box.

Three steps later, he pulled up short. The Achilles tendon in his left leg severed, Maloney had to be carried off the field and was virtually through for the season.

There it was again. The injury jinx that had been living with the Red pitchers for so many years had struck again. The team with the strongest bats and the frailest pitching arms in baseball was in trouble once more.

But this time it was to be different. By the time the inevitable pitching injuries came to Cincinnati in abundance, the Big Red Machine was rolling at such a clip even the highway patrol couldn't catch it.

The accumulated pitching problems eventually did wipe out the Reds, but it didn't happen until the team was facing the Orioles in the World Series. And if it had to happen, the World Series was a great place for it. At least, the team already had won the league championship and. furthermore, there would be universal sympathy for the problem.

Before the season was over, Manager Sparky Anderson would lose, for extended periods, the services of Jim Merritt, the team's only 20-game winner; Wayne Simpson, the rookie sensation; Jim McGlothlin, who physically was battered twice; and Clay Carroll, half of the best bullpen tandem in the league.

There are many reasons why this team was able to overcome the pitching infirmities and go on to a club record 102 victories as well as a three-game sweep over Pittsburgh in the Championship Series for the N. L. flag.

Any time a team wins, a lot of players have to have big years. But you only have to examine that very game in which Maloney was hurt to find some of them.

Anderson, who hit the jackpot in his first season as a major league manager, checked Maloney's injury, then pointed to the bullpen for Don Gullett.

This lefthanded pitcher was a lad of 19. A year earlier he still had been in high school. His pro experience consisted of 11 games for the

Reds' Sioux Falls team in the Northern league after being the club's first choice in the June draft of free agents.

But when Gullett made a big impression in spring training, Anderson didn't hesitate to promote him to the varsity roster. Gullett proved right away it was a good move. The quiet youngster worked five innings against the Dodgers, stopping them with three hits as he picked up his first major league victory on April 16.

It was this faith in young ballplayers that was a major factor in Anderson's successful debut as a manager. Sparky carried six rookies all season, probably an unprecedented situation for a championship team, and he put them to good use.

Two of them, Bernie Carbo and Hal McRae, platooned in left field, where they combined for 29 homers and 86 RBIs. Dave Concepcion was a part-time regular at shortstop. Simpson, possibly the best pitcher in the league the first half of the season, was a regular starter. Gullett became a top-notch "short" man in the bullpen. And Angel Bravo was a valuable pinch-hitter.

There were some other notable events on that fateful night of April 16 that were to portend well for the future. Tony Perez slammed a double and a two-run homer and Lee May bashed a grand-slammer as the Reds routed Dodger ace Bill Singer.

The Big Red Machine was rolling in high gear and it wasn't to slow down for a long, long time. About the only absentee from that onslaught was Johnny Bench, who took the collar in five trips to the plate.

That was a mere oversight. Bench, premier catcher in the majors at the tender age of 22, went on to have a year every player dreams about.

He hit .293 and led the majors with 45 homers and 148 RBIs. For his incredible performance, Bench was given almost everything but the Heisman Trophy. Among other things, he was voted the outstanding player in the majors as well as the National League MVP.

He also convinced his manager that he is the "greatest athlete who ever played the game of baseball." Actually, Sparky didn't need much convincing. He said in spring training that Bench was so versatile he would use him at various other positions to give Bench a little rest from the strain of everyday catching.

Bench eventually played all three outfield positions as well as first and third bases. He played them all as though he had been there all his life.

Winning the West Division title, as the Reds did by 14½ games, was almost ridiculously easy. The team took over first place on Opening Day when Jim Merritt pitched a three-hitter against Montreal while May, Carbo and Bobby Tolan hit home runs.

The team was out of the lead only one day all season. That was April 11, when the Reds lost to the Giants in San Francisco. But the club bounced back to win a doubleheader the next afternoon and never was headed again until the Orioles smashed them in five games in the World Series.

Every time a western rival made a run at the Reds, Cincinnati would go on a streak of its own and the lead kept widening and widening.

The Reds were bombarding pitchers from almost every spot in the batting order, but the big gun was Perez. In April, when the team built a five-game lead, Tony batted .455, swatted 10 homers and drove in 26 runs.

Cincinnati players slowly leave the playing field after the last game ever to be played in Crosley Field, longtime home of the Reds.   They beat the Giants, 5-4, on June 24, 1970.

By the All-Star break, the third baseman was still sizzling with 29 homers and 90 RBIs to go with his .356 average. The Reds were in front by 10 games and their margin dipped under that mark only once the rest of the way.

There was one question around the league that had to be answered, however. The Reds had fantastic success in Crosley Field, the cozy little park that was pure delight for the robust Cincinnati hitting.

When the Reds played there for the last time on June 24, beating Juan Marichal on back-to-back homers in the eighth by Bench and May, the Crosley record was 28-8.

Would the Reds still be as potent when they moved to the New Riverfront Stadium with its far more spacious dimensions?

The answer was no. The Reds hit only one homer in the first seven games there and that was stroked by Tommy Helms, who would rather not talk at all about his hitting in 1970. But the Reds won five of those seven games, anyway. The adjustments were made with a minimum of trouble.

Pete Rose found the AstroTurf to his liking. He didn't get his third straight batting championship, but met his annual goal of 200 hits with five to spare as he batted .316. Tolan matched that .316 and Perez was a point higher. Carbo joined them in the .300 club with a .310 mark. Sluggers Bench, Perez and May combined for 119 homers and 371 RBIs.

The AstroTurf, with its perfect hops, also gave Helms, an All-Star

Mr. Everything of 1970—Johnny Bench shows how it's done.

Fielding team member at second base, a chance to show off his superb skills. And Woody Woodward showed his best defensive play ever.

The one traumatic period for the Reds came in August in Los Angeles during a four-game series with the Dodgers. In the first game of the set, Clay Carroll was spiked on the ankle while covering first. He missed two weeks, which threw the bullpen load even heavier on Wayne Granger, but the skinny righthander had no trouble taking it. The N. L. Fireman of the Year winner finished with 35 saves to go with his six victories.

Two days after Carroll was spiked, Billy Grabarkewitz smashed a line drive that hit Jim McGlothlin just above the right eye. It was the second setback for McGlothlin, an off-season addition from the American League. He missed 11 days in July after being hit on the knee by a line drive. This time he was out 10 days. More importantly, Jim never really was effective again, after posting an 11-4 record prior to his first injury.

Complicating the situation was the shoulder problem that had hit Simpson two weeks earlier. The strapping righthander won 13 of his first 14 decisions (losing when a dropped pop fly let in two unearned runs), and they included a one-hitter, a two-hitter and a three-hitter. But he made only two token appearances after July.

But Merritt, Gary Nolan and Tony Cloninger kept the Reds firmly in command. Merritt's elbow trouble didn't emerge until September. And the lefthander had become a 20-game winner before the end of August, winning five times that critical month.

Nolan, with a history of arm trouble throughout his career, avoided it all year and emerged as the club's pitching leader. He posted an 18-7 record, plus a half-dozen games in which he limited the opposition to two or fewer runs for seven innings without getting a decision.

Cloninger, battered freely as a mopup relief man in the early season, earned his letter when the team needed pitching in the last half. He became a regular starter through necessity in mid-July and was a real saver for the staff.

His record as a regular starter was 8-6. Two of the losses were by 2-1 scores and he also pitched eight shutout innings in one game without getting a decision.

And so the Reds were able to glide through the closing days of the season without a challenge, clinching the West title on September 17.

SCORES OF CINCINNATI REDS' 1970 GAMES

APRIL—		Winner	Loser	MAY—		Winner	Loser
6—Montreal	W 5-1	Merritt	Sparma	1—Pitts.	W 6-4	Simpson	Ellis
7—At L. A.	W 4-0	Nolan	Osteen	2—Pitts.	W 7-2	McGlothlin	Veale
8—At L. A.	W 5-2	McGlothlin	Singer	3—Pitts.	W 11-7	Merritt	Blass
9—At L. A.	W 3-0	Simpson	Sutton	4—St. Louis	W 7-3	Nolan	Torrez
10—At S. F.	L 3-4	Linzy	Granger	5—St. Louis	W 5-1	Simpson	Carlton
11—At S. F.	L 1-2	Perry	Merritt	7—At Chi.	W 5-2	McGlothlin	Decker
12—At S. F.	W 6-5	Cloninger	McCormick	8—At Chi.	L 7-10	Holtzman	Merritt
12—At S. F.	W 5-2	Nolan	Bryant	9—At Chi.	L 1-8	Hands	Nolan
13—S. Diego	L 1-3	Santorini	McGlothlin	10—At Chi.	W 7-6	Carroll	Jenkins
14—S. Diego	W 6-1	Simpson	Kirby	11—At Pitts.	L 1-4	Veale	McGlothlin
15—Los Ang.	W 3-2	Merritt	Osteen	12—At Pitts.	W 5-3	Merritt	Blass
16—Los Ang.	W 12-2	Gullett	Singer	15—Atlanta	L 1-3	Nash	Nolan
17—S. Fran.	W 8-5	Granger	McMahon	16—Atlanta	W 2-0	McGlothlin	Niekro
18—S. Fran.	L 9-16	Jim Johnson	Cloninger	17—Atlanta	W 5-1	Merritt	Jarvis
19—S. Fran.	W 6-0	Simpson	Perry	17—Atlanta	W 7-6z	Gullett	Neibauer
20—At Atl.	W 6-2	Merritt	Stone	18—Chicago	L 5-12	Hands	Washburn
21—At Atl.	W 13-8	Nolan	Niekro	19—Chicago	W 3-1	Nolan	Decker
24—At St. L.	L 1-3	Culver	Simpson	21—At Hous.	W 3-0	McGlothlin	Lemaster
25—At St. L.	W 3-2	Merritt	Carlton	22—At Hous.	W 5-2	Merritt	Dierker
26—At St. L.	L 1-4	Gibson	McGlothlin	23—At Hous.	W 14-3	Simpson	Wilson
28—Houston	W 4-2	Nolan	Lemaster	24—At Hous.	L 7-10	Gladding	Carroll
29—Houston	W 5-3	Merritt	Griffin	25—At S. D.	W 2-1	McGlothlin	Kirby

MAY—			Winner	Loser
26—At S. D.	L	1-8	Corkins	Merritt
26—At S. D.	L	1-4	Coombs	Borbon
27—At S. D.	W	6-4	Carroll	Dukes
29—Montreal	W	6-4	Carroll	Raymond
30—Montreal	W	5-4‡	Granger	Dillman
31—Montreal	W	6-4	Merritt	Reed
JUNE—				
2—Phila.	W	7-2*	Simpson	Fryman
3—Phila.	L	4-11	Bunning	Borbon
5—N. York	W	5-4†	McGlothlin	Ryan
6—N. York	W	5-1	Merritt	Sadecki
7—N. York	W	10-2	Simpson	Gentry
9—At Mon.	W	6-4	Nolan	Moore
10—At Mon.	W	7-0	McGlothlin	Wegener
11—At Mon.	L	4-8	Morton	Merritt
12—At Phila.	W	3-1	Simpson	Fryman
13—At Phila.	L	3-6	Bunning	Nolan
14—At Phila.	W	10-1	McGlothlin	Short
16—At N. Y.	L	1-3	McAndrew	Merritt
17—At N. Y.	W	7-4	Carroll	Taylor
19—Los Ang.	L	1-6	Singer	Nolan
20—Los Ang.	W	5-4	McGlothlin	Moeller
21—Los Ang.	L	3-9	Sutton	Merritt
21—Los Ang.	W	9-3	Simpson	Osteen
22—S. Fran.	L	6-13	Robertson	Gullett
23—S. Fran.	W	5-3	Nolan	McCormick
24—S. Fran.	W	5-4	Granger	Marichal
26—At Hous.	W	3-2	Simpson	Bouton
27—At Hous.	W	5-2	Merritt	Griffin
28—At Hous.	W	3-2	Carroll	Wilson
30—Atlanta	L	2-8	Jarvis	McGlothlin
JULY—				
1—Atlanta	W	9-2	Simpson	Reed
2—Atlanta	W	2-1	Merritt	Stone
3—Houston	W	3-0	Nolan	Wilson
3—Houston	L	4-10	Griffin	Cloninger
4—Houston	W	3-0	McGlothlin	Billingham
5—Houston	W	3-1	Simpson	Lemaster
6—S. Diego	W	5-0	Merritt	Santorini
7—S. Diego	W	3-0	Nolan	Dobson
8—S. Diego	L	1-3	Kirby	Washburn
9—S. Diego	L	9-10‡	Ross	Granger
10—At Atl.	L	3-11	Reed	Merritt
10—At Atl.	W	3-1	Cloninger	Stone
11—At Atl.	W	7-6	Nolan	Niekro
12—At Atl.	W	6-5	Washburn	Jarvis
16—At Pitts.	W	3-2	Carroll	Ellis
17—At Pitts.	L	3-4	Giusti	Simpson
18—At Pitts.	W	3-1‡	Merritt	Giusti
19—At Pitts.	L	3-7	Walker	Gullett
20—At St. L.	W	4-3	Nolan	Reuss
20—At St. L.	W	4-0‡	Granger	Chlupsa
21—At St. L.	W	6-5	Carroll	Carlton
22—At Chi.	L	2-10	Hands	Merritt
23—At Chi.	L	0-1	Pappas	Carroll
24—St. Louis	W	4-0	Nolan	Torrez
25—St. Louis	W	5-3	Cloninger	Reuss
26—St. Louis	W	12-5	Simpson	Carlton
27—St. Louis	L	9-16	Taylor	Merritt
28—Pitts.	L	3-4	Dal Canton	McGlothlin
29—Pitts.	W	4-3	Nolan	Ellis
30—Pitts.	W	8-4	Cloninger	Veale

JULY—			Winner	Loser
31—Chicago	L	1-7	Hands	Simpson
31—Chicago	L	7-11	Rodriquez	Merritt
AUGUST—				
1—Chicago	W	6-4	Granger	Regan
2—Chicago	W	4-3§	Granger	Colborn
3—At S. D.	L	3-10	Kirby	Cloninger
4—At S. D.	W	12-1	Merritt	Dobson
5—At S. F.	L	3-5	Perry	McGlothlin
6—At S. F.	L	3-9	Reberger	Washburn
7—At L. A.	W	4-2	Carroll	Moeller
8—At L. A.	W	10-5	Cloninger	Singer
9—At L. A.	L	3-7	Brewer	Washburn
9—At L. A.	L	3-13	Foster	McGlothlin
11—N. York	W	8-1	Nolan	McAndrew
12—N. York	L	1-2	Gentry	Cloninger
13—N. York	W	6-1	Merritt	Sadecki
14—Phila.	L	4-5	Wise	Behney
15—Phila.	W	5-4y	Washburn	Champion
16—Phila.	W	4-2	Cloninger	Bunning
17—Phila.	W	9-3	Merritt	G. Jackson
18—Montreal	L	4-7	Renko	Behney
19—Montreal	W	6-8	Marshall	Nolan
21—At N. Y.	L	1-4	Koosman	Cloninger
22—At N. Y.	W	3-2	Merritt	McGraw
23—At N. Y.	L	4-5	Taylor	Granger
23—At N. Y.	W	7-5	Gullett	Seaver
25—At Phila.	L	2-3x	Selma	Granger
26—At Phila.	W	6-5	Merritt	Bunning
27—At Phila.	L	3-6	G. Jackson	McGlothlin
28—At Mon.	L	3-4‡	Raymond	Granger
29—At Mon.	W	4-3§	Carroll	Morton
30—At Mon.	L	1-5	Renko	Merritt
SEPTEMBER—				
1—S. Fran.	L	3-5	Perry	Carroll
2—S. Fran.	W	2-0	Nolan	Marichal
3—S. Fran.	W	7-3	Cloninger	Pitlock
4—S. Diego	L	2-15	Corkins	Merritt
5—S. Diego	W	6-2	Wilcox	Roberts
6—S. Diego	W	6-5	McGlothlin	Dobson
7—At S. F.	L	3-6	Marichal	Nolan
7—At S. F.	L	3-4	Cumberland	Carroll
8—At S. F.	W	5-2	Washburn	Reberger
9—At L. A.	W	6-0	Wilcox	Osteen
10—At L. A.	W	13-4	McGlothlin	Moeller
11—At S. D.	L	2-3	Dobson	Nolan
11—At S. D.	L	2-4	Coombs	Cloninger
13—At S. D.	L	4-5	Kirby	Wilcox
15—At Hous.	L	2-9	Dierker	McGlothlin
16—At Hous.	W	3-2	Nolan	Blasingame
18—At Atl.	W	11-6	Cloninger	Jarvis
19—At Atl.	W	7-4	McGlothlin	Barber
20—At Atl.	L	2-11	Reed	Maloney
21—Houston	W	2-0	Gullett	Forsch
22—Houston	W	6-5	Wilcox	Gladding
23—Houston	W	6-2	Cloninger	Billingham
25—Los Ang.	L	3-9	Osteen	McGlothlin
26—Los Ang.	W	6-3	Gullett	Sutton
27—Los Ang.	W	8-5	Nolan	Strahler
29—Atlanta	W	2-1	McQueen	Cloninger
OCTOBER—				
1—Atlanta	W	4-1	Washburn	Jarvis

* Game halted by rain with one out in top of eighth. † Game halted by rain with one out in bottom of eighth. ‡ 10 innings. § 11 innings. x 12 innings. y 14 innings. z 15 innings.

Dodgers Did As Well As They Could

By BOB HUNTER

Something happened to the Dodgers on their way down Pennant Boulevard early in 1970.

They were run over by the Big Red Machine at the first intersection they crossed paths.

Walter Alston's Los Angeles entry had the best record among National League clubs in the spring, they swept the Angels three games, had a

couple of hot-hitting rookies, and went into the regular season at full speed.

But Cincinnati's Big Red Machine bowled 'em over in the opening three games in Dodger Stadium, and they never recovered, finally being hard-pressed to save second place from San Francisco, finishing 14½ games back.

After the Reds ruined their opening series, then the San Diego Padres came in and stretched the Dodgers' losses to five before they scored their first triumph of 1970.

They never did catch the machine that hit them, but still they played as well as it was possible for them to play, making it an exciting season before almost 1,700,000 paying fans at home.

Several factors, in addition to the Cincinnati powerhouse, prevented the Dodgers from coming closer than they did. They couldn't win at home, finishing three games under .500, while eating up the opposition on the road. Also they were without the pitching of Bill Singer much of the season.

Ironically, it was The Singer Throwing Machine who brought the Dodgers their first victory of 1970 by delivering a 6-0 shutout over the Padres in the sixth game.

Soon they were 8-7 on the young season, but the Reds were 14-5, never looking back as Singer suddenly joined reliever Pete Mikkelsen in the hospital with hepatitis. Singer missed 52 days at that time, then finished the last seven weeks on the disabled list with a broken finger.

Despite the illness of the two "hep-cats," there were upbeat notes that splattered sunshine through the clouds.

In between appearances at the infirmary, Singer highlighted the season by no-hitting the Phils July 20.

Wes Parker, the All-Star fielding team perennial, blossomed as one of the league's outstanding clutch hitters, knocking in 111 runs with a .319 average and leading the majors in two-base hits, although hitting only 10 homers in his cleanup spot.

"I was especially pleased to bat in that many runs with so few homers, because it showed I was coming through with hits in the key situations," explained the velvet-smooth first baseman.

He was the first Dodger to knock in more than 100 tallies since Frank Howard and Tommy Davis did it in 1962.

Parker's bat not only gave him his peak all-round season, but almost won the team batting title for the first time since the slam-bang 1955 Brooklyn club hit .271.

Ted Sizemore hit .306 and Willie Davis and Manny Mota each batted .305 to give the usually docile-hitting Dodgers four .300 batters.

Their amazing team average of .2702 was a fraction of a decimal under Cincinnati's .2703.

One more hit would have made them the batting champs, and the irony of it is they had that hit—for 24 hours. Then the San Francisco scorer sent word he was taking a hit away from Davis and ruling an error on the play.

While they had 233 doubles and 67 triples, more than they ever had hit on the West Coast, they recorded only 87 homers, lowest in the majors.

Perhaps the biggest single surprise was Billy Grabarkewitz, who was in the Top Ten most of the season, and a strong offensive weapon all season.

LOS ANGELES DODGERS, 1970

Front row—Norman, Lefebvre, Ozark, Walker, coach; Hartsfield, coach; Alston, manager; Adams, coach; Beringer, coach; Gilliam, coach; Sizemore, Garvey, Buckner. Second row—Bonfils, batboy; Brewer, Parker, Kosco, Torborg, Foster, Mota, Davis, Singer, Stinson, Wills, Joshua. Third row—Franks, McDermott and Beaver, batboys; Ferguson, Paciorek, Sutton, Osteen, Sudakis, Lamb, Hough, Russell, Grabarkewitz, Dr. Woods, team physician. Back row—Buhler, trainer; Scott, traveling secretary; Dr. Jobe, team physician; Crawford, Gabrielson, Haller, Mikkelsen, Moeller, Stephenson, Strahler, Vance, Kawano, equipment manager.

However, the usually impeccable Dodger pitching dropped to fifth in the league with a 3.82 earned-run average, but the year did provide an opportunity for several young hurlers—Sandy Vance, Joe Moeller, Ray Lamb and Alan Foster—to mature.

So, 1970 was not a lost cause, with the bright spots outnumbering the dark ones.

SCORES OF LOS ANGELES DODGERS' 1970 GAMES

APRIL—			Winner	Loser
7—Cinn.	L	0-4	Nolan	Osteen
8—Cinn.	L	2-5	McGlothlin	Singer
9—Cinn.	L	0-3	Simpson	Sutton
10—S. Diego	L	2-7	Roberts	Foster
11—S. Diego	L	0-4	Coombs	Osteen
12—S. Diego	W	6-0	Singer	Dobson
13—At Hous.	W	2-0	Osteen	Lemaster
14—At Hous.	W	3-2	Foster	Ray
15—At Cinn.	L	2-3	Merritt	Osteen
16—At Cinn.	L	2-12	Gullett	Singer
18—At Atl.	W	5-4	Sutton	Jarvis
19—At Atl.	W	10-1	Foster	Nash
22—At Mon.	W	9-2	Sutton	Stoneman
24—N. York	W	1-0y	Lamb	Taylor
25—N. York	W	1-0	Osteen	Ryan
26—N. York	L	1-3	Seaver	Vance
27—Phila.	L	3-4	Wise	Sutton
28—Phila.	L	2-3†	Selma	Foster
29—Phila.	W	6-1	Osteen	G. Jackson
30—Montreal	W	2-1	Vance	Stoneman

MAY—				
1—Montreal	L	1-3	Morton	Sutton
2—Montreal	W	7-3	Moeller	Waslewski
3—Montreal	W	15-1	Osteen	Renko
4—At N. Y.	W	4-0	Vance	Ryan
6—At N. Y.	L	4-5	Seaver	Sutton
7—At N. Y.	W	7-4†	Lamb	McAndrew
8—At Phila.	W	8-4§	Pena	Hoerner
9—At Phila.	W	9-4x	Norman	Selma
10—At Phila.	W	7-0	Sutton	G. Jackson
12—Houston	L	3-8	Wilson	Foster
13—Houston	L	5-6	Lemaster	Osteen
14—S. Fran.	W	6-3	Vance	Marichal
15—S. Fran.	W	11-5	Sutton	Puente
16—S. Fran.	L	4-5	Perry	Foster
17—S. Fran.	W	8-0	Osteen	Robertson
18—At S. D.	W	4-3	Vance	Coombs
19—At S. D.	W	8-3	Sutton	Kirby
20—At S. D.	L	4-10	Roberts	Foster
21—Atlanta	W	6-3	Osteen	Niekro
22—Atlanta	L	0-1	Jarvis	Vance
23—Atlanta	L	1-5	Stone	Sutton
24—Atlanta	W	8-1	Foster	Pappas
26—At S. F.	W	19-3	Osteen	Robertson
27—At S. F.	L	3-11	Marichal	Vance
28—At S. F.	L	3-4	Perry	Brewer
29—At St. L.	W	8-6	Pena	McCool
30—At St. L.	W	7-6	Osteen	Guzman
31—At St. L.	W	8-6‡	Pena	Culver

JUNE—				
1—At Chi.	W	5-4*	Sutton	Hands
3—At Chi.	L	5-6‡	Aguirre	Pena
4—At Pitts.	W	5-0	Osteen	Blass
5—At Pitts.	L	0-3	Moose	Moeller
6—At Pitts.	L	6-7§	Giusti	Pena
7—At Pitts.	L	1-3	Veale	Foster
9—St. Louis	L	0-4	Taylor	Osteen
10—St. Louis	W	4-2	Moeller	Torrez
11—St. Louis	W	2-1§	Brewer	Linzy
12—Chicago	L	1-2	Holtzman	Foster
12—Chicago	L	1-7	Jenkins	Osteen
14—Chicago	W	5-4	Brewer	Regan
15—Pitts.	L	2-5	Nelson	Moeller
16—Pitts.	W	1-0	Sutton	Veale
17—Pitts.	W	4-0	Osteen	Ellis
19—At Cinn.	W	6-1	Singer	Nolan
20—At Cinn.	L	4-5	McGlothlin	Moeller
21—At Cinn.	W	9-3	Sutton	Merritt
21—At Cinn.	L	3-9	Simpson	Osteen
22—At Atl.	W	4-2	Foster	Niekro

JUNE—			Winner	Loser
23—At Atl.	W	7-0	Singer	McQueen
24—At Atl.	W	7-0	Moeller	Jarvis
26—S. Diego	W	4-1	Osteen	Kirby
27—S. Diego	W	7-5	Sutton	Dobson
28—S. Diego	W	2-0	Foster	Roberts
29—Houston	L	5-10	Billingham	Singer
30—Houston	L	2-6	Lemaster	Moeller

JULY—				
1—Houston	W	6-3	Osteen	Gladding
3—At S. F.	W	8-6	Brewer	Davison
4—At S. F.	W	7-2	Foster	Perry
5—At S. F.	W	4-0	Singer	McCormick
6—At Hous.	W	10-8†	Brewer	Bouton
7—At Hous.	W	7-2	Moeller	Griffin
8—At Hous.	W	6-5	Lamb	DiLauro
9—At Hous.	L	5-9	Billingham	Foster
10—At S. D.	W	9-7	Singer	Coombs
11—At S. D.	L	3-4	Herbel	Brewer
12—At S. D.	L	1-4	Kirby	Sutton
16—N. York	W	3-1	Singer	McAndrew
17—N. York	L	1-0†	Sutton	McGraw
18—N. York	L	3-4	Frisella	Brewer
19—Phila.	L	4-9	Wenz	Brewer
19—Phila.	L	2-4	Lersch	Mikkelsen
20—Phila.	W	5-0	Singer	Fryman
21—Montreal	L	2-5	Morton	Sutton
22—Montreal	W	12-10	Pena	Raymond
24—At N. Y.	L	1-2†	McGraw	Brewer
25—At N. Y.	L	4-6	Frisella	Pena
26—At N. Y.	W	5-3	Sutton	Gentry
27—At Phila.	L	3-10	Fryman	Osteen
28—At Phila.	W	6-2	Moeller	Bunning
30—At Mon.	W	7-3	Singer	McGinn
31—At Mon.	W	8-5	Sutton	Marshall

AUGUST—				
1—At Mon.	L	6-11	Nye	Foster
1—At Mon.	W	6-3	Renko	Osteen
2—At Mon.	W	6-3	Lamb	Strohmayer
3—S. Fran.	L	2-5	Pitlock	Singer
4—S. Fran.	L	4-11	Marichal	Sutton
5—Atlanta	W	12-2	Foster	Stone
6—Atlanta	L	1-4	Nash	Osteen
7—Cinn.	L	2-4	Carroll	Moeller
8—Cinn.	L	5-10	Cloninger	Singer
9—Cinn.	W	7-3	Brewer	Washburn
9—Cinn.	W	13-3	Foster	McGlothlin
11—At Pitts.	W	5-4	Osteen	Dal Canton
12—At Pitts.	W	11-4	Mikkelsen	Moose
13—At Chi.	L	4-5	Norman	Gura
15—At Chi.	W	9-7	Mikkelsen	Jenkins
15—At Chi.	L	2-13	Holtzman	Moeller
16—At Chi.	L	2-5	Hands	Osteen
17—At St. L.	L	8-11	Gibson	Sutton
18—At St. L.	W	7-2	Vance	Reuss
19—At St. L.	W	4-2	Brewer	Carlton
21—Pitts.	W	2-1	Osteen	Veale
22—Pitts.	L	1-2z	Dal Canton	Mikkelsen
23—Pitts.	L	0-11	Blass	Foster
24—Chicago	L	2-4	Jenkins	Vance
25—Chicago	W	4-1	Moeller	Hands
26—Chicago	W	8-5	Osteen	Holtzman
28—St. Louis	L	0-1	Reuss	Sutton
29—St. Louis	L	2-3	Taylor	Brewer
30—St. Louis	L	1-2	Carlton	Vance

SEPTEMBER—				
1—At Atl.	W	6-3	Lamb	Niekro
1—At Atl.	W	3-2	Moeller	Reed
2—At Atl.	L	3-4	Wilhelm	Sutton
3—At Atl.	L	4-11	Stone	Foster
4—At Hous.	L	3-7	Wilson	Vance

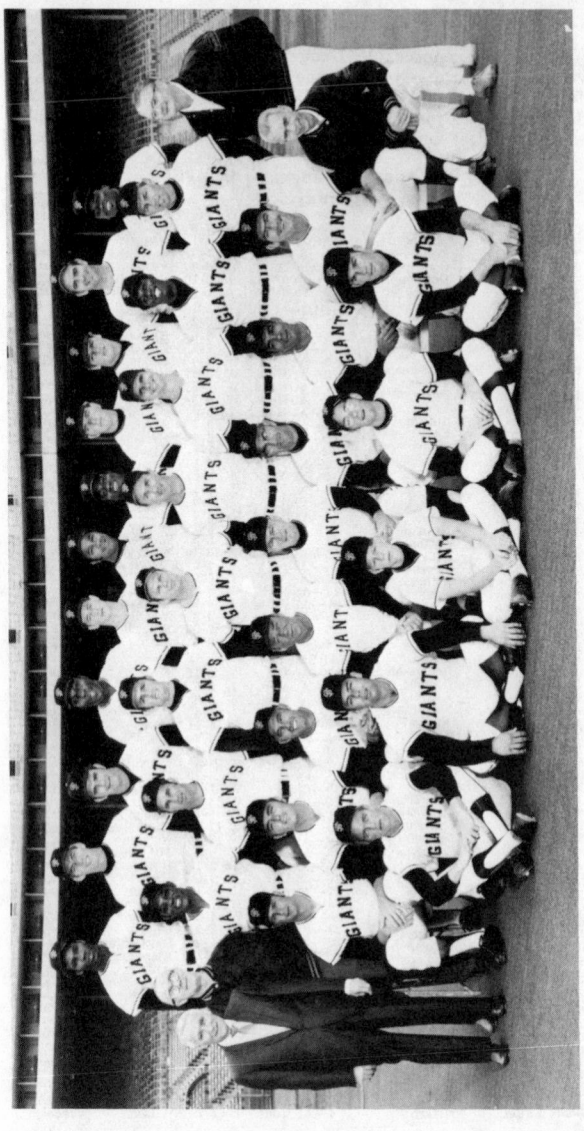

SAN FRANCISCO GIANTS, 1970

Front row—Mason, Hunt, Saunders and Sockolov, batboys; Heise. Second row—Davison, Bryant, Davenport, coach; Westrum, coach; Fox, manager; Virgil, coach; Jansen, coach; Dietz; Wylder, trainer. Third row—Bergonzi, traveling secretary; Logan, equipment manager; Mays, Stephenson, Robertson, Gallagher, McMahon, Henderson, F. Johnson, Lanier, Hughes, trainer. Back row—Bonds, Reberger, Gibson, McCovey, Pitlock, Marichal, Hart, Carrithers, Jerry Johnson, Perry, Fuentes.

SEPTEMBER—		Winner	Loser		SEPTEMBER—		Winner	Loser
5—At Hous.	L 2-7	Dierker	Osteen		18—Houston	W 3-2	Vance	Billingham
6—At Hous.	W 4-3	Mikkelsen	Gladding		19—Houston	W 6-5	Strahler	Wilson
7—Atlanta	W 4-3	Sutton	Nash		20—Houston	W 7-6x	Lamb	Culver
7—Atlanta	W 6-1	Foster	Jarvis		21—S. Fran.	L 0-7	Marichal	Moeller
8—Atlanta	L 2-3	Stone	Vance		22—S. Fran.	W 1-0	Foster	Bryant
9—Cinn.	L 0-6	Wilcox	Osteen		23—S. Fran.	L 10-14†	Robertson	Lamb
10—Cinn.	L 4-13	McGlothlin	Moeller		25—At Cinn.	W 9-3	Osteen	McGlothlin
11—At S. F.	L 3-4	Marichal	Sutton		26—At Cinn.	L 3-6	Gullett	Sutton
12—At S. F.	L 3-8	Pitlock	Foster		27—At Cinn.	L 5-8	Nolan	Strahler
13—At S. F.	W 5-3†	Brewer	Bryant		29—At S. D.	W 8-2	Vance	Roberts
14—S. Diego	W 12-4	Osteen	Nyman		30—At S. D.	L 1-2	Dobson	Osteen
15—S. Diego	W 5-4	Mikkelsen	Dukes					
16—S. Diego	L 0-4	Roberts	Moeller		OCTOBER—			
17—Houston	L 5-10	Cook	Foster		1—At S. D.	W 7-4	Sutton	Dukes

* Game halted by rain with two outs in top of seventh.   † 10 innings.   ‡ 11 innings.   § 12 innings.   x 14 innings.   y 15 innings.   z 16 innings.

Giants Escape Bridesmaid Role—To Third

By PAT FRIZZELL

Off to a slow start, the Giants played almost .600 baseball over the last half of the season and still finished third in the West Division.

This was a drop from second, where San Francisco clubs had wound up five consecutive times.

A sixth successive runner-up finish appeared in prospect when the Giants made up a 10½-game deficit and passed the Dodgers with four games to play.

But four defeats by Houston in the final series at the Astrodome, where the Giants stand 3-15 over the past two seasons, spelled third place.

Charlie Fox became manager May 24, succeeding Clyde King, when the club stood 19-23.

Under Fox, the Giants' record was 67-53. They were 45-32 after the All-Star Game break.

Illness which rendered Juan Marichal virtually valueless until after midseason tossed the club's pitching rotation out of kilter.

Gaylord Perry was the only consistent winner over the entire campaign. Marichal returned to the rotation later and proved effective in the closing months, finishing with a 12-10 record.

Juan became ill following the Giants' unprecedented and somewhat controversial spring trip to Japan, where they lost six of nine games.

Perry was outstanding, compiling a 23-13 record, pitching five shutouts and leading the league again in innings worked with 329. He was second to Bob Gibson in voting for the N. L. Cy Young Award.

Willie McCovey, although plagued by injuries and frequent walks, managed 39 home runs and 126 runs batted in, exactly matching his league-leading 1969 RBI total.

McCovey lost the homer and RBI championships he had held for two years, but he took the slugging title for a third consecutive season with a mark of .612.

McCovey drew 137 walks, 40 intentional, most in the league, while batting .289.

Bobby Bonds, Dick Dietz, Ken Henderson, Willie Mays and McCovey all were outstanding at bat as the Giants led both major leagues in runs scored with 831.

Bonds raised his batting average 43 points to .302 while becoming the first Giant to achieve 200 hits since Mays in 1958.

Bonds also scored 134 runs, clouted 26 homers, stole 48 bases and broke his own major league strikeout record with 189.

Dietz batted an even .300, with 22 homers and 107 RBIs, while appearing in 148 games.

Henderson hit .294 with 17 home runs and came into his own as a full-fledged regular outfielder.

Mays produced his 3,000th career base-hit, joining only nine others in major league history, against Montreal at Candlestick Park July 18. He finished the year with 3,065 hits. of which 628 have been home runs.

Willie's 28 homers, .291 average and 83 RBIs in 139 games, plus continued fielding brilliance at 39, amounted to his best season since 1966.

Second only to May's 3,000th hit as an event was Marichal's 200th Giant victory, accomplished against Pittsburgh August 28, also at Candlestick.

Juan became the eighth big league pitcher to win 200 games as early in his career as his 11th season. He was only the 10th to register No. 200 in the past 20 years.

Athough the pitching staff tied with Montreal for the league's highest earned-run average, 4.50, Don McMahon was exceptionally effective in relief.

McMahon, at 40, worked in 61 games, compiling a 9-5 record with a 2.97 ERA and 19 saves.

Ron Hunt led the league for the third consecutive year in the hit-by-pitched-ball department. He was plunked by 26 pitches.

SCORES OF SAN FRANCISCO GIANTS' 1970 GAMES

APRIL—		Winner	Loser
7—Houston	L 5-8	Dierker	Perry
8—Houston	W 5-4	McMahon	DiLauro
9—Houston	W 7-4	Bryant	DiLauro
10—Cinn.	W 4-3	Linzy	Granger
11—Cinn.	W 2-1	Perry	Merritt
12—Cinn.	L 5-6	Cloninger	McCormick
12—Cinn.	L 2-5	Nolan	Bryant
13—At Atl.	L 3-9	Jarvis	Reberger
14—At Atl.	W 15-11	McMahon	Neibauer
15—At Hous.	L 6-7*	Gladding	Bryant
16—At Hous.	W 11-9*	Bryant	Osinski
17—At Cinn.	L 5-8	Granger	McMahon
18—At Cinn.	W 16-9	Jim Johnson	Cloninger
19—At Cinn.	L 0-6	Simpson	Perry
22—At Phila.	L 1-6	Fryman	Robertson
24—Montreal	W 12-3	Perry	McGinn
25—Montreal	L 3-7	McGinn	Bryant
26—Montreal	W 11-1	McCormick	Stoneman
26—Montreal	L 2-3	Morton	Robertson
28—N. York	L 2-5	Gentry	Perry
29—N. York	W 8-6	Linzy	Taylor
30—N. York	L 1-4	Ryan	McCormick

MAY—			
1—Phila.	W 3-1	Robertson	Bunning
2—Phila.	W 7-1	Perry	Short
3—Phila.	L 6-8‡	Hoerner	Bryant
3—Phila.	L 6-13	Palmer	Reberger
5—At Mon.	W 4-1	Robertson	Stoneman
7—At Mon.	L 8-15	Morton	Perry
8—At N. Y.	W 7-1	Puente	Gentry
9—At N. Y.	L 5-14	Koosman	Linzy
10—At N. Y.	W 11-7	Marichal	Ryan
11—At S. D.	W 6-5§	Perry	Ross
12—At S. D.	L 5-6	Corkins	Puente
13—At S. D.	W 5-1	Robertson	Coombs
14—At L. A.	L 3-6	Vance	Marichal
15—At L. A.	L 5-11	Sutton	Puente
16—At L. A.	W 5-4	Perry	Foster

MAY—		Winner	Loser
17—At L. A.	L 0-8	Osteen	Robertson
19—Atlanta	L 2-4	Pappas	Marichal
20—Atlanta	L 1-6†	Wilhelm	Perry
22—S. Diego	W 9-4	Robertson	Corkins
23—S. Diego	L 16-17x	Coombs	Puente
24—S. Diego	W 6-1	Perry	Herbel
24—S. Diego	W 7-6	McCormick	Dobson
26—Los Ang.	L 3-19	Osteen	Robertson
27—Los Ang.	W 11-3	Marichal	Vance
28—Los Ang.	W 4-3	Perry	Brewer
29—At Pitts.	L 3-6	Veale	Robertson
30—At Pitts.	W 13-11	Bryant	Blass
31—At Pitts.	L 3-7	Moose	Marichal

JUNE—			
2—At St. L.	L 1-12	Carlton	Perry
3—At St. L.	L 5-6	Gibson	Reberger
5—At Chi.	L 8-12	Jenkins	Marichal
6—At Chi.	W 5-3	Perry	Hands
7—At Chi.	L 4-8	Regan	Davison
9—Pitts.	L 1-5	Blass	Marichal
10—Pitts.	W 4-2	Perry	Moose
12—St. Louis	L 1-4	Gilson	Pitlock
13—St. Louis	W 6-5	McMahon	Canpisi
14—St. Louis	W 7-4	Marichal	Taylor
16—Chicago	W 3-2	Perry	Hands
17—Chicago	L 1-6	Holtzman	Pitlock
18—Chicago	L 0-6	Jenkins	Robertson
19—At S. D.	L 3-6	Herbel	Marichal
20—At S. D.	W 7-1	Perry	Kirby
21—At S. D.	W 7-2	Reberger	Dobson
22—At Cinn.	W 13-6	Robertson	Gullett
23—At Cinn.	L 3-5	Nolan	McCormick
24—At Cinn.	L 4-5	Granger	Marichal
26—Atlanta	W 4-1	Perry	Reed
27—Atlanta	W 3-0	Pitlock	Stone
28—Atlanta	W 6-4*	McMahon	Priddy
28—Atlanta	W 4-3	Robertson	Niekro
30—S. Diego	L 2-3	Coombs	Perry

JULY—		Winner	Loser
1—S. Diego	W 12-7	McCormick	Santorini
3—Los Ang.	L 6-8	Brewer	Davison
4—Los Ang.	L 2-7	Foster	Perry
5—Los Ang.	L 0-4	Singer	McCormick
6—At Atl.	L 4-12	Stone	Jerry J'son
7—At Atl.	W 8-5	Jerry J'nson	Priddy
8—At Atl.	W 13-0	Perry	Niekro
9—At Atl.	W 7-6†	McMahon	Priddy
10—At Hous.	W 8-5	Reberger	Lemaster
11—At Hous.	L 4-5§	Bouton	Davison
12—At Hous.	L 7-8	Ray	McMahon
17—Montreal	L 3-7	Morton	Marichal
18—Montreal	W 10-1	Perry	Wegener
19—N. York	W 5-3	McMahon	Taylor
19—N. York	L 6-7*	Taylor	McMahon
20—N. York	W 7-4	Davison	Folkers
21—Phila.	L 6-9	Wise	Marichal
22—Phila.	L 2-5	Bunning	Perry
24—At Mon.	W 8-7	Davison	Renko
24—At Mon.	L 5-7	Reed	Pitlock
25—At Mon.	L 5-10	Morton	Reberger
26—At Mon.	W 6-2	Marichal	Marshall
27—At N. Y.	L 3-5	Seaver	Perry
28—At N. Y.	L 2-12	McAndrew	Robertson
29—At N. Y.	W 4-2	Pitlock	Folkers
31—At Phila.	W 8-3	Marichal	G. Jackson
31—At Phila.	W 7-2	Reberger	Short
AUGUST—			
1—At Phila.	L 5-6†	Selma	Jerry J'son
1—At Phila.	L 1-6	Wise	Carrithers
2—At Phila.	L 6-7	Wenz	Davison
3—At L. A.	W 5-2	Pitlock	Singer
4—At L. A.	W 11-4	Marichal	Sutton
5—Cinn.	W 5-3	Perry	McGlothlin
6—Cinn.	W 9-3	Reberger	Washburn
7—Houston	L 2-11	Dierker	Bryant
8—Houston	W 6-5	McMahon	Culver
9—Houston	L 5-7*	DiLauro	Robertson
9—Houston	W 6-1	Perry	Griffin
11—At Chi.	L 1-4	Jenkins	Reberger
12—At Chi.	L 6-3	Carrithers	Hands
13—At Chi.	L 3-6	Pappas	Perry
14—At St. L.	L 1-2‡	Taylor	McMahon
14—At St. L.	W 5-4*	McMahon	Hilgendorf
15—At St. L.	W 3-2	Carrithers	Briles
16—At St. L.	W 5-2	Bryant	Cleveland

AUGUST—		Winner	Loser
17—At Pitts.	W 5-4	Perry	Dal Canton
18—At Pitts.	L 2-6	Blass	Pitlock
19—At Pitts.	W 7-4	Marichal	Walker
21—Chicago	W 5-1	Reberger	Hands
22—Chicago	L 0-15	Holtzman	Perry
23—Chicago	W 4-3	Marichal	Pappas
25—St. Louis	W 4-2	Pitlock	Carlton
26—St. Louis	W 8-7	Davison	Hilgendorf
27—St. Louis	L 1-4	Gibson	Perry
28—Pitts.	W 5-1	Marichal	Moose
29—Pitts.	W 10-9*	McMahon	Dal Canton
30—Pitts.	W 7-3	Jerry J'nson	Walker
30—Pitts.	W 2-1	Bryant	Giusti
SEPTEMBER—			
1—At Cinn.	W 5-3	Perry	Carroll
2—At Cinn.	L 0-2	Nolan	Marichal
3—At Cinn.	L 3-7	Cloninger	Pitlock
4—At Atl.	L 2-5	Niekro	Jerry J'son
5—At Atl.	L 3-5	Cardwell	Robertson
6—At Atl.	W 1-0	Perry	Reed
7—Cinn.	W 6-3	Marichal	Nolan
7—Cinn.	W 3-1	Cumberland	Carroll
8—Cinn.	L 2-5	Washburn	Reberger
9—Houston	W 9-5	Jerry J'son	Dierker
10—Houston	W 11-0	Perry	Blasingame
11—Los Ang.	W 4-3	Marichal	Sutton
12—Los Ang.	W 8-3	Pitlock	Foster
13—Los Ang.	L 3-5*	Brewer	Bryant
14—Atlanta	W 7-5	Reberger	McQueen
15—Atlanta	W 8-0	Perry	Reed
16—Atlanta	L 7-10	Niekro	Jerry J'son
17—At S. D.	W 4-3	Robertson	Dobson
18—At S. D.	W 3-2*	Reberger	Coombs
19—At S. D.	W 3-0	Perry	Kirby
21—At L. A.	W 7-0	Marichal	Moeller
22—At L. A.	L 0-1	Foster	Bryant
23—At L. A.	W 14-10*	Robertson	Lamb
25—S. Diego	L 4-7	Dobson	Reberger
26—S. Diego	W 7-6	Cumberland	Doyle
27—S. Diego	W 3-2	Perry	Coombs
28—At Hous.	L 0-3	Billingham	Bryant
29—At Hous.	L 1-3	Wilson	Reberger
30—At Hous.	L 3-4	Dierker	McMahon
OCTOBER—			
1—At Hous.	L 4-5	Gladding	Davison

* 10 innings.   † 11 innings.   ‡ 13 innings.   § 14 innings.   x 15 innings.

Midseason Countdown Benefited Astros

By JOHN WILSON

The failure of the Houston Astros' mound staff to live up to the high goals set for it doomed any chances the Spacemen might have had for being a pennant contender in the National League West. For the first time in their nine-year history, the Astros actually were looked upon in the spring as a potential contender.

Pitching was not the Astros' only failure over the first half of the season. The club couldn't put anything together. An overhauling of the team at midseason proved to be highly beneficial and the Astros turned a disappointing season into one that at least again offered hope "for next year."

The Astros finished fourth in the West, overtaking the 1969 division champion, Atlanta, in the final week of the campaign. The 79-83 record represented two fewer wins than the .500 fifth-place finish of the year before. But the Astros posted a better won-lost percentage than five teams in the league, the best showing yet in that respect.

Houston won 42 games and lost 32 after the All-Star Game, and only the Giants did better than that, including the teams from both divisions.

HOUSTON ASTROS, 1970

Front row—Canales, assistant trainer; Edwards, Parker, coach; McGaha, coach; Walker, manager; Hancken, coach; Owens, coach; Pepitone, Diskin, equipment manager. Second row—Ewell, trainer; Miller, Wynn, McFadden, Rader, Menke, Beauchamp, Watson, Martinez, Alou, Mayberry, Davis. Back row—Lampard, Wilson, Gladding, Bouton, Cook, DiLauro, Morgan, Billingham, Griffin, Dierker, Ray, Lemaster. Seated in front—Dushkin, Tiller, batboys.

Manager Harry Walker's job appeared to be in jeopardy as the team stumbled through June, but Spec Richardson, the general manager, announced he was going to stick with The Hat the rest of the way. On two dates in the first week of July, the team dropped 16 games under .500, but began to make up a little ground and was a much more cohesive ball club the rest of the way.

However, the disappointment in the season overall left considerable doubt about the status of Manager Walker. The Astros finished the season by winning their last seven games, passing the Braves when they won three straight at Atlanta and then knocking the Giants out of second place with a four-game sweep in the Dome. It wasn't until only two games remained on the schedule that Richardson announced that Walker and his coaches were being retained for another season.

Larry Dierker, the 20-game winner of 1969, got off to a fast start for an 8-2 record, but then went 10 consecutive starts without picking up a win. He finished the season with a 16-12 mark and pitched 17 complete games.

Don Wilson, who had climbed with 10, 13 and 16 wins over the past three years, was on the disabled list at the start of the season. He came back and did creditably well without his formerly blazing fast ball and posted an 11-6 record.

Tom Griffin, the league's "Rookie Pitcher of the Year" in 1969 when he had an 11-10 record, couldn't get going this time and ended with a 3-13 mark. He was sent back to Triple A in August.

Jack Billingham came out of the bullpen to take a starting role when the Astros were stumbling and the 27-year-old righthander took up some of the slack with a 13-9 record.

The bullpen was inconsistent the entire season and the Astros saw a lot of games get away from them when Manager Walker had to summon help for the starter.

Houston had started the season with Tommy Davis in left field, Joe Pepitone in right and rookie John Mayberry at first base.

With the team floundering from the start, the management couldn't wait on Mayberry to get his bearings in the majors and he was gone to Oklahoma City by the time the season was a month old. Before June was out, veteran Davis was waived to Oakland in the American League as 19-year-old Cesar Cedeno, who was having phenomenal success at Oklahoma City, was called up.

On July 21, Pepitone, who had been out of the lineup for most of the preceding month for a variety of reasons, walked out on the team and went home to Brooklyn. He was suspended and eventually sold to the Cubs on waivers.

But the Astros by then had the team that was going to make a respectable showing the rest of the season and offer hope for the future. Cedeno entered the lineup on June 20 and, after experiencing some difficulties the first couple of weeks, came on to become the best-looking prospect the organization yet had produced.

Cedeno hit .310 and as soon as it was certain he would stay, Jim Wynn was moved to left field to make room for the aggressive Dominican in center.

Bob Watson took over first base at the same time Cedeno came up and batted in 61 runs for the season as he gave the club a strong bat in the

No. 4 spot. And Jesus Alou, finally getting a chance to play right field regularly after midseason, batted .306.

Denis Menke had his first .300 season as the veteran shortstop batted .304 and knocked in a career high 92 runs. Doug Rader was one of the league's outstanding gloves at third base and knocked in 87 runs, with 25 homers, on a .252 average. Joe Morgan had his best year at second base.

Jim Wynn hit 27 homers and knocked in 88 runs.

The Astros finished with a .259 team batting average and 129 home runs, each a club record.

SCORES OF HOUSTON ASTROS' 1970 GAMES

APRIL—	Winner	Loser
7—At S. F. W 8-5	Dierker	Perry
8—At S. F. L 4-5	McMahon	DiLauro
9—At S. F. L 4-7	Bryant	DiLauro
10—Atlanta L 0-5	Stone	Griffin
11—Atlanta W 8-7	Bouton	Pappas
12—Atlanta W 8-3	Dierker	Niekro
13—Los Ang. L 0-2	Sutton	Lemaster
14—Los Ang. L 2-3	Foster	Ray
15—S. Fran. W 7-6*	Gladding	Bryant
16—S. Fran. L 9-11*	Bryant	Osinski
17—S. Diego W 4-1	Dierker	Roberts
18—S. Diego W 4-3	Lemaster	Ross
19—S. Diego W 5-1	Griffin	Santorini
20—At Pitts. L 1-3	Ellis	Bouton
21—At Pitts. L 8-9	Veale	Dierker
22—At Pitts. L 1-6	Blass	Lemaster
24—At Chi. L 3-6	Holtzman	Griffin
25—At Chi. L 5-11	Hands	Bouton
26—At Chi. L 3-6	Jenkins	Dierker
28—At Cinn. L 2-4	Nolan	Lemaster
29—At Cinn. L 3-5	Merritt	Griffin
MAY—		
1—At St. L. W 9-3	Dierker	Carlton
2—At St. L. W 5-3*	Gladding	Hilgendorf
3—At St. L. L 4-7	Briles	Griffin
3—At St. L. W 8-1	Lemaster	Culver
4—Chicago W 7-2	Bouton	Hands
5—Chicago L 1-3	Dierker	Jenkins
7—Pitts. L 5-9	Walker	Bouton
8—Pitts. W 7-5	Ray	Blass
9—Pitts. L 3-6	Moose	Griffin
10—Pitts. W 9-2	Dierker	Ellis
12—At L. A. W 8-3	Wilson	Foster
13—At L. A. W 6-5	Lemaster	Osteen
14—At S. D. W 3-1	Dierker	Kirby
15—At S. D. L 8-10*	Coombs	Ray
16—At S. D. W 9-7	Billingham	Dobson
17—At S. D. L 3-5	Corkins	Lemaster
18—St. Louis W 6-0	Dierker	Gibson
19—St. Louis L 3-12	Guzman	Spinks
20—St. Louis L 2-3	Torrez	Griffin
21—Cinn. L 0-3	McGlothlin	Lemaster
22—Cinn. L 2-5	Merritt	Dierker
23—Cinn. L 3-14	Simpson	Wilson
24—Cinn. W 10-7	Gladding	Carroll
26—At Atl. L 3-5	Nash	Dierker
27—At Atl. L 1-8	Niekro	Lemaster
29—At N. Y. W 5-0	Billingham	Seaver
30—At N. Y. L 3-4	Ryan	Dierker
31—At N. Y. L 4-14	Sadecki	Lemaster
31—At N. Y. L 3-4x	McGraw	Lemaster
JUNE—		
2—Montreal W 6-4	Ray	Morton
3—Montreal W 5-0	Billingham	Moore
4—Montreal W 8-0	Griffin	McGinn
5—Phila. W 7-8†	Ray	Selma
6—Phila. L 3-7	Wise	Wilson
7—Phila. L 3-10	Fryman	Dierker
8—N. York L 0-2	McAndrew	Billingham
9—N. York L 1-2	Seaver	Griffin
10—N. York W 3-5	Lemaster	Ryan
12—At Mon. L 6-7	Reed	Marshall
13—At Mon. W 5-2	Billingham	Stoneman
14—At Mon. L 1-2	Renko	Lemaster
16—At Phila. L 1-2§	Hoerner	Bouton

JUNE—	Winner	Loser
17—At Phila. L 2-4	Fryman	Dierker
19—At Atl. L 6-7	Reed	Ray
19—At Atl. L 2-4	Jarvis	Lemaster
20—At Atl. W 9-6	Bouton	Stone
21—At Atl. L 4-6	Nash	Dierker
22—S. Diego W 4-1	Wilson	Roberts
23—S. Diego W 2-1	Billingham	Coombs
24—S. Diego W 5-4	Lemaster	Santorini
26—Cinn. L 2-3	Simpson	Bouton
27—Cinn. L 2-5	Merritt	Griffin
28—Cinn. L 2-3	Carroll	Wilson
29—At L. A. W 10-5	Billingham	Singer
30—At L. A. W 6-2	Lemaster	Moeller
JULY—		
1—At L. A. L 3-6	Osteen	Gladding
3—At Cinn. L 0-3	Nolan	Wilson
3—At Cinn. W 10-4	Griffin	Cloninger
4—At Cinn. L 0-3	McGlothlin	Billingham
4—At Cinn. L 0-3	Simpson	Lemaster
6—Los Ang. L 8-10*	Brewer	Bouton
7—Los Ang. L 2-7	Moeller	Griffin
9—Los Ang. W 9-5	Billingham	Foster
10—S. Fran. L 5-8	Reberger	Lemaster
11—S. Fran. W 5-4x	Bouton	Davison
12—S. Fran. W 8-7	Ray	McMahon
16—Chicago W 2-1	Wilson	Holtzman
17—Chicago W 5-2	Dierker	Jenkins
18—Chicago L 3-7	Hands	Billingham
19—Chicago W 5-4‡	Pappas	Griffin
20—Pitts. W 5-4‡	Cook	Dal Canton
21—Pitts. W 3-1	Wilson	Nelson
22—At St. L. W 13-9	Culver	Briles
23—At St. L. W 3-2	Billingham	Gibson
24—At Pitts. L 0-11	Ellis	Griffin
25—At Pitts. W 8-4	Cook	Veale
26—At Pitts. W 6-4*	Lemaster	Giusti
28—At Chi. W 10-4	Billingham	Pappas
29—At Chi. L 2-9	Holtzman	Dierker
30—At Chi. L 3-6	Jenkins	Griffin
31—St. Louis L 1-5	Carlton	Cook
AUGUST—		
1—St. Louis L 7-14	Briles	Wilson
2—St. Louis L 2-3	Gibson	Billingham
3—Atlanta W 7-5	Culver	Niekro
3—Atlanta L 1-3	Reed	Dierker
4—Atlanta L 1-6	Jarvis	Cook
5—At S. D. W 4-3*	Gladding	Dukes
6—At S. D. W 8-6	Billingham	Coombs
7—At S. F. W 11-2	Dierker	Bryant
8—At S. F. L 5-6	McMahon	Culver
9—At S. F. W 7-5*	DiLauro	Robertson
9—At S. F. L 1-6	Perry	Griffin
11—Phila. L 5-6	Bunning	Billingham
12—Phila. W 4-0	Dierker	G. Jackson
13—Phila. W 4-3	Ray	Selma
14—Montreal L 2-10	Renko	Cook
15—Montreal W 7-3	Wilson	Morton
16—Montreal L 3-5	Raymond	Cook
18—At N. Y. L 1-7	Gentry	Dierker
19—At N. Y. W 9-4	Blasingame	Seaver
21—At Phila. L 3-9	Bunning	Billingham
21—At Phila. W 9-1	Wilson	G. Jackson
22—At Phila. L 1-2	Hoerner	Gladding
23—At Phila. L 0-4	Wise	Blasingame

AUGUST—				Winner	Loser
25—At Mon.	W	6-3§		Cook	Marshall
26—At Mon.	W	5-4		Gladding	Renko
27—At Mon.	W	5-4		Dierker	Wegener
28—N. York	W	2-1		Blasingame	Seaver
29—N. York	W	9-8*		Culver	McGraw
30—N. York	W	9-5		Wilson	Ryan
SEPTEMBER—					
1—S. Diego	L	1-2*		Dobson	Culver
2—S. Diego	W	2-1		Blasingame	Coombs
3—S. Diego	L	0-4		Kirby	Billingham
4—Los Ang.	W	7-3		Wilson	Vance
5—Los Ang.	W	7-2		Dierker	Osteen
6—Los Ang.	L	3-4		Mikkelsen	Gladding
7—At S. D.	W	10-5		Forsch	Nyman
7—At S. D.	W	9-4		Billingham	Coombs
8—At S. D.	W	8-7		Wilson	Kirby
9—At S. F.	L	5-9		Jerry J'nson	Dierker
10—At S. F.	L	0-11		Perry	Blasingame
11—Atlanta	W	3-2		Billingham	Wilhelm

SEPTEMBER—				Winner	Loser
12—Atlanta	L	3-5		Jarvis	Forsch
13—Atlanta	W	10-6		Wilson	Stone
15—Cinn.	W	9-2		Dierker	McGlothlin
16—Cinn.	L	2-3		Nolan	Blasingame
17—At L. A.	W	10-5		Cook	Foster
18—At L. A.	L	2-3		Vance	Billingham
19—At L. A.	L	5-6		Strahler	Wilson
20—At L. A.	L	6-7x		Lamb	Culver
21—At Cinn.	L	0-2		Gullett	Forsch
22—At Cinn.	L	5-6		Wilcox	Gladding
23—At Cinn.	L	2-6		Cloninger	Billingham
25—At Atl.	W	7-4‡		Gladding	Jarvis
26—At Atl.	W	5-2		Dierker	Stone
27—At Atl.	W	10-7		Ray	Nash
28—S. Fran.	W	3-0		Billingham	Bryant
29—S. Fran.	W	3-1		Wilson	Reberger
30—S. Fran.	W	4-3		Dierker	McMahon
OCTOBER—					
1—S. Fran.	W	5-4		Gladding	Davison

* 10 innings.   † 11 innings.   ‡ 12 innings.   § 13 innings. x 14 innings.

Injuries, Poor Defense Offset Good Efforts

By WAYNE MINSHEW

Statistics definitely do not tell the story for the 1970 Braves.

For example, the defending National League West Division champs had three players who batted .300 or better, three who hit 25 or more homers apiece and three who knocked in more than 100 runs each.

They also received more complete games from their pitching staff and more shutouts.

Still, the 1970 Braves plunged from first to a dismal fifth in the West Division, which wasn't nearly so wild as the year previous when the Georgians reeled off 10 straight victories near the end to win the title.

There were reasons, of course, for the Braves' fall.

Foremost were injuries to key pitching personnel. Relief ace Cecil Upshaw missed the entire season after suffering a severe finger injury following the team's opening game of the year at San Diego. Returning 18-game winner Ron Reed broke his collarbone in spring training and missed the first nine weeks of the campaign.

Then there was the defense, or the lack of same, which probably made the pitching look worse than it really was.

Balls fell in the outfield which should have been caught, the infield as a unit lacked range and did not make the tough double play and opposing runners stole bases at an alarming rate as they got big jumps on pitchers and slid under inaccurate catchers' throws.

On the positive side of the ledger, the Braves had the major league batting champ who compiled the highest average in the bigs since 1957, when Ted Williams hit .388.

That would be Rico Carty, who won the crown with relative ease with a .366 average. Other .300 hitters were Orlando Cepeda (.305) and Felix Millan (.311). Carty, Cepeda and Hank Aaron each drove in better than 100 runs.

Pat Jarvis led the pitching staff with 16 victories. But he also lost 16. Jim Nash, after compiling a 10-2 record by the All-Star Game break, sputtered the second half and finished at 13-9, while George Stone was 11-11.

The biggest disappointment was Phil Niekro, a 23-game winner last year, who managed only a 12-18 record this time around and served up 40

ATLANTA BRAVES, 1970

Front row—Davidson, traveling secretary; Garrido, Didier, Jackson, Goodman, coach; Busby, coach; Harris, manager; Silvestri, coach; Dorish, coach; House, Jarvis, Millan, McCammon, McQueen. Second row—Pursley, trainer; Lum, Garr, Gonzalez, Wilhelm, Priddy, King, T. Aaron, Aspromonte, Boyer, Evans, Bell, Hill, Kester, H. Aaron, Baker, Gladulich, equipment manager. Back row—Brown, Pappas, Breazeale, Mitchell, Murphy, Jaster, Nash, Reed, Neibauer, Schueler, Upshaw, Stone, Niekro, Tillman, Britton.

home-run balls. Things got so bad that Manager Luman Harris finally relegated the 1969 ace to the bullpen, then sent him to Arizona for extra work in preparation for the 1971 season.

Highlights were few for the Braves, who delighted their fans early in the year by reeling off an 11-game winning streak. Also, Mike Lum smashed three homers in a single game, against San Diego on July 3, and Orlando Cepeda turned the same trick, July 26, against the Cubs at Chicago.

Carty put together a 31-game hitting streak and batted over .400 until mid June. He also hit three homers in one game against the Phillies on May 31.

But pitching and defensive woes, particularly at shortstop, catcher and center field, did in the Braves early. They finished with a 76-86 record, their worst in five years in Atlanta.

SCORES OF ATLANTA BRAVES' 1970 GAMES

			Winner	Loser
APRIL—				
7—At S. D.	L	3-8	Dobson	Niekro
8—At S. D.	W	6-1	Jarvis	Santorini
9—At S. D.	W	6-1	Nash	Kirby
10—At Hous.	W	5-0	Stone	Griffin
11—At Hous.	L	7-8	Bouton	Pappas
12—At Hous.	L	3-8	Dierker	Niekro
13—S. Fran.	W	9-3	Jarvis	Iteberger
14—S. Fran.	L	11-15	McMahon	Neibauer
15—S. Diego	W	7-5	Stone	Corkins
16—S. Diego	L	4-5†	Ross	Niekro
18—Los Ang.	L	4-5	Sutton	Jarvis
19—Los Ang.	L	1-10	Foster	Nash
20—Cinn.	L	2-6	Merritt	Stone
21—Cinn.	L	8-13	Nolan	Niekro
23—At Pitts.	L	6-8	Walker	Jarvis
24—At Pitts.	W	9-0	Nash	Moose
25—At Pitts.	L	7-8	Giusti	Wilhelm
26—At Pitts.	W	2-0	Niekro	Veale
28—At St. L.	W	3-2	Wilhelm	Torrez
29—At St. L.	W	10-6	Priddy	Taylor
30—Chicago	W	9-2	Stone	Jenkins
MAY—				
1—Chicago	W	3-2	Niekro	Decker
2—Chicago	W	4-2	Jarvis	Holtzman
4—Pitts.	W	5-3	Nash	Walker
5—Pitts.	W	12-6	Stone	Moose
6—Pitts.	W	3-0	Niekro	Ellis
8—St. Louis	W	8-7	Priddy	Taylor
9—St. Louis	W	5-3	Nash	Culver
10—St. Louis	L	5-6	Johnson	Priddy
11—At Chi.	W	7-6†	Niekro	Reynolds
12—At Chi.	L	3-4‡	Regan	Priddy
15—At Cinn.	W	3-1	Nash	Nolan
16—At Cinn.	L	0-2	McGlothlin	Niekro
17—At Cinn.	L	1-5	Merritt	Jarvis
17—At Cinn.	L	6-7x	Gillett	Neibauer
19—At S. F.	W	4-2	Pappas	Marichal
20—At S.F.	W	6-1‡	Wilhelm	Perry
21—At L. A.	L	3-6	Osteen	Niekro
22—At L. A.	W	1-0	Jarvis	Vance
23—At L. A.	W	5-1	Stone	Sutton
24—At L. A.	L	1-8	Foster	Pappas
26—Houston	W	5-3	Nash	Dierker
27—Houston	W	8-1	Niekro	Lemaster
29—Phila.	W	5-2	Jarvis	Short
30—Phila.	L	5-7	Bunning	Neibauer
31—Phila.	W	9-1	Nash	Wise
JUNE—				
2—N. York	W	4-1	Niekro	Gentry
4—N. York	W	3-1	Jarvis	Seaver
5—Montreal	L	2-3	Dillman	Wilhelm
6—Montreal	L	4-12	Stoneman	Nash
7—Montreal	L	1-10	Morton	Niekro
9—At Phila.	L	1-2	Bunning	Jarvis
10—At Phila.	W	5-1	Stone	Short
11—At Phila.	W	6-4	Nash	Wise
12—At N. Y.	L	1-8	Gentry	Niekro
13—At N. Y.	L	1-4	Sadecki	McQueen
14—At N. Y.	L	5-7	Seaver	Jarvis

			Winner	Loser
JUNE—				
16—At Mon.	W	7-5	Pappas	Morton
17—At Mon.	W	6-5	Jaster	Raymond
18—At Mon.	L	7-10	Stoneman	Jaster
19—Houston	W	7-6	Reed	Ray
19—Houston	L	4-2	Jarvis	Lemaster
20—Houston	L	6-9	Bouton	Stone
21—Houston	W	6-4	Nash	Dierker
22—Los Ang.	L	2-4	Foster	Niekro
23—Los Ang.	L	0-7	Singer	McQueen
24—Los Ang.	L	0-7	Moeller	Jarvis
26—At S. F.	L	1-4	Perry	Reed
27—At S. F.	L	0-3	Pitlock	Stone
28—At S. F.	L	4-6†	McMahon	Priddy
28—At S. F.	L	3-4	Robertson	Niekro
30—At Cinn.	W	8-2	Jarvis	McGlothlin
JULY—				
1—At Cinn.	L	2-9	Simpson	Reed
2—At Cinn.	L	1-2	Merritt	Stone
3—S. Diego	W	8-1	Nash	Kirby
3—S. Diego	W	9-4	Niekro	Dobson
4—S. Diego	W	2-1	Jarvis	Roberts
5—S. Diego	L	5-6	Willis	Wilhelm
6—S. Fran.	W	12-4	Stone	Jerry J'son
7—S. Fran.	L	5-8	Jerry J'son	Priddy
8—S. Fran.	L	0-13	Perry	Niekro
9—S. Fran.	L	6-7‡	McMahon	Priddy
10—Cinn.	W	11-9	Reed	Merritt
10—Cinn.	L	1-3	Cloninger	Stone
11—Cinn.	L	6-7	Nolan	Niekro
12—Cinn.	L	5-6	Washburn	Jarvis
16—At St. L.	W	7-3	Jarvis	Carlton
17—At St. L.	L	6-11	Briles	Stone
18—At St. L.	W	8-7‡	Wilhelm	Linzy
19—At St. L.	L	1-3	Torrez	Reed
20—Chicago	W	3-1	Niekro	Holtzman
20—Chicago	W	5-0*	Cardwell	Decker
21—Chicago	L	2-8	Jenkins	Jarvis
22—At Pitts.	L	3-5	Dal Canton	Stone
23—At Pitts.	L	5-6	Colpaert	McQueen
24—At Chi.	L	1-11	Holtzman	Reed
25—At Chi.	W	9-0	Niekro	Jenkins
26—At Chi.	W	8-3	Jarvis	Hands
26—At Chi.	L	6-7	Colborn	Cardwell
28—St. Louis	W	4-6	Gibson	Nash
29—St. Louis	W	9-7	Reed	Linzy
30—St. Louis	L	2-4	Reuss	Niekro
31—Pitts.	W	4-3	Jarvis	Nelson
AUGUST—				
1—Pitts.	L	10-20	Pena	Stone
2—Pitts.	L	7-10	Ellis	Nash
3—At Hous.	L	5-7	Culver	Niekro
3—At Hous.	W	3-1	Reed	Dierker
4—At Hous.	W	6-1	Jarvis	Cook
5—At L. A.	L	2-12	Foster	Stone
6—At L. A.	W	4-1	Nash	Osteen
7—At S. D.	W	8-2	Niekro	Roberts
7—At S. D.	L	1-6	Kirby	Reed
9—At S. D.	L	2-4	Dobson	Jarvis
11—Montreal	W	1-0	Nash	Morton

SAN DIEGO PADRES, 1970

Front row—Cannizzaro, Willis, Campbell, Wietelmann, coach; Skinner, coach; Gomez, manager; Craig, coach; Garcia, coach; Colbert, Stahl. Second row—Mattei, trainer; Ferrara, Dobson, Kirby, Dukes, Roberts, Gaston, Slocum, Murrell, Coombs, Brown, Peralta, equipment manager. Back row—Wilson, Webster, Spiezio, Baldschun, Arcia, Huntz, Dean, Barton, Herbel, Tunis, assistant trainer.

AUGUST—		Winner	Loser	SEPTEMBER—		Winner	Loser
12—Montreal	W 8-7	Priddy	Stoneman	6—S. Fran.	L 0-1	Perry	Reed
13—Montreal	W 4-1	Stone	Wegener	7—At L. A.	L 3-4	Sutton	Nash
14—N. York	W 10-2	Reed	Ryan	7—At L. A.	L 1-6	Foster	Jarvis
14—N. York	L 2-4	Koosman	Jarvis	8—At L. A.	W 3-2	Stone	Vance
15—N. York	W 3-2	Wilhelm	Seaver	9—At S. D.	W 6-3‡	Priddy	Dukes
16—N. York	L 1-2	McAndrew	Nash	9—At S. D.	L 4-7	Wilson	Niekro
18—Phila.	W 3-2	Wilhelm	Short	10—At S. D.	L 2-3	Roberts	Reed
19—Phila.	W 3-2	Jarvis	Wise	11—At Hous.	L 2-3	Billingham	Wilhelm
20—Phila.	W 6-2	Reed	Lersch	12—At Hous.	W 5-3	Jarvis	Forsch
21—At Mon.	L 4-6	Morton	Niekro	13—At Hous.	L 6-10	Wilson	Stone
22—At Mon.	L 1-4	Renko	Nash	14—At S. F.	L 5-7	Reberger	McQueen
24—At Mon.	W 6-0	Stone	Stoneman	15—At S. F.	L 0-8	Perry	Reed
25—At N. Y.	W 7-6	Jarvis	Ryan	16—At S. F.	W 10-7	Niekro	Jerry J'son
26—At N. Y.	W 9-7	Priddy	Gentry	18—Cinn.	L 6-11	Cloninger	Jarvis
27—At N. Y.	L 1-5	McAndrew	Niekro	19—Cinn.	L 4-7	McGlothlin	Barber
28—At Phila.	L 2-5	Short	Nash	20—Cinn.	W 11-2	Reed	Maloney
29—At Phila.	L 9-10	Hoerner	Reed	22—S. Diego	W 3-2	Nash	Wilson
30—At Phila.	L 2-4	Lersch	Jarvis	23—S. Diego	L 0-2	Arlin	Jarvis
SEPTEMBER—				24—S. Diego	L 0-5	Roberts	McQueen
1—Los Ang.	L 3-6	Lamb	Niekro	25—Houston	L 4-7§	Gladding	Jarvis
1—Los Ang.	L 2-3	Moeller	Reed	26—Houston	L 2-5	Dierker	Stone
2—Los Ang.	W 4-3	Wilhelm	Sutton	27—Houston	L 7-10	Ray	Nash
3—Los Ang.	W 11-4	Stone	Foster	29—At Cinn.	W 2-1	McQueen	Cloninger
5—S. Fran.	W 5-2	Niekro	Jerry J'son	OCTOBER—			
5—S. Fran.	W 5-3	Cardwell	Robertson	1—At Cinn.	L 1-4	Washburn	Jarvis

* Game halted by rain with two outs in top of sixth. † 10 innings. ‡ 11 innings. § 12 innings. x 15 innings.

Tough Padres Penance for Pennant Clubs

By PAUL COUR

It was George (Sparky) Anderson, manager of the pennant-winning Reds, who paid the San Diego Padres the highest compliment on their second year in the National League.

"I'm glad we don't have to face the Padres in a playoff for the pennant," said the former San Diego third base coach. "They have one of the best offenses in baseball."

Anderson had good reason for his remarks.

The Padres beat the runaway West Division champions 10 out of 18 times. The only other club in the senior circuit to hold a series edge over the Big Red Machine was the Cubs, who had a 7-5 advantage.

In winning 11 more games—63—than in their expansion season, the Padres also were rough on East Division champion Pittsburgh, breaking even with the Pirates, 6-6. And they were 6-6 against the dethroned world champion Mets.

The Padres were a vastly improved offensive unit over their maiden season. Their 172 home runs ranked third in the league behind the Reds (191) and Cubs (179). And their .246 team batting average was 21 points higher than in 1969.

In center fielder Clarence Gaston, the Padres had one of the bright young stars in the majors. Coming off a rookie year when he hit only .230 with two homers and 28 runs batted in, the 26-year-old former Atlanta chattel jumped his average to .318, knocked in 93 runs and poled 29 homers. He was the club's representative on the All-Star team in July.

First baseman Nate Colbert led the club in homers with 38 and knocked in 86 runs. Right fielder Ollie Brown, for whom stardom was predicted when he broke into the majors with the Giants in 1965, had his best year. He hit .292 with 23 homers and 89 RBIs.

Catcher Chris Cannizzaro was one of the club's most consistent per-

formers. Up around the .300 mark for most of the season, the veteran receiver finished at .279—59 points above his 1969 average.

Other Padres finishing in double home-run figures were Al Ferrara (13), Dave Campbell (12), Ivan Murrell (12), Ed Spiezio (12) and Steve Huntz (11).

Pat Dobson, acquired from Detroit last winter, was the bellwether of the pitching staff with a 14-15 record and 3.76 earned-run average. The veteran righthander had eight complete games, tops on the staff, and was the workhorse with 251 innings pitched.

Righthander Clay Kirby (10-16) was involved in the Padres' biggest controversy of the season on July 21 at San Diego Stadium.

Kirby had a no-hitter going for eight innings when Manager Preston Gomez lifted him for a pinch-hitter with two out in the eighth and the Padres trailing the Mets, 1-0.

The Mets went on to win, 3-0, and the second guessers had a field day.

Gomez withstood the storm and was rehired to manage the club again in 1971.

"I was hoping for 70 wins," said Gomez, "and we finished with 63. That's 11 more than we won in 1969 and what is more important to me, the players improved themselves and their team even more than they did their record."

Attendance was up 130,709 to 643,679.

SCORES OF SAN DIEGO PADRES' 1970 GAMES

APRIL—		Winner	Loser
7—Atlanta	W 8-3	Dobson	Niekro
8—Atlanta	L 1-6	Jarvis	Santorini
9—Atlanta	L 1-6	Nash	Kirby
10—At L. A.	W 7-2	Roberts	Foster
11—At L. A.	W 4-0	Coombs	Osteen
12—At L. A.	L 0-6	Singer	Dobson
13—At Cinn.	W 3-1	Santorini	McGlothlin
14—At Cinn.	L 1-6	Simpson	Kirby
15—At Atl.	L 5-7	Stone	Corkins
16—At Atl.	W 5-4*	Ross	Niekro
17—At Hous.	L 1-4	Dierker	Roberts
18—At Hous.	L 3-4	Lemaster	Ross
19—At Hous.	L 1-5	Griffin	Santorini
21—At N. Y.	W 5-3	Herbel	Koonce
22—At N. Y.	L 1-2	Seaver	Corkins
24—Phila.	L 4-5	G. Jackson	Dobson
25—Phila.	L 0-1	Bunning	Santorini
26—Phila.	L 2-3	Short	Roberts
28—Montreal	L 2-4	Reed	Corkins
28—Montreal	L 3-7	Renko	Coombs
29—Montreal	W 10-0	Dobson	Sparma
MAY—			
1—N. York	L 1-2	Seaver	Santorini
2—N. York	W 5-4	Kirby	McAndrew
3—N. York	W 4-3*	Roberts	Koonce
3—N. York	L 2-3	Gentry	Dobson
5—At Phila.	W 11-8	Roberts	Selma
6—At Phila.	L 3-4	Selma	Kirby
7—At Phila.	W 8-2	Dobson	Short
8—At Mon.	W 11-1	Corkins	Waslewski
8—At Mon.	L 6-7†	Raymond	Ross
9—At Mon.	W 6-0	Coombs	Stoneman
10—At Mon.	W 5-4	Kirby	Reed
11—S. Fran.	L 5-6‡	Perry	Ross
12—S. Fran.	W 6-5	Corkins	Puente
13—S. Fran.	L 1-5	Robertson	Coombs
14—Houston	L 1-3	Dierker	Kirby
15—Houston	W 10-8*	Coombs	Ray
16—Houston	L 7-9	Billingham	Dobson
17—Houston	W 5-3	Corkins	Lemaster
18—Los Ang.	L 3-4	Vance	Coombs
19—Los Ang.	L 3-8	Sutton	Kirby

MAY—		Winner	Loser
20—Los Ang.	W 10-4	Roberts	Foster
22—At S. F.	L 4-9	Robertson	Corkins
23—At S. F.	W 17-16§	Coombs	Puente
24—At S. F.	L 1-6	Perry	Herbel
24—At S. F.	L 6-7	McCormick	Dobson
25—Cinn.	L 1-2	McGlothlin	Kirby
26—Cinn.	W 8-1	Corkins	Merritt
26—Cinn.	W 4-1	Coombs	Borbon
27—Cinn.	L 4-6	Carroll	Dukes
30—At Chi.	W 11-4	Herbel	Dunegan
30—At Chi.	L 7-8	Regan	Dukes
31—At Chi.	L 4-7	Jenkins	Corkins
JUNE—			
1—At Pitts.	L 1-5	Ellis	Coombs
2—At Pitts.	W 14-8	Herbel	Veale
5—At St. L.	W 3-2	Dobson	Torrez
6—At St. L.	W 5-4	Herbel	Carlton
7—At St. L.	L 7-10	Gibson	Herbel
9—Chicago	L 3-7	Jenkins	Kirby
10—Chicago	W 11-8	Dobson	Dunegan
11—Chicago	L 1-7	Hands	Corkins
12—Pitts.	L 0-2	Ellis	Roberts
12—Pitts.	W 5-2	Coombs	Veale
13—Pitts.	L 2-7	Blass	Santorini
14—Pitts.	W 2-1	Kirby	Moose
15—St. Louis	L 1-6	Torrez	Dobson
16—St. Louis	W 4-0	Roberts	Carlton
17—St. Louis	L 0-8	Gibson	Coombs
19—S. Fran.	W 6-3	Herbel	Marichal
20—S. Fran.	L 1-7	Perry	Kirby
21—S. Fran.	L 2-7	Reberger	Dobson
22—At Hous.	L 1-4	Wilson	Roberts
23—At Hous.	L 1-2	Billingham	Coombs
24—At Hous.	L 4-5	Lemaster	Santorini
26—At L. A.	L 1-4	Osteen	Kirby
27—At L. A.	L 5-7	Sutton	Dobson
28—At L. A.	L 0-2	Foster	Roberts
30—At S. F.	W 3-2	Coombs	Perry
JULY—			
1—At S. F.	L 7-12	McCormick	Santorini
3—At Atl.	L 1-8	Nash	Kirby

JULY—			Winner	Loser	AUGUST—			Winner	Loser
3—At Atl.	L	4-9	Niekro	Dobson	18—At Chi.	W	11-3	Dobson	Decker
4—At Atl.	L	1-2	Jarvis	Roberts	19—At Chi.	L	2-12	Jenkins	Roberts
5—At Atl.	W	6-5	Willis	Wilhelm	21—St. Louis	L	8-14	Briles	Wilson
6—At Cinn.	L	0-5	Merritt	Santorini	22—St. Louis	L	0-7	Gibson	Coombs
7—At Cinn.	L	0-3	Nolan	Dobson	23—St. Louis	L	7-8	Linzy	Dobson
8—At Cinn.	W	3-1	Kirby	Washburn	25—Pitts.	W	4-3	Dukes	Cambria
9—At Cinn.	W	10-9*	Ross	Granger	26—Pitts.	W	2-1	Dobson	Wilson
10—Los Ang.	L	7-9	Singer	Coombs	27—Chicago	L	1-5	Pappas	Wilson
11—Los Ang.	W	4-3	Herbel	Brewer	28—Chicago	L	4-8	Jenkins	Doyle
12—Los Ang.	W	4-1	Kirby	Sutton	30—Chicago	L	0-3	Hands	Roberts
16—Phila.	L	7-10	Selma	Willis					
17—Phila.	L	3-8	Wise	Kirby	SEPTEMBER—				
18—Phila.	L	4-7	Bunning	Wilson	1—At Hous.	W	2-1*	Dobson	Culver
19—Montreal	W	6-5	Coombs	Renko	2—At Hous.	W	1-2	Blasingame	Coombs
19—Montreal	L	5-6	Strohmayer	Roberts	3—At Hous.	W	4-0	Kirby	Billingham
20—Montreal	W	3-1	Dobson	Marshall	4—At Cinn.	W	15-2	Corkins	Merritt
21—N. York	L	0-3	McAndrew	Kirby	5—At Cinn.	L	2-6	Wilcox	Roberts
22—N. York	W	5-4*	Baldschun	Ryan	6—At Cinn.	L	5-6	McGlothlin	Dobson
24—At Phila.	L	3-4	G. Jackson	Herbel	7—Houston	L	5-10	Forsch	Nyman
25—At Phila.	L	2-9	Lersch	Roberts	7—Houston	L	4-9	Billingham	Coombs
26—At Phila.	W	16-2	Dobson	Wise	8—Houston	L	7-8	Wilson	Kirby
28—At Mon.	L	4-5	Strohmayer	Coombs	9—Atlanta	L	3-6†	Priddy	Dukes
29—At Mon.	L	3-4	Morton	Kirby	9—Atlanta	W	7-4	Wilson	Niekro
31—At N. Y.	L	5-6	Frisella	Herbel	10—Atlanta	W	3-2	Roberts	Reed
					11—Cinn.	W	3-2	Dobson	Nolan
AUGUST—					12—Cinn.	W	4-2	Coombs	Cloninger
1—At N. Y.	L	2-4	Seaver	Wilson	13—Cinn.	W	5-4	Kirby	Wilcox
2—At N. Y.	W	3-0	Coombs	McAndrew	14—At L. A.	L	4-12	Osteen	Nyman
2—At N. Y.	W	4-2	Willis	Frisella	15—At L. A.	L	4-5	Mikkelsen	Dukes
3—Cinn.	W	10-3	Kirby	Cloninger	16—At L. A.	W	4-0	Roberts	Moeller
4—Cinn.	L	1-12	Merritt	Dobson	17—S. Fran.	L	3-4	Robertson	Dobson
5—Houston	L	3-4*	Gladding	Dukes	18—S. Fran.	L	2-3*	Reberger	Coombs
6—Houston	L	6-8	Billingham	Coombs	19—S. Fran.	L	0-3	Perry	Kirby
7—Atlanta	L	2-8	Niekro	Roberts	22—At Atl.	L	2-3	Nash	Wilson
7—Atlanta	W	6-1	Kirby	Reed	23—At Atl	W	2-0	Arlin	Jarvis
9—Atlanta	W	4-2	Dobson	Jarvis	24—At Atl.	W	5-0	Roberts	McQueen
11—At St. L.	L	10-11	Parker	Herbel	25—At S. F.	W	7-4	Dobson	Reberger
12—At St. L.	L	4-5‡	Gibson	Willis	26—At S. F.	L	6-7	Cumberland	Doyle
13—At St. L.	W	9-7	Kirby	Cleveland	27—At S. F.	L	2-3	Perry	Coombs
14—At Pitts.	L	1-2	Pena	Roberts	29—Los Ang.	L	2-8	Vance	Roberts
14—At Pitts.	L	1-10	Walker	Dobson	30—Los Ang.	W	2-1	Dobson	Osteen
15—At Pitts.	L	3-9	Veale	Wilson					
16—At Pitts.	W	8-6	Herbel	Pena	OCTOBER—				
17—At Chi.	L	0-7	Pappas	Kirby	1—Los Ang.	L	4-7	Sutton	Dukes

* 10 innings.   † 11 innings.   ‡ 14 innings.   § 15 innings.

Major League Baseball Players Association

Marvin J. Miller—Executive Director

Richard M. Moss—Legal Counsel

EXECUTIVE BOARD

Steve Hamilton—American League representative
Tom Haller—National League representative
Jim Bunning—Pension Committee
Brooks Robinson—Pension Committee
Plus all remaining player representatives

NATIONAL LEAGUE PLAYER REPRESENTATIVES

Tom Haller, Los Angeles Dodgers, National League representative

Cecil Upshaw—Atlanta Braves
Jim Colborn—Chicago Cubs
Woody Woodward—Cincinnati Reds
Denny Lemaster—Houston Astros
Wes Parker—Los Angeles Dodgers
Bob Bailey—Montreal Expos

Tom Seaver—New York Mets
Terry Harmon—Philadelphia Phillies
Dave Giusti—Pittsburgh Pirates
Dal Maxvill—St. Louis Cardinals
Ed Spiezio—San Diego Padres
Gaylord Perry—San Francisco Giants

RICO CARTY
• BRAVES •
BATTING CHAMPION
(.366)

BILLY WILLIAMS
• CUBS •
RUNS (137)
HITS (205-tied)

JOHNNY BENCH
• REDS •
HOME RUNS (45)
RUNS BATTED IN (148)

1970 NATIONAL LEAGUE LEADERS

TOM SEAVER
• METS •
EARNED-RUN AVERAGE
(2.81)
STRIKEOUTS (283)

GAYLORD PERRY
• GIANTS •
WINS (23-tied)
SHUTOUTS (5), GAMES
STARTED (41), INNINGS
PITCHED (329)

FERGIE JENKINS
• CUBS •
COMPLETE GAMES (24)

National League Averages for 1970

CHAMPIONSHIP WINNERS IN PREVIOUS YEARS

1876—Chicago .788	1907—Chicago .704	1939—Cincinnati .630
1877—Boston .646	1908—Chicago .643	1940—Cincinnati .654
1878—Boston .683	1909—Pittsburgh .724	1941—Brooklyn .649
1879—Providence .705	1910—Chicago .675	1942—St. Louis .688
1880—Chicago .798	1911—New York .647	1943—St. Louis .682
1881—Chicago .667	1912—New York .682	1944—St. Louis .682
1882—Chicago .655	1913—New York .664	1945—Chicago .636
1883—Boston .643	1914—Boston .614	1946—St. Louis* .628
1884—Providence .750	1915—Philadelphia .592	1947—Brooklyn .610
1885—Chicago .777	1916—Brooklyn .610	1948—Boston .595
1886—Chicago .726	1917—New York .636	1949—Brooklyn .630
1887—Detroit .637	1918—Chicago .651	1950—Philadelphia .591
1888—New York .641	1919—Cincinnati .686	1951—New York† .624
1889—New York .659	1920—Brooklyn .604	1952—Brooklyn .627
1890—Brooklyn .667	1921—New York .614	1953—Brooklyn .682
1891—Boston .630	1922—New York .604	1954—New York .630
1892—Boston .680	1923—New York .621	1955—Brooklyn .641
1893—Boston .662	1924—New York .608	1956—Brooklyn .604
1894—Baltimore .695	1925—Pittsburgh .621	1957—Milwaukee .617
1895—Baltimore .669	1926—St. Louis .578	1958—Milwaukee .597
1896—Baltimore .698	1927—Pittsburgh .610	1959—Los Angeles‡ .564
1897—Boston .705	1928—St. Louis .617	1960—Pittsburgh .617
1898—Boston .685	1929—Chicago .645	1961—Cincinnati .604
1899—Brooklyn .677	1930—St. Louis .597	1962—San Francisco§ .624
1900—Brooklyn .603	1931—St. Louis .656	1963—Los Angeles .611
1901—Pittsburgh .647	1932—Chicago .584	1964—St. Louis .574
1902—Pittsburgh .741	1933—New York .599	1965—Los Angeles .599
1903—Pittsburgh .650	1934—New York .621	1966—Los Angeles .586
1904—New York .693	1935—Chicago .649	1967—St. Louis .627
1905—New York .686	1936—New York .597	1968—St. Louis .599
1906—Chicago .763	1937—New York .625	1969—New York (East)a . .617
	1938—Chicago .586	

*Defeated Brooklyn, two games to none, in playoff for pennant. †Defeated Brooklyn, two games to one, in playoff for pennant. ‡Defeated Milwaukee, two games to none, in playoff for pennant. §Defeated Los Angeles, two games to one, in playoff for pennant. aDefeated Atlanta (West) in Championship Series.

STANDING OF CLUBS AT CLOSE OF SEASON

EAST DIVISION

Club	Pitt.	Chi.	N.Y.	St.L.	Phil.	Mon.	Cin.	L.A.	S.F.	Hou.	Atl.	S.D.	W.	L.	Pct.	G.B.
Pittsburgh	..	10	12	12	14	9	4	6	4	6	6	6	89	73	.549	....
Chicago	8	..	7	7	9	13	7	4	7	4	9	8	84	78	.519	5
New York	6	11	..	12	13	8	4	5	6	6	6	6	83	79	.512	6
St. Louis	6	11	6	..	10	11	3	5	5	6	5	8	76	86	.469	13
Philadelphia	4	9	5	8	..	7	5	5	8	5	9	9	73	88	.453	15½
Montreal	9	5	10	7	11	..	5	4	6	4	6	6	73	89	.451	16

WEST DIVISION

Club	Cin.	L.A.	S.F.	Hou.	Atl.	S.D.	Pitt.	Chi.	N.Y.	St.L.	Phil.	Mon.	W.	L.	Pct.	G.B.
Cincinnati	..	13	9	15	13	8	8	5	8	9	7	7	102	60	.630	....
Los Angeles	5	..	9	10	12	11	6	6	7	7	6	8	87	74	.540	14½
San Francisco	9	9	..	8	11	13	8	5	6	7	6	4	86	76	.531	16
Houston	3	8	10	..	9	14	6	5	6	6	4	8	79	83	.488	23
Atlanta	5	6	7	9	..	9	6	8	6	7	7	6	76	86	.469	26
San Diego	10	7	5	4	9	..	6	4	3	6	6	3	63	99	.389	39

CANCELLED GAME—Los Angeles at Philadelphia, July 29 (rain).

CHAMPIONSHIP SERIES—Cincinnati defeated Pittsburgh, three games to none.

RECORD AT HOME

EAST DIVISION

Club	Pitt.	Chi.	N.Y.	Phil.	Mon.	St.L.	Cin.	S.F.	Hou.	Atl.	L.A.	S.D.	W.	L.	Pct.
Pittsburgh	..-..	5-4	6-3	8-1	5-5	5-4	3-3	3-3	4-2	4-2	3-3	4-2	50	32	.610
Chicago	4-5	..-..	1-7	7-2	7-2	4-5	4-2	4-2	5-1	3-3	3-3	4-2	46	34	.575
New York	3-6	4-6	..-..	6-3	5-4	6-3	3-3	3-3	4-2	4-2	3-3	3-3	44	38	.537
Philadelphia	3-6	7-2	2-7	..-..	4-5	4-5	3-3	4-2	5-1	4-2	1-4	3-3	40	40	.500
Montreal	4-4	3-6	6-3	6-3	..-..	4-5	3-3	3-3	2-4	3-3	2-4	3-3	39	41	.488
St. Louis	2-7	6-3	3-6	5-4	6-3	..-..	2-4	3-3	1-5	2-4	1-5	3-3	34	47	.420

WEST DIVISION

Club	Cin.	S.F.	Hou.	Atl.	L.A.	S.D.	Pitt.	Chi.	N.Y.	Phil.	Mon.	St.L.	W.	L.	Pct.
Cincinnati	..-..	6-3	8-1	6-3	6-3	5-4	5-1	3-3	5-1	4-2	4-2	5-1	57	24	.704
San Francisco	6-3	..-..	6-3	6-3	4-5	6-3	5-1	3-3	3-3	2-4	3-3	4-2	48	33	.593
Houston	2-7	7-2	..-..	5-4	3-6	7-2	4-2	4-2	4-2	3-3	4-2	1-5	44	37	.543
Atlanta	2-7	4-5	5-4	..-..	2-7	5-4	4-2	5-1	4-2	5-1	3-3	3-3	42	39	.519
Los Angeles	2-7	4-5	4-5	5-4	..-..	4-5	6-3	3-3	3-3	4-2	2-4	2-4	39	42	.481
San Diego	6-3	2-7	2-7	5-4	4-5	..-..	4-2	1-5	3-3	0-6	3-1	1-5	31	50	.383

NOTE—New York at Chicago, September 3, postponed, played at New York, September 22; Pittsburgh at Montreal, September 6, postponed, played at Pittsburgh, September 28, as part of a doubleheader.

RECORD ABROAD

EAST DIVISION

Club	St.L.	N.Y.	Pitt.	Chi.	Mon.	Phil.	L.A.	Cin.	S.F.	Hou.	Atl.	S.D.	W.	L.	Pct.
St. Louis	..-..	3-6	4-5	5-4	5-4	5-4	4-2	1-5	2-4	5-1	3-3	5-1	42	39	.519
New York	6-3	..-..	3-6	7-1	3-6	7-2	2-4	1-5	3-3	2-4	2-4	3-3	39	41	.488
Pittsburgh	7-2	6-3	..-..	5-4	4-4	6-3	3-3	1-5	1-5	2-4	2-4	2-4	39	41	.488
Chicago	3-6	6-4	4-5	..-..	6-3	2-7	3-3	3-3	3-3	2-4	1-5	5-1	38	44	.463
Montreal	3-6	4-5	5-5	2-7	..-..	5-4	2-4	2-4	3-3	2-4	3-3	3-3	34	48	.415
Philadelphia	4-5	3-6	1-8	2-7	3-6	..-..	4-2	2-4	4-2	3-3	1-5	6-0	33	48	.407

WEST DIVISION

Club	L.A.	Cinn.	S.F.	Hou.	Atl.	S.D.	St.L.	N.Y.	Pitt.	Chi.	Mon.	Phil.	W.	L.	Pct.
Los Angeles	..-..	3-6	5-4	6-3	7-2	5-4	5-1	3-3	3-3	3-3	4-2	4-1	48	32	.600
Cincinnati	7-2	..-..	3-6	7-2	7-2	3-6	4-2	3-3	2-4	3-3	3-3	4-5	45	36	.556
San Francisco	5-4	3-6	..-..	2-7	5-4	7-2	3-3	3-3	3-3	2-4	3-2	2-4	38	43	.469
Houston	5-4	1-8	3-6	..-..	4-5	7-2	5-1	2-4	2-4	1-5	4-2	1-5	35	46	.432
Atlanta	4-5	3-6	3-6	4-5	..-..	4-5	4-2	2-4	2-4	3-3	3-3	2-4	34	47	.420
San Diego	3-6	4-5	3-6	2-7	4-5	..-..	3-3	3-3	2-4	2-4	3-3	3-2	32	49	.395

SHUTOUT GAMES

Club	Cin.	L.A.	Pitt.	N.Y.	Atl.	Chi.	S.F.	St.L.	Mon.	S.D.	Hou.	Phila.	W.	L.	Pct.
Cincinnati	....	3	0	0	1	0	2	2	1	2	4	0	15	1	.938
Los Angeles	0	..	3	4	2	0	3	0	0	2	1	2	17	11	.607
Pittsburgh	0	2	..	0	0	1	0	3	2	1	1	3	13	12	.520
New York	0	0	0	..	0	2	0	2	0	1	1	4	10	10	.500
Atlanta	0	1	3	0	..	2	0	0	2	0	1	0	9	9	.500
Chicago	1	0	1	1	0	..	..	0	0	2	0	1	9	9	.500
San Francisco	0	1	0	0	4	0	..	0	0	1	1	0	7	8	.467
St. Louis	0	2	0	1	0	2	0	..	2	2	0	2	11	13	.458
Montreal	0	0	2	2	0	1	0	3	..	0	0	2	10	13	.435
San Diego	0	2	0	1	2	0	0	1	2	..	1	0	9	12	.429
Houston	0	0	0	1	0	0	1	1	0	2	..	1	6	11	.353
Philadelphia	0	0	3	0	0	1	0	0	2	1	1	..	8	15	.348

OFFICIAL NATIONAL LEAGUE BATTING AVERAGES

Compiled by Elias Sports Bureau, New York, N. Y.

CLUB BATTING

Club	G.	AB.	R.	OR.	H.	TB.	2B.	3B.	HR.	RBI.	SH.	SF.	SB.	CS.	LOB.	Pct.
Cinn.	162	5540	775	681	1498	2414	253	45	191	726	58	48	115	52	1178	.2703
L. A.	161	5606	749	684	1515	2143	233	67	87	695	72	50	138	57	1185	.2702
Pitts.	162	5637	729	664	1522	2287	235	70	130	676	53	53	66	34	1177	.2700
Atl.	162	5546	736	772	1495	2238	215	24	160	692	54	42	58	34	1157	.2695
St. L.	162	5689	744	747	1497	2156	218	51	113	688	52	40	117	47	1199	.263
S. F.	162	5578	831	826	1460	2282	257	35	165	773	66	40	83	27	1275	.262
Hous.	162	5574	744	763	1446	2177	250	47	129	694	63	43	114	41	1186	.259
Chi.	162	5491	806	679	1424	2277	228	44	179	761	75	36	39	16	1130	.259
N. Y.	162	5443	695	630	1358	2013	211	42	120	640	74	48	118	54	1211	.249
S. D.	162	5494	681	788	1353	2149	208	36	172	629	83	29	60	45	1093	.246
Phila.	161	5456	594	730	1299	1942	224	58	101	553	62	37	72	64	1093	.238
Mont.	162	5411	687	807	1284	1973	211	35	136	646	107	35	65	45	1219	.237
Tot.		66465	8771	8771	17151	26051	2743	554	1683	8173	819	501	1045	516	14103	.258

INDIVIDUAL BATTING

(Top Fifteen Qualifiers for Batting Championship—502 or More Plate Appearances)

*Bats lefthanded. †Switch-hitter.

Player and Club	G.	AB.	R.	H.	TB.	2B.	3B.	HR.	RBI.	SH.	SF.	SB.	CS.	Pct.
Carty, Ricardo, Atlanta	136	478	84	175	279	23	3	25	101	0	3	1	2	.366
Torre, Joseph, St. Louis	161	624	89	203	311	27	9	21	100	0	3	2	2	.325
Sanguillen, Manuel, Pittsburgh	128	486	63	158	216	19	9	7	61	1	6	2	3	.325
Williams, Billy, Chicago*	161	636	137	205	373	34	4	42	129	0	4	7	1	.322
Parker, M. Wesley, Los Ang†	161	614	84	196	281	47	4	10	111	4	8	8	2	.319
Gaston, Clarence, San Diego	146	584	92	186	317	26	9	29	93	0	2	4	1	.318
Perez, Atanasio, Cincinnati	158	587	107	186	346	28	6	40	129	0	7	8	3	.317
Rose, Peter, Cincinnati†	159	649	120	205	305	37	9	15	52	0	4	12	7	.316
Tolan, Robert, Cincinnati*	152	569	112	186	280	34	6	16	80	9	7	57	20	.316
Hickman, James, Chicago	149	514	102	162	299	33	4	32	115	2	3	0	1	.315
Millan, Felix, Atlanta	142	590	100	183	224	25	5	2	37	9	3	16	5	.310
Davis, William, Los Angeles*	146	593	92	181	260	23	16	8	93	8	6	38	14	.305
Cepeda, Orlando, Atlanta	148	567	87	173	308	33	0	34	111	0	4	6	5	.305
Menke, Denis, Houston	154	562	82	171	248	26	6	13	92	7	9	6	5	.304
Brock, Louis, St. Louis*	155	664	114	202	280	29	5	13	57	1	3	51	15	.304

DEPARTMENTAL LEADERS: G—Wes Parker, Torre, Billy Williams, 161; AB—Mateo Alou, 677; R—Billy Williams, 137; H—Rose, Billy Williams, 205; TB—Billy Williams, 373; 2B—Wes Parker, 47; 3B—William Davis, 16; HR—Bench, 45; RBI—Bench, 148; SH—Dobson, 19; SF—Bench, 11; SB—Tolan, 57; CS—Tolan, 20.

(All Players in Ten or More Games—Listed Alphabetically)

Player and Club	G.	AB.	R.	H.	TB.	2B.	3B.	HR.	RBI.	SH.	SF.	SB.	CS.	Pct.
Aaron, Henry, Atlanta	150	516	103	154	296	26	1	38	118	0	6	9	0	.298
Aaron, Tommie, Atlanta	44	63	3	13	21	2	0	2	7	0	0	0	0	.206
Abernathy, Ted, 11 Chi-11 StL	22	3	0	0	0	0	0	0	0	0	0	0	0	.000
Agee, Tommie, New York	153	636	107	182	298	30	7	24	75	1	2	31	15	.286
Aguirre, Henry, Chicago†	17	2	0	0	0	0	0	0	0	0	0	0	0	.000
Allen, Richard, St. Louis	122	459	88	128	257	17	5	34	101	0	1	5	4	.279
Alley, L. Eugene, Pittsburgh	121	426	46	104	154	16	5	8	41	2	4	7	3	.244
Alou, Jesus, Houston	117	458	59	140	176	27	3	1	44	3	4	3	2	.306
Alou, Mateo, Pittsburgh*	155	677	97	201	241	21	8	1	47	4	3	19	11	.297
Arcia, Jose, San Diego	114	229	28	51	66	9	3	0	17	4	0	3	6	.223
Aspromonte, Robert, Atlanta	62	127	5	27	30	3	0	0	7	0	2	0	0	.213
Bailey, Robert, Montreal	131	352	77	101	210	19	3	28	84	2	2	5	3	.287
Baker, Johnnie, Atlanta	13	24	3	7	7	0	0	0	4	0	1	0	0	.292
Baldschun, Jack, San Diego	12	0	0	0	0	0	0	0	0	0	0	0	0	.000
Banks, Ernest, Chicago	72	222	25	56	102	6	2	12	44	1	3	0	0	.252
Barber, Stephen, 5 Chi-5 Atl*	10	4	0	1	1	0	0	0	0	0	0	0	0	.250
Barton, Robert, San Diego	61	188	15	41	59	6	0	4	16	1	1	1	1	.218
Bateman, John, Montreal	139	520	51	123	199	21	5	15	68	5	3	8	4	.237
Bates, Delbert, Philadelphia*	22	60	1	8	10	2	0	0	1	0	0	0	1	.133

Player and Club	G.	AB.	R.	H.	TB.	2B.	3B.	HR.	RBI.	SH.	SF.	SB.	CS.	Pct.
Beauchamp, James, 31Hou-44StL	75	84	11	20	28	2	0	2	10	0	2	2	1	.238
Beckert, Glenn, Chicago	143	591	99	170	206	15	6	3	36	6	3	4	1	.288
Bench, Johnny, Cincinnati	158	605	97	177	355	35	4	45	148	1	11	5	2	.293
Billingham, John, Houston	46	58	2	6	6	0	0	0	1	7	0	0	0	.103
Blasingame, Wade, Houston☆	13	24	0	2	2	0	0	0	2	0	0	0	0	.083
Blass, Stephen, Pittsburgh	32	70	3	8	9	1	0	0	2	3	1	0	0	.114
Boccabella, John, Montreal	61	145	18	39	59	3	1	5	17	0	0	0	1	.269
Bonds, Bobby, San Francisco	157	663	134	200	334	36	10	26	78	1	2	48	10	.302
Borbon, Pedro, Cincinnati	12	3	0	0	0	0	0	0	0	0	0	0	0	.000
Boswell, Kenneth, New York☆	105	351	32	89	121	13	2	5	44	3	5	5	4	.254
Bouton, James, Houston	29	17	3	6	6	0	0	0	2	1	0	0	0	.353
Bowa, Lawrence, Philadelphia†	145	547	50	137	166	17	6	0	34	6	3	24	13	.250
Boyer, Cletis, Atlanta	134	475	44	117	181	14	1	16	62	3	5	2	5	.246
Brand, Ronald, Montreal	72	126	10	30	38	2	3	0	9	4	1	2	1	.238
Bravo, Angel, Cincinnati☆	65	65	10	18	21	1	1	0	3	4	0	0	1	.277
Brewer, James, Los Angeles☆	58	12	0	1	1	0	0	0	1	1	0	1	0	.083
Briggs, John, Philadelphia☆	110	341	43	92	148	15	7	9	47	4	3	5	4	.270
Briles, Nelson, St. Louis	30	39	4	7	12	1	2	0	3	3	0	0	0	.179
Brock, Louis, St. Louis☆	155	664	114	202	280	29	5	13	57	1	3	51	15	.304
Brown, Ollie, San Diego	139	534	79	156	261	34	1	23	89	3	6	5	3	.292
Brown, Oscar, Atlanta	28	47	6	18	25	2	1	1	7	1	1	0	2	.383
Browne, Byron, Philadelphia	104	270	29	67	118	17	2	10	36	1	3	1	2	.248
Brunet, George, Pittsburgh	12	4	0	0	0	0	0	0	0	0	0	0	0	.000
Bryant, Donald, Houston	15	24	2	5	5	0	0	0	3	0	1	0	0	.208
Bryant, Ronald, San Francisco†	34	27	0	3	3	0	0	0	2	2	0	0	0	.111
Buckner, William, Los Angeles☆	28	68	6	13	18	3	1	0	4	0	0	0	1	.191
Bunning, James, Philadelphia	35	71	1	9	9	0	0	0	6	3	1	0	0	.127
Burda, E. Robert, San Francisco☆	28	23	1	6	6	0	0	0	3	0	0	0	0	.261
Callison, John, Chicago☆	147	477	65	126	210	23	2	19	68	0	3	7	2	.264
Campbell, David, San Diego	154	581	71	127	195	28	2	12	40	9	4	18	6	.219
Campbell, James, St. Louis☆	13	13	0	3	3	0	0	0	1	0	0	0	0	.231
Campisi, Salvatore, St. Louis	37	1	0	0	0	0	0	0	0	0	0	0	0	.000
Cannizzaro, Christopher, S D	111	341	27	95	129	13	3	5	42	4	3	2	7	.279
Carbo, Bernardo, Cincinnati☆	125	365	54	113	201	19	3	21	63	2	2	10	4	.310
Cardenal, Jose, St. Louis	148	552	73	162	236	32	6	10	74	1	0	26	9	.293
Cardwell, Donald, 16 NY-16 Atl	32	10	1	2	2	0	0	0	1	0	1	0	0	.200
Carlton, Steven, St. Louis☆	34	80	4	16	18	2	0	0	4	3	0	1	1	.200
Carrithers, Donald, San Francisco	11	6	0	0	0	0	0	0	0	0	0	0	0	.000
Carroll, Clay, Cincinnati	65	14	1	1	1	0	0	0	0	0	0	0	0	.071
Carty, Ricardo, Atlanta	136	478	84	175	279	23	3	25	101	0	3	1	2	.366
Cash, David, Pittsburgh	64	210	30	66	88	7	6	1	28	0	2	5	2	.314
Cedeno, Cesar, Houston	90	355	46	110	160	21	4	7	42	3	2	17	4	.310
Cepeda, Orlando, Atlanta	148	567	87	173	308	33	0	34	111	0	4	6	5	.305
Chaney, Darrel, Cincinnati†	57	95	7	22	28	3	0	1	4	2	0	1	1	.232
Chlupsa, Robert, St. Louis	14	0	0	0	0	0	0	0	0	0	0	0	0	.000
Clemente, Roberto, Pittsburgh	108	412	65	145	229	22	10	14	60	1	2	3	0	.352
Clendenon, Donn, New York	121	396	65	114	204	18	3	22	97	0	7	4	1	.288
Cleveland, Reginald, St. Louis	16	4	0	1	1	0	0	0	0	0	0	0	0	.250
Cline, Tyrone, 2 Mont-48 Cin☆	50	65	13	18	27	7	1	0	8	3	0	1	2	.277
Clines, Eugene, Pittsburgh	31	37	4	15	17	2	0	0	3	0	0	2	1	.405
Cloninger, Tony, Cincinnati	30	47	7	10	18	2	0	2	3	2	0	0	0	.213
Colbert, Nathan, San Diego	156	572	84	148	291	17	6	38	86	1	3	3	5	.259
Colborn, James, Chicago	34	15	0	1	1	0	0	0	1	1	0	0	0	.067
Compton, Michael, Philadelphia	47	110	8	18	23	0	1	1	7	0	0	0	0	.164
Concepcion, David, Cincinnati	101	265	38	69	84	6	3	1	19	3	2	10	2	.260
Cook, Ronald, Houston☆	43	17	2	4	8	0	2	0	1	1	0	0	0	.235
Coombs, Daniel, San Diego	35	52	3	5	7	2	0	0	1	7	0	0	0	.096
Corkins, Michael, San Diego	25	37	6	8	12	1	0	1	4	5	0	0	0	.216
Corrales, Patrick, Cincinnati	43	106	9	25	35	5	1	1	10	0	0	0	0	.236
Crawford, Willie, Los Angeles☆	109	299	48	70	114	8	6	8	40	0	2	4	4	.234
Crosby, Edward, St. Louis☆	38	95	9	24	30	4	1	0	6	1	1	0	0	.253
Culver, George, 11 StL-32 Hou	43	21	3	4	6	0	1	0	6	2	2	1	0	.190
Dal Canton, J. Bruce, Pittsburgh	41	16	0	0	0	0	0	0	0	0	1	0	0	.000
Davalillo, Victor, St. Louis☆	111	183	29	57	80	14	3	1	33	2	1	4	1	.311
DaVanon, F. Gerald, St. Louis	11	18	2	2	3	1	0	0	0	0	0	0	0	.111
Davenport, James, San Francisco	22	37	3	9	10	1	0	0	4	1	1	0	0	.243
Davis, H. Thomas, 57 Hou-11 Chi	68	255	28	71	104	14	2	5	38	0	0	8	3	.278

Player and Club	G.	AB.	R.	H.	TB.	2B.	3B.	HR.	RBI.	SH.	SF.	SB.	CS.	Pct.
Davis, William, Los Angeles*	146	593	92	181	260	23	16	8	93	8	6	38	14	.305
Davison, Michael, San Francisco*	31	1	1	0	0	0	0	0	0	0	0	0	0	.000
Day, Charles, 11 Chi-41 Mont*	52	116	16	31	35	4	0	0	5	4	0	3	2	.267
Dean, Tommy, San Diego	61	158	18	35	48	5	1	2	13	7	1	2	0	.222
Decker, George, Chicago	24	34	3	6	10	1	0	1	3	2	0	0	0	.176
Didier, Robert, Atlanta†	57	168	9	25	29	2	1	0	7	2	0	1	0	.149
Dierker, Lawrence, Houston	37	92	7	16	18	2	0	0	4	9	1	0	0	.174
Dietz, Richard, San Francisco	148	493	82	148	254	36	2	22	107	2	5	0	1	.300
DiLauro, Jack, Houston†	43	2	0	0	0	0	0	0	0	0	0	0	0	.000
Dillman, William, Montreal	18	2	0	0	0	0	0	0	0	0	0	0	0	.000
Dobson, Patrick, San Diego	40	71	5	10	11	1	0	0	4	19	0	0	1	.141
Doyle, R. Dennis, Philadelphia*	112	413	43	86	116	10	7	2	16	1	2	6	5	.208
Dukes, Thomas, San Diego	53	7	0	0	0	0	0	0	0	0	0	0	0	.000
Dunegan, James, Chicago	10	4	0	1	2	1	0	0	2	0	0	0	0	.250
Dyer, Donald, New York	59	148	8	31	38	1	0	2	12	1	0	1	1	.209
Edwards, Howard, Phil	35	78	5	21	21	0	0	0	6	3	0	0	0	.269
Edwards, John, Houston*	140	458	46	101	146	16	4	7	49	3	2	1	0	.221
Ellis, Dock, Pittsburgh†	38	70	9	7	8	1	0	0	1	4	0	1	0	.100
Evans, Darrell, Atlanta*	12	44	4	14	17	1	1	0	9	0	0	0	0	.318
Fairey, James, Montreal	92	211	35	51	75	9	3	3	25	2	2	1	3	.242
Fairly, Ronald, Montreal*	119	385	54	111	175	19	0	15	61	6	4	10	2	.288
Ferrara, Alfred, San Diego	138	372	44	103	165	15	4	13	51	0	1	0	0	.277
Folkers, Richard, New York*	16	6	1	2	2	0	0	0	0	3	0	0	0	.333
Foster, Alan, Los Angeles	33	64	4	7	7	0	0	0	6	8	1	0	0	.109
Foy, Joseph, New York	99	322	39	76	106	12	0	6	37	2	3	22	13	.236
Frisella, Daniel, New York*	30	13	0	4	4	0	0	0	1	1	0	0	0	.308
Fryman, Woodrow, Philadelphia	27	39	2	5	5	0	0	0	1	3	0	0	0	.128
Fuentes, Rigoberto, San Fran†	123	435	49	116	149	13	7	2	32	10	6	4	5	.267
Gabrielson, Leonard, Los Ang*	43	42	1	8	10	2	0	0	6	0	1	0	0	.190
Gagliano, Philip, 18St. L-26Chi	44	72	5	12	12	0	0	0	7	1	0	0	1	.167
Gallagher, Alan, San Francisco	109	282	31	75	106	15	2	4	28	5	1	2	1	.266
Gamble, Oscar, Philadelphia*	88	275	31	72	95	12	4	1	19	2	0	5	4	.262
Garber, H. Eugene, Pittsburgh	14	3	1	2	2	0	0	0	0	0	0	0	0	.667
Garr, Ralph, Atlanta*	37	96	18	27	30	3	0	0	8	0	1	5	2	.281
Garrett, R. Wayne, New York*	114	366	74	93	154	17	4	12	45	3	2	5	1	.254
Garrido, Gil, Atlanta	101	367	38	97	113	5	4	1	19	3	4	0	2	.264
Garvey, Steven, Los Angeles	34	93	8	25	33	5	0	1	6	0	1	1	1	.269
Gaspar, Rodney, New York†	11	14	4	0	0	0	0	0	0	0	0	1	0	.000
Gaston, Clarence, San Diego	146	584	92	186	317	26	9	29	93	0	2	4	1	.318
Gentry, Gary, New York	32	59	2	4	6	2	0	0	2	5	0	0	1	.068
Geronimo, Cesar, Houston*	47	37	5	9	9	0	0	0	2	1	0	0	0	.243
Gibson, Joseph, Pittsburgh	41	3	0	0	0	0	0	0	0	0	0	0	0	.000
Gibson, J. Russell, San Fran	24	69	3	16	22	6	0	0	6	0	0	0	0	.232
Gibson, Robert, St.L	40	109	14	33	44	3	1	2	19	6	1	0	2	.303
Giusti, David, Pittsburgh	66	16	1	3	5	0	1	0	3	1	0	0	0	.188
Gladding, Fred, Houston*	63	6	0	0	0	0	0	0	0	1	0	0	0	.000
Gonzalez, A. Antonio, Atl*	123	430	57	114	157	18	2	7	55	0	3	3	5	.265
Gosger, James, Montreal*	91	274	38	72	102	11	2	5	37	2	0	5	3	.263
Grabarkewitz, Billy, Los Ang	156	529	92	153	240	20	8	17	84	3	7	19	9	.289
Granger, Wayne, Cincinnati	67	10	0	1	1	0	0	0	0	3	0	0	0	.100
Griffin, Thomas, Houston	23	33	1	2	3	1	0	0	1	4	0	0	0	.061
Grote, Gerald, New York	126	415	38	106	128	14	1	2	34	6	5	2	1	.255
Gullett, Donald, Cincinnati	44	19	3	4	6	0	1	0	2	0	0	1	0	.211
Gura, Lawrence, Chicago	20	10	0	0	0	0	0	0	0	1	0	0	0	.000
Hague, Joe, St. Louis*	139	451	58	122	188	16	4	14	68	4	5	2	1	.271
Hahn, Donald, Montreal	82	149	22	38	46	8	0	0	8	8	1	4	2	.255
Hall, Jimmie, 28 Chi-39 Atl*	67	79	9	13	22	3	0	2	5	0	0	0	0	.165
Haller, Thomas, Los Angeles*	112	325	47	93	151	16	6	10	47	3	3	3	0	.286
Hands, William, Chicago	39	75	6	10	12	2	0	0	6	9	2	0	0	.133
Harmon, Terry, Philadelphia	71	129	16	32	42	2	4	0	7	3	1	6	3	.248
Harrelson, Derrel, New York†	157	564	72	137	174	18	8	1	42	12	8	23	4	.243
Hart, James, San Francisco	76	255	30	72	110	12	1	8	37	0	4	0	0	.282
Hartenstein, Charles, 17 Pitt-6 StL	23	3	1	0	0	0	0	0	0	0	0	0	0	.000
Hebner, Richard, Pittsburgh*	120	420	60	122	195	24	8	11	46	3	3	2	3	.290
Heise, Robert, San Francisco	67	154	15	36	46	5	1	1	22	5	1	0	1	.234
Helms, Tommy, Cincinnati	150	575	42	136	162	21	1	1	45	5	4	2	2	.237

Player and Club	G.	AB.	R.	H.	TB.	2B.	3B.	HR.	RBI.	SH.	SF.	SB.	CS.	Pct.
Henderson, Kenneth, San Fran†	148	554	104	163	255	35	3	17	88	1	2	20	3	.294
Herbel, Ronald, 64 SD-12 NY	76	13	0	0	0	0	0	0	0	0	0	0	0	.000
Hiatt, Jack, 17 Mont-66 Chi	83	221	23	57	79	14	1	2	29	5	1	0	0	.258
Hickman, James, Chicago	149	514	102	162	299	33	4	32	115	2	3	0	1	.315
Hilgendorf, Thomas, St. Louis†	23	1	0	0	0	0	0	0	0	0	0	0	0	.000
Hisle, Larry, Philadelphia	126	405	52	83	143	22	4	10	44	3	4	5	5	.205
Hoerner, Joseph, Philadelphia	44	10	0	2	3	1	0	0	0	0	0	0	0	.200
Holtzman, Kenneth, Chicago	40	105	6	21	26	5	0	0	6	8	0	0	0	.200
Howard, Larry, Houston	31	88	11	27	39	6	0	2	16	0	0	0	0	.307
Hrabosky, Alan, St. Louis	16	3	0	0	0	0	0	0	0	0	0	0	0	.000
Hundley, C. Randolph, Chicago	73	250	13	61	87	5	0	7	36	4	1	0	1	.244
Hunt, Ronald, San Francisco	117	367	70	103	140	17	1	6	41	3	2	1	2	.281
Huntz, Stephen, San Diego†	106	352	54	77	118	8	0	11	37	5	3	0	3	.219
Hutto, James, Philadelphia	57	92	7	17	28	2	0	3	12	2	2	0	0	.185
Jackson, Grant, Philadelphia*	52	44	9	4	4	0	0	0	1	1	0	0	0	.091
Jackson, Roland, Atlanta*	103	328	60	85	105	14	3	0	20	3	3	11	4	.259
James, Cleo, Chicago	100	176	33	37	57	7	2	3	14	2	0	5	0	.210
Jarvis, R. Patrick, Atlanta	36	82	6	15	17	2	0	0	2	11	0	0	0	.183
Jaster, Larry, Atlanta*	14	3	0	0	0	0	0	0	0	0	0	0	0	.000
Javier, M. Julian, St. Louis	139	513	62	129	157	16	3	2	42	9	4	6	4	.251
Jenkins, Ferguson, Chicago	40	113	4	14	25	2	0	3	11	10	2	0	0	.124
Jeter, John, Pittsburgh	85	126	27	30	43	3	2	2	12	0	0	9	5	.238
Johnson, Deron, Philadelphia	159	574	66	147	262	28	3	27	93	2	2	0	0	.256
Johnson, Frank, San Francisco	67	161	25	44	58	1	2	3	31	2	0	1	1	.273
Johnson, Jerry, 7 StL-33 SF	40	16	1	1	1	0	0	0	0	0	0	0	0	.063
Jones, Cleon, New York	134	506	71	140	211	25	8	10	63	0	6	12	3	.277
Jones, Mack, Montreal*	108	271	51	65	124	11	3	14	32	1	1	5	3	.240
Jorgensen, Michael, New York*	76	87	15	17	31	3	1	3	4	1	0	2	2	.195
Joseph, Ricardo, Philadelphia	71	119	7	27	40	2	1	3	10	0	0	0	0	.227
Joshua, Von, Los Angeles*	72	109	23	29	39	1	3	1	8	0	1	2	2	.266
Kelly, Van, San Diego*	38	89	9	15	21	3	0	1	9	1	0	0	1	.169
Kennedy, James, St. Louis*	12	24	1	3	3	0	0	0	0	0	0	0	0	.125
Kessinger, Donald, Chicago‡	154	631	100	168	220	21	14	1	39	10	2	12	6	.266
Kester, Richard, Atlanta	15	9	0	0	0	0	0	0	0	0	0	0	0	.000
King, Harold, Atlanta*	89	204	29	53	94	8	0	11	30	0	1	1	0	.260
Kirby, Clayton, San Diego	36	74	4	11	12	1	0	0	1	3	0	0	0	.149
Koonce, Calvin, New York	13	1	0	0	0	0	0	0	0	0	0	0	0	.000
Koosman, Jerry, New York	30	70	5	6	7	1	0	0	4	8	0	0	0	.086
Kopacz, George, Pittsburgh*	10	16	1	3	3	0	0	0	0	1	0	0	0	.188
Kosco, Andrew, Los Angeles	74	224	21	51	87	12	0	8	27	2	1	1	1	.228
Kranepool, Edward, New York*	43	47	2	8	8	0	0	0	3	0	0	0	0	.170
Laboy, Jose, Montreal	137	432	37	86	129	26	1	5	53	7	4	0	2	.199
Lamb, John, Pittsburgh	23	3	0	0	0	0	0	0	0	0	0	0	0	.000
Lamb, Raymond, Los Angeles	35	4	0	0	0	0	0	0	0	0	0	0	0	.000
Lampard, C. Keith, Houston*	53	72	8	17	27	8	1	0	5	2	0	0	0	.236
Lanier, Harold, San Francisco†	134	438	33	101	122	13	1	2	41	2	2	1	2	.231
Lee, Leron, St. Louis*	121	264	28	60	93	13	1	6	23	1	4	5	1	.227
Lefebvre, James, Los Angeles†	109	314	33	79	108	15	1	4	44	4	3	1	1	.252
Lemaster, Denver, Houston	39	45	3	8	11	0	0	1	7	3	1	0	0	.178
Lersch, Barry, Philadelphia	42	31	3	2	2	0	0	0	1	5	1	0	0	.065
Linzy, Frank, 20 SF-47 StL	67	11	0	0	0	0	0	0	0	0	0	0	0	.000
Lis, Joseph, Philadelphia	13	37	1	7	12	2	0	1	4	0	0	0	0	.189
Lum, Michael, Atlanta*	123	291	25	74	116	17	2	7	28	2	1	3	2	.254
Marichal, Juan, San Francisco	34	85	5	5	5	0	0	0	3	5	1	0	0	.059
Marshall, David, New York*	92	189	21	46	76	10	1	6	29	0	1	4	1	.243
Marshall, Michael, 4 Hou-24 Mon	28	11	0	1	1	0	0	0	1	2	1	0	0	.091
Martin, Joseph, Chicago*	40	77	11	12	16	1	0	1	4	1	1	0	0	.156
Martinez, Jose, Pittsburgh	19	20	1	1	1	0	0	0	0	1	0	0	0	.050
Martinez, Orlando, Houston†	75	150	12	33	36	3	0	0	12	0	0	0	0	.220
Mashore, Clyde, Montreal	13	25	2	4	7	0	0	1	3	0	0	0	0	.160
Mason, Donald, San Francisco*	46	36	4	5	5	0	0	0	1	0	0	0	0	.139
Maxvill, C. Dallan, St. Louis	152	399	35	80	89	5	2	0	28	9	7	0	0	.201
May, Jerry, Pittsburgh	51	139	13	29	40	4	2	1	16	0	2	0	0	.209
May, Lee, Cincinnati	153	605	78	153	293	34	2	34	94	0	4	1	1	.253
Mayberry, John, Houston*	50	148	23	32	54	3	2	5	14	1	2	1	1	.216
Mays, Willie, San Francisco	139	478	94	139	242	15	2	28	83	0	6	5	0	.291
Mazeroski, William, Pittsburgh	112	367	29	84	119	14	0	7	39	5	3	2	0	.229

Player and Club	G.	AB.	R.	H.	TB.	2B.	3B.	HR.	RBI.	SH.	SF.	SB.	CS.	Pct.
McAndrew, James, New York	32	54	6	8	11	3	0	0	2	8	0	0	0	.148
McCarver, J. Timothy, Phila*	44	164	16	47	72	11	1	4	14	1	0	2	2	.287
McCool, William, St. Louis	18	4	0	0	0	0	0	0	0	1	0	0	0	.000
McCormick, Michael, San Fran*	23	25	5	4	5	1	0	0	2	0	0	0	0	.160
McCovey, Willie, San Fran*	152	495	98	143	303	39	2	39	126	0	3	0	0	.289
McGinn, Daniel, Montreal*	52	35	2	4	4	0	0	0	1	3	0	0	0	.114
McGlothlin, James, Cincinnati	35	66	5	8	14	1	1	1	6	4	0	0	0	.121
McGraw, Frank, New York	57	13	1	4	5	1	0	0	5	0	1	0	0	.308
McMahon, Donald, San Francisco	61	14	1	2	2	0	0	0	1	1	0	0	0	.143
McQueen, Michael, Atlanta*	22	20	2	6	8	2	0	0	2	0	0	0	0	.300
McRae, Harold, Cincinnati	70	165	18	41	73	6	1	8	23	0	1	0	2	.248
Melendez, Luis, St. Louis	21	70	11	21	22	1	0	0	8	6	1	3	0	.300
Menke, Denis, Houston	154	562	82	171	248	26	6	13	92	7	9	6	5	.304
Merritt, James, Cincinnati*	35	83	7	14	23	0	0	3	6	6	0	0	0	.169
Mikkelsen, Peter, Los Angeles ..	33	6	0	2	2	0	0	0	1	1	0	0	0	.333
Millan, Felix, Atlanta	142	590	100	183	224	25	5	2	37	9	3	16	5	.310
Miller, Norman, Houston*	90	226	29	54	75	9	0	4	29	0	1	3	1	.239
Moeller, Joseph, Los Angeles	31	39	2	6	6	0	0	0	2	3	0	0	0	.154
Money, Donald, Philadelphia	120	447	66	132	207	25	4	14	66	3	7	4	7	.295
Montanez, Guillermo, Phila*	18	25	3	6	6	0	0	0	3	0	0	0	0	.240
Moose, Robert, Pittsburgh	29	66	5	12	16	2	1	0	2	4	0	0	0	.182
Morales, Julio, San Diego	28	58	6	9	14	0	1	1	4	0	0	0	0	.155
Morgan, Joe, Houston*	144	548	102	147	217	28	9	8	52	5	2	42	13	.268
Morton, Carl, Montreal	43	93	6	15	23	2	0	2	7	11	2	0	0	.161
Mota, Manuel, Los Angeles	124	417	63	127	160	12	6	3	37	12	2	11	6	.305
Murrell, Ivan, San Diego	125	347	43	85	136	9	3	12	35	1	1	9	7	.245
Nash, James, Atlanta	34	80	5	7	14	1	0	2	3	3	0	0	0	.088
Navarro, Julio, Atlanta	17	6	0	1	1	0	0	0	0	0	0	0	0	.167
Nelson, James, Pittsburgh	15	20	1	4	4	0	0	0	3	1	1	0	0	.200
Niekro, Philip, Atlanta	34	79	5	12	15	0	0	1	3	6	1	0	0	.152
Nolan, Gary, Cincinnati	37	82	4	13	16	1	1	0	6	9	1	0	0	.159
Norman, Fredie, 30 LA-1 StL* ..	31	7	1	1	1	0	0	0	0	2	0	0	0	.143
Nye, Richard, 6 StL-10 Mont* ..	16	19	2	4	4	0	0	0	0	1	0	0	1	.211
Oliver, Albert, Pittsburgh*	151	551	63	149	228	33	5	12	83	2	7	1	1	.270
Osteen, Claude, Los Angeles* ..	39	93	10	19	27	5	0	1	9	1	2	0	0	.204
Pagan, Jose, Pittsburgh	95	230	21	61	98	14	1	7	29	0	2	1	1	.265
Palmer, Lowell, Philadelphia	38	27	4	4	7	3	0	0	4	1	0	0	0	.148
Pappas, Milton, 11 Atl-21 Chi ..	32	60	7	12	22	2	1	2	5	1	1	0	0	.200
Parker, M. Wesley, Los Ang†	161	614	84	196	281	47	4	10	111	4	8	8	2	.319
Parrilla, Samuel, Philadelphia ..	11	16	0	2	3	1	0	0	0	0	0	0	0	.125
Pascual, Camilo, Los Angeles ..	10	0	0	0	0	0	0	0	0	0	0	0	0	.000
Patek, Freddie, Pittsburgh	84	237	42	58	81	10	5	1	19	6	4	8	2	.245
Pena, Jose, Los Angeles	29	8	1	1	1	0	0	0	0	3	0	0	0	.125
Pena, Orlando, Pittsburgh	23	6	0	0	0	0	0	0	0	1	0	0	0	.000
Pepitone, Joseph, 75Hou-56Chi*	131	492	82	127	237	18	7	26	79	4	3	5	4	.258
Perez, Atanasio, Cincinnati	158	587	107	186	346	28	6	40	129	0	7	8	3	.317
Perry, Gaylord, San Francisco ..	41	120	7	14	20	3	0	1	7	10	1	0	0	.117
Phillips, Adolfo, Montreal	92	214	36	51	81	6	3	6	21	1	1	7	1	.238
Pitlock, Lee, San Francisco*	18	25	2	2	6	1	0	1	2	1	0	0	0	.080
Pizarro, Juan, Chicago ☆..........	12	3	0	0	0	0	0	0	0	0	0	0	0	.000
Popovich, Paul, Chicago†	78	186	22	47	66	5	1	4	20	2	1	0	1	.253
Priddy, Robert, Atlanta	41	15	0	3	3	0	0	0	3	2	0	0	0	.200
Rader, Douglas, Houston	156	554	90	145	251	25	3	25	87	4	3	3	2	.252
Ramirez, Milton, St. Louis	62	79	8	15	19	2	1	0	3	0	0	0	1	.190
Ray, James, Houston	52	27	1	5	5	0	0	0	2	0	0	0	1	.185
Raymond, J. Claude, Montreal ..	59	11	0	0	0	0	0	0	0	2	0	0	0	.000
Reberger, Frank, San Francisco*	48	47	7	11	12	1	0	0	2	3	0	0	0	.234
Reed, Howard, Montreal	57	10	0	0	0	0	0	0	0	1	0	0	0	.000
Reed, Ronald, Atlanta	22	44	3	4	5	1	0	0	4	5	0	0	0	.091
Regan, Philip, Chicago	54	9	1	0	0	0	0	0	0	3	0	0	0	.000
Reid, Scott, Philadelphia*	25	49	5	6	7	1	0	0	1	0	0	0	0	.122
Renko, Steve, Montreal	41	80	8	16	22	3	0	1	6	3	0	0	0	.200
Reuss, Jerry, St. Louis*	20	40	3	2	2	0	0	0	1	5	0	1	0	.050
Ricketts, David, Pittsburgh†	14	11	0	2	2	0	0	0	0	0	0	0	0	.182
Roberts, David, San Diego*	43	59	6	9	16	1	0	2	3	6	0	0	0	.153
Robertson, Richard, San Francisco	41	59	4	6	14	2	0	2	3	7	0	0	0	.102
Robertson, Robert, Pittsburgh	117	390	69	112	220	19	4	27	82	1	7	4	1	.287

Player and Club	G.	AB.	R.	H.	TB.	2B.	3B.	HR.	RBI.	SH.	SF.	SB.	CS.	Pct.
Robinson, David, San Diego†	15	38	5	12	20	2	0	2	6	0	0	2	0	.316
Robles, Rafael, San Diego	23	89	5	19	20	1	0	0	3	2	0	3	0	.213
Rodriquez, Roberto, 1OSD-26Chi.	36	11	1	1	4	0	0	1	1	0	0	0	0	.091
Rojas, Octavio, St. Louis	23	47	2	5	5	0	0	0	2	0	0	0	0	.106
Rose, Peter, Cincinnati†	159	649	120	205	305	37	9	15	52	0	4	12	7	.316
Ross, Gary, San Diego	33	8	1	4	5	1	0	0	2	2	0	0	0	.500
Rudolph, Kenneth, Chicago	20	40	1	4	5	1	0	0	2	2	0	0	0	.100
Russell, William, Los Angeles	81	278	30	72	101	11	9	0	28	4	3	9	1	.259
Ryan, L. Nolan, New York	27	45	2	8	8	0	0	0	2	0	1	0	0	.178
Ryan, Michael, Philadelphia	46	134	14	24	38	8	0	2	11	1	1	0	0	.179
Sadecki, Raymond, New York☆	28	39	2	8	8	0	0	0	3	8	0	0	0	.205
Sanguillen, Manuel, Pittsburgh	.128	486	63	158	216	19	9	7	61	1	6	2	3	.325
Santo, Ronald, Chicago	154	555	83	148	264	30	4	26	114	1	6	2	0	.267
Santorini, Alan, San Diego	21	18	0	0	0	0	0	0	0	1	0	0	0	.000
Seaver, G. Thomas, New York	42	95	9	17	23	1	1	1	10	7	0	0	0	.179
Selma, Richard, Philadelphia	73	20	1	3	4	1	0	0	2	1	0	0	0	.150
Shamsky, Arthur, New York☆	122	403	48	118	174	19	2	11	49	0	3	1	1	.293
Shannon, T. Michael, St. Louis	55	174	18	37	50	9	2	0	22	0	3	1	1	.213
Short, Christopher, Philadelphia.	36	61	0	3	3	0	0	0	2	7	1	0	0	.049
Simmons, Ted, St. Louis†	82	284	29	69	90	8	2	3	24	0	1	2	2	.243
Simpson, Wayne, Cincinnati	27	64	4	6	6	0	0	0	1	5	0	0	0	.094
Singer, William, Los Angeles	16	38	4	5	6	1	0	0	1	1	0	0	0	.132
Singleton, Kenneth, New York†	69	198	22	52	75	8	0	5	26	4	1	1	1	.263
Sizemore, Ted, Los Angeles	96	340	40	104	119	10	1	1	34	0	2	5	1	.306
Slocum, Ronald, San Diego	60	71	8	10	19	2	2	1	11	2	0	1	1	.141
Smith, Willie, Chicago☆	87	167	15	36	62	9	1	5	24	2	1	2	1	.216
Spangler, Albert, Chicago☆	21	14	2	2	6	1	0	1	1	0	0	0	0	.143
Spiezio, Edward, San Diego	110	316	45	90	145	18	1	12	42	2	4	4	0	.285
Staehle, Marvin, Montreal☆	104	321	41	70	81	9	1	0	26	6	3	1	3	.218
Stahl, Larry, San Diego☆	52	66	5	12	14	2	0	0	3	0	0	2	2	.182
Stargell, Wilver, Pittsburgh☆	136	474	70	125	242	18	3	31	85	0	6	0	1	.264
Staub, Daniel, Montreal☆	160	569	98	156	283	23	7	30	94	11	4	12	11	.274
Stephenson, John, San Fran☆	23	43	3	3	4	1	0	0	6	0	1	0	0	.070
Stewart, James, Cincinnati†	101	105	15	28	36	3	1	1	8	1	1	5	3	.267
Stone, George, Atlanta☆	35	72	9	17	19	2	0	0	5	3	0	0	0	.236
Stone, H. Ronald, Philadelphia☆	123	321	30	84	115	12	5	3	39	2	4	5	6	.262
Stoneman, William, Montreal	42	60	0	6	8	2	0	0	0	4	0	0	0	.100
Strohmayer, John, Montreal	42	6	1	1	1	0	0	0	0	1	0	0	0	.167
Sudakis, William, Los Angeles†	94	269	37	71	124	11	0	14	44	1	3	4	0	.264
Sutherland, Gary, Montreal	116	359	37	74	93	10	0	3	26	7	3	2	2	.206
Sutton, Donald, Los Angeles	40	84	6	13	17	2	1	0	6	5	0	1	0	.155
Swoboda, Ronald, New York	115	245	29	57	96	8	2	9	40	1	2	2	4	.233
Taylor, Antonio, Philadelphia	124	439	74	132	203	26	4	9	55	1	2	9	11	.301
Taylor, Carl, St. Louis	104	245	39	61	95	12	2	6	45	0	1	5	2	.249
Taylor, Charles, St. Louis	56	26	3	3	4	1	0	0	3	3	0	0	0	.115
Taylor, Robert, San Francisco☆	63	84	12	16	22	0	0	2	10	0	0	0	0	.190
Taylor, Ronald, New York	57	4	0	0	0	0	0	0	0	1	0	0	0	.000
Tillman, J. Robert, Atlanta	71	223	19	53	91	5	0	11	30	1	1	0	0	.238
Tolan, Robert, Cincinnati☆	152	589	112	186	280	34	6	16	80	9	7	57	20	.316
Torborg, Jeffrey, Los Angeles	64	134	11	31	42	6	0	1	17	0	2	1	1	.231
Torre, Joseph, St. Louis	161	624	89	203	311	27	9	21	100	0	3	2	2	.325
Torres, Hector, Houston	31	65	6	16	21	1	2	0	5	0	0	0	0	.246
Torrez, Michael, St. Louis	30	63	4	17	21	2	1	0	5	2	0	0	0	.270
Vance, Gene, Los Angeles	20	37	2	7	8	1	0	0	2	4	0	0	0	.189
Veale, Robert, Pittsburgh†	34	67	5	11	15	4	0	0	6	1	0	0	0	.164
Walker, J. Luke, Pittsburgh☆	42	46	0	6	6	0	0	0	5	8	0	0	0	.130
Washburn, Ray, Cincinnati	35	13	0	0	0	0	0	0	1	1	0	0	0	.000
Watson, Robert, Houston	97	327	48	89	145	19	2	11	61	1	6	1	1	.272
Webster, Ramon, San Diego☆	95	116	12	30	39	3	0	2	11	0	0	1	1	.259
Wegener, Michael, Montreal	25	34	1	4	4	0	0	0	2	4	0	0	0	.118
Weis, Albert, New York	75	121	20	25	37	7	1	1	11	0	1	1	1	.207
Wenz, Frederick, Philadelphia	22	5	0	0	0	0	0	0	0	0	0	0	0	.000
Whitaker, Steve, San Francisco☆	16	27	3	3	4	1	0	0	4	0	1	0	0	.111
Wilhelm, J. Hoyt, 50 Atl-3 Chi	53	11	0	1	1	0	0	0	1	0	0	0	0	.091
Williams, Billy, Chicago☆	161	636	137	205	373	34	4	42	129	0	4	7	1	.322
Williams, Earl, Atlanta	10	19	4	7	11	4	0	0	5	0	2	0	0	.368
Williams, James, San Diego	11	14	4	4	4	0	0	0	0	0	1	0	0	.286

Player and Club	G.	AB.	R.	H.	TB.	2B.	3B.	HR.	RBI.	SH.	SF.	SB.	CS.	Pct.
Willis, Ronald, San Diego	42	5	0	0	0	0	0	0	0	0	0	0	0	.000
Wills, Maurice, Los Angeles†	132	522	77	141	166	19	3	0	34	5	1	28	13	.270
Wilson, Donald, Houston	30	69	1	8	10	2	0	0	4	3	0	0	0	.116
Wilson, R. Earl, San Diego	15	17	2	1	4	0	0	1	2	0	0	0	0	.059
Wilson, William, Philadelphia	37	4	0	1	1	0	0	0	1	0	0	0	0	.250
Wine, Robert, Montreal	159	501	40	116	152	21	3	3	51	10	3	0	1	.232
Wise, Richard, Philadelphia	37	75	6	15	25	4	0	2	10	6	0	0	0	.200
Woodward, William, Cincinnati	100	264	23	59	76	8	3	1	14	0	3	1	2	.223
Wynn, James, Houston	157	554	82	156	273	32	2	27	88	0	7	24	5	.282

(Fewer Than Ten Games)

Player and Club	G.	AB.	R.	H.	TB.	2B.	3B.	HR.	RBI.	SH.	SF.	SB.	CS.	Pct.
Acosta, Eduardo, Pittsburgh	3	0	0	0	0	0	0	0	0	0	0	0	0	.000
Arlin, Stephen, San Diego	2	5	0	0	0	0	0	0	0	0	0	0	0	.000
Behney, Melvin, Cincinnati*	5	1	0	0	0	0	0	0	0	0	0	0	0	.000
Belinsky, Robert, Cincinnati*	3	1	0	1	1	0	0	0	0	0	0	0	0	1.000
Bertaina, Frank, St. Louis*	8	7	0	1	1	0	0	0	0	0	0	0	0	.143
Cambria, Frederick, Pittsburgh	6	10	1	2	2	0	0	0	1	2	0	0	0	.200
Champion, B. Billy, Philadelphia	7	3	0	0	0	0	0	0	0	0	0	0	0	.000
Chance, W. Dean, New York	3	0	0	0	0	0	0	0	0	0	0	0	0	.000
Colpaert, Richard, Pittsburgh	4	0	0	0	0	0	0	0	0	0	0	0	0	.000
Cosman, James, Chicago	1	0	0	0	0	0	0	0	0	0	0	0	0	.000
Cruz, Jose, St. Louis*	6	17	2	6	7	1	0	0	1	0	0	0	0	.353
Cumberland, John, San Francisco	7	1	0	0	0	0	0	0	0	0	0	0	0	.000
Davis, B. Brock, Chicago*	6	3	0	0	0	0	0	0	0	0	0	0	0	.000
Doyle, Paul, San Diego*	9	1	0	0	0	0	0	0	0	0	0	0	0	.000
Duffy, Frank, Cincinnati	6	11	1	2	4	2	0	0	0	0	0	1	0	.182
Faul, William, San Francisco	7	0	0	0	0	0	0	0	0	0	0	0	0	.000
Ferguson, Joe, Los Angeles	5	4	0	1	1	0	0	0	1	0	1	0	0	.250
Foli, Timothy, New York	5	11	0	4	4	0	0	0	1	0	0	0	0	.364
Forsch, Kenneth, Houston	4	6	0	0	0	0	0	0	0	3	0	0	0	.000
Foster, George, San Francisco	9	19	2	6	12	1	1	1	4	0	0	0	0	.316
Garrett, H. Adrian, Chi*	3	3	0	0	0	0	0	0	0	0	0	0	0	.000
Gatewood, Aubrey, Atlanta	3	0	0	0	0	0	0	0	0	0	0	0	0	.000
Geiger, Gary, Houston*	5	4	0	1	1	0	0	0	0	0	0	0	0	.250
Goodson, J. Edward, San Fran*.	7	11	1	3	3	0	0	0	0	0	0	0	0	.273
Grant, James, Pittsburgh	8	2	0	0	0	0	0	0	0	0	0	0	0	.000
Guzman, Santiago, St. Louis	8	5	1	1	1	0	0	0	0	1	0	0	0	.200
Harris, Walter, Houston	2	1	0	0	0	0	0	0	0	0	0	0	0	.000
Hermoso, Angel, Montreal	4	1	0	0	0	0	0	0	0	0	0	0	0	.000
Herrera, Jose, Montreal	1	1	0	0	0	0	0	0	0	0	0	0	0	.000
Hough, Charles, Los Angeles	8	3	0	1	1	0	0	0	0	0	0	0	0	.333
Hughes, Terry, Chicago	2	3	0	1	1	0	0	0	0	0	0	0	0	.333
Jackson, Michael, Philadelphia*	5	1	0	1	1	0	0	0	0	0	0	0	0	1.000
Johnson, James, San Francisco* .	3	2	0	0	0	0	0	0	0	0	0	0	0	.000
Johnson, Kenneth, Montreal	3	0	0	0	0	0	0	0	0	0	0	0	0	.000
Kendall, Fred, San Diego	4	9	0	0	0	0	0	0	0	1	0	0	0	.000
Kline, Ronald, Atlanta	5	0	0	0	0	0	0	0	0	0	0	0	0	.000
Laxton, William, Philadelphia*	2	0	0	0	0	0	0	0	0	0	0	0	0	.000
Luzinski, Gregory, Philadelphia	8	12	0	2	2	0	0	0	0	0	0	0	1	.167
Maloney, James, Cincinnati*	7	3	0	0	0	0	0	0	0	0	0	0	0	.000
Marone, Louis, Pittsburgh	1	0	0	0	0	0	0	0	0	0	0	0	0	.000
Martinez, Teodoro, New York	4	16	0	1	1	0	0	0	0	0	0	0	0	.063
May, Milton, Pittsburgh*	5	4	1	2	3	1	0	0	2	0	0	0	0	.500
McBean, Alvin, 1 LA-7 Pitt	8	1	0	0	0	0	0	0	0	0	0	0	0	.000
McFadden, Leon, Houston	2	0	0	0	0	0	0	0	0	0	0	0	0	.000
Metzger, Roger, Chicago*	1	2	0	0	0	0	0	0	0	0	0	0	0	.000
Miller, Robert, Chicago	7	0	0	0	0	0	0	0	0	0	0	0	0	.000
Moore, Balor, Montreal*	6	3	0	1	1	0	0	0	0	0	0	0	0	.333
Moore, Gary, Los Angeles	7	16	2	3	7	0	2	0	0	0	0	1	0	.188
Neibauer, Gary, Atlanta	7	2	0	0	0	0	0	0	0	0	0	0	0	.000
Noriega, John, Cincinnati	8	4	0	1	1	0	0	0	0	0	0	0	0	.250
Nossek, Joseph, St. Louis	1	1	0	0	0	0	0	0	0	0	0	0	0	.000
Nyman, Gerry, San Diego*	3	0	0	0	0	0	0	0	0	0	0	0	0	.000
O'Donoghue, John, Montreal	9	4	0	0	0	0	0	0	0	0	0	0	0	.000
Osinski, Daniel, Houston	3	0	0	0	0	0	0	0	0	0	0	0	0	.000

Player and Club	G.	AB.	R.	H.	TB.	2B.	3B.	HR.	RBI.	SH.	SF.	SB.	CS.	Pct.
Paciorek, Thomas, Los Angeles ..	8	9	2	2	3	1	0	0	0	0	0	0	0	.222
Parker, Harry, St. Louis ...	7	8	1	2	2	1	0	0	0	0	0	0	0	.250
Plummer, William, Cincinnati ..	4	8	0	1	1	0	0	0	0	0	0	0	0	.125
Puente, Miguel, San Francisco	6	7	0	0	0	0	0	0	0	0	1	0	0	.000
Qualls, James, Montreal†	9	9	1	1	1	0	0	0	1	0	0	0	0	.111
Reynolds, Archie, Chicago	7	2	0	0	0	0	0	0	0	0	0	0	0	.000
Reynolds, Kenneth, Philadelphia*	4	0	0	0	0	0	0	0	0	0	0	0	0	.000
Roque, Jorge, St. Louis	5	1	2	0	0	0	0	0	0	0	0	0	0	.000
Sembera, Carroll, Montreal	5	0	0	0	0	0	0	0	0	0	0	0	0	.000
Skidmore, R. Roe, Chicago	1	1	0	1	1	0	0	0	0	0	0	0	0	1.000
Sparma, Joseph, Montreal	9	6	0	0	0	0	0	0	0	0	0	0	1	.000
Spinks, Scipio, Houston	6	3	1	0	0	0	0	0	0	0	1	0	0	.000
Stanton, Leroy, New York	4	4	0	1	3	0	1	0	0	0	0	0	0	.250
Stephenson, Jerry, Los Angeles*	3	1	0	0	0	0	0	0	0	0	0	0	0	.000
Stinson, G. Robert, Los Ang†	4	3	1	0	0	0	0	0	0	0	0	0	0	.000
Strahler, Michael, Los Angeles	6	8	1	2	2	0	0	0	2	0	0	0	0	.250
Vukovich, John, Philadelphia	3	8	1	1	1	0	0	0	0	0	0	0	0	.125
Ward, John, Cincinnati	6	3	0	0	0	0	0	0	0	0	0	0	0	.000
Waslewski, Gary, Montreal	6	6	0	0	0	0	0	0	0	0	1	0	0	.000
Whitfield, Fred, Montreal*	4	15	0	1	1	0	0	0	0	0	0	0	0	.067
Wilcox, Milton, Cincinnati	5	5	0	1	1	0	0	0	1	1	0	0	0	.200
Williams, Bernard, San Francisco	7	16	2	5	7	2	0	0	1	0	0	1	1	.313
Zeller, Barton, St. Louis	1	0	0	0	0	0	0	0	0	0	0	0	0	.000

AWARDED FIRST BASE ON INTERFERENCE—Short, Phila. 3 (Sanguillen, J. R. Gibson, Tillman); Helms, Cin. 2 (Torre, Martin); Rose, Cin. 2 (J. R. Gibson, Martin); Corrales, Cin (Dietz); Javier, St. L. (King); Carl Taylor, St. L. (Barton); Torres, Hou. (Bateman); Webster, S. D. (Dyer).

PLAYERS WITH TWO OR MORE CLUBS DURING 1970 SEASON

(Alphabetically arranged with first club on top)

Player and Club	G.	AB.	R.	H.	TB.	2B.	3B.	HR.	RBI.	SH.	SF.	Tot. Int. BB.	BB.	HP.	SO.	SB.	CS.	GI DP.	Pct.
Abernathy, Chicago	11	0	0	0	0	0	0	0	0	0	0	0	0	0	0	0	0	0	.000
Abernathy, St. Louis	11	3	0	0	0	0	0	0	0	0	0	0	0	0	2	0	0	0	.000
Barber, Chicago	5	0	0	0	0	0	0	0	0	0	0	0	0	0	2	0	0	0	.000
Barber, Atlanta	5	4	0	1	1	0	0	0	0	0	0	0	0	0	3	0	0	0	.250
Beauchamp, Houston	31	26	3	5	8	0	0	1	4	0	0	3	0	0	7	0	1	1	.192
Beauchamp, St. Louis	44	58	8	15	20	2	0	1	6	0	2	8	0	0	11	2	0	0	.259
Cardwell, New York	16	5	0	0	0	0	0	0	1	0	1	0	0	0	3	0	0	0	.000
Cardwell, Atlanta	16	5	1	2	2	0	0	0	0	0	0	0	0	0	3	0	0	0	.400
Cline, Montreal	2	2	0	1	1	0	0	0	0	0	0	0	0	0	0	0	0	0	.500
Cline, Cincinnati	48	63	13	17	26	7	1	0	8	3	0	12	1	0	11	1	2	0	.270
Culver, St. Louis	11	17	2	3	5	0	1	0	6	1	2	0	0	0	5	1	0	0	.176
Culver, Houston	32	4	1	1	1	0	0	0	0	0	0	0	0	0	2	0	0	0	.250
H. T. Davis, Houston	57	213	24	60	85	12	2	3	30	0	0	7	1	0	25	8	3	3	.282
H. T. Davis, Chicago	11	42	4	11	19	2	0	2	8	0	0	1	0	0	1	0	0	0	.262
Day, Chicago	11	8	2	2	2	0	0	0	0	0	0	0	0	0	3	0	0	1	.250
Day, Montreal	41	108	14	29	33	4	0	0	5	4	0	6	2	0	18	3	2	2	.269
Gagliano, St. Louis	18	32	0	6	6	0	0	0	2	0	0	1	0	0	3	0	0	1	.188
Gagliano, Chicago	26	40	5	6	6	0	0	0	5	1	0	5	0	0	5	0	0	1	.150
Hall, Chicago	28	32	2	3	4	1	0	0	1	0	0	4	1	0	12	0	0	0	.094
Hall, Atlanta	39	47	7	10	18	2	0	2	4	0	0	2	1	0	14	0	0	1	.213
Hartenstein, Pittsburgh	17	1	1	0	0	0	0	0	0	0	0	0	0	0	0	0	0	0	.000
Hartenstein, St. Louis ..	6	2	0	0	0	0	0	0	0	0	0	1	0	0	2	0	0	0	.000
Herbel, San Diego	64	13	0	0	0	0	0	0	0	0	0	1	0	0	8	0	0	0	.000
Herbel, New York	12	0	0	0	0	0	0	0	0	0	0	0	0	0	0	0	0	0	.000
Hiatt, Montreal	17	43	4	14	16	2	0	0	7	0	0	14	0	0	14	0	0	1	.326
Hiatt, Chicago	66	178	19	43	63	12	1	2	22	5	1	31	2	0	48	0	0	6	.242
Jerry Johnson, St. Louis	7	1	1	0	0	0	0	0	0	0	0	0	1	0	0	0	0	0	.000
Jerry Johnson, San Fran	33	15	0	1	1	0	0	0	0	0	0	0	0	0	5	0	0	0	.067
Linzy, San Francisco	20	4	0	0	0	0	0	0	0	0	0	0	0	0	3	0	0	0	.000
Linzy, St. Louis	47	7	0	0	0	0	0	0	0	0	0	0	0	0	5	0	0	0	.000

Player and Club	G.	AB.	R.	H.	TB.	2B.	3B.	HR.	RBI.	SH.	SF.	BB.	Int.BB.	SO.	SB.	CS.	GI DP.	Pct.
Marshall, Houston	4	0	0	0	0	0	0	0	0	0	0	0	0	0	0	0	0	.000
Marshall, Montreal	24	11	0	1	1	0	0	0	1	2	1	2	0	1	2	0	1	.091
McBean, Los Angeles	1	0	0	0	0	0	0	0	0	0	0	0	0	0	0	0	0	.000
McBean, Pittsburgh	7	1	0	0	0	0	0	0	0	0	0	0	0	0	0	0	0	.000
Norman, Los Angeles	30	7	1	1	1	0	0	0	2	0	2	0	0	4	0	0	0	.143
Norman, St. Louis	1	0	0	0	0	0	0	0	0	0	0	0	0	0	0	0	0	.000
Nye, St. Louis	6	2	0	1	1	0	0	0	0	0	0	1	0	0	0	0	0	.500
Nye, Montreal	10	17	2	3	3	0	0	0	1	0	1	0	0	4	0	1	0	.176
Pappas, Atlanta	11	10	0	0	0	0	0	0	0	0	0	0	0	3	0	0	0	.000
Pappas, Chicago	21	50	7	12	22	2	1	2	5	1	1	2	0	17	0	0	0	.240
Pepitone, Houston	75	279	44	70	131	9	5	14	35	0	1	18	9	28	5	2	7	.251
Pepitone, Chicago	56	213	38	57	106	9	2	12	44	4	2	15	2	15	0	2	2	.268
Rodriquez, San Diego	10	3	0	0	0	0	0	0	0	0	0	0	0	0	0	0	0	.000
Rodriquez, Chicago	26	8	1	1	4	0	0	1	1	0	0	1	0	1	0	0	0	.125
Wilhelm, Atlanta	50	11	0	1	1	0	0	0	1	0	0	2	0	6	0	0	0	.091
Wilhelm, Chicago	3	0	0	0	0	0	0	0	0	0	0	0	0	0	0	0	0	.000

MISCELLANEOUS NATIONAL LEAGUE BATTING RECORDS

CLUB MISCELLANEOUS RECORDS

Club	G.	AB.	TB.	Pct.	TBB.	IBB.	HP.	SO.	GIDP.	ShO.
Cincinnati	162	5540	2414	.436	547	70	29	984	119	1
Chicago	162	5491	2277	.415	607	65	20	844	110	9
San Francisco	162	5578	2282	.409	729	95	56	1005	143	8
Pittsburgh	162	5637	2287	.406	444	82	44	871	117	12
Atlanta	162	5546	2238	.404	522	72	38	736	140	9
San Diego	162	5494	2149	.391	500	46	39	1164	111	12
Houston	162	5574	2177	.391	598	81	27	911	144	11
Los Angeles	161	5606	2143	.382	541	67	24	841	114	11
St. Louis	162	5689	2156	.379	569	65	26	961	138	13
New York	162	5443	2013	.370	684	60	26	1062	139	10
Montreal	162	5411	1973	.365	659	64	39	972	106	13
Philadelphia	161	5456	1942	.356	519	59	25	1066	133	15
Totals		66465	26051	.392	6919	826	393	11417	1514	124

INDIVIDUAL MISCELLANEOUS RECORDS

(Fifteen Top Qualifiers for Slugging Championship)

Player and Club	G.	AB.	TB.	Pct.	Tot. BB.	Int. BB.	HP.	SO.	GI DP.
McCovey, San Francisco	152	495	303	.612	137	40	3	75	13
Perez, Cincinnati	158	587	346	.589	83	13	4	134	15
Bench, Cincinnati	158	605	355	.587	54	9	0	102	12
Williams, Chicago	161	636	373	.586	72	9	2	65	13
Carty, Atlanta	136	478	279	.584	77	6	2	46	19
Hickman, Chicago	149	514	299	.582	93	8	1	99	10
H. Aaron, Atlanta	150	516	296	.574	74	15	2	63	13
Allen, St. Louis	122	459	257	.560	71	16	2	118	9
Cepeda, Atlanta	148	567	308	.543	47	11	9	75	15
Gaston, San Diego	146	584	317	.543	41	2	2	142	16
Dietz, San Francisco	148	493	254	.515	109	10	3	106	16
Stargell, Pittsburgh	136	474	242	.511	44	11	5	119	14
Colbert, San Diego	156	572	291	.509	56	8	4	150	11
Mays, San Francisco	139	478	242	.506	79	3	3	90	7
Bonds, San Francisco	157	663	334	.504	77	7	2	189	6

DEPARTMENTAL LEADERS: TBB—McCovey, 137; IBB—McCovey, 40; HP—Hunt, 26; SO—Bonds, 189; GIDP—Cleon Jones, 26.

(All Players in Ten or More Games—Listed Alphabetically)

Player and Club	G.	AB.	TB.	Pct.	Tot. BB.	Int. BB.	HP.	SO.	GI DP.
H. Aaron, Atlanta	150	516	296	.574	74	15	2	63	13
T. Aaron, Atlanta	44	63	21	.333	3	0	0	10	5
Abernathy, Chicago-St. Louis	22	3	0	.000	0	0	0	2	0
Agee, New York	153	636	298	.469	55	3	2	156	11
Aguirre, Chicago	17	2	0	.000	0	0	0	2	0
Allen, St. Louis	122	459	257	.560	71	16	2	118	9
Alley, Pittsburgh	121	426	154	.362	31	9	3	70	6
Alou, Houston	117	458	176	.384	21	4	1	15	15
Alou, Pittsburgh	155	677	241	.356	30	3	4	18	9
Arcia, San Diego	114	229	66	.288	12	1	7	36	3
Aspromonte, Atlanta	62	127	30	.236	13	0	0	13	4
Bailey, Montreal	131	352	210	.597	72	8	1	70	12
Baker, Atlanta	13	24	7	.292	2	0	0	4	1
Baldschun, San Diego	12	0	0	.000	0	0	0	0	0
Banks, Chicago	72	222	102	.459	20	3	1	33	5
Barber, Chicago-Atlanta	10	4	1	.250	0	0	0	3	0
Barton, San Diego	61	188	59	.314	15	2	1	37	4
Bateman, Montreal	139	520	199	.383	28	9	1	75	15
Bates, Philadelphia	22	60	10	.167	6	1	4	15	2
Beauchamp, Houston-St. Louis	75	84	28	.333	11	0	0	18	1
Beckert, Chicago	143	591	206	.349	32	0	0	22	13
Bench, Cincinnati	158	605	355	.587	54	9	0	102	12
Billingham, Houston	46	58	6	.103	4	0	0	27	1
Blasingame, Houston	13	24	2	.083	4	0	0	10	1
Blass, Pittsburgh	32	70	9	.129	2	0	0	15	2
Boccabella, Montreal	61	145	59	.407	11	2	0	24	3
Bonds, San Francisco	157	663	334	.504	77	7	2	189	6
Borbon, Cincinnati	12	3	0	.000	0	0	0	2	0
Boswell, New York	105	351	121	.345	41	8	2	32	13
Bouton, Houston	29	17	6	.353	1	0	1	6	1
Bowa, Philadelphia	145	547	166	.303	21	1	1	48	8
Boyer, Atlanta	134	475	181	.381	41	8	1	71	11
Brand, Montreal	72	126	38	.302	9	0	0	16	0
Bravo, Cincinnati	65	65	21	.323	9	0	0	13	0
Brewer, Los Angeles	58	12	1	.083	1	0	0	6	0
Briggs, Philadelphia	110	341	148	.434	39	5	0	65	14
Briles, St. Louis	30	39	12	.308	1	0	0	14	0
Brock, St. Louis	155	664	280	.422	60	12	1	99	10
Brown, San Diego	139	534	261	.489	34	8	0	78	14
Brown, Atlanta	28	47	25	.532	7	0	1	7	1
Browne, Philadelphia	104	270	118	.437	33	5	0	72	12
Brunet, Pittsburgh	12	4	0	.000	0	0	0	2	0
Bryant, Houston	15	24	5	.208	1	0	0	8	0
Bryant, San Francisco	34	27	3	.111	1	0	0	6	0
Buckner, Los Angeles	28	68	18	.265	3	1	0	7	0
Bunning, Philadelphia	35	71	9	.127	2	0	0	18	2
Burda, San Francisco	28	23	6	.261	5	2	1	2	0
Callison, Chicago	147	477	210	.440	60	11	3	63	10
Campbell, San Diego	154	581	195	.336	40	2	1	115	7
Campbell, St. Louis	13	13	3	.231	0	0	0	3	0
Campisi, St. Louis	37	1	0	.000	0	0	0	1	0
Cannizzaro, San Diego	111	341	129	.378	48	8	1	49	9
Carbo, Cincinnati	125	365	201	.551	94	9	4	77	6
Cardenal, St. Louis	148	552	236	.428	45	0	1	70	14
Cardwell, New York-Atlanta	32	10	2	.200	1	0	0	6	0
Carlton, St. Louis	34	80	18	.225	1	0	4	28	1
Carrithers, San Francisco	11	6	0	.000	1	0	0	4	0
Carroll, Cincinnati	65	14	1	.071	1	0	0	4	1
Carty, Atlanta	136	478	279	.584	77	6	2	46	19
Cash, Pittsburgh	64	210	88	.419	17	3	1	25	9
Cedeno, Houston	90	355	160	.451	15	2	2	57	8
Cepeda, Atlanta	148	567	308	.543	47	11	9	75	15
Chaney, Cincinnati	57	95	28	.295	3	1	1	26	0
Chlupsa, St. Louis	14	0	0	.000	0	0	0	0	0
Clemente, Pittsburgh	108	412	229	.556	38	14	2	66	7
Clendenon, New York	121	396	204	.515	39	4	1	91	15

Player and Club	G.	AB.	TB.	Pct.	Tot. BB.	Int. BB.	HP.	SO.	GI DP.
Cleveland, St. Louis	16	4	1	.250	0	0	0	2	0
Cline, Montreal-Cincinnati	50	65	27	.415	12	1	0	11	0
Clines, Pittsburgh	31	37	17	.459	2	0	0	5	2
Cloninger, Cincinnati	30	47	18	.383	0	0	0	16	1
Colbert, San Diego	156	572	291	.509	56	8	4	150	11
Colborn, Chicago	34	15	1	.067	1	0	0	11	0
Compton, Philadelphia	47	110	23	.209	9	3	2	22	1
Concepcion, Cincinnati	101	265	84	.317	23	5	3	45	10
Cook, Houston	43	17	8	.471	1	0	0	11	0
Coombs, San Diego	35	52	7	.135	3	0	0	29	1
Corkins, San Diego	25	37	12	.324	2	0	0	23	1
Corrales, Cincinnati	43	106	35	.330	8	1	0	22	4
Crawford, Los Angeles	109	299	114	.381	33	4	2	88	5
Crosby, St. Louis	38	95	30	.316	7	0	1	5	1
Culver, St. Louis-Houston	43	21	6	.286	0	0	0	7	0
Dal Canton, Pittsburgh	41	16	0	.000	2	0	1	9	1
Davalillo, St. Louis	111	183	80	.437	13	1	0	19	4
DaVanon, St. Louis	11	18	3	.167	2	0	0	5	1
Davenport, San Francisco	22	37	10	.270	7	1	0	6	0
H. T. Davis, Houston-Chicago	68	255	104	.408	8	1	0	26	3
Davis, Los Angeles	146	593	260	.438	29	2	1	54	6
Davison, San Francisco	31	1	0	.000	1	0	0	1	0
Day, Chicago-Montreal	52	116	35	.302	6	2	0	21	3
Dean, San Diego	61	158	48	.304	11	3	0	29	4
Decker, Chicago	24	34	10	.294	2	0	0	16	0
Didier, Atlanta	57	168	29	.173	12	4	1	11	3
Dierker, Houston	37	92	18	.196	1	0	0	37	2
Dietz, San Francisco	148	493	254	.515	109	10	3	106	16
DiLauro, Houston	43	2	0	.000	0	0	0	1	0
Dillman, Montreal	18	2	0	.000	0	0	0	1	0
Dobson, San Diego	40	71	11	.155	5	0	1	17	2
Doyle, Philadelphia	112	413	116	.281	33	3	0	64	6
Dukes, San Diego	53	7	0	.000	0	0	0	5	0
Dunegan, Chicago	10	4	2	.500	0	0	0	2	0
Dyer, New York	59	148	38	.257	21	4	0	32	5
Edwards, Philadelphia	35	78	21	.269	4	3	1	10	4
Edwards, Houston	140	458	146	.319	51	16	1	63	9
Ellis, Pittsburgh	38	70	8	.114	2	0	0	37	0
Evans, Atlanta	12	44	17	.386	7	0	1	5	2
Fairey, Montreal	92	211	75	.355	14	4	2	38	5
Fairly, Montreal	119	385	175	.455	72	9	4	64	9
Ferrara, San Diego	138	372	165	.444	46	2	11	63	8
Folkers, New York	16	6	2	.333	0	0	0	4	0
Foster, Los Angeles	33	64	7	.109	5	0	0	13	1
Foy, New York	99	322	106	.329	68	5	4	58	4
Frisella, New York	30	13	4	.308	1	0	0	4	0
Fryman, Philadelphia	27	39	5	.128	0	0	0	12	0
Fuentes, San Francisco	123	435	149	.343	36	3	3	52	7
Gabrielson, Los Angeles	43	42	10	.238	1	0	0	15	0
Gagliano, St. Louis-Chicago	44	72	12	.167	6	0	0	8	1
Gallagher, San Francisco	109	282	106	.376	30	4	0	37	9
Gamble, Philadelphia	88	275	95	.345	27	3	1	37	8
Garber, Pittsburgh	14	3	2	.667	0	0	0	0	0
Garr, Atlanta	37	96	30	.313	5	1	0	12	3
Garrett, New York	114	366	154	.421	81	6	2	60	4
Garrido, Atlanta	101	367	113	.308	15	3	0	16	18
Garvey, Los Angeles	34	93	33	.355	6	0	0	17	3
Gaspar, New York	11	14	0	.000	1	0	0	4	0
Gaston, San Diego	146	584	317	.543	41	2	2	142	16
Gentry, New York	32	59	6	.102	5	0	0	39	0
Geronimo, Houston	47	37	9	.243	2	0	1	5	2
Gibbon, Pittsburgh	41	3	0	.000	0	0	0	1	0
Gibson, San Francisco	24	69	22	.319	7	1	0	12	4
Gibson, St. Louis	40	109	44	.404	8	0	0	25	4
Giusti, Pittsburgh	66	16	5	.313	3	0	0	6	0
Gladding, Houston	63	6	0	.000	0	0	0	6	0
Gonzalez, Atlanta	123	430	157	.365	46	10	8	45	10

Player and Club	G.	AB.	TB.	Pct.	Tot. BB.	Int. BB.	HP.	SO.	GI DP.
Gosger, Montreal	91	274	102	.372	35	3	1	35	4
Grabarkewitz, Los Angeles	156	529	240	.454	95	8	6	149	8
Granger, Cincinnati	67	10	1	.100	0	0	0	4	0
Griffin, Houston	23	33	3	.091	1	0	0	13	0
Grote, New York	126	415	128	.308	36	8	3	39	14
Gullett, Cincinnati	44	19	6	.316	1	0	1	6	0
Gura, Chicago	20	10	0	.000	0	0	0	5	0
Hague, St. Louis	139	451	188	.417	63	3	1	87	12
Hahn, Montreal	82	149	46	.309	27	1	2	27	1
Hall, Chicago-Atlanta	67	79	22	.278	6	2	0	26	1
Haller, Los Angeles	112	325	151	.465	32	7	2	35	6
Hands, Chicago	39	75	12	.160	15	0	0	33	0
Harmon, Philadelphia	71	129	42	.326	12	1	1	22	0
Harrelson, New York	157	564	174	.309	95	4	3	74	9
Hart, San Francisco	76	255	110	.431	30	6	3	29	12
Hartenstein, Pittsburgh-St. Louis	23	3	0	.000	1	0	0	2	0
Hebner, Pittsburgh	120	420	195	.464	42	5	7	48	8
Heise, San Francisco	67	154	46	.299	5	0	0	13	3
Helms, Cincinnati	150	575	162	.282	21	4	0	33	18
Henderson, San Francisco	148	554	255	.460	87	9	5	78	14
Herbel, San Diego-New York	76	13	0	.000	1	0	0	8	0
Hiatt, Montreal-Chicago	83	221	79	.357	45	2	0	62	7
Hickman, Chicago	149	514	299	.582	93	8	1	99	10
Hilgendorf, St. Louis	23	1	0	.000	0	0	0	0	0
Hisle, Philadelphia	126	405	143	.353	53	2	3	139	9
Hoerner, Philadelphia	44	10	3	.300	2	0	0	4	0
Holtzman, Chicago	40	105	26	.248	5	0	0	22	3
Howard, Houston	31	88	39	.443	10	3	0	23	2
Hrabosky, St. Louis	16	3	0	.000	0	0	0	0	0
Hundley, Chicago	73	250	87	.348	16	0	0	52	5
Hunt, San Francisco	117	367	140	.381	44	1	26	29	9
Huntz, San Diego	106	352	118	.335	66	1	1	69	5
Hutto, Philadelphia	57	92	28	.304	5	0	0	20	3
G. Jackson, Philadelphia	52	44	4	.091	1	0	1	15	1
Jackson, Atlanta	103	328	105	.320	45	1	1	27	3
James, Chicago	100	176	57	.324	17	5	5	24	3
Jarvis, Atlanta	36	82	17	.207	2	0	0	28	0
Jaster, Atlanta	14	3	0	.000	0	0	0	1	0
Javier, St. Louis	139	513	157	.306	24	6	1	70	14
Jenkins, Chicago	40	113	25	.221	1	0	0	36	1
Jeter, Pittsburgh	85	126	43	.341	13	1	1	34	3
Johnson, Philadelphia	159	574	262	.456	72	7	0	132	13
F. Johnson, San Francisco	67	161	58	.360	19	3	2	18	12
Jerry Johnson, St. Louis-San Francisco	40	16	1	.063	1	0	0	5	0
Jones, New York	134	506	211	.417	57	2	5	87	26
Jones, Montreal	108	271	124	.458	59	0	13	74	2
Jorgensen, New York	76	87	31	.356	10	1	0	23	0
Joseph, Philadelphia	71	119	40	.336	6	1	0	28	5
Joshua, Los Angeles	72	109	39	.358	6	2	0	24	0
Kelly, San Diego	38	89	21	.236	15	0	0	21	1
Kennedy, St. Louis	12	24	3	.125	0	0	0	0	0
Kessinger, Chicago	154	631	220	.349	66	6	2	59	12
Kester, Atlanta	15	9	0	.000	0	0	0	1	0
King, Atlanta	89	204	94	.461	32	6	2	41	5
Kirby, San Diego	36	74	12	.162	5	0	0	38	0
Koonce, New York	13	1	0	.000	0	0	0	1	0
Koosman, New York	30	70	7	.100	8	0	0	46	2
Kopacz, Pittsburgh	10	16	3	.188	0	0	0	5	0
Kosco, Los Angeles	74	224	87	.388	1	0	0	40	7
Kranepool, New York	43	47	8	.170	5	0	0	2	0
Laboy, Montreal	137	432	129	.299	31	5	2	81	12
Lamb, Pittsburgh	23	3	0	.000	0	0	0	2	0
Lamb, Los Angeles	35	4	0	.000	0	0	0	2	0
Lampard, Houston	53	72	27	.375	5	0	1	24	3
Lanier, San Francisco	134	438	122	.279	21	4	0	41	20

Player and Club	G.	AB.	TB.	Pct.	Tot. BB.	Int. BB.	HP.	SO.	GI DP.
Lee, St. Louis	121	264	93	.352	24	4	1	66	4
Lefebvre, Los Angeles	109	314	108	.344	29	2	1	42	7
Lemaster, Houston	39	45	11	.244	5	0	0	13	0
Lersch, Philadelphia	42	31	2	.065	2	0	0	11	0
Linzy, San Francisco-St. Louis	67	11	0	.000	0	0	0	8	0
Lis, Philadelphia	13	37	12	.324	5	0	0	11	0
Lum, Atlanta	123	291	116	.399	17	0	5	43	3
Marichal, San Francisco	34	85	5	.059	2	0	0	21	0
Marshall, New York	92	189	76	.402	17	0	0	43	4
Marshall, Houston-Montreal	28	11	1	.091	2	0	1	2	1
Martin, Chicago	40	77	16	.208	20	7	1	11	2
Martinez, Pittsburgh	19	20	1	.050	1	0	0	5	1
Martinez, Houston	75	150	36	.240	9	0	0	22	3
Mashore, Montreal	13	25	7	.280	4	2	0	11	0
Mason, San Francisco	46	36	5	.139	5	0	0	7	3
Maxvill, St. Louis	152	399	89	.223	51	3	0	56	8
J. May, Pittsburgh	51	139	40	.288	21	6	1	25	3
May, Cincinnati	153	605	293	.484	38	5	2	125	19
Mayberry, Houston	50	148	54	.365	21	6	2	33	6
Mays, San Francisco	139	478	242	.506	79	3	3	90	7
Mazeroski, Pittsburgh	112	367	119	.324	27	9	2	40	6
McAndrew, New York	32	54	11	.204	5	0	0	17	1
McCarver, Philadelphia	44	164	72	.439	14	4	1	10	3
McCool, St. Louis	18	4	0	.000	0	0	0	1	0
McCormick, San Francisco	23	25	5	.200	1	0	0	6	0
McCovey, San Francisco	152	495	303	.612	137	40	3	75	13
McGinn, Montreal	52	35	4	.114	0	0	0	14	1
McGlothlin, Cincinnati	35	66	14	.212	7	0	0	26	1
McGraw, New York	57	13	5	.385	1	0	0	2	0
McMahon, San Francisco	61	14	2	.143	2	0	0	9	0
McQueen, Atlanta	22	20	8	.400	1	0	0	3	0
McRae, Cincinnati	70	165	73	.442	15	2	1	23	6
Melendez, St. Louis	21	70	22	.314	2	0	0	12	3
Menke, Houston	154	562	248	.441	82	10	5	80	8
Merritt, Cincinnati	35	83	23	.277	4	0	0	42	0
Mikkelsen, Los Angeles	33	6	2	.333	0	0	0	3	0
Millan, Atlanta	142	590	224	.380	35	2	5	23	15
Miller, Houston	90	226	75	.332	41	7	1	33	5
Moeller, Los Angeles	31	39	6	.154	3	0	0	21	1
Money, Philadelphia	120	447	207	.463	43	6	7	68	7
Montanez, Philadelphia	18	25	6	.240	1	1	0	4	0
Moose, Pittsburgh	29	66	16	.242	6	0	0	18	1
Morales, San Diego	28	58	14	.241	3	0	0	11	2
Morgan, Houston	144	548	217	.396	102	3	1	55	11
Morton, Montreal	43	93	23	.247	6	0	0	29	0
Mota, Los Angeles	124	417	160	.384	47	4	3	37	13
Murrell, San Diego	125	347	136	.392	17	5	4	93	7
Nash, Atlanta	34	80	14	.175	2	0	0	38	1
Navarro, Atlanta	17	6	1	.167	0	0	0	3	1
Nelson, Pittsburgh	15	20	4	.200	1	0	0	6	0
Niekro, Atlanta	34	79	15	.190	2	0	0	17	1
Nolan, Cincinnati	37	82	16	.195	5	0	0	27	3
Norman, Los Angeles-St. Louis	31	7	1	.143	2	0	0	4	0
Nye, St. Louis-Montreal	16	19	4	.211	1	0	0	4	0
Oliver, Pittsburgh	151	551	228	.414	35	8	14	35	10
Osteen, Los Angeles	39	93	27	.290	3	0	1	20	0
Pagan, Pittsburgh	95	230	98	.426	20	1	0	24	6
Palmer, Philadelphia	38	27	7	.259	2	0	0	15	0
Pappas, Atlanta-Chicago	32	60	22	.367	2	0	1	20	0
Parker, Los Angeles	161	614	281	.458	79	18	0	70	14
Parrilla, Philadelphia	11	16	3	.188	1	0	0	4	0
Pascual, Los Angeles	10	0	0	.000	0	0	0	0	0
Patek, Pittsburgh	84	237	81	.342	29	1	0	46	2
Pena, Los Angeles	29	8	1	.125	2	0	0	1	0
Pena, Pittsburgh	23	6	0	.000	0	0	0	3	0

Player and Club	G.	AB.	TB.	Pct.	Tot. BB.	Int. BB.	HP.	SO.	GI DP.
Pepitone, Houston-Chicago	131	492	237	.482	33	11	1	43	9
Perez, Cincinnati	158	587	346	.589	83	13	4	134	15
Perry, San Francisco	41	120	20	.167	0	0	1	47	1
Phillips, Montreal	92	214	81	.379	36	1	2	51	5
Pitlock, San Francisco	18	25	6	.240	1	0	0	18	0
Pizarro, Chicago	12	3	0	.000	1	0	0	3	0
Popovich, Chicago	78	186	66	.355	18	4	2	18	3
Priddy, Atlanta	41	15	3	.200	1	0	0	11	0
Rader, Houston	156	576	251	.436	57	7	4	102	23
Ramirez, St. Louis	62	79	19	.241	8	1	0	9	4
Ray, Houston	52	27	5	.185	0	0	0	9	2
Raymond, Montreal	59	11	0	.000	1	0	0	7	0
Reberger, San Francisco	48	47	12	.255	0	0	0	18	0
Reed, Montreal	57	10	0	.000	3	0	0	6	0
Reed, Atlanta	22	44	5	.114	1	0	0	14	0
Regan, Chicago	54	9	0	.000	1	0	0	7	0
Reid, Philadelphia	25	49	7	.143	11	0	0	22	1
Renko, Montreal	41	80	22	.275	2	0	0	18	1
Reuss, St. Louis	20	40	2	.050	3	0	0	32	0
Ricketts, Pittsburgh	14	11	2	.182	1	0	0	3	0
Roberts, San Diego	43	59	16	.271	1	0	0	16	1
Robertson, San Francisco	41	59	14	.237	1	0	0	33	0
Robertson, Pittsburgh	117	390	220	.564	51	2	2	98	8
Robinson, San Diego	15	38	20	.526	5	1	0	4	2
Robles, San Diego	23	89	20	.225	5	0	1	11	1
Rodriquez, San Diego-Chicago	36	11	4	.364	1	0	0	1	0
Rojas, St. Louis	23	47	5	.106	3	0	1	4	1
Rose, Cincinnati	159	649	305	.470	73	10	2	64	7
Ross, San Diego	33	8	5	.625	0	0	0	1	1
Rudolph, Chicago	20	40	5	.125	1	1	0	12	1
Russell, Los Angeles	81	278	101	.363	16	1	3	28	5
Ryan, New York	27	45	8	.178	0	0	0	21	0
Ryan, Philadelphia	46	134	38	.284	16	3	0	24	8
Sadecki, New York	28	39	8	.205	2	0	0	10	1
Sanguillen, Pittsburgh	128	486	216	.444	17	9	6	45	15
Santo, Chicago	154	555	264	.476	92	6	1	108	17
Santorini, San Diego	21	18	0	.000	1	0	0	9	0
Seaver, New York	42	95	23	.242	10	0	0	31	1
Selma, Philadelphia	73	20	4	.200	1	0	0	8	1
Shamsky, New York	122	403	174	.432	49	13	3	33	11
Shannon, St. Louis	55	174	50	.287	16	4	0	20	3
Short, Phil	36	61	3	.049	1	0	0	20	3
Simmons, St. Louis	82	284	90	.317	37	5	2	37	5
Simpson, Cincinnati	27	64	6	.094	1	0	0	34	0
Singer, Los Angeles	16	38	6	.158	2	0	0	10	1
Singleton, New York	69	198	75	.379	30	1	1	48	5
Sizemore, Los Angeles	96	340	119	.350	34	6	0	19	15
Slocum, San Diego	60	71	19	.268	8	1	1	24	2
Smith, Chicago	87	167	62	.371	11	0	1	32	2
Spangler, Chicago	21	14	6	.429	3	0	0	3	0
Spiezio, San Diego	110	316	146	.462	43	2	4	42	7
Staehle, Montreal	104	321	81	.252	39	1	3	21	6
Stahl, San Diego	52	66	14	.212	2	0	0	14	0
Stargell, Pittsburgh	136	474	242	.511	44	11	5	119	14
Staub, Montreal	160	569	283	.497	112	11	3	93	7
Stephenson, San Francisco	23	43	4	.093	2	0	0	7	1
Stewart, Cincinnati	101	105	36	.343	8	1	1	13	2
Stone, Atlanta	35	72	19	.264	8	0	0	8	2
Stone, Philadelphia	123	321	115	.358	38	1	1	45	5
Stoneman, Montreal	42	60	8	.133	1	0	1	31	0
Strohmayer, Montreal	42	6	1	.167	0	0	0	1	0
Sudakis, Los Angeles	94	269	124	.461	35	4	3	46	7
Sutherland, Montreal	116	359	93	.259	31	1	2	22	8
Sutton, Los Angeles	40	84	17	.202	10	0	1	22	1
Swoboda, New York	115	245	96	.392	40	0	1	72	7

Player and Club	G.	AB.	TB.	Pct.	Tot. BB.	Int. BB.	HP.	SO.	GI DP.
Taylor, Philadelphia	124	439	203	.462	50	9	3	67	14
Carl Taylor, St. Louis	104	245	95	.388	41	0	1	30	11
Charles Taylor, St. Louis	56	26	4	.154	1	0	0	7	2
Taylor, San Francisco	63	84	22	.262	12	0	4	13	3
Taylor, New York	57	4	0	.000	1	0	0	4	0
Tillman, Atlanta	71	223	91	.408	20	4	0	66	2
Tolan, Cincinnati	152	589	280	.475	62	3	8	94	9
Torborg, Los Angeles	64	134	42	.313	14	6	0	15	2
Torre, St. Louis	161	624	311	.498	70	10	7	91	23
Torres, Houston	31	65	21	.323	6	0	0	8	2
Torrez, St. Louis	30	63	21	.333	0	0	1	18	2
Vance, Los Angeles	20	37	8	.216	1	0	0	9	0
Veale, Pittsburgh	34	67	15	.224	4	0	0	34	2
Walker, Pittsburgh	42	46	6	.130	3	0	0	26	0
Washburn, Cincinnati	35	13	0	.000	1	0	0	10	0
Watson, Houston	97	327	145	.443	24	1	4	59	10
Webster, San Diego	95	116	39	.336	11	0	0	12	2
Wegener, Montreal	25	34	4	.118	0	0	0	14	0
Weis, New York	75	121	37	.306	7	1	1	21	5
Wenz, Philadelphia	22	5	0	.000	0	0	0	5	0
Whitaker, San Francisco	16	27	4	.148	2	0	0	14	1
Wilhelm, Atlanta-Chicago	53	11	1	.091	2	0	0	6	0
Williams, Chicago	161	636	373	.586	72	9	2	65	13
Williams, Atlanta	10	19	11	.579	3	0	0	4	1
Williams, San Diego	11	14	4	.286	1	0	0	3	0
Willis, San Diego	42	5	0	.000	0	0	0	2	0
Wills, Los Angeles	132	522	166	.318	50	2	0	34	10
Wilson, Houston	30	69	10	.145	0	0	1	28	3
Wilson, San Diego	15	17	4	.235	2	0	0	12	0
Wilson, Philadelphia	37	4	1	.250	1	0	0	2	0
Wine, Montreal	159	501	152	.303	39	5	1	94	10
Wise, Philadelphia	37	75	25	.333	4	0	0	20	2
Woodward, Cincinnati	100	264	76	.288	20	6	2	21	5
Wynn, Houston	157	554	273	.493	106	12	1	96	16

(Fewer Than Ten Games)

Player and Club	G.	AB.	TB.	Pct.	Tot. BB.	Int. BB.	HP.	SO.	GI DP.
Acosta, Pittsburgh	3	0	0	.000	0	0	0	0	0
Arlin, San Diego	2	5	0	.000	0	0	0	1	0
Behney, Cincinnati	5	1	0	.000	0	0	0	1	0
Belinsky, Cincinnati	3	1	1	1.000	0	0	0	0	0
Bertaina, St. Louis	8	7	1	.143	2	0	0	0	1
Cambria, Pittsburgh	6	10	2	.200	2	0	0	1	1
Champion, Philadelphia	7	3	0	.000	0	0	0	2	0
Chance, New York	3	0	0	.000	0	0	0	0	0
Colpaert, Pittsburgh	8	0	0	.000	0	0	0	0	0
Cosman, Chicago	1	0	0	.000	0	0	0	0	1
Cruz, St. Louis	6	17	7	.412	4	0	1	0	0
Cumberland, San Francisco	7	1	0	.000	0	0	0	1	0
B. B. Davis, Chicago	6	3	1	.000	0	0	0	1	0
Doyle, San Diego	9	1	0	.000	0	0	0	0	0
Duffy, Cincinnati	6	11	4	.364	1	0	0	2	0
Faul, San Francisco	7	0	0	.000	0	0	0	0	0
Ferguson, Los Angeles	5	4	1	.250	2	0	0	2	0
Foli, New York	5	11	4	.364	0	0	0	2	0
Forsch, Houston	4	6	0	.000	0	0	0	4	0
Foster, San Francisco	9	19	12	.632	2	1	0	5	1
Garrett, Chicago	3	3	0	.000	0	0	0	3	0
Gatewood, Atlanta	3	0	0	.000	0	0	0	0	0
Geiger, Houston	5	4	1	.250	0	0	0	0	0
Goodson, San Francisco	7	11	3	.273	0	0	0	2	0
Grant, Pittsburgh	8	2	0	.000	0	0	0	0	1
Guzman, St. Louis	8	5	1	.200	0	0	0	1	0
Harris, Houston	2	1	0	.000	0	0	0	1	0
Hermoso, Montreal	4	1	0	.000	0	0	0	0	0
Herrera, Montreal	1	1	0	.000	0	0	0	1	0
Hough, Los Angeles	8	3	1	.333	0	0	0	0	0

Player and Club	G.	AB.	TB.	Pct.	Tot. BB.	Int. BB.	HP.	SO.	GI DP.
Hughes, Chicago	2	3	1	.333	0	0	0	0	0
M. Jackson, Philadelphia	5	1	1	1.000	0	0	0	0	0
James Johnson, San Francisco	3	2	0	.000	1	0	0	1	0
Johnson, Montreal	3	0	0	.000	0	0	0	0	0
Kendall, San Diego	4	9	0	.000	0	0	0	0	0
Kline, Atlanta	5	0	0	.000	0	0	0	0	0
Laxton, Philadelphia	2	0	0	.000	0	0	0	0	0
Luzinski, Philadelphia	8	12	2	.167	3	0	0	5	1
Maloney, Cincinnati	7	3	0	.000	0	0	0	1	0
Marone, Pittsburgh	1	0	0	.000	0	0	0	0	0
Martinez, New York	4	16	1	.063	0	0	0	3	0
M. May, Pittsburgh	5	4	3	.750	0	0	1	0	0
McBean, Los Angeles-Pittsburgh	8	1	0	.000	0	0	0	0	0
McFadden, Houston	2	0	0	.000	0	0	0	0	0
Metzger, Chicago	1	2	0	.000	0	0	0	0	0
Miller, Chicago	7	0	0	.000	0	0	0	0	0
Moore, Montreal	6	3	1	.333	0	0	0	1	0
Moore, Los Angeles	7	16	7	.438	0	0	0	1	2
Neibauer, Atlanta	7	2	0	.000	0	0	0	1	0
Noriega, Cincinnati	8	4	1	.250	0	0	0	2	0
Nossek, St. Louis	1	1	0	.000	0	0	0	0	0
Nyman, San Diego	3	0	0	.000	1	0	0	0	0
O'Donoghue, Montreal	9	4	0	.000	1	0	0	4	0
Osinski, Houston	3	0	0	.000	0	0	0	0	0
Paciorek, Los Angeles	8	9	3	.333	0	0	1	3	0
Parker, St. Louis	7	8	2	.250	0	0	0	2	0
Plummer, Cincinnati	4	8	1	.125	0	0	1	2	0
Puente, San Francisco	6	7	0	.000	0	0	0	5	0
Qualls, Montreal	9	9	1	.111	0	0	0	0	0
Reynolds, Chicago	7	2	0	.000	1	0	0	0	0
Reynolds, Philadelphia	4	0	0	.000	0	0	0	0	0
Roque, St. Louis	5	1	0	.000	0	0	1	1	0
Sembera, Montreal	5	0	0	.000	0	0	0	0	0
Skidmore, Chicago	1	1	1	1.000	0	0	0	0	0
Sparma, Montreal	9	6	0	.000	1	0	0	2	0
Spinks, Houston	6	3	0	.000	0	0	0	1	0
Stanton, New York	4	4	3	.750	0	0	0	0	1
Stephenson, Los Angeles	3	1	0	.000	0	0	0	0	0
Stinson, Los Angeles	4	3	0	.000	0	0	0	1	0
Strahler, Los Angeles	6	8	2	.250	0	0	0	3	0
Vukovich, Philadelphia	3	8	1	.125	0	0	0	0	0
Ward, Cincinnati	6	3	0	.000	2	0	0	1	0
Waslewski, Montreal	6	6	0	.000	1	0	0	6	0
Whitfield, Montreal	4	15	1	.067	1	0	0	3	1
Wilcox, Cincinnati	5	5	1	.200	0	0	0	1	0
Williams, San Francisco	7	16	7	.438	2	0	0	1	1
Zeller, St. Louis	1	0	0	.000	0	0	0	0	0

NATIONAL LEAGUE FIELDING AVERAGES

CLUB FIELDING

Club	G.	PO.	A.	E.	TC.	DP.	TP.	PB.	Pct.
Philadelphia	161	4383	1568	114	6065	134	0	19	.981
New York	162	4379	1514	124	6017	136	0	6	.979
Pittsburgh	162	4361	1930	137	6428	195	1	20	.979
Los Angeles	161	4376	1768	135	6279	135	0	17	.978
Chicago	162	4305	1791	137	6233	146	0	19	.978
Houston	162	4368	1791	140	6299	144	0	12	.978
Montreal	162	4316	1751	141	6208	193	0	12	.977
Atlanta	162	4292	1684	141	6117	118	0	30	.977
St. Louis	162	4427	1834	150	6411	159	0	20	.977
Cincinnati	162	4334	1835	151	6320	173	0	10	.976
San Diego	162	4321	1798	158	6277	159	0	3	.975
San Francisco	162	4373	1774	170	6317	153	0	30	.973
Totals		52235	21038	1698	74971	1845	1	198	.977

INDIVIDUAL FIELDING
(Ten or More Games)
(Position Leader in Capitals)

*Throws lefthanded.

FIRST BASEMEN

Player and Club	G.	PO.	A.	E.	DP.	Pct.	Player and Club	G.	PO.	A.	E.	DP.	Pct.
Hutto, Phil	12	31	1	0	4	1.000	Watson, Hou	83	695	39	6	54	.992
Parker, L A*	161	1498	125	7	116	.996	Jorgensen, N Y*	50	116	12	1	9	.992
Johnson, Phil	154	1178	73	6	104	.995	Colbert, S. D.	153	1406	90	14	126	.991
Fairly, Mont*	118	944	90	5	112	.995	Clendenon, N Y	100	722	62	7	72	.991
Robertson, Pitt	99	907	78	5	107	.995	Bailey, Mont	18	98	13	1	12	.991
Pepitone, 50 Hou-							Hickman, Chi	74	563	60	6	46	.990
13 Chi*	63	403	31	2	45	.995	McCovey, SF *	146	1217	134	15	117	.989
Shamsky, N Y*	56	378	35	2	29	.995	Oliver, Pitt*	77	582	48	7	68	.989
Mayberry, Hou*	45	371	35	2	29	.995	Bench, Cin	12	74	4	1	7	.987
Hague, St L*	82	672	48	4	65	.994	Henry Aaron, Atl	11	73	4	1	6	.987
Smith, Chi*	43	318	11	2	32	.994	Carl Taylor, St L.	15	109	6	2	10	.983
May, Cin	153	1362	109	10	143	.993	Webster, S D*	15	99	7	2	14	.981
Allen, St L	79	676	41	5	67	.993	Gosger, Mont*	19	128	7	3	14	.978
Banks, Chi	62	528	35	4	53	.993	Frank Johnson, SF	27	155	12	4	15	.977
Boccabella, Mont.	33	234	33	2	25	.993	Joseph, Phil	10	54	1	2	4	.965
Cepeda, Atl	148	1288	112	12	100	.992	Tommie Aaron, At	16	40	2	2	1	.955

(Fewer Than Ten Games)

Player and Club	G.	PO.	A.	E.	DP.	Pct.	Player and Club	G.	PO.	A.	E.	DP.	Pct.
Kranepool, N Y*	8	47	3	0	5	1.000	Sudakis, L A	1	4	1	0	0	1.000
Perez, Cin	8	36	6	0	4	1.000	Moore, L A *	1	4	0	0	0	1.000
Mays, S F	5	34	3	0	3	1.000	Gabrielson, L A	1	2	1	0	1	1.000
Beauchamp, St L.	5	26	3	0	1	1.000	Rader, Hou	1	2	0	0	0	1.000
Gagliano, 3 St L-							Ward, Cin	1	2	0	0	1	1.000
1 Chi	4	27	0	0	2	1.000	Kendall, S D	1	1	0	0	0	1.000
Luzinski, Phil	3	20	3	0	1	1.000	Murrell, S D	1	1	0	0	1	1.000
Williams, Atl	4	20	1	0	1	1.000	Pagan, Pitt	1	1	0	0	0	1.000
Kopacz, Pitts*	3	17	0	0	2	1.000	Stargell, Pitt*	1	0	1	0	0	1.000
Menke, Hou	5	14	0	0	0	1.000	Buckner, L A*	1	1	0	0	0	1.000
Hiatt, 2 Mont-							Kosco, L A	1	1	0	0	0	1.000
2 Chi	4	13	1	0	0	1.000	Whitfield, Mont*	4	34	7	1	3	.976
Torre, StL	1	12	0	0	0	1.000	Stone, Phil*	6	16	0	1	1	.941
Montanez, Phil*	5	7	2	0	3	1.000	Goodson, S F	2	14	2	1	1	.941
Lefebvre, L A	1	6	1	0	3	1.000	Burda, S F*	8	14	0	1	1	.933
Cline, Cin*	2	6	0	0	0	1.000	Stewart, Cin	1	4	0	2	0	.667
Howard, Hou	2	5	1	0	0	1.000	Martin, Chi	3	1	1	2	0	.500
Woodward, Cin	2	6	0	0	1	1.000	Aspromonte, Atla	1	0	0	0	0	.000
Lampard, Hou	2	5	0	0	0	1.000	Selma, Phil	1	0	0	0	0	.000
Lanier, S F	2	4	1	0	1	1.000							

Triple Play—Oliver.

SECOND BASEMEN

Player and Club	G.	PO.	A.	E.	DP.	Pct.	Player and Club	G.	PO.	A.	E.	DP.	Pct.
Arcia, S D	20	44	40	0	15	1.000	Javier, St L.	137	329	413	15	84	.980
Rojas, St L	10	22	30	0	9	1.000	Gagliano, 2 St L-						
Harmon, Phil	14	26	24	0	6	1.000	16 Chi	18	19	29	1	3	.980
Stewart, Cin	18	19	18	0	3	1.000	Morgan, Hou	142	349	430	17	98	.979
Woodward, Cin	10	17	13	0	3	1.000	Millan, Atl	142	337	359	15	83	.979
Boswell, N Y	101	204	244	2	49	.996	Doyle, Phil	103	251	228	11	55	.978
Taylor, Phil	59	151	132	1	41	.996	Sutherland, Mont	97	178	254	11	72	.975
Menke, Hou	21	51	62	1	14	.991	Campbell, S D	153	359	455	22	96	.974
Maxvill, St. L.	22	44	59	1	11	.990	Cash, Pitt	55	147	156	8	46	.974
Garrido, Atl	26	43	59	1	10	.990	Beckert, Chi	138	302	412	22	88	.970
Popovich, Chi	22	42	58	1	18	.990	Hunt, S F	85	162	173	11	38	.968
Garrett, N Y	45	94	92	2	28	.989	Fuentes, S F	78	141	205	12	41	.966
Lefebvre, L A	70	142	177	4	34	.988	Staehle, Mont	91	152	208	14	53	.963
Grabarkewitz, L A	20	43	42	1	10	.988	Heise, S F	28	53	52	4	10	.963
Mazeroski, Pitt	102	227	325	7	87	.987	Weis, N Y	44	60	59	6	10	.952
Sizemore, L A	86	194	232	5	47	.984	Mason, S F	14	11	8	1	1	.950
Helms, Cin	148	350	410	13	107	.983	Chaney, Cin	18	28	38	4	10	.943

SECOND BASEMEN—Continued
(Fewer Than Ten Games)

Player and Club	G.	PO.	A.	E.	DP.	Pct.	Player and Club	G.	PO.	A.	E.	DP.	Pct.
Alley, Pitt	8	13	30	0	4	1.000	Brand, Mont	3	1	1	0	0	1.000
Slocum, S D	9	13	22	0	4	1.000	Hermoso, Mont	1	0	1	0	0	1.000
Martinez, N Y	4	8	7	0	3	1.000	McRae, Cin	1	0	1	0	0	1.000
Torres, Hou	6	8	6	0	2	1.000	Kennedy, St L	5	10	9	2	3	.905
Concepcion, Cin	3	7	3	0	0	1.000	Martinez, Pitt	4	11	15	3	4	.897
DaVanon, St L	3	2	8	0	0	1.000	Crosby, St L	2	4	1	1	1	.833
Laboy, Mont	3	2	6	0	1	1.000	Bowa, Phil	1	0	0	0	0	.000
Martinez, Hou	4	5	3	0	1	1.000	Garvey, L A	1	0	0	0	0	.000
Lanier, S F	4	3	1	0	1	1.000	Pagan, Pitt	1	0	0	0	0	.000
Qualls, Mont	2	2	2	0	0	1.000	Ward, Cin	1	0	0	0	0	.000
Kelly, S D	1	1	2	0	1	1.000							

THIRD BASEMEN

Player and Club	G.	PO.	A.	E.	DP.	Pct.	Player and Club	G.	PO.	A.	E.	DP.	Pct.
Woodward, Cin	20	7	11	0	3	1.000	Santo, Chi	152	143	320	27	36	.945
Martinez, Hou	10	6	11	0	0	1.000	Garrett, N Y	70	57	113	10	6	.944
Davenport, S F	10	7	7	0	0	1.000	Garvey, L A	27	23	59	5	4	.943
Gallagher, S F	91	70	128	6	12	.971	Fuentes, S F	24	20	45	4	4	.942
Kelly, S D	27	22	44	2	2	.971	Evans, Atl	12	6	26	2	0	.941
Taylor, Phil	38	41	81	4	7	.968	Hebner, Pitt	117	64	235	19	24	.940
Rader, Hou	154	147	357	18	39	.966	Aspromonte, Atl	30	27	49	5	5	.938
Lefebvre, L A	21	20	34	2	4	.964	Foy, N Y	97	90	179	18	20	.937
Money, Phil	119	131	236	15	27	.961	Huntz, S D	51	32	91	9	7	.932
Grabarkewitz, L A	97	88	190	12	19	.959	Perez, Cin	153	131	286	35	34	.923
Pagan, Pitt	53	43	91	6	14	.957	Shannon, St L	51	32	59	8	4	.919
Popovich, Chi	16	9	12	1	1	.955	Hunt, S F	16	10	33	4	1	.915
Boyer, Atl	126	107	268	18	21	.954	Sudakis, L A	37	27	85	11	8	.911
Spiezio, S D	93	66	178	12	10	.953	Hart, S F	56	39	69	11	2	.908
Bailey, Mont	48	31	71	5	5	.953	Allen, St L	38	27	67	11	3	.895
Torre, St L	73	68	133	11	12	.948	Brand, Mont	12	6	18	3	0	.889
Laboy, Mont	132	105	194	17	19	.946	Slocum, S D	11	9	23	5	3	.865

(Fewer Than Ten Games)

Player and Club	G.	PO.	A.	E.	DP.	Pct.	Player and Club	G.	PO.	A.	E.	DP.	Pct.
DaVanon, St L	5	6	6	0	3	1.000	Stewart, Cin	9	6	17	1	5	.958
Williams, Atl	3	3	7	0	3	1.000	Gagliano, 6 St L-						
McRae, Cin	6	1	5	0	1	1.000	1 Chi	7	3	4	1	1	.875
Crosby, St L	3	3	3	0	1	1.000	Robertson, Pitt	5	4	3	1	1	.875
Foli, N Y	2	3	3	0	1	1.000	Joseph, Phil	9	3	7	2	1	.833
Vukovich, Phil	1	1	4	0	0	1.000	Menke, Hou	5	1	4	1	1	.833
Johnson, Phil	3	2	1	0	0	1.000	Harmon, Phil	2	1	1	1	0	.667
Ward, Cin	2	2	1	0	0	1.000	Arcia, S D	9	1	3	4	0	.500
Carl Taylor, St L	1	1	2	0	0	1.000	Chaney, Cin	3	0	0	0	0	.000
Martinez, Pitt	7	1	1	0	0	1.000	Heise, S F	2	0	0	0	0	.000
Alley, Pitt	2	1	1	0	0	1.000	Selma, Phil	2	0	0	0	0	.000
Boccabella, Mont	1	1	1	0	0	1.000	Colbert, S D	1	0	0	0	0	.000
Wills, L A	4	0	1	0	0	1.000	Hughes, Chi	1	0	0	0	0	.000
Bench, Cin	1	1	0	0	0	1.000	Hutto, Phil	1	0	0	0	0	.000
Hermoso, Mont	1	1	0	0	0	1.000	Sutherland, Mont	1	0	0	0	0	.000
Mota, L A	1	0	1	0	0	1.000	Ramirez, St L	1	0	0	1	0	.000

Triple Play—Hebner.

SHORTSTOPS

Player and Club	G.	PO.	A.	E.	DP.	Pct.	Player and Club	G.	PO.	A.	E.	DP.	Pct.
Helms, Cin	12	3	2	0	0	1.000	Fuentes, S F	36	41	74	3	12	.975
Martinez, Hou	29	34	64	1	9	.990	Dean, S D	55	84	143	6	30	.974
Harmon, Phil	35	37	56	1	10	.989	Woodward, Cin	77	101	226	9	48	.973
Maxvill, St L	136	216	426	12	80	.982	Kessinger, Chi	154	257	501	22	86	.972
Bowa, Phil	143	202	418	13	69	.979	Harrelson, N Y	156	305	401	21	84	.971
Wine, Mont	159	284	481	19	137	.976	Patek, Pitts	65	122	212	10	42	.971
Alley, Pitt	108	202	381	15	84	.975	Robles, S D	23	38	83	4	14	.968
Garrido, Atl	80	119	233	9	36	.975	Lanier, S F	130	256	397	22	83	.967

SHORTSTOPS—Continued

Player and Club	G.	PO.	A.	E.	DP.	Pct.
Popovich, Chi	17	24	27	2	7	.962
Wills, L A	126	171	396	24	58	.959
Huntz, S D	57	86	166	11	32	.958
Grabarkewitz, L A	50	47	135	8	16	.958
Arcia, S D	67	89	146	11	32	.958
Menke, Hou	133	192	394	28	66	.954
Crosby, St L.....	35	37	87	6	15	.954
Brand, Mont	19	22	37	3	8	.952
Slocum, S D	17	8	11	1	2	.950
Weis, N Y	15	15	22	2	3	.949
Torres, Hou	22	26	45	4	7	.947
Concepcion, Cin..	93	137	244	22	51	.945
Chaney, Cin	30	28	52	5	5	.941
Jackson, Atl	87	123	240	26	40	.933
Sutherland, Mont	15	4	10	1	1	.933
Ramirez, St L	59	63	92	13	25	.923
Heise, S F	33	25	72	9	14	.915

(Fewer Than Ten Games)

Player and Club	G.	PO.	A.	E.	DP.	Pct.
Duffy, Cin	5	4	12	0	4	1.000
Foli, N Y	2	1	7	0	0	1.000
Aspromonte, Atl..	4	1	4	0	0	1.000
Martinez, N Y	1	1	4	0	1	1.000
Staehle, Mont	1	1	2	0	0	1.000
Money, Phil	2	2	0	0	1	1.000
Russell, L A	1	0	2	0	0	1.000
Rojas, St L	2	1	0	0	0	1.000
Garrett, N Y.....	1	1	0	0	0	1.000
Martinez, Pitt	1	0	1	0	0	1.000
Taylor, Phil	1	0	1	0	0	1.000
Boyer, Atl	5	6	12	1	1	.947
Sizemore, L A....	2	6	5	1	3	.917
Kennedy, St L ...	7	9	11	2	2	.909
Metzger, Chi	1	1	4	1	1	.833
Vukovich, Phil ..	2	3	4	2	1	.778

Triple Play—Alley.

OUTFIELDERS

Player and Club	G.	PO.	A.	E.	DP.	Pct.
Gosger, Mont*...	71	124	5	0	1	1.000
James, Chi	90	115	5	0	1	1.000
Shamsky, N Y*...	58	104	2	0	1	1.000
Jeter, Pitt	56	53	2	0	0	1.000
Garr, Atl	21	43	0	0	0	1.000
Buckner, L A*....	20	36	1	0	1	1.000
Reid, Phil	18	28	6	0	1	1.000
Melendez, St L...	18	31	2	0	0	1.000
Taylor, Phil	18	28	1	0	0	1.000
Hall, 8 Chi-28 Atl	36	27	1	0	0	1.000
Taylor, S F.......	26	26	1	0	1	1.000
Hutto, Mont	22	25	2	0	0	1.000
Beauchamp, 16 Hou-10 St L..	26	23	1	0	0	1.000
Robinson, S D*..	13	22	1	0	0	1.000
Lampard, Hou ...	16	20	2	0	0	1.000
Stahl, S D*........	20	16	1	0	0	1.000
Stewart, Cin	48	15	1	0	0	1.000
Tommie Aaron, Atl	12	13	0	0	0	1.000
Mashore, Mont...	10	12	0	0	0	1.000
Montanez, Phil*..	10	8	1	0	0	1.000
Rose, Cin	159	309	8	1	2	.997
Davis, L A*.......	143	342	12	3	4	.992
Williams, Chi ..	160	259	13	3	1	.989
Pepitone, 28 Hou-56 Chi*..	84	173	2	2	0	.989
Lum, Atl*	98	168	3	2	0	.988
Hague, St L*.....	52	77	3	1	1	.988
Wynn, Hou	151	293	14	4	4	.987
Gonzalez, Atl	119	235	1	3	0	.987
Oliver, Pitts*....	80	136	4	2	1	.986
Hahn, Mont	61	65	5	1	1	.986
Carl Taylor, StL..	46	66	3	1	1	.986
Staub, Mont	160	308	14	5	4	.985
Phillips, Mont ...	75	130	1	2	0	.985
Swoboda, N Y...	100	117	3	2	1	.984
Russell, L A	79	167	8	3	1	.983
Jones, N Y*.....	130	243	10	5	3	.981
Kosco, L A	58	101	2	2	0	.981
McRae, Cin	46	52	1	1	0	.981
Briggs, Phil*.....	95	188	7	4	1	.980
Carbo, Cin	119	177	8	4	2	.979
Frank Johnson, SF	33	44	2	1	1	.979
Tolan, Cin*	150	349	7	8	0	.978
Hisle, Phil	121	262	5	6	0	.978
Fairey, Mont*....	59	86	1	2	0	.978
Henry Aaron, Atl.	125	246	6	6	1	.977
Stargell, Pitt*....	125	184	16	5	1	.976
Day, 7 Chi-35 Mont*	42	81	2	2	0	.976
Gaston, S D......	142	310	7	8	0	.975
Alou, Pitt*.......	153	297	15	8	1	.975
Mays, S F	129	269	6	7	3	.975
Browne, Phil	88	150	4	4	1	.975
Carty, Atl	133	219	5	6	0	.974
Hickman, Chi ...	79	143	7	4	1	.974
Callison, Chi	144	244	8	7	3	.973
Mota, L A	111	172	8	5	3	.973
Marshall, N Y ...	43	71	2	2	0	.973
Davalillo, St L*..	54	67	3	2	1	.972
Murrell, S D	101	183	8	6	2	.970
Bonds, S F	157	326	14	11	7	.969
Cardenal, St L ..	134	276	6	9	0	.969
Lee, St L	77	120	3	4	0	.969
Cedeno, Hou	90	211	1	7	0	.968
Stone, Phil*	99	148	5	5	0	.968
Ferrara, S D	96	119	2	4	0	.968
Jones, Mont	87	118	3	4	1	.968
Singleton, N Y ..	51	90	1	3	0	.968
Agee, N Y	150	374	4	13	3	.967
Henderson, S F..	146	272	15	10	2	.966
Clemente, Pitt ...	104	189	12	7	2	.966
Cline, Cin*	20	27	1	1	1	.966
Brown, S D	137	258	12	10	3	.964
Bailey, Mont	44	50	2	2	1	.963
Brock, St L*	152	247	9	10	2	.962
Alou, Hou.	108	169	6	7	2	.962
Crawford, L A*..	94	160	9	7	1	.960

OUTFIELDERS—Continued

Player—Club	G.	PO.	A.	E.	DP.	Pct.	Player and Club	G.	PO.	A.	E.	DP.	Pct.
Brown, Atl	25	24	0	1	0	.960	Joshua, L A*	41	47	1	3	1	.941
Hart, S F	18	21	2	1	0	.958	Jorgensen, N Y*	10	29	0	2	0	.935
Gamble, Phil	74	148	4	7	0	.956	Morales, S D	26	25	0	2	0	.926
Miller, Hou	72	101	6	6	1	.947	Geronimo, Hou*	26	23	0	2	0	.920
H. Thomas Davis,							Joseph, Phil	12	11	0	1	0	.917
53 Hou-10 Chi.	63	86	4	5	1	.947	Bench, Cin	23	20	1	2	0	.913
Bravo, Cin*	22	17	1	1	0	.947	Baker, Atl	11	11	1	3	0	.800

(Fewer Than Ten Games)

Player and Club	G.	PO.	A.	E.	DP.	Pct.	Player and Club	G.	PO.	A.	E.	DP.	Pct.
Cruz, St L*	4	16	0	0	0	1.000	Beckert, Chi	1	1	0	0	0	1.000
Gaspar, N Y*	8	13	0	0	0	1.000	Kendall, S D	1	1	0	0	0	1.000
Foster, S F	7	10	0	0	0	1.000	Santo, Chi	1	1	0	0	0	1.000
Williams, S F	6	9	1	0	1	1.000	Stanton, N Y	1	1	0	0	0	1.000
Williams, S D	6	6	0	0	0	1.000	Watson, Hou	1	1	0	0	0	1.000
Spangler, Chi*	6	5	0	0	0	1.000	Lis, Phil	9	18	0	1	0	.947
Moore, L A*	5	5	0	0	0	1.000	Sizemore, L A	9	9	2	1	0	.917
Parrilla, Phil	3	5	0	0	0	1.000	Whitaker, S F	9	6	0	1	0	.857
Clines, Pitt	7	4	0	0	0	1.000	Allen, StL	3	5	1	2	0	.750
Menke, Hou	3	4	0	0	0	1.000	Robertson, Pitt	3	4	0	2	0	.667
Arcia, S D	7	3	0	0	0	1.000	Qualls, Mont	2	0	0	0	0	.000
Pagan, Pitt	4	3	0	0	0	1.000	B. Brock Davis,						
Sudakis, L A	3	2	0	0	0	1.000	Chi*	1	0	0	0	0	.000
Burda, S F*	1	2	0	0	0	1.000	Granger Cin	1	0	0	0	0	.000
Brand, Mont	5	1	0	0	0	1.000	Howard, Hou	1	0	0	0	0	.000
Fairly, Mont*	4	1	0	0	0	1.000	Hughes, Chi	1	0	0	0	0	.000
Paciorek, L A	3	1	0	0	0	1.000	Roque, St L	1	0	0	0	0	.000
Rojas, St L	3	1	0	0	0	1.000	Smith, Chi*	1	0	0	0	0	.000
Gabrielson, L A	2	1	0	0	0	1.000	Stephenson, S F.	1	0	0	0	0	.000
Geiger, Hou	2	1	0	0	0	1.000	Webster, S. D.*	1	0	0	0	0	.000
Aspromonte, Atl.	1	1	0	0	0	1.000							

CATCHERS

Player—Club	G.	PO.	A.	E.	PB.	DP.	Pct.	Player—Club	G.	PO.	A.	E.	PB.	DP.	Pct.
Rudolph, Chi	16	67	6	0	1	1	1.000	Torre, St L	90	571	29	8	5	4	.987
Edwards, Hou	139	854	74	5	6	11	.995	Bench, Cin	140	759	73	12	9	12	.986
Barton, S D	59	347	28	2	1	5	.995	Hiatt, 12 Mont-							
Jerry May, Pitt	45	280	32	2	6	2	.994	63 Chi	75	453	23	7	9	1	.986
Haller, L A	106	524	26	4	9	7	.993	Compton, Phil	40	265	13	4	5	1	.986
Howard, Hou	26	125	11	1	1	0	.993	King, Atl	62	316	14	5	10	1	.985
Ryan, Phil	46	238	15	2	2	1	.992	Dietz, S F	139	820	58	14	25	9	.984
Bates, Phil	20	116	8	1	5	0	.992	Bateman, Mont	137	824	62	15	9	19	.983
Grote, N Y	125	855	46	8	6	12	.991	Torborg, L A	63	275	16	5	1	2	.983
McCarver, Phil.	44	314	18	3	2	2	.991	Corrales, Cin	42	167	11	3	1	3	.983
Dyer, N Y	57	294	20	3	0	6	.991	Martin, Chi	36	163	15	3	6	2	.983
Simmons, St L.	79	466	37	5	15	2	.990	Sudakis, L A	38	161	14	3	7	1	.983
Hundley, Chi	73	455	26	5	5	2	.990	Cannizzaro, S D.	110	559	44	12	2	5	.980
Boccabella, Mont	24	79	10	1	0	2	.989	Slocum, S D	19	42	2	1	0	0	.978
Sanguillen, Pitt.	125	775	66	10	14	12	.988	Gibson, S F	23	126	7	4	5	1	.971
Tillman, Atl	70	404	22	5	10	0	.988	Edwards, Phil	34	177	19	6	3	6	.970
Didier, Atl	57	297	25	4	10	3	.988	Bryant, Hou	13	42	2	2	3	0	.957

(Fewer Than Ten Games)

Player—Club	G.	PO.	A.	E.	PB.	DP.	Pct.	Player—Club	G.	PO.	A.	E.	PB.	DP.	Pct.
Stephenson, S F	9	52	8	0	1	1	1.000	Stewart, Cin	1	2	0	0	0	0	1.000
Hutto, Phil	5	15	1	0	2	0	1.000	Taylor, S F	1	1	0	0	0	0	1.000
Watson, Hou	6	11	1	0	1	0	1.000	Zeller, St L	1	1	0	0	0	0	1.000
Ferguson, L A.	3	9	0	0	1	0	1.000	Brand, Mont	9	30	1	1	1	0	.969
Kendall, S D	2	5	1	0	0	0	1.000	Martinez, Hou	6	12	0	1	1	0	.923
Stinson, L A	3	3	0	0	0	0	1.000	Ricketts, Pitt	7	8	2	1	0	0	.909
Miller, Hou.	1	2	0	0	0	0	1.000	Plummer, Cin	4	6	0	1	0	0	.857

PITCHERS

Player and Club	G.	PO.	A.	E.	DP.	Pct.
McGlothlin, Cin..	35	16	55	0	6	1.000
Dobson, S D.......	40	17	31	0	2	1.000
Stoneman, Mont..	40	10	22	0	1	1.000
Charles Taylor, St. L	56	7	23	0	1	1.000
McAndrew, N Y*....	32	13	17	0	1	1.000
Koosman, N Y*....	30	7	20	0	1	1.000
Regan, Chi	54	7	18	0	3	1.000
Coombs, S D*.....	35	4	20	0	1	1.000
Bryant, S F*	34	4	20	0	0	1.000
Marshall, 4 Hou-24 Mont	28	4	20	0	2	1.000
Linzy, 20 S F-47 St L	67	3	20	0	1	1.000
Willis, S D	42	9	13	0	1	1.000
Fryman, Phil*	27	5	17	0	1	1.000
Wegener, Mont...	25	7	14	0	0	1.000
Reed, Mont	57	7	13	0	2	1.000
Giusti, Pitt	66	5	14	0	1	1.000
McCormick, S F*..	23	4	15	0	2	1.000
Pitlock, S. F*...	18	3	15	0	0	1.000
McMahon, S F	61	8	9	0	0	1.000
Taylor, N Y	57	5	12	0	0	1.000
Palmer, Phil	38	7	10	0	1	1.000
Mikkelsen, L A...	33	5	10	0	0	1.000
Ross, S D	33	3	12	0	1	1.000
Pena, L A	29	1	14	0	0	1.000
Strohmayer, Mont	42	7	7	0	0	1.000
Dal Canton, Pitt..	41	3	10	0	2	1.000
Davison, S F*....	31	4	9	0	1	1.000
Briles, St L......	30	6	7	0	0	1.000
Borbon, Cin	12	2	11	0	1	1.000
Nye, 6 St. L-8 Mont*	14	5	7	0	1	1.000
Frisella, N York	30	3	8	0	1	1.000
Rodriquez, 10 SD-26 Chi..	36	2	8	0	1	1.000
Folkers, N Y*....	16	0	10	0	2	1.000
Campisi, St. L ..	37	1	8	0	0	1.000
Santorini, SD ...	21	2	7	0	1	1.000
Dillman, Montreal	18	3	6	0	0	1.000
Garber, Pitt	14	2	7	0	2	1.000
Jaster, Atl*	14	0	8	0	0	1.000
Gullett, Cin*	44	2	5	0	1	1.000
Gura, Chicago*...	20	1	6	0	1	1.000
Lamb, Los Ang ..	35	3	3	0	1	1.000
Chlupsa, St. L...	14	1	5	0	1	1.000
Hilgendorf, St.L*	23	0	5	0	0	1.000
McCool, St. L*...	18	0	5	0	0	1.000
Navarro, Atlanta..	17	2	3	0	0	1.000
Koonce, N York..	13	0	5	0	0	1.000
Pizarro, Chi*.....	12	0	4	0	0	1.000
Carrithers, SF...	11	1	3	0	0	1.000
Pascual, LA	10	1	3	0	1	1.000
Lamb, Pittsburgh	23	0	2	0	0	1.000
Wenz, Phil	22	1	1	0	0	1.000
Barber, 5 Chi-5 Atl*	10	0	2	0	0	1.000
Hrabosky, St.L*..	16	1	0	0	0	1.000
Baldschun, SD ...	12	0	1	0	0	1.000
Marichal, SF	34	25	43	1	1	.986
Jarvis, Atlanta ..	36	29	38	1	0	.985
Wise, Phila	35	17	35	1	3	.981
Niekro, Atlanta..	34	14	38	1	4	.981
Osteen, Los Ang*	37	10	40	1	5	.980

Player—Club	G.	PO.	A.	E.	DP.	Pct.
Nolan, Cincinnati	37	17	28	1	1	.978
Morton, Mont	43	29	42	2	2	.973
Roberts, SD*	43	5	29	1	3	.971
Grant Jackson, Philadelphia* ..	32	13	21	1	0	.971
Torrez, St. L	30	7	27	1	2	.971
Reed, Atlanta ...	21	10	24	1	2	.971
Pappas, 11 Atl-21 Chi	32	12	21	1	4	.971
Selma, Phila	73	8	24	1	3	.970
Gentry, N York ..	32	15	17	1	1	.970
Short, Phila*	36	10	18	1	1	.966
Holtzman, Chi*...	39	11	44	2	1	.965
Ellis, Pittsburgh..	30	21	34	2	3	.965
Walker, Pitt*	42	3	24	1	3	.964
Simpson, Cinn ...	26	22	30	2	2	.963
Reuss, St.L*	20	8	18	1	0	.963
Lemaster, Hou* ..	39	8	17	1	1	.962
Perry, San Fran..	41	30	67	4	5	.960
Blass, Pittsburgh	31	21	26	2	1	.959
Nash, Atlanta ...	34	18	27	2	1	.957
Cloninger, Cinn ..	30	13	31	2	5	.957
Gladding, Hou ...	63	7	15	1	1	.957
Seaver, N York ..	37	19	46	3	3	.956
Billingham, Hou..	46	13	30	2	1	.956
Hands, Chi	39	22	42	3	2	.955
Ray, Houston	52	4	17	1	1	.955
Priddy, Atlanta ..	41	7	14	1	0	.955
Foster, Los Ang ..	33	17	23	2	4	.952
Wilhelm, 50 Atl-3 Chi ..	53	4	16	1	0	.952
Bunning, Phila ..	34	12	27	2	1	.951
Stone, Atlanta*..	35	14	42	3	3	.949
Robertson, SF ...	41	14	23	2	3	.949
Griffin, Houston..	23	8	10	1	0	.947
Merritt, Cinn*...	35	5	30	2	1	.946
Colborn, Chi	34	4	13	1	1	.944
Blasingame, Hou*	13	2	15	1	0	.944
Dierker, Hou	37	19	31	3	3	.943
Sutton, Los Ang..	38	21	28	3	1	.942
Carroll, Cinn	65	8	22	2	1	.938
Kirby, San Diego	36	6	23	2	1	.935
Brewer, Los Ang*	58	0	14	1	0	.933
Gibson, St. L	34	22	32	4	3	.931
Culver, 11 StL-32 Hou	43	8	19	2	2	.931
Jenkins, Chicago..	40	14	39	4	1	.930
Cardwell, 16 NY-16 Atl..	32	1	12	1	2	.929
Abernathy, 11 Chi-11 St.L	22	1	12	1	1	.929
Herbel, 64 SD-12 NY..	76	8	17	2	0	.926
Lersch, Phila	42	6	18	2	3	.923
Jerry Johnson, 7 StL-33 SF ..	40	3	9	1	0	.923
Hartenstein, 17 Pitt-6 StL	23	2	10	1	1	.923
McGinn, Mont* ..	52	6	29	3	1	.921
Wilson, Houston..	29	6	17	2	2	.920
Carlton, St L* ...	34	6	38	4	1	.917
Moose, Pitt	28	10	22	3	2	.914
Moeller, LA	31	6	15	2	1	.913
Washburn, Cinn ..	35	7	13	2	2	.909
Dukes, SD	53	2	8	1	1	.909
Gibbon, Pitt*	41	3	7	1	0	.909

PITCHERS—Continued

Player and Club	G.	PO.	A.	E.	DP.	Pct.
Wilson, Phila	37	0	9	1	1	.900
McGraw, NY*	57	9	17	3	0	.897
Reberger, SF	45	15	19	4	1	.895
Cook, Houston* ..	41	3	13	2	1	.889
Veale, Pitt*	34	0	23	3	1	.885
Granger, Cinn	67	8	22	4	4	.882
Vance, Los Ang ...	20	6	8	2	0	.875
McQueen, Atl*	22	0	7	1	0	.875
Wilson, SD	15	2	5	1	0	.875
Renko, Montreal..	41	17	31	7	3	.873
Singer, Los Ang..	16	8	12	3	0	.870
Corkins, SD	24	8	10	3	1	.857
Decker, Chicago ..	24	4	14	3	0	.857
Nelson, Pitts	15	7	4	2	1	.846

Player and Club	G.	PO.	A.	E.	DP.	Pct.
Ryan, New York..	27	11	10	4	2	.840
Bouton, Hous	29	4	11	3	0	.833
Sadecki, NY*	28	3	13	4	0	.800
Pena, Pitts	23	4	8	3	1	.800
Brunet, Pitts*	12	0	4	1	0	.800
Norman,						
30 L A-1 St L*	31	2	8	3	0	.769
Raymond, Mont ..	59	6	7	4	0	.765
DiLauro, Hou*	42	2	4	2	0	.750
Hoerner, Phila* ..	44	2	1	1	0	.750
Cleveland, St.L ..	16	1	1	1	0	.667
Kester, Atlanta ..	15	0	3	2	0	.600
Aguirre, Chicago*	17	0	2	3	0	.400

(Fewer Than Ten Games)

Player and Club	G.	PO.	A.	E.	DP.	Pct.
Noriega, Cinn	8	1	7	0	0	1.000
Parker, St.L	7	4	4	0	0	1.000
Cambria, Pitts ..	6	1	6	0	1	1.000
Waslewski, Mont..	6	2	5	0	1	1.000
Doyle, SD*	9	0	6	0	1	1.000
Grant, Pitts	8	4	2	0	0	1.000
Wilcox, Cinn	5	1	5	0	0	1.000
Bertaina, St.L* ..	8	0	5	0	0	1.000
Dunegan, Chi	7	1	4	0	0	1.000
Maloney, Cinn	7	0	5	0	0	1.000
Strahler, LA	6	3	2	0	0	1.000
O'Donoghue,						
Mont*	9	0	4	0	1	1.000
Hough, LA	8	1	3	0	0	1.000
Forsch, Hou	4	2	2	0	1	1.000
Arlin, SD	2	0	4	0	0	1.000
Champion, Phila..	7	0	3	0	0	1.000
Miller, Chicago ..	7	1	2	0	0	1.000
Colpaert, Pitts	8	2	0	0	0	1.000
Guzman, St.L	8	0	2	0	0	1.000
McBean,						
1 LA-7 Pitt ..	8	0	2	0	1	1.000
Cumberland, S F*	7	0	2	0	0	1.000
Gatewood, Atl	3	1	1	0	0	1.000
James Johnson,						
S. F.*	3	0	2	0	0	1.000

Player and Club	G.	PO.	A.	E.	DP.	Pct.
Johnson, Mont	3	1	1	0	0	1.000
Neibauer, Atl	7	0	1	0	0	1.000
Reynolds, Chi	7	0	1	0	1	1.000
Behney, Cin*	5	0	1	0	0	1.000
Michael Jackson,						
Phil*	5	0	1	0	0	1.000
Sembera, Mont....	5	0	1	0	0	1.000
Chance, N Y	3	0	1	0	0	1.000
Harris, Hou	2	1	0	0	0	1.000
Puente, S F	6	1	4	1	0	.833
Moore, Mont*	6	1	2	1	1	.750
Sparma, Mont	9	2	3	2	0	.714
Reynolds, Phil* ..	4	1	1	1	0	.667
Faul, S F	7	0	0	0	0	.000
Kline, Atl	5	0	0	0	0	.000
Spinks, Hou	5	0	0	0	0	.000
Acosta, Pitt	3	0	0	0	0	.000
Belinsky, Cin*....	3	0	0	0	0	.000
Osinski, Hou	3	0	0	0	0	.000
Stephenson, L. A.	3	0	0	0	0	.000
Laxton, Phil*	2	0	0	0	0	.000
Nyman, S D*	2	0	0	0	0	.000
Cosman, Chi	1	0	0	0	0	.000
Marone, Pitt*......	1	0	0	0	0	.000

1969-70 Comparison of Game's Direction

Here are a few key areas of comparison by which we can look at what happened performance-wise in 1970 as against the pattern followed the previous season. Note the American League's increase in power but decline in defense and how closely the National League follows the same pattern, with one main exception—stolen bases—and a minor shift in the direction of strikeouts.

	BA.	Hits	HR.	SB.	Runs	ERA.	SO.
American League—1969	.246	16,120	1649	1033	7960	3.62	10,845
1970	.250	16,404	1746	863	8109	3.71	10,957
National League—1969	.250	16,461	1470	817	7890	3.59	11,628
1970	.258	17,151	1683	1045	8771	4.05	11,417

NATIONAL LEAGUE PITCHING AVERAGES

Compiled by Elias Sports Bureau, New York, N. Y.

CLUB PITCHING RECORDS

Club	G	CG	Sv.	ShO.	IP.	H.	BFP.	R.	ER.	HR.	SH.	SF.	Tot. BB.	Int. BB.	HB.	SO.	WP.	Bk.	ERA.
New York	162	47	32	10	1460	1260	6134	630	559	135	80	42	575	96	26	1064	48	7	3.45
Cincinnati	162	32	60	15	1445	1370	6184	681	592	118	67	42	592	74	29	843	43	9	3.69
Pittsburgh	162	36	43	13	1454	1386	6197	664	597	106	64	34	625	84	36	990	35	4	3.70
Chicago	162	59	25	9	1435	1402	6086	679	599	143	66	34	475	58	25	1000	40	4	3.76
Los Angeles	161	37	42	17	1459	1394	6192	684	619	164	63	34	496	49	34	880	49	6	3.82
St. Louis	162	51	20	11	1476	1483	6425	747	665	102	82	51	632	102	22	960	66	7	4.05
Philadelphia	161	24	36	8	1461	1483	6294	730	677	132	75	53	538	51	33	1047	52	7	4.17
Houston	162	36	35	6	1456	1491	6337	763	685	131	64	37	577	45	41	942	91	5	4.23
Atlanta	162	45	24	9	1431	1451	6179	772	688	185	66	37	478	42	30	960	44	5	4.33
San Diego	162	24	32	9	1440	1483	6326	788	697	149	75	57	611	92	38	886	39	7	4.36
San Francisco	162	50	30	7	1458	1514	6408	826	729	156	70	43	604	57	38	931	76	5	4.50
Montreal	162	29	32	10	1439	1434	6347	807	720	162	47	40	716	76	49	914	49	6	4.50
Totals		470	411	124	17412	17151	75109	8771	7827	1683	819	501	6919	826	393	11417	632	73	4.05

BFP total includes 12 batsmen awarded first base because of interference or obstruction.

NOTE—Totals for earned runs for several clubs do not agree with the composite totals for all pitchers of each respective club due to instances in which provisions of Section 10.18 (i) of the Scoring Rules were applied. The following differences are to be noted: Atlanta, the pitchers add to 691; Chicago, 600; Cincinnati, 595; Los Angeles, 620; Montreal, 721; New York, 561; Pittsburgh, 599; San Diego, 700.

PITCHERS' RECORDS

(Top Fifteen Qualifiers for Earned-Run Leadership—162 or More Innings)

Pitcher and Club	G.	GS.	CG.	GF.	Sv.	ShO.	W.	L.	Pct.	IP.	H.	BFP.	R.	ER.	HR.	SH.	SF.	Tot. BB.	Int. BB.	HB.	SO.	WP.	Bk.	ERA.
Seaver, G. Thomas, New York	37	36	19	1	0	2	18	12	.600	291	230	1173	103	91	21	9	4	83	8	4	283	6	0	2.81
Simpson, Wayne, Cincinnati	26	26	10	0	0	3	14	3	.824	176	125	730	73	59	15	4	3	81	3	9	119	6	6	3.02
Walker, J. Luke, Pittsburgh*	42	19	5	15	13	3	15	6	.714	163	129	684	56	55	13	6	1	102	1	5	111	4	2	3.04
Gibson, Robert, St. Louis	34	34	23	0	0	3	23	7	.767	294	262	1213	111	102	13	10	3	88	8	8	274	5	1	3.12
Koosman, Jerry, New York*	30	29	5	1	0	0	12	7	.632	212	189	884	87	74	22	7	7	84	8	8	118	11	0	3.14
Perry, Gaylord, San Francisco	41	41	23	0	0	5	23	13	.639	329	292	1336	138	117	27	7	7	87	1	10	214	11	0	3.20
Ellis, Dock, Pittsburgh	30	30	9	0	0	4	13	10	.565	202	194	863	81	72	9	6	5	96	9	1	128	3	8	3.21
Nolan, Gary, Cincinnati	37	37	8	0	0	2	18	7	.720	251	226	1052	102	91	25	12	6	82	9	1	181	8	2	3.26
Coombs, Daniel, San Diego*	35	27	5	6	0	1	10	14	.417	188	185	817	83	69	12	11	2	76	14	2	105	3	3	3.30

*Throws lefthanded.

Pitcher and Club	G.	GS.	CG.	GF.	Sv.	ShO.	W.	L.	Pct.	IP.	H.	BFP.	R.	ER.	HR.	SH.	SF.	Tot. BB.	Int. BB.	HB.	SO.	WP.	Bk.	ERA.
Pappas, Milton, 11 Atl-21 Chi	32	23	7	3	0	0	12	10	.545	180	179	752	78	67	20	6	6	43	10	2	105	4	1	3.35
Holtzman, Kenneth, Chicago*	39	38	15	0	0	2	17	11	.607	288	271	1208	125	108	30	10	7	94	6	3	202	12	—	3.38
Jenkins, Ferguson, Chicago	40	39	24	1	0	0	22	16	.579	313	265	1265	125	118	40	6	4	60	6	7	274	0	1	3.39
Blass, Stephen, Pittsburgh	31	31	6	0	0	0	10	12	.455	197	187	824	92	77	14	6	6	73	8	5	120	2	0	3.52
McAndrew, James, New York	32	27	9	3	1	0	10	14	.417	184	166	745	77	73	18	6	7	38	6	3	120	2	0	3.57
McGlothlin, James, Cincinnati	35	34	5	1	0	3	14	10	.583	211	192	893	91	84	19	12	5	86	8	3	97	2	0	3.58

DEPARTMENTAL LEADERS: G—Herbel, 76; GS—Perry, 41; CG—Jenkins, 24; ShO—Perry, 5; W—Gibson, Perry, 23; L—Carlton, 19; Sv—Granger, 35; Pct.—Simpson, .824; IP—Perry, 329; H—Perry, 292; AB—Perry, 1336; R. Perry, 138; ER—Jenkins, Sutton, 118; HR—Niekro, 40; SH—Carlton, Nash, 14; SF—Bunning, Kirby, 11; BB—Morton, 125; IBB—McGraw, Morton, 17; HB—Stoneman, 14; SO—Seaver, 283; WP—Robertson, 18; Bk—Fryman, Herbel, Koosman, Morton, 3.

(All Pitchers—Listed Alphabetically)

*Throws lefthanded.

Pitcher and Club	G.	GS.	CG.	GF.	Sv.	ShO.	W.	L.	Pct.	IP.	H.	BFP.	R.	ER.	HR.	SH.	SF.	Tot. BB.	Int. BB.	HB.	SO.	WP.	Bk.	ERA.
Abernathy, Ted, 11 Chi-11 StL	22	0	0	6	2	0	1	0	1.000	27	24	122	8	8	0	6	2	17	5	1	10	1	0	2.67
Acosta, Eduardo, Pittsburgh	3	0	0	2	1	0	0	0	.000	3	5	16	4	4	0	2	0	1	0	1	1	0	0	12.00
Aguirre, Henry, Chicago*	17	0	0	3	1	0	0	0	1.000	14	13	64	10	7	3	0	0	9	4	0	11	0	0	4.50
Arlin, Stephen, San Diego	2	2	0	0	0	0	0	0	1.000	13	13	56	5	5	0	2	1	8	1	0	3	0	0	2.77
Baldschun, Jack, San Diego	12	0	0	8	0	0	0	0	.000	20	27	97	14	12	2	0	0	11	3	0	12	0	0	10.38
Barber, Stephen, 5 Chi-5 Atl*	10	2	0	2	0	0	2	0	1.000	20	15	97	16	14	4	1	2	14	4	0	14	0	0	6.30
Behney, Melvin, Cincinnati*	3	1	0	0	0	0	0	2	.000	8	10	40	6	4	0	0	0	8	3	0	6	3	0	4.50
Belinsky, Robert, Cincinnati*	5	0	0	1	0	0	0	0	.000	8	10	40	6	4	0	0	0	8	3	0	6	3	0	4.50
Bertaina, Frank, St. Louis*	8	5	1	0	0	0	2	4	.333	31	36	142	19	13	3	1	3	15	3	1	19	0	0	3.19
Billingham, John, Houston	46	24	8	7	0	0	13	9	.591	188	190	818	102	83	10	9	2	63	10	1	134	11	1	3.97
Blasingame, Wade, Houston*	13	13	1	0	0	0	5	5	.500	78	76	320	34	30	7	6	4	23	8	0	55	4	1	3.46
Blass, Stephen, Pittsburgh	31	31	6	0	0	0	10	12	.455	197	187	824	92	77	14	6	6	73	8	5	120	2	0	3.52
Borbon, Pedro, Cincinnati	12	0	0	6	1	0	2	1	.455	17	21	79	15	13	2	1	0	6	3	0	49	0	0	6.88
Bouton, James, Houston	29	6	0	7	1	0	4	6	.400	73	84	336	53	44	7	7	1	33	9	1	91	6	0	5.42
Brewer, James, Los Angeles*	58	0	0	41	24	0	7	6	.538	89	66	361	36	31	6	5	0	36	7	1	91	8	0	3.13
Briles, Nelson, St. Louis	30	19	6	1	0	2	6	7	.462	107	129	484	84	74	14	6	2	39	1	0	49	3	0	6.22
Brunet, George, Pittsburgh*	12	11	0	0	0	0	1	1	.500	17	19	75	5	5	1	0	0	9	0	0	17	0	0	2.65
Bryant, Ronald, San Francisco*	34	11	1	7	0	0	5	8	.385	96	103	425	58	51	7	3	0	38	5	0	59	4	0	4.78
Bunning, James, Philadelphia	34	33	4	0	0	2	10	15	.400	219	233	937	111	100	19	12	11	56	0	8	147	1	0	4.11
Cambria, Frederick, Pittsburgh	6	2	0	0	0	0	0	2	.000	33	37	150	15	13	2	2	0	9	1	1	14	0	0	3.55
Campisi, Salvatore, St. Louis	37	0	0	15	3	0	3	3	.500	49	53	232	19	16	2	4	0	37	11	3	26	2	0	2.94
Cardwell, Donald, 16 NY-16 Atl	32	10	0	10	2	0	2	3	.400	48	62	223	42	41	8	3	2	19	3	1	26	3	1	7.69
Carlton, Steven, St. Louis*	34	33	13	0	4	0	10	19	.345	254	239	1086	123	105	25	14	7	109	16	3	193	14	0	3.72
Carrithers, Donald, San Francisco	11	0	0	2	0	0	2	1	.667	22	31	108	19	18	5	4	1	14	7	2	12	1	0	7.36
Carroll, Clay, Cincinnati	65	0	0	31	16	0	9	4	.692	104	104	437	38	30	14	6	0	27	9	1	63	2	0	2.60
Champion, B. Billy, Philadelphia	7	1	0	0	0	0	0	1	.000	10	14	70	14	14	3	0	2	10	1	0	12	1	0	9.00
Chance, W. Dean, New York	1	0	0	1	0	0	0	0	.000	2	3	10	3	3	0	2	0	2	0	0	1	0	0	13.50
Chlupsa, Robert, St. Louis	14	0	0	5	0	0	2	0	1.000	16	26	83	16	16	2	1	0	9	3	0	10	2	0	9.00
Cleveland, Reginald, St. Louis	16	1	0	0	0	0	0	0	.000	26	31	129	27	22	3	0	1	18	6	0	22	0	0	7.62
Cloninger, Tony, Cincinnati	30	18	3	1	0	0	9	7	.563	148	136	637	69	63	10	7	3	78	6	4	56	7	0	3.83

Pitcher and Club	G.	GS.	CG.	GF.	Sv.	ShO.	W.	L.	Pct.	IP.	H.	BFP.	R.	ER.	HR.	SH.	SF.	Tot. BB.	Int. BB.	HB.	SO.	WP.	Bk.	ERA.
Colborn, James, Chicago	34	5	0	11	4	0	3	1	.750	73	88	327	37	29	3	4	4	23	6	1	50	1	0	3.58
Colpaert, Richard, Pittsburgh	8	0	0	2	0	0	1	0	1.000	11	8	47	7	7	3	1	0	6	2	0	6	1	1	5.73
Cook, Ronald, Houston*	41	0	0	26	6	0	5	6	.455	82	80	350	37	34	3	11	4	42	14	2	50	1	1	3.73
Coombs, Daniel, San Diego*	35	27	5	1	0	0	10	14	.417	188	185	817	83	69	12	11	6	76	14	2	105	1	1	3.30
Corkins, Michael, San Diego	24	18	0	6	3	0	5	6	.455	111	109	518	62	57	11	9	3	79	10	4	75	0	1	4.62
Cosman, James, Chicago	1	0	0	1	0	0	0	0	.000	1	6	9	3	3	0	1	0	4	0	0	0	0	0	27.00
Culver, George, 11 StL-32 Hou	43	7	0	16	6	0	6	6	.500	102	108	452	48	45	7	3	1	45	6	0	54	11	0	3.97
Cumberland, John, San Francisco*	7	0	0	2	0	0	3	0	1.000	11	8	44	2	1	1	2	1	8	0	0	6	0	0	0.82
Dal Canton, J. Bruce, Pittsburgh	41	6	1	14	1	0	9	4	.692	85	94	379	48	43	7	1	2	39	8	0	53	1	0	4.55
Davison, Michael, San Francisco*	31	0	0	16	1	0	3	5	.375	36	46	171	29	26	4	5	2	22	4	0	21	5	0	6.50
Decker, George, Chicago	24	17	1	1	0	0	2	7	.222	109	108	482	64	56	12	5	2	56	4	0	79	8	0	4.62
Dierker, Lawrence, Houston	37	36	17	0	0	3	16	12	.571	270	263	1132	124	116	31	7	5	82	6	4	191	3	1	3.87
DiLauro, Jack, Houston*	42	0	0	16	4	0	1	3	.250	34	34	152	23	16	4	5	3	17	4	0	23	0	0	4.24
Dillman, William, Montreal	18	0	0	10	1	0	2	3	.400	31	28	134	24	18	9	7	3	18	13	1	17	3	0	5.23
Dobson, Patrick, San Diego	40	34	8	3	0	4	14	15	.483	251	257	1073	126	105	28	12	9	78	1	0	185	0	0	3.76
Doyle, Paul, San Diego*	9	0	0	5	2	0	0	2	.000	7	5	32	5	5	0	0	0	6	1	0	2	0	0	6.43
Dukes, Thomas, San Diego	53	0	0	26	10	0	1	6	.143	69	62	288	39	31	7	2	1	25	3	1	56	0	0	4.04
Dunegan, James, Chicago	7	0	0	2	0	0	0	2	.000	13	13	63	8	7	0	0	0	12	1	0	13	0	0	4.85
Ellis, Dock, Pittsburgh	30	30	8	0	0	2	13	10	.565	202	194	863	81	72	9	6	2	87	11	10	128	3	0	3.21
Faul, William, San Francisco	16	1	0	7	0	0	0	2	.000	10	15	49	9	8	1	4	0	5	0	0	13	0	0	7.20
Folkers, Richard, New York*	8	1	0	0	0	0	1	2	.333	29	36	145	21	21	6	0	1	25	4	0	15	0	0	6.52
Forsch, Kenneth, Houston	6	0	0	2	0	0	0	2	.000	16	15	63	10	10	1	0	0	5	0	0	13	0	0	5.63
Foster, Alan, Los Angeles	33	20	4	7	1	0	8	3	.727	128	122	532	61	58	11	2	3	43	2	1	97	5	3	4.25
Frisella, Daniel, New York	30	0	0	14	5	0	8	6	.571	66	49	279	23	22	4	11	3	34	11	2	54	3	0	3.00
Fryman, Woodrow, Philadelphia*	32	29	7	3	0	1	8	8	.500	188	198	798	95	85	19	7	6	86	7	2	134	6	1	4.08
Garber, H. Eugene, Pittsburgh	14	0	0	5	1	0	0	0	.000	41	44	190	25	24	4	4	0	24	8	1	26	5	0	5.32
Gatewood, Aubrey, Atlanta	3	0	0	1	0	0	0	0	.000	6	6	14	3	3	0	0	0	2	1	0	4	0	0	4.50
Gentry, Gary, New York	34	32	6	1	0	1	9	9	.500	215	190	857	88	88	13	4	4	72	3	1	134	8	0	3.69
Gibbon, Joseph, Pittsburgh*	34	0	0	13	5	0	2	3	.400	41	44	190	26	22	4	8	0	24	8	1	26	5	0	4.83
Gibson, Robert, St. Louis	34	34	23	0	0	3	23	7	.767	294	262	1213	111	102	13	6	10	88	8	3	274	5	0	3.12
Giusti, David, Pittsburgh	66	1	0	47	26	0	9	3	.750	103	98	428	38	35	7	6	1	39	8	3	85	5	0	3.06
Gladding, Fred, Houston	63	0	0	44	18	0	7	4	.636	85	84	324	39	32	4	9	2	24	8	0	46	7	0	4.06
Granger, Wayne, Cincinnati	67	0	0	59	35	0	6	5	.545	85	79	352	33	25	5	8	0	27	8	0	38	3	0	2.65
Grant, James, Pittsburgh	8	0	0	2	2	0	2	1	.667	16	14	64	4	4	0	0	0	2	1	0	9	0	0	2.25
Griffin, Thomas, Houston	23	20	2	2	0	0	3	13	.188	111	118	511	72	71	21	4	1	72	13	3	118	9	0	5.76
Gullett, Donald, Cincinnati *	44	2	1	10	6	0	5	2	.714	78	54	323	23	21	3	2	1	44	6	1	76	6	0	2.42
Gura, Lawrence, Chicago*	20	3	1	1	0	0	1	3	.250	38	35	167	18	16	4	5	0	23	1	0	21	0	0	3.79
Guzman, Santiago, St. Louis	8	1	0	1	1	0	1	1	.500	14	14	64	12	11	0	1	0	13	0	0	9	1	0	7.07
Hands, William, Chicago	39	38	12	0	0	2	18	15	.545	265	278	1127	121	109	20	10	5	76	8	0	170	0	1	3.70
Harris, Walter, Houston	3	0	0	0	0	0	0	1	.000	6	6	25	4	4	0	0	0	2	0	0	2	0	0	6.00
Hartenstein, Charles, 17 Pitt-6 StL.23	23	0	0	13	1	0	1	1	.500	37	49	174	28	25	4	5	2	13	4	0	23	1	1	6.08

Pitcher and Club	G.	GS.	CG.	GF.	Sv.	ShO.	W.	L.	Pct.	IP.	H.	BFP.	R.	ER.	HR.	SH.	SF.	Tot. BB.	Int. BB.	HB.	SO.	WP.	Bk.	ERA.
Herbel, Ronald, 64 SD-12 NY	76	1	0	38	10	0	9	7	.563	124	128	535	72	63	15	6	5	41	11	4	61	4	3	4.57
Hilgendorf, Thomas, St. Louis*	23	0	0	12	3	0	0	0	.000	21	22	97	11	9	1	6	1	13	5	0	13	3	1	3.86
Hoerner, Joseph, Philadelphia*	44	0	0	28	9	0	9	5	.643	58	53	245	20	17	5	4	5	20	7	0	39	1	0	2.64
Holtzman, Kenneth, Chicago*	39	38	15	0	0	3	17	11	.607	288	248	1208	125	108	30	10	4	94	6	3	202	12	0	3.38
Hough, Charles, Los Angeles	8	0	0	5	1	0	0	0	.000	17	18	79	11	10	2	1	0	11	1	0	8	0	0	5.29
Hrabosky, Alan, St. Louis*	16	0	0	7	1	0	2	1	.667	19	17	85	11	10	1	0	0	7	1	1	12	1	0	4.74
Jackson, Grant, Philadelphia*	32	23	4	0	0	1	5	15	.250	150	170	669	94	88	17	13	4	61	3	0	104	2	0	5.28
Jackson, Michael, Philadelphia*	5	1	0	1	0	0	1	1	.500	6	6	25	1	1	0	1	0	4	0	0	4	0	0	1.50
Jarvis, R. Patrick, Atlanta	36	34	11	0	0	6	16	16	.500	254	240	1062	110	102	21	9	8	72	5	0	173	5	1	3.61
Jaster, Larry, Atlanta*	14	0	0	6	1	0	1	1	.500	22	33	105	18	17	5	3	2	8	6	0	9	0	0	6.95
Jenkins, Ferguson, Chicago	40	39	24	0	0	3	22	16	.579	313	265	1265	128	118	30	6	7	60	1	7	274	2	1	3.39
Johnson, James, San Francisco	40	0	0	14	1	0	5	4	.556	77	73	340	43	35	6	5	0	41	2	1	49	4	0	4.09
Johnson, Jerry, 7 StL-33 SF	40	0	0	14	3	0	0	4	.000	32	31	149	24	20	5	2	1	19	2	0	20	1	0	7.71
Johnson, Kenneth, Montreal	1	0	0	0	0	0	0	0	.000	9	9	30	5	5	1	0	0	5	0	0	1	0	0	7.50
Kester, Richard, Atlanta	15	0	0	2	0	0	0	0	.000	32	36	99	24	20	4	2	1	10	1	0	20	1	0	5.63
Kirby, Clayton, San Diego	36	34	5	2	0	1	10	16	.385	215	198	949	118	108	29	9	4	71	5	2	154	7	0	4.52
Kline, Ronald, Atlanta	5	0	0	0	0	0	0	0	.000	9	11	30	5	5	1	1	0	3	0	0	10	0	0	7.50
Koonce, Calvin, New York	13	0	0	8	1	0	6	3	.667	31	25	99	14	10	2	2	1	14	1	1	43	0	0	3.27
Koosman, Jerry, New York*	30	29	6	0	0	3	12	7	.632	215	189	884	87	74	22	9	5	71	14	2	118	6	0	3.14
Lamb, John, Pittsburgh	23	0	0	15	0	0	1	3	.250	32	23	127	10	10	4	1	2	13	1	1	24	0	0	2.81
Lamb, Raymond, Los Angeles	35	0	0	8	1	0	6	1	.857	57	57	250	27	24	5	5	4	27	9	4	32	3	0	3.79
Laxton, William, Philadelphia*	2	0	0	0	0	0	0	1	.000	2	7	11	3	3	0	0	0	2	0	0	1	0	0	13.50
Lemaster, Denver, Houston*	39	21	3	3	0	0	7	12	.368	162	169	709	88	82	22	5	6	65	9	2	103	12	0	4.56
Lersch, Barry, Philadelphia	42	11	3	14	0	0	7	4	.632	138	119	573	52	50	17	8	6	47	5	1	92	4	1	3.26
Linzy, Frank, 20 SF-47 StL	67	0	0	30	9	0	5	6	.455	87	99	380	46	45	11	6	5	34	14	2	35	7	0	4.66
Maloney, James, Cincinnati	7	3	0	0	0	0	0	2	.000	26	26	92	27	27	3	4	0	15	0	1	7	1	1	11.12
Marichal, Juan, San Francisco	34	33	14	0	0	2	12	10	.545	243	269	1035	128	111	28	9	3	48	2	3	123	4	0	4.11
Marone, Louis, Pittsburgh*	34	0	0	13	0	0	0	0	.000	70	64	308	39	30	1	4	0	33	6	0	43	0	0	4.50
Marshall, Michael, 4 Hou-24 Mont	28	5	0	11	3	0	3	8	.273	184	166	745	77	73	18	6	3	38	6	0	111	4	0	3.86
McAndrew, James, New York	32	27	3	1	0	0	6	7	.417	184	166	745	77	73	18	6	3	51	1	1	111	6	0	3.57
McBean, Alvin, 1 LA-7 Pitt	8	0	0	1	0	0	0	1	.000	11	14	51	9	8	0	0	0	3	0	0	3	0	0	7.36
McCool, William, St. Louis*	18	0	0	7	1	0	0	0	.000	22	20	99	15	15	5	1	0	16	2	0	12	0	0	6.14
McCormick, Michael, San Fran*	23	11	3	3	0	0	3	4	.429	78	80	351	58	54	15	8	7	36	4	0	37	6	0	6.23
McGinn, Daniel, Montreal*	52	0	0	12	1	0	7	10	.412	131	154	615	88	84	13	8	8	88	8	3	83	6	0	5.43
McGlothlin, James, Cincinnati	35	19	5	3	0	2	14	10	.583	211	192	893	91	84	19	12	6	49	17	1	97	2	0	3.58
McGraw, Frank, New York*	57	0	0	32	10	0	4	6	.400	91	77	398	40	33	6	11	5	49	13	0	81	4	1	3.26
McMahon, Donald, San Francisco	61	0	0	44	19	0	9	5	.643	94	70	399	32	31	7	9	3	41	12	1	74	2	0	2.97
McQueen, Michael, Atlanta*	22	8	1	6	0	0	2	5	.286	91	95	291	48	41	11	5	2	53	5	2	54	4	0	5.59
Merritt, James, Cincinnati*	35	35	12	0	0	4	20	12	.625	234	248	984	114	106	21	10	3	53	12	4	136	4	0	4.08
Mikkelsen, Peter, Los Angeles	33	0	0	22	6	0	4	5	.444	62	48	255	20	19	5	4	1	20	6	1	47	1	0	2.76
Miller, Robert, Chicago	7	1	0	2	0	0	0	0	.000	9	9	39	5	5	3	1	0	4	0	0	4	0	0	5.00

Pitcher and Club	G.	GS.	CG.	GF.	Sv.	ShO.	W.	L.	Pct.	IP.	H.	BFP.	R.	ER.	HR.	SH.	SF.	Tot. BB.	Int. BB.	HB.	SO.	WP.	Bk.	ERA.
Moeller, Joseph, Los Angeles	31	19	2	7	4	1	7	9	.438	135	131	578	63	59	16	4	2	43	3	1	63	2	0	3.93
Moore, Balor, Montreal*	6	2	0	2	0	0	2	2	.500	10	14	48	8	8	0	0	1	5	0	0	6	0	2	7.20
Moose, Robert, Pittsburgh	28	27	2	0	0	2	11	10	.524	190	186	784	88	84	14	5	5	64	5	3	119	0	0	3.98
Morton, Carl, Montreal	43	37	10	1	0	0	18	11	.621	285	281	1218	123	114	27	6	6	125	17	2	154	2	2	3.60
Nash, James, Atlanta	34	33	6	0	0	2	13	9	.591	212	211	936	105	96	22	14	4	90	7	1	153	1	3	4.08
Navarro, Julio, Atlanta	17	0	0	10	0	0	0	0	.000	26	24	105	12	12	7	0	0	10	1	0	21	0	0	4.15
Neibauer, Gary, Atlanta	7	6	0	0	0	0	0	1	.000	13	7	56	7	5	0	2	0	8	5	0	9	2	0	3.44
Nelson, James, Pittsburgh	15	10	1	1	0	1	4	2	.667	68	64	298	32	26	5	4	4	38	5	3	42	8	1	3.44
Niekro, Philip, Atlanta	34	32	10	1	0	0	12	18	.400	230	222	980	124	109	40	6	6	68	9	1	168	6	0	4.27
Nolan, Gary, Cincinnati	37	37	8	0	0	2	18	7	.720	251	226	1052	102	91	25	7	7	96	5	2	181	8	1	3.26
Noriega, John, Cincinnati	8	0	0	4	0	0	0	0	.000	18	25	90	17	16	0	2	1	10	1	0	6	1	0	8.00
Norman, Fredie, 30 LA-1 StL*	31	6	0	11	0	3	1	1	1.000	63	66	286	40	36	8	1	1	33	1	2	47	10	0	5.14
Nye, Richard, 6 StL-8 Mont*	14	6	0	2	0	0	0	2	.000	54	60	246	28	25	5	3	4	26	4	0	26	0	0	4.17
Nyman, Gerry, San Diego*	9	3	0	3	0	0	0	3	.000	5	3	26	9	9	1	1	0	11	0	0	2	0	1	16.20
O'Donoghue, John, Montreal*	9	0	0	3	0	0	2	3	.400	22	20	94	14	13	2	2	1	11	2	0	6	0	0	5.32
Osinski, Daniel, Houston	9	0	0	3	0	0	0	0	.000	22	20	94	14	13	2	2	1	11	2	0	6	0	0	9.00
Osteen, Claude, Los Angeles*	37	37	11	0	0	4	16	14	.533	259	280	1085	121	110	24	9	4	52	3	1	114	1	0	3.82
Palmer, Lowell, Philadelphia	38	5	0	10	0	0	2	4	.333	102	98	451	66	62	15	4	5	55	5	4	85	14	1	5.47
Pappas, Milton, 11 Atl-21 Chi	32	23	7	1	0	2	12	10	.545	180	179	752	78	67	20	6	4	43	10	0	105	4	0	3.35
Parker, Harry, St. Louis	10	0	0	5	0	0	1	1	.500	14	24	105	13	8	1	0	0	15	0	0	8	0	1	3.27
Pascual, Camilo, Los Angeles	29	0	0	3	0	0	4	3	.571	35	51	251	32	28	8	0	1	29	5	1	31	1	0	2.57
Pena, Jose, Los Angeles	23	0	0	7	0	0	4	3	.667	38	38	152	21	20	2	1	1	7	2	0	25	0	1	4.42
Pena, Orlando, Pittsburgh	41	0	0	24	8	0	5	5	.639	39	29	329	138	117	6	7	2	84	8	8	214	11	0	4.74
Perry, Gaylord, San Francisco	41	41	23	0	0	5	23	13	.639	329	292	1336	138	117	27	7	2	84	8	8	214	11	0	3.20
Pitlock, Lee, San Francisco*	18	15	1	0	0	0	5	5	.500	87	93	394	48	45	13	4	2	48	2	1	56	3	1	4.66
Pizarro, Juan, Chicago*	12	0	0	4	0	0	0	0	.000	16	16	73	9	8	2	2	0	9	0	0	14	0	0	4.50
Priddy, Robert, Atlanta	41	0	0	24	6	0	5	5	.500	73	75	313	46	44	5	5	3	24	2	3	32	7	0	5.42
Puente, Miguel, San Francisco	6	2	0	1	0	0	1	3	.250	19	25	93	18	17	3	5	1	11	2	0	14	0	0	8.05
Ray, James, Houston	52	0	0	16	5	0	7	6	.462	105	97	443	39	38	13	4	2	49	2	1	67	4	0	3.26
Raymond, J. Claude, Montreal	59	0	0	43	23	0	6	7	.462	83	76	354	48	41	13	5	4	27	4	0	68	4	0	4.45
Reberger, Frank, San Francisco	45	18	3	7	2	0	7	8	.467	152	178	727	108	94	13	10	3	98	6	1	117	15	0	5.57
Reed, Howard, Montreal	57	0	0	20	5	0	6	5	.545	89	81	368	34	31	13	4	2	40	5	1	42	2	0	3.13
Reed, Ronald, Atlanta	21	18	8	0	0	3	7	10	.412	135	140	572	69	66	16	1	5	39	2	1	68	5	0	4.40
Regan, Philip, Chicago	41	0	0	40	12	0	5	9	.357	76	81	324	43	40	8	5	3	32	4	1	31	0	0	4.74
Renko, Steve, Montreal	41	33	7	4	0	1	13	11	.542	223	203	962	121	107	27	7	6	104	7	1	142	8	0	4.32
Reuss, Jerry, St. Louis*	20	20	5	0	0	0	7	8	.467	127	132	548	62	58	13	8	0	49	6	1	74	8	0	4.11
Reynolds, Archie, Chicago	4	0	0	2	0	0	0	0	.000	17	17	67	11	11	2	0	0	11	0	0	10	1	1	6.60
Reynolds, Kenneth, Philadelphia*	3	1	0	0	0	0	2	0	.000	13	10	13	0	0	0	0	0	0	0	0	0	0	0	0.00
Roberts, David, San Diego*	43	21	11	11	8	0	8	14	.364	182	182	753	80	77	16	9	3	43	11	0	102	3	0	3.81
Robertson, Richard, San Francisco	41	26	6	4	1	0	9	9	.471	184	199	830	113	99	22	6	3	96	3	1	121	18	0	4.84
Rodriquez, Roberto, 10 SD-26 Chi	36	0	0	16	5	0	3	2	.600	60	76	270	49	40	7	3	3	26	2	0	54	3	0	6.00

Pitcher and Club	G.	GS.	CG.	GF.	Sv.	ShO.	W.	L.	Pct.	IP.	H.	BFP.	R.	ER.	HR.	SH.	SF.	Tot. BB.	Int. BB.	HB.	SO.	WP.	Bk.	ERA.
Ross, Gary, San Diego	33	2	0	11	1	0	2	3	.400	62	72	282	37	36	8	6	1	36	10	2	39	4	0	5.23
Ryan, L. Nolan, New York	27	19	5	4	1	2	7	11	.389	132	86	570	59	50	10	8	4	97	2	8	125	8	0	3.41
Sadecki, Raymond, New York	28	19	4	2	0	1	8	4	.667	139	134	592	67	60	18	10	4	52	9	0	89	5	0	3.88
Santorini, Alan, San Diego	21	12	2	5	1	0	1	8	.111	76	91	360	56	51	11	1	3	43	6	3	41	6	0	6.04
Seaver, G. Thomas, New York	37	36	19	0	0	2	18	12	.600	291	230	1173	103	91	21	9	4	83	6	8	283	5	0	2.81
Selma, Richard, Philadelphia	73	0	0	47	22	0	8	9	.471	134	108	552	48	41	11	9	3	59	11	3	153	10	0	2.75
Sembera, Carroll, Montreal	5	0	0	2	0	0	1	0	1.000	7	11	46	14	14	0	0	0	11	3	0	6	1	0	18.00
Short, Christopher, Philadelphia*	36	34	7	2	0	1	9	16	.360	199	211	863	103	95	13	6	10	66	3	2	133	2	1	4.30
Simpson, Wayne, Cincinnati	26	26	10	0	0	2	14	3	.824	176	125	730	73	59	15	4	8	81	2	6	119	1	2	3.02
Singer, William, Los Angeles	16	16	5	0	0	1	8	5	.615	99	93	428	42	35	7	5	4	32	2	3	93	2	1	3.14
Sparma, Joseph, Montreal	9	6	1	2	0	0	0	4	.000	29	34	146	25	23	5	1	3	25	3	2	23	4	1	7.14
Spinks, Scipio, Houston	5	2	0	0	0	0	2	0	1.000	14	11	67	17	15	1	0	0	10	2	0	6	1	0	9.64
Stephenson, Jerry, Los Angeles	3	0	0	1	0	0	0	1	.000	7	9	34	8	7	0	0	0	4	3	0	6	1	0	9.00
Stone, George, Atlanta*	35	30	9	0	0	1	11	11	.500	207	218	890	111	89	27	13	3	50	8	3	131	2	0	3.87
Stoneman, William, Montreal	40	30	9	2	0	1	7	15	.318	208	209	928	118	106	26	6	5	78	0	8	176	9	0	4.59
Strahler, Michael, Los Angeles	6	0	0	2	0	0	3	1	.750	19	13	77	6	3	0	0	0	10	3	0	11	1	0	1.42
Strohmayer, John, Montreal	42	0	0	22	4	0	7	7	.500	76	85	349	48	41	10	9	7	31	7	3	74	9	1	4.86
Sutton, Donald, Los Angeles	38	38	10	0	0	4	15	13	.536	260	251	1109	127	118	38	9	7	78	10	3	201	9	0	4.08
Taylor, Charles, St. Louis	56	0	0	40	13	0	6	7	.462	124	116	500	47	43	5	5	9	31	10	2	64	3	0	3.12
Taylor, Ronald, New York	57	0	0	40	13	0	5	4	.556	66	68	275	31	29	5	3	2	16	3	1	28	3	0	3.95
Torrez, Michael, St. Louis	30	18	4	5	0	1	8	10	.444	179	168	799	96	84	12	9	3	103	3	7	100	5	0	4.22
Vance, Gene, Los Angeles	20	0	0	13	0	0	1	1	.500	115	100	484	47	40	5	3	2	37	2	1	45	5	0	3.13
Veale, Robert, Pittsburgh*	34	32	11	0	0	3	10	15	.400	202	189	882	99	88	8	13	4	94	11	3	178	6	0	3.92
Walker, J. Luke, Pittsburgh*	42	20	5	13	0	3	15	6	.714	163	129	684	56	55	15	3	2	89	8	0	124	6	0	3.04
Washburn, Ray, Cincinnati	35	8	1	5	0	0	4	4	.500	66	79	331	61	51	7	6	0	48	3	1	37	1	0	6.95
Waslewski, Gary, Montreal	6	4	0	4	0	0	0	2	.000	25	27	109	16	14	2	3	2	15	0	1	19	4	0	5.04
Wegener, Michael, Montreal	25	16	4	0	0	0	3	6	.333	104	97	461	74	61	14	2	3	56	4	3	35	4	0	5.28
Wenz, Frederick, Montreal	22	0	0	11	1	0	1	0	1.000	22	20	133	9	6	3	2	1	13	3	0	13	2	0	2.45
Wilcox, Milton, Cincinnati	6	2	0	0	0	0	3	1	.750	16	13	92	9	8	2	1	0	7	1	0	7	1	0	3.40
Wilhelm, J. Hoyt, 50 Atl-3 Chi	53	0	0	39	13	0	6	5	.545	82	73	357	33	31	8	3	4	42	7	2	68	4	0	4.50
Willis, Ronald, San Diego	42	0	0	20	5	0	5	5	.500	56	53	254	33	25	3	1	5	28	5	4	24	4	0	4.02
Wilson, Donald, Houston	29	27	11	0	0	2	11	6	.647	184	153	806	90	80	15	6	7	94	4	3	94	15	1	3.91
Wilson, R. Earl, San Diego	15	9	0	0	0	0	1	6	.143	65	58	258	36	35	8	2	2	19	2	1	29	0	0	4.85
Wilson, William, Philadelphia	37	0	0	11	0	0	1	0	1.000	50	45	220	29	27	5	1	0	11	3	0	41	0	0	4.81
Wise, Richard, Philadelphia	35	34	13	0	0	4	13	14	.481	220	253	962	115	102	15	9	4	65	7	3	113	3	1	4.17

NOTE—Following pitchers combined to pitch shutout games: Chicago (1)—Decker, Aguirre and Regan; Cincinnati (6)—Nolan and Granger 2, Cloninger and Granger, Gullett, Carroll and Granger, McGlothlin and Granger, Nolan and Carroll; Houston (1)—Griffin and Billingham; Los Angeles (4)—Foster, Brewer and Lamb, Foster and Brewer, Singer and Mikkelsen, Vance and Norman; Philadelphia (2)—Bunning and Selma; Wise, Hoerner and Selma; Pittsburgh (1)—Walker and Hartenstein; St. Louis (1)—Torrez and McCool; San Diego (3)—Coombs and Dukes, Coombs and Herbel, Corkins and Roberts; San Francisco (1)—Pitlock, Reberger and McMahon.

PITCHERS WITH TWO OR MORE CLUBS DURING 1970 SEASON

(Alphabetically Arranged With Pitcher's First Club on Top)

Pitcher and Club	G.	GS.	CG.	GF.	Sv.	ShO.	W.	L.	Pct.	IP.	H.	BFP.	R.	ER.	HR.	SH.	SF.	Tot. BB.	Int. BB.	HB.	SO.	WP.	Bk.	ERA.
Abernathy, Chicago	11	0	0	3	1	0	0	0	.000	9	9	40	2	2	0	2	0	5	1	1	2	0	0	2.00
Abernathy, St. Louis	11	0	0	3	1	0	1	0	1.000	18⅓	15	82	6	6	0	4	2	12	4	3	8	1	0	3.00
Barber, Chicago	5	0	0	4	0	0	0	1	.000	5⅔	10	31	6	6	0	1	0	6	3	0	3	1	0	9.00
Barber, Atlanta	5	2	0	2	0	0	0	1	.000	14⅔	17	66	10	8	3	1	0	5	0	1	11	2	0	4.80
Cardwell, New York	16	1	0	2	0	0	0	2	.000	25	31	112	19	18	3	2	3	6	1	3	8	1	0	6.48
Cardwell, Atlanta	16	2	1	8	0	1	2	1	.667	23	31	111	23	23	5	1	1	13	2	1	16	1	1	9.00
Culver, St. Louis	11	7	2	1	0	0	3	3	.500	56⅔	64	252	31	29	6	1	1	24	4	1	23	3	0	4.58
Culver, Houston	32	0	0	15	3	0	3	3	.500	45	44	200	17	16	1	2	1	21	2	3	31	8	0	3.20
Hartenstein, Pittsburgh	17	0	0	5	1	0	1	1	.500	23⅔	25	103	15	12	3	4	1	8	4	0	14	0	1	4.50
Hartenstein, St. Louis	6	0	0	1	0	0	0	0	.000	13⅓	24	71	13	13	1	1	1	5	0	0	9	1	0	9.00
Herbel, San Diego	64	1	0	31	9	0	7	5	.583	111	114	481	69	61	14	5	5	39	5	4	53	4	3	4.95
Herbel, New York	12	0	0	7	1	0	2	2	.500	13	14	54	3	2	1	1	0	2	1	0	8	0	0	1.38
Jerry Johnson, St. Louis	7	0	0	3	1	0	2	0	1.000	11⅓	6	44	4	4	1	0	0	3	0	0	5	0	0	3.27
Jerry Johnson, San Francisco	33	1	0	11	3	0	3	4	.429	65⅓	67	296	39	31	5	5	0	38	2	1	44	4	0	4.29
Linzy, San Francisco	20	0	0	9	1	0	2	1	.667	25⅔	33	117	20	20	2	2	2	11	4	1	16	0	0	6.92
Linzy, St. Louis	47	0	0	21	2	0	3	5	.375	61⅓	66	263	26	25	3	4	2	23	10	0	19	2	0	3.69
Marshall, Houston	4	0	0	0	0	0	0	1	.000	5⅓	8	27	5	5	0	2	0	4	0	1	5	2	0	9.00
Marshall, Montreal	24	5	0	11	3	0	3	7	.300	64⅔	56	281	34	25	4	2	1	29	4	0	38	4	0	3.46
McBean, Los Angeles	1	0	0	1	0	0	0	0	.000	1	1	3	0	0	0	0	0	0	0	0	0	0	0	0.00
McBean, Pittsburgh	7	0	0	3	1	0	0	0	.000	10	13	48	11	9	2	0	0	7	0	0	3	0	0	8.10
Norman, Los Angeles	30	0	0	11	1	0	2	0	1.000	62	65	282	40	36	8	7	2	33	1	2	47	10	1	5.23
Norman, St. Louis	1	0	0	0	0	0	0	0	.000	1	1	4	0	0	0	0	1	0	0	0	0	0	0	0.00
Nye, St. Louis	6	0	0	2	0	0	0	0	.000	8	13	43	5	4	2	1	1	6	1	0	5	0	0	4.50
Nye, Montreal	8	6	2	0	0	0	3	2	.600	46⅓	47	203	23	21	3	0	2	20	3	0	21	0	0	4.11
Pappas, Atlanta	11	3	1	2	0	0	2	2	.500	35⅔	44	160	25	24	6	0	1	7	1	2	25	4	0	6.00
Pappas, Chicago	21	20	6	1	0	2	10	8	.556	144⅔	135	592	53	43	14	6	5	36	9	0	80	0	1	2.67
Rodriquez, San Diego	10	0	0	4	3	0	0	0	.000	16⅓	26	77	16	12	1	1	0	5	0	0	8	2	0	6.75
Rodriquez, Chicago	26	0	0	12	2	0	3	2	.600	43⅓	50	193	33	28	6	2	3	15	2	0	46	1	0	5.86
Wilhelm, Atlanta	50	0	0	37	13	0	6	4	.600	78⅓	69	339	29	27	7	2	2	39	7	1	67	4	0	3.12
Wilhelm, Chicago	3	0	0	2	0	0	0	1	.000	3⅔	4	18	4	4	1	1	0	3	0	0	1	0	0	9.00

1970 N. L. Pitching Against Each Club

ATLANTA—76-86

Pitcher	Chi. W—L	Cin. W—L	Hou. W—L	L.A. W—L	Mont. W—L	N.Y. W—L	Phila. W—L	Pitts. W—L	St.L. W—L	S.D. W—L	S.F. W—L	Totals W—L
Barber	0—0	0—1	0—0	0—0	0—0	0—0	0—0	0—0	0—0	0—0	0—0	0—1
Cardwell	1—1	0—0	0—0	0—0	0—0	0—0	0—0	0—0	0—0	1—0	0—0	2—1
Jarvis	2—1	1—4	3—1	1—3	0—0	2—2	2—2	1—1	1—0	2—2	1—0	16—16
Jaster	0—0	0—0	0—0	0—1	1—1	0—0	0—0	0—0	0—0	0—0	0—0	1—1
McQueen	0—0	1—0	0—0	0—1	0—0	0—1	0—0	0—1	0—0	0—1	0—1	1—5
Nash	0—0	1—0	2—1	1—2	1—2	0—1	2—1	2—1	1—1	3—0	0—0	13—9
Neibauer	0—0	0—1	0—0	0—0	0—0	0—0	0—1	0—0	0—0	0—0	0—0	0—3
Niekro	4—0	0—3	1—2	0—3	0—2	1—2	0—0	2—0	0—1	2—3	2—2	12—18
Pappas	0—0	0—0	0—1	0—1	1—0	0—0	0—0	0—0	0—1	0—0	0—0	1—3
Priddy	0—1	0—0	0—0	0—0	1—0	1—0	0—0	0—0	0—0	0—0	1—0	2—1
Reed	0—1	2—1	2—0	0—1	0—0	0—1	1—0	0—0	2—1	1—0	0—3	5—5
Stone	1—0	0—3	1—3	3—1	2—0	0—0	1—1	0—0	1—1	0—2	0—3	7—10
Wilhelm	0—0	0—0	0—1	1—0	0—1	1—0	1—0	0—1	1—2	0—1	1—1	6—4
Totals	8—4	5—13	9—9	6—12	6—6	6—6	7—5	6—6	7—5	9—9	7—11	76—86

No Decisions—Gatewood, Kester, Kline, Navarro.

CHICAGO—84-78

Pitcher	Atl. W—L	Cin. W—L	Hou. W—L	L.A. W—L	Mont. W—L	N.Y. W—L	Phila. W—L	Pitts. W—L	St.L. W—L	S.D. W—L	S.F. W—L	Totals W—L
Aguirre	0—0	0—0	0—0	1—0	1—0	0—0	1—0	0—0	0—0	0—0	0—0	3—0
Barber	0—0	0—0	0—0	0—0	0—0	0—0	0—0	0—1	0—0	0—0	0—0	0—1
Colborn	1—0	0—1	0—0	0—0	0—0	1—0	0—0	1—0	0—0	0—0	0—0	3—1
Decker	0—2	0—2	0—0	0—0	1—0	0—2	0—0	1—0	0—0	0—1	0—0	2—7
Dunegan	0—0	0—0	0—0	0—0	0—0	0—0	0—0	0—0	0—2	0—0	0—0	0—2
Gura	0—0	0—0	0—0	0—1	1—0	0—0	0—1	0—0	0—1	0—0	0—0	1—3
Hands	0—1	4—0	2—1	1—2	1—0	2—2	1—2	3—1	2—2	2—0	0—4	18—15
Holtzman	1—2	1—0	2—1	2—1	3—1	0—2	2—1	1—2	3—1	0—0	2—0	17—11
Jenkins	1—2	1—0	2—2	2—1	1—1	3—1	3—2	1—4	2—2	4—0	3—0	22—16
Pappas	0—0	1—0	1—1	0—0	2—1	0—1	2—1	1—2	0—1	2—0	1—1	10—8
Regan	1—0	0—0	0—0	0—1	2—1	0—0	1—0	0—1	0—3	1—0	1—0	5—9
Reynolds	0—1	0—0	0—0	0—0	0—0	0—1	0—0	0—0	0—0	1—0	0—0	0—2
Rodriquez	0—0	1—0	0—0	0—0	1—1	1—0	0—0	0—0	0—0	0—0	0—0	3—2
Wilhelm	0—0	0—0	0—0	0—0	0—0	0—1	0—0	0—0	0—0	0—0	0—0	0—1
Totals	4—8	7—5	7—5	6—6	13—5	7—11	9—9	8—10	7—11	9—3	7—5	84—78

No Decisions—Abernathy, Cosman, Miller, Pizarro.

CINCINNATI—102-60

Pitcher	Atl. W—L	Chi. W—L	Hou. W—L	L.A. W—L	Mont. W—L	N.Y. W—L	Phila. W—L	Pitts. W—L	St.L. W—L	S.D. W—L	S.F. W—L	Totals W—L
Behney	0—0	0—0	0—0	0—0	0—1	0—0	0—1	0—0	0—0	0—0	0—0	0—2
Borbon	0—0	0—0	0—0	0—0	0—0	0—0	0—1	0—0	0—0	0—1	0—0	0—2
Carroll	0—0	1—1	1—1	1—0	2—0	1—0	0—0	1—0	1—0	1—0	0—2	9—4
Cloninger	2—1	0—0	1—1	1—0	0—0	0—2	1—0	1—0	1—0	0—2	2—1	9—7
Granger	0—0	2—0	0—0	0—0	1—1	0—1	0—0	0—1	1—0	0—1	2—1	6—5
Gullett	0—0	0—0	1—0	2—0	0—0	1—0	0—0	0—1	0—0	0—0	0—1	5—2
Maloney	0—1	0—0	0—0	0—0	0—0	0—0	0—0	0—0	0—0	0—0	0—0	0—1
McGlothlin	2—1	1—0	2—1	3—2	1—0	1—0	1—1	1—2	0—1	2—1	0—1	14—10
Merritt	3—1	0—3	3—0	1—1	2—2	3—1	2—0	3—0	1—1	2—2	0—1	20—12
Nolan	2—1	1—1	3—0	2—1	1—1	1—0	0—1	1—0	3—0	1—1	3—1	18—7
Simpson	1—0	0—1	3—0	2—0	0—0	1—0	2—0	1—1	2—1	1—0	0—0	13—3
Washburn	2—1	0—0	0—0	0—1	0—0	0—0	1—0	0—0	0—0	0—0	1—1	4—4
Wilcox	0—0	0—0	1—0	1—0	0—0	0—0	0—0	0—0	0—0	1—1	0—0	3—1
Totals	13—5	5—7	15—3	13—5	7—5	8—4	7—5	8—4	9—3	8—10	9—9	102—60

No Decisions—Belinsky, Noriega.

HOUSTON—79-83

Pitcher	Atl. W–L	Chi. W–L	Cin. W–L	L.A. W–L	Mont. W–L	N.Y. W–L	Phila. W–L	Pitts. W–L	St.L. W–L	S.D. W–L	S.F. W–L	Totals W–L
Billingham .	1–0	1–1	0–2	2–1	2–0	1–1	0–2	0–0	1–1	4–1	1–0	13– 9
Blasingame .	0–0	0–0	0–1	0–0	0–0	2–0	0–1	0–0	0–0	1–0	0–1	3– 3
Bouton	2–0	1–1	0–1	0–1	0–0	0–0	0–1	0–2	0–0	0–0	1–0	4– 6
Cook	0–1	0–0	0–0	1–0	1–2	0–0	0–0	2–0	0–1	0–0	0–0	4– 4
Culver	1–0	0–0	0–0	0–1	0–0	1–0	0–0	0–0	1–0	0–1	0–1	3– 3
Dierker	2–3	2–2	1–1	1–0	1–0	0–2	1–2	1–1	2–0	2–0	3–1	16–12
DiLauro	0–0	0–0	0–0	0–1	0–0	0–0	0–0	0–0	0–0	0–0	1–2	1– 3
Forsch	0–1	0–0	0–1	0–0	0–0	0–0	0–0	0–0	1–0	0–0	0–0	1– 2
Gladding ...	1–0	0–0	1–1	0–2	1–0	0–0	0–1	0–0	1–0	1–0	2–0	7– 4
Griffin	0–1	0–3	1–2	0–1	1–0	0–1	0–0	0–2	0–2	1–0	0–1	3–13
Lemaster ...	0–2	0–0	0–3	2–1	0–1	1–2	0–0	1–1	1–0	2–1	0–1	7–12
Marshall ...	0–0	0–0	0–0	0–0	0–1	0–0	0–0	0–0	0–0	0–0	0–0	0– 1
Osinski	0–0	0–0	0–0	0–0	0–0	0–0	0–0	0–0	0–0	0–0	0–1	0– 1
Ray	1–1	0–0	0–0	0–1	1–0	0–0	2–0	1–0	0–0	0–1	1–0	6– 3
Spinks	0–0	0–0	0–0	0–0	0–0	0–0	0–0	0–0	0–1	0–0	0–0	0– 1
Wilson	1–0	1–0	0–3	2–1	1–0	1–0	1–1	1–0	0–1	2–0	1–0	11– 6
Totals ..	9–9	5–7	3–15	8–10	8–4	6–6	4–8	6–6	6–6	14–4	10–8	79–83

No Decisions—Harris.

LOS ANGELES—87-74

Pitcher	Atl. W–L	Chi. W–L	Cin. W–L	Hou. W–L	Mont. W–L	N.Y. W–L	Phila. W–L	Pitts. W–L	St.L. W–L	S.D. W–L	S.F. W–L	Totals W–L
Brewer	0–0	1–0	1–0	1–0	0–0	0–2	0–1	0–0	2–1	0–1	2–1	7– 6
Foster	5–1	0–1	1–0	1–3	0–1	0–0	0–1	0–2	0–0	1–2	2–2	10–13
Lamb	1–0	0–0	0–0	2–0	1–0	2–0	0–0	0–0	0–0	0–0	0–1	6– 1
Mikkelsen ..	0–0	1–0	0–0	1–0	0–0	0–0	0–1	1–1	0–0	1–0	0–0	4– 2
Moeller	2–0	0–1	0–3	1–1	1–0	0–0	1–0	0–2	1–0	0–1	0–1	7– 9
Norman	0–0	1–0	0–0	0–0	0–0	0–0	1–0	0–0	0–0	0–0	0–0	2– 0
Osteen	1–1	1–2	1–4	1–2	1–1	1–0	1–1	4–0	1–1	2–2	2–0	16–14
Pena	0–0	0–1	0–0	0–0	1–0	0–1	1–0	0–1	2–0	0–0	0–0	4– 3
Singer	1–0	0–0	1–3	0–1	1–0	1–0	1–0	0–0	0–0	2–0	1–1	8– 5
Strahler ...	0–0	0–0	0–1	1–0	0–0	0–0	0–0	0–0	0–0	0–0	0–0	1– 1
Sutton	2–2	1–0	1–2	1–0	2–2	2–1	1–1	1–0	0–2	3–1	1–2	15–13
Vance	0–2	0–1	0–0	1–1	1–0	1–1	0–0	0–0	1–1	2–0	1–1	7– 7
Totals ..	12–6	6–6	5–13	10–8	8–4	7–5	6–5	6–6	7–5	11–7	9–9	87–74

No Decisions—Hough, McBean, Pascual, Stephenson.

MONTREAL—73-89

Pitcher	Atl. W–L	Chi. W–L	Cin. W–L	Hou. W–L	L.A. W–L	N.Y. W–L	Phila. W–L	Pitts. W–L	St.L. W–L	S.D. W–L	S.F. W–L	Totals W–L
Dillman	1–0	0–0	0–1	0–0	0–0	0–0	0–1	1–1	0–0	0–0	0–0	2– 3
Marshall ...	0–0	1–0	1–0	0–1	0–1	0–2	0–0	1–1	0–0	0–1	0–1	3– 7
McGinn	0–0	1–0	0–0	0–1	0–1	1–3	2–1	2–1	0–2	0–0	1–1	7–10
Moore	0–0	0–0	0–1	0–1	0–0	0–0	0–0	0–0	0–0	0–0	0–0	0– 2
Morton	2–2	0–3	1–1	0–2	2–0	3–1	2–0	1–2	2–0	1–0	4–0	18–11
Nye	0–0	0–0	0–0	0–0	1–0	0–1	1–0	1–0	0–1	0–0	0–0	3– 2
O'Donoghue .	0–0	0–2	0–0	0–0	0–0	1–0	1–0	0–0	0–1	0–0	0–0	2– 3
Raymond	0–1	0–1	1–1	1–0	0–1	0–1	1–1	0–1	1–1	1–0	0–0	6– 7
Reed	0–0	1–1	0–1	1–0	0–0	0–1	0–0	0–0	1–1	1–1	1–0	6– 5
Renko	1–0	0–3	2–0	2–1	1–1	2–1	3–1	0–0	1–1	1–1	0–1	13–11
Sparma	0–0	0–1	0–1	0–0	0–0	0–0	0–0	0–0	0–1	0–0	0–0	0– 4
Stoneman ...	2–2	1–1	0–0	0–1	0–2	0–0	1–2	2–1	1–3	0–1	0–2	7–15
Strohmayer .	0–0	0–0	0–0	0–0	0–1	0–0	0–0	1–0	0–0	2–0	0–0	3– 1
Waslewski ..	0–0	0–0	0–0	0–0	0–1	0–0	0–0	0–0	0–1	0–0	0–0	0– 2
Wegener	0–1	1–1	0–1	0–1	0–0	1–0	0–0	0–1	1–0	0–0	0–1	3– 6
Totals ..	6–6	5–13	5–7	4–8	4–8	10–8	11–7	9–9	7–11	6–6	6–6	73–89

No Decisions—Johnson, Sembera.

NEW YORK—83-79

Pitcher	Atl. W—L	Chi. W—L	Cin. W—L	Hou. W—L	L.A. W—L	Mont. W—L	Phila. W—L	Pitts. W—L	St.L. W—L	S.D. W—L	S.F. W—L	Totals W—L
Cardwell	0—0	0—0	0—0	0—0	0—0	0—0	0—1	0—1	0—0	0—0	0—0	0—2
Chance	0—0	0—0	0—0	0—0	0—0	0—0	0—0	0—0	0—1	0—0	0—0	0—1
Folkers	0—0	0—0	0—0	0—0	0—0	0—0	0—0	0—0	0—0	0—0	0—2	0—2
Frisella	0—1	1—1	0—0	0—0	2—0	2—0	0—1	0—0	2—0	1—1	0—0	8—3
Gentry	1—2	1—1	1—1	1—0	0—1	1—0	0—1	2—1	1—0	1—1		9—9
Herbel	0—0	0—0	0—0	0—0	0—0	0—0	1—0	1—1	0—0	0—0	0—0	2—2
Koonce	0—0	0—0	0—0	0—0	0—0	0—0	0—0	0—0	0—2	0—0	0—0	0—2
Koosman	1—0	3—2	1—0	0—0	0—0	0—2	2—2	3—1	1—0	0—0	1—0	12—7
McAndrew	2—0	0—1	1—1	1—0	0—2	1—2	1—0	0—4	2—2	1—2	1—0	10—14
McGraw	0—0	0—0	0—1	1—1	1—1	1—1	1—0	0—2	0—0	0—0	0—0	4—6
Ryan	0—2	3—1	0—1	1—2	0—2	0—0	2—0	0—0	1—0	0—1	1—1	7—11
Sadecki	1—0	0—0	0—2	1—0	0—0	2—2	2—0	0—0	2—0	0—0	0—0	8—4
Seaver	1—2	1—1	0—1	1—3	2—0	1—3	4—0	2—0	2—2	3—0	1—0	18—12
Taylor	0—0	2—0	1—1	0—0	0—0	0—0	0—0	1—0	0—0	0—0	1—2	5—4
Totals	6—6	11—7	4—8	6—6	5—7	8—10	13—5	6—12	12—6	6—6	6—6	83—79

No Decisions—None.

PHILADELPHIA—73-88

Pitcher	Atl. W—L	Chi. W—L	Cin. W—L	Hou. W—L	L.A. W—L	Mont. W—L	N.Y. W—L	Pitts. W—L	St.L. W—L	S.D. W—L	S.F. W—L	Totals W—L
Bunning	2—0	0—1	2—2	2—0	0—1	0—1	1—2	0—5	0—2	2—0	1—1	10—15
Champion	0—0	0—0	0—0	0—0	0—0	0—0	0—0	0—1	0—0	0—0	0—0	0—2
Fryman	0—0	1—0	0—2	2—0	1—1	2—1	0—2	1—0	0—0	0—0	1—0	8—6
Hoerner	1—0	1—1	0—0	2—0	0—1	2—1	0—1	0—0	2—1	0—0	1—0	9—5
G. Jackson	0—0	1—2	1—1	0—2	0—2	0—1	0—4	0—1	1—1	2—0	0—1	5—15
M. Jackson	0—0	0—0	0—0	0—0	0—0	0—0	0—0	0—0	1—1	0—0	0—0	1—1
Lersch	1—1	2—0	0—0	0—0	1—0	0—0	1—0	0—0	0—0	1—0	0—0	6—3
Palmer	0—0	0—0	0—0	0—0	0—0	0—1	1—0	0—0	0—0	1—0	0—0	1—2
Selma	0—0	0—0	1—0	0—2	1—1	1—0	0—2	0—2	2—1	2—1	1—0	8—9
Short	1—3	2—3	0—1	0—0	0—0	0—3	2—1	2—1	1—1	1—1	0—2	9—16
Wenz	0—0	0—0	0—0	0—0	1—0	0—0	0—0	0—0	0—0	0—0	1—0	2—0
Wilson	0—0	0—0	0—0	0—0	0—0	0—0	0—0	0—0	0—0	0—0	0—0	1—0
Wise	0—3	1—2	1—0	2—0	1—0	2—3	1—1	1—2	1—2	1—1	2—0	13—14
Totals	5—7	9—9	5—7	8—4	5—6	7—11	5—13	4—14	8—10	9—3	8—4	73—88

No Decisions—Laxton, Reynolds.

PITTSBURGH—89-73

Pitcher	Atl. W—L	Chi. W—L	Cin. W—L	Hou. W—L	L.A. W—L	Mont. W—L	N.Y. W—L	Phila. W—L	St.L. W—L	S.D. W—L	S.F. W—L	Totals W—L
Blass	0—0	1—4	0—2	1—1	1—1	1—0	1—1	2—1	0—1	1—0	2—1	10—12
Brunet	0—0	0—0	0—0	0—0	0—0	0—0	0—1	0—0	1—0	0—0	0—0	1—1
Cambria	0—0	0—0	0—0	0—0	0—0	0—0	0—0	1—0	0—1	0—1	0—0	1—2
Colpaert	1—0	0—0	0—0	0—0	0—0	0—0	0—0	0—0	0—0	0—0	0—0	1—0
Dal Canton	1—0	0—0	1—0	0—1	1—1	1—0	1—0	2—0	2—0	0—0	0—2	9—4
Ellis	1—1	2—0	0—3	2—1	0—1	1—1	3—1	1—1	1—1	2—0	0—0	13—10
Garber	0—0	0—1	0—0	0—0	0—0	0—0	0—0	0—0	0—1	0—0	0—0	0—3
Gibbon	0—0	0—0	0—0	0—0	0—0	0—1	0—0	0—0	0—0	0—0	0—0	0—1
Giusti	1—0	2—0	1—1	0—1	1—0	0—0	0—0	3—0	0—0	0—1	1—0	9—3
Grant	0—0	0—0	0—0	0—0	0—0	0—0	2—0	0—0	0—1	0—0	0—0	2—1
Hartenstein	0—0	0—0	0—0	0—0	0—0	1—1	0—0	0—0	0—0	0—0	0—0	1—1
Lamb	0—0	0—0	0—0	0—0	0—0	0—0	0—1	0—0	0—0	0—0	0—0	0—1
Moose	0—2	3—1	0—0	1—0	1—1	0—2	1—1	2—0	2—0	0—1	1—2	11—10
Nelson	0—1	1—0	0—0	0—1	1—0	0—0	0—0	0—0	1—0	0—0	0—0	2—1
Pena	1—0	0—0	0—0	0—0	0—0	0—0	0—0	0—0	0—0	1—1	0—0	2—1
Veale	0—1	0—2	1—2	1—1	1—2	4—2	0—2	1—1	0—0	1—2	1—0	10—15
Walker	1—1	1—0	1—0	1—0	0—0	2—1	2—0	4—0	2—1	1—1	0—2	15—6
Totals	6—6	10—8	4—8	6—6	6—6	9—9	12—6	14—4	12—6	6—6	4—8	89—73

No Decisions—Acosta, Marone, McBean.

ST. LOUIS—76-86

Pitcher	Atl. W—L	Chi. W—L	Cin. W—L	Hou. W—L	L.A. W—L	Mont. W—L	N.Y. W—L	Phila. W—L	Pitts. W—L	S.D. W—L	S.F. W—L	Totals W—L
Abernathy ..	0—0	0—0	0—0	0—0	0—0	0—0	0—0	1—0	0—0	0—0	0—0	1—0
Bertaina ...	0—0	0—0	0—0	0—0	0—0	0—1	0—0	0—1	1—0	0—0	0—0	1—2
Briles	1—0	0—0	0—0	2—1	0—0	0—0	1—3	0—1	1—1	1—0	0—1	6—7
Campisi	0—0	1—0	0—0	0—0	0—0	1—0	0—1	0—0	0—0	0—0	0—1	2—2
Carlton	0—1	2—2	0—4	1—1	1—1	1—2	1—3	2—0	1—2	0—2	1—1	10—19
Chlupsa	0—0	0—1	0—0	0—0	0—0	0—0	0—0	0—1	0—0	0—0	0—0	0—2
Cleveland ..	0—0	0—0	0—0	0—0	0—0	0—1	0—0	0—0	0—1	0—1	0—1	0—4
Culver	0—1	0—0	1—0	0—0	0—1	0—1	0—0	1—0	0—0	1—0	0—0	3—3
Gibson	1—0	4—1	1—0	1—2	1—0	4—0	2—1	2—0	0—3	4—0	3—0	23—7
Guzman	0—0	0—0	0—0	1—0	0—1	0—0	0—0	0—0	0—0	0—0	1—0	1—1
Hilgendorf .	0—0	0—0	0—0	0—1	0—0	0—1	0—0	0—0	0—0	0—2	0—0	0—4
Hrabosky ..	0—0	1—0	0—0	0—0	0—0	1—0	0—0	0—0	0—1	0—0	0—0	2—1
Johnson	1—0	0—0	0—0	0—0	0—0	0—0	0—0	1—0	0—0	0—0	0—0	2—0
Linzy	0—2	0—0	0—0	0—0	0—1	0—0	1—1	1—1	0—1	1—0	0—1	3—5
McCool	0—0	0—0	0—0	0—0	0—1	0—0	0—0	0—1	0—1	0—0	0—0	0—3
Parker	0—0	0—0	0—0	0—0	0—0	0—0	0—0	0—0	1—0	0—0	0—0	1—1
Reuss	1—0	2—1	0—2	0—0	1—1	1—0	0—3	1—1	1—0	0—0	0—0	7—8
Taylor	0—2	0—0	1—0	0—0	2—0	1—1	0—0	1—1	0—2	0—0	1—1	6—7
Torrez	1—1	1—3	0—2	1—0	0—1	2—1	0—1	2—0	0—0	0—0	1—1	8—10
Totals ..	5—7	11—7	3—9	6—6	5—7	11—7	6—12	10—8	6—12	8—4	5—7	76—86

No Decisions—Hartenstein, Norman, Nye.

SAN DIEGO—63-99

Pitcher	Atl. W—L	Chi. W—L	Cin. W—L	Hou. W—L	L.A. W—L	Mont. W—L	N.Y. W—L	Phila. W—L	Pitts. W—L	St.L. W—L	S.F. W—L	Totals W—L
Arlin	1—0	0—0	0—0	0—0	0—0	0—0	0—0	0—0	0—0	0—0	0—0	1—0
Baldschun ..	0—0	0—0	0—0	0—0	0—0	0—0	1—0	0—0	0—0	0—0	0—0	1—0
Coombs	0—0	0—0	0—0	1—4	1—2	2—2	1—0	0—0	1—1	0—2	2—3	10—14
Corkins	0—1	0—2	2—0	1—0	0—0	1—1	0—1	0—0	0—0	0—0	1—1	5—6
Dobson	2—1	2—0	1—3	1—1	1—2	2—0	0—1	2—1	1—1	1—2	1—3	14—15
Doyle	0—0	0—1	0—0	0—0	0—0	0—0	0—0	0—0	0—0	0—0	0—1	0—2
Dukes	0—1	0—1	0—1	0—1	0—2	0—0	0—0	0—0	1—0	0—0	0—0	1—6
Herbel	0—0	1—0	0—0	0—0	1—0	0—0	1—1	0—1	2—0	1—2	1—1	7—5
Kirby	1—2	0—2	3—2	1—2	1—2	1—1	1—1	0—2	1—0	1—0	0—2	10—16
Nyman	0—0	0—0	0—0	0—1	0—1	0—0	0—0	0—0	0—0	0—0	0—0	0—2
Roberts	2—2	0—2	0—1	0—2	3—2	0—1	1—0	1—2	0—2	1—0	0—0	8—14
Ross	1—0	0—0	1—0	0—1	0—0	0—1	0—0	0—0	0—0	0—0	0—1	2—3
Santorini ..	0—1	0—0	1—1	0—2	0—0	0—0	0—1	0—1	0—1	0—0	0—1	1—8
Willis	1—0	0—0	0—0	0—0	0—0	0—0	1—0	0—1	0—0	0—1	0—0	1—2
Wilson	1—1	0—1	0—0	0—0	0—0	0—0	0—1	0—1	0—1	0—1	0—0	1—6
Totals ..	9—9	3—9	10—8	4—14	7—11	6—6	6—6	3—9	6—6	4—8	5—13	63—99

No Decisions—Rodriquez.

SAN FRANCISCO—86-76

Pitcher	Atl. W—L	Chi. W—L	Cin. W—L	Hou. W—L	L.A. W—L	Mont. W—L	N.Y. W—L	Phila. W—L	Pitts. W—L	St.L. W—L	S.D. W—L	Totals W—L
Bryant	0—0	0—0	0—0	2—3	0—2	0—1	0—0	0—1	2—0	1—0	0—0	5—8
Carrithers ..	0—0	1—0	0—0	0—0	0—0	0—0	0—1	0—0	1—0	0—0	0—0	2—1
Cumberland .	0—0	0—0	1—0	0—0	0—0	0—0	0—0	0—0	0—0	0—0	1—0	2—0
Davison	0—0	0—1	0—0	0—2	0—1	1—0	1—0	0—0	0—0	1—0	0—0	3—5
Jim Johnson	0—0	0—0	1—0	0—0	0—0	0—0	0—0	0—0	0—0	0—0	0—0	1—0
Jerry Johnson	1—3	0—0	0—0	1—0	0—0	0—0	0—0	0—1	1—0	0—0	0—0	3—4
Linzy	0—0	0—0	1—0	0—0	0—0	0—0	1—1	0—0	0—0	0—0	0—0	2—1
Marichal ...	0—1	1—1	1—2	0—0	4—1	1—1	1—0	1—1	2—2	1—0	0—1	12—10
McCormick ..	0—0	0—0	0—2	0—0	0—1	1—0	0—1	0—0	0—0	0—0	2—0	3—4
McMahon ..	3—0	0—0	0—1	2—2	0—0	0—0	1—1	0—0	1—0	2—1	0—0	9—5
Perry	4—1	2—2	3—1	2—1	2—1	2—1	0—2	1—1	2—0	0—2	5—1	23—13
Pitlock	1—0	0—1	0—1	0—0	2—0	0—1	1—0	0—0	1—1	0—0	0—0	5—5
Puente	0—0	0—0	0—0	0—0	0—1	0—0	1—0	0—0	0—0	0—0	0—2	1—3
Reberger ...	1—1	1—1	1—1	1—1	0—0	0—1	0—0	1—1	0—0	0—1	2—1	7—8
Robertson ..	1—1	0—1	1—0	0—1	1—2	1—1	0—1	1—1	0—1	0—0	3—0	8—9
Totals ..	11—7	5—7	9—9	8—10	9—9	6—6	6—6	4—8	8—4	7—5	13—5	86—76

No Decisions—Faul.

NATIONAL LEAGUE YEARLY FINISHES

Year	Atl.	Chi.	Cin.	Hous.	L.A.	N.Y.	Phil.	Pitt.	St.L.	S.F.
1900	*4	x5	7	..	†1	..	3	2	x5	‡8
1901	*5	6	8	..	†1	..	2	1	4	‡7
1902	*3	5	4	..	†2	..	7	1	6	‡8
1903	*6	3	4	..	†5	..	7	1	8	‡2
1904	*7	2	3	..	†6	..	4	4	5	‡1
1905	*7	3	5	..	†8	..	4	2	6	‡1
1906	*8	1	6	..	†5	..	4	3	7	‡2
1907	*7	1	6	..	†5	..	3	2	8	‡4
1908	*6	1	5	..	†7	..	4	x2	8	x‡2
1909	*8	2	4	..	†6	..	5	1	7	‡3
1910	*8	1	5	..	†6	..	4	3	7	‡2
1911	*8	2	6	..	†7	..	4	3	5	‡1
1912	*8	3	4	..	†7	..	5	2	6	‡1
1913	*5	3	7	..	†6	..	2	4	8	‡1
1914	*1	4	8	..	†5	..	6	7	3	‡2
1915	*2	4	7	..	†3	..	1	5	6	‡8
1916	*3	5	x7	..	†1	..	2	6	x7	‡4
1917	*6	5	4	..	†7	..	2	8	3	‡1
1918	*7	1	3	..	†5	..	6	4	8	‡2
1919	*6	3	1	..	†5	..	8	4	7	‡2
1920	*7	x5	3	..	†1	..	8	4	x5	‡2
1921	*4	7	6	..	†5	..	8	2	3	‡1
1922	*8	5	2	..	†6	..	7	x3	x3	‡1
1923	*7	4	2	..	†6	..	8	3	5	‡1
1924	*8	5	4	..	†2	..	7	3	6	‡1
1925	*5	8	3	..	x†6	..	x6	1	4	‡2
1926	*7	4	2	..	†6	..	8	3	1	‡5
1927	*7	4	5	..	†6	..	8	1	2	‡3
1928	*7	3	5	..	†6	..	8	4	1	‡2
1929	*8	1	7	..	†6	..	5	2	4	‡3
1930	*6	2	7	..	†4	..	8	5	1	‡3
1931	*7	3	8	..	†4	..	6	5	1	‡2
1932	*5	1	8	..	†3	..	4	2	x6	x‡6
1933	*4	3	8	..	†6	..	7	2	5	‡1
1934	*4	3	8	..	†6	..	7	5	1	‡2
1935	*8	1	6	..	†5	..	7	4	2	‡3
1936	*6	x2	5	..	†7	..	8	7	x2	‡1
1937	*5	2	8	..	†6	..	7	3	4	‡1
1938	*5	1	4	..	†7	..	8	2	6	‡3
1939	*7	4	1	..	†3	..	8	6	2	‡5
1940	*7	5	1	..	†2	..	8	4	3	‡6
1941	*7	6	3	..	†1	..	8	4	2	‡5
1942	*7	6	4	..	†2	..	8	5	1	‡3
1943	*6	5	2	..	†3	..	7	4	1	‡8
1944	*6	4	3	..	†7	..	8	2	1	‡5
1945	*6	1	7	..	†3	..	8	4	2	‡5
1946	*4	3	6	..	†2	..	5	7	1	‡8
1947	*3	6	5	..	†1	..	x7	x7	2	‡4
1948	*1	8	7	..	†3	..	6	4	2	‡5
1949	*4	8	7	..	†1	..	3	6	2	‡5
1950	*4	7	6	..	†2	..	1	8	5	‡3
1951	*4	8	6	..	†2	..	5	7	3	‡1
1952	*7	5	6	..	†1	..	4	8	3	‡2
1953	*2	7	6	..	†1	..	x3	8	x3	‡5
1954	*3	7	5	..	†2	..	4	8	6	‡1
1955	*2	8	5	..	†1	..	4	8	7	‡3
1956	*2	8	3	..	†1	..	5	7	4	‡6
1957	*1	x7	4	..	†3	..	8	x7	2	‡6
1958	*1	x5	4	..	7	..	8	2	x5	3
1959	*2	x5	x5	..	1	..	8	4	7	3
1960	*2	7	6	..	4	..	8	1	3	5
1961	*4	7	1	..	2	..	8	6	5	3
1962	*5	9	3	8	2	10	7	4	6	1
1963	*6	7	5	9	1	10	4	8	2	3
1964	*5	8	x2	9	x6	10	x2	x6	1	4
1965	*5	8	4	9	1	10	6	3	7	2
1966	5	10	7	8	1	9	4	3	6	2
1967	7	3	4	10	x7	9	5	6	1	2
1968	5	3	4	10	x7	9	7	6	1	2

	EAST DIVISION						WEST DIVISION					
Year	Chi.	Mon.	N.Y.	Phila.	Pitts.	St.L	Atl.	Cin.	Hous.	L.A.	S.D.	S.F.
1969	2	6	1	5	3	4	1	3	5	4	6	2
1970	2	6	3	5	1	4	5	1	4	2	6	3

*Record of predecessor Boston (1900-1952) and Milwaukee (1953-1965) clubs; †Brooklyn club; ‡New York Giants.
xTied for position.

NATIONAL LEAGUE PENNANT WINNERS

Year Club	Manager	W.	L.	Pct.	*G.A.
1900—Brooklyn	Edward (Ned) Hanlon	82	54	.603	4½
1901—Pittsburgh	Frederick Clarke	90	49	.647	7½
1902—Pittsburgh	Frederick Clarke	103	36	.741	27½
1903—Pittsburgh	Frederick Clarke	91	49	.650	6½
1904—New York	John McGraw	106	47	.693	13
1905—New York	John McGraw	105	48	.686	9
1906—Chicago	Frank Chance	116	36	.763	20
1907—Chicago	Frank Chance	107	45	.704	17
1908—Chicago	Frank Chance	99	55	.643	1
1909—Pittsburgh	Frederick Clarke	110	42	.724	6½
1910—Chicago	Frank Chance	104	50	.675	13
1911—New York	John McGraw	99	54	.647	7½
1912—New York	John McGraw	103	48	.682	10
1913—New York	John McGraw	101	51	.664	12½
1914—Boston	George Stallings	94	59	.614	10½
1915—Philadelphia	Patrick Moran	90	62	.592	7
1916—Brooklyn	Wilbert Robinson	94	60	.610	2½
1917—New York	John McGraw	98	56	.636	10
1918—Chicago	Fred Mitchell	84	45	.651	10½
1919—Cincinnati	Patrick Moran	96	44	.686	9
1920—Brooklyn	Wilbert Robinson	93	61	.604	7
1921—New York	John McGraw	94	59	.614	4
1922—New York	John McGraw	93	61	.604	7
1923—New York	John McGraw	95	58	.621	4½
1924—New York	John McGraw	93	60	.608	1½
1925—Pittsburgh	William McKechnie	95	58	.621	8½
1926—St. Louis	Rogers Hornsby	89	65	.578	2
1927—Pittsburgh	Owen (Donie) Bush	94	60	.610	1½
1928—St. Louis	William McKechnie	95	59	.617	2
1929—Chicago	Joseph McCarthy	98	54	.645	10½
1930—St. Louis	Charles (Gabby) Street	92	62	.597	2
1931—St. Louis	Charles (Gabby) Street	101	53	.656	13
1932—Chicago	Charles Grimm	90	64	.584	4
1933—New York	William Terry	91	61	.599	5
1934—St. Louis	Frank Frisch	95	58	.621	2
1935—Chicago	Charles Grimm	100	54	.649	4
1936—New York	William Terry	92	62	.597	5
1937—New York	William Terry	95	57	.625	3
1938—Chicago	Charles (Gabby) Hartnett	89	63	.586	2
1939—Cincinnati	William McKechnie	97	57	.630	4½
1940—Cincinnati	William McKechnie	100	53	.654	12
1941—Brooklyn	Leo Durocher	100	54	.649	2½
1942—St. Louis	William Southworth	106	48	.688	2
1943—St. Louis	William Southworth	105	49	.682	18
1944—St. Louis	William Southworth	105	49	.682	14½
1945—Chicago	Charles Grimm	98	56	.636	3
1946—St. Louis†	Edwin Dyer	98	58	.628	2
1947—Brooklyn	Burton Shotton	94	60	.610	5
1948—Boston	William Southworth	91	62	.595	6½
1949—Brooklyn	Burton Shotton	97	57	.630	1
1950—Philadelphia	Edwin Sawyer	91	63	.591	2
1951—New York‡	Leo Durocher	98	59	.624	1
1952—Brooklyn	Charles Dressen	96	57	.627	4½
1953—Brooklyn	Charles Dressen	105	49	.682	13
1954—New York	Leo Durocher	97	57	.630	5
1955—Brooklyn	Walter Alston	98	55	.641	13½
1956—Brooklyn	Walter Alston	93	61	.604	1
1957—Milwaukee	Fred Haney	95	59	.617	8
1958—Milwaukee	Fred Haney	92	62	.597	8
1959—Los Angeles§	Walter Alston	88	68	.564	2
1960—Pittsburgh	Daniel Murtaugh	95	59	.617	7
1961—Cincinnati	Frederick Hutchinson	93	61	.604	4
1962—San Francisco x	Alvin Dark	103	62	.624	1
1963—Los Angeles	Walter Alston	99	63	.611	6
1964—St. Louis	John Keane	93	69	.574	1
1965—Los Angeles	Walter Alston	97	65	.599	2
1966—Los Angeles	Walter Alston	95	67	.586	1½
1967—St. Louis	Albert (Red) Schoendienst	101	60	.627	10½
1968—St. Louis	Albert (Red) Schoendienst	97	65	.599	9
1969—New York (E)**	Gilbert Hodges	100	62	.617	8
1970—Cincinnati (W)**	George (Sparky) Anderson	102	60	.630	14½

*Games ahead of second-place club. †Defeated Brooklyn, two games to none, in playoff for pennant. ‡Defeated Brooklyn, two games to one, in playoff for pennant. §Defeated Milwaukee, two games to none, in playoff for pennant. xDefeated Los Angeles, two games to one, in playoff for pennant.

**Won Championship Series.

PRE-1900 NATIONAL LEAGUE PENNANT WINNERS

Year	Club	Manager	W.	L.	Pct.	Year	Club	Manager	W.	L.	Pct.
1876	Chi.	Albert Spalding	52	14	.788	1888	N. Y.	James Mutrie	84	47	.641
1877	Bos.	Harry Wright	31	17	.646	1889	N.Y.	James Mutrie	83	43	.659
1878	Bos.	Harry Wright	41	19	.683	1890	Bkyn.	Wm. McGunnigle	86	43	.667
1879	Prov.	George Wright	55	23	.705	1891	Bos.	Frank Selee	87	51	.630
1880	Chi.	Adrian Anson	67	17	.798	1892	Bos.	Frank Selee	102	48	.680
1881	Chi.	Adrian Anson	56	28	.667	1893	Bos.	Frank Selee	86	44	.662
1882	Chi.	Adrian Anson	55	29	.655	1894	Balt.	Edward Hanlon	89	39	.695
1883	Bos.	John Morrill	63	35	.643	1895	Balt.	Edward Hanlon	87	43	.669
1884	Prov.	Frank Bancroft	84	28	.750	1896	Balt.	Edward Hanlon	90	39	.698
1885	Chi.	Adrian Anson	87	25	.777	1897	Bos.	Frank Selee	93	39	.705
1886	Chi.	Adrian Anson	90	34	.726	1898	Bos.	Frank Selee	102	47	.685
1887	Det.	Wm. Watkins	79	45	.637	1899	Bkyn.	Edward Hanlon	88	42	.677

PRE-1900 NATIONAL LEAGUE YEARLY FINISHES

	Chi.	Cin.	N.Y.	Phil.	Pit.	St.L.	Bal.	Bos.	Bkn.	Buf.	Cle.	Det.	Ind.	Lou.	Prov.	Troy	Was.	Wor.
1876	1	8	6	7	..	3	..	4	..	..	..	..	..	..	5	..	..	..
1877	5	..	..	..	4	..	1	..	..	..	..	..	..	6	3	..	..
1878	4	2	..	..	..	..	1	..	..	..	..	5	..	3	..	..	..
1879	*3	5	..	..	..	2	..	*3	6	..	..	1	7	..	..
1880	1	8	..	..	..	6	..	7	3	..	..	2	4	..	5
1881	1	..	..	..	..	6	..	3	7	4	..	2	5	..	8
1882	1	..	..	..	..	*3	..	*3	5	6	..	2	7	..	8
1883	2	..	6	8	..	..	1	..	5	4	7	..	3	..	..
1884	*4	..	*4	6	..	..	2	..	3	7	8	..	1	..	..
1885	1	..	2	3	..	8	..	5	7	..	6	..	4	..	..
1886	1	..	3	4	..	6	..	5	..	..	2	..	..	8	..
1887	3	..	4	2	6	..	..	5	..	..	1	8	..	7	..
1888	2	..	1	3	6	..	..	4	..	..	5	7	..	8	..
1889	3	..	1	4	5	..	..	2	..	..	6	..	..	8	..
1890	2	4	6	3	8	..	..	5	1	..	7	..	..	..	..
1891	2	7	3	4	8	..	..	1	6	..	5	..	..	..	..
1892	7	5	2	4	6	11	12	1	3	..	2	..	9	..	10	..
1893	9	*6	5	4	2	10	8	1	*6	..	3	..	11	..	12	..
1894	8	10	2	4	7	9	1	3	5	..	6	..	12	..	11	..
1895	4	8	9	3	7	11	1	*5	*5	..	2	..	12	..	10	..
1896	5	3	7	8	6	11	1	4	*9	..	2	..	12	..	*9	..
1897	9	4	3	10	8	12	2	1	*6	..	5	..	11	..	*6	..
1898	4	3	7	6	8	12	2	1	10	..	5	..	9	..	11	..
1899	8	6	10	3	7	5	4	2	1	..	12	..	9	..	11	..
1900	*5	7	8	3	2	*5	..	4	1	..	..	..	..	..	..

*Tie.

Note—Hartford was second in 1876, third in 1877; Milwaukee was sixth in 1878; Syracuse was eighth in 1879; Kansas City was seventh in 1886.

PRE-1900 NATIONAL LEAGUE PITCHING LEADERS
(15 OR MORE VICTORIES)

Year	Pitcher and Club	W.	L.	Pct.	Year	Pitcher and Club	W.	L.	Pct.
1876	Albert Spalding, Chi	47	13	.783	1888	Timothy Keefe, N. Y.	35	12	.745
1877	Thomas Bond, Boston	31	17	.646	1889	John Clarkson, Boston	49	19	.721
1878	Thomas Bond, Boston	40	19	.678	1890	Thomas Lovett, Brooklyn	32	11	.744
1879	John M. Ward, Prov	44	18	.710	1891	John Ewing, N. Y.	22	8	.733
1880	Fred Goldsmith, Chicago	22	3	.880	1892	Denton (Cy) Young, Clev.	36	11	.766
1881	Chas. Radbourn, Prov	25	11	.694	1893	Frank Killen, Pittsburgh	34	10	.773
1882	Lawrence Corcoran, Chi	27	13	.675	1894	Jouett Meekin, N. Y.	34	9	.791
1883	James McCormick, Clev	27	13	.675	1895	William Hoffer, Balt	30	7	.811
1884	Chas. Radbourn, Prov	60	12	.833	1896	William Hoffer, Balt	26	7	.788
1885	Michael Welch, N. Y.	44	11	.800	1897	Amos Rusie, New York	29	8	.784
1886	John Flynn, Chicago	24	6	.800	1898	Edward Lewis, Boston	25	8	.758
1887	Charles Getzein, Detroit	29	13	.690	1899	James Hughes, Brooklyn	28	6	.824

PRE-1900 NATIONAL LEAGUE LEADERS

LEADING BATSMEN

Year—Player	Club	G.	H.	Pct.
1876—Barnes,	Chicago	66	138	.404
1877—White,	Boston	48	82	.385
1878—Dalrymple,	Milwaukee	60	95	.356
1879—Anson,	Chicago	49	90	.407
1880—Gore,	Chicago	75	114	.365
1881—Anson,	Chicago	84	137	.399
1882—Brouthers,	Buffalo	84	129	.367
1883—Brouthers,	Buffalo	97	156	.371
1884—O'Rourke,	Buffalo	104	157	.350
1885—Connor,	New York	110	169	.371
1886—Kelly,	Chicago	118	175	.388
1887—Anson,	Chicago	122	*224	.421
1888—Anson,	Chicago	134	177	.343
1889—Brouthers,	Boston	126	181	.373
1890—Glasscock,	New York	124	172	.336
1891—Hamilton,	Phila.	133	179	.338
1892—Brouthers,	Brooklyn	152	197	.335
	Childs, Cleveland	144	185	.335
1893—Duffy,	Boston	131	203	.378
1894—Duffy,	Boston	124	236	.438
1895—Burkett,	Cleveland	132	235	.423
1896—Burkett,	Cleveland	133	240	.410
1897—Keeler,	Baltimore	128	243	.432
1898—Keeler,	Baltimore	128	214	.379
1899—Delahanty,	Phila.	145	234	.408

*Bases on balls counted as hits.

TWO-BASE HIT LEADERS

Year		2B.
1876—Roscoe Barnes, Chicago		23
1877—Adrian (Cap) Anson, Chicago		20
1878—Lewis Brown, Providence		18
1879—Charles Eden, Cleveland		31
1880—Fred Dunlap, Cleveland		27
1881—Michael (King) Kelly, Chicago		25
1882—Michael (King) Kelly, Chicago		36
1883—Edward Williamson, Chicago		50
1884—Paul Hines, Providence		34
1885—Adrian (Cap) Anson, Chicago		35
1886—Dennis (Dan) Brouthers, Detroit		41
1887—Dennis (Dan) Brouthers, Detroit		35
1888—James Ryan, Chicago		37
1889—John Glasscock, Indianapolis		39
1890—Samuel Thompson, Philadelphia		38
1891—Michael Griffin, Brooklyn		36
1892—Brouthers, Bkn.-Delahanty, Phil.		33
1893—Oliver (Pat) Tebeau, Cleveland		35
1894—Hugh Duffy, Boston		50
1895—Edward Delahanty, Philadelphia		47
1896—Edward Delahanty, Philadelphia		42
1897—Jacob Stenzel, Baltimore		40
1898—Napoleon Lajoie, Philadelphia		40
1899—Edward Delahanty, Philadelphia		56

THREE-BASE HIT LEADERS

Year		3B.
1876—George Hall, Athletics		12
1877—Brown, Bos-McVey, Chi-White, Bos		9
1878—Thomas York, Providence		9
1879—L. Dickerson, Cin.-M. Kelly, Cin.		14
1880—Harry Stovey, Worcester		14
1881—John Rowe, Buffalo		11
1882—Roger Connor, Troy		17
1883—Dennis (Dan) Brouthers, Buffalo		17
1884—William (Buck) Ewing, New York		18
1885—R. Connor, N.Y.-J. O'Rourke, N.Y.		15
1886—Roger Connor, New York		19
1887—Samuel Thompson, Detroit		23
1888—R. Connor, N.Y.-R. Johnston, Bos.		17
1889—Connor, NY-Fogarty, Ph-Wilmot, W		17
1890—John McPhee, Cincinnati		25
1891—Jacob Beckley, Pittsburgh		20
1892—Dennis (Dan) Brouthers, Brooklyn		20
1893—Perry Werden, St. Louis		33
1894—Henry Reitz, Baltimore		29
1895—A. Seloach, Wash-S. Thompson, Phil		22
1896—McCreery, Lou-G. Van Haltren, N.Y.		21
1897—Harry Davis, Pittsburgh		28
1898—John Anderson, Bkn.-Wash.		19
1899—James Williams, Pittsburgh		27

HOME RUN LEADERS

Year		HR.
1876—George Hall, Athletics		5
1877—George Shaffer, Louisville		3
1878—Paul Hines, Providence		4
1879—Charles Jones, Boston		9
1880—J. O'Rourke, Bos.-H. Stovey, Wor.		6
1881—Dennis (Dan) Brouthers, Buffalo		8
1882—George Wood, Detroit		7
1883—William (Buck) Ewing, New York		10
1884—Edward Williamson, Chicago		27
1885—Abner Dalrymple, Chicago		11
1886—Harding Richardson, Detroit		11
1887—R. Connor, N.Y.-T. O'Brien, Wash.		17
1888—Roger Connor, New York		14
1889—Samuel Thompson, Philadelphia		20
1890—T. Burns, Bkn.-M. Tiernan, N.Y.		13
1891—H. Stovey, Bos.-M. Tiernan, N.Y.		16
1892—James Holliday, Cincinnati		13
1893—Edward Delahanty, Philadelphia		19
1894—H. Duffy, Boston; R. Lowe, Boston		18
1895—William Joyce, Washington		17
1896—Delahanty, Phil.-S. Thompson, Phil.		13
1897—Napoleon Lajoie, Philadelphia		10
1898—James Collins, Boston		14
1899—John (Buck) Freeman, Washington		25

STOLEN BASE LEADERS

Year		SB.
1886—George Andrews, Philadelphia		56
1887—John M. Ward, New York		111
1888—William (Dummy) Hoy, Wash.		82
1889—James Fogarty, Philadelphia		99
1890—William Hamilton, Philadelphia		102
1891—William Hamilton, Philadelphia		115
1892—John M. Ward, Brooklyn		94
1893—John M. Ward, New York		72
1894—William Hamilton, Philadelphia		99
1895—William Hamilton, Philadelphia		95
1896—William Lange, Chicago		100
1897—William Lange, Chicago		83
1898—Frederick Clarke, Louisville		66
1899—James Sheckard, Baltimore		78

NATIONAL LEAGUE LEADING BATSMEN

Year—Player and Club	G.	AB.	R.	H.	TB.	2B.	3B.	HR.	RBI.	B.A.
1900—John (Honus) Wagner, Pittsburgh..134	528	107	201	302	45	22	4	..	.381
1901—Jesse Burkett, St. Louis 142	597	139	228	313	21	17	10	..	.382
1902—Clarence Beaumont, Pittsburgh 131	544	101	194	227	21	6	0	..	.357
1903—John (Honus) Wagner, Pittsburgh..129	512	97	182	265	30	19	5	..	.355
1904—John (Honus) Wagner, Pittsburgh..132	490	97	171	255	44	14	4	..	.349
1905—J. Bentley Seymour, Cincinnati...149	581	95	219	325	40	21	8	..	.377
1906—John (Honus) Wagner, Pittsburgh..140	516	103	175	237	38	9	2	..	.339
1907—John (Honus) Wagner, Pittsburgh..142	515	98	180	264	38	14	6	91	.350
1908—John (Honus) Wagner, Pittsburgh..151	568	100	201	308	39	19	10	106	.354
1909—John (Honus) Wagner, Pittsburgh..137	495	92	168	242	39	10	5	102	.339
1910—Sherwood Magee, Philadelphia 154	519	110	172	263	39	17	6	116	.331
1911—John (Honus) Wagner, Pittsburgh..130	473	87	158	240	23	16	9	108	.334
1912—Henry Zimmerman, Chicago 145	557	95	207	318	41	14	14	98	.372
1913—Jacob Daubert, Brooklyn 139	508	76	178	215	17	7	2	46	.350
1914—Jacob Daubert, Brooklyn 126	474	89	156	205	17	7	6	44	.329
1915—Lawrence Doyle, New York 150	591	86	189	261	40	10	4	68	.320
1916—Harold Chase, Cincinnati 142	542	66	184	249	29	12	4	84	.339
1917—Edd Roush, Cincinnati 136	522	82	178	237	19	14	4	62	.341
1918—Zachariah Wheat, Brooklyn 105	409	39	137	158	15	3	0	48	.335
1919—Edd Roush, Cincinnati 133	504	73	162	216	19	13	3	69	.321
1920—Rogers Hornsby, St. Louis 149	589	96	218	329	44	20	9	94	.370
1921—Rogers Hornsby, St. Louis 154	592	131	235	378	44	18	21	126	.397
1922—Rogers Hornsby, St. Louis 154	623	141	250	450	46	14	42	152	.401
1923—Rogers Hornsby, St. Louis 107	424	89	163	266	32	10	17	83	.384
1924—Rogers Hornsby, St. Louis 143	536	121	227	373	43	14	25	94	.424
1925—Rogers Hornsby, St. Louis 138	504	133	203	381	41	10	39	143	.403
1926—Eugene Hargrave, Cincinnati 105	326	42	115	171	22	8	6	62	.353
1927—Paul Waner, Pittsburgh 155	623	113	237	338	40	17	9	131	.380
1928—Rogers Hornsby, Boston 140	486	99	188	307	42	7	21	94	.387
1929—Frank O'Doul, Philadelphia 154	638	152	254	397	35	6	32	122	.398
1930—William Terry, New York 154	633	139	254	392	39	15	23	129	.401
1931—Chas. (Chick) Hafey, St. Louis ..122	450	94	157	256	35	8	16	95	.349
1932—Frank O'Doul, Brooklyn 148	595	120	219	330	32	8	21	90	.368
1933—Charles Klein, Philadelphia 152	606	101	223	365	44	7	28	120	.368
1934—Paul Waner, Pittsburgh 146	599	122	217	323	32	16	14	90	.362
1935—J. Floyd (Arky) Vaughan, Pitt....137	499	108	192	303	34	10	19	99	.385
1936—Paul Waner, Pittsburgh 148	585	107	218	304	53	9	5	94	.373
1937—Joseph Medwick, St. Louis 156	633	111	237	406	56	10	31	154	.374
1938—Ernest Lombardi, Cincinnati 129	489	60	167	256	30	1	19	95	.342
1939—John Mize, St. Louis 153	564	104	197	353	44	14	28	108	.349
1940—Debs Garms, Pittsburgh 103	358	76	127	179	23	7	5	57	.355
1941—Harold (Pete) Reiser, Brooklyn ..137	536	117	184	299	39	17	14	76	.343
1942—Ernest Lombardi, Boston 105	309	32	102	149	14	0	11	46	.330
1943—Stanley Musial, St. Louis 157	617	108	220	347	48	20	13	81	.357
1944—Fred (Dixie) Walker, Brooklyn ...147	535	77	191	283	37	8	13	91	.357
1945—Philip Cavarretta, Chicago 132	498	94	177	249	34	10	6	97	.355
1946—Stanley Musial, St. Louis 156	624	124	228	366	50	20	16	103	.365
1947—Harry Walker, St. Louis-Phila....140	513	81	186	250	29	16	1	41	.363
1948—Stanley Musial, St. Louis 155	611	135	230	429	46	18	39	131	.376
1949—Jack Robinson, Brooklyn 156	593	122	203	313	38	12	16	124	.342
1950—Stanley Musial, St. Louis 146	555	105	192	331	41	7	28	109	.346
1951—Stanley Musial, St. Louis 152	578	124	205	355	30	12	32	108	.355
1952—Stanley Musial, St. Louis 154	578	105	194	311	42	6	21	91	.336
1953—Carl Furillo, Brooklyn 132	479	82	165	278	38	6	21	92	.344
1954—Willie Mays, New York 151	565	119	195	377	33	13	41	110	.345
1955—Richie Ashburn, Philadelphia 140	533	91	180	239	32	9	3	42	.338
1956—Henry Aaron, Milwaukee 153	609	106	200	340	34	14	26	92	.328
1957—Stanley Musial, St. Louis 134	502	82	176	307	38	3	29	102	.351
1958—Richie Ashburn, Philadelphia 152	615	98	215	271	24	13	2	33	.350
1959—Henry Aaron, Milwaukee 154	629	116	223	400	46	7	39	123	.355
1960—Richard Groat, Pittsburgh 138	573	85	186	226	26	4	2	50	.325
1961—Roberto Clemente, Pittsburgh 146	572	100	201	320	30	10	23	89	.351
1962—H. Thomas Davis, Los Angeles ...163	665	120	230	356	27	9	27	153	.346
1963—H. Thomas Davis, Los Angeles ...146	556	69	181	254	19	3	16	88	.326
1964—Roberto Clemente, Pittsburgh 155	622	95	211	301	40	7	12	87	.339
1965—Roberto Clemente, Pittsburgh 152	589	91	194	275	21	14	10	65	.329
1966—Mateo Alou, Pittsburgh 141	535	86	183	225	18	9	2	27	.342
1967—Roberto Clemente, Pittsburgh 147	585	103	209	324	26	10	23	110	.357
1968—Peter Rose, Cincinnati 149	626	94	210	294	42	6	10	49	.335
1969—Peter Rose, Cincinnati 156	627	120	218	321	33	11	16	82	.348
1970—Ricardo Carty, Atlanta 136	478	84	175	279	23	3	25	101	.366

LEADING PITCHERS—NATIONAL LEAGUE

(15 OR MORE VICTORIES)

Year	Pitcher	Club	Won	Lost	Pct.
1900	Joseph McGinnity	Brooklyn	29	9	.763
1901	John Chesbro	Pittsburgh	21	9	.700
1902	John Chesbro	Pittsburgh	28	6	.824
1903	Samuel Leever	Pittsburgh	25	7	.781
1904	Joseph McGinnity	New York	35	8	.814
1905	Samuel Leever	Pittsburgh	20	5	.800
1906	Edward Reulbach	Chicago	19	4	.826
1907	Edward Reulbach	Chicago	17	4	.810
1908	Edward Reulbach	Chicago	24	7	.774
1909	Christy Mathewson	New York	25	6	.806
	Howard Camnitz	Pittsburgh	25	6	.806
1910	Leonard Cole	Chicago	20	4	.833
1911	Richard (Rube) Marquard	New York	24	7	.774
1912	Claude Hendrix	Pittsburgh	24	9	.727
1913	Albert Humphries	Chicago	16	4	.800
1914	William James	Boston	26	7	.788
1915	Grover Alexander	Philadelphia	31	10	.756
1916	Thomas Hughes	Boston	16	3	.842
1917	Ferdinand Schupp	New York	21	7	.750
1918	Claude Hendrix	Chicago	20	7	.741
1919	Walter Ruether	Cincinnati	19	6	.760
1920	Burleigh Grimes	Brooklyn	23	11	.676
1921	Arthur Nehf	New York	20	10	.667
1922	Peter Donohue	Cincinnati	18	9	.667
1923	Adolfo Luque	Cincinnati	27	8	.771
1924	Emil Yde	Pittsburgh	16	3	.842
1925	William Sherdel	St. Louis	15	6	.714
1926	Ray Kremer	Pittsburgh	20	6	.769
1927	Lawrence Benton	New York	17	7	.708
1928	Lawrence Benton	New York	25	9	.735
1929	Charles Root	Chicago	19	6	.760
1930	Fred Fitzsimmons	New York	19	7	.731
1931	Paul Derringer	St. Louis	18	8	.692
1932	Lonnie Warneke	Chicago	22	6	.786
1933	Benjamin Cantwell	Boston	20	10	.667
1934	Jerome (Dizzy) Dean	St. Louis	30	7	.811
1935	William Lee	Chicago	20	6	.769
1936	Carl Hubbell	New York	26	6	.813
1937	Carl Hubbell	New York	22	8	.733
1938	William Lee	Chicago	22	9	.710
1939	Paul Derringer	Cincinnati	25	7	.781
1940	Fred Fitzsimmons	Brooklyn	16	2	.889
1941	Elmer Riddle	Cincinnati	19	4	.826
1942	Lawrence French	Brooklyn	15	4	.789
1943	Morton Cooper	St. Louis	21	8	.724
1944	Theodore Wilks	St. Louis	17	4	.810
1945	Harry Brecheen	St. Louis	15	4	.789
1946	Murry Dickson	St. Louis	15	6	.714
1947	Lawrence Jansen	New York	21	5	.808
1948	Harry Brecheen	St. Louis	20	7	.741
1949	Elwin (Preacher) Roe	Brooklyn	15	6	.714
1950	Salvatore Maglie	New York	18	4	.818
1951	Elwin (Preacher) Roe	Brooklyn	22	3	.880
1952	J. Hoyt Wilhelm	New York	15	3	.833
1953	Carl Erskine	Brooklyn	20	6	.769
1954	John Antonelli	New York	21	7	.750
1955	Donald Newcombe	Brooklyn	20	5	.800
1956	Donald Newcombe	Brooklyn	27	7	.794
1957	Robert Buhl	Milwaukee	18	7	.720
1958	Warren E. Spahn	Milwaukee	22	11	.667
	S. Lewis Burdette	Milwaukee	20	10	.667
1959	ElRoy Face	Pittsburgh	18	1	.947
1960	Ernest Broglio	St. Louis	21	9	.700
1961	John Podres	Los Angeles	18	5	.783
1962	Robert Purkey	Cincinnati	23	5	.821
1963	Ronald Perranoski	Los Angeles	16	3	.842
1964	Sanford Koufax	Los Angeles	19	5	.792
1965	Sanford Koufax	Los Angeles	26	8	.765
1966	Juan Marichal	San Francisco	25	6	.806
1967	Richard Hughes	St. Louis	16	6	.727
1968	Stephen R. Blass	Pittsburgh	18	6	.750
1969	G. Thomas Seaver	New York	25	7	.781
1970	Robert Gibson	St. Louis	23	7	.767

Earl Weaver—Championship Series are made for him

SECOND CHAMPIONSHIP SERIES

Including

A. L. Playoff Review

A. L. Game Box Scores

A. L. Composite Box Score

N. L. Playoff Review

N. L. Game Box Scores

N. L. Composite Box Score

Birds Rule Roost Again

By LOWELL REIDENBAUGH

Sweeping success was once more the name of the game for the Baltimore Orioles in the 1970 American League Championship Series.

And for the Minnesota Twins, it was again dismal defeat in three games.

But, whereas the Orioles' victory flight of 1969 included two one-run squeakers, their 1970 conquest was accomplished with relative ease. The games were decided by margins of four, eight and five runs.

For Manager Earl Weaver's Baltimore brigade, which won a total of 217 games in two seasons, the playoff sweep was a continuation of their winning ways in the regular A. L. campaign, which finished with 11 consecutive victories.

For Bill Rigney's Twins, the closing note closely resembled the sour chord on which their season had commenced. In the Florida exhibition season, the Twins lost their first nine decisions before finding the winning touch.

Prospects for a more impressive Twin performance in the playoffs had been enhanced by their seven victories in 12 regular-season meetings with Baltimore. On paper, in all departments, the clubs were fairly evenly matched. On the field, it was a different matter. The Orioles outhit, outpitched and outfielded their rivals from the West Division by a wide margin.

The Twins enjoyed the lead only once, a 1-0 edge in the very first inning of the opening game. Their only tie was forged one inning later. At all other points, the Baltimore behemoths dominated action.

Rigney employed 14 pitchers in a bid to stay the tide, but at the finish the Birds had collected 36 hits and 27 runs. A year earlier, the Orioles had feasted on 36 hits and 16 runs.

By comparison, Weaver called on only four pitchers. Their yield was 24 hits and 10 runs. A year earlier, seven Oriole hurlers had given up only 17 hits and five runs.

Mike Cuellar, half of Baltimore's 24-win duo, received the Oriole opening game assignment in the Twin Cities. Although staked to an early 9-3 lead, the Cuban lefthander was unable to attain maximum efficiency on the cool and windy afternoon and departed in the fifth inning. Dick Hall, 40-year-old relief specialist, allowed only one hit in the final 4⅔ innings to pick up the victory.

With the teams deadlocked, 2-2, the Orioles put the game beyond Minnesota reach in the fourth inning, aided considerably by Cuellar's bat and the lusty blasts of a strong wind blowing across Metropolitan Stadium from right field.

Two singles and Brooks Robinson's sacrifice fly produced one fourth-inning run off Jim Perry, the Twins' 24-game winner, and the Orioles then loaded the bases with one out.

The lefthanded-hitting Cuellar, with an .089 batting average and seven RBIs to show for his season's efforts, then pulled a Perry pitch toward foul territory in right field. As the ball passed first base it was patently foul,

Twins' catcher Paul Ratliff dives for ball as Orioles' Brooks Robinson scores in finale.

maybe as much as 15 feet. Cuellar, himself, stood transfixed at the plate, watching the pellet transcribe a high parabola in the direction of the right field seats.

As the ball soared into the 29-mile-an-hour current, however, it started drifting toward fair territory. Cuellar started jogging from the plate. By the time he arrived at first base, the wind had worked its deviltry against the home forces, depositing the ball over the fence in fair territory, and giving Cuellar a grand-slam homer.

Before the inning was completed, Don Buford cuffed Perry for a knockout homer and Bill Zepp yielded a left-field round-tripper to southpaw-swinging Boog Powell to complete the seven-run outburst.

The Twins recovered one tally in their half of the fourth inning, before shelling Cuellar in the fifth. Mike, who completed 21 of his 40 starting assignments in regular campaigning, gave up three runs. one on Harmon Killebrew's homer. But any flickering hopes among the 26,847 for a Twin triumph were quickly extinguished when Hall entered the game and threw a first-pitch, double-play ball to Danny Thompson.

Hall himself scored the final run in the 10-6 victory in the sixth inning. He singled, equaling his entire regular season's output, advanced on a walk and crossed the plate on Powell's single.

The game was not without its defensive brilliance. Paul Blair, held hitless in five trips to the plate, more than compensated for the Orioles. In the first inning, he speared Tony Oliva's wicked liner. In the seventh, he raced toward the center

GAME OF SATURDAY, OCTOBER 3, AT MINNESOTA

Baltimore	AB.	R.	H.	RBI.	PO.	A.
Buford, lf	3	1	1	0	0	0
Blair, cf	5	0	0	0	3	0
Powell, 1b	5	1	2	2	10	1
F. Robinson, rf	4	1	1	0	0	0
Hendricks, c	5	2	2	0	5	0
B. Robinson, 3b	3	1	3	1	2	1
Johnson, 2b	3	1	1	0	4	2
Belanger, ss	4	1	1	1	2	5
Cuellar, p	2	1	1	4	1	3
Hall, p	2	1	1	0	0	0
Totals	36	10	13	9	27	12

Minnesota	AB.	R.	H.	RBI.	PO.	A.
Tovar, cf-2b	5	1	2	1	1	0
Cardenas, ss	4	0	0	0	2	5
Killebrew, 3b	5	1	2	2	1	1
Oliva, rf	4	1	3	0	3	0
Alyea, lf	3	1	0	0	0	0
Reese, 1b	4	0	0	0	10	1
Mitterwald, c	4	2	3	2	7	1
Thompson, 2b	3	0	1	0	1	3
Williams, p	0	0	0	0	0	0
Holt, ph-cf	1	0	0	0	0	0
Perry, p	1	0	0	1	1	0
Zepp, p	0	0	0	0	0	0
Allison, ph	1	0	0	0	0	0
Woodson, p	0	0	0	0	0	0
Quilici, 2b	1	0	0	0	1	1
Carew, ph	1	0	0	0	0	0
Perranoski, p	0	0	0	0	0	0
Totals	37	6	11	6	27	12

Baltimore									
Baltimore	0	2	0	7	0	1	0	0	0—10
Minnesota	1	1	0	1	3	0	0	0	0— 6

Baltimore	IP.	H.	R.	ER.	HR.	BB.	SO.
Cuellar	4⅓	10	6	6	1	3	0
Hall (Winner)	4⅔	1	0	0	0	1	3

Minnesota	IP.	H.	R.	ER.	HR.	BB.	SO.
Perry (Loser)	3⅓	8	8	7	2	1	1
Zepp	⅔	1	1	1	1	0	2
Woodson	1*	1	1	1	0	0	0
Williams	3	2	0	0	0	1	1
Perranoski	1	0	0	0	0	0	2

*Pitched to two batters in sixth.

Errors—Thompson, Killebrew. Double plays—Baltimore 1, Minnesota 3. Left on bases—Baltimore 4, Minnesota 6. Two-base hits—Thompson, Oliva 2, B. Robinson. Home runs—Cuellar, Buford, Powell, Killebrew. Sacrifice hit—Cardenas. Sacrifice fly—B. Robinson. Hit by pitcher—By Perry (Johnson). Umpires—Stevens, Deegan, Satchell and Berry. Time of game—2:36. Attendance—26,847.

field fence for Brant Alyea's smash, flicked the ball with the heel of his glove and then grabbed it with his bare hand.

In Blair's book, the Oliva catch was the more difficult "because it was hit right at me."

Alyea's drive, he reported, was driven by the wind "and I had to turn twice, but I felt all along that I'd catch it."

Dave McNally, who registered a ten-inning, 1-0 three-hitter in the second game of the 1969 playoffs, received the second-game assignment again and once more responded with victory, although with considerably more ease.

The other half of the Birds' 24-win combo, McNally allowed only six hits, two in the fourth inning when the Twins scored all their runs in an 11-3 setback.

The Birds handed McNally a four-run cushion. Powell doubled home Mark Belanger in the first inning, Frank Robinson homered with Belanger aboard in the third and McNally himself singled home Andy Etchebarren in the fourth.

The Twins nearly erased that lead with two swings of the bat in their turn, Killebrew connecting for a homer after a pass to Leo Cardenas and Tony Oliva hitting a solo smash.

GAME OF SUNDAY, OCTOBER 4, AT MINNESOTA

Baltimore	AB	R.	H.	RBI.	PO.	A.	Minnesota	AB.	R.	H.	RBI.	PO.	A.
Belanger, ss	4	3	3	0	1	5	Tovar, cf-lf	4	0	1	0	2	0
Blair, cf	4	0	0	0	0	0	Cardenas, ss	3	1	1	0	4	3
F. Robinson, rf	3	2	1	2	1	0	Killebrew, 1b	3	1	1	2	7	0
Powell, 1b	5	1	3	3	9	0	Oliva, rf	4	1	1	1	4	2
Rettenmund, lf	3	1	1	1	3	1	Alyea, lf	3	0	0	0	0	0
B. Robinson, 3b	5	1	1	0	1	4	Holt, pr-cf	0	0	0	0	0	0
Johnson, 2b	5	1	1	3	5	1	Mitterwald, c	4	0	1	0	9	0
Etchebarren, c	5	1	1	0	7	0	Renick, 3b	4	0	1	0	1	3
McNally, p	5	1	2	1	0	0	Thompson, 2b	4	0	0	0	0	0
							Hall, p	1	0	0	0	0	0
							Zepp, p	0	0	0	0	0	0
							Williams, p	0	0	0	0	0	0
							Allison, ph	0	0	0	0	0	0
							Perranoski, p	0	0	0	0	0	1
							Tiant, p	0	0	0	0	0	0
							Quilici, ph	1	0	0	0	0	0
Totals	39	11	13	10	27	11	Totals	31	3	6	3	27	9

Baltimore	1	0	2	1	0	0	0	7—11	
Minnesota	0	0	0	3	0	0	0	0— 3	

Baltimore	IP.	H.	R.	ER.	HR.	BB.	SO.
McNally (Winner)	9	6	3	3	2	5	5

Minnesota	IP.	H.	R.	ER.	HR.	BB.	SO.
Hall (Loser)	3⅓	6	4	4	1	3	4
Zepp	⅔*	1	0	0	0	2	0
Williams	3	0	0	0	0	0	1
Perranoski	1⅓	5	5	5	0	1	1
Tiant	⅔	1	2	1	1	0	0

*Pitched to three batters in fifth.
Errors—Cardenas 2. Double plays—Baltimore 1, Minnesota 2. Left on bases—Baltimore 7, Minnesota 6. Two-base hits—Powell 2, Mitterwald, McNally. Home runs—F. Robinson, Killebrew, Oliva, Johnson. Stolen base—Rettenmund. Umpires—Haller, Odom, Neudecker, Honochick, Goetz and Springstead. Time of game—2:59. Attendance—27,490.

Stan Williams, following Tom Hall and Bill Zepp to the Twin mound, blanked Baltimore the next three frames and Ron Perranoski zeroed the visitors in the eighth before the East Division champs erupted for their second seven-run rally in the series.

McNally's bat ignited the conflagration with a wrong-field double and Dave Johnson concluded it with a three-run homer. All the Birds except

Blair participated in the 13-hit feast, Belanger and Powell accounting for three apiece.

Minnesota fans were hardly in a reflective mood after a second consecutive rebuff, but they did gain a titillating respite in the eighth inning when Perranoski entered the game.

As the southpaw fireman approached the mound, Baltimore Manager Earl Weaver asked umpire Bill Haller to check the pitcher's hand. Haller discovered a foreign substance and ordered it removed.

When a towel failed to do the job, Perranoski shuffled to the clubhouse for soap and water. Returning minutes later, Perranoski strolled to the plate, extended his hands, palms up, much like a chastised schoolboy, and received the arbiter's gold star for cleanliness.

Explaining the Orioles' suspicions, Weaver said: "Yesterday, our bullpen coach, Jim Frey, noticed Perranoski, in the adjoining bullpen, applying something to his hands. Today we asked the umpire to check it."

What had Haller found?

"Pine tar," said the ump, referring to an illegal substance.

"It was resin," deadpanned Perranoski.

The incident was another in the Weaver-Perranoski feud, which had its inception in the summer of 1970, when Earl failed to name the pitcher to the American League All-Star squad, an omission that elicited some fiery observations from Perranoski.

When the series shifted to Baltimore, October 5, Weaver called on his workhorse, Jim Palmer, to wrap it all up.

GAME OF MONDAY, OCTOBER 5, AT BALTIMORE

Minnesota	AB.	R.	H.	RBI.	PO.	A.
Tovar, lf	4	1	2	0	3	0
Cardenas, ss	4	0	1	1	0	3
Oliva, rf	4	0	2	0	3	0
Killebrew, 3b	3	0	0	0	0	3
Holt, cf	4	0	0	0	3	0
Ratliff, c	4	0	1	0	7	0
Reese, 1b	3	0	1	0	6	1
Tiant, pr	0	0	0	0	0	0
Thompson, 2b	1	0	0	0	1	0
Allison, ph	1	0	0	0	0	0
Quilici, 2b	0	0	0	0	0	0
Alyea, ph	1	0	0	0	0	0
Kaat, p	1	0	0	0	0	0
Blyleven, p	0	0	0	0	1	0
Manuel, ph	1	0	0	0	0	0
Hall, p	0	0	0	0	0	0
Carew, ph	1	0	0	0	0	0
Perry, p	0	0	0	0	0	0
Renick, ph	1	0	0	0	0	0
Totals	33	1	7	1	24	7

Baltimore	AB.	R.	H.	RBI.	PO.	A.
Buford, lf	4	1	2	2	2	0
Blair, cf	4	0	1	0	1	0
F. Robinson, rf	3	0	0	0	1	0
Powell, 1b	4	0	1	1	5	0
B. Robinson, 3b	4	1	3	0	0	0
Johnson, 2b	3	2	2	1	2	1
Etchebarren, c	4	0	0	0	12	0
Belanger, ss	4	1	0	0	3	4
Palmer, p	4	1	1	1	1	1
Totals	34	6	10	5	27	6

Minnesota	0	0	0	1	0	0	0	0—1
Baltimore	1	1	3	0	0	0	1	0	x—6

Minnesota	IP.	H.	R.	ER.	HR.	BB.	SO.
Kaat (Loser)	2*	6	4	2	0	2	1
Blyleven	2	2	1	0	0	0	2
Hall	2	0	0	0	0	1	2
Perry	2	2	1	1	1	0	2

Baltimore	IP.	H.	R.	ER.	HR.	BB.	SO.
Palmer (Winner)	9	7	1	1	0	3	12

*Pitched to two batters in third.

Errors—Holt, Ratliff. Double play—Baltimore 1. Left on bases—Minnesota 8, Baltimore 9. Two-base hits—Buford, B. Robinson, Palmer. Three-base hit—Tovar. Home run—Johnson. Sacrifice hit—Blair. Sacrifice fly—Buford. Umpires—Odom, Neudecker, Springstead, Honochick, Haller and Goetz. Time of game—2:20. Attendance—27,608.

The big righthander, just ten days short of his twenty-fifth birthday and two years removed from an arm ailment that threatened his career, was razor-sharp, scattering seven hits.

In fairness, Palmer was entitled to a shutout. A brilliant sun blinded Frank Robinson while he was tracking down Cesar Tovar's fifth-inning fly that fell for a triple. Cardenas' single produced a run, but that was all for the Twins.

A 20-game winner with a 2.71 ERA in regular play, Palmer set a personal career high of 12 strikeouts and issued only three walks.

He also laced a double and figured prominently in the second-inning Oriole run when his looper to short center field was misplayed for a two-base error. Palmer subsequently scored on Buford's double.

The Minnesota starting assignment went to Jim Kaat, a 14-game winner who had been handicapped by late-season arm miseries. The lefthander departed with none out in the third after yielding six hits. By that time the trend of the game had been established and three successors, while more effective, were helpless to change the outcome, the Birds cruising to an easy 6-1 victory.

Two singles, around a sacrifice, netted one Oriole run in the opening frame and Palmer made the score 2-0 in the second. A double by Brooks Robinson and Johnson's single shelled Kaat in the third. With 19-year-old Bert Blyleven on duty, Etchebarren grounded to Cardenas. The shortstop's throw to the plate was in time, but Robbie's crunching slide dislodged the ball from Paul Ratliff's mitt. Palmer's double made the score, 4-0, and Buford's sacrifice fly plated a fifth run.

Johnson's second homer of the series concluded the scoring in the seventh inning.

The Orioles experienced an anxious moment in the second inning when Ratliff lined savagely back to the box. The ball knocked Palmer to the turf as it ricocheted 20 feet toward first base. An examination revealed no great damage to the pitcher and he resumed action.

Attendance for the three games totaled only about 57 percent of the two parks' combined capacity. The series drew 81,945, whereas a total of 143,965 seats were available, 91,828 for two games in Minnesota and 52,137 in Baltimore.

In 1969, when the first two games were played in Baltimore, the gate was 113,763 out of a possible 150,188.

BALTIMORE ORIOLES' BATTING AND FIELDING AVERAGES

Player—Position	G.	AB.	R.	H.	TB.	2B.	3B.	HR.	RBI.	B.A.	PO.	A.	E.	F.A.
B. Robinson, 3b	3	12	3	7	9	2	0	0	1	.583	3	5	0	1.000
Cuellar, p	1	2	1	1	4	0	0	1	4	.500	1	3	0	1.000
R. Hall, p	1	2	1	1	1	0	0	0	0	.500	0	0	0	.000
Powell, 1b	3	14	2	6	11	2	0	1	6	.429	24	1	0	1.000
Buford, lf	2	7	2	3	7	1	0	1	3	.429	2	0	0	1.000
Hendricks, c	1	5	2	2	2	0	0	0	0	.400	5	0	0	1.000
McNally, p	1	5	1	2	3	1	0	0	1	.400	0	0	0	.000
Johnson, 2b	3	11	4	4	10	0	0	2	4	.364	11	4	0	1.000
Belanger, ss	3	12	5	4	4	0	0	0	1	.333	6	14	0	1.000
Rettenmund, lf	1	3	1	1	1	0	0	0	1	.333	3	1	0	1.000
Palmer, p	1	4	1	1	2	1	0	0	1	.250	1	1	0	1.000
F. Robinson, rf	3	10	3	2	5	0	0	1	2	.200	2	0	0	1.000
Etchebarren, c	2	9	1	1	1	0	0	0	0	.111	19	0	0	1.000
Blair, cf	3	13	0	1	1	0	0	0	0	.077	4	0	0	1.000
Totals	3	109	27	36	61	7	0	6	24	.330	81	29	0	1.000

MINNESOTA TWINS' BATTING AND FIELDING AVERAGES

Player—Position	G.	AB.	R.	H.	TB.	2B.	3B.	HR.	RBI.	B.A.	PO.	A.	E.	F.A.
Oliva, rf	3	12	2	6	11	2	0	1	1	.500	10	2	0	1.000
Mitterwald, c	2	8	2	4	5	1	0	0	2	.500	16	1	0	1.000
Tovar, cf-2b-lf	3	13	2	5	7	0	1	0	1	.385	6	0	0	1.000
Killebrew, 3b-1b	3	11	2	3	9	0	0	2	4	.273	8	4	1	.923
Ratliff, c	1	4	0	1	1	0	0	0	0	.250	7	0	1	.875
Renick, 3b-ph	2	5	0	1	1	0	0	0	0	.200	1	3	0	1.000
Cardenas, ss	3	11	1	2	2	0	0	0	1	.182	6	11	2	.895
Reese, 1b	2	7	0	1	1	0	0	0	0	.143	16	2	0	1.000
Thompson, 2b	3	8	0	1	2	1	0	0	0	.125	2	3	1	.833
Blyleven, p	1	0	0	0	0	0	0	0	0	.000	1	0	0	1.000
Perranoski, p	2	0	0	0	0	0	0	0	0	.000	0	1	0	1.000
Tiant, p-pr	2	0	0	0	0	0	0	0	0	.000	0	0	0	.000
Williams, p	2	0	0	0	0	0	0	0	0	.000	0	0	0	.000
Woodson, p	1	0	0	0	0	0	0	0	0	.000	0	0	0	.000
Zepp, p	2	0	0	0	0	0	0	0	0	.000	0	0	0	.000
T. Hall, p	2	1	0	0	0	0	0	0	0	.000	0	0	0	.000
Kaat, p	1	1	0	0	0	0	0	0	0	.000	0	0	0	.000
Manuel, ph	1	1	0	0	0	0	0	0	0	.000	1	0	0	1.000
Perry, p	2	1	0	0	0	0	0	0	1	.000	0	0	0	.000
Allison, ph	3	2	0	0	0	0	0	0	0	.000	0	0	0	.000
Carew, ph	3	2	0	0	0	0	0	0	0	.000	1	1	0	1.000
Quilici, 2b-ph	3	5	0	0	0	0	0	0	0	.000	3	0	1	.750
Holt, ph-cf-pr	3	5	0	0	0	0	0	0	0	.000	0	0	0	.000
Alyea, lf-ph	3	7	1	0	0	0	0	0	0	.000	0	0	0	.000
Totals	3	101	10	24	39	4	1	3	10	.238	78	28	6	.946

BALTIMORE ORIOLES' PITCHING RECORDS

Pitcher	G.	GS.	CG.	IP.	H.	R.	ER.	SO.	BB.	HB.	WP.	W.	L.	Pct.	ERA.
R. Hall	1	0	0	4⅔	1	0	0	3	0	0	1	0	1.000	0.00
Palmer	1	1	1	9	7	1	1	12	3	0	0	1	0	1.000	1.00
McNally	1	1	1	9	6	3	3	5	5	0	0	1	0	1.000	3.00
Cuellar	1	1	0	4⅓	10	6	6	2	1	0	0	0	0	.000	12.46
Totals	3	3	2	27	24	10	10	22	9	0	0	3	0	1.000	3.33

MINNESOTA TWINS' PITCHING RECORDS

Pitcher	G.	GS.	CG.	IP.	H.	R.	ER.	SO.	BB.	HB.	WP.	W.	L.	Pct.	ERA.
Williams	2	0	0	6	2	0	0	2	1	0	0	0	0	.000	0.00
Blyleven	1	0	0	2	2	1	0	2	0	0	0	0	0	.000	0.00
T. Hall	2	1	0	5⅓	6	4	4	6	4	0	0	0	1	.000	6.75
Zepp	2	0	0	1⅓	2	1	1	2	2	0	0	0	0	.000	6.75
Kaat	1	1	0	2	6	4	2	1	2	0	0	0	1	.000	9.00
Woodson	1	0	0	1	2	1	1	0	1	0	0	0	0	.000	9.00
Perry	2	1	0	5⅓	10	9	8	3	1	1	0	0	1	.000	13.50
Tiant	1	0	0	⅔	1	2	1	0	0	0	0	0	0	.000	13.50
Perranoski	2	0	0	2⅓	5	5	5	3	1	0	0	0	0	.000	19.29
Totals	3	3	0	26	36	27	22	19	12	1	0	0	3	.000	7.62

COMPOSITE SCORE BY INNINGS

Baltimore		2	3	5		8	0	1		1	0	7—27
Minnesota		1	1	0		4	4	0		0	0	0—10

Sacrifice hits—Cardenas, Blair.

Sacrifice flies—B. Robinson, Buford.

Stolen base—Rettenmund.

Double plays—Johnson, Belanger and Powell 2; Belanger, Johnson and Powell; Thompson, Cardenas and Reese; Reese, Mitterwald and Reese; Cardenas, Quilici and Reese; Oliva and Mitterwald; Perranoski, Cardenas and Killebrew.

Hit batsman—By Perry (Johnson).

Left on bases—Baltimore 20—4, 7, 9; Minnesota 20—6, 6, 8.

Time of games—First game, 2:36; second game, 2:59; third game, 2:20.

Attendance—First game, 26,847; second game, 27,490; third game, 27,608.

Umpires—Stevens, Deegan, Satchell and Berry (first game); Haller, Odom, Neudecker, Honochick.

Official scorers—Tom Briere, Minneapolis Tribune; Phil Jackman, Baltimore Evening Sun. Goetz and Springstead (second and third games).

Big Red Machine Runs Over Pirates

By RALPH RAY

A potent attack and a question-mark pitching staff. That was the consensus view of the Cincinnati Reds as the 1970 National League Championship Series began in Pittsburgh's Three Rivers Stadium October 3. Two days later, it was all over. The Reds reigned as National League champions, but not because of their menacing bats. It was that shaky pitching staff which carried the Reds to three successive victories over the Pirates.

Cincinnati sluggers had whacked 191 home runs in cruising to the West Division title by 14½ games. East Division champ Pittsburgh wasn't that easy for the Reds, despite their three-game sweep. The Reds had all they could handle in each conquest, particularly the finale, in which the Pirates repeatedly threatened but could not deliver.

Pittsburgh's presence in the showdown series was a surprise to most observers. Both the New York Mets and Chicago Cubs had been rated better bets to prevail in a torrid three-way battle for the N. L. East title. The Pirates, it was said, lacked pitching. Pittsburgh's pitching proved better than the Reds expected—but not quite good enough.

Both the Reds and Pirates displayed plenty of thump in winning division titles. The pennant playoff was something else. The Reds scored nine runs and belted 22 hits in their three playoff victories. The Pirates managed to get only three runs on 23 hits and were especially impotent with runners aboard, leaving 29 stranded.

Cincinnati boasted dual heroes in subduing the Pirates, 3-0, in 10 innings in the playoff opener. Gary Nolan, an 18-game winner during the regular season, pitched nine shutout innings to edge Dock Ellis. Nolan departed for pinch-hitter Ty Cline in the 10th, which turned out to be a stroke of genius by Red Manager Sparky Anderson. Cline socked a triple to lead off the inning. He scored the decisive run on Pete Rose's single, and Lee May doubled to provide two insurance tallies, sealing Ellis' fate.

GAME OF SATURDAY, OCTOBER 3, AT PITTSBURGH

Cincinnati	AB.	R.	H.	RBI.	PO.	A.		Pittsburgh	AB.	R.	H.	RBI.	PO.	A.
Rose, rf	5	1	2	1	1	0		Alou, cf	3	0	2	0	4	0
Tolan, cf	5	0	1	0	2	0		Cash, 2b	5	0	0	0	3	3
Perez, 3b-1b	4	0	1	0	1	1		Clemente, rf	5	0	0	0	3	0
Bench, c	3	1	0	0	8	3		Stargell, lf	4	0	3	0	2	0
May, 1b	5	0	1	2	9	0		Jeter, pr-lf	1	0	0	0	2	0
Concepcion, pr-ss	0	0	0	0	0	0		Oliver, 1b	3	0	0	0	10	0
Carbo, lf	3	0	0	0	0	0		Sanguillen, c	4	0	1	0	2	0
McRae, ph	1	0	0	0	0	0		Hebner, 3b	4	0	2	0	0	2
Carroll, p	0	0	0	0	0	0		Alley, ss	3	0	0	0	4	3
Helms, 2b	4	0	2	0	5	5		Ellis, p	2	0	0	0	0	3
Woodward, ss-3b	4	0	0	0	4	4		Gibbon, p	0	0	0	0	0	0
Nolan, p	3	0	1	0	0	2								
Cline, ph-lf	1	1	1	0	0	0								
Totals	38	3	9	3	30	15		Totals	34	0	8	0	30	11

```
Cincinnati ........ 0  0  0      0  0    0  0  0    3—3
Pittsburgh ........ 0  0  0      0  0    0  0  0    0—0
```

Cincinnati	IP.	H.	R.	ER.	HR.	BB.	SO.
Nolan (Winner)	9	8	0	0	0	4	6
Carroll (Save)	1	0	0	0	0	0	2

Pittsburgh	IP.	H.	R.	ER.	HR.	BB.	SO.
Ellis (Loser)	9⅔	9	3	3	0	4	6
Gibbon	⅓	0	0	0	0	0	1

Errors—None. Double play—Pittsburgh 1. Left on bases—Cincinnati 9, Pittsburgh 10. Two-base hits—Alou, Perez, Stargell, May. Three-base hit—Cline. Sacrifice hits—Ellis 2. Umpires—Grimsley, Blandford, Morgenweck and Grygiel. Time—2:23. Attendance—33,088.

Reliever Clay Carroll protected Nolan's victory by holding Pittsburgh hitless in the 10th.

Another key contributor to the Reds' opening triumph was second baseman Tommy Helms. With Pirate runners on second and third and two out in the third inning, Dave Cash rifled a shot to Helms' right. Tommy's diving stop and quick throw to first prevented two Buc runs.

Four minor league umpires worked the opener while the regularly assigned arbiters (and several others) picketed the Pittsburgh park. The umps were striking for higher pay in the pennant playoffs and World Series. An hour before game two was scheduled to start, the striking umps reached an agreement with the major leagues and returned to work.

The Reds didn't cut it quite as close in game two. They led from the third inning on, but never by much, in posting a 3-1 victory. Pittsburgh's chief tormentors in this one were Bobby Tolan, the swift center fielder, and Don Gullett, 19-year-old fireballing reliever.

Tolan was a complete mystery to Buc starter Luke Walker. Bobby began his three-hit salvo with a single in the third inning. He stole second base and wound up at third on catcher Manny Sanguillen's wild peg into center field. Walker's wild pitch permitted Tolan to score. Bobby delivered his kayo punch in the fifth, belting a home run over the wall in right-center, and capped his big day with a single off reliever Dave Giusti in the eighth. Tolan's three runs accounted for all the Cincinnati scoring.

GAME OF SUNDAY, OCTOBER 4, AT PITTSBURGH

Cincinnati	AB.	R.	H.	RBI.	PO.	A.	Pittsburgh	AB.	R.	H.	RBI.	PO.	A.
Rose, rf	4	0	0	0	2	0	Alou, cf	4	0	0	0	1	0
Tolan, cf	4	3	3	1	2	0	Cash, 2b	3	1	1	0	3	5
Perez, 3b	4	0	2	1	2	3	Clemente, rf	4	0	1	1	2	0
Concepcion, ss	0	0	0	0	1	1	Sanguillen, c	4	0	1	0	6	0
Bench, c	3	0	0	0	5	0	Robertson, 1b	4	0	1	0	11	1
May, 1b	4	0	1	0	10	0	Stargell, lf	4	0	0	0	1	0
McRae, lf	3	0	0	0	2	0	Pagan, 3b	3	0	1	0	0	4
Carroll, p	0	0	0	0	0	0	Alley, ss	4	0	0	0	2	4
Gullett, p	1	0	0	0	0	0	Walker, p	2	0	0	0	0	0
Helms, 2b	4	0	1	0	3	3	Jeter, ph	1	0	0	0	0	0
Woodward, ss-3b	3	0	1	0	0	2	Giusti, p	0	0	0	0	1	0
Merritt, p	2	0	0	0	0	2							
Stewart, lf	2	0	0	0	0	0	Totals	33	1	5	1	27	14
Totals	34	3	8	2	27	11							

Cincinnati	0	0	1	0	1	0	0	1	0—3
Pittsburgh	0	0	0	0	0	1	0	0	0—1

Cincinnati	IP.	H.	R.	ER.	HR.	BB.	SO.
Merritt (Winner)	5⅓	3	1	1	0	0	2
Carroll	⅓	2	0	0	0	0	0
Gullett (Save)	3⅓	0	0	0	0	2	3

Pittsburgh	IP.	H.	R.	ER.	HR.	BB.	SO.
Walker (Loser)	7	5	2	1	1	1	5
Giusti	2	3	1	1	0	1	1

Errors—Walker, Perez, Sanguillen. Double plays—Pittsburgh 2. Left on bases—Cincinnati 6, Pittsburgh 7. Two-base hits—Robertson, Cash, Perez. Home run—Tolan. Stolen base—Tolan. Wild pitch—Walker. Umpires—Landes, Pryor, Harvey, Engel, Wendelstedt and Colosi. Time of game—2:10. Attendance—39,317.

Lefty Jim Merritt, Cincinnati's lone 20-game winner, was the second-game starter. Arm trouble had kept Merritt on the shelf in the closing weeks of the regular season, but Manager Anderson had precedent going for him in this case. Merritt had beaten the Pirates six times in six starts over a two-year period. He made it seven for seven by lasting 5⅓ innings this time. Carroll relieved Merritt in the sixth, but gave up two hits and had retired only one batter when Anderson signaled for Gullett.

That did it. Gullett shut off the Pirate threat right now, struck out the side in the seventh and finished the job with 3⅓ hitless rounds. Red

Ty Cline, Reds, beats late throw to Bucs' Manny Sanguillen in eighth to clinch N. L. flag.

catcher Johnny Bench found no dissenters to his post-game appraisal of Gullett's efforts: "This boy has super stuff."

When the scene shifted to Cincinnati for game three, the Reds wrapped it up, 3-2, but not without a struggle. The Pirates scored a run in the first inning off Tony Cloninger, who averted disaster three times before Anderson finally yanked him for a pinch-hitter in the fifth with the score 2-2.

The slugging Reds uncorked their only power show of the playoffs in the first inning, Tony Perez and Bench smacking successive homers off Pirate starter Bob Moose. Pirate starter Moose showed more courage than stuff in the early going. But he hung on and proceeded to halt the Reds until he had two out in the eighth. Then he walked pinch-hitter Cline and gave up a single to Rose.

With Tolan coming up, Pirate Manager Danny Murtaugh brought in lefty Joe Gibbon. Tolan whacked a single to left. Cline took off from second and sped for the plate. He arrived just a hair ahead of Willie Stargell's peg, and the Reds had a 3-2 lead. As it turned out, that was enough, and for the second successive day, Tolan was Cincinnati's hitting hero.

The Reds had a pitching star in this one, too, young Milt Wilcox, who worked three shutout innings in relief of Cloninger and earned the victory.

GAME OF MONDAY, OCTOBER 5, AT CINCINNATI

Pittsburgh	AB.	R.	H.	RBI.	PO.	A.		Cincinnati	AB.	R.	H.	RBI.	PO.	A.
Patek, ss	3	0	0	0	1	2		Rose, rf	4	0	1	0	0	0
Robertson, ph	1	0	0	0	0	0		Tolan, cf	3	0	1	1	1	0
Alou, cf	5	1	1	0	1	0		Perez, 3b	4	1	1	1	3	2
Clemente, rf	5	1	2	0	2	0		Granger, p	0	0	0	0	0	0
Stargell, lf	4	0	3	1	1	0		Gullett, p	0	0	0	0	0	0
Jeter, pr	0	0	0	0	0	0		Bench, c	3	1	2	1	7	0
Oliver, 1b	5	0	2	1	12	1		May, 1b	3	0	0	0	12	1
Sanguillen, c	4	0	0	0	5	1		Carbo, lf	3	0	0	0	0	0
Hebner, 3b	2	0	2	0	0	2		Helms, 2b	3	0	0	0	3	4
Mazeroski, 2b	2	0	0	0	1	4		Woodward, ss-3b	3	0	0	0	1	3
Moose, p	4	0	0	0	1	2		Cloninger, p	1	0	0	0	0	2
Gibbon, p	0	0	0	0	0	0		Bravo, ph	1	0	0	0	0	0
Giusti, p	0	0	0	0	0	0		Wilcox, p	0	0	0	0	0	1
								Cline, ph	0	1	0	0	0	0
								Concepcion, ss	0	0	0	0	0	0
Totals	35	2	10	2	24	12		Totals	28	3	5	3	27	13

Pittsburgh	1	0	0	0	1	0	0	0	0—2
Cincinnati	2	0	0	0	0	0	0	1	x—3

Pittsburgh	IP.	H.	R.	ER.	HR.	BB.	SO.
Moose (Loser)	7⅔	4	3	3	2	2	4
Gibbon	0*	1	0	0	0	0	0
Giusti	⅓	0	0	0	0	0	1

Cincinnati	IP.	H.	R.	ER.	HR.	BB.	SO.
Cloninger	5	7	2	2	0	4	1
Wilcox (Winner)	3	1	0	0	0	2	5
Granger	⅔	1	1	0	0	0	0
Gullett (Save)	⅓	1	0	0	0	0	0

*Pitched to one batter in eighth.

Errors—None. Double play—Cincinnati 1. Left on bases—Pittsburgh 12, Cincinnati 3. Two-base hits—Hebner 2. Home runs—Perez, Bench. Wild pitch—Cloninger. Umpires—Pryor, Harvey, Engel, Wendelstedt, Colosi and Landes. Time of game—2:38. Attendance—40,538.

Wilcox vanished for pinch-hitter Cline in the eighth. Wayne Granger tried to protect the Reds' 3-2 lead in the ninth, but was removed with two down and a runner on first. Gullett was Anderson's choice to wrap it up. The teen-ager wasn't invincible this time, yielding a single to Stargell. But with runners on first and third, Al Oliver swung at Gullett's first pitch and grounded to Helms. The Reds were National League champs.

CINCINNATI REDS' BATTING AND FIELDING AVERAGES

Player—Position	G.	AB.	R.	H.	TB.	2B.	3B.	HR.	RBI.	B.A.	PO.	A.	E.	F.A.
Cline, ph-lf	2	1	2	1	3	0	1	0	1	1.000	0	0	0	.000
Tolan, cf	3	12	3	5	8	0	0	1	2	.417	5	0	0	1.000
Perez, 3b-1b	3	12	1	4	9	2	0	1	2	.333	6	6	1	.923
Nolan, p	1	3	0	1	1	0	0	0	0	.333	0	2	0	1.000
Helms, 2b	3	11	0	3	3	0	0	0	0	.273	11	12	0	1.000
Rose, rf	3	13	1	3	3	0	0	0	1	.231	3	0	0	1.000
Bench, c	3	9	2	2	5	0	0	1	1	.222	20	3	0	1.000
May, 1b	3	12	0	2	3	1	0	0	2	.167	31	1	0	1.000
Woodward, ss-3b	3	10	0	1	1	0	0	0	0	.100	5	9	0	1.000
Carroll, p	2	0	0	0	0	0	0	0	0	.000	0	0	0	.000
Concepcion, pr-ss	3	0	0	0	0	0	0	0	0	.000	1	1	0	1.000
Granger, p	1	0	0	0	0	0	0	0	0	.000	0	0	0	.000
Wilcox, p	1	0	0	0	0	0	0	0	0	.000	0	1	0	1.000
Bravo, ph	1	1	0	0	0	0	0	0	0	.000	0	0	0	.000
Cloninger, p	1	1	0	0	0	0	0	0	0	.000	0	2	0	1.000
Gullett, p	2	1	0	0	0	0	0	0	0	.000	0	0	0	.000
Merritt, p	1	2	0	0	0	0	0	0	0	.000	0	2	0	1.000
Stewart, lf	1	2	0	0	0	0	0	0	0	.000	0	0	0	.000
McRae, ph-lf	2	4	0	0	0	0	0	0	0	.000	2	0	0	1.000
Carbo, lf	2	6	0	0	0	0	0	0	0	.000	0	0	0	.000
Totals	3	100	9	22	36	3	1	3	8	.220	84	39	1	.992

PITTSBURGH PIRATES' BATTING AND FIELDING AVERAGES

Player—Position	G.	AB.	R.	H.	TB.	2B.	3B.	HR.	RBI.	B.A.	PO.	A.	E.	F.A.
Hebner, 3b	2	6	0	4	6	2	0	0	0	.667	0	4	0	1.000
Stargell, lf	3	12	0	6	7	1	0	0	1	.500	4	0	0	1.000
Pagan, 3b	1	3	0	1	1	0	0	0	0	.333	0	4	0	1.000
Alou, cf	3	12	1	3	4	1	0	0	0	.250	6	0	0	1.000
Oliver, 1b	3	12	1	3	4	1	0	0	1	.250	22	1	0	1.000
Clemente, rf	3	14	1	3	3	0	0	0	1	.214	7	0	0	1.000
Robertson, 1b-ph	2	5	0	1	2	1	0	0	0	.200	11	1	0	1.000
Sanguillen, c	3	12	0	2	2	0	0	0	0	.167	13	1	1	.933
Cash, 2b	2	8	1	1	2	1	0	0	0	.125	6	8	0	1.000
Gibbon, p	2	0	0	0	0	0	0	0	0	.000	0	0	0	.000
Giusti, p	2	0	0	0	0	0	0	0	0	.000	1	0	0	1.000
Ellis, p	1	2	0	0	0	0	0	0	0	.000	0	3	0	1.000
Jeter, pr-lf-ph	3	2	0	0	0	0	0	0	0	.000	2	0	0	1.000
Mazeroski, 2b	1	2	0	0	0	0	0	0	0	.000	1	4	0	1.000
Walker, p	1	2	0	0	0	0	0	0	0	.000	0	0	1	.000
Patek, ss	1	3	0	0	0	0	0	0	0	.000	1	2	0	1.000
Moose, p	1	4	0	0	0	0	0	0	0	.000	1	2	0	1.000
Alley, ss	2	7	0	0	0	0	0	0	0	.000	6	7	0	1.000
Totals	3	102	3	23	29	6	0	0	3	.225	81	37	2	.983

CINCINNATI REDS' PITCHING RECORDS

Pitcher	G.	GS.	CG.	IP.	H.	R.	ER.	SO.	BB.	HB.	WP.	W.	L.	Pct.	ERA.
Nolan	1	1	0	9	8	0	0	6	4	0	0	1	0	1.000	0.00
Gullett	2	0	0	3⅔	1	0	0	3	2	0	0	0	0	.000	0.00
Wilcox	1	0	0	3	1	0	0	3	2	0	0	1	0	1.000	0.00
Carroll	2	0	0	1⅓	2	0	0	2	0	0	0	0	0	.000	0.00
Granger	1	0	0	⅔	1	0	0	0	0	0	0	0	0	.000	0.00
Merritt	1	1	0	5⅓	3	1	1	2	0	0	1	0	1	.000	1.69
Cloninger	1	1	0	5	7	2	2	1	4	0	1	0	0	.000	3.60
Totals	3	3	0	28	23	3	3	19	12	0	1	3	0	1.000	0.96

Saves—Carroll, Gullett 2.

PITTSBURGH PIRATES' PITCHING RECORDS

Pitcher	G.	GS.	CG.	IP.	H.	R.	ER.	SO.	BB.	HB.	WP.	W.	L.	Pct.	ERA.
Gibbon	2	0	0	⅓	1	0	0	1	0	0	0	0	0	.000	0.00
Walker	1	1	0	7	5	2	1	5	1	0	1	0	1	.000	1.29
Ellis	1	1	0	9⅔	9	3	3	4	4	0	0	0	1	.000	2.79
Moose	1	1	0	7⅔	4	3	3	4	2	0	0	0	1	.000	3.52
Giusti	2	0	0	2⅓	3	1	1	1	1	0	0	0	0	.000	3.86
Totals	3	3	0	27	22	9	8	12	8	0	1	0	3	.000	2.67

COMPOSITE SCORE BY INNINGS

Cincinnati	2	0	1	0	1	0	0	2	0		3—9
Pittsburgh	1	0	0	0	1	1	0	0	0		0—3

Sacrifice hits—Ellis 2.

Stolen base—Tolan.

Double plays—Alley, Cash and Oliver; Alley and Cash; Alley, Cash and Robertson; Perez, Helms and May.

Left on bases—Cincinnati 18—9, 6, 3; Pittsburgh 29—10, 7, 12.

Time of games—First game, 2:23; second game, 2:10; third game, 2:38.

Attendance—First game, 33,088; second game, 39,317; third game, 40,538.

Umpires—Grimsley, Blandford, Morgenweck and Grygiel (first game); Landes, Pryor, Harvey, Engel, Wendelstedt and Colosi (second and third games).

Official scorers—Charles Feeney, Pittsburgh Post-Gazette; Earl Lawson, Cincinnati Post and Times-Star.

1970 WORLD SERIES

Including

Review of '70 Series

Pictures of Key Plays

Official Play-By-Play, Each Game

Official Composite Box Score

World Series Tables—Attendance, Money,
    Results

World Series

WORLD SERIES CHAMPIONS, 1903-1970

New York, A. L.	20	1923-27-28-32-36-37-38-39-41-43-47-49-50-51-52-53-56-58-61-62
St. Louis, N. L.	8	1926-31-34-42-44-46-64-67
Philadelphia, A.L.	5	1910-11-13-29-30
Boston, A. L.	5	1903-12-15-16-18
New York, N.L.	6	1905-21-22-33-54 (Giants). 1969 (Mets)
Pittsburgh, N.L.	3	1909-25-60
Los Angeles N.L.	3	1959-63-65
Detroit, A. L.	3	1935-45-68
Chicago, A. L.	2	1906-17
Chicago, N. L.	2	1907-08
Cincinnati, N.L.	2	1919-40
Cleveland, A.L.	2	1920-48
Baltimore, A.L.	2	1966-70
Boston, N. L.	1	1914
Washington, A.L.	1	1924
Brooklyn, N. L.	1	1955
Milwaukee, N.L.	1	1957

American League has won 40, National League 27.

RESULTS OF WORLD SERIES GAMES OF 1970

Game	Where Played	Date	Winner	Score	Winner	Loser	Att.
First	Cincinnati	Oct. 10	Baltimore	4-3	Palmer	Nolan	51,531
Second	Cincinnati	Oct. 11	Baltimore	6-5	Phoebus	Wilcox	51,531
Third	Baltimore	Oct. 13	Baltimore	9-3	McNally	Cloninger	51,773
Fourth	Baltimore	Oct. 14	Cincinnati	6-5	Carroll	Watt	53,007
Fifth	Baltimore	Oct. 15	Baltimore	9-3	Cuellar	Merritt	45,341

ROSTERS OF ELIGIBLES FOR WORLD SERIES

Baltimore Orioles—Mark H. Belanger, Paul L. D. Blair, Donald A. Buford, Terrence M. Crowley, Miguel A. Cuellar, Myron W. Drabowsky, Andrew A. Etchebarren, Robert A. Grich, Richard W. Hall, James W. Hardin, Elrod J. Hendricks, David A. Johnson, David P. Leonhard, Marcelino P. Lopez, David A. McNally, Curtell H. Motton, James A. Palmer, Thomas H. Phoebus, John W. Powell, Mervin W. Rettenmund, Peter G. Richert, Brooks C. Robinson, Frank Robinson, Ruthford Salmon, Eddie D. Watt, Earl S. Weaver, manager; George Bamberger, James Frey, G. William Hunter, George Staller, coaches; Ralph Salvon, trainer.

Cincinnati Reds—Melvin B. Behney, Johnny L. Bench, Angel Bravo, Bernardo Carbo, Clay P. Carroll, Darrell L. Chaney, Tony L. Cloninger, David Concepcion, Patrick Corrales, Wayne A. Granger, Donald E. Gullett, Tommy V. Helms, Lee A. May, James M. McGlothlin, Harold A. McRae, James Merritt, Tyrone A. Cline, Gary L. Nolan, Atanasio Perez, Peter E. Rose, James F. Stewart, Robert Tolan, Ray C. Washburn, Milton Wilcox, William F. Woodward, George L. Anderson, manager; Alex P. Grammas, Ted Kluszewski, George Scherger, Lawrence Shepard, coaches; William Cooper, trainer.

By BEN HENKEY

Sobered by memories of what could be called nothing other than humiliation at the hands of the Miracle Mets the previous October, the American League champion Baltimore Orioles approached the 67th World Series with about the same personnel and performance records, but in a slightly different frame of mind.

The Orioles were anxious to redeem themselves, and the 1970 opposition —the Cincinnati Reds—appeared more formidable than had New York's 1969 National League representatives. Clearly, a difficult task lay ahead.

Baltimore felt it had the tools for the job. Included was a trio of pitchers, lefthanders Mike Cuellar and Dave McNally and righthander Jim Palmer, which had accounted for 68 victories during the regular season. Each was a 20-game winner in his own right, and the triumvirate had become the first to reach those heights since 1956 when Bob Lemon, Early Wynn and Herb Score of the Indians had accomplished it.

The Baltimores had only one .300 hitter—outfielder Frank Robinson— but there was excellent power and balance up and down the lineup and the Orioles, anchored by all-star fielding third baseman Brooks Robinson, were solid defensively. And they'd clearly proven their mettle in the A. L. East by a whopping 15 games and then brushing aside Western champion Minnesota in three straight playoff games.

If the 1970 edition of the Orioles lacked one thing, it was overconfidence, which had been a costly commodity against the Mets a year earlier.

A look at the Cincinnati club statistics for 1970 was not apt to inspire overconfidence in an opponent. The Reds, who'd won the N. L. West title by a 14½-game margin under freshman Manager Sparky Anderson, then eliminated Eastern titlist Pittsburgh in three games for the league championship, had led the senior circuit in batting, total bases and home runs. They boasted the major leagues' RBI and home-run champion in youthful catcher Johnny Bench, the stolen base leader in outfielder Bobby Tolan and three .300-plus hitters in Tolan, third baseman Tony Perez and outfielder Pete Rose.

Making their first Series appearance since 1961, when they'd lost to the Yankees in five games, the Reds had a lefthanded ace of their own in Jim Merritt. But Merritt, the first Cincinnati southpaw to win 20 games in a single season in 45 years, had come down with tendinitis in his left elbow.

Indeed, injuries and ailments seemed to have plagued the Reds' pitching staff much of the season, but particularly over the final month. Veteran Jim Maloney, who ruptured an Achilles tendon April 16, didn't get back on the active list until September 3, then was ruled ineligible for the Series.

Young righthander Wayne Simpson (14-3) suffered a hemorrhage in his right shoulder September 17 and righthander Jim McGlothlin, another 14-game winner, was not 100 percent fit. But if the Reds' staff had been weakened, it wasn't apparent in the N. L. playoffs, where Cincinnati pitchers had limited the Pirates to just three runs in as many contests.

Anderson chose 18-game winner Gary Nolan as the Reds' leadoff hurler in the opening Series game in Cincinnati's new Riverfront Stadium October 10. Baltimore pilot Earl Weaver countered with Palmer (20-10), and the Cincinnati club wasted no time in showing Palmer why it had been dubbed the Big Red Machine. The Reds broke the Series scoring ice in the very first inning on Tolan's double and a single by Bench and led 3-0 in the third

after Tolan walked and first baseman Lee May deposited a Palmer pitch over the left field barrier.

But the Orioles made a 3-2 game of it in the fourth when outfielder Paul Blair beat out a slow roller and first baseman Boog Powell followed with an opposite-field homer to left. When catcher Ellie Hendricks greeted Nolan with a leadoff home run in the fifth, it was a tie game.

Brooks Robinson, getting away to a quick start in what was to be one of the most outstanding individual performances by a player in a Series, unknotted the tie with yet another bases-empty homer in the seventh.

The blow by Robinson, who'd robbed May of an extra-base hit in the sixth with a sparkling defensive play at third, was the game decider and pinned the defeat on Nolan, who'd given up an average of only one home run for each 10 innings on the mound during the N. L. season, but was touched for three in less than seven frames by Baltimore.

Robinson's play on the ball hit by May in the sixth inning took on added importance as the result of a controversial play at the plate later in the frame involving Hendricks, the Reds' Bernie Carbo and umpire Ken Burkhart.

Carbo had walked and moved to third on Tommy Helms' single, and when Ty Cline hit a chopper in front of the plate, Carbo attempted to score. Neither Burkhart nor the Orioles (or the Reds, for that matter) were expecting Carbo to try for the plate. The umpire straddled the third base foul line and signaled "fair ball." Hendricks fielded the squibber, cocked his arm and prepared to throw to first base.

Palmer, spotting Carbo on the way to the plate, screamed a warning to his batterymate. Hendricks whirled and dove for the sliding Carbo, but collided with the umpire instead. The Orioles' catcher managed to tag Carbo, whose path to the plate was blocked by Burkhart, with his glove hand, although sequence photos of the play later showed that Hendricks had held the ball in his bare hand during the action. Burkhart, sitting in the cloud of dust raised by the three-way collision, called Carbo out.

The Reds' outfielder and Anderson protested, but not too strenuously, and Burkhart's ruling stood. And the Reds lost a run which would have changed the complexion of the game and perhaps the Series itself.

Palmer needed two-out relief from Pete Richert in the ninth, but had silenced the Big Red Machine on one hit after the third inning and gotten Baltimore off on the right foot with a 4-3 victory.

Some unexpectedly shoddy fielding behind Oriole starter Cuellar in the first inning helped the Reds get away to another 3-0 lead in the second game. Shortstop Mark Belanger kicked Rose's routine grounder. Tolan forced Rose, but Perez lined a single to center. May doubled into left center scoring Tolan and Perez and, when Blair bobbled the ball, May wound up at third. He scored on Hal McRae's perfectly-placed bunt single down the third base line.

Cuellar was dispatched to an early shower by Tolan's leadoff homer and a walk to Bench in the third, but the O's began to peck away at Reds' starter McGlothlin in the next inning. Powell cracked a tremendous solo homer which carried to the second tier beyond the center field wall.

McGlothlin escaped further immediate damage, but was batted out in the fifth when Chico Salmon, Don Buford, Blair, Powell and Brooks Robinson all laced singles and Hendricks tacked on a double to account for five runs and a 6-4 Baltimore advantage.

The Reds battled back on Bench's solo homer off Moe Drabowsky in the sixth. Drabowsky got into further difficulty in the seventh, but 40-year-old reliever Dick Hall came to the rescue and held Cincinnati hitless the rest of the way. Baltimore had scored its second one-run victory, 6-5. Rookie Milt Wilcox, who had been touched for Hendricks' decisive double in the fifth, was saddled with the defeat.

Thus the Reds found themselves in the unenviable position of having lost the first two games in their own park. No club ever had done that and come back to win a Series.

Following a day off for travel, the league champions resumed play October 13 in Baltimore. The Orioles, with Brooks Robinson and McNally playing leading roles, altered the script somewhat, with the same results.

Brooks's two-out, two-run double in the first against Tony Cloninger gave Baltimore the scoring jump for the first time in the Series. McNally, bailed out of early trouble by a Robinson-instigated double play, took a 4-1 lead into the sixth, thanks to bases-empty home runs by Frank Robinson and Buford. The Oriole starter stepped in to face Cincinnati's ace reliever Wayne Granger in a bases-loaded situation in the sixth. A strikeout victim his first two trips, McNally picked on a 2-and-2 pitch and rode it 360 feet into the left field bleachers. The grand slam made it 8-1.

The Reds scored two in their half of the seventh, but Baltimore got one of them back in the same frame and McNally coasted in a 9-3 winner. He'd allowed the Reds nine hits, but all of them had been singles and Brooks Robinson had taken away at least two others with outstanding defensive plays at third base.

Looking to complete a four-game sweep before the home fans October 14—something which would have matched their 1966 effort against the Dodgers—the Orioles sent first-game winner Palmer against the Reds, and Jim was working on a 5-3 lead in the eighth.

Weaver detected a certain weariness after Palmer walked Perez and gave up a single to Bench. The Oriole manager called Eddie Watt in from the bullpen to pitch to May. Watt hadn't worked in 14 days, and his first offering to the Reds' first baseman landed in the left field bleachers.

May's clutch three-run homer and the follow-up relief pitching of Clay Carroll, who clung to a 6-5 lead the rest of the way, enabled the Reds to avoid a wipeout. It was the first defeat for Baltimore since September 19.

Cincinnati had gotten out in front again in the fourth game. Young Dave Concepcion had touched Palmer for a run-scoring triple in the second, but Brooks Robinson, by now assured of winning Series most valuable player honors regardless of the outcome, tied the score with a solo home run off Reds' starter Nolan in the home half of the second.

After Cincinnati had forged ahead 2-1 in the third on a walk to Tolan and singles by Rose and May, Baltimore tilted the game in the opposite direction with a three-run third. Palmer got it started with a single. Powell drew a two-out walk and suddenly Nolan could get nobody out. Frank Robinson's single tied the score, Brooks Robinson's single made it 3-2 and Hendricks gave the O's a two-run advantage with yet another single.

The Reds' Rose turned in the game's key defensive play on Hendricks' hit, however. The right fielder's throw to the plate cut down Brooks Robinson trying to score. Rose contributed offensively in the fifth with a bases-empty home run which narrowed Baltimore's lead to 4-3.

But his throwing error in the sixth allowed Brooks Robinson to score what looked like an insurance run at the time. Robinson and Hendricks had tagged reliever Don Gullett for singles, and Rose's throw to third in an effort to nip Brooks had skipped past Perez.

Carroll, who was to finish the Series with the most impressive set of mound statistics for either club, took over at this point and pitched 3⅔ innings of shutout relief to claim what was to be the Reds' only victory.

Cuellar, a 24-game winner during the regular season who had been strangely ineffective in the playoffs and Series, took the hill October 15 in an effort to wrap up the title for Baltimore.

The Cuban lefthander's most effective pitch, a screwball, hadn't worked well for him in recent outings, but he stuck with it long enough to find himself in a 3-0 hole after half an inning. For the third time in the Series, Cincinnati got away to a three-run lead as Bench singled and Rose, May and McRae each knocked doubles. Weaver, on the verge of yanking his struggling ace, let Mike work on Tommy Helms with two out, and Cuellar got Helms on a grounder to short.

Weaver's patience was rewarded. A dugout conference involving Cuellar, Weaver, pitching coach George Bamberger and catcher Andy Etchebarren resulted in a decision to scrap the screwball. Cuellar would rely on his curve and slider instead. The switch paid dividends.

But before it did, the Orioles struck back. They picked up two quick runs in the first on a Blair single and Frank Robinson's homer, his sixth in Series play. Behind by one instead of three, Cuellar retired the Cincinnati side in order in the second. And he went on to get seven more Red hitters in order before walking pinch-hitter Angel Bravo in the fifth.

With his pitching staff in dire straits, Cincinnati's Anderson had fallen back on Merritt as the fifth-game starter. Having worked only eight innings in the past five weeks and still bothered by that tender elbow, Merritt tried gamely but lasted less than two innings. He came out in the second while the Orioles were in the process of scoring what were to be the decisive runs on RBI singles by Belanger and Blair, both struck against reliever Granger.

Granger was touched for two more runs in the third when Powell doubled and Merv Rettenmund and Dave Johnson singled around a ground out. The Reds got still another taste of Oriole depth in the fifth when outfielder Rettenmund, who played in only two of the five games, homered off Cloninger, boosting Baltimore's lead to 7-3.

Meanwhile, Cuellar was breezing. He surrendered harmless singles to Helms and Concepcion in the seventh and took a 9-3 cushion to the ninth after the O's had completed their rough-up of six Cincinnati pitchers with two more markers off Ray Washburn on eighth-inning singles by Blair, Frank Robinson and Johnson. Sandwiched among the hits was a ground out by Powell on which Blair scooted around from second to score.

Brooks Robinson had one more fielding gem up his sleeve, saving it for the final inning as he stole another hit from Bench when he dove for the Red catcher's line drive down the line and wound up lying in foul territory—but with the ball clutched in his glove. Moments later, Brooks fielded Pat Corrales' routine grounder, flipped to first base and the Orioles were 9-3 winners and world champions.

The batting goat of the '69 Series against the Mets when he had one single in 19 at-bats, Brooks went 9-for-21, two homers included, against

the Reds. His .429 average was second only to teammate Blair's .474. Both tied a five-game Series record by getting nine hits each. And, as a club, the Orioles hit .292, setting a five-game record by clouting 10 home runs.

If it hadn't been for May's .389 average—the Cincinnati first sacker was the only player on either club to hit safely in every game—the Reds' batting totals would have been even more anemic than the final .213 figure. May was the Series' top RBI man with eight, tying the five-game mark.

There was an even bigger disparity between the clubs' final pitching figures. The Orioles' composite 3.40 ERA wasn't too far off their American League-leading 3.15, but the Cincinnati staff could do no better than 6.70, compared with 3.69 during the N. L. season.

Anderson, however, refused to point the finger at his pitching staff. "It's the same pitching that held Pittsburgh to three runs when we beat them in the playoffs," he said. But, with the exception of Carroll, who struck out 11 in nine scoreless innings of relief, it obviously wasn't.

Frank Robinson, who was hitless in the first two games but a tough out in the last three, perhaps best summed up the Orioles' success secret. "The difference this year," he said, "was better preparation on our part, mentally and physically. We didn't relax or take time off after we won our division. We didn't make the mistake of letting down this year."

The monetary rewards for the 1970 classic fell short of the record set a year earlier, since there were numerous empty seats at league playoff games and at each of the three Series contests played in Baltimore. But each of the 31 Orioles voted a full share pocketed $18,215.78. The Reds voted 32 full shares, each worth $13,687.59.

Baltimore's total cut of the receipts was $617,149.85, Cincinnati's $462,-862.39. As divisional champions, Minnesota and Pittsburgh club shares came to $214,288.14 each.

Attendance for the five games was 253,183, with a disappointing 45,341 turning out for the final game in Baltimore.

AT CINCINNATI   GAME 1   OCTOBER 10

Baltimore	AB.	R.	H.	PO.	A.	E.
Buford, lf	4	0	1	1	0	0
Blair, cf	4	1	1	7	0	0
Powell, 1b	3	1	1	6	0	0
F. Robinson, rf	4	0	0	2	0	0
B. Robinson, 3b	4	1	1	3	3	1
Hendricks, c	4	1	1	4	1	1
Johnson, 2b	3	0	1	2	0	0
Belanger, ss	3	0	1	2	3	0
Palmer, p	4	0	0	0	0	0
Richert, p	0	0	0	0	0	0
Totals	33	4	7	27	7	2

Cincinnati	AB.	R.	H.	PO.	A.	E.
xRose, rf	3	0	0	3	0	0
Tolan, cf	4	2	1	0	0	0
Perez, 3b	3	0	0	0	3	0
Bench, c	4	0	1	12	0	0
May, 1b	4	1	2	7	1	0
Carbo, lf	2	0	0	2	0	0
Helms, 2b	4	0	1	1	1	0
Woodward, ss	2	0	0	2	1	0
aCline	1	0	0	0	0	0
Chaney, ss	1	0	0	0	0	0
bStewart	1	0	0	0	0	0
Nolan, p	2	0	0	0	0	0
Carroll, p	0	0	0	0	0	0
cBravo	1	0	0	0	0	0
Totals	31	3	5	27	6	0

Baltimore	0	0	0	2	1	0	1	0	0—4
Cincinnati	1	0	2	0	0	0	0	0	0—3

Baltimore	IP.	H.	R.	ER.	HR.	SO.	BB.
Palmer (Winner)	8⅔	5	3	3	1	2	5
Richert (Save)	⅓	0	0	0	0	0	0

Cincinnati	IP.	H.	R.	ER.	HR.	SO.	BB.
Nolan (Loser)	6⅔	5	4	4	3	7	1
Carroll	2⅓	2	0	0	0	4	2

xAwarded first base on catcher's interference. aGrounded into fielder's choice for Woodward in sixth. bStruck out for Chaney in ninth. cStruck out for Carroll in ninth. Runs batted in—

Powell 2, B. Robinson, Hendricks, Bench, May 2. Two-base hits—Tolan, Johnson. Home runs—May, Powell, Hendricks, B. Robinson. Stolen base—Tolan. Caught stealing—Carbo. Sacrifice hit—Nolan. Wild pitch—Palmer. Double play—May, Woodward and May. Left on bases—Baltimore 5, Cincinnati 8. Bases on balls—Off Nolan 1 (Johnson), off Carroll 2 (Powell, Belanger), off Palmer 5 (Tolan, Carbo 2, Perez, Rose). Struck out—By Nolan 7 (Powell, Belanger 2, Johnson, Palmer, Blair, Hendricks), by Carroll 4 (Palmer, F. Robinson, B. Robinson, Hendricks), by Palmer 2 (Stewart, Bravo). Umpires—Burkhart (NL) plate, Flaherty (AL) first base, Venzon (NL) second base, Stewart (AL) third base, Williams (NL) left field, Ashford (AL) right field. Time—2:24. Attendance—51,531.

FIRST INNING

Baltimore—Buford fouled to Bench. Blair popped to Woodward. Powell was called out on strikes. No runs, no hits, no errors, none left.

Cincinnati—Rose grounded to Belanger. Tolan doubled to right-center. Perez flied deep to F. Robinson, Tolan advancing to third after the catch. Bench lined a single to left, Tolan scoring. May singled to left, Bench stopping at second. Carbo lined to B. Robinson. One run. three hits, no errors, two left.

SECOND INNING

Baltimore—F. Robinson flied to Carbo. B. Robinson grounded to Perez. Hendricks fouled to May. No runs, no hits, no errors, none left.

Cincinnati—Helms popped to B. Robinson. Woodward bounced to B. Robinson and was safe at first when the throw pulled Powell off the bag. Nolan sacrificed, B. Robinson to Johnson covering first. Rose grounded to Belanger. No runs, no hits, one error, one left.

Elrod Hendricks, Baltimore catcher, with ball in hand and empty glove, tries to tag Red outfielder Bernie Carbo. Umpire Ken Burkhart, blocking home plate, had knelt to judge chopper in front of plate by Ty Cline in sixth. Hendricks put empty glove on Carbo, but Burkhart called him out.

THIRD INNING

Baltimore—Johnson popped to Helms. Belanger fanned. Palmer grounded to Helms. No runs, no hits, no errors, none left.

Cincinnati—Tolan walked. Tolan stole second. Perez flied to F. Robinson. Bench popped to Johnson in short right. May lined a homer over the left field wall near the foul line, Tolan scoring ahead of him. Carbo walked. Carbo was out attempting to steal, Hendricks to Belanger. Two runs, one hit, no errors, none left.

FOURTH INNING

Baltimore—Buford flied to Rose. Blair beat out a roller down the third base line. Powell homered over the left field wall, Blair scoring ahead of him. F. Robinson flied to Rose. B. Robinson bounced to Perez. Two runs, two hits, no errors, none left.

Cincinnati—Helms flied to Blair. Woodward fouled to Powell. Nolan flied to Blair. No runs, no hits, no errors, none left.

FIFTH INNING

Baltimore—Hendricks lined a homer over the right field wall. Johnson struck out. Belanger was called out on strikes. Palmer fanned. One run, one hit, no errors, none left.

Cincinnati—Rose was awarded first base when catcher Hendricks interfered with his swing. Hendricks was charged with an error. Tolan flied to Blair. Perez flied to Blair. Bench fouled to Hendricks. No runs, no hits, one error, one left.

SIXTH INNING

Baltimore—Buford singled to center. Blair fanned. Powell grounded into double play, May to Woodward to May. No runs, one hit, no errors, none left.

Cincinnati—May smashed a ground ball just inside the third base bag. B. Robinson made a backhand stop and, while moving into foul territory, whirled and made a one-bounce throw to first, getting May by a stride. Carbo walked. Helms singled to center, Carbo going to third. Cline batted for Woodward and chopped a high bouncer in front of the plate. Hendricks fielded the ball and tagged Carbo, attempting to score, with empty glove. Umpire Burkhart, who blocked plate on play, called Carbo out, Helms stopping at second. Nolan flied to Blair. No runs, one hit, no errors, two left.

SEVENTH INNING

Baltimore—Chaney went to shortstop for Cincinnati. F. Robinson popped to May. B. Robinson homered over the left field fence. Hendricks struck out. Johnson walked. Carroll replaced Nolan on the mound for Cincinnati. Belanger singled to right, Johnson moving to second. Palmer was called out on strikes. One run, two hits, no errors, two left.

Cincinnati—Rose flied to Blair. Tolan flied to Buford. Perez walked. Perez went to second on a wild pitch. Bench grounded to B. Robinson. No runs, no hits, no errors, one left.

EIGHTH INNING

Baltimore—Buford flied to Carbo in short left-center. Blair grounded to Perez. Powell walked. F. Robinson was called out on strikes. No runs, no hits, no errors, one left.

Cincinnati—May grounded to Belanger. Carbo lined to B. Robinson. Helms flied to Blair. No runs, no hits, no errors, none left.

NINTH INNING

Baltimore—B. Robinson was called out on strikes. Hendricks fanned. Johnson doubled to center. Belanger was purposely passed. Palmer flied to Rose. No runs, one hit, no errors, two left.

Cincinnati—Stewart batted for Chaney and struck out. Bravo batted for Carroll and fanned. Rose walked. Richert replaced Palmer on the mound for Baltimore. Tolan lined softly to Belanger. No runs, no hits, no errors, one left.

Game No. 2's heroes—Brooks Robinson, who carried a magic glove, and Elrod Hendricks, who had a two-run double—show victory smiles.

AT CINCINNATI GAME 2 OCTOBER 11

Baltimore	AB.	R.	H.	PO.	A.	E.
Buford, lf	4	1	2	1	0	0
Blair, cf	5	1	2	6	0	1
Powell, 1b	3	2	2	9	2	0
F. Robinson, rf	5	0	0	1	0	0
B. Robinson, 3b	4	1	1	1	6	0
Johnson, 2b	3	0	1	3	0	0
Hendricks, c	3	0	1	5	3	0
Belanger, ss	4	0	0	0	3	1
Cuellar, p	1	0	0	0	0	0
Phoebus, p	0	0	0	0	0	0
aSalmon	1	1	1	0	0	0
Drabowsky, p	1	0	0	1	0	0
Lopez, p	0	0	0	0	0	0
Hall, p	1	0	0	0	0	0
Totals	35	6	10	27	14	2

Cincinnati	AB.	R.	H.	PO.	A.	E.
Rose, rf	3	0	3	0	0	0
Tolan, cf	4	2	1	0	0	0
Perez, 3b	4	1	1	0	3	0
Bench, c	3	1	1	5	0	0
May, 1b	4	1	1	13	1	0
McRae, lf	4	0	2	0	0	0
Helms, 2b	4	0	0	4	4	0
Woodward, ss	2	0	0	2	4	0
bCline	1	0	1	0	0	0
Chaney, ss	0	0	0	1	0	0
dCarbo	1	0	0	0	0	0
McGlothlin, p	2	0	0	0	0	0
Wilcox, p	0	0	0	0	0	0
Carroll, p	0	0	0	0	0	0
cBravo	0	0	0	0	0	0
Gullett, p	0	0	0	0	0	0
eStewart	1	0	0	0	0	0
Totals	33	5	7	27	13	0

Baltimore			0	0	0		1	5	0		0	0	0—6
Cincinnati			3	0	1		0	0	1		0	0	0—5

Baltimore	IP.	H.	R.	ER.	HR.	SO.	BB.
Cuellar	2⅓	4	4	1	1	1	1
Phoebus (Winner)	1⅔	1	0	0	0	0	0
Drabowsky	2⅓	2	1	1	0	1	1
Lopez	⅓	0	0	0	0	0	0
Hall (Save)	2⅓	0	0	0	0	0	0

Cincinnati	IP.	H.	R.	ER.	HR.	SO.	BB.
McGlothlin	4½	6	4	4	1	2	2
Wilcox (Loser)	⅓	3	2	2	0	0	0
Carroll	2⅓	1	0	0	0	1	0
Gullett	2	0	0	0	0	2	3

aSingled for Phoebus in fifth. bSingled for Woodward in seventh. cSacrificed for Carroll in seventh. dGrounded out for Chaney in ninth. eFlied out for Gullett in ninth. Runs batted in—Blair, Powell 2, B. Robinson, Hendricks 2, Tolan, Bench, May 2, McRae. Two-base hits—May, McRae,

Brooks Robinson making brilliant stop of a savage smash by Cincinnati's Lee May in the third inning. Brooks managed to right himself and started a double play to kill off a dangerous Red rally.

Hendricks. Home runs—Tolan, Powell, Bench. Sacrifice hit—Bravo. Double plays—Woodward, Helms Powell), off Cuellar 1 (Bench), off Drabowsky 1 (Rose). Struck out—By McGlothlin 2 (F. Robinson, and May; B. Robinson, Johnson and Powell; May, Woodward and May. Left on bases—Baltimore 7, Cincinnati 4. Bases on balls—Off McGlothlin 2 (Powell, Hendricks), off Gullett 3 (Johnson, Buford, Cuellar), by Carroll 1 (Drabowsky), by Gullett 2 (Hall, F. Robinson), by Cuellar 1 (McGlothlin), by Drabowsky 1 (Perez). Umpires—Flaherty (AL) plate, Venzon (NL), first base, Stewart (AL) second base, Williams (NL) third base, Ashford (AL) left field, Burkhart (NL) right field. Time—2:26. Attendance—51,531.

FIRST INNING

Baltimore—Buford popped a single over Perez' head. Blair grounded into a double play, Woodward to Helms to May. Powell walked. F. Robinson was called out on strikes. No runs, one hit, no errors, one left.

Cincinnati—Rose was safe at first when Belanger fumbled his ground ball. Tolan forced Rose, B. Robinson to Johnson. Perez singled to center, Tolan stopping at second. Bench flied to F. Robinson, Tolan going to third after the catch. May lined a double to left-center scoring Tolan and Perez and continued on to third when Blair had trouble picking up the ball. McRae bunted safely down the third base line, May scoring. Helms forced McRae, B. Robinson to Johnson. Three runs, three hits, two errors, one left.

SECOND INNING

Baltimore—B. Robinson popped to May. Hendricks grounded out to May unassisted. Johnson singled to left. Belanger fouled to May. No runs, one hit, no errors, one left.

Cincinnati—Woodward flied to Blair. McGlothlin struck out. Rose grounded to B. Robinson. No runs, no hits, no errors, none left.

THIRD INNING

Baltimore—Cuellar struck out. Buford flied deep to Rose. Blair grounded to Woodward. No runs, no hits, no errors, none left.

Cincinnati — Tolan homered over the right field wall. Perez fouled to Hendricks near the Cincinnati dugout. Bench walked. Phoebus replaced Cuellar on the mound for Baltimore. May smashed a hot grounder to B. Robinson who made a backhand stop and started a double play via Johnson and Powell. One run, one hit, no errors, none left.

FOURTH INNING

Baltimore—Powell homered into the second tier of the center field stands. F. Robinson grounded to Woodward in deep short. The throw pulled May off the bag but he tagged F. Robinson for the out. B. Robinson bounced to Perez. Hendricks walked. Johnson forced Hendricks, Perez to Helms. One run, one hit, no errors, one left.

Cincinnati—McRae lined a double down the left field line. Helms grounded to Johnson, McRae holding second. Woodward flied to Blair. McGlothlin grounded to Belanger. No runs, one hit, no errors, one left.

FIFTH INNING

Baltimore—Belanger popped to Woodward. Salmon batted for Phoebus and singled to center. Buford singled to right, Salmon moving to second. Blair singled to left, Salmon scoring and Buford stopping at second. Wilcox replaced McGlothlin on the mound for Cincinnati. Powell singled to left scoring Buford, Blair going to second. F. Robinson flied to Rose in deep right, Blair advancing to third after the catch. B. Robinson grounded a single to right, Blair scoring and Powell stopping at second. Hendricks lined a double into the left field corner scoring Powell and B. Robinson. Wilcox was removed and Carroll took the mound for Cincinnati. Johnson bounced to Helms. Five runs, six hits, no errors, one left.

Cincinnati—Drabowsky was the new pitcher for Baltimore. Rose bounced to Powell who threw to Drabowsky covering first for the out. Tolan grounded to Johnson. Perez struck out. No runs, no hits, no errors, none left.

SIXTH INNING

Baltimore—Belanger grounded to Helms. Drabowsky struck out. Buford bounced to Helms. No runs, no hits, no errors, none left.

Cincinnati—Bench lined a homer over the left wall. May flied to Blair. McRae grounded to B. Robinson. Helms flied to Blair. One run, one hit, no errors, none left.

SEVENTH INNING

Baltimore—Blair singled to center. Powell bounced into a double play, May to Woodward to May. F. Robinson grounded out to May unassisted. No runs, one hit, no errors, none left.

Cincinnati—Cline batted for Woodward and lined a single to left. Bravo batted for Carroll and sacrificed, Powell to Johnson covering first. Rose walked. Lopez replaced Drabowsky on the mound for Baltimore. Tolan forced to B. Robinson. Hall replaced Lopez as the Baltimore pitcher. Perez forced Rose, B. Robinson to Johnson. No runs, one hit, no errors, two left.

EIGHTH INNING

Baltimore—Chaney went to short and Gullett was the new pitcher for Cincinnati. B. Robinson grounded to Chaney. Hendricks lined to Helms. Johnson walked. Belanger forced Johnson, Perez to Helms. No runs, no hits, no errors, one left.

Cincinnati—Bench flied to Blair. May grounded to Belanger. McRae flied to Buford. No runs, no hits, no errors, none left.

NINTH INNING

Baltimore—Hall fanned. Buford walked. Blair flied to Rose. Powell walked. F. Robinson took a called third strike. No runs, no hits, no errors, two left.

Cincinnati—Helms grounded to Belanger. Carbo batted for Chaney and grounded out to Powell unassisted. Stewart batted for Gullett and flied deep to Blair. No runs, no hits, no errors, none left.

AT BALTIMORE   GAME 3   OCTOBER 13

Cincinnati	AB.	R.	H.	PO.	A.	E.
Rose, rf	5	0	2	4	0	0
Tolan, cf	4	0	1	2	0	0
Perez, 3b	3	0	0	0	2	0
Bench, c	4	0	0	5	2	0
May, 1b	3	1	1	9	0	0
McRae, lf	4	1	2	1	1	0
Helms, 2b	4	1	1	3	1	0
Concepcion, ss	3	0	1	0	2	0
Cloninger, p	2	0	0	0	0	0
Granger, p	0	0	0	0	1	0
aWoodward	1	0	1	0	0	0
Gullett, p	0	0	0	0	0	0
bCline	1	0	0	0	0	0
Totals	34	3	9	24	9	0

Baltimore	AB.	R.	H.	PO.	A.	E.
Buford, lf	3	2	1	3	0	0
Belanger, ss	4	0	0	2	3	0
Powell, 1b	2	1	0	8	0	0
F. Robinson, rf	4	2	3	2	0	0
Blair, cf	3	1	3	0	0	0
B. Robinson, 3b	4	1	2	3	3	0
Johnson, 2b	2	1	0	4	2	0
Etchebarren, c	4	0	0	5	0	1
McNally, p	4	1	1	0	1	0
Totals	31	9	10	27	9	1

```
Cincinnati .................. 0   1   0      0   0   0      2   0   0—3
Baltimore .................. 2   0   1      0   1   4      1   0   x—9
```

Cincinnati	IP.	H.	R.	ER.	HR.	SO.	BB.
Cloninger (Loser)	5⅓	6	5	5	2	3	3
Granger	⅔	2	3	3	1	1	1
Gullett	2	2	1	1	0	0	1

Baltimore	IP.	H.	R.	ER.	HR.	SO.	BB.
McNally (Winner)	9	9	3	3	0	5	2

aSingled for Granger in seventh. bGrounded into force play for Gullett in ninth. Runs batted in—Rose, Concepcion 2, Buford, F. Robinson, Blair, B. Robinson 2, McNally 4. Two-base hits—B. Robinson 2, Blair. Home runs—F. Robinson, Buford, McNally. Sacrifice fly—Concepcion. Caught stealing—Blair, Johnson. Double plays—B. Robinson and Powell; Bench and Helms. Left on bases—Cincinnati 7, Baltimore 3. Bases on balls—Off McNally 2 (Perez, May), off Cloninger 3 (Buford, Blair, Johnson), off Granger 1 (Johnson), off Gullett 1 (Powell). Struck out—By McNally 5 (May, Cloninger, McRae, Perez, Bench), by Cloninger 3 (McNally 2, Etchebarren), by Granger 1 (Etchebarren). Umpires—Venzon (NL) plate, Stewart (AL) first base, Williams (NL) second base, Ashford (AL) third base, Burkhart (NL) left field, Flaherty (AL) right field. Time—2:09. Attendance—51,773.

FIRST INNING

Cincinnati—Rose grounded a single to center. Tolan beat out a bunt down the third base line, Rose stopping at second. Perez bounced to B. Robinson who stepped on third, forcing Rose, and threw to first for the double play. Bench lined to B. Robinson. No runs, two hits, no errors, one left.

Baltimore—Buford walked. Belanger flied to Rose in short right. Powell fouled to Bench between home and third. F. Robinson singled to right, Buford racing to third. Blair walked, loading the bases. B. Robinson lined a double to left-center scoring Buford and F. Robinson, Blair stopping at third. Johnson flied to Tolan. Two runs, two hits, no errors, two left.

SECOND INNING

Cincinnati—May was called out on strikes. McRae looped a single to center. Helms topped a roller down the third base line and was out at first on a good play by B. Robinson, McRae moving to second. Concepcion lined a single to right scoring McRae and when Etchebarren let F. Robinson's throw get past him for an error Concepcion went to second. Cloninger was called out on strikes. One run, two hits, one error, one left.

Baltimore—Etchebarren bounced to Perez. McNally was called out on strikes. Buford flied to Rose. No runs, no hits, no errors, none left.

THIRD INNING

Cincinnati—Rose smashed a liner headed for right-center but Johnson made a leaping onehanded catch. Tolan grounded to Johnson. Perez walked. Bench fouled to Powell in front of the Cincinnati dugout. No runs, no hits, no errors, one left.

Baltimore—Belanger fouled to May. Powell grounded to Concepcion. F. Robinson homered over the center field fence. Blair singled to center. Blair was out stealing, Bench to Helms. One run, two hits, no errors, none left.

Brooks Robinson signals "out" after grabbing Johnny Bench's liner in sixth inning.

Oriole second baseman Dave Johnson lets out a loud yell after being called out on an attempt to steal second base in the fourth inning. Red second sacker Tommy Helms, at right, made the tag and umpire Bill Williams made the call. Shortstop Dave Concepcion lopes in at left.

FOURTH INNING

Cincinnati—May grounded to B. Robinson. McRae fanned. Helms flied to Buford in deep left-center. No runs, no hits, no errors, none left.

Baltimore—B. Robinson bounced to Perez. Johnson walked. Etchebarren struck out and Johnson was doubled attempting to steal, Bench to Helms. No runs, no hits, no errors, none left.

FIFTH INNING

Cincinnati—Concepcion lined to Buford. Cloninger bounced to McNally. Rose grounded to Belanger. No runs, no hits, no errors, none left.

Baltimore—McNally was called out on strikes. Buford homered over the right field fence. Belanger flied to Rose in short right. Powell grounded out to May unassisted. One run, one hit, no errors, none left.

SIXTH INNING

Cincinnati—Tolan flied to Buford. Perez struck out. Bench lined to B. Robinson who made a diving catch to his left. No runs, no hits, no errors, none left.

Baltimore—F. Robinson flied to Tolan in left-center. Blair singled to center. Granger replaced Cloninger on the mound for Cincinnati. B. Robinson doubled off the left field fence, Blair stopping at third. Johnson was intentionally passed, filling the bases. Etchebarren struck out. McNally homered

into the left field bleachers, Blair, B. Robinson, and Johnson scoring ahead of him. Buford bounced to Granger. Four runs, three hits, no errors, none left.

SEVENTH INNING

Cincinnati—May walked. McRae singled to left-center, May going to second. Helms forced McRae, Belanger to Johnson, May moving to third. Concepcion flied to F. Robinson, May scoring after the catch. Woodward batted for Granger and popped a single to short left, Helms advancing to second. Rose singled to right scoring Helms, Woodward stopping at second. Tolan popped to Belanger behind third. Two runs, three hits, no errors, two left.

Baltimore—Gullett was the new pitcher for Cincinnati. Belanger grounded to Helms. Powell walked. F. Robinson singled to left but was out attempting to stretch his hit, McRae to Helms, Powell going to third. Blair doubled down the left field line scoring Powell. B. Robinson fouled to May. One run, two hits, no errors, one left.

EIGHTH INNING

Cincinnati—Perez popped to Powell. Bench was called out on strikes. May lined a single to left. McRae popped to Johnson in short right. No runs, one hit, no errors, one left.

Baltimore—Johnson flied to Rose in short right. Etchebarren grounded to Concepcion. McNally flied to McRae. No runs, no hits, no errors, none left.

NINTH INNING

Cincinnati—Helms singled to center. Concepcion lined to F. Robinson. Cline batted for Gullett and forced Helms, Johnson to Belanger. Rose forced Cline, Belanger to Johnson. No runs, one hit, no errors, one left.

AT BALTIMORE   GAME 4   OCTOBER 14

Cincinnati	AB.	R.	H.	PO.	A.	E.	Baltimore	AB.	R.	H.	PO.	A.	E.
Tolan, cf	3	1	1	1	0	1	Buford, lf	4	0	0	1	0	0
Rose, rf	5	1	2	1	1	1	Blair, cf	3	0	0	3	0	0
Perez, 3b	4	1	0	0	3	1	Powell, 1b	3	1	0	6	0	0
Bench, c	4	1	1	8	1	0	F. Robinson, rf	4	1	1	1	0	0
May, 1b	3	2	2	13	0	0	B. Robinson, 3b	4	2	4	1	0	0
Carbo, lf	4	0	0	2	0	0	Hendricks, c	4	0	2	10	1	0
Helms, 2b	3	0	1	1	3	0	Johnson, 2b	4	0	0	2	3	0
Concepcion, ss	3	0	1	0	0	0	Belanger, ss	3	0	0	3	1	0
Carroll, p	1	0	0	0	0	0	bCrowley	1	0	0	0	0	0
Nolan, p	1	0	0	0	1	0	Palmer, p	3	1	1	0	0	0
Gullett, p	1	0	0	0	0	0	Watt, p	0	0	0	0	0	0
Woodward, ss	0	0	0	0	0	0	Drabowsky, p	0	0	0	0	0	0
aBravo	1	0	0	0	0	0	cRettenmund	1	0	0	0	0	0
Chaney, ss	1	0	0	1	1	0							
							Totals	34	5	8	27	5	0
Totals	34	6	8	27	10	3							

Cincinnati		0	1	1	0 1 0	0 3	0—6
Baltimore		0	1	3	0 0 1	0 0	0—5

Cincinnati	IP.	H.	R.	ER.	HR.	SO.	BB.
Nolan	2⅔	4	4	4	1	2	2
Gullett	2⅔	3	1	0	0	2	0
Carroll (Winner)	3⅔	1	0	0	0	4	0

Baltimore	IP.	H.	R.	ER.	HR.	SO.	BB.
Palmer	7*	6	5	5	1	7	4
Watt (Loser)	1†	2	1	1	1	3	1
Drabowsky	1	0	0	0	0	0	0

*Pitched to two batters in eighth.
†Pitched to one batter in ninth.

aPopped out for Woodward in seventh. bGrounded out for Belanger in ninth. cReached first on Perez' throwing error for Drabowsky in ninth. Runs batted in—Rose, May 4, Concepcion, F. Robinson, B. Robinson 2, Hendricks. Three-base hit—Concepcion. Home runs—B. Robinson, Rose, May. Sacrifice hit—Blair. Caught stealing—Tolan. Left on bases—Cincinnati 6, Baltimore 5. Bases on balls—Off Palmer 4 (May, Tolan, Helms, Perez), off Watt 1 (Tolan), off Nolan 2 (Buford, Powell). Struck out—By Palmer 7 (Perez 2, Carbo 2, Helms, Gullett, Tolan), by Watt 3 (Carbo, Carroll, Chaney), by Nolan 2 (F. Robinson, Blair), by Gullett 2 (Palmer, Powell), by Carroll 4 (Johnson, Buford 2, Blair). Umpires—Stewart (AL) plate, Williams (NL) first base, Ashford (AL) second base, Burkhart (NL) third base, Flaherty (AL) left field, Venzon (NL) right field. Time—2:26. Attendance—53,007.

Lee May hits game-deciding, three-run homer in eighth inning.

FIRST INNING

Cincinnati—Tolan singled to right. Rose grounded out, Johnson to Powell, Tolan going to second. Perez fanned. Bench fouled to Powell at the edge of the Cincinnati dugout. No runs, one hit, no errors, one left.

Baltimore—Buford walked. Blair sacrificed, Perez to May. Powell grounded out to May unassisted, Buford moving to third. F. Robinson was called out on strikes. No runs, no hits, no errors, one left.

SECOND INNING

Cincinnati—May walked. Carbo struck out. Helms also fanned. Concepcion tripled to the wall in right scoring May. Nolan grounded to Johnson. One run, one hit, no errors, one left.

Baltimore—B. Robinson homered into the left field stands. Hendricks grounded to Helms. Johnson bounced to Nolan. Belanger flied to Tolan. One run, one hit, no errors, none left.

THIRD INNING

Cincinnati—Tolan walked. Rose singled to center, Tolan racing to third. Perez struck out. Bench popped to Belanger in short left. May was credited with a hit on a grounder to Belanger who made the stop behind second base but was unable to make a play, Tolan scoring and Rose stopping at second. Carbo forced Rose, B. Robinson unassisted. One run, two hits, no errors, two left.

Baltimore—Palmer singled to center. Buford bounced out to May unassisted, Palmer going to second. Blair struck out. Powell walked. F. Robinson grounded a single to left, Palmer scoring and Powell advancing to second. B. Robinson singled to center scoring Powell and when Tolan fumbled the ball F. Robinson went to third and B. Robinson to second. Gullett replaced Nolan on the mound for Cincinnati. Hendricks singled to right scoring F. Robinson but B. Robinson was out at the plate, Rose to Bench. Three runs, four hits, one error, one left.

FOURTH INNING

Cincinnati—Helms lined to F. Robinson. Concepcion grounded to Johnson. Gullett struck out. No runs, no hits, no errors, none left.

Baltimore—Johnson flied to Rose. Belanger smashed a ground ball to the right of second base but Helms made a backhand stop and threw to May for the out. Palmer fanned. No runs, no hits, no errors, none left.

FIFTH INNING

Cincinnati—Tolan popped to Belanger in short left. Rose homered over the fence in left-center. Perez flied deep to Blair. Bench flied to Buford. One run, one hit, no errors, none left.

Baltimore—Buford grounded to Helms. Blair bounced to Perez. Powell struck out. No runs, no hits, no errors, none left.

SIXTH INNING

Cincinnati—May grounded to Belanger. Carbo struck out. Helms walked. Concepcion lined to Belanger. No runs, no hits, no errors, one left.

Baltimore—F. Robinson lined to Carbo. B. Robinson grounded a single to left. Hendricks singled to right and when Rose's throw to third went into the Baltimore dugout B. Robinson scored and Hendricks went all the way to third. Carroll replaced Gullett on the mound and Woodward replaced Concepcion at short for Cincinnati. Johnson struck out. Belanger popped to Perez but the play was voided because time had been called by the left field umpire. Belanger then flied to Carbo. One run, two hits, one error, one left.

SEVENTH INNING

Cincinnati—Bravo batted for Woodward and popped to Johnson. Tolan struck out. Rose grounded out to Powell unassisted. No runs, no hits, no errors, none left.

Baltimore—Chaney went to shortstop for Cincinnati. Palmer popped to Helms. Buford fanned but Bench dropped the third strike and had to throw

The only winning battery shot possible for the Reds in the 1970 Series shows the happy catcher Johnny Bench (left) and reliever Clay Carroll after 6-5 victory in the fourth game.

to May for the out. Blair was called out on strikes. No runs, no hits, no errors, none left.

EIGHTH INNING

Cincinnati—Perez walked. Bench lined a single off the left field wall, Perez going to third. Watt replaced Palmer on the mound for Baltimore. May homered into the left field stands, Perez and Bench scoring ahead of him. Carbo struck out. Helms beat out a single to deep short. Belanger made the stop to his right but could not make a play. Carroll bunted foul on the third strike for a strikeout. Chaney fanned. Three runs, three hits, no errors, one left.

Baltimore—Powell grounded sharply to Perez who made a backhand stop. The throw to first pulled May off the bag but he tagged Powell for the out. F. Robinson grounded to Chaney. B. Robinson singled to center. Hendricks grounded out to May unassisted. No runs, one hit, no errors, one left.

NINTH INNING

Cincinnati—Tolan walked. Drabowsky replaced Watt on the mound for Baltimore. Rose flied to Blair. Tolan was out attempting to steal, Hendricks to Johnson. Perez flied to Blair. No runs, no hits, no errors, none left.

Baltimore—Johnson fouled to Chaney behind third. Crowley batted for Belanger and grounded out to May unassisted. Rettenmund batted for Drabowsky and was safe at first when Perez threw badly after fielding his ground ball. Buford struck out. No runs, no hits, one error, one left.

AT BALTIMORE   GAME 5   OCTOBER 15

Cincinnati	AB.	R.	H.	PO.	A.	E.
Tolan, cf	4	0	0	1	0	0
Rose, rf	4	1	1	3	0	0
Perez, 3b	4	0	0	3	2	0
Bench, c	4	1	1	6	1	0
May, 1b	4	1	1	6	1	0
McRae, lf	3	0	1	1	0	0
cCorrales	1	0	0	0	0	0
Helms, 2b	3	0	1	1	4	0
Concepcion, ss	3	0	1	2	0	0
Merritt, p	1	0	0	0	0	0
Granger, p	0	0	0	0	0	0
Wilcox, p	0	0	0	0	1	0
aBravo	0	0	0	0	0	0
Cloninger, p	0	0	0	0	1	0
bCarbo	1	0	0	0	0	0
Washburn, p	0	0	0	1	3	0
Carroll, p	0	0	0	0	0	0
Totals	32	3	6	24	12	0

Baltimore	AB.	R.	H.	PO.	A.	E.
Belanger, ss	5	0	1	4	4	0
Blair, cf	4	2	3	2	0	0
F. Robinson, rf	5	2	2	1	0	0
Powell, 1b	5	1	2	9	0	0
Rettenmund, lf	4	2	2	3	0	0
B. Robinson, 3b	5	0	1	1	2	0
Johnson, 2b	4	1	3	2	1	0
Etchebarren, c	3	1	1	5	0	0
Cuellar, p	3	0	0	0	1	0
Totals	38	9	15	27	8	0

```
Cincinnati ............... 3 0 0   0 0   0 0 0—3
Baltimore ................ 2 2 2   0 1   0 0 2 x—9
```

Cincinnati	IP.	H.	R.	ER.	HR.	SO.	BB.
Merritt (Loser)	1⅔	3	4	4	1	0	1
Granger	⅔	5	2	2	0	0	0
Wilcox	1⅓	0	0	0	0	2	0
Cloninger	2	4	1	1	1	1	2
Washburn	1⅓	2	2	2	0	0	2
Carroll	⅔	1	0	0	0	2	0

Baltimore	IP.	H.	R.	ER.	HR.	SO.	BB.
Cuellar (Winner)	9	8	3	3	2	4	1

aWalked for Wilcox in fifth. bGrounded into double play for Cloninger in seventh. cGrounded out for McRae in ninth. Runs batted in—Bench, McRae, Blair, Belanger, Blair, F. Robinson 2, Powell, Rettenmund 2, Johnson 2. Two-base hits—Rose, May, McRae, Powell, Johnson. Home runs—F. Robinson, Rettenmund. Sacrifice hit—Cuellar. Double play—Cuellar, Belanger and Powell. Left on bases—Cincinnati 3, Baltimore 11. Bases on balls—Off Cuellar 1 (Bravo), off Merritt 1 (Johnson), off Cloninger 2 (Etchebarren, Blair), off Washburn 2 (Etchebarren, Rettenmund). Struck out—By Cuellar 4 (Tolan, Merritt, Bench, May), by Wilcox 2 (Cuellar, Blair), by Cloninger 1 (F. Robinson), by Carroll 2 (B. Robinson, Etchebarren). Umpires—Williams (NL), plate, Ashford (AL) first base, Burkhart (NL) second base, Flaherty (AL) third base, Venzon (NL) left field, Stewart (AL) right field. Time—2:35. Attendance—45,341.

FIRST INNING

Cincinnati—Tolan struck out. Rose popped a double down the right field line. Perez flied to Rettenmund. Bench singled to right-center scoring Rose. May doubled off the left field wall, Bench stopping at third. McRae doubled to center, Bench and May scoring. Helms grounded to Belanger. Three runs, four hits, no errors, one left.

Baltimore—Belanger fouled to Perez. Blair lined a single to left. F. Robinson hit a home run into the left field stands, Blair scoring ahead of him. Powell looped a fly to left-center where Concepcion made a backhand catch. Rettenmund popped to Concepcion behind third. Two runs, two hits, no errors, none left.

SECOND INNING

Cincinnati—Concepcion popped to Johnson in short right. Merritt struck out. Tolan bounced out to Powell unassisted. No runs, no hits, no errors, none left.

Baltimore—B. Robinson flied to McRae. Johnson walked. Etchebarren grounded a single to center, Johnson stopping at second. Cuellar lined to Rose. Granger replaced Merritt on the mound for Cincinnati. Belanger singled on the ground between third and short, Johnson scoring and Etchebarren moving to second. Blair singled to left scoring Etchebarren and advancing Belanger to second. F. Robinson flied to Tolan. Two runs, three hits, no errors, two left.

THIRD INNING

Cincinnati—Rose bounced to Johnson. Perez lined to Rettenmund. Bench fanned. No runs, no hits, no errors, none left.

Baltimore—Powell lined a double to right. Rettenmund singled to center scoring Powell and went to second on Tolan's throw to the plate. B. Robin-

Frank Robinson's two-run homer sets tempo of Orioles' clincher

Elrod Hendricks (with bottle), Pete Richert (rear), Curt Motton (with mock white face of shave cream) and promotions director Bud Freeman rap happily.

son's hot smash bounced off Helms' shoulder but the second baseman recovered in time to make the throw to May for the out, Rettenmund going to third. Johnson singled to left scoring Rettenmund. Wilcox replaced Granger on the mound for Cincinnati. Etchebarren flied to Rose. Cuellar struck out. Two runs, three hits, no errors, one left.

FOURTH INNING

Cincinnati—May grounded to B. Robinson. McRae popped to Belanger. Helms popped to Powell. No runs, no hits, no errors, none left.

Baltimore—Belanger bounced to Helms. Blair fanned. F. Robinson lined a drive off Wilcox' hip, the ball rebounding to Perez who threw to first for the out. No runs, no hits, no errors, none left.

FIFTH INNING

Cincinnati—Concepcion grounded to Belanger. Bravo batted for Wilcox and walked. Tolan flied to Rettenmund. Rose flied to F. Robinson. No runs, no hits, no errors, one left.

Baltimore—Cloninger was the new pitcher for Cincinnati. Powell popped to Perez. Rettenmund homered over the fence in right just inside the foul pole. B. Robinson popped a single to center. Johnson doubled down the left field line, B. Robinson stopping at third. Etchebarren was intentionally passed, loading the bases. Cuellar tapped to Cloninger who threw to Bench forcing B. Robinson at the plate. Belanger flied to Rose. One run, three hits, no errors, three left.

SIXTH INNING

Cincinnati—Perez lined to Belanger who made a leaping catch. Bench popped to Johnson. May flied deep to Blair. No runs, no hits, no errors, none left.

Baltimore—Blair walked. F. Robinson struck out. Powell singled to left-center, Blair racing to third. Rettenmund fouled to Perez. B. Robinson forced Powell, Perez to Helms. No runs, one hit, no errors, two left.

SEVENTH INNING

Cincinnati—McRae fouled to Etchebarren. Helms singled off Johnson's glove. Concepcion singled to right, Helms stopping at second. Carbo batted for Cloninger and bounced into a double play, Cuellar to Belanger to Powell. No runs, two hits, no errors, one left.

Baltimore—Washburn took the mound for Cincinnati. Johnson bounced to Washburn. Etchebarren walked. Cuellar sacrificed, Washburn to May. Belanger's grounder was deflected by Washburn to Helms who threw to first for the out. No runs, no hits, no errors, one left.

EIGHTH INNING

Cincinnati—Tolan flied to Blair. Rose grounded to Belanger. Perez popped to Belanger. No runs, no hits, no errors, none left.

Baltimore—Blair beat out a grounder to deep short. F. Robinson singled to right, Blair going to second. Powell hit a ground smash to May who fell after blocking the ball. Helms retrieved the ball and threw to Washburn covering first for the out, Blair scoring all the way from second base and F. Robinson moving to second. Rettenmund walked. Carroll replaced Washburn on the mound for Cincinnati. B. Robinson was called out on strikes. Johnson singled to center, F. Robinson scoring and Rettenmund stopping at second. Etchebarren struck out. Two runs, three hits, no errors, two left.

NINTH INNING

Cincinnati—Bench lined to B. Robinson who dove to his right to make the catch. May struck out. Corrales batted for McRae and grounded to B. Robinson. No runs, no hits, no errors, none left.

BALTIMORE ORIOLES' BATTING AND FIELDING AVERAGES

Player-Position	G.	AB.	R.	H.	TB.	2B.	3B.	HR.	RBI.	SO.	BB.	IBB.	B.A.	PO.	A.	E.	F.A.
Salmon, ph	1	1	1	1	1	0	0	0	0	0	0	0	1.000	0	0	0	.000
Blair, cf	5	19	5	9	10	1	0	0	3	4	2	0	.474	18	0	1	.947
B. Robinson, 3b	5	21	5	9	17	2	0	2	6	2	0	0	.429	9	14	1	.958
Rettenmund, ph-lf	2	5	2	2	5	0	0	1	2	0	1	0	.400	3	0	0	1.000
Hendricks, c	3	11	1	4	8	1	0	1	4	2	1	0	.364	17	2	1	.950
Johnson, 2b	5	16	2	5	7	2	0	0	2	4	3	0	.313	15	9	0	1.000
Powell, 1b	5	17	6	5	12	1	0	2	5	2	5	1	.294	38	2	0	1.000
F. Robinson, rf	5	22	5	6	12	0	0	2	4	5	0	0	.273	7	0	0	1.000
Buford, lf	4	15	3	4	7	0	0	1	1	2	3	0	.267	6	0	0	1.000
McNally, p	1	4	1	1	4	0	0	1	4	2	0	0	.250	0	1	0	1.000
Etchebarren, c	2	7	1	1	1	0	0	0	0	3	2	1	.143	10	0	1	.909
Palmer, p	2	7	1	1	1	0	0	0	3	0	0	0	.143	0	0	0	.000
Belanger, ss	5	19	0	2	2	0	0	0	1	2	1	1	.105	11	14	1	.962
Drabowsky, p	2	1	0	0	0	0	0	0	1	0	0	0	.000	1	0	0	1.000
Crowley, ph	1	1	0	0	0	0	0	0	0	0	0	0	.000	0	0	0	.000
Hall, p	1	1	0	0	0	0	0	0	0	1	0	0	.000	0	0	0	.000
Cuellar, p	2	4	0	0	0	0	0	0	0	2	0	0	.000	0	1	0	1.000
Lopez, p	1	0	0	0	0	0	0	0	0	0	0	0	.000	0	0	0	.000
Phoebus, p	1	0	0	0	0	0	0	0	0	0	0	0	.000	0	0	0	.000
Richert, p	1	0	0	0	0	0	0	0	0	0	0	0	.000	0	0	0	.000
Watt, p	1	0	0	0	0	0	0	0	0	0	0	0	.000	0	0	0	.000
Totals	5	171	33	50	87	7	0	10	32	33	20	3	.292	135	43	5	.973

Salmon singled for Phoebus in fifth inning of second game.
Crowley grounded out for Belanger in ninth inning of fourth game.
Rettenmund reached first on Perez' throwing error for Drabowsky in ninth inning of fourth game.

CINCINNATI REDS' BATTING AND FIELDING AVERAGES

Player-Position	G.	AB.	R.	H.	TB.	2B.	3B.	HR.	RBI.	SO.	BB.	IBB.	B.A.	PO.	A.	E.	F.A.
McRae, lf	3	11	1	5	7	2	0	0	3	1	0	0	.455	2	1	0	1.000
May, 1b	5	18	6	7	15	2	0	2	8	2	2	0	.389	48	3	0	1.000
Concepcion, ss	3	9	0	3	5	0	1	0	3	0	0	0	.333	2	2	0	1.000
Cline, ph	3	3	0	1	1	0	0	0	0	0	0	0	.333	0	0	0	.000
Rose, rf	5	20	2	5	9	1	0	1	2	0	2	0	.250	14	1	1	.938
Helms, 2b	5	18	1	4	4	0	0	0	1	1	0	0	.222	10	13	0	1.000
Bench, c	5	19	3	4	7	0	0	1	3	2	1	0	.211	36	3	0	1.000
Tolan, cf	5	19	5	4	7	0	0	1	1	2	3	0	.211	4	0	1	.800
Woodward, ss-ph	5	5	0	1	1	0	0	0	0	2	3	0	.200	4	5	0	1.000
Perez, 3b	5	18	2	1	1	0	0	0	4	3	0	0	.056	3	13	1	.941
Carroll, p	4	1	0	0	0	0	0	0	1	0	0	0	.000	0	0	0	.000
Chaney, ss	3	1	0	0	0	0	0	0	0	1	0	0	.000	1	2	0	1.000
Gullett, p	3	1	0	0	0	0	0	0	1	0	0	0	.000	0	0	0	.000
Corrales, ph	1	1	0	0	0	0	0	0	0	0	0	0	.000	0	0	0	.000
Merritt, p	1	1	0	0	0	0	0	0	0	0	0	0	.000	0	0	0	.000
Bravo, ph	4	2	0	0	0	0	0	0	0	1	1	0	.000	0	0	0	.000
Cloninger, p	2	2	0	0	0	0	0	0	0	1	0	0	.000	0	1	0	1.000
Stewart, ph	2	2	0	0	0	0	0	0	0	1	0	0	.000	0	0	0	.000
McGlothlin, p	1	2	0	0	0	0	0	0	0	1	0	0	.000	0	0	0	.000

Player-Position	G.	AB.	R.	H.	TB.	2B.	3B.	HR.	RBI.	SO.	BB.	IBB.	B.A.	PO.	A.	E.	F.A.
Nolan, p	2	3	0	0	0	0	0	0	0	0	0	0	.000	0	1	0	1.000
Carbo, lf-ph	4	8	0	0	0	0	0	0	3	2	0	0	.000	4	0	0	1.000
Granger, p	2	0	0	0	0	0	0	0	0	0	0	0	.000	0	1	0	1.000
Wilcox, p	2	0	0	0	0	0	0	0	0	0	0	0	.000	0	1	0	1.000
Washburn, p	1	0	0	0	0	0	0	0	0	0	0	0	.000	1	3	0	1.000
Totals	5	164	20	35	58	6	1	5	20	23	15	0	.213	129	50	3	.984

Cline grounded into fielder's choice for Woodward in sixth inning of first game; singled for Woodward in seventh inning of second game; grounded into force play for Gullett in ninth inning of third game.

Stewart struck out for Chaney in ninth inning of first game; flied out for Gullett in ninth inning of second game.

Bravo struck out for Carroll in ninth inning of first game; sacrificed for Carroll in seventh inning of second game; popped out for Woodward in seventh inning of fourth game; walked for Wilcox in fifth inning of fifth game.

Carbo grounded out for Chaney in ninth inning of second game; grounded into double play for Cloninger in seventh inning of fifth game.

Woodward singled for Granger in seventh inning of third game.

Corrales grounded out for McRae in ninth inning of fifth game.

BALTIMORE ORIOLES' PITCHING RECORDS

Pitcher	G.	GS.	CG.	IP.	H.	R.	ER.	HR.	SO.	BB.	IBB.	HB.	WP.	Bk.	W.	L.	Pct.	ERA.
Hall	1	0	0	2⅓	0	0	0	0	0	0	0	0	0	0	0	0	.000	0.00
Phoebus	1	0	0	1⅔	1	0	0	0	0	0	0	0	0	1	0	0	1.000	0.00
Lopez	1	0	0	⅓	0	0	0	0	0	0	0	0	0	0	0	0	.000	0.00
Richert	1	0	0	⅓	0	0	0	0	0	0	0	0	0	0	0	0	.000	0.00
Drabowsky	2	0	0	3⅓	2	1	1	1	4	0	0	0	0	0	0	0	.000	2.70
McNally	1	1	1	9	9	3	3	0	5	2	0	0	0	0	1	0	1.000	3.00
Cuellar	2	2	1	11⅓	10	7	4	1	5	2	0	0	0	0	1	0	1.000	3.18
Palmer	2	2	0	15⅔	11	8	8	2	9	9	0	0	1	0	1	1	1.000	4.60
Watt	1	0	0	1	2	1	1	1	3	1	0	0	0	0	0	0	.000	9.00
Totals	5	5	2	45	35	20	17	5	23	15	0	0	1	0	4	1	.800	3.40

Saves—Richert 1, Hall 1.

CINCINNATI REDS' PITCHING RECORDS

Pitcher	G.	GS.	CG.	IP.	H.	R.	ER.	HR.	SO.	BB.	IBB.	HB.	WP.	Bk.	W.	L.	Pct.	ERA.
Carroll	4	0	0	9	5	0	0	0	11	2	1	0	0	0	1	0	1.000	0.00
Gullett	3	0	0	6⅔	5	2	1	0	4	4	0	0	0	0	0	0	.000	1.35
Cloninger	2	1	0	7⅓	10	6	6	3	4	5	1	0	0	0	0	1	.000	7.36
Nolan	2	2	0	9⅓	9	8	8	4	2	5	0	0	0	0	0	1	.000	7.71
McGlothlin	1	1	0	4⅓	6	4	4	1	2	2	0	0	0	0	0	0	.000	8.31
Wilcox	2	0	0	2	3	2	2	0	0	2	0	0	0	1	0	0	.000	9.00
Washburn	1	0	0	1½	2	2	2	0	0	1	0	0	0	0	0	0	.000	13.50
Merritt	1	1	0	1⅔	3	4	4	1	0	1	0	0	0	0	0	0	.000	21.60
Granger	2	0	0	1⅓	7	5	5	1	1	1	0	0	0	0	0	0	.000	33.75
Totals	5	5	0	43	50	33	32	10	33	23	0	0	0	1	4	.200	6.70

COMPOSITE SCORE BY INNINGS

Baltimore	4	3	6	3	8	5		2	2	0—	33
Cincinnati	7	2	4	0	1	1		2	3	0—	20

Sacrifice hits—Nolan, Bravo, Blair, Cuellar.

Sacrifice fly—Concepcion.

Stolen base—Tolan.

Caught stealing—Carbo, Blair, Johnson, Tolan.

Awarded first base on catcher's interference—Rose.

Double plays—May, Woodward and May 2; Helms and May; Bench and Helms; B. Robinson, Johnson and Powell; B. Robinson and Powell; Cuellar, Belanger and Powell.

Strikeouts—By Nolan 9 (Powell, Belanger 2, Johnson, Palmer, Blair 2, Hendricks, F. Robinson); by Carroll 11 (Palmer, B. Robinson 3, Hendricks, B. Robinson, Drabowsky, Johnson, Buford 2, Blair, Etchebarren); by McGlothlin 2 (F. Robinson, Cuellar); by Gullett 4 (Hall, F. Robinson, Palmer, Powell); by Cloninger 4 (McNally 2, Etchebarren, F. Robinson); by Granger 1 (Etchebarren); by Wilcox 2 (Cuellar, Blair); by Palmer 9 (Stewart, Bravo, Perez 2, Carbo 2, Helms, Gullett, Tolan); by Cuellar 5 (McGlothlin, Tolan, Merritt, Bench, May); by Drabowsky 4 (Perez); by McNally 5 (May, Cloninger, McRae, Perez, Bench); by Watt 3 (Carbo, Carroll, Chaney).

Bases on balls—Off Nolan 3 (Johnson, Buford, Powell); off Carroll 2 (Powell, Belanger); off McGlothlin 2 (Powell, Hendricks); off Gullett 4 (Johnson, Buford, Powell 2); off Cloninger 5 (Buford, Blair 2, Johnson, Etchebarren); off Granger 1 (Johnson); off Merritt 1 (Johnson); off Washburn 2 (Etchebarren, Rettenmund); off Palmer 9 (Tolan 2, Carbo 2, Perez 2, Rose, May, Helms); off Cuellar 2 (Bench, Bravo); off McNally 2 (Perez, May); off Watt 1 (Tolan).

Left on bases—Baltimore 31—5, 7, 3, 5, 11; Cincinnati 28—8, 4, 7, 6, 3.

Time of games—First game, 2:24; second game, 2:09; third game, 2:09; fourth game, 2:26; fifth game, 2:35.

Attendance—First game, 51,531; second game, 51,531; third game, 51,773; fourth game, 53,007; fifth game, 45,341. Total—253,183.

Umpires—Burkhart (NL), Flaherty (AL), Venzon (NL), Stewart (AL), Williams (NL) and Ashford (AL).

Official scorers—Bob Hunter, Los Angeles Herald-Examiner; Jim Elliot, Baltimore Sun, and Bob Hertzel, Cincinnati Enquirer.

WORLD SERIES RESULTS

Year—Winner   Loser
1903—Boston A. L., 5 games; Pittsburgh N. L., 3 games.
1904—No Series.
1905—New York N. L., 4 games; Philadelphia A. L., 1 game.
1906—Chicago A. L., 4 games; Chicago N. L., 2 games.
1907—Chicago N. L., 4 games; Detroit A. L., 0 game; 1 tie.
1908—Chicago N. L. 4 games; Detroit A. L., 1 game.
1909—Pittsburgh N. L., 4 games; Detroit A. L., 3 games.
1910—Philadelphia A. L., 4 games; Chicago N. L., 1 game.
1911—Philadelphia A. L., 4 games; New York N. L., 2 games.
1912—Boston A. L., 4 games; New York N. L., 3 games; 1 tie.
1913—Philadelphia A. L., 4 games; New York N. L., 1 game.
1914—Boston N. L., 4 games; Philadelphia A. L., 0 game.
1915—Boston A. L., 4 games; Philadelphia N. L., 1 game.
1916—Boston A. L., 4 games; Brooklyn N. L., 1 game.
1917—Chicago A. L., 4 games; New York N. L., 2 games.
1918—Boston A. L., 4 games; Chicago N. L., 2 games.
1919—Cincinnati N. L., 5 games; Chicago A. L., 3 games.
1920—Cleveland A. L., 5 games; Brooklyn N. L., 2 games.
1921—New York N. L., 5 games; New York A. L., 3 games.
1922—New York N. L., 4 games; New York A. L., 0 game; 1 tie.
1923—New York A. L., 4 games; New York N. L., 2 games.
1924—Washington A. L., 4 games; New York N. L., 3 games.
1925—Pittsburgh N. L., 4 games; Washington A. L., 3 games.
1926—St. Louis N. L., 4 games; New York A. L., 3 games.
1927—New York A. L., 4 games; Pittsburgh N. L., 0 game.
1928—New York A. L., 4 games; St. Louis N. L., 0 game.
1929—Philadelphia A. L., 4 games; Chicago N. L., 1 game.
1930—Philadelphia A. L., 4 games; St. Louis N. L., 2 games.
1931—St. Louis N. L., 4 games; Philadelphia A. L., 3 games.
1932—New York A. L., 4 games; Chicago N. L., 0 game.
1933—New York N. L., 4 games; Washington A. L., 1 game.
1934—St. Louis N. L., 4 games; Detroit A. L., 3 games.
1935—Detroit A. L. 4 games; Chicago N. L., 2 games.
1936—New York A. L., 4 games; New York N. L., 2 games.
1937—New York A. L., 4 games; New York N. L., 1 game.
1938—New York A. L., 4 games; Chicago N. L., 0 game.
1939—New York A. L., 4 games; Cincinnati N. L., 0 game.
1940—Cincinnati N. L., 4 games; Detroit A. L., 3 games.
1941—New York A. L., 4 games; Brooklyn N. L., 1 game.
1942—St. Louis N. L., 4 games; New York A. L., 1 game.
1943—New York A. L., 4 games; St. Louis N. L., 1 game
1944—St. Louis N. L., 4 games; St. Louis A. L., 2 games.
1945—Detroit A. L., 4 games; Chicago N. L., 3 games.
1946—St. Louis N. L., 4 games; Boston A. L., 3 games.
1947—New York A. L., 4 games; Brooklyn, N. L., 3 games.
1948—Cleveland A. L., 4 games; Boston N. L., 2 games.
1949—New York A. L., 4 games; Brooklyn N. L., 1 game.
1950—New York A. L., 4 games; Philadelphia N. L., 0 game.
1951—New York A. L., 4 games; New York N. L., 2 games.
1952—New York A. L., 4 games; Brooklyn N. L., 3 games.
1953—New York A. L., 4 games; Brooklyn N. L., 2 games.
1954—New York N. L., 4 games; Cleveland A. L., 0 game.
1955—Brooklyn N. L., 4 games; New York A. L., 3 games.
1956—New York A. L., 4 games; Brooklyn N. L., 3 games.
1957—Milwaukee N. L., 4 games; New York A. L., 3 games.
1958—New York A. L., 4 games; Milwaukee N. L., 3 games.
1959—Los Angeles N. L., 4 games; Chicago A. L., 2 games.
1960—Pittsburgh N. L., 4 games; New York A. L., 3 games.
1961—New York A. L., 4 games; Cincinnati N. L., 1 game.
1962—New York A. L., 4 games; San Francisco N. L., 3 games.
1963—Los Angeles N. L., 4 games; New York A. L., 0 game.
1964—St. Louis N. L., 4 games; New York A. L., 3 games.
1965—Los Angeles N. L., 4 games; Minnesota A. L., 3 games.
1966—Baltimore A. L., 4 games; Los Angeles N. L., 0 game.
1967—St. Louis N. L., 4 games; Boston A. L., 3 games.
1968—Detroit A. L., 4 games; St. Louis N. L., 3 games.
1969—New York N. L., 4 games, Baltimore A. L., 1 game.
1970—Baltimore A. L., 4 games; Cincinnati N. L., 1 game.

WORLD SERIES ATTENDANCE, MONEY

Year	Games	Attendance	Gate Receipts	Players' Tot.	W. Share	L. Share
1903	8	100,429	$ 50,000.00	$ 32,612.00	$ 1,182.00	$1,316.25
1905	5	91,723	68,436.81	27,394.20	1,142.00	832.22
1906	6	99,845	106,550.00	33,401.70	1,874.63	439.50
1907	5	78.068	101,728.50	54,933.39	2,142.85	1,945.96
1908	5	62,232	94,975.50	46,114.92	1,317.58	870.00
1909	7	145,295	188,302.50	66,924.90	1,825.22	1,274.76
1910	5	124,222	178,980.00	79,071.93	2,062.79	1,375.16
1911	6	179,851	342,364.50	127,910.61	3,654.58	2,436.39
1912	8	252,037	490,833.00	147,572.28	4,024.68	2,566.47
1913	5	151,000	325,980.00	135,164.16	3,246.36	2,164.22
1914	4	111,009	225,739.00	121,898.94	2,812.28	2,031.65
1915	5	143,351	320,361.50	144,899.55	3,780.25	2,520.17
1916	5	162,859	385,590.50	162,927.45	3,910.26	2,834.82
1917	6	186,654	425,878.00	152,888.58	3,669.32	2,442.21
1918	6	128,483	179,619.00	69,527.70	1,102.51	671.09
1919	8	236,928	722,414.00	260,349.66	5,207.07	3,254.36
1920	7	178,737	564,800.00	214,882.74	4,168.00	2,419.60
1921	8	269,976	900,233.00	292,522.23	5,265.00	3,510.00
1922	5	185,947	605,475.00	247,309.71	4,545.71	2,842.86
1923	6	301,430	1,063,815.00	368,783.04	6,143.49	4,112.88
1924	7	283,665	1,093,104.00	331,092.51	5,959.64	3,820.29
1925	7	282,848	1,182,854.00	339,644.19	5,332.72	3,734.60
1926	7	328,051	1,207,864.00	372,300.51	5,584.51	3,417.75
1927	4	201,705	783,217.00	399,440.67	5,782.24	3,985.47
1928	4	199,072	777,290.00	419,736.60	5,813.20	4,181.30
1929	5	190,490	859,494.00	388,086.66	5,620.57	3,782.01
1930	6	212,619	953,772.00	323,865.00	5,038.07	3,536.68
1931	7	231,567	1,030,723.00	320,303.46	4,467.59	3,023.09
1932	4	191,998	713,377.00	363,822.27	5,231.77	4,244.60
1933	5	163,076	679,365.00	284,665.68	4,256.72	3,019.86
1934	7	281,510	1,031,341.00	327,950.46	5,389.57	3,354.68
1935	6	286,672	1,073,794.00	397,360.24	6,544.76	4,198.53
1936	6	302,924	1,204,399.00	460,002.66	6,430.55	4,655.58
1937	5	238,142	985,994.00	459,629.35	6,471.11	4,489.96
1938	4	200,833	851,166.00	434,094.66	5,728.76	4,674.87
1939	4	183,849	745,329.09	431,117.84	5,541.89	4,193.39
1940	7	281,927	1,222,328.21	474,184.54	5,803.62	3,531.41
1941	5	235,773	1,007,762.00	474,184.54	5,943.31	4,829.40
1942	5	277,101	1,105,249.00	427,573.41	6,192.53	3,351.77
1943	5	277,312	1,105,784.00	488,005.74	6,139.46	4,321.96
1944	6	206,708	906,122.00	309,590.91	4,626.01	2,743.79
1945	7	333,457	1,492,454.00	475,579.04	6,443.34	3,930.22
1946	7	250,071	1,052,900.00	304,141.05	3,742.34	2,140.89
1947	7	389,763	1,781,348.92	493,674.82	5,830.03	4,081.19
1948	6	358,362	1,633,685.56	548,214.99	6,772.07	4,570.73
1949	5	236,716	1,129,627.88	490,855.84	5,626.74	4,272.74
1950	4	196,009	953,669.03	486,371.21	5,737.95	4,081.34
1951	6	341,977	1,633,457.47	560,562.37	6,446.09	4,951.03
1952	7	340,706	1,622,753.01	500,003.28	5,982.65	4,200.64
1953	6	307,350	1,779,269.44	691,341.61	8,280.68	6,178.42
1954	4	251,507	1,566,203.38	881,763.72	11,147.90	6,712.50
1955	7	362,310	2,337,515.34	737,853.59	9,768.21	5,598.58
1956	7	345,903	2,183,254.59	758,561.63	8,714.76	6,934.34
1957	7	394,712	2,475,978.94	709,027.55	8,924.36	5,606.06
1958	7	393,909	2,397,223.03	726,044.55	8,759.10	5,896.08
1959	6	420,784	2,628,809.44	893,301.40	11,231.18	7,257.17
1960	7	349,813	2,230,627.88	682,144.82	8,417.94	5,214.64
1961	5	223,247	1,480,059.95	645,928.28	7,389.13	5,356.37
1962	7	376,864	2,878,891.11	863,281.71	9,882.74	7,291.49
1963	4	247,279	1,995,189.09	1,017,546.43	12,794.00	7,874.32
1964	7	321,807	2,243,187.96	696,520.15	8,622.19	5,309.29
1965	7	364,326	2,975,041.60	885,612.21	10,297.43	6,634.36
1966	4	220,791	2,047,142.46	1,044,042.65	11,683.04	8,189.36
1967	7	304,085	2,350,607.10	705,878.44	8,314.81	5,115.23
1968	7	379,670	3,018,113.40	879,761.08	10,936.66	7,078.71
1969	5	272,378	2,857,782.78	1,142,200.93	13,259.65	9,349.58
1970	5	253,183	2,599,170.26	1,098,631.14	*18,338.18	*14,904.21
					*18,215.78	*13,687.59

*Total combined figures for World Series and League Championship Series.

NOTE—Losers' shares in 1903-05-07 and winners' in 1906-07 include club owners' slices which were added to their teams' player pools.

Two National Leaders—President Richard Nixon and Baseball Commissioner Bowie Kuhn.

1970 ALL-STAR GAME

Including

Review of '70 Game

Official Box Score

Official Play-By-Play

Results of Previous Games

Pete Rose crashes into catcher Ray Fosse to score winning run for N. L.

Pete's Run Wins All-Star Game for N. L.

By BEN HENKEY

For the first time since 1957, when folk in Cincinnati had stuffed the ballot boxes, selection of the starting lineups for the All-Star Game was placed back in the hands of the nation's baseball fans—with appropriate safeguards against what had transpired 13 years earlier.

The site of the 1970 game, coincidentally, was Cincinnati's new Riverfront Stadium, where 51,838 fans, including President Nixon, gathered on a sweltering July 14 evening to watch the fans' choices—plus 40 other athletes added to the rosters by Managers Earl Weaver of Baltimore (American) and Gil Hodges of New York (National)—do battle.

Just three outs away from a 4-1 triumph, the Americans fell, 5-4 in 12 innings, before a National League comeback capped, fittingly, by a game-winning blow delivered by the Cubs' Jim Hickman. The Chicago outfielder had been a late addition to the N. L. roster, and was to go on to win THE SPORTING NEWS' Comeback award.

Through eight innings, it appeared as if the American Leaguers would reverse the trend of the '60s, which had seen the Nationals go five games up in a series where the A. L. had won 12 of the first 16 games.

Excellent pitching by starter Jim Palmer of the Orioles, the Indians' Sam McDowell and Jim Perry of the Twins limited the N. L.'s premier batsmen to just three hits. Up to that point, N. L. hurlers were just as effective. Starter Tom Seaver of the Mets and the Reds' Jim Merritt worked five scoreless innings between them.

The N. L. half of the Perry brothers' All-Star pitching act, San Francisco's Gaylord Perry, was tapped for the game's first run in the top of the sixth. Cleveland's Ray Fosse singled, moved to second on a perfect sacrifice bunt by McDowell and rode home on another single by Boston's Carl Yastrzemski, who was to gather four hits—and Most Valuable Player honors—in the game.

The Americans increased their lead to 2-0 in the seventh on a one-out single by Baltimore's Brooks Robinson, a walk to Tony Oliva of the Twins, an infield hit by Oriole Dave Johnson and Fosse's sacrifice fly, all against Perry.

The Nationals threatened to have a big inning in their half but scored only once. They quickly loaded the bases with none out when Bud Harrelson of the Mets singled, the Padres' Clarence Gaston walked and Denis Menke of the Astros was hit by a pitched ball. The rally fizzled out when Giant slugger Willie McCovey hit into a double play, Harrelson scoring.

Bob Gibson took the mound for the N. L. in the eighth inning, and the American Leaguers hit the St. Louis righthander hard. Yastrzemski and Detroit's Willie Horton delivered singles and, with two out, Brooks Robinson made it a 4-1 contest when he tripled over Gaston's head in center.

A few of the fans in the predominantly-N. L. crowd began heading for the exits at this point, but Giants' catcher Dick Dietz, who'd entered the game in the seventh, sent them back to their seats with a leadoff home run over the 404-foot mark in center field off new A. L. pitcher Jim Hunter of the Athletics. Singles by Bud Harrelson and Houston's Joe Morgan, the latter with one out, prompted Weaver to lift Hunter in favor of the Yankees' Fritz Peterson.

Willie McCovey greeted the lefthanded Peterson with an RBI single. Suddenly, it was a one-run ball game and Morgan, representing the tying run for the Nationals, stood on third base.

On came another Yankee, Mel Stottlemyre, to face Pittsburgh's Roberto Clemente. The Pirate outfielder lined hard to Kansas City's Amos Otis in right-center, and Morgan scored the tying run easily after the catch.

The National League, which had won all of the five All-Star games which had gone into extra innings, ran true to form again. American League threats in the 10th, 11th and 12th innings against reliever Claude Osteen of the Dodgers produced no runs, and it looked like extended overtime in the bottom of the 12th after the first two N. L. hitters were retired by the seventh hurler for the Americans, California's Clyde Wright.

But the Reds' Pete Rose, twice a strikeout victim, kept things alive with a single to center. Billy Grabarkewitz of the Dodgers lined a hit to left, Rose stopping at second.

Hickman, who'd gone to left field for the N. L. in the fifth and then moved to first base in the 10th, singled to center. Rose headed for the plate and beat Otis' strong throw to score the winning run, bowling over catcher Fosse in a collision which left both players bruised and sore for a week—but saddled the American League with its eighth straight All-Star Game defeat, and its 12th setback in the 14 games played since 1960.

Americans	AB.	R.	H.	RBI.	PO.	A.
Aparicio (White Sox), ss	6	0	0	0	1	4
Yastrzemski						
(Red Sox), cf-1b	6	1	4	1	8	0
F. Robinson						
(Orioles), rf-lf	3	0	0	0	1	0
Horton (Tigers), lf	2	1	2	0	1	0
Powell (Orioles), 1b	3	0	0	0	5	0
Otis (Royals), cf	3	0	0	0	2	0
Killebrew (Twins), 3b	2	0	1	0	0	0
bHarper (Brewers)	0	0	0	0	0	0
B. Robinson (Orioles), 3b	3	1	2	2	1	1
Howard (Senators), lf	2	0	0	0	0	0
Oliva (Twins), rf	2	0	1	0	0	0
D. Johnson (Orioles), 2b	5	0	1	0	5	1
Wright (Angels), p	0	0	0	0	0	0
Freehan (Tigers), c	1	0	0	0	4	0
Fosse (Indians), c	2	1	1	1	7	0
Palmer (Orioles), p	1	0	0	0	0	0
McDowell (Indians), p	0	0	0	0	0	0
dA. Johnson (Angels)	1	0	0	0	0	0
J. Perry (Twins), p	0	0	0	0	0	0
fFregosi (Angels)	1	0	0	0	0	0
Hunter (Athletics), p	0	0	0	0	0	0
Peterson (Yankees), p	0	0	0	0	0	0
Stottlemyre (Yankees), p	0	0	0	0	0	0
Alomar (Angels), 2b	1	0	0	0	0	2
Totals	**44**	**4**	**12**	**4**	**†35**	**11**

Nationals	AB.	R.	H.	RBI.	PO.	A.
Mays (Giants), cf	3	0	0	0	3	0
G. Perry (Giants), p	0	0	0	0	0	2
eMcCovey (Giants), 1b	2	0	1	1	0	0
gOsteen (Dodgers), p	0	0	0	0	1	0
iTorre (Cardinals)	1	0	0	0	0	0
Allen (Cardinals), 1b	3	0	0	0	4	0
Gibson (Cardinals), p	0	0	0	0	0	0
hClemente (Pirates), rf	1	0	0	1	2	0
Aaron (Braves), rf	2	0	0	0	1	0
Rose (Reds), rf-lf	3	1	1	0	3	0
Perez (Reds), 3b	2	0	0	0	1	1
Grabarkewitz						
(Dodgers), 3b	3	0	1	0	0	1
Carty (Braves), lf	2	0	0	0	1	0
Hickman (Cubs), lf-1b	4	0	1	1	6	1
Bench (Reds), c	3	0	0	0	5	1
Dietz (Giants), c	2	1	1	1	2	0
Kessinger (Cubs), ss	2	0	2	0	0	0
Harrelson (Mets), ss	3	2	2	0	0	4
Beckert (Cubs), 2b	2	0	0	0	2	1
Gaston (Padres), cf	2	0	0	0	2	0
Seaver (Mets), p	0	0	0	0	0	0
aStaub (Expos)	1	0	0	0	0	0
Merritt (Reds), p	0	0	0	0	0	0
cMenke (Astros), 2b	0	0	0	0	2	1
Morgan (Astros), 2b	2	1	1	0	1	2
Totals	**43**	**5**	**10**	**4**	**36**	**14**

Americans	0	0	0	0	0	1 2 0 0 0 0—4	
Nationals	0	0	0	0	0	1 0 3 0 0 1—5	

†Two out when winning run scored.

Americans	IP.	H.	R.	ER.	SO.	BB.
Palmer (Orioles)	3	1	0	0	3	1
McDowell (Indians)	3	1	0	0	3	3
J. Perry (Twins)	2	1	1	1	3	1
Hunter (Athletics)	⅓	3	3	3	0	0
Peterson (Yankees)	0*	1	0	0	0	0
Stottlemyre (Yankees)	1⅔	0	0	0	2	0
Wright (Angels)	1⅔	3	1	1	0	0

Nationals	IP.	H.	R.	ER.	SO.	BB.
Seaver (Mets)	3	1	0	0	4	0
Merritt (Reds)	2	1	0	0	1	0
G. Perry (Giants)	2	4	2	2	0	1
Gibson (Cardinals)	2	3	2	2	2	1
Osteen (Dodgers)	3	3	0	0	0	1

*Pitched to one batter in ninth.

Winning pitcher—Osteen. Losing pitcher—Wright.

aFlied out for Seaver in third. bRan for Killebrew in fifth. cWalked for Merritt in fifth. dHit into force play for McDowell in seventh. eGrounded into double play for G. Perry in seventh. fFlied out for J. Perry in ninth. gRan for McCovey in ninth. hHit sacrifice fly for Gibson in ninth. iGrounded out for Osteen in twelfth. Errors—None. Double plays—Aparicio and Yastrzemski; Harrelson, Morgan and Hickman. Left on bases—Americans 9, Nationals 10. Two-base hits—Oliva,

Yastrzemski. Three-base hit—B. Robinson. Home run—Dietz. Sacrifice hit—McDowell. Sacrifice flies—Fosse, Clemente. Caught stealing—Harper. Struck out—By Palmer 3 (Mays, Bench, Perez), by McDowell 3 (Perez, Bench 2), by J. Perry 3 (Allen, Rose, Hickman), by Stottlemyre 2 (Rose, Hickman), by Seaver 4 (Aparicio, F. Robinson, Killebrew, Howard), by Merritt 1 (F. Robinson), by Gibson 2 (D. Johnson, Aparicio). Bases on balls—Off Palmer 1 (Carty), off McDowell 3 (Menke, Allen, Rose), off J. Perry 1 (Gaston), off G. Perry 1 (Oliva), off Gibson 1 (Fosse), off Osteen 1 (Horton). Hit by pitcher—By J. Perry (Menke). Umpires—Barlick (NL) plate, Rice (AL) first base, Secory (NL) second base, Haller (AL) third base, Dezelan (NL) left field, Goetz (AL) right field. Official scorers—Bob Hunter, Los Angeles Herald Examiner; Earl Lawson, Cincinnati Post and Times-Star; Si Burick, Dayton News. Time of game—3:19. Attendance—51,838.

FIRST INNING

Americans—Aparicio struck out. Yastrzemski grounded a single to center. F. Robinson fanned. Powell popped to Perez. No runs, one hit, no errors, one left.

Nationals—Mays struck out. Allen flied deep to F. Robinson. Aaron grounded to Aparicio. No runs, no hits, no errors, none left.

SECOND INNING

Americans—Killebrew struck out. Howard also fanned. D. Johnson flied to Aaron. No runs, no hits, no errors, none left.

Nationals—Perez struck out. Carty walked on four pitches. Bench fanned. Kessinger singled to center, Carty stopping at second. Beckert bounced to D. Johnson. No runs, one hit, no errors, two left.

THIRD INNING

Americans—Freehan lined to Mays. Palmer bunted down the third base line but Perez made a barehand pickup and threw to Allen for the out. Aparicio grounded to Beckert. No runs, no hits, no errors, none left.

Nationals—Staub batted for Seaver and flied to Yastrzemski in short center. Mays fouled to Powell. Allen lined to D. Johnson. No runs, no hits, no errors, none left.

FOURTH INNING

Americans—Merritt was the new pitcher for the Nationals. Yastrzemski lined deep to Mays. F. Robinson was called out on strikes. Powell flied to Mays in deep left-center. No runs, no hits, no errors, none left.

Nationals—McDowell took the mound for the Americans. Aaron tapped a roller down the third base line and McDowell threw him out on a close play. Perez struck out. Carty bounced to McDowell. No runs, no hits, no errors, none left.

FIFTH INNING

Americans—Rose went to right field and Hickman to left field for the Nationals. Killebrew grounded a single to left. Harper ran for Killebrew. Howard flied to Hickman in short left. D. Johnson fouled to Beckert behind first base. Harper was out attempting to steal, Bench to Beckert. No runs, one hit, no errors, none left.

Nationals—Fosse was the new catcher, B. Robinson went to third base and Oliva went to right field with F. Robinson moving to left field and Howard leaving the game for the Americans. Bench struck out. Kessinger lined a single to center. Beckert's ground ball was deflected by McDowell to D. Johnson who stepped on second, forcing Kessinger. Menke batted for Merritt and walked. Mays fouled to B. Robinson. No runs, one hit, no errors, two left.

SIXTH INNING

Americans—Menke remained in the game at second base, Gaston went to center field and G. Perry was the new pitcher for the Nationals. Fosse lined a single to right. McDowell sacrificed, G. Perry to Menke, who covered first. Aparicio flied to Rose. Yastrzemski looped a single to right-center scoring Fosse. F. Robinson grounded to Menke. One run, two hits, no errors, one left.

Nationals—Horton replaced F. Robinson in left field for the Americans. Allen walked. Rose also walked. Perez popped to D. Johnson. Hickman also popped to D. Johnson. Bench struck out. No runs, no hits, no errors, two left.

SEVENTH INNING

Americans—Grabarkewitz went to third base, Harrelson to shortstop and Dietz behind the plate for the Nationals. Powell bounced to G. Perry. B. Robinson singled to center. Oliva walked. D. Johnson smashed a ground ball

to Harrelson who made the stop behind second but could not make a play and it went for a hit, loading the bases. Fosse lined deep to Gaston, B. Robinson scoring and Oliva advancing to third after the catch. A. Johnson batted for McDowell and forced D. Johnson, Harrelson to Menke. One run, two hits, no errors, two left.

Nationals—Yastrzemski moved to first base, Otis went to center field and J. Perry came in to pitch for the Americans. Harrelson singled to right. Gaston walked. Menke was hit by a pitched ball, filling the bases. McCovey batted for G. Perry and bounced to Aparicio who fielded the ball in front of second base, tagged Menke and threw to first for the double play, Harrelson scoring and Gaston going to third. Allen was called out on strikes. One run, one hit, no errors, one left.

EIGHTH INNING

Americans—McCovey remained in the game at first base, Morgan went to second base and Gibson took the mound for the Nationals. Aparicio grounded to Morgan. Yastrzemski singled to right. Horton singled to center, Yastrzemski stopping at second. Otis flied to Rose, Yastrzemski going to third after the catch. B. Robinson tripled over Gaston's head to the center field wall, Yastrzemski and Horton scoring. Oliva flied to Rose. Two runs, three hits, no errors, one left.

Nationals—Rose fanned. Grabarkewitz flied to Horton in short left. Hickman struck out. No runs, no hits, no errors, none left.

NINTH INNING

Americans—D. Johnson struck out. Fosse walked. Fregosi batted for J. Perry and flied deep to Hickman. Aparicio struck out. No runs, no hits, no errors, one left.

Nationals—Hunter was the new pitcher for the Americans. Dietz homered over the center field fence. Harrelson singled to left. Gaston popped to Yastrzemski. Morgan singled to right, Harrelson moving to second. Peterson replaced Hunter on the mound for the Americans. McCovey grounded a single to center, Harrelson scoring and Morgan racing to third. Osteen ran for McCovey and Clemente batted for Gibson. Stottlemyre replaced Peterson on the mound for the Americans. Clemente lined to Otis in right-center, Morgan scoring after the catch. Rose struck out. Three runs, four hits, no errors, one left.

TENTH INNING

Americans—Clemente remained in the game in right field, Rose moved to left field, Hickman moved to first base and Osteen remained in the game as the new pitcher for the Nationals. Yastrzemski grounded out, Hickman to Osteen who covered first. Horton lined a drive off the right field fence but was held to a single when Clemente played the carom perfectly and threw quickly to second base. Otis grounded into a double play, Harrelson to Morgan to Hickman. No runs, one hit, no errors, none left.

Nationals—Grabarkewitz grounded to Aparicio. Hickman struck out. Dietz lined to D. Johnson. No runs, no hits, no errors, none left.

ELEVENTH INNING

Americans—B. Robinson bounced to Harrelson. Oliva doubled into the right field corner. D. Johnson grounded to Grabarkewitz, Oliva holding second. Fosse grounded to Harrelson. No runs, one hit, no errors, one left.

Nationals—Alomar went to second base and Wright was the new pitcher for the Americans. Harrelson flied to Otis. Gaston grounded to Alomar. Morgan grounded to Aparicio. No runs, no hits, no errors, none left.

TWELFTH INNING

Americans—Alomar flied to Clemente. Aparicio lined to Gaston. Yastrzemski was credited with a double when Gaston missed a shoestring catch of his line drive. Horton was purposely passed. Otis lined to Clemente. No runs, one hit, no errors, two left.

Nationals—Torre batted for Osteen and grounded to B. Robinson whose throw was high but Yastrzemski made a leaping catch and tagged Torre for the out. Clemente grounded to Alomar. Rose singled to center. Grabarkewitz singled to left, Rose stopping at second. Hickman lined a single to center, Rose scoring the winning run. One run, three hits, no errors, two left.

RESULTS OF PREVIOUS GAMES

1933—At Comiskey Park, Chicago, July 6. Americans 4, Nationals 2. Managers—Connie Mack, John McGraw. Winning pitcher—Lefty Gomez. Losing pitcher—Bill Hallahan. Attendance—47,595.

1934—At Polo Grounds, New York, July 10. Americans 9, Nationals 7. Managers—Joe Cronin, Bill Terry. Winning pitcher—Mel Harder. Losing pitcher—Van Mungo. Attendance—48,363.

1935—At Municipal Stadium, Cleveland, July 8. Americans 4, Nationals 1. Managers—Mickey Cochrane, Frankie Frisch. Winning pitcher—Lefty Gomez. Losing pitcher—Bill Walker. Attendance—69,831.

1936—At Braves Field, Boston, July 7. Nationals 4, Americans 3. Managers—Charlie Grimm, Joe McCarthy. Winning pitcher—Dizzy Dean. Losing pitcher—Lefty Grove. Attendance—25,556.

1937—At Griffith Stadium, Washington, July 7. Americans 8, Nationals 3. Managers—Joe McCarthy, Bill Terry. Winning pitcher—Lefty Gomez. Losing pitcher—Dizzy Dean. Attendance—31,391.

1938—At Crosley Field, Cincinnati, July 6. Nationals 4, Americans 1. Managers—Bill Terry, Joe McCarthy. Winning pitcher—Johnny Vander Meer. Losing pitcher—Lefty Gomez. Attendance—27,067.

1939—At Yankee Stadium, New York, July 11. Americans 3, Nationals 1. Managers—Joe McCarthy, Gabby Hartnett. Winning pitcher—Tommy Bridges. Losing pitcher—Bill Lee. Attendance—62,892.

1940—At Sportsman's Park, St. Louis, July 9. Nationals 4, Americans 0. Managers—Bill McKechnie, Joe Cronin. Winning pitcher—Paul Derringer. Losing pitcher—Red Ruffing. Attendance—32,373.

1941—At Briggs Stadium, Detroit, July 8. Americans 7, Nationals 5. Managers—Del Baker, Bill McKechnie. Winning pitcher—Ed Smith. Losing pitcher—Claude Passeau. Attendance—54,674.

1942—At Polo Grounds, New York, July 6. Americans 3, Nationals 1. Managers—Joe Cronin, Leo Durocher. Winning pitcher—Spud Chandler. Losing pitcher—Mort Cooper. Attendance—34,178.

1943—At Shibe Park, Philadelphia, July 13 (night game). Americans 5, Nationals 3. Managers—Joe McCarthy, Billy Southworth. Winning pitcher—Dutch Leonard. Losing pitcher—Mort Cooper. Attendance—31,938.

1944—At Forbes Field, Pittsburgh, July 11 (night game). Nationals 7, Americans 1. Managers—Billy Southworth, Joe McCarthy. Winning pitcher—Ken Raffensberger. Losing pitcher—Tex Hughson. Attendance—29,589.

1945—No game played.

1946—At Fenway Park, Boston, July 9. Americans 12, Nationals 0. Managers—Steve O'Neill, Charlie Grimm. Winning pitcher—Bob Feller. Losing pitcher—Claude Passeau. Attendance—34,906.

1947—At Wrigley Field, Chicago, July 8. Americans 2, Nationals 1. Managers—Joe Cronin, Eddie Dyer. Winning pitcher—Frank Shea. Losing pitcher—Johnny Sain. Attendance—41,123.

1948—At Sportsman's Park, St. Louis, July 13. Americans 5, Nationals 2. Managers—Bucky Harris, Leo Durocher. Winning pitcher—Vic Raschi. Losing pitcher—Johnny Schmitz. Attendance—34,009.

1949—At Ebbets Field, Brooklyn, July 12. Americans 11, Nationals 7. Managers—Lou Boudreau, Billy Southworth. Winning pitcher—Virgil Trucks. Losing pitcher—Don Newcombe. Attendance—32,577.

1950—At Comiskey Park, Chicago, July 11. Nationals 4, Americans 3 (14 innings). Managers—Burt Shotton, Casey Stengel. Winning pitcher—Ewell Blackwell. Losing pitcher—Ted Gray. Attendance—46,127.

1951—At Briggs Stadium, Detroit, July 10. Nationals 8, Americans 3. Managers—Eddie Sawyer, Casey Stengel. Winning pitcher—Sal Maglie. Losing pitcher—Ed Lopat. Attendance—52,075.

1952—At Shibe Park, Philadelphia, July 8. Nationals 3, Americans 2 (five innings—rain). Managers—Leo Durocher, Casey Stengel. Winning pitcher—Bob Rush. Losing pitcher—Bob Lemon. Attendance—32,785.

1953—At Crosley Field, Cincinnati, July 14. Nationals 5, Americans 1. Managers—Chuck Dressen, Casey Stengel. Winning pitcher—Warren Spahn. Losing pitcher—Allie Reynolds. Attendance—30,846.

1954—At Municipal Stadium, Cleveland, July 13. Americans 11, Nationals 9. Managers—Casey Stengel, Walter Alston. Winning pitcher—Dean Stone. Losing pitcher—Gene Conley. Attendance—68,751.

1955—At Milwaukee County Stadium, Milwaukee, July 12. Nationals 6, Americans 5 (12 innings). Managers—Leo Durocher, Al Lopez. Winning pitcher—Gene Conley. Losing pitcher—Frank Sullivan. Attendance—45,643.

1956—At Griffith Stadium, Washington, July 10. Nationals 7, Americans 3. Managers—Walter Alston, Casey Stengel. Winning pitcher—Bob Friend. Losing pitcher—Billy Pierce. Attendance—28,843.

1957—At Busch Stadium, St. Louis, July 9. Americans 6, Nationals 5. Managers—Casey Stengel, Walter Alston. Winning pitcher—Jim Bunning. Losing pitcher—Curt Simmons. Attendance—30,693.

1958—At Memorial Stadium, Baltimore, July 8. Americans 4, Nationals 3. Managers—Casey Stengel, Fred Haney. Winning pitcher—Early Wynn. Losing pitcher—Bob Friend. Attendance—48,829.

1959 (first game)—At Forbes Field, Pittsburgh, July 7. Nationals 5, Americans 4. Managers—Fred Haney, Casey Stengel. Winning pitcher—Johnny Antonelli. Losing pitcher—Whitey Ford. Attendance—35,277.

1959 (second game)—At Memorial Coliseum, Los Angeles, August 3. Americans 5, Nationals 3. Managers—Casey Stengel, Fred Haney. Winning pitcher—Jerry Walker. Losing pitcher—Don Drysdale. Attendance—55,105.

1960 (first game)—At Municipal Stadium, Kansas City, July 11. Nationals 5, Americans 3. Managers—Walter Alston, Al Lopez. Winning pitcher—Bob Friend. Losing pitcher—Bill Monbouquette. Attendance—30,619.

1960 (second game)—At Yankee Stadium, New York, July 13. Nationals 6, Americans 0. Managers—Walter Alston, Al Lopez. Winning pitcher—Vern Law. Losing pitcher—Whitey Ford. Attendance—38,362.

1961 (first game)—At Candlestick Park, San Francisco, July 11. Nationals 5, Americans 4 (10 innings). Managers—Danny Murtaugh, Paul Richards. Winning pitcher—Stu Miller. Losing pitcher—Hoyt Wilhelm. Attendance—44,115.

1961 (second game)—At Fenway Park, Boston, July 31. Americans 1, Nationals 1 (nine-inning tie, stopped by rain). Managers—Paul Richards, Danny Murtaugh. Attendance—31,851.

1962 (first game)—At District of Columbia Stadium, Washington, July 10. Nationals 3, Americans 1. Managers—Fred Hutchinson, Ralph Houk. Winning pitcher—Juan Marichal. Losing pitcher—Camilo Pascual. Attendance—45,480.

1962 (second game)—At Wrigley Field, Chicago, July 30. Americans 9, Nationals 4. Managers—Ralph Houk, Fred Hutchinson. Winning pitcher—Ray Herbert. Losing pitcher—Art Mahaffey. Attendance—38,359.

1963—At Municipal Stadium, Cleveland, July 9. Nationals 5, Americans 3. Managers—Alvin Dark, Ralph Houk. Winning pitcher—Larry Jackson. Losing pitcher—Jim Bunning. Attendance—44,160.

1964—At Shea Stadium, New York, July 7. Nationals 7, Americans 4. Managers—Walter Alston, Al Lopez. Winning pitcher—Juan Marichal. Losing pitcher—Dick Radatz. Attendance—50,850.

1965—At Metropolitan Stadium, Bloomington (Minnesota), July 13. Nationals 6, Americans 5. Managers—Gene Mauch, Al Lopez. Winning pitcher—Sandy Koufax. Losing pitcher—Sam McDowell. Attendance—46,706.

1966—At Busch Memorial Stadium, St. Louis, July 12. Nationals 2, Americans 1 (10 innngs). Managers—Walter Alston, Sam Mele. Winning pitcher—Gaylord Perry. Losing pitcher—Pete Richert. Attendance—49,936.

1967—At Anaheim Stadium, Anaheim (California), July 11. Nationals 2, Americans 1 (15 innings). Managers—Walter Alston, Hank Bauer. Winning pitcher—Don Drysdale. Losing pitcher—Jim Hunter. Attendance—46,309.

1968—At Astrodome, Houston, July 9. Nationals 1, Americans 0. Managers—Red Schoendienst, Dick Williams. Winning pitcher—Don Drysdale. Losing pitcher—Luis Tiant. Attendance—48,321.

1969—At Robert F. Kennedy Memorial Stadium, Washington, July 23, Nationals 9, Americans 3. Managers—Red Schoendienst, Mayo Smith. Winning pitcher—Steve Carlton. Losing pitcher—Mel Stottlemyre. Attendance—45,259.

JOHNNY BENCH
• CINCINNATI REDS •
PLAYER OF THE YEAR

HARRY DALTON
• BALTIMORE ORIOLES •
MAJOR LEAGUE EXECUTIVE

DANNY MURTAUGH
• PITTSBURGH PIRATES •
MAJOR LEAGUE MANAGER

TOM LASORDA
• SPOKANE •
MINOR LEAGUE MANAGER

DICK KING
• WICHITA •
MINOR LEAGUE EXECUTIVE
IN CLASS AAA

DON BAYLOR
• ROCHESTER •
MINOR LEAGUE PLAYER
OF THE YEAR

CARL SAWATSKI
• ARKANSAS •
MINOR LEAGUE EXECUTIVE
IN CLASS AA

NO. 1
MEN
OF
1970

Selected by

The Sporting News

as

Outstanding for Year

BOB WILLIAMS
• BAKERSFIELD •
MINOR LEAGUE EXECUTIVE
IN CLASS A

Hank Aaron receives first Commissioner's Award from Bowie Kuhn as leading vote-getter in All-Star poll.

REVIEW OF 1970

Including

No. 1 Men of 1970

Summation of Year's Activities

Pictures of Key People and Events

MVP Tables, All-Star Teams

Major League Leaders in Performance
Tables

Homers by Parks

Commissioner Bowie Kuhn announces Denny McLain's six-month sabbatical.

Players, Umpires, Books, Law Suits . . .

By JEROME HOLTZMAN

Attendance and litigation were up in 1970. The 24 major league clubs drew a total of 28 million paid admissions, an all-time record. The new Seattle franchise, after much legal skirmishing, was transferred to Milwaukee, which had been abandoned by the Braves and without baseball since 1965. Two new major league parks were opened, Riverfront Stadium in Cincinnati and Three Rivers Stadium in Pittsburgh, and the tenants of both responded by winning divisional championships.

Pitcher Denny McLain was suspended three times, twice by Commissioner Bowie Kuhn, believed to be a record for the most suspensions, one season, one player. The umpires staged a one-day strike, another record. Jim Bouton, a veteran pitcher, wrote a book titled "Ball Four," which drew the censure of Commissioner Kuhn and many of the players. Immediately, the book soared to record sales. Veteran outfielder Curt Flood, after losing his multi-million dollar suit vs. baseball, continued challenging the reserve clause by appealing to a higher court and, in November, abruptly ended his baseball sabbatical by signing a 1971 contract with the Washington Senators, who had acquired negotiation rights to him—a surprising and dizzying turn of events that somehow seemed appropriate. It was that kind of year.

McLain, the super pitcher of the Detroit Tigers and a two-time winner of the Cy Young Award, was the year's biggest baseball newsmaker. Seldom, if ever, did baseball have a "bad boy" to match him. He was suspended the first time for allegedly consorting with gamblers and participating in a 1967 Flint (Mich.) bookmaking operation. This suspension was for half the season and was lifted on July 1 when he made a dramatic return that attracted Detroit's biggest home crowd in nine years, plus 71 sportswriters who came to cover the event. Later, McLain was suspended by the Detroit club for dousing two baseball writers with a bucket of ice water. McLain drew suspension No. 3 for carrying a gun. On the eve of the World Series, McLain was in the news again: The Tigers traded him to the Washington Senators in an eight-player deal.

Magazine Blows Whistle on McLain's Gambling

McLain's season of woe began when Sports Illustrated Magazine, in a copyrighted story, revealed he had been ". . . a partner in a bookmaking operation during the 1967 season and had become inextricably involved with mobsters." The story ran about 2,500 words and was featured in the issue dated February 23 which hit the newsstands February 17. The magazine had McLain's picture on the cover and titled its expose—"Baseball's Big Scandal—Denny McLain and the Mob."

Described as "poor, dumb Denny McLain," the story told how he allegedly became involved in a Flint (Mich.) gambling operation. McLain, reportedly, put up money to back Jiggs Gazell, who in turn was "sponsored by members of a Syrian mob with Cosa Nostra connections." Said the magazine: "This sordid and tangled tale has been pieced together from information supplied by several law enforcement agencies and by Lawrence A. Burns, a one-time Detroit Mafia and Teamster lawyer."

According to the story, which was never verified but nonetheless pro-

Denny McLain, caught in life's revolving door, enters building where he received verdict considered too light for his capers.

vided the thrust of the investigation, McLain and one of his friends, Edwin K. Schober, then an executive with a soft-drink company, were persuaded to put up money to back Gazell, but were treated as "chumps" by their hoodlum partners. They were billed by the handbook when the bookies lost, but were not informed when the handbook had a winner.

"Heavy pressure was put on both McLain and his executive friend in August and September of 1967 to make good on a $46,600 loss suffered when a Battle Creek (Mich.) plunger scored heavily on an allowance race at the Detroit Race Course." A year later, the plunger, identified as Ed Voshen, was killed in an auto accident when his car crashed into a tree on "a lonely stretch" of highway. Prior to his death, Voshen had collected $1,000 of the $46,600 allegedly owed him.

It was further stated that McLain and Schober did raise some of the money to pay Voshen, but the magazine did not mention a specific amount, or offer a guess. Also, according to Sports Illustrated, Voshen had gone ". . . from mobster to mobster, seeking influence to enable him to collect his money and finally was granted an audience with Tony Giacalone," the so-called enforcer of the Detroit underworld.

McLain was taken before Giacalone. In this confrontation, the magazine intimated that Giacalone brought his heel down on McLain's foot, dislocating several of McLain's toes, an injury which forced him to miss two or three pitching starts. Sports Illustrated admitted somewhat tacitly it had no proof that this actually happened, but offered this as one of the five versions of how McLain injured his toes. McLain had given two previous explanations: (1) he stubbed his toes after falling asleep while watching television and (2) he angrily kicked the lockers in the clubhouse.

Kuhn, Denny Say Charges 80 Percent False

McLain and Commissioner Kuhn, when confronted with the Sports Illustrated expose, denied that the story was true. They both were quoted, in separate interviews, insisting that 80 percent of the story was false. Unfortunately, neither McLain nor the commissioner ever was to tell the public which 20 percent they regarded as true.

Precisely four days before the Sports Illustrated story was circulated, Commissioner Kuhn ordered McLain to his New York office. The commissioner made this move on February 13, possibly after he had been informed that the story was in type and about to break. Whatever the reason, it was the first indication that McLain was in trouble. After this initial meeting with McLain, the commissioner issued this statement to the press:

"This office has been reviewing certain off-the-field activities of Denny McLain which occurred in 1967. I had a conference today with Mr. McLain and his attorney and we discussed the matter fully. They are giving this office their cooperation and have assured me of their continuing willingness to do so.

"There is no indication that these activities in any way involved the playing or the outcome of baseball games. When all the pertinent facts and circumstances have been determined and evaluated, I will have a further statement to make."

McLain was back in Detroit on February 18, testifying for 45 minutes before a special United States Grand Jury investigating an alleged nationwide sports betting ring. James Brickley, U. S. attorney for Eastern Michigan, said McLain appeared as a witness voluntarily and was "very cooperative." Brickley also emphasized that McLain had not been charged ". . . and is free to go as he pleases." Told that the Tigers were scheduled to open spring training the next day, Brickley said: "I know of no reason for him (McLain) not to show up."

Detroit Hurler Suspended Indefinitely

But the next day, in mid-afternoon on February 19, Commissioner Kuhn announced from his New York office that he was suspending McLain from baseball for an indefinite period. Immediately prior to this announcement, Kuhn had held another meeting with McLain, who had flown in from Detroit. This session lasted 5½ hours. Also in attendance were McLain's attorney, William Aiken of Detroit; Henry Fitzgibbon,

As news broke about Denny McLain's involvement in bookmaking operations in the Detroit area, the Tiger hurler, besieged by network airmen, prophetically has baseball scene in background—not future.

baseball's new security chief, and Charles Segar, baseball's secretary-treasurer. At the conclusion of this meeting, Kuhn gave McLain the following letter:

"This is to advise you that you are herewith suspended from all Organized Baseball activities pending the completion of the recently announced review which this office is conducting regarding certain of your personal activities. You and I have discussed today the reasons which required this action."

Denny Nailed by Revelations to Kuhn

The commissioner then appeared before the press and said:

"I had further conferences today with Denny McLain and his attorneys on the general subject matter covered by our conference of last Friday (February 13). I have decided on the basis of facts developed at these conferences that McLain's involvement in 1967 bookmaking activities and his associations at that time leave me no alternative but to suspend him from all Organized Baseball activities pending the completion of my review of his situation."

Commissioner Kuhn also made it clear "that the action taken today is based substantially on certain admissions made candidly to me by Mr.

McLain and not on allegations contained in a recent magazine article, many of which I believe to be unfounded. I cannot at this time indicate when that review might be completed."

In Lakeland, Fla., where the Tigers were opening their spring training camp, Detroit Manager Mayo Smith was asked for his comment. Replied Smith: "Sure, I think we can win the pennant without McLain, but it will be tougher without him. Anyone would recognize that."

McLain immediately went to Lakeland, where he has a home, and began expressing remorse. "All I can say," he told Jerry Green of the Detroit News, "is I'm very sorry I've embarrassed baseball to a certain extent. I'm asking for the benefit of the doubt. I apologize to the commissioner. I'm sorry anything like this had to happen."

Commissioner Kuhn searches for words which would not reveal facts he was determined to withhold at the time of the gambling mess.

McLain indicated he felt he would be reinstated within a month and said, "My immediate problem is getting a job. I'm in financial trouble. What am I going to do for money? I've got a family to take care of. Contrary to belief, 99 percent of my problems stem from business. I made a lot of bad investments."

Commissioner Refuses to Reveal Facts

Week after week passed with still no further announcement from the commissioner's office. Red Smith of New York, who is nationally syndicated and one of the nation's most influential sports columnists, warned: "The longer Bowie Kuhn puts off letting the public in on the facts about Denny McLain, the more baseball and everybody concerned will suffer. . . . The commissioner neither denies nor confirms the implications. He does not maintain silence. He says too little, which is worse. He is purposely vague. He is bound by his duty to baseball to make the fullest possible disclosure of facts at the earliest possible moment."

Marvin Miller, executive director of the Major League Baseball Players Association, said that McLain, in effect, had been judged guilty before all the facts were in. Miller declared that the commissioner should have given McLain a statement of charges. Said Miller: "McLain is the victim of self-incrimination. Bowie called him into his office for an informal dis-

Marvin Miller, director of Players Association, said Kuhn acted like "forgiving Dutch uncle" to McLain, then lowered boom when Denny spilled.

cussion and said, in the manner of a forgiving Dutch uncle, 'Tell me all about it, Denny.' Then Denny speaks and discovers he has incriminated himself."

The commissioner, in the meantime, began touring the Florida and Arizona spring training camps. Almost wherever he went, he held press conferences, but warned the writers in advance that he couldn't discuss the McLain case. Columnist Smith, attending one such "weekly half hour of silence," observed: "Triple ax murders have been solved in less time than has been consumed getting answers to simple questions. Kuhn is determined not to make a final ruling until he has all the facts. This is wise, but the weeks go by and delay invites public suspicion."

Hurler Works Out at Florida Home

Expecting to be eligible for the Tigers' American League opener, Mc-Lain engaged in mild workouts at his Lakeland home and also played golf. Under the terms of his suspension, he was not allowed to go to the ball park. On March 14, catcher Jim Price, the Tigers' player representative, invited him to the club's annual spring meeting with Marvin Miller of the Players Association. The meeting was held at a motel. McLain was delighted with the invitation, but did not participate in the discussion. "Denny was very quiet," Price said later. "But it did give him a chance to see all the guys."

The newspapers seemed to be carrying daily bulletins on McLain's tangled finances. Though he had been recently earning at the rate of $200,000 a year, McLain's total debts, according to a bankruptcy petition later filed in Detroit, came to a whopping $446,069, of which $273,500 he was contesting in a variety of court suits. Attorney Aiken listed McLain's assets at $413, with which he was supposed to pay off 86 creditors, ranging from friends who had loaned him money to corporations which honored his credit cards. The Tigers were among his creditors and were down for $39,386, which had been given as a 1970 salary advance.

On March 19, a month after his suspension, the furniture in McLain's rented home in Beverly Hills, a Detroit suburb, was seized by the Internal Revenue Service to satisfy $9,460 in income taxes owed for 1968. The IRS sold the furnishings at an auction which brought $5,852. Included in that total was $3,400 paid by Charles Walker, a Detroit salesman, for McLain's Hammond organ. McLain, also a professional organist, later said the organ didn't belong to him, but was loaned to him by the Hammond Organ Company.

Nixon Shows Much Interest in McLain Case

Commissioner Kuhn made the traditional visit to the White House on March 31, the annual occasion when the President is given a baseball pass for the coming season. President Richard Nixon, an ardent fan, accepted the pass and also several autographed baseballs and a New York Mets' world championship ring. During this visit, President Nixon asked Kuhn if he had reached a decision on McLain.

"Yes, I have, Mr. President," Commissioner Kuhn replied to the inquiring Chief Executive.

The commissioner advised the President that McLain would be suspended for approximately half of the championship season and would be eligible

Exiled McLain loosens up with brother as catcher beside Florida residence the bankrupt hurler used as do-it-yourself spring base.

to return on July 1. Telling about this conversation later, Kuhn said: "In the President's judgment, the decision was a fair one."

On April 1, six days before the Presidential opener in Washington, D. C. — ironically, Detroit was the visiting team — Commissioner Kuhn announced his decision to the press. The complete text of the commissioner's ruling follows:

"On February 19, 1970, I suspended Denny McLain from all Organized Baseball activities pending the completion of further investigation and my review of the facts obtained therefrom. I based the initial suspension substantially upon certain admissions made candidly to me by McLain. These admissions related to his involvement in purported bookmaking activities in 1967 and his associations at that time.

Kuhn Details McLain's Involvement

"My investigation has continued since that date regarding McLain's activities in 1967 and subsequent years. I am satisfied at this time my investigation has been thorough and has developed all pertinent information available. Pursuant to my powers under the Major League Agreement and Rules, I have now made the following findings and conclusions:

"In January, 1967, McLain played an engagement at a bar in Flint, Mich., and there became acquainted with certain gamblers said to be involved in a bookmaking operation. McLain at that time commenced placing basketball bets with this operation and subsequently he was persuaded to make financial contributions totaling approximately $5,700. While McLain believed he had become a partner in this operation and has so admitted to me in the presence of his personal attorney, it would appear that in fact he was the victim of a confidence scheme. I would thus conclude that McLain was never a partner and had no proprietary interest in the bookmaking operation. The fair inference is that his own gullibility and avarice had committed him to become a dupe of the gamblers with whom he associated. This, of course, does not remove the serious dereliction on McLain's part of associating with the Flint gamblers.

"A thorough investigation has not revealed any other material facts beyond those I have described. There is no evidence to indicate that McLain ever bet on a baseball game involving the Detroit Tigers or any other team. There is no evidence to indicate that McLain gave less than his best effort at any time while performing for the Detroit Tigers. There is no evidence that McLain in 1967 or subsequently has been guilty of any misconduct involving baseball or the playing of baseball games.

"Irresponsible in Personal Affairs"

"McLain's association in 1967 with gamblers was contrary to his obligation as a professional baseball player to conform to high standards of personal conduct, and it is my judgment that this conduct was not in the best interests of baseball. It therefore must be made the subject of discipline. In reaching my conclusions, consideration has been given to the fact that no evidence has been developed by my investigation that McLain's conduct apart from his 1967 associations has been inconsistent with his duties and obligations as a baseball player. While it is true that in 1967 and subsequently McLain has been irresponsible in his personal financial affairs, and that this is a source of serious concern, I have not in this particular

case based my disciplinary action on such irresponsibility, although the probationary aspects of my action are related thereto.

"Under the circumstances, it is my judgment that McLain's suspension should be continued to July 1. 1970. In the meantime, his disassociation from all Organized Baseball activities must continue. In addition, McLain will be placed on a probationary status and required to provide this office periodically with such data on his financial affairs as may be requested. The purpose of this data is to satisfy this office that personal financial irresponsibility will not again contribute to leading McLain into such a situation as involved him in 1967."

Difference? "Murder and Attempted Murder"

As soon as Kuhn finished reading this statement, he was asked by a reporter to explain the difference in attempting to become a bookmaker, as McLain had done, and actually being one. Replied Kuhn, in what was to become a widely quoted statement: "I think you have to consider the difference is the same as between murder and attempted murder."

The reaction to Commissioner Kuhn's decision was mixed. McLain and Tiger officials were delighted. Joseph Durso of the New York Times, who was among the dozens of writers camping at McLain's Lakeland home, reported that McLain, when hearing the news, ". . . put down the phone, gave a deep sigh that sagged his chest and shoulders, caught his wife Sharyn in a bear-hug, and like a man reprieved, exclaimed, 'Till July first, till July first.'"

Tiger catcher Bill Freehan, McLain's batterymate, seemed puzzled and said, shaking his head, "Half a season? Funny. It's like saying he almost did something wrong." Dick McAuliffe, veteran Tiger infielder, also expressed surprise. "If Denny's innocent," McAuliffe said, "it should be nothing. If he's guilty, then this is not enough."

Another reaction, also somewhat typical, was registered by Jim Price, the Tigers' second-string catcher and player representative. Said Price, who was McLain's closest friend on the club: "Most of the guys thought Denny would get one or two years, or nothing at all. The three-month suspension is as close to nothing as you could get."

Penalty Panned as Too Light by News Media

Jim Campbell, the Tigers' general manager, complimented Kuhn. "He did a thorough job," Campbell told newsmen, "and I think he did what is right. I think it's very fair. I'm certainly pleased the suspension isn't any longer."

Like the players, most sportswriters regarded Kuhn's penalty too lenient. Dick Young of the New York Daily News, the nation's most widely quoted baseball writer, referred to Commissioner Kuhn as "Bowie the Benign" and wrote:

"The fans, most of them, will boo the decision of Bowie the Benign. He let them down. This was his chance to be a stern commissioner, a severe commissioner. Baseball is something special in American society because it has a mystique of purity. The seeming paradox of all life is that more money is bet on baseball than on any other sport because it is honest. The people know it is honest. The people want to keep it that way, even if it takes an occasional scalp or two."

Harried G. M. Jim Campbell of Tigers tries to dry up water damage caused by McLain's dousing of two unsuspecting Detroit sportswriters.

Columnist Pete Waldmeir of the Detroit News, who helped gather much of the background material for the Sports Illustrated story, commented: "How do you spell travesty? Better yet, what's the definition of white-wash? Kuhn ought to have a ready answer in the wake of his slap-on-the-wrist penalty."

Joe Falls, columnist and sports editor of the Detroit Free Press, also

was critical. Wrote Falls: "Nobody here can quite believe the stand that Kuhn took in handing down his sentence—just 12 weeks and McLain can play again. Kuhn took the easy way out—a penalty, but not one that fits the tradition of the game."

The erudite Robert Lipsyte of the New York Times commented: "Mc-Lain, it can be argued, must have considered himself at least a rookie bookmaker. As such, he knew he was violating some of the strictest laws and customs in baseball and endangering his team and the sport as well as his own career. But his venture into crime did not pay off, he was suckered and saved. His intent was criminal, but his technique inept; therefore, he will miss less than three months of the season."

Smith Names Denny Starter on July 1 vs. Yankees

Said Tiger Manager Mayo Smith: "We'll start him July 1 against the Yankees in Detroit and, knowing Denny, he'll probably pitch a shutout."

McLain missed the Tigers' first 71 games and then, as Manager Smith said he would, pitched against the Yankees on July 1. But there was no shutout. He was knocked out after 5⅓ innings, gave up eight hits, three of them homers, and was jolted for five earned runs. When McLain departed, the Yankees were leading, 5-3, but the Tigers tied it up and won, 6-5, in 11 innings. Reliever Tom Timmerman was the winning pitcher.

More significant is that the game drew a crowd of 53,863 paid, the largest crowd at Tiger Stadium since 1961 and bigger than the Tigers were to have on Al Kaline Day in mid-August. A total of 71 writers covered the game, or rather McLain, giving the scene a World Series atmosphere. The crowd gave McLain a warm embrace and cheered him throughout. Said McLain after the game: "I'm not an emotional man. But I thought I was going to cry when I heard those cheers. I didn't know what to expect. I almost had to swallow my tongue to hold myself together."

The honeymoon was brief. McLain made four more starts without success, then won two games in succession, both with relief help. It wasn't until his 13th start, on August 22 against Milwaukee, that McLain was able to go the distance and win. It was the third and final victory of his brief season.

McLain was in trouble and in the headlines on August 28 when he doused a pair of Detroit baseball writers with a bucket of ice water. McLain got them one at a time, first soaking rookie Jim Hawkins of the Free Press and then Watson Spoelstra of the News, a former president of the Baseball Writers' Association of America. Tiger General Manager Jim Campbell immediately suspended McLain for a period not to exceed 30 days at $500 per day.

Scribes Hawkins, Spoelstra Doused by Water

Hawkins had gone to the Detroit clubhouse about an hour before a night game with Oakland and asked McLain about an Associated Press story quoting McLain as evading a question by saying, "Go ask Bill Freehan, he wrote the damn book." As Hawkins prepared to leave, pitcher Joe Niekro, who was at the next locker, said, "Sit down for a few minutes." Hawkins sat down. McLain then wielded the water bucket behind Hawkins' back and doused him over the head and shoulders.

About a half-hour later, Spoelstra received a message that McLain wanted to see him. Spoelstra was in the umpires' room, visiting with Hank

Soar, an old friend. McLain greeted Spoelstra cordially and then said, "I didn't like the headlines in your paper." The conversation continued for several minutes, but ended on a pleasant note with Spoelstra and McLain shaking hands. Then, as soon as Spoelstra's back was turned, McLain gave him a soaking.

Another Suspension Follows 'Clowning' on the Square

Spoelstra immediately reported the incident to General Manager Campbell, who apologized for the club and suspended McLain. McLain was amazed at Campbell's action and insisted, "I was just clowning around, that was easy to see." But writer Hawkins disputed this and said that after his dousing, McLain told him: "I'm going to get all you guys. So don't say I didn't warn you. And I'd like to throw all of you, one by one, into the whirlpool before the season is over."

McLain's Florida domicile with identification alteration.

Technically, this second suspension was for seven days and ended on September 5, but on September 4 Commissioner Kuhn advised the Detroit club that he wanted to see McLain and several club officials when they arrived in New York on September 9 for a regularly-scheduled series against the Yankees. Kuhn acknowledged that the club was re-instating McLain as of September 5, but said he didn't want McLain reactivated until after the hearing in New York.

The hearing was held, as scheduled, and lasted two hours. Attending were McLain and his attorneys, William Aiken and William Carpenter; General Manager Campbell, Manager Mayo Smith; Tiger Farm Director Walter (Hoot) Evers; baseball attorney Paul Porter; Henry Fitzgibbon, baseball's security chief; Charles Segar, and Commissioner Kuhn, who presided over the hearing.

Then came another bombshell. The commissioner suspended McLain again, this time for carrying a gun and breaking probation. This suspension was for the remainder of the 1970 season. Kuhn said he had information that McLain had carried a gun during the Tigers' August 6-19 trip and that this was "not consistent with his probationary status." Kuhn also said that on at least one occasion, in an unidentified Chicago restaurant, McLain removed the gun from its holster and showed it to several team-mates.

The season-long perils of Denny McLain had been such that the reaction by fans and baseball alike was one of general relief. At last, it appeared, the Denny McLain story had run its course, at least for this season, anyway. But there was still one more chapter to go — one final

Back in business again at the old stand . . . nothing really happened . . . just about 18 starts missed . . . peanuts, popcorn, cold beer here . . .

touch of drama which was to be just as surprising and unexpected as all the events that had gone before.

This time McLain, with the help of Commissioner Kuhn, actually up-staged the opening game of the World Series.

It is October 9, 4 p.m. in Cincinnati, the day before the Baltimore Ori-oles and Cincinnati Reds are to meet for the world championship. Kuhn, presiding at a hastily-called press conference at World Series headquar-ters, steps to the front of the room—flanked by Jim Campbell of the Tigers and Bob Short, owner of the Washington Senators.

"Gentlemen," Kuhn begins, and he then announces that Denny McLain has been sent to Washington in a eight-player deal. Reporters rush to the telephones and to their typewriters and suddenly the anticipated Game 1 World Series match between the Orioles and the Reds is secondary. Mc-Lain is in the headlines once again.

Trade Causes Suspension Termination

It was believed to be the first time a trade was announced by a com-missioner, but Kuhn explained there were unusual circumstances. The Detroit and Washington clubs had been talking trade, seriously, for more than a week, but a player cannot be traded so long as he is on the sus-pended list. Hence, Kuhn revealed, he secretly had lifted McLain's sus-pension as of October 1, which was the last day of the regular season.

Commissioner Kuhn also revealed that sometime in mid-September—he wasn't sure of the date—McLain had agreed to undergo a series of tests ". . . by a very eminent psychiatrist." Kuhn didn't further identify the psychiatrist, nor did he say who footed the bill, but the psychiatrist, after observing and examining McLain, made a two-page report to the commissioner, declaring that McLain ". . . is not mentally ill and not in need of such service."

The commissioner also said, in explanation of McLain's toting a gun, ". . . he was merely manifesting a kind of flamboyance typical of his personality and has been the victim of emotional stress by a conglomera-tion of problems." Kuhn predicted "a change of location might be bene-ficial."

Campbell of the Tigers then explained that for the 178-day season just completed, McLain was in uniform and paid for only 58 days and said, in farewell, "I wish Denny and his family well. He's one heckuva fine pitcher. I'll have no further comments." Washington Owner Short, asked why he made the deal, replied: "I think he is the greatest pitcher in base-ball. This is my trade."

Williams Not Pleased By Loss of Key Players

The trade was as follows: McLain and Norman McRae, also a pitcher, and infielders Don Wert and Elliott Maddox to the Senators in exchange for infielders Ed Brinkman and Aurelio Rodriguez and pitchers Joe Cole-man and Jim Hannan. Before the press conference was over, Owner Short admitted that Ted Williams, his field manager, didn't approve of the deal and was of the opinion that too much talent was given up for McLain. But there was this consolation: The 1970 Denny McLain story had come to an end.

Four nights later, on October 13 — and after Baltimore had won the first three World Series games against Cincinnati — Washington Owner

"The bull ends here." In a move that upstaged the World Series, McLain was traded to the Senators, whose manager, Ted Williams, was not thrilled at the loss of key Washington players the deal cost him.

Bob Short was involved in another significant announcement. Short revealed he had spoken to John Quinn, general manager and vice-president of the Phillies, and had obtained negotiation rights to outfielder Curt Flood who, with the full support of the Major League Baseball Players Association, had filed a $4.1 million suit vs. baseball, challenging the legality of the reserve clause.

Judge Cooper Reaffirms Antitrust Tradition

Flood had been traded the previous October by the Cardinals and had been sent to the Phillies in what was originally a seven-player deal. Flood refused to report to the Phillies and, instead, initiated legal action vs. baseball. Judge Irving Ben Cooper of the United States District Court in New York City heard the case without a jury and on August 12, in a 47-page opinion, upheld the defense argument that federal antitrust laws do not apply to baseball. Judge Cooper, however, also said he did believe modifications in the reserve system could and should be achieved in negotiations between the players and club owners, and without court action. Flood's attorneys appealed. The case is now before the Second Circuit Court of Appeals and is likely to go all the way to the United States Supreme Court.

As he vowed he would, Flood sat out the entire 1970 season at a considerable financial sacrifice. The Phillies had offered him a $90,000 contract, plus $8,000 in expenses. Flood rejected the offer and on more than one occasion indicated he would not return to baseball until his suit was settled.

Flood Enjoys Sabbatical in Denmark

Flood spent much of his summer in Denmark, where he worked as a portrait painter and also opened a restaurant-lounge. It was obvious, however, that he was short on funds. In August, the United States Internal Revenue Service, citing non-payment of $6,888 in taxes on Flood's portrait business in St. Louis, auctioned off a camera and stand from his studio.

While in Denmark, Flood was convinced he would be blackballed from baseball. Even if he did have the urge to play again, he believed no owner would sign him to a contract. "Fortunately," Flood said later, "that didn't happen. After I found my playing baseball would not prejudice the litigation, I said, 'Why not?' Heck, I'm a baseball player. I don't know anything else."

Flood and Owner Short met on the weekend of October 23, in New York City. A salary agreement — reported at $110,000 for the 1971 season — was quickly reached. But Flood had had prior discussions with Marvin Miller and Dick Moss, director and attorney of the Players Association. They advised Flood he should not sign unless his contract included certain exceptions. One was that his return would not prejudice his appeal.

Short apparently approved these exceptions, but later withdrew approval after consulting with Commissioner Kuhn. The commissioner insisted that Flood's contract must contain the standard reserve clause, without modification. Kuhn, however, did agree that the contract could contain a covenant stipulating that Flood's return to baseball would not be prejudicial to the issues under dispute in court.

Curt Reveals "Unwritten" Agreement

While the fine print in his contract was being negotiated, Flood quoted Short as telling him:

"I promise that I won't trade you. And I guarantee you the full year's pay no matter what happens. And at the end of the year, if we don't agree on terms for the following season, I'll make you a free agent so you can work out a deal with another club. But I can't put any of this in writing. And if anybody says that I agreed to such an arrangement, I'll deny it."

These quotes were in the original galley proofs of Flood's book, "The Way It Is," but were deleted prior to publication. Flood, however, does tell of this conversation with Short, but merely toned down the language.

It was subsequently pointed out that these concessions, if promised by Short, contravene conditions of the reserve system which are part of the standard player's contract One of the long-range interpretations was that if Short did enter into such a clandestine agreement, he was, in effect, modifying the reserve clause—and seemingly strengthening Flood's original stance. Some observers, however, regarded Flood's return as a weakening of his case since he was once again willing to be subjected to "slavery and bondage," etc.

Originally, Owner Short had agreed to give the Phillies one player

merely for the right to negotiate for Flood. But Commissioner Kuhn ruled against this. As a result, no trade agreement was reached until Flood signed—and then the Senators sent three minor league players to the Phillies in exchange. Earlier in the year the Phillies had received minor league first baseman Guillermo Montanez and pitcher-shortstop Jim Browning from the Cardinals as compensation for Flood's refusal to report.

Big Names Testify at Flood Trial

Flood's action vs. baseball was among the highlights of the year's off-the-field activities. The suit, a civil action, was filed on January 16, 1970, in New York City's Federal Court. The trial ran three weeks, from May 19 to June 10. Judge Cooper heard testimony from a veritable "Who's Who in Baseball." Future historians may wish to note that 22 persons testified, 11 for each side. The cost of a single copy of the entire transcript was $2,200.

Judge Cooper often used baseball cliches in conversing with the lawyers and witnesses. At the outset, he likened himself to "a man in blue" and said he would "call them as I see them." After hearing the opening arguments from both sides, the judge thanked the attorneys for the clarity of their presentations and said, "You have thrown the ball to me and I hope I don't fluff it."

Former Supreme Court Justice Arthur Goldberg, on a different bench, confers with Flood in New York. Goldberg took Flood's case vs. reserve clause.

Since the case was heard without a jury, it was up to Judge Cooper to decide two basic points: Do the antitrust laws apply to baseball, despite previous Supreme Court rulings granting baseball exemption from them? And are the reserve arrangements which bind a player to a club indefinitely, in themselves, "reasonable" as a necessity to keep the baseball business sound?

The defense used four squads of attorneys, and Flood three. The best-known among them was Arthur Goldberg, a former labor official, former United States Supreme Court Justice, and also formerly the United States Ambassador to the United Nations. Goldberg, additionally, was at the time campaigning for election as the Democratic candidate for governor of New York. At the end of the summer, attorney Goldberg had gone 0-for-2. He lost out as governor and also lost the Flood hearing at the District Court level.

Goldberg Cites British Soccer's Survival

In his opening statement, Goldberg said the previous Supreme Court decisions "do not apply now because times have changed." He said the reserve clause not only violated federal and state antitrust laws, but also the 13th Amendment to the Constitution, which prohibits "involuntary servitude."

Goldberg pointed out that football, boxing and the theater all have come under federal antitrust laws and "they seem to be doing all right." He also called Judge Cooper's attention to the successful attack in Great Britain on a soccer reserve clause similar to baseball's and said, "They (the British soccer leagues) don't seem to be suffering any harm."

Attorneys Mark Hughes, representing the Phillies, and Paul Porter, representing the commissioner's office, gave the opening arguments for baseball. Hughes said Flood was not being treated as "a slave, or peon, or as a chattel," considering that he was paid $90,000 to play baseball for the Cardinals in 1969 and was being offered at least the same salary by the Phillies.

League Presidents Uphold Need for Reserve Clause

Hughes and Porter contended that past Supreme Court decisions, going back to Justice Oliver Wendell Holmes' famous ruling in 1922, still were valid. Hughes also stressed that essentially a labor dispute was involved and that Flood's recourse was to the National Labor Relations Board and not to the federal court.

Commissioner Kuhn was among those testifying in behalf of baseball. Kuhn told Judge Cooper that "baseball could not operate on a league basis without the reserve clause." The commissioner traced the history of the game, told of the chaotic conditions that threatened baseball between 1871 and 1879, when there was no reserve system, and declared it would be "impossible to maintain the integrity of the game and maintain honesty among clubs and players" without the reserve system.

Joe Cronin and Charles (Chub) Feeney, presidents of the American and National leagues, also testified, and essentially took the same position. So did such club executives as John McHale of the Montreal Expos, Francis Dale of the Cincinnati Reds, Bob Reynolds of the California Angels and Bing Devine of the St. Louis Cardinals. Ewing Kauffman, owner of the Kansas City Royals, testified but took a somewhat softer line.

Cronin, a Hall of Famer and long-time baseball mogul, had one rather embarrassing moment. He had extolled the late Clark Griffith as his teacher and friend, as well as his employer in Washington in the 1930s. When cross-examined by defense attorney Jay Topkis, Cronin repeated his warm regard for Griffith's judgment.

Devine Holds Dealing "Essential Element"

"And you said he was one of the pioneers of the American League?" Topkis asked.

"Yes," Cronin replied.

"But didn't you know, Mr. Cronin," Topkis said, "that Clark Griffith jumped his National League reserve to come into the American in 1901?"

"No, sir," said Cronin. "I don't think I knew that."

Bing Devine, vice-president and general manager of the Cardinals and the man who engineered Flood's trade to the Phillies, told Judge Cooper that the trading of baseball players is an essential element of the sport. The 1964 pennant-winning Cardinals, Devine said, included six key players acquired in trades—Flood, Lou Brock, Bill White, Julian Javier, Dick Groat and Barney Schultz.

The testimony of Ewing Kauffman, the new Kansas City owner, was regarded as somewhat damaging to baseball. Though a defense witness, Kauffman conceded under cross-examination that he would pay Flood $100,000 to $125,000 a year, and possibly more, if Flood were under a long-term contract to play with his club. This was an admission that a player, bound by the reserve system to one club, is not always able to reach his maximum salary potential. Kauffman also said a rule that provided for yearly salary escalation (with the player becoming a free agent if the club didn't want to meet the scale set) "wouldn't hurt at all."

Joe Garagiola, a former major league catcher and now a network television and radio personality, also appeared as a defense witness. Garagiola, a baseball comic and storyteller, opened with a joke, prompting Judge Cooper to ask: "Do you always smile?"

"When you have one of those bad years, you have to laugh through them," Garagiola replied.

"That's what I do in a bad case, too," Judge Cooper confided.

"I wish you were on a bubble gum card," Garagiola said. "I'd have you."

"Thanks," Judge Cooper said.

Garagiola joked about his .257 lifetime batting average and, encouraged by the laughter of Judge Cooper and the spectators, went on to explain his understanding of the reserve clause.

"You sign a contract and are with them (the ball club) until they get rid of you and they got rid of me several times. But to me it's the best system. If you changed the name, everybody probably would be happy."

Garagiola Part-Time Testifier, Too

When Flood's attorneys declined to cross-examine, Garagiola was dismissed and Judge Cooper told him, cheerfully, "You were on for 13 minutes."

"Yeah," replied Garagiola in mock chagrin, "but I can't even get to play a full game here."

Two Hall of Famers, Jackie Robinson and Hank Greenberg, testified in behalf of Flood. Robinson, who broke the color line in 1947, character-

ized the reserve clause as "one-sided in favor of the owners" and said it should be modified "to give the player more control over his destiny." Greenberg, who had been a player, club executive and owner, agreed and said the reserve clause should be eliminated and replaced by a provision that gives the signing club control for a certain number of years, but not for the total duration of the player's career. Greenberg also called the reserve clause "obsolete and antiquated."

Jim Brosnan, a former pitcher and baseball author, told of player hardship and related a little story which brought laughter to the courtroom. Brosnan told of the time his contract had been transferred and he came home to tell his wife they had to pack up and move on. "My wife threatened to divorce me," Brosnan explained. "She had just bought two weeks of steaks to put in the freezer. She wanted to know what to do with the steaks."

And, asked counsel, could Brosnan say what she finally did with the steaks.

"She gave them," said Brosnan, "to the player who reported in my place."

Veeck Offers Reserve Clause Modifications

Former major league owner Bill Veeck, also appearing in Flood's behalf, suggested modifications of the reserve clause and recommended three alternate provisions. Veeck's alternatives were:

1—A form of the contract used in the motion picture industry, enabling a studio to hold rights to a performer for a specified period, usually seven years, with the contract calling for scheduled raises at intervals during the contract period.

2—A form of professional football's option clause, in which a player can become a free agent by playing out the option year of his contract with the exception that compensation be in the form of cash rather than in a player of equivalent quality.

3—Some form of combination contract, covering first a specific period during which management could maintain its hold on a player's services in the minors, and another contract for an undetermined length of time to hold his services after he reached the major league level.

Economists Take Opposite Views On Reserve Clause

Two economists, one for each side, also appeared. Robert P. Nathan said the reserve system "tends to depress wage levels because there is no opportunity to negotiate with alternative users of the services." Dr. John Clark took an opposite view and said players in 1965 were earning an average of $19,500 in salary and that this rose to $24,957 in 1969 and to $28,088 in 1970, or 44 percent overall. It was pointed out that Flood, himself, was the beneficiary of steady annual salary increases, to his peak of $90,000 paid to him by the Cardinals in 1969.

Flood also took the stand and said he resented being traded because "I don't think I should be traded and treated like a piece of property." Flood conceded that the Phillies offered him "a little more than $90,000 in salary," plus $8,000 spring training expenses, but said he didn't want to play for the Phillies because "I don't want to move my businesses and family into another part of the United States."

One of the interesting aspects of the trial was that though Flood had the unanimous support of the Players Association, not a single active player testified in his behalf. Flood refused to put the knock on his fellow players and said he understood the lack of player volunteers. "If a guy (a player) comes here and publicly says I'm right," Flood explained, "he could be risking his future career in baseball."

Heads of Other Major Pro Sports Testify

In completing their presentation, Flood's lawyers called Walter Kennedy, commissioner of the National Basketball Association; Pete Rozelle, commissioner of the National Football League; Clarence Campbell, president of the National Hockey League, and Alan Eagleson, director of the National Hockey League Players' Association, to show that the reserve systems in these sports were less restrictive than baseball's, but still permitted those sports to prosper.

Judge Cooper announced his decision on August 12 and ruled in favor of baseball on all causes of the action, including Flood's assertion the system amounted to "peonage and involuntary servitude." But Judge Cooper also conceded he was "impressed with Flood's argument" and suggested that modifications in the reserve clause could be reconciled through negotiation.

"Clearly the preponderance of credible proof does not favor elimination of the reserve clause," Judge Cooper wrote. Instead, the judge said, the evidence suggested that "arbitration or negotiation" might modify the system to satisfy all parties.

Judge Cooper thus upheld the defense argument that federal antitrust laws do not apply to baseball because of Supreme Court decisions in 1953 and 1957. Only the Supreme Court itself can change the situation, he said, in the absence of action by Congress.

The loss at the District Court level was anticipated by the Players Association. Dick Moss, attorney for the players, announced that there would be an immediate appeal and called the decision "the end of the first inning." Said Moss: "The next inning will be in the Court of Appeals."

Marvin Miller, executive director of the players' organization, said, "All that Judge Cooper held is that it is up to the Supreme Court to overrule the Supreme Court. I think everyone knew it would be difficult for a District Court to overrule the Supreme Court."

Bargaining Seen as Best Vehicle for Change

Commissioner Bowie Kuhn, asked for his comments, said: "I am particularly pleased that the court has recognized the need for a reserve system. I have constantly maintained that the clubs and players can bargain out solutions to any problems that arise. I share Judge Cooper's conclusion that any change necessary in the reserve system can be achieved by bargaining."

In retrospect, the Flood trial was tame and quite orderly compared with baseball's other 1970 major legal entanglement. There was considerably more heat, and almost constant action, or the threat of action, in the transfer of the American League's ailing Seattle franchise to Milwaukee. Baseball also won this legal battle and was permitted to have the franchise sold to the highest bidder, a group from Milwaukee, but only after advancing through a gauntlet of legal maneuverings.

It had been apparent the previous summer that the Seattle franchise was in financial difficulty. Though expected to be a rousing success, the Seattle team, an expansion club, had an unsuccessful maiden season. This was baseball's first venture into the Great Northwest, at the major league level, but the Pilots didn't draw well at the gate and had only 677,944 paid admissions. This caused financial losses estimated at $850,000. The team also finished last in the American League West, as anticipated. The area suffered a general economy slump.

Clevelander Daley Holder of Important Shares in Pilots

The Seattle club, moreover, had the additional burden of what was principally absentee ownership. William Daley, one-time chairman of the board of the Cleveland Indians, owned 47 percent of the club and controlled an additional 13 percent held by fellow Clevelanders Greg Devine and Alan Fritschey. The three Soriano brothers, Max, Dewey and Milton, owned or controlled 34 percent. Like Daley, they also wanted to sell. The remaining six percent was held by Vern Coulon, a Seattle realtor; Dr. William Hutchinson, also of Seattle, and by Chinn Ho, a Honolulu businessman.

The American League, as early as the previous October (see the 1969 Review of the Year), was encouraging Seattle investors to purchase the club, or at the minimum, controlling interest since Daley was agreeable to remain as a minor stockholder. These attempts had failed and on January 16 the American League issued another ultimatum: A purchase group purportedly organized earlier by Fred Danz would now have until January 22 to buy the club from Pacific Northwest Sports, Inc., which was the Daley-Soriano combine.

Injunction Issued to Prevent Move

Twenty-four hours before this deadline, Seattle Mayor Wes Uhlman announced that if the club was moved to another city, the American League owners, and the Daley-Soriano group, would "be defendants in a multi-million dollar lawsuit." On January 23, Judge F. A. Walterskirchen of the Superior Court in Seattle ordered Pacific Northwest "to show cause" why he should not grant Mayor Uhlman's request for a preliminary injunction that would bar removal of the franchise.

A committee of American Leaguers, headed by A. L. President Joe Cronin, met the prospective buyers on January 27-28 in Oakland, Calif. To help facilitate the sale, Daley lowered the asking price for the franchise from a reported $10,300,000 to $9,000,000. A new purchase group also surfaced, headed by Edward Carlson, a multi-millionaire Seattle hotel magnate.

Representatives from Milwaukee and Dallas were also at this two-day meeting, but were advised by Cronin that there would be no sale to outside interests. Once again, the American League would do all it could to keep the franchise in Seattle. Local buyers would be given every preference.

Carlson returned to Seattle and huddled with officials of the Bank of California, which had been insisting on payment of an overdue note for $3,500,000 from Pacific Northwest. A spokesman for the bank then indicated that the note was negotiable and said the bank "would do anything within reason to keep the team in Seattle."

An intensive fund-raising campaign followed, mostly to convince bank officials that the Carlson group would have a sound financial base. But in-

vestors were slow to step forward. When Carlson realized he couldn't raise the necessary monies through the normal private equity channels, he restructured the group into a non-profit organization.

On February 11, at a full membership meeting of American League owners, Carlson presented his non-profit proposal. The owners turned him down on the basis that financial pledges were not enough. The franchise must have investors ready to risk further losses. Said Owner John Allyn of the Chicago White Sox, himself an investment expert: "They have not produced anyone who would display a continuing financial responsibility."

Cronin advised Carlson that his proposal was "honorable but not palatable" and the American League owners then agreed they would, to keep the franchise afloat, extend a loan of $650,000 to Pacific Northwest. This money was for past-due salary payments to club employes, for past-due player bonus payments, and also for spring training expenses.

American League Appoints Roy Hamey 'Overseer'

Carlson said he was "extremely pleased with the league's decision to keep the franchise in Seattle, even if we (his group) are not a part of it." But not all of the A. L. owners were satisfied with this sudden arrangement which, in effect, was league subsidization of the Seattle franchise. Frank Cashen, vice-president of the Orioles, warned that the Seattle losses for the full 1971 season could reach $2,000,000.

On February 14, the league appointed Roy Hamey, a long-time baseball executive, as the general overseer of the Seattle franchise. For the next several weeks, there was silence. The Pilots began their spring training exercises in Tempe, Ariz., and all seemed well. But, as time wore on, the American League owners began coming to the realization that additional financing would be necessary and there were some expressions that the league would not commit itself beyond its original $650,000 loan.

Another American League owners' meeting was scheduled for March 10 in Tampa, Fla., but this meeting suddenly was postponed. The reason given was that the 78-year-old Daley had entered a hospital in Cleveland and could not attend. However, Daley revealed he had gone to the hospital only for a check-up and said: "I think they kind of used me as an excuse to cancel the meeting."

One of the factors that apparently caused postponement was a threat issued 24 hours earlier by Senator Warren G. Magnuson of Washington, who said if the franchise were moved, he would ask Congress to strip baseball of its immunity from the antitrust laws. Magnuson declared, "When you move these franchises around like pawns, just because you think you'll do better in some other town, then you're running a business, not a sport."

Seattle Attorney Throws Wrench Into Machinery

On March 13, Alfred J. Schweppe, a Seattle attorney and legal scholar and curmudgeon, asked for and was granted a temporary restraining order barring the American League from relocating the Seattle franchise. Schweppe said he was acting on behalf of "his outraged self and all other outraged persons" and contended he would suffer damages if the team was transferred because he already had purchased two season tickets and parking privileges at Sicks' Stadium, where the Pilots played their home games.

Three days later, on March 16, the American League suffered still another jolt. The State of Washington and the City of Seattle filed a suit vs.

the A. L. owners and Daley and the Sorianos, asking more than $80 million in damages if the franchise was moved. The suit was based on $25 million to the state, $2,500,500 to the city and an unspecified amount of other damage to the general public. Under the State of Washington's antitrust laws, the damages are trebled.

Owners Served With Restraining Order

The A. L. owners met in Tampa the next morning, and to their surprise, a temporary injunction had been granted against them by a Hillsborough County (Fla.) judge, who had acted at the request of Attorney Schweppe. As the owners arrived at the International Inn, they were greeted by Milt Gaston, a former major league pitcher and now a deputy sheriff of Hillsborough County.

Irony of ironies! Gaston, who had served up four of Babe Ruth's 1927 home runs, now was serving processes on Cronin, a former teammate, and all of the A. L. owners. He handed each of them a subpoena which advised them that they faced the threat of a jail sentence if they ignored the Florida injunction and went ahead with plans to shift the Seattle franchise to Milwaukee.

The owners met for 7½ hours and as A. L. President Joe Cronin was to

Joe Cronin, president of the American League, explaining the myriad problems faced in transferring the Seattle franchise to Milwaukee.

say later, "It was a day for the lawyers." The magnates obviously couldn't approve of a sale to the Milwaukee group, which was headed by Allan (Bud) Selig, and ready for action.

Instead, Alexander (Sandy) Hadden, one of the American League's attorneys, read the following statement:

"The American League is now under a legal restraint whereby it cannot approve transfer of the Seattle franchise to any other city of the United States. But for that restraint, at this meeting, it would have given consideration to such a transfer.

Hadden Reads American League Statement On Seattle

"There are valid and substantial legal and practical reasons why the American League and its constituent members cannot continue financial support of the Seattle Pilots beyond the amount already committed for that purpose.

"Even with the amount already committed by the American League, Pacific Northwest Sports, Inc., appears to be financially incapable of continuing its baseball operation in Seattle for the 1970 season, and at the present time there is no proposal for any Seattle interests to continue the Pilots in Seattle.

"It has therefore been resolved that (a) the American League instruct its counsel to proceed with all possible speed in using every tool at their command to have these restraints lifted and removed in order that the American League can conduct its business of playing baseball beginning on April 6 with 12 teams, and (b) when all legal restraint has been lifted so that Pacific Northwest Sports, Inc. may transfer the Seattle franchise to a city other than Seattle and the American League may approve such a transfer, without violating any court order, and if at that time there is no opportunity to transfer the ownership of the Seattle Pilots on a reasonable basis to a responsible party who will continue its operation in Seattle, the American League will give favorable consideration to any responsible proposal providing for its transfer to another city."

Bankruptcy Proceedings Against Pilots' Owners

This statement failed to emphasize one significant point—that the A. L. owners, in effect, were ready to sit by and watch, with immunity, as the franchise collapsed into bankruptcy. The next day, on March 18, the possibility of bankruptcy proceedings was mentioned for the first time when the Bank of California, still holding the $3,500,000 note owed by the baseball club, filed a motion in Seattle's Superior Court, joining the American League in seeking to dissolve legal restraints from transferring the franchise.

Suddenly, the ball was bouncing the other way and on March 19 attorneys for Pacific Northwest petitioned the Federal court in Seattle to order the sale of the club under the Bankruptcy Act. The petition was granted and the restraining orders became academic as the case moved into the bankruptcy court where Max Soriano, secretary-treasurer of the club, stated the club had only $91,000 in cash while operating expenses totaled $12,500 per day. It would be a "catastrophe," Soriano said, to keep the team in Seattle.

On March 13, Sidney C. Volinn of Seattle, a federal bankruptcy referee, cleared the way for the sale to Milwaukee interests. Volinn told a packed

courtroom, "I am constrained to find and conclude" that Pacific Northwest Sports, Inc., accept a $10.8 million offer from the Milwaukee Brewers Baseball Club, Inc. Volinn said it was clear that the Pilots could not meet their debts as they matured and that the club would soon become insolvent.

"The debtor is without funds to operate," said Volinn, "and helpless to get more." He said to saddle the American League with the obligation of carrying the team through the 1970 season would force the league into deficit financing that could amount to over $5 million in the next three years.

Selig-Fitzgerald Group Pays $10.8 Million for Club

The next day, on April 1 the Milwaukee Brewers Baseball Club, Inc., headed by Bud Selig and Ed Fitzgerald, both of Milwaukee, purchased the Seattle Pilots for $10.8 million. "Baseball To Return Here," trumpeted the Milwaukee Sentinel and "We're Big League Again" reported the Milwaukee Journal. Tickets went on sale 24 hours later and on April 7, the new Milwaukee Brewers, formerly the Seattle Pilots, opened their home American League season at County Stadium and, despite raw weather, drew a crowd of 37,237. Major league baseball had returned to Milwaukee.

The American League also won another significant court battle in 1970 when a trial examiner for the National Labor Relations Board recommended dismissal of the complaints of former umpires Al Salerno and Bill Valentine, both of whom had lodged charges of unfair labor practices. It was a milestone hearing and the first time the NLRB assumed jurisdiction in a dispute involving baseball, an action interpreted by the baseball unionists that the game was slowly, but inevitably losing its antitrust immunity.

The NLRB, starting on July 7, conducted nine days of hearings on the Salerno and Valentine charges. Four months later, on November 19, David S. Davidson, the NLRB's New England trial examiner who heard the case in Boston, recommended dismissal, ruling there was not sufficient evidence that the umpires had been fired by American League President Joe Cronin because of their activities in helping the American League umpires form a union. Attorneys for the umpires immediately filed exceptions to the trial examiner's recommendation and the case is now before the five-man NLRB group in Washington, D. C., which is the final arbitrator.

Cronin had fired Salerno and Valentine two years earlier, on September 16, 1968, for incompetence, claiming, "They are lousy umpires, that's all." Ever since, both umpires insisted they were discharged solely because of their union activities. Two weeks after these firings, on September 30, 1968, the American League umpires joined the union formed five years earlier by the National League umpires. The organization is still in effect and has since been known as the Major League Umpires Association.

Umpire Case Offers "Insufficient Evidence"

Trial Examiner Davidson, in his recommendation that the charges be dismissed, said that the umpires' counsel had failed to establish that the American League had knowledge of union activities "beyond mere suspicion or surmise" and that "the evidence is not sufficient to permit the inference that Cronin and Cal Hubbard (then the supervisor of the A. L.'s umpire staff) knew of the organizational efforts of Salerno and Valentine before their contracts were terminated."

Three American League managers, or former managers, testified in behalf of the umpires. They were Alvin Dark of the Cleveland Indians, Eddie

Stanky, formerly of the Chicago White Sox, and Dick Williams, formerly of the Boston Red Sox. John Flaherty, a veteran American League umpire and a crew chief, also supported the umpires. "Both were very good umpires," Flaherty said. "They more than held their own on the ball field."

Dark told the hearing that "every man has a different opinion of what an umpire should do" but Salerno and Valentine "had the courage to do what they thought was right . . . and they handled the ball game." Dark also said if he had to grade the two umpires in relation to other umpires, he would put them in the top half.

Stanky Testifies Arbiters Are 'Competent'

Stanky, a long-time umpire baiter on the field, called umpires, policemen and baseball managers the most underpaid professionals in the country. "When umpires come to the majors, they are competent," he said. Asked to define competence, Stanky replied: "Knowing the rules and calling them the same way in every city, playing no favorites."

Williams categorized Salerno and Valentine as strong-willed and admitted he had trouble with them and their crews. "Some crews you just have trouble with," Williams said. "But it doesn't mean they're bad. It just turns out that way."

Valentine and Salerno also were called to the stand. Valentine broke

Umpires Al Salerno (left) and Bill Valentine, who lost their court appeal for reinstatement at all levels of law, even the Supreme Court.

down while relating the details of the telephone call in which Cronin advised him of his dismissal. "I told him," said Valentine, " 'All of a sudden, after six years in the league, I'm a bad umpire.' He said, 'You've always been a bad umpire.' " Tears began to stream down Valentine's face and a 15-minute recess was called.

Cronin Describes Umps as "Arrogant"

The next day, Salerno took the stand and spent two hours explaining the developments that led to his dismissal. Salerno generally backed Valentine's recollection of events and explained they talked to at least 15 umpires and almost every one was in favor of organizing.

Cronin was among the last to testify and mentioned various incidents which he gave as illustrations of Salerno's and Valentine's incompetence. Said Cronin: "Salerno and Valentine often inflamed arguments instead of stopping them." Cronin also described them as "arrogant" and said that at the All-Star Game all he heard "was complaints about Salerno and Valentine."

Tom Yawkey, owner of the Boston Red Sox, testified and revealed that Cronin had told him in August, more than a month before the firings, that Salerno and Valentine "would not be back next year." Yawkey said

Alexander (Sandy) Hadden, then A. L. attorney and now the game's General Counsel and Secretary-Treasurer, had key role in Seattle and umpire discussions.

Cronin gave him this information after he had called the league office to find out if Red Sox star Carl Yastrzemski would be fined or suspended after having a row with Salerno the day before.

The NLRB verdict against the umpires came as a surprise, particularly to Salerno. So certain was Salerno and his attorney, Joe Kelner of New York City, of an NLRB victory that Salerno rejected a succession of secret settlement agreements offered by the American League which, if accepted, would have led to the complete reinstatement of both umpires.

Tentative Agreement Reached, But Rejected

The basic agreement, as revealed by the Chicago Sun-Times, was worked out between Jack Reynolds, counsel for the Major League Umpires Association, and Alexander Hadden, attorney for the American League. The agreement contained seven clauses. The fifth clause read as follows:

"There shall be no public comments by any of the parties regarding the circumstances, terms and conditions of this settlement, provided, however, that a single public announcement with regard thereto, in form approved by the parties, shall be made by the American League office."

No such public announcement was necessary because Salerno, after expressing approval, refused to sign on the subsequent advice of his attorney. Valentine signed and later journeyed across the country to Salerno's home in Utica, N. Y., in a futile effort to change his mind. Terms of the agreement insisted upon approval by both umpires. This was in March.

In essence, the agreement stated that Salerno and Valentine would cancel the impending NLRB hearing and also drop their two court actions vs. baseball which, together, were for damages of approximately $4 million. One of these suits challenged baseball's antitrust immunity; the other was vs. the American League and Cronin for "defamation of character."

So anxious was the league to avoid litigation that Salerno and Valentine were to be reinstated at the salary rate of $20,000 a year. This was the current scale for umpires in their experience classification but, nonetheless, was $8,000 more than they were being paid at the time of their dismissal.

Umpires Would Open '70 Season in Minors

The plan was for both umpires to open the 1970 season in the minor leagues. Salerno would be assigned to the International League and Valentine to the Texas League. After approximately two months in the minors, both umpires were to undergo a "review" by Cronin. This "review" or "tryout" was to make it appear they had improved as umpires and was designed as a face-saving gesture for Cronin and the American League.

Automatic reinstatement was scheduled to follow. Salerno and Valentine also were to be recompensed the sum of $10,000 each, as salary for the 1969 season which they missed. Additionally, they were to receive full pension benefits retroactive to the date of their dismissal.

According to Valentine the American League, through its attorneys, made four different attempts at settlement. The first two of these secret agreements were drawn up and rejected during spring training. The third and fourth attempts occurred on July 6 in Boston, a day before the NLRB hearings.

The July 6 agreements were basically the same, though this time Salerno and Valentine would receive settlements of $20,000 each and were promised reinstatement prior to the 1971 season. Again Valentine accepted, but Salerno refused and, according to Valentine, told the attorneys, "Heck, I owe more than that. I owe $40,000."

Valentine Only One Attempting Settlement

Valentine, in recalling the incident months later, said, "I even agreed I would give Alex (Salerno) $8,000 to $10,000 from my $20,000. I told him, 'Alex, that'll give you $28 to $30,000. That ought to be enough to bail you out.'

"But Alex said, 'No, I want big money. I don't want to umpire anymore. I want $50,000.' He said, 'Tell them (the American League attorneys) if they give me $50,000, they won't have to worry about me anymore. I'm going to quit umpiring, anyway."

According to Valentine, the four lawyers huddled again. They were Hadden and Arthur Hayes, representing the American League; Reynolds from the Umpires' Association, and Henry Kelleher, the general counsel for the NLRB, who also was pushing for a settlement.

Another settlement offer was made. This time, Salerno was told he would be given $37,500 with the stipulation he would no longer seek reinstatement. "But Salerno refused this offer, too," Valentine said. Alex said, 'They've got to be kidding. I wouldn't take less than $100,000 to quit.' "

According to Valentine, Salerno was supported by Attorney Kelner in the belief he was going to win "big money" from the A. L. Kelner assured Salerno he would gain reinstatement via the NLRB and, in addition, predicted baseball eventually would agree to an out-of-court settlement of about $250,000 for each umpire on their antitrust and defamation of character suits.

At the year's end, Kelner was batting .000. The antitrust litigation, which originally was filed in 1969, was dismissed on motion, at the District Court level. The umpires appealed, but the Second Circuit Court of Appeals also dismissed the suit. A final appeal was made to the Supreme Court, but the nation's highest tribunal refused to hear the case.

Otherwise, it was a good year for the major league umpires. The men in blue won salary increases, for the regular season, of approximately $2,500 per man. This raise lifted some of the senior umpires, in both leagues, slightly above the $25,000-a-year bracket, a rather handsome figure. The umpires, through their association, also won increased pension benefits and a pre-retirement insurance plan was also inaugurated. In addition, the umpires received an increase in per diem expenses from $30 to $40 for each day of spring training and the regular championship season.

Playoffs Scene of Unprecedented Arbiter Strike

The umpires also won across-the-board increases for the championship playoffs, the World Series and All-Star games. These increases, however, were awarded after the umpires staged an unprecedented one-day strike. The strike occurred on October 3, a Saturday, which was the first day of the National and American League playoffs. All twelve of the umpires assigned to the playoffs (six for each game) struck and had the support of the Major League Umpires Association. A strike vote taken earlier by

the 52-man association was as follows: 37 in favor of a strike and 12 against. Three members did not appear at this meeting.

The strike wasn't a total surprise. There had been murmurs of a walk-out several days before, when negotiations on these issues were reaching an impasse. Both league offices secretly prepared against such an eventuality and decided that if there was a strike, minor league umpires would be used. Negotiations broke off on October 2, on the eve of the playoffs, and the league presidents assured the fans (and the television networks) that the playoffs would proceed as scheduled. Said N. L. President Chub Feeney: "We'll have the games played and we'll have four competent umpires." Declared Joe Cronin, the A. L. president: "Don't worry. There will be a ball game."

Picketing by Umpires Outside Pittsburgh Ballpark

The National League playoffs (Cincinnati vs. Pittsburgh) opened in Pittsburgh, a strong union city and which, coincidentally, was also the scene of a near-player strike in 1946. The American League playoffs (Baltimore vs. Minnesota) opened in Minnesota. The 12 regularly-assigned umpires did not go home and sulk. Instead, they went to the city where they had been assigned. They did this to emphasize their willingness to work and also to be ready, if and when league officials met their demands.

Most of the strike action, insofar as news stories, photographs—and the eventual resumption of negotiations—occurred in Pittsburgh. The umpires assigned there were at the new Three Rivers Stadium in the early morning, dressed in their working blue serge suits, complete with caps. As the crowd began arriving, there was this unusual sight: The umpires had split into pairs and were walking a picket line. Several umpires carried signs which read: "Major League Umpires on Strike for Wages." There was no picketing, however, at Minnesota's Metropolitan Stadium. The six American League umpires assigned there simply remained in their hotel rooms.

Four Minor League Arbiters Begin Playoffs

The games went on as scheduled. Four minor league umpires worked the Cincinnati-Pittsburgh game. They were John Grimsley and Fred Blandford of the American Association and Hank Morgenweck and George Grygiel of the International League. The substitute umpires at Minnesota were Bill Deegan of the American Association, Derold Satchel of the International League, and John Stevens and Charlie Berry, both veteran American League umpires who were still on the A. L. staff, Stevens as a swing-man, and Berry in a supervisory capacity. Before the games, the players and managers on all four clubs were told by league officials to go easy and, if at all possible, to refrain from criticizing an umpire's decision. Both games were played without any incidents involving the umpires.

The newspaper and television reports on the opening of the playoffs were highlighted by the umpires' strike. In many instances, the playoff games were the secondary story. The umpires in the picket line submitted, gladly, to numerous interviews. Harry Wendelstedt, one of the six umpires assigned to the National League playoffs and the president of the umpires' organization, told newsmen: "I'm a professional man. I don't want to be doing something like this. I want to be inside working.

I'm ashamed to be out here. We want to be properly compensated, that's all."

Significantly, the players, who themselves are highly organized, didn't express much sympathy. Marvin Miller and Dick Moss, the executive director and chief counsel for the Players Association, insisted the players were sympathetic but said they couldn't walk out since "a secondary boycott is illegal." Miller and Moss also pointed out that the Players Association must live up to its own contract with the major leagues.

Players Laud Efforts by Minor League Substitutes

The players, in post-game interviews, were high in their praise of the substitute umpires. Cincinnati catcher Johnny Bench lauded Grimsley, who worked the plate, and said, "You couldn't call a better game." Bench's comment was typical. Pete Rose, Cincinnati's All-Star outfielder, was one of the few players who seemed to be in genuine sympathy with the striking umpires. Said Rose: "Sure they (the substitutes) did a good job. But I'm sure the regular guys would have done a good job, too."

The striking umpires were on the picket line as early as 5 o'clock the next morning. By 8 o'clock officials from other unions also had gathered at the stadium and it was becoming apparent that the union members, whether employed by the Pirates or the county and working at Three Rivers Stadium, would honor the picket line. At approximately 11 o'clock, negotiations re-opened between National League President Feeney and Jack Reynolds, the counsel for the umpires' organization.

While Feeney and Reynolds were hammering out a temporary compromise, the ball park was virtually empty. City bus drivers, members of the Teamsters Union, refused to wheel the special busses into the stadium area. Members of the Building Service unions also remained outside. Ticket sellers and electricians would not cross the picket line. The grounds crew even refused to remove the tarpaulin from the infield.

At 11:30, Umpire Wendelstedt telephoned Bill Haller, the umpire in charge of the American League crew in Minneapolis, and told him to get his men together because they might be going to work in a matter of minutes. At 11:57, a unior leader of one of the Pittsburgh locals emerged from the Pirates' office and instructed his men to go to work.

An agreement had been reached. By this time, there were about 2,000 people standing outside the lower level of the stadium. A cheer went up. Said veteran National League umpire Al Barlick: "Give the people of Pittsburgh the credit. They're the greatest."

Hike Fees for World Series, Playoffs and All-Star Game

The agreement, which was finalized several days later, was for four years and was as follows: The pay scale for the playoffs was raised from $2,500 to $3,000 per man; the World Series, from $6,500 to $7,500 for 1970 and 1971, then to $8,000 in 1972 and 1973; and a flat $1,000 fee for the All-Star Game, which represented an increase of $500. The entire sum amounted to $81,000 in increased wages.

Historians may wish to note that the substitute umpires, though they worked only one game, were paid in full at the new playoff rate of $3,000 per man. The 12 striking umpires, all of whom returned to work, were Wendelstedt, Stan Landes, Nick Colosi, Bob Engel, Doug Harvey and Paul Pryor of the National League, and Haller, Jim Honochick, Russell Goetz,

Jerry Neudecker, James Odom and Marty Springstead of the American League.

There was also some labor vs. management difficulty between the owners and players. This dispute was to include a threat by the players of a one-day boycott, a "demonstration strike" which, it was reported, would occur on a Saturday or Sunday in May. But, in retrospect, this was an idle threat. The majority of the players appeared to be against a strike, though a strike vote never was taken. At the end, both sides agreed to a new contract with the hope that they would live happily ever after.

The dispute centered around the Basic Agreement which covers virtually all aspects of owner-player relations except the pension plan. The Basic Agreement expired on December 31, 1969, and was to have been replaced by April 5, the day before the season opened. When a new settlement was not reached by that date, the players agreed to give the owners a 30-day extension, until May 5. The vote to grant the owners the extra 30 days was taken, by teams, and passed 23 to 1.

The team against the extension was the Oakland Athletics. Infielder Bob Johnson, the A's player representative, revealed that 23 of the 25 Oakland players voted against the extension. Johnson emphasized, however, that this vote was not a reflection against Charlie Finley, the Oakland owner. "Mr. Finley called me and asked about it," Johnson said, "and I told him, 'Mr. Finley, we are not trying to single you out or ostracize you in any way. The players feel that the owners had been given enough time to work out a new agreement.'"

Other Oakland players were more outspoken. Said veteran outfielder Tito Francona: "The owners had all winter to sit down and talk. I don't see why we had to give them an extra 30 days. I think the owners haven't shown good faith. They've been stalling."

Don Mincher, Oakland's husky first baseman, agreed and declared: "This is all a stall by the owners. They're just beating Marvin Miller around the bush." Said veteran pitcher Jim (Mudcat) Grant: "An owner has never attended a single negotiation session. If we give them those 30 extra days, they'll just stall like they did before."

Negotiations resumed and on May 1 the owners submitted a "final" proposal. Miller summarized this proposal, which was 34 pages long, and mailed it to the players. Miller insisted he was sending this report to the players "without any recommendation," i.e., he was not offering advice. It would be up to the players to accept or reject.

99 Percent of Players Vote on Agreement Issue

The players rejected by an overwhelming margin. The vote, which was revealed by The Chicago Sun-Times, was 503-89, with 99 percent of the players voting, and 85 percent of them against acceptance. The only club in favor of acceptance was the Philadelphia Phillies. A club-by-club breakdown of this vote follows:

American League

California Angels	23-1	Baltimore Orioles	14-11
Chicago White Sox	23-0	Cleveland Indians	23-2
Kansas City Royals	25-0	Boston Red Sox	21-4
Minnesota Twins	23-1	Detroit Tigers	23-2
Oakland Athletics	25-0	New York Yankees	20-5
Milwaukee Brewers	18-7	Washington Senators	22-3

National League

Atlanta Braves	22-2	New York Mets	25-0
Chicago Cubs	22-3	Philadelphia Phillies	5-19
Cincinnati Reds	17-9	Pittsburgh Pirates	23-1
Houston Astros	25-0	St. Louis Cardinals	24-1
Los Angeles Dodgers	19-6	San Diego Padres	21-4
Montreal Expos	17-8	San Francisco Giants	23-0

At this point, there had been 35 negotiation sessions (since the previous October) between the owner and player groups and there were only three major areas of disagreement: 1, the length of the season; 2, playoff compensation, and 3, termination pay.

Agreement had been reached on increases in minimum salaries, and also on a fundamental change in the procedure of grievance cases in which Commissioner Bowie Kuhn no longer would be the final authority in all disputes, but only in those concerning the "integrity of the game." Other cases would go to an outside arbitrator, hired and approved by both parties.

The presence of an outside arbitrator was not new, though knowledge of this was not widespread. Dick Young of the New York Daily News, a long-time baseball watcher, when learning of this new clause in the Basic Agreement, accused the owners of "selling out" Commissioner Kuhn and lamented the diminution of his powers. Kuhn replied that this was done with his knowledge and approval and pointed out that the authority of the commissioner remained unchanged in cases involving the integrity of the game and that this is a key function of his office.

Kuhn Agrees With Wisdom of Outside Arbitrator

Said Kuhn: "I am of the opinion that the use of an outside arbitrator in all other matters will be helpful. It will remove a source of agitation between players and club owners and will make for a better understanding and a more efficient operation."

Further player-owner negotiations followed, and on May 23 Miller announced that a preliminary settlement had been reached, but was subject to ratification by the Players Association. Miller recommended acceptance and on June 8 the temporary agreement was made permanent. The players voted to accept by a 541-54 majority.

Under the new contract, which was for three years, the length of the season remained at 162 games (the players had been asking for a shorter, 154-game schedule) but the players won many gains, nonetheless. The new contract gave them an additional $4 million in benefits, of which $800,000 was to be realized the first year.

Some of the player gains follow:

•An increase in minimum salaries, from $10,000 to $12,000 in 1970, to $12,500 in 1971, and to $13,500 in 1972.

•An increase in the players' share of the playoff pool, from 50 to 60 percent, with all expenses coming out of the owners' share and not off the top as they did in 1969 when expenses amounted to $212,000.

•Players would receive 30 days' salary (one-sixth of the season) if cut during spring training, and 60 days' pay (one-third of the season) if cut during the regular season. Additionally, starting in 1972, a player cut after May 15 would receive his entire salary in full. Previously, a player re-

ceived nothing if dropped during spring training and only 30 days' pay if he was cut after the season had begun.

•An increase in spring training allowances from $15 to $16 in 1971, and to $17 in future years, plus a provision for cost of living increases.

A new limit on the amount a player's salary could be cut. The prior one-year limit of 20 percent remained, but the total cut over a two-year span can not be more than 30 percent.

Minor improvements in the scheduling of games so that "getaway" games must start no later than 5 p.m. (instead of 6 p.m.) if a team has a day game in another city the next day.

Players Association Gains Sole Bargaining Position

The owners recognized the Players Association as the sole and exclusive bargaining agent for all major league players and for individuals who may become major league players, with regard to all terms and conditions of employment, except (1) individual salaries over and above the minimum established and (2) special covenants to be included in the player's contract, which actually or potentially provide additional benefits to the player.

A player may be accompanied, if he so desires, by a representative of his choice to assist him in negotiating his individual salary with his employing club.

Also agreed upon was that until the final unappealable adjudication (or voluntary discontinuance) of Flood vs. Kuhn et al., now pending in the courts, neither of the parties would resort to any form of concerted action with respect to the reserve system.

One further aspect of the player-owner relations in 1970 is also worthy of mention. On June 22, the Players Association, after filing a grievance, won a total of $82,240 for additional World Series shares for the four second-place finishers of the previous season. The players involved were from the Detroit Tigers and the Oakland Athletics of the American League and the San Francisco Giants and Chicago Cubs of the National League.

The Players Association had claimed that a unilateral change in the player pool rule early in the 1969 season had reduced the benefits for some teams and charged this was in violation of the Basic Agreement. Arbitrator David L. Cole heard the grievance and ruled in favor of the players and the shares of the affected players were virtually doubled. The full shares for each of the players was increased by these amounts: Cubs $551; Giants $598; Tigers $623, and Athletics $595.

Player Salaries Climb to All-Time Peak

Player salaries in 1970 continued to spiral upward. According to published estimates, six players were earning at the rate of $125,000 a year. They were Frank Robinson, Baltimore; Carl Yastrzemski, Boston, and Frank Howard, Washington, of the American League; and Willie Mays, San Francisco; Hank Aaron, Atlanta, and Bob Gibson, St. Louis of the National League. Pete Rose of Cincinnati, Roberto Clemente of Pittsburgh and Juan Marichal and Willie McCovey of San Francisco were also reported in the $100,000 bracket.

Some owners did try to hold the line on salaries and, as a result, there was an uncommonly large number of holdouts, i.e., players who had not

signed on or before the official March 1 spring training reporting date. The holdouts included second baseman Davey Johnson of the Baltimore Orioles; first baseman Orlando Cepeda of the Atlanta Braves; outfielder Jim Wynn of the Houston Astros; outfielder Reggie Jackson of the Oakland Athletics, and pitcher Steve Carlton and outfielder-first baseman Richie Allen of the St. Louis Cardinals.

Late Signers Wage Tough Battle for Bucks

Cepeda and Johnson signed on March 3, Cepeda for an estimated $80,000 and Johnson for $35,000. Allen capitulated for a reported $90,000 on March 12 and five days later the Cardinals also signed Carlton, who agreed to a two-year pact that was said to call for $32,000 for 1970 and $40,000 for 1971. Wynn signed for $60,000 on March 22. Jackson was the last to submit and signed for $45,000 on March 25, considerably less than the $75,000 he had been asking for, but still $20,000 more than he had earned the season before. As a bonus, Oakland Owner Charlie Finley also gave Jackson a rent-free apartment.

The Carlton and Jackson holdouts were rather bitter and many angry words were exchanged. Cardinal Owner Gussie Busch indicated that Carlton was seeking a 100 percent raise, from $25,000 to $50,000. After one particularly frustrating negotiating session, Busch said, "I don't care if he (Carlton) ever pitches another damn ball for us." Owner Finley and Jackson also hurled unkind epithets at each other in a feud that lasted into the championship season.

Busch's anger went deeper than the mere fact he was confronted with holdouts Allen and Carlton. Busch seemed infuriated by the rebellious times and admitted to disillusionment. "I can't understand it," Busch said. "The player contracts are at their best, the pension plan is the finest, and the fringe benefits are better than ever. Yet, the players think that we (the owners) are a bunch of stupid asses."

In rebuttal to the soaring salaries, a total of 11 major league clubs increased ticket prices, though some of the increases were nominal. The Boston Red Sox, for example, boosted their reserve seat price by only 25 cents. One club, the Cleveland Indians, cut prices and reduced by $1 the cost of all reserved seats for children under 12.

N. L. Attendance Hits New High—16,662,198

Attendance continued to climb. The National League set another all-time record with 16,662,198 paid admissions, an increase of 1,567,252 over the previous season. The American League, however, suffered a slight decline and drew 12,085,135, a drop of 45,684 from its 1969 total. The 1970 aggregate major league gate was a record 28,747,333 and represented an increase of 1,521,568 from the previous season.

Nine of the National League clubs passed the million mark, headed by the New York Mets who set a club and New York major league record with 2,697,479 admissions. The Mets probably would have broken the all-time, single-team record had they been able to hang in the pennant race a day or two longer. As it was, they fell only 57,705 short of the record high of 2,755,184 set by the 1962 Los Angeles Dodgers.

The Cincinnati Reds, who had the double advantage of winning a pennant and playing in a new park, and the Montreal Expos were the only other major league teams to set club records. The league champion

Reggie Jackson, in casual splendor, arrives at camp following bitter haggling over salary with A's Owner Charlie Finley.

The National Anthem is being sung prior to the first ball ever pitched in the Reds' new Riverfront Stadium June 30. Atlanta was the visiting club.

Reds drew 1,803,568—a whopping 677,640 admissions beyond their previous record of 1,125,928 set in 1956. The Expos, playing in a park with a seating capacity of only 28,000, attracted 1,424,683.

The Boston Red Sox, with the smallest park in the league, only 33,000 seats, led the American League with 1,595,278 admissions, a remarkable total considering that the Red Sox were seldom in contention. The California Angels were the biggest gainer in the A. L. and showed an increase of 319,353 from the previous season. The Milwaukee Brewers, in their maiden A. L. season, drew 933,690, almost 300,000 more than the same club drew in Seattle the season before.

The benefits that can be gained by a new stadium were well illustrated in Cincinnati and Pittsburgh. These clubs ranked 1-2 in the majors insofar as the biggest gate increases from the previous season, the Reds showing a gain of 815,577 and the Pirates 572,578. Pittsburgh's total gate was 1,341,947—the Pirates' largest since 1960.

The Reds moved into their new park first, on June 30, and on the first night set a new single-game club record by drawing 51,050 fans. All of the National League's top officials were on hand for the opening. Commissioner Bowie Kuhn was among the dignitaries and said, "Ball parks like this are an exquisite addition to baseball. I'm delighted with it." So were the Cincinnati fans. The Reds' average gate for 34 dates at Crosley Field, before the switch, was 16,704; for 43 openings at their new Riverfront Stadium, the average was 28,735.

The Pirates played their first game at their new Three Rivers Stadium on July 16 and drew a crowd of 48,846. Like the Reds before them, the Pirates also lost their new-park opener. To coincide with this gala opening, the Pirates also introduced new buttonless uniforms made of stretchable lightweight nylon and cotton. The shirts are slipovers and the pants resemble ski slacks.

The Philadelphia Phillies also were expected to move into their new park in 1970. This stadium was to have been ready for opening day, but construction was delayed by bad weather. A second opening-date of May 9 was scheduled, but the stadium was further delayed by a strike of non-skilled construction workers.

There was considerable nostalgia when the Reds and Pirates played their final games in their old home parks, but the biggest, or certainly the most violent, farewell occurred in Philadelphia on the night of October 1 when the Phillies said adieu to Connie Mack Stadium, the major league's oldest park, which was opened as Shibe Park on April 12, 1909.

The Phillies, who now will be moving into their new park in 1971, drew their largest crowd of the season, 31,822, in this farewell. To mark the occasion, club officials had planned to give away a total of 62 prizes in post-game drawings, but the crowd was so wild that the drawings had to be postponed until the next day.

Fans Demolished Stands of Dying Phillie Park

Veteran Philadelphia scribe Allen Lewis, writing about the Phillies' farewell in THE SPORTING NEWS, reported that ". . . after the last fan had departed, the park wasn't good for much more than a junkyard. They ripped up their seats, ransacked the dugouts, ripped off the railings and billboards and tore off the doors." Lewis also wrote that one fan even carried off a toilet.

Connie Mack, Jr., son of the famed manager, came up from his Florida home for the occasion. When introduced to the crowd, he said: "I wasn't sure I was in Philadelphia until I heard the boos."

Artificial turf, the newest thing in baseball, was used in the new Cincinnati and Pittsburgh parks and, immediately prior to the 1970 season, also had been installed at Busch Memorial Stadium in St. Louis and at Candlestick Park in San Francisco. This brought to six the number of major league stadiums with ersatz grass. The two others are the Astrodome in Houston, which pioneered in this area, and Comiskey Park in Chicago, the home of the White Sox, who put in an artificial grass infield in 1969.

Baseball people, owners and players alike, seemed to be divided on whether or not the artificial turf was beneficial to the game. The new carpet virtually eliminated the bad hop, which met with the unanimous approval of the infielders. The ball also seemed to skip through the infield with greater speed. This gave the hitters an advantage, but angered the pitchers. There also was some fear that because of the fast surface the bunt would become extinct.

AstroTurf was used in Cincinnati's Riverfront Stadium and covered the entire field, including the baselines. The entire playing surface resembled one large pool table. The only patches of dirt were around the bases and on the pitcher's mound. Tartan-Turf was installed in the Three

Rivers Stadium in Pittsburgh which, however, retained the dirt baselines and the skin part of the infield.

Some players complained that there wasn't enough "give" in the artificial turf and that it was hard on the legs, a belief corroborated by Don Seger, trainer for the Philadelphia Phillies who said because of a ". . . greater pounding effect, some of my players would ache, be sore in the calves of their legs and in Achilles tendon area." Other players complained about the heat and contended that the artificial carpet was considerably hotter than the conventional grass.

Football Presses for Wider Use of Artificial Turf

Still another controversial aspect was that the professional football teams, which share most of the new stadiums with baseball, were constantly pushing for artificial turf. This was especially apparent in Minneapolis where the football Vikings advised civic officials that artificial grass was a necessity. Calvin Griffith, president of the Minnesota Twins, took an opposite view and, as the prime tenant of Metropolitan Stadium, said he wanted the Twins to continue playing on the traditional grass.

The one area in which everyone seemed to agree was that the ersatz grass helped the batting averages. Carl Yastrzemski of the Boston Red Sox, after playing in the All-Star Game which was held at the Riverfront Stadium, said, "It's great for the hitters. It's got to help some guys 30 points on their batting averages and a lot of other guys at least 15 points. You can't believe the speed the ball picks up when it hits the surface."

The use of synthetic grass coincided with the movement by Commissioner Kuhn, and others, for higher batting averages. There was no new legislation against the pitchers in 1970, as there had been the season before, but there was a notable 1970 spring training experiment in which a lively ball was introduced. This ball, called X-5, because it was five percent livelier, was to be used in all Wednesday spring training games.

The experiment was a success in the sense that there was a decisive reaction. Almost everyone, except the hitters, was against X-5. Though only five percent livelier, the ball soared into the wild blue yonder with tremendous speed. Scores were higher and tape-measure home runs became somewhat commonplace.

X-5 Ball Enters Orbit—Experiment Dropped

The reaction against X-5 was so intense that Commissioner Kuhn discontinued the experiment after only two Wednesdays of competition. The commissioner noted that 22 games had been played with X-5 and that this constituted an "adequate test basis" for analysis of the ball's effect and for comparison with any future experiments. Kuhn said a "substantial quantity of data on the ball's characteristics" had been collected and that a report would be made public when the analysis was complete.

The players and managers, however, had seen enough. One of the comments against X-5, and which was typical, was voiced by veteran Manager Leo Durocher of the Chicago Cubs, who declared: "If they use that ball on AstroTurf or Tartan-Turf, somebody will get killed." Significantly, the commissioner's office never made public its findings on X-5. Explained Kuhn later: "There wasn't any need. Everyone was against it."

THE SPORTING NEWS also urged abandonment of the X-5 pellet and in an editorial said: "What baseball needs is more batters making contact with the ball, not batters aiming for the fences. Singles, doubles and triples are where the action is. A livelier ball is not the answer to the shortages in those departments. There's not much exciting about a steady stream of strikeouts."

As THE SPORTING NEWS and Commissioner Kuhn hoped they would, the batting averages continued to rise. The major league batting average in 1970 was .253 compared with .248 in 1969 and .237 in 1968. Run production was also up. An average of 8.68 runs were scored (by both teams) in one game compared with 8.16 and 6.84 the previous two years. There was also a slight increase in home runs and a decrease in shutouts.

Other experiments designed mostly to escalate run production, also were tested, though at the minor league level. These experiments included the use of a designated pinch-batter who could hit for the pitcher at any time, without forcing the pitcher to leave the game, an automatic intentional walk, on the word of the manager and without pitches being thrown, and expanded foul lines that increased the fair territory area.

The Eastern League used the pinch-batting experiment, which was later rejected by the Playing Rules Committee. The automatic walk was tested in the New York-Pennsylvania League and also met with disfavor. Charles Segar, chairman of the Rules Committee, said that according to reports the automatic walk speeded up the game by only a few seconds and was almost always greeted by boos from the fans.

Wider Foul Lines For More 'Hit' Area Sidelined

The wider foul lines constituted a definite change in the playing field. The foul lines "flared out" beyond first and third bases by three degrees. This produced 12 extra feet of fair territory at each outfield corner (assuming the fences were 320 feet distant) and added a total of 2,771 square feet to fair territory, an increase of 2.8 percent. The idea was to help the offense by making more space for fair balls and force the outfielders either to spread out or leave the foul lines less guarded. This experiment, used on only one Gulf Coast Rookie League field, was soundly rejected.

Also rejected by the Playing Rules Committee was the recommendation, by Oakland Owner Charlie Finley, of the use of colored bases and colored foul lines. Finley did gain approval from Commissioner Kuhn to use gold colored bases, which glowed under the lights, for Oakland's opening game. But permission was limited to this one game only and the Rules Committee subsequently vetoed this suggestion. The trend, however, was to color. At season's end, three clubs—the Red Sox, White Sox and Phillies—announced they would be using red shoes, with white stripes, in 1971.

Clearly, Commissioner Kuhn, plus some owners and general managers, were eager to explore all possible new avenues that might make the game more attractive. Kuhn was also in favor of greater spectator involvement and in mid-March announced that the starting teams for the midseason All-Star Game would be selected by the fans. This, in itself, was not new; fans had participated in previous All-Star polls, which usually were conducted with the assistance of newspapers.

It was the system of selection that was a departure from the past. The Gillette Company underwrote all costs and placed ballots in some 75,000 stores from coast to coast. Ballots also were available at 150 major

Controversial All-Star ballots, from noted fans (from left) then Sen. Eugene McCarthy, former Chief Justice Earl Warren and former Presidential candidate Hubert Humphrey and shot of actor Cary Grant casting his ballot in California, all held by Commissioner Kuhn.

and minor league parks. The ballots actually were punch cards and were processed by computer. Each ballot included six nominees for each infield position and catcher, and 18 outfielders. The pitchers and reserves, as in the past, were selected by the All-Star managers. The voting period was from May 30 through June 28.

A king-sized rhubarb, one of the biggest of the season, resulted when it was discovered the names of some potential All-Stars were omitted from the ballots. This flaw was due to an early deadline. Because of the printing and distribution problems, Gillette had advised the commissioner's office that the ballots had to be completed by late February. Thus, the decision as to which 96 players (48 from each league) were to be listed had to be made even before spring training.

The commissioner's office then asked the player representatives from each team to submit the names of players whom they thought would be most likely deserving of All-Star recognition. Some but not all of the player reps responded and filled out these questionnaires. Managers were also consulted. Aware there would be other deserving players, some of them rookies, space was left on each ballot for write-in candidates.

The foresight to provide write-in space helped save the day because

there was an immediate avalanche of criticism when it was learned, for example, that outfielder Rico Carty of the Atlanta Braves did not make the printed list. Atlantans reacted as if the Yankees were coming. Within hours after this slight was revealed, the Braves received more than 200 telephone calls from angry fans. Carty, at the time, was leading both leagues with a .421 average and had batted safely in 28 consecutive games.

On May 10, when the ballots were made public, six of the National League's top ten hitters were not listed. Among the missing were such potential All-Stars as Al Kaline of Detroit; Ray Fosse and Vada Pinson, Cleveland; Dick Dietz, San Francisco; Bill Grabarkewitz, Los Angeles; Alex Johnson, California Angels; Doug Rader, Houston; Don Money, Phillies, and Nate Colbert, San Diego. Compounding the situation was the fact that Ken Harrelson of Cleveland and Mike Shannon of St. Louis, both disabled because of spring training tragedies, were on the list. But luckily, Carty received enough write-in votes to win a starting berth.

Fading Bouton's Book Fires Up Major Controversy

Another of the year's biggest rhubarbs involved a player who didn't have a chance to make the All-Star team. At the center of this swirling controversy, which lasted through the season, was Jim Bouton, a tousle-haired 31-year-old relief pitcher who was hanging onto the fringes of the major leagues by his fingertips. A 21-game winner with the New York Yankees in 1963 and victorious in two 1964 World Series games, Bouton was sent to the minors when he lost his fast ball. He spent most of the 1968 season in the bushes and was then rescued by the Seattle Pilots, one of the American League's new expansion teams.

Bouton joined Seattle at its 1969 spring training camp and began keeping a diary. This was not a little-girl diary, to be hidden under his pillow and for no one else to see. The intention, from the beginning, was to publish. Bouton took notes. In addition, he often spoke into a tape recorder and mailed the casettes to Leonard Shecter, a former baseball writer for the New York Post who had agreed and sought the collaboration. The result was a blockbuster of a book, titled "Ball Four," and sub-titled "My Life and Hard Times Throwing the Knuckleball in the Big Leagues."

Seldom, if ever, did a sports book cause such a stir. Look Magazine, where Shecter was a senior editor, ran two lengthy pre-publication excerpts. The baseball establishment reacted in horror. The diary was a veritable "kiss and tell" expose written from the inside. The private lives of some players were included, with a healthy portion of sex. Bouton told how some of the players were Peeping Toms and of the chicanery of some general managers when negotiating salaries with their players. He also tilted the halo of Mickey Mantle, his long-time teammate with the Yankees.

Of Mantle, Bouton wrote:

". . . . There were all of those times he'd push little kids aside when they wanted his autograph and the times when he was snooty to reporters, just about making them crawl and beg for a minute of his time. I've seen him slam a bus window on kids trying to get autographs. And I hated that *look* of his, when he'd get angry at somebody and cut him down with a glare.

"Like everybody else on the club, I ached with Mantle when he had one of his numerous and extremely painful injuries. I often wondered, though, if he might have healed quicker if he'd been sleeping more and

Jim Bouton visited the new offices of THE SPORTING NEWS and signed a copy of "Ball Four" for Managing Editor Lowell Reidenbaugh.

loosening up with the boys at the bar less. I guess we'll never know. What we do know, though, is that the face he showed in the clubhouse, as opposed to the one he reserved for the outside world, was often one of great merriment.

"I remember one time he'd been injured and didn't expect to play, and I guess he got himself smashed. The next day, he was hung over out of his mind and was sent up to pinch-hit. He could hardly see. So he staggered to the plate and hit a tremendous drive to left field for a home run. When he came back into the dugout, everybody shook his hand and leaped all over him, and all the time he was getting a standing ovation from the crowd. He squinted out at the stands and said, 'Those people don't know how tough that really was.' "

In defense of his diary, and himself, Bouton admitted, "It is not a normal baseball book, like 'The Perfect Game' or 'How I Became A Great Star,' " and emphasized that his was not a totally clandestine undertaking.

In a radio interview in St. Louis during the summer while visiting with the Astros, Bouton said: "I didn't masquerade . . . . I kept a note pad with me wherever I went. The players knew I was writing a book. Sometimes the players would come to me and say, 'Hey, I got something for your book. Write this down!' Or, I'd be sitting at a bar and they'd say 'Did you get that?' Or someone would make a funny comment and one of

the players would remark, 'There goes Bouton writing it down again.' So they knew I was writing a book. They just had no idea of the contents.

"I wasn't trying to prove anything, good or bad. I happen to like playing baseball. I like quite a bit about the game and wanted to share the fun that I've had in the game with the fans, showing them what the game is really like, good parts and bad."

Leo Durocher, manager of the Cubs, said he wouldn't have Bouton on his club, and the San Diego Padres, demonstrating disapproval, burned a copy of the book and left the charred pages and binding in a heap in the visitors' clubhouse in Los Angeles, for Bouton to see. Telling about this later, Bouton said, laughing, "Everyone wants to have their book banned in Boston, but the next best thing is to have someone burn it."

In a sense, the book was banned by baseball. Before publication, just after the excerpts had appeared in Look, Commissioner Bowie Kuhn had Bouton on the carpet. Bouton was ordered to report to Kuhn's New York office on June 1. Bouton complied and brought with him Marvin Miller and Dick Moss, the executive director and counsel for the Players Association. This meeting lasted for two hours.

Kuhn Scolds Author, But Doesn't Spank

Kuhn emerged and read this statement: "I met today with Jim Bouton for the purpose of discussing recently published writings co-authored by him.

"I advised Mr. Bouton of my displeasure with these writings and have warned him against future writings of this character.

"Under all the circumstances, I have concluded that no other action was necessary."

Bouton's publishers greeted this announcement with unrestrained glee. Thereafter "Ball Four" was advertised as "The Book Baseball Tried To Ban." Commissioner Kuhn's censure merely stimulated sales and at the year's end, the book, which was to have had an original printing of 10,000, had sales in excess of 100,000 copies in hard cover and was expected to become the best-selling sports book ever.

As for pitcher Bouton, he encountered hard times. He couldn't control his knuckleball and on July 31 the Houston club sent him to their Oklahoma City farm club in the American Association. Bouton departed with a 4-6 record and with a 5.42 earned-run average for 73 innings of toil. He took the demotion gracefully and said, "If anything, I probably stayed up here (in the majors) longer because of the book. The Houston executives bent over backward to show people they weren't worried about what I had written." Bouton made two appearances for Oklahoma City and then retired from the game. Later, he took a job as a sports television announcer in New York City and revealed he was busy writing another book, this one to be titled, "I Hope You Didn't Take It Personally."

Bouton wasn't the year's only player-author. Bill Freehan, star catcher of the Tigers, also lugged a tape recorder and, like Bouton, kept a diary of the 1969 season. This dear diary, entitled "Behind The Mask," hit the book stalls in March and created a stir, though it was a mere ripple compared with Bouton's book. "Behind the Mask" was an artistic and financial flop and sold about 20,000, which is about normal for a sports book.

Whereas Bouton stood his ground and said he wasn't sorry, Freehan was ashamed of his work and vowed never to do it again. Excerpts of

Even though scowling in the midst of a heated argument in '69 with umpire Bill Kinnamon, these were happier times for Bill Freehan (left) and Mayo Smith (center)—before Bill's book came out. Mickey Lolich eyes the crabgrass.

Freehan's book appeared initially in Sports Illustrated and, in the main, were limited to Freehan's critical comments on Tiger pitcher Denny McLain and Mayo Smith, the Tigers' veteran manager. Freehan told how McLain was able to come and go as he pleased and pictured Smith as a nice guy but ineffective manager, who supposedly had one set of rules for McLain and another set for the 24 other Tiger players.

Freehan apparently went into this venture with considerable naivete and came out with a red face. He didn't want to discuss the book with writers and avoided as many interviews as possible. "Why don't you ease up and just let me play baseball," Freehan told several scribes on one occasion. When confronted again, Freehan said: "Let's talk about what's happening on the field. We're trying to win (the pennant) this year. What's done is done as far as the book is concerned."

Freehan apologized to McLain and Smith and said he was sorry during a heated clubhouse exchange with Grover Resinger, the Tigers' third base coach. Resinger accused him of disloyalty to his club and was so upset he informed Manager Smith he was quitting at the end of the season because he "couldn't keep working with someone who had written things about his teammates." Freehan told Resinger he was sorry and said,

"I didn't mean it to come out that way." Resinger quit the Tigers in October, as he said he would.

It was also the last year for Smith at the Detroit helm. Smith was to be one of five managers who were fired in 1970, either during the season, or immediately thereafter. Others who got the axe were Clyde King of the Giants; Charlie Metro of the Royals, Don Gutteridge of the White Sox and John McNamara of the Athletics.

King was the first to go. He was given the boot on May 23, his 46th birthday, after a 17-16, 15-inning loss to the Padres. Horace Stoneham, Giant owner, expressed great regret: 'I have just finished an unpleasant task. I told Clyde I thought we could improve the situation, or whatever you want to call it, if we changed managers."

Fox, Russ Hodges Veterans of Giants' Organization

King, who had directed the Giants to their fifth consecutive second-place finish in 1969, was replaced by Charlie Fox, a long-time organization man. Fox had been managing the Giants' Phoenix (Pacific Coast) farm club. Under King, the Giants had a 19-23 won-and-lost record. They improved and were 67-53 under Fox' guidance but, nonetheless, finished third in the National League West. Russ Hodges, voice of the Giants for 22 years, quit the mike and joined the club's P. R. department. Hodges witnessed every Mays homer (628).

Metro also was the victim of an early bounce. The Royals fired him on June 9. Cedric Tallis, the Royals' executive vice-president, voiced the traditional regrets. Some friction had developed between Metro and his players, but Tallis insisted that was not a factor in the dismissal. Said Tallis: "I think there's a great misconception about managers—that the players have to like the manager. I think the club was hustling. Charlie did his utmost. It took a lot of soul-searching to reach this decision."

Bob Lemon, who was Metro's pitching coach, became the new Kansas City manager. A one-time pitching star with the Indians (207 major league victories), Lemon had spent four years managing minor league teams and four more years as a major league coach, but never was a manager before. The Royals were 19-33 under Metro and 46-64 under Lemon.

The White Sox, who underwent the biggest shakeup, fired Gutteridge September 2. At the time, the Chisox had a 49-87 chart and were in last place in the A. L. West. Third base coach Bill Adair was named interim manager for 10 games, during which time the Sox were 4-6.

Tanner Had Led Hawaii to PCL Division Title

Owner John Allyn, stressing youth, then appointed Chuck Tanner as the club's field manager. Tanner, 41, a one-time outfielder with the cross-town Cubs, had been managing minor league clubs for the previous eight seasons and just had led Hawaii to a Pacific Coast League divisional title. He took over as Chicago's new boss on September 14. The Sox were 3-13 under Tanner and finished with a club record of 106 losses.

Detroit fired Smith on October 1, immediately after the Tigers' final game. Smith had handled the Tigers for four years and guided them to the 1968 pennant. He departed with kind words for his employers and for Denny McLain, who spent most of the season under suspension. Said Smith, pointing to his World Series ring, "That man (McLain) helped put that ring on my finger and I'm very proud of that ring."

Firebrand Billy Martin, who had a choice of several managing jobs, was revealed as Smith's successor the next day. At his first press conference, Martin paid homage to Smith and said: "I know I'm taking a wonderful man's spot by replacing Mayo Smith. I've admired him all my life." It was Martin's second major league managing job. He had directed Minnesota to the A. L.'s West Division title in 1969, but was fired, nonetheless.

The fifth and last managerial change was at Oakland. Owner Charlie Finley broke the bad news to McNamara on October 2. Finley thus kept his record intact of never having a manager last as long as two years. Oakland finished second in the American League West under McNamara and won 89 games, most victories by an Athletic team since 1932.

It was the 11th managerial change for Finley since he bought the club in 1960. Finley chose Dick Williams as McNamara's successor. Williams had spent the 1970 season as a coach with the Expos, had previous managerial experience in the American League, and had his biggest success in 1967 when he managed the Red Sox to their first pennant in 22 years.

As in the past, there were speculative stories about the possibility of a Negro manager. A non-profit organization, Race Relations Information Center of Nashville, Tenn., took a survey forecast that there would be a black manager within the next three years and predicted the honor was most

Familiar No. 7 in an unfamiliar role. Mickey Mantle on his first day as a first-base coach August 30, has his first baserunner, Bobby Murcer.

likely to go to Willie Mays of the Giants, Ernie Banks of the Cubs or Maury Wills of the Dodgers.

Mickey Mantle, the Yankee super star who retired as a player prior to the 1969 season, also appeared to be interested in returning to the majors as a manager. Mantle revealed his managerial ambitions in midsummer and, on August 29, rejoined the Yankees as a coach, presumably to begin an apprenticeship that eventually would allow him to succeed Ralph Houk as the Yankee pilot. Mantle finished the season with the Bombers, but was not expected to return as a full-time coach in 1971.

Chisox Shake Up Front-Office Personnel

Of all the major league clubs, the White Sox made the most changes at the management level. In addition to the firing of Gutteridge, Owner John Allyn dismissed Ed Short, a longtime Chisox employe who had risen through the ranks to become the club's trade-maker and vice-president in charge of player personnel. Explained Owner Allyn: "Short worked hard at his job. But it was imperative that we change the image of the ball club."

Stu Holcomb, a former nationally-known college football coach and previously a vice-president in charge of White Sox public relations, emerged as the new front-office chief. Holcomb then hired Roland Hemond, 42, as the Chisox' director of player personnel and trade-maker. Hemond came highly recommended. He had served a long and distinguished apprenticeship and was hired away from the Angels, where he had been the farm and scouting director.

The Mets also underwent some executive changes, though this was the result of the death of Johnny Murphy, who had been the Mets' general manager. Bob Scheffing, a former major league catcher who had been Murphy's assistant, took over as the Met g.m. Said M. Donald Grant, the Mets' chairman of the board: "Mr. Scheffing was our only serious candidate. We all felt we had the right man." This change occurred in mid-January, shortly after Murphy's death.

Marvin Milkes resigned as executive vice-president and general manager of the Brewers. Milkes, who retained his position during the Seattle-Milwaukee transfer, was given a new five-year contract on May 4, but announced his resignation on December 17. Milkes did agree, however, to remain with the Brewers as a special-assignment scout in Southern California. He later was succeeded by Frank Lane.

Young O'Malley and Galbreath Take Over From Dads

Peter O'Malley, the boss' son, continued to win promotion and in March was named president of the Dodgers. Peter succeeded his father, Walter, 66, who stepped down as president, but remained as chairman of the board. A month later, the elder O'Malley underwent abdominal surgery.

A similar change occurred in Pittsurgh. John Galbreath, 72, resigned as the club president and was succeeded by his son, Dan, 41. The elder Galbreath, who had been the Pirates' chief executive officer for 23 years, was elected chairman of the board and, in announcing the change, said: "I decided to put some young and more active people in the picture."

Age also finally caught up with Bill Skiff, 75, and brought to an end his 55-year career in baseball when he resigned as a super-scout for the Brewers. Skiff had been a player for 18 years, a minor league manager and

farm director and major league scout. He was the farm supervisor for the Yankees in 1938, when the Bombers had 21 teams and the most extensive minor league operation at the time.

Joe DiMaggio, another baseball old-timer, resigned as a coach with the Athletics. DiMaggio departed immediately after spring training and with kind words for Charlie Finley, the controversial Oakland owner. DiMaggio later turned down a job offered to him by Commissioner Kuhn and explained he did not plan to stay in baseball because he was weary of the travel.

Indians Sail 'Tight Ship' Course of Operation

The Cleveland Indians, who were losing money at a rapid rate, cut their scouting budget and during the World Series announced the release of six scouts in what was described as an economy move. Given the bounce were Henry (Dutch) Dotterer of Syracuse; Benny Zientara and Jerry Krause of Chicago; Ed McCarrick, Long Island; Ray Mueller, Steelton, Pa., and Tony Stiel, Pontiac.

While Cleveland was cutting down, other organizations were expanding. The Pirates, who were moving into a new stadium, beefed up their executive staff by hiring Bill Guilfoile to head up their public relations department. Guilfoile, a graduate of Notre Dame, had been a p.r. man with the Yankees since 1960.

The Dodgers added Don Newcombe, their one-time pitching ace, to their front office. In one of his first moves as club president, young Peter O'Malley appointed Newcombe to a newly-created post as the Dodgers' director of community relations. "I know Don will be a great help to us," said O'Malley.

The Washington Senators, though troubled financially, also found a spot for David Eisenhower, grandson of former President Dwight Eisenhower and the son-in-law of President Richard Nixon. David, an avid baseball fan, requested and was given a summer job as a statistician and kept tabs on all Washington players plus the 120 players with the organization's five minor league teams. David also made several trips with the Senators.

The Atlanta Braves showed no such sentiment and instead achieved something of a first. In an effort to provide scribes with quicker statistical data, the Braves leased an IBM computer and fed it all of the available data. "We are only scratching the surface," said Lee Walburn, the Braves' publicity man. "We hope to show that major league baseball can formulate a joint computer program that will add accuracy, immediacy and volume to the current methods of baseball data processing."

Sandy Hadden New General Counsel and Secretary-Treasurer

Commissioner Kuhn's staff also was expanded. Alexander (Sandy) Hadden, for the last five years an attorney for the American League, joined the commissioner's office as general counsel and secretary-treasurer. Johnny Johnson, previously of the Yankees, where he had served as director of player procurement and development, was hired as an administrator by the commissioner and assigned a variety of duties including "matters relating to player sources and development covering all minor leagues, amateur baseball and foreign groups; and external relations with other sports, both amateur and professional."

Robert C. Shea was appointed executive director of the Major League

Bob Short (center), owner of the Senators and Washington's No. 1 foe of unemployment, hired David Eisenhower, grandson of the late President, as a public relations assistant. At right is young Pete Bavasi, son of the owner of the Padres and minor league director of the San Diego club.

Baseball Promotion Corporation, which works closely with the commissioner's office. Shea's assignment included responsibility for promoting baseball on a national level, the supervision of licensing and merchandising activities and the development of new marketing approaches with particular emphasis on the use of movies, radio, television and the printed media.

Also joining the commissioner's staff was Henry A. Fitzgibbon, who was appointed the Director of Security for baseball. Formerly with the Federal Bureau of Investigation, Fitzgibbon was assigned the task of patrolling all 24 major league clubs. Later, two other security officers, Francis J. Gallant and Buck Greene, also were hired by Commissioner Kuhn. The security men had a busy rookie season.

Anonymous threats were made on the lives of several players in 1970. Ernie Banks, longtime star of the Cubs, received threatening phone calls from Chicago while at the Bruins' Scottsdale (Ariz.) spring training camp. Banks was advised to leave the field in the midst of a workout and spent several days in seclusion while the FBI made arrests. Banks returned to uniform without further incident.

Baseball's new security officers also investigated a threat on the life of Cleon Jones, star left fielder of the Mets. Jones received an anonymous

letter advising him he would be shot at Shea Stadium on September 29 "with one out in the top of the first inning." The letter also stated "See you in the graveyard" and was signed "Chicago No. 1." Jones disregarded the letter.

Also threatened by mail was Ron Santo, the All-Star third baseman of the Cubs. Santo was warned he would be shot if he played in the Cubs' final series, which was against the Mets at Shea Stadium. Fitzgibbon, plus a squad of FBI agents, accompanied Santo and the Cubs to the ball park. An hour before game-time, it was decided that since the pennant already had been clinched (by Pittsburgh), Santo should not play and instead returned to Chicago. Hence, Santo missed the Cubs' final four games.

Clemente Reveals '69 Kidnapping Experience in San Diego

Roberto Clemente, star Pittsburgh outfielder, revealed that he had been kidnapped in May, 1969, while in San Diego for a series with the Padres. Clemente didn't tell of the circumstances of the kidnapping until August 11, 1970, when he mentioned it to baseball writer Bill Christine of the Pittsburgh Press.

Clemente said he was returning to the El Cortez Hotel with a bag of fried chicken at about 1 a.m., after a night game. About two blocks from the hotel, four men forced him into a car at gun-point. They drove to an isolated mountain area and ordered Clemente to strip to his undershorts and took his wallet, All-Star ring and about $250 in cash.

"This is where I figure they are going to shoot me and throw me into the woods," Clemente explained. "They already had the pistol inside my mouth." Two of his captors spoke Spanish and Clemente, also speaking Spanish, pleaded for his life and told them he was a baseball player with the San Diego Padres, on the hope that they might be baseball fans.

The kidnappers deliberated and spoke among themselves for several minutes. They returned his possessions and drove Clemente back to the hotel unharmed and even gave him his bag of fried chicken which had not been opened. A San Diego detective, when told the story, said he believed it was true because of the accuracy of Clemente's description where he was taken.

Clemente, as usual, was among the year's leading performers. Though injured and used sparingly late in the season, Clemente set a modern major league record in August by knocking out 10 hits in two consecutive games. He also continued approaching the 3,000-hit plateau and had 145 hits for the season to increase his career total to 2,704.

Mays, Aaron Join 3,000-Hit Club in Span of Two Months

Two players, Hank Aaron of the Braves and Willie Mays of the Giants, joined the 3,000-hit club in 1970. Aaron's 3000th hit came May 17 and was a single off Wayne Simpson of Cincinnati. Mays reached this milestone on July 18 when he singled off Mike Wegener of the Expos.

Mays and Aaron were the ninth and tenth players to reach the 3,000-hit level and also continued as baseball's most productive home-run hitters, with the exception of Babe Ruth. Mays slammed 28 homers to increase his career total to 628 and Aaron had 38 to lift his total to 592. Ernie Banks of the Cubs joined the 500-homer club on May 12 when he connected against Atlanta's Pat Jarvis. Banks finished the season with a career total of 509 homers, putting him ninth among the all-time sluggers.

Cesar Gutierrez, Detroit shortstop, became the first player in modern major league history to knock out seven consecutive hits in one game. He had six singles and a double in seven trips in a 12-inning, second game of a June 21 doubleheader at Cleveland. The only other player to go 7-for-7 was Wilbert Robinson of the Baltimore National League club in 1892. Robinson's performance, however, came in a nine-inning game.

Vic Davalillo of the St. Louis Cardinals tied a major league record and set an N. L. mark by connecting for 24 hits as a pinch-batter. Dave Philley had set the record in 1961 while with Baltimore. The previous N. L. mark was 22, set by Sam Leslie of the 1932 New York Giants and tied by Red Schoendienst of the 1962 Cardinals.

American League records were tied by Bobby Murcer of the Yankees, four home runs in a doubleheader, and by Rich Reese of Minnesota who hit the second grand-slam homer of his career as a pinch-batter. Rick Monday of Oakland and Bill Melton of Chicago also equaled A. L. records, Monday by striking out in seven consecutive times at bat and Melton by striking out in 11 consecutive *official* times at bat.

Billy Williams of the Chicago Cubs stopped his Iron-Man streak at 1,117 games, longest in National League annals and third longest in baseball history. Williams benched himself on September 3, saying, "I'm pooped. A day of rest ought to do me some good." Billy's streak began September 22, 1963.

Billy Williams, in jacket, walks to dugout from clubhouse, where he spent his first inactive game, breaking streak. Fans stand in acclaim.

The pitchers also were busy setting records in 1970. The ageless Hoyt Wilhelm of the Braves became the first player in baseball history to pitch in 1,000 games and reached this milestone on May 10 when he relieved against the Cardinals. The crowd gave Wilhelm a standing ovation. Later, asked if he had any special feeling, Hoyt said, "Not a heck of a lot."

Bunning Wins 100 in Each Major League

Jim Bunning of the Phillies also appeared to be unimpressed when he became the first pitcher since the legendary Cy Young to win 100 games in each major league. Bunning, who captured 118 victories with Detroit in the American League, notched his 100th National League triumph on August 11 when he pitched the Phillies to a 6-5 decision over Houston. "All it means," said Bunning, "is that only one other pitcher ever got traded to a different league when he was still capable of winning 100 more games."

Tom Seaver of the Mets broke one major league record and tied another when he struck out 19 San Diego batters on April 22. The 19 Ks equaled the mark established in 1969 by Steve Carlton of St. Louis. Seaver struck out the last 10 San Diego batters to better the previous modern mark of eight in a row, set by Max Surkont of the Milwaukee Braves and later equaled by Johnny Podres of the Los Angeles Dodgers, Jim Maloney of the Reds and Don Wilson of the Astros.

Though he dropped to 18 victories, seven fewer than he won in 1969, Seaver led the National League in earned-run average with a 2.81 figure for 291 innings pitched. He also led in strikeouts with 283. Bob Gibson of the Cardinals and Gaylord Perry of the Giants tied for most victories with 23. Gibson was 23-7 and Perry 23-13.

Diego Segui of Oakland, who worked as both a starter and reliever, won the American League's earned-run title with 2.56. Segui pitched 162 innings, the precise minimum for qualification. Sam McDowell of Cleveland led in strikeouts for the third year in succession with 304. The top winners were Mike Cuellar and Dave McNally, both of Baltimore, and Jim Perry of Minnesota, each with 24 victories.

Rico Carty of Atlanta won the National League batting championship with a .366 average, highest in the N. L. since Stan Musial's .376 in 1948. Alex Johnson of the Angels and Carl Yastrzemski of the Red Sox waged a close battle for the American League bat title Johnson led by a razor-thin margin of .0003. Johnson finished at .3289 compared with .3286 for Yaz. It was the A. L.'s tightest race since 1949, when George Kell nipped Ted Williams by .0002.

Johnson Won Bat Title With Two Hits in Finale

Yastrzemski finished the season a day earlier. Johnson trailed by .0013 going into his final game, which was against the White Sox, and needed a 2-for-2, 2-for-3, 3-for-4, or 3-for-5 performance to win the title, He batted leadoff and grounded out in the first inning, but rapped out singles in his next two trips, which were in the third and fifth innings, and was then taken out for a pinch-runner by Lefty Phillips, the Angels' manager.

That Johnson didn't finish the game irked the Boston press and some of the Back Bay scribes criticized the action. Manager Phillips defended his move and said: "I took Alex out without asking him and I'll argue

Portrait of an Artist—The Soft Look of a Batting Champion—Rico Carty

with anyone who is upset by it. When a man goes to bat 600 times and collects more than 200 hits, as Alex did, he deserves to be the batting champion."

The top power men were Johnny Bench of the Reds in the National League and Frank Howard of the Senators in the American. Bench was the N. L. and major league leader in homers with 45 and in runs batted in with 148. Howard led the A. L. in homers with 44 and in RBIs with 126. Howard also led in walks with 132. Willie McCovey of the Giants was the N. L. leader in walks with 137.

Some but not all of these stars were honored in an unprecedented dinner sponsored by the commissioner's office during the winter meeting in Los Angeles on December 13. It was an academy awards-type festival held at the plush Beverly Hilton Hotel and, though priced at $50 per plate, drew a capacity crowd of 1,200. Portions of the dinner were later seen as a 90-

Publisher C. C. Johnson Spink presents citations for honored service to baseball to Phil Piton (left), minors' boss, and Charley Segar, retiring secretary-treasurer of baseball, at the awards dinner during the convention.

minute network television special on the Merv Griffin Show, giving the game tremendous publicity in the dead of winter. Merv emceed the dinner.

Commissioner Kuhn appointed a special panel of voters who decided on the award winners. Cincinnati's Bench was acclaimed as player of the year, and Gibson of St. Louis as the pitcher of the year. Other winners were Brooks Robinson of Baltimore, defensive player of the year; Willie Mays, San Francisco, the player best typifying the game, on and off the field; Danny Murtaugh, Pittsburgh, manager of the year, and General Manager Harry Dalton of Baltimore, executive of the year.

Spink Honors Piton, Retiring Segar

C. C. Johnson Spink, editor and publisher of THE SPORTING NEWS, was among the honored guests and presented special awards to Charley Segar, the long-time secretary-treasurer of baseball, who was retiring, and to Phil Piton, president of the National Association since 1963. A World Series trophy was presented to Jerry Hoffberger, owner of the world champion Orioles.

Astronaut James Lovell, representing President Nixon's Council on Health and Physical Fitness, presented a special award to Sadaharu Oh, the Babe Ruth of Japanese baseball. Many of the game's best-known celebri-

ties attended the dinner, including such Hall of Famers as Carl Hubbell, Stan Musial, Roy Campanella, Casey Stengel, Joe Cronin and Joe DiMaggio.

The balloting that determined the winners for the television spectacular was in no way connected with the voting for the annual awards made by THE SPORTING NEWS, or those chosen by a selected membership of the Baseball Writers' Association of Amercia. However, there was considerable similarity.

TSN Picks Bench, Gibson, Killebrew, McDowell

As is its custom, THE SPORTING NEWS chose a Player of the Year and a Pitcher of the Year in each league. Bench of Cincinnati and Gibson of St. Louis won these honors in the National League. Harmon Killebrew of Minnesota was selected Player of the Year and Sam McDowell of Cleveland was Pitcher of the Year in the American League.

Rookie Player and Rookie Pitcher awards in each league again were made by THE SPORTING NEWS. Winners in the American League were outfielder Roy Foster of the Indians and righthander Bert Blyleven of the Twins. Reds' outfielder Bernie Carbo and Carl Morton, righthanded ace of the Expos, were honored in the National League.

Winners of THE SPORTING NEWS' Comeback of the Year trophies were pitcher Clyde Wright of the Angels in the American League and outfielder Jim Hickman of the Cubs in the National. Wright, 1-8 in 1969, rocketed to a 22-12 record in 1970. Hickman, who was used sparingly in 1969, when he batted only .237, was among the 1970 slugging stars and batted .315 with 32 homers and 115 runs batted in.

Danny Murtaugh of the National League champion Pirates won selection as Manager of the Year in a poll of major league managers conducted by THE SPORTING NEWS. The managers were allowed to vote only for opponents. Murtaugh led with eight votes. Ralph Houk of the Yankees was second with five, and Sparky Anderson of Cincinnati third with four. Earl Weaver of Baltimore received three votes. Four other pilots received one vote each.

Harry Dalton, the Baltimore general manager, won selection as the major league's Executive of the Year in another poll conducted by THE SPORTING NEWS. Dalton edged Bob Howsam of Cincinnati, 12 votes to 10. John Holland of the Cubs finished third and Joe Brown of the Pirates was fourth.

The BBWAA awards were as follows: American League—John (Boog) Powell, Baltimore first baseman, Most Valuable Player; Thurman Munson, Yankee catcher, Rookie of the Year, and Jim Perry, Minnesota, the Cy Young award winner. National League—Bench of Cincinnati, MVP; Morton of Montreal, Rookie of the Year, and Gibson of St. Louis, Cy Young award.

Powell Decisive Winner in MVP Poll

The 29-year-old Powell, who was instrumental in helping Baltimore win the American League pennant and the World Series, was a decisive winner and polled 234 points. Tony Oliva and Harmon Killebrew, both of Minnesota, were second and third, respectively, Oliva polling 157 points and Killebrew 152. Carl Yastrzemski of Boston was fourth with 136 and Frank Howard of Washington fifth with 91.

Eight players received first-place votes. Powell had 11, more than twice as many as Oliva, who had five. Others who received first-place recognition were Yastrzemski and Brooks Robinson of Baltimore, two each; and Killebrew, Howard, Tommy Harper of Milwaukee and Ron Perranoski of Minnesota, one each. Powell was named on 23 of the 24 ballots.

Bench was also a landslide MVP winner in the National League and, at 22, became the youngest player so honored. He polled 22 of a possible 24 first-place votes. Billy Williams of the Cubs was the only other player to receive first-place mention.

Bench wound up with 326 points, only 10 short of the maximum.

Besides being the youngest player to win an MVP award, Bench was the first catcher to win in the N. L. since Roy Campanella of the 1955 Brooklyn Dodgers. Said Bench: "It's a dream come true."

Complete Tabulation of MVP Voting

The results of the MVP balloting in each league, with 14 points awarded for each first-place vote, nine for second, eight for third, etc., follow:

AMERICAN LEAGUE

Player	1	2	3	4	5	6	7	8	9	10	Pts.
Boog Powell	11	4	2	1	1	2	0	1	1	0	234
Tony Oliva	5	4	2	1	3	1	0	1	0		157
Harmon Killebrew	1	8	3	2	2	2	0	0	3	0	152
Carl Yastrzemski	2	2	2	3	4	3	1	2	1	2	136
Frank Howard	1	1	1	2	1	4	2	1	3	3	91
Tommy Harper	1	1	3	1	0	2	2	1	1	1	78
Brooks Robinson	2	1	1	3	0	0	2	0	0	1	75
Alex Johnson	0	1	2	1	5	0	0	2	1	0	70
Jim Perry	0	0	1	2	1	3	2	2	2		63
Frank Robinson	0	0	2	2	1	2	2	2	0		60
Mike Cuellar	0	0	1	3	0	0	2	0	4	0	45
Ron Perranoski	1	1	1	0	0	0	1	0		1	35
Jim Fregosi	0	1	1	1	1	0	0	1	1	0	35
Luis Aparicio	0	0	0	0	1	1	4	2	1	0	35
Roy White	0	0	0	1	2	2	0	0	1		25
Dave McNally	0	0	1	0	1	0	0	1	1	3	22
Sam McDowell	0	0	0	1	1	2	0	1	1		22
Cesar Tovar	0	0	1	0	0	1	1	0	2		16
Thurman Munson	0	0	0	0	1	1	2	0	0		15
Don Buford	0	0	0	1	0	0	0	1	1	0	12
Clyde Wright	0	0	1	0	0	0	0	0		0	8
Lindy McDaniel	0	0	0	1	0	0	0	1	0		8
Ray Fosse	0	0	0	0	0	1	2	0		7
Campy Campaneris	0	0	0	0	0	1	0	2		5
Jim Palmer	0	0	0	0	0	1	0	0	0		4
Reggie Smith	0	0	0	0	0	1	0	0		3
Sal Bando	0	0	0	0	0	0	0	0	1	1	3
Tony Horton	0	0	0	0	0	0	0	0	1	1	1
Bob Oliver	0	0	0	0	0	0	0	0	0	1	1

NATIONAL LEAGUE

Player	1	2	3	4	5	6	7	8	9	10	Pts.
Johnny Bench	22	2	0	0	0	0	0	0	0	0	326
Billy Williams	2	17	3	1	1	0	0	0	0		218
Tony Perez	0	2	11	3	2	0	0	1	3	0	149
Bob Gibson	0	0	4	2	6	1	3	1	2	4	110
Wes Parker	0	0	1	4	2	4	3	3	1	0	91
Dave Giusti	0	0	1	3	0	4	1	3	0	1	72
Pete Rose	0	0	1	3	1	1	1	2		2	54
Jim Hickman	0	0	1	1	2	2	1	2	2	1	52
Willie McCovey	0	0	1	1	2	0	3	2	1	0	47
Rico Carty	0	0	0	2	3	2	2	1	0	0	43
Manny Sanguillen	0	1	3	0	0	1	1	0		0	36
R. Clemente	0	1	0	1	1	2	0	0	0	1	33
Donn Clendenon	0	0	0	0	3	2	0	1		1	26
Gaylord Perry	0	0	0	1	1	1	0	3	3	3	24
Willie Stargell	0	0	0	2	1	0	0	0	0		20
Bobby Tolan	0	1	0	0	0	1	0	1	0		17
Hank Aaron	0	0	0	0	1	1	1	2	0		16
Joe Torre	0	0	0	1	0	0	1	3	0		15
Tommie Agee	0	0	0	0	1	0	0	1	1	2	13
Bud Harrelson	0	0	0	0	0	0	2	0	1	0	10
Fergie Jenkins	0	0	0	0	0	1	0	0	1	1	8
Jim Merritt	0	0	0	0	0	1	1	0	1		8
Don Kessinger	0	0	0	0	1	0	0	0	0		6
Clarence Gaston	0	0	0	0	0	0	0	1	3	5	5
Deron Johnson	0	0	0	0	0	0	1	0	0		4
Luke Walker	0	0	0	0	0	0	1	0	0		4
Carl Morton	0	0	0	0	0	0	1	0	0		3
Bob Robertson	0	0	0	0	0	0	0	1	0	0	3
Tom Seaver	0	0	0	0	0	0	0	0	0	2	2
Wayne Granger	0	0	0	0	0	0	0	0	1	1	1

Gibson was an almost unanimous winner for the N. L.'s Cy Young award and drew 23 first-place votes and one second for a total of 118 points. Gaylord Perry of San Francisco, who like Gibson also won 23 games, was a distant second with 51 points. He had the other No. 1 vote. In all, ten N. L. pitchers were mentioned.

The voting, for the first time, was conducted on the basis whereby each writer was allowed to list three pitchers. Five points were awarded for first, three for second and one for third.

The balloting for the Cy Young award in the American League was

extremely close. Jim Perry of Minnesota, Gaylord's brother, polled 55 points, barely edging Dave McNally of Baltimore, who had 47 points. Sam McDowell of Cleveland was third with 45 and Mike Cuellar of Baltimore fourth with 44. Perry and Cuellar led in first-place votes (6).

The voting for the BBWAA's Rookie of the Year awards remained unchanged and each of the selectors was allowed to list only one player. Munson of the Yankees received 23 of the 24 American League votes, the other one going to outfielder Roy Foster of Cleveland.

Morton, an 18-game winner for Montreal, led in the National League balloting with 11 votes. Cincinnati outfielder Bernie Carbo was a close second with eight votes. Larry Bowa, Philadelphia shortstop, drew three votes. Pitcher Dick Simpson of Cincinnati and outfielder Cesar Cedeno of Houston had one vote each.

All-Star Teams And Top Fielders, Too

Major league All-Star teams were again selected by THE SPORTING NEWS. As in the past, these teams were chosen by the players, coaches and managers who could vote only for opponents.

The American League All-Star team was as follows: 1b—Boog Powell, Orioles; 2b—Dave Johnson, Orioles; 3b—Harmon Killebrew, Twins, ss—Luis Aparicio, White Sox; lf—Frank Howard, Senators; cf—Reggie Smith, Red Sox; rf—Tony Oliva, Twins; c—Ray Fosse, Indians; righthanded pitcher—Jim Perry, Twins; lefthanded pitcher—Sam McDowell, Indians.

The National League All-Star team: 1b—Willie McCovey, Giants; 2b—Glenn Beckert, Cubs; 3b—Tony Perez, Reds; ss—Don Kessinger, Cubs; lf—Billy Williams, Cubs; cf—Bobby Tolan, Reds; rf—Hank Aaron, Braves; c—Johnny Bench, Reds; righthanded pitcher—Bob Gibson, Cardinals; lefthanded pitcher—Jim Merritt, Reds.

Selected for THE SPORTING NEWS, by the major league managers and coaches, were the following All-Star fielding teams:

American League: 1b—Jim Spencer, Angels; 2b—Dave Johnson, Orioles; 3b—Brooks Robinson, Orioles; ss—Luis Aparicio, White Sox; of—Mickey Stanley, Tigers; Paul Blair, Orioles, and Ken Berry, White Sox; c—Ray Fosse, Indians; p—Jim Kaat, Twins.

National League: 1b—Wes Parker, Dodgers; 2b—Tommy Helms, Reds; 3b—Doug Rader, Astros; ss—Don Kessinger, Cubs; of—Pete Rose, Reds; Roberto Clemente, Pirates, and Tommie Agee, Mets; c—Johnny Bench, Reds; p—Bob Gibson, Cardinals.

And, finally, the review of the year would not be complete without a mention of Miss Morganna Roberts, a bosomy strip teaser who made the big league scene by repeatedly leaping over box seat railings and running onto the playing field where she embraced and kissed several ballplayers.

Miss Roberts began her season on Opening Day when she kissed Frank Howard of the Senators. She made two strikes on the West Coast, nailing Billy Cowan of the Angels at Anaheim and Wes Parker of the Dodgers in Los Angeles. She then announced she also would appear at the All-Star Game in Cincinnati, which was on national television. But the gendarmes, thus pre-warned, apprehended the shapely gal as she leaped onto the field and took her to court.

That's the shape and direction the game took in 1970, too.

LEADING PITCHERS—EARNED-RUN AVERAGE

(Based on Ten Complete Games Thru 1950, Then 154 Innings Until A. L. Expanded in '61, N. L. in '62, When It Became 162 Innings)

AMERICAN LEAGUE

Year	Pitcher and Club	G.	IP.	ERA.	Year	Pitcher and Club	G.	IP.	ERA.
1913	Johnson, Washington	48	346	1.14	1942	Lyons, Chicago	20	180	2.10
1914	Leonard, Boston	35	222	1.01	1943	Chandler, New York	30	253	1.64
1915	Wood, Boston	25	157	1.49	1944	Trout, Detroit	40	352	2.12
1916	Ruth, Boston	44	324	1.75	1945	Newhouser, Detroit	40	313	1.81
1917	Cicotte, Chicago	49	346	1.53	1946	Newhouser, Detroit	37	293	1.94
1918	Johnson, Washington	39	325	1.27	1947	Chandler, New York	17	128	2.46
1919	Johnson, Washington	39	290	1.49	1948	Bearden, Cleveland	37	230	2.43
1920	Shawkey, New York	38	267	2.46	1949	Parnell, Boston	39	295	2.78
1921	Faber, Chicago	43	331	2.47	1950	Wynn, Cleveland	32	214	3.20
1922	Faber, Chicago	43	353	2.80	1951	Rogovin, Det.-Chi.	27	217	2.78
1923	S. Coveleski, Cleveland	33	228	2.76	1952	Reynolds, New York	35	244	2.07
1924	Johnson, Washington	38	278	2.72	1953	Lopat, New York	25	178	2.43
1925	S. Coveleski, Wash.	32	241	2.84	1954	Garcia, Cleveland	45	259	2.64
1926	Grove, Philadelphia	45	258	2.51	1955	Pierce, Chicago	33	206	1.97
1927	Moore, New York	50	213	2.28	1956	Ford, New York	31	226	2.47
1928	Braxton, Washington	38	218	2.52	1957	Shantz, New York	30	173	2.45
1929	Grove, Philadelphia	42	275	2.81	1958	Ford, New York	30	219	2.01
1930	Grove, Philadelphia	50	291	2.54	1959	Wilhelm, Baltimore	32	226	2.19
1931	Grove, Philadelphia	41	289	2.06	1960	Baumann, Chicago	47	185	2.68
1932	Grove, Philadelphia	44	292	2.84	1961	Donovan, Washington	23	169	2.40
1933	Pearson, Cleveland	19	135	2.33	1962	Aguirre, Detroit	42	216	2.21
1934	Gomez, New York	38	282	2.33	1963	Peters, Chicago	41	243	2.33
1935	Grove, Boston	35	273	2.70	1964	Chance, Los Angeles	46	278	1.65
1936	Grove, Boston	35	253	2.81	1965	McDowell, Cleveland	42	273	2.18
1937	Gomez, New York	34	278	2.33	1966	Peters, Chicago	30	205	1.98
1938	Grove, Boston	24	164	3.07	1967	Horlen, Chicago	35	258	2.06
1939	Grove, Boston	23	191	2.54	1968	Tiant, Cleveland	34	258	1.60
1940	Feller, Cleveland	43	320	2.62	1969	Bosman, Washington	31	193	2.19
1941	T. Lee, Chicago	35	300	2.37	1970	Segui, Oakland	47	162	2.56

Note—Wilcy Moore pitched only six complete games—he started 12—in 1927, but was recognized as leader because of 213 innings pitched; Ernie Bonham, New York, had 1.91 ERA and ten complete games in 1940, but appeared in only 12 games and 99 innings, and Bob Feller was recognized as leader.

NATIONAL LEAGUE

Year	Pitcher and Club	G.	IP.	ERA.	Year	Pitcher and Club	G.	IP.	ERA.
1912	Tesreau, New York	36	243	1.96	1942	M. Cooper, St. Louis	37	279	1.77
1913	Mathewson, New York	40	306	2.06	1943	Pollet, St. Louis	16	118	1.75
1914	Doak, St. Louis	36	256	1.72	1944	Heusser, Cincinnati	30	193	2.38
1915	Alexander, Phila.	49	376	1.22	1945	Borowy, Chicago	15	122	2.14
1916	Alexander, Phila.	48	390	1.55	1946	Pollet, St. Louis	40	266	2.10
1917	Alexander, Phila.	45	388	1.83	1947	Spahn, Boston	40	290	2.33
1918	Vaughn, Chicago	35	290	1.74	1948	Brecheen, St. Louis	33	233	2.24
1919	Alexander, Chicago	30	235	1.72	1949	Koslo, New York	38	212	2.50
1920	Alexander, Chicago	46	363	1.91	1950	Hearn, St. L.-N.Y.	22	134	2.49
1921	Doak, St. Louis	32	209	2.58	1951	Nichols, Boston	33	156	2.88
1922	Ryan, New York	46	192	3.00	1952	Wilhelm, New York	71	159	2.43
1923	Luque, Cincinnati	41	322	1.93	1953	Spahn, Milwaukee	35	266	2.10
1924	Vance, Brooklyn	35	309	2.16	1954	Antonelli, New York	39	259	2.29
1925	Luque, Cincinnati	36	291	2.63	1955	Friend, Pittsburgh	44	200	2.84
1926	Kremer, Pittsburgh	37	231	2.61	1956	Burdette, Milwaukee	39	256	2.71
1927	Kremer, Pittsburgh	35	226	2.47	1957	Podres, Brooklyn	31	196	2.66
1928	Vance, Brooklyn	38	280	2.09	1958	Miller, San Francisco	41	182	2.47
1929	Walker, New York	29	178	3.08	1959	S. Jones, San Francisco	50	271	2.82
1930	Vance, Brooklyn	35	259	2.61	1960	McCormick, San Fran.	40	253	2.70
1931	Walker, New York	37	239	2.26	1961	Spahn, Milwaukee	38	263	3.01
1932	Warneke, Chicago	35	277	2.37	1962	Koufax, Los Angeles	28	184	2.54
1933	Hubbell, New York	45	309	1.66	1963	Koufax, Los Angeles	40	311	1.88
1934	Hubbell, New York	49	313	2.30	1964	Koufax, Los Angeles	29	223	1.74
1935	Blanton, Pittsburgh	35	254	2.59	1965	Koufax, Los Angeles	43	336	2.04
1936	Hubbell, New York	42	304	2.31	1966	Koufax, Los Angeles	41	323	1.73
1937	Turner, Boston	33	257	2.38	1967	P. Niekro, Atlanta	46	207	1.87
1938	W. Lee, Chicago	44	291	2.66	1968	Gibson, St. Louis	34	305	1.12
1939	Walters, Cincinnati	39	319	2.29	1969	Marichal, San Francisco	37	300	2.10
1940	Walters, Cincinnati	36	305	2.48	1970	Seaver, New York	37	291	2.81
1941	E. Riddle, Cincinnati	33	217	2.24					

Note—Earned-run records not tabulated in American League prior to 1913 and in National League prior to 1912.

STRIKEOUT LEADERS—PITCHING

AMERICAN LEAGUE		NATIONAL LEAGUE	
Year—Pitcher and Club	SO.	Year—Pitcher and Club	SO.
1900—Not a major league.		1900—George (Rube) Waddell, Pitts.	.133
1901—Denton (Cy) Young, Boston	.159	1901—Frank (Noodles) Hahn, Cinn.	.233
1902—George (Rube) Waddell, Phila.	.210	1902—Victor Willis, Boston	.226
1903—George (Rube) Waddell, Phila.	.301	1903—Christopher Mathewson, New York	267
1904—George (Rube) Waddell, Phila.	.349	1904—Christopher Mathewson, New York	212
1905—George (Rube) Waddell, Phila.	.286	1905—Christopher Mathewson, New York	206
1906—George (Rube) Waddell, Phila.	.203	1906—Frederick Beebe, Chicago-St. L.	.171
1907—George (Rube) Waddell, Phila.	.226	1907—Christopher Mathewson, New York	178
1908—Edward Walsh, Chicago	269	1908—Christopher Mathewson, New York	259
1909—Frank Smith, Chicago	.177	1909—Orval Overall, Chicago	.205
1910—Walter Johnson, Washington	.313	1910—Christopher Mathewson, New York	190
1911—Edward Walsh, Chicago	.255	1911—Richard (Rube) Marquard, N. Y.	237
1912—Walter Johnson, Washington	.303	1912—Grover Alexander, Philadelphia	.195
1913—Walter Johnson, Washington	.243	1913—Thomas Seaton, Philadelphia	.168
1914—Walter Johnson, Washington	.225	1914—Grover Alexander, Philadelphia	.214
1915—Walter Johnson, Washington	.203	1915—Grover Alexander, Philadelphia	.241
1916—Walter Johnson, Washington	.228	1916—Grover Alexander, Philadelphia	.167
1917—Walter Johnson, Washington	.188	1917—Grover Alexander, Philadelphia	.200
1918—Walter Johnson, Washington	.162	1918—James (Hippo) Vaughn, Chicago	.148
1919—Walter Johnson, Washington	.147	1919—James (Hippo) Vaughn, Chicago	.141
1920—Stanley Coveleski, Cleveland	.133	1920—Grover Alexander, Chicago	.173
1921—Walter Johnson, Washington	.143	1921—Burleigh Grimes, Brooklyn	.136
1922—Urban Shocker, St. Louis	.149	1922—Arthur (Dazzy) Vance, Brooklyn	.134
1923—Walter Johnson, Washington	.130	1923—Arthur (Dazzy) Vance, Brooklyn	.197
1924—Walter Johnson, Washington	.158	1924—Arthur (Dazzy) Vance, Brooklyn	.262
1925—Robert Grove, Philadelphia	.116	1925—Arthur (Dazzy) Vance, Brooklyn	.221
1926—Robert Grove, Philadelphia	.194	1926—Arthur (Dazzy) Vance, Brooklyn	.140
1927—Robert Grove, Philadelphia	.174	1927—Arthur (Dazzy) Vance, Brooklyn	.184
1928—Robert Grove, Philadelphia	.183	1928—Arthur (Dazzy) Vance, Brooklyn	.200
1929—Robert Grove, Philadelphia	.170	1929—Perce (Pat) Malone, Chicago	.166
1930—Robert Grove, Philadelphia	.209	1930—William Hallahan, St. Louis	.177
1931—Robert Grove, Philadelphia	.175	1931—William Hallahan, St. Louis	.159
1932—Charles (Red) Ruffing, New York	190	1932—Jerome (Dizzy) Dean, St. Louis	.191
1933—Vernon Gomez, New York	.163	1933—Jerome (Dizzy) Dean, St. Louis	.199
1934—Vernon Gomez, New York	.158	1934—Jerome (Dizzy) Dean, St. Louis	.195
1935—Thomas Bridges, Detroit	.163	1935—Jerome (Dizzy) Dean, St. Louis	.182
1936—Thomas Bridges, Detroit	.175	1936—Van Lingle Mungo, Brooklyn	.238
1937—Vernon Gomez, New York	.194	1937—Carl Hubbell, New York	.159
1938—Robert Feller, Cleveland	.240	1938—Claiborne Bryant, Chicago	.135
1939—Robert Feller, Cleveland	.246	1939—Claude Passeau, Phila.-Chi.	.137
		Wm. (Bucky) Walters, Cincinnati	137
1940—Robert Feller, Cleveland	.261	1940—W. Kirby Higbe, Philadelphia	.137
1941—Robert Feller, Cleveland	.260	1941—John Vander Meer, Cincinnati	.202
1942—Louis (Bobo) Newsom, Wash.	.113	1942—John Vander Meer, Cincinnati	.186
Cecil (Tex) Hughson, Boston	113		
1943—Allie Reynolds, Cleveland	.151	1943—John Vander Meer, Cincinnati	.174
1944—Harold Newhouser, Detroit	.187	1944—William Voiselle, New York	.161
1945—Harold Newhouser, Detroit	.212	1945—Elwin (Preacher) Roe, Pittsburgh	148
1946—Robert Feller, Cleveland	.348	1946—John Schmitz, Chicago	.135
1947—Robert Feller, Cleveland	.196	1947—Ewell Blackwell, Cincinnati	.193
1948—Robert Feller, Cleveland	.164	1948—Harry Brecheen, St. Louis	.149
1949—Virgil Trucks, Detroit	.153	1949—Warren Spahn, Boston	.151
1950—Robert Lemon, Cleveland	.170	1950—Warren Spahn, Boston	.191
1951—Victor Raschi, New York	.164	1951—Warren Spahn, Boston	.164
		Donald Newcombe, Brooklyn	164
1952—Allie Reynolds, New York	.160	1952—Warren Spahn, Boston	.183
1953—W. William Pierce, Chicago	.186	1953—Robin Roberts, Philadelphia	.198
1954—Robert Turley, Baltimore	.185	1954—Robin Roberts, Philadelphia	.185
1955—Herbert Score, Cleveland	.245	1955—Samuel Jones, Chicago	.198
1956—Herbert Score, Cleveland	.263	1956—Samuel Jones, Chicago	.176
1957—Early Wynn, Cleveland	.184	1957—John Sanford, Philadelphia	.188
1958—Early Wynn, Chicago	.179	1958—Samuel Jones, St. Louis	.225
1959—James Bunning, Detroit	.201	1959—Donald Drysdale, Los Angeles	.242
1960—James Bunning, Detroit	.201	1960—Donald Drysdale, Los Angeles	.246
1961—Camilo Pascual, Minnesota	.221	1961—Sanford Koufax, Los Angeles	.269
1962—Camilo Pascual, Minnesota	.206	1962—Donald Drysdale, Los Angeles	.232
1963—Camilo Pascual, Minnesota	.202	1963—Sanford Koufax, Los Angeles	.306
1964—Alphonso Downing, New York	.217	1964—Robert Veale, Pittsburgh	.250
1965—Samuel McDowell, Cleveland	.325	1965—Sanford Koufax, Los Angeles	.382
1966—Samuel McDowell, Cleveland	.225	1966—Sanford Koufax, Los Angeles	.317
1967—James Lonborg, Boston	.246	1967—James Bunning, Philadelphia	.253
1968—Samuel McDowell, Cleveland	.283	1968—Robert Gibson, St. Louis	.268
1969—Samuel McDowell, Cleveland	.279	1969—Ferguson Jenkins, Chicago	.273
1970—Samuel McDowell, Cleveland	.304	1970—G. Thomas Seaver, New York	.283

LEADERS IN RUNS SCORED

AMERICAN LEAGUE		NATIONAL LEAGUE	
Year Player—Club	Runs	Year Player—Club	Runs
1900—(Not classed as major)		1900—Roy Thomas, Philadelphia	131
1901—Napoleon Lajoie, Philadelphia	145	1901—Jesse Burkett, St. Louis	139
1902—David Fultz, Philadelphia	110	1902—John (Honus) Wagner, Pitts.	105
1903—Patrick Dougherty, Boston	108	1903—Clarence Beaumont, Pittsburgh	137
1904—Patrick Dougherty, Bos.-N. Y.	113	1904—George Browne, New York	99
1905—Harry Davis, Philadelphia	92	1905—Michael Donlin, New York	124
1906—Elmer Flick, Cleveland	98	1906—John (Honus) Wagner, Pitts.	103
		Frank Chance, Chicago	103
1907—Samuel Crawford, Detroit	102	1907—W. Porter Shannon, New York	104
1908—Matthew McIntyre, Detroit	105	1908—Frederick Tenney, New York	101
1909—Tyrus Cobb, Detroit	116	1909—Thomas Leach, Pittsburgh	126
1910—Tyrus Cobb, Detroit	106	1910—Sherwood Magee, Philadelphia	110
1911—Tyrus Cobb, Detroit	147	1911—James Sheckard, Chicago	121
1912—Edward Collins, Philadelphia	137	1912—Robert Bescher, Cincinnati	120
1913—Edward Collins, Philadelphia	125	1913—Thomas Leach, Chicago	99
		Max Carey, Pittsburgh	99
1914—Edward Collins, Philadelphia	122	1914—George Burns, New York	100
1915—Tyrus Cobb, Detroit	144	1915—Cliff. (Gavvy) Cravath, Phila.	89
1916—Tyrus Cobb, Detroit	113	1916—George Burns, New York	105
1917—Owen (Donie) Bush, Detroit	112	1917—George Burns, New York	103
1918—Raymond Chapman, Cleveland	84	1918—Henry Groh, Cincinnati	88
1919—George (Babe) Ruth, Boston	103	1919—George Burns, New York	86
1920—George (Babe) Ruth, New York	158	1920—George Burns, New York	115
1921—George (Babe) Ruth, New York	177	1921—Rogers Hornsby, St. Louis	131
1922—George Sisler, St. Louis	134	1922—Rogers Hornsby, St. Louis	141
1923—George (Babe) Ruth, New York	151	1923—Ross Youngs, New York	121
1924—George (Babe) Ruth, New York	143	1924—Frank Frisch, New York	121
1925—John Mostil, Chicago	135	Rogers Hornsby, St. Louis	121
1926—George (Babe) Ruth, New York	139	1925—Hazen (Kiki) Cuyler, Pittsburgh	144
1927—George (Babe) Ruth, New York	158	1926—Hazen (Kiki) Cuyler, Pittsburgh	113
1928—George (Babe) Ruth, New York	163	1927—Lloyd Waner, Pittsburgh	133
1929—Charles Gehringer, Detroit	131	Rogers Hornsby, New York	133
1930—Aloysius Simmons, Philadelphia	152	1928—Paul Waner, Pittsburgh	142
1931—H. Louis Gehrig, New York	163	1929—Rogers Hornsby, Chicago	156
1932—James Foxx, Philadelphia	151	1930—Charles (Chuck) Klein, Phila.	158
1933—H. Louis Gehrig, New York	138	1931—Terry, N. Y.-Klein, Phila.	121
1934—Charles Gehringer, Detroit	134	1932—Charles (Chuck) Klein, Phila.	152
		1933—John (Pepper) Martin, St. Louis	122
1935—H. Louis Gehrig, New York	125	1934—Paul Waner, Pittsburgh	122
1936—H. Louis Gehrig, New York	167	1935—August Galan, Chicago	133
1937—Joseph DiMaggio, New York	151	1936—J. Floyd (Arky) Vaughan, Pitts.	122
		1937—Joseph Medwick, St. Louis	111
1938—Henry Greenberg, Detroit	144	1938—Melvin Ott, New York	116
1939—Robert (Red) Rolfe, New York	139	1939—William Werber, Cincinnati	115
1940—Theodore Williams, Boston	134	1940—J. Floyd (Arky) Vaughan, Pitts.	113
1941—Theodore Williams, Boston	135	1941—Harold (Pete) Reiser, Brooklyn	117
1942—Theodore Williams, Boston	141	1942—Melvin Ott, New York	118
1943—George Case, Washington	102	1943—J. Floyd (Arky) Vaughan, Brk.	112
1944—George Stirnweiss, New York	125	1944—William Nicholson, Chicago	116
1945—George Stirnweiss, New York	107	1945—Edward Stanky, Brooklyn	128
1946—Theodore Williams, Boston	142	1946—Stanley Musial, St. Louis	124
1947—Theodore Williams, Boston	125	1947—John Mize, New York	137
1948—Thomas Henrich, New York	138	1948—Stanley Musial, St. Louis	135
1949—Theodore Williams, Boston	150	1949—Harold (Pee Wee) Reese, Brk.	132
1950—Dominic DiMaggio, Boston	131	1950—C. Earl Torgeson, Boston	120
1951—Dominic DiMaggio, Boston	104	1951—Musial, St. L.-Kiner, Pitt.	124
1952—Lawrence Doby, Cleveland	105	1952—Musial, St. L.-Hemus, St. L.	105
1953—Albert Rosen, Cleveland	115	1953—Edwin (Duke) Snider, Brooklyn	132
1954—Mickey Mantle, New York	129	1954—Musial, St. L.-Snider, Brk.	120
1955—Alphonse Smith, Cleveland	123	1955—Edwin (Duke) Snider, Brooklyn	126
1956—Mickey Mantle, New York	132	1956—Frank Robinson, Cincinnati	122
1957—Mickey Mantle, New York	121	1957—Henry Aaron, Milwaukee	118
1958—Mickey Mantle, New York	127	1958—Willie Mays, San Francisco	121
1959—Edward Yost, Detroit	115	1959—Vada Pinson, Cincinnati	131
1960—Mickey Mantle, New York	119	1960—William Bruton, Milwaukee	112
1961—Mantle, N. Y.-Maris, N. Y.	132	1961—Willie Mays, San Francisco	129
1962—Albert G. Pearson, Los Angeles	115	1962—Frank Robinson, Cincinnati	134
1963—W. Robert Allison, Minnesota	99	1963—Henry Aaron, Milwaukee	121
1964—Pedro (Tony) Oliva, Minnesota	109	1964—Richard Allen, Philadelphia	125
1965—Zoilo Versalles, Minnesota	126	1965—Tommy Harper, Cincinnati	126
1966—Frank Robinson, Baltimore	122	1966—Felipe Alou, Atlanta	122
1967—Carl Yastrzemski, Boston	112	1967—Henry Aaron, Milwaukee	113
		Louis Brock, St. Louis	113
1968—Richard McAuliffe, Detroit	95	1968—Glenn Beckert, Chicago	98
1969—Reginald Jackson, Oakland	123	1969—Bobby Bonds, San Francisco	120
		Pete Rose, Cincinnati	120
1970—Carl Yastrzemski, Boston	125	1970—Billy Williams, Chicago	137

LEADERS IN HITS

Year	AMERICAN LEAGUE Player and Club	Hits	Year	NATIONAL LEAGUE Player and Club	Hits
1900—	(Not classed as major)		1900—	William Keeler, Brooklyn	208
1901—	Napoleon Lajoie, Philadelphia	229	1901—	Jesse Burkett, St. Louis	228
1902—	Charles Hickman, Cleveland	194	1902—	Clarence Beaumont, Pittsburgh	194
1903—	Patrick Dougherty, Boston	195	1903—	Clarence Beaumont, Pittsburgh	209
1904—	Napoleon Lajoie, Cleveland	211	1904—	Clarence Beaumont, Pittsburgh	185
1905—	George Stone, St. Louis	187	1905—	J. Bentley Seymour, Cincinnati	219
1906—	Napoleon Lajoie, Cleveland	214	1906—	Harry Steinfeldt, Chicago	176
1907—	Tyrus Cobb, Detroit	212	1907—	Clarence Beaumont, Boston	187
1908—	Tyrus Cobb, Detroit	188	1908—	John (Honus) Wagner, Pittsburgh	201
1909—	Tyrus Cobb, Detroit	216	1909—	Lawrence Doyle, New York	172
1910—	Napoleon Lajoie, Cleveland	227	1910—	Wagner, Pitt.—Robt. Byrne, Pitt.	178
1911—	Tyrus Cobb, Detroit	248	1911—	Roy Miller, Boston	192
1912—	Tyrus Cobb, Detroit	227	1912—	Henry Zimmerman, Chicago	207
1913—	Joseph Jackson, Cleveland	197	1913—	Cliff (Gavvy) Cravath, Phila.	179
1914—	Tristram Speaker, Boston	193	1914—	Sherwood Magee, Philadelphia	171
1915—	Tyrus Cobb, Detroit	208	1915—	Lawrence Doyle, New York	189
1916—	Tristram Speaker, Cleveland	211	1916—	Harold Chase, Cincinnati	184
1917—	Tyrus Cobb, Detroit	225	1917—	Henry Groh, Cincinnati	182
1918—	George Burns, Philadelphia	178	1918—	Charles Hollocher, Chicago	161
1919—	Cobb, Det.—Robert Veach, Det.	191	1919—	Ivy Olson, Brooklyn	164
1920—	George Sisler, St. Louis	257	1920—	Rogers Hornsby, St. Louis	218
1921—	Harry Heilmann, Detroit	237	1921—	Rogers Hornsby, St. Louis	235
1922—	George Sisler, St. Louis	246	1922—	Rogers Hornsby, St. Louis	250
1923—	Charles Jamieson, Cleveland	222	1923—	Frank Frisch, New York	223
1924—	Edgar (Sam) Rice, Washington	216	1924—	Rogers Hornsby, St. Louis	227
1925—	Aloysius Simmons, Philadelphia	253	1925—	James Bottomley, St. Louis	227
1926—	George Burns, Cleveland	216	1926—	Edward Brown, Boston	201
	Edgar (Sam) Rice, Washington	216			
1927—	Earle Combs, New York	231	1927—	Paul Waner, Pittsburgh	237
1928—	Henry Manush, St. Louis	241	1928—	Fred Lindstrom, New York	231
1929—	Dale Alexander, Detroit	215	1929—	Frank O'Doul, Philadelphia	254
	Charles Gehringer, Detroit	215			
1930—	U. John Hodapp, Cleveland	225	1930—	William Terry, New York	254
1931—	H. Louis Gehrig, New York	211	1931—	Lloyd Waner, Pittsburgh	214
1932—	Aloysius Simmons, Philadelphia	216	1932—	Charles Klein, Philadelphia	226
1933—	Henry Manush, Washington	221	1933—	Charles Klein, Philadelphia	223
1934—	Charles Gehringer, Detroit	214	1934—	Paul Waner, Pittsburgh	217
1935—	Joseph Vosmik, Cleveland	216	1935—	William Herman, Chicago	227
1936—	H. Earl Averill, Cleveland	232	1936—	Joseph Medwick, St. Louis	223
1937—	Roy (Beau) Bell, St. Louis	218	1937—	Joseph Medwick, St. Louis	237
1938—	Joseph Vosmik, Boston	201	1938—	Frank McCormick, Cincinnati	209
1939—	Robert (Red) Rolfe, New York	213	1939—	Frank McCormick, Cincinnati	209
1940—	Raymond (Rip) Radcliff, St. L.	200	1940—	Stanley Hack, Chicago	191
	W. Barney McCosky, Detroit	200		Frank McCormick, Cincinnati	191
	Roger (Doc) Cramer, Boston	200			
1941—	Cecil Travis, Washington	218	1941—	Stanley Hack, Chicago	186
1942—	John Pesky, Boston	205	1942—	Enos Slaughter, St. Louis	188
1943—	Richard Wakefield, Detroit	200	1943—	Stanley Musial, St. Louis	220
1944—	George Stirnweiss, New York	205	1944—	Musial, St. L.—Cavarretta, Chi.	197
1945—	George Stirnweiss, New York	195	1945—	Thomas Holmes, Boston	224
1946—	John Pesky, Boston	208	1946—	Stanley Musial, St. Louis	228
1947—	John Pesky, Boston	207	1947—	Thomas Holmes, Boston	191
1948—	Robert Dillinger, St. Louis	207	1948—	Stanley Musial, St. Louis	230
1949—	L. Dale Mitchell, Cleveland	203	1949—	Stanley Musial, St. Louis	207
1950—	George Kell, Detroit	218	1950—	Edwin (Duke) Snider, Brooklyn	199
1951—	George Kell, Detroit	191	1951—	Richie Ashburn, Philadelphia	221
1952—	J. Nelson Fox, Chicago	192	1952—	Stanley Musial, St. Louis	194
1953—	Harvey Kuenn, Detroit	209	1953—	Richie Ashburn, Philadelphia	205
1954—	Fox, Chicago—Kuenn, Detroit	201	1954—	Donald Mueller, New York	212
1955—	Albert Kaline, Detroit	200	1955—	Theodore Kluszewski, Cincinnati	192
1956—	Harvey Kuenn, Detroit	196	1956—	Henry Aaron, Milwaukee	200
1957—	J. Nelson Fox, Chicago	196	1957—	Al (Red) Schoendienst, N.Y.-Mil.	200
1958—	J. Nelson Fox, Chicago	187	1958—	Richie Ashburn, Philadelphia	215
1959—	Harvey Kuenn, Detroit	198	1959—	Henry Aaron, Milwaukee	223
1960—	Orestes (Minnie) Minoso, Chicago	184	1960—	Willie Mays, San Francisco	190
1961—	Norman Cash, Detroit	193	1961—	Vada Pinson, Cincinnati	208
1962—	Robert Richardson, New York	209	1962—	H. Thomas Davis, Los Angeles	230
1963—	Carl Yastrzemski, Boston	183	1963—	Vada Pinson, Cincinnati	204
1964—	Pedro (Tony) Oliva, Minnesota	217	1964—	Clemente, Pitt.—Flood, St. Louis	211
1965—	Pedro (Tony) Oliva, Minnesota	185	1965—	Peter Rose, Cincinnati	209
1966—	Pedro (Tony) Oliva, Minnesota	191	1966—	Felipe Alou, Atlanta	218
1967—	Carl Yastrzemski, Boston	189	1967—	Roberto Clemente, Pittsburgh	209
1968—	Dagoberto Campaneris, Oakland	177	1968—	Felipe Alou, Atlanta	210
				Peter Rose, Cincinnati	210
1969—	Pedro (Tony) Oliva, Minnesota	197	1969—	Mateo Alou, Pittsburgh	231
1970—	Pedro (Tony) Oliva, Minnesota	204	1970—	Peter Rose, Cincinnati	205
				Billy Williams, Chicago	205

LEADERS IN TOTAL BASES

Year	AMERICAN LEAGUE	T.B.
1900	(Not classed as major)	
1901	Napoleon Lajoie, Philadelphia	342
1902	John (Buck) Freeman, Boston	287
1903	John (Buck) Freeman, Boston	281
1904	Napoleon Lajoie, Cleveland	304
1905	George Stone, St. Louis	260
1906	George Stone, St. Louis	288
1907	Tyrus Cobb, Detroit	286
1908	Tyrus Cobb, Detroit	276
1909	Tyrus Cobb, Detroit	296
1910	Napoleon Lajoie, Cleveland	304
1911	Tyrus Cobb, Detroit	367
1912	Joseph Jackson, Cleveland	331
1913	Samuel Crawford, Detroit	298
1914	Tristram Speaker, Boston	287
1915	Tyrus Cobb, Detroit	274
1916	Joseph Jackson, Chicago	293
1917	Tyrus Cobb, Detroit	336
1918	George Burns, Philadelphia	236
1919	George (Babe) Ruth, Boston	284
1920	George Sisler, St. Louis	399
1921	George (Babe) Ruth, New York	457
1922	Kenneth Williams, St. Louis	367
1923	George (Babe) Ruth, New York	399
1924	George (Babe) Ruth, New York	391
1925	Aloysius Simmons, Philadelphia	392
1926	George (Babe) Ruth, New York	365
1927	H. Louis Gehrig, New York	447
1928	George (Babe) Ruth, New York	380
1929	Aloysius Simmons, Philadelphia	373
1930	H. Louis Gehrig, New York	419
1931	H. Louis Gehrig, New York	410
1932	James Foxx, Philadelphia	438
1933	James Foxx, Philadelphia	403
1934	H. Louis Gehrig, New York	409
1935	Henry Greenberg, Detroit	389
1936	Harold Trosky, Cleveland	405
1937	Joseph DiMaggio, New York	418
1938	James Foxx, Boston	398
1939	Theodore Williams, Boston	344
1940	Henry Greenberg, Detroit	384
1941	Joseph DiMaggio, New York	348
1942	Theodore Williams, Boston	338
1943	Rudolph York, Detroit	301
1944	John Lindell, New York	297
1945	George Stirnweiss, New York	301
1946	Theodore Williams, Boston	343
1947	Theodore Williams, Boston	335
1948	Joseph DiMaggio, New York	355
1949	Theodore Williams, Boston	368
1950	Walter Dropo, Boston	326
1951	Theodore Williams, Boston	295
1952	Albert Rosen, Cleveland	297
1953	Albert Rosen, Cleveland	367
1954	Orestes (Minnie) Minoso, Chicago	304
1955	Albert Kaline, Detroit	321
1956	Mickey Mantle, New York	376
1957	Roy Sievers, Washington	331
1958	Mickey Mantle, New York	307
1959	Rocco Colavito, Cleveland	301
1960	Mickey Mantle, New York	294
1961	Roger Maris, New York	366
1962	Rocco Colavito, Detroit	309
1963	Richard Stuart, Boston	319
1964	Pedro (Tony) Oliva, Minnesota	374
1965	Zoilo Versalles, Minnesota	308
1966	Frank Robinson, Baltimore	367
1967	Carl Yastrzemski, Boston	360
1968	Frank Howard, Washington	330
1969	Frank Howard, Washington	340
1970	Carl Yastrzemski, Boston	335

Year	NATIONAL LEAGUE	T.B.
1900	John (Honus) Wagner, Pitt.	302
	Elmer Flick, Philadelphia	302
1901	Jesse Burkett, St. Louis	314
1902	Samuel Crawford, Cincinnati	256
1903	Clarence Beaumont, Pittsburgh	272
1904	John (Honus) Wagner, Pittsburgh	255
1905	J. Bentley Seymour, Cincinnati	325
1906	John (Honus) Wagner, Pittsburgh	237
1907	John (Honus) Wagner, Pittsburgh	264
1908	John (Honus) Wagner, Pittsburgh	308
1909	John (Honus) Wagner, Pittsburgh	242
1910	Sherwood Magee, Philadelphia	263
1911	Frank Schulte, Chicago	308
1912	Henry Zimmerman, Chicago	318
1913	Cliff. (Gavvy) Cravath, Phila.	298
1914	Sherwood Magee, Philadelphia	277
1915	Cliff. (Gavvy) Cravath, Phila.	266
1916	Zachariah Wheat, Brooklyn	262
1917	Rogers Hornsby, St. Louis	253
1918	Charles Hollocher, Chicago	202
1919	Henry (Hi) Myers, Brooklyn	223
1920	Rogers Hornsby, St. Louis	329
1921	Rogers Hornsby, St. Louis	378
1922	Rogers Hornsby, St. Louis	450
1923	Frank Frisch, New York	311
1924	Rogers Hornsby, St. Louis	373
1925	Rogers Hornsby, St. Louis	381
1926	James Bottomley, St. Louis	305
1927	Paul Waner, Pittsburgh	338
1928	James Bottomley, St. Louis	362
1929	Rogers Hornsby, Chicago	410
1930	Charles Klein, Philadelphia	445
1931	Charles Klein, Philadelphia	347
1932	Charles Klein, Philadelphia	420
1933	Charles Klein, Philadelphia	365
1934	James (Rip) Collins, St. Louis	369
1935	Joseph Medwick, St. Louis	365
1936	Joseph Medwick, St. Louis	367
1937	Joseph Medwick, St. Louis	406
1938	John Mize, St. Louis	326
1939	John Mize, St. Louis	353
1940	John Mize, St. Louis	368
1941	Harold (Pete) Reiser, Brooklyn	299
1942	Enos Slaughter, St. Louis	292
1943	Stanley Musial, St. Louis	347
1944	William Nicholson, Chicago	317
1945	Thomas Holmes, Boston	367
1946	Stanley Musial, St. Louis	366
1947	Ralph Kiner, Pittsburgh	361
1948	Stanley Musial, St. Louis	429
1949	Stanley Musial, St. Louis	382
1950	Edwin (Duke) Snider, Brooklyn	343
1951	Stanley Musial, St. Louis	355
1952	Stanley Musial, St. Louis	311
1953	Edwin (Duke) Snider, Brooklyn	370
1954	Edwin (Duke) Snider, Brooklyn	378
1955	Willie Mays, New York	382
1956	Henry Aaron, Milwaukee	340
1957	Henry Aaron, Milwaukee	369
1958	Ernest Banks, Chicago	379
1959	Henry Aaron, Milwaukee	400
1960	Henry Aaron, Milwaukee	334
1961	Henry Aaron, Milwaukee	358
1962	Willie Mays, San Francisco	382
1963	Henry Aaron, Milwaukee	370
1964	Richard Allen, Philadelphia	352
1965	Willie Mays, San Francisco	360
1966	Felipe Alou, Atlanta	355
1967	Henry Aaron, Atlanta	344
1968	Billy Williams, Chicago	321
1969	Henry Aaron, Atlanta	332
1970	Billy Williams, Chicago	373

TWO-BASE HIT LEADERS

Year	AMERICAN LEAGUE	2B.
1900	—(Not classed as major)	
1901	—Napoleon Lajoie, Philadelphia	48
1902	—Harry Davis, Philadelphia	43
1903	—Ralph Seybold, Philadelphia	43
1904	—Napoleon Lajoie, Cleveland	50
1905	—Harry Davis, Philadelphia	47
1906	—Napoleon Lajoie, Cleveland	49
1907	—Harry Davis, Philadelphia	37
1908	—Tyrus Cobb, Detroit	36
1909	—Samuel Crawford, Detroit	35
1910	—Napoleon Lajoie, Cleveland	51
1911	—Tyrus Cobb, Detroit	47
1912	—Tristram Speaker, Boston	53
1913	—Joseph Jackson, Cleveland	39
1914	—Tristram Speaker, Boston	46
1915	—Robert Veach, Detroit	40
1916	—Graney, Cleve.-Speaker, Cleve.	41
1917	—Tyrus Cobb, Detroit	44
1918	—Tristram Speaker, Cleveland	33
1919	—Robert Veach, Detroit	45
1920	—Tristram Speaker, Cleveland	50
1921	—Tristram Speaker, Cleveland	52
1922	—Tristram Speaker, Cleveland	48
1923	—Tristram Speaker, Cleveland	59
1924	—J. Sewell, Cleve.-Heilmann, Det.	45
1925	—Martin McManus, St. Louis	44
1926	—George Burns, Cleveland	64
1927	—H. Louis Gehrig, New York	52
1928	—Manush, St. L.-Gehrig, N. Y.	47
1929	—Manush, St.L.-R. Johnson, Det.- Gehringer, Detroit	45
1930	—U. John Hodapp, Cleveland	51
1931	—Earl Webb, Boston	67
1932	—Eric McNair, Philadelphia	47
1933	—Joseph Cronin, Washington	45
1934	—Henry Greenberg, Detroit	63
1935	—Joseph Vosmik, Cleveland	47
1936	—Charles Gehringer, Detroit	60
1937	—Roy (Beau) Bell, St. Louis	51
1938	—Joseph Cronin, Boston	51
1939	—Robert (Red) Rolfe, New York	46
1940	—Henry Greenberg, Detroit	50
1941	—Louis Boudreau, Cleveland	45
1942	—Donald Kolloway, Chicago	40
1943	—Richard Wakefield, Detroit	38
1944	—Louis Boudreau, Cleveland	45
1945	—Wallace Moses, Chicago	35
1946	—Jas. (Mickey) Vernon, Washington	51
1947	—Louis Boudreau, Cleveland	45
1948	—Theodore Williams, Boston	44
1949	—Theodore Williams, Boston	39
1950	—George Kell, Detroit	56
1951	—Kell, Det.-Yost. Wash.-Mele, Wash.	36
1952	—Ferris Fain, Philadelphia	43
1953	—Jas. (Mickey) Vernon, Washington	43
1954	—Jas. (Mickey) Vernon, Washington	33
1955	—Harvey Kuenn, Detroit	38
1956	—James Piersall, Boston	40
1957	—Minoso, Chi.-Gardner, Balt.	36
1958	—Harvey Kuenn, Detroit	39
1959	—Harvey Kuenn, Detroit	42
1960	—John (Tito) Francona, Cleveland	36
1961	—Albert Kaline, Detroit	41
1962	—Floyd Robinson, Chicago	45
1963	—Carl Yastrzemski, Boston	40
1964	—Pedro (Tony) Oliva, Minnesota	43
1965	—Zoilo Versalles, Minnesota	45
	Carl Yastrzemski, Boston	45
1966	—Carl Yastrzemski, Boston	39
1967	—Pedro (Tony) Oliva, Minnesota	34
1968	—C. Reginald Smith, Boston	37
1969	—Pedro (Tony) Oliva, Minnesota	39
1970	—Pedro (Tony) Oliva, Minnesota	36
	Amos Otis, Kansas City	36
	Cesar Tovar, Minnesota	36

Year	NATIONAL LEAGUE	2B.
1900	—John (Honus) Wagner, Pittsburgh	45
1901	—Wagner, Pitts.-Beckley, Cinn.	39
1902	—John (Honus) Wagner, Pittsburgh	33
1903	—Clarke,Pit-MertesNY-Steinfeldt,Ci	32
1904	—John (Honus) Wagner, Pittsburgh	44
1905	—J. Bentley Seymour, Cincinnati	40
1906	—John (Honus) Wagner, Pittsburgh	38
1907	—John (Honus) Wagner, Pittsburgh	38
1908	—John (Honus) Wagner, Pittsburgh	39
1909	—John (Honus) Wagner, Pittsburgh	39
1910	—Robert Byrne, Pittsburgh	43
1911	—Edward Konetchy, St. Louis	38
1912	—Henry Zimmerman, Chicago	41
1913	—J. Carlisle Smith, Brooklyn	40
1914	—Sherwood Magee, Philadelphia	39
1915	—Lawrence Doyle, New York	40
1916	—J. Albert Niehoff, Philadelphia	42
1917	—Henry Groh, Cincinnati	39
1918	—Henry Groh, Cincinnati	28
1919	—Ross Youngs, New York	31
1920	—Rogers Hornsby, St. Louis	44
1921	—Rogers Hornsby, St. Louis	44
1922	—Rogers Hornsby, St. Louis	46
1923	—Edd Roush, Cincinnati	41
1924	—Rogers Hornsby, St. Louis	43
1925	—James Bottomley, St. Louis	44
1926	—James Bottomley, St. Louis	40
1927	—J. Riggs Stephenson, Chicago	46
1928	—Paul Waner, Pittsburgh	50
1929	—John Frederick, Brooklyn	52
1930	—Charles Klein, Philadelphia	59
1931	—Earl (Sparky) Adams, St. Louis	46
1932	—Paul Waner, Pittsburgh	62
1933	—Charles Klein, Philadelphia	44
1934	—Cuyler, Chicago-Allen, Philadelphia	42
1935	—William Herman, Chicago	57
1936	—Joseph Medwick, St. Louis	64
1937	—Joseph Medwick, St. Louis	56
1938	—Joseph Medwick, St. Louis	47
1939	—Enos Slaughter, St. Louis	52
1940	—Frank McCormick, Cincinnati	44
1941	—Reiser, Brooklyn-Mize, St. Louis	39
1942	—Martin Marion, St. Louis	38
1943	—Stanley Musial, St. Louis	48
1944	—Stanley Musial, St. Louis	51
1945	—Thomas Holmes, Boston	47
1946	—Stanley Musial, St. Louis	50
1947	—Edward Miller, Cincinnati	38
1948	—Stanley Musial, St. Louis	46
1949	—Stanley Musial, St. Louis	41
1950	—Al. (Red) Schoendienst, St. Louis	43
1951	—Alvin Dark, New York	41
1952	—Stanley Musial, St. Louis	42
1953	—Stanley Musial, St. Louis	53
1954	—Stanley Musial, St. Louis	41
1955	—Logan, Milw.-Aaron, Milw.	37
1956	—Henry Aaron, Milwaukee	34
1957	—Donald Hoak, Cincinnati	39
1958	—Orlando Cepeda, San Francisco	38
1959	—Vada Pinson, Cincinnati	47
1960	—Vada Pinson, Cincinnati	37
1961	—Henry Aaron, Milwaukee	39
1962	—Frank Robinson, Cincinnati	51
1963	—Richard Groat, St. Louis	43
1964	—A. Lee Maye, Milwaukee	44
1965	—Henry Aaron, Milwaukee	40
1966	—John Callison, Philadelphia	40
1967	—Daniel Staub, Houston	44
1968	—Louis Brock, St. Louis	46
1969	—Mateo Alou, Pittsburgh	41
1970	—M. Wesley Parker, Los Angeles	47

THREE-BASE HIT LEADERS

Year	AMERICAN LEAGUE	3B.
1900	(Not classed as major)	
1901	James Williams, Baltimore	22
1902	James Williams, Baltimore	23
1903	Samuel Crawford, Detroit	25
1904	Charles (Chick) Stahl, Boston	22
1905	Elmer Flick, Cleveland	19
1906	Elmer Flick, Cleveland	22
1907	Elmer Flick, Cleveland	18
1908	Tyrus Cobb, Detroit	20
1909	J. Franklin Baker, Philadelphia	19
1910	Samuel Crawford, Detroit	19
1911	Tyrus Cobb, Detroit	24
1912	Joseph Jackson, Cleveland	26
1913	Samuel Crawford, Detroit	23
1914	Samuel Crawford, Detroit	26
1915	Samuel Crawford, Detroit	19
1916	Joseph Jackson, Chicago	21
1917	Tyrus Cobb, Detroit	23
1918	Tyrus Cobb, Detroit	14
1919	Robert Veach, Detroit	17
1920	Joseph Jackson, Chicago	20
1921	Howard Shanks, Washington	19
1922	George Sisler, St. Louis	18
1923	Rice, Wash.-Goslin, Wash.	18
1924	Walter Pipp, New York	19
1925	Leon (Goose) Goslin, Washington	20
1926	H. Louis Gehrig, New York	20
1927	Earle Combs, New York	23
1928	Earle Combs, New York	21
1929	Charles Gehringer, Detroit	19
1930	Earle Combs, New York	22
1931	Roy Johnson, Detroit	19
1932	Joseph Cronin, Washington	18
1933	Henry Manush, Washington	17
1934	W. Benjamin Chapman, New York	13
1935	Joseph Vosmik, Cleveland	20
1936	Averill,Clev.-F.DiMaggio, Rolfe, NY.	15
1937	F. Walker, Chi.-Kreevich, Chi.	16
1938	J. Geoffrey Heath, Cleveland	18
1939	John (Buddy) Lewis, Washington	16
1940	Barney McCosky, Detroit	19
1941	J. Geoffrey Heath, Cleveland	20
1942	Stanley Spence, Washington	15
1943	Lindell, New York-Moses, Chicago	12
1944	Lindell, N. Y.-Stirnweiss, N. Y.	15
1945	George Stirnweiss, New York	22
1946	Henry Edwards, Cleveland	16
1947	Thomas Henrich, New York	13
1948	Thomas Henrich, New York	14
1949	L. Dale Mitchell, Cleveland	23
1950	D. DiMaggio,Doerr,Bos-Evers, Det.	11
1951	Orestes (Minnie) Minoso, Cle.-Chi.	14
1952	Roberto Avila, Cleveland	11
1953	Manuel (Jim) Rivera, Chicago	16
1954	Orestes (Minnie) Minoso, Chicago	18
1955	Mantle, N. Y.-Carey, N. Y.	11
1956	Minoso, Chi.-Jensen, Bos.-Simpson, Kan. City-Lemon, Wash.	11
1957	McDougald, Bauer, Simpson, N. Y.	9
1958	Victor Power, K. C.-Cleve.	10
1959	W. Robert Allison, Washington	9
1960	J. Nelson Fox, Chicago	10
1961	Jacob Wood, Detroit	14
1962	Gino Cimoli, Kansas City	15
1963	Zoilo Versalles, Minnesota	13
1964	Rich. Rollins, Versalles, Minn.	10
1965	Dagoberto Campaneris, Kansas City.	12
	Zoilo Versalles, Minnesota	12
1966	Robert Knoop, California	11
1967	Paul L. Blair, Baltimore	12
1968	James Fregosi, California	13
1969	Delbert Unser, Washington	8
1970	Cesar Tovar, Minnesota	13

Year	NATIONAL LEAGUE	3B.
1900	John (Honus) Wagner, Pittsburgh	22
1901	James Sheckard, Brooklyn	21
1902	Samuel Crawford, Cincinnati	23
1903	John (Honus) Wagner, Pittsburgh	19
1904	Harry Lumley, Brooklyn	18
1905	J. Bentley Seymour, Cincinnati	21
1906	Clarke, Pitt.-Schulte, Chi.	13
1907	Ganzel, Cinn.-Alperman, Bkn.	16
1908	John (Honus) Wagner, Pittsburgh	19
1909	Michael Mitchell, Cincinnati	17
1910	Michael Mitchell, Cincinnati	18
1911	Lawrence Doyle, New York	25
1912	John (Chief) Wilson, Pittsburgh	36
1913	Victor Saier, Chicago	21
1914	Max Carey, Pittsburgh	17
1915	Thomas Long, St. Louis	25
1916	William Hinchman, Pittsburgh	16
1917	Rogers Hornsby, St. Louis	17
1918	Jacob Daubert, Brooklyn	15
1919	Hi Myers, Brkn.-Southworth, Pitt.	14
1920	Henry (Hi) Myers, Brooklyn	22
1921	Hornsby, St. Louis-Powell, Bos	18
1922	Jacob Daubert, Cincinnati	22
1923	Carey, Pitt.-Traynor, Pitt.	19
1924	Edd Roush, Cincinnati	21
1925	Hazen (Kiki) Cuyler, Pittsburgh	26
1926	Paul Waner, Pittsburgh	22
1927	Paul Waner, Pittsburgh	17
1928	James Bottomley, St. Louis	20
1929	Lloyd Waner, Pittsburgh	20
1930	Adam Comorosky, Pittsburgh	23
1931	William Terry, New York	20
1932	Floyd (Babe) Herman, Cincinnati	19
1933	J. Floyd (Arky) Vaughan, Pitt.	19
1934	Joseph Medwick, St. Louis	18
1935	Ival Goodman, Cincinnati	18
1936	Ival Goodman, Cincinnati	14
1937	J. Floyd (Arky) Vaughan, Pitt.	17
1938	John Mize, St. Louis	16
1939	William Herman, Chicago	18
1940	J. Floyd (Arky) Vaughan, Pitt.	15
1941	Harold (Pete) Reiser, Brooklyn	17
1942	Enos Slaughter, St. Louis	17
1943	Stanley Musial, St. Louis	20
1944	John Barrett, Pittsburgh	19
1945	Luis Olmo, Brooklyn	13
1946	Stanley Musial, St. Louis	20
1947	Harry Walker, St. Louis-Phila.	16
1948	Stanley Musial, St. Louis	18
1949	Musial, St. L.-Slaughter, St. L.	13
1950	Richie Ashburn, Philadelphia	14
1951	Musial, St. L.-Bell, Pitts.	12
1952	Robert Thomson, New York	14
1953	James Gilliam, Brooklyn	17
1954	Willie Mays, New York	13
1955	Mays, N. Y.-Long, Pitts.	13
1956	William Bruton, Milwaukee	15
1957	Willie Mays, New York	20
1958	Richie Ashburn, Philadelphia	13
1959	Moon, L. A.-Neal, L. A.	11
1960	William Bruton, Milwaukee	13
1961	George Altman, Chicago	12
1962	Callison, Phila.-Virdon, Pitt.-W. Davis, Wills, Los Ang.	10
1963	Vada Pinson, Cincinnati	14
1964	Allen, Phila.-Santo, Chicago	13
1965	John Callison, Philadelphia	16
1966	J. Timothy McCarver, St. Louis	13
1967	Vada Pinson, Cincinnati	13
1968	Louis Brock, St. Louis	14
1969	Roberto Clemente, Pittsburgh	12
1970	William Davis, Los Angeles	16

HOME RUN LEADERS

Year	AMERICAN LEAGUE	HR.
1900—	(Not classed as major.)	
1901—	Napoleon Lajoie, Philadelphia	13
1902—	Ralph (Socks) Seybold, Phila.	16
1903—	John (Buck) Freeman, Boston	13
1904—	Harry Davis, Philadelphia	10
1905—	Harry Davis, Philadelphia	8
1906—	Harry Davis, Philadelphia	12
1907—	Harry Davis, Philadelphia	8
1908—	Samuel Crawford, Detroit	7
1909—	Tyrus Cobb, Detroit	9
1910—	J. Garland (Jake) Stahl, Boston	10
1911—	J. Franklin Baker, Philadelphia	9
1912—	J. Franklin Baker, Philadelphia	10
1913—	J. Franklin Baker, Philadelphia	12
1914—	Baker, Phil.-Crawford, Detroit	8
1915—	Robert Roth, Chicago-Cleveland	7
1916—	Walter Pipp, New York	12
1917—	Walter Pipp, New York	9
1918—	Ruth, Bos.-Tilly Walker, Phila.	11
1919—	George (Babe) Ruth, Boston	29
1920—	George (Babe) Ruth, New York	54
1921—	George (Babe) Ruth, New York	59
1922—	Kenneth Williams, St. Louis	39
1923—	George (Babe) Ruth, New York	41
1924—	George (Babe) Ruth, New York	46
1925—	Robert Meusel, New York	33
1926—	George (Babe) Ruth, New York	47
1927—	George (Babe) Ruth, New York	60
1928—	George (Babe) Ruth, New York	54
1929—	George (Babe) Ruth, New York	46
1930—	George (Babe) Ruth, New York	49
1931—	Ruth, N. Y.-Gehrig, N. Y.	46
1932—	James Foxx, Philadelphia	58
1933—	James Foxx, Philadelphia	48
1934—	H. Louis Gehrig, New York	49
1935—	Foxx, Phil.-Greenberg, Detroit	36
1936—	H. Louis Gehrig, New York	49
1937—	Joseph DiMaggio, New York	46
1938—	Henry Greenberg, Detroit	58
1939—	James Foxx, Boston	35
1940—	Henry Greenberg, Detroit	41
1941—	Theodore Williams, Boston	37
1942—	Theodore Williams, Boston	36
1943—	Rudolph York, Detroit	34
1944—	Nicholas Etten, New York	22
1945—	Vernon Stephens, St. Louis	24
1946—	Henry Greenberg, Detroit	44
1947—	Theodore Williams, Boston	32
1948—	Joseph DiMaggio, New York	39
1949—	Theodore Williams, Boston	43
1950—	Albert Rosen, Cleveland	37
1951—	Gus Zernial, Chi.-Phila.	33
1952—	Lawrence Doby, Cleveland	32
1953—	Albert Rosen, Cleveland	43
1954—	Lawrence Doby, Cleveland	32
1955—	Mickey Mantle, New York	37
1956—	Mickey Mantle, New York	52
1957—	Roy Sievers, Washington	42
1958—	Mickey Mantle, New York	42
1959—	Colavito, Cleve.-Killebrew, Wash.	42
1960—	Mickey Mantle, New York	40
1961—	Roger Maris, New York	61
1962—	Harmon Killebrew, Minnesota	48
1963—	Harmon Killebrew, Minnesota	45
1964—	Harmon Killebrew, Minnesota	49
1965—	Anthony Conigliaro, Boston	32
1966—	Frank Robinson, Baltimore	49
1967—	Harmon Killebrew, Minnesota	44
	Carl Yastrzemski, Boston	44
1968—	Frank Howard, Washington	44
1969—	Harmon Killebrew, Minnesota	49
1970—	Frank Howard, Washington	44

Year	NATIONAL LEAGUE	HR.
1900—	Herman Long, Boston	12
1901—	Samuel Crawford, Cincinnati	16
1902—	Thomas Leach, Pittsburgh	6
1903—	James Sheckard, Brooklyn	9
1904—	Harry Lumley, Brooklyn	9
1905—	Fred Odwell, Cincinnati	9
1906—	Timothy Jordan, Brooklyn	12
1907—	David Brain, Boston	10
1908—	Timothy Jordan, Brooklyn	12
1909—	John (Red) Murray, New York	7
1910—	Fred Beck, Bos.-F. Schulte, Chi.	10
1911—	Frank Schulte, Chicago	21
1912—	Henry Zimmerman, Chicago	14
1913—	Cliff. (Gavvy) Cravath, Phila.	19
1914—	Cliff. (Gavvy) Cravath, Phila.	19
1915—	Cliff. (Gavvy) Cravath, Phila.	24
1916—	Robertson, N. Y.-Williams, Chi.	12
1917—	Robertson, N. Y.-Cravath, Phila.	12
1918—	Cliff. (Gavvy) Cravath, Phila.	8
1919—	Cliff. (Gavvy) Cravath, Phila.	12
1920—	Fred (Cy) Williams, Philadelphia.	15
1921—	George Kelly, New York	23
1922—	Rogers Hornsby, St. Louis	42
1923—	Fred (Cy) Williams, Philadelphia.	41
1924—	Jacques Fournier, Brooklyn	27
1925—	Rogers Hornsby, St. Louis	39
1926—	Lewis (Hack) Wilson, Chicago	21
1927—	Wilson, Chi.-Williams, Phila.	30
1928—	Wilson, Chi.-Bottomley, St. L.	31
1929—	Charles Klein, Philadelphia	43
1930—	Lewis (Hack) Wilson, Chicago	56
1931—	Charles Klein, Philadelphia	31
1932—	Klein, Philadelphia-Ott, New York.	38
1933—	Charles Klein, Philadelphia	28
1934—	Collins, St. Louis-Ott, New York	35
1935—	Walter Berger, Boston	34
1936—	Melvin Ott, New York	33
1937—	Ott, New York-Medwick, St. Louis	31
1938—	Melvin Ott, New York	36
1939—	John Mize, St. Louis	28
1940—	John Mize, St. Louis	43
1941—	Adolph Camilli, Brooklyn	34
1942—	Melvin Ott, New York	30
1943—	William Nicholson, Chicago	29
1944—	William Nicholson, Chicago	33
1945—	Thomas Holmes, Boston	28
1946—	Ralph Kiner, Pittsburgh	23
1947—	Kiner, Pittsburgh-Mize, New York	51
1948—	Kiner, Pittsburgh-Mize, New York	40
1949—	Ralph Kiner, Pittsburgh	54
1950—	Ralph Kiner, Pittsburgh	47
1951—	Ralph Kiner, Pittsburgh	42
1952—	Kiner, Pittsburgh-Sauer, Chicago	37
1953—	Edwin Mathews, Milwaukee	47
1954—	Theodore Kluszewski, Cincinnati	49
1955—	Willie Mays, New York	51
1956—	Edwin (Duke) Snider, Brooklyn	43
1957—	Henry Aaron, Milwaukee	44
1958—	Ernest Banks, Chicago	47
1959—	Edwin Mathews, Milwaukee	46
1960—	Ernest Banks, Chicago	41
1961—	Orlando Cepeda, San Francisco	46
1962—	Willie Mays, San Francisco	49
1963—	H. Aaron, Mil.-McCovey, San Fran.	44
1964—	Willie Mays, San Francisco	47
1965—	Willie Mays, San Francisco	52
1966—	Henry Aaron, Atlanta	44
1967—	Henry Aaron, Atlanta	39
1968—	Willie McCovey, San Francisco	36
1969—	Willie McCovey, San Francisco	45
1970—	Johnny Bench, Cincinnati	45

RUNS BATTED IN LEADERS

Year	AMERICAN LEAGUE	RBI	Year	NATIONAL LEAGUE	RBI
1907	Tyrus Cobb, Detroit	116	1907	John (Honus) Wagner, Pittsburgh	91
1908	Tyrus Cobb, Detroit	101	1908	John (Honus) Wagner, Pittsburgh	106
1909	Tyrus Cobb, Detroit	115	1909	John (Honus) Wagner, Pittsburgh	102
1910	Samuel Crawford, Detroit	115	1910	Sherwood Magee, Philadelphia	116
1911	Tyrus Cobb, Detroit	144	1911	Frank Schulte, Chicago	121
1912	J. Franklin Baker, Philadelphia	133	1912	Henry Zimmerman, Chicago	98
1913	J. Franklin Baker, Philadelphia	126	1913	Cliff. (Gavvy) Cravath, Phila.	118
1914	Samuel Crawford, Detroit	112	1914	Sherwood Magee, Philadelphia	101
1915	Samuel Crawford, Detroit	116	1915	Cliff. (Gavvy) Cravath, Phila.	118
1916	Walter Pipp, New York	99	1916	Harold Chase, Cincinnati	84
1917	Robert Veach, Detroit	115	1917	Henry Zimmerman, New York	100
1918	George Burns, Philadelphia	74	1918	Frederick Merkle, Chicago	71
	Robert Veach, Detroit	74			
1919	George (Babe) Ruth, Boston	112	1919	Henry (Hi) Myers, Brooklyn	72
1920	George (Babe) Ruth, New York	137	1920	George Kelly, New York	94
				Rogers Hornsby, St. Louis	94
1921	George (Babe) Ruth, New York	170	1921	Rogers Hornsby, St. Louis	126
1922	Kenneth Williams, St. Louis	155	1922	Rogers Hornsby, St. Louis	152
1923	George (Babe) Ruth, New York	130	1923	Emil Meusel, New York	125
	Tristram Speaker, Cleveland	130			
1924	Leon (Goose) Goslin, Washington	129	1924	George Kelly, New York	136
1925	Robert Meusel, New York	138	1925	Rogers Hornsby, St. Louis	143
1926	George (Babe) Ruth, New York	155	1926	James Bottomley, St. Louis	120
1927	H. Louis Gehrig, New York	175	1927	Paul Waner, Pittsburgh	131
1928	George (Babe) Ruth, New York	142	1928	James Bottomley, St. Louis	136
	H. Louis Gehrig, New York	142			
1929	Aloysius Simmons, Philadelphia	157	1929	Lewis (Hack) Wilson, Chicago	159
1930	H. Louis Gehrig, New York	174	1930	Lewis (Hack) Wilson, Chicago	190
1931	H. Louis Gehrig, New York	184	1931	Charles Klein, Philadelphia	121
1932	James Foxx, Philadelphia	169	1932	Frank (Don) Hurst, Philadelphia	143
1933	James Foxx, Philadelphia	163	1933	Charles Klein, Philadelphia	120
1934	H. Louis Gehrig, New York	165	1934	Melvin Ott, New York	135
1935	Henry Greenberg, Detroit	170	1935	Walter Berger, Boston	130
1936	Harold Trosky, Cleveland	162	1936	Joseph Medwick, St. Louis	138
1937	Henry Greenberg, Detroit	183	1937	Joseph Medwick, St. Louis	154
1938	James Foxx, Boston	175	1938	Joseph Medwick, St. Louis	122
1939	Theodore Williams, Boston	145	1939	Frank McCormick, Cincinnati	128
1940	Henry Greenberg, Detroit	150	1940	John Mize, St. Louis	137
1941	Joseph DiMaggio, New York	125	1941	Adolph Camilli, Brooklyn	120
1942	Theodore Williams, Boston	137	1942	John Mize, New York	110
1943	Rudolph York, Detroit	118	1943	William Nicholson, Chicago	128
1944	Vernon Stephens, St. Louis	109	1944	William Nicholson, Chicago	122
1945	Nicholas Etten, New York	111	1945	Fred (Dixie) Walker, Brooklyn	124
1946	Henry Greenberg, Detroit	127	1946	Enos Slaughter, St. Louis	130
1947	Theodore Williams, Boston	114	1947	John Mize, New York	138
1948	Joseph DiMaggio, New York	155	1948	Stanley Musial, St. Louis	131
1949	Theodore Williams, Boston	159	1949	Ralph Kiner, Pittsburgh	127
	Vernon Stephens, Boston	159			
1950	Walter Dropo, Boston	144	1950	Delmer Ennis, Philadelphia	126
	Vernon Stephens, Boston	144			
1951	Gus Zernial, Chi.-Phila.	129	1951	Monford Irvin, New York	121
1952	Albert Rosen, Cleveland	105	1952	Henry Sauer, Chicago	121
1953	Albert Rosen, Cleveland	145	1953	Roy Campanella, Brooklyn	142
1954	Lawrence Doby, Cleveland	126	1954	Theodore Kluszewski, Cincinnati	141
1955	Raymond Boone, Detroit	116	1955	Edwin (Duke) Snider, Brooklyn	136
	Jack Jensen, Boston	116			
1956	Mickey Mantle, New York	130	1956	Stanley Musial, St. Louis	109
1957	Roy Sievers, Washington	114	1957	Henry Aaron, Milwaukee	132
1958	Jack Jensen, Boston	122	1958	Ernest Banks, Chicago	129
1959	Jack Jensen, Boston	112	1959	Ernest Banks, Chicago	143
1960	Roger Maris, New York	112	1960	Henry Aaron, Milwaukee	126
1961	Roger Maris, New York	142	1961	Orlando Cepeda, San Francisco	142
1962	Harmon Killebrew, Minnesota	126	1962	H. Thomas Davis, Los Angeles	153
1963	Richard Stuart, Boston	118	1963	Henry Aaron, Milwaukee	130
1964	Brooks Robinson, Baltimore	118	1964	Kenton Boyer, St. Louis	119
1965	Rocco Colavito, Cleveland	108	1965	Deron Johnson, Cincinnati	130
1966	Frank Robinson, Baltimore	122	1966	Henry Aaron, Atlanta	127
1967	Carl Yastrzemski, Boston	121	1967	Orlando Cepeda, St. Louis	111
1968	Kenneth Harrelson, Boston	109	1968	Willie McCovey, San Francisco	105
1969	Harmon Killebrew, Minnesota	140	1969	Willie McCovey, San Francisco	126
1970	Frank Howard, Washington	126	1970	Johnny Bench, Cincinnati	148

Note—Runs batted in not compiled prior to 1907; officially adopted in 1920.

LEADING BASE STEALERS

AMERICAN LEAGUE		NATIONAL LEAGUE	
Year Player—Club	SB.	Year Player—Club	SB.
1900—Not classed as major league.		1900—James Barrett, Cincinnati	46
1901—Frank Isbell, Chicago	48	1901—John (Honus) Wagner, Pittsburgh.	48
1902—Fred (Topsy) Hartsel, Philadelphia	54	1902—John (Honus) Wagner, Pittsburgh.	43
1903—Harry Bay, Cleveland	46	1903—Sheckard, Brooklyn-Chance, Chicago	67
1904—Elmer Flick, Clev.-Harry Bay, Clev.	42	1904—John (Honus) Wagner, Pittsburgh.	53
1905—Daniel Hoffman, Philadelphia	46	1905—Maloney, Chi.-Devlin, N. York	59
1906—Flick, Cleve.-Anderson, Wash.	39	1906—Frank Chance, Chicago	57
1907—Tyrus Cobb, Detroit	49	1907—John (Honus) Wagner, Pittsburgh.	61
1908—Patrick Dougherty, Chicago	47	1908—John (Honus) Wagner, Pittsburgh.	53
1909—Tyrus Cobb, Detroit	76	1909—Robert Bescher, Cincinnati	54
1910—Edward Collins, Philadelphia	81	1910—Robert Bescher, Cincinnati	70
1911—Tyrus Cobb, Detroit	83	1911—Robert Bescher, Cincinnati	80
1912—J. Clyde Milan, Washington	88	1912—Robert Bescher, Cincinnati	67
1913—J. Clyde Milan, Washington	74	1913—Max Carey, Pittsburgh	61
1914—Frederick Maisel, New York	74	1914—George Burns, New York	62
1915—Tyrus Cobb, Detroit	96	1915—Max Carey, Pittsburgh	36
1916—Tyrus Cobb, Detroit	68	1916—Max Carey, Pittsburgh	63
1917—Tyrus Cobb, Detroit	55	1917—Max Carey, Pittsburgh	46
1918—George Sisler, St. Louis	45	1918—Max Carey, Pittsburgh	58
1919—Edward Collins, Chicago	33	1919—George Burns, New York	40
1920—Edgar (Sam) Rice, Washington	63	1920—Max Carey, Pittsburgh	52
1921—George Sisler, St. Louis	35	1921—Frank Frisch, New York	49
1922—George Sisler, St. Louis	51	1922—Max Carey, Pittsburgh	51
1923—Edward Collins, Chicago	49	1923—Max Carey, Pittsburgh	51
1924—Edward Collins, Chicago	42	1924—Max Carey, Pittsburgh	49
1925—John Mostil, Chicago	43	1925—Max Carey, Pittsburgh	46
1926—John Mostil, Chicago	35	1926—Hazen (Kiki) Cuyler, Pittsburgh.	35
1927—George Sisler, St. Louis	27	1927—Frank Frisch, St. Louis	48
1928—Charles (Buddy) Myer, Boston.	30	1928—Hazen (Kiki) Cuyler, Chicago.	37
1929—Charles Gehringer, Detroit	27	1929—Hazen (Kiki) Cuyler, Chicago.	43
1930—Martin McManus, Detroit	23	1930—Hazen (Kiki) Cuyler, Chicago.	37
1931—W. Benjamin Chapman, N. York.	61	1931—Frank Frisch, St. Louis	28
1932—W. Benjamin Chapman, N. York.	38	1932—Charles Klein, Philadelphia	20
1933—W. Benjamin Chapman, N. York.	27	1933—John (Pepper) Martin, St. Louis.	26
1934—William Werber, Boston	40	1934—John (Pepper) Martin, St. Louis.	23
1935—William Werber, Boston	29	1935—August Galan, Chicago	22
1936—Lynford Lary, St. Louis	37	1936—John (Pepper) Martin, St. Louis.	23
1937—Werber, Phila.-Chapman, Wa.-Bos.	35	1937—August Galan, Chicago	23
1938—Frank Crosetti, New York	27	1938—Stanley Hack, Chicago	16
1939—George Case, Washington	51	1939—Hack, Chicago-Handley, Pittsburgh	17
1940—George Case, Washington	35	1940—Linus Frey, Cincinnati	22
1941—George Case, Washington	33	1941—Daniel Murtaugh, Philadelphia	18
1942—George Case, Washington	44	1942—Harold (Pete) Reiser, Brooklyn	20
1943—George Case, Washington	61	1943—J. Floyd (Arky) Vaughan, Brooklyn	20
1944—George Stirnweiss, New York	55	1944—John Barrett, Pittsburgh	28
1945—George Stirnweiss, New York	33	1945—Al. (Red) Schoendienst, St. Louis	26
1946—George Case, Cleveland	28	1946—Harold (Pete) Reiser, Brooklyn.	34
1947—Robert Dillinger, St. Louis	34	1947—Jack Robinson, Brooklyn	29
1948—Robert Dillinger, St. Louis	28	1948—Richie Ashburn, Philadelphia	32
1949—Robert Dillinger, St. Louis	20	1949—Jack Robinson, Brooklyn	37
1950—Dominic DiMaggio, Boston	15	1950—Samuel Jethroe, Boston	35
1951—Orestes (Minnie) Minoso, Cle.-Chi.	31	1951—Samuel Jethroe, Boston	35
1952—Orestes (Minnie) Minoso, Chicago.	22	1952—Harold (Pee Wee) Reese, Brooklyn	30
1953—Orestes (Minnie) Minoso, Chicago.	25	1953—William Bruton, Milwaukee	26
1954—Jack Jensen, Boston	22	1954—William Bruton, Milwaukee	34
1955—Manuel (Jim) Rivera, Chicago.	25	1955—William Bruton, Milwaukee	25
1956—Luis Aparicio, Chicago	21	1956—Willie Mays, New York	40
1957—Luis Aparicio, Chicago	28	1957—Willie Mays, New York	38
1958—Luis Aparicio, Chicago	29	1958—Willie Mays, San Francisco	31
1959—Luis Aparicio, Chicago	56	1959—Willie Mays, San Francisco	27
1960—Luis Aparicio, Chicago	51	1960—Maurice Wills, Los Angeles	50
1961—Luis Aparicio, Chicago	53	1961—Maurice Wills, Los Angeles	35
1962—Luis Aparicio, Chicago	31	1962—Maurice Wills, Los Angeles	104
1963—Luis Aparicio, Baltimore	40	1963—Maurice Wills, Los Angeles	40
1964—Luis Aparicio, Baltimore	57	1964—Maurice Wills, Los Angeles	53
1965—Dagoberto Campaneris, Kan. City.	51	1965—Maurice Wills, Los Angeles	94
1966—Dagoberto Campaneris, Kan. City.	52	1966—Louis Brock, St. Louis	74
1967—Dagoberto Campaneris, Kan. City.	55	1967—Louis Brock, St. Louis	52
1968—Dagoberto Campaneris, Oakland	62	1968—Louis Brock, St. Louis	62
1969—Tommy Harper, Seattle	73	1969—Louis Brock, St. Louis	53
1970—Dagoberto Campaneris, Oakland ..	42	1970—Robert Tolan, Cincinnati	57

SLUGGING LEADERS

AMERICAN LEAGUE		NATIONAL LEAGUE	
Year Player—Club	Slug. Avg.	Year Player—Club	Slug. Avg.
1900—Not classed as major league.		1900—John (Honus) Wagner, Pittsburgh	.572
1901—Napoleon Lajoie, Philadelphia	.630	1901—James Sheckard, Brooklyn	.536
1902—Edward Delahanty, Washington	.589	1902—John (Honus) Wagner, Pittsburgh	.467
1903—Napoleon Lajoie, Cleveland	.533	1903—Fred Clarke, Pittsburgh	.532
1904—Napoleon Lajoie, Cleveland	.549	1904—John (Honus) Wagner, Pittsburgh	.520
1905—Elmer Flick, Cleveland	.466	1905—J. Bentley Seymour, Cincinnati	.559
1906—George Stone, St. Louis	.496	1906—Harry Lumley, Brooklyn	.477
1907—Tyrus Cobb, Detroit	.473	1907—John (Honus) Wagner, Pittsburgh	.513
1908—Tyrus Cobb, Detroit	.475	1908—John (Honus) Wagner, Pittsburgh	.542
1909—Tyrus Cobb, Detroit	.517	1909—John (Honus) Wagner, Pittsburgh	.489
1910—Tyrus Cobb, Detroit	.554	1910—Sherwood Magee, Philadelphia	.507
1911—Tyrus Cobb, Detroit	.621	1911—Frank Schulte, Chicago	.534
1912—Tyrus Cobb, Detroit	.586	1912—Henry Zimmerman, Chicago	.571
1913—Joseph Jackson, Cleveland	.551	1913—Cliff. (Gavvy) Cravath, Phila.	.568
1914—Tyrus Cobb, Detroit	.513	1914—Sherwood Magee, Philadelphia	.501
1915—Tyrus Cobb, Detroit	.487	1915—Cliff. (Gavvy) Cravath, Phila.	.510
1916—Tristram Speaker, Cleveland	.502	1916—Zachariah Wheat, Brooklyn	.461
1917—Tyrus Cobb, Detroit	.571	1917—Rogers Hornsby, St. Louis	.484
1918—George (Babe) Ruth, Boston	.555	1918—Edd Roush, Cincinnati	.455
1919—George (Babe) Ruth, Boston	.657	1919—Henry (Hi) Myers, Brooklyn	.436
1920—George (Babe) Ruth, New York	.847	1920—Rogers Hornsby, St. Louis	.559
1921—George (Babe) Ruth, New York	.846	1921—Rogers Hornsby, St. Louis	.659
1922—George (Babe) Ruth, New York	.672	1922—Rogers Hornsby, St. Louis	.722
1923—George (Babe) Ruth, New York	.764	1923—Rogers Hornsby, St. Louis	.627
1924—George (Babe) Ruth, New York	.739	1924—Rogers Hornsby, St. Louis	.696
1925—Kenneth Williams, St. Louis	.613	1925—Rogers Hornsby, St. Louis	.756
1926—George (Babe) Ruth, New York	.737	1926—Fred Williams, Philadelphia	.569
1927—George (Babe) Ruth, New York	.772	1927—Charles Hafey, St. Louis	.590
1928—George (Babe) Ruth, New York	.709	1928—Rogers Hornsby, Boston	.632
1929—George (Babe) Ruth, New York	.697	1929—Rogers Hornsby, Chicago	.681
1930—George (Babe) Ruth, New York	.732	1930—Lewis (Hack) Wilson, Chicago	.723
1931—George (Babe) Ruth, New York	.700	1931—Charles Klein, Philadelphia	.584
1932—James Foxx, Philadelphia	.749	1932—Charles Klein, Philadelphia	.646
1933—James Foxx, Philadelphia	.703	1933—Charles Klein, Philadelphia	.602
1934—H. Louis Gehrig, New York	.706	1934—James (Rip) Collins, St. Louis	.615
1935—James Foxx, Philadelphia	.636	1935—J. Floyd (Arky) Vaughan, Pitts.	.607
1936—H. Louis Gehrig, New York	.696	1936—Melvin Ott, New York	.588
1937—Joseph DiMaggio, New York	.673	1937—Joseph Medwick, St. Louis	.641
1938—James Foxx, Boston	.704	1938—John Mize, St. Louis	.614
1939—James Foxx, Boston	.694	1939—John Mize, St. Louis	.626
1940—Henry Greenberg, Detroit	.670	1940—John Mize, St. Louis	.636
1941—Theodore Williams, Boston	.735	1941—Harold (Pete) Reiser, Brooklyn	.588
1942—Theodore Williams, Boston	.648	1942—John Mize, New York	.521
1943—Rudolph York, Detroit	.527	1943—Stanley Musial, St. Louis	.562
1944—Robert Doerr, Boston	.5278	1944—Stanley Musial, St. Louis	.549
1945—George Stirnweiss, New York	.476	1945—Tommy Holmes, Boston	.577
1946—Theodore Williams, Boston	.667	1946—Stanley Musial, St. Louis	.587
1947—Theodore Williams, Boston	.634	1947—Ralph Kiner, Pittsburgh	.639
1948—Theodore Williams, Boston	.615	1948—Stanley Musial, St. Louis	.702
1949—Theodore Williams, Boston	.650	1949—Ralph Kiner, Pittsburgh	.658
1950—Joseph DiMaggio, New York	.585	1950—Stanley Musial, St. Louis	.596
1951—Theodore Williams, Boston	.556	1951—Ralph Kiner, Pittsburgh	.627
1952—Lawrence Doby, Cleveland	.541	1952—Stanley Musial, St. Louis	.538
1953—Albert Rosen, Cleveland	.613	1953—Edwin (Duke) Snider, Brooklyn	.6271
1954—Theodore Williams, Boston	.635	1954—Willie Mays, New York	.667
1955—Mickey Mantle, New York	.611	1955—Willie Mays, New York	.659
1956—Mickey Mantle, New York	.705	1956—Edwin (Duke) Snider, Brooklyn	.598
1957—Theodore Williams, Boston	.731	1957—Willie Mays, New York	.626
1958—Rocco Colavito, Cleveland	.620	1958—Ernest Banks, Chicago	.614
1959—Albert Kaline, Detroit	.530	1959—Henry Aaron, Milwaukee	.636
1960—Roger Maris, New York	.581	1960—Frank Robinson, Cincinnati	.595
1961—Mickey Mantle, New York	.687	1961—Frank Robinson, Cincinnati	.611
1962—Mickey Mantle, New York	.605	1962—Frank Robinson, Cincinnati	.624
1963—Harmon Killebrew, Minnesota	.555	1963—Henry Aaron, Milwaukee	.586
1964—John (Boog) Powell, Baltimore	.606	1964—Willie Mays, San Francisco	.607
1965—Carl Yastrzemski, Boston	.536	1965—Willie Mays, San Francisco	.645
1966—Frank Robinson, Baltimore	.637	1966—Richard Allen, Philadelphia	.632
1967—Carl Yastrzemski, Boston	.622	1967—Henry Aaron, Atlanta	.573
1968—Frank Howard, Washington	.552	1968—Willie McCovey, San Francisco	.545
1969—Reginald Jackson, Oakland	.608	1969—Willie McCovey, San Francisco	.656
1970—Carl Yastrzemski, Boston	.592	1970—Willie McCovey, San Francisco	.612

BATTERS LEADING IN BASES ON BALLS

AMERICAN LEAGUE

Year	Player and Club	BB	Year	Player and Club	BB
1913	Burton Shotton, St. Louis	102	1941	Theodore Williams, Boston	145
1914	Owen (Donie) Bush, Detroit	112	1942	Theodore Williams, Boston	145
1915	Edward Collins, Chicago	119	1943	Charles Keller, New York	106
1916	Burton Shotton, St. Louis	111	1944	Nicholas Etten, New York	97
1917	John Graney, Cleveland	94	1945	Roy Cullenbine, Cleve.-Detroit	112
1918	Raymond Chapman, Cleveland	84	1946	Theodore Williams, Boston	156
1919	John Graney, Cleveland	105	1947	Theodore Williams, Boston	162
1920	George (Babe) Ruth, New York	148	1948	Theodore Williams, Boston	126
1921	George (Babe) Ruth, New York	144	1949	Theodore Williams, Boston	162
1922	L. W. (Whitey) Witt, New York	89	1950	Edward Yost, Washington	141
1923	George (Babe) Ruth, New York	170	1951	Theodore Williams, Boston	143
1924	George (Babe) Ruth, New York	142	1952	Edward Yost, Washington	129
1925	William Kamm, Chicago	90	1953	Edward Yost, Washington	123
	John Mostil, Chicago	90	1954	Theodore Williams, Boston	136
1926	George (Babe) Ruth, New York	144	1955	Mickey Mantle, New York	113
1927	George (Babe) Ruth, New York	138	1956	Edward Yost, Washington	151
1928	George (Babe) Ruth, New York	135	1957	Mickey Mantle, New York	146
1929	Max Bishop, Philadelphia	128	1958	Mickey Mantle, New York	129
1930	George (Babe) Ruth, New York	136	1959	Edward Yost, Detroit	135
1931	George (Babe) Ruth, New York	128	1960	Edward Yost, Detroit	125
1932	George (Babe) Ruth, New York	130	1961	Mickey Mantle, New York	126
1933	George (Babe) Ruth, New York	114	1962	Mickey Mantle, New York	122
1934	James Foxx, Philadelphia	111	1963	Carl Yastrzemski, Boston	95
1935	H. Louis Gehrig, New York	132	1964	Norman Siebern, Baltimore	106
1936	H. Louis Gehrig, New York	130	1965	Rocco Colavito, Cleveland	93
1937	H. Louis Gehrig, New York	127	1966	Harmon Killebrew, Minnesota	103
1938	James Foxx, Boston	119	1967	Harmon Killebrew, Minnesota	131
	Henry Greenberg, Detroit	119	1968	Carl Yastrzemski, Boston	119
1939	Harfold Clift, St. Louis	111	1969	Harmon Killebrew, Minnesota	145
1940	Charles Keller, New York	106	1970	Frank Howard, Washington	132

NATIONAL LEAGUE

Year	Player and Club	BB	Year	Player and Club	BB
1910	Miller Huggins, St. Louis	116	1942	Eelvin Ott, New York	109
1911	James Sheckard, Chicago	147	1943	August Galan, Brooklyn	103
1912	James Sheckard, Chicago	122	1944	August Galan, Brooklyn	101
1913	Robert Bescher, Cincinnati	94	1945	Edward Stanky, Brooklyn	148
1914	Miller Huggins, St. Louis	105	1946	Edward Stanky, Brooklyn	137
1915	Cliff. (Gavvy) Cravath, Phila.	86	1947	Henry Greenberg, Pittsburgh	104
1916	Henry Groh, Cincinnati	84		Harold (Pee Wee) Reese, Brook.	104*
1917	George Burns, New York	75	1948	Robert Elliott, Boston	131
1918	Max Carey, Pittsburgh	62	1949	Ralph Kiner, Pittsburgh	117
1919	George Burns, New York	82	1950	Edward Stanky, New York	144
1920	George Burns, New York	76	1951	Ralph Kiner, Pittsburgh	137
1921	George Burns, New York	80	1952	Ralph Kiner, Pittsburgh	110
1922	Max Carey, Pittsburgh	80	1953	Stanley Musial, St. Louis	105
1923	George Burns, New York	101	1954	Richie Ashburn, Philadelphia	125
1924	Rogers Hornsby, St. Louis	89	1955	Edwin Mathews, Milwaukee	109
1925	Jacques Fournier, Brooklyn	86	1956	Edwin (Duke) Snider, Brooklyn	99
1926	Lewis (Hack) Wilson, Chicago	69	1957	Richie Ashburn, Philadelphia	94
1927	Rogers Hornsby, New York	86		John Temple, Cincinnati	94
1928	Rogers Hornsby, Boston	107	1958	Richie Ashburn, Philadelphia	97
1929	Melvin Ott, New York	113	1959	James Gilliam, Los Angeles	96
1930	Lewis (Hack) Wilson, Chicago	105	1960	Richie Ashburn, Chicago	116
1931	Melvin Ott, New York	80	1961	Edwin Mathews, Milwaukee	93
1932	Melvin Ott, New York	100	1962	Edwin Mathews, Milwaukee	101
1933	Melvin Ott, New York	75	1963	Edwin Mathews, Milwaukee	124
1934	J. Floyd (Arky) Vaughan, Pitts.	94	1964	Ronald Santo, Chicago	86
1935	J. Floyd (Arky) Vaughan, Pitts.	97	1965	Joe Morgan, Houston	97
1936	J. Floyd (Arky) Vaughan, Pitts.	118	1966	Ronald Santo, Chicago	95
1937	Melvin Ott, New York	102	1967	Ronald Santo, Chicago	96
1938	Adolph Camilli, Brooklyn	119	1968	Ronald Santo, Chicago	96
1939	Adolph Camilli, Brooklyn	110	1969	James Wynn, Houston	148
1940	Elburt Fletcher, Pittsburgh	119	1970	Willie McCovey, San Francisco	137
1941	Elburt Fletcher, Pittsburgh	118			

Note—Bases on balls not included in batting records in American League prior to 1913 and in National League prior to 1910.

BATTERS LEADING IN STRIKEOUTS

AMERICAN LEAGUE

Year	Player—Club	SO.
1913	Daniel Moeller, Washington	106
1914	August Williams, St. Louis	120
1915	John Lavan, St. Louis	83
1916	Walter Pipp, New York	82
1917	Robert Roth, Cleveland	73
1918	George (Babe) Ruth, Boston	58
1919	Maurice Shannon, Phila.-Boston	70
1920	Aaron Ward, New York	84
1921	Robert Meusel, New York	88
1922	James Dykes, Philadelphia	98
1923	George (Babe) Ruth, New York	93
1924	George (Babe) Ruth, New York	81
1925	Martin McManus, St. Louis	69
1926	Anthony Lazzeri, New York	96
1927	George (Babe) Ruth, New York	89
1928	George (Babe) Ruth, New York	87
1929	James Foxx, Philadelphia	70
1930	James Foxx, Philadelphia	66
	Edward Morgan, Cleveland	66
1931	James Foxx, Philadelphia	84
1932	Bruce Campbell, Chic.-St. Louis	104
1933	James Foxx, Philadelphia	93
1934	Harlond Clift, St. Louis	100
1935	James Foxx, Philadelphia	99
1936	James Foxx, Boston	119
1937	Frank Crosetti, New York	105
1938	Frank Crosetti, New York	97
1939	Hank Greenberg, Detroit	95
1940	Samuel Chapman, Philadelphia	96
1941	James Foxx, Boston	103
1942	Joseph Gordon, New York	95

Year	Player—Club	SO.
1943	Chester Laabs, St. Louis	105
1944	J. Patrick Seerey, Cleveland	99
1945	J. Patrick Seerey, Cleveland	97
1946	Charles Keller, New York	101
	J. Patrick Seerey, Cleveland	101
1947	Edwin Joost, Philadelphia	110
1948	J. Patrick Seerey, Cleve.-Chicago	102
1949	Richard Kokos, St. Louis	91
1950	Gus Zernial, Chicago	110
1951	Gus Zernial, Chic.-Phila.	101
1952	Lawrence Doby, Cleveland	111
	Mickey Mantle, New York	111
1953	Lawrence Doby, Cleveland	121
1954	Mickey Mantle, New York	107
1955	Norbert Zauchin, Boston	105
1956	James Lemon, Washington	138
1957	James Lemon, Washington	94
1958	James Lemon, Washington	120
	Mickey Mantle, New York	120
1959	Mickey Mantle, New York	126
1960	Mickey Mantle, New York	125
1961	Jacob Wood, Detroit	141
1962	Harmon Killebrew, Minnesota	142
1963	David Nicholson, Chicago	175
1964	Nelson Mathews, Kansas City	143
1965	Zoilo Versalles, Minnesota	122
1966	George Scott, Boston	152
1967	Frank Howard, Washington	155
1968	Reginald Jackson, Oakland	171
1969	Reginald Jackson, Oakland	142
1970	Reginald Jackson, Oakland	135

NATIONAL LEAGUE

Year	Player—Club	SO.
1910	John Hummell, Brooklyn	81
1911	Robert Coulson, Brooklyn	78
	Robert Bescher, Cincinnati	78
1912	Edward McDonald, Boston	91
1913	George Burns, New York	74
1914	Frederick Merkle, New York	80
1915	H. Douglass Baird, Pittsburgh	88
1916	Cliff. (Gavvy) Cravath, Phila.	89
1917	Fred Williams, Chicago	78
1918	Ross Youngs, New York	49
	George Paskert, Chicago	49
1919	Raymond Powell, Boston	79
1920	George Kelly, New York	92
1921	Raymond Powell, Boston	85
1922	Frank Parkinson, Philadelphia	93
1923	George Grantham, Chicago	92
1924	George Grantham, Chicago	63
1925	Chas. (Gabby) Hartnett, Chicago	77
1926	Bernard Friberg, Philadelphia	77
1927	Lewis (Hack) Wilson, Chicago	70
1928	Lewis (Hack) Wilson, Chicago	94
1929	Lewis (Hack) Wilson, Chicago	83
1930	Lewis (Hack) Wilson, Chicago	84
1931	H. Nicholas Cullop, Cincinnati	86
1932	Lewis (Hack) Wilson, Brooklyn	85
1933	Walter Berger, Boston	77
1934	Adolph Camilli, Chi.-Phila.	94
1935	Adolph Camilli, Philadelphia	113
1936	Wilbur Brubaker, Pittsburgh	96
1937	Vincent DiMaggio, Boston	134
1938	Vincent DiMaggio, Boston	111
1939	Adolph Camilli, Brooklyn	107

Year	Player—Club	SO.
1940	Chester Ross, Boston	128
1941	Adolph Camilli, Brooklyn	115
1942	Vincent DiMaggio, Pittsburgh	87
1943	Vincent DiMaggio, Pittsburgh	126
1944	Vincent DiMaggio, Pittsburgh	83
1945	Vincent DiMaggio, Philadelphia	91
1946	Ralph Kiner, Pittsburgh	109
1947	William Nicholson, Chicago	83
1948	Henry Sauer, Cincinnati	85
1949	Edwin (Duke) Snider, Brooklyn	92
1950	Roy Smalley, Chicago	114
1951	Gilbert Hodges, Brooklyn	99
1952	Edwin Mathews, Boston	115
1953	Stephen Bilko, St. Louis	125
1954	Edwin (Duke) Snider, Brooklyn	96
1955	Walter Post, Cincinnati	102
1956	Walter Post, Cincinnati	124
1957	Edwin (Duke) Snider, Brooklyn	104
1958	Harry Anderson, Philadelphia	95
1959	Walter Post, Philadelphia	101
1960	J. Francisco Herrera, Phila.	136
1961	Richard Stuart, Pittsburgh	121
1962	Kenneth Hubbs, Chicago	129
1963	Donn Clendenon, Pittsburgh	136
1964	Richard Allen, Philadelphia	138
1965	Richard Allen, Philadelphia	150
1966	Byron Browne, Chicago	143
1967	James Wynn, Houston	137
1968	Donn Clendenon, Pittsburgh	163
1969	Bobby Bonds, San Francisco	187
1970	Bobby Bonds, San Francisco	189

Note—Strikeouts not included in batting records in American League prior to 1913 and in National League prior to 1910.

Homers by Parks for 1970

AMERICAN LEAGUE

	At Balt.	At Bos.	At Calif.	At Chi.	At Clev.	At Det.	At K.C.	At Milw.	At Minn.	At N.Y.	At Oak.	At Wash.	Totals 1970	1969
Baltimore	88	16	6	12	10	12	8	8	3	7	4	5	179	175
Boston	5	117	8	12	13	10	5	9	3	4	8	9	203	197
California	4	6	41	9	7	11	7	6	8	3	6	6	114	88
Chicago	2	4	6	78	2	5	1	3	5	3	9	5	123	113
Cleveland	6	7	2	3	133	4	2	10	2	3	2	9	183	119
Detroit	2	10	4	9	12	86	3	3	5	5	6	3	148	182
Kansas City	3	6	0	6	8	6	46	7	2	1	6	6	97	98
Milwaukee	5	5	2	8	9	4	4	68	7	5	4	5	126	*125
Minnesota	9	7	10	13	9	10	9	9	66	1	7	3	153	163
New York	7	3	2	4	10	8	3	2	4	60	4	4	111	94
Oakland	9	9	11	12	10	7	4	9	8	3	83	6	171	148
Washington	6	2	8	9	13	9	2	6	6	5	0	72	138	148
1970 Totals	146	192	100	175	236	172	94	140	119	100	139	133	1746	....
1969 Totals	133	183	114	141	116	176	102	*167	140	95	143	139	....	1649

1970 Totals: 938 by home clubs; 808 by visiting clubs.

*1969 totals are for Seattle.

AT BALTIMORE (146): Baltimore (88)—Powell 18, F. Robinson 12, Buford 10, B. Robinson 9. Blair 8, Rettenmund 7, Johnson 5, Hendricks 5, Etchebarren 3, Salmon 3, Crowley 2, Motton 2, Belanger, Dalrymple, May, McNally, Palmer. **Boston (5)**—Scott 2, Kennedy, Montgomery, Yastrzemski. **California (4)**—Johnstone, McMullen, Repoz, Spencer. **Chicago (2)**—Herrmann, May. **Cleveland (6)**—Fosse, Foster, Horton, Leon, Pinson, Sims. **Detroit (2)**—Cash, Stanley. **Kansas City (3)**—Kelly, Oliver, Otis. **Milwaukee (5)**—Hegan 3, Harper, Roof. **Minnesota (9)**—Killebrew 4. Mitterwald, Oliva, Quilici, Reese, Tovar. **New York (7)**—Blefary, Clarke, Ellis, Gibbs, Munson, Stottlemyre, Woods. **Oakland (9)**—Campaneris 2, Alou, Fernandez, Green, Jackson, Mincher, Monday, Rudi. **Washington (6)**—Epstein 2, Howard 2, B. Allen, Casanova.

AT BOSTON (192): Baltimore (16)—Johnson 3, B. Robinson 3, Blair 2, F. Robinson 2. Buford, Hendricks, Motton, Powell, Rettenmund, Salmon. **Boston (117)**—Yastrzemski 22, Petrocelli 20, A. Conigliaro 18, W. Conigliaro 14, Smith 14, Andrews 10, Scott 8, Moses 3, Kennedy 2, Alvarado, Brett, Lahoud, Lonborg, Romo, Thomas. **California (6)**—Egan 2, Repoz 2, Johnstone, K. Tatum. **Chicago (4)**—Melton 4. **Cleveland (7)**—Fosse 2, Nettles 2, Fuller, Harrelson, Rollins. **Detroit (10)**—Cash 2, Northrup 2, Price 2, G. Brown, Lamont, McAuliffe, Stanley. **Kansas City (6)**—Oliver 3. Hernandez, Kelly, Kirkpatrick. **Milwaukee (5)**—Harper 2, Kubiak, McNertney, Walton. **Minnesota (7)**—Alyea 3, Killebrew, Mitterwald, Oliva, Tovar. **New York (3)**—Blefary, Cater, White. **Oakland (9)**—Fernandez 3, Alou, Campaneris, Francona, Mincher, Monday, Rudi. **Washington (2)**—Rodriguez, Unser.

AT CALIFORNIA (100): Baltimore (6)—Powell 2, Blair, Etchebarren, B. Robinson, F. Robinson. **Boston (8)**—A. Conigliaro 4, Yastrzemski 2, Andrews, Moses. **California (41)**—Fregosi 10, McMullen 6, Spencer 5, Johnstone 4, Cowan 3, Johnson 3, Repoz 3, Alomar, Egan, Gonzalez, Messersmith, Reynolds, Voss, Wright. **Chicago (6)**—Melton 4, McCraw, Williams. **Cleveland (2)**—Nettles, Pinson. **Detroit (4)**—G. Brown, I. Brown, Kaline, Northrup. **Kansas City (0)**. **Milwaukee (2)**—Roof, Walton. **Minnesota (10)**—Cardenas 3, Alyea 2, Killebrew 2, Tovar 2, Oliva, Nixon. **New York (2)**—Munson, Woods. **Oakland (11)**—Jackson 3, Bando 2, Tenace 2, Campaneris, Fernandez, Lewis, Rudi. **Washington (8)**—Howard 4, Epstein 3, Reichardt.

AT CHICAGO (175): Baltimore (12)—Blair 3, Hendricks 3, Powell 3, Rettenmund, B. Robinson, F. Robinson. **Boston (12)**—Petrocelli 3, Yastrzemski, Andrews 2, Scott 2, A. Conigliaro, Smith. **California (9)**—Repoz 3, Johnson 2, Egan, Fregosi, Johnstone, McMullen. **Chicago (78)**—Melton 23, Herrmann 9, May 9, Berry 6, O'Brien 6, Aparicio 4, Knoop 4, McKinney 3, Hopkins 3, Josephson 3, Spence 3, Christian, Matias, Murphy, Williams. **Cleveland (3)**—Foster, Horton, Sims. **Detroit (9)**—Freehan 2, Kaline 2, Cash, Horton, McAuliffe, Stanley, Wert. **Kansas City (6)**—Kelly, Kirkpatrick, Oliver, Rodriguez, Schaal, Spriggs. **Milwaukee (8)**—Walton 3, Alvis, Gil, Koegel, Lauzerique, Wicker. **Minnesota (13)**—Oliva 4, Killebrew 2, Alyea 2, Mitterwald, Ratliff, Reese, Tovar. **New York (4)**—Murcer 2, Michael, White. **Oakland (9)**—Campaneris 2, Jackson 2, Rudi 2, Alou, Bando, Blue, Donaldson, Mincher, Odom. **Washington (9)**—Rodriguez 4, Howard 2, Epstein, French, Unser.

AT CLEVELAND (236): Baltimore (10)—Blair 2, Buford 2, F. Robinson 2, Crowley, Johnson, Powell, Rettenmund. **Boston (13)**—A. Conigliaro 2, Petrocelli 2, Yastrzemski 2, Brett, W. Conigliaro, Kennedy, Lahoud, Satriano, Scott, Smith. **California (7)**—Alomar, Johnson, Johnstone, McMullen, Repoz, Spencer, Voss. **Chicago (2)**—Herrmann, May. **Cleveland (133)**—Foster 19, Pinson 19. Sims 15, Horton 14, Nettles 13, Fosse 12, Uhlaender 11, Leon 9, Hinton 8, Bradford 6, Heidemann

4, Lowenstein, McDowell, Rollins. **Detroit** (12)—Northrup 4, Kaline 2, Stanley 2, Cash, McAuliffe, Price, Wilson. **Kansas City** (8)—Oliver 3, Otis 2, Piniella, Rojas, Rooker. **Milwaukee** (9)—Harper 3, Walton 2, Hegan, Pena, Smith, Snyder. **Minnesota** (9)—Killebrew 3, Oliva 2, Alyea, Cardenas, Mitterwald, Ratliff. **New York** (10)—Ellis 2, Munson 2, White 2, Clarke, Hansen, Murcer, Woods. **Oakland** (10)—Mincher 2, Aloʋ, Bando, Campaneris, Hunter, Monday, Odom, Rudi, Tenace. **Washington** (13)—Howard 4, Reichardt 3, Brinkman, Casanova, Epstein, Grieve, Rodriguez, Roseboro.

AT DETROIT (172): Baltimore (12)—Powell 3, Rettenmund 3, Hendricks 2, Blair, Crowley, Cuellar, F. Robinson. **Boston** (10)—Smith 3, Andrews 2, A. Conigliaro 2, Petrocelli, Schofield, Yastrzemski. **California** (11)—Fregosi 3, Cowan 2, Johnson 2, Repoz 2, Johnstone, McMullen. **Chicago** (5)—Herrmann 2, Aparicio, Hopkins, McCraw. **Cleveland** (4)—Ford, Foster, Pinson, Sims. **Detroit** (86)—Horton 13, Northrup 13, Freehan 10, Kaline 9, Cash 7, McAuliffe 7, Stanley 6, Jones 4, Wert 4, I. Brown 3, Szotkiewicz 3, Maddox 2, Price 2, G. Brown, Cain, Collins. **Kansas City** (6)—Kirkpatrick 2, Oliver 2, Keough, Otis. **Milwaukee** (4)—Harper, Hegan, May, Roof. **Minnesota** (10)—Killebrew 4, Oliva 4, Allison, Manuel. **New York** (8)—Murcer 2, Woods 2, Ellis, Kenney, Munson, White. **Oakland** (7)—Campaneris, Davis, Fernandez, Jackson, Mincher, Monday, Tenace. **Washington** (9)—Reichardt 3, B. Allen 2, Rodriguez 2, Epstein, Howard.

AT KANSAS CITY (94): Baltimore (8)—F. Robinson 2, Blair, Buford, Cuellar, Johnson, Powell, B. Robinson. **Boston** (5)—Smith 2, Andrews, A. Conigliaro, Petrocelli. **California** (7)—Fregosi 2, Johnson 2, Repoz 2, Azcue. **Chicago** (1)—McCraw. **Cleveland** (2)—Nettles 2. **Detroit** (3)—Horton, Kaline, Maddox. **Kansas City** (46)—Oliver 11, Kirkpatrick 10, Piniella 7, Otis 6, Campanis 2, Kelly 2, Keough 2, Sorroll 2, Alcaraz, Hernandez, Schaal, Severson. **Milwaukee** (4)—Burda, Harper, Hegan, Savage. **Minnesota** (9)—Carew 3, Cardenas 2, Killebrew 2, Ratliff, Reese. **New York** (3)—Kenney, Murcer, White. **Oakland** (3)—Jackson 2, Bando, Mincher. **Washington** (2)—Howard, Unser.

AT MILWAUKEE (140): Baltimore (8)—Rettenmund 3, Powell 2, Hendricks, F. Robinson, Salmon. **Boston** (9)—Yastrzemski 3, A. Conigliaro 2, W. Conigliaro 2, Moses, Thomas. **California** (6)—Fregosi 2, Johnson, Johnstone, Murphy, Repoz. **Chicago** (3)—Herrmann 2, May. **Cleveland** (10)—Sims 4, Nettles 3, Fosse 2, Bradford. **Detroit** (3)—Kaline, Northrup, Wert. **Kansas City** (7)—Piniella 3, Kelly, Oliver, Schaal, Sorrell. **Milwaukee** (68)—Harper 18, Roof 9, Savage 7, Walton 6, Hegan 5, May 5, Kubiak 3, Alvis 2, Kennedy 2, McNertney 2, Pena 2, Snyder 2, Bolin, Burda, Goossen, Hershberger, Lockwood. **Minnesota** (9)—Killebrew 4, Alyea 2, Carew, Mitterwald, Oliva. **New York** (2)—Gibbs, White. **Oakland** (9)—Campaneris 3, Mincher 2, Bando, Duncan, Fingers, Jackson. **Washington** (6)—Epstein 2, Howard 2, Reichardt 2.

AT MINNESOTA (119): Baltimore (3)—Buford 2, Powell. **Boston** (3)—A. Conigliaro, Petrocelli, Satriano. **California** (8)—Spencer 3, Fregosi, Johnson, McMullen, Repoz, Voss. **Chicago** (5)—Herrmann, Hopkins, Knoop, Morales, O'Brien. **Cleveland** (2)—Nettles 2. **Detroit** (5)—Freehan, Horton, McAuliffe, Northrup, Stanley. **Kansas City** (2)—Oliver, Schaal. **Milwaukee** (7)—Harper 3, Burda, Roof, Snyder, Walton. **Minnesota** (66)—Killebrew 16, Mitterwald 9, Oliva 6, Renick 6, Alyea 5, Cardenas 5, Reese 5, Tovar 5, Holt 3, Haydel, Kaat, Perry, Quilici, Ratliff, Tischinski. **New York** (4)—Cater, Ellis, Ward, White. **Oakland** (8)—Mincher 3, Bando 2, Campaneris, Jackson, Monday. **Washington** (6)—Howard 4, Rodriguez, Unser.

AT NEW YORK (100): Baltimore (7)—Powell 2, Crowley, Hendricks, Rettenmund, B. Robinson, Salmon. **Boston** (4)—W. Conigliaro, Satriano, Scott, Yastrzemski. **California** (3)—McMullen 2, Spencer. **Chicago** (3)—Berry, Herrmann, McCraw. **CLEVELAND** (3)—Klimchock, Nagelson, Nettles. **Detroit** (5)—Hosley, Jones, McAuliffe, Northrup, Stanley. **Kansas City** (1)—Otis. **Milwaukee** (5)—McNertney 2, Burda, Savage, Walton. **Minnesota** (1)—Ratliff. **New York** (60)—Murcer 16, White 12, Blefary 7, Gibbs 6, Cater 3, Lyttle 3, Clarke 2, Ellis 2, Peterson 2, Woods 2, Hansen, Kenney, Michael, Munson, Stottlemyre. **Oakland** (3)—Fernandez, Jackson, Mincher. **Washingtno** (5)—Epstein 2, B. Allen, Billings, Unser.

AT OAKLAND (139): Baltimore (4)—Rettenmund, B. Robinson, F. Robinson, Salmon. **Boston** (8)—Yastrzemski 4, A. Conigliaro 2, Petrocelli, Smith. **California** (6)—Johnson 2, Fregosi, Johnstone, McMullen, Spencer. **Chicago** (9)—Bradford 2, Hopkins, Josephson, Matias, McCraw, Melton, O'Brien, Spence. **Cleveland** (2)—Fosse, Pinson. **Detroit** (6)—Cash 2, Freehan 2, Horton, Jones. **Kansas City** (4)—Kirkoatrick 2, Oliver 2, Rojas, Sorrell. **Milwaukee** (4)—Harper, May, McNertney, Savage. **Minnesota** (7)—Oliva 3, Alyea, Mitterwald, Reese, Renick. **New York** (4)—White 2, Hansen, Kenney. **Oakland** (83)—Mincher 14, Bando 11, Campaneris 10, Duncan 9, Fernandez 8, Jackson 8, Monday 5, Rudi 5, Alou 3, Tenace 3, Brooks 2, Green 2, Driscoll, Johnson, Odom. **Washington** (0).

AT WASHINGTON (133): Baltimore (5)—F. Robinson 2, Buford, Powell, B. Robinson. **Boston** (9)—A. Conigliaro 3, Scott 2, Andrews, Moses, Peters, Yastrzemski. **California** (6)—Fregosi 2, Repoz 2, Azcue, Wright. **Chicago** (5)—Herrmann 2, McCraw, Melton, Williams. **Cleveland** (9)—Heidemann 2, Nettles 2, Foster, Hinton, Horton, Pinson, Sims. **Detroit** (3)—Cash, Freehan, Northrup. **Kansas City** (6)—Kirkpatrick 2, Oliver 2, Keough, Schaal. **Milwaukee** (5)—Savage 2, Walton 2, Harper. **Minnesota** (3)—Killebrew 2, Reese. **New York** (5)—Cater, Hansen, Murcer, Woods. **Oakland** (6)—Jackson 2, Alou, Bando, Green. **Washington** (72)—Howard 24, Rodriguez 10, Epstein 8, Maye 7, Reichardt 6, Stroud 5, B. Allen 4, Casanova 4, Grieve 2, Brunet, Cullen.

A. L. Homer King—Frank Howard, Senators—44

N. L. Homer King—Johnny Bench, Reds—45

NATIONAL LEAGUE

	At Atl.	At Chi.	At Cin.	At Hou.	At L.A.	At Mon.	At N.Y.	At Phil.	At Pitt.	At St.L.	At S.D.	At S.F.	Totals 1970	1969
Atlanta	92	7	6	7	8	5	8	4	5	4	9	5	160	141
Chicago	7	109	3	2	7	10	7	5	10	4	7	8	179	142
Cincinnati	21	11	100	11	12	8	4	4	3	3	7	7	191	171
Houston	14	8	5	51	10	6	6	2	5	5	9	9	129	104
Los Angeles	10	7	6	4	35	5	5	4	1	3	2	5	87	97
Montreal	9	7	5	6	6	77	10	6	4	1	3	2	136	125
New York	5	7	4	4	3	16	63	4	2	2	1	9	120	109
Philadelphia	6	7	4	3	6	5	3	48	3	4	6	6	101	137
Pittsburgh	9	16	4	8	3	11	10	8	43	9	5	4	130	119
St. Louis	9	6	4	2	3	10	6	9	3	51	3	7	113	90
San Diego	18	8	9	7	10	10	6	14	2	4	68	16	172	99
San Francisco	11	8	8	10	14	5	10	3	3	5	84		165	136
1970 Totals	211	201	158	115	117	168	138	111	84	95	124	161	1683	....
1969 Totals	161	148	171	90	96	160	115	139	74	84	94	138	....	1470

AT ATLANTA (211): Atlanta (92)—H. Aaron 23, Carty 19, Cepeda 14, Boyer 8, Gonzalez 5, King 5, Lum 5, Tillman 5, Hall 2, Millan 2, T. Aaron, Garrido, Nash, Niekro. **Chicago (7)**—Santo 2, Decker, Hickman, Hundley, Jenkins, Williams. **Cincinnati (21)**—Carbo 4, Bench 3, Perez 3, May 2, Rose 2, Concepcion, Corrales, McGlothlin, McRae, Merritt, Tolan, Woodward. **Houston (14)**—Watson 4, Rader 3, Cedeno 2, Edwards, Menke, Miller, Pepitone, Wynn. **Los Angeles (10)**—Parker 3, Sudakis 2, Davis, Grabarkewitz, Haller, Kosco, Lefebvre. **Montreal (9)**—Bailey 3, Laboy 3, Boccabella, Jones, Staub. **New York (5)**—Agee, Clendenon, Dyer, Garrett, Jones. **Philadelphia (6)** —Browne 2, Hisle, Johnson, Taylor, Wise. **Pittsburgh (9)**—Robertson 5, Stargell 2, Jeter, Pagan. **St. Louis (9)**—Allen 2, Brock 2, Torre 2, Davalillo, Hague, Javier. **San Diego (18)**—Gaston 6, Colbert 4, Brown 2, Campbell, Dean, Huntz, Murrell, Spiezio, Webster. **San Francisco (11)**—Dietz 3, Bonds 2, McCovey 2, Hart, Henderson, Mays, Robertson.

AT CHICAGO (201): Atlanta (7)—Cepeda 4, H. Aaron 2, King. **Chicago (109)**—Williams 28, Hickman 19, Santo 16, Callison 12, Banks 7, Hundley 6, Pepitone 4, Beckert 3, James 3, Pappas 2, Smith 2, Hiatt, Jenkins, Kessinger, Martin, Popovich, Rodriquez, Spangler. **Cincinnati (11)**—Bench 2, Carbo 2, May 2, McRae 2, Perez 2, Rose. **Houston (8)**—Edwards 2, Rader 2, Wynn 2, Cedeno, Menke. **Los Angeles (4)**—Grabarkewitz 3, Crawford 2, Kosco, Lefebvre. **Montreal (7)**—Bailey 4, Staub 2, Fairly. **New York (7)**—Shamsky 2, Agee, Clendenon, Dyer, Garrett, Marshall. **Philadelphia (7)**— Gamble, Hisle, Johnson, Joseph, McCarver, Money, Wise. **Pittsburgh (16)**—Clemente 4, Alley 3, Robertson 3, Stargell 2, Hebner, Mazeroski, Oliver, Sanguillen. **St. Louis (6)**—Torre 3, Cardenal, Lee, Simmons. **San Diego (8)**—Gaston 2, Barton, Brown, Colbert, Ferrara, Huntz, Spiezio. **San Francisco (8)**—McCovey 3, Bonds, Dietz, Gallagher, Henderson, Mays.

AT CINCINNATI (158): Atlanta (6)—H. Aaron 4, Carty, King. **Chicago (3)**—Hickman, Smith, Williams. **Cincinnati (100)**—Bench 30, May 21, Perez 19, Tolan 8, Rose 7, Carbo 6, McRae 5, Cloninger 2, Helms, Merritt. **Houston (5)**—Watson 2, Mayberry, Morgan, Pepitone. **Los Angeles (6)**— Kosco 2, Grabarkewitz, Haller, Parker, Sudakis. **Montreal (5)**—Staub 2, Bailey, Bateman, Jones. **New York (4)**—Agee, Boswell, Foy, Jones. **Philadelphia (4)**—Briggs, Doyle, Joseph, Taylor. **Pittsburgh (4)** —Mazeroski, Oliver, Robertson, Stargell. **St. Louis (2)**—Allen 3, Torre. **San Diego (7)**—Gaston 2, Campbell Colbert, Corkins, Dean, Ferrara, Roberts, Spiezio. **San Francisco (8)**—Mays 2, McCovey 2, Bonds, Dietz, Hunt, Robertson.

Note—Figures include 87 home runs at old Crosley Field as follows: **Atlanta (2)**—H. Aaron 2. **Chicago (0)**. **Cincinnati (57)**—Bench 15, May 14, Perez 12, McRae 5, Rose 5, Tolan 5, Carbo. **Houston (2)**—Mayberry, Pepitone. **Los Angeles (4)**—Kosco 2, Haller, Parker. **Montreal (4)**—Staub 2, Bateman, Jones. **New York (3)**—Agee, Boswell, Foy. **Philadelphia (2)**—Doyle, Taylor. **Pittsburgh (3)** —Oliver, Robertson, Stargell. **St. Louis (2)**—Allen, Torre. **San Diego (1)**—Dean. **San Francisco (7)**— Mays 2, McCovey 2, Dietz, Hunt, Robertson.

AT HOUSTON (115): Atlanta (8)—Cepeda 3, H. Aaron, Carty, Gonzalez, King. **Chicago (2)**— Hickman, Santo. **Cincinnati (11)**—Perez 4, Carbo 3, Tolan 2, Bench, Rose. **Houston (51)**—Wynn 13, Rader 11, Menke 7, Pepitone 6, Morgan 4, Cedeno 2, Mayberry 2, Miller 2, Alou, Davis, Edwards, Watson. **Los Angeles (4)**—Crawford, Davis, Haller, Kosco. **Montreal (6)**—Staub 3, Bailey 2, Phillips. **New York (4)**—Agee, Clendenon, Garrett, Shamsky. **Philadelphia (3)**—Browne, Hisle, Johnson. **Pittsburgh (8)**—Robertson 4, Stargell 2, Alley, Clemente. **St. Louis (2)**—Allen 2. **San Diego (7)**— Brown 2, Gaston 2, Barton, Ferrara, Morales. **San Francisco (10)**—McCovey 3, Bonds 2, Mays 2, Dietz, Fuentes, Hunt.

AT LOS ANGELES (117): Atlanta (8)—Cepeda 5, Boyer 3. **Chicago (7)**—Banks 2, Hickman 2, Callison, Hiatt, Pepitone. **Cincinnati (12)**—Bench 3, May 3, Rose 3, Perez 2, Carbo. **Houston (10)**— Menke 2, Pepitone 2, Rader 2, Watson 2, Edwards, Lemaster. **Los Angeles (35)**—Grabarkewitz 8, Sudakis 7, Davis 4, Haller 3, Kosco 3, Parker 3, Crawford 2, Mota 2, Garvey, Joshua, Lefebvre. **Montreal (6)**—Fairly 2, Bailey, Morton, Staub, Wine. **New York (3)**—Clendenon, Jones, Jorgensen.

Philadelphia (6)—Johnson 2, Hisle, Hutto, Joseph, Ryan. **Pittsburgh (3)**—Clemente, Oliver, Stargell. **St. Louis (3)**—Brock, Lee, Torre. **San Diego (10)**—Colbert 4, Campbell 2, Ferrara, Gaston, Murrell, Spiezio. **San Francisco (14)**—Mays 4, McCovey 4, Dietz 2, Hart 2, Henderson, F. Johnson.

AT MONTREAL (168): Atlanta (5)—H. Aaron, Boyer, Lum, Nash, Tillman. **Chicago (10)**—Callison 3, Williams 3, Hickman 2, Pepitone, Santo. **Cincinnati (8)**—Carbo 2, May 2, Perez 2, Bench, Tolan. **Houston (6)**—Cedeno, Davis, Mayberry, Menke, Morgan, Wynn. **Los Angeles (5)**—Haller 2, Crawford, Sudakis, Torborg. **Montreal (77)**—Bailey 13, Staub 13, Bateman 11, Fairly 10, Jones 8, Boccabella 4, Gosger 4, Phillips 4, Sutherland 3, Fairey 2, Laboy 2, Mashore, Morton, Renko. **New York (16)**—Agee 4, Marshall 3, Clendenon 2, Shamsky 2, Foy, Grote, Jones, Singleton, Swoboda. **Philadelphia (5)**—Taylor 3, Briggs, Johnson. **Pittsburgh (11)**—Alley 2, Robertson 2, Alou, Clemente, Jeter, Mazeroski, Oliver, Sanguillen, Stargell. **St. Louis (10)**—Hague 3, Allen 2, Brock 2, Lee, Carl Taylor, Torre. **San Diego (10)**—Campbell 2, Ferrara 2, Barton, Cannizzaro, Colbert, Kelly, Murrell, Roberts. **San Francisco (5)**—Hart 3, Mays, McCovey.

AT NEW YORK (138): Atlanta (8)—Cepeda 3, Tillman 2, H. Aaron, Boyer, King. **Chicago (7)**—Hickman 2, Williams 2, Callison 2, T. Davis, Pepitone. **Cincinnati (4)**—Bench 2, May, Stewart. **Houston (6)**—Wynn 3, Davis, Pepitone, Rader. **Los Angeles (5)**—Crawford, Davis, Haller, Parker, Sizemore. **Montreal (10)**—Staub 3, Bailey 2, Bateman, Fairey, Gosger, Phillips, Wine. **New York (63)**—Agee 13, Clendenon 10, Garrett 8, Jones 6, Shamsky 6, Swoboda 6, Boswell 4, Singleton 3, Foy 2, Grote, Harrelson, Jorgensen, Marshall, Seaver. **Philadelphia (3)**—Briggs, McCarver, Money. **Pittsburgh (10)**—Oliver 2, Pagan 2, Robertson 2, Stargell 2, Alley, Hebner 2. **St. Louis (6)**—Hague 2, Allen, Cardenal, Carl Taylor, Torre. **San Diego (6)**—Colbert 2, Brown, Campbell, Ferrara, Spiezio. **San Francisco (10)**—Bonds 4, Henderson 2, Mays 2, McCovey 2.

AT PHILADELPHIA (111): Atlanta (4)—Boyer, Cepeda, Lum, Tillman. **Chicago (5)**—Callison, T. Davis, Hickman, Pepitone, Santo. **Cincinnati (4)**—Perez 2, Bench, Carbo. **Houston (2)**—Rader, Wynn. **Los Angeles (4)**—Parker 2, Grabarkewitz, Sudakis. **Montreal (6)**—Bateman 2, Staub 2, Bailey, Jones. **New York (4)**—Clendenon 3, Swoboda. **Philadelphia (48)**—Johnson 16, Money 8, Browne 5, Briggs 4, Hisle 4, Taylor 4, Stone 2, Compton, Hutto, Lis, McCarver, Ryan. **Pittsburgh (8)**—Hebner 2, Mazeroski 2, Clemente, Pagan, Robertson, Stargell. **St. Louis (9)**—Allen 4, Carl Taylor 2, Cardenal, Javier, Torre. **San Diego (14)**—Colbert 5, Ferrara 3, Huntz 3, Brown 2, Gaston. **San Francisco (3)**—Henderson 2, McCovey.

AT PITTSBURGH (84): Atlanta (5)—H. Aaron, T. Aaron, Carty, Cepeda, Gonzalez. **Chicago (10)**—Williams 3, Santo 2, Smith 2, Hickman, Jenkins, Pepitone. **Cincinnati (3)**—Bench, May, Perez. **Houston (5)**—Wynn 3, Cedeno, Watson. **Los Angeles (1)**—Grabarkewitz. **Montreal (4)**—Staub 2, Jones, Wine. **New York (2)**—Clendenon 2. **Philadelphia (3)**—Briggs, Browne, McCarver. **Pittsburgh (43)**—Stargell 13, Robertson 7, Clemente 6, Hebner 5, Sanguillen 4, Oliver 2, Pagan 2, Alley, Cash, Mazeroski, Patek. **St. Louis (3)**—Allen 2, Carl Taylor. **San Diego (2)**—Gaston, Spiezio. **San Francisco (3)**—McCovey 2, Hart.

Note—Figures include 34 home runs at old Forbes Field as follows: **Atlanta (5)**—H. Aaron, T. Aaron, Carty, Cepeda, Gonzalez. **Chicago (3)**—Hickman, Smith, Williams. **Cincinnati (2)**—Bench, May. **Houston (1)**—Wynn. **Los Angeles (0)**. **Montreal (4)**—Staub 2, Jones, Wine. **New York (0)**. **Philadelphia (1)**—Browne. **Pittsburgh (14)**—Stargell 4, Clemente 3, Sanguillen 3, Alley, Hebner, Oliver, Robertson. **St. Louis (3)**—Allen 2, Carl Taylor. **San Diego (1)**—Gaston. **San Francisco (0)**.

AT ST. LOUIS (95): Atlanta (4)—H. Aaron 2, Boyer 2. **Chicago (4)**—Banks 2, Pepitone, Williams. **Cincinnati (3)**—May, Perez, Tolan. **Houston (5)**—Edwards 2, Menke, Pepitone, Wynn. **Los Angeles (3)**—Crawford, Grabarkewitz, Mota. **Montreal (1)**—Staub. **New York (2)**—Agee, Weis. **Philadelphia (4)**—Hisle, Johnson, Money, Stone. **Pittsburgh (9)**—Oliver 3, Hebner 2, Stargell 2, J. May, Mazeroski. **St. Louis (51)**—Allen 17, Brock 7, Hague 7, Torre 7, Cardenal 5, Lee 3, Simmons 2, Beauchamp, Gibson, Carl Taylor. **San Diego (4)**—Brown 2, Colbert, Gaston. **San Francisco (5)**—McCovey 2, Bonds, Henderson, Hunt.

AT SAN DIEGO (124): Atlanta (9)—H. Aaron 3, Cepeda 2, Tillman 2, Brown, Carty. **Chicago (7)**—Hickman 2, Popovich 2, Callison, Pepitone, Williams. **Cincinnati (7)**—Bench, Carbo, May, Merritt, Perez, Rose, Tolan. **Houston (9)**—Howard 2, Pepitone 2, Rader 2, Morgan, Watson, Wynn. **Los Angeles (2)**—Sudakis 2. **Montreal (3)**—Fairly 2, Bailey. **New York (1)**—Agee. **Philadelphia (6)**—Johnson 2, Money 2, Browne, Doyle. **Pittsburgh (5)**—Stargell 3, Oliver, Robertson. **St. Louis (3)**—Torre 2, Cardenal. **San Diego (68)**—Colbert 16, Gaston 12, Brown 11, Murrell 8, Campbell 5, Spiezio 5, Cannizzaro 3, Ferrara 3, Huntz 2, Webster, Wilson. **San Francisco (4)**—Bonds, Dietz, Fuentes, McCovey.

AT SAN FRANCISCO (161): Atlanta (5)—Carty 2, King 2, Cepeda. **Chicago (8)**—Santo 3, Williams 2, Banks, Pepitone, Popovich. **Cincinnati (7)**—Perez 3, Tolan 2, Carbo, Chaney. **Houston (8)**—Rader 3, Beauchamp, Mayberry, Miller, Morgan, Wynn. **Los Angeles (5)**—Davis, Grabarkewitz, Haller, Lefebvre, Osteen. **Montreal (2)**—Jones 2. **New York (9)**—Foy 2, Agee, Clendenon, Garrett, Jorgensen, Marshall, Singleton, Swoboda. **Philadelphia (6)**—Johnson 2, Briggs, Hisle, Hutto, Money. **Pittsburgh (4)**—Pagan, Robertson, Sanguillen, Stargell. **St. Louis (7)**—Torre 2, Allen, Brock, Cardenal, Gibson, Hague. **San Diego (16)**—Colbert 3, Huntz 3, Brown 2, Robinson 2, Barton, Cannizzaro, Gaston, Murrell, Slocum, Spiezio. **San Francisco (84)**—McCovey 16, Mays 15, Bonds 14, Dietz 13, Henderson 9, Gallagher 3, Hunt 3, F. Johnson 2, Lanier 2, Taylor 2, Foster, Hart, Heise, Perry, Pitlock.

NO-HITTERS

Including

Review of Four '70 No-Hitters

Official Box Scores of Each

Key Picture of Each

BATTING, PITCHING FEATURES

THE SPORTING NEWS AWARDS

Including

BBWAA Awards

HALL OF FAME ELECTION

Including

Feature on Electees

All Hall of Famers Listed According to
    Years Selected

MAJOR LEAGUE DRAFT

Four No-Hitters Spice '70 Season

By BEN HENKEY

A refugee from the disabled list, a rookie, a righthander having trouble with his control and a hurler coming off a 1-8 record the previous season achieved the ultimate in pitching glory in 1970 by authoring major league no-hit games.

For each of the pitchers—Pittsburgh's Dock Ellis, California's Clyde Wright, Los Angeles' Bill Singer and Oakland's Vida Blue—the no-hit efforts were their first in the big leagues.

The season was a little more than two months old when Ellis, facing the San Diego Padres for the second time in two weeks, got the season's string of mound masterpieces started with a 2-0 victory in enemy territory over San Diego June 12.

Eleven days earlier in Pittsburgh, the 25-year-old righthander had whipped San Diego, 5-1, on a six-hitter. Both Ellis and the Padres agreed that he'd thrown harder in that victory than he did while fashioning the no-hitter, and he'd certainly had better control.

The Padres had nine baserunners, eight on walks and a ninth as the result of a hit batsman, as Ellis struggled to find the plate while holding San Diego hitless.

The only out-of-the-ordinary assistance he needed was a diving backhanded grab of pinch-hitter Ramon Webster's line drive by second baseman Bill Mazeroski in the seventh inning.

The catch helped Ellis retire the side in order, something he did only three times during the game. The Padres got good wood on the ball on only two other occasions, but both were line drives directly at center fielder Matty Alou.

Ellis, who'd taken a 4-4 record into the contest, which was the first game of a doubleheader, struck out six and had Willie Stargell to thank for his victory margin. Stargell hit bases-empty home runs in the second and seventh innings.

AT SAN DIEGO—JUNE 12

Pittsburgh	AB.	R.	H.	RBI.	E.	San Diego	AB.	R.	H.	RBI.	E.
Alou, cf	4	0	0	0	0	Campbell, 2b	3	0	0	0	0
Alley, ss	4	0	1	0	0	Huntz, 3b	1	0	0	0	0
Clemente, rf	4	0	0	0	0	Ferrara, lf	4	0	0	0	0
Robertson, 3b	3	0	0	0	0	Colbert, 1b	2	0	0	0	0
Pagan, 3b	1	0	0	0	0	Brown, rf	3	0	0	0	0
Stargell, lf	3	2	2	2	0	Murrell, cf	3	0	0	0	0
May, c	3	0	0	0	0	Cannizzaro, c	3	0	0	0	0
Oliver, 1b	3	0	2	0	0	Dean, ss	3	0	0	0	0
Mazeroski, 2b	3	0	0	0	0	Kelly, ph	1	0	0	0	0
ELLIS, p	3	0	0	0	0	Roberts, p	2	0	0	0	0
						Webster, ph	1	0	0	0	0
						Herbel, p	0	0	0	0	0
						Spiezio, ph	1	0	0	0	0
Totals	31	2	5	2	0	Totals	27	0	0	0	0

Pittsburgh	0	1	0	0	0	0	1	0	0—2
San Diego	0	0	0	0	0	0	0	0	0—0

Pittsburgh	IP.	H.	R.	ER.	BB.	SO.
ELLIS (W. 5-4)	9	0	0	0	8	6

San Diego	IP.	H.	R.	ER.	BB.	SO.
Roberts (L. 4-3)	7	5	2	2	0	7
Herbel	2	0	0	0	0	0

Left on bases—Pittsburgh 2, San Diego 9. Home runs—Stargell 2 (12). Stolen bases—Murrell, Campbell, Colbert. Hit by pitcher—By ELLIS (Murrell). Umpires—Venzon, Secory, Engel and Wendelstedt. Time of game—2:13. Attendance—9,903.

When two do the sweating, two should take the cheering, and this is what the joyous pair—catcher Jerry May and pitcher Dock Ellis—are doing after the Buc hurler no-hitted the Padres June 12.

Wright tossed the American League's first no-no of 1970 against Oakland at Anaheim July 3, after being inducted into the NAIA hall of fame in pre-game ceremonies.

The 27-year-old lefthander, who'd won just one of nine decisions with the Angels in 1969, proceeded to toss a routine no-hitter, if there is such a thing. He faced only 29 batters, retiring 15 on ground balls, five on fly balls, four on infield flies, two on line drives and one, Reggie Jackson, on a strikeout. He walked three and threw just 98 pitches in a game which was crisply played in 1:51.

Jackson came close to breaking up the no-hitter in the seventh inning when he backed center fielder Jay Johnstone to within two feet of the wall in a home-run bid.

The game's only homer accounted for most of the scoring in Wright's 4-0 triumph. Angel third baseman Ken McMullen connected with two teammates on base in the fourth inning.

AT CALIFORNIA—JULY 3

Oakland	AB.	R.	H.	RBI.	E.
Campaneris, ss	4	0	0	0	0
Alou, rf	4	0	0	0	0
Jackson, cf	3	0	0	0	0
Bando, 3b	2	0	0	0	0
Davis, lf	3	0	0	0	0
Rudi, 1b	3	0	0	0	0
Duncan, c	2	0	0	0	0
Green, 2b	3	0	0	0	0
Dobson, p	1	0	0	0	0
LaRussa, ph	1	0	0	0	0
Roland, p	0	0	0	0	0
Fernandez, ph	0	0	0	0	0
Tartabull, pr	0	0	0	0	0
Totals	26	0	0	0	

California	AB.	R.	H.	RBI.	E.
Alomar, 2b	4	0	0	0	0
Repoz, rf	3	1	1	0	0
Fregosi, ss	4	0	1	0	0
Johnson, lf	3	1	1	0	0
Tatum, lf	0	0	0	0	0
Spencer, 1b	3	1	1	0	0
McMullen, 3b	3	1	1	3	0
Azcue, c	3	0	1	0	0
Johnstone, cf	3	0	0	0	0
WRIGHT, p	3	0	0	0	0
Totals	29	4	5	4	0

Oakland	0	0	0	0	0	0	0	0	0—0
California	1	0	0	3	0	0	0	0	x—4

Oakland	IP.	H.	R.	ER.	BB.	SO.
Dobson (L. 7-9)	5	4	4	4	2	2
Roland	3	1	0	0	0	2

California	IP.	H.	R.	ER.	BB.	SO.
WRIGHT (W. 12-5)	9	0	0	0	3	1

Double play—California 1. Left on bases—Oakland 2, California 3. Two-base hit—Spencer. Three-base hit—Repoz. Home run—McMullen (9). Umpires—Napp, Rice, Springstead and Barnett. Time of game—1:51. Attendance—12,131.

Bare-chested Clyde Wright is surrounded by gleeful mates after his masterpiece over the Athletics July 3. Clockwise are Joe Azcue, Jim Fregosi at the top and Ken McMullen.

The victory was Wright's 12th against five losses, marking the half-way point in a season where he eventually was to accumulate 22 victories and be named the American League's Comeback Player of the Year by THE SPORTING NEWS.

Less than three weeks later, on July 20, in Los Angeles, Dodger fans got their first look at a no-hit pitcher since the days of Sandy Koufax when Singer silenced the Phillies, 5-0.

A 26-year-old righthander who'd won 20 for L. A. the previous year, Singer had been sidelined by a bout with hepatitis, but had come back strong, winning six, including a pair of two-hitters, since being taken off the disabled list.

He reached the pinnacle by striking out 10 and getting three key defensive plays on the infield. Third baseman Steve Garvey took a hit away from Oscar Gamble in the fourth inning, Singer himself made an outstanding play on a ball hit by Larry Hisle in the next frame, and Maury Wills, who had been inserted at third in the eighth, robbed Hisle a second time in that inning.

It was the first no-hit effort by a Dodger pitcher since Koufax' perfect game five years earlier. Jeff Torborg, who performed the catching chores in the last of Sandy's four masterpieces, was behind the plate for Singer's effort, as well.

AT LOS ANGELES—JULY 20

Philadelphia	AB.	R.	H.	RBI.	E.	Los Angeles	AB.	R.	H.	RBI.	E.
Doyle, 2b	4	0	0	0	0	Grabarkewitz, ss	4	1	1	0	0
Gamble, rf	1	0	0	0	0	Sizemore, lf	4	1	1	0	0
Browne, rf	2	0	0	0	0	Wills, 3b	0	0	0	0	0
Money, 3b	3	0	0	0	1	Davis, cf	3	1	1	1	0
Johnson, 1b	3	0	0	0	0	Parker, 1b	4	1	2	1	0
Briggs, lf	3	0	0	0	0	Lefebvre, 2b	4	0	3	1	0
Hisle, cf	3	0	0	0	0	Garvey, 3b	4	1	0	0	0
Bowa, ss	3	0	0	0	1	Joshua, lf	0	0	0	0	0
Ryan, c	3	0	0	0	0	Russell, rf	4	0	2	2	0
Fryman, p	1	0	0	0	0	Torborg, c	4	0	1	0	0
Palmer, p	1	0	0	0	0	SINGER, p	4	0	0	0	2
Harmon, ph	1	0	0	0	0						
Totals	28	0	0	0	2	Totals	35	5	11	5	2

Philadelphia	0	0	1	0 0 0	0 0	0—0
Los Angeles	2	0	1	0 2 0	0 0	x—5

Philadelphia	IP.	H.	R.	ER.	BB.	SO.	Los Angeles	IP.	H.	R.	ER.	BB.	SO.
Fryman (L. 6-6)	4⅔	10	5	5	0	3	SINGER (W. 7-3)	9	0	0	0	0	10
Palmer	3⅓	1	0	0	0	5							

Left on bases—Philadelphia 2, Los Angeles 7. Two-base hits—Parker, Russell. Stolen bases—Davis, Parker. Sacrifice fly—Davis. Hit by pitcher—By SINGER (Gamble). Umpires—Sudol, Steiner, Williams and Colosi. Time of game—2:10. Attendance—12,454.

Oakland's Blue prefaced his no-hitter—tossed at the Minnesota Twins September 21—with a one-hit victory.

The 21-year-old rookie lefthander, just recalled fom Iowa (American Association) where he had compiled a 12-3 record and led the league in strikeouts with 165 in only 133 innings despite numerous military service interruptions, hurled a one-hitter in his second start against Kansas City September 11.

Ten days later, he drew the starting assignment against the Twins, who needed one victory to wrap up a divisional title in the American League West. Relying on a live fast ball for about 90 percent of the 114 pitches he threw, Blue delayed the Minnesota celebration, temporarily, 6-0.

Bill Singer, who just had finished his no-hitter against the Phillies July 20, gives a big wave to the cheering fans after he had donned his blue Dodger warmup jacket.

He missed throwing a perfect game by walking Harmon Killebrew with two out in the fourth, and got key support in the field while the game itself still hung in the balance.

Shortstop Bert Campaneris backhanded George Mitterwald's line drive in the fifth, and third baseman Sal Bando managed to knock down another hard smash off Mitterwald's bat in the eighth and throw out the Twins' catcher.

Blue held a 1-0 lead at that point, but the Athletics, playing before only 4,284 fans, left the rookie free to concentrate on the no-hitter by scoring five times in the bottom of the eighth. Campaneris struck the key blow, a three-run homer.

Singer and Blue had been down the no-hit trail earlier in their careers, but never in the majors. Singer threw a seven-inning no-hitter while with the Dodgers' Pacific Coast League club in Spokane, and Blue tossed a seven-inning no-no at Burlington (Midwest) in 1968.

AT OAKLAND—SEPTEMBER 21

Minnesota	AB.	R.	H.	RBI.	E.
Tovar, cf-lf	4	0	0	0	0
Cardenas, ss	3	0	0	0	0
Killebrew, 1b	2	0	0	0	0
Oliva, rf	3	0	0	0	0
Alyea, lf	3	0	0	0	0
Holt, cf	0	0	0	0	0
Renick, 3b	3	0	0	0	0
Mitterwald, c	3	0	0	0	0
Thompson, 2b	3	0	0	0	1
Perry, p	2	0	0	0	0
Allison, ph	1	0	0	0	0
Totals	27	0	0	0	1

Oakland	AB.	R.	H.	RBI.	E.
Campaneris, ss	5	2	2	3	0
Rudi, lf	2	0	1	0	0
Hovley, cf	2	0	1	0	0
Alou, rf-lf	4	0	1	0	0
Mincher, 1b	3	1	2	0	0
Bando, 3b	3	1	1	0	0
Jackson, cf-rf	3	0	0	0	0
Tenace, c	2	1	1	0	0
Green, 2b	4	1	1	1	0
BLUE, p	2	0	0	0	0
Totals	30	6	9	4	0

```
Minnesota ........  0  0  0    0  0  0    0  0  0—0
Oakland   ........  1  0  0    0  0  0    0  5  x—6
```

Minnesota	IP.	H.	R.	ER.	BB.	SO.
Perry (L. 23-12)	8	9	6	2	5	3

Oakland	IP.	H.	R.	ER.	BB.	SO.
BLUE (W. 2-0)	9	0	0	0	1	9

Double play—Minnesota 1. Left on bases—Minnesota 1. Oakland 8. Two-base hit—Alou. Three-base hit—Campaneris. Home run—Campaneris (21). Sacrifice hit—BLUE. Hit by pitcher—By Perry (Mincher, Bando). Umpires—Napp, Rice, Springstead and Barnett. Time of game—2:21. Attendance—4,284.

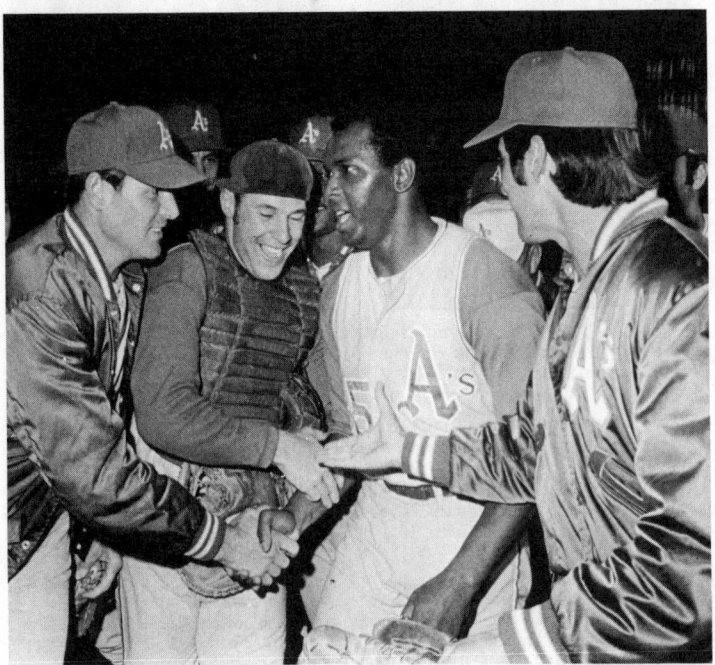

Vida Blue gets the five-by-five routine from his mates after his no-hitter against the Twins September 21. From left is pitcher Paul Lindblad, catcher Gene Tenace and pitcher Dooley Womack.

69 Low-Hit Games in '70

By CHRIS ROEWE

Low-hit pitching efforts experienced a decline in the majors in 1970 with a total of 69 games in which one team was held to fewer than three hits as compared with 77 the previous year. Each league had two no-hit games. There were 15 one-hitters, eight by National League moundsmen. The N. L. also had the edge in two-hit games with 26, two more than were fashioned by American League hurlers.

Nolan Ryan, hard-throwing righthander of the Mets, whose record was a disappointing 7-11 for the season, topped all pitchers in number of low-hit jobs. On April 18, before a hometown crowd, Ryan yielded a single to leadoff man Denny Doyle and then set down the Phillies without another hit, winning, 7-0, and striking out 15. A week later he permitted only two safeties but lost to the Dodgers at Los Angeles, 1-0, when Maury Wills singled home the only run of the game in the third. Ryan pitched his second two-hitter on May 24, beating the Cubs in the second game of a doubleheader at Shea Stadium, 3-1. On June 24 he went seven innings for the win as the Cubs again were the victims in the second game of a bargain bill, this time at Wrigley Field. Tug McGraw saved the 6-1 victory. Ryan was to win only two more games in the remaining three months of the campaign.

Bill Singer of the Dodgers and Bob Gibson of the Cardinals each had three low-hit wins. Singer pitched a no-hit game against the Phillies on July 20 and was the winner in two games in which the opposition got only two safeties. Gibson had to be content with a one-hitter on June 17 when Ivan Murrell of the Padres singled with two out in the eighth and Bob later added two-hit victories over the Padres and Cubs.

No American League hurler notched more than two wins in which he permitted less than three hits. Sam McDowell of the Indians hurled two-hitters in successive starts, beating the Athletics on May 29 and the Brewers on June 2.

Vida Blue, rookie lefthander of the Athletics, hurled a one-hit shutout over the Royals in his sixth starting assignment in the majors on September 11 and 10 days later joined the elite corps of no-hit pitchers when he blanked the hard-hitting Twins, 6-0, at Oakland.

Ken Holtzman's one-hit victory over the Giants on August 22 was unusual in that the score was 15-0 and the Cubs were nine runs ahead after two innings. Despite his tremendous lead, the Chicago lefthander pitched hitless ball until Hal Lanier singled with one out in the eighth.

The following is the complete list of one-hit and two-hit games in the majors in 1970:

AMERICAN LEAGUE
One-Hit Games

May 24—Dobson, Oakland vs. Chicago, 5-1 (first game)—Hopkins, single in first.
July 2—Niekro, Detroit vs. New York, 5-0—Clarke, single in ninth.
July 31—Siebert, Boston vs. California, 2-0—Johnstone, single in third.
Aug. 13—Bosman, Washington vs. Minnesota, 1-0—Tovar, single in first.
Aug. 17—Hannan, Washington vs. Kansas City, 7-0—Schaal, triple in fifth.
Aug. 28—Hand, Cleveland vs. California, 5-1 (second game)—Repoz, homer in first.
Sept. 11—Blue, Oakland vs. Kansas City, 3-0—Kelly, single in eighth.

Two-Hit Games

April 9—Phoebus, Baltimore vs. Cleveland, 13-1—Pinson, single in fourth and homer in ninth.
May 19—May, California vs. Chicago, 3-0—Berry, single in second; Williams, single in ninth.
May 24—Cuellar (nine innings) and Watt (one inning), Baltimore vs. Boston, 2-1 (first game)—Scott, homer in second; Petrocelli, single in fourth.

May 29—McDowell, Cleveland vs. Oakland, 2-1—Rudi, homer in fourth; Alou, single in seventh.
June 2—McDowell, Cleveland vs. Milwaukee, 4-1 (first game)—Walton, double in eighth; Pena, single in eighth.
June 11—Cuellar, Baltimore vs. California, 9-1—J. Tatum, double in first; Alomar, single in third.
June 12—John, Chicago vs. Washington, 6-0—Comer, single in fifth; Brinkman, single in ninth.
June 24—Queen (six innings) and Fisher (three innings), California vs. Chicago, 2-1 (second game)— O'Brien, single in fourth; Josephson, double in fourth.
June 27—Blyleven, Minnesota vs. Chicago, 9-1—McCraw, single in first; Spence, homer in eighth.
July 4—Siebert, Boston vs. Cleveland, 5-1—Fosse, homer in seventh; Klimchock, single in eighth.
July 17—Dunning (eight innings) and Hennigan (one inning), Cleveland vs. Kansas City, 6-0— Campanis, single in sixth; Piniella, single in seventh.
July 18—Hargan, Cleveland vs. Kansas City, 4-1—Kelly, single in first; Sorrell, homer in fifth.
July 20—Downing (seven innings) and Sanders (one inning), Milwaukee vs. Washington, lost, 2-0— Cullen, single in first; Howard, homer in ninth.
July 22—Perry (Seven and two-thirds innings) and Perranoski (one and one-third innings), Minnesota vs. Detroit, 2-1—Wert, single in sixth and double in eighth.
July 25—Shellenback, Washington vs. California, 5-0—J. Tatum, single in second; Johnson, single in fourth.
July 28—Downing, Milwaukee vs. Washington, 5-1—Grieve, single in third; Cullen, single in fifth.
Aug. 23—Lolich (eight innings) and Timmerman (one inning), Detroit vs. Milwaukee, 1-0—Kubiak, single in fourth; Smith, double in seventh.
Aug. 23—Johnson, Kansas City vs. Boston, 4-3—A. Conigliaro, homer in fourth; Smith, double in ninth.
Sept. 6—Odom, Oakland vs. Kansas City, 7-1—Sorrell, homer in second; Piniella, double in ninth.
Sept. 13—Hargan, Cleveland vs. New York, 3-1—White, single in fourth; Cater, single in eighth.
Sept. 15—Lockwood, Milwaukee vs. Oakland, 1-0 (first game)—Campaneris, single in first; Duncan, single in second.
Sept. 23—Hall (seven and two-thirds innings) and Zepp (one and one-third innings) Minnesota vs. Oakland, 7-4—Campaneris, homer in seventh; Duncan, homer in eighth.
Sept. 25—Perry, Minnesota vs. Kansas City, 1-0—Rojas, singles in sixth and eighth.
Oct.   1—Hiller, Detroit vs. Cleveland, 1-0—Sims, single in first; Fuller, single in sixth.

NATIONAL LEAGUE

One-Hit Games

April 15—Torrez, St. Louis vs. Montreal, 10-0—Phillips, single in eighth.
April 18—Ryan, New York vs. Philadelphia, 7-0—Doyle, single in first.
April 19—Simpson, Cincinnati vs. San Francisco, 6-0—Henderson, double in first.
May 13—Gentry, New York vs. Chicago, 4-0—Banks, single in eighth.
May 15—Seaver, New York vs. Philadelphia, 4-0—Compton, single in third.
June 17—Gibson, St. Louis vs. San Diego, 8-0—Murrell, single in eighth.
Aug. 22—Holtzman, Chicago vs. San Francisco, 15-0—Lanier, single in eighth.

Two-Hit Games

April 7—Nolan, Cincinnati vs. Los Angeles, 4-0—Crawford, singles in fourth and ninth.
April 9—Simpson, Cincinnati vs. Los Angeles, 3-0—Sizemore, single in sixth; Crawford, single in seventh.
April 13—Sutton, Los Angeles vs. Houston, 2-0—Menke, double in second; Miller, single in sixth.
April 22—Seaver, New York vs. San Diego, 2-1—Ferrara, homer in second; Campbell, single in fourth.
April 25—Ryan, New York vs. Los Angeles, lost, 1-0—Sizemore, single in first; Wills, single in ninth.
April 26—Niekro, Atlanta vs. Pittsburgh, 2-0—Sanguillen, single in seventh; Alou, single in eighth.
May 1—Robertson, San Francisco vs. Philadelphia, 3-1—Doyle, double in fifth; Johnson, single in eighth.
May 5—Coombs, San Diego vs. Montreal, 6-0—Hahn, single in third; Bailey, single in fourth.
May 21—McGlothlin, Cincinnati vs. Houston, 3-0—Morgan, single in first; Alou, single in fourth.
May 24—Ryan, New York vs. Chicago, 3-1 (second game)—Kessinger, single in first; Williams, single in third.
June 9—Bunning (five and one-third innings) and Selma (three and two-thirds innings), Philadelphia vs. Atlanta, 2-1—Boyer, homer in sixth; Garrido, single in ninth.
June 23—Singer (seven and two-thirds innings) and Mikkelsen (one and one-third innings), Los Angeles vs. Atlanta, 7-0—Boyer, single in eighth; Garrido, single in ninth.
June 24—Ryan (seven innings) and McGraw (two innings), New York vs. Chicago, 6-1 (second game)— Kessinger, single in first; Banks, single in eighth.
July 5—Singer, Los Angeles vs. San Francisco, 4-0—Heise, single in first; McCovey, single in fourth.
July 16—Holtzman (seven innings) and Regan (one inning), Chicago vs. Houston, lost, 2-1—Wynn, single in third; Cedeno, double in seventh.
July 25—Niekro, Atlanta vs. Chicago, 9-0—Williams, singles in fourth and seventh.
Aug. 5—Walker, Pittsburgh vs. Philadelphia, 4-0—Hutto and Ryan, singles in sixth.
Aug. 9—Reuss, St. Louis vs. Montreal, 4-0 (second game)—Staub, single in fourth; Bateman, single in seventh.
Aug. 22—Walker, St. Louis vs. San Diego, 7-0—Spiezio, singles in sixth and eighth.
Aug. 28—Reuss, St. Louis vs. Los Angeles, 1-0—Sudakis, singles in fourth and seventh.
Sept. 10—Walker, Pittsburgh vs. St. Louis, 2-0—Maxvill, single in third; Beauchamp, single in fifth.
Sept. 11—Morton, Montreal vs. Philadelphia, 1-0—Short, single in third; Luzinski, single in seventh.
Sept. 11—Dobson, San Diego vs. Cincinnati, 3-2—Perez, triple in second; Rose, double in ninth.
Sept. 20—Koosman, New York vs. Pittsburgh, 4-1 (first game)—Pagan, homer in sixth; Stargell, single in eighth.
Sept. 23—Gibson, St. Louis vs. Chicago, 2-1 (first game)—Beckert, triple in fourth; Pepitone, single in seventh.
Oct.   1—Jenkins, Chicago vs. New York, 4-1—Singleton, doubles in seventh and ninth.

Gibson Cracks 200-Mark Eighth Time

By LARRY WIGGE

Bob Gibson definitely put himself in some elite company in 1970. He achieved a personal high of 274 strikeouts, which aided his climb to tenth place on the all-time strikeout list with 2,393. His season's total also established a standard-bearing mark of eight years with 200 or more whiffs. Only a broken ankle in 1967 prevented Gibson from putting together a longer string and eclipsing the seven-season records of Walter Johnson and Rube Waddell that had withstood the assaults of baseball's greatest hurlers for more than fifty years.

Gibson's pitching feats in 1970 were not the only strikeout heroics of the year.

When the smoke cleared in Cleveland, Sam McDowell again had topped the majors in total strikeouts as he added 304 A. L. batters to his collection. The Mets' Tom Seaver tied a single-game record by fanning 19 San Diego Padres on April 22 and his 283 seasonal whiffs gave him the N. L. leadership. Unlike McDowell, who won his crown over Mickey Lolich by 74 lengths, the 1969 N. L. Cy Young winner had only nine more strikeouts than did Gibson and Chicago's Ferguson Jenkins.

Gibson, McDowell and Seaver formed a tough threesome in other respects as well. In 1970, there were eight games in which pitchers found the hitters so much to their liking that 15 strikeouts were on the menu. Each of our sterling trio was able to dig in for a second helping. Nolan Ryan of the Mets and Steve Carlton of the Cardinals also partook in these festivities.

Following is a complete record of these contests:

Date	Pitcher-Club—Opposition	Place	IP.	H.	R.	ER.	BB.	SO.	Result
Apr. 18	—Ryan, Mets vs. Phillies	H	9	1	0	0	6	15	W 7-0
Apr. 22	—Seaver, Mets vs. Padres	H	9	2	1	1	2	19	W 2-1
Apr. 26	—Gibson, Cardinals vs. Reds	H	9	5	1	1	2	15	W 4-1
May 6	—McDowell, Indians vs. White Sox	A	8⅓	5	2	1	2	15	L 2-1
May 15	—Seaver, Mets vs. Phillies	A	9	1	0	0	3	15	W 4-0
May 21	—*Carlton, Cardinals vs. Phillies	A	8	9	3	3	2	16	L 4-3
May 23	—Gibson, Cardinals vs. Phillies	A	9	4	1	1	1	16	W 3-1
July 6	—McDowell, Indians vs. Senators	H	8⅔	11	4	4	5	15	W 6-4

*Was not charged with the loss.

Stylish Seaver tossed the most ten-strikeout games in the big leagues in 1970. His 12 trips into double-figures were challenged only by lefty McDowell, who paced the A. L. with ten similar performances.

In the following are listed the hurlers who had games of ten or more strikeouts in 1970 and the number of times each accomplished the feat:

AMERICAN LEAGUE: Baltimore (5)—Cuellar 2, McNally 2, Palmer. Boston (3)—Brett, Culp, Siebert. California (3)—Messersmith 2, May. Chicago (1)—Johnson. Cleveland (11)—McDowell 10, Dunning. Detroit (8)—Lolich 4, Cain 2, Hiller, Kilkenny. Kansas City (5)—Johnson 5. Milwaukee (4)—Pattin 2, Bolin, Lockwood. Minnesota (4)—Blyleven 2, Hall 2. New York (1)—Bahnsen. Oakland (3)—Dobson, Hunter, Odom. Washington (1)—Brunet.

NATIONAL LEAGUE: Atlanta (5)—Jarvis, McQueen, Nash, Niekro, Stone. Chicago (13)—Jenkins 9, Holtzman 3, Hands. Cincinnati (2)—Merritt, Simpson. Houston (5)—Billingham 3, Dierker 2. Los Angeles (3)—Singer 2, Sutton. Montreal (3)—Morton, Renko, Stoneman. New York (19)—Seaver 12, Ryan 5, Koosman, Sadecki. Philadelphia (2)—Palmer, Short. Pittsburgh (7)—Veale 3, Ellis 2, Blass, Moose. St. Louis (11)—Gibson 7, Carlton 3, Torrez. San Diego (4)—Kirby 2, Dobson, Roberts. San Francisco (8)—Perry 5, Robertson 3.

Perranoski, Granger No. 1 Firemen Again

For the first time since 1960, when THE SPORTING NEWS began awarding trophies to the Fireman of the Year, the previous year's winners repeated, not just in one league, but in both circuits.

Wayne Granger of the Reds and Ron Perranoski of the Twins notched their second successive titles in 1970.

With one point awarded for a relief victory, and one for a game saved, both leaders totaled a record 41 points. Granger recorded 35 saves, also a record number, and six victories, while Perranoski had 34 saves and seven wins. The previous top point total was 40, amassed by Dick Radatz of the Red Sox in winning the American League award in 1964 and tied by Perranoski in 1969.

The National League derby this year never was a contest with Granger, the slim rescue artist of the pennant-winning Reds, in front all of the way. Dave Giusti of the Pirates came on strong in the stretch to finish second with 35 points.

In the A. L., Lindy McDaniel of the Yankees was in contention from the start and finished a close second to Perranoski with 38 points.

Stan Williams of the Twins and Dick Hall of the Orioles were tops in victories in relief, racking up 10 apiece.

No National League reliever won ten games. Dave Giusti, Pittsburgh; Don McMahon, San Francisco; Clay Carroll, Cincinnati; Ron Herbel, San Diego-New York, and Joe Hoerner, Philadelphia, were tied for the lead with nine wins.

The importance of the relief pitcher was clearly demonstrated in 1970's Fireman Derby. League winners Granger and Perranoski and the N. L. runner-up, Giusti, all worked for clubs that won their divisional titles, while McDaniel, the runner-up in the A. L., was the bullpen ace for the Yankees, who finished second in the A. L. East Division.

A complete list of saves and victories by major league relief pitchers follows:

NATIONAL LEAGUE

Pitcher—Club	Saves	Relief Wins	Tot. Pts.	Pitcher—Club	Saves	Relief Wins	Tot. Pts.
Granger, Cincinnati	35	6	41	Herbel, S. Diego-N. York	10	9	19
Giusti, Pittsburgh	26	9	35	Wilhelm, Atlanta-Chicago	13	6	19
Brewer, Los Angeles	24	7	31	Hoerner, Philadelphia	9	9	18
Selma, Philadelphia	22	8	30	Taylor, New York	13	5	18
Raymond, Montreal	23	6	29	Regan, Chicago	12	5	17
McMahon, San Francisco	19	9	28	McGraw, New York	10	4	14
Carroll, Cincinnati	16	9	25	Priddy, Atlanta	8	5	13
Gladding, Houston	18	7	25	Dukes, San Diego	10	1	11

Wayne Granger—NL

Ron Perranoski—AL

Pitcher—Club	Saves	Relief Wins	Tot. Pts.
Ray, Houston	5	6	11
Reed, Montreal	5	6	11
Chuck Taylor, St. Louis	8	3	11
Gullett, Cincinnati	6	4	10
Mikkelsen, Los Angeles	6	4	10
Jerry Johnson, St. L.-S. F.	4	5	9
Frisella, New York	1	7	8
Linzy, S. F.-St. Louis	3	5	8
Pena, Los Angeles	4	4	8
Rodriquez, S. Diego-Chi.	5	3	8
Dal Canton, Pittsburgh	1	6	7
Campisi, St. Louis	4	2	6
Colborn, Chicago	4	2	6
Culver, St. Louis-Houston	3	3	6
Lamb, Los Angeles	0	6	6
Marshall, Hous.-Mont.	3	3	6
Walker, Pittsburgh	3	3	6
Willis, San Diego	4	2	6
Cook, Houston	2	3	5
Gibbon, Pittsburgh	5	0	5
Lersch, Philadelphia	3	2	5
Moeller, Los Angeles	4	1	5
Roberts, San Diego	1	4	5
Aguirre, Chicago	1	3	4
Davison, San Francisco	1	3	4
DiLauro, Houston	3	1	4
Lemaster, Houston	3	1	4
Pena, Pittsburgh	2	2	4
Washburn, Cincinnati	0	4	4
Abernathy, Chi-St. Louis	2	1	3
Bryant, San Francisco	0	3	3

Pitcher—Club	Saves	Relief Wins	Tot. Pts.
Hilgendorf, St. Louis	3	0	3
Lamb, Pittsburgh	3	0	3
Norman, Los A.-St. Louis	1	2	3
Reberger, San Francisco	2	1	3
Ross, San Diego	1	2	3
Strohmayer, Montreal	0	3	3
Wenz, Philadelphia	1	2	3
Billingham, Houston	0	2	2
Bouton, Houston	0	2	2
Carrithers, San Francisco	0	2	2
Cloninger, Cincinnati	1	1	2
Coombs, San Diego	0	2	2
Cumberland, San Francisco	0	2	2
Dillman, Montreal	0	2	2
Doyle, San Diego	2	0	2
Folkers, New York	2	0	2
Grant, Pittsburgh	0	2	2
Hartenstein, Pitts.-St. L.	1	1	2
Hough, Los Angeles	2	0	2
Hrabosky, St. Louis	0	2	2
G. Jackson, Philadelphia	0	2	2
McAndrew, New York	2	0	2
McCormick, San Francisco	2	0	2
McGinn, Montreal	0	2	2
Miller, Chicago	2	0	2
O'Donoghue, Montreal	0	2	2
Robertson, San Francisco	1	1	2
Ryan, New York	1	1	2
Strahler, Los Angeles	1	1	2
Wilcox, Cincinnati	1	1	2

One Relief Win, No Saves

Baldschun, S a n Diego; Briles, St. Louis; Brunet, Pittsburgh; Cardwell, N e w York-Atlanta; Colpaert, Pittsburgh; F r y m a n, Philadelphia; M. Jackson, Philadelphia; Jaster, Atlanta; Jim Hannan, San F r a n c i s c o; Niekro, Atlanta; Palmer, Philadelphia; Pappas, Atlanta-Chicago; Parker, St. Louis; Reed, Atlanta; Stoneman, Montreal; R. E. Wilson, San Diego; W. Wilson, Philadelphia.

One Save, No Relief Wins

Acosta, Pittsburgh; Chance, N e w York; Dierker, Houston; Dobson, San Diego; Faul, San Francisco; Gentry, New York; Gura, Chicago; H a n d s, Chicago; K l i n e, Atlanta; Maloney, Cincinnati; McBean, L o s Angeles-Pittsburgh; McCool, St. Louis; Mc-Q u e e n, Atlanta; Navarro, Atlanta; Pizarro, Chicago; R e n k o, Montreal; Santorini, San Diego; Short, Philadelphia.

AMERICAN LEAGUE

Pitcher—Club	Saves	Relief Wins	Tot. Pts.		Pitcher—Club	Saves	Relief Wins	Tot. Pts.
Perranoski, Minnesota	34	7	41		Zepp, Minnesota	2	3	5
McDaniel, New York	29	9	38		Austin, Cleveland	3	1	4
Timmerman, Detroit	27	6	33		Garrett, California	0	4	4
Grant, Oakland	24	6	30		Hannan, Washington	0	4	4
Wood, Chicago	21	9	30		Hardin, Baltimore	1	3	4
Knowles, Washington	27	2	29		Humphreys, Wash.-Milw.	3	1	4
Williams, Minnesota	15	10	25		Johnson, Kansas City	4	0	4
K. Tatum, California	17	7	24		Segui, Oakland	2	2	4
Abernathy, Kansas City	12	9	21		Wright, Kansas City	3	1	4
Lyle, Boston	20	1	21		Baldwin, Milwaukee	1	2	3
Aker, New York	16	4	20		Colbert, Cleveland	2	1	3
Richert, Baltimore	13	7	20		Hand, Cleveland	3	0	3
Watt, Baltimore	12	7	19		Miller, Cleveland-Chicago	1	2	3
Sanders, Milwaukee	13	5	18		Reed, Detroit	2	1	3
Higgins, Cleveland	11	4	15		Shellenback, Washington	0	3	3
Hall, Baltimore	3	10	13		Barber, Minnesota	2	0	2
Fisher, California	8	4	12		Brabender, Milwaukee	1	1	2
Romo, Boston	6	6	12		Cumberland, New York	0	2	2
Lindblad, Oakland	3	8	11		Haydel, Minnesota	0	2	2
Pina, Washington	6	5	11		Hedlund, Kansas City	0	2	2
Queen, California	9	2	11		Kealey, California	1	1	2
Lasher, Detroit-Cleveland	8	2	10		Koonce, Boston	2	0	2
Locker, Milwaukee-Oak.	7	3	10		Lonborg, Boston	0	2	2
Wagner, Boston	7	3	10		Mingori, Cleveland	1	1	2
Hennigan, Cleveland	3	6	9		O'Donoghue, Milwaukee	0	2	2
Patterson, Detroit	2	7	9		Pattin, Milwaukee	0	2	2
Chance, Cleveland	4	4	8		Rooker, Kansas City	1	1	2
Doyle, California	5	3	8		Saunders, Detroit	1	1	2
Drabowsky, K. C.-Balt.	3	5	8		Woodson, Minnesota	1	1	2
Gelnar, Milwaukee	4	4	8					
Grzenda, Washington	6	2	8					
Hall, Minnesota	4	4	8					

One Save, No Relief Wins

Cox, Washington; Hartenstein, Boston; L e e, Boston; Leonhard, Baltimore; Morehead, Kansas City; Santiago, Boston.

Pitcher—Club	Saves	Relief Wins	Tot. Pts.
Hiller, Detroit	3	5	8
LaRoche, California	4	4	8
Messersmith, California	5	3	8
Burgmeier, Kansas City	1	6	7
Hamilton, New York-Chi.	3	4	7
Murphy, Chicago	5	2	7
Bolin, Milwaukee-Boston	3	3	6
Crider, Chicago	4	2	6
Klimkowski, New York	1	5	6
Lachemann, Oakland	3	3	6
Brett, Boston	2	3	5
Ellsworth, Cleve-Milw	3	2	5
Fingers, Oakland	2	3	5
Fitzmorris, Kansas City	1	4	5
Roland, Oakland	2	3	5
Scherman, Detroit	1	4	5
Stange, Boston-Chicago	2	3	5

One Relief Win, No Saves

Brown, Washington; Brunet, Washington; Kaat, Minnesota; Kilkenny, Detroit; May, California; McCormick, New York; Monteagudo, Kansas City; M o r e t, Boston; Morris, Milwaukee; Niekro, Detroit; Peterson, New York; Sisk, Chicago; Such, Washington; Verbanic, New York; Waslewski, N e w York; Weaver, Chicago; York, Kansas City.

32 1-0 Tilts in Majors-Drop of 24 From '69

By CHRIS ROEWE

Only 32 1-0 games were played in the majors in 1970 as the dominance of the pitchers continued the decline that began in the preceding season. The skimpy total represented a 24-game decrease from 1969 and was 50 games fewer than the 82 one-run games hurled by big league pitchers in 1968.

The Dodgers, whose staff led the majors in shutouts with 17, were involved in the most minimum-score games, seven, and had the highest win total, five. The Tigers had the best record in the American League, winning both of their 1-0 games. The Astros were the only club to finish the season without playing a single game in which only one run was scored.

Carl Morton of the Expos and Don Sutton of the Dodgers were the only pitchers to register two 1-0 victories. Morton blanked the Phillies on September 11 and 16 days later went all the way to beat the Cardinals when the Expos pushed over a run in the 11th inning. Sutton's first 1-0 win came on June 16 at the expense of the Pirates and a month later on July 17 he prevailed over the Mets in ten innings.

The Mets, who lost all three one-run games in which they participated, were the losers in the longest 1-0 contest of the year when the Dodgers finally scored in the bottom of the 15th on April 24.

Six 1-0 games were decided by homers. Don Mincher homered with two out in the bottom of the ninth to give the Athletics a win in the second game of a doubleheader against the Senators on August 2. Joe Torre's homer in the ninth provided the margin in Jerry Reuss' win for the Cardinals over the Dodgers at Dodger Stadium on August 28. Other game-winning homers were hit by Deron Johnson, Phillies, April 25; Billy Grabarkewitz, Dodgers, June 16; Tony Conigliaro, Red Sox, August 25; Bobby Bonds, Giants, September 6.

The complete list of 1-0 games, including the inning in which the run was scored, follows:

AMERICAN LEAGUE (15)

Date	Winner	Loser	Inning
APRIL—			
29	—*Kaat, Minnesota	*Hand, Cleveland	3
30	Bahnsen, New York	*May, California	3
MAY—			
13	—*Fitzmorris, Kan C	*Hennigan, Cleve	12
JULY—			
7‡	— Krausse, Milwaukee	*Horlen, Chicago	7
25	— Segui, Oakland	*Peterson, N Y	1
AUGUST—			
2‡	—*Grant, Oakland	*Pina, Washington	9
13	— Bosman, Wash	Kaat, Minnesota	1
23	—*Lolich, Detroit	Pattin, Mil	6
25	—*Brett, Boston	*Hall, Minnesota	8
SEPTEMBER—			
3	— Bradley, California	Rooker, Kan C	2
9	— Cuellar, Baltimore	*Kline, New York	6
15†	— Lockwood, Mil	Odom, Oakland	5
25	— Perry, Minnesota	Bunker, Kan C	5
28	—*Hall, Minnesota	*Drago, Kan C	5
OCTOBER—			
1	— Hiller, Detroit	*Paul, Cleveland	1

NATIONAL LEAGUE (17)

Date	Winner	Loser	Inning
APRIL—			
24	—*Lamb, Los Angeles	*Taylor, New York	15
25	— Osteen, Los Angeles	Ryan, New York	3
25	—*Bunning, Phila	*Santorini, S D	4
27	—*Decker, Chicago	*Blass, Pittsburgh	3
MAY—			
15	—*Torrez, St. Louis	*Regan, Chicago	7
22	— Jarvis, Atlanta	*Vance, Los Ang	3
JUNE—			
16	— Sutton, Los Angeles	*Veale, Pittsburgh	4
22‡	— Nelson, Pittsburgh	*Linzy, St. Louis	10
JULY—			
17	— Sutton, Los Angeles	*McGraw, N Y	10
23	— Pappas, Chicago	*Carroll, Cincinnati	8
AUGUST—			
11	— Nash, Atlanta	*Morton, Montreal	5
28	— Reuss, St. Louis	Sutton, Los Ang	9
SEPTEMBER—			
6	— Perry, San Fran	*Reed, Atlanta	3
11	— Morton, Montreal	Short, Phila	8
22‡	— Stoneman, Montreal	*Ellis, Pittsburgh	6
22	— Foster, Los Angeles	*Bryant, S F	2
27	— Morton, Montreal	*Hilgendorf, S L	11

*Did not pitch complete game. †First game of doubleheader. ‡Second game of doubleheader.

Eight Sluggers Produce 3-Homer Games

By LARRY WIGGE

Not since 1955, when eight players also connected for three-homer games, have sluggers worked so vigorously. Each league split the honors: Paul Blair (Orioles), Tony Horton (Indians), Willie Horton (Tigers) and Bobby Murcer (Yankees) hit for the A. L. National League sluggers included three members of the Braves: Rico Carty, Mike Lum and Orlando Cepeda, while Johnny Bench provided the final burst for the Reds.

Blair started it all on April 29 with a power performance in Chicago, 18-2. A trend was reversed when his club lost, 8-7, while Tony Horton had his big day in the second game of a doubleheader against the Yankees on May 24. Willie Horton floored Milwaukee with three blasts in an 8-3 victory on June 9 at Detroit. Bobby Murcer had a trio of homers in the second game against Cleveland on June 24 at Yankee Stadium in a 5-4 win.

Carty's shots lifted the Braves to a 9-1 win over Philadelphia on May 31 in Atlanta. Atlanta Stadium yielded to Mike Lum in an 8-1 triumph over the Padres on July 3 in the opener of a twin bill. Orlando Cepeda socked three homers in an 8-3 conquest in the lidlifter at Chicago on July 26. On the same day, Johnny Bench did the Cardinals in with three clouts in a 12-5 victory at Cincinnati.

The records of the eight players and their three-homer games follow:

Date	Player—Opposition	Place	AB	R	H	2B	3B	HR	RBI	Result
April 29	—Blair, Orioles vs. White Sox	A	6	3	3	0	0	3	6	W 18-2
May 24†	—T. Horton, Indians vs. Yankees (11 inn.)	H	4	3	3	0	0	3	4	L 8-7
May 31	—Carty, Braves vs. Phillies	H	4	4	4	0	0	3	6	W 9-1
June 9	—W. Horton, Tigers vs. Brewers	H	4	3	3	0	0	3	7	W 8-3
June 24†	—Murcer, Yankees vs. Indians	H	3	3	3	0	0	3	4	W 5-4
July 3*	—Lum, Braves vs. Padres	H	3	3	3	0	0	3	5	W 8-1
July 26	—Bench, Reds vs. Cardinals	H	5	3	4	0	0	3	7	W 12-5
July 26*	—Cepeda, Braves vs. Cubs	A	5	3	4	0	0	3	7	W 8-3

*First game of doubleheader. †Second game of doubleheader.

The league leader in multiple-homer games was Duke Sims of the Cleveland Indians with six. A list of the players who hit two or more homers in a game and the number of times follows:

AMERICAN LEAGUE: Baltimore (9)—Blair 3, F. Robinson 3, Buford, Powell, B. Robinson. Boston (10)—A. Conigliaro 4, Yastrzemski 3, W. Conigliaro, Petrocelli, Scott. California (6)—Fregosi 3, Spencer 2, Johnson. Chicago (4)—Melton 2, Berry, Herrmann. Cleveland (14)—Sims 6, Foster 2, Horton 2, Bradford, Fosse, Nettles, Pinson. Detroit (11)—Horton 4, Northrup 2, I. Brown, Cash, Freehan, McAuliffe, Stanley. Kansas City (5)—Oliver 3, Kirkpatrick, Otis. Milwaukee (4)—Harper 2, Walton 2. Minnesota (5)—Alyea 2, Killebrew 2, Renick. New York (4)—Murcer 2, Gibbs, White. Oakland (5)—Mincher 3, Bando, Campaneris. Washington (6)—Howard 3, Epstein 2, Reichardt.

NATIONAL LEAGUE: Atlanta (12)—H. Aaron 3, Cepeda 3, Boyer 2, Carty 2, Lum, Tillman. Chicago (8)—Williams 3, Hickman 2, Santo 2, Banks. Cincinnati (11)—Bench 3, Perez 3, May 2, Carbo, McRae, Rose. Houston (6)—Wynn 3, Howard, Mayberry, Menke, Rader. Los Angeles (1)—Grabarkewitz. Montreal (9)—Staub 4, Jones 3, Bailey, Fairly. New York (8)—Agee 3, Clendenon, Foy, Garrett, Shamsky, Swoboda. Philadelphia (5)—Money 2, Briggs, Johnson, Taylor. Pittsburgh (11)—Stargell 3, Clemente 2, Robertson 2, Alley, Hebner, Pagan, Sanguillen. St. Louis (6)—Allen 4, Brock, Hague. San Diego (8)—Colbert 5, Brown, Ferrara, Murrell. San Francisco (13)—Mays 5, McCovey 5, Bonds 2, Hart.

Mays, Aaron Collect 3,000 Hits

By LARRY WIGGE

Through the history of baseball many lights have shone. The memory recalls names like Ruth, Gehrig, Hornsby and old Double-X. Their spirits did not ease away from the game, but the old bones told them that a new era had arrived. Indeed they were all stars, but the new age of statistical-conscious performers was at hand.

The one horizon that remained untouched by even these immortals wasn't part of their nature. Whether ancients had two, three or four thousand hits didn't matter. Personal achievements were secondary. The game itself was stressed as most important.

Only eight men had accumulated three thousand career hits prior to the 1970 season—Ty Cobb heads the list with 4,191 base hits—when two of the most luminous athletes of the present era, or any for that matter, joined that grouping. The names Mays and Aaron are destined to join their predecessors in the Hall of Fame. And when they do, the year 1970—the year both achieved the 3,000-hit plateau—will be noted also.

Hank Aaron came into '70 with a 30-hit edge on Willie Mays, thus it was his honor to be the first since Stan Musial in 1958 to join the select circle. Musial, the only living member of the initial eight, was on hand at the doubleheader in Cincinnati on May 17 to see Hammerin' Hank dribble his momentous hit up the middle. Next to Ty Cobb (at age 34), the Braves' great outfielder at 36 was the youngest to reach the figure.

Two months later, on July 18, the Say-Hey Kid bounced No. 3,000 off Candlestick Park's new artificial turf and through the left side of the Expos's infield. He was now the first player ever to have 600 home runs and 3,000 hits.

The careers of both Mays and Aaron have run parallel in that each has been with one club through his entire major league career. Each is from the state of Alabama and each is known for his power-hitting ability, being ranked right behind Babe Ruth on the home-run totem pole. And oddly enough, each achieved his 3,000th hit on ground singles.

It is difficult to say just how long both Mays and Aaron can continue. They are physical marvels and seem to be able to push themselves longer and harder than other players of their time. Already they have assured themselves of a place amongst the game's greatest stars, of any era.

Following is a list of statistics for the 3,000-hit members:

	G.	AB.	R.	H.	2B.	3B.	HR.	Avg.	Age*
Ty Cobb (1905-1928)	3033	11429	2244	4191	724	297	118	.367	34
Stan Musial (1941-1963)	3026	10972	1949	3630	725	177	475	.331	37
Tris Speaker (1907-1928)	2789	10208	1881	3515	793	224	115	.344	37
Honus Wagner (1897-1917)	2785	10427	1740	3430	651	252	101	.329	40
Eddie Collins (1906-1930)	2826	9949	1818	3311	437	186	47	.333	38
Nap Lajoie (1896-1916)	2475	9589	1503	3251	650	162	82	.339	39
Paul Waner (1926-1945)	2549	9459	1626	3152	603	190	112	.333	39
Hank Aaron (1954-1970)	2576	9952	1806	3110	540	92	592	.313	36
Cap Anson (1876-1897)	2253	9084	1712	3081	530	129	92	.339	45
Willie Mays (1951-1970)	2702	10011	1921	3065	478	134	628	.306	39

*Age when achieved 3,000th hit.

Gutierrez Lone 7-Hit Producer

By CHRIS ROEWE

Cesar Gutierrez, little shortstop of the Tigers, who had made only 20 hits in the major leagues when the 1970 season began, became the first American League player in history to get seven hits in seven times at bat when he had six singles and a double as Detroit outlasted the Indians, 9-8, in the second game of a doubleheader at Cleveland, June 21. Gutierrez had singles in the first, third and fifth innings, doubled in the seventh and singled in the eighth, tenth and twelfth. He made at least one hit off each of the five hurlers employed by the Indians. The only other major leaguer to hit 7-for-7 was Wilbert Robinson, National League catcher and manager and a member of the Hall of Fame, who also had six singles and a double for the old Baltimore Orioles in the first game of a doubleheader on June 10, 1892.

Atlanta second baseman Felix Millan joined the ranks of the "6-for-6" club on July 6 when he had a triple, double and four singles as the Braves trounced San Francisco at Atlanta, 12-4. Millan singled in the first, tripled in the third, singled in the fourth and fifth, doubled in the seventh and singled in the eighth. He was the first National leaguer to accomplish this feat since Joe Morgan made six hits in six trips to the plate for Houston on July 8, 1965. Millan also had five hits as the Braves beat the Dodgers, 4-1, on August 6.

Roberto Clemente set a modern National League record for most hits in two consecutive games when he had five safeties in each contest as the Pirates won from the Dodgers at Dodger Stadium on August 22-23. The great Pittsburgh right fielder drove in the first run and scored the second as the Pirates edged the Dodgers, 2-1, in 16 innings on Saturday night, August 22. The following day, Clemente had five more blows as the Pirates waltzed to a 11-0 win.

A total of 29 players enjoyed five-hit games in 1970 as compared with only 12 in 1969. Millan and Clemente were the only hitters to get five or more hits on more than one occasion.

Willie Stargell staged the top slugging exhibition of the season when he had two homers and three doubles to lead the Pirates to a 20-10 mauling of the Braves on August 1. His five extra-base hits equaled the major league record. Teammate Bob Robertson had five hits in the same game. Luis Aparicio and Walt Williams of the White Sox also had five hits in the same game as Chicago outlasted the Red Sox, 22-13, on May 31.

The records of all players making five or more hits in one game follow:

Date	Player—Opposition	Place	AB	R	H	2B	3B	HR	RBI	Result
April 18	—Carew, Twins vs. Athletics	A	5	2	5	0	0	0	0	W 11-5
April 19†	—Clarke, Yankees vs. Orioles	A	6	0	5	0	0	0	1	W 8-5
April 24	—Kaline, Tigers vs. Twins	A	5	1	5	2	0	0	1	W 8-6
May 1	—Otis, Royals vs. Indians	H	5	2	5	1	0	0	0	L 7-5
May 17†	—Perez, Reds vs. Braves (15 innings)	H	7	2	5	1	0	0	0	W 7-6
May 23	—Colbert, Padres vs. Giants (15 innings)	A	8	2	5	0	0	1	4	W 17-16

Date	Player—Opposition	Place	AB	R	H	2B	3B	HR	RBI	Result
May 27	—Uhlaender, Indians vs. Orioles	A	5	2	5	1	0	0	0	L 5-4
May 30	—Staub, Expos vs. Reds (10 innings)	A	5	1	5	1	0	1	1	L 5-4
May 31	—Aparicio, White Sox vs. Red Sox	A	5	3	5	0	1	0	3	W 22-13
May 31	—Williams, White Sox vs. Red Sox	A	7	5	5	1	0	0	2	W 22-13
June 13	—White, Yankees vs. Royals (12 innings)	A	6	2	5	0	0	1	2	W 9-4
June 21	—Cater, Yankees vs. Red Sox (11 innings)	A	6	2	5	1	0	0	3	W 14-10
June 21†	—Gutierrez, Tigers vs. Indians (12 innings)	A	7	3	7	1	0	0	1	W 9-8
June 28*	—Heidemann, Indians vs. Tigers	A	5	2	5	0	0	0	1	W 8-2
July 6	—Millan, Braves vs. Giants	H	6	2	6	1	1	0	4	W 12-4
July 10†	—Rose, Reds vs. Braves	A	5	0	5	0	0	0	0	W 3-1
July 19†	—Foy, Mets vs. Giants (10 innings)	A	5	2	5	1	0	2	5	W 7-6
July 26†	—Beckert, Cubs vs. Braves	H	5	1	5	2	0	0	1	W 7-6
Aug. 1	—Robertson, Pirates vs. Braves	A	6	4	5	1	0	1	3	W 20-10
Aug. 1	—Stargell, Pirates vs. Braves	A	6	5	5	3	0	2	6	W 20-10
Aug. 6	—Millan, Braves vs. Dodgers	A	5	0	5	2	0	0	2	W 4-1
Aug. 8	—Agee, Mets vs. Pirates	A	6	4	5	2	1	0	2	W 12-9
Aug. 14	—Wills, Dodgers vs. Cubs	A	5	2	5	1	0	0	1	W 13-9
Aug. 19	—Alou, Pirates vs. Giants	H	5	0	5	0	0	0	0	L 7-4
Aug. 22	—Clemente, Pirates vs. Dodgers (16 innings)	A	7	1	5	0	0	0	1	W 2-1
Aug. 23	—Clemente, Pirates vs. Dodgers	A	6	4	5	1	0	1	3	W 11-10
Sept. 4	—B. Robinson, Orioles vs. Red Sox	A	5	3	5	1	0	2	4	W 8-6
Sept. 6	—Howard, Senators vs. Tigers (12 innings)	H	6	2	5	0	0	2	5	L 8-7
Sept. 7†	—Morgan, Astros vs. Padres	A	6	0	5	2	0	0	2	W 9-4
Sept. 22	—Rudi, Athletics vs. Twins	H	5	0	5	2	0	0	1	L 5-3
Sept. 29	—Cardenas, Twins vs. Royals (12 innings)	H	6	2	5	0	0	0	4	L 14-13

*First game of doubleheader. †Second game of doubleheader.

National League batting champion Rico Carty hit safely in 31 consecutive games, the longest batting streak of the year. Carty began his string in the Braves' second game of the season on April 8 and was not stopped until May 16 when he failed to hit safely in four tries against Jim McGlothlin of the Reds who blanked the Braves, 2-0. Carty batted a hefty .451 in this stretch with 51 hits in 113 at-bats. Included in his blows were eight homers and nine doubles and he batted in 30 runs while crossing the plate 31 times.

The best American League streak was fashioned by Ray Fosse, young Indian catcher, who hit safely in 23 straight games from June 9 through July 2, a remarkable string for a player catching every day. Fosse had 35 hits in 93 times at bat in his skein for a .376 mark. Five of his blows were homers as he batted in 16 runs.

Cleon Jones of the Mets also had a 23-game streak which extended from August 25 through September 15th. Sandy Alomar of the Angels had the second-best American League streak, a 22-game string from June 3 through June 27. Tommie Agee hit in 20 straight games from April 16 through May 9 and later had a skein of 19 straight from June 22 through July 8.

There were a total of 21 streaks of 15 games or more in the majors, twelve of them by National Leaguers. In addition to those noted above the

following is the complete list: 18 games—Larry Bowa, Phillies; 17 games—Bobby Bonds, Giants; Tito Fuentes, Giants; Jim Hickman, Cubs; Doug Rader, Astros; Tony Oliva, Twins; 16 games—Willie Horton, Tigers; Sonny Jackson, Braves; 15 games—Lou Brock, Cardinals; Ted Sizemore, Dodgers; Ken Berry, White Sox; Leo Cardenas, Twins; Reggie Smith, Red Sox; Cesar Tovar, Twins; Carl Yastrzemski, Red Sox.

Glenn Beckert, Cub second baseman, made four or more hits in one game six times to lead the majors in this department in 1970. Beckert had five hits as the Cubs nosed out the Braves 7-6, in the second game of a doubleheader on July 26 and had four safeties in one contest on five occasions.

Another second baseman, Sandy Alomar of the Angels, was the American League leader in this category with five four-hit games. Other National Leaguers with five multiple-hit games were: Tommie Agee, Mets; Lou Brock, Cardinals; Roberto Clemente, Pirates; Clarence Gaston, Padres and Billy Williams, Cubs. No other American League player had more than four.

Pittsburgh had the best team total with 20 four-or-more-hit efforts. The Chicago Cubs were second with 19. The best American League total was 17, a mark reached by Baltimore and California.

The complete list of players who made four or more hits in a game follows:

AMERICAN LEAGUE: Baltimore (17)—Buford 4, Rettenmund 3, Blair 2, B. Robinson 2, F. Robinson 2, Belanger, Hendricks, Powell, Salmon. Boston (10)—Andrews 3, A. Conigliaro 2, Scott 2, Smith 2, Petrocelli. California (17) —Alomar 5, Fregosi 2, Johnson 2, Azcue, Egan, Johnstone, McMullen, Rodriguez, Spencer, J. Tatum, Voss. Chicago (13)—Aparicio 3, Berry 3, Josephson 2, Williams 2, Knoop, Melton, Spence. Cleveland (9)—Foster 2, Heidemann 2, Horton 2, Uhlaender 2, Sims. Detroit (5)—McAuliffe 2, Gutierrez, Kaline, Maddox. Kansas City (13)—Otis 2, Piniella 2, Rojas 2, Floyd, Keough, Kirkpatrick, Oliver, Schaal, Severson, Spriggs. Milwaukee (6)—Harper 4, Kubiak, Snyder. Minnesota (14)—Oliva 4, Cardenas 3, Carew 3, Alyea, Reese, Thompson, Tovar. New York (11)—Munson 4, Clarke 3, Cater 2, Lyttle, White. Oakland (7)—Campaneris 2, Bando, Duncan, Jackson, Monday, Rudi. Washington (11)—Rodriguez 3, Brinkman 2, Howard 2, Epstein, Maye, Stroud, Unser.

NATIONAL LEAGUE: Atlanta (12)—Millan 3, Carty 2, H. Aaron, T. Aaron, Baker, Boyer, Cepeda, Garr, Garrido. Chicago (19)—Beckert 6, Williams 5, Callison 2, Hickman 2, Santo 2, Kessinger, Smith. Cincinnati (13)—Perez 4, Bench 3, May 2, Rose 2, Concepcion, Helms. Houston (10)—Morgan 3, Alou 2, Menke 2, Wynn 2, Edwards. Los Angeles (16)—Davis 4, Parker 4, Mota 2, Wills 2, Garvey, Haller, Osteen, Sizemore. Montreal (3)—Gosger 2, Staub. New York (9)—Agee 5, Boswell, Foy, Garrett, Grote. Philadelphia (8)—Bowa 2, Briggs, Browne, Doyle, Money, Stone, Taylor. Pittsburgh (20)—Clemente 5, Alou 3, Robertson 3, Oliver 2, Pagan 2, Alley, Mazeroski, Patek, Sanguillen, Stargell. St. Louis (15)—Brock 5, Torre 4, Allen, Hague, Javier, Maxvill, Melendez, Torrez. San Diego (13)—Gaston 5, Colbert 3, Arcia, Brown, Dean, Huntz, Murrell. San Francisco (13)—Bonds 3, Hunt 3, Henderson 2, Mays 2, Dietz, Gallagher, Hart.

Pinch-Homers in '70 Hit New High—94

By CHRIS ROEWE

The pinch-hit homer proved a lethal weapon in the majors in 1970. A total of 94 circuit clouts were hit by emergency swingers, 49 by American Leaguers, breaking the old mark of 84, set in 1962 in 10-club leagues.

Five players led the way with three pinch-homers each: Frank Fernandez of the Athletics, Ted Uhlaender of the Indians, Rick Reichardt of the Senators, Rick Joseph of the Phillies and Bob Bailey of the Expos. Joseph only three homers for the entire season and all came while pinch-hitting.

Bailey also accounted for one of the seven grand-slam homers hit by pinch-hitters. Others were produced by Rich Reese and Rick Renick of the Twins, Reggie Jackson of the Athletics, Jim Hutto of the Phillies, Tom Haller of the Dodgers and Carl Taylor of the Cardinals.

A complete list of pinch-homers, including the innings in which they were hit and the number of men on base, follows:

AMERICAN LEAGUE (49)

APRIL—
29 —Francona, Oakland vs. Boston ...... (7-0)
30 —Fernandez, Oakland vs. Boston ...... (8-0)
MAY—
3†—McNertney, Milwaukee vs. New York. (7-1)
10*—Reichardt, Washington vs. Milwaukee (7-1)
12 —Alvis, Milwaukee vs. New York ...... (8-0)
20 —Christian, Chicago vs. California .... (9-1)
21 —Nettles, Cleveland vs. Boston ...... (5-0)
22 —Donaldson, Oakland vs. Chicago .... (6-2)
31 —Ward, New York vs. Minnesota ...... (7-0)
JUNE—
3 —G. Brown, Detroit vs. California .... (9-0)
7 —Reese, Minnesota vs. Washington .. (6-3)
7 —Roof, Milwaukee vs. Baltimore ...... (8-2)
7 —Rudi, Oakland vs. Detroit .... (9-2)
11 —Hinton, Cleveland vs. Oakland ...... (9-1)
22 —Fernandez, Oakland vs. Kansas City (9-0)
23 —Cowan, California vs. Chicago ...... (7-1)
24*—Blefary, New York vs. Cleveland ...... (8-0)
28 —Reichardt, Washington vs. Baltimore (12-1)
30 —Renick, Minnesota vs. Kansas City .. (6-3)
JULY—
4 —Cash, Detroit vs. Baltimore .... (9-1)
4 —Piniella, Kansas City vs. Milwaukee. (9-2)
5 —Rollins, Cleveland vs. Boston ...... (6-0)
5 —Kennedy, Boston vs. Cleveland ...... (5-0)
7†—Roseboro, Washington vs. Cleveland . (7-0)
7*—Savage, Milwaukee vs. Chicago ...... (12-0)
8 —Reichardt, Washington vs. Cleveland. (8-0)
9 —Uhlaender, Cleveland vs. Washington (8-0)
12 —Hansen, New York vs. Washington .. (9-1)
24†—Horton, Cleveland vs. Kansas City .. (6-0)
3: —Allison, Minnesota vs. Detroit ...... (9-1)
31 —Manuel, Minnesota vs. Detroit ...... (8-0)
AUGUST—
8 —Hinton, Cleveland vs. Washington .. (9-1)
16 —Moses, Boston vs. Minnesota ...... (8-0)
18 —Maye, Washington vs. Kansas City .. (7-2)
25†—Collins, Detroit vs. California ...... (8-2)
26 —Uhlaender, Cleveland vs. Milwaukee (7-0)
28*—Hendricks, Baltimore vs. Milwaukee. (8-0)
30 —Jackson, Oakland vs. Detroit ...... (8-1)
SEPTEMBER—
1 —Hopkins, Chicago vs. Oakland ...... (9-1)
3 —Alyea, Minnesota vs. Milwaukee .... (7-1)
3 —Fernandez, Oakland vs. Chicago .... (9-2)
5 —Jackson, Oakland vs. Kansas City .. (8-3)
12 —Nettles, Cleveland vs. New York .... (8-1)
15†—Blefary, New York vs. Boston ...... (9-2)
21 —Johnstone, California vs. Milwaukee. (7-1)
25*—Hansen, New York vs. Detroit ...... (5-0)
25*—Koegel, Milwaukee vs. Chicago ...... (9-0)
25 —Uhlaender, Cleveland vs. Baltimore . (9-2)
30 —Ratliff, Minnesota vs. Kansas City .. (9-2)

NATIONAL LEAGUE (45)

APRIL—
7 —Miller, Houston vs. San Francisco .. (7-2)
8 —Beauchamp, Houston vs. San Fran. . (8-0)
14 —Joseph, Philadelphia vs. Chicago ... (9-1)
16 —Murrell, San Diego vs. Atlanta ....(10-0)
17 —McRae, Cincinnati vs. San Francisco (9-0)
28 —Joseph, Philadelphia vs. Los Angeles (10-0)
28 —Mayberry, Houston vs. Cincinnati ... (9-0)
MAY—
3*—Johnson, Philadelphia vs. San Fran. (8-2)
9 —Davalillo, St. Louis vs. Atlanta ...... (7-1)
18 —Bailey, Montreal vs. New York ...... (9-3)
19 —Boccabella, Montreal vs. New York .. (9-0)
JUNE—
7 —Gallagher, San Francisco vs. Chicago (7-0)
11 —Bailey, Montreal vs. Cincinnati ...... (6-1)
11 —Hutto, Philadelphia vs. Atlanta ...... (9-0)
14 —Sudakis, Los Angeles vs. Chicago ... (9-1)
22 —Clendenon, New York vs. Chicago .. (8-2)
24*—Banks, Chicago vs. New York .... (9-2)
26 —Sutherland, Montreal vs. New York . (4-1)
33 —Cardenal, St. Louis vs. Chicago ...... (9-0)
JULY—
3 —Taylor, San Francisco vs. Los Angeles (6-2)
3†—Webster, San Diego vs. Atlanta ...... (5-0)
6*—Bailey, Montreal vs. Chicago .... (8-0)
8 —Wynn, Houston vs. Los Angeles ...... (9-0)
9 —Carbo, Cincinnati vs. San Diego .... (8-2)
10†—Hall, Atlanta vs. Cincinnati .... (9-0)
18 —Spiezio, San Diego vs. Philadelphia . (9-0)
19*—Hutto, Philadelphia vs. Los Angeles . (9-3)
22 —Haller, Los Angeles vs. Montreal ... (7-3)
25 —Marshall, New York vs. Los Angeles . (7-2)
28 —Spangler, Chicago vs. Houston ...... (6-0)
29 —Hague, St. Louis vs. Atlanta .... (9-0)
AUGUST—
2†—Swoboda, New York vs. San Diego .. (7-0)
11 —Carl Taylor, St. Louis vs. San Diego. (9-3)
14†—Hunt, San Francisco vs. St. Louis ... (8-1)
17 —Joseph, Philadelphia vs. Cincinnati . (8-1)
23†—Stewart, Cincinnati vs. New York .... (7-2)
SEPTEMBER—
2 —Robertson, Pittsburgh vs. Montreal .. (9-0)
4 —Cardenal, St. Louis vs. Montreal ....(10-1)
6 —Miller, Houston vs. Los Angeles ...... (8-1)
7*—Smith, Chicago vs. Pittsburgh ...... (7-1)
13 —Haller, Los Angeles vs. San Fran. ..(10-2)
15 —Marshall, New York vs. Montreal .... (8-0)
18*—Fairey, Montreal vs. Chicago .... (8-0)
19 —Edwards, Houston vs. Los Angeles .. (9-1)
25 —Foster, San Francisco vs. San Diego . (7-0)

*First game of doubleheader. Second game of doubleheader.

Grand Slam Marks Shattered

By CHRIS ROEWE

For the second year in a row National League batsmen broke the league record for grand-slam homers in a season with a whopping total of 49, nine more than 1969's record-breaking figure. A. L. hitters had 39 bases-loaded circuit clouts for a record combined total of 88.

Frank Robinson of the Orioles added another to his list of slugging achievements when he smashed bases-loaded homers in the fifth and sixth innings as Baltimore mauled the Senators, 12-2, on June 26. Frank joined five other American League players and one National Leaguer as co-holders of the record for most grand-slam homers in one game.

Lee May was the top producer of grand-slams in 1970 with three. The burly first baseman of the National League champion Reds connected against the Dodgers on April 16, the Cardinals in the second game of a doubleheader on July 20 and the Dodgers again on September 10.

A complete list of grand-slam homers, with the inning in which each was hit in parentheses, follows:

AMERICAN LEAGUE (39)

APRIL.—
15 —Alyea, Minn. vs. Messersmith, Calif. (6)
18 —Voss, Calif. vs. Bunker, Kansas City (5)
18 —Renick, Minnesota vs. Downing, Oak. (4)
MAY.—
21 —Fosse, Cleveland vs. Romo, Boston (5)
24 —Reichardt, Wash. vs. Lolich, Detroit (2)
30 —Pena, Milwaukee vs. Cain, Detroit (1)
JUNE—
7†—Petrocelli, Bos. vs. Fitzmorris, K. C. (8)
7 —Reese, Minnesota vs. Bosman, Wash. (6)
9 —Horton, Detroit vs. Lockwood, Mil. (1)
10 —Petrocelli, Boston vs. Horlen, Chicago (4)
12 —Northrup, Det. vs. O'Donoghue, Mil. (8)
12 —Snyder, Mil. vs. Hand, Cleveland (8)
15 —McAuliffe, Detroit vs. Dobson, Oak. (2)
15 —Fernandez, Oakland vs. Lolich, Det. (3)
15 —Rettenmund, Baltimore vs. Bolin, Mil. (1)
16 —Andrews, Boston vs. Johnson, K. C. (9)
19*—Epstein, Wash. vs. Drabowsky, Balt. (7)
21†—Horton, Cleve. vs. Kilkenny, Detroit (1)
26 —F. Robinson, Balt. vs. Coleman, Wash. (5)
26 —F. Robinson, Balt. vs. Grzenda, Wash. (6)
30 —Renick, Minnesota vs. Johnson, K. C. (6)
JULY.—
7 —B. Robinson, Balt. vs. McDaniel, N.Y. (10)
8 —Bradford, Cleve. vs. Knowles, Wash. (8)
18 —Kubiak, Milwaukee vs. Phillips, Bos. (9)
20 —Hendricks, Baltimore vs. Moore, Chi. (7)
26 —Powell, Baltimore vs. Woodson, Minn. (8)
29 —Pinson, Cleveland vs. Hamm, Minn. (3)
AUGUST—
5 —Herrmann, Chi. vs. Brabender, Mil. (1)
13 —Kirkpatrick, K. C. vs. Curtis, Boston (8)
25†—Johnstone, Calif. vs. LaGrow, Detroit (8)
28†—Buford, Balt. vs. Baldwin, Milwaukee (6)
29 —Herrmann, Chi. vs. Hartenstein, Boston (6)
30 —White, N. Y. vs. Blyleven, Minnesota (1)
SEPTEMBER—
1 —A. Conigliaro, Boston vs. Hiller, Det. (2)
1 —Price, Detroit vs. Siebert, Boston (4)
4 —A. Conigliaro, Bos. vs. Cuellar, Balt. (1)
5 —Jackson, Oak. vs. Burgmeier, K. C. (8)
7*—Alyea, Minnesota vs. Krausse, Mil. (1)
15*—Cardenas, Minn. vs. Bradley, Calif. (2)

NATIONAL LEAGUE (49)

APRIL—
10 —H. Aaron, Atl. vs. Griffin, Houston (3)
14 —Henderson, San Fran. vs. Pappas, Atl. (9)
14 —Tolan, Cin. vs. Coombs, San Diego (7)
16 —May, Cincinnati vs. Norman, L. A. (5)
18 —Hunt, San Fran. vs. Cloninger, Cin. (6)
23 —Cepeda, Atl. vs. Hartenstein, Pitts. (8)
26†—Dietz, San Fran. vs. Sembera, Mont. (8)
26 —Santo, Chicago vs. Dierker, Houston (6)
26*—McCovey, San F. vs. Stoneman, Mont. (1)
28 —Marshall, N. Y. vs. Perry, San Fran. (1)
30 —Carty, Atlanta vs. Jenkins, Chicago (1)
MAY—
1 —Stargell, Pitts. vs. Simpson, Cin. (7)
10 —McCovey, San F. vs. McGraw, N. Y. (4)
13 —Oliver, Pitts. vs. Gibson, St. Louis (6)
18 —Bailey, Montreal vs. Koonce, N. Y. (9)
22 —Henderson, San F. vs. Dukes, San D. (8)
JUNE—
2 —Allen, St. L. vs. Jerry Johnson, S.F. (8)
4 —Rader, Houston vs. McGinn, Montreal (1)
6 —Staub, Montreal vs. Kline, Atlanta (8)
10 —Pepitone, Houston vs. Ryan, N. Y. (4)
13 —Robertson, Pitts. vs. Dukes, San Diego (7)
18 —Fairly, Montreal vs. Jaster, Atlanta (8)
JULY—
2 —Bateman, Mont. vs. Torrez, St. Louis (1)
3 —Williams, Chicago vs. Gibbon, Pitts. (2)
6†—Santo, Chicago vs. Wegener, Montreal (1)
9 —Menke, Hous. vs. Foster, Los Angeles (1)
9 —Swoboda, New York vs. Nye, Montreal (3)
16 —Browne, Phila. vs. Willis, San Diego (9)
19*—Hutto, San Diego vs. Brewer, Los Angeles (9)
20†—May, Cin. vs. Chlupsa, St. Louis (10)
22 —Haller, L. A. vs. Raymond, Montreal (7)
25 —Fairly, Mont. vs. Reberger, San Fran. (4)
26*—Cepeda, Atlanta vs. Hands, Chicago (5)
AUGUST—
1 —Allen, St. Louis vs. DiLauro, Hous. (7)
2 —Taylor, Phil. vs. Davison, San Fran. (9)
5 —Davis, Los Angeles vs. Cardwell, Atl. (5)
11 —Perez, Cincinnati vs. McAndrew, N. Y. (2)
11 —Carl Taylor, St. L. vs. Herbel, San D. (9)
14 —Pepitone, Chicago vs. Sutton, L. A. (1)
14*—King, Atlanta vs. McGraw, New York (7)
18 —Spiezio, San Diego vs. Rodriquez, Chi. (6)
SEPTEMBER—
2 —King, Atlanta vs. Sutton, Los Angeles (1)
3 —Alley, Pittsburgh vs. Morton, Mont. (6)
4 —Corkins, San Diego vs. Merritt, Cin. (4)
7*—Watson, Houston vs. Willis, San Diego (6)
7*—Webster, San Diego vs. Forsch, Hous. (9)
10 —May, Cin. vs. Moeller, Los Angeles (1)
17 —Watson, Hous. vs. Brewer, Los Angeles (7)
23 —Dietz, San Fran. vs. Brewer, L.A. (7)
*First game of doubleheader. †Second game of doubleheader.

35 Pinch-Hitters Topped .300

JOSE CARDENAL, NL
Cardinal Jolter

JOHN DONALDSON, AL
Oakland Dandy

AMERICAN LEAGUE
(Compiled By Howe News Bureau)
(Ten or More At-Bats)

Player—Club	G.	AB.	H.	HR.	RBI.	Pct.
Donaldson, Oakland ..	16	13	6	1	4	.462
Uhlaender, Cleveland .	15	11	5	3	6	.455
Duncan, Oakland	13	10	4	0	0	.400
Alyea, Minnesota ...	19	18	7	1	4	.389
Josephson, Chicago ...	19	13	5	0	3	.385
Burda, Milwaukee	15	13	5	0	1	.385
Jones, Detroit	37	29	11	0	7	.379
Tepedino, New York ..	14	11	4	0	2	.364
Fernandez, Oakland ..	17	14	5	3	5	.357
Hegan, Milwaukee	17	14	5	0	1	.357
Cash, Detroit	21	17	6	1	4	.353
Allison, Minnesota ...	24	20	7	1	6	.350
I. Brown, Detroit	29	21	7	0	3	.333
Reese, Minnesota	16	12	4	1	9	.333
Stroud, Washington ..	20	19	6	0	2	.316
Hinton, Cleveland ...	39	37	11	2	10	.297
Rettenmund, Baltimore	19	17	5	0	1	.294
Smith, Milwaukee	17	17	5	0	0	.294
Crowley, Baltimore ...	39	31	9	0	2	.290
Cowan, California	41	39	11	1	7	.282
Hopkins, Chicago	42	36	10	1	5	.278
Gil, Milwaukee	15	11	3	0	4	.273
Renick, Minnesota ...	36	26	7	1	8	.269
Goossen, Mil-Wash ...	20	19	5	0	0	.263
Sorrell, Kansas City .	25	23	6	0	3	.261
Francona, Oak-Mil ...	68	59	15	1	7	.254
McCraw, Chicago	37	32	8	0	5	.250
Williams, Chicago ...	32	28	7	0	1	.250
Hovley, Mil-Oak	32	28	7	0	0	.250
Blefary, New York ...	17	12	3	2	6	.250
G. Brown, Detroit	55	41	10	1	13	.244
Voss, California	30	26	6	0	5	.231
Ward, New York	53	44	10	1	10	.227
Brown, Cleveland	24	22	5	0	1	.227
McNertney, Milwaukee	20	18	4	1	3	.222
Johnstone, California .	28	23	5	1	8	.217
Snyder, Milwaukee ...	33	28	6	0	3	.214
Holt, Minnesota	15	14	3	0	4	.214
Manuel, Minnesota ...	52	43	9	1	5	.209
Alvis, Milwaukee	15	15	3	1	2	.200
Buford, Baltimore	14	10	2	0	0	.200
Spriggs, Kansas City .	13	10	2	0	1	.200
Taylor, Kansas City ..	54	46	9	0	6	.196
Savage, Milwaukee ...	44	31	6	1	3	.194
Nagelson, Clev-Det ...	37	31	6	0	3	.194
Fiore, KC-Bos........	30	26	5	0	3	.192
Reichardt, Cal-Wash .	50	42	8	3	8	.190
Rollins, Mil-Clev	45	42	8	1	4	.190
Collins, Detroit	24	21	4	1	3	.190
Kirkpatrick, Kan City	23	21	4	0	1	.190
Hendricks, Baltimore .	19	16	3	1	2	.188
Hershberger, Milw ...	19	16	3	0	0	.188
Blanco, Chicago	18	16	3	0	2	.188
Matias, Chicago	29	27	5	0	1	.185
Ratliff, Minnesota ...	24	22	4	1	3	.182
Nelson, Washington ...	14	11	2	0	0	.182
Pena, Oak-Mil	13	11	2	0	0	.182
LaRussa, Oakland	11	11	2	0	0	.182
Maye, Wash-Chi	42	39	7	1	8	.179
Roseboro, Washington	21	17	3	1	1	.176
Schaal, Kansas City ..	19	17	3	0	0	.176
Reynolds, California ..	29	24	4	0	0	.167
Bradford, Chi-Clev ...	20	18	3	0	0	.167
Grieve, Washington ..	12	12	2	0	3	.167
Schofield, Boston	49	43	7	0	2	.163
Woods, New York	26	19	3	0	3	.158

Player—Club	G.	AB.	H.	HR.	RBI.	Pct.
Johnson, Oakland	23	19	3	0	1	.158
Motton, Baltimore	31	26	4	0	4	.154
Salmon, Baltimore	14	13	2	0	2	.154
Repoz, California	20	20	3	0	1	.150
Hansen, New York	36	28	4	2	6	.143
H. Allen, Wash-Mil	17	14	2	0	0	.143
Klimchock, Cleveland	33	30	4	0	0	.133
Wert, Detroit	16	15	2	0	0	.133
B. Allen, Washington	27	23	3	0	0	.130
Davis, Oakland	16	16	2	0	1	.125
Comer, Mil-Wash	30	26	3	0	4	.115
Rudi, Oakland	20	18	2	1	4	.111
Epstein, Washington	20	18	2	0	1	.111
Ruiz, California	35	30	3	0	2	.100
Maddox, Detroit	24	20	2	0	1	.100
Ellis, New York	20	20	2	0	2	.100
Unser, Washington	28	21	2	0	2	.095
Derrick, Boston	21	21	2	0	0	.095
Price, Detroit	15	12	1	0	1	.083
Cullen, Washington	13	12	1	0	0	.083
Ford, Cleveland	13	12	1	0	0	.083
J. Tatum, California	14	13	1	0	0	.077
May, Balt-Mil	21	15	1	0	0	.067
Campanis, Kansas City	17	16	1	0	0	.063
Kelly, Kansas City	19	17	1	0	0	.059
Matchick, Bos-KC	14	12	0	0	0	.000
Silverio, California	11	10	0	0	0	.000

NATIONAL LEAGUE
(Compiled by Elias Sports Bureau)
(Ten or More At-Bats)

Player—Club	G.	AB.	H.	HR.	RBI.	Pct.
Cardenal, St. L.	17	16	8	2	6	.500
Taylor, Philadelphia	17	14	6	0	5	.429
Haller, Los Angeles	14	12	5	2	8	.417
Hague, St. Louis	19	17	7	1	7	.412
Clines, Pittsburgh	22	20	8	0	2	.400
Briggs, Philadelphia	18	15	6	0	4	.400
Gallagher, San Fran.	20	18	7	1	3	.389
Watson, Houston	14	13	5	0	2	.385
Fairey, Montreal	41	37	14	1	8	.378
Mota, Los Angeles	20	16	6	0	5	.375
Jones, Montreal	38	27	10	0	4	.370
Geronimo, Houston	14	11	4	0	1	.364
Stewart, Cincinnati	42	39	13	1	6	.333
Bailey, Montreal	43	36	12	3	8	.333
Spiezio, San Diego	25	21	7	1	2	.333
Davalillo, St. Louis	76	73	24	1	20	.329
Lum, Atlanta	32	28	9	0	3	.321
Bravo, Cincinnati	49	42	13	0	3	.310
Hunt, San Francisco	26	23	7	1	4	.304
Garvey, Los Angeles	10	10	3	0	1	.300
Joseph, Philadelphia	43	37	11	3	7	.297
Jeter, Pittsburgh	19	17	5	0	4	.294
Gamble, Philadelphia	14	14	4	0	3	.286
Hahn, Montreal	27	18	5	0	0	.278
Davenport, San Fran.	14	11	3	0	2	.273
F. Johnson, San Fran.	14	11	3	0	3	.273
Patek, Pittsburgh	13	11	3	0	0	.273
Cline, Mont-Cin	33	26	7	0	7	.269
Miller, Houston	24	19	5	2	6	.263
McRae, Cincinnati	21	19	5	1	4	.263
Carl Taylor, St. Louis	48	42	11	1	12	.262
Pagan, Pittsburgh	32	35	9	0	6	.257
Marshall, New York	50	44	11	2	4	.250
Ferrara, San Diego	44	36	9	0	3	.250
Swoboda, New York	26	20	5	1	2	.250
Webster, San Diego	80	70	17	1	6	.243
Beauchamp, Hou-St.L.	43	37	9	1	4	.243
Sudakis, Los Angeles	26	21	5	1	7	.238
Joshua, Los Angeles	22	21	5	0	1	.238
Lee, St. Louis	46	38	9	0	6	.237
Lampard, Houston	43	38	9	0	3	.237
Martinez, Houston	30	38	9	0	3	.237
King, Atlanta	30	26	6	0	3	.231
Hutto, Philadelphia	28	26	6	2	6	.231
Day, Chi-Mont	14	13	3	0	0	.231
Campbell, St. Louis	13	13	3	0	1	.231
Clendenon, New York	25	22	5	1	8	.227
Smith, Chicago	46	40	9	1	7	.225
Browne, Philadelphia	25	18	4	0	2	.222
Singleton, New York	20	18	4	0	1	.222
Taylor, San Francisco	36	28	6	1	6	.214
Burda, San Francisco	19	14	3	0	3	.214
Stephenson, San Fran.	15	14	3	0	3	.214
Stahl, San Diego	33	33	7	0	3	.212
Gabrielson, Los Ang	40	38	8	0	6	.211
Brand, Montreal	39	35	7	0	4	.200
Crawford, Los Angeles	20	15	3	0	1	.200
Mays, San Francisco	13	10	2	0	0	.200
Rojas, St. Louis	10	10	2	0	1	.200
Gagliano, St. L-Chi	17	16	3	0	3	.188
Aspromonte, Atl	29	27	5	0	2	.185
Spangler, Chicago	14	11	2	1	1	.182
Shamsky, New York	13	11	2	0	1	.182
Alou, Houston	11	11	2	0	1	.182
Lefebvre, Los Angeles	24	17	3	0	1	.176
Stone, Philadelphia	30	23	4	0	6	.174
Sutherland, Mont	25	23	4	1	2	.174
Murrell, San Diego	24	24	4	1	3	.167
Phillips, Montreal	25	18	3	0	1	.167
Staehle, Montreal	19	13	2	0	0	.154
Hall, Chi-Atl	30	29	4	1	2	.138
Jorgensen, New York	18	15	2	0	0	.133
Kranepool, New York	36	31	4	0	2	.129
Gosger, Los Angeles	19	16	2	0	0	.125
T. Aaron, Atlanta	17	16	2	0	0	.125
Gosger, Montreal	14	10	1	0	1	.100
Garr, Atlanta	11	10	1	0	0	.100
Kelly, San Diego	15	11	1	0	1	.091
Popovich, Chicago	28	26	2	0	1	.077
Mason, San Francisco	23	20	1	0	0	.050

NATIONAL LEAGUE CLUB PINCH-HITTING

Club	AB.	H.	HR.	RBI.	Pct.
St. Louis	273	82	5	58	.300
Pittsburgh	164	49	1	26	.299
Cincinnati	167	46	3	26	.275
Houston	181	47	6	25	.260
Montreal	274	70	6	32	.255
Los Angeles	204	50	3	37	.245
Philadelphia	206	50	6	41	.243
San Francisco	203	46	4	36	.227
Atlanta	155	35	1	12	.226
San Diego	232	49	3	22	.211
New York	196	38	4	22	.194
Chicago	151	24	3	17	.159
Totals	2406	586	45	354	.244

AMERICAN LEAGUE CLUB PINCH-HITTING

Club	AB.	H.	HR.	RBI.	Pct.
Chicago	226	55	2	26	.243
Detroit	224	54	3	36	.241
Oakland	194	46	8	28	.237
Minnesota	194	46	6	42	.237
Milwaukee	284	65	5	27	.229
New York	172	39	5	36	.227
Baltimore	161	35	1	13	.217
Cleveland	237	46	9	28	.194
California	237	45	2	28	.190
Kansas City	196	35	1	16	.179
Boston	146	26	2	11	.178
Washington	271	45	5	28	.166
Totals	2542	537	49	319	.211

The Sporting News AWARDS
THE SPORTING NEWS MVP AWARDS

AMERICAN LEAGUE				NATIONAL LEAGUE		
Year	Player	Club	Points	Player	Club	Points
1929	Al Simmons, Philadelphia, of ..		40	No selection		
1930	Joseph Cronin, Washington, ss		52	William Terry, New York, 1b		47
1931	H. Louis Gehrig, New York, 1b		40	Charles Klein, Philadelphia, of		40
1932	James Foxx, Philadelphia, 1b....		56	Charles Klein, Philadelphia, of		46
1933	James Foxx, Philadelphia, 1b		49	Carl Hubbell, New York, p		64
1934	H. Louis Gehrig, New York, 1b		51	Jerome Dean, St. Louis, p		57
1935	Henry Greenberg, Detroit, 1b ..		64	J. Floyd Vaughan, Pitts., ss		42
1936	H. Louis Gehrig, New York, 1b		55	Carl Hubbell, New York, p		61
1937	Charles Gehringer, Detroit, 2b		78	Joseph Medwick, St. Louis, of		70
1938	James Foxx, Boston, 1b		305	Ernest Lombardi, Cincinnati, c ...229		
1939	Joseph DiMaggio, N. York, of ..280			William Walters, Cincinnati, p ...303		
1940	Henry Greenberg, Detroit, of ..292			Frank McCormick, Cinn., 1b 274		
1941	Joseph DiMaggio, N. York, of ..291			Adolph Camilli, Brooklyn, 1b 300		
1942	Joseph Gordon, New York, 2b ..270			Morton Cooper, St. Louis, p........263		
1943	Spurgeon Chandler, N. Y., p ..246			Stanley Musial, St. Louis, of 267		
1944	Robert Doerr, Boston, 2b			Martin Marion, St. Louis, ss		
1945	Edward J. Mayo, Detroit, 2b			Thomas Holmes, Boston, of		

THE SPORTING NEWS PLAYER, PITCHER OF YEAR

1948—Louis Boudreau, Cleveland, ss Robert Lemon, Cleveland, p	1948—Stanley Musial, St. Louis, of-1b John Sain, Boston, p
1949—Theodore Williams, Boston, of Ellis Kinder, Boston, p	1949—Enos Slaughter, St. Louis, of Howard Pollet, St. Louis, p
1950—Philip Rizzuto, New York, ss Robert Lemon, Cleveland, p	1950—Ralph Kiner, Pittsburgh, of C. James Konstanty, Phila., p
1951—Ferris Fain, Philadelphia, 1b Robert Feller, Cleveland, p	1951—Stanley Musial, St. Louis, of Elwin Roe, Brooklyn, p
1952—Luscious Easter, Cleveland, 1b Robert Shantz, Philadelphia, p	1952—Henry Sauer, Chicago, of Robin Roberts, Philadelphia, p
1953—Albert Rosen, Cleveland, 3b Erv (Bob) Porterfield, Wash., p	1953—Roy Campanella, Brooklyn, c Warren Spahn, Milwaukee, p
1954—Roberto Avila, Cleveland, 2b Robert Lemon, Cleveland, p	1954—Willie Mays, New York, of John Antonelli, New York, p
1955—Albert Kaline, Detroit, of Edward Ford, New York, p	1955—Edwin Snider, Brooklyn, of Robin Roberts, Philadelphia, p
1956—Mickey Mantle, New York, of W. William Pierce, Chicago, p	1956—Henry Aaron, Milwaukee, of Donald Newcombe, Brooklyn, p
1957—Theodore Williams, Boston, of W. William Pierce, Chicago, p	1957—Stanley Musial, St. Louis, 1b Warren Spahn, Milwaukee, p
1958—Jack Jensen, Boston, of Robert Turley, New York, p	1958—Ernest Banks, Chicago, ss Warren Spahn, Milwaukee, p
1959—J. Nelson Fox, Chicago, 2b Early Wynn, Chicago, p	1959—Ernest Banks, Chicago, ss Samuel Jones, San Francisco, p
1960—Roger Maris, New York, of Charles Estrada, Baltimore, p	1960—Richard Groat, Pittsburgh, ss Vernon Law, Pittsburgh, p
1961—Roger Maris, New York, of Edward Ford, New York, p	1961—Frank Robinson, Cincinnati, of Warren Spahn, Milwaukee, p
1962—Mickey Mantle, New York, of Richard Donovan, Cleveland, p	1962—Maurice Wills, Los Angeles, ss Donald Drysdale, Los Angeles, p
1963—Albert Kaline, Detroit, of Edward Ford, New York, p	1963—Henry Aaron, Milwaukee, of Sanford Koufax, Los Angeles, p
1964—Brooks Robinson, Baltimore, 3b Dean Chance, Los Angeles, p	1964—Kenton Boyer, St. Louis, 3b Sanford Koufax, Los Angeles, p
1965—Pedro (Tony) Oliva, Minn., of James Grant, Minnesota, p	1965—Willie Mays, San Francisco, of Sanford Koufax, Los Angeles, p
1966—Frank Robinson, Baltimore, of James Kaat, Minnesota, p	1966—Roberto Clemente, Pittsburgh, of Sanford Koufax, Los Angeles, p
1967—Carl Yastrzemski, Boston, of Jim Lonborg, Boston, p	1967—Orlando Cepeda, St. Louis, 1b Mike McCormick, San Fran. p
1968—Ken Harrelson, Boston, of Denny McLain, Detroit, p	1968—Pete Rose, Cincinnati, of Bob Gibson, St. Louis, p

PLAYER, PITCHER OF YEAR—Continued

1969—Harmon Killebrew, Minn., 1b-3b
    Denny McLain, Detroit, p
1970—Harmon Killebrew, Minn., 3b
    Sam McDowell, Cleveland, p

1969—Willie McCovey, San Fran., 1b
    Tom Seaver, New York, p
1970—Johnny Bench, Cin., c
    Bob Gibson, St. Louis, p

THE SPORTING NEWS ROOKIE AWARDS

1946—Combined selection—Delmer Ennis, Philadelphia, N. L., of
1947—Combined selection—Jack Robinson, Brooklyn, 1b
1948—Combined selection—Richie Ashburn, Philadelphia, N. L., of

	AMERICAN LEAGUE		NATIONAL LEAGUE	
Year	Player	Club	Player	Club
1949	Roy Sievers, St. Louis, of		Donald Newcombe, Brooklyn, p	
1950	Combined selection—Edward Ford, New York, A. L., p			
1951	Orestes Minoso, Chicago, of		Willie Mays, New York, of	
1952	Clinton Courtney, St. Louis, c		Joseph Black, Brooklyn, p	
1953	Harvey Kuenn, Detroit, ss		James Gilliam, Brooklyn, 2b	
1954	Robert Grim, New York, p		Wallace Moon, St. Louis, of	
1955	Herbert Score, Cleveland, p		William Virdon, St. Louis, of	
1956	Luis Aparicio, Chicago, ss		Frank Robinson, Cincinnati, of	
1957	Anthony Kubek, New York, inf-of		Edward Bouchee, Philadelphia, 1b	
	(No pitcher named)		Jack Sanford, Philadelphia, p	
1958	Albert Pearson, Washington, of		Orlando Cepeda, San Francisco, 1b	
	Ryne Duren, New York, p		Carlton Willey, Milwaukee, p	
1959	W. Robert Allison, Washington, of		Willie McCovey, San Francisco, 1b	
1960	Ronald Hansen, Baltimore, ss		Frank Howard, Los Angeles, of	
1961	Richard Howser, Kansas City, ss		Billy Williams, Chicago, of	
	Donald Schwall, Boston, p		Kenneth Hunt, Cincinnati, p	
1962	Thomas Tresh, New York, of-ss		Kenneth Hubbs, Chicago, 2b	
1963	Peter Ward, Chicago, 3b		Peter Rose, Cincinnati, 2b	
	Gary Peters, Chicago, p		Raymond Culp, Philadelphia, p	
1964	Pedro (Tony) Oliva, Minn., of		Richard Allen, Philadelphia, 3b	
	Wallace Bunker, Baltimore, p		William McCool, Cincinnati, p	
1965	Curtis Blefary, Baltimore, of		Joseph Morgan, Houston, 2b	
	Marcelino Lopez, California, p		Frank Linzy, San Francisco, p	
1966	Tommie Agee, Chicago, of		Tommy Helms, Cincinnati, 3b	
	James Nash, Kansas City, p		Donald Sutton, Los Angeles, p	
1967	Rod Carew, Minnesota, 2b		Lee May, Cincinnati, 1b	
	Tom Phoebus, Baltimore, p		Dick Hughes, St. Louis, p	
1968	Del Unser, Washington, of		Johnny Bench, Cincinnati, c	
	Stan Bahnsen, New York, p		Jerry Koosman, New York, p	
1969	Carlos May, Chicago, of		Coco Laboy, Montreal, 3b	
	Mike Nagy, Boston, p		Tom Griffin, Houston, p	
1970	Roy Foster, Cleveland, of		Bernie Carbo, Cincinnati, of	
	Bert Blyleven, Minnesota, p		Carl Morton, Montreal, p	

MAJOR LEAGUE EXECUTIVE

Year	Executive	Club	Year	Executive	Club
1936	Branch Rickey, St. Louis NL		1954	Horace Stoneham, N. York NL	
1937	Edward Barrow, New York AL		1955	Walter O'Malley, Brooklyn NL	
1938	Warren Giles, Cincinnati NL		1956	Gabe Paul, Cincinnati NL	
1939	Larry MacPhail, Brooklyn NL		1957	Frank Lane, St. Louis NL	
1940	W. O. Briggs, Sr., Detroit AL		1958	Joe L. Brown, Pittsburgh NL	
1941	Edward Barrow, New York AL		1959	E. J. (Buzzie) Bavasi, L. A. NL	
1942	Branch Rickey, St. Louis NL		1960	George Weiss, New York AL	
1943	Clark Griffith, Washington		1961	Dan Topping, New York AL	
1944	Wm. O. DeWitt, St. Louis AL		1962	Fred Haney, Los Angeles AL	
1945	Philip K. Wrigley, Chicago NL		1963	Vaughan (Bing) Devine, St. L. NL	
1946	Thomas A. Yawkey, Boston AL		1964	Vaughan (Bing) Devine, St. L. NL	
1947	Branch Rickey, Brooklyn NL		1965	Calvin Griffith, Minnesota AL	
1948	Bill Veeck, Cleveland AL		1966	Lee MacPhail, Commissioner's	
1949	Robt. Carpenter, Phila'phia NL			Office	
1950	George Weiss, New York AL		1967	Dick O'Connell, Boston AL	
1951	George Weiss, New York AL		1968	James Campbell, Detroit AL	
1952	George Weiss, New York AL		1969	John Murphy, New York NL	
1953	Louis Perini, Milwaukee NL		1970	Harry Dalton, Baltimore AL	

MAJOR LEAGUE MANAGER

Year	Manager	Club
1936	Joe McCarthy, New York AL	
1937	Bill McKechnie, Boston NL	
1938	Joe McCarthy, New York AL	
1939	Leo Durocher, Brooklyn NL	
1940	Bill McKechnie, Cincinnati NL	
1941	Billy Southworth, St. Louis NL	
1942	Billy Southworth, St. Louis NL	
1943	Joe McCarthy, New York AL	
1944	Luke Sewell, St. Louis AL	
1945	Ossie Bluege, Washington AL	
1946	Eddie Dyer, St. Louis NL	
1947	Bucky Harris, New York AL	
1948	Bill Meyer, Pittsburgh NL	
1949	Casey Stengel, New York AL	
1950	Red Rolfe, Detroit AL	
1951	Leo Durocher, New York NL	
1952	Eddie Stanky, St. Louis NL	
1953	Casey Stengel, New York AL	
1954	Leo Durocher, New York NL	
1955	Walter Alston, Brooklyn NL	
1956	Birdie Tebbetts, Cincinnati NL	
1957	Fred Hutchinson, St. Louis NL	
1958	Casey Stengel, New York AL	
1959	Walter Alston, Los Angeles NL	
1960	Danny Murtaugh, Pitts. NL	
1961	Ralph Houk, New York AL	
1962	Bill Rigney, Los Angeles AL	
1963	Walter Alston, Los Angeles NL	
1964	Johnny Keane, St. Louis NL	
1965	Sam Mele, Minnesota AL	
1966	Hank Bauer, Baltimore AL	
1967	Dick Williams, Boston AL	
1968	Mayo Smith, Detroit AL	
1969	Gil Hodges, New York NL	
1970	Danny Murtaugh, Pittsburgh NL	

MAJOR LEAGUE PLAYER

Year	Player	Club
1936	Carl Hubbell, New York NL	
1937	Johnny Allen, Cleveland AL	
1938	Johnny Vander Meer, Cinn. NL	
1939	Joe DiMaggio, New York AL	
1940	Bob Feller, Cleveland AL	
1941	Ted Williams, Boston AL	
1942	Ted Williams, Boston AL	
1943	Spud Chandler, New York AL	
1944	Marty Marion, St. Louis NL	
1945	Hal Newhouser, Detroit AL	
1946	Stan Musial, St. Louis NL	
1947	Ted Williams, Boston AL	
1948	Lou Boudreau, Cleveland AL	
1949	Ted Williams, Boston AL	
1950	Phil Rizzuto, New York AL	
1951	Stan Musial, St. Louis NL	
1952	Robin Roberts, Philadelphia NL	
1953	Al Rosen, Cleveland AL	
1954	Willie Mays, New York NL	
1955	Duke Snider, Brooklyn NL	
1956	Mickey Mantle, New York AL	
1957	Ted Williams, Boston AL	
1958	Bob Turley, New York AL	
1959	Early Wynn, Chicago AL	
1960	Bill Mazeroski, Pittsburgh NL	
1961	Roger Maris, New York AL	
1962	Maury Wills, Los Angeles NL	
	Don Drysdale, Los Angeles NL	
1963	Sandy Koufax, Los Angeles NL	
1964	Ken Boyer, St. Louis NL	
1965	Sandy Koufax, Los Angeles NL	
1966	Frank Robinson, Baltimore AL	
1967	Carl Yastrzemski, Boston AL	
1968	Denny McLain, Detroit AL	
1969	Willie McCovey, San Fran. NL	
1970	Johnny Bench, Cin. NL	

MINOR LEAGUE EXECUTIVE (HIGHER CLASSIFICATIONS)

(Restricted to Class AAA Starting in 1963)

Year	Executive	Club
1936	Earl Mann, Atlanta, Southern	
1937	Robt. LaMotte, Savannah, Sally	
1938	Louis McKenna, St. Paul, A.A.	
1939	Bruce Dudley, Louisville, A.A.	
1940	Roy Hamey, Kansas City, A.A.	
1941	Emil Sick, Seattle, PCL	
1942	Bill Veeck, Milwaukee, A.A.	
1943	Clar. Rowland, Los Angeles, PCL	
1944	William Mulligan, Seattle, PCL	
1945	Bruce Dudley, Louisville, A.A.	
1946	Earl Mann, Atlanta, Southern	
1947	Wm. Purnhage, Waterloo, Midw.	
1948	Ed. Glennon, Bir'ham, Southern	
1949	Ted Sullivan, Indianapolis, A.A.	
1950	Cl. (Brick) Laws, Oakland, PCL	
1951	Robert Howsam, Denver, West.	
1952	Jack Cooke, Toronto, Int.	
1953	Richard Burnett, Dallas, Texas	
1954	Edward Stumpf, Indpls., A.A.	
1955	Dewey Soriano, Seattle, PCL	
1956	Robert Howsam, Denver, A.A.	
1957	John Stiglmeier, Buffalo, Int.	
1958	Ed. Glennon, Bir'ham, Southern	
1959	Ed Leishman, Salt Lake, PCL	
1960	Ray Winder, Little R., Southern	
1961	Elten Schiller, Omaha, A.A.	
1962	George Sisler, Rochester, Int.	
1963	Lewis Matlin, Hawaii, PCL	
1964	Ed. Leishman, San Diego, PCL	
1965	Harold Cooper, Columbus, Int.	
1966	John Quinn, Jr., Hawaii, PCL	
1967	Hillman Lyons, Richmond, Int.	
1968	Gabe Paul, Jr., Tulsa, PCL	
1969	Bill Gardner, Louisville, Int.	
1970	Dick King, Wichita, A.A.	

MINOR LEAGUE EXECUTIVE (LOWER CLASSIFICATIONS)

(Separate Awards for Class AA and Class A Started in 1963)

Year	Executive	Club
1950—H. Cooper, Hutch'son, West. A.
1951—O. W. (Bill) Hayes, T'ple, B.S.
1952—Hillman Lyons, Danville, MOV
1953—Carl Roth, Peoria, III
1954—James Meaghan, Cedar R., III
1955—John Petrakis, Dubuque, MOV
1956—Marvin Milkes, Fresno, Calif.
1957—Richard Wagner, L'coln, West.
1958—Gerald Waring, Macon, Sally
1959—Clay Dennis, Des Moines, III
1960—Hubert Kittle, Yakima, Northw.
1961—David Steele, Fresno, California
1962—John Quinn, Jr., S. Jose, Calif.
1963—Hugh Finnerty, Tulsa, Texas
Ben Jewell, M. Valley, Pioneer

Year	Executive	Club
1964—Glynn West, B'ham, Southern
Jas. Bayens, Rock Hill, W. Car.
1965—Dick Butler, Dallas-Ft.W., Tex.
Ken. Blackman, Quad C., Midw.
1966—Tom Fleming, Evansville, South.
Cappy Harada, Lodi, California
1967—Robt. Quinn, Reading, East.
Pat Williams, Spar'burg, W. C.
1968—Phil Howser, Charlotte, South.
Merle Miller, Burlington, Midw.
1969—Charlie Blaney, Albuq., Tex.
Bill Gorman, Visalia, Calif.
1970—Carl Sawatski, Arkansas, Tex.
Bob Williams, Bakersfield, Calif.

MINOR LEAGUE MANAGER

Year	Manager	Club
1936—Al Sothoron, Milwaukee, A.A.
1937—Jake Flowers, Salis'y, East. Sh.
1938—Paul Richards, Atlanta, South.
1939—Bill Meyer, Kansas City, A.A.
1940—Larry Gilbert, Nashville, South.
1941—Burt Shotton, Columbus, A.A.
1942—Eddie Dyer, Columbus, A.A.
1943—Nick Cullop, Columbus, A.A.
1944—Al Thomas, Baltimore, Int.
1945—Lefty O'Doul, San Fran., PCL
1946—Clay Hopper, Montreal, Int.
1947—Nick Cullop, Milwaukee, A.A.
1948—Casey Stengel, Oakland, PCL
1949—Fred Haney, Hollywood, PCL
1950—Rollie Hemsley, Columbus, A.A.
1951—Charlie Grimm, Milw., A.A.
1952—Luke Appling, Memphis, South.

Year	Manager	Club
1953—Bobby Bragan, Hollywood, PCL
1954—Kerby Farrell, Indpls., A.A.
1955—Bill Rigney, Minneapolis, A.A.
1956—Kerby Farrell, Indpls., A.A.
1957—Ben Geraghty, Wichita, A.A.
1958—Cal Ermer, Birmingham, South.
1959—Pete Reiser, Victoria, Texas
1960—Mel McGaha, Toronto, Int.
1961—Kerby Farrell, Buffalo, Int.
1962—Ben Geraghty, Jackson'le., Int.
1963—Rollie Hemsley, Indpls., Int.
1964—Harry Walker, Jacks'vle., Int.
1965—Grady Hatton, Okla. City, PCL
1966—Bob Lemon, Seattle, PCL
1967—Bob Skinner, San Diego, PCL
1968—Jack Tighe, Toledo, Int.
1969—Clyde McCullough, Tide., Int.
1970—Tom Lasorda, Spokane, PCL

MINOR LEAGUE PLAYER

Year	Player	Club
1936—Jn. Vander Meer Durham, Pied.
1937—Charlie Keller, Newark, Int.
1938—Fred Hutchinson, Seattle, PCL
1939—Lou Novikoff, Tulsa-Los A'les.
1940—Phil Rizzuto, Kansas City, A.A.
1941—John Lindell, Newark, Int.
1942—Dick Barrett, Seattle, PCL
1943—Chet Covington, Scranton, East.
1944—Rip Collins, Albany, Eastern
1945—Gil Coan, Chattanooga, South.
1946—Sibby Sisti, Indianapolis, A. A.
1947—Hank Sauer, Syracuse, Int.
1948—Gene Woodling, S. F., PCL
1949—Orie Arntzen, Albany, Eastern
1950—Frank Saucier, San Ant'o, Tex.
1951—Gene Conley, Hartford, Eastern
1952—Bill Skowron, Kans. City, A.A.

Year	Player	Club
1953—Gene Conley, Toledo, A.A.
1954—Herb Score, Indianapolis, A.A.
1955—John Murff, Dallas, Texas
1956—Steve Bilko, Los Angeles, PCL
1957—Norm Siebern, Denver, A.A.
1958—Jim O'Toole, Nashville, South.
1959—Frank Howard, Victoria-Spok.
1960—Willie Davis, Spokane, PCL
1961—Howie Koplitz, Bir'ham, South.
1962—Bob Bailey, Columbus, Int.
1963—Don Buford, Indianapolis, Int.
1964—Mel Stottlemyre, Richm'd., Int.
1965—Joe Foy, Toronto, International
1966—Mike Epstein, Rochester, Int.
1967—John Bench, Buffalo, Int.
1968—Merv Rettenmund, Roch'ter, Int.
1969—Danny Walton, Okla. City, A.A.
1970—Don Baylor, Rochester, Int.

BASEBALL WRITERS' ASSOCIATION AWARDS
Most Valuable Player Citations

CHALMERS AWARD

AMERICAN LEAGUE			NATIONAL LEAGUE		
Year	Player Club	Points	Player Club		Points
1911	Tyrus Cobb, Detroit, of	64	Frank Schulte, Chicago, of		29
1912	Tristram Speaker, Boston, of	59	Lawrence Doyle, N. Y., 2b		48
1913	Walter Johnson, Washington, p	54	Jacob Daubert, Brooklyn, 1b		50
1914	Edward Collins, Phila., 2b	63	John Evers, Boston, 2b		50

LEAGUE AWARDS

AMERICAN LEAGUE			NATIONAL LEAGUE		
Year	Player Club	Points	Player Club		Points
1922	George Sisler, St. Louis, 1b	59	No selection		
1923	George Ruth, New York, of	64	No selection		
1924	Walter Johnson, Washington, p	55	Arthur Vance, Brooklyn, p		74
1925	Roger Peckinpaugh, Wash., ss	45	Rogers Hornsby, St. Louis, 2b		73
1926	George Burns, Cleveland, 1b	63	Robert O'Farrell, St. Louis, c		79
1927	H. Louis Gehrig, New York, 1b	56	Paul Waner, Pittsburgh, of		72
1928	Gordon Cochrane, Phila., c	53	James Bottomley, St. Louis, 1b		76
1929	No selection		Rogers Hornsby, Chicago, 2b		60

BASEBALL WRITERS' ASSOCIATION MVP AWARDS

AMERICAN LEAGUE			NATIONAL LEAGUE		
Year	Player Club	Points	Player Club		Points
1931	Robert Grove, Philadelphia, p	78	Frank Frisch, St. Louis, 2b		65
1932	James Foxx, Philadelphia, 1b	75	Charles Klein, Phila., of		78
1933	James Foxx, Philadelphia, 1b	74	Carl Hubbell, New York, p		77
1934	Gordon Cochrane, Detroit, c	67	Jerome Dean, St. Louis, p		78
1935	Henry Greenberg, Detroit, 1b	*80	Charles Hartnett, Chicago, c		75
1936	H. Louis Gehrig, New York, 1b	73	Carl Hubbell, New York, p		60
1937	Charles Gehringer, Detroit, 2b	78	Joseph Medwick, St. Louis, of		70
1938	James Foxx, Boston, 1b	305	Ernest Lombardi, Cinn., c		229
1939	Joseph DiMaggio, N. York, of	280	William Walters, Cinn., p		303
1940	Henry Greenberg, Detroit, of	292	Frank McCormick, Cinn., 1b		274
1941	Joseph DiMaggio, N. York, of	291	Adolph Camilli, Brooklyn, 1b		300
1942	Joseph Gordon, New York, 2b	270	Morton Cooper, St. Louis, p		263
1943	Spurgeon Chandler, N. Y., p	246	Stanley Musial, St. Louis, of		267
1944	Harold Newhouser, Detroit, p	236	Martin Marion, St. Louis, ss		190
1945	Harold Newhouser, Detroit, p	236	Philip Cavarretta, Chicago, 1b		279
1946	Theodore Williams, Boston, of	224	Stanley Musial, St. Louis, 1b		319
1947	Joseph DiMaggio, N. York, of	202	Robert Elliott, Boston, 3b		205
1948	Louis Boudreau, Cleveland, ss	324	Stanley Musial, St. Louis, of		303
1949	Theodore Williams, Boston, of	272	Jack Robinson, Brooklyn, 2b		264
1950	Philip Rizzuto, New York, ss	284	C. James Konstanty, Phila., p		286
1951	Lawrence Berra, New York, c	184	Roy Campanella, Brooklyn, c		243
1952	Robert Shantz, Phila., p	280	Henry Sauer, Chicago, of		226
1953	Albert Rosen, Cleveland, 3b	*336	Roy Campanella, Brooklyn, c		297

BASEBALL WRITERS' ASSOCIATION MVP AWARDS—Cont.

AMERICAN LEAGUE			NATIONAL LEAGUE		
Year	Player Club	Points	Player Club		Points
1954	Lawrence Berra, New York, c	230	Willie Mays, New York, of		283
1955	Lawrence Berra, New York, c	218	Roy Campanella, Brooklyn, c		226
1956	Mickey Mantle, N. Y., of	*336	Donald Newcombe, Brkn., p		223
1957	Mickey Mantle, New York, of	233	Henry Aaron, Milwaukee, of		239
1958	Jack Jensen, Boston, of	233	Ernest Banks, Chicago, ss		283
1959	J. Nelson Fox, Chicago, 2b	295	Ernest Banks, Chicago, ss		232½
1960	Roger Maris, New York, of	225	Richard Groat, Pittsburgh, ss		276
1961	Roger Maris, New York, of	202	Frank Robinson, Cinn., of		219
1962	Mickey Mantle, New York, of	234	Maurice Wills, Los Angeles, ss		209
1963	Elston Howard, New York, c	248	Sanford Koufax, Los Ang., p		237
1964	Brooks Robinson, Balti., 3b	269	Kenton Boyer, St. Louis, 3b		243
1965	Zoilo Versalles, Minn., ss	275	Willie Mays, San Francisco, of		224
1966	Frank Robinson, Balti., of	*280	Roberto Clemente, Pitts., of		218
1967	Carl Yastrzemski, Boston, of	275	Orlando Cepeda, St. Louis, 1b		*280
1968	Dennis McLain, Detroit, p	*280	Robert Gibson, St. Louis, p		242
1969	Harmon Killebrew, Minn., 1-3b	294	Willie McCovey, San Fran., 1b		265
1970	John (Boog) Powell, Balti., 1b	234	Johnny Bench, Cincinnati, c		326

*Unanimous selection.

BASEBALL WRITERS' ASSOCIATION ROOKIE AWARDS

1947—Combined selection—Jack Robinson, Brooklyn, 1b.
1948—Combined selection—Alvin Dark, Boston, N. L., ss.

AMERICAN LEAGUE			NATIONAL LEAGUE		
Year	Player Club	Points	Player Club		Votes
1949	Roy Sievers, St. Louis, of	10	Donald Newcombe, Brklyn., p		21
1950	Walter Dropo, Boston, 1b	15	Samuel Jethroe, Boston, of		11
1951	Gilbert McDougald, N. Y., 3b	13	Willie Mays, New York, of		18
1952	Harry Byrd, Philadelphia, p	9	Joseph Black, Brooklyn, p		19
1953	Harvey Kuenn, Detroit, ss	23	James Gilliam, Brooklyn, 2b		11
1954	Robert Grim, New York, p	15	Wallace Moon, St. Louis, of		17
1955	Herbert Score, Cleveland, p	18	William Virdon, St. Louis, of		15
1956	Luis Aparicio, Chicago, ss	22	Frank Robinson, Cinn., of		*24
1957	Anthony Kubek, N. Y., inf-of	23	John Sanford, Philadelphia, p		16
1958	Albert Pearson, Washington, of	14	Orlando Cepeda, San Fran., 1b		*†21
1959	W. Robert Allison, Wash., of	18	Willie McCovey, San Fran., 1b		*24
1960	Ronald Hensen, Baltimore, ss	22	Frank Howard, Los Angeles, of		12
1961	Donald Schwall, Boston, p	7	Billy Williams, Chicago, of		10
1962	Thomas Tresh, New York, of-ss	13	Kenneth Hubbs, Chicago, 2b		19
1963	Gary Peters, Chicago, p	10	Peter Rose, Cincinnati, 2b		17
1964	Pedro (Tony) Oliva, Minn., of	19	Richard Allen, Philadelphia, 3b		18
1965	Curtis Blefary, Baltimore, of	12	James Lefebvre, Los Ang., 2b		13
1966	Tommie Agee, Chicago, of	16	Tommy Helms, Cincinnati, 3b		12
1967	Rod Carew, Minnesota, 2b	19	Tom Seaver, New York, p		11
1968	Stan Bahnsen, New York, p	17	Johnny Bench, Cincinnati, c		10½
1969	Lou Piniella, Kansas City, of	9	Ted Sizemore, Los Angeles, 2b		14
1970	Thurman Munson, N. Y., c	23	Carl Morton, Montreal, p		11

*Unanimous selection. †Three writers did not vote.

CY YOUNG MEMORIAL AWARD

Year	Pitcher Club	Votes	Year	Pitcher Club	Votes
1956	Donald Newcombe, Brooklyn	10	1966	Sanford Koufax, L. A., N. L.	*20
1957	Warren Spahn, Milwaukee	15	1967	A. L.—Jim Lonborg, Boston	18
1958	Robert Turley, N. Y., A. L.	5		N. L.—M. McCormick, S. F.	18
1959	Early Wynn, Chicago, A. L.	13	1968	A. L.—Dennis McLain, Det.	*20
1960	Vernon Law, Pittsburgh	8		N. L.—Robert Gibson, St. L.	*20
1961	Edward Ford, N. Y., A. L.	9	1969	A. L.—Dennis McLain, Det.	10
1962	Donald Drysdale, L. A., N. L.	14		Mike Cuellar, Balt.	10
1963	Sanford Koufax, L. A., N. L.	*20		N. L.—Tom Seaver, N. Y.	23
1964	Dean Chance, L. A., A. L.	17	1970	A. L.—Jim Perry, Minn.	†55
1965	Sanford Koufax, L. A., N. L.	*20		N. L.—Bob Gibson, St. L.	†118

*Unanimous selection. †Point system used.

Vets' Seven Save Cooperstown Show

The 1971 voting on Hall of Fame candidates by qualified members of the Baseball Writers' Association of America drew the largest number of ballots ever cast, but they failed to elect a single player. Yogi Berra, catcher of the Yankees and a first-time eligible, was the closest with 242 votes out of 360 cast. He was 28 shy of the required 270, or 75 percent.

However, the Committee on Veterans, doubtless conscious that there would be no live bodies at Cooperstown, added seven to the rolls.

Originally planning to examine the pre-1900 acients for the purpose of naming, once and for all, whatever eligibles remained un-Shrined from baseball's gaslight era, a change in plans was apparent when the committee expanded its concept of "old-timers" to include players who competed as late as 1925. From this category, they named first baseman Jake Beckley, outfielder Joe Kelley, both pre-1900 players, and outfielder Harry Hooper and pitcher Rube Marquard, both of whom competed until 1925. The more modern ones added included outfielder Chick Hafey, short-stop Davey Bancroft and Yankee executive George Weiss.

Five of the seven electees were living at the time of their election January 31. Only Beckley and Kelley were deceased.

Beckley, whose election was long overdue, still holds the major league records for first basemen in most games played, most putouts, most chances accepted and is tied for the major league lead with Bill Terry for most years leading majors in chances accepted. He batted .309 and had 2,930 hits. Kelley, also a major league manager, coach and scout, had a .321 lifetime major league batting average and had 458 stolen bases.

Harry Hooper, the third member of the famed Tris Speaker and Duffy Lewis, Boston outfield combination, had an exceptional arm with 344 assists, was a consistent batter with 2,466 hits in 2308 games and batted .281 for his big-time career. Marquard, who had 201 victories as a Giant, Dodger, Red and Brave, was most remembered for his 1912 season, when he won 26 games, with 19 of them coming in succession. He also pitched a no-hitter against Brooklyn, April 15, 1915.

Chick Hafey, a bespectacled fielding demon with a powerful arm, had a lifetime .317 batting average, and Davey Bancroft, who also was called "Beauty" by his confreres, was a long-time shortstop with the Braves, Phillies, Dodgers and Giants. He consistently led in putouts, assists and total chances, including the major mark of 984 chances accepted in 1922.

Weiss, a long-time Yankee farm director, became general manager of the major league club in 1947, hired Casey Stengel and they both rode high, wide and handsome via pennants all the way to Cooperstown.

Following is a complete list of those enshrined in the Hall of Fame prior to 1971, with the vote by which each was elected:

1936—Tyrus Cobb (222), John (Honus) Wagner (215), George (Babe) Ruth (215), Christy Mathewson (205), Walter Johnson (189), named by Baseball Writers' Association of America. Total ballots cast, (226).

1937—Napoleon Lajoie (168), Tristram Speaker (165), Denton (Cy) Young (153), named by the BBWAA. Total ballots cast, 201. George Wright, Morgan G. Bulkeley, Byron Bancroft Johnson, John J. McGraw, Cornelius McGillicuddy (Connie Mack), named by Centennial Commission.

1938—Grover C. Alexander (212), named by BBWAA. Total ballots, 262.

1971 electees——Top row: Chick Hafey, Rube Marquard, Joe Kelley.
Bottom row: George Weiss, Dave Bancroft, Harry Hooper, Jake Beckley.

Henry Chadwick, Alexander J. Cartwright, named by Centennial Commission.

1939—Geroge Sisler (235), Edward Collins (213), William Keeler (207), Louis Gehrig, named by BBWAA. (Gehrig by special election after retirement from game was announced). Total ballots cast, 274. Albert G. Spalding, Adrian C. Anson, Charles A. Comiskey, William (Buck) Ewing, Charles Radbourn, William A. (Candy) Cummings named by committee of old-time players and writers.

1942—Rogers Hornsby (182) named by BBWAA. Total ballots cast, 233.

1944—Judge Kenesaw M. Landis, named by committee on old timers.

1945—Hugh Duffy, Jimmy Collins, Hugh Jennings, Ed Delahanty, Fred Clarke, Mike Kelly, Wilbert Robinson, Jim O'Rourke, Dennis (Dan) Brouthers and Roger Bresnahan, named by committee on old-timers.

1946—Jesse Burkett, Frank Chance, Jack Chesbro, Johnny Evers, Clark Griffith, Tom McCarthy, Joe McGinnity, Eddie Plank, Joe Tinker, Rube Waddell and Ed Walsh, named by committee on old timers.

1947—Carl Hubbell (140), Frank Frisch (136), Gordon (Mickey) Cochrane (128), and Robert (Lefty) Grove (123), named by BBWAA. Total ballots, 161.

1948—Herbert J. Pennock (94) and Harold (Pie) Traynor (93), named by BBWAA. Total ballots cast, 121.

1949—Charles Gehringer (159), named by BBWAA. Total ballots cast, 187. Charles (Kid) Nichols and Mordecai (Three-Finger) Brown, named by committee on old-timers.

1951—Mel Ott (197) and Jimmie Foxx (179), named by BBWAA. Total ballots cast, 226.

1952—Harry Heilmann (203) and Paul Waner (195), named by BBWAA. Total ballots cast, 234.

1953—Jerome (Dizzy) Dean (209) and Al Simmons (199), named by BBWAA. Total ballots cast, 264. Charles Albert (Chief) Bender, Roderick (Bobby) Wallace, William Klem, Tom Connolly, Edward G. Barrow and William Henry (Harry) Wright, named by the new Committee on Veterans.

1954—Walter (Rabbit) Maranville (209), William Dickey (202) and William Terry (195), named by BBWAA. Total ballots cast, 252.

1955—Joe DiMaggio (223), Ted Lyons (217), Arthur (Dazzy) Vance (205) and Charles (Gabby) Hartnett (195), named by BBWAA. Total ballots cast, 251. J. Franklin (Home Run) Baker and Ray Schalk, named by Committee on Veterans.

1956—Hank Greenberg (164) and Joe Cronin (152), named by BBWAA. Total ballots cast, 193.

1957—Joseph V. McCarthy and Sam Crawford, named by Committee on Veterans.

1959—Zachariah (Zack) Wheat, named by Committee on Veterans.

1961—Max Carey and William Hamilton, named by Committee on Veterans.

1962—Bob Feller (150) and Jackie Robinson (124), named by BBWAA. Total ballots cast, 160. Bill McKechnie and Edd Roush, named by Committee on Veterans.

1963—Eppa Rixey, Edgar (Sam) Rice, Elmer Flick and John Clarkson, named by Committee on Veterans.

1964—Luke Appling (189), named by BBWAA in runoff election. Total ballots cast, 225. Urban (Red) Faber, Burleigh Grimes, Tim Keefe, Heinie Manush, Miller Huggins and John Montgomery Ward, named by Committee on Veterans.

1965—James (Pud) Galvin, named by Committee on Veterans.

1966—Ted Williams (282), named by BBWAA. Total ballots cast, 302. Casey Stengel, named by Committee on Veterans.

1967—Charles (Red) Ruffing (226), named by BBWAA. Total ballots cast, 306. Branch Rickey and Lloyd Waner, named by Committee on Veterans.

1968—Joseph (Ducky) Medwick (240), named by BBWAA. Total ballots cast, 283. Leon (Goose) Goslin and Hazen (Kiki) Cuyler, named by Committee on Veterans.

1969—Stan (The Man) Musial (317) and Roy Campanella (270), named by BBWAA. Total ballots cast, 340. Stan Coveleski and Waite Hoyt, named by Committee on Veterans.

1970—Lou Boudreau (232), named by BBWAA. Total ballots cast, 300. Earle Combs, Jesse Haines and Ford Frick, named by Committee on Veterans.

Only Eight Players Taken in Draft

By LARRY WIGGE

For the past three years, the source of possible steals at the annual winter meetings has diminished to practically nothing. At the 1970 conference of baseball's talent seekers, only eight players were selected by the 24 major league clubs. Of those clubs, only seven participated, and the California Angels were the only interested buyers in the second round. It was estimated that the entire proceedings at the ballroom of the Biltmore Hotel in Los Angeles lasted only 18 minutes.

In the past three years, the entire drafting procedures have consumed a little over an hour in time and have involved 27, 19 and eight players respectively. The primary complaint during this time has been the dilution of talent due to the last expansion.

In 1970, however, a change in the draft rules was cited as another contributing factor to the drop-off. The new rule made it possible for a young player to really show himself to the management by not allowing the majors to draft any such performers under contract for less than three years.

The 1970 assembly marked the least number of players secured via draft on record. The previous low came in 1956, when only nine players were chosen.

By virtue of having the worst record in the National League in 1970, the San Diego Padres were given first choice, and grabbed Bill Laxton, a lefthanded hurler from the Eugene club. Veterans John Stephenson, Fred Lasher and Joe Foy also were among the eight selected for the $25,000 fee.

Minor league drafting suffered as well with only 20 total players being grabbed by 18 of a possible 56 participating Double-A and Triple-A clubs. The cost of these 20 players was $168,000, for men with only limited quality. From that grouping can be found former big leaguers Dan Osinski, Federico Velazquez, Frank Coggins and Julio Gotay.

REGULAR DRAFT

American League: California—Pitcher Fred Lasher from Wichita and catcher John Stephenson from Phoenix; Chicago—Pitcher Alfredo Mariscal from Spokane; Washington—Infielder Joe Foy from Tidewater.

National League: Atlanta—Outfielder Guy Rose from Spokane; Chicago—Pitcher Ron Tompkins from Portland; St. Louis—Outfielder Cecil Cooper from Louisville; San Diego—Pitcher Bill Laxton from Eugene.

Cubs' Deals Fail in Elusive Quest

By CHRIS ROEWE

Only one trade of any consequence was made by major league clubs while the 1970 season was in progress. On April 27 the Angels sent third baseman Aurelio Rodriguez and outfielder Rick Reichardt to the Senators in exchange for third baseman Ken McMullen. Rodriguez played well for his new club but was traded again after the season ended. Both Reichardt and McMullen had disappointing years.

The Cubs spent considerable money buying veteran players in a vain attempt to capture the first-place rung in the National League's East Division. Pitcher Milt Pappas was purchased from the Braves on June 25, first baseman-outfielder Joe Pepitone from the Astros on July 29, pitcher Bob Miller from the White Sox on September 1, outfielder Tommy Davis from the Athletics on September 16 and pitcher Hoyt Wilhelm from the Braves on September 21. The first two acquisitions made significant contributions to the Cubs' down-to-the-wire pennant fight. Pappas won 10 games, including two shutouts, after being installed in the starting rotation. Pepitone was a productive hitter and solved the center field problem that had plagued the Cubs the first half of the season.

Curt Flood, former star National League center fielder, who sat out the entire 1970 campaign while testing Organized Ball's reserve clause in the courts, was induced to return to active play by Bob Short, Washington Senators' owner. The Phillies, to whom Flood technically belonged, agreed to a deal in which they received three minor league players as compensation.

There was a flurry of activity after the season ended. In the biggest trade of the year the Tigers, on October 9, dealt controversial pitching star Denny McLain, third baseman Don Wert, pitcher Norm McRae and third baseman-outfielder Elliott Maddox to the Senators for shortstop Eddie Brinkman, third baseman Aurelio Rodriguez and pitchers Joe Coleman and Jim Hannan.

In other late-season moves, the Cardinals traded slugging first baseman Richie Allen, acquired only the year before from the Phillies, to the Dodgers for infielder Ted Sizemore and catcher Bob Stinson; the Red Sox sent popular outfielder Tony Conigliaro to the Angels in a deal involving six players and traded regular second baseman Mike Andrews and young infielder Luis Alvarado to the White Sox for 36-year-old shortstop Luis Aparicio.

A list of the principal major league transactions of 1970 follows:

January 14—Reds traded pitcher Jack Fisher to Angels for pitcher Bill Harrelson and infielder Dan Loomer, both assigned from Hawaii to Indianapolis.

January 15—Athletics traded catcher Phil Roof, outfielder Mike Hershberger and pitchers Lew Krausse and Ken Sanders (latter assigned from Iowa to Portland) to Brewers for first baseman Don Mincher and third baseman Ron Clark.

February 28—Yankees purchased infielder Ron Hansen from White Sox.

March 9—White Sox acquired pitcher Gerry Janeski from Red Sox as replacement for pitcher Billy Farmer who was included in four-player deal between the two clubs on December 13, 1969 and had announced retirement.

March 21—Senators traded outfielder Brant Alyea to Twins for pitchers Joe Grzenda and Charlie Walters, latter assigned from Evansville to Denver.

March 24—Padres traded infielder Roberto Pena to Athletics for first baseman Ramon Webster.

March 24—Cubs released outfielder Al Spangler who signed with Tacoma as a player-coach; returned to Cubs June 29; released as player and signed as Cub coach September 8.

March 29—Mets traded catcher J. C. Martin to Cubs for catcher Randy Bobb.

March 30—Senators signed pitcher Pedro Ramos, a free agent.

March 30—White Sox traded pitcher Gerry Nyman to Padres for pitcher Tommie Sisk.

March 31—Cardinals released pitcher Ramon Hernandez.

April 1—Brewers released pitcher Stephen D. Barber.

April 2—Cardinals traded shortstop Steve Huntz to Padres for pitcher Billy McCool who was assigned to Tulsa.

April 4—Indians traded third baseman Max Alvis and outfielder Russ Snyder to Brewers for outfielder Roy Foster, infielder Frank Coggins and cash; Coggins was assigned to Wichita.

April 4—Giants purchased catcher Russ Gibson from Red Sox.

April 5—Brewers purchased outfielder Ted Savage from Reds.

April 5—Padres released pitcher Jack Baldschun.

April 6—Expos purchased catcher Jack Hiatt from Giants.

April 6—Senators released shortstop Zoilo Versalles.

April 6—Twins released pitcher Darrell Brandon.

April 7—Angels released pitcher Jack Fisher.

April 8—Phillies acquired first baseman Guillermo Montanez from Cardinals as partial compensation for their loss in the deal of October 7, 1969 in which they obtained outfielder Curt Flood who remained out of baseball for the entire season; Montanez was assigned to Eugene.

April 8—Tigers released outfielder Tom Tresh.

April 8—Expos signed pitcher Ken Johnson, released by Cubs.

April 13—Reds released pitcher Al Jackson.

April 13—Dodgers signed pitcher Camilo Pascual, released by Reds.

April 17—Angels purchased shortstop Ray Oyler from Athletics.

April 20—Braves signed pitcher Dick Farrell, a free agent.

April 20—Expos purchased outfielder Jim Gosger from Giants and assigned him to Buffalo.

April 22—Expos purchased outfielder Jim Qualls from Cubs.

April 23—Cubs signed pitcher Stephen D. Barber, a free agent, and assigned him to Tacoma; placed on Cub roster May 14; released June 30.

April 24—Pirates signed pitcher Al McBean, released by Dodgers.

April 27—Angels traded third baseman Aurelio Rodriguez and outfielder Rick Reichardt to Senators for third baseman Ken McMullen.

April 27—Senators released pitcher Pedro Ramos.

April 28—Expos released pitcher Ken Johnson.

April 30—Braves signed pitcher Ron Kline, a free agent.

May 5—Athletics released pitcher Tony Pierce.

May 6—Braves released pitcher Dick Farrell.

May 11—Brewers traded outfielder Wayne Comer to Senators for outfielder Hank Allen and infielder Ron Theobald, latter assigned from Denver to Indianapolis.

May 12—Royals released second baseman Jerry Adair.

May 12—Cubs traded outfielder Charles (Boots) Day to Expos for catcher Jack Hiatt.

May 13—Indians signed third baseman Rich Rollins, released by Brewers.

May 15—Expos purchased pitcher Rich Nye from Cardinals and assigned him to Buffalo.

May 15—Yankees traded first baseman Dave McDonald to Expos for pitcher Gary Waslewski; McDonald was assigned to Buffalo.

May 16—Angels purchased outfielder Tom Reynolds from Athletics.

May 18—Pirates released pitcher Al McBean.

May 18—Brewers traded second baseman John Donaldson to Athletics for infielder Roberto Pena.

May 19—Cardinals traded pitcher Jerry Johnson to Giants for pitcher Frank Linzy.

May 22—Tigers traded pitcher Fred Lasher to Indians for outfielder Russ Nagelson, assigned to Toledo, and pitcher Bill Rohr, assigned from Wichita to Toledo.

May 26—Padres purchased pitcher Roberto Rodriguez from Iowa, Athletics' AAA affiliate.

May 28—Red Sox traded infielder Tom Matchick to Royals for first baseman Mike Fiore.

May 29—Cardinals traded infielder Phil Gagliano to Cubs for pitcher Ted Abernathy.

June 6—Phillies signed coach Howard (Doc) Edwards to a player contract; returned to coach status October 7.

June 8—Red Sox purchased pitcher Cal Koonce from Mets.

June 8—Cardinals released catcher Bart Zeller as a player and signed him as a coach.

June 9—Pirates signed pitcher Orlando Pena, a free agent.

June 9—Brewers purchased outfielder-first baseman Bob Burda from Giants and assigned him to Portland.

June 10—Red Sox signed coach George Thomas to a player contract.

June 11—Athletics traded pitcher Al Downing and first baseman-outfielder John (Tito) Francona to Brewers for outfielder Steve Hovley.

June 13—Cardinals traded pitcher George Culver to Astros for outfielder-first baseman Jim Beauchamp and shortstop Leon McFadden, latter assigned from Oklahoma City to Tulsa.

June 13—Cardinals traded second baseman Octavio (Cookie) Rojas to Royals for outfielder Fred Rico, assigned from Omaha to Tulsa.

June 15—Expos purchased pitcher John O'Donoghue from Brewers.

June 15—Brewers signed pitcher Bob Humphreys, released by Senators.

June 15—Expos traded outfielder Ty Cline to Reds for outfielder Clyde Mashore, recalled from Indianapolis and assigned to Winnipeg.

June 15—Orioles traded outfielder Dave May to Brewers for pitchers Dick Baney and Louis (Buzz) Stephen, both assigned from Portland to Rochester.

June 15—White Sox traded outfielder Charles (Buddy) Bradford to Indians for pitchers Barry Moore and Robert L. Miller.

June 15—Athletics purchased pitcher Bob Locker from Brewers.

June 15—Orioles traded infielder Bobby Floyd to Royals for pitcher Myron (Moe) Drabowsky.

June 22—Braves released pitcher Ron Kline.

June 22—Athletics purchased outfielder Tommy Davis from Astros.

June 22—Cardinals purchased pitcher Charles (Chuck) Hartenstein from Pirates.

June 23—Cubs purchased pitcher Roberto Rodriguez from Padres.

June 25—Cubs purchased pitcher Milt Pappas from Braves.

June 26—Red Sox purchased infielder John Kennedy from Brewers.

June 29—Braves purchased outfielder Jimmie Hall from Cubs.

June 29—White Sox purchased pitcher Lee Stange from Red Sox.

July 1—Cardinals traded pitcher Ted Abernathy to Royals for pitcher Chris Zachary, assigned from Omaha to Tulsa.

July 5—Braves signed pitcher Stephen D. Barber, a free agent, and assigned him to Richmond.

July 6—Cubs released pitcher Hank Aguirre.

July 8—Athletics released infielder Robert W. Johnson.

July 9—Angels traded pitcher Juan Pizarro, on Hawaii roster, to Cubs for pitcher Archie Reynolds, assigned to Hawaii.

July 12—Braves purchased pitcher Don Cardwell from Mets.

July 13—Giants released third baseman Jim Davenport as a player and signed him as a coach.

July 15—Padres purchased pitcher Earl Wilson from Tigers.

July 20—Giants traded pitcher Mike McCormick to Yankees for pitcher John Cumberland.

July 21—Red Sox signed pitcher Charles (Chuck) Hartenstein, released by Cardinals, and assigned him to Louisville.

July 29—Cubs purchased first baseman-outfielder Joe Pepitone from Astros.

August 7—Brewers purchased pitcher Dick Ellsworth from Indians.

August 11—Indians released infielder Lou Klimchock.

August 14—Cardinals purchased pitcher Frank Bertaina from Rochester, Baltimore affiliate.

August 19—Senators released catcher John Roseboro as a player and signed him as a coach.

August 25—Padres purchased pitcher Paul Doyle from Angels.

August 25—Dodgers released pitcher Camilo Pascual.

August 26—Pirates released pitcher Orlando Pena.

August 30—Phillies acquired pitcher Jim Browning from Cardinals as final payment in the Curt Flood deal of October 7, 1969; Browning was assigned from St. Petersburg to the Peninsula club of the Carolina League.

August 31—Angels purchased outfielder Tony Gonzalez from Braves.

August 31—Senators traded pitcher George Brunet to Pirates for pitcher Dennis Riddleberger, on Columbus, O. roster, and cash.

September 1—Expos signed pitcher Ron Piche, a free agent, to enable him to qualify for a major league player's pension; released him October 15.

September 1—Mets purchased pitcher Ron Herbel from Padres; deal was completed when Mets sent outfielder Rod Gaspar to Padres on October 20.

September 1—Cubs purchased pitcher Robert L. Miller from White Sox.

September 9—Pirates released catcher Dave Ricketts as a player and signed him as a coach.

September 9—White Sox purchased pitcher Steve Hamilton from Yankees.

September 10—Red Sox purchased pitcher Bob Bolin from Brewers.

September 11—White Sox purchased outfielder Lee Maye from Senators.

September 14—Pirates purchased pitcher Jim Grant from Athletics; Pirates assigned outfielder Angel Mangual to Athletics on October 20 to complete deal.

September 15—Brewers purchased infielder Juan Rios from Royals and assigned him to Portland.

September 16—Cubs purchased outfielder Tommy Davis from Athletics.

September 17—Cardinals purchased pitcher Fred Reahm from Mets.

September 18—Mets purchased pitcher Dean Chance from Indians.

September 21—Cubs purchased pitcher Hoyt Wilhelm from Braves.

September 28—Cardinals purchased pitcher Fredie Norman from Dodgers.

October 5—Cardinals traded first baseman-third baseman Richie Allen to Dodgers for infielder Ted Sizemore and catcher Bob Stinson.

October 9—Tigers traded pitcher Denny McLain, third baseman Don Wert, pitcher Norm McRae and third baseman-outfielder Elliott Maddox to Senators for shortstop Eddie Brinkman, third baseman Aurelio Rodriguez and pitchers Joe Coleman and Jim Hannan.

October 11—Red Sox traded outfielder Tony Conigliaro, pitcher Ray Jarvis and catcher Gerry Moses to Angels for pitcher Ken Tatum, outfielder Jarvis Tatum and second baseman Doug Griffin.

October 12—Astros traded shortstop Hector Torres to Cubs for infielder Roger Metzger.

October 13—Royals traded outfielder Pat Kelly and pitcher Don O'Riley to White Sox for first baseman-catcher Gail Hopkins and outfielder-first baseman John Matias.

October 19—Athletics purchased first baseman Ramon Webster from Padres and assigned him to Iowa.

October 20—Cardinals traded pitcher Sal Campisi and infielder Jim Kennedy, latter on Tulsa roster, to Twins for outfielder Herman Hill and outfielder Charles Wissler, latter assigned from Evansville to Tulsa.

October 20—Reds purchased pitcher Ed Sprague from Athletics.

October 20—Brewers released third baseman Max Alvis.

October 20—Cardinals traded outfielder-first baseman Carl Taylor and pitcher Jim Ellis, latter assigned from Arkansas to Portland, to Brewers for catcher Gerry McNertney and pitchers George Lauzerique and Jesse Huggins, latter two assigned from Portland to Tulsa.

October 21—Angels traded shortstop Marty Perez to Braves for catcher John Burns, assigned from Shreveport to El Paso.

October 21—Red Sox traded infielder Dick Schofield to Cardinals for first baseman Jim Campbell, assigned from Tulsa to Louisville.

October 23—Senators purchased outfielder Richie Scheinblum, on Wichita roster, from Indians.

October 26—Pirates released pitcher Joe Gibbon.

October 27—Brewers released first baseman-outfielder John (Tito) Francona.

October 28—Braves released outfielder Jimmie Hall.

November 3—Phillies traded outfielder Curt Flood, inactive for entire 1970 season, to Senators for first baseman-catcher Greg Goossen, pitcher Jeff Terpko and first baseman Gene Martin, latter on Denver roster; Phillies assigned all three players to Eugene.

November 10—Brewers released outfielder Mike Hershberger.

November 30—Cubs traded pitcher Hoyt Wilhelm to Braves for first baseman Hal Breeden.

November 30—Cubs traded outfielder-first baseman Willie Smith to Reds for catcher Dan Breeden, assigned to Tacoma.

November 30—Orioles traded pitcher Myron (Moe) Drabowsky to Cardinals for infielder Jerry DaVanon.

November 30—Cubs traded pitchers Pat Jacquez and Dave Lemonds and first baseman Roe Skidmore to White Sox for outfielder Jose Ortiz and first baseman Ossie Blanco, latter assigned from Tucson to Tacoma.

November 30—White Sox traded outfielder Ken Berry, second baseman Syd O'Brien and pitcher Billy Wynne to Angels for outfielder Jay Johnstone, catcher Tom Egan and pitcher Tom Bradley.

December 1—Astros purchased catcher Jack Hiatt from Cubs.

December 1—Mets traded pitcher Ron Herbel to Braves for third baseman Bob Aspromonte.

December 1—Orioles traded pitchers Tom Phoebus, Al Severinsen and Fred Beene and shortstop Enzo Hernandez to Padres for pitchers Pat Dobson and Tom Dukes.

December 1—Red Sox traded second baseman Mike Andrews and shortstop Luis Alvarado to White Sox for shortstop Luis Aparicio.

December 2—Braves traded catcher Bob Tillman to Brewers for outfielder Hank Allen, pitcher Paul Click and infielder John Ryan; Allen and Click were assigned to Richmond and Ryan to Savannah.

December 2—Pirates traded shortstop Fred Patek, pitcher Bruce Dal Canton and catcher Jerry May to Royals for pitcher Bob Johnson, shortstop Jackie Hernandez and catcher Jim Campanis, latter assigned from Omaha to Columbus, O.

December 3—Cubs traded infielder Phil Gagliano to Red Sox for third baseman Carmen Fanzone, assigned to Tacoma.

December 4—Giants traded second baseman Don Mason and pitcher Bill Frost, latter on Phoenix roster, to Padres, for infielder Steve Huntz; Frost was assigned to Hawaii.

December 11—Dodgers traded pitchers Alan Foster and Ray Lamb to Indians for catcher Duke Sims.

December 15—Reds traded pitcher Jim Maloney to Angels for pitcher Greg Garrett.

December 16—Orioles traded outfielder Roger Freed to Phillies for pitcher Grant Jackson, outfielder-first baseman Jim Hutto and outfielder Sam Parrilla, latter on Eugene roster; Hutto and Parrilla were placed on Rochester roster.

December 22—Braves released pitcher Don Cardwell.

December 28—Cubs released outfielder Tommy Davis.

December 30—Giants traded second baseman Ron Hunt to Expos for first baseman Dave McDonald.

Hotels of Major League Teams

AMERICAN LEAGUE

AT BALTIMORE: Baltimore-Hilton—Boston, California, Cleveland, Chicago, Detroit, Kansas City, Minnesota, New York, Oakland. **Holiday Inn**—Milwaukee. **Lord Baltimore**—Washington.

AT BOSTON: Statler-Hilton—Baltimore, Chicago, Cleveland, Detroit, Kansas City, Minnesota, Oakland, New York. **Sheraton-Plaza**—Milwaukee, Washington. **Parker House**—California.

AT CALIFORNIA: Grand—Baltimore, Boston, Cleveland, Chicago, Detroit, Kansas City, Milwaukee, Minnesota, New York, Oakland. **Royal Coach**—Washington.

AT CHICAGO: Executive House—Baltimore, Boston, California, Detroit, Kansas City, Milwaukee, Washington. **Sheraton**—Minnesota. **Conrad Hilton**—Cleveland. **Ambassador East**—Oakland. **Ambassador West**—New York.

AT CLEVELAND: Hollenden House—Baltimore, Boston, California, Kansas City, Milwaukee, Minnesota, New York, Washington. **Sheraton-Cleveland**—Chicago, Detroit, Oakland.

AT DETROIT: Sheraton-Cadillac—All clubs.

AT KANSAS CITY: Muehlebach—All clubs.

AT MILWAUKEE: Schroeder—Boston, Detroit, Minnesota. **Pfister**—Baltimore, California, Cleveland, Kansas City, New York, Oakland. **Holiday Inn**—Chicago. **Downtowner Inn**—Washington.

AT MINNESOTA: Radisson (Minneapolis)—California. **Leamington (Minneapolis)**—Baltimore, Boston, Chicago, Cleveland, Detroit, Kansas City, Milwaukee, New York, Oakland, Washington.

AT NEW YORK: Roosevelt—Baltimore, California, Chicago, Detroit, Minnesota, Washington. **Waldorf**—Boston. **Biltmore**—Milwaukee. **Americana**—Kansas City, Oakland. **Summit**—Cleveland.

AT OAKLAND: Edgewater—All clubs.

AT WASHINGTON: Washington-Hilton—Boston, California, Chicago, Cleveland, Kansas City, Minnesota. **Shoreham**—Baltimore, Detroit, Milwaukee, New York, Oakland.

NATIONAL LEAGUE

AT ATLANTA: Marriott—All clubs.

AT CHICAGO: Executive House—Cincinnati, Houston, Los Angeles, Montreal, New York, Philadelphia, Pittsburgh, St. Louis, San Diego, San Francisco. **Ambassador East**—Atlanta.

AT CINCINNATI: Sheraton-Gibson—Atlanta. **Terrace-Hilton**—San Francisco. **Netherland**—Chicago, Houston, Los Angeles, New York, Philadelphia, Pittsburgh, St. Louis, San Diego. **Stouffer's Inn**—Montreal.

AT HOUSTON: Marriott—All clubs.

AT LOS ANGELES: Ambassador—San Francisco. **Sheraton West**—Atlanta, Montreal, San Diego. **Wilshire Hyatt House**—Philadelphia. **Biltmore**—Chicago, Cincinnati, Houston, New York, Pittsburgh, St. Louis.

AT MONTREAL: Queen Elizabeth—All clubs.

AT NEW YORK: Biltmore—Cincinnati, Montreal, St. Louis, San Diego, San Francisco. **Roosevelt**—Atlanta, Houston. **Waldorf-Astoria**—Chicago. **Summit**—Philadelphia, Pittsburgh. **Hilton**—Los Angeles.

AT PHILADELPHIA: Bellevue-Stratford—Atlanta, Chicago, Cincinnati, Houston, Los Angeles, Pittsburgh, San Diego, San Francisco. **Marriott**—Montreal. **Warwick**—New York. **Holiday Inn**—St. Louis.

AT PITTSBURGH: Hilton—Chicago, Cincinnati, Los Angeles, New York, St. Louis, San Diego, San Francisco. **William Penn**—Atlanta, Houston, Montreal, Philadelphia.

AT ST. LOUIS: Chase-Park Plaza—Atlanta, Chicago, Cincinnati, Houston, Los Angeles, San Diego, San Francisco. **Stouffer's Inn**—Montreal, New York, Philadelphia, Pittsburgh.

AT SAN DIEGO: El Cortez—Chicago, Houston, New York, St. Louis. **Hanalei**—San Francisco. **Town and Country**—Cincinnati, Los Angeles. **Villa Fontana**—Atlanta, Montreal, Philadelphia, Pittsburgh.

AT SAN FRANCISCO: Palace—Houston, Los Angeles, New York, St. Louis. **Jack Tar**—Atlanta, Chicago, Cincinnati, Montreal, Philadelphia, Pittsburgh, San Diego.

Hall of Famer Schalk Led Valhalla Parade

By CHRIS ROEWE

Ray Schalk, star catcher for the Chicago White Sox from 1912 through 1928 and a member of the Hall of Fame, was the most noted baseball personality to die in 1970. Schalk, player-manager of the White Sox in 1927-28, still holds several major league records for defensive brilliance, including most years leading catchers in fielding percentage (8) and most consecutive years leading in fielding percentage (5). Ray passed away at Chicago May 19.

In addition to Schalk, who caught all eight games for the White Sox, three other men involved in the ill-starred World Series of 1919 between Cincinnati and Chicago were among the decedents: Chick Gandil, White Sox first baseman, one of eight Sox players banned for life from Organized Ball, died at Calistoga, Calif., December 13; Walter (Dutch) Ruether, left-hander who led the National League in winning percentage with .760 (19-6) as one of the aces of the Reds' staff in 1919, died at Phoenix, Ariz., May 16; Abe Attell, former featherweight boxing champion and one of the "fixers," succumbed at Liberty, N. Y., February 6.

Two former players who moved up to responsible front-office jobs in the major leagues were 1970 victims. Johnny Murphy, a ten-year relief star for the New York Yankees, who served as farm director for the Boston Red Sox from 1948 through 1960 and who, as general manager of the New York Mets, put together the world champion club of 1969, died of a heart attack at New York City, January 14. Sherry Robertson, an outfielder-infielder with Washington and the Philadelphia Athletics in the period from 1940 through 1952 and a brother of Calvin Griffith, president of the Minnesota Twins, who had been farm director for the Senators and Twins since 1958, was killed in an auto accident near Houghton, S. D., October 23.

Other familiar names found in the obituary notices included: Rudy York, slugging first baseman, who hit 277 regular-season home runs in an American League career from 1934 through 1948; Eddie Rommel, one of first major league pitchers to throw the knuckleball, who later umpired in the American League for 22 years; Jim (Rip) Collins, National League first baseman with the Cardinals, Cubs and Pirates, who tied for the league lead in home runs in 1934; Fred Mitchell, player and manager who skippered the pennant-winning Cubs of 1918; Johnny Mostil, rated one of the game's greatest defensive center fielders while with the White Sox in the 1920s; Charlie Root, winner of 201 major league games in a pitching career that stretched from 1923 through 1941; Dave Robertson, National League outfielder for nearly ten years, who tied for the major league lead in home runs in 1916-17; Nap Rucker, Dodger fireballer of the early 1900s, who numbered 38 shutouts among his 134 big league victories; Lefty Leifield, major league pitcher for 12 seasons, who hurled three one-hit games in the majors.

Several well known minor league figures were called out for the last time. Bob Cobb, longtime owner of the Hollywood Stars of the Pacific Coast League, died March 21; Edwin C. Johnson, president of the Western League from 1947 through 1955 and a former governor of Colorado and U. S. Senator, succumbed May 30 and Tommy Richardson, who served for many years as president of the Eastern and International loops, died November 13.

A list of baseball deaths in 1970 follows:

Spencer Dewey Adams, 73, infielder with four major league clubs in the period from 1923 through 1927, at Salt Lake City, U., November 25.

Ivy Paul Andrews, 63, pitcher with the New York Yankees in 1931-32, the Boston Red Sox in 1932-33, the St. Louis Browns in 1934-35-36, Cleveland in 1937 and the Yankees in 1937-38, at Dora, Ala., November 23.

Orie Edgar (Old Folks) Arntzen, 60, pitcher with the Philadelphia Athletics in 1943, at Cedar Rapids, Ia., January 28; pitched in Organized Ball from 1931 through 1952; named Minor League Player of the Year by THE SPORTING NEWS in 1949 when he had a 25-2 record for Albany of the Eastern League.

Robert Anthony (Asby) Asbjornson, 60, catcher with the Boston Red Sox in 1928-29 and Cincinnati in 1931-32, at Williamsport, Pa., January 21.

Abe Attell, 85, former featherweight boxing champion and one of the principals in the Chicago "Black Sox" scandal of 1919, at Liberty, N. Y., February 6.

Stanley Bell, 23, pitcher with Shreveport of the Texas League in 1970, at Atlanta, Ga., September 20, of injuries suffered in automobile accident the previous day.

Herbert Eugene Benninghoven, 73, scout for the St. Louis Cardinals from 1936 through 1960 and Kansas City from November, 1968 until his death at Lakeside, Calif., January 27.

Edgar G. Brands, 82, an authority on baseball history and administration and editor of THE SPORTING NEWS from 1930 to June, 1954, at St. Louis, Mo., November 26.

Edwin H. Brauner, 70, scout for various major league clubs, including San Francisco from 1968 until his death at Eugene, Ore., September 10.

Frank B. Bridges, 79, scout for the Chicago White Sox in 1947-48-49, the Philadelphia Athletics in 1950-51 and Detroit in 1952 and a college coach in various sports in the Southwest Conference for many years, at San Antonio, Tex., June 10.

Walter Owen (Spike) Briggs, Jr., 58, member of the Briggs family that controlled the Detroit Tigers from 1935 to 1956 and president of the club from 1952 through June, 1956, at Detroit, Mich., July 3.

Richard Ernest Brown, 35, catcher with Cleveland in 1957-58-59, the Chicago White Sox in 1960, Detroit in 1961-62 and Baltimore in 1963-64-65 and a brother of Larry Brown, Cleveland infielder, at Baltimore, Md., April 12.

Thomas Francis (Scoops) Carey, 61, infielder with the St. Louis Browns in 1935-36-37 and the Boston Red Sox from 1939 through 1942 and in 1946, at Rochester, N. Y., February 21.

Clarence Chun Hoon, 59, scout for the New York and San Francisco Giants from 1955 until his death at New York City, February 16.

Robert H. (Bob) Cobb, 71, principal stockholder in the Hollywood Stars of the Pacific Coast League from 1938 through 1957 and owner of the Brown Derby restaurant chain, at Los Angeles, Calif., March 21.

James Anthony (Rip) Collins, 65, first baseman with the St. Louis Cardinals from 1931 through 1936, the Chicago Cubs in 1937-38 and Pittsburgh in 1941, at New Haven, N. Y., April 16; tied for league lead in home runs (35) in 1934; served as player-manager of Albany in Eastern League from 1942 through 1946, winning batting title in 1944 with .396 mark; coached for the Cubs in 1961-62-63.

Raymond Williston Collins, 82, pitcher with the Boston Red Sox from 1909 through 1915, at Burlington, Vt., January 9; won 20 games in 1914.

Richard Conger, 48, pitcher who saw brief service with Detroit in 1940, Pittsburgh in 1941-42 and the Philadelphia Phillies in 1943, at Los Angeles, Calif., February 16.

Thomas M. Conroy, 73, secretary-treasurer of the Cincinnati Reds from 1934 through 1966, at Belleaire, Fla., March 13.

Michael John Cvengros, 68, pitcher with the New York Giants in 1922, the Chicago White Sox in 1923-24-25, Pittsburgh in 1927 and the Chicago Cubs in 1929, at Hot Springs, Ark., August 2.

David Charles Danforth, 80, pitcher with the Philadelphia Athletics in 1911-12, the Chicago White Sox from 1916 through 1919 and the St. Louis Browns from 1922 through 1925, at Baltimore, Md., September 19.

Alfred Lovill (Chubby) Dean, 54, pitcher-first baseman with the Philadelphia Athletics from 1936 through 1941 and Cleveland in 1941-42-43, at Riverside, N. J., December 21.

Arthur D. Delaney, 73, pitcher with the St. Louis Cardinals in 1924 and the Boston Braves in 1928-29, at Hayward, Calif., May 2.

Claude J. (Dutch) Dietrich, 78, scout for various major league clubs from 1950 through 1968 and the Major League Scouting Bureau from 1969 until his death at Farmington, N. M., August 29.

Thomas Charles Downey, 83, scout for Brooklyn, Pittsburgh, Cleveland, the Boston Red Sox, Los Angeles Angels and Chicago Cubs from 1938 through 1963, at San Diego, Calif., May 20.

Calvin Troy Drummond, 52, American League umpire from 1960 through 1969, at Des Moines, Ia., May 3; suffered head injury when struck by foul tip in June, 1969, and was out of action for balance of year; joined American Association staff May 1, 1970 and collapsed while working game at Des Moines on May 2.

Malcolm Wayne Eason, 91, pitcher with the Chicago Cubs in 1900-01-02, the Boston Braves in 1902, Detroit in 1903 and Brooklyn in 1905-06, at Douglas, Ariz., April 16; pitched a no-hit game on July 20, 1906; umpired in the National League from 1910 through 1915 and the Pacific Coast League from 1919 through 1922.

Paul Michael Edmondson, 27, pitcher with the Chicago White Sox in 1969, in auto crash near Santa Barbara, Calif., February 13.

James Thomas (Jumbo Jim) Elliott, 69, pitcher with the St. Louis Browns in 1923, Brooklyn in 1925 and from 1927 through 1930, the Philadelphia Phillies from 1931 through 1934 and the Boston Braves in 1934, at Terre Haute, Ind., January 7.

Reuben Ewing, 70, infielder who appeared in three games for the St. Louis Cardinals in 1921, at West Hartford, Conn., October 5.

Floyd Haskell (Jack) Farmer, 77, infielder-outfielder with Pittsburgh in 1916 and Cleveland in 1918, at Columbia, La., May 21.

Thomas G. Fisher, 70, scout for the Philadelphia Phillies in 1954-55 and the Washington Senators and Minnesota Twins from 1956 until his death at Milwaukee, Wis., December 22.

Harvey B. Freeman, 72, pitcher with the Philadelphia Athletics in 1921, at Kalamazoo, Mich., January 10.

Arthur Edwin (Cy) Fried, 73, pitcher with Detroit briefly in 1920, at San Antonio, Tex., October 10.

Miguel Fuentes, 21, pitcher with Seattle in 1969, of gunshot wounds in tavern fight at Loiza Aldea, Puerto Rico, January 29.

Lester LeRoy Fusselman, 49, catcher with the St. Louis Cardinals in 1952-53, at Cleveland, O., May 21.

Harold Dennis (Chick) Gagnon, 72, shortstop who saw brief service with Detroit in 1922 and Washington in 1924, at Wilmington, Del., April 30.

Charles Arnold (Chick) Gandil, 83, first baseman with the Chicago White Sox in 1910, Washington from 1912 through 1915, Cleveland in 1916 and the White Sox in 1917-18-19, and one of eight Chicago players banned from Organized Ball for life for conspiring to lose the 1919 World Series, at Calistoga, Calif., December 13.

Walter Paul (Doc) Gautreau, 66, second baseman with the Philadelphia Athletics in 1925 and the Boston Braves from 1925 through 1928, at Salt Lake City, U., August 23; scouted for the Boston and Milwaukee Braves from 1952 through 1961 and the California Angels from 1962 through 1969; worked for the Major League Scouting Bureau in 1970.

James Charles Grant, 51, third baseman with the Chicago White Sox in 1942-43 and Cleveland in 1943-44, at Rochester, Minn., July 8.

Howard Watterson Gregory, 83, pitcher in three games with the St. Louis Browns in 1911, at Tulsa, Okla., May 30.

Lee Elmer (Jeep) Handley, 56, infielder with Cincinnati in 1936, Pittsburgh from 1937 through 1941 and in 1944-45-46 and the Philadelphia Phillies in 1947 and a brother of Eugene Handley, former American League infielder, at Pittsburgh, Pa., April 8.

Harry Hesse, 71, scout for the New York Yankees from 1948 until his death at New York City, June 10.

Joseph William Heving, 69, pitcher with five major league clubs in the period from 1930 through 1945 and a brother of John Heving, former American League catcher, at Covington, Ky., April 11.

Herman Alexander Hill, 25, outfielder with Minnesota in 1969-70, a drowning victim in the Caribbean Sea near Valencia, Venezuela, December 14.

David Taylor Hoskins, 47, pitcher with Cleveland in 1953-54 and the first Negro to play in the Texas League when he pitched for Dallas in 1952, at Flint, Mich., April 2.

John Wilson Hudson, 58, infielder with Brooklyn from 1936 through 1940, the Chicago Cubs in 1941 and the New York Giants in 1945 and a scout for the Giants from 1949 until his death at Bryan, Tex., November 7.

Herbert Harrison Hunter, 74, infielder with four major league clubs briefly in the period from 1916 through 1921 and an umpire and club owner in the minor leagues, at Orlando, Fla., July 25; had great interest in Japanese baseball and in 1931 took an all-star major league group to that country; served as baseball coach at six universities in Japan.

Edwin Carl Johnson, 86, president of the Western League from 1947 through 1955 and a former governor of Colorado and U. S. senator from that state, at Denver, Colo., May 30.

John Walter (Red) Juelich, 54, infielder with Pittsburgh briefly in 1939, at St. Louis, Mo., December 25.

Donald Stafford Kellett, 61, infielder with the Boston Red Sox briefly in 1934 and the general manager of the Baltimore Colts of the National Football League from 1953 through 1966, at Fort Lauderdale, Fla., November 5.

Wayman William Kerksieck, 56, pitcher for the Philadelphia Phillies in 1939, at Little Rock, Ark., March 11.

Wathen R. Knebelkamp, 69, an official and part-owner of the Louisville club of the American Association from 1921 through 1938 and a former president of Churchill Downs race track, at Louisville, Ky., July 3.

Kurt Ferdinand Krieger, 43, pitcher with the St. Louis Cardinals briefly in 1949 and 1951, at St. Louis, Mo., August 16.

William Harmong Lamar, 73, outfielder with the New York Yankees in 1917-18-19, the Boston Red Sox in 1920, Brooklyn in 1920-21 and the Philadelphia Athletics from 1924 through 1927, at Rockport, Mass., July 19.

Frederick Arthur Lamline, 83, pitcher who saw brief service with the Chicago White Sox in 1912 and the St. Louis Cardinals in 1915, at Port Huron, Mich., September 20.

Walter Laskowski, 56, scout for Cleveland from 1939 through 1954, the Chicago White Sox in 1955-56, the Philadelphia Phillies from 1957 through 1961 and Houston from 1962 until his death in auto crash near Monterrey, Mex., February 14.

William Wallace Leard, 84, infielder with Brooklyn briefly in 1917, at San Francisco, Calif., January 15.

Albert Peter (Lefty) Leifield, 87, pitcher with Pittsburgh from 1905 through 1912, the Chicago Cubs in 1912-13 and the St. Louis Browns in 1918-19-20, at Alexandria, Va., October 10; coached for the Browns in 1921-22-23, the Boston Red Sox in 1924-25-26 and Detroit in 1927-28; managed Oklahoma City of the Western League in 1929 and St. Paul of the American Association in 1930-31-32; pitched three one-hit games in the majors.

James Julius Levey, 63, shortstop with the St. Louis Browns from 1930 through 1933 and a halfback with Pittsburgh of the National Football League in 1934-35-36, at Dallas, Tex., March 14.

Robert Clarendon (Bob) Lewis, 72, traveling secretary of the Chicago Cubs from 1927 through 1959, at Chicago, Ill., August 6.

Clarence F. Lloyd, 82, traveling secretary of the St. Louis Cardinals from 1919 through 1937, at Dublin, Ga., October 9.

James Albert Long, 72, catcher with the Chicago White Sox briefly in 1922, at Fort Dodge, Ia., September 8.

John Charles (Buster) Lucas, 62, outfielder with the Boston Red Sox briefly in 1931-32, at Maryville, Ill., October 31.

Frank Spruiell (Jakie) May, 74, pitcher with the St. Louis Cardinals from 1917 through 1921, Cincinnati from 1924 through 1930 and the Chicago Cubs in 1931-32, at Wendell, N. C., June 3.

William Lusk McAllester, 80, catcher with the St. Louis Browns in 1913, at Chattanooga, Tenn., March 3.

Harold Leroy McKain, 63, pitcher with Cleveland in 1927 and the Chicago White Sox from 1929 through 1932, at Sacramento, Calif., January 24.

Joseph W. McKenney, 51, public relations director for the American League from 1959 through 1966, at Cambridge, Mass., July 21.

John Davis Meador, 77, pitcher with Pittsburgh briefly in 1920, at Winston-Salem, N. C., April 11.

Rufus Rivers Meadows, 62, pitcher in one game with Cincinnati in 1926, at Wichita, Kan., May 10.

Frederick Francis Mitchell, 92, major league player, manager and coach, at Newton, Mass., October 13; pitcher, catcher and infielder with six big league clubs in the period from 1901 through 1913; coached for the Boston Braves in 1914-15-16; managed the Chicago Cubs from 1917 through 1920, winning the pennant in 1918, and the Braves in 1921-22-23; worked as relief pitcher in first American League game ever played by the Boston Red Sox on April 26, 1901.

Leo Moon, 71, pitcher in one game with Cleveland in 1932 who had a long career in the high minor leagues, at New Orleans, La., August 25.

J. T. (Jake) Mooty, 57, pitcher with Cincinnati in 1936-37, the Chicago Cubs from 1940 through 1943 and Detroit in 1944, at Fort Worth, Tex., April 20.

John Anthony (Bananas) Mostil, 74, outfielder with the Chicago White Sox in 1918 and from 1921 through 1929, at Midlothian, Ill., December 10; rated one of greatest defensive center fielders of all time; made 11 put-outs on May 22, 1928, an American League record for a nine-inning game shared with three other outfielders; scouted for the White Sox from 1949 through 1968.

John Joseph (Grandma) Murphy, 61, pitcher and front-office executive, at New York City, January 14; one of majors' greatest relief pitchers with a 93-53 record in service with the New York Yankees in 1932 and from 1934 through 1943 and once more in 1946; also pitched for the Boston Red Sox in 1947; scouted for the Red Sox in 1948 and was named farm system director in October, 1948, a position he held through 1960; scouted for the New York Mets in 1961 and served as assistant to the general manager from 1962 through 1967; was named general manager in 1968 and remained in that position until his death.

Alexander Dominick Mustaikis, 60, pitcher in six games with the Boston Red Sox in 1940, at Scranton, Pa., January 17.

Louis Alexander Novikoff, 54, outfielder with the Chicago Cubs from 1941 through 1944 and the Philadelphia Phillies in 1946, at South Gate, Calif., September 30; won batting championship four times in five-year minor league career—Three I League 1938, Texas League 1939, Pacific Coast League 1940 and American Association 1941.

Emilio A. Palmero, 75, pitcher who saw brief service with four major league clubs in the period from 1915 through 1928 and one of the first Cubans to play in the big leagues, at Toledo, O., July 15; had long career in the high minors, winning 28 games for Omaha of the Western League in 1920.

Urban Hugh Pickering, 71, third baseman with the Boston Red Sox in 1931-32, at Modesto, Calif., May 13.

Mizell George (Whitey) Platt, 49, outfielder with the Chicago Cubs in 1942-43, the Chicago White Sox in 1946 and the St. Louis Browns in 1948-49, at West Palm Beach, Fla., July 27.

John William Richardson, 78, outfielder with the Philadelphia Athletics briefly in 1915-16, at Marion, Ill., January 18.

Thomas H. (Tommy) Richardson, 75, president of the Eastern League from 1937 through 1960, International League from 1961 through 1965 and Eastern League from 1968 until retirement in September, 1970, at Williamsport, Pa., November 13.

Leon Francis Riley, 64, infielder-outfielder in four games with the Philadelphia Phillies in 1944 and a minor league player and manager for more than 20 years, at Schenectady, N. Y., September 13.

Davis Aydelotte Robertson, 81, outfielder with the New York Giants in 1912 and from 1914 through 1919, the Chicago Cubs in 1919-20-21, Pittsburgh in 1921 and the Giants in 1922, at Virginia Beach, Va., November 5; tied for major league lead in home runs in 1916 and 1917, hitting 12 each year; batted .500 in the 1917 World Series against the Chicago White Sox with 11 hits in 22 times at bat, a record batting average for a six-game Series that has been tied but never exceeded.

Sherrard Alexander (Sherry) Robertson, 51, former major league infielder-outfielder and vice-president and farm director of the Minnesota Twins and a brother of Calvin Griffith, Twins' president, in automobile accident near Houghton, S. D., October 23; played with Washington in 1940-41, 1943 and from 1946 through 1952 and the Philadelphia Athletics in 1952; served as farm director for Washington in 1958-59-60 and the Twins from 1961 until his death.

Edwin Americus (Eddie) Rommel, 72, major league pitcher, coach and umpire, at Baltimore, Md., August 26; pitched for the Philadelphia Athletics from 1920 through 1932; one of first pitchers to use the knuckleball, he won 27 games in 1922 and 21 in 1925; coached for the Athletics in 1933-34; worked as an umpire in American League from 1938 through 1959.

Charles Henry (Chinski) Root, 71, pitcher who won 201 games in the major leagues, at Hollister, Calif., November 5; pitched for the St. Louis Browns in 1923 and the Chicago Cubs from 1926 through 1941; led league in victories (26) and innings pitched (309) in 1927 and in winning percentage (.760) in 1929; managed Hollywood of Pacific Coast League in 1943-44, Columbus of American Association in 1945-46 and Des Moines of the Western League in 1950; coached for the Cubs in 1951-52-53, Milwaukee in 1956-57 and the Cubs in 1960.

George (Nap) Rucker, 86, pitcher with Brooklyn from 1907 through 1916, at Alpharetta, Ga., December 19; pitched no-hit game against Boston on September 5, 1908; struck out 16 in one game on July 24, 1909; won 134 games in the major leagues, including 38 shutouts.

Walter Henry (Dutch) Ruether, 76, pitcher with the Chicago Cubs in 1917, Cincinnati from 1917 through 1920, Brooklyn from 1921 through 1924, Washington in 1925-26 and the New York Yankees in 1926-27; worked for 33 years as a major league scout for various clubs, including the New York and San Francisco Giants from 1947 until his death at Phoenix, Ariz., May 16; led league in winning percentage with .760 (19-6) in 1919; won 21 games in 1922.

Raymond William (Cracker) Schalk, 77, major league catcher and manager and member of Hall of Fame, at Chicago, Ill., May 19; played with the Chicago White Sox from 1912 through 1928 and the New York Giants in 1929; managed the White Sox in 1927-28, Buffalo of the International League from 1932 through 1937, Indianapolis of the American Association in 1938-39, Milwaukee of the American Association in 1940 and Buffalo in 1950; holds major league records for most years leading catchers in fielding percentage (8) and most consecutive years leading in fielding percentage (5); caught four no-hit games by White Sox pitchers, including Charlie Robertson's perfect game on April 30, 1922; named to Hall of Fame in 1955.

Matty Schwab, Sr., 90, groundskeeper for Cincinnati at National League parks for more than 60 years, at Cincinnati, O., April 8.

Maurice Joseph (Red) Shannon, 75, infielder who saw brief service with four major league clubs in the period from 1915 through 1926, at Jersey City, N. J., April 12; twin brother, Joseph, was teammate on the Boston Red Sox in 1915.

Joseph Benjamin Shaute, 70, pitcher with Cleveland from 1922 through 1930, Brooklyn in 1931-32-33 and Cincinnati in 1934, at Scranton, Pa., February 21; won 20 games in 1924.

Raymond Curtis Shook, 80, catcher with the Chicago White Sox briefly in 1916, at South Bend, Ind., September 16.

Harry Graydon Shriver, 73, pitcher with Brooklyn in 1922-23, at Morgantown, W. Va., January 21.

Mrs. J. G. Taylor Spink, 77, widow of the longtime publisher of THE SPORTING NEWS and mother of the present publisher, C. C. Johnson Spink, at St. Louis, Mo., December 25.

Bradford Louis Springer, 65, pitcher briefly with the St. Louis Browns in 1925 and Cincinnati in 1926, at Birmingham, Mich., January 4.

Fred Spurgeon, 69, second baseman with Cleveland from 1924 through 1927, at Kalamazoo, Mich., November 5.

Eugene Gass Steinbrenner, 77, infielder with the Philadelphia Phillies briefly in 1912, at Pittsburgh, Pa., April 25.

John Davis Stuart, 69, pitcher with the St. Louis Cardinals from 1922 through 1925, at Charleston, W. Va., May 13; pitched and won complete-game victories in both games of a doubleheader on July 10, 1923.

Arthur J. Sullivan, 62, controller for the American League from 1959 until his death at Boston, Mass., March 29.

Ray R. Swallow, 45, front-office official for the Kansas City and Oakland Athletics from 1962 through 1968 and a scout for Cleveland in 1969-70, a drowning victim in an apparent accident at Huntington Beach, Calif., December 16.

Walter Joseph Tragesser, 83, catcher with the Boston Braves in 1913 and from 1915 through 1919 and the Philadelphia Phillies in 1919-20, at Lafayette, Ind., December 14.

Walter Joseph VanUum, 81, scout for Cleveland from 1948 until his death at Cleveland, O., April 28.

George Archibald (Watty) Watkins, 67, outfielder with the St. Louis Cardinals from 1930 through 1933, the New York Giants in 1934, the Philadelphia Phillies in 1935-36 and Brooklyn in 1936, at Houston, Tex., June 1; batted .373 in 119 games in his first year in the majors; hit three homers in one game on June 24, 1931.

Clinton Earl Wolgamot, 75, coach for Cleveland in 1931-32-33 and a minor league catcher and manager who spent 32 years in Organized Ball, at Independence, Ia., April 25.

Harry Meigs Wolter, 85, pitcher-outfielder with six major league clubs in the period from 1907 through 1917, at Palo Alto, Calif., July 7; led Pacific Coast League in batting in 1914-15 while playing for Los Angeles; coached the baseball team at Stanford U. from 1923 through 1949.

George (Yats) Wuestling, 66, shortstop with Detroit in 1929-30 and the New York Yankees in 1930, at St. Louis, Mo., April 26.

Rudolph Preston York, 56, first baseman, at Rome, Ga., February 5; played with Detroit in 1934 and from 1937 through 1945, the Boston Red Sox in 1946-47, the Chicago White Sox in 1947 and the Philadelphia Athletics in 1948; coached for the Red Sox from 1959 through 1962; hit 277 home runs in majors and led the league in homers (34) and runs batted in (118) in 1943; hit three homers in World Series play with Detroit in 1940 and 1945 and Boston in 1946.

George Washington (Zip) Zabel, 79, pitcher with the Chicago Cubs in 1913-14-15, at Beloit, Wis., May 31; set major league record that still stands for most innings pitched in one game by a relief pitcher who finished the contest when he went 18 and one-third innings to beat Brooklyn on June 17, 1915.

Major League Farm Systems for 1971

*Indicates working agreement. All other clubs owned outright.

AMERICAN LEAGUE

BALTIMORE (6): AAA—*Rochester. AA—*Dallas-Fort Worth. A—*Stockton, Miami, *Aberdeen. Rookie—Bluefield.

BOSTON (6): AAA—*Louisville. AA—*Pawtucket. A—*Winston-Salem, *Greenville, *Winter Haven, *Williamsport.

CALIFORNIA (4): AAA—*Salt Lake City. AA—*Shreveport. A—*Quad Cities. Rookie—*Idaho Falls.

CHICAGO (4): AAA—*Tucson. AA—Asheville. A—*Appleton. Rookie—Sarasota.

CLEVELAND (4): AAA—*Wichita. AA—*Jacksonville. A—*Reno. Rookie—Sarasota.

DETROIT (6): AAA—*Toledo. AA—*Montgomery. A—*Batavia, Lakeland, *Rocky Mount. Rookie—Bristol.

KANSAS CITY (7): AAA—Omaha. AA—Elmira. A—*San Jose, *Waterloo. Rookie—Kingsport, *Billings, Sarasota.

MILWAUKEE (3): AAA—*Evansville. A—*Danville, *Newark.

MINNESOTA (8): AAA—*Portland. AA—Charlotte. A—*Lynchburg, Orlando, *Wisconsin Rapids, *St. Cloud, *Auburn. Rookie—Sarasota.

NEW YORK (6): AAA—*Syracuse. AA—*Manchester. A—*Kinston, Fort Lauderdale, *Oneonta. Rookie—Johnson City.

OAKLAND (4): AAA—*Iowa. AA—Birmingham. A—*Burlington, Ia., Coos Bay-North Bend.

WASHINGTON (5): AAA—*Denver. AA—*Pittsfield. A—*Burlington, N. C., *Anderson. Rookie—*Geneva.

NATIONAL LEAGUE

ATLANTA (4): AAA—Richmond. AA—Savannah. A—Greenwood. Rookie—Wytheville.

CHICAGO (4): AAA—Tacoma. AA—San Antonio. A—*Quincy. Rookie—Caldwell.

CINCINNATI (5): AAA—*Indianapolis. AA—*Three Rivers. A—*Tampa, *Sioux Falls. Rookie—Bradenton.

HOUSTON (5): AAA—*Oklahoma City. AA—*Columbus, Ga. A—Cocoa, *Sumter. Rookie—*Covington.

LOS ANGELES (6): AAA—Spokane. AA—Albuquerque. A—*Bakersfield, Daytona Beach, *Medford. Rookie—Ogden.

MONTREAL (6): AAA—Winnipeg. AA—*Quebec City. A—West Palm Beach, *Jamestown, Watertown. Rookie—Bradenton.

NEW YORK (6): AAA—*Tidewater. AA—*Memphis. A—Visalia, *Lewiston (shares working agreement with St. Louis), *Pompano Beach. Rookie—Marion.

PHILADELPHIA (6): AAA—*Eugene. AA—Reading. A—*Newport News, Spartanburg, *Walla Walla. Rookie—*Pulaski.

PITTSBURGH (6): AAA—*Charleston. AA—*Waterbury. A—Monroe, *Niagara Falls, *Salem, Va. Rookie—Bradenton.

ST. LOUIS (7): AAA—*Tulsa. AA—*Arkansas. A—*St. Petersburg, *Cedar Rapids, *Modesto, *Lewiston, (shares working agreement with New York Mets). Rookie—Sarasota.

SAN DIEGO (3): AAA—*Hawaii. A—Lodi, *Tri-City.

SAN FRANCISCO (5): AAA—Phoenix. AA—Amarillo. A—*Fresno, *Decatur. Rookie—Great Falls.

KEY TO 1970 FARM CLUB SETUP

1—Baltimore Orioles	9—Minnesota Twins	17—Los Angeles Dodgers
2—Boston Red Sox	10—New York Yankees	18—Montreal Expos
3—California Angels	11—Oakland Athletics	19—New York Mets
4—Chicago White Sox	12—Washington Senators	20—Philadelphia Phillies
5—Cleveland Indians	13—Atlanta Braves	21—Pittsburgh Pirates
6—Detroit Tigers	14—Chicago Cubs	22—St. Louis Cardinals
7—Kansas City Royals	15—Cincinnati Reds	23—San Diego Padres
8—Milwaukee Brewers	16—Houston Astros	24—San Francisco Giants

SUMMER COLLEGE LEAGUES

Kent Froede of the National City club of the California Collegiate League was the top hitter in summer college ball with a .421 mark. Biggest winner among the pitchers was Henry Bunnell of New Market in the Shenandoah Valley League with 13 victories.

BASIN LEAGUE

Club	W.	L.	Pct.	G.B.
Chamberlain	27	21	.563	....
Rapid City	27	21	.563	....
Mobridge	23	25	.479	4
Pierre	23	25	.479	4
Sturgis	20	28	.417	7

Managers—Chamberlain, Terry Schliessler; Mobridge, Dell Youngblood; Pierre, Jack Stallings; Rapid City, Gary Adams; Sturgis, Larry Cochell.

Leading Batters

Player—Club	AB.	H.	HR.	RBI.	Pct.
Ron Cash, Mobridge	173	66	5	50	.382
Tony Hewitt, Rapid City	188	66	5	47	.351
Chris Cammack, Pierre	181	63	3	25	.348
Mike Gerakos, Rapid City	197	68	1	32	.345
R. J. Englert, Mobridge	217	73	1	19	.336
Greg Gromek, Mobridge	197	66	7	35	.335
Dudley Mitchell, Cha'lain	182	59	10	38	.324
Jim Corcoran, Mobridge	192	61	4	23	.318
Jim Seida, Rapid City	166	51	2	13	.307
Chris Sans, Mobridge	180	55	6	37	.306
Rocky Craig, Rapid City	191	58	5	24	.304
Bill Stearns, Chamberlain	181	53	4	35	.293
Greg Pryor, Pierre	189	55	7	28	.291
Ken Doria, Pierre	183	53	8	39	.290
Mike Cubbage, Pierre	174	50	8	39	.287

Leading Pitchers

Pitcher—Club	IP.	SO.	W.	L.	ERA.
Larry Ike, Sturgis	94	75	7	3	1.82
Barry Sbraigia, Mobridge	51	48	8	0	2.12
David Weaver, Cham	98	82	7	4	2.48
Joe Blake, Rapid City	61	35	5	2	2.51
Barry Bagley, Cham	78	65	5	4	2.88
Steve Lacki, Mobridge	107	94	7	4	2.94
Bob Apodaca, Cham	97	74	9	2	2.97
Rusty Gerhardt, Sturgis	65	73	1	6	3.05
Mike McKay, Cham	67	68	2	6	3.36
Bill Hall, Mobridge	89	73	3	8	3.54

CAPE COD LEAGUE

Club	W.	L.	Pct.	G.B.
Falmouth	25	16	.610	....
Wareham	25	16	.610	....
Orleans	23	16	.590	1
Cotuit	23	19	.548	2½
Chatham	21	20	.512	4
Yarmouth	13	26	.333	11
Harwich	11	28	.282	13

Playoffs—Falmouth defeated Cotuit, two games to none; Orleans defeated Wareham, two games to one; Falmouth defeated Orleans, two games to none.

Managers: Falmouth, William Livesey; Wareham, Ed Lyons; Orleans, Tony Williams; Cotuit, Jack McCarthy; Chatham, Doug Holmquist; Yarmouth, Merrill Wilson; Harwich, Don Stanford.

Leading Batters

Player—Club	AB.	H.	HR.	RBI.	Pct.
Mike Eden, Orleans	119	45	2	15	.378
Gary Boyce, Chatham	149	53	6	30	.356
Jim Prete, Wareham	137	46	2	17	.336
Jim Norris, Orleans	138	46	1	22	.333
Dan Radison, Harwich	142	47	4	15	.331
Dave Landers, Chatham	159	51	0	15	.321
Jim Eschen, Yarmouth	147	46	1	12	.313
Tom Henner, Cotuit	131	41	5	31	.313
Ray O'Brien, Falmouth	125	39	0	7	.312
Jack Gillis, Falmouth	150	46	5	29	.307
Don Robinson, Chatham	128	39	4	22	.305
Nat Calamis, Cotuit	155	46	0	13	.297
Scott Rahl, Orleans	130	38	4	22	.292
Brian Martin, Yarmouth	139	40	6	26	.288
Terry Wedgewood, Fal	167	48	6	37	.287
Doug Davies, Wareham	143	41	3	26	.287

Leading Pitchers

Pitcher—Club	IP.	SO.	W.	L.	ERA.
Jeff Peeples, Wareham	91	86	8	4	1.38
Paul Mitchell, Falmouth	86	105	8	1	1.47
John Petronaci, Orleans	69	50	6	1	1.96
John Fischetti, Wareham	72	57	6	2	2.13
Sonny Robinson, Wareham	52	43	4	3	2.25
Gary Huhn, Orleans	43	9	4	1	2.30
Jim Jachym, Falmouth	82	84	6	4	2.41
Tom White, Orleans	67	74	4	3	2.42
Dan Wallace, Chatham	92	71	5	5	2.45
Jim VanDerBeek, Ware	60	84	4	3	2.55

CALIFORNIA COLLEGIATE LEAGUE

Northern Division

Club	W.	L.	Pct.	G.B.
Long Beach	27	13	.675	....
San Fernando	26	14	.650	1
Downey	23	17	.575	4
La Crescenta	10	30	.250	17

Southern Division

Club	W.	L.	Pct.	G.B.
National City	27	12	.692	....
San Bernardino	21	19	.525	6½
La Mesa	18	21	.462	9
Ontario	7	33	.175	20½

Tie—La Mesa and National City.

Playoff—Long Beach defeated National City, three games to none.

Managers: Downey, Al Verdun; La Crescenta, Joe Cicero; La Mesa, Milo Lizalde; Long Beach, Joe Hicks; National City, John Cunningham; Ontario, Arlen Downs; San Bernardino, Steve Smith; San Fernando, Brent Nickoloff.

Leading Batters

*Bats lefthanded.

Player—Club	AB.	H.	HR.	RBI.	Pct.
Kent Froede, National C	140	59	5	35	.421
Richard Dauer, San Bern	133	54	2	31	.406
David Ravare, San Fer	124	49	3	32	.395
William Baker, Long Bch	147	57	1	15	.388
John D. Wathan, Nat City	151	57	1	23	.377
David Zall, San Fer*	120	43	1	26	.358
Steve Liebeck, Long Bch	127	44	2	20	.346
Greg Warzecka, Ontario	142	49	1	28	.345
Danathan Noonan, La Cres	119	41	3	28	.345
Douglas Redican, Downey	119	41	1	27	.345
Craig Perkins, Long Bch	111	38	9	41	.342
William McCorkle, Ont	124	42	1	19	.339
James Ramos, San Bern*	139	47	0	9	.338
Daniel Coronado, La Mesa	135	45	5	20	.333
Steve Ludwig, Downey	133	44	0	15	.331

Leading Pitchers

*Throws lefthanded.

Pitcher—Club	IP.	SO.	W.	L.	ERA.
Bruce Cooke, Long Beach	47	37	3	0	1.53
Kenneth Koske, Nat City	81	40	8	1	1.67
Gary R. Myron, Nat City	47	55	3	1	1.91
Curran Percival, Nat City	70	50	7	4	1.93
Ken Kollmyer, Nat City*	62	46	6	2	2.03
Eugene Kerr, Downey	83	42	7	5	2.39
Roger Fechner, Downey	67	47	6	3	2.82
Peter Martinez, Long Bch	100	86	10	2	2.88
Mark Fishback, San Fern	48	27	4	2	3.19
Glenn Burns, Downey	47	24	4	1	3.26

No-hit game—Percival, National City, defeated Long Beach, 3-0, August 16 (seven innings).

SHENANDOAH VALLEY LEAGUE

Club	W.	L.	Pct.	G.B.
Harrisonburg	26	15	.634	....
New Market	23	18	.561	3
Madison	22	19	.537	4
Waynesboro	21	22	.488	6
Charlottesville	20	23	.465	7
Shenandoah	18	23	.439	8
Staunton	16	26	.381	10½

Playoffs—New Market defeated Madison, three games to one; Harrisonburg defeated Waynesboro, three games to none; Harrisonburg defeated New Market, four games to one.

Managers: Harrisonburg, Ed D a u b; New Market, Thomas Martz; Madison, Bill Mitchell; Waynesboro, John Whitesell; Charlottesville, Jim West; Shenandoah, Larry Dofflemoyer; Staunton, James Zerilla.

Leading Batters

Player—Club	AB.	H.	HR.	RBI.	Pct.
Horace Richardson, Staun.	160	56	1	11	.350
James Procopio, Waynes	107	37	8	31	.346
Edward Palat, Harrison	169	57	7	31	.337
Craig White, Charlottes	.153	50	5	29	.327
Larry Kiser, New Market	.153	50	2	31	.327
Roger McSwain, Harrison	.155	50	8	35	.323
Michael Aldridge, N Mkt	.100	32	2	11	.320
Butch Anderson, Madison	.148	46	7	26	.311
Thomas Cassell, Waynes	.165	51	1	23	.309
Theodore Zink, Staunton	.130	40	1	29	.308
Henry Bunnell, New Mkrk	.164	50	4	39	.305
Ronald Hodges, Harrison	.168	51	4	23	.304
James Richardson, Harris	.160	47	6	24	.294
Stephen Estep, N Market	.166	48	0	9	.289
Daniel Baker, Charlottes	.140	40	1	17	.286

Leading Pitchers

Pitcher—Club	IP.	SO.	W.	L.	ERA.
Frank Carpin, Madison	. 60	60	5	2	1.65
Henry Bunnell, N Market	.133	167	13	3	1.69
George Beam, Madison	.. 73	78	3	4	1.73
Robin Flake, Charlottes	. 52	75	3	2	1.73
William Moran, Shenan	. 59	39	2	4	1.98
Larry Erbaugh, Harrison	. 74	84	5	1	2.07
Robert Becher, Shenandoah	66	53	4	3	2.18
Richard Fillings, Madison.	84	67	6	3	2.36
Harold Baird, Charlottes	.102	106	7	4	2.56
Mark Tschopp, Staunton	. 76	51	4	5	2.61

CENTRAL ILLINOIS COLLEGIATE LEAGUE

Standing at Close of First Half

Club	W.	L.	Pct.	G.B.
Springfield	17	9	.654	....
Bloomington	15	10	.600	1½
Galesburg	13	13	.500	4
Peoria	10	15	.400	6½
Macomb	9	17	.346	8

Standing at Close of Second Half

Club	W.	L.	Pct.	G.B.
Galesburg	17	9	.654	....
Macomb	13	12	.520	3½
*Bloomington	12	12	.500	4
Springfield	12	13	.480	4½
*Peoria	6	16	.273	9

*Forfeit — Doubleheader between Bloomington and Peoria, August 14, canceled. League ruled a loss to be added to each club.

Playoffs—Springfield defeated Galesburg, two games to none.

Managers: Bloomington, J a c k Horenberger; Galesburg, Jim Wasem; Macomb, Richard Pawlow; Peoria, Larry Schmittou; Springfield, Bud Middaugh.

Leading Batters

*Bats lefthanded.

Player—Club	AB.	H.	HR.	RBI.	Pct.
Sam Ewing, Peoria*	142	53	5	17	.373
Bob Prokopowicz, Gales*	.165	61	3	30	.370
Jim Cox, Bloomington	..192	67	9	39	.349
Ron Pruitt, Bloomington	.157	53	6	38	.338
Rob Ellis, Bloomington	.176	57	7	27	.324
Jim Dwyer, Springfield*	.193	61	4	14	.316
Randy Swanson, Macomb	.131	41	3	21	.313
Bob Blakley, Macomb*	..142	44	0	21	.310
Rick Valley, Galesburg	.181	54	4	36	.298
Tony Dobies, Springfield	.171	51	3	29	.298
Phil Rashead, Springfield	.158	47	1	19	.297
Dave Banko, Macomb	...183	53	1	22	.290
Larry Corrigan, Bloom*	.142	41	6	31	.289
Mike Hannah, Bloom	...153	44	3	27	.288
Ed Dixon, Macomb*	...159	45	2	22	.283

Leading Pitchers

*Throws lefthanded.

Pitcher—Club	IP.	SO.	W.	L.	ERA.
Lee Hansen, Springfield	.. 54	43	8	1	1.50
Doug Wessel, Peoria	.. 52	65	3	5	2.42
Frank Bjork, Bloom	 89	83	5	5	2.63
Bruce Katt, Galesburg*	.. 94	81	9	3	2.68
Bernie Strawn, Peoria	.. 75	65	3	4	2.90
Steve Foran, Galesburg*	. 85	79	6	5	2.96
Steve Valadez, Macomb	. 97	44	8	4	3.06
Jeff Lessig, Peoria	 63	56	1	6	3.29
Steve Greenough, Spring*	. 67	59	5	3	3.36
Bill Slevcove, Macomb*	. 54	29	5	1	3.50

No-hit games—Katt, Galesburg, defeated Peoria, 2-0, July 4 (seven innings).

ATLANTIC COLLEGIATE LEAGUE

Club	W.	L.	Pct.	G.B.
Staten Island	18	9	.667	....
Mount Vernon	15	12	.556	3
Long Island	13	15	.464	5½
Jersey City	12	14	.462	5½
Brooklyn-Queens	10	18	.357	8½

Managers — Brooklyn-Queens, James Apicella; Jersey City, John Kucks; Long Island, Al Goldis; Mount Vernon, Jack Lyons; Staten Island, Tony Russo.

Leading Batters

Player—Club	AB.	H.	HR.	RBI.	Pct.
Gil Hodges, Jr., Staten Is	85	32	0	11	.376
Lou Anemone, Staten Is	..102	38	0	20	.373
John Yeglinski, Staten Is.	. 98	34	1	16	.347
Larry Liedy, Staten Is	.. 67	23	2	21	.343
Joe Chiaramonte, Mt. V	.. 60	27	1	21	.338
Al Volpe, Brooklyn-Queens	67	22	0	10	.328
Marc Rubin, Mt. Vernon	.. 76	24	1	16	.316
Tony Giordano, Staten Is.	. 96	30	2	24	.313
Russ Bove, Long Island	.. 87	27	0	16	.310
Skip Borowicz, Long Is	..105	32	1	14	.305
Nick Fanelli, Mt. Vernon	. 99	30	3	25	.303
Harry Hess, Brooklyn-Que	80	24	0	7	.300
Bob Borowicz, Long Is	.. 97	29	0	12	.299
Vincent Camuto, B-Queens	88	26	1	11	.295
Dennis Mendoza, Long Is.	. 95	28	1	6	.295

Leading Pitchers

Pitcher—Club	IP.	SO.	W.	L.	ERA.
Bill Dotter, Long Island	.. 35	26	1	3	1.03
Terry Blitz, Mt. Vernon	.. 60	46	6	2	1.65
Mike Salogub, Jersey City.	64	56	4	2	1.69
Bob MacDonald, Long Is..	63	36	4	2	1.71
Jeff Sartorius, Staten Is..	47	23	4	2	2.30
Bob Nelson, Long Island	. 34	15	2	3	2.65
Larry Nickol, Long Island.	68	33	5	3	2.78
Marty Dwonarski, Staten Is	80	53	7	4	2.93
Larry Aubel, Jersey City	. 35	20	2	3	3.09
Steve Broege, Mt. Vernon.	45	46	3	3	3.80

West Covina Post No. 790: Front row—Manny Estrada, Mark Marcus, Art Bauer, Frank O'Connor, Mike Quinley, Bill Devine. Second row—Ernie Sanchez, Coley Smith, Bill Pico, Joe Opatkiewicz, Jr., Burl Truesdale, Jesus Mendoza. Back row—Don Sealy, manager; Ward Lyons, Dan Watters, Mike McManus, Greg Terlecky, Craig Barnes, Randy Haas, Joe Opatkiewicz, Sr., coach. Seated in front—Glen Barnes and Tom Cunningham, batboys.

West Covina, Calif., '70 Legion Champs

By LARRY WIGGE

Never before was the old phrase "Pitching is 75 percent of the game" so evident as it was in 1970, when Klamath Falls, Ore., hosted the American Legion Championship.

If any manager were told he could go into a four-game series and have to call upon only three pitchers to sweep the entire set, he would immediately turn his back on you. However, Don Sealy, manager of the 1970 American Legion champion club from West Covina, Calif., faced such an experience head-on. Sealy's hurlers recorded three shutouts in four games and, in just 41 innings, they mesmerized opposition batsmen into 61 strikeouts.

For the first time in the history of Legion tournaments, an all-star team was selected, and the complete dominance of the West Covina pitching staff was further exemplified with the placing of Greg Terlecky and Coley Smith on that squad. Smith and Frank O'Connor turned in complete-game shutouts for Post No. 790, while Smith and Terlecky combined to blank Manchester in a 14-inning affair.

Kiger Stadium in Klamath Falls yielded 14 homers in as many games. With the robust strokes taken at the offerings served up to the plate, nine contests involved pitchers who fanned ten or more batters. Coley Smith whiffed 18 batters in his 12 innings of that shutout game against Manchester, while Terlecky fanned 17 Wilmington hitters in the only game West Covina allowed a score.

Tulsa's Carson-Wilson Post No. 1 engineered the greatest rout of the tournament, when it smashed Manchester, 19-0. Carroll Watts chipped in with four hits in that game and had a .421 average for regional and tournament play. For this he was selected Player of the Year.

The Phoenix entry contributed two honors to its luggage after a fourth-place finish. Leadoff batter Ron Brown had the highest average (.429) in the postseason games and shortstop Gil Stafford won the James Daniel Award for sportsmanship. The Phoenix cleanup hitter suffered a badly injured leg, but still hit .316 to earn the award.

West Covina went undefeated in the World Series, and claimed the crown with a resounding 10-0 victory over Levittown, whom they had beaten in their previous encounter, 7-0. This was the 12th time a California entry had won the title in the 45 years it has been run.

Here are the scores as they occurred:

Levittown 5, New Castle 4	West Covina 6, Wilmington 3
Omaha 2, Phoenix 1	Phoenix 10, Wilmington 9
Wilmington 11, Tulsa 2	Tulsa 10, Omaha 8
West Covina 1, Manchester 0	West Covina 7, Levittown 0
Phoenix 5, New Castle 3	Tulsa 6, Phoenix 2
Tulsa 19, Manchester 0	Levittown 3, Tulsa 2
Levittown 6, Omaha 2	West Covina 10, Levittown 0

The avid Legion fans in Klamath Falls rolled up an attendance figure of 22,379.

Presidents of Minor Leagues for '71

CLASS AAA

American Association—Allie Reynolds, P. O. Box 16696, Oklahoma City, Okla. 73116

International League—George H. Sisler, Jr., International Suite, Sheraton Hotel, Rochester, N. Y. 14604

Mexican League—Antonio Ramirez (Muro), Av. Baja California 177-103, Mexico 7, D. F., Mex.

Pacific Coast League—William B. McKechnie, Jr., P. O. Box 5560, Phoenix, Ariz. 85010

CLASS AA

Eastern League—Roy Jackson, Box 530, Paoli, Pa. 19301

Southern League—Sam C. Smith, Jr., 4205 Holston Hills Road, Knoxville, Tenn. 37914

Texas League—Robert R. Bragan, 910 Mallick Tower, Fort Worth, Tex. 76102. (Texas and Southern leagues have combined to form the Dixie Association.)

CLASS A

California League—Edward J. Mulligan, 18 Corte Dorado, Millbrae, Calif. 94030

Carolina League—Wallace McKenna, P. O. Box 1326, Lynchburg, Va. 24505

Florida State League—George MacDonald, P. O. Box 414, Lakeland, Fla. 33802

Mexican Center League—Antonio Ramirez (Muro), Av. Baja California 177-103, Mexico 7, D. F., Mex.

Mexican Northern League—Horacio Lopez, Plutarco Elias Calles No. 100 Altos, Hermosillo, Sonora, Mex.

Midwest League—Jim Doster, 10 Fair Oaks Drive, Decatur, Ill. 62225

New York-Pennsylvania League—Vincent M. McNamara, Box 109, Orchard Park, N. Y. 14127

Northern League—A. O. White, 1946 Johnson Drive, Sioux Falls, S. D. 57105

Northwest League—John L. Carbray, 1849 Willamette St., Eugene, Ore. 97401

Western Carolinas League—John H. Moss, P. O. Box 49, Kings Mountain, N. C. 28086

ROOKIE CLASSIFICATION

Appalachian League—Chauncey DeVault, 14 Lee St., Bristol, Va. 24201

Gulf Coast League—George MacDonald, P. O. Box 414, Lakeland, Fla. 33802

Pioneer League—Claude Engberg, 1500 Walker Bank Building, Salt Lake City, Utah

PHILLIP PITON
President of National Association

Official Minor League Averages

Including

1970 Junior World Series

Official Averages Of All Triple A, Double A and A Leagues, Plus Appalachian, Gulf Coast and Pioneer Rookie Leagues

Syracuse 'Reigns' in Junior World Series

By BEN HENKEY

Revived after a seven-year hiatus, baseball's Junior World Series, which 46 times previously had matched playoff winners from the International League, once known as the Eastern League, and American Association, had all the makings of a class confrontation in 1970 until an uncontrollable factor—the weather—turned the comeback of the Triple-A classic into a soggy patchwork affair.

Syracuse's Chiefs, after winning their first International League pennant since 1897, had qualified for a fifth JWS appearance by eliminating Tidewater and Columbus in the Int's drawn-out Shaughnessy playoffs.

The American Association representative was Omaha, twice a pennant winner since the league had been resurrected in 1969. The Royals had captured the AA's Eastern flag, then disposed of West winner Denver in just five games of a best-of-seven playoff.

The Chiefs were to prove the superior club, but not before a damp and sometimes stormy series of events—including a near rebellion by the players involved and a "shutout" in Omaha—left a rather bad taste in the mouths of all concerned.

Omaha was to be the site of the first three games in the best-of-seven series, with the opener scheduled September 13. But a cold rain washed out the contest and the field at Rosenblatt Stadium, unaccountably, was left uncovered.

When it became apparent the next day that the field could not be put into playable condition, the three-man committee in charge of the series (National Association President Phil Piton and Presidents George Sisler Jr. of the International League and Allie Reynolds of the American Association) huddled and announced that the first three games were being shifted to Syracuse.

Another factor in the decision was the apparent lack of interest on the part of Omaha fans. Less than 200 tickets had been sold in four days.

As the players boarded a flight for Syracuse, there were rumors that the committee had reached a decision to play the series in its entirety at MacArthur Stadium.

The weather in Syracuse wasn't much of an improvement over Omaha's when the Royals and Chiefs resumed play September 15. A cold rain fell in the New York city, but it had stopped by game time.

The Royals, facing Syracuse lefthander Rob Gardner, never got started in the openre. They were limited to one hit by the 25-year-old former Met, who claimed his 19th victory of the season and his third in the playoffs, 2-0. Luis Alcaraz' fifth-inning double spoiled Gardner's no-hit bid, while in the same inning a squeeze bunt by Matt Galante and a wild pitch by loser Mike Hedlund accounted for both of the Chiefs' runs.

Omaha scored its first run of the series in the opening inning of the second game the next day—then was blanked the rest of the way by Alan Closter. The Chiefs, with the help of three unearned sixth-inning runs on a pair of two-base errors by outfielder Ted Parks, made it two straight, 5-1.

Weather and attendance improved September 17, and so did the Royals. They drove Syracuse starter Thad Tillotson from the box with a four-run

outburst in the third inning. But the Chiefs rebounded with five runs in the home half of the fourth inning, including solo home runs by Bill Robinson and Tony Solaita. Royal relievers checked the Chiefs the rest of the way, however, and Omaha sewed up an 11-5 victory with four runs in the eighth, two driven home by Charlie Day's triple.

The series committee at this point announced that the fourth and fifth games would be played in Syracuse, and that if additional contests were necessary, the clubs would return to Omaha. The arrangement met with approval by the players, who were to receive 70 percent of the receipts from the first four games and had been pleased with attendance for the first three.

But the announcement drew protests and complaints from Omaha. "I can't believe this could happen," said Mayor Eugene Leahy, who added that he would ask the National Association office for a full report of the circumstances leading to the decision.

Meanwhile, the rain moved back into Syracuse. Showers fell all day September 18 and the MacArthur Stadium field remained covered. Another postponement seemed likely. Fewer than 1,500 fans were in the park at the scheduled 7:30 starting time, and about half of those departed while players from both clubs and the series committee argued over whether or not to start the game.

The committee didn't want another delay; the players balked because it was to be the final game in which they got a share of the gate receipts.

However, the series committee was insistent, and at 9:16 the fourth game got under way, with Omaha batting as the home club.

Syracuse grabbed a 4-1 lead after only two innings, but the Royals fought back to tie the score in the fourth. But the Chiefs finally won it, 6-5, on a run driven home in the eighth by George Pena, and took a commanding 3-1 lead.

Game five was played in Syracuse September 19—following an announcement by the series committee that if a sixth and seventh game were necessary, they would be contested in Omaha.

But Royals' fans were not to get the opportunity to see the club in series action at home; the Chiefs closed out the season with a 5-3, 11-inning victory to claim their first JWS title.

Syracuse's Pena untied a 3-3 knot in the top of the 11th (the Royals again were batting as the home team) with a triple which scored Bobby Cox, who had walked. Winning pitcher Hal Reniff, appearing in relief for the third straight night, then lofted a sacrifice fly to get Pena home with an insurance run.

Omaha had taken a 2-0 lead in the first against Syracuse starter Gary Jones, who had control problems, hitting a batter, throwing two wild pitches and giving up a single and sacrifice fly before settling down to work six scoreless innings.

The Chiefs used the long ball to battle back. Bobby Mitchell, Cox and Robinson hit bases-empty home runs in the third, fifth and eighth innings, Robinson's giving Syracuse a 3-2 lead. The Royals' Luis Alcaraz sent the game into extra innings with a run-scoring double in the bottom of the ninth.

Robinson finished as the batting star of the series, going 8-for-17, in-

BILL ROBINSON
Batting Star

HAL RENIFF
Copped Finale

cluding two homers and three doubles, although Syracuse hit only .224 as a club, compared with .233 for Omaha.

A $25,416.97 players' pool was split 60-40 by the participants, with the victorious Chiefs dividing up $15,250.18, largest amount in the last 15 series. Attendance for the five games, despite the weather, was 20,427.

Game of September 15

Omaha	0	0	0	0	0	0	0	0	0—0	1	0
Syracuse	0	0	0	0	2	0	0	0	x—2	4	1

Hedlund, York (8) and Healy; Gardner and Pena. W—Gardner. L— Hedlund. HR—None. A—3,662.

Game of September 16

Omaha	1	0	0	0	0	0	0	0	0—1	7	2
Syracuse	0	0	0	1	0	3	1	0	x—5	7	0

Splittorff, Gladden (8) and Healy; Closter and Pena. W—Closter. L—Splittorff. HR—None. A—4,035.

Game of September 17

Omaha	0	0	4	0	2	0	0	4	1—11	13	0
Syracuse	0	0	0	5	0	0	0	0	0—5	7	1

O'Riley, Gladden (4). York (8) and Sullivan; Tillotson, Burbach (3), Reniff (5), Jones (8), Spier (8) and Pena. W—Gladden. L—Reniff. HR—Syracuse, Robinson, Solaita. A—5,357.

Game of September 18

Syracuse	1	3	0		0	1	0		0	1	0—6	10	2
Omaha	0	1	2		1	0	0		0	1	0—5	10	2

Game played at Syracuse; Omaha home club.

Schoen, Reniff (6) and Pena; Cram, Clemons (4), Cisco (5), York (8) and Sullivan, Healy (8). W—Schoen. L—Clemons. HR—Omaha, Sullivan. A—1,483.

Game of September 19

Syracuse	0	0	1		0	1	0		0	1	0		0	2—5	9	2
Omaha	2	0	0		0	0	0		0	0	1		0	0—3	9	0

Game played at Syracuse; Omaha home club.

Jones, Tillotson (8), Reniff (8) and Pena; Hedlund, Gladden (7), Splittorff (10) and Healy. W—Reniff. L—Splittorff. HR—Syracuse, Mitchell, Cox, Robinson. A—5,890.

All-Time Finalists in Jr. World Series

Year	Winner—Manager	Loser—Manager	Outcome
1904	Buffalo E.L. (George Stallings)	St. Paul A.A. (Mike Kelley)	2-1
1906	Buffalo E.L. (George Stallings)	Columbus A.A. (Bill Clymer)	*3-2
1907	Toronto E.L. (Joe Kelley)	Columbus A.A. (Bill Clymer)	4-1
1917	Indianapolis A.A. (J. Hendricks)	Toronto I.L. (Nap Lajoie)	4-1
1920	Baltimore I.L. (Jack Dunn)	St. Paul A.A. (Mike Kelley)	5-1
1921	Louisville A.A. (Joe McCarthy)	Baltimore I.L. (Jack Dunn)	5-3
1922	Baltimore I.L. (Jack Dunn)	St. Paul A.A. (Mike Kelley)	5-2
1923	Kansas City A.A. (Wilbur Good)	Baltimore I.L. (Jack Dunn)	5-4
1924	St. Paul A.A. (Nick Allen)	Baltimore I.L. (Jack Dunn)	*5-4
1925	Baltimore I.L. (Jack Dunn)	Louisville A.A. (Joe McCarthy)	5-3
1926	Toronto I.L. (Dan Howley)	Louisville A.A. (Bill Meyer)	5-0
1927	Toledo A.A. (Casey Stengel)	Buffalo I.L. (Bill Clymer)	5-1
1928	Indianapolis A.A. (Bruno Betzel)	Rochester I.L. (Billy Southworth)	*5-1
1929	Kan. City A.A. (Dutch Zwilling)	Rochester I.L. (Billy Southworth)	5-4
1930	Rochester I.L. (Billy Southworth)	Louisville A.A. (Al Sothoron)	5-3
1931	Rochester I.L. (Billy Southworth)	St. Paul A.A. (Al Leifield)	5-3
1932	Newark I.L. (Al Mamaux)	Minneapolis A.A. (Donie Bush)	4-2
1933	Columbus A.A. (Ray Blades)	Buffalo I.L. (Ray Schalk)	5-3
1934	Columbus A.A. (Ray Blades)	Toronto I.L. (Ike Boone)	5-4
1935	No series played.		
1936	Milwaukee A.A. (Al Sothoron)	Buffalo I.L. (Ray Schalk)	4-1
1937	Newark I.L. (Oscar Vitt)	Columbus A.A. (Burt Shotton)	4-3
1938	Kansas City A.A. (Bill Meyer)	Newark I.L. (Johnny Neun)	4-3
1939	Louisville A.A. (Bill Burwell)	Rochester I.L. (Billy Southworth)	4-3
1940	Newark I.L. (Johnny Neun)	Louisville A.A. (Bill Burwell)	4-2
1941	Columbus A.A. (Burt Shotton)	Montreal I.L. (Clyde Sukeforth)	4-2
1942	Columbus A.A. (Eddie Dyer)	Syracuse I.L. (Jewel Ens)	4-1
1943	Columbus A.A. (Nick Cullop)	Syracuse I.L. (Jewel Ens)	4-1
1944	Baltimore I.L. (Tommy Thomas)	Louisville A.A. (Harry Leibold)	4-2
1945	Louisville A.A. (Harry Leibold)	Newark I.L. (Bill Meyer)	4-2
1946	Montreal I.L. (Clay Hopper)	Louisville A.A. (Harry Leibold)	4-2
1947	Milwaukee A.A. (Nick Cullop)	Syracuse I.L. (Jewel Ens)	4-3
1948	Montreal I.L. (Clay Hopper)	St. Paul A.A. (Walter Alston)	4-1
1949	Indianapolis A.A. (Al Lopez)	Montreal I.L. (Clay Hopper)	4-2
1950	Columbus A.A. (Rollie Hemsley)	Baltimore I.L. (Nick Cullop)	4-1
1951	Milwaukee A.A. (Chas. Grimm)	Montreal I.L. (Walter Alston)	4-2
1952	Rochester I.L.(Harry Walker)	Kansas City A.A. (George Selkirk)	4-3
1953	Montreal I.L. (Walter Alston)	Kansas City A.A. (Harry Craft)	4-1
1954	Louisville A.A. (Mike Higgins)	Syracuse I.L. (Skeeter Newsome)	4-2
1955	Minneapolis A.A.(Bill Rigney)	Rochester I.L. (Dixie Walker)	4-3
1956	Ind'napolis A.A. (Kerby Farrell)	Rochester I.L. (Dixie Walker)	4-0
1957	Denver A.A. (Ralph Houk)	Buffalo I.L. (Phil Cavarretta)	4-1
1958	Minneapolis A.A. (Gene Mauch)	Montreal I.L. (Clay Bryant)	4-0
1959	Havana I.L (Preston Gomez)	Minneapolis A.A. (Gene Mauch)	4-3
1960	Louisville A.A. (Bill Adair)	Toronto I.L. (Mel McGaha)	4-2
1961	Buffalo I.L. (Kerby Farrell)	Louisville A.A. (Ben Geraghty)	4-0
1962	Atlanta I.L. (Joe Schultz)	Louisville A.A. (Jack Tighe)	4-3

Note—Asterisk (*) indicates one tie game.

American Association

Leading Batter	League President	Leading Pitcher
CHRIS CHAMBLISS	ALLIE REYNOLDS	ROSS GRIMSLEY
Wichita		Indianapolis

CHAMPIONSHIP WINNERS IN PREVIOUS YEARS

1902—Indianapolis .... .683	1931—St. Paul .... .623	1949—St. Paul .... .608
1903—St. Paul .... .657	1932—Minneapolis .... .595	Indianapolis (2nd)‡ .604
1904—St. Paul .... .646	1933—Columbus* .... .604	1950—Minneapolis .... .584
1905—Columbus .... .658	Minneapolis .... .562	Columbus (3rd)‡ .. .549
1906—Columbus .... .615	1934—Minneapolis .... .570	1951—Milwaukee† .... .623
1907—Columbus .... .584	Columbus* .... .556	1952—Milwaukee .... .656
1908—Indianapolis ...... .601	1935—Minneapolis .... .591	Kansas City (2nd)‡ .578
1909—Louisville .... .554	1936—Milwaukee† .... .584	1953—Toledo .... .584
1910—Minneapolis ...... .637	1937—Columbus† .... .584	Kansas City (2nd)‡ .571
1911—Minneapolis ...... .600	1938—St. Paul .... .596	1954—Indianapolis ...... .625
1912—Minneapolis ...... .636	Kansas City (2nd)‡ .. .556	Louisville (2nd)‡ .. .556
1913—Milwaukee .... .599	1939—Kansas City ...... .695	1955—Minneapolis† ...... .597
1914—Milwaukee .... .590	Louisville (4th)‡ .. .490	1956—Indianapolis† ..... .597
1915—Minneapolis ...... .597	1940—Kansas City ...... .625	1957—Wichita .... .604
1916—Louisville .... .605	Louisville (4th)‡ .. .500	Denver (2nd)‡ .... .584
1917—Indianapolis ...... .588	1941—Columbus† .... .621	1958—Charleston .... .589
1918—Kansas City ...... .589	1942—Kansas City ...... .549	Minneapolis (3rd)‡ .. .536
1919—St. Paul .... .610	Columbus (3rd)‡ .. .532	1959—Louisville§ .... .599
1920—St. Paul .... .701	1943—Milwaukee .... .596	Omaha§ .... .516
1921—Louisville .... .583	Columbus (3rd)‡ .. .532	Minneapolis (2nd)‡ .58c
1922—St. Paul .... .641	1944—Milwaukee ... .667	1960—Denver .... .571
1923—Kansas City ...... .675	Louisville (3rd)‡ .. .574	Louisville (2nd)‡ .. .556
1924—St. Paul .... .578	1945—Milwaukee .... .604	1961—Indianapolis ..... .573
1925—Louisville .... .635	Louisville (3rd)‡ .. .545	Louisville (2nd)‡ .. .533
1926—Louisville .... .629	1946—Louisville† .... .601	1962—Indianapolis ..... .605
1927—Toledo .... .601	1947—Kansas City ...... .608	Louisville (4th)‡ .. .486
1928—Indianapolis ...... .593	Milwaukee (3rd)‡ .. .513	1963-68—Did not operate.
1929—Kansas City ...... .665	1948—Indianapolis ...... .649	1969—Omaha .... .607
1930—Louisville .... .608	St. Paul (3rd)‡ ... .558	

*Won playoff (East vs. West). †Won championship and four-team playoff. ‡Won four-team
playoff. §Respective Eastern and Western Division winners.

STANDING OF CLUBS AT CLOSE OF SEASON, SEPTEMBER 3

EASTERN DIVISION

Club	Omaha	Iowa	Ind.	Evan.	Den.	Tul.	O.C.	Wich.	W.	L.	T.	Pct.	G.B.
Omaha (7)	..	7	12	14	12	11	6	11	73	65	1	.529	....
†Iowa (11*)	15	..	11	13	8	11	8	4	70	68	1	.507	3
Indianapolis (15*)	12	13	..	14	8	7	8	9	71	69	0	.507	3
Evansville (9*)	10	11	10	..	8	7	13	8	67	71	0	.486	6

WESTERN DIVISION

Denver (12*)	5	9	9	8	..	13	11	15	70	69	0	.504	....
Tulsa (22*)	6	6	10	10	11	..	15	12	70	70	0	.500	½
Oklahoma City (16)	11	9	9	3	13	9	..	14	68	71	0	.489	2
Wichita (5*)	6	13	8	9	9	12	10	..	67	73	0	.479	3½

†Represented Des Moines, Iowa.

Key to major league farm teams (indicated by numbers after clubs in standing) shown on Page 384.

Playoff—Omaha defeated Denver, four games to one.

Regular Season Attendance—Denver, 175,746; Des Moines, 133,929; Evansville, 130,809; Indianapolis, 150,807; Oklahoma City, 157,728; Omaha, 196,086; Tulsa, 151,258; Wichita, 256,824. Total, 1,353,187. All-star game, 4,286. Playoff, 9,144.

Managers: Denver—George (Whitey) Kurowski, Art Fowler (interim); Dick Gernert; Evansville—Ralph Rowe; Indianapolis—Vern Rapp; Iowa—Sherm Lollar; Oklahoma City—Hub Kittle; Omaha—Jack McKeon; Tulsa—Warren Spahn; Wichita—Ken Aspromonte.

All-Star Team: 1B—Marquez, Iowa; 2B—Glover, Evansville; 3B—Lowenstein, Wichita; SS—Duffy, Indianapolis; OF—Scheinblum, Wichita; Melendez, Tulsa; Spriggs, Omaha; C—Tenace, Iowa; Suarez, Wichita; P—Blue, Iowa; Wilcox, Indianapolis; Manager—Jack McKeon, Omaha.

(Compiled by William J. Weiss, League Statistician, San Mateo, Calif.)

CLUB BATTING

Club	G.	AB.	R.	OR.	H.	TB.	2B.	3B.	HR.	RBI.	SH.	Int. SF.	BB.	HP.	SO.	SB.	CS.	LOB.	Pct.
Wichita ..	140	4663	655	646	1319	1946	216	36	113	586	54	41	484	43	27	804	60	59	982	.283
Okla. City	139	4594	642	641	1268	1817	195	57	80	572	59	24	485	42	45	797	77	59	1051	.276
Iowa	139	4692	677	655	1272	1954	220	21	140	620	44	28	539	45	57	1023	49	31	1084	.271
Denver ..	139	4655	668	684	1248	1838	193	49	103	612	57	50	520	36	38	961	75	28	1062	.268
Omaha ..	139	4534	602	567	1191	1707	199	46	75	537	78	40	522	49	30	786	69	46	1009	.263
Tulsa	140	4484	571	605	1155	1648	203	34	74	516	40	40	511	43	37	783	65	46	997	.258
Indi'apolis	140	4542	544	542	1152	1615	173	28	78	486	67	43	405	49	42	819	113	71	923	.254
Evansville	138	4416	521	537	1119	1635	169	34	93	470	39	31	406	48	23	843	72	40	915	.253

INDIVIDUAL BATTING

(Leading Qualifiers for Batting Championship—434 or More Plate Appearances)

*Bats lefthanded.   †Switch-hitter.

Player and Club	G.	AB.	R.	H.	TB.	2B.	3B.	HR.	RBI.	SH.	SF.	BB.	HP.	SO.	SB.	CS.	Pct.
Chambliss, C. Christopher, Wichita*	105	383	60	131	185	17	8	7	52	2	3	46	2	62	14	5	.342
Marquez, Gonzalo, Iowa* ...	115	449	56	153	193	16	3	6	60	2	3	23	0	55	8	9	.341
Scheinblum, Richard, Wich†	.133	460	79	155	265	32	3	24	84	3	6	72	2	54	4	8	.337
Nettles, James, Evansville*	.112	385	62	122	174	22	3	8	34	1	3	55	0	64	4	4	.317
Melendez, Luis, Tulsa	140	507	77	155	244	34	8	13	71	2	5	51	2	64	14	5	.306
Patterson, Joe, Denver* ...	.124	409	76	125	173	21	6	5	55	4	3	60	3	69	26	4	.306
Billings, Richard, Denver ..	.112	387	60	118	181	14	2	15	67	0	2	43	5	67	4	1	.305
Chiles, Richard, Okla C* ...	.108	414	56	126	175	24	11	1	36	1	2	35	6	32	9	11	.304
Spriggs, George, Omaha* ...	.105	386	71	116	193	26	9	11	43	1	1	46	0	83	29	13	.301
McNulty, William, Iowa	.106	386	53	114	203	19	2	22	73	1	5	49	3	105	2	2	.295
Lowenstein, John, Wichita*	.108	369	63	109	190	15	6	18	52	4	3	59	3	64	10	10	.295

Departmental Leaders: G—Melendez, 140; AB—Melendez, 507; R—Scheinblum, 79; H—Melendez, Scheinblum, 155; TB—Scheinblum, 265; 2B—Melendez, 34; 3B—Chiles, 11; HR—Nash, 33; RBI—Scheinblum, 84; SH—Duffy, 11; SF—Rico, 7; BB—Brooks, 82; HP—Ragland, 10; SO—Dwain Anderson, 134; SB—Spriggs, 29; CS—Hill, Spriggs, 13.

(All Players—Listed Alphabetically)

Player and Club	G.	AB.	R.	H.	TB.	2B.	3B.	HR.	RBI.	SH.	SF.	BB.	HP.	SO.	SB.	CS.	Pct.
Adair, K. Jerry, Tulsa	33	77	5	23	28	5	0	0	7	0	2	9	2	8	0	0	.299
Alcaraz, A. Luis, Omaha ..	77	263	30	67	102	11	3	6	29	8	2	39	3	41	1	0	.255
Allen, Robert, Wichita* ...	8	1	0	0	0	0	0	0	0	0	0	0	0	1	0	0	.000
Almonte, Secundino, Okla C	.35	23	6	5	7	0	1	0	0	0	0	2	0	12	0	0	.217
Anderson, Donald, Ind.* ...	.117	358	46	102	154	21	5	7	44	0	2	38	2	55	3	0	.285
Anderson, Dwain, Iowa	.130	456	62	115	178	14	2	15	60	5	2	50	2	134	3	1	.252
Armstrong, James, Ind	.102	328	30	81	91	5	1	1	30	3	4	28	3	48	2	7	.247
Austin, Rick, Wichita	6	17	1	3	3	0	0	0	4	0	1	2	0	9	0	0	.176
Bailey, Steven, OC-17 Tul	38	52	5	10	14	4	0	0	6	4	0	2	0	16	0	0	.192
Bakenhaster, David, Tulsa ..	44	11	1	2	3	1	0	0	1	1	0	2	0	6	0	0	.182
Baker, Frank, Wichita*	108	341	50	97	159	20	3	12	46	1	3	33	2	72	3	6	.284

Player and Club	G.	AB.	R.	H.	TB.	2B.	3B.	HR.	RBI.	SH.	SF.	BB.	HP.	SO.	SB.	CS.	Pct.
Baldwin, Richard, Denver* ..	84	176	21	40	51	5	3	0	20	2	5	8	2	41	5	1	.227
Barber, Steven, Evansville† ..	12	5	0	1	2	1	0	0	0	1	0	0	0	2	0	0	.200
Barrett, Alexander, Okla C ..	12	26	5	5	9	1	0	1	3	0	0	3	0	5	0	0	.192
Bates, Delbert, Wichita*	21	65	7	18	25	2	1	1	6	0	0	11	1	18	1	0	.277
Batista, Rafael, Okla C*	90	234	33	72	104	8	6	4	36	2	1	29	1	49	5	3	.308
Beckner, Bobbye, Evansville .	18	55	8	9	12	3	0	0	3	1	0	9	0	16	1	0	.164
Behney, Melvin, Indianapolis*	4	10	1	3	3	0	0	0	0	0	0	0	0	1	0	0	.300
Belinsky, Robert, Ind*	16	27	1	4	5	1	0	0	1	0	0	6	0	9	0	0	.148
Bevacqua, Kurt, Ind 135	135	482	62	126	207	26	5	15	67	7	2	31	5	96	12	9	.261
Bickerton, Brien, Iowa*	17	12	2	2	5	0	0	1	3	1	0	3	0	4	0	0	.167
Billings, Richard, Denver ...112	112	387	60	118	181	14	2	15	67	0	2	43	5	67	4	1	.305
Blackmon, Jimmy, Denver ..	24	4	0	3	3	0	0	0	1	0	0	0	0	0	0	0	.750
Blasingame, Wade, Okla C* .	16	34	4	7	9	2	0	0	6	0	0	9	0	14	0	0	.206
Blateric, Stephen, Ind	4	1	0	0	0	0	0	0	0	0	0	0	0	0	0	0	.000
Blue, Vida, Iowa†	17	45	2	5	6	1	0	0	2	3	0	5	0	28	0	0	.111
Blyleven, Rikalbert, Evan ..	8	21	1	4	4	0	0	0	0	1	0	0	0	11	0	0	.190
Bobb, M. Randall, Tulsa 50	50	170	19	51	87	10	1	8	18	0	0	4	0	30	1	2	.300
Boehmer, Bernard, Iowa	1	2	0	0	0	0	0	0	0	0	0	0	0	0	0	0	.000
Bogle, Warren, Iowa*	18	11	0	2	2	0	0	0	0	0	0	0	0	6	0	0	.182
Borbon, Pedro, Indianapolis .	32	11	1	1	1	0	0	0	1	0	0	0	0	3	0	0	.091
Bosch, Donald, Okla City† ..	25	92	14	18	28	4	0	2	5	0	0	6	0	13	4	2	.196
Bouton, James, Okla City ..	2	1	0	0	0	0	0	0	0	0	0	0	0	1	0	0	.000
Bowlin, L. Weldon, Evan ...	87	252	26	67	81	8	3	0	28	0	3	24	0	32	2	0	.266
Boyd, A. LaDon, Iowa	13	19	0	2	2	0	0	0	1	1	0	0	0	8	0	0	.105
Boyles, Thomas, Wichita	1	1	0	0	0	0	0	0	0	0	0	0	0	0	0	0	.000
Braxton, James, Wichita	32	18	1	1	2	1	0	0	0	0	0	1	0	9	0	0	.056
Breeden, Danny, Ind	60	155	19	39	58	8	1	3	13	2	0	14	2	37	0	0	.252
Brohamer, John, Wichita* ...	40	146	24	34	49	7	1	2	17	0	2	18	0	15	2	2	.233
Brooks, Robert, Iowa 124	124	447	72	128	205	28	2	15	60	3	0	82	0	112	4	3	.286
Brown, Jackie, Denver	12	26	3	3	3	0	0	0	1	0	0	2	0	12	0	0	.115
Brumley, T. Mike, Okla C* .	80	244	28	72	98	15	1	3	38	1	2	42	1	22	0	0	.295
Bryant, Donald, Okla City ..	30	46	5	9	9	0	0	0	3	0	0	9	0	11	1	0	.196
Burchart, Larry, Wichita ...	27	32	1	9	9	0	0	0	2	3	1	0	0	12	0	0	.281
Burgmeier, Thomas, Omaha*	10	8	1	2	2	0	0	0	0	0	0	2	0	3	1	0	.250
Burroughs, Jeffrey, Denver .115	115	390	64	105	185	17	6	17	71	2	6	70	3	117	4	5	.269
Butler, William, Omaha*	4	5	1	0	0	0	0	0	0	0	0	3	0	3	0	0	.000
Camacho, Jacinto, Wichita ..	37	14	0	2	2	0	0	0	0	0	0	0	0	6	0	0	.143
Camilli, Louis, Wichita† 100	100	386	50	113	158	20	2	7	30	6	1	39	2	40	5	7	.293
Campbell, James, Tulsa*	80	229	38	58	104	10	3	10	31	0	2	23	5	41	2	2	.253
Carlos, Francisco, Denver ..	32	69	6	14	16	2	0	0	9	7	2	3	0	21	0	0	.203
Carruthers, Michael, Wich* .102	102	324	32	102	142	21	2	5	46	5	1	23	1	56	0	0	.315
Castle, Donald, Denver*	26	89	6	19	28	2	2	1	10	0	1	8	0	19	0	1	.213
Cedeno, Cesar, Okla City ...54	54	233	47	87	161	14	9	14	61	1	1	8	4	26	9	6	.373
Chambliss, C. Christopher, Wichita* 105	105	383	60	131	185	17	8	7	52	2	3	46	2	62	14	5	.342
Chiles, Richard, Okla C* ...108	108	414	56	126	175	24	11	1	36	1	2	35	6	32	9	11	.304
Chlupsa, Robert, Tulsa	21	8	0	2	3	1	0	0	0	0	0	0	0	4	0	0	.250
Cisco, Galen, Omaha†	24	20	1	3	4	1	0	0	1	3	0	0	0	3	0	0	.150
Clark, Ronald, B., Iowa 117	117	441	65	120	166	18	2	8	55	2	3	60	2	73	1	4	.272
Clemons, Lance, Omaha*	16	18	0	3	3	0	0	0	1	0	0	0	0	8	0	0	.167
Cleveland, Reginald, Tulsa .	24	54	7	11	13	2	0	0	2	5	0	1	0	19	0	1	.204
Coggins, Franklin, Wichita† .	25	47	6	9	10	1	0	0	4	0	0	4	0	10	0	0	.191
Colbert, Vincent, Wichita* .	28	17	1	0	0	0	0	0	0	0	0	2	0	7	0	0	.000
Conde, Ramon, Indianapolis .	14	16	0	2	2	0	0	0	1	0	0	1	2	0	0	0	.125
Conger, Gregory, Iowa*	21	33	5	7	13	1	1	1	6	1	2	5	0	15	0	0	.212
Coulter, Thomas, Tulsa†	21	72	7	18	21	3	0	0	6	1	2	4	1	11	4	1	.250
Cram, Gerald, Omaha	35	55	6	11	12	1	0	0	3	7	0	2	0	15	0	0	.200
Crawford, Alfred, Ind 127	127	455	57	117	154	16	6	3	36	5	3	28	6	81	18	12	.257
DaVanon, F. Gerald, Tulsa .	76	254	33	59	83	9	3	3	27	0	0	36	2	39	8	5	.232
Day, Charles E., Omaha 85	85	312	38	97	122	14	4	1	40	2	2	19	3	19	2	2	.311
de la Hoz, Miguel, Ind 53	53	152	15	41	50	6	0	1	17	0	2	9	3	10	0	0	.270
Demeter, Steve, Tulsa	26	50	2	11	15	1	0	1	6	0	2	2	0	10	0	0	.220
Dickson, James, Okla City* .	39	9	2	2	3	1	0	0	1	0	0	1	0	2	0	0	.222
Donnelly, Richard, Denver* .	62	111	13	26	31	3	1	0	6	2	1	13	1	13	0	0	.234
Driscoll, James, Iowa*	76	297	44	90	133	18	2	7	37	4	3	27	7	35	0	4	.303
Duffalo, James, Okla City ..	40	9	0	0	0	0	0	0	0	0	0	0	0	6	0	0	.000
Duffy, Frank, Indianapolis ..117	117	415	57	109	145	11	2	7	33	11	5	39	1	68	17	5	.263
Dukes, N. Jan, Denver*	29	38	4	16	21	0	1	1	6	2	0	1	0	5	0	0	.421
Dusan, Gene, Iowa†	10	18	3	5	5	0	0	0	1	0	0	1	0	5	0	0	.278
Ellis, James, Tulsa	22	16	3	3	5	2	0	0	1	1	0	0	0	8	0	0	.188
Ellis, Samuel, Tulsa*	7	8	0	3	4	1	0	0	1	0	0	0	0	3	0	0	.375
Engbers, Donald, Tulsa†	18	26	1	5	7	2	0	0	3	0	0	0	0	4	0	0	.192
Estelle, Richard, Evan†	35	59	2	10	13	1	1	0	3	3	0	0	0	31	0	0	.169
Etheridge, Bobby, Tulsa	42	106	11	24	33	3	0	2	13	1	2	13	2	25	1	2	.226
Evans, Richard, Okla City* .	13	4	0	1	1	0	0	0	1	0	0	0	0	1	0	0	.250
Farmer, Edward, Wichita ...	23	42	2	4	4	0	0	0	3	0	1	0	2	12	0	0	.095
Finafrock, Carl, Evansville .	28	25	1	8	8	0	0	0	3	1	1	1	0	8	0	0	.320
Fisher, John, Tulsa	9	6	1	1	1	0	0	0	1	0	0	1	0	1	0	0	.167
Floyd, Robert, Omaha	62	236	36	69	88	11	1	2	32	4	4	19	0	35	0	0	.292
Ford, Theodore, Wichita ...106	106	383	63	125	181	12	4	12	57	0	5	15	2	71	4	7	.326
Forsch, Kenneth, Okla C	5	15	0	0	0	0	0	0	2	0	0	0	0	7	0	0	.000

Player and Club	G.	AB.	R.	H.	TB.	2B.	3B.	HR.	RBI.	SH.	SF.	BB.	HP.	SO.	SB.	CS.	Pct.
Fowler, J. Arthur, Denver ..	45	7	0	0	0	0	0	0	0	0	0	1	0	7	0	0	.000
Gebhard, Robert, Evansville .	44	12	1	2	2	0	0	0	1	2	0	1	0	4	0	0	.167
Geiger, Gary, Okla City*	105	304	44	86	126	14	4	6	36	1	3	62	2	67	1	5	.283
Geishert, Vernon, Ind	31	69	3	7	9	2	0	0	4	2	1	2	0	24	0	0	.101
Gilhooley, Robert, Iowa	23	45	2	3	3	0	0	0	0	0	0	7	1	7	0	0	.067
Gladden, Lloyd, Omaha ...	3	1	0	0	0	0	0	0	0	0	0	0	0	0	0	0	.000
Glover, James, Evansville .	115	432	41	112	132	8	3	2	36	3	2	24	2	46	3	3	.259
Godby, Danny, Indianapolis .	17	58	4	20	25	2	0	1	8	0	0	1	0	6	1	1	.345
Gonzalez, Pedro, Wichita ...	90	329	36	89	120	15	2	4	32	7	2	17	4	35	7	7	.271
Gotay, Julio, Okla City ...	85	280	34	78	99	6	0	5	42	2	1	21	4	34	2	1	.279
Green, Lee, Omaha*	77	152	20	37	52	6	3	1	17	6	0	29	1	35	2	1	.243
Grieve, Thomas, Denver ..	51	182	39	51	98	4	2	13	29	0	1	30	2	61	2	0	.280
Griffin, Thomas, Okla City ..	5	10	1	3	3	0	0	0	0	2	0	0	0	5	0	0	.300
Grimsley, Ross, Ind*	30	62	5	11	11	0	0	0	4	6	1	2	0	20	0	0	.177
Guindon, Robert, Tulsa* ...	94	254	31	70	118	13	4	9	48	0	4	33	3	57	3	4	.276
Guinn, Drannon, Okla City ..	32	37	4	9	9	0	0	0	2	3	0	1	0	4	0	1	.243
Guzman, Santiago, Tulsa ...	22	25	3	3	4	1	0	0	0	3	0	3	0	9	0	0	.120
Hamende, Joseph, Ind	48	7	2	1	1	0	0	0	0	1	0	1	0	3	0	1	.143
Hamm, Peter, Evansville ..	15	34	0	6	9	1	1	0	0	1	0	1	0	3	0	1	.176
Handrahan, J. Vernon, Iowa*	8	3	0	2	2	0	0	0	0	0	0	0	0	0	0	0	.667
Hargan, Steven, Wichita ...	14	21	5	6	8	0	1	0	4	0	0	1	0	10	0	0	.286
Harrelson, William, Ind† ...	23	30	1	6	7	1	0	0	2	0	0	3	0	14	0	1	.200
Harris, J. William, Omaha*..	73	149	21	30	39	7	1	0	7	1	0	13	0	36	2	2	.201
Harrison, Charles, Omaha ...	109	387	69	108	191	18	1	21	65	2	3	59	6	38	1	0	.279
Haydel, J. Harold, Evan .	28	66	6	6	11	0	1	1	5	5	0	3	0	33	0	0	.091
Healy, Francis, Omaha ..	82	252	35	74	103	12	1	5	36	2	1	53	0	62	5	3	.294
Hedlund, Michael, Omaha† ..	28	44	2	5	10	0	1	1	2	2	0	1	0	24	0	0	.114
Hefferon, John, Iowa	9	3	0	0	0	0	0	0	0	0	0	0	0	1	0	0	.000
Hennigan, Phillip, Wichita ..	7	12	0	1	1	0	0	0	1	0	0	1	0	5	0	0	.083
Henninger, Richard, Denver	9	17	1	0	0	0	0	0	0	0	0	0	0	16	0	0	.000
Hense, Richard, Denver	65	190	26	56	81	8	1	5	32	1	0	9	2	36	1	1	.295
Hilgendorf, Thomas, Tulsa† .	28	29	5	7	8	1	0	0	1	1	0	3	0	10	0	0	.241
Hill, Herman, Evansville* .	112	452	50	112	152	15	8	3	35	1	1	31	0	99	24	13	.248
Hinsley, Jerry, Wichita	10	8	0	2	2	0	0	0	1	0	0	0	0	2	0	0	.250
House, Patrick, 32 In-24 Den*	56	7	1	1	1	0	0	0	0	0	0	1	1	5	0	0	.143
Howard, Lawrence, Okla C ..	83	268	46	81	140	21	4	12	51	1	3	41	1	51	1	3	.302
Humphreys, Robert, Denver .	3	0	0	0	0	0	0	0	0	0	0	0	1	0	0	0	.000
Isaac, Luis, Wichita	52	135	15	30	33	3	0	0	12	1	1	20	3	30	1	2	.222
Jagutis, H. John, Iowa†	2	4	0	1	1	0	0	0	0	0	0	0	0	1	0	0	.250
James, William, Wichita ...	15	3	0	0	0	0	0	0	0	0	0	0	0	2	0	0	.000
Jaster, Daniel, Tulsa	7	2	0	0	0	0	0	0	0	0	0	1	0	1	0	0	.000
Jimenez, P. Elvio, 59 Denver-49 Ind	108	386	33	106	159	14	3	11	51	4	2	12	3	29	5	1	.275
Johnson, Clifford, Okla C ..	22	55	12	21	30	4	1	1	5	0	0	5	1	5	0	0	.382
Johnson, Jerry, Tulsa	2	3	1	2	2	0	0	0	0	0	0	0	0	0	0	0	.667
Johnson, Robert W., Iowa ..	8	38	4	11	15	2	1	0	6	0	0	1	0	4	1	0	.289
Jones, Steven, Omaha	41	12	0	1	1	0	0	0	0	0	0	0	0	3	0	0	.083
Joyce, Thomas, Omaha	38	117	18	27	38	1	5	0	12	1	2	18	2	26	1	2	.231
Kaiser, Robert, Wichita	10	10	1	1	1	0	0	0	1	0	0	2	0	5	0	0	.100
Kennedy, James, Tulsa*	73	229	31	63	80	13	2	0	20	1	1	26	2	22	6	3	.275
Kernek, George, Ind*	78	157	14	33	42	6	0	1	16	1	4	15	1	23	1	4	.210
Klimchock, Louis, Denver* ..	20	73	13	18	29	5	0	2	7	0	1	6	0	6	0	1	.247
Krebs, Kristopher, Denver ..	61	179	26	51	69	9	3	1	24	3	3	17	0	34	5	1	.285
Kuhn, Charles, Denver*	7	3	0	0	0	0	0	0	0	0	0	1	0	0	0	0	.000
Lachemann, Marcel, Iowa ...	11	5	1	1	1	0	0	0	0	0	0	0	1	0	0	0	.200
Lachemann, Rene, Iowa	61	171	25	44	69	10	1	0	5	20	1	22	2	36	0	0	.257
Lampard, C. Keith, Okla C* .	14	14	3	1	1	0	0	0	1	0	0	1	0	2	0	0	.071
LaRussa, Anthony, Iowa	22	88	13	22	33	5	0	2	5	0	0	9	2	14	0	0	.250
Law, Ronald, Denver	35	72	4	12	16	2	1	0	5	2	0	1	0	19	0	0	.167
Lewis, Allen, Iowa†	71	230	36	52	72	6	4	2	12	3	0	8	3	38	17	4	.226
Lind, Jackson, Okla City† ..	82	254	29	52	68	8	4	0	14	7	0	27	2	70	0	0	.205
Look, Bruce, Evansville* ...	99	284	17	69	91	14	1	2	23	0	2	27	2	34	0	1	.243
Lowenstein, John, Wichita* .	108	369	69	109	190	15	6	18	52	4	3	59	3	64	10	10	.295
Mairena, Alfonso, Tulsa	11	10	1	1	1	0	0	0	1	0	0	1	0	2	0	0	.100
Major, John, Iowa	7	2	1	1	1	0	0	0	0	0	0	0	0	1	0	0	.500
Manuel, Charles, Evansville*	21	70	13	23	46	5	0	6	26	0	0	6	1	5	0	0	.329
Marquez, Gonzalo, Iowa* ...	115	449	56	153	193	16	3	6	60	2	3	23	0	55	8	9	.341
Marshall, Michael G., O C ..	16	15	0	0	0	0	0	0	1	1	0	1	0	2	0	0	.000
Martin, M. LeRoy, Okla C ..	4	1	0	0	0	0	0	0	0	0	0	0	0	0	0	0	.000
Martin, T. Eugene, Denver* .	86	318	43	81	149	13	2	17	63	1	3	21	2	86	0	1	.255
Mashore, Clyde, Ind	48	177	28	34	53	7	0	4	20	1	2	27	0	40	11	6	.192
Mason, James, Denver*	110	382	50	92	144	16	6	8	43	1	6	55	1	86	8	5	.241
Mason, John E., Okla	101	367	40	105	126	13	1	2	40	3	2	17	4	51	9	3	.286
Mayberry, John, Okla City* .	70	231	55	63	115	7	3	13	38	2	3	49	5	41	5	0	.273
McCool, William, Tulsa	11	7	1	0	0	0	0	0	0	0	0	2	0	5	0	0	.000
McFadden, Leon, 16OC-74Tul	90	313	48	83	103	8	3	2	28	7	0	39	5	50	11	4	.265
McKenzie, George D., Evan .	13	28	3	6	7	1	0	0	1	0	0	1	0	8	0	0	.214
McMillan, Steven, Omaha ...	77	234	27	63	75	5	2	1	26	1	3	24	4	38	2	2	.269
McNulty, William, Iowa	106	386	53	114	203	19	2	22	73	1	5	49	3	105	2	2	.295
Melendez, Luis, Tulsa	140	507	77	155	244	34	8	13	71	2	5	51	2	64	14	5	.306
Mendoza, C. Rigoberto, Evan	84	314	37	87	107	14	0	2	16	3	1	17	0	16	8	6	.277
Miles, James, Denver	25	17	0	2	2	0	0	0	1	1	0	1	0	13	1	0	.118

Player and Club	G.	AB.	R.	H.	TB.	2B.	3B.	HR.	RBI.	SH.	SF.	BB.	HP.	SO.	SB.	CS.	Pct.
Miller, Raymond, Wichita	56	26	1	2	3	1	0	0	2	0	0	0	0	12	0	0	.077
Mingori, Stephen, Wichita* ..	16	4	0	0	0	0	0	0	0	1	0	0	0	1	0	0	.000
Monteagudo, Aurelio, Omaha	14	5	0	2	2	0	0	0	3	1	0	0	0	2	0	1	.400
Montgomery, Monty, Omaha .	26	45	2	4	5	1	0	0	2	8	1	0	0	18	0	0	.089
Morales, Jose, Iowa	93	229	36	70	120	14	0	12	31	1	1	36	2	58	1	1	.306
Morris, Danny, Evansville ..	35	63	4	9	9	0	0	0	5	2	1	4	0	26	0	0	.143
Murphy, William, Tulsa	35	74	8	14	18	1	0	1	7	0	2	7	0	18	0	1	.189
Nash, Charles, Evansville ..	120	383	60	97	208	12	0	33	83	1	4	55	3	90	5	2	.253
Nasif, Ralph, Evansville ...	5	4	0	0	0	0	0	0	0	0	0	0	0	1	0	0	.000
Nelson, David, Denver	53	206	36	76	111	17	6	2	20	5	4	20	1	18	8	2	.369
Nen, Richard, Denver*	101	294	41	92	137	18	3	7	48	0	5	47	3	41	1	2	.313
Nettles, James, Evansville* .	112	385	62	122	174	22	3	8	34	1	3	55	0	64	4	4	.317
Nordberg, Alan, Evansville* .	33	57	5	9	10	1	0	0	1	0	0	9	0	10	1	0	.158
Noriega, John, Indianapolis .	24	34	3	2	2	0	0	0	1	0	0	1	0	22	0	0	.059
Northey, Scott, Omaha	31	93	12	21	35	2	2	2	8	1	1	16	2	23	4	4	.226
Norton, Wayne, Iowa*	117	345	54	84	141	15	0	14	42	2	5	51	1	57	0	0	.243
Nossek, Joseph, Tulsa	116	356	35	81	100	11	1	2	30	4	1	32	2	54	2	10	.228
Olerud, John, Tulsa	103	311	34	80	93	9	2	0	32	0	2	35	2	58	2	1	.257
Olivo, Milciades, Iowa	34	39	1	5	6	1	0	0	2	2	1	0	0	11	0	0	.128
O'Riley, Donald, Omaha ..	17	34	0	5	5	0	0	0	1	3	0	0	0	16	0	0	.147
Osborn, Danny, Indianapolis	15	8	1	1	4	0	0	1	1	0	0	1	0	3	0	0	.125
Osinski, Daniel, Okla C ..	45	17	1	4	4	0	0	0	1	0	0	0	0	2	0	0	.235
Osteen, M. Darrell, Iowa ..	21	36	3	6	8	2	0	0	1	2	0	6	0	15	1	0	.167
Paepke, Dennis, Omaha	93	305	36	80	118	16	2	6	44	2	2	29	2	46	3	0	.262
Panther, James, Iowa	35	8	0	0	0	0	0	0	0	0	0	1	0	5	0	0	.000
Parker, Harry, Tulsa	26	39	1	6	6	0	0	0	2	4	0	5	0	18	1	0	.154
Parker, John, Denver	9	10	1	2	2	0	0	0	0	0	0	3	0	4	0	0	.200
Parks, Theodore, Omaha ..	84	257	30	67	96	11	3	4	27	5	6	25	1	48	2	1	.261
Patterson, Joe, Denver†	124	409	76	125	173	21	4	5	55	4	3	60	3	69	26	4	.306
Paul, Michael, Wichita*	10	23	3	2	3	1	0	0	1	1	0	3	0	6	0	0	.087
Peterson, Charles, Wichita ..	101	288	52	84	113	12	1	5	44	0	6	38	1	29	2	2	.292
Peterson, Richard, Evan ..	17	14	0	0	0	0	0	0	0	1	0	1	0	8	0	0	.000
Pitts, Gaylen, Tulsa	115	364	51	86	133	14	3	9	39	2	3	46	5	71	5	2	.236
Pizarro, Juan, Iowa*	5	13	3	5	7	2	0	0	3	0	0	1	0	4	0	0	.385
Plummer, William, Ind	115	365	37	95	130	12	1	7	42	6	5	40	6	71	1	6	.260
Powell, Paul, Evansville ..	86	254	47	74	126	15	2	11	33	0	1	17	2	66	7	3	.291
Ragland, Thomas, Denver ..	126	424	73	110	137	19	1	2	40	6	2	61	10	79	3	2	.259
Randle, Leonard, Denver† ..	46	101	14	21	24	3	0	0	5	3	0	12	1	15	3	1	.208
Ranew, Merritt, Denver* ..	6	19	0	4	4	0	0	0	1	0	1	2	0	7	0	0	.211
Reuss, Jerry, Tulsa*	11	30	3	3	4	1	0	0	1	0	1	0	0	19	0	0	.100
Reynolds, Thomas, Iowa‡ ..	23	94	25	36	51	9	0	2	19	0	0	7	1	6	1	0	.383
Rico, Alfredo, 46 Om-85 Tul .	131	441	58	117	174	20	5	9	66	0	0	67	1	74	8	3	.265
Rios, Juan, Omaha	27	99	5	22	25	3	0	0	11	0	1	1	1	7	0	1	.222
Ritter, B. Douglas, Denver*	34	4	0	0	0	0	0	0	0	1	0	0	0	2	0	0	.000
Rittwage, James, Wichita ..	35	48	5	10	11	1	0	0	1	0	0	0	0	17	1	0	.208
Rohr, William, Wichita* ..	7	9	0	0	0	0	0	0	1	1	0	0	0	3	0	0	.000
Roos, Leslie, Omaha	28	56	7	9	11	0	1	0	8	1	0	12	0	9	1	0	.161
Russell, Donald, Okla City ..	15	32	3	4	6	2	0	0	2	0	0	2	0	9	0	0	.125
Rusteck, Richard, Evan ..	30	20	1	3	5	0	1	0	5	0	0	0	0	10	0	0	.150
Salvato, Steve, Denver ..	16	12	2	1	1	0	0	0	1	0	0	1	0	2	0	0	.083
Schaeffer, Mark, Okla C* ..	26	39	0	10	12	2	0	0	9	2	0	1	0	4	0	0	.256
Scheinblum, Richard, Wich† .	133	460	79	155	265	32	3	24	84	3	6	72	2	54	4	8	.337
Schneider, Daniel, Tulsa* ..	34	10	5	3	4	1	0	0	0	1	0	3	0	4	0	0	.158
Schubert, Gregory, Iowa* ..	19	54	6	14	20	3	0	1	4	0	0	8	0	4	1	0	.259
Scott, G. Robert, Okla C ..	35	25	1	5	6	1	0	0	2	2	1	0	0	2	0	0	.200
Scruggs, John, Wichita ..	59	131	28	35	74	7	1	10	30	0	2	12	3	38	3	1	.267
Sembera, Carroll, Tulsa ..	34	4	0	1	2	1	0	0	0	0	0	0	0	2	0	0	.250
Sevcik, John, Evansville ..	69	196	19	55	75	12	1	2	31	2	5	19	3	24	1	0	.281
Shaw, Donald, Tulsa*	2	1	0	0	0	0	0	0	0	0	0	0	0	1	0	0	.000
Shifflett, Garland, Evan ..	53	28	6	5	5	0	0	0	2	1	0	5	0	10	0	0	.179
Simmons, Ted, Tulsa†	15	51	10	19	28	4	1	1	8	0	1	11	0	2	1	0	.373
Simon, Thomas, Okla City* ..	105	271	33	68	83	9	3	0	22	6	1	22	6	48	10	7	.251
Sims, Gregory, Okla City† ..	88	263	44	80	127	19	2	8	37	0	0	54	0	46	5	1	.304
Sisk, Tommie, Wichita	20	16	1	2	2	0	0	0	1	0	2	0	0	4	0	0	.125
Skrable, Patrick, Omaha ..	74	188	28	54	80	14	0	4	25	6	2	22	1	30	6	6	.287
Smith, Richard K., Denver ..	20	71	8	19	29	2	1	2	7	0	1	7	0	11	0	0	.268
Soderholm, Eric, Evansville .	98	310	44	77	139	11	3	15	42	1	3	42	5	58	7	2	.248
Sorrell, Bill, Omaha*	37	136	18	49	64	5	2	2	17	1	1	15	1	12	0	2	.360
Southard, Edward, Wichita	70	205	30	48	66	5	2	3	23	4	1	21	0	23	3	2	.234
Spinks, Scipio, Okla City ..	26	60	7	10	14	1	0	1	7	1	0	2	0	30	0	0	.167
Splittorff, Paul, Omaha* ..	28	53	3	10	11	1	0	0	5	2	0	2	0	14	1	0	.189
Sprague, Edward, Iowa ..	33	61	6	15	30	3	0	4	14	0	0	1	0	24	0	0	.246
Sprague, Gary, Wichita* ..	19	36	6	9	10	1	0	0	7	0	1	4	1	10	0	1	.250
Spriggs, George, Omaha* ..	105	386	71	116	193	26	9	11	43	1	1	46	0	83	29	13	.301
Stickels, Robert, Iowa	49	21	1	5	6	1	0	0	3	0	0	0	0	5	0	0	.238
Suarez, Kenneth, Wichita ..	84	269	24	81	112	22	0	3	28	0	2	35	1	28	0	0	.301
Such, Richard, Denver* ..	13	22	3	4	4	0	0	0	1	1	0	0	0	6	0	0	.182
Sullivan, John P., Omaha* ..	64	160	10	41	56	12	0	1	20	9	6	21	0	18	0	1	.256
Swanson, Stanley, Ind	120	431	62	122	174	19	3	9	51	5	6	49	4	54	26	10	.283
Talbot, Fred, Iowa	27	62	6	14	21	1	0	2	5	4	0	6	0	26	0	0	.226
Tartabull, Jose, Iowa*	38	98	19	24	29	2	0	1	7	0	0	7	0	6	4	0	.245
Tatis, Fernando, Okla C	36	119	13	36	42	4	1	0	18	3	2	4	0	22	1	1	.303

Player and Club	G.	AB.	R.	H.	TB.	2B.	3B.	HR.	RBI.	SH.	SF.	BB.	HP.	SO.	SB.	CS.	Pct.
Tenace, F. Gene, Iowa	93	319	54	90	164	24	1	16	63	1	1	49	4	81	5	1	.282
Theobald, Ronald, 29Den-64In	93	285	38	88	108	18	1	0	28	8	5	25	2	31	12	5	.309
Thomas, Derrel, Okla City† .	75	272	39	73	102	5	6	4	21	6	0	18	3	53	11	2	.268
Thomas, J. Leroy, Tulsa* ..	135	477	67	128	175	23	0	8	66	2	5	55	5	48	2	1	.268
Thompson, Danny, Evan	58	215	26	53	72	13	3	0	18	3	0	16	2	29	5	1	.247
Thompson, Michael, Denver ..	5	4	0	1	1	0	0	0	0	0	0	0	0	2	0	0	.250
Tidrow, Richard, Wichita ..	19	26	2	1	1	0	0	0	1	2	1	1	0	12	0	0	.038
Torres, Hector, Okla City ...	38	151	15	46	65	7	3	2	20	3	1	6	1	19	1	0	.305
Valdespino, Hilario, Omaha*	54	213	42	64	87	11	3	2	27	3	1	29	2	22	3	4	.300
Vasser, Lucious, Evan*	109	261	30	69	105	11	2	7	29	0	3	17	0	54	2	2	.264
Vaughan, Charles, Omaha† ..	5	2	0	0	0	0	0	0	0	0	0	0	0	0	0	0	.000
Walters, Charles, Denver ...	15	8	1	1	1	0	0	0	1	0	0	0	0	2	0	0	.125
Ward, John, Indianapolis ..	92	276	44	67	113	8	1	12	45	4	1	44	3	71	7	3	.243
Watkins, Robert, Okla C	20	33	5	7	10	0	0	1	3	3	1	2	0	9	0	1	.212
Welsch, Ronald, Indianapolis	34	10	0	0	0	0	0	0	0	0	0	1	0	3	0	0	.000
Whitby, William, Denver ...	9	5	0	0	0	0	0	0	0	0	0	0	0	2	0	0	.000
Wilcox, Milton, Ind	38	52	6	9	9	0	0	0	3	2	0	3	1	14	0	1	.173
Willhite, J. Nicholas, Omaha*	6	1	1	1	1	0	0	0	1	0	0	0	0	0	0	0	1.000
Wissler, C. Robert, Evan* ..	47	109	11	22	28	1	1	1	12	0	1	20	3	28	2	2	.202
Wolff, William, Tulsa*	16	24	3	6	9	3	0	0	1	1	0	4	0	4	1	0	.250
Womack, Horace, Ind*	49	12	3	3	6	1	1	0	2	2	0	0	4	1	0	0	.250
Woodson, George, Denver ...	41	43	2	5	6	1	0	0	4	7	1	1	0	17	0	0	.116
Woodson, Richard, Evan	9	7	0	0	0	0	0	0	0	0	0	0	0	3	0	0	.000
York, James, Omaha	41	14	0	2	2	0	0	0	1	2	0	2	0	4	0	0	.143
Young, Donald, Iowa	32	107	18	23	42	5	1	4	17	2	2	14	1	36	1	1	.215
Zachary, W. Chris, 16 Omaha-17 Tulsa*	33	82	10	15	23	5	0	1	6	1	0	1	0	25	0	0	.183
Zuber, Ronald, Wichita	12	15	0	4	4	0	0	0	1	0	0	0	0	6	0	0	.267

The following players had no plate appearances (listed alphabetically by clubs, games in parentheses):

EVANSVILLE—Baker, E. Gene (4).

IOWA—Rodriquez, Roberto (2).

OKLAHOMA CITY—Penalver, Luis (1).

OMAHA—Hudgins, Jerry (8); Wright, Stephen (7).

TULSA—Campisi, Salvatore (4); Dillman, William (4); Marion, Gary* (1); Seminoff, Richard (5).

GRAND-SLAM HOME RUNS—Dwain Anderson, 3; Cedeno, Melendez, 2 each; Bevacqua, Billings, Burroughs, Ford, Harrison, Howard, Lowenstein, Norton, Scruggs, Young, 1 each.

AWARDED FIRST BASE ON INTERFERENCE—Alcaraz (Tenace), Hense (Sevcik), Shifflett (Billings).

CLUB FIELDING

Club	G.	PO.	A.	E.	DP.	PB.	Pct.	Club	G.	PO.	A.	E.	DP.	PB.	Pct.
Indianapolis ..	140	3638	1463	136	135	10	.9740	Omaha	139	3598	1421	185	126	10	.964
Evansville ..	138	3463	1502	133	154	8	.9739	Denver	139	3588	1679	196	144	30	.964
Wichita ...	140	3620	1480	162	119	19	.969	Oklahoma City .	139	3517	1332	184	116	17	.963
Tulsa ...	140	3553	1439	164	120	27	.968	Iowa	139	3591	1399	203	132	29	.961

Triple Plays—Tulsa, Denver, 1 each.

INDIVIDUAL FIELDING
(Ten or More Games)

*Throws lefthanded.

FIRST BASEMEN

Player and Club	G.	PO.	A.	E.	DP.	Pct.	Player and Club	G.	PO.	A.	E.	DP.	Pct.
Castle, Denver*	13	124	12	0	7	1.000	Peterson, Wichita ..	25	162	20	2	16	.989
Kernek, Ind*	52	230	13	1	28	.996	Anderson, Ind*	100	737	55	10	66	.988
Carruthers, Wichita ..	88	688	57	4	55	.995	Batista, Okla City* ..	61	426	35	6	40	.987
Vasser, Evansville* ..	23	136	10	1	14	.993	Ward, Indianapolis .	27	209	21	3	26	.987
HARRISON, Omaha .107		846	91	7	82	.993	R. Lachemann, Iowa .43		362	18	5	36	.987
Nash, Evansville ...108		818	68	7	98	.992	Mayberry, Okla C* ..	70	536	30	8	50	.986
Nen, Denver	88	739	75	7	69	.991	Harris, Omaha	13	61	9	1	7	.986
Martin, Denver	37	312	19	3	43	.991	Guindon, Tulsa*	23	178	15	3	12	.985
Burroughs, Denver ..	12	106	2	1	10	.991	Chambliss, Wichita .	48	323	18	6	25	.983
Sorrell, Omaha	11	100	2	1	13	.990	Paepke, Omaha	17	119	9	3	10	.977
Thomas, Tulsa	98	739	61	8	79	.990	Nordberg, Evan*	21	112	8	3	16	.976
Marquez, Iowa* 109		852	61	10	81	.989	Campbell, Tulsa	21	146	11	6	14	.963

Triple Plays—Nen, Campbell.

(Fewer Than Ten Games)

Player and Club	G.	PO.	A.	E.	DP.	Pct.	Player and Club	G.	PO.	A.	E.	DP.	Pct.
Bobb, Tulsa	6	48	4	0	3	1.000	Adair, Tulsa	1	4	0	0	0	1.000
Sevcik, Evansville ..	3	24	1	0	2	1.000	Demeter, Tulsa	1	2	1	0	1	1.000
Bevacqua, Ind	3	17	2	0	2	1.000	Billings, Denver	1	1	0	0	0	1.000
Geiger, Okla City ..	3	13	1	0	0	1.000	Plummer, Ind	1	1	0	0	0	1.000
Engbers, Tulsa*	3	10	1	0	1	1.000	Howard, Okla City ..	5	38	4	1	1	.977
Nossek, Tulsa	1	9	0	0	1	1.000	Mason, Okla City ...	5	34	7	1	6	.976
Johnson, Okla City .	1	5	0	0	0	1.000	Manuel, Evansville ..	2	18	3	1	3	.955

SECOND BASEMEN

Player and Club	G.	PO.	A.	E.	DP.	Pct.
Harris, Omaha	23	39	42	0	8	1.000
Parks, Omaha	23	35	45	1	11	.988
Alcaraz, Omaha ..	61	105	155	4	23	.985
McMillan, Omaha ..	27	69	89	3	23	.981
Ragland, Denver ..	87	197	266	10	58	.979
GLOVER, Evan ...	111	281	285	13	84	.978
Pitts, Tulsa	41	64	106	4	20	.977
Theobald, Den-Ind .	61	112	173	7	42	.976
Randle, Denver	34	68	89	4	20	.975
LaRussa, Iowa	32	52	59	3	11	.974
Southard, Wichita .	53	102	117	6	26	.973
DaVanon, Tulsa ...	52	115	161	8	37	.972
Adair, Tulsa	23	43	52	3	13	.969
Nelson, Denver	18	36	58	3	12	.969
Gonzalez,. Wichita .	87	184	246	14	50	.968
Coulter, Tulsa	20	50	57	4	11	.964
Armstrong, Ind	94	209	271	18	58	.964
Clark, Iowa	55	99	129	9	25	.962
Gotay, Okla City ..	72	130	161	12	35	.960
Mason, Okla City .	58	94	135	10	31	.958
Bowlin, Evansville .	25	56	58	5	17	.958
Driscoll, Iowa	61	145	187	15	46	.957
Kennedy, Tulsa	15	20	28	3	6	.941
Lind, Oklahoma City	13	24	31	4	4	.932
Sorrell, Omaha	12	33	23	5	7	.918

Triple Play—Adair.

(Fewer Than Ten Games)

Player and Club	G.	PO.	A.	E.	DP.	Pct.
Mairena, Tulsa	5	6	13	0	3	1.000
Bevacqua, Ind	3	8	10	0	1	1.000
Mendoza, Evansville	4	6	11	0	4	1.000
Ward, Indianapolis .	3	7	9	0	2	1.000
Suarez, Wichita ...	1	9	5	0	3	1.000
McFadden, Tulsa ...	1	3	3	0	1	1.000
Gilhooley, Iowa ...	2	1	5	0	0	1.000
Roos, Omaha	2	1	4	0	1	1.000
Conde, Indianapolis .	1	3	1	0	1	1.000
Coggins, Wichita ...	3	2	2	0	0	1.000
Boyles, Wichita	1	1	1	0	1	1.000
Sprague, Iowa	1	1	1	0	0	1.000
Lowenstein, Wichita .	1	1	0	0	0	1.000
Rios, Omaha	2	0	1	0	0	1.000
Marion, Tulsa	1	1	0	0	0	1.000
Brohamer, Wichita .	7	15	25	1	4	.976
Joyce, Omaha	4	10	7	1	3	.944
Thomas, Okla City .	5	8	7	2	1	.882
Krebs, Denver	2	4	10	2	2	.875
Nossek, Tulsa	3	3	4	1	0	.875
R. Lachemann, Iowa	1	3	1	2	1	.750
Rico, Omaha	2	1	0	1	0	.500

THIRD BASEMEN

Player and Club	G.	PO.	A.	E.	DP.	Pct.
Brohamer, Wichita .	20	18	24	1	2	.977
Mendoza, Evansville	79	63	193	7	25	.970
Etheridge, Tulsa ...	35	18	37	2	3	.965
Nossek, Tulsa	26	24	31	2	5	.965
Pitts, Tulsa	72	60	120	7	8	.963
Lowenstein, Wichita .	72	61	132	8	14	.960
Demeter, Tulsa	11	6	17	1	2	.958
BEVACQUA, Ind ...	95	73	168	12	26	.953
Bowlin, Evansville .	17	17	39	3	1	.949
Soderholm, Evan ...	21	28	36	4	4	.941
Ward, Indianapolis .	20	15	16	2	3	.939
Clark, Iowa	55	39	111	10	13	.938
de la Hoz, Ind	41	34	64	7	3	.933
Krebs, Denver	37	23	61	6	7	.933
Mason, Okla City ..	36	37	57	7	5	.931
McMillan, Omaha ..	40	39	62	8	6	.92?
Beckner, Evansville .	17	7	28	3	4	.921
Peterson, Wichita ..	39	27	59	8	6	.915
Alcaraz, Omaha	15	9	33	4	4	.913
Driscoll, Iowa	14	17	33	5	2	.909
Tatis, Okla City ...	28	24	35	6	1	.908
Nelson, Denver	35	24	54	8	5	.907
Lind, Okla City ...	42	33	62	10	9	.905
Klimchock, Denver .	18	11	35	5	3	.902
McNulty, Iowa	58	46	136	21	13	.897
Rico, Omaha-Tulsa .	57	35	98	16	5	.893
Parks, Omaha	48	41	75	14	6	.892
Howard, Okla City .	20	14	32	6	1	.885
Sprague, Wichita ..	10	7	20	4	1	.871
Hense, Denver	23	11	36	8	1	.855
Burroughs, Denver .	28	18	40	10	3	.853
Russell, Okla City .	11	9	15	5	3	.828

Triple Play—Klimchock.

(Fewer Than Ten Games)

Player and Club	G.	PO.	A.	E.	DP.	Pct.
Coggins, Wichita ...	4	2	10	0	0	1.000
Gilhooley, Iowa	7	3	5	0	0	1.000
Gotay, Okla City ...	1	0	6	0	0	1.000
Gonzalez, Wichita ..	3	0	5	0	0	1.000
Swanson, Ind	4	0	3	0	0	1.000
Mairena, Tulsa	6	1	1	0	0	1.000
Sevcik, Evansville ..	3	1	1	0	0	1.000
Bosch, Okla City ...	2	0	1	0	0	1.000
Jacutis, Iowa	1	0	1	0	0	1.000
McKenzie, Evan	7	8	8	1	1	.941
McFadden, Okla City	9	10	20	2	2	.938
R. Lachemann, Iowa	5	2	9	1	2	.917
Theobald, Denver ..	6	3	7	1	1	.909
Sorrell, Omaha	9	7	11	2	2	.900
Johnson, Iowa	8	5	13	2	2	.900
Barrett, Okla City ..	8	4	8	2	0	.857
Powell, Evansville ..	2	1	5	2	0	.750
Camilli, Wichita	3	1	1	1	0	.667
Harris, Omaha	2	0	2	2	1	.500
Carruthers, Wichita .	1	0	1	1	0	.500
Roos, Omaha	2	0	1	2	0	.333

SHORTSTOPS

Player and Club	G.	PO.	A.	E.	DP.	Pct.
Tatis, Okla City ...	10	20	15	0	1	1.000
Thompson, Evan ...	58	94	181	5	34	.982
DUFFY, Ind	116	208	335	16	64	.971
Roos, Omaha	19	33	66	3	17	.971
Soderholm, Evan ...	75	140	243	14	53	.965
Lowenstein, Wichita	30	51	86	5	13	.965
Torres, Okla City ..	38	65	126	9	24	.955
McFadden, OC-Tul .	76	131	215	18	48	.951
Lind, Oklahoma City	24	40	77	6	17	.951
Camilli, Wichita ...	96	161	289	27	53	.943
Floyd, Omaha	62	92	160	17	36	.937
Thomas, Okla City .	68	111	149	18	32	.935
Kennedy, Tulsa	47	73	129	14	22	.935
Ragland, Denver ...	31	59	93	11	17	.933
Mason, Denver ...	109	220	408	48	78	.929
Joyce, Omaha	34	58	93	12	17	.926
Anderson, Iowa ...	129	223	378	49	79	.925
DaVanon, Tulsa ...	26	54	77	11	14	.923
Rios, Omaha	24	28	82	12	11	.902
Bevacqua, Ind	17	30	33	7	7	.900
Brohamer, Wichita .	13	25	29	6	6	.900

Triple Play—Mason.

(Fewer Than Ten Games)

Player and Club	G.	PO.	A.	E.	DP.	Pct.
Ward, Indianapolis ..	3	3	6	0	0	1.000
Glover, Evansville ..	2	2	3	0	0	1.000
Randle, Denver	1	0	3	0	0	1.000
Peterson, Wichita ..	1	2	0	0	0	1.000
Rico, Tulsa	1	0	2	0	0	1.000
Sorrell, Omaha	1	1	0	0	0	1.000
Theobald, Ind	9	16	23	2	9	.951
Bowlin, Evansville ..	3	9	8	1	2	.944
Parks, Omaha	5	5	19	2	2	.923
Clark, Iowa	7	8	20	3	1	.903
Gilhooley, Iowa	6	8	11	4	2	.826
Coggins, Wichita ...	4	10	9	5	2	.792
Driscoll, Iowa	3	0	3	1	1	.750
Pitts, Tulsa	5	2	10	5	0	.706
Nasif, Evansville ...	3	2	1	2	0	.600

OUTFIELDERS

Player and Club	G.	PO.	A.	E.	DP.	Pct.
Valdespino, Omaha* ..	54	103	4	0	0	1.000
Tartabull, Iowa* ...	22	38	0	0	0	1.000
Peterson, Wichita ..	22	17	1	0	0	1.000
Bobb, Tulsa	15	15	0	0	0	1.000
Salvato, Denver	13	12	0	0	0	1.000
NORTON, Iowa 110		182	10	1	0	.995
Jimenez, Den-Ind ..	96	148	0	1	2	.994
Lewis, Iowa	56	111	0	1	0	.991
Skrable, Omaha ...	58	97	3	1	1	.990
Swanson, Ind 120		252	12	3	1	.989
Geiger, Okla City ..	89	171	3	2	0	.989
Baker, Wichita ...	96	185	10	3	1	.985
Simon, Okla City* ..	82	123	5	2	2	.985
Day, Omaha	84	204	7	4	2	.981
Baldwin, Denver* ..	72	96	9	2	2	.981
Nossek, Tulsa	96	129	5	3	1	.978
Bowlin, Evansville ..	26	41	3	1	2	.978
Patterson, Denver ..110		195	16	5	1	.977
Chiles, Okla City* ..106		150	9	4	2	.975
Ford, Wichita 101		182	10	5	5	.975
Powell, Evansville ..	72	104	8	3	1	.974
Young, Iowa	31	65	2	2	0	.971
Mashore, Ind	48	94	1	3	0	.969
Green, Omaha*	42	63	0	2	0	.969
Hill, Evansville 112		268	14	9	2	.969
Cedeno, Okla City ..	53	113	6	4	1	.967
Godby, Indianapolis .	17	28	1	1	0	.967
Nettles, Evansville* ..110		156	15	6	4	.966
Burroughs, Denver ..	77	126	10	5	3	.965
Schubert, Iowa*	16	27	0	1	0	.964
Brooks, Iowa 124		227	13	9	3	.964
Paepke, Omaha ..	48	77	3	3	0	.964
Melendez, Tulsa ...137		268	8	11	1	.962
Ward, Indianapolis ..	37	44	2	2	0	.958
Reynolds, Iowa ...	23	43	2	2	0	.957
Grieve, Denver ...	51	123	5	6	1	.955
Martin, Denver	49	61	3	3	0	.955
Sims, Oklahoma ..	75	116	11	6	5	.955
Rico, Omaha-Tulsa ..	30	78	6	4	2	.955
Murphy, Tulsa	22	17	4	1	0	.955
Kernek, Ind*	21	19	1	1	0	.952
Wissler, Evansville .	42	57	2	3	1	.952
Bosch, Okla City ...	22	38	1	2	0	.951
Spriggs, Omaha ...	101	195	16	11	1	.950
Scheinblum, Wichita .127		215	13	13	3	.946
Hense, Denver	24	32	2	2	1	.944
Crawford, Ind 126		191	8	12	2	.943
Bevacqua, Ind	24	29	3	2	0	.941
Scruggs, Wichita ..	39	57	3	4	0	.938
Campbell, Tulsa	48	66	3	5	0	.932
Chambliss, Wichita .	64	90	3	7	0	.930
Thomas, Tulsa	38	48	4	4	0	.929
Vasser, Evansville* .	57	62	11	6	2	.924
Guindon, Tulsa* ...	53	70	2	6	0	.923
Northey, Omaha ...	29	52	1	5	0	.914
McNulty, Iowa ...	49	64	6	7	0	.909
Harris, Omaha	13	20	0	2	0	.909
Manuel, Evansville .	18	25	3	3	0	.903
Smith, Denver	18	16	1	2	0	.895
Tenace, Iowa	13	5	1	1	0	.857

(Fewer Than Ten Games)

Player and Club	G.	PO.	A.	E.	DP.	Pct.
Lowenstein, Wichita .	8	17	0	0	0	1.000
Johnson, Okla City ..	7	14	1	0	0	1.000
Plummer, Ind	8	11	0	0	0	1.000
Parks, Omaha	7	9	0	0	0	1.000
Castle, Denver* ...	9	8	1	0	0	1.000
Lampard, Okla City .	4	8	1	0	0	1.000
Thomas, Okla City ..	3	7	0	0	0	1.000
Engbers, Tulsa* ...	5	5	0	0	0	1.000
Gilhooley, Iowa	3	5	0	0	0	1.000
Armstrong, Ind	4	3	0	0	0	1.000
Howard, Okla City ..	3	3	0	0	0	1.000
Batista, Okla City* ..	1	3	0	0	0	1.000
Anderson, Ind*	2	2	0	0	0	1.000
Billings, Denver	2	2	0	0	0	1.000
Pitts, Tulsa	1	2	0	0	0	1.000
Kennedy, Tulsa	1	1	0	0	0	1.000
Watkins, Okla City ..	1	1	0	0	0	1.000
Wolff, Tulsa	6	10	1	1	0	.917
Nash, Evansville ...	8	8	0	1	0	.889
Sorrell, Omaha	6	7	0	1	0	.875
Marquez, Iowa* ...	6	7	0	2	0	.778
Barrett, Okla City ..	1	0	1	0	0	.500

CATCHERS

Player and Club	G.	PO.	A.	E.	DP.	PB.	Pct.
Paepke, Omaha ..	22	134	4	0	1	0	1.000
Bryant, Okla C ..	17	107	6	0	0	2	1.000
Simmons, Tulsa ..	15	99	7	0	0	4	1.000
Donnelly, Den ..	56	166	23	1	1	7	.995
Bobb, Tulsa ...	29	167	17	1	3	4	.995
PLUMMER, Ind ..102		641	52	4	5	5	.994
Sullivan, Omaha .	51	287	31	2	3	4	.994
Isaac, Wichita ..	50	242	19	2	2	10	.992
Breeden, Ind ..	51	277	26	3	2	5	.990
Look, Evan ..	96	519	73	6	11	3	.990
Bates, Wichita ..	21	140	9	2	0	6	.987
Tenace, Iowa ...	81	529	56	8	5	17	.987
Suarez, Wichita ..	83	537	68	9	9	3	.985
Olerud, Iowa ..	68	634	45	11	5	18	.984
Brumley, O C ..	70	516	28	9	5	8	.984
Sevcik, Evan ...	58	322	20	6	4	5	.983
Morales, Iowa ..	61	327	31	6	3	10	.975
Billings, Den ..106		566	63	16	8	21	.975
Healy, Omaha ..	81	480	44	15	4	6	.972
Howard, Okla C ..	55	366	42	12	9	5	.971

(Fewer Than Ten Games)

Player and Club	G.	PO.	A.	E.	DP.	PB.	Pct.
Murphy, Tulsa ..	8	51	8	0	0	1	1.000
Ranew, Denver ..	6	29	0	0	0	2	1.000
Rico, Om-Tul ..	3	15	2	0	0	0	1.000
Mason, Okla C ..	1	1	0	0	0	0	1.000
Boehmer, Iowa ..	1	0	1	0	0	0	1.000
Dusan, Iowa	7	34	3	1	1	2	.974
Johnson, Okla C .	7	44	8	2	1	2	.963

PITCHERS

Player and Club	G.	PO.	A.	E.	DP.	Pct.
MORRIS, Evansville .	35	12	30	0	6	1.000
Talbot, Iowa	25	15	20	0	1	1.000
Cleveland, Tulsa .	24	16	19	0	1	1.000
Dukes, Denver*	28	7	26	0	2	1.000
Osteen, Iowa	20	6	22	0	1	1.000
Parker, Tulsa	25	10	15	0	2	1.000
O'Riley, Omaha ...	17	9	16	0	3	1.000
Borbon, Ind	32	7	16	0	2	1.000
Colbert, Wichita ..	28	5	16	0	1	1.000
Hilgendorf, Tulsa* ..	23	2	18	0	0	1.000
Hamm, Evansville .	15	7	12	0	0	1.000
Marshall, Okla City.	16	5	14	0	2	1.000
Finafrock, Evan ...	23	5	14	0	1	1.000
House, Ind-Denver*.	56	4	12	0	2	1.000
Reuss, Tulsa*	11	1	15	0	0	1.000
Dickson, Okla City .	39	6	7	0	0	1.000
Paul, Wichita*	10	6	6	0	0	1.000
Chlupsa, Tulsa	21	3	8	0	2	1.000
Osinski, Okla City .	45	2	9	0	0	1.000
Osborn, Ind	15	3	5	0	0	1.000
Peterson, Evan* ...	17	2	6	0	0	1.000
Bogle, Iowa*	18	3	4	0	1	1.000
Walters, Denver ...	15	1	6	0	0	1.000
Mingori, Wichita* ..	16	3	3	0	0	1.000
Ritter, Denver*	34	2	4	0	1	1.000
McCool, Tulsa*	10	3	2	0	0	1.000
James, Wichita	15	3	1	0	0	1.000
Evans, Okla City* ..	13	1	3	0	0	1.000
Hinsley, Wichita ...	10	1	3	0	0	1.000
Kaiser, Wichita* ...	10	1	3	0	0	1.000
M. Lachemann, Iowa	11	0	4	0	1	1.000
Barber, Evansville .	12	0	2	0	0	1.000
Zachary, Omaha-Tul.	27	14	23	1	2	.974
Geishert, Ind	29	11	25	1	1	.973
Womack, Ind	17	11	19	1	4	.968
Rittwage, Wichita ..	32	5	25	1	1	.968
Blasingame, Okla C*	16	4	23	1	1	.964
Montgomery, Omaha .	25	10	15	1	3	.962
Wilcox, Ind	28	12	35	2	4	.959
Splittorff, Omaha* .	28	6	15	1	1	.955
Guinn, Okla City* ..	29	4	17	1	0	.955
Burchart, Wichita ..	27	4	17	1	0	.955
J. Ellis, Tulsa*	22	1	20	1	0	.955
Law, Denver	32	17	44	3	3	.953
Cisco, Omaha	24	11	9	1	0	.952
Schneider, Tulsa* ..	31	5	15	1	1	.952
Tidrow, Wichita ...	18	10	18	1	0	.947
Carlos, Denver	32	12	39	3	3	.944
Noriega, Ind	24	8	25	2	1	.943
Brown, Denver	12	10	6	1	0	.941
Fowler, Denver ...	45	4	11	1	0	.938
Panther, Iowa	35	3	12	1	1	.938
Miller, Wichita ...	56	7	7	1	0	.933
Blue, Iowa*	17	5	9	1	1	.933
Almonte, Okla City .	35	3	11	1	0	.933
Farmer, Wichita ...	23	13	28	3	1	.932
Burgmeier, Omaha*.	10	5	8	1	2	.929
Camacho, Wichita* .	37	2	11	1	0	.929
Sembera, Tulsa	34	1	12	1	0	.929
Haydel, Evansville .	28	16	35	4	3	.927
Sprague, Iowa	26	7	31	3	1	.927
Estelle, Evan*	29	6	42	4	3	.923
Shifflett, Evan	50	11	24	3	3	.921
Scott, Okla City ...	35	3	20	2	2	.920
Grimsley, Ind*	29	3	19	2	2	.917
Woodson, Denver ..	39	13	29	4	2	.913
Conger, Iowa*	20	4	27	3	1	.912
Bakenhaster, Tulsa .	44	6	4	1	1	.909
Zuber, Wichita	12	4	6	1	2	.909
Sisk, Wichita	20	7	12	2	1	.905
Schaeffer, Okla C* .	25	5	14	2	0	.905
York, Omaha	41	4	5	1	0	.900
Jones, Omaha*	41	4	13	2	1	.895
Hedlund, Omaha ..	28	10	14	3	0	.889
Monteagudo, Omaha .	14	1	7	1	0	.889
Braxton, Wichita ..	32	7	8	2	0	.882
Belinsky, Ind*	16	4	11	2	0	.882
Cram, Omaha	30	21	23	6	1	.880
Olivo, Iowa	34	8	14	3	2	.880
Harrelson, Ind	22	8	14	3	1	.880
Such, Denver	12	4	10	2	0	.875
Stickels, Iowa	49	3	17	3	2	.870
Guzman, Tulsa	18	7	5	2	0	.857
Gebhard, Evansville .	44	3	9	2	1	.857
Boyd, Iowa	13	1	11	2	0	.857
Miles, Denver	25	8	9	3	1	.850
Rusteck, Evan*	30	1	15	3	5	.842
Bailey, OC-Tulsa ..	36	7	19	5	1	.839
Duffalo, Okla City .	40	4	11	3	0	.833
Clemons, Omaha* ..	16	1	8	2	1	.818
Blackmon, Denver ..	24	0	4	1	0	.800
Hamende, Ind*	48	6	13	5	0	.792
Spinks, Okla City ..	23	7	23	8	1	.789
Bickerton, Iowa* ...	17	0	7	2	0	.778
Watkins, Okla City .	18	2	6	3	0	.727
Welsch, Ind	34	2	7	4	0	.692

Triple Play—Cleveland.

(Fewer Than Ten Games)

Player and Club	G.	PO.	A.	E.	DP.	Pct.
Parker, Denver	9	1	7	0	1	1.000
Behney, Ind*	4	1	7	0	1	1.000
Forsch, Okla City ..	5	2	5	0	0	1.000
Allen, Wichita* ...	8	1	6	0	0	1.000
Whitby, Denver ...	9	2	4	0	1	1.000
Hefferon, Iowa ...	9	1	4	0	1	1.000
Major, Iowa*	9	1	4	0	1	1.000
Griffin, Okla City ..	5	1	4	0	0	1.000
Blateric, Ind	4	1	4	0	1	1.000
Hennigan, Wichita .	7	1	3	0	0	1.000
Humphreys, Denver .	3	1	3	0	0	1.000
Gladden, Omaha ..	3	0	4	0	0	1.000
Vaughan, Omaha* ..	5	1	2	0	0	1.000
Hudgins, Omaha ..	8	0	3	0	0	1.000
Johnson, Tulsa	2	2	0	0	0	1.000
Dillman, Tulsa	4	0	2	0	1	1.000
Handrahan, Iowa ..	8	1	1	0	0	1.000
Guindon, Tulsa* ...	4	1	1	0	0	1.000
Wright, Omaha	7	1	0	0	0	1.000
Shaw, Tulsa*	2	1	0	0	0	1.000
Baldwin, Denver* ..	1	1	0	0	0	1.000
Willhite, Omaha* ..	6	0	1	0	0	1.000
Rodriquez, Iowa ..	2	0	1	0	0	1.000
Kernek, Ind	1	0	1	0	0	1.000
Hargan, Wichita ...	9	3	13	1	1	.941
Blyleven, Evan	8	6	9	1	0	.938
Austin, Wichita* ..	6	3	7	1	0	.909
Henninger, Denver .	9	3	4	1	2	.875
Pizarro, Iowa*	5	3	4	1	1	.875
Woodson, Evan	9	3	3	1	0	.857
Fisher, Tulsa	9	4	3	2	0	.778
S. Ellis, Tulsa	7	0	3	1	0	.750
Rohr, Wichita*	7	1	6	3	0	.700
Campisi, Tulsa	4	0	2	1	0	.667
Thompson, Denver .	5	2	2	3	0	.571
Butler, Omaha* ...	4	0	2	2	0	.500
Seminoff, Tulsa ...	5	1	0	1	0	.500
Bouton, Okla City ..	2	0	1	1	0	.500
Kuhn, Denver*	7	0	0	2	0	.000

The following players do not have any recorded accepted chances at the positions indicated; therefore, are not listed in the fielding averages for those particular positions: E. Baker, p; Billings, 3b; Clark, p; DaVanon, 1b; Estelle, of; Gonzalez, 1b; Harris, p; Hense, 1b; Jagutis, of; Jaster*, p; R. Lachemann, c; M. Martin, p; McKenzie, 2b; McMillan, ss; Mendoza, ss; Nasif, of; Penalver, p; Ragland, 3b; Scheinblum, p; Spriggs, 2b.

CLUB PITCHING

Club	G.	CG.	ShO.	Sv.	IP.	H.	R.	ER.	HR.	BB.	Int. BB.	HB.	SO.	WP.	Bk.	ERA.
Omaha	139	38	7	26	1199	1197	567	455	91	417	34	29	845	32	4	3.42
Indianapolis	140	29	17	32	1213	1154	542	489	105	471	50	32	871	56	2	3.63
Evansville	138	40	10	27	1154	1178	537	466	83	472	38	28	776	45	3	3.63
Tulsa	140	42	9	21	1184	1211	605	512	100	413	28	35	917	65	8	3.89
Oklahoma City	139	32	5	30	1172	1182	641	513	92	577	56	29	995	75	3	3.94
Wichita	140	22	4	27	1207	1237	646	537	102	571	61	36	884	42	5	4.00
Iowa	139	38	10	29	1197	1241	658	541	105	478	37	43	850	71	3	4.07
Denver	139	34	4	27	1196	1316	684	553	78	476	57	41	714	47	3	4.16

PITCHERS' RECORDS

(Leading Qualifiers for Earned-Run Average Leadership—140 or More Innings)

*Throws lefthanded.

Pitcher—Club	G.	GS.	CG.	ShO.	W.	L.	Sv.	Pct.	IP.	H.	R.	ER.	HR.	BB.	Int. BB.	HB.	SO.	WP.	ERA.
Grimsley, Ind*	29	28	8	4	11	8	0	.579	188	140	65	57	19	59	1	3	162	4	2.73
Wilcox, Ind	28	26	7	5	12	10	0	.545	168	144	58	53	14	53	5	6	110	7	2.84
Cram, Omaha	30	27	8	3	7	9	0	.438	171	190	80	61	13	57	7	2	115	7	3.21
Spinks, Okla City	23	23	10	0	9	12	0	.429	158	138	80	58	13	77	2	7	153	17	3.30
Haydel, Evansville	28	26	9	2	12	12	0	.500	196	185	80	73	13	92	5	6	152	9	3.35
Carlos, Denver	32	28	9	0	13	9	1	.591	204	212	102	77	12	62	4	5	103	5	3.40
Montgomery, Oma	25	22	6	0	11	6	0	.647	140	142	66	55	8	31	0	2	95	0	3.54
Zachary, 14 Omaha-13 Tulsa	27	26	16	2	12	13	0	.480	192	204	89	76	19	48	5	2	152	11	3.56
H. Parker, Tulsa	25	23	4	0	8	6	0	.571	148	153	72	59	11	48	2	5	117	4	3.59
Estelle, Evan*	29	28	7	1	9	11	0	.450	169	181	75	70	14	63	7	2	81	3	3.73

Departmental Leaders: G—House, Miller, 56; GS—Morris, 30; CG—Zachary, 16; ShO—Wilcox, 5; W—Carlos, 13; L—Morris, 16; Sv—Fowler, Shifflett, Stickels, 15; Pct.—Blue, .800; IP—Carlos, 204; H—Geishert, 223; R—Geishert, 107; ER—Morris, 98; HR—Olivo, 21; BB—Haydel, 92; IBB—Osinski, 12; HB—Sprague, 10; SO—Blue, 165; WP—Bailey, 21.

(All Pitchers—Listed Alphabetically)

Pitcher—Club	G.	GS.	CG.	ShO.	W.	L.	Sv.	Pct.	IP.	H.	R.	ER.	HR.	BB.	Int. BB.	HB.	SO.	WP.	ERA.
Allen, Wichita*	8	0	0	0	1	1	0	1.000	13	13	7	7	0	5	0	0	5	0	4.85
Almonte, Okla City	35	7	1	0	5	3	0	.625	79	90	45	38	4	40	2	4	59	3	4.33
Austin, Wichita*	6	6	2	1	4	1	0	.800	48	43	15	13	3	18	0	0	36	0	2.44
Bailey, 21 Okla C-15 Tulsa	36	22	5	0	8	7	2	.533	154	150	72	69	8	75	8	3	136	21	4.03
Bakenhaster, Tulsa	44	2	0	0	2	4	7	.333	68	79	41	32	6	22	3	1	44	5	4.24
Baker, Evansville	4	0	0	0	0	0	0	.000	4	13	11	7	1	3	1	2	6	0	15.75
Baldwin, Denver*	1	0	0	0	0	0	0	.000	1	0	0	0	0	0	0	0	0	0	0.00
Barber, Evansville	12	1	0	0	0	0	0	.000	24	30	17	16	4	16	0	0	18	1	6.00
Behney, Ind*	4	3	2	1	3	0	0	1.000	25	16	4	4	2	12	0	0	15	1	1.44
Belinsky, Ind*	16	16	4	2	7	6	0	.538	91	73	50	45	9	64	1	3	95	11	4.45
Bickerton, Iowa*	17	6	1	1	2	2	0	.500	46	43	37	34	2	53	1	3	32	6	6.65
Blackmon, Denver	21	0	0	0	1	3	0	.250	30	43	26	23	4	16	3	2	15	2	6.90
Blasingame, O C*	16	16	4	1	8	2	0	.800	101	102	39	35	6	23	2	4	96	4	3.12
Blateric, Ind	4	1	0	0	1	0	0	.000	9	13	4	4	1	2	0	0	5	1	4.00
Blue, Iowa*	17	17	9	4	12	3	0	.800	133	88	40	32	8	55	0	5	165	7	2.17
Blyleven, Evan	8	7	2	1	4	2	0	.667	54	48	18	15	1	12	0	0	63	1	2.50
Bogle, Iowa*	18	2	0	0	3	1	1	.750	38	54	37	28	6	17	1	6	20	2	6.63
Borbon, Ind	32	2	0	0	5	2	4	.714	71	81	27	26	3	29	8	0	53	5	3.30
Bouton, Okla City	2	2	0	0	0	2	0	.000	6	14	11	11	3	2	0	1	6	0	16.50
Boyd, Iowa	13	8	1	0	3	3	2	.500	60	64	30	25	10	15	5	1	47	2	3.75
Braxton, Wichita	32	4	0	0	7	3	2	.700	80	78	35	30	6	39	7	5	63	1	3.38
Brown, Denver	12	9	3	1	6	1	0	.857	71	68	24	20	5	27	2	0	56	4	2.54
Burchart, Wichita	27	14	5	0	7	6	0	.538	106	117	74	57	11	61	5	6	55	6	4.84
Burgmeier, Oma*	10	0	0	0	3	1	2	.750	22	10	3	3	0	7	1	0	9	1	1.23
Butler, Omaha*	4	4	1	1	1	0	0	.500	20	15	7	5	4	6	0	0	10	0	2.25
Camacho, Wichita*	37	0	0	0	2	1	2	.667	57	60	25	22	7	27	2	0	39	2	3.47
Campisi, Tulsa	4	1	0	0	0	1	0	.000	7	9	6	5	0	3	1	0	3	4	6.43
Carlos, Denver	32	28	9	0	13	9	1	.591	204	212	102	77	12	62	4	5	103	5	3.40
Chlupsa, Tulsa	21	0	0	0	4	1	3	.800	36	36	5	5	0	9	1	3	23	0	1.25
Cisco, Omaha	24	4	1	0	6	3	2	.667	76	63	25	21	6	17	2	3	49	0	2.49
Clark, Iowa	4	0	0	0	0	0	0	.000	4	4	4	4	1	3	0	0	3	0	9.00
Clemons, Omaha*	16	8	0	0	1	2	0	.333	52	57	32	27	3	36	1	1	51	3	4.67
Cleveland, Tulsa	24	23	8	2	12	8	0	.600	155	165	78	69	15	49	0	6	106	5	4.01
Colbert, Wichita	28	2	0	0	8	3	0	.727	64	49	22	18	1	27	5	0	64	1	2.53
Conger, Iowa*	20	15	5	0	8	6	0	.571	102	103	40	37	8	32	4	8	59	4	3.26
Cram, Omaha	30	27	8	3	7	9	0	.438	171	190	80	61	13	57	7	2	115	7	3.21
Dickson, Okla City	39	1	0	0	5	4	3	.556	58	70	38	32	6	21	3	1	48	2	4.97
Dillman, Tulsa	4	0	0	0	0	0	0	.000	4	1	2	2	1	3	0	0	4	0	4.50
Duffalo, Okla City	40	0	0	0	3	2	1	.600	64	66	38	31	2	28	4	0	41	2	4.36
Dukes, Denver*	28	14	2	0	5	7	0	.417	112	127	70	51	6	26	1	4	65	1	4.10
J. Ellis, Tulsa*	22	6	2	1	5	4	3	.556	59	63	37	30	4	30	3	2	39	4	4.58

Pitcher—Club	G	GS	CG	ShO	W	L	Sv	Pct.	IP	H	R	ER	HR	BB	Int. BB	HB	SO	WP	ERA
S. Ellis, Tulsa	7	7	0	0	0	4	0	.000	33	42	28	24	12	14	0	0	15	0	6.55
Estelle, Evan*	29	28	7	1	9	11	0	.450	169	181	75	70	14	63	7	2	81	9	3.73
Evans, Okla City*	.13	5	0	0	0	2	2	.000	24	21	22	17	0	35	1	0	24	4	6.38
Farmer, Wichita .	.23	21	3	0	5	7	0	.417	121	114	64	54	9	70	6	4	69	5	4.02
Finafrock, Evan .	.23	6	0	0	4	4	0	.500	71	84	36	31	4	24	1	4	43	3	3.93
Fisher, Tulsa	9	2	1	1	3	2	2	.600	25	28	11	9	2	5	1	0	16	2	3.24
Forsch, Okla City .	5	5	4	2	3	4	0	1.000	40	25	7	7	2	10	0	1	37	1	1.58
Fowler, Denver ..	.45	0	0	0	9	5	15	.643	68	67	22	12	0	16	6	0	30	3	1.59
Gebhard, Evan ..	44	0	0	0	1	5	7	.167	68	60	34	24	5	28	6	2	57	1	3.18
Geishert, Ind ...	.29	28	3	0	12	13	0	.480	184	223	107	97	19	30	3	3	120	0	4.74
Gladden, Omaha ..	3	0	0	0	0	1	0	1.000	8	8	2	2	0	5	2	0	3	0	2.25
Griffin, Okla City .	5	5	1	0	3	2	0	.600	28	23	14	4	1	16	0	1	27	3	1.29
Grimsley, Ind* ..	.29	28	8	4	11	8	0	.579	188	140	65	57	19	59	1	3	162	4	2.73
Guindon, Tulsa* .	4	0	0	0	0	0	0	.000	6	6	2	2	1	2	1	1	4	0	3.00
Guinn, Okla City*	.29	14	3	0	4	8	3	.333	117	120	57	50	13	48	5	0	116	2	3.85
Guzman, Tulsa ..	.18	14	4	1	5	6	0	.455	96	89	44	34	4	38	1	4	84	8	3.19
Hamende, Ind* ..	.48	0	0	0	4	6	4	.333	68	78	33	27	5	35	8	6	41	4	3.57
Hamm, Evansville	.15	13	6	1	8	4	0	.667	95	83	32	30	5	33	3	2	66	3	2.84
Handrahan, Iowa .	8	0	0	0	0	1	0	.000	11	19	12	8	0	11	2	0	3	0	6.55
Hargan, Wichita .	9	8	3	0	4	2	0	.667	53	58	25	22	4	13	1	1	27	2	3.74
Harrelson, Ind ..	.22	17	1	1	3	8	1	.273	87	86	59	53	7	62	0	5	62	10	5.48
Haydel, Evansville	.28	26	9	2	12	12	0	.500	196	185	80	73	13	92	5	6	152	9	3.35
Hedlund, Omaha .	.28	17	5	0	9	4	0	.692	131	119	59	49	14	31	4	3	81	1	3.37
Hefferon, Iowa ..	9	0	0	0	1	3	0	.250	12	12	4	4	0	4	1	2	9	3	3.00
Hennigan, Wichita.	7	6	0	0	2	2	0	.500	27	41	24	24	4	12	1	2	16	1	8.00
Henninger, Denver .	9	7	3	2	3	3	0	.500	52	46	19	14	2	16	1	0	38	5	2.42
Hilgendorf, Tulsa*.	.23	9	5	2	4	5	2	.444	91	79	39	35	12	20	0	2	83	1	3.46
Hinsley, Wichita .	.10	4	0	0	1	6	0	.143	33	34	20	16	4	11	0	0	27	2	4.36
House, 32 Ind-																			
24 Denver*	.56	0	0	0	3	3	10	.500	80	82	35	27	4	28	4	4	66	2	3.04
Hudgins, Omaha ..	8	0	0	0	2	0	0	.000	9	14	8	7	1	5	0	0	7	1	7.00
Humphreys, Denver	3	0	0	0	0	0	0	.000	8	14	5	5	1	0	0	0	3	1	5.63
James, Wichita ..	.15	0	0	0	1	0	4	1.000	16	13	10	10	0	2	10	4	2	13	1	5.63
Jaster, Tulsa* ...	7	1	0	0	1	0	0	1.000	12	10	6	5	0	6	0	1	7	1	3.75
Johnson, Tulsa ..	2	1	0	0	1	0	0	1.000	7	12	4	4	1	1	0	0	4	0	5.14
Jones, Omaha* ..	.41	0	0	0	3	4	8	.429	68	62	32	22	6	28	1	1	67	0	2.91
Kaiser, Wichita* .	.10	8	0	0	5	1	0	.000	42	46	23	18	0	25	6	0	33	5	3.86
Kernek, Ind*	1	0	0	0	0	0	0	.000	1	1	0	0	0	0	0	0	2	0	0.00
Kuhn, Denver* ...	7	0	0	0	0	0	0	.000	14	11	12	10	0	8	0	3	13	3	6.43
M. Lachemann, Ia	.11	0	0	0	3	2	4	.600	22	25	8	6	0	7	3	1	17	1	2.45
Law, Denver	.32	27	8	1	12	13	0	.480	189	203	104	92	14	67	8	8	119	4	4.38
Major, Iowa*	9	0	0	0	1	0	0	.000	16	22	16	11	1	19	1	0	12	2	6.19
Marshall, Okla C	.16	3	2	0	4	3	3	.571	45	32	11	8	0	16	1	1	42	5	1.60
Martin, Okla City .	4	0	0	0	0	0	0	.000	7	6	4	3	0	6	1	0	5	0	3.86
McCool, Tulsa* ..	.10	5	0	0	2	3	0	.400	36	28	22	21	1	18	1	3	36	5	5.25
Miles, Denver ...	.25	7	2	0	3	4	2	.429	61	73	37	35	1	33	8	6	37	1	5.16
Miller, Wichita ..	.56	1	0	0	6	6	7	.500	98	94	49	40	7	46	6	1	87	4	3.67
Mingori, Wichita*.	.16	0	0	0	0	1	0	.000	21	23	14	10	3	11	1	2	21	2	4.29
Monteagudo, Oma	.14	0	0	0	3	1	3	.750	28	22	9	8	0	8	2	0	28	0	2.57
Montgomery, Oma	.25	22	6	0	11	6	0	.647	140	142	66	55	8	31	0	2	95	0	3.54
Morris, Evansville	.35	30	10	2	10	16	1	.385	181	222	103	98	18	57	4	1	103	4	4.87
Noriega, Ind	.24	15	4	2	6	6	0	.500	106	96	42	41	7	37	6	3	57	1	3.48
Olivo, Iowa	.34	20	5	1	8	13	0	.381	134	153	88	71	21	40	1	1	63	2	4.77
O'Riley, Omaha ..	.17	3	1	5	8	0	0	.385	110	102	54	44	8	50	1	5	68	4	3.60
Osborn, Ind	.15	4	0	0	1	1	1	.500	34	34	20	15	5	16	1	0	20	1	3.97
Osinski, Okla City	.45	0	0	0	6	8	11	.429	67	55	30	18	6	33	12	1	50	0	2.42
Osteen, Oma	.20	18	3	0	6	7	0	.462	110	128	76	64	10	52	3	0	85	10	5.24
Panther, Iowa ...	.35	0	0	1	1	6	.500	58	50	21	17	0	29	2	3	38	2	2.64
H. Parker, Tulsa .	.25	23	4	0	8	6	0	.571	148	153	73	59	11	48	2	5	117	4	3.59
J. Parker, Denver .	9	7	1	0	1	4	0	.200	40	57	29	29	3	18	6	2	23	3	6.53
Paul, Wichita* ..	.10	9	3	0	6	1	0	.857	71	60	19	17	4	15	3	3	46	0	2.15
Penalver, Okla C .	1	0	0	0	0	0	0	.000	2	3	3	3	1	0	0	0	2	0	13.50
Peterson, Evan* ..	.17	8	1	1	3	2	0	.600	55	57	28	26	6	32	0	4	28	7	4.25
Pizarro, Iowa* ...	5	5	1	0	2	2	0	.500	37	48	27	20	4	12	0	0	25	0	4.86
Reuss, Tulsa* ...	.11	4	0	0	7	2	0	.778	85	69	26	20	0	28	0	0	69	7	2.12
Ritter, Denver* ..	.34	1	0	0	2	3	0	.400	44	49	35	30	6	29	4	3	31	4	6.14
Rittwage, Wichita	.32	16	3	0	6	6	0	.500	134	119	66	54	13	71	5	4	88	2	3.63
Rodriquez, Iowa ..	2	0	0	0	1	0	0	1.000	3	2	0	0	0	0	0	0	3	0	0.00
Rohr, Wichita* ..	7	0	0	1	6	3	0	.143	33	45	23	16	3	16	0	0	27	3	4.36
Rusteck, Evan* ..	.30	12	3	1	6	5	3	.545	53	60	42	29	6	50	1	0	48	2	2.81
Schaeffer, Okla C*	.25	22	2	1	4	7	0	.364	107	120	79	62	6	79	5	4	78	10	5.21
Scheinblum, Wich	.1	0	0	0	0	0	0	.000	1	2	0	0	0	1	0	0	1	0	0.00
Schneider, Tulsa*	.31	10	3	0	3	7	1	.300	81	107	55	47	9	27	3	3	48	1	5.22
Scott, Okla City ..	.35	8	2	0	3	7	5	.300	98	112	53	40	10	30	11	2	81	1	3.67
Sembera, Tulsa ..	.34	0	0	0	3	4	2	.429	55	63	40	33	6	29	4	3	62	6	5.40
Seminoff, Tulsa ...	5	0	0	0	1	0	0	1.000	4	13	11	5	1	3	0	0	2	1	11.25
Shaw, Tulsa*	2	0	0	0	1	0	0	1.000	7	2	1	1	0	3	0	0	11	0	1.29
Shifflett, Evan ...	.50	2	0	2	8	7	15	.533	117	103	40	29	4	43	8	3	80	3	2.23
Sisk, Wichita	.20	9	1	0	3	8	2	.273	55	63	38	31	2	33	5	1	25	3	5.07
Spinks, Okla City .	.23	23	10	0	9	12	0	.429	158	138	80	58	13	77	2	7	153	17	3.30
Splittorff, Omaha*	.28	25	6	1	8	12	1	.400	162	192	87	69	10	55	3	3	91	2	3.83

| | | | | | | | | | | | | | | | Int. | | | | |
Pitcher—Club	G.	GS.	CG.	ShO.	W.	L.	Sv.	Pct.	IP.	H.	R.	ER.	HR.	BB.	BB.	HB.	SO.	WP.	ERA.
Sprague, Iowa 26	21	9	3	8	9	0	.471	150	156	80	65	11	48	4	10	95	13	3.90	
Stickels, Iowa 49	1	0	0	3	7	15	.300	83	76	37	34	7	44	4	1	70	8	3.69	
Such, Denver 12	9	2	0	2	2	1	.500	48	54	35	28	7	34	3	2	37	1	5.25	
Talbot, Iowa 25	25	4	1	9	8	0	.529	174	192	101	81	15	47	5	3	107	9	4.19	
Thompson, Denver . 5	3	0	0	0	2	0	.000	13	16	17	15	0	14	0	1	7	2	10.38	
Tidrow, Wichita ...18	15	2	0	3	4	0	.429	83	99	49	47	7	29	3	5	71	2	5.10	
Vaughan, Omaha* . 5	2	0	0	0	2	0	.000	11	11	11	6	1	6	0	4	9	1	4.91	
Walters, Denver ...15	1	0	0	1	1	0	.500	30	39	17	13	2	12	3	0	11	1	3.90	
Watkins, Okla City 18	18	1	0	6	7	0	.462	93	99	68	55	12	72	1	1	57	6	5.32	
Welsch, Ind 34	0	0	0	1	4	0	.200	57	57	35	31	8	26	10	0	32	4	4.89	
Whitby, Denver ... 9	3	1	0	1	2	0	.333	26	39	23	14	5	14	1	0	12	1	4.85	
Wilcox, Ind 28	26	7	5	12	10	0	.545	168	144	58	53	14	53	5	6	110	7	2.84	
Willhite, Omaha* . 6	0	0	0	0	0	0	.000	13	15	9	8	3	6	0	0	7	2	5.54	
Womack, Ind 47	0	0	0	6	3	14	.667	74	59	18	18	2	29	4	1	53	6	2.19	
Woodson, Denver .39	23	3	0	10	10	2	.500	157	169	91	76	10	73	6	3	92	5	4.36	
Woodson, Evan 9	5	0	0	2	3	1	.400	28	32	20	18	2	19	2	2	31	2	5.79	
Wright, Omaha ... 7	0	0	0	0	1	0	.000	10	14	9	8	1	11	0	0	5	1	7.20	
York, Omaha 41	0	0	0	8	5	9	.615	68	51	30	26	4	31	8	4	77	2	3.44	
Zachary, 14 Omaha-																			
13 Tulsa 27	26	16	2	12	13	0	.480	192	204	89	76	19	48	5	2	152	11	3.56	
Zuber, Wichita ...12	10	0	0	1	4	0	.200	51	66	44	31	10	31	1	0	33	0	5.47	

BALKS—Guzman, 3; Blyleven, Conger, Montgomery, Zachary, Zuber, 2 each; Almonte, Bailey, Braxton, Carlos, Cram, J. Ellis, Farmer, Grimsley, Guinn, Hinsley, Kuhn, McCool, Noriega, J. Parker, Rusteck, Schaeffer, Sprague, York, 1 each.

COMBINATION SHUTOUTS—Estelle-Shifflett, Evansville; Grimsley-Womack, Wilcox-Womack, Indianapolis; Blasingame-Osinski, Oklahoma City; Hilgendorf-McCool-J. Ellis-Guzman, Tulsa; Farmer-Miller, Hargan-Camacho, Paul-James, Wichita.

NO-HIT GAME—Wilcox, Indianapolis, defeated Evansville, 2-0 July 4 (seven innings).

ALONG THE MINOR LEAGUE TRAIL . . . .

Don Zimmer, when named manager of Salt Lake (Pacific Coast) last spring, addressed the local fans before the opener and said: "I know I will do a few things out on the field you guys won't agree with. . . ." He sure did. The Padres finished 52½ games behind in the Southern Division. . . . Mexico is a land of siestas and slow-moving burros—to some—but to veteran Ronnie Camacho and front-office executive Cesar Faz, it was like the Los Angeles Freeway at 5 p. m. Instead of waiting until the season was completed to compile a record, on March 25 Camacho blasted two homers to top his own league HR mark and scored twice to set a new Mexican League record for total runs tallied. Faz, g.m. at slow-starting Monterrey (5-17), said he was fired; the club president said Faz had resigned. The only thing certain was that Victor Ortega was collecting pay in Faz' old chair. Proof of the fast pace of the Mexican way, the Mexico City Reds planned to have three managers, one at home and two on the road. . . . Sometimes we can't escape the fact we aren't loved. Take Toledo, for instance. G. M. Charlie Senger tried to sell the Mud Hens' games via radio, but no station in northwest Ohio would listen. He even offered to buy the radio time and sell the advertising, but was told there was no time available to the ball club. . . . When a club opens its season with a rash of homers, the fans have visions of fireworks night after night until September. But what kind of nightmares did the Lodi (California) fans have after the

(Continued on page 430)

International League

CLASS AAA

Leading Batter
RALPH GARR
Richmond

League President
GEORGE SISLER, JR.

Leading Pitcher
ROB GARDNER
Syracuse

CHAMPIONSHIP WINNERS IN PREVIOUS YEARS

Year	Winner	Pct.
1884	Trenton	.520
1885	Syracuse	.584
1886	Utica	.646
1887	Toronto	.644
1888	Syracuse	.723
1889	Detroit	.649
1890	Detroit	.617
1891	Buffalo (reg. season)	.727
	Buffalo (supplem'l)	.680
1892	Providence	.615
	Binghamton*	.667
1893	Erie	.606
1894	Providence	.696
1895	Springfield	.687
1896	Providence	.602
1897	Syracuse	.632
1898	Montreal	.586
1899	Rochester	.624
1900	Providence	.616
1901	Rochester	.642
1902	Toronto	.669
1903	Jersey City	.642
1904	Buffalo	.657
1905	Providence	.638
1906	Buffalo	.607
1907	Toronto	.619
1908	Baltimore	.593
1909	Rochester	.596
1910	Rochester	.601
1911	Rochester	.645
1912	Toronto	.595
1913	Newark	.625
1914	Providence	.617
1915	Buffalo	.632
1916	Buffalo	.586
1917	Toronto	.604
1918	Toronto	.693
1919	Baltimore	.671

Year	Winner	Pct.
1920	Baltimore	.719
1921	Baltimore	.717
1922	Baltimore	.689
1923	Baltimore	.677
1924	Baltimore	.709
1925	Baltimore	.633
1926	Toronto	.657
1927	Buffalo	.667
1928	Rochester	.549
1929	Rochester	.613
1930	Rochester	.629
1931	Rochester	.601
1932	Newark	.649
1933	Newark	.622
	Buffalo (4th)†	.494
1934	Newark	.608
	Toronto (3rd)†	.559
1935	Montreal	.597
	Syracuse (2nd)†	.565
1936	Buffalo‡	.610
1937	Newark‡	.717
1938	Newark‡	.684
1939	Jersey City	.582
	Rochester (2nd)†	.556
1940	Rochester	.611
	Newark (2nd)†	.594
1941	Newark	.649
	Montreal (2nd)†	.584
1942	Newark	.601
	Syracuse (3rd)†	.513
1943	Toronto	.625
	Syracuse (3rd)†	.536
1944	Baltimore‡	.553
1945	Montreal	.621
	Newark (2nd)†	.582
1946	Montreal‡	.649
1947	Jersey City	.610
	Syracuse (3rd)†	.575
1948	Montreal‡	.614

Year	Winner	Pct.
1949	Buffalo	.584
	Montreal (3rd)†	.545
1950	Rochester	.609
	Baltimore (3rd)†	.556
1951	Montreal‡	.617
1952	Montreal	.629
	Rochester (3rd)†	.619
1953	Rochester	.630
	Montreal (2nd)†	.586
1954	Toronto	.630
	Syracuse (4th)§	.510
1955	Montreal	.617
	Rochester (4th)†	.497
1956	Toronto	.566
	Rochester (2nd)†	.553
1957	Toronto	.575
	Buffalo (2nd)†	.571
1958	Montreal‡	.588
1959	Buffalo	.582
	Havana (3rd)†	.523
1960	Toronto‡	.649
1961	Columbus	.597
	Buffalo (3rd)†	.559
1962	Jacksonville	.610
	Atlanta (3rd)†	.539
1963	Syracuse x	.533
	Indianapolis†	.562
1964	Jacksonville	.589
	Rochester (4th)†	.532
1965	Columbus	.582
	Toronto (3rd)†	.556
1966	Rochester	.565
	Toronto (2nd-tied)†	.558
1967	Richmond	.574
	Toledo (3rd)†	.525
1968	Toledo	.565
	Jacksonville (4th)†	.514
1969	Tidewater	.563
	Syracuse (3rd)†	.536

*Won split-season playoff. †Won four-team playoff. ‡Won championship and four-game playoff. §Defeated Havana in game to decide fourth place, then won four-team playoff. xLeague was divided into Northern, Southern divisions. (NOTE—Known as Eastern League in 1884, New York State League in 1885, International League in 1886-87, International Association in 1888, International League in 1889-90, Eastern Association in 1891, and Eastern League from 1892 until 1912.)

STANDING OF CLUBS AT CLOSE OF SEASON, SEPTEMBER 3

Club	Syr.	Col.	Roch.	Tide.	Rich.	Lou.	Wpg.	Tol.	W.	L.	T.	Pct.	G.B.
Syracuse (10*)	..	11	10	13	10	16	10	14	84	56	0	.600	....
Columbus (21*)	9	..	8	9	13	12	15	15	81	59	0	.579	3
Rochester (1*)	10	12	..	7	10	8	16	13	76	64	0	.543	8
†Tidewater (19*)	7	11	13	..	8	8	15	12	74	66	0	.529	10
Richmond (13)	10	7	10	12	..	13	10	11	73	67	0	.521	11
Louisville (2*)	4	8	12	12	7	..	12	14	69	71	0	.493	15
‡Winnipeg (18*)	10	5	4	5	10	8	..	10	52	88	0	.371	32
Toledo (6*)	6	5	7	8	9	6	10	..	51	89	0	.364	33

†Tidewater club represented Norfolk, Va.

‡Buffalo franchise was transferred to Winnipeg, June 11.

Key to major league farm teams (indicated by numbers after clubs in standing) shown on Page 384.

Playoffs—Syracuse defeated Tidewater, three games to none; Columbus defeated Rochester, three games to two; Syracuse defeated Columbus, three games to one.

Syracuse defeated Omaha, American Association, four games to one.

Regular-Season Attendance—Columbus, 140,700; Louisville, 136,439; Richmond, 120,928; Rochester, 323,743; Syracuse, 221,376; Tidewater, 142,290; Toledo, 86,428; Winnipeg, 89,901.   Total, 1,261,805. All-Star Game, 6,338. Playoffs, 33,860. Inter-League Series, 19,846.

Managers: Columbus—Joe Morgan; Louisville—Billy Gardner; Richmond—Mickey Vernon; Rochester—Cal Ripken; Syracuse—Frank Verdi; Tidewater—Chuck Hiller; Toledo—Frank Carswell; Winnipeg—Clyde McCullough.

All-Star Team: 1B—Kopacz, Columbus; 2B—Boehmer, Syracuse; 3B—Ferraro, Richmond; SS—Baker, Syracuse; OF—Freed, Rochester; Baylor, Rochester; Garr, Richmond; C—Montgomery, Louisville; May, Columbus; P—Reniff, Syracuse; McAnally, Winnipeg; Gardner, Syracuse; Manager—Verdi, Syracuse.

(Compiled by Elias Sports Bureau, New York, N. Y.)

CLUB BATTING

Club	G.	AB.	R.	OR.	H.	TB.	2B.	3B.	HR.	RBI.	SH.	SF.	BB.	Int. BB.	HP.	SO.	SB.	CS.	LOB.	Pct.
Rochester ..	140	4592	757	635	1317	1983	237	45	113	697	73	39	593	57	46	745	108	53	1065	.287
Tidewater ..	140	4592	641	614	1278	1844	184	29	108	583	53	28	518	47	24	725	68	56	989	.280
Richmond ..	140	4592	694	596	1282	1904	205	21	125	630	70	41	585	59	27	726	80	37	1058	.279
Columbus ..	140	4622	673	612	1254	1854	175	43	113	619	43	54	552	46	22	754	97	49	1017	.271
Louisville ..	140	4561	695	679	1213	1841	205	48	109	660	34	38	649	44	22	812	23	20	1062	.266
Syracuse ..	140	4453	646	550	1128	1748	187	29	125	586	66	35	610	75	26	831	69	46	1023	.253
Winnipeg ..	140	4318	535	753	1066	1646	156	20	128	480	31	25	450	34	23	798	77	51	866	.247
Toledo	140	4431	546	748	1058	1552	159	16	101	494	23	21	492	27	22	903	37	20	918	.239

INDIVIDUAL BATTING

(Leading Qualifiers for Batting Championship—434 or More Plate Appearances)

*Bats lefthanded.   †Switch-hitter.

Player and Club	G.	AB.	R.	H.	TB.	2B.	3B.	HR.	RBI.	SH.	SF.	BB.	HP.	SO.	SB.	CS.	Pct.
Garr, Ralph, Richmond* ...	98	391	83	151	204	26	3	7	51	5	5	29	2	43	39	9	.386
Freed, Roger, Rochester ..	138	503	96	168	282	30	6	24	130	0	5	82	3	92	6	2	.334
Lanier, Lorenzo, Columbus*	129	434	58	143	182	14	8	3	36	2	5	113	2	45	20	12	.329
Baylor, Donald, Rochester ..	140	508	127	166	296	34	15	22	107	2	6	76	19	99	26	5	.327
Baker, Johnnie, Richmond ..	118	461	97	150	218	29	3	11	51	3	3	53	6	45	10	8	.325
Montgomery, Robert, Lou ...	131	487	71	158	236	30	3	14	89	1	5	38	4	46	10	0	.324
Gaspar, Rodney, Tidewater†	131	468	81	149	173	17	2	1	37	4	3	84	5	25	13	13	.318
Kopacz, George, Columbus*	135	497	100	154	268	19	4	29	115	2	11	71	1	81	11	2	.310
Solaita, Tolja, Syracuse* ..	130	396	62	122	207	24	2	19	87	3	4	95	3	89	3	2	.308
Martinez, Teodoro, Tide	116	438	62	134	181	20	9	3	36	2	1	11	1	53	13	9	.306

Garr did not have the required number of plate appearances, but when charged with two official at bats to reach the qualification plateau, he thus became the leader with a .384 average. Under the provisions of scoring rule 10.23a, Garr qualified for the batting championship.

Departmental Leaders: G—Baylor, Kalafatis, 140; AB—Mangual, 509; R—Baylor, 127; H—Freed; 168; TB—Baylor, 296; 2B—Baylor, 34; 3B—Baylor, 15; HR—Breeden, 37; RBI—Freed, 130; SH—Damaska, 13; SF—Kopacz, 11; BB—Lahoud, 116; HP—Baylor, 19; SO—Lopez, 132; SB—Garr, 39; CS—Shopay, 15.

(All Players—Listed Alphabetically)

Player and Club	G.	AB.	R.	H.	TB.	2B.	3B.	HR.	RBI.	SH.	SF.	BB.	HP.	SO.	SB.	CS.	Pct.
Acosta, Eduardo, Columbus .	28	24	1	2	2	0	0	0	0	1	0	0	0	11	1	0	.083
Adamson, John, Rochester ..	9	26	3	4	5	1	0	0	1	0	3	0	12	0	0		.154
Allen, Harold, Rochester ...	57	181	21	63	81	10	1	2	24	0	0	21	0	27	6	3	.348
Allen, Raymond, Tidewater .	17	6	1	1	1	0	0	0	0	0	0	2	0	4	0	0	.167
Allen, Ronald F., Tide*	103	358	50	91	164	13	0	20	76	2	4	56	4	90	0	0	.254
Alvarado, Luis, Louisville ..	69	294	43	59	79	12	1	2	23	3	3	22	0	28	4	2	.201
Arrington, David, Columbus .	26	81	8	21	34	2	1	3	12	0	0	2	0	17	2	0	.259
Baker, Frank, Syracuse* ..	104	332	47	86	112	11	3	3	40	3	3	49	4	54	3	5	.259
Baker, Johnnie, Richmond ..	118	461	97	150	218	29	3	11	51	3	3	53	6	45	10	8	.325
Baney, Richard, Rochester ..	15	26	1	6	8	0	1	0	3	0	0	0	1	9	0	0	.231
Barber, Stephen, Richmond*.	13	17	4	2	2	0	0	0	1	0	2	0	3	0	1	0	.118
Barski, Martin, Toledo	3	10	2	3	3	0	0	0	0	0	0	0	0	5	0	0	.300
Bateman, John, Winnipeg ..	7	24	4	3	12	1	0	1	5	0	0	0	0	5	0	0	.125
Baylor, Donald, Rochester .	140	508	127	166	296	34	15	22	107	2	6	76	19	99	26	5	.327
Bearnarth, Lawrence, Tide .	30	27	3	8	10	0	1	0	4	0	0	1	0	2	0	0	.296
Beckett, Douglas, Louisville .	21	4	1	0	0	0	0	0	0	0	0	1	0	2	0	0	.000
Beene, Fred, Rochester† ...	18	39	4	8	8	0	0	0	2	1	0	2	0	10	0	0	.205
Bertaina, Frank, Rochester*.	30	66	12	22	31	3	0	2	13	1	2	3	0	3	0	0	.333

Player and Club	G.	AB.	R.	H.	TB.	2B.	3B.	HR.	RBI.	SH.	SF.	BB.	HP.	SO.	SB.	CS.	Pct.
Bladt, Richard, Syracuse ...117	328	51	85	132	15	4	8	34	4	0	43	4	51	10	2	.259
Blanco, Gilbert, Winnipeg* . 33	25	0	5	5	0	0	0	1	1	0	2	0	7	0	0	.200
Blomberg, Ronald, Syracuse* 92	289	50	79	126	13	2	10	38	0	1	47	1	44	10	6	.273
Bobb, M. Randall, Tidewater 17	57	6	13	26	4	0	3	6	0	0	7	0	7	0	0	.228
Boehmer, Leonard, Syracuse.123	417	45	120	163	10	0	11	67	8	5	26	1	29	0	3	.288
Booker, Richard, SSRi-14Col* 72	181	15	37	47	6	2	0	12	3	4	22	1	26	1	0	.204
Bosch, Donald, Winnipeg† ... 51	173	22	46	70	5	2	5	15	1	1	25	1	33	5	4	.266
Bowens, Samuel, Columbus . 35	86	9	20	32	5	0	3	9	0	2	15	0	17	2	0	.233
Breazeale, James, Rich* 101	341	45	98	153	22	0	11	46	0	1	26	3	32	3	0	.287
Breeden, Harold, Richmond .136	450	75	132	261	16	1	37	116	1	5	85	4	86	1	2	.293
Brosseau, Franklin, Col 19	29	0	6	6	0	0	0	4	1	0	2	0	10	0	0	.207
Brown, Curtis, Tidewater ... 12	26	4	9	16	1	0	2	9	0	0	1	0	2	0	0	.346
Brown, James, Toledo 4	1	0	0	0	0	0	0	0	0	0	0	0	0	0	0	.000
Brown, Oscar, Richmond 22	88	13	19	24	2	0	1	5	2	1	6	0	12	5	1	.216
Brunsberg, Arlo, Toledo 28	46	9	17	34	2	0	5	18	0	0	3	1	13	0	0	.370
Burbach, William, Syracuse . 21	39	0	3	4	1	0	0	4	0	0	0	0	15	0	0	.077
Cain, Leslie, Toledo* 4	11	1	3	4	1	0	0	2	0	0	0	0	6	0	0	.273
Calero, Jose, Louisville 74	195	12	37	44	4	1	0	16	0	1	9	1	19	0	1	.296
Cambria, Frederick, Col 26	55	5	12	21	6	0	1	3	3	0	4	1	19	0	0	.218
Campbell, Ronald, Columbus 96	253	18	60	91	10	0	7	29	2	3	21	0	29	0	3	.237
Camy, Donald, Tidewater ... 2	2	0	0	0	0	0	0	0	0	0	0	0	0	0	0	.000
Canzano, Anthony, Tide† ... 59	143	13	27	35	6	1	0	5	4	0	19	0	35	5	0	.189
Carden, William, Winnipeg . 8	7	0	0	0	0	0	0	0	0	0	3	0	5	0	0	.000
Cash, David, Columbus 35	128	20	40	50	3	2	1	16	1	2	20	0	16	5	1	.313
Castiglione, Robert, 2Ri-10Ti 12	19	1	4	4	0	0	0	1	1	1	1	0	6	0	0	.211
Cernich, Joseph, Louisville* 31	61	1	7	8	1	0	0	7	0	0	5	0	16	0	0	.115
Chandler, Ronnie, Toledo ... 29	38	2	8	14	0	0	2	2	0	2	0	0	15	0	0	.211
Chavarria, Osvaldo, Syr 123	399	42	103	153	20	3	8	49	1	3	40	0	68	1	3	.258
Chilcott, Steven, 3Win-19Ti* 22	70	12	18	37	2	1	5	8	1	0	4	0	27	1	1	.257
Clark, Rickey, Toledo 13	1	0	0	0	0	0	0	0	0	0	0	0	1	0	0	.000
Clifford, Arthur, Toledo 3	4	0	1	1	0	0	0	0	0	0	0	0	1	0	0	.250
Closter, Alan, Syracuse* ... 19	35	3	6	7	1	0	0	1	2	0	4	0	17	0	1	.171
Coggins, Richard, Rochester . 43	165	27	46	66	7	2	3	19	2	1	19	1	19	2	2	.279
Coletta, Christopher, Lou* ..107	304	54	101	137	18	6	2	40	0	3	31	1	26	0	0	.332
Collins, Kevin, Winnipeg* .. 73	242	39	84	134	12	1	12	41	0	1	18	2	37	1	2	.347
Colpaert, Richard, Col 46	12	0	1	1	0	0	0	0	4	0	3	0	4	0	0	.083
Cook, Donald, Louisville 60	14	1	3	7	1	0	1	6	2	0	3	0	7	0	0	.214
Cox, Robert, Syracuse 90	251	34	55	97	15	0	9	30	1	2	49	2	40	0	1	.219
Crist, Jack, Richmond 81	184	34	41	77	12	0	8	23	2	0	42	1	50	1	1	.223
Cruz, Pablo, Columbus 134	479	75	129	157	22	3	0	36	7	2	54	5	52	15	7	.269
Cullen, John, Richmond 10	6	0	1	2	1	0	0	1	0	0	1	0	2	0	0	.167
Damaska, Jack, Richmond ..117	419	43	113	144	10	0	7	64	13	9	36	2	33	5	3	.270
Davis, Ronald, Columbus ...132	430	59	114	177	17	2	14	47	2	3	36	1	92	12	6	.265
Dawson, J. Arthur, Syr* 9	3	0	0	0	0	0	0	0	0	0	1	0	2	0	0	.000
Day, Charles F., Winnipeg* . 84	313	46	92	151	19	5	10	39	4	2	25	0	62	5	5	.294
Delgado, Ricardo, Rochester 31	29	3	2	4	2	0	0	0	2	0	5	0	14	0	0	.069
DeNeff, James, Toledo 79	184	28	41	74	12	0	7	29	0	0	33	1	55	2	0	.223
Denehy, William, Tidewater* 16	40	6	5	5	0	0	0	4	4	0	3	0	13	0	0	.125
Derrick, J. Michael, Lou* .. 43	117	34	39	66	8	2	5	31	0	1	29	0	27	2	1	.333
Didier, Robert, Richmond† . 46	152	21	47	58	8	0	1	16	4	1	19	0	10	0	1	.309
Dillman, William, Win 16	19	0	2	2	0	0	0	0	2	0	1	0	12	0	0	.105
Dix, James, Winnipeg† 29	65	6	14	21	1	0	2	5	0	1	5	0	20	0	1	.215
Duliba, Robert, Richmond .. 43	12	1	1	1	0	0	0	2	5	0	1	0	5	0	0	.083
Engbers, Donald, Tide† 28	103	16	30	42	6	0	2	10	0	0	10	0	7	0	0	.291
Evans, Darrell, Richmond* ..120	447	92	134	228	20	7	20	83	2	5	73	3	80	1	4	.300
Fanzone, Carmen, Lou 101	344	70	100	188	27	2	19	78	1	5	77	4	80	1	5	.291
Farmer, Billy, Louisville ... 14	16	2	5	6	1	0	0	2	1	0	0	0	8	0	0	.313
Farrell, Richard, Richmond . 15	5	0	0	0	0	0	0	0	2	0	0	0	4	0	0	.000
Farson, George, Rochester .. 50	118	4	28	38	10	0	0	10	1	1	15	0	26	0	0	.237
Fazio, Donato, Louisville ...125	404	55	95	129	9	5	5	44	0	3	92	3	75	3	0	.235
Ferraro, Michael, Rochester .135	474	57	144	193	29	1	6	70	2	7	62	1	47	2	6	.304
Fisher, John, Rochester 8	20	4	6	7	1	0	0	5	3	0	1	0	4	0	0	.300
Fiskland, Edward, Syracuse . 7	2	0	0	0	0	0	0	0	0	0	0	0	2	0	0	.000
Fitzer, Lyn, Columbus 8	6	1	2	2	1	0	0	0	0	0	0	0	0	0	0	.300
Fitzmaurice, Shaun, Rich ...106	312	43	82	124	12	3	8	44	2	3	56	1	61	3	2	.167
Floyd, Robert, Rochester ... 35	131	12	38	52	7	2	1	14	2	0	15	1	23	2	3	.263
Foli, Timothy, Tidewater ...103	375	63	98	134	10	4	6	30	8	0	38	1	39	0	4	.290
Folkers, Richard, Tide* 5	12	1	5	5	0	0	0	1	0	0	0	0	1	0	0	.417
Foshie, Brent, Winnipeg 4	1	0	0	0	0	0	0	0	0	0	0	0	0	0	0	.000
Freed, Roger, Rochester 138	503	96	168	282	30	6	24	130	0	5	82	3	92	8	2	.334
Frensley, James, Toledo 3	10	1	3	3	0	0	0	1	0	0	0	0	5	0	0	.300
Frisella, Daniel, Tide* 13	38	3	9	12	0	0	1	6	1	0	0	0	13	0	0	.237
Frondorf, Thomas, Columbus 38	24	2	1	1	0	0	0	1	6	1	0	0	13	0	0	.042
Frontino, Frank, Columbus . 3	1	0	0	0	0	0	0	0	1	0	0	0	1	0	0	.000
Fulk, William, Toledo 5	13	1	3	3	0	0	0	1	1	0	5	0	5	0	0	.231
Galante, Matthew, Syracuse . 66	175	29	42	50	4	2	0	19	1	3	29	0	11	3	1	.240
Garber, H. Eugene, Col 33	23	4	1	1	0	0	0	0	1	0	0	0	5	0	0	.043
Gardner, Richard, Syracuse . 30	65	4	8	9	1	0	0	11	1	1	6	0	31	0	0	.123
Garman, Michael, Louisville 28	57	5	8	9	1	0	0	1	1	1	0	0	12	0	0	.140
Garr, Ralph, Richmond* 98	391	83	151	204	26	3	7	51	5	5	29	2	43	39	9	.386
Gaspar, Rodney, Tidewater†.131	468	81	149	173	17	2	1	37	4	3	84	5	25	13	13	.318
Gatewood, Aubrey, Richmond 5	4	0	1	1	0	0	0	0	0	0	0	0	0	0	0	.250
Gilhooley, Robert, Toledo ... 29	72	11	17	24	4	0	1	6	0	1	9	1	8	0	1	.236

Player and Club	G.	AB.	R.	H.	TB.	2B.	3B.	HR.	RBI.	SH.	SF.	BB.	HP.	SO.	SB.	CS.	Pct.
Glass, John, Winnipeg	7	6	0	1	1	0	0	0	0	0	0	0	0	5	0	0	.167
Goggin, Charles, Columbus	62	145	14	31	45	6	1	2	14	0	0	10	2	35	1	0	.214
Gosger, James, Winnipeg*	30	110	14	36	64	2	1	8	20	0	0	13	0	13	3	3	.327
Gourleux, David, Richmond	10	4	0	1	1	0	0	0	1	0	0	1	0	2	0	0	.250
Gregory, John, Toledo	65	59	7	14	24	1	0	3	11	0	1	1	0	21	0	0	.237
Grich, Robert, Rochester	63	235	67	90	134	11	3	9	42	1	1	57	1	42	10	5	.383
Hahn, Donald, Winnipeg	5	18	1	6	7	1	0	0	1	0	0	0	1	0	1	0	.333
Hammond, Wilbert, Columbus	45	70	8	14	18	2	1	0	7	0	0	6	0	14	4	3	.200
Handrahan, J. Vernon, Tol*	21	19	1	3	4	1	0	0	0	1	0	1	0	6	0	0	.158
Haney, W. Larry, Winnipeg	81	251	21	55	76	8	2	3	26	0	0	19	0	31	5	2	.219
Hansen, Douglas, Syracuse	20	3	0	0	0	0	0	0	0	0	1	0	0	4	0	0	.000
Hermoso, Angel, Winnipeg	.100	313	37	66	69	3	0	0	12	3	1	39	4	40	14	9	.211
Hernandez, Enzo, Rochester	.100	372	61	99	120	10	4	1	39	12	1	33	1	22	11	4	.266
Herrera, Jose, Winnipeg	47	147	14	31	44	8	1	1	15	0	1	3	4	12	2	0	.211
Hill, Garry, Richmond	24	36	7	9	14	2	0	1	3	3	0	4	0	5	0	0	.250
House, Thomas, Richmond*	47	22	1	6	8	2	0	0	3	1	0	1	0	3	0	0	.273
Hudson, Jessie, Tidewater*	28	34	5	10	11	1	0	0	5	2	0	0	0	5	0	0	.294
Huyke, Elwood, Columbus	11	31	2	7	14	1	0	2	5	0	2	0	0	7	1	0	.226
Jack, Zelman, Columbus	9	16	0	3	4	1	0	0	0	0	0	2	0	2	1	0	.188
Jarvis, Raymond, Louisville	17	25	1	2	2	0	0	0	1	4	0	2	0	12	0	1	.080
Jaster, Larry, Richmond*	18	35	1	4	5	1	0	0	2	0	0	1	0	9	0	0	.114
Jenke, Noel, Louisville*	17	38	9	10	17	1	2	1	7	1	0	5	1	5	2	1	.263
Jestadt, Garry, Winnipeg	2	8	0	2	2	0	0	0	0	0	0	0	0	1	0	0	.250
Johnson, Donald, Winnipeg	11	18	2	0	0	0	0	0	0	0	0	3	0	12	0	0	.000
Johnson, Elijah, Rochester	.138	505	75	137	234	31	3	20	104	4	4	39	8	87	0	5	.271
Jones, Gary, Syracuse*	49	15	3	2	2	0	0	0	41	1	1	2	0	2	0	0	.133
Jones, Steven, Rochester*	8	2	0	1	1	0	0	0	0	0	0	0	0	1	0	0	.500
Kalafatis, George, Toledo*	.140	468	79	114	217	17	1	28	92	1	3	85	4	131	6	6	.244
Kelley, Thomas, Richmond	12	11	0	1	1	0	0	0	0	0	0	0	0	4	0	0	.091
Kendrick, Harry, Toledo	10	27	3	3	3	0	0	0	0	0	0	7	0	5	0	0	.111
Kester, Richard, Richmond	20	43	1	9	9	0	0	0	3	0	1	0	1	12	0	0	.209
Killingsworth, Larry, Col	25	50	6	8	8	0	0	0	2	3	0	0	1	16	0	0	.160
Kirkpatrick, William, Roch	27	39	8	8	9	1	0	0	3	4	0	8	0	11	0	0	.205
Kline, Steven, Syracuse	11	25	4	5	6	1	0	0	5	2	1	3	1	2	0	0	.200
Knechtges, Paul, Winnipeg*	36	7	1	1	1	0	0	0	0	0	0	2	0	5	0	0	.143
Kolb, Gary, Columbus*	.104	319	50	85	109	11	2	3	42	1	4	52	4	46	12	2	.266
Kopacz, George, Columbus*	.135	497	100	154	268	19	4	29	115	2	11	71	1	81	11	2	.310
Korince, George, 8 Tol-3Wpg	11	1	0	1	1	0	0	0	1	0	0	0	0	0	0	0	1.000
Kovach, Vaughn, Rochester	7	1	0	0	0	0	0	0	1	0	0	1	0	0	0	0	.000
Kranepool, Edward, Tide*	47	174	29	54	89	8	3	7	45	0	2	30	0	11	2	1	.310
Krull, David, Winnipeg	26	75	7	20	25	2	0	1	11	0	2	16	0	26	3	2	.267
Kuhn, Charles, Toledo*	43	14	2	3	3	0	0	0	0	0	0	0	0	3	0	0	.214
Lahoud, Joseph, Louisville*	.136	454	92	136	220	19	7	17	93	0	4	116	2	45	3	2	.300
Lamb, John, Columbus	9	4	0	1	1	0	0	0	0	1	0	3	0	1	0	1	.250
Lamont, Gene, Toledo†	74	230	27	61	84	9	1	4	32	0	3	19	1	46	1	0	.265
Landis, William, Louisville*	28	31	2	4	4	0	0	0	1	3	0	3	0	6	0	0	.129
Lanier, Lorenzo, Columbus*	129	434	98	143	182	14	8	3	36	4	5	113	2	45	20	12	.329
LaRose, Victor, Richmond	81	246	27	55	71	2	1	4	24	2	1	42	0	56	4	2	.224
Lehrer, Albert, Louisville	30	86	11	14	18	4	0	0	5	0	0	9	1	8	0	1	.163
Lock, Don, Louisville	99	257	40	61	119	11	1	15	41	0	4	62	0	100	2	1	.237
Lonborg, James, Louisville	2	2	0	0	0	0	0	0	0	0	0	0	0	0	0	0	.215
Lopez, Emerito, Toledo	.139	456	51	98	163	14	0	17	58	2	3	61	1	132	0	0	1.000
Loughlin, Larry, Winnipeg*	11	1	0	1	1	0	0	0	0	0	0	0	0	0	0	0	.212
Maduro, Jorge, Syracuse	35	104	8	22	26	2	1	0	9	2	0	10	1	20	1	0	.212
Mangual, Angel, Columbus	.135	509	74	143	240	19	9	20	87	0	7	43	2	77	4	6	.281
Maras, Edwin, Rochester	44	19	2	2	3	1	0	0	3	0	0	2	0	4	0	0	.105
Marone, Louis, Columbus	6	3	1	2	4	2	0	0	0	0	0	2	0	0	0	0	.667
Marshall, Michael, Winnipeg	12	15	0	0	0	0	0	0	1	0	0	2	0	7	0	0	.000
Martinez, Jose, Columbus	91	333	52	103	143	18	5	4	51	3	5	40	1	60	4	4	.309
Martinez, Teodoro, Tide	.116	438	62	134	181	20	4	3	36	2	1	11	1	53	13	9	.306
Marting, Timothy, Toledo	.118	413	46	115	141	19	2	1	23	2	0	33	0	51	0	1	.278
Mashore, Clyde, Winnipeg	57	169	36	52	94	9	0	11	27	0	1	29	0	43	4	0	.308
Mason, John R. B., Lou	80	225	29	52	75	10	2	3	27	0	2	26	1	34	2	2	.231
Matlack, Jonathan, Tide*	26	59	2	5	5	0	0	0	5	2	0	8	0	34	0	0	.085
Maxie, Larry, Richmond	24	34	3	3	7	1	1	1	5	0	4	0	20	0	0	.088
May, Milton, Columbus*	.111	397	49	111	194	14	3	21	86	1	7	35	1	49	1	0	.280
McAnally, Ernest, Winnipeg	34	70	8	11	22	2	0	3	12	2	0	3	0	20	1	0	.157
McDonald, David, Wpg*	.121	376	59	96	178	13	0	23	64	1	1	58	2	68	7	7	.255
McFarlane, Orlando, Tide	65	313	33	58	88	9	0	7	20	1	1	19	0	55	0	0	.266
McKenzie, George, D. Toledo	14	46	3	11	11	0	0	0	3	1	0	3	0	5	0	0	.239
McQueen, Michael, Rich*	8	15	2	7	7	0	0	0	2	0	0	1	0	5	0	0	.467
McRae, Norman, Toledo	44	24	1	4	6	2	0	0	2	0	1	0	0	13	0	0	.167
Mills, Richard, Louisville	27	51	3	4	5	1	0	0	0	2	0	3	0	32	0	0	.078
Miranda, Arturo, Roch	48	99	9	17	19	0	1	0	5	2	1	12	1	23	0	0	.172
Mitchell, Robert, Syracuse	.107	384	68	103	176	18	4	13	57	1	5	40	1	75	18	3	.268
Montague, John, Rochester	26	43	2	2	2	0	0	0	1	7	0	5	0	14	0	0	.047
Montgomery, Robert, Lou	.131	487	71	158	236	30	3	14	89	1	5	38	4	86	0	0	.324
Moock, Joseph, Winnipeg*	18	29	1	2	3	1	0	0	2	1	0	2	1	8	1	0	.108
Moore, Balor, Winnipeg*	22	37	4	4	5	1	0	0	3	0	0	1	0	12	0	0	.108
Moore, Tommy, Tidewater	4	1	0	0	0	0	0	0	0	0	0	0	0	0	0	0	.000
Morgan, R. Barry, Toledo*	93	289	41	69	96	9	0	6	41	1	3	50	5	46	3	1	.239
Moulder, Frederick, Toledo	.106	384	27	90	107	13	2	0	34	0	1	14	2	41	4	5	.234
Murphy, Brian, 52Lu-50Wi	.102	270	30	65	77	10	1	0	22	2	4	29	2	41	2	5	.241

Player and Club	G.	AB.	R.	H.	TB.	2B.	3B.	HR.	RBI.	SH.	SF.	BB.	HP.	SO.	SB.	CS.	Pct.
Murphy, Marlan, Richmond	2	6	1	1	2	1	0	0	1	0	0	2	0	3	0	0	.167
Muser, Anthony, Louisville*	114	462	66	130	184	25	7	5	45	2	1	38	0	49	1	2	.281
Musgraves, Dennis, Tide	39	7	0	1	1	0	0	0	1	0	0	0	0	2	0	0	.143
Nagelson, Russell, Toledo*	64	215	24	63	104	9	4	8	41	0	2	32	0	40	0	0	.293
Nagy, Michael, Louisville	2	6	0	1	1	0	0	0	0	0	0	0	0	4	0	0	.167
Navarro, Julio, Richmond	16	34	5	8	9	1	0	0	4	0	0	4	0	8	0	0	.235
Neibauer, Gary, Richmond	20	27	2	3	3	0	0	0	1	0	0	5	0	15	0	0	.111
Nelson, Brian, Richmond*	6	2	0	0	0	0	0	0	0	0	0	0	0	1	0	0	.000
Nelson, James, Columbus	11	12	1	3	4	1	0	0	0	0	0	1	0	4	0	0	.250
Nelson, Melvin, Richmond	39	26	7	6	10	1	0	1	5	0	0	0	0	4	0	0	.231
Nitschke, David, Tidewater	16	48	5	9	11	2	0	0	0	0	0	6	0	9	0	0	.188
Noessel, Conrad, Toledo	1	1	0	0	0	0	0	0	0	0	0	0	0	0	0	0	.000
Nye, Richard, Winnipeg*	5	10	1	1	1	0	0	0	0	0	0	0	0	2	0	0	.100
Oates, Johnny, Rochester	9	16	1	6	7	1	0	0	4	0	0	4	0	2	0	0	.375
Obregon, Francisco, Rich	113	329	44	99	127	21	2	1	35	4	1	38	2	22	3	3	.301
O'Donoghue, John, Wpg	18	39	2	5	8	0	0	1	1	0	0	2	0	16	0	2	.128
Ortiz, Alfredo, Winnipeg	7	13	1	3	6	0	0	1	1	0	0	1	0	4	0	0	.231
Paul, Ronald, Tidewater	33	22	3	2	2	0	0	0	1	0	0	3	0	10	0	0	.091
Pavelko, Paul, Toledo*	130	479	68	124	157	16	4	3	31	4	0	50	3	36	7	1	.259
Pena, George, Syracuse	87	264	38	65	124	10	2	15	41	1	1	37	0	55	0	0	.246
Pfeiffer, G. Charles, Lou	50	18	2	4	4	0	0	0	0	0	0	1	0	11	0	0	.222
Pfeil, Robert, Tidewater	37	156	16	47	58	8	0	1	19	0	0	4	0	13	1	2	.301
Phillips, Norman E., Lou	11	16	0	1	1	0	0	0	0	0	1	1	0	6	0	0	.063
Piche, Ronald, 12 Syr-5 Wpg	17	5	1	0	0	0	0	0	0	2	0	1	0	2	0	0	.000
Prediger, Charles, Louisville	5	1	0	1	1	0	0	0	0	0	0	0	0	0	0	0	1.000
Qualls, James Winnipeg†	67	231	23	65	89	7	4	3	22	0	0	12	2	24	8	3	.281
Raziano, Barry, Tidewater†	35	47	9	12	16	1	0	1	5	2	0	3	1	14	0	0	.255
Reahm, Frederick, Tide*	10	12	0	3	3	0	0	0	2	2	0	0	0	7	0	0	.250
Reams, Leroy, Toledo*	42	102	8	19	25	0	0	2	10	1	0	6	1	18	0	0	.186
Redmond, H. Wayne, Toledo	17	58	12	13	30	2	0	5	8	0	0	11	0	15	0	0	.224
Reed, Robert, Toledo	24	44	1	1	1	0	0	0	0	2	0	3	0	31	0	0	.023
Reniff, Harold, Syracuse	58	28	4	2	2	0	0	0	0	2	0	3	0	15	0	0	.071
Reynolds, Robert, Winnipeg	43	40	0	2	2	0	0	0	0	1	0	0	0	15	0	0	.050
Ribant, Dennis, Columbus	32	71	5	18	22	2	1	0	7	3	0	5	0	19	0	0	.254
Riddleberger, Dennis, Col	60	8	0	1	1	0	0	0	0	0	0	0	0	5	0	0	.125
Ritchie, Jay, 3 Rich-41 Lou	44	19	1	4	4	0	0	0	2	4	0	1	0	7	0	0	.211
Rivas, Danilo, Columbus	25	41	5	8	8	0	0	0	4	2	1	2	0	7	0	0	.195
Robertson, Jerry, Toledo†	18	24	0	1	1	0	0	0	1	2	0	0	0	10	0	0	.042
Robinson, William, Syr	115	372	68	96	155	20	0	13	43	4	4	46	2	66	12	10	.258
Rohr, Les, Tidewater*	17	37	2	8	9	0	0	0	4	1	0	0	0	14	0	0	.216
Rohr, William, Toledo*	23	37	4	3	3	0	0	0	1	0	0	0	0	12	0	0	.111
Sands, Charles, Syracuse*	41	105	15	25	41	4	0	4	8	0	0	3	1	11	0	0	.238
Santiago, Jose, Louisville	24	35	1	12	16	1	0	1	8	1	2	4	0	4	0	0	.343
Santos, Miguel, Columbus*	8	22	2	4	4	0	0	0	0	1	0	0	0	10	0	1	.182
Sauget, Richard, Richmond	3	4	0	1	1	0	0	0	0	0	0	0	0	1	0	0	.250
Saunders, Dennis, Toledo†	10	15	0	3	3	0	0	0	0	0	0	1	0	4	0	0	.200
Schaffer, Jimmie, Rochester	118	376	52	95	157	21	1	13	48	2	2	52	2	71	2	0	.253
Schoen, Gerald, 6 Ro-18 Syr	24	28	1	1	1	0	0	0	0	3	0	2	0	14	0	0	.036
Scott, Ralph, Rochester*	43	10	2	2	2	0	0	0	0	0	0	1	0	3	0	0	.200
Scripture, E. William, Tide	73	152	27	42	67	10	0	5	32	1	6	27	5	27	0	1	.276
Seelbach, Charles, Toledo	18	18	1	2	2	0	0	0	1	1	0	0	0	9	0	0	.111
Severinsen, Albert, Roch	45	21	4	5	10	2	0	1	3	0	0	0	0	11	0	0	.238
Shea, Steven, Winnipeg	51	19	0	1	1	0	0	0	3	2	1	2	0	9	0	0	.053
Shelton, Ronald, Rochester	13	29	2	6	6	0	0	0	1	2	0	3	0	8	0	0	.207
Shopay, Thomas, Rochester*	88	343	76	111	158	14	6	7	34	6	6	49	4	27	37	15	.324
Singleton, Kenneth, Tide†	64	219	48	85	154	16	1	17	46	0	1	57	0	26	3	3	.388
Smith, Richard, Winnipeg	82	262	33	65	101	9	0	9	30	1	2	33	0	33	4	2	.248
Solaita, Tolia, Syracuse*	130	396	62	122	207	24	2	19	87	3	4	95	3	89	3	2	.308
Solimine, Joseph, Winnipeg*	35	50	2	4	5	1	0	0	3	0	0	7	0	13	0	0	.080
Sparma, Joseph, Winnipeg	25	36	0	3	3	0	0	0	1	5	1	1	0	10	0	1	.083
Spier, Dale, Syracuse	27	29	3	1	1	0	0	0	1	6	0	1	0	15	0	0	.034
Sprague, Gary, Tidewater*	84	275	34	78	99	8	2	3	27	7	3	27	0	21	3	7	.284
Staab, Lawrence, Rochester	19	16	1	0	0	0	0	0	0	2	0	1	0	9	0	0	.000
Stanton, Leroy, Tidewater	133	498	66	151	238	20	5	19	94	1	2	41	4	96	15	9	.303
Stennett, Renaldo, Col	4	4	1	2	3	1	0	0	0	0	0	0	0	1	0	0	.500
Stitzel, Glenn, Tidewater	59	144	17	37	51	8	0	2	13	0	1	18	1	11	0	2	.257
Stone, Gary, Tidewater	43	122	13	31	48	5	0	4	16	0	3	13	0	29	0	0	.254
Taylor, Gary, Toledo	30	48	5	9	12	1	1	0	3	0	1	2	0	10	0	1	.188
Tepedino, Frank, Syracuse*	31	107	20	38	62	9	0	5	15	0	0	8	2	15	2	0	.355
Thibdeau, John, Louisville*	36	21	2	5	6	0	0	0	0	1	0	1	0	8	0	0	.238
Tillotson, Thaddeus, Syr	45	34	5	5	5	0	0	0	3	5	0	9	0	12	0	0	.147
Timmerman, Thomas, Toledo	6	16	1	1	1	0	0	0	0	0	0	0	0	10	0	0	.063
Tompkins, Ronald, Richmond	12	3	0	0	0	0	0	0	0	0	0	0	0	0	0	0	.000
Tracy, John, Rochester	45	151	20	33	45	9	0	1	11	1	0	17	1	19	1	2	.219
Turzilli, Robert, Richmond	60	195	20	44	55	8	0	1	23	2	1	16	0	42	3	1	.226
Valle, Hector, Toledo	80	236	17	52	71	7	0	4	20	1	0	21	0	18	0	0	.220
Vanzin, Frank, Rochester*	20	21	4	2	5	0	0	1	3	1	1	3	0	8	0	0	.095
Vaughan, Charles, Rich	2	1	0	0	0	0	0	0	0	0	0	0	0	0	0	0	.000
Velazquez, Federico, Wpg	33	89	11	25	40	7	1	5	20	0	3	9	0	17	1	1	.281
Verbanic, Joseph, Syracuse	19	23	4	3	4	1	0	0	2	0	1	0	0	6	0	0	.130
Vidal, Jose, Syracuse	73	195	36	51	83	7	2	7	22	2	0	37	0	48	6	3	.262
Wagner, Gary, Louisville	14	29	2	4	9	0	1	1	4	2	0	2	0	11	0	0	.138
Wagner, Steven, Winnipeg*	10	11	2	3	4	1	0	0	2	0	0	2	0	3	0	0	.273

Player and Club	G.	AB.	R.	H.	TB.	2B.	3B.	HR.	RBI.	SH.	SF.	BB.	HP.	SO.	SB.	CS.	Pct.
Wallin, Larry, Winnipeg* ...	68	157	25	42	75	6	0	9	25	0	1	20	1	38	1	2	.268
Washington, Ivy, Louisville*	8	8	1	0	0	0	0	0	0	0	0	2	0	7	0	0	.000
Whitfield, Fred, Winnipeg*	.102	309	41	82	143	12	2	15	48	1	3	32	3	59	3	0	.265
Williams, Earl, Richmond ..	22	68	10	18	34	1	0	5	15	0	1	3	2	13	1	0	.265
Williams, James F., Wpg ..	109	361	49	83	107	15	0	3	18	2	3	34	2	48	5	3	.230
Wilshusen, Terry, Rochester	12	4	0	0	0	0	0	0	0	0	0	1	0	2	0	0	.000
Wolcott, Frederick, Toledo	.116	328	62	85	122	20	1	5	25	0	3	34	0	74	14	3	.259
Wolff, William, Tidewater*	.74	168	25	50	62	9	0	1	17	0	0	24	2	18	3	4	.298
Yates, Albert, Louisville ...	.131	444	73	135	225	20	11	16	77	3	2	60	3	69	3	4	.304

The following pitchers had no plate appearances (listed alphabetically by clubs, games in parentheses):

LOUISVILLE—Hartenstein, Charles (3).

ROCHESTER—Stephen, Louis (4).

TOLEDO—Coleman, Paul (8); Fremuth, Michael (3); Todtenhausen, Arthur (7); Whillock, Jack (7).

WINNIPEG—Cisterna, Joseph (8); Hartman, David* (3); Marentette, Leo (9); Sembera, Carroll (2); Shaw, Donald* (12).

GRAND-SLAM HOME RUNS—Collins, Pena, Solaita, 2 each; J. Baker, Blomberg, Breeden, Calero, Campbell, Chavarria, Crist, Evans, Ferraro, Kopacz, Lock, Lopez, May, McDonald, Mitchell, Montgomery, 1 each.

AWARDED FIRST BASE ON INTERFERENCE—DeNeff 2 (Chilcott, Haney); Frondorf (Montgomery), Solaita (Booker), Tillotson (Chilcott), Tracy (Stone), Velazquez (Turzilli).

CLUB FIELDING

Club	G.	PO.	A.	E.	DP.	PB.	Pct.	Club	G.	PO.	A.	E.	DP.	PB.	Pct.
Tidewater	.140	3552	1428	127	138	19	.975	Columbus	140	3640	1426	154	155	18	.970
Syracuse	140	3567	1519	134	149	11	.974	Richmond	140	3573	1389	152	131	11	.970
Rochester	140	3509	1458	138	143	8	.973	Toledo	140	3474	1490	165	151	16	.968
Louisville	.140	3543	1461	142	171	11	.972	Winnipeg	140	3398	1386	189	155	19	.962

Triple Play—Rochester.

INDIVIDUAL FIELDING
(Ten or More Games)

*Throws lefthanded.

FIRST BASEMEN

Player and Club	G.	PO.	A.	E.	DP.	Pct.	Player and Club	G.	PO.	A.	E.	DP.	Pct.
Calero, Louisville ..	18	130	10	0	17	1.000	Kalafatis, Toledo*	.140	1160	107	16	126	.988
Breazeale, Rich ...	15	122	3	0	10	1.000	Johnson, Rochester	.137	1095	111	16	120	.987
Engbers, Tide*	28	213	22	1	30	.996	Ron Allen, Tide ..	.102	841	62	12	72	.987
Boehmer, Syracuse	25	194	17	1	23	.995	Solaita, Syracuse*	.129	1097	69	16	113	.986
MUSER, Lou*	.114	1013	45	9	119	.992	McDonald, Wpg ..	.47	337	21	5	38	.986
Kopacz, Columbus*	.135	1136	77	11	126	.991	Breeden, Rich* ...	.126	1033	51	16	98	.985
Whitfield, Wpg* ...	.87	639	63	7	73	.990	Derrick, Louisville ..	15	107	3	2	10	.982

Triple Play—Johnson.

(Fewer Than Ten Games)

Player and Club	G.	PO.	A.	E.	DP.	Pct.	Player and Club	G.	PO.	A.	E.	DP.	Pct.
Jack, Columbus	5	29	4	0	6	1.000	McFarlane, Tide ..	2	6	0	0	2	1.000
Kranepool, Tide* ...	4	22	0	0	3	1.000	M. Nelson, Rich* ..	1	2	0	0	1	1.000
Dix, Winnipeg*	3	18	4	0	2	1.000	Haney, Winnipeg ..	1	1	0	0	0	1.000
Bateman, Winnipeg .	3	16	2	0	2	1.000	Crist, Richmond ...	1	1	0	0	0	1.000
Tepedino, Syr*	2	15	1	0	0	1.000	Freed, Rochester ..	7	50	2	1	7	.981
Wagner, Winnipeg* .	4	11	0	0	1	1.000	Brown, Tidewater ..	4	34	4	1	5	.974
Williams, Rich	2	9	0	0	1	1.000	Kolb, Columbus ...	4	30	2	1	6	.970
Collins, Winnipeg ...	1	9	0	0	1	1.000	Scripture, Tide	9	54	4	2	6	.967
Evans, Richmond ...	4	7	0	0	1	1.000	Wallin, Winnipeg ..	2	18	3	2	3	.913

SECOND BASEMEN

Player and Club	G.	PO.	A.	E.	DP.	Pct.	Player and Club	G.	PO.	A.	E.	DP.	Pct.
Obregon, Richmond .	11	15	17	0	1	1.000	Herrera, Winnipeg ..	10	17	17	1	5	.971
Crist, Richmond ...	25	45	51	1	10	.990	Marting, Toledo ...	99	200	290	16	63	.968
Boehmer, Syracuse ..	54	109	141	3	38	.988	Miranda, Rochester ..	14	28	28	2	7	.966
Tracy, Rochester ...	39	89	101	3	22	.984	Allen, Rochester ...	25	58	51	4	12	.965
Canzano, Tidewater .	37	88	87	3	18	.983	Mason, Louisville ..	62	98	179	11	38	.962
Murphy, Lou-Wpg ..	89	188	218	7	69	.983	Fazio, Louisville ...	32	64	86	6	27	.962
Galante, Syracuse ..	55	95	152	5	33	.980	Qualls, Winnipeg ...	51	84	133	10	25	.956
Williams, Wpg	16	42	43	2	10	.977	Goggin, Columbus ..	20	32	42	4	7	.949
Martinez, Tide	75	139	179	8	46	.975	Lehrer, Louisville ..	25	51	55	6	18	.946
DAMASKA, Rich	.110	270	332	16	80	.974	Stitzel, Tidewater ..	27	51	72	7	16	.946
Grich, Rochester ...	62	144	195	9	59	.974	Gilhooley, Toledo ...	11	21	27	3	4	.941
Chavarria, Syr	52	96	129	6	33	.974	Wolcott, Toledo ...	25	55	54	8	18	.932
Martinez, Columbus .	76	152	207	10	52	.973	Kolb, Columbus ...	22	40	48	8	9	.917
Cash, Columbus	35	89	86	5	29	.972	Hermoso, Winnipeg .	10	14	21	4	6	.897

(Fewer Than Ten Games)

Player and Club	G.	PO.	A.	E.	DP.	Pct.	Player and Club	G.	PO.	A.	E.	DP.	Pct.
Ortiz, Winnipeg	4	6	6	0	3	1.000	Collins, Winnipeg ...	8	17	17	1	8	.971
Smith, Winnipeg	3	8	6	0	1	1.000	Foli, Tidewater	3	5	10	1	3	.938
Scripture, Tide	2	2	4	0	1	1.000	Moulder, Toledo ...	7	18	16	3	4	.919
Jestadt, Winnipeg ...	2	4	5	0	0	1.000	Shelton, Rochester ..	3	3	6	1	2	.900
Hernandez, Roch	2	2	3	0	0	1.000	Barski, Toledo	3	6	7	2	1	.867
McKenzie, Toledo ...	1	1	2	0	0	1.000	Stennett, Columbus .	1	5	1	1	2	.857
Moock, Winnipeg	1	0	3	0	0	1.000	Campbell, Columbus .	1	2	3	1	1	.833
Pfeil, Tidewater ...	8	21	15	1	5	.973							

THIRD BASEMEN

Player and Club	G.	PO.	A.	E.	DP.	Pct.
Lanier, Columbus ..	15	12	10	0	2	1.000
Fazio, Louisville ..	20	18	31	1	7	.980
Pfeil, Tidewater ..	32	31	76	3	15	.973
Moulder, Toledo ..	47	54	73	4	13	.969
Goggin, Columbus ..	16	14	15	1	0	.967
Campbell, Columbus .	83	52	144	8	11	.961
Cox, Syracuse ..	77	83	157	11	28	.956
EVANS, Richmond .120		92	220	16	12	.951
Obregon, Rich ..	15	14	23	2	3	.949
Derrick, Lou ..	14	10	26	2	4	.947
Fanzone, Lou ..101		82	195	17	23	.942
Chavarria, Syr ..	65	38	114	10	16	.938
Sprague, Tidewater .	76	44	133	12	14	.937
Ferraro, Rochester ..133		99	267	27	24	.931
Kolb, Columbus ..	53	34	74	8	10	.931
Lopez, Toledo ..	56	35	111	11	9	.930
Williams, Wpg ..	15	14	24	3	0	.927
Herrera, Winnipeg ..	16	14	39	5	3	.914
Collins, Winnipeg ..	49	22	73	9	10	.913
Scripture, Tide ..	25	12	39	5	3	.911
Hermoso, Winnipeg ..	19	13	38	5	8	.911
Mashore, Winnipeg ..	16	18	30	5	4	.906
McKenzie, Toledo ..	11	9	22	4	4	.886
Wolcott, Toledo ..	10	14	11	4	0	.862
McDonald, Wpg ..	10	9	8	3	2	.850

(Fewer Than Ten Games)

Player and Club	G.	PO.	A.	E.	DP.	Pct.
Martinez, Tide	4	4	15	0	2	1.000
Galante, Syracuse ..	6	6	12	0	2	1.000
Stitzel, Tidewater ..	9	5	10	0	1	1.000
Boehmer, Syracuse ..	6	4	9	0	1	1.000
Calero, Louisville ..	5	5	8	0	1	1.000
Allen, Rochester ...	5	4	7	0	0	1.000
Martinez, Columbus ..	6	5	5	0	0	1.000
Miranda, Roch	3	1	6	0	2	1.000
Bladt, Syracuse ...	4	1	3	0	0	1.000
Crist, Richmond ...	4	1	1	0	0	1.000
Haney, Winnipeg ...	2	0	1	0	0	1.000
Pena, Syracuse	1	0	1	0	0	1.000
Wolff, Tidewater ...	1	0	1	0	0	1.000
DeNeff, Toledo	7	8	9	1	0	.944
Smith, Winnipeg ...	9	4	11	1	0	.938
Lamont, Toledo	8	9	20	2	1	.935
Williams, Rich	8	8	17	2	4	.926
Canzano, Tidewater .	7	4	19	2	1	.920
Murphy, Winnipeg ..	4	1	7	1	2	.889
Marting, Toledo ...	2	1	7	1	0	.875
Tracy, Rochester ...	1	2	3	1	0	.833
Bosch, Winnipeg ...	7	5	9	4	0	.778
Shelton, Rochester .	1	3	2	2	1	.714
Velazquez, Wpg	1	1	1	2	0	.500
Ortiz, Winnipeg	2	1	0	2	0	.333

SHORTSTOPS

Player and Club	G.	PO.	A.	E.	DP.	Pct.
Boehmer, Syracuse ..	51	71	126	4	21	.980
Martinez, Tide ..	40	58	113	6	21	.966
Fazio, Louisville ..	71	138	253	14	69	.965
BAKER, Syracuse ..104		172	301	17	63	.965
Alvarado, Lou ..	69	95	210	11	55	.965
Obregon, Rich ..	70	92	231	13	50	.961
Poli, Tidewater ..100		176	279	19	58	.960
Moulder, Toledo ..	50	102	173	12	35	.958
Floyd, Rochester ..	34	78	116	9	35	.956
Lopez, Toledo ..	81	141	244	18	63	.955
Martinez, Columbus ..	15	25	38	3	9	.955
Hernandez, Roch ..	98	178	273	26	60	.945
Cruz, Columbus ..133		208	362	34	79	.944
Hermoso, Wpg ..	60	106	162	18	43	.937
Marting, Toledo ..	14	20	42	5	8	.925
Williams, Wpg ..	73	122	177	25	43	.923
LaRose, Richmond ..	69	117	179	27	34	.916

Triple Play—Hernandez.

(Fewer Than Ten Games)

Player and Club	G.	PO.	A.	E.	DP.	Pct.
Canzano, Tide	5	6	8	0	0	1.000
Collins, Winnipeg ..	2	3	4	0	0	1.000
Chavarria, Syr	2	2	3	0	0	1.000
Grich, Rochester ..	2	0	4	0	0	1.000
Campbell, Columbus .	3	2	0	0	0	1.000
Wolcott, Toledo ...	1	1	1	0	0	1.000
Fitzmaurice, Rich ..	1	1	0	0	0	1.000
Stitzel, Tidewater ..	1	0	1	0	0	1.000
Crist, Richmond ...	9	10	22	2	7	.941
Murphy, Winnipeg ..	4	8	12	2	3	.909
Qualls, Winnipeg ...	8	10	19	3	3	.906
Miranda, Rochester .	8	7	25	4	3	.889
Cox, Syracuse	4	3	6	2	2	.818
Calero, Louisville ..	1	0	1	1	0	.500

OUTFIELDERS

Player and Club	G.	PO.	A.	E.	DP.	Pct.
DAVIS, Columbus ..126		254	18	0	5	1.000
Bosch, Winnipeg ..	43	89	4	0	2	1.000
Bowens, Columbus ..	27	49	0	0	0	1.000
Reams, Toledo ..	24	42	1	0	0	1.000
Crist, Richmond ..	19	36	0	0	0	1.000
Krull, Winnipeg ..	24	24	1	0	1	1.000
Scripture, Tide ..	16	21	0	0	0	1.000
Gaspar, Tide* ..129		313	23	1	8	.997
Freed, Rochester .133		193	11	2	6	.990
Robinson, Syracuse .102		166	6	2	1	.989
Lock, Louisville ..	83	147	5	2	0	.987
Gosger, Winnipeg* ..	30	63	2	1	0	.985
Wolff, Tidewater ..	52	57	4	1	1	.984
Shopay, Rochester ..	87	159	12	3	1	.983
Pavelko, Toledo ..128		288	13	6	2	.980
Mitchell, Syracuse ..	99	234	11	5	2	.980
Singleton, Tide ..	64	92	4	2	1	.980
Coggins, Rochester ..	43	93	2	2	0	.979
Fitzmaurice, Rich ..	98	186	2	4	0	.979
Tepedino, Syr* ..128		44	2	1	0	.979
Arrington, Col ..	20	42	2	1	0	.978
Baylor, Rochester ..137		286	5	7	1	.977
Stanton, Tidewater .133		233	8	6	3	.976
Day, Winnipeg* ..	84	187	13	5	3	.976
Yates, Louisville ..128		257	4	7	0	.974
Nagelson, Toledo ..	62	101	10	3	1	.974
Baker, Richmond ..114		236	10	7	2	.972
Kranepool, Tide* ..	46	69	1	2	0	.972
Blomberg, Syr ..	80	124	11	4	2	.971
Allen, Rochester ..	21	30	2	1	0	.970
Redmond, Toledo ..	17	28	4	1	0	.970
Garr, Richmond ..	96	182	7	6	3	.969
Dix, Winnipeg* ..	14	30	1	1	0	.969
Coletta, Lou* ..	82	111	3	4	0	.966
Mangual, Columbus .135		270	12	11	8	.962
Mashore, Winnipeg ..	39	46	3	2	1	.961
Herrera, Winnipeg ..	14	22	2	1	1	.960
Brown, Richmond ..	21	46	0	2	0	.958
Laboud, Louisville* .132		220	4	10	3	.957
Morgan, Toledo ..	88	102	6	5	2	.956
McDonald, Wpg ..	62	95	8	5	4	.954
Bladt, Syracuse ..	93	161	8	9	3	.949
Lanier, Columbus ..110		185	12	11	3	.947
Breazeale, Rich ..	73	81	8	5	0	.947
Wolcott, Toledo ..	71	98	5	6	2	.945
DeNeff, Toledo ..	54	75	4	5	0	.940
Smith, Winnipeg ..	70	96	3	7	1	.934
Vidal, Syracuse ..	60	73	1	6	1	.925
Jenke, Louisville* ..	10	11	0	1	0	.917
Wallin, Winnipeg ..	16	24	3	3	0	.900
Hammond, Col ..	20	17	1	4	1	.818
Collins, Winnipeg ..	10	9	0	2	0	.818
Solimine, Wpg* ..	10	7	1	2	0	.800

OUTFIELDERS—Continued
(Fewer Than Ten Games)

Player and Club	G.	P.O.	A.	E.	DP.	Pct.
Gilhooley, Toledo ...	7	10	1	0	0	1.000
Santos, Columbus* ..	7	11	0	0	0	1.000
Williams, Rich	8	10	0	0	0	1.000
Qualls, Winnipeg ..	8	9	0	0	0	1.000
Shelton, Rochester ..	5	9	0	0	0	1.000
Hahn, Winnipeg ..	5	7	0	0	0	1.000
LaRose, Richmond ..	4	6	0	0	0	1.000
Derrick, Louisville ..	3	5	1	0	1	1.000
Lamont, Toledo	5	5	0	0	0	1.000
Brown, Tidewater ..	3	5	0	0	0	1.000
Vanzin, Rochester ..	2	5	0	0	0	1.000
Moeck, Winnipeg ...	6	4	0	0	0	1.000
Brunsberg, Toledo ..	4	4	0	0	0	1.000
Taylor, Toledo	1	4	0	0	0	1.000
Calero, Louisville ..	3	3	0	0	0	1.000
Murphy, Richmond ..	2	3	0	0	0	1.000
Velazquez, Wpg ...	2	3	0	0	0	1.000
Montgomery, Lou ...	1	2	0	0	0	1.000
O'Donoghue, Wpg* ..	2	1	0	0	0	1.000
McKenzie, Toledo ..	1	1	0	0	0	1.000
Stitzel, Tidewater ..	1	1	0	0	0	1.000
Turzilli, Richmond .	7	6	2	1	0	.889

CATCHERS

Player and Club	G.	PO.	A.	E.	DP.	PB.	Pct.
Didier, Rich ...	46	242	16	1	1	2	.996
Wallin, Wpg ...	31	198	21	1	10	2	.995
McFarlane, Tide ..	60	346	22	2	8	8	.995
SCHAFFER, Ro .109		607	48	4	8	3	.994
Bobb, Tidewater .	17	110	9	1	1	1	.992
Lamont, Toledo ..	57	299	39	3	9	6	.991
Farson, Roch ...	32	195	17	2	2	4	.991
Velazquez, Wpg ..	27	150	24	2	0	7	.989
Stone, Tide	40	219	13	3	2	7	.987
Valle, Toledo ...	70	389	42	6	5	7	.986
Haney, Wpg	74	458	43	8	7	7	.984
Nitschke, Tide ..	16	119	5	2	1	0	.984
Pena, Syracuse ..	80	394	35	7	4	4	.984
Booker, Rich-Col	53	336	23	6	5	5	.984
Chilcott, Wpg-Tide	21	107	10	2	0	5	.983
Montgomery, Lou .127		748	63	16	11	10	.981
May, Columbus ..108		688	68	15	10	10	.981
Turzilli, Rich ...	55	320	26	7	3	2	.980
Kolb, Columbus .	19	77	7	2	0	5	.977
Maduro, Syr	32	144	13	4	3	0	.975
Sands, Syracuse .	37	180	15	5		7	.975
Huyke, Col	11	61	9	3	1	2	.959
Cernich, Lou ...	19	86	8	6	2	1	.940

(Fewer Than Ten Games)

Player and Club	G.	PO.	A.	E.	DP.	PB.	Pct.
Kendrick, Tol	9	46	7	0	0	1	1.000
Johnson, Wpg	8	36	2	0	1	1	1.000
Oates, Roch	5	24	2	0	0	1	1.000
Bateman, Wpg ...	4	23	3	0	2	0	1.000
Frensley, Toledo .	3	21	1	0	0	0	1.000
Breazeale, Rich ..	3	19	1	0	0	2	1.000
Goggin, Col	4	16	0	0	1	1	1.000
Brunsberg, Toledo	4	14	5	0	0	1	1.000
Sauget, Rich	1	6	0	0	0	0	1.000
DeNeff, Toledo ..	1	2	0	0	0	0	1.000
Moock, Wpg	1	1	0	0	0	0	1.000
Fulk, Toledo	5	23	1	1	0	1	.960

PITCHERS

Player and Club	G.	PO.	A.	E.	DP.	Pct.
GARBER, Col	30	12	17	0	1	1.000
Maxie, Richmond ..	24	5	19	0	0	1.000
Beene, Rochester ..	13	10	14	0	0	1.000
Shea, Winnipeg ...	49	5	18	0	0	1.000
Severinsen, Roch ...	45	9	14	0	1	1.000
Delgado, Rochester .	31	10	13	0	2	1.000
Duliba, Richmond ..	43	9	11	0	1	1.000
Frondorf, Columbus .	38	6	14	0	1	1.000
O'Donoghue, Wpg* ..	15	11	9	0	1	1.000
Pfeiffer, Louisville .	50	3	16	0	0	1.000
Killingsworth, Col ...	25	7	12	0	0	1.000
Adamson, Rochester .	27	5	13	0	0	1.000
Handrahan, Toledo ..	21	4	14	0	0	1.000
Santiago, Lou	19	4	14	0	0	1.000
Schoen, Roch-Syr ..	24	4	12	0	1	1.000
Seelbach, Toledo ...	18	6	10	0	1	1.000
Jarvis, Louisville ..	17	5	11	0	1	1.000
Phillips, Louisville ..	11	5	10	0	1	1.000
Jones, Syracuse* ...	49	2	12	0	1	1.000
Farmer, Louisville ..	14	9	5	0	0	1.000
Colpaert, Columbus .	46	3	10	0	1	1.000
Neibauer, Richmond .	20	3	10	0	0	1.000
Nelson, Columbus ..	11	3	8	0	3	1.000
Farrell, Richmond ..	15	1	6	0	1	1.000
Wilshusen, Roch ...	12	2	5	0	0	1.000
Reahm, Tidewater* ..	10	1	5	0	0	1.000
Beckett, Lou	21	1	4	0	0	1.000
Ray Allen, Tide ...	17	2	2	0	0	1.000
Cullen, Richmond ...	10	0	3	0	0	1.000
Shaw, Winnipeg* ...	12	1	1	0	0	1.000
Gourieux, Rich	10	1	1	0	0	1.000
Korince, Tol-Wpg ..	11	0	1	0	0	1.000
Ribant, Columbus ...	28	9	36	1	5	.978
Bearnarth, Tide	30	11	22	1	1	.971
Burbach, Syracuse ..	21	9	24	1	2	.971
Bertaina, Roch*	22	11	20	1	1	.969
Kline, Syracuse	11	6	24	1	1	.968
Raziano, Tidewater .	32	11	17	1	1	.966
Hudson, Tide*	26	7	21	1	1	.966
Kirkpatrick, Roch ...	24	13	15	1	0	.966
Wagner, Louisville ..	13	4	24	1	2	.966
Taylor, Toledo	29	10	17	1	1	.964
Mills, Louisville	27	7	18	1	3	.962
McRae, Toledo	44	11	13	1	1	.960
Montague, Roch	26	13	11	1	1	.960
Reniff, Syracuse	58	10	13	1	0	.958
Reed, Toledo	24	3	18	1	1	.955
Cambria, Columbus .	26	17	23	2	4	.952
Scott, Rochester* ...	43	6	14	1	0	.952
Rivas, Columbus* ...	25	2	17	1	3	.950
Spier, Syracuse	27	1	15	1	2	.941
Landis, Louisville* ..	28	2	13	1	1	.938
Closter, Syracuse* ..	19	6	9	1	0	.938
Dillman, Wpg	16	6	9	1	0	.938
Gardner, Syracuse* .	30	3	25	2	0	.933
Navarro, Richmond ..	15	6	8	1	2	.933
Castiglione, Rich-Tide	12	5	9	1	2	.933
Denehy, Tidewater ..	16	9	18	2	1	.931
Riddleberger, Col* ..	60	3	10	1	0	.929
Hansen, Syracuse ...	20	3	10	1	1	.929
Knechtges, Wpg* ...	36	3	9	1	1	.923
Sparma, Winnipeg ..	24	3	9	1	1	.923
Rohr, Tidewater* ...	15	4	8	1	1	.923
Baney, Rochester ...	13	6	6	1	1	.923
Ritchie, Rich-Lou ..	44	2	9	1	0	.917
Kester, Richmond ...	19	6	5	1	0	.917
Cook, Louisville	60	4	6	1	0	.909
Brosseau, Columbus .	19	1	9	1	2	.909
McAnally, Wpg	31	23	36	6	3	.908
Matlack, Tide*	26	7	22	3	1	.906
Garman, Louisville ..	28	6	22	3	1	.903
Moore, Winnipeg* ..	18	10	27	4	3	.902
Robertson, Toledo ..	18	3	6	1	0	.900
Kelley, Richmond ...	12	4	5	1	1	.900
Tillotson, Syr	45	8	17	3	1	.893
Saunders, Toledo ...	10	3	5	1	1	.889

PITCHERS—Continued

Player and Club	G.	PO.	A.	E.	DP.	Pct.	Player and Club	G.	PO.	A.	E.	DP.	Pct.
Gregory, Toledo	48	9	14	3	2	.885	Tompkins, Rich	12	2	7	2	1	.818
Reynolds, Wpg	43	18	12	4	1	.882	Paul, Tidewater	33	2	15	4	1	.810
Jaster, Richmond	18	1	14	2	3	.882	Musgraves, Tide	39	3	9	3	0	.800
Barber, Richmond*	13	1	13	2	2	.875	Loughlin, Wpg*	11	2	2	1	0	.800
Piche, Syr-Wpg	17	2	5	1	1	.875	Acosta, Columbus	28	6	13	5	2	.792
House, Richmond*	44	1	12	2	0	.867	Rohr, Toledo*	23	6	13	5	1	.792
M. Nelson, Rich*	37	2	11	2	2	.867	Hill, Richmond	24	4	11	4	2	.789
Blanco, Winnipeg*	33	7	12	3	0	.864	Frisella, Tide	13	3	19	6	1	.786
Maras, Rochester	43	5	7	2	0	.857	Kuhn, Toledo*	40	2	5	2	0	.778
Chandler, Toledo	25	4	12	3	1	.842	Staab, Rochester*	19	1	11	4	1	.750
Verbanic, Syracuse	15	8	10	4	2	.818	Thibdeau, Lou*	36	0	9	4	1	.692

(Fewer Than Ten Games)

Player and Club	G.	PO.	A.	E.	DP.	Pct.	Player and Club	G.	PO.	A.	E.	DP.	Pct.
Fisher, Rochester	8	5	13	0	2	1.000	Fiskland, Syracuse	7	0	1	0	0	1.000
Timmerman, Toledo	5	3	9	0	1	1.000	Kovach, Rochester	7	0	1	0	0	1.000
Fitzer, Columbus	8	2	9	0	0	1.000	B. Nelson, Rich*	6	1	0	0	0	1.000
Marentette, Wpg	9	2	5	0	0	1.000	Marone, Columbus*	6	1	0	0	0	1.000
Washington, Lou	8	1	6	0	1	1.000	Prediger, Lou	5	0	1	0	0	1.000
McQueen, Rich*	7	1	6	0	0	1.000	Brown, Toledo	4	0	1	0	0	1.000
Folkers, Tide*	5	2	4	0	0	1.000	Crist, Richmond	4	1	0	0	0	1.000
Glass, Winnipeg	6	1	3	0	0	1.000	Foshie, Winnipeg	4	0	1	0	0	1.000
Dawson, Syracuse*	5	0	4	0	0	1.000	Frontino, Columbus	3	1	0	0	0	1.000
Gatewood, Rich	5	0	3	0	0	1.000	Camy, Tidewater	2	0	1	0	0	1.000
Moore, Tidewater	4	0	3	0	0	1.000	Lonborg, Lou	2	0	1	0	0	1.000
Hartman, Wpg*	3	1	2	0	2	1.000	Marshall, Winnipeg	9	8	8	1	1	.941
Whillock, Toledo	7	1	1	0	0	1.000	Carden, Winnipeg	8	1	4	1	0	.833
Clifford, Toledo	3	1	1	0	0	1.000	Cain, Toledo*	3	0	4	1	0	.800
Fremuth, Toledo	3	1	1	0	0	1.000	Nagy, Louisville	2	2	2	1	0	.800
Hartenstein, Lou	3	0	2	0	1	1.000	Nye, Winnipeg*	4	1	2	1	1	.750
Sembera, Wpg	2	2	0	0	0	1.000	Jones, Rochester*	8	1	1	1	0	.667
Lamb, Columbus	9	1	0	0	0	1.000	Cisterna, Winnipeg	8	0	1	1	1	.500
Coleman, Toledo	8	0	1	0	0	1.000							

The following players do not have any recorded accepted chances at the positions indicated; therefore, are not listed in the fielding averages for those particular positions: Boehmer, p; Booker, p; Breazeale, 2b; Breeden*, of; Chavarria, c; Clark, p; Cox, 2b; Crist, c; Evans, of; Fitzmaurice, 3b; House*, of; Kolb, p; Kuhn*, of; Maduro, 3b-of; McAnally, of; McDonald, p; Noessel, p; Robinson, 3b; Schaffer, of; Scripture, p; Stephen, p; Todtenhausen, p; Valle, 2b; Vaughan*, p.

CLUB PITCHING

Club	G.	CG.	ShO.	Sv.	IP.	H.	R.	ER.	HR.	BB.	Int. BB.	HB.	SO.	WP.	Bk.	ERA.
Syracuse	140	36	14	35	1189	1177	550	483	116	429	43	17	671	49	5	3.66
Columbus	140	32	9	37	1213	1164	612	540	134	559	70	36	824	48	7	4.01
Tidewater	140	46	9	24	1184	1147	614	542	129	529	38	23	820	45	6	4.12
Richmond	140	30	9	37	1191	1216	596	549	101	460	25	23	848	51	4	4.15
Rochester	140	39	8	34	1180	1220	635	556	138	466	36	23	761	54	3	4.24
Louisville	140	23	10	30	1181	1200	679	562	84	662	74	32	782	91	5	4.28
Toledo	140	34	6	19	1158	1267	748	644	118	629	57	17	739	59	3	5.01
Winnipeg	140	35	5	14	1133	1205	753	639	111	715	46	41	849	70	3	5.08

PITCHERS' RECORDS

(Leading Qualifiers for Earned-Run Average Leadership—140 or More Innings)

*Throws lefthanded.

Pitcher—Club	G.	GS.	CG.	ShO.	W.	L.	Sv.	Pct.	IP.	H.	R.	ER.	HR.	BB.	Int. BB.	HB.	SO.	WP.	ERA.
Gardner, Syracuse*	.30	24	13	4	16	5	2	.762	192	162	59	54	16	53	2	4	126	6	2.53
Reed, Toledo	.24	20	9	1	9	9	2	.500	143	138	57	45	12	49	3	0	58	4	2.83
Mills, Louisville	.27	27	4	2	6	6	0	.500	153	162	71	60	6	71	2	1	96	12	3.53
Bertaina, Roch*	.22	22	11	1	12	3	0	.800	152	131	69	62	15	61	0	1	108	10	3.67
Ribant, Columbus	.28	27	8	0	14	9	0	.609	189	194	96	80	23	50	7	4	102	1	3.81
Matlack, Tide*	.26	26	9	1	12	11	0	.522	183	168	94	84	14	90	1	2	146	10	4.13
Cambria, Columbus	.26	26	9	2	12	7	0	.632	164	167	81	76	23	57	9	3	91	2	4.17
Tillotson, Syr	.45	11	1	1	11	9	8	.550	142	144	77	70	17	41	3	1	72	4	4.44
Raziano, Tide	.32	16	4	0	8	10	6	.444	141	145	82	70	15	68	3	3	84	5	4.47
McAnally, Win	.31	29	14	0	12	13	0	.480	192	173	116	100	12	144	6	8	178	9	4.69

Departmental Leaders: G—Cook, Riddleberger, 60; GS—McAnally, 29; CG—McAnally, 14; ShO—Gardner, 4; W—Gardner, 16; L—Reynolds, 15; Sv—Severinsen, 22; Pct.—Bertaina, Colpaert, .800; IP—Gardner, McAnally, 192; H—Ribant, 194; R—Sparma, 120; ER—Sparma, 106; HR—Cambria, Ribant, 23; BB—McAnally, 144; IBB—Pfeiffer, 14; HB—Sparma, 9; SO—McAnally, 178; WP—Garman, Sparma, 19.

(All Pitchers—Listed Alphabetically)

Pitcher—Club	G	GS	CG	ShO	W	L	Sv	Pct.	IP	H	R	ER	HR	BB	Int. BB	HB	SO	WP	ERA
Acosta, Columbus	28	7	1	0	5	2	4	.714	82	69	32	27	7	53	8	2	57	7	2.96
Adamson, Roch	27	14	1	0	4	5	4	.444	95	90	48	46	12	47	1	0	60	7	4.36
Ray Allen, Tide	17	0	0	0	3	4	0	.429	36	44	28	27	4	20	2	0	26	0	6.75
Baney, Rochester	13	13	1	0	4	4	0	.500	70	89	47	41	9	25	0	0	37	3	5.27
Barber, Richmond*	13	10	5	1	7	1	1	.875	67	62	27	25	1	31	1	1	43	3	3.36
Bearnarth, Tide	30	10	4	1	6	6	3	.500	96	98	53	42	8	25	6	3	54	0	3.94
Beckett, Louis	21	1	0	0	1	0	1	1.000	31	34	23	21	2	22	3	1	20	1	6.10
Beene, Rochester	13	13	8	0	9	3	0	.750	90	95	37	32	9	26	1	0	63	1	3.20
Bertaina, Roch*	22	22	11	1	12	3	0	.800	152	131	69	62	15	61	0	1	108	10	3.67
Blanco, Winnipeg*	33	13	1	0	4	9	1	.308	93	85	60	47	7	72	4	3	66	6	4.55
Boehmer, Syracuse	2	0	0	0	0	0	0	.000	2	0	0	0	0	1	1	0	1	0	0.00
Brosseau, Col	19	16	0	0	4	8	0	.333	91	84	53	49	9	44	5	2	71	1	4.85
Brown, Toledo	4	0	0	0	0	0	0	.000	8	4	2	2	0	1	0	0	4	0	2.25
Burbach, Syracuse	21	21	7	2	5	10	0	.333	127	134	70	61	12	56	5	2	43	5	4.32
Cain, Toledo*	3	3	2	1	2	0	0	1.000	25	13	4	4	1	10	0	0	19	0	1.44
Cambria, Columbus	26	26	9	2	12	7	0	.632	164	167	81	76	23	57	9	3	91	2	4.17
Camy, Tidewater	2	2	0	0	0	1	0	.000	7	12	10	10	4	3	0	0	3	1	12.86
Carden, Winnipeg	8	4	0	0	1	2	0	.333	27	49	31	27	4	7	1	2	20	1	9.00
Castiglione, 2 Rich-10 Tide	12	10	4	2	5	2	0	.714	57	51	27	23	4	21	0	1	41	3	3.63
Chandler, Toledo	25	20	2	0	2	11	0	.154	114	138	100	97	9	89	4	2	63	6	7.66
Cisterna, Winnipeg	8	0	0	0	1	0	0	1.000	15	9	7	1	6	1	0	3	1		7.00
Clark, Toledo	13	0	0	0	1	2	2	.333	16	17	11	9	1	18	1	0	12	3	5.06
Clifford, Toledo	3	3	0	0	0	3	0	.000	10	16	12	12	2	5	1	1	5	0	10.80
Closter, Syracuse*	19	19	3	1	8	3	0	.727	95	108	60	54	9	50	1	2	66	5	5.12
Coleman, Toledo	8	0	0	0	0	0	0	.000	14	14	10	10	2	12	0	0	8	1	6.43
Colpaert, Columbus	46	0	0	0	12	3	10	.800	79	64	27	20	3	45	9	1	59	8	2.28
Cook, Louisville	60	0	0	0	9	4	9	.692	89	66	44	33	4	55	9	1	59	8	3.34
Crist, Richmond	4	0	0	0	0	0	0	.000	5	1	1	0	0	4	0	0	2	0	0.00
Cullen, Richmond	11	1	0	0	2	1	1	.667	23	20	13	11	1	5	1	0	15	0	4.30
Dawson, Syracuse*	5	2	1	0	1	1	0	.500	16	15	9	9	3	8	0	0	5	2	5.06
Delgado, Roch	31	8	3	2	7	8	0	.467	96	99	43	34	10	24	1	1	58	1	3.19
Denehy, Tidewater	16	16	8	1	7	4	0	.636	123	124	50	45	7	51	1	3	104	4	3.29
Dillman, Win	16	8	2	0	2	5	1	.286	66	71	45	32	10	30	2	0	46	0	4.36
Duliba, Richmond	43	0	0	0	4	6	14	.400	78	73	29	22	4	18	2	0	57	1	2.54
Farmer, Louisville	14	5	1	1	3	2	0	.600	49	49	27	24	6	13	1	2	40	5	4.41
Farrell, Richmond	15	2	0	0	0	1	3	.000	33	43	23	23	4	11	0	0	17	1	6.27
Fisher, Rochester	8	5	1	0	4	4	0	.500	51	66	34	25	7	9	1	6	34	1	4.41
Fiskland, Syracuse	7	0	0	0	0	1	0	.000	22	31	23	21	3	17	0	0	14	5	8.59
Fitzer, Columbus	8	3	0	0	0	1	0	.000	31	27	15	11	5	5	1	0	28	0	3.19
Folkers, Tide*	5	5	1	1	4	0	0	1.000											
Foshie, Winnipeg	4	0	0	0	0	0	0	.000	5	4	1	1	0	6	1	0	3	1	1.80
Fremuth, Toledo	3	0	0	0	0	1	0	.000	5	12	10	10	3	4	0	0	1	0	18.00
Frisella, Tide	13	13	5	2	7	3	0	.700	98	95	37	36	10	37	0	0	81	9	3.31
Frondorf, Col	38	8	1	0	5	5	2	.500	92	88	44	40	11	40	7	5	63	1	3.91
Frontino, Col	3	0	0	0	0	1	0	.000	3	4	2	1	1	2	2	0	2	0	3.00
Garber, Columbus	30	10	4	1	5	2	4	.714	96	96	57	50	13	38	5	1	75	9	4.71
Gardner, Syracuse*	30	24	13	4	16	5	2	.762	192	162	59	54	16	53	2	4	126	6	2.53
Garman, Lou	28	27	4	0	7	13	0	.350	156	154	103	83	9	132	4	2	127	19	4.79
Gatewood, Rich	5	3	0	0	1	1	0	.500	15	15	9	8	1	10	0	2	9	1	4.80
Glass, Winnipeg	6	4	0	0	0	4	0	.000	21	34	28	28	4	19	0	1	7	0	12.00
Gourieux, Rich	10	1	0	0	1	0	1	1.000	20	18	14	13	3	1	1	0	13	0	5.85
Gregory, Toledo	48	0	0	0	6	6	3	.500	122	132	63	56	21	64	8	1	88	3	4.13
Handrahan, Toledo	21	9	1	1	3	6	0	.333	70	73	49	43	4	50	6	0	39	0	5.53
Hansen, Syracuse	20	9	0	0	0	7	0	.000	52	60	36	33	7	23	5	0	34	1	5.71
Hartenstein, Lou	3	0	0	0	0	0	0	.000	4	5	1	1	0	1	0	0	3	2	2.25
Hartman, Winnipeg*	3	0	0	0	0	0	0	.000	6	4	4	3	1	1	5	0	0	3	4.50
Hill, Richmond	24	15	2	0	6	8	1	.429	109	108	64	60	11	57	1	1	59	2	4.95
House, Richmond*	44	4	1	0	6	5	7	.545	83	89	40	38	7	29	5	0	45	8	4.12
Hudson, Tide*	26	13	5	0	6	7	6	.462	107	85	41	34	11	48	4	3	70	1	2.86
Jarvis, Louisville	17	13	3	0	4	6	2	.400	81	75	51	47	6	52	1	5	43	12	5.22
Jaster, Richmond*	18	15	4	1	7	5	1	.583	97	118	48	44	14	37	3	3	56	5	4.08
Jones, Syracuse*	49	4	1	0	7	5	8	.583	79	74	29	27	3	30	5	1	43	5	3.08
Jones, Rochester*	8	0	0	0	1	0	1	1.000	17	17	13	13	3	10	0	1	16	1	6.88
Kelley, Richmond	12	10	2	0	2	6	0	.250	43	50	31	30	4	32	0	1	43	3	6.28
Kester, Richmond	19	19	5	1	8	6	0	.571	126	113	48	48	8	41	0	3	114	3	3.43
Killingsworth, Col	25	24	4	2	10	5	0	.667	138	127	76	70	10	97	6	8	103	9	4.57
Kirkpatrick, Roch	24	23	3	0	7	8	0	.467	134	156	70	67	13	46	5	5	70	6	4.50
Kline, Syracuse	11	11	4	2	8	2	0	.800	78	78	27	22	5	13	1	1	54	2	2.54
Knechtges, Win*	36	0	0	0	4	3	2	.571	59	61	24	20	6	26	8	0	43	2	3.05
Kolb, Columbus	5	0	0	0	0	0	0	.000	8	12	5	5	0	8	0	0	5	0	5.63
Korinec, 8 Tol-3 Wpg	11	1	0	0	0	2	0	.000	16	18	20	16	3	20	1	1	8	0	9.00
Kovach, Rochester	7	0	0	0	1	0	0	1.000	11	12	11	11	2	9	2	1	7	0	9.00
Kuhn, Toledo*	40	1	0	0	3	3	2	.500	68	67	45	33	4	54	6	3	50	10	4.37
Lamb, Columbus	9	0	0	0	0	4	1	.000	20	19	11	1	0	4	2	0	19	1	0.45
Landis, Lou*	28	15	1	0	5	9	1	.357	101	115	69	50	10	62	8	4	72	3	4.46
Lonborg, Lou	2	2	0	0	1	1	0	.500	10	12	5	5	1	6	2	0	8	2	4.50
Loughlin, Wpg*	11	1	0	0	0	1	0	.500	14	22	16	12	2	10	2	0	11	2	7.71
Maras, Rochester	43	1	0	0	5	2	4	.714	78	71	38	30	6	37	8	1	52	6	3.46
Marenette, Wpg	9	0	0	0	0	1	0	.000	12	18	12	12	3	9	3	0	3	3	9.00

Pitcher—Club	G	GS	CG	ShO	W	L	Sv	Pct	IP	H	R	ER	HR	BB	Int. BB	HB	SO	WP	ERA
Marone, Columbus*	6	0	0	0	0	2	1	.000	10	15	10	10	3	7	2	1	4	0	9.00
Marshall, Wpg	9	5	2	0	2	1	4	.667	41	30	13	10	3	19	2	0	23	1	2.20
Matlack, Tide*	26	26	9	1	12	11	0	.522	183	168	94	84	14	90	1	2	146	10	4.13
Maxie, Richmond	24	21	3	2	8	4	0	.667	123	134	57	53	11	46	2	2	109	5	3.88
McAnally, Wpg	31	29	14	0	12	13	0	.480	192	173	116	100	12	144	6	8	178	14	4.69
McDonald, Wpg	2	0	0	0	0	0	0	.000	2	6	7	7	2	3	0	0	1	0	31.50
McQueen, Rich*	7	7	0	0	5	2	0	.714	42	43	17	16	4	21	0	1	44	7	3.43
McRae, Toledo	44	7	1	0	6	11	5	.353	95	108	75	62	5	63	11	1	76	10	5.87
Mills, Louisville	27	27	4	2	6	6	0	.500	153	162	71	60	6	71	2	1	96	12	3.53
Montague, Roch	26	26	5	2	6	6	0	.400	139	137	82	75	18	60	3	5	102	8	4.86
Moore, Winnipeg*	18	18	6	1	4	9	0	.308	119	107	67	59	13	99	0	5	100	11	4.46
Moore, Tidewater	4	1	0	0	0	0	0	.000	12	17	13	13	3	10	0	1	11	0	9.75
Musgraves, Tide	39	0	0	0	5	8	7	.385	63	54	30	27	4	38	12	1	46	5	3.86
Nagy, Louisville	2	2	1	2	0	0	1	1.000	15	12	1	0	0	0	0	0	12	0	0.00
Navarro, Rich	15	5	1	1	6	0	0	1.000	75	75	48	44	5	42	4	3	45	2	5.28
Neibauer, Rich	11	2	1	1	4	3	1	.571	75	75	48	44	5	42	4	3	45	2	5.28
B. Nelson, Rich*	6	1	0	0	0	0	0	.000	10	14	7	5	2	3	0	0	9	0	4.50
Nelson, Columbus	11	5	1	0	3	2	1	.600	35	37	17	14	0	28	3	4	31	2	3.60
M. Nelson, Rich*	37	3	1	0	6	8	5	.429	93	100	53	47	7	30	1	0	59	1	4.55
Noessel, Toledo	1	0	0	0	0	0	0	.000	2	1	0	0	0	1	0	1	1	0	0.00
Nye, Winnipeg*	4	4	1	1	2	0	0	.333	25	22	8	6	2	10	1	1	25	1	2.16
O'Donoghue, Wpg*	15	12	4	2	6	5	0	.545	86	77	30	27	3	35	4	5	59	3	2.83
Paul, Tidewater*	33	11	3	1	7	3	1	.700	104	95	53	44	8	41	2	0	62	2	3.81
Pfeiffer, Louisville	50	0	0	0	6	5	6	.545	82	90	50	42	6	40	14	2	60	5	4.61
Phillips, Lou	11	10	1	0	1	5	1	.167	53	68	44	39	12	23	3	4	29	1	6.62
Piche, 12 Syr— 5 Wpg	17	2	0	0	3	0	1	1.000	28	39	23	16	5	12	1	1	13	1	5.14
Prediger, Lou	5	1	0	0	0	0	0	.000	11	15	8	8	2	6	0	0	4	0	6.55
Raziano, Tide	32	16	4	0	8	10	6	.444	141	145	82	70	15	68	3	3	84	5	4.47
Reahm, Tide*	10	6	0	0	1	3	0	.250	46	43	26	23	6	28	1	2	29	3	4.50
Reed, Toledo	24	20	9	1	9	9	2	.500	143	138	57	45	12	49	3	0	58	4	2.83
Reniff, Syracuse	58	1	0	0	10	3	13	.769	120	109	38	32	4	57	8	2	61	8	2.40
Reynolds, Wpg	43	16	4	0	7	15	0	.318	133	142	93	77	9	60	5	5	117	7	5.21
Ribant, Columbus	28	27	8	0	14	9	0	.609	189	194	96	80	23	50	7	4	102	1	3.81
Riddleberger, Col*	60	0	0	0	3	4	9	.429	72	57	22	19	9	23	6	2	42	2	2.38
Ritchie, 3 Rich— 41 Lou	44	0	0	0	5	6	7	.455	90	103	39	31	5	29	8	4	59	6	3.10
Rivas, Columbus*	25	14	4	2	7	8	2	.467	114	110	66	57	16	49	4	3	77	1	4.50
Robertson, Toledo	18	11	2	1	4	4	0	.500	71	74	39	38	7	31	3	1	68	4	4.82
L. Rohr, Tide*	15	13	1	0	4	4	0	.500	86	96	55	54	16	45	5	4	54	2	5.65
W. Rohr, Toledo*	23	14	2	0	3	9	1	.250	90	93	66	53	8	56	1	4	62	6	5.30
Santiago, Lou	19	9	1	0	7	4	1	.636	77	80	42	31	5	33	5	2	47	3	3.62
Saunders, Toledo	10	8	3	0	2	4	1	.400	46	47	25	23	6	18	2	0	28	2	4.50
Schoen, 6 Roch— 18 Syr	24	10	1	1	5	2	1	.714	90	88	44	35	20	24	3	0	57	2	3.50
Scott, Rochester*	43	1	0	0	6	3	3	.667	65	73	43	36	10	25	5	0	43	1	4.98
Scripture, Tide	2	0	0	0	0	0	0	.000	0	0	0	0	0	0	0	0	0	0	22.50
Seelbach, Toledo	18	5	2	0	1	4	0	.200	59	44	23	18	7	32	0	1	46	3	2.75
Sembera, Wpg	2	0	0	0	0	1	0	.000	4	3	3	2	0	2	0	0	9	0	6.75
Severinsen, Roch	45	0	0	0	4	6	22	.400	81	68	33	29	5	35	5	2	49	3	3.22
Shaw, Winnipeg*	12	0	0	0	0	1	0	.000	10	12	8	6	1	7	0	0	8	0	5.40
Shea, Winnipeg	49	3	0	0	3	3	2	.500	88	101	51	43	12	48	2	2	47	3	4.40
Sparma, Winnipeg	24	23	1	0	3	13	0	.188	116	157	120	106	10	92	3	9	76	19	8.22
Spier, Syracuse	27	14	3	1	7	5	2	.583	103	104	42	40	13	26	3	3	74	1	3.50
Staab, Rochester*	19	10	2	1	4	6	0	.400	64	72	39	32	7	30	2	1	33	4	4.50
Stephen, Roch	4	0	0	0	1	0	0	.000	5	6	5	4	1	6	1	0	1	0	7.20
Taylor, Toledo	29	25	6	1	6	14	1	.300	133	192	103	90	15	37	5	1	56	5	6.09
Thibdeau, Lou*	36	11	2	1	5	5	0	.500	78	75	49	44	7	50	6	2	45	8	5.08
Tillotson, Syr	45	11	1	1	11	8	6	.550	142	144	77	70	17	41	3	1	72	4	4.41
Timmerman, Toledo	5	4	1	0	3	1	0	.750	38	30	11	7	3	12	0	0	36	1	1.66
Todtenhausen, Tol	7	0	0	0	0	0	0	.000	9	12	11	9	3	7	0	0	5	0	9.00
Tompkins, Rich	2	0	0	0	0	0	2	.000	20	29	13	10	1	7	0	1	7	1	4.50
Vaughan, Rich*	2	0	0	0	0	0	0	.000	2	1	1	0	2	1	0	0	2	1	4.50
Verbanic, Syracuse	15	13	2	1	5	4	0	.556	75	77	39	33	6	33	3	0	32	7	3.96
Wagner, Lou	13	13	3	2	6	5	0	.545	82	81	39	33	4	35	1	1	43	3	3.62
Washington, Lou	8	4	0	0	2	1	1	.667	28	24	16	13	1	25	4	0	20	4	4.18
Whillock, Toledo	7	0	0	0	0	2	1	.000	11	17	11	11	3	10	0	0	12	0	9.00
Wilshusen, Roch	12	0	0	0	2	1	0	.500	17	16	13	13	6	13	1	1	17	2	6.88

BALKS—Cambria, Mills, 3 each; Adamson, Garman, Handrahan, Hudson, Kline, 2 each; Baney, Boehmer, Brosseau, Cullen, Folkers, Frondorf, Gatewood, Hill, Lamb, McDonald, Moore (Wpg), Musgraves, Paul, Rivas, L. Rohr, W. Rohr, Schoen, Shea, Vaughan, Verbanic, 1 each.

COMBINATION SHUTOUTS—Nelson-Riddleberger, Brosseau-Riddleberger, Columbus; Santiago-Cook, Landis-Cook, Louisville; Maxie-M. Nelson, McQueen-Duliba, Richmond; Beene-Severinsen, Rochester; Burbach-Jones-Reniff, Syracuse; O'Donoghue-Knechtges, Winnipeg.

NO-HIT GAME—Farmer, Louisville, defeated Toledo, 8-0, August 24 (seven innings).

Mexican League

CLASS AAA

Leading Batter	League President	Leading Pitcher
FRANCISCO CAMPOS	ANTONIO RAMIREZ M.	ALFREDO MARISCAL
Jalisco		Yucatan

CHAMPIONSHIP WINNERS IN PREVIOUS YEARS

1955—Mexico City Tigers* .539
1956—Mexico City Reds .. .692
1957—Yucatan .... .567
    Mex. C. Reds (2nd)† .550
1958—Nuevo Laredo ...... .625
1959—Poza Rica .... .575
    Mex. C. Reds (3rd)† .507

1960—Mexico City Tigers . .538
1961—Veracruz .... .575
1962—Monterrey .... .592
1963—Puebla .... .606
1964—Mexico City Reds .. .586
1965—Mexico City Tigers . .590

1966—Mexico City Tigers‡ .614
    Mexico City Reds .. .571
1967—Jalisco .... .607
1968—Mexico City Reds .. .586
1969—Reynosa .... .591

*Defeated Nuevo Laredo, two games to none, in playoff for pennant. †Won four-team playoff.
‡Won split-season playoff.

STANDING OF CLUBS AT CLOSE OF SEASON, AUGUST 23

NORTHERN DIVISION

Club	M.R.	Rey.	G.P.	Mon.	Sal.	Ag.	Jal.	Yuc.	M.T.	P.R.	W.	L.	T.	Pct.	G.B.
Mexico C. Reds	..	10	13	14	15	8	6	10	4	11	91	59	0	.607	....
Reynosa	10	..	12	12	9	5	6	7	6	9	76	72	4	.514	14
§Gomez Palacio	7	8	..	12	8	5	6	5	12	5	68	82	0	.453	23
Monterrey	6	8	8	..	7	3	10	9	4	12	67	81	0	.453	23
Saltillo	5	11	12	13	..	6	3	4	5	8	67	83	1	.447	24

SOUTHERN DIVISION

	M.R.	Rey.	G.P.	Mon.	Sal.	Ag.	Jal.	Yuc.	M.T.	P.R.	W.	L.	T.	Pct.	G.B.
†Aguila	6	9	9	11	8	..	9	12	10	13	87	63	1	.580	....
‡Jalisco	8	7	8	4	11	11	..	13	10	11	83	66	1	.557	3½
Yucatan	4	7	9	5	10	8	7	..	13	14	77	73	1	.513	10
Mexico C. T.	..	10	7	2	8	9	10	10	..	10	73	74	0	.497	12½
Poza Rica	..	3	5	9	2	6	7	9	6	10	57	93	4	.380	30

Forfeit—Mexico City Tigers forfeited to Yucatan, April 1.
†Aguila club represented Veracruz.
‡Jalisco club represented Guadalajara, Jalisco.
§Gomez Palacio club represented area known as Union Laguna.
Playoff—Aguila defeated Mexico City Reds, four games to two.
Regular-Season Attendance—Aguila, 122,663; Gomez Palacio, 211,879; Jalisco, 170,055; Mexico City Reds, 275,815; Mexico City Tigers, 200,936; Monterrey, 244,594; Poza Rica, 143,398; Reynosa, 123,239; Saltillo, 256,595; Yucatan, 130,369. Total, 1,879,543. Playoffs, 86,569.
Managers: Gomez Palacio, Minnie Minoso; Jalisco, Guillermo Garibay; Mexico City Reds, Jose Guerrero; Mexico City Tigers, Jose Luis Garcia; Monterrey, Vinicio Garcia, Rodolfo Alvarado; Poza

Rica, David Garcia; Reynosa, Miguel Sotelo; Saltillo, Tomas Herrera, Andres Tanaka; Veracruz, Enrique Izquierdo; Yucatan, Tony Castano, Luis Esma.

All-Star Team: 1B—Campos, Jalisco; 2B—F. Chavez, Aguila; 3B—Sanchez, Tigers; SS—F. Rodriguez, Aguila; OF—Garcia, Gomez Palacio· Sosa, Aguila; Montoya, Reds; C—Estrada, Reds; Luque, Tigers; P—Mazon, Agtila; Mariscal, Yucatan; Manager—Izquierdo, Aguila.

(Compiled by Raul Mendoza, League Statistician. Mexico, D. F.)

CLUB BATTING

Club	G.	AB.	R.	OR.	H.	TB.	2B.	3B.	HR.	RBI.	SH.	Int. SF.	BB.	HP.	SO.	SB.	CS.	LOB.	Pct.
Jalisco ...	150	4671	689	569	1349	1973	226	52	98	654	62	62	510	74	50	709	62	61	1019	.289
Mex. Reds	150	4800	714	610	1379	1915	168	76	72	645	85	46	430	67	37	587	67	39	1018	.287
Gomez Pal.	150	4808	655	686	1365	1996	217	39	112	572	75	42	422	79	33	588	75	33	1005	.284
Mex. Tig.	146	4557	534	587	1248	1609	170	40	37	479	103	39	338	65	37	505	36	44	978	.274
Saltillo ...	151	4758	612	667	1287	1776	175	34	82	559	64	41	432	47	33	775	58	64	960	.270
Reynosa	152	4710	597	596	1272	1747	177	53	64	524	66	40	515	58	27	776	121	61	1063	.270
Monterrey	148	4699	557	622	1269	1807	159	41	99	503	47	35	353	59	36	731	35	28	949	.270
Aguila ...	151	4752	640	475	1278	1855	163	33	116	570	64	17	458	65	36	782	55	38	1001	.269
Yucatan ...	150	4555	519	567	1180	1557	183	34	42	453	69	30	448	77	28	640	72	49	960	.259
Poza Rica	154	4557	445	583	1149	1478	170	24	37	404	68	40	445	53	21	585	28	39	1025	.252

INDIVIDUAL BATTING

(Leading Qualifiers for Batting Championship—465 or More Plate Appearances)

*Bats lefthanded. †Switch-hitter.

Player and Club	G.	AB.	R.	H.	TB.	2B.	3B.	HR.	RBI.	SH.	SF.	BB.	HP.	SO.	SB.	CS.	Pct.
Campos, Francisco, Jalisco	.138	453	83	162	248	23	12	13	94	3	7	59	8	47	0	7	.358
Garcia, Francisco, G P	.149	535	120	185	335	44	11	28	90	3	8	61	4	58	31	3	.346
Sparks, Oliverio, Monterrey	140	459	83	159	253	20	7	20	85	4	3	49	9	91	6	3	.346
Acosta, Teolindo, Yucatan*	140	469	76	158	221	26	14	3	55	2	3	54	6	26	14	12	.337
Sosa, Emilio, 98 PR-42 Agu.	140	491	70	161	193	21	1	31	5	1	57	1	22	3	5	.328
Ruiz, Ildefonso, Gomez Pal.*	150	479	73	156	255	15	1	24	99	4	4	90	2	113	4	1	.326
Ponce, Manuel, Mex. Tigers	137	461	61	150	165	15	0	42	13	4	35	3	24	2	7	.325
Vega, Abelardo, Mexico Reds	133	440	70	142	261	20	12	5	68	9	1	40	6	67	17	4	.323
Cerda, Benjamin, Jalisco	.148	506	69	162	216	29	2	7	78	4	15	47	3	27	1	5	.320
Montoya, Ramon, Mex. Reds	142	503	86	161	240	24	8	13	84	10	8	50	8	25	13	7	.320
Rubio, Ramiro, Saltillo	.149	525	70	168	222	14	5	10	75	4	1	42	1	73	5	9	.320

Departmental Leaders: G—Mendoza, 153; AB—A. Garcia, 606; R—F. Garcia, 120; T—F. Garcia, 185; TB—F. Garcia, 335; 2B—F. Garcia, 44; 3B—T. Acosta, 14; HR—R. Alvarez, 33; RBI—I. Ruiz, 99; SH—Mendoza, 16; SF—Cerda, 15; BB—Parlier, 131; HP—Mendez, 21; SO—Parlier, 131; SB—Macias, 35; CS—Macias, 16.

(All Players—Listed Alphabetically)

Player and Club	G.	AB.	R.	H.	TB.	2B.	3B.	HR.	RBI.	SH.	SF.	BB.	HP.	SO.	SB.	CS.	Pct.
Abreu, Andres, Monterrey ...	5	7	0	1	1	0	0	0	1	0	0	1	0	0	1	0	.143
Acosta, Cecilio, Jalisco ...	45	20	1	3	3	0	0	0	0	1	0	1	0	7	0	0	.150
Acosta, Ramon, Reynosa ...	23	15	0	3	4	1	0	0	1	0	1	0	6	0	0	.200
Acosta, Teolino, Yucatan*	.140	469	76	158	221	26	14	3	55	2	3	54	6	26	14	12	.337
Adame, Arnulfo, Gomez Pal.	39	74	3	7	7	0	0	0	4	10	1	4	0	27	0	3	.095
Aguilar, Jose Luis, Saltillo*	6	11	1	2	2	0	0	0	1	0	0	0	3	0	0	.182
Agundez, Victor, 18 Gomez Palacio-20 Mexico Tigers	38	14	4	4	4	0	0	0	2	3	0	0	2	0	0	.286
Ahumada, Alejo, Reynosa ...	10	6	1	0	0	0	0	0	1	0	2	0	0	0	0	.000
Alfonso, Julio, Mexico Reds	7	15	1	1	1	0	0	0	0	1	0	3	0	0	.067
Almada, Guillermo, Mex. T.*	5	4	0	0	0	0	0	0	0	0	0	0	2	0	0	.000
Alvarado, Natanael, Aguila	5	5	0	0	0	0	0	0	0	0	0	0	2	0	.000
Alvarez, Arturo, Yucatan*	.118	380	54	127	172	29	5	2	33	4	4	41	0	43	18	6	.334
Alvarez, Rogelio, Aguila	.146	465	66	134	249	16	0	33	93	2	7	87	2	91	0	0	.288
Antonety, Felipe, Aguila	5	5	1	1	1	0	0	0	0	0	1	0	2	0	0	.200
Aquino, Carmelo, Saltillo ...	46	41	4	7	9	2	0	0	7	2	2	1	0	13	0	0	.171
Arano, Ramon, Mexico Reds	36	66	5	11	14	0	0	1	10	3	0	4	2	24	0	2	.167
Arano, Wilfredo, Aguila ...	.151	553	87	153	201	19	4	7	35	11	5	50	12	57	10	13	.277
Arce, Alberto, Mexico Tigers	11	3	0	0	0	0	0	0	0	0	0	0	1	0	0	.000
Argumedo, Antonio, Mont.	.107	265	25	64	87	11	3	2	26	3	2	30	3	56	0	2	.242
Armas, Tomas, Jalisco*	21	1	0	0	0	0	0	0	0	0	0	0	0	0	.000
Ayon, Andres, Jalisco	46	65	10	14	20	3	0	1	5	2	0	9	0	23	1	1	.215
Azcarraga, Ernesto, Mex. R.	30	16	1	3	3	0	0	0	3	0	0	3	0	0	0	.188
Balcazar, Raul, Aguila	36	13	1	4	4	0	0	0	2	0	0	0	0	0	0	.308
Baretty, Santiago, Gomez Pal.	12	4	1	1	1	0	0	0	0	0	0	0	0	0	0	.250
Bauta, Eduardo, Poza Rica	54	44	2	5	7	2	0	0	2	1	0	0	0	18	0	1	.114
Bedolla, Eduardo, Gomez Pal.	27	7	0	0	0	0	0	0	0	0	1	0	0	0	.000
Berzunza, William, Reynosa*	125	388	33	121	143	13	3	1	35	8	5	43	1	35	2	2	.312
Betancourt, Simon, G P	38	37	2	5	5	0	0	3	1	0	3	0	15	0	0	.135
Bojorquez, Jose, Poza Rica*	81	235	17	63	79	6	2	2	21	5	2	21	0	30	3	2	.268
Bouye, Lucas, Saltillo	37	112	14	30	44	6	1	2	18	0	2	J6	1	29	2	1	.268
Brito, Hector, Aguila	21	41	5	4	5	1	0	0	1	0	0	0	0	0	0	.098
Brown, Winston, Poza Rica	34	55	9	12	16	1	0	1	3	0	1	0	0	0	0	.218
Buentello, Israel, Reynosa	41	33	5	8	9	1	0	0	1	0	0	6	0	0	.242
Burgos, Antonio, Yucatan	.132	394	52	96	114	16	1	0	20	4	1	17	2	40	11	7	.244
Burgos, Carlos, 6 Jal-3 Agu.	9	0	0	0	0	0	0	0	1	0	0	0	0	0	.000
Caceres, Porfirio, Saltillo ...	40	76	7	19	30	2	0	3	12	3	0	2	0	41	0	0	.250
Calvo, Jorge, Saltillo	33	70	13	24	37	4	0	3	10	3	1	13	1	11	0	2	.343

Player and Club	G.	AB.	R.	H.	TB.	2B.	3B.	HR.	RBI.	SH.	SF.	BB.	HP.	SO.	SB.	CS.	Pct.
Camacho, Moises, Poza Rica	129	391	35	85	114	17	0	4	46	4	5	57	3	30	0	2	.217
Camacho, Ronaldo, Yucatan	141	439	58	106	172	19	1	15	77	4	4	73	2	70	1	1	.241
Camarero, Rolando, Aguila	.151	543	91	165	272	22	2	27	91	5	4	36	2	102	2	4	.304
Campos, Francisco, Jalisco	.138	453	83	162	248	23	12	13	94	3	7	59	8	47	0	7	.358
Cancino, Guadalupe, Saltillo	31	94	12	29	32	3	0	0	7	0	2	6	1	9	0	2	.309
Cano, Raul, Mexico Reds	..	2	1	0	0	0	0	0	0	0	0	0	0	0	0	0	.000
Carrasco, Carlos, Jalisco	..	26	19	3	5	5	0	0	0	2	1	0	1	0	7	0	0	.263
Carrillo, Lucio, Poza Rica	35	16	0	4	4	0	0	0	1	2	0	0	0	4	1	0	.250
Castillo, Enrique, Saltillo	48	51	2	10	13	3	0	0	6	4	0	2	2	21	0	0	.196
Castillo, Roberto, Gomez P.	34	24	5	2	2	0	0	0	1	1	0	2	2	9	0	0	.083
Castro, Arnoldo, Mexico T.	.137	437	50	106	141	20	0	5	45	13	4	30	3	46	2	5	.243
Castro, Fernando, Gomez P.	122	264	30	58	84	13	2	3	23	5	1	21	1	32	2	0	.220
Cerda, Benjamin, Jalisco	.148	506	69	162	216	29	2	7	78	4	15	47	3	27	1	5	.320
Chavez, Francisco, Aguila	.124	410	48	111	144	15	3	4	45	1	4	31	2	81	2	4	.271
Chavez, J. Guadalupe, Salt.	137	457	56	117	161	22	2	6	47	10	3	45	1	76	3	12	.256
Chavez, Rene, Aguila	52	31	1	4	4	0	0	0	3	0	1	0	0	9	0	0	.129
Cisneros, Alfonso, Monterrey	19	7	0	0	0	0	0	0	0	1	0	0	0	3	0	0	.000
Coleman, Clarence, Mex. R.*	142	511	85	150	229	23	7	14	75	6	3	43	8	64	1	4	.294
Conde, Ramon, Saltillo	..	77	8	20	24	4	0	0	4	1	0	5	0	5	0	0	.260
Conkle, Francisco, Saltillo	34	90	6	23	33	5	1	1	8	3	1	5	0	13	0	1	.256
Contreras, Adalberto, M R	115	349	45	100	123	9	7	0	51	9	7	26	1	36	2	3	.287
Contreras, Jesus, Gomez Pal.	84	232	21	62	76	8	0	2	23	4	2	24	2	26	1	2	.267
Cordova, Ernesto, Jalisco	..	23	13	1	1	2	1	0	0	0	0	0	0	0	5	0	0	.077
Corella, Jaime, Jalisco	.102	230	22	60	86	17	0	3	29	2	4	41	1	21	0	0	.261
Cortes, Ruben, Monterrey*	..	24	15	0	0	0	0	0	0	0	1	0	1	0	5	0	0	.000
Cota, Sergio, Yucatan	..	3	1	0	0	0	0	0	0	0	0	0	0	0	0	0	0	.000
Cruz, Concepcion, Mex. T.	..	42	32	1	6	7	1	0	0	0	0	0	0	0	8	0	0	.188
Davila, L. Alberto, Mont.	.106	268	33	66	91	10	6	1	30	4	3	26	0	52	6	3	.246
Davis, Jaime, Reynosa	..	56	8	23	27	2	1	0	5	0	0	11	1	5	0	0	.411
Diaz, Cesar, Aguila	..	56	47	10	7	7	0	0	1	2	0	0	2	0	29	2	0	.149
Diaz, Hector M., Me. T.	..	28	19	1	1	1	0	0	0	1	0	0	0	0	9	0	0	.053
Diaz, M. Antonio, Poza Rica	113	321	18	86	99	11	1	0	47	3	10	26	1	23	1	0	.268
Elizalde, Eusebio, Reynosa	6	2	0	0	0	0	0	0	0	0	0	0	0	1	0	0	.000
Enriquez, Graciano, Yucatan	125	385	30	80	104	10	1	4	32	1	5	27	3	67	4	7	.208
Esma, Luis, Yucatan	76	151	9	36	41	5	0	0	14	3	1	16	0	19	0	0	.238
Espino, Hector, Monterrey	.136	432	86	138	213	17	2	18	47	0	1	75	10	51	3	5	.319
Espinoza, Ernesto, Me R	106	291	51	83	103	9	4	1	24	6	3	18	2	40	4	3	.285
Esquivel, Ramiro, Mont.	..	46	117	7	27	31	2	1	0	11	2	0	8	1	17	1	1	.231
Esquivias, Ruben, M Tigers*	120	336	47	97	152	18	2	11	55	2	4	48	3	38	1	0	.289
Estrada, Francisco, M. Reds	138	442	83	134	234	24	11	18	85	2	7	72	4	53	1	0	.303
Fabela, Jaime, Poza Rica	.110	306	31	82	93	11	0	0	17	4	1	21	1	37	0	2	.268
Fabela, Victor, 65 Jal-69 Sal	134	368	50	83	125	19	1	7	47	5	2	45	5	83	7	5	.226
Fajardo, Ignacio, Mex. Reds	34	10	0	0	0	0	0	0	0	1	0	0	0	3	0	0	.000
Ferguson M., Leonardo, Yuc	15	21	0	5	6	1	0	0	2	0	0	1	0	3	0	0	.238
Fernandez, Rogelio, Yuca	144	450	62	114	148	20	4	2	34	12	3	40	4	62	8	5	.253
Figueroa, Agustin, Gomez P.	40	76	3	8	11	3	0	0	3	3	0	1	1	28	0	0	.105
Fitch, Jorge, Reynosa	.137	433	59	118	151	15	3	4	54	10	5	63	2	44	6	4	.273
Fuentes, Antonio, Poza Rica	24	54	11	15	17	2	0	0	1	4	0	5	0	9	2	7	.283
Galindo, Guillermo, G. P.	.102	205	24	58	80	6	2	4	23	5	2	15	0	27	1	2	.283
Gamez, Raul, Saltillo*	..	49	27	6	6	8	2	0	0	1	0	0	2	0	8	0	0	.222
Garcia, Alonso, Reynosa	.152	606	91	171	221	14	12	4	42	5	5	46	3	114	31	11	.282
Garcia, Ernesto, Aguila	..	2	3	0	0	0	0	0	0	0	0	0	1	0	1	0	0	.000
Garcia, Francisco, G P	.149	535	120	185	335	44	11	28	90	3	8	61	4	58	31	3	.346
Garcia, Humberto, Reynosa	.102	248	31	55	95	15	5	4	32	1	2	29	1	63	6	3	.234
Garcia, Nicolas, Mex. Tigers	63	65	1	10	13	1	1	0	4	1	0	2	0	16	0	0	.154
Garcia, Oscar, Saltillo	..	4	0	1	0	0	0	0	0	0	0	0	0	0	0	0	0	.000
Garcia, Sergio, Monterrey	..	5	0	1	1	0	0	0	0	1	0	0	0	0	0	0	.200
Garcia, Victor, Mexico Reds	37	27	7	8	11	1	0	1	1	0	1	0	1	6	0	0	.296
Garcia, Vinicio, 11-Mon.-1 Mex. T.	..	12	11	2	4	7	0	0	1	3	0	0	2	0	0	0	0	.364
Garibay, Jose, Mexico Reds*	126	408	50	114	139	14	4	1	49	6	4	31	0	27	2	3	.279
Garza, Adolfo, Reynosa	..	5	2	2	4	2	0	0	0	0	0	1	0	1	0	0	.400
Garza, Carlos, Me Tigers†	.	37	65	10	16	19	3	0	0	3	0	1	10	0	10	0	1	.246
Garza, Gustavo, Mex. Tigers*	110	303	44	91	121	10	7	2	31	8	4	32	3	19	1	7	.300
Garza, Ricardo, Mex T†	..	7	2	0	0	0	0	0	0	1	0	0	0	4	1	3	0	.000
Gaspar, Miguel, Gomez Pal.	94	267	21	78	95	11	0	2	27	1	2	19	3	6	1	0	.292
Geigel, J. Manuel, Poza Rica*	35	56	5	12	18	1	1	1	11	3	0	1	0	10	0	0	.214
Gleason, Roy W., Jalisco*	52	127	21	29	55	1	2	7	21	0	1	16	2	55	0	1	.228
Gonzalez, Ernesto, Reynosa	45	88	9	24	27	3	0	0	5	2	0	2	0	16	1	0	.273
Goycolea, Gerardo, Gomez P.	16	4	0	1	1	0	0	0	1	0	0	0	0	0	0	0	.250
Guerra, Eugenio, Jalisco	..	2	2	1	1	1	0	0	0	0	0	0	0	0	0	0	0	.500
Guerrero, J. Angel, Jalisco	..	28	39	2	11	11	0	0	0	5	1	0	3	1	4	0	1	.282
Guerrero, Jose, Mexico Reds	2	5	0	0	0	0	0	0	0	0	0	2	0	0	0	0	.000
Gutierrez, Cesar, 6 PR-41 Yuc	47	15	0	0	0	0	0	0	0	0	1	0	6	0	0	.000
Gutierrez, Gerardo, Mex T	.	11	17	1	4	4	0	0	0	2	0	0	0	1	6	0	0	.235
Gutierrez, M. Angel, Yuc*	.	4	3	1	2	3	1	0	0	0	0	0	1	0	0	0	.667
Gutierrez, Pablo, Reynosa	..	44	21	1	1	1	0	0	0	0	0	2	1	2	0	0	.048
Hernandez, Javier, Poza Rica	97	289	35	84	107	9	4	2	39	2	7	19	2	33	4	4	.291
Hernandez, J. Manuel, Aguila	11	23	2	6	9	0	0	1	2	0	0	1	0	7	0	1	.261
Hernandez, Juan, Monterrey	.	23	4	0	0	0	0	0	0	0	0	0	1	0	0	0	0	.000
Hernandez, G., Ramon, MR†	32	20	1	4	5	1	0	0	6	0	0	1	0	7	0	0	.200

Player and Club	G.	AB.	R.	H.	TB.	2B.	3B.	HR.	RBI.	SH.	SF.	BB.	HP.	SO.	SB.	CS.	Pct.
Hernandez, Z., Ramon, MR	137	536	79	146	169	11	6	0	37	5	5	37	1	25	16	7	.272
Herrera, Francisco, Saltillo	32	86	13	25	40	4	1	3	12	0	0	16	3	20	1	2	.291
Herrera, Roberto, Yucatan	123	327	37	102	152	15	1	11	66	0	3	87	5	54	5	3	.312
Horsford, James, Monterrey	28	51	3	10	11	1	0	0	2	0	1	4	0	15	0	0	.196
Huerta, Hector, Mex. Tigers	78	167	14	47	58	7	2	0	14	8	1	6	4	25	1	3	.281
Hurtado, Ruben, Reynosa	93	250	29	66	99	10	7	3	29	3	2	36	0	53	3	2	.264
Icedo, Enrique, Mexico T.	49	15	0	2	2	0	0	0	0	1	0	2	0	8	0	0	.133
Imbert, Julio, C., Yucatan*	42	81	9	19	23	4	0	0	6	7	0	2	0	19	0	0	.235
Izquierdo, Enrique, Aguila	98	223	17	60	71	11	0	0	28	4	1	16	1	24	0	0	.269
Jimenez, Manuel, Reynosa*	50	148	18	45	71	8	0	6	28	0	0	23	3	10	0	0	.304
Johnson, Theodore, Reynosa	24	77	9	15	19	4	0	0	4	1	0	6	0	19	1	0	.195
Jusino, Ramon, Gomez Pal.	55	59	5	15	20	2	0	1	6	6	0	1	1	10	0	0	.254
Lagunas, Crescencio, PR	33	33	3	7	8	1	0	0	1	1	0	3	1	9	0	0	.212
Lara, Armando, Mex. Tigers	22	32	5	5	6	1	0	0	2	0	0	0	0	4	0	0	.156
Lazo, Esteban, Monterrey	68	150	10	31	36	3	1	0	10	0	0	10	1	25	0	0	.207
Leal, Felipe, Mexico Reds	69	122	23	42	63	5	5	2	24	2	0	6	0	11	0	0	.344
Leal, Jesus, Saltillo	44	92	10	15	16	1	0	0	5	0	1	12	0	15	1	2	.163
Leon, Maximino, Jalisco	40	72	2	11	13	2	0	0	0	3	0	0	0	18	0	0	.153
Leyva, Jose, Gomez Palacio*	10	8	2	4	4	0	0	0	1	0	0	0	0	2	0	0	.500
Lilly, James, Gomez Palacio	3	2	1	0	0	0	0	0	0	0	0	0	1	1	0	0	.000
Lira, Jorge, Poza Rica	21	16	2	3	3	0	0	0	3	0	0	3	0	5	0	0	.188
Lizarraga, Roberto, M Reds	81	258	25	69	83	8	0	2	27	7	3	19	0	26	4	1	.267
Lopez, Aurelio, Mexico Reds	38	57	2	4	4	0	0	0	1	5	0	2	0	38	0	1	.070
Lopez, Ernesto, Monterrey	37	22	0	0	0	0	0	0	0	0	0	2	0	9	0	0	.000
Lopez, Francisco, Aguila	11	3	0	0	0	0	0	0	0	0	0	1	0	1	0	0	.000
Lopez, Jose Ramon, Mon	35	75	5	13	21	5	0	1	2	0	0	2	0	29	0	0	.173
Lopez, Lorenzo, Monterrey	104	297	31	67	106	9	0	10	23	2	5	35	2	64	0	1	.226
Lopez, Manuel, 12Yuc-83PR	95	234	18	62	69	5	1	0	21	1	5	23	1	18	0	0	.265
Lopez, Rigoberto, 7 Rey-13S	20	16	0	2	3	1	0	0	1	1	0	2	0	6	0	0	.125
Lozano, Pedro, Monterrey	10	11	0	3	4	1	0	0	4	0	0	1	0	0	0	0	.273
Lugo, Gabriel, Jalisco	148	560	99	176	258	30	11	10	80	3	8	28	4	38	25	11	.314
Lugo, Manuel, Jalisco	57	37	4	6	8	0	1	0	5	1	0	1	0	20	0	0	.162
Lugo, Urbano, Yucatan	15	6	1	0	0	0	0	0	0	0	0	0	0	5	0	0	.000
Luque, Gregorio, M Tigers	117	327	22	84	96	8	2	0	32	8	2	15	2	7	1	1	.257
Macias, Angel, Reynosa*	151	516	74	136	195	25	8	6	68	7	6	76	1	89	35	16	.264
Madrigal, Hector, P Rica	44	27	1	1	1	0	0	0	0	0	0	4	0	15	0	0	.037
Malpica, Luis, Aguila	26	51	5	13	14	1	0	0	7	2	1	5	0	16	0	0	.255
Manrique, Gerardo, Mont	10	3	0	0	0	0	0	0	0	0	0	0	0	1	0	0	.000
Mariscal, Alfredo, Yucatan*	45	79	8	20	24	4	0	0	7	3	0	4	1	15	0	0	.253
Marquez, Francisco, Reynosa	97	247	26	71	94	8	3	3	32	0	0	9	4	43	8	5	.287
Marquez, Prudencio, P Rica	1	1	0	0	0	0	0	0	0	0	0	0	0	1	0	0	.000
Martinez, Francisco, Mon*	33	28	0	3	3	0	0	0	1	0	0	0	0	17	0	0	.107
Martinez, Javier, Yucatan	32	29	4	1	1	0	0	0	1	0	1	0	0	8	0	0	.034
Mason, Larry, Monterrey	14	8	1	0	0	0	0	0	0	0	0	0	0	6	0	0	.000
Mata, Jorge, Monterrey	12	16	2	2	2	0	0	0	0	0	0	1	0	4	0	0	.125
Maytorena, Francisco, Me T	39	44	2	6	6	0	0	0	4	6	0	5	0	18	0	0	.136
Mazon, Blas, Aguila	33	52	3	11	14	1	1	0	3	3	5	2	0	19	0	0	.212
Mena, Rigoberto, Mon	129	459	49	129	164	16	5	3	67	8	7	15	0	17	0	2	.281
Menchaca, J. Francisco, Jal	128	368	41	111	162	18	3	9	66	5	9	20	0	52	1	5	.302
Mendez, Roberto, Jalisco	150	545	97	172	227	38	7	1	41	12	2	63	21	65	8	3	.316
Mendivil, Rafael, Mex Reds	16	29	2	7	7	0	0	0	2	0	3	0	0	6	1	0	.241
Mendoza, Saul, Poza Rica	153	471	58	128	189	22	3	11	41	16	3	61	3	81	9	8	.272
Mere, Luis, Yucatan	18	4	0	0	0	0	0	0	0	0	0	0	0	0	0	0	1.000
Meza, Alfredo, Jalisco*	20	12	0	3	3	0	0	0	1	0	0	3	0	3	0	0	.250
Meza, Gonzalo, Saltillo	46	12	2	3	3	0	0	0	0	0	0	5	0	2	0	0	.250
Minoso, Orestes, Gomez Pal.	40	47	6	22	34	6	0	2	17	0	2	3	1	3	0	0	.468
Moncayo, Bernardo, 26 Y-10 S	36	31	3	5	5	0	0	0	0	0	2	1	12	0	0		.161
Montoya, Ramon, Mex Reds	142	503	86	161	240	24	8	13	84	10	8	50	8	25	13	7	.320
Montoya, Raul, Reynosa	117	351	49	105	127	8	7	0	26	10	2	16	3	36	12	8	.299
Mora, Jesus, Jalisco	149	563	63	148	190	17	8	3	46	9	4	30	5	44	9	12	.263
Morejon, Daniel, Saltillo	151	536	78	165	245	33	7	11	73	3	3	63	2	55	17	5	.308
Moreno, Eleazar, Mex Reds	7	3	0	0	0	0	0	0	0	0	0	0	0	0	0	0	.000
Moreno, Victor M., Mon	5	2	0	0	0	0	0	0	0	0	0	0	0	1	0	0	.000
Mota, Francisco, Yucatan	2	1	0	0	0	0	0	0	0	0	0	0	0	1	0	0	.000
Munoz, Romulo, Mex Tigers	14	14	2	1	1	0	0	0	1	0	0	0	0	0	0	0	.071
Munro, Ernesto, Monterrey	20	14	0	4	4	0	0	0	0	0	0	0	0	4	0	0	.286
Murillo, Armando, Gomez P.	76	237	36	59	78	11	1	2	25	3	3	20	1	13	2	3	.249
Murillo, Sergio, 15 Gomez Pal.-35 Mex T	50	14	1	2	2	0	0	0	0	1	0	1	0	3	0	0	.143
Murrieta, Carlos, Mon*	1	1	0	0	0	0	0	0	0	0	0	0	0	0	0	0	.000
Naranjo, Jose Luis, Saltillo*	102	180	22	40	68	5	1	7	26	1	1	32	2	30	1	1	.222
Navarrete, Juan, Saltillo	11	9	1	1	1	0	0	0	0	0	0	0	0	5	0	0	.111
Nazario, Victor, Poza Rica	31	102	11	29	32	3	0	0	9	0	0	6	0	19	1	2	.284
Nieblas, Manuel de J., MR	5	15	6	4	9	0	1	1	3	1	0	3	0	0	0	0	.267
Nuno, Ramiro, Aguila*	28	26	0	1	1	0	0	0	1	1	0	2	0	16	0	1	.038
Ochoa, David, Jalisco	20	17	3	3	3	0	0	0	1	0	2	0	16	0	0		.176
Olivares, Alonso, Poza Rica	1	1	0	0	0	0	0	0	0	0	0	4	0	4	0	0	.000
Ornelas, Rafael, Mexico Reds	2	5	1	2	2	0	0	0	0	0	0	0	1	0	1	0	.400
Orozco, Octavio, Aguila*	4	2	0	2	2	0	0	0	0	0	0	1	0	0	0	0	1.000
Orozco, Victor, Saltillo	98	227	30	53	66	2	1	3	19	3	3	25	2	41	0	5	.233
Ortega, Raul, Saltillo	3	2	0	1	1	0	0	0	0	0	0	1	0	0	0	0	.500

Player and Club	G.	AB.	R.	H.	TB.	2B.	3B.	HR.	RBI.	SH.	SF.	BB.	HP.	SO.	SB.	CS.	Pct.
Ortiz, Alfredo, Mex Reds* ..	44	61	7	16	19	1	1	0	11	1	0	8	3	16	0	0	.262
Ortiz, Jose Manuel, Mon	147	595	78	168	226	15	8	9	40	6	3	22	6	56	13	8	.282
Ortiz, Roberto, Aguila	149	489	94	140	230	18	6	20	81	8	6	90	7	72	5	3	.286
Osorio, Alberto, Aguila	22	51	2	9	9	0	0	0	5	2	0	0	0	8	0	0	.176
Osuna, Carlos, Poza Rica ..	56	159	13	29	39	7	0	1	10	0	2	13	3	37	0	2	.182
Osuna, Elpidio, Monterrey ..	139	501	55	150	224	22	2	16	50	7	2	22	2	68	4	3	.299
Pacheco, Jesus, Mexico Reds	3	2	0	0	0	0	0	0	0	0	0	0	0	0	0	0	.000
Palomino, Alfredo, Poza R*	103	282	25	72	97	14	1	3	18	6	2	26	0	35	3	7	.255
Paredes, Rene, Saltillo	30	46	4	11	13	2	0	0	2	2	0	1	0	8	0	0	.239
Parlier, William, Jalisco† ..	145	422	100	125	240	22	3	29	97	0	9	131	6	131	11	6	.296
Parra, Graciliano,																	
14 Saltillo-12 Gomez Pal.	26	28	0	3	4	1	0	0	1	0	1	0	0	9	0	0	.107
Penalver, Luis, Monterrey ..	23	54	6	11	18	2	1	1	4	0	1	2	0	14	0	0	.204
Pereira, Miguel, M Tigers ..	50	49	4	10	14	0	2	0	5	2	0	3	0	13	0	0	.204
Perez Torres, Miguel, PR*	.110	286	25	75	103	15	5	1	16	2	0	26	0	14	2	1	.262
Plascencia, Obed, M Tigers	.105	319	30	95	114	9	2	2	39	3	2	28	2	25	2	2	.298
Plascencia, Rigoberto, Yuc .	25	49	5	11	14	1	1	0	3	1	0	1	0	10	0	0	.224
Pollorena, Antonio, Jalisco .	41	50	7	14	17	3	0	0	3	7	0	2	0	12	0	1	.280
Ponce, Manuel, Mex Tigers	.137	461	61	150	165	15	0	0	42	13	4	35	3	24	2	7	.325
Preciado, Alfredo, M Tigers	89	220	26	68	98	14	5	2	37	4	3	19	3	38	0	1	.309
Prescott, George, Poza Rica	57	166	14	45	70	8	1	5	27	0	1	19	0	25	0	1	.271
Quintana, Juan de Jesus,																	
10-Aguila-13 Gomez Pal	23	28	2	5	9	1	0	1	2	1	0	0	1	10	0	0	.179
Quiroz, Juan Ramon, Yucatan	45	73	8	9	13	2	1	0	5	1	0	2	0	26	1	1	.123
Ramirez, Alfredo, Saltillo	.136	493	76	139	189	18	4	8	59	4	4	47	5	62	9	5	.282
Ramirez, Francisco, M Reds	4	1	0	0	0	0	0	0	0	0	0	0	0	0	0	0	.000
Ramirez, Gustavo, Gomez P	129	393	45	102	138	10	7	4	35	3	4	29	6	49	2	3	.260
Ramirez, Pascual, Saltillo ..	3	9	1	1	1	0	0	0	0	0	0	2	0	2	0	0	.111
Ramirez, Victor, Reynosa	.133	437	74	133	225	18	4	22	76	1	5	67	3	60	9	6	.304
Ramos, Pedro, Jalisco†	21	43	4	7	13	0	0	2	2	3	0	4	0	16	0	0	.163
Ramos, Roman, Yucatan	9	1	0	0	0	0	0	0	0	0	0	0	0	0	0	0	.000
Raygoza, German,																	
19 M Tigers-24 Gomez P	43	11	3	0	0	0	0	0	0	3	0	0	0	4	0	0	.000
Reinoso, Ramon, Reynosa .	40	53	12	10	10	0	0	0	2	2	0	8	0	14	0	0	.189
Remes, Fernando, M Tigers	133	429	40	101	119	12	3	0	38	14	5	42	0	34	4	5	.235
Rendon, Alberto, Reynosa .	26	48	7	12	12	0	0	0	3	0	0	3	0	13	3	2	.250
Rey, Arturo, Poza Rica ...	87	222	14	49	58	6	0	1	17	3	2	13	2	27	2	2	.221
Reyes, Cruz, Yucatan	8	4	0	0	0	0	0	0	0	1	0	0	0	2	0	0	.000
Reyes, Jose, Aguila	38	64	6	13	14	1	0	0	2	0	0	3	1	15	0	0	.203
Reyes, Rosario, Yucatan	5	4	2	2	2	0	0	0	0	0	0	1	0	0	0	0	.500
Reyes, Rufino, 34 Ag-37 PR	71	139	16	30	38	4	2	0	5	4	1	14	1	36	1	3	.216
Richardson, Martin, P Rica	41	139	13	30	47	6	1	3	12	0	0	13	1	19	0	0	.216
Rios, Alfredo, Gomez Pal.	131	468	51	128	161	14	2	5	43	5	4	16	5	13	3	0	.274
Rivas, Danilo, Mexico Reds	.	1	1	1	1	0	0	0	1	0	0	0	0	0	0	0	.333
Rivas, F. Rolando, Saltillo*	37	52	2	3	3	0	0	0	3	5	1	2	1	18	0	0	.058
Rivera, Andres, 21 S-6 MT	27	57	8	12	16	1	0	1	4	0	2	8	0	13	0	0	.211
Rivera, Domingo, Saltillo	.121	409	49	113	146	15	3	4	33	11	4	17	2	42	2	6	.276
Rivera, Enrique, Saltillo .	46	163	24	47	66	5	1	4	15	2	2	7	1	12	4	0	.288
Rizales, Jesus, Aguila	30	52	4	7	7	0	0	0	3	0	1	0	1	16	0	0	.135
Robinson, Joe, Reynosa	6	15	0	1	2	1	0	0	0	0	0	0	0	7	0	0	.067
Robles, Alejandro, M Reds*	72	196	30	58	69	3	1	2	20	4	3	22	2	15	5	1	.296
Rodgers, Norbert, Reynosa .	55	34	2	6	6	0	0	0	2	5	0	0	0	14	0	0	.176
Rodriguez, Francisco, Ag .	.149	570	69	159	206	27	4	4	57	5	4	35	0	64	8	7	.275
Rodriguez, Gerardo, Mont .	47	78	5	11	12	1	0	0	3	1	0	8	0	29	0	0	.141
Rodriguez M., Hector, Ag ..	4	4	0	0	0	0	0	0	0	0	0	0	0	2	0	0	.000
Rodriguez, Jose																	
37 Jalisco-42 Saltillo ..	79	248	27	71	113	9	3	9	52	4	5	14	1	42	2	2	.286
Rodriguez, Pilar, Mont ...	15	15	0	1	1	0	0	0	0	0	0	0	3	0	0	0	.067
Rojas, Olinto, Aguila	1	2	0	0	0	0	0	0	0	0	0	0	1	0	0	0	.000
Romo, Enrique, Jalisco	35	59	1	11	13	0	1	0	10	2	0	5	0	18	0	0	.186
Rosas, Clemente, Jalisco ...	52	126	13	32	55	6	1	5	21	1	1	11	0	32	1	1	.254
Rubio, Ramiro, Saltillo	.149	525	70	168	222	14	5	10	75	4	1	42	1	73	5	9	.320
Ruelas, Heriberto, Sal*	44	32	6	8	11	3	0	0	7	0	1	2	0	6	0	1	.250
Ruiz, Ildefonso, G Palacio*	.150	479	73	156	255	25	1	24	99	4	4	90	2	113	4	1	.326
Ruiz, Porfirio, Aguila	.117	347	44	80	119	9	6	6	42	1	2	29	1	39	1	1	.231
Salgado, Octavio, Aguila ..	21	10	0	0	0	0	0	0	0	0	0	0	0	3	0	0	.000
Salinas, Hilario, Saltillo ..	.127	392	49	114	154	10	3	8	51	2	3	27	2	65	9	8	.291
Salinas, Juan Manuel, Yuc .	.137	429	39	119	145	16	2	2	50	6	3	41	1	23	3	3	.277
Sanchez, Carlos, Monterrey .	41	69	3	9	9	0	0	0	2	4	0	1	2	20	0	1	.130
Sanchez, Celerino, M Tigers	.114	383	58	132	192	20	5	10	53	1	6	41	7	44	6	4	.345
Sanchez, Salvador, Reynosa*	.67	113	5	27	31	4	0	0	10	1	0	2	0	27	1	0	.239
Sandoval, Carlos, Yucatan .	86	249	20	56	62	4	1	0	11	5	1	8	0	32	2	1	.252
Sandoval, Rodolfo, Reynosa	.117	349	40	88	140	19	0	11	57	4	7	54	2	46	1	0	.252
Sandoval, Rodrigo, G Pal .	41	26	1	2	2	0	0	0	1	2	1	0	0	8	0	0	.077
Sandoval, Tomas, Reynosa .	13	28	4	6	8	2	0	0	3	0	0	3	0	14	0	0	.214
Santiago, Joaquin, Aguila .	19	37	1	6	8	0	1	0	4	3	0	5	0	7	0	0	.162
Santos, Tobias, Aguila	3	9	1	2	2	0	0	0	0	0	0	3	0	8	0	1	.235
Sed, Oscar Rey, Mont	20	51	4	12	14	2	0	0	3	0	0	3	0	8	0	1	.235
Serna, Antonio, M Tigers* .	1	1	0	0	0	0	0	0	0	0	1	0	0	0	0	0	.000
Silva, Raymundo, Reynosa .	1	0	0	0	0	0	0	0	0	0	0	1	0	0	0	0	.000
Solano, Horacio, Mex Tigers	14	8	1	1	2	1	0	0	1	1	0	1	0	4	0	0	.125
Solis, Jesus, Saltillo	14	14	0	0	0	0	0	0	0	0	0	1	0	4	0	0	.000

Player and Club	G.	AB.	R.	H.	TB.	2B.	3B.	HR.	RBI.	SH.	SF.	BB.	HP.	SO.	SB.	CS.	Pct.
Sommers, Jesus, Yucatan	92	265	27	66	85	8	1	3	22	6	0	18	0	46	3	2	.249
Soqui, Ruben, Mex Reds*	37	27	2	5	8	1	1	0	7	1	0	1	0	8	0	0	.185
Sosa, Emilio, 98 PR-42 Ag	.140	491	70	161	193	21	4	1	31	5	1	57	1	22	3	5	.328
Soto, Hector, Poza Rica	5	9	0	1	1	0	0	0	0	0	0	1	0	2	0	0	.111
Soto, Jose, Poza Rica*	68	73	15	17	18	1	0	0	8	2	0	12	0	11	0	0	.233
Sparks, Oliverio, Mont	.140	459	83	159	253	20	7	20	85	4	3	49	9	91	6	3	.346
Suby, Juan, Mexico Tigers	58	66	5	11	12	1	0	0	4	6	0	0	1	19	6	0	.167
Tiburcio, Edgar, M Tigers	83	159	22	42	57	5	2	2	18	0	1	19	1	27	1	0	.264
Torres, Reyes, Yucatan	61	68	7	12	13	1	0	0	0	2	0	4	1	14	2	1	.176
Torres, Victor, Monterrey	95	353	56	125	188	20	5	11	55	2	3	22	0	22	2	0	.354
Tovar, Jose de Jesus, Rey	56	116	7	20	23	3	0	0	8	3	0	10	1	28	2	1	.172
Trevino, Carlos, Mex Reds	.103	362	50	112	177	15	7	12	61	1	1	35	1	75	1	3	.309
Urbano, Hector, Yucatan	16	8	1	3	3	0	0	0	0	0	0	0	0	1	0	0	.375
Uriarte, Manuel,																	
16 M Tigers-18 Yucatan	34	44	3	10	12	0	1	0	5	2	0	1	0	8	0	0	.227
Urias, Eladio, G Palacio	.121	406	63	130	174	20	3	6	34	4	2	28	1	21	8	6	.320
Uzcanga, Lazaro, Yucatan	46	23	0	5	5	0	0	0	4	0	1	0	0	12	0	0	.217
Valenzuela, Hector, M Reds	8	4	1	1	1	0	0	0	0	0	0	0	0	0	0	0	.250
Valenzuela, Ramon, G Pal	7	1	0	0	0	0	0	0	0	0	0	1	0	0	0	0	.000
Valtierra, Esteban, Aguila*	5	11	1	0	0	0	0	0	0	0	0	0	1	0	0	0	.000
Vazquez, Nicolas,																	
107 Aguila-38 P Rica	.145	499	62	145	213	17	3	15	62	1	4	46	9	60	5	3	.291
Vega, Abelardo, Mex Reds	.133	440	70	142	201	20	12	5	68	9	1	40	6	67	17	4	.323
Vega, Fidel, 9 Jal-14 GP	.23	9	0	1	1	0	0	0	0	0	0	0	0	5	0	0	.111
Vega, Valenciano, Yucatan	16	36	3	9	12	1	1	0	1	2	0	1	0	8	0	0	.250
Velazquez, Manuel, M Reds	42	14	0	1	1	0	0	0	0	1	0	0	0	9	0	0	.071
Velez, Juan Enrique, Yuc	.17	39	3	9	9	0	0	0	2	1	0	3	0	9	0	0	.231
Versalles, Zoilo, Gomez Pal	.163	371	58	121	210	16	5	21	67	1	3	37	2	49	7	3	.326
Villa, Alberto, Monterrey	6	5	0	1	1	0	0	0	0	0	0	1	0	2	0	0	.200
Villalobos, Gonzalo, G Pal	.138	535	78	152	209	23	5	8	45	7	3	41	0	52	13	7	.284
Villalobos, Lauro, Jalisco	22	27	4	7	8	1	0	0	0	0	1	0	0	2	0	3	.259
Villarreal, Juan de Dios, Mon	87	250	13	59	80	3	0	6	33	2	3	9	0	28	0	0	.236
Zamudio, Hector, M Tigers	.138	534	74	152	201	24	8	3	41	4	3	14	5	43	15	8	.285
Zavala, Manrique, P Rica	.33	36	2	5	7	0	1	0	3	0	2	0	0	18	0	0	.139
Zazueta, Alejandro, Reynosa	5	17	0	2	2	0	0	0	1	0	0	1	0	4	0	1	.118

The following players had no plate appearances (listed alphabetically by club, games in parentheses):

JALISCO—Boehlert, William* (2).
MEXICO CITY TIGERS—Delfin, Justino (2).
MONTERREY—Alvarado, Rodolfo (2).
POZA RICA—Colis, Exiquio (2); Howden, Huey (1).
REYNOSA—Cano, Jose Paz (2); Rubio, Jorge (1).
SALTILLO—Merla, Rafael (7).
YUCATAN—Franco, Antonio (1); Peraza, Alejandro (1); Uzcanga, Carlos (3).
GRAND-SLAM HOME RUNS—R. Ortiz, 2; R. Alvarez, W. Arano, Camarero, F. Castro, Esquivias, Galindo, G. Lugo, Richardson, I. Ruiz, P. Ruiz, Sparks, Vazquez, A. Vega, 1 each.
AWARDED FIRST BASE ON INTERFERENCE—Javier Hernandez 2 (P. Ruiz, Rosas); Ahumada (Gaspar), F. Castro (Luque), Corella (Luque), Luque (P. Ruiz), Macias (Villarreal), Morejon (G. Rodriguez).

CLUB FIELDING

Club	G.	PO.	A.	E.	DP.	PB.	Pct.	Club	G.	PO.	A.	E.	DP.	PB.	Pct.
Aguila	153	3746	1687	129	168	20	.977	Mexico Reds	150	3695	1616	179	189	13	.967
Mexico Tigers	.146	3588	1571	131	134	11	.975	Saltillo	153	3735	1677	192	166	30	.966
Poza Rica	154	3599	1504	138	120	22	.974	Reynosa	152	3717	1573	191	152	18	.965
Monterrey	148	3650	1668	170	145	17	.969	Yucatan	150	3647	1547	188	135	17	.965
Jalisco	150	3672	1657	171	125	25	.969	Gomez Palacio	.150	3705	1549	243	171	17	.956

Triple Plays—Gomez Palacio, Jalisco, Poza Rica, Reynosa, Yucatan, 1 each.

INDIVIDUAL FIELDING
(Ten or More Games)

*Throws lefthanded.

FIRST BASEMEN

Player and Club	G.	PO.	A.	E.	DP.	Pct.	Player and Club	G.	PO.	A.	E.	DP.	Pct.
Argumedo, Mon	19	168	15	0	15	1.000	Diaz, Poza Rica	14	87	2	1	7	.989
Robles, Mex Reds*	17	117	7	0	15	1.000	Conde, Saltillo	18	147	11	2	15	.988
Calvo, Saltillo	11	67	0	0	6	1.000	Camacho, Poza Rica	21	152	6	2	14	.988
Izquierdo, Aguila	14	36	2	0	5	1.000	Coleman, Mex Reds	.123	908	54	13	128	.987
ALVAREZ, Aguila	.145	1207	59	7	142	.995	Trevino, Mex Reds	11	65	5	1	10	.986
Prescott, PR	50	382	17	2	38	.995	Herrera, Saltillo	28	247	15	4	25	.985
Perez Torres, PR*	86	625	29	4	53	.994	C. Garza, Tigers	23	131	4	2	12	.985
Esquivias, Tigers*	72	483	16	3	44	.994	Espino, Monterrey	.129	1119	93	20	116	.984
Camacho, Yucatan	.134	1006	54	9	103	.992	H. Garcia, Reynosa	42	251	14	5	28	.981
Berzunza, Reynosa*	.119	943	58	10	109	.990	A. Alvarez, Yuc*	26	122	13	3	18	.978
Plascencia, Tigers	74	546	43	6	56	.990	Camarero, Aguila	11	42	3	1	1	.978
Naranjo, Saltillo*	54	376	29	4	39	.990	I. Ruiz, GP*	.149	1161	77	29	148	.977
V. Fabela, Jal-Sal	.105	786	29	9	84	.989	Menchaca, Jalisco	12	79	2	2	9	.976
Campos, Jalisco	89	751	32	9	76	.989	Bouye, Saltillo	10	77	9	5	12	.945

Triple Plays—Perez Torres, Berzunza, V. Fabela, A. Alvarez, I. Ruiz.

FIRST BASEMEN—Continued
(Fewer Than Ten Games)

Player and Club	G.	PO.	A.	E.	DP.	Pct.	Player and Club	G.	PO.	A.	E.	DP.	Pct.
Parlier, Jalisco	5	32	0	0	4	1.000	Ortiz, Mex Reds*	2	4	0	0	1	1.000
Alfonso, Mex Reds	4	26	2	0	1	1.000	Sandoval, Yucatan	1	4	0	0	1	1.000
Rubio, Saltillo	4	22	4	0	1	1.000	Sparks, Monterrey	1	4	0	0	0	1.000
Fabela, Poza Rica	5	19	0	0	1	1.000	R. Reyes, Aguila*	1	3	1	0	0	1.000
Palomino, Poza Rica*	4	16	0	0	2	1.000	Osorio, Aguila	1	3	0	0	0	1.000
Santiago, Aguila	2	14	1	0	3	1.000	Hernandez, PR	1	3	0	0	0	1.000
Rosas, Jalisco	1	13	1	0	0	1.000	Vega, Jal-GP	2	2	0	0	0	1.000
Garcia, Aguila	1	12	1	0	0	1.000	Leal, Mex Reds	1	1	0	0	0	1.000
Marquez, Reynosa	2	12	0	0	0	1.000	Esma, Yucatan	1	1	0	0	0	1.000
Jimenez, Reynosa	2	11	1	0	0	1.000	R. Sandoval, Rey	7	48	6	1	5	.982
Acosta, Yucatan*	1	11	0	0	3	1.000	Sanchez, Mex Tigers.	8	52	2	1	6	.982
V. Garcia, Mon	1	9	2	0	1	1.000	Minoso, Gomez Pal	9	25	1	1	1	.963
E. Rivera, Saltillo	1	6	4	0	1	1.000	Estrada, Mex Reds	6	35	5	2	6	.952
Valtierra, Aguila*	1	9	0	0	1	1.000	G. Garza, Tigers	2	10	0	1	0	.909
Fitch, Reynosa	2	9	0	0	1	1.000	Castro, Gomez Pal	2	4	1	1	1	.833
Guerrero, Jalisco	1	8	1	0	1	1.000	Urias, Gomez Pal	4	4	1	1	1	.833
F. Chavez, Aguila	1	6	0	0	1	1.000	Herrera, Yucatan	1	5	0	1	1	.833
Gaspar, Gomez Pal	2	5	1	0	1	1.000	Mariscal, Yucatan*	2	3	0	1	0	.750
Ruelas, Saltillo*	1	4	1	0	1	1.000							

SECOND BASEMEN

Player and Club	G.	PO.	A.	E.	DP.	Pct.	Player and Club	G.	PO.	A.	E.	DP.	Pct.
Camacho, Poza Rica.	23	20	26	0	2	1.000	Garibay, Mex Reds	.106	246	239	16	80	.968
Hernandez Z., Reds .	65	142	144	4	56	.986	Camacho, Poza Rica	.82	150	188	12	46	.966
CASTRO, M. Tigers.	127	276	303	9	76	.985	Lopez, Yuc-PR	27	50	48	4	13	.961
Camarero, Aguila	22	50	49	2	13	.980	G. Lugo, Jalisco	.146	375	410	33	88	.960
Torres, Yucatan	14	29	13	1	3	.977	Galindo, GP	.50	58	90	7	22	.955
Fernandez, Yucatan	.140	353	353	18	95	.975	A. Garcia, Reynosa	.152	387	343	36	98	.953
D Rivera, Saltillo	.118	277	309	15	82	.975	Leal, Saltillo	19	36	37	4	8	.948
Ortiz, Monterrey	.146	407	404	24	108	.971	Preciado, Tigers	32	52	53	6	14	.946
F. Chavez, Aguila	.119	271	328	18	80	.971	Sommers, Yucatan	13	32	15	3	7	.940
Rios, Gomez Pal	.126	300	305	19	96	.970	Hernandez, PR	11	21	19	5	4	.889
Richardson, PR	41	74	83	5	11	.969							

Triple Plays—Fernandez, Rios, Richardson.

(Fewer Than Ten Games)

Player and Club	G.	PO.	A.	E.	DP.	Pct.	Player and Club	G.	PO.	A.	E.	DP.	Pct.
J. Reyes, Aguila	9	23	19	0	6	1.000	Espinoza, Mex Reds.	1	1	1	0	1	1.000
Osuna, Poza Rica	2	7	9	0	2	1.000	Vega, Mex Reds	1	0	1	0	0	1.000
Villalobos, Jalisco	4	5	9	0	2	1.000	Hurtado, Reynosa	1	1	0	0	0	1.000
Huerta, Mex Tigers	3	8	6	0	3	1.000	Guerrero, Jalisco	9	12	9	1	2	.955
Mena, Monterrey	3	5	2	0	2	1.000	Santiago, Aguila	6	18	18	2	2	.947
Ruiz, Aguila	1	2	3	0	1	1.000	Navarrete, Sal	3	2	2	2	0	.667
Chavez, Saltillo	1	0	2	0	0	1.000	Torres, Monterrey	2	1	1	1	0	.667

THIRD BASEMEN

Player and Club	G.	PO.	A.	E.	DP.	Pct.	Player and Club	G.	PO.	A.	E.	DP.	Pct.
Camacho, Poz Rica.	23	20	26	0	2	1.000	Hernandez, PR	31	27	45	6	3	.923
Galindo, GP	16	15	32	1	5	.979	Huerta, Mex Tigers	29	13	47	5	2	.923
Mena, Monterrey	23	15	26	1	3	.976	Garibay, Mex Reds	14	13	23	3	4	.923
Osuna, Poza Rica	17	9	24	1	0	.971	H. Garcia, Reynosa	33	25	56	7	5	.920
SANCHEZ, Tigers	.107	85	210	11	12	.964	Conkle, Saltillo	28	19	50	6	7	.920
A. Ramirez, Sal	81	64	190	10	14	.962	Espinoza, Mex Reds.	27	18	48	6	5	.917
Ortiz, Aguila	.149	123	350	19	31	.961	Ramirez, GP	39	38	59	9	10	.915
Plascencia, Tigers	21	17	32	2	3	.961	Montoya, Reynosa	.105	68	168	24	19	.908
Leal, Saltillo	11	6	16	1	1	.957	Ramirez, Reynosa	18	9	38	5	2	.904
Fuentes, Poza Rica	21	19	23	2	1	.955	E. Rivera, Saltillo	41	38	84	14	6	.897
R. Torres, Yucatan	39	16	25	2	2	.953	Sommers, Yucatan	57	35	65	12	7	.896
Fitch, Reynosa	14	9	32	2	5	.953	Lopez, Yucatan-PR	44	23	53	9	7	.894
Torres, Monterrey	92	58	179	12	20	.952	Versailles, GP	35	26	56	10	9	.891
Sandoval, Yucatan	78	67	122	10	13	.950	Mendoza, Poza Rica.	34	24	54	10	7	.886
Cerda, Jalisco	.147	110	305	26	19	.941	Argumedo, Mon	38	15	67	13	5	.863
Vega, Mex Reds	.117	99	219	21	29	.938	Velez, Yucatan	15	7	18	4	2	.862
A. Murillo, GP	67	54	121	14	15	.926							

Triple Plays—Osuna, R. Torres, Cerda.

(Fewer Than Ten Games)

Player and Club	G.	PO.	A.	E.	DP.	Pct.	Player and Club	G.	PO.	A.	E.	DP.	Pct.
J. Reyes, Aguila	4	5	9	0	1	1.000	Lozano, Monterrey	3	1	2	0	0	1.000
Fernandez, Yucatan	5	1	5	0	0	1.000	Prescott, Poza Rica.	1	0	2	0	0	1.000
Hurtado, Reynosa	1	4	1	0	0	1.000	Villalobos, Jalisco	4	0	2	0	0	1.000
Conde, Saltillo	3	0	5	0	0	1.000	Preciado, Tigers	2	0	1	0	0	1.000
Santiago, Aguila	1	1	4	0	0	1.000	Guerrero, Mex Reds	1	0	1	0	0	1.000
Diaz, Poza Rica	2	1	2	0	0	1.000	Camacho, Yucatan	1	0	1	0	0	1.000

THIRD BASEMEN—Continued

Player and Club	G.	PO.	A.	E.	DP.	Pct.
Esquivel, Monterrey	1	0	1	0	0	1.000
Guerrero, Jalisco	6	4	7	1	0	.917
Camarero, Aguila	3	6	4	1	0	.909
Burgos, Yucatan	8	3	6	1	0	.900
Mata, Monterrey	8	5	10	3	2	.833
Estrada, Mex Reds	3	2	3	1	0	.833
Castro, Mex Tigers	3	0	2	1	1	.667
F. Chavez, Aguila	1	1	0	1	0	.500
Guerra, Jalisco	1	0	0	1	0	.000
Morejon, Saltillo	1	0	0	1	0	.000

SHORTSTOPS

Player and Club	G.	PO.	A.	E.	DP.	Pct.
F. RODRIGUEZ, A	149	297	493	22	118	.973
Mendoza, Poza Rica	119	229	386	19	67	.970
Remes, Mex Tigers	129	219	427	24	70	.964
Osuna, Poza Rica	39	61	119	7	24	.963
Mena, Monterrey	108	156	356	23	60	.957
Vega, Yucatan	13	15	28	2	4	.956
Mendez, Jalisco	149	246	495	35	78	.955
Huerta, Mex Tigers	34	36	65	5	13	.943
Fitch, Reynosa	121	171	390	28	81	.952
Versalles, GP	66	108	201	18	44	.945
Salinas, Yucatan	136	188	419	36	82	.944
Hernandez Z., Reds	86	146	268	25	60	.943
Vega, Mex Reds	14	19	45	4	13	.941
Chavez, Saltillo	129	199	399	38	89	.940
Tovar, Reynosa	42	61	120	12	19	.938
Espinoza, Mex Reds	73	88	181	18	50	.937
A. Ramirez, Sal	34	37	95	9	21	.936
Galindo, GP	12	21	32	4	12	.930
Lazo, Monterrey	52	58	148	16	21	.928
G. Ramirez, GP	84	148	251	33	50	.924

Triple Plays—Fitch, G. Ramirez.

(Fewer Than Ten Games)

Player and Club	G.	PO.	A.	E.	DP.	Pct.
Ortiz, Monterrey	3	5	8	0	3	1.000
Castro, Mex Tigers	4	2	8	0	2	1.000
J. Reyes, Aguila	1	1	3	0	1	1.000
Hernandez, PR	1	0	3	0	0	1.000
H. Garcia, Reynosa	1	0	2	0	1	1.000
Burgos, Yucatan	2	1	1	0	0	1.000
Torres, Monterrey	1	1	1	0	1	1.000
Santiago, Aguila	1	0	1	0	0	1.000
E. Rivera, Saltillo	1	0	1	0	0	1.000
Torres, Yucatan	6	8	11	1	4	.950
Fernandez, Yucatan	2	5	16	2	0	.913
Navarrete, Saltillo	2	1	3	1	0	.800
Villalobos, Jalisco	2	1	3	1	0	.800
Sandoval, Yucatan	1	0	0	1	0	.000

OUTFIELDERS

Player and Club	G.	PO.	A.	E.	DP.	Pct.
Esquivias, Tigers*	46	64	4	0	0	1.000
Johnson, Reynosa	24	41	2	0	0	1.000
Argumedo, Montcrrey	31	38	1	0	0	1.000
Plascencia, Yucatan	19	25	0	0	0	1.000
Lara, Mex Tigers	16	25	0	0	0	1.000
Fabela, Jalisco-Sal	14	15	0	0	0	1.000
ARANO, Aguila	147	325	15	4	2	.988
Osuna, Monterrey	134	289	16	4	0	.987
Hernandez, PR	48	63	3	1	0	.985
Sosa, Poza Rica-Ag	139	288	12	5	1	.984
Hurtado, Reynosa	80	117	6	2	0	.984
Nazario, Poza Rica	29	59	2	1	0	.984
Ramirez, Reynosa	122	212	9	4	1	.982
Zamudio, Mex Tigers	135	292	24	6	8	.981
Rodriguez, Jal-Sal	74	151	4	3	1	.981
Salinas, Saltillo	70	149	6	3	1	.981
Morejon, Saltillo	150	292	17	7	2	.978
Montoya, Mex Reds	139	314	17	8	5	.976
Macias, Reynosa	150	306	13	8	1	.976
Sparks, Monterrey	134	216	25	6	3	.976
Sommers, Yucatan	22	37	3	1	0	.976
Burgos, Yucatan	111	178	16	5	2	.975
Contreras, Mex Reds	100	190	9	6	4	.971
Fabela, Poza Rica	92	132	4	4	0	.971
L. Lopez, Monterrey	90	153	7	5	0	.971
Acosta, Yucatan*	135	259	18	9	1	.969
Davila, Monterrey	81	151	7	5	2	.969
Bojorquez, PR	74	150	7	5	0	.969
Vazquez, Aguila-PR	144	380	14	13	3	.968
Ponce, Mex Tigers	135	310	8	11	1	.967
Palomino, PR*	86	190	11	7	0	.966
Rendon, Reynosa	18	25	3	1	0	.966
Rubio, Saltillo	143	204	9	8	1	.964
Camarero, Aguila	125	199	13	8	0	.964
Castro, Gomez Pal	96	134	12	6	2	.961
Mora, Jalisco	147	297	15	13	2	.960
Robles, Mex Reds*	49	94	2	4	0	.960
Calvo, Saltillo	14	22	1	1	0	.958
Lizarraga, Mex Reds	74	149	7	7	3	.957
R. Reyes, Aguila-PR*	52	64	3	3	0	.957
Orozco, Saltillo	37	39	5	2	0	.957
H. Garcia, Reynosa	21	16	5	1	0	.955
Izquierdo, Aguila	12	19	2	1	0	.955
Garcia, Gomez Pal	149	354	10	18	2	.953
Parlier, Jalisco	138	185	16	10	1	.953
Gleason, Jalisco	44	56	5	3	0	.953
Menchaca, Jalisco	101	170	8	9	1	.952
Alvarez, Yucatan	148	148	11	8	1	.952
A. Rivera, Sal-Tigers	16	38	2	2	1	.952
Enriquez, Yucatan	119	236	14	13	7	.951
Villalobos, GP	137	361	22	22	5	.946
Urias, Gomez Pala'io	105	176	6	11	0	.943
Jimenez, Reynosa	42	59	5	4	0	.941
Preciado, Mex Tigers	45	45	3	3	0	.941
Trevino, Mex Reds	92	106	12	8	2	.937
Davis, Reynosa	19	39	2	3	0	.932
Campos, Jalisco	11	11	1	1	0	.923
Marquez, Reynosa	16	11	0	1	0	.917
G. Garza, Mex Tigers	86	123	6	12	0	.915

(Fewer Than Ten Games)

Player and Club	G.	PO.	A.	E.	DP.	Pct.
Hernandez, Aguila	8	15	1	0	0	1.000
H. Soto, Poza Rica	4	7	0	0	0	1.000
Ochoa, Jalisco	7	7	0	0	0	1.000
Zazueta, Reynosa	5	6	1	0	0	1.000
J. Reyes, Aguila	2	6	0	0	0	1.000
Munoz, Mex Tigers	7	4	0	0	0	1.000
R. Sandoval, Rey	4	4	0	0	0	1.000
E. Rivera, Saltillo	1	4	0	0	0	1.000
R. Chavez, Aguila	3	2	1	0	0	1.000
Sed, Monterrey	2	3	0	0	0	1.000
Nieblas, Mex Reds	5	2	0	0	0	1.000
Leal, Mexico Reds	4	2	0	0	0	1.000
Huerta, Mex Tigers	1	1	0	0	0	1.000
Mariscal, Yucatan*	1	2	0	0	0	1.000
Santiago, Aguila	1	1	0	0	0	1.000
Sandoval, Yucatan	1	1	0	0	0	1.000
Villalobos, Jalisco	1	1	0	0	0	1.000
Torres, Monterrey	1	1	0	0	0	1.000
Valtierra, Aguila*	2	1	0	0	0	1.000
Ornelas, Mex Reds	2	1	0	0	0	1.000
Bouye, Saltillo	4	9	0	1	0	.900
Vega, Mex Reds	5	4	1	1	0	.833
Alfonso, Mex Reds	3	4	1	1	0	.833
Hernandez G., Reds*	2	3	1	1	0	.800
Perez Torres, PR*	3	0	1	1	0	.500

CATCHERS

Player and Club	G.	PO.	A.	E.	DP.	PB.	Pct.
Mendivil, Reds .	16	67	3	0	1	0	1.000
CORELLA, Jalisco	99	429	52	1	3	12	.998
Esquivel, Mon .	41	188	25	1	2	2	.995
Diaz, Poza Rica.	89	360	46	3	6	6	.993
R. Sandoval, Rey.	104	527	55	5	2	10	.991
Rosas, Jalisco ..	40	184	13	2	2	7	.990
Estrada, Mex R.	128	694	100	9	15	11	.989
Luque, Mex T .	112	541	75	9	12	7	.986
Ruiz, Aguila ...	110	431	65	7	8	15	.986
Cancino, Saltillo .	29	128	14	2	1	6	.986
Bouye, Saltillo ..	22	96	7	2	2	4	.981
G. Rodrig'z, Mon	42	128	19	3	0	9	.980
Villarreal, Mon ..	82	335	46	8	4	4	.979
Gaspar, Gomez Pal	85	227	40	6	6	7	.978
Salinas, Saltillo.	54	277	27	7	4	3	.977
Campos, Jalisco .	44	181	17	5	1	6	.975
Rey, Poza Rica .	83	298	26	9	1	14	.973
Herrera, Yucatan.	114	581	62	19	0	10	.971
Orozco, Saltillo ..	55	235	29	8	4	14	.971
Sed, Monterrey ..	15	58	8	2	0	2	.971
Tiburcio, Tigers .	52	181	16	6	0	2	.970
Marquez, Reynosa.	60	275	26	10	5	8	.968
Izquierdo, Aguila.	50	157	24	6	5	3	.968
Esma, Yucatan ...	61	302	23	8	4	7	.966
Contreras, GP ...	77	323	38	13	8	10	.965
Coleman, Mex R .	23	92	12	4	1	2	.963

Triple Play—Rey.

(Fewer Than Ten Games)

Player and Club	G.	PO.	A.	E.	DP.	PB.	Pct.
Santos, Aguila ...	3	13	1	0	0	0	1.000
Castro, GP	2	5	0	0	0	0	1.000
Alvarado, Aguila.	2	4	0	0	0	0	1.000
J. Reyes, Aguila .	1	2	0	0	0	2	1.000
Rojas, Aguila	1	1	0	0	0	0	1.000
Aguilar, Saltillo .	5	16	6	1	0	0	.957
Gutierrez, Tigers .	7	22	1	2	1	2	.920
P. Ramirez Sal ..	3	7	1	1	0	3	.889
Sosa, Poza Rica .	1	0	0	0	0	2	.000

PITCHERS

Player and Club	G.	PO.	A.	E.	DP.	Pct.
J. SOTO, Poza Rica*.	33	4	52	0	6	1.000
Geigel, Poza Rica* .	28	4	44	0	1	1.000
Leal, Mexico Reds .	34	11	36	0	3	1.000
M. Lugo, Jalisco ...	57	3	31	0	1	1.000
Pereira, Tigers	39	8	25	0	0	1.000
Maytorena, Tigers ..	39	3	27	0	2	1.000
Diaz, Aguila	31	5	23	0	4	1.000
Castillo, Saltillo ...	48	7	17	0	2	1.000
T.Sandoval, Rey ...	12	6	16	0	0	1.000
Ruelas, Saltillo* ...	41	5	16	0	3	1.000
Velazquez, Mex Reds.	42	5	13	0	4	1.000
S. Murillo, GP-Tig .	44	4	12	0	0	1.000
Ferguson J, Yucatan	14	5	10	0	2	1.000
Cruz, Mex Tigers ..	42	1	13	0	0	1.000
Cortes, Monterrey* ..	24	4	10	0	0	1.000
Lira, Poza Rica	19	0	14	0	2	1.000
Hernandez G., Reds*	32	0	14	0	1	1.000
Nuno, Aguila	28	4	9	0	1	1.000
Fajardo, Mex Reds ..	34	3	10	0	0	1.000
Icedo, Mex Tigers* ..	48	2	10	0	0	1.000
Meza, Jalisco*	20	4	8	0	0	1.000
Solano, Mex Tigers .	14	5	6	0	0	1.000
Arce, Mex Tigers ...	11	5	7	0	1	1.000
Mere, Yucatan	12	3	3	0	0	1.000
Lugo, Yucatan	14	1	5	0	0	1.000
Cordova, Jalisco	23	1	5	0	0	1.000
P. Rodriguez, Mon ..	15	1	5	0	1	1.000
S. Garcia, Mon	14	0	5	0	0	1.000
Lopez, Aguila	11	0	4	0	0	1.000
Goycolea, GP	16	0	4	0	0	1.000
Bedolla, GP	23	0	4	0	0	1.000
Baretty, GP	11	2	1	0	0	1.000
Urbano, Yucatan ...	13	1	2	0	0	1.000
Armas, Jalisco*	21	0	3	0	0	1.000
Solis, Saltillo	14	0	2	0	0	1.000
N. Garcia, Tigers ..	61	5	48	1	8	.981
Ayon, Jalisco	31	5	45	1	5	.980
Brito, Aguila	20	6	35	1	2	.976
Gutierrez, Reynosa .	43	10	29	1	1	.975
Mariscal, Yucatan* .	35	6	33	1	1	.975
Uriarte, Tigers-Yuc .	34	4	34	1	1	.974
Pollorena, Jalisco ..	27	11	27	1	3	.974
Suby, Mex Tigers ..	58	8	27	1	3	.972
Romo, Jalisco	36	7	28	1	0	.972
Brown, Poza Rica ..	29	2	33	1	1	.972
Castillo, GP	29	8	24	1	3	.970
Adame, Gomez Pal .	39	5	46	2	4	.962
Quiroz, Yucatan ...	34	11	36	2	3	.959
Sanchez, Monterrey .	41	9	37	2	1	.958
Lagunas, Poza Rica .	42	2	21	1	2	.958
R. Chavez, Aguila ..	47	4	18	1	1	.957
Diaz, Mex Tigers ..	27	6	15	1	3	.955
Moncayo, Yuc-Sal ..	32	4	17	1	3	.955
C. Gutierrez, PR-Y .	47	2	18	1	0	.952
Meza, Saltillo	46	7	13	1	1	.952
Soqui, Mex Reds* ..	34	5	15	1		.952
Leon, Jalisco	37	10	48	3	2	.951
Aquino, Saltillo	46	9	29	2	2	.950
Raygoza, Tigers-GP .	40	5	14	1	2	.950
Osorio, Aguila	20	1	18	1	2	.950
Sandoval, GP	41	5	13	1	1	.947
Mazon, Aguila	32	5	12	1	3	.944
Reinoso, Reynosa ..	34	8	24	2	2	.941
Acosta, Reynosa ...	23	4	12	1	0	.941
Gonzalez, Reynosa ..	43	18	44	4	7	.939
Zavala, Poza Rica ..	33	5	26	2	0	.939
Bauta, Poza Rica ..	54	5	37	3	5	.933
Carrillo, Poza Rica .	34	5	9	1	1	.933
Lopez, Reynosa-Sal ..	20	1	13	0	0	.933
Carrasco, Jalisco ...	25	2	11	1	1	.929
Lopez, Mexico Reds..	37	8	30	3	2	.927
Horsford, Monterrey .	24	11	27	3	1	.927
Penalver, Monterrey .	23	10	28	3	3	.927
Paredes, Saltillo	30	3	22	2	0	.926
Jusino, Gomez Pal ..	49	3	33	3	3	.923
E. Lopez, Monterrey .	37	2	10	1	2	.923
Ramos, Jalisco	21	2	21	2	1	.920
Madrigal, Poza Rica.	44	2	19	2	1	.913
Imbert, Yucatan* ...	40	4	37	4	1	.911
Rizales, Aguila	26	5	24	3	1	.906
Sanchez, Reynosa* ..	49	10	47	6	4	.905
J. R. Lopez, Mon ...	33	8	29	4	1	.902
Azcarraga, Mex Reds.	27	1	8	1	1	.900
Hernandez, Mon	23	2	7	1	1	.900
Figueroa, GP	39	12	23	4	1	.897
Malpica, Aguila	25	12	30	5	2	.894
Arano, Mexico Reds .	36	3	37	5	4	.889
Rivas, Saltillo*	33	6	26	4	1	.889
Quintana, Aguila-GP.	22	2	14	2	1	.889
Cacerez, Saltillo	40	9	38	6	0	.887
Garcia, Mex Reds ...	29	4	10	2	0	.875
Salgado, Aguila	14	0	7	1	0	.875
Martinez, Yucatan ..	25	2	18	3	2	.870
Gamez, Saltillo* ...	45	4	20	4	4	.857
Buentello, Reynosa ..	39	5	13	3	0	.857
Munro, Monterrey ..	20	1	5	1	0	.857
L. Uzcanga, Yucatan	46	0	11	2	1	.846
Agundez, GP-Tigers.	38	0	11	2	3	.846
Ortiz, Mexico Reds*.	21	4	12	3	0	.842
Acosta, Jalisco	45	1	9	2	0	.833
Rodgers, Reynosa ..	55	3	15	4	0	.818
Parra, Saltillo-GP ..	25	4	9	3	2	.813
Betancourt, GP	38	2	11	3	0	.813
Martinez, Mon*	34	0	13	3	0	.813
Cisneros, Monterrey .	19	1	7	2	0	.800
Garza, Reynosa	12	2	2	1	0	.800
Balcazar, Aguila ...	36	1	6	2	0	.778
Vega, Jalisco-GP ...	13	1	2	1	1	.750

PITCHERS—Continued
(Fewer Than Ten Games)

Player and Club	G.	PO.	A.	E.	DP.	Pct.
Mason, Monterrey ..	7	3	5	0	0	1.000
Ahumada, Reynosa ..	9	3	3	0	0	1.000
Manrique, Monterrey*	7	0	4	0	0	1.000
Burgos, Jalisco-Ag* .	9	1	3	0	1	1.000
Moreno, Mexico Reds	7	1	3	0	0	1.000
Valenzuela, GP	7	1	3	0	0	1.000
Moreno, Monterrey ..	5	1	3	0	0	1.000
Antonety, Aguila ...	5	1	2	0	0	1.000
R. Reyes, Yucatan ..	2	0	3	0	0	1.000
Valenzuela, Mex Reds	8	0	2	0	0	1.000
Robinson, Reynosa ..	6	0	2	0	0	1.000
Elizalde, Reynosa ...	6	0	2	0	0	1.000
Serna, Mex Tigers* .	4	0	2	0	0	1.000
Ramirez, Mex Reds..	4	1	1	0	0	1.000
Almada, Mex Tigers*	8	0	1	0	0	1.000
Merla, Saltillo	7	0	1	0	0	1.000
Lilly, Gomez Palacio	3	0	1	0	1	1.000
Garcia, Saltillo	3	0	1	0	0	1.000
Palomino, Poza Rica*	3	0	1	0	0	1.000
Pacheco, Mex Reds ..	3	0	1	0	0	1.000
Colis, Poza Rica	2	0	1	0	0	1.000
Delfin, Mex Tigers ..	2	0	1	0	0	1.000
Rivas, Mexico Reds*	1	0	1	0	0	1.000
Camarero, Aguila ...	1	0	1	0	0	1.000
Sandoval, Yucatan ...	1	0	1	0	0	1.000
Howden, Poza Rica ..	1	0	1	0	0	1.000
C. Uzcanga, Yucatan .	3	1	0	0	0	1.000
Villa, Monterrey	6	0	5	1	1	.833
C. Reyes, Yucatan ...	8	0	2	1	0	.667
Ramos, Yucatan	9	0	4	2	0	.667
Leyva, Gomez Pal*..	8	0	1	0	0	.500
Abreu, Monterrey ...	5	0	0	2	0	.000

The following players do not have any recorded accepted chances at the positions indicated; therefore, are not listed in the fielding averages at those particular positions: R. Alvarado, p; Ayon, of; Boehlert*, p; Brito, 1b; J. P. Cano, p; R. Cano, p; A. Contreras, c; Cota, c-p; Cruz, 1b; Esquivias*, p; Franco, p; Gamez*, of; A. Garcia, c; Gleason, p; J. A. Guerrero, of; Lazo, 3b; Minoso, of; Moncayo, of; Raul Montoya, ss-of; Mota, p; Naranjo*, of; Ochoa, 3b; Olivares, p; O. Orozco, 1b-of; Ortega, ss; Peraza, p; O. Plascencia, of; Pollorena, 3b; Quiroz, of; G. Ramirez, of; Reinoso, of; Rendon, 1b; F. Rodriguez, of; J. Rodriguez, 2b; J. Rubio, p; Salgado, of; Silva, p; R. Torres, of; F. Vega, c; Velez, shortstop.

PITCHERS' RECORDS
(Leading Qualifiers for Earned-Run Average Leadership—150 or More Innings)
*Throws lefthanded.

Pitcher and Club	G.	GS.	CG.	ShO	W.	L.	Pct.	IP.	H.	R.	ER.	HR.	BB.	Int. BB.	HB.	SO.	WP.	ERA.
Mariscal, Yucatan* ...35	28	16	4	21	7		.750	200	180	60	41	8	51	12	1	147	1	1.85
Castillo, Saltillo 48	16	9	2	14	5		.737	176	150	56	48	8	56	5	10	119	2	2.45
Gonzalez, Reynosa 43	31	13	5	17	12		.586	230	232	93	71	13	64	17	9	109	2	2.78
Romo, Jalisco 36	23	8	2	10	9		.526	155	159	67	48	3	50	10	4	79	5	2.79
Mazon, Aguila 32	16	8	2	13	3		.813	154	125	58	48	11	81	5	3	92	4	2.81
J. R. Lopez, Monterrey.33	25	18	6	16	13		.552	205	204	74	64	8	51	6	5	152	3	2.81
Pollorena, Jalisco 27	24	8	3	10	5		.667	154	151	59	49	7	39	4	6	79	5	2.86
Leon, Jalisco 37	28	10	3	14	9		.609	182	185	75	58	8	42	5	4	138	7	2.87
Malpica, Aguila 25	24	10	3	9	9		.500	158	160	61	51	6	45	11	1	56	4	2.91
Geigel, Poza Rica* 28	28	15	4	12	11		.522	167	132	60	54	3	62	3	1	68	5	2.91

DEPARTMENTAL LEADERS: G—N. Garcia, 61; GS—S. Sanchez, 39; CG—S. Sanchez, 21; ShO —J. R. Lopez, Sanchez, 6; W—Mariscal, 21; L—Aquino, Figueroa, 17; Pct.—Mazon, .813; IP—S. Sanchez, 250; H—Figueroa, 251; R—Cacerez, 119; ER—Leal, C. Sanchez, 97; HR—Adame, 21; BB—S. Sanchez, 114; IBB—N. Garcia, 19; HB—Madrigal, 12; SO—Leal, 170; WP—S. Sanchez, 17.

(All Pitchers—Listed Alphabetically)

Pitcher and Club	G.	GS.	CG.	ShO	W.	L.	Pct.	IP.	H.	R.	ER.	HR.	BB.	Int. BB.	HB.	SO.	WP.	ERA.
Abreu, Monterrey 5	5	0	0	0	1		.000	21	26	16	13	2	14	0	0	7	0	5.57
C. Acosta, Jalisco ...45	2	1	0	9	3		.750	85	70	34	24	3	36	6	4	99	2	2.54
Acosta, Reynosa 23	8	1	1	2	2		.500	72	78	30	30	3	30	6	3	36	3	4.58
Adame, Gomez Palacio .39	31	14	3	19	14		.576	222	219	107	95	21	55	7	2	94	3	3.89
Agundez, 18 GP-20 Tig.38	2	0	0	2	4		.333	70	76	51	36	5	14	5	0	31	5	4.63
Ahumada, Reynosa 9	3	0	0	2	1		.500	32	35	19	19	2	14	1	1	17	3	5.34
Almada, Mex Tigers* ..8	2	0	0	0	2		.000	17	22	7	5	0	11	3	0	10	3	2.65
Alvarado, Monterrey ..2	0	0	0	0	0		.000	3	7	2	2	0	0	0	0	0	0	6.00
Antonety, Aguila 5	0	0	0	0	0		.000	18	19	14	9	0	13	0	1	7	2	4.50
Aquino, Saltillo......46	18	3	1	5	17		.227	142	160	76	64	8	48	9	8	50	3	4.06
Arano, Mexico Reds ...36	35	5	1	15	14		.517	198	242	108	87	10	47	3	9	114	5	3.95
Arce, Mexico Tigers ..11	1	0	0	1	2		.333	18	14	7	6	0	10	1	0	8	0	3.00
Armas, Jalisco* 21	0	0	0	0	0		1.000	20	17	9	7	1	6	3	0	13	0	3.15
Ayon, Jalisco 31	25	12	0	14	14		.440	176	205	85	68	13	51	9	0	58	5	3.48
Azcarraga, Mexico Reds.27	2	1	0	5	1		.833	62	63	23	19	2	17	3	4	36	2	2.76
Balcazar, Aguila 36	0	0	0	5	5		.500	71	60	28	23	4	21	5	1	21	8	2.92
Baretty, Gomez Palacio.11	0	0	0	1	0		1.000	25	26	11	10	3	9	1	0	8	1	3.60
Bauta, Poza Rica 54	8	3	2	9	8		.529	158	171	73	55	5	32	9	2	92	2	3.13
Bedolla, Gomez Palacio.23	0	0	0	2	0		1.000	35	22	9	9	1	20	2	1	19	0	2.31
Betancourt, Gomez Pal.38	21	4	0	3	11		.214	125	157	79	61	13	59	10	4	52	1	4.39
Boehlert, Jalisco* ...2	0	0	0	0	0		.000	1	1	3	3	0	4	0	0	0	0	27.00
Brito, Aguila 20	20	9	2	7	8		.467	121	116	44	39	6	25	3	3	48	11	2.90
Brown, Poza Rica 29	26	6	1	7	14		.333	160	185	85	76	15	40	3	1	85	5	4.28
Buentello, Reynosa ...39	9	2	1	6	8		.429	86	107	60	49	5	48	8	5	58	8	5.13
Burgos, 6 Jal-3 Ag* ..9	0	0	0	0	1		.000	12	16	6	5	1	6	1	0	10	1	3.75
Cacerez, Saltillo 40	36	8	2	19	12		.571	211	210	119	92	11	86	5	6	130	12	3.92
Camarero, Aguila 1	0	0	0	0	0		.000	1	0	0	0	0	0	0	0	0	0	18.00
Cano, Reynosa 2	0	0	0	0	0		.000	2	5	4	1	0	2	0	0	1	2	4.50
Cano, Mexico Reds 2	1	0	0	0	0		.000	4	10	6	6	1	4	0	0	1	0	13.50
Carrasco, Jalisco 25	6	2	1	4	2		.667	69	80	34	28	4	23	4	1	33	2	3.65

Pitcher and Club	G	GS	CG	ShO	W	L	Pct.	IP	H	R	ER	HR	BB	Int. BB	HB	SO	WP	ERA
Carrillo, Poza Rica .34	6	2	1	2	3	.400	85	94	48	44	7	18	3	2	45	2	4.66
Castillo, Saltillo 48	16	9	2	14	5	.737	176	150	56	48	8	56	5	10	119	7	2.45
Castillo, Gomez Pal .29	9	4	1	7	6	.538	89	94	52	44	1	26	7	5	93	2	4.45
R. Chavez, Aguila ...47	0	0	0	6	6	.500	84	61	24	23	5	53	10	2	40	9	2.04
Cisneros, Monterrey ..19	0	0	0	1	2	.333	36	36	18	10	2	17	1	4	29	3	2.50
Colis, Poza Rica ... 2	0	0	0	0	0	.000	1	3	5	5	0	1	0	1	0	2	45.00
Cordova, Jalisco 23	6	0	0	0	5	.000	51	61	42	35	9	19	6	2	32	1	6.18
Cortes, Monterrey* ..24	7	1	0	1	8	.111	57	67	42	38	5	18	4	1	23	5	6.00
Cota, Yucatan 1	0	0	0	0	0	.000	1	2	2	2	0	0	0	0	0	0	0.00
Cruz, Mexico Tigers .42	18	2	1	5	11	.313	109	116	59	57	4	56	16	1	42	3	4.71
Delfin, Mexico Tigers . 2	0	0	0	0	0	.000	2	3	1	1	0	2	0	1	3	0	4.50
Diaz, Aguila 31	22	7	3	10	8	.556	149	158	69	60	4	51	4	7	84	8	3.62
Diaz, Mexico Tigers ..27	8	2	0	3	5	.375	78	67	27	21	3	33	5	0	38	6	2.42
Elizalde, Reynosa ... 6	0	0	0	1	1	.500	6	13	8	6	0	5	2	1	3	1	9.00
Esquivias, Mex Tigers* 2	0	0	0	0	0	.000	½	1	1	1	1	0	0	0	0	1	27.00
Fajardo, Mexico Reds .34	0	0	0	2	1	.667	61	62	28	21	4	27	7	0	28	2	3.10
Ferguson M., Yucatan.14	7	3	2	5	2	.714	60	49	15	12	1	14	4	1	33	1	1.80
Figueroa, G Palacio ..39	31	10	1	15	17	.469	209	251	116	91	16	45	13	3	77	2	3.92
Franco, Yucatan 1	0	0	0	0	0	.000	1	1	0	0	0	0	0	0	1	0	0.00
Gamez, Saltillo* 45	7	1	0	7	6	.538	109	121	61	54	15	30	3	3	89	6	4.46
N. Garcia, M. Tigers ..61	14	3	1	11	6	.647	189	186	77	68	10	62	19	7	109	3	3.24
Garcia, Saltillo 3	0	0	0	0	0	.000	5	7	2	2	1	2	0	0	4	0	3.60
S. Garcia, Monterrey .14	1	0	0	0	0	.000	31	39	18	15	2	7	0	0	14	2	4.35
Garcia, Mexico Reds ..29	13	4	1	5	5	.500	96	120	63	52	8	34	2	3	42	2	4.88
Garza, Reynosa 12	2	0	0	1	2	.333	21	25	12	10	1	10	1	1	8	1	4.29
Geigel, Poza Rica* ..28	28	15	4	12	11	.522	167	132	60	54	3	62	3	1	68	5	2.91
Gleason, Jalisco 1	0	0	0	0	0	.000	3	4	1	1	0	4	0	0	1	0	3.00
Gonzalez, Reynosa ...43	31	13	5	17	12	.586	230	232	93	71	13	64	17	9	109	2	2.78
Goycolea, Gomez Pal ..16	0	0	0	0	0	.000	23	19	13	10	3	11	3	3	5	4	3.91
C. Gutierrez, 6PR-41Y47	0	0	0	6	6	.500	85	93	40	34	6	32	10	3	46	2	3.60
P. Gutierrez, Reynosa .43	1	0	0	4	2	.667	97	98	45	41	3	29	6	6	51	10	3.80
Hernandez, Monterrey .23	1	0	0	1	2	.333	33	44	17	8	3	3	1	2	19	0	2.18
Hernandez G., M R* .22	2	1	0	5	3	.625	79	87	18	16	0	9	1	1	56	3	1.82
Horsford, Monterrey .24	22	8	2	6	12	.333	131	158	87	75	6	49	6	7	50	5	5.15
Howden, Poza Rica ... 1	0	0	0	0	1	.000	2	4	3	3	0	1	0	0	1	0	13.50
Icedo, Mexico Tigers* .48	5	1	1	4	4	.500	67	72	41	36	3	36	4	2	34	4	4.84
Imbert, Yucatan* 40	31	11	5	14	11	.560	221	221	84	74	11	75	10	3	119	4	3.01
Jusino, Gomez Palacio .49	26	10	2	8	13	.381	185	215	116	89	19	66	16	6	132	4	4.33
Lagunas, Poza Rica .42	15	3	1	5	12	.294	120	130	59	53	6	31	4	1	57	1	3.98
Leal, Mexico Reds ...34	33	19	1	18	10	.643	223	220	111	97	14	91	4	8	170	7	3.92
Leon, Jalisco 37	28	10	3	14	9	.609	182	185	75	58	8	42	5	1	138	7	2.87
Leyva, Gomez Palacio* 8	4	1	0	1	1	.500	17	22	10	8	3	5	1	1	6	0	4.24
Lilly, Gomez Palacio . 3	1	0	0	0	1	.000	10	5	6	3	0	7	2	0	4	0	2.70
Lira, Poza Rica 19	3	0	0	1	5	.167	60	70	39	34	9	16	1	2	26	3	5.10
A. Lopez, Mex Reds .37	24	14	4	16	11	.593	172	153	64	57	3	100	7	6	127	15	2.98
E. Lopez, Monterrey .37	4	2	0	8	4	.667	83	88	32	29	5	27	7	7	37	1	3.14
Lopez, Aguila 3	0	0	0	2	0	1.000	21	15	8	6	0	11	6	3	7	0	2.57
J. R. Lopez, Mont ...33	25	18	6	16	13	.552	205	204	74	64	8	51	6	5	152	3	2.81
Lopez, 7 Rey-12 Sal .20	9	2	4	5	4	.444	61	76	41	35	6	15	2	2	32	0	5.16
M. Lugo, Jalisco 57	13	3	1	9	12	.429	133	136	65	57	7	55	12	1	74	4	3.86
Lugo, Yucatan 14	1	0	0	1	3	.250	23	31	22	19	4	12	2	2	9	1	7.43
Madrigal, Poza Rica .44	17	4	3	4	11	.267	132	130	60	50	9	41	2	12	59	6	3.41
Malpica, Aguila 25	24	10	3	9	9	.500	158	160	61	51	6	45	11	1	56	4	2.91
Manrique, Monterrey* 7	2	0	0	0	2	.000	17	14	11	9	2	13	1	1	7	6	4.76
Mariscal, Yucatan* ..35	28	16	4	21	7	.750	200	180	60	41	8	51	12	1	147	1	1.85
Martinez, Monterrey* 34	9	2	1	4	4	.500	85	87	40	37	5	34	2	4	48	1	3.92
J. Martinez, Yucatan .25	16	3	0	3	7	.300	85	106	57	45	7	33	3	6	55	1	4.76
Mason, Monterrey ... 7	6	0	0	0	6	.000	25	26	17	13	2	14	1	0	5	3	4.68
Maytorena, Mex T ...39	29	5	2	11	9	.550	165	146	80	71	7	84	11	6	134	13	3.87
Mazon, Aguila 30	16	8	2	13	3	.813	154	125	58	48	11	81	5	3	92	4	2.81
Mere, Yucatan 12	4	0	0	1	1	.500	21	23	13	10	0	15	2	0	14	1	4.29
Merla, Saltillo 7	0	0	0	1	1	.500	8	18	11	10	0	4	1	0	4	1	11.25
Meza, Jalisco* 20	5	1	0	2	1	.667	51	64	36	30	2	23	8	2	31	5	5.29
G. Meza, Saltillo 46	4	0	0	4	6	.400	89	106	63	57	9	20	3	4	39	3	5.76
Moncayo, 22 Y-10 S 32	15	3	0	2	7	.222	101	128	59	54	10	36	7	0	39	4	4.81
Moreno, Mex Reds .. 7	0	0	0	0	0	.000	8	10	1	1	0	8	3	0	4	0	1.13
V. M. Moreno, Mont . 5	1	0	0	1	0	1.000	12	14	7	5	0	3	0	4	0	0.75	
Mota, Yucatan 1	0	0	0	0	0	.000	3	7	4	4	1	0	0	0	1	12.00	
Munro, Monterrey ...20	2	0	0	2	1	.667	49	50	17	17	4	19	4	2	30	1	3.12
S. Murillo, 14 GP-30 T ..44	3	0	0	6	5	.545	73	75	40	36	4	52	10	0	34	9	4.44
Nuno, Aguila 28	9	4	1	6	2	.750	95	66	23	21	4	43	5	2	55	2	1.99
Olivares, Poza Rica .. 1	0	0	0	0	1	.000	2	4	5	5	0	4	0	0	1	0	22.50
Ortiz, Mex Reds* ...21	20	8	1	10	3	.769	115	138	56	46	8	22	2	0	69	0	3.60
Osorio, Aguila 20	19	12	4	10	7	.588	133	149	44	42	15	26	9	0	42	4	2.84
Pacheco, Mex Reds .. 3	1	0	0	0	1	.000	6	10	4	4	2	2	0	0	4	0	6.00
Palomino, Poza Rica* 3	0	0	0	0	0	.000	4	4	3	3	1	2	0	0	1	0	6.75
Paredes, Saltillo 30	23	4	1	7	13	.350	131	153	73	62	8	55	7	2	69	1	4.26
Parra, 14 Sal-11 GP .25	18	4	1	3	7	.300	86	98	60	44	5	55	1	4	46	2	4.60
Penalver, Monterrey ..23	20	12	2	10	9	.526	152	170	71	60	13	29	4	2	86	0	3.55
Peraza, Yucatan 1	0	0	0	0	0	.000	1	3	2	2	0	0	0	0	0	0	18.00

Pitcher and Club	G	GS	CG	ShO	W	L	Pct.	IP	H	R	ER	HR	BB	Int. BB	HB	SO	WP	ERA
Pereira, Mex Tigers	43	26	7	2	12	11	.522	149	156	65	59	10	77	8	5	61	4	3.56
Pollorena, Jalisco	27	24	8	3	10	5	.667	154	151	59	49	7	39	4	6	79	5	2.86
Quintana, 10 Ag-12 GP	22	17	3	1	4	7	.364	94	94	45	36	8	37	5	2	44	3	3.45
Quiroz, Yucatan	34	28	11	4	12	11	.522	193	186	86	68	14	80	11	5	117	3	3.17
Ramirez, Mex Reds*	4	0	0	0	0	0	.000	7	7	5	1	1	1		0	6	0	1.29
Ramos, Jalisco	21	17	7	2	12	6	.667	120	105	41	34	6	19	9	4	76	1	2.55
Ramos, Yucatan	9	0	0	0	0	0	.000	14	11	9	8	0	7	4	1	3	0	5.14
Raygoza, 17 Tigers-23 GP	40	3	0	0	2	4	.333	78	89	38		7	40	6	1	30	8	4.68
Reinoso, Reynosa	34	29	6	2	10	9	.526	164	169	85	80	9	58	6	3	77	1	4.39
C. Reyes, Yucatan	8	0	0	0	0	0	.000	13	18	11	9	3	2	1	0	4	1	6.23
R. Reyes, Yucatan	2	0	0	0	0	0	.000	7	8	5	5	2	3	1	0	5	2	6.43
Rivas, Mex Reds*	1	1	0	0	1	0	1.000	8	1	1	1	0	7	0	0	4	0	1.29
F. R. Rivas, Saltillo*	33	24	5	1	8	15	.348	146	145	72	64	10	41	4	4	66	6	3.95
Rizales, Aguila	26	25	8	1	12	6	.667	161	167	63	53	13	33	6	4	43	1	2.96
Robinson, Reynosa	6	3	1	0	4	1	.800	44	35	16	13	2	22	1	1	27	2	2.66
Rodgers, Reynosa	55	6	3	0	7	10	.412	128	102	50	43	9	48	14	4	108	3	3.02
P. Rodriguez, Mont	15	7	1	1	3	2	.600	54	53	22	20	6	24	2	1	21	3	3.33
Romo, Jalisco	36	23	8	2	10	9	.526	155	159	67	48	3	50	10	4	79	5	2.79
Rubio, Reynosa	1	0	0	0	0	0	.000	1	1	0	0	0	0	0	0	2	0	0.00
Ruelas, Saltillo*	41	10	1	1	6	3	.667	114	109	56	48	6	45	3	5	94	6	3.79
Salgado, Aguila	14	1	1	1	4	2	.667	28	20	8	8	1	6	1	0	14	1	2.57
C. Sanchez, Monterrey	41	24	13	2	14	12	.538	204	215	114	97	16	89	12	3	113	8	4.28
S. Sanchez, Reynosa*	49	39	21	6	16	15	.516	250	228	104	83	7	114	12	3	154	17	2.99
Sandoval, Yucatan	1	0	0	0	0	0	.000	1/3	0	0	0	0	0	0	0	0	0	0.00
Sandoval, Gomez Pal	41	9	2	0	5	8	.385	103	102	45	36	7	42	9	1	45	1	3.15
T. Sandoval, Reynosa	12	11	6	0	4	7	.364	78	71	32	19	4	18	5	0	55	1	2.19
Serna, Mex Tigers*	1	0	0	0	0	0	.000	6	5	1	1	0	3	0	0	5	0	1.50
Silva, Reynosa	1	0	0	0	0	0	.000	3	1	1	1	0	2	0	0	1	0	3.00
Solano, Mex Tigers	14	2	0	0	0	1	.000	23	40	24	19	5	11	1	0	15	1	6.11
Solis, Saltillo	14	0	0	0	0	0	.000	26	33	18	15	1	8	1	2	14	1	5.19
Soqui, Mexico Reds*	34	16	2	0	5	6	.455	103	110	66	53	10	54	2	4	68	3	4.63
J. Soto, Poza Rica*	33	25	15	4	10	16	.385	176	193	73	63	9	50	2	1	74	4	3.22
Suby, Mexico Tigers	58	26	8	4	20	14	.588	214	219	98	85	17	58	14	1	139	2	3.57
Urbano, Yucatan	3	2	0	0	2	4	.333	22	27	19	14	1	14	2	2	13	3	5.73
Uriarte, 16 T-18 Y	34	23	6	3	8	10	.444	134	117	61	46	8	65	2	2	89	7	3.09
C. Uzcanga, Yucatan	3	0	0	0	0	0	.000	3	2	2	2	0	2	1	0	2	0	6.00
L. Uzcanga, Yucatan	46	2	0	0	3	6	.333	89	116	54	47	3	21	7	2	39	1	4.75
Valenzuela, Mex Reds	8	1	0	0	1	0	1.000	18	27	13	11	2	3	0	0	11	0	5.50
Valenzuela, Gomez Pal	7	1	0	0	0	0	.000	11	14	7	7	0	4	0	0	5	0	5.73
Vega, 7 Jalisco-6 GP	13	0	0	0	0	0	.000	26	39	15	12	0	8	1	0	12	4	4.15
Velazquez, Mex Reds	42	0	0	0	8	4	.667	73	79	42	35	1	44	3	2	39	5	4.32
Villa, Monterrey	6	3	1	0	1	2	.333	18	24	14	10	1	4	0	1	9	1	5.00
Zavala, Poza Rica	33	19	5	1	7	10	.413	119	129	65	52	4	44	3	1	49	5	3.93

BALKS—Paredes, 5; F. R. Rivas, 3; Cisneros, Gamez, N. Garcia, A. Lopez, M. Lugo, J. Martinez, G. Meza, Pereira, S. Sanchez, 2 each; C. Acosta, Adame, Ahumada, Azcarraga, Balcazar, Baretty, Buentello, Burgos, Cacerez, Garza, C. Gutierrez, P. Gutierrez, Leal, Leon, E. Lopez, Malpica, Maytorena, Mazon, Moncayo, V. M. Moreno, Nuno, Osorio, Rizales, Salgado, 1 each.

COMBINATION SHUTOUTS—Osorio-R. Chavez, Diaz-Nuno, Mazon-Balcazar, Aguila; Ramos-Armas, Jalisco; Arano-Fajardo, Ortiz-Velazquez, Mexico Reds; N. Garcia-Uriarte, Diaz-Diaz-Suby, Suby-Icedo, Serna-S. Murillo, N. Garcia-Pereira-Suby, Mexico Tigers; P. Rodriguez-E. Lopez, Monterrey; Geigel-Bauta, Poza Rica; Quiroz-C. Gutierrez, Quiroz-Mariscal, Yucatan.

NO-HIT GAMES—J. R. Lopez, Monterrey, defeated Jalisco, 1-0, July 11, (seven innings); Madrigal, Poza Rica, defeated Jalisco, 2-0, July 29.

ALONG THE MINOR LEAGUE TRAIL . . . .

(Continued from page 407)

"Crushers" won their opener—with two runs in the 10th to win, 8-7? Here's how the power went: Two bases on balls, a fielder's choice grounder, a hit batsman and a sacrifice fly. . . . Vinegar Bend Mizell, who threw his share of wild ones as a National League lefthander, tossed one of his most errant ones via phone from Washington, D.C., where he now is a Congressman, to Memphis, Tenn., where a banquet was being held to honor the

(Continued on page 442)

Pacific Coast League

CLASS AAA

Leading Batter
BOB VALENTINE
Spokane

League President
BILL McKECHNIE, JR.

Leading Pitcher
JERRY STEPHENSON
Spokane

CHAMPIONSHIP WINNERS IN PREVIOUS YEARS

1903—Los Angeles .... .630	1928—San Francisco* .... .630	1946—San Francisco‡ .... .628
1904—Tacoma .... .589	Sacramento§§ .... .626	1947—Los Angeles†† .... .567
Tacoma§ .... .571	San Francisco§§ ... .626	1948—Oakland‡ .... .606
Los Angeles§ .... .571	1929—Mission .... .643	1949—Hollywood‡ .... .583
1905—Tacoma .... .583	Hollywood* .... .592	1950—Oakland .... .590
Los Angeles* .... .604	1930—Los Angeles .... .576	1951—Seattle‡ .... .593
1906—Portland .... .657	Hollywood* .... .650	1952—Hollywood .... .606
1907—Los Angeles ...... .608	1931—Hollywood .... .626	1953—Hollywood .... .589
1908—Los Angeles ...... .585	San Francisco* .... .608	1954—San Diego y ...... .604
1909—San Francisco .... .623	1932—Portland .... .587	1955—Seattle .... .552
1910—Portland .... .567	1933—Los Angeles ...... .610	1956—Los Angeles ...... .637
1911—Portland .... .589	1934—Los Angeles z .... .786	1957—San Francisco .... .601
1912—Oakland .... .591	Los Angeles z .... .689	1958—Phoenix .... .578
1913—Portland .... .559	1935—Los Angeles ...... .648	1959—Salt Lake City ... .552
1914—Portland .... .574	San Francisco* .... .608	1960—Spokane .... .601
1915—San Francisco .... .570	1936—Portland‡ .... .549	1961—Tacoma .... .630
1916—San Francisco .... .601	1937—Sacramento ...... .573	1962—San Diego .... .604
1917—San Francisco .... .561	San Diego (3rd)† ... .545	1963—Spokane .... .620
1918—Vernon .... .569	1938—Los Angeles ...... .590	Oklahoma City a ... .532
Los Angeles (2nd)x. .548	Sacramento (3rd)†.. .537	1964—Arkansas .... .609
1919—Vernon .... .613	1939—Seattle .... .580	San Diego a .... .576
1920—Vernon .... .556	Sacramento (4th)† .. .500	1965—Oklahoma City a ... .628
1921—Los Angeles ...... .574	1940—Seattle‡ .... .629	Portland .... .547
1922—San Francisco .... .638	1941—Seattle‡ .... .598	1966—Seattle a .... .561
1923—San Francisco .... .617	1942—Sacramento ...... .590	Tulsa .... .578
1924—Seattle .... .545	Seattle (3rd)† .... .539	1967—San Diego a ...... .574
1925—San Francisco .... .643	1943—Los Angeles ...... .710	Spokane .... .541
1926—Los Angeles ...... .599	S. Francisco (2nd)† .574	1968—Tulsa a .... .642
1927—Oakland .... .615	1944—Los Angeles ...... .586	Spokane .... .586
	S. Francisco (3rd)† .509	1969—Tacoma a .... .589
	1945—Portland .... .622	Eugene .... .603
	S. Francisco (4th)† .525	

*Won split-season playoff. †Won four-team playoff. ‡Won pennant and four-team playoff.
§Tied for second-half title with Tacoma winning playoff. §§Tied for second-half title, with Sacramento winning playoff. ††Ended regular season in tie with San Francisco and won one-game playoff for pennant, then won four-club playoff. xWon playoff from first-place Vernon and awarded championship. yDefeated Hollywood in one-game playoff for pennant. zWon both halves, no playoff.
aLeague was divided into Northern, Southern divisions in 1963 and Eastern, Western divisions in 1964-65-66-67-68-69; won two-team playoff. NOTE—Championship awarded to playoff winner, 1936-37.

aLeague was divided into Northern, Southern divisions in 1963, 1969-70, and Eastern, Western divisions in 1964-65-66-67-68; won two-team playoff.

STANDING OF CLUBS AT CLOSE OF SEASON, SEPTEMBER 2

NORTHERN DIVISION

Club	Spo.	Port.	Eug.	Tac.	Haw.	Phx.	Tuc.	S.L.C.	W.	L.	T.	Pct.	G.B.
Spokane (17)	..	15	17	19	9	11	10	13	94	52	0	.644	....
Portland (8)	7	..	8	13	8	7	10	15	68	78	0	.466	26
Eugene (20*)	5	14	..	16	6	5	7	13	66	80	0	.452	28
Tacoma (14)	3	9	6	..	6	6	6	9	45	98	0	.315	47½

SOUTHERN DIVISION

Club	Spo.	Port.	Eug.	Tac.	Haw.	Phx.	Tuc.	S.L.C.	W.	L.	T.	Pct.	G.B.
†Hawaii (3*)	11	12	14	14	..	14	14	19	98	48	1	.671	....
Phoenix (24)	9	13	15	14	8	..	14	13	85	61	0	.582	13
Tucson (4*)	10	10	13	14	8	9	..	17	81	65	1	.555	17
Salt Lake City (23)	7	5	7	8	3	9	5	..	44	99	0	.308	52½

†Hawaii club represented Honolulu, Hawaii.

Key to major league farm teams (indicated by numbers after clubs in standing) shown on Page 384.

Playoff—Spokane defeated Hawaii, four games to none.

Regular-Season Attendance—Hawaii, 467,217; Tucson, 164,072; Spokane, 151,394; Tacoma, 137,-891; Phoenix, 122,213; Portland, 119,906; Eugene, 101,142; Salt Lake City, 100,373. Total, 1,364,208. Playoffs, 40,056. No all-star game.

Managers: Eugene—Bob Wellman, Lou Kahn; Hawaii—Chuck Tanner; Phoenix—Charlie Fox, Bob Garibaldi, Hank Sauer; Portland—Al Federoff; Salt Lake City—Don Zimmer; Spokane—Tom Lasorda; Tacoma—Whitey Lockman; Tucson—Gordon Maltzberger.

All-Star Team: 1B—Hutton, Spokane; 2B—Griffin, Hawaii; 3B—Garvey, Spokane; SS—Valentine, Spokane; OF—Lis, Eugene; Llenas, Hawaii; Buckner, Spokane; C—Felske, Portland; P—Garibaldi, Phoenix; O'Brien, Spokane; Manager—Lasorda, Spokane; Tanner, Hawaii.

(Compiled by William J. Weiss, League Statistician, San Mateo, Calif.)

CLUB BATTING

Club	G.	AB.	R.	OR.	H.	TB.	2B.	3B.	HR.	RBI.	SH.	SF.	Int. BB.	HP.	SO.	SB.	CS.	LOB.	Pct.
Spokane ..	146	5033	799	590	1503	2191	277	75	87	730	66	48	480	70	34	684	95	41	1092	.299
Tucson ...	147	5032	643	651	1386	1886	214	50	62	573	77	29	421	49	36	745	53	20	1125	.275
Portland ..	146	4881	710	747	1343	2015	220	34	128	653	57	36	547	48	33	879	54	38	1088	.275
Hawaii ...	147	4852	812	595	1328	1985	175	37	136	732	72	48	659	57	35	959	94	49	1077	.274
Phoenix ..	146	4958	694	558	1341	1871	181	68	71	628	59	55	515	56	37	712	66	35	1097	.270
Eugene ...	146	4837	732	743	1294	2070	213	46	157	669	55	45	576	64	46	844	63	39	1068	.268
Salt L. C.	143	4623	549	813	1170	1667	183	43	76	503	30	30	515	40	22	774	63	39	897	.253
Tacoma ...	143	4728	512	754	1190	1646	178	40	66	457	38	43	437	33	26	843	62	24	1017	.252

INDIVIDUAL BATTING

(Leading Qualifiers for Batting Championship—453 or More Plate Appearances)

*Bats lefthanded. †Switch-hitter.

Player and Club	G.	AB.	R.	H.	TB.	2B.	3B.	HR.	RBI.	SH.	SF.	BB.	HP.	SO.	SB.	CS.	Pct.
Valentine, Robert, Spokane .146	621	122	211	324	39	16	14	80	4	10	47	9	51	29	10	.340
Llenas, Winston, Hawaii ...140	542	93	184	275	25	3	20	108	2	7	35	5	59	7	6	.339
Buckner, William, Spokane*.111	465	78	156	202	33	2	3	74	1	8	31	0	25	10	1	.335
Davis, Bryshear, Tacoma* ...133	500	77	166	198	20	6	0	47	1	5	50	1	48	17	5	.332
Wicker, Floyd, Portland* ...115	386	69	127	201	28	2	14	73	2	3	78	2	84	8	2	.329
Griffin, Douglas, Hawaii ...139	552	119	180	241	20	7	9	60	8	5	46	2	34	35	8	.326
Paciorek, Thomas, Spokane .146	549	88	179	290	36	12	17	101	2	6	54	5	92	1	0	.326
Lis, Joseph, Eugene 139	487	102	158	300	24	5	36	107	2	7	89	5	84	6	3	.324
Felske, John, Portland 131	432	70	136	219	25	2	18	75	2	6	64	5	77	1	1	.315
Foster, George, Phoenix 114	403	54	124	178	18	6	8	66	1	6	41	5	57	1	2	.308
Ortiz, Jose, Tucson 143	611	97	188	224	32	2	0	42	9	1	32	9	43	20	6	.308

Departmental Leaders: G—Paciorek, Valentine, 146; AB—Valentine, 621; R—Valentine, 122; H—Valentine, 211; TB—Valentine, 324; 2B—Valentine, 39; 3B—Valentine, 16; HR—Lis, 36; RBI—Llenas, 108; SH—Brinkman, 13; SF—Valentine, 10; BB—Werhas, 98; HP—Ortiz, Valentine, 9; SO—Barry, 121; SB—Griffin, 35; CS—Robles, Smith, 11.

(All Players—Listed Alphabetically)

Player and Club	G.	AB.	R.	H.	TB.	2B.	3B.	HR.	RBI.	SH.	SF.	BB.	HP.	SO.	SB.	CS.	Pct.
Adams, Daniel, Portland ...	11	44	1	4	11	0	0	0	1	0	1	1	0	1	0	0	.091
Adams, H. Douglas, Tucson*.	82	256	30	64	99	14	3	5	29	1	1	37	1	61	1	0	.250
Adlesh, David, Hawaii	50	134	8	20	24	4	0	0	13	0	2	14	2	45	0	0	.149
Albury, Victor, Salt Lake C*	22	15	1	4	6	2	0	0	0	1	0	1	0	2	0	0	.267
Alexander, Doyle, Spokane .	19	52	5	13	14	1	0	0	4	6	0	0	1	9	0	0	.250
Allen, Robert, Hawaii*	34	12	3	1	1	0	0	0	0	0	0	3	0	8	0	0	.083
Amaro, Ruben, Eugene 106	310	54	72	95	11	3	2	17	7	2	66	1	31	9	0	.232
Arlin, Stephen, Salt Lake C.	16	31	1	7	8	1	0	0	1	1	0	1	0	8	0	0	.226
Armstrong, Richard, Spokane	36	8	0	2	2	0	0	0	1	4	0	1	0	5	0	0	.250
Arnold, Christopher, Phoenix	4	6	1	3	6	1	1	0	2	0	0	0	0	2	0	0	.500
Arrigo, Gerald, Tucson*	12	16	1	4	4	0	0	0	0	2	0	1	0	8	0	0	.250
Auerbach, Frederick, Port ...	80	300	52	90	118	15	2	3	19	5	3	37	3	31	17	3	.300
Baca, Johnny, Salt Lake City	14	23	0	4	4	0	0	0	1	0	0	3	0	5	0	0	.174
Bailey, Calvin, Salt Lake C.	20	9	1	0	0	0	0	0	0	0	0	3	0	4	0	0	.000

The Sporting News
SPORTS PUBLICATIONS
authored and researched by nationally-known sports experts and statisticians

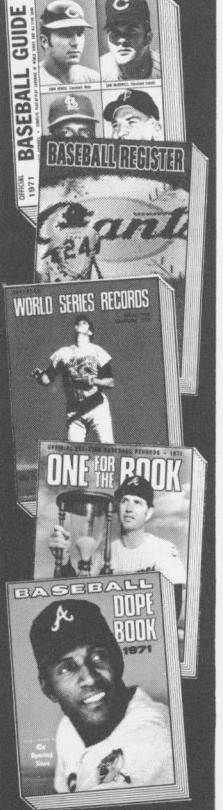

OFFICIAL BASEBALL GUIDE
Contains complete official major and minor league averages, directory of major league club officials, photographs of all major league clubs and stories on pennant races. Also Review of the Year, All-Star Game, Hall of Fame and farm systems. Published annually on April 1. Price *$2.00.

BASEBALL REGISTER
Complete season-by-season records and personal data of more than 1,000 active major league players, managers, coaches and former umpires. The Register will be published and delivered in June after player changes have been made, bringing player personnel up to date. Price *$5.00

OFFICIAL WORLD SERIES RECORDS
Box scores, summary and composite batting and pitching averages of all World Series games played from 1903 through current Series. Includes all Series individual and club batting, fielding and pitching records. Also lists all player and manager participants in over 380 pages. Annually in December. Price *$3.00.

ONE FOR THE BOOK
All-time major league baseball club and individual performance records. Completely indexed for easy reference. Used by sports writers and broadcasters. Published annually in March. Price *$2.00.

THE DOPE BOOK
Rosters of all major league clubs, diagrams of ball parks, All-Star Game records and player averages and many more important facts in handy pocket-size form. Published annually on April 15. Price *$1.00.

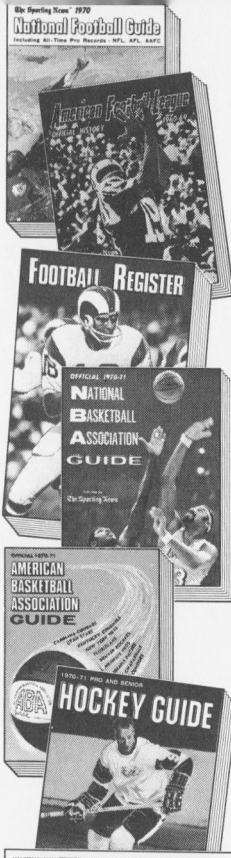

THE SPORTING NEWS' NATIONAL FOOTBALL GUIDE

Club directories of 26 NFL teams, complete NFL statistics. Diagrams of NFL stadia. All-time records and many other features, plus photos. Annually in July.

Price *$2.00

OFFICIAL AMERICAN FOOTBALL LEAGUE HISTORY

Complete statistics and review of 1969 season, team records, 1960-69; all-time AFL records, records of championship, All-Star and Super-Bowl Games. Price *$2.00.

FOOTBALL REGISTER

Complete season-by-season records of all active National Football League players and coaches. Photos of top stars. Annually in October. Price *$5.00.

OFFICIAL NATIONAL BASKETBALL ASSOCIATION GUIDE

All N.B.A. records since 1946 including playoffs, championship, team and individual records. Complete listing of active players and their playing statistics plus directory of club officials. Past season team records against each other and current season schedules. Over 300 pages. Available Oct. 15. Price *$1.50.

OFFICIAL AMERICAN BASKETBALL ASSOCIATION GUIDE

Contains team directories, schedules, player records, statistics and rules. Annual edition available in November. Price *$1.50.

HOCKEY GUIDE

Over 500 pages . Photos, Player Records and Statistics. Names of League and Team Officials. Final Team Standings. Annually in November. Price *$2.00.

The Sporting News

America's national sports weekly — established in 1886. Jampacked with data, feature articles a n d breezy baseball gossip from all points of the compass. Special sections cover professional and collegiate football and basketball a n d other professional sports in season. This authoritative publication sent to subscribers post-age-paid. One-year subscription $12.00. Six-month subscription $6.25.

USE HANDY ORDER FORA

Player and Club	G.	AB.	R.	H.	TB.	2B.	3B.	HR.	RBI.	SH.	SF.	BB.	HP.	SO.	SB.	CS.	Pct.
Baldschun, Jack, Salt Lake C	41	11	1	2	2	0	0	0	0	0	0	1	0	4	0	0	.182
Baldwin, David G., Portland	15	4	0	0	0	0	0	0	0	0	0	0	0	4	0	0	.000
Baney, Richard, Portland ...	9	10	0	0	0	0	0	0	0	0	0	0	0	4	0	0	.000
Barber, Stephen D., Tacoma*	4	5	0	1	1	0	0	0	0	2	0	2	0	1	0	0	.200
Barry, Richard, Hawaii	123	435	73	120	209	27	4	18	85	1	5	79	6	121	7	7	.276
Bates, C. Richard, Portland*	3	2	0	0	0	0	0	0	0	0	0	0	0	0	0	0	.000
Bates, Delbert, Eugene*	49	127	21	38	62	8	2	4	18	0	1	21	2	31	0	0	.299
Bell, Gary, Hawaii	5	7	2	1	1	0	0	0	1	0	0	1	0	3	0	0	.143
Bennett, Dennis, Hawaii*..	44	87	10	15	23	2	0	2	11	2	1	7	0	30	0	0	.172
Bielski, Daniel, Salt Lake C	4	7	0	0	0	0	0	0	0	0	0	0	0	5	0	0	.000
Blanco, C. Oswaldo, Tucson	45	176	53	66	112	15	2	9	33	0	2	25	1	23	2	0	.375
Blanco, Damaso, Phoenix ...	142	499	51	119	143	16	4	0	40	1	4	30	4	34	20	6	.238
Bobb, M. Randall, Portland .	19	61	8	18	27	6	0	1	5	0	0	2	0	14	0	0	.295
Bollo, Gregory, Tucson	19	13	1	1	1	0	0	0	0	0	0	0	0	5	0	0	.077
Borunda, Elias, Salt Lake C .	17	14	0	0	0	0	0	0	1	1	0	1	0	9	0	0	.000
Bradley, Thomas, Hawaii ...	16	39	3	6	6	0	0	1	7	0	1	1	1	10	0	0	.154
Brandon, Darrell, Tucson ...	41	85	9	22	35	4	0	3	16	4	1	4	0	26	0	0	.259
Brinkman, Charles, Tucson ..	117	415	30	96	114	14	2	0	30	13	2	24	2	27	0	0	.231
Brown, E. Randolph, Hawaii*	30	69	7	17	23	3	0	1	5	0	0	13	0	12	0	1	.246
Brubaker, Bruce, Portland ..	32	71	6	12	17	2	0	1	4	6	0	3	0	26	0	0	.169
Bryant, Ronald, Phoenix* ..	7	11	1	1	1	0	0	0	2	1	0	0	0	3	0	0	.091
Buckner, William, Spokane*.	111	465	78	156	202	33	2	3	74	1	8	21	0	25	10	1	.335
Burk, Dean, Tacoma	31	31	1	2	5	0	0	1	3	0	0	1	0	13	0	0	.065
Carrithers, Donald, Phoenix .	24	19	4	6	6	0	0	0	3	0	0	0	0	9	0	0	.316
Castiglione, Robert, SLC ...	14	9	1	1	1	0	0	0	0	0	0	2	0	2	0	0	.111
Chacon, Elio, Portland	59	84	8	18	26	5	0	1	10	1	0	15	0	24	0	0	.214
Champion, B. Billy, Eugene .	24	61	7	14	20	1	1	1	4	3	0	1	0	13	0	0	.230
Christian, Robert, Tucson ..	62	218	34	73	97	16	4	0	40	0	0	27	4	9	0	0	.335
Christino, Michael, Spokane*	8	12	0	1	1	0	0	0	2	0	1	2	0	3	0	0	.083
Church, Leonard, Tacoma† ..	41	14	1	2	2	0	0	0	0	4	0	4	1	6	0	0	.143
Cisterna, Joseph, Salt Lake C†	7	0	0	0	0	0	0	0	0	0	0	0	0	2	0	0	.000
Clark, Rickey, Hawaii	6	7	2	2	2	0	0	0	0	0	0	0	0	0	0	0	.286
Click, Paul, Portland	24	21	1	4	4	0	0	0	1	0	0	0	0	8	0	0	.190
Coates, James, Hawaii	47	28	2	3	3	0	0	0	1	1	0	0	0	12	0	0	.107
Colton, Lawrence, Tacoma*.	32	70	7	12	19	2	1	1	10	5	0	7	0	21	0	0	.171
Compton, Michael, Eugene .	27	88	8	17	24	1	0	2	8	1	0	13	0	15	0	0	.193
Corkins, Michael, SLC	5	13	0	3	4	1	0	0	1	1	0	0	0	3	0	0	.231
Cosman, James, Tacoma	31	19	1	6	8	2	0	0	2	0	0	2	0	5	0	1	.316
Costello, Joseph, Phoenix ..	45	8	0	0	0	0	0	0	0	0	0	0	0	6	0	0	.000
Coward, Stirling, Eugene ...	69	113	13	26	31	3	1	0	7	1	1	5	0	8	2	1	.230
Cox, Larry, Eugene	16	40	4	5	7	2	0	0	0	0	0	6	0	3	0	0	.125
Crider, Jerry, Tucson	5	15	0	2	2	0	0	0	0	0	0	0	1	0	0	0	.133
Cumberland, John, Phoenix .	7	13	1	1	3	0	1	0	0	0	0	0	0	6	0	0	.077
Davis, Bryshear, Tacoma*...	133	500	77	166	198	20	6	0	47	1	5	50	1	48	17	5	.332
Davison, Michael, Phoenix*..	15	2	0	0	0	0	0	0	0	0	0	0	0	0	0	0	.000
DeCastris, Frank, Eugene*..	100	378	74	109	186	16	2	19	52	2	2	36	7	62	5	7	.288
DeNeff, James, Hawaii	19	55	6	9	13	1	0	1	8	0	0	6	0	20	2	7	.164
Distaso, Alec, Tacoma	7	3	0	1	1	0	0	0	0	0	0	0	0	0	0	0	.333
Donaldson, John, Portland*.	32	120	10	29	32	3	0	0	7	1	2	17	0	10	0	3	.242
Drake, Ronald, Salt Lake C .	91	258	18	47	61	3	1	3	27	4	2	26	2	51	1	0	.182
Dudek, John, Tacoma	25	73	10	20	34	5	0	3	14	1	0	2	0	9	0	0	.274
Dunegan, James, Tacoma ...	18	39	7	9	12	0	0	1	2	0	1	5	1	8	0	0	.231
Eddy, Donald, Tucson	34	13	0	1	1	0	0	0	0	0	0	0	0	5	0	0	.077
Edgerton, William, Portland*	38	8	0	2	2	0	0	0	1	0	1	1	0	4	0	0	.250
Etheridge, Bobby, Salt Lake C	36	107	10	30	44	3	1	3	19	1	2	15	0	20	0	0	.280
Face, El Roy, Hawaii†	8	2	0	0	0	0	0	0	0	0	0	0	0	0	0	0	.000
Fast, Darcy, 5 Tac-20 SLC* .	25	30	1	4	5	1	0	0	1	1	0	3	0	12	0	0	.133
Faul, William, Phoenix	36	9	1	1	1	0	0	0	0	0	0	0	0	3	0	0	.111
Felske, John, Portland	131	432	70	136	219	25	2	18	75	2	6	64	5	77	1	1	.315
Fenwick, Robert, Phoenix ..	94	305	40	95	124	13	5	2	37	4	5	30	1	38	4	4	.311
Ferrell, William, Portland .	34	8	0	1	1	0	0	0	0	0	0	0	0	3	0	0	.125
Fisher, Thomas, Portland ...	34	5	0	0	0	0	0	0	0	0	1	0	4	0	0	0	.000
Fitzer, Lyn, Tacoma	18	19	2	1	1	0	0	0	0	0	0	0	0	13	0	1	.053
Foster, George, Phoenix ...	114	403	54	124	178	18	6	8	66	1	6	41	5	57	1	2	.308
Francis, John, Eugene	4	7	1	0	0	0	0	0	0	0	0	0	0	0	0	0	.000
Frost, William, Phoenix ...	25	10	0	1	1	0	0	0	0	1	0	0	0	2	0	0	.100
Galliher, Marvin, Spokane .	62	208	37	67	94	12	6	1	31	3	1	28	1	21	1	0	.322
Gamble, Oscar, Eugene* ...	28	108	26	32	46	7	2	1	8	1	2	6	0	14	5	0	.296
Garibaldi, Robert, Phoenix*	42	96	14	9	12	0	0	1	6	2	0	16	0	36	0	0	.100
Garvey, Steven, Spokane ...	95	376	71	120	201	26	5	15	87	1	6	34	4	51	13	0	.319
Gil, T. Gustavo, Portland ..	30	93	11	27	36	1	1	2	18	2	0	14	1	11	0	0	.290
Goossen, Gregory, Portland .	77	281	45	84	153	9	0	20	69	1	5	44	2	59	0	1	.299
Gosger, James, Phoenix* ...	8	16	3	3	6	0	0	1	2	0	0	2	0	1	0	0	.188
Gray, David, Salt Lake City .	15	7	1	1	1	0	0	0	1	0	0	1	0	2	0	0	.143
Griffin, Douglas, Hawaii ...	139	552	119	180	241	20	7	9	60	8	5	46	2	34	35	8	.326
Gura, Lawrence, Tacoma ...	11	20	4	2	2	0	0	0	0	0	0	0	0	9	0	0	.100
Hairston, John, Tacoma	44	153	13	36	61	6	2	5	21	0	1	12	2	39	0	0	.235
Hamilton, Jack, Tucson	30	38	1	5	6	1	0	0	0	0	0	3	0	14	0	0	.132
Hansen, Robert, Portland* ..	33	127	20	41	63	2	1	6	24	0	0	5	1	11	0	1	.323
Harrell, John, Phoenix	18	43	2	3	5	0	1	0	3	0	0	11	0	9	0	0	.070
Harrison, Roric, Portland ..	41	53	12	11	23	3	0	3	10	1	0	4	0	20	0	0	.208
Hart, James, Phoenix	67	164	32	52	88	8	2	8	37	0	6	48	2	29	0	1	.317

Player and Club	G.	AB.	R.	H.	TB.	2B.	3B.	HR.	RBI.	SH.	SF.	BB.	HP.	SO.	SB.	CS.	Pct.
Heath, William, Tacoma*	37	99	12	17	27	4	0	2	10	1	1	11	1	11	0	0	.172
Herrera, Jose, Portland	70	272	36	73	118	8	2	11	40	2	3	11	3	28	2	1	.268
Herron, Gerald, Eugene	4	1	0	0	0	0	0	0	0	0	0	1	0	1	0	0	.000
Hibbs, James, Tacoma	54	180	16	47	59	6	0	2	20	1	2	6	2	25	1	1	.261
Hicks, James, Hawaii	86	262	44	81	135	10	4	12	63	1	3	52	4	77	4	3	.309
Hinton, Richard, Tucson*	44	77	11	18	26	2	0	2	8	4	0	6	0	23	0	0	.234
Hiser, Gene, Tacoma*	66	232	23	58	71	7	0	2	22	1	2	26	1	40	6	3	.250
Hough, Charles, Spokane	49	33	1	6	9	0	0	1	3	3	0	5	0	8	0	0	.182
Howard, Wilbur, Portland†	7	27	3	9	11	2	0	0	2	0	0	3	0	7	1	1	.333
Hriniak, Walter, SLC*	121	410	49	101	136	21	4	2	36	3	4	66	1	64	3	3	.246
Huggins, Jesse, Portland*	13	11	0	2	2	0	0	0	0	0	0	0	0	3	0	0	.182
Hughes, Terry, Tacoma	104	395	33	113	161	25	4	5	44	1	5	18	4	75	1	0	.286
Humphreys, Robert, Portland	6	5	0	0	0	0	0	0	0	0	0	0	0	2	0	0	.000
Huntz, Stephen, Salt Lake C†	7	26	3	8	9	1	0	0	2	0	0	1	0	5	0	0	.308
Hutton, Thomas, Spokane*	90	310	51	100	152	21	5	7	56	2	4	44	0	17	3	5	.323
Jackson, Michael, Eugene*	32	58	9	2	4	2	0	0	1	5	0	6	1	30	0	0	.034
Jacobsen, Gary, Phoenix	45	114	10	26	32	1	1	1	12	0	2	8	2	22	1	1	.228
Jacquez, Patrick, Tacoma	6	12	0	2	2	0	0	0	0	0	0	0	0	0	0	0	.167
Jagutis, H. John, Eugene†	2	9	1	0	0	0	0	0	0	0	0	0	0	0	0	0	.000
James, Jeffrey, Eugene	34	55	4	7	10	0	0	1	4	2	0	1	0	23	0	0	.127
Jenkins, Warren, Spokane	35	32	3	7	12	2	0	1	4	1	0	0	0	18	0	0	.219
Jestadt, Garry, Tacoma	92	338	39	97	115	6	3	2	27	1	6	27	2	28	2	1	.287
Johnson, C. Barth, Tucson	10	21	0	4	5	1	0	0	3	2	0	1	0	4	0	0	.190
Johnson, Frank, Phoenix	29	116	20	41	49	1	2	1	13	3	0	8	1	9	1	1	.353
Johnson, James, Phoenix*	28	29	3	10	11	1	0	0	4	2	0	2	0	6	1	0	.345
Johnson, Larry, Portland	71	260	33	84	108	13	1	3	33	2	3	5	1	12	0	0	.323
Jones, Stephen, Portland	70	217	36	56	94	13	2	7	23	1	2	19	3	57	4	4	.258
Joshua, Von, Spokane*	16	53	7	19	28	4	1	1	9	0	3	0	8	2	6		.358
Kealey, Steven, Hawaii	24	13	0	0	0	0	0	0	0	0	0	0	0	7	0	0	.000
Kelly, Robert, Eugene*	27	73	7	19	23	4	0	0	4	0	0	3	0	6	1	2	.260
Kelly, Van, Salt Lake City*	72	248	29	66	82	14	1	0	25	1	1	34	1	51	3	3	.266
Kendall, Fred, Salt Lake C	115	391	49	120	165	14	2	9	48	0	2	25	1	33	2	1	.307
Kennedy, John, Portland	31	118	19	29	48	7	3	2	17	0	0	9	1	21	2	0	.246
Kenworthy, Richard, Tucson	67	267	37	97	129	14	3	4	44	3	3	35	1	49	3	2	.264
Kline, Ronald, Hawaii	16	7	1	0	0	0	0	0	1	3	0	0	0	5	0	0	.000
Knuckles, Philip, SLC	45	43	5	4	8	1	0	1	4	1	0	1	0	16	0	0	.093
Knutson, Gordon, Eugene*	21	13	1	1	1	0	0	0	1	1	0	4	0	5	0	0	.077
Koegel, Peter, Portland	55	200	37	54	108	12	0	14	40	1	1	26	3	35	0	0	.270
Krawczyk, Thomas, SLC	33	71	10	15	23	3	1	1	8	2	0	6	0	11	0	0	.211
Kroll, Gary, Hawaii	16	7	1	1	1	0	0	0	0	0	0	0	0	1	0	0	.143
Lanning, Gerald, Eugene*	18	14	1	2	2	0	0	0	0	1	0	1	0	5	0	0	.143
LaRoche, David, Hawaii*	24	17	2	0	0	0	0	0	1	0	0	3	0	6	0	0	.000
Lauzerique, George, Port	22	42	6	5	6	1	0	0	5	4	1	3	0	15	0	0	.119
Laxton, William, Eugene*	9	11	0	2	2	0	0	0	0	0	0	2	0	3	0	0	.182
Lazar, J. Daniel, Tucson*	6	14	1	4	4	0	0	0	2	0	0	0	0	4	0	0	.286
LeMay, Richard, Tacoma*	53	19	1	2	3	1	0	0	2	0	0	0	0	6	1	0	.105
Lemonds, David, Tacoma*	24	46	4	5	9	0	1	0	3	2	0	6	0	24	2	0	.109
Linares, Julio, Phoenix	128	455	55	124	172	15	12	3	63	6	6	19	1	47	4	4	.273
Lis, Joseph, Eugene	139	487	102	158	300	24	5	36	107	2	7	89	5	84	6	3	.324
Llenas, Winston, Hawaii	140	542	93	184	275	25	3	20	108	2	7	35	5	59	7	6	.339
Lockwood, Claude, Portland	5	14	0	2	2	0	0	0	0	1	0	0	0	7	0	0	.143
Lolich, Ronald, Tucson	108	383	68	112	187	21	3	16	67	3	3	49	6	57	0	1	.292
Lopes, David, Spokane	100	343	48	90	131	15	4	6	35	4	1	37	3	65	11	4	.262
Lott, George, Spokane†	89	188	22	45	71	8	3	4	28	0	2	17	0	37	3	4	.239
Loughlin, Larry, Hawaii*	10	1	0	0	0	0	0	0	0	0	0	0	0	0	0	0	.000
Lund, Gordon, Hawaii	71	194	21	46	50	4	0	0	17	4	0	34	0	31	2	1	.237
Lung, John, Tacoma	83	275	41	69	100	13	3	4	24	2	1	19	0	66	2	2	.251
Mariscal, Alfredo, Spokane*	6	4	1	2	2	0	0	0	1	0	0	1	0	2	0	0	.500
Matias, John, Tucson*	97	255	30	82	111	7	2	6	41	2	3	16	2	24	0	2	.322
McBean, Alvin, Eugene	7	13	1	2	5	0	0	1	2	0	0	0	0	5	0	0	.154
McGraw, Henry, 82Eug-16Ta	98	306	52	93	167	22	2	16	59	1	6	38	4	62	1	4	.304
McGuire, M. C., Tucson	107	395	43	110	132	11	4	1	33	5	1	17	0	17	0	0	.278
McKinney, C. Richard, Tuc	62	251	35	76	122	14	7	6	41	1	1	15	1	31	1	2	.303
McKnight, James, Phoenix	130	481	59	133	195	29	3	9	76	0	8	25	7	61	1	2	.277
McLaughlin, Richard, Spo*	64	117	21	30	40	7	0	1	14	0	0	16	1	11	4	1	.256
McMath, Jimmy, Eugene*	51	136	14	29	49	7	2	3	11	0	0	13	0	40	3	0	.213
Merrill, Carl, Eugene*	55	111	12	29	33	4	0	0	12	1	0	27	3	12	1	1	.261
Messerly, Jerry, Eugene†	60	16	1	3	3	0	0	0	0	1	0	3	0	8	0	0	.188
Metzger, Roger, Tacoma*	134	492	59	133	170	20	7	1	32	1	3	48	1	44	12	6	.270
Moloney, Richard, Tucson	25	7	0	0	0	0	0	0	0	0	0	0	0	1	2	0	.000
Montanez, Guillermo, Eug*	119	434	65	120	210	24	9	16	80	2	6	44	6	66	2	1	.276
Montreuil, Allan, Tacoma	89	239	19	66	85	11	1	2	27	4	4	24	1	21	2	1	.276
Morales, Julio, Salt Lake C	109	433	50	107	159	20	7	6	35	0	3	31	2	60	16	7	.247
Moyer, James, Phoenix	33	62	5	7	12	2	0	1	3	0	0	4	0	34	0	0	.113
Mulcahey, Robert, SLC	5	5	1	1	1	0	0	0	0	0	0	0	0	1	0	0	.200
Murphy, William, 12Por-22Ta	34	104	11	27	31	2	1	0	8	0	1	4	2	15	1	0	.260
Napier, James, Tucson	50	125	15	36	47	5	0	2	16	0	3	17	0	30	2	1	.288
Newman, Raymond, Tacoma*	14	3	0	2	2	0	0	0	0	0	0	0	0	0	0	0	.667
Nutter, Jack, Eugene	29	37	1	8	10	2	0	0	1	0	0	4	0	10	0	0	.216
Nyman, Gerald, SLC*	38	59	3	5	5	0	0	0	2	1	0	5	0	41	0	0	.085
O'Brien, Robert, Spokane*	31	60	11	12	13	1	0	0	5	0	1	8	0	0	0		.200
Ogier, Maurice, Salt Lake C	18	16	3	5	8	1	1	0	1	0	0	2	0	4	0	0	.313

Player and Club	G	AB	R	H	TB	2B	3B	HR	RBI	SH	SF	BB	HP	SO	SB	CS	Pct.
Oliver, Nathaniel, 45Ta-25Ha	70	176	27	46	55	6	0	1	13	0	2	23	0	26	10	4	.261
Ortega, Filomeno, Hawaii ...	15	12	0	1	1	0	0	0	0	0	0	0	0	5	0	0	.083
Ortiz, Jose, Tucson	143	611	97	188	224	32	2	0	42	9	1	32	9	43	20	6	.308
Oyler, Raymond, Hawaii	2	7	1	2	2	0	0	0	0	0	0	0	0	4	0	0	.286
Paciorek, Thomas, Spokane .146	549	88	179	290	36	12	17	101	2	6	54	5	92	1	0	.326
Parrilla, Samuel, Eugene ..	67	224	31	74	99	12	2	3	34	1	2	17	1	38	0	0	.330
Parsons, William, Portland .	4	7	2	1	2	1	0	0	0	1	0	4	0	3	0	0	.143
Pena, Jose, Spokane	10	6	0	1	1	0	0	0	0	1	0	2	0	1	0	0	.167
Pentland, Jeffrey, SLC*	98	212	22	64	78	11	0	1	27	2	1	31	2	26	0	1	.302
Perez, Martin, Hawaii	105	406	54	114	135	12	3	1	33	12	4	36	1	35	8	9	.281
Perry, Melvin, Portland	6	10	1	2	2	0	0	0	0	0	0	1	1	3	0	0	.200
Perzanowski, Stanley, Tuc† .	4	4	0	0	0	0	0	0	0	0	0	0	0	3	0	0	.000
Peters, Francis, Portland ..122	422	59	105	143	21	4	3	48	2	1	34	0	38	2	2	.249
Peters, Raymond, Portland ..	25	43	1	4	7	0	0	1	5	3	0	5	0	26	0	1	.093
Pfeil, Robert, Eugene	96	371	55	103	145	16	4	6	36	10	4	27	5	27	4	0	.278
Pitlock, Lee, Phoenix*	14	38	3	3	4	1	0	0	4	0	3	0	16	0	0		.079
Pizarro, Juan, Hawaii*	19	40	6	10	20	4	0	2	6	3	0	0	1	12	0	0	.250
Puente, Miguel, Phoenix	14	25	2	6	6	0	0	0	3	0	1	0	6	0	0		.240
Purdin, John, 25 Spo-12 Haw	37	56	3	7	9	0	1	0	3	6	0	3	0	15	0	0	.125
Qualls, James, Oakland†	9	30	2	3	5	2	0	0	1	0	1	2	0	1	2	0	.100
Raffo, Albert, Eugene	15	4	1	1	1	0	0	0	0	0	0	1	0	1	0	0	.250
Ranew, Merritt, Hawaii* ...	95	309	49	86	117	14	1	5	45	0	3	53	3	54	0	0	.278
Rath, Frederick, Tucson	16	14	2	1	1	0	0	0	2	0	0	2	0	4	0	0	.071
Redmond, H. Wayne, Hawaii	89	279	48	71	135	7	3	17	47	1	2	28	1	95	6	2	.254
Reichenbach, Harold, Tuc ...	55	170	21	38	48	5	1	1	18	2	2	13	1	24	1	0	.224
Reid, Scott, Eugene*	79	253	56	74	138	10	6	14	46	1	1	59	5	61	6	7	.292
Reser, Philip, Tacoma*	21	35	3	5	7	0	1	0	1	0	0	5	0	12	0	0	.143
Reynolds, Archie, Hawaii ...	16	36	2	3	3	0	0	0	0	7	0	0	0	13	0	0	.083
Reynolds, Kenneth, Eugene*.	37	77	5	17	24	2	1	1	8	5	1	4	0	14	2	0	.221
Richard, Lee, Tucson	69	239	30	68	92	10	7	0	28	7	1	15	1	41	1	2	.285
Rickey, Ralph, Tacoma†	50	179	14	39	62	6	1	5	19	0	1	29	1	69	1	1	.218
Roberts, Dale, 4 Haw-7 Eug .	11	3	0	0	0	0	0	0	0	0	0	1	0	2	0	0	.000
Robinson, David, SLC†	135	445	73	114	192	17	11	13	58	0	3	57	3	58	7	5	.256
Robles, Rafael, Salt Lake C	143	602	63	157	199	22	4	4	41	6	3	8	3	58	5	11	.261
Rosario, Angel, Phoenix† ...112	448	94	135	176	19	11	0	33	3	1	76	2	46	19	6	.301
Ross, Gary, Salt Lake City ..	8	18	0	2	2	0	0	0	1	0	0	0	0	6	0	0	.111
Rounsaville, Virle, Tucson ..	27	30	5	10	16	3	0	1	2	0	0	1	0	8	0	0	.333
Russell, William, Spokane ..	55	237	48	86	118	13	5	3	30	3	1	11	3	26	12	3	.363
Sadek, Michael, Phoenix	74	197	29	48	62	5	3	1	25	1	4	39	1	34	1	0	.244
Sanders, Kenneth, Portland .	14	8	0	0	0	0	0	0	1	0	1	0	1	4	0	0	.000
Santorini, Alan, SLC	7	15	1	0	0	0	0	0	0	0	0	0	0	8	0	0	.000
Saul, James, 8 Haw-40 Tac* .	48	90	11	20	27	1	0	2	5	1	0	28	2	21	0	0	.222
Scarpati, Peter, Spokane ...	11	7	1	0	0	0	0	0	0	0	0	2	0	3	0	0	.000
Scharringhausen, Gilbert, SLC	11	11	0	0	0	0	0	0	0	1	0	1	0	6	0	0	.000
Schlesinger, William, Eug ...	29	58	4	11	13	2	0	0	4	1	0	10	0	22	4	1	.190
Schroder, Robert, Phoenix* .115	439	63	126	142	10	3	0	33	5	3	42	3	29	3	4	.287
Secrist, Donald, Tucson* ...	22	35	2	8	13	0	1	1	3	1	0	0	0	12	0	0	.229
Shank, Harvey, Hawaii	40	23	4	5	6	1	0	0	1	1	0	0	0	8	1	0	.217
Sheldon, Roland, 10T-24SLC	34	41	2	4	4	0	0	0	2	1	0	2	0	19	0	0	.098
Sherrod, George, Tacoma ...	27	28	2	3	4	1	0	0	2	3	0	1	0	15	0	0	.107
Shirley, Barton, Spokane ...139	418	58	125	157	21	4	1	53	5	1	71	1	54	0	0	.299
Silverio, Tomas, Hawaii* ...	82	238	53	70	108	6	7	6	45	3	1	49	0	41	8	2	.294
Simpson, Richard, Phoenix .	45	88	10	31	45	2	0	4	22	0	0	7	0	15	0	0	.352
Sipin, John, Salt Lake City .135	465	74	140	237	31	3	20	80	0	4	40	1	75	9	3	.301
Skidmore, R. Roe, Tacoma ..	78	295	23	61	104	8	1	11	37	0	2	12	0	32	0	0	.207
Smith, C. Bernard, Port	98	403	75	133	200	18	5	13	49	2	1	44	2	46	11	11	.330
Sogge, Steven, Spokane	86	288	32	79	112	9	3	6	43	2	3	21	1	32	1	5	.274
Spangler, Albert, Tacoma* ..	26	35	4	11	18	3	2	0	5	0	1	8	0	5	0	0	.314
Spence, J. Robert, Tucson* .	25	92	17	28	39	4	2	1	12	0	1	16	0	21	0	0	.304
Sposito, Gustavo, Spokane .	56	112	16	25	35	6	2	0	7	1	1	11	1	15	0	0	.223
Staab, Lawrence, Spokane ..	17	6	0	0	0	0	0	0	0	0	0	0	0	3	0	0	.000
Stahl, Larry, Salt Lake C* ..	48	140	24	47	66	5	1	4	23	0	3	9	1	15	10	1	.336
Stanley, Frederick, Port† ...	88	291	26	78	94	8	4	0	33	2	1	40	2	54	1	1	.268
Stephenson, Jerry, Spokane*	30	70	9	16	21	1	2	0	6	5	0	7	0	20	0	0	.229
Stephenson, John, Phoenix*.	44	163	22	51	78	13	1	4	29	2	4	11	1	13	0	1	.313
Stinson, G. Robert, Spo† ...101	315	56	94	139	19	4	6	53	4	3	31	2	42	6	2	.298
Stone, Steven, Phoenix	8	21	2	1	2	1	0	0	0	0	0	1	0	10	0	0	.048
Strahler, Michael, Spokane .	30	63	8	11	14	3	0	0	5	0	2	5	0	29	0	0	.175
Sukla, Edward, 3 Haw-36 Eug	39	6	0	0	0	0	0	0	1	0	0	0	0	3	0	0	.000
Tatum, Jarvis, Hawaii*	13	49	13	17	35	3	0	5	11	0	0	8	1	9	1	2	.347
Thompson, Albert, SLC	35	69	9	15	20	2	0	1	8	0	0	8	1	22	2	0	.217
Timberlake, Gary, Portland .	8	5	0	0	0	0	0	0	0	0	0	1	0	3	0	0	.000
Tompkins, Ronald, Portland .	19	4	0	0	0	0	0	0	0	2	0	0	0	2	0	0	.000
Twitchell, Wayne, Portland .	27	49	2	3	4	1	0	0	2	0	0	2	0	30	0	0	.061
Valdespino, Hilario, Port* ..	59	186	30	52	64	10	1	0	18	1	0	20	0	25	4	5	.280
Valentine, Robert, Spokane .146	621	122	211	324	39	16	14	80	4	10	47	9	51	29	10	.340
Vance, Gene, Spokane	13	33	0	1	1	0	0	0	0	2	0	1	0	9	0	0	.030
Vaughns, Clarence, Port	51	163	23	39	61	6	2	4	14	0	1	21	2	39	1	1	.239
Vega, Fernando, Salt Lake C	2	0	0	0	0	0	0	0	0	0	0	0	0	0	0	0	.000
Vinson, Charles, Hawaii* ...134	440	80	118	203	15	2	22	91	0	3	76	6	94	4	1	.268
Vopicka, James, Eugene 136	482	64	123	194	21	4	14	63	5	3	45	4	101	7	5	.255
Vukovich, John, Eugene 138	520	58	143	236	21	3	22	96	0	6	38	2	81	7	8	.275

Player and Club	G.	AB.	R.	H.	TB.	2B.	3B.	HR.	RBI.	SH.	SF.	BB.	HP.	SO.	SB.	CS.	Pct.
Wagner, Leon, Phoenix*	45	53	4	10	20	2	1	2	8	0	6	0	10	0	0		.189
Wallin, Larry, Portland* ...	13	20	2	4	9	0	1	1	5	1	1	6	1	8	0	0	.200
Ward, Chris, Tacoma*	2	1	0	0	0	0	0	0	0	0	0	0	0	1	0	0	.000
Washburn, Gregory, Hawaii ..	29	51	5	6	8	2	0	0	6	0	0	0		11	0	0	.118
Weaver, D. Floyd, Tucson ..	15	5	0	0	0	0	0	0	0	0	0	0		4	0	0	.000
Wenz, Frederick, Eugene ..	13	0	0	0	0	0	0	0	0	0	0	0	0	0	0		.000
Werhas, John, Hawaii 111		382	83	108	161	13	2	12	62	1	7	98	2	58	5	2	.283
Whitaker, Steve, Phoenix* ..	83	224	31	52	111	7	2	16	53	1	3	27	1	45	0	0	.232
Wicker, Floyd, Portland* ..115		386	69	127	201	28	2	14	73	2	3	78	2	84	8	2	.329
Wilkinson, Don, 3Haw-70Tac	73	259	32	63	112	8	4	11	37	0	2	31	5	77	0	0	.243
Williams, Bernard, Phoenix .113		346	71	107	165	15	8	9	47	4	5	57	0	50	9	3	.309
Williams, James A., SLC ..	119	376	46	92	137	9	6	8	47	2	2	32	4	72	4	4	.245
Willoughby, James, Phoenix .	30	61	5	13	15	0	1	0	9	7	1	4	2	21	0	0	.213
Wilson, William, Eugene ..	11	5	1	3	4	1	0	0	0	0	0	0	0	0	0		.600
Winston, Fred, Tucson	78	257	34	66	91	9	2	4	26	0	0	36	3	85	19	3	.257
Wolf, Walter, Hawaii	12	2	0	0	0	0	0	0	1	0	0	0		0	0	0	.000
Wolfe, William, Eugene	19	13	0	2	3	1	0	0	3	0	0	0		7	0	0	.154
Wynne, Billy, Tucson†	23	38	5	8	11	1	1	0	2	0	4	0		12	0	0	.211
Young, Donald, Tacoma	48	137	10	30	47	7	2	2	17	2	3	17	0	32	2	1	.219
Young, Robert, Tucson 114		384	49	96	116	12	4	0	32	9	4	24	3	55	3	1	.250
Zahn, Geoffrey, Spokane* ..	27	20	2	3	3	0	0	0	0	0	1	1	6	0	0		.150
Zinniger, Richard, SLC	9	8	0	2	2	0	0	0	0	1	0	1	0	0			.250

The following pitchers had no plate appearances (listed alphabetically by club, games in parentheses):

PORTLAND—Stephen, Louis (4).

SALT LAKE CITY—Katawczik, Fred (3); Kelley, Richard (1).

SPOKANE—Rau, Douglas* (1).

TACOMA—James, Richard (3); Nottebart, Donald (3).

GRAND-SLAM HOME RUNS—Goossen, Hicks, Valentine, Vinson, 2 each; Compton, Hart, Lis, McGraw, McKinney, Napier, R. Peters, Pfeil, Redmond, Reid, Tatum, Vopicka, Wicker, B. Williams, 1 each.

AWARDED FIRST BASE ON INTERFERENCE—Stinson 4 (Drake, Pfeil, Ranew, Stephenson).

CLUB FIELDING

Club	G.	PO.	A.	E.	DP.	PB.	Pct.	Club	G.	PO.	A.	E.	DP.	PB.	Pct.
Salt Lake City .143		3608	1589	138	139	35	.974	Eugene 146		3739	1592	173	157	24	.969
Hawaii 147		3856	1494	155	133	25	.972	Tacoma 143		3664	1662	180	145	15	.967
Portland 146		3746	1487	152	140	23	.972	Tucson 147		3841	1768	191	156	22	.967
Phoenix 146		3864	1558	175	133	30	.969	Spokane 146		3847	1577	190	153	51	.966

Triple Plays—Eugene, Spokane, Tucson, 1 each.

INDIVIDUAL FIELDING
(Ten or More Games)

*Throws lefthanded.

FIRST BASEMEN

Player and Club	G.	PO.	A.	E.	DP.	Pct.	Player and Club	G.	PO.	A.	E.	DP.	Pct.
VINSON, Hawaii* ..131		1023	55	4	101	.996	Rickey, Tacoma	50	409	29	5	46	.989
Montanez, Eugene* ..100		813	65	4	98	.995	Blanco, Tucson	40	407	24	5	48	.989
Stahl, Salt Lake City*	25	183	13	1	16	.995	Goossen, Portland ..	42	325	30	4	39	.989
Hicks, Hawaii	26	184	8	1	16	.995	Thompson, SLC* ...	11	81	3	1	10	.988
McKnight, Phoenix ..	99	826	55	6	76	.993	McGraw, Eug-Haw ..	38	283	19	4	30	.987
Skidmore, Tacoma ..	73	709	37	5	70	.993	Pentland, SLC* ...	54	394	33	6	29	.986
Matias, Tucson*	66	567	26	5	47	.992	Spence, Tucson	25	254	11	4	23	.985
Sipin, Salt Lake C ..	30	245	10	2	22	.992	Hansen, Portland* ..	30	238	21	4	25	.985
Buckner, Spokane* ..	65	512	22	5	52	.991	F. Johnson, Phoe ...	28	239	13	4	20	.984
Hutton, Spokane* ...	90	768	57	8	84	.990	Hughes, Tacoma	18	163	2	3	13	.982
Kendall, SLC	44	377	21	4	41	.990	Johnson, Portland ..	64	526	38	11	53	.981
Pfeil, Eugene	15	100	1	1	10	.990	Linares, Phoenix ...	17	128	5	3	17	.978

Triple Plays—Hutton, Matias, Montanez.

(Fewer Than Ten Games)

Player and Club	G.	PO.	A.	E.	DP.	Pct.	Player and Club	G.	PO.	A.	E.	DP.	Pct.
Reichenbach, Tuc ..	8	79	2	0	12	1.000	Drake, Salt Lake C ..	1	2	1	0	1	1.000
F. Peters, Portland ..	7	56	8	0	10	1.000	Vukovich, Eugene ..	1	2	0	0	1	1.000
Hairston, Tacoma ..	4	45	1	0	3	1.000	Whitaker, Phoenix ..	1	2	0	0	1	1.000
Coward, Eugene ...	8	41	3	0	5	1.000	Amaro, Eugene	1	1	0	0	0	1.000
Christian, Tucson ..	6	30	4	0	5	1.000	Bates, Eugene	1	1	0	0	0	1.000
Gosger, Phoenix* ..	3	33	0	0	1	1.000	Nyman, SLC*	1	0	1	0	0	1.000
Winston, Tucson ...	3	23	1	0	2	1.000	Lis, Eugene	3	25	1	1	4	.963
Young, Tucson	4	23	0	0	3	1.000	Napier, Tucson	1	13	2	1	2	.938
Koegel, Portland ...	2	16	2	0	2	1.000	Wagner, Phoenix ...	1	11	0	1	0	.917
Lott, Spokane	2	14	0	0	0	1.000	Vaughns, Portland ..	2	9	0	1	0	.900
McLaughlin, Spo* ..	2	9	2	0	1	1.000	Hart, Phoenix	1	9	0	1	1	.900
Felske, Portland	1	9	0	0	1	1.000	Parrilla, Eugene ...	3	15	0	2	3	.882
Murphy, Tacoma ...	1	7	0	0	1	1.000	Vopicka, Eugene ...	1	1	0	1	0	.500
Lolich, Tucson	1	3	0	0	0	1.000							

SECOND BASEMEN

Player and Club	G.	PO.	A.	E.	DP.	Pct.
Gil, Portland	15	32	44	0	13	1.000
Linares, Phoenix	12	8	14	0	0	1.000
F. Peters, Portland	85	188	224	4	58	.990
McGuire, Tucson	77	203	250	6	64	.987
SCHRODER, Phoe	.109	240	283	10	69	.981
Vopicka, Eugene	.130	328	319	17	92	.974
Shirley, Spokane	.139	302	374	19	106	.973
Hriniak, SLC	.118	284	330	19	90	.970
Oliver, Tac-Haw	42	103	124	7	37	.970
Krawczyk, SLC	13	27	38	2	6	.970
Griffin, Hawaii	.134	295	330	23	82	.965
Young, Tucson	73	210	218	16	62	.964
Montreuil, Tacoma	54	110	149	10	35	.963
Stanley, Portland	19	37	42	3	6	.963
Donaldson, Port	15	33	43	3	6	.962
Kennedy, Portland	11	23	28	2	3	.962
Llenas, Hawaii	16	26	18	2	3	.957
Chacon, Portland	12	22	21	2	5	.956
Fenwick, Phoenix	46	76	87	8	17	.953
Sipin, Salt Lake City	14	35	24	3	4	.952
Sposito, Spokane	17	21	18	2	4	.951
Jestadt, Tacoma	58	135	133	14	41	.950
Pfeil, Eugene	15	25	20	3	8	.938
Galliher, Spokane	11	15	19	4	4	.895

Triple Plays—Vopicka, Young.

(Fewer Than Ten Games)

Player and Club	G.	PO.	A.	E.	DP.	Pct.
Kelly, Salt Lake City	2	3	8	0	1	1.000
Lund, Hawaii	1	3	3	0	0	1.000
Kelly, Eugene	5	14	9	1	4	.958
Oyler, Hawaii	2	2	8	1	1	.909
Coward, Eugene	6	10	15	3	4	.893
Garvey, Spokane	6	7	9	2	2	.889
Lopes, Spokane	3	3	9	2	0	.857
Wilkinson, Hawaii	1	0	0	1	0	.000

THIRD BASEMEN

Player and Club	G.	PO.	A.	E.	DP.	Pct.
F. Peters, Portland	14	9	16	0	1	1.000
Herrera, Portland	65	54	118	5	12	.972
Etheridge, SLC	31	27	70	4	11	.960
Reichenbach, Tuc	17	12	34	2	7	.958
VUKOVICH, Eug	.138	122	334	22	29	.954
Llenas, Hawaii	32	31	66	5	6	.951
Werhas, Hawaii	.110	106	224	18	24	.948
Kelly, Salt Lake City	70	41	155	11	22	.947
Sposito, Spokane	27	16	37	3	5	.946
Sipin, Salt Lake City	33	18	67	5	5	.944
Kenworthy, Tucson	89	49	195	15	18	.942
Blanco, Phoenix	28	21	59	5	5	.941
Russell, Spokane	19	11	35	3	3	.939
Hughes, Tacoma	47	40	96	9	12	.938
Montreuil, Tacoma	11	10	20	2	4	.938
Jestadt, Tacoma	22	19	40	4	1	.937
Lung, Tacoma	72	61	186	17	17	.936
Hart, Phoenix	53	30	81	8	4	.933
Linares, Phoenix	92	45	128	13	11	.930
Young, Tucson	23	16	57	6	5	.924
McGuire, Tucson	23	25	47	6	4	.923
Galliher, Spokane	20	13	32	4	2	.918
Garvey, Spokane	93	96	169	24	23	.917
Smith, Portland	14	10	23	3	1	.917
Donaldson, Port	17	13	36	5	3	.907
Kennedy, Portland	23	16	22	5	3	.884
Gil, Portland	12	6	15	4	1	.840
Schroder, Phoenix	11	3	7	2	0	.833

Triple Play—McGuire.

(Fewer Than Ten Games)

Player and Club	G.	PO.	A.	E.	DP.	Pct.
Huntz, Salt Lake City	7	6	15	0	1	1.000
Krawczyk, SLC	8	5	7	0	2	1.000
Vaughns, Portland	5	5	4	0	1	1.000
Lott, Spokane	2	2	5	0	0	1.000
Pfeil, Eugene	8	1	6	0	0	1.000
Drake, Salt Lake City	2	2	0	0	1	1.000
Chacon, Portland	3	1	3	0	1	1.000
Stinson, Spokane	2	0	3	0	0	1.000
Lis, Eugene	1	1	1	0	1	1.000
McGraw, Eugene	1	0	1	0	0	1.000
Sadek, Phoenix	1	0	1	0	0	1.000
Lund, Hawaii	7	4	11	1	0	.938
Murphy, Tacoma	4	5	4	2	0	.818
Fenwick, Phoenix	3	1	2	1	0	.750
Arnold, Phoenix	1	2	1	1	0	.750
Coward, Eugene	3	1	3	2	1	.667
F. Johnson, Phoenix	1	1	1	1	1	.667
Sogge, Spokane	1	0	1	1	0	.500

SHORTSTOPS

Player and Club	G.	PO.	A.	E.	DP.	Pct.
Stanley, Portland	64	110	181	10	37	.967
ROBLES, SLC	.143	211	472	31	67	.957
Pfeil, Eugene	52	79	158	11	33	.956
Perez, Hawaii	.100	141	313	22	55	.954
Blanco, Phoenix	.116	194	392	30	70	.951
Metzger, Tacoma	.133	212	483	37	88	.949
McKinney, Tucson	62	101	261	21	45	.945
Amaro, Eugene	.104	142	300	26	66	.944
Jestadt, Tacoma	12	20	23	3	3	.935
Auerbach, Portland	76	119	242	26	47	.933
Lund, Hawaii	48	60	137	15	26	.929
Valentine, Spokane	.146	217	474	54	106	.928
Fenwick, Phoenix	39	65	122	19	29	.908
Richard, Tucson	69	90	232	35	30	.902
Reichenbach, Tuc	18	23	63	14	12	.860

Triple Plays—Amaro, Richard, Valentine.

(Fewer Than Ten Games)

Player and Club	G.	PO.	A.	E.	DP.	Pct.
F. Peters, Portland	7	9	20	0	4	1.000
Lung, Tacoma	2	3	11	0	1	1.000
Griffin, Hawaii	5	4	7	0	2	1.000
Young, Tucson	1	2	4	0	1	1.000
Schroder, Phoenix	1	1	3	0	0	1.000
Linares, Phoenix	1	2	0	0	0	1.000
Arnold, Phoenix	1	1	1	0	0	1.000
Oliver, Hawaii	3	0	1	0	0	1.000
Russell, Spokane	1	1	0	0	0	1.000
Vopicka, Eugene	6	11	18	6	4	.829
Adams, Portland	3	2	7	2	0	.818
Jagutis, Eugene	2	0	7	2	1	.778
Coward, Eugene	1	0	0	1	0	.000

OUTFIELDERS

Player and Club	G.	PO.	A.	E.	DP.	Pct.
Koegel, Portland ...	49	88	4	0	0	1.000
Gamble, Eugene ...	26	54	3	0	1	1.000
Joshua, Spokane* ..	15	27	2	0	1	1.000
Jones, Portland ...	57	91	5	1	1	.990
Adams, Tucson ...	48	69	8	1	1	.987
Redmond, Hawaii ..	82	188	7	3	1	.985
MORALES, SLC ...	109	237	7	4	1	.984
Hiser, Tacoma ...	65	178	3	3	1	.984
Young, Tacoma ...	48	121	3	2	1	.984
Napier, Tucson ..	24	45	2	1	1	.979
Paciorek, Spokane .	145	262	5	6	0	.978
Lott, Spokane ...	67	87	3	2	1	.978
Lolich, Tucson ..	104	185	15	5	3	.976
Galliher, Spokane .	38	40	1	1	0	.976
McLaughlin, Spo* ..	33	39	0	1	0	.975
Silverio, Hawaii* ..	76	173	8	5	2	.973
Rosario, Phoenix ..	111	272	10	8	3	.972
Robinson, SLC* ...	130	231	12	7	2	.972
Davis, Tacoma* ..	131	204	8	6	0	.972
Christian, Tucson ..	51	99	7	3	1	.972
Buckner, Spokane* .	57	70	0	2	0	.972
Russell, Spokane ..	41	101	3	3	1	.972
Williams, Phoenix .	105	230	3	7	0	.971
Hicks, Hawaii ...	57	95	4	3	0	.971
Vaughns, Portland .	39	62	5	2	0	.971
Linares, Phoenix ..	29	31	3	1	0	.971
Ortiz, Tucson ..	142	309	16	10	2	.970
Wicker, Portland ..	109	239	12	8	3	.969
Wilkinson, Tacoma .	69	116	9	4	3	.969
Valdespino, Port* ..	51	87	4	3	1	.968
Montanez, Eugene* ..	16	29	1	1	0	.968
Barry, Hawaii ..	120	222	5	8	1	.966
Lis, Eugene	135	258	16	10	4	.965
McMath, Tacoma* ..	44	76	7	3	2	.965
Goossen, Portland ..	36	51	2	2	0	.964
Simpson, Phoenix ..	18	26	1	1	0	.964
Reid, Eugene	78	117	13	5	2	.963
DeCastris, Eugene .	97	238	9	10	0	.961
Smith, Portland ...	86	208	15	9	4	.961
Foster, Phoenix ..	111	202	5	9	2	.958
Pteil, Eugene	14	22	1	1	0	.958
Parrilla, Eugene ..	56	86	2	4	0	.957
Lopes, Spokane ...	98	199	10	10	1	.954
Williams, SLC ...	105	187	13	10	2	.952
Sipin, SLC	61	90	9	5	2	.952
Whitaker, Phoenix ..	65	111	4	6	1	.950
Schlesinger, Eugene	20	38	0	2	0	.950
DeNeff, Hawaii ...	17	36	1	2	0	.949
Llenas, Hawaii ...	95	163	3	10	0	.943
McKnight, Phoenix .	24	32	1	2	0	.943
Stahl, Salt Lake City*	19	29	3	2	0	.941
Hughes, Tacoma ...	44	66	11	5	1	.939
Reser, Tacoma ...	12	12	3	1	1	.938
Winston, Tucson ...	70	107	7	8	0	.934
Kelly, Eugene	10	26	0	2	0	.929
Coward, Eugene ...	10	13	0	1	0	.929
Tatum, Hawaii ...	13	20	0	2	0	.909
Murphy, Port-Tac ..	19	26	1	3	0	.900
McGraw, Eug-Haw .	13	23	1	3	1	.889
Stinson, Spokane ..	19	24	1	4	1	.862

Triple Play—Lolich.

(Fewer Than Ten Games)

Player and Club	G.	PO.	A.	E.	DP.	Pct.
Reichenbach, Tuc ..	4	16	0	0	0	1.000
Qualls, Tacoma ...	9	13	0	0	0	1.000
Chacon, Portland ..	6	13	0	0	0	1.000
Perez, Hawaii	4	10	0	0	0	1.000
Hairston, Tacoma ..	8	7	1	0	0	1.000
Spangler, Tacoma* .	8	7	0	0	0	1.000
Wagner, Phoenix ..	5	7	0	0	0	1.000
Thompson, SLC* ...	7	6	1	0	0	1.000
Herrera, Portland ..	8	6	1	0	0	1.000
Oliver, Tac-Haw ..	6	5	0	0	0	1.000
Hinton, Tucson* ...	1	5	0	0	0	1.000
Drake, Salt Lake City	5	4	0	0	0	1.000
Brandon, Tucson ..	2	4	0	0	0	1.000
Christino, Spokane* .	4	3	1	0	0	1.000
Sadek, Phoenix	3	3	0	0	0	1.000
Pentland, SLC*	5	2	0	0	0	1.000
Hart, Phoenix	2	2	0	0	0	1.000
Gosger, Phoenix* ..	1	2	0	0	0	1.000
Hibbs, Tacoma	1	2	0	0	0	1.000
Perry, Portland ...	2	2	0	0	0	1.000
Stephenson, Phoe ..	2	1	0	0	0	1.000
Stanley, Portland ..	1	1	0	0	0	1.000
Howard, Portland ..	6	18	1	1	0	.950
Blanco, Tucson ...	6	10	1	1	0	.917
Bobb, Portland ...	5	5	1	1	0	.857

CATCHERS

Player and Club	G.	PO.	A.	E.	DP.	PB.	Pct.
Kendall, SLC ...	65	352	31	0	6	16	1.000
Brown, Hawaii ..	21	127	11	0	1	4	1.000
Harrell, Phoe ...	17	104	7	0	0	3	1.000
Bobb, Portland ..	11	67	3	0	0	1	1.000
Napier, Tucson ..	11	59	5	0	1	2	1.000
Jacobsen, Phoe ..	41	198	18	1	3	9	.995
Merrill, Eugene ..	41	176	21	1	2	2	.995
Hairston, Tac ...	30	156	18	1	3	4	.994
Heath, Tacoma ..	27	126	17	1	2	4	.993
Hibbs, Tacoma ..	47	222	32	2	3	2	.992
Bates, Eugene ...	37	199	22	2	2	9	.991
STINSON, Spo ..	73	447	43	5	6	19	.990
Felske, Portland .	125	769	60	10	7	16	.988
Sogge, Spokane ..	79	470	42	6	3	32	.988
Ranew, Hawaii ..	91	561	55	8	7	15	.987
Drake, SLC	81	416	51	6	8	18	.987
Brinkman, Tuc ..	116	631	75	10	11	17	.986
Cox, Eugene	15	62	6	1		3	.986
Adams, Tucson ..	29	113	14	2	0	3	.984
Adlesh, Hawaii ..	46	229	9	4	2	6	.983
Compton, Eugene .	27	149	12	3	1	2	.982
Baca, SLC	13	40	5	1	0	1	.978
Stephenson, Phx .	41	269	18	7	3	5	.975
Sadek, Phoenix ..	68	351	36	10	3	12	.975
McGraw, Eugene .	36	200	18	7	1	6	.969
Saul, Tacoma ...	26	125	14	5	0	3	.965
Dudek, Tacoma ..	20	97	5	5	0	3	.953

Triple Plays—Adams, Bates.

(Fewer Than Ten Games)

Player and Club	G.	PO.	A.	E.	DP.	PB.	Pct.
Wallin, Port	8	40	3	0	0	2	1.000
Murphy, Port-Tac .	6	28	2	0	0	1	1.000
Francis, Eug	4	18	2	0	0	0	1.000
Hriniak, SLC	1	1	0	0	0	0	1.000
Schroder, Phx ...	1	1	0	0	0	1	1.000
Koegel, Port	6	29	2	1	0	1	.969
Pfeil, Eugene ...	6	10	3	1	0	2	.929

PITCHERS

Player and Club	G.	PO.	A.	E.	DP.	Pct.
SHELDON, Tuc-SLC	34	8	31	0	4	1.000
Champion, Eugene .	23	11	22	0	3	1.000
Lauzerique, Port ..	21	11	20	0	3	1.000
Stephenson, Spo ..	28	4	26	0	0	1.000
O'Brien, Spokane* .	29	5	23	0	4	1.000
J. Johnson, Phoenix*.	22	4	22	0	0	1.000
Sukla, Haw-Eug ..	39	6	16	0	5	1.000
Puente, Phoenix ...	13	4	18	0	0	1.000
Dunegan, Tacoma ..	15	5	15	0	1	1.000
Arlin, Salt Lake C ..	16	8	11	0	1	1.000
Moloney, Tucson ..	25	4	13	0	2	1.000
Allen, Hawaii*	33	4	13	0	3	1.000
Carrithers, Phoenix .	24	2	15	0	3	1.000
Costello, Phoenix ..	45	3	11	0	2	1.000

PITCHERS—Continued

Player and Club	G.	PO.	A.	E.	DP.	Pct.	Player and Club	G.	PO.	A.	E.	DP.	Pct.
Ortega, Hawaii	15	5	8	0	1	1.000	Frost, Phoenix	24	8	7	1	1	.938
Baldschun, SLC	41	3	9	0	0	1.000	Gura, Tacoma*	10	4	11	1	0	.938
Bollo, Tucson	19	2	10	0	1	1.000	Albury, SLC*	21	3	12	1	0	.938
Knutson, Eugene*	21	3	8	0	0	1.000	Strahler, Spokane	28	13	31	3	3	.936
Raffo, Eugene	15	3	8	0	0	1.000	Hamilton, Tucson	20	5	21	2	0	.929
Click, Portland	24	2	9	0	0	1.000	Pizarro, Hawaii*	13	1	12	1	0	.929
Wolf, Hawaii	12	4	6	0	0	1.000	Sherrod, Tacoma	27	4	21	2	2	.926
Ogier, Salt Lake C	12	3	7	0	1	1.000	Reynolds, Hawaii	14	8	16	2	0	.923
Staab, Spokane*	17	2	8	0	2	1.000	Colton, Tacoma	32	11	24	3	3	.921
Castiglione, SLC	14	2	8	0	1	1.000	Hough, Spokane	49	7	28	3	3	.921
Ferrell, Portland	34	3	6	0	0	1.000	Church, Tacoma	41	9	14	2	1	.920
Kealey, Hawaii	24	2	7	0	0	1.000	Fitzer, Tacoma	18	1	10	1	0	.917
Eddy, Tucson *	34	1	8	0	2	1.000	Rath, Tucson	14	0	11	1	0	.917
Lanning, Eugene*	18	0	9	0	1	1.000	Nutter, Eugene	26	6	15	2	2	.913
Faul, Phoenix	36	1	7	0	1	1.000	Burk, Tacoma	31	8	22	3	3	.909
Vance, Spokane	13	0	8	0	1	1.000	Scharringhausen, SLC	59	7	13	2	1	.909
Pentland, SLC*	20	2	5	0	2	1.000	Tompkins, Portland	19	1	9	1	0	.909
Kline, Hawaii	15	2	5	0	1	1.000	LeMay, Tacoma*	13	8	21	3	0	.906
Newman, Tacoma *.	14	1	6	0	1	1.000	R. Peters, Portland	25	7	22	3	1	.906
Kroll, Hawaii	16	0	6	0	0	1.000	Washburn, Hawaii	24	9	19	3	1	.903
Bailey, Salt Lake C	20	3	2	0	0	1.000	Purdin, Spo-Haw	36	8	19	3	2	.900
Wilson, Eugene	11	1	4	0	0	1.000	Davison, Phoenix*	15	2	7	1	0	.900
Baldwin, Portland	15	0	5	0	1	1.000	Twitchell, Portland	27	6	18	3	0	.889
Pena, Spokane	10	0	5	0	1	1.000	Sanders, Portland	14	2	14	2	1	.889
Weaver, Tucson	15	1	3	0	0	1.000	Wolfe, Eugene	19	1	7	1	1	.889
LaRoche, Hawaii*	22	0	4	0	0	1.000	Johnson, Tucson	10	0	7	1	0	.875
Wenz, Eugene	13	0	4	0	0	1.000	Fast, Tac-SLC*	24	4	23	4	1	.871
Willoughby, Phx	29	11	36	1	0	.979	Rounsaville, Tucson	27	4	16	3	1	.870
Alexander, Spokane	19	13	31	1	1	.978	Messerly, Eugene	60	10	9	3	3	.864
Brandon, Tucson	35	17	22	1	2	.975	Nyman, SLC*	37	6	19	4	0	.862
Hinton, Tucson*	31	11	21	1	3	.970	Harrison, Portland	31	7	11	3	1	.857
Moyer, Phoenix	33	11	20	1	1	.969	Coates, Hawaii	47	2	16	3	0	.857
Bennett, Hawaii*	33	4	23	1	3	.964	Pitlock, Phoenix*	13	2	10	2	0	.857
Wynne, Tucson	20	10	16	1	1	.963	Lemonds, Tacoma*..	22	2	18	4	1	.833
Jackson, Eugene*	28	8	18	1	2	.963	Gray, Salt Lake City	15	1	4	1	0	.833
Knuckles, SLC	41	7	19	1	1	.963	Fisher, Portland	34	4	5	2	0	.818
Brubaker, Portland	32	21	29	2	1	.962	Edgerton, Portland*	37	2	5	2	0	.778
James, Eugene	34	12	13	1	2	.962	Borunda, SLC	17	1	6	2	0	.778
Shank, Hawaii	40	6	19	1	0	.962	Jenkins, Spokane	34	2	11	4	0	.765
Cosman, Tacoma	51	6	17	1	3	.958	Scarpati, Spokane	11	0	6	2	0	.750
Reynolds, Eugene*	29	5	32	2	3	.949	Roberts, Haw-Eug*	11	1	2	1	0	.750
Secrist, Tucson*	21	3	15	1	1	.947	Armstrong, Spokane	36	3	5	3	0	.727
Bradley, Hawaii	16	10	25	2	3	.946	Huggins, Portland*	13	2	3	2	0	.714
Garibaldi, Phx	32	17	29	3	4	.939	Zahn, Spokane*	27	2	5	3	0	.700

(Fewer Than Ten Games)

Player and Club	G.	PO.	A.	E.	DP.	Pct.	Player and Club	G.	PO.	A.	E.	DP.	Pct.
McBean, Eugene	7	6	9	0	1	1.000	Timberlake, Port*	8	0	2	0	0	1.000
Ross, Salt Lake City	8	5	7	0	0	1.000	Corkins, SLC	5	0	2	0	0	1.000
Santorini, SLC	6	3	7	0	1	1.000	Herron, Eugene	4	0	2	0	0	1.000
Lockwood, Portland	5	3	7	0	1	1.000	Stephen, Portland	4	1	0	0	0	1.000
Crider, Tucson	5	1	8	0	0	1.000	Coward, Eugene	2	1	0	0	0	1.000
Baney, Portland	9	4	3	0	0	1.000	Vega, Salt Lake City	2	1	0	0	0	1.000
Zinniger, SLC*	7	0	7	0	0	1.000	Cisterna, SLC	7	0	1	0	0	1.000
Mulcahey, SLC	4	4	2	0	0	1.000	Bates, Portland	3	0	1	0	0	1.000
Bell, Hawaii	5	0	6	0	0	1.000	Nottebart, Tacoma	3	0	1	0	0	1.000
Bielski, SLC	4	3	2	0	0	1.000	Jacquez, Tacoma	6	4	9	1	1	.929
Arrigo, Tucson*	9	1	4	0	0	1.000	Cumberland, Phx*	7	2	5	1	0	.875
Stone, Phoenix	8	1	4	0	0	1.000	Laxton, Eugene*	9	1	6	1	0	.875
Distaso, Tacoma	7	1	3	0	1	1.000	Barber, Tacoma*	4	1	5	1	0	.857
Parsons, Portland	4	1	3	0	0	1.000	Bryant, Phoenix*	7	0	6	1	1	.857
Lazar, Tucson*	6	0	3	0	0	1.000	Clark, Hawaii	5	0	4	1	0	.800
Kelley, Salt Lake C*.	1	0	3	0	0	1.000	Humphreys, Portland	5	0	3	1	1	.750
Mariscal, Spokane*	6	1	1	0	0	1.000	Perzanowski, Tuc	4	0	2	0	0	.500
James, Tacoma	3	1	1	0	0	1.000	Face, Hawaii	8	1	0	1	0	.500

The following players do not have any recorded accepted chances at the positions indicated; therefore, are not listed in the fielding averages for those particular positions: D. Bates, of; Bradley, of; Chacon, ss; Garvey, of; Hough, 1b-of; Jenkins, of; Jones, 1b; Katawczik*, p; Kendall, 3b; Kline, 3b; Krawczyk, ss; Loughlin*, p; McGuire, c; Napier, p; Purdin, of; Ranew, of; Rau*, p; Rosario, 3b; Sheldon, 1b-3b; Sposito, ss; Valentine, 2b; Ward*, of; Zahn*, 1b.

CLUB PITCHING

Club	G.	CG.	ShO.	Sv.	IP.	H.	R.	ER.	HR.	BB.	Int. BB.	HB.	SO.	WP.	Bk.	ERA.
Phoenix	146	57	10	26	1288	1279	558	460	64	419	57	27	860	36	6	3.21
Spokane	146	42	13	41	1282	1215	590	471	72	520	46	29	881	74	4	3.31
Hawaii	147	44	9	38	1280	1242	595	528	114	443	57	26	886	53	8	3.70
Tuscon	147	49	5	24	1281	1362	631	531	92	419	36	30	747	48	6	3.73
Eugene	146	33	6	22	1246	1322	743	631	100	575	52	35	780	72	4	4.56
Portland	146	33	11	24	1249	1376	747	642	105	560	47	48	852	68	7	4.63
Tacoma	143	29	9	19	1221	1361	754	652	107	487	44	44	658	81	4	4.81
Salt Lake City	143	21	5	26	1203	1411	813	715	125	625	85	23	771	75	12	5.35

PITCHERS' RECORDS

(Leading Qualifiers for Earned-Run Average Leadership—146 or More Innings)

*Throws lefthanded.

Pitcher—Club	G.	GS.	CG.	ShO.	W.	L.	Sv.	Pct.	IP.	H.	R.	ER.	HR.	BB.	Int. BB.	HB.	SO.	WP.	ERA.
Stephenson, Spo	28	28	7	3	18	5	0	.783	182	155	75	57	11	82	3	2	151	10	2.82
Garibaldi, Phx	32	32	20	3	15	10	0	.600	254	248	105	81	15	52	7	3	131	3	2.87
Strahler, Spokane	28	28	7	0	15	5	0	.750	175	155	66	58	4	87	4	5	100	9	2.98
Purdin, 25Sp-11Ha	36	25	9	2	11	10	5	.524	177	172	71	60	6	51	10	3	119	10	3.05
Moyer, Phoenix	33	30	10	3	12	14	0	.462	206	189	88	74	11	82	7	1	149	8	3.23
Willoughby, Phx	29	26	9	1	11	9	0	.550	190	211	84	69	8	39	5	2	116	6	3.27
O'Brien, Spokane*	29	27	9	4	13	3	0	.813	164	163	71	62	13	52	2	3	117	7	3.40
K. Reynolds, Eug*	29	28	12	1	13	10	0	.565	202	175	95	77	18	106	2	0	143	9	3.43
Brandon, Tucson	35	28	14	2	15	10	0	.600	214	211	106	93	23	83	2	13	167	8	3.91
Hinton, Tucson*	31	30	7	1	10	12	0	.455	196	216	106	88	11	43	3	1	103	3	4.04

Departmental Leaders: G—Messerly, 60; GS—Bennett, Garibaldi, 32; CG—Garibaldi, 20; ShO—O'Brien, 4; W—Bennett, Stephenson, 18; L—Colton, J. James, Moyer, 14; Sv—Hough, 18; Pct.—O'Brien, .813; IP—Garibaldi, 254; H—Garibaldi, 248; R—J. James, 121; ER—Colton, 104; HR—Bennett, 27; BB—K. Reynolds, 106; IBB—Nyman, 16; HB—Brandon, J. James, 13; SO—Brandon, 167; WP—Colton, 17.

(All Pitchers—Listed Alphabetically)

Pitcher—Club	G.	GS.	CG.	ShO.	W.	L.	Sv.	Pct.	IP.	H.	R.	ER.	HR.	BB.	Int. BB.	HB.	SO.	WP.	ERA.
Albury, SLC*	21	5	1	1	2	4	0	.333	47	69	47	44	9	33	3	1	27	1	8.43
Alexander, Spo	19	19	9	1	9	7	0	.563	137	137	66	55	8	26	2	3	78	3	3.61
Allen, Hawaii*	33	0	0	0	6	1	5	.857	52	57	23	20	3	22	7	0	18	5	3.46
Arlin, SLC	16	14	4	0	5	7	0	.417	87	99	67	59	6	50	6	1	52	5	6.10
Armstrong, Spo	36	1	0	0	4	5	9	.444	58	47	24	19	4	33	6	2	50	4	2.95
Arrigo, Tucson*	9	7	1	0	3	3	0	.500	38	50	28	26	6	16	1	2	18	4	6.16
Bailey, SLC	20	0	0	0	2	4	0	.333	40	50	34	25	8	21	3	2	26	0	5.63
Baldschun, SLC	41	0	0	0	4	7	15	.364	60	56	28	24	4	24	3	0	62	6	3.60
Baldwin, Portland	15	0	0	0	1	4	5	.200	27	22	10	4	0	13	3	2	28	2	1.33
Baney, Portland	9	3	0	1	1	1	0	.500	29	40	18	16	2	13	1	2	11	0	4.97
Barber, Tacoma*	4	5	1	1	1	1	0	.500	29	26	7	5	0	7	0	3	17	0	1.55
Bates, Portland	3	0	0	0	1	0	0	.000	7	12	5	5	0	0	0	0	2	0	6.43
Bell, Hawaii	5	5	0	0	0	2	0	.000	26	34	26	24	6	13	1	1	14	1	8.31
Bennett, Hawaii*	33	32	9	0	18	8	0	.692	200	228	106	100	27	44	1	3	145	5	4.50
Bielski, SLC	4	3	0	0	1	0	0	.000	15	18	14	13	3	18	2	0	5	1	7.80
Bollo, Tucson	19	3	0	0	2	1	0	.667	44	52	38	30	3	29	0	3	30	5	6.14
Borunda, SLC	17	12	1	0	0	9	1	.000	50	87	53	50	5	39	4	1	31	5	9.00
Bradley, Hawaii	16	16	7	2	11	1	0	.917	114	96	37	32	1	32	1	0	92	5	2.53
Brandon, Tucson	35	28	14	2	15	10	0	.600	214	211	106	93	23	83	2	13	167	8	3.91
Brubaker, Portland	32	30	6	1	9	12	0	.429	200	231	107	94	16	46	5	5	121	10	4.11
Bryant, Phoenix*	7	4	1	0	1	2	0	.333	29	38	21	19	4	8	0	0	24	2	5.90
Burk, Tacoma	31	18	0	0	2	11	0	.154	106	130	89	78	14	50	3	5	48	6	6.62
Carrithers, Phoenix	24	2	1	0	9	1	1	.900	67	70	19	16	0	20	6	2	52	2	2.15
Castiglione, SLC	14	5	1	0	2	3	0	.400	41	32	14	13	2	13	0	5	24	1	2.85
Champion, Eugene	23	23	7	0	8	11	0	.421	152	165	99	84	9	70	6	3	96	10	4.97
Church, Tacoma	41	10	1	1	2	7	1	.222	102	128	60	53	6	29	2	0	49	6	4.68
Cisterna, SLC	7	0	0	0	1	0	0	1.000	11	11	3	3	1	5	2	0	6	0	2.45
Clark, Hawaii	5	5	0	0	0	1	0	.000	17	19	16	16	3	15	0	0	15	1	8.47
Click, Portland	24	1	0	0	4	3	0	.571	67	85	34	31	3	21	3	2	45	2	4.16
Coates, Hawaii	47	7	2	1	8	5	17	.615	109	86	40	34	9	45	10	3	73	6	2.81
Colton, Tacoma	32	28	12	2	12	14	1	.462	221	226	116	104	24	76	7	2	118	17	4.24
Corkins, SLC	5	5	1	0	3	1	0	.750	35	23	6	5	2	6	0	0	34	0	1.29
Cosman, SLC	1	1	0	0	0	3	5	1	.375	77	95	58	52	5	32	6	0	38	9	6.08
Costello, Phoenix	15	0	0	0	6	2	4	.750	70	72	28	23	2	24	7	4	42	1	2.96
Coward, Eugene	2	0	0	0	0	0	0	.000	7	8	3	3	0	2	1	0	2	0	3.86
Crider, Tucson	5	4	2	1	3	0	0	1.000	36	34	10	8	0	15	1	0	15	0	2.00
Cumberland, Phoe*	7	7	0	0	0	3	0	.000	42	53	27	22	2	12	1	0	19	1	4.71
Davison, Phoenix*	15	0	0	0	2	1	6	.667	20	16	5	2	0	8	4	0	10	1	0.90
Distaso, Tacoma	7	3	0	0	0	5	0	.000	14	37	29	26	3	8	1	2	5	1	16.71
Dunegan, Tacoma	15	15	4	0	5	7	0	.417	105	121	67	64	13	62	2	7	61	7	5.49
Eddy, Tucson*	34	1	0	0	10	4	9	.714	59	41	10	9	2	21	3	0	36	2	1.37
Edgerton, Port*	37	1	0	0	3	3	6	.500	55	59	29	23	2	31	3	3	31	3	3.76
Face, Hawaii	8	1	0	0	1	1	0	1.000	10	10	5	5	1	3	0	0	9	0	4.50
Fast, 5 Tac- 19 Hawaii	24	20	2	0	2	13	0	.133	108	128	87	60	13	62	4	3	64	7	5.00
Faul, Phoenix	36	0	0	0	4	2	12	.667	46	39	12	11	2	19	5	5	34	2	2.15
Ferrell, Portland	34	1	0	0	1	4	4	.200	54	62	35	30	5	22	3	1	41	3	5.00
Fisher, Portland	34	1	0	0	2	4	3	.333	51	70	42	35	5	17	2	0	31	1	6.18
Fitzer, Tacoma	18	10	0	0	4	7	0	.364	73	81	39	35	4	25	2	2	36	8	4.32
Frost, Phoenix	24	2	0	0	1	3	1	.250	42	49	28	25	3	18	2	0	21	1	5.36
Garibaldi, Phoe	32	32	20	3	15	10	0	.600	254	248	105	81	15	52	7	3	131	3	2.87
Gray, SLC	15	4	0	0	1	4	0	.500	26	40	25	25	4	19	3	2	20	5	8.65
Gura, Tacoma*	10	10	2	2	3	4	0	.429	61	55	32	27	4	17	3	3	32	1	3.98
Hamilton, Tucson	30	13	5	0	5	7	2	.417	119	118	56	45	3	54	4	2	75	6	3.40
Harrison, Portland	31	25	4	2	6	11	0	.353	152	183	112	94	15	98	7	9	102	10	5.57
Herron, Eugene	4	0	0	0	1	0	1	1.000	7	2	0	0	0	2	0	0	3	0	0.00

Pitcher—Club	G.	GS.	CG.	ShO.	W.	L.	Sv.	Pct.	IP.	H.	R.	ER.	HR.	BB.	Int. BB.	HB.	SO.	WP.	ERA.
Hinton, Tucson*	31	30	7	1	10	12	0	.455	196	216	106	88	11	43	3	1	103	3	4.04
Hough, Spokane	49	3	2	0	12	8	18	.600	134	98	43	29	8	44	6	6	90	3	1.95
Huggins, Portland*	13	5	0	0	1	0	1	1.000	36	27	17	12	0	26	1	3	22	1	3.00
Humphreys, Port	6	1	1	0	0	2	0	.000	17	13	6	5	0	9	4	2	13	0	2.65
Jackson, Eugene*	28	24	6	1	8	10	0	.444	164	168	92	85	16	82	4	0	117	4	4.66
Jacquez, Tacoma	6	6	1	0	1	4	0	.200	37	42	25	25	4	18	1	3	20	1	6.08
J. James, Eugene	34	26	4	2	6	14	2	.300	156	182	121	103	8	79	5	13	99	13	5.94
R. James, Tacoma	3	1	0	0	0	1	0	.000	4	10	9	9	1	3	0	0	0	2	20.25
Jenkins, Spokane	34	5	0	0	4	2	3	.667	95	101	58	43	2	65	6	0	67	9	4.07
C. Johnson, Tucson	10	7	5	0	6	3	0	.667	61	61	25	19	3	22	1	0	50	0	2.80
J. Johnson, Phoe	22	10	2	0	6	5	2	.545	83	95	59	47	8	45	9	5	71	3	5.10
Katawczik, SLC*	3	1	0	0	1	0	0	.000	3	8	6	6	1	1	0	1	0	1	18.00
Kealey, Hawaii*	24	3	1	1	4	3	7	.571	57	53	24	22	2	10	2	1	48	0	3.47
Kelley, SLC*	1	1	0	0	0	1	0	.000	4	4	1	1	0	3	1	0	2	0	2.25
Kline, Hawaii	15	3	0	0	4	0	0	1.000	33	34	14	12	0	20	5	1	17	2	3.27
Knuckles, SLC	41	10	2	0	2	9	3	.182	122	144	80	74	10	84	11	1	87	10	5.46
Knutson, Eugene*	21	9	2	1	2	5	1	.286	61	52	26	25	3	27	6	0	46	4	3.69
Kroll, Hawaii	16	2	0	0	1	0	0	1.000	28	28	22	14	3	20	0	2	29	4	4.50
Lanning, Eugene*	18	7	0	0	2	1	0	.667	51	61	36	32	11	24	0	1	17	1	5.65
LaRoche, Hawaii*	22	1	0	0	0	0	5	1.000	58	31	11	8	2	19	3	0	67	4	1.24
Lauzerique, Port	21	18	6	0	8	6	1	.571	122	135	80	75	17	49	3	5	86	11	5.53
Laxton, Eugene*	9	5	0	0	1	3	0	.250	37	36	24	23	0	32	0	5	39	4	5.59
Lazar, Tucson*	6	6	0	0	2	0	0	.000	37	48	20	13	3	9	2	0	16	4	3.16
LeMay, Tacoma*	53	0	0	0	6	10	13	.375	103	103	53	46	8	32	7	2	61	7	4.02
Lemonds, Tacoma	22	22	5	1	5	9	0	.357	137	134	85	62	10	65	4	3	106	7	4.07
Lockwood, Portland	5	5	4	1	4	1	0	.800	34	29	13	10	1	9	1	1	24	0	2.65
Loughlin, Hawaii*	10	0	0	0	2	1	0	.667	13	16	7	3	2	7	1	0	8	1	2.08
Mariscal, Spokane*	6	2	1	1	2	0	0	1.000	15	5	1	1	0	7	1	5	1	1	2	4.20
McBean, Eugene	7	6	1	0	3	3	0	.500	34	43	24	19	4	12	0	0	15	0	5.03
Messerly, Eugene	60	1	0	0	7	8	8	.467	105	116	46	34	4	46	14	2	49	12	2.91
Moloney, Tucson	25	0	0	0	3	2	4	.600	43	55	22	21	1	16	4	0	16	1	4.40
Moyer, Phoenix	33	30	10	3	12	14	0	.462	206	189	88	74	11	82	7	1	149	8	3.23
Mulcahey, SLC	4	0	0	0	0	0	0	.000	14	16	9	9	2	6	0	0	7	3	5.79
Napier, Tucson	1	0	0	0	0	0	0	.000	4	5	2	2	1	2	0	0	2	1	4.50
Newman, Tacoma*	14	1	0	0	1	0	2	1.000	25	25	8	7	1	11	1	0	21	4	2.52
Nottebart, Tacoma	3	0	0	0	0	0	0	.000	4	8	6	6	0	5	0	0	2	0	13.50
Nutter, Eugene	26	11	1	1	5	7	1	.417	104	118	70	49	9	30	3	3	53	2	4.24
Nyman, SLC*	37	29	7	2	9	13	2	.409	187	200	100	85	13	99	16	3	101	8	4.09
O'Brien, Spokane*	29	27	9	4	13	3	0	.813	164	163	71	62	13	52	2	3	117	7	3.40
Ogier, SLC	12	8	0	0	1	6	0	.143	39	41	42	38	7	29	3	0	19	10	8.77
Ortega, Hawaii	15	9	0	0	2	5	1	.286	51	53	24	22	9	18	5	1	25	2	3.88
Parsons, Portland	4	4	2	2	3	0	0	1.000	28	19	7	7	1	10	0	1	26	0	2.25
Pena, Spokane	10	1	0	0	2	2	5	.500	25	24	12	9	3	9	0	2	20	6	3.24
Pentland, SLC*	20	0	0	0	0	0	0	.000	47	59	34	30	6	17	0	1	28	1	5.74
Perzanowski, Tucson	4	2	1	0	0	1	0	.000	13	13	11	9	0	11	1	2	13	1	6.23
R. Peters, Portland	25	24	6	2	7	10	0	.412	134	144	93	86	19	72	3	4	109	11	5.78
Pitlock, Phoenix*	13	13	8	1	10	3	0	.769	106	78	34	29	4	43	1	2	92	1	2.46
Pizarro, Hawaii*	13	12	4	1	9	0	0	1.000	89	78	33	32	9	22	2	0	67	1	3.24
Puente, Phoenix	13	12	2	0	3	3	0	.500	75	75	35	31	1	26	2	3	49	3	3.72
Purdin, 25Sp-11Ha	36	25	9	2	11	10	5	.524	177	172	71	60	6	51	10	3	119	10	3.05
Raffo, Eugene	15	0	0	0	3	1	0	.750	22	27	20	15	3	16	4	3	7	4	6.14
Rath, Tucson	14	4	1	0	2	2	0	.500	47	55	25	22	4	14	3	1	25	2	4.21
Rau, Spokane*	1	1	0	0	0	0	0	.000	1	7	6	5	0	0	0	0	1	1	45.00
A. Reynolds, Haw	14	12	6	1	7	3	0	.700	103	88	35	30	7	37	2	2	72	1	2.62
K. Reynolds, Eug*	29	28	12	1	13	10	0	.565	202	175	95	77	18	106	2	0	143	9	3.43
Roberts, 4 Haw- 7 Eug	11	0	0	0	2	1	0	.000	15	23	14	13	3	4	1	2	6	1	7.80
Ross, SLC	8	8	0	1	4	0	0	.200	45	63	34	29	2	16	3	1	24	4	5.80
Rounsaville, Tuc	27	8	1	0	3	5	5	.375	91	101	45	33	8	17	2	3	25	1	3.26
Sanders, Portland	14	0	0	0	4	1	2	.800	34	21	5	4	0	10	3	0	21	4	1.06
Santorini, SLC	6	3	0	0	2	2	0	.500	40	47	18	17	1	16	0	1	31	0	3.83
Scarpati, Spokane	11	0	0	0	1	0	0	1.000	28	31	17	14	2	9	0	0	20	2	4.50
Scharringhausen, SLC	59	1	0	0	5	7	3	.417	83	103	54	50	10	29	12	1	51	2	5.42
Secrist, Tucson*	21	11	4	0	3	7	0	.300	99	108	52	46	9	25	1	1	70	3	4.18
Shank, Hawaii	40	6	2	0	7	3	2	.700	82	79	47	39	8	36	10	5	60	4	4.28
Sheldon, 10 Tuc- 24 SLC	34	16	0	0	3	10	2	.231	127	160	85	75	15	48	8	3	75	10	5.31
Sherrod, Tacoma	27	7	2	0	9	1	0	.000	104	114	52	40	8	32	4	1	33	2	3.46
Staab, Spokane*	17	2	0	0	1	4	1	.200	28	32	18	16	2	16	4	1	15	6	5.14
Stephen, Portland	4	0	0	0	0	0	0	.000	4	4	4	4	0	3	0	0	1	0	9.00
Stephenson, Spo	28	28	7	3	18	5	0	.783	182	155	75	57	11	82	3	2	151	10	2.82
Stone, Phoenix	8	8	1	5	3	0	0	.625	58	46	13	11	4	23	1	0	52	1	1.71
Strahler, Spokane	23	28	7	0	15	5	0	.750	175	155	66	58	4	87	4	5	100	9	2.98
Sukla, 3 Haw- 36 Eug	39	0	0	0	4	2	4	.667	55	63	28	27	5	9	2	2	29	0	4.42
Timberlake, Port*	8	1	0	0	0	2	0	.000	21	28	13	11	4	7	1	1	11	0	4.71
Tompkins, Portland	19	0	0	0	5	3	2	.625	29	27	11	9	2	17	4	2	24	0	2.79
Twitchell, Portland	27	26	4	2	9	12	0	.429	144	163	106	87	13	93	2	6	103	10	5.44
Vance, Spokane	13	12	3	1	5	4	0	.556	89	83	39	28	5	29	3	0	67	7	2.83
Vega, SLC	2	2	0	0	0	0	0	.000	7	11	6	6	3	1	0	0	5	0	7.71

Pitcher—Club	G.	GS.	CG.	ShO.	W.	L.	Sv.	Pct.	IP.	H.	R.	ER.	HR.	BB.	Int. BB.	HB.	SO.	WP.	ERA.
Washburn, Hawaii ..	24	22	7	0	8	8	0	.500	140	142	80	72	16	42	1	3	63	4	4.63
Weaver, Tucson ...	15	0	0	0	4	1	3	.800	22	18	6	3	0	4	2	0	12	0	1.23
Wenz, Eugene	13	0	0	0	1	1	1	.500	16	9	5	5	0	9	2	0	14	2	2.81
Willoughby, Phoe .	29	26	9	1	11	9	0	.550	190	211	84	69	8	39	5	2	116	6	3.27
Wilson, Eugene ...	11	0	0	0	1	1	2	.500	20	27	15	13	2	13	1	0	17	3	5.85
Wolf, Hawaii	12	0	0	0	0	1	0	.000	19	18	12	11	3	13	0	1	16	2	5.21
Wolfe, Eugene ...	19	2	0	0	1	2	1	.333	45	62	34	33	6	17	3	3	30	4	6.60
Wynne, Tucson ..	20	16	8	1	11	2	1	.846	117	121	55	35	8	33	6	1	58	2	2.69
Zahn, Spokane* ..	27	3	1	0	1	1	0	.500	53	67	41	32	5	32	3	2	22	1	5.43
Zinniger, SLC* ..	7	5	0	0	0	3	0	.000	25	23	18	16	7	11	2	0	18	4	5.76

BALKS—Borunda, Brubaker, Colton, Fast, Faul, Huggins, Sheldon, 2 each; Arrigo, Bailey, Bennett, Bollo, Cisterna, Click, Coates, Cosman, Crider, Gray, J. Johnson, LaRoche, Laxton, Lazar, Loughlin, Mariscal, Messerly, Moloney, Moyer, Nutter, Nyman, Ogier, Ortega, Pentland, Peters, Puente, Purdin, Raffo, Rounsaville, Stephenson, Strahler, Twitchell, Washburn, Willoughby, Wolf, Zahn, Zinniger, 1 each.

COMBINATION SHUTOUTS—Bennett-Kealey, Bradley-LaRoche, Hawaii; Willoughby-Carrithers, Phoenix; Brubaker-Baldwin, Portland; Castiglione-Scharringhausen-Baldschun, Nyman-Baldschun, Salt Lake City; Strahler-Hough, Strahler-Purdin, Spokane; Fitzer-Cosman-LeMay, Lemonds-LeMay, Tacoma.

NO-HIT GAMES—Jackson, Eugene, defeated Tucson, 5-0, June 11 (seven innings).

ALONG THE MINOR LEAGUE TRAIL . . . .

(Continued from page 430)

new Blues' manager, Johnny Antonelli. "I used to get my share of hits off you," quipped Mizell, "and you got yours off me, Johnny." The wild pitch was that the Johnny Antonelli he was talking to was the former infielder of the Cardinals and Phillies, not the Johnny Antonelli who faced Wilmer as a pitcher for the Braves and Giants. . . . Another politician blew one when Iowa Governor Robert Ray urged the spectators to support the "Iowa Hawks." Of course, the Iowa "Oaks" didn't take the error too kindly—in fact, five errors cropped up in the American Association game that followed. . . . In the same league. Jim Burris, Denver's g.m., solved his crowd control problem before any mass exodus from the stands ever began—he obtained a live bear to keep on display. . . . Way out in Hawaii (Pacific Coast), Jarvis Tatum started out like the bear was chasing him. In the season opener, he slammed a bases-loaded homer and a solo in the eighth inning, hit one the next day and also the next. . . . Danny Rivas of Columbus (International) didn't take his eyes off his catcher until he left for Mexico. It seems that catcher Gary Kolb, just before the opener, was catching Rivas' slants. A foul ball went over Kolb's head and he was given a new ball almost immediately. Kolb fired the ball back to Rivas, who was not looking. It hit Danny over the eye and knocked him cold, cost five stitches and a night in the hospital. . . . Eddie Williams must have felt strange in his Miami (Florida State) uniform. He was the first lefthanded starter for the Marlins since 1968. . . . Rich Coggins, Dallas-Fort Worth (Texas) center fielder, worked hard at the plate. He fouled off five pitches before he

(Continued on page 461)

Eastern League

CLASS AA

Leading Batter	League President	Leading Pitcher
GREG LUZINSKI	TOMMY RICHARDSON	DAVE BENNETT
Reading		Waterbury

CHAMPIONSHIP WINNERS IN PREVIOUS YEARS

1923—Williamsport ...... .661	1941—Wilkes-Barre ...... .630	1955—Reading .... .613
1924—Williamsport ...... .654	Elmira (3rd)‡ ..... .514	Allentown (2nd)‡ .. .565
1925—York§ .... .583	1942—Albany .... .600	1956—Schenectady† ..... .609
Williamsport§ ...... .583	Scranton (2nd)† ... .593	1957—Binghamton ...... .607
1926—Scranton .... .627	1943—Scranton .... .630	Reading (3rd)‡ .... .529
1927—Harrisburg .... .630	Elmira (2nd)‡ ..... .568	1958—Lancaster x ...... .568
1928—Harrisburg .... .603	1944—Hartford .... .723	Binghamton (6th)‡. .493
1929—Binghamton .... .597	Binghamton (4th)‡. .474	1959—Springfield† ...... .607
1930—Wilkes-Barre ...... .572	1945—Utica .... .615	1960—Williamsport y ... .551
1931—Harrisburg .... .597	Albany (3rd)‡ ..... .564	Springfieldl (3rd)y. .496
1932—Wilkes-Barre ...... .561	1946—Scranton† .... .691	1961—Springfield .... .612
1933—Binghamton .... .690	1947—Utica† .... .652	1962—Williamsport ..... .593
1934—Binghamton .... .694	1948—Scranton† .... .636	Elmira (2nd)‡ ..... .514
Williamsport* ...... .603	1949—Albany .... .664	1963—Charleston .... .593
1935—Scranton .... .657	Binghamton (4th)‡. .500	1964—Elmira .... .586
Binghamton* ...... .580	1950—Wilkes-Barre‡ .... .652	1965—Pittsfield .... .607
1936—Scranton* .... .609	1951—Wikles-Barre ..... .612	1966—Elmira .... .633
Elmira .... .629	Scranton (2nd)† ... .562	1967—Binghamton z ..... .586
1937—Elmira† .... .622	1952—Albany .... .603	Elmira .... .532
1938—Binghamton .... .622	Binghamton (2nd)‡. .562	1968—Pittsfield .... .604
Elmira (3rd)‡ ..... .522	1953—Reading .... .682	Reading (2nd)‡ .... .579
1939—Scranton† .... .571	Binghamton (2nd)‡. .636	1969—York .... .640
1940—Scranton .... .568	1954—Wilkes-Barre ...... .576	Springfield (3rd)y . .496
Binghamton (2nd)‡. .554	Albany (3rd)‡ ..... .540	

*Won split-season playoff. †Won championship and four-team playoff. ‡Won four-team playoff. §Tied for pennant, York winning playoff. xLeague was divided into Northern, Southern divisions and played a split season; Lancaster over-all season leader. yPlayoff finals canceled after one game because of rain with Williamsport and Springfield declared playoff co-champions. zLeague was divided into Eastern, Western divisions; Binghamton won playoff. (NOTE—Known as New York-Pennsylvania League prior to 1938.)

STANDING OF CLUBS AT CLOSE OF SEASON, SEPTEMBER 7

Club	Wat.	Read.	Pitt.	Paw.	Man.	Elm.	W.	L.	T.	Pct.	G.B.
†Waterbury (21*)	...	15	13	17	17	17	79	62	0	.560	....
†Reading (20)	14	...	14	20	13	17	78	63	0	.553	1
Pittsfield (12*)	15	14	...	11	16	16	72	66	0	.522	5½
Pawtucket (2*)	11	8	16	...	17	16	68	70	0	.493	9½
Manchester (10*)	11	15	12	10	...	18	66	73	0	.475	12
Elmira (7/23*)	11	11	11	12	10	...	55	84	0	.396	23

†Tied at end of season. Waterbury defeated Reading, 3-2, September 8, to determine pennant winner. All statistics of this game included in averages.

Key to major league farm teams (indicated by numbers after clubs in standing) shown on Page 384.

Playoff—None.

Regular-Season Attendance—Pawtucket, 105,027; Reading, 96,684; Waterbury, 70,031; Elmira, 51,907; Pittsfield, 49,875; Manchester, 36,928. Total, 410,452. Playoff for pennant winner, 3,043. All-star game (at Philadelphia), no attendance figure available.

Managers: Elmira—Harry Malmberg; Manchester—Gene Hassell; Pawtucket—Matt Sczesny; Pittsfield—Dick Gernert, Joe Klein; Reading—Andy Seminick; Waterbury—John (Red) Davis.

All-Star Team: 1B—Luzinski, Reading; 2B—Hunter, Pawtucket; 3B—Quinn, Waterbury; SS—Harrah, Pittsfield; OF—Baldridge, Manchester; Clines, Waterbury; Civil, Waterbury; C—Stelmaszek, Pittsfield; P—Gogolewski, Pittsfield; Curtis, Pawtucket; Manager—Davis, Waterbury.

(Compiled by Elias Sports Bureau, New York, N. Y.)

CLUB BATTING

Club	G.	AB.	R.	OR.	H.	TB.	2B.	3B.	HR.	RBI.	SH.	Int. SF. BB.	BB.	HP.	SO.	SB.	CS.	LOB.	Pct.
Pittsfield	138	4340	628	595	1117	1740	166	44	123	564	48	40	628	46	55	724	63	23	1067	.257
Waterbury	141	4425	629	522	1135	1772	173	28	136	590	57	31	608	48	30	731	108	49	1029	.256
Reading	141	4343	636	613	1108	1646	158	49	94	551	74	30	562	44	46	861	83	34	974	.255
Pawtucket	138	4276	669	624	1074	1564	162	20	96	592	42	34	717	37	39	686	105	48	1037	.251
Elmira	139	4422	483	611	1104	1491	156	33	55	426	80	28	420	35	21	602	50	19	987	.250
Manchester	139	4352	587	667	1075	1576	151	13	108	509	57	35	628	53	34	693	47	29	1025	.247

INDIVIDUAL BATTING

(Leading Qualifiers for Batting Championship—434 or More Plate Appearances)

*Bats lefthanded. †Switch-hitter.

Player and Club	G.	AB.	R.	H.	TB.	2B.	3B.	HR.	RBI.	SH.	SF.	BB.	HP.	SO.	SB.	CS.	Pct.
Luzinski, Gregory, Reading	.141	471	94	153	287	25	5	33	120	0	2	85	12	148	4	3	.3248
Biittner, Larry, Pitt*	.102	388	51	126	192	27	6	9	62	1	3	44	1	37	3	2	.3247
Huebner, Kenneth, Elmira*	.135	508	61	156	201	23	5	4	67	3	2	31	0	15	5	0	.307
Zisk, Richard, Waterbury	.125	450	83	133	264	17	6	34	88	2	0	57	3	110	5	1	.296
Hunter, Harold, Pawtucket	.133	444	81	130	189	18	1	13	71	3	2	80	7	67	2	3	.293
Torchia, Anthony, Paw	.137	492	81	144	214	29	1	13	68	3	4	62	2	53	4	1	.293
Kelly, Robert, Reading*	.109	408	73	118	153	11	6	4	43	3	1	52	2	35	8	2	.289
Pactwa, Joseph, Man*	.102	368	88	105	200	16	2	25	74	1	2	128	8	106	14	5	.285
Kolinsky, Steven, Paw	.118	411	72	117	189	16	4	16	70	1	6	62	7	80	11	7	.285
Civil, Melwood, Waterbury	.139	489	70	138	204	25	4	11	69	7	4	88	5	80	29	4	.282

Departmental Leaders: G—Luzinski, 141; AB—Guerrero, 555; R—Luzinski, 94; H—Huebner, 156; TB—Luzinski, 287; 2B—Howard, 30; 3B—Rogodzinski, 11; Hit—Zisk, 34; RBI—Luzinski, 120; SH—Marshall, 16; SF—G. Washington, 9; BB—Pactwa, 128; HP—Luzinski, 12; SO—Luzinski, 148; SB—Clines, 32; CS—Clines, 16.

(All Players—Listed Alphabetically)

Player and Club	G.	AB.	R.	H.	TB.	2B.	3B.	HR.	RBI.	SH.	SF.	BB.	HP.	SO.	SB.	CS.	Pct.
Arsenuk, Michael, Elmira	.74	299	20	42	57	9	0	2	17	4	0	23	4	26	0	0	.201
Austin, Frank, Pawtucket	.6	19	4	2	3	1	0	0	0	0	0	3	0	3	0	0	.105
Bagwell, Louis, Pittsfield*	.6	19	1	2	2	0	0	0	1	0	0	0	0	3	0	0	.105
Bailey, Calvin, Waterbury	.21	1	0	0	0	0	0	0	0	0	0	0	0	0	0	0	.000
Baldridge, Dennis, Man	.105	359	57	88	151	9	0	18	53	3	4	39	5	79	2	0	.245
Baldwin, Richard, Pitt*	.12	41	6	10	11	1	0	0	1	0	0	4	0	3	1	0	.244
Beckner, Bobbye, Pittsfield	.14	37	4	7	14	1	0	2	5	0	1	8	1	11	1	0	.189
Beniquez, Juan, Pawtucket	.56	233	29	58	81	5	3	4	25	1	1	15	2	41	13	2	.249
Biittner, Larry, Pittsfield*	.102	388	51	126	192	27	6	9	62	1	3	44	1	37	3	2	.325
Bongiovanni, Terry, Man	.20	3	0	0	0	0	0	0	1	0	0	1	0	2	0	0	.000
Boone, Robert, Reading	.20	80	12	23	31	2	0	2	10	1	0	7	1	9	0	0	.288
Bottoms, James, Pitt*	.3	9	2	3	3	0	0	0	0	0	0	0	2	4	1	0	.333
Bowers, Otho, Pittsfield	.74	230	16	40	55	4	1	3	18	4	1	25	0	45	1	0	.174
Branch, Jerry, Waterbury*	.78	224	28	50	61	8	0	1	15	1	2	49	1	38	1	1	.223
Brown, Darrell, Waterbury	.117	369	34	84	122	17	6	3	42	10	2	41	1	54	3	2	.228
Campanis, James, Elmira	.32	111	13	32	40	5	0	1	8	0	2	13	0	12	0	1	.288
Carson, Robert, Manchester	.24	67	13	16	31	4	1	3	11	0	2	16	2	13	2	1	.239
Castle, Donald, Pittsfield*	.94	338	53	106	162	13	5	11	47	4	4	38	2	54	1	3	.314
Civil, Melwood, Waterbury	.139	489	70	138	204	25	4	11	69	7	4	88	5	80	29	4	.282
Clark, Brian, Manchester	.26	5	0	0	0	0	0	0	0	0	0	0	0	0	0	0	.000
Clines, Eugene, Waterbury	.95	371	62	115	158	19	3	6	42	8	4	39	2	46	32	16	.310
Coccia, Louis, Manchester	.63	175	19	39	65	6	1	6	20	5	0	31	1	52	1	0	.223

Player and Club	G.	AB.	R.	H.	TB.	2B.	3B.	HR.	RBI.	SH.	SF.	BB.	HP.	SO.	SB.	CS.	Pct.
Collins, Michael, Reading†	17	35	6	5	5	0	0	0	1	0	0	14	0	10	0	0	.143
Colson, Loyd, Manchester	48	2	0	0	0	0	0	0	0	0	0	0	0	0	0	0	.000
Cox, Larry, Reading	59	189	22	41	61	3	1	5	27	5	1	22	1	36	4	0	.217
Cox, Ronald, Reading	131	457	62	116	169	17	0	12	55	6	7	58	1	70	5	6	.254
Crespo, Manuel, Pawtucket	105	333	35	80	97	8	3	1	47	4	4	39	1	30	8	4	.240
Croken, William, Pawtucket.	6	14	3	2	2	0	0	0	1	0	0	3	0	2	0	0	.143
Dawson, J. Arthur, Man*	21	3	0	0	0	0	0	0	0	0	0	1	0	1	0	0	.000
Day, Charles E., Elmira	28	106	12	28	42	5	3	1	13	3	2	12	1	9	2	0	.264
DeCastris, Frank, Reading*	17	59	8	17	25	3	1	1	8	1	0	8	2	6	0	2	.288
Demery, Art, Elmira*	7	0	1	0	0	0	0	0	0	0	0	0	0	0	0	0	.000
Dettore, Thomas, Wat*	27	11	0	1	1	0	0	0	0	0	0	2	0	4	1	0	.091
Dilly, Donald, Pawtucket	93	275	42	62	97	12	1	7	47	5	3	48	3	48	4	4	.225
Donnelly, Richard, Pitt*	1	4	0	1	1	0	0	0	0	0	0	0	0	0	0	0	.250
Drew, C. Ollie, Elmira*	36	142	18	34	47	4	3	1	11	1	0	16	0	20	2	0	.239
Dugan, James, Elmira	58	194	22	49	80	7	0	8	27	0	3	25	0	38	3	3	.253
Dunn, Perry, Waterbury*	17	61	7	16	22	4	1	0	7	0	1	3	0	8	1	2	.262
Ferraro, Thomas, Elmira	26	1	0	0	0	0	0	0	0	0	0	0	0	0	0	0	.000
Fisk, Carlton, Pawtucket	93	284	43	65	121	18	1	12	44	1	1	42	5	66	6	5	.229
Fiskland, Edward, Man	20	2	1	0	0	0	0	0	0	0	0	1	0	1	0	0	.000
Francis, John, Reading	52	148	8	32	39	7	0	0	17	6	0	17	0	27	1	0	.216
Gaines, Jack, Pawtucket	23	0	1	0	0	0	0	0	0	0	0	0	0	0	0	0	.000
Gibson, Roy, Pittsfield	11	25	4	5	6	1	0	0	1	1	1	3	3	9	2	0	.200
Gifford, Roger, Pittsfield*	1	5	1	0	0	0	0	0	0	0	0	0	0	3	0	0	.000
Goldstone, Edward, Reading	1	1	0	0	0	0	0	0	0	0	0	0	0	1	0	0	.000
Grate, D. Jeffrey, Pawtucket	71	204	30	42	58	6	2	2	24	10	2	64	1	51	8	8	.206
Guerrero, Mario, Man	139	555	57	134	161	19	1	2	38	9	5	43	3	32	6	3	.241
Hammond, Wilbert, Wat	18	57	9	13	21	0	1	2	5	0	0	8	0	8	1	1	.228
Hansen, Brian, Reading	1	2	0	0	0	0	0	0	0	0	0	0	0	1	0	0	.000
Harmon, Thomas, Elmira*	77	287	37	80	94	9	1	1	21	5	3	15	4	21	0	0	.279
Harrah, Colbert, Pittsfield	95	359	57	99	128	18	1	3	37	7	4	54	4	46	27	6	.276
Haynes, W. Daniel, Elmira	88	288	33	65	101	12	0	8	29	3	4	33	2	59	4	0	.226
Herrera, Hector, Waterbury	27	72	5	13	17	4	0	0	5	3	0	2	1	11	0	2	.181
Hoots, Wayne, Pittsfield*	50	138	17	32	42	5	1	1	13	2	0	18	0	33	0	0	.232
Howard, Charles, Wat†	135	489	83	130	235	30	0	25	85	1	5	98	3	71	12	4	.266
Huebner, Kenneth, Elmira*	135	508	61	156	201	22	5	4	67	3	2	31	0	15	5	0	.307
Hunter, Harold, Pawtucket	133	444	81	130	189	18	1	13	71	3	2	80	7	67	2	3	.293
Huyke, Elwood, Waterbury	70	232	18	53	81	4	0	8	36	2	3	12	0	22	3	2	.228
Jack, Zelman, Waterbury	78	264	47	64	120	4	2	16	51	0	3	40	0	69	8	3	.242
Jackson, Richard, Paw*	56	177	21	44	53	6	0	1	22	1	0	27	2	22	0	0	.249
Jones, Dallas, Manchester*	73	256	34	53	71	6	0	4	27	2	2	36	3	35	3	3	.207
Joyce, Thomas, Elmira	78	243	25	64	74	6	2	0	16	11	0	26	1	49	4	3	.263
Kelly, Robert, Reading*	109	408	73	118	153	11	6	4	43	3	1	52	2	35	8	2	.289
Kent, A. David, Man	48	159	22	45	79	8	1	8	29	1	3	19	2	30	0	0	.283
Kolinsky, Steven, Paw	118	411	72	117	189	16	4	16	70	1	6	62	7	80	11	7	.285
Lange, Kenneth, Man	38	2	0	0	0	0	0	0	0	0	0	0	0	2	0	0	.000
Locanto, Patrick, Reading	2	6	2	0	0	0	0	0	0	0	1	0	0	2	1	0	.000
Luzinski, Gregory, Reading	141	471	94	153	287	25	5	33	120	0	2	85	12	148	4	3	.325
Lyscio, Gerald, Elmira	11	0	0	0	0	0	0	0	0	0	0	1	0	0	0	0	.000
Maduro, Jorge, Manchester	52	160	16	41	50	4	1	1	18	1	1	19	0	10	0	0	.256
Marshall, Keith, Elmira	127	413	40	89	116	13	1	4	29	16	2	44	3	78	10	6	.215
Martin, T. Eugene, Pitt*	32	126	21	40	80	5	1	11	29	2	0	15	3	27	0	1	.317
Mason, John R. B., Paw	16	56	14	15	21	0	0	2	17	0	0	11	0	6	0	0	.268
McDaniel, Robert, Man*	12	35	2	6	10	1	0	1	3	0	1	6	0	6	4	1	.171
Medich, George, Man	8	2	0	0	0	0	0	0	0	0	0	0	0	0	0	0	.000
Meier, F. Calvin, Elmira	26	73	5	13	21	1	2	1	6	2	1	9	0	12	0	0	.178
Mello, Edward, Pawtucket	3	8	2	3	4	1	0	0	0	0	0	1	0	2	0	0	.375
Merlet, Gerald, Pittsfield	73	206	22	39	57	4	1	4	16	6	0	20	4	30	2	1	.189
Merlet, John, Pittsfield	102	386	51	90	138	14	2	10	43	2	3	32	6	49	2	4	.233
Miller, Richard A., Paw*	113	381	69	94	154	16	4	12	56	4	2	75	4	77	10	4	.247
Minster, Michael, Elmira	22	50	1	10	15	3	1	0	6	1	2	6	0	9	0	0	.200
Moates, David, Pittsfield*	2	10	2	4	6	0	1	0	1	0	0	0	0	4	1	0	.400
Moret, Rogelio, Pawtucket*	27	0	1	0	0	0	0	0	0	0	0	0	0	0	0	0	.000
Mountain, John, Pawtucket*	84	280	32	59	74	6	0	3	31	3	3	41	0	33	4	2	.211
Murtaugh, Timothy, Wat†	23	66	11	13	15	2	0	0	2	2	0	21	0	7	0	0	.197
Northey, Scott, Elmira	102	363	53	86	106	7	2	3	21	6	0	42	3	81	14	1	.237
O'Connell, Timothy, Man*	122	427	54	119	159	16	0	8	46	5	2	60	2	62	5	2	.279
O'Donnell, Kenneth, Elmira	26	75	10	16	18	2	0	0	4	2	2	9	0	12	0	1	.213
Oglivie, Benjamin, Paw*	115	391	62	91	136	15	0	10	51	0	5	76	2	78	12	5	.233
Pacheco, Joseph, Man*	41	140	12	29	39	4	0	2	8	1	0	9	3	21	1	1	.207
Pactwa, Joseph, Elmira	132	368	88	105	200	16	2	25	74	1	2	128	8	106	14	5	.285
Phillips, H. Dale, Elmira	54	182	18	38	54	6	5	0	7	5	0	13	0	39	0	0	.209
Pirtle, Gerald, Manchester	34	9	1	2	2	0	0	0	2	1	0	0	0	1	0	1	.222
Pyle, Lawrence, Manchester	47	153	23	34	53	4	0	5	14	1	0	32	0	35	2	1	.222
Quinn, Luther, Waterbury	118	416	76	115	203	16	0	24	75	2	3	58	4	99	6	3	.276
Ratliff, Gary, Pittsfield	112	366	45	71	121	9	1	13	43	3	4	63	8	121	8	3	.194
Rios, Juan, Elmira	92	306	28	76	90	6	4	0	20	10	1	15	2	25	3	2	.248
Roberts, Melvin, Reading	22	34	4	12	12	0	0	0	1	1	0	6	1	7	0	0	.353
Robinson, Craig, Reading	89	272	34	57	77	7	5	1	16	10	2	26	4	73	4	1	.210
Rodriguez, Gerardo, Read	60	179	29	39	67	6	2	6	21	3	4	16	2	52	3	0	.218
Rogers, Rickey, Pittsfield	3	8	3	2	2	0	0	0	0	4	0	0	0	0	0	0	.250
Rogodzinski, Michael, Read*	128	413	57	105	181	18	11	12	81	6	4	57	3	129	5	7	.254
Rojas, Hilario, Reading	87	240	25	43	61	5	2	3	17	6	1	26	3	59	6	3	.179
Salas, Jose, Elmira	4	3	0	1	1	0	0	0	0	0	0	1	0	0	0	0	.333

Player and Club	G.	AB.	R.	H.	TB.	2B.	3B.	HR.	RBI.	SH.	SF.	BB.	HP.	SO.	SB.	CS.	Pct.
Salvato, Steve, Pittsfield ...	14	38	4	4	8	2	1	0	4	2	0	3	0	6	0	0	.105
Sands, Charles, Man*	46	138	16	30	40	4	0	2	9	1	0	32	1	29	0	0	.217
Sanserino, Gary, Elmira ...	132	456	45	112	156	21	1	7	56	6	3	41	0	45	3	2	.246
Santana, Felix, Waterbury ..	64	187	24	45	59	4	2	2	17	10	1	26	2	31	1	2	.241
Santos, Miguel, Waterbury* ..	38	130	21	29	40	4	2	1	11	4	1	22	2	15	4	4	.223
Schultz, Jerry, Manchester*	127	436	42	99	116	9	1	2	39	10	0	46	1	37	3	4	.227
Sheridan, Roger, Pittsfield* ..	95	343	67	103	151	16	7	6	35	7	3	58	4	34	3	3	.300
Shitanishi, Katsuhiro, Paw ..	86	273	46	66	71	5	0	0	19	5	1	68	3	27	23	3	.242
Shoemaker, Charles, Wat* ..	116	396	39	94	110	11	1	1	32	4	2	43	3	37	0	1	.237
Silicato, Thomas, Reading ..	111	385	50	95	122	13	7	0	37	12	2	48	5	40	10	1	.247
Slough, Leslie, Pawtucket ...	1	1	0	0	0	0	0	0	0	0	0	0	0	1	0	0	.000
Smith, Tommie, Elmira*	121	412	40	113	178	17	3	14	68	2	1	45	1	58	0	0	.274
Starnes, Raymond, Reading ..	131	438	88	113	141	16	3	2	37	9	3	65	7	65	25	3	.258
Stelmaszek, Richard, Pitt ..	128	386	50	95	126	11	4	4	47	6	7	98	4	41	1	0	.246
Terlecki, Robert, Reading ..	29	0	1	0	0	0	0	0	0	0	0	0	0	0	0	0	.000
Thompson, Albert, Pitt	93	313	70	102	208	17	4	27	87	0	3	65	5	59	5	0	.326
Torchia, Anthony, Paw	137	492	81	144	214	29	1	13	68	3	4	62	2	53	4	1	.293
Torres, Rosendo, Man*	41	127	21	31	45	5	0	3	16	1	1	27	0	26	0	4	.244
Urrieta, Eulises, Reading ..	65	178	16	30	39	5	0	0	15	2	0	16	0	34	3	3	.169
Vega, Fernando, Elmira	28	0	1	0	0	0	0	0	0	0	0	0	0	0	0	0	.000
Walker, James, Pittsfield ...	54	136	19	30	53	7	2	4	24	0	2	15	0	36	1	0	.221
Washington, Gary, Man*	131	455	66	123	199	20	3	15	60	6	9	68	5	62	6	1	.270
Wissel, Richard, Reading* ..	102	348	45	109	176	20	4	13	45	2	3	37	2	57	4	3	.313
Wockenfuss, Johnny, Pitt ...	123	429	65	106	174	11	6	15	47	0	4	63	10	69	3	0	.247
Yawn, James, Manchester ...	126	454	55	110	149	20	2	5	45	8	3	24	1	68	3	0	.242
Zisk, Richard, Waterbury ...	125	450	83	133	264	17	6	34	88	2	0	57	3	110	5	1	.296

The following pitchers had no plate appearances primarily through use of wild card pinch-hitters (listed alphabetically by club, games in parentheses):

ELMIRA—Assaf, Edward (24); Balderson, Richard (21); Brookens, Edward (1); Chlan, Gregory (17); DeBenedetti, Gary (15); Gladden, Lloyd (34); Myers, Steven (14); Pasierb, John (19); Salazar, Rafael* (5); Sommer, Timothy (30); Weaver, James B.* (13); Wright, Stephen (18); York, James (14).

MANCHESTER—Drummond, William (14); Gowell, Lawrence (30); Johnson, Kenneth A.* (6); Ley, Terrence* (6); Olson, Bruce (11); Ordway, Richard (5).

PAWTUCKET—Beckett, Douglas (22); Boteze, Carl (15); Clifton, John* (9); Curtis, John* (21); Dowd, Paul* (5); LaRose, H. John* (22); Lohfink, Glenn (40); Mercado, Raul (23); Prediger, Charles (18); Robinson, G. Cecil* (26); Sanossian, Gary† (22); Thomas, James L.† (31); Washington, Ivy* (13); Williams, Terry (16).

PITTSFIELD—Blackmon, Jimmy (14); Campbell, Paul A. (26); Constantino, Ronald (4); Foucault, Steven* (2); Gogolewski, William* (21); Henninger, Richard (18); Janek, Jeffery* (20); Parchem, Robert* (2); Redmon, James (1); Scally, Mark (9); Shutts, Robert (37); Sierra, Pedro (37); Slade, Michael (9); Szado, Edward* (13); Terpko, Jeffrey (20); Thompson, Michael (19); Valesente, George (4); Vollweiler, Jeffrey (3); Whitson, Michael (14).

READING—Bayless, Patrick (24); Cates, Steve* (13); Champion, B. Billy (3); Clem, Harold (14); Foreman, Jack (26); Holland, G. Smith (23); Horne, Thomas* (20); Laxton, William* (15); Muniz, Manuel (28); Nutter, Jack (7); Penn, A. John (37); Raffo, Albert (13); Scramuzzo, Craig (2); Wolfe, William (13).

WATERBURY—Acosta, Eduardo (5); Bennett, David (29); Cluck, Robert* (22); Cordeiro, Raymond* (36); Hayward, Roger (7); Hendrix, Richard (26); Houser, Barry* (22); Kison, Bruce (20); Lamb, John (30); Marrujo, Jimmie (13); Quezada, Silvano (26); Sells, D. Alvin (12).

GRAND-SLAM HOME RUNS—Luzinski, 4; Pactwa, 3; Hunter, Miller, Quinn, 2 each; Howard, Huebner, Jones, Rogodzinski, A. Thompson, Walker, Wissel, 1 each.

AWARDED FIRST BASE ON INTERFERENCE—Civil 2 (Croken, Fisk); R. Cox (Walker), Luzinski (Coccia), Quinn (Fisk), Schultz (Huyke).

CLUB FIELDING

Club	G.	PO.	A.	E.	DP.	PB.	Pct.		Club	G.	PO.	A.	E.	DP.	PB.	Pct.
Pittsfield	138	3442	1388	167	120	19	.967		Waterbury	141	3516	1462	181	133	18	.965
Pawtucket	138	3408	1453	169	131	24	.966		Elmira	139	3450	1413	184	129	8	.964
Reading	141	3461	1355	170	132	12	.966		Manchester	139	3480	1457	188	134	28	.963

Triple Plays—Pawtucket, 2; Pittsfield, 1.

INDIVIDUAL FIELDING
(Ten or More Games)

*Throws lefthanded.

FIRST BASEMEN

Player and Club	G.	PO.	A.	E.	DP.	Pct.		Player and Club	G.	PO.	A.	E.	DP.	Pct.
Blittner, Pitt* ...	76	637	44	4	53	.994		Luzinski, Reading ..	141	1122	65	21	119	.983
TORCHIA, Paw* ...	133	1123	73	8	107	.993		Huebner, Elmira* ..	13	95	17	2	10	.982
Haynes, Elmira ...	85	698	51	10	64	.987		Campanis, Elmira ..	31	249	25	6	26	.979
Howard, Waterbury ..116		1002	81	16	105	.985		Castle, Pittsfield ..	24	169	15	5	22	.974
Washington, Man* ..130		1145	81	19	104	.985		A. Thompson, Pitt* ..	24	180	11	6	15	.970
Martin, Pittsfield ...	18	178	10	3	17	.984		Arsenuk, Elmira	12	101	5	4	9	.964
Jack, Waterbury	23	173	14	3	14	.984								

Triple Plays—Thompson, Torchia, 1 each.

FIRST BASEMEN—Continued
(Fewer Than Ten Games)

Player and Club	G.	PO.	A.	E.	DP.	Pct.	Player and Club	G.	PO.	A.	E.	DP.	Pct.
Pactwa, Man*	7	62	3	0	8	1.000	Dilly, Pawtucket	1	2	0	0	0	1.000
Quinn, Waterbury	6	33	1	0	2	1.000	Jackson, Paw	1	1	0	0	0	1.000
O'Connell, Man*	5	22	5	0	1	1.000	Slough, Pawtucket	1	1	0	0	0	1.000
Mountain, Paw*	4	24	2	0	6	1.000	Smith, Elmira	1	1	0	0	0	1.000
Santos, Waterbury*	1	5	0	0	0	1.000	Austin, Pawtucket	4	24	2	1	3	.963

SECOND BASEMEN

Player and Club	G.	PO.	A.	E.	DP.	Pct.	Player and Club	G.	PO.	A.	E.	DP.	Pct.
O'Donnell, Elmira	13	30	35	1	8	.985	Schultz, Man	22	45	53	4	20	.961
SHOEMAKER, Wat	.103	273	279	12	64	.979	Rios, Elmira	10	20	25	2	7	.957
Silicato, Reading	..108	267	259	14	59	.974	Joyce, Elmira	40	81	90	8	21	.955
Yawn, Manchester	..119	269	313	17	76	.972	Urrieta, Reading	10	18	22	2	8	.952
Rojas, Reading	25	45	58	3	14	.972	Phillips, Elmira	54	104	141	14	27	.946
J. Merlet, Pitt	..102	231	276	16	66	.969	Quinn, Waterbury	37	69	88	9	21	.946
Hunter, Pawtucket	.131	298	334	20	78	.969	Arsenuk, Elmira	29	47	59	8	22	.930
Bowers, Pittsfield	25	55	48	4	11	.963							

Triple Plays—Hunter, J. Merlet, 1 each.

(Fewer Than Ten Games)

Player and Club	G.	PO.	A.	E.	DP.	Pct.	Player and Club	G.	PO.	A.	E.	DP.	Pct.
Bagwell, Pitt	6	11	17	0	5	1.000	Wockenfuss, Pitt	2	1	0	0	0	1.000
Rogers, Pittsfield	3	3	6	0	0	1.000	Shitanishi, Paw	6	13	7	1	4	.952
Mello, Pawtucket	2	4	4	0	2	1.000	Sheridan, Pitt	3	12	8	1	1	.952
Santana, Waterbury	1	2	4	0	2	1.000	Locanto, Reading	2	7	1	1	0	.889
Beckner, Pitt	1	1	1	0	1	1.000	Howard, Waterbury	3	9	8	3	1	.850

THIRD BASEMEN

Player and Club	G.	PO.	A.	E.	DP.	Pct.	Player and Club	G.	PO.	A.	E.	DP.	Pct.
Santana, Waterbury	28	24	66	4	6	.957	Sanserino, Elmira	..110	94	219	24	25	.929
Sheridan, Pitt	58	51	111	9	10	.947	R. Cox, Reading	95	94	149	19	18	.927
SCHULTZ, Man	..104	95	234	19	28	.945	Pacheco, Waterbury	33	22	60	8	7	.911
Rojas, Reading	28	29	48	5	6	.939	Jones, Manchester	24	16	54	7	5	.909
Arsenuk, Elmira	30	10	35	3	2	.938	Boone, Reading	20	28	38	7	5	.904
G. Merlet, Pitt	60	45	97	10	14	.934	Shitanishi, Paw	43	31	73	12	3	.897
Crespo, Pawtucket	.103	102	227	24	33	.932	Quinn, Waterbury	76	64	139	32	12	.864
Bowers, Pittsfield	20	19	34	4	1	.930	Gibson, Pittsfield	11	3	13	5	1	.762

Triple Play—Crespo.

(Fewer Than Ten Games)

Player and Club	G.	PO.	A.	E.	DP.	Pct.	Player and Club	G.	PO.	A.	E.	DP.	Pct.
Mason, Pawtucket	3	1	6	0	0	1.000	Kent, Manchester	4	2	8	1	0	.909
Harrah, Pittsfield	1	2	1	0	0	1.000	Civil, Waterbury	8	10	12	3	0	.880
Shoemaker, Wat	1	2	1	0	0	1.000	Wockenfuss, Pitt	2	4	3	1	1	.875
Salas, Elmira	3	1	1	0	0	1.000	Hunter, Pawtucket	1	3	3	1	0	.857
Collins, Reading	1	0	1	0	0	1.000	Baldridge, Man	7	4	16	4	3	.833
Meier, Elmira	1	1	0	0	0	1.000	Beckner, Pitt	2	1	2	1	1	.750
Rios, Elmira	7	8	16	2	2	.923							

SHORTSTOPS

Player and Club	G.	PO.	A.	E.	DP.	Pct.	Player and Club	G.	PO.	A.	E.	DP.	Pct.
Robinson, Reading	89	142	282	10	53	.977	Grate, Pawtucket	71	107	200	21	42	.936
BROWN, Wat	..117	155	340	16	82	.969	Urrieta, Reading	49	86	145	16	34	.935
Santana, Waterbury	22	30	53	3	12	.965	Guerrero, Man	..139	225	355	44	72	.929
Rios, Elmira	73	106	183	17	30	.944	Rojas, Reading	11	12	27	3	4	.929
Harrah, Pittsfield	94	157	292	27	59	.943	Bowers, Pittsfield	28	29	76	10	14	.913
Shitanishi, Paw	11	13	20	2	4	.943	Joyce, Elmira	31	51	73	13	17	.905
Sheridan, Pitt	18	25	51	5	3	.938	Beniquez, Paw	56	105	167	29	35	.904
Meier, Elmira	25	49	72	8	20	.938							

Triple Plays—Bowers, Grate, 1 each.

(Fewer Than Ten Games)

Player and Club	G.	PO.	A.	E.	DP.	Pct.	Player and Club	G.	PO.	A.	E.	DP.	Pct.
Shoemaker, Wat	1	1	0	0	0	1.000	Crespo, Pawtucket	2	0	9	1	0	.900
O'Donnell, Elmira	7	18	17	1	7	.972	Schultz, Man	3	3	2	1	0	.833
Pacheco, Waterbury	5	8	10	1	2	.947	Arsenuk, Elmira	1	0	2	1	0	.667
Sanserino, Elmira	9	18	21	3	3	.929							

OUTFIELDERS

Player and Club	G.	PO.	A.	E.	DP.	Pct.	Player and Club	G.	PO.	A.	E.	DP.	Pct.
Sanserino, Elmira	25	36	2	0	1	1.000	Kolinsky, Paw	34	39	1	1	0	.976
Baldwin, Pitt*	11	16	3	0	0	1.000	Baldridge, Man	70	113	4	3	1	.975
Salvato, Pitt	13	17	0	0	0	1.000	Oglivie, Paw*	..114	172	14	5	5	.974
Howard, Waterbury	11	16	0	0	0	1.000	Castle, Pitt*	71	108	3	3	0	.974
WOCKENFUSS, Pit.121		214	8	3	3	.987	Carson, Manchester	23	33	4	1	1	.974
Clines, Waterbury	95	233	15	5	2	.980	Dilly, Pawtucket	93	126	2	4	0	.970
Huebner, Elmira*	.113	179	8	4	0	.979	Starnes, Reading	.129	325	8	11	0	.968
Marshall, Elmira	.127	266	13	6	1	.979	Civil, Waterbury	.132	261	10	9	1	.968
Miller, Pawtucket*	.107	227	5	5	0	.979	Pactwa, Man*	.116	233	7	8	0	.968
Kelly, Reading	.106	209	8	5	0	.977	Torres, Man	41	86	2	3	0	.967

OUTFIELDERS—Continued

Player and Club	G.	PO.	A.	E.	DP.	Pct.
O'Connell, Man* 100	164	9	6	2	.966	
Mountain, Paw* ..	76	122	7	5	0	.963
Zisk, Waterbury ..122	175	10	2	1	.959	
Jones, Manchester ..	25	43	3	2	1	.958
Ratliff, Pittsfield ..112	189	10	9	2	.957	
Hoots, Pittsfield ..	40	60	1	3	0	.953
Pyle, Manchester ..	45	74	4	4	1	.951
Rogodzinski, Read .120	197	15	11	2	.951	
Martin, Pittsfield ..	15	18	1	1	0	.950
Northey, Elmira ..102	214	10	12	1	.949	
Kent, Manchester ..	15	17	1	1	0	.947

Player and Club	G.	PO.	A.	E.	DP.	Pct.
R. Cox, Reading	36	70	1	4	1	.947
Santos, Waterbury*	33	52	1	3	0	.946
Day, Elmira	28	44	8	3	2	.945
Drew, Elmira	36	62	4	4	2	.943
DeCastris, Reading .	17	25	6	2	0	.939
Sheridan, Pitt	21	29	0	2	0	.935
Blittner, Pitt*	12	21	2	2	0	.920
Roberts, Reading ..	14	18	0	2	0	.900
Dunn, Waterbury ..	16	17	0	2	0	.895
Jack, Waterbury ...	15	23	1	3	0	.889

(Fewer Than Ten Games)

Player and Club	G.	PO.	A.	E.	DP.	Pct.
Wissel, Reading ...	7	10	2	0	1	1.000
Beckner, Pitt	3	7	0	0	0	1.000
Rodriguez, Reading .	3	6	1	0	0	1.000
Moates, Pitt*	2	6	0	0	0	1.000
Silicato, Reading ..	2	4	0	0	0	1.000
Dugan, Elmira	5	5	0	0	0	1.000
Fisk, Pawtucket ...	3	3	0	0	0	1.000
Walker, Pittsfield ..	2	3	0	0	0	1.000

Player and Club	G.	PO.	A.	E.	DP.	Pct.
Bottoms, Pitt	3	2	0	0	0	1.000
Gifford, Pitt	1	2	0	0	0	1.000
A. Thompson, Pitt*.	5	1	0	0	0	1.000
Campanis, Elmira ..	1	1	0	0	0	1.000
Hammond, Waterbury	6	5	1	1	0	.857
O'Donnell, Elmira ..	4	3	0	1	0	.750
Torchia, Paw*	4	3	0	1	0	.750

CATCHERS

Player and Club	G.	PO.	A.	E.	DP.	PB.	Pct.
Jackson, Paw	50	296	22	2	3	10	.994
SMITH, Elmira ..	70	396	47	5	8	4	.989
Fisk, Pawtucket ..	44	479	50	7	7	10	.987
Huyke, Waterbury	66	336	21	5	3	1	.986
Harmon, Elmira ..	58	260	59	5	5	2	.985
Rodriguez, Read ..	54	258	41	5	2	5	.984
Branch, Water ...	56	313	39	6	5	13	.983
Minster, Elmira ..	22	102	8	2	1	2	.982

Player and Club	G.	PO.	A.	E.	DP.	PB.	Pct.
Stelmaszek, Pitt .127	782	67	17	8	12	.980	
Maduro, Man ...	51	242	37	6	3	13	.979
L. Cox, Reading .	57	289	25	7	2	2	.978
Coccia, Man	53	279	19	10	3	9	.968
Sands, Manchester	40	211	16	8	4	6	.966
Walker, Pittsfield	19	77	5	3	1	7	.965
Murtaugh, Wat ..	17	97	5	4	1	2	.962
Francis, Reading .	27	103	11	6	2	4	.950

Triple Play—Fisk.

(Fewer Than Ten Games)

Player and Club	G.	PO.	A.	E.	DP.	PB.	Pct.
Herrera, Waterbury	8	36	4	0	0	2	1.000
Donnelly, Pitt ...	1	14	1	0	0	0	1.000
Jones, Manchester.	2	3	0	0	0	0	1.000
Salas, Elmira ...	1	2	0	0	0	0	1.000

Player and Club	G.	PO.	A.	E.	DP.	PB.	Pct.
Collins, Reading .	7	37	3	1	1	1	.976
Croken, Pawtucket	6	19	2	3	1	4	.875
Hansen, Reading .	1	2	0	1	0	0	.667

PITCHERS

Player and Club	G.	PO.	A.	E.	DP.	Pct.
LANGE, Elmira .	38	9	24	0	2	1.000
Pasierb, Elmira ..	19	8	24	0	1	1.000
Colson, Manchester	48	4	27	0	0	1.000
Terlecki, Reading .	27	9	18	0	2	1.000
Henninger, Pitt ..	18	4	20	0	1	1.000
Foreman, Reading .	26	5	16	0	1	1.000
Lohfink, Pawtucket	40	5	14	0	1	1.000
Mercado, Pawtucket	23	7	12	0	1	1.000
Terpko, Pittsfield .	20	3	14	0	1	1.000
Weaver, Elmira* ..	13	5	11	0	0	1.000
York, Elmira	14	6	9	0	0	1.000
Sommer, Elmira ..	30	7	6	0	0	1.000
Boteze, Pawtucket .	15	3	8	0	0	1.000
Olson, Manchester .	11	5	6	0	0	1.000
Muniz, Reading ...	27	2	7	0	1	1.000
Drummond, Man ..	14	1	7	0	1	1.000
Blackmon, Pitt ...	14	0	7	0	0	1.000
Beckett, Pawtucket .	22	2	4	0	1	1.000
Horne, Reading* ..	20	0	6	0	0	1.000
Myers, Elmira	14	2	3	0	0	1.000
Janek, Pittsfield* ..	20	1	2	0	0	1.000
Campbell, Pitt ...	24	12	27	1	1	.975
Quezada, Waterbury	26	10	28	1	2	.974
Dawson, Man* ...	19	7	28	1	2	.972
Prediger, Paw ...	18	8	23	1	2	.969
M. Thompson, Pitt	19	1	24	1	0	.962
Moret, Pawtucket* .	25	7	39	2	6	.958
Penn, Reading ...	37	6	16	1	1	.957
Hendrix, Waterbury	26	6	15	1	1	.955
Bayless, Reading ..	24	7	13	1	0	.952
Gogolewski, Pitt ..	21	19	20	2	1	.951
Kison, Waterbury ..	19	10	29	2	1	.951
Balderson, Elmira .	21	8	11	1	1	.950
Fiskland, Man	18	5	13	1	1	.947
Assaf, Elmira	24	17	18	2	0	.946

Player and Club	G.	PO.	A.	E.	DP.	Pct.
Washington, Paw ..	13	6	10	1	1	.941
Houser, Waterbury*	22	11	19	2	2	.938
Sierra, Pittsfield ...	37	5	24	2	0	.935
Wright, Elmira ...	18	12	2	1	0	.933
Vega, Elmira	26	7	20	2	1	.931
Pirtle, Manchester .	27	26	27	4	2	.930
Bongiovanni, Man .	20	5	21	2	0	.929
Gaines, Pawtucket* .	22	2	11	1	0	.929
Whitson, Pitt	14	5	8	1	0	.929
Bennett, Water ...	29	14	24	3	1	.927
Laxton, Reading* ..	11	6	6	1	0	.923
Raffo, Reading ...	12	8	15	2	0	.920
Gladden, Elmira ..	34	8	26	3	1	.919
Robinson, Paw ...	26	13	32	4	2	.918
Thomas, Pawtucket* .	31	2	9	1	0	.917
Lamb, Waterbury ..	30	1	10	1	0	.917
Cates, Reading* ...	13	1	10	1	1	.917
Sells, Manchester ..	12	1	10	1	0	.917
Gowell, Manchester .	30	16	38	5	2	.915
Clark, Manchester .	26	12	18	3	1	.909
Dettore, Waterbury .	23	10	20	3	0	.909
Clem, Reading	16	4	16	2	2	.909
Curtis, Pawtucket* .	21	5	33	4	1	.905
Williams, Paw ...	16	4	13	2	3	.895
DeBenedictis, Elmira	15	7	10	2	6	.895
Shutts, Pittsfield ..	37	4	4	1	0	.889
Ferraro, Elmira* ..	24	4	4	1	1	.889
Szado, Pittsfield* ..	13	3	5	1	0	.889
Bailey, Waterbury .	20	2	12	2	1	.875
Chlan, Elmira	17	3	9	2	1	.857
Wolfe, Reading ...	13	3	9	2	0	.857
Cordeiro, Wat*	36	1	9	2	0	.833
Cluck, Waterbury* .	22	6	13	4	2	.826
Holland, Reading ..	22	7	4	3	0	.786
Marrujo, Waterbury.	13	0	3	1	0	.750

PITCHERS—Continued
(Fewer Than Ten Games)

Player and Club	G.	PO.	A.	E.	DP.	Pct.
Lyscio, Elmira	9	6	9	0	1	1.000
Clifton, Paw*	9	4	10	0	0	1.000
Salazar, Elmira* ..	4	0	4	0	0	1.000
Dowd, Pawtucket ..	5	1	2	0	0	1.000
LaRose, Pawtucket* .	2	1	2	0	0	1.000
Ordway, Manchester .	5	1	2	0	1	1.000
Vollweiler, Pitt ..	3	1	2	0	0	1.000
Constantino, Pitt .	4	0	1	0	0	1.000
Parchem, Pitt*	2	0	1	0	1	1.000
Sanossian, Paw	2	0	1	0	0	1.000
Medich, Manchester .	8	3	10	1	0	.929
Scally, Pittsfield ...	9	3	8	2	0	.846
Acosta, Waterbury ..	5	0	4	1	0	.800
Slade, Pittsfield	9	1	2	1	0	.750
Hayward, Waterbury	7	0	3	1	0	.750
Ley, Manchester* ...	6	0	3	1	0	.750
Champion, Reading .	3	0	3	1	0	.750
Valesente, Pitt	4	0	2	1	0	.667
O'Connell, Man*	2	0	2	1	0	.667
Demery, Elmira* ...	5	0	1	1	0	.500
Johnson, Man	5	0	1	1	0	.500

The following players do not have any recorded accepted chances at the positions indicated; therefore, are not listed in the fielding averages for those particular positions: Brookens, p; Fisk, 1b; Foucault, p; Herrera, of; Minster, of; Mountain*, p; Nutter, p; Redmon, p; Scramuzzo, p; Shitanishi, of; Smith, p; Urrieta, 3b.

CLUB PITCHING

Club	G.	CG.	ShO.	Sv.	IP.	H.	R.	ER.	HR.	BB.	Int. BB.	HB.	SO.	WP.	Bk.	ERA.
Waterbury	141	45	17	28	1172	1065	522	421	89	533	51	51	719	28	1	3.23
Elmira	139	53	13	14	1150	1101	611	509	102	630	56	33	701	54	7	3.98
Pittsfield	138	51	14	18	1147	1080	595	508	95	604	39	39	821	74	1	3.99
Reading	141	59	6	20	1154	1181	613	522	95	613	58	27	636	77	3	4.07
Manchester	139	39	12	22	1160	1133	667	539	115	541	31	40	672	78	1	4.18
Pawtucket	138	56	7	20	1136	1053	624	535	116	642	28	35	748	79	2	4.24

PITCHERS' RECORDS

(Leading Qualifiers for Earned-Run Average Leadership—140 or More Innings)
*Throws lefthanded.

Pitcher—Club	G.	GS.	CG.	ShO.	W.	L.	Sv.	Pct.	IP.	H.	R.	ER.	HR.	BB.	Int. BB.	HB.	SO.	WP.	ERA.
Bennett, Waterbury 29	22	10	4		12	7	2	.632	154	132	59	38	8	59	5	6	96	5	2.22
Quezada, Water .26	16	7	4		10	7	4	.588	143	130	45	37	10	25	6	1	72	1	2.33
Gogolewski, Pitt .21	21	15	2		14	5	0	.737	171	136	51	47	15	36	1	2	146	6	2.47
Moret, Pawtucket* .25	23	9	1		11	7	0	.611	158	130	66	55	13	97	0	4	124	8	3.13
Gowell, Manchester 30	29	11	1		12	11	1	.522	190	159	102	75	10	96	1	10	129	13	3.55
Assaf, Elmira 24	24	12	2		11	12	0	.478	160	144	77	67	12	82	4	2	111	13	3.77
Robinson, Paw 26	26	14	1		13	9	0	.591	176	186	99	78	15	53	7	5	81	7	3.99
Bayless, Reading .24	24	11	1		8	11	0	.421	150	150	90	67	16	88	7	0	79	7	4.02
Pirtle, Manchester .27	26	15	4		10	14	1	.417	179	166	89	80	14	69	5	3	114	7	4.02
Campbell, Pitt ...24	22	7	3		9	7	0	.563	149	151	75	70	16	75	5	5	75	11	4.23

Departmental Leaders: G—Colson, 48; GS—Gowell, 29; CG—Gogolewski, Pirtle, 15; ShO—Bennett, Pirtle, Quezada, 4; W—Gogolewski, Terlecki, 14; L—Pirtle, 14; Sv—Colson, 16; Pct.—Gogolewski, .737; IP—Gowell, 190; H—Robinson, 186; R—Gowell, 102; ER—Terlecki, 81; HR—Clark, 24; BB—Moret, 97; IBB—Cluck, 12; HB—Kison, 21; SO—Gogolewski, 146; WP—Assaf, Gowell, Terlecki, 13.

(All Pitchers—Listed Alphabetically)

Pitcher—Club	G.	GS.	CG.	ShO.	W.	L.	Sv.	Pct.	IP.	H.	R.	ER.	HR.	BB.	Int. BB.	HB.	SO.	WP.	ERA.
Acosta, Waterbury . 5	5	1	0		1	4	0	.200	24	22	15	14	3	11	1	2	20	2	5.25
Assaf, Elmira 24	24	12	2		11	12	0	.478	160	144	77	67	12	82	4	2	111	13	3.77
Bailey, Manchester .20	6	1	0		5	5	0	.500	65	63	36	28	2	45	3	4	29	3	3.88
Balderson, Elmira .21	5	2	2		4	4	0	.500	73	58	43	38	6	59	6	5	46	2	4.68
Bayless, Reading .24	24	11	1		8	11	0	.421	150	150	90	67	16	88	7	0	79	7	4.02
Beckett, Pawtucket 22	3	0	0		2	6	3	.250	43	36	41	38	6	45	1	5	28	8	7.95
Bennett, Wat 29	22	10	4		12	7	2	.632	154	132	59	38	8	59	5	6	96	5	2.22
Blackmon, Pitt ..14	1	0	0		2	1	3	.667	34	38	16	12	1	17	2	1	21	1	3.18
Bongiovanni, Man .20	20	4	1		8	8	0	.500	110	106	68	55	9	58	3	4	79	9	4.50
Boteze, Pawtucket .15	4	0	0		1	2	0	.333	39	42	20	18	1	25	0	0	17	4	4.15
Brookens, Elmira . 1	1	0	0		0	0	0	.000	7	8	3	3	1	3	1	0	3	1	3.86
Campbell, Pitt ...24	22	7	3		9	7	0	.563	149	151	75	70	16	75	5	5	75	11	4.23
Cates, Reading* .13	11	3	0		2	5	0	.286	58	59	39	29	7	42	4	0	34	4	4.50
Champion, Reading. 3	3	2	0		2	1	0	.667	17	16	9	9	0	6	0	0	9	1	4.24
Chlan, Elmira ...17	16	7	1		5	8	0	.385	106	89	48	37	8	59	3	3	58	7	3.14
Clark, Manchester .26	9	2	0		5	3	0	.625	98	102	70	65	24	31	2	3	21	5	5.97
Clem, Reading ...14	13	9	1		9	2	0	.818	92	78	33	27	9	28	0	2	34	0	2.64
Clifton, Pawtucket*. 9	8	4	0		2	3	0	.286	52	53	26	17	3	27	1	2	29	4	2.94
Cluck, Waterbury*.22	8	4	1		5	3	2	.625	90	70	38	31	6	55	12	1	56	4	3.10
Colson, Man 48	2	0	0		5		16	.583	102	85	46	36	13	48	8	0	66	5	3.18
Constantino, Pitt . 4	0	0	0		1	0	0	.000	14	16	18	16	1	18	1	2	7	0	10.29
Cordeiro, Wat* ...36	6	0	0		2	3	7	.400	60	43	25	18	4	42	3	1	87	1	2.70
Curtis, Pawtucket*.21	19	9	0		9	8	0	.529	138	113	65	57	11	75	2	2	114	6	3.72
Dawson, Man* ...19	19	2	2		7	9	0	.438	111	120	65	42	9	36	4	3	68	8	3.41
DeBenedetti, Elm .15	15	7	1		4	9	0	.308	93	98	45	40	8	36	7	1	45	2	3.87

Pitcher—Club	G.	GS.	CG.	ShO.	W.	L.	Sv.	Pct.	IP.	H.	R.	ER.	HR.	BB.	Int. BB.	HB.	SO.	WP.	ERA.
Demery, Elmira*	5	5	0	0	0	4	0	.000	17	22	20	16	1	20	2	1	14	1	8.47
Dettore, Wat	23	22	5	2	6	11	0	.353	125	142	82	70	16	61	3	5	58	3	5.04
Dowd, Pawtucket	5	0	0	0	0	1	1	.000	10	15	13	13	4	6	0	0	6	1	11.70
Drummond, Man	14	0	0	0	1	0	0	1.000	39	53	36	27	6	24	1	6	19	10	6.23
Ferraro, Elmira*	24	0	0	0	1	2	1	.333	21	17	11	9	3	11	1	1	7	2	3.86
Fiskland, Man	18	11	2	0	3	7	0	.300	85	95	58	50	6	45	1	4	46	4	5.29
Foreman, Reading	26	6	1	0	3	3	2	.500	93	110	54	51	9	42	7	1	36	5	4.94
Foucault, Pitt	2	0	0	0	0	0	0	.000	2	3	1	1	0	0	0	0	3	1	4.50
Gaines, Pawtucket	22	10	1	1	2	4	2	.333	54	63	53	49	8	40	2	6	35	8	8.17
Gladden, Elmira	34	13	5	1	4	7	6	.364	112	115	57	47	11	54	6	2	63	5	3.78
Gogolewski, Pitt	21	21	15	2	14	5	0	.737	171	136	51	47	15	36	1	2	146	6	2.47
Gowell, Manchester	30	29	11	1	12	11	1	.522	190	159	102	75	10	96	1	10	129	13	3.55
Hayward, Wat	7	5	0	0	0	2	0	.000	18	27	20	20	4	16	1	1	8	1	10.00
Hendrix, Wat	26	4	1	1	9	3	0	.750	98	91	37	33	7	27	7	2	57	1	3.03
Henninger, Pitt	18	17	10	2	9	7	0	.563	107	119	51	46	8	38	4	2	70	4	3.70
Holland, Reading	22	6	3	0	6	6	0	.500	82	117	59	48	10	51	7	2	48	10	5.27
Horne, Reading*	20	3	1	0	2	4	0	.333	49	44	24	22	2	22	7	0	14	2	4.04
Houser, Wat*	22	22	6	2	9	6	0	.600	123	138	62	46	10	67	2	4	62	3	3.37
Janek, Pittsfield*	20	1	0	0	1	1	2	.500	33	30	18	18	4	22	1	0	13	5	4.91
Johnson, Man	5	0	0	0	0	0	0	.000	11	20	11	9	1	14	0	0	2	0	7.36
Kison, Waterbury	19	19	10	3	10	4	0	.714	130	93	42	33	3	54	2	21	82	2	2.28
Lamb, Waterbury	30	0	0	0	5	2	11	.714	49	27	8	8	3	25	2	1	39	1	1.47
Lange, Manchester	38	0	0	0	7	4	4	.636	87	80	35	24	7	16	4	2	58	3	2.48
LaRose, Pawtucket*	2	2	2	2	0	0	0	1.000	18	7	0	0	0	8	0	1	9	0	0.00
Laxton, Reading*	15	15	4	1	6	5	0	.545	78	58	41	31	2	93	2	9	63	11	3.58
Ley, Manchester*	6	4	0	0	0	3	0	.000	14	20	19	18	5	23	0	1	11	0	11.57
Lohfink, Paw	40	3	1	0	5	6	8	.455	77	76	37	35	11	47	1	0	64	7	4.09
Lyscio, Elmira	9	3	0	1	7	0	0	.125	54	61	34	31	9	22	1	3	34	0	5.17
Marrujo, Wat	13	0	0	0	2	0	1	1.000	33	27	9	8	3	10	2	0	22	0	2.18
Medich, Man	8	1	0	0	5	0	0	.000	42	47	28	23	3	21	0	0	18	7	4.93
Mercado, Paw	23	1	0	0	2	3	0	.400	51	59	28	24	10	15	3	0	20	1	4.24
Moret, Pawtucket*	25	23	9	1	11	7	0	.611	158	130	66	55	13	97	0	4	124	8	3.13
Mountain, Paw*	5	0	0	0	0	0	0	.000	3	4	1	2	0	2	0	0	2	0	6.00
Muniz, Reading	27	5	2	1	4	3	6	.571	86	77	33	29	11	42	3	2	54	2	3.03
Myers, Elmira	14	0	0	0	0	1	1	.000	35	32	18	16	3	14	1	3	28	3	4.11
Nutter, Reading	4	4	3	0	3	1	0	.750	29	27	8	7	0	5	0	1	24	1	2.17
O'Connell, Man*	2	0	0	0	1	0	0	1.000	7	4	2	2	0	5	0	1	4	1	2.57
Olson, Manchester	11	11	2	1	4	4	0	.500	70	66	34	30	8	42	1	2	31	6	3.86
Ordway, Man	5	0	0	0	1	0	0	1.000	15	10	4	3	0	13	1	1	6	0	1.80
Parchem, Pitt*	2	1	0	0	1	0	0	1.000	7	6	2	2	0	7	0	2	3	2	2.57
Pasierb, Elmira	19	19	4	1	4	10	0	.286	107	114	64	52	11	32	4	0	62	4	4.37
Penn, Reading	37	1	0	0	8	4	11	.667	85	101	45	39	2	49	11	2	60	7	4.13
Pirtle, Manchester	27	26	15	4	10	14	1	.417	179	166	89	80	14	69	5	3	114	7	4.02
Prediger, Paw	18	14	7	1	7	5	0	.583	98	84	46	40	12	47	1	5	51	5	3.67
Quezada, Wat	26	16	7	0	10	7	5	.588	143	130	45	37	10	25	6	1	72	1	2.33
Raffo, Reading	12	12	5	0	3	8	0	.273	83	93	53	49	12	45	5	2	26	10	5.31
Redmon, Pittsfield	1	1	0	0	0	1	0	.000	2	2	2	2	0	0	2	0	1	1	9.00
Robinson, Paw	26	26	14	1	13	9	0	.591	176	186	99	78	15	53	7	5	81	7	3.99
Salazar, Elmira*	4	0	0	0	0	0	0	.000	9	20	15	8	0	11	0	2	1	2	8.00
Sanossian, Paw	2	0	0	0	0	1	0	.000	2	4	6	6	1	3	1	1	1	1	27.00
Scally, Pittsfield	9	2	0	0	1	1	0	.500	50	51	27	24	3	26	3	0	27	6	4.32
Scramuzzo, Reading	2	2	1	0	1	1	0	.500	15	14	6	5	0	2	1	0	9	1	3.00
Sells, Waterbury	12	12	0	0	3	5	0	.375	61	60	44	40	12	36	4	2	33	1	5.90
Shutts, Pittsfield	37	0	0	0	4	6	8	.400	62	57	32	23	5	50	7	4	63	3	4.06
Sierra, Pittsfield	37	7	1	1	6	4	0	.600	111	64	50	15	43	3	1	65	4	5.56
Slade, Pittsfield	9	4	1	1	2	5	0	.400	36	28	24	8	3	13	1	4	25	4	2.00
Smith, Elmira	1	0	0	0	0	0	0	.000	1	1	0	0	0	1	0	0	0	0	0.00
Sommer, Elmira	30	4	1	0	3	7	1	.300	92	102	60	51	11	44	7	2	64	3	4.99
Szado, Pittsfield*	13	10	2	1	3	4	0	.429	54	44	24	21	4	50	2	0	55	4	3.50
Terlecki, Reading	27	24	8	1	14	7	1	.667	160	165	88	81	13	89	3	3	88	13	4.56
Terpko, Pittsfield	20	16	4	1	6	10	0	.375	97	92	61	48	7	66	4	7	78	6	4.45
Thomas, Paw*	31	4	0	0	3	4	4	.429	61	52	34	28	6	34	4	2	33	3	4.13
M. Thompson, Pitt	19	18	6	1	5	9	0	.643	110	101	70	65	10	77	2	3	102	10	5.32
Valesente, Pitt	4	0	0	0	2	0	0	1.000	23	20	10	10	4	13	0	0	12	2	3.91
Vega, Elmira	26	19	8	2	8	7	0	.533	128	131	63	58	13	88	3	2	71	4	4.08
Vollweiler, Pitt	3	3	0	0	0	1	0	.000	9	12	8	8	0	11	0	0	4	3	0.00
Washington, Paw	13	9	6	1	5	2	0	.625	86	53	32	28	4	60	4	0	96	3	2.93
Weaver, Elmira*	13	6	3	0	3	3	1	.500	68	33	16	11	2	35	3	2	25	2	2.06
Whitson, Pitt	14	11	5	1	4	3	1	.571	65	64	37	34	4	38	3	2	65	1	4.71
Williams, Paw	16	12	3	0	4	6	0	.400	72	72	52	47	11	58	1	2	38	5	5.88
Wolfe, Reading	13	12	6	1	7	2	0	.778	76	72	31	29	4	29	2	2	58	2	3.43
Wright, Elmira	18	3	0	0	2	3	2	.400	51	37	30	21	1	40	2	0	45	3	3.71
York, Elmira	14	0	0	0	5	0	2	1.000	34	19	7	4	2	19	5	4	24	0	1.06

BALKS—DeBenedetti, Vega, 2 each; Bongiovanni, Demery, Gladden, Horne, Lamb, Raffo, Robinson, Scramuzzo, Sommer, Valesente, Washington, 1 each.

COMBINATION SHUTOUTS — DeBenedetti-Ferraro, Pasierb-Weaver-Gladden, Vega-Gladden, Elmira; Bongiovanni-Colson, Dawson-Lange, Fiskland-Colson, Manchester; Szado-Sierra, Pittsfield.

NO-HIT GAMES—Whitson, Pittsfield, defeated Waterbury, 4-0, May 29 (seven innings).

Southern League

Leading Batter
STEVE BRYE
Chattanooga

League President
SAM C. SMITH

Leading Pitcher
DAVE HARTMAN
Jacksonville

CHAMPIONSHIP WINNERS IN PREVIOUS YEARS

Year	Team	Pct.	Year	Team	Pct.
1904	Macon	.598	1925	Spartanburg	.620
1905	Macon	.625	1926	Greenville	.662
1906	Savannah	.637	1927	Greenville	.622
1907	Charleston	.620	1928	Asheville	.664
1908	Jacksonville	.694	1929	Asheville	.605
1909	Chattanooga*	.738		Knoxville*	.634
	Augusta	.702	1930	Greenville*	.620
1910	Columbus	.588		Macon	.643
1911	Columbus*	.681	1931-32-33-34-35	Did not	
	Columbia	.710		operate.	
1912	Jacksonville*	.679	1936	Jacksonville	.652
	Columbus	.632		Columbus*	.650
1913	Savannah	.754	1937	Columbus	.572
	Savannah	.593		Savannah (3rd)†	.565
1914	Savannah*	.667	1938	Savannah	.574
	Albany	.650		Macon (2nd)†	.570
1915	Macon	.588	1939	Columbus	.601
	Columbus*	.686		Augusta (2nd)†	.597
1916	Augusta*	.617	1940	Savannah	.627
	Columbia	.631		Columbia (2nd)†	.583
1917	Charleston	.741	1941	Macon	.643
	Columbia*	.667		Columbia (2nd)†	.636
1918	Did not operate.		1942	Charleston	.620
1919	Columbia	.585		Macon (2nd)†	.585
1920	Columbia	.633	1943-44-45	Did not operate.	
1921	Columbia	.642	1946	Columbus	.568
1922	Charleston	.625		Augusta (4th)†	.547
1923	Charlotte*	.653	1947	Columbus	.563
	Macon	.580		Savannah (2nd)†	.563
1924	Augusta	.612	1948	Charleston	.572
				Greenville (3rd)†	.549

Year	Team	Pct.
1949	Macon‡	.623
1950	Macon‡	.588
1951	Montgomery	.607
1952	Columbia	.649
	Montgomery (3rd)†	.558
1953	Jacksonville	.679
	Savannah (2nd)†	.571
1954	Jacksonville	.593
	Savannah (2nd)†	.571
1955	Columbia	.636
	Augusta (3rd)†	.543
1956	Jacksonville‡	.621
1957	Augusta	.636
	Charlotte (2nd)†	.562
1958	Augusta	.550
	Macon (3rd)†	.500
1959	Knoxville	.557
	Gastonia (4th)†	.504
1960	Columbia	.597
	Savannah (3rd)†	.561
1961	Asheville	.635
1962	Savannah	.662
	Macon (3rd)†	.576
1963	Augusta*	.661
	Lynchburg	.662
1964	Lynchburg	.579
1965	Columbus	.572
1966	Mobile	.629
1967	Birmingham	.604
1968	Asheville	.614
1969	Charlotte	.579

*Won split-season playoff. †Won four-club playoff. ‡Won championship and four-club playoff.
(NOTE—Known as South Atlantic League from 1904 through 1963.)

STANDING OF CLUBS AT CLOSE OF SEASON, SEPTEMBER 4

Club	Col.	Mty.	Birm.	Sav.	Jax.	Char.	Mob.	Ash.	W.	L.	T.	Pct.	G.B.
Columbus (16*)	..	10	10	10	9	11	13	15	78	59	0	.569	....
Montgomery (6*)	10	..	13	11	10	11	12	12	79	60	0	.568	..
Birmingham (11)	9	7	..	7	15	15	9	11	73	65	0	.529	5½
Savannah (5*)	10	9	13	..	9	6	12	12	71	67	1	.514	7½
Jacksonville (8/18*)	9	10	5	10	..	14	10	9	67	70	0	.489	11
Charlotte (9)	9	9	5	14	6	..	13	10	66	73	1	.475	13
Mobile (4*)	7	7	10	7	10	7	..	11	59	78	0	.431	19
Asheville (15)	5	8	9	8	11	9	9	..	59	80	0	.424	20

Key to major league farm teams (indicated by numbers after clubs in standing) shown on Page 384. Playoff—None.

Regular-Season Attendance—Asheville, 28,720; Birmingham, 39,787; Charlotte, 57,107; Columbus, 40,758; Jacksonville, 64,722; Mobile, 35,775; Montgomery, 57,631; Savannah, 33,854. Total, 358,354. All-star game, 6,598. No playoff.

Managers: Asheville—James R. Snyder; Birmingham—Phil Cavarretta; Charlotte—Harry Warner, Pete Appleton; Columbus—Jim Williams; Jacksonville—Gus Niarhos; Mobile—Tom Saffell, Larry Sherry; Montgomery—Frank Overmire; Savannah—Ray Hathaway.

All-Star Team: 1B—Dolinsek, Columbus; 2B—Andersen, Montgomery; 3B—Hodge, Savannah; SS—Busse, Columbus; OF—Covington, Jacksonville, Clark, Birmingham, Brye, Charlotte; C—Dempsey, Charlotte; Ferguson, Asheville; P—C. Swanson, Montgomery; LaGrow, Montgomery; Manager —Williams, Columbus.

(Compiled by Howe News Bureau, Chicago, Ill.)

CLUB BATTING

Club	G.	AB.	R.	OR.	H.	TB.	2B.	3B.	HR.	RBI.	SH.	SF.	BB.	Int. BB.	HP.	SO.	SB.	CS.	LOB.	Pct.
Birm'gham	138	4451	529	511	1114	1517	170	31	57	480	44	34	398	21	27	711	55	41	929	.250
Charlotte	.140	4505	465	502	1111	1453	150	27	43	412	83	27	539	42	32	756	77	58	1087	.247
Columbus	.137	4427	477	426	1072	1439	139	54	60	406	67	34	368	50	41	803	69	44	913	.242
Jacks'ville	.137	4539	532	512	1092	1563	135	29	86	481	65	39	472	52	40	812	82	28	989	.241
M'tgomery	.139	4470	493	410	1055	1527	170	29	62	399	42	33	800	58	28	928				.236
Asheville	.139	4436	404	498	998	1363	175	23	48	348	49	29	355	39	31	749	100	56	876	.225
Mobile	139	4263	376	441	959	1244	131	17	40	328	74	27	424	41	33	730	62	42	922	.225
Savannah	.139	4349	478	454	970	1444	161	38	79	424	63	26	450	42	55	901	71	40	900	.223

INDIVIDUAL BATTING

(Leading Qualifiers for Batting Championship—434 or More Plate Appearances)

*Bats lefthanded. †Switch-hitter.

Player and Club	G.	AB.	R.	H.	TB.	2B.	3B.	HR.	RBI.	SH.	SF.	BB.	HP.	SO.	SB.	CS.	Pct.
Brye, Stephen, Charlotte	106	374	52	115	170	17	10	6	48	3	5	53	4	39	3	8	.307
Clark, James, Birmingham	.133	443	71	132	195	30	6	7	73	0	9	74	5	77	6	7	.298
Dolinsek, John, Columbus*	.137	469	61	139	203	20	10	8	57	4	9	64	8	53	6	8	.296
Hodge, Harold, Savannah†	.138	506	72	147	214	28	6	9	66	1	4	43	11	78	13	5	.291
Monzon, Daniel, Charlotte	.138	517	69	149	185	19	1	5	45	5	4	72	7	40	20	19	.288
Ferguson, William, Asheville	.123	414	49	116	171	50	2	7	51	1	3	38	8	58	6	5	.280
Lisetski, Michael, Asheville	.119	390	44	103	150	19	5	6	40	0	5	52	1	56	7	4	.264
Busse, Raymond, Columbus	.105	402	48	106	146	13	3	7	49	6	1	26	2	70	5	8	.264
Pamlanye, James, Birm	.104	415	58	107	137	17	2	3	19	5	2	20	7	78	3	1	.258
Covington, James, Jax*	.127	417	70	106	194	15	5	21	65	4	4	76	3	98	6	2	.254
Frias, Jesus, Jacksonville	.136	492	42	125	142	13	2	0	44	10	5	25	3	73	8	3	.254

Departmental Leaders: G—Hodge, Monzon, 138; AB—Monzon, 517; R—Hodge, F. Smith, 72; H—Monzon, 149; TB—Hodge, 214; 2B—James Clark, Ferguson, 30; 3B—Brye, Dolinsek, 10; HR—Covington, 21; RBI—James Clark, Sanders, 73; SH—Kolb, 12; SF—Dolinsek, 9; BB—Covington, 76; HP—F. Smith, 13; SO—Young, 124; SB—Andersen, 24; CS—Monzon, 19.

(All Players—Listed Alphabetically)

Player and Club	G.	AB.	R.	H.	TB.	2B.	3B.	HR.	RBI.	SH.	SF.	BB.	HP.	SO.	SB.	CS.	Pct.
Abbott, Lawrence, Birm†	..	33	53	3	12	13	1	0	0	3	3	0	0	19	0	0	.226
Adams, Glenn C., Col*	..	83	234	32	69	89	10	2	2	20	1	0	16	7	15	2	1	.295
Adkins, William, Birm*	..	32	291	47	79	102	10	2	3	30	3	1	34	0	11	12	11	.271
Allen, Ronald C., Savannah	.116	411	56	98	160	11	9	11	51	6	5	32	8	86	9	8	.238
Ammann, Eugene, Jax	..	11	9	0	0	0	0	0	0	0	0	1	0	1	0	3	0	.000
Andersen, Hagan, Mty	.131	507	68	127	168	20	0	7	33	5	1	47	8	49	24	8	.250
Andrens, Sheldon, Ash*	.130	423	44	101	122	10	1	3	30	5	4	27	4	17	14	17	.239
Apellaniz, Domingo, Jax	..	3	3	1	1	4	0	1	0	1	3	0	0	0	1	1	0	.333
Armbrister, Edison, Col	.127	428	58	102	155	13	8	8	46	3	6	22	5	57	9	5	.238
Arruda, Thomas, Charlotte	. 51	10	0	1	2	1	0	0	1	1	0	0	0	6	0	0	.100
Ash, Robert, Savannah	..	4	5	0	0	0	0	0	0	0	0	0	0	0	0	0	.000
Baldwin, Michael, Mobile*	..	14	23	0	1	1	0	0	0	2	0	0	0	0	13	0	0	.043
Barrett, Alexander, Col	....	8	21	2	3	3	0	0	0	1	0	0	3	1	3	0	1	.143
Barski, Martin, Montgomery	.110	336	47	89	119	7	1	7	27	2	2	32	1	43	2	1	.265
Bates, Charles, Jax*	..	18	29	1	5	6	1	0	0	3	0	0	4	0	8	0	0	.172
Bauer, John, Mobile*	..	45	12	1	2	2	0	0	0	1	1	0	1	0	2	0	0	.167
Belinsky, Robert, Asheville*	. 5	7	1	1	1	0	0	0	1	0	0	2	1	0	.143
Belloir, Robert, Savannah	.18	47	3	10	12	0	1	0	5	3	0	6	2	7	1	0	.213
Bertino, Charles, Jax	.24	22	1	3	4	1	0	0	1	4	1	0	0	6	0	0	.136

Player and Club	G.	AB.	R.	H.	TB.	2B.	3B.	HR.	RBI.	SH.	SF.	BB.	HP.	SO.	SB.	CS.	Pct.
Bethell, Roy, Columbus†	2	1	0	0	0	0	0	0	0	0	0	0	0	0	0	0	.000
Bickerton, Brien, Birm*	9	7	0	2	2	0	0	1	0	0	0	0	0	4	0	0	.286
Blanco, C. Oswaldo, Mobile .	54	184	21	55	85	12	3	4	22	2	0	21	3	36	1	1	.299
Blanken, Randy, Asheville .	17	5	0	0	0	0	0	0	0	0	0	0	0	1	0	0	.000
Blateric, Stephen, Ash	37	29	3	2	2	0	0	0	0	0	0	2	0	15	0	0	.069
Blessitt, Isaiah, Mty 104	345	37	89	136	14	6	7	36	2	2	31	3	87	12	4		.258
Bond, Jerry, Savannah	14	37	4	5	8	0	0	1	3	0	0	1	4	11	1	0	.135
Boyd, Gary, Savannah	29	43	6	11	21	2	1	2	6	2	0	1	0	15	0	0	.256
Branscomb, Marvin, Ash ..119	371	31	77	102	17	1	2	23	5	1	18	2	57	6	5		.208
Braxton, James, Savannah .	9	24	0	3	3	0	0	0	1	0	1	0	0	10	0	0	.125
Brohamer, John, Savannah†	75	269	31	63	102	17	5	4	22	6	2	24	2	31	3	2	.234
Bryant, Donald, Columbus .	17	71	6	16	24	2	0	2	9	0	0	6	0	14	0	0	.225
Brye, Stephen, Charlotte ..106	374	52	115	170	17	10	6	48	3	5	53	4	39	3	8		.307
Busse, Raymond, Columbus .105	402	48	106	146	13	3	7	49	6	1	26	2	70	5	8		.264
Camacho, Jacinto, Sav*	9	12	2	3	3	0	0	0	1	1	0	1	0	7	0	0	.250
Campbell, Dayle, Mobile .	17	53	6	10	17	1	0	2	6	0	0	8	1	7	0	1	.189
Carden, William, Jax	18	39	2	2	2	0	0	0	0	4	0	3	0	16	0	0	.051
Chambers, Ronald, Mty* ..	77	198	20	47	57	7	0	1	12	3	0	30	5	36	1	0	.237
Christman, Gerald, Char ..	14	27	1	1	1	0	0	0	0	4	0	2	0	10	0	0	.037
Clark, Glen, Columbus† ..	35	82	6	18	26	4	2	0	12	0	1	6	0	20	0	0	.220
Clark, James, Birmingham ..133	443	71	132	195	30	6	7	73	0	0	74	5	77	6	7		.298
Clark, Jerry, Savannah† ..	39	130	23	33	45	5	2	1	7	3	0	20	3	20	4	2	.254
Clark, William, Mobile ..	35	80	4	12	16	4	0	0	4	1	0	11	0	29	0	1	.150
Click, Paul, Jacksonville .	3	5	1	0	0	0	0	0	0	0	0	1	0	2	0	0	.000
Coggins, Franklin, Sav† ..	62	211	20	52	79	10	4	3	15	1	0	21	2	45	2	3	.246
Coleman, Paul, Montgomery .	1	1	0	0	0	0	0	0	0	0	0	0	0	0	0	0	.000
Conde, Ramon, Asheville ..	32	64	2	16	19	3	0	0	5	1	0	5	0	11	1	1	.250
Conger, Gregory, Birm* ..	14	27	4	4	8	1	0	1	3	1	0	4	1	14	0	0	.148
Cook, David M., Mty	25	15	0	0	0	0	0	0	0	0	0	0	0	9	0	0	.000
Cook, Tom D., Birmingham .	71	196	21	40	55	8	2	1	16	1	0	34	1	55	0	0	.204
Cooper, Clarence, Ash*	6	7	0	1	1	0	0	0	0	1	0	0	0	4	0	0	.143
Cooper, Durant, 13 Mob-30 Char	43	52	6	11	13	0	1	0	4	5	0	3	0	7	0	0	.212
Copeland, Howell, Birm† ..	4	7	1	1	1	0	0	0	0	0	0	0	0	2	0	0	.143
Corbin, A. Ray, Charlotte .	32	79	5	13	15	2	0	0	7	4	0	0	0	19	0	0	.165
Correa, Maximo A. Mobile* ..	79	191	20	36	37	1	0	0	7	5	0	36	0	33	9	6	.188
Correll, Victor, Savannah ..116	371	31	85	130	15	3	8	41	1	3	38	1	77	2	1		.229
Covington, James, Mty* ..127	417	70	106	194	15	5	21	65	4	4	76	3	98	6	2		.254
Crook, Ronald, Asheville .	27	43	2	4	5	0	0	1	4	1	2	0	2	21	0	0	.093
Crossan, Lawrence, Sav ..	22	32	1	4	5	1	0	0	1	2	0	3	0	17	0	0	.125
Cunnyngham, R. Gregg, Sav.	31	17	0	1	1	0	0	0	0	2	0	0	0	11	0	0	.059
Cushmore, Stephen, Mty* ..	17	22	1	1	1	0	0	0	1	4	0	1	0	8	0	0	.045
Dailey, Terry, Jax	16	44	3	10	15	5	0	0	4	1	0	7	0	12	0	0	.227
Dempsey, J. Rikard, Char ..105	351	28	86	130	20	6	4	42	2	1	35	1	66	4	1		.245
Dickinson, Richard, Sav* ..	74	218	11	51	58	5	1	0	15	3	3	22	0	22	1	3	.234
Dolinsek, John, Columbus* ..137	469	61	139	203	20	10	8	57	4	9	64	8	53	6	8		.296
Dominguez, Marcelino, Mob .	39	38	0	5	5	0	0	0	0	0	0	2	0	9	0	0	.132
Donahue, Jerome, Mty*	37	9	0	1	1	0	0	0	1	0	0	1	0	5	0	0	.111
Dreier, Douglas, Asheville .	30	34	1	1	2	1	0	0	0	4	0	1	0	19	0	0	.029
Ezell, Glenn, Charlotte ..	49	117	13	35	50	3	0	4	21	0	1	20	2	23	0	0	.299
Ferguson, William, Ash ..123	414	49	116	171	30	2	7	51	1	3	38	8	58	6	5		.280
Ferrell, William, Jax	4	8	0	1	1	0	0	0	1	1	0	0	0	2	0	0	.125
Fisher, Thomas, Jax	4	0	1	0	0	0	0	0	0	0	0	0	0	0	0	0	.000
Fitzgerald, William, Birm .	15	47	6	12	15	3	0	0	7	0	0	4	1	10	0	0	.255
Flanagan, Michael A., Col ..	25	51	6	9	19	4	0	2	5	8	1	1	0	20	0	0	.176
Foor, James, Montgomery* ..	20	52	1	7	8	1	0	0	2	2	0	3	0	18	0	0	.135
Forsch, Kenneth, Columbus .	22	48	2	4	4	0	0	0	2	7	0	4	1	21	0	0	.083
Foshie, Brent, Jacksonville .	32	12	0	0	0	0	0	0	0	0	0	0	0	2	0	0	.000
Foster, Clifford, Charlotte* .	62	150	20	36	57	8	3	1	14	2	0	25	4	52	1	0	.240
Frailing, Kenneth, Mobile† .	37	59	1	14	18	1	0	1	5	5	0	4	2	11	0	0	.237
Francingues, Wayne, Mobile .	18	49	1	11	12	1	0	0	4	0	0	3	1	12	1	1	.224
Frias, Jesus, Jacksonville ..136	492	42	125	142	13	2	0	44	10	5	25	3	73	8	3		.254
Geronimo, Cesar, Columbus* .	74	264	26	71	88	9	4	0	21	2	5	17	2	46	5	4	.269
Gilbreth, William, Mty* ..	40	76	5	10	11	1	0	0	0	2	1	0	1	26	0	0	.132
Gill, Kenneth, Charlotte ..	42	46	2	9	11	2	0	0	5	4	1	1	0	21	0	0	.196
Glass, John, Jacksonville ..	18	31	2	1	1	0	0	0	0	5	0	4	0	10	0	0	.032
Glassco, Craig, Jacksonville .	31	11	0	0	0	0	0	0	0	0	0	1	0	1	0	0	.000
Godby, Danny, Asheville ..	92	341	39	89	132	20	4	5	33	1	3	29	2	59	15	8	.261
Goltz, David, Charlotte .	1	1	0	0	0	0	0	0	0	0	0	0	0	1	0	0	.000
Gomez, Juan, Birmingham .	64	214	13	51	60	7	1	0	15	4	4	13	2	32	0	0	.238
Grangaard, David, Columbus.	58	179	18	40	62	7	3	3	22	0	2	33	1	48	0	0	.223
Grayson, Thomas, Mty* ..123	447	56	113	176	19	1	14	61	0	3	30	1	50	2	0		.253
Greif, William, Columbus† ..	27	65	2	9	9	0	0	2	0	1	0	0	0	28	0	0	.138
Haggard, Jerry, Savannah* .	47	137	5	22	26	4	0	0	6	3	0	13	2	23	2	1	.161
Hahn, William, Charlotte* ..122	389	33	93	141	20	2	8	63	2	4	35	3	70	0	0		.239
Hamilton, David, Birm* ..	21	26	3	7	7	0	0	0	1	0	0	8	0	10	0	0	.269
Hamm, Peter, Charlotte ..	10	29	0	5	5	0	0	0	1	3	1	0	0	6	0	0	.172
Hankammer, John, Mobile .	16	10	0	1	1	0	0	0	0	1	0	0	0	3	0	0	.100
Harris, Walter, Columbus .	25	64	0	3	4	0	0	0	0	1	2	1	0	34	0	0	.047
Hart, Ronald, Savannah .	9	22	1	6	7	1	0	0	3	0	1	3	0	3	0	0	.273
Hartman, David, Jax*	22	49	10	10	15	3	1	0	5	2	1	7	0	20	1	0	.204
Harvey, Slidell, Columbus* .	74	223	34	63	87	3	3	5	31	2	2	24	1	44	3	0	.283

Player and Club	G.	AB.	R.	H.	TB.	2B.	3B.	HR.	RBI.	SH.	SF.	BB.	HP.	SO.	SB.	CS.	Pct.
Haynes, Bruce, Charlotte ...	27	44	3	6	6	0	0	0	3	5	1	4	0	15	0	0	.136
Hebert, Gerald, Jacksonville.	5	3	0	0	0	0	0	0	0	0	0	0	0	0	0	0	.000
Hefferon, John, Birm ...	17	4	0	1	1	0	0	0	0	0	0	0	0	2	0	0	.250
Hendrick, George, Birm	54	199	30	57	87	12	0	6	20	0	2	17	1	34	1	4	.286
Herrera, Jose, Jacksonville .	8	27	6	6	6	0	0	0	2	0	0	1	0	4	0	0	.222
Higgins, Charles, Ash* ...	39	40	6	4	7	0	0	1	5	1	0	5	0	19	0	0	.100
Hill, David Eddie, Ash* ..	36	20	2	4	7	0	0	1	1	1	1	3	0	7	0	0	.200
Hinsley, Jerry, Savannah ...	10	25	1	4	4	0	0	0	0	0	0	1	0	6	0	0	.160
Hodge, Harold, Savannah† ..	138	506	72	147	214	28	6	9	66	1	4	43	11	78	13	5	.291
Hoff, James, Asheville	126	398	41	91	110	12	2	1	23	4	4	31	5	17	11	3	.229
Holland, Gary, Jacksonville .	84	271	31	58	86	7	0	7	28	2	3	37	4	51	6	2	.214
Hosley, Timothy, Mty	110	326	41	70	147	15	1	20	50	2	5	46	5	99	4	0	.215
Hottman, Kenneth, Mobile .	19	50	4	6	8	2	0	0	2	0	1	8	1	13	0	0	.120
Howell, Gregory, Mobile* ..	119	358	30	92	103	11	0	0	26	2	5	33	3	21	0	2	.257
Howell, John, Savannah* ..	5	2	0	0	0	0	0	0	0	0	0	0	0	0	0	0	.000
Huggins, Jesse, Jax* ...	8	18	3	1	1	0	0	0	0	0	0	0	0	1	0	0	.056
Humphrey, John, Columbus	28	5	0	0	0	0	0	0	0	1	0	1	0	4	0	0	.000
Humphrey, Terryal, Jax ...	101	345	36	98	147	21	2	8	44	1	2	25	2	38	3	1	.284
Jagutis, H. John, Birm ...	69	245	27	58	70	7	1	1	12	2	2	16	1	23	3	2	.237
James, Willie, Jax ...	112	390	62	85	123	13	5	5	36	3	5	51	3	77	8	4	.218
Jata, Paul, Montgomery ...	101	358	43	106	160	26	2	8	52	2	1	22	2	16	0	1	.296
Jedelsky, James, Mobile† ..	84	295	23	75	84	6	1	6	26	0	3	26	2	52	2	7	.254
Johnson, C. Barth, Mobile .	5	11	0	3	3	0	0	0	2	1	0	0	0	2	0	0	.273
Johnson, Donald, Jax	38	75	6	19	27	2	0	2	13	0	1	16	0	25	1	1	.253
Johnson, Michael, Asheville .	54	5	0	0	0	0	0	0	1	0	0	0	0	3	0	0	.000
Jones, Stephen, Jacksonville .	53	213	29	64	90	12	1	4	22	4	1	10	5	46	10	2	.300
Kaiser, Robert, Savannah* .	20	37	2	6	7	1	0	0	2	0	0	0	0	16	0	0	.162
Kampf, Frederick, Birm ...	23	55	7	2	2	0	0	0	1	2	0	4	0	35	0	0	.036
Kelly, J Thomas, Jax* ...	93	266	33	64	100	10	1	8	38	0	2	41	3	37	2	4	.241
Kelso, William, Birmingham	37	64	8	16	27	2	0	3	15	1	0	4	0	13	0	0	.250
Kendrick, Harry, Mty	18	55	5	13	14	1	0	0	0	0	1	4	1	7	0	3	.236
Kennedy, Donald, Savannah .	7	2	0	0	0	0	0	0	0	0	0	0	0	1	0	0	.000
Killion, Bruce, Savannah ...	27	44	0	3	3	0	0	0	2	3	0	3	0	19	0	0	.068
Kimball, Frank, Asheville ..	104	256	21	63	91	7	0	7	31	0	3	44	1	51	1	0	.246
King, Douglas, Birmingham .	10	30	4	7	8	1	0	0	5	0	0	2	0	9	1	0	.233
Klinger, Donald, Jacksonville	3	6	1	2	5	1	1	0	0	0	0	1	0	3	0	0	.333
Koegel, Peter, Jacksonville .	78	293	49	83	143	15	3	13	51	1	4	32	7	51	6	0	.283
Kolb, Jeffery, Mobile*	83	151	17	28	29	1	0	0	8	12	1	28	1	31	6	1	.185
Kryczkowski, John. Col* ...	22	3	0	0	0	0	0	0	0	0	0	1	0	3	0	0	.000
Kurtz, Kenneth, Jacksonville*	80	301	30	79	93	12	1	0	16	1	2	26	2	29	18*	6	.262
Kusnyer, Arthur, Mobile ...	122	396	43	99	153	14	2	12	49	3	5	23	3	67	5	3	.250
LaGrow, Lerrin, Montgomery	19	54	1	9	10	1	0	0	5	2	0	0	0	16	0	0	.167
LaPointe, David, Jax*	29	75	8	14	16	2	0	0	3	0	0	8	0	17	1	0	.187
Lee, Clifford, Savannah* ...	26	35	4	7	8	1	0	0	1	1	0	7	0	12	0	0	.200
Lee, Won Kuk, Savannah ..	30	34	1	4	4	0	0	0	5	0	0	6	0	17	0	1	.118
LeFevre, Keith, Jacksonville .	34	8	0	1	1	0	0	0	1	0	1	0	0	2	0	0	.125
Leyland, James, Montgomery	2	3	0	0	0	0	0	0	0	1	0	1	0	2	0	0	.000
Limke, James, Mobile ...	31	9	0	2	2	0	0	0	1	0	0	0	0	5	0	0	.222
Lisetski, Michael, Ash ...	119	390	44	103	150	19	5	6	40	0	5	52	1	56	7	4	.264
Locke, Ronald, Jacksonville*	30	3	0	1	1	0	0	0	0	0	0	1	0	0	0	0	.333
Locklear, Gene, Asheville ..	46	122	6	20	30	4	0	2	7	0	0	6	0	37	0	1	.164
Lohse, Donald, Birmingham .	4	0	0	0	0	0	0	0	0	0	0	0	0	0	0	0	.000
Loomer, Daniel, Asheville ..	47	87	9	13	19	1	1	1	4	1	1	9	0	14	1	0	.149
Lovelace, Samuel, Birm ...	77	269	21	55	71	7	3	1	23	6	2	15	1	29	6	5	.204
MacDonnell, James, Mobile*	9	15	0	1	1	0	0	0	0	0	0	0	0	9	0	0	.067
Machemehl, Charles, Sav ...	33	35	2	3	3	0	0	0	1	0	0	4	0	20	0	0	.086
Magness, Jerry, Charlotte ..	30	11	0	1	1	0	0	0	1	0	0	1	0	3	0	0	.091
Magnuson, James, Mobile ..	13	31	2	1	1	0	0	0	2	0	1	0	1	11	0	0	.032
Major, John, Birmingham* .	9	12	1	1	4	0	0	1	4	0	0	1	0	8	0	0	.083
Marcano, Gilberto, Birm ...	21	16	3	1	1	0	0	0	0	0	2	2	0	5	0	0	.063
Marcano, Robert, Savannah .	54	122	9	19	30	1	2	9	3	0	12	1	36	3	0		.156
Marquess, Mark, Mobile †..	82	272	30	65	78	7	3	0	15	7	0	56	4	23	7	3	.239
Martinez, Anselmo, 47 Birm-54 Mobile† ..	101	307	26	61	80	13	0	2	27	5	3	21	1	44	1	2	.199
Mastin, P. Stephen, Birm .	34	8	1	2	3	1	0	0	0	0	0	3	0	4	0	0	.250
Mata, Virgilio, Asheville ..	74	213	18	43	47	4	0	0	12	3	1	13	0	32	12	4	.202
McConnell, Jerry, Sav†	43	32	3	1	2	1	0	0	1	0	0	0	0	9	0	0	.031
McDonald, James, Mobile* .	99	346	37	94	112	13	1	1	27	0	3	37	2	37	19	7	.272
McKenzie, George, Mty ...	56	202	25	48	64	8	1	2	18	3	4	16	2	19	1	0	.238
McMasters, Joel, Columbus .	23	16	1	5	6	1	0	0	1	3	0	1	1	5	0	0	.313
Mingori, Stephen, Savannah*	10	19	0	4	5	1	0	0	2	1	0	2	0	5	0	1	.211
Minster, Michael, Char ...	10	22	3	6	6	0	0	0	1	0	0	4	0	5	0	0	.273
Molinaro, Robert, Mty* ...	96	335	30	82	108	15	4	1	35	2	3	21	2	43	1	2	.245
Moloney, Richard, Mobile ..	20	4	0	1	1	0	0	0	0	1	0	0	1	0	0	0	.250
Monty, Joseph, Mobile	38	119	12	32	38	3	0	1	7	1	0	9	0	9	6	1	.269
Monzon, Daniel, Charlotte ..	138	517	69	149	185	19	1	5	45	5	4	72	7	40	20	19	.288
Morales, Neudo, Columbus .	86	312	29	72	78	6	0	0	15	3	3	25	4	33	4	4	.231
Mueller, Jim A., Mobile .*	32	128	12	35	39	4	0	0	6	1	0	10	3	22	3	2	.273
Murray, Michael, Mty ...	59	158	9	30	37	4	0	1	10	4	0	14	0	23	0	0	.190
Myette, Kenneth, Ash* ...	6	2	0	1	1	0	0	0	1	0	0	0	0	0	0	0	.500
Neumeier, Daniel, Mobile ..	18	28	1	1	1	0	0	0	0	3	0	1	0	14	0	0	.036
Nichols, Thomas, Char† ...	121	365	35	84	111	10	1	5	34	1	6	66	0	80	0	3	.230

Player and Club	G.	AB.	R.	H.	TB.	2B.	3B.	HR.	RBI.	SH.	SF.	BB.	HP.	SO.	SB.	CS.	Pct.
Nordberg, Alan, Charlotte*	66	217	17	54	59	5	0	0	14	7	2	18	0	19	2	1	.249
Nunn, William M., Char*	19	52	1	9	11	2	0	0	0	0	0	5	0	16	0	0	.173
O'Connor, Michael, Ash†	32	7	0	0	0	0	0	0	0	0	0	2	0	2	0	0	.000
Osborn, Danny L., Asheville	27	47	5	9	16	2	1	1	4	1	0	3	0	16	0	0	.191
O'Sullivan, Barry, Mobile	89	258	22	54	85	10	0	7	29	6	4	20	0	46	4	1	.209
O'Toole, Dennis, Mobile	28	53	3	13	13	0	0	0	8	1	0	5	0	10	0	0	.245
Pamlanye, James, Birm	104	415	58	107	137	17	2	3	19	5	2	20	7	18	3	1	.258
Pena, Norbert M., Birm	5	2	0	0	0	0	0	0	0	0	0	0	0	1	0	0	.000
Peters, Raymond, Jax	3	6	0	1	1	0	0	0	0	0	1	0	0	3	0	0	.167
Propst, Jack, Birmingham	23	17	0	3	3	0	0	0	2	0	0	0	0	3	0	0	.176
Radakovic, Nikola, Col	9	9	0	1	1	0	0	0	0	0	0	0	0	2	0	0	.111
Randolph, John, Charlotte*	31	19	0	2	2	0	0	0	1	1	0	1	0	11	0	0	.105
Rathje, Larry, Charlotte*	93	239	24	49	56	7	0	0	11	1	0	29	2	33	10	7	.205
Reams, Leroy, Montgomery*	4	7	0	2	5	1	1	0	3	0	0	0	0	0	0	0	.286
Redmon, Glenn, Mobile	134	412	35	84	106	13	0	3	20	5	1	34	4	71	3	3	.204
Redmon, James, Mobile	52	177	19	34	47	10	0	1	8	1	2	8	2	22	4	2	.192
Renfroe, Dalton, Savannah	90	236	24	56	80	10	1	4	25	3	2	22	0	37	0	0	.237
Richard, Lee, Mobile	13	30	2	9	9	0	0	0	2	0	0	0	0	9	1	2	.300
Richardson, Carl, Columbus	117	443	48	101	125	11	5	1	19	8	2	40	0	46	22	13	.228
Riddoch, Gregory, Asheville	132	448	25	92	113	16	1	1	22	11	3	19	3	87	9	6	.205
Robson, Thomas, Jacksonville	81	226	21	52	70	6	0	4	31	0	4	22	1	37	1	2	.230
Rowell, Alexander, Char	2	6	0	1	1	0	0	0	0	0	0	0	0	0	0	0	.167
Ruberto, John, Asheville	37	102	4	28	33	5	0	0	7	0	0	6	0	16	1	0	.275
Ruddell, J. Preston, Char*	23	72	7	16	18	2	0	0	4	0	0	3	1	16	3	2	.222
Ruddell, Michael, Asheville	17	32	2	5	6	1	0	0	3	1	0	0	0	8	0	0	.156
Runk, George, Asheville	4	9	0	1	2	1	0	0	1	0	0	0	0	1	0	0	.111
Ryan, Dana, Mobile*	18	52	5	11	11	0	0	0	2	1	0	2	0	6	1	1	.212
Ryan, John, Jacksonville	118	408	40	98	135	8	4	7	43	3	1	44	4	35	3	6	.240
Sanders, Reginald, Birm	128	477	50	114	173	16	5	11	73	0	4	16	1	77	5	3	.239
Saunders, Dennis, Mty†	4	13	1	1	1	0	0	0	0	0	0	2	0	10	0	0	.077
Schlueter, Jay Columbus	110	387	33	85	139	14	5	10	44	3	1	26	3	102	6	1	.220
Schmidt, David, Charlotte	116	381	51	83	98	11	1	1	18	7	1	53	3	53	7	3	.218
Schubert, Gregory, Birm*	74	227	18	60	86	9	1	5	33	1	0	23	2	50	6	3	.264
Schwartz, Richard, Sav*	25	18	1	2	2	0	0	0	2	0	2	0	0	8	0	1	.111
Scrivener, Wayne, Mty	82	243	31	57	87	13	1	5	25	7	0	22	0	34	1	0	.235
Sexton, Jackson, Savannah	111	335	42	71	125	21	0	11	39	3	4	46	4	82	4	4	.212
Shaughnessy, Harry, Sav†	12	35	1	5	5	0	0	0	1	0	2	0	0	9	1	0	.143
Sherry, Lawrence, Mobile	27	7	0	1	2	1	0	0	0	0	0	1	0	0	0	0	.143
Shoup, Raymond, Char*	106	356	31	104	116	10	1	0	20	6	0	41	0	34	6	7	.292
Sires, Richard, Asheville	3	9	0	0	0	0	0	0	0	0	0	0	0	4	0	0	.000
Slape, Gregg, Asheville*	113	360	35	88	139	13	4	10	33	2	1	37	3	61	13	9	.244
Smith, Eddie, Mobile	31	39	1	4	4	0	0	0	3	0	0	0	0	16	0	0	.103
Smith, Frederick, Savannah	131	471	72	111	139	14	1	4	26	7	1	47	13	51	22	10	.236
Smith, Thomas, Birm	19	39	3	10	11	1	0	0	4	4	0	0	0	11	0	0	.256
Smith, Tommy A., Savannah*	4	17	1	5	8	0	0	1	5	0	0	0	0	3	1	0	.294
Southard, Edward, Savannah	6	16	1	1	1	0	0	0	1	0	0	3	0	5	0	0	.063
Spicer, Keith, Montgomery	32	30	4	6	8	2	0	0	3	3	0	3	0	9	0	0	.200
Stanhouse, Donald, Birm	17	28	2	8	11	0	0	1	5	1	0	3	0	8	0	0	.286
Staples, Edwin, Savannah	15	20	2	5	7	2	0	0	5	0	0	4	0	8	0	0	.250
Stephen, Louis, Jax	8	12	1	3	3	0	0	0	1	1	0	0	0	4	0	0	.250
Strable, Raymond, Char	56	34	1	5	6	1	0	0	5	3	1	0	0	12	0	0	.147
Strampe, Robert, Mty†	25	53	6	7	11	1	0	1	2	6	0	3	0	22	0	0	.132
Swanson, Charles, Mty	24	38	0	4	4	0	0	0	1	3	1	4	0	26	0	0	.105
Thomas, Derrel, Columbus†	38	156	24	38	63	5	4	4	12	1	1	7	3	27	4	2	.244
Thornton, Otis, Columbus	96	322	29	88	125	14	4	5	27	2	0	27	1	60	0	0	.273
Timberlake, Gary, Jax	10	22	1	1	1	0	0	0	1	2	0	1	0	10	0	0	.045
Tomasovich, Theodore, Ash*	34	107	7	18	24	4	1	0	7	0	0	3	1	33	2	3	.168
Tomlin, David, Asheville*	33	48	5	7	11	2	1	0	3	1	0	0	0	14	0	0	.146
Trillo, Jesus, Birmingham	84	241	26	63	81	10	1	2	19	2	6	14	3	40	5	0	.261
Vaughns, Clarence, Jax	71	267	28	69	87	6	3	2	15	1	2	16	1	42	6	4	.258
Velazquez, Federico, Jax	36	99	9	25	39	2	0	4	11	2	1	6	2	13	0	2	.253
Walls, Richard, Mty	31	103	6	17	26	7	1	0	5	0	1	9	0	19	0	1	.165
Ware, Robert, Montgomery	4	1	0	0	0	0	0	0	1	0	0	0	0	0	0	0	.000
Washington, Roger, 89 Birm-23 Mobile†	112	364	43	96	121	15	2	2	43	2	6	48	1	64	5	8	.264
Watkins, Robert, Columbus	5	14	2	4	4	0	0	0	0	0	0	0	0	0	2	0	.286
Weatherford, Forrest, Col	34	79	8	18	31	2	1	3	14	0	1	9	1	22	0	0	.228
Weaver, R. Michael, Sav*	7	13	0	8	8	0	0	0	3	2	0	0	0	1	0	0	.615
Weimer, George, Mobile	15	3	0	1	1	0	0	0	1	0	0	1	0	1	0	0	.333
Weisenberg, Robert, Char	13	25	3	5	6	1	0	0	2	2	0	1	0	8	0	0	.200
Whillock, Jack, Montgomery	27	12	0	1	1	0	0	0	1	0	0	0	0	6	0	0	.083
Winston, Fred, Mobile	28	92	15	24	47	6	1	5	13	0	0	13	0	25	5	2	.261
Wissler, C. Robert, Char*	55	176	22	40	68	6	2	6	20	3	1	33	2	50	3	0	.227
Wojcik, Stanley, Birm	111	328	44	92	132	9	5	7	42	0	2	34	0	42	3	0	.280
Wolfe, Gary, Charlotte	6	11	0	0	0	0	0	0	1	0	0	1	0	3	0	0	.000
Wood, Howard, Mobile*	118	354	35	93	127	13	6	3	33	3	3	39	5	60	6	2	.263
Wrenn, Stephen, Savannah*	104	323	46	64	132	7	2	19	59	1	1	65	2	89	1	0	.198
Yingling, Donald, Birm†	13	4	1	1	1	0	0	0	0	0	0	1	0	0	0	1	.250
Young, John, Montgomery	128	470	53	118	166	15	3	9	50	7	1	55	2	124	10	7	.251
Yount, Lawrence, Columbus	26	66	3	7	7	0	0	0	2	3	0	4	0	18	0	0	.106
Zamora, Oscar, Columbus	43	11	0	1	1	0	0	0	1	1	0	0	0	5	0	0	.091
Zuber, Ronald, Savannah	16	19	0	1	1	0	0	0	0	2	0	0	0	8	0	0	.053

The following pitchers had no plate appearances (listed alphabetically by club, games in parentheses):

CHARLOTTE—O'Neill, Raymond* (3).
COLUMBUS—McFarland, Michael (7).
JACKSONVILLE—Kline, Dennis (2).
MONTGOMERY—Helwig, Arnold (5); Meeler, C. Philip (3); Voss, Eugene (1).
SAVANNAH—Blake, Michael (3).
GRAND-SLAM HOME RUNS—Sanders, 2; Adams, Allen, Andersen, Barski, Covington, Kelly, Major, Robson, 1 each.
AWARDED FIRST BASE ON INTERFERENCE—McConnell (Hosley 2); Martinez (Hosley), Stephen (Weatherford).

CLUB FIELDING

Club	G.	PO.	A.	E.	DP.	PB.	Pct.	Club	G.	PO.	A.	E.	DP.	PB.	Pct.
Montgomery	139	3599	1428	142	95	26	.973	Savannah	139	3575	1405	158	82	13	.969
Birmingham	138	3510	1345	144	109	18	.971	Asheville	139	3585	1550	164	120	12	.969
Charlotte	140	3622	1541	159	124	20	.970	Jacksonville	137	3632	1519	187	114	17	.965
Columbus	137	3577	1356	155	91	13	.970	Mobile	137	3493	1509	190	126	18	.963

Triple Plays—None.

INDIVIDUAL FIELDING
(Ten or More Games)

*Throws lefthanded.

FIRST BASEMEN

Player and Club	G.	PO.	A.	E.	DP.	Pct.	Player and Club	G.	PO.	A.	E.	DP.	Pct.
Jata, Montgomery	11	86	4	0	8	1.000	Wrenn, Savannah*	102	829	62	11	55	.988
Ferguson, Asheville	11	76	5	0	6	1.000	Sanders, Birm	127	996	53	14	87	.987
Covington, Jax*	30	289	21	1	17	.997	Branscomb, Ash	48	365	22	5	24	.987
Foster, Charlotte*	35	267	15	1	16	.996	Hodge, Savannah	45	353	24	5	22	.987
O'Sullivan, Mobile	18	155	9	1	15	.994	Kimball, Asheville	53	407	26	6	38	.986
DOLINSEK, Col*	137	1221	80	9	78	.993	Tomasovich, Ash	28	221	22	4	19	.984
Hahn, Charlotte*	98	822	74	8	69	.991	Vaughns, Jax	41	256	28	5	39	.983
Robson, Jacksonville	59	517	38	5	39	.991	Howell, Mobile	75	576	47	13	53	.980
Conde, Asheville	16	105	9	1	7	.991	Nordberg, Char*	24	178	17	6	20	.970
Marquess, Mobile	33	263	20	3	23	.990	Kelly, Jax*	11	81	6	4	3	.956
Young, Montgomery*	127	1087	62	13	74	.989							

(Fewer Than Ten Games)

Player and Club	G.	PO.	A.	E.	DP.	Pct.	Player and Club	G.	PO.	A.	E.	DP.	Pct.
Campbell, Mobile	9	91	10	0	7	1.000	Kolb, Mobile	1	1	0	0	0	1.000
Pamlanye, Birm	7	65	2	0	6	1.000	Loomer, Asheville	1	1	0	0	0	1.000
Blanco, Mobile	8	56	4	0	9	1.000	Slape, Asheville	1	1	0	0	0	1.000
Wojcik, Birmingham	5	44	6	0	5	1.000	Martinez, Birm-Mob.	7	85	4	2	7	.978
Humphrey, Jax	5	19	1	0	2	1.000	Hosley, Montgomery	5	34	1	2	4	.946
King, Birmingham	2	8	1	0	1	1.000	Ezell, Charlotte	1	12	0	1	1	.923
Koegel, Jax	1	2	0	0	0	1.000							

SECOND BASEMEN

Player and Club	G.	PO.	A.	E.	DP.	Pct.	Player and Club	G.	PO.	A.	E.	DP.	Pct.
Trillo, Birmingham	21	37	50	0	12	1.000	Ryan, Jacksonville	88	199	252	14	47	.970
Haggard, Savannah	41	85	114	1	14	.995	Richardson, Col	112	189	307	17	41	.967
HOFF, Asheville	122	283	340	10	73	.984	Kolb, Mobile	14	12	16	1	3	.966
Grayson, Mty	29	69	83	3	16	.981	Coggins, Savannah	49	113	121	9	18	.963
Schmidt, Charlotte	110	292	299	12	63	.980	Barski, Montgomery	18	37	34	3	6	.959
Lovelace, Birm	50	101	121	5	24	.978	Loomer, Asheville	20	32	36	3	11	.958
McDonald, Char	38	97	66	4	29	.976	Brohamer, Savannah	10	16	24	2	2	.952
Lisetski, Asheville	10	17	24	1	3	.976	Marcano, Savannah	35	69	68	7	15	.951
G. Redmon, Mobile	134	292	358	18	84	.973	Kurtz, Jacksonville	44	117	118	14	27	.944
Adkins, Birmingham	74	189	203	11	43	.973	Morales, Columbus	25	49	67	7	10	.943
Andersen, Mty	95	202	230	13	43	.971							

(Fewer Than Ten Games)

Player and Club	G.	PO.	A.	E.	DP.	Pct.	Player and Club	G.	PO.	A.	E.	DP.	Pct.
Martinez, Birm-Mob.	5	3	5	0	1	1.000	Runk, Asheville	1	0	1	0	0	1.000
Klinger, Jacksonville	2	4	2	0	1	1.000	Shaughnessy, Sav	4	13	15	1	3	.966
Thomas, Columbus	2	3	3	0	0	1.000	Ryan, Mobile	7	5	11	1	1	.941
Dempsey, Charlotte	1	4	1	0	0	1.000	LaPointe, Jax	8	13	15	2	2	.933
Clark, Mobile	2	3	0	0	0	1.000	Southard, Savannah	4	6	4	1	1	.909
Monty, Mobile	3	2	1	0	0	1.000	Lee, Savannah	4	3	5	2	1	.800
Mata, Asheville	3	1	1	0	1	1.000	Vaughns, Jax	1	0	4	1	0	.800

THIRD BASEMEN

Player and Club	G.	PO.	A.	E.	DP.	Pct.	Player and Club	G.	PO.	A.	E.	DP.	Pct.
Busse, Columbus	26	28	54	2	2	.976	Monzon, Charlotte	136	121	303	31	33	.932
McKenzie, Mty	55	39	120	7	11	.958	Jedelsky, Mobile	38	24	72	7	10	.932
HODGE, Savannah	100	86	177	14	13	.949	Vaughns, Jax	19	16	37	4	4	.930
Riddoch, Asheville	121	112	262	21	21	.947	Renfroe, Savannah	41	41	62	9	7	.920
Pamlanye, Birm	54	80	198	16	13	.946	Holland, Jax	77	68	163	22	15	.913
Ruberto, Mobile	19	18	35	3	3	.946	Francingues, Mob	18	8	44	5	5	.912
Grayson, Mty	82	59	149	13	9	.941	Lovelace, Birm	16	15	24	4	3	.907
Morales, Columbus	35	32	61	6	4	.939	Grangaard, Col	56	43	90	14	6	.905
Ryan, Jacksonville	17	14	31	3	5	.938	O'Sullivan, Mobile	38	28	69	12	7	.890

THIRD BASEMEN—Continued

Player and Club	G.	PO.	A.	E.	DP.	Pct.	Player and Club	G.	PO.	A.	E.	DP.	Pct.
LaPointe, Jax	15	12	28	5	3	.889	Armbrister, Col	17	12	27	8	1	.830
Clark, Mobile	27	20	49	9	5	.885	Ryan, Mobile	11	4	24	6	2	.824
Trillo, Birmingham	35	28	29	8	3	.877	Dailey, Jacksonville	10	10	12	5	0	.815
Kolb, Mobile	17	12	25	6	3	.860							

(Fewer Than Ten Games)

Player and Club	G.	PO.	A.	E.	DP.	Pct.	Player and Club	G.	PO.	A.	E.	DP.	Pct.
Barrett, Columbus	5	6	7	0	1	1.000	Richard, Mobile	2	1	0	0	0	1.000
Runk, Asheville	2	4	2	0	2	1.000	Monty, Mobile	7	5	15	1	2	.952
Weaver, Savannah	2	3	2	0	0	1.000	McDonald, Char	6	5	10	1	0	.938
Marquess, Mobile*	1	0	4	0	0	1.000	Herrera, Jax	6	8	5	1	0	.929
Clark, Columbus	2	1	2	0	1	1.000	Marcano, Savannah	5	3	5	1	2	.889
Ezell, Charlotte	1	1	2	0	0	1.000	Martinez, Birm-Mob	7	4	15	3	1	.864
Conde, Asheville	2	1	1	0	0	1.000	Barski, Montgomery	7	4	5	2	0	.818
Hoff, Asheville	1	2	0	0	0	1.000	Lee, Savannah	6	1	2	2	0	.600
Wissler, Charlotte	1	0	2	0	0	1.000	Howell, Mobile	1	0	0	1	0	.000

SHORTSTOPS

Player and Club	G.	PO.	A.	E.	DP.	Pct.	Player and Club	G.	PO.	A.	E.	DP.	Pct.
Belloir, Savannah	17	28	42	2	7	.972	Andersen, Mty	39	60	117	12	9	.937
Scrivener, Mty	76	102	243	11	44	.969	Trillo, Birmingham	21	36	51	6	10	.935
Jagutis, Birm	68	111	195	10	33	.968	Clark, Savannah	38	55	98	11	11	.933
McDonald, Charlotte	31	48	98	5	19	.967	Monty, Mobile	28	45	81	9	17	.933
Coggins, Savannah	13	19	40	2	7	.967	Martinez, Birm-Mob	71	117	202	24	36	.930
Riddoch, Asheville	10	13	30	2	5	.956	Morales, Columbus	20	31	42	6	9	.924
FRIAS, Jax	136	204	432	32	68	.952	J. Redmon, Mobile	47	82	118	17	27	.922
Lisetski, Asheville	71	81	227	16	33	.951	Kolb, Mobile	30	37	81	11	21	.915
Busse, Columbus	79	124	253	21	33	.947	Thomas, Columbus	35	57	92	14	14	.914
Nichols, Charlotte	115	171	360	31	55	.945	Mata, Asheville	59	90	163	24	33	.913
Brohamer, Savannah	63	89	164	15	22	.944	Jedelsky, Mobile	12	10	31	4	5	.911
Walls, Montgomery	31	35	85	8	7	.938							

(Fewer Than Ten Games)

Player and Club	G.	PO.	A.	E.	DP.	Pct.	Player and Club	G.	PO.	A.	E.	DP.	Pct.
Holland, Jax	3	4	7	0	1	1.000	Hart, Savannah	7	7	16	2	2	.920
Barrett, Columbus	3	3	7	0	0	1.000	Shaughnessy, Sav	7	9	20	3	7	.906
Grangaard, Columbus	1	1	2	0	1	1.000	Marcano, Savannah	4	3	7	2	0	.833
Loomer, Asheville	9	15	14	2	3	.935	Lovelace, Birm	3	1	12	3	1	.813
Richard, Mobile	8	10	16	2	2	.929							

OUTFIELDERS

Player and Club	G.	PO.	A.	E.	DP.	Pct.	Player and Club	G.	PO.	A.	E.	DP.	Pct.
Kelly, Jacksonville*	76	123	13	0	3	1.000	Washington, Bir-Mo	100	141	12	5	0	.968
Dickinson, Sav	68	113	9	0	1	1.000	McDonald, Char	31	55	3	2	1	.967
Jedelsky, Mobile	44	72	1	0	1	1.000	Jones, Jacksonville	53	82	3	3	1	.966
Mueller, Mobile*	32	59	2	0	1	1.000	Clark, Birmingham	129	235	13	9	4	.965
Lisetski, Asheville	32	38	1	0	1	1.000	Brye, Charlotte	105	212	6	8	0	.965
Hottman, Mobile	17	23	2	0	0	1.000	Molinaro, Mty	92	150	8	6	0	.963
Clark, Columbus	14	19	3	0	1	1.000	Hosley, Montgomery	20	26	0	1	0	.963
Grayson, Mont	11	13	1	0	0	1.000	James, Jacksonville	103	200	4	8	1	.962
Rathje, Charlotte*	83	152	2	1	0	.994	Correa, Mobile*	76	117	10	5	2	.962
SCHLUETER, Col	109	264	9	2	3	.993	Harvey, Columbus*	60	97	1	3	0	.961
Wood, Mobile	103	203	7	2	1	.991	Armbrister, Col	107	201	13	9	4	.960
Branscomb, Ash	66	98	6	1	1	.990	Hendrick, Birm	54	115	4	5	0	.960
Sexton, Savannah	102	170	7	2	1	.989	Chambers, Mty	62	91	5	4	0	.960
Andrens, Asheville*	117	260	12	4	1	.986	Wissler, Charlotte	52	90	2	4	0	.958
Geronimo, Col*	73	113	8	2	3	.984	O'Sullivan, Mobile	24	21	0	1	0	.955
Wojcik, Birm	93	155	7	3	1	.982	Koegel, Jacksonville	55	96	1	5	0	.951
Jata, Montgomery	86	147	9	3	3	.981	Nordberg, Char*	40	54	4	3	0	.951
Barski, Montgomery	69	97	6	2	1	.981	Locklear, Asheville	39	52	3	3	1	.948
Covington, Jax*	90	190	9	4	1	.980	Winston, Mobile	28	46	3	3	0	.942
Blessitt, Mty	101	226	6	5	0	.979	Godby, Asheville	91	167	9	11	3	.941
Marquess, Mobile*	53	85	6	2	1	.978	Adams, Columbus	57	74	6	5	1	.941
Allen, Savannah	116	314	8	8	0	.976	Hahn, Charlotte*	19	15	1	1	0	.941
Blanco, Mobile	47	79	2	2	0	.974	Velazquez, Jax	18	25	3	2	1	.933
Slape, Asheville	107	210	14	6	4	.974	Kurtz, Jacksonville	31	45	1	4	1	.920
Schubert, Birm*	69	145	14	4	0	.974	Ruddell, Charlotte	21	29	2	3	0	.912
F. Smith, Savannah	124	199	7	6	0	.972	Bond, Savannah	10	15	1	2	0	.889
Shoup, Charlotte	94	166	4	5	1	.971	Kolb, Mobile	10	6	1	1	1	.875

(Fewer Than Ten Games)

Player and Club	G.	PO.	A.	E.	DP.	Pct.	Player and Club	G.	PO.	A.	E.	DP.	Pct.
Foster, Charlotte*	8	12	1	0	0	1.000	Apellaniz, Jax	1	2	0	0	0	1.000
Lee, Savannah	7	11	0	0	0	1.000	Renfroe, Savannah	1	3	0	0	0	1.000
King, Birmingham	6	8	0	0	0	1.000	Southard, Savannah	2	1	0	0	0	1.000
Rowell, Charlotte	2	4	0	0	0	1.000	Reams, Montgomery	1	1	0	0	0	1.000
Weaver, Savannah	1	3	1	0	0	1.000	Dempsey, Charlotte	8	12	2	2	0	.875
T. Smith, Savannah	4	3	0	0	0	1.000	Vaughns, Jax	9	13	1	3	0	.824
Kimball, Asheville	3	2	0	0	0	1.000	Campbell, Mobile	5	7	1	2	0	.800
Richardson, Col	3	2	0	0	0	1.000	Tomasovich, Ash	2	3	0	1	0	.750
Pamlanye, Birm	2	2	0	0	0	1.000							

CATCHERS

Player and Club	G.	PO.	A.	E.	DP.	PB.	Pct.	Player and Club	G.	PO.	A.	E.	DP.	PB.	Pct.
Johnson, Jax	22	105	14	0	1	3	1.000	Thornton, Col	94	656	63	13	7	13	.982
Cook, Birm	65	384	38	3	2	6	.993	Hosley, Mty	81	590	55	12	4	14	.982
Bryant, Columbus	17	135	7	1	0	0	.993	Renfroe, Sav	29	140	17	3	0	6	.981
Gomez, Birm	63	409	39	5	1	8	.989	Correll, Savannah	111	647	71	17	5	7	.977
FERGUSON, As	111	615	57	8	15	9	.988	Koegel, Jax	21	115	15	3	1	3	.977
Murray, Mty	44	274	14	4	0	9	.986	Kimball, Asheville	31	155	11	4	3	3	.976
Weatherford, Col	22	134	8	2	0	0	.986	Fitzgerald, Birm	12	77	4	2	1	4	.976
Ezell, Charlotte	30	123	7	2	1	2	.985	Kendrick, Mty	18	103	6	3	1	3	.973
Humphrey, Jax	93	563	46	10	9	11	.984	Dempsey, Char	91	490	73	16	11	12	.972
Kusnyer, Mobile	111	650	88	13	10	14	.983	Nunn, Charlotte	16	64	5	2	0	5	.972
Howell, Mobile	32	155	23	3	3	3	.983	Ruberto, Ash	12	37	12	2	1	0	.961

(Fewer Than Ten Games)

Player and Club	G.	PO.	A.	E.	DP.	PB.	Pct.	Player and Club	G.	PO.	A.	E.	DP.	PB.	Pct.
Clark, Columbus	6	21	2	0	0	0	1.000	Staples, Savannah	5	34	2	1	0	0	.973
Wolfe, Charlotte	2	21	0	0	0	0	1.000	Minster, Charlotte	8	24	3	1	0	1	.964
Monzon, Charlotte	1	3	0	0	0	0	1.000	Wood, Mobile	2	10	1	1	0	0	.917
Velazquez, Jax	8	55	5	1	0	0	.984	Leyland, Mty	2	6	0	1	0	0	.857

PITCHERS

Player and Club	G.	PO.	A.	E.	DP.	Pct.	Player and Club	G.	PO.	A.	E.	DP.	Pct.
SMITH, Mobile	24	12	26	0	1	1.000	Sires, Asheville	20	6	11	1	1	.944
Gill, Charlotte	42	9	20	0	2	1.000	Smith, Birmingham	19	5	12	1	0	.944
Harris, Columbus	25	12	17	0	1	1.000	Crook, Asheville*	27	5	28	2	0	.943
Carden, Jax	18	13	13	0	1	1.000	Conger, Birm*	12	6	26	2	1	.941
Mingori, Savannah*	10	7	11	0	1	1.000	Flanagan, Columbus	24	7	24	2	2	.939
Weisenberg, Char	13	7	10	0	0	1.000	Forsch, Columbus	22	9	21	2	3	.938
Cook, Montgomery	25	5	11	0	0	1.000	Haynes, Charlotte	27	15	15	2	0	.938
Randolph, Char*	31	2	14	0	0	1.000	Schwartz, Savannah*	25	1	14	1	1	.938
Arruda, Charlotte	51	6	9	0	0	1.000	Abbott, Birm	33	13	30	3	2	.935
Bates, Jax	18	8	7	0	0	1.000	Yount, Columbus	26	8	21	2	0	.935
Hinsley, Savannah	10	5	9	0	0	1.000	Hill, Asheville	32	12	16	2	2	.933
Donahue, Mty	37	5	8	0	0	1.000	LaGrow, Mty	19	7	21	2	1	.933
Whillock, Mty	27	4	7	0	0	1.000	Hamilton, Birm*	51	0	14	1	2	.933
Bauer, Mobile*	43	2	7	0	0	1.000	Swanson, Mty	23	9	18	2	2	.931
Glassco, Jax	31	3	6	0	0	1.000	Bertino, Jax	23	8	18	2	4	.929
LeFevre, Jax	34	5	4	0	0	1.000	Gilbreth, Mty*	30	9	28	3	1	.925
Baldwin, Mobile*	14	4	4	0	0	1.000	Ammann, Jax	11	4	8	1	0	.923
Hankammer, Mobile	16	1	7	0	0	1.000	Locke, Jacksonville*	30	3	9	1	0	.923
Hefferon, Birm	17	2	5	0	0	1.000	Magness, Charlotte	28	6	6	1	0	.923
Humphrey, Columbus	28	2	5	0	0	1.000	Propst, Birmingham	23	4	8	1	1	.923
Limke, Mobile	31	2	5	0	0	1.000	Stanhouse, Birm	16	4	8	1	0	.923
Moloney, Mobile	20	3	4	0	0	1.000	Spicer, Montgomery	26	6	17	2	1	.920
O'Connor, Ash*	32	3	4	0	0	1.000	Hartman, Jax*	21	11	30	4	1	.911
Blanken, Asheville	17	2	3	0	0	1.000	Marcano, Birmingham	21	9	1	1	0	.909
Kryczkowski, Col*	21	2	3	0	0	1.000	Sherry, Mobile	26	2	8	1	0	.909
Mastin, Birmingham	34	1	4	0	0	1.000	Christman, Char*	14	7	12	2	3	.905
Weimer, Mobile	15	0	3	0	0	1.000	Hamm, Charlotte	10	2	16	2	0	.900
Yingling, Birm	13	0	3	0	0	1.000	Glass, Jacksonville	18	7	19	3	0	.897
Corbin, Charlotte	32	24	35	1	1	.983	Johnson, Asheville	54	5	12	2	0	.895
Tomlin, Asheville*	25	7	42	1	3	.980	Magnuson, Mobile*	13	5	11	2	1	.889
Osborn, Asheville	19	11	31	1	4	.977	Dominguez, Mobile	38	10	20	4	0	.882
Machemehl, Savannah	32	14	25	1	1	.975	Greif, Columbus	27	5	25	4	0	.882
Killion, Savannah	27	11	27	1	1	.974	Ruddell, Asheville	17	3	12	2	1	.882
McConnell, Savannah	38	10	22	1	1	.970	Higgins, Asheville	30	14	29	6	2	.878
Foor, Montgomery*	29	7	24	1	3	.969	O'Toole, Mobile	25	10	17	4	0	.871
Lee, Jacksonville	30	4	24	1	0	.966	Blateric, Asheville	36	4	33	5	3	.870
Strampe, Mty	25	7	19	1	1	.963	Kampf, Birmingham	22	5	21	4	1	.867
Cooper, Mobile-Char	31	11	14	1	0	.962	Dreier, Asheville	30	11	21	5	0	.865
Kelso, Birmingham	26	11	11	1	0	.957	Frailing, Mobile*	22	8	23	5	3	.861
Kaiser, Savannah*	16	2	18	1	0	.952	Crossan, Savannah	22	5	19	4	2	.857
McMasters, Col	23	7	13	1	1	.952	Neumeier, Mobile	18	3	9	2	0	.857
Strable, Charlotte	56	5	13	1	1	.947	Cushmore, Mty*	17	3	8	2	0	.846
Boyd, Savannah	27	9	8	1	0	.944	Zuber, Savannah	16	2	8	2	0	.833
Cunnyngham, Sav	31	4	13	1	1	.944	Zamora, Columbus	43	4	5	2	0	.818
Foshie, Jax	32	8	9	1	1	.944	Timberlake, Jax*	10	1	9	4	1	.714

(Fewer Than Ten Games)

Player and Club	G.	PO.	A.	E.	DP.	Pct.	Player and Club	G.	PO.	A.	E.	DP.	Pct.
Braxton, Savannah	9	7	16	0	0	1.000	Watkins, Columbus	5	2	2	0	0	1.000
Ferrell, Jax	4	1	9	0	0	1.000	Ash, Savannah	4	3	0	0	0	1.000
MacDonnell, Mobile*	9	0	10	0	1	1.000	Helwig, Montgomery*	5	1	2	0	0	1.000
Johnson, Mobile	4	5	4	0	0	1.000	Click, Jacksonville	3	1	1	0	0	1.000
Radakovic, Col	9	3	6	0	0	1.000	Copeland, Birm	4	0	2	0	0	1.000
Saunders, Mty	4	0	8	0	0	1.000	Hebert, Jax	5	0	2	0	0	1.000
Peters, Jax	3	2	5	0	0	1.000	Kennedy, Sav*	7	0	2	0	0	1.000
Major, Birm*	9	3	2	0	0	1.000	Meeler, Mty	5	0	2	0	0	1.000
Belinsky, Ash*	5	0	4	0	0	1.000	Blake, Savannah	3	1	0	0	0	1.000
Fisher, Jax	4	0	4	0	0	1.000	Lohse, Birmingham	4	1	0	0	0	1.000
Pena, Birmingham	5	2	2	0	0	1.000	McFarland, Col	7	1	0	0	0	1.000

PITCHERS—Continued

Player and Club	G.	PO.	A.	E.	DP.	Pct.
O'Neill, Charlotte*	3	0	1	0	0	1.000
Wrenn, Savannah*	5	0	1	0	1	1.000
Huggins, Jax*	8	0	14	1	0	.933
Bickerton, Birm*	9	1	5	1	0	.857
Camacho, Savannah*	9	4	9	3	0	.813
Howell, Savannah*	5	2	2	1	0	.800

Player and Club	G.	PO.	A.	E.	DP.	Pct.
Ware, Montgomery	4	0	3	1	0	.750
Stephen, Jax	8	5	6	4	0	.733
Cooper, Asheville*	5	0	2	1	0	.667
Kline, Jacksonville	1	0	2	1	0	.667
Myette, Asheville	6	0	2	1	0	.667

The following pitchers do not have any recorded accepted chances; therefore are not listed in the fielding averages: Bethell, Coleman, Goltz, Kimball, Nichols, Voss.

CLUB PITCHING

Club	G.	CG.	ShO.	Sv.	IP.	H.	R.	ER.	HR.	BB.	Int. BB.	HB.	SO.	WP.	Bk.	ERA.
Montgomery	139	55	16	23	1200	990	410	336	49	424	41	33	922	63	10	2.52
Columbus	137	51	18	26	1192	975	426	341	56	373	14	19	892	66	1	2.57
Mobile	137	25	16	31	1164	1028	441	337	36	398	40	37	747	52	5	2.61
Savannah	139	46	23	25	1192	993	454	361	72	420	65	33	759	42	5	2.73
Charlotte	140	34	15	17	1207	1107	502	406	60	393	37	46	675	58	6	3.03
Jacksonville	137	35	13	31	1211	1097	512	411	70	393	32	42	761	61	4	3.05
Asheville	139	24	7	23	1195	1085	498	410	75	554	71	52	695	62	8	3.09
Birmingham	138	47	9	21	1170	1096	511	416	78	450	29	30	811	74	5	3.20

PITCHERS' RECORDS

(Leading Qualifiers for Earned-Run Average Leadership—140 or More Innings)

*Throws lefthanded.

Pitcher—Club	G.	GS.	CG.	ShO.	W.	L.	Sv.	Pct.	IP.	H.	R.	ER.	HR.	BB.	Int. BB.	HB.	SO.	WP.	ERA.
Hartman, Jax*	21	21	11	3	9	10	0	.474	157	130	45	35	6	41	4	3	77	6	2.01
Harris, Columbus	25	25	13	1	11	9	0	.550	205	134	59	46	12	43	2	1	159	14	2.02
Forsch, Columbus	22	22	9	5	13	8	0	.619	167	135	48	38	6	39	2	2	152	3	2.05
Foor, Montgomery	20	19	7	2	10	6	0	.625	151	104	45	35	6	53	1	10	122	9	2.09
LaGrow, Mty	19	19	11	0	11	4	0	.733	146	111	49	34	8	49	3	4	126	7	2.10
Killion, Savannah	27	18	7	3	10	7	1	.588	140	105	37	33	4	39	5	1	63	2	2.12
Crook, Asheville*	27	21	2	0	8	10	0	.444	145	122	51	38	8	60	3	4	86	5	2.36
Gilbreth, Mty*	30	30	11	3	13	11	0	.542	221	166	71	61	9	75	2	8	192	14	2.48
Flanagan, Col	24	24	5	1	11	5	0	.688	160	131	57	45	9	48	1	0	99	5	2.53
Frailing, Mobile*	22	22	6	1	4	9	0	.308	146	141	55	44	3	40	2	4	77	9	2.71

Departmental Leaders: G—Strable, 56; GS—Corbin, 32; CG—Harris, 13; ShO—Forsch, 5; W—Forsch, Gilbreth, 13; L—Haynes, 15; Sv—Whillock, 12; Pct.—LaGrow, .733; IP—Gilbreth, 221; H—Greif, 177; R—Greif, 82; ER—Corbin, 66; HR—Greif, 13; BB—Corbin, 86; IBB—M. Johnson, 14; HB—Bertino, M. Johnson, 11; SO—Gilbreth, 192; WP—Yount, 16.

(All Pitchers—Listed Alphabetically)

Pitcher—Club	G.	GS.	CG.	ShO.	W.	L.	Sv.	Pct.	IP.	H.	R.	ER.	HR.	BB.	Int. BB.	HB.	SO.	WP.	ERA.
Abbott, Birm	33	20	4	0	7	12	2	.368	160	173	70	59	10	28	5	3	86	9	3.32
Ammann, Jax	11	6	1	1	1	5	1	.167	41	41	24	13	3	15	1	0	36	3	2.85
Arruda, Charlotte	51	1	0	0	5	2	3	.714	81	71	23	14	3	36	5	5	55	8	1.56
Ash, Savannah	4	1	0	0	0	1	0	.000	12	15	12	12	1	8	1	1	5	1	9.00
Baldwin, Mobile*	14	13	2	0	5	3	0	.625	69	45	21	15	6	30	0	4	60	3	1.96
Bates, Jax*	18	15	5	1	7	6	1	.538	100	103	50	43	7	19	0	1	45	2	3.87
Bauer, Mobile*	43	0	0	0	3	2	10	.600	61	57	26	20	3	17	4	0	35	1	2.95
Belinsky, Ash*	5	3	0	0	0	2	0	.000	25	22	9	8	0	9	1	2	24	3	2.88
Bertino, Jax	23	12	1	0	2	5	0	.286	88	80	46	39	3	42	0	11	55	6	3.99
Bethell, Columbus	2	0	0	0	1	0	0	.000	2	4	2	2	1	3	1	0	3	0	9.00
Bickerton, Birm*	9	3	0	0	1	3	0	.250	26	26	13	11	0	24	1	0	24	5	3.81
Blake, Savannah	3	0	0	0	0	0	0	.000	2	1	0	0	0	1	0	0	1	2	0.00
Blanken, Ash	17	1	0	0	2	1	1	.667	31	30	13	13	2	10	3	0	18	0	3.77
Blateric, Ash	36	10	2	0	6	10	8	.375	107	81	39	31	5	39	5	4	85	3	2.61
Boyd, Savannah	27	17	4	1	9	8	1	.529	128	125	64	51	10	49	4	2	93	8	3.59
Braxton, Sav	9	9	6	4	6	2	0	.750	71	53	19	17	4	22	8	3	56	1	2.15
Camacho, Sav*	9	4	2	1	2	2	0	.500	35	23	9	5	1	9	1	0	20	0	1.29
Carden, Jax	18	18	3	1	8	7	0	.533	121	119	64	52	10	28	1	3	66	9	3.87
Christman, Char*	14	14	3	1	5	5	0	.500	72	65	32	30	4	38	0	4	32	5	3.75
Click, Jax	3	2	1	1	2	0	0	1.000	18	14	4	4	1	5	1	0	12	0	2.00
Coleman, Mty	1	1	0	0	0	1	0	.000	3	6	3	3	0	4	0	1	2	0	9.00
Conger, Birm	12	12	4	0	5	6	0	.455	78	78	34	27	4	35	1	3	58	6	3.12
Cook, Montgomery	25	0	0	0	3	1	0	.750	66	66	29	25	3	33	6	3	34	3	3.41
Cooper, Ash*	5	4	2	1	1	2	0	.333	24	16	5	4	0	8	1	2	16	0	1.50
Cooper, 13 Mobile—18 Char	31	19	3	1	10	8	2	.556	147	137	67	52	6	58	6	7	52	3	3.18
Copeland, Birm	4	3	1	0	1	1	0	.500	22	15	6	6	2	16	0	0	11	3	2.45
Corbin, Charlotte	32	32	10	4	11	14	0	.440	208	174	80	66	7	86	5	8	149	9	2.86
Crook, Asheville*	27	21	2	0	8	10	0	.444	145	122	51	38	8	60	3	4	86	5	2.36
Crossan, Sav	22	21	4	2	6	10	0	.375	119	101	61	46	9	53	5	6	74	7	3.48

Pitcher—Club	G	GS	CG	ShO	W	L	Sv	Pct.	IP	H	R	ER	HR	BB	Int.BB	HB	SO	WP	ERA
Cunnyngham, Sav	31	0	0	0	3	6	6	.333	62	54	21	17	6	25	8	7	46	1	2.47
Cushmore, Mty*	17	13	2	1	4	6	0	.400	77	60	31	27	2	38	1	1	47	5	3.16
Dominguez, Mob	38	10	3	1	7	7	1	.500	123	122	51	37	4	32	1	7	92	4	2.71
Donahue, Mty	37	0	0	0	5	3	7	.625	60	39	14	11	0	30	10	1	45	5	1.65
Dreier, Asheville	30	24	2	1	5	8	1	.385	127	129	60	57	11	38	3	2	49	3	4.04
Ferrell, Jax	4	4	1	0	1	1	0	.500	25	32	14	11	2	6	1	2	14	5	3.96
Fisher, Jax	4	0	0	0	1	0	1	1.000	6	3	1	1	0	1	1	0	7	0	1.50
Flanagan, Col	24	24	5	1	11	5	0	.688	160	131	57	45	9	48	1	0	99	5	2.53
Foor, Montgomery*	20	19	7	2	10	6	0	.625	151	104	45	35	6	53	1	10	122	9	2.09
Forsch, Columbus	22	22	9	5	13	8	0	.619	167	135	48	38	6	39	2	2	152	3	2.05
Foshie, Jax	32	0	0	0	6	3	8	.667	64	42	19	18	5	20	5	1	59	2	2.53
Frailing, Mobile*	22	22	6	1	4	9	0	.308	146	141	55	44	3	40	3	4	77	9	2.71
Gilbreth, Mty*	30	11	3		13	11	0	.542	221	166	71	61	9	75	2	8	192	14	2.48
Gill, Charlotte	42	17	5	3	11	9	3	.550	163	142	62	54	10	37	8	5	87	8	2.98
Glass, Jax	18	18	4	2	8	8	0	.500	116	117	56	47	5	31	3	7	53	6	3.65
Glassco, Jax*	31	1	0	0	2	3	6	.400	55	49	22	21	3	16	2	0	47	4	3.44
Goltz, Charlotte	1	1	0	0	1	0	0	.000	2	1	1	0	0	1	0	0	1	0	0.00
Greif, Columbus	27	10	3		10	12	0	.455	190	177	82	61	13	54	1	4	131	10	2.89
Hamilton, Birm*	21	14	5	2	6	4	1	.600	104	89	39	28	10	32	2	3	86	1	2.42
Hamm, Charlotte	10	10	5	1	6	2	0	.750	80	58	17	15	2	16	1	1	53	1	1.69
Hankammer, Mob	16	2	0	0	1	2	1	.333	46	46	19	17	3	17	0	3	29	1	3.33
Harris, Columbus	25	25	13	1	11	9	0	.550	205	134	59	46	12	43	3	1	159	14	2.02
Hartman, Jax*	21	21	11	3	9	10	0	.474	157	130	45	35	6	41	4	3	77	6	2.01
Haynes, Charlotte	27	25	4	1	4	15	0	.211	150	159	72	59	11	28	4	2	72	3	3.54
Hebert, Jax	5	0	0	0	0	3	1	.000	12	14	5	4	0	9	1	0	13	0	3.00
Hefferon, Birm	17	0	0	0	2	2	1	.500	28	22	12	8	4	12	2	1	14	2	2.57
Helwig, Mty*	5	0	0	0	0	0	0	.000	5	1	1	0	0	0		1	6	1	1.29
Higgins,	30	17	6	2	11	7	0	.611	135	125	51	48	8	48	6	10	57	8	3.20
Hill, Asheville	32	1	0	0	7	2	2	.778	77	63	27	22	6	30	7	0	36	9	2.57
Hinsley, Sav	10	10	4	1	3	4	0	.429	71	65	31	27	7	20	9	0	30	3	3.42
Howell, Sav*	5	2	0	0	0	0	0	.000	10	14	10	5	2	4	0	4	1		4.50
Huggins, Jax*	8	8	1	0	4	1	0	.800	57	48	18	13	2	22	0	2	43	0	2.05
Humphrey, Col	28	0	0	0	4	2	10	.667	43	30	16	12	2	16	1	1	31	3	3.35
M. Johnson, Ash	54	1	0	0	4	8	7	.333	80	77	29	17	3	45	14	11	44	2	1.91
Johnson, Mobile	4	4	0	0	1	1	0	.500	29	24	5	5	1	7	1	1	21	0	1.55
Kaiser, Sav*	16	16	3	0	7	5	0	.583	99	71	28	22	3	31	1	1	65	4	2.00
Kampf, Birm	22	22	10	0	10	8	0	.556	155	144	65	59	12	56	2	1	93	5	3.43
Kelso, Birm	26	19	8	1	10	6	2	.625	144	136	65	47	7	40	2	5	107	5	2.94
Kennedy, Sav*	1	1	0	0	0	0	0	.000	11	16	11	11	0	9	1	2	0	8	8.18
Killion, Savannah	27	18	7	3	10	7	1	.588	140	105	37	33	4	39	5	1	63	2	2.12
Kimball, Ash	1	0	0	0	0	0	0	.000	1	2	2	2	0	2	0	0	1	0	18.00
Kline, Jax	1	0	0	0	0	1	0	.000	1	2	2	2	0	2	0	1	1	0	4.50
Kryczkowski, Col*	21	0	0	0	0	4	3	.571	24	25	9	9	1	20	1	1	26	2	3.38
LaGrow, Mty	19	19	11	0	11	4	0	.733	146	111	49	34	8	49	3	4	126	7	2.10
Lee, Jacksonville	30	14	1	0	4	7	0	.364	114	111	55	47	9	37	3	5	65	5	3.71
LeFevre, Jax	34	0	0	0	2	3		.333	59	50	22	14	5	30	3	1	48	1	2.14
Limke, Mobile	31	0	0	0	2	7	6	.222	44	46	16	15	0	16	3	0	36	1	3.07
Locke, Jax*	30	1	0	0	3	3	10	.500	45	35	15	10	3	20	3		33	1	2.00
Lohse, Birmingham	4	1	0	0	0	0	0	1.000	7	7	4	3	1	5	3	0	3	1	3.86
MacDonnell, Mob*	9	9	3	0	1	4	0	.200	48	41	10	10	0	13	0	1	25	3	1.88
Machemehl, Sav	32	8	6	2	6	6	7	.500	112	90	47	32	8	44	4	7	60	2	2.57
Magness, Char	28	5	0	0	1	3	3	.250	59	60	30	32	4	23	1	5	38	6	4.58
Magnuson, Mob*	13	13	2	1	5	5	0	.500	88	72	24	19	3	14	1	1	48	6	1.94
Major, Birm*	9	8	1	0	3	5	0	.400	40	42	27	21	3	28	3	1	36	9	4.73
Marcano, Birm	21	5	1	0	5	1	1	.833	44	46	27	21	4	24	1	2	39	5	2.95
Mastin, Birm	34	0	0	0	6	2	7	.750	56	56	18	16	3	27	2	3	29	3	2.57
McConnell, Sav	38	3	0		3	7	5	.300	106	108	47	32	7	20	7	1	62	1	2.72
McFarland, Col	7	0	0	0	0	2	0	.000	12	12	9	4	0	12	1	1	9	2	3.00
McMasters, Col	23	5	1	0	4	3	1	.333	68	76	36	29	1	27	1	1	38	2	3.84
Meeler, Mty	3	0	0	0	1	0	0	.000	3	1	1	0	0	3	0	1	1	0	3.00
Mingori, Sav*	10	8	5	4	6	0	1	1.000	65	38	6	6	0	8	1	2	50	1	0.83
Moloney, Mobile	20	0	0	0	2	3	2	.400	30	31	18	12	1	18	3	2	20	1	3.60
Myette, Asheville	6	0	0	0	0	0	0	.000	9	11	6	6	1	7	3	3	6		6.00
Neumeier, Mobile	18	18	1	1	4	7	0	.364	97	81	43	37	1	37	2	2	68	6	3.43
Nichols, Char	2	0	0	0	0	0	0	.000	2	0	0	0	0	0	0	0	0	0	0.00
O'Connor, Ash*	32	1	0	0	0	0	3	.000	41	32	27	21	1	58	0	6	25	4	4.61
O'Neill, Char*	3	0	0	0	0	0	0	.000	0	0	0	0	0	0	0	0	0	0	0.00
Osborn, Ash	19	19	7	0	3	7	0	.300	120	122	50	38	7	33	2	3	75	4	2.65
O'Toole, Mobile	25	24	7	1	8	12	0	.400	154	131	66	51	5	62	4	5	85	8	2.98
Pena, Birmingham	5	0	0	0	0	1	0	.000	10	15	10	7	1	6	0	0	3	2	6.30
Peters, Jax	3	3	1	1	0	1	0	1.000	20	12	6	1	0	9	0	2	14	0	0.45
Propst, Birm	23	5	0	0	2	5	4	.286	58	66	34	29	4	11	2	3	43	6	4.50
Radakovic, Col	9	0	0	0	1	2	1	.333	32	27	9	9	0	18	1	0	22	3	2.53
Randolph, Char*	31	7	1	0	2	6	1	.250	83	81	39	31	4	36	1	5	53	7	3.36
Ruddell, Ash	17	15	1	0	4	6	0	.400	89	74	40	35	8	76	1	2	79	8	3.54
Saunders, Mty	4	4	4	0	0	1	0	1.000	36	22	6	6	1	5	0	0	24	0	1.50
Schwartz, Sav*	25	10	0	0	6	4	2	.600	68	59	26	24	5	32	3	1	48	3	3.18
Sherry, Mobile	26	0	0	0	6	4	6	.429	33	36	14	9	1	13	5	0	24	2	2.45
Sires, Asheville	20	0	0	0	2	3	0	.000	37	44	24	22	3	33	4	0	21	7	5.35
Smith, Birm	10	18	8	4	8	6	0	.571	117	108	50	44	10	52	2	0	93	5	3.38
Smith, Mobile	24	17	1	1	5	6	0	.455	128	95	44	26	3	53	7	5	84	5	1.83

Pitcher—Club	G.	GS.	CG.	ShO.	W.	L.	Sv.	Pct.	IP.	H.	R.	ER.	HR.	BB.	Int. BB.	HB.	SO.	WP.	ERA.
Spicer, Mty 26	8	4	2	4	4	3	.500	84	70	29	20	5	25	3	2	46	1	2.14
Stanhouse, Birm ..16	11	5	0	7	5	1	.583	84	57	27	21	3	42	3	4	80	6	2.25
Stephen, Jax 8	4	3	2	3	2	0	.600	38	28	11	8	1	12	2	0	24	3	1.89
Strable, Char 56	2	1	0	11	5	6	.688	128	110	57	39	5	37	6	4	69	2	2.74
Strampe, Mty 25	25	7	4	9	12	0	.429	157	159	67	57	6	49	2	2	134	11	3.27
Swanson, Mty 23	18	9	3	12	5	0	.706	134	120	35	28	6	26	2	0	102	4	1.88
Timberlake, Jax* ..10	10	2	1		4	3	0	.571	73	64	32	29	5	29	0	1	49	6	3.58
Tomlin, Ash* 25	22	2	0	6	10	1	.375	139	135	62	48	12	58	11	3	73	5	3.11
Voss, Montgomery* . 1	0	0	0	0	0	0	.000	⅓	2	1	1	0	1	0	0	1	0	27.00
Ware, Montgomery . 4	2	0	0	0	0	0	.000	10	12	10	9	1	12	0	0	5	0	8.10
Watkins, Col 5	5	2	0	2	1	0	.667	37	24	15	8	1	23	0	0	29	6	1.95
Weimer, Mobile ...15	0	0	0	5	3	3	.625	22	19	4	3	1	9	3	0	16	1	1.23
Weisenberg, Char ..13	12	2	0	3	6	1	.333	78	88	42	32	5	13	2	2	38	11	3.69
Whillock, Mty ...27	0	0	0	4	6	12	.400	45	45	18	17	2	19	8	0	35	2	3.40
Wrenn, Savannah* . 5	0	0	0	0	0	0	.000	7	4	2	1	1	2	0	0	3	1	1.29
Yingling, Birm ...13	0	0	0	1	1	0	.500	19	15	10	9	0	12	1	1	6	1	4.26
Yount, Columbus ..26	26	11	3	12	8	0	.600	184	148	66	58	7	58	1	8	149	16	2.84
Zamora, Columbus .43	0	0	0	8	4	11	.667	70	52	18	12	3	12	1	0	44	0	1.54
Zuber, Savannah ..16	11	5	3	4	4	1	.500	73	51	23	21	2	43	2	1	71	2	2.59

BALKS—Strampe, 4; Haynes, Hill, Swanson, Zuber, 3 each; LeFevre, Moloney, 2 each; Abbott, Bates, Bertino, Bickerton, Christman, Cook, Crook, Crossan, Dominguez, Frailing, Gilbreth, Gill, Greif, Higgins, Hinsley, M. Johnson, Kampf, LaGrow, Limke, Magness, O'Connor, Stanhouse, Tomlin, Yingling, 1 each.

COMBINATION SHUTOUTS—Dreier-Johnson-Blateric, Tomlin-Blateric, Higgins-Hill, Asheville; Propst-Mastin, Hamilton-Mastin, Birmingham; Hamm-Arruda-Gill, Magness-Randolph, Gill-Strable, Charlotte; Yount-Humphrey (2), Harris-Kryczkowski-Zamora, Harris-Humphrey, Greif-Zamora, Columbus; Frailing-Sherry, Neumeier-Limke-Sherry, O'Toole-Bauer, Magnuson-Limke, Baldwin-Weimer, MacDonnell-Dominguez, Smith-Weimer-Bauer, Smith-Weimer, O'Toole-Hankammer, Smith-Bauer-Weimer, Mobile; Cushmore-Whillock, Montgomery; Killion-Mingori, Hinsley-Boyd, Savannah.

NO-HIT GAME—Swanson, Montgomery, defeated Savannah, 3-0, August 14 (perfect game).

ALONG THE MINOR LEAGUE TRAIL ....

(Continued from page 442)

drew a walk. As he grinned while jogging down the line, General Manager Joe Macko scowled, muttering, "That walk cost us $16." .... How could Steve Green, Coggins' teammate, feel snooty after hitting only one homer? Well, if you lived in the Snooty Fox Apartments, as did Steve and other Dallas players, it's easy. The Snooty Fox manager offered free rent for a week to any of the player tenants who hit a homer. ... Something must be wrong with the scheduling when Pittsfield (Eastern) Owner Pat McKernan came up with this gimmick for fan comfort—wool blankets issued free to the shivering spectators. ... The Evansville (American Association) Triplets had a contest for batboys and who won? A set of triplets—14-year-old Danny, Don and Doug Huff. ... If you want to make things easy for yourself, just ask Jim Glover of Evansville how to do it. In 1969, Jim hit only one homer, so on April 22, first inning, he hit one, thus giving him 135 games to set a new personal high. ... Old Soupy Suby was at it again. The Mexican League hurler, who previously had admitted over the air that he threw a wet one, started off the season with three consecutive shutouts. Juan was accused once more of practicing ball doctoring—without a license. He won 20 games over the season, but the heat must have dried some saliva

(Continued on page 473)

Texas League

CLASS AA

Leading Batter
JOHNNY RIVERS
El Paso

League President
BOBBY BRAGAN

Leading Pitcher
GEORGE MANZ
Dallas-Ft. Worth

CHAMPIONSHIP WINNERS IN PREVIOUS YEARS

1888—Dallas .... .671	1920—Fort Worth .... .703	1946—Fort Worth .... .656
1889—Houston .... .551	Fort Worth .... .750	Dallas (2nd) § ..... .591
1890—Galveston .... .705	1921—Fort Worth .... .691	1947—Houston‡ .... .623
1892—Houston .... .741	Fort Worth .... .662	1948—Fort Worth‡ ..... .601
Houston .... .913	1922—Fort Worth .... .694	1949—Fort Worth ...... .649
1895—Dallas .... .754	Fort Worth .... .711	Tulsa (2nd) § ..... .584
Fort Worth* ...... .750	1923—Fort Worth .... .632	1950—Beaumont .... .595
1896—Fort Worth ...... .757	1924—Fort Worth .... .689	San Antonio (4th)§ .513
Houston* .... .679	Fort Worth .... .763	1951—Houston‡ .... .619
Galveston .... .548	1925—Fort Worth .... .711	1952—Dallas .... .571
1897—San Antonio† ..... .657	Fort Worth y ...... .653	Shreveport (3rd) § . .522
Galveston† .... .717	1926—Dallas .... .574	1953—Dallas‡ .... .571
1898—League disbanded.	1927—Wichita Falls .... .654	1954—Shreveport ...... .559
1899—Galveston .... .632	1928—Houston* .... .679	Houston (2nd)§ ... .553
Galveston .... .762	Wichita Falls .... .731	1955—Dallas .... .581
1900-01—Did not operate.	1929—Dallas* .... .588	Shreveport (3rd)§ . .540
1902—Corsicana .... .866	Wichita Falls .... .620	1956—Houston‡ .... .623
Corsicana .... .682	1930—Wichita Falls .... .697	1957—Dallas .... .662
1903—Paris-Waco .... .615	Fort Worth* ...... .632	Houston (2nd)§ ... .630
Dallas* .... .648	1931—Houston** .... .625	1958—Fort Worth ...... .582
1904—Corsicana* ...... .615	Houston .... .734	Cor. Christi (3rd) .507
Fort Worth .... .800	1932—Beaumont* .... .640	1959—Victoria .... .589
1905—Fort Worth ...... .545	Dallas .... .727	Austin (2nd)§ .... .548
1906—Fort Worth ...... .677	1933—Houston .... .623	1960—Rio Grande Valley .590
Cleburne x .... .609	San Antonio (4th)§ .523	Tulsa (3rd)§ ..... .528
1907—Austin .... .629	1934—Galveston‡ ...... .523	1961—Amarillo .... .643
1908—San Antonio ..... .664	1935—Oklahoma City‡ .. .590	San Antonio (3rd)§ .532
1909—Houston .... .601	1936—Dallas .... .604	1962—El Paso .... .571
1910—Dallas† .... .586	Tulsa (3rd)§ ..... .519	Tulsa (2nd)§ ..... .550
Houston† .... .586	1937—Oklahoma City ... .635	1963—San Antonio ..... .564
1911—Austin .... .575	Fort Worth (3rd)§ .535	Tulsa (3rd)§ ..... .529
1912—Houston .... .626	1938—Beaumont .... .635	1964—San Antonio‡ .... .607
1913—Houston .... .620	1939—Houston .... .606	1965—Tulsa .... .574
1914—Houston† .... .671	Fort Worth (4th)§. .540	Albuquerque xx ... .550
Waco† .... .671	1940—Houston‡ .... .652	1966—Arkansas .... .579
1915—Waco .... .592	1941—Houston .... .673	1967—Albuquerque ..... .557
1916—Waco .... .587	Dallas (4th)§ .... .519	1968—Arkansas .... .586
1917—Dallas .... .600	1942—Beaumont .... .605	El Paso xx .... .562
1918—Dallas .... .584	Shreveport (2nd)§ . .576	1969—Amarillo .... .593
1919—Shreveport* ..... .677	1943-44-45—Did not operate.	Memphis xx .... .504
Fort Worth .... .651		

*Won split-season playoff.   †No playoff for title.   ‡Finished first and won four-club playoff.

STANDING OF CLUBS AT CLOSE OF SEASON, SEPTEMBER 7

EASTERN DIVISION

Club	Mem.	Ark.	S.A.	Shrev.	Alb.	ElP.	D-FtW.	Amar.	W.	L.	T.	Pct.	G.B.
Memphis (19*)	..	14	7	15	7	4	9	13	69	67	0	.507	....
†Arkansas (22*)	10	..	15	13	7	8	6	8	67	67	0	.500	1
San Antonio (14)	17	9	..	11	6	7	8	9	67	69	0	.493	2
Shreveport (13)	9	10	13	..	5	4	8	9	58	76	0	.433	10

WESTERN DIVISION

Club	Mem.	Ark.	S.A.	Shrev.	Alb.	ElP.	D-FtW.	Amar.	W.	L.	T.	Pct.	G.B.
Albuquerque (17)	9	8	10	11	..	11	17	17	83	52	0	.615	....
El Paso (3)	12	8	9	12	13	..	13	10	77	59	0	.566	6½
Dallas-Fort Worth (1*) ...	7	10	8	8	7	11	..	12	63	73	0	.463	20½
Amarillo (24)	3	8	7	6	7	14	12	..	57	78	0	.422	26

†Arkansas club represented Little Rock, Ark.
Key to major league farm teams (indicated by numbers after clubs in standing) shown on Page 384.
Playoff—Albuquerque defeated Memphis, three games to one.
Regular-Season Attendance—Albuquerque, 177,747; Amarillo, 58,027; Arkansas, 119,554; Dallas-Fort Worth, 182,743; El Paso, 37,337; Memphis, 107,584; San Antonio, 44,271; Shreveport, 42,807. Total, 770,070. Playoff, 13,617. All-star game, 6,047.
Managers: Albuquerque—Del Crandall; Amarillo—Andy Gilbert; Arkansas—Ken Boyer; Dallas-Fort Worth—Joe Altobelli; El Paso—Del Rice; Memphis—Johnny Antonelli; San Antonio—Jim Marshall; Shreveport—Lou Fitzgerald, Clint Courtney.
All-Star Team: 1B—Milner, Memphis; 2B—Eckenrode, Albuquerque; 3B—Cey, Albuquerque; SS—Speier, Amarillo; OF—Rivers, El Paso; Gallagher, Albuquerque; Cruz, Arkansas; Garrett, San Antonio; C—Ferguson, Albuquerque; Jutze, Arkansas; P—Flynn, Albuquerque; Ellingsen, Albuquerque; L. Allen, El Paso; Hassler, El Paso; C. Williams, Memphis; Jacquez, San Antonio; D. Miller, Dallas-Fort Worth; Manager—Crandall, Albuquerque; Rice, El Paso.
(Compiled by Friend News Service, Blytheville, Ark.)

CLUB BATTING

Club	G.	AB.	R.	OR.	H.	TB.	2B.	3B.	HR.	RBI.	SH.	Int SF.BB.		HP.	SO.	SB.	CS.	LOB.	Pct.
Albuq'rque	135	4522	677	513	1257	1808	226	62	67	588	58	43	526	44	26	757	161	60	995	.278
El Paso ..	136	4503	746	673	1216	1889	238	39	119	672	59	39	594	41	46	1010	102	56	992	.270
Memphis .	136	4366	587	562	1141	1652	177	44	82	504	52	36	487	35	47	837	85	25	1015	.261
Arkansas	134	4457	660	664	1167	1687	172	38	92	529	52	39	460	32	41	757	60	51	973	.261
Amarillo	135	4506	596	657	1165	1662	166	53	75	523	41	28	510	33	42	740	37	26	1013	.259
D.-Ft.W.	136	4534	564	579	1132	1549	150	50	49	497	47	27	462	33	53	786	95	52	972	.250
Shreveport	134	4307	497	654	1050	1530	167	32	83	431	32	27	423	35	44	844	97	54	895	.244
S. Antonio	136	4417	557	562	1030	1511	149	34	88	486	59	27	527	29	49	891	54	32	974	.233

INDIVIDUAL BATTING

(Leading Qualifiers for Batting Championship—422 or More Plate Appearances)

*Bats lefthanded. †Switch-hitter.

Player and Club	G.	AB.	R.	H.	TB.	2B.	3B.	HR.	RBI.	SH.	SF.	BB.	HP.	SO.	SB.	CS.	Pct.
Rivers, John, El Paso*	114	449	99	154	241	25	10	14	56	2	1	66	4	62	30	13	.343
Gallagher, Robert, Alb*	101	378	51	127	167	16	9	2	41	8	7	34	0	65	15	3	.336
Moore, Gary, Albuquerque ..	104	402	68	132	205	23	7	12	67	3	5	28	1	41	20	10	.328
Diaz, Arsenio, Memphis	134	497	65	154	238	28	4	16	102	3	10	29	6	91	7	1	.310
Alderete, Paul, El Paso	115	376	57	115	166	25	1	8	71	0	4	55	1	64	7	2	.306
Ferguson, Joe, Albuquerque .	109	364	72	111	187	20	4	16	65	1	1	66	2	73	14	2	.305
Eckenrode, Larry, Alb*	107	393	65	119	157	20	3	4	46	4	3	53	1	41	30	8	.303
Cruz, Jose, Arkansas*	133	493	89	148	254	29	7	21	90	3	6	73	3	60	11	8	.300
Milner, John, Memphis*	136	461	88	137	232	19	8	20	71	1	2	100	4	59	27	8	.297
Rosario, Santiago, Shrev*	122	446	66	130	177	25	5	4	45	1	6	61	4	81	16	5	.291

Departmental Leaders: G—Milner, 136; AB—Diaz, 497; R—Rivers, 99; H—Diaz, Rivers, 154; TB—Cruz, 254; 2B—Cruz, 29; 3B—G. Rose, 11; HR—Garrett, 29; RBI—Diaz, 102; SH—Evans, Shelton, Shibley, 9; SF—Diaz, 10; BB—Milner, 100; HP—Matney, 13; SO—Parker, 126; SB—G. Rose, 37; CS—Howarth, G. Rose, 13.

(All Players—Listed Alphabetically)

Player and Club	G.	AB.	R.	H.	TB.	2B.	3B.	HR.	RBI.	SH.	SF.	BB.	HP.	SO.	SB.	CS.	Pct.
Abreu, Manuel, Arkansas ...	19	68	3	18	20	2	0	0	5	0	3	1	7	2	0		.265
Alderete, Paul, El Paso*	115	376	57	115	166	25	1	8	71	0	4	55	1	64	7	2	.306
Alexander, Doyle, Alb	11	26	2	8	13	2	0	1	10	1	0	1	0	9	0		.308
Allen, David, Albuquerque* ..	14	26	2	3	5	2	0	0	2	0	3	0	0	12	0		.115
Allen, Lloyd, El Paso	27	61	4	7	8	1	0	0	5	3	1	4	1	27	0		.115
Allen, Raymond, Memphis ...	19	12	0	2	2	0	0	0	0	0	0	2	0	4	0	0	.167
Allen, Ronald, Memphis*	24	83	9	23	32	6	0	1	13	0	1	13	0	20	2	0	.277
Altobelli, Joseph, D-FtW*	11	11	1	4	4	0	0	0	3	0	0	2	0	1	0		.364
Amman, David,																	
3 San An-8 Amar	11	11	0	0	0	0	0	0	0	0	0	0	0	1	0		.000
Arnold, Christopher, Amar. ..	66	242	42	66	105	8	5	7	33	1	1	18	3	48	3	2	.273
Arnold, Gregory, D-FtW	12	21	4	9	10	1	0	0	1	0	1	0	3	0	3	0	.429
Auferio, Anthony, Arkansas ..	11	26	1	5	5	0	0	0	1	0	0	6	0	8	0	0	.192
Barbosa, Anthony, El Paso* ..	16	26	2	5	5	0	0	0	3	0	0	1	0	2	0		.192
Bare, Raymond, Arkansas	29	57	7	4	4	0	0	0	4	0	6	0	0	31	0	0	.070
Barnes, Luther, Memphis ...	121	458	60	133	158	15	2	2	31	4	4	28	4	69	12	4	.290
Barr, James, Amarillo	14	33	4	9	14	5	0	0	3	0	2	0	0	11	0	0	.273
Barry, William, Shreveport ..	1	1	0	0	0	0	0	0	0	0	0	0	0	1	0		.000

Player and Club	G.	AB.	R.	H.	TB.	2B.	3B.	HR.	RBI.	SH.	SF.	BB.	HP.	SO.	SB.	CS.	Pct.
Bashore, Theodore, Mem*	105	291	39	88	141	16	5	9	52	3	2	61	2	40	3	1	.302
Beasley, Lewis, D-FtW*	107	410	42	115	143	16	6	0	41	2	1	23	2	52	14	8	.280
Bell, Barton, Arkansas	6	7	0	1	1	0	0	0	1	0	0	0	0	1	0	0	.143
Bell, Stanley, Shreveport	24	38	2	8	10	2	0	0	4	2	0	2	0	19	0	0	.211
Bethke, James, Memphis	37	13	0	1	1	0	0	0	0	0	0	0	0	6	0	0	.077
Bigone, Vincent, El Paso	16	58	11	18	31	6	2	1	7	0	0	7	1	9	0	2	.310
Binkowski, Thomas, San An*	88	285	43	71	105	11	4	5	35	5	0	41	3	37	8	4	.249
Bowens, Samuel, Shrev	34	123	19	31	40	3	0	2	11	0	0	15	3	33	1	0	.252
Boyer, Leonard, Arkansas*	24	87	10	20	35	4	1	3	6	1	0	6	0	17	1	0	.230
Bradley, Thomas, El Paso	4	12	1	2	2	0	0	0	0	0	0	1	0	5	0	0	.167
Breitzman, Robert, San An*	55	133	18	34	40	4	1	0	11	2	1	11	0	18	4	5	.256
Britton, Jimmy, Shrev*	32	24	1	3	4	1	0	0	2	1	0	3	0	12	0	0	.125
Brown, Curtis, Memphis	104	371	52	102	148	19	6	5	37	1	3	37	5	48	5	4	.275
Brown, E. Randolph, ElP*	48	166	35	51	84	15	3	4	30	2	4	30	0	32	4	1	.307
Brown, Oscar, Shreveport	30	114	19	40	53	7	0	2	9	0	0	7	1	19	1	0	.351
Brunette, James, San An	118	421	60	119	183	18	2	14	53	0	2	43	7	103	7	5	.283
Bryan, James, San Antonio	16	32	0	6	7	1	0	0	2	1	0	2	0	5	0	0	.188
Burgos, Celestino																	
35 Am-34 Shrev-24 Mem	93	265	28	61	79	9	3	1	24	3	2	26	6	43	0	1	.230
Burns, John, Shreveport*	59	118	12	21	30	3	0	2	14	2	2	8	0	22	0	0	.178
Cambero, Alberto, Shrev	59	193	23	42	56	6	4	0	5	0	0	9	1	22	7	3	.218
Camp, Michael, San Antonio	2	0	0	0	0	0	0	0	0	1	0	0	0	1	0	0	.000
Campbell, Dayle, El Paso	57	172	30	46	93	12	1	11	36	0	1	17	1	42	4	2	.267
Campbell, J. Jeffrey, Amar*	23	5	1	0	0	0	0	0	0	0	0	2	0	2	0	0	.000
Campbell, Tommie, Memphis	116	338	38	68	94	6	4	4	28	3	2	31	4	112	7	3	.201
Camy, Donald, Memphis	6	18	3	4	6	1	0	0	1	0	0	2	0	4	0	0	.222
Canada, Romel, Alb*	24	59	10	16	20	1	0	1	4	0	0	10	1	5	3	0	.271
Cann, Stuart, Shreveport*	98	309	31	65	87	8	1	4	20	4	2	37	5	36	7	5	.210
Carnegie, Christopher, DFW	111	308	35	83	110	15	0	4	31	4	2	23	2	49	3	2	.269
Carthel, Billy, Memphis	105	331	39	81	128	14	0	11	45	5	3	41	6	77	1	1	.245
Cedeno, Rosendo, Amarillo*	94	264	41	66	104	9	1	9	32	0	1	37	4	44	0	1	.250
Cey, Ronald, Albuquerque	71	239	31	79	115	22	4	2	56	1	4	33	2	38	1	2	.331
Chilcott, Steven, Memphis*	50	129	20	27	50	3	1	6	20	0	1	29	2	33	0	0	.209
Childers, Terry, San An	17	37	5	1	1	0	0	0	0	2	0	8	0	19	1	0	.027
Chlupsa, Robert, Arkansas	7	3	0	1	1	0	0	0	0	0	0	0	0	1	0	0	.333
Christino, Michael, Alb*	9	22	4	3	3	0	0	0	0	0	0	4	0	2	0	0	.136
Clark, Rickey, El Paso	15	27	1	3	3	0	0	0	1	0	0	4	0	9	0	0	.111
Cleary, Arthur, Amarillo*	96	340	46	91	118	13	4	2	25	2	1	43	2	37	11	1	.268
Clements, Allan, Memphis	33	36	3	4	4	0	0	0	3	0	0	2	0	13	0	0	.111
Coggins, Richard, D-FtW	86	316	41	87	140	14	9	7	37	2	4	28	2	45	3	4	.275
Cohen, Randy, Dal-FtW	32	45	4	4	5	1	0	0	3	4	1	8	0	26	0	0	.089
Coil, Charles, Amarillo	40	106	10	30	45	7	1	2	15	0	3	11	0	17	0	0	.283
Coleman, Garrett, Shrev	30	60	3	13	16	3	0	0	9	0	0	9	1	9	1	0	.217
Contreras, Efrain, El Paso	18	8	1	1	1	0	0	0	1	0	0	1	0	1	0	0	.125
Coulter, Thomas, Arkansas	48	180	29	50	61	5	0	2	15	2	1	27	4	36	4	4	.278
Cox, Terry, El Paso	32	38	3	10	16	3	0	1	7	4	0	2	1	8	0	0	.263
Crandall, Delmar, Alb	2	4	0	0	0	0	0	0	0	0	0	0	0	0	0	0	.000
Creola, Thomas, Dal-FtW*	32	81	6	25	30	3	1	0	17	0	1	8	1	15	0	0	.309
Crosby, Edward, Arkansas*	78	300	40	90	132	17	5	5	31	2	2	20	4	23	4	7	.300
Cruz, Jose, Arkansas*	133	493	89	148	254	29	7	21	90	3	6	73	3	60	11	8	.300
Cummings, Robert, Alb	14	46	4	11	14	1	1	0	5	1	0	0	0	2	0	0	.239
Daboll, Dennis, Arkansas	9	16	1	2	3	1	0	0	1	1	0	6	0	6	0	0	.125
DeClinces, Douglas, D-FtW	11	35	3	6	7	1	0	0	1	0	0	2	0	6	1	0	.171
Decker, George, San An	2	5	0	0	0	0	0	0	0	0	0	1	0	2	0	0	.000
Dees, Wayne, Arkansas*	100	356	50	99	164	14	3	15	65	0	3	41	6	36	3	2	.278
Dehn, Gregory, El Paso	22	75	2	13	16	3	0	0	6	3	0	4	0	24	0	1	.173
DeLong, Robert, Amarillo*	22	47	4	8	9	1	0	0	1	0	0	6	0	20	0	0	.170
Del Orbe, Lazaro, D-FtW	14	50	2	9	9	0	0	0	4	0	1	4	0	6	1	0	.180
Denehy, William, Memphis*	7	14	0	3	4	1	0	0	1	2	0	0	0	4	0	0	.214
Detter, Roger, San Antonio	109	328	22	71	89	6	0	4	28	2	3	32	7	61	3	3	.216
DeWald, Terry, Memphis	93	295	35	68	86	11	2	1	22	2	2	23	4	38	10	0	.231
Diaz, Arsenio, Memphis	134	497	65	154	238	28	4	16	102	3	10	29	6	91	7	1	.310
Dickerson, Donald, Mem*	4	3	0	0	0	0	0	0	0	0	0	1	1	3	0	0	.000
DiFabio, Joseph, Arkansas	26	55	4	9	15	3	0	1	5	0	1	2	0	11	0	0	.164
Distaso, Alec, San Antonio	6	4	0	0	0	0	0	0	1	0	0	0	0	4	0	0	.000
Dix, James, Memphis†	23	61	12	18	31	6	2	1	3	0	1	10	0	7	2	0	.295
Dodder, Joseph, Alb*	10	27	4	3	6	0	0	1	2	0	0	7	1	7	2	0	.111
Doherty, John, El Paso*	6	21	1	5	7	2	0	0	0	0	0	0	0	2	0	0	.238
Downing, Ronald, Alb†	84	238	20	62	81	14	1	1	32	3	2	18	0	38	1	4	.261
Dudek, John, San Antonio	22	43	2	9	12	0	0	1	4	0	0	0	1	8	0	0	.209
Dunegan, James, San An	12	28	4	7	9	2	0	0	2	0	0	2	0	10	0	0	.250
Eckenrode, Larry, Alb*	107	393	65	119	157	20	4	3	46	4	3	53	1	41	30	8	.303
Ellingsen, H. Bruce, Alb*	28	59	5	7	7	0	0	0	3	1	0	3	1	30	0	0	.119
Encerti, Gary, San Antonio	24	6	0	0	0	0	0	0	0	0	0	3	0	3	0	0	.000
Engbers, Donald, Arkansas†	12	24	0	1	1	0	0	0	0	0	0	1	0	15	0	0	.042
Engelhardt, James, El Paso	26	24	0	0	0	0	0	0	0	0	0	0	0	12	0	0	.000
Evans, Steven, Arkansas	16	46	1	6	7	1	0	0	5	0	1	0	1	21	0	1	.130
Ewing, Ray, Memphis†	16	14	0	1	1	0	0	0	2	1	0	0	0	7	0	0	.071
Feldman, Jerry, El Paso*	111	366	68	106	155	19	3	8	72	5	3	84	3	55	19	6	.290
Ferguson, Joe, Albuquerque	109	364	72	111	187	20	4	16	65	1	1	66	2	73	14	2	.305
Floyd, G. Michael, El Paso	99	329	49	98	178	24	4	16	65	1	5	52	11	77	5	4	.298
Flynn, James, Albuquerque†	32	76	11	18	22	4	0	0	10	4	2	5	2	20	1	0	.237
Ford, Percival, Shreveport	45	38	3	10	11	1	0	0	3	1	0	1	0	11	0	1	.263

Player and Club	G.	AB.	R.	H.	TB.	2B.	3B.	HR.	RBI.	SH.	SF.	BB.	HP.	SO.	SB.	CS.	Pct.
Foster, Leonard, Shrev	69	251	35	66	97	9	5	4	15	2	1	16	2	43	16	7	.263
Frazier, Dyain, San An	2	1	0	0	0	0	0	0	0	0	0	0	0	1	0	0	.000
Frazier, Robert, Amarillo ..	87	257	43	68	106	10	2	8	39	1	3	25	4	64	0	0	.265
Frost, David, El Paso	8	4	0	0	0	0	0	0	0	2	0	0	0	2	0	0	.000
Gagle, Edward, Arkansas ..	79	252	41	69	135	12	3	16	44	1	1	42	4	100	0	2	.274
Gallagher, Robert, Alb*	101	378	51	127	167	16	9	2	41	8	7	34	0	65	15	3	.336
Galliher, Marvin, Alb	24	56	10	14	17	1	1	0	2	0	0	11	1	7	0	1	.250
Garland, Marcus W., D-FtW	21	48	5	8	12	1	0	1	3	1	0	5	0	22	0	0	.167
Garrett, H. Adrian, San An*	128	448	82	124	238	21	3	29	86	1	3	64	5	91	4	0	.277
Gatewood, Aubrey, Shrev ..	14	19	0	2	2	0	0	0	1	2	0	1	0	9	0	0	.105
Gonzalez, Dionicio, Ark* ...	10	10	2	2	2	0	0	0	0	0	0	0	0	0	0	0	.200
Gourleux, David, Shrev	8	13	1	4	4	0	0	0	1	1	0	3	0	3	0	0	.308
Grant, W. Richard, Shrev*	69	164	22	36	72	6	0	10	27	0	0	18	0	38	1	0	.220
Green, Steven, Dal-FtW ...	118	420	52	119	162	19	6	4	53	0	4	46	7	64	17	10	.283
Guth, Charles, Shreveport .	11	29	3	3	4	1	0	0	1	0	0	2	0	7	0	2	.103
Hacker, Richard, Memphis .	13	43	7	14	19	2	0	1	3	0	0	6	0	6	0	0	.326
Hanson, Larry, El Paso	44	146	25	42	71	9	1	6	32	0	2	20	0	49	0	2	.288
Hassler, Andrew, El Paso* ..	22	48	7	7	12	2	0	1	6	1	0	5	0	23	0	1	.146
Haynes, LeRoy, San An ..	7	14	1	3	4	1	0	0	0	0	0	3	0	5	1	0	.214
Henderson, Joseph, ElP* ...	37	68	7	13	19	1	1	1	5	1	0	3	0	27	1	0	.191
Hernandez, David, Amarillo*	45	13	1	4	4	0	0	0	2	1	0	0	0	3	0	0	.308
Hernandez, Enzo, Dal-FtW	42	156	27	44	54	8	1	0	9	4	1	8	0	9	6	3	.282
Herson, Michael, Dal-FtW ..	24	39	2	3	3	0	0	0	2	0	0	7	0	24	0	0	.077
Hickey, Donald, Dal-FtW ..	8	26	1	6	6	0	0	0	4	1	0	0	0	3	0	0	.231
Hill, Gary, Memphis	12	23	1	5	5	0	0	0	0	0	1	0	0	3	0	1	.217
Holbert, Robert, Amarillo .	75	238	24	58	74	5	4	1	26	0	2	18	2	22	2	0	.244
Holland, Albert, El Paso* ..	53	146	24	38	64	9	4	3	23	2	0	19	1	30	1	4	.260
Howard, Douglas, El Paso ..	16	55	6	11	15	1	0	1	4	0	1	2	1	8	0	0	.200
Howarth, James, Amarillo*	122	466	72	119	158	20	8	1	38	4	2	64	4	43	5	13	.255
Hrabosky, Alan, Arkansas .	15	32	5	6	8	2	0	0	5	0	0	5	1	14	0	0	.188
Huckle, Wilbur, Memphis ..	49	185	31	51	61	6	2	0	14	2	0	9	1	12	7	0	.276
Hudson, Charles, Memphis* .	33	19	3	1	1	0	0	0	2	0	0	0	0	12	0	0	.053
Huisman, William, San An .	76	244	42	53	79	9	4	3	20	1	2	30	1	35	6	3	.217
Hutton, Lawrence, Alb	21	0	0	0	0	0	0	0	0	1	0	0	0	0	0	0	.000
Jacquez, Patrick, San An ..	19	50	2	6	7	1	0	0	4	3	1	2	0	12	0	0	.120
Jagutis, H. John, El Paso†	13	36	2	10	12	2	0	0	6	1	0	0	0	6	0	0	.278
James, Richard, San An ...	13	7	0	0	0	0	0	0	0	1	0	0	0	2	0	0	.000
Jaster, Daniel, Arkansas ..	4	3	0	1	1	0	0	0	0	0	0	0	0	2	0	0	.333
Jeffcoat, Harold, Amar* ...	37	38	2	9	9	0	0	0	5	1	0	1	0	10	0	0	.237
Jestadt, Garry, San An ...	19	75	8	17	24	2	1	1	6	0	1	1	0	6	1	1	.227
Johnson, Timothy, Alb†	102	361	45	95	146	17	8	6	40	3	2	24	3	58	5	2	.263
Jones, Ronald, San An* ...	3	0	0	0	0	0	0	0	0	0	0	0	0	0	0	0	.000
Jones, Terry, Dal-FtW	6	23	2	6	7	1	0	0	1	0	0	2	0	3	1	0	.261
Jutze, Alfred, Arkansas ...	117	412	49	100	140	17	4	5	41	3	3	37	3	58	2	1	.243
Kazmarek, George, Memphis.	8	21	4	6	7	1	0	0	0	0	0	0	0	8	0	0	.286
Kelleher, Michael, Ark ...	21	83	12	18	23	3	1	0	3	1	1	6	2	7	1	1	.217
Keller, Daniel, El Paso ...	33	15	0	0	0	0	0	0	6	0	2	0	0	11	0	0	.000
Kelley, Thomas, Shreveport .	12	28	1	3	5	2	0	0	1	0	0	2	0	10	0	0	.107
Kelly, James, Dal-FtW	18	42	3	5	8	0	0	1	3	1	0	8	0	16	0	0	.119
Kennedy, Junior, Dal-FtW .	3	9	1	3	3	0	0	0	2	0	0	1	0	0	0	0	.333
King, G. Anthony, Shrev ...	10	7	0	1	2	1	0	0	0	0	0	0	0	3	0	0	.143
King, Jeffrey, Dal-FtW	12	3	0	2	2	0	0	0	0	0	0	0	0	1	0	0	.667
King, Travis, Albuquerque .	31	56	7	9	12	1	1	0	4	3	0	7	0	28	1	0	.161
Kingman, David, Amarillo .	60	210	41	62	118	6	1	15	41	1	0	37	1	64	3	1	.295
Knutzen, Patrick, El Paso*	15	3	0	0	0	0	0	0	0	0	0	0	0	2	0	0	.000
Koonce, Donald, Memphis* .	32	13	3	5	6	1	0	0	0	1	0	1	0	4	0	0	.385
Kovach, Vaughn, Dal-FtW .	19	9	0	0	0	0	0	0	0	0	0	1	0	9	0	0	.000
Krawczyk, Thomas, San An .	6	16	2	3	5	0	1	0	1	0	0	3	0	4	0	0	.188
Lavelle, Gary, Amarillo† ..	22	33	1	5	5	0	0	0	1	1	3	0	18	0	0	.152
Lisetski, Michael, San An ..	7	25	3	8	18	4	0	2	9	0	0	3	0	5	0	0	.320
Lobb, David, Shreveport ...	43	45	1	4	6	0	1	0	1	2	0	5	0	16	0	0	.089
Lombardo, Earl, San An ...	2	9	4	5	8	0	0	1	2	0	0	1	0	1	0	0	.556
Long, Robert, Albuquerque*	71	199	35	44	71	12	3	3	24	1	1	23	0	32	6	1	.221
Lowe, Q. V., San Antonio .	34	23	1	5	5	0	0	0	3	0	0	1	0	8	0	0	.217
Lundstedt, Thomas, San An .	36	94	8	12	17	2	0	1	4	0	0	11	0	31	0	0	.128
Macko, Joseph, Dal-FtW** .	4	10	0	0	0	0	0	0	0	0	0	1	0	4	0	0	.000
Mairena, Alfonso, Arkansas.	15	29	3	6	10	1	0	1	4	1	0	1	0	3	0	0	.207
Mallon, James, Amarillo* ..	105	377	39	111	128	13	2	0	45	1	4	29	1	38	2	0	.294
Manfredi, Ralph, Dal-FtW .	106	340	46	85	116	15	5	2	44	0	1	35	0	40	0	1	.250
Mang, Fabien, Shreveport* .	51	169	14	38	51	7	0	2	12	1	0	25	3	31	3	2	.225
Manz, George, Dl1as-FtW ..	21	58	4	7	7	0	0	0	4	1	0	1	0	17	0	0	.121
Marikos, David, El Paso ..	1	1	0	0	0	0	0	0	0	0	0	0	0	1	0	0	.000
Marion, Gary, Arkansas* ..	5	13	2	3	3	0	0	0	1	0	0	0	0	5	0	0	.231
Marquez, Francisco, ElP ...	11	29	4	9	13	2	1	0	3	0	0	2	1	3	1	0	.310
Marsden, John, Amarillo* .	91	296	42	75	104	15	4	2	24	2	0	36	2	50	5	2	.253
Martin, Stanley, Dal-FtW† .	34	116	16	24	29	3	1	0	8	2	2	12	1	11	8	3	.207
Massarand, William, San An	21	61	4	9	14	1	2	0	5	0	2	0	0	22	0	0	.148
Mathwig, Michael, Alb	39	16	4	2	3	1	0	0	1	0	4	0	2	0	0	.125
Matney, Ronnie, San An† ..	98	296	46	74	105	13	3	4	27	7	0	34	13	64	2	3	.250
Matthew, Clifton, Dal-FtW	115	348	47	87	135	15	7	8	44	2	3	68	2	100	9	3	.250
Mazzone, Leo, Amarillo* ..	9	1	0	0	0	0	0	0	0	0	0	0	0	1	0	0	.000
McCammon, Michael, Shrev.	3	2	0	0	0	0	0	1	0	1	0	0	0	0	0	0	.000
McCord, Gilbert, El Paso ...	109	426	79	118	167	20	1	9	65	4	6	35	2	50	3	6	.277

Player and Club	G.	AB.	R.	H.	TB.	2B.	3B.	HR.	RBI.	SH.	SF.	BB.	HP.	SO.	SB.	CS.	Pct.
McDonald, Michael, Ark	41	91	11	26	54	6	1	9	1	0	19	0	19	0	1	.286
McDonald, Scott, Dal-FtW .	125	428	62	101	155	19	4	9	60	2	9	52	1	72	5	1	.236
McDowell, Larry, Alb	27	57	4	13	17	2	1	0	6	3	0	3	0	10	0	1	.228
McLeod, Robert, Memphis ..	28	52	4	11	16	2	0	1	6	7	0	3	0	13	1	0	.212
Meoli, Rudolph, El Paso* ..	7	24	3	7	11	1	0	1	3	2	0	1	0	5	1	2	.292
Miller, Dyar, Dal-FtW	31	60	4	11	18	2	1	1	7	3	1	1	2	24	0	0	.183
Miller, Martin, San Ant ..	130	439	55	105	127	13	3	1	47	2	5	79	2	17	5	0	.239
Milner, John, Memphis* .	136	481	98	137	232	19	8	20	71	1	2	100	6	59	27	8	.297
Moock, Joseph, Shreveport*	20	49	8	15	20	2	0	1	6	0	0	8	0	10	1	2	.306
Moore, Gary, Albuquerque ..	104	402	68	132	205	23	7	12	67	3	5	28	1	41	20	10	.328
Moore, Tommy, Memphis ..	9	15	0	1	3	0	1	0	2	0	1	2	0	6	0	0	.067
Moschetti, Matthew, ElP ..	100	309	48	78	106	12	2	4	41	3	1	61	2	65	0	4	.252
Moulden, C. Carroll, DFW .	37	8	0	0	0	0	0	0	0	1	0	1	0	6	0	0	.000
Mull, Jack, San Antonio ..	73	174	15	34	46	1	1	3	17	2	2	13	4	58	1	1	.195
Mullen, Michael, San An ..	28	14	1	3	5	0	1	0	1	3	0	2	1	8	0	0	.214
Murphy, Marian, Shreveport.	102	323	50	76	121	11	2	10	43	3	3	50	7	100	25	6	.235
Napoleon, Daniel, Arkansas .	105	364	62	106	168	16	5	12	64	1	1	34	1	54	2	4	.291
Nelson, Brian, Shreveport* .	14	9	0	0	0	0	0	0	0	0	1	0	0	7	0	0	.000
Nelson, Frederick, Alb	56	137	19	29	36	5	1	0	9	0	3	16	1	21	3	1	.212
Newman, Raymond, San Ant	27	12	0	2	2	0	0	0	0	1	0	1	0	6	0	0	.167
Newson, Michael, Shrev ..	103	314	21	62	80	6	3	2	17	1	1	21	5	71	9	6	.197
Niles, Randall, El Paso ..	38	131	18	40	60	11	0	3	20	0	0	8	1	42	0	0	.305
Nitschke, David, Memphis ..	62	174	17	50	63	11	1	0	19	1	1	22	1	27	0	0	.287
Nordbrook, Timothy, DFW ..	25	69	7	7	13	1	1	0	7	0	0	8	1	20	1	0	.101
North, William, San An ..	25	77	14	16	20	2	1	0	3	1	0	13	0	20	8	2	.208
Nottebart, Donald, San An .	40	10	0	0	0	0	0	0	0	0	0	0	0	6	0	0	.000
Nunn, William, El Paso* ..	42	106	14	16	26	4	0	2	11	1	1	17	2	44	0	1	.151
Parker, William, El Paso .	116	436	72	125	220	26	3	21	71	0	5	39	9	126	9	2	.287
Perkins, Jerry, Memphis ..	45	9	1	1	1	0	0	0	1	3	0	2	0	6	0	0	.111
Plodinec, Timothy, Ark ..	13	9	0	1	1	0	0	0	0	3	0	0	0	4	0	0	.111
Porter, Horace, San An* ..	36	90	12	21	27	2	2	0	5	1	1	11	1	12	0	1	.233
Powell, Grover, Shrev* ..	12	4	0	0	0	0	0	0	0	0	0	0	0	3	0	0	.000
Rader, David, Amarillo ..	92	282	44	68	115	9	4	10	41	0	1	45	8	38	0	0	.241
Ralston, William, Alb	111	307	50	88	129	24	4	3	37	8	3	36	2	53	2	4	.287
Raynor, James, Albuquerque.	26	23	1	3	3	0	0	0	3	1	1	3	0	3	0	1	.130
Reahm, Frederick, Memphis*	12	17	1	1	1	0	0	0	0	0	0	0	0	10	0	0	.059
Reed, Ronald, Shreveport .	2	2	0	0	0	0	0	0	0	0	0	0	0	0	0	0	.000
Reuschel, Paul, San An ..	33	57	5	10	14	1	0	1	4	7	0	7	0	20	0	0	.175
Rice, Delbert, El Paso ..	3	3	0	2	2	0	0	0	1	0	0	1	0	0	0	0	.667
Rickey, Ralph, San An ..	69	221	34	46	85	10	1	9	35	1	0	50	4	85	0	1	.208
Rivera, Enrique, Arkansas ..	46	157	18	48	63	6	3	1	17	2	4	10	0	8	4	0	.306
Rivera, Gilberto, San An ..	27	25	2	4	4	0	0	0	3	0	1	1	0	7	0	0	.160
Rivers, John, El Paso*	114	449	99	154	241	25	10	14	56	2	1	66	4	62	30	13	.343
Roberts, Dale, Shreveport .	34	13	1	0	0	0	0	0	0	0	0	0	0	5	0	0	.000
Rohr, Leslie, Memphis* ..	10	21	4	4	4	0	0	0	0	3	0	1	0	7	0	0	.190
Rosario, Santiago, Shrev* .	122	446	66	130	177	25	5	4	45	1	6	61	4	81	16	5	.291
Rose, Donald, Memphis ..	30	51	6	6	9	3	0	0	3	0	7	0	20	0	0	.118
Rose, Guy, Albuquerque .	118	383	59	106	158	15	11	5	45	0	6	66	2	67	37	13	.277
Rosello, David, San Antonio	64	209	22	49	67	7	1	3	16	7	0	20	0	22	2	1	.234
Rudolph, Kenneth, San An .	36	120	11	30	38	6	1	0	7	1	1	14	0	28	0	2	.250
Ryerson, Gary, Amarillo ..	34	55	4	5	8	1	1	0	4	5	0	4	1	21	0	0	.091
Sadek, Michael, Amarillo ..	17	46	6	9	11	2	0	0	3	0	0	9	0	11	0	0	.196
St. Clair, Ronnie, El Paso ..	27	11	1	2	2	0	0	0	1	0	1	0	4	0	0	.182
Santiago, Roberto, 34 Amar-46 Shrev	80	228	18	54	74	6	1	4	24	1	2	22	8	40	0	1	.237
Sauget, Richard, Shrev	49	135	13	36	59	6	1	5	16	0	1	13	3	32	0	0	.267
Saul, James, San Antonio* .	5	11	1	1	1	0	0	0	0	0	0	0	3	0	0	.091
Schroeppel, John, Ark*	35	29	3	5	5	0	0	0	2	1	0	3	0	8	0	0	.172
Schueler, Ronald, Shrev ..	29	44	2	10	15	1	2	0	2	1	1	1	0	6	1	1	.227
Scott, Leslie, Amarillo ..	39	60	5	14	18	2	1	0	3	1	0	4	0	8	0	0	.233
Sells, David W., El Paso ..	57	14	4	5	8	0	0	1	2	3	0	0	6	0	0	.357
Seminoff, Richard, Ark ..	43	26	0	3	3	0	0	0	0	2	0	0	14	1	0	.115
Shelton, Ronald, D-FtW .	104	398	55	97	119	15	2	1	24	9	4	52	4	37	22	11	.244
Shibley, Richard, El Paso ..	75	218	39	47	59	2	2	2	15	9	1	45	3	51	14	4	.216
Skidmore, R. Roe, San An ..	52	209	25	66	98	10	2	6	39	0	3	11	0	25	0	0	.316
Sowinski, Thomas, Alb	23	19	1	4	4	0	0	0	0	2	0	1	0	6	0	0	.211
Speier, Chris, Amarillo ..	129	460	44	130	178	20	5	6	66	8	2	54	2	56	2	4	.283
Spellman, T. Michael, El Paso	9	6	0	0	0	0	0	0	0	1	0	0	0	4	0	0	.000
Sprinkle, Charles, Shrev ..	43	24	3	3	5	2	0	0	0	3	0	3	0	6	0	0	.125
Stein, William, Arkansas .	114	429	56	124	173	21	2	8	52	5	3	38	2	63	1	6	.289
Stephen, Louis, Dal-FtW ..	10	9	0	2	2	0	0	0	1	0	0	5	0	0	.222
Stephenson, C. Earl, S A* ..	22	13	1	1	1	0	0	0	2	1	0	0	6	0	0	.077
Stewart, S. Charles, Ark* .	104	339	58	83	86	1	1	0	17	1	1	33	4	53	24	11	.245
Stitzel, Glenn, Memphis* ..	7	13	0	2	2	0	0	0	0	0	0	0	0	5	0	0	.154
Stone, Steven, Amarillo ..	19	45	7	7	11	0	2	0	6	1	0	5	0	16	0	0	.156
Stover, Joseph, San An ..	27	8	1	1	1	0	0	0	1	1	0	0	1	2	0	0	.125
Strickland, James, Alb* ..	3	5	0	0	0	0	0	0	0	0	0	2	0	3	0	0	.000
Swanson, Charles, Shrev ..	3	2	0	0	0	0	0	0	0	0	0	0	0	0	0	0	.000
Thompson, Charles, Ark* ..	35	13	2	2	3	1	0	0	3	0	0	0	3	0	0	.154
Thompson, Lucky, Arkansas	80	272	30	68	75	5	1	0	23	6	1	38	4	38	3	1	.250
Thoms, Richard, Dal-FtW* .	40	24	0	3	4	1	0	0	0	1	0	3	0	15	0	0	.125
Todd, James, San Antonio* .	19	39	1	4	5	1	0	0	3	0	2	0	17	1	0	.103
Tolliver, Larry, Amarillo ..	7	5	0	0	0	0	0	0	0	0	0	0	4	0	0	.000

Player and Club	G.	AB.	R.	H.	TB.	2B.	3B.	HR.	RBI.	SH.	SF.	BB.	HP.	SO.	SB.	CS.	Pct.
Toney, Robert, Shreveport	53	191	18	52	73	7	4	2	26	1	1	12	0	21	1	2	.272
Towers, Richard, Shrev	9	7	0	1	1	0	0	0	0	0	0	0	0	5	0	0	.143
Upton, Gary, Memphis	15	45	4	10	18	0	1	2	6	0	0	0	0	10	0	0	.222
Vanzin, Frank, 21 Ark-42 Dal-FtW	63	200	27	57	85	12	2	4	25	0	0	27	0	31	1	2	.285
Vaughan, Charles, Shrev†	18	16	5	5	12	1	0	2	4	1	0	0	0	2	0	0	.313
Von Hoff, Bruce, Arkansas	18	27	1	4	5	1	0	0	4	1	0	2	0	9	0	0	.148
Walseth, Michael, Shrev*	63	236	31	70	99	11	0	6	29	0	0	18	1	30	1	2	.297
Watts, Edward, Dal-FtW	117	462	65	125	168	14	4	7	62	3	2	26	8	54	4	6	.271
White, Leland, Arkansas	1	1	0	1	1	0	0	0	1	0	0	0	0	0	0	0	1.000
White, Richard, Amarillo*	.100	365	54	102	154	10	6	10	54	2	4	30	2	57	4	2	.279
Wilkinson, Don, El Paso	18	60	11	12	16	1	0	1	3	0	0	8	1	18	2	0	.200
Williams, Bernard, Amar	2	8	1	3	3	0	0	0	0	0	0	1	0	2	0	0	.375
Williams, Charles P., Mem	27	53	4	7	8	1	0	0	2	7	1	2	1	29	0	0	.132
Williams, Earl, Shreveport	89	330	53	105	187	21	2	19	63	1	3	37	1	36	6	5	.318
Williams, James O., Alb†	113	393	70	109	152	18	5	5	47	1	1	46	2	43	18	5	.277
Williams, Thomas, Memphis†	36	106	12	31	46	3	3	2	10	0	0	15	1	23	0	2	.292
Williamson, Jeffrey, D-FtW	10	7	0	0	0	0	0	0	0	0	0	0	0	6	0	0	.000
Willis, Ronald, Arkansas	26	7	0	1	1	0	0	0	0	0	1	0	3	0	0	0	.143
Wilshusen, Terry, D-FtW	32	16	1	4	5	1	0	0	0	0	0	0	0	5	0	0	.250
Winslow, George, Arkansas*	51	70	6	16	25	1	1	2	6	0	0	0	0	14	1	0	.229
Wysocki, Michael, Amarillo	44	17	0	1	1	0	0	0	0	1	0	0	0	3	0	0	.059
Yeager, Stephen, Alb	55	151	23	42	58	5	1	3	24	1	1	19	1	39	2	1	.278
Zabala, Faustino, Shrev	72	201	20	46	66	9	1	3	26	1	5	23	2	35	1	3	.229

The following pitchers had no plate appearances (listed alphabetically by club, games in parentheses):

ALBUQUERQUE—Dermody, Norman† (6); Price, Michael (2).
AMARILLO—Sosa, Elias (3).
ARKANSAS—Ford, Daniel (1).
DALLAS-FORT WORTH—Grant, Herman (2).
EL PASO—Ogier, Maurice (1).
SHREVEPORT—Wilson, Richard (4).
GRAND-SLAM HOME RUNS—D. Campbell, Floyd, Garrett, 2 each; Alderete, Alexander, Binkowski, Brunette, Gagle, W. Grant, Jutze, Manfredi, Moock, Murphy, Napoleon, Rickey, Rivers, Watts, Yeager, 1 each.
AWARDED FIRST BASE ON INTERFERENCE—Shelton 2 (Ferguson, Jutze); Barnes (Santiago), Binkowski (Zabala), Cann (Carthel), Green (E. Brown), S. McDonald (Ferguson), Murphy (Carthel).

CLUB FIELDING

Club	G.	PO.	A.	E.	DP.	PB.	Pct.	Club	G.	PO.	A.	E.	DP.	PB.	Pct.
Albuquerque	135	3552	1581	132	149	20	.975	El Paso	136	3538	1512	192	130	33	.963
Dal-Fort Worth	136	3563	1305	146	91	32	.971	Memphis	136	3409	1331	184	108	24	.963
Arkansas	134	3461	1470	177	132	35	.965	Amarillo	135	3494	1391	192	110	34	.962
San Antonio	136	3577	1591	189	139	28	.965	Shreveport	134	3402	1429	202	113	48	.960

Triple Play—Shreveport.

INDIVIDUAL FIELDING
(Ten or More Games)

*Throws lefthanded.

FIRST BASEMEN

Player and Club	G.	PO.	A.	E.	DP.	Pct.	Player and Club	G.	PO.	A.	E.	DP.	Pct.
Kingman, Amarillo	21	160	4	0	14	1.000	Skidmore, San An	52	519	42	7	47	.988
Howard, El Paso	13	135	5	0	6	1.000	Milner, Memphis*	87	714	34	10	57	.987
Alderete, El Paso	13	112	12	0	8	1.000	Ron Allen, Memphis	24	214	14	3	11	.987
McDONALD, D-FW	119	959	78	6	56	.994	Binkowski, San An*	16	140	5	2	8	.986
Walseth, Shrev	15	139	9	1	12	.993	Moore, Albuquerque*	91	645	54	10	72	.986
Dees, Arkansas*	74	676	47	6	65	.992	Feldman, El Paso*	106	1002	60	16	98	.985
Rosario, Shreveport	75	550	42	5	46	.992	Gagle, Arkansas	41	338	20	6	35	.984
Coil, Amarillo	18	101	7	1	8	.991	Rickey, San An	69	649	35	12	55	.983
Manfredi, D-FtW	15	97	11	1	9	.991	Boyer, Arkansas	12	102	8	2	8	.982
Mallon, Amarillo*	.101	870	63	9	69	.990	Grant, Shreveport*	43	298	27	6	23	.982
Williams, Shrev	14	92	5	1	9	.990	Bashore, Memphis*	24	174	23	6	18	.970
Downing, Alb	59	460	33	6	58	.988							

Triple Play—Grant.

(Fewer Than Ten Games)

Player and Club	G.	PO.	A.	E.	DP.	Pct.	Player and Club	G.	PO.	A.	E.	DP.	Pct.
Christino, Alb*	8	66	3	0	5	1.000	Coleman, Shreveport	2	4	0	0	1	1.000
Matthew, D-FtW	6	32	2	0	3	1.000	Campbell, El Paso	9	61	4	1	5	.985
Sauget, Shreveport	4	29	2	0	2	1.000	Dodder, Alb*	8	85	6	2	9	.978
Winslow, Arkansas*	4	13	1	0	2	1.000	Engbers, Arkansas*	5	32	2	1	7	.971
Miller, San An*	1	13	0	0	3	1.000	Mairena, Arkansas	2	16	0	1	0	.941
Macko, D-FtW	3	11	1	0	1	1.000	Diaz, Memphis	3	23	3	2	6	.929
Cedeno, Amarillo*	3	9	0	0	0	1.000	Auferio, Arkansas	2	19	3	2	1	.917
Mang, Shreveport*	1	6	3	0	1	1.000	Altobelli, D-FtW*	3	17	1	2	2	.900
Ralston, Alb	1	6	0	0	0	1.000	Schroeppel, Ark*	1	9	0	1	1	.900
Garrett, San An	2	5	0	0	0	1.000	Toney, Shreveport	1	3	3	1	0	.857
Rivera, Arkansas	1	5	0	0	0	1.000	Detter, San Antonio	1	0	0	1	0	.000

SECOND BASEMEN

Player and Club	G.	PO.	A.	E.	DP.	Pct.
ECKENRODE, Alb .106	229	293	9	82	.983	
Holbert, Amarillo .. 69	116	159	6	28	.979	
Shelton, D-FtW 103	228	255	11	38	.978	
Detter, San Antonio . 20	35	52	2	6	.978	
Coulter, Arkansas .. 48	125	165	7	40	.976	
Cann, Shreveport .. 27	53	59	3	11	.974	
Shibley, El Paso .. 58	101	173	10	31	.965	
Jestadt, San An 19	50	58	4	11	.964	
Carthel, Memphis .. 22	38	43	3	8	.964	
DeWald, Memphis .. 76	127	162	11	23	.963	
Moschetti, El Paso . 33	61	95	6	20	.963	
Nelson, Albuquerque . 37	59	90	6	20	.961	
Barnes, Memphis ... 45	86	130	9	24	.960	

Triple Play—Cann.

Player and Club	G.	PO.	A.	E.	DP.	Pct.
Stein, Arkansas 60	106	167	12	32	.958	
Huisman, San An ... 62	152	209	16	46	.958	
Martin, Dal-FtW ... 29	55	80	7	16	.951	
Arnold, Amarillo ... 34	89	82	10	22	.945	
McCord, El Paso ... 48	85	133	13	26	.944	
L. Thompson, Ark .. 13	30	37	4	7	.944	
Porter, San An 11	27	39	4	9	.943	
Cambero, Shreveport 22	31	49	5	9	.941	
Newson, Shreveport . 99	236	236	30	48	.940	
Breitzman, San An .. 26	53	72	9	15	.933	
Burgos, Am-Shr-Mem 31	52	69	10	19	.924	
Frazier, Amarillo .. 17	26	34	5	7	.923	

(Fewer Than Ten Games)

Player and Club	G.	PO.	A.	E.	DP.	Pct.
Kennedy, Dal-FtW .. 3	7	14	0	2	1.000	
Marion, Arkansas ... 3	7	8	0	2	1.000	
Manfredi, Dal-FtW .. 5	4	8	0	1	1.000	
Toney, Shreveport .. 2	3	4	0	1	1.000	
Dudek, San Antonio . 1	3	1	0	0	1.000	
Abreu, Arkansas ... 1	0	2	0	0	1.000	
Foster, Shreveport .. 1	1	1	0	0	1.000	
Brown, Shreveport .. 1	2	0	0	1	1.000	

Player and Club	G.	PO.	A.	E.	DP.	Pct.
Lisetski, San An 7	11	21	1	7	.970	
Mairena, Arkansas .. 6	10	20	1	3	.968	
Ralston, Alb 8	17	9	2	0	.929	
Rivera, Arkansas ... 9	15	24	4	5	.907	
Jagutis, El Paso 7	7	19	4	4	.867	
Cleary, Amarillo ... 1	4	2	1	1	.857	
Lombardo, San An .. 2	2	1	1	0	.750	

THIRD BASEMEN

Player and Club	G.	PO.	A.	E.	DP.	Pct.
Toney, Shreveport .. 39	34	68	3	6	.971	
McDonald, Arkansas . 15	14	16	1	2	.968	
Zabala, Shreveport .. 10	8	13	1	2	.955	
GREEN, Dal-FtW ..109	90	194	15	12	.950	
Carthel, Memphis .. 48	48	64	6	6	.949	
Ralston, Alb 70	33	114	8	6	.948	
Cey, Albuquerque .. 70	44	132	10	14	.946	
Moschetti, El Paso .. 55	27	99	8	7	.944	
Diaz, Memphis 76	64	151	15	11	.935	
Hanson, El Paso 42	34	95	9	6	.935	
Arnold, Amarillo ... 13	15	27	3	3	.933	
Frazier, Amarillo .. 51	41	65	8	10	.930	

Player and Club	G.	PO.	A.	E.	DP.	Pct.
Cummings, Alb 14	5	21	2	1	.929	
Detter, San An 11	13	25	3	0	.927	
Brunette, San An ..116	89	184	22	18	.925	
McCord, El Paso ... 37	26	59	7	2	.924	
Cleary, Amarillo ... 70	72	130	18	10	.918	
Rivera, Arkansas ... 32	21	46	6	9	.918	
Manfredi, D-FtW ... 20	18	26	4	1	.917	
L. Thompson, Ark .. 47	40	84	13	12	.905	
Williams, Shrev 82	58	116	20	10	.897	
Gagle, Arkansas 32	28	56	11	5	.884	
Boyer, Arkansas 12	12	14	4	2	.867	
Barnes, Memphis ... 15	7	24	6	2	.838	

(Fewer Than Ten Games)

Player and Club	G.	PO.	A.	E.	DP.	Pct.
Porter, San An 4	4	10	0	1	1.000	
Ferguson, Alb 3	2	5	0	1	1.000	
Marsden, Amarillo .. 3	4	3	0	0	1.000	
McDonald, Dal-FtW . 2	2	3	0	2	1.000	
Speier, Amarillo ... 2	1	2	0	0	1.000	
Brown, Memphis ... 1	0	1	0	0	1.000	
Campbell, Memphis . 1	0	1	0	0	1.000	
Cann, Shreveport .. 3	1	0	0	0	1.000	
Huckle, Memphis ... 1	0	0	0	0	1.000	
Coil, Amarillo 2	0	1	0	0	1.000	
Carnegie, Dal-FtW .. 9	8	14	1	1	.957	
Long, Albuquerque .. 7	6	8	1	2	.933	

Player and Club	G.	PO.	A.	E.	DP.	Pct.
Breitzman, San An .. 5	3	8	1	1	.917	
Burgos, Amarillo ... 7	3	7	1	1	.909	
Downing, Alb 7	2	14	2	1	.889	
Cambero, Shrev 8	8	14	4	2	.846	
Stitzel, Memphis ... 3	6	5	2	2	.846	
Shibley, El Paso 5	4	6	2	0	.833	
Garrett, San An 7	1	8	3	0	.750	
Alderete, El Paso ... 3	3	3	2	1	.750	
Nelson, Alb 3	0	1	1	0	.500	
Bell, Arkansas 1	0	1	1	0	.500	
Yeager, Alb 1	0	0	0	0	.000	
Niles, El Paso 2	0	0	0	0	.000	

SHORTSTOPS

Player and Club	G.	PO.	A.	E.	DP.	Pct.
Cann, Shreveport .. 19	22	42	1	10	.985	
Porter, San Antonio . 15	23	26	1	4	.980	
JOHNSON, Alb 100	177	315	11	71	.978	
Abreu, Arkansas ... 18	31	58	2	10	.978	
L. Thompson, Ark .. 13	28	44	2	4	.973	
Moschetti, El Paso . 21	16	20	1	4	.973	
Huckle, Memphis .. 46	91	130	7	20	.969	
Hacker, Memphis ... 13	14	37	2	7	.962	
Manfredi, D-FtW ... 51	72	100	8	13	.956	
Ralston, Alb 42	75	125	10	32	.952	
Hernandez, D-FtW .. 42	95	98	10	23	.951	
Crosby, Arkansas .. 78	150	225	20	49	.949	
Kelleher, Arkansas . 21	44	68	6	21	.949	
Rosello, San An 60	101	192	18	40	.942	

Triple Play—Foster.

Player and Club	G.	PO.	A.	E.	DP.	Pct.
Guth, Shreveport ... 10	16	15	2	1	.939	
Burgos, Am-Shr-Mem 49	65	126	13	35	.936	
DeCinces, D-FtW ... 11	25	19	3	6	.936	
Speier, Amarillo ...121	223	325	38	65	.935	
Detter, San An 76	120	207	23	47	.934	
Nordbrook, D-FtW .. 24	39	55	7	9	.931	
Parker, El Paso ...109	181	312	43	75	.920	
Barnes, Memphis ... 57	90	157	23	20	.915	
Foster, Shreveport .. 63	78	178	26	20	.908	
Toney, Shreveport .. 19	17	32	5	5	.907	
Cambero, Shrev 24	34	43	8	12	.906	
McCord, El Paso ... 14	17	42	7	7	.894	
Del Orbe, D-FtW ... 14	21	40	8	3	.884	
Cleary, Amarillo ... 16	26	41	9	9	.882	

SHORTSTOPS—Continued

(Fewer Than Ten Games)

Player and Club	G.	PO.	A.	E.	DP.	Pct.	Player and Club	G.	PO.	A.	E.	DP.	Pct.
Meoli, El Paso	7	5	17	0	2	1.000	Jagutis, El Paso	2	0	1	0	0	1.000
Hanson, El Paso	1	0	3	0	1	1.000	Krawczyk, San An	6	4	20	2	1	.923
Carthel, Memphis	1	2	1	0	0	1.000	Stein, Arkansas	6	7	21	4	1	.875
Gagle, Arkansas	1	0	3	0	0	1.000	Arnold, Amarillo	1	3	7	2	2	.833
Williams, Shrev	1	1	1	0	0	1.000	Nelson, Alb	2	4	5	3	1	.750
Martin, Dal-FtW	1	0	2	0	1	1.000	Green, Dal-FtW	1	0	0	1	0	.000
Huisman, San An	1	0	1	0	0	1.000	Brunette, San An	1	0	0	1	0	.000

OUTFIELDERS

Player and Club	G.	PO.	A.	E.	DP.	Pct.	Player and Club	G.	PO.	A.	E.	DP.	Pct.
Milner, Memphis*	49	78	2	0	1	1.000	Alderete, El Paso	89	113	8	5	2	.960
Moore, Albuquerque*	26	35	1	0	0	1.000	Cruz, Arkansas*	133	276	10	12	0	.960
Moock, Shreveport	17	15	1	0	0	1.000	Murphy, Shreveport	99	184	7	8	1	.960
Zabala, Shreveport	14	19	2	0	0	1.000	Campbell, Memphis	108	217	12	10	2	.958
McCord, El Paso	13	14	2	0	0	1.000	Watts, Dal-FtW	117	180	16	9	5	.956
HOWARTH, Amar*	.119	265	26	1	5	.997	Holland, El Paso*	44	61	4	3	0	.956
Long, Albuquerque	55	95	4	1	0	.990	Vanzin, Ark-D-FW	52	84	2	4	0	.956
Gallagher, Alb*	98	224	11	3	0	.987	Rivers, El Paso*	113	235	13	12	3	.954
Stein, Arkansas	49	66	10	1	2	.987	Coggins, Dal-FtW	85	195	9	10	2	.953
Matney, San An*	74	142	9	2	0	.987	Rose, Albuquerque*	.107	177	6	9	1	.953
Mang, Shreveport*	50	99	7	2	0	.981	Diaz, Memphis	50	72	4	4	2	.951
Beasley, Dal-FtW	97	199	7	4	1	.981	Massarand, San A	16	18	1	1	0	.950
Cann, Shreveport	59	89	8	2	0	.980	Carnegie, Dal-FtW	75	119	7	7	1	.947
Bashore, Memphis*	72	92	1	2	0	.979	North, San Antonio	22	50	2	3	3	.945
Floyd, El Paso	92	121	6	3	2	.977	Stewart, Arkansas	87	139	10	9	1	.943
Dees, Arkansas*	31	34	7	1	0	.976	Dix, Memphis*	14	29	4	2	1	.943
Rosario, Shreveport	58	72	7	2	1	.975	T. Williams, Mem	31	44	5	3	0	.942
Napoleon, Arkansas	53	118	7	4	1	.969	Brown, Shreveport	29	51	6	4	0	.934
Binkowski, San An*	64	114	5	4	2	.967	Bowens, Shreveport	24	51	4	4	1	.932
Miller, San An*	.124	191	14	7	1	.967	Brown, Memphis	103	149	6	12	1	.928
Marsden, Amarillo	72	111	5	4	1	.967	White, Amarillo*	95	131	5	13	1	.913
Walseth, Shreveport	51	55	3	2	1	.967	Canada, Alb	18	15	3	2	0	.900
Williams, Alb	.106	163	8	6	0	.966	Galliher, Alb	16	18	0	2	0	.900
Cedeno, Amarillo*	68	109	2	4	0	.965	Kingman, Amarillo	38	66	5	9	0	.888
Garrett, San An	.120	168	10	7	2	.962	Wilkinson, El Paso	17	17	0	3	0	.850
Campbell, El Paso	37	47	3	2	0	.962	Arnold, Amarillo	16	18	1	6	1	.760

(Fewer Than Ten Games)

Player and Club	G.	PO.	A.	E.	DP.	Pct.	Player and Club	G.	PO.	A.	E.	DP.	Pct.
Bigone, El Paso	9	15	0	0	0	1.000	Downing, Alb	2	2	0	0	0	1.000
Moore, Memphis	4	11	3	0	0	1.000	Manfredi, Dal-FtW	1	2	0	0	0	1.000
Burns, Shreveport	9	13	0	0	0	1.000	Rivera, Arkansas	2	2	0	0	0	1.000
Parker, El Paso	7	13	0	0	0	1.000	Sauget, Shreveport	1	2	0	0	0	1.000
Breitzman, San An	6	10	0	0	0	1.000	Yeager, Albuquerque	1	2	0	0	0	1.000
Matthew, Dal-FtW	6	9	0	0	0	1.000	Ford, Shreveport	5	1	0	0	0	1.000
Doherty, El Paso*	5	8	0	0	0	1.000	Howard, El Paso	1	1	0	0	0	1.000
Foster, Shreveport	4	6	2	0	1	1.000	Mathwig, Alb	1	1	0	0	0	1.000
Coil, Amarillo	1	6	0	0	0	1.000	Newson, Shrev	1	0	1	0	0	1.000
Frazier, Amarillo	6	6	0	0	0	1.000	Jones, Dal-FtW	6	13	0	1	0	.929
Kazmarek, Memphis	5	6	0	0	0	1.000	Coleman, Shrev	7	7	0	1	0	.875
Ferguson, Alb	9	5	0	0	0	1.000	Hill, Memphis	6	5	1	2	0	.750
Martin, Dal-FtW	4	5	0	0	0	1.000	Williams, Amarillo	2	3	0	1	0	.750
Haynes, San An	5	4	0	0	0	1.000	Grant, Shreveport*	1	1	0	1	0	.500
L. Thompson, Ark	2	4	0	0	0	1.000							

CATCHERS

Player and Club	G.	PO.	A.	E.	DP.	PB.	Pct.	Player and Club	G.	PO.	A.	E.	DP.	PB.	Pct.
Creola, Dal-FtW	27	157	16	1	2	5	.994	Marquez, El Paso	11	59	2	1	1	1	.984
Dehn, El Paso	21	127	14	1	3	1	.993	Santiago, Ama-Shr	73	509	53	10	8	18	.983
Chilcott, Mem	38	256	16	2	1	6	.993	Matthew, D-FtW	90	650	62	13	6	20	.982
Nunn, El Paso	31	205	22	2	2	10	.991	Niles, San An	32	220	33	5	3	7	.981
Childers, San An	17	80	16	1	2	5	.990	Dudek, San An	13	44	6	1	1	4	.980
Kelly, D-FtW	14	90	5	1	2	7	.990	Lundstedt, San An	31	129	16	3	3	2	.980
FERGUSON, Alb	.100	599	78	8	4	12	.988	Rudolph, San An	36	203	17	5	2	7	.978
Upton, Mem	11	77	6	1	3	3	.988	Rader, Amarillo	89	519	63	14	9	17	.977
Brown, El Paso	47	300	26	4	2	12	.988	Scuget, Shrev	45	220	22	6	2	15	.976
Jutze, Arkansas	.116	715	87	11	9	28	.986	Nitschke, Mem	50	330	26	9	2	6	.975
Coil, Amarillo	12	67	4	1	1	6	.986	Zabala, Shrev	43	219	32	7	2	15	.973
Carthel, Mem	34	181	26	3	4	6	.986	Coleman, Shrev	10	27	4	1	1	1	.969
Mull, San An	64	309	31	5	9	10	.986	Burns, Shreveport	27	122	14	5	1	5	.965
Sadek, Amarillo	14	116	17	2	2	5	.985	McDonald, Ark	18	93	7	5	0	5	.952
Yeager, Alb	40	222	29	4	3	8	.984								

(Fewer Than Ten Games)

Player and Club	G.	PO.	A.	E.	DP.	PB.	Pct.	Player and Club	G.	PO.	A.	E.	DP.	PB.	Pct.
Bigone, El Paso	7	37	3	0	1	2	1.000	Auferio, Ark	7	44	8	1	0	2	.981
Dickerson, Mem	3	8	0	0	0	0	1.000	Hickey, Dal-FtW	8	42	7	1	2	0	.980
Canada, Alb	1	7	0	0	0	0	1.000	Diaz, Memphis	5	36	4	1	1	1	.976
Alderete, El P	2	1	1	0	0	0	1.000	Saul, San An	4	14	1	1	1	0	.938
Moock, Shrev	1	1	0	0	0	0	1.000	T. Williams, Mem	2	5	1	1	0	2	.857

PITCHERS

Player and Club	G.	PO.	A.	E.	DP.	Pct.		Player and Club	G.	PO.	A.	E.	DP.	Pct.
McDOWELL, Alb ...	27	13	38	0	2	1.000		Bethke, Memphis ...	37	3	17	1	1	.952
C. Williams, Mem ...	26	14	21	0	2	1.000		Bryan, San Antonio .	16	4	16	1	1	.952
Stone, Amarillo ...	19	8	20	0	1	1.000		Gatewood, Shreveport	13	4	16	1	0	.952
Keller, El Paso ...	33	3	21	0	0	1.000		Britton, Shreveport*	32	5	14	1	0	.950
Nottebart, San An ...	40	4	17	0	2	1.000		King, Albuquerque .	31	15	41	3	4	.949
Rivera, San Antonio .	24	1	19	0	2	1.000		Ford, Shreveport ...	51	11	25	2	1	.947
Sprinkle, Shreveport .	38	2	16	0	2	1.000		Hassler, El Paso* ...	32	5	27	2	3	.941
Schroeppel, Ark* ...	34	5	12	0	1	1.000		Rose, Memphis ...	25	16	30	3	1	.939
Barbosa, El Paso* ...	16	1	15	0	0	1.000		Garland, Dal-FtW ...	21	6	24	2	0	.938
Mullen, San Antonio	26	3	13	0	0	1.000		Allen, Albuquerque*.	12	0	15	1	0	.938
Mathwig, Alb ...	38	5	9	0	1	1.000		Hudson, Memphis* ...	32	5	10	1	1	.938
Moulden, Dal-FtW ...	37	5	8	0	1	1.000		Raynor, Albuquerque	26	5	9	1	1	.933
Plodinec, Arkansas .	12	2	11	0	1	1.000		Winslow, Arkansas* .	20	5	21	2	2	.929
Sowinski, Alb ...	22	3	10	0	1	1.000		Vaughan, Shreveport*	13	6	15	2	1	.913
Wilshusen, Dal-FtW.	31	6	7	0	1	1.000		DiFabio, Arkansas ...	26	15	16	3	0	.912
Von Hoff, Arkansas .	18	2	10	0	1	1.000		C. Thompson, Ark* ...	34	3	7	1	1	.909
Hrabosky, Arkansas*	15	3	8	0	0	1.000		Grant, Shreveport* ...	12	2	8	1	1	.909
Contreras, El Paso ...	18	2	8	0	0	1.000		Stephenson, San An* .	21	2	8	1	1	.909
Encerti, San Antonio	24	2	8	0	2	1.000		Cohen, Dal-FtW ...	31	10	29	4	0	.907
Koonce, Memphis ...	32	3	7	0	1	1.000		Ryerson, Amarillo* ...	34	11	46	6	2	.905
James, San Antonio .	13	6	3	0	0	1.000		Jeffcoat, Amarillo ...	37	6	21	3	5	.900
King, Shreveport ...	10	7	2	0	0	1.000		Campbell, Amarillo ...	22	3	6	1	0	.900
Kovach, Dal-FtW ...	19	3	4	0	0	1.000		Strickland, Alb* ...	38	2	17	2	1	.900
Stover, San Antonio .	27	2	5	0	0	1.000		Flynn, Albuquerque .	31	7	36	5	2	.896
Arnold, Dal-FtW ...	11	2	3	0	0	1.000		Allen, El Paso ...	25	5	29	4	3	.895
King, Dal-FtW ...	12	2	2	0	1	1.000		Bell, Shreveport* ...	23	4	21	3	2	.893
Williamson, Dal-FtW	10	1	3	0	0	1.000		Miller, Dal-FtW ...	26	8	25	4	2	.892
Hutton, Albuquerque	21	0	2	0	0	1.000		Henderson, El Paso .	27	15	26	5	0	.891
Bare, Arkansas ...	29	14	43	1	1	.983		DeLong, Amarillo* ...	22	2	30	4	0	.889
Scott, Amarillo ...	31	14	36	1	2	.980		Evans, Arkansas ...	23	8	16	3	1	.889
Jacquez, San An ...	19	16	22	1	1	.974		Roberts, Shreveport*	33	3	13	2	0	.889
Lobb, Shreveport ...	43	16	54	2	4	.972		Sells, El Paso ...	57	4	11	2	1	.882
Schueler, Shrev ...	26	8	26	1	0	.971		Willis, Arkansas ...	26	5	9	2	0	.875
Alexander, Alb ...	10	4	29	1	1	.971		Nelson, Shreveport* .	13	1	6	1	1	.875
Lowe, San Antonio ...	33	8	22	1	2	.968		Gonzalez, Ark* ...	10	1	6	1	0	.875
Manz, Dal-FtW ...	21	7	23	1	1	.968		Powell, Shreveport* .	11	3	4	1	1	.875
McLeod, Memphis ...	25	15	17	1	2	.966		Perkins, Memphis* ...	45	3	16	3	2	.864
Cox, El Paso ...	31	4	23	1	3	.964		St. Clair, El Paso ...	27	3	9	2	0	.857
Thoma, Dal-FtW* ...	40	7	20	1	2	.964		Kelley, Shreveport ...	11	5	6	2	0	.846
Clements, Memphis ...	27	5	21	1	0	.963		Matney, San An* ...	14	0	10	2	0	.833
Lavelle, Amarillo* ...	22	5	20	1	2	.962		Ray Allen, Memphis.	18	1	4	1	0	.833
Ellingsen, Alb* ...	28	8	16	1	0	.960		Newman, San An* ...	26	8	9	5	0	.773
Engelhardt, El Paso*	26	5	19	1	1	.960		Hernandez, Amarillo.	45	1	8	3	0	.750
Herson, Dal-FtW ...	21	5	19	1	1	.960		Reahm, Memphis* ...	11	1	8	3	0	.750
Reuschel, San An ...	32	9	38	2	6	.959		Ewing, Memphis* ...	16	1	7	3	1	.727
Clark, El Paso ...	14	3	19	1	0	.957		Wysocki, Amarillo ...	44	3	7	5	0	.667
Seminoff, Arkansas .	43	3	19	1	5	.957		Amman, San An-Am.	11	1	0	1	0	.500
Todd, San Antonio ...	18	8	34	2	3	.955		Knutzen, El Paso* ..	15	0	0	1	0	.000

(Fewer Than Ten Games)

Player and Club	G.	PO.	A.	E.	DP.	Pct.		Player and Club	G.	PO.	A.	E.	DP.	Pct.
Dunegan, San An ...	8	4	11	0	0	1.000		Sosa, Amarillo	3	1	1	0	1	1.000
Decker, San An	2	4	6	0	0	1.000		Dermody, Alb	6	0	1	0	0	1.000
Gourieux, Shrev ...	8	2	5	0	0	1.000		Frazier, San An* ...	2	0	1	0	0	1.000
Tolliver, Amarillo ...	7	2	4	0	0	1.000		Denehy, Memphis ...	7	5	8	1	1	.929
Frost, El Paso	8	1	4	0	1	1.000		Rohr, Memphis* ...	7	8	4	1	2	.923
Marsden, Amarillo ...	2	1	4	0	0	1.000		Camy, Memphis ...	6	2	6	1	1	.889
Spellman, El Paso ...	9	3	2	0	0	1.000		Stephen, Dal-FtW* ...	9	0	8	1	0	.889
Chlupsa, Arkansas ...	7	1	3	0	0	1.000		Bradley, El Paso ...	4	3	4	1	2	.875
Swanson, Shreveport.	3	1	3	0	0	1.000		Distaso, San An ...	6	1	3	1	0	.800
Daboll, Arkansas ...	8	1	2	0	0	1.000		Towers, Shreveport.	9	1	3	1	1	.800
McCammon, Shrev .	3	0	3	0	1	1.000		Reed, Shreveport ...	2	1	0	1	0	.500
Camp, San Antonio .	2	1	1	0	0	1.000		Mazzone, Amarillo* .	9	0	0	1	0	.000

The following players do not have any recorded accepted chances at the positions indicated; therefore, are not listed in the fielding averages for those particular positions: Altobelli, p; Barry, p; Coleman, 3b; Crandall, 3b-p; DeWald, 3b; Diaz, p; Dodder*, of; D. Ford, p; P. Ford, 2b; H. Grant, p; Jaster*, p; R. Jones*, p; Long, ss; Lowe, of; Lundstedt, of; Mathwig, 1b; Mull, of; B. Nelson*, of; Newson, p; Nitschke, of; Nunn, 2b; Ogier, p; Powell*, of; Price*, p; Rice, p; Roberts*, p; Rosario*, p; Speier, of; Sprinkle, of; C. Thompson*, c; Towers, of; L. White*, p; Wilson, p.

CLUB PITCHING

Club	G.	CG.	ShO.	Sv.	IP.	H.	R.	ER.	HR.	BB.	Int. BB.	HB.	SO.	WP.	Bk.	ERA.
Albuquerque 135		47	20	28	1184	1132	513	437	89	410	36	40	782	52	2	3.32
San Antonio 136		26	12	32	1192	1172	562	450	73	451	37	46	731	50	4	3.40
Memphis 136		35	11	15	1136	1027	562	464	81	481	43	31	828	46	4	3.68
Dallas-Fort Worth ...136		40	9	21	1188	1120	579	493	65	559	30	31	871	61	9	3.73
Arkansas 134		33	12	26	1154	1204	624	511	86	414	22	33	811	70	2	3.99
Amarillo 135		41	5	13	1165	1165	657	522	84	542	52	35	871	72	8	4.03
Shreveport 134		23	11	20	1134	1152	654	517	93	507	28	60	824	78	6	4.10
El Paso 136		26	8	39	1179	1182	673	558	84	625	34	52	904	69	10	4.26

PITCHERS' RECORDS

(Leading Qualifiers for Earned-Run Average Leadership—136 or More Innings)

*Throws lefthanded.

Pitcher—Club	G	GS	CG	ShO	W	L	Sv	Pct.	IP	H	R	ER	HR	BB	Int. BB	HB	SO	WP	ERA
Manz, D-FtW 21	19	8	0	7	4	0	.636	154	125	46	34	4	61	5	1	99	6	1.99
Flynn, Alb 31	31	15	3	19	4	0	.826	228	204	78	67	15	77	6	5	135	18	2.64
Rose, Memphis ..25	25	8	2	7	11	0	.389	160	149	76	55	8	56	3	0	88	10	3.09
Ellingsen, Alb* ..28	21	10	1	12	5	0	.706	167	169	73	59	16	47	5	0	109	1	3.18
McDowell, Alb ..27	21	5	3	10	9	0	.526	161	132	66	57	10	58	5	9	127	6	3.19
Reuschel, San An .32	27	7	2	10	10	0	.500	184	198	80	66	13	59	5	3	79	4	3.23
Miller, D-FtW ...26	25	10	2	12	10	0	.545	170	149	69	61	5	83	2	4	102	7	3.23
C. Williams, Mem .26	24	8	4	12	5	1	.706	158	136	67	57	8	61	1	4	128	7	3.25
DiFabio, Ark ...26	23	6	2	10	7	0	.588	160	152	73	58	10	55	1	3	108	5	3.26
Scott, Amarillo ..31	22	8	1	6	15	0	.286	171	119	87	67	8	93	10	5	137	12	3.53

Departmental Leaders: G—Sells, 57; GS—Flynn, 31; CG—Flynn, 15; ShO—King (Alb), 6; W—Flynn, 19; L—Scott, 15; Sv—Nottebart, Sells, Strickland, 15; Pct.—Flynn, .826; IP—Flynn, 228; H—Flynn, 204; R—Ryerson, 102; ER—Cohen, 81; HR—Evans, 17; BB—Scott, 93; IBB—Clements, Scott, 10; HB—Allen (ElP), 10; SO—Cohen, 151; WP—DeLong, 19.

(All Pitchers—Listed Alphabetically)

Pitcher—Club	G	GS	CG	ShO	W	L	Sv	Pct.	IP	H	R	ER	HR	BB	Int. BB	HB	SO	WP	ERA
Alexander, Alb .. 10	10	3	2	4	3	0	.571	80	72	29	28	5	20	0	3	60	1	3.15
Allen, Alb* 12	12	3	2	6	5	0	.545	87	76	32	25	10	29	2	3	66	4	2.59
Allen, El Paso ..25	25	5	0	12	8	0	.600	152	152	92	77	8	81	3	10	116	10	4.56
Ray Allen, Mem ..18	0	0	0	2	3	1	.400	34	25	16	13	3	19	7	2	28	1	3.44
Altobelli, D-FtW* . 2	0	0	0	0	0	0	.000	4	5	8	6	2	3	0	2	1	0	13.50
Amman, 3 SA-																		
8 Amar 11	0	0	0	1	0	0	1.000	14	18	14	13	3	10	1	0	9	4	8.36
Arnold, D-FtW ...11	11	2	0	5	3	0	.625	59	57	38	36	1	51	0	1	53	5	5.49
Barbosa, El Paso* .16	14	1	0	3	5	1	.375	75	83	36	32	6	26	2	3	65	4	3.84
Bare, Arkansas ..29	26	11	3	10	13	0	.435	179	195	86	78	12	55	4	2	98	7	3.92
Barr, Amarillo ...14	14	6	0	6	5	0	.545	98	107	51	36	6	23	4	2	48	2	3.31
Barry, Shreveport . 1	0	0	0	0	0	0	.000	1	1	0	0	0	0	1	1	0	0	0.00
Bell, Shreveport ..23	19	3	2	9	8	1	.529	111	112	61	52	9	43	1	7	86	7	4.22
Bethke, Memphis .37	1	0	0	2	7	2	.222	67	57	27	20	3	26	3	4	46	2	2.69
Bradley, El Paso .. 4	4	2	0	3	0	0	1.000	31	30	7	7	1	8	0	1	38	0	2.03
Britton, Shrev* ..32	8	0	0	6	7	2	.462	91	100	48	41	11	32	3	1	54	3	4.05
Bryan, San An ...16	15	3	1	8	4	0	.667	106	101	34	32	7	20	2	1	54	3	2.72
Camp, San An .. 2	1	0	0	1	0	0	1.000	7	3	0	0	0	1	0	0	4	0	0.00
Campbell, Amar ..22	0	0	0	2	0	0	.000	36	34	22	18	3	19	3	1	24	3	4.50
Camy, Memphis .. 6	6	2	0	4	0	0	1.000	44	42	17	15	2	15	0	0	20	0	3.07
Chlupsa, Arkansas . 7	0	0	0	1	0	0	1.000	12	16	7	4	0	3	1	0	10	1	3.00
Clark, El Paso ...14	12	4	1	5	7	1	.417	86	85	44	41	4	45	2	3	59	6	4.29
Clements, Memphis 27	16	1	0	5	7	0	.417	107	113	78	68	15	62	10	2	68	8	5.72
Cohen, D-FtW* ..31	25	7	1	8	13	0	.381	170	172	97	81	11	74	2	5	151	11	4.29
Contreras, ElP ...18	0	0	0	2	2	2	.500	38	45	28	20	3	21	1	1	24	1	4.74
Cox, El Paso ...31	16	4	1	7	5	6	.583	124	118	79	67	14	51	4	7	82	6	4.86
Crandall, Alb 2	0	0	0	1	0	0	1.000	3	2	0	0	0	2	0	0	2	0	0.00
Daboll, Arkansas . 8	4	3	0	3	2	0	.600	45	29	10	6	1	8	0	0	47	2	1.20
Decker, San An .. 2	2	1	0	1	0	0	1.000	18	9	1	1	1	6	0	1	18	0	0.50
DeLong, Amar* ..22	22	6	0	7	9	0	.438	143	138	76	64	6	84	4	9	105	19	4.03
Denehy, Memphis . 7	7	3	1	3	4	0	.429	46	26	17	16	4	18	0	3	49	0	3.13
Dermody, Alb 6	0	0	0	0	1	1	.000	8	4	3	3	0	1	0	0	6	1	3.38
Diaz, Memphis ... 3	0	0	0	0	0	0	.000	6	2	1	1	0	3	0	1	4	0	1.50
DiFabio, Arkansas .26	23	6	2	10	7	0	.588	160	152	73	58	10	55	1	3	108	5	3.26
Distaso, San An .. 6	5	0	0	3	0	0	.000	14	27	25	22	0	19	0	2	6	1	14.14
Dunegn, San An .. 8	8	2	0	3	2	0	.600	57	47	21	17	2	30	0	1	60	5	2.68
Ellingsen, Alb* ...28	21	10	1	12	5	0	.706	167	169	73	59	16	47	5	0	109	1	3.18
Encerti, San An ..24	0	0	0	2	5	7	.286	35	36	16	14	1	16	6	2	14	2	3.60
Engelhardt, ElP* ..26	8	1	1	3	2	5	.600	82	83	38	31	2	23	1	2	73	1	3.40
Evans, Arkansas ..23	22	3	0	8	10	0	.444	139	144	87	76	17	41	1	8	109	14	4.92
Ewing, Memphis* ..16	11	0	0	1	4	0	.200	54	69	48	40	3	30	1	3	35	6	6.67
Flynn, Alb 31	31	15	3	19	4	0	.826	228	204	78	67	15	77	6	5	135	18	2.64
Ford, Arkansas .. 1	0	0	0	0	0	0	.000	1	3	4	3	1	2	0	0	1	0	27.00
Ford, Shreveport .31	13	4	1	3	8	0	.273	102	126	72	54	8	37	9	3	52	4	4.76
Frazier, San An* .. 2	1	0	0	0	1	0	.000	6	2	2	1	3	0	1	6	0	3.00
Frost, El Paso .. 8	2	0	0	1	1	0	.500	21	18	11	9	1	19	0	1	18	0	3.86
Garland, D-FtW ..21	4	0	7	10	0	.412	140	122	63	55	6	63	2	3	107	10	3.54
Gatewood, Shrev .13	10	1	1	2	6	1	.250	59	52	44	32	6	29	1	3	50	9	4.88
Gonzalez, Ark* ...10	2	1	1	1	0	0	1.000	29	32	14	11	0	11	0	1	18	1	3.41
Gourieux, Shrev .. 8	7	2	1	4	4	0	.500	45	36	19	14	7	15	2	2	28	0	2.80
Grant, D-FtW 1	0	0	0	0	0	0	.000	2	3	3	3	0	2	0	0	2	0	13.50

Pitcher—Club	G	GS	CG	ShO	W	L	Sv	Pct.	IP	H	R	ER	HR	BB	Int. BB	HB	SO	WP	ERA
Grant, Shreveport*	12	3	0	0	2	1	0	.667	50	32	22	17	1	36	0	7	38	11	3.06
Hassler, El Paso*	22	22	4	0	10	7	0	.588	144	138	80	62	10	87	3	6	122	7	3.88
Henderson, ElP	27	27	4	2	12	7	0	.632	163	165	89	76	13	89	2	3	124	6	4.20
Hernandez, Amar	45	1	0	0	4	5	5	.444	71	72	37	29	6	22	6	2	76	2	3.68
Herson, D-FtW	21	21	7	0	4	14	0	.222	135	130	73	56	8	71	5	6	113	7	3.73
Hrabosky, Ark*	15	14	3	0	8	1	0	.889	91	80	36	33	7	33	0	6	68	3	3.26
Hudson, Memphis*	32	5	1	0	3	5	2	.375	79	68	33	26	2	39	8	1	79	2	2.96
Hutton, Alb	21	0	0	0	2	4	3	.333	22	30	18	16	0	20	0	2	18	4	6.55
Jacquez, San An	19	18	5	1	10	5	0	.667	133	132	60	48	6	35	0	9	79	6	3.25
James, San An	13	5	0	0	1	4	0	.200	36	41	19	14	1	13	1	1	12	1	3.50
Jaster, Arkansas*	3	1	0	0	0	1	0	.000	5	7	6	6	0	6	0	0	6	1	10.80
Jeffcoat, Amar	37	11	3	0	6	6	2	.500	118	121	66	52	12	45	2	0	66	5	3.97
Jones, San An*	3	1	0	0	0	1	0	.000	7	10	7	5	1	0	0	1	6	0	6.43
Keller, El Paso	33	4	1	0	5	5	2	.500	85	81	53	42	6	57	2	5	68	11	4.45
Kelley, Shreveport	11	10	4	1	7	1	0	.875	76	47	28	22	5	34	0	2	98	4	2.61
King, Shreveport	10	0	0	0	1	0	2	1.000	21	23	8	7	1	7	1	1	11	1	3.00
King, D-FtW	12	0	0	0	1	2	0	.333	22	29	13	13	1	3	1	2	14	1	5.32
King, Alb	31	26	9	6	12	9	0	.571	167	158	75	67	11	60	5	7	64	5	3.61
Knutzen, El Paso*	15	0	0	0	1	0	3	1.000	20	19	19	19	0	20	2	0	15	5	8.55
Koonce, Memphis	32	0	0	0	5	3	3	.625	61	50	22	22	5	28	5	1	42	1	3.25
Kovach, D-FtW	19	1	0	0	2	4	2	.333	41	52	34	31	7	29	3	1	30	4	6.80
Lavelle, Amar*	22	18	2	1	6	12	0	.333	100	99	75	60	12	72	6	2	64	9	5.40
Lobb, Shreveport	43	18	3	1	7	9	3	.438	155	158	84	70	10	50	0	8	90	9	4.06
Lowe, San An	33	7	3	0	7	4	1	.636	89	65	23	19	5	30	2	3	61	4	1.92
Manz, D-FtW	21	19	8	0	7	4	0	.636	154	125	46	34	4	61	5	1	99	6	1.99
Marsden, Amarillo	2	0	0	0	0	0	0	.000	8	12	9	8	1	2	1	1	5	0	9.00
Mathwig, Alb	38	3	1	1	4	3	8	.571	62	66	39	20	5	21	3	7	63	2	2.90
Matney, San An*	14	1	0	0	1	2	1	.333	34	26	13	10	2	22	1	1	25	2	2.65
Mazzone, Amar*	9	0	0	0	0	0	0	.000	14	15	7	7	0	4	0	1	11	0	4.50
McCammon, Shrev	3	1	0	0	0	0	0	.000	11	10	6	3	1	6	0	0	5	1	2.45
McDowell, Alb	27	21	5	3	10	9	0	.526	161	132	66	57	10	58	5	9	127	6	3.19
McLeod, Memphis	25	24	6	2	10	8	0	.556	144	134	69	61	16	29	2	3	86	2	3.81
Miller, D-FtW	26	25	10	2	12	10	0	.545	170	149	69	61	5	83	2	4	102	7	3.23
Moulden, D-FtW	37	0	0	0	4	1	4	.800	62	52	21	18	4	14	2	0	39	0	2.61
Mullen, San An	26	2	0	0	2	3	1	.400	55	67	35	29	5	21	1	1	33	2	4.75
Nelson, Shrev*	13	5	0	0	1	3	0	.250	35	45	27	20	1	21	3	0	28	3	5.14
Newman, San An*	26	3	1	0	1	4	1	.200	59	58	39	24	6	26	3	7	56	5	3.66
Newson, Shrev	2	0	0	0	0	0	0	.000	5	2	0	0	0	4	0	0	5	1	0.00
Nottebart, San An	40	0	0	0	7	3	15	.700	63	46	20	13	4	22	6	2	51	1	1.86
Ogier, El Paso	1	0	0	0	0	0	0	.000	0	1	1	1	0	2	1	1	0	0	9.00
Perkins, Memphis*	45	0	0	0	8	2	6	.800	73	57	26	22	3	32	0	2	60	1	2.71
Plodinec, Ark	12	2	0	0	1	2	0	.333	31	29	22	19	4	15	1	2	24	1	5.52
Powell, Shrev*	11	0	0	0	1	0	0	.000	18	19	12	10	0	13	3	1	10	4	5.00
Price, Alb*	2	0	0	0	0	1	0	.000	1	3	1	1	0	4	0	0	1		9.00
Raynor, Alb	26	9	1	0	5	3	1	.625	86	97	52	46	8	33	6	2	46	3	4.81
Reahm, Memphis*	11	11	2	0	3	5	0	.375	51	50	44	31	4	53	3	3	53	4	5.47
Reed, Shreveport	2	2	0	0	0	0	0	.000	7	5	2	2	0	2	0	1	6	1	2.57
Reuschel, San An	32	27	7	2	10	10	0	.500	184	198	80	66	13	59	5	3	79	4	3.23
Rice, El Paso	2	0	0	0	1	0	0	1.000	3	4	0	0	1	0	0	0	0	0	0.00
Rivera, San An	24	16	2	2	3	5	0	.375	89	80	48	42	6	38	2	2	40	3	4.25
Roberts, Shrev*	33	0	0	0	4	6	6	.400	61	75	31	19	6	16	1	3	41	1	2.80
Rohr, Memphis*	7	6	4	0	4	3	0	.571	53	49	21	17	5	10	0	2	42	2	2.89
Rosario, Shrev*	3	0	0	0	0	0	0	.000	3	1	1	1	0	2	0	0	3	0	12.00
Rose, Memphis	25	25	8	2	7	11	0	.389	160	149	76	55	8	56	3	0	88	10	3.09
Ryerson, Amarillo*	34	25	9	0	7	13	1	.350	176	191	102	79	12	57	4	3	123	4	4.04
St. Clair, El Paso	27	1	0	0	4	4	0	.500	63	65	35	27	7	29	5	1	41	1	3.86
Schroeppel, Ark*	34	8	1	0	4	3	2	.571	90	121	54	40	7	24	2	1	41	5	4.00
Schueler, Shrev	26	19	3	1	6	10	1	.375	115	112	66	57	11	61	1	4	93	10	4.46
Scott, Amarillo	31	22	8	1	6	15	0	.286	171	149	87	67	8	93	10	5	137	12	3.53
Sells, El Paso	57	0	0	0	7	4	15	.636	71	70	53	39	6	60	5	4	47	11	4.94
Seminoff, Ark	43	7	1	0	4	5	7	.444	96	101	53	42	10	28	1	5	65	3	3.94
Sosa, Amarillo	3	0	0	0	0	0	0	.000	5	3	2	1	1	4	0	0	2		1.80
Sowinski, Alb	22	2	0	0	3	4	0	.429	65	76	37	33	5	21	2	0	34	3	4.57
Spellman, El Paso	9	1	0		1	2	3	.333	22	19	8	8	2	9		3	9	0	3.27
Sprinkle, Shrev	38	9	2	1	4	6	1	.400	93	107	58	47	12	48	1	7	80	3	4.55
Stephen, D-FtW	9	7	0	0	2	4	0	.333	29	42	30	31	7	23	2		7	4	9.62
Stephenson, SA*	21	8	0	0	3	1	0	.500	49	66	41	35	7	33	3	6	42	4	6.43
Stone, Amarillo	19	18	7	1	9	5	0	.643	114	103	55	50	7	59	2	1	108	3	3.95
Stover, San An	27	0	0	0	2	4	5	.333	42	39	26	21	2	19	2	1	35	2	4.50
Strickland, Alb*	38	0	0	0	5	1	15	.833	46	39	18	15	2	21	2	2	52	3	2.93
Swanson, Shrev	3	0	0	0	0	0	0	.000	7	5	3	3	0	2	1	2	4	0	3.86
C. Thompson, Ark*	34	0	0	0	5	3	4	.625	63	79	42	33	1	28	5	1	49	7	4.71

Pitcher—Club	G.	GS.	CG.	ShO.	W.	L.	Sv.	Pct.	IP.	H.	R.	ER.	HR.	Int. BB.	BB.	HB.	SO.	WP.	ERA.
Thoms, D-FtW* ..40	5	2	0	8	4	6	.667	106	100	40	36	4	44	3	1	75	4	3.06
Todd, San An 18	16	2	1	5	6	0	.455	106	107	50	34	2	36	2	1	48	4	2.89
Tolliver, Amarillo. 7	4	0	0	2	3	0	.460	23	24	11	9	0	12	2	2	20	1	3.52
Towers, Shrev 9	2	0	0	0	1	0	.000	22	28	20	14	1	7	1	5	13	1	5.73
Vaughan, Shrev* ..13	8	1	0	2	4	0	.333	40	40	30	21	3	36	0	2	26	4	4.73
Von Hoff, Ark 18	10	0	0	2	7	0	.222	79	96	61	50	8	41	1	2	61	9	5.70
White, Arkansas* . 1	0	0	0	0	0	0	.000	4	7	3	2	0	2	0	0	3	0	4.50
C. Williams, Mem.26	24	8	4	12	5	1	.706	158	136	67	57	8	61	1	4	128	7	3.25
Williamson, DFW .10	1	0	0	0	0	0	.000	29	34	15	14	1	13	0	0	19	0	4.34
Willis, Arkansas ..26	0	0	0	2	4	13	.333	43	25	11	8	3	15	3	0	22	0	1.67
Wilshusen, D-FtW.31	0	0	0	3	4	9	.429	66	48	20	18	3	25	3	3	59	2	2.45
Wilson, Shrev 4	0	0	0	0	0	0	.000	6	10	8	4	0	6	1	0	2	1	12.00
Winslow, Ark* ...20	15	4	2	8	9	0	.471	88	88	55	42	5	47	2	2	81	11	4.30
Wysocki, Amar ...44	0	0	0	3	3	5	.500	77	81	45	31	8	38	6	6	75	4	3.62

BALKS—Keller, 3; Arnold, Barbosa, Daboll, Garland, Jacquez, Lavelle, Miller, Scott, 2 each; Bell, Bethke, DeLong, Distaso, Engelhardt, Gatewood, Grant (Shrev), Hassler, Henderson, Hernandez, Herson, King (Alb), Manz, Mullen, Nelson, Reahm, Roberts, Rohr, Ryerson, St. Clair, Sells, Sowinski, Sprinkle, Thoms, Tolliver, Williams, 1 each.

COMBINATION SHUTOUTS—McDowell-Strickland, Flynn-Strickland-Mathwig, Albuquerque; Lavelle-Jeffcoat, Stone-Hernandez, Amarillo; DiFabio-Seminoff, Evans-Willis, Hrabosky-Willis, Schroeppel-Daboll, Arkansas; Arnold-Moulden, Manz-Thoms (2), Manz-Wilshusen-Moulden, Stephen-Thoms, Miller-Wilshusen, Dallas-Fort Worth; Clark-Cox, Clark-Sells, Cox-Contreras, El Paso; Williams-Perkins (2), Memphis; Bryan-Stover-Nottebart, Lowe-Stover, Reuschel-Encerti, Reuschel-Nottebart (2), San Antonio; Bell-King, Britton-Ford, Shreveport.

NO-HIT GAMES—Miller, Dallas-Fort Worth, defeated Amarillo, 10-0, May 9 (seven innings); McDowell, Albuquerque, defeated Amarillo, 12-0, August 4; Schueler, Shreveport, defeated San Antonio, 2-0, September 7.

ALONG THE MINOR LEAGUE TRAIL . . . .

(Continued from page 461)

—he was defeated 14 times. . . . Rusty Klobas, 19-year-old Spartanburg (Western Carolinas) rookie, did a service to all beginners in professional ball—he set a pattern for them on how to perform in their first game. He tied a league record for extra-base hits—three doubles and a home run. . . . To say a rookie's life is made up of high spots and low spots is saying a mouthful. Note 18-year-old Joel Youngblood, rookie shortstop of Tampa (Florida State). On April 23, he had a perfect night, five for five, and the next night he took a bad hop in the mouth, chipped a tooth, cut his lip and had six stitches. . . . . Texas League President Bobby Bragan revived a good thing and allowed players again to work off their fines. Each thumbing was an automatic $25 whack and a player could deduct $12.50 each time he made a public appearance in behalf of baseball. The previous season (1969), out of 35 ejections, all but two players worked off their penalties. In 1970, of 39 ejections, 37 players wiped out their fines by PR work for their clubs. . . . Many ballplayers secretly maintain that the fans are all wet, and Ruben Amaro did his bit to prove them correct. The Eugene (Pacific Coast) shortstop, batting in the rain-soaked Northwest climate, fouled off a pitch and the ball hit a rain gutter along the grand-

(Continued on page 484)

California League

CLASS A

CHAMPIONSHIP WINNERS IN PREVIOUS YEARS

1914—Fresno	.571	1951—Santa Barbara‡	.599	1962—San José§	.686
1915—Modesto	.857	1952—Fresno‡	.629	Reno	.587
1916-40—Did not operate.		1953—San José‡	.664	1963—Modesto	.589
1941—Fresno	.643	1954—Modesto‡	.623	Stockton§	.687
S. Barbara (2nd)*	.597	1955—Stockton	.733	1964—Fresno	.638
1942—Santa Barbara†	.642	Fresno§	.718	Fresno	.600
1943-44-45—Did not operate.		1956—Fresno‡	.650	1965—San José	.586
1946—Stockton‡	.600	1957—Visalia x	.622	Stockton§	.614
1947—Stockton‡	.679	Salinas (4th)*	.504	1966—Modesto	.577
S. Barbara (3rd)*	.529	1958—Fresno*	.639	Modesto	.671
1948—Fresno	.607	Bakersfield	.672	1967—San José§	.676
1949—Bakersfield	.612	1959—Bakersfield	.592	Modesto	.586
San José (4th*)	.543	Modesto§	.643	1968—San José	.629
1950—Ventura	.607	1960—Reno	.614	Fresno§	.623
Modesto (2nd)*	.586	Reno	.657	1969—Stockton§	.600
		1961—Reno	.743	Visalia	.614
		Reno	.643		

*Won four-club playoff. †League disbanded June 28. ‡Won championship and four-club playoff. §Won split-season playoff. xWon both halves of split-season.

STANDING OF CLUBS AT CLOSE OF FIRST HALF, JUNE 25

Club	W.	L.	T.	Pct.	G.B.	Club	W.	L.	T.	Pct.	G.B.
Bakersfield (17*)	46	23	0	.667	....	Fresno (24*)	36	33	0	.522	10
Reno (5*)	39	31	0	.557	7½	Visalia (19)	33	37	0	.471	13½
San José (7*)	38	32	0	.543	8½	Stockton (1*)	29	41	0	.414	17½
Modesto (22*)	38	32	0	.543	8½	Lodi (23)	20	50	0	.286	26½

STANDING OF CLUBS AT CLOSE OF SECOND HALF, SEPTEMBER 2

Club	W.	L.	T.	Pct.	G.B.	Club	W.	L.	T.	Pct.	G.B.
Bakersfield (17*)	47	23	0	.671	....	Fresno (24*)	35	35	0	.500	12
Reno (5*)	40	30	0	.571	7	Visalia (19)	33	37	0	.471	14
San José (7*)	39	31	0	.557	8	Stockton (1*)	25	45	0	.357	22
Modesto (22*)	38	32	0	.543	9	Lodi (23)	23	47	0	.329	24

COMPOSITE STANDING OF CLUBS AT CLOSE OF SEASON, SEPTEMBER 2

Club	Bak.	Reno	S.J.	Mod.	Fr.	Vis.	Sto.	Lodi	W.	L.	T.	Pct.	G.B.
Bakersfield (17*)	..	12	12	10	11	16	17	15	93	46	0	.669	....
Reno (5*)	8	..	9	13	9	12	12	16	79	61	0	.564	14½
San José (7*)	8	11	..	10	11	10	13	14	77	63	0	.550	16½
Modesto (22*)	10	7	10	..	10	11	13	15	76	64	0	.543	17½
Fresno (24*)	8	11	9	10	..	8	10	15	71	68	0	.511	22
Visalia (19)	4	8	10	9	12	..	13	10	66	74	0	.471	27½
Stockton (1*)	3	8	7	7	10	7	..	12	54	86	0	.386	39½
Lodi (23)	5	4	6	5	5	10	8	..	43	97	0	.307	50½

Key to major league farm teams (indicated by numbers after clubs in standing) shown on Page 384.

Playoff—None.

Regular-Season Attendance—Bakersfield, 88,784; San José, 71,303; Modesto, 57,332; Fresno, 54,872; Stockton, 46,167; Visalia, 42,344; Reno, 29,887; Lodi, 18,285. Total, 408,974. No playoff. No all-star game.

Managers: Bakersfield—Don LeJohn; Fresno—Dennis Sommer; Lodi—John (Sonny) Ruberto, Ken Bracey; Modesto—Jack Krol; Reno—Merrill (Pinky) May; San José—Buddy Peterson; Stockton—Bill Werle; Visalia—Joe Frazier.

All-Star Team: 1B—Goodson, Fresno; 2B—Timmons, Visalia; 3B—Cummings, Bakersfield; SS—Lacy, Bakersfield; OF—Johnson, Bakersfield; Kazmarek, Visalia; J. Roque, Modesto; Utility—Stillman, Bakersfield; C—Brown, Fresno; P—Rau, Bakersfield; Dawson, Bakersfield; Hood, Stockton; Kokor, Fresno; Manager—LeJohn, Bakersfield.

(Compiled by William J. Weiss, League Statistician, San Mateo, Calif.)

CLUB BATTING

Club	G.	AB.	R.	OR.	H.	TB.	2B.	3B.	HR.	RBI.	SH.	SF.	BB.	Int. BB.	HP.	SO.	SB.	CS.	LOB.	Pct.
Bakersfield	139	4704	766	562	1353	1903	203	31	95	651	51	45	472	32	44	1098	183	75	983	.288
Visalia	140	4713	720	739	1244	1949	183	24	158	633	15	24	571	18	31	1140	67	38	1048	.264
Reno	140	4617	699	599	1215	1797	181	61	93	605	46	43	567	36	32	1157	201	53	1054	.263
Modesto	140	4752	684	593	1184	1772	177	39	111	600	50	27	613	40	51	1266	80	24	1112	.249
Fresno	139	4675	620	617	1149	1698	160	49	97	542	50	34	487	29	38	1216	100	24	1031	.246
Lodi	140	4620	565	879	1118	1658	144	30	112	689	25	26	442	19	19	1300	85	52	954	.242
Stockton	140	4564	537	662	1070	1428	140	34	50	454	44	21	489	24	67	1193	138	66	1007	.234
San Jose	140	4480	573	513	1044	1521	147	39	84	486	44	37	526	26	40	1222	84	49	970	.233

INDIVIDUAL BATTING

(Leading Qualifiers for Batting Championship—434 or More Plate Appearances)

*Bats lefthanded. †Switch-hitter.

Player and Club	G.	AB.	R.	H.	TB.	2B.	3B.	HR.	RBI.	SH.	SF.	BB.	HP.	SO.	SB.	CS.	Pct.
Johnson, Paul, Bak*	113	452	89	158	221	28	4	9	68	1	5	24	7	94	44	11	.350
Kazmarek, George, Visalia	115	448	79	143	241	23	3	23	82	0	1	45	1	115	9	2	.319
Cummings, Robert, Bak	114	457	87	144	179	20	3	3	45	6	5	40	2	53	33	6	.315
Goodson, J. Edward, Fresno*	127	506	66	159	254	28	5	19	94	2	8	33	1	74	3	0	.314
Theodore, George, Visalia	123	454	68	140	199	15	1	14	69	1	1	48	5	77	9	9	.308
Roque, Jorge, Modesto	137	538	101	165	268	24	11	19	82	2	2	57	7	121	16	2	.307
Greer, George, Modesto*	115	448	69	136	221	16	3	21	96	0	4	49	4	98	0	1	.304
Lacy, Leondaus, Bakersfield	124	502	96	151	192	19	5	4	49	3	2	59	5	91	21	12	.301
Thomas, Reginald, Reno	109	384	75	110	189	12	14	13	64	1	3	55	6	121	40	10	.286
Cabell, Enos, Stockton	138	517	78	147	214	25	6	10	67	0	4	52	8	103	24	10	.284

Departmental Leaders: G—L. Brown, 140; AB—L. Brown, 572; R—J. Roque, 101; H—J. Roque, 165; TB—J. Roque, 268; 2B—Goodson, Paul Johnson, 28; 3B—Bond, 16; HR—Fritz, 24; RBI—Greer, 96; SH—L. Brown, 9; SF—Goodson, Stillman, 8; BB—T. Thompson, 83; HP—Winters, 15; SO—Nelson, 164; SB—L. Brown, 51; CS—L. Brown, 19.

(All Players—Listed Alphabetically)

Player and Club	G.	AB.	R.	H.	TB.	2B.	3B.	HR.	RBI.	SH.	SF.	BB.	HP.	SO.	SB.	CS.	Pct.
Abreu, Manuel, Modesto	78	257	28	55	60	1	2	0	17	0	2	28	2	52	5	1	.214
Acosta, Eduardo, Bakersfield	10	4	0	1	0	0	0	0	1	0	0	1	0	0	0	0	.250
Adams, Jackie, Visalia	55	173	30	41	68	3	3	6	20	0	1	27	0	59	8	3	.237
Albury, Victor, Lodi*	21	33	9	8	13	0	1	1	2	1	1	5	0	7	0	0	.242
Alger, Thomas, Modesto	3	1	0	0	0	0	0	0	1	0	0	1	0	0	0	0	.000
Allen, David, Bakersfield	17	49	6	13	15	2	0	0	5	1	0	3	0	19	0	0	.265
Allen, Gregory, Visalia	29	77	13	17	32	0	0	5	14	0	0	14	1	28	2	1	.221
Allen, James, Bakersfield*	25	10	1	2	2	0	0	0	0	0	0	2	0	7	0	0	.200
Ambrose, Victor, Reno*	116	409	74	102	132	14	5	2	29	6	0	64	2	102	41	12	.249
Angelini, Norman, Jose*	21	37	3	5	7	2	0	0	1	4	1	7	0	14	0	0	.135
Arendell, Richard, Lodi	19	49	4	7	11	1	0	1	5	0	1	7	0	18	1	0	.143
Aristimuno, Jesus, Fresno	111	402	53	110	160	16	1	3	40	7	3	31	2	50	13	2	.274
Ashby, Alan, Reno†	40	121	15	23	39	5	1	3	18	1	3	18	2	31	1	0	.190
Baca, Johnny, Lodi	76	229	24	58	77	7	0	4	18	0	2	25	2	35	1	1	.253
Bach, Brian, Modesto	20	36	4	2	2	0	0	0	2	0	0	10	0	22	0	0	.056
Ballard, Steven, Modesto	36	104	13	22	24	2	0	0	6	0	0	19	2	22	0	0	.212
Ballinger, Mark, Reno	27	59	7	16	24	3	1	1	7	2	0	3	0	24	0	0	.271
Bartlett, Robert, Visalia*	12	21	2	5	6	1	0	0	2	0	0	1	0	9	0	0	.238
Beitey, Michael, Stockton†	37	111	8	24	27	1	1	0	13	1	0	8	2	29	0	1	.216
Bennett, Russell, Modesto*	38	130	18	28	42	2	0	4	14	0	0	11	3	40	3	1	.215
Bielski, Daniel, Lodi	32	40	2	2	2	0	0	0	0	1	0	3	0	20	0	0	.050
Biko, Michael, Reno	30	23	5	5	6	1	0	0	2	0	0	0	0	7	0	0	.217
Bird, J. Douglas, San Jose	3	2	0	0	0	0	0	0	0	0	0	1	0	0	0	0	.000
Bishop, Robert, Visalia	33	34	4	5	11	3	0	1	3	0	0	5	0	18	0	0	.147
Bloom, Joseph, Stockton	7	2	0	0	0	0	0	0	0	0	0	2	0	1	0	0	.000
Bond, Jerry, Reno	112	420	73	115	197	11	16	13	64	1	7	21	5	104	32	5	.274
Bosch, Gerald, Fresno*	81	295	51	82	98	10	3	0	11	1	1	49	9	34	13	3	.278
Boyer, Leonard, Modesto*	63	232	36	54	84	10	1	6	26	3	1	40	1	44	5	0	.233
Boyles, Thomas, Reno	75	209	19	47	52	2	0	1	22	3	3	17	1	31	1	1	.225
Brenner, Glenn, Visalia	3	4	1	2	5	0	0	1	2	0	0	0	0	1	0	0	.500
Brookens, Edward, San Jose	30	25	1	1	1	0	0	0	0	2	0	1	0	14	0	0	.040
Brooks, William, Modesto*	82	262	46	72	100	7	3	5	30	0	1	34	0	81	22	6	.275
Brown, Bruce, Visalia*	12	14	2	1	1	0	0	0	0	0	0	0	0	9	0	0	.071
Brown, Jerald, Fresno	119	428	58	111	188	14	6	17	58	1	0	36	3	129	17	6	.259
Brown, Leon, Stockton	140	572	78	154	195	21	4	4	49	9	1	34	8	84	51	19	.269
Buckner, Robert, Bak	71	196	28	49	60	9	1	0	17	1	0	24	1	36	4	5	.250
Burrows, Robert, San Jose	113	404	59	97	144	15	4	8	57	2	6	37	0	128	3	2	.240
Cabell, Enos, Stockton	138	517	78	147	214	25	6	10	67	0	4	52	8	103	24	10	.284
Camy, Donald, Visalia	19	61	7	13	18	2	0	1	6	0	1	0	0	24	0	0	.213
Canada, Romel, Bakersfield*	93	330	77	110	191	25	4	16	84	2	3	44	5	61	23	11	.333
Cappelli, Peter, San Jose†	29	81	10	17	24	4	0	1	6	0	1	2	1	17	0	0	.210
Capra, Lee, Visalia	24	46	6	6	7	1	0	0	2	1	0	8	0	16	0	0	.130
Chapman, Michael, Lodi	21	35	1	6	6	0	0	0	5	0	0	3	0	12	3	0	.171
Chlan, Gregory, San Jose	13	18	0	2	2	0	0	0	0	0	0	1	0	4	0	0	.111
Clark, Jerry, Reno	57	226	37	73	94	9	0	4	41	3	4	27	2	52	14	2	.323
Coleman, W. Frank, Stockton	11	2	0	0	0	0	0	0	0	0	0	0	0	0	0	0	.000
Collins, Ronald, Visalia	65	242	39	58	91	9	3	6	30	0	1	28	4	64	4	1	.240

Player and Club	G.	AB.	R.	H.	TB.	2B.	3B.	HR.	RBI.	SH.	SF.	BB.	HP.	SO.	SB.	CS.	Pct.
Cook, Eugene, Fresno	117	410	58	93	126	9	6	4	36	7	2	36	4	100	7	2	.227
Cornell, Kenneth, Fresno*	59	138	14	36	44	4	2	0	14	0	1	41	1	38	1	1	.261
Corona, Thomas, Stockton	69	195	22	53	70	7	2	2	24	1	1	35	4	59	7	7	.272
Cotton, William, Visalia	81	257	27	65	109	11	0	11	41	0	3	31	2	68	2	0	.253
Cousins, Derryl, Reno	15	40	3	9	12	0	0	1	2	0	0	4	0	8	0	0	.225
Cowgill, Alan, Fresno	26	44	2	4	5	1	0	0	5	1	1	8	0	25	0	0	.091
Crain, J. Kevin, Reno	30	27	1	4	4	0	0	0	0	4	0	2	0	8	0	0	.148
Creola, Thomas, Stockton	11	21	2	5	6	1	0	0	0	0	0	7	0	6	0	0	.238
Crichton, Thomas, San Jose	.135	472	84	127	236	25	9	22	77	0	2	59	13	112	23	5	.269
Cummings, Robert, Bak	114	457	87	144	179	20	3	3	45	6	5	40	2	53	33	6	.315
Daboll, Dennis, Modesto	21	20	3	8	9	1	0	0	3	2	0	0	0	2	0	0	.400
Darwin, A. Bobby, Bak	86	303	52	90	170	9	1	23	70	1	1	28	5	127	10	2	.297
Davies, Steven, Fresno	10	13	2	3	4	1	0	0	2	1	0	1	0	5	0	0	.231
Dawson, Albert, Bakersfield	28	71	6	10	13	3	0	0	3	3	7	1	3	0	35	0	.141
DeBenedetti, Gary, San Jose	12	29	2	5	6	1	0	0	6	3	0	4	0	15	0	0	.172
DeCaminada, Timothy, Vis*	.30	73	10	11	12	1	0	0	3	0	0	11	2	29	0	0	.151
Del Orbe, Lazaro, Stockton	.34	106	11	24	25	1	0	0	9	1	0	5	2	18	3	1	.226
Demery, Art, San Jose*	12	24	2	2	2	0	0	0	2	0	0	1	1	8	0	0	.083
Dermody, Norman, Bak†	25	9	3	2	2	0	0	0	0	0	0	2	0	3	0	0	.222
Dickerson, Donald, Visalia	58	158	23	34	43	6	0	1	14	0	1	33	0	56	0	1	.215
DiSarcina, Joseph, Lodi	.103	352	49	71	107	11	5	5	33	1	1	39	0	97	12	6	.202
Dodder, Joseph, Bak*	86	282	39	87	124	11	1	8	44	0	3	24	1	78	0	2	.309
Dorn, Robert, Bakersfield*	6	0	0	0	0	0	0	0	0	0	0	0	0	0	0	0	.000
Downen, Martin, San Jose	6	9	0	1	2	1	0	0	2	0	0	0	0	6	0	0	.111
Drew, C. Ollie, San Jose*	76	288	31	82	102	13	2	1	28	4	1	19	0	76	7	8	.285
Duncan, Peter, San Jose	62	217	26	52	88	7	4	7	28	0	1	16	2	61	1	1	.240
Dunn, Ronald, Stockton	132	475	49	111	151	14	7	4	53	2	6	47	4	134	6	5	.234
Eargle, Guy, Lodi	133	482	58	124	206	16	3	20	77	3	2	47	2	140	8	7	.257
Easom, Michael, Reno*	87	279	38	84	122	16	5	4	45	0	2	25	0	48	2	1	.301
Elliott, Randy, Lodi	.132	481	68	135	209	20	6	14	51	0	4	43	1	109	10	9	.281
Ervin, Elvin, Bakersfield*	6	0	0	0	0	0	0	0	0	0	0	0	0	0	0	0	.000
Esposito, Kenneth, Visalia	17	10	2	3	4	1	0	0	0	0	0	0	0	4	0	0	.300
Estes, Ronald, Bakersfield	54	170	40	58	93	5	3	8	34	0	2	15	3	40	12	4	.341
Ewing, Ray, Visalia†	8	23	4	4	7	0	0	1	5	0	0	2	0	11	1	0	.174
Felderman, Douglas, Stockton	17	26	0	2	3	1	0	0	0	0	0	5	0	16	0	0	.077
Figueroa, Eduardo, Fresno	14	14	0	0	0	0	0	0	0	1	0	1	0	0	0	0	.000
Filbeck, Leon, Reno	17	34	3	4	6	0	0	0	1	2	0	2	0	11	0	0	.118
Finlay, Andrew, Lodi	83	221	19	46	71	8	1	5	23	0	1	32	1	85	4	1	.208
Fitzgerald, Emmanuel, Sto	41	52	7	17	22	0	1	1	5	4	0	5	0	15	0	0	.327
Fitzgerald, Joseph, Visalia	28	24	1	3	3	0	0	0	0	0	0	1	0	7	0	0	.125
Foderaro, Robert, Visalia	27	14	0	2	3	1	0	0	0	1	0	0	0	7	0	0	.143
Ford, Daniel, Modesto	13	4	0	0	0	0	0	0	0	0	2	0	0	2	0	0	.000
Forsch, Robert, Modesto	20	47	4	7	13	3	0	1	1	0	0	7	0	21	0	0	.149
Fritz, Lawrence, Visalia*	80	295	65	89	174	9	2	24	73	1	1	54	1	88	3	3	.302
Frye, James, Bakersfield	36	23	2	2	5	0	0	1	2	1	0	3	0	16	0	0	.087
Furlong, Nicholas, Visalia	3	2	0	0	0	0	0	0	0	0	0	1	0	2	0	0	.000
Gagliano, Ralph, Reno*	.104	320	39	88	125	18	2	5	45	2	2	78	0	54	4	1	.275
Gambero, Darrell, San Jose	12	19	0	1	6	0	0	2	3	0	1	0	0	10	0	1	.053
Garcia, Ralph, Lodi	13	30	1	8	9	1	0	0	1	0	0	1	0	10	0	0	.267
Gardner, Terry, Lodi	8	3	0	0	0	0	0	0	1	0	0	1	0	0	0	0	.000
Gilje, Theodore, Bak*	29	64	5	10	13	0	0	1	4	1	0	5	1	35	1	0	.156
Giresi, Anthony, Stockton*	3	3	0	1	1	0	0	0	0	0	0	0	0	0	0	0	.333
Globokar, Richard, Visalia*	10	15	3	1	2	1	0	0	3	1	0	3	0	4	0	0	.067
Gonzalez, R. Randy, Mod*	12	16	1	1	1	0	0	0	1	1	0	1	0	12	0	0	.063
Goodson, J. Edward, Fresno*	.127	506	66	159	254	28	5	19	94	2	8	33	1	74	3	0	.314
Gordon, Howard, Modesto*	69	228	35	58	101	8	1	11	52	1	0	52	2	82	1	0	.254
Grant, Herman, Stockton*	1	1	0	0	0	0	0	0	0	0	0	0	1	0	0	0	.000
Graves, William, Bakersfield	22	8	1	0	0	0	0	0	0	2	0	0	0	0	0	0	.000
Gray, Rickey, Stockton†	.108	337	33	71	85	6	1	2	23	1	1	37	3	101	7	7	.211
Green, John, Lodi	31	22	1	2	2	0	0	0	1	0	0	2	0	16	0	0	.091
Greer, George, Modesto*	.115	448	69	136	221	16	3	21	96	0	4	49	4	98	0	1	.304
Gregg, Roger, Lodi	57	162	21	28	50	5	1	5	14	1	2	31	1	88	3	1	.173
Haines, Robert, Visalia	21	13	1	2	2	0	0	0	0	1	0	0	1	7	0	0	.154
Hairston, James, Modesto*	18	52	4	8	12	1	0	1	6	0	0	5	0	18	0	2	.154
Hansen, Guy, San Jose	36	17	2	2	2	0	0	0	0	0	0	0	0	6	0	0	.118
Hardy, H. Lawrence, Lodi	11	28	4	7	12	2	0	1	5	2	0	1	0	11	0	0	.250
Harkey, Bruce, Visalia	5	4	1	0	0	0	0	0	0	0	0	2	0	4	0	0	.000
Harrell, John, Fresno	32	97	7	17	19	2	0	0	6	0	0	11	1	33	1	0	.175
Harrison, J. Patrick, Bak	24	76	11	22	23	1	0	0	7	3	1	12	0	19	1	0	.289
Hill, Gary, Visalia	86	281	35	78	116	9	1	9	38	1	4	40	5	41	8	3	.278
Hines, Marvin, Stockton	12	11	2	4	4	0	0	0	0	0	0	1	0	2	0	0	.364
Hoban, Richard, Reno*	30	57	8	19	31	4	0	2	19	0	1	3	0	26	0	0	.333
Hofferd, John, San Jose	24	27	3	3	4	1	0	0	1	2	0	2	0	15	0	0	.111
Homik, William, Bakersfield	93	319	40	93	129	18	0	6	49	5	4	28	1	87	3	3	.292
Homoly, Guy, Fresno	3	11	4	2	3	1	0	0	0	0	0	2	0	4	0	0	.182
Hood, Donald, Stockton*	32	72	11	19	25	1	1	1	7	1	0	7	1	13	0	0	.264
Howard, Fred, Visalia	7	23	4	7	12	2	0	1	3	0	0	2	0	10	0	0	.304
Howell, John, Reno*	34	32	0	7	9	1	0	0	3	0	0	3	0	12	0	0	.219
Huckle, Wilbur, Visalia	38	161	25	49	80	11	1	6	23	0	1	11	1	15	4	4	.304
Hughes, Michael, Bakersfield	16	16	1	3	7	1	0	1	4	0	1	1	1	5	0	0	.188
Iskierka, Dennis, Visalia	15	44	2	5	10	2	0	1	3	1	0	5	1	26	0	0	.114
Isom, Curtis, San Jose*	12	17	2	2	2	0	0	0	2	0	0	1	1	11	0	0	.118

Player and Club	G.	AB.	R.	H.	TB.	2B.	3B.	HR.	RBI.	SH.	SF.	BB.	HP.	SO.	SB.	CS.	Pct.
Jacobsen, Gary, Fresno	30	89	14	21	37	3	2	3	12	0	1	16	1	27	1	0	.236
Jakubs, David, Lodi	98	273	27	62	81	3	2	4	24	2	0	19	0	99	4	7	.227
James, Dennis, Bakersfield†	24	47	3	7	8	1	0	0	3	2	0	1	0	25	0	0	.149
James, William, Reno†	33	17	2	3	3	0	0	0	1	0	0	3	0	10	0	0	.176
Jaster, Daniel, Modesto	10	16	1	0	0	0	0	0	1	0	2	0	9	0	0	.000
Jefferson, Jesse, Stockton	27	53	5	3	3	0	0	0	2	2	0	4	0	35	0	0	.057
Johnson, David, Stockton	31	18	3	5	9	1	0	1	2	0	0	0	8	0	0	.278
Johnson, Larry, Reno	89	293	36	76	105	13	5	2	31	1	1	32	2	56	6	3	.259
Johnson, Paul, Bak*	113	452	89	158	221	28	4	9	68	1	5	24	7	94	44	11	.350
Johnson, Philip, Fresno	20	5	1	1	1	0	0	0	0	0	0	0	0	2	0	0	.200
Johnson, Ray, Reno	97	346	49	99	158	17	3	12	52	2	5	33	2	71	1	1	.286
Karp, Julian, San Jose*	8	5	1	0	0	0	0	1	1	0	1	0	2	0	0	.000
Katawczik, Fred, Lodi	23	7	1	1	4	0	0	1	1	0	0	0	3	0	0	.143
Kazmarek, George, Visalia	115	448	79	143	241	23	3	23	82	0	1	45	1	115	9	2	.319
Keister, Craig, Stockton	28	48	3	2	2	0	0	0	0	3	0	2	1	27	0	0	.042
Kern, James, Reno	4	5	0	1	1	0	0	0	1	0	0	1	0	1	0	0	.200
Kinnaugh, Arthur, Fresno*	8	23	4	7	7	0	0	0	3	0	1	2	0	6	1	0	.304
Kirkland, Donald, Modesto	104	398	70	106	147	24	1	5	31	4	4	54	5	100	2	2	.266
Knight, Robert, Lodi†	11	31	5	2	3	1	0	0	0	0	0	6	1	14	1	0	.065
Koch, Lawrence, Modesto	16	33	4	9	10	1	0	0	5	0	1	2	0	17	0	0	.273
Kokor, Steven, Fresno	52	17	1	2	3	1	0	0	0	6	0	1	0	9	0	0	.118
Krawiecki, John, Lodi	15	14	1	2	3	1	0	0	0	0	0	0	7	0	0	.143
Kyle, William, Reno*	18	60	9	11	18	4	0	1	4	0	1	8	0	23	0	1	.183
Lacy, Leondaus, Bakersfield	124	502	96	151	192	19	5	4	49	3	2	59	5	91	21	12	.301
Lagunas, Luis, San Jose	112	345	49	72	124	15	2	11	50	1	1	61	4	102	0	1	.209
Leonard, Marvin, Visalia*	5	4	2	1	1	0	0	0	0	0	0	1	0	0	0	0	.250
Libran, Francisco, Lodi	117	404	64	101	157	15	1	13	46	3	1	77	0	108	8	5	.250
Lightfoot, Lloyd, San Jose	134	439	45	112	134	15	2	1	36	4	4	42	5	85	3	3	.255
Llanos, Rosario, Modesto	7	10	0	0	0	0	0	0	0	0	2	0	5	0	0	.000
Lolich, Frank, Visalia	11	8	0	0	0	0	0	0	0	0	0	4	0	0	.000
Looper, Benny, Modesto	21	63	5	11	15	4	0	0	3	0	0	10	1	25	0	1	.175
Maine, J. Kevin, Visalia	11	2	0	0	0	0	0	0	0	0	0	0	0	2	0	0	.000
Manahan, Patrick, Bak*	50	107	9	30	35	5	0	0	10	2	1	15	1	14	1	3	.280
Marion, Gary, Modesto*	10	36	4	6	9	1	1	0	4	0	9	2	7	0	0	.167
Martin, Stanley, Stockton†	94	379	56	104	128	12	3	2	27	3	2	34	0	85	30	8	.274
Matte, Bruce, Visalia†	4	4	0	0	0	0	0	0	0	0	0	0	3	0	0	.000
Matthews, Gary, Fresno	117	380	76	106	196	11	5	23	74	4	4	58	3	120	20	5	.279
McBride, Arnold, Modesto*	26	85	17	25	33	4	2	0	7	0	1	8	5	24	9	1	.294
McGhee, Wayne, Modesto	94	290	34	67	90	10	2	3	25	6	2	21	5	67	11	2	.231
McGrew, Alvin, Reno	74	239	49	57	111	3	3	15	40	0	1	30	2	100	11	2	.238
McVay, Richard, Modesto	11	12	2	1	1	0	0	0	1	0	0	0	2	0	0	.083
Medina, Efrain, Lodi†	82	208	15	54	68	9	1	1	18	0	1	20	2	39	2	4	.260
Meschuk, Mark, Bakersfield	24	32	1	2	3	1	0	0	1	0	2	0	26	0	0	.063
Miller, Richard, Fresno	88	208	29	70	116	15	2	9	39	0	1	23	0	88	0	0	.235
Moffitt, Randall, Fresno	18	46	5	4	6	2	0	0	4	0	3	0	19	0	0	.087
Mohler, Randall, Fresno	117	402	51	94	156	14	6	12	56	2	4	43	5	115	3	0	.234
Moore, Steven, San Jose*	117	342	48	76	122	11	4	9	54	1	6	64	4	103	6	3	.222
Morrell, William, Lodi	13	14	3	2	3	1	0	0	1	0	0	0	6	0	0	.143
Mulcahey, Robert, Lodi	20	7	1	2	2	0	0	0	0	0	0	1	0	0	.286
Murray, Charles, San Jose	8	1	0	0	0	0	0	0	0	0	0	0	0	0	0	0	.000
Myers, Steven, San Jose	20	8	1	3	3	0	0	0	3	1	0	0	2	0	0	.375
Nelson, Johnnie, San Jose†	126	466	54	106	144	8	3	8	34	0	0	50	2	164	16	0	.227
Nichols, Grady, Lodi*	104	344	45	100	173	13	3	18	59	1	2	20	1	111	1	1	.291
Nielsen, Steven, San Jose*	8	0	0	0	0	0	0	0	0	0	0	0	0	0	0	.000
Nordbrook, Timothy, Stockton	23	63	4	11	12	1	0	0	1	2	0	11	1	33	1	1	.175
O'Brien, R. Patrick, Lodi*	27	76	13	26	42	2	1	4	15	1	1	4	0	9	2	0	.342
O'Connor, William, Stockton*	26	63	5	8	9	1	0	0	4	0	12	2	25	0	0	.127
O'Donnell, Kenneth, San Jose	22	67	8	15	17	0	1	0	4	0	0	10	0	10	1	1	.224
Oliva, Ernest, Lodi†	7	0	0	0	0	0	0	0	0	0	0	0	0	0	0	.000
Parks, Dennis, Modesto	92	322	39	86	131	19	1	8	57	1	3	32	3	61	1	1	.267
Parks, Theodore, San Jose	44	180	29	59	75	7	3	1	16	1	1	17	2	26	5	4	.328
Peden, Michael, Modesto	19	47	3	6	9	0	1	3	0	1	1	1	16	0	0	.128
Phillips, Michael, Fresno*	94	318	26	79	101	7	3	3	21	0	1	18	0	69	7	1	.248
Pierce, W. Grady, Stockton	29	29	4	3	4	1	0	0	3	4	0	0	16	0	0	.103
Pietila, Ronald, Reno	54	186	23	57	77	5	0	5	34	1	3	13	1	25	2	3	.306
Plant, James, Visalia	107	395	54	103	184	16	1	21	64	1	3	30	4	119	2	2	.261
Plodinec, Timothy, Modesto	39	25	2	5	9	1	0	1	3	1	0	2	0	7	0	0	.200
Poteete, Rodney, Bakersfield	1	1	0	0	0	0	0	0	0	0	0	0	0	1	0	.000
Preston, John, Lodi	28	22	1	3	3	0	0	0	2	0	12	0	1	.136
Preston, William, Lodi	10	23	1	4	4	0	0	2	0	1	0	13	0	0	.174
Price, Michael, Bakersfield	20	19	0	0	0	0	0	0	0	0	2	0	15	0	0	.000
Prieto, Michael, San Jose	59	131	13	24	35	1	2	2	12	0	2	15	2	47	1	2	.183
Pullins, Gary, Bakersfield	12	31	2	2	2	0	0	0	3	0	15	0	1	.065
Pullman, Jerry, Fresno†	70	203	18	31	39	2	3	0	14	1	0	17	0	63	4	0	.322
Putnam, Christopher, Visalia	34	59	10	19	23	0	2	0	7	1	0	5	0	9	0	0	.322
Putz, G. Alan, Modesto*	98	291	49	79	143	14	4	14	53	1	1	58	4	70	0	0	.271
Queen, Dennis, Reno	8	19	0	2	2	0	0	0	2	1	0	0	14	0	0	.105
Randall, Robert, Bakersfield	98	362	48	97	126	14	3	3	39	1	3	30	5	51	11	5	.268
Rankhorn, C. Wayne, Reno	9	29	4	4	5	1	0	0	0	0	5	1	12	3	0	.138
Rau, Douglas, Bakersfield*	15	43	6	5	6	1	0	2	3	0	4	1	11	0	0	.116
Rauch, Robert, Bakersfield	25	26	0	2	3	1	0	2	0	0	0	16	0	0	.077

Player and Club	G.	AB.	R.	H.	TB.	2B.	3B.	HR.	RBI.	SH.	SF.	BB.	HP.	SO.	SB.	CS.	Pct.
Reeve, Dennis, Stockton†	32	99	9	23	32	5	2	0	20	1	0	11	1	23	2	2	.232
Rivera, Emiliano, Fresno	4	4	1	1	1	0	0	0	1	0	1	0	0	2	0	0	.250
Rivera, Jorge, San Jose	3	6	0	0	0	0	0	0	1	0	1	0	0	2	0	0	.000
Robinson, Herman, Lodi	122	464	64	115	169	10	4	12	52	3	1	24	1	116	8	6	.248
Robles, Sergio, Bakersfield	99	350	44	88	115	14	2	3	34	4	5	22	2	61	5	5	.251
Roos, Leslie, San Jose	49	177	28	45	51	1	1	1	9	3	1	32	2	29	9	4	.254
Roque, Felix, Modesto	52	9	0	1	1	0	0	0	0	0	0	1	0	8	0	0	.111
Roque, Jorge, Modesto	137	538	101	165	268	24	11	19	82	2	2	57	7	121	16	2	.307
Ruberto, John, Lodi	1	3	0	0	0	0	0	0	0	0	0	1	0	1	0	0	.000
Sanders, Willie, San Jose	33	31	2	3	3	0	0	0	0	2	0	2	0	8	1	1	.097
Sawyer, Richard, Reno	24	49	6	13	17	4	0	0	5	1	0	4	1	15	1	0	.265
Schofield, Terry, San Jose*	11	34	1	6	7	1	0	0	1	0	0	5	0	13	0	0	.176
Schwartz, Richard, Reno*	5	8	1	1	1	0	0	0	1	0	0	2	0	2	0	0	.125
Shaughnessy, Harry, Reno†	37	131	20	35	50	10	1	1	13	2	4	16	1	33	8	4	.267
Sheppard, Tommie, Visalia	17	11	1	1	4	0	0	1	1	0	0	0	0	6	0	0	.091
Sherzer, Marvin, Lodi	24	32	2	3	4	1	0	0	1	0	3	0	20	1	0		.094
Sibley, Steven, Fresno*	35	19	3	3	3	0	0	0	2	1	0	7	0	0	1		.158
Sielicki, John, Fresno†	28	46	6	7	1	0	0	6	5	0	10	0	33	0	0		.130
Simendinger, Gregory, Sto	8	6	0	0	0	0	0	0	0	1	0	1	0	6	0	0	.000
Sinclair, Gregory, Lodi	48	22	1	2	2	0	0	0	1	1	0	0	0	13	0	0	.091
Smith, Herbert, Lodi†	8	1	0	0	0	0	0	0	0	0	0	0	0	1	0	0	.000
Smith, James A., San Jose	4	3	0	0	0	0	0	0	0	0	0	0	0	3	0	0	.000
Snyder, James C., San Jose	10	20	2	4	4	0	0	0	1	0	0	5	0	7	0	0	.200
Sosa, Elias, Fresno	21	31	4	3	3	0	0	0	1	2	0	2	0	16	0	0	.097
Southard, Edward, Reno	24	90	22	33	47	6	1	2	12	0	0	12	1	8	5	1	.367
Souza, Thomas, Stockton	62	176	14	32	36	4	0	0	13	0	1	14	0	53	0	1	.182
Stafford, James, Stockton†	31	101	11	20	30	3	2	1	11	0	0	7	2	48	0	1	.198
Staiger, Roy, Visalia	76	297	37	71	105	13	0	7	34	0	3	20	0	56	4	2	.239
Stark, Clinton, Modesto	40	93	11	19	29	1	0	3	13	4	0	3	1	32	1	0	.204
Stensland, George, Modesto*	20	29	3	4	8	1	0	1	8	2	1	1	0	18	0	0	.138
Sterling, Randall, Visalia†	5	10	1	1	2	1	0	0	1	0	0	2	0	6	0	0	.100
Stewart, Ronald, Visalia*	7	9	0	1	1	0	0	0	1	0	1	0	5	0	0		.111
Stillman, Royle, Bak*	163	336	68	115	165	15	4	9	76	0	8	73	2	63	15	5	.342
Stitzel, Glenn, Visalia*	24	84	22	33	44	2	0	3	10	0	0	24	0	5	2	1	.393
Stoligrosz, Daniel, Reno†	63	187	25	42	70	8	1	6	27	1	1	55	2	59	1	1	.225
Stripling, Jackie, Modesto	11	21	2	3	4	0	0	0	1	0	1	0	10	0	0		.143
Strom, Brent, Visalia	10	28	3	6	7	1	0	0	3	1	0	1	0	12	0	0	.214
Stureman, Richard, Visalia	9	22	2	1	3	0	1	0	0	0	0	3	0	10	1	0	.045
Taylor, Charles, Lodi*	21	12	0	1	1	0	0	0	1	0	0	4	0	6	0	0	.083
Theodore, George, Visalia	123	454	68	140	199	15	1	14	69	1	1	48	5	77	9	9	.308
Thomas, Reginald, Reno	109	384	75	110	189	12	14	13	64	1	3	55	6	121	40	10	.286
Thompson, Marvin, Lodi	5	5	1	1	1	0	0	0	0	0	0	0	0	2	0	0	.200
Thompson, Thomas, Modesto	125	447	66	115	165	21	7	5	39	4	3	83	3	131	17	6	.257
Tidrow, Richard, Reno	6	10	1	1	1	0	0	0	0	1	0	2	0	3	0	0	.100
Timmons, Jimmy, Visalia*	96	341	56	96	120	17	2	1	25	0	2	48	0	28	4	3	.282
Trombino, Philip, Modesto	13	38	6	9	12	0	0	1	6	0	0	0	2	6	0	0	.237
Tsoukalas, William, Reno*	39	42	5	9	11	2	0	0	4	0	0	3	0	11	0	1	.214
Turigliatto, Steven, Sto†	99	275	40	77	112	10	2	7	36	0	0	60	5	57	4	3	.280
Tyler, Timothy, Lodi*	12	1	0	0	0	0	0	0	0	0	0	0	0	1	0	0	.000
Ulrich, Robert, Fresno	29	46	1	4	4	0	0	0	2	3	1	1	0	18	0	0	.087
Upton, Gary, Visalia	34	105	19	28	58	7	1	7	16	1	0	11	0	26	0	0	.267
Van Lue, Nick, San Jose*	84	276	33	60	105	13	1	10	33	0	5	45	1	57	3	2	.217
Vicente, Juan, Modesto*	5	18	0	3	3	0	0	0	0	0	0	0	0	4	0	0	.167
Vidrio, Gilbert, Lodi†	114	450	55	125	149	16	1	2	27	1	5	20	0	52	13	4	.278
Waldeck, Martin, Fresno	22	47	4	3	4	1	0	0	1	0	0	3	0	24	0	0	.064
Walker, R. Thomas, Stockton	21	46	1	5	8	0	0	1	4	1	0	0	0	13	0	0	.109
Wallace, Dean, Fresno	38	10	1	3	4	1	0	0	0	0	0	0	0	3	0	0	.300
Warden, Jonathan, San Jose†	17	29	3	4	5	1	0	0	3	1	0	5	0	20	0	0	.103
Watts, Edward, Stockton	13	52	14	17	32	4	1	3	13	0	1	2	11	1	1		.327
Weaver, R. Michael, Reno*	67	242	50	63	77	10	2	0	17	7	1	26	1	57	28	4	.260
Wedel, Gary, Bakersfield	7	6	0	0	0	0	0	0	0	0	0	1	0	0	0	0	.000
Weems, Mark, Stockton	48	14	4	4	13	0	0	3	6	1	0	1	0	4	0	0	.286
Welker, Michael, Fresno	6	3	1	1	2	1	0	0	0	0	0	0	0	1	0	0	.333
Whisman, Jimmy, San Jose	36	44	4	11	12	1	0	0	6	1	0	8	0	0			.250
White, Leland, Modesto	25	26	0	3	3	0	0	0	2	4	0	1	0	7	0	0	.115
Whiteside, Lawrence, Lodi†	6	3	1	1	1	0	0	0	1	0	0	1	2	0	0		.333
Wihtol, Alan, Visalia†	14	32	1	4	5	1	0	0	2	0	1	0	17	0	0		.125
Williamson, Jeffrey, Sto	20	31	0	3	3	0	0	0	4	0	1	0	15	0	0		.097
Winfield, Max, Reno	37	24	0	2	2	0	0	0	0	1	0	0	17	0	0		.083
Winters, James, Stockton*	129	400	45	78	111	15	0	6	48	1	3	71	15	95	2	0	.195
Woolsey, Jack, Fresno*	93	324	60	93	130	15	5	4	39	2	1	37	5	99	9	4	.287
Wright, Donald, San Jose*	70	181	27	45	57	4	1	2	13	0	3	19	0	37	6	1	.249
Wright, Larry, Modesto	5	3	0	0	0	0	0	0	0	0	0	0	0	3	0	0	.000
Wukits, Richard, Stockton	65	208	18	44	57	5	1	2	17	1	1	12	2	56	0	1	.212
Young, Danny, Lodi	17	23	2	2	5	0	0	1	2	0	1	0	16	0	0		.087
Ziegler, James, Visalia†	106	331	58	95	136	14	3	7	40	0	2	52	3	36	4	2	.287
Zinniger, Richard, Lodi	5	11	1	7	8	1	0	0	4	0	0	0	0	2	0	0	.636

GRAND-SLAM HOME RUNS—Matthews, 2; Boyer, L. Brown, Burrows, Cotton, Fritz, Gagliano, Gordon, Hoban, Lagunas, Robinson, Stensland, Theodore, Thomas, Van Lue, Vidrio, Walker, 1 each.

AWARDED FIRST BASE ON INTERFERENCE—Crichton 5 (Baca, Jacobsen, L. Johnson, Turigliatto, Upton); Pullman 5 (Robles 2, Gregg, Homik, L. Johnson); Jacobsen 2 (Robles 2); Gray (Cotton), Nichols (Cotton), Weaver (Baca).

CLUB FIELDING

Club	G.	PO.	A.	E.	DP.	PB.	Pct.	Club	G.	PO.	A.	E.	DP.	PB.	Pct.
Modesto	140	3712	1328	178	87	39	.966	Fresno	139	2643	1528	248	109	28	.954
San Jose	140	3605	1423	187	93	36	.964	Lodi	140	3547	1334	240	95	42	.953
Reno	140	3569	1347	198	103	49	.961	Stockton	140	3592	1291	247	96	41	.952
Visalia	140	3583	1440	207	123	44	.960	Bakersfield	139	3632	1346	257	99	24	.951

Triple Play—Fresno.

INDIVIDUAL FIELDING
(Ten or More Games)

*Throws lefthanded.

FIRST BASEMEN

Player and Club	G.	PO.	A.	E.	DP.	Pct.	Player and Club	G.	PO.	A.	E.	DP.	Pct.
DeCaminada, Vis*	21	146	10	0	21	1.000	Easom, Reno	15	116	2	2	12	.983
Cornell, Fresno	10	79	2	0	5	1.000	Lagunas, San Jose	14	102	10	2	7	.982
Greer, Modesto	69	506	25	4	39	.993	Ziegler, Visalia	20	151	11	3	9	.982
Van Lue, San Jose*	82	691	34	7	54	.990	Estes, Bakersfield	15	94	8	2	8	.981
GOODSON, Fresno	.125	1121	55	14	84	.988	Dickerson, Visalia	50	383	19	9	33	.978
Gagliano, Reno	22	159	8	2	9	.988	R. Johnson, Reno	93	701	49	17	63	.978
Gordon, Modesto	64	460	32	6	27	.988	Eargle, Lodi	52	393	36	10	24	.977
Kyle, Reno*	10	75	3	1	3	.987	Homik, Bakersfield	48	363	26	10	31	.975
Nichols, Lodi*	91	642	46	9	54	.987	Moore, San Jose*	46	395	17	11	22	.974
Dodder, Bak*	68	535	33	8	42	.986	Cabell, Stockton	114	803	80	26	69	.971
Fritz, Visalia*	58	446	33	8	46	.984	Stafford, Stockton*	28	195	15	8	13	.963

Triple Play—Goodson.

(Fewer Than Ten Games)

Player and Club	G.	PO.	A.	E.	DP.	Pct.	Player and Club	G.	PO.	A.	E.	DP.	Pct.
Howard, Visalia*	6	40	1	0	6	1.000	Miller, Fresno	7	53	2	1	4	.982
Boyer, Modesto	4	26	1	0	2	1.000	Buckner, Bak	6	41	0	1	1	.976
Duncan, San Jose	2	17	1	0	1	1.000	Parks, Modesto	5	29	2	1	4	.969
Pietila, Reno	3	16	0	0	0	1.000	Libran, Lodi	4	28	2	1	1	.968
Kirkland, Modesto	1	12	0	0	1	1.000	Stark, Modesto*	3	25	1	1	2	.963
Turigliatto, Sto	1	5	2	0	0	1.000	Theodore, Visalia	3	22	0	1	2	.957
Creola, Stockton	1	5	0	0	1	1.000	Putz, Modesto	3	19	2	1	4	.955
Darwin, Bak	9	81	5	1	4	.989	Elliott, Lodi	1	8	0	1	0	.889

SECOND BASEMEN

Player and Club	G.	PO.	A.	E.	DP.	Pct.	Player and Club	G.	PO.	A.	E.	DP.	Pct
Kirkland, Modesto	20	48	42	1	7	.989	Timmons, Visalia	79	159	229	16	54	.960
Stalger, Visalia	27	56	75	2	18	.985	O'Donnell, San Jose	17	23	45	3	7	.958
Lagunas, San Jose	15	32	38	2	12	.972	DiSarcina, Lodi	98	171	267	20	46	.956
Roos, San Jose	45	89	120	6	17	.972	Easom, Reno	46	86	114	10	17	.952
Dunn, Stockton	41	95	94	6	16	.969	Cook, Fresno	108	222	317	27	58	.952
Huckle, Visalia	13	25	36	2	4	.968	Wright, San Jose	12	28	50	5	5	.940
RANDALL, Bak	96	174	272	15	51	.967	Gray, Stockton	74	94	145	19	25	.936
Martin, Stockton	26	46	64	4	9	.965	Collins, Visalia	23	42	54	7	13	.932
Pullman, Fresno	27	60	76	5	7	.965	Boyles, Reno	33	58	68	10	19	.926
Shaughnessy, Reno	32	73	86	6	15	.964	Ambrose, Reno	15	32	35	7	5	.905
Parks, San Jose	44	97	132	9	24	.962	Jakubs, Lodi	33	59	65	14	13	.899
Thompson, Modesto	121	293	283	23	57	.962	Buckner, Bak	21	34	44	9	7	.897
Southard, Reno	17	38	35	3	10	.961	Harrison, Bak	24	42	52	13	12	.879

Triple Play—Cook.

(Fewer Than Ten Games)

Player and Club	G.	PO.	A.	E.	DP.	Pct.	Player and Club	G.	PO.	A.	E.	DP.	Pct.
Manahan, Bak	2	3	4	0	0	1.000	Libran, Lodi	7	22	19	2	3	.953
Reeve, Stockton	1	4	1	0	1	1.000	Stitzel, Visalia	7	11	20	2	5	.939
Marion, Modesto	2	2	2	0	0	1.000	Souza, Stockton	3	2	10	1	0	.923
Medina, Lodi	2	2	1	0	0	1.000	Aristimuno, Fresno	8	24	19	4	6	.915
Phillips, Fresno	1	2	0	0	0	1.000	Knight, Lodi	8	13	22	4	2	.897
Del Orbe, Stockton	1	1	0	0	0	1.000	Ruberto, Lodi	1	5	3	1	1	.889
Parks, Modesto	1	0	1	0	0	1.000							

THIRD BASEMEN

Player and Club	G.	PO.	A.	E.	DP.	Pct.	Player and Club	G.	PO.	A.	E.	DP.	Pct.
Pullman, Fresno	14	7	20	0	3	1.000	Stoligrosz, Reno	62	30	115	15	3	.906
Vidrio, Lodi	17	9	18	1	1	.964	Trombino, Modesto	11	7	12	2	2	.905
Easom, Reno	11	10	14	1	4	.960	Manahan, Bak	24	14	42	6	3	.903
Stalger, Visalia	11	6	17	1	4	.958	Mohler, Fresno	110	88	199	31	14	.903
Lagunas, San Jose	73	54	111	9	9	.948	Medina, Lodi	44	30	65	11	2	.896
Ziegler, Visalia	10	6	11	1	1	.944	Kirkland, Modesto	19	9	25	4	1	.895
Reeve, Stockton	20	32	95	3	1	.941	Weaver, Reno	18	12	28	5	2	.889
Boyer, Modesto	58	48	103	10	7	.938	Gagliano, Reno	12	3	20	3	0	.885
Jakubs, Lodi	29	18	41	4	2	.937	Plant, Visalia	103	70	169	32	14	.882
Ballard, Modesto	27	20	52	5	3	.935	Libran, Lodi	45	36	70	16	6	.869
Pietila, Reno	43	40	74	8	7	.934	Buckner, Bak	16	12	27	6	1	.867
Dunn, Stockton	91	66	140	15	17	.932	Souza, Stockton	10	5	7	2	0	.857
CUMMINGS, Bak	94	65	161	17	15	.930	Aristimuno, Fresno	15	4	20	5	0	.828
Forsch, Modesto	16	19	19	3	1	.927	Wright, San Jose	13	7	14	5	0	.808
Duncan, San Jose	59	31	120	12	8	.926	Winters, Stockton	30	21	40	15	2	.803
Putz, Modesto	12	4	18	2	2	.917	Arendell, Lodi	16	7	20	11	3	.711
Lacy, Bakersfield	12	7	24	3	5	.912							

Triple Play—Mohler.

THIRD BASEMEN—Continued
(Fewer Than Ten Games)

Player and Club	G.	PO.	A.	E.	DP.	Pct.	Player and Club	G.	PO.	A.	E.	DP.	Pct.
Parks, Modesto	7	3	10	0	1	1.000	Coodson, Fresno	1	0	2	0	1	1.000
Globokar, Visalia	6	4	4	0	0	1.000	Marion, Modesto	8	2	18	1	2	.952
Stitzel, Visalia	5	3	4	0	0	1.000	Timmons, Visalia	5	2	6	1	0	.889
DiSarcina, Lodi	4	2	4	0	1	1.000	Stureman, Visalia	8	4	4	2	0	.800
Miller, Fresno	2	2	3	0	1	1.000	Jacobsen, Fresno	1	1	1	2	0	.500
Burrows, San Jose	2	1	4	0	0	1.000	Crichton, San Jose	3	0	1	1	0	.500
Knight, Lodi	2	1	1	0	0	1.000							

SHORTSTOPS

Player and Club	G.	PO.	A.	E.	DP.	Pct.	Player and Club	G.	PO.	A.	E.	DP.	Pct.
Nordbrook, Stockton	21	37	53	3	3	.968	Reeve, Stockton	12	15	28	4	4	.915
Kirkland, Modesto	71	89	181	15	27	.947	Abreu, Modesto	70	81	184	25	22	.914
Libran, Lodi	63	105	147	14	27	.947	Stitzel, Visalia	12	18	33	5	8	.911
Staiger, Visalia	38	58	102	9	19	.947	Gray, Stockton	26	43	51	10	9	.904
Collins, Visalia	42	56	135	12	27	.941	Del Orbe, Stockton	31	45	74	13	8	.902
Vidrio, Lodi	79	130	201	23	29	.935	Clark, Reno	57	62	157	24	24	.901
Huckle, Visalia	24	35	65	7	14	.935	Cummings, Bak	22	20	51	9	7	.888
Pullins, Bak	11	18	24	3	7	.933	Souza, Stockton	33	31	68	13	16	.884
Ambrose, Reno	13	21	33	4	9	.931	Lacy, Bakersfield	111	182	267	63	45	.877
LIGHTFOOT, S Jose	134	190	389	46	57	.926	Hill, Visalia	28	31	79	16	18	.873
Gagliano, Reno	63	68	184	20	28	.926	Pullman, Fresno	12	18	39	9	3	.864
Aristimuno, Fresno	48	77	157	19	22	.925	Martin, Stockton	31	41	64	18	18	.854
Phillips, Fresno	84	131	264	34	48	.921							

(Fewer Than Ten Games)

Player and Club	G.	PO.	A.	E.	DP.	Pct.	Player and Club	G.	PO.	A.	E.	DP.	Pct.
Shaughnessy, Reno	5	7	17	0	4	1.000	Lagunas, San Jose	1	1	0	0		1.000
Roos, San Jose	3	2	8	0	1	1.000	Wright, San Jose	3	2	16	1	1	.947
Randall, Bak	1	2	2	0	1	1.000	Pietila, Reno	4	6	5	2	1	.846
Boyer, Modesto	2	0	4	0	0	1.000	Ballard, Modesto	6	5	15	4	1	.833
Jakubs, Lodi	1	2	2	0	1	1.000	Parks, San Jose	1	0	0	1	0	.000

OUTFIELDERS

Player and Club	G.	PO.	A.	E.	DP.	Pct.	Player and Club	G.	PO.	A.	E.	DP.	Pct.
Putz, Modesto	69	77	3	0	0	1.000	Finlay, Lodi	59	97	7	5	1	.954
Bennett, Modesto	35	44	5	0	1	1.000	O'Connor, Stockton	19	18	2	1	1	.952
Vidrio, Lodi	14	17	1	0	1	1.000	Estes, Bakersfield	33	37	2	2	0	.951
Chapman, Lodi	12	13	0	0	0	1.000	Bosch, Fresno*	75	127	9	7	1	.951
Buckner, Bak	12	11	1	0	0	1.000	Thomas, Reno	104	148	7	8	1	.951
CRICHTON, S Jose	131	259	6	3	0	.989	Brooks, Modesto*	63	83	3	5	1	.945
Ambrose, Reno	83	127	9	2	2	.986	Watts, Stockton	13	12	5	1	0	.944
McGrew, Reno	65	128	4	2	0	.985	Robinson, Lodi	117	182	17	12	3	.943
Weaver, Reno	46	52	3	1	0	.982	Hill, Visalia	55	99	0	6	0	.943
Aristimuno, Fresno	30	47	4	1	0	.981	Fritz, Visalia*	31	30	3	2	1	.943
Nelson, San Jose	119	157	7	4	1	.976	Prieto, San Jose	32	47	2	3	1	.942
Stillman, Bak*	100	139	3	4	0	.973	Ziegler, Visalia	64	62	3	4	0	.942
Theodore, Visalia	118	186	18	6	0	.971	Darwin, Bakersfield	71	59	4	4	1	.940
Adams, Visalia	49	63	2	2	0	.970	Hairston, Modesto	14	15	0	1	0	.938
Woolsey, Fresno*	85	125	4	4	1	.970	Moore, San Jose*	58	96	7	7	1	.936
Brown, Stockton	140	274	15	9	3	.966	Johnson, Bak	111	135	5	10	2	.933
Elliott, Lodi	126	233	21	9	3	.966	Miller, Fresno	70	82	9	7	0	.929
Drew, San Jose	75	106	5	4	0	.965	Brown, Fresno	26	25	1	2	0	.929
Bond, Reno	105	151	13	6	3	.965	Cornell, Fresno	34	23	1	2	0	.923
Greer, Modesto	50	67	5	3	0	.960	Canada, Bakersfield	90	106	10	10	3	.921
Corona, Stockton	62	89	4	4	1	.959	Matthews, Fresno	104	183	15	15	3	.908
Kazmarek, Visalia	115	150	10	7	2	.958	O'Brien, Lodi*	13	17	0	2	0	.895
Parks, Modesto	43	57	9	3	2	.957	Martin, Stockton	40	41	7	6	1	.889
J. Roque, Modesto	135	267	12	13	2	.955	McBride, Modesto	22	26	1	4	0	.871
Eargle, Lodi	84	101	6	5	1	.955	Cabell, Stockton	27	41	1	7	0	.857
Winters, Stockton	89	115	10	6	0	.954	Beitey, Stockton	30	26	4	5	1	.857

(Fewer Than Ten Games)

Player and Club	G.	PO.	A.	E.	DP.	Pct.	Player and Club	G.	PO.	A.	E.	DP.	Pct.
Souza, Stockton	9	13	1	0	0	1.000	Brown, Visalia*	2	2	0	0	0	1.000
Boyles, Reno	9	13	0	0	0	1.000	Gordon, Modesto	2	2	0	0	0	1.000
Wright, San Jose	9	9	1	0	0	1.000	L. Johnson, Reno	2	2	0	0	0	1.000
Southard, Reno	7	7	0	0	0	1.000	Hines, Stockton	1	1	0	0	0	1.000
Kyle, Reno*	6	7	0	0	0	1.000	Hoban, Reno*	1	1	0	0	0	1.000
Snyder, San Jose	6	7	0	0	0	1.000	Upton, Visalia	1	1	0	0	0	1.000
Medina, Lodi	5	7	0	0	0	1.000	Forsch, Modesto	1	0	1	0	0	1.000
Rankhorn, Reno	3	6	0	0	0	1.000	Kinnaugh, Fresno	5	8	1	1	0	.900
McGhee, Modesto	3	6	0	0	0	1.000	Timmons, Visalia	5	7	1	1	0	.889
DeCaminada, Vis*	4	5	0	0	0	1.000	Turigliatto, Sto	9	8	0	2	0	.800
Homoly, Fresno	3	4	1	0	0	1.000	Jakubs, Lodi	6	4	0	1	0	.800
Manahan, Bak	4	3	0	0	0	1.000							

CATCHERS

Player and Club	G.	PO.	A.	E.	DP.	PB.	Pct.
Cousins, Reno ...	12	96	8	0	2	1	1.000
Schofield, S J ...	11	77	7	0	0	4	1.000
Cappelli, S J ..	22	175	18	2	0	8	.990
McGHEE, Mod ..	82	713	55	8	5	20	.990
Wukits, Stockton .	60	505	50	6	2	9	.989
Allen, Visalia ..	29	188	14	3	0	12	.985
L. Johnson, Reno	85	745	63	14	8	25	.983
Peden, Modesto .	14	99	10	2	0	5	.982
Harrell, Fresno .	27	232	31	5	5	6	.981
Parks, Modesto ..	41	336	25	7	3	10	.981
Upton, Visalia .	28	234	18	5	0	5	.981
Ashby, Reno	38	321	27	7	2	10	.980
Robles, Bak	98	955	63	23	8	11	.978
Looper, Modesto .	18	158	17	4	1	3	.978
Turigliatto, Sto ..	76	639	57	16	6	25	.978
Cotton, Visalia ..	77	574	58	15	5	19	.977
Baca, Lodi	72	564	46	15	6	7	.976
Homik, Bak	45	420	34	12	5	12	.974
Iskierka, Vis	14	101	6	3	0	7	.973
Burrows, S J	107	836	83	27	6	23	.971
Jacobsen, Fresno .	25	191	29	7	1	5	.969
Brown, Fresno ..	87	688	79	25	7	17	.968
Gregg, Lodi	54	390	41	16	2	18	.964
Boyles, Reno ...	12	101	6	4	0	12	.964
Jakubs, Lodi	17	106	4	5	0	14	.957
Felderman, Sto ..	11	71	5	5	1	5	.938

Triple Play—Brown.

(Fewer Than Ten Games)

Player and Club	G.	PO.	A.	E.	DP.	PB.	Pct.
Hughes, Bak	4	49	1	0	1	1	1.000
Bishop, Visalia ..	2	20	2	0	0	1	1.000
Dickerson, Vis ..	3	15	1	0	0	0	1.000
Smith, San Jose .	1	2	0	0	0	0	1.000
W. Preston, Lodi	9	70	4	3	0	3	.961
Creola, Stockton .	9	58	6	3	2	2	.955
Rivera, San Jose .	3	18	2	1	0	1	.952
Vicente, Mod	2	13	3	1	0	1	.941

PITCHERS

Player and Club	G.	PO.	A.	E.	DP.	Pct.
MOFFITT, Fresno .	18	7	23	0	3	1.000
WHISMAN, San Jose	34	6	24	0	1	1.000
Fitzgerald, Stockton .	33	5	17	0	1	1.000
Hoban, Reno*	25	3	19	0	1	1.000
Howell, Reno*	33	6	15	0	2	1.000
Angelini, San Jose* .	21	4	17	0	1	1.000
Pierce, Stockton ...	29	5	12	0	1	1.000
Strom, Visalia* ...	10	1	15	0	0	1.000
Sinclair, Lodi	48	0	16	0	0	1.000
Williamson, Sto	19	3	12	0	0	1.000
Garcia, Lodi	13	3	10	0	0	1.000
Biko, Reno	28	5	7	0	0	1.000
Gambero, San Jose ..	12	4	8	0	0	1.000
Chlan, San Jose ...	13	2	10	0	0	1.000
Foderaro, Visalia ..	27	5	6	0	1	1.000
Johnson, Fresno	20	3	7	0	1	1.000
Morrell, Lodi*	11	1	8	0	0	1.000
Mulcahey, Lodi	20	3	5	0	1	1.000
Ford, Modesto	13	2	5	0	1	1.000
Daboll, Modesto ...	21	1	6	0	0	1.000
Davies, Fresno	10	3	3	0	0	1.000
Myers, San Jose	20	0	6	0	0	1.000
Jaster, Modesto* ...	10	0	6	0	0	1.000
Esposito, Visalia* ..	17	1	4	0	0	1.000
Lolich, Visalia	11	3	1	0	0	1.000
Katawczik, Lodi* ...	23	1	3	0	0	1.000
Tyler, Lodi*	12	0	3	0	0	1.000
Acosta, Bakersfield .	10	0	1	0	0	1.000
Ulrich, Fresno	28	10	22	1	2	.970
Sawyer, Reno	23	10	21	1	0	.969
Capra, Visalia	24	11	18	1	0	.967
Sherzer, Lodi	23	10	17	1	0	.964
Warden, San Jose *.	27	6	21	1	2	.964
Stark, Modesto* ...	33	6	20	1	0	.963
Crain, Reno	30	5	19	1	1	.960
Bishop, Visalia	29	13	9	1	0	.957
White, Modesto* ...	25	4	17	1	1	.955
Filbeck, Reno	17	8	12	1	0	.952
Putnam, Visalia ...	31	9	30	2	0	.951
Rauch, Bakersfield ..	25	5	14	1	1	.950
Dawson, Bakersfield .	28	11	25	2	0	.947
Camy, Visalia	19	13	22	2	3	.946
Johnson, Stockton .	31	7	10	1	0	.944
J. Allen, Bak*	25	3	13	1	0	.941
Hood, Stockton* ...	28	12	31	3	2	.935
Kokor, Fresno	52	5	9	1	1	.933
DeBenedetti, S J ..	12	3	11	1	0	.933
Demery, San Jose* ..	11	4	9	1	0	.929
Sibley, Fresno*	33	1	12	1	2	.929
Wallace, Fresno	38	4	21	2	0	.926
D. Allen, Bak*	17	4	21	2	0	.926
J. Preston, Lodi ...	28	6	6	1	0	.923
Bach, Modesto	19	4	8	1	0	.923
Hofferd, San Jose ..	24	2	10	1	1	.923
Gilje, Bakersfield* .	28	7	27	3	1	.919
Winfield, Reno	37	3	8	1	1	.917
Keister, Stockton* .	28	6	26	3	2	.914
Walker, Stockton ...	21	9	12	2	0	.913
Sielicki, Fresno* ...	28	4	17	2	0	.913
Plodinec, Modesto .	39	7	13	2	0	.909
Cowgill, Fresno	26	7	13	2	1	.909
Dermody, Bak	25	4	6	1	0	.909
Fitzgerald, Visalia .	28	3	7	1	0	.909
Bartlett, Visalia ...	12	0	10	1	1	.909
Meschuk, Bak	24	8	11	2	0	.905
Tsoukalas, Reno* ...	38	6	13	2	4	.905
Meredith, Modesto* .	28	3	16	2	2	.905
Waldeck, Fresno ...	22	8	20	3	3	.903
Stripling, Modesto .	11	10	7	2	0	.895
Wihtol, Visalia	14	5	11	2	2	.889
Green, Lodi	31	5	3	1	0	.889
Isom, San Jose* ...	10	3	5	1	0	.889
Brookens, San Jose .	30	5	18	3	0	.885
Albury, Lodi*	17	2	12	2	0	.875
Young, Lodi	17	5	2	1	0	.875
James, Reno	33	2	5	1	0	.875
Graves, Bakersfield .	22	2	5	1	0	.875
Krawiecki, Lodi ...	15	2	5	1	1	.875
McVay, Modesto ...	11	0	7	1	1	.875
Bielski, Lodi	22	11	30	6	4	.872
Jefferson, Stockton .	26	14	20	6	3	.850
Sanders, San Jose ..	27	9	19	5	3	.848
Ballinger, Reno ...	27	5	23	5	1	.848
Stensland, Mod* ...	17	4	7	2	0	.846
Hansen, San Jose ..	35	2	9	2	0	.846
Rau, Bakersfield* ..	15	4	11	3	2	.833
Weems, Stockton ...	48	2	13	3	1	.833
Price, Bakersfield* .	20	4	6	2	1	.833
Haines, Visalia	21	2	3	1	0	.833
James, Bakersfield* .	24	7	17	5	1	.828
Frye, Bakersfield ..	36	3	11	3	1	.824
Koch, Modesto	15	2	12	3	2	.824
Hardy, Lodi	11	8	5	3	0	.813
Sheppard, Visalia ..	17	1	7	2	0	.800
F. Roque, Modesto .	52	0	8	2	0	.800
Figueroa, Fresno ...	14	0	8	2	1	.800
O'Brien, Lodi*	12	2	13	5	0	.750
Gonzalez, Mod* ...	10	2	6	3	0	.727
Sosa, Fresno	21	3	10	6	1	.684
Taylor, Lodi*	21	1	3	2	0	.667
Coleman, Stockton .	11	1	1	1	0	.667
Maine, Visalia	11	0	1	1	0	.500

PITCHERS—Continued
(Fewer Than Ten Games)

Player and Club	G.	PO.	A.	E.	DP.	Pct.
Schwartz, Reno* ...	5	1	10	0	1	1.000
Sterling, Visalia ...	5	2	8	0	1	1.000
Stewart, Visalia* ...	7	1	8	0	0	1.000
Downen, San Jose ...	6	2	6	0	0	1.000
Rivera, Fresno	4	2	5	0	0	1.000
Zinniger, Lodi* ...	5	1	6	0	1	1.000
Harkey, Visalia ...	5	0	7	0	0	1.000
Llanos, Modesto ...	6	0	6	0	0	1.000
Simendinger, Sto ...	8	0	5	0	2	1.000
Karp, San Jose ...	8	1	3	0	0	1.000
Tidrow, Reno	6	1	3	0	0	1.000
Brenner, Visalia ...	3	1	3	0	0	1.000
Poteete, Bak	1	1	3	0	0	1.000
Thompson, Lodi ...	5	0	4	0	0	1.000
Alger, Modesto* ...	3	0	4	0	0	1.000
Nielsen, San Jose* ...	8	0	3	0	0	1.000
Ervin, Bakersfield* .	6	0	3	0	0	1.000
Grant, Stockton	1	0	3	0	0	1.000
Welker, Fresno*	6	1	1	0	0	1.000
Smith, Lodi	8	0	2	0	0	1.000
Leonard, Visalia* ..	5	0	1	0	1	1.000
Dorn, Bakersfield* .	4	0	1	0	1	1.000
Ewing, Visalia*	8	0	8	2	0	.800
Queen, Reno*	8	1	3	1	1	.800
Furlong, Visalia ...	3	1	3	1	0	.800
Matte, Visalia	6	0	4	1	0	.800
Whiteside, Lodi	6	2	2	2	0	.667
Murray, San Jose ..	8	1	1	1	0	.667
Kern, Reno	4	0	2	1	0	.667
Bloom, Stockton ...	7	0	1	1	0	.500
Brown, Visalia*	6	0	1	1	0	.500

The following players do not have any recorded accepted chances at the positions indicated; therefore, are not listed in the fielding averages for those particular positions: Bach, of; Bird, p; Bishop, 2b; Chapman, 3b; DiSarcina, ss; Gardner, p; Giresi*, p; J. Howell*, of; Nichols*, p; Oliva, p; Plant, of; Stark*, of; Vicente, of; L. Wright*, p.

PITCHERS' RECORDS

(Leading Qualifiers for Earned-Run Average Leadership—140 or More Innings)

*Throws lefthanded.

Pitcher—Club	G.	GS.	CG.	ShO.	W.	L.	Sv.	Pct.	IP.	H.	R.	ER.	HR.	BB.	Int. BB.	HB.	SO.	WP.	ERA.
Dawson, Bak ...	28	27	9	4	17	6	0	.739	182	134	72	50	10	100	0	4	244	12	2.47
Hood, Stockton* ..	28	27	13	5	10	10	0	.500	178	165	78	57	13	66	0	6	196	9	2.88
Gilje, Bak* ...	28	24	11	0	14	8	1	.636	183	151	78	60	14	69	6	5	235	7	2.95
Camy, Visalia ...	19	19	13	4	12	7	0	.632	148	130	61	49	9	45	3	7	142	9	2.98
Stark, Modesto* ..	33	24	15	5	14	9	1	.609	209	191	85	72	14	51	2	9	202	7	3.10
Ulrich, Fresno ...	28	19	4	1	7	7	0	.500	142	150	78	54	14	45	4	4	134	3	3.42
Keister, Stockton* .	28	25	4	3	7	12	0	.368	149	183	89	59	9	71	3	8	127	12	3.56
Meredith, Mod* ..	28	28	6	4	10	8	0	.556	158	146	82	64	16	67	0	2	193	13	3.65
Jefferson, Sto ...	26	26	9	3	8	16	0	.333	157	129	89	64	6	123	0	8	177	18	3.67
E. Fitzgerald, Sto .	33	13	4	0	4	6	0	.400	144	128	77	59	13	85	1	1	177	12	3.69

Departmental Leaders: G—Kokor, Roque, 52; GS—Meredith, 28; CG—Stark, 15; ShO—Hood, Stark, 5; W—Dawson, 17; L—Jefferson, 16; Sv—Kokor, Roque, 12; Pct.—D. Allen, .923; IP—Stark, 209; H—Stark, 191; R—Ballinger, 94; ER—Preston, 74; HR—J. Fitzgerald, 19; BB—Jefferson, 123; IBB—Frye, 11; HB—Stark, 9; SO—Dawson, 244; WP—Ballinger, 26.

(All Pitchers—Listed Alphabetically)

Pitcher—Club	G.	GS.	CG.	ShO.	W.	L.	Sv.	Pct.	IP.	H.	R.	ER.	HR.	BB.	Int. BB.	HB.	SO.	WP.	ERA.
Acosta, Bak ...	10	0	0	0	1	0	1	.000	17	13	5	3	0	11	0	0	23	3	1.59
Albury, Lodi* ...	17	10	6	0	5	6	0	.455	92	103	54	46	10	36	0	1	80	4	4.50
Alger, Modesto* ..	3	0	0	0	1	0	0	1.000	5	5	1	1	0	6	0	0	5	0	1.80
D. Allen, Bak* ...	17	17	8	2	12	1	0	.923	122	101	47	40	7	44	2	2	143	3	2.95
J. Allen, Bak* ...	25	1	1	1	1	2	8	.333	48	32	9	8	3	19	3	1	55	5	1.50
Angelini, S Jose* .	21	17	7	2	8	8	0	.500	129	115	47	38	7	34	2	3	136	4	2.65
Bach, Modesto ...	19	18	4	0	6	6	0	.455	114	116	57	45	16	25	1	2	96	5	3.55
Ballinger, Reno ...	27	27	4	1	9	8	0	.529	147	128	91	71	13	114	1	8	180	26	4.35
Bartlett, Visalia .	12	9	2	1	2	5	0	.286	58	60	33	24	4	23	1	7	45	1	3.72
Bielski, Lodi ...	22	19	5	0	4	13	0	.235	123	151	85	50	5	51	3	3	70	11	4.35
Biko, Reno ...	28	2	0	0	6	4	2	.600	71	85	50	44	11	43	2	3	70	3	5.58
Bird, San Jose ..	3	2	0	0	0	2	0	.000	10	10	10	7	1	3	0	0	14	0	6.30
Bishop, Visalia ..	29	2	1	0	6	3	11	.667	74	51	27	19	6	44	0	4	68	8	2.31
Bloom, Stockton ..	7	0	0	0	0	1	0	.000	17	15	21	17	3	19	0	3	16	2	9.00
Brenner, Visalia .	3	2	0	0	1	1	0	.500	9	13	9	8	1	5	0	1	4	1	8.00
Brookens, S Jose .	30	7	1	1	4	2	2	.667	95	81	42	33	5	49	3	3	91	11	3.13
Brown, Visalia* ..	6	0	0	0	0	0	9	.000	9	15	13	11	3	5	0	0	9	3	11.00
Camy, Visalia ...	19	19	13	4	12	7	0	.632	148	130	61	49	9	45	3	7	142	9	2.98
Capra, Visalia ...	24	14	6	2	9	5	3	.643	129	106	56	46	15	30	0	1	157	8	3.21
Chlan, San Jose ..	13	6	4	2	6	0	1	1.000	60	37	11	11	1	21	0	2	48	4	1.65
Coleman, Stockton .11		0	0	0	0	2	3	.000	17	23	24	19	3	16	2	1	13	0	10.06
Cowgill, Fresno ..	26	21	6	0	7	8	1	.467	135	158	80	61	12	69	0	6	81	6	4.07
Crain, Reno ...	30	14	3	2	7	6	3	.538	93	95	53	38	4	37	3	4	83	3	3.68
Daboll, Modesto ..	10	0	0	0	4	2	4	.667	60	43	14	10	3	15	0	1	76	4	1.50
Davies, Fresno ...	10	10	0	0	1	7	0	.125	39	44	44	32	4	31	0	1	34	5	7.38
Dawson, Bak ...	28	27	9	4	17	6	0	.739	182	134	72	50	10	100	0	4	244	12	2.47
DeBenedetti, S J ..	12	11	7	4	8	1	0	.889	88	72	20	17	3	19	2	0	58	1	1.74
Demery, San Jose* .	11	10	3	2	3	4	0	.429	76	59	25	15	1	28	3	3	114	8	1.78
Dermody, Bak ...	25	0	0	0	4	3	9	.571	42	45	24	17	5	17	6	1	32	2	3.64
Dorn, Bakersfield* .	4	0	0	0	0	0	0	.000	5	5	1	1	0	3	0	0	4	0	1.80
Downen, San Jose .	6	6	1	1	1	3	0	.250	29	29	18	11	3	19	0	0	26	2	3.41
Ervin, Bak* ...	6	1	0	0	0	0	1	.000	7	13	7	7	1	2	0	0	11	1	9.00

Pitcher—Club	G.	GS.	CG.	ShO.	W.	L.	Sv.	Pct.	IP.	H.	R.	ER.	HR.	BB.	Int.BB.	HB.	SO.	WP.	ERA.
Esposito, Visalia*	.17	1	0	0	0	2	1	.000	40	34	29	23	6	13	1	3	37	7	5.18
Ewing, Visalia*	.. 8	8	1	0	4	2	0	.667	51	52	36	26	5	38	0	3	50	4	4.59
Figueroa, Fresno	.14	5	1	0	1	5	0	.167	51	55	27	25	1	18	1	1	47	2	4.41
Filbeck, Reno	...17	14	2	2	8	5	0	.615	97	87	46	36	8	30	0	2	78	2	3.34
E. Fitzgerald, Sto	.33	13	4	0	4	6	0	.400	144	128	77	59	13	85	1	1	177	12	3.69
J. Fitzgerald, Vis	.28	9	0	0	4	7	1	.364	78	84	52	38	19	46	0	3	60	7	4.38
Foderaro, Visalia	.27	2	0	0	2	4	3	.333	55	62	35	29	11	34	0	6	67	1	4.75
Ford, Modesto	..13	0	0	0	1	3	0	.000	23	21	8	4	0	5	1	0	42	0	1.29
Frye, Bakersfield	.36	2	0	0	8	6	6	.571	80	69	41	32	4	41	11	1	84	4	3.60
Furlong, Visalia	.. 8	3	0	0	1	0	0	1.000	8	7	7	6	1	5	0	0	13	0	6.75
Gambero, San Jose	.12	11	1	1	5	2	0	.714	62	61	30	24	4	18	1	0	46	5	3.48
Garcia, Lodi	..13	13	5	0	3	6	0	.333	84	78	46	39	7	53	2	4	108	12	4.18
Gardner, Lodi	 8	1	0	0	1	1	0	.500	13	25	15	15	2	6	0	1	14	3	10.38
Gilje, Bak*	28	24	11	0	14	8	1	.636	183	151	78	60	14	69	6	5	235	7	2.95
Giresi, Stockton*	.. 3	1	0	0	0	0	0	.000	9	9	7	1	0	10	0	0	12	1	7.00
Gonzalez, Mod*	...10	10	1	0	2	4	0	.333	49	57	34	24	4	26	2	1	27	1	4.41
Grant, Stockton	.. 1	0	0	0	0	0	0	.000	4	5	2	1	0	1	1	0	3	0	2.25
Graves, Bak	22	0	0	0	1	1	2	.500	34	48	27	22	2	15	1	2	29	3	5.82
Green, Lodi	31	8	1	0	2	6	1	.250	94	85	50	47	6	62	7	5	119	18	4.50
Haines, Visalia	..21	2	0	0	1	4	2	.200	51	73	50	46	9	26	1	6	49	3	8.12
Hansen, San Jose	.35	0	0	0	7	3	7	.700	63	39	22	13	2	29	6	4	50	6	1.86
Hardy, Lodi	11	11	8	1	3	8	0	.273	83	95	52	39	2	22	1	2	77	5	4.23
Harkey, Visalia	.. 5	1	0	0	1	0	0	1.000	14	14	6	6	2	6	1	1	9	2	3.86
Hoban, Reno*	25	19	5	0	10	9	0	.526	134	121	68	56	10	86	0	1	145	18	3.76
Hofferd, San Jose	.24	10	4	1	3	5	1	.375	93	89	43	33	8	31	1	7	91	7	3.19
Hood, Stockton*	.28	27	13	5	10	10	0	.500	178	165	78	57	13	66	0	6	196	9	2.88
Howell, Reno*	...33	10	5	0	4	7	9	.364	103	97	47	38	6	36	1	1	94	5	3.32
Isom, San Jose*	...10	10	0	0	3	3	0	.500	47	44	28	24	3	38	0	0	36	9	4.60
D. James, Bak*	...24	20	6	1	6	5	0	.545	130	121	72	50	12	62	3	8	158	16	3.46
W. James, Reno	..33	0	0	0	4	2	11	.667	63	34	8	3	1	9	0	0	71	1	0.43
Jaster, Modesto*	..10	7	3	1	3	3	0	.500	52	46	29	22	5	18	2	2	49	6	3.81
Jefferson, Sto	...26	26	9	3	8	16	0	.333	157	129	89	64	6	123	0	8	177	18	3.67
D. Johnson, Sto	..31	2	0	0	4	4	0	.500	76	56	35	23	2	33	2	4	81	6	2.72
P. Johnson, Fresno	.20	0	0	0	2	1	0	.667	39	29	17	13	3	19	3	3	39	4	3.00
Karp, San Jose	.. 8	4	0	0	1	2	0	.333	22	28	20	12	2	10	2	3	15	2	4.91
Katawczik, Lodi*	.23	0	0	0	4	1	2	.800	32	30	15	13	5	21	2	1	23	5	3.66
Keister, Stockton*	.28	25	4	3	7	12	0	.368	149	163	89	59	9	71	3	8	127	12	3.56
Kern, Reno	 4	0	0	0	0	0	0	.000	15	9	12	10	0	20	0	3	20	4	6.00
Koch, Modesto	..15	12	3	1	4	5	0	.444	82	83	46	30	10	33	2	4	95	10	3.29
Kokor, Fresno	...52	0	0	0	8	4	12	.667	101	66	27	18	3	37	5	3	120	1	1.60
Krawiecki, Lodi	..15	1	0	0	2	2	0	.500	46	68	39	24	4	14	1	1	22	2	4.70
Leonard, Visalia*	. 5	3	0	0	1	0	0	1.000	14	11	8	6	1	10	0	0	13	1	3.86
Llanos, Modesto	.. 6	6	1	0	2	2	0	.500	36	37	22	18	4	8	0	1	33	0	4.50
Lolich, Visalia	..11	5	1	1	2	1	3	.667	30	26	17	14	4	6	0	3	24	1	4.20
Maine, Visalia	...11	0	0	0	0	1	0	.000	14	12	12	8	3	10	0	1	11	0	5.14
Matte, Visalia	.. 4	4	0	0	0	4	0	.000	14	21	16	16	6	13	0	1	14	1	10.29
McVay, Modesto	..11	4	1	1	4	1	0	.800	41	35	12	10	1	13	0	1	35	1	2.20
Meredith, Mod*	...28	28	6	4	10	8	0	.556	158	146	82	64	16	67	0	2	193	13	3.65
Meschuk, Bak	...24	19	5	0	9	5	0	.643	100	108	77	65	16	39	1	7	109	3	5.85
Moffitt, Fresno	..18	16	9	4	9	6	0	.600	135	91	35	24	6	23	0	6	149	8	1.60
Morrell, Lodi*	...11	7	0	0	4	4	0	.000	41	59	42	40	6	36	1	2	49	5	8.78
Mulcahey, Lodi	..20	0	0	0	1	1	4	.500	27	41	24	21	3	19	7	2	20	1	7.00
Murray, San Jose	. 8	0	0	0	2	1	0	.667	12	8	2	2	1	4	0	0	12	1	1.50
Myers, San Jose	..20	0	0	0	2	2	4	.500	46	34	11	10	3	14	4	2	58	0	1.96
Nichols, Lodi*	 1	0	0	0	0	0	0	.000	⅔	0	0	0	0	0	0	0	1	0	0.00
Nielsen, San Jose*	. 8	0	0	0	0	2	0	.000	10	11	9	9	1	5	0	1	10	1	8.10
O'Brien, Lodi*	..12	3	0	0	2	3	0	.400	58	60	49	34	6	34	0	0	21	5	5.28
Oliva, Lodi	 5	0	0	0	0	1	0	.000	7	11	12	11	2	7	0	1	10	3	14.14
Pierce, Stockton	..29	8	1	0	4	9	0	.308	107	136	75	65	11	26	2	2	96	3	5.47
Plodinec, Modesto	.39	0	0	0	5	2	8	.714	84	66	32	27	5	25	7	4	93	6	2.89
Poteete, Bak	 1	0	0	0	0	0	0	.000	4	3	4	1	0	1	0	0	3	1	2.25
J. Preston, Lodi	..28	14	1	0	4	10	0	.286	73	92	88	74	5	88	2	4	76	18	9.12
Price, Bak*	29	7	1	1	5	2	1	.714	62	65	28	21	4	20	2	1	62	7	3.05
Putnam, Visalia	.31	16	7	0	7	8	3	.467	135	148	89	67	14	58	1	1	83	13	4.47
Queen, Reno*	... 8	8	1	1	4	2	0	.667	53	43	21	18	8	26	0	1	80	6	3.06
Rau, Bakersfield*	.15	15	11	2	12	2	0	.857	113	86	34	22	5	18	3	1	140	0	1.75
Rauch, Bak	25	1	0	0	4	4	3	.500	83	68	36	26	5	41	3	2	91	6	2.82
Rivera, Fresno	... 4	3	1	1	1	2	0	.333	17	18	11	10	3	5	0	2	23	1	5.29
F. Roque, Mod	..52	0	0	0	6	6	12	.500	75	74	34	31	7	25	6	1	62	4	3.72
Sanders, San Jose	.27	12	2	1	5	8	1	.385	103	98	56	34	7	41	8	0	75	6	2.97
Sawyer, Reno	...23	19	5	2	10	5	0	.667	130	125	60	49	10	42	2	7	122	4	3.39
Schwartz, Reno*	. 5	5	2	1	2	1	0	.667	31	18	8	8	2	14	0	2	27	0	2.32
Sheppard, Visalia	.17	5	0	0	1	3	1	.250	44	46	31	27	6	27	0	4	59	3	5.52
Sherzer, Lodi	...23	19	4	0	3	14	1	.176	109	135	80	60	8	41	1	2	94	11	4.95
Sibley, Fresno*	...33	4	1	0	6	4	2	.600	75	80	35	25	3	32	2	3	54	1	3.00
Sielicki, Fresno*	.28	26	7	3	10	8	0	.556	155	172	87	64	7	50	0	2	132	7	3.72
Simendinger, Sto	.. 8	7	0	0	0	6	0	.000	27	38	33	28	3	25	0	0	24	1	9.33
Sinclair, Lodi	...48	8	3	0	3	6	11	.333	101	110	50	41	9	29	8	3	104	5	3.65
Smith, Lodi	 8	0	0	0	1	1	0	.500	13	7	4	6	1	13	3	0	9	2	4.15
Sosa, Fresno	21	15	3	1	6	8	0	.429	102	119	66	58	10	39	0	2	95	7	5.12

| | | | | | | | | | | | | | | Int. | | | | | |
Pitcher—Club	G.	GS.	CG.	ShO.	W.	L.	Sv.	Pct.	IP.	H.	R.	ER.	HR.	BB.	BB.	HB.	SO.	WP.	ERA.
Stark, Modesto* ...33	24	15	5	14	9	1		.609	209	191	85	72	14	51	2	9	202	7	3.10
Stensland, Mod* ..17	12	3	0	5	7	0		.417	85	100	58	51	14	37	4	1	75	10	5.40
Sterling, Visalia .. 5	1	0	2	2	0			.500	30	41	27	21	7	17	0	2	28	6	6.30
Stewart, Visalia* .. 7	7	0	0	2	4	0		.333	29	42	30	23	3	22	0	1	20	5	7.14
Stripling, Mod 11	9	1	1	4	3	0		.571	59	52	22	18	2	23	2	0	59	6	2.75
Strom, Visalia* ...10	10	3	1	4	5	0		.444	72	65	32	30	6	22	2	1	79	4	3.75
Taylor, Lodi* 21	7	0	0	1	4	0		.200	57	76	48	37	9	37	1	3	46	7	5.84
Thompson, Lodi ...5	1	0	0	0	2	0		.000	12	14	17	16	0	13	2	0	13	1	12.00
Tidrow, Reno 6	4	0	0	2	2	0		.500	35	35	16	10	4	12	0	0	33	1	2.57
Tsoukalas, Reno* ..38	11	3	2	2	5	4		.615	128	131	66	47	10	43	1	8	151	7	3.30
Tyler, Lodi* 12	0	0	0	0	1	2		.000	14	25	9	7	2	6	2	0	9	0	4.50
Ulrich, Fresno ...28	19	4	1	7	7	0		.500	142	150	78	54	14	45	4	4	134	3	3.42
Waldeck, Fresno ..22	19	7	1	11	4	0		.733	137	147	58	46	10	51	0	1	132	8	3.02
Walker, Stockton ..21	16	9	0	8	8	1		.500	125	113	53	39	12	39	3	2	129	7	2.81
Wallace, Fresno .. 38	0	0	0	2	4	4		.333	69	84	42	35	9	18	3	2	62	2	4.57
Warden, San Jose* .27	22	2	0	6	10	0		.375	126	148	78	57	14	59	4	5	90	6	4.07
Weems, Stockton ..48	0	0	0	5	4	6		.556	82	56	26	17	4	37	5	3	113	8	1.87
Welker, Fresno* ... 6	0	0	0	0	1	0		.000	11	14	10	7	1	8	0	0	8	5	5.73
Whisman, S Jose ..34	12	6	1	13	7	6		.650	131	108	41	34	7	37	3	3	113	9	2.34
White, Modesto* ..25	8	1	0	6	4	0		.600	91	99	43	39	4	31	2	2	106	7	3.86
Whiteside, Lodi ... 6	5	0	0	1	4	0		.200	18	21	23	24	2	28	1	1	14	6	12.00
Wihtol, Visalia ...14	13	2	2	4	6	0		.400	91	109	65	55	9	28	0	2	76	5	5.44
Williamson, Sto ...19	15	3	1	4	8	0		.333	103	102	51	34	10	30	2	1	90	3	2.97
Winfield, Reno ...37	3	0	0	5	5	6		.500	94	86	53	34	13	28	3	4	114	6	3.26
Wright, Modesto .. 5	2	0	0	1	1	0		.500	9	10	14	11	0	12	1	0	10	2	11.00
Young, Lodi 17	3	0	0	1	2	0		.333	51	67	54	51	5	51	2	4	61	7	9.00
Zinniger, Lodi* ... 5	4	1	0	2	2	0		.500	36	27	16	15	4	17	1	1	37	4	3.75

BALKS—Pierce, 4; Ballinger, Bielski, Brookens, Capra, Dawson, Dorn, Garcia, Gilje, Hood, Rauch, Sherzer, Sinclair, Stensland, Strom, Taylor, Weems, Whiteside, Wihtol, 2 each; D. Allen, Angelini, Bishop, Bloom, Camy, Chlan, E. Fitzgerald, Frye, Giresi, Green, Hardy, Isom, W. James, Jefferson, D. Johnson, Katawczik, Keister, Maine, Mulcahey, Price, Roque, Sawyer, Schwartz, Waldeck, Williamson, 1 each.

COMBINATION SHUTOUTS—Dawson-Rauch, Bakersfield; Ulrich-Johnson-Kokor, Fresno; Green-Smith-Mulcahey, Lodi; Angelini-Brookens, Gambero-Myers, San Jose; Sheppard-Bishop, Visalia.

NO-HIT GAMES—Ballinger, Reno, defeated San Jose, 4-0, July 19 (seven innings).

ALONG THE MINOR LEAGUE TRAIL . . . .

(Continued from page 473)

stand roof. The gutter broke and water cascaded down on the fans below, thoroughly dousing them in 40-degree temperatures. . . . Pawtucket (Eastern) pulled a rare triple play—the batter didn't hit the ball. Instead, the batter fanned, a runner was thrown out attempting to steal second and the relay nailed a runner from third trying to score. . . . Steve Shea, a pitcher for Buffalo (International), found a way to cure calcium deposits in his right shoulder, a run-of-the-mill malady of pitchers, but enough to end most careers. Wanna do what Steve did? He joined the Hartford Charter Oaks of the Continental Football League and later said, "The buffeting I took on that shoulder playing safety broke down the calcium and I was able to pitch again." All sore-armed pitchers who want to play pro football form a line to the right. . . . Dyar Miller figured he couldn't hit, so he discarded his catching tools and became a pitcher. On May 9, he fired a seven-inning no-hitter for Dallas-Fort Worth (Texas) over Amarillo. A good move, huh? At bat, he drove in three runs with a homer and single. . . . What's a communications gap? Try this one: Manager Billy Gardner of

(Continued on page 495)

Carolina League

CLASS A
CHAMPIONSHIP WINNERS IN PREVIOUS YEARS

1945—Danville* .... .681	1955—HP-Thomasville ... .580	1964—Kinston§ .... .572
1946—Greensboro .... .599	Danville (2nd)† .... .533	Winston-Salem§† ... .590
Raleigh (2nd)† .... .563	1956—HP-Thomasville ... .591	1965—Peninsula§ .... .597
1947—Burlington .... .613	Fayetteville (4th)†.. .523	Durham§ .... .580
Raleigh (3rd)† .... .574	1957—Durham .... .632	Tidewater† .... .528
1948—Raleigh .... .592	HP-Thomasville .... .622	1966—Kinston§ .... .547
Martinsville (2nd)† .570	1958—Danville .... .576	Winston-Salem§ ... .586
1949—Danville .... .601	Burlington (4th)† ... .511	Rocky Mount† ..... .533
Burlington (4th)† ... .500	1959—Raleigh .... .600	1967—Durham x (West.) .. .536
1950—Winston-Salem* ... .693	Wilson (2nd)† ..... .550	Raleigh (East.) .... .542
1951—Durham .... .600	1960—Greensboro‡ ...... .636	1968—Salem (West.) .... .607
Wins-Salem (2nd)† .583	Burlington .... .586	Ral-Dur (East.) .... .597
1952—Raleigh .... .581	1961—Wilson .... .594	H P-Thom. y (W.) .493
Reidsville (4th)† ... .536	1962—Durham .... .636	1969—Rocky M (East.) .. .569
1953—Raleigh .... .593	Wilson .... .600	Salem (West.) .... .542
Danville (2nd)† ... .572	Kinston (2nd)† .... .593	Ral-Dur z (East.) .. .560
1954—Fayetteville* ...... .628	1963—Kinston§ .... .538	
	Greensboro§ .... .590	
	Wilson (2nd)† ..... .535	

*Won championship and four-club playoff.   †Won four-club playoff.   ‡Won split-season playoff.
§League was divided into Eastern, Western divisions.   xWon eight-club, two-division playoff.
yWon eight-club, two-division playoff against Raleigh-Durham.
zWon eight-club, two-division playoff against Burlington.

STANDING OF CLUBS AT CLOSE OF FIRST HALF, JUNE 24

Club	W.	L.	T.	Pct.	G.B.	Club	W.	L.	T.	Pct.	G.B.
†Winston-Salem (2*) ...41	29	1	.586	....		Rocky Mount (6*) 34	36	0	.486	7
‡Peninsula (20*) 41	29	0	.586	....		Burlington (12*) 32	38	0	.457	9
Raleigh-Durham 40	30	1	.571	1		Salem (21*) 29	41	0	.414	12
Kinston (10*) 39	31	0	.557	2		Lynchburg (9*) 24	46	0	.343	17

†Winston-Salem defeated Peninsula 9 to 1 on June 26 in playoff for first-half championship.

STANDING OF CLUBS AT CLOSE OF SECOND HALF, SEPTEMBER 2

Club	W.	L.	T.	Pct.	G.B.	Club	W.	L.	T.	Pct.	G.B.
Burlington (12*) 40	27	0	.597	....		Kinston (10*) 33	34	0	.493	7
Winston-Salem (2*) ...38	29	0	.567	2		Lynchburg (9*) 33	37	0	.471	8½
Rocky Mount (6*) 36	32	0	.529	4½		Salem (21*) 31	39	0	.443	10½
Raleigh-Durham 37	33	0	.529	4½		‡Peninsula (20*) 26	43	0	.377	15

COMPOSITE STANDING OF CLUBS AT CLOSE OF SEASON, SEPTEMBER 2

Club	W-S.	R.D.	Bur.	Kin.	RM.	Pen.	Sal.	Lyn.	W.	L.	T.	Pct.	G.B.
Winston-Salem (2*)	..	9	13	12	11	10	12	13	80	58	1	.580	....
Raleigh-Durham 11	..	7	11	10	12	13	13	77	63	1	.550	4
Burlington (12*) 7	13	..	9	10	10	12	11	72	65	0	.526	7½
Kinston (10*) 6	9	10	..	7	13	14	13	72	65	0	.526	7½
Rocky Mount (6*) 8	10	9	13	..	7	10	13	70	68	0	.507	10
‡Peninsula (20*) 11	8	9	7	13	..	10	9	67	73	0	.479	14
Salem (21*) 8	7	8	6	10	11	..	10	60	80	0	.429	21
Lynchburg (9*) 7	7	7	9	7	10	10	..	57	83	0	.407	24

‡Represents Newport News and Hampton, Va.
Key to major league farm teams (indicated by numbers after clubs in standing) shown on Page 384.
First half championship game won-lost record included in composite standing for Winston-Salem and Peninsula.   Game statistics also included in club and individual averages.
Playoff—Winston-Salem defeated Burlington, two games to none.
Regular-Season Attendance—Burlington, 33,406; Kinston, 49,949; Lynchburg, 42,326; Peninsula, 65,114; Raleigh-Durham, 56,138; Rocky Mount, 34,062; Salem, 50,076; Winston-Salem, 36,923. Total, 367,994.   All-star game, 2,054.   Playoffs, 1,849.
Managers: Burlington—Joe Klein, Whitey Kurowski; Kinston—Alex Cosmidis; Lynchburg—Tommy Umphlett, Spencer (Red) Robbins; Peninsula—Nolan Campbell; Raleigh-Durham—Cliff Davis; Rocky Mount—Max Lanier; Salem—Bill Klaus; Winston-Salem—Bill Slack.
All-Star Team: 1B—Anderson, Peninsula; 2B—Adams, Rocky Mount; Frazier, Kinston; 3B—Braun, Lynchburg; SS—Beniquez, Winston-Salem; OF—Moates, Burlington; Stennett, Salem; Storm, Lynchburg; C—C. Johnson, Raleigh-Durham; P—Olsen, Kinston; McGlothen, Winston-Salem; Manager —Davis, Raleigh-Durham.

(Compiled by Howe News Bureau, Chicago, Ill.)

CLUB BATTING

Club	G.	AB.	R.	OR.	H.	TB.	2B.	3B.	HR.	RBI.	SH.	SF.	BB.	Int. BB.	HP.	SO.	SB.	CS.	LOB.	Pct.
Ral-Dur	141	4550	652	574	1189	1664	191	19	82	563	58	43	574	31	51	786	90	46	1059	.261
Kinston	137	4447	557	472	1124	1490	165	21	53	492	81	29	510	24	40	783	82	28	1051	.253
Salem	140	4596	542	645	1144	1637	148	45	85	470	45	15	469	29	40	901	71	35	999	.249
Burlington	137	4312	582	552	1068	1378	150	29	34	497	56	37	517	26	33	795	102	33	956	.248
Win-Salem	139	4579	554	489	1109	1505	146	35	60	487	58	39	552	42	33	903	168	60	1061	.242
Peninsula	140	4474	472	506	1077	1437	147	18	59	408	57	36	529	31	35	856	68	29	1046	.241
Lynchburg	140	4545	497	603	1063	1449	181	23	53	429	76	35	569	24	52	886	58	41	1099	.234
Rocky Mt	138	4282	470	485	965	1325	146	17	60	417	60	36	600	22	45	815	55	23	963	.225

INDIVIDUAL BATTING

(Leading Qualifiers for Batting Championship—434 or More Plate Appearances)

*Bats lefthanded. †Switch-hitter.

Player and Club	G.	AB.	R.	H.	TB.	2B.	3B.	HR.	RBI.	SH.	SF.	BB.	HP.	SO.	SB.	CS.	Pct.
Stennett, Renaldo, Salem	131	540	65	176	229	20	9	5	50	4	0	26	1	46	9	11	.326
Anderson, Michael, Pen	118	402	77	126	219	19	4	22	67	1	2	81	2	79	16	3	.313
Moates, David, Burlington*	121	440	76	137	180	14	7	5	70	5	5	34	3	48	44	6	.311
Fenderson, Johnnie, Kinston	113	389	65	114	173	20	3	11	59	2	4	40	5	84	6	0	.293
Mello, Edward, Ral-Dur	120	389	64	113	137	15	3	1	40	3	3	87	5	39	9		.290
Oliveras, Max, Wins-Salem	113	402	52	115	137	13	3	1	33	6	3	32	2	59	17	9	.286
Frazier, Frederic, Kinston	137	528	92	151	196	25	1	6	49	14	2	59	12	55	33	10	.286
Dixon, Jasper, Burlington*	124	465	81	132	147	9	3	0	31	2	1	56	9	94	25	8	.284
Brown, Willie, Burlington	115	403	53	114	151	16	3	5	63	5	8	21	2	43	7		.283
Braun, Stephen, Lynchburg*	118	387	52	108	146	24	1	4	43	2	2	71	6	47	6	4	.279
Terrell, Jerry, Lynchburg	118	463	60	129	158	16	5	1	36	9	4	42	3	43	17	7	.279

Departmental Leaders: G—Frazier, Powell, 137; AB—Stennett, 540; R—Frazier, 92; H—Stennett, 176; TB—Stennett, 229; 2B—Storm, 28; 3B—Stennett, 9; HR—C. Johnson, 27; RBI—C. Johnson, 91; SH—Frazier, 14; SF—Powell, 10; BB—Sharkey, 89; HP—Obradovich, 13; SO—Obradovich, 107; SB—R. Nelson, 45; CS—R. Nelson, 18.

(All Players—Listed Alphabetically)

Player and Club	G.	AB.	R.	H.	TB.	2B.	3B.	HR.	RBI.	SH.	SF.	BB.	HP.	SO.	SB.	CS.	Pct.
Adams, Robert, Rocky Mt	117	388	60	108	186	18	3	18	68	2	4	87	6	74	23	5	.278
Aguirre, Ernest, Peninsula	73	248	20	55	63	3	1	1	21	2	3	33	2	41	2	2	.222
Anderson, Michael, Pen	118	402	77	126	219	19	4	22	67	1	2	81	2	79	16	3	.313
Angelier, Mitchel, Rocky Mt	10	5	0	0	0	0	0	0	0	0	0	0	0	3	0	0	.000
Apellaniz, Domingo, Ral-Dur	76	256	40	66	78	8	2	0	21	2	2	18	8	36	10	5	.258
Austin, Frank, Wins-Salem	58	166	20	42	67	7	0	6	26	3	2	29	1	30	0	0	.253
Baker, E. Gene, Lynchburg	47	30	1	5	7	0	1	0	1	4	0	1	0	8	0	0	.167
Baker, Michael, Rocky Mt*	16	39	2	6	8	2	0	0	1	0	1	0	1	11	0	0	.154
Bandy, Bert, Pen†	40	9	3	1	1	0	0	0	1	0	0	0	0	6	0	0	.111
Baretta, Paul, Kinston	126	453	46	112	133	15	3	0	27	8	1	58	2	44	6	3	.247
Barranca, Guillermo, Kinston	25	41	4	5	5	0	0	0	2	4	0	2	0	23	0	0	.122
Barrett, Alexander, Ral-Dur	23	73	5	15	22	1	0	2	9	0	3	0		20	1	0	.205
Barrientos, Virgilio, Pen	8	0	0	0	0	0	0	0	0	0	0	0	0	0	0	0	.000
Beckman, Rodger, Rocky Mt	45	87	6	14	15	1	0	0	11	0	3	19	1	25	0	0	.161
Beniquez, Juan, Wins-Salem	92	335	53	91	134	12	2	9	37	4	2	38	2	68	30	5	.272
Bethell, Roy, Ral-Dur*	29	54	6	12	16	1	0	1	2	1	0	4	0	19	1	0	.222
Bevil, John, Rocky Mount*	19	18	1	7	8	1	0	0	5	1	0	2	1	7	0	0	.389
Biedenbach, John, Bur*	103	291	27	70	88	12	3	0	31	2	2	28	6	39	2	1	.241
Bike, David, Rocky Mount	120	409	42	88	126	11	0	9	47	2	7	48	7	48	0	0	.215
Blackman, Edward, Salem	92	226	26	46	78	8	0	8	31	2	4	26	4	48	1	0	.204
Boer, Martin, Ral-Dur	7	22	2	6	7	0	0	0	2	0	1	2	0	3	1	1	.273
Bolick, Frank, Burlington	17	34	2	5	6	1	0	0	2	1	0	3	0	12	0	0	.147
Bonalewicz, Robert, Lynch	92	298	34	67	96	11	0	6	35	1	4	46	4	56	1	1	.225
Bonfonte, Frank, Lynchburg	47	147	15	27	33	3	0	1	12	0	1	22	2	47	1	2	.184
Bootcheck, Daniel, Ry Mt*	23	60	6	16	16	0	0	0	3	0	0	5	0	16	0	0	.267
Bowers, Allen, Peninsula	126	467	47	127	147	14	0	2	44	0	5	37	1	63	12	6	.272
Bowlby, Charles, Ral-Dur	40	23	4	5	12	1	0	0	7	1	0	1	0	13	0	0	.217
Brandt, John G. Ral-Dur	4	8	1	3	4	1	0	0	2	0	0	2	0	3	0	0	.375
Braun, Stephen, Lynchburg*	118	387	52	108	146	24	1	4	43	2	2	71	6	47	6	4	.279
Brechtel, Wayne, Ral-Dur	14	20	1	0	0	0	0	0	0	0	0	1	0	9	0	0	.000
Brescher, Wayne, Burlington	28	57	8	9	12	1	0	1	3	0	0	17	0	22	0	0	.158
Brown, William L., Burl	115	403	53	114	151	16	3	5	63	5	8	21	2	43	7	7	.283
Bryan, James, Kinston	5	2	0	0	0	0	0	0	0	0	0	0	0	2	0	0	.000
Bryant, Steve, Lynchburg*	53	184	27	46	57	6	1	1	11	4	1	29	1	37	2	5	.250
Brykczynski, William, Bur	1	0	0	0	0	0	0	0	0	0	0	0	0	0	0	0	.000
Buskey, Thomas, Kinston	2	5	0	0	0	0	0	0	0	0	0	1	0	2	0	0	.000
Cabral, John, Salem*	16	5	0	1	1	0	0	0	0	0	0	0	1	3	0	0	.000
Cambero, Alberto, Ral-Dur	45	141	22	38	46	2	3	0	19	0	1	12	5	10	6	2	.270
Camp, Hudie, Salem*	60	216	22	64	88	8	2	4	23	1	1	12	1	25	5	2	.296
Campbell, Nolan, Peninsula	7	5	1	0	0	0	0	0	0	0	0	1	0	0	0	0	.000
Canty, John, Ral-Dur*	16	20	2	5	6	1	0	0	1	3	0	5	0		0		.250
Cappelli, Peter, Ral-Dur†	1	3	0	0	0	0	0	0	0	0	0	0	0	1	0	0	.000
Carson, Robert, Kinston	21	57	4	8	9	1	0	0	4	3	0	12	2	17	0	1	.140
Carter, Ezell, Lynchburg	103	306	34	79	114	16	2	5	42	4	2	33	1	57	13	2	.258
Carter, Gary, Burlington*	18	18	4	2	6	1	0	1	2	1	0	7	0	9	0	0	.111
Cates, Steve, Peninsula*	10	20	1	5	5	0	0	0	3	0	1	0	2	0	0		.250
Choate, Lee. Kintson*	15	23	2	3	4	1	0	0	0	0	0	12	0	7	1	0	.130
Christman, Gerald, Lynch	21	26	4	3	3	0	0	0	1	0	1	2	1	10	0	0	.115
Cichon, Michael, Lynchburg	5	2	0	0	0	0	0	0	0	0	0	0	0	0	0	0	.000

Player and Club	G.	AB.	R.	H.	TB.	2B.	3B.	HR.	RBI.	SH.	SF.	BB.	HP.	SO.	SB.	CS.	Pct.
Clifford, Arthur, Rocky Mt	9	15	2	2	2	0	0	1	3	0	0	4	0	0			.133
Clifton, John, Wins-Salem*	23	47	2	3	3	0	0	0	1	4	0	5	1	16	0	0	.064
Cluney, Patrick, Kinston	119	449	46	122	170	15	6	7	69	3	5	37	4	45	8	1	.272
Coble, Michael, Peninsula	6	12	2	3	3	0	0	0	1	0	0	1	0	5	0	0	.250
Cole, Robert, Rocky Mount	8	27	2	4	5	1	0	0	1	1	0	3	0	5	0	0	.148
Coley, Steve, Winston-Salem	79	247	39	70	83	7	3	0	33	3	4	20	2	34	10	3	.283
Colunio, John, Kinston	77	213	23	50	60	7	0	1	19	4	2	10	1	39	3	2	.235
Corddry, Philip, Win-Salem†	31	23	3	2	2	0	0	0	0	2	0	4	2	3	0	0	.087
Covey, Frederick, Peninsula	32	21	2	2	3	1	0	0	1	2	0	1	0	7	0	0	.095
Croken, William, Win-Salem	6	6	0	0	0	0	0	0	0	0	0	2	0	5	0	0	.000
Crosby, Kenneth, Kinston	18	34	1	1	1	0	0	0	1	3	0	5	1	20	0	0	.029
Crosby, Robert, Lynchburg	8	2	0	0	0	0	0	0	0	0	0	0	0	1	0	0	.000
Crowder, Wayne, Kinston	4	5	1	2	2	0	0	0	0	0	0	0	0	0	0	0	.400
Cushmore, Stephen, Ry Mt*	3	6	1	0	0	0	0	0	1	2	0	3	0	3	0	0	.000
Dalton, Dennis, Burlington	19	29	1	3	3	0	0	0	2	2	1	4	0	10	0	0	.103
Darcy, Patrick, Ral-Dur	4	10	0	0	0	0	0	0	0	0	0	0	0	4	0	0	.000
Dare, Richard, Salem*	35	19	1	6	7	1	0	0	1	0	0	0	0	5	1	0	.316
Davidson, Ralph, Burlington	2	1	0	0	0	0	0	0	0	0	0	0	0	1	0	0	.000
Davis, E. Clifford, Ral-Dur	32	76	7	17	22	2	0	1	8	0	0	3	1	16	0	1	.224
Deidel, James, Kinston	71	241	24	57	76	11	1	2	29	0	2	18	1	42	1	0	.237
Dennington, John, Burling	14	6	1	0	0	0	0	0	1	0	0	0	1	0	0	0	.000
Dickey, Barney, Peninsula	44	142	14	35	50	4	1	3	19	1	2	12	2	24	1	1	.246
Dietz, James C., Peninsula	115	377	28	96	117	16	1	1	31	5	4	38	1	50	5	2	.255
Dietz James J., Ral-Dur*	2	0	0	0	0	0	0	0	0	0	0	0	0	0	0	0	.000
Diorio, Ronald, Peninsula	21	7	1	1	1	0	0	0	0	1	0	1	0	3	0	0	.143
DiPace, Daniel, 13 Burlington-6 Lynch	19	57	3	7	10	1	1	0	11	2	2	7	0	11	1	0	.123
Disher, Jackie, Peninsula*	56	174	23	35	56	5	2	4	19	0	0	30	1	56	0	1	.201
Dixon, Jasper, Burlington	124	465	81	132	147	9	3	0	31	2	1	56	9	94	25	8	.284
Dunn, Perry, Salem*	70	242	28	67	96	11	3	4	12	0	1	10	2	37	3	2	.277
Durham, Harry R., Pen*	80	172	19	45	69	5	2	5	18	1	0	33	2	47	0	0	.262
Eagan, Stephen, Wins-Salem	69	206	11	40	57	6	1	3	20	1	1	16	1	42	0	0	.194
Elliott, Robert, Kinston	15	28	2	7	11	1	0	1	5	1	0	1	0	8	0	0	.250
Enewold, Dan, Salem*	55	150	16	26	39	4	3	1	10	1	0	34	3	35	0	0	.173
Evans, Richard, Ral-Dur*	10	21	3	1	1	0	0	0	2	0	0	6	0	6	0	0	.048
Everett, Michael, Salem	33	27	4	3	6	1	1	0	4	4	0	6	0	8	0	0	.111
Evert, Steve, Salem	68	217	29	44	77	4	4	7	18	2	1	26	7	68	5	0	.203
Fahey, William, Burling*	118	377	49	92	115	10	2	3	36	3	2	54	0	73	2	0	.244
Farrell, Ben K., Ral-Dur*	79	249	22	49	61	4	1	2	16	4	0	16	4	38	1	4	.197
Fenderson, Johnnie, Kinston	113	389	65	114	173	20	3	11	59	2	4	40	5	84	6	0	.293
Finkbeiner, Bruce, Ry Mt†	36	91	10	14	19	3	1	0	9	0	1	19	0	19	2	0	.154
Fore, David, Rocky Mount	65	168	11	32	41	3	0	2	15	0	0	16	3	22	0	1	.190
Foster, Clifford, Lynchburg*	22	59	5	14	21	2	1	1	5	1	0	5	0	15	0	0	.237
Foucher, Raymond, Ry Mt*	50	29	4	5	5	0	0	0	0	0	0	3	0	9	0	1	.172
Francis, DeGold, Salem	48	115	18	29	43	5	0	3	16	0	0	12	0	35	0	0	.252
Frazier, Frederic, Kinston	137	528	92	151	196	25	1	6	49	14	2	59	12	55	33	10	.286
Fremuth, Michael, Rocky Mt	20	10	0	0	0	0	0	0	1	0	0	0	8	0	0		.000
Frontino, Frank, Salem	38	23	0	0	0	0	0	0	0	1	0	5	0	11	0	0	.000
Fryar, John, Winston-Salem	38	43	4	10	11	1	0	0	2	1	0	1	0	17	0	0	.233
Fuchs, Michael, Salem*	23	28	4	3	3	0	0	0	1	0	4	0	15	0	0		.107
Giallella, Richard, Pen*	87	331	43	95	116	14	2	1	29	4	3	34	11	27	10	3	.287
Gifford, Roger, Burlington*	35	58	7	11	11	0	0	0	6	0	1	11	0	21	1	0	.190
Giron, Manuel, Salem	15	30	1	4	5	1	0	0	1	0	1	0	16	0	0		.133
Grate, D. Jeffrey, Wins-S†	10	36	4	6	8	0	0	0	1	0	0	5	0	8	0	0	.167
Gregory, Elmer, Lynchburg	18	19	1	3	3	0	0	0	1	0	0	2	0	10	0	0	.158
Grotemeyer, Steven, Kinston	64	191	27	43	56	5	1	2	21	2	0	29	2	63	1	0	.225
Gruber, James, Salem	14	33	6	13	14	1	0	0	2	0	0	7	0	6	1	0	.394
Guarnera, Richard, Bur	134	463	70	120	148	10	6	2	55	6	3	75	1	69	4	5	.259
Guerrero, Daniel, Lynchburg	13	42	2	8	9	1	0	0	1	0	1	6	0	12	0	0	.190
Guth, Charles, Lynchburg	37	141	21	33	52	2	1	5	10	3	0	10	0	30	3	2	.234
Hambright, Roger, Kinston	45	20	1	2	2	0	0	0	2	1	0	9	0	0			.100
Handel, Roy A., Wins-Salem	1	0	0	0	0	0	0	0	0	0	0	0	0	0			.000
Hankins, Terry, Ral-Dur	126	429	52	112	143	17	1	4	41	2	4	45	4	42	9	2	.261
Hansen, Brian, Peninsula	24	65	7	16	20	1	0	1	5	1	1	6	2	14	0	0	.246
Harkness, Michael, Lynch	10	1	0	0	0	0	0	0	0	1	0	2	0	0	0	0	.000
Harris, Alonzo, Ral-Dur*	96	354	65	107	135	12	5	2	20	2	0	49	0	56	28	13	.302
Harris, James, Rocky Mount	9	27	2	5	6	1	0	0	1	0	0	0	0	8	1	1	.185
Heger, Dennis, Lynchburg†	7	12	0	2	2	0	0	0	1	2	0	0	0	6	0	0	.167
Helwig, Arnold, Rocky Mt	17	26	2	3	3	0	0	0	1	3	0	1	0	16	1	0	.115
Hepler, William, Bur*	5	4	0	0	0	0	0	0	0	0	0	1	0	1	0	0	.000
Herrera, Hector, Salem	34	96	6	24	31	2	1	1	7	2	0	6	1	15	2	2	.250
Herron, Gerald, Peninsula	37	13	0	2	3	1	0	0	1	0	1	0	7	0	0		.154
Hetrick, John, Ral-Dur	17	48	12	18	20	2	0	0	3	2	0	5	0	4	1	1	.375
Hillstrom, Kim, Burlington	33	34	4	3	3	0	0	0	0	5	0	4	0	21	0	0	.088
Holliday, Richard, Rocky Mt	7	10	1	2	2	0	0	0	1	0	0	0	0	2	0	0	.200
Holt, W. Kenneth, Bur*	18	8	2	2	3	1	0	0	1	0	0	1	0	3	0	0	.250
Hummell, R. Shane, Ral-D	45	129	7	34	39	2	0	1	14	0	3	10	0	16	1	0	.264
Ignasiak, Gary, Rocky Mount	9	8	1	0	0	0	0	0	0	0	0	0	0	2	0	0	.000
Jacquez, Henry, Peninsula	40	103	10	19	25	3	0	1	5	1	2	9	1	23	2	3	.184
Jenke, Noel, Wins-Salem*	13	32	2	5	6	1	0	0	3	1	0	8	0	5	1	0	.156
Jenkins, James, Lynchburg	32	35	5	3	6	0	0	1	3	1	0	2	0	8	0	0	.086
Johnson, Clifford, Ral-Dur	102	343	74	114	219	24	0	27	91	0	1	68	6	51	6	1	.332
Johnson, Howard, Rocky Mt	129	387	37	93	109	16	0	0	38	4	6	42	1	58	0	0	.240

Player and Club	G.	AB.	R.	H.	TB.	2B.	3B.	HR.	RBI.	SH.	SF.	BB.	HP.	SO.	SB.	CS.	Pct.
Johnson, James C., Lynch	26	79	4	16	18	2	0	0	6	0	0	3	0	15	0	0	.203
Johnson, James L., Ral-Dur	111	397	53	106	139	27	0	2	44	1	3	41	3	69	8	4	.267
Johnson, Kenneth, Kinston	74	266	28	67	84	14	0	1	21	6	3	48	2	55	13	7	.252
Johnston, Robert, Salem	3	1	0	0	0	0	0	0	0	0	0	1	0	0	0	0	.000
Jones, J. Thomas, Wins-Sal	13	7	0	2	2	0	0	0	2	1	0	0	0	1	0	0	.286
Kelly, Edward, Peninsula	10	22	0	0	0	0	0	0	0	0	0	1	0	14	0	0	.000
Kelly, James, Peninsula	15	36	3	4	5	1	0	0	0	0	0	7	0	12	0	0	.111
Kent, A. David, Kinston	31	87	12	17	32	3	0	4	13	2	2	15	1	14	0	0	.195
Ketter, Lonnie, Wins-Salem*	64	217	22	40	49	5	2	0	12	1	3	32	4	54	6	6	.184
Kirik, John, Peninsula	19	30	2	3	3	0	0	0	0	0	0	8	0	7	0	0	.100
Kison, Bruce, Salem	6	9	0	1	1	0	0	0	1	0	0	0	0	5	0	0	.111
Kobi, James, Rocky Mount	.112	328	32	65	75	5	1	1	22	4	2	36	7	46	6	0	.198
Koering, James, Lynchburg	.31	72	6	15	16	1	0	0	2	6	0	4	0	19	0	0	.208
Kogut, S. Craig, Kinston*	. 13	40	4	10	14	2	1	0	5	0	0	4	1	5	0	0	.250
Koritko, Michael, Wins-Sal	101	352	40	88	130	17	2	7	36	1	3	43	2	58	12	4	.250
Kotzin, Michael, Rocky Mt*	4	6	0	0	0	0	0	0	0	0	0	2	0	2	0	0	.000
Krebs, Kristopher, Bur	20	70	11	19	23	4	0	0	1	0	0	12	0	14	4	1	.271
Kuehner, James, Bur†	.125	390	59	94	131	23	1	4	60	2	5	83	4	64	0	0	.241
Leatherwood, Robert, Pen†	95	299	29	68	79	8	0	1	16	3	2	49	1	28	1	1	.227
LeBright, Daniel, Ral-Dur	25	24	2	5	6	1	0	0	0	0	0	2	0	7	0	0	.208
Leshnock, Donald, Rocky Mt	28	36	3	4	4	0	0	0	2	4	0	2	0	19	0	0	.111
Lewis, Gary, Lynchburg	29	72	2	9	11	2	0	0	1	1	0	9	1	11	0	0	.125
Ley, Terrence, Kinston*	20	14	1	2	3	1	0	0	1	3	0	0	0	8	0	0	.143
Licini, Richard, Wins-Sal*	102	342	34	83	125	19	1	7	53	1	5	51	1	87	1	1	.243
Lightford, Eugene, Bur†	7	9	0	1	2	1	0	0	0	0	0	1	0	2	0	0	.111
Lohse, Lary, Rocky Mt*	16	23	2	2	2	0	0	0	0	1	0	1	0	13	0	0	.087
Love, Robert, Burlington	12	5	0	0	0	0	0	0	0	0	1	0	0	2	0	0	.000
Lovitto, Joseph, Bur*	.101	372	42	99	138	18	3	5	45	4	4	22	2	56	13	5	.266
Lyles, John, Salem	.131	452	48	116	163	10	5	3	59	4	3	42	7	91	7	3	.257
Mack, James, Lynchburg	15	25	2	2	3	1	0	0	0	0	0	2	0	7	0	0	.080
Mackanin, Peter, Burlington	105	361	39	73	96	9	1	4	42	1	5	31	4	84	0	0	.202
Maggard, Thomas, Wins-Sal	81	280	30	71	110	13	1	8	37	1	1	30	4	85	0	0	.254
Malcolm, Robert, Peninsula	6	10	1	1	1	0	0	0	1	2	0	1	0	4	0	0	.100
Mannerino, Frank, Wins-Sal	102	315	38	83	103	7	2	3	45	0	5	32	6	42	12	4	.263
Mansfield, Larry, Ral-Dur*	27	89	11	19	32	4	0	3	17	0	1	14	0	22	0	0	.213
Mappin, Timothy, Lynchburg	32	136	10	36	45	5	2	0	6	0	0	9	1	22	0	4	.265
Marsden, John, Wins-Salem*	22	11	0	1	1	0	0	0	1	0	4	0	5	0	0	.091
Mason, DeWayne, Salem	17	39	3	8	8	0	0	0	2	0	2	0	5	0	0	.205
Mazerall, Michael, W-S	31	13	1	1	1	0	0	0	1	1	0	3	1	6	0	0	.077
McBrayer, Michael, Salem	68	249	28	58	78	8	3	2	26	4	3	30	1	25	3	1	.233
McCall, Michael, Peninsula*	11	39	4	8	11	3	0	0	1	0	0	7	0	4	1	0	.205
McCullough, Joseph, W-S	.126	438	57	112	164	17	7	7	64	6	6	65	1	66	11	8	.256
McDaniel, Robert, Kinston	91	311	51	89	110	12	0	3	36	1	0	46	6	55	1	2	.286
McDonald, Leroy, Lynchburg	54	172	8	32	40	4	2	0	15	5	0	14	2	38	0	5	.186
McFarland, Michael, R-D	13	30	2	2	3	1	0	0	1	1	0	3	1	10	0	0	.067
McGlothen, Lynn, Wins-Sal*	32	83	7	13	16	1	1	0	3	3	0	5	0	21	0	0	.157
McKee, James, Salem	26	58	4	7	8	1	0	0	1	0	0	4	1	31	0	0	.121
McLachlin, Robert, Pen*	22	47	1	4	5	1	0	0	3	2	0	4	0	26	0	0	.085
Medina, Miguel, Rocky Mt	8	17	0	3	3	0	0	0	0	0	0	2	0	3	0	0	.176
Mello, Edward, Ral-Dur	.120	389	64	113	137	15	3	1	40	3	3	87	5	39	9	9	.290
Mercado, Francisco, W-S*	23	36	1	4	4	0	0	0	4	1	0	3	0	25	0	0	.111
Meyer, Philip, Peninsula*	10	18	2	5	5	0	0	0	1	0	0	2	0	2	0	0	.278
Miller, Robert, Burlington	60	147	19	40	54	8	0	2	22	2	0	26	0	19	0	0	.272
Minshall, James, Salem	26	37	3	1	1	0	0	0	0	1	0	3	0	20	0	0	.027
Moates, David, Burlington*	121	440	76	137	180	14	7	5	70	5	5	34	3	48	44	6	.311
Morgan, Wayne, Ral-Dur	25	43	4	9	13	2	1	0	4	6	0	0	0	12	0	0	.209
Muniz, Angel, Kinston*	57	171	20	39	45	2	2	0	10	0	0	12	1	14	2	1	.228
Munoz, Mark, Burlington	13	21	3	5	7	2	0	0	1	0	1	2	1	6	0	0	.238
Murphy, George, Rocky Mt*	8	13	1	2	3	1	0	0	0	1	0	2	0	1	0	0	.154
Nelson, Louis, Lynchburg	62	172	19	42	55	4	3	1	24	3	2	37	0	27	0	1	.244
Nelson, Roger, Wins-Salem	122	442	67	123	165	7	7	7	44	3	5	58	0	52	45	18	.278
Newhauser, Donald, W-S	14	9	0	0	0	0	0	0	0	0	0	0	0	4	0	0	.000
Nichols, Richard, Wins-Sal	37	118	16	22	32	3	2	1	9	1	1	16	1	20	4	1	.186
Nordhagen, Wayne, Kinston	88	283	31	65	87	10	3	2	30	0	5	25	3	50	2	0	.230
Nottle, Edward, Lynchburg	42	25	3	6	6	0	0	0	0	3	0	2	0	8	0	0	.240
Obradovich, James, Lynch*	124	392	57	89	136	16	2	9	44	3	6	76	13	107	4	2	.227
Oglesby, Ronald, Lynchburg	24	33	0	0	0	0	0	0	0	1	0	2	0	13	0	0	.000
Oliveras, Max, Wins-Salem	.113	402	52	115	137	13	3	1	33	6	3	32	2	59	17	9	.286
Olsen, William, Kinston*	. 23	62	7	18	25	1	0	2	6	6	0	2	1	8	0	1	.290
Pacheco, Edwin, Salem	47	159	16	35	50	7	1	2	18	0	1	9	2	26	5	3	.220
Padron, Jose, Peninsula	.123	464	43	116	131	13	1	0	33	5	4	38	1	42	1	1	.250
Parchem, Robert, Bur*	20	22	1	5	6	1	0	0	5	1	1	2	0	5	0	0	.227
Parker, John, Burlington	21	25	1	2	2	0	0	0	1	0	3	0	15	0	0	.080
Passarella, Gilbert, Kinston	48	176	19	53	75	10	0	4	26	1	2	12	0	24	1	0	.301
Pierce, Michael, Peninsula*	27	45	4	11	12	1	0	0	2	6	0	3	0	18	0	0	.244
Pole, Richard, Wins-Salem	3	0	0	0	0	0	0	0	0	0	0	0	0	0	0	0	.000
Poulsen, Ken, Kinston*	37	65	4	16	22	3	0	1	10	4	0	4	0	19	0	0	.246
Powell, J. Edward, Ral-Dur	137	467	84	126	221	19	2	24	86	7	10	83	6	102	1	0	.270
Pyle, Lawrence, Kinston	42	149	22	37	54	2	0	5	26	1	0	38	0	33	2	1	.248
Ramirez, Alonzo, Kinston*	17	3	1	0	0	0	0	0	0	0	0	3	2	0	0	.000
Remington, Ted, Lynchburg	16	28	2	2	3	1	0	0	2	3	0	6	0	12	0	0	.071

Player and Club	G.	AB.	R.	H.	TB.	2B.	3B.	HR.	RBI.	SH.	SF.	BB.	HP.	SO.	SB.	CS.	Pct.
Roberts, Melvin, Peninsula .	25	62	2	11	14	3	0	0	7	0	1	6	0	15	0	1	.177
Robinson, Beau, Kinston* ..	12	16	2	3	7	1	0	1	4	1	0	4	0	2	1	0	.188
Robinson, Robert, Ry Mt*	101	352	42	91	121	18	3	2	31	1	1	43	0	57	2	3	.259
Robinson, Stanley, Ral-Dur	7	12	1	1	1	0	0	0	0	0	0	0	0	5	0	0	.083
Rothermel, Russell, Ral-Dur*	22	45	3	9	9	0	0	0	2	8	0	1	0	21	0	0	.200
Rusco, David, Peninsula ..1	106	388	41	97	141	16	2	8	46	1	2	31	3	86	6	5	.250
Rusnak, Kevin, Peninsula ..	2	4	0	0	0	0	0	0	0	0	0	0	0	2	0	0	.000
Salvato, Steve, Burlington	2	7	4	1	1	0	0	0	0	0	0	3	1	0	0	0	.143
Sanders, James, Ral-Dur	6	14	1	0	0	0	0	0	0	0	0	2	0	10	0	0	.000
Santana, Felix, Salem	62	227	22	61	76	10	1	1	21	4	0	22	2	23	2	0	.269
Santos, Miguel, Salem*	77	239	36	62	88	7	2	5	26	0	0	34	1	37	3	2	.259
Sauget, Richard, Ral-Dur .	14	42	2	6	10	1	0	1	4	1	0	7	0	8	0	0	.143
Schirripa, Dante, Kinston .	26	30	3	3	3	0	0	0	0	4	0	1	0	2	0	0	.100
Schlegelmilch, Jerry, Lynch	89	299	29	79	115	17	2	5	36	4	1	34	3	43	2	1	.264
Schlieve, Gary, Peninsula .	28	52	0	7	9	2	0	0	2	6	0	4	0	23	0	0	.135
Scramuzzo, Craig, Pen	30	71	3	5	5	0	0	0	1	7	0	2	2	30	0	0	.070
Scrivener, Wayne, Rocky Mt	11	23	2	2	3	1	0	0	0	0	0	4	1	5	1	0	.087
Seifert, John, Ral-Dur* ...	6	14	0	4	6	2	0	0	2	0	0	0	0	8	0	0	.286
Sellers, Danny, Ral-Dur ...	2	9	1	3	4	1	0	0	2	0	0	0	0	1	0	0	.333
Sells, D. Alvin, Salem	12	32	2	6	7	1	0	0	5	1	0	0	1	13	0	0	.188
Senger, Frederick, Ral-Dur	3	4	0	1	1	0	0	0	1	0	0	1	1	1	0	0	.250
Settle, Robert, Salem	24	47	3	7	10	1	1	0	1	3	0	1	0	18	0	0	.149
Sharkey, John, Rocky Mt*	.136	443	52	100	139	17	5	4	33	11	4	89	1	74	10	7	.226
Sharon, Richard, Salem ..1	132	464	78	118	212	18	5	22	71	1	0	57	0	106	14	5	.254
Sheftall, Michael, Lynchburg	37	53	1	6	8	2	0	0	6	0	0	1	0	22	0	0	.113
Shields, Donald, Burlington	4	4	0	0	0	0	0	0	0	0	0	0	0	2	0	0	.000
Shreve, Charles, Ral-Dur ..	28	50	1	2	2	0	0	0	1	6	0	5	0	30	0	0	.040
Sinclair, John, Wins-Salem*	10	30	5	8	9	1	0	0	3	0	0	2	0	4	2	0	.267
Singleton, Norman, Ry Mt*	108	258	32	56	74	9	0	3	14	3	0	54	3	60	0	0	.217
Slayback, William, Rocky Mt	14	29	2	5	5	0	0	0	3	5	0	1	1	4	0	0	.172
Smallwood, Wallace, Bur ..	28	58	6	11	15	4	0	0	2	0	0	2	0	18	0	0	.190
Smith, Stephen, Rocky Mt ..	67	259	18	68	102	15	2	5	35	0	4	14	0	50	0	0	.263
Snyder, Robert, Wins-Sal†	35	52	5	11	14	3	0	0	5	2	0	4	0	13	0	0	.212
Spatz, Eugene, Rocky Mount	83	258	39	74	85	11	0	0	17	5	0	39	7	28	8	2	.287
Speer, Robert, Lynchburg ..	28	73	4	13	19	4	1	0	9	0	1	13	1	8	1	1	.178
Stennett, Renaldo, Salem ..1	131	540	65	176	229	20	9	5	50	4	0	26	1	46	9	11	.326
Storm, Robert, Lynchburg .1	130	461	66	122	183	28	0	11	57	5	5	46	8	102	7	3	.265
Strampe, Robert, Rocky Mt†	4	4	0	1	1	0	0	0	0	0	0	0	0	0	0	0	.250
Susce, John, Burlington ...	28	10	0	0	0	0	0	0	0	0	0	1	0	7	0	0	.000
Suskiewich, James, Kinston*	25	34	9	13	15	2	0	0	7	0	0	5	0	10	0	0	.382
Swanson, Neil, Kinston* ..	3	1	0	0	0	0	0	0	0	0	0	0	0	1	0	0	.000
Tekulve, Kenton, Salem ...	42	20	0	4	4	0	0	0	0	1	0	0	0	11	0	0	.200
Terrell, Jerry, Lynchburg ..1	118	463	60	129	158	16	5	1	36	9	4	42	3	43	17	7	.279
Thomas, Ronald, Rocky Mt .	10	1	0	0	0	0	0	0	0	0	0	0	0	0	0	0	.000
Thornton, Andre, Peninsula	67	193	24	48	74	7	2	5	23	1	5	41	1	40	8	0	.249
Thornton, James, Wins-Sal	44	20	0	4	4	0	0	0	6	0	1	0	0	12	0	0	.200
Thornton, Otis, Ral-Dur ...	18	74	12	17	28	2	0	3	16	1	0	5	0	12	1	1	.230
Tissot, Stephen, Rocky Mt .	50	19	3	2	3	1	0	0	0	0	0	3	0	5	0	0	.105
Toney, Robert, Ral-Dur ...	77	287	58	105	142	25	0	4	51	5	7	39	2	16	5	4	.366
Torres, Maximo, Salem	23	83	8	14	22	0	1	2	9	0	0	6	0	23	2	0	.169
Valesente, George, Bur	13	35	5	3	3	0	0	0	1	0	0	3	0	13	0	0	.086
Vance, John, Salem*	83	250	34	69	98	10	2	5	37	0	0	57	5	57	0	1	.276
Velazquez, Nestor, Lyncn .	88	255	22	58	72	12	1	0	18	3	2	34	3	37	2	0	.227
Vickery, Billy, Burlington .	5	19	1	3	3	0	0	0	2	1	0	2	0	0	0	0	.158
Vollweiler, Jeffrey, Bur ...	19	46	2	8	10	2	0	0	4	3	0	0	0	14	0	0	.174
Walls, Richard, Salem	70	233	30	66	89	9	1	4	27	2	1	26	0	32	8	3	.283
Walters, Walter, Kinston ..	23	58	6	14	15	1	0	0	8	6	0	2	0	12	0	0	.241
Wang, Geoffrey, Peninsula	39	92	10	19	32	4	0	3	7	9	0	3	0	37	4	0	.207
Ware, Robert, Rocky Mount	19	33	1	7	7	0	0	0	4	1	1	0	0	10	0	0	.212
White, Ronald, Wins-Sal* .	9	1	0	0	0	0	0	0	0	0	0	0	0	0	0	0	.000
Whitson, Michael, Bur	5	8	2	2	2	0	0	0	1	0	0	2	0	4	0	0	.250
Williams, Terry, Wins-Salem	9	22	2	2	2	0	0	0	0	1	0	1	0	8	0	0	.091
Wolger, George, Ral-Dur ..	12	14	1	3	3	0	0	0	3	1	0	1	0	8	0	0	.214
Wosman, James, Rocky Mt	110	367	51	85	148	11	2	16	52	0	2	58	5	96	0	0	.232
Ybes, Carmelo, Salem	14	30	0	5	5	0	0	0	2	1	0	2	0	5	0	0	.167
Yoakum, David, Ral-Dur ..	85	269	27	56	75	11	1	2	27	2	4	36	2	51	1	0	.208
Zgorzelski, James, W-S* ..	88	237	37	56	63	14	0	1	10	4	0	42	3	44	17	2	.236
Zuniga, Ralph, Lynchburg*	10	4	0	3	3	0	0	0	0	0	0	1	0	0	0	0	.750

GRAND SLAM HOME RUNS—C. Johnson, 3; Adams, Deidel, 2 each; Barrett, Bowlby, Brescher, E. Carter, Cluney, Gialella, Kuehner, Licini, Maggard, Mansfield, Poulsen, Pyle, Rusco, Santos, 1 each.

AWARDED FIRST BASE ON INTERFERENCE—Guarnera, 2 (Deidel, Eagan); Anderson (Fahey), Blackman (Fore), Deidel (Vance), Hansen (Deidel), Hetrick (Vance), Mello (Vance), Padron (Vance).

CLUB FIELDING

Club	G.	PO.	A.	E.	DP.	PB.	Pct.	Club	G.	PO.	A.	E.	DP.	PB.	Pct.
Peninsula	140	3597	1477	155	93	23	.970	Raleigh-Dur	141	3595	1466	193	111	31	.963
Winston-Salem	139	3664	1508	178	125	30	.967	Kinston	137	3526	1415	195	126	15	.962
Rocky Mount	138	3485	1512	176	118	11	.966	Lynchburg	140	3629	1506	219	131	16	.959
Burlington	137	3436	1457	186	129	21	.963	Salem	140	3608	1417	247	107	35	.953

Triple Plays—Raleigh-Durham, 2; Winston-Salem, Burlington, Salem, 1 each.

INDIVIDUAL FIELDING

(Ten or More Games)

*Throws lefthanded.

FIRST BASEMEN

Player and Club	G.	PO.	A.	E.	DP.	Pct.	Player and Club	G.	PO.	A.	E.	DP.	Pct.
Passarella, Kinston .	12	95	6	0	8	1.000	Kuehner, Burlington	122	1020	60	18	95	.984
Anderson, Peninsula	41	371	19	1	28	.997	Cluney, Kinston* ..	119	993	68	17	96	.984
Austin, Wins-Salem	28	249	13	1	15	.996	Oliveras, W-S	22	159	17	3	9	.983
Santos, Salem* ..	36	289	12	2	23	.993	Wosman, R Mount .	108	880	38	17	77	.982
OBRADOVICH, L.*	111	928	44	8	80	.992	Camp, Salem*	55	459	26	10	40	.980
Thornton, Peninsula	60	499	30	5	37	.991	Enewold, Salem* ..	46	361	24	8	24	.980
Licini, Wins-Salem	94	790	47	8	90	.991	Schlegelmilch, Lyn .	20	188	8	5	25	.975
Blackman, Salem .	10	88	1	1	9	.989	Mansfield, Ral-Dur*	25	183	9	6	16	.970
Singleton, R Mount	20	159	8	2	9	.988	Fore, Rocky Mount	16	140	4	6	11	.960
Powell, Ral-Dur ...	112	943	65	13	76	.987	Miller, Burlington .	10	70	6	4	8	.950
Durham, Peninsula	43	342	29	5	22	.987							

Triple Plays—Powell, 2; Austin, Kuehner, 1 each.

(Fewer Than Ten Games)

Player and Club	G.	PO.	A.	E.	DP.	Pct.	Player and Club	G.	PO.	A.	E.	DP.	Pct.
Guarnera, Bur	4	33	4	0	2	1.000	Davis, Raleigh-Dur	1	1	0	0	0	1.000
Moates, Burlington*	5	28	1	0	5	1.000	Carson, Kinston .	5	37	2	1	4	.975
Foster, Lynchburg*	4	27	0	0	2	1.000	Vickery, Burlington	4	31	1	1	2	.970
Brandt, Raleigh-Dur	4	15	1	0	3	1.000	Choate, Kinston* ..	3	25	6	1	1	.969
Kotzin, R Mount* .	1	10	0	0	1	1.000	Nelson, Lynchburg .	5	27	3	1	4	.968
Bike, Rocky Mount	1	7	2	0	1	1.000	Velazquez, Lynch .	8	48	2	2	9	.962
Poulsen, Kinston ...	2	5	1	0	1	1.000	Koritko, Wins-Salem	3	22	1	1	2	.958
Kent, Kinston	2	1	0	0	1	1.000	Nordhagen, Kinston	1	6	0	1	1	.857
Bowlby, Raleigh-Dur	1	1	0	0		1.000							

SECOND BASEMEN

Player and Club	G.	PO.	A.	E.	DP.	Pct.	Player and Club	G.	PO.	A.	E.	DP.	Pct.
Yoakum, Ral-Dur .	21	40	49	1	11	.989	Lovitto, Burlington	59	132	158	10	35	.967
Kobi, Rocky Mount	11	27	33	1	10	.984	Oliveras, W-S	51	135	155	10	38	.967
Santana, Salem ...	56	101	143	5	22	.980	McDonald, Lynch ..	11	30	26	2	5	.966
Ketter, Wins-Salem	60	149	159	8	35	.975	Mello, Raleigh-Dur	116	290	322	24	67	.962
Nichols, Wins-Salem	32	70	86	4	12	.975	Adams, Rocky Mt .	115	310	310	27	61	.958
Leatherwood, Pen .	87	199	203	11	36	.973	McBrayer, Salem ..	68	138	176	14	38	.957
TERRELL, Lynch .	117	332	341	20	81	.971	Krebs, Burlington ..	15	26	41	3	6	.957
Guarnera, Bur	61	154	180	10	49	.971	Frazier, Kinston ..	137	321	345	39	90	.945
Padron, Peninsula .	53	121	113	7	26	.971	Gruber, Salem	10	14	13	2	3	.931
Beckman, Rocky Mt	14	35	32	2	6	.971							

Triple Plays—Mello, 2; Ketter, Lovitto, 1 each.

(Fewer Than Ten Games)

Player and Club	G.	PO.	A.	E.	DP.	Pct.	Player and Club	G.	PO.	A.	E.	DP.	Pct.
Pacheco, Salem ...	6	20	15	0	5	1.000	Miller, Burlington .	1	0	1	0	0	1.000
Scrivener, Rocky Mt	3	12	11	0	3	1.000	Hankins, Ral-Dur .	4	9	10	1	5	.950
Nelson, Lynchburg .	4	10	10	0	2	1.000	Dunn, Salem	7	10	13	2	3	.920
Braun, Lynchburg .	2	2	2	0	0	1.000	Velazquez, Lynch .	9	20	24	4	7	.917
Davis, Raleigh-Dur	1	4	0	0	1	1.000	J. Johnson, R-D ...	1	3	3	1	1	.857
Roberts, Peninsula .	1	1	3	0	0	1.000	Biedenbach, Bur ...	4	4	6	3	0	.769
Campbell, Peninsula	1	2	0	0	0	1.000	Colunio, Kinston ..	2	1	1	2	0	.500
Bonalewicz, Lynch .	1	1	0	0	0	1.000							

THIRD BASEMEN

Player and Club	G.	PO.	A.	E.	DP.	Pct.	Player and Club	G.	PO.	A.	E.	DP.	Pct.
Hankins, Ral-Dur ..	18	21	36	1	3	.983	McCall, Peninsula .	11	7	14	2	0	.913
Passarella, Kinston	35	21	63	4	6	.955	Lyles, Salem	112	110	265	36	27	.912
McCullough, W-S ..	37	27	76	6	4	.945	Smith, Rocky Mount	65	59	127	18	14	.912
Beckman, Rocky Mt	11	9	32	2	1	.953	Rusco, Peninsula ..	32	27	58	10	3	.895
Cambero, Ral-Dur .	37	27	76	6	4	.945	Gifford, Burlington	11	5	19	3	1	.889
Yoakum, Ral-Dur ..	56	31	104	8	8	.944	Colunio, Kinston ..	44	29	85	15	9	.884
Koritko, Wins-Sal .	55	57	105	10	17	.942	Mackanin, Bur	39	18	78	13	7	.881
Kobi, Rocky Mount	62	40	131	12	6	.934	Anderson, Peninsula	22	14	30	6	1	.880
Biedenbach, Bur ...	84	54	144	15	18	.930	Johnson, Kinston ..	64	57	120	25	9	.876
BRAUN, Lynchburg .	112	107	251	29	24	.925	Dunn, Salem	20	17	44	9	3	.871
Toney, Raleigh-Dur	33	26	55	7	6	.920	Nelson, Lynchburg .	28	27	55	13	8	.863
Aguirre, Peninsula .	72	44	143	17	6	.917	Pacheco, Salem	12	13	17	7	1	.811

Triple Plays—Yoakum, Koritko.

(Fewer Than Ten Games)

Player and Club	G.	PO.	A.	E.	DP.	Pct.	Player and Club	G.	PO.	A.	E.	DP.	Pct.
Velazquez, Lynch ..	3	2	5	0	0	1.000	Harris, Rocky Mt ..	8	8	20	2	3	.933
Singleton, Rocky Mt	1	0	5	0	0	1.000	Roberts, Peninsula .	3	3	7	1	0	.909
Herrera, Salem	2	2	2	0	1	1.000	Oliveras, W-S	9	6	14	3	3	.870
Storm, Lynchburg .	1	1	2	0	0	1.000	Miller, Burlington .	9	4	17	4	2	.840
McDonald, Lynchburg	1	1	1	0	0	1.000	Barrett, Ral-Dur ..	3	2	3	1	0	.833
Kent, Kinston	2	1	0	0	0	1.000							

SHORTSTOPS

Player and Club	G.	PO.	A.	E.	DP.	Pct.
Padron, Peninsula	72	127	242	5	35	.987
Kobi, Rocky Mount	16	18	26	1	4	.978
BARETTA, Kinston	126	172	395	20	70	.966
Guarnera, Bur	71	114	249	18	32	.953
Hankins, Ral-Dur	31	49	93	8	16	.947
Johnson, Rocky Mt	129	175	380	33	59	.944
Walls, Salem	69	99	205	18	39	.944
Velazquez, Lynch	42	76	112	12	14	.940
Guth, Lynchburg	37	40	124	11	20	.937
McCullough, W-S	41	57	101	11	16	.935
Mackanin, Bur	65	104	180	22	35	.928
Rusco, Peninsula	76	100	241	27	34	.927
Beniquez, W-S	91	144	275	35	49	.923
McDonald, Lynch	39	60	106	14	19	.922
Grate, Wins-Salem	10	13	31	4	10	.917
Pacheco, Salem	29	38	86	12	11	.912
J. Johnson, R-D	108	171	342	51	51	.910
Mappin, Lynchburg	29	46	92	16	22	.896
Colunio, Kinston	13	13	29	5	7	.894
Torres, Salem	22	30	46	11	3	.874
Lyles, Salem	19	22	41	10	4	.863

Triple Plays—Guarnera, Walls, J. Johnson.

(Fewer Than Ten Games)

Player and Club	G.	PO.	A.	E.	DP.	Pct.
Sellers, Ral-Dur	2	3	6	0	2	1.000
Adams, Rocky Mount	4	2	4	0	0	1.000
Santana, Salem	3	8	15	2	2	.900
Cambero, Ral-Dur	3	1	7	1	0	.889
Scrivener, Rocky Mt	7	5	17	3	2	.880
Krebs, Burlington	5	5	12	4	1	.810
Oliveras, W-S	1	2	0	2	0	.500
Ketter, Wins-Salem	1	0	1	3	0	.250

OUTFIELDERS

Player and Club	G.	PO.	A.	E.	DP.	Pct.
Spatz, Rocky Mount	75	135	8	0	1	1.000
Wang, Peninsula	27	38	1	0	0	1.000
Roberts, Peninsula	16	33	0	0	0	1.000
Choate, Kinston*	10	10	0	0	1	1.000
Hankins, Ral-Dur	70	121	2	1	1	.992
Bryant, Lynchburg	53	88	5	1	0	.989
Mannerino, W-S	85	126	7	2	3	.985
Disher, Peninsula*	47	63	3	1	0	.985
Apellaniz, Ral-Dur	72	106	4	2	3	.982
Giallella, Pen*	86	227	8	5	2	.979
Muniz, Kinston	46	87	3	2	1	.978
Pyle, Kinston	42	82	8	2	2	.978
Koritko, Wins-Salem	41	79	7	2	1	.977
Jacquez, Peninsula	30	41	2	1	0	.977
Miller, Burlington	26	41	2	1	1	.977
MOATES, Bur*	112	231	15	6	3	.976
Sharkey, Rocky Mt*	134	249	14	7	3	.974
Zgorzelski, W-S*	71	104	6	3	1	.973
Storm, Lynchburg	135	272	10	9	3	.969
Anderson, Peninsula	56	120	4	4	1	.969
Nelson, Wins-Salem	113	232	6	8	1	.967
Dixon, Burlington	122	167	11	6	2	.967
Carter, Lynchburg	77	165	6	6	0	.966
Dickey, Peninsula	40	53	3	2	2	.966
Brown, Burlington	106	181	10	7	3	.965
Harris, Raleigh-Dur	96	202	13	8	1	.964
Finkbeiner, R Mt	31	43	7	2	0	.962
Fenderson, Kinston	108	161	12	7	1	.961
Robinson, Rocky Mt	94	113	9	5	2	.961
Evert, Salem	64	116	4	5	3	.960
Coley, Wins-Salem	72	110	9	5	0	.960
Singleton, R Mt	63	88	7	4	1	.960
Blackman, Salem	51	91	3	4	0	.959
Kent, Kinston	27	43	2	2	0	.957
Carson, Kinston	15	21	1	1	1	.957
Foster, Lynchburg*	14	18	4	1	0	.957
Bonfonte, Lynch	42	63	2	3	1	.956
Stennett, Salem	130	201	13	10	2	.955
Toney, Raleigh-Dur	41	76	9	4	1	.955
DiPace, Bur-Lynch	17	20	1	1	0	.955
Santos, Salem*	31	59	3	3	1	.954
Nordhagen, Kinston	85	169	9	9	2	.952
Velazquez, Lynch	14	19	1	1	0	.952
Sharon, Salem	130	268	13	16	2	.946
Bowers, Peninsula	123	205	16	13	1	.944
McDaniel, Kinston	88	143	8	9	1	.944
Jenke, Wins-Salem*	10	16	1	1	1	.944
Powell, Raleigh-Dur	21	33	0	2	0	.943
Lovitto, Burlington	42	72	6	5	1	.940
C. Johnson, Ral-Dur	26	45	1	3	0	.939
Kobi, Rocky Mount	22	27	4	2	1	.939
Dunn, Salem	38	40	3	3	0	.935
Schlegelmilch, Lyn	65	92	7	8	1	.925
Davis, Raleigh-Dur	13	23	1	2	0	.923
Farrell, Ral-Dur	65	80	3	7	1	.922
Austin, Wins-Salem	20	22	1	2	0	.920
Hetrick, Ral-Dur	17	22	0	2	0	.917
Oliveras, W-S	31	38	1	4	0	.907
Speer, Lynchburg	19	27	2	3	1	.906
Barrett, Ral-Dur	19	19	0	3	0	.864
Nelson, Lynchburg	13	15	0	3	0	.833

Triple Play—Stennett.

(Fewer Than Ten Games)

Player and Club	G.	PO.	A.	E.	DP.	Pct.
Matson, Peninsula	8	17	1	0	1	1.000
Boer, Raleigh-Dur	6	16	2	0	1	1.000
Medina, Rocky Mt	7	10	1	0	1	1.000
Sinclair, W-S	8	10	0	0	1	1.000
Gifford, Bur	8	8	0	0	0	1.000
Johnson, Kinston	7	7	0	0	0	1.000
Robinson, Kinston	6	7	0	0	0	1.000
Hummell, Ral-Dur	5	6	0	0	0	1.000
Colunio, Kinston	5	4	0	0	0	1.000
Fore, Rocky Mount	4	3	1	0	0	1.000
Bethell, Ral-Dur	3	4	0	0	1	1.000
Lightfoot, Bur	2	4	0	0	0	1.000
Passarella, Kinston	2	3	1	0	0	1.000
Salvato, Burlington	2	4	0	0	0	1.000
Campbell, Peninsula	1	1	0	0	1	1.000
Grotemeyer, Kinston	1	2	0	0	1	1.000
Rusnak, Peninsula	1	2	0	0	0	1.000
Bonalewicz, Lynch	1	1	0	0	0	1.000
Baker, Rocky Mount	9	13	0	1	0	.929
Obradovich, Lynch*	6	12	1	1	0	.929
Cole, Rocky Mount	8	15	1	2	0	.889
McDonald, Lynch	1	3	0	1	0	.750

CATCHERS

Player and Club	G.	PO.	A.	E.	DP.	PB.	Pct.
Kirik, Peninsula	12	45	3	0	0	2	1.000
BIKE, Rocky Mt	114	686	78	5	12	7	.993
Johnson, Lynch	25	109	17	1	0	1	.992
Lewis, Lynchburg	24	113	6	1	1	1	.992
Hummell, Ral-Dur	35	204	25	2	2	8	.991
Fahey, Bur	117	724	76	10	11	16	.988
Dietz, Peninsula	104	621	57	9	5	15	.987
C. Johnson, R-D	71	429	39	6	5	11	.987
Grotemeyer, Kin	60	385	32	6	3	5	.986
Maggard, Wins-S	80	538	58	10	4	20	.983
Hansen, Peninsula	18	111	7	2	1	6	.983
Fore, Rocky Mt	31	150	18	3	0	3	.982
Francis, Salem	37	193	16	4	0	8	.981
Deidel, Kinston	70	488	41	11	7	7	.980
Eagan, Wins-Sal	60	396	38	9	6	8	.980
Vance, Salem	80	544	40	13	6	19	.978
Guerrero, Lynch	13	67	15	2	1	2	.976
Thornton, Ral-Dur	18	149	7	4	1	8	.975
Kogut, Kinston	11	75	4	2	2	3	.975
J. Kelly, Pen	14	72	4	2	1	0	.974

CATCHERS—Continued

Player and Club	G.	PO.	A.	E.	DP.	PB.	Pct.		Player and Club	G.	PO.	A.	E.	DP.	PB.	Pct.
Sauget, Ral-Dur	13	75	1	2	0	2	.974		Ybes, Salem	10	68	4	3	1	5	.960
Bonalewicz, Lynch	83	520	68	17	10	12	.972		Brescher, Bur	18	93	13	5	3	5	.955
Herrera, Salem	25	161	14	5	2	3	.972									

Triple Plays—Hummell, Vance.

(Fewer Than Ten Games)

Player and Club	G.	PO.	A.	E.	DP.	PB.	Pct.		Player and Club	G.	PO.	A.	E.	DP.	PB.	Pct.
Powell, Ral-Dur	7	31	4	0	0	2	1.000		Handel, Wins-Sal	1	1	0	0	0	1	1.000
Munoz, Burlington	7	25	2	0	0	0	1.000		Senger, Ral-Dur	3	13	3	1	0	0	.941
Vickery, Bur	1	9	1	0	0	0	1.000		Singleton, R Mt	3	15	1	1	1	1	.941
Croken, Wins-Sal	3	9	0	0	0	1	1.000		Cappelli, Ral-Dur	1	7	1	1	0	0	.889

PITCHERS

Player and Club	G.	PO.	A.	E.	DP.	Pct.		Player and Club	G.	PO.	A.	E.	DP.	Pct.
SCHLIEVE, Pen	27	12	25	0	0	1.000		Lohse, Rocky Mount*	16	2	11	1	0	.929
Shreve, Ral-Dur	28	14	18	0	1	1.000		Wolger, Ral-Dur	12	2	11	1	0	.929
Olsen, Kinston*	23	8	23	0	2	1.000		Settle, Salem	22	9	15	2	1	.923
Slayback, Rocky Mt	14	4	23	0	1	1.000		Poulsen, Kinston	27	5	7	1	0	.923
Everett, Salem*	33	7	16	0	0	1.000		Helwig, Rocky Mt*	17	5	10	1	1	.923
Jenkins, Lynchburg	29	9	14	0	1	1.000		Herron, Peninsula	37	5	18	2	0	.920
Valesente, Bur	13	1	19	0	3	1.000		Leshnock, Rocky Mt*	25	5	18	2	1	.920
Meyer, Peninsula*	10	5	13	0	1	1.000		Vollweiler, Bur	19	4	19	2	0	.920
Morgan, Ral-Dur	24	1	16	0	1	1.000		Parchem, Bur*	19	1	10	1	1	.917
Bolick, Burlington	17	6	11	0	0	1.000		Susce, Burlington	28	4	6	1	1	.909
Tissot, Rocky Mt	49	5	10	0	1	1.000		Koering, Lynchburg	31	8	41	5	2	.907
Canty, Ral-Dur*	12	4	11	0	0	1.000		Sheftall, Lynchburg	36	3	16	2	0	.905
Brechtel, Ral-Dur	14	5	9	0	0	1.000		Mercado, W-S*	22	6	13	2	0	.905
Elliott, Kinston	14	2	9	0	0	1.000		Covey, Peninsula	32	6	22	3	0	.903
Baker, Lynchburg	47	6	4	0	0	1.000		Barranca, Kinston	23	2	25	3	0	.900
Love, Kinston*	12	1	7	0	0	1.000		Parker, Burlington	21	4	14	2	2	.900
Ley, Kinston*	20	2	5	0	0	1.000		Ware, Rocky Mount	18	2	16	2	2	.900
Giron, Salem	14	0	7	0	0	1.000		Christman, Lynch*	15	3	15	2	1	.900
Bandy, Peninsula	39	0	6	0	0	1.000		Fremuth, Rocky Mt	20	2	7	1	0	.900
Cabral, Salem*	16	1	4	0	0	1.000		Dennington, Bur	14	1	8	1	2	.900
Ramirez, Kinston	16	1	4	0	0	1.000		Foucher, Rocky Mt	44	6	20	3	2	.897
Davis, Raleigh-Dur	10	2	3	0	2	1.000		Smallwood, Bur	25	7	19	3	1	.897
Thomas, Rocky Mt	10	0	5	0	0	1.000		Diorio, Peninsula	21	2	15	2	2	.895
Zuniga, Lynchburg	10	1	3	0	0	1.000		Sells, Salem	11	6	11	2	0	.895
Harkness, Lynch	10	0	3	0	0	1.000		Hambright, Kinston	45	5	3	1	0	.889
Newhauser, W-S	14	0	2	0	0	1.000		Cates, Peninsula*	10	1	7	1	0	.889
Scramuzzo, Pen	30	10	36	1	4	.979		Tekulve, Salem	41	4	19	3	1	.885
Clifton, W-S*	21	5	25	1	0	.968		Corddry, W-S*	31	2	13	2	0	.882
Frontino, Salem	38	7	21	1	0	.966		Mason, Salem	12	2	12	2	0	.875
Thornton, W-S	44	5	18	1	2	.958		Mazerall, W-S	31	3	4	1	0	.875
Pierce, Peninsula*	27	7	38	2	2	.957		Holt, Burlington*	17	3	4	1	1	.875
Hillstrom, Bur	32	4	17	1	1	.955		Schirripa, Kin	26	4	9	2	1	.867
McGlothen, W-S	31	15	25	2	1	.952		Nottle, Lynchburg	42	5	13	3	2	.857
Bethell, Ral-Dur	20	9	11	1	1	.952		Minshall, Salem	26	4	13	3	0	.850
Snyder, Wins-Sal*	34	5	33	2	2	.950		Bowlby, Ral-Dur	38	3	13	3	1	.842
Oglesby, Lynchburg	22	3	16	1	0	.950		Marsden, Wins-Salem	22	3	7	2	0	.833
Walters, Kinston	23	18	38	3	3	.949		Dalton, Burlington	19	5	14	4	0	.826
Crosby, Kinston	18	5	13	1	1	.947		E. Kelly, Peninsula	10	4	5	2	0	.818
Bootcheck, R Mt*	23	7	25	2	3	.941		Remington, Lynch	16	5	11	4	0	.800
McLachlin, Pen*	22	8	23	2	0	.939		Jones, Wins-Salem	13	1	3	1	0	.800
Gregory, Lynchburg	18	3	12	1	1	.938		McKee, Salem	26	7	12	5	0	.792
Evans, Ral-Dur*	10	7	8	1	1	.938		Mack, Lynchburg*	15	5	9	4	1	.778
Suskiewich, Kin*	21	4	25	2	1	.935		McFarland, Ral-Dur	13	4	11	5	0	.750
Rothermel, Ral-Dur*	21	6	22	2	2	.933		Nevil, Rocky Mount*	19	1	7	3	0	.727
LeBright, Ral-Dur	25	4	10	1	0	.933		Angelier, Rocky Mt	10	1	1	1	0	.667
Carter, Burlington	18	5	9	1	0	.933		Dare, Salem*	35	1	6	4	0	.636
Fryar, Wins-Salem	27	10	17	2	1	.931		Fuchs, Salem*	22	1	9	7	1	.588

(Fewer Than Ten Games)

Player and Club	G.	PO.	A.	E.	DP.	Pct.		Player and Club	G.	PO.	A.	E.	DP.	Pct.
Williams, W-S	9	4	11	0	1	1.000		Hepler, Burlington*	5	1	1	0	0	1.000
Malcolm, Peninsula	6	1	9	0	0	1.000		Bryan, Kinston	5	0	1	0	0	1.000
Kison, Salem	5	1	5	0	0	1.000		Johnston, Salem	3	0	1	0	0	1.000
Whitson, Burlington	5	3	4	0	0	1.000		Clifford, Rocky Mt	9	4	6	1	1	.909
Sanders, Ral-Dur	6	2	3	0	0	1.000		Murphy, Rocky Mt*	7	6	7	1	1	.875
Crowder, Kinston	4	0	5	0	0	1.000		Seifert, Ral-Dur	6	0	6	1	0	.857
Darcy, Raleigh-Dur	4	0	5	0	0	1.000		Robinson, Ral-Dur	7	2	5	2	0	.778
Cushmore, Rocky Mt*	3	1	4	0	1	1.000		Holliday, Rocky Mt	7	1	8	3	0	.750
Durham, Peninsula	3	1	4	0	0	1.000		Ignasiak, Rocky Mt*	7	0	3	1	0	.750
Swanson, Kinston	3	2	3	0	0	1.000		Coble, Peninsula	6	0	3	1	0	.750
White, Wins-Salem*	8	0	3	0	0	1.000		Shields, Burlington	4	1	1	1	0	.667
Buskey, Kinston	3	2	1	0	0	1.000		Strampe, Rocky Mt	4	1	1	1	0	.667
Crosby, Lynchburg	2	0	2	0	0	1.000		Heger, Lynchburg	7	0	1	1	0	.500
Zgorzelski, W-S*	7	0	2	0	0	1.000		Pole, Winston-Salem	3	1	0	1	0	.500

The following players do not have any recorded accepted chances; therefore are not listed in the fielding average in their respective positions: Barrientos, p; Brykczynski, p; Bowers, p; Campbell, p; Cichon, p; Davidson, p; James J. Dietz, p*.

CLUB PITCHING

Club	G.	CG.	ShO.	Sv.	IP.	H.	R.	ER.	HR.	BB.	Int. BB.	HB.	SO.	WP.	Bk.	ERA.
Kinston	137	47	12	26	1175	1024	472	355	67	451	38	26	883	79	3	2.72
Winston-Salem	139	50	13	18	1221	1035	489	393	50	653	40	49	909	95	6	2.90
Rocky Mount	138	43	16	20	1162	1019	485	375	44	574	32	29	773	50	4	2.91
Peninsula	140	44	16	24	1199	1054	506	411	59	467	29	43	803	71	1	3.09
Raleigh-Durham	141	60	18	22	1198	1109	574	468	67	634	24	49	855	89	6	3.51
Burlington	137	52	16	17	1145	1093	552	452	65	515	12	30	801	69	1	3.55
Salem	140	39	7	21	1203	1124	645	478	71	588	24	60	932	100	5	3.58
Lynchburg	140	39	11	20	1210	1281	603	481	63	438	30	49	769	70	9	3.58

PITCHERS' RECORDS

(Leading Qualifiers for Earned-Run Average Leadership—140 or More Innings)

*Throws lefthanded.

Pitcher—Club	G.	GS.	CG.	ShO.	W.	L.	Sv.	Pct.	IP.	H.	R.	ER.	HR.	BB.	Int. BB.	HB.	SO.	WP.	ERA.
Bootcheck, R Mt* .23	23	15	5	13	8	0	.619	173	135	47	37	6	47	0	1	88	6	1.92
McGlothen, W-S	31	29	16	5	15	7	1	.682	229	166	63	57	8	91	6	7	202	8	2.24
Olsen, Kinston* .23	23	12	5	13	5	0	.722	171	148	52	43	15	24	2	0	131	3	2.26
Clifton, Wins-S*	21	20	9	0	8	6	0	.571	147	100	42	38	8	76	1	7	88	9	2.33
Schlieve, Pen ..27	22	12	3	8	10	1	.444	172	136	53	45	7	32	4	5	121	5	2.35
Walters, Kinston	23	22	10	1	11	7	0	.611	162	145	61	43	5	45	7	5	69	5	2.39
Rothermel, R-D* .21	20	12	2	8	10	0	.444	150	129	58	43	7	55	3	1	97	9	2.58
Scramuzzo, Pen .30	29	14	3	8	16	0	.333	222	182	78	68	14	86	7	5	153	6	2.76
Snyder, Wins-S*	34	17	7	2	13	5	3	.722	146	134	56	45	6	63	4	5	94	13	2.77
Keoring, Lynch ..31	29	9	3	12	13	0	.480	220	234	87	71	5	78	2	5	113	10	2.90

Departmental Leaders: G—Tissot, 49; GS—Koering, McGlothen, Scramuzzo, 29; CG—McGlothen, 16; ShO—Bootcheck, Evans, McGlothen, Olsen, 5; W—McGlothen, 15; L—Scramuzzo, 16; Sv—Bowlby, Hambright, 15; Pct.—Suskiewich, .750; IP—McGlothen, 229; H—Koering, 234; R—McKee, 93; ER—Koering, 71; HR—Olsen, 15; BB—Bethell, 93; IBB—Thornton, Tissot, 9; HB—Oglesby, 9; SO—McGlothen, 202; WP—McKee, Schirripa, Vollweiler, 17.

(All Pitchers—Listed Alphabetically)

Pitcher—Club	G.	GS.	CG.	ShO.	W.	L.	Sv.	Pct.	IP.	H.	R.	ER.	HR.	BB.	Int. BB.	HB.	SO.	WP.	ERA.
Angelier, Ry Mt* .10	0	0	0	2	1	0	.667	15	16	12	6	2	13	2	0	12	1	3.60
Baker, Lynchburg	47	3	3	0	11	5	9	.688	110	105	32	27	7	28	4	7	95	3	2.21
Bandy, Peninsula	39	0	0	5	3	9	5	.625	62	48	22	20	3	18	2	3	52	0	2.90
Barranca, Kinston	23	21	3	0	7	6	0	.538	134	119	61	34	8	56	3	2	107	15	2.28
Barrientos, Pen	8	0	0	0	0	1	0	.000	11	15	10	7	2	10	0	0	9	0	5.73
Bethell, Ral-Dur	20	20	6	1	7	0	0	.438	115	109	68	57	6	93	2	7	89	12	4.46
Bevil, Rocky Mt*	19	10	1	1	1	5	1	.167	66	70	36	27	2	28	0	3	44	2	3.68
Bolick, Burlington	17	13	8	3	8	5	1	.615	102	99	43	39	6	24	0	2	75	1	3.44
Bootcheck, R Mt*	23	23	15	5	13	8	0	.619	173	135	47	37	6	47	0	1	88	6	1.92
Bowers, Peninsula	1	0	0	0	0	1	0	.000	1	2	2	1	0	0	0	0	2	0	9.00
Bowlby, Ral-Dur .38	1	0	0	7	4	15	.636	75	51	24	21	3	37	2	4	46	4	2.52
Brechtel, Ral-Dur	14	9	0	0	3	1	0	.750	68	65	28	23	2	26	2	4	58	1	3.04
Bryan, Kinston ..	5	0	0	0	0	2	0	.000	6	6	3	1	0	6	0	1	5	0	1.50
Brykczynski, Bur .	1	0	0	0	0	0	0	.000	1	2	2	2	1	1	0	0	0	0	18.00
Buskey, Kinston .	2	1	0	0	1	1	0	.500	13	7	2	2	1	3	0	0	5	0	1.38
Cabral, Salem* ..16	1	0	0	0	2	0	0	.000	32	31	19	19	2	23	0	3	26	2	5.34
Campbell, Pen ...	1	1	0	0	0	0	0	.000	0	3	0	0	0	5	0	0	0	0	0.00
Canty, Ral-Dur* ..12	7	1	3	2	2	1	.600	50	63	45	35	5	27	1	5	23	9	6.30
Carter, Burling .18	9	2	0	2	6	2	.250	76	79	42	32	3	40	2	0	41	7	3.79
Cates, Peninsula*	10	10	4	2	3	5	0	.375	59	60	30	22	5	26	1	2	24	8	3.36
Christman, Lynch*	15	15	1	0	3	7	0	.300	83	82	49	39	6	46	2	2	58	5	4.23
Cichon, Lynchburg	5	0	0	0	0	0	0	.000	7	14	12	11	2	6	1	0	5	1	14.14
Clifford, Rocky Mt	9	7	3	0	3	3	0	.500	52	54	16	12	3	11	3	2	27	0	2.08
Clifton, Wins-S*	21	20	9	0	8	6	0	.571	147	100	42	38	8	76	1	7	88	9	2.33
Coble, Peninsula	6	6	1	1	2	3	0	.400	29	42	22	15	1	7	0	1	18	0	4.66
Corddry, Wins-S*	31	11	3	2	5	4	0	.556	100	79	42	32	4	78	3	8	88	10	2.88
Covey, Peninsula .32	4	1	1	6	3	1	.667	86	73	32	31	5	30	3	5	49	11	3.24
Crosby, Kinston ..18	17	2	1	5	8	0	.385	113	103	53	49	6	46	3	2	94	5	3.90
Crosby, Lynchburg	8	0	0	0	2	2	0	.000	11	19	12	10	1	7	1	0	5	0	8.18
Crowder, Kinston	4	2	0	0	1	0	1	1.000	15	15	10	5	1	3	0	1	12	0	3.00
Cushmore, Ry Mt*	2	2	2	2	2	0	0	1.000	26	11	2	2	1	6	0	0	17	0	0.69
Dalton, Burlington	19	16	5	1	5	8	1	.385	108	101	51	45	4	61	3	3	90	3	3.75
Darcy, Ral-Dur .	4	4	1	0	1	2	0	.333	27	25	7	4	0	14	1	0	11	1	1.33
Dare, Salem* ..35	2	1	0	1	6	4	.143	62	52	39	31	3	43	1	6	48	5	4.50
Davidson, Bur ...	2	0	0	0	0	0	0	.000	.1	.1	2	2	0	3	0	0	2	2	18.00
Davis, Ral-Dur .10	2	1	1	1	0	0	1.000	34	32	15	12	3	17	3	2	30	1	3.18
Dennington, Bur .14	1	0	0	0	1	0	.000	33	35	20	15	2	20	0	2	16	3	4.09
Dietz, Ral-Dur* .	2	0	0	0	0	0	0	.000	2	4	3	2	2	0	0	4	2	0	9.00
Diorio, Peninsula	21	0	0	0	1	3	0	.250	49	29	22	10	4	12	3	5	35	4	1.84
Durham, Pen 3	0	0	0	0	0	0	0	.000	8	11	8	6	2	1	0	0	8	0	6.75
Elliott, Kinston ..14	11	3	1	5	4	1	.556	72	61	39	32	6	42	0	3	69	6	4.00
Evans, Ral-Dur* .10	10	7	5	8	2	0	.800	78	54	15	14	3	38	0	2	70	8	1.62

Pitcher—Club	G	GS	CG	ShO	W	L	Sv	Pct.	IP	H	R	ER	HR	BB	Int. BB	HB	SO	WP	ERA
Everett, Salem*	.33	13	2	1	9	5	4	.643	111	103	54	38	9	53	1	5	98	15	3.08
Foucher, Ry Mt	.44	2	1	0	4	4	2	.500	109	97	48	42	5	56	5	7	86	7	3.47
Fremuth, Ry Mt	.20	0	0	0	6	1	5	.857	48	30	10	7	0	18	2	1	66	1	1.31
Frontino, Salem	.38	2	0	0	4	7	5	.364	100	95	44	35	4	36	5	3	78	7	3.15
Fryar, Wins-S	...27	20	7	2	8	8	0	.500	125	105	67	49	6	92	3	0	74	14	3.53
Fuchs, Salem*	.22	17	1	0	4	8	1	.333	83	108	82	59	4	65	1	4	63	8	6.40
Giron, Salem	...14	11	2	0	5	4	0	.556	75	71	41	28	5	32	2	1	65	4	3.36
Gregory, Lynch	.18	9	4	1	3	7	1	.300	76	88	50	38	9	21	1	3	46	2	4.50
Hambright, Kins	.45	1	1	0	6	6	15	.500	93	65	19	16	4	34	3	2	96	7	1.55
Harkness, Lynch	.10	0	0	0	0	0	0	.000	16	9	8	1	0	9	0	0	14	0	3.60
Heger, Lynchburg	7	1	0	1	5	0	1	.167	39	38	25	19	2	27	0	4	43	5	4.38
Helwig, Ry Mt*	.17	11	4	0	6	6	0	.500	80	80	38	34	8	19	2	0	36	1	3.83
Hepler, Burling*	5	1	0	0	1	2	0	.333	8	6	8	1	9	0	1	6	2	9.00
Herron, Pen	37	1	0	0	12	8	3	.600	72	59	25	12	3	26	3	3	65	5	1.50
Hillstrom, Bur	.32	12	5	0	8	8	3	.500	114	105	51	40	5	60	1	1	95	2	3.16
Holliday, Ry Mt	.7	5	0	0	0	5	0	.000	33	37	21	12	1	8	0	0	16	1	3.27
Holt, Burlington*	17	3	1	1	1	2	1	.333	37	30	26	22	4	31	1	0	23	2	5.35
Ignasiak, Ry Mt*	7	7	1	0	2	1	0	.667	29	27	18	16	0	30	0	1	21	5	4.97
Jenkins, Lynch	.29	8	4	2	6	2	2	.750	102	87	39	33	2	42	2	4	78	13	2.91
Johnston, Salem	.3	0	0	0	0	0	0	.000	6	8	6	4	0	2	0	1	5	0	6.00
Jones, Wins-Sal	.13	4	0	0	2	2	0	.500	27	19	11	8	1	19	0	1	24	0	2.67
E. Kelly, Pen	...10	10	0	0	3	4	0	.429	56	53	32	28	0	32	0	2	42	9	4.50
Kison, Salem	.. 5	4	2	0	3	1	0	.750	33	17	5	3	0	7	1	7	26	2	0.82
Koering, Lynch	.31	29	9	3	12	13	0	.480	220	234	87	71	5	78	2	5	113	10	2.90
LeBright, R-D	.25	6	4	0	6	5	3	.545	83	90	43	36	8	27	2	6	41	0	3.90
Leshnock, Ry Mt*	25	21	4	2	6	8	0	.429	116	104	67	52	5	82	1	1	81	7	4.03
Ley, Kinston*	...20	6	1	0	1	5	4	.167	51	49	30	19	2	41	2	3	54	7	3.35
Lohse, Rocky Mt*	16	12	3	0	4	3	1	.571	75	78	34	25	4	37	1	0	34	7	3.00
Love, Burlington	.12	3	1	1	1	2	0	.333	33	38	15	15	2	17	1	1	31	4	4.09
Mack, Lynchburg*	15	12	2	1	3	9	0	.250	61	73	42	32	3	39	1	1	35	8	4.72
Malcolm, Pen	.. 6	6	0	0	2	0	0	1.000	33	13	13	2	14	0	0	11	0	3.66
Marsden, Wins-S	22	6	0	0	2	6	2	.250	61	69	33	25	2	21	2	5	27	5	3.69
Mason, Salem	...16	16	7	1	4	7	0	.364	110	97	58	37	6	39	1	5	82	3	3.03
Mazerall, Wins-S	31	1	0	0	2	3	3	.400	55	58	28	24	3	16	4	1	48	4	3.93
McFarland, R-D	.13	12	9	1	6	6	0	.500	94	80	41	29	6	39	0	1	54	3	2.78
McGlothen, W-S	.31	29	16	5	15	7	1	.682	229	166	63	57	8	91	6	7	202	8	2.24
McKee, Salem	..26	26	10	1	8	15	0	.348	173	155	93	69	9	88	1	7	170	17	3.59
McLachlin, Pen*	.22	22	4	0	8	8	0	.500	138	127	65	51	3	70	1	6	97	8	3.33
Mercado, Wins-S*	22	18	4	2	8	6	0	.571	107	106	48	43	4	55	2	7	97	8	3.62
Meyer, Pen*	...10	9	2	1	1	3	0	.250	55	49	28	22	1	28	2	2	33	3	3.60
Minshall, Salem	.26	18	4	1	5	8	0	.385	124	124	66	57	6	74	2	4	62	12	4.14
Morgan, Ral-Dur	24	16	5	1	5	5	1	.500	120	124	79	66	2	79	2	5	90	15	4.95
Murphy, Ry Mt*	.7	7	2	1	1	5	0	.167	43	41	18	14	0	27	1	1	18	0	2.93
Newhauser, W-S	.14	1	0	0	3	1	0	.750	25	28	18	15	4	26	3	0	23	2	5.40
Nottle, Lynchburg	42	5	2	0	6	2	4	.750	86	88	37	26	6	20	5	4	40	1	2.72
Oglesby, Lynch	..22	15	3	0	2	10	2	.167	106	118	56	48	5	29	9	6	65	6	4.08
Olsen, Kinston*	.23	23	12	5	13	5	0	.722	171	148	52	43	15	24	2	0	131	3	2.26
Parchem, Bur*	.19	9	4	0	5	5	1	.500	80	80	34	28	7	42	0	2	43	6	3.15
Parker, Burling	.21	9	3	1	7	4	2	.636	91	90	38	32	6	29	0	0	68	1	3.16
Pierce, Pen*	...27	20	6	2	8	5	1	.615	146	142	64	60	7	64	3	4	86	10	3.70
Pole, Wins-Salem	3	3	1	0	1	2	0	.333	20	21	13	11	0	8	0	1	18	3	4.95
Poulsen, Kinston	.27	13	8	0	7	9	1	.438	134	129	54	42	9	45	6	4	95	4	2.82
Ramirez, Kinston	16	0	0	0	1	1	2	.500	25	29	14	12	0	20	5	0	13	5	4.32
Remington, Lynch	16	5	4	1	4	7	0	.364	90	97	46	41	3	32	3	3	64	7	4.10
Robinson, R-D	.7	2	1	0	2	2	0	.500	30	36	29	23	2	35	1	1	26	6	6.90
Rothermel, R-D*	.21	20	12	2	8	10	0	.444	150	129	58	43	7	55	3	1	97	9	2.58
Sanders, Ral-Dur	6	5	2	1	3	1	0	.750	37	44	21	21	4	15	0	1	37	3	5.11
Schirripa, Kinston	26	9	2	0	5	7	2	.417	94	78	39	29	5	52	5	2	65	17	2.78
Schlieve, Pen	...27	22	12	3	8	10	1	.444	172	136	53	45	7	32	4	5	121	5	2.35
Scramuzzo, Pen	.30	29	14	3	8	16	0	.333	222	182	78	68	14	86	7	5	153	6	2.76
Seifert, Ral-Dur	6	4	4	3	4	1	1	.800	34	17	7	6	1	14	0	1	14	0	1.59
Sells, Salem	11	11	5	1	6	4	0	.600	84	73	46	32	9	18	3	2	54	3	3.43
Settle, Salem	...22	19	5	1	7	7	0	.500	131	122	63	49	11	57	0	6	80	14	3.37
Sheftall, Lynch	.36	22	6	2	6	12	0	.333	178	187	91	66	9	45	4	7	99	9	3.34
Shields, Burling	4	0	0	0	0	0	0	.000	13	20	23	12	0	13	0	1	5	0	8.31
Shreve, Ral-Dur	28	18	7	1	10	11	1	.476	163	151	70	58	12	82	5	6	138	9	3.20
Slayback, Ry Mt	14	14	4	1	5	5	0	.500	89	60	40	26	3	55	2	8	63	3	2.63
Smallwood, Bur	.25	19	6	4	9	6	1	.600	136	122	66	49	8	51	0	1	131	9	3.24
Snyder, Wins*	34	17	7	2	13	5	3	.722	146	134	56	45	6	63	4	5	94	13	2.77
Strampe, Ry Mt	.4	1	1	1	2	0	0	1.000	14	3	2	2	0	8	0	0	11	0	1.29
Susce, Burlington	28	1	0	0	6	2	2	.750	58	56	24	21	4	27	3	5	47	5	3.26
Suskiewich, Kin*	21	10	4	2	9	3	0	.750	88	72	26	20	3	31	2	6	64	4	2.05

Pitcher—Club	G.	GS.	CG.	ShO.	W.	L.	Sv.	Pct.	IP.	H.	R.	ER.	HR.	BB.	Int.BB.	HB.	SO.	WP.	ERA.
Swanson, Kins*	..3	1	0	0	1	0	0	.000	6	7	9	8	2	8	0	0	3	1	12.00
Tekulve, Salem	..41	0	0	0	4	6	7	.400	79	68	29	17	3	51	6	6	75	8	1.94
Thomas, Rocky Mt	10	0	0	0	2	1	1	.667	15	15	5	5	1	15	3	0	14	1	3.00
Thornton, Wins-S	44	0	0	0	8	7	9	.533	93	78	30	21	2	43	9	1	67	7	2.03
Tissot, Rocky Mt	49	1	0	0	5	7	8	.417	88	71	28	18	0	64	9	1	75	5	1.84
Valesente, Bur	..13	13	7	1	8	1	0	.889	95	90	38	31	5	37	0	4	37	5	2.94
Vollweiler, Bur	.19	19	8	2	7	10	0	.412	129	116	62	53	7	40	1	5	78	17	3.70
Walters, Kins	...23	22	10	1	11	7	0	.611	162	145	61	43	5	45	7	5	69	5	2.39
Ware, Rocky Mt	.18	14	2	1	6	5	2	.545	91	90	43	38	3	50	1	3	64	3	3.76
White, Wins-S*	.8	0	0	0	1	1	0	.500	10	4	4	2	0	14	0	1	7	1	1.80
Whitson, Burling	5	5	2	1	4	0	0	1.000	29	23	7	6	0	10	0	2	13	0	1.86
Williams, Wins-S	9	9	3	0	4	0	0	1.000	67	57	19	15	2	33	3	3	38	3	2.01
Wolger, Ral-Dur	.12	5	0	0	3	1	0	.750	37	35	21	18	1	34	1	3	27	6	4.38
Zgorzelski, W-S*	7	0	0	0	0	0	0	.000	10	11	15	8	0	18	0	2	14	8	7.20
Zuniga, Lynch	...10	0	0	0	0	2	0	.000	20	25	16	12	2	9	2	0	9	0	5.40

BALKS—Bethell, 4; Fryar, Zuniga, 3 each; Marsden, Remington, Tissot, 2 each; Cabral, Carter, Crowder, Dare, Foucher, Hambright, Harkness, Ignasiak, Jenkins, Mack, McKee, Minshall, Morgan, Schirripa, Scramuzzo, Settle, Sheftall, Snyder, Wolger, 1 each.

COMBINATION SHUTOUTS—Parchem-Dennington, Burlington; Barranca-Schirripa, Crosby-Hambright, Kinston; Nottle-Gregory, Lynchburg; McLachlin-Herron, Schlieve-Herron, Scramuzzo-Herron, Peninsula; Brechtel-Rothermel-Bowiby, Raleigh-Durham; Bootcheck-Tissot, Ignasiak-Fremuth, Rocky Mount; Giron-Cabral-Dare, Salem.

NO-HIT GAMES—Olsen, Kinston, defeated Burlington, 2-0, May 11; Smallwood, Burlington, defeated Salem, 5-0, June 1 (seven innings); Elliott, Kinston, defeated Lynchburg, 5-0, June 14 (seven innings); Leshnock, Rocky Mount, defeated Peninsula, 4-0, June 28.

ALONG THE MINOR LEAGUE TRAIL . . . .

(Continued from page 484)

Louisville (International) went out to the mound to talk to young Mike Garman, who had gotten into trouble. "He was trying to overthrow the ball, so I went out and told him just to relax." Garman did, too much. He proceeded to throw two wild pitches and lose the game. . . . Writer George McClelland's solution to Buffalo's park problem: "Bring in 50 bulldozers and level everything within five blocks of the stadium. Because it is not a bad place to play baseball or to watch a game. It's the coming and going that gets you." . . . . Shreveport (Texas) was awarded one of the most unique "outs" in history when President Bobby Bragan gave the Braves a one-time postponement okay of a scheduled May 16-17 weekend series with Memphis. Reason? Eight Shreveport players were away on military duty. . . . Professional soccer, which can't get arrested in the United States, stole fans from the Mexico City clubs and got away with it. With World Cup matches in progress there, a key Reds' game against Poza Rica drew only 1,200 fans. Ordinarily you can find these many around one taco stand in the park. . . . When 47-year-old Art Fowler threw his first pitch in relief the night of May 24 for Denver vs Wichita, it marked the 1,000th game of his professional career. . . . Once a thief, always a thief, so it says. Well, for the Waterbury Pirates that holds true Last year, playing at York, they led the Eastern League with 186 thefts. Now at Waterbury, they stole

(Continued on page 521)

Florida State League

CLASS A

CHAMPIONSHIP WINNERS IN PREVIOUS YEARS

1919—Sanford* .... .605	1941—St. Augustine .... .659	1958—St. Petersburg .... .732
Orlando* .... .703	Leesburg (4th)‡ .... .488	St. Petersburg .... .681
1920—Tampa .... .654	1942-45—Did not operate.	1959—Tampa .... .591
Tampa .... .722	1946—Orlando§ .... .681	St. Petersburg† .... .612
1921—Orlando .... .635	1947—St. Augustine .... .625	1960—Lakeland .... .731
St. Petersburg .... .618	Gainesville (2nd)‡ .. .584	Palatka† .... .614
1922—St. Petersburg .... .503	1948—Orlando .... .643	1961—Tampa† .... .710
St. Petersburg .... .618	Daytona B'ch (2nd)‡ .616	Sarasota .... .696
1923—Orlando .... .667	1949—Gainesville .... .635	1962—Sarasota .... .689
Orlando .... .678	St. Augustine (3rd)‡ .556	Fort Lauderdale† .... .623
1924—Lakeland .... .695	1950—Orlando .... .629	1963—Sarasota .... .645
Lakeland .... .683	DeLand (3rd)‡ .... .590	Sarasota .... .667
1925—St. Petersburg .... .667	1951—DeLand§ .... .643	1964—Fort Lauderdale† .... .629
Tampa† .... .696	Palatka (3rd)‡ .... .704	St. Petersburg .... .594
1926—Sanford .... .647	1952—DeLand x .... .704	1965—Fort Lauderdale .... .627
Sanford .... .623	Palatka (3rd)‡ .... .569	Fort Lauderdale .... .634
1927—Orlando† .... .600	1953—Daytona Beach† .... .657	1966—Leesburg† .... .781
Miami .... .661	DeLand .... .703	St. Petersburg .... .700
1928-35—Did not operate.	1954—Jacksonville Beach .629	1967—St. Petersburg y .... .691
1936—Gainesville .... .542	Lakeland† .... .594	Orlando .... .638
St. Augustine (4th)† .492	1955—Orlando .... .671	1968—Miami .... .613
1937—Gainesville§ .... .616	Orlando .... .643	Orlando z .... .579
1938—Cocoa .... .626	1956—Cocoa .... .614	1969—Miami a .... .606
Gainesville (2nd)‡ .615	Cocoa .... .671	Orlando .... .606
1939—Sanford .... .787	1957—Palatka .... .629	
Orlando (4th)‡ .... .507	Tampa† .... .681	
1940—Daytona Beach .... .619		

*Split-season playoff abandoned after each team won three games. †Won split-season playoff.
‡Won four-club playoff. §Won championship and four-club playoff. xWon both halves of split-season.
yLeague divided into Eastern and Western divisions with split-season. St. Petersburg and Orlando won both halves of split season; St. Petersburg won playoff.
zLeague divided into Eastern and Western divisions. Miami won regular-season pennant on basis of highest won-lost percentage. Orlando won four-club playoff involving first two teams in each division.
aLeague divided into Southern and Central divisions. Miami won playoff between division leaders.
(NOTE—Pennant awarded to playoff winner in 1936.)

COMPOSITE STANDING OF CLUBS AT CLOSE OF SEASON, AUGUST 29

EASTERN DIVISION

Club	Mia.	WPB.	DB.	PB.	FtL.	Coa.	StP.	Lak.	Tam.	WH.	Orl.	DeL.	W.	L.	T.	Pct.	G.B.
†Miami (1*) .. .		13	13	13	16	15	3	4	4	1	3	3	88	45	0	.662	....
W. Palm B.(18)	9		9	15	15	15	2	3	3	3	3	2	79	50	0	.612	7
Daytona B.(17)	9	11		15	13	16	2	4	1	1	3	1	76	55	0	.580	11
Pomp. B.(19*)	8	7	7		15	9	2	2	1	3	2	2	58	70	0	.453	27½
Ft. Laud.(10)	6	7	8	7		14	1	2	2	2	4	3	56	76	0	.424	31½
Cocoa (16) ...	7	5	6	10	7		1	2	1	1	1	2	43	84	0	.339	42

WESTERN DIVISION

Club	Mia.	WPB.	DB.	PB.	FtL.	Coa.	StP.	Lak.	Tam.	WH.	Orl.	DeL.	W.	L.	T.	Pct.	G.B.
St. Pete.(22*)	1	2	2	2	3	2		16	15	14	8	13	78	52	0	.600	....
Lakeland (6) ..	0	1	0	2	2	2	6		14	14	16	12	69	64	0	.519	10½
Tampa (15*) ..	0	1	3	2	2	3	6	8		13	12	14	64	68	0	.485	15
Winter H.(2*)	3	1	3	1	2	3	7	7	9		13	12	61	71	0	.462	18
Orlando (9) ..	1	0	1	2	0	3	14	6	10	9		13	59	74	0	.444	20½
DeLand (C-op)	1	2	3	1	1	2	8	10	8	10	9		55	77	0	.417	24

†Miami won regular-season pennant on basis of highest won-lost percentage.
Key to major league farm teams (indicated by numbers after clubs in standing) shown on Page 384.
Playoffs—Miami defeated Lakeland, two games to none. St. Petersburg defeated West Palm Beach, two games to one. Miami defeated St. Petersburg, two games to none.
Regular-Season Attendance—Cocoa, 22,166; Daytona Beach, 31,371; DeLand, 16,357; Ft. Lauderdale, 51,063; Lakeland, 15,524; Miami, 74,235; Orlando, 51,931; Pompano Beach, 14,759; St. Petersburg, 104,485; Tampa. 32,408; West Palm Beach, 50,620; Winter Haven, 15,684. Total, 480,603. Playoffs, 8,523. No all-star game.
Managers: Cocoa—Tony Pacheco; Daytona Beach—Stan Wasiak; DeLand—Malcolm (Bunky) Warren; Ft. Lauderdale—Lamar North; Lakeland—Dick Tracewski; Miami—Woody Smith; Orlando—

Jackie Ferrell; Pompano Beach—Gordon MacKenzie; St. Petersburg—Joe Cunningham; Tampa—Dick Kennedy; West Palm Beach—J. W. Porter; Winter Haven—John K. Butler.

All-Star Team: 1B—Staton, Lakeland; 2B—Stroman, West Palm Beach; 3B—Reitz, St. Petersburg; SS—Garcia, Orlando; OF—Caldarella, St. Petersburg; Mangual, West Palm Beach; Reinbach, Miami; C—McDermott, Daytona Beach; P—Luebber, Orlando; Hebert, Miami; Manager—Dick Tracewski, Lakeland.

(Compiled by Howe News Bureau, Chicago, Ill).

CLUB BATTING

Club	G.	AB.	R.	OR.	H.	TB.	2B.	3B.	HR.	RBI.	SH.	SF.	BB.	Int. BB.	HP.	SO.	SB.	CS.	LOB.	Pct.
Daytona B.	131	4079	584	462	1054	1389	132	64	25	465	61	30	477	34	30	667	127	60	921	.258
Miami ...	133	4073	554	419	1014	1334	133	62	21	481	60	46	594	36	36	648	124	47	925	.249
St. Pete. ..	130	4256	489	416	1055	1344	135	38	26	426	79	37	464	37	53	670	48	37	1028	.248
DeLand ..	132	4227	506	620	1022	1324	149	42	23	430	74	31	485	27	29	867	85	38	925	.242
Lakeland ..	133	4240	486	491	1004	1247	114	36	19	411	44	37	468	30	36	755	99	26	949	.237
W. Palm B.	129	3979	493	387	937	1173	101	51	11	421	82	37	584	20	46	744	123	37	986	.235
Tampa ...	132	4120	433	452	967	1189	108	36	14	353	81	40	457	21	32	752	122	51	954	.235
Orlando ..	133	4254	476	458	983	1320	130	33	47	460	88	33	467	39	34	850	109	34	931	.231
Win. Haven	132	4219	441	481	964	1271	141	35	32	380	62	30	522	29	31	965	83	58	1003	.228
Ft. Laud.	132	4116	473	555	937	1248	119	39	38	394	54	40	538	25	43	813	133	45	973	.228
Pompano B.	128	3814	480	524	851	1103	105	39	23	379	51	25	456	15	26	809	89	32	809	.223
Cocoa ...	127	3841	366	516	823	1018	96	36	9	287	35	22	469	19	47	831	71	40	892	.214

Missing games at Pompano Beach unobtainable and not included: August 21, Pompano Beach 3, Daytona Beach 1; August 23, Daytona Beach 6-5, Pompano Beach 4-4.

INDIVIDUAL BATTING

(Leading Qualifiers for Batting Championship—415 or More Plate Appearances)

*Bats lefthanded. †Switch-hitter.

Player and Club	G.	AB.	R.	H.	TB.	2B.	3B.	HR.	RBI.	SH.	SF.	BB.	HP.	SO.	SB.	CS.	Pct.
Staton, Joseph, Lakeland*	.126	462	80	160	207	22	2	7	59	5	4	45	6	47	42	7	.346
Mangual, Jose, W Palm B	.124	415	73	137	203	18	18	4	69	0	7	82	1	87	15	5	.330
Robinson, Lee, Daytona B	.126	450	81	138	201	18	12	7	86	5	5	61	2	51	15	8	.307
Klitsner, John, W Haven*	.125	456	55	137	168	17	7	0	35	8	2	49	1	63	6	7	.300
Stroman, Kenneth, WPB*	.115	390	74	115	127	10	1	0	29	6	0	95	8	32	33	9	.295
Reinbach, Michael, Miami*	.126	422	87	124	157	14	8	1	44	3	4	87	3	40	34	9	.294
Reitz, Kenneth, St. Pete	.127	513	51	149	202	33	1	6	75	7	8	17	0	38	1	0	.290
Flesner, Paul, Miami	.113	382	50	110	134	18	3	0	57	5	5	61	0	47	5	2	.288
Andino, Javier, Miami*	.117	411	58	118	152	12	11	0	41	2	7	42	2	25	16	4	.287
Spencer, H. Thomas, Tampa	.130	571	52	134	166	13	5	3	50	7	11	41	1	37	21	11	.285

Departmental Leaders: G—Garcia, 133; AB—Reitz, 513; R—Gamble, 99; H—Staton, 160; TB—E. Hill, 230; 2B—Reitz, 33; 3B—Mangual, 18; HR—E. Hill, 22; RBI—L. Robinson, 86; SH—Pearlman, 18; SF—Spencer, 11; BB—Pearlman, Stroman, 95; HP—W. Ray, 13; SO—Spikes, 157; SB—Gamble, 60; CS—Gamble, 15.

(All Players—Listed Alphabetically)

Player and Club	G.	AB.	R.	H.	TB.	2B.	3B.	HR.	RBI.	SH.	SF.	BB.	HP.	SO.	SB.	CS.	Pct.
Acosta, Eduardo, Day Bch	17	11	1	1	1	0	0	0	0	2	0	1	0	9	0	0	.091
Adams, Lynn, Lakeland*	89	294	44	64	80	7	3	1	21	3	3	46	3	62	3	2	.218
Adey, Walter, Daytona B*	8	5	0	0	0	0	0	0	0	1	0	1	0	2	0	0	.000
Albury, Vincent, W Haven	99	345	22	82	92	10	0	0	28	7	2	22	2	60	5	7	.238
Alfonso, Carlos, Cocoa	37	57	5	8	8	0	0	0	3	3	0	7	0	16	0	0	.140
Alvarez, Jesus, Daytona B	76	203	30	48	65	8	3	2	23	0	0	26	1	44	2	1	.236
Amman, David, Cocoa	21	5	1	1	1	0	0	0	0	0	0	0	0	2	0	0	.200
Amyotte, Wayne, Lakeland	27	54	4	6	7	1	0	0	6	5	0	7	0	24	0	0	.111
Andino, Javier, Miami*	117	411	58	118	152	12	11	0	41	2	7	42	2	25	16	4	.287
Angelier, Mitchel, Lake	22	32	3	3	3	0	0	0	2	5	0	4	0	11	0	0	.094
Angelo, Steven, 7WPB-18DeL	25	71	10	16	22	2	2	0	7	2	0	3	0	16	1	1	.225
Arce, Felix, West Palm Bch	11	19	1	3	3	0	0	0	1	0	0	1	0	7	0	0	.158
Auferio, Anthony, St. Pete	79	251	25	65	75	7	0	1	25	4	4	34	7	21	1	0	.259
Austin, John, Miami	25	49	7	18	30	3	3	1	9	4	0	4	1	13	0	0	.367
Avalos, Richard, Pompano B	95	335	39	76	97	16	1	1	40	0	0	14	3	90	11	2	.227
Babcock, Phillip, DeLand	26	27	2	3	3	0	0	0	1	2	0	1	0	10	0	0	.111
Babcock, Robert, W Palm B	19	42	1	11	11	0	0	0	2	3	0	2	0	22	1	0	.262
Babyak, James, Ft. Land	81	271	20	64	77	7	3	0	32	2	2	31	1	34	4	1	.236
Baker, Michael, Lakeland*	41	153	20	39	51	4	4	0	14	2	0	5	0	29	2	1	.255
Barakat, Gary, St. Pete	6	26	4	5	6	1	0	0	1	0	0	3	0	7	1	0	.192
Barisoff, Robert, Day Bch	7	4	0	0	0	0	0	0	0	0	0	0	0	4	0	0	.000
Barlow, Billy, Miami	42	127	7	28	39	3	1	2	16	0	1	18	0	20	0	0	.220
Bartee, Jerry, St. Pete*	.115	366	55	88	110	14	4	0	25	6	2	52	6	48	16	9	.240
Bayer, Randall, Day Bch*	81	290	48	83	118	10	11	1	29	4	1	32	3	35	7	5	.286
Beckman, Bernard, Lake*	30	69	3	5	5	0	0	0	2	1	0	10	0	30	0	0	.072
Belair, J. C. Richard, PB*	98	325	40	83	107	12	3	2	31	8	0	41	1	52	3	1	.255
Belcik, Michael, Lakeland*	11	30	4	7	10	1	1	0	7	0	1	4	2	9	0	0	.233
Bell, Barton, St. Petersburg	13	28	2	3	4	1	0	0	3	1	0	4	2	1	0	0	.107
Bellm, Lawrence, W Haven	17	5	0	0	0	0	0	0	0	1	0	0	3	0	0	.000

Player and Club	G.	AB.	R.	H.	TB.	2B.	3B.	HR.	RBI.	SH.	SF.	BB.	HP.	SO.	SB.	CS.	Pct.
Bereguete, Demetrio, Day B*	22	22	2	7	7	0	0	0	3	1	0	3	2	4	0	0	.318
Beresford, Gary, W Palm B*	.100	317	34	67	88	12	3	1	39	3	2	52	2	48	6	1	.211
Bergholtz, James, Lakeland	40	112	8	22	25	3	0	0	8	0	2	17	1	24	2	0	.196
Bertino, Charles, WPB	5	6	2	2	7	0	1	1	3	0	0	1	0	1	0	0	.333
Bettis, Terrill, WPB*	30	8	0	2	2	0	0	0	0	1	0	0	0	4	0	0	.250
Boer, Martin, Cocoa	109	365	33	65	77	6	3	0	22	4	4	35	3	66	9	9	.178
Bograkos, Timothy, Pom B	36	90	11	13	15	2	0	0	4	0	0	11	0	28	1	0	.144
Bonfonte, Frank, Orlando	42	125	11	32	37	2	0	1	8	0	1	25	1	29	4	1	.256
Borowy, Joseph, DeLand	3	1	1	0	0	0	0	0	1	0	0	0	0	0	0	0	.000
Botterman, Barry, WPB	29	61	3	14	15	1	0	0	6	0	1	4	1	10	0	0	.230
Boyett, Wade, St. Pete	14	28	2	5	5	0	0	0	1	3	0	0	0	5	0	0	.179
Brandt, John G., Cocoa	61	90	17	26	36	1	3	1	11	0	0	17	0	7	1	0	.289
Brandt, Michael, St. Pete*	30	59	6	9	9	0	0	0	2	12	0	3	0	11	0	0	.153
Breese, Richard, Pom Beach	15	14	0	2	2	0	0	0	2	1	0	2	0	4	0	0	.143
Brenner, Glenn, Pompano B	8	12	1	2	2	0	0	0	0	3	0	2	0	4	0	0	.167
Bright, William, St. Pete*	53	186	20	62	79	10	2	1	19	2	1	17	0	15	3	2	.333
Brown, Arthur, St. Pete	10	21	0	2	2	0	0	0	0	0	0	1	0	6	0	0	.095
Brown, David P., Ft. Laud	21	67	9	12	15	0	0	1	6	1	0	13	0	19	3	1	.179
Brown, Gary, W Palm B	17	8	0	0	0	0	0	0	0	1	0	0	0	5	0	0	.000
Brown, Lewis, Cocoa	56	157	12	38	51	7	3	0	15	0	1	11	2	28	5	1	.242
Brown, Willie A., WPB†	.113	409	52	101	133	11	9	1	63	0	6	32	7	70	19	6	.247
Browning, James, St. Pete	1	4	0	0	0	0	0	0	0	0	0	0	0	2	0	0	.000
Brunner, Randolph, WPB*	2	6	0	1	1	0	0	0	1	0	0	0	0	2	0	0	.167
Bruntrager, Frederick, Lake*	10	1	0	0	0	0	0	0	0	1	0	1	0	1	0	0	.000
Bryant, James, W Haven	6	0	0	0	0	0	0	0	0	0	0	1	0	0	0	0	.000
Burch, Richard, Tampa	64	142	14	27	28	1	0	0	10	7	1	20	3	34	7	2	.190
Burdick, Kent, Tampa	36	134	14	27	34	2	1	1	10	4	2	8	1	38	6	1	.201
Burleson, Richard, W H	.118	419	42	92	116	13	4	1	29	6	5	49	6	72	6	12	.220
Bushey, Dennis, Lakeland*	5	1	0	0	0	0	0	0	0	0	0	0	0	1	0	0	.000
Buskey, Thomas, Ft. Laud	18	43	1	4	4	0	0	0	2	0	0	8	2	16	0	0	.093
Butler, John K., W Haven	1	0	0	0	0	0	0	0	0	0	0	1	0	0	0	0	.000
Buys, Gregory, Ft. Laud	8	3	0	0	0	0	0	0	0	0	0	0	0	1	0	0	.000
Bynon, Charles, DeLand	22	44	4	9	9	0	0	0	3	5	1	5	0	9	0	0	.205
Caldarella, Russell, StP	.128	462	65	126	188	17	9	9	72	1	7	63	3	89	13	6	.273
Cardasis, James, Daytona B	84	250	26	58	75	6	1	3	35	0	1	23	2	41	3	0	.232
Carey, Daniel, 1 PB-18 DeL*	19	35	6	7	8	1	0	0	1	1	0	4	0	13	0	0	.200
Casablanca, Fernando, DeL	11	27	8	6	6	0	0	0	0	0	0	6	0	6	0	2	.222
Castellanos, Nelson, Orl	.118	451	55	105	138	13	4	4	43	2	5	41	1	51	16	7	.233
Castillo, Ruben, Miami*	20	31	0	7	8	1	0	0	3	3	1	3	0	7	1	0	.226
Chadwick, Winfield, FtL	14	11	1	0	0	0	0	0	0	0	0	1	0	4	1	0	.000
Chew, David, Pompano Beach	7	16	1	2	2	0	0	0	0	1	0	1	0	3	0	0	.125
Choate, Lee, Ft. Lauderdale*	48	132	17	26	42	4	3	2	11	1	0	21	0	39	1	2	.197
Christopher, Steven, 10 PB-2 DeLand	12	4	2	1	1	0	0	0	0	0	1	0	0	1	0	0	.250
Cichon, Michael, DeLand	2	1	0	0	0	0	0	0	0	1	0	0	0	1	0	0	.000
Clapp, Terry, Miami*	47	154	15	31	43	3	3	1	22	2	2	28	1	27	2	2	.201
Clark, Ronald R., Day B	3	1	0	0	0	0	0	0	0	0	0	0	0	0	0	0	.000
Clayton, Henry, Miami	7	4	0	0	0	0	0	0	0	0	0	0	0	4	0	0	.000
Clifford, Arthur, Lakeland	16	25	2	7	7	0	0	0	1	2	0	1	0	8	0	0	.280
Cogan, Brian, Ft. Laud	26	20	0	1	1	0	0	0	0	2	0	1	0	11	0	0	.050
Cole, Thomas, St. Pete†	24	16	1	2	2	0	0	0	1	0	0	1	0	7	0	0	.125
Coleman, David, W. Haven	94	354	48	93	134	13	5	6	51	1	4	33	0	95	11	6	.263
Colin, Edward, St. Pete	84	192	21	40	48	6	1	0	18	0	4	27	5	39	3	2	.208
Collier, Ronald, Ft. Laud	29	19	0	2	2	0	0	0	1	0	3	0	0	11	0	0	.105
Collins, Allen, W Haven	35	100	5	24	28	1	0	1	5	0	1	17	1	20	1	1	.240
Collins, Donnie, Miami	77	235	23	62	84	4	3	4	39	1	3	27	0	38	1	4	.264
Collins, Garrett, St. Pete	11	30	2	3	7	1	0	1	5	1	0	2	2	9	0	0	.100
Combs, Charles, Ft. Laud	34	92	4	14	15	1	0	0	4	0	1	10	0	22	1	0	.152
Connors, William, Pom Bch	24	13	4	4	4	0	0	0	3	0	0	2	0	0	0	0	.308
Contreras, Arnaldo, Tampa†	22	28	2	4	4	0	0	0	3	0	0	6	0	8	0	0	.143
Cooper, Clarence, Tampa*	20	36	7	10	11	1	0	0	2	3	1	7	0	11	0	0	.278
Cosgrove, Michael, Cocoa*	35	37	7	12	14	0	1	0	2	4	0	2	0	7	0	0	.324
Costa, William, Cocoa	22	53	12	7	11	4	0	0	3	1	0	15	0	19	1	1	.132
Cott, Martin, Cocoa*	32	91	5	13	17	4	0	0	5	0	0	15	0	29	0	0	.143
Cousino, Brian, Lakeland	8	1	0	0	0	0	0	0	0	0	0	0	0	0	0	0	.000
Cross, Christopher, W Haven	89	255	24	49	87	14	3	6	31	3	2	57	2	49	2	3	.192
Crowder, Wayne, Ft. Laud	15	29	2	4	5	1	0	0	2	1	0	3	0	12	0	0	.138
Dailey, Terry, W Palm B	95	333	34	82	119	15	8	2	50	1	4	24	4	46	2	0	.246
Davis, Garnett, Pom Beach	95	302	41	61	89	9	2	5	34	0	1	33	7	85	5	0	.202
Davis, Gerald, Pompano Bch	67	204	35	43	61	4	4	2	23	1	4	43	0	48	1	0	.211
DeJesus, Ivan, Daytona Bch	.123	396	51	92	124	12	7	2	28	3	3	49	4	88	5	6	.232
Del Busto, Oscar, Miami	83	243	31	58	72	8	0	2	20	2	2	25	1	37	3	1	.239
Del Orbe, Lazaro, Miami	43	114	18	32	35	3	0	0	9	3	1	7	1	10	1	2	.281
Del Papa, Ronald, Lakeland	20	53	2	6	7	1	0	0	2	0	1	7	0	9	0	0	.113
Denbow, Donnie, Daytona B	1	1	0	1	1	0	0	0	0	0	0	0	0	0	0	0	1.000
Deremer, Terry, Pom Bch	59	188	15	39	40	1	0	0	11	1	2	24	1	44	1	2	.207
DeRiggi, Raymond, Ft. Laud*	66	174	6	42	47	3	1	0	14	2	0	28	3	37	0	3	.241
Dews, Robert, St. Pete	15	31	5	10	11	1	0	0	3	2	0	5	0	2	0	0	.323
Diaz, Erasmo, Cocoa	36	11	1	2	2	0	0	0	1	0	0	3	0	5	0	0	.182
Diaz, Francisco, Cocoa	13	19	3	2	3	1	0	0	2	1	0	3	0	6	0	0	.105
Diaz, Victor, St. Pete	60	150	21	30	32	2	0	0	5	12	0	13	0	12	0	0	.200
Dickerson, Donald, Pom B*	14	36	10	14	19	5	0	0	7	0	0	13	1	11	1	0	.389
Didleo, James, Pompano B	14	46	2	6	9	1	1	0	9	0	1	2	0	13	0	0	.130

Player and Club	G.	AB.	R.	H.	TB.	2B.	3B.	HR.	RBI.	SH.	SF.	BB.	HP.	SO.	SB.	CS.	Pct.
Dittmar, Thomas, Tampa*	51	187	19	54	69	7	4	0	15	2	1	18	0	23	6	3	.289
Dix, James, Pompano Bch†	15	50	10	16	18	2	0	0	3	0	1	7	0	4	5	1	.320
Dodson, Alan, Pompano B	10	9	0	1	1	0	0	0	1	1	0	2	0	4	0	0	.111
Dorsch, Richard, Daytona B	42	6	1	1	1	0	0	0	0	1	0	1	0	2	0	0	.167
Down, Richard, W Palm B	109	358	43	85	110	12	5	1	34	2	4	46	7	75	15	3	.237
Driessen, Daniel, Tampa*	93	242	28	54	58	2	1	0	20	2	3	27	2	32	9	4	.223
Driscoll, Mark, St. Pete	17	28	4	3	3	0	0	0	2	0	0	2	0	4	0	0	.107
Earley, Dennis, DeLand	11	5	0	0	0	0	0	0	0	0	0	0	0	2	0	0	.000
Easler, Michael, Cocoa*	96	314	30	79	101	11	4	1	24	3	1	25	4	39	8	7	.252
Eastwick, Rawlins, Tampa	37	20	2	3	3	0	0	0	1	2	0	2	0	12	0	0	.150
Ebner, Ronald, St. Pete	57	21	0	2	2	0	0	0	4	3	1	1	0	3	0	0	.095
Edge, Leo, Winter Haven	39	11	0	0	0	0	0	0	0	0	0	0	0	4	0	0	.000
Egnatchik, Peter, DeLand	4	5	0	0	0	0	0	0	0	0	0	2	0	4	0	0	.000
Elenes, Larry, Cocoa	13	25	1	5	5	0	0	0	2	0	0	0	0	9	0	0	.200
Emard, Richard, Miami	75	241	42	75	91	14	1	0	37	2	2	37	3	19	5	4	.311
Enyart, Terry, Orlando	35	55	2	5	6	1	0	0	1	2	0	3	0	22	0	0	.091
Ervin, Elvin, Daytona B*	15	28	1	4	4	0	0	0	0	2	0	0	0	8	0	0	.143
Escoe, Orlando, Pom Bch	29	98	15	22	26	2	1	0	7	0	0	6	0	20	1	0	.224
Fairbanks, Randall, Day B	10	11	3	3	3	0	0	0	2	1	0	4	0	3	0	0	.273
Fairbanks, Richard, Lake	72	245	33	61	73	5	2	1	23	2	1	22	2	29	5	2	.249
Farley, Benny, St. Pete*	21	24	3	4	4	0	0	0	3	1	0	1	0	8	0	0	.167
Farmer, Billy, Winter H	7	8	0	0	0	0	0	0	0	1	0	1	0	5	0	0	.000
Fenton, Stanley, St. Pete	11	28	1	4	4	0	0	0	1	0	1	1	0	3	0	0	.143
Finkbeiner, Bruce, Lake†	78	243	26	62	81	10	3	1	22	0	4	34	2	28	4	3	.255
Fisher, Frank, Lakeland	45	9	1	1	1	0	0	0	0	1	0	1	0	7	0	0	.111
Fisher, Mark, Lakeland*	22	10	2	3	3	0	0	0	4	0	0	2	0	2	0	0	.300
Flesner, Paul, Miami	113	382	50	110	134	18	3	0	57	5	5	61	0	47	5	2	.288
Foor, James, Lakeland*	5	3	0	1	1	0	0	0	0	0	0	0	0	1	0	0	.333
Ford, Gary, DeLand	71	194	22	51	63	8	2	0	30	3	2	38	2	48	2	0	.263
Foust, Robert, Tampa	11	4	0	1	2	1	0	0	0	0	0	1	0	0	1	0	.250
Franklin, Anthony, Tampa	113	378	50	78	82	2	1	0	19	10	0	72	1	88	20	4	.206
Freeman, Mario, Cocoa	15	43	1	10	11	1	0	0	1	0	0	4	0	5	3	0	.233
Frensley, James, Lakeland	12	37	1	7	7	0	0	0	3	0	1	2	1	12	0	0	.189
Fricchione, Paul, Ft. Laud	12	7	0	0	0	0	0	0	0	1	0	2	0	3	0	0	.000
Frick, Gregory, W Palm B	47	92	13	24	35	2	3	1	10	0	2	23	2	27	1	0	.261
Fulk, William, Lakeland	2	2	0	0	0	0	0	0	0	0	0	0	0	1	0	0	.000
Fuller, James, Miami	114	373	42	92	151	20	6	9	64	0	9	40	2	83	2	0	.247
Fuller, Joseph, St. Pete*	9	14	0	0	0	0	0	0	1	0	0	0	0	8	0	1	.000
Gable, Larry, Tampa	49	11	0	1	1	0	0	0	0	0	0	1	0	3	0	0	.091
Gallagher, Robert, Tampa	17	37	7	3	4	1	0	0	3	0	1	10	0	11	0	0	.081
Gamble, John, Daytona B	126	484	99	125	144	7	6	0	28	4	1	59	2	47	60	15	.258
Garcia, Robert, Orlando*	133	478	45	117	153	20	5	2	41	5	0	70	4	98	16	10	.245
Gardner, Steven, Cocoa	127	440	43	91	118	12	3	3	42	0	3	41	4	85	16	4	.207
Gardner, William L., FtL*	59	166	35	45	55	8	1	0	7	5	0	20	6	23	14	1	.271
Gentile, John, W Palm B	8	19	1	5	5	0	0	0	1	0	0	0	4	0	0	0	.263
Giegler, Mark, Lakeland	40	127	14	30	37	5	1	0	11	1	1	10	1	31	5	2	.236
Gilman, Richard, Winter H	29	43	2	10	12	0	1	0	4	1	0	4	0	12	0	0	.233
Goodman, William L., Orl	109	361	50	82	115	8	8	3	29	4	2	43	4	68	13	5	.227
Goodwin, Donnell, 16 Ta-6 Mi	22	25	0	3	3	0	0	0	1	2	0	1	0	6	0	0	.120
Goodwin, Scott, 25 DeL-5 PB	30	23	0	1	1	0	0	0	0	0	0	0	0	11	0	0	.043
Gorsuch, Timothy, Miami†	95	285	40	54	60	4	1	0	16	6	2	42	2	55	11	2	.189
Graham, Michael, Pom Beach	61	191	23	40	62	6	5	2	22	1	2	19	1	35	4	4	.209
Grant, Timothy, Tampa*	38	70	9	21	32	1	5	0	8	3	1	3	0	10	2	0	.300
Grassing, Arthur, Lakeland	33	45	3	12	14	2	0	0	6	2	1	2	0	10	1	0	.267
Grigsby, Charles, Cocoa	30	17	2	4	5	1	0	0	3	1	0	3	0	4	0	0	.235
Grindle, Robert, Tampa	30	20	2	2	2	0	0	0	3	1	0	1	0	5	0	0	.100
Grover, Stephen, Cocoa*	14	5	0	0	0	0	0	0	0	0	0	1	0	2	0	0	.000
Guerrero, Daniel, Orlando	31	72	5	14	19	5	0	0	4	0	1	11	0	18	0	0	.194
Hairston, James, St. Pete*	44	140	17	39	45	4	1	0	14	1	1	9	1	24	1	1	.279
Hall, Kara, Daytona Beach	60	129	11	28	35	1	0	2	14	0	2	16	2	24	1	1	.217
Hallmark, Daryl, DeLand	19	25	5	4	4	0	0	0	2	0	3	0	2	12	0	0	.160
Hansen, David, St. Pete	30	25	3	3	3	0	0	0	2	1	0	2	0	11	0	0	.120
Hardiman, Kerry, Tampa	20	14	1	3	3	0	0	0	0	0	0	1	0	2	0	0	.214
Haren, Dennis, Daytona Bch	4	5	0	1	1	0	0	0	0	0	0	0	0	2	0	0	.200
Harkey, Bruce, Pompano Bch	26	23	3	6	6	0	0	0	6	0	0	0	0	10	0	0	.261
Harris, Thomas, Tampa	72	231	23	53	68	2	5	1	19	6	3	15	0	41	4	2	.229
Hart, John, WPB	98	305	25	67	73	4	1	0	25	4	3	24	4	25	2	1	.220
Hartig, Mark, Orlando	16	23	1	2	2	0	0	0	0	0	0	2	2	9	0	0	.087
Harts, Gregory, Pom Beach*	52	173	15	37	49	3	0	3	11	3	1	15	0	39	1	3	.214
Harvison, Michael, W Haven	11	13	3	1	2	1	0	0	1	0	1	3	0	7	0	0	.077
Hazelip, David, Ft. Laud	33	67	4	11	19	4	2	0	12	6	0	10	1	14	0	1	.164
Hebert, Michael, Miami*	23	12	1	2	2	0	0	0	0	0	0	1	0	4	0	0	.167
Hefflinger, James, Ft. Laud	38	109	20	25	38	4	3	1	10	3	0	33	0	31	9	3	.229
Helton, Ronnie, Winter H*.	5	10	0	3	3	0	0	0	1	0	0	3	0	6	0	0	.300
Hemenway, Ted, St. Pete	24	15	0	3	3	0	0	0	1	1	0	3	0	7	0	0	.186
Hernandez, Julio, Ft. Laud	17	43	0	8	11	3	0	0	3	2	0	4	0	19	0	0	.173
Herrmann, Conrad, Miami	21	52	5	9	9	0	0	0	3	2	0	4	0	3	1	0	.280
Hether, Donald, Lakeland	8	25	3	7	9	2	0	0	8	2	0	12	3	24	1	0	.243
Hetman, Michael, Winter H	48	103	15	25	28	3	0	0	8	2	6	29	4	116	18	3	.274
Hill, Elmore, Orlando	129	485	68	133	230	19	6	22	84	2	0	1	0	0	0	0	.000
Hill, Norwood, Winter H	21	2	0	0	0	0	0	0	0	2	0	1	0	0	0	0	.000
Hoelzer, William, Tampa*	80	247	22	54	66	8	2	0	23	6	0	34	0	62	8	3	.219
Hogan, Jeffrey, Lakeland	130	470	55	121	156	20	6	1	65	2	7	45	0	31	13	4	.257

Player and Club	G.	AB.	R.	H.	TB.	2B.	3B.	HR.	RBI.	SH.	SF.	BB.	HP.	SO.	SB.	CS.	Pct.
Holdsworth, Frederick, Lake.	3	2	0	0	0	0	0	0	0	0	0	0	0	2	0	0	.000
Holtberg, Arnold, Ft. Laud.	38	107	7	18	21	0	0	1	8	0	0	12	1	19	1	0	.168
Hoops, Alan, WPB	19	43	0	6	7	1	0	0	4	2	0	1	0	14	0	0	.140
Howard, Gary, Cocoa	58	159	19	34	48	5	0	3	15	0	1	24	4	58	1	1	.214
Hubbard, David, W Haven*	26	43	8	10	14	4	0	0	4	1	0	10	1	19	2	1	.233
Hughes, James, Orlando	12	19	0	1	1	0	0	0	0	0	2	0	0	11	0	0	.053
Hughes, John, Day Beach*	37	94	13	17	18	1	0	0	5	4	1	8	1	14	3	1	.181
Hughes, Michael, Day Beach	8	19	1	4	6	2	0	0	0	0	0	4	0	3	0	0	.211
Hurley, John, Orlando	17	33	2	6	7	1	0	0	3	4	0	3	0	6	1	0	.182
Ignasiak, Gary, Lakeland	15	26	1	3	4	1	0	0	3	1	0	2	1	5	0	0	.115
Iskierka, Dennis, Pom Bch	4	11	3	0	0	0	0	0	1	0	0	3	0	8	0	0	.000
Jackson, John, Tampa	13	21	4	2	2	0	0	0	0	0	0	2	9	1	0	.095
Jacobsen, Joseph, Orlando	.131	472	44	113	146	14	2	5	54	6	9	34	9	67	3	2	.239
Johnson, James C., Orlando	64	181	15	49	58	6	0	1	24	3	0	28	2	31	1	1	.271
Johnson, Robert M., DB*	29	5	0	1	1	0	0	0	1	1	0	0	3	0	0	.200
Jones, John, Cocoa*	61	169	16	29	38	2	2	1	12	0	0	32	0	60	1	1	.172
Joseph, David, 8 WH-25 DeL	33	17	2	3	3	0	0	0	1	1	0	9	0	7	0	0	.176
Kaminski, Albert, Lakeland	71	230	18	41	46	2	0	1	9	1	1	29	3	46	5	1	.178
Kavanaugh, Ronald, Miami*	6	1	0	0	0	0	0	0	0	0	0	1	0	0	0	0	.000
Keller, Stephen, WPB	24	43	4	9	9	0	0	0	4	0	3	0	19	0	0	.209
Kelley, William, Miami	24	47	6	8	8	0	0	0	1	6	0	6	1	9	0	0	.170
Kelly, Milton, Orlando	33	47	8	13	13	0	0	0	1	4	0	3	0	18	0	0	.277
Ker, Clifford, WPB	3	6	1	1	1	0	0	0	0	1	0	0	0	1	0	0	.167
Kerr, Robert, Winter Haven	24	19	0	1	1	0	0	0	1	0	0	1	0	11	0	0	.053
Kessler, Robert, Pom Bch*	22	41	1	8	8	0	0	0	1	3	0	7	0	18	0	0	.195
Kilgore, David, DeLand*	68	196	27	49	78	10	2	5	27	0	2	22	0	38	0	2	.250
Kilgore, Thomas, Pom Beach	55	164	16	31	35	4	0	0	16	3	2	17	0	32	2	0	.189
Killian, Jerry, Lakeland†	9	3	0	0	0	0	0	0	0	0	0	0	0	3	0	0	.000
Kimbrell, Michael, Day Bch.	12	18	2	3	5	2	0	0	3	0	1	3	0	5	0	0	.167
Kinder, Bruce, WPB	31	96	12	21	23	2	0	0	8	1	0	9	0	13	1	0	.219
King, Jeffrey, Miami	16	11	2	0	0	0	0	0	0	0	0	2	0	6	0	0	.000
Kinner, Ronald, St. Pete	17	60	6	14	16	2	0	0	4	2	0	1	0	17	1	1	.233
Kinney, Ronald, St. Pete*	24	40	3	5	5	0	0	0	5	0	3	0	18	0	0	.125
Klastava, David, W Haven	24	33	2	9	10	1	0	0	2	3	0	5	1	11	0	2	.273
Kleem, Larry, WPB*	19	10	0	0	0	0	0	0	0	0	0	1	0	5	0	0	.000
Kleibl, Mark, Winter Haven	24	30	2	3	3	0	0	0	3	0	4	0	7	0	0	.100
Kline, Dennis, WPB	27	7	2	0	0	0	0	0	1	0	0	5	0	0	0	.000
Klitsner, John, W Haven*	.125	456	55	137	168	17	7	0	35	8	2	49	1	63	6	7	.300
Kmet, Michael, Tampa†	3	6	2	2	4	0	1	0	1	0	0	1	0	0	0	.333
Kogut, S. Craig, Ft. Laud*	43	106	5	23	28	3	1	0	9	1	2	19	2	9	1	1	.217
Kohn, Randolph, Day Beach*	23	56	4	7	11	0	2	0	5	0	14	0	19	0	1	.125
Kooyman, Kevin, Tampa	13	41	5	6	7	1	0	0	3	2	0	1	0	4	0	0	.146
Kramer, Thomas, W Haven	3	4	1	0	0	0	0	0	0	0	0	0	1	0	0	.000
Kurtzman, Harold, DeLand	96	365	43	88	103	13	1	0	19	1	3	31	4	34	11	6	.241
Lane, Marvin, Lakeland	94	361	52	83	105	4	6	2	30	0	4	35	6	47	12	7	.230
LaRusso, James, DeLand*	14	51	13	16	19	3	0	0	6	1	1	7	0	5	4	1	.314
Lehman, Thomas, Cocoa*	27	28	1	4	4	0	0	0	1	4	0	4	1	11	1	0	.143
Lemery, Ronald, Lakeland	7	15	3	3	3	0	0	0	3	0	0	1	0	6	0	0	.200
Leon, Richard, DeLand†	97	324	37	100	128	20	4	0	50	5	4	42	2	60	4	6	.309
Lewis, James, Orlando	82	217	18	44	62	7	1	3	20	1	1	13	4	36	3	1	.203
Lewis, Jerry, Cocoa*	21	44	2	6	6	0	0	0	3	0	0	6	1	24	0	0	.136
Locascio, Alan, Lakeland	19	54	6	11	12	1	0	0	5	0	0	9	1	17	0	0	.204
Lohse, Lary, Lakeland*	6	6	0	0	0	0	0	0	0	0	0	0	0	2	0	0	.000
Long, Robert, Daytona Bch*	30	105	22	35	55	8	6	0	14	0	0	19	0	16	5	5	.333
Lopez, Jose A., Cocoa	91	237	23	58	72	6	4	0	21	1	0	25	3	48	1	1	.245
Luebber, Stephen, Orlando	34	81	6	8	11	1	1	0	3	7	0	3	0	30	0	0	.099
Lugo, Luis, DeLand†	76	228	14	45	66	4	4	3	24	1	2	11	2	45	2	0	.197
Mack, James, Orlando	10	4	0	1	1	0	0	0	0	0	0	1	0	1	0	0	.250
Maine, J. Kevin, DeLand	7	5	0	1	1	0	0	0	0	0	0	1	0	3	0	0	.200
Mairena, Alfonso, St. Pete	65	241	26	69	82	3	5	0	20	3	2	17	1	19	1	3	.286
Manderbach, Gary, Ft. Laud	21	39	1	1	2	1	0	0	1	0	3	0	23	0	0	.026
Mangual, Jose, WPB	.124	415	73	137	203	18	18	4	69	0	7	82	1	87	15	5	.330
Marrero, Antonio, PB	3	8	1	0	0	0	0	0	0	2	0	1	0	0	0	.000
Marshall, Jerry, Orlando	51	147	12	28	42	3	1	3	20	1	0	9	1	28	3	0	.190
Mason, David, Lakeland	5	3	1	0	0	0	0	0	0	0	2	0	2	0	0	.000
Mason, Jeffrey, Ft. Laud	76	250	28	73	95	9	2	3	38	0	5	31	1	15	3	1	.292
Mata, Virgilio, Tampa	1	1	0	0	0	0	0	0	0	0	0	0	0	0	0	.000
Matheson, Thomas, Ft. Laud.	17	48	2	7	13	1	1	1	4	0	1	5	1	13	0	0	.146
Mays, Jerry, Lakeland	32	28	1	4	4	0	0	0	3	0	2	0	5	0	0	.143
McClain, Jerry, WPB	9	15	1	3	3	0	0	0	2	0	0	1	0	5	0	0	.200
McConnaughy, Robert, Miami	52	149	21	31	44	5	4	0	11	3	1	27	1	27	4	3	.208
McDermott, Terrence, DB	97	348	47	112	146	22	3	2	51	3	2	28	1	36	10	7	.322
McDonald, Michael, St. P*	28	82	8	21	24	3	0	0	4	0	0	13	1	7	1	1	.256
McEnderfer, Timothy, St. P†	24	58	5	6	7	1	0	0	2	0	13	2	15	0	0	.103
McLaughlin, Donnie, Cocoa	72	236	23	56	79	7	8	0	21	0	3	17	1	25	3	0	.237
Meeler, C. Philip, Lake.	17	4	1	1	1	0	0	0	0	0	0	0	0	1	0	0	.250
Milam, Wayne, Winter Haven	21	40	3	9	11	2	0	0	3	0	3	0	14	0	0	.225
Millan, Jorge, St. Pete	11	34	3	7	9	1	0	4	4	0	1	0	9	0	0	.206
Miller, Rowe, Tampa	31	91	8	25	27	2	0	0	6	1	1	9	3	19	0	0	.275
Miller, Steven K., Tampa	19	34	2	4	4	0	0	0	2	1	0	2	1	18	0	0	.118
Miller, Steven O., W Haven	.114	379	40	89	126	15	2	6	46	2	2	49	2	111	2	3	.235
Mims, Edward, Cocoa	15	17	0	0	0	0	0	0	1	1	0	1	9	0	0	.000

Player and Club	G.	AB.	R.	H.	TB.	2B.	3B.	HR.	RBI.	SH.	SF.	BB.	HP.	SO.	SB.	CS.	Pct.
Montalvo, Nestor, Lakeland	37	92	7	23	25	2	0	0	11	0	0	6	1	11	0	0	.250
Moore, Balor, WPB*	3	9	3	3	3	0	0	0	2	1	0	0	0	0	0	0	.333
Moore, Henry, Cocoa*	12	9	0	3	3	0	0	0	0	0	0	0	0	4	0	0	.333
Moore, Tommy, Pom Beach	23	55	3	17	24	0	2	1	8	0	1	1	1	10	0	0	.309
Mora, Nephtale, Ft. Laud	26	79	11	15	24	3	0	2	13	0	2	8	0	22	0	0	.190
Morgan, Robert, DeLand	23	36	1	3	3	0	0	0	2	7	0	3	0	6	0	0	.083
Morris, Avery, Orlando	56	157	24	30	34	4	0	0	8	4	0	38	2	41	8	0	.191
Murphy, Daniel, Pom Beach	4	3	0	0	0	0	0	0	0	0	0	0	0	3	0	0	.000
Murray, Dale, WPB	4	3	0	1	1	0	0	0	0	0	0	0	0	2	0	0	.333
Murray, Joseph, DeLand	30	30	1	2	2	0	0	0	2	4	0	2	0	15	0	0	.067
Myers, Gary, Winter Haven	37	117	9	28	37	5	2	0	10	1	0	11	0	29	3	2	.239
Nagy, Michael, W Haven	3	2	0	0	0	0	0	0	0	0	0	0	1	0	0	0	.000
Navarro, Hector, DeLand	128	467	37	114	150	16	7	2	42	4	2	8	1	81	2	0	.244
Nichols, George T., Lake	76	226	19	59	75	7	3	1	32	2	3	33	1	37	2	0	.261
Nichols, Richard, W Haven	10	32	3	9	12	3	0	0	4	0	1	3	0	7	3	0	.281
Nixon, John, St. Pete*	44	142	24	33	42	4	1	1	7	1	1	38	4	51	4	4	.232
Nolan, Joseph, Pom Beach*	95	281	38	65	79	6	4	0	30	3	3	50	1	22	3	2	.231
Nordbrook, Timothy, Miami	9	24	5	3	3	0	0	0	1	0	1	9	0	5	0	1	.125
Norton, William, W Haven*	23	58	3	12	12	0	0	0	3	0	0	3	1	5	1	0	.207
Nowlin, Donald, W Haven	60	154	10	22	27	2	0	1	9	1	2	17	2	44	0	2	.143
O'Brien, Rodney, W Haven	27	59	9	8	9	1	0	0	3	1	0	9	0	18	2	1	.136
O'Connor, Michael, Tampa*	8	1	0	0	0	0	0	0	0	0	0	0	1	1	0	0	.000
O'Connor, Thomas, Ft. L*	43	144	13	28	37	5	2	0	17	2	3	17	4	17	6	0	.194
Olson, Mitchell, Pom Beach	16	27	4	4	7	1	1	0	2	3	0	3	0	7	0	0	.148
O'Neil, Phillip, St. Pete*	23	66	9	16	23	3	2	0	7	0	0	10	1	6	0	1	.242
Orozco, W. Bolivar, Cocoa	9	9	1	1	1	0	0	0	1	0	1	0	1	0	0	0	.111
Ortiz, Alfredo R., 1 WPB-28 DeLand	29	68	5	16	16	0	0	0	4	0	0	7	1	15	1	0	.235
Ostrosser, Brian, Pom Bch*	17	54	4	6	8	0	1	0	2	2	2	4	3	10	2	1	.111
Outten, Sidney, WPB	5	12	0	4	5	1	0	0	2	0	0	1	0	2	0	0	.333
Palas, Lee, DeLand	12	2	0	0	0	0	0	0	0	0	0	0	0	2	0	0	.000
Palmer, Donald, DeLand	83	266	33	72	98	8	3	4	35	1	1	16	0	62	4	2	.271
Papi, Stanley, Cocoa	91	300	24	72	78	4	1	0	16	2	1	45	3	58	6	4	.240
Passarella, Gilbert, Ft. L	29	103	10	27	41	8	0	2	16	0	2	5	0	14	1	1	.262
Pauls, Arthur, Day Beach	11	21	2	6	10	1	0	1	3	0	0	1	0	7	0	0	.286
Pearlman, Lawrence, WPB	122	378	64	76	78	2	0	0	21	18	1	95	6	52	19	8	.201
Peery, Richard, Orlando*	24	11	0	1	1	0	0	0	0	1	0	2	0	6	0	0	.091
Phillips, Samuel, W Haven	16	19	0	3	3	0	0	0	3	3	0	1	0	9	0	0	.158
Pichardo, Nelson, Pom Bch	109	400	37	78	88	6	2	0	23	7	0	28	0	47	29	10	.195
Pieve, Carlos, Ft. Laud	20	62	5	14	15	1	0	0	10	2	1	1	0	9	1	0	.226
Pinnick, Leo, Orlando*	22	36	0	2	2	0	0	0	1	5	1	2	0	13	0	0	.056
Pitcock, G. Wayne, Ft. L*	117	399	45	103	134	18	5	1	36	3	5	37	2	26	17	8	.258
Pitruzzello, Michael, Mia*	17	49	6	5	7	2	0	0	4	0	1	5	0	11	2	0	.102
Pizarro, Jose, Pom Beach	6	6	0	0	0	0	0	0	0	0	0	0	0	2	0	0	.000
Polcari, David, St. Pete*	37	91	10	21	32	1	2	2	10	0	0	10	2	12	0	0	.231
Pole, Richard, W Haven	19	28	1	3	4	1	0	0	1	2	0	2	0	7	0	0	.107
Pompa, Eliseo, WPB*	13	27	4	6	7	1	0	0	2	0	0	1	0	4	3	1	.222
Potash, Lawrence, Pom Bch*	20	9	0	0	0	0	0	0	1	1	0	2	0	5	0	0	.000
Powell, Barry, Tampa	12	33	1	4	5	1	0	0	3	2	0	2	0	10	0	0	.121
Price, Jack, St. Pete*	3	1	0	0	0	0	0	0	0	0	0	0	0	1	0	0	.000
Prince, Marion, Ft. Laud	44	123	16	20	27	5	1	0	3	2	0	26	3	28	1	1	.163
Pruett, Jerome, St. Pete	2	2	1	1	1	0	0	0	0	0	0	1	0	0	0	0	.500
Pullins, Gary, Daytona Bch	19	22	5	5	5	0	0	0	2	0	1	4	0	3	0	1	.227
Punko, Michael, Ft. Laud	34	93	26	25	33	2	3	0	3	2	1	34	3	22	13	3	.269
Quinones, Carlos, Lakeland	38	117	9	22	23	1	0	0	8	2	1	4	0	18	0	0	.188
Raible, Bruce, Day Beach*	8	7	1	0	0	0	0	0	0	2	0	4	0	4	0	0	.000
Ramirez, Alonzo, Ft. Laud*	11	14	2	4	4	0	0	0	4	2	0	2	2	1	0	0	.286
Ray, Jerry, DeLand*	22	49	1	6	9	1	1	0	2	8	0	1	0	16	1	0	.122
Ray, William, Miami*	130	435	69	117	155	9	13	1	64	3	4	56	13	63	38	9	.269
Reid, John, WPB	16	43	3	11	11	0	0	0	4	2	0	11	0	4	0	0	.256
Reinbach, Michael, Miami*	126	422	87	124	157	14	8	1	44	3	4	87	3	40	34	9	.294
Reitz, Kenneth, St. Pete	127	513	51	149	202	33	1	6	75	7	8	17	0	38	1	0	.290
Remson, Robert, W Haven	32	7	0	3	3	0	0	0	1	0	0	0	0	2	0	0	.429
Reynolds, Cecil, Pom Bch	10	14	2	1	1	0	0	0	0	3	1	9	0	0	0	0	.071
Richard, James R., Cocoa	20	38	2	7	10	3	0	0	3	2	0	3	0	11	0	0	.184
Robinson, Beau, Ft. Laud*	47	147	16	31	41	4	3	0	6	1	0	20	0	23	7	2	.211
Robinson, Edmond, Pom Bch*	26	18	5	4	4	0	0	0	1	1	0	3	0	7	0	0	.222
Robinson, Lee, Daytona Bch	126	450	81	138	201	18	12	7	86	5	5	61	2	51	15	8	.307
Robson, Thomas, WPB	12	44	4	9	12	1	1	0	4	0	0	4	1	9	0	0	.205
Rodriguez, Luis, Cocoa	36	85	4	14	15	1	0	0	2	0	0	5	3	28	0	0	.165
Rohde, Theodore, DeLand	74	220	31	54	81	15	0	4	25	1	0	25	1	68	15	3	.236
Rondon, Alfio, Cocoa	17	34	6	5	5	0	0	0	0	0	0	4	0	9	0	0	.147
Rosiek, Matthew, Cocoa	53	33	1	7	7	0	0	0	4	4	0	0	0	6	0	0	.212
Ruddell, Michael, Tampa	12	25	2	1	1	0	0	0	0	0	0	9	0	0	0	0	.040
Runk, George, Tampa	95	336	33	99	131	14	3	4	48	4	4	33	1	38	5	2	.295
Russell, Donald, Cocoa	11	33	4	4	5	1	0	0	1	0	0	6	1	6	1	0	.121
Russell, Patrick, WPB	25	56	2	7	8	1	0	0	9	6	0	4	0	21	0	0	.125
Russell, William, DeLand	84	250	43	56	79	8	3	3	28	3	1	45	9	64	18	2	.224
St. John, Michael, St. P	9	12	0	4	4	0	0	0	0	0	0	1	0	2	0	0	.333
Salazar, William, WPB	12	14	0	1	1	0	0	0	1	0	0	1	0	3	0	0	.071
Sanders, Clement, Ft. Laud	102	337	46	90	127	6	8	5	50	2	4	42	1	73	15	3	.267
Sankey, Robert, St. Pete	8	18	1	0	0	0	0	0	0	0	0	2	1	2	1	0	.000

Player and Club	G.	AB.	R.	H.	TB.	2B.	3B.	HR.	RBI.	SH.	SF.	BB.	HP.	SO.	SB.	CS.	Pct.
Sathre, James, Orlando	38	28	2	0	0	0	0	0	0	0		3	0	19	0	0	.000
Savold, Edmund, Orlando	23	11	2	2	2	0	0	0	1	2	0	3	0	2	0	0	.182
Schleider, Robert, WPB	4	3	1	0	0	0	0	0	0	0		0	1	0	3	0	.000
Schlesiger, John, Ft. Laud ..	18	42	0	7	7	0	0	0	0	1	0	3	0	11	1	0	.167
Schroeder, Donald, Ft. Laud	25	49	4	4	4	0	0	0	1	6	0	5	0	22	0	0	.082
Schultz, Robert, W Haven* .	93	258	31	60	72	6	3	0	13	0	5	34	1	19	12	7	.233
Scott, Anthony, WPB	3	2	0	1	1	0	0	0	0	0		1	0	1	1	0	.500
Scott, Leonard, Miami	52	21	1	1	2	1	0	0	2	0	0	0	0	10	0	0	.048
Seifert, John, Day Beach* ..	25	13	1	3	3	0	0	0	1	1	0	1	0	4	0	0	.231
Seltzer, William, Miami	27	62	5	8	9	1	0	0	4	0	0	12	0	12	0	0	.129
Senger, Frederick, Pom Bch .	36	119	14	38	59	6	3	3	22	0	0	18	2	15	0	0	.319
Sheanshang, Larry, Cocoa ..	5	2	0	0	0	0	0	0	0	0	0	0	0	2	0	0	.000
Shearer, Robert, Cocoa*	58	145	14	33	40	5	1	0	6	3	0	42	2	16	2	1	.228
Shepley, Lowell, DeLand* ...	79	258	36	61	74	7	3	0	22	3	3	37	2	43	9	5	.236
Shown, Larry, Ft. Laud	36	25	0	9	10	1	0	0	3	1	1	2	0	6	0	0	.360
Simmons, Philip, Ft. Laud ..	18	13	0	3	4	1	0	0	1	1	0	0	0	5	0	0	.231
Sires, Richard, Tampa	11	20	2	6	6	0	0	0	2	0	0	3	0	6	0	0	.300
Sitarz, John, Winter Haven .	8	23	3	4	5	1	0	0	0	0	0	2	0	7	1	0	.174
Slayback, William, Lake	3	2	0	0	0	0	0	0	0	0	0	0	0	0	0	0	.000
Small, Donald, W Haven	21	45	2	5	5	0	0	0	5	1	0	2	0	23	1	0	.111
Smith, James T., St. Pete ...	28	60	4	8	9	1	0	0	1	3	0	1	0	21	0	0	.133
Smith, James, Orlando	11	12	0	2	2	0	0	0	1	0	0	3	0	5	0	0	.167
Smith, Randy, Daytona Bch†	48	134	15	37	44	5	1	0	19	0	1	12	0	29	0	0	.276
Smith, Stephen, Lakeland ..	46	174	25	54	65	5	3	0	20	0	1	16	0	26	0	0	.310
Smithson, Alan, Pom Beach .	26	16	0	2	2	0	0	0	0	1	0	0	0	7	0	1	.125
Snowdon, Jeffrey, 16 Orl-10 DeLand*	26	27	3	1	1	0	0	0	1	3	1	4	0	11	0	0	.037
Soderholm, Eric, Orlando ...	25	90	17	20	29	4	1	1	9	0	2	10	0	18	0	0	.222
Solomon, Eddie, Day Bch† ..	22	60	3	8	8	0	0	0	2	4	1	1	0	13	0	0	.133
Sonnichsen, Keith, Orlando .	53	161	15	37	42	3	1	0	11	3	0	33	0	26	7	4	.230
Sorrentino, Robert, Miami* ..	4	6	0	0	0	0	0	0	0	0		3	0	3	0	0	.000
Spencer, H. Thomas, Tampa .130	471	52	134	166	13	5	3	50	7	11	41	1	37	21	11	.285
Spikes, Leslie, Ft. Laud 127	422	71	100	173	12	2	19	62	0	6	62	11	157	22	6	.237
Spilman, James, WPB*	37	56	9	8	9	1	0	0	6	0	0	12	2	21	1	0	.143
Staton, Joseph, Lakeland ...126	462	80	160	207	22	2	7	59	5	4	45	6	47	42	7	.346
Steele, Ronald, Tampa	6	12	0	0	0	0	0	0	0	0		2	1	4	1	1	.000
Stennett, Jose, Orlando 126	467	69	129	159	18	3	2	36	3	2	34	0	52	18	10	.276
Stewart, Ronald, DeLand* ..	5	10	1	2	2	0	0	0	0	0		1	0	6	0	0	.200
Stodgel, Douglas, Ft. Laud ..	74	284	50	90	104	8	3	0	11	7	0	28	0	19	19	5	.317
Stroman, Kenneth, WPB* ...115	390	74	115	127	10	1	0	29	6	0	95	8	32	33	9	.295
Sturman, Richard, Pom Bch	80	250	36	56	75	8	1	3	20	2	1	40	2	62	10	3	.224
Sturtevant, Anthony, Coa* ..	73	159	18	32	36	4	0	0	13	2	2	23	4	42	2	1	.201
Suchan, Curtis, W Haven 118	423	64	108	168	22	4	10	53	1	1	46	4	86	20	5	.255
Sudzina, G. Nicholas, Lake .	51	152	13	32	44	2	2	2	13	1	0	10	3	24	5	1	.211
Sulprizio, Scott, St. Pete ...	10	26	1	7	8	1	0	0	3	0	0	5	1	3	0	0	.269
Swanson, Paul, Ft. Laud	14	6	0	0	0	0	0	0	0	0		0	0	4	0	0	.000
Swiss, Douglas, Lakeland ...	80	240	20	44	55	5	0	2	14	1	2	31	3	58	0	0	.183
Tanner, James, Lakeland	4	5	1	2	2	0	0	0	0	0	0	0	0	2	0	0	.400
Tatis, Fernando, Cocoa	96	366	34	94	113	11	4	0	35	0	1	42	7	59	14	11	.257
Taylor, Charles, Cocoa	16	10	2	2	2	0	0	0	1	0		0	0	6	0	0	.200
Thompson, Richard, D Bch.113	369	38	90	106	10	3	0	37	6	2	50	0	54	7	6	.244
Todd, Stanley, WPB	1	1	0	1	1	0	0	0	0	0	0	0	0	0	0	0	1.000
Tomasovich, Theodore, Tam*	13	35	2	5	7	2	0	0	3	1	0	5	1	13	2	0	.143
Trombino, Philip, St. Pete .	80	257	31	87	111	9	6	1	41	2	3	49	5	21	0	0	.339
Tuck, Terry, WPB	58	140	16	29	33	4	0	0	18	1	5	15	1	34	2	1	.207
Turner, Richard, WPB	24	53	5	7	10	1	1	0	3	0	0	3	1	15	0	1	.132
Tyson, Michael, St. Pete ...109	400	47	98	126	10	3	4	37	3	3	26	8	52	2	5	.245
Valenzuela, Ramon C., WPB	28	71	5	6	6	0	0	0	3	0	0	15	0	23	2	2	.085
Veintidos, Juan, Pom Beach.	26	61	5	12	14	2	0	0	5	6	0	4	0	14	0	0	.197
Velez, Otoniel, Ft. Laud	20	54	7	9	11	0	1	0	4	1	2	11	1	14	0	1	.167
Vicente, Juan, DeLand	5	14	0	1	1	0	0	0	1	0	0	1	0	7	0	0	.071
Vickery, O. Glenn, WPB	8	9	0	2	2	0	0	0	2	0	0	2	0	5	0	0	.222
Viefhaus, Randolph, WPB*.	7	18	0	4	4	0	0	0	0	0	0	2	0	3	0	0	.222
Villalobos, Milton, Cocoa ...	7	3	0	0	0	0	0	0	1	0	0	0	0	1	0	0	.000
Vogler, Gary, DeLand 130	485	72	121	157	18	6	2	41	8	5	78	3	104	9	6	.249
Volkening, Larry, St. Pete ..	4	4	1	1	1	0	0	0	0	0	0	0	0	0	0	0	.250
VonHoff, Bruce, St. Pete ...	4	0	0	0	0	0	0	0	0	0		2	0	0	0	0	.000
Wagner, Steven, DeLand* ...120	411	48	114	134	14	3	0	51	5	2	64	2	36	1	1	.277
Wall, Stanley, Day Beach* .	24	56	4	15	17	0	1	0	6	3	1	0	0	11	0	0	.268
Ward, Wm. Frank, W Haven	25	53	2	7	9	0	1	0	4	0	1	1	0	20	0	0	.132
Warren, Malcolm, DeLand* .	22	13	0	1	1	0	0	0	1	0	1	0	0	6	0	0	.077
Washington, Manuel, Day B.111	384	56	108	151	14	7	5	56	5	5	38	9	54	12	5	.281
Wayne, Thomas. Orlando ...	6	5	2	2	3	1	0	0	0	0	0	3	0	2	0	0	.400
Webb, Henry, Pompano Bch.	11	22	2	7	7	0	0	0	2	0	0	3	0	5	0	0	.318
Wellman, Gregory, Day Bch*	18	28	1	5	6	1	0	0	5	0	0	0	0	10	0	0	.179
Welsh, Robert, Tampa 107	358	33	71	92	14	2	1	26	2	4	46	2	73	13	6	.198
West, Richard, Tampa† 129	462	55	119	156	25	3	2	52	6	3	35	7	49	20	7	.258
White, Timothy, Tampa ...	98	301	25	78	100	9	3	2	19	1	3	45	1	62	4	4	.259
Williams, Eddie, Miami*	23	41	6	8	11	3	0	0	1	5	0	13	2	13	0	0	.195
Williams, Henry, Day Bch ..	34	45	5	7	10	1	1	0	1	2	0	4	0	14	0	0	.156
Williams, Robert L., WPB ..	31	14	0	3	3	0	0	0	1	0	0	1	0	6	0	0	.214
Williams, Thomas, Pom B† ..	84	293	50	91	130	11	8	4	41	3	4	36	2	56	14	7	.311

Player and Club	G.	AB.	R.	H.	TB.	2B.	3B.	HR.	RBI.	SH.	SF.	BB.	HP.	SO.	SB.	CS.	Pct.
Wilson, Gary Ft. Laud	22	51	5	13	17	1	0	1	8	0	0	10	2	11	4	0	.255
Wolfenbarger, Alan, W H* ..	7	17	2	3	4	1	0	0	1	0	1	2	0	2	0	0	.176
Wyche, Robert, DeLand*	1	5	1	2	4	0	1	0	2	0	0	0	0	2	0	0	.400
Youngblood, Joel, Tampa ...	17	54	7	12	12	0	0	0	3	0	0	4	2	9	3	0	.222
Zaskoda, Wayne, Miami	8	26	3	4	6	0	1	0	1	0	0	3	0	5	1	1	.154
Zuniga, Ralph, Orlando*	21	11	0	1	1	0	0	0	1	0	2	0	3	0	0	.091

The following pitchers had no plate appearances (listed alphabetically by clubs, games in parentheses):
FORT LAUDERDALE—Vargason, Terry* (4).
LAKELAND—Smith, Millard (1).
MIAMI—Norris, Ronald (2); Seidel, Norman (2).
ORLANDO—Goltz, David (1); Norton, Thomas (3), Stathos, William (2).
POMPANO BEACH—Betts, Gary* (2); Esposito, Kenneth (2); Hartman, Bryan (3).
ST. PETERSBURG—Doggett, Charles (4).
TAMPA—Kmet, Stanley (1); Sawyer, Richard (1).
WEST PALM BEACH—Kopylow, Boris (2).
GRAND-SLAM HOME RUNS—Coleman, D. Collins, Garnett Davis, Marshall, S. O. Miller, Reitz, L. Robinson, Runk, 1 each.
AWARDED FIRST BASE ON INTERFERENCE—Giegler 2 (Jas. Lewis, McDonald); Sturtevant 2 (Del Busto, Lugo); Belair (Lemery), W. Brown (Barlow), DeJesus (Holtberg), W. Ray (Senger), Sonnichsen (Auferio). OBSTRUCTION—Shown (McDermott).

CLUB FIELDING

Club	G.	PO.	A.	E.	DP.	PB.	Pct.	Club	G.	PO.	A.	E.	DP.	PB.	Pct.
W. Palm Beach	129	3271	1379	141	87	29	.971	St. Petersburg .	130	3434	1267	187	103	19	.962
Orlando	133	3451	1369	178	99	19	.964	Tampa	132	3328	1231	189	98	31	.960
Lakeland	133	3398	1388	179	82	28	.964	Pompano Beach	128	3061	1125	181	105	25	.959
Daytona Beach	131	3215	1359	171	103	37	.964	DeLand	132	3332	1329	206	78	48	.958
Miami	133	3407	1455	186	118	30	.963	Ft. Lauderdale	132	3315	1460	226	100	35	.955
Winter Haven .	132	3415	1519	195	94	37	.962	Cocoa	127	3106	1229	249	87	65	.946

Triple Plays—West Palm Beach, Daytona Beach, St. Petersburg, 1 each.

INDIVIDUAL FIELDING
(Ten or More Games)

*Throws lefthanded.

FIRST BASEMEN

Player and Club	G.	PO.	A.	E.	DP.	Pct.	Player and Club	G.	PO.	A.	E.	DP.	Pct.
Cardasis, Day Bch* .	13	92	9	0	9	1.000	Bartee, St. Pete	43	279	25	5	21	.984
WAGNER, DeLand* ..	118	981	75	6	61	.994	Trombino, St. Pete ..	65	523	29	10	46	.982
Norton, W Haven ...	15	114	11	1	15	.992	Miller, W Haven	109	922	60	18	58	.982
O'Neil, St. Pete*	18	121	4	1	5	.992	Fuller, Miami	102	864	53	17	66	.982
Robson, W Palm B ..	12	98	11	1	6	.991	Andino, Miami*	38	202	14	6	27	.981
Belair, Pompano B* .	95	682	54	7	62	.990	Gardner, Cocoa	54	376	41	9	29	.979
Jacobsen, Orlando ..	126	1051	69	11	75	.990	Kohn, Daytona Bch .	15	133	4	3	12	.979
Driessen, Tampa ...	61	473	37	5	43	.990	Hoelzer, Tampa	68	469	25	11	33	.978
Collins, St. Pete	10	81	1	1	6	.988	Brown, Cocoa	20	139	8	4	13	.974
J. Hughes, Day B* ..	36	226	14	3	18	.988	Williams, Pom Bch .	10	67	6	2	10	.973
Choate, Ft. Laud* ..	36	296	20	4	25	.988	O'Connor, Ft. Laud .	41	372	21	11	24	.973
Brandt, Cocoa	27	142	10	2	2	.987	Staton, Lakeland* ..	123	1060	50	32	52	.972
DeRiggi, Ft. Laud* .	52	477	25	7	31	.986	Lewis, Cocoa*	14	95	9	3	5	.972
Spilman, W Palm B*	26	136	7	2	11	.986	Howard, Cocoa	20	124	10	7	12	.950
Bograkos, Pompano B	18	115	14	2	17	.985	Giegler, Lakeland ...	11	71	4	4	6	.949
Beresford, WPB* ...	98	831	59	14	52	.984	Cott, Cocoa	12	84	7	5	6	.948
Bayer, Daytona B* ..	81	654	40	11	53	.984							

Triple Plays—Beresford, Bayer.

(Fewer Than Ten Games)

Player and Club	G.	PO.	A.	E.	DP.	Pct.	Player and Club	G.	PO.	A.	E.	DP.	Pct.
Klitsner, W Haven* .	9	69	6	0	2	1.000	Collins, W Haven ...	2	4	1	0	0	1.000
Casablanca, DeLand .	9	65	3	0	3	1.000	Smith, Orlando*	2	3	0	0	1	1.000
Tomasovich, Tampa .	6	40	2	0	4	1.000	Harris, Tampa	1	2	0	0	0	1.000
Palmer, DeLand	5	28	0	0	2	1.000	Boer, Cocoa	1	1	0	0	0	1.000
West, Tampa	2	20	1	0	2	1.000	Viefhaus, W. Palm B	5	41	5	1	1	.979
Dickerson, Pom B ...	3	19	1	0	1	1.000	Dix, Pompano Beach*	4	38	4	1	2	.977
Montalvo, Lakeland .	2	16	3	0	0	1.000	Robinson, Ft. Laud .	8	61	7	2	5	.971
Brunner, W Palm B .	2	13	1	0	3	1.000	Down, W Palm B ...	3	24	0	1	0	.960
Reid, W Palm B	1	12	1	0	4	1.000	Babyak, Ft. Laud ...	3	21	0	1	1	.955
Wyche, DeLand	1	11	0	0	1	1.000	Hill, Orlando	6	41	0	2	1	.953
Rohde, DeLand	2	9	0	0	1	1.000	Warren, DeLand	3	27	1	3	2	.903
O'Brien, W Haven ..	3	6	0	0	1	1.000	Reitz, St. Petersburg	4	22	1	4	2	.852

SECOND BASEMEN

Player and Club	G.	PO.	A.	E.	DP.	Pct.	Player and Club	G.	PO.	A.	E.	DP.	Pct.
Montalvo, Lakeland .	14	30	28	0	2	1.000	CASTELLANOS, Or	.118	302	282	17	60	.972
Schultz, W. Haven ..	26	34	48	1	7	.988	Schlesiger, Ft. Laud	14	36	29	2	4	.970
Gorsuch, Miami	19	35	44	1	5	.988	Stroman, W Palm B	.111	251	307	20	51	.965
Mairena, St. Pete ...	39	83	91	3	20	.983	Nowlin, W Haven ...	24	47	64	4	10	.965
Diaz, St. Petersburg	46	120	93	4	19	.982	Flesner, Miami	49	120	123	9	26	.964
Stodgel, Ft. Laud ..	72	140	245	8	43	.980	Kurtzman, DeLand .	91	230	218	17	34	.963
Emard, Miami	70	149	173	8	41	.976	Marshall, Orlando ..	16	25	27	2	2	.963

SECOND BASEMEN—Continued

Player and Club	G.	PO.	A.	E.	DP.	Pct.
Thompson, Day Bch	.109	229	307	21	61	.962
Deremer, Pompano B	49	91	120	10	32	.957
Franklin, Tampa	..103	276	224	23	49	.956
Harvison, W Haven	. 48	103	108	10	15	.955
Babyak, Ft. Laud	.. 47	91	116	10	28	.954
Adams, Lakeland	.. 71	185	182	19	27	.951
Kinder, W Palm B	19	39	57	5	14	.950
Bergholtz, Lakeland	. 36	83	82	9	10	.948
McLaughlin, Cocoa	.. 72	161	164	18	34	.948
Hall, Daytona Beach	23	28	61	5	9	.947
Ger. Davis, Pom B	. 60	131	151	16	30	.946
Papi, Cocoa	51	101	122	13	15	.945
Harris, Tampa	35	57	74	8	10	.942
Helton, W Haven	28	78	74	11	21	.933
Kilgore, Pompano B	17	42	37	6	6	.929
Giegler, Lakeland	17	54	46	8	8	.926
Angelo, WPB-DeL	11	21	25	4	1	.920
LaRusso, Deland	14	32	31	6	9	.913
Passarella, Ft. Laud	12	9	30	5	1	.886
Driscoll, St. Pete	13	9	12	3	2	.875
Ortiz, WPB-DeL	19	40	38	12	6	.867

Triple Plays—Diaz (St. Pete), Thompson.

(Fewer Than Ten Games)

Player and Club	G.	PO.	A.	E.	DP.	Pct.
Dews, St. Petersburg	9	25	17	0	4	1.000
Nichols, W Haven	7	17	17	0	5	1.000
Rondon, Cocoa	8	17	13	0	5	1.000
Nixon, St. Pete	4	7	12	0	2	1.000
Gamble, Daytona B	3	4	8	0	0	1.000
Millan, St. Pete	3	6	3	0	2	1.000
Navarro, DeLand	1	2	5	0	1	1.000
Costa, Cocoa	1	2	2	0	1	1.000
Sonnichsen, Orlando	2	0	4	0	0	1.000
Pearlman, W Palm B	1	1	1	0	0	1.000
Breese, Pompano B	1	1	0	0	0	1.000
Sankey, St. Pete	6	19	6	1	5	.962
Pichardo, Pompano B	7	12	11	1	2	.960
Wolfenbarger, W H	5	16	7	1	1	.958
Zaskoda, Miami	3	11	9	1	4	.952
Strazz, Winter Haven	5	12	13	2	2	.926
Bell, St. Petersburg	9	21	24	4	6	.918
Pullins, Daytona B	9	12	10	2	2	.917
Hether, Lakeland	3	6	5	1	2	.917
Hernandez, Ft. Laud	2	5	4	1	0	.900
Barakat, St. Pete	6	16	7	3	3	.885
Shepley, DeLand	4	7	8	2	1	.882
Tyson, St. Pete	4	11	11	3	2	.880
F. Diaz, Cocoa	4	6	10	3	1	.842
Alfonso, Cocoa	4	7	12	4	2	.826
Wayne, Orlando	3	1	2	3	0	.500

THIRD BASEMEN

Player and Club	G.	PO.	A.	E.	DP.	Pct.
Tuck, West Palm Bch	35	24	52	2	1	.974
Schultz, W Haven	24	17	45	2	1	.969
RUNK, Tampa	93	79	195	10	15	.965
S. Smith, Lakeland	46	45	90	6	8	.957
Flesner, Miami	63	41	136	8	9	.957
Soderholm, Orlando	24	20	55	4	0	.949
Mairena, St. Pete	17	21	30	3	0	.944
Gamble, Daytona B	.113	108	229	20	23	.944
Hill, Orlando	27	29	52	5	5	.942
Reitz, St. Pete	.124	128	240	23	15	.941
Hogan, Lakeland	76	49	158	13	11	.941
Dailey, W Palm B	93	67	154	14	13	.940
Navarro, DeLand	.127	130	258	27	16	.935
Sonnichsen, Orlando	46	43	97	10	11	.933
Marshall, Orlando	28	23	60	6	4	.933
Gardner, Cocoa	26	26	41	5	5	.931
Passarella, Ft Laud	16	6	32	3	2	.927
Kilgore, Pompano B	34	24	51	6	3	.926
Babyak, Ft. Laud	28	25	54	7	4	.919
Stureman, Pom Bch	75	69	105	16	12	.916
Clapp, Miami	47	48	96	14	12	.911
Papi, Cocoa	22	26	65	9	8	.910
DiDleo, Pompano B	12	9	21	3	2	.909
Coleman, W Haven	88	73	184	28	7	.902
Nowlin, W Haven	20	17	38	6	3	.902
Shearer, Cocoa	46	32	84	13	9	.899
Welsh, Tampa	11	12	20	3	5	.865
Prince, Ft. Laud	13	12	13	4	0	.862
Hall, Daytona Bch	14	4	20	4	1	.857
Spikes, Ft. Laud	68	53	126	30	8	.856
Burch, Tampa	16	8	20	5	4	.848
Costa, Cocoa	19	17	26	8	1	.843
Bonfonte, Orlando	13	7	23	8	2	.789

Triple Plays—Gamble, Reitz, Dailey.

(Fewer Than Ten Games)

Player and Club	G.	PO.	A.	E.	DP.	Pct.
Nolan, Pompano Bch	4	7	8	0	0	1.000
Franklin, Tampa	6	5	6	0	0	1.000
Valenzuela, W P B	2	5	6	0	0	1.000
Chew, Pompano Bch	4	3	3	0	0	1.000
Salazar, W Palm B	4	2	2	0	1	1.000
Garcia, Orlando	1	1	2	0	1	1.000
Pullins, Daytona B	1	1	2	0	1	1.000
Castellanos, Orl	2	1	2	0	1	1.000
Helton, W Haven	1	1	1	0	0	1.000
Wayne, Orlando	1	1	1	0	0	1.000
Rondon, Cocoa	3	0	2	0	0	1.000
Hoelzer, Tampa	1	0	1	0	0	1.000
Pearlman, W P B	1	0	1	0	1	1.000
Powell, Tampa	8	3	11	1	0	.933
O'Brien, W Haven	5	2	11	1	1	.929
Robinson, Ft. Laud	7	6	14	2	0	.909
Angelo, WPB-DeL	7	4	18	3	2	.880
Gorsuch, Miami	7	3	11	2	0	.875
Del Orbe, Miami	7	9	9	3	2	.857
Collins, Miami	9	5	15	4	0	.833
Russell, Cocoa	4	0	14	3	0	.824
Zaskoda, Miami	5	3	10	3	0	.813
Montalvo, Lakeland	8	5	17	6	0	.786
Caldarella, St. Pete	4	1	2	1	0	.750
Brandt, Cocoa	2	1	1	1	0	.667
Nichols, W Haven	2	1	1	2	0	.500
F. Diaz, Cocoa	3	1	1	2	0	.500
Adams, Lakeland	2	0	1	1	0	.500
Emard, Miami	1	0	1	3	0	.250

SHORTSTOPS

Player and Club	G.	PO.	A.	E.	DP.	Pct.
McConnaughy, Miami	47	67	131	9	18	.957
Deremer, Pompano B	10	16	28	2	2	.957
Ostrosser, Pom B	17	28	36	3	9	.955
Pieve, Ft. Laud	18	15	46	3	5	.953
Hogan, Lakeland	53	56	162	11	16	.952
Schultz, W Haven	13	22	36	3	3	.951
Reid, West Palm Bch	11	10	28	2	1	.950
Mairena, St. Pete	15	20	36	3	8	.949
PEARLMAN, WPB	.118	200	386	32	53	.948
Burleson, W Haven	..117	188	400	38	50	.939
Gorsuch, Miami	66	96	181	18	37	.939
DeJesus, Daytona B	.122	164	361	38	56	.933
Mason, Ft. Laud	75	92	224	23	35	.932
Tyson, St. Pete	.104	166	265	40	48	.931
Garcia, Orlando	132	198	367	42	50	.931
Vogler, DeLand	.127	196	355	43	45	.928
Pichardo, Day B	100	168	269	36	51	.924
Gamble, Daytona B	11	12	24	3	2	.923

SHORTSTOPS—Continued

Player and Club	G.	PO.	A.	E.	DP.	Pct.
Kaminski, Lakeland .	70	79	191	23	17	.922
Prince, Ft. Laud ..	30	41	73	11	12	.912
Del Orbe, Miami ..	22	35	77	11	10	.911
Hernandez, Ft. Laud	14	21	40	6	5	.910
Tatis, Cocoa	96	137	231	38	30	.906
Freeman, Cocoa ..	15	28	26	7	4	.885
Welsh, Tampa	94	122	218	45	34	.883
Youngblood, Tampa .	14	22	40	9	6	.873
Adams, Lakeland ..	10	14	20	5	3	.872
Harris, Tampa	25	23	60	14	7	.856
Nixon, St. Pete	11	17	40	12	5	.826

(Fewer Than Ten Games)

Player and Club	G.	PO.	A.	E.	DP.	Pct.
Russell, Cocoa	7	8	17	0	2	1.000
Kurtzman, DeLand .	3	5	8	0	2	1.000
Flesner, Miami	2	6	5	0	2	1.000
Runk, Tampa	2	3	6	0	1	1.000
Sitarz, Winter Haven	2	2	5	0	0	1.000
Sonnichsen, Orlando	1	2	4	0	2	1.000
Mangual, W Palm B .	2	2	3	0	1	1.000
Dews, St. Pete	1	1	2	0	0	1.000
Ortiz, DeLand	2	1	2	0	0	1.000
Giegler, Lakeland ..	1	1	1	0	0	1.000
Mata, Tampa	1	0	2	0	0	1.000
Montalvo, Lakeland .	1	1	0	0	0	1.000
Stureman, Pom B ...	1	0	1	0	0	1.000
Valenzuela, W P B .	1	0	1	0	0	1.000
Papi, Cocoa	7	17	29	2	4	.958
Nowlin, W. Haven ..	4	7	16	1	4	.958
Hether, Lakeland ...	5	8	15	2	0	.920
Nordbrook, Miami ..	9	13	37	5	4	.909
Millan, St. Pete	8	15	24	4	2	.907
Stodgel, Ft. Laud ..	3	3	6	1	1	.900
Diaz, St. Petersburg	4	0	7	1	1	.875
Kinder, W Palm B ..	9	9	25	5	2	.872
Rondon, Cocoa	4	3	2	1	0	.833

OUTFIELDERS

Player and Club	G.	PO.	A.	E.	DP.	Pct.
Brown, Ft. Laud	19	26	2	0	1	1.000
Nolan, Pompano B ..	14	22	5	0	1	1.000
Trombino, St. Pete ..	13	22	0	0	0	1.000
Wilson, Ft. Laud ...	17	18	2	0	0	1.000
Hubbard, W Haven* .	15	17	1	0	0	1.000
Botterman, W P B ..	19	17	0	0	0	1.000
Tuck, West Palm Bch	18	13	2	0	0	1.000
Gallagher, Tampa ..	13	13	1	0	0	1.000
HILL, Orlando	96	196	14	1	1	.995
Graham, Pompano B	58	112	5	1	0	.992
Mangual, W P B ...	119	212	10	2	3	.991
Lane, Lakeland	93	189	6	2	1	.990
Leon, DeLand*	91	164	5	2	0	.988
Dittmar, Tampa ...	50	73	2	1	1	.987
Boer, Cocoa	108	210	8	3	2	.986
Sudzina, Lakeland ..	41	63	4	1	1	.985
Down, W Palm B ...	105	193	6	3	1	.985
Fairbanks, Lakeland	66	126	3	2	1	.985
Palmer, DeLand	69	128	1	2	1	.985
Finkbeiner, Lakeland	68	111	6	2	1	.983
Bartee, St. Pete	63	108	4	2	0	.982
Burch, Tampa	31	51	0	1	0	.981
Avalos, Pompano B*..	89	181	6	4	1	.979
Nichols, Lakeland ..	66	82	8	2	1	.978
Morris, Orlando ...	52	80	6	2	1	.977
Polcari, St. Pete* ..	29	41	2	1	0	.977
Alvarez, Daytona B.	62	80	5	2	2	.977
West, Tampa	128	203	7	5	1	.977
Bonfonte, Orlando .	29	37	4	1	2	.976
Long, Daytona Bch ..	30	41	0	1	0	.976
Burdick, Tampa ...	36	73	6	2	1	.975
Cardasis, Day Bch* .	60	72	6	2	1	.975
Caldarella, St. P ...	127	303	7	8	0	.975
Spencer, Tampa ...	130	294	11	8	2	.974
Andino, Miami*	75	105	5	3	0	.973
Gardner, Ft. Laud ..	45	63	3	2	0	.971
Washington, Day B .	108	190	7	6	0	.970
W. Brown, W P B ..	111	177	6	6	0	.968
Rav, Miami*	128	282	10	10	1	.967
Colin, St. Petersburg	72	106	7	4	2	.966
Klitsner, W Haven* .	116	150	19	6	2	.966
Pitcock, Ft. Laud ..	110	183	7	7	1	.964
Collins, Miami	60	99	7	4	3	.964
Bright, St. Pete	52	77	2	3	0	.963
Punko, Ft. Laud ...	29	48	4	2	0	.963
Baker, Lakeland ...	38	47	5	2	0	.963
Goodman, Orlando ..	100	182	17	8	4	.961
Williams, Pom B ...	69	164	9	7	2	.961
Quinones, Lakeland ..	31	43	5	2	0	.960
Dix, Pompano Beach*	10	21	3	1	0	.960
Stennett, Orlando ..	119	179	8	8	2	.959
Shepley, DeLand ...	71	133	6	6	1	.959
Reinbach, Miami ...	126	175	10	8	0	.959
Russell, DeLand ...	76	195	7	9	1	.957
Gar. Davis Pom B ..	95	167	11	8	1	.957
Robinson, Day B ...	101	142	5	7	1	.955
Easler, Cocoa	30	40	2	2	0	.952
Myers, Winter Haven	35	49	7	3	1	.949
Sturtevant, Cocoa ..	56	51	3	3	0	.947
Suchan, W Haven ...	115	195	9	12	1	.944
Rohde, DeLand	59	97	5	6	0	.944
Robinson, Ft. Laud .	26	31	3	2	0	.944
Hairston, St. Pete ..	35	45	2	3	0	.940
Valenzuela, WPB ...	20	15	0	1	0	.938
Velez, Ft. Lauderdale	17	27	2	2	1	.935
Rodriguez, Cocoa ...	29	28	1	2	0	.935
Sanders, Ft. Laud ..	91	136	7	10	3	.935
Kinner, St. Pete	17	28	0	2	0	.933
Giegler, Lakeland ...	12	14	0	1	0	.933
Escoe, Pompano Bch	28	52	1	4	0	.930
O'Brien, W Haven ...	16	24	2	2	0	.929
Pitruzzello, Miami* .	12	12	0	1	0	.923
Lopez, Cocoa	63	68	2	6	0	.921
Bograkos, Pom B ...	10	21	2	2	0	.920
Howard, Cocoa	11	11	0	1	0	.917
Kilgore, DeLand	55	86	1	8	0	.916
Nixon, St. Petersburg	28	48	5	5	2	.914
Albury, W Haven ...	87	121	5	12	2	.913
Gardner, Cocoa	50	67	6	7	0	.913
Spikes, Ft. Laud ...	58	79	9	10	0	.898
Small, Winter Haven	58	15	1	2	1	.889
Schultz, W Haven ..	13	14	1	2	0	.882
Smith, Daytona Bch .	32	42	2	6	0	.880

(Fewer Than Ten Games)

Player and Club	G.	PO.	A.	E.	DP.	Pct.
Pompa, W Palm B ..	8	16	0	0	0	1.000
Coleman, W Haven ..	4	6	2	0	0	1.000
Shearer, Cocoa	6	8	0	0	0	1.000
Choate, Ft. Laud* ..	9	7	1	0	1	1.000
Harts, Pompano Bch*	4	7	0	0	0	1.000
Hartig, Orlando	6	7	0	0	0	1.000
White, Tampa	4	6	0	0	0	1.000
Kimbrell, Daytona B	5	6	0	0	0	1.000
Hetman, W Haven ..	4	5	0	0	0	1.000
Arce, W Palm B	6	5	0	0	0	1.000
Tomasovich, Tampa .	6	4	1	0	0	1.000
Cross, Winter Haven	4	4	0	0	0	1.000
Fuller, Miami	8	3	1	0	0	1.000
Tanner, Lakeland ...	2	3	0	0	0	1.000
Orozco, Cocoa	4	3	0	0	0	1.000
Passarella, Ft. Laud	1	2	0	0	0	1.000
Pullins, Daytona Bch	1	2	0	0	0	1.000
Smith, Orlando*	1	2	0	0	0	1.000
Hoelzer, Tampa	3	2	0	0	0	1.000
Pinnick, Orlando* ..	3	2	0	0	0	1.000
Reid, W Palm Beach	3	2	0	0	0	1.000
Klastava, W Haven ..	1	1	0	0	0	1.000
Zuniga, Orlando	1	0	1	0	0	1.000
Joseph, DeLand	2	1	0	0	0	1.000

OUTFIELDERS—Continued

(Fewer Than Ten Games)

Player and Club	G.	PO.	A.	E.	DP.	Pct.
Scott, West Palm Bch	2	1	0	0	0	1.000
Brandt, Cocoa	3	1	0	0	0	1.000
Moore, Pompano B ..	6	17	1	1	0	.947
Steele, Tampa	4	6	0	3	0	.667
Lewis, Orlando	1	1	0	1	0	.500
Gamble, Daytona B ..	1	1	0	2	0	.333
Dailey, W Palm B ..	1	0	0	1	0	.000

CATCHERS

Player and Club	G.	PO.	A.	E.	DP.	PB.	Pct.
Locascio, Lake ..	18	78	8	0	1	2	1.000
Frensley, Lake ..	11	60	10	0	0	5	1.000
SWISS, Lake ..	80	478	49	3	3	12	.994
Hetman, W H ..	27	140	17	1	1	6	.994
Hart, W P B ..	98	559	51	5	6	24	.992
Johnson, Orlando .	54	392	32	5	6	6	.988
Kooyman, Tampa .	14	78	3	1	1	3	.988
White, Tampa ...	95	620	83	9	9	21	.987
Del Papa, Lake ..	17	70	8	1	0	6	.987
Seltzer, Miami ..	21	141	10	2	1	7	.987
McDermott, D B .	92	635	42	9	5	26	.987
Senger, P B ...	35	300	16	3	0	5	.986
R. Miller, Tampa	31	197	16	3	1	7	.986
Kogut, Ft. Laud .	41	228	22	4	5	10	.984
Robinson, D B ..	26	165	20	3	0	7	.984
McEnderfer, StP .	19	113	10	2	1	4	.984
Auferio, St. Pete .	77	469	59	9	0	3	.983
Frick, W P B	37	167	14	4	0	3	.978
Collins, W H ...	30	158	22	4	2	12	.978
Barlow, Miami ..	42	226	22	6	2	8	.976
McDonald, StP ..	26	146	18	4	0	9	.976
Brown, Cocoa ...	32	213	16	6	0	11	.974
Del Busto, Miami	79	448	44	13	9	15	.974
Matheson, FtL ..	15	105	7	3	0	2	.974
Combs, Ft. Laud .	30	167	19	5	1	4	.974
Lewis, Orlando ..	56	387	41	12	3	7	.973
Jones, Cocoa	58	322	46	11	4	24	.971
Cott, Cocoa	16	136	12	5	1	10	.967
Lugo, DeLand ...	71	331	47	13	2	22	.967
Ford, DeLand ...	68	344	46	14	3	19	.965
Howard, Cocoa ..	26	130	9	5	1	13	.965
Nolan, P B	74	490	46	18	6	15	.962
Holtberg, FtL ...	36	174	22	8	0	10	.961
Cross, W Haven .	82	147	57	9	6	18	.958
Guerrero, Orlando	23	119	17	6	1	5	.958
Mora, Ft. Laud ..	26	160	12	9	2	9	.950
Lopez, Cocoa	10	69	7	8	1	7	.905
Fenton, St. Pete .	10	28	0	6	0	1	.824

(Fewer Than Ten Games)

Player and Club	G.	PO.	A.	E.	DP.	PB.	Pct.
Sulprizio, StP	9	56	5	0	0	2	1.000
Kohn, Daytona B .	8	47	1	0	0	3	1.000
Williams, P B	4	31	4	0	0	1	1.000
M. Hughes, D B ..	8	30	4	0	0	1	1.000
Jacobsen, Orlando	5	24	1	0	0	1	1.000
Miller, W Haven .	5	19	1	0	1	1	1.000
Iskierka, P B	4	17	0	0	0	2	1.000
Vicente, DeLand .	3	11	4	0	0	1	1.000
Marrero, P B	2	11	0	0	0	0	1.000
Vogler, DeLand ..	3	6	0	0	0	3	1.000
Haren, Day B ...	1	4	0	0	0	0	1.000
Todd, W Palm B	1	3	0	0	0	0	1.000
Kramer, W Haven	2	1	1	0	0	0	1.000
Gentile, WPB ...	7	33	4	1	0	2	.974
Lemery, Lake ...	5	21	4	1	0	1	.962
Outten, W Palm B	5	17	3	1	0	0	.952
Belcik, Lakeland .	8	56	3	3	0	2	.952
Dickerson, P B ..	8	49	8	4	0	4	.934

PITCHERS

Player and Club	G.	PO.	A.	E.	DP.	Pct.
MORGAN, DeLand ..	23	8	27	0	4	1.000
Klastava, W Haven .	23	13	19	0	2	1.000
Amyotte, Lakeland .	27	8	23	0	0	1.000
Rosiek, Cocoa	22	8	19	0	3	1.000
Contreras, Tampa ...	22	8	16	0	1	1.000
Chadwick, Ft. Laud .	14	10	13	0	1	1.000
Babcock, W Palm B .	19	5	17	0	0	1.000
Hoops, W Palm B ..	18	5	16	0	0	1.000
Herrmann, Miami ..	21	6	15	0	2	1.000
Joseph, WH-DeL ..	31	5	15	0	0	1.000
Sires, Tampa	11	6	13	0	3	1.000
Kleibl, Winter Haven	22	7	11	0	0	1.000
Seifert, Daytona B .	25	7	10	0	0	1.000
Gable, Tampa	49	5	12	0	0	1.000
Hemenway, St. Pete .	24	5	10	0	0	1.000
Shown, Ft. Laud ...	36	1	13	0	0	1.000
Edge, Winter Haven .	39	1	13	0	0	1.000
Clifford, Lakeland ..	16	4	9	0	0	1.000
Cole, St. Petersburg .	24	3	9	0	1	1.000
Amman, Cocoa	20	4	7	0	1	1.000
Kessler, Pompano B* .	21	1	10	0	0	1.000
Connors, Pompano B .	24	1	9	0	0	1.000
Hughes, Orlando ...	12	3	6	0	0	1.000
Warren, DeLand ...	19	2	7	0	1	1.000
Hardiman, Tampa ...	20	3	6	0	0	1.000
Remson, W Haven* ..	32	3	6	0	0	1.000
Brown, St. Pete	10	2	6	0	0	1.000
Breese, Pompano B .	14	2	5	0	0	1.000
Hefflinger, Ft. Laud*	23	1	6	0	0	1.000
Foust, Tampa	11	3	3	0	0	1.000
Palas, DeLand*	12	2	4	0	0	1.000
Grover, Cocoa*	14	2	4	0	0	1.000
Smithson, Pompano B	26	1	4	0	0	1.000
Bruntrager, Lake* ...	10	1	3	0	0	1.000
Swanson, Ft. Laud ..	14	2	2	0	0	1.000
Bellm, Winter Haven	17	0	2	0	0	1.000
Kline, W Palm B ...	24	1	1	0	0	1.000
Earley, DeLand	11	0	1	0	0	1.000
Ray, DeLand*	22	4	27	1	0	.969
Grant, Tampa	27	12	17	1	3	.967
Brandt, St. Pete* ...	26	3	23	1	1	.963
S. Miller, Tampa ...	19	5	20	1	0	.962
Mays, Lakeland	32	10	14	1	0	.960
Bynon, DeLand	22	9	14	1	1	.958
Milam, Winter Haven	21	5	16	1	1	.955
Scott, Miami	52	8	13	1	2	.955
Turner, W Palm B ..	24	11	29	2	2	.952
Jackson, Tampa	13	10	10	1	0	.952
Bereguete, Day B* ..	22	4	16	1	2	.952
Bettis, W Palm B* ..	30	3	14	1	0	.944
Hebert, Miami*	33	4	61	4	2	.942
King, Miami	16	3	13	1	0	.941
Goodwin, Tampa-Mia	22	3	13	1	0	.941
Ebner, St. Pete	57	4	12	1	1	.941
Ward, Winter Haven	25	8	22	2	2	.938
Ignasiak, Lakeland* .	15	1	14	1	0	.938
Pole, Winter Haven .	19	5	10	1	2	.938
Kerr, Winter Haven .	24	1	14	1	0	.938
Solomon, Daytona B	22	13	31	3	1	.936
Kelly, Orlando	30	3	25	2	0	.933
Olson, Pompano B ...	16	2	12	1	1	.933
Phillips, W Haven ..	16	6	8	1	1	.933
Smith, St. Petersburg	28	9	18	2	2	.931
Buskey, Ft. Laud ...	18	15	24	3	1	.929
Crowder, Ft. Laud ..	15	5	19	2	0	.923
Pauls, Daytona Bch .	11	3	9	1	0	.923
Taylor, Cocoa	15	4	8	1	0	.923
Williams, W Palm B	30	4	8	1	0	.923
Austin, Miami	22	7	28	3	0	.921
Elenes, Cocoa	12	5	18	2	1	.920
Pinnick, Orlando* ..	19	5	18	2	0	.920
Veintidos, Pom B	26	11	23	3	3	.919
Schroeder, Ft. Laud	25	13	20	3	1	.917
Hurley, Orlando ...	16	8	14	2	0	.917
Grassing, Lakeland .	30	3	19	2	0	.917
Enyart, Orlando* ...	33	3	19	2	3	.917

PITCHERS—Continued

Player and Club	G	PO	A	E	DP	Pct.
Fricchione, FtL	12	0	11	1	0	.917
Angelier, Lakeland ..	21	6	15	2	0	.913
Keller, W Palm B ...	24	9	22	3	1	.912
Wall, Daytona Bch* ..	23	5	25	3	1	.909
Kelley, Miami	24	5	25	3	1	.909
Hansen, St. Pete ...	30	5	15	2	1	.909
Moore, Cocoa*	12	4	6	1	0	.909
G. Brown, W Palm B	17	3	7	1	0	.909
Williams, Daytona B	33	7	22	3	2	.906
Castillo, Miami* ...	20	3	15	2	0	.900
Murray, DeLand	30	4	14	2	1	.900
Boyett, St. Pete ...	13	2	7	1	0	.900
Gilman, W Haven ...	27	7	35	5	3	.894
Wellman, Daytona B*	17	1	7	1	1	.889
Peery, Orlando*	24	2	6	1	0	.889
F. Fisher, Lakeland	45	2	6	1	0	.889
Snowdon, Orl-DeL*..	26	6	17	3	0	.885
Beckman, Lakeland* .	30	7	23	4	0	.882
Ramirez, Ft. Laud ..	11	7	8	2	0	.882
Ervin, Daytona B* ..	14	2	13	2	0	.882
Russell, W Palm B ..	25	7	29	5	0	.878
Cooper, Tampa*	19	5	16	3	1	.875
Eastwick, Tampa ...	37	3	11	2	1	.875
Savold, Orlando	19	2	5	1	0	.875
M. Fisher, Lake* ...	21	0	7	1	0	.875
Harkey, Pompano B .	26	0	7	1	0	.875
Williams, Miami* ...	23	4	23	4	3	.871
Manderbach, FtL* ...	21	3	23	4	0	.867
Moore, Pompano B ..	16	4	9	2	0	.867
Lehman, Cocoa*	27	8	17	4	0	.862
Carey, PB-DeL*	18	2	16	3	2	.857
Mims, Cocoa	15	4	8	2	0	.857

Player and Club	G	PO	A	E	DP	Pct.
Dorsch, Daytona B ..	42	1	11	2	0	.857
Fairbanks, Day B* ..	10	1	5	1	0	.857
Johnson, Daytona B*	29	2	4	1	1	.857
Cogan, Ft. Laud* ...	26	6	17	4	1	.852
Grigsby, Cocoa	30	6	17	4	0	.852
Kinney, St. Pete* ...	23	2	15	3	0	.850
Simmons, Ft. Laud ..	18	3	8	2	0	.846
Hallmark, DeLand ..	19	3	13	3	1	.842
E. Diaz, Cocoa	35	5	11	3	0	.842
Sathre, Orlando	38	2	13	3	1	.833
Robinson, Pom B* ...	22	2	3	1	0	.833
Luebber, Orlando ...	34	10	34	10	1	.815
Collier, Ft. Laud ...	29	2	15	4	0	.810
Cosgrove, Cocoa* ...	30	3	18	5	0	.808
Richard, Cocoa*	19	6	10	4	1	.800
Meeler, Lakeland ...	17	3	5	2	0	.800
Hill, Winter Haven .	21	2	6	2	1	.800
Reynolds, Pom Bch ..	10	1	3	1	0	.800
Acosta, Daytona B ..	17	1	3	1	0	.800
Grindle, Tampa	30	6	14	6	0	.769
Potash, Pompano B* .	20	3	7	3	1	.769
Goodwin, DeL-PB ...	30	4	8	4	0	.750
Hazelip, Ft. Laud ..	11	1	5	2	0	.750
Babcock, DeLand ...	26	5	9	5	2	.737
Farley, St. Pete* ...	21	1	10	4	0	.733
Alfonso, Cocoa	23	4	26	11	1	.732
Kleem, W Palm B* ..	18	2	6	3	1	.727
Ruddell, Tampa	12	2	8	4	2	.714
Dodson, Pompano B .	10	2	3	3	1	.625
Webb, Pompano B ...	11	1	4	3	0	.625
Zuniga, Orlando	19	0	3	2	0	.600

(Fewer Than Ten Games)

Player and Club	G	PO	A	E	DP	Pct.
Vickery, W Palm B ..	8	2	5	0	0	1.000
Ker, West Palm Bch	3	1	4	0	0	1.000
M. Kmet, Tampa ...	3	2	3	0	0	1.000
VonHoff, St. Pete ..	3	4	1	0	0	1.000
Sorrentino, Miami* ..	4	0	5	0	0	1.000
Lohse, Lakeland* ...	6	1	4	0	0	1.000
Barisoff, Daytona B .	7	1	4	0	0	1.000
Farmer, W Haven ..	7	1	4	0	0	1.000
Fuller, St. Pete	9	3	2	0	0	1.000
McClain, W P B	9	3	2	0	0	1.000
DeRiggi, Ft. Laud* ..	6	0	4	0	0	1.000
Villalobos, Cocoa ...	6	1	3	0	0	1.000
Vargason, Ft. Laud* .	4	0	3	0	0	1.000
Brandt, Cocoa	7	1	2	0	0	1.000
Raible, Daytona B ..	8	0	3	0	0	1.000
Mack, Orlando*	9	1	2	0	0	1.000
Holdsworth, Lake ...	3	0	2	0	0	1.000
Slayback, Lakeland ..	3	0	2	0	0	1.000
Bushey, Lakeland* ..	4	0	2	0	0	1.000
Volkening, St. Pete .	4	0	2	0	0	1.000
Bertino, W Palm B .	5	0	2	0	0	1.000
Foor, Lakeland*	5	1	1	0	1	1.000
Buys, Ft. Lauderdale	8	0	2	0	0	1.000
Browning, St. Pete .	1	0	1	0	0	1.000
Choate, Ft. Laud* ..	1	0	1	0	0	1.000
M. Smith, Lakeland .	1	1	0	0	0	1.000

Player and Club	G	PO	A	E	DP	Pct.
Stroman, W Palm B .	1	0	1	0	0	1.000
Betts, Pompano B* ..	2	0	1	0	0	1.000
Kopylow, W Palm B	2	0	1	0	0	1.000
Norris, Miami	3	1	0	0	0	1.000
Clark, Daytona B ...	3	1	0	0	0	1.000
Hartman, Pompano B	4	0	1	0	0	1.000
Doggett, St. Pete ...	4	1	0	0	0	1.000
Murphy, Pompano B .	4	0	1	0	0	1.000
Schleider, W P B ...	4	1	0	0	0	1.000
Stewart, DeLand* ...	5	3	5	1	0	.889
Brenner, Pompano B	8	3	2	1	0	.833
Maine, DeLand	7	3	1	1	0	.800
Mason, Lakeland* ..	5	2	4	2	1	.750
O'Connor, Tampa* ..	8	2	4	2	0	.750
Clayton, Miami	7	0	3	1	0	.750
St. John, St. Pete ..	9	1	4	2	0	.714
Moore, W Palm B* ..	8	1	1	1	0	.667
Nagy, Winter Haven	3	0	2	1	0	.667
Killian, Lakeland* ..	8	1	1	1	1	.667
Cousino, Lakeland ..	8	0	3	2	0	.600
Egnatchik, DeLand .	5	0	1	1	0	.500
Sheanshang, Cocoa .	5	0	1	1	0	.500
Kavanaugh, Miami* .	4	0	1	2	0	.333
Adey, Daytona B* ...	4	0	3	0	0	.250
Stathos, Orlando ...	2	0	0	1	0	.000

The following players do not have any recorded accepted chances at the positions indicated; therefore, are not listed in the fielding averages for those particular positions: Borowy, p; Braynt, p; Butler, ph; Christopher,* p; Cichon, p; Denbow, ph; Esposito,* p; Fulk, ph; Goltz, p; S. Kmet, p; D. Murray, of; T. Norton, p; Pizarro, ph; Price,* p; Pruett, ph; Quinones, 3b; Sawyer, p; Schlesiger, p; Seidel, p; Tuck, p.

CLUB PITCHING

*Throws lefthanded.

Club	G.	CG.	ShO.	Sv.	IP.	H.	R.	ER.	HR.	BB.	Int. BB.	HB.	SO.	WP.	Bk.	ERA.
St. Petersburg	130	28	15	39	1145	1006	416	316	26	377	29	28	779	45	3	2.48
Miami	133	66	20	20	1136	954	419	317	16	473	18	30	791	49	0	2.51
West Palm Beach	129	51	20	24	1090	866	387	305	11	477	10	43	728	59	4	2.52
Daytona Beach	131	44	11	24	1072	934	462	333	25	462	43	25	840	73	7	2.80
Orlando	133	50	13	19	1150	991	458	360	32	548	18	43	860	81	4	2.82
Winter Haven	132	35	15	23	1138	1039	481	368	23	461	13	42	803	59	5	2.91
Tampa	132	29	14	29	1109	854	452	364	31	572	89	40	858	66	7	2.95
Cocoa	127	28	13	18	1035	905	516	354	19	520	39	44	817	102	10	3.08
Lakeland	133	37	13	26	1333	1016	491	388	23	499	27	27	762	48	11	3.08
Fort Lauderdale	132	37	14	13	1105	963	555	401	18	561	22	42	781	87	3	3.27
Pompano Beach	128	34	10	12	1020	979	524	406	26	542	13	43	670	68	2	3.58
DeLand	132	32	7	23	1111	1104	620	496	38	486	11	36	682	96	6	4.02

PITCHERS' RECORDS

(Leading Qualifiers for Earned-Run Average Leadership—134 or More Innings)

*Throws lefthanded.

Pitcher—Club	G	GS	CG	ShO	W	L	Sv	Pct.	IP	H	R	ER	HR	BB	Int. BB	HB	SO	WP	ERA
Hebert, Miami* .33	23	20	5	21	7	2	.750	219	173	54	35	2	56	7	9	135	3	1.44
Luebber, Orlando .34	30	17	4	17	11	1	.607	237	184	70	47	7	79	3	0	172	13	1.78
Kelley, Miami .24	22	11	3	12	6	1	.667	154	132	53	35	0	80	3	5	63	14	2.05
Brandt, St. Pete* .26	26	11	2	11	11	0	.500	194	160	65	45	6	57	4	4	101	1	2.09
Keller, W Palm B .24	21	8	4	11	7	0	.611	142	98	44	33	3	57	0	3	106	7	2.09
Ward, W Haven .25	23	10	3	11	8	0	.579	166	147	52	40	5	42	0	5	103	4	2.17
Turner, W Palm B .24	24	7	3	12	8	0	.600	157	111	54	38	1	56	1	6	100	9	2.18
Solomon, Day B .22	22	11	3	11	7	0	.611	156	131	61	41	2	72	2	5	104	10	2.37
Ray, DeLand* .22	21	4	0	9	9	0	.500	148	135	59	39	6	62	2	6	84	5	2.37
Veintidos, Pom B .26	26	12	4	12	11	0	.522	188	148	57	51	4	88	1	8	134	8	2.44

Departmental Leaders: G—Ebner, 57; GS—Luebber, 30; CG—Hebert, 20; ShO—Buskey, Hebert, Milam, 5; W—Hebert, 21; L—Alfonso, Amyotte, Beckman, 13; Sv—Ebner, 28; Pct.—J. Smith, .765; IP—Luebber, 237; H—Beckman, 185; R—Amyotte, 93; ER—Amyotte, 80; HR—Bynon, 8; BB—Grant, 89; IBB—Gable, 17; HB—Kelly, 12; SO—Luebber, 172; WP—Cosgrove, 22.

(All Pitchers—Listed Alphabetically)

Pitcher—Club	G	GS	CG	ShO	W	L	Sv	Pct.	IP	H	R	ER	HR	BB	Int. BB	HB	SO	WP	ERA
Acosta, Daytona B .17	2	0	0	5	2	0	.714	36	37	23	21	1	14	2	3	33	7	5.25
Adey, Daytona B* .8	2	0	0	1	2	1	.333	21	12	6	3	0	12	2	0	13	0	1.29
Alfonso, Cocoa ...23	19	2	0	3	13	0	.188	134	133	70	47	1	51	5	7	104	11	3.16
Amman, Cocoa ...20	0	0	0	3	7	0	.400	28	36	17	13	1	12	3	2	14	1	4.18
Amyotte, Lakeland .27	27	6	2	8	13	0	.381	168	161	93	80	5	84	3	0	121	8	4.29
Angelier, Lakeland .21	14	7	2	9	3	0	.750	118	88	32	21	2	49	1	0	64	2	1.60
Austin, Miami 23	19	5	2	10	7	0	.588	130	109	75	59	3	78	1	7	78	8	3.81
P. Babcock, DeL .26	10	2	0	3	6	1	.333	93	125	59	48	2	27	2	1	41	3	4.65
R. Babcock, WPB .19	19	10	2	10	7	0	.588	126	89	41	28	0	59	1	8	70	8	2.00
Barisoff, Day B .. 7	2	0	0	0	0	0	.000	14	13	9	7	1	12	0	0	7	1	4.50
Beckman, Lake* .30	29	7	1	13	13	0	.500	212	185	86	67	7	87	8	4	152	8	2.84
Belim, W Haven .17	1	0	0	1	2	5	.333	25	26	11	9	2	7	1	0	16	1	3.24
Bereguete, Day B* .22	13	2	0	3	4	1	.429	90	93	36	23	2	20	6	0	60	3	2.30
Bertino, W Palm B 5	0	0	0	1	2	0	.000	11	6	7	7	0	10	1	4	7	3	5.73
Bettis, W Palm B* .30	0	0	0	3	1	6	.750	54	35	14	8	0	27	2	1	44	4	1.33
Betts, Pompano B* . 2	0	0	0	0	0	0	.000	2	0	0	0	0	2	0	0	0	0	0.00
Borowy, DeLand .. 3	0	0	0	2	0	0	.000	14	17	14	12	1	18	0	3	7	2	7.71
Boyett, St. Pete .13	11	2	1	5	3	0	.625	75	69	34	24	1	25	2	2	47	6	2.88
Brandt, Cocoa ... 7	0	0	0	1	2	0	.000	12	12	8	4	1	7	1	1	10	4	3.00
Brandt, St. Pete* .26	26	11	2	11	11	0	.500	194	160	65	45	6	57	4	4	101	1	2.09
Breese, Pom B ..14	6	0	0	0	8	0	.286	48	53	19	12	0	21	1	0	29	2	2.25
Brenner, Pom B .. 8	7	0	0	2	3	0	.400	45	35	26	22	2	26	0	2	39	7	4.40
A. Brown, StP ...10	9	2	1	2	1	0	.667	54	48	17	11	0	18	1	2	41	3	1.65
G. Brown, WPB ...17	1	0	0	2	1	0	.667	33	31	20	18	1	18	0	0	13	1	4.91
Browning, St. Pete . 1	1	1	0	1	0	0	1.000	7	5	1	1	0	1	0	0	6	1	1.29
Bruntrager, Lake* .10	0	0	0	1	0	0	.000	14	16	15	14	0	6	1	3	11	3	9.00
Bryant, W Haven .. 6	0	0	0	1	0	0	.000	8	5	3	2	0	10	2	0	6	1	2.25
Bushey, Lakeland . 4	0	0	0	0	1	0	.000	8	11	7	7	1	11	1	0	7	2	7.88
Buskey, Ft. Laud .18	15	10	5	10	5	1	.667	133	98	37	29	2	19	1	7	81	2	1.96
Buys, Ft. Laud .. 8	3	0	0	0	2	0	.000	14	11	13	12	0	6	1	1	11	5	7.07
Bynon, DeLand ...22	18	3	1	9	5	0	.643	136	121	53	42	8	29	3	4	59	3	2.78
Carey, 1PB-17DeL* .18	16	5	0	7	9	0	.438	105	101	64	53	5	56	0	3	79	12	4.54
Castillo, Miami* ...20	15	7	2	4	10	0	.400	109	96	46	34	4	39	0	1	79	3	2.81
Chadwick, FtL ...14	9	1	2	2	5	0	.286	43	47	35	26	1	33	0	1	21	0	5.44
Choate, Ft. Laud* . 1	0	0	0	0	0	0	.000	0	0	0	0	0	0	0	0	0	0	0.00
Christopher, 9 PB-2 DeL* .11	1	0	0	1	1	0	.500	15	15	13	11	0	18	1	1	12	7	6.60
Cichon, DeLand .. 2	0	0	0	0	4	0	.000	4	7	5	5	0	3	0	0	6	0	11.25
Clark, Daytona B . 3	0	0	0	0	0	0	.000	15	15	8	6	0	11	0	0	6	0	3.60
Clayton, Miami .. 7	0	0	0	0	3	0	.000	15	15	8	3	2	6	1	0	3	1	3.00
Clifford, Lakeland .16	8	5	2	9	1	2	.900	79	57	11	8	0	11	0	0	52	0	0.91
Cogan, Ft. Laud* .26	9	2	0	4	8	1	.200	86	81	55	38	2	66	0	2	47	10	3.98
Cole, St. Pete ...24	0	0	0	4	3	4	.571	62	49	19	14	0	21	2	5	39	4	2.00
Collier, Ft. Laud .29	2	0	0	1	3	2	.250	88	71	27	21	0	65	3	1	89	11	2.15
Connors, Pom B ..24	3	1	0	4	3	0	.571	43	43	27	19	1	22	4	0	22	2	3.98
Contreras, Tampa .22	18	2	0	3	10	0	.231	108	89	56	46	5	59	4	7	75	9	3.83
Cooper, Tampa* ...19	18	2	1	7	9	0	.438	117	79	47	37	5	64	9	4	95	6	2.85
Cosgrove, Cocoa* .30	19	3	1	7	11	0	.389	113	112	62	50	3	81	4	4	81	22	3.98
Cousino, Lakeland . 8	0	0	1	0	1	0	1.000	12	7	2	2	0	0	0	0	5	0	1.50
Crowder, Ft. Laud .15	14	6	1	6	6	0	.500	89	70	34	28	2	36	0	7	73	4	2.83
DeRiggi, Ft. Laud* . 4	0	0	0	3	0	0	.000	14	20	16	9	1	3	0	0	7	2	5.79
E. Diaz, Cocoa ...35	0	0	0	3	3	3	.333	71	49	31	20	0	33	6	8	48	2	2.54
Dodson, Pom B ...10	6	0	0	1	3	0	.333	50	35	26	18	1	18	0	1	16	2	5.40
Doggett, St. Pete . 4	0	0	0	1	0	0	.000	4	6	6	6	0	0	0	0	4	0	13.50
Dorsch, Daytona B .42	0	0	0	5	4	12	.556	61	44	28	15	3	21	5	5	69	5	2.21
Earley, DeLand ...11	4	0	0	1	2	0	.333	19	26	21	14	0	14	0	4	12	4	6.63
Eastwick, Tampa .37	7	0	0	2	9	3	.182	101	93	53	39	5	45	11	1	70	7	3.48
Ebner, St. Pete ...57	0	0	0	9	6	28	.600	105	89	18	15	1	19	9	1	109	1	1.29
Edge, W Haven ...39	0	0	0	4	1	20	.200	63	39	20	19	1	38	1	4	50	2	2.71
Egnatchik, DeL .. 4	1	0	0	1	0	0	.000	17	14	3	3	1	4	0	0	13	1	1.59
Elenes, Cocoa ...12	11	3	0	3	7	0	.300	70	61	35	24	2	37	3	0	55	2	3.09

Pitcher—Club	G	GS	CG	ShO	W	L	Sv	Pct.	IP	H	R	ER	HR	BB	Int. BB	HB	SO	WP	ERA
Enyart, Orlando* ..33	21	4	1	7	11	1		.389	159	144	69	61	5	84	5	7	141	9	3.45
Ervin, Day B* ...14	14	5	1	4	8	0		.333	85	71	33	27	4	38	1	2	64	2	2.86
Esposito, Pom B* .. 2	0	0	0	0	1	0		.000	1	3	1	1	0	1	0	0	0	0	9.00
Fairbanks, D B* ...10	10	2	1	4	5	0		.444	44	41	23	20	1	31	1	2	25	4	4.09
Farley, St. Pete* ..21	10	1	1	3	4	1		.429	81	79	38	27	3	32	2	2	41	6	3.00
Farmer, W Haven .. 7	7	0	0	0	2	0		.000	33	46	23	21	2	6	0	2	27	3	5.73
F. Fisher, Lake ..45	2	1	1	5	5	5		.500	63	77	29	22	0	22	3	2	42	3	3.14
M. Fisher, Lake* ..21	4	1	0	2	5	2		.286	48	47	22	14	0	17	4	1	30	1	2.63
Foor, Lakeland* .. 5	1	0	0	1	0	1		1.000	12	7	2	0	0	7	0	2	7	0	0.00
Foust, Tampa ...11	3	0	0	1	5	0		.167	21	34	22	19	1	17	8	3	14	2	8.14
Fricchione, FtL ...12	5	1	1	2	5	0		.286	42	41	20	12	1	12	1	2	29	3	2.57
Fuller, St. Pete ..19	6	1	0	3	3	0		.500	45	43	16	15	1	8	0	0	25	3	2.00
Gable, Tampa ...49	0	0	0	6	6	14		.500	74	63	24	18	2	38	17	0	82	3	2.19
Gilman, W Haven ..27	18	4	1	5	11	0		.313	144	144	65	48	0	58	1	4	98	9	3.00
Goltz, Orlando ... 1	1	0	0	0	1	0		.000	3	4	4	4	1	6	0	0	2	0	6.00
D. Goodwin, 16 Tam-6 Mia .22	10	1	0	3	7	1		.300	86	78	48	37	1	42	7	3	80	10	3.87
S. Goodwin, 25 DeL-5 PB ..30	8	0	0	3	7	4		.300	74	62	53	49	3	80	1	6	65	19	5.96
Grant, Tampa ...27	24	5	0	11	7	0		.611	167	130	73	64	7	89	7	6	116	8	3.45
Grassing, Lake ..30	16	3	0	6	4	1		.600	122	112	55	46	3	56	2	2	87	5	3.39
Grigsby, Cocoa ..30	5	0	0	3	6	1		.333	80	63	44	30	1	46	3	5	54	13	3.38
Grindle, Tampa ..30	7	3	1	6	3	3		.667	88	73	25	20	1	45	9	7	41	6	2.05
Grover, Cocoa* ...14	4	0	0	0	3	0		.000	27	24	24	12	0	27	1	2	24	5	4.00
Hallmark, DeL ...19	7	3	0	6	3	1		.727	77	66	31	31	0	30	0	2	78	6	3.62
Hansen, St. Pete ..30	7	1	0	8	3	5		.727	81	70	29	23	1	19	2	3	64	5	2.56
Hardiman, Tampa ..20	2	1	0	6	1	4		.857	51	36	10	8	0	14	1	4	53	3	1.41
Harkey, Pom B ..26	4	2	1	4	6	2		.400	66	71	33	26	0	36	1	7	44	5	3.55
Hartman, Pom B .. 3	0	0	0	0	0	0		.000	3	1	2	0	0	2	0	0	2	0	0.00
Hazelip, Ft. Laud .11	11	1	1	2	4	0		.333	52	53	31	26	1	22	1	1	39	2	4.50
Hebert, Miami* ..33	23	20	5	21	7	2		.750	219	173	54	35	2	56	7	9	135	3	1.44
Hefflinger, FtL* ..23	2	0	0	1	3	0		.250	50	49	33	24	2	30	1	1	40	3	4.32
Hemenway, StP ...24	4	0	0	5	1	0		.833	68	47	20	15	1	25	2	1	59	2	1.99
Herrmann, Miami .21	21	11	4	10	6	0		.625	149	140	57	43	1	67	2	4	103	2	2.60
Hill, Winter Haven .21	0	0	0	3	1	0		.750	29	33	20	11	3	14	2	2	29	1	3.41
Holdsworth, Lake .. 3	1	0	0	0	1	1		.000	7	7	5	2	1	3	0	0	5	2	2.57
Hoops, W Palm B .18	17	10	2	9	5	0		.643	120	102	38	37	2	40	1	3	86	2	2.78
Hughes, Orlando ..12	7	0	0	1	4	0		.200	53	50	35	24	2	30	1	4	49	9	4.08
Hurley, Orlando ...16	13	8	2	9	4	1		.692	101	62	29	22	2	47	0	3	89	14	1.96
Ignasiak, Lake* ...15	3	2	2	4	5	0		.444	76	62	40	30	1	55	0	5	53	7	3.55
Jackson, Tampa ..13	11	2	0	3	4	1		.429	76	65	29	21	2	19	5	0	50	1	2.49
Johnson, Day B* ..29	0	0	0	1	2	3		.333	46	40	23	18	2	21	4	1	48	6	3.52
Joseph, 8WH-23De .31	2	1	0	5	5	3		.500	74	91	49	35	4	18	4	3	29	2	4.26
Kavanaugh, Miami* 4	0	0	0	0	0	0		.000	7	12	9	8	1	1	0	0	6	0	10.29
Keller, W Palm B .24	21	8	4	11	7	0		.611	142	98	44	33	3	57	0	3	106	7	2.09
Kelley, Miami ...24	22	11	3	12	6	1		.667	154	132	53	35	0	80	3	5	63	14	2.05
Kelly, Orlando ...30	19	8	3	8	7	1		.533	155	135	54	46	4	67	0	12	105	8	2.67
Ker, W Palm B .. 3	2	1	0	1	0	1		1.000	19	11	3	3	1	9	0	2	11	2	1.42
Kerr, W Haven ..24	8	0	0	2	8	1		.200	74	86	58	51	1	53	2	1	60	12	6.20
Kessler, Pom B* ..21	18	3	1	7	8	0		.467	124	139	60	51	4	39	0	3	74	3	3.70
Killian, Lakeland* . 8	1	0	0	1	3	1		.250	18	16	8	6	0	12	1	0	13	0	3.00
King, Miami ...16	2	1	0	5	0	2		1.000	44	42	23	23	0	18	1	1	18	1	4.70
Kinney, St. Pete* ..23	19	2	0	8	9	0		.471	131	137	60	41	5	54	2	1	84	6	2.82
Klastava, W Haven .23	18	6	2	7	6	1		.538	128	111	40	29	2	37	2	7	84	1	2.04
Kleem, W Palm B* .18	2	0	0	4	4	4		.667	38	27	16	13	0	36	0	4	20	6	3.08
Kleibl, W Haven ..22	10	3	0	6	5	1		.545	103	85	39	26	1	51	0	3	58	5	2.27
Kline, W Palm B ..24	0	0	0	3	2	0		.600	40	50	23	21	0	29	2	1	28	1	4.73
M. Kmet, Tampa .. 3	0	1	1	2	0	0		.667	15	10	3	3	0	5	0	0	10	0	1.80
S. Kmet, Tampa .. 1	0	0	0	0	0	0		.000	2	2	0	0	0	2	0	1	0	0	27.00
Kopylow, WPB ... 2	0	0	0	0	0	0		.000	⅔	4	2	2	0	2	0	1	0	0	27.00
Lehman, Cocoa* ...27	15	8	2	7	6	4		.538	125	107	41	32	2	31	3	1	73	3	2.30
Lohse, Lakeland* .. 6	4	0	0	1	2	1		.333	21	17	11	10	0	16	0	0	12	2	4.29
Luebber, Orlando ..34	30	17	4	17	11	1		.607	237	184	70	47	7	79	3	0	172	13	1.78
Mack, Orlando* ... 9	1	0	0	0	3	0		.000	19	23	17	13	2	12	0	1	11	2	6.16
Maine, DeLand .. 7	0	0	0	0	3	0		.000	15	19	16	14	0	10	0	0	13	3	8.40
Manderbach, FtL* .21	13	5	1	7	8	0		.467	115	96	50	40	1	74	1	4	76	10	3.13
Mason, Lakeland* .. 5	3	0	0	2	1	0		.667	21	17	6	6	0	13	0	1	10	0	2.57
Mays, Lakeland .. 32	8	4	1	4	5	2		.444	100	97	43	37	2	23	0	6	61	5	3.33
McClain, WPB ... 9	7	1	0	5	1	0		.833	43	53	22	14	0	15	0	1	28	2	2.93
Meeler, Lakeland ..17	0	0	0	2	5	0		.667	24	20	14	8	0	15	4	2	18	0	3.00
Milam, W Haven ..21	20	6	3	9	8	0		.529	127	112	45	35	3	40	0	3	80	6	2.48
S. Miller, Tampa ..19	15	4	2	4	6	0		.600	94	54	31	24	1	67	2	1	56	6	2.30
Mims, Cocoa ...15	9	2	1	4	4	1		.500	35	35	22	15	0	45	3	6	15	0	1.96
B. Moore, WPB* .. 3	3	2	1	0	2	5		1.000	25	12	3	2	0	9	0	0	31	2	0.72
H. Moore, Cocoa* ..12	4	0	0	1	2	0		.333	35	35	20	14	0	21	1	1	25	6	3.60
T. Moore, Pom B .16	13	5	0	3	8	0		.273	82	75	43	33	4	51	1	6	63	3	3.62
Morgan, DeLand ..23	22	6	3	6	12	0		.333	128	151	77	63	5	36	0	1	44	12	4.43
Murphy, Pom B ... 1	0	0	0	1	0	0		.000	9	4	2	2	0	7	0	3	2	0	2.00
Murray, DeLand ..30	14	5	0	3	9	4		.250	116	117	71	60	1	64	0	1	74	13	4.66
Nagy, W Haven ... 5	0	0	0	0	0	0		.000	11	14	6	3	0	7	0	3	13	0	2.45
Norris, Miami 2	0	0	0	0	0	0		.000	3	3	2	2	0	0	0	3	0	6.00

Pitcher—Club	G	GS	CG	ShO	W	L	Sv	Pct.	IP	H	R	ER	HR	BB	Int. BB	HB	SO	WP	ERA
Norton, Orlando ... 3	0	0	0	0	0	0		.000	2	5	4	2	0	2	0	0	1		9.00
O'Connor, Tampa* . 8	0	0	0	0		1	0	.000	12	8	5	1	0	13	1	0	11	2	0.75
Olson, Pom B ...16	13	4	0		4	8	0	.333	84	85	56	39	3	36	2	2	40	4	4.18
Palas, DeLand* ...12	0	0	0		1	0	1	1.000	17	16	14	11	0	14	0	0	11	5	5.82
Pauls, Daytona B ..11	10	3	0		5	3	0	.625	58	49	28	16	1	37	1	1	36	4	2.48
Peery, Orlando* ...24	2	0	0		0	2		.000	51	52	16	15	0	35	1	1	60	9	2.65
Phillips, W Haven .16	10	2	0		6	4	1	.600	67	58	35	26	2	52	0	5	45	7	3.49
Pinnick, Orlando* .19	16	8	0		4	11	0	.267	112	111	50	43	5	50	1	5	56	3	3.46
Pole, W Haven ...19	15	4	3		6	7	1	.462	99	72	42	33	1	28	0	3	79	2	3.00
Potash, Pom B*...20	1	0	0		4	0		1.000	41	32	12	12	0	19	0	2	28	1	2.63
Price, St. Pete* ... 3	0	0	0	0		0		.000	4	8	4	4	0	1	0	1	3	1	9.00
Raible, Daytona B . 8	6	2	1		3	1	0	.750	34	34	13	13	1	15	0	1	23	6	3.44
Ramirez, Ft. Laud .11	7	3	0		3	4	1	.429	51	41	23	15	1	26	2	1	29	2	2.65
Ray, DeLand* 22	21	4	0		9	9	0	.500	148	135	59	39	6	62	2	6	84	5	2.37
Remson, W Haven*.32	8	3	0		2	3	3	.500	51	42	12	10	0	15	1	0	50	0	1.76
Richard, Cocoa* .19	14	4	2		4	11	0	.267	109	67	53	29	1	68	2	3	138	20	2.39
Robinson, Pom B*.26	5	1	0		3	1		.667	66	45	31	21	2	60	2	4	49	9	2.86
Rosiek, Cocoa 15		2	1		4	9		.308	102	98	53	37	7	31	3	4	61	6	3.26
Ruddell, Tampa .12	12	2	1		6	9		.714	72	34	31	26	1	49	6	4	99	3	3.25
Russell, WPB 25	25	11	4	14		9	0	.609	170	145	64	53	2	72	0	5	99	3	2.81
St. John, St. Pete . 9	6	0	0		3	1		.750	38	37	17	15	0	18	0	0	24	3	3.55
Sathre, Orlando .38	14	5	1		6	8		.429	118	97	48	37	2	57	3	1	87	6	2.82
Savold, Orlando ...19	0	0	0		3	4		.429	35	32	19	12	1	13	0	3	31	1	3.09
Sawyer, Tampa ... 1	0	0	0	0				.000	1	2	1	1	0	1	0	0	0		9.00
Schleider, WPB . 4	1	0	0	0		0		.000	12	10	1	1	0	3	0	1	7	3	0.75
Schlesiger, FtL .. 1	0	0	0	0		0		.000	1	1	1	1	0	1	0	0	1		...
Schroeder, FtL ..25	25	8	4	11		9	0	.550	155	129	68	54	1	58	0	7	139	9	3.14
Scott, Miami ...52	3	1	1		7	7	15	.500	97	65	25	18	2	38	3	2	119	7	1.67
Seidel, Miami . 2	0	0	0	0		0		.000	3	3	0	0	0	1	0	0	2		0.00
Seifert, Day B ...	1	0	0	0		1		.000	1	1	0	0	0	1	0	0	2		0.00
Sheanshang, Cocoa . 5	2	0	0		2	1		.600	59	40	19	16	0	23	2	1	44	4	2.44
Shown, Ft. Laud .36	1	0	0		1	0		.000	8	13	12	9	0	7	0	0	3		10.13
Simmons, FtL ...18	7	0	0		1	6		.143	52	52	43	25	0	22	3	0	38	7	4.33
Sires, Tampa ...11	7	6	3		6	1		.357	53	28	7	7	0	22	1	0	37	2	1.09
Slayback, Lake . 3	1	0	0	0		1		.800	10	9	5	3	0	5	0	1	12	2	2.70
J. Smith, St. Pete .28	23	6	3	13		4		.765	156	129	62	51	0	51	1	4	111	2	2.94
M. Smith, Lake . 1	0	0	0	0		1		.800	⅔	3	5	5	0	4	0	0	1		67.50
Smithson, Pom B .26	2	0	0		0	1	4	.000	53	58	37	33	3	34	0	0	28	4	5.60
Snowdon, 16 Orl-10 DeL*.26	13	2	0		5	7	1	.417	99	81	43	29	2	63	0	5	53	10	2.64
Solomon, Day B .22	22	11	3	11		7	0	.611	156	131	61	41	2	72	5	2	104	10	2.37
Sorrentino, Miami* . 4	3	1	1		1	0		1.000	15	7	3	3	0	9	0	1	15	1	1.80
Stathos, Orlando .. 2	0	0	0	0		2		.000	2	4	4	4	0	4	0	0	1		18.00
Stewart, DeLand* . 5	0	0	0	0		0		.000	29	27	21	17	1	17	0	2	26	10	5.28
Stroman, WPB .. 1	1	0	0	0		0		.000	1	0	0	0	0	0	0	0	0		0.00
Swanson, Ft. Laud .14	0	0	0		1	0		1.000	31	35	22	15	1	14	3	1	15	2	4.35
Taylor, Cocoa ...15	5	3	2		2	1	0	.667	43	45	14	12	0	15	1	8	1	15	2	4.35
Tuck, W Palm B . 1	0	0	0	0			4	.000	4	3	2	2	0	2	0	0	4		4.50
Turner, W Palm B .24	24	7	3	12		8		.600	157	111	54	38	1	56	0	9	100	5	2.18
Vargason, FtL* .. 4	0	0	0	0		4		.000	4	4	4	4	0	5	0	0	2		9.00
Veintidos, Pom B .26	26	12	4	12		11		.522	188	148	57	51	4	88	1	8	134	8	2.44
Vickery, W Palm B . 8	5	1	1		2	2	0	.333	30	30	17	11	0	10	0	0	16	5	3.30
Villalobos, Cocoa .. 6	0	0	0	0		9		.000	9	15	10	8	0	5	0	0	8		8.00
Volkening, StP ... 4	3	1	1		1	1	0	.500	12	16	8	8	2	4	0	0	7	1	6.00
VonHoff, St. Pete . 3	0	0	0	0		2		.667	20	14	2	1	0	12	0	0	15		0.45
Wall, Daytona B*.23	23	10	1	11		6	0	.647	150	141	62	43	2	64	4	5	120	5	2.58
Ward, W Haven ...25	23	10	3	11		8	0	.579	166	147	52	40	5	42	0	5	103	4	2.17
Warren, DeLand .19	0	0	0		2	1	9	.667	27	11	4	2	0	3	0	1	9		0.67
Webb, Pompano B .11	9	3	1		5	2	1	.714	58	57	26	18	1	27	0	2	43	3	2.79
Wellman, Day B*..17	13	2	1		9	2	0	.818	75	67	33	24	1	34	0	0	64	6	2.88
Williams, Miami* .23	21	8	1	15		5	0	.750	159	132	52	47	3	56	0	9	127	3	2.66
Williams, Day B .33	10	2	0		9	6	7	.600	135	113	51	46	4	42	7	2	122	9	3.07
Williams, WPB ...33	1	0	0	0		3	5	9	.375	65	48	16	14	0	25	1	3	62	1	1.94
Zuniga, Orlando ...19	1	0	0	0		2		.000	42	42	21	16	0	20	4	2	26	2	3.43

BALKS—Alfonso, Amyotte, Grassing, 3 each; Angelier, P. Babcock, R. Babcock, Cosgrove, Ervin, Hardiman, Ignasiak, Richard, 2 each; Bereguete, Boyett, A. Brown, G. Brown, Bushey, Carey, Connors, Contreras, Dorsch, Earley, Egnatchik, Fairbanks, Fuller, Gilman, D. Goodwin, Grant, Grigsby, Kelly, Legohn, Manderbach, Milam, Miller, H. Moore, Pauls, Phillips, Pinnick, Pole, Ray, Rosiek, Russell, Sathre, Shown, Simmons, Sires, Veintidos, Wall, Ward, 1 each.

COMBINATION SHUTOUTS—Alfonso-Lehman, Moore-Amman, Cosgrove-Amman, Lehman-Grover-Mims-E. Diaz, Cocoa; Wellman-Williams, Daytona Beach; Morgan-Murray, Ray-Goodwin, Carey-Warren, DeLand; Grassing-F. Fisher, Grassing-M. Fisher-F. Fisher, Lakeland; Williams-Scott, Miami; Snowdon-Kelly-Peery, Snowdon-Enyart-Luebber, Orlando; Reynolds-Christopher, Brenner-Connors, Veintidos-Connors, Pompano Beach; St. John-Ebner, Kinney-Ebner, Boyett-Smith, VonHoff-Ebner, Smith-Ebner, Cole-Ebner, St. Petersburg; Cooper-Gable, Ruddell-O'Connor, Grant-Gable, Cooper-Eastwick, Hardiman-Gable. Tampa; Russell-Williams, Turner-Betts, Turner-Williams, West Palm Beach; Gilman-Edge, Winter Haven.

NO-HIT GAMES—Kleem (3⅔ innings), Kline (½ inning), and Williams (3 innings), West Palm Beach, defeated Pompano Beach, 5-2, July 2 (seven innings); Kelly, Orlando, defeated DeLand, 2-0, August 28 (seven innings); Richard, Cocoa, defeated Daytona Beach, 2-0, August 28 (seven innings).

Mexican Center League

CLASS A

CHAMPIONSHIP WINNERS IN PREVIOUS YEARS

1960—Salamanca	.582	1966—Guanajuato*	.701
1961—Aguascalientes	.567	San Luis Potosi	.750
1962—Fresnillo	.588	1967—Leon	.604
1963—Guanajuato	.627	1968—Saltillo	.648
1964—Leon	.630	1969—San Luis Potosi*	.705
1965—San Luis Potosi	.633	Zacatecas	.667

*Won split-season playoff.

STANDING OF CLUBS AT CLOSE OF FIRST HALF, MAY 4

Club	W.	L.	T.	Pct.	G.B.	Club	W.	L.	T.	Pct.	G.B.
Ciudad Madero						San Luis Potosi					
(Yucatan)	43	25	2	.632	....	(Jalisco)	36	34	0	.514	8
Zacatecas (Poza Rica)	38	32	0	.543	6	Aguascalientes					
Tampico						(Mexico City Tigers)	35	35	0	.500	9
(Mexico City Reds)	37	32	1	.536	6½	Monterrey (Monterrey)	27	42	1	.391	16½
Ciudad Mante (Reynosa)	37	32	1	.536	6½	Leon (Veracruz)	24	45	1	.348	19½

STANDING OF CLUBS AT CLOSE OF SECOND HALF, JUNE 21

Club	W.	L.	T.	Pct.	G.B.	Club	W.	L.	T.	Pct.	G.B.
Ciudad Madero						Ciudad Mante (Reynosa)	25	29	1	.463	10½
(Yucatan)	36	19	0	.655	....	Leon (Veracruz)	25	30	0	.455	11
Monterrey (Monterrey)	33	22	0	.600	3	Aguascalientes					
Tampico						(Mexico City Tigers)	20	35	0	.364	16
(Mexico City Reds)	32	24	0	.571	4½	Zacatecas (Poza Rica)	19	35	1	.352	16½
San Luis Potosi (Jalisco)	30	26	0	.536	6½						

Farm clubs of Mexican League teams as shown in parentheses.

Playoff—None.

Regular-Season Attendance—Aguascalientes, 24,011; Leon, 10,290; C. Madero, 98,857; C. Mante, 37,767; Monterrey, 20,605; San Luis Potosi, 19,542; Tampico, 25,034; Zacatecas, 18,088. Total, 254,194. No playoff. No all-star game.

Managers: Aguascalientes—Jesus Valenzuela; C. Madero—Rene Friol; C. Mante—Agustin Enriquez; Leon—Hector Rodriguez; Monterrey—Javier Espinosa; San Luis Potosi—Benjamin Reyes; Tampico—Francisco Martinez; Zacatecas—Jose Villegas.

All-Star Team: 1B—Martinez, Zacatecas; 2B—Garcia, Mante; 3B—Guerra, San Luis Potosi; SS—V. Vega, Madero; OF—Suarez, Tampico; Rendon, Mante; Sauceda, San Luis Potosi; C—Mendivil, Tampico; Feliciano, Aguascalientes; P—P. Salomon, Mante; J. Reyes, San Luis Potosi; Manager—Friol, Madero.

(Compiled by Raul Mendoza, League Statistician, Mexico, D. F.)

CLUB BATTING

Club	G.	AB.	R.	OR.	H.	TB.	2B.	3B.	HR.	RBI.	SH.	Int. SF.	BB.	BB.	HP.	SO.	SB.	CS.	LOB.	Pct.
S. L. Pot.	126	4004	660	622	1176	1743	224	53	79	634	55	35	351	52	54	628	85	46	805	.294
Ciud. Mad.	125	4061	732	565	1173	1825	169	21	147	712	44	31	439	52	58	503	77	22	877	.289
Leon	125	3887	660	793	1141	1632	205	41	68	632	35	20	338	25	46	596	59	16	816	.286
Zacatecas	125	3922	620	661	1104	1587	200	47	63	612	76	47	456	54	35	602	74	22	883	.281
Monterrey	125	3901	541	541	1076	1462	131	27	67	523	61	35	375	44	29	554	85	20	871	.276
Ciud. Man.	125	3862	591	562	1060	1563	153	34	94	573	83	40	458	48	52	770	90	26	882	.274
Tampico	126	3918	633	635	1064	1508	172	16	80	603	71	31	396	39	39	674	91	25	768	.272
Aguasca.	125	3893	597	665	1035	1451	148	56	52	559	62	28	374	38	46	653	50	19	832	.266

INDIVIDUAL BATTING

(Leading Qualifiers for Batting Championship—391 or More Plate Appearances)

*Bats lefthanded. †Switch-hitter.

Player and Club	G.	AB.	R.	H.	TB.	2B.	3B.	HR.	RBI.	SH.	SF.	BB.	HP.	SO.	SB.	CS.	Pct.
Suarez, Miguel, Tampico*	.126	460	105	181	268	37	4	14	101	7	6	36	6	20	15	4	.393
Cardona, Trinidad, C Mad	104	370	89	141	252	24	0	29	101	2	3	31	3	45	5	0	.381
Castellon, Roberto, SLP	.108	400	73	152	206	20	11	4	69	4	5	33	3	38	14	3	.380
Rendon, Alberto, C Mante	.120	432	120	156	245	23	6	18	63	5	4	72	6	65	47	13	.361
Martinez H., Juan, Zac	.117	370	67	129	206	25	8	12	104	7	8	54	6	60	3	1	.349
Lujan, Felipe, Agua	.114	386	65	134	204	20	4	14	93	4	5	34	6	41	3	5	.347
Guerra, Eugenio, S L P	.116	405	93	129	230	30	8	15	97	1	5	54	1	32	10	9	.343
Zazueta, Alejandro, C M	.104	340	74	115	206	17	4	22	95	0	7	70	5	34	3	1	.338
Lozano, Pedro, Monterrey	.116	387	76	128	220	22	2	22	85	0	4	55	4	33	4	2	.331
Martinez C., Juan, C M	.115	386	73	125	239	30	3	26	117	3	6	55	3	107	9	2	.324

Departmental Leaders: G—Suarez, 126; AB—Suarez, 460; R—Rendon, 120; H—Suarez, 181; TB—Suarez, 268; 2B—Suarez, 37; 3B—Castellon, Dominguez, J. Valdez, 11; HR—Cardona, 29; RBI—Martinez C., 117; SH—P. Martinez, 15; SF—Martinez H., 8; BB—Rendon, 72; HP—Sauceda, 17; SO—Martinez C., 107; SB—Rendon, 47; CS—Rendon, 13.

(All Players—Listed Alphabetically)

Player and Club	G.	AB.	R.	H.	TB.	2B.	3B.	HR.	RBI.	SH.	SF.	BB.	HP.	SO.	SB.	CS.	Pct.
Ahumada, Jose Luis, Zac ..	4	3	0	1	1	0	0	0	1	0	0	0	0	0	0	0	.333
Alanis, Felix, Zacatecas ..	62	132	19	20	35	3	0	4	14	3	2	14	2	29	1	0	.152
Almada, Guillermo, Aguas*	41	58	7	19	26	5	1	0	12	0	0	4	0	14	0	0	.328
Almeida, Ramon, Aguas ...	8	24	6	11	19	2	0	2	8	0	2	0	0	3	1	0	.458
Alvarado, Natanael, Leon .	27	58	7	11	12	1	0	0	6	0	0	7	0	20	0	0	.190
Alvarez, Jose F., Tampico ..	1	0	0	0	0	0	0	0	0	1	0	0	0	0	0	0	.000
Arizpe, Cesar, Monterrey ..	98	293	44	90	119	10	2	5	56	2	1	31	1	23	2	2	.307
Arreguin, Enrique, Zac ...	21	58	7	17	17	0	0	0	4	0	0	5	1	5	0	1	.293
Arreguin, Jesus, Leon ...	64	130	16	27	44	6	1	3	25	0	1	12	4	34	0	1	.208
Arroyo, Abelardo, SLP ...	24	13	3	3	7	1	0	1	2	1	0	1	0	0	0	0	.231
Arvizu, Hector, Aguas ...	30	15	1	0	0	0	0	0	0	0	0	1	0	8	0	0	.000
Arvizu, Juan, Aguas ...	117	399	66	120	150	13	1	5	59	4	2	45	1	55	6	2	.301
Avila, Abelardo, Aguas ..	107	365	68	110	156	18	5	6	74	5	6	35	3	48	9	2	.301
Avila, Gabriel, Zacatecas .	9	28	2	6	10	1	0	1	8	0	1	2	1	8	2	0	.214
Ayala, Gregorio, C Madero	51	156	14	33	44	3	1	2	21	1	0	6	1	26	0	0	.212
Barajas, Nestor, 19 Tampico-1 C Madero	20	15	2	1	1	0	0	0	0	0	0	3	0	6	0	0	.067
Barandica, Jesus, Zacatecas	12	1	1	1	1	0	0	0	1	0	0	0	0	0	0	0	1.000
Basanez, Alejandro, C M ..	8	1	0	0	0	0	0	0	0	0	0	0	0	0	0	0	.000
Benitez, Jose Luis, Tampico	72	160	25	33	39	3	0	1	20	3	0	25	0	38	3	2	.206
Berlanga, Pedro, S L P ..	27	75	14	21	24	5	0	0	7	1	0	6	1	14	0	1	.280
Bernal, Manuel, S L P ...	49	165	9	28	39	6	1	1	20	1	1	8	1	24	0	0	.267
Bojorquez, Jose, Zacatecas .	11	40	4	9	12	1	1	0	3	0	0	3	1	4	2	0	.225
Bourguet, Alfonso, Tampico	22	33	4	8	12	1	0	1	4	1	0	3	0	13	0	0	.242
Briones, Eleazar, Monterrey	45	77	6	26	28	2	0	0	4	1	0	10	0	10	1	0	.338
Buendia, Ramiro, Monterrey	1	1	1	1	4	0	0	0	0	0	0	0	0	0	0	0	1.000
Camacho, Antonio, Monterrey	6	9	1	1	4	0	0	1	3	0	0	0	0	5	0	0	.111
Campos, Carlos, Leon	87	256	44	83	122	20	2	5	52	3	2	21	1	23	3	1	.324
Campoy, Alejandro, Tampico	24	31	2	3	4	1	0	0	1	0	0	3	0	13	0	0	.097
Cano, Jose Paz, C Mante ..	27	54	6	8	8	0	0	0	1	0	0	3	0	21	0	0	.148
Cano, Raul, Tampico	19	16	1	1	1	0	0	0	1	0	0	1	0	4	0	0	.063
Cardona, Trinidad, C M ..	104	370	89	141	252	24	0	29	101	2	3	31	3	45	5	0	.381
Carpio, Ruben, Leon	11	8	0	0	0	0	0	0	0	0	0	1	0	3	0	0	.000
Carrazco, Ramon, C Mante	39	116	12	30	35	3	1	0	11	1	0	14	2	21	1	1	.259
Carrera, J. Carmen, Zac* ..	3	2	0	0	0	0	0	0	0	0	0	0	0	0	0	0	.000
Castaneda, Edmundo, SLP .	13	32	2	6	7	1	0	0	2	0	0	3	0	2	0	0	.188
Castellon, Roberto, SLP ..	108	400	73	152	206	20	11	4	69	4	5	33	3	38	14	3	.380
Castillo, Luis Lauro, Mon .	78	227	29	64	74	1	3	1	22	4	3	10	0	23	10	0	.282
Castillo, Romulo, C Mante .	16	35	5	6	8	2	0	0	2	0	0	6	0	11	0	0	.171
Castro, Mario, Aguas	25	49	5	14	20	3	0	1	6	1	0	1	0	9	0	0	.286
Celestino, Victor, Leon ...	36	44	2	9	11	0	1	0	1	1	0	3	0	12	0	0	.205
Contreras, Celso, Leon ...	1	2	0	0	0	0	0	0	0	0	0	0	0	0	0	0	.000
Contreras, Tomas, Zacatecas	18	36	1	5	8	3	0	0	2	0	0	1	0	8	0	0	.139
Coronado, Edmundo, C M	68	187	17	61	86	10	0	5	27	1	3	22	3	14	0	0	.326
Cortez, Ricardo, C Mante ..	8	15	1	2	2	0	0	0	0	0	0	5	0	4	0	0	.133
Cortez, Ruben, Monterrey* .	8	12	1	2	5	1	1	0	2	0	0	0	0	2	0	0	.167
Cruz, Eleuterio, Zacatecas .	56	108	12	24	29	1	2	0	10	3	0	13	1	21	2	3	.222
De la Torre, Adolfo, SLP .	35	19	4	2	5	0	0	1	2	0	1	0	0	10	0	0	.105
De Leon, Miguel, C Mante	16	47	4	11	12	1	0	0	1	2	0	4	1	12	2	0	.234
Delfin, Jose, Ciudad Madero	28	54	4	4	4	0	0	0	2	0	0	3	0	20	0	0	.074
Delgado, Jose Luis, Mon ..	101	280	36	79	133	14	2	12	63	2	6	33	3	45	4	2	.282
Delgado, Pedro, S L Potosi	45	104	10	29	36	7	0	0	10	0	2	7	0	28	1	0	.279
Diaz, Albino, Zacatecas ..	4	5	1	1	1	0	0	0	1	0	0	0	0	2	0	0	.200
Diaz, Lorenzo, Aguas* ...	1	1	0	0	0	0	0	0	0	0	0	0	0	0	0	0	.000
Dominguez, Hector, Leon ..	117	407	77	121	189	16	11	10	88	4	4	25	6	64	5	1	.297
Dumer, Jorge, Zacatecas ...	9	11	2	3	3	0	0	0	0	0	0	2	0	0	0	0	.273
Elias Diaz, Ramiro, Mon* ..	42	38	4	7	11	1	0	1	3	1	0	5	0	12	0	0	.184
Escalante, Felix, C Mante .	57	179	19	37	43	3	0	1	18	1	1	17	1	48	1	2	.207
Escalante, Refugio, Aguas .	25	22	4	4	5	1	0	0	3	0	0	1	1	4	0	0	.182
Escalante, Sergio, Aguas* .	31	13	0	3	3	0	0	0	2	2	0	2	0	6	0	1	.231
Escalante, Victor, C M ..	108	343	52	89	107	12	0	2	40	5	4	52	4	57	5	6	.259
Esparza, Jesus, C. Madero ..	3	3	0	1	1	0	0	0	0	0	0	0	0	2	0	0	.333
Espinoza, Jose, C Madero* .	110	353	63	93	161	17	0	17	70	1	4	45	3	69	0	0	.263
Esquivel, Ramiro, Monterrey	55	163	18	43	64	7	1	4	24	2	1	16	2	26	2	0	.264
Esteves, Gumersindo, Leon	32	78	5	20	27	1	0	2	11	0	0	3	3	10	0	0	.250
Feliciano, Magdaleno, A ..	109	346	51	87	133	17	7	5	43	7	3	28	7	40	1	0	.251
Felix, Arnoldo, Tampico ...	52	72	12	10	11	1	0	0	3	2	0	19	0	16	2	0	.139
Fierro, Javier, S L Potosi .	74	184	21	51	69	10	1	2	27	2	0	13	4	27	3	1	.277
Flores, Alberto, Zacatecas .	5	4	0	1	1	0	0	0	0	0	0	0	0	2	0	0	.250
Flores, Fidel, Leon	19	29	5	7	10	3	0	0	4	0	0	1	0	6	0	0	.241
Fragosa, Francisco, C Mad	59	110	18	41	56	9	0	2	18	0	1	16	2	13	6	3	.373
Friol, Rene, Ciudad Madero	90	242	64	101	180	10	0	23	90	0	5	69	5	21	5	1	.417
Fuentes, Antonio, Zacatecas	60	200	37	67	91	16	1	2	27	3	3	30	2	12	5	0	.335
Fuentes, Martin, Monterrey	31	9	4	2	2	0	0	0	0	0	1	4	0	3	0	0	.222
Galaviz, Efren, Tampico ...	10	5	0	1	1	0	0	0	1	0	0	0	0	3	0	0	.200
Gallardo, Antonio, C Madero	11	17	2	6	8	0	1	0	0	0	0	2	0	4	0	0	.353
Gallegos, Leonardo, Mon ..	110	376	67	97	107	4	3	9	19	7	1	23	7	34	28	4	.258
Gamez, Godofredo, Aguas†	38	18	2	2	2	0	0	0	1	3	0	2	0	11	0	0	.111
Gamoundi, Timoteo, Zac ...	72	211	34	57	79	10	3	2	36	4	2	28	1	42	5	1	.270
Garcia, Bulmaro, C Mante ..	117	388	50	120	164	19	8	3	50	9	5	25	6	52	8	2	.309
Garcia, Enrique, C Madero	9	5	0	0	0	0	0	0	0	0	0	0	0	4	0	0	.000

Player and Club	G.	AB.	R.	H.	TB.	2B.	3B.	HR.	RBI.	SH.	SF.	BB.	HP.	SO.	SB.	CS.	Pct.
Garcia, Guillermo, Mon*	.103	302	48	85	107	14	1	2	30	2	4	22	1	31	7	3	.281
Garcia, Jesus, C Madero	.30	58	6	10	11	1	0	0	4	1	1	8	0	13	0	0	.172
Garcia, Sergio, Monterrey	.24	26	3	2	2	0	0	0	0	0	0	3	0	8	0	0	.077
Garza, Javier, Monterrey	.26	15	3	1	1	0	0	0	3	0	2	4	0	0	0	0	.067
Gomez, Carlos, S L Potosi	.13	21	1	4	4	0	0	0	1	4	1	1	0	7	0	0	.190
Gonzalez, Esteban, Aguas*	84	234	40	60	71	5	3	0	25	1	0	37	6	48	6	0	.256
Gonzalez, Gonzalo, Aguas†	103	297	45	66	99	14	5	3	28	3	0	25	5	85	1	2	.222
Gozzalez, J. Manuel, C Mte	4	3	0	1	1	0	0	0	0	0	0	1	0	1	0	0	.333
Gonzalez, Roberto, C Mante	14	23	2	5	5	0	0	0	3	0	0	2	0	4	0	0	.217
Gonzalez, Wenceslao, Tam*	22	34	1	5	6	1	0	0	3	0	4	0	10	0	1		.147
Guerra, Eugenio, S L P	.116	405	93	139	230	30	8	15	97	1	5	54	1	32	10	9	.343
Guerrero, Gustavo, C Mad*	22	28	7	8	11	3	0	0	3	1	1	4	0	1	0	0	.286
Guerrero, Inocencio, C Mte	1	1	0	0	0	0	0	0	0	0	0	0	0	0	0	0	.000
Guerrero, Leobardo, SLP	.115	245	52	95	123	17	1	3	47	4	5	28	4	33	7	5	.275
Guillen, Norberto, Aguas	40	80	5	13	19	3	0	1	9	1	0	7	2	29	0	0	.163
Guirardo, Juan Manuel, Zac	4	4	0	0	0	0	0	0	0	0	0	1	0	1	0	0	.000
Hernandez, Angel, Zacatecas	42	34	1	2	3	1	0	0	1	2	0	5	0	6	0	0	.959
Hernandez, David, Zacatecas	63	229	39	63	91	10	3	4	38	1	3	19	2	27	3	0	.275
Hernandez, Guadalupe, Mon	25	14	3	5	5	0	0	0	1	2	0	0	3	0	1		.357
Hernandez, Israel, Aguas	42	27	3	4	7	0	0	1	5	2	0	1	1	9	0	0	.148
Hernandez, Jose M., Leon*	75	247	49	85	136	10	4	9	47	0	1	26	4	43	4	1	.344
Hernandez, Juan, Monterrey	1	0	0	0	0	0	0	0	0	0	0	1	0	0	0	0	.000
Hernandez, Pedro, Aguas	21	6	0	0	0	0	0	0	0	0	0	1	0	1	0	0	.000
Hernandez, Rodolfo, SLP	80	275	50	91	157	23	2	13	65	6	3	21	3	39	8	1	.331
Horsford, James, Monterrey	5	16	0	4	5	1	0	0	3	0	0	1	0	4	0	0	.250
Ibarra, Humberto, SLP*	.106	324	37	102	129	12	3	3	44	3	2	21	4	23	2	4	.315
Jaime, Antonio, Aguas	2	2	0	0	0	0	0	0	0	0	0	0	0	0	0	0	.000
Jasso, Raul, Ciudad Mante	11	21	1	1	1	0	0	0	0	0	0	3	0	7	0	0	.048
Jimenez, Enrique, Aguas	8	15	4	3	6	0	0	1	3	0	1	0	0	4	0	0	.200
Jordan, Enrique, Tampico*	109	314	41	84	127	16	3	7	56	6	1	26	2	69	2	2	.268
Juarez, Luis, Tampico	.18	30	1	6	9	0	0	1	3	5	0	0	14	0	0		.200
Lazaro, Alfredo, C Mante	5	16	4	6	6	0	0	0	3	0	0	3	0	1	0	0	.375
Leal, Alvaro, Tampico	52	111	13	23	31	3	1	1	8	1	0	12	1	42	0	1	.207
Lerma, Salvador, C Madero	2	1	0	0	0	0	0	0	0	0	0	1	0	0	0	0	.000
Leyva, Leonel, Ciudad Mante	36	117	9	31	41	6	2	0	15	2	2	9	3	24	3	1	.265
Leyva, Ramon, Aguas*	38	16	1	2	2	0	0	0	1	1	0	1	0	6	0	0	.125
Lizarraga, Ernesto, SLP	.24	20	2	5	6	1	0	0	4	0	0	2	0	6	0	0	.250
Lizarraga, Miguel, Tampico	104	295	36	64	97	15	0	6	40	4	6	19	1	72	3	0	.217
Lopez, Ernesto, Monterrey	16	5	0	1	1	0	0	0	1	0	0	0	2	0	0		.200
Lopez, Francisco, Leon	12	19	1	0	0	0	0	0	0	0	0	0	1	0	0	0	.000
Lopez, Jose Luis, C Madero	17	35	9	11	21	2	1	2	6	0	0	3	0	5	0	0	.314
Lopez, Leobardo, Zacatecas	106	314	34	83	108	12	2	3	45	8	4	19	5	59	5	2	.264
Loya, Gustavo, Tampico	.16	36	3	7	11	1	0	1	6	0	0	1	0	17	0	0	.194
Lozano, Pedro, Monterrey	.116	387	76	128	220	22	2	22	85	0	4	55	4	33	4	2	.331
Lujan, Felipe, Aguas	.114	386	65	134	204	20	4	14	93	4	5	36	4	41	3	5	.347
Macias, Juan, Ciudad Mante	44	108	22	32	49	5	4	0	16	3	0	11	1	24	2	1	.296
Magana, Gabriel, S L Potosi	77	208	36	57	78	13	4	0	17	6	1	21	2	33	4	4	.274
Malagon, Manuel, Leon	.116	400	67	126	191	28	5	9	92	3	0	43	5	53	2	1	.315
Mandujano, Ranulfo, Tam	24	42	2	3	4	1	0	0	2	0	1	0	12	0	0		.071
Manrique, Gerardo, Mon	.30	48	5	13	17	2	1	0	7	0	0	0	0	7	0	1	.271
Manrique, Othon, Aguas	.26	14	0	0	0	0	0	0	0	0	0	2	0	5	0	0	.000
Marquez, Prudencio, Zac	.77	216	28	60	82	13	3	1	32	3	0	27	3	41	2	2	.278
Marquez, Rufino, Zacatecas	1	1	0	0	0	0	0	0	0	1	0	0	0	0	0	0	.000
Martinez, Antonio, Aguas†	55	190	32	56	102	7	6	9	41	0	0	20	2	21	1	0	.295
Martinez, Fidencio, Tam*	14	11	3	2	2	0	0	0	2	0	1	3	0	3	0	0	.182
Martinez, Francisco, Mon	1	1	0	0	0	0	0	0	0	1	0	0	0	1	0	0	.000
Martinez C., Juan, C M	.115	386	73	125	239	30	3	26	117	3	6	55	3	107	9	2	.324
Martinez H., Juan, Zac	.117	370	67	129	206	25	8	12	104	7	8	54	6	60	3	1	.349
Martinez, Pedro, C Mante	.110	361	53	93	107	12	1	0	31	15	5	36	1	41	5	3	.258
Mason, Larry, Monterrey	2	5	0	0	0	0	0	0	0	0	1	0	0	4	0	0	.000
Mata, Jorge, Monterrey	69	209	30	71	96	14	1	3	39	1	3	24	0	28	2	0	.340
Medina, Pedro, C Madero	.17	17	1	4	5	1	0	0	4	2	0	2	4	0	0		.235
Medrano, Francisco, Zac*	.119	409	87	131	181	22	5	6	61	11	3	56	3	45	9	4	.320
Mallado, Oscar, Tampico	.28	29	2	5	5	0	0	0	2	0	0	0	9	0	0		.172
Mendia, Homero, Zacatecas	55	110	11	32	47	6	3	1	17	1	0	1	0	25	1	0	.291
Mendiola, Angel, S L P	.10	8	2	2	2	0	0	0	1	0	0	0	0	3	0	0	.250
Mendivil, Rafael, Tampico	101	303	61	95	172	15	1	20	81	1	3	44	7	47	8	0	.314
Mendoza, Jose Luis, Aguas	1	2	0	1	1	0	0	0	0	0	0	0	0	0	0	0	.500
Mendoza, Rosendo, Aguas	25	37	5	3	3	0	0	0	2	1	4	0	15	0	0		.081
Menendez, Jose Luis, Leon	16	50	5	8	9	1	0	1	0	0	5	0	15	1	0		.160
Mercado, Ruben, Zacatecas	4	2	0	0	0	0	0	0	0	0	0	1	0	0	0	0	.000
Minjarez, Ruben, Aguas	32	28	2	3	4	1	0	0	0	2	1	0	6	0	1		.107
Mojica, Bartolo, C Mante	43	104	7	18	23	3	1	0	6	0	0	13	3	39	0	0	.173
Montero, Castulo, C Madero	6	16	2	3	3	0	0	0	0	0	0	3	0	3	0	0	.188
Montero, Hernan, C Mante	22	57	5	10	14	1	0	1	4	0	0	4	0	32	0	0	.175
Mora, Carlos, S L Potosi	31	38	7	10	12	0	1	0	1	4	0	3	0	6	0	0	.263
Moreno, Lorenzo, Aguas	.52	173	19	44	58	8	3	0	30	4	2	9	4	32	3	0	.254
Moreno, Pedro, Monterrey	.98	273	19	63	80	12	1	1	24	4	2	22	0	47	5	3	.231
Moreno, Victor M., Mon	.25	39	0	2	2	0	0	0	3	0	0	3	0	11	0	0	.051
Moroyoqui, Regino, Zac	.31	23	3	4	6	2	0	0	1	0	0	0	0	2	0	0	.174
Munoz, Adan, C Mante	.29	45	3	8	11	0	0	1	3	5	0	5	0	17	0	0	.178
Munoz, Concepcion, Zac*	.30	37	3	8	10	2	0	0	3	1	0	8	0	13	1	0	.216

Player and Club	G.	AB.	R.	H.	TB.	2B.	3B.	HR.	RBI.	SH.	SF.	BB.	HP.	SO.	SB.	CS.	Pct.
Munro, Ernesto, Monterrey	10	16	1	2	2	0	0	0	0	0	0	2	0	6	0	0	.125
Murrieta, Manuel, C M	60	209	35	69	135	14	2	16	58	1	3	21	3	46	4	0	.330
Nevarez, Arturo, Zacatecas	27	83	6	14	24	5	1	1	14	1	0	8	0	18	0	0	.169
Nevarez, Casiano, Zacatecas	19	30	4	8	10	2	0	0	3	1	0	0	0	6	0	0	.267
Olguin, Leonardo, Leon	33	29	1	4	4	0	0	0	3	1	0	2	0	11	1	0	.138
Orduno, Juan, Tampico	90	282	34	71	87	10	0	2	48	6	0	16	3	33	6	0	.252
Orea, Diacono, Leon	32	60	10	16	23	4	0	1	8	2	0	5	1	11	0	0	.267
Ornelas, Rafael, Tampico ..119		401	76	115	178	18	3	13	84	4	6	48	9	65	13	4	.287
Orozco, Octavio, Leon*	31	78	14	17	25	2	3	0	11	2	1	12	2	12	2	0	.218
Ortega, Dario, Aguas	27	43	8	8	8	0	0	0	3	1	0	7	0	8	2	1	.186
Ortega, Ignacio, C Mante .	27	17	2	1	1	0	0	0	1	0	0	0	0	9	0	0	.059
Ortiz, Armando, Tampico ..109		372	63	100	125	18	2	1	45	7	6	49	2	66	16	7	.269
Ortiz, David, Ciudad Mante	10	22	4	3	4	1	0	0	1	1	1	3	2	10	1	0	.136
Osorio, Raul, Ciudad Madero	23	49	10	14	20	3	0	1	6	1	0	3	0	9	1	0	.286
Osuna, Filiberto, C Mante*	24	31	6	9	11	2	0	0	3	3	0	8	2	12	0	0	.290
Pacheco, Enrique, Tampico	72	176	24	51	66	4	1	3	20	3	0	18	2	21	2	1	.290
Pacheco, Jose Luis, Tampico	16	7	0	0	0	0	0	0	0	0	0	1	0	4	0	0	.000
Pacheco, Teodoro, Tampico*	32	35	9	11	12	1	0	0	3	1	0	4	0	8	1	1	.314
Pantoja, Fidel, Aguas†	61	211	35	56	70	5	3	1	30	2	2	30	0	24	5	0	.265
Paredes, Jesus, C Madero ..	41	83	13	16	21	2	0	1	9	2	0	13	1	12	4	2	.193
Perez, Edgardo, C Madero .	21	7	1	0	0	0	0	0	0	0	0	1	0	1	0	0	.000
Perez, Jose Luis, Monterrey	5	2	0	0	0	0	0	0	0	0	0	0	0	1	0	0	.000
Perezchica, Guadalupe, Tam	116	430	77	130	165	15	1	6	53	4	1	40	4	39	15	3	.302
Perez de los Santos, Juan, Ciudal Mante	33	64	7	14	17	1	1	0	5	0	1	3	0	15	0	0	.219
Perez Dominguez, Juan, Ciudal Mante	12	14	0	0	0	0	0	0	0	2	0	0	0	2	0	0	.000
Pichardo, Antonio, Aguas .	5	7	1	3	3	0	0	0	0	0	0	1	0	2	0	0	.429
Picos, Loreto, Ciudad Mante	12	31	8	9	12	1	1	0	6	1	0	1	6	6	0	0	.290
Pina, Francisco, Zacatecas	83	291	69	112	166	22	7	6	51	6	6	42	1	24	10	6	.385
Pinon, Eduardo, C Madero .	10	25	0	3	3	0	0	0	1	0	0	0	0	7	0	0	.120
Plascencia, Rigoberto, C M	22	79	20	27	47	2	0	6	20	0	0	5	3	11	1	0	.342
Ponce, Francisco, Mon*	29	19	1	1	1	0	0	0	0	0	0	4	0	12	0	0	.053
Prado, Mario, Leon	28	51	8	7	11	1	0	1	5	0	0	2	1	14	0	0	.137
Pratts, Efrain, S L Potosi	48	155	28	45	62	6	4	1	14	2	0	12	1	17	6	3	.290
Preciado, Alfonso, Zac 117		398	61	123	155	18	1	4	64	3	5	70	4	26	9	0	.309
Quintana, Jacinto, Aguas ..112		342	46	91	115	20	2	0	31	3	1	24	6	50	7	3	.266
Quiroz, Amado, Leon	38	46	9	11	14	1	1	0	8	0	0	4	0	13	0	0	.239
Ramirez, Francisco, Tampico	5	11	2	3	3	0	0	0	1	0	0	1	0	1	0	0	.273
Ramirez, Guillermo, C M ..	24	11	0	2	3	1	0	0	1	1	0	0	0	6	0	0	.182
Ramirez, Raymundo, Mont	21	5	0	3	3	0	0	0	1	0	0	0	0	0	0	0	.600
Ramos, Alfonso, S L Potosi	28	20	5	6	9	0	2	1	0	3	0	4	2	4	0	0	.300
Rendon, Alberto, C Mante .120		432	120	156	245	23	6	18	63	5	4	72	6	63	47	13	.361
Reyes, Alfonso, S L Potosi	5	3	0	1	1	0	0	0	0	0	0	0	0	1	0	0	.333
Reyes, Cruz, Ciudad Madero	10	22	1	2	3	1	0	0	2	0	0	0	0	6	0	0	.091
Reyes, Javier, S L Potosi*	48	73	12	14	18	2	1	0	7	1	0	8	0	21	0	0	.192
Reyes, Rosario, C Madero .	27	54	7	13	14	1	0	0	9	3	0	1	0	3	1	0	.241
Reyes, Ruben, Ciudad Mante	14	10	1	1	1	0	0	0	0	0	0	0	0	1	0	0	.100
Reyes, Rufino, Leon*	17	60	7	17	26	1	1	2	8	0	0	6	0	9	1	1	.283
Reza, Juan Manuel, C M ..	12	10	1	1	1	0	0	0	0	0	0	2	0	4	0	0	.100
Rivera, Eduardo, S L Potosi	83	211	24	36	51	4	1	3	14	3	0	13	3	55	0	3	.171
Rivera, Enrique, S L Potosi	7	5	1	2	3	1	0	0	0	0	0	0	0	2	0	0	.400
Rivera, Martin, C Mante ..	27	87	15	21	28	2	1	1	17	2	0	9	0	13	4	0	.241
Robles, Julio, Leon 115		428	60	138	177	22	1	5	67	3	5	9	1	58	6	2	.322
Rocha, Armando, C Mante .	2	3	0	0	0	0	0	0	0	0	0	0	0	1	0	0	.000
Rodriguez, Adolfo, Zac	25	40	5	7	12	2	0	1	8	3	1	6	0	15	0	0	.175
Rodriguez, Antonio, Mon ..	17	29	3	7	7	0	0	0	3	0	0	1	0	5	1	0	.241
Rodriguez S., Antonio, C M	16	37	0	9	10	1	0	0	4	2	0	2	0	4	2	0	.243
Rodriguez, Eduardo, C Mad.	10	15	0	1	1	0	0	0	0	0	0	0	0	5	0	0	.067
Rodriguez, Gerardo, Mon ..	8	16	2	5	6	1	0	0	0	0	0	4	0	2	1	0	.313
Rodriguez M., Hector, Leon	4	7	1	0	0	0	0	0	0	2	0	1	0	0	0	0	.000
Rodriguez, Juan, Tampico	49	154	33	46	65	10	0	3	23	2	1	14	1	10	4	0	.299
Rodriguez, Manuel, C M ..	3	0	1	0	0	0	0	0	0	0	0	1	0	0	0	0	.000
Rodriguez G., Manuel, SLP	46	176	33	44	65	6	3	3	15	3	0	23	4	38	5	3	.250
Rodriguez, L., Manuel, Tam.	16	32	1	1	1	0	0	0	0	0	0	2	1	16	1	0	.031
Rodriguez, Pilar, Monterrey	20	35	7	6	6	0	0	0	3	3	0	4	1	11	0	0	.171
Saiz, Francisco, C Mad*	118	429	96	129	215	23	6	17	76	2	0	51	4	42	20	6	.301
Salazar, Jose Luis, Mon ..	25	11	0	1	1	0	0	0	0	0	0	1	0	6	0	0	.091
Salcido, Crispin, C Madero	52	29	7	6	9	0	0	1	3	1	0	5	0	12	0	0	.207
Saldana, Antonio, Aguas ..	26	51	4	7	11	0	2	0	2	0	0	4	1	17	0	1	.137
Saldana, Ruben, Monterrey	121	325	40	87	109	12	2	2	43	8	3	26	2	37	4	0	.268
Saldivar, Arturo, Zacatecas	24	18	3	3	3	0	0	0	1	2	0	0	2	0	0	0	.167
Salomon, Porfirio, C Mante	24	56	8	16	19	0	0	1	4	5	0	2	0	16	0	0	.286
Salomon, Saturnino, C Mte	22	43	2	3	7	1	0	1	1	1	0	5	0	23	0	0	.070
Sanchez, Carlos, Leon†	24	46	4	9	14	2	0	1	4	0	0	1	1	11	0	0	.196
Santamaria, Andres, Leon .	10	0	0	0	0	0	0	0	0	2	0	0	0	0	0	0	.000
Santiago, Joaquin, Leon	30	105	7	24	25	1	0	0	7	1	0	5	0	14	2	1	.229
Santos, Tobias, Leon	65	228	39	73	115	17	2	7	45	2	3	11	3	46	1	0	.320
Santos, Victor, Zacatecas ..	34	47	8	4	8	1	0	1	2	2	0	3	0	12	0	0	.085
Santoyo, Arturo, Leon 120		435	84	130	164	25	3	1	43	6	1	38	4	35	10	4	.299
Sauceda, Victor, S L Potosi	115	383	64	117	188	30	4	11	89	2	5	30	17	64	13	5	.305
Sed, Oscar Rey, Monterrey	50	131	19	47	79	7	2	7	29	1	0	17	4	16	2	1	.359

Player and Club	G.	AB.	R.	H.	TB.	2B.	3B.	HR.	RBI.	SH.	SF.	BB.	HP.	SO.	SB.	CS.	Pct.
Serna, Antonio, Aguas* ...	33	32	6	5	13	0	1	2	4	1	1	4	0	15	0	0	.156
Serna, Joel, Monterrey ...	75	272	42	85	115	9	3	5	34	10	1	27	1	39	4	0	.313
Silva, Raymundo, C Mante	4	7	3	4	4	0	0	0	2	0	0	0	0	2	0	0	.571
Soria, Angel, Zacatecas	99	326	57	85	146	20	4	11	38	8	4	30	1	82	10	1	.261
Suarez, Miguel, Tampico*	.126	460	105	181	268	37	4	14	101	7	6	36	6	20	15	4	.393
Torres, Mauro, Monterrey .	31	27	4	5	5	0	0	0	2	2	0	3	0	8	0	0	.185
Torres, Ricardo, Montcrrey	51	166	23	40	48	0	1	2	20	1	3	19	2	42	8	1	.241
Torres, Salvador, Leon ...	32	48	7	12	22	5	1	1	2	0	0	4	0	7	0	0	.250
Valdez, Jose Felix, Aguas	.101	369	63	104	136	7	11	1	48	5	2	37	3	18	10	0	.282
Valdez, Manuel, C Mante	.113	367	40	89	140	13	4	10	64	11	3	35	11	58	1	0	.243
Valenzuela, Benjamin, Aguas	1	1	0	1	1	0	0	0	0	0	0	0	0	0	0	0	1.000
Valenzuela, Carlos, C Mad .	25	47	9	7	7	0	0	0	2	0	0	4	2	18	1	0	.149
Valenzuela, Humberto, SLP*	22	14	0	1	1	0	0	0	1	0	0	0	0	2	0	0	.071
Valenzuela, Jesus, Aguas .	21	16	1	2	2	0	0	0	0	1	0	0	0	5	0	0	.125
Valtierra, Esteban, Leon* ...	88	297	69	95	157	23	3	11	48	2	0	46	5	31	12	1	.320
Vega, Fernando, Zacatecas .	36	71	15	19	25	2	2	0	6	0	0	3	1	20	1	1	.268
Vega, Fidel, S L Potosi .	81	224	45	66	132	14	2	16	47	2	0	21	5	82	5	2	.295
Vega, Jose Luis, Leon ...	89	326	56	91	111	16	2	0	42	2	2	37	4	32	10	2	.279
Vega, Rogelio, C Madero	.115	423	74	131	177	19	3	7	60	5	3	29	1	38	13	1	.310
Vega, Valenciano, C Mad	.122	419	69	121	164	18	5	5	43	8	2	25	2	38	9	1	.289
Velez, Juan E., C Madero	79	260	47	72	128	7	2	15	46	0	3	30	1	25	2	1	.277
Verdugo, Froilan, C Madero	29	70	4	8	12	1	0	1	5	0	1	2	0	25	0	0	.114
Verdugo, Roberto, C Madero	40	31	6	9	9	0	0	0	8	4	0	1	0	3	1	1	.290
Villa, Alberto, Monterrey .	5	11	1	4	5	1	0	0	1	1	1	1	0	2	0	0	.364
Villa, Carlos, S L Potosi .	74	156	33	46	68	13	3	1	31	1	3	20	0	20	8	1	.295
Villegas, Jose, Zacatecas ...	26	39	8	15	28	4	0	3	14	0	1	7	0	10	3	0	.385
Zamarron, Enrique, C Mante	5	12	0	1	1	0	0	0	1	0	0	1	0	3	0	0	.083
Zatarain, Ariel, S L Potosi	7	6	0	1	1	0	0	0	0	0	0	0	0	0	0	0	.167
Zazueta, Alejandro, C Man	104	340	74	115	206	17	4	22	95	0	7	70	5	34	3	1	.338
Zazueta, Alsadio, C Mante*	8	3	0	0	0	0	0	0	0	0	0	0	0	3	0	0	.000
Zazueta, Ernesto, Leon	15	13	1	0	0	0	0	0	0	0	0	0	1	0	5	0	0	.000

The following players had no plate appearances (listed alphabetically by club, games in parentheses) :

AGUASCALIENTES: De la Rosa, Roberto* (3).
CIUDAD MADERO: Lopez, Marco* (6); Lopez, Rigoberto (2).
MONTERREY: Espinoza, Javier (1).
TAMPICO: Gallegos, Gonzalo (1).
ZACATECAS: Garcia, Rafael (3); Lopez, Gumaro (1).

GRAND-SLAM HOME RUNS—Saiz, 4; Murrieta, Sauceda, 2 each; Cardona, Castellon, J. L. Delgado, Esquivel, Friol, J. M. Hernandez, R. Hernandez, Lozano, Malagon, Martinez C., Mendivil, Pantoja, Rendion, J. Rodriguez, M. Valdez, 1 each.

AWARDED FIRST BASE ON INTERFERENCE—L. Gallegos (T. Santos), Lozano (T. Santos), A. Ortiz (T. Santos), Quintana (Guerra), Robles (Mendivil), Sed (T. Santos), A. Villa (Feliciano).

CLUB FIELDING

Club	G.	PO.	A.	E.	DP.	PB.	Pct.	Club	G.	PO.	A.	E.	DP.	PB.	Pct.
S. L. Potosi ..	126	3016	1432	159	101	24	.9654	Ciudad Madero	125	3061	1275	172	82	16	.962
Ciudad Mante	125	3051	1329	158	79	23	.9651	Tampico	126	3070	1270	180	56	23	.960
Zacatecas	125	3009	1275	156	74	30	.9648	Leon	125	2924	1270	206	97	17	.953
Monterrey	125	2972	1392	159	85	14	.9648	Aguascalientes	125	2954	1397	215	92	41	.953

Triple Play—Aguascalientes.

INDIVIDUAL FIELDING
(Ten or More Games)

*Throws lefthanded.

FIRST BASEMEN

Player and Club	G.	PO.	A.	E.	DP.	Pct.	Player and Club	G.	PO.	A.	E.	DP.	Pct.
Perez de los Santos, C Mante	19	105	8	0	6	1.000	Espinoza, C Madero*	97	737	39	12	50	.985
Cardona, C Madero ...	12	77	4	0	3	1.000	Jordan, Tampico ...	98	772	30	13	38	.984
Friol, C Madero	11	69	4	0	6	1.000	Coronado, C Mante .	12	106	4	2	6	.982
A. ZAZUETA, CM	90	739	36	4	42	.995	Ibarra, S L Potosi .	89	720	36	15	62	.981
Arizpe, Monterrey ...	63	498	46	3	26	.995	G. Garcia, Monterrey	14	84	6	2	5	.978
Villa, S L Potosi ...	35	218	7	2	17	.991	Malagon, Leon ...	84	704	24	17	51	.977
Preciado, Zacatecas .	13	90	8	1	2	.990	Lozano, Monterrey ...	55	391	22	11	31	.974
Sanchez, Leon	14	79	2	1	3	.988	A. Martinez, Aguas	42	352	21	10	26	.974
Valtierra, Leon* ...	26	234	6	3	19	.988	Mendia, Zacatecas .	12	64	5	2	1	.972
Ortega, Aguas	13	73	1	1	5	.987	Alanis, Zacatecas	10	63	5	3	2	.967
Lizarraga, Tampico .	23	127	10	2	4	.986	F. Verdugo, C Mad	22	154	9	6	16	.964
Martinez H., Zac ...	96	874	34	14	49	.985	Avila, Aguas	13	112	4	5	3	.959

Triple Play—A. Martinez.

(Fewer Than Ten Games)

Player and Club	G.	PO.	A.	E.	DP.	Pct.	Player and Club	G.	PO.	A.	E.	DP.	Pct.
Castellon, SLP	9	55	3	0	4	1.000	Medrano, Zacatecas*	2	21	2	0	1	1.000
Jasso, Ciudad Mante	6	35	2	0	0	1.000	Hernandez, Leon	3	16	0	0	0	1.000
Villegas, Zacatecas .	6	28	1	0	3	1.000	D. Hernandez, Zac ..	2	11	1	0	0	1.000
Sed, Monterrey	3	27	0	0	1	1.000	Orduno, Tampico ...	2	10	1	0	0	1.000

FIRST BASEMEN—Continued

Player and Club	G.	PO.	A.	E.	DP.	Pct.
Martinez C., C Mte .	1	10	0	0	0	1.000
Pina, Zacatecas	2	8	0	0	0	1.000
Bojorquez, Zacatecas	1	5	1	0	0	1.000
Soria, Zacatecas ...	1	5	0	0	1	1.000
B. Valenzuela, Aguas	1	2	2	0	0	1.000
C. Nevarez, Zac	1	4	0	0	1	1.000
Flores, Leon	1	4	0	0	0	1.000
E. Pacheco, Tampico	1	4	0	0	1	1.000
Orozco, Leon	1	3	0	0	1	1.000
Macias, Ciudad Mante	1	3	0	0	0	1.000
Almeida, Aguas ...	1	2	0	0	0	1.000
J. Garcia, C Madero	1	2	0	0	0	1.000
J. L. Lopez, C Mad	1	2	0	0	0	1.000
Esteves, Leon	1	2	0	0	1	1.000
Alvarado, Leon	1	2	0	0	0	1.000
A. Rodriguez, Mon .	1	2	0	0	0	1.000
Vega, Zacatecas ...	1	1	0	0	0	1.000
E. Rodriguez, C Mad	1	1	0	0	0	1.000
Saldana, Monterrey .	1	1	0	0	0	1.000
Manrique, Mon* ...	1	1	0	0	0	1.000
Rodriguez L., Tam ...	1	1	0	0	0	1.000
Guerra, S L Potosi .	9	70	6	1	4	.987
Vega, S L Potosi ...	7	50	0	1	3	.980
Mata, Monterrey ...	4	31	3	1	1	.971
Ornelas, Tampico ...	9	71	2	3	5	.961
Arreguin, Leon ...	2	19	1	1	0	.952
Benitez, Tampico ...	2	13	0	1	0	.929
Mendivil, Tampico ...	7	30	1	3	1	.912
Rodriguez M., Leon .	2	10	0	1	1	.909
Ramirez, Monterrey .	6	18	1	2	2	.905
Bernal, S L Potosi .	1	6	0	1	0	.857
T. Pacheco, Tampico .	1	6	0	2	0	.750
Campos, Leon	1	2	0	1	0	.667

SECOND BASEMEN

Player and Club	G.	PO.	A.	E.	DP.	Pct.
Robles, Leon	11	27	24	0	2	1.000
Castellon, SLP	48	87	130	4	25	.982
Valdez, Aguas	34	78	74	3	9	.981
Preciado, Zacatecas .	38	63	70	3	9	.978
GARCIA, C Mante .	117	225	274	15	43	.971
P. Moreno, Mon ...	86	194	193	12	31	.970
D. Hernandez, Zac .	58	131	152	9	38	.969
Escalante, C Madero	97	229	209	14	38	.969
L. Moreno, Aguas .	50	129	108	8	28	.967
A. Nevarez, Zac ...	26	51	66	4	9	.967
Santoyo, Leon	113	302	303	21	66	.966
Serna, Monterrey ..	17	37	48	3	9	.966
Magana, S L Potosi	55	113	113	8	26	.966
R. Vega, C Madero .	10	29	26	2	4	.965
R. Torres, Mon ...	26	56	85	6	13	.959
Pantoja, Aguas ...	38	82	99	8	14	.958
Villa, S L Potosi ..	12	11	9	1	1	.952
Perezchica, Tampico	87	179	218	22	27	.947
Pratts, S L Potosi .	29	40	46	7	8	.925
Leal, Tampico	36	62	46	9	10	.923
Fragosa, C Madero .	27	35	54	11	12	.890

Triple Play—L. Moreno.

(Fewer Than Ten Games)

Player and Club	G.	PO.	A.	E.	DP.	Pct.
Berlanga, SLP	8	12	25	0	7	1.000
E. Pacheco, Tampico	7	22	15	0	2	1.000
Fuentes, Zacatecas ..	5	15	14	0	2	1.000
De Leon, C Mante .	7	11	13	0	2	1.000
Malagon, Leon	2	4	7	0	0	1.000
Saldana, Monterrey .	5	4	6	0	0	1.000
Saldana, Aguas	1	2	4	0	3	1.000
Rodriguez S., CMte	1	1	3	0	0	1.000
R. Verdugo, C Mad .	2	0	4	0	0	1.000
Hernandez, SLP ...	2	2	1	0	0	1.000
Manrique, Aguas ...	1	2	0	1	0	1.000
Fierro, S L Potosi .	1	2	0	0	0	1.000
T. Pacheco, Tampico	1	0	2	0	0	1.000
Villegas, Zacatecas .	1	1	0	0	0	1.000
Lizarraga, Tampico ..	1	1	0	0	0	1.000
G. Garcia, Mon	1	1	0	0	0	1.000
A. Rodriguez, Mon .	2	0	1	0	1	1.000
Orduno, Tampico ...	7	17	13	1	2	.968
Avila, Aguas	9	9	15	1	1	.960
Alanis, Zacatecas ...	9	18	16	2	2	.944
Ortiz, Ciudad Mante	2	5	3	1	0	.889
Lazaro, C Mante ...	4	16	9	5	3	.833

THIRD BASEMEN

Player and Club	G.	PO.	A.	E.	DP.	Pct.
Castellon, SLP	13	12	30	0	1	1.000
Perezchica, Tampico	11	11	24	1	2	.972
Velez, Ciudad Mad	78	62	163	11	9	.953
Orduno, Tampico ...	76	88	152	12	8	.952
VALDEZ, C Mte ...	94	81	198	15	17	.949
Fuentes, Zacatecas .	54	47	91	8	3	.945
J. Arvizu, Aguas ...	33	78	195	19	9	.935
Malagon, Leon	29	29	54	6	1	.933
Guerra, S L Potosi .	97	83	226	23	13	.931
Mata, Monterrey .	61	38	116	12	3	.928
Pratts, S L Potosi .	12	13	12	2	1	.926
Saldana, Monterrey .	59	46	114	13	9	.925
Preciado, Zacatecas .	36	38	70	9	9	.923
E. Pacheco, Tampico	34	20	31	5	2	.911
Robles, Leon	98	91	174	27	12	.908
R. Vega, C Madero .	38	35	78	12	6	.904
Rivera, Ciudad Mante	17	23	41	8	2	.889
Plascencia, C Madero	10	4	19	3	2	.885
Pantoja, Aguas	17	13	31	6	0	.880
Gamboul, Zacatecas	26	14	34	9	5	.842
Castro, Aguas	12	11	20	6	1	.838
Avila, Aguas	22	14	37	12	4	.810

(Fewer Than Ten Games)

Player and Club	G.	PO.	A.	E.	DP.	Pct.
Loya, Tampico	9	5	13	0	1	1.000
Sed, Monterrey	4	3	8	0	0	1.000
Ed. Rivera, SLP ..	1	8	2	0	1	1.000
Camacho, Monterrey	2	5	0	0	0	1.000
Martinez H., Zac ..	5	1	4	0	1	1.000
A. Rodriguez, Mon .	2	0	4	0	0	1.000
Martinez C., C Mte .	2	1	0	0	0	1.000
Lozano, Monterrey ..	1	1	2	0	1	1.000
Mendia, Zacatecas ..	1	0	2	0	0	1.000
Perez de los Santos, Ciudad Mante ...	1	1	1	0		1.000
Villa, S L Potosi ...	1	0	2	0	0	1.000
Esteves, Leon	1	1	0	0	0	1.000
Ramirez, C Mante ..	1	0	1	0	0	1.000
Rodriguez M., Leon .	1	0	1	0	1	1.000
Vega, Leon	1	0	1	0	0	1.000
P. Moreno, Mon ...	3	5	11	1	2	.941
Serna, Monterrey ..	8	6	24	3	0	.909
Alanis, Zacatecas ...	6	6	4	1	0	.909
Escalante, C Madero	3	4	6	1	0	.909
Magana, S L Potosi	8	12	15	3	1	.900
Avila, Zacatecas ...	6	2	12	2	0	.875
Berlanga, SLP	5	4	9	2	0	.867
Leal, Tampico	8	4	14	3	0	.857
Fragosa, C Madero .	4	3	3	1	1	.857
Rodriguez S., CMte .	4	2	3	1	0	.833
Cortez, C Mante ...	3	7	10	4	0	.810
Jordan, Tampico ...	1	0	4	1	0	.800
Escalante, C Mante .	2	6	3	3	0	.750
De Leon, C Mante .	1	0	3	1	0	.750
Ortiz, Tampico	1	2	1	1	0	.750

SHORTSTOPS

Player and Club	G.	PO.	A.	E.	DP.	Pct.
Saldana, Monterrey .	46	57	123	6	11	.968
Santiago, Leon	30	34	107	6	15	.959
R. Torres, Mon	27	38	73	6	9	.949
J. Arvizu, Aguas ...	40	48	116	9	12	.948
Hernandez, SLP	74	126	215	19	36	.947
L. LOPEZ, Zacatec	109	96	305	23	27	.946
Valdez, C Mante ..	12	10	23	2	5	.943
Perezchica, Tampico	21	22	60	5	4	.943
Castellon, SLP	47	73	171	16	24	.938
Carrazco, C Mante .	37	55	103	11	13	.935
V. Vega, C Madero .121	189	338	38	48	.933
Ortiz, Tampico 109	149	315	35	30	.930
Valdez, Aguas	68	127	243	28	41	.930
Escalante, C Madero	49	58	140	16	7	.925
Preciado, Zacatecas .	34	44	95	13	14	.914
Serna, Monterrey ..	51	103	168	27	26	.909
Vega, Leon	87	106	298	44	30	.902
Escalante, C Madero	10	14	25	6	2	.867
Saldana, Aguas	16	22	37	11	5	.843

(Fewer Than Ten Games)

Player and Club	G.	PO.	A.	E.	DP.	Pct.
Fuentes, Zacatecas .	3	5	6	0	2	1.000
Loya, Tampico	3	1	7	0	1	1.000
Rodriguez S., C Mt .	3	2	2	0	1	1.000
Pichardo, Aguas ...	2	2	2	0	0	1.000
Velez, C Madero ...	1	3	1	0	1	1.000
Robles, Leon	1	3	0	0	0	1.000
Esparza, C Madero .	2	0	3	0	0	1.000
Alanis, Zacatecas ...	1	0	2	0	1	1.000
Leal, Tampico	2	0	2	0	0	1.000
Macias, C Mante ...	1	0	2	0	0	1.000
Pantoja, Aguas	9	11	24	1	0	.972
Berlanga, SLP	9	6	17	1	6	.958
Santoyo, Leon	7	15	30	3	0	.938
Pratts, S L Potosi .	4	8	7	1	2	.938
De Leon, C Mante .	8	5	27	3	3	.914
Avila, Zacatecas ...	3	3	7	1	0	.909
Cortez, C Mante ...	4	4	5	1	1	.900
Mendia, Zacatecas ..	2	4	5	1	0	.900
Rivera, C Mante ...	5	12	9	3	1	.875
P. Moreno, Monterrey	8	12	14	4	3	.867
Avila, Aguas	1	3	2	1	0	.833
Castro, Aguas	2	1	3	1	2	.800
Ortiz, Ciudad Mante	8	12	18	8	3	.789
Zamarron, C Mante	3	1	9	3	2	.769

OUTFIELDERS

Player and Club	G.	PO.	A.	E.	DP.	Pct.
Lozano, Monterrey .	70	72	4	0	0	1.000
Reyes, Leon*	16	29	2	0	1	1.000
Bojorquez, Zac	10	18	3	0	1	1.000
Mendia, Zacatecas	10	17	1	0	0	1.000
E. Pacheco, Tampico	15	14	0	0	0	1.000
R. Vega, C Madero	64	80	2	1	2	.985
SAUCEDA, S L P .108	251	14	4	2	.985
Fierro, S L Potosi .	61	62	8	1	0	.985
Soria, Zacatecas ...	92	142	6	3	0	.980
Felix, Tampico	26	36	3	1	0	.975
Rodriguez G., SLP .	46	71	6	2	0	.975
Rendon, C Mante .115	234	27	7	0	.974
Cardona, C Madero .	92	141	8	4	1	.974
Paredes, C Madero .	35	34	3	1	0	.974
Martinez C., C Mte .104	125	13	4	0	.971
P. Martinez, C Mte	99	154	12	5	0	.971
Gallegos, Monterrey	105	182	7	6	3	.969
Rodriguez, Tampico .	44	83	9	3	0	.968
Delgado, Monterrey	93	107	11	4	2	.967
Ornelas, Tampico ...113	170	19	7	0	.964
Plascencia, C Mad .	14	23	3	1	0	.963
G. Garcia, Mon ...	73	95	5	4	1	.962
Macias, C Mante ...	28	48	2	2	0	.962
G. Gonzalez, Aguas	95	160	12	7	0	.961
Castillo, Monterrey .	66	91	6	4	1	.960
Saiz, C Madero* ..115	217	20	10	1	.960
Pina, Zacatecas	76	102	14	5	1	.959
Delgado, S L Potosi.	35	42	4	2	2	.958
Osorio, C Madero ..	14	21	2	1	0	.958
Dominguez, Leon ..115	261	11	12	2	.958
Lujan, Aguas	50	64	4	3	0	.958
Quintana, Aguas ...107	142	13	7	0	.957
Medrano, Zacatecas* 116	205	12	10	2	.956
Murrieta, C Madero	57	78	7	4	0	.955
Lizarraga, Tampico .	72	82	8	5	0	.947
Martinez H., Zac ...	22	18	0	1	0	.947
Valtierra, Leon*	61	86	3	5	0	.947
Cruz, Zacatecas	23	33	2	2	0	.946
Gamoundi, Zacatecas	45	79	5	5	0	.944
Suarez, Tampico* 126	209	15	14	1	.941
Guerrero, S L P .106	128	11	10	1	.933
Avila, Aguas	64	71	6	6	1	.928
Martinez, Aguas ...	14	22	2	2	0	.923
Campos, Leon	78	102	18	11	2	.916
Esteves, Leon	20	29	3	3	0	.914
Orozco, Leon	26	26	6	3	0	.914
E. Gonzalez, Aguas*	78	100	10	11	0	.909
Bernal, S L Potosi .	30	26	1	3	0	.900
Hernandez, Leon ...	69	92	6	11	0	.899
Alej. Zazueta, C Mte	11	11	0	2	0	.840

(Fewer Than Ten Games)

Player and Club	G.	PO.	A.	E.	DP.	Pct.
Almeida, Aguas	5	10	0	0	0	1.000
Alanis, Zacatecas ...	7	8	0	0	0	1.000
R. Gonzalez, C Mante 5	7	1	0	0	1.000
Sed, Monterrey	6	7	0	0	0	1.000
Montero, C Madero	4	3	2	0	0	1.000
Robles, Leon	3	4	0	0	0	1.000
Magana, S L Potosi	3	3	1	0	0	1.000
L. Lopez, Zacatecas	1	2	2	0	0	1.000
Villa, S L Potosi ...	5	3	0	0	0	1.000
E. Rodriguez, C Mad	4	3	0	0	0	1.000
Fragosa, C Madero .	4	2	1	0	0	1.000
Orduno, Tampico ...	1	2	0	0	0	1.000
J. Reyes, SLP*	1	2	0	0	0	1.000
Vega, Zacatecas	1	1	1	0	0	1.000
Espinoza, C Madero*	6	1	0	0	0	1.000
Ortega, Aguas	1	1	0	0	0	1.000
J. Arvizu, Aguas ...	1	1	0	0	0	1.000
Saldivar, Zacatecas .	2	1	0	0	0	1.000
Diaz, Zacatecas	3	1	0	0	0	1.000
M. Rodriguez, C Mad	1	1	0	0	0	1.000
Pratts, S L Potosi .	9	14	2	1	2	.941
Picos, Ciudad Mante	9	15	0	1	0	.938
A. Rodriguez, Mon .	9	13	0	1	0	.929
Guillen, Aguas	4	7	1	1	0	.889
Vega, S L Potosi ...	5	6	0	1	1	.857
Castaneda, SLP	3	6	0	1	0	.857
Cano, Ciudad Mante	5	5	0	1	0	.833
T. Pacheco, Tampico	4	4	0	1	0	.800
Dumer, Zacatecas ..	4	2	1	1	0	.750
Serna, Aguas*	1	2	0	1	0	.667
Ibarra, S L Potosi .	1	1	0	1	0	.500
S. Escalante, Aguas*	1	1	0	1	0	.500

CATCHERS

Player and Club	G.	PO.	A.	E.	DP.	PB.	Pct.
Ayala, C Madero	46	226	21	0	1	6	1.000
Arreguin, Zac	17	71	8	0	0	2	1.000
Villegas, Zac	10	25	3	0	0	0	1.000
Coronado, C Mte	39	223	36	1	1	3	.996
Leyva, C Mante	33	165	29	1	2	2	.995
Sed, Monterrey	30	159	18	1	2	2	.994
Castillo, C Mte	13	87	18	1	0	8	.991
Vega, S L Potosi	46	238	25	3	4	9	.989
Esquivel, Mon	49	284	24	4	0	1	.987
Contreras, Zac	18	70	6	1	0	3	.987
SANTOS, Leon	65	311	28	5	3	9	.985
Alvarado, Leon	18	64	3	1	0	4	.985
Arizpe, Mon	23	104	26	2	3	2	.985
Menendez, Leon	15	61	4	1	0	2	.985

Triple Play—Feliciano.

Player and Club	G.	PO.	A.	E.	DP.	PB.	Pct.
Guerra, SLP	15	53	9	1	0	4	.984
J. L. Lopez, CMad	13	54	6	1	0	0	.984
Mendivil, Tam	86	547	74	11	2	15	.983
Mojica, C Mante	37	233	20	5	1	9	.981
Feliciano, Aguas	108	483	112	12	11	26	.980
Benitez, Tampico	52	246	29	6	1	8	.979
Ed. Rivera, SLP	78	217	42	6	1	10	.977
Friol, C Madero	68	429	36	11	2	8	.977
P. Marquez, Zac	73	388	33	11	4	17	.975
Guillen, Aguas	24	92	15	4	2	15	.964
Briones, Mon	31	129	31	6	1	9	.964
Arreguin, Leon	36	122	11	5	0	2	.964
Vega, Zacatecas	25	111	17	5	1	7	.962

(Fewer Than Ten Games)

Player and Club	G.	PO.	A.	E.	DP.	PB.	Pct.
Preciado, Zac	9	50	1	0	0	1	1.000
Pinon, C Madero	9	41	5	0	0	2	1.000
G. Rodriguez, Mon	7	37	5	0	0	0	1.000
Rodriguez S., CMte	5	28	2	0	0	1	1.000
Rocha, C Mante	3	3	2	0	0	1	1.000
Ibarra, S L Potosi	2	5	1	0	0	0	1.000
A. Hernandez, Zac	1	5	0	0	0	1	1.000
Alanis, Zacatecas	1	4	0	0	0	1	1.000

Player and Club	G.	PO.	A.	E.	DP.	PB.	Pct.
Pratts, S L Potosi	1	3	0	0	0	0	1.000
En. Rivera, SLP	1	2	0	0	0	0	1.000
Campos, Leon	1	1	0	0	0	0	1.000
Felix, Tampico	1	1	0	0	0	0	1.000
Castaneda, SLP	7	21	6	1	1	1	.964
R. Vega, C Madero	3	11	1	1	0	0	.923
Jimenez, Aguas	4	9	2	2	0	0	.846

PITCHERS

Player and Club	G.	PO.	A.	E.	DP.	Pct.
DELFIN, C Madero	26	6	30	0	1	1.000
Mandujano, Tampico	22	3	29	0	0	1.000
Vega, S L Potosi	29	6	25	0	1	1.000
Cruz, Zacatecas	26	10	18	0	1	1.000
V. M. Moreno, Mon	25	4	23	0	1	1.000
S. Salomon, C Mante	22	4	23	0	0	1.000
Torres, Leon	32	5	19	0	2	1.000
Almada, Aguas*	23	4	20	0	0	1.000
P. Rodriguez, Mon	20	2	19	0	0	1.000
Juarez, Tampico	18	4	16	0	2	1.000
I. Hernandez, Aguas	11	4	18	0	2	1.000
Gonzalez, Tampico*	21	3	14	0	0	1.000
Ortega, C Mante	25	6	9	0	1	1.000
Lizarraga, SLP	24	6	9	0	0	1.000
Valenzuela, SLP*	21	3	11	0	0	1.000
P. Hernandez, Aguas	21	2	11	0	0	1.000
Bernal, S L Potosi	10	1	12	0	0	1.000
Ibarra, S L Potosi	12	1	12	0	0	1.000
Gallardo, C Madero	11	3	9	0	1	1.000
Moroyoqui, Zac	31	3	9	0	0	1.000
Flores, Leon	17	4	8	0	1	1.000
Galaviz, Tampico	10	3	8	0	0	1.000
E. Pacheco, Tampico	13	3	8	0	0	1.000
Garza, Monterrey	34	1	10	0	0	1.000
Saldivar, Zacatecas	22	3	6	0	1	1.000
Lopez, Leon	12	3	6	0	0	1.000
Martinez, Tampico*	14	1	7	0	0	1.000
T. Pacheco, Tampico	16	1	6	0	0	1.000
Perez de los Santos, Ciudad Mante	10	0	7	0	0	1.000
J. Pacheco, Tampico	16	2	4	0	0	1.000
Ramirez, Monterrey	18	1	5	0	0	1.000
Barandica, Zac	10	0	3	0	0	1.000
Reyes, Ciudad Mante	12	0	1	0	0	1.000
P. Salomon, Aguas	23	7	31	1	2	.974
Munoz, Ciudad Mante	29	7	29	1	0	.973
Salcido, C Madero	52	6	23	1	4	.967
Rodriguez, Zacatecas	25	9	20	1	0	.967
Quiroz, Leon	38	5	21	1	2	.963
J. Reyes, SLP*	43	4	46	2	3	.962
Celestino, Leon	36	1	22	1	1	.958
Alanis, Zacatecas	10	3	19	1	1	.957
Rodriguez L., Tam	14	10	12	1	0	.957
Mora, S L Potosi	31	6	36	2	3	.955
C. Nevarez, Zac	15	1	20	1	0	.955
Manrique, Mont*	20	1	19	1	0	.952
R. Reyes, C Madero	24	7	13	1	0	.952
R. Escalante, Aguas	25	4	16	1	1	.952

Triple Play—Leyva.

Player and Club	G.	PO.	A.	E.	DP.	Pct.
De la Torre, SLP	34	6	13	1	1	.950
Gomez, S L Potosi	13	4	15	1	0	.950
Osuna, Ciudad Mte*	21	7	12	1	1	.950
Santos, Zacatecas	33	2	17	1	1	.950
Ponce, Monterrey*	29	6	12	1	1	.947
Ramos, S L Potosi	27	4	14	1	0	.947
Campoy, Tampico	24	7	10	1	0	.944
Salazar, Monterrey	24	4	13	1	0	.944
Mendia, Zacatecas	19	1	15	1	0	.941
J. Valenzuela, Aguas	21	2	13	1	1	.938
Fuentes, Monterrey	23	3	12	1	2	.938
Gamez, Aguas	38	6	9	1	0	.938
Cano, Ciudad Mante	18	2	22	2	0	.923
Arroyo, S L Potosi	24	4	8	1	0	.923
Prado, Leon	28	4	19	2	0	.920
Munoz, Zacatecas*	30	2	19	2	0	.913
Medina, C Madero	17	6	15	2	0	.913
Minjarez, Aguas	30	7	14	2	2	.913
Mellado, Tampico	28	2	18	2	1	.909
R. Mendoza, Aguas	20	5	15	2	1	.909
Valenzuela, C Mad	24	3	25	3	1	.903
Reza, Ciudad Mante	12	2	7	1	0	.900
Orea, Leon	32	11	29	5	2	.889
R. Verdugo, C Mad	29	3	13	2	0	.889
Leyva, Aguas*	24	4	8	1	0	.889
G. Hernandez, Mon	24	2	6	1	0	.889
Cano, Tampico	19	1	7	1	0	.889
Montero, C Mante	22	2	21	3	0	.885
Serna, Aguas*	26	2	13	2	0	.882
H. Arvizu, Aguas	30	2	13	2	0	.882
Ramirez, C Mante	23	2	5	1	0	.875
M. Torres, Monterrey	30	1	12	2	1	.867
Manrique, Aguas	26	3	9	2	0	.857
C. Reyes, C Madero	10	1	5	1	0	.857
Mendiola, S L P	12	1	5	1	1	.857
Lopez, Monterrey	16	3	3	1	0	.857
Olguin, Leon	33	2	14	3	0	.842
Bourguet, Tampico	22	5	5	2	0	.833
A. Hernandez, Zac	38	3	7	2	0	.833
J. Garcia, C Madero	16	4	19	5	4	.821
Guerrero, C Madero*	16	2	11	3	1	.813
S. Escalante, Aguas*	30	5	8	3	2	.813
S. Garcia, Monterrey	24	2	15	4	2	.810
Perez, Ciudad Mad	21	1	3	1	0	.800
Diaz, Aguas*	12	0	3	1	0	.750
Zazueta, Leon	15	3	3	3	0	.667
Carpio, Leon	11	0	2	1	0	.667
Barajas, Tam-C Mad	19	1	4	5	0	.500

PITCHERS—Continued
(Fewer Than Ten Games)

Player and Club	G.	PO.	A.	E.	DP.	Pct.	Player and Club	G.	PO.	A.	E.	DP.	Pct.
Cortez, Monterrey*	8	1	9	0	0	1.000	Perez, Monterrey	3	3	0	0	0	1.000
Horsford, Monterrey	5	3	5	0	0	1.000	R. Marquez, Zac	3	1	0	0	0	1.000
Villa, Monterrey	5	2	6	0	1	1.000	Alvarez, Tampico	1	0	1	0	0	1.000
A. Reyes, S L Potosi	5	1	5	0	0	1.000	Contreras, Leon	1	0	1	0	0	1.000
Magana, S L Potosi	4	1	3	0	0	1.000	Guerrero, C Mante	1	0	1	0	0	1.000
Als. Zazueta, C Mte*	8	0	3	0	0	1.000	J. Hernandez, Mon	1	0	1	0	0	1.000
Silva, Ciudad Mante	4	0	3	0	0	1.000	J. L. Mendoza, Aguas	1	0	1	0	0	1.000
Mason, Monterrey	2	0	3	0	0	1.000	P. Moreno, Monterrey	1	0	1	0	0	1.000
E. Garcia, C Madero	8	1	2	0	0	1.000	Sed, Monterrey	1	0	1	0	0	1.000
Flores, Zacatecas	5	1	2	0	0	1.000	Saldana, Monterrey	1	0	1	0	0	1.000
Jaime, Aguas	3	1	2	0	0	1.000	Ramirez, Tampico	5	1	5	1	0	.857
Martinez, Monterrey*	1	0	2	0	1	1.000	Munro, Monterrey	8	1	5	2	0	.750
M. Lopez, C Madero*	6	1	0	0	0	1.000	Basanez, C Madero	8	0	2	1	0	.667
J. M. Gonzalez, CMte	4	0	1	0	0	1.000	Zatarain, SLP	7	0	3	2	0	.600
Guirardo, Zacatecas	4	0	1	0	0	1.000	En. Rivera, SLP	6	0	3	2	0	.600
Quintana, Aguas	3	0	1	0	0	1.000	Mata, Monterrey	3	0	1	2	0	.333

The following players do not have any recorded accepted chances at the positions indicated: therefore, are not listed in the fielding averages for those particular positions: Ahumada, p; J. Arreguin, p; Carrera*, p; Castaneda, p; De la Rosa*, p; Javier Espinoza, p; Fierro, c; G. Gallegos, p; R. Garcia, p; Lerma, p; R. Lopez, p; Mercado, p; D. Ortega, p; Perez Dominguez, 1b-3b; Santamaria, p.

PITCHERS' RECORDS
(Leading Qualifiers for Earned-Run Average Leadership—126 or More Innings)
*Throws lefthanded.

Pitcher and Club	G.	GS.	CG.	ShO.	W.	L.	Pct.	IP.	H.	R.	ER.	HR.	BB.	Int. BB.	HB.	SO.	WP.	ERA.
P. Salomon, C Mante	23	19	15	4	13	6	.684	157	136	56	31	7	53	6	0	111	4	1.78
J. Garcia, C Madero	26	16	10	2	13	4	.765	138	138	53	34	5	30	3	9	83	2	2.23
Montero, C Mante	22	20	13	1	13	7	.650	153	137	62	43	7	65	4	4	119	6	2.53
J. Reyes, SLP*	43	25	13	1	17	9	.654	178	174	85	53	10	86	10	4	87	4	2.68
Vega, S L Potosi	29	10	8	2	12	8	.600	131	116	57	40	5	35	7	2	112	1	2.75
Delfin, C Madero	26	21	9	0	14	3	.824	143	138	60	46	8	49	6	6	96	6	2.90
R. Reyes, C Madero	24	19	9	1	15	3	.833	132	136	64	47	10	28	3	4	147	3	3.20
Orea, Leon	32	22	7	0	13	12	.520	162	199	107	68	16	44	7	5	110	3	3.78
A. Munoz, C Mante	29	15	6	1	6	11	.353	135	153	85	58	10	64	6	6	117	3	3.87
Quiros, Leon	38	7	4	0	9	8	.529	129	170	102	58	10	39	6	8	57	3	4.05

Departmental Leaders: G—Salcido, 52; GS—J. Reyes, 25; CG—Salomon, 15; ShO—P. Salomon, 4; W—J. Reyes, 17; L—Prado, C. Munoz, 13; Pct.—R. Reyes, .833; IP—J. Reyes, 178; H—Orea, 199; R—Prado, 122; ER—Celestino, 84; HR—Prado, 19; BB—J. Reyes, 86; IBB—R. Mendoza, 13; HB—Prado, 13; SO—R. Reyes, 147; WP—Prado 9.

(All Pitchers—Listed Alphabetically)

Pitcher and Club	G.	GS.	CG.	ShO	W.	L.	Pct.	IP.	H.	R.	ER.	HR.	BB.	Int. BB.	HB.	SO.	WP.	ERA.
Ahumada, Zacatecas	4	4	0	0	1	0	1.000	9	25	14	14	1	3	0	0	3	0	14.00
Alanis, Zacatecas	19	10	3	0	6	6	.500	96	101	68	48	8	38	5	7	80	2	4.50
Almada, Aguas*	23	17	8	3	10	6	.625	101	117	63	39	2	36	8	6	77	6	3.48
Alvarez, Tampico	1	0	0	0	0	1	.000	5	7	4	4	2	2	0	0	2	0	7.20
Arreguin, Leon	3	0	0	0	0	0	.000	9	11	6	4	1	2	0	1	2	0	4.00
Arroyo, S L Potosi	24	6	1	0	3	7	.300	49	51	36	26	8	26	6	3	20	2	4.78
H. Arvizu, Aguas	30	10	2	0	5	4	.556	62	92	55	38	5	30	4	1	17	5	5.52
Barajas, 18 Tam-1 C Mad	19	5	1	0	2	3	.400	45	66	43	25	3	21	1	3	19	5	5.00
Barandica, Zacatecas	12	0	0	0	1	0	1.000	13	13	8	7	2	7	0	1	7	0	4.85
Basanez, C Madero	8	0	0	0	0	0	.000	5	7	5	2	0	6	1	0	5	1	3.60
Bernal, S L Potosi	10	6	2	0	1	3	.250	51	47	28	16	0	18	1	1	35	4	2.82
Bourguet, Tampico	22	12	7	0	7	4	.636	98	97	51	36	7	34	1	4	55	3	3.31
Campoy, Tampico	24	19	7	1	8	8	.500	102	103	57	35	5	37	1	4	109	3	3.09
Cano, Ciudad Mante	18	16	5	1	4	8	.333	95	96	69	45	6	61	5	3	86	4	4.26
Cano, Tampico	19	7	2	1	4	4	.500	47	58	39	25	8	23	4	3	20	5	4.79
Carpio, Leon	11	0	0	0	1	1	.500	25	39	23	16	3	13	2	0	9	2	5.78
Carrera, Zacatecas*	3	0	0	0	0	0	.000	8	13	8	3	2	0	0	0	2	0	9.00
Castaneda, S L Potosi	1	0	0	0	0	0	.000	½	2	1	1	0	1	0	0	1	1	27.00
Celestino, Leon	36	16	1	0	3	10	.231	126	163	119	84	13	33	3	4	53	4	6.00
Contreras, Leon	1	1	0	0	1	0	1.000	7	9	3	2	1	0	0	0	4	0	2.57
Cortez, Monterrey*	8	5	2	1	1	3	.250	33	38	17	14	2	5	1	1	25	0	3.82
Cruz, Zacatecas	26	15	7	0	5	7	.417	110	119	65	41	10	20	1	5	68	4	3.35
De la Rosa, Aguas*	3	0	0	0	0	0	.000	4	5	1	1	0	1	0	0	2	0	2.25
De la Torre, SLP	34	5	4	0	4	4	.556	77	86	41	31	2	26	6	2	37	1	3.62
Delfin, C Madero	26	21	9	0	14	3	.824	143	138	60	46	8	49	6	6	96	6	2.90
Diaz, Aguascalientes*	12	2	0	0	1	2	.333	14	21	13	10	1	8	0	0	9	1	6.43
R. Escalante, Aguas	25	13	3	1	3	9	.250	69	80	54	39	6	23	0	3	32	2	5.09
S. Escalante, Aguas*	30	7	0	0	1	2	.333	53	68	40	26	3	29	7	7	31	4	4.42
Espinoza, Monterrey	1	0	0	0	0	0	.000	1	2	4	3	0	1	0	0	1	0	18.00
Flores, Zacatecas	5	0	0	0	0	0	.000	7	7	3	3	0	1	0	1	3	0	3.86
Flores, Leon	17	12	3	1	5	3	.625	72	97	56	34	5	20	0	2	40	5	4.25
Fuentes, Monterrey	23	8	0	1	4	4	.200	46	61	35	25	5	19	5	3	33	2	4.89

Pitcher and Club	G	GS	CG	ShO	W	L	Pct.	IP	H	R	ER	HR	BB	Int.BB	HB	SO	WP	ERA.
Galaviz, Tampico 10	6	2	0	2		5	.286	42	48	27	20	5	18	2	1	21	1	4.29
Gallardo, C Madero ..11	9	1	0	2		6	.250	46	52	30	23	6	29	3	2	20	2	4.50
Gallegos, Tampico 1	1	0	0	0	1		1.000	1	4	3	3	0	0		0	1	0	27.00
Gamez, Aguascalientes 38	3	0	0		4		.500	80	80	55	45	9	42	9	2	45	2	5.06
E. Garcia, C Madero . 8	0	0	0	0	0		.000	10	13	5	4	0	4	0	0	3	2	3.60
J. Garcia, C Madero .26	16	10	2		13	4	.765	138	138	53	34	5	30	3	9	83	2	2.22
Garcia, Zacatecas 3	0	0	0	0	0		.000	4	5	3	3	0	1	0	2	3	2	6.75
S. Garcia, Monterrey .24	14	3	2		6	8	.429	95	97	57	31	6	38	5	2	51	1	2.94
Garza, Monterrey ...24	5	1	0	2	2		.500	63	81	45	37	7	34	1	3	35	1	5.29
Gomez, S L Potosi ...13	12	4	0	5		0	1.000	65	58	34	26	3	41	3	2	46	3	3.60
J. M. Gonzalez, C Mte 4	1	0	0	0	0		.000	11	13	10	5	2	4	0	2	6	1	4.09
Gonzalez, Tampico* ..21	11	7	1		8	4	.667	102	97	45	28	10	23	3	1	75	4	2.47
Guerrero, C Madero* .16	1	1	0	2	3		.400	51	50	23	19	3	16	2	0	15	4	3.35
Guerrero, C Mante . 1	0	0	0	0		1	.000	3	7	4	3	0	0	0		1	0	9.00
Guirardo, Zacatecas .. 4	3	0	0	0	1		.000	13	15	8	5	2	4	0	1	7	1	3.46
A. Hernandez, Zac ..38	4	1	0	4		7	.364	106	99	63	50	9	21	3	1	103	2	4.25
G. Hernandez, Mon ..24	6	0	0	3		4	.429	48	68	43	39	5	20	2	3	17	7	7.31
I. Hernandez, Aguas .41	4	0	0	3		5	.444	87	84	48	39	9	53	10	3	27	4	4.03
J. Hernandez, Mon .. 1	1	0	0	0	1		.000	5	6	3	3	1	1	0	0	3	0	5.40
P. Hernandez, Aguas .21	5	0	0	0		3	.000	33	44	28	17	4	10	1	6	8	1	4.64
Horsford, Monterrey . 5	5	4	1	3	2		.600	39	34	14	10	3	15	1	1	41	0	2.31
Ibarra, S L Potosi .12	5	1	0	1	2		.333	45	48	24	18	0	24	2	3	36	0	3.60
Jaime, Aguascalientes . 2	0	0	0	0	0		.000	5	4	3	2	1	3	0	1	1	0	3.60
Juarez, Tampico 18	15	8	1		9	2	.818	89	103	54	41	8	39	3	6	77	3	4.15
Lerma, Ciudad Madero 2	0	0	0	0		1	.000	5	8	5	5	2	4	1	0	1	0	9.00
Leyva, Aguas* 34	8	2	0	4		6	.400	48	46	30	33	3	45	12	0	26	2	6.19
Lizarraga, S L Potosi 24	8	1	1	5		4	.556	76	95	42	32	3	29	2	2	46	0	3.79
E. Lopez, Monterrey .16	0	0	0	0		3	.000	29	28	20	17	2	15	3	3	22	0	5.28
F. Lopez, Leon 12	8	4	0	2		6	.250	52	67	32	25	10	22	1	0	35	2	4.33
M. Lopez, C Mad* .. 6	0	0	0	0		1	.000	8	10	5	4	0	3	0	0	4	0	4.50
R. Lopez, C Madero . 2	0	0	0	0	0		.000	5	6	4	4	0	0	0	0	4	0	7.20
Magana, S L Potosi . 4	0	0	0	0		1	.000	18	20	11	9	1	6	0	0	10	0	4.50
Mandujano, Tampico .22	16	5	0	6		8	.429	125	113	62	45	12	37	3	6	101	6	3.24
G. Manrique, Mon* ..20	13	8	3	12	4		.750	100	83	44	34	8	39	2	2	54	5	.306
O. Manrique, Aguas .26	8	1	0	2		5	.286	66	84	48	31	3	27	0	6	29	7	4.23
R. Marquez, Zacatecas 3	1	0	0	1	0		1.000	8	16	11	9	0	6	0	1	2	0	10.13
Martinez, Tampico* ..14	6	2	1	3		4	.429	48	47	44	29	2	36	2	4	27	4	5.44
Martinez, Monterrey* . 1	0	0	0	0		1	.000	5	6	4	4	0	2	1	1	3	0	7.20
Mason, Monterrey .. 2	2	1	0	1	1		.500	13	8	6	5	0	8	0	0	7	0	3.46
Mata, Monterrey 3	0	0	0	0	0		.000	3	5	5	2	0	2	0	0	3	0	6.00
Medina, C Madero .17	15	2	1		2	6	.250	71	80	56	35	8	27	2	6	46	4	4.44
Mellado, Tampico ..28	3	1	0	5	1		.833	91	95	56	45	9	26	2	2	63	1	4.45
Mendia, Zacatecas ..19	15	5	1	5		10	.333	90	93	56	38	6	43	3	2	46	3	3.80
Mendiola, S L Potosi 10	3	1	0	1	2		.333	25	29	26	15	4	10	1	0	8	0	5.40
J. L. Mendoza, Aguas 1	0	0	0	0	0		.000	2	4	3	3	0	2	0	0	3	1	13.50
R. Mendoza, Aguas .20	16	5	0	7		5	.583	105	97	57	46	6	55	13	3	58	8	3.94
Mercado, Zacatecas .. 4	1	0	0	0		1	.000	5	3	4	1	0	2	0	0	5	0	1.80
Minjarez, Aguas 30	13	6	1	5	9		.357	109	107	51	38	6	39	9	0	72	3	3.14
Montero, C Mante .22	20	13	1		13	7	.650	153	137	62	43	7	65	4	4	119	6	2.53
Mora, S Luis Potosi 31	23	7	1	6		12	.333	130	130	94	69	10	69	8	3	60	5	4.78
P. Moreno, Monterrey 1	0	0	0	0	0		.000	1	1	0	0	0	1	0	0	0	0	0.00
V. M. Moreno, Mon ..25	14	5	3	5		8	.385	106	95	40	26	5	27	3	5	76	5	2.21
A. Munoz, C Mante .29	15	6	1	6		11	.353	139	153	85	58	10	64	6	6	117	3	3.87
C. Munoz, Zacatecas* 30	19	6	0	6		13	.316	116	144	78	49	6	47	0	4	89	7	3.80
Munro, Monterrey ... 8	6	2	0	3	4		.429	49	48	14	13	1	7	1	2	33	2	2.39
C. Nevarez, Zacatecas 15	11	3	0	3	2		.600	68	63	45	36	8	25	3	4	25	0	5.79
Olguin, Leon 33	15	4	0	3		7	.300	86	137	84	60	11	41	5	6	30	8	6.23
Orea, Leon 32	22	7	0	13		12	.520	162	199	107	68	16	44	7	5	110	3	3.78
Ortega, Aguas 1	0	0	0	0	0		.000	1	2	0	0	0	0	0	0	0	0	0.00
Ortega, Ciudad Mante 25	1	0	0	2	2		.500	55	63	29	20	5	27	5	5	25	3	3.27
Osuna, Ciudad Mante* 21	17	7	2	9	6		.600	103	92	48	32	10	34	2	6	64	2	2.80
E. Pacheco, Tampico .12	6	3	1	3		4	.429	51	48	27	21	4	22	1	4	42	2	3.71
J. L. Pacheco, Tam .16	1	0	0	0		2	.000	27	37	32	24	5	22	0	4	15	0	8.00
T. Pacheco, Tampico .16	4	1	1	1	1		.500	39	56	39	28	6	22	2	4	22	1	6.46
E. Perez, C Madero .21	1	1	0	1	1		.500	31	40	24	20	4	15	2	0	20	1	5.81
Perez, Monterrey 3	0	0	0	0	0		.000	4	2	1	1	0	1	0	1	1	0	2.25
Perez de los Santos, Ciudad Mante 10	6	4	0	2		3	.400	45	53	20	13	2	14	1	1	28	2	2.60
Ponce, Monterrey* ..29	9	3	1	3	4		.429	59	61	30	24	2	19	3	0	42	1	3.66
Prado, Leon 28	24	9	1	8		13	.381	128	167	122	78	19	64	7	13	84	9	5.48
Quintana, Aguas 3	1	0	0	0		1	.000	8	9	4	4	0	3	1	0	9	0	4.50
Quiroz, Leon 38	7	4	0	9		8	.529	129	170	102	58	10	39	6	8	57	3	4.05
Ramirez, Tampico . 5	3	1	0	3	0		1.000	28	18	9	1	1	3	0	0	18	0	0.32
Ramirez, C Mante ..23	3	1	0	1		4	.200	50	66	35	27	6	26	3	1	31	2	4.86
Ramirez, Monterrey .18	0	0	0	1	2		.667	22	29	18	17	5	11	0	1	17	2	6.95
Ramos, S L Potosi ..27	7	0	0	4		3	.571	75	101	65	54	8	28	5	3	41	0	6.48
A. Reyes, S L Potosi . 5	3	0	0	0		1	.000	10	18	12	9	3	3	0	3	0	2	8.10
C. Reyes, C Madero .10	10	3	0	4		3	.571	56	57	34	24	7	12	3	3	37	2	3.86
J. Reyes, S L Potosi* 43	25	13	1	17	9		.654	178	174	85	53	10	86	10	4	87	4	2.68
R. Reyes, C Madero .24	19	9	1	15	3		.833	132	136	64	47	10	28	3	4	147	3	3.20

Pitcher and Club	G	GS	CG	ShO	W	L	Pct.	IP	H	R	ER	HR	BB	Int. BB	HB	SO	WP	ERA
Reyes, Ciudad Mante ..12	0	0	0	1	0		1.000	19	34	27	18	5	8	0	5	11	3	8.53
Reza, Ciudad Mante ..12	7	1	0	2	4		.333	35	51	41	27	7	22	1	1	23	1	6.94
En. Rivera, SLP 6	3	0	0	2	2		.500	10	13	14	10	1	9	1	0	3	0	9.00
Rodriguez, Zacatecas ..25	18	5	1	6	10		.375	116	166	84	53	14	29	3	1	59	3	4.11
Rodriguez L., Tam .14	11	5	1	8	4		.667	90	88	43	35	12	30	2	4	58	0	3.50
P. Rodriguez, Mon ..20	16	7	1	9	3		.750	98	88	50	37	5	39	1	7	85	5	3.40
Salazar, Monterrey ...24	4	0	0	1	2		.333	43	59	23	16	1	16	3	6	33	1	3.35
Salcido, C Madero ..52	1	0	0	11	5		.688	107	99	58	42	8	54	5	4	91	5	3.53
Saldana, Monterrey .. 1	0	0	0	0	0		.000	¾	0	0	0	0	0	0	0	0	0	0.00
Saldivar, Zacatecas ..22	6	1	0	4	2		.667	50	52	25	20	2	33	2	4	18	4	3.60
P. Salomon, C Mante 23	19	15	4	13	6		.684	157	136	56	31	7	53	6	0	111	4	1.78
S. Salomon, C Mante 22	18	10	3	7	9		.438	120	104	53	44	4	55	4	6	80	1	3.30
Santamaria, Leon ...10	3	0	0	0	2		.000	7	12	11	8	3	12	1	0	2	4	10.29
Santos, Zacatecas ...33	14	8	6	9	5		.643	125	142	75	61	10	37	2	3	74	0	4.39
Sed, Monterrey 1	0	0	0	0	0		.000	2	1	0	0	0	0	0	1	1	0	0.00
Serna, Aguas* 26	14	1	0	4	6		.400	75	103	78	55	6	54	7	1	34	5	6.60
Silva, Ciudad Mante . 4	2	1	0	2	0		1.000	14	22	12	9	2	7	0	0	9	0	5.79
M. Torres, Monterrey .30	12	4	0	5	8		.385	93	104	54	37	5	41	2	6	70	1	3.58
S. Torres, Leon 32	16	4	0	5	11		.313	131	175	99	68	12	58	8	4	65	5	4.67
Valenzuela, C Madero 24	21	7	0	11	4		.733	123	133	78	53	11	45	2	1	62	1	3.88
H. Valenzuela, SLP* 21	2	0	0	1	1		.500	44	53	32	25	0	18	3	3	22	2	5.11
J. Valenzuela, Aguas 21	4	3	2	3	3		.625	53	68	26	20	2	14	6	2	37	1	3.40
Vega, S L Potosi ...29	10	8	2	12	8		.600	131	116	57	40	5	35	7	2	112	1	2.75
R. Verdugo, C Madero 29	9	2	0	4	4		.500	85	89	61	47	14	40	1	5	47	4	4.98
Villa, Monterrey 5	4	3	1	3	1		.750	36	29	9	6	2	4	0	0	20	0	1.50
Zatarain, SLP 7	5	0	0	3	1		.750	21	28	20	10	1	8	1	4	9	2	4.29
Als. Zazueta, C Mte* . 8	0	0	0	0	0		.000	16	17	11	11	3	5	0	0	15	2	6.19
E. Zazueta, Leon 15	1	0	0	0	0		.000	36	39	29	24	6	16	2	2	16	5	6.00

BALKS—Mandujano, S. Torres, H. Valenzuela, R. Verdugo, 2 each; Almada, Barandica, De la Torre, Garza, I. Hernandez, Juarez, Lizarraga, E. Lopez, G. Manrique, O. Manrique, Minjarez, Montero, Moroyoqui, C. Munoz, E. Perez, P. Salomon, Santos, E Zazueta, 1 each.

COMBINATION SHUTOUTS—Serna-R. Escalante, Aguascalientes; Valenzuela-Salcido, Ciudad Madero; Osuna-Ramirez, Ciudad Mante; Ponce-Garza-G. Hernandez, Monterrey; C. Munoz-Alanis. Saldivar-Cruz, Zacatecas.

NO-HIT GAMES—None.

ALONG THE MINOR LEAGUE TRAIL....

(Continued from page 495)

25 bases in their first 18 games. When the final averages came out, they showed the Pirates had led the loop again, with 108. Gene Clines repeated his theft title with 32 stolen bases for Waterbury. ... Rochester (International) fans were treated to a "Guaranteed Win" night May 19. If the Reds Wings, didn't win, they'd get to see another game free. So what did the Wings do? They buried Buffalo, 27-4, making dead sure all stubs were worthless. ... Dalton Renfro of Savannah (Southern) received two RBIs on one sacrifice fly, a rare thing Against Columbus May 19, he whacked a long fly to left, but the fielder hit the wall and dropped in pain The runners on second and third scampered home on the fly. ... Kenny Boyer, longtime third base great for the St Louis Cardinals, made his toughest play as manager of Arkansas (Texas) It was his sad move to have to ship out his younger brother, Lenny, who had been hitting a poor .228 and needed more experience. ... Tom Shopay, sidelined with a badly-sprained wrist, had to fill in for a substitute who hadn't yet arrived Batting for Rochester (International), Shopay led off with a homer, hit a three-run

(Continued on page 541)

Mexican Southeast League

CLASS A

CHAMPIONSHIP WINNERS IN PREVIOUS YEARS

1964—Tabasco* .... .636	1967—Campeche† .... .610
Campeche .... .591	1968—Campeche .... .633
1965—Tabasco .... .600	Carmen‡ .... .628
Campeche* .... .643	1969—Campeche§ .... .620
1966—Puerto Mexico* ... .589	
Campeche .... .661	

*Won split-season playoff. †Won championship and four-club playoff. ‡Won three-club playoff. §Won championship and two-club playoff.

STANDING OF CLUBS AT CLOSE OF FIRST HALF, APRIL 28

Club	W.	L.	T.	Pct.	G.B.
Puerto Mexico (Jalisco)	33	20	1	.623	...
Campeche (Mexico City Reds)	30	23	2	.566	3
Ciudad del Carmen (Yucatan)	23	31	1	.426	10½
Tabasco (Mexico City Tigers)	21	33	0	.389	12½

STANDING OF CLUBS AT CLOSE OF SECOND HALF, JUNE 17

Club	W.	L.	T.	Pct.	G.B.
Campeche (Mexico City Reds)	34	15	1	.694	...
Puerto Mexico (Jalisco)	26	23	0	.531	8
Ciudad del Carmen (Yucatan)	25	27	2	.481	10½
Tabasco (Mexico City Tigers)	16	36	1	.308	19½

Farm clubs of Mexican League teams as shown in parentheses.

Playoff—Puerto Mexico defeated Campeche, four games to none.

Regular-Season Attendance—Campeche, 35,959; Ciudad del Carmen, 31,311; Puerto Mexico, 9,503; Tabasco, 11,803. Total, 88,576. Playoffs, 2,319.

Managers: Campeche—Mario Pelaez; Ciudad del Carmen—Leonel Aldama; Puerto Mexico—Felipe Hernandez; Tabasco—Luis Montes de Oca.

All-Star Team: 1B—Lopez, Puerto Mexico; 2B—Flores, Puerto Mexico; 3B—Osuna, Puerto Mexico; SS—Conkle, Campeche; OF—L. Peralta, Campeche; Ochoa, Puerto Mexico; Salazar, Puerto Mexico; C—Orozco, Campeche; Jackson, Puerto Mexico; P—Ferguson, Campeche; Ruiz, Tabasco; Manager—Pelaez, Campeche.

(Compiled by Raul Mendoza, League Statistician, Mexico, D. F.)

CLUB BATTING

Club	G.	AB.	R.	OR.	H.	TB.	2B.	3B.	HR.	RBI.	SH.	SF.	BB.	Int BB.	HP.	SO.	SB.	CS.	LOB.	Pct.
Puerto Mex	103	3297	437	345	918	1270	114	56	42	424	68	34	251	50	25	507	99	67	643	.278
Campeche	...105	3313	462	331	887	1203	128	31	42	443	107	34	379	72	43	506	60	41	780	.268
C'ad del C.	109	3425	346	466	846	1125	131	23	34	335	58	20	357	44	31	618	69	34	779	.247
Tabasco	...107	3343	327	430	795	989	71	39	15	306	71	20	261	32	27	550	77	37	673	.238

INDIVIDUAL BATTING

(Leading Qualifiers for Batting Championship—335 or More Plate Appearances)

*Bats lefthanded. †Switch-hitter.

Player and Club	G.	AB.	R.	H.	TB.	2B.	3B.	HR.	RBI.	SH.	SF.	BB.	HP.	SO.	SB.	CS.	Pct.
Conkle, Francisco, Cam ...	97	320	57	114	149	14	3	5	55	8	3	70	6	32	3	3	.356
Peralta, Luis, Campeche ...	93	312	62	105	164	17	0	14	65	9	5	42	3	41	5	5	.337
Flores, Teodoro, P Mexico	97	339	57	107	125	6	6	0	27	8	0	26	1	50	16	9	.316
Villalobos, Lauro, P Mexico	101	351	44	109	144	12	4	5	51	9	2	13	1	21	7	9	.311
Gutierrez, M. Angel, Car*	. 95	293	38	88	126	21	4	3	50	5	4	35	2	19	0	4	.300
Salazar, Mario, P Mexico	.102	344	41	100	131	13	6	2	56	5	7	29	1	29	13	9	.291
Osuna, Carlos, P Mexico	. 99	348	54	99	143	12	7	6	50	5	5	28	5	60	11	6	.284
Ochoa, David, P Mexico	... 91	317	60	90	151	12	8	11	63	2	7	26	3	52	15	9	.284
Romellon, Jose Angel, Car	101	336	43	94	143	19	0	10	50	0	3	38	1	70	12	4	.280
Barajas, Armando, Cam	...100	353	43	98	119	14	2	1	43	19	1	36	3	27	4	4	.278

Department Leaders: G—F. Rodriguez, 108; AB—F. Rodriguez, 380; R—L. Peralta, 62; H—Conkle, 114; TB—L. Peralta, 164; 2B—M. A. Gutierrez, 21; 3B—Garza, Ochoa, 8; HR—L. Peralta, 14; RBI—L. Peralta, 65; SH—Barajas, 19; SF—Ochoa, Salazar, 7; BB—Conkle, 70; HP—Orozco, 11; SO—M. Parra, 73; SB—Alvarado, 19; CS—Alvarado, 10.

(All Players—Listed Alphabetically)

Player and Club	G.	AB.	R.	H.	TB.	2B.	3B.	HR.	RBI.	SH.	SF.	BB.	HP.	SO.	SB.	CS.	Pct.
Aguilera, Jorge, Tabasco	74	255	29	58	87	7	5	4	30	0	1	13	3	56	10	2	.227
Almeida, Ramon, Tabasco	30	78	11	23	29	1	1	1	13	1	1	13	1	23	3	0	.295
Alvarado, Alejandro, PM*	97	272	38	70	85	11	2	0	21	3	3	36	6	22	19	10	.257
Andrade, Manuel, Campeche	5	3	0	0	0	0	0	0	0	0	0	0	0	0	0	0	.000
Arce, Alberto, Tabasco	17	32	2	3	3	0	0	0	2	1	0	3	0	12	0	0	.094
Armas, Tomas, Puerto M*	14	30	2	1	1	0	0	0	1	2	0	1	1	18	0	0	.033
Armendariz, Waldo, Tab*	16	8	0	0	0	0	0	0	0	0	0	0	0	0	0	0	.000
Arroyo, Abelardo, P Mexico	11	15	1	3	5	0	1	0	0	2	0	0	0	5	0	0	.200
Ayala, Gregorio, Carmen	15	39	2	6	7	1	0	0	2	0	0	3	0	6	0	0	.154
Barajas, Armando, Cam	100	353	43	98	119	14	2	1	43	19	1	36	3	27	4	4	.278
Bonilla, Antelmo, Carmen	92	341	38	83	107	15	3	1	18	3	0	33	3	43	14	2	.243
Bouye, Lucas, 31 Car-24 Ca	55	187	32	62	82	6	4	2	25	0	1	33	3	32	16	3	.332
Burgos, Juan, Carmen	1	2	1	0	0	0	0	0	0	0	0	1	0	0	0	0	.000
Camarero, Genaro, Tabasco	83	209	14	46	53	7	0	0	18	2	1	8	1	48	8	1	.220
Carrasco, Carlos, P Mexico	9	22	0	5	5	0	0	0	2	0	0	1	0	5	0	0	.227
Castro, Gilberto, Tabasco	23	31	2	3	3	0	0	0	4	0	2	0	0	14	0	0	.097
Castro, Jose Luis, Carmen	21	22	2	4	5	1	0	0	2	0	0	2	0	13	0	0	.182
Cedillo, Genaro, Carmen	7	10	1	1	1	0	0	0	0	0	0	1	0	2	1	0	.100
Conkle, Francisco, Camp	97	320	57	114	149	14	3	5	55	8	3	70	6	32	3	3	.356
Contreras, Adan, Tabasco	101	324	28	83	107	10	7	0	35	3	1	43	1	27	11	3	.250
Contreras, Celso, Carmen	7	9	0	1	1	0	0	0	1	0	0	0	0	5	0	0	.111
Cordero, Cesar, Campeche*	36	18	1	0	0	0	0	0	3	3	1	1	0	4	0	0	.000
Cordova, Ernesto, P Mexico	3	6	0	0	0	0	0	0	0	0	0	0	0	2	0	0	.000
Cota, Sergio, Carmen	32	81	2	13	14	1	0	0	4	0	0	2	1	19	0	1	.160
Delfin, Justino, Tabasco	18	19	4	4	4	0	0	0	0	0	0	2	0	7	0	0	.211
Diaz, Hector M., Tabasco	18	31	4	7	12	3	1	0	0	2	0	3	0	8	0	0	.226
Ek B., Eleazar, Campeche	33	15	1	1	1	0	0	0	1	0	0	0	0	6	0	0	.067
Escamilla, Hector, Tabasco	14	46	3	9	10	1	0	0	4	1	0	3	0	5	1	1	.196
Espinosa, Cruz, Campeche	88	299	27	79	115	16	7	2	40	9	2	20	4	52	6	2	.264
Espinosa, Roberto, Carmen	91	281	23	72	79	5	1	0	20	8	1	22	2	34	5	4	.256
Fabela, Wilfredo, Campeche	24	42	6	9	9	0	0	0	2	4	0	1	0	8	0	0	.214
Fajardo, Ignacio, Campeche	9	9	1	0	0	0	0	0	1	0	0	0	0	4	0	0	.000
Ferguson, M., L'nardo, Cam	42	85	7	17	22	1	2	0	7	1	1	4	0	8	1	0	.200
Figueroa, Victor M., Carmen	81	228	15	50	59	7	1	0	22	1	1	20	2	67	0	0	.219
Flores, Teodoro, P Mexico	97	339	57	107	125	6	6	0	27	8	0	26	1	50	16	9	.316
Franco, David, Tabasco	22	10	2	2	2	0	0	0	0	0	0	1	0	6	0	0	.000
Galaviz, Efren, 4 Cam-7 Tab	11	16	1	3	3	0	0	0	0	1	0	0	0	1	0	0	.188
Garza, Carlos, Tabasco†	68	227	33	65	92	5	8	2	31	1	4	20	2	33	0	5	.286
Gonzalez, Sergio, Tabasco†	11	16	1	3	3	0	0	0	0	0	0	2	0	3	0	1	.188
Goycolea, Gerardo, Tabasco	7	2	0	0	0	0	0	0	1	0	1	0	1	0	0	0	.000
Guerrero, Jesus, Carmen	17	48	4	12	15	3	0	0	4	3	0	4	1	5	0	1	.250
Guillen, Juan, P Mexico	17	22	1	5	5	0	0	0	3	4	0	0	7	0	0	0	.227
Gutierrez, Gerardo, Tabasco	99	301	22	82	100	10	1	2	35	1	1	22	1	44	5	3	.272
Gutierrez, M. Angel, Car*	95	293	38	88	126	21	1	3	50	5	4	35	2	19	0	4	.300
Herrera, Francisco, Carmen	50	157	32	56	97	9	1	10	36	0	3	42	2	26	1	3	.357
Jackson, Alfonso, P Mexico	81	258	27	74	99	14	1	3	30	2	2	20	1	33	3	5	.287
Lara, Armando, Tabasco	107	379	39	93	114	7	7	0	37	5	4	29	5	45	10	5	.245
Lilly, James, Campeche	2	1	0	0	0	0	0	0	0	0	0	1	0	1	0	0	.000
Lizarraga, Roberto, Camp	34	132	28	40	49	7	1	0	13	3	2	15	1	10	4	1	.303
Lopez, Armando, Campeche	83	284	31	83	109	12	1	4	35	9	4	14	2	40	7	7	.292
Lopez, Carlos, Tabasco	79	296	29	84	93	6	0	1	13	8	0	16	4	46	13	8	.284
Lopez, Jaime, P Mexico*	89	285	34	93	112	9	5	0	31	7	1	26	0	14	4	4	.326
Lopez, Marco, Carmen*	9	3	0	0	0	0	0	0	0	0	0	0	0	0	0	0	.000
Lugo, Urbano, Carmen	11	7	1	1	1	0	0	0	0	0	0	0	0	4	0	0	.143
Mendez, Vicente, P Mexico	25	29	4	3	3	0	0	0	0	0	0	3	0	13	0	0	.103
Mendiola, Angel, P Mexico	13	10	1	2	2	0	0	0	1	0	1	0	0	4	0	0	.200
Mere, Luis, Carmen	44	65	9	16	18	2	0	0	3	1	0	3	0	14	4	0	.246
Montero, Fausto, Carmen	27	30	1	6	6	0	0	0	3	6	0	0	0	7	0	0	.200
Montoya, Saul, Campeche*	19	41	7	8	9	1	0	0	7	6	1	6	0	15	0	0	.195
Moreno, Eleazar, Campeche	12	21	2	4	4	0	0	0	2	5	0	2	0	6	1	0	.190
Moreno, Juan, Carmen	80	234	16	54	68	4	2	2	21	4	0	11	0	47	0	1	.231
Mota, Francisco, Carmen	24	37	5	4	5	1	0	0	2	3	0	4	0	12	0	0	.108
Munoz, Romulo, Tabasco	49	144	21	41	55	3	1	3	24	5	2	11	0	20	2	1	.285
Murrieta, Manuel, Carmen	43	119	4	25	30	3	1	0	9	2	1	7	1	32	2	0	.210
Nieblas S., Jesus, Tabasco	57	156	13	31	36	1	2	0	9	2	2	7	1	32	1	0	.199
Nieblas, Manuel de J., Cam	73	248	26	65	81	6	2	2	37	6	4	33	3	12	1	2	.262
Ochoa, David, P Mexico	91	317	60	90	151	12	8	11	63	2	7	26	3	52	15	9	.284
Orozco, Arturo, Campeche	95	268	45	60	100	20	1	6	38	2	4	50	11	71	8	6	.224
Orta, Jorge, Puerto Mexico*	18	43	6	13	14	1	0	0	3	0	0	2	0	7	6	1	.302
Osorio, Francisco, P Mex*	25	41	6	6	11	1	2	0	5	2	0	0	0	9	0	0	.146
Osorio, Raul, Carmen	24	35	2	2	2	0	0	0	2	0	0	3	0	11	0	0	.057
Osuna, Carlos, P Mexico	99	348	54	99	143	12	7	6	50	5	5	28	5	60	11	6	.284
Pacheco, Jesus, Campeche	12	19	3	2	2	0	0	0	0	0	0	5	0	5	1	0	.105
Pantoja, Fidel, Tabasco†	22	55	9	11	16	3	1	0	5	1	0	2	0	7	2	2	.200
Parra, Manuel, P Mexico	80	223	20	56	98	10	4	8	40	1	4	15	1	73	0	1	.251
Parra, Raymundo, Carmen*	20	42	1	7	9	0	1	0	4	0	2	2	11	0	0	0	.167
Pena, Hilario, Campeche†	24	84	13	24	26	2	0	0	11	3	3	12	0	7	1	1	.286
Peralta, Alfredo, Campeche	43	110	12	28	38	3	2	1	11	0	2	9	1	29	1	1	.255
Peralta, Luis, Campeche	93	312	62	105	164	17	0	14	65	9	5	42	3	41	5	5	.337
Peralta, Vicente, Tabasco	79	224	19	55	65	3	2	1	20	7	1	15	1	27	7	6	.246
Peraza, Alejandro, Carmen	18	24	2	3	4	1	0	0	3	0	0	1	0	9	0	0	.125

Player and Club	G.	AB.	R.	H.	TB.	2B.	3B.	HR.	RBI.	S.	SF.	BB.	HP.	SO.	SB.	CS.	Pct.
Perea, Francisco, Tabasco	15	10	2	3	3	0	0	0	0		0	0	2	0	0		.300
Perea, Tomas, Carmen	80	270	34	70	97	14	2	3	25		2	25	4	42	9	6	.259
Ramos, Roman, Carmen ..	25	15	0	0	0	0	0	0	0		1	0	3	0	0		.000
Raygoza, German, Tabasco	3	5	0	0	0	0	0	0	0		0	0	2	0	0		.000
Reyes, Benjamin, P Mexico	17	20	0	6	7	1	0	0	1		0	2	0	3	0	0	.300
Rocha, Jose Ramon, Carmen	17	13	1	2	2	0	0	1	0		0	2	0	4	0	0	.154
Rodriguez, Eduardo, Carmen	12	15	1	2	2	0	0	0	0		0	1	1	7	0	0	.133
Rodriguez, Federico, Car	108	380	30	87	109	12	5	0	30	6	4	44	3	40	6	7	.229
Rodriguez, Juan, Campeche	7	21	1	5	6	1	0	0	1		0	0	0	1	0	0	.238
Rodriguez, Manuel, Camp	6	8	0	1	1	0	0	0	1	1	0	0	1	0	0		.125
Rojas, Olinto, Campeche ..	38	125	16	34	56	3	2	5	23	1	1	9	3	18	0	3	.272
Romellon, Jose Angel, Car	.101	336	43	94	143	19	0	10	50	0	3	38	1	70	12	4	.280
Romero, Guadalupe, Tabasco	26	18	2	3	6	0	0	1	1	0	0	0	9	0	0		.167
Rosas, Clemente, P Mexico	66	230	36	63	106	11	7	6	36	2	2	21	3	36	3	3	.286
Ruiz, Roberto, Tabasco* ..	33	47	2	12	15	1	1	0	5	1	0	6	0	13	0	0	.255
Sainz, Roberto, Tabasco ..	12	12	0	0	0	0	0	0	1	0	0	1	0	6	0	0	.000
Salas, Jose Luis, Campeche	31	87	9	19	21	2	0	0	7	2	0	5	0	6	0	1	.218
Salazar, Mario, P Mexico	.102	344	41	100	131	13	6	2	56	5	7	29	1	29	13	9	.291
San Miguel, Jesus, Tabasco	31	23	0	1	1	0	0	0	0	2	0	4	0	5	0	0	.043
Sanudo, Hector, Carmen ..	19	61	10	18	28	4	0	2	11	0	0	15	1	6	1	1	.295
Simental, Ramiro, P Mexico	21	35	3	5	9	0	0	2	6	0	2	6	1	11	0	0	.143
Solano, Horacio, Tabasco .	10	19	1	3	3	0	0	2	1	1	4	0	2	0	0		.158
Sommers, Jesus, Carmen ..	20	73	9	16	26	4	0	2	9	1	0	10	1	15	3	3	.219
Tamez, Juan Jose, Campeche	77	272	42	54	74	6	4	2	22	5	0	30	5	71	12	4	.199
Tovar, Esteban, Campeche ..	9	12	0	2	2	0	0	0	0	0	0	0	4	0	0		.167
Urbano, Hector, Carmen ..	2	3	0	1	1	0	0	0	0	0	0	1	0	0			.333
Uzcanga, Carlos, Carmen ..	27	27	1	2	2	0	0	0	0	0	0	16	0	0			.074
Valenzuela, Hector, Camp ..	26	38	7	7	7	0	0	0	2	0	1	5	0	0			.184
Valenzuela, Humberto, PM*	10	20	1	2	3	1	0	0	2	0	1	5	0	0			.100
Valenzuela, Ramon, P Mex	24	39	1	5	5	0	0	0	4	0	1	8	0	0			.128
Verdugo, Enrique, Tabasco	105	350	35	71	78	3	2	0	23	13	1	21	6	37	6	2	.203
Verdugo, Froilan, Carmen .	11	18	0	2	4	0	1	0	0	0	3	0	13	0	0		.111
Villalobos, Lauro, P Mex	101	351	44	109	144	12	4	5	51	9	2	13	1	21	7	9	.311
Zatarain, Ariel, P Mexico .	6	10	0	0	0	0	0	0	0		0	0	6	0	0		.000

The following pitchers had no plate appearances (listed alphabetically by club, games in parentheses):

CAMPECHE—Gallegos, Gonzalo (1); Pastrana, Maximino (4).

PUERTO MEXICO—Mendiolea, Jaime (1).

GRAND-SLAM HOME RUNS—C. Espinosa, Herrera, J. Moreno, Rojas, Romellon, 1 each.

AWARDED FIRST BASE ON INTERFERENCE—None.

CLUB FIELDING

Club	G.	PO.	A.	E.	DP.	PB.	Pct.	Club	G.	PO.	A.	E.	DP.	PB.	Pct.
Campeche	105	2689	1056	129	73	16	.967	Carmen	109	2744	1161	152	52	14	.963
Puerto Mexico	103	2607	1152	146	87	8	.963	Tabasco	107	2677	1169	165	79	11	.959

Triple Plays—None.

INDIVIDUAL FIELDING
(Ten or More Games)

*Throws lefthanded.

FIRST BASEMEN

Player and Club	G.	PO.	A.	E.	DP.	Pct.	Player and Club	G.	PO.	A.	E.	DP.	Pct.
L. Peralta, Campeche	17	167	3	0	14	1.000	Romellon, Carmen	52	426	17	6	26	.987
Pena, Campeche	14	94	5	1	9	.990	Bouye, Carmen-Camp	25	186	9	3	17	.985
LOPEZ, P Mexico*	72	523	30	6	47	.989	Herrera, Carmen	48	401	27	7	17	.984
Camarero, Tabasco ..	14	81	8	1	10	.989	A. Peralta, Campeche	19	117	9	3	2	.977
Nieblas, Campeche ..	14	75	3	1	7	.987	Rojas, Campeche ..	37	271	12	7	26	.976
Garza, Tabasco ...	64	512	30	7	30	.987	Peralta, Tabasco ..	14	126	5	4	11	.970
Parra, Puerto Mexico	50	361	19	5	29	.987	Aguilera, Tabasco ..	11	90	5	7	8	.931

(Fewer Than Ten Games)

Player and Club	G.	PO.	A.	E.	DP.	Pct.	Player and Club	G.	PO.	A.	E.	DP.	Pct.
Verdugo, Carmen ...	5	37	1	0	1	1.000	Ferguson, Campeche	2	2	0	0	0	1.000
Murrieta, Carmen ..	5	20	0	0	0	1.000	Diaz, Tabasco	1	1	0	0	0	1.000
Gonzalez, Tabasco ..	1	12	0	0	1	1.000	Moreno, Carmen ..	6	47	3	2	0	.962
Verdugo, Tabasco ..	1	7	0	0	1	1.000	Almeida, Tabasco ..	9	63	4	3	3	.957
Rosas, Puerto Mexico	1	5	0	0	1	1.000	Mendez, P Mexico ..	1	1	0	1	0	.500

SECOND BASEMEN

Player and Club	G.	PO.	A.	E.	DP.	Pct.	Player and Club	G.	PO.	A.	E.	DP.	Pct.
BARAJAS, Campeche	99	238	217	10	47	.978	Bonilla, Carmen	88	228	189	16	31	.963
Orta, Puerto Mexico	13	26	16	1	8	.977	Pantoja, Tabasco ..	17	29	27	3	6	.949
Verdugo, Tabasco ...	82	232	188	13	37	.970	Figueroa, Carmen ..	26	47	42	7	5	.927
Flores, P Mexico ...	89	225	192	13	49	.970	Escamilla, Tabasco .	13	27	15	6	3	.875

(Fewer Than Ten Games)

Player and Club	G.	PO.	A.	E.	DP.	Pct.	Player and Club	G.	PO.	A.	E.	DP.	Pct.
Osuna, P Mexico .	9	23	17	0	6	1.000	Villalobos, P Mexico	3	5	8	2	1	.867
Pena, Campeche	5	10	9	0	0	1.000	Ochoa, P Mexico ...	4	9	7	3	1	.842
Sommers, Carmen .	1	2	1	0	0	1.000	F. Rodriguez, Car .	1	1	3	1	1	.800
Conkle, Campeche ...	7	13	8	2	3	.913							

THIRD BASEMEN

Player and Club	G.	PO.	A.	E.	DP.	Pct.	Player and Club	G.	PO.	A.	E.	DP.	Pct.
Sanudo, Carmen	19	20	46	2	2	.971	OSUNA, P Mexico .	86	70	186	22	12	.921
Guerrero, Carmen ..	15	15	24	2	0	.951	Pena, Campeche ..	12	10	24	3	1	.919
Contreras, Tabasco .	57	50	120	10	10	.944	Conkle, Campeche .	37	29	68	9	7	.915
L. Peralta, Camp ..	15	14	18	2	1	.941	Espinosa, Campeche	31	22	64	8	5	.915
Camarero, Tabasco ..	39	35	75	8	7	.932	Rosas, Puerto Mexico	17	10	32	5	2	.894
Figueroa, Carmen ..	48	31	99	10	9	.929	Salas, Campeche ..	20	11	22	5	2	.868
Peralta, Tabasco ...	13	10	15	2	2	.926	Perea, Carmen	14	9	15	4	0	.857
Sommers, Carmen ..	20	24	37	5	4	.924							

(Fewer Than Ten Games)

Player and Club	G.	PO.	A.	E.	DP.	Pct.	Player and Club	G.	PO.	A.	E.	DP.	Pct.
Solano, Tabasco	3	4	12	0	0	1.000	Jackson, P Mexico ..	1	1	0	0	0	1.000
Verdugo, Tabasco ..	2	1	6	0	1	1.000	Flores, P Mexico ...	5	4	11	2	0	.882
Aguilera, Tabasco ..	3	1	3	0	0	1.000	Ochoa, P Mexico ...	9	4	8	2	1	.857

SHORTSTOPS

Player and Club	G.	PO.	A.	E.	DP.	Pct.	Player and Club	G.	PO.	A.	E.	DP.	Pct.
Conkle, Campeche .	59	82	172	11	22	.958	Espinosa, Campeche .	50	80	122	19	19	.914
Contreras, Tabasco .	46	64	151	14	14	.939	Verdugo, Tabasco ...	20	26	27	5	6	.914
F. RODR'UEZ, Car	107	170	350	38	27	.932	Nieblas S., Tabasco	53	71	134	20	11	.911
Villalobos, P Mexico	97	206	322	39	48	.931							

(Fewer Than Ten Games)

Player and Club	G.	PO.	A.	E.	DP.	Pct.	Player and Club	G.	PO.	A.	E.	DP.	Pct.
Bonilla, Carmen	5	2	16	0	0	1.000	Osuna, P Mexico ...	8	5	21	3	4	.897
Orta, Puerto Mexico	3	3	12	0	1	1.000	Salas, Campeche ...	6	6	11	2	1	.895
Escamilla, Tabasco .	1	1	0	0	0	1.000	Flores, P Mexico ...	6	7	15	3	1	.880
Camarero, Tabasco ..	1	0	1	0		1.000							

OUTFIELDERS

Player and Club	G.	PO.	A.	E.	DP.	Pct.	Player and Club	G.	PO.	A.	E.	DP.	Pct.
Almeida, P Mexico .	18	32	2	0	0	1.000	Peralta, Tabasco	17	25	4	1	1	.967
Lopez, P Mexico* ..	19	24	2	0	0	1.000	Salazar, P Mexico ..	102	210	13	8	0	.965
Rosas, Puerto Mexico	18	20	1	0	0	1.000	Gutierrez, Carmen* .	94	179	10	7	1	.964
Osorio, Carmen	13	16	1	0	0	1.000	Perea, Carmen	66	137	7	7	0	.954
LARA, Tabasco	107	207	15	3	5	.987	Alvarado, P Mexico*	92	118	14	7	1	.950
Ochoa, Puerto Mexico	82	134	11	2	0	.986	Lopez, Tabasco	78	158	11	10	2	.944
Murrieta, Carmen ..	37	58	4	1	2	.984	Espinosa, Carmen ..	80	122	9	8	2	.943
Nieblas, Campeche .	65	115	10	3	3	.977	Parra, P Mexico ...	25	28	1	2	1	.935
Lizarraga, Campeche	34	74	3	2	0	.975	Aguilera, Tabasco ..	58	92	5	8	3	.924
Tamez, Campeche ..	72	133	8	4	3	.972	Romellon, Carmen ..	57	61	9	6	1	.921
L. Peralta, Camp ..	64	90	6	3	1	.970	Munoz, Tabasco	42	53	5	5	0	.921
Lopez, Campeche ...	80	153	6	5	1	.970	Bouye, Car-Camp ..	16	20	2	2	0	.917

(Fewer Than Ten Games)

Player and Club	G.	PO.	A.	E.	DP.	Pct.	Player and Club	G.	PO.	A.	E.	DP.	Pct.
J. Rodriguez, Camp	7	11	2	0	0	1.000	Flores, P Mexico ...	2	3	0	0	0	1.000
Camarero, Tabasco .	6	11	0	0	0	1.000	Gonzalez, Tabasco ..	1	2	1	0	1	1.000
Mere, Carmen	5	7	0	0	0	1.000	Garza, Tabasco	2	2	0	0	0	1.000
Gutierrez, Tabasco .	4	6	0	0	0	1.000	Ferguson, Camp ...	3	1	0	0	0	1.000
Cedillo, Carmen ...	5	4	0	0	1	1.000	E. Rodriguez, Car .	5	1	0	0	0	1.000
Villalobos, P Mexico	2	4	0	0	0	1.000	Jackson, P Mexico ..	5	9	0	1	0	.900
Reyes, P Mexico ...	2	3	0	0		1.000	Espinosa, Camp	8	5	0	1	0	.833

CATCHERS

Player and Club	G.	PO.	A.	E.	DP.	PB.	Pct.	Player and Club	G.	PO.	A.	E	DP.	PB.	Pct.
Cota, Carmen	29	136	14	2	0	4	.987	Gutierrez, Tabasco	83	471	76	10	16	7	.982
OROZCO, Camp .	91	539	64	9	6	12	.9852	Bouye, Car-Camp	20	103	24	3	0	2	.977
Moreno, Carmen	66	334	55	6	1	10	.9848	Rosas, P Mexico	37	175	20	5	1	3	.975
Jackson, P Mex .	70	340	38	6	5	3	.984	Peralta, Tabasco ..	22	111	23	6	0	3	.957
Ayala, Carmen ..	14	50	12	1	0	0	.984	Camarero, Tab ..	11	28	8	3	0	1	.923
A. Peralta, Camp	21	97	13	2	1	1	.982								

(Fewer Than Ten Games)

Player and Club	G.	PO.	A.	E.	DP.	PB.	Pct.	Player and Club	G.	PO.	A.	E.	DP.	PB.	Pct.
Osuna, P Mexico	5	24	1	0	0	2	1.000	Rojas, Campeche	1	2	0	1	0	1	.667
Gonzalez, Tab ...	2	3	1	0	0		1.000								

PITCHERS

Player and Club	G.	PO.	A.	E.	DP.	Pct.
Osorio, P Mexico*	18	3	30	0	2	1.000
Fabela, Campeche	17	4	24	0	0	1.000
Montoya, Campeche*	19	4	20	0	1	1.000
San Miguel, Tabasco	31	2	21	0	2	1.000
Parra, Carmen*	20	5	18	0	0	1.000
Peraza, Carmen	15	2	15	0	0	1.000
Mota, Carmen	23	5	8	0	1	1.000
Uzcanga, Carmen	27	3	10	0	0	1.000
Ek B., Campeche	32	2	11	0	0	1.000
Perea, Tabasco	15	0	12	0	0	1.000
Armas, P Mexico*	14	0	12	0	0	1.000
Lugo, Carmen	11	2	8	0	0	1.000
Moreno, Campeche	12	0	10	0	2	1.000
Arroyo, P Mexico	11	0	9	0	0	1.000
H. Valenzuela, PM*	10	2	7	0	1	1.000
Sainz, Tabasco	12	1	6	0	0	1.000
Galaviz, Camp-Tab	11	0	6	0	1	1.000
Ferguson, Campeche	22	7	33	1	3	.976
Simental, P Mexico	19	4	18	1	1	.957
Diaz, Tabasco	14	3	17	1	1	.952
Montero, Carmen	26	1	18	1	1	.950
Franco, Tabasco	22	3	15	1	0	.947
Castro, Carmen	21	4	12	1	0	.941
Cordero, Campeche*	36	1	24	2	0	.933
Ramos, Carmen	35	2	12	1	0	.933
Romero, Tabasco	26	2	11	1	0	.929
Valenzuela, Camp	23	2	11	1	0	.929
Mendez, P Mexico	25	6	19	2	1	.926
R. Valenzuela, PM	24	4	20	2	2	.923
Castro, Tabasco	22	7	31	4	1	.905
Mere, Carmen	26	10	21	3	0	.912
Arce, Tabasco	17	3	16	2	1	.905
Rocha, Carmen	17	1	8	1	0	.900
Armendariz, Tab*	16	2	7	1	2	.900
Ruiz, Tabasco*	27	3	21	3	1	.889
Guillen, P Mexico	17	3	13	2	1	.889
Mendiola, P Mexico	12	3	5	1	1	.889
Delfin, Tabasco	18	1	14	2	0	.882
Pacheco, Campeche	12	0	9	4	0	.692

(Fewer Than Ten Games)

Player and Club	G.	PO.	A.	E.	DP.	Pct.
Solano, Tabasco	6	0	13	0	1	1.000
Zatarain, P Mexico	6	1	6	0	1	1.000
Goycolea, Tabasco	7	2	4	0	0	1.000
Contreras, Carmen	5	1	5	0	0	1.000
M. Rodriguez, Camp	6	0	4	0	0	1.000
Tovar, Campeche	9	1	2	0	0	1.000
Burgos, Carmen	1	0	3	0	0	1.000
Camarero, Tabasco	2	1	1	0	1	1.000
Pastrana, Campeche	4	1	1	0	1	1.000
Reyes, P Mexico	8	1	1	0	0	1.000
A. Peralta, Camp	1	1	0	0	0	1.000
Flores, P Mexico	1	1	0	0	0	1.000
Rojas, Campeche	1	0	1	0	0	1.000
Jackson, P Mexico	2	0	1	0	0	1.000
Mendiolea, P Mex	1	0	1	0	0	1.000
Cordova, P Mexico	3	0	1	0	0	1.000
Villalobos, P Mex	2	0	1	0	1	1.000
Carrasco, P Mexico	8	1	11	1	1	.923
Fajardo, Campeche	9	1	6	1	0	.875
M. Lopez, Carmen*	9	0	5	1	0	.833
Raygoza, Tabasco	3	1	4	1	0	.833
Cota, Carmen	3	2	0	1	0	.667
Andrade, Campeche	5	0	2	1	0	.667
Lilly, Campeche	2	0	1	1	0	.500

The following players did not have any recorded accepted chances at the positions indicated; therefore, are not listed in the fielding averages for those particular positions: Alvarado*, p; Cedillo, 3b, p; Gallegos, p; J. Lopez*, p; Mendez, of; Mendiola, of; Nieblas S., 2b; Reyes, c; Sanudo, p; Simental, of; Urbano, p.

PITCHERS' RECORDS

(Leading Qualifiers for Earned-Run Average Leadership—108 or More Innings)

*Throws lefthanded.

Pitcher and Club	G.	GS.	CG.	ShO	W.	L.	Pct.	IP.	H.	R.	ER.	HR.	BB.	Int. BB.	HB.	SO.	WP.	ERA.
Ferguson, Campeche	22	19	14	4	13	6	.684	158	126	39	32	9	36	13	3	128	6	1.82
R. Valenzuela, P Mex	24	13	8	1	9	6	.600	118	100	43	26	2	31	1	8	48	2	1.98
Ruiz, Tabasco*	27	18	5	1	6	9	.400	130	127	55	30	3	25	1	1	77	5	2.08
Fabela, Campeche	17	17	6	3	8	4	.667	122	99	43	30	5	39	7	8	84	4	2.21
Simental, P Mexico	19	13	6	2	5	6	.455	108	90	41	27	4	50	1	5	60	6	2.25
Mota, Carmen	23	16	6	2	6	6	.500	108	116	48	29	4	36	3	3	80	3	2.42
Mere, Carmen	26	20	9	2	8	9	.471	153	151	71	45	4	50	7	5	101	6	2.65
Parra, Carmen*	20	17	7	2	7	8	.467	121	113	59	36	8	26	4	1	90	2	2.68
Castro, Tabasco	22	16	6	1	5	9	.357	110	93	53	34	2	41	4	4	76	7	2.78
Montoya, Campeche*	19	19	6	3	8	5	.615	127	104	64	41	6	62	7	6	114	7	2.91

Departmental Leaders: G—Cordero, 36; GS—Mere, 20; CG—Ferguson, 14; ShO—Ferguson, 4; W—Ferguson, 13; L—Arce, 10; Pct.—Valenzuela (Campeche), .818; IP—Ferguson, 158; H—Mere, 151; R— Mere, 71; ER—Mere, 45; HR—Ferguson, 9; BB—Montoya, 62; IBB—Ferguson, 13; HB—Fabela, San Miguel, R. Valenzuela, 8; SO—Ferguson, 128; WP—Rocha, 8.

(All Pitchers—Listed Alphabetically)

Pitcher and Club	G.	GS.	CG.	ShO	W.	L.	Pct.	IP.	H.	R.	ER.	HR.	BB.	Int. BB.	HB.	SO.	WP.	ERA.
Alvarado, P Mexico*	2	0	0	0	0	0	.000	⅓	0	1	0	0	1	0	0	0	0	0.00
Andrade, Campeche	5	0	0	0	0	1	.000	8	11	6	4	1	6	3	0	4	4	4.50
Arce, Tabasco	17	13	4	1	4	10	.286	92	96	39	27	1	36	8	6	55	1	2.64
Armas, P Mexico*	14	10	4	1	7	1	.875	85	79	15	12	3	8	1	0	38	1	1.27
Armendariz, Tabasco*	16	3	0	0	2	4	.333	36	46	21	14	0	14	3	1	24	4	3.50
Arroyo, P Mexico	11	4	2	0	2	3	.400	42	64	36	18	4	23	2	6	27	2	3.86
Burgos, Carmen	1	0	0	0	0	0	.000	5	2	1	1	0	1	0	0	0	3	1.80
Camarero, Tabasco	2	0	0	0	0	0	.000	2	1	0	0	0	0	0	0	1	0	0.00
Carrasco, P Mexico	8	6	4	0	6	1	.857	56	42	19	12	2	18	5	1	41	1	1.93
Castro, Tabasco	22	16	6	1	5	9	.357	110	93	53	34	2	41	4	4	76	7	2.78
Castro, Carmen	21	3	2	1	2	3	.400	70	85	38	24	4	17	4	2	30	3	3.09
Cedillo, Carmen	1	0	0	0	0	0	.000	2	5	3	3	0	0	1	0	5		13.50
Contreras, Carmen	5	4	0	0	1	1	.500	21	22	9	5	1	4	1	0	6	0	2.14
Cordero, Campeche*	36	1	0	0	6	7	.462	72	64	30	24	1	36	12	1	61	4	3.00
Cordova, P Mexico*	3	2	2	1	1	2	.333	17	16	3	2	0	3	0	1	19	1	1.06
Cota, Carmen	3	1	0	0	0	1	.000	5	8	3	3	1	5	0	1	5	3	5.40

Pitcher and Club	G	GS	CG	ShO	W	L	Pct.	IP	H	R	ER	HR	BB	Int. BB	HB	SO	WP	ERA
Delfin, Tabasco	18	8	3	1	5	4	.556	75	65	30	15	1	28	2	1	50	3	1.80
Diaz, Tabasco ..	14	11	4	1	5	4	.556	88	77	28	22	0	28	7	6	62	3	2.25
Ek B., Campeche	32	0	0	0	5	2	.714	60	46	9	7	1	19	10	0	39	1	1.05
Fabela, Campeche	17	17	6	3	8	4	.667	122	99	43	30	5	39	7	8	84	4	2.21
Fajardo, Campeche .	9	1	0	0	2	2	.500	32	29	11	5	0	10	2	0	14	2	1.41
Ferguson, Campeche .	22	19	14	4	13	6	.684	158	126	39	32	9	36	13	3	128	6	1.82
Flores, P Mexico	1	1	1	1	1	0	1.000	7	1	0	0	0	3	0	1	2	0	0.00
Franco, Tabasco ..	22	2	0	0	0	2	.000	35	51	35	22	2	20	1	1	16	5	5.66
Galaviz, 4 Cam-7 Tab	11	3	0	0	0	2	.000	28	33	15	11	1	11	5	0	15	2	3.54
Gallegos, Campeche .	1	0	0	0	0	0	.000	2	5	6	4	1	4	0	0	1	1	18.00
Goycolea, Tabasco ...	7	3	1	1	1	2	.333	22	21	10	7	0	11	3	4	12	3	2.80
Guillen, P Mexico	17	10	4	1	6	6	.500	75	69	34	19	1	35	2	4	41	4	2.28
Jackson, P Mexico ..	2	0	0	0	1	0	1.000	7	7	2	1	0	7	0	0	5	1	1.29
Lilly, Campeche	2	2	0	0	1	0	1.000	8	11	4	3	0	2	0	0	6	2	3.38
Lopez, P Mexico* ..	1	0	0	0	0	0	.000	½	0	0	0	0	0	0	0	0	0	0.00
Lopez, Carmen*	9	0	0	0	0	0	.000	16	29	18	13	3	7	0	0	6	0	7.31
Lugo, Carmen ...	11	5	0	0	0	5	.000	34	37	23	14	0	11	4	0	19	3	3.71
Mendez, Carmen .	25	11	3	1	4	6	.400	97	98	40	28	3	42	3	7	54	5	2.60
Mendiola, P Mexico	12	5	2	1	3	3	.500	36	43	21	19	2	9	1	2	20	2	4.75
Mendiolea, P Mexico	1	0	0	0	0	0	.000	2	2	2	2	0	1	0	0	1	0	9.00
Mere, Carmen .	26	20	9	2	8	9	.471	153	151	71	45	4	50	7	5	101	6	2.65
Montero, Carmen	26	15	1	0	6	6	.500	97	111	55	40	3	37	10	1	50	3	3.71
Montoya, Campeche	19	19	6	3	8	5	.615	127	104	64	41	6	62	7	6	114	7	2.91
Moreno, Campeche	12	11	5	2	6	2	.750	66	65	23	20	5	18	2	1	56	1	2.73
Mota, Carmen ...	23	16	6	2	6	6	.500	108	116	48	29	4	36	3	8	80	3	2.42
Osorio, P Mexico* ..	18	17	9	2	10	3	.769	107	106	36	29	5	32	2	1	64	4	2.44
Pacheco, Campeche	13	9	2	1	4	3	.571	61	51	22	13	1	31	2	0	42	2	1.92
Parra, Carmen*	20	17	7	2	7	8	.467	121	113	59	36	8	26	4	1	90	2	2.68
Pastrana, Campeche .	4	1	0	0	0	0	.000	4	6	1	1	0	1	0	0	2	1	2.25
A. Peralta, Campeche	1	0	0	0	0	0	.000	½	0	0	0	0	0	0	0	0	0	0.00
Peraza, Carmen ...	15	12	4	2	3	8	.273	78	74	34	17	2	28	7	0	30	0	1.96
Perea, Tabasco ...	15	6	1	0	1	4	.200	41	41	25	19	2	11	3	3	24	1	4.17
Raygoza, Tabasco ..	3	1	0	0	0	2	.000	10	5	8	5	0	9	1	1	4	0	4.50
Ramos, Carmen ...	25	0	0	0	5	4	.556	56	51	16	10	1	9	2	0	28	0	1.61
Reyes, Puerto Mexico	4	1	0	0	0	3	.000	22	31	18	13	2	9	1	0	8	0	5.32
Rocha, Carmen	17	10	1	0	2	3	.400	51	56	41	29	0	33	2	1	26	1	5.12
M. Rodriguez, Camp .	6	4	0	0	0	2	.000	23	34	16	11	0	9	2	4	7	1	4.30
Rojas, Campeche .	7	0	0	0	0	0	.000	3	1	1	1	0	1	0	1	1	0	3.00
Romero, Tabasco ..	26	7	0	0	1	7	.125	64	77	44	29	5	25	6	0	47	5	4.08
Ruiz, Tabasco*	27	18	5	1	6	9	.400	130	127	55	30	3	25	3	1	77	5	2.08
Sainz, Tabasco	12	2	0	0	0	2	.000	37	41	15	12	0	21	6	2	13	0	2.92
San Miguel, Tabasco	31	10	4	0	4	8	.333	98	93	40	31	5	27	6	8	42	3	2.85
Sanudo, Carmen	1	0	0	0	0	0	.000	½	0	4	0	0	0	0	0	0	0	0.00
Simental, P Mexico	19	14	6	2	5	6	.455	108	90	41	27	4	50	1	5	60	6	2.25
Solano, Tabasco	6	5	3	1	3	1	.750	36	39	16	10	1	7	3	1	10	0	2.50
Tovar, Campeche ...	9	6	2	0	2	1	.667	36	39	13	11	1	19	3	1	25	2	2.75
Urbano, Carmen	2	2	1	0	0	1	.000	8	11	6	6	1	4	1	1	8	1	6.75
Uzcanga, Carmen	27	4	3	1	8	3	.727	88	60	30	20	3	42	6	4	69	5	2.05
Valenzuela, Camp ..	23	14	9	1	9	2	.818	103	76	28	16	4	20	3	7	48	2	1.40
H. Valenzuela, PM* .	10	5	3	0	4	3	.571	57	66	26	17	3	17	2	2	25	1	2.68
R. Valenzuela, P M	24	13	8	1	9	6	.600	118	100	43	26	2	31	1	3	48	2	1.98
Villalobos, P Mexico	2	0	0	0	0	0	.000	4	4	1	1	0	0	0	0	4	0	2.25
Zatarain, P Mexico ..	6	4	0	0	0	0	.000	30	24	7	6	2	13	1	0	15	3	1.80

BALKS—Arce, 3; Guillen, Ruiz, 2 each; Diaz, Fajardo, Jackson, Montoya, Mota, Pacheco, Reyes, Romero, Uzcanga, Villalobos, 1 each.

COMBINATION SHUTOUTS—Lilly-Tovar-Cordero, Ferguson-Ek B.-Cordero, Fabela-Ek B.-Cordero, Fabela-Ek B., Campeche; Montero-Ramos, Ciudad del Carmen; Zatarain-Osorio-Guillen, Armas-Mendiola, Mendez-Arroyo, Puerto Mexico; Delfin-Arce, Tabasco.

NO-HIT GAMES—Montoya, Campeche, defeated Tabasco, 5-0, May 24. Ferguson, Campeche, defeated Puerto Mexico, 2-0, June 11 (seven innings)-(Perfect Game).

Midwest League

CLASS A

CHAMPIONSHIP WINNERS IN PREVIOUS YEARS

1947—Belleville	.667	1956—Paris y	.656	1963—Clinton	.710
Belleville	.672	Dubuque	.603	Clinton	.629
1948—West Frankfort*	.708	1957—Decatur y	.683	1964—Clinton	.667
1949—Centralia	.627	Clinton	.623	Fox Cities	.667
Paducah (4th)†	.454	1958—Michigan City	.623	1965—Burlington	.667
1950—Centralia‡	.675	Waterloo	.613	Burlington	.677
1951—Paris§	.700	1959—Waterloo	.613	1966—Fox Cities z	.689
Danville (4th)†	.432	Waterloo	.613	Cedar Rapids	.762
1952—Danville x	.685	1960—Waterloo	.629	1967—Wisconsin Rapids	.685
Decatur (3rd)†	.584	Waterloo	.677	Appleton z	.587
1953—Decatur*	.576	1961—Waterloo	.613	1968—Decatur	.656
1954—Decatur	.587	Quincy z	.594	Quad Cities z	.648
Danville (2nd)‡	.528	1962—Dubuque z	.667	1969—Appleton	.648
1955—Dubuque*	.587	Waterloo	.625	Appleton	.690

*Won championship and four-club playoff. †Won four-club playoff. ‡Playoff finals cancelled because of bad weather. xWon first half of split-season and tied Paris for second-half title. yWon first-half title and four-team playoff. zWon split-season playoff. (NOTE—Known as Illinois State League in 1947-48 and Mississippi-Ohio Valley League from 1949 through 1955.)

STANDING OF CLUBS AT CLOSE OF FIRST HALF, JUNE 27

Club	W.	L.	T.	Pct.	G.B.	Club	W.	L.	T.	Pct.	G.B.
Quincy (14*)	38	17	0	.691		Decatur (24*)	27	29	0	.482	11½
†Quad Cities (3*)	31	27	0	.534	8½	Wisconsin Rapids (9*)	27	31	0	.466	12½
Danville (Co-op)	32	28	0	.533	8½	Burlington (11*)	28	34	0	.452	13½
Appleton (4*)	32	30	0	.516	9½	Cedar Rapids (22*)	25	33	0	.431	14½
Clinton (8*)	31	30	0	.508	10	Waterloo (7*)	25	37	0	.403	16½

STANDING OF CLUBS AT CLOSE OF SECOND HALF, AUGUST 31

Club	W.	L.	T.	Pct.	G.B.	Club	W.	L.	T.	Pct.	G.B.
††Quad Cities (3*)	36	26	0	.581		Cedar Rapids (22*)	32	31	0	.508	4½
Decatur (24*)	36	26	0	.581		Danville (Co-op)	32	31	0	.508	4½
Wisconsin Rapids (9*)	32	29	0	.525	3½	Burlington (11*)	28	34	0	.452	8
Quincy (14*)	30	28	0	.517	4	Clinton (8*)	26	37	0	.413	10½
Appleton (4*)	32	30	0	.516	4	Waterloo (7*)	24	36	0	.400	11

‡Quad Cities defeated Decatur 8 to 5 on September 1 in playoff for second-half championship.

COMPOSITE STANDING OF CLUBS AT CLOSE OF SEASON, AUGUST 31

Club	Qui.	Q.C.	Dec.	Dan.	Apl.	W.R.	C.R.	Cln.	Bur.	Wat.	W.	L.	T.	Pct.	G.B.
Quincy (14*)		5	4	11	6	6	5	12	11	8	68	45	0	.602	...
†Quad Cities (3*)	7		10	6	9	6	6	5	10	9	68	53	0	.562	4
Decatur (24*)	8	5		5	8	6	10	5	7	9	63	56	0	.529	8
Danville (Co-op)	3	7	9		8	6	7	6	9	9	64	59	0	.520	9
Appleton (4*)	8	5	4	6		9	8	9	5	10	64	60	0	.516	9½
Wisconsin Rapids (9*)	6	5	7	8	5		8	7	9	4	59	60	0	.496	12
Cedar Rapids (22*)	5	8	4	6	6	6		6	7	9	57	64	0	.471	15
Clinton (8*)	2	9	7	8	5	7	4		5	6	57	67	0	.460	16½
Burlington (11*)	3	4	6	5	9	4	8	9		5	56	68	0	.452	17½
Waterloo (7*)	3	5	5	4	4	10	5	8	5		49	73	0	.402	23½

†Quad Cities represented Davenport and Bettendorf, Ia, and Moline and Rock Island, Ill.

Key to major league farm teams (indicated by numbers after clubs in standing) shown on Page 384.

Second-half championship game won-lost record included in composite standing for Quad Cities and Decatur. Game statistics also included in club and individual averages.

Playoff—Quincy defeated Quad Cities, two games to none.

Regular-season attendance—Appleton, 83,818; Burlington, 35,017; Cedar Rapids, 42,724; Clinton, 59,610; Decatur, 67,091; Davenport, 70,089; Decatur, 47,633; Quincy, 46,932; Waterloo, 33,541; Wisconsin Rapids, 45,579. Total, 532,034. All-star game, 1,228. Playoff, 2,758.

Managers: Appleton—Ira Hutchinson; Burlington—Roy Sievers; Cedar Rapids—Roy Majtyka; Clinton—Earl Torgeson; Danville—Bobby Bauer; Decatur—Frank Funk; Quad Cities—James (Mike) Stubbins; Quincy—Walt Dixon; Waterloo—Steve Boros; Wisconsin Rapids—John Goryl.

All-Star Team: 1B—Cooper, Danville; 2B—Ashford, Davenport; 3B—Ransom, Danville; SS—Hansen, Clinton; OF—Howard, Clinton; Bowen, Danville; Cain, Burlington; C—Davini, Appleton; Dusan, Burlington; Rodriguez, Decatur; P—Jones, Quincy; Stover, Quincy; Manager—Calo, Danville.

(Compiled by Howe News Bureau, Chicago, Ill.)

CLUB BATTING

Club	G.	AB.	R.	OR.	H.	TB.	2B.	3B.	HR.	RBI.	SH.	SF.	Int. BB.	BB.	HP.	SO.	SB.	CS.	LOB.	Pct.
Danville ...	123	3977	619	562	1050	1470	168	36	60	525	46	37	527	52	37	815	77	36	915	.264
Quad Cities	121	3929	530	490	978	1417	167	46	60	467	41	39	383	33	32	817	138	50	818	.249
Quincy ...	113	3631	510	413	895	1261	129	33	57	430	63	26	507	40	32	780	83	36	884	.246
Wis. Rapids	119	3844	510	531	938	1395	137	28	88	450	36	23	478	32	35	951	70	33	846	.244
Burlington	124	3992	460	547	959	1325	132	18	66	411	68	26	398	23	36	851	56	22	874	.240
Decatur ...	119	3838	442	478	916	1297	134	32	61	367	34	23	454	22	34	772	89	33	908	.239
Ced. Rapids	121	3819	430	450	908	1175	119	32	28	388	82	29	517	33	53	744	94	50	956	.238
Appleton ..	124	3989	451	475	946	1262	126	38	38	372	62	27	430	29	44	735	87	65	913	.237
Waterloo ...	122	3983	469	499	943	1333	147	39	55	392	46	23	430	29	41	840	50	28	920	.237
Clinton ...	124	3959	494	520	917	1318	152	33	61	427	34	33	494	39	35	987	121	40	906	.232

INDIVIDUAL BATTING
(Leading Qualifiers for Batting Championship—391 or More Plate Appearances)

*Bats lefthanded.   †Switch-hitter

Player and Club	G.	AB.	R.	H.	TB.	2B.	3B.	HR.	RBI.	SH.	SF.	BB.	HP.	SO.	SB.	CS.	Pct.
Cooper, Cecil, Danville*	114	420	86	141	182	16	8	3	39	4	3	57	2	65	28	12	.336
Bourque, Patrick, Quincy* ..	107	359	68	117	178	18	2	13	77	2	6	72	5	28	3	1	.326
McDonald, Ronald, Wis R ..	106	374	56	117	175	15	2	12	53	0	1	35	0	95	3	2	.313
Cunnigan, Donald, Danville .	119	429	86	133	201	25	5	11	67	1	4	52	6	75	8	5	.310
Ransom, Walter, Danville ..	123	459	91	141	161	14	3	0	38	6	1	72	3	60	17	4	.307
Howard, Wilbur, Clinton ...	117	469	70	142	182	17	7	3	34	1	2	34	5	90	40	13	.303
Bowen, Joseph, Danville ..	120	457	66	138	187	31	3	4	83	3	3	37	1	61	4	3	.302
Lombardo, Earl, Quincy ...	110	428	55	125	178	18	7	7	63	7	4	24	5	91	14	3	.292
Combs, Thomas, Waterloo ..	116	441	70	128	187	18	4	11	55	2	5	42	7	72	14	12	.290
Price, Michael, Cedar Rap ..	119	399	55	115	143	11	7	1	56	6	8	64	8	74	18	8	.288
Knight, Kenneth, Wis Rap* .	103	337	45	97	143	14	1	10	43	2	4	48	3	55	2	2	.288

Departmental Leaders: G—Cain, Ransom, 123; AB—Minor, 483; R—Ransom, 91; H—W. Howard, 142; TB—Cain, 203; 2B—Bowen, 31; 3B—Meoli, 12; HR—Cain, 23; RBI—Bowen, 83; SH—Minor, 12; SF—Ashford, Doherty, O. McCowan, 7; BB—Calderan, 77; HP—Isakson, 12; SO—Cain, 127; SB—Minor, 67; CS—W. Howard, Thomasson, 13.

(All Players—Listed Alphabetically)

Player and Club	G.	AB.	R.	H.	TB.	2B.	3B.	HR.	RBI.	SH.	SF.	BB.	HP.	SO.	SB.	CS.	Pct.
Abreu, Manuel, Cedar R ..	18	65	8	18	18	0	0	0	7	0	0	2	0	10	4	1	.277
Adams, Daniel, Clinton ...	69	256	29	61	77	6	2	2	17	2	2	17	1	34	6	3	.238
Agrella, Larry, Waterloo ..	40	116	8	25	31	6	0	0	13	2	2	13	2	22	0	0	.216
Alcaide, Jose, Clinton* ..	69	186	19	41	61	7	2	3	22	0	3	26	1	37	4	2	.220
Alger, Thomas, Cedar R. ..	22	28	2	5	6	1	0	0	3	5	1	1	0	9	0	0	.179
Almquist, Russell, Bur* ..	6	4	1	0	0	0	0	0	0	0	0	0	0	1	0	0	.000
Aloway, Tommy, Cedar R* .	37	116	13	22	34	6	0	2	11	0	1	11	1	32	0	2	.190
Arbogast, Richard, Quincy .	21	34	2	3	3	0	0	0	1	2	0	1	0	15	0	0	.088
Arteaga, Edito, Appleton ..	51	182	21	44	58	8	3	0	19	1	0	4	3	25	1	2	.242
Ashford, Sam, Quad Cities*	116	405	60	109	161	18	5	8	59	2	7	38	7	90	13	10	.269
Atkinson, Michael, Appleton	9	15	1	1	1	0	0	0	2	2	0	3	0	9	0	0	.067
Auerbach, Frederick, Clinton	28	117	26	38	48	5	1	1	5	0	0	12	1	12	16	1	.325
Auger, Robert, Cedar Rapids	10	31	3	6	11	2	0	1	1	0	0	0	0	12	0	1	.194
Austerman, Carl, Clinton ..	11	14	1	1	1	0	0	0	1	1	0	1	0	9	0	0	.071
Austin, Augusto, Danville .	116	367	46	95	137	16	4	6	42	8	2	48	4	60	2	4	.259
Autry, Albert, Waterloo ...	3	3	0	0	0	0	0	0	0	0	1	0	0	3	0	0	.000
Avila, Edgardo, Decatur* ..	115	424	55	114	182	17	6	13	68	0	4	50	3	42	9	5	.269
Bachman, John, Danville ..	47	97	7	22	29	2	1	1	18	1	3	21	4	20	0	0	.227
Bailey, Richard, Quad Cities	60	150	21	28	38	1	3	1	9	2	1	39	1	44	6	3	.187
Baker, Jon, Cedar Rapids .	5	1	0	0	0	0	0	0	0	0	0	1	0	0	0	0	.000
Bannon, Mel, Wis Rapids *	10	8	0	1	1	0	0	0	0	0	0	2	0	3	0	0	.125
Barnes, Richard, Quincy* .	10	1	0	0	0	0	0	0	0	0	0	0	0	1	0	0	.000
Barrientos, Virgilio, QC ..	20	18	1	1	1	0	0	0	0	0	0	5	0	8	0	0	.056
Beasley, Steve, Clinton* ..	18	31	3	5	6	1	0	0	3	0	0	5	0	13	0	0	.161
Beckett, Thomas, Decatur .	60	193	19	36	42	6	0	0	13	0	0	43	1	56	5	1	.187
Beebe, Kenneth, Cedar R ..	41	15	3	1	1	0	0	0	0	0	0	4	0	10	0	0	.067
Beech, F. Charles, Quincy .	31	99	14	23	42	7	0	4	19	0	1	12	1	21	3	1	.232
Bell, Jerry, Clinton	28	66	4	7	7	0	0	0	4	4	0	5	0	42	0	1	.106
Benedickt, Thomas, Quad C*	6	3	0	0	0	0	0	0	0	0	0	0	0	2	0	0	.000
Berg, Charles, Decatur* ...	24	70	3	15	15	0	0	0	3	1	0	9	0	14	0	0	.214
Biercevicz, Joseph, Quincy .	3	3	0	0	0	0	0	0	1	0	0	0	0	0	0	0	.000
Bigone, Vincent, Quad C* .	92	310	49	94	158	25	3	11	64	0	4	27	8	33	5	3	.303
Billmeier, Louis, Appleton .	15	10	2	4	7	0	0	1	3	0	0	0	0	2	0	0	.400
Bird, J. Douglas, Waterloo .	24	55	2	15	21	4	1	0	7	2	0	1	0	19	0	0	.273
Boehmer, Bernard, Bur	42	123	11	31	37	4	1	0	15	1	1	14	0	24	1	0	.252
Bourque, Patrick, Quincy* .	107	359	68	117	178	18	2	13	77	2	6	72	5	28	3	1	.326
Bowen, Joseph, Danville ..	120	457	66	138	187	31	3	4	83	3	3	37	1	61	4	3	.302
Brenner, Ronald, Burlington	12	6	0	1	1	0	0	0	0	0	0	0	0	2	0	0	.167
Breshears, Gary, Cedar R .	56	184	18	41	49	3	1	1	12	2	1	18	5	20	5	0	.223
Brooks, Michael, Wis Rapids	67	265	39	76	114	11	3	7	28	1	1	9	1	42	10	5	.287
Brown, Arthur, Cedar R ..	14	25	4	4	4	0	0	0	1	0	0	1	0	8	0	0	.160
Brown, Bruce, Danville* ...	28	53	7	17	18	1	0	0	2	0	0	8	0	13	0	1	.321
Brown, Richard, Cedar R* .	8	12	0	3	3	0	0	0	1	0	0	2	0	3	0	0	.250
Brown, Steven, Waterloo ...	3	1	0	0	0	0	0	0	0	0	0	0	0	0	0	0	.000
Bunch, Louie, Quad Cities .	2	3	1	0	0	0	0	0	0	0	0	0	0	0	0	0	.000

Player and Club	G.	AB.	R.	H.	TB.	2B.	3B.	HR.	RBI.	SH.	SF.	BB.	HP.	SO.	SB.	CS.	Pct.
Burgos, Jaime, Clinton*	14	10	1	0	0	0	0	0	0	0	0	0	0	5	0	0	.000
Burke, Patrick, Danville	41	70	16	16	30	2	0	4	14	2	0	5	0	19	0	0	.229
Burr, Clinton, Clinton	24	24	1	2	2	0	0	0	2	4	0	3	0	15	0	0	.083
Burrows, Robert, Waterloo	4	14	1	2	5	0	0	1	5	0	1	2	0	6	0	0	.143
Cain, Roger, Burlington	123	416	62	109	203	17	4	23	56	4	3	62	8	127	13	2	.262
Calderan, Kent, Cedar R.	103	316	48	78	94	7	0	3	28	6	4	77	6	51	9	6	.247
Campbell, Dayle, Quad C.	14	38	2	8	14	1	1	1	9	0	0	5	1	10	0	2	.211
Campos, Juan, Burlington	4	1	0	0	0	0	0	0	0	0	0	0	0	1	0	0	.000
Cassis, John, Quad Cities	96	302	40	79	108	10	5	3	26	0	3	35	1	49	5	0	.262
Caudell, William, Cedar R.	13	23	2	3	5	0	1	0	1	0	0	2	0	4	0	1	.130
Caudle, Kenneth, Decatur	27	100	11	20	26	3	0	1	6	0	0	6	2	18	3	0	.200
Cavanaugh, Michael, Wis R.	29	107	23	29	37	1	2	1	9	1	0	19	0	19	7	3	.271
Chaney, Charles, Burlington	39	137	18	40	63	8	0	5	19	0	2	8	1	47	8	2	.292
Chorley, David, Quad C.	116	419	51	113	161	26	2	6	63	2	5	38	3	78	11	3	.270
Ciganovich, Peter, Waterloo	30	14	1	3	4	1	0	0	2	0	0	0	0	3	0	0	.214
Clark, William, Appleton	25	60	5	15	23	3	1	1	4	1	0	7	1	12	0	0	.250
Clemons, Lance, Waterloo*	22	12	1	2	2	0	0	0	1	0	1	0	4	4	0	0	.167
Clouser, James, Quincy	14	30	8	8	10	0	1	0	4	0	0	12	0	7	0	2	.267
Coleman, Garrett, Burlington	6	16	0	3	3	0	0	0	2	0	0	0	0	1	0	0	.188
Collette, Steven, Quincy	107	413	63	115	146	9	5	1	46	4	2	55	1	55	18	7	.280
Collins, Garrett, Cedar R.	13	39	4	7	11	1	0	1	4	0	1	2	0	11	0	0	.179
Coluccio, Robert, Clinton	63	238	37	66	102	11	2	7	37	0	3	25	1	36	0	3	.277
Combs, Thomas, Waterloo	116	441	70	128	187	18	4	11	55	2	5	42	7	72	14	12	.290
Compton, R. Clinton, QC*	21	22	1	0	0	0	0	0	0	0	5	0	2	7	0	0	.000
Conzatti, John, Clinton	29	37	4	3	4	1	0	0	0	1	0	3	0	17	0	0	.081
Cooley, Stephen, Burlington*	31	95	10	20	30	1	0	3	11	1	0	16	2	12	0	1	.211
Cooper, Cecil, Danville*	114	420	86	141	182	16	8	3	39	4	3	57	2	65	28	12	.336
Cope, William, Wis Rapids	39	13	3	5	5	2	0	0	0	0	0	2	0	5	0	0	.231
Copeland, Howell, Burt	9	16	0	2	2	0	0	0	1	0	0	5	0	6	0	0	.125
Corder, Daniel, Quincy	34	35	2	2	4	0	1	0	1	2	0	3	0	17	0	0	.057
Corro, Alexis, Burlington	85	282	32	65	84	7	3	2	19	6	0	35	2	51	5	5	.230
Cotto, Jose, Cedar Rapids	76	220	17	61	75	7	2	1	29	5	2	13	4	15	1	1	.277
Coull, Dennis, Burlington	26	34	3	4	4	0	0	0	2	0	4	0	19	0	0		.118
Cromer, Charlie, Appleton	10	4	1	0	0	0	0	0	0	0	0	1	0	0	0	0	.000
Crossan, Marshall, Bur.	23	46	8	6	6	0	0	1	3	0	7	0	24	0	0		.130
Cruz, Hector, Cedar Rapids	24	41	8	6	8	0	1	0	1	0	0	10	2	14	0	3	.146
Cuddy, Fred, Cedar Rapids	15	42	3	11	12	1	0	0	6	1	1	2	0	5	1	0	.262
Cunnigan, Donald, Danville	119	429	86	133	201	25	5	11	67	1	4	52	6	75	8	5	.310
Curnutt, Ronald, Wis Rapids	14	10	0	3	3	0	0	0	2	0	0	0	0	4	0	0	.300
Daboll, Dennis, Cedar R.	18	12	1	2	2	0	0	0	4	1	2	1	0	6	0	0	.167
Daniel, Alan, Danville	13	10	0	1	1	0	0	0	1	0	0	0	0	3	0	0	.100
Darrow, Darrell, Quad C.	5	10	0	0	0	0	0	0	0	0	0	1	0	5	0	0	.000
Davies, Steven, Decatur	2	1	0	0	0	0	0	0	0	0	0	0	0	0	0	0	.000
Davini, Ronald, Appleton	91	331	37	75	106	10	3	5	29	3	3	27	6	43	10	3	.227
Davis, James, Quincy*	16	45	4	10	11	1	0	0	6	1	6	1	14	0	0		.222
Deck, Dennis, Appleton*	28	56	0	8	9	1	0	0	2	4	0	4	0	14	0	0	.143
Dehn, Gregory, Quad Cities	47	146	14	27	40	4	0	3	19	1	1	7	0	28	4	0	.185
Dent, Russell, Appleton	39	163	23	42	59	4	2	3	12	5	0	20	1	21	3	5	.258
Derr, Michael, Quincy	7	9	1	1	1	0	0	0	1	0	0	0	4	0	0		.111
Dick, Ralph, Wis Rapids	20	57	5	8	8	0	0	0	5	0	0	4	0	13	2	3	.140
Dickson, John, Quad Cities	17	38	3	11	15	2	1	0	4	0	0	1	1	5	1	1	.289
Distaso, Alec, Quincy	4	10	0	0	0	0	0	0	0	0	1	1	6	0	0		.000
Dixon, John, Waterloo	43	17	0	0	0	0	0	0	0	1	0	0	8	0	0		.000
Doherty, John, Quad Cities*	93	331	40	101	145	16	5	6	42	0	7	32	0	46	2	1	.305
Donahue, Patrick, Burlington	68	235	23	49	59	8	1	0	10	1	0	33	2	55	6	2	.209
Dunbar, Samuel, Appleton	9	16	2	2	2	0	0	0	1	0	1	0	0	6	0	0	.125
Dunham, Dale, Decatur	13	25	0	3	3	0	0	0	1	3	0	0	0	8	0	0	.120
Dunham, Donald, Cedar R.	12	23	3	4	6	1	1	0	1	1	0	1	0	6	0	0	.174
Dusan, Gene, Burlington*	63	207	18	54	61	4	0	1	16	7	0	15	3	35	1	0	.261
Dyson, Ronald, Cedar Rapids	22	84	13	21	25	4	0	0	11	0	0	5	0	17	0	0	.250
Edwards, Phillip, Wis R.	39	50	11	8	13	3	1	0	5	0	0	11	1	16	1	0	.169
Emerson, Neil, Wis Rapids*	30	12	4	2	3	0	0	0	0	0	0	2	0	5	0	0	.167
Erautt, James, Quad Cities	5	10	0	1	2	1	0	0	2	0	0	0	0	6	0	0	.067
Erickson, Virgil, Cedar R.	19	38	4	5	7	2	0	0	2	0	0	9	0	10	0	0	.132
Evans, Daniel, Danville	18	27	1	3	4	1	0	0	1	0	0	2	0	14	0	0	.111
Feldhaus, Timothy, Quincy	38	119	6	24	26	2	0	0	7	3	0	5	0	29	2	1	.202
Figueroa, Eduardo, Decatur	13	39	2	10	10	0	0	0	4	0	0	1	0	10	0	0	.256
Fitzgerald, William, Bur.	46	138	19	32	37	5	2	0	14	4	0	18	1	14	1	1	.232
Flanagan, Michael S., D*	35	52	7	11	11	0	0	0	5	0	1	12	0	6	1	0	.212
Flodin, Philip, Wis Rapids	21	53	2	8	9	1	0	0	5	0	1	2	0	22	0	0	.151
Floethe, Christopher, Bur.	16	29	1	5	5	0	0	0	1	0	0	0	0	13	0	0	.172
Florez, Roy, Cedar Rapids	5	8	0	0	0	0	0	0	1	0	0	0	4	0	0		.000
Forsch, Robert, Cedar R.	19	34	2	3	5	2	0	0	1	3	0	3	1	19	0	0	.088
Forster, Terry, Appleton*	16	28	2	6	7	1	0	0	5	2	0	0	0	2	0	0	.214
Foss, William, Quincy	58	170	10	39	58	7	3	2	27	2	2	9	0	36	1	0	.229
Franceschi, Stephen, Decatur	9	13	1	1	1	0	0	0	0	0	0	0	0	8	0	0	.077
Francingues, Wayne, Apple.	88	296	36	65	85	11	3	1	19	3	1	30	1	54	9	3	.220
Frost, David, Quad Cities	16	40	1	10	13	3	0	0	3	1	0	0	0	10	0	0	.250
Garcia, Pedro, Clinton	54	181	26	44	61	5	0	4	16	1	1	26	4	48	5	3	.243
Geiger, William, Burlington	40	33	0	5	6	1	0	0	1	0	0	1	0	14	0	0	.152
Geist, Robert, Cedar Rapids*	6	15	0	1	1	0	0	0	0	0	0	1	0	3	0	0	.067
Gideon, Dennis, Decatur*	28	5	1	1	1	0	0	0	0	0	0	0	0	4	0	0	.200

Player and Club	G.	AB.	R.	H.	TB.	2B.	3B.	HR.	RBI.	SH.	SF.	BB.	HP.	SO.	SB.	CS.	Pct.
Gills, C. Wayne, Cedar R†	10	1	0	0	0	0	0	0	0	0	0	0	0	0	0	0	.000
Glover, Jack, Burlington* ..	36	51	6	17	19	2	0	0	5	2	0	2	0	10	0	0	.333
Gonsalves, Larry, Decatur ..	28	75	4	7	8	1	0	0	3	2	0	5	1	31	0	0	.093
Gonzalez, Dionicio, Cedar R*	3	3	0	0	0	0	0	0	0	0	0	0	0	1	1	0	.000
Gossage, Richard, Appleton	10	9	0	1	1	0	0	0	1	1	0	2	0	6	0	0	.111
Groth, Robert, Quad Cities*	1	3	1	1	2	1	0	0	0	0	0	1	0	1	0	0	.333
Grout, Stanley, Waterloo ..	17	18	1	2	2	0	0	0	2	0	1	0	0	10	0	0	.111
Hale, Mark, Cedar Rapids* .	32	102	14	24	29	3	1	0	11	0	0	10	2	19	1	0	.235
Hamilton, Hugh, Decatur ...	9	7	0	0	0	0	0	0	0	0	0	1	0	6	0	0	.000
Hansen, Brian, Danville ...	30	95	13	25	32	2	1	1	13	0	2	7	1	19	0	1	.263
Hansen, Richard, Quad C ..	24	24	2	1	2	1	0	0	1	1	0	0	0	19	0	0	.042
Hansen, Robert, Clinton* ...	90	308	36	78	125	19	2	8	47	0	4	47	1	49	2	0	.253
Hansen, Terry, Decatur	28	64	8	9	11	2	0	0	5	2	1	3	0	17	0	0	.141
Hanson, Larry, Quad Cities	60	215	31	57	97	13	0	9	37	2	4	19	0	51	3	6	.265
Hardin, Steve, Wis Rapids	29	70	4	6	6	0	0	0	2	3	0	2	0	34	0	0	.086
Harkness, Michael, WR	18	3	0	1	1	0	0	0	0	0	0	0	0	0	0	0	.333
Harvey, Stephen, Clinton ..	21	38	2	4	4	0	0	0	1	4	0	5	0	21	0	0	.105
Haugen, David, Cedar R* ..	2	1	0	0	0	0	0	0	0	0	0	0	0	1	0	0	.000
Heath, Toby, Waterloo* ...	118	355	41	92	143	20	5	7	60	1	2	69	2	57	2	2	.259
Hebert, Gerald, Clinton ...	21	16	0	0	0	0	0	0	0	1	0	2	0	5	0	0	.000
Heinbechner, Bruce, Q C* .	38	56	8	17	26	6	0	1	7	0	0	3	0	13	0	0	.304
Heinitz, Michael, Burlington	31	16	0	3	3	0	0	0	2	0	1	1	0	4	0	0	.188
Henderson, James, WR*	29	42	1	5	5	0	0	0	0	3	0	0	0	19	0	0	.119
Hendrick, George, Bur	54	198	37	61	112	9	3	12	43	0	2	19	1	19	1	0	.308
Higgins, Joseph, Decatur ..	17	73	8	15	19	0	1	0	3	0	0	7	0	14	0	2	.205
Hill, Jesse, Quincy	22	47	4	7	12	0	1	1	6	4	0	4	0	29	0	1	.149
Hofvendahl, Herbert, C R	45	124	24	33	53	4	2	4	24	0	0	21	3	35	5	2	.266
Holbrook, Michael, Quincy	.85	249	49	52	98	11	4	9	32	3	0	42	4	99	7	3	.209
Hoppe, James, Wis Rapids	.115	425	65	118	189	20	6	13	57	3	5	53	4	84	21	2	.278
Hottman, Kenneth, Appleton	82	292	47	91	161	22	3	14	54	0	4	39	4	60	6	5	.312
Houston, Gary, Waterloo ...	6	8	2	2	3	1	0	0	3	0	0	2	0	5	0	0	.250
Howard, Douglas, Quad C	52	187	33	55	72	9	1	2	17	1	2	20	3	23	3	1	.294
Howard, Wilbur, Clinton	.117	469	70	142	182	17	7	3	34	1	2	34	5	90	40	13	.303
Isakson, Gary, Appleton	.100	355	43	81	106	13	3	2	18	3	1	35	12	72	10	10	.228
Isom, Curtis, Waterloo*	7	4	0	0	0	0	0	0	0	1	0	0	0	4	0	0	.000
Jackson, Cleothus, Appleton	10	4	0	0	0	0	0	0	0	1	0	0	0	3	0	0	.000
Jackson, Jimmie, Cedar R .	26	41	1	4	4	0	0	0	1	5	0	0	0	22	0	0	.098
James, Gary, Quincy†	15	16	1	1	1	0	0	0	0	1	0	0	0	5	0	0	.063
Jaycox, Gregory, Wis Rapids	25	52	8	11	16	2	0	1	5	7	0	1	0	15	0	0	.212
Johannes, Arnold, Wis R ..	29	65	4	10	14	1	0	1	5	1	0	1	0	22	0	0	.154
Johnson, James, A., Quincy*	50	132	13	29	30	1	0	0	11	5	1	16	1	22	2	0	.220
Johnson, Lamar, Appleton	7	13	0	3	3	0	0	0	0	0	0	1	0	0	0	0	.231
Jones, E. Dennis, Bur*	17	7	0	0	0	0	0	0	1	1	0	0	0	3	0	0	.000
Jones, Ronald, Quincy	21	48	5	12	15	1	1	0	7	0	0	5	0	14	0	0	.250
Jones, Terrell, Quincy*	19	36	3	4	7	0	0	1	4	0	1	13	2	18	0	0	.111
Jordan, Milton, Clinton	12	15	1	2	2	0	0	0	0	1	0	4	0	7	0	0	.133
Kapano, Randolph, Decatur	53	155	18	39	63	12	0	4	23	2	3	16	0	45	1	1	.252
Kelleher, Michael, Cedar R	59	188	23	50	66	10	3	0	27	4	3	25	5	17	6	5	.266
Key, Bobby, Cedar Rapids .	8	2	0	0	0	0	0	0	0	0	0	0	0	2	0	0	.000
Kimm, Bruce, Appleton ...	3	8	0	1	1	0	0	0	0	0	0	0	0	3	0	0	.125
Kissock, Larry, Clinton ...	49	67	4	17	19	2	0	0	6	0	0	12	0	18	0	0	.254
Kitchen, John, Cedar Rapids	9	3	0	1	1	0	0	0	1	0	0	0	0	2	0	0	.333
Kleckley, James, Waterloo†	28	30	2	2	2	0	0	0	2	3	0	2	0	13	0	0	.067
Knight, Kenneth, Wis R*†	103	337	45	97	143	14	1	10	43	2	4	48	3	55	2	2	.288
Koon, Eugene, Appleton .	45	9	0	1	1	0	0	0	1	0	0	0	0	3	0	0	.111
Kropfelder, David, Clinton	17	40	4	4	11	1	0	2	7	0	0	10	1	21	0	0	.100
Krumm, Richard, Decatur .	7	12	1	3	6	0	0	1	1	0	0	0	0	7	0	0	.250
Kurtz, Scott, Danville*	6	14	0	0	0	0	0	0	1	1	0	1	0	11	0	0	.000
LaCock, Peter, Quincy	18	13	3	1	1	0	0	0	2	1	0	3	0	1	0	0	.077
LaFrance, Robert, Danville	81	224	26	43	69	9	1	5	25	2	1	27	5	65	1	0	.192
La Gore, Philip, Burlington*	26	23	1	5	6	1	0	0	3	0	1	0	0	4	0	0	.217
Lambert, Thomas, Cedar R*	100	330	46	91	106	10	1	1	18	4	1	48	2	53	9	5	.276
Lasorsa, Joseph, Burlington	11	12	0	0	0	0	0	0	0	2	0	0	0	3	0	0	.000
Lawhorn, Leroy, Quad Cities	2	1	0	0	0	0	0	0	0	0	0	0	0	0	0	0	.000
Leifer, Clare, Decatur	72	204	14	56	65	5	2	0	11	0	1	21	4	42	3	0	.275
Limke, James, Appleton ...	3	4	1	1	2	1	0	0	0	0	0	0	0	3	0	0	.250
Lindsey, David, Danville*	101	253	37	69	99	15	3	3	39	1	4	26	3	41	6	1	.273
Linville, Larry, Appleton .	38	108	12	19	24	3	1	0	5	0	2	18	0	28	2	2	.176
Lizak, Steven, Waterloo ...	20	74	8	18	22	1	0	1	6	0	0	3	2	13	0	1	.243
Llanos, Rosario, Cedar R ..	21	47	6	11	16	2	0	1	5	0	1	0	0	13	0	0	.234
Lombardo, Earl, Quincy	110	428	55	125	178	18	7	7	63	7	4	24	5	91	14	3	.292
Loseth, Charles, Clinton ..	26	12	4	2	2	0	0	0	1	1	0	1	0	7	0	0	.167
Luck, Thomas, Waterloo ...	35	11	0	1	1	0	0	0	0	0	0	0	0	4	0	0	.091
Lundgren, Thomas, Quad C*	2	2	0	0	0	0	0	0	0	0	0	0	0	2	0	0	.000
Lundstedt, Thomas, Quincy	78	18	2	1	1	0	0	0	0	0	0	1	5	0	0	0	.056
MacDonnell, James, Apple*	12	16	1	1	1	0	0	0	0	0	0	4	2	12	0	0	.063
Mahoney, James, Appleton .	3	5	1	2	2	0	0	0	0	0	0	2	0	1	0	0	.400
Malone, James, Danville ...	25	36	3	7	7	0	0	0	2	4	0	3	0	22	0	0	.194
Mansfield, Larry, Danville*	57	158	26	31	69	3	1	11	32	0	4	32	0	51	1	0	.196
Mappin, Timothy, Wis R*.	84	273	28	68	89	5	2	4	32	1	2	40	6	39	7	5	.249
Marcano, Gilberto, Bur	7	13	1	1	0	0	0	0	1	0	0	0	0	4	0	0	.077

Player and Club	G.	AB.	R.	H.	TB.	2B.	3B.	HR.	RBI.	SH.	SF.	BB.	HP.	SO.	SB.	CS.	Pct.
Marceno, Carmine, Bur*	61	190	23	48	66	6	0	4	20	5	3	13	2	40	1	2	.253
Marikos, David, Quad Cities	2	3	1	0	0	0	0	0	0	0	0	1	0	2	0	0	.000
Marion, Gary, Cedar R*	57	169	23	37	51	6	4	0	21	4	3	40	3	24	2	2	.219
Marks, Gary, Cedar Rapids*	10	5	0	1	2	1	0	0	0	0	0	0	0	1	0	0	.200
Martin, M. Leroy, Danville	46	22	2	2	3	1	0	0	1	3	0	3	0	10	0	0	.091
Martorella, Michael, QC*	25	41	4	8	10	2	0	0	3	0	0	2	0	12	0	0	.195
Martz, Gary, Clinton	77	256	33	62	92	9	3	5	36	1	4	30	4	73	1	0	.242
Maselbas, Michael, Cedar R	25	47	10	9	16	2	1	1	3	2	1	3	1	14	0	0	.191
Massarand, William, Quincy	53	159	23	39	62	10	2	3	24	5	1	22	1	32	0	0	.245
Massaro, Leonard, Appleton	15	13	2	0	0	0	0	0	0	0	0	0	0	9	0	0	.000
Mata, Lazaro, Wis Rapids	25	78	9	13	16	3	0	0	4	0	0	9	1	27	0	0	.167
May, Edward, Danville	29	15	4	0	0	0	0	0	0	5	0	1	0	7	2	0	.000
May, Larry, Clinton	4	0	0	0	0	0	0	0	0	0	0	0	0	3	0	0	.000
McCartney, Stephen, Clin	76	264	27	51	82	18	2	3	36	3	5	25	1	82	4	2	.193
McCowan, John, Quad Cities	36	61	15	12	17	1	2	0	1	0	0	6	0	15	3	2	.197
McCowan, Odis, Clinton	108	374	55	91	134	16	3	7	47	0	7	66	3	72	24	7	.243
McDonald, Ronald, Wis R	106	374	56	117	175	18	2	12	53	0	1	35	2	95	3	2	.313
McFarland, Edward, Water	47	132	17	27	35	4	2	0	12	1	1	23	0	27	0	0	.205
McGowen, Cecil, Cedar R	8	3	0	0	0	0	0	0	0	0	0	0	0	2	0	0	.000
McGrath, Michael, Waterloo*	22	45	2	5	7	2	0	0	1	2	0	3	0	10	0	0	.111
McKinley, Donald, Waterloo	20	52	5	5	6	1	0	0	4	0	1	9	0	24	0	0	.096
McTheny, Guy, Clinton	20	51	6	13	20	3	2	0	8	0	0	11	0	9	0	0	.255
Medlock, Kennard, Decatur	61	142	20	38	54	7	0	3	9	0	0	9	1	35	0	0	.268
Meier, F. Calvin, Waterloo	20	74	7	19	24	3	1	0	7	1	0	16	0	14	3	0	.257
Meier, Richard, Burlington*	31	80	7	16	24	2	0	2	9	1	2	12	0	23	1	0	.200
Melum, David, Appleton	6	23	3	5	6	1	0	0	1	0	0	1	0	6	0	1	.217
Meoli, Rudolph, Quad C*	110	400	56	103	165	14	12	8	59	1	4	52	1	74	15	5	.258
Merkerson, Gregory, Apple	17	46	6	10	13	0	0	1	4	0	1	5	0	9	3	1	.217
Meyer, John, Quincy*	28	24	0	4	4	0	0	0	3	1	1	0	0	8	0	0	.167
Meyer, Russell, Waterloo	65	172	20	28	41	4	3	1	16	0	0	26	3	35	0	1	.163
Miali, Thomas, Quad Cities	25	11	1	2	3	1	0	0	1	0	0	0	0	4	0	0	.182
Miklos, John, Clinton*	11	12	0	2	2	0	0	0	2	1	0	3	1	6	0	0	.167
Millan, Jorge, Cedar Rapids	2	2	0	0	0	0	0	0	0	0	0	0	0	1	0	0	.000
Mingo, Ronald, Danville	34	64	5	13	17	4	0	0	5	0	0	1	3	25	1	0	.203
Minor, Roger, QC	121	483	81	102	117	9	3	0	25	12	1	32	5	97	67	11	.211
Monty, Joseph, Appleton	37	133	12	32	45	3	2	2	18	0	2	9	4	16	3	1	.241
Morelli, Michael, Clinton	2	9	0	0	0	0	0	0	0	0	0	0	0	0	0	0	.000
Morgan, Philip, Danville	34	122	13	38	50	4	1	2	22	1	4	13	0	12	0	0	.309
Mottine, James, Quincy	22	12	2	1	1	0	0	0	0	0	0	0	0	5	0	0	.083
Muir, Brian, Clinton	7	15	2	4	6	2	0	0	1	0	0	0	0	2	0	0	.267
Mullen, Michael, Quincy	14	6	0	2	2	0	0	0	0	0	0	0	0	2	0	1	.333
Murnahan, Phillip, Bur	25	18	0	1	1	0	0	0	0	2	0	1	0	8	1	0	.056
Nasif, Ralph, Wis Rapids	49	190	28	60	71	4	2	1	18	4	0	28	0	35	3	2	.316
Nichols, George L., Waterloo	11	44	10	13	19	1	1	1	2	0	0	1	1	8	4	0	.295
Nicholson, Theodore, Appleton	36	125	9	25	29	4	0	0	11	0	2	8	1	40	2	0	.200
Nixon, John, Cedar Rapids	52	139	21	30	42	3	0	3	16	3	0	37	5	34	2	7	.216
North, William, Quincy	42	144	31	42	66	6	3	4	10	1	1	44	4	33	15	5	.292
Nunn, Joseph, Waterloo	33	65	0	9	9	0	0	0	1	3	0	1	0	13	0	0	.138
O'Brien, K. Michael, Dec	6	3	0	0	0	0	0	0	0	0	0	1	0	1	0	0	.000
Olson, Martin, Burlington	2	9	1	1	1	0	0	0	1	0	1	0	2	0	0	0	.111
O'Neil, Phillip, Cedar R*	6	14	2	3	3	0	0	0	3	0	0	4	0	5	0	0	.214
O'Neill, Raymond, WR*	22	53	7	12	19	2	1	1	3	0	0	1	0	15	0	0	.226
Ontiveros, Steven, Decatur	117	417	64	114	176	23	3	11	52	0	2	65	3	78	4	0	.273
Opatkiewicz, Ronald, Wat*	115	393	41	75	91	8	1	2	24	1	2	43	4	57	4	2	.191
Ortiz, Reyes, Burlington	84	266	25	58	81	8	0	5	29	0	1	16	0	24	0	1	.218
O'Sullivan, Barry, Appleton	22	87	10	21	34	4	3	1	11	2	0	7	0	20	0	0	.241
Paganucci, Allan, Appleton	16	13	1	3	4	1	0	0	1	0	0	0	0	6	0	0	.231
Parent, Gerald, Cedar Rapids	20	1	0	0	0	0	0	0	0	1	0	0	0	0	0	0	.000
Pasierb, Louis, Decatur*	9	13	2	2	5	0	0	1	2	0	0	3	0	2	0	0	.154
Pastrovich, Mark, WR*	7	2	0	0	0	0	0	0	0	0	0	1	0	1	0	0	.000
Pavlik, Martin, 9QC—4Dec*	13	6	2	1	1	0	0	0	0	1	0	1	0	1	0	0	.167
Payne, Arthur, Waterloo	9	17	0	1	1	0	0	0	1	2	0	1	0	5	0	0	.059
Peden, Michael, Burlington	4	3	0	1	1	0	0	0	0	1	0	0	0	0	0	0	.333
Perzanowski, Stanley, Apl	23	44	2	6	6	0	0	0	1	5	0	3	0	17	0	0	.136
Pettaway, Nathaniel, Apl*	15	37	3	8	10	2	0	0	1	0	0	11	0	15	1	1	.216
Pettigrew, Melvin, CR	35	117	17	33	53	2	3	4	13	1	0	18	1	27	8	2	.282
Pettis, Robert, Waterloo*	5	4	2	1	1	0	0	0	0	0	0	1	1	1	0	0	.250
Phillips, H. Dale, Waterloo	53	210	31	67	91	8	2	2	29	2	3	24	2	46	2	0	.319
Plummer, R. Wayne, 7 Decatur—12 WR	19	5	2	0	0	0	0	0	0	0	0	2	0	4	0	0	.000
Poepping, Michael, WR	17	44	7	8	14	1	1	1	7	0	0	9	0	21	0	0	.182
Poris, Barry, CR*	43	131	15	30	39	6	0	1	15	1	0	23	0	28	5	1	.229
Porter, Darrell, Clinton*	62	185	24	37	60	11	0	4	21	0	1	50	1	52	1	2	.200
Price, Jack, Cedar Rapids.*	10	1	1	1	1	0	0	0	0	0	0	0	0	0	0	0	1.000
Price, Michael, CR	119	399	55	115	143	11	7	1	56	6	6	64	8	74	18	8	.288
Primeau, Dennis, Burlington	53	203	23	50	66	8	1	2	25	3	2	29	3	51	4	4	.246
Pryor, Paul J., Quad Cities	24	43	4	5	9	0	0	1	2	0	1	0	8	0	0	0	.116
Ransom, Walter, Danville	.123	459	91	141	161	14	3	0	38	6	1	72	3	60	17	4	.307
Redmon, James, Appleton	9	40	9	10	18	0	1	2	5	0	0	0	0	4	0	0	.250
Reid, James D., Wat*	9	8	0	1	1	0	0	0	1	0	0	1	0	5	0	0	.125
Reid, Roger, Appleton	94	304	37	70	82	8	2	0	26	5	3	48	1	29	9	8	.230
Reser, Philip, Quincy*	54	186	31	53	73	11	0	3	16	3	1	29	1	31	5	2	.285

Player and Club	G.	AB.	R.	H.	TB.	2B.	3B.	HR.	RBI.	SH.	SF.	BB.	HP.	SO.	SB.	CS.	Pct.
Riggin, Nathaniel, Waterloo	7	16	1	3	4	1	0	0	0	0	0	1	0	5	1	0	.188
Riggins, Franklin, QC*	8	20	3	7	8	1	0	0	2	0	0	6	0	5	1	1	.350
Rinaldi, Eugene, Decatur	77	317	44	80	95	6	3	1	12	4	1	22	2	35	5	3	.252
Rivera, Emiliano, Decatur	17	27	0	3	3	0	0	0	2	0	2	2	0	13	0	0	.111
Rivera, Jorge, Waterloo	95	355	40	97	123	15	4	1	16	1	0	17	3	44	3	3	.273
Robinson, Allen, Quincy*	19	68	10	22	31	1	1	2	5	0	0	9	0	11	3	2	.324
Robinson, Joseph, Bur	120	458	47	119	139	15	1	1	45	11	5	28	2	74	5	1	.260
Rodriguez, Adriano, Decatur	64	207	15	58	79	9	3	2	28	3	3	11	0	25	1	0	.280
Rodriguez, Anthony, Apl	5	10	1	2	2	0	0	0	2	0	0	1	0	4	0	0	.200
Roe, Michael, Quincy	16	17	2	2	3	1	0	0	2	0	4	0	5	0	0	.118
Rosello, David, Quincy	51	165	33	42	60	6	0	4	16	0	1	25	2	21	5	1	.255
Ross, Douglas, Quincy*	23	12	3	3	3	0	0	0	4	4	0	3	0	4	0	0	.250
Ryan, Dana, Appleton*	49	179	19	53	63	6	2	0	17	2	1	14	1	6	7	4	.296
Rybicki, Lawrence, Danville	4	3	0	1	2	1	0	0	1	0	0	0	0	0	0	0	.333
Sabourin, Jerry, CR*	4	1	0	0	0	0	0	0	0	0	0	0	0	0	0	0	.000
Sagaser, David, CR*	8	5	1	3	4	1	0	0	2	0	0	1	0	2	0	0	.600
St. Clair, Ronnie, QC	6	4	0	0	0	0	0	0	0	0	0	0	0	4	0	0	.000
Salado, Jose, Clinton	80	232	27	51	64	7	3	0	21	1	0	35	3	45	2	1	.220
Salata, Stephen, Quincy	74	214	21	44	54	8	1	0	22	2	2	39	1	60	1	0	.206
Sanchez, Porfirio, Clinton	40	21	1	3	5	2	0	0	0	0	0	0	0	6	0	0	.143
Sandt, Thomas, Burlington	26	118	18	34	38	4	0	0	4	0	0	5	1	11	7	0	.288
Sankey, Robert, CR	28	69	12	10	13	1	1	0	1	2	0	12	0	13	6	1	.145
Sapp, Ross, Appleton*	90	307	38	81	97	3	5	1	30	7	4	23	2	36	12	4	.264
Schell, Robert, Quincy	10	24	1	2	2	0	0	0	0	0	1	0	7	0	0	.083
Schroeder, Richard, Dec*	59	197	9	29	39	3	2	1	8	5	1	22	1	53	2	1	.147
Scott, J. Marlyn, WR	86	252	19	45	56	8	0	1	19	4	2	42	3	53	0	1	.179
Sennett, Edward, Decatur	9	3	1	1	1	0	0	0	1	0	0	0	0	0	0	0	.333
Shafer, John, Waterloo*	52	146	10	27	31	1	0	1	5	2	0	10	5	21	1	2	.185
Shaffer, Duane, Appleton	27	50	6	7	14	1	0	2	6	4	0	3	0	26	0	0	.140
Shearer, John, Burlington*	6	2	0	0	0	0	0	0	0	0	0	0	0	0	0	0	.000
Shields, Michael, WR*	15	3	0	0	0	0	0	0	0	0	0	0	0	2	0	0	.000
Shotts, Ronnie, WR	100	254	49	57	117	7	4	15	51	0	4	60	7	100	2	2	.224
Singleton, Stuart, Appleton*	115	381	30	90	111	9	3	2	35	2	2	64	5	70	4	9	.236
Siracusa, Edward, Waterloo	.110	388	50	94	143	22	3	7	48	2	3	25	1	84	3	0	.242
Skogan, Thor, 20Dan-15QC	35	47	2	4	5	1	0	0	2	0	3	0	16	0	0	.085
Slaton, James, Clinton	2	7	2	2	2	0	0	0	2	1	0	0	0	0	0	.286
Smith, Patrick, WR	82	249	32	56	77	12	0	3	20	4	1	31	3	47	4	0	.225
Smith, Thomas, Burlington	9	15	2	0	0	0	0	0	0	2	0	1	0	3	0	0	.000
Spain, Donald, Decatur	20	34	3	3	3	0	0	0	2	1	0	0	1	12	0	0	.088
Spanich, Stephen, Appleton	13	26	3	7	7	0	0	0	4	0	0	3	0	4	0	0	.269
Speed, Horace, Decatur	109	363	46	96	153	14	5	11	46	0	4	50	7	94	12	7	.264
Spellman, T. Michael, QC*	43	17	1	1	1	0	0	0	2	0	3	0	9	0	0	.059
Sperry, Paul, Decatur	25	5	0	1	1	0	0	0	1	0	0	2	0	3	0	0	.200
Stankey, John, Waterloo	106	350	57	97	157	19	7	9	49	5	2	58	4	66	6	1	.277
Stedman, James, CR	10	21	1	2	3	1	0	0	1	0	0	0	8	0	0	.095
Steele, Clyde, Danville*	7	3	0	0	0	0	0	0	0	0	0	1	0	2	0	0	.000
Stewart, Ronald, Danville*	21	15	2	1	1	0	0	0	0	0	0	0	0	5	0	0	.067
Stover, Joseph, Quincy	26	6	4	3	3	0	0	0	1	3	0	1	0	3	0	0	.500
Streett, Edward, Danville	29	12	0	0	0	0	0	0	0	0	1	1	8	0	0	.000
Sulprizio, Scott, CR	79	251	24	58	73	11	2	0	23	6	1	21	1	51	5	0	.231
Suzuki, Hiroshi, Decatur*	15	18	0	2	2	0	0	0	0	0	1	2	7	0	0	.111
Swain, Ralph M., Clinton	18	14	1	5	9	1	0	1	6	2	0	1	0	4	0	0	.357
Talley, Joseph, Appleton	33	111	13	32	39	5	1	0	13	0	0	23	0	22	2	3	.288
Tanner, James, Danville	53	127	19	26	37	4	2	1	11	0	0	21	2	41	8	2	.205
Tatom, Patrick, Burlington	9	8	2	2	2	0	0	0	0	0	0	0	0	3	0	0	.250
Tecklenberg, Jeffrey, Wat*	3	1	0	0	0	0	0	0	0	0	0	0	0	0	0	0	.000
Texdahl, David, Bur	81	259	36	64	88	15	0	3	31	3	0	37	4	48	1	0	.247
Texidor, Estaban, Quincy	13	29	4	4	6	2	0	0	0	0	0	2	0	5	0	0	.138
Thomas, James G., Clinton	85	297	35	63	100	5	4	8	39	1	1	30	1	98	7	3	.212
Thomasson, Gary, Decatur*	115	424	76	115	169	18	4	8	53	2	2	65	2	56	37	13	.271
Thompson, John, Waterloo	76	230	31	60	96	6	3	8	28	1	1	25	2	81	6	3	.261
Todd, James, Quincy*	11	26	3	6	8	2	0	0	1	3	0	1	0	9	0	0	.231
Torres, Gilberto, Quad Cities	21	30	4	13	18	1	2	0	5	0	0	0	0	5	0	0	.433
Traffenstedt, Jack, Bur	3	11	1	4	4	0	0	0	1	0	0	1	0	0	0	0	.364
Travers, William, Clinton*	10	13	0	2	2	0	0	0	0	0	2	0	1	0	7	0	0	.154
Tucker, Wayne, Danville	18	41	4	7	12	3	1	0	5	0	1	8	1	17	0	2	.171
Tuley, Terry, Quad Cities	31	23	2	2	5	0	0	1	2	1	0	5	0	10	0	1	.087
Van Camp, Charles, Dan*	96	284	50	67	109	14	2	8	50	1	3	66	1	61	5	1	.236
Vandehey, Michael, Apl*	3	1	0	0	0	0	0	0	0	0	0	0	0	0	0	0	.000
Velazquez, Carlos, Clinton	29	19	4	5	5	0	0	0	1	0	3	0	4	0	0	.263
Vicente, Juan, CR†	1	4	0	0	0	0	0	0	0	0	0	0	0	2	0	0	.000
Waln, Hugh, Waterloo*	18	19	0	2	2	0	0	0	0	0	0	2	0	12	0	0	.105
Walter, Robert, WR*	76	242	23	54	76	11	1	3	27	1	1	27	3	44	5	2	.223
Ward, Chris, Quincy*	70	226	26	51	60	7	1	0	15	3	1	42	1	21	4	7	.226
Warner, Fred, Cedar Rapids	13	12	1	1	1	0	0	0	0	3	0	0	0	4	0	0	.083
Weimer, George, Appleton	10	1	0	0	0	0	0	0	0	0	1	0	0	0	0	0	.000
Wells, Allen, Waterloo	12	39	3	10	11	1	0	0	0	1	0	2	1	6	1	0	.256
Westerhouse, Charles, Dan	19	13	1	1	1	0	0	0	0	2	0	1	0	9	0	0	.077
Whitley, Buddy, WR	82	259	37	62	118	13	2	13	48	1	0	37	1	89	2	4	.239
Williams, Charles E., Clin	.25	65	4	9	19	4	0	2	5	0	0	4	0	33	0	0	.138
Williams, James, CR†	57	212	27	59	77	8	2	2	25	2	2	19	3	19	1	2	.278
Williams, Robert, Burlington	3	11	1	3	3	0	0	0	3	0	0	2	0	3	0	0	.273

Player and Club	G.	AB.	R.	H.	TB.	2B.	3B.	HR.	RBI.	SH.	SF.	BB.	HP.	SO.	SB.	CS.	Pct.
Williamson, Michael, Bur	61	198	22	45	68	8	3	3	22	1	2	12	3	49	1	1	.227
Woods, Gary, Decatur	70	205	18	45	62	8	0	3	14	4	1	38	4	35	0	0	.220
Yancy, Hugh, Appleton	28	74	12	21	22	1	0	0	10	1	0	19	0	9	4	2	.284
Yard, Dennis, Clinton	2	3	0	0	0	0	0	0	0	0	0	1	0	3	0	0	.000
Young, Richard, QC*	30	37	3	6	8	0	1	0	3	2	0	3	0	11	0	1	.162
Zontini, Anthony, Waterloo	23	55	4	9	16	0	2	1	3	1	0	6	0	16	0	0	.164

The following players had no plate appearances (listed alphabetically by club, games in parentheses):

APPLETON—Kenary, Adrian (3).
BURLINGTON—Thomas, Darryl* (2).
CEDAR RAPIDS—Valdes, Juan (1); Velazquez, Anastasio (7).
CLINTON—McGrath, Garry (5).
DECATUR—Hiranuma, Kazuo† (12); Huff, James (1); McAlpine, William (3).
QUAD CITIES—Stubbins, James (1).
WATERLOO—Hein, Rex (1); Pounders, Fredrick* (1).
WISCONSIN RAPIDS—Farmer, Clifford† (6).
GRAND-SLAM HOME RUNS—Holbrook, 2; Austin, Beech, Burrows, Cunnigan, LaFrance, Mansfield, Mappin, McCartney, O. McCowan, Shotts, Siracusa, Texdahl, J. Thomas, Whitley, 1 each.
AWARDED FIRST BASE ON INTERFERENCE—B. Hansen 2, (Bigone, Dusan); Cain (Arteaga), Cunnigan (Salata), Francingues (Salata), LaFrance (Foss), Mappin (Salata), Marion (Dusan), Maselbas (Salado), McCartney (LaFrance), Pettis (Arteaga), Wells (Boehmer).
The following players are listed in the batting averages, but have no chances in the field: Baker, S. Brown, Davies, Hein, Huff, McAlpine, G. McGrath, Millan, Morelli, Peden, Pounders, Stubbins, Vandehey.

CLUB FIELDING

Club	G.	PO.	A.	E.	DP.	PB.	Pct.	Club	G.	PO.	A.	E.	DP.	PB.	Pct.
Cedar Rapids .121	3041	1154	145	86	28	.967	Danville	123	3106	1247	206	89	35	.955
Waterloo	122	3110	1211	175	101	37	.961	Quincy	113	2917	1256	202	90	20	.954
Quad Cities .121	3102	1235	182	106	38	.960	Decatur	119	3020	1267	208	88	31	.954
Clinton	124	3137	1178	185	96	37	.959	Wis Rapids	119	3058	1348	226	93	33	.951
Appleton	124	3205	1343	197	99	27	.958	Burlington	124	3162	1160	239	96	23	.948

Triple Plays—None.

INDIVIDUAL FIELDING
(Ten or More Games)

*Throws lefthanded.
FIRST BASEMEN

Player and Club	G.	PO.	A.	E.	DP.	Pct.	Player and Club	G.	PO.	A.	E.	DP.	Pct.
Collins, Cedar R	10	64	5	0	6	1.000	M. Price, Cedar R	17	147	7	3	8	.981
Bourque, Quincy*	61	529	36	4	42	.993	McDonald, Wis R	49	451	27	10	36	.980
O'Sullivan, Appleton	12	99	8	1	6	.991	Martorella, Quad C*	10	47	1	1	2	.980
Davis, Quincy*	13	93	7	1	13	.990	Walter, Wis Rapids*	60	520	31	12	35	.979
Dusan, Burlington	11	88	3	1	7	.989	Williamson, Bur	28	215	13	5	21	.979
Cooper, Danville*	72	483	31	6	35	.988	Hanson, Quad Cities	53	439	24	11	31	.977
Marceno, Burlington*	59	442	37	6	39	.988	Mansfield, Danville*	45	351	34	9	35	.977
Van Camp, Danville	18	153	4	2	9	.987	Martz, Clinton	35	280	14	7	24	.977
Hale, Cedar Rapids*	32	195	9	3	18	.986	Poris, Cedar R*	33	256	8	7	18	.974
Siracusa, Waterloo	24	129	7	2	11	.986	Ortiz, Burlington	15	104	8	3	5	.974
HEATH, Waterloo*	114	863	70	14	78	.985	Holbrook, Quincy	29	247	10	7	19	.973
Nixon, Cedar Rapids	10	65	2	1	6	.985	Sulprizio, Cedar R	22	159	9	5	13	.971
Singleton, Appleton	95	851	49	15	76	.984	T. Jones, Quincy	11	96	3	3	9	.971
Avila, Decatur*	114	1013	70	17	70	.983	Texdahl, Burlington	13	78	6	3	7	.966
Hansen, Clinton*	88	631	64	12	60	.983	Poepping, Wis R	15	130	9	6	12	.959
Howard, Quad Cities	52	426	19	8	42	.982							

(Fewer Than Ten Games)

Player and Club	G.	PO.	A.	E.	DP.	Pct.	Player and Club	G.	PO.	A.	E.	DP.	Pct.
Chorley, Quad Cities	7	47	2	0	6	1.000	Auger, Cedar Rapids	7	56	3	2	4	.967
Bigone, Quad Cities	7	46	0	0	6	1.000	Melum, Appleton	6	53	4	2	3	.966
Johnson, Quincy	1	7	2	0	0	1.000	Cain, Burlington	3	25	3	1	0	.966
Forsch, Cedar Rapids	2	3	0	0	2	1.000	Suzuki, Decatur*	3	22	0	1	0	.957
Coleman, Burlington	1	2	0	0	0	1.000	Texidor, Quincy	7	39	0	2	1	.951
Beasley, Clinton*	8	43	1	1	4	.978	Johnson, Appleton	2	11	4	1	1	.938
O'Neil, Cedar R*	6	33	2	1	1	.972	Pettaway, Appleton*	9	74	3	6	4	.928
Medlock, Decatur	4	30	1	1	3	.969	Aloway, Cedar R	3	24	1	2	4	.926
Mingo, Danville	4	29	1	1	1	.968	Glover, Burlington*	1	6	1	1	0	.875

SECOND BASEMEN

Player and Club	G.	PO.	A.	E.	DP.	Pct.	Player and Club	G.	PO.	A.	E.	DP.	Pct.
Cuddy, Cedar Rapids	10	25	28	0	7	1.000	Reid, Appleton	58	131	169	10	32	.968
Shafer, Waterloo	38	65	75	2	14	.986	Robinson, Burlington	68	145	178	12	41	.964
McFarland, Waterloo	11	21	28	1	4	.980	Primeau, Burlington	15	40	35	3	8	.962
Marion, Cedar R	54	116	109	5	27	.978	LOMBARDO, Q	103	250	292	22	58	.961
Breshears, Cedar R	34	66	69	3	16	.978	Coluccio, Clinton	63	132	160	12	30	.961
Lizak, Waterloo	11	20	20	1	3	.976	Phillips, Waterloo	52	129	142	11	43	.961
Garcia, Clinton	53	96	119	6	27	.973	Ryan, Appleton	47	91	149	10	26	.960

SECOND BASEMEN—Continued

Player and Club	G.	PO.	A.	E.	DP.	Pct.	Player and Club	G.	PO.	A.	E.	DP.	Pct.
Tucker, Danville	10	25	21	2	5	.958	Beckett, Decatur	22	43	41	6	5	.933
Ransom, Danville .	87	208	224	20	52	.956	Schroeder, Decatur	59	127	145	21	33	.928
Smith, Wis Rapids .	55	112	162	14	24	.951	Austin, Danville	32	61	43	9	6	.920
Brooks, Wis Rapids	59	164	158	17	32	.950	Higgins, Decatur ...	17	34	43	7	5	.917
Ashford, Quad Cities	114	273	295	35	74	.942	Corro, Burlington ..	25	40	35	7	10	.915
Donahue, Burlington	13	19	29	3	8	.941	Caudle, Decatur ...	21	38	46	14	3	.857
Calderan, Cedar R	27	55	80	9	13	.938							

(Fewer Than Ten Games)

Player and Club	G.	PO.	A.	E.	DP.	Pct.	Player and Club	G.	PO.	A.	E.	DP.	Pct.
Darrow, Quad Cities	3	1	11	0	0	1.000	Johnson, Quincy	7	10	18	1	0	.966
Mappin, Wis Rapids	2	2	7	0	1	1.000	Sankey, Cedar Rapids	7	14	14	1	5	.966
Feldhaus, Quincy ...	2	5	2	0	1	1.000	Cassis, Quad Cities .	8	6	18	1	5	.960
Schell, Quincy	2	3	4	0	2	1.000	Dent, Appleton	5	7	15	1	1	.957
McCartney, Clinton .	1	2	4	0	1	1.000	Monty, Appleton	6	13	18	2	2	.939
Alcaide, Clinton* ..	1	0	5	0	1	1.000	Traffenstedt, Bur ..	3	9	6	1	0	.938
Meoli, Quad Cities ..	1	1	2	0	1	1.000	Riggin, Waterloo ...	5	4	8	1	1	.923
Thomas, Clinton	1	1	2	0	1	1.000	Adams, Clinton	5	9	12	2	2	.913
Ontiveros, Decatur .	3	1	1	0	0	1.000	Edwards, Wis Rapids	7	20	10	4	4	.882
Opatkiewicz, Wat ...	1	1	1	0	1	1.000	Collette, Quincy	3	4	3	1	1	.875
Tanner, Danville ...	1	1	0	0	0	1.000	Yancy, Appleton	8	16	16	5	7	.865
Zontini, Waterloo ..	6	13	18	1	4	.969	Derr, Quincy	2	5	3	2	2	.800
Agrella, Waterloo ..	6	14	15	1	3	.967	Salado, Clinton	2	6	1	4	1	.636

THIRD BASEMEN

Player and Club	G.	PO.	A.	E.	DP.	Pct.	Player and Club	G.	PO.	A.	E.	DP.	Pct.
O'Sullivan, Appleton	10	8	20	1	0	.966	Forsch, Cedar Rapids	13	6	18	3	3	.889
Minor, Quad Cities .	24	17	48	3	1	.956	Johnson, Quincy ...	32	23	47	9	2	.886
Morgan, Danville .	34	21	77	5	7	.951	Collette, Quincy ..	91	64	160	30	10	.882
Cassis, Quad Cities .	69	43	124	9	16	.949	McCartney, Clinton .	55	47	64	15	10	.881
Francingues, Apl .	78	48	158	12	10	.945	Agrella, Waterloo .	31	16	47	9	5	.875
M. Price, Cedar R .	26	17	48	4	3	.942	Primeau, Burlington	40	36	60	14	5	.873
Mappin, Wis Rapids	39	20	92	8	4	.933	Bailey, Quad Cities .	22	28	65	8	0	.869
Williams, Cedar R .	55	48	105	13	10	.922	McDonald, Wis R ..	48	34	103	21	7	.867
Monty, Appleton ...	15	14	33	3	2	.922	Williamson, Bur ...	29	23	39	10	5	.861
Clark, Appleton	14	15	19	3	0	.919	Donahue, Burlington	50	50	93	25	10	.851
McFarland, Waterloo	30	25	42	6	4	.918	Smith, Wis Rapids .	10	6	11	3	1	.850
Salado, Clinton	17	12	33	4	1	.918	Shotts, Wis Rapids .	21	19	35	10	3	.844
ONTIVEROS, Dec .	108	93	219	29	18	.915	Combs, Waterloo ...	15	8	24	6	4	.842
Adams, Clinton	22	24	41	7	7	.903	Medlock, Decatur ..	12	4	11	3	0	.833
Calderan, Cedar R ..	30	22	43	7	3	.903	Rivera, Waterloo ..	26	12	35	11	4	.810
Van Camp, Danville .	71	58	89	16	8	.902	Mingo, Danville ...	18	10	19	10	2	.744
Thomas, Clinton ...	30	17	53	8	5	.897							

(Fewer Than Ten Games)

Player and Club	G.	PO.	A.	E.	DP.	Pct.	Player and Club	G.	PO.	A.	E.	DP.	Pct.
Bigone, Quad Cities .	6	5	13	0	2	1.000	Texidor, Quincy	4	4	4	1	0	.889
Tucker, Danville ...	5	3	7	0	0	1.000	Rodriguez, Decatur .	4	6	7	2	1	.867
Caudle, Decatur ...	3	3	1	0	0	1.000	Massarand, Quincy .	1	1	4	1	1	.833
Ortiz, Burlington ...	3	3	1	0	0	1.000	Meier, Waterloo ...	9	6	17	5	3	.821
Edwards, Wis R ...	8	1	1	0	0	1.000	Cavanaugh, Wis R .	3	2	5	2	1	.778
Phillips, Waterloo ..	1	1	1	0	0	1.000	Shafer, Waterloo ...	6	3	10	4	0	.765
Ashford, Quad Cities	1	0	1	0	0	1.000	McTheny, Clinton ..	2	2	1	1	0	.750
Kropfelder, Clinton .	1	1	0	0	0	1.000	Yancy, Appleton ...	1	0	3	1	0	.750
Lambert, Cedar R ..	2	0	1	0	0	1.000	Zontini, Waterloo ..	2	2	7	4	1	.692
Merkerson, Appleton	1	0	1	0	0	1.000	Corro, Burlington ..	9	2	14	8	0	.667
Hanson, Quad Cities	8	12	15	1	2	.964	Jordan, Clinton	4	4	3	4	0	.636
Lizak, Waterloo	6	4	12	1	1	.941	Siracusa, Waterloo .	2	0	2	2	0	.500
Arteaga, Appleton ..	6	7	16	2	4	.920	Austin, Danville ...	3	0	1	1	0	.500
Brooks, Wis Rapids .	9	6	17	2	2	.920	Olson, Burlington ..	1	0	1	1	1	.500
Tanner, Danville ...	9	8	17	3	1	.893	Cuddy, Cedar Rapids	1	0	0	1	0	.000

SHORTSTOPS

Player and Club	G.	PO.	A.	E.	DP.	Pct.	Player and Club	G.	PO.	A.	E.	DP.	Pct.
Abreu, Cedar Rapids	17	23	40	1	5	.984	Rosello, Quincy	51	78	172	23	28	.916
Reid, Appleton	34	53	96	5	14	.968	Thomas, Clinton ...	56	87	131	20	26	.916
Kelleher, Cedar R .	58	85	157	10	29	.960	Feldhaus, Quincy ..	35	60	102	15	20	.915
Nasif, Wis Rapids ..	48	87	169	11	26	.959	Ransom, Danville ..	38	46	121	17	6	.908
OPATKIEWICZ, W.	109	171	320	24	61	.953	Monty, Appleton ...	16	27	50	8	10	.906
Auerbach, Clinton .	28	53	79	7	15	.950	Dent, Appleton	34	46	101	16	15	.902
Rinaldi, Decatur .	77	123	269	23	41	.945	Mappin, Wis Rapids	37	44	114	18	16	.898
Breshears, Cedar R .	21	34	50	5	9	.944	Sandt, Burlington ..	29	50	89	16	19	.897
Adams, Clinton ...	39	58	106	10	14	.943	Yancy, Appleton ...	14	17	31	6	7	.889
Robinson, Burlington	50	63	137	13	21	.939	Beckett, Decatur ..	38	50	96	19	14	.885
Meoli, Quad Cities .	109	148	305	32	59	.934	Merkerson, Appleton	11	14	32	6	9	.885
Austin, Danville ..	80	105	243	26	41	.930	Collette, Quincy ...	24	30	66	13	8	.881
Calderan, Cedar R .	22	26	40	5	7	.930	Corro, Burlington ..	47	75	91	23	20	.878
Meier, Waterloo ...	12	6	34	3	4	.930	Cavanaugh, Wis R .	25	34	81	16	11	.878
Cassis, Quad Cities .	13	10	41	4	12	.929	Tanner, Danville ...	11	4	18	5	3	.815

SHORTSTOPS—Continued

(Fewer Than Ten Games)

Player and Club	G.	PO.	A.	E.	DP.	Pct.	Player and Club	G.	PO.	A.	E.	DP.	Pct.
Schell, Quincy	7	9	13	0	2	1.000	Redmon, Appleton	9	20	31	3	7	.944
Francingues, Apl	3	1	10	0	1	1.000	Sankey, Cedar R	7	8	14	2	0	.917
Ontiveros, Decatur	6	5	6	0	1	1.000	McCartney, Clinton	3	3	8	1	2	.917
Mahoney, Appleton	2	4	3	0	2	1.000	Lombardo, Quincy	7	14	18	3	1	.914
McFarland, Waterloo	1	2	1	0	0	1.000	Shafer, Waterloo	4	4	6	1	2	.909
Garcia, Clinton	1	1	1	0	1	1.000	M. Price, Cedar R	3	0	8	1	1	.889
Lizak, Waterloo	3	1	1	0	0	1.000	Rodriguez, Appleton	2	5	2	1	0	.875
Marion, Cedar R	1	0	1	0	1	1.000	Florez, Cedar R	5	2	4	2	1	.750
Smith, Wis Rapids	7	9	30	2	4	.951	Bannon, Wis Rapids	2	1	2	1	1	.750

OUTFIELDERS

Player and Club	G.	PO.	A.	E.	DP.	Pct.	Player and Club	G.	PO.	A.	E.	DP.	Pct.
Kapano, Decatur	44	72	3	0	0	1.000	McCartney, Clinton	17	22	2	1	0	.960
Cruz, Cedar Rapids	23	35	2	0	0	1.000	Hoppe, Wis Rapids	.114	202	6	9	2	.959
Aloway, Cedar R	34	32	0	0	0	1.000	Shotts, Wis Rapids	71	88	5	4	0	.959
Berg, Decatur*	21	28	1	0	0	1.000	McCowan, Quad C	17	23	0	1	0	.958
McTheny, Clinton	17	25	2	0	1	1.000	Alcaide, Clinton*	56	84	3	4	0	.956
Campbell, Quad C	13	16	0	0	0	1.000	Texdahl, Burlington	61	76	6	4	2	.953
Walter, Wis Rapids*	12	8	1	0	0	1.000	Linville, Appleton	32	54	4	3	1	.951
LaCock, Quincy	10	5	0	0	0	1.000	Combs, Waterloo	.101	185	4	10	1	.950
Leifer, Decatur	54	80	5	1	2	.988	Speed, Decatur	.107	233	9	13	1	.949
Thompson, Waterloo	66	78	5	1	0	.988	Isakson, Appleton	96	159	10	9	2	.949
MINOR, Quad Cities	99	181	10	3	3	.985	Nicholson, Appleton	34	51	5	3	0	.949
Bailey, Cedar R	31	62	4	1	2	.985	Cunnigan, Danville	.118	258	8	15	0	.947
McCowan, Clinton*	.108	173	9	3	1	.984	Bourque, Quincy*	46	69	1	4	0	.946
Lambert, Cedar R	95	170	11	3	1	.984	Hendrick, Burlington	53	80	1	5	0	.942
Pettigrew, Cedar R	32	57	0	1	0	.983	Stankey, Waterloo	.102	146	10	10	2	.940
Hottman, Appleton	82	159	3	3	0	.982	Massarand, Quincy	46	60	3	4	0	.940
Doherty, Quad C*	90	133	2	3	0	.978	Singleton, Appleton	15	15	0	1	0	.938
Siracusa, Waterloo	90	126	6	3	1	.978	Beech, Quincy*	28	37	7	3	0	.936
North, Quincy	42	86	5	2	2	.978	Sapp, Appleton	78	140	4	10	0	.935
Ward, Quincy*	69	120	5	3	1	.977	Lindsey, Danville	73	91	8	7	1	.934
Howard, Clinton	.117	252	6	7	3	.974	Ortiz, Burlington	56	93	6	7	0	.934
Reser, Quincy	52	62	9	2	2	.973	Nixon, Cedar Rapids	36	39	3	3	0	.933
Bowen, Danville	.117	177	15	6	1	.970	Chorley, Quad Cities	.110	139	4	12	1	.923
Tanner, Danville	28	28	4	1	2	.970	Talley, Appleton	31	52	6	5	1	.921
Williams, Clinton*	21	32	0	1	0	.970	Robinson, Quincy	18	23	0	2	0	.920
Holbrook, Quincy	46	56	6	2	4	.969	Dyson, Cedar Rapids	20	28	4	3	0	.914
M. Price, Cedar R	76	120	2	4	0	.968	Medlock, Decatur	22	30	2	3	0	.914
Meier, Burlington	24	28	2	1	1	.968	Cooper, Danville*	47	52	2	6	0	.900
Knight, Wis Rapids*	96	134	9	5	1	.966	Cooley, Burlington	28	36	4	5	0	.889
Hofvendahl, Cedar R	38	53	3	2	0	.966	Nichols, Waterloo	10	16	0	2	0	.889
Whitley, Wis Rapids	70	82	1	3	0	.965	Brown, Danville*	14	7	0	1	0	.875
Calderan, Cedar R	12	26	1	1	0	.964	Clouser, Quincy	.111	11	2	2	1	.867
Martz, Clinton	43	49	1	2	0	.962	Chaney, Burlington	37	36	5	8	1	.837
Cain, Burlington	.120	276	14	12	2	.960	Dick, Wis Rapids	16	14	1	3	1	.833
Thomasson, Decatur*	114	179	14	8	4	.960	Poris, Cedar Rapids*	12	8	0	2	0	.800

(Fewer Than Ten Games)

Player and Club	G.	PO.	A.	E.	DP.	Pct.	Player and Club	G.	PO.	A.	E.	DP.	Pct.
Wells, Waterloo	9	13	4	0	1	1.000	Hale, Cedar Rapids*	4	1	0	0	1	1.000
Torres, Quad Cities	8	7	0	0	1	1.000	Robinson, Bur	1	1	0	0	0	1.000
Waln, Waterloo	6	6	0	0	1	1.000	Salata, Quincy	1	1	0	0	0	1.000
R. Brown, Cedar R*	4	4	1	0	0	1.000	Salado, Clinton	9	10	0	1	0	.909
Geist, Cedar Rapids*	5	5	0	0	0	1.000	Arteaga, Appleton	5	8	1	1	0	.900
Riggins, Quad C*	6	4	1	0	1	1.000	Muir, Clinton	3	8	0	1	0	.889
Olson, Burlington	2	4	0	0	0	1.000	Sankey, Cedar Rapids	8	7	1	1	0	.889
Beasley, Clinton*	3	3	0	0	0	1.000	Bigone, Quad Cities	5	4	3	1	0	.875
Johnson, Quincy	5	2	1	0	1	1.000	Donahue, Burlington	2	4	0	1	0	.800
Martorella, QC*	2	3	0	0	0	1.000	Rivera, Waterloo	3	3	0	1	0	.750
Curnutt, Wis Rapids	8	2	0	0	0	1.000	McKinley, Waterloo	3	5	0	2	0	.714
Garcia, Clinton	1	2	0	0	0	1.000	Zontini, Waterloo	4	5	0	2	0	.714
Groth, Quad Cities	2	1	0	0	0	1.000	Francingues, Apl	1	2	0	2	0	.500
LaFrance, Danville	6	2	0	0	0	1.000	Avila, Decatur*	2	0	0	1	0	.000

CATCHERS

Player and Club	G.	PO.	A.	E.	DP.	PB.	Pct.	Player and Club	G.	PO.	A.	E.	DP.	PB.	Pct.
Hansen, Danville	29	191	15	0	2	5	1.000	Sulprizio, CR	51	311	33	3	2	5	.991
Kropfelder, Clin	.15	123	6	0	3	4	1.000	Dehn, Quad Cities	46	355	38	4	2	6	.990
Erickson, CR	16	78	6	0	0	3	1.000	Boehmer, Bur	33	259	27	3	4	5	.990
Meyer, Waterloo	51	400	37	3	0	12	.993	Bachman, Dan	35	246	25	3	0	11	.989
SCOTT, WR	86	562	57	5	4	23	.992	Rivera, Wat	62	438	45	6	5	21	.988

CATCHERS—Continued

Player and Club	G.	PO.	A.	E.	DP.	PB.	Pct.
Salado, Clinton	47	316	27	4	2	8	.988
Kissock, Clin	14	65	12	1	0	1	.987
Davini, Appleton	87	606	61	11	4	13	.984
Dusan, Burlington	42	347	32	6	4	12	.984
Salata, Quincy	70	447	47	9	2	12	.982
Cotto, CR	66	432	37	8	1	14	.982
LaFrance, Dan	67	407	28	8	4	18	.982
McKinley, Wat	14	91	6	2	0	3	.980
Fitzgerald, Bur	43	293	17	7	1	5	.978
Bigone, QC	73	510	49	13	7	29	.977
Rodriguez, Dec	57	376	54	10	2	15	.977
Porter, Clinton	58	380	42	10	4	24	.977
Arteaga, Apl	37	249	27	7	3	14	.975
Woods, Decatur	68	376	38	12	6	16	.972
Foss, Quincy	48	276	26	10	4	7	.968
Mata, WR	25	164	20	7	2	3	.963
Dickson, QC	14	67	6	4	2	2	.948
Flodin, WR	19	99	9	6	1	7	.947

(Fewer Than Ten Games)

Player and Club	G.	PO.	A.	E.	DP.	PB.	Pct.
Burrows, Wat	4	34	1	0	0	1	1.000
Kimm, Apl	3	32	1	0	1	0	1.000
Caudell, CR	7	30	0	0	0	4	1.000
Burke, Danville	4	27	1	0	0	1	1.000
Williams, Bur	3	24	4	0	0	0	1.000
Dyson, CR	2	16	2	0	0	2	1.000
Shafer, Waterloo	1	5	0	0	0	0	1.000
Marikos, QC	2	4	0	0	0	0	1.000
Lawhorn, QC	1	1	0	0	0	0	1.000
Coleman, Bur	5	26	4	1	0	1	.968
Lundstedt, Quin	6	23	3	1	0	1	.963
Vicente, CR	1	7	0	1	0	0	.875
Bunch, QC	2	2	1	1	0	1	.750

PITCHERS

Player and Club	G.	PO.	A.	E.	DP.	Pct
HANSEN, Decatur	26	14	39	0	2	1.000
Flanagan, Danville*	29	9	30	0	3	1.000
Shaffer, Appleton	26	6	28	0	1	1.000
Harvey, Clinton	20	4	15	0	1	1.000
Stedman, CR	10	4	14	0	2	1.000
Arbogast, Quincy	20	8	9	0	2	1.000
Austerman, Clinton	11	8	9	0	1	1.000
La Gore, Burlington	26	6	11	0	4	1.000
A. Brown, CR	11	1	15	0	0	1.000
Compton, QC*	21	2	14	0	0	1.000
Beebe, Cedar Rapids	41	4	10	0	0	1.000
Forster, Appleton*	10	4	10	0	2	1.000
Swain, Clinton	17	9	5	0	0	1.000
Jackson, CR*	26	5	8	0	1	1.000
Durham, CR	12	2	10	0	0	1.000
Emerson, WR *	30	3	7	0	1	1.000
Stewart, Danville*	21	2	8	0	0	1.000
Barrientos, QC	20	2	7	0	0	1.000
Daboll, CR	16	3	6	0	0	1.000
Luck, Waterloo	35	3	6	0	1	1.000
Heinitz, Bur	31	1	7	0	0	1.000
Jones, Burlington*	17	2	6	0	0	1.000
Weimer, Appleton	10	3	4	0	0	1.000
Ciganovich, Wat	30	2	4	0	0	1.000
J. Price, CR*	10	2	4	0	0	1.000
Cromer, Appleton	10	0	3	0	0	1.000
Gills, Cedar Rapids	10	0	3	0	0	1.000
Mullen, Quincy	14	0	3	0	0	1.000
Brenner, Burlington	11	0	2	0	0	1.000
Hebert, Clinton	21	0	2	0	0	1.000
Hiranuma, Decatur	12	0	2	0	0	1.000
Tuley, Quad Cities	30	9	17	0	0	.963
Gonsalves, Decatur	28	13	36	2	1	.961
Figueroa, Decatur	13	4	19	1	1	.958
Alger, Cedar Rapids*	22	3	19	1	1	.957
Geiger, Burlington	40	4	15	1	1	.950
R. Jones, Quincy*	19	6	31	2	2	.949
Hill, Quincy	22	8	28	2	0	.947
Dixon, Waterloo	43	8	10	1	0	.947
Spanich, Appleton	13	7	11	1	0	.947
Velazquez, Clinton	29	4	14	1	0	.947
Perzanowski, Apl	22	10	24	2	3	.944
Rivera, Decatur	13	3	14	1	2	.944
Spellman, QC	42	4	13	1	0	.944
Sperry, Decatur	25	1	15	1	3	.941
Westerhouse, Dan	19	3	13	1	0	.941
Billmeier, Appleton	14	4	11	1	0	.938
Todd, Quincy	11	4	11	1	0	.938
Henderson, WR*	29	5	24	2	1	.935
Streett, Danville*	28	3	11	1	0	.933
Bird, Waterloo	22	8	19	2	2	.931
Jaycox, Wis Rapids	25	8	32	3	4	.930
Daniel, Danville	13	3	10	1	0	.929
Meyer, Quincy*	28	4	21	2	1	.926
Nunn, Waterloo	25	11	37	4	2	.923
Dunham, Decatur	13	3	9	1	0	.923
James, Quincy*	15	1	11	1	1	.923
Sanchez, Clinville	40	4	8	1	0	.923
Malone, Danville	25	10	13	2	0	.920
Koon, Appleton	45	2	9	1	0	.917
Ross, Quincy*	21	4	7	1	0	.917
Warner, Cedar R	13	1	10	1	1	.917
Coull, Burlington	26	6	15	2	1	.913
Frost, Quad Cities	16	9	12	2	2	.913
Deck, Appleton*	26	3	28	3	0	.912
Massaro, Appleton	14	4	6	1	0	.909
Travers, Clinton*	10	2	8	1	0	.909
Young, Quad Cities*	21	1	18	2	0	.905
Burke, Danville	26	8	38	5	1	.902
Maselbas, Cedar R	24	3	34	4	2	.902
Skogan, Dan-QC*	33	3	24	3	4	.900
Cope, Wis Rapids	39	3	15	2	2	.900
Floethe, Burlington	16	2	16	2	1	.900
Spain, Decatur	20	7	10	2	0	.895
McGrath, Wat*	22	4	21	3	2	.893
Miali, Quad Cities*	25	1	7	1	0	.889
Mottine, Quincy	22	2	6	1	1	.889
Parent, Cedar R	20	1	7	1	0	.889
Stover, Quincy	26	2	6	1	1	.889
Johannes, WR	29	7	24	4	1	.886
Evans, Danville*	18	6	17	3	1	.885
Hardin, Wis Rapids	29	6	32	5	1	.884
Bell, Clinton	26	19	38	8	3	.877
Corder, Quincy	33	7	21	4	3	.875
Grout, Waterloo	17	1	13	2	0	.875
Roe, Quincy	16	7	7	2	1	.875
Pavlik, QC-Dec*	13	0	7	1	1	.875
Crossan, Burlington	23	15	26	6	2	.872
Heinbechner, QC*	27	1	9	0	0	.870
Conzatti, Clinton	27	1	18	4	1	.867
O'Neill, Wis Rapids*	22	4	25	5	1	.853
Lasorsa, Burlington	11	3	8	2	0	.840
Llanos, Cedar Rapids	20	7	14	4	0	.840
Paganucci, Appleton	16	5	5	2	1	.833
Hansen, Quad Cities	24	4	15	4	0	.826
MacDonnell, Apl*	12	2	17	4	0	.826
Kleckley, Waterloo	28	4	14	4	1	.818
Plummer, Dec-WR	19	1	8	2	0	.818
Loseth, Clinton	16	0	13	3	0	.813
Murnahan, Bur	25	5	12	4	0	.810
Burr, Clinton	24	3	7	5	3	.800
Miklos, Clinton*	11	2	10	3	1	.800
Clemons, Waterloo*	10	0	8	2	0	.800
Harkness, WR	18	1	3	1	0	.800
Glover, Burlington*	15	1	10	3	0	.786
Gideon, Decatur*	28	3	5	3	0	.727
Pryor, Quad Cities	23	2	20	9	0	.710
Gossage, Appleton	10	2	6	4	1	.667
May, Danville*	18	1	7	4	1	.667
Burgos, Clinton*	13	0	4	2	0	.667
Barnes, Quincy*	10	1	1	1	0	.667
Jackson, Appleton*	10	0	2	1	0	.667
Martin, Danville	46	2	13	8	0	.652
Shields, Wis Rapids*	15	1	2	2	1	.600

PITCHERS—Continued
(Fewer Than Ten Games)

Player and Club	G.	PO.	A.	E.	DP.	Pct.
Distaso, Quincy	4	5	7	0	1	1.000
Franceschi, Decatur	9	2	10	0	0	1.000
Smith, Burlington ..	9	4	8	0	0	1.000
Copeland, Burlington	9	2	8	0	1	1.000
Atkinson, Appleton .	9	0	6	0	0	1.000
Hamilton, Decatur* .	9	1	5	0	0	1.000
Slaton, Clinton	2	2	4	0	0	1.000
Benedickt, Quad C* .	6	0	5	0	0	1.000
Kurtz, Danville*	6	0	5	0	0	1.000
Limke, Appleton	9	0	5	0	0	1.000
St. Clair, Quad C ..	6	2	3	0	0	1.000
May, Clinton	4	1	3	0	0	1.000
O'Brien, Decatur ...	6	1	3	0	1	1.000
Velazquez, Cedar R .	7	0	4	0	0	1.000
Kitchen, Cedar R ...	9	1	2	0	0	1.000
Pettis, Waterloo* ..	5	0	3	0	0	1.000
Sagaser, Cedar R* ..	7	0	3	0	0	1.000
Shearer, Burlington*	6	0	3	0	0	1.000
Tecklenberg, Wat* ..	3	0	3	0	0	1.000
Autry, Waterloo	3	1	1	0	0	1.000
Haugen, Cedar R* ...	2	1	1	0	0	1.000
Kenary, Appleton ...	3	0	1	0	2	1.000
Key, Cedar Rapids ..	8	1	1	0	0	1.000
Marks, Cedar Rapids*	7	1	1	0	0	1.000
Reid, Waterloo*	9	0	2	0	0	1.000
Campos, Burlington .	4	0	1	0	0	1.000
Forsch, Cedar Rapids	1	0	1	0	0	1.000
Lindsey, Danville ...	3	0	1	0	0	1.000
Lundgren, Quad C* ..	2	0	1	0	1	1.000
McGowen, Cedar R ...	7	1	0	0	0	1.000
Rybicki, Danville ...	4	0	1	0	0	1.000
Thomas, Burlington*	2	0	1	0	0	1.000
Valdes, Cedar Rapids	1	0	1	0	0	1.000
Yard, Clinton	2	0	1	0	0	1.000
Erautt, Quad Cities	9	1	9	1	0	.909
Pasierb, Decatur* ..	5	1	9	1	2	.909
Marcano, Burlington	7	2	7	1	1	.900
Tatom, Burlington ..	9	3	4	1	0	.875
Dunbar, Appleton ...	9	1	3	1	0	.800
Krumm, Decatur	7	0	4	1	0	.800
Pastrovich, WR*	7	2	2	1	0	.800
Payne, Waterloo	9	5	5	3	0	.769
Gonzalez, Cedar R* .	3	0	3	1	0	.750
Houston, Waterloo ..	6	0	3	1	0	.750
Sennett, Decatur ...	8	1	2	1	0	.750
Steele, Danville* ...	3	0	3	1	0	.750
Farmer, Wis Rapids	6	0	2	1	0	.667
Sabourin, Cedar R* .	4	0	2	1	0	.667
Biercevicz, Quincy ..	3	3	2	0	0	.600
Dickson, Quad C	1	0	1	1	0	.500
Isom, Waterloo*	7	0	1	1	0	.500
Almquist, Bur*	6	0	0	1	0	.000

CLUB PITCHING

Club	G.	CG.	ShO.	Sv.	IP.	H.	R.	ER.	HR.	BB.	Int. BB.	HB.	SO.	WP.	Bk.	ERA.
Quincy	113	31	11	27	972	929	413	305	45	320	35	23	736	61	6	2.82
Appleton	124	37	8	21	1068	950	475	351	53	473	51	27	840	55	4	2.96
Decatur	119	48	10	20	1007	906	450	344	57	350	27	37	685	55	6	3.08
Clinton	124	34	9	23	1046	941	520	377	65	522	29	54	849	66	6	3.24
Cedar Rapids	121	29	10	21	1014	906	450	575	65	443	29	43	815	43	4	3.33
Burlington	124	31	15	23	1054	975	547	390	62	536	26	29	897	58	6	3.33
Waterloo	122	32	9	15	1037	899	499	384	55	550	30	35	935	59	13	3.33
Quad Cities	121	20	9	38	1034	898	490	389	42	514	15	53	893	74	9	3.39
Wisconsin Rapids	119	47	8	22	1019	954	531	393	78	451	41	32	814	59	9	3.47
Danville	123	40	3	20	1035	1029	562	435	52	457	29	46	808	53	15	3.78

PITCHERS' RECORDS

(Leading Qualifiers for Earned-Run Average Leadership—126 or More Innings)
*Throws lefthanded.

Pitcher—Club	G.	GS.	CG.	ShO.	W.	L.	Sv.	Pct.	IP.	H.	R.	ER.	HR.	BB.	Int. BB.	HB.	SO.	WP.	ERA.
Bird, Waterloo ..22	22	7	1	11	9	0	.550	147	122	49	30	5	32	6	6	149	7	1.84
Bell, Clinton ...26	23	15	2	12	12	2	.500	192	166	67	45	11	47	4	3	123	8	2.11
Perzanowski, Apl .22	16	11	2	9	8	1	.529	139	109	42	33	6	53	2	9	118	2	2.14
Gonsalves, Decatur 28	27	12	2	12	12	1	.500	207	205	83	50	12	42	2	2	128	6	2.17
O'Neill, Wis R* ..29	16	7	2	11	6	4	.647	139	104	48	34	6	66	3	1	129	6	2.20
Nunn, Waterloo ..25	23	12	1	10	11	2	.476	170	159	58	43	10	49	2	2	100	8	2.28
Llanos, C Rapids ..20	19	3	1	9	5	0	.643	136	118	53	37	14	38	1	5	91	2	2.45
R. Jones, Quincy* 19	18	6	1	9	3	0	.750	126	110	49	35	7	47	2	3	98	17	2.50
Hill, Quincy ...22	18	6	2	11	6	0	.647	142	152	60	40	6	30	3	2	82	6	2.54
Hansen, Decatur 26	21	9	1	11	7	0	.611	177	151	75	53	5	57	4	10	118	11	2.69

Departmental Leaders: G—Martin, 46; GS—Hardin, 28; CG—Bell, 15; ShO—Conzatti, Figueroa, Jaycox, MacDonnell, 3; W—Bell, Conzatti, Gonsalves, Hardin, Johannes, 12; L—Bell, Gonsalves, Hardin, Henderson, Maselbas, 12; Sv—Spellman, 17; Pct.—Conzatti, Johannes, .750; IP—Gonsalves, 207; H—Gonsalves, 206; R—Hardin, 96; ER—Flanagan, 76; HR—Llanos, 14; BB—Heinbechner, 91; IBB—Hardin, 10; HB—Crossan, T. Hansen, 10; SO—Hardin, 161; WP—R. Jones, 17.

(All Pitchers—Listed Alphabetically)

Pitcher—Club	G.	GS.	CG.	ShO.	W.	L.	Sv.	Pct.	IP.	H.	R.	ER.	HR.	BB.	Int. BB.	HB.	SO.	WP.	ERA.
Alger, C Rapids* 22	12	1	1	6	5	0	.545	88	82	37	33	4	37	1	4	67	5	3.38
Almquist, Bur* . 6	2	0	0	1	2	0	.333	12	10	9	6	1	15	0	0	13	2	4.50
Arbogast, Quincy .20	15	5	2	6	5	1	.545	98	100	53	41	5	42	1	4	66	7	3.77
Atkinson, Appleton 9	9	3	0	3	4	0	.429	58	54	25	17	5	27	3	1	52	3	2.64
Austerman, Clin .11	11	0	0	2	4	0	.333	51	33	17		4	49	0	1	31	3	3.00
Autry, Waterloo . 3	3	0	0	1	0	0	1.000	11	13	8	6	1	10	0	0	15	1	4.91
Avila, Decatur* . 1	0	0	0	0	0	0	.000	2	1	0	0	0	0	0	0	2	0	0.00
Bachman, Danville 1	0	0	0	0	1	0	.000	4	5	1	1		0	0	0	2	0	2.25
Baker, C Rapids . 5	0	0	0	0	1	0	.000	7	17	8	7	1	3	0	0	8	4	9.00
Barnes, Quincy* .10	0	0		1	1		.500	11	6	4	2	1	5	1	0	14	0	1.64

Pitcher—Club	G.	GS.	CG.	ShO.	W.	L.	Sv.	Pct.	IP.	H.	R.	ER.	HR.	BB.	Int. BB.	HB.	SO.	WP.	ERA.
Barrientos, Q C ...20	4	0	0	5	1	5	.833	60	51	21	21	5	21	2	0	52	1	3.15
Beebe, C Rapids ..41	2	1	0	2	3	7	.400	84	72	34	27	4	34	4	6	61	8	2.89
Bell, Clinton 26	23	15	2	12	12	2	.500	192	166	67	45	11	47	4	3	123	8	2.11
Benedickt, Q C* . 6	0	0	0	1	0	1	1.000	12	12	2	1	0	3	0	1	10	4	0.75
Biercevicz, Quincy 3	0	0	0	0	1	0	.000	8	6	5	4	1	5	0	0	10	1	4.50
Billmeier, Apl 14	1	0	0	3	0	0	.600	33	31	17	14	2	18	2	0	23	1	3.82
Bird, Waterloo ...22	22	7	1	11	9	0	.550	147	122	49	30	5	32	6	6	149	7	1.84
Brenner, Bur 11	0	0	0	1	0	2	1.000	23	21	11	8	1	16	2	3	24	2	3.13
A. Brown, C R ..11	11	4	1	5	4	0	.556	67	55	24	22	2	26	1	3	57	4	2.96
Burgos, Clinton* ..13	2	0	0	1	2	1	.333	24	29	29	17	1	25	1	1	16	2	6.38
Burke, Danville ..26	17	8	0	9	8	0	.529	140	156	69	56	2	51	3	5	96	6	3.60
Burr, Clinton ...24	13	2	1	5	8	1	.385	98	94	50	37	5	46	6	4	98	5	3.40
Campos, Bur 4	0	0	0	0	1	0	.000	7	10	4	4	0	2	0	0	7	0	5.14
Ciganovich, Wat ..30	0	0	0	3	2	3	.600	48	34	21	19	1	28	4	4	46	3	3.56
Clemons, Wat* .. 18	0	0	0	1	2	3	.333	30	18	19	9	2	23	0	2	43	4	2.70
Compton, Quad C* 21	14	1	0	7	5	1	.583	79	67	48	43	4	51	0	3	72	6	4.90
Conzatti, Clinton 27	15	5	3	12	4	2	.750	118	98	43	34	7	47	7	5	114	4	2.59
Cope, Wis Rapids.39	4	0	0	6	3	6	.667	68	63	37	28	7	36	2	2	39	2	3.71
Copeland, Bur ... 9	0	5	2	8	3	0	.667	56	48	19	12	2	28	0	1	60	12	1.93
Corder, Quincy ...33	12	3	0	8	4	6	.667	103	101	47	40	3	20	2	5	72	3	3.50
Coull, Burlington 26	9	3	0	5	2	2	.714	112	98	50	37	6	45	2	0	93	4	2.97
Cromer, Appleton 10	0	0	0	1	1	1	.500	24	22	14	10	2	10	2	1	16	0	3.75
Crossan, Bur 23	23	7	1	6	11	0	.353	146	139	80	59	8	64	4	10	99	6	3.64
Daboll, C Rapids 16	5	3	0	4	2	5	.667	52	31	13	13	5	21	2	0	49	2	2.25
Daniel, Danville ..13	1	0	0	3	2	1	.600	32	35	24	18	5	12	0	2	33	3	5.06
Davies, Decatur .. 2	1	0	0	0	0	0	.000	2	3	4	3	1	3	0	1	2	1	13.50
Deck, Appleton* ..26	24	7	1	8	9	1	.471	161	133	79	55	6	61	4	5	124	9	3.07
Dickson, Quad C .1	0	0	0	0	0	0	.000	3	5	8	5	0	3	0	2	1	0	15.00
Distaso, Quincy .. 4	1	0	0	4	0	0	1.000	28	26	8	4	1	8	0	1	17	2	1.29
Dixon, Waterloo ..43	1	0	0	3	5	4	.375	92	71	37	27	4	49	4	2	96	5	2.64
Donahue, Bur ... 1	0	0	0	0	0	0	.000	1	1	0	0	0	0	0	0	0	0	0.00
Dunbar, Appleton 9	8	1	0	1	3	0	.250	50	54	25	17	2	16	1	1	46	2	3.06
Dunham, Decatur 13	12	2	1	5	5	0	.500	74	62	33	26	4	36	1	1	30	1	3.16
Durham, C Rapids 12	8	5	2	5	:	1	.833	68	51	14	12	1	16	1	2	62	0	1.59
Emerson, Wis R* ..30	3	0	0	2	5	5	.286	62	52	39	26	6	43	4	5	59	9	3.77
Erautt, Quad C .. 9	1	1	1	5	0	0	1.000	48	30	15	11	0	23	1	0	36	4	2.06
Evans, Danville* ..18	14	6	0	6	2	0	.750	90	79	45	30	4	44	0	5	63	6	3.00
Farmer, Wis R .. 6	0	0	0	0	0	0	.000	4	13	17	16	3	4	1	1	5	1	36.00
Figueroa, Decatur 13	13	8	3	8	3	0	.727	102	86	33	22	3	23	2	1	85	0	1.94
Flanagan, Dan* ..29	13	0	1	11	11	0	.500	155	168	94	76	10	63	2	2	97	6	4.41
Floethe, Bur 16	14	4	1	5	5	0	.500	94	70	35	28	5	60	2	0	87	3	2.68
Forsch, C Rapids 1	0	0	0	0	0	0	.000	3	6	4	1	2	0	0	1	0	0.00
Forster, Appleton* 10	9	1	0	6	1	0	.857	54	30	11	8	0	29	1	0	42	3	1.33
Foss, Quincy 1	1	0	0	1	0	0	.000	5	3	1	1	0	5	0	0	3	1	1.00
Franceschi, Dec 9	5	2	0	2	2	0	.500	40	24	10	8	3	17	3	1	19	0	1.80
Frost, Quad C ...16	16	2	2	5	7	0	.417	106	79	46	31	3	51	1	9	91	7	2.63
Geiger, Burlington 40	7	1	1	8	5	7	.615	123	93	49	33	7	56	3	2	110	3	2.41
Gideon, Decatur* .28	0	0	0	3	1	7	.750	35	27	11	5	2	17	3	2	50	3	1.29
Gills, C Rapids ..10	0	0	0	0	2	1	.000	10	9	5	4	1	2	0	0	4	1	3.60
Glover, Bur* 15	14	3	1	4	6	0	.400	70	85	49	30	1	30	0	1	35	5	3.86
Gonsalves, Decatur 28	27	12	2	12	12	1	.500	207	206	83	50	12	42	2	2	128	6	2.17
Gonzalez, C R* .. 3	0	0	0	0	0	1	.000	8	15	11	9	1	3	0	2	8	0	10.13
Gossage, Appleton 10	5	0	0	3	6	0	.000	35	41	27	23	3	19	4	3	21	2	5.91
Grout, Waterloo ..17	8	1	0	2	5	0	.286	67	61	37	31	5	43	0	2	43	7	4.16
Hamilton, Dec* .. 9	1	0	0	1	1	0	.500	27	33	12	9	1	7	2	0	10	0	3.00
R. Hansen, Q C 24	10	1	1	5	4	1	.555	82	72	35	29	3	41	0	5	73	3	3.18
T. Hansen, Dec 26	21	1	1	11	7	0	.611	177	151	75	55	5	57	4	10	118	11	2.69
Hardin, Wis R .29	28	13	1	12	12	0	.560	195	190	96	75	10	80	10	5	161	12	3.46
Harkness, Wis R ..18	0	0	0	1	2	6	.333	23	19	13	11	1	15	1	0	19	2	4.30
Harvey, Clinton ..20	19	1	0	5	5	0	.500	115	90	61	46	4	63	1	9	99	12	3.60
Haugen, Cedar R* 2	1	0	0	1	0	0	.000	5	4	4	0	5	0	0	2	1	7.20
Hebert, Clinton ..21	2	1	0	4	2	4	.667	58	46	19	13	2	30	3	3	58	2	2.02
Hein, Waterloo .. 1	0	0	0	0	0	0	.000	1	1	1	0	0	4	0	0	1	0	9.00
Heinbechner, Q C* 27	21	6	0	6	9	3	.400	126	122	89	67	11	91	1	9	94	14	4.79
Heinitz, Bur 31	1	0	0	6	3	6	.667	61	67	28	25	2	25	3	1	56	1	3.69
Henderson, WR* .29	18	9	1	12	9	12	.250	135	130	78	56	13	62	5	5	107	10	3.73
Hill, Quincy 22	18	6	2	11	6	0	.647	142	152	60	40	6	30	3	2	82	6	2.54
Hiranuma, Decatur 12	0	0	0	0	2	3	.000	11	12	7	6	2	3	1	0	6	0	4.91
Houston, Waterloo 6	5	1	1	1	3	0	.250	28	32	17	14	2	19	0	0	16	2	4.50
Huff, Decatur ... 1	0	0	0	0	0	0	.000	1	2	7	1	1	2	0	0	0	0	9.00
Isom, Waterloo* .. 7	7	0	0	0	2	3	.000	18	20	25	16	2	33	0	1	18	0	8.00
Jackson, Appleton* 10	0	0	0	0	1	0	.000	21	29	16	11	0	15	1	0	19	3	4.71
J. Jackson, C R* .26	16	3	1	7	9	0	.438	116	100	46	42	7	70	5	3	95	3	3.26
James, Quincy* ..15	8	1	1	3	4	1	.429	53	52	24	20	1	17	1	1	45	0	3.40
Jaycox, Wis R ...25	22	12	3	11	10	3	.524	162	145	70	52	12	53	5	4	122	7	2.89
Johannes, Wis R .29	23	6	1	12	4	0	.750	174	172	73	57	12	55	4	4	131	3	2.95
Jones, Bur* 17	1	0	0	2	3	0	.500	30	26	17	11	4	16	0	1	27	2	3.30
R. Jones, Quincy* 19	18	6	1	9	3	0	.750	126	110	49	35	7	47	2	3	98	17	2.50
Kenary, Appleton . 3	0	0	0	1	0	0	1.000	3	2	1	1	0	3	0	0	2	0	3.00
Key, Cedar Rapids 8	1	0	0	0	0	2	.000	12	21	14	11	0	9	1	3	9	0	8.25
Kitchen, Cedar R 9	1	0	0	1	1	2	.333	15	13	9	8	0	12	1	0	12	0	4.80

Pitcher—Club	G	GS	CG	ShO	W	L	Sv	Pct.	IP	H	R	ER	HR	BB	Int. BB	HB	SO	WP	ERA
Kleckley, Waterloo	28	12	2	0	5	10	2	.333	105	84	49	41	6	55	3	2	96	6	3.51
Koon, Appleton	.45	0	6	0	4	8	14	.333	74	50	19	15	3	36	6	2	69	3	1.82
Krumm, Decatur	.7	7	1	0	2	2	0	.500	32	44	32	24	9	13	2	0	27	5	6.75
Kurtz, Danville*	.6	6	1	0	2	2	0	.500	41	40	21	16	1	16	1	1	45	1	3.51
La Gore, Bur	.26	7	1	1	4	4	3	.500	80	81	28	21	4	24	5	3	56	1	2.36
Lasorsa, Bur	..11	5	1	0	0	7	0	.000	43	54	41	27	3	19	1	2	43	3	5.65
Limke, Appleton	.9	0	0	0	3	1	0	.750	16	16	5	2	0	8	3	1	11	0	1.13
Lindsey, Danville	.3	0	0	0	0	0	0	.000	5	3	1	1	0	3	0	0	6	0	1.80
Llanos, Cedar R	.20	19	3	1	9	5	0	.643	136	118	53	37	14	38	1	5	91	2	2.45
Loseth, Clinton	.16	10	2	0	3	4	0	.429	48	36	18	15	1	43	0	3	42	5	2.81
Luck, Waterloo*	.35	0	0	0	5	4	1	.556	63	57	51	39	3	54	2	1	71	8	5.57
Lundgren, Q C*	.2	0	0	0	0	0	0	.000	5	10	7	3	0	3	0	1	2	1	5.40
MacDonnell, Apl*	.12	11	5	3	6	3	0	.667	78	58	25	19	3	22	0	0	66	7	2.19
Malone, Danville	.25	15	5	1	8	6	0	.571	118	120	50	42	5	38	4	3	88	8	3.20
Marcano, Bur	... 7	6	3	1	1	4	0	.200	40	36	24	11	5	12	1	0	37	0	2.44
Marks, Cedar R*	.7	2	0	0	0	2	0	.000	15	14	10	10	3	9	0	1	12	2	6.00
Martin, Danville	.46	7	2	0	5	10	1	.643	98	79	45	38	3	58	9	9	102	7	3.49
Maselbas, Cedar R	24	21	6	1	8	12	0	.400	143	124	75	57	11	70	6	4	141	4	3.59
Massaro, Appleton	14	5	0	0	1	3	2	.250	41	33	19	12	1	23	1	0	33	0	2.63
May, Clinton	..4	0	0	0	0	0	0	.000	9	11	7	3	1	6	1	1	3	1	3.00
May, Danville*	..18	6	1	0	2	4	0	.333	57	52	28	18	3	18	2	2	39	3	2.84
McAlpine, Decatur	3	0	0	0	0	0	0	.000	3	2	6	4	0	6	0	1	1	0	12.00
McGowen, Cedar R	7	1	0	0	1	0	0	1.000	15	13	6	4	1	6	0	0	9	0	2.40
McGrath, Clinton	.5	0	0	0	1	0	0	1.000	9	18	10	10	2	6	1	1	3	0	10.00
M. McGrath, W*	22	21	2	1	4	10	0	.286	130	122	60	48	4	58	5	5	107	2	3.32
McKinley, Wat	..3	0	0	0	0	0	0	.000	5	5	2	2	0	5	0	0	4	0	3.60
Meyer, Quincy*	.28	13	0	0	3	5	1	.375	81	102	48	37	8	36	6	0	59	9	4.11
Miali, Quad C*	.25	3	1	0	2	3	3	.400	48	44	39	25	1	23	0	0	41	7	4.69
Miklos, Clinton*	.11	8	3	1	2	4	0	.333	47	42	35	28	0	29	0	8	27	6	5.36
Mottine, Quincy	.22	2	1	0	2	2	0	.500	52	44	15	11	1	24	5	4	40	2	1.90
Mullen, Quincy	.14	0	0	0	0	3	1	.000	24	15	7	6	2	6	2	0	21	3	2.25
Murnahan, Bur	..25	16	1	0	3	10	0	.231	67	77	66	54	6	59	1	2	51	9	7.25
Nunn, Waterloo	.25	23	12	1	10	11	2	.476	170	159	58	43	10	49	2	2	100	8	2.28
O'Brien, Decatur	.6	2	1	0	0	2	0	.000	17	22	14	11	2	11	0	2	15	3	5.82
O'Neill, Wis R*	.22	19	7	2	11	6	0	.647	139	104	48	34	6	66	3	1	129	6	2.20
Paganucci, Apl	..16	2	0	0	2	4	2	.333	41	47	23	13	0	13	4	1	22	2	2.85
Parent, Cedar R	.20	0	0	0	2	0	1	1.000	28	27	11	9	2	6	1	0	22	1	2.89
Pasierb, Decatur*	.5	5	2	0	2	2	0	.500	26	39	26	20	2	14	0	1	13	3	6.92
Pastrovich, WR*	.7	1	0	0	0	3	0	.000	16	17	18	15	4	16	0	2	15	2	8.44
Pavlik, 9 QC-4D*	13	3	0	0	1	2	0	.333	34	42	27	26	1	15	0	4	33	3	6.88
Payne, Waterloo	.9	8	2	1	2	3	0	.400	55	38	31	24	6	48	0	3	67	4	3.93
Perzanowski, Apl	.22	16	11	2	9	8	1	.529	139	109	42	33	6	53	2	9	118	7	2.14
Pettis, Waterloo*	5	5	0	0	0	4	0	.000	19	24	19	18	3	16	3	3	13	1	8.53
Plummer, 7-Dec 12 WR	19	1	0	0	0	3	0	.000	39	49	28	17	4	12	0	2	18	0	3.92
Pounders, Wat*	..1	0	0	0	0	0	0	.000	2	2	1	1	0	2	0	0	4	0	4.50
J. Price, Cedar R*	10	0	0	0	1	2	1	.333	13	11	3	3	0	11	3	0	7	0	2.08
Pryor, Quad Cities	23	18	5	0	6	9	2	.400	127	121	54	46	5	63	0	3	131	8	3.26
Reid, Waterloo*	..9	4	0	1	2	4	0	.333	29	18	13	10	2	18	1	2	35	1	3.10
Rivera, Decatur	.13	12	5	2	4	6	0	.400	83	70	34	28	2	41	0	4	51	8	3.04
Roe, Quincy	..16	9	2	1	2	5	4	.286	64	76	37	31	2	21	4	2	42	2	4.36
Ross, Quincy*	..21	3	0	0	5	3	3	.625	57	44	16	11	4	23	1	0	55	3	1.74
Rybicki, Danville	4	1	0	0	1	0	0	.000	12	12	10	10	1	7	0	1	4	0	7.50
Sabourin, C R*	.4	0	0	0	0	0	0	.000	4	3	1	1	1	2	0	0	5	0	2.25
Sagaser, Cedar R*	7	1	0	0	1	0	2	1.000	18	17	10	10	0	10	0	0	16	3	5.00
St. Clair, Quad C	6	0	0	0	1	0	1	1.000	15	11	5	3	1	6	2	1	11	0	1.80
Sanchez, Clinton	.40	0	0	0	4	2	7	.667	80	65	32	20	7	43	3	7	72	6	2.25
Sennett, Decatur	.8	0	0	0	1	2	1	.333	16	15	10	9	2	6	1	1	16	3	5.06
Shaffer, Appleton	26	21	6	0	10	5	0	.667	151	148	74	55	10	68	9	1	124	6	3.28
Shearer, Bur*	...6	0	0	0	0	0	0	.000	13	7	2	0	0	11	1	1	10	1	0.00
Shields, Wis R*	.15	0	0	0	0	1	0	.000	19	23	22	14	0	14	1	2	19	5	6.63
Skogan, 18 Da-15 QC*	33	17	7	0	7	8	3	.467	138	130	69	52	6	51	3	4	138	5	3.39
Slaton, Clinton	..2	2	2	0	1	1	0	.500	18	9	4	3	0	5	0	1	15	0	1.50
Smith, Burlington	.9	8	2	1	3	2	0	.600	46	32	22	18	4	33	0	1	61	1	3.52
Spain, Decatur	..20	13	6	0	6	7	1	.462	99	109	57	41	5	34	6	7	72	7	3.73
Spanich, Appleton	13	13	3	1	4	3	0	.571	70	75	45	40	7	39	5	2	38	5	5.14
Spellman, Quad C	42	0	0	0	8	4	17	.667	80	64	20	12	3	25	5	2	55	3	1.35
Sperry, Decatur	..25	0	0	0	7	1	0	.857	33	30	9	9	0	8	0	2	26	3	2.45
Stedman, Cedar R	10	9	2	1	2	6	0	.250	59	49	24	21	5	13	0	2	41	0	3.20
Steele, Danville*	..6	2	0	0	1	1	0	.500	17	15	10	6	3	8	0	3	16	0	3.18
Stewart, Danville*	21	8	1	1	2	5	1	.286	54	60	45	36	0	38	2	3	54	3	6.00
Stover, Quincy	..26	0	0	0	7	1	9	.875	41	30	12	6	2	13	5	0	45	0	1.32
Streett, Danville*	28	6	0	0	4	3	0	.571	60	55	36	29	4	46	3	3	30	4	4.35
Stubbins, Quad C	1	0	0	0	0	0	0	.000	1	1	0	0	0	0	0	0	0	0	0.00
Swain, Clinton	..17	6	0	0	4	0	0	.333	47	47	32	23	7	27	1	1	33	4	4.40
Tanner, Danville	.. 1	0	0	0	0	0	0	.000	1	2	3	2	0	4	0	0	0	0	18.00
Tatom, Burlington	9	2	0	0	1	1	0	.500	28	18	9	5	1	19	1	0	27	3	1.61
Tecklenberg, Wat*	3	1	0	0	1	0	0	.000	17	18	10	5	0	6	0	0	8	0	2.65
Thomas, Bur*	2	0	0	0	0	0	0	.000	1	2	2	1	1	2	0	1	0	0	9.00
Todd, Quincy	11	11	6	2	7	2	0	.778	82	65	28	17	1	21	2	1	67	5	1.87

| | | | | | | | | | | | | | Int. | | | | |
| Pitcher—Club | G. | GS. | CG.ShO. | W. | L. | Sv. | Pct. | IP. | H. | R. | ER. | HR. | BB. | BB.HB.SO.WP.ERA. |

Pitcher—Club	G.	GS.	CG.	ShO.	W.	L.	Sv.	Pct.	IP.	H.	R.	ER.	HR.	BB.	Int.BB.	HB.	SO.	WP.	ERA.
Travers, Clinton*	.10	8	2	0	1	6	1	.143	48	53	35	30	8	26	0	3	38	1	5.63
Tuley, Quad Cities	30	11	1	1	6	4	1	.600	96	81	46	39	2	48	1	4	71	9	3.66
Valdes, Cedar R	1	0	0	0	0	0	0	.000	1	1	0	0	0	2	1	0	2	0	0.00
Vandehey, Apl*	2	0	0	0	0	0	0	.000	3	4	3	3	0	4	0	3	2	9.00
Velazquez, Cedar R	7	0	0	3	0	0	0	.000	9	9	5	4	1	5	1	3	8	1	4.00
Velazquez, Clinton	29	3	1	0	1	8	5	.111	68	76	38	34	5	25	5	2	63	2	4.50
Warner, Cedar R	13	8	0	3	4	0	.429	37	40	29	23	0	31	0	5	27	2	5.59
Weimer, Appleton	10	0	0	2	1	0	.667	17	14	5	4	3	9	3	0	11	0	2.12
Westerhouse, Dan	19	3	0	4	2	3	.667	50	41	21	14	6	15	1	5	33	2	2.52
Yard, Clinton	2	2	0	1	1	0	.500	14	10	2	2	0	5	0	1	14	0	1.29
Young, Quad C*	21	7	0	5	4	0	.556	79	71	35	24	4	37	2	7	86	2	2.73

BALKS—Westerhouse, 4; Flanagan, Meyer, 3 each; Ciganovich, Glover, Grout, T. Hansen, Hardin, Harvey, Henderson, Johannes, Key, Kleckley, Marcano, Rivera, Young, 2 each; Arbogast, Barnes, Barrientos, Burke, Burr, Compton, Coull, Daboll, Daniel, Dunbar, Erautt, Frost, R. Hansen, Hebert, Heinbechner, Heinitz, Isom, J. Jackson, Jaycox, Koon, Lindsey, Luck, Martin, M. McGrath, Miali, Miklos, Nunn, O'Brien, Paganucci, Pastrovich, Payne, Reid, Shaffer, Shields, Skogan, Spain, Steele, Stewart, Streett, Tecklenberg, Todd, Yard, 1 each.

COMBINATION SHUTOUTS—Forster-Koon, Appleton; Crossan-Heinitz (2), Geiger-Coull (2), Murnahan-Geiger, Floethe-La Gore, Burlington; Jackson-Beebe, Durham-Maselbas, Cedar Rapids; Burr-Conzatti, Swain-Sanchez, Clinton; Dunham-Gideon-Sperry, Decatur; Frost-Hansen-Spellman, Heinbechner-Barrientos-Miali, Barrientos-Spellman, Heinbechner-Spellman, Quad Cities; James-Stover, Jones-Stover, Quincy; Bird-Dixon (2), Reid-Ciganovich, Bird-Kleckley, Waterloo.

NO-HIT GAME—Conzatti, Clinton defeated Quad Cities, 2-0, August 7 (6 innings).

ALONG THE MINOR LEAGUE TRAIL . . . .

(Continued from page 521)

blast in the sixth, stole a base and ended up with five RBIs. . . . When Greg Luzinski got hot, whether it was he hit you or you hit him, it made no difference. The Reading (Eastern) slugger went on a spree May 26 with four singles and two homers, one a grand slam, for 7 RBIs. Waterbury changed strategy the next game by walking him three times and beaning him twice. However, he scored three runs and had one RBI on a bases-loaded walk. The next night, Waterbury switched and pitched, but Greg hit his second grand slam in three days and won the game with his ninth-inning smash. Waterbury got one break—the schedule called for them to leave town. . . . Iowa's Vida Blue had rung up six consecutive victories in the American Association, but he got it from both ends of the calendar when he faced Denver May 31. Rookie Jeff Burroughs, 19, hit a key double and homer against Blue and 47-year-old Art Fowler, the Methuselah of the Minors, saved the game with a shutout ninth inning. . . . Bill Gogolewski of Pittsfield (Eastern) was waiting for his wife to deliver their first child. To make the time fly, he pitched a three-hitter against Elmira June 4. But before he took the mound, he asked Owner Pat McKernan to telephone the hospital to inquire about his wife's condition. While McKernan was on the phone, the ice man came in for the night's order. "Three-hundred pounds," said McKernan. "Wha-a-a-a-a-a-t?" gasped the fainting pitcher, who thought the owner was talking to the hospital. . . . Louisville (American Association) took to the air headed for a game at Rochester. Engine trouble

(Continued on page 574)

New York-Pennsylvania League

CLASS A

CHAMPIONSHIP WINNERS IN PREVIOUS YEARS

1939—Olean* .... .631	1950—Hornell .... .653	1961—Geneva .... .616
1940—Olean* .... .625	Olean (2nd)† ...... .568	Olean (4th)† ...... .512
1941—Jamestown .... .618	1951—Olean .... .622	1962—Jamestown .... .580
Bradford (2nd)† ... .549	Hornell (3rd)† ...... .568	**Auburn (3rd)†** .... .521
1942—Hamilton* .... .672	1952—Hamilton .... .659	1963—Auburn .... .585
1943—Lockport .... .591	Jamestown (2nd)† .. .643	Batavia (3rd)† ...... .485
Wellsville (3rd)† .. .532	1953—Jamestown* .... .704	1964—Auburn§ .... .622
1944—Lockport .... .608	1954—Corning* .... .621	1965—Binghamton .... .677
Jamestown (2nd)† .. .565	1955—Hamilton* .... .656	Binghamton .... .607
1945—Batavia* .... .677	1956—Wellsville* .... .617	1966—Auburn x .... .620
1946—Jamestown‡ .... .672	1957—Wellsville .... **.632**	Binghamton .... .646
Batavia‡ .... .672	Erie (2nd)† ...... .598	1967—Auburn .... .667
1947—Jamestown* .... .690	1958—Wellsville .... .556	1968—Auburn .... .645
1948—Lockport* .... .603	Geneva (2nd)† .. .548	Oneonta (2nd)† .. .558
1949—Bradford* .... .635	1959—Wellsville† .... .635	1969—Oneonta .... .662
	1960—Erie .... .643	
	Wellsville (2nd)† .. **.535**	

*Won championship and four-club playoff. †Won four-club playoff. ‡Jamestown and Batavia declared co-champions; Batavia defeated Jamestown in final of four-club playoff. §Won championship and two-club playoff. xWon split-season playoff. (NOTE—Known as Pennsylvania-Ontario-New York League from 1929 through 1956.)

STANDING OF CLUBS AT CLOSE OF SEASON, AUGUST 30

Club	Aub.	One.	Bat.	New.	Gen.	Jtn.	N.F.	Wmpt.	W.	L.	T.	Pct.	G.B.
Auburn (9*)	..	6	8	4	7	7	7	4	43	26	1	.623	....
Oneonta (10*)	4	..	6	6	4	8	5	8	41	28	1	.594	2
Batavia (6*)	2	4	..	5	6	5	8	7	37	32	1	.536	6
Newark (8*)	6	3	5	..	5	5	6	6	36	33	0	.522	7
Geneva (12*)	3	6	3	5	..	7	2	7	33	35	1	.485	9½
Jamestown (2*)	3	2	5	5	3	..	6	6	30	40	0	.429	13½
Niagara Falls (21*)	2	5	2	4	7	4	..	4	28	40	0	.412	14½
Williamsport (16*)	6	2	3	4	3	4	6	..	28	42	0	.400	15½

Key to major league farm teams (indicated by numbers after clubs in standing) shown on Page 384.

Playoff—None.

Regular-Season Attendance—Auburn, 32,383; Batavia, 50,977; Geneva, 21,466; Jamestown, 25,260; Newark, 20,988; Niagara Falls, 60,962; Oneonta, 23,015; Williamsport, 43,599. Total, 278,650. No playoff. No all-star game.

Managers: Auburn—Boyd Coffie; Batavia—Joe Lewis; Geneva—Bill Haywood; Jamestown—Jackie Jensen; Newark—Sandy Johnson; Niagara Falls—Irv Noren; Oneonta—George Case; Williamsport—Richard (Dick) Bogard.

All-Star Team: 1B—Cott, Williamsport; 2B—Blood, Auburn; 3B—O'Keefe, Williamsport; SS—Garcia, Newark; OF—Sinclair, Jamestown; Ford, Williamsport; Miller, Auburn; Lambe, Batavia; C—Walsh, Newark; Smithson, Auburn; P—Wiley, Auburn; Leinheiser, Newark; DeFilippis, Geneva; LaRose, Jamestown; Manager—Case, Oneonta.

(Compiled by Howe News Bureau, Chicago, Ill.)

CLUB BATTING

Club	G.	AB.	R.	OR.	H.	TB.	2B.	3B.	HR.	RBI.	SH.	SF.	Int. BB.	BB.	HP.	SO.	SB.	CS.	LOB.	Pct.
Oneonta	70	2253	381	320	601	812	71	34	24	310	18	24	283	13	24	456	88	23	513	.267
Auburn	70	2252	346	257	596	812	88	13	34	290	24	16	289	6	22	479	60	17	537	.265
Geneva	69	2151	300	325	556	768	75	16	35	252	27	14	271	14	25	510	50	21	517	.258
Batavia	70	2214	323	316	557	765	70	18	34	260	33	16	281	20	24	478	92	29	507	.252
Williamsport ..	70	2210	303	327	553	779	91	15	35	254	40	9	256	16	7	559	40	20	478	.250
Jamestown ...	70	2195	292	341	548	712	70	20	18	222	27	26	309	18	14	497	67	15	542	.250
Newark	69	2179	329	300	544	804	69	13	55	289	11	13	264	9	36	623	37	13	501	.250
Niagara Falls .	68	2087	292	320	439	596	60	17	21	246	31	20	280	9	20	585	57	20	450	.210

INDIVIDUAL BATTING

(Leading Qualifiers for Batting Championship—217 or More Plate Appearances)

*Bats lefthanded. †Switch-hitter.

Player and Club	G.	AB.	R.	H.	TB.	2B.	3B.	HR.	RBI.	SH.	SF.	BB.	HP.	SO.	SB.	CS.	Pct
Ford, Lambert, Wmpt*	67	239	40	88	128	12	5	6	39	3	2	49	0	49	12	7	.368
Jackson, Marion, Newark*	52	197	39	66	80	3	1	3	24	0	0	24	2	29	13	2	.335
Miller, E. Jackson, Auburn*	69	264	52	88	118	14	2	4	35	2	1	40	2	32	20	4	.333
Thomas, Price, Newark	60	231	33	75	93	6	3	2	28	0	3	12	3	38	2	2	.325
Swindler, S. Major, Gen*	66	203	30	65	80	9	3	0	25	0	1	43	1	55	3	2	.320
Knox, John, Batavia*	70	254	51	80	99	10	3	1	14	6	1	54	2	33	23	12	.315
Lambe, Bryan, Batavia	70	274	51	86	121	8	6	5	38	3	1	30	1	40	24	4	.314
Blood, Daniel, Auburn	65	225	44	70	109	11	2	8	35	2	4	28	1	35	6	1	.311
Casablanca, Fernando, Jtn	65	211	25	64	102	7	2	9	34	0	2	41	1	30	0	2	.303
Giegler, Mark, Batavia	70	279	40	83	103	10	2	2	40	2	4	9	4	29	22	6	.297

Departmental Leaders: G—Giegler, Knox, Lambe, Roderick, Smith, 70; AB—Giegler, 279; R—O'Connor, 56; H—Ford, E. Miller, 88; TB—Ford, 128; 2B—Cott, 16; 3B—O'Connor, 9; HR—Garcia, 14; RBI—Cott, 52; SH—Dixon, Fernley, 7; SF—Auckland, Beckman, Blood, Giegler, O'Connor, Sanderson, Waters, 4; BB—Knox, 54; HP—Garcia, 11; SO—Beasley, 76; SB—Lambe, 24; CS—Knox, 12.

(All Players—Listed Alphabetically)

Player and Club	G.	AB.	R.	H.	TB.	2B.	3B.	HR.	RBI.	SH.	SF.	BB.	HP.	SO.	SB.	CS.	Pct.
Abbott, Donald, Batavia	47	90	8	22	27	2	0	1	14	0	2	5	1	23	0	1	.244
Adkins, Kenneth, Jtn*	21	31	3	7	7	0	0	0	1	0	1	4	1	7	0	0	.226
Allen, Gordon, Wmpt*	41	86	10	10	21	3	1	2	13	0	1	14	0	44	1	1	.116
Arrendale, Charles, NF	12	20	1	0	0	0	0	0	1	2	1	3	0	6	1	0	.000
Astor, Richard, Niagara Falls	36	83	6	16	22	4	1	0	17	0	2	16	1	44	2	2	.193
Auckland, R. Dennis, Gen*	50	162	22	49	61	8	2	0	19	1	4	23	5	32	1	2	.302
Babbitt, Clark, Oneonta	19	11	5	3	3	0	0	0	1	1	0	2	0	5	0	0	.273
Bagwell, Louis, Geneva*	4	13	1	3	3	0	0	0	1	1	1	1	0	1	0	0	.231
Baker, Michael, Batavia*	17	50	4	9	11	2	0	0	1	1	0	10	2	20	1	1	.180
Bakis, John, Oneonta	68	246	38	64	97	13	4	4	38	1	2	29	4	73	12	2	.260
Barker, Christopher, Oneonta	9	13	1	0	0	0	0	0	0	2	0	2	0	10	0	0	.000
Barnes, William, Auburn*	9	10	0	1	1	0	0	0	0	0	0	2	0	7	0	0	.100
Barton, David, Jamestown†	15	24	2	2	2	0	0	0	2	2	1	3	0	9	0	0	.083
Baxley, Lenny, Batavia*	7	16	2	3	5	2	0	0	1	1	0	2	1	3	0	0	.188
Baye, David, Batavia	12	15	2	4	4	0	0	0	1	0	3	0	4	4	0	0	.267
Beasley, L. Steven, Newark*	69	239	31	56	84	11	1	5	37	0	3	28	4	76	1	0	.234
Beattie, George, Oneonta	26	56	6	10	12	2	0	0	3	0	1	3	0	16	2	0	.179
Beckman, Rodger, Batavia	61	218	36	63	88	8	1	5	39	1	4	24	1	35	5	4	.289
Bedenkop, Eric, Williamsport	23	21	1	0	0	0	0	0	3	0	0	0	0	8	0	0	.000
Bergholtz, James, Batavia	2	5	0	1	1	0	0	0	0	0	0	0	0	1	0	0	.200
Billings, Bobby, Geneva*	65	238	34	52	79	5	2	6	20	3	2	14	3	41	13	7	.218
Blackwell, Timothy, Jtn*	28	81	8	19	26	3	2	0	10	3	0	12	0	27	1	0	.235
Blood, Daniel, Auburn	65	225	44	70	109	11	2	8	35	2	4	28	1	35	6	1	.311
Boggs, Harold, Williamsport	9	5	0	1	1	0	0	0	0	0	1	0	0	2	0	0	.200
Bradshaw, Gary, Newark	12	29	3	4	4	0	0	0	2	1	0	2	0	14	0	0	.138
Broseker, Gordon, Geneva	41	133	25	45	54	4	1	1	12	1	0	12	1	20	3	2	.338
Brown, John M., Geneva	14	32	5	5	6	1	0	0	4	1	0	4	0	10	0	0	.156
Brykczynski, William, Gen†	9	18	2	1	1	0	0	0	1	0	0	0	0	7	0	0	.056
Bushey, Dennis, Batavia*	13	6	0	1	1	0	0	0	1	0	0	0	0	4	0	0	.167
Caballero, Robert, Jtn*	49	149	19	36	39	1	1	0	18	1	1	26	0	19	7	0	.242
Cameron, Archibald, Geneva	1	2	0	0	0	0	0	0	0	0	0	0	0	2	0	0	.000
Canty, John, Williamsport*	18	16	1	2	3	1	0	0	2	0	1	0	0	4	0	0	.125
Cappello, Charles, Newark*	13	20	1	5	5	0	0	0	1	0	0	2	0	3	0	0	.250
Casablanca, Fernando, Jtn	65	211	25	64	102	7	2	9	34	0	2	41	1	30	0	2	.303
Cavanaugh, Carl, Batavia	22	33	0	4	4	0	0	0	2	4	0	5	0	16	0	0	.121
Ciaramella, Frank, Auburn	48	154	18	36	43	4	0	1	16	1	0	27	1	31	0	0	.234
Cichon, Michael, Auburn	6	3	1	1	1	0	0	0	0	0	0	0	1	0	0	0	.333
Clites, Robert, Niagara Falls	4	3	0	0	0	0	0	0	0	0	0	1	0	1	0	0	.000
Collins, Kenneth, Newark	5	0	0	0	0	0	0	0	0	0	0	0	0	0	0	0	.000
Cott, Martin, Williamsport*	68	243	33	63	105	16	1	8	52	0	2	34	1	58	3	2	.259
Couples, Thomas, Oneonta	12	13	2	4	4	0	0	0	1	1	0	0	0	6	0	0	.308
Crable, John, Geneva*	31	101	19	27	42	6	0	3	9	1	0	23	1	30	6	1	.267
Crane, Gordon, Wmpt	17	17	0	1	1	0	0	0	1	2	0	0	0	7	0	0	.059
Criscione, David, Geneva	42	113	18	33	44	5	0	2	14	0	0	20	1	16	2	0	.292
Crowley, William, Batavia	4	8	0	1	1	0	0	0	0	0	0	1	0	7	0	0	.125
Cupples, Terence, Auburn*	10	1	0	1	1	0	0	0	0	0	0	0	0	1	0	0	1.000
Curnutt, Ronald, Auburn	63	222	25	52	65	11	1	0	25	2	2	32	1	50	9	2	.234
Currence, D. Lafayette, NF*	7	13	0	3	3	0	0	0	0	0	1	0	0	6	0	0	.231
Dalonzo, Danny, Oneonta	20	19	5	3	3	0	0	0	2	1	1	0	0	6	0	0	.158
Darcy, Patrick, Williamsport	19	18	4	4	4	0	0	0	1	2	0	1	0	9	0	0	.222
DeFilippis, Arthur, Geneva*	25	44	9	17	27	4	2	11	0	0	9	0	6	0	0		.386
DeLuca, David, Batavia	14	27	6	4	7	0	0	1	9	0	0	5	1	14	0	0	.148
Dixon, George, Auburn*	14	37	5	9	9	0	0	3	7	0	3	0	1	0	0		.243
Dudley, Donald, Jamestown	11	15	2	4	5	1	0	0	2	0	1	1	0	7	0	0	.267
Dukes, Michael, Nia Falls	11	35	9	8	13	2	0	1	4	0	0	4	0	10	0	0	.229
Dumaw, Anthony, Jamestown	15	6	0	1	1	0	0	0	0	0	0	0	0	2	0	0	.167
Durant, Keith, Jamestown	6	11	0	0	0	0	0	0	0	0	0	4	0	9	0	1	.000
Dwyer, Michael, Batavia	17	28	5	6	9	1	1	0	4	0	1	0	0	12	0	0	.214
Dye, Wayne, Newark*	16	30	3	3	3	0	0	0	1	0	0	5	0	15	0	0	.100
Dzitko, Vincent, Jtn*	18	5	0	1	1	0	0	0	1	0	0	0	0	2	0	0	.200
Elenes, Larry, Williamsport	14	15	3	8	11	1	0	2	0	0	0	0	3	0	0		.533

Player and Club	G.	AB.	R.	H.	TB.	2B.	3B.	HR.	RBI.	SH.	SF.	BB.	HP.	SO.	SB.	CS.	Pct.
Fernley, Robert, Wmpt*	59	210	25	60	69	4	1	1	21	7	0	18	0	24	7	1	.286
Fink, Ian, Batavia	6	2	1	0	0	0	0	0	0	0	0	1	0	0	0	0	.000
Flores, Jess, Auburn	10	3	0	0	0	0	0	0	0	0	0	0	0	3	0	0	.000
Ford, Lambert, Wmpt*	67	239	40	88	128	12	5	6	39	3	2	49	0	49	12	7	.368
Forsythe, Steven, Batavia	64	192	28	37	51	3	1	2	26	0	3	41	7	39	4	0	.193
Foulk, Richard, Batavia*	12	5	0	2	2	0	0	0	1	0	0	2	0	2	0	0	.400
French, Timothy, Geneva*	2	0	0	0	0	0	0	0	0	0	0	0	0	0	0	0	.000
Frensley, James, Batavia	35	100	10	13	17	1	0	1	6	1	1	1	1	57	0	0	.130
Garcia, Pedro, Newark	51	164	46	50	111	9	5	14	36	0	1	27	11	44	6	2	.305
Gasque, John, Geneva	13	10	0	1	1	0	0	0	1	0	0	0	0	2	0	0	.100
Giegler, Mark, Batavia	70	279	40	83	103	10	2	2	40	2	4	9	4	29	22	6	.297
Gilbert, W. Earl, Newark	15	5	0	0	0	0	0	0	0	0	0	0	0	4	0	0	.000
Giliberti, Robert, Wmpt	10	17	1	1	2	1	0	0	3	0	0	1	0	13	0	0	.059
Ginter, Gerald, Geneva	13	13	0	1	1	0	0	0	1	0	1	0	1	10	0	0	.077
Gouin, Richard, Auburn*	37	79	14	24	27	3	0	0	11	1	0	14	2	16	4	0	.304
Goularte, Gregory, Auburn†	63	229	36	64	107	9	2	10	36	0	1	11	2	64	12	0	.279
Grant, D. Patrick, Bat*	43	124	15	32	46	8	0	2	12	2	0	25	0	28	0	0	.258
Greenberg, Stephen, Geneva	50	155	26	43	69	6	1	6	24	2	1	29	1	25	2	1	.277
Grover, Robert, Auburn*	13	29	5	6	7	1	0	0	4	1	1	5	0	11	0	0	.207
Gunter, Chester, Nia Falls	4	8	0	5	5	0	0	0	1	0	1	0	1	1	0	0	.625
Hamilton, Wayne, Geneva*	6	5	0	0	0	0	0	0	0	0	0	0	0	3	0	0	.000
Handel, Roy, Jamestown	11	28	4	4	5	1	0	0	2	0	0	5	0	5	1	0	.143
Hannibal, Thomas, One*	10	13	4	4	4	0	0	0	1	1	0	0	0	4	0	0	.308
Harred, Ronald, Newark	22	43	3	8	14	0	0	2	7	0	0	9	0	11	0	0	.186
Hazelip, David, Oneonta	10	20	1	3	3	0	0	0	2	1	0	0	0	10	0	0	.150
Helton, Ronnie, Jtn*	34	109	19	34	40	4	1	0	12	1	2	10	0	19	4	2	.312
Hernandez, Miguel, Wpt*	32	88	18	15	17	2	0	0	3	0	0	13	0	11	2	3	.170
Herzog, James, Geneva*	4	2	1	0	0	0	0	0	0	0	0	0	0	2	0	0	.000
Hetman, Michael, Jtn	2	8	3	3	4	1	0	0	5	0	1	0	0	2	0	0	.375
Hicks, Richard, Williamsport	28	6	0	1	1	0	0	0	1	0	0	0	0	4	0	0	.167
Hill, Norman, Newark†	67	243	33	58	64	6	0	0	15	1	1	19	5	71	4	6	.239
Hippi, Robin, Oneonta	12	16	1	0	0	0	0	0	0	0	0	2	0	10	0	0	.000
Hoellwarth, Raylan, Wmpt	11	33	3	6	7	1	0	0	2	1	0	4	0	12	0	0	.182
Holmberg, Dennis, Newark*	67	214	35	56	75	1	0	6	25	0	0	45	5	53	3	1	.262
Homs, Irving, Oneonta*	47	150	24	47	57	3	2	1	26	0	2	9	2	18	5	1	.313
Hubbard, David, Jtn*	44	104	18	27	34	7	0	0	12	0	1	16	1	19	3	0	.260
Hyde, Henry, Niagara Falls*	15	3	1	0	0	0	0	0	0	0	0	2	0	1	0	0	.000
Jackson, Alan, Jamestown†	13	29	1	5	5	0	0	0	2	1	0	2	0	10	0	0	.172
Jackson, Gary, Geneva*	5	8	0	1	1	0	0	0	0	0	0	2	0	4	0	0	.125
Jackson, Marion, Newark	52	197	39	66	80	3	1	3	24	0	0	24	2	29	13	2	.335
Jacobs, Michael, Batavia	10	28	4	7	11	1	1	1	4	0	0	8	1	8	1	0	.250
Johnson, Christopher, NF*	16	29	4	7	8	1	0	0	2	0	0	2	0	6	0	0	.241
Johnson, Gerald, Wmpt	2	2	0	0	0	0	0	0	0	0	0	0	0	1	0	0	.000
Johnson, Jerrold, Oneonta*	15	20	2	4	4	0	0	0	1	1	0	1	0	8	0	0	.200
Johnson, Thomas, Auburn	15	8	0	1	1	0	0	0	0	0	0	1	0	0	0	0	.125
Johnson, W. Scott, NF	7	20	1	1	1	0	0	0	0	0	0	0	0	6	0	0	.050
Joiner, Terry, Jamestown	18	6	3	2	4	0	1	0	0	0	0	0	0	2	0	0	.333
Jordan, H. Curtis, Wmpt	53	179	24	42	64	7	0	5	32	1	1	16	1	51	6	0	.235
Karmelich, F. Philip, Gen	39	107	9	19	31	3	0	3	11	1	1	12	0	37	1	1	.178
Kemp, Richard, Geneva*	2	4	1	2	2	0	0	0	2	0	0	0	0	0	0	0	.500
Kidd, John, Niagara Falls	22	6	0	1	1	0	0	0	1	2	0	2	0	3	0	0	.167
Knox, John, Batavia*	70	254	51	80	99	10	3	1	14	6	1	54	3	33	23	12	.315
Koschak, Seth, Jamestown*	41	97	14	26	29	3	0	0	8	0	2	18	0	28	1	1	.268
Kouns, William, Jamestown	11	18	1	1	1	0	0	0	0	0	0	0	0	8	0	0	.056
Kriz, Ricky, Oneonta*	30	91	10	26	29	3	0	0	1	3	1	2	13	1	20	0	2	.286
Laborio, Edward, Batavia	29	5	0	0	0	0	0	0	0	0	0	1	0	1	0	0	.000
Lambe, Bryan, Batavia	70	274	51	86	121	8	6	5	38	3	1	30	1	40	24	4	.314
Lambert, Nils, Batavia*	2	6	1	3	3	0	0	0	1	0	0	0	0	2	0	0	.500
Lang, Paul, Newark	17	19	3	2	2	0	0	0	1	0	0	0	0	11	0	0	.105
LaRose, H. John, Jtn*	14	26	5	7	10	3	0	0	0	3	0	0	0	7	1	0	.269
Lawson, Joseph, Newark	9	14	0	1	1	0	0	0	0	0	0	0	0	7	0	0	.071
Leaver, Alberto, NF	64	195	30	39	48	2	2	1	25	3	1	14	3	74	18	5	.200
Lee, David, Niagara Falls	7	2	0	1	1	0	0	0	0	0	0	0	0	0	0	0	.500
Leffel, Michael, Geneva*	17	29	3	4	6	2	0	0	3	1	0	6	0	10	0	0	.138
Leinheiser, William, Newark	11	31	2	3	4	1	0	0	4	1	0	1	0	16	0	0	.097
Lightford, Eugene, Gen†	38	76	10	15	24	2	2	1	8	1	0	9	0	29	2	0	.197
Locascio, Alan, Batavia	18	30	2	3	7	1	0	1	1	0	0	5	0	13	0	0	.100
Lopez, Francisco, Wmpt	19	60	3	8	9	1	0	0	2	0	0	6	0	29	1	0	.133
Madlock, Bill, Geneva	66	234	44	63	88	5	1	6	29	2	2	32	3	46	16	4	.269
Maluzhinsky, Daniel, Batavia	12	3	0	0	0	0	0	0	0	0	0	0	0	2	0	0	.000
Mason, David, Batavia*	15	11	0	0	0	0	0	0	0	0	0	1	0	6	0	0	.000
Matheson, Thomas, Oneonta	23	42	4	8	10	2	0	0	6	0	0	5	0	9	0	0	.190
Maxwell, Charles, Geneva*	40	119	14	25	36	8	0	1	14	1	1	9	1	35	0	0	.210
May, Larry, Newark	5	1	0	0	0	0	0	0	0	0	0	0	0	0	0	0	.000
Mazza, Matthew, NF	4	1	0	0	0	0	0	0	0	0	0	0	0	0	0	0	.000
McCartney, Stephen, Newark	35	115	22	35	62	7	1	6	29	1	0	24	0	30	1	0	.304
McGrath, Garry, Newark	3	4	0	0	0	0	0	0	0	0	0	0	0	1	0	0	.000
McIlvaine, Joseph, Batavia	3	8	1	1	4	0	0	1	1	0	0	2	0	5	0	0	.125
McLin, Anthony, Jamestown	33	109	12	29	34	3	1	0	4	1	1	5	1	10	5	0	.266
McRoberts, Brad, Wmpt	15	32	6	9	17	2	0	2	3	1	0	2	1	15	0	0	.281
McRoberts, Robert, Wmpt*	41	100	13	32	42	4	0	2	17	0	0	15	0	17	1	3	.320
McTheny, Guy, Newark	16	28	2	4	5	1	0	0	2	0	1	2	1	8	0	0	.143
Medich, George, Oneonta	4	8	0	1	2	1	0	0	0	4	0	0	0	0	0	0	.125

Player and Club	G.	AB.	R.	H.	TB.	2B.	3B.	HR.	RBI.	SH.	SF.	BB.	HP.	SO.	SB.	CS.	Pct.
Melton, Bruce, Geneva†	3	1	0	0	0	0	0	0	0	0	0	0	0	0	0	0	.000
Meyer, Gary, Niagara Falls	9	19	1	2	2	0	0	0	0	3	0	2	0	4	0	0	.105
Miller, E. Jackson, Auburn*	69	264	52	88	118	14	2	4	25	2	1	40	2	32	20	4	.333
Miller, Samuel, Geneva	8	2	1	1	1	0	0	0	0	0	0	0	0	1	0	0	.500
Miller, Steven J., Wmpt*	4	1	0	0	0	0	0	0	0	0	0	0	0	1	0	0	.000
Mora, Nephtale, Oneonta	33	91	11	27	44	4	2	3	19	0	0	5	0	21	0	0	.297
Moreno, Omar, NF*	10	23	1	4	4	0	0	0	3	0	0	3	0	8	0	1	.174
Morrison, Ronald, Batavia	9	3	1	1	1	0	0	0	1	1	0	2	0	2	0	0	.333
Muir, Brian, Newark	13	25	2	3	3	0	0	0	1	0	0	2	0	7	0	0	.120
Muniz, Angel, Oneonta*	42	157	32	61	77	6	5	0	31	1	2	8	0	8	10	3	.389
Munoz, Mark, Geneva	2	2	0	0	0	0	0	0	0	0	0	0	0	1	0	0	.000
Nielsen, Chad, Jamestown	20	35	4	4	8	1	0	1	3	0	0	4	0	15	0	0	.114
Nielsen, Robert, Oneonta	52	140	13	32	37	3	1	0	19	0	2	24	2	39	5	3	.229
Niles, Reginald, Jamestown	21	60	5	16	17	1	0	0	10	0	3	5	1	13	1	1	.267
Norton, Thomas, Auburn	13	43	5	10	15	2	0	1	6	0	1	1	0	11	0	0	.233
O'Connor, Thomas, Oneonta*	69	253	56	70	115	6	9	7	50	1	4	37	7	51	7	0	.277
O'Keefe, Patrick, Wmpt	51	180	28	51	73	12	2	2	20	3	1	19	0	34	1	0	.283
O'Neill, G. Charles, Newark*	9	18	0	0	0	0	0	0	0	2	0	0	0	11	0	0	.000
Ott, Edward, Niagara Falls*	61	206	38	60	79	9	5	0	24	3	0	34	2	43	6	1	.291
Ovca, J. Michael, Newark	3	7	0	0	0	0	0	0	0	0	0	1	0	4	0	0	.000
Owens, James, Batavia	2	1	1	0	0	0	0	0	0	0	0	1	0	1	0	0	.000
Pagan, David, Oneonta	9	23	1	4	4	0	0	0	0	0	0	0	0	4	0	0	.174
Peckham, Peter, Jtn*	14	14	1	3	4	1	0	0	0	1	0	0	0	4	0	0	.214
Perrotta, Carmine, Batavia	17	14	1	2	2	0	0	0	0	3	0	0	0	8	0	0	.143
Pettit, Michael, Geneva ..	24	11	1	1	1	0	0	0	0	1	0	1	0	7	0	0	.091
Prince, Marion, Oneonta	63	201	29	41	53	7	1	1	23	0	2	48	3	37	5	3	.204
Provenzano, James, Wmpt	4	3	0	0	0	0	0	0	0	0	0	0	0	2	0	0	.000
Punko, Michael, Oneonta	50	125	32	37	54	4	2	3	17	0	0	33	4	33	11	1	.296
Quinn, Daniel, Niagara Falls	14	6	0	0	0	0	0	0	0	0	0	0	0	5	0	0	.000
Redmon, James, Geneva	19	44	5	13	19	1	1	1	6	3	0	3	0	11	0	0	.295
Regent, John, Niagara Falls*	48	104	19	27	46	5	1	4	24	1	1	19	4	35	0	1	.260
Rhyne, Kenneth, Geneva*	6	17	3	5	6	1	0	0	3	1	0	2	2	5	0	0	.294
Robbins, Edward, NF	12	20	3	4	6	2	0	0	4	3	2	1	0	5	0	0	.133
Robinson, Beau, Oneonta*	32	119	24	38	63	6	2	5	18	0	1	16	1	18	7	0	.319
Robinson, James, Auburn*	29	66	9	18	22	1	0	1	10	1	0	10	0	14	1	0	.273
Roderick, Barry, Auburn	70	275	50	73	89	5	1	3	19	2	3	35	7	32	3	8	.265
Rodriguez, Antonio, Jtn	55	181	23	42	54	6	3	0	13	1	3	26	4	32	5	2	.232
Rondon, Alfio, Wmpt	52	171	26	47	60	5	1	2	10	3	0	3	1	31	2	1	.275
Roswald, Scott, Niagara Falls	48	161	23	30	38	3	1	1	15	1	2	21	1	30	6	2	.186
Rowe, Richard, Geneva*	50	168	15	52	71	6	2	3	28	1	1	14	4	25	1	1	.310
Ruth, Daniel, Batavia*	65	227	31	53	85	7	2	7	29	1	0	27	1	56	1	0	.233
Saatzer, Vernon, Geneva*	9	4	0	0	0	0	0	0	0	0	0	1	0	0	0	0	.000
Sage, Lee, Batavia*	1	1	0	0	0	0	0	0	0	0	0	0	0	0	0	0	.000
Salado, Jose, Newark	5	18	7	7	12	2	0	1	5	0	0	2	0	2	0	0	.389
Sanderson, James, NF*	56	171	20	37	47	4	0	2	25	2	4	18	3	42	2	0	.216
Sanford, James, Niagara Falls	12	20	0	6	6	0	0	0	2	1	0	1	0	2	0	0	.300
Schmonsky, Donald, Newark	10	11	1	0	0	0	0	0	1	0	0	4	0	9	0	0	.000
Scoville, Mark, Auburn	22	59	9	12	15	3	0	0	5	0	0	10	0	13	2	1	.203
Semp, Michael, Niagara Falls	23	80	20	23	43	1	2	5	17	0	0	13	2	13	0	0	.288
Shaw, John, Oneonta	32	127	31	37	47	2	4	0	9	0	1	16	0	10	10	4	.291
Sheanshang, Larry, Wmpt	12	16	1	1	1	0	0	0	1	0	0	0	0	9	0	0	.063
Sherlin, Edward, NF	62	237	35	49	63	7	2	1	14	1	2	28	0	73	8	3	.207
Sinclair, John, Jtn*	54	171	35	63	91	13	3	3	26	3	2	28	1	28	17	3	.368
Sitarz, John, Jamestown	48	142	15	34	38	2	1	0	9	2	0	31	0	28	7	1	.239
Slagle, Dennis, Niagara Falls	8	15	2	3	4	1	0	0	2	2	1	1	0	9	0	0	.200
Slough, Leslie, Jamestown	23	66	10	17	28	2	0	3	9	1	0	7	0	22	0	0	.258
Small, Donald, Jamestown	5	11	1	3	4	1	0	0	0	0	0	0	0	6	0	0	.273
Smith, James, Auburn	70	242	40	65	95	14	2	4	49	2	1	49	1	60	0	0	.269
Smithson, Thomas, Auburn	45	139	13	31	43	6	3	0	20	2	2	6	0	30	2	1	.223
Snyder, Steven, Oneonta*	16	10	2	3	3	0	0	0	1	0	0	1	0	4	0	0	.300
Spadola, Francis, Jamestown	31	94	12	21	23	2	0	0	9	1	2	18	0	28	2	1	.223
Spencer, Gerald, Jamestown	12	32	2	10	14	4	0	0	4	0	0	1	0	11	0	0	.313
Standart, Richard, NF	63	223	24	50	64	9	1	1	25	0	0	27	1	45	10	1	.224
Stathos, William, Auburn	11	16	3	3	3	0	0	0	5	1	0	0	0	3	0	0	.188
Stedman, Thomas, Newark	34	79	12	21	26	5	0	0	5	1	0	10	0	15	1	0	.266
Steen, Darryl, Newark	5	10	0	1	1	0	0	0	0	0	0	0	0	3	0	0	.100
Stonum, Richard, Newark	20	6	1	1	2	1	0	0	1	2	1	0	0	3	0	0	.167
Strickland, Rudi, NF†	44	102	16	20	34	2	0	4	14	1	0	25	0	34	0	1	.196
Sudzina, G. Nicholas, Bat	36	115	18	28	42	4	2	2	16	2	0	7	1	15	9	1	.243
Sullivan, John, Niagara Falls	53	146	21	15	19	2	1	0	12	2	3	27	2	45	9	3	.103
Swindler, S. Major, Gen*	66	203	30	65	80	9	3	0	25	0	1	43	1	55	3	2	.320
Sydnor, Bruce, Geneva ..	8	13	1	2	4	1	0	0	1	0	0	0	0	6	0	0	.154
Szado, Edward, Geneva*	1	2	0	0	0	0	0	0	0	0	1	0	0	1	0	0	.000
Tanner, James, Batavia	10	31	5	8	13	2	0	1	2	0	0	7	0	6	2	0	.258
Tetrault, Alan, Oneonta*	6	7	1	2	2	0	0	0	1	0	0	0	0	5	0	0	.286
Thomas, Donald, Geneva†	7	2	0	0	0	0	0	0	0	0	0	0	0	0	0	0	.000
Thomas, Price, Newark	60	231	33	75	93	6	3	2	28	0	3	12	3	38	2	1	.325
Vargason, Terry, Oneonta*	13	1	0	0	0	0	0	0	0	0	0	0	0	0	0	0	.000
Vasquez, George, Wmpt	55	159	26	43	64	9	0	4	13	2	1	37	3	51	0	0	.270
Veleas, Leo, Jamestown	32	67	9	12	25	1	3	2	9	0	0	14	1	28	1	1	.179
Walsh, John E., Newark*	54	178	24	39	69	9	0	7	31	0	1	27	2	61	1	0	.219
Ward, Roger, Jamestown*	1	0	0	0	0	0	0	0	0	0	0	0	0	0	0	0	.000

Player and Club	G.	AB.	R.	H.	TB.	2B.	3B.	HR.	RBI.	SH.	SF.	BB.	HP.	SO.	SB.	CS.	Pct.
Waters, Edwin, Oneonta* ...	69	278	45	72	84	8	2	29	1	4	27	0	30	14	4	.259
Wayne, Thomas, Auburn	1	3	0	0	0	0	0	0	0	0	0	0	0	0	0	.000
Wegner, Frederick, Jtn	36	101	16	16	21	1	2	0	6	0	2	0	36	5	0	.158
Wick, Jack, Jamestown	43	122	14	27	28	1	0	0	10	4	1	8	1	17	4	0	.221
Wiley, Mark, Auburn	15	54	5	11	15	1	0	1	5	1	0	1	0	16	0	0	.204
Williams, Charles E., Newark	57	185	24	45	82	9	2	8	33	0	1	16	2	71	5	1	.243
Wing, David, Williamsport ..	53	194	26	35	45	8	1	0	8	2	1	7	0	48	4	2	.180
Wise, Thomas, Williamsport	24	80	8	22	29	2	1	1	8	2	0	10	0	14	0	0	.275
Wisniewski, David, Geneva ..	33	97	4	15	16	1	0	0	9	1	0	8	1	21	0	0	.155
Wolfe, Gary, Auburn	30	91	12	20	26	3	0	1	5	0	0	13	5	38	0	0	.220
Wolger, George, Williamsport	19	20	3	3	5	0	1	0	1	3	0	3	0	8	0	0	.150
Wright, James, Jamestown ..	3	2	0	0	0	0	0	0	0	0	0	0	0	2	0	0	.000
Yard, Dennis, Newark	11	16	2	1	1	0	0	1	0	1	0	0	4	0	0	.063
Ybes, Carmelo, Niagara Falls	39	94	14	24	33	4	1	1	12	1	0	5	0	24	4	0	.255
Young, Blaine, Jamestown ..	6	2	0	0	0	0	0	0	0	0	0	0	0	0	0	.000
Zbercot, John, Jamestown ...	18	29	4	8	8	0	0	3	0	1	1	1	6	0	0	.276

The following players had no plate appearances (listed alphabetically by clubs, games in parentheses):

BATAVIA—Killian, Jerry* (2).

GENEVA—Bruce, Wayne (2); McLane, David* (2).

JAMESTOWN—Beck, Stanley (4); Bryant, James (2).

NIAGARA FALLS—Wastradowski, Kenneth* (4).

WILLIAMSPORT—Keller, Harlan (1).

GRAND-SLAM HOME RUNS—Allen, Cott, Ford, Jordan, Lambe, Rowe, Smith, Williams, 1 each.

AWARDED FIRST BASE ON INTERFERENCE—Beckman (Walsh), Dukes (Smithson), Madlock (Walsh), Mason (Walsh), Sullivan (Criscione), Swindler (Cott).

CLUB FIELDING

Club	G.	PO.	A.	E.	DP.	PB.	Pct.	Club	G.	PO.	A.	E.	DP.	PB.	Pct.
Auburn	70	1743	691	100	42	11	.961	Williamsport	70	1718	608	130	49	17	.947
Batavia	70	1749	627	106	52	18	.957	Jamestown	70	1724	632	132	44	22	.947
Oneonta	70	1725	647	107	38	24	.957	Geneva	69	1667	577	127	37	17	.946
Newark	69	1676	547	103	45	20	.956	Niagara Falls	68	1685	608	156	47	12	.936

Triple Play—None.

INDIVIDUAL FIELDING
(Ten or More Games)

*Throws lefthanded.

FIRST BASEMEN

Player and Club	G.	PO.	A.	E.	DP.	Pct.	Player and Club	G.	PO.	A.	E.	DP.	Pct.
Greenberg, Geneva ..	18	134	4	1	10	.993	Beasley, Newark* ..	69	479	36	10	44	.981
RUTH, Batavia*	64	480	31	4	36	.992	Casablanca, Jtn	64	471	31	10	35	.980
Semp, Niagara Falls	23	185	13	2	15	.990	Auckland, Geneva* ..	49	311	20	7	15	.979
Nielsen, Jtn	14	68	6	1	3	.987	Cott, Williamsport ..	60	413	29	12	38	.974
O'Connor, Oneonta ..	69	564	41	9	34	.985	Sanderson, NF*	47	301	27	11	20	.968
Smith, Auburn*	70	560	38	10	36	.984							

(Fewer Than Ten Games)

Player and Club	G.	PO.	A.	E.	DP.	Pct.	Player and Club	G.	PO.	A.	E.	DP.	Pct.
O'Keefe, Wmpt	7	58	2	0	7	1.000	Hubbard, Jtn*	1	2	1	0	0	1.000
Baxley, Batavia*	4	35	0	0	6	1.000	Abbott, Batavia	4	25	2	1	1	.964
Jordan, Wmpt	2	15	2	0	1	1.000	Broseker, Geneva ...	9	38	3	2	3	.953
Wise, Williamsport ..	1	6	0	0	1	1.000	Nielsen, Oneonta ...	3	11	1	1	0	.923
Maxwell, Geneva ...	1	5	0	0	1	1.000	Strickland, NF*	3	9	1	3	1	.769

SECOND BASEMEN

Player and Club	G.	PO.	A.	E.	DP.	Pct.	Player and Club	G.	PO.	A.	E.	DP.	Pct.
Bakis, Oneonta	10	17	24	0	1	1.000	Wisniewski, Geneva .	22	28	37	4	3	.942
Rondon, Wmpt	12	32	30	2	8	.969	Hill, Newark	67	119	166	18	28	.941
BLOOD, Auburn	62	121	155	12	24	.958	Rowe, Geneva	48	87	121	14	19	.937
Fernley, Wmpt	57	116	131	13	24	.950	Shaw, Oneonta	32	70	68	10	10	.932
Sitarz, Jamestown ..	25	51	57	6	9	.947	Helton, Jamestown ..	30	54	47	9	8	.918
Knox, Batavia	70	148	184	19	37	.946	Sherlin, NF	62	106	133	25	27	.905
Rodriguez, Jtn	25	56	48	6	12	.945	Robinson, Auburn ..	10	20	16	5	5	.878
Robinson, Oneonta ..	31	55	75	8	9	.942							

(Fewer Than Ten Games)

Player and Club	G.	PO.	A.	E.	DP.	Pct.	Player and Club	G.	PO.	A.	E.	DP.	Pct.
Garcia, Newark	3	2	5	0	1	1.000	Lopez, Wmpt	1	2	3	1	2	.833
Bagwell, Geneva	1	0	5	0	0	1.000	Wayne, Auburn	1	1	4	1	0	.833
Stedman, Newark ...	1	0	1	0	0	1.000	Roswald, NF	4	11	6	4	1	.810
Herzog, Geneva	2	0	1	0	0	1.000	Leffel, Niagara Falls	1	2	0	1	0	.667
C. Johnson, NF	4	4	4	1	2	.889							

THIRD BASEMEN

Player and Club	G.	PO.	A.	E.	DP.	Pct.
Madlock, Geneva ...	10	16	10	1	2	.963
Holmberg, Newark .	36	34	38	6	3	.923
BECKMAN, Bat ..	56	35	83	10	5	.922
O'Keefe, Wmpt	40	35	51	8	4	.915
Wick, Jamestown ...	20	16	36	5	3	.912
Blackwell, Jtn	24	23	29	5	1	.912
Prince, Oneonta ...	62	42	102	14	6	.911
Wing, Williamsport .	23	16	25	4	1	.911
Abbott, Batavia	14	10	9	2	2	.905
McCartney, Newark ..	17	16	19	4	1	.897
Maxwell, Geneva	34	34	41	9	3	.893
Ciaramella, Auburn .	46	28	80	14	4	.885
Spadola, Jtn	29	25	43	9	1	.883
Greenberg, Geneva ..	32	28	32	8	1	.882
Roswald, NF	30	41	47	12	3	.880
Astor, Niagara Falls .	29	28	37	12	5	.844
Scoville, Auburn ...	16	10	19	8	3	.784

(Fewer Than Ten Games)

Player and Club	G.	PO.	A.	E.	DP.	Pct.
C. Johnson, NF	5	8	5	0	1	1.000
Dye, Newark	9	7	6	0	1	1.000
Crowley, Batavia ...	3	3	5	0	0	1.000
Leffel, Niagara Falls .	1	0	3	0	0	1.000
Stedman, Newark ...	1	0	1	0	0	1.000
Garcia, Newark	9	5	11	2	2	.889
Rondon, Wmpt	2	3	5	1	0	.889
Bakis, Oneonta	3	0	7	1	1	.875
Nielsen, Oneonta ...	3	2	4	1	0	.857
Wise, Williamsport .	4	5	1	1	0	.857
Robinson, Auburn ..	9	3	17	4	1	.833
Punko, Oneonta	1	2	1	1	1	.750
Dukes, Niagara Falls	8	8	13	7	1	.735
Rodriguez, Jtn	1	1	4	2	0	.714
Kriz, Oneonta	1	0	2	1	0	.667
Lopez, Williamsport .	1	1	1	1	0	.667

SHORTSTOPS

Player and Club	G.	PO.	A.	E.	DP.	Pct.
Garcia, Newark	39	59	76	9	15	.938
McCartney, Newark .	14	29	28	4	6	.934
RODERICK, Aub .	70	104	215	23	22	.933
Rondon, Wmpt	31	62	91	12	15	.927
Bakis, Oneonta	57	79	156	20	22	.922
Wick, Jamestown ...	22	33	37	6	4	.921
Wisniewski, Gen ...	10	14	20	3	3	.919
Wing, Williamsport .	24	29	48	7	11	.917
Lopez, Wmpt	14	22	31	5	8	.914
Rodriguez, Jtn	27	41	67	11	12	.908
Madlock, Geneva ..	57	107	122	25	23	.902
Standart, NF	62	95	136	28	25	.892
Forsythe, Batavia ..	63	101	140	30	29	.889
Stedman, Newark ..	28	32	48	10	10	.889
Beattie, Oneonta ..	16	17	31	7	2	.873
Sitarz, Jamestown ..	22	21	37	10	7	.853

(Fewer Than Ten Games)

Player and Club	G.	PO.	A.	E.	DP.	Pct.
Bagwell, Geneva	3	8	3	0	1	1.000
Abbott, Batavia	1	0	3	0	0	1.000
Dukes, NF	1	2	1	0	0	1.000
Robinson, Auburn ..	1	2	1	0	0	1.000
Bergholtz, Bat	1	1	1	0	0	1.000
Beckman, Batavia ...	6	15	12	4	1	.871
Helton, Jamestown ..	3	5	8	2	4	.867
Leffel, Niagara Falls	6	5	13	3	2	.857
Maxwell, Geneva ...	3	0	5	1	0	.833
Wegner, Jamestown .	5	4	8	3	3	.800

OUTFIELDERS

Player and Club	G.	PO.	A.	E.	DP.	Pct.
Baker, Batavia	17	22	1	0	1	1.000
Adkins, Jamestown* .	10	9	0	0	0	1.000
WATERS, Oneonta* .	69	124	6	1	1	.992
Lambe, Batavia	70	97	11	1	3	.991
Caballero, Jamestown	44	75	1	1	0	.987
Holmberg, Newark ..	41	45	5	1	0	.980
Ott, Niagara Falls ..	61	84	8	2	2	.979
Sudzina, Batavia ...	32	44	3	1	1	.979
Miller, Auburn	68	82	6	2	2	.978
Lightford, Geneva .	25	43	2	1	0	.978
Wegner, Jamestown .	29	42	3	1	0	.978
Leaver, Niagara Falls	62	112	8	3	1	.976
R. McRoberts, Wmpt	28	32	4	1	0	.973
Jackson, Newark ...	51	97	1	4	0	.961
Punko, Oneonta ...	39	45	1	2	0	.958
Roswald, NF	13	22	0	1	0	.957
Curnutt, Auburn ...	63	98	11	5	2	.956
Crable, Geneva	30	37	2	2	0	.951
McLin, Jamestown ..	32	34	3	2	0	.949
Giegler, Batavia ...	70	110	10	7	2	.945
Ford, Wmpt	67	128	8	8	0	.944
Swindler, Geneva* .	65	112	7	7	1	.944
Kriz, Oneonta	25	29	3	2	2	.941
Goularte, Auburn ..	62	61	1	4	0	.939
Gouin, Auburn* ...	25	11	4	1	0	.938
Hubbard, Jamestown*	27	26	3	2	0	.935
Thomas, Newark ...	60	86	1	7	0	.926
Muniz, Oneonta ...	42	57	3	5	0	.923
Nielsen, Oneonta ..	36	43	5	4	0	.923
Regent, NF*	40	37	5	4	1	.913
Williams, Newark* .	52	98	4	10	0	.911
Billings, Geneva ...	64	84	9	10	0	.903
Jordan, Wmpt	23	36	0	4	0	.900
Allen, Wmpt	22	58	9	7	0	.900
Veleas, Jamestown ..	23	13	3	2	1	.889
Niles, Jamestown ...	18	19	3	3	0	.880
Sinclair, Jamestown .	49	73	3	11	0	.874
Jacobs, Batavia	10	13	0	2	0	.867
Hernandez, Wmpt* ..	28	48	3	8	0	.864
Tanner, Batavia	10	17	2	3	0	.864
Broseker, Geneva ...	31	27	6	6	1	.846
Wise, Wmpt	18	18	2	4	0	.833
Strickland, NF*	31	19	0	5	0	.792

(Fewer Than Ten Games)

Player and Club	G.	PO.	A.	E.	DP.	Pct.
Moreno, NF*	8	10	0	0	0	1.000
McCartney, Newark .	5	9	0	0	0	1.000
Giliberti, Wmpt	7	7	0	0	0	1.000
Small, Jamestown ..	4	6	0	0	0	1.000
McTheny, Newark ..	5	5	0	0	0	1.000
Homs, Oneonta	3	3	1	0	0	1.000
Abbott, Batavia	4	4	0	0	0	1.000
Muir, Newark	6	4	0	0	0	1.000
Ciaramella, Auburn .	1	1	0	0	0	1.000
Quinn, Niagara Falls	1	1	0	0	0	1.000
Ruth, Batavia*	1	1	0	0	0	1.000
Astor, Niagara Falls.	2	1	0	0	0	1.000
Cott, Wmpt	2	1	0	0	0	1.000
Ybes, Niagara Falls..	8	9	0	1	0	.900
Maxwell, Geneva ...	2	4	0	1	0	.800
Durant, Jamestown ..	4	7	0	3	0	.700
Karmelich, Geneva .	3	2	0	1	0	.667
Rondon, Wmpt	4	3	0	2	0	.600
Sanderson, NF*	6	1	0	1	0	.500
Locascio, Batavia ...	1	0	0	2	0	.000

CATCHERS

Player and Club	G.	PO.	A.	E.	DP.	PB.	Pct.
Harred, Newark	12	84	5	0	0	4	1.000
Matheson, Oneonta	12	60	3	0	0	3	1.000
Wolfe, Auburn	30	265	19	2	3	5	.993
SMITHSON, Aub.	44	336	24	3	3	6	.992
Frensley, Batavia	30	220	17	2	1	6	.992
Karmelich, Gen	33	240	25	4	4	7	.985
Homs, Oneonta	40	286	22	5	0	17	.984
Ybes, NF	22	189	14	3	1	3	.982
Koschak, Jtn	38	235	25	5	1	6	.981
Grant, Batavia	40	274	11	6	2	10	.979
Vasquez, Wmpt	55	403	36	10	2	12	.978
Walsh, Newark	51	395	27	10	1	12	.977
Sullivan, NF	53	365	36	10	2	9	.976
Mora, Oneonta	23	178	14	5	2	4	.975
Handel, Jtn	10	67	12	2	0	5	.975
Slough, Jtn	19	131	11	4	0	5	.973
Locascio, Batavia	10	70	2	2	0	2	.973
Criscione, Geneva	32	240	17	8	3	8	.970
Hoellwarth, Wmpt	11	94	4	3	0	3	.970

(Fewer Than Ten Games)

Player and Club	G.	PO.	A.	E.	DP.	PB.	Pct.
Zbercot, Jtn	9	45	4	0	0	1	1.000
Rhyne, Geneva	4	42	2	0	0	1	1.000
Salado, Newark	5	36	2	0	0	3	1.000
Hetman, Jtn	2	14	2	0	1	1	1.000
Blackwell, Jtn	2	10	1	0	0	1	1.000
Proseker, Geneva	1	8	0	0	0	1	1.000
Ovca, Newark	2	8	0	0	0	1	1.000
Munoz, Geneva	1	2	0	0	0	0	1.000
Cott, Wmpt	5	37	3	2	0	2	.952
Sydnor, Geneva	4	14	3	1	0	0	.944
Miller, Auburn	2	8	0	1	0	0	.889
Joiner, Jtn	1	13	0	2	0	4	.867

PITCHERS

Player and Club	G.	PO.	A.	E.	DP.	Pct.
DWYER, Batavia	15	3	18	0	2	1.000
DeLuca, Batavia	14	3	17	0	1	1.000
Jackson, Jtn	13	3	15	0	2	1.000
Johnson, Oneonta*	15	2	14	0	0	1.000
Hicks, Wmpt	28	4	10	0	0	1.000
McIlvaine, Batavia	12	0	13	0	0	1.000
Hippi, Oneonta	12	4	8	0	0	1.000
Sheanshang, Wmpt	12	2	9	0	0	1.000
Peckham, Jtn*	14	2	8	0	0	1.000
Johnson, Auburn	15	1	9	0	0	1.000
Laborio, Batavia	29	1	9	0	0	1.000
Cappello, Newark*	13	1	8	0	0	1.000
Baye, Batavia	12	2	6	0	0	1.000
Joiner, Jtn	17	2	6	0	0	1.000
Yard, Newark	11	2	5	0	0	1.000
Schmonsky, Newark	10	1	5	0	0	1.000
Stathos, Auburn	10	3	3	0	0	1.000
Dzitko, Jtn*	18	1	4	0	0	1.000
Flores, Auburn	10	1	2	0	0	1.000
Cupples, Auburn	10	0	2	0	0	1.000
Snyder, Oneonta*	16	0	2	0	1	1.000
Robbins, NF	12	16	18	1	1	.971
Wiley, Auburn	15	9	22	1	0	.969
Dixon, Auburn*	14	7	18	1	0	.962
Barton, Jtn	14	3	18	1	0	.955
Pettit, Geneva	24	2	18	1	1	.952
B. McRoberts, Wmpt	15	7	12	1	0	.950
Dalonzo, Oneonta	20	9	10	1	0	.950
Sanford, NF	12	7	10	1	1	.944
Leinheiser, Newark	11	3	10	1	2	.929
DeFilippis, Gen*	13	4	9	1	0	.929
Lang, Newark	16	3	10	1	0	.929
Couples, Oneonta	12	4	7	1	1	.917
Perrotta, Batavia	12	1	10	1	1	.917
Babbitt, Oneonta	10	4	7	1	1	.917
Norton, Auburn	13	8	12	2	0	.909
Gasque, Geneva	13	2	8	1	0	.909
Redmon, Geneva	13	3	7	1	0	.909
Canty, Wmpt*	18	2	8	1	0	.909
Cavanaugh, Bat	21	11	17	3	0	.903
Grover, Auburn*	13	0	9	1	1	.900
Kouns, Jamestown	13	3	13	2	0	.889
Kidd, Niagara Falls	22	2	6	1	0	.889
Arrendale, NF	12	6	9	2	0	.882
Spencer, Jtn	12	3	12	2	0	.882
Wolger, Wmpt	19	6	16	3	0	.880
LaRose, Jtn*	14	4	10	2	0	.875
Hazelip, Oneonta	10	3	4	1	0	.875
Bradshaw, Newark	11	4	3	1	2	.875
Quinn, Niagara Falls	14	2	4	1	0	.857
Bedenkop, Wmpt	23	3	14	3	0	.850
Elenes, Wmpt	13	3	8	2	1	.846
Crane, Wmpt	17	3	8	2	0	.846
Gilbert, Newark	15	2	3	1	1	.833
Brown, Geneva	15	2	11	3	0	.813
Bushey, Batavia	12	1	3	1	0	.800
Dudley, Jtn	11	3	4	2	1	.778
Vargason, One*	13	0	3	1	0	.750
Stonum, Newark	20	3	0	1	0	.750
Dumaw, Jtn	14	1	4	2	0	.714
Mason, Batavia*	15	0	5	2	0	.714
Ginter, Geneva	10	0	7	3	0	.700
Maluzhinsky, Bat	12	0	2	1	0	.667
Hyde, Niagara Falls*	15	0	4	5	0	.444

(Fewer Than Ten Games)

Player and Club	G.	PO.	A.	E.	DP.	Pct.
Darcy, Wmpt	9	3	11	0	1	1.000
Meyer, Niagara Falls	9	8	4	0	0	1.000
Medich, Oneonta	4	7	3	0	0	1.000
Steen, Newark	4	2	4	0	0	1.000
Tetrault, One*	6	4	3	0	1	1.000
Young, Jamestown*	5	1	4	0	0	1.000
Kemp, Geneva*	2	1	3	0	0	1.000
Barnes, Auburn*	9	1	3	0	0	1.000
Bryant, Jamestown	2	0	3	0	0	1.000
Wright, Jamestown	3	1	2	0	0	1.000
Clites, Niagara Falls	4	1	2	0	0	1.000
Lee, Niagara Falls	7	1	2	0	0	1.000
Brykczynski, Geneva	9	0	3	0	0	1.000
Lambert, Batavia*	2	0	3	0	0	1.000
McGrath, Batavia	3	0	2	0	0	1.000
Wastradowski, NF*	4	0	2	0	0	1.000
Cichon, Auburn	6	2	0	0	0	1.000
Thomas, Geneva	1	1	0	0	0	1.000
Saatzer, Geneva*	9	0	2	0	0	1.000
Cameron, Geneva	1	0	1	0	0	1.000
Szado, Geneva*	1	0	1	0	0	1.000
French, Geneva*	2	1	0	0	0	1.000
Johnson, Wmpt	2	0	1	0	0	1.000
McLane, Geneva*	2	0	1	0	0	1.000
Melton, Geneva*	3	0	1	0	0	1.000
Beck, Jamestown	4	0	1	0	0	1.000
Miller, Wmpt*	4	0	1	0	0	1.000
W. Johnson, NF	7	1	10	1	0	.917
Slagle, Niagara Falls	8	3	8	1	0	.909
O'Neill, Newark*	9	0	10	1	0	.909
Pagan, Oneonta	9	2	8	1	1	.909
Hannibal, One*	8	2	5	1	0	.875
Currence, NF*	4	1	5	1	0	.857
Fink, Batavia	6	1	5	1	0	.857
Jackson, Geneva*	4	0	6	1	0	.857
Strickland, NF*	7	0	5	1	0	.833
Lawson, Newark	3	3	2	1	0	.833
Gunter, NF	4	1	3	1	0	.800
Morrison, Batavia	3	1	3	1	0	.800
Barker, Oneonta	4	1	4	2	0	.714
Mazza, NF	4	1	1	1	0	.667
Provenzano, Wmpt*	4	1	0	1	0	.500
Miller, Geneva	4	0	0	1	0	.000
Boggs, Wmpt	9	0	0	1	0	.000

The following players do not have any recorded accepted chances at the positions indicated; therefore are not listed in the fielding averages for those particular positions: Allen, p; Bruce, p; Collins, p; Foulk, p; Hamilton, of; Keller, pr; Killian, p; May, p; O'Keefe, ss; Owens, ph; Sage, ph; Ward, p.

CLUB PITCHING

Club	G.	CG.	ShO.	Sv.	IP.	H.	R.	ER.	HR.	BB.	Int.BB.	HB.	SO.	WP.	Bk.	ERA.
Auburn	70	41	12	6	581	504	257	183	29	246	4	18	588	69	1	2.83
Niagara Falls	67	27	2	7	562	543	320	221	27	296	25	14	514	39	1	3.54
Batavia	70	17	4	12	583	569	316	240	61	254	29	14	552	47	2	3.70
Oneonta	70	23	4	12	575	564	320	240	29	258	9	15	499	34	3	3.76
Geneva	69	30	4	5	556	511	325	237	29	309	13	30	519	29	2	3.84
Newark	69	23	10	16	559	552	300	242	32	243	7	22	513	30	1	3.90
Jamestown	70	19	4	9	575	576	341	250	28	275	9	32	493	25	1	3.91
Williamsport	70	11	3	11	573	575	387	307	21	352	9	27	509	44	0	4.82

PITCHERS' RECORDS

(Leading Qualifiers for Earned-Run Average Leadership—70 or More Innings)

*Throws lefthanded.

Pitcher—Club	G.	GS.	CG.	ShO.	W.	L.	Sv.	Pct.	IP.	H.	R.	ER.	HR.	BB.	Int.BB.	HB.	SO.	WP.	ERA.
Leinheiser, Newark	.11	11	10	4	9	2	0	.818	89	50	17	10	4	31	0	0	90	2	1.01
Wiley, Auburn	.15	15	14	6	10	3	0	.769	127	87	29	21	3	33	1	1	144	11	1.49
DeFilippis, Gen*	.13	12	9	2	9	2	0	.818	95	46	27	17	4	54	1	5	139	5	1.61
Dixon, Auburn*	.14	14	11	3	8	4	0	.667	109	88	38	27	7	20	0	2	105	4	2.23
Dwyer, Batavia	.15	11	2	1	5	5	0	.500	80	63	29	23	7	24	2	5	65	4	2.59
Arrendale, NF	.12	11	5	1	5	5	0	.500	79	59	36	23	5	40	1	2	86	6	2.62
Norton, Auburn	.13	13	10	0	9	4	0	.692	102	90	47	30	2	45	0	5	90	11	2.65
Grover, Auburn*	.13	13	5	2	7	6	0	.538	89	73	36	28	2	57	0	1	86	14	2.83
Cavanaugh, Bat	.21	14	7	2	8	6	2	.571	112	101	48	36	10	33	7	3	125	5	2.89
DeLuca, Batavia	.14	12	4	1	6	3	0	.667	77	77	33	25	8	26	0	0	66	0	2.92

Departmental Leaders: G—Laborio, 29; GS—Wiley, 15; CG—Wiley, 14; ShO—Wiley, 6; W—Wiley, 10; L—Jackson (Jtn), 9; Sv—Stonum, 9; Pct.—DeFilippis, Leinheiser, .818; IP—Wiley, 127; H—Cavanaugh, 101; R—Jackson (Jtn), 61; ER—Canty, 40; HR—Cavanaugh, 10; BB—Wolger, 58; IBB—Baye, Cavanaugh, 7; HB—Brown, 8; SO—Wiley, 144; WP—Grover, 14.

(All Pitchers—Listed Alphabetically)

Pitcher—Club	G.	GS.	CG.	ShO.	W.	L.	Sv.	Pct.	IP.	H.	R.	ER.	HR.	BB.	Int.BB.	HB.	SO.	WP.	ERA.
Allen, Williamsport	.1	0	0	0	0	0	0	.000	⅔	0	0	0	0	1	0	0	0	0	0.00
Arrendale, NF	.12	11	5	1	5	5	0	.500	79	59	36	23	5	40	1	2	86	6	2.62
Babbitt, Oneonta	.19	3	1	0	4	1	1	.800	42	47	25	16	0	15	1	0	20	4	3.43
Barker, Oneonta	.9	7	1	0	2	4	1	.333	44	49	28	22	2	27	1	1	27	2	4.50
Barnes, Auburn*	.9	6	1	1	2	1	0	.667	36	31	19	15	4	21	0	1	36	6	3.75
Barton, Jamestown	.14	8	1	0	4	3	0	.571	64	62	30	24	5	14	0	3	42	0	3.38
Baye, Batavia	.12	5	2	0	5	2	1	.714	49	41	28	26	6	25	7	1	48	2	4.78
Beck, Jamestown	.4	1	0	0	0	1	0	.000	8	14	6	4	0	3	0	1	4	0	4.50
Bedenkop, Wmpt	.23	8	1	3	4	4	1	.500	66	73	41	33	9	41	4	3	54	3	4.50
Boggs, Williamsport	9	5	1	0	0	0	0	.000	23	23	32	25	1	43	0	1	24	2	9.78
Bradshaw, Newark	.11	11	5	1	5	3	0	.625	75	81	36	30	6	24	1	2	52	3	3.60
Brown, Geneva	.13	13	6	1	7	4	0	.636	84	67	42	34	2	56	0	8	77	7	3.64
Bruce, Geneva	.2	0	0	0	0	0	0	.000	4	8	5	5	0	3	0	1	2	1	15.00
Bryant, Jamestown	.2	0	0	0	0	0	0	.000	4	4	1	0	0	3	0	1	1	0	0.00
Brykczynski, Gen	.9	4	0	0	1	2	0	.333	35	45	38	28	4	21	0	1	25	4	7.20
Bushey, Batavia*	.12	2	0	0	1	1	0	.500	20	18	15	7	4	11	0	1	23	6	3.15
Cameron, Geneva	.1	0	0	0	0	0	0	.000	7	3	3	1	5	0	0	0	6	0	4.50
Canty, Wmpt*	.18	6	1	0	2	4	2	.333	56	70	44	40	4	24	1	6	58	3	6.43
Cappello, Newark*	.13	8	2	1	3	5	0	.375	57	54	29	24	2	21	2	3	65	1	3.79
Cavanaugh, Bat	.21	14	7	2	8	6	2	.571	112	101	48	36	10	33	7	3	125	5	2.89
Cichon, Auburn	.6	0	0	0	4	0	1	1.000	13	10	3	3	0	9	0	0	9	0	2.08
Clites, Niagara Falls	4	3	0	0	0	0	0	.000	10	21	25	15	1	15	0	1	5	2	13.50
Collins, Newark	.5	0	0	0	0	0	0	.000	5	8	5	5	0	2	0	0	5	3	9.00
Couples, Oneonta	.12	5	2	0	4	1	1	.800	59	52	33	22	2	18	1	2	34	2	4.04
Crane, Wmpt	.17	6	1	1	2	4	0	.333	59	51	35	26	4	28	0	4	60	6	3.97
Cupples, Auburn	.10	0	0	0	1	0	0	1.000	10	6	7	4	0	15	1	3	9	4	3.60
Currence, NF*	.4	1	0	0	0	0	0	.000	25	27	13	10	1	19	4	0	26	3	3.60
Dalonzo, Oneonta	.20	3	1	0	4	2	3	.667	56	54	23	20	0	29	1	1	50	3	3.21
Darcy, Wmpt	.9	3	1	0	4	3	0	.571	56	42	28	23	3	36	0	1	56	7	3.70
DeFilippis, Gen*	.13	12	9	2	9	2	0	.818	95	46	27	17	4	54	1	5	139	5	1.61
DeLuca, Batavia	.14	12	4	1	6	3	0	.667	77	77	33	25	8	26	0	0	66	0	2.92
Dixon, Auburn*	.14	14	11	3	8	4	0	.667	109	88	38	27	7	20	0	2	105	4	2.23
Dudley, Jamestown	.11	8	1	1	2	6	0	.250	45	54	36	32	2	14	2	1	18	1	4.32
Dumaw, Jtn	.14	0	0	0	1	1	0	.500	25	27	14	12	2	14	2	1	15	4	4.32
Dwyer, Batavia	.15	11	2	1	5	5	0	.500	80	63	29	23	7	24	2	5	65	4	2.59
Dzitko, Jtn*	.18	0	0	0	1	4	0	.533	44	56	36	27	1	25	2	5	35	4	5.52
Elenes, Wmpt	.13	7	1	0	2	4	0	.000	10	13	15	12	1	8	0	1	6	4	10.80
Fink, Batavia	.6	0	0	0	2	0	0	.000	19	25	26	17	4	13	0	3	22	6	8.05
Flores, Auburn	.10	0	0	0	0	0	0	.000	10	12	13	9	2	8	2	1	7	1	8.00
Foulk, Batavia*	.6	0	0	0	1	0	1	1.000	9	8	8	8	2	9	2	1	7	1	8.00
French, Geneva*	.2	1	0	0	0	0	0	.000	3	6	4	4	1	4	0	0	1	2	12.00
Gasque, Geneva	.13	1	0	0	2	1	0	.667	41	37	17	13	2	14	0	2	20	1	2.85
Gilbert, Newark	.15	0	0	0	3	0	2	1.000	24	24	8	3	1	9	2	0	18	1	1.13

Pitcher—Club	G	GS	CG	ShO	W	L	Sv	Pct.	IP	H	R	ER	HR	BB	Int.BB	HB	SO	WP	ERA
Ginter, Geneva	10	9	1	0	0	6	0	.000	43	49	36	24	2	34	1	3	30	4	5.02
Grover, Auburn*	13	13	5	2	7	6	0	.538	92	73	36	28	2	57	0	1	86	14	2.83
Gunter, NF	4	4	2	0	1	2	0	.333	24	20	11	4	2	8	0	2	24	0	1.50
Hannibal, One*	8	6	1	0	3	1	0	.750	38	30	21	17	3	34	0	2	38	4	4.03
Hazelip, Oneonta	10	9	2	0	5	2	0	.714	57	60	27	19	2	21	0	1	49	3	3.00
Hicks, Wmpt	28	1	0	0	1	4	5	.200	43	47	24	22	2	22	1	0	33	1	4.60
Hippi, Oneonta	12	9	4	1	4	4	0	.500	65	53	30	22	4	38	0	3	74	2	3.74
Hyde, Nia Falls*	15	0	0	0	2	2	1	.500	27	33	18	9	1	14	1	1	40	2	3.00
Jackson, Geneva*	6	6	2	0	2	3	0	.400	31	33	26	15	0	22	0	3	32	1	4.35
Jackson, Jtn*	13	13	4	0	4	9	0	.308	79	80	61	37	5	45	0	5	69	1	4.22
Johnson, Auburn	15	3	0	0	1	3	0	.250	34	49	25	17	5	14	0	0	38	3	4.50
W. Johnson, NF	7	7	3	0	2	2	0	.500	46	34	27	20	4	35	2	1	24	3	3.91
Johnson, One*	15	10	2	0	2	5	3	.286	69	69	41	32	6	21	1	1	62	1	4.17
Johnson, Wmpt	2	0	0	0	0	0	0	.000	4	6	9	9	0	10	0	0	6	0	20.25
Joiner, Jtn	17	0	0	0	3	1	3	.750	25	25	15	11	2	19	2	1	18	0	3.96
Kemp, Geneva*	2	1	0	0	1	1	0	.500	10	9	6	4	0	6	0	0	12	0	3.60
Kidd, Niagara F	22	1	0	0	3	1	2	.750	36	35	24	16	2	19	2	2	29	1	4.00
Killian, Batavia*	2	0	0	0	0	0	0	.000	3	7	5	2	0	2	0	1	3	0	6.00
Kouns, Jamestown	11	9	3	0	4	4	0	.500	61	60	27	24	2	10	1	4	46	0	3.54
Laborio, Batavia	29	0	0	0	3	2	6	.600	44	47	19	14	4	18	3	0	32	4	2.86
Lambert, Batavia*	2	2	1	0	1	0	0	1.000	14	11	10	8	2	9	0	0	19	3	5.14
Lang, Newark	16	5	1	1	5	5	0	.500	57	42	19	13	1	24	0	4	57	6	2.05
LaRose, Jtn*	14	14	4	1	4	4	0	.500	83	82	43	31	3	39	2	1	87	3	3.36
Lawson, Newark	9	7	2	0	1	6	0	.143	37	50	42	37	4	18	0	1	31	4	9.00
Lee, Niagara Falls	7	0	0	0	0	1	0	.000	12	12	14	12	0	13	1	0	12	0	9.00
Leinheiser, Newark	11	11	10	4	9	2	0	.818	89	50	17	10	4	31	0	0	90	2	1.01
Maluzhinsky, Bat	12	0	0	0	2	1	2	.667	18	20	10	9	4	9	2	0	13	1	4.50
Mason, Batavia*	15	7	0	0	2	3	0	.400	43	45	35	24	4	22	0	1	51	5	5.02
May, Newark	5	0	0	0	0	0	0	.000	9	12	11	11	0	8	0	1	5	1	11.00
Mazza, Niagara F	4	1	0	0	0	1	0	.000	8	9	7	6	0	7	0	0	8	6	6.75
McGrath, Newark	3	0	0	0	0	3	0	.000	12	23	16	14	2	3	0	1	11	4	10.50
McIlvaine, Bat	12	5	1	0	0	3	1	.000	36	43	27	16	7	21	1	1	27	5	4.00
McLane, Geneva*	2	0	0	0	0	0	0	.000	2	4	1	1	0	1	0	0	2	0	0.00
B. McRoberts, Wpt	15	12	2	1	5	4	0	.556	85	77	53	38	1	35	0	1	61	4	4.02
Medich, Oneonta	4	4	3	1	3	1	0	.750	31	16	10	5	2	14	0	0	32	0	1.45
Melton, Geneva	3	1	0	0	0	1	0	.000	5	9	5	5	0	1	0	0	3	0	9.00
Meyer, Niagara F.	9	9	4	1	2	7	0	.222	66	59	20	16	1	20	3	0	53	3	2.18
Miller, Geneva	8	4	0	0	0	3	0	.000	18	25	18	8	0	12	2	0	11	0	4.00
Miller, Wmpt	4	0	0	0	0	1	0	.000	7	12	13	11	1	9	0	1	5	1	14.14
Morrison, Batavia	9	3	0	0	1	3	0	.250	19	27	17	13	1	9	1	1	11	2	6.16
Norton, Auburn	13	13	10	0	9	4	0	.692	102	90	47	30	2	45	0	5	90	11	2.65
O'Neill, Newark*	9	7	1	1	4	1	0	.800	50	40	22	17	3	35	0	0	44	1	3.06
Pagan, Oneonta	9	7	4	0	4	3	0	.571	58	54	26	19	1	31	1	2	56	1	2.95
Peckham, Jtn*	14	5	0	0	3	6	1	.333	48	58	45	32	3	36	0	4	48	3	6.00
Perrotta, Batavia	17	6	0	0	2	1	0	.667	49	47	20	17	1	29	3	0	55	6	3.12
Pettit, Geneva	24	2	1	0	1	7	3	.125	52	56	28	22	3	22	6	4	44	1	3.81
Provenzano, Wmpt*	4	1	0	0	0	1	0	.000	12	7	4	4	0	8	0	0	13	0	3.00
Quinn, Niagara F	14	2	0	0	0	2	1	.000	26	27	22	14	1	20	2	2	24	2	4.85
Redmon, Geneva	13	13	9	1	9	3	0	.750	96	80	46	38	8	32	1	1	81	3	3.56
Robbins, NF	12	12	7	0	4	7	0	.364	96	92	39	34	3	28	3	2	79	2	3.19
Saatzer, Geneva*	9	0	0	0	0	0	0	.000	15	17	10	7	0	11	2	2	19	1	4.20
Sanford, NF	12	2	0	0	5	3	0	.625	50	49	24	17	2	18	4	1	56	3	3.06
Schmonsky, New	10	6	1	1	3	3	0	.500	40	43	25	20	4	18	0	2	33	0	4.50
Sheanshang, Wmpt	12	6	2	1	6	3	0	.667	48	45	21	14	1	13	0	1	32	1	2.63
Slagle, Niagara F	8	3	0	0	3	3	0	.500	43	46	30	19	3	33	1	1	39	5	3.98
Snyder, Oneonta*	16	4	1	0	2	3	0	.400	30	39	27	22	5	18	1	0	20	8	6.60
Spencer, Jtn	12	12	6	1	5	6	0	.455	81	66	34	28	1	32	1	5	78	5	3.11
Stathos, Auburn	10	6	0	0	2	3	0	.400	42	45	27	21	2	21	1	1	45	9	4.50
Steen, Newark	4	4	0	0	2	1	0	.667	24	26	16	12	3	11	0	0	8	0	4.50
Stonum, Newark	20	0	0	0	0	0	9	.000	32	33	19	17	1	13	0	1	36	1	4.78
Strickland, NF*	7	0	0	0	1	0	0	1.000	11	14	8	4	0	2	0	0	6	1	3.27
Szado, Geneva*	1	1	0	0	1	0	0	1.000	7	2	2	2	0	5	0	0	9	0	2.57
Tetrault, Oneonta	3	1	0	0	3	1	0	.750	23	25	17	10	0	5	0	0	16	2	3.91
Thomas, Geneva	7	0	0	0	0	1	0	.000	11	15	8	8	2	6	0	0	7	0	6.55
Vargason, One*	13	0	0	0	1	0	0	1.000	13	16	12	9	0	6	1	1	15	2	6.23
Ward, Jamestown*	1	0	0	0	0	0	0	.000	2	4	4	4	0	0	0	1	1	0	18.00
Wastradowski, NF*	4	1	0	0	0	0	0	.000	4	4	2	2	1	5	0	0	3	0	4.50
Wiley, Auburn	15	15	14	6	10	3	0	.769	127	87	29	21	3	33	1	1	144	11	1.49
Wolger, Wmpt	19	9	1	0	3	7	0	.300	69	66	47	35	0	58	1	3	72	12	4.57
Wright, Jtn	7	0	0	0	0	1	0	.000	8	1	1	0	0	4	0	1	4	1	1.13
Yard, Newark	11	7	0	0	1	3	0	.250	47	57	35	29	1	26	2	4	58	3	5.55
Young, Jamestown*	5	0	0	0	0	1	0	.000	10	12	10	6	0	6	0	1	7	1	5.40

BALKS—Barnes, Baye, Brown, Dalonzo, Hippi, W. Johnson, Johnson (One), Laborio, LaRose, O'Neill, Thomas, 1 each.

COMBINATION SHUTOUTS—Barton-Dudley-Wright, Jamestown; O'Neill-Stonum, Newark; Hazelip-Snyder, Hannibal-Couples, Oneonta.

NO-HIT GAME—Arrendale, Niagara Falls, defeated Newark, 1-0, July 23.

Northern League

CLASS A

CHAMPIONSHIP WINNERS IN PREVIOUS YEARS

1902—Winnipeg .... .649
1903—Winnipeg .... .690
1904—Duluth .... .720
1905—Duluth .... .653
1906—Calumet .... .620
1907—Winnipeg .... .722
1908—Brandon .... .617
1909—Duluth .... .556
1910—Eau Claire .... .642
1911—Superior .... .667
1912—Disbanded in June.
1913—Winona .... .686
1914—Duluth .... .656
1915—Fargo-Moorhead ... .602
1916—Winnipeg§ .. .574
   Fargo-Moorhead§ .. .679
1917—Fargo .... .667
1918-32—Did not operate.
1933—Superior* .... .647
   Brandon .... .672
1934—Superior .... .639
   Fargo-Moorhead* .. .610
1935—Winnipeg* .... .772
   Fargo-Moorhead ... .700

1936—Jamestown .... .598
   Eau Claire (2nd)‡. .563
1937—Duluth† .... .675
1938—Superior .... .684
   Duluth (2nd)‡ ... .621
1939—Winnipeg‡ .... .610
1940—Grand Forks† .... .642
1941—Wausau .... .640
   Eau Claire (4th)‡ ... .536
1942—Eau Claire .... .664
   Winnipeg (2nd)‡ .. .661
1943-44-45—Did not operate.
1946—St. Cloud† .... .702
1947—Aberdeen .... .695
   Sioux Falls (2nd)‡. .636
1948—Grand Forks† .... .672
1949—Eau Claire .... .577
   Aberdeen (2nd)‡ .. .568
1950—St. Cloud .... .585
   Sioux Falls (3rd)‡.. .560
1951—Eau Claire .... .636
   Grand Forks (4th)‡. .508
1952—Superior† .... .659
1953—Fargo-Moorhead† .. .688

1954—Fargo-Moorhead† .. .607
1955—Eau Claire .... .653
   St. Cloud (2nd)‡ .. .624
1956—Eau Claire .... .574
   Duluth-Sup'r (3rd)‡ .529
1957—Duluth-Superior ... .625
   Winnipeg* .... .593
1958—St. Cloud .... .590
   Fargo-Moor. (2nd)‡ .585
1959—Winnipeg† .... .661
1960—Winnipeg† .... .585
1961—Duluth-Superior ... .594
   Aberdeen (2nd)‡ ... .578
1962—Grand Forks .... .581
   Eau Claire (3rd)‡ .. .524
1963—Duluth-Superior ... .642
   Grand Forks (5th)x .. .458
1964—Aberdeen y .... .684
1965—St. Cloud .... .652
1966—St. Cloud .... .731
1967—St. Cloud .... .629
1968—St. Cloud .... .614
1969—Duluth-Superior ... .667

*Won split-season playoff. †Won championship and four-team playoff. ‡Won four-team playoff. §Playoff between first and second-half winners abandoned after each club won two games. xWon Baukol playoff based on last 30 games of season. yWon championship and Baukol playoff. (NOTE–Known as Northern Copper County League in 1906-07 and as Minnesota-Wisconsin League from 1909 to 1912.)

STANDING OF CLUBS AT CLOSE OF SEASON, SEPTEMBER 7

Club	D.-S.	Hur.	Abe.	Wtn.	St.C.	S.F.	W.	L.	T.	Pct.	G.B.
Duluth-Superior (4*)	..	8	7	9	11	13	48	21	0	.696	....
Huron (14*)	5	..	5	9	10	8	37	31	0	.544	10½
Aberdeen (1*)	7	8	..	5	7	9	36	33	0	.522	12
Watertown (18*)	5	5	9	..	7	6	32	38	0	.457	16½
St. Cloud (9*)	3	4	7	7	..	10	31	39	0	.443	17½
Sioux Falls (15*)	1	6	5	8	4	..	24	46	0	.343	24½

Key to major league farm teams (indicated by numbers after clubs in standing) shown on Page 384.

Playoff—None.

Regular-Season Attendance—Aberdeen, 20,880; Duluth, 22,747; Huron, 23,997; St. Cloud, 27,581; Sioux Falls, 21,477; Watertown, 14,475. Total, 131,157. No playoff. No all-star game.

Managers: Aberdeen—Ken Rowe; Duluth-Superior—Joe Sparks; Huron—George Freese; St. Cloud —Jim Merrick; Sioux Falls—Russ Nixon; Watertown—Bobby Malkmus.

All-Star Team: None selected.

(Compiled by Howe News Bureau, Chicago, Ill.)

CLUB BATTING

Club	G.	AB.	R.	OR.	H.	TB.	2B.	3B.	HR.	RBI.	SH.	SF.	BB.	Int. BB.	HP.	SO.	SB.	CS.	LOB.	Pct.
Duluth-Superior	69	2410	469	335	695	996	114	29	43	383	28	27	339	17	18	438	91	23	580	.288
Aberdeen	68	2368	407	433	632	898	94	14	48	334	41	17	363	18	17	591	47	32	577	.267
Watertown	70	2404	375	427	614	858	87	11	45	319	33	18	342	7	16	589	69	28	584	.255
St. Cloud	70	2402	372	370	603	871	96	14	48	307	23	22	343	13	15	588	81	24	579	.251
Huron	68	2207	378	313	549	733	83	17	53	323	18	26	382	15	21	501	20	5	577	.249
Sioux Falls	70	2257	283	406	493	663	70	14	24	238	30	16	307	7	17	608	103	35	526	.218

INDIVIDUAL BATTING

(Leading Qualifiers for Batting Championship—217 or More Plate Appearances)

*Bats lefthanded. †Switch-hitter.

Player and Club	G.	AB.	R.	H.	TB.	2B.	3B.	HR.	RBI.	SH.	SF.	BB.	HP.	SO.	SB.	CS.	Pct.
Houck, Steven, D-S*	58	219	51	80	116	12	6	4	41	0	1	50	2	37	14	4	.365
O'Connor, William M., Abe*	52	204	44	71	106	9	4	6	46	0	1	39	3	30	4	2	.348
Watson, Robert, Huron	64	237	59	81	131	19	5	7	40	2	3	37	2	37	8	0	.342
Yancy, Hugh, Dul-Superior	66	243	56	81	113	11	6	3	40	3	2	36	1	22	22	5	.333
Cavanaugh, Michael, St. C	61	222	46	73	97	8	2	4	33	1	3	28	1	43	14	1	.329
Johnson, Lamar, D-S	55	221	35	71	103	10	2	6	44	0	4	16	2	31	4	1	.321
Stafford, James, Aberdeen†	69	264	57	82	148	15	0	17	56	0	1	34	1	94	1	4	.311
Clapp, Terry, Aberdeen*	66	268	47	82	124	14	2	8	51	0	1	33	0	46	3	2	.306
Graham, Daniel, Aberdeen†	66	246	51	75	115	13	3	7	36	2	1	52	1	49	5	7	.305
Hale, Frank, Watertown	61	204	40	62	86	7	1	5	36	1	2	30	0	36	2	0	.304
Angelo, Steven, Watertown	68	283	43	86	113	15	0	4	35	1	2	22	1	30	6	4	.304

Departmental Leaders: G—Poepping, 70; AB—Angelo, 283; R—Rourke, 74; H—Angelo, 86; TB—Stafford, 148; 2B—Watson, 19; 3B—Houck, Yancy, 6; HR—Stafford, 17; RBI—Stafford, 56; SH—Rourke, 9; SF—Linville, C. Miller, 5; BB—Bianchi, 56; HP—Arce, Youngblood, 5; SO—Poepping, Stafford, 94; SB—Yancy, 22; CS—Bekeza, 10.

(All Players—Listed Alphabetically)

Player and Club	G.	AB.	R.	H.	TB.	2B.	3B.	HR.	RBI.	SH.	SF.	BB.	HP.	SO.	SB.	CS.	Pct.
Abraham, Brian, Wtn*	13	27	2	3	3	0	0	0	1	0	3	0	9	0	0		.111
Allen, David, St. Cloud*	13	30	3	5	7	2	0	0	4	2	0	2	0	15	0	0	.167
Angelo, Steven, Watertown	68	283	43	86	113	15	0	4	35	1	2	22	1	30	6	4	.304
Arce, Felix, Watertown	58	206	25	55	70	8	2	1	21	0	0	16	5	64	9	2	.267
Aschermann, Kurt, Huron	1	3	2	1	1	0	0	0	1	0	0	1	0	2	0	0	.333
Atkinson, Michael, D-S	13	40	4	8	9	1	0	0	3	1	1	1	2	19	0	0	.200
Badcock, W. Thomas, Huron*	12	29	1	3	3	0	0	0	2	0	0	0	0	13	0	0	.103
Bannon, Mel, St. Cloud	38	82	8	17	24	4	0	1	10	0	1	16	0	41	3	0	.207
Barker, Gary, St. Cloud	13	39	2	9	13	2	1	0	4	2	0	3	0	15	1	0	.231
Barnes, Richard, Huron	14	14	2	3	7	1	0	1	3	0	0	2	0	1	0	0	.214
Beech, F. Charles, Huron	3	10	1	1	1	0	0	0	1	0	0	1	0	4	0	0	.100
Beerbower, Dan, Aberdeen	35	108	14	30	32	2	0	0	10	3	1	8	1	21	7	2	.278
Bekeza, Patrick, St. Cloud*	55	200	31	53	60	3	2	0	16	1	0	28	0	33	19	10	.265
Belluomini, Donald, Abe*	2	17	0	2	2	0	0	0	1	0	0	0	0	4	0	0	.118
Bianchi, James, Huron	55	162	29	26	40	6	1	2	14	2	3	56	4	59	0	0	.160
Biercevicz, Joseph, Huron	3	4	0	1	1	0	0	0	0	0	0	0	0	3	0	0	.250
Billmeier, Louis, D-S	20	45	3	9	11	2	0	0	6	0	0	3	0	0	0	0	.200
Blackard, Gordon, St. Cloud	24	17	3	4	5	1	0	0	2	0	1	5	0	5	0	0	.235
Blackstone, Richard, SF*	58	197	36	54	68	6	1	2	25	0	1	23	2	54	11	1	.274
Blake, Edward, Aberdeen	16	18	0	3	3	0	0	0	4	0	3	0	8	0	0		.167
Bonardel, Jeffrey, Abe	15	5	0	1	1	0	0	0	0	1	0	0	0	4	0	0	.200
Bonham, William, Huron	18	10	0	3	4	1	0	0	3	0	0	0	2	0	0	0	.300
Bourg, William, D-S	15	31	5	11	13	2	0	0	3	2	1	1	0	10	0	0	.355
Bracamontes, Ignacio, Huron*	13	28	5	5	11	0	0	2	6	1	2	5	2	13	0	0	.179
Breshers, Lloyd, Aberdeen	42	141	27	40	55	5	2	2	15	1	1	22	0	46	3	2	.284
Brooks, William, Aberdeen	6	2	0	0	0	0	0	0	0	0	0	0	0	2	0	0	.000
Brunick, Lloyd, St. Cloud	10	2	1	0	0	0	0	0	0	0	0	0	0	0	0	0	.000
Brunner, Randolph, Wtn*	33	46	2	9	12	1	1	0	0	0	0	2	0	12	0	0	.196
Buchan, R. Frank, D-S*	1	3	0	1	1	0	0	0	0	0	0	0	0	1	0	0	.333
Cain, Thomas, St. Cloud	12	9	2	3	3	0	0	0	1	0	0	0	0	1	0	0	.333
Carroll, Thomas, Sioux F*	12	26	1	3	4	1	0	0	2	3	1	0	1	7	0	0	.115
Case, Robert, St. Cloud	49	129	18	22	38	5	1	3	13	0	1	27	1	47	1	1	.171
Caudle, S. Ronald, Abe*	56	203	31	53	68	7	1	2	26	5	2	26	2	42	4	5	.261
Cavanaugh, Michael, St. C	61	222	46	73	97	8	2	4	33	1	3	28	1	43	14	1	.329
Champion, Carl, D-S	14	23	2	6	7	1	0	0	1	0	0	1	0	6	1	0	.261
Chrisman, Steven, Abe	18	7	1	1	1	0	0	0	2	0	0	0	0	3	0	0	.143
Clapp, Terry, Aberdeen*	66	268	47	82	124	14	2	8	51	2	1	33	0	46	3	2	.306
Clark, Lincoln, Watertown	17	56	8	14	24	1	0	3	8	1	1	11	1	23	2	1	.250
Clayton, Henry, Aberdeen	22	28	2	2	3	1	0	0	1	2	0	1	0	5	0	0	.071
Clouser, James, Huron	52	157	35	43	76	8	2	7	34	0	2	46	1	27	0	0	.274
Crews, Randolph, Huron	37	98	10	32	52	8	4	4	22	0	0	7	0	13	0	0	.327
Davis, James, Huron*	44	132	21	30	40	4	0	2	20	2	1	19	0	25	0	0	.227
DeGuire, Derry, St. Cloud	56	214	25	49	63	6	1	2	12	4	2	23	0	24	3	2	.229
Derr, Michael, Huron	62	247	50	70	104	9	5	5	22	1	3	22	3	50	7	4	.283
Dick, Ralph, St. Cloud	68	266	38	76	112	18	0	6	53	2	2	26	4	45	8	3	.286
Dreher, Robert, Sioux Falls†	50	141	18	26	42	4	0	4	21	0	2	34	1	59	2	1	.184
Duhe, Gene, Dul-Sup	10	24	4	3	3	0	0	0	0	2	0	4	0	4	0	0	.125
Durand, Dionel, Huron	36	99	13	17	29	1	1	3	14	0	1	13	2	39	1	1	.172
Faix, Albert, Sioux Falls	22	14	2	3	3	0	0	0	1	0	0	1	0	6	0	0	.214
Fiene, John, Dul-Sup	12	30	4	6	6	0	0	0	5	0	1	2	0	13	0	0	.200
Foust, Robert, Sioux Falls	19	7	1	1	1	0	0	0	1	0	0	2	1	3	0	0	.143
Frayser, William, Wtn†	46	144	23	34	47	7	0	2	18	3	0	40	1	29	4	1	.236
Gallagher, Robert, Sioux F	43	150	21	29	47	3	0	5	17	0	1	29	1	38	10	4	.193
Gause, Robert, St. Cloud*	10	3	1	1	1	0	0	0	0	0	0	1	0	1	0	0	.333
Giesler, Robert, D-S	13	11	0	0	0	0	0	0	0	0	0	0	0	4	0	0	.000
Gonzalez, Hector, Watertown	58	199	32	52	73	7	1	4	30	2	1	23	2	55	6	2	.261
Graham, Daniel, Abe†	66	246	51	75	115	13	3	7	36	2	1	52	1	49	5	7	.305
Griffy, G. Kenneth, SF*	51	164	20	40	50	2	1	2	24	2	2	23	1	41	10	7	.244
Guenther, Garret, Huron	28	100	13	22	25	3	0	0	8	0	1	8	3	18	1	0	.220

Player and Club	G.	AB.	R.	H.	TB.	2B.	3B.	HR.	RBI.	SH.	SF.	BB.	HP.	SO.	SB.	CS.	Pct.
Hagadorn, David, Sioux F	19	9	0	1	1	0	0	0	0	1	0	0	0	3	0	0	.111
Hale, Frank, Watertown ...	61	204	40	62	86	7	1	5	36	1	2	30	0	36	2	0	.304
Harkness, Michael, St. Cloud	8	11	1	2	2	0	0	0	0	0	0	1	0	3	0	0	.182
Harrington, Dale, Wtn	22	34	5	8	10	2	0	0	3	3	0	1	0	7	0	0	.235
Hasbrouck, Jack, St. Cloud*	58	166	30	39	65	12	1	4	23	1	3	37	1	47	0	0	.235
Hecomovich, Frank,																	
6 Huron-7 St. Cloud* ..	13	15	0	0	0	0	0	0	0	0	0	2	0	13	0	0	.000
Hildebrandt, Bruce, Huron*	23	67	14	13	24	2	0	3	9	0	0	14	0	26	0	0	.194
Hines, Marvin A., Aberdeen	56	220	31	53	68	6	0	3	20	4	1	23	1	36	9	5	.241
Hoffman, Ross, Watertown*	35	62	10	16	23	4	0	1	9	2	0	14	0	13	1	1	.258
Houck, Steven, D-S*	58	219	51	80	116	12	6	4	41	0	1	50	2	37	14	4	.365
Hughes, James, St. Cloud ..	14	23	1	1	1	0	0	0	3	3	0	2	0	10	1	0	.043
Hundley, Kenneth, Huron ..	8	19	2	4	7	0	0	1	3	0	0	2	1	7	0	0	.211
Jackson, Rex, Sioux Falls ..	20	23	3	8	9	1	0	0	2	0	0	0	0	5	0	0	.348
James, Gary, Huron†	9	9	0	2	3	1	0	0	1	0	0	2	0	3	0	0	.222
Johnson, Lamar, D-S	55	221	35	71	103	10	2	6	44	0	4	16	2	31	4	1	.321
Jones, Christopher, SF	62	192	37	57	87	8	2	6	31	0	1	35	1	57	14	2	.297
Jones, Terrell, Huron*	29	70	13	17	31	5	0	3	16	1	1	18	0	17	0	0	.243
Juniel, James, Aberdeen ...	49	113	32	24	33	4	1	1	14	0	1	42	3	34	9	1	.212
Kenary, Adrian, D-S	20	20	5	6	10	2	1	0	2	1	0	3	0	2	0	0	.300
Kernan, William, Abe	29	13	0	0	0	0	0	0	0	1	0	2	0	10	0	0	.000
Kimm, Bruce, Dul-Sup	64	238	50	64	87	12	1	3	43	2	1	47	0	35	7	1	.269
Kopylow, Boris, Watertown .	6	1	0	0	0	0	0	0	0	0	0	0	0	0	0	0	.000
Krull, David, Watertown ...	30	103	28	28	36	2	0	2	7	0	0	18	0	19	8	3	.272
Kusick, Craig, St. Cloud ..	61	201	35	59	93	13	0	7	41	0	2	46	2	31	3	1	.294
LaPointe, David, Watertown*	19	52	10	10	13	0	0	1	7	2	1	13	0	14	2	1	.192
Lee, R. William, Aberdeen†.	8	15	2	1	1	0	0	0	0	2	0	1	0	9	0	0	.067
Leopaldi, Anthony, Abe	25	64	14	16	22	1	1	1	5	0	0	3	2	18	1	0	.250
Liebeck, Michael, Watertown	56	190	31	45	59	2	0	4	15	0	1	29	0	55	5	3	.237
Linville, Larry, D-S	35	115	31	38	69	8	1	7	31	0	5	27	2	17	4	2	.330
Locklear, Gene, Sioux Falls*	23	83	12	24	33	5	2	0	14	1	0	14	0	19	0	0	.289
Loewe, Dennis, St. Cloud ..	36	52	11	13	24	2	0	3	8	0	1	10	1	19	2	1	.250
Lucke, Richard, Dul-Sup* ..	45	129	24	33	48	3	0	4	27	1	1	26	2	23	2	1	.256
Madison, Lyle, Wtn	18	5	0	0	0	0	0	0	0	0	0	0	0	5	0	0	.000
Martin, Frank, Sioux Falls .	20	13	2	2	3	1	0	0	1	1	0	4	0	7	0	0	.154
Mavroleon, James, Sioux F .	13	24	2	5	7	2	0	0	2	0	0	1	0	7	0	0	.208
McElroy, Thomas, Abe*	27	17	3	5	5	0	0	0	1	1	0	2	0	4	0	0	.294
McEnaney, William, Sioux F	16	30	7	4	4	0	0	0	1	2	0	2	0	8	0	0	.133
Melum, David, Dul-Sup	17	47	9	16	22	4	1	0	10	0	0	4	0	13	0	0	.340
Miller, Charles, B., D-S ...	69	257	43	71	99	15	2	3	37	4	5	31	1	40	6	2	.276
Miller, N. Peter, Aberdeen .	32	77	10	14	15	1	0	0	8	2	1	15	0	27	0	1	.182
Mitchell, Emery, D-S	4	5	1	2	2	0	0	0	1	0	0	2	0	0	0	0	.400
Motsinger, Richard, D-S ...	35	102	11	22	29	5	1	0	15	0	1	9	0	11	3	0	.216
Murray, Dale, Watertown ..	22	12	1	2	2	0	0	0	1	4	0	0	0	4	0	0	.167
Nicholson, Theodore, D-S ..	54	217	38	63	111	11	5	9	37	0	0	13	2	63	0	1	.290
Norman, Stan, Sioux Falls .	27	63	3	9	11	2	0	0	8	0	1	11	1	21	0	1	.143
O'Connor, William M., Abe*	52	204	44	71	106	9	4	6	46	0	1	39	3	30	4	2	.348
Osentowski, Richard, St. C .	47	163	32	45	70	5	4	4	23	0	3	18	1	43	7	1	.276
Pastrovich, Mark, St. C* ...	15	17	1	3	3	0	0	0	1	2	0	2	0	5	0	0	.176
Patterson, Chester, Wtn ...	20	8	1	1	1	0	0	0	0	0	0	2	0	4	0	0	.125
Pinkham, L. William, SF ..	12	44	2	11	13	2	0	0	0	1	0	3	0	9	2	1	.250
Pipes, Ralph, Huron	18	11	1	3	3	0	0	0	2	0	0	0	0	1	0	0	.273
Platt, Robert, Aberdeen ...	14	25	1	5	6	1	0	0	1	0	1	3	0	9	0	0	.200
Poepping, Michael, St. Cloud	70	259	35	58	112	8	2	14	43	1	1	33	2	94	6	0	.224
Polczynski, Gary, Sioux F .	68	242	25	36	46	5	1	1	14	4	1	43	3	90	13	7	.149
Powell, Barry, Sioux Falls .	40	112	10	21	29	3	1	1	10	1	0	12	0	26	3	0	.188
Propson, Richard, D-S	10	2	0	1	1	0	0	0	0	0	0	0	0	1	0	0	.500
Reid, John, Watertown	43	144	22	39	50	5	0	2	27	0	3	32	0	27	4	2	.271
Reiten, Gary, Dul-Sup	12	18	2	5	5	0	0	0	1	0	0	0	0	3	1	0	.278
Reuschel, Rick, Huron	14	39	7	9	12	0	0	1	4	0	0	5	0	11	0	0	.231
Rolandson, Russell, St. C ..	61	237	41	61	65	4	0	0	15	4	1	25	2	29	12	3	.257
Rourke, Daniel, D-S	69	275	74	66	90	11	2	3	19	9	4	50	2	43	21	5	.240
Salazar, William, Watertown	16	42	6	7	11	1	0	1	3	1	1	12	1	9	0	0	.167
Satterlee, Michael, Abe ...	36	95	17	28	37	9	0	0	17	0	0	23	1	24	0	0	.295
Scanlon, J. Patrick, Wtn* ..	39	131	21	36	58	6	2	4	26	1	1	24	1	38	3	2	.275
Scherer, Michael, Watertown	16	20	5	4	4	0	0	0	2	0	0	1	0	6	0	0	.200
Schleider, Robert, Watertown	15	25	2	7	9	2	0	0	4	2	0	1	0	8	1	0	.280
Schmidt, Thomas, St. Cloud.	12	24	3	5	5	0	0	0	1	0	0	4	0	10	0	0	.208
Schwerman, Craig, Huron ..	14	23	1	6	6	0	0	0	4	0	0	1	0	5	0	0	.261
Scott, Anthony, Watertown .	63	243	41	61	104	9	2	10	46	3	3	27	1	70	13	4	.251
Seidel, Norman, Aberdeen ..	11	25	1	3	3	0	0	0	1	2	0	0	0	8	0	0	.120
Siereveld, Gregory, SF	56	181	15	37	46	5	2	0	15	4	2	17	0	49	8	5	.204
Skog, David, St. Cloud*	4	2	2	1	2	1	0	0	0	0	0	1	0	0	0	0	.500
Stafford, James, Aberdeen†	69	264	57	82	148	15	0	17	56	0	1	34	1	94	1	4	.311
Starkovich, Paul, Aberdeen .	16	32	3	3	5	2	0	0	2	0	0	4	0	15	0	0	.094
Steele, Steve, Watertown ..	45	129	12	31	46	8	2	1	19	1	2	14	3	28	1	1	.240
Steitz, Stephen, Huron*	35	101	27	29	55	5	1	3	28	0	3	31	2	18	0	0	.287
Stinson, Glenn, Huron	46	155	21	37	63	9	1	5	23	1	1	23	0	36	0	0	.239
Sublett, Harold, Aberdeen ..	2	1	1	0	0	0	0	0	0	0	0	0	0	0	0	0	.000
Sullivan, Paul, Watertown .	19	24	3	4	4	0	0	0	2	0	0	4	0	9	0	0	.167
Szorc, Stephen, D-S	24	11	2	0	0	0	0	0	0	0	0	2	1	7	0	0	.000
Talley, Joseph, Dul-Sup* ..	17	66	15	31	40	4	1	1	16	1	0	11	0	4	3	1	.470

Player and Club	G.	AB.	R.	H.	TB.	2B.	3B.	HR.	RBI.	SH.	SF.	BB.	HP.	SO.	SB.	CS.	Pct.
Thomas, Mark, Huron	10	16	0	0	0	0	0	0	0	1	0	0	1	5	0	0	.000
Tiemeier, Steven, D-S	13	6	0	1	1	0	0	0	0	0	0	0	0	5	0	0	.167
Tominesian, Greg, SF	10	28	5	5	6	1	0	0	4	0	1	7	0	7	2	0	.179
Ulsh, Barry, Sioux Falls* ..	61	241	31	61	84	8	3	3	21	4	2	22	0	34	14	1	.253
Upstone, E. Thomas, Huron*	11	6	0	0	0	0	0	0	0	0	0	0	0	4	0	0	.000
Urbanovich, Joseph, Huron .	32	81	15	21	28	1	0	2	14	1	2	24	0	14	0	0	.259
Vickery, O. Glenn, Wtn	18	13	2	0	0	0	0	0	0	0	1	2	0	8	0	0	.000
Vossler, Danny, St. Cloud† .	19	22	1	4	6	2	0	0	2	0	0	3	0	8	0	0	.182
Wall, H. William, Sioux F ..	16	29	1	2	2	0	0	0	1	0	0	0	0	14	0	0	.069
Watson, Robert, Huron	64	237	59	81	131	19	5	7	40	2	3	37	2	37	8	0	.342
White, Robert, Huron*	61	209	32	56	72	8	1	2	27	2	2	35	3	32	2	0	.268
Wood, William, Aberdeen .	46	134	20	36	43	4	0	1	19	0	2	25	2	30	2	0	.269
Woods, Robert, Huron	12	30	4	5	5	0	0	0	2	0	0	4	0	6	1	0	.167
Wooten, William, Aberdeen*	10	18	2	2	2	0	0	0	2	2	0	4	0	7	0	0	.111
Yaccarino, Daniel, Abe	12	4	0	0	0	0	0	0	0	0	0	1	0	0	0	0	.000
Yancy, Hugh, Dul-Sup	66	243	56	81	113	11	6	3	40	3	2	36	1	22	22	5	.333
Young, Michael, Huron	3	1	0	0	0	0	0	0	0	0	0	0	0	1	0	0	.000
Youngblood, Joel, Sioux F .	65	236	27	53	66	11	1	0	17	3	1	18	5	40	4	5	.225
Zachry, Patrick, SF	3	8	1	1	1	0	0	0	0	0	0	1	0	0	0	0	.125

GRAND-SLAM HOME RUNS—Davis, Dick, Lucke, Osentowski, Scanlon, Scott, Steitz, Watson, 1 each.

AWARDED FIRST BASE ON INTERFERENCE—Rourke 2 (Barker, Hasbrouck); Clouser (Kimm); Lucke (Hale); Yancy (Dreher).

CLUB FIELDING

Club	G.	PO.	A.	E.	DP.	PB.	Pct.
Duluth-Superior	69	1823	672	121	58	22	.954
St. Cloud	70	1835	680	125	50	31	.953
Huron	68	1712	678	130	39	34	.948
Aberdeen	69	1824	694	148	39	25	.944
Watertown	70	1845	783	165	63	27	.941
Sioux Falls	70	1788	660	156	42	26	.940

Triple Play—St. Cloud.

INDIVIDUAL FIELDING
(Ten or More Games)

*Throws lefthanded.

FIRST BASEMEN

Player and Club	G.	PO.	A.	E.	DP.	Pct.
Melum, Duluth-Sup .	13	69	4	1	3	.986
Jones, Huron	17	112	8	2	6	.984
Crews, Huron	24	154	4	3	12	.981
Steele, Watertown .	26	149	15	4	18	.976
Davis, Huron*	34	275	10	7	17	.976
POEPPING, St. C ..	69	537	22	14	42	.976
Johnson, Duluth-Sup	54	411	27	12	44	.973
Stafford, Aberdeen* .	68	510	31	19	32	.966
Hoffman, Watertown*	21	109	4	4	7	.966
Ulsh, Sioux Falls* ..	61	457	37	18	31	.965
Gonzalez, Watertown	24	171	13	8	18	.958
Blackstone, Sioux F.	12	83	4	5	8	.946

Triple Play—Poepping.

(Fewer Than Ten Games)

Player and Club	G.	PO.	A.	E.	DP.	Pct.
Champion, Dul-Sup .	3	18	0	0	1	1.000
Hale, Watertown ...	4	16	0	0	1	1.000
Juniel, Aberdeen ...	4	15	0	0	0	1.000
Miller, Aberdeen ...	2	13	1	0	0	1.000
Mitchell, Dul-Sup ..	1	12	0	0	0	1.000
Talley, Duluth-Sup .	1	8	0	0	0	1.000
DeGuire, St. Cloud .	1	6	0	0	1	1.000
Dick, St. Cloud	1	3	1	0	0	1.000
LaPointe, Watertown.	9	69	4	2	7	.973
Brunner, Watertown.	9	69	5	4	7	.949

SECOND BASEMEN

Player and Club	G.	PO.	A.	E.	DP.	Pct.
Frayser, Watertown .	30	53	74	3	11	.977
Bekeza, St. Cloud ..	30	73	55	4	12	.970
Rolandson, St. Cloud	34	78	76	6	18	.963
ROURKE, Dul-Sup .	69	169	171	14	39	.960
Siereveld, Sioux Falls	32	76	69	7	13	.954
Graham, Aberdeen ..	65	152	139	17	22	.945
Derr, Huron	46	98	120	16	17	.932
Angelo, Watertown ..	36	83	83	13	17	.927
Youngblood, SF	41	88	94	19	20	.905
Guenther, Huron ...	26	52	57	14	13	.886

(Fewer Than Ten Games)

Player and Club	G.	PO.	A.	E.	DP.	Pct.
Steele, Watertown ..	1	3	2	0	1	1.000
DeGuire, St. Cloud .	9	25	16	2	4	.953
Miller, Aberdeen ...	6	8	7	1	3	.938
Salazar, Watertown .	9	24	17	4	6	.911
Beerbower, Aberdeen.	1	2	1	1	0	.750

THIRD BASEMEN

Player and Club	G.	PO.	A.	E.	DP.	Pct.
Cavanaugh, St. Cloud	30	58		6	3	.936
WATSON, Huron ...	60	47	125	15	7	.920
Motsinger, Dul-Sup .	29	27	52	8	4	.908
DeGuire, St. Cloud .	22	11	38	5	6	.907
Youngblood, SF	22	20	38	6	1	.906
Angelo, Watertown .	32	24	65	10	6	.899
Powell, Sioux Falls .	35	26	63	10	7	.899
Siereveld, SF	22	24	35	7	1	.894
Case, St. Cloud	19	13	28	5	3	.891
Clapp, Aberdeen ...	66	65	176	32	11	.883
Scanlon, Watertown .	34	36	69	17	4	.861
Yancy, Duluth-Sup .	45	43	71	21	4	.844

Triple Play—Cavanaugh.

THIRD BASEMEN—Continued
(Fewer Than Ten Games)

Player and Club	G.	PO.	A.	E.	DP.	Pct.	Player and Club	G.	PO.	A.	E.	DP.	Pct.
Salazar, Watertown .	3	2	5	0	0	1.000	Steele, Watertown ..	2	0	2	0	0	1.000
Miller, Aberdeen	3	3	2	0	0	1.000	Woods, Huron	8	2	11	1	0	.929
LaPointe, Watertown	1	0	4	0	0	1.000	Hasbrouck, St. Cloud	1	0	3	1	0	.750
Bannon, St. Cloud ..	2	1	3	0	0	1.000	Liebeck, Watertown .	1	3	1	2	0	.667

SHORTSTOPS

Player and Club	G.	PO.	A.	E.	DP.	Pct.	Player and Club	G.	PO.	A.	E.	DP.	Pct.
Beerbower, Aberdeen.	26	30	77	7	10	.939	Bianchi, Huron	55	62	143	27	19	.884
Cavanaugh, St. Cloud	28	37	80	9	6	.929	Breshers, Aberdeen .	40	58	93	20	11	.883
DeGuire, St. Cloud ..	22	36	68	8	14	.929	Polczynski, SF	68	102	149	36	22	.875
Reid, Watertown	43	77	142	18	29	.924	Clark, Watertown ..	17	19	48	11	8	.859
Rolandson, St. Cloud	25	27	81	12	13	.900	Derr, Huron	16	15	31	9	6	.836
MILLER, Dul-Sup ..	69	107	159	30	32	.899	Frayser, Watertown	10	17	28	9	4	.833

(Fewer Than Ten Games)

Player and Club	G.	PO.	A.	E.	DP.	Pct.	Player and Club	G.	PO.	A.	E.	DP.	Pct.
Miller, Aberdeen	8	12	19	3	4	.912	Kusick, St. Cloud ..	1	3	0	1	0	.750
Salazar, Watertown .	3	4	5	1	1	.900	Yancy, Duluth-Sup	1	1	1	1	0	.667
Youngblood, SF	2	2	2	1	1	.800	Bannon, St. Cloud ..	1	1	0	2	0	.333

OUTFIELDERS

Player and Club	G.	PO.	A.	E.	DP.	Pct.	Player and Club	G.	PO.	A.	E.	DP.	Pct.
Lucke, Duluth-Sup* .	34	43	2	0	1	1.000	Durand, Huron	30	32	2	2	0	.944
Hildebrandt, Huron .	22	28	4	0	0	1.000	Nicholson, D-S	54	63	4	4	0	.944
Bekeza, St. Cloud ..	21	28	0	0	0	1.000	Osentowski, St. Cloud	41	65	1	4	0	.943
Leopaldi, Aberdeen .	19	25	1	0	0	1.000	Stinson, Huron	44	47	2	3	0	.942
Talley, Duluth-Sup .	17	21	2	0	0	1.000	Bannon, St. Cloud ..	21	27	2	2	1	.935
CLOUSER, Huron ..	51	97	3	1	0	.990	Linville, Duluth-Sup	34	36	6	3	1	.933
White, Huron	60	75	9	2	2	.977	Scott, Watertown ..	62	108	12	9	0	.930
Gallagher, SF	42	76	4	2	1	.976	Blackstone, SF	42	78	1	6	0	.929
Houck, Duluth-Sup*.	58	108	6	3	2	.974	Liebeck, Watertown .	50	64	3	6	0	.918
Dick, St. Cloud	66	127	5	5	2	.964	Criffey, Sioux Falls*	48	76	2	7	0	.918
Juniel, Aberdeen ...	36	50	1	2	1	.962	Yancy, Duluth-Sup .	20	29	2	3	0	.912
Jones, Sioux Falls ..	52	111	4	5	0	.958	Norman, Sioux Falls	12	9	0	1	0	.900
Krull, Watertown ..	27	41	2	2	1	.956	Arce, Watertown ...	49	68	3	8	1	.899
Loewe, St. Cloud ...	19	21	0	1	0	.955	Gonzalez, Watertown	34	38	4	5	1	.894
Lockbear, Sioux Falls	23	39	1	2	0	.952	Caudle, Aberdeen* ..	50	81	2	10	0	.892
Hines, Aberdeen	55	95	3	5	0	.951	Kusick, St. Cloud ..	55	73	7	11	1	.879
O'Connor, Aberdeen .	52	73	2	4	1	.949							

(Fewer Than Ten Games)

Player and Club	G.	PO.	A.	E.	DP.	Pct.	Player and Club	G.	PO.	A.	E.	DP.	Pct.
Miller, Aberdeen ...	6	8	0	0	0	1.000	Buchan, D-S	1	2	0	0	0	1.000
Jones, Huron	6	6	0	0	0	1.000	Rolandson, St. Cloud	1	2	0	0	0	1.000
Champion, Dul-Sup .	1	3	1	0	0	1.000	Steele, Watertown ..	1	1	0	0	0	1.000
Angelo, Watertown .	1	3	0	0	0	1.000	Cavanaugh, St. Cloud	2	1	0	0	0	1.000
Beech, Huron*	2	3	0	0	0	1.000	Case, St. Cloud	7	3	1	1	0	.800

CATCHERS

Player and Club	G.	PO.	A.	E.	DP.	PB.	Pct.	Player and Club	G.	PO.	A.	E.	DP.	PB.	Pct.
Case, St. Cloud	14	106	10	0	0	8	1.000	Steele, Watertown	18	107	15	3	1	2	.976
Urbanovich, Hur.	28	220	12	1	3	7	.996	Tominesian, SF ..	10	73	6	2	0	3	.975
KIMM, Dul-Sup .	64	571	54	6	8	20	.990	Dreher, SF	47	295	22	10	3	12	.969
Hale, Watertown .	55	424	40	6	2	23	.987	Satterlee, Aber .	29	245	19	10	1	8	.964
Pinkham, SF	11	79	9	2	0	4	.978	Steitz, Huron ...	39	301	15	13	0	22	.960
Wood, Aberdeen .	41	270	29	7	1	17	.977	Barker, St. Cloud.	13	96	15	5	2	6	.957
Hasbrouck, St. C.	54	381	31	10	4	17	.976								

(Fewer Than Ten Games)

Player and Club	G.	PO.	A.	E.	DP.	PB.	Pct.	Player and Club	G.	PO.	A.	E.	DP.	PB.	Pct.
Fiene, Duluth-Sup	7	55	1	0	0	2	1.000	Hundley, Huron .	7	51	3	1	0	4	.982
Wooten, Aberdeen.	6	42	0	0	0	0	1.000	Norman, Sioux F.	6	35	7	1	0	7	.977
LaPointe, Wtn ...	6	36	3	0	0	2	1.000	Platt, Aberdeen .	6	36	2	1	1	0	.974
Aschermann, Hur.	1	10	4	0	0	1	1.000								

PITCHERS

Player and Club	G.	PO.	A.	E.	DP.	Pct.	Player and Club	G.	PO.	A.	E.	DP.	Pct.
WALL, Sioux Falls .	16	8	18	0	1	1.000	Martin, Sioux Falls*	19	1	8	0	1	1.000
Faix, Sioux Falls* ..	22	4	12	0	0	1.000	Abraham, Watertown*	13	3	5	0	0	1.000
Atkinson, D-S	13	2	13	0	1	1.000	Belluomini, Abe* ...	12	1	5	0	1	1.000
Foust, Sioux Falls .	19	5	10	0	1	1.000	Loewe, St. Cloud ...	15	2	0	0	0	1.000
Vossler, St. Cloud ..	19	4	11	0	0	1.000	Cain, St. Cloud	11	0	5	0	1	1.000
Kernan, Aberdeen ..	29	5	10	0	0	1.000	Tiemeier, D-S*	13	1	4	0	0	1.000
Schmidt, St. Cloud .	12	0	10	0	0	1.000	Hoffman, Watertown*	16	1	4	0	1	1.000
Brunner, Watertown.	23	4	6	0	1	1.000	Bonardel, Aberdeen .	15	0	3	0	0	1.000
Chrisman, Aberdeen*	18	0	9	0	0	1.000	Bonham, Huron	18	0	3	0	0	1.000

PITCHERS—Continued

Player and Club	G.	PO.	A.	E.	DP.	Pct.
Madison, Watertown.	18	0	3	0	0	1.000
Propson, D-S*	10	0	1	0	0	1.000
Yaccarino, Aberdeen	12	0	1	0	0	1.000
Clayton, Aberdeen	22	10	14	1	0	.960
Kenary, Dul-Sup	20	8	15	1	1	.958
McEnaney, SF	15	4	16	1	0	.952
Starkovich, Abe	16	5	14	1	1	.950
Harrington, Wtn	22	2	16	1	2	.947
Schwerman, Huron	13	1	14	1	1	.938
Blake, Aberdeen	16	5	9	1	0	.933
Reuschel, Huron	14	4	22	2	1	.929
Blackard, St. Cloud	24	2	11	1	0	.929
Pipes, Huron	18	2	10	1	1	.923
Schleider, Watertown	15	2	21	2	2	.920
Mavroleon, SF	13	7	14	2	1	.913
Bourg, Dul-Sup	15	4	17	2	2	.913
Bracamontes, Hur*	13	2	18	2	0	.909
Pastrovich, St. C*	11	3	7	1	0	.909
Jackson, Sioux Falls	12	1	9	1	3	.909
Barnes, Huron*	14	2	8	1	0	.909
Seidel, Aberdeen	11	1	8	1	0	.900
Allen, St. Cloud*	13	2	7	1	0	.900
McElroy, Aberdeen*	27	1	8	1	0	.900
Badcock, Huron*	12	2	14	2	0	.889
Giesler, Dul-Sup*	13	1	7	1	1	.889
Hecomovich, Hu-StC*	13	0	8	1	0	.889
Vickery, Watertown.	18	2	6	1	0	.889
Reiten, D-S	12	3	11	2	0	.875
Upstone, Huron	11	1	6	1	0	.875
Hagadorn, SF	19	3	10	2	0	.867
Murray, Watertown	22	2	11	2	0	.867
Carroll, Sioux Falls.	12	6	12	3	0	.857
Szorc, Dul-Sup	24	0	6	1	1	.857
Hughes, St. Cloud	14	3	8	2	0	.846
Sullivan, Watertown	19	7	20	5	2	.844
Scherer, Watertown	11	2	14	3	3	.842
Billmeier, D-S	20	5	23	7	4	.800
Gause, St. Cloud	10	1	3	1	0	.800
Patterson, Watertown	20	0	8	3	1	.727
Thomas, Huron	10	2	2	2	0	.667

(Fewer Than Ten Games)

Player and Club	G.	PO.	A.	E.	DP.	Pct.
Lee, Aberdeen*	8	0	5	0	0	1.000
Zachry, Sioux Falls.	3	1	3	0	0	1.000
Biercevicz, Huron	3	0	2	0	0	1.000
Skog, St. Cloud*	4	1	1	0	1	1.000
Fiene, Dul-Sup	2	0	1	0	0	1.000
Brunick, St. Cloud	8	0	1	0	0	1.000
Duhe, Dul-Sup	9	3	10	1	0	.929
James, Huron*	9	0	5	1	0	.833
Harkness, St. Cloud	8	0	5	3	1	.625
Brooks, Aberdeen	6	2	2	3	0	.571
Jones, Sioux Falls	1	0	1	1	1	.500
Dick, St. Cloud	1	0	0	1	0	.000
Kopylow, Watertown.	6	0	0	1	0	.000

The following players do not have any recorded accepted chances at the positions indicated; therefore, are not listed in the fielding averages for those particular positions: Blackstone, p; Poepping, p; Siereveld, p; Stafford*, p; Sublett, ph; Young, p.

CLUB PITCHING

Club	G.	CG.	ShO.	Sv.	IP.	H.	R.	ER.	HR.	BB.	Int. BB.	HB.	SO.	WP.	Bk.	ERA.
Huron	68	22	6	12	571	519	313	227	33	291	7	11	570	56	2	3.58
Duluth-Superior	69	24	3	17	608	572	355	257	38	357	9	16	599	47	4	3.80
St. Cloud	70	20	1	8	612	587	370	269	40	365	8	19	571	40	5	3.96
Watertown	70	15	4	11	615	671	427	317	59	361	23	28	527	57	2	4.64
Sioux Falls	70	17	3	8	596	586	406	309	36	358	21	16	470	56	3	4.67
Aberdeen	69	11	1	15	608	651	433	333	55	344	9	14	578	60	3	4.93

PITCHERS' RECORDS

(Leading Qualifiers for Earned-Run Average Leadership—70 or More Innings)

*Throws lefthanded.

Pitcher-Club	G.	GS.	CG.	ShO.	W.	L.	Sv.	Pct.	IP.	H.	R.	ER.	HR.	BB.	Int. BB.	HB.	SO.	WP.	ERA.
Sullivan, Wtn	19	11	6	1	5	5	2	.500	86	85	37	19	2	25	2	2	68	5	1.99
Bracamontes, Hur*	13	13	5	3	7	3	0	.700	86	76	38	23	8	47	0	1	80	6	2.41
Kenary, D-S	20	5	3	0	7	1	3	.875	71	53	33	21	4	38	1	3	77	6	2.66
Bourg, D-S	15	10	4	2	5	3	3	.625	88	79	37	27	3	44	1	3	110	3	2.76
Carroll, SF	12	12	4	0	4	5	0	.444	86	69	51	27	2	54	2	0	63	10	2.83
Billmeier, D-S	20	14	6	1	11	3	3	.786	105	98	51	33	7	47	3	2	112	10	2.83
Vossler, St. Cloud	19	5	2	0	5	3	0	.625	70	55	31	22	2	31	1	3	75	5	2.83
Badcock, Huron*	12	10	5	0	6	4	1	.600	76	59	37	25	2	35	0	2	74	8	2.96
Harrington, Wtn	22	10	5	1	9	2	4	.818	101	99	43	34	4	39	2	4	103	7	3.03
Wall, Sioux Falls	16	10	2	0	4	2	1	.667	81	55	35	29	3	36	0	4	77	4	3.22

Departmental Leaders: G—Kernan, 29; GS—Billmeier, Clayton, McEnaney, Reuschel, 14; CG—Reuschel, 7; ShO—Bracamontes, 3; W—Billmeier, 11; L—McEnaney, 10; Sv—Kernan, Szorc, 7; Pct.—Kenary, .875; IP—Billmeier, 105; H—McEnaney, 104; R—McEnaney, 65; ER—McEnaney, 50; HR—Allen, Vickery, 9; BB—Hughes, 66; IBB—Murray, 6; HB—Hughes, 6; SO—Billmeier, 112; WP—Scherer, 15.

(All Pitchers—Listed Alphabetically)

Pitcher-Club	G.	GS.	CG.	ShO.	W.	L.	Sv.	Pct.	IP.	H.	R.	ER.	HR.	BB.	Int. BB.	HB.	SO.	WP.	ERA.
Abraham, Wtn*	13	12	3	1	5	3	0	.625	76	73	45	32	8	38	0	0	71	1	3.79
Allen, St. Cloud*	13	12	2	1	5	4	0	.400	79	88	49	37	9	42	1	1	68	9	4.22
Atkinson, D-S	13	13	5	0	8	3	0	.727	97	92	54	45	6	57	2	1	106	5	4.18
Badcock, Huron*	12	10	5	0	6	4	1	.600	76	59	37	25	2	35	0	2	74	8	2.96
Barnes, Huron*	14	4	2	0	4	2	0	.667	44	41	18	15	3	24	2	1	33	4	3.07
Belluomini, Abe*	12	4	0	0	2	2	0	.500	41	36	16	14	5	18	0	0	48	5	3.07

Pitcher—Club	G	GS	CG	ShO	W	L	Sv	Pct.	IP	H	R	ER	HR	BB	Int. BB	HB	SO	WP	ERA
Biercevicz, Huron	3	2	0	0	0	0	0	.000	11	7	2	2	0	11	0	1	4	2	1.64
Billmeier, D-S	20	14	6	1	11	3	0	.786	105	98	51	33	7	47	3	2	112	10	2.83
Blackard, St. C	24	4	2	0	7	4	2	.636	69	60	26	20	4	24	2	0	75	3	2.61
Blackstone, SF	2	0	0	0	0	0	0	.000	4	10	9	6	2	3	0	2	1	0	13.50
Blake, Aberdeen	16	11	1	0	1	3	1	.250	65	84	51	46	7	37	0	1	65	0	6.37
Bonardel, Abe	15	0	0	0	1	0	1	1.000	24	24	22	18	6	18	0	0	20	4	6.75
Bonham, Huron	18	2	0	0	3	3	6	.500	39	27	20	13	0	24	0	1	69	3	3.00
Bourg, D-S	15	10	4	2	5	3	3	.625	88	79	37	27	3	44	1	3	110	3	2.76
Bracamontes, Hur*	13	13	5	3	7	3	0	.700	86	76	38	23	8	47	0	1	80	6	2.41
Brooks, Aberdeen	6	0	0	0	0	0	0	.000	12	13	12	8	1	11	0	0	9	1	6.00
Brunick, St. Cloud	8	0	0	0	0	0	0	.000	16	13	5	5	1	7	0	2	14	2	2.81
Brunner, Wtn	23	1	0	0	3	3	2	.000	34	28	22	12	3	34	1	3	44	1	3.18
Cain, St. Cloud	11	5	0	0	0	3	0	.000	31	38	22	16	2	13	0	0	27	1	4.65
Carroll, Sioux F	12	12	4	0	4	5	0	.444	86	69	51	27	2	54	2	0	63	10	2.83
Chrisman, Abe*	2	0	0	0	2	1	2	.667	32	39	29	20	3	21	2	2	24	2	5.63
Clayton, Abe	22	14	2	0	5	5	1	.500	88	88	60	43	6	48	1	2	63	4	4.40
Dick, St. Cloud	1	1	0	0	1	0	0	1.000	9	9	7	4	2	2	0	0	8	1	4.50
Duhe, Dul-Sup	9	9	5	0	6	2	0	.750	62	52	27	15	2	25	0	1	39	5	2.18
Faix, Sioux Falls*	22	3	0	3	4	0	3	.429	56	55	32	29	6	35	4	1	42	4	4.66
Fiene, Dul-Sup	2	1	0	0	0	0	0	.000	6	2	1	1	0	9	0	1	2	0	1.50
Foust, Sioux Falls	19	2	2	1	3	5	1	.375	45	32	19	16	1	23	2	0	27	8	3.20
Gause, St. Cloud	10	0	0	0	1	4	0	.200	19	26	14	9	1	4	0	1	16	0	4.26
Giesler, D-S*	13	5	1	0	1	4	0	.200	38	42	33	27	6	22	2	2	23	3	6.39
Hagadorn, SF	19	2	1	0	0	2	3	.000	41	45	42	23	3	28	3	5	26	10	5.05
Harkness, St. C	8	3	2	0	2	2	1	.500	33	18	16	9	1	19	1	1	24	0	2.45
Harrington, Wtn	22	10	5	1	9	2	4	.818	101	99	43	34	4	39	2	4	103	7	3.03
Hecomovich, 6 Hur-7 St.C*	13	6	1	0	2	4	1	.333	49	55	30	25	3	31	0	0	42	6	4.59
Hoffman, Wtn*	16	0	0	0	0	1	0	.000	30	32	24	19	2	27	4	2	23	2	5.70
Hughes, St. Cloud	14	13	3	1	2	4	0	.333	71	65	47	33	5	66	1	6	75	6	4.18
Jackson, Sioux F	12	10	1	1	1	7	0	.125	54	53	55	47	6	63	1	2	48	7	7.83
James, Huron*	9	6	1	0	1	6	0	.143	33	34	29	19	4	23	1	0	41	3	5.18
Jones, Sioux Falls	1	0	0	0	0	0	0	.000	⅔	0	0	0	0	1	0	0	0	0	0.00
Kenary, Dul-Sup	20	9	3	0	7	1	3	.875	71	53	33	21	4	38	1	3	77	6	2.66
Kernan, Aberdeen	29	1	0	0	5	4	7	.556	55	62	35	21	6	15	4	2	46	4	3.44
Kopylow, Wtn	6	0	0	0	0	0	0	.000	6	15	11	9	3	5	0	1	5	2	13.50
Lee, Aberdeen*	8	8	0	0	2	4	0	.333	43	51	32	25	2	43	0	2	27	3	5.23
Loewe, St. Cloud	15	0	0	0	4	1	0	.800	43	46	30	26	5	19	1	2	31	2	5.44
Madison, Wtn	18	1	0	0	0	2	1	.000	25	38	27	24	5	15	2	1	17	1	8.64
Martin, Sioux F*	9	3	1	0	3	4	2	.429	57	70	46	36	3	45	5	0	51	5	5.68
Mavroleon, SF	13	11	2	0	1	6	1	.143	65	73	43	38	4	32	3	1	45	3	5.26
McElroy, Abe*	27	5	0	0	5	7	1	.417	67	66	51	41	1	40	0	2	84	12	5.51
McEnaney, SF	15	14	1	0	3	10	0	.231	87	104	65	50	5	33	1	1	71	3	5.17
Murray, Wtn	22	4	0	4	6	1	0	.400	51	50	41	32	6	39	6	1	48	4	5.65
Pastrovich, St.C*	11	9	2	0	2	4	0	.333	40	52	43	34	3	52	1	3	54	5	5.10
Patterson, Wtn	20	3	0	0	4	5	0	.444	39	57	41	33	3	31	3	4	29	3	7.62
Pipes, Huron	18	0	0	0	1	0	2	1.000	44	44	27	21	2	17	0	1	55	5	4.30
Poepping, St. C	1	0	0	0	1	0	0	1.000	1	0	0	0	0	1	0	0	2	1	0.00
Propson, D-S*	10	0	0	0	0	0	0	.000	16	16	12	11	2	20	0	1	21	3	6.19
Reiten, D-S	12	9	0	0	2	0	0	1.000	47	55	38	35	5	36	0	1	31	6	6.70
Reuschel, Huron	14	14	7	0	9	2	0	.818	102	96	52	40	7	22	0	0	88	5	3.53
Scherer, Wtn	11	1	0	1	3	0	0	.250	51	57	43	35	6	48	1	4	40	15	6.18
Schleider, Wtn	15	13	0	0	3	4	0	.429	69	87	60	40	8	33	1	2	37	8	5.22
Schmidt, St. Cloud	12	12	3	0	2	5	0	.286	67	66	55	34	3	60	0	0	65	1	4.57
Schwerman, Huron	13	8	2	1	3	6	0	.333	57	49	32	26	1	36	2	3	42	11	4.11
Seidel, Aberdeen	11	11	5	1	5	3	0	.625	68	63	43	34	4	32	1	2	72	9	4.50
Siereveld, SF	1	0	0	0	0	0	0	.000	⅓	0	0	0	0	0	0	0	0	0	0.00
Skog, St. Cloud*	4	1	0	0	0	0	0	.000	9	12	6	4	0	8	0	0	9	1	4.00
Stafford, Abe*	1	0	0	0	0	0	0	.000	2	8	6	6	3	0	0	2	0	0	27.00
Starkovich, Abe	16	13	3	0	6	4	2	.600	91	89	54	41	2	45	1	1	98	7	4.05
Sullivan, Wtn	19	11	6	1	5	5	2	.500	86	85	37	19	2	25	2	2	68	5	1.99
Szorc, Dul-Sup	24	2	0	0	5	4	7	.55¢	56	63	33	27	2	36	2	1	56	2	4.34
Thomas, Huron	10	8	0	0	2	1	0	.667	40	46	31	20	1	28	1	0	37	4	4.50
Tiemeier, D-S*	13	1	0	0	3	1	0	.750	23	20	16	15	1	23	0	0	22	4	5.87
Upstone, Huron	11	0	0	0	2	3	0	.000	24	16	10	8	2	8	1	1	28	2	3.00
Vickery, Wtn	18	5	0	0	1	4	1	.200	47	50	33	28	9	27	1	4	42	8	5.36
Vossler, St. Cloud	19	5	2	0	5	3	3	.625	70	55	31	22	2	31	1	3	75	5	2.83
Wall, Sioux Falls	16	10	2	0	4	2	1	.667	81	55	35	29	3	36	0	4	77	4	3.22
Yaccarino, Abe	12	0	0	0	2	0	1	1.000	20	27	22	16	6	13	0	0	20	1	7.20
Young, Huron	3	0	0	0	0	3	0	.000	3	8	6	6	2	0	0	5	0	18.00
Zachry, Sioux F	3	3	1	1	2	1	0	.667	21	20	9	8	1	5	0	0	19	2	3.43

BALKS—Cain, Fiene, 2 each; Atkinson, Bracamontes, Brooks, Clayton, Faix, Hagadorn, Harrington, Kernan, Madison, Pastrovich, Pipes, Schmidt, Szorc, Vossler, Wall, 1 each.

COMBINATION SHUTOUTS — Badcock-Upstone, Thomas-Bonham, Huron; Abraham-Sullivan, Watertown.

NO-HIT GAME—None.

Northwest League

CLASS A

CHAMPIONSHIP WINNERS IN PREVIOUS YEARS

1901—Portland 675	1937—Wenatchee 603	1956—Yakima 691
1902—Butte 608	Tacoma* 627	Yakima 619
1903—Butte 578	1938—Yakima 583	1957—Eugene 576
1904—Boise 625	Bellingham (2nd)† ..511	Wenatchee* 647
1905—Vancouver 586	1939—Wenatchee 601	1958—Lewiston 621
Everett* 667	Tacoma (2nd)†† 533	Yakima* 594
1906—Tacoma 600	1940—Spokane 587	1959—Salem 623
1907—Aberdeen 625	Tacoma (4th)† 500	Yakima* 563
1908—Vancouver 578	1941—Spokane 669	1960—Yakima‡ 638
1909—Seattle 653	1942—Vancouver 594	Yakima 562
1910—Spokane 596	1943-44-45—Did not operate.	1961—Lewiston* 621
1911—Vancouver 628	1946—Wenatchee 622	Yakima 600
1912—Seattle 600	1947—Vancouver 566	1962—Wenatchee* 574
1913—Vancouver 600	1948—Spokane 614	Tri-City 580
1914—Vancouver 632	1949—Yakima 660	1963—Lewiston 594
1915—Seattle 564	Vancouver (2nd)† ..615	Yakima* 613
1916—Spokane 622	1950—Yakima 613	1964—Eugene 636
1917—Great Falls 592	1951—Spokane 655	Yakima* 611
1918—Seattle 588	1952—Victoria 631	1965—Lewiston 667
1919—Seattle 590	1953—Salem 635	Tri-City* 681
1920—Victoria 600	Spokane* 590	1966—Tri-City 679
1921—Yakima 710	1954—Vancouver* 636	1967—Medford 607
Yakima 660	Lewiston 629	1968—Tri-City 600
1922—Calgary§ 600	1955—Salem 646	1969—Rogue Valley 633
1923-36—Did not operate.	Eugene* 639	

*Won split-season playoff. †Won four-club playoff. §League disbanded June 18. (NOTE—Known as Pacific Northwest League 1901-02. Pacific National League 1903-04. Northwestern League 1905-18. Pacific Coast International League 1919-22 and Western International League 1937-54.)

STANDING OF CLUBS AT CLOSE OF SEASON, AUGUST 31

NORTHERN DIVISION

Club	Lew.	W.W.	T.-C.	C.B.	-N.B.	Bend	Med.	W.	L.	T.	Pct.	G.B.
††Lewiston (22*)	..	8	9	8	9	8	9	43	37	0	.538	....
Walla Walla (20*)	8	..	8	7	8	8	8	39	41	0	.488	4
§Tri-City (23*)	7	8	..	7	7	7	9	38	42	0	.475	5

SOUTHERN DIVISION

Club								W.	L.	T.	Pct.	G.B.
Coos Bay-North Bend (11)	7	9	9	..	11	9	45	35	0	.563	....	
Bend (Hawaii)	8	8	9	5	..	9	39	41	0	.488	6	
Medford (17*)	7	8	7	7	7	..	36	44	0	.450	9	

†Lewiston declared champion on basis of regular season record against Coos Bay-North Bend.
‡Lewiston represented Lewiston, Idaho and Clarkston, Washington.
§Tri-City represented Kennewick, Pasco and Richland, Washington.
Key to major league farm teams (indicated by numbers after clubs in standing) shown on Page 384.
Playoff—None.
Regular-Season Attendance—Bend, 21,677; Coos Bay-North Bend, 14,817; Lewiston, 22,395; Medford, 19,687; Tri-City, 30,320; Walla Walla, 32,043. Total, 140,939. No playoff. All-Star game at Kennewick, 1,637.
Managers: Bend—Charlie Silvera; Coos Bay-North Bend—Harry Bright; Lewiston—Fred Hatfield; Medford—Bill Berrier; Tri-City—Marty Keough; Walla Walla—R. G. Powel.
All-Star Team: 1B—Beall, Walla Walla; 2B—Van Wyck, Bend; 3B—Joost, Coos Bay-North Bend; SS—Ristig, Medford; OF—Hutchinson, Walla Walla; Bushman, Bend; Hunt, Tri-City; C—Ivie, Tri-City; Krines, Medford; P—Spillner, Tri-City; Millikan, Lewiston; Manager—Fred Hatfield, Lewiston.

(Compiled by William J. Weiss, League Statistician, San Mateo, Calif.)

CLUB BATTING

Club	G.	AB.	R.	OR.	H.	TB.	2B.	3B.	HR.	RBI.	SH.	SF.	BB.	Int. BB.	HP.	SO.	SB.	CS.	LOB.	Pct.
C. B.-N. B. ..	80	2735	478	459	744	1101	111	15	72	407	31	20	343	24	35	559	79	18	659	.272
Medford	80	2638	418	494	711	1031	116	24	52	357	28	23	304	11	21	558	56	26	617	.270
Lewiston	80	2608	468	405	699	1009	101	19	57	409	30	19	327	7	25	510	80	30	575	.268
Walla Walla .	80	2683	458	469	712	1085	124	15	73	395	22	22	381	5	28	581	83	20	656	.265
Tri-City	80	2663	484	465	702	1050	131	23	57	390	15	26	338	15	17	581	124	29	571	.264
Bend	80	2589	471	485	681	980	116	24	45	403	16	27	416	11	31	556	113	21	619	.263

INDIVIDUAL BATTING

(Leading Qualifiers for Batting Championship—248 or More Plate Appearances)

*Bats lefthanded. †Switch-hitter.

Player and Club	G.	AB.	R.	H.	TB.	2B.	3B.	HR.	RBI.	SH.	SF.	BB.	HP.	SO.	SB.	CS.	Pct.
Beall, Robert, Walla Walla†	80	262	81	102	149	17	3	8	55	0	2	95	6	50	14	4	.389
Poris, Barry, Lewiston*	74	251	54	89	127	12	7	4	48	3	2	48	2	28	12	7	.355
Thompson, Terry L., Bend	58	223	44	74	131	15	3	12	49	0	4	30	0	34	4	1	.332
Harris, Victor, CB-NB†	75	288	63	94	127	12	0	7	53	2	3	33	0	37	30	4	.326
Bushman, Philip, Bend*	68	276	69	87	121	7	6	5	48	0	1	34	2	43	36	4	.315
Chant, Charles, CB-NB	76	284	50	89	129	12	2	8	38	1	1	27	4	45	8	3	.313
Burney, O. Wayne, Medford*	73	278	48	86	135	17	4	8	53	4	3	32	3	57	11	4	.309
Ristig, W. David, Medford	71	236	34	73	105	8	3	6	24	2	3	31	2	49	5	5	.309
Hutchinson, Lloyd W W†	72	287	47	88	151	17	2	14	64	1	4	30	3	54	4	1	.307
Steer, Grant, Tri-City*	80	295	54	89	137	14	5	8	51	2	4	52	1	51	21	6	.302

Departmental Leaders: G—Beall, Steer, Wise, 80; AB—Steer, 295; R—Beall, 81; H—Beall, 102; TB—Hutchinson, 151; 2B—Wise, 22; 3B—Poris, 7; HR—Hutchinson, Sanner, Santana, 14; RBI—Wise, 65; SH—Cecil, Millan, 5; SF—Joost, Scott, Stewart, Suzuki, Van Wyck, 5; BB—Beall, 95; HP—Cruz, 7; SO—Millan, 85; SB—Bushman, 36; CS—Poris, 7.

(All Players—Listed Alphabetically)

Player and Club	G.	AB.	R.	H.	TB.	2B.	3B.	HR.	RBI.	SH.	SF.	BB.	HP.	SO.	SB.	CS.	Pct.
Abbott, W. Glenn, CB-NB	14	39	4	5	5	0	0	0	2	0	0	2	0	23	0	0	.128
Almquist, Russell, CB-NB*	15	9	0	2	2	0	0	0	1	1	0	0	1	4	0	0	.222
Arroyo, Rudolph, Lewiston*	12	20	3	5	6	1	0	0	2	1	0	8	0	4	0	0	.250
Baasse, James, Walla Walla*	40	59	8	11	15	1	0	1	9	1	1	7	2	18	1	1	.186
Ballou, Clifford,																	
1 Walla Walla-1 Bend	2	2	0	0	0	0	0	0	0	0	0	0	0	1	0	0	.000
Barker, Douglas, W	10	6	1	1	4	0	0	1	5	1	0	1	0	3	0	0	.167
Barlow, Michael, CB-NB*	16	24	3	2	7	0	1	1	4	3	0	1	1	15	0	0	.083
Barry, Peter, Medford†	58	185	33	58	66	6	1	0	22	2	0	29	1	23	3	3	.314
Beall, Robert, Walla Walla†	80	262	81	102	149	17	3	8	55	0	2	95	6	50	14	4	.389
Bell, Barton, Lewiston	42	139	20	37	45	5	0	1	24	1	0	20	0	18	5	1	.266
Benedickt, Thomas, Bend*	7	13	3	5	8	3	0	0	3	0	0	2	0	2	0	0	.385
Benson, Gary, Bend	13	2	0	0	0	0	0	0	0	0	0	0	0	0	0	0	.000
Bethel, Kevin, Medford	11	4	1	1	2	1	0	0	0	0	0	0	0	3	0	0	.250
Bodkin, Russell, Lewiston	76	275	67	74	113	11	2	8	35	3	2	56	0	75	15	3	.269
Borges, Edward, Bend	76	284	54	81	114	17	2	4	42	1	1	31	4	35	7	3	.285
Borning, William, Bend	5	6	0	0	0	0	0	0	0	0	0	1	0	3	0	0	.000
Bozeman, Douglas, CB-NB†	5	19	3	5	8	1	1	0	1	0	0	2	0	7	0	0	.263
Bradford, Christopher, W W	19	38	8	6	6	0	0	0	2	1	1	1	0	19	0	0	.158
Brooks, Larry, Bend	16	6	0	1	1	0	0	0	0	0	0	0	0	4	0	0	.167
Brown, Norman, Medford	74	258	43	77	99	9	2	3	32	1	4	25	3	52	9	5	.298
Brown, Richard R., T-C*	29	33	5	7	14	1	0	2	5	1	0	2	0	13	0	0	.212
Brown, Richard W., Lew*	54	132	30	36	45	4	1	1	23	0	1	32	3	15	6	5	.273
Brown, Stephen, Bend*	39	124	22	33	61	8	1	6	25	0	1	29	1	31	2	0	.266
Burney, O. Wayne, Medford*	73	278	48	86	135	17	4	8	53	4	3	32	3	57	11	4	.309
Bushman, Philip, Bend*	68	276	69	87	121	7	6	5	48	0	1	34	2	43	36	4	.315
Butler, Bruce, Walla Walla*	70	221	42	56	97	12	1	9	48	3	4	39	1	55	7	3	.253
Butorac, Jack, Lewiston	2	1	0	1	1	0	0	0	0	0	0	1	0	0	0	0	1.000
Capehart, James, CB-NB*	49	184	33	57	76	6	2	3	23	2	2	16	2	31	8	4	.310
Carr, Gerald, Lewiston	9	1	0	0	0	0	0	0	0	0	0	0	0	1	0	0	.000
Castro, Alan, CB-NB	13	20	4	5	6	1	0	0	1	0	0	9	0	3	0	0	.250
Cecil, Edward, Bend	27	32	6	3	4	1	0	0	4	5	0	7	0	12	0	0	.094
Chant, Charles, CB-NB	76	284	50	89	129	12	2	8	38	1	1	27	4	45	8	3	.313
Chapman, Michael, Tri-City	52	149	16	40	57	9	1	2	27	1	0	2	0	23	7	1	.268
Cichon, David, Lewiston	1	1	0	0	0	0	0	0	0	0	0	0	0	0	0	0	.000
Ciotti, James, Lewiston	1	0	0	0	0	0	0	0	0	0	0	0	0	0	0	0	.000
Cole, Wilbur, Walla Walla	10	26	0	5	6	1	0	0	4	0	0	2	0	9	0	0	.192
Coplin, Thomas, W W†	6	7	1	1	1	0	0	0	1	0	1	0	4	0	0	.143
Cruz, Cirilo, Lewiston*	43	144	27	44	69	8	1	5	22	1	0	7	7	14	5	0	.306
Cuddy, Fred, Lewiston	7	22	2	3	3	0	0	0	0	1	0	0	0	1	0	2	.136
Culpepper, David, Medford	23	16	1	2	2	0	0	0	1	0	0	1	0	5	0	0	.125
Cunningham, Gary, Tri-City	5	6	2	0	0	0	0	0	0	0	0	1	0	0	0	0	.000
Daniel, Alan, Walla Walla	17	5	1	2	3	1	0	0	1	0	0	0	0	1	0	0	.400
Daugherty, Henry, Lewiston	9	28	4	7	8	1	0	0	2	0	0	3	0	4	1	0	.250
Davis, Robert, Tri-City	77	279	58	82	135	14	3	11	48	0	4	18	1	60	5	0	.294
Desmond, Dennis, CB-NB	40	115	28	24	31	2	1	1	14	1	2	14	2	26	8	1	.209
Downs, David, Walla Walla	14	26	0	3	3	0	0	0	1	3	0	0	16	0	0	.115
DuBois, Steven, Medford*	16	41	5	9	9	0	0	0	6	0	0	4	1	14	0	1	.220
Dyson, Ronald, Lewiston	65	240	40	68	89	9	0	4	35	2	1	21	3	24	3	4	.283
Emer, Joseph, Walla Walla	5	13	2	2	2	0	0	0	1	0	0	4	0	2	0	0	.154
Erickson, Charles, Lewiston	8	13	0	0	0	0	0	0	0	0	0	5	0	6	0	0	.000
Evilsizor, Edward, Tri-City†	67	234	44	61	107	12	5	8	46	0	2	32	1	80	5	0	.261
Field, Daniel, Walla Walla*	22	48	3	9	13	1	0	1	4	0	0	1	1	7	0	0	.188
Fingers, Gordon, CB-NB	9	1	0	0	0	0	0	0	0	0	0	0	0	0	0	0	.000
Fitzgerald, R. Dennis, T-C†	30	17	3	5	10	5	0	0	2	0	0	1	0	1	0	0	.294
Forsch, Robert, Lewiston	18	30	5	4	6	0	1	0	3	0	0	2	0	12	2	0	.133
Foster, Richard, Bend	22	26	5	4	6	2	0	0	0	0	0	9	1	12	0	0	.154
Fuller, Kenneth, Walla Walla	21	35	6	7	8	1	0	0	2	2	0	6	0	16	0	0	.200
Garcia, Ralph, Tri-City	2	4	1	2	2	0	0	0	0	0	0	1	0	0	0	0	.500
Geitz, William, Walla Walla*	23	19	0	2	2	0	0	0	0	0	1	0	0	11	0	0	.105

Player and Club	G.	AB.	R.	H.	TB.	2B.	3B.	HR.	RBI.	SH.	SF.	BB.	HP.	SO.	SB.	CS.	Pct.
Gibson, Robert W., Tri-City	17	9	2	2	4	2	0	0	3	0	0	2	0	6	0	0	.222
Gills, C. Wayne, Lewiston†	14	11	0	2	2	0	0	0	1	0	0	0	0	4	1	0	.182
Gonzalez, R. Randy, Lew*	14	11	1	4	5	1	0	0	2	3	0	2	0	4	0	0	.364
Graczyk, John, Tri-City	18	11	1	1	1	0	0	0	1	0	0	5	0	5	0	0	.091
Greenwood, Allen, W W	6	1	0	0	0	0	0	0	0	0	0	2	0	1	0	0	.000
Griffin, Alan, CB-NB	9	15	1	2	2	0	0	0	1	1	0	0	0	2	0	0	.133
Groth, Robert, Bend*	42	170	36	52	73	7	4	2	25	0	2	17	2	25	14	2	.306
Hagen, Frank, Walla Walla	1	0	0	0	0	0	0	0	0	0	0	0	0	0	0	0	.000
Hall, Ronald, Medford	15	39	8	7	8	1	0	0	3	0	0	3	0	19	0	0	.179
Hamilton, Marvin, W W†	17	35	1	6	7	1	0	0	1	0	1	3	0	14	1	1	.171
Hardy, H. Lawrence, T-C.	1	3	0	1	2	1	0	0	0	0	0	0	0	0	0	0	.333
Harms, Edward, CB-NB	3	1	0	0	0	0	0	0	0	0	0	0	0	0	0	0	.000
Harris, Victor, CB-NB†	75	288	63	94	127	12	0	7	53	2	3	33	0	37	30	4	.326
Harrison, J. Patrick, Med	71	254	41	67	101	10	3	6	35	2	2	34	1	64	3	0	.264
Harvey, L. M. Scott, Lew	57	198	34	55	87	9	1	7	43	1	3	19	1	28	3	0	.278
Hellen, Harwood, Medford	19	9	1	1	1	0	0	0	1	0	3	0	5	0	0	.111
Howard, John, Lewiston*	6	4	0	0	0	0	0	0	0	0	1	0	3	0	0	.000
Howder, Stephen, Medford	7	26	1	5	7	2	0	0	7	0	1	1	0	11	0	0	.192
Hunt, Douglas, Tri-City†	67	248	58	74	91	12	1	1	22	1	0	45	0	45	18	5	.298
Hutchinson, Lloyd W W†	72	287	47	88	151	17	2	14	64	1	4	30	3	54	4	1	.307
Iverson, Dennis, Walla Walla	14	7	2	1	1	0	0	0	1	0	0	1	0	1	0	.143
Ivie, Michael, Tri-City	56	198	29	51	70	10	0	3	25	0	3	22	4	39	5	2	.258
Jackson, Chester, Lewiston	8	22	3	3	7	1	0	1	3	0	0	1	0	9	0	0	.136
Johnson, James L., Medford*	52	122	24	26	37	4	2	1	16	1	0	17	1	26	2	0	.213
Johnson, Michael J., Med*	18	10	0	0	0	0	0	0	0	0	0	1	0	8	0	0	.000
Johnson, Robert F., Bend	11	24	2	4	7	0	0	1	2	0	0	1	0	11	0	0	.167
Jones, J. Philip, W W	65	203	27	49	67	10	1	2	16	1	0	39	1	52	3	0	.241
Jones, Willie, Walla Walla	68	281	66	71	91	12	4	0	17	1	1	28	1	54	27	1	.253
Joost, Dean, CB-NB	78	291	44	77	121	10	2	10	64	0	5	30	6	65	3	3	.265
Keenan, Don, Bend	43	116	15	20	24	1	0	1	12	0	0	15	1	28	0	0	.172
Keller, Philip, Medford	4	3	1	1	1	0	0	0	1	0	0	3	0	1	0	0	.333
Knutsen, Jack, 2 CB-NB, 22 Bend	24	28	3	7	9	2	0	0	2	0	0	3	0	7	0	0	.250
Krawiecki, John, Tri-City	3	2	1	1	1	0	0	0	0	0	0	0	0	0	0	0	.500
Krines, Stephen, Medford	66	217	36	65	113	15	0	11	41	0	2	23	0	34	3	0	.300
Lang, Richard, Walla Walla*	4	1	0	0	0	0	0	0	0	0	0	2	0	0	0	0	.000
Lanning, Craig, Medford	23	62	11	13	18	2	0	1	8	0	3	9	0	9	3	1	.210
Lawson, Steven, CB-NB	12	21	3	7	12	2	0	1	3	3	0	0	0	8	0	0	.333
Lewis, Gerald, Bend	16	39	7	7	8	1	0	0	4	2	0	5	0	3	1	0	.179
Linehan, William, CB-NB	1	0	0	0	0	0	0	0	0	0	0	0	0	0	0	0	.000
Logelin, Michael, CB-NB	55	188	27	44	50	6	0	0	13	0	0	15	2	16	6	1	.234
Longhurst, Richard, Bend	22	47	4	10	13	3	0	0	3	1	0	4	0	27	0	0	.213
Lucas, William, CB-NB*	42	101	22	29	38	3	0	2	18	1	1	22	2	29	0	1	.287
Lynch, Charles, CB-NB	3	1	0	0	0	0	0	0	0	0	0	0	0	0	0	0	.000
Marks, Gary, Lewiston	14	8	2	2	2	0	0	0	1	0	0	0	0	5	0	0	.250
Marrero, Wilfredo, W W	27	8	0	0	0	0	0	0	1	0	0	0	0	6	0	0	.000
McClintock, Donald, CB-NB	25	62	12	15	18	3	0	0	3	1	0	17	0	15	1	1	.242
McMonigle, William, W W	74	272	31	67	84	15	1	0	23	4	3	16	3	25	2	2	.246
Meier, Richard, CB-NB*	12	42	8	11	23	2	2	2	4	0	0	4	1	15	1	0	.262
Messier, Paul, Medford	7	3	0	1	1	0	0	0	2	0	0	0	0	2	0	0	.333
Millan, Jorge, Medford	78	257	59	66	107	9	1	10	39	5	1	37	5	85	15	1	.257
Miller, Albert, C., W W	6	2	0	0	0	0	0	0	0	0	0	0	0	1	0	0	.000
Millikan, Gregory, Lewiston*	15	39	4	10	16	0	0	2	10	1	0	1	0	8	0	0	.256
Morrell, William, Tri-City	3	5	1	2	2	0	0	0	0	0	0	1	0	1	0	0	.400
Morrison, Michael, CB-NB*	20	20	3	4	4	0	0	0	2	0	0	1	0	8	0	0	.200
Mould, Gary, Lewiston	45	142	18	34	43	4	1	1	18	0	1	9	0	30	3	4	.239
Myers, Dennis, CB-NB	10	33	5	15	22	1	0	2	8	1	0	3	0	3	0	0	.455
Myers, Michael, Lewiston	37	101	13	30	37	5	1	0	13	0	0	6	0	17	0	3	.297
O'Brien, Kenneth, Medford	14	30	1	1	1	0	0	0	1	0	0	1	0	17	0	0	.033
Olson, Ronald, Tri-City†	14	13	2	0	0	0	0	0	1	0	3	0	7	0	0	.000
Pandis, John, Walla Walla	29	77	5	19	31	3	0	3	9	0	1	7	0	27	0	1	.247
Payette, Michel, W W†	1	1	0	0	0	0	0	0	0	0	0	0	0	0	0	0	.000
Perlozzo, Nicholas, T-C*	78	269	49	74	115	13	2	8	44	0	2	41	1	50	18	3	.275
Perry, Tony, Walla Walla	18	32	4	5	5	0	0	4	3	1	5	0	9	1	0	.156
Phillips, John, CB-NB	8	14	2	3	4	1	0	0	1	0	0	3	0	2	1	0	.214
Plunkett, Michael, Medford	14	26	1	6	7	1	0	0	1	4	0	1	0	12	0	1	.231
Poris, Barry, Lewiston*	74	251	54	89	127	12	7	4	48	3	2	48	2	28	12	7	.355
Poteete, Rodney, Medford	23	13	1	3	4	1	0	0	0	0	0	1	0	8	0	0	.231
President, Larry, Medford*	11	10	1	1	1	0	0	1	1	0	0	1	0	1	0	.100
Preston, William, Tri-City	4	8	1	1	1	0	0	0	1	0	0	1	0	5	0	0	.125
Price, V. Bruce, Medford	3	0	0	0	0	0	0	0	0	0	0	0	1	0	0	.000
Pstragowski, Michael, CB-NB	5	1	0	1	2	1	0	0	0	0	0	0	0	0	0	1	1.000
Rainer, Wilson, CB-NB*	10	3	0	1	1	0	0	0	0	0	0	0	0	0	0	0	.333
Rettig, Wayne, Tri-City	24	10	1	0	0	0	0	0	0	0	1	0	7	0	0	.000
Richardson, Robert, Lewiston	19	11	2	1	1	0	0	0	0	0	0	0	0	7	0	0	.091
Ristig, W. David, Medford	71	236	34	73	105	8	3	6	24	2	3	31	2	49	5	5	.309
Rogers, Leslie, Medford	72	268	44	75	115	13	3	7	39	0	2	36	0	38	6	2	.280
Ross, Douglas A., CB-NB*	5	7	0	1	1	0	0	0	1	0	0	0	0	2	0	0	.143
Russell, Stanley, Medford	70	264	39	72	107	11	3	6	32	0	1	25	4	42	9	3	.273
Sagaser, David, Lewiston*	7	9	0	0	0	0	0	0	0	0	0	0	0	2	0	0	.000
St. George, John, Lewiston	5	10	0	1	1	0	0	0	1	0	0	1	0	0	0	0	.100
St. John, Michael, Lewiston.	15	26	3	5	5	0	0	0	2	2	0	3	1	14	0	0	.192

Player and Club	G.	AB.	R.	H.	TB.	2B.	3B.	HR	RBI.	SH.	SF.	BB.	HP.	SO.	SB.	CS.	Pct.
Salas, Robert, Bend*	9	3	3	1	1	0	0	0	0	0	0	1	0	1	0	0	.333
Sanner, Dale, CB-NB*	72	273	54	82	137	9	2	14	53	0	1	36	2	82	10	0	.300
Santana, Blas, Walla Walla	70	285	60	76	139	13	4	14	53	2	1	24	4	51	11	1	.267
Santiago, Luis, Lewiston	10	3	1	1	2	1	0	0	2	0	0	1	0	1	0	0	.333
Saylor, Bruce, Lewiston	33	102	21	28	48	3	1	5	23	1	2	10	0	17	2	1	.275
Schumacher, Alex, CB-NB*	74	237	36	61	95	10	0	8	35	3	3	37	5	23	0	1	.257
Scott, John, Tri-City	65	215	31	58	86	12	2	4	31	0	5	27	1	41	6	2	.270
Seibly, Frederick, Tri-City	18	33	5	10	16	3	0	1	4	2	0	2	0	5	0	0	.303
Selinsky, David, W W*	3	3	0	1	1	0	0	0	1	1	0	0	0	1	0	0	.333
Shanahan, Paul, Medford	14	24	3	4	6	2	0	0	3	4	0	3	0	13	0	0	.167
Shetler, Keith, Bend*	25	30	4	5	5	0	0	0	3	2	0	19	1	20	0	0	.167
Sievers, Robin, Lewiston*	43	144	21	42	62	11	0	3	24	0	1	9	2	18	2	3	.292
Silverio, Juan, Bend	20	42	5	3	3	0	0	0	2	0	0	7	1	15	6	0	.071
Simpson, Steven, Tri-City	19	25	8	10	17	1	0	2	5	0	0	5	0	8	0	0	.400
Sinclair, H. Wayne, CB-NB	33	17	3	3	4	1	0	0	1	2	0	2	0	8	0	0	.176
Sledge, Willie, Walla Walla*	36	98	13	17	31	2	0	4	12	0	0	9	1	20	3	3	.173
Smith, Michael, Tri-City	58	153	28	38	60	7	0	5	30	0	1	36	3	49	3	3	.248
Smoot, Malcolm, W W*	60	177	25	64	106	9	0	11	39	0	3	28	3	22	3	1	.362
Spicher, S. Gerald, CB-NB	12	5	0	0	0	0	0	0	0	0	0	0	0	2	0	0	.000
Spillner, Daniel, Tri-City	7	12	1	0	0	0	0	0	0	1	0	1	0	8	0	0	.000
Steer, Grant, Tri-City*	80	295	54	89	137	14	5	8	51	2	4	52	2	51	21	6	.302
Stewart, Daniel, Lewiston	52	155	31	41	62	7	1	4	29	1	5	29	2	31	2	0	.265
Stripling, Jackie, Lewiston	5	8	2	1	1	0	0	0	1	0	0	0	0	2	0	0	.125
Suzuki, Yuki, Bend	69	201	26	46	63	10	2	1	29	0	5	28	4	63	0	0	.229
Swope, Billy, Bend	17	7	1	1	1	0	0	0	1	0	0	3	0	3	0	0	.143
Szakacs, Gary, 2 WW-10 Ben	12	33	6	8	11	3	0	0	4	0	0	6	1	18	0	0	.242
Thompson, Terry L., Bend	58	225	44	74	151	15	3	12	49	0	4	30	0	34	4	1	.329
Tikker, Thomas, CB-NB	45	132	21	33	50	10	2	1	18	2	1	29	1	24	1	0	.250
Tomasetti, Steven, CB-NB	8	13	0	1	1	0	0	0	0	2	0	0	0	4	0	0	.077
Treblehorn, Thomas, Bend*	68	198	33	48	66	4	1	4	32	0	3	42	5	49	3	0	.242
Urquhart, Thomas, W W	33	22	1	3	4	1	0	0	2	0	0	1	1	10	0	0	.136
Van Wyck, James, Bend	76	270	55	76	99	9	4	2	32	1	5	38	4	28	10	4	.281
Vaughn, Ronald, Medford	53	169	28	46	59	9	2	0	16	0	1	16	5	29	6	2	.272
Velazquez, Anastasio, Lew	22	11	0	2	2	0	0	0	0	0	0	0	0	3	0	0	.182
Wedel, Gary, Medford	11	32	6	6	12	1	1	1	9	0	1	7	0	8	0	0	.188
Werdick, Gregory, Tri-City	23	43	4	8	11	0	0	1	7	0	0	5	0	8	1	1	.186
Whiteside, Lawrence, 8 Tri-City-10 CB-NB†	18	17	4	5	9	1	0	1	2	0	0	0	0	5	0	0	.294
Williams, Robert E., CB-NB	60	195	35	59	100	14	0	9	31	0	1	19	1	27	1	0	.303
Williamson, J. Darrell, CB-NB*	39	56	8	9	17	2	0	2	5	1	0	18	4	19	1	0	.161
Wilson, Robert G., W W	4	7	2	1	1	0	0	0	0	0	0	3	1	3	0	0	.143
Wilson, Ulysses, Tri-City	74	289	60	67	86	8	4	1	31	2	4	25	3	53	25	4	.232
Wise, Alan, Bend*	80	283	44	79	124	22	1	7	65	0	4	55	4	54	19	6	.279
Wright, Larry, Lewiston	16	39	3	2	2	0	0	0	4	0	2	0	0	20	0	0	.051
Wyatt, John, Medford*	16	18	4	5	13	2	0	2	6	0	0	1	0	4	0	0	.278
Wynne, Ronnie, CB-NB	3	11	2	0	0	0	0	0	0	0	0	2	0	3	1	0	.000
Yates, David, Walla Walla	32	110	17	33	53	5	0	5	20	0	0	13	0	19	4	1	.300
Yeargan, Henry, Tri-City†	35	78	17	12	17	5	0	0	6	0	0	14	1	11	4	2	.154
Young, Danny, Tri-City	12	22	2	4	5	1	0	0	3	0	0	0	0	9	0	0	.182
Zamora, Robert, Bend	40	109	21	26	27	1	0	0	13	3	1	21	0	26	10	1	.239

GRAND-SLAM HOME RUNS—Harris, 2; Barker, S. Brown, Burney, Bushman, Millikan, Schumacher, Tikker, 1 each.

AWARDED FIRST BASE ON INTERFERENCE—Smith (Dyson), Vaughn (Treblehorn), Williams (Treblehorn).

CLUB FIELDING

Club	G.	PO.	A.	E.	DP.	PB.	Pct.	Club	G.	PO.	A.	E.	DP.	PB.	Pct.
Walla Walla	80	2032	851	149	53	30	.951	Tri-City	80	1996	696	164	43	22	.943
Medford	80	1967	821	153	58	53	.948	Lewiston	80	1978	803	172	63	34	.942
C. Bay-N. Bend	80	2035	801	164	49	32	.945	Bend	80	1969	873	189	53	20	.938

Triple Play—None.

INDIVIDUAL FIELDING
(Ten or More Games)

*Throws lefthanded.

FIRST BASEMEN

Player and Club	G.	PO.	A.	E.	DP.	Pct.	Player and Club	G.	PO.	A.	E.	DP.	Pct.
Burney, Medford*	20	150	5	1	13	.994	Brown, Bend*	23	188	12	5	12	.976
Williamson, CB-NB	20	123	10	1	10	.993	Poris, Lewiston*	71	544	32	15	47	.975
RUSSELL, Bend*	59	505	39	9	35	.984	Schumacher, CB-NB*	60	429	32	13	28	.973
Beall, Walla Walla*	80	715	40	17	47	.978	Thompson, Bend	58	552	37	21	35	.966
Perlozzo, Tri-City*	76	543	45	14	36	.977							

(Fewer Than Ten Games)

Player and Club	G.	PO.	A.	E.	DP.	Pct.	Player and Club	G.	PO.	A.	E.	DP.	Pct.
Castro, CB-NB	5	35	0	0	3	1.000	Smith, Tri-City	5	25	1	1	0	.963
J. Johnson, Medford	1	11	0	0	0	1.000	Harvey, Lewiston	3	26	0	1	2	.963
Mould, Lewiston	1	5	1	0	0	1.000	Tikker, CB-NB	9	43	3	2	2	.958
Suzuki, Bend	2	3	0	0	1	1.000	Barry, Medford	2	19	2	1	1	.955
Cruz, Lewiston*	1	1	0	0	1	1.000	Dyson, Lewiston	2	9	1	1	0	.909
Szakacs, Walla Walla	1	1	0	0	0	1.000	Werdick, Tri-City	1	7	0	1	0	.875
Stewart, Lewiston	5	45	1	1	4	.979							

SECOND BASEMEN

Player and Club	G.	PO.	A.	E.	DP.	Pct.	Player and Club	G.	PO.	A.	E.	DP.	Pct.
Harvey, Lewiston ...	13	23	23	1	5	.979	Bell, Lewiston	42	79	112	13	22	.936
HARRIS, CB-NB ...	67	150	191	19	34	.947	Barry, Medford	10	18	22	3	4	.930
McMonigle, W W ..	74	152	197	20	37	.946	Davis, Tri-City	22	32	47	6	6	.929
Van Wyck, Bend	39	66	111	11	19	.941	Logelin, CB-NB	12	21	26	4	2	.922
Harrison, Medford ..	69	131	185	20	36	.940	Groth, Bend	33	76	89	18	12	.902
Evilsizor, Tri-City ..	48	85	95	12	16	.938							

(Fewer Than Ten Games)

Player and Club	G.	PO.	A.	E.	DP.	Pct.	Player and Club	G.	PO.	A.	E.	DP.	Pct.
Bozeman, CB-NB ...	4	8	6	0	1	1.000	Treblehorn, Bend ...	4	6	13	1	1	.950
Werdick, Tri-City ..	4	6	8	0	1	1.000	Emer, Walla Walla ..	5	7	7	1	1	.933
Forsch, Lewiston ...	3	4	5	0	1	1.000	Cuddy, Lewiston ...	7	12	15	2	2	.931
Erickson, Lewiston ..	2	3	5	0	0	1.000	Daugherty, Lewiston .	9	15	21	4	5	.900
Wedel, Lewiston ...	1	3	3	0	0	1.000	St. George, Lew	5	8	9	2	3	.895
McClintock, CB-NB .	1	1	3	0	0	1.000	Borges, Bend	3	12	3	2	0	.882
J. P. Jones, W W ...	1	0	3	0	0	1.000	Yeargan, Tri-City ...	9	14	24	6	1	.864
Lucas, CB-NB	1	1	0	0	1	1.000	Zamora, Bend	5	3	9	3	0	.800
Tikker, CB-NB	1	0	1	0	0	1.000	Baasse, Walla Walla .	3	1	6	3	1	.700
Stewart, Lewiston ...	8	12	16	1	4	.966	Hagen, Walla Walla .	1	2	0	1	0	.667

THIRD BASEMEN

Player and Club	G.	PO.	A.	E.	DP.	Pct.	Player and Club	G.	PO.	A.	E.	DP.	Pct.
Sievers, Lewiston ...	39	30	50	6	5	.930	Wilson, Tri-City	12	8	16	3	0	.889
JOOST, CB-NB	76	59	110	14	4	.923	Harvey, Lewiston ...	35	33	66	13	7	.884
Barry, Medford	15	4	19	2	1	.920	Davis, Tri-City	54	70	85	22	4	.876
Santana, Walla Walla	59	55	130	20	7	.902	Yates, Walla Walla ..	21	9	37	7	0	.868
Rogers, Medford	43	33	82	14	6	.891	Borges, Bend	74	66	135	31	6	.866
Krines, Medford	21	10	39	6	4	.891							

(Fewer Than Ten Games)

Player and Club	G.	PO.	A.	E.	DP.	Pct.	Player and Club	G.	PO.	A.	E.	DP.	Pct.
Werdick, Tri-City ..	3	3	2	0	1	1.000	Evilsizor, Tri-City ..	7	3	10	3	0	.813
Hutchinson, W W ...	1	3	0	0	0	1.000	Longhurst, Bend	2	3	1	1	0	.800
Forsch, Lewiston ...	2	0	1	0	0	1.000	Erickson, Lewiston ..	2	1	2	1	0	.750
Stewart, Lewiston ...	7	6	10	1	1	.941	Scott, Tri-City	4	2	6	4	0	.667
Zamora, Bend	6	0	10	1	0	.909	Dyson, Lewiston	4	1	3	2	0	.667
Treblehorn, Bend ...	6	2	5	1	0	.875	Baasse, Walla Walla .	3	1	3	2	0	.667
Lucas, CB-NB	8	5	5	2	0	.833	J. Johnson, Medford .	2	2	0	1	0	.667

SHORTSTOPS

Player and Club	G.	PO.	A.	E.	DP.	Pct.	Player and Club	G.	PO.	A.	E.	DP.	Pct.
Santana, Walla Walla	12	22	40	3	2	.954	Millan, Lewiston	77	122	230	38	39	.903
Barry, Medford	15	15	44	3	3	.952	Ristig, Medford	67	106	186	32	29	.901
Van Wyck, Bend ...	33	73	107	11	14	.942	Scott, Tri-City	14	18	27	6	5	.882
Zamora, Bend	30	51	77	10	13	.928	McClintock, CB-NB .	21	27	42	10	9	.873
J. P. JONES, W W ..	63	93	170	26	30	.910	Lucas, CB-NB	19	28	46	13	7	.851
Logelin, CB-NB	41	63	126	19	16	.909	Silverio, Bend	18	19	41	12	5	.833
Wilson, Tri-City	61	103	150	26	24	.907							

(Fewer Than Ten Games)

Player and Club	G.	PO.	A.	E.	DP.	Pct.	Player and Club	G.	PO.	A.	E.	DP.	Pct.
Yates, Walla Walla ..	3	5	8	0	3	1.000	Forsch, Lewiston ...	3	3	5	3	1	.727
Werdick, Tri-City ..	2	2	1	0	0	1.000	Wynne, CB-NB	3	4	5	4	0	.692
Yeargan, Tri-City ..	9	14	22	1	3	.974	Sievers, Lewiston ...	1	1	1	2	1	.500
Harris, CB-NB	5	7	12	1	2	.950	Chant, CB-NB	1	1	0	1	0	.500
Baasse, Walla Walla	7	11	8	1	1	.864	Harvey, Lewiston ...	1	0	0	2	0	.000
Groth, Bend	8	9	18	5	5	.844							

OUTFIELDERS

Player and Club	G.	PO.	A.	E.	DP.	Pct.	Player and Club	G.	PO.	A.	E.	DP.	Pct.
Vaughn, Medford ...	32	48	1	0	0	1.000	Hunt, Tri-City	64	88	5	7	2	.930
Smith, Tri-City	16	16	2	0	0	1.000	Sanner, CB-NB	72	123	4	10	1	.927
Evilsizor, Tri-City ..	11	16	0	0	0	1.000	Hutchinson, W W ...	71	111	8	8	2	.925
Longhurst, Bend	13	13	0	0	0	1.000	Cruz, Lewiston*	40	45	3	4	0	.923
Szakacs, Bend	10	8	1	0	0	1.000	Chant, CB-NB	75	96	13	10	0	.916
STEER, Tri-City* ...	80	178	6	3	0	.984	Mould, Lewiston	36	31	1	3	0	.914
Bushman, Bend	68	134	6	3	1	.979	Saylor, Lewiston	28	35	3	4	1	.905
Burney, Medford* ..	53	78	4	2	0	.976	Desmond, CB-NB ...	30	34	3	4	0	.902
Bodkin, Lewiston ...	74	148	3	4	0	.974	Brown, Bend*	14	17	1	2	1	.900
Capehart, CB-NB ...	47	65	3	2	0	.971	Dyson, Lewiston	27	25	4	4	1	.879
Wise, Bend	80	118	7	5	1	.962	Suzuki, Bend	59	60	5	9	0	.878
W. Jones, W W*	65	141	5	7	0	.954	J. Johnson, Medford .	25	26	2	4	0	.875
Butler, Walla Walla*	65	77	2	4	0	.952	Lanning, Medford ...	18	19	2	3	0	.875
Brown, Lewiston* ...	41	56	3	3	2	.952	Meier, CB-NB	12	14	0	2	0	.875
Scott, Tri-City	41	55	1	3	1	.949	Rogers, Medford	22	29	3	5	1	.865
Brown, Medford	68	111	9	8	2	.938	Sledge, Walla Walla*	25	41	0	7	0	.854
Chapman, Tri-City ..	34	39	1	3	0	.930	Schumacher, CB-NB*	17	9	0	2	0	.818

OUTFIELDERS—Continued

(Fewer Than Ten Games)

Player and Club	G.	PO.	A.	E.	DP.	Pct.	Player and Club	G.	PO.	A.	E.	DP.	Pct.
Russell, Medford	9	11	0	0	0	1.000	Lang, Walla Walla*	1	1	0	0	0	1.000
Baasse, Walla Walla	6	6	0	0	0	1.000	Williamson, CB-NB	1	1	0	0	0	1.000
Harvey, Lewiston	4	5	1	0	0	1.000	Barry, Medford	7	5	1	1	1	.857
Hamilton, W W	9	4	1	0	0	1.000	Yates, Walla Walla	6	6	0	1	0	.857
Wedel, Medford	3	3	0	0	0	1.000	Stewart, Lewiston	9	3	1	1	0	.800
Wilson, Walla Walla	2	3	0	0	0	1.000	Jackson, Lewiston	6	6	0	2	0	.750
Cole, Walla Walla	5	2	0	0	0	1.000	Tomasetti, CB-NB	5	3	0	1	0	.750
Ivie, Tri-City	1	2	0	0	0	1.000	Treblehorn, Bend	3	3	0	1	0	.750
Howder, Medford	1	1	1	0	0	1.000	Krines, Medford	6	2	0	2	0	.500
Shetler, Bend*	2	1	0	0	0	1.000	Groth, Bend	1	1	0	2	0	.333
Keenan, Bend	1	1	0	0	0	1.000							

CATCHERS

Player and Club	G.	PO.	A.	E.	DP.	PB.	Pct.	Player and Club	G.	PO.	A.	E.	DP.	PB.	Pct.
WILLIAMS, CB-NB	50	391	28	6	3	16	.986	Smith, Tri-City	29	200	13	6	2	4	.973
Smoot, W W	50	318	42	6	1	15	.984	Treblehorn, Bend	49	285	30	9	5	9	.972
Vaughn, Med	21	159	18	4	3	16	.978	Krines, Medford	35	227	19	8	1	16	.969
Stewart, Lew	23	157	13	4	0	7	.977	Ivie, Tri-City	52	417	34	15	3	18	.968
Pandis, W W	21	112	14	3	1	6	.977	Field, W W	14	72	10	3	1	8	.965
Myers, Lewiston	32	187	21	5	2	9	.977	Keenan, Bend	36	151	17	7	1	11	.960
Tikker, CB-NB	34	264	21	7	1	16	.976	Dyson, Lewiston	36	259	17	12	2	17	.958
								DuBois, Med	15	94	3	6	2	6	.942

(Fewer Than Ten Games)

Player and Club	G.	PO.	A.	E.	DP.	PB.	Pct.	Player and Club	G.	PO.	A.	E.	DP.	PB.	Pct.
Cole, Walla Walla	3	29	1	0	0	1	1.000	Tomasetti, CB-NB	1	2	0	0	0	0	1.000
Rogers, Med	5	24	0	0	0	4	1.000	Wedel, Med	6	36	8	1	1	2	.978
Preston, Tri-City	2	15	1	0	0	0	1.000	Howder, Med	6	48	7	3	0	9	.948
Castro, CB-NB	1	6	1	0	0	0	1.000	Werdick, T-C	1	0	2	1	0	0	.667
Cichon, Lew	1	2	0	0	0	0	1.000	Gills, Lew	1	0	0	0	1	0	.000

PITCHERS

Player and Club	G.	PO.	A.	E.	DP.	Pct.	Player and Club	G.	PO.	A.	E.	DP.	Pct.
BRADFORD, W W	18	3	20	0	0	1.000	Downs, Walla Walla	14	2	15	2	0	.895
Fuller, Walla Walla	19	10	12	0	1	1.000	Richardson, Lew	19	3	5	1	2	.889
St. John, Lewiston	15	7	8	0	0	1.000	Swope, Bend	17	1	7	1	3	.889
Velazquez, Lewiston	22	2	12	0	1	1.000	Benson, Bend	13	1	7	1	1	.889
Morrison, CB-NB*	17	3	7	0	0	1.000	Lawson, CB-NB*	12	5	10	2	1	.882
Brooks, Bend	16	2	8	0	0	1.000	Geitz, Walla Walla*	23	2	13	2	0	.882
Marrero, Walla Walla	27	1	9	0	1	1.000	Culpepper, Med	23	4	10	2	2	.875
Wyatt, Medford	11	1	9	0	1	1.000	Olson, Tri-City	13	1	6	1	0	.875
Graczyk, Tri-City	18	3	4	0	0	1.000	Iverson, Walla Walla	14	1	5	1	2	.857
Marks, Lewiston	11	1	5	0	0	1.000	Hall, Medford*	14	3	19	4	0	.846
Spicher, CB-NB	11	1	5	0	0	1.000	Gibson, Tri-City	17	6	5	2	0	.846
Barker, Walla Walla	10	2	3	0	0	1.000	Young, Tri-City	12	5	6	2	1	.846
M. Johnson, Medford	18	0	5	0	1	1.000	Sinclair, CB-NB	33	3	8	2	1	.846
Rainer, CB-NB	10	0	2	0	0	1.000	Perry, Walla Walla	18	5	11	3	0	.842
Santiago, Lewis	10	0	2	0	0	1.000	Barlow, CB-NB	16	1	15	3	2	.842
Abbott, CB-NB	14	3	19	1	0	.957	Wright, Lewiston	16	6	14	4	1	.833
Arroyo, Lewiston*	12	0	22	1	1	.957	Plunkett, Medford	14	6	14	4	0	.833
Cecil, Bend	27	7	33	2	0	.952	Fitzgerald, Tri-City	30	4	6	2	0	.833
Myers, CB-NB	14	5	15	1	0	.952	Gonzalez, Lewiston*	14	0	5	1	0	.833
Millikan, Lew*	15	4	15	1	1	.950	Shetler, Bend*	15	3	24	6	1	.818
Lewis, Bend	14	5	13	1	0	.947	Simpson, Tri-City	19	1	8	2	1	.818
O'Brien, Medford	14	4	13	1	0	.944	Foster, Bend	22	8	13	5	1	.807
Knutsen, CB-NB-Bnd	21	4	12	1	1	.941	Whiteside, TC-CB-NB	18	0	4	1	0	.800
Urquhart, W W	32	3	13	1	0	.941	President, Medford*	10	3	6	3	0	.750
Brown, Tri-City*	27	6	21	2	1	.931	Daniel, Walla Walla	17	1	2	1	0	.750
Seibly, Tri-City	17	7	19	2	1	.929	Gills, Lewiston	13	0	7	3	1	.700
Poteete, Medford	23	5	5	1	3	.909	Almquist, CB-NB*	15	1	3	4	0	.500
Hellen, Medford	19	2	8	1	0	.909	Rettig, Tri-City*	24	1	2	4	0	.429
Shanahan, Medford	14	6	21	3	2	.900							

(Fewer Than Ten Games)

Player and Club	G.	PO.	A.	E.	DP.	Pct.	Player and Club	G.	PO.	A.	E.	DP.	Pct.
Stripling, Lewiston	3	4	7	0	2	1.000	Ross, CB-NB	5	1	2	0	0	1.000
Griffin, CB-NB	9	3	5	0	1	1.000	Price, Medford	3	1	1	0	0	1.000
Phillips, CB-NB	8	1	7	0	0	1.000	Ballou, WW-Bend	2	1	1	0	0	1.000
Borning, Bend	5	3	4	0	1	1.000	Butorac, Lewiston	2	1	1	0	0	1.000
Krawiecki, Tri-City	3	1	4	0	0	1.000	Pstragowski, CB-NB	5	0	2	0	0	1.000
Selinsky, W W*	3	2	2	0	0	1.000	Keller, Medford	3	0	2	0	0	1.000
Messier, Medford	7	0	4	0	0	1.000	Lynch, CB-NB	3	0	2	0	0	1.000
Bethel, Medford	9	1	2	0	0	1.000	Hardy, Tri-City	1	0	2	0	0	1.000

PITCHERS—Continued

(Fewer Than Ten Games)

Player and Club	G.	PO.	A.	E.	DP.	Pct.	Player and Club	G.	PO.	A.	E.	DP.	Pct.
Greenwood, W W	6	0	1	0	0	1.000	Morrell, Tri-City*	3	0	4	1	0	.800
Miller, Walla Walla*	6	0	1	0	0	1.000	Coplin, Walla Walla*	6	1	2	1	0	.750
Harms, CB-NB	3	0	1	0	0	1.000	Sagaser, Lewiston*	7	0	3	1	0	.750
Burney, Medford*	1	0	1	0	0	1.000	Howard, Lewiston*	6	2	0	1	0	.667
Johnson, Bend	7	2	5	1	0	.875	Forsch, Lewiston	7	2	2	3	1	.571
Benedickt, Bend*	5	1	7	2	0	.800	Salas, Bend*	9	0	1	1	0	.500
Spillner, Tri-City	7	3	1	1	0	.800	Fingers, CB-NB	8	0	1	1	0	.500

The following players do not have any recorded accepted chances at the positions indicated; therefore, are not listed in the fielding averages for those particular positions: Bozeman, 3b-ss; R. Brown, of; Carr, p; Clotti, p; Cunningham, of; DuBois, of; Dyson, 2b-ss; Garcia, p; Harvey, p; Hutchinson, p; Logelin, 3b; Payette, p; Perlozzo, of; Schumacher, p; Sievers, 2b; Wyatt, of; Yeargan, 3b.

PITCHERS' RECORDS

(Leading Qualifiers for Earned-Run Average Leadership—80 or More Innings)

*Throws lefthanded.

Pitcher—Club	G.	GS.	CG.	ShO.	W.	L.	Sv.	Pct.	IP.	H.	R.	ER.	HR.	Int. BB.	BB.	HB.	SO.	WP.	ERA.
Hall, Medford*	14	14	8	2	8	4	0	.667	104	86	58	35	5	48	2	1	104	17	3.03
Millikan, Lew*	15	15	4	0	6	4	0	.600	100	94	50	38	4	44	2	2	105	7	3.42
Wright, Lewiston	16	13	3	0	7	2	0	.778	102	96	56	39	5	70	3	3	111	17	3.44
Brown, Tri-City*	27	11	2	1	5	6	6	.455	112	88	61	43	12	40	3	1	120	4	3.46
Shanahan, Med	14	13	3	0	5	5	0	.500	86	76	46	35	9	25	0	3	85	8	3.66
Abbott, CB-NB	14	14	7	1	8	3	0	.727	101	106	55	43	11	40	0	3	92	5	3.83
St. John, Lewiston	15	12	3	0	6	6	1	.500	80	73	44	38	5	33	3	5	57	6	4.28
Foster, Bend	22	13	5	0	5	8	0	.385	96	124	64	46	6	33	0	1	51	4	4.31
Fuller, W W	19	17	6	0	8	5	0	.615	100	94	54	48	8	44	1	4	94	6	4.32
Lewis, Bend	14	14	5	1	7	4	0	.636	99	114	54	48	7	16	2	4	62	3	4.36

Departmental Leaders: G—Sinclair, 33; GS—Fuller, 17; CG—Hall, 8; ShO—Hall, Young, 2; W—Cecil, Sinclair, 10; L—Foster, Plunkett, 8; Sv—Daniel, Sinclair, 8; Pct.—Wright, .778; IP—Cecil, 114; H—Cecil, 128; R—Shetler, 76; ER—Shetler, 60; HR—Perry, 17; BB—Wright, 70; IBB—Shetler, 5; HB—Downs, Gibson, 7; SO—Brown, 120; WP—Hall, Wright, 17.

(All Pitchers—Listed Alphabetically)

Pitcher—Club	G.	GS.	CG.	ShO.	W.	L.	Sv.	Pct.	IP.	H.	R.	ER.	HR.	Int. BB.	BB.	HB.	SO.	WP.	ERA.
Abbott, CB-NB	14	14	7	1	8	3	0	.727	101	106	55	43	11	40	0	3	92	5	3.83
Almquist, CB-NB*	15	5	0	0	1	1	0	.000	36	49	36	27	5	28	0	2	24	2	6.75
Arroyo, Lewiston*	12	11	5	1	6	4	0	.600	75	63	39	30	3	40	1	1	74	5	3.60
Ballou, 1W W-1Bend	2	0	0	0	0	0	0	.000	6	9	2	2	0	2	0	0	6	0	3.00
Barker, W W	10	0	0	0	1	0	1	1.000	23	10	8	6	1	6	0	1	23	1	2.35
Barlow, W W	16	10	2	1	4	3	0	.571	74	72	47	36	7	33	4	3	58	4	4.38
Benedickt, Bend*	5	4	2	0	3	2	0	.600	28	33	22	13	1	23	1	1	21	3	4.82
Benson, Bend	13	0	0	0	1	1	0	1.000	21	25	18	13	0	8	0	1	13	2	5.57
Bethel, Medford	9	1	0	0	1	3	0	.000	15	32	22	17	2	5	0	0	4	2	10.20
Borning, Bend	5	5	0	0	0	3	0	.000	19	30	27	25	4	21	1	1	11	4	11.84
Bradford, W W	18	12	3	1	5	6	0	.455	93	111	63	53	8	39	0	3	52	2	5.13
Brooks, Bend	16	3	1	0	3	0	0	.000	33	51	41	34	8	23	1	2	15	2	9.27
Brown, Tri-City*	27	11	2	1	5	6	6	.455	112	88	61	43	12	40	3	1	120	4	3.46
Burney, Medford*	1	0	0	0	0	0	0	.000	4	3	2	2	1	2	0	0	4	1	4.50
Butorac, Lewiston	2	0	0	0	0	0	0	.000	1	4	2	2	0	1	0	0	1	0	18.00
Carr, Lewiston	9	0	0	0	2	0	0	1.000	10	8	3	2	0	4	0	1	16	2	1.80
Cecil, Bend	27	13	7	1	10	7	4	.588	114	128	73	59	14	39	4	2	58	9	4.66
Clotti, Lewiston	1	0	0	0	0	0	0	.000	⅓	2	2	2	0	0	0	0	0	0	54.00
Coplin, W W*	6	5	0	0	0	2	0	.000	25	26	22	20	3	13	0	0	18	1	7.20
Culpepper, Med	23	1	0	0	3	4	2	.429	47	58	40	32	6	17	0	0	32	6	6.13
Daniel, W W	17	0	0	0	0	0	8	.000	20	12	15	12	1	6	0	2	17	0	5.40
Downs, W W	14	14	2	0	5	7	0	.417	80	103	58	50	10	26	1	7	52	6	5.63
Fingers, CB-NB	8	0	0	0	1	1	0	.500	8	10	6	5	1	6	2	0	1	1	5.63
Fitzgerald, T-C	30	0	0	0	3	2	0	.600	56	57	39	25	6	43	2	6	35	12	4.02
Forsch, Lewiston	7	5	0	0	2	3	0	.400	28	32	22	13	0	17	1	0	15	4	4.13
Foster, Bend	22	13	5	0	5	8	0	.385	96	124	64	46	6	33	0	1	51	4	4.31
Fuller, W W	19	17	6	0	8	5	0	.615	100	94	54	48	8	44	1	4	94	6	4.32
Garcia, Tri-City	2	0	0	0	1	0	0	.000	7	9	10	3	0	9	0	3	16	1	3.86
Geitz, W W*	23	6	1	0	2	2	1	.500	71	76	36	33	10	34	0	1	47	4	4.18
Gibson, Tri-City	17	7	0	0	2	3	0	.400	47	54	47	37	4	36	1	7	26	1	7.09
Gills, Lewiston	13	3	0	0	0	2	0	.000	34	45	36	30	1	28	1	4	26	4	7.94
Gonzalez, Lew*	14	5	1	1	3	2	0	.250	38	34	25	16	0	26	0	1	35	8	3.79
Graczyk, Tri-City	18	2	0	0	1	4	0	.200	38	30	32	27	5	36	1	2	49	8	6.39
Greenwood, W W	6	3	0	0	0	2	0	.000	8	12	20	18	1	18	0	1	4	2	20.25
Griffin, CB-NB	9	9	1	1	3	4	0	.429	45	50	32	30	6	18	0	0	49	1	6.00
Hall, Medford*	14	14	8	2	8	4	0	.667	104	86	58	35	5	48	2	1	104	17	3.03
Hardy, Tri-City	1	1	0	0	1	0	0	.000	5	7	2	2	1	0	0	0	10	0	2.25
Harms, CB-NB	3	0	0	0	1	1	0	.500	5	6	5	3	2	2	0	0	3	0	5.40
Harvey, Lewiston	5	1	0	0	1	0	0	1.000	10	13	11	6	1	5	0	0	17	1	5.40
Hellen, Medford	19	4	1	0	3	1	0	.500	46	36	33	22	3	35	0	4	54	6	4.30
Howard, Lewiston*	6	3	0	0	0	3	0	.000	14	21	18	14	0	11	1	1	9	2	9.00

Pitcher—Club	G.	GS.	CG.	ShO.	W.	L.	Sv.	Pct.	IP.	H.	R.	ER.	HR.	BB.	Int. BB.	HB.	SO.	WP.	ERA.
Hutchinson, W W .	1	1	0	0	0	0	0	.000	4	3	2	2	1	1	0	0	5	0	4.50
Iverson, W W	14	0	0	0	1	1	0	.500	27	30	16	15	2	16	2	3	18	0	5.00
M. Johnson, Med ..	18	4	1	0	1	6	0	.143	47	55	43	36	7	30	0	2	55	5	6.89
Johnson, Bend	7	6	6	1	4	2	0	.667	48	31	22	14	2	27	0	3	48	2	2.63
Keller, Medford ..	3	2	0	0	0	1	0	.000	14	14	10	7	1	4	0	0	19	2	4.50
Knutsen, 2 CB-NB-																			
19 Bend	21	8	0	3	2	2	2	.600	73	80	53	40	5	50	1	1	46	7	4.93
Krawiecki, Tri-City	3	1	0	0	0	0	0	.000	9	8	6	3	1	0	0	0	5	1	3.00
Lawson, CB-NB* ..	12	11	3	1	3	4	0	.429	66	64	39	27	3	34	1	2	71	12	3.68
Lewis, Bend	14	14	5	1	7	4	0	.636	99	114	54	48	7	16	2	4	62	3	4.36
Lynch, CB-NB* ...	3	1	0	0	0	1	0	.000	7	12	10	9	0	4	0	1	3	1	11.57
Marks, Lewiston* ..	11	2	0	0	1	2	0	.333	18	25	21	18	1	11	2	0	16	1	9.00
Marrero, W W	27	1	0	0	3	5	1	.375	40	50	28	25	5	19	0	2	32	1	5.63
Messier, Medford ..	7	0	0	0	2	0	0	1.000	12	12	19	13	3	19	0	2	8	3	9.75
Miller, W W*	6	0	0	0	0	0	0	.000	6	9	15	12	1	7	0	0	6	0	18.00
Millikan, Lew* ...	15	4	0	6	4	0	0	.600	100	94	50	38	4	44	2	2	105	7	3.42
Morrell, Tri-City* .	3	2	0	0	1	0	0	1.000	15	13	9	7	0	8	1	0	15	1	4.20
Morrison, CB-NB* .	17	6	1	1	7	1	1	.875	52	54	34	24	3	34	2	1	54	4	4.15
Myers, CB-NB	14	4	0	4	5	0	0	.444	88	81	53	46	8	50	0	2	81	12	4.70
O'Brien, Medford .	14	13	4	1	4	7	0	.364	87	103	70	50	7	48	0	4	78	6	5.17
Olson, Tri-City ..	13	5	0	0	3	1	0	.750	41	37	24	23	2	30	1	4	34	11	5.05
Payette, W W	1	0	0	0	0	0	0	.000	2	4	3	3	0	1	0	0	2	1	13.50
Perry, W W	18	14	3	0	9	4	0	.692	97	98	66	50	17	37	0	4	75	4	4.64
Phillips, Lew	8	5	1	0	1	1	1	.500	39	48	24	20	4	17	0	0	36	1	4.62
Plunkett, Medford .	14	13	4	1	5	8	0	.385	86	108	63	48	6	44	0	2	65	8	5.02
Poteete, Medford .	23	2	0	3	0	5	1	1.000	38	44	22	20	2	19	0	6	34	4	4.74
President, Med* ..	10	8	2	1	3	0	0	.250	37	38	24	14	2	26	0	0	24	8	3.41
Price, Medford ...	3	2	0	0	1	0	0	.000	7	10	9	8	0	5	0	2	3	1	10.29
Pstragowski, CB-NB	5	0	0	0	0	0	0	.000	5	9	6	6	0	5	0	0	4	0	10.80
Rainer, CB-NB ...	10	0	0	0	1	1	0	.500	17	27	20	16	0	9	0	0	10	1	8.47
Rettig, Tri-City* .	24	5	1	1	4	5	3	.444	50	49	36	30	7	32	3	1	40	2	5.40
Richardson, Lew ..	19	0	0	4	3	7	1	.571	38	33	16	13	2	19	0	2	24	4	3.08
Ross, CB-NB	5	1	0	1	0	0	1	1.000	17	15	12	6	1	7	0	1	14	0	3.18
Sagaser, Lewiston* .	7	4	1	0	2	2	1	.500	24	21	18	9	1	14	1	1	28	2	3.38
St. John, Lewiston .15	15	12	3	0	6	6	1	.500	80	73	44	38	5	33	3	5	57	6	4.28
Salas, Bend*	9	0	0	1	0	2	0	.333	13	13	13	11	0	11	2	0	14	4	7.62
Santiago, Lew	10	3	0	0	1	1	0	.500	19	30	18	16	2	11	1	1	9	2	7.58
Schumacher,																			
CB-NB*	1	0	0	0	0	0	0	.000	2	2	1	1	0	1	0	0	1	0	4.50
Seibly, Tri-City ...	17	14	2	0	6	4	0	.600	88	91	64	51	12	53	1	2	83	5	5.22
Selinsky, W W ...	3	2	0	0	0	2	0	.000	10	18	15	12	0	8	0	0	7	1	10.80
Shanahan, Med ...	14	13	3	0	5	5	0	.500	86	76	46	35	9	25	0	3	85	8	3.66
Shetler, Bend* ...	15	14	5	0	4	6	0	.400	92	118	76	60	15	37	5	0	74	4	5.87
Simpson, Tri-City	19	11	3	1	8	5	1	.615	80	68	52	39	5	59	2	4	82	7	4.39
Sinclair, CB-NB ..	33	1	0	0	10	6	8	.625	61	61	29	27	7	29	3	1	73	5	3.98
Spicher, CB-NB ...	11	0	0	0	1	2	1	.333	19	20	16	13	1	13	1	1	19	4	6.16
Spillner, Tri-City .	7	6	1	0	1	1	0	.500	29	37	21	18	2	15	0	1	21	2	5.59
Stripling, Lew	3	3	3	0	3	0	0	1.000	23	18	5	3	0	8	1	0	12	0	1.17
Swope, Bend	17	2	1	0	2	1	0	.667	32	38	25	23	6	25	1	1	13	6	6.47
Urquhart, W W ..	32	0	0	4	5	4	3	.444	67	79	48	33	3	26	0	2	54	2	4.43
Velazquez, Lew ...	22	0	0	2	2	4	0	.500	44	32	19	15	2	17	3	1	41	1	3.07
Whiteside, 8 T-C-																			
10 CB-NB	18	3	0	1	3	0	0	.250	47	51	37	33	4	46	1	4	43	6	6.32
Wright, Lewiston ..	16	13	3	0	7	2	2	.778	102	96	56	39	5	70	3	3	111	17	3.44
Wyatt, Medford ...	11	3	0	1	1	0	0	.500	27	41	33	31	1	17	0	2	24	5	10.33
Young, Tri-City ...	12	11	3	2	3	6	0	.333	66	70	49	40	6	47	0	3	49	5	5.45

BALKS—Griffin, 4; Bradford, Morrison, Perry, 2 each; Barker, Borning, Brooks, Brown, Fitzgerald, Foster, Hall, Knutsen, Lewis, Myers, O'Brien, Plunkett, Rettig, St. John, Salas, Santiago, Seibly, Selinsky, Shetler, Simpson, Spicher, 1 each.

COMBINATION SHUTOUTS—Millikan-Richardson, St. John-Wright, Lewiston.

NO-HIT GAME—Rettig (two-thirds inning), and Seibly (six and one-third innings), Tri-City, lost to Bend, 0-2, July 17 (seven innings).

Western Carolinas League

CLASS A

CHAMPIONSHIP WINNERS IN PREVIOUS YEARS

1948—Lincolnton* .... .627	1960—Lexington .... .707	1965—Salisbury .... .641
1949—Newton-Conover ... .667	Salisbury (2nd)† .. .650	Rock Hill‡ ..... .603
Ruth'ford Co. (2nd)† .627	1961—Salisbury .... .627	1966—Spartanburg ...... .682
1950—Newton-Conover .... .627	Shelby (4th)† ...... .481	Spartanburg ...... .767
Lenoir (2nd)† ...... .626	1962—Statesville .... .563	1967—Spartanburg ...... .730
1951—Morganton .... .645	Statesville .... .700	Spartanburg ...... .567
Shelby (2nd)† ...... .604	1963—Greenville† .... .576	1968—Spartanburg ...... .597
1952—Lincolnton .... .649	Salisbury .... .631	Greenwood‡ .... .597
Shelby (2nd)† ...... .645	1964—Rock Hill .... .672	1969—Greenwood‡ .... .587
1953-59—League inactive.	Salisbury‡ .... .631	Shelby .... .565

*Won championship and four-club playoff. †Won four-club playoff. ‡Won split-season playoff.
(NOTE—Known as Western Carolina League from 1948 through 1962.)

STANDING OF CLUBS AT CLOSE OF FIRST HALF, JUNE 22

Club	W.	L.	T.	Pct.	G.B.	Club	W.	L.	T.	Pct.	G.B.
†Greenville (2*)	38	28	1	.576	....	Spartanburg (20)	33	32	0	.508	4½
Greenwood (13)	37	29	0	.561	1	Gastonia (21)	30	35	2	.462	7½
Anderson (12*)	35	30	1	.538	2½	Sumter (5*)	23	42	0	.354	14½

†Greenville defeated Greenwood 1 to 0 on June 27 in playoff for first-half championship.

STANDING OF CLUBS AT CLOSE OF SECOND HALF, AUGUST 26

Club	W.	L.	T.	Pct.	G.B.	Club	W.	L.	T.	Pct.	G.B.
Greenville (2*)	39	24	0	.619	....	Spartanburg (20)	31	32	0	.492	8
Sumter (5*)	38	26	0	.594	1½	Anderson (12*)	26	39	0	.400	14
Greenwood (13)	33	31	0	.516	6½	Gastonia (21)	25	40	0	.385	15

COMPOSITE STANDING OF CLUBS AT CLOSE OF SEASON, AUGUST 26

Club	Grnv.	Grnw.	Spar.	Sum.	And.	Gas.	W.	L.	T.	Pct.	G.B.
Greenville (2*)	..	15	17	11	18	16	77	52	1	.597	....
Greenwood (13)	11	..	15	15	15	14	70	60	0	.538	7½
Spartanburg (20)	8	11	..	13	14	18	64	64	0	.500	12½
Sumter (5*)	15	11	12	..	9	14	61	68	0	.473	16
Anderson (12*)	8	11	12	17	..	13	61	69	1	.469	16½
Gastonia (21)	10	12	8	12	13	..	55	75	2	.423	22½

Key to major league farm teams (indicated by numbers after clubs in standing) shown on Page 384.
Playoffs—None.
Regular-Season Attendance—Anderson, 184,212; Gastonia, 27,381; Greenville, 46,245; Greenwood, 48,648; Spartanburg, 29,743; Sumter, 33,196. Total, 369,425. No playoff. All-star game at Greenville, 1,216.
Managers: Anderson—Frank Gable; Gastonia—Ed Hobaugh; Greenville—Rac Slider; Greenwood—Eddie Haas; Spartanburg—Howie Bedell; Sumter—Len Johnston.
All-Star Team: 1B—Covert, Sumter; 2B—Coker, Spartanburg; 3B—Hodge, Spartanburg; SS—Taveras, Gastonia; Utility—Blanks, Greenwood; OF—Garcia, Spartanburg; Bottoms, Anderson; Matson, Spartanburg; Utility—Gibson, Anderson; C—Hancock, Anderson; Benoit, Spartanburg; P—Sparkman, Greenville; Gratz, Gastonia; Manager—Rac Slider, Greenville.

(Compiled by Howe News Bureau, Chicago, Ill.)

CLUB BATTING

Club	G.	AB.	R.	OR.	H.	TB.	2B.	3B.	HR.	RBI.	SH.	Int. SF.	BB.	BB.	HP.	SO.	SB.	CS.	LOB.	Pct
Spartanburg	128	4186	647	649	1124	1681	197	48	88	558	54	31	445	17	29	699	138	52	870	.269
Greenville	130	4158	699	567	1093	1535	166	60	52	601	38	52	647	12	38	765	95	37	1008	.263
Greenwood	130	4255	691	645	1089	1609	190	33	88	595	31	38	567	16	42	827	127	24	990	.256
Sumter	129	4078	648	694	1031	1460	160	31	69	540	51	23	614	12	30	850	108	21	946	.253
Gastonia	132	4195	571	651	1060	1426	129	30	54	483	48	36	500	11	38	861	169	38	950	.253
Anderson	131	4209	687	737	1062	1529	158	39	77	565	43	33	641	18	27	787	180	28	1004	.252

Averages are incomplete owing to the fact that NO official scores were received from Sumter since June 30. A total of 29 reports were not filed, 27 of which were compiled from newspaper box scores and two (August 15th doubleheader) are missing altogether.

INDIVIDUAL BATTING
(Leading Qualifiers for Batting Championship—403 or More Plate Appearances)

*Bats lefthanded. †Switch-hitter.

Player and Club	G.	AB.	R.	H.	TB.	2B.	3B.	HR.	RBI.	SH.	SF.	BB.	HP.	SO.	SB.	CS.	Pct.
Hodge, George, Spartanburg	.111	403	88	144	217	25	3	14	82	0	4	50	3	51	13	5	.357
Garcia, Nelson, Spartanburg	.101	363	82	115	177	23	6	9	44	4	1	30	3	55	20	7	.317
Cummings, Michael, Grnv		98	379	81	119	144	13	6	0	40	5	3	37	3	17	48	7	.314
Stephen, John, Greenville	.111	365	73	108	177	15	9	12	77	0	6	80	0	66	6	2	.296
Covert, Danay, Sumter	.111	386	84	114	180	21	3	16	69	0	0	58	6	44	8	1	.295
Smith, Larry, Gastonia	.105	364	50	107	145	10	2	8	51	1	3	40	3	78	19	5	.294
Bottoms, James, Anderson*	.117	382	104	112	144	13	5	3	41	3	3	114	3	50	66	5	.293
Hanegan, Tommy, Grnv*	.112	370	70	107	157	21	4	7	59	1	7	69	2	68	2	5	.289
Casey, Kevin, Sumter	.119	427	48	123	172	20	1	9	78	2	4	22	4	60	1	1	.288
Davis, LaMar, Anderson*	.95	346	64	99	180	19	7	16	88	0	3	72	3	32	9	2	.286
Fuller, John E., Grnw*	.118	424	64	118	170	27	2	7	65	2	3	41	4	65	7	2	.278

Departmental Leaders: G—Taveras, 122; AB—Michael, 450; R—Bottoms, 104; H—Hodge, 144; TB—Hodge, 217; 2B—Fuller, 27; 3B—Evans, 11; HR—Gibson, 18; RBI—Davis, 88; SH—Coker, 9; SF—Evans, 8; BB—Bottoms, 114; HP—Neat, 14; SO—Gibson, 110; SB—Bottoms, 66; CS—Coker, 9.

(All Players—Listed Alphabetically)

Player and Club	G.	AB.	R.	H.	TB.	2B.	3B.	HR.	RBI.	SH.	SF.	BB.	HP.	SO.	SB.	CS.	Pct.
Abram, Gary, Gastonia	4	5	0	2	2	0	0	0	0	1	0	0	0	2	0	0	.400
Augustine, David, Gastonia	86	259	35	80	103	13	2	2	26	1	3	23	2	30	10	3	.309
Aviles, Ramon, Greenville	94	304	47	90	103	9	2	0	38	5	3	47	1	34	5	5	.296
Bagwell, Louis, Anderson*	.46	156	22	43	51	8	0	0	14	1	3	16	0	11	8	2	.276
Banks, Farley, Anderson	.23	60	5	12	17	2	0	1	7	1	0	6	0	11	0	0	.200
Barker, Douglas, Spartanburg	11	12	1	1	1	0	0	0	0	0	0	3	0	4	0	0	.083
Barr, Steven, Greenville*	.15	30	4	5	5	0	0	0	0	0	0	1	0	9	0	0	.167
Barringer, Doyle S., Grnw	.9	4	0	0	0	0	0	0	0	0	0	1	0	4	0	0	.000
Barry, William, Greenville	.24	9	0	0	0	0	0	0	0	1	0	2	0	4	0	0	.000
Beard, Donald, Gastonia*	.32	12	2	3	3	0	0	0	1	3	0	1	0	9	0	0	.250
Bell, David, Sumter	.121	442	81	117	178	19	3	12	75	2	2	44	1	43	9	3	.265
Benoit, Dan, Spartanburg	.80	246	28	59	84	15	2	2	31	3	1	30	2	31	4	3	.240
Blanks, Larvell, Greenwood	.116	437	79	121	188	16	3	15	69	2	5	48	12	45	19	3	.277
Bogard, James, Sumter*	.83	242	20	62	71	6	0	1	14	1	2	19	1	27	1	0	.256
Bottoms, James, Anderson*	.117	382	104	112	144	13	5	3	41	3	3	114	3	50	66	5	.293
Bozich, Tommie, Sumter	.34	107	8	25	34	6	0	1	12	2	0	5	0	24	0	0	.234
Brenner, Glenn, Spartanburg	7	2	0	0	0	0	0	0	0	0	0	0	0	0	0	0	.000
Brescher, Wayne, Anderson	.11	31	8	9	23	1	2	3	7	0	0	3	0	11	0	0	.290
Brown, William E., Grnv*	.98	329	64	96	156	16	4	12	63	0	5	49	0	45	0	0	.292
Bryan, Billy, Spartanburg*	.18	46	6	11	20	0	0	3	8	0	1	11	0	11	0	0	.239
Burger, Michael, Sumter	.78	251	46	56	106	11	3	11	34	2	0	25	1	55	9	0	.223
Cabral, John, Gastonia*	.21	10	3	1	1	0	0	0	0	0	0	2	1	3	0	0	.100
Cameron, Archibald, And	.8	5	0	1	2	-1	0	0	1	0	0	1	0	3	0	0	.200
Camp, Hudie, Gastonia*	.51	180	30	62	81	12	2	1	31	0	1	17	0	27	13	0	.344
Campos, Melvin, Anderson	.15	30	4	4	6	0	1	0	2	0	0	5	0	8	1	0	.133
Cana, Nelson, Greenwood	.26	42	13	9	12	1	1	0	5	0	0	9	0	14	1	0	.214
Cannon, Bruce, Sumter	.19	46	3	9	13	1	0	1	5	0	0	2	0	29	0	0	.196
Casey, Kevin, Sumter	.119	427	48	123	172	20	1	9	78	2	4	22	4	60	1	1	.288
Clay, James, Gastonia*	.90	272	31	64	87	6	5	5	45	1	4	38	5	35	4	1	.235
Cleary, James, Anderson*	.66	166	21	34	46	9	0	1	17	3	0	29	0	31	4	0	.205
Coble, Michael, Spar†	.7	10	0	1	1	0	0	0	0	0	0	1	0	3	0	0	.100
Coker, Jerry, Spartanburg	.105	365	47	97	112	9	3	0	36	9	4	28	2	31	25	9	.266
Coleman, Douglas, Gas*	.73	277	44	75	82	3	2	0	18	0	3	15	1	25	13	1	.271
Coplin, Thomas, Spar†	.12	17	1	5	6	1	0	0	4	3	0	0	0	4	0	0	.294
Covert, Danay, Sumter	.111	386	84	114	189	21	3	16	69	0	0	58	6	44	8	1	.295
Criscione, David, Anderson	.10	20	0	3	4	1	0	0	1	0	0	0	0	0	0	0	.150
Croken, William, Grnv	.21	56	10	14	17	1	1	0	7	0	0	13	1	20	0	1	.250
Cummings, Michael, Grnv	.98	379	81	119	144	13	6	0	40	5	3	37	3	17	48	7	.314
Daniel, Alan, Spartanburg	.11	1	0	0	0	0	0	0	0	0	0	0	0	0	0	0	.000
Danson, Kenneth, Sumter	.113	361	59	75	104	9	4	4	38	7	1	72	6	75	19	6	.208
Davidson, Ralph, Anderson	.15	21	2	1	2	1	0	0	1	2	0	2	0	6	0	0	.048
Davis, LaMar, Anderson*	.95	346	64	99	180	19	7	16	88	0	3	72	3	32	9	2	.286
Derrickson, Richard, Sum	.19	30	4	2	2	0	0	0	1	2	0	1	0	2	0	0	.067
Detter, John, Sumter	.23	33	2	5	8	0	0	1	1	0	3	0	15	0	0	.152
Dietz, James J., Spar*	.18	2	0	0	0	0	0	0	0	0	0	0	0	1	0	0	.000
Dillon, Russell, Grnw†	.24	36	2	1	2	1	0	0	4	0	0	3	0	6	0	0	.028
Eldridge, Robert, Sumter	.14	25	6	6	10	1	0	1	6	1	1	1	0	2	0	0	.240
Elgin, Thomas, Anderson*	.11	2	0	0	0	0	0	0	0	0	0	1	0	2	0	0	.000
Enewold, Dan, Gastonia	.48	144	19	35	44	4	1	1	20	1	3	24	1	19	3	0	.243
Essian, James, Spartanburg	.35	119	19	35	65	8	2	6	20	0	0	4	2	14	3	1	.294
Estrellas, Thomas, Gas*	.14	1	0	0	0	0	0	0	0	0	0	0	0	0	0	0	.000
Evans, Dwight, Greenville	.108	355	69	98	155	14	11	7	68	1	8	55	2	66	1	1	.276
Figueroa, Domingo, Grnw*	.23	11	0	1	1	0	0	0	2	0	2	1	3	0	0	.091
Fletcher, John, Grnv*	.53	163	16	34	46	5	2	1	29	0	3	12	0	39	0	0	.209
Foucault, Steven, And*	.45	41	4	14	15	1	0	0	1	1	0	1	0	5	0	0	.341
Freeman, Jimmy, Greenwood*	.22	38	2	7	9	2	0	0	4	0	0	4	0	9	0	0	.184
Fry, Harry, Sumter	.6	2	0	0	0	0	0	0	0	0	0	0	1	0	0	.000
Fuller, John E., Grnw*	.118	424	64	118	170	27	2	7	65	2	3	41	4	65	7	2	.278
Galindo, Anthony, Sumter	.21	59	5	9	10	1	0	0	1	0	0	9	0	12	0	0	.153
Gallagher, Larry, Sumter	.5	1	0	0	0	0	0	0	0	0	0	0	0	0	0	0	.000
Garcia, Nelson, Spar	.101	363	82	115	177	23	6	9	44	4	1	30	3	55	20	7	.317

Player and Club	G.	AB.	R.	H.	TB.	2B.	3B.	HR.	RBI.	SH.	SF.	BB.	HP.	SO.	SB.	CS.	Pct.
Gentry, Ralph, Spar*	91	277	50	67	97	7	7	3	30	8	1	26	2	44	19	6	.242
Gibson, Roy, Anderson	111	394	61	97	171	16	2	18	80	0	6	50	5	110	6	3	.246
Goldstone, Edward, Spar	40	132	19	35	61	6	1	6	24	0	0	9	2	19	3	1	.265
Gonzalez, Ednio, Gastonia*	2	5	0	1	1	0	0	0	0	0	0	0	0	1	0	0	.200
Goodwin, James, Spar	16	3	0	0	0	0	0	0	0	1	0	0	0	3	0	0	.000
Goodwin, Scott, Greenwood	13	9	1	1	1	0	0	0	0	0	0	0	0	5	0	0	.111
Gorski, Robert, Gastonia	14	8	0	0	0	0	0	0	0	2	0	1	0	5	0	0	.000
Gourieux, David, Greenwood	15	31	3	6	7	1	0	0	4	3	0	5	0	10	0	0	.194
Gratz, Bradford, Gastonia	31	60	11	11	14	1	1	0	3	3	0	1	0	24	0	0	.183
Green, Gordon, Gastonia†	18	7	2	1	1	0	0	0	1	0	1	0	1	0	0	0	.143
Grigas, Joseph, Gastonia*	21	66	10	19	32	4	0	3	11	0	1	6	1	10	2	1	.288
Guenther, Jeffrey, Grnv	7	1	0	0	0	0	0	0	0	0	0	0	0	0	0	0	.000
Hamilton, John, Greenville	61	166	17	39	48	6	0	1	14	2	2	21	1	27	0	3	.235
Hancock, William A., And	84	265	45	72	114	9	3	9	33	1	2	39	1	56	1	0	.272
Handel, Roy, Greenville†	11	28	3	2	3	1	0	0	1	0	0	4	1	11	0	0	.071
Hanegan, Tommy, Grnv*	112	370	70	107	157	21	4	7	59	1	7	69	2	68	2	5	.289
Hansen, Brian, Spar	7	21	3	8	12	1	0	1	3	0	0	4	0	2	0	1	.381
Harris, Harold, Sumter	49	161	19	42	53	3	1	2	23	3	0	8	0	18	1	1	.261
Hatchell, Daniel, Sumter	24	53	3	6	6	0	0	0	4	3	0	1	0	22	0	0	.113
Heintz, David, Greenwood	95	326	52	96	117	19	1	0	33	0	3	40	0	26	6	1	.294
Hendricks, William, Sumter*	22	30	2	2	3	1	0	0	1	0	0	3	0	12	0	0	.067
Hernandez, William, Sumter	22	32	7	10	12	2	0	0	5	0	1	5	0	11	0	0	.313
Hill, Norwood, Greenville	12	19	3	4	7	0	0	1	3	0	0	0	0	2	0	0	.211
Hockett, Nicholas, Sumter*	29	39	5	2	2	0	0	0	0	5	0	1	0	14	1	0	.051
Hodge, George, Spartanburg.	111	403	88	144	217	25	3	14	82	0	4	50	3	51	13	5	.357
Holbert, Eugene, Grnw†	86	274	36	70	96	14	3	2	49	1	5	34	2	59	1	0	.255
Holt, W. Kenneth, And*	1	2	0	0	0	0	0	0	0	0	0	0	0	0	0	0	.000
Hose, Edward, Anderson*	17	6	0	0	0	0	0	0	0	0	0	0	0	4	0	0	.000
Hotchkiss, Bruce, Spar*	103	322	54	84	135	11	5	10	44	1	2	50	4	65	4	4	.261
Houston, Rex, Greenwood	104	351	68	94	123	12	7	1	32	3	0	43	1	85	41	5	.268
Iverson, Dennis, Spar	11	2	0	0	0	0	0	0	0	0	0	0	0	1	0	0	.000
Ivie, Conn C., Gastonia	3	1	0	1	1	0	0	0	0	0	0	1	0	0	0	0	1.000
Jackson, James L., Grnv	48	33	4	4	6	2	0	0	2	3	1	4	0	15	0	0	.121
Jacome, David, Sumter	10	18	0	2	2	0	0	0	1	0	0	2	0	2	0	0	.111
Jimenez, Juan, Spartanburg	27	55	3	11	14	3	0	0	4	5	0	3	0	14	0	0	.200
Johnson, James H., Gas	76	233	25	48	75	9	0	6	34	1	3	30	1	81	4	2	.206
Jones, Wallace, Greenwood	9	15	0	3	3	0	0	0	2	0	0	1	0	4	0	0	.200
Jones, Willie, Spar*	37	100	10	28	40	6	3	0	7	0	0	2	0	14	5	0	.280
Kaaihue, Kala, Gastonia	86	242	27	62	80	10	1	2	35	7	2	30	3	64	1	1	.256
Keenan, James, Anderson	28	25	3	1	1	0	0	0	1	1	0	3	0	10	0	0	.040
Keeter, Lonnie, Grnv*	31	86	20	21	30	2	2	1	16	1	2	16	2	16	5	0	.244
Kelly, Calvin, Greenwood	12	23	5	3	4	1	0	0	1	0	0	5	0	7	0	0	.130
Kelly, Edward, Spartanburg.	18	33	2	2	2	0	0	0	1	2	1	4	0	15	0	0	.061
Kelly, James, Spartanburg	4	3	1	1	1	0	0	0	0	0	0	0	0	2	0	0	.333
Kemp, Richard, Anderson*	9	19	1	3	6	1	1	0	2	0	0	0	0	5	0	0	.158
Kern, James, Sumter	14	28	2	4	5	1	0	0	2	1	1	0	0	10	0	0	.143
King, Bruce, Spartanburg	30	9	2	2	3	1	0	0	0	3	0	4	1	0	.222
King, Gary, C., Sumter	30	91	10	18	20	2	0	0	6	0	2	11	1	17	2	0	.198
King, George A., Greenwood	28	20	4	6	6	0	0	0	4	2	0	6	0	5	0	0	.300
Kinzel, Donald, Spar	69	214	26	45	64	8	1	3	20	4	2	30	1	49	7	3	.210
Klobas, Russell, Spar	88	317	51	94	147	15	4	10	62	1	3	30	1	36	15	3	.297
Kniffin, Charles, Spar	15	14	3	6	12	3	0	1	2	0	0	5	0	3	0	0	.429
Koch, James, Sumter	58	169	24	48	60	8	2	0	24	1	2	25	0	15	1	0	.284
Krivda, Louis, Sumter	2	3	0	0	0	0	0	0	0	0	0	0	0	2	0	0	.000
LaGarde, Larry, Greenwood	96	323	51	86	138	14	4	10	47	0	3	28	4	40	16	5	.266
Landis, Danny, Greenwood	23	24	1	1	1	0	0	0	3	0	2	1	0	10	0	0	.042
Lash, William, Spartanburg	48	127	24	34	50	5	1	3	6	0	0	4	0	20	3	2	.268
Law, Emmett, Anderson	22	24	1	5	5	0	0	0	0	0	1	0	11	0	0	.208
Layman, Edwin, Anderson	11	20	4	7	11	1	0	1	6	1	0	5	0	7	0	0	.350
Lee, David, Gastonia	11	8	0	1	1	0	0	0	0	0	0	3	0	3	0	0	.125
Lee, John, Spartanburg	24	7	0	0	0	0	0	0	0	2	0	0	0	4	0	0	.000
Little, William, Greenwood	30	77	8	15	16	1	0	0	5	2	1	25	1	18	0	0	.195
Llenas, Gustavo, Spar	9	28	5	5	6	1	0	0	1	1	0	2	0	4	0	0	.179
Love, Robert, Anderson	14	29	2	3	3	0	0	0	3	0	0	4	0	10	0	0	.103
Lovett, Horace, Greenwood	31	83	19	21	33	3	0	3	15	0	3	9	0	28	2	0	.253
Lowe, David, Sumter	12	11	0	3	4	1	0	0	1	2	0	2	0	7	0	0	.273
Lyman, Scott, Gastonia	24	32	1	2	2	0	0	0	3	0	0	0	0	18	0	0	.063
Machado, Omar, 15 Gas-23 Sum	38	16	0	2	2	0	0	0	4	0	0	2	0	5	0	0	.125
Magness, Michael, Grnw	15	38	5	10	12	2	0	0	4	1	0	2	0	11	0	0	.263
Majoras, Ernest, Sumter*	3	1	0	0	0	0	0	0	0	0	0	0	0	0	0	0	.000
Malcolm, Robert, Spar	17	8	2	4	4	0	0	0	1	0	0	2	0	1	1	0	.500
Maldonado, Felix, Grnv	35	93	11	23	31	4	2	0	12	1	2	6	3	6	3	0	.247
Marine, Michael, Gastonia	12	21	0	0	0	0	0	0	0	0	0	0	0	4	0	0	.000
Marrero, Wilfredo, Spar	2	1	0	0	0	0	0	0	0	0	0	0	0	0	0	0	.000
Mason, DeWayne, Gastonia	8	20	0	2	2	0	0	0	1	0	0	0	0	5	0	0	.100
Matson, Allan, Spar*	94	332	61	107	168	20	4	11	57	2	3	34	3	44	8	2	.322
May, Robert, Gastonia	13	24	4	6	6	0	0	0	1	2	1	1	0	3	1	0	.250
McCall, Michael, Spar*	69	198	25	48	71	14	3	1	36	0	7	38	2	26	5	4	.242
McCammon, Michael, Grnw	22	24	1	3	4	1	0	0	4	1	0	2	1	9	0	0	.125
McCormick, Kenneth, Grnv	100	339	67	99	144	18	9	3	50	2	1	49	1	38	13	4	.292
McCullough, Edgar, Grnw	11	1	0	0	0	0	0	0	0	0	0	2	0	1	0	0	.000

Player and Club	G.	AB.	R.	H.	TB.	2B.	3B.	HR.	RBI.	SH.	SF.	BB.	HP.	SO.	SB.	CS.	Pct.
McFarland, Steve, Gastonia .	97	309	34	84	108	12	3	2	24	2	3	31	1	40	8	7	.272
McKee, Robert, Gastonia* ..	4	1	0	0	0	0	0	0	0	0	0	0	0	0	0	0	.000
McLane, David, Anderson* ..	4	1	0	0	0	0	0	0	0	0	0	0	0	0	0	0	.000
McRobie, William, Spar .	3	8	1	2	5	0	0	1	1	0	0	1	0	2	0	0	.250
Meyer, Gary, Gastonia	8	6	0	0	0	0	0	0	0	1	0	0	0	3	0	0	.000
Michael, John, Anderson ..	120	450	85	116	161	17	5	6	62	5	4	50	4	41	10	1	.258
Miller, Samuel, Anderson ...	10	14	0	1	1	0	0	0	0	1	0	0	0	3	0	0	.071
Mitchell, Ronald, Gastonia	110	371	71	97	154	7	4	14	51	1	2	62	2	80	30	4	.261
Moore, Curtis, Greenwood*	85	251	71	77	131	15	3	11	42	0	1	72	1	48	10	2	.307
Moreno, Carlos, Greenwood .	21	6	0	1	1	0	0	0	1	0	0	0	0	0	0	0	.167
Morgan, Philip, Spartanburg	42	131	15	32	46	8	0	2	15	0	1	4	2	8	1	1	.244
Morlan, John, Gastonia	65	221	27	49	79	6	3	6	30	0	2	22	7	54	3	1	.222
Murtaugh, Timothy, Gas†	36	77	10	29	41	4	1	2	14	0	1	10	1	6	2	0	.377
Nageleisen, James, Grnw ..	35	128	16	27	38	4	2	1	13	1	0	12	1	29	11	2	.211
Napoleon, Edward, Gastonia	24	50	12	15	21	3	0	1	5	0	2	8	0	2	1	0	.300
Neal, Michael, Grnv*	34	27	2	8	10	2	0	0	2	1	0	3	0	4	0	0	.296
Neat, Scott, Greenville* ..	92	305	57	85	115	13	4	3	51	1	6	50	14	34	7	2	.279
Ormond, Robert, Anderson*	22	25	0	4	4	0	0	0	0	1	0	1	0	8	0	0	.160
Pandis, John, Spartanburg .	5	7	0	3	4	1	0	0	0	0	0	0	0	1	0	0	.429
Peguero, Nelson, Sumter ...	101	343	53	98	120	21	2	2	53	6	4	36	5	19	19	1	.286
Pettit, Michael, Anderson .	5	5	0	0	0	0	0	0	0	0	0	0	0	2	0	0	.000
Powell, Grover, Greenwood*	4	3	1	2	2	0	0	0	0	0	0	0	0	0	0	0	.667
Powers, James, Greenville .	65	209	26	48	61	5	1	2	29	2	1	29	3	39	2	0	.230
Price, Lawrence, Sumter ...	15	24	2	4	4	0	0	0	1	0	1	3	0	8	1	1	.167
Proulx, Bennie, Spartanburg	13	3	0	0	0	0	0	0	0	0	0	0	0	2	0	0	.000
Ray, Richard, Sumter	49	21	2	6	10	1	0	1	3	1	0	2	0	4	0	0	.286
Rhyne, Kenneth, Anderson*	19	54	5	12	18	3	0	1	6	0	0	5	0	15	0	0	.222
Richards, Albert,																	
19 And-20 Sumter	39	90	10	16	19	3	0	0	4	2	0	10	0	21	0	0	.178
Roadarmel, Robert, Gas ...	3	2	0	0	0	0	0	0	0	0	0	1	0	1	0	0	.000
Robertson, Michael, And*	73	179	23	52	65	10	0	1	19	0	1	23	5	26	0	3	.291
Robison, Jerry, Greenwood	85	317	42	77	100	13	2	5	54	4	6	37	3	31	7	2	.243
Rodriguez, Antonio, Grnv .	19	60	7	10	13	3	0	0	3	2	0	8	1	15	1	1	.167
Rogers, Rickey, Anderson .	69	220	29	51	79	9	2	5	26	0	3	22	1	30	12	4	.232
Roswald, Scott, Gastonia .	67	187	31	42	57	4	4	1	17	1	1	32	6	34	15	2	.225
Ruby, Joseph, Sumter*	35	20	5	5	6	1	0	0	2	0	0	0	0	5	0	0	.250
Ruiz, Manuel, Greenwood .	31	82	8	15	18	1	1	0	6	0	1	6	1	13	0	0	.183
Sadler, Richard, Spar	13	24	0	2	3	1	0	0	2	1	0	1	0	10	0	0	.083
Sadowski, James, Gastonia .	18	38	2	7	7	0	0	0	2	3	0	2	1	6	1	0	.184
Salvato, Steve, Anderson .	66	240	35	78	95	9	4	0	31	1	0	16	1	14	1	4	.325
Sandate, Richard, Grnw*	20	26	0	5	6	1	0	0	2	0	0	3	0	13	0	0	.192
Sandstedt, William, Grnv*	34	22	1	4	6	2	0	0	3	0	0	1	0	3	0	0	.182
Santana, Blas, Spartanburg	11	28	4	7	12	1	2	0	3	0	0	0	0	3	0	0	.250
Santiago, Fernando, Grnv*	65	154	20	29	37	4	2	0	12	2	1	28	0	29	1	2	.188
Schneider, Dean, Sumter* .	15	14	2	3	5	0	1	0	1	0	0	4	0	3	0	0	.214
Sevillano, Jose, Greenwood .	22	35	2	7	7	0	0	0	1	0	3	0	0	10	0	0	.200
Shade, Craig, Gastonia ...	13	27	1	2	3	1	0	0	1	0	3	0	0	9	2	0	.074
Shaw, Larry, Sumter*	107	354	86	94	127	11	5	4	31	1	0	66	3	62	30	5	.266
Shields, Donald, Anderson .	25	35	1	3	4	1	0	0	2	0	0	2	0	21	0	0	.086
Skok, Craig, Greenville	32	61	9	11	15	2	1	0	4	2	0	4	2	30	0	1	.180
Slagle, Dennis, Gastonia ..	10	10	0	0	0	0	0	0	0	0	0	0	0	6	0	0	.000
Smith, Larry, Gastonia	105	364	50	107	145	10	2	8	51	1	3	40	3	78	19	5	.294
Smith, Tommy A., Sumter*	53	183	27	67	98	10	6	3	43	2	2	8	1	10	7	1	.366
Southworth, James, And ...	17	44	2	7	7	0	0	0	2	0	0	1	1	10	0	0	.159
Spadola, Francis, Grnv	19	50	3	11	18	1	0	2	6	0	0	6	0	20	1	0	.220
Sparkman, Paul, Grnv*	40	46	9	9	12	3	0	0	5	0	0	5	0	17	0	0	.196
Spottke, John, Greenwood .	90	285	56	71	124	15	1	12	45	1	4	37	2	52	4	2	.249
Stach, Robert, Anderson ..	34	97	17	18	32	1	2	3	14	0	2	10	1	30	3	0	.186
Stephen, John, Greenville ..	111	365	73	108	177	15	9	12	77	0	6	80	0	66	6	2	.296
Stevens, Robert, Sumter ...	5	3	0	1	1	0	0	0	0	0	0	0	0	1	0	0	.333
Strickland, Rudi, Gas*	49	152	21	33	54	7	1	4	19	0	0	17	1	50	1	1	.217
Suarez, Carlos, Sumter* ...	5	4	1	1	1	0	0	0	1	0	0	1	0	0	0	0	.250
Taveras, Franklin, Gastonia	122	442	67	115	135	13	2	1	41	1	0	42	0	65	35	6	.260
Taylor, John, Anderson* ..	99	308	67	75	94	7	3	2	41	1	2	64	2	48	41	4	.244
Terral, Charles, Spar	6	2	0	0	0	0	0	0	0	0	0	0	0	0	0	0	.000
Terry, Keith, Greenville ...	34	43	3	7	8	1	0	0	4	4	1	2	1	12	0	0	.163
Torrealba, Pablo, Grnw* ...	41	20	4	7	7	0	0	0	2	2	0	0	0	6	0	0	.350
Vandewater, Mark, Grnw ..	81	245	32	54	89	12	1	7	35	2	2	29	2	82	0	0	.220
Vickery, Billy, Anderson ..	34	68	9	24	29	2	0	1	10	0	1	13	0	6	0	0	.353
Vingle, Gary, Gastonia	12	19	0	0	0	0	0	0	1	0	0	0	0	5	0	0	.000
Waits, Michael, Anderson*	9	13	1	1	1	0	0	0	0	0	0	1	0	7	0	0	.077
Wallace, David, Spar	25	55	6	6	9	0	0	1	4	2	0	2	0	14	0	0	.109
Wallace, Michael, Spar* ...	25	54	1	6	6	0	0	0	1	3	0	4	0	17	0	0	.111
Walseth, Michael, Grnw* ..	66	239	43	76	135	13	2	14	44	0	2	20	6	23	3	1	.318
Walsh, Thomas J., Grnv ...	33	38	1	4	5	1	0	0	2	0	0	3	0	22	0	0	.105
Walters, Keith, Greenwood .	6	6	1	0	0	0	0	0	0	0	0	0	0	0	0	0	.000
Wang, Geoffrey, Spar	8	21	2	4	7	0	0	1	2	0	0	0	0	6	2	0	.190
Wanless, Richard, Gastonia .	6	1	0	0	0	0	0	0	0	0	0	0	0	1	0	0	.000
Warmbrod, David, Gastonia	29	24	1	3	4	1	0	0	2	0	0	2	0	6	0	0	.125
Watkins, Kenneth, Grnv ...	15	20	2	4	4	0	0	0	1	0	0	1	0	7	0	0	.200
Weiner, Dennis, Spar*	23	70	5	15	21	4	1	0	7	0	0	2	0	11	1	0	.214

Player and Club	G.	AB.	R.	H.	TB.	2B.	3B.	HR.	RBI.	SH.	SF.	BB.	HP.	SO.	SB.	CS.	Pct.
Westerhouse, Charles, Grnw.	4	2	0	0	0	0	0	0	0	0	0	1	0	1	0	0	.000
Whalin, Michael, Spar*	1	0	0	0	0	0	0	0	0	0	0	0	0	0	0	0	.000
Wiley, Eugene, Anderson	15	18	3	2	3	0	0	0	1	3	0	2	0	7	0	0	.167
Williams, Fred, Anderson	33	15	0	2	2	0	0	0	5	0	1	0	4	0	0	.133
Williams, Melvin, And*	.93	319	44	87	123	16	1	6	45	1	2	21	2	50	16	1	.273
Young, Michael L., Sumter*	38	11	2	3	3	0	0	0	1	0	3	0	2	0	0	.273

GRAND-SLAM HOME RUNS—Casey, Davis, Hodge, 2 each; Bell, Blanks, Brown, Gibson, Taveras, 1 each.

AWARDED FIRST BASE ON INTERFERENCE—Aviles (Hancock), Hotchkiss (Bogard), Shaw (Hancock).

CLUB FIELDING

Club	G.	PO.	A.	E.	DP.	PB.	Pct.	Club	G.	PO.	A.	E.	DP.	PB.	Pct.
Greenville	130	3270	1433	187	120	34	.962	Gastonia	132	3266	1348	230	102	34	.953
Greenwood	130	3274	1295	210	98	34	.956	Anderson	131	3261	1313	241	98	29	.950
Spartanburg	..128	3239	1286	215	109	20	.955	Sumter	129	3227	1325	246	96	29	.949

Triple Play—Gastonia.

INDIVIDUAL FIELDING
(Ten or More Games)

*Throws lefthanded.

FIRST BASEMEN

Player and Club	G.	PO.	A.	E.	DP.	Pct.	Player and Club	G.	PO.	A.	E.	DP.	Pct.
Clay, Gastonia*	72	507	42	3	38	.995	Cleary, Anderson*	28	195	10	4	17	.981
DAVIS, Anderson*	94	766	45	9	50	.989	Covert, Sumter	109	705	70	16	72	.980
Weiner, Spar*	20	144	10	2	20	.987	McCall, Spartanburg	61	451	34	10	40	.980
Enewold, Gastonia*	28	191	9	3	24	.985	Hodge, Spartanburg	20	120	9	3	9	.977
Fuller, Greenwood*	.113	891	51	16	73	.983	Walseth, Greenwood	19	109	7	3	9	.975
Santiago, Grnv*	41	316	20	6	29	.982	Strickland, Gas*	29	242	11	9	21	.966
Brown, Greenville*	.93	782	45	15	73	.982	Casey, Sumter	17	94	10	4	4	.963
Goldstone, Spar	38	256	11	5	13	.982							

Triple Play—Clay.

(Fewer Than Ten Games)

Player and Club	G.	PO.	A.	E.	DP.	Pct.	Player and Club	G.	PO.	A.	E.	DP.	Pct.
Maldonado, Grnv	4	30	0	0	1	1.000	Gibson, Anderson	1	2	0	0	1	1.000
Shade, Gastonia	4	20	1	0	0	1.000	Murtaugh, Gastonia	1	1	0	0	0	1.000
Spottke, Greenwood	2	8	2	0	1	1.000	Camp, Gastonia*	5	45	2	2	2	.959
Schneider, Sumter	4	6	0	0	1	1.000	Vickery, Anderson	9	67	3	4	9	.946
Johnson, Gastonia	1	3	0	0	0	1.000	Nageleisen, Grnw	4	15	0	1	0	.938

SECOND BASEMEN

Player and Club	G.	PO.	A.	E.	DP.	Pct.	Player and Club	G.	PO.	A.	E.	DP.	Pct.
Rodriguez, Grnv	10	16	27	1	5	.977	Keeter, Greenville	10	19	32	3	13	.944
Richards, And-Sum	17	16	23	1	4	.975	McFarland, Gas	64	107	146	15	32	.944
Blanks, Greenwood	27	41	71	3	14	.974	Coker, Spartanburg	.105	187	248	26	44	.944
Ruiz, Greenwood	14	27	42	2	6	.972	Taylor, Anderson	14	20	30	3	5	.943
McCORMICK, Grnv	.96	199	264	17	52	.965	King, Sumter	17	39	41	5	10	.941
Robison, Greenwood	80	197	187	18	46	.955	Bell, Sumter	38	71	95	12	17	.933
Coleman, Gastonia	49	94	112	11	21	.949	Peguero, Sumter	64	69	109	18	23	.908
Robertson, And	50	74	109	10	25	.948	Rogers, Anderson	62	116	134	27	23	.903
Kinzel, Spartanburg	19	29	42	4	19	.947	Augustine, Gas	24	42	46	11	4	.889

Triple Play—McFarland.

(Fewer Than Ten Games)

Player and Club	G.	PO.	A.	E.	DP.	Pct.	Player and Club	G.	PO.	A.	E.	DP.	Pct.
Klobas, Spar	2	4	6	0	1	1.000	Spottke, Greenwood	6	8	14	1	3	.957
Harris, Sumter	2	4	4	0	1	1.000	Llenas, Spar	7	18	23	2	10	.932
Galindo, Sumter	2	0	6	0	3	1.000	Aviles, Greenwood	7	12	14	2	4	.929
Bagwell, Anderson	8	13	18	1	2	.969	Kelly, Greenwood	8	5	14	2	2	.905
Hanegan, Grnv	8	10	18	1	2	.966	Burger, Sumter	2	3	4	3	1	.700

THIRD BASEMEN

Player and Club	G.	PO.	A.	E.	DP.	Pct.	Player and Club	G.	PO.	A.	E.	DP.	Pct.
HANEGAN, Grnv	.99	66	183	12	27	.954	Bell, Sumter	82	44	94	15	3	.902
Coleman, Gastonia	21	23	28	3	4	.944	Morgan, Spar	41	31	75	12	8	.898
Blanks, Grnw	88	60	159	13	11	.944	Lovett, Greenwood	24	8	38	6	2	.885
Napoleon, Gastonia	12	8	8	1	0	.941	Harris, Sumter	39	39	60	13	1	.884
Spottke, Grnw	18	8	21	2	2	.935	Taylor, Anderson	47	35	72	15	7	.877
Hodge, Spartanburg	91	78	144	19	13	.921	Michael, Anderson	67	50	96	21	10	.874
McFarland, Gastonia	18	15	20	3	1	.921	Augustine, Gastonia	49	40	83	21	7	.854
Keeter, Greenville	15	9	23	3	1	.914	Roswald, Gastonia	34	24	41	12	1	.844
Spadola, Greenville	13	9	20	3	1	.906	Gibson, Anderson	21	11	18	7	2	.806

(Fewer Than Ten Games)

Player and Club	G.	PO.	A.	E.	DP.	Pct.	Player and Club	G.	PO.	A.	E.	DP.	Pct.
Robison, Greenwood	2	5	4	0	0	1.000	McCall, Spartanburg	1	1	1	0	0	1.000
Shade, Gastonia	6	0	8	0	0	1.000	Hamilton, Grnv	6	2	11	1	0	.929
Santana, Spar	2	3	1	0	1	1.000	Foucault, Anderson	3	2	6	1	0	.889
Richards, And-Sum	3	1	3	0	0	1.000	Smith, Gastonia	8	5	9	2	2	.875
Cummings, Greenville	1	1	2	0	0	1.000	King, Sumter	9	12	16	7	2	.800
Burger, Sumter	1	0	2	0	0	1.000	Ruiz, Greenwood	5	2	6	3	0	.727
Kinzel, Spartanburg	1	0	2	0	0	1.000	Evans, Greenville	2	1	1	1	0	.667

SHORTSTOPS

Player and Club	G.	PO.	A.	E.	DP.	Pct.
TAVERAS, Gastonia	122	193	337	37	56	.935
Taylor, Anderson	26	38	67	8	11	.929
Richards, And.-Sum	12	13	25	3	5	.927
Aviles, Greenville	85	124	231	30	40	.922
Hamilton, Grnv	45	50	115	14	21	.922
Heintz, Greenwood	93	122	275	37	44	.915
Kinzel, Spartanburg	48	81	121	20	19	.910
Bagwell, Anderson	37	40	77	12	17	.907
Michael, Anderson	54	78	138	23	18	.904
Klobas, Spartanburg	79	138	207	39	47	.898
Campos, Anderson	11	16	28	5	6	.898
Spottke, Greenwood	38	49	81	15	16	.897
Burger, Sumter	74	84	119	24	29	.894
Bozich, Sumter	32	64	82	21	20	.874
Galindo, Sumter	15	23	39	10	12	.861
McFarland, Gastonia	15	14	22	7	2	.837

Triple Play—Taveras.

(Fewer Than Ten Games)

Player and Club	G.	PO.	A.	E.	DP.	Pct
Blanks, Greenwood	1	3	2	0	0	1.000
Garcia, Spartanburg	1	0	2	0	0	1.000
Bell, Sumter	1	1	0	0	0	1.000
Rodriguez, Grnv	7	16	21	1	2	.974
Rogers, Anderson	2	3	8	1	3	.917
Harris, Sumter	2	5	5	1	2	.909
Cana, Greenwood	8	8	14	3	3	.880
Santana, Spar	5	8	14	6	2	.786
Jacome, Sumter	4	1	4	2	0	.714
McCormick, Grnv	1	0	1	1	0	.500

OUTFIELDERS

Player and Club	G.	PO.	A.	E.	DP.	Pct.
Strickland, Gas*	11	15	1	0	0	1.000
Spottke, Greenwood	23	37	3	1	0	.976
Neat, Greenville	82	99	4	3	2	.972
Salvato, Anderson	62	93	6	3	1	.971
GENTRY, Spar	74	138	7	5	1	.967
LaGarde, Greenwood	87	135	3	5	0	.965
Garcia, Spartanburg	89	182	10	7	1	.965
Morlan, Gastonia	65	74	7	3	2	.964
Jones, Spartanburg*	23	25	2	1	0	.964
Walseth, Greenwood	50	72	1	3	0	.961
Peguero, Sumter	28	44	4	2	2	.960
M. Williams, And*	89	137	5	6	3	.959
Evans, Greenville	100	129	10	6	2	.959
Houston, Greenwood	96	151	5	7	1	.957
Hotchkiss, Spar*	90	126	4	6	0	.956
Grigas, Gastonia*	20	19	2	1	1	.955
Smith, Gastonia	96	146	8	8	3	.951
Cannon, Sumter	16	18	1	1	0	.950
Nageleisen, Grnw	29	53	2	3	0	.948
Mitchell, Gastonia	107	171	9	10	1	.947
Cummings, Greenville	92	182	13	11	2	.947
Casey, Sumter	101	110	7	7	1	.944
Enewold, Gastonia*	15	16	0	1	0	.941
Lash, Spartanburg	34	43	3	3	0	.939
Camp, Gastonia*	42	73	3	5	0	.938
Stephen, Greenville	103	123	8	9	0	.936
Maldonado, Grnv	24	27	2	2	0	.935
Bottoms, Anderson	107	161	10	12	2	.934
Gibson, Anderson	88	118	6	10	0	.925
Danson, Sumter	109	165	8	14	1	.925
Roswald, Gastonia	24	29	3	3	1	.914
Shaw, Sumter*	96	132	5	13	0	.913
Vandewater, Grnw	49	80	3	8	1	.912
Moore, Greenwood	77	89	2	9	0	.910
Matson, Spartanburg	87	129	11	14	1	.909
Stach, Anderson	27	38	5	5	1	.896
Johnson, Gastonia	33	40	3	6	1	.878
Cleary, Anderson*	27	33	2	5	0	.875
Cana, Greenwood	13	7	0	1	0	.875
Smith, Sumter	47	37	1	7	1	.844

(Fewer Than Ten Games)

Player and Club	G.	PO.	A.	E.	DP.	Pct.
Wang, Spartanburg	5	16	1	0	0	1.000
Klobas, Spartanburg	4	9	0	0	0	1.000
Augustine, Gastonia	1	1	0	0	0	1.000
Davis, Anderson*	1	1	0	0	0	1.000
Santiago, Grnv*	2	1	0	0	0	1.000
Taylor, Anderson	4	1	0	0	0	1.000
Clay, Gastonia*	7	9	1	1	0	.909
Foucault, Anderson	3	5	0	1	0	.833
Price, Sumter	4	6	1	2	0	.778

CATCHERS

Player and Club	G.	PO.	A.	E.	DP.	PB.	Pct.
Vickery, Anderson	13	60	10	0	0	1	1.000
BENOIT, Spar	77	437	50	5	7	7	.990
Bryan, Spar	16	81	7	1	3		.989
Koch, Sumter	56	223	27	4	3	8	.984
Little, Grnw	30	169	13	3	1	7	.984
Brescher, And	10	53	1	1	1	3	.982
Essian, Spar	31	204	21	5	5	5	.978
Croken, Grnv	19	104	13	3	1	4	.975
Holbert, Grnw	83	500	29	14	4	22	.974
Hancock, And	78	467	43	14	6	15	.973
Rhyne, And	18	93	13	3	1	2	.972
Johnson, Gas	40	248	29	8	4	14	.972
Kaaihue, Gas	81	466	43	17	3	17	.968
Powers, Grnv	62	367	45	14	3	15	.967
Bogard, Sumter	73	355	48	15	2	14	.964
Fletcher, Grnv	46	253	16	11	0	11	.961
Murtaugh, Gas	18	129	18	6	0	3	.961
Vandewater, Grnw	24	146	7	7	1	5	.956
Handel, Grnv	10	68	7	4	1	4	.949
Banks, Anderson	20	88	6	7	0	6	.931

(Fewer Than Ten Games)

Player and Club	G.	PO.	A.	E.	DP.	PB.	Pct.
McRobie, Spar	3	11	0	0	0	3	1.000
Pandis, Spar	2	6	0	0	0		1.000
J. Kelly, Spar	2	1	0	0	0		1.000
Hernandez, Sum	9	25	0	1	0	7	.962
Hansen, Spar	7	41	3	2	0	2	.957
Criscione, And	7	24	2	2	0	2	.929

PITCHERS

Player and Club	G.	PO.	A.	E.	DP.	Pct.
JACKSON, Grnv*	47	11	20	0	2	1.000
Love, Anderson	14	5	20	0	0	1.000
Hockett, Sumter*	29	2	18	0	0	1.000
Watkins, Greenville	15	2	17	0	1	1.000
Young, Sumter	33	8	11	0	0	1.000
Hill, Greenville	12	1	17	0	1	1.000
Ormond, Anderson*	22	3	15	0	0	1.000
Sandstedt, Grnv*	34	6	12	0	2	1.000
Torrealba, Grnw*	40	2	13	0	0	1.000
Marine, Gastonia	12	3	11	0	1	1.000
Davidson, Anderson	15	4	10	0	0	1.000
Barry, Greenville	14	1	12	0	1	1.000
F. Williams, And	33	4	8	0	1	1.000
Vingle, Gastonia	12	3	8	0	1	1.000
Figueroa, Grnw*	23	2	8	0	1	1.000
Lee, Gastonia	11	0	9	0	1	1.000

PITCHERS—Continued

Player and Club	G.	PO.	A.	E.	DP.	Pct.
Ruby, Sumter*	31	3	6	0	0	1.000
Foucault, Anderson	33	2	7	0	1	1.000
Goodwin, Spar	16	0	7	0	2	1.000
Green, Gastonia	17	2	5	0	1	1.000
Proulx, Spartanburg	13	1	2	0	0	1.000
Gorski, Gastonia	14	1	2	0	1	1.000
Dietz, Spartanburg*	13	0	3	0	0	1.000
Daniel, Spar	11	1	1	0	0	1.000
Iverson, Spar	11	0	2	0	0	1.000
McCullough, Grnw	11	0	2	0	0	1.000
Terry, Greenville	34	8	29	1	1	.974
Jimenez, Spar	27	6	27	1	1	.971
Walsh, Greenville	33	4	24	1	2	.966
Sparkman, Grnv	40	8	18	1	0	.963
Southworth, And	17	7	40	2	0	.959
Lyman, Gastonia	24	3	19	1	1	.957
Gourieux, Grnw	15	8	12	1	1	.952
Gratz, Gastonia*	22	9	29	2	2	.950
Sadler, Spartanburg	13	7	10	1	0	.944
Sevillano, Grnw	22	7	10	1	0	.944
Skok, Greenville*	32	9	23	2	2	.941
Ray, Sumter	48	7	9	1	0	.941
Kniffin, Spar*	15	4	10	1	0	.933
Law, Anderson	22	2	12	1	2	.933
Shields, Anderson	24	6	8	1	1	.933
Machado, Gas-Sum	38	4	9	1	1	.929
M. Wallace, Spar*	25	7	17	2	2	.923
Moreno, Greenwood	20	1	10	1	1	.917
E. Kelly, Spar	18	3	18	2	1	.913
Slagle, Gastonia	10	1	9	1	0	.909
Sadowski, Gastonia	17	9	20	3	2	.906
Warmbrod, Gastonia	29	3	26	3	1	.906
Magness, Grnw	15	3	16	2	1	.905
Wiley, Anderson	15	2	7	1	0	.900
King, Greenwood	28	2	7	1	2	.900
Hatchell, Sumter	24	10	24	4	1	.895
Derrickson, Sumter	17	2	15	2	0	.895
Malcolm, Spar	17	1	7	1	0	.889
Barr, Greenville*	15	4	19	3	1	.885
Neal, Greenville*	33	1	21	3	0	.880
D. Wallace, Spar	24	6	15	3	0	.875
Goodwin, Grnw	13	2	5	1	0	.875
King, Spartanburg	30	2	5	1	0	.875
McCammon, Grnw	22	5	8	2	0	.867
Freeman, Grnw*	22	1	31	5	1	.865
Dillon, Greenwood*	16	4	14	3	0	.857
Detter, Sumter	23	4	14	3	1	.857
Keenan, Anderson	28	5	13	3	2	.857
Beard, Gastonia*	31	1	11	2	1	.857
Barker, Spartanburg	11	1	5	1	0	.857
Hendricks, Sum*	22	5	12	3	2	.850
Lowe, Sumter	12	2	9	2	0	.846
Landis, Greenwood	23	4	7	2	0	.846
Miller, Anderson	10	1	8	2	0	.818
Cabral, Gastonia*	21	0	13	3	2	.813
Elgin, Anderson*	11	0	4	1	0	.800
Eldridge, Sumter	14	3	10	4	1	.765
Coplin, Spartanburg*	12	4	8	4	0	.750
Lee, Spartanburg	24	3	6	3	0	.750
Kern, Sumter	14	2	8	4	1	.714
Roane, Anderson	17	0	5	2	0	.714
Sandate, Grnw*	20	2	7	5	0	.643

(Fewer Than Ten Games)

Player and Club	G.	PO.	A.	E.	DP.	Pct.
Layman, Anderson	9	2	6	0	0	1.000
Walters, Grnw	6	1	5	0	2	1.000
Jones, Greenwood	9	4	2	0	0	1.000
Suarez, Sumter*	5	0	5	0	1	1.000
Abram, Gastonia	4	0	4	0	0	1.000
Coble, Spartanburg	6	2	2	0	1	1.000
Strickland, Gas*	1	1	2	0	0	1.000
Murtaugh, Gastonia	2	1	2	0	1	1.000
Powell, Greenwood*	4	1	2	0	0	1.000
Gallagher, Sumter	5	0	3	0	0	1.000
Cameron, Anderson	8	0	3	0	0	1.000
Gonzalez, Gastonia*	2	0	2	0	0	1.000
Ivie, Gastonia	3	2	0	0	0	1.000
Napoleon, Gastonia	3	1	1	0	0	1.000
Westerhouse, Grnw	4	0	2	0	0	1.000
Guenther, Grnv	7	0	2	0	0	1.000
Krivda, Sumter	2	0	1	0	0	1.000
Marrero, Spar	2	0	1	0	0	1.000
Stevens, Sumter*	5	0	1	0	0	1.000
Fry, Sumter	6	1	0	0	0	1.000
Terral, Spartanburg	6	1	0	0	0	1.000
Barringer, Grnw	9	0	1	0	0	1.000
Waits, Anderson*	9	1	16	1	0	.944
Kemp, Anderson*	9	3	11	1	0	.933
May, Gastonia	9	3	18	2	0	.913
Wanless, Gastonia	6	2	4	1	0	.857
Mason, Gastonia	8	2	9	2	0	.846
Meyer, Gastonia	8	0	3	1	0	.750
Majoras, Sumter*	3	1	0	1	0	.500
Pettit, Anderson	5	1	0	1	0	.500
Roadarmel, Gas	3	1	0	2	0	.333

The following pitchers do not have any recorded accepted chances; therefore, are not listed in the fielding averages: Brenner, Estrellas*, Holt*, McKee*, McLane*, Michael, Taylor, Whalin*.

CLUB PITCHING

Club	G.	CG.	ShO.	Sv.	IP.	H.	R.	ER.	HR.	BB.	Int. BB.	HB.	SO.	WP.	Bk.	ERA.
Greenville	130	22	8	45	1090	1027	567	448	58	531	13	40	800	81	5	3.70
Greenwood	130	13	8	41	1091	1092	645	515	76	512	23	35	822	79	3	4.25
Gastonia	132	36	13	16	1089	1002	651	514	66	690	18	38	869	113	8	4.25
Anderson	131	33	4	21	1087	1113	737	526	73	572	6	42	803	87	6	4.36
Spartanburg	128	44	6	17	1080	1127	649	527	75	525	21	22	747	70	3	4.39
Sumter	129	24	3	30	1076	1098	694	544	85	584	5	27	748	109	7	4.55

PITCHERS' RECORDS

(Leading Qualifiers for Earned-Run Average Leadership—130 or More Innings)

*Throws lefthanded.

Pitcher—Club	G.	GS.	CG.	ShO.	W.	L.	Sv.	Pct.	IP.	H.	R.	ER.	HR.	BB.	Int. BB.	HB.	SO.	WP.	ERA.
Gratz, Gastonia*	22	21	14	5	12	6	0	.667	163	116	52	41	6	80	0	2	160	16	2.26
Skok, Greenville*	32	23	7	2	14	4	0	.778	167	130	54	47	6	43	1	2	134	4	2.53
Jimenez, Spar	27	20	9	2	10	8	0	.556	171	166	63	51	5	33	1	3	99	7	2.68
Hatchell, Sumter	24	22	5	0	10	5	1	.667	144	129	72	52	12	57	0	0	92	5	3.25
Sparkman, Grnv	40	11	4	0	16	5	9	.762	138	112	67	54	7	56	0	3	87	8	3.52
Hockett, Sumter*	29	15	5	0	10	12	0	.455	132	137	71	52	7	52	1	2	83	5	3.55
M. Wallace, Spar*	25	15	10	2	8	8	0	.500	167	150	95	68	10	72	3	0	157	2	3.66
D. Wallace, Spar	24	24	7	0	8	8	0	.500	150	154	101	86	10	89	6	5	104	12	5.16

Departmental Leaders: G—Ray, 48; GS—M. Wallace, 25; CG—Gratz, 14; ShO—Gratz, 5; W—Sparkman, 16; L—Hockett, 12; Sv—Ray, 13; Pct.—Skok, .778; IP—Jimenez, 171; H—Jimenez, 166; R—D. Wallace, 101; ER—D. Wallace, 86; HR—Coplin, Hatchell, 12; BB—D. Wallace, 89; IBB—D. Wallace, 6; HB—Terry, 13; SO—Gratz, 160; WP—Kern, 25.

(All Pitchers—Listed Alphabetically)

Pitcher—Club	G.	GS.	CG.	ShO.	W.	L.	Sv.	Pct.	IP.	H.	R.	ER.	HR.	BB.	Int. BB.	HB.	SO.	WP.	ERA.
Abram, Gastonia ..	4	3	1	0	1	2	0	.333	18	21	16	13	1	16	0	0	16	1	6.50
Barker, Spar	11	4	3	1	2	4	0	.333	45	33	16	13	1	22	1	0	31	4	2.60
Barr, Greenville* ..	15	15	1	0	3	4	0	.429	74	72	52	36	6	55	0	1	61	14	4.38
Barringer, Grnw ..	9	0	0	0	2	1	1	.667	23	27	18	18	3	9	1	2	23	2	7.04
Barry, Greenville ..	24	4	0	0	4	2	6	.667	44	40	22	15	1	26	0	0	30	8	3.07
Beard, Gastonia* ..	31	3	0	3	6	2	2	.333	60	55	49	37	2	42	2	1	42	11	5.55
Brenner, Spar	7	0	0	0	1	0	0	1.000	9	2	3	3	0	9	0	0	8	0	3.00
Cabral, Gastonia* ..	21	5	2	0	1	5	1	.167	51	43	37	37	5	62	2	5	47	3	6.53
Cameron, Anderson	8	1	0	0	0	2	0	.000	17	26	20	18	1	26	0	0	12	4	9.53
Coble, Spartanburg	6	4	1	1	2	0	0	1.000	24	28	9	7	2	5	0	2	12	2	2.63
Coplin, Spar*	12	10	1	0	2	4	0	.333	59	73	44	38	12	36	0	2	28	2	5.80
Daniel, Spar	11	0	0	0	1	2	0	.000	17	20	18	14	2	11	0	0	14	3	7.41
Davidson, And ...	15	14	1	0	3	8	0	.273	67	69	55	41	5	60	0	3	54	6	5.51
Derrickson, Sum ..	17	15	5	1	6	8	0	.429	99	106	63	49	8	59	0	2	89	9	4.45
Detter, Sumter ...	23	16	3	1	6	8	1	.429	102	105	62	49	3	59	1	6	70	15	4.32
Dietz, Spar*	18	0	0	0	3	2	0	.600	19	29	19	14	0	13	0	0	17	2	6.63
Dillon, Grnw*	16	15	0	0	3	5	0	.375	75	84	50	41	3	42	1	1	63	11	4.92
Eldridge, Sum	14	12	0	0	5	2	0	.714	74	64	41	33	5	57	0	4	56	8	4.01
Elgin, Anderson* ..	11	0	0	0	0	2	0	.000	20	22	19	12	3	7	0	1	9	4	5.40
Estrellas, Gas*	14	0	0	0	1	3	1	.250	12	14	13	7	1	11	1	1	5	1	5.25
Figueroa, Grnw* ..	23	1	0	0	4	0	1	1.000	43	38	23	20	2	35	0	1	26	2	4.19
Foucault, And	33	0	0	0	3	5	6	.500	65	49	25	10	1	25	0	2	58	1	1.38
Freeman, Grnw* ..	22	22	2	1	8	7	0	.533	115	105	66	54	10	54	1	2	85	9	4.23
Fry, Sumter	6	0	0	0	2	0	0	.000	12	10	7	7	3	3	0	0	13	0	5.25
Gallagher, Sumter .	5	0	0	0	1	1	0	.500	6	10	11	9	1	6	0	1	5	1	13.50
Gonzalez, Gas*	2	0	0	0	0	0	0	.000	15	8	7	6	1	10	0	0	14	2	3.60
Goodwin, Spar	16	0	0	0	3	0	1	1.000	25	22	10	7	1	12	0	0	16	2	2.52
Goodwin, Grnw ...	13	0	0	0	1	4	0	.500	31	36	26	20	2	20	1	1	16	3	5.81
Gorski, Gastonia ..	14	5	2	1	1	4	0	.200	38	33	27	23	1	30	1	0	30	3	5.45
Gourieux, Grnw ..	15	14	1	1	8	5	1	.615	98	82	42	29	6	21	0	4	84	5	2.66
Gratz, Gastonia* ..	22	21	14	5	12	6	0	.667	163	116	52	41	6	80	0	2	160	16	2.26
Green, Gastonia ..	17	2	0	0	1	3	1	.250	31	26	15	12	0	27	1	3	29	2	3.48
Guenther, Grnw ...	7	0	0	0	0	1	0	.000	10	17	10	6	3	7	0	0	5	0	5.40
Hatchell, Sumter ..	24	22	5	0	10	5	1	.667	144	129	72	52	12	57	0	0	92	5	3.25
Hendricks, Sum* ..	22	13	1	0	2	7	0	.222	93	103	63	53	11	50	0	2	46	4	5.13
Hill, Greenville ...	12	8	1	0	4	4	0	.500	59	58	25	30	2	41	2	4	34	4	4.58
Hockett, Sumter* ..	29	15	5	0	10	12	2	.455	132	137	71	52	7	52	1	2	83	5	3.55
Holt, Anderson* ...	1	0	0	0	0	0	0	.000	5	3	2	0	3	0	0	5	1	3.60
Hose, Anderson ...	17	1	0	0	1	2	0	.333	32	33	18	17	1	18	1	3	29	2	4.78
Iverson, Spar	11	0	0	0	2	0	1	1.000	9	11	3	3	1	7	0	0	7	2	3.00
Ivie, Gastonia	3	0	0	0	0	1	1	.000	11	17	12	10	2	1	0	0	5	1	8.18
Jackson, Grnv*	47	8	2	1	6	6	9	.500	127	115	55	39	6	40	2	3	67	3	2.76
Jimenez, Spar	27	20	9	2	10	8	0	.556	171	166	63	51	5	33	1	3	99	7	2.68
Jones, Greenwood .	9	8	0	0	2	3	1	.400	44	56	33	25	4	23	0	2	26	5	5.11
Keenan, Anderson .	28	10	4	1	6	6	3	.500	90	121	80	57	8	31	0	4	58	3	5.70
E. Kelly, Spar ...	18	17	5	1	7	4	0	.636	92	90	52	46	4	55	0	4	54	12	4.50
Kemp, Anderson* .	9	8	1	0	3	4	0	.429	51	52	30	24	0	33	0	2	24	3	3.53
Kern, Sumter	14	13	2	0	5	6	0	.455	72	57	47	39	3	70	0	3	71	25	4.88
King, Spartanburg .	32	0	0	0	6	5	5	.545	49	54	33	30	4	29	2	4	54	2	5.51
King, Greenwood ..	28	2	0	0	7	3	8	.700	66	66	24	17	4	29	1	4	49	3	2.32
Kniffin, Spar*	15	6	2	0	2	4	1	.333	53	59	37	33	6	13	2	2	33	4	5.60
Krivda, Sumter ...	2	0	0	0	0	0	0	.000	9	12	8	7	1	5	0	0	2	2	7.00
Landis, Greenwood	23	10	2	1	4	2	0	.667	78	80	63	49	5	49	2	0	50	14	5.65
Law, Anderson ...	22	7	4	1	3	3	1	.500	66	83	55	47	10	36	0	2	33	6	6.41
Layman, And	9	8	3	0	3	4	0	.429	55	49	38	30	4	35	0	2	54	3	4.91
Lee, Gastonia	11	1	0	0	2	1	0	.667	26	16	10	8	2	22	0	1	17	2	2.77
Lee, Spartanburg ..	24	4	2	0	2	5	4	.286	47	59	39	35	2	27	3	0	24	3	4.98
Love, Anderson ...	13	4	1	5	5	0	.500	87	89	53	35	4	35	1	3	53	11	3.62
Lowe, Sumter	12	7	1	0	1	1	0	.500	41	53	37	30	7	25	1	1	25	4	6.59
Lyman, Gastonia ..	24	15	4	0	4	10	0	.286	105	94	68	53	8	71	1	5	87	15	4.54
Machado, 15 Gas- 23 Sumter ...	38	0	0	0	8	2	7	.800	76	76	49	41	9	25	2	5	60	5	4.86
Magness, Grnw ...	15	15	4	1	6	6	0	.500	93	97	51	38	7	31	1	2	65	0	3.68
Majoras, Sumter* ..	3	0	0	0	1	0	0	.000	7	15	14	8	2	5	0	0	5	3	10.29
Malcolm, Spar ...	17	3	0	0	2	2	2	.500	34	42	36	30	2	31	2	1	23	5	7.94
Marine, Gastonia ..	12	12	1	0	4	5	0	.444	64	61	38	31	6	45	1	2	58	5	4.36
Marrero, Spar	2	0	0	0	0	1	0	.000	4	3	0	0	0	4	0	0	2	0	0.00
Mason, Gastonia ..	8	4	3	5	1	0	.833	61	37	17	13	0	31	1	0	60	6	1.92
May, Gastonia ...	9	9	1	0	3	2	0	.600	62	64	36	29	6	28	2	1	42	7	4.21
McCammon, Grnw .	22	8	2	2	7	2	5	.778	78	60	29	22	4	37	2	3	62	4	2.54
McCullough, Grnw	11	0	0	0	0	3	0	.000	17	21	10	5	0	6	0	0	7	0	2.65
McKee, Gastonia* ..	4	0	0	0	1	0	0	1.000	5	4	2	2	0	5	0	0	3	0	3.60
McLane, And*	4	1	0	0	0	1	0	.000	5	8	11	10	2	7	0	0	5	4	18.00
Meyer, Gastonia ..	8	5	0	0	1	3	0	.250	29	36	24	21	1	16	0	0	24	8	6.52
Michael, And	1	0	0	0	0	0	0	.000	2	4	4	4	1	1	0	0	1	5	18.00
Miller, Anderson ..	10	4	1	0	2	2	1	.500	39	34	14	11	1	32	0	1	32	2	2.54
Moreno, Grnw	20	0	0	0	4	4	0	.000	34	35	23	22	4	23	1	1	33	3	5.82
Murtaugh, Gastonia	2	0	0	0	0	0	0	.000	5	4	4	0	0	0	0	0	0	0.00
Napoleon, Gastonia .	3	0	0	0	1	0	0	1.000	5	4	4	3	0	5	0	0	0	5.40
Neal, Greenville* ..	33	12	2	0	8	4	6	.667	88	80	52	37	4	65	3	7	84	6	3.78

Pitcher—Club	G.	GS.	CG.	ShO.	W.	L.	Sv.	Pct.	IP.	H.	R.	ER.	HR.	BB.	Int.BB.	HB.	SO.	WP.	ERA.
Ormond, Anderson*.22	10	1	0	2	7	0	.222	75	88	52	40	4	26	2	2	43	0	4.80
Pettit, Anderson .. 5	3	1	0	1	2	1	.333	12	26	22	12	5	4	0	1	9	0	9.00
Powell, Grnw* 4	2	0	0	0	3	0	.000	13	17	11	11	0	12	3	0	9	4	7.62
Proulx, Spar 13	0	0	0	1	4	0	.200	22	25	12	12	2	7	0	1	13	1	4.91
Ray, Sumter 8	2	1	0	3	3	13	.500	83	68	41	37	4	31	1	0	77	5	4.01
Roadarmel, Gas .. 3	1	0	0	0	0	1	.000	7	9	7	7	0	6	1	0	5	1	9.00
Ruby, Sumter* ...31	5	1	0	4	5	1	.444	67	94	57	43	3	46	0	2	33	8	5.78
Sadler, Spar 13	9	4	0	4	5	0	.444	75	100	50	38	7	24	0	0	45	5	4.56
Sadowski, Gas ...17	16	2	0	4	7	0	.364	104	96	69	49	6	65	1	3	77	9	4.24
Sandate, Grnw* ...20	13	0	0	3	7	1	.300	82	88	53	38	9	32	0	1	63	7	4.17
Sandstedt, Grnv* .34	6	0	0	5	3	0	.500	80	98	50	44	8	31	1	3	49	7	4.95
Sevillano, Grnw ..22	16	2	1	8	7	0	.533	97	100	62	54	5	53	2	8	64	2	5.01
Shields, Anderson 24	11	3	0	8	5	5	.615	101	84	50	41	3	53	0	5	83	9	3.65
Skok, Greenville* .32	23	7	2	14	4	4	.778	167	138	54	47	6	43	1	2	134	4	2.53
Slagle, Gastonia ..10	4	1	1	2	1	0	.667	35	45	25	21	2	22	1	1	24	5	5.40
Southworth, And ..17	16	9	1	10	3	0	.769	124	111	51	37	5	31	0	2	115	10	2.69
Sparkman, Grnv ..40	11	4	0	16	5	9	.762	138	112	67	54	7	56	0	3	87	8	3.52
Stevens, Sumter* .. 5	1	0	0	1	0	0	1.000	10	12	6	6	1	4	0	0	6	4	5.40
Strickland, Gas* .. 1	1	0	0	1	0	0	1.000	7	5	1	1	0	3	0	0	4	0	1.29
Suarez, Sumter* .. 5	3	0	0	0	2	1	.000	12	18	16	14	1	17	0	0	4	3	10.50
Taylor, Anderson ..2	0	0	0	0	0	0	.000	3	4	4	1	0	1	0	0	1	0	3.00
Terral, Spar 6	0	0	0	0	2	0	.000	8	7	9	6	0	6	0	0	6	0	6.75
Terry, Greenville .34	17	4	1	11	8	5	.579	127	129	78	63	7	61	2	13	107	17	4.46
Torrealba, Grnw* .40	0	0	0	7	3	11	.700	76	65	41	33	6	22	2	6	78	4	3.91
Vingle, Gastonia ..12	9	1	0	3	5	0	.375	53	61	41	34	5	33	0	2	43	6	5.77
Waits, Anderson* .. 9	8	1	0	2	3	0	.400	42	27	25	22	2	33	0	2	37	3	4.71
D. Wallace, Spar ..24	24	7	0	8	8	0	.500	150	154	101	86	10	89	6	5	104	12	5.16
M. Wallace, Spar* .25	25	10	2	8	8	0	.500	167	150	95	68	10	72	3	0	157	2	3.66
Walsh, Greenville .33	18	0	0	2	8	2	.200	118	108	63	50	3	80	2	2	96	8	3.81
Walters, Grnw ... 6	4	0	0	0	1	0	.000	21	26	17	16	2	12	1	0	13	1	6.86
Vanless, Gastonia .. 6	2	0	0	0	2	0	.000	12	19	17	11	1	10	0	4	5	3	8.25
Warmbrod, Gas ...29	8	2	1	3	7	4	.500	82	75	36	26	2	40	2	2	42	4	2.85
Watkins, Grnv 15	8	1	1	4	2	0	.667	59	60	29	27	5	26	0	2	46	2	4.12
Westerhouse, Grnw 4	0	0	0	0	1	0	1.000	7	9	4	3	0	2	1	0	6	0	3.86
Whalin, Spar* 1	0	0	0	0	0	0	.000	0	1	2	2	1	2	0	0	0	0	...
Wiley, Anderson .15	11	0	0	3	4	0	.429	54	66	43	33	6	36	0	1	39	3	5.50
F. Williams, And ..33	2	0	0	5	2	4	.714	75	63	41	26	3	39	2	6	49	11	3.12
Young, Sumter ...38	1	0	0	1	3	7	.250	65	69	42	34	6	26	0	2	36	5	4.71

BALKS—Lyman, 6; F. Williams, 3; Barry, Ruby, 2 each; Barr, Beard, Detter, Eldridge, Gratz, Hill, Hockett, Jimenez, Kern, Landis, Law, Magness, Sevillano, Shields, Sparkman, D. Wallace, M. Wallace, Wiley, Young, 1 each.

COMBINATION SHUTOUTS—Marine-Machado, Vingle-Gorski-Warmbrod, Gastonia; Skok-Sparkman (3), Greenville; Freeman-King, Greenwood; Hatchell-Ray, Sumter.

NO-HIT GAME—Gorski, Gastonia, defeated Greenwood, 4-0, August 5 (seven innings).

ALONG THE MINOR LEAGUE TRAIL . . . .

(Continued from page 541)

forced the plane to land in Columbus, O., and no other planes were available to fly them on. But Rochester couldn't pick up a forfeit because it rained there later in the day and no game could have been played. . . . The first week of June was a sad one for the minor leagues. Buffalo, a member of Organized Baseball for 93 years, was forced to give up its franchise, which was moved to Winnipeg by the Montreal Expos, who took over the expense of the shift. . . . When you nail down a championship, you should nail it down good, like Leonardo Martinez Ferguson of Campeche (Mexican Southeast). A victory would assure the Pirates of the second-half championship, so Fergie proceeds to wrap up the title with a perfect game over first-half champ Puerto Mexico June 11. . . . John Glass, who was 0-4 be-

(Continued on page 583)

Appalachian League

ROOKIE CLASSIFICATION

CHAMPIONSHIP WINNERS IN PREVIOUS YEARS

1921—Greenville .... .608	1942—Bristol .... .667	1954—Bluefield‡ .... .619
Johnson City* ..... .627	Bristol x .... .660	1955—Salem** .... .689
1922—Bristol .... .557	1943—Bristol .... .755	1956—Did not operate.
1923—Knoxville .... .635	Bristol y .... .617	1957—Bluefield .... .701
1924—Knoxville* .... .642	1944—Kingsport‡ .... .575	1958—Johnson City ...... .662
Bristol .... .607	1945—Kingsport‡ .... .670	1959—Morristown .... .603
1925—Greenville .... .667	1946—New River‡ .... .675	1960—Wytheville .... .614
1926-36—Did not operate.	1947—Pulaski .... .648	1961—Middlesboro .... .591
1937—Elizabethton ...... .559	New River (3rd)† ... .516	1962—Bluefield .... .671
Pennington Gap* .... .580	1948—Pulaski‡ .... .680	1963—Bluefield .... .652
1938—Elizabethton ...... .664	1949—Bluefield‡ .... .721	1964—Johnson City ...... .662
Greenville (3rd)† .. .571	1950—Bluefield .... .600	1965—Salem .... .614
1939—Elizabethton‡ ..... .597	Bluefield z .... .745	1966—Marion .... .623
1940—Johnson City§ ..... .726	1951—Kingsport‡ .... .659	1967—Bluefield .... .627
Elizabethton .... .750	1952—Johnson City ...... .595	1968—Marion .... .583
1941—Johnson City ...... .614	Welch (3rd)† .... .509	1969—Pulaski a .... .576
Elizabethton* ...... .661	1953—Welch‡ .... .705	Johnson City ...... .544
	Johnson City ...... .672	

*Won split-season playoff. †Won four-team playoff. ‡Won championship and four-team playoff.
§Johnson City, first-half winner, won playoff involving six clubs. xWon both halves and defeated
second-place Elizabethton in playoff. yWon both halves, but Erwin won four-team playoff. zWon
both halves, but Bristol won two-club playoff. **Salem and Johnson City declared playoff co-champions
when weather forced cancellation of final series. aNorthern Division Pulaski declared pennant winner,
based on highest won-lost percentage.

STANDING OF CLUBS AT CLOSE OF SEASON, AUGUST 27

Club	Blu.	Cov.	J.C.	Pul.	Bris.	Kgpt.	Mar.	W.	L.	T.	Pct.	G.B.
Bluefield (1)	..	3	6	5	8	8	7	37	21	0	.638	....
Covington (16*)	5	..	4	6	5	5	7	32	24	0	.571	4
Johnson City (10)	4	6	..	2	4	5	7	28	27	0	.509	7½
Pulaski (20*)	5	2	6	..	5	6	3	27	28	1	.491	8½
Bristol (6)	2	5	3	5	..	5	6	26	30	0	.464	10
Kingsport (7)	2	5	5	3	5	..	7	27	32	1	.458	10½
Marion (19)	3	3	3	7	3	3	..	22	37	0	.373	15½

Key to major league farm teams (indicated by numbers after clubs in standing) shown on Page 384.

Playoff—None.

Regular-Season Attendance—Kingsport, 22,572; Covington, 20,870; Bluefield, 19,306; Pulaski,
16,699; Bristol, 15,520; Johnson City, 14,199; Marion, 10,786. Total, 119,952. No playoff. No all-
star game.

Managers: Bluefield—Ray Malgradi; Bristol—Al Lakeman; Covington—Dick Smith; Johnson City—
Jerry Walker; Kingsport—Owen Friend; Marion—Terry Christman; Pulaski—Brandy Davis.

All-Star Team: 1B—Jackson, Kingsport; 2B—Serna, Covington; 3B—Velez, Johnson City; SS—
DeCinces, Bluefield; OF—Gross, Covington; Jones, Bluefield; Bennett, Johnson City; C—Essian,
Pulaski; P—Holdsworth, Bristol; Cheadle, Johnson City; Manager—Malgradi, Bluefield.

(Compiled by Howe News Bureau, Chicago, Ill.)

CLUB BATTING

Club	G.	AB.	R.	OR.	H.	TB.	2B.	3B.	HR.	RBI.	SH.	SF.	BB.	Int. BB.	HP.	SO.	SB.	CS.	LOB.	Pct.
Covington ...	56	1829	286	263	484	689	64	12	39	233	16	17	202	5	21	404	45	21	424	.265
Bluefield ...	58	1846	270	226	470	653	72	9	31	218	22	23	171	6	11	418	93	16	388	.255
Johnson City ..	55	1790	290	284	453	677	61	14	45	238	13	10	250	5	26	394	35	10	428	.253
Pulaski	56	1818	278	243	447	644	82	14	29	237	18	15	202	6	13	428	49	12	367	.246
Marion	59	1898	278	329	433	667	73	22	39	229	21	13	222	3	18	538	48	19	413	.228
Kingsport ...	60	1907	264	259	432	602	64	8	30	213	16	15	238	8	33	479	49	20	429	.227
Bristol	56	1751	208	270	393	494	43	11	12	157	25	11	222	6	24	407	63	11	415	.224

INDIVIDUAL BATTING

(Leading Qualifiers for Batting Championship—186 or More Plate Appearances)

*Bats lefthanded.   †Switch-hitter.

Player and Club	G.	AB.	R.	H.	TB.	2B.	3B.	HR.	RBI.	SH.	SF.	BB.	HP.	SO.	SB.	CS.	Pct.
Velez, Otoniel, Johnson City	53	176	49	65	104	10	4	7	44	1	1	33	2	36	8	1	.369
Gross, Gregory, Covington*	54	211	40	74	94	8	3	2	27	4	1	17	0	27	12	4	.351
Jackson, Stanley, Kingsport	57	192	38	65	107	7	4	9	37	1	2	39	7	49	8	3	.339
Hallums, Thomas, Marion	54	195	38	61	113	6	2	14	44	0	1	18	2	53	0	0	.313
Andrews, Freddie, Pulaski	53	194	36	60	75	10	1	1	24	6	2	11	0	29	6	4	.309
Sanderlin, Richard, Cov	47	177	32	54	82	8	1	6	28	0	1	24	2	39	12	1	.305
DeCinces, Douglas, Bluefield	54	164	28	48	70	10	0	4	27	2	2	21	0	38	8	1	.293
Jones, Terry, Bluefield	54	179	33	51	88	7	3	8	32	0	7	18	1	25	11	1	.285
Pavic, Donald, Bristol	50	180	26	51	60	5	2	0	17	6	1	14	1	16	14	2	.283
Quinones, Carlos, Bristol	50	171	21	48	58	1	3	1	11	1	1	14	1	24	11	2	.281

Departmental Leaders: G—Johnson, 60; AB—Johnson, 218; R—Velez, 49; H—Gross, 74; TB—Hallums, 113; 2B—De La Rosa, 12; 3B—Bennett, 6; HR—Hallums, 14; RBI—Hallums, Velez, 44; SH—Andrews, Pavic, 6; SF—Jones, 7; BB—Jackson, Van Denburg, 39; HP—Jackson, Ostrosser, J. Salas, 7; SO—Goodson, 69; SB—Newhook, 210; CS—Harts, J. Williams, 6.

(All Players—Listed Alphabetically)

Player and Club	G.	AB.	R.	H.	TB.	2B.	3B.	HR.	RBI.	SH.	SF.	BB.	HP.	SO.	SB.	CS.	Pct.
Agosto, Victor, Bluefield	14	20	1	0	0	0	0	0	0	0	0	2	0	6	1	0	.000
Allen, David, Kingsport*	8	15	3	1	1	0	0	0	0	0	0	5	0	9	0	0	.067
Andrews, Freddie, Pulaski	53	194	36	60	75	10	1	1	24	6	2	11	0	29	6	4	.309
Armstrong, Clyde, Johnson C*	11	1	0	1	1	0	0	0	0	0	0	1	0	0	0	0	1.000
Arroyo, Fred, Bristol	11	28	1	5	6	1	0	0	4	0	0	0	0	6	0	0	.179
Bailor, Robert, Bluefield†	46	121	18	33	36	3	0	0	8	1	1	6	0	14	11	1	.273
Barb, David, Marion	12	19	1	2	2	0	0	0	1	1	0	0	0	8	0	0	.105
Bartlett, Robert, Marion*	3	5	0	0	0	0	0	0	0	0	0	0	0	1	0	0	.000
Barton, Keith, Marion*	12	5	1	2	4	0	1	0	0	0	0	1	0	0	0	0	.400
Baxley, Lenny, Bristol*	36	114	13	22	37	2	0	3	17	2	0	11	3	28	0	1	.193
Bebout, James, Bristol	40	105	10	19	27	2	0	2	7	1	0	12	1	38	2	1	.181
Behar, Robert, Johnson City	12	3	0	0	0	0	0	0	0	0	0	1	0	2	0	0	.000
Beitey, Michael, Bluefield†	13	21	1	4	5	1	0	0	3	0	0	1	0	8	1	0	.190
Bennett, Kenneth, J C*	45	171	36	46	86	10	6	6	25	0	2	16	2	27	6	2	.269
Bianchi, Richard, J C†	16	43	7	13	17	4	0	0	10	0	0	10	1	11	0	0	.302
Bingham, Wayman, Bluefield	23	44	5	9	9	0	0	0	4	0	0	5	0	22	1	0	.205
Blackwood, James, Blu*	47	131	25	35	45	8	1	0	13	1	1	7	0	14	9	2	.267
Boisclair, Bruce, Marion	40	117	15	33	42	5	2	0	10	2	1	10	0	33	6	1	.282
Bonardel, Jeffrey, Bluefield	8	1	0	0	0	0	0	0	0	0	0	0	0	0	0	0	.000
Brady, Morgan, Marion	1	1	0	0	0	0	0	0	0	0	0	0	0	1	0	0	.000
Brazell, Ted, Bristol	45	157	17	42	50	5	0	1	20	0	1	16	4	24	6	0	.268
Briddell, Donald, Bluefield†	3	3	0	0	0	0	0	0	0	0	0	0	0	2	0	0	.000
Brown, Bruce, Marion*	6	16	1	5	7	2	0	0	3	0	0	4	0	2	1	0	.313
Brown, Mark, Pulaski	10	8	0	2	2	0	0	0	1	2	0	0	0	0	0	0	.250
Brown, Steven, Kingsport	11	16	2	2	4	0	1	0	1	0	0	7	0	5	0	0	.125
Bruntrager, Frederick, Bris*	6	4	0	0	0	0	0	0	0	0	0	0	0	4	0	0	.000
Bucciarelli, Giovanni, Blu	2	2	0	0	0	0	0	0	0	0	0	0	0	0	0	0	.000
Buist, Lawrence, Bristol	7	3	0	0	0	0	0	0	0	0	0	0	0	3	0	0	.000
Busby, Richard, Covington	47	151	28	45	68	5	3	4	18	1	3	21	0	32	5	2	.298
Buys, Gregory, Johnson City	8	17	0	6	7	1	0	0	0	0	0	3	0	2	0	0	.353
Buzzard, James, Kingsport	11	31	3	4	4	0	0	0	5	0	0	6	0	7	1	1	.129
Cheadle, David, Johnson C*	9	20	4	6	10	1	0	1	1	0	0	3	0	6	0	0	.300
Chew, David, Marion	8	19	6	8	13	0	1	1	2	0	0	2	0	2	1	0	.421
Cichon, E. Scott, Marion*	13	15	3	5	5	1	0	0	5	1	0	1	0	5	1	0	.333
Clark, Dickie, Johnson City*	20	59	2	7	9	2	0	0	2	0	0	6	2	32	0	0	.119
Clark, Gerald, Kingsport	5	4	0	1	2	1	0	0	2	0	0	1	0	2	0	0	.250
Cooper, Michael, Marion*	9	3	1	0	0	0	0	0	0	0	0	1	0	2	0	0	.000
Crews, Christopher, Kgpt	46	154	14	34	41	5	1	0	17	2	3	9	0	29	0	0	.221
Cruet, Arnold, Kingsport†	32	106	12	27	32	5	0	0	11	0	0	4	1	15	1	3	.255
Davis, Leonnard, Covington	20	47	7	9	22	2	1	3	10	0	0	13	0	23	0	1	.191
DeCaminada, Timothy, Mar*	23	76	16	27	44	6	4	1	11	0	1	17	1	11	1	0	.355
DeCinces, Douglas, Bluefield	54	164	28	48	70	10	0	4	27	2	2	21	0	38	8	1	.293
DeJean, Ronald, Covington	11	25	5	7	7	0	0	0	4	0	2	5	0	8	0	0	.280
De La Rosa, Jesus, Cov	54	209	32	55	85	12	0	6	28	0	1	9	3	41	4	0	.263
DeMola, Donald, Johnson C	10	22	1	1	1	0	0	0	0	1	0	0	0	14	0	1	.045
Denison, Stephen, Kingsport	18	14	1	4	4	0	0	0	0	1	0	2	0	4	0	0	.286
DeTray, Joel, Johnson City	13	2	0	0	0	0	0	0	0	0	0	0	0	0	0	0	.000
Diaz, Juan, Covington	2	1	0	0	0	0	0	0	0	0	0	0	0	1	0	0	.000
Donaire, William, Pulaski*	28	73	9	12	18	1	1	1	7	0	2	5	3	30	3	0	.164
DuBois, David, Bristol†	7	4	0	1	1	0	0	0	1	0	0	0	0	1	0	0	.250
Dunn, Emory, Kingsport	36	109	14	22	37	3	0	4	13	0	2	24	0	28	1	0	.202
Dusenbury, John, Pulaski	31	72	6	14	19	3	1	0	8	0	2	12	0	17	1	0	.194
Earle, Richard, Johnson City	9	29	5	5	11	0	0	2	4	1	0	4	0	4	0	0	.172
Eldridge, Larry, Covington	4	1	0	0	0	0	0	0	0	0	0	0	0	0	0	0	.000
Escoe, Orlando, Marion	39	121	24	28	40	2	2	2	14	1	1	11	2	28	5	2	.231
Essian, James, Pulaski	36	119	17	36	69	9	0	5	30	0	0	11	2	18	0	1	.303
Feiler, James, Kingsport	13	6	1	1	2	1	0	0	0	0	0	1	0	1	0	0	.167
Fields, James, Bluefield*	45	127	19	33	46	3	2	2	12	1	1	10	1	15	7	2	.260
Fields, Robert, Bluefield	13	7	1	1	1	0	0	0	1	0	0	3	0	3	0	1	.143
Finch, Donald, Bluefield*	11	22	4	1	3	0	1	0	0	0	0	1	0	9	0	0	.045
Forfar, Kenneth, Bristol	7	9	0	0	0	0	0	0	0	0	0	0	0	6	0	0	.000
Fowler, Kenneth, Pulaski	12	3	1	1	1	0	0	0	0	0	0	1	0	0	0	0	.333

Player and Club	G.	AB.	R.	H.	TB.	2B.	3B.	HR.	RBI.	SH.	SF.	BB.	HP.	SO.	SB.	CS.	Pct.
Freeman, Mario, Covington ..	16	35	4	9	9	0	0	0	0	0	0	2	0	7	1	0	.257
Fusari, Richard, Pulaski	18	33	6	9	10	1	0	0	3	0	0	2	0	8	0	0	.273
Gaffey, Gregory, Johnson C .	36	93	7	17	29	3	0	3	12	0	0	8	0	20	0	0	.183
Galasso, Robert, Bluefield*	24	31	5	7	12	2	0	1	6	0	1	3	0	11	0	0	.226
Gardner, William, Covington	8	11	4	2	2	0	0	0	1	1	0	0	0	2	0	0	.182
Gearhart, Steven, Marion ...	4	8	3	2	4	2	0	0	2	0	0	0	0	2	0	0	.250
Gillies, Clark, Covington * ..	5	13	0	1	1	0	0	0	0	0	0	0	0	10	0	0	.077
Globokar, Richard, Marion* .	11	35	4	6	7	1	0	0	1	0	0	5	0	9	0	0	.171
Goodson, Rex, Kingsport ...	55	210	31	53	86	9	0	8	31	2	1	24	4	69	7	1	.252
Grady, C. Edward, Marion* ...	16	28	1	4	6	2	0	0	1	0	0	1	0	12	0	0	.143
Greenwood, Allen, Pulaski ..	4	2	0	1	1	0	0	0	0	0	0	1	0	0	0	0	.500
Griggs, Bruce, Kingsport ...	12	28	1	4	5	1	0	0	2	0	0	4	0	15	0	0	.143
Gross, Gregory, Covington* ..	54	211	40	74	94	8	3	2	27	0	1	17	0	27	12	4	.351
Grout, Stanley, Kingsport ..	5	10	1	2	3	1	0	0	1	0	0	1	0	4	0	0	.200
Hagen, Frank, Pulaski	21	60	7	14	21	4	0	1	7	0	0	11	0	21	0	0	.233
Hallums, Thomas, Marion ..	54	195	38	61	113	6	2	14	44	0	1	18	2	53	0	0	.313
Hammon, Randal, Kingsport	6	12	0	2	2	0	0	0	1	0	0	1	0	4	0	0	.167
Hammond, David, Bristol* ...	12	8	1	1	1	0	0	0	0	0	0	1	0	3	1	0	.125
Harris, James C., Bristol ..	30	97	16	25	29	1	0	1	13	1	1	19	4	24	2	0	.258
Harris, James F., Bristol ..	16	9	0	0	0	0	0	0	1	3	0	2	0	3	0	0	.000
Hartman, Bryan, Marion	12	23	3	6	8	2	0	0	3	1	0	2	0	8	0	0	.261
Harts, Gregory, Marion*	54	189	21	45	63	6	3	2	20	1	0	17	1	43	7	6	.238
Hickey, Donald, Bluefield ..	53	164	21	43	59	4	0	4	23	1	2	7	1	25	10	1	.262
Hinckley, Ronald, Johnson C	8	4	1	1	1	0	0	0	0	0	0	2	0	2	0	0	.250
Holdsworth, Frederick, Bris	8	23	3	5	5	0	0	0	2	0	2	0	0	6	0	0	.217
Horn, Spencer, Bristol	33	80	13	13	14	1	0	0	5	2	1	13	2	22	0	1	.163
Horton, David, Bristol	7	4	0	1	1	0	0	0	0	0	0	0	0	0	0	0	.250
House, Edward, Bluefield† ..	15	19	1	6	6	0	0	0	1	1	0	0	0	4	1	0	.316
Hurst, John, Kingsport	38	120	6	13	15	2	0	0	9	5	2	8	1	41	3	0	.108
Hutson, G. Herbert, Blu	24	27	4	8	11	3	0	0	2	4	0	2	0	6	0	0	.296
Iskierka, Dennis, Marion ...	16	41	4	8	12	2	1	0	7	0	2	8	0	17	0	0	.195
Isom, Curtis, Kingsport* ...	7	10	2	2	2	0	0	0	1	0	0	4	0	8	0	0	.200
Ivancin, Michael, Bluefield*	12	8	1	0	0	0	0	0	0	1	0	0	0	7	0	0	.000
Jackson, Stanley, Kingsport	57	192	38	65	107	7	4	9	37	1	2	39	7	49	8	3	.339
Johnson, John C., Kingsport	60	218	29	45	54	9	0	0	22	1	1	19	0	39	4	4	.206
Johnston, Gordon, Bluefield	11	8	1	1	2	1	0	0	0	0	0	1	0	6	0	0	.125
Jones, Terry, Bluefield	54	179	33	51	88	7	3	8	32	0	7	18	1	25	11	1	.285
Joyce, Allen, Pulaski	24	68	6	13	17	2	1	0	3	0	0	6	0	22	1	0	.191
Keener, Larry, Pulaski†	27	81	11	20	35	3	0	4	19	0	1	6	1	38	2	0	.247
Keister, Robert, Pulaski	19	7	1	0	0	0	0	0	0	0	0	1	0	5	0	0	.000
Knowlton, Steven, Bristol* ..	6	5	1	1	1	0	0	0	0	0	0	1	0	0	0	0	.107
Kostrba, William, Johnson C*	9	7	1	3	3	0	0	0	0	0	0	0	0	3	0	0	.429
Kowalski, Michael, Marion ..	15	3	1	2	3	1	0	0	4	0	0	1	0	1	0	0	.667
Lang, Anthony, Covington* ..	7	7	0	1	1	0	0	0	0	0	0	1	0	4	0	0	.143
Lang, Richard, Pulaski*	37	129	35	43	57	4	2	2	9	1	0	18	1	11	13	3	.333
Lantz, Thomas, Bristol*	7	13	2	2	2	0	0	0	2	0	2	0	0	6	0	0	.154
Lawson, David, Johnson City	7	12	0	2	2	0	0	0	0	1	0	0	0	6	0	0	.167
Leckrone, George, Marion* ..	4	8	0	1	1	0	0	0	1	0	0	0	0	5	0	0	.125
Lee, R. William, Bluefield† ..	11	4	0	0	0	0	0	0	0	0	0	0	0	0	0	0	.000
Leopaldi, Anthony, Bluefield	19	45	6	12	14	0	1	0	4	0	0	6	1	11	1	0	.267
Lincon, George, Bluefield ...	1	1	0	0	0	0	0	0	0	0	0	0	0	1	0	0	.000
Llenas, Gustavo, Pulaski ...	48	149	16	29	32	3	0	0	8	1	0	8	0	22	2	0	.195
Logan, Sterling, Marion* ...	23	55	9	11	21	5	1	1	4	0	0	3	0	21	1	2	.200
Lopez, Edgar, Pulaski	5	13	1	1	1	0	0	0	1	0	1	5	0	8	0	0	.077
Lopez, Francisco, Cov	10	29	4	9	10	1	0	0	4	0	0	1	0	4	0	0	.310
Maine, J. Kevin, Marion ...	12	5	1	0	0	0	0	0	0	0	0	0	0	2	0	0	.000
Mair, Randall, Bristol*	8	4	1	1	2	1	0	0	0	0	0	0	0	2	0	0	.250
Mappin, Terry, Bristol*	43	132	19	33	52	5	1	4	18	0	3	31	1	39	1	0	.250
Martin, J. Michael, Pulaski*	12	24	3	3	3	0	0	0	1	0	0	3	0	12	1	0	.125
Masteller, Robert, Pulaski* .	17	8	0	1	1	0	0	0	0	0	0	1	0	4	1	0	.125
McDonald, R. Gary, Blu* ...	37	96	14	29	33	2	1	0	6	0	1	7	1	6	8	2	.302
McDonald, Robert, Kingsport	12	19	1	1	1	0	0	0	2	0	0	4	0	8	0	0	.053
McGuire, James, Pulaski* ...	4	5	1	0	0	0	0	0	0	0	0	0	0	2	0	0	.000
McLaren, John, Covington ...	40	121	22	29	40	2	0	3	11	2	1	20	2	22	0	1	.240
McRobie, W. Brian, Pulaski	10	21	0	3	4	1	0	0	2	0	0	2	0	5	0	0	.143
Melendez, William, Covington	17	57	7	8	10	0	1	0	3	0	0	9	1	17	0	0	.140
Mercado, John, Johnson City†	48	127	22	32	53	1	1	6	23	0	2	28	3	25	0	0	.252
Midura, John, Covington ...	8	11	2	3	4	1	0	0	0	0	0	4	0	3	0	0	.273
Montalvo, Nestor, Bristol ...	22	75	8	23	27	4	0	0	6	0	0	4	0	10	1	0	.307
Mooney, John, Pulaski	39	126	18	31	40	4	1	1	11	0	1	19	1	33	5	3	.246
Moore, Henry, Covington* ...	10	24	1	4	5	1	0	0	2	1	0	0	0	8	1	1	.167
Moser, Eugene, Johnson City	34	112	12	28	33	2	0	1	14	0	1	11	2	12	1	1	.250
Murphy, Daniel, Marion ...	6	6	0	0	0	0	0	0	0	0	0	2	0	1	4	0	.000
Newhook, James, Bristol ...	53	177	28	40	47	5	1	0	8	0	0	24	0	40	20	2	.226
Ostrosser, Brian, Marion* ...	57	183	30	41	63	7	0	5	23	1	0	36	7	33	3	4	.224
Pagan, David, Johnson C ..	4	10	0	0	0	0	0	0	0	0	0	0	0	2	0	0	.000
Paglierani, Charles, Pul* ..	39	92	27	27	53	6	1	6	27	0	2	20	0	20	2	0	.293
Pappas, James, Kingsport ...	1	1	0	0	0	0	0	0	0	0	0	0	0	1	0	0	.000
Pavic, Donald, Bristol	50	180	26	51	60	5	2	0	17	6	1	14	1	16	14	2	.283
Peck, Jeffrey, Pulaski*	1	4	1	2	2	0	0	0	0	0	0	0	0	1	0	0	.500
Pfenninger, Martin, Blu* ...	46	111	17	22	27	5	0	0	10	1	3	12	1	21	6	0	.198
Phelps, Rex, Marion	9	7	0	0	0	0	0	0	1	0	1	0	0	6	0	0	.000
Pieve, Carlos, Johnson City .	34	114	12	27	29	2	0	0	4	3	0	11	2	12	2	1	.237

Player and Club	G.	AB.	R.	H.	TB.	2B.	3B.	HR.	RBI.	SH.	SF.	BB.	HP.	SO.	SB.	CS.	Pct.
Pivec, Michael, Bristol	31	77	10	15	20	3	1	0	6	0		13	1	24	0		.195
Pizarro, Jose, Marion*	29	90	14	25	30	3	1	0	9	0		10	2	22	3	1	.278
Poquette, Thomas, Kgpt* ...	56	209	41	57	90	7	1	8	18	1	1	24	5	27	2	2	.273
Potash, Lawrence, Marion* ..	2	2	0	1	1	0	0	0	0	0		0	0	0	0		.500
Price, Victor, Kingsport	26	77	13	15	23	5	0	1	4	0		7	2	29	5	1	.195
Pugh, Randolph, Marion ..	12	13	0	0	0	0	0	0	0	3		0	0	4	0		.000
Quinones, Carlos, Bristol ..	50	171	21	48	58	1	3	1	11	1		14	1	24	11	2	.281
Rafferty, Alan, Pulaski	31	62	16	15	23	4	2	0	5	1	0	11	1	14	1	0	.242
Reid, James, Kingsport ...	12	32	2	9	11	2	0	0	4	1		3	1	11	0	1	.281
Renfro, Claude, Bluefield ..	46	133	18	28	58	5	0	5	20	0	0	21	0	42	7	2	.286
Reynolds, Cecil, Marion ...	12	27	3	1	1	0	0	0	0	3		0	1	11	0	0	.037
Rivas, Bernardino, Marion .	11	24	4	6	7	1	0	0	2	0	0	4	0	8	2	0	.250
Rizzardi, Joseph, Bristol* ..	12	7	0	1	1	0	0	0	0	0	2	0	1	0	5	0	.143
Robbins, T. Randolph, J C*.	33	113	29	38	58	4	2	4	10	0	0	9	3	15	6	0	.336
Robins, Douglas, Johnson C.	30	89	5	18	26	5	0	1	9	1	0	13	3	15	0	0	.202
Rodrigues, James, Bristol ..	37	121	8	21	24	3	0	0	11	0	2	13	2	25	2	1	.174
Rodriguez, Carlos, Jchnson C	32	116	24	32	48	5	1	3	13	1	1	7	2	28	0	1	.276
Rodriguez, Luis, Covington ..	41	138	22	36	53	5	0	4	23	1	1	7	5	24	1	0	.261
Rooker, Bradley, Kingsport .	10	14	0	2	2	0	0	0	2	0	0	1	0	6	0	0	.143
Rusnak, Kevin, Pulaski ...	28	92	8	18	24	6	0	0	9	1	0	7	1	20	3	0	.196
Russell, Donald, Covington ..	12	36	8	13	20	4	0	1	11	0	2	11	0	3	1	1	.361
Salas, Jose, Kingsport*	32	94	19	24	29	4	0	0	15	0	0	16	7	20	9	0	.255
Salas, Robert, Kingsport* ..	10	5	0	0	0	0	0	0	0	0	0	1	0	1	0	0	.000
Salmon, Gene, Bluefield* ...	6	15	1	3	5	2	0	0	2	0	0	2	0	6	0	0	.200
Sanderlin, Richard, Cov	49	177	32	54	82	8	1	6	28	0	1	24	2	39	12	1	.305
Schlesiger, John, Johnson C.	47	157	18	34	38	4	0	0	16	1	1	24	2	38	2	0	.217
Schmitt, Roman, Marion ...	37	112	12	15	21	3	0	1	7	1	2	4	0	38	0	1	.134
Schroerlucke, Richard, Bris .	2	7	0	1	1	0	0	0	0	0		0	0	2	0		.143
Seltzer, William, Bluefield .	26	59	6	11	13	2	0	0	2	0	0	4	0	11	1	0	.186
Serna, Joel, Covington	46	170	24	47	57	3	2	1	21	3	2	16	2	18	6	2	.276
Seroka, Andrew, Bristol	27	57	4	8	10	2	0	0	8	0	1	12	1	13	3	0	.140
Shaw, Richard, Johnson City*	6	1	0	0	0	0	0	0	0	0		0	0	1	0		.000
Sheets, William, Johnson C*.	8	9	0	2	2	0	0	0	0	0		0	0	2	0		.222
Shook, Kyle, Covington	8	16	5	6	10	1	0	1	2	0	0	0	0	4	0		.375
Simendinger, Gregory, Blu ..	8	12	2	3	3	0	0	0	0	0	3	0	4	0	5	0	.250
Simon, Arthur, Bluefield ...	2	5	1	1	1	0	0	0	0	0		0	1	0	0		.200
Simpson, Richard, Kingsport	32	104	16	20	24	2	1	0	9	1	2	12	3	17	2	0	.192
Sosa, Jose, Covington	10	21	2	6	6	0	0	0	0	0	0	0	0	6	1		.286
Sosa, Miguel, Kingsport	6	2	0	0	0	0	0	0	0	0		0	0	0	0		.000
Stefany, Hector, Covington ..	8	15	0	2	2	0	0	0	1	0	0	1	0	8	0	0	.133
Stenglein, J. Greg, Blu	39	81	11	22	32	4	0	2	17	1	0	15	1	23	4	0	.272
Stratton, R. Donald, Cov ...	12	35	3	6	8	2	0	0	3	1	1	2	0	9	0	0	.171
Streleski, James, Covington* .	5	5	1	1	2	1	0	0	0	0		0	0	4	0		.200
Talbert, Carroll, Marion ...	41	124	17	25	46	4	1	5	20	0	2	10	1	46	3	1	.202
Thomason, Fred, Pulaski* ...	12	23	4	6	9	0	0	1	1	2	0	1	0	9	0		.261
Thomason, M Erskine, Pul ..	17	35	5	5	5	0	0	0	1	4	2	0	1	0	9	0	.143
Tregilgus, John, Marion ...	6	11	2	0	0	0	0	0	1	0	1	2	0	5	1	0	.000
Underwood, George, Blu	17	15	1	3	3	0	0	0	2	3	0	1	0	10	0		.200
Urquiola, Efrain, Covington .	11	5	0	0	0	0	0	0	0	1	0	1	0	4	0	0	.000
Van Denburg, Wesley, J C .	46	129	30	28	43	3	0	4	20	1	1	39	0	47	7	1	.217
Vargason, Terry, Johnson C* .	5	0	0	0	0	0	0	0	0	0		2	0	0	0		.000
Velez, Otoniel, Johnson City	53	176	49	65	104	10	4	7	44	1	1	33	2	36	8	1	.369
Villalobos, Elvin, Covington .	7	6	1	1	1	0	0	0	0	0		1	0	0	0		.167
Villalobos, Milton, Cov	19	9	1	2	2	0	0	0	0	0		3	0	0	0		.222
Walker, Dale, Marion	8	9	1	1	1	0	0	0	0	0	2	0	1	0	7	0	.111
Wahn, Hugh, Kingsport ...	17	32	5	5	5	0	0	0	0	0	0	7	1	10	5	1	.156
Wamble, Kenneth, Marion ..	46	148	18	29	57	6	2	6	19	2	0	30	0	58	7	0	.196
Ward, Michael, Kingsport ...	15	5	2	2	2	0	0	0	1	0	0	0	0	3	0		.400
Warden, Steven, Marion ...	38	109	12	20	27	2	1	1	8	0	1	18	1	25	6	0	.183
Weiner, Dennis, Pulaski* ...	41	144	21	42	71	9	1	6	40	0	3	13	0	12	2	0	.292
Welch, Gary, Marion*	14	45	11	12	16	4	0	0	5	0	1	4	1	10	0	1	.267
Wells, B. Alan, Kingsport ..	16	58	7	15	15	0	0	0	6	0	0	4	1	9	2	3	.259
West, James, Bluefield† ...	50	144	23	42	64	10	4	0	20	0	2	16	3	45	6	2	.292
Whalin, Michael, Pulaski* ..	15	10	3	3	5	0	1	0	3	1	0	2	0	2	0	0	.300
Williams, Bryan, Marion	1	1	1	1	1	0	0	0	0	0		0	0	0	0		1.000
Williams, J. Alton, Cov*	53	186	23	38	60	5	1	5	24	1	3	27	2	62	3	6	.204
Williams, Richard, Marion ..	13	9	0	1	1	0	0	0	0	0	0	1	0	2	0		.111
Wilson, Gary, Johnson City .	48	154	25	41	66	4	0	7	31	1	0	25	2	25	3	2	.266
Wilson, Robert, Pulaski	48	156	19	33	47	10	2	0	13	1	1	23	3	55	6	1	.212
Wise, Thomas, Covington ...	23	57	8	16	28	2	0	0	10	0	0	11	4	10	0	0	.281
Wisniewski, Robert, Bristol .	26	67	5	13	17	2	1	0	4	0	0	17	1	23	0	0	.194
Witkowski, Michael, Bristol	10	3	0	0	0	0	0	0	0	0		0	0	0	0		.000
Wooten, William, Bluefield*	13	20	1	4	7	0	0	1	3	0	1	2	0	4	0		.200
Zailchas, Daniel, Pulaski ...	4	6	0	3	4	1	0	0	0	0	0	1	0	1	0		.500

The following players had no plate appearances (listed alphabetically by clubs, games in parentheses):
JOHNSON CITY—Campbell, Bruce* (7); Velander, Daniel (2).
KINGSPORT—Chandler, Andrew (1); Hausaman, David (1).
MARION—Betts, Gary (2).
PULASKI—Barrios, Andres* (3); Utz, Lawrence (1).
GRAND-SLAM HOME RUNS—Jackson, Stenglein, 1 each.
AWARDED FIRST BASE ON INTERFERENCE—None.

CLUB FIELDING

Club	G.	PO.	A.	E.	DP.	PB.	Pct.	Club	G.	PO.	A.	E.	DP.	PB.	Pct.
Bluefield	58	1441	489	100	37	19	.951	Marion	59	1457	566	129	35	24	.940
Johnson City	55	1371	544	104	39	38	.948	Kingsport	60	1517	555	143	43	26	.935
Pulaski	56	1411	499	107	43	23	.947	Covington	56	1394	511	138	28	28	.932
Bristol	56	1398	487	112	40	20	.944								

Triple Play—Bluefield.

INDIVIDUAL FIELDING
(Ten or More Games)

*Throws lefthanded.

FIRST BASEMEN

Player and Club	G.	PO.	A.	E.	DP.	Pct.	Player and Club	G.	PO.	A.	E.	DP.	Pct.
Montalvo, Bristol	13	86	5	1	5	.989	Keener, Pulaski	18	117	9	4	16	.969
Gaffey, Johnson C*	22	167	6	2	11	.989	Mercado, Johnson C.	36	293	12	10	18	.968
Baxley, Bristol*	34	264	22	4	20	.986	De La Rosa, Cov	54	356	38	19	19	.954
JACKSON, Kgpt*	57	456	27	8	35	.984	Renfro, Bluefield	39	248	8	13	15	.952
Weiner, Pulaski*	39	282	9	5	25	.983	West, Bluefield	13	89	5	7	6	.931
Hallums, Marion	51	428	24	14	27	.970							

Triple Play—Renfro.

(Fewer Than Ten Games)

Player and Club	G.	PO.	A.	E.	DP.	Pct.	Player and Club	G.	PO.	A.	E.	DP.	Pct.
DeCaminada, Marion*	9	68	3	0	5	1.000	DeCinces, Bluefield	7	22	1	1	3	.958
Jones, Bluefield	3	10	2	0	1	1.000	Wisniewski, Bristol	4	40	0	2	1	.952
Cruet, Kingsport	1	5	0	0	1	1.000	Brown, Kingsport	2	17	1	1	0	.947
Russell, Covington	2	5	0	0	2	1.000	Gillies, Covington	2	8	2	1	1	.909
Lang, Covington*	1	1	0	0	1	1.000	Quinones, Bristol	2	7	3	1	1	.909
Mappin, Bristol	6	54	0	1	4	.982	Seroka, Bristol	1	7	0	2	1	.778
Salmon, Bluefield*	4	21	3	1	2	.960							

SECOND BASEMEN

Player and Club	G.	PO.	A.	E.	DP.	Pct.	Player and Club	G.	PO.	A.	E.	DP.	Pct.
Brazell, Bristol	15	24	33	2	4	.966	Wamble, Marion	34	54	75	10	19	.928
SCHLESIGER, J C	47	84	124	9	19	.959	Llenas, Pulaski	45	88	95	17	27	.915
Blackwood, Bluefield	29	51	72	6	11	.953	McDonald, Bluefield	12	13	18	3	4	.912
Joyce, Pulaski	13	24	35	3	6	.952	Hurst, Kingsport	38	78	96	17	21	.911
Bailor, Bluefield	23	27	31	4	7	.935	Velez, Johnson City	11	26	22	5	4	.906
Quinones, Bristol	12	14	27	3	2	.932	Talbert, Marion	23	36	43	9	3	.898
Serna, Covington	45	105	95	15	16	.930	Cruet, Kingsport	17	27	46	9	7	.890
Rodrigues, Bristol	31	58	71	10	14	.928							

(Fewer Than Ten Games)

Player and Club	G.	PO.	A.	E.	DP.	Pct.	Player and Club	G.	PO.	A.	E.	DP.	Pct.
Leckrone, Marion	2	3	5	0	0	1.000	Freeman, Covington	7	17	16	3	2	.917
DeCinces, Bluefield	1	2	3	0	0	1.000	Hagen, Pulaski	3	8	11	2	2	.905
Stenglein, Bluefield	1	1	0	0	0	1.000	Pavic, Bristol	5	10	9	2	5	.905
Tregilgus, Marion	1	0	1	0	0	1.000	Pfenninger, Bluefield	7	3	5	1	1	.889
Busby, Covington	5	11	13	2	3	.923	Chew, Marion	2	5	7	3	0	.800
Buzzard, Kingsport	9	15	20	3	7	.921	Hickey, Bluefield	1	2	0	2	0	.500

THIRD BASEMEN

Player and Club	G.	PO.	A.	E.	DP.	Pct.	Player and Club	G.	PO.	A.	E.	DP.	Pct.
Russell, Covington	10	18	17	1	3	.972	Moser, Johnson City	15	13	22	4	3	.897
WARDEN, Marion	33	48	62	5	9	.957	J. C. Harris, Bristol	30	26	46	10	7	.878
Hickey, Bluefield	42	25	56	4	7	.953	Brazell, Bristol	11	6	14	3	1	.870
Wilson, Pulaski	34	26	44	6	6	.921	Hagen, Pulaski	16	12	26	6	3	.864
McDonald, Bluefield	17	12	32	8	1	.921	Busby, Covington	23	21	42	10	5	.863
Williams, Covington	24	24	41	6	3	.915	Crews, Kingsport	45	36	76	20	8	.848
Globokar, Marion	10	6	14	2	2	.909	Talbert, Marion	13	12	15	5	1	.844
Velez, Johnson City	42	33	61	10	3	.904							

(Fewer Than Ten Games)

Player and Club	G.	PO.	A.	E.	DP.	Pct.	Player and Club	G.	PO.	A.	E.	DP.	Pct.
Finch, Bluefield	3	2	4	0	0	1.000	Joyce, Pulaski	4	3	6	1	2	.900
Freeman, Covington	3	1	5	0	0	1.000	J. Salas, Kingsport	9	9	11	3	0	.870
Renfro, Bluefield	2	2	2	0	0	1.000	Quinones, Bristol	3	1	5	1	1	.857
Pieve, Johnson City	3	0	4	0	0	1.000	Wamble, Marion	7	7	19	5	0	.839
Andrews, Pulaski	1	1	1	0	0	1.000	Horn, Bristol	1	1	4	1	0	.833
Brady, Marion	1	1	0	0	0	1.000	Pfenninger, Blu	3	1	3	1	1	.800
DeCinces, Bluefield	1	1	0	0	0	1.000	Peck, Pulaski	1	1	4	2	2	.714
Essian, Pulaski	2	0	1	0	0	1.000	Cruet, Kingsport	7	3	14	7	4	.708
Rodrigues, Bristol	7	6	11	1	0	.944	Chew, Marion	1	1	2	2	0	.600
Montalvo, Bristol	7	7	9	1	1	.941	Rafferty, Pulaski	4	2	2	3	1	.571
Bailor, Bluefield	7	3	7	1	2	.909							

SHORTSTOPS

Player and Club	G.	PO.	A.	E.	DP.	Pct.	Player and Club	G.	PO.	A.	E.	DP.	Pct.
OSTROSSER, Marion	57	102	171	21	20	.929	Johnson, Kingsport	60	88	158	29	20	.895
DeCinces, Bluefield	46	80	93	16	14	.915	Andrews, Pulaski	51	61	111	21	13	.891
Busby, Covington	17	25	59	6	3	.914	Pavic, Bristol	46	70	108	23	16	.886
Pieve, Johnson City	28	40	71	12	10	.902	Pfenninger, Blu	12	10	27	5	3	.881
Rodriguez, Johnson C	30	45	88	15	11	.899	Williams, Covington	29	31	48	24	3	.767

Triple Play—DeCinces.

(Fewer Than Ten Games)

Player and Club	G.	PO.	A.	E.	DP.	Pct.
Bailor, Bluefield ...	5	7	5	0	3	1.000
Horn, Bristol ...	2	4	6	0	1	1.000
Brazell, Bristol ...	2	1	4	0	1	1.000
Wilson, Pulaski ...	5	1	3	0	0	1.000
Hickey, Bluefield ...	1	1	1	0	0	1.000
Llenas, Pulaski ...	1	1	0	0	0	1.000
Joyce, Pulaski ...	6	8	12	2	2	.909
Quinones, Bristol ..	7	9	15	3	2	.889
Stefany, Covington ..	7	8	6	2	3	.875
Schroerlucke, Bris ..	2	4	3	1	1	.875
Lopez, Covington ...	9	15	19	7	2	.829
Simon, Bluefield ...	2	2	6	2	0	.800
Chew, Marion ...	1	3	1	1	0	.800
Wamble, Marion ...	3	2	4	4	0	.600

OUTFIELDERS

Player and Club	G.	PO.	A.	E.	DP.	Pct.
Boisclair, Marion* ..	33	49	1	0	0	1.000
Leopaldi, Bluefield .	17	30	0	0	0	1.000
Pfenninger, Blu ...	24	27	2	0	2	1.000
Wilson, Pulaski ...	13	26	1	0	0	1.000
Price, Kingsport ...	19	19	1	0	1	1.000
Bailor, Bluefield ...	11	16	0	0	0	1.000
Mappin, Bristol ...	11	9	1	0	0	1.000
Wain, Kingsport ...	11	8	0	0	0	1.000
NEWHOOK, Bristol .	50	97	0	1	0	.990
Jones, Bluefield ...	51	72	6	1	1	.987
Escoe, Marion ...	36	42	0	1	0	.977
Rodriguez, Covington	50	40	2	1	0	.977
Gross, Covington* ..	54	93	10	3	3	.972
Pizarro, Marion* ...	23	33	1	1	0	.971
Simpson, Kingsport .	30	32	0	1	0	.970
Lang, Pulaski* ...	36	56	5	2	1	.968
Robbins, Johnson C .	29	29	1	1	0	.968
Rusnak, Pulaski ...	27	50	4	2	2	.964
J Fields, Bluefield .	41	69	5	3	0	.961
Stenglein, Bluefield .	35	46	2	2	1	.960
Wells, Kingsport ...	16	19	2	1	1	.955
Van Denburg, J C ..	40	58	3	3	2	.953
Brazell, Bristol ...	19	32	4	2	0	.947
DeCaminada, Marion*	13	14	1	1	0	.938
Goodson, Kingsport .	54	79	6	6	0	.934
Wilson, Johnson City	47	49	7	4	3	.933
Bennett, Johnson C*.	45	63	6	5	2	.932
Poquette, Kingsport .	55	81	5	7	2	.925
Horn, Bristol ...	22	34	2	3	0	.923
Quinones, Bristol ...	23	32	1	3	0	.917
Harts, Marion* ...	51	90	3	9	1	.912
Logan, Marion* ...	14	20	0	2	0	.909
Sanderlin, Covington .	46	60	9	7	0	.908
Paglierani, Pulaski .	31	25	3	3	0	.903
Bingham, Bluefield .	22	15	0	2	0	.882
Mooney, Pulaski ...	26	42	2	6	0	.880
Bebout, Bristol ...	33	27	1	4	0	.875
Wise, Covington ...	18	18	2	3	1	.870
Donaire, Pulaski* ..	22	29	1	5	0	.857
Grady, Marion ...	11	6	0	1	0	.857
Moser, Johnson City .	17	18	5	4	0	.852
Rafferty, Pulaski ..	21	21	1	4	0	.846
Beitey, Bluefield ..	13	10	0	2	0	.833
Pivec, Bristol ...	20	19	1	5	0	.800
Davis, Covington ...	19	14	4	6	0	.750

(Fewer Than Ten Games)

Player and Club	G.	PO.	A.	E.	DP.	Pct.
Brown, Marion* ...	4	4	1	0	0	1.000
Finch, Bluefield ...	4	4	0	0	0	1.000
Seroka, Bristol ...	4	4	0	0	0	1.000
Keener, Pulaski ...	6	4	0	0	0	1.000
Velez, Johnson City .	1	2	0	0	0	1.000
Gearhart, Marion ..	2	2	0	0	0	1.000
Gillies, Covington ..	1	1	0	0	0	1.000
Warden, Marion ...	1	1	0	0	0	1.000
Zeilchas, Pulaski ...	1	1	0	0	0	1.000
Brown, Kingsport ..	2	1	0	0	0	1.000
Hickey, Bluefield ...	2	1	0	0	0	1.000
Galasso, Bluefield ..	2	0	1	0	0	1.000
Renfro, Bluefield ...	2	1	0	0	0	1.000
Rivas, Marion ...	9	10	1	1	0	.917
McDonald, Bluefield.	6	8	0	1	0	.889
Lopez, Pulaski ...	4	6	0	2	0	.750
Lang, Covington* ...	4	3	0	1	0	.750
Tregilgus, Marion ..	4	3	0	1	0	.750

CATCHERS

Player and Club	G.	PO.	A.	E.	DP.	PB.	Pct.
ESSIAN, Pulaski.	33	243	20	2	1	6	.992
Seltzer, Bluefield .	26	151	11	2	3	3	.988
Dusenbury, Pul ..	25	207	14	3	1	12	.987
McLaren, Cov ...	39	333	28	6	0	15	.984
Melendez, Cov ...	17	158	5	3	2	13	.982
J. Salas, Kgpt ...	23	197	18	4	2	3	.982
Iskierka, Marion .	16	84	4	2	0	7	.978
Robins, Johnson C	29	197	17	5	2	9	.977
Dunn, Kingsport .	35	279	15	7	1	15	.977
West, Bluefield .	33	228	20	6	3	13	.976
Clark, Johnson C .	17	138	8	4	1	19	.973
Seroka, Bristol ..	14	71	2	2	0	2	.973
Mappin, Bristol ..	25	186	6	6	3	12	.970
Wisniewski, Bris	21	158	11	6	4	5	.966
Schmitt, Marion .	36	207	9	8	1	11	.964
Welch, Marion ..	14	92	4	5	0	6	.950
Bianchi, John C.	11	67	5	4	1	10	.947

(Fewer Than Ten Games)

Player and Club	G.	PO.	A.	E.	DP.	PB.	Pct.
Hickey, Blue ...	9	42	7	0	0		1.000
McDonald, Kgpt.	6	39	1	0	0	3	1.000
Pivec, Bristol ...	2	6	0	0	0		1.000
J. Fields, Blu ...	1	5	0	0	0	1	1.000
Lopez, Pulaski ...	1	1	0	0	0	0	1.000
Wooten, Bluefield	8	38	5	1	1	2	.977
McRobie, Pulaski.	7	49	6	3	0	5	.948

PITCHERS

Player and Club	G.	PO.	A.	E.	DP.	Pct.
STRATTON, Cov ..	12	6	14	0	1	1.000
Fusari, Pulaski ...	14	4	12	0	1	1.000
Pugh, Marion ...	12	4	8	0	1	1.000
DeMola, Johnson C .	10	4	7	0	1	1.000
Hutson, Bluefield ..	22	4	7	0	1	1.000
Martin, Pulaski* ...	11	0	10	0	1	1.000
Masteller, Pulaski* ..	16	1	8	0	0	1.000
Barb, Marion ...	11	1	7	0	0	1.000
Whalin, Pulaski* ...	13	0	8	0	0	1.000
Moore, Covington* ..	10	3	4	0	0	1.000
DeTray, Johnson C .	13	1	6	0	0	1.000
Feiler, Kingsport* ..	13	3	4	0	0	1.000
R. Salas, Kingsport*.	10	2	4	0	1	1.000
Rizzardi, Bristol ...	12	3	3	0	0	1.000
Brown, Pulaski ...	10	1	4	0	0	1.000
Urquiola, Covington.	11	1	4	0	0	1.000
Lee, Bluefield* ...	10	0	4	0	0	1.000
Johnston, Bluefield .	10	1	2	0	0	1.000
Fowler, Pulaski ...	11	0	3	0	0	1.000
Barton, Marion* ...	12	0	3	0	0	1.000

PITCHERS—Continued

Player and Club	G.	PO.	A.	E.	DP.	Pct.
Maine, Marion	12	2	1	0	0	1.000
Agosto, Bluefield	14	0	3	0	0	1.000
Ivancin, Bluefield*	12	0	2	0	0	1.000
Hammond, Bristol	10	1	0	0	0	1.000
M. E. Thomason, Pul	14	6	11	1	0	.944
M. Villalobos, Cov	13	5	8	1	0	.929
DeJean, Covington	9	0	7	1	1	.917
Hartman, Marion	12	5	15	2	1	.909
F. Thomason, Pul*	11	2	8	1	1	.909
Keister, Pulaski	19	3	7	1	0	.909
Cichon, Marion*	13	8	1	1	0	.900
Denison, Kingsport	8	3	5	1	1	.889
Kowalski, Marion	15	3	4	1	0	.875
J. F. Harris, Bristol	16	2	11	2	0	.867

Player and Club	G.	PO.	A.	E.	DP.	Pct.
Behar, Johnson City	12	1	5	1	0	.857
Reynolds, Marion	12	4	13	3	0	.850
R. Williams, Marion	10	2	10	2	0	.833
Witkowski, Bristol	10	2	3	1	0	.833
Armstrong, J C*	11	0	5	1	0	.833
Galasso, Bluefield	10	2	5	2	0	.778
House, Bluefield*	11	1	6	2	0	.778
Griggs, Kingsport	12	5	5	3	0	.769
Underwood, Blu	17	2	4	2	0	.750
Reid, Kingsport*	12	2	8	4	0	.714
Sosa, Covington	10	3	8	5	0	.688
Ward, Kingsport	14	1	4	3	2	.625
R. Fields, Bluefield	11	0	2	2	0	.500

(Fewer Than Ten Games)

Player and Club	G.	PO.	A.	E.	DP.	Pct.
Allen, Kingsport*	8	8	10	0	2	1.000
Arroyo, Bristol	9	8	6	0	1	1.000
Holdsworth, Bristol	8	3	9	0	0	1.000
Rooker, Kingsport	9	2	8	0	1	1.000
Forfar, Bristol	7	2	6	0	1	1.000
Simendinger, Blu	7	1	6	0	3	1.000
Earle, Johnson City	9	0	7	0	1	1.000
Pagan, Johnson City	4	2	4	0	2	1.000
Bonardel, Bluefield	7	4	2	0	0	1.000
Gardner, Covington	8	2	3	0	0	1.000
Horton, Bristol	7	0	4	0	1	1.000
Hinckley, Johnson C	8	0	4	0	1	1.000
Vargason, Johnson C*	5	0	3	0	0	1.000
Buist, Bristol	7	0	3	0	0	1.000
Mair, Bristol	8	0	3	0	0	1.000
Walker, Bristol	8	0	3	0	0	1.000
Bolsclair, Marion*	1	0	2	0	0	1.000
Betts, Marion*	2	0	2	0	0	1.000
Horn, Bristol	2	2	0	0	0	1.000
Briddell, Bristol	3	0	2	0	0	1.000
Eldridge, Covington	4	1	1	0	0	1.000
Greenwood, Pulaski	4	0	2	0	0	1.000
Shaw, Johnson City*	6	1	1	0	0	1.000
Sheets, Johnson C*	8	1	0	0	0	1.000
Chandler, Kingsport	1	0	1	0	0	1.000

Player and Club	G.	PO.	A.	E.	DP.	Pct.
Gillies, Covington	1	0	1	0	0	1.000
Potash, Marion*	2	0	1	0	0	1.000
Velander, Johnson C	2	0	1	0	0	1.000
Bruntrager, Bristol*	6	0	1	0	0	1.000
Cheadle, Johnson C*	9	5	10	1	1	.938
Buys, Johnson City	8	0	7	1	0	.875
Phelps, Marion	9	0	7	1	0	.875
Hammon, Kingsport	7	1	5	1	0	.857
Lawson, Johnson C	7	1	5	1	0	.857
Midura, Covington	8	1	10	2	0	.846
Shook, Covington	8	1	8	2	0	.818
Bartlett, Marion	3	2	4	2	0	.750
Murphy, Marion	6	2	4	2	0	.750
Lantz, Bristol	7	1	5	2	0	.750
Cooper, Marion*	9	0	6	2	0	.750
Streleski, Cov*	5	1	2	1	0	.750
Kostrba, Johnson C*	9	0	3	1	0	.750
DuBois, Bristol*	7	0	4	2	0	.667
Knowlton, Bristol*	5	0	2	1	0	.667
Campbell, Johnson C*	7	0	2	1	0	.667
Grout, Kingsport	5	1	2	2	0	.600
DeCinces, Bluefield	5	1	1	1	0	.500
Isom, Kingsport*	6	1	2	3	0	.375
Bailor, Bluefield	5	0	1	1	0	.000
Hausaman, Kgpt	1	0	1	0	0	.000

The following players do not have any recorded accepted chances at the positions indicated; therefore, are not listed in the fielding averages for those particular positions: Barrios*, p; Bucciarelli, p; Clark, ph; Diaz, p; Dusenbury, p; Hickey, p; Lincon, 3b; McGuire, of; Pappas, ph; Pfenninger, p; Renfro, p; Rivas, p; Sosa, Kingsport, p; Utz, p; E. Villalobos, of; B. Williams, ph.

CLUB PITCHING

Club	G.	CG.	ShO.	Sv.	IP.	H.	R.	ER.	HR.	BB.	Int. BB.	HB.	SO.	WP.	Bk.	ERA.
Bluefield	58	14	5	14	480	417	226	163	26	236	4	14	450	46	6	3.06
Kingsport	60	23	5	9	506	425	259	178	33	243	2	29	498	46	6	3.17
Pulaski	56	16	6	11	470	441	243	286	33	199	10	25	487	34	3	3.56
Covington	56	17	2	18	465	422	263	185	27	217	1	18	464	20	1	3.58
Bristol	56	14	5	8	466	441	270	201	37	200	5	17	400	40	2	3.88
Johnson City	55	10	5	12	457	447	284	206	29	187	1	17	403	38	3	4.06
Marion	59	8	3	13	486	519	329	255	40	225	16	26	366	47	1	4.72

PITCHERS' RECORDS

(Leading Qualifiers for Earned-Run Average Leadership—60 or More Innings)

*Throws lefthanded.

Pitcher—Club	G.	GS.	CG.	ShO.	W.	L.	Sv.	Pct.	IP.	H.	R.	ER.	HR.	BB.	Int. BB.	HB.	SO.	WP.	ERA.
Holdsworth, Bristol	8	8	4	1	5	1	0	.833	62	56	14	9	1	15	0	0	64	7	1.31
Hutson, Bluefield	22	6	4	1	9	1	8	.900	83	50	20	16	4	16	0	2	78	3	1.73
Arroyo, Bristol	9	8	5	0	4	1	0	.800	61	45	28	14	3	21	0	3	53	2	2.07
Agosto, Bluefield	14	3	1	4	3	1	1	.571	65	72	25	18	2	11	0	5	54	0	2.49
Griggs, Kingsport	12	12	6	1	3	5	0	.375	82	50	29	23	6	68	0	2	86	14	2.52
Reynolds, Marion	12	11	6	1	7	3	0	.700	80	67	29	23	5	13	0	3	74	5	2.59
Martin, Pulaski*	11	11	2	1	6	2	0	.750	65	42	25	20	6	42	2	1	76	9	2.77
Stratton, Covington	12	12	8	0	7	5	0	.583	93	87	39	29	5	20	0	4	107	2	2.81
Fusari, Pulaski	14	10	4	1	6	3	0	.667	80	80	38	25	4	16	1	2	84	4	2.81
M. E. Thomason, P.	14	12	4	1	4	5	1	.444	85	72	34	27	4	26	1	3	77	5	2.86

Departmental Leaders: G—Hutson, 22; GS—Griggs, Stratton, M. E. Thomason, 12; CG—Stratton, 8; ShO—Reid, 2; W—Hutson, 9; L—Harris, Stratton, Rooker, 6; Sv—Villalobos, 11; Pct.—Hutson, .900; IP—Stratton, 93; H—Stratton, 87; R—DeJean, 46; ER—DeJean, 30; HR—DeMola, Earle, Reid, Walker, 7; BB—Griggs, 68; IBB—Keister, 4; HB—Rooker, 10; SO—Stratton, 107; WP—Griggs, 14.

(All Pitchers—Listed Alphabetically)

Pitcher—Club	G	GS	CG	ShO	W	L	Sv	Pct.	IP	H	R	ER	HR	BB	Int. BB	HB	SO	WP	ERA
Agosto, Bluefield .14	11	3	1	4	3	1	.571	65	72	25	18	2	11	0	5	54	0	2.49
Allen, Kingsport* .. 8	8	2	0	2	3	0	.500	56	47	23	21	2	27	0	2	41	7	3.38
Armstrong, J C* ..11	0	0	0	1	1	0	.500	18	21	19	10	1	11	0	1	25	1	5.00
Arroyo, Bristol ... 9	8	5	0	4	1	0	.800	61	45	28	14	3	21	0	3	53	2	2.07
Bailor, Bluefield .. 1	0	0	0	0	0	0	.000	1	7	8	8	0	2	0	0	1	0	72.00
Barb, Marion 11	8	0	0	3	3	0	.500	50	54	31	25	4	19	2	2	30	3	4.50
Barrios, Pulaski* .. 3	0	0	0	1	0	0	.000	4	10	8	5	1	3	0	1	5	0	11.25
Bartlett, Marion . 3	2	0	0	1	1	0	.500	15	13	7	4	1	5	0	0	10	1	2.40
Barton, Marion .12	0	0	0	1	1	0	1.000	16	25	19	16	1	21	2	1	10	5	9.00
Behar, Johnson C .12	0	0	0	2	1	4	.667	23	19	12	8	0	7	0	1	20	2	3.13
Betts, Marion* ... 2	0	0	0	1	0	0	.000	4	7	5	5	2	2	0	0	3	0	11.25
Boisclair, Marion*. 1	0	0	0	0	0	0	.000	4	7	5	5	2	2	0	1	0	1	11.25
Bonardel, Bluefield. 7	4	0	0	2	2	0	.500	23	37	17	12	2	6	0	0	16	3	3.86
Briddell, Bluefield. 3	1	0	0	0	0	0	.000	9	10	7	2	0	5	0	0	4	1	2.00
Brown, Pulaski 10	8	0	0	2	1	0	.667	35	33	20	14	2	18	0	2	48	3	3.60
Bruntrager, Bristol* 6	1	0	0	1	1	2	.500	10	14	7	3	0	5	0	0	15	0	2.70
Bucciarelli, Blu .. 2	0	0	0	1	0	0	1.000	5	6	2	2	1	5	0	0	3	1	3.60
Buist, Bristol ... 7	1	0	0	1	0	0	1.000	15	20	10	8	1	7	1	0	10	0	4.80
Buys, Johnson City. 8	8	0	0	1	2	0	.333	42	50	35	25	1	17	0	3	33	4	5.36
Campbell, J C* ... 7	0	0	0	1	1	0	.500	10	5	2	2	1	2	0	0	9	1	1.80
Chandler, Kgpt ... 1	0	0	0	0	0	0	.000	2	4	3	3	2	1	0	0	1	0	13.50
Cheadle, Johnson C* 9	9	3	1	5	3	0	.625	57	47	22	12	4	26	1	1	50	2	1.89
Cichon, Marion* ..13	6	0	0	1	5	3	.167	44	49	29	25	5	21	3	3	51	2	5.11
Cooper, Marion* ... 9	0	0	0	2	1	0	.000	19	9	12	6	1	9	0	0	15	4	7.11
DeCinces, Bluefield 1	0	0	0	1	0	0	.000	2	3	2	1	0	2	0	0	1	0	0.00
DeJean, Covington .11	10	1	0	7	7	0	.778	71	73	46	30	4	30	0	2	59	3	3.80
DeMola, Johnson C.10	10	1	1	3	4	0	.429	62	54	39	28	7	26	0	1	67	7	4.06
Denison, Kingsport 18	3	2	1	4	2	2	.667	58	47	23	18	4	13	1	0	75	0	2.79
DeTray, Johnson C.13	0	0	0	3	1	5	.750	21	16	9	6	1	9	0	1	23	1	2.57
Diaz, Covington .. 2	0	0	0	0	0	0	.000	4	3	2	0	0	2	0	0	1	0	0.00
DuBois, Bristol* .. 7	3	0	0	3	0	0	.000	12	19	29	22	4	16	0	1	14	3	16.50
Dusenbury, Marion. 1	0	0	0	0	0	0	.000	1	1	1	1	0	1	0	0	0	0	9.00
Earle, Johnson City 9	9	3	1	6	2	0	.750	66	61	31	26	7	23	0	1	55	4	3.55
Eldridge, Cov 4	0	0	0	0	0	0	.000	6	5	3	1	0	5	0	1	7	1	1.50
Feiler, Kingsport* .13	0	0	0	2	0	1	1.000	24	23	13	9	2	9	0	0	28	3	3.38
R. Fields, Blu 11	3	0	0	3	4	0	.429	27	25	17	17	2	24	0	1	30	5	5.67
Forfar, Bristol ... 7	3	0	0	2	2	0	.500	28	28	12	10	2	9	0	0	14	4	3.21
Fowler, Pulaski ...11	0	0	0	3	0	3	.000	19	21	14	14	5	8	0	0	16	1	6.63
Fusari, Pulaski ..14	10	4	1	6	3	0	.667	80	80	38	25	4	16	1	2	84	4	2.81
Galasso, Bluefield .10	7	1	0	3	3	0	.500	43	33	25	17	0	39	2	1	32	11	3.56
Gardner, Covington. 8	4	0	0	2	0	0	1.000	29	34	16	15	3	16	0	0	22	1	4.66
Gillies, Covington . 1	0	0	0	0	0	0	.000	6	3	2	2	0	3	0	1	5	0	0.00
Greenwood, Pulaski. 4	0	0	0	1	0	0	1.000	8	7	5	4	2	6	0	2	5	1	4.50
Griggs, Kingsport .12	12	6	1	3	5	0	.375	82	50	29	23	6	68	0	2	86	14	2.52
Grout, Kingsport .. 5	5	1	0	2	2	0	.500	26	23	17	11	2	9	0	1	18	2	3.81
Hammon, Kingsport 6	6	2	1	1	3	0	.250	36	39	17	13	1	11	0	1	39	1	3.25
Hammond, Bristol .10	0	0	0	0	0	1	.000	19	31	22	20	3	9	0	0	14	2	9.47
J. F. Harris, Bris .16	8	1	0	2	6	4	.250	59	50	29	22	2	29	2	3	61	5	3.36
Hartman, Marion .12	11	1	1	4	5	0	.444	70	76	43	29	3	24	1	1	34	4	3.73
Hausaman, Kgpt .. 1	0	0	0	0	0	0	.000	1	1	0	0	0	1	0	0	2	0	0.00
Hickey, Bluefield .. 2	1	0	0	0	0	0	.000	2	0	1	0	0	3	0	0	1	2	0.00
Hinckley, Johnson C 8	3	0	0	0	2	1	.000	25	31	21	18	3	9	0	2	13	2	6.48
Holdsworth, Bristol. 8	8	4	1	5	1	0	.833	62	56	14	9	1	15	0	0	64	7	1.31
Horn, Bristol 7	3	0	0	2	1	0	1.000	13	8	3	3	1	3	0	2	4	1	2.08
Horton, Bristol ... 7	4	0	0	3	4	0	.000	16	27	21	18	3	12	0	3	9	1	10.13
House, Bluefield ..11	8	2	0	4	4	0	.500	50	38	32	16	4	37	0	1	67	7	2.88
Hutson, Bluefield .22	6	4	1	9	1	3	.900	83	50	20	16	3	14	0	0	78	3	1.73
Isom, Kingsport* .. 6	6	2	0	2	3	0	.400	31	29	35	25	4	30	0	3	34	5	7.26
Ivancin, Bluefield .12	0	0	0	1	0	1	1.000	24	29	20	15	2	9	0	1	21	7	5.63
Johnston, Bluefield.10	1	0	0	0	2	0	.000	24	21	6	6	3	8	1	0	34	2	2.25
Keister, Pulaski ..19	1	0	0	6	1	0	.000	38	44	25	18	2	29	4	2	38	1	4.26
Knowlton, Bristol* . 6	2	1	1	2	0	0	1.000	22	5	0	0	0	12	0	0	26	3	0.00
Kostrba, Johnson C* 9	1	0	0	1	1	0	.500	22	17	12	10	1	12	0	2	20	1	4.09
Kowalski, Marion .15	3	0	0	3	1	0	.250	28	34	33	21	3	17	2	3	20	2	6.75
Lantz, Bristol ... 7	7	1	1	3	0	0	.500	39	26	24	18	1	27	1	2	45	5	4.15
Lawson, Johnson C. 7	7	1	1	5	0	0	.167	36	42	32	20	0	10	0	0	22	4	5.00
Lee, Bluefield* ...10	1	0	0	0	0	0	.000	16	13	5	3	0	9	0	1	8	0	1.69
Maine, Marion 12	0	0	0	2	0	0	.000	26	29	21	15	4	15	0	1	16	4	5.19
Mair, Bristol 8	1	0	0	1	0	0	.000	20	23	14	14	5	3	0	0	2	4	6.30
Martin, Pulaski ..11	11	2	1	6	2	0	.750	65	62	43	25	0	42	2	1	76	9	2.77
Masteller, Pulaski*.16	3	0	0	0	2	5	.000	33	25	12	12	2	17	0	1	36	2	3.27
Midura, Covington . 8	6	2	0	2	1	0	.500	37	46	33	27	4	13	0	1	37	0	6.57
Moore, Covington* .10	7	2	0	4	2	0	.667	57	39	27	16	4	20	0	0	68	1	2.53
Murphy, Marion .. 6	3	0	0	3	1	0	.500	26	27	17	10	1	7	1	0	21	1	3.46
Pagan, Johnson City 4	4	1	0	1	1	0	.500	25	26	16	14	1	12	0	3	26	2	5.04
Pfenninger, Blue .. 1	0	0	0	0	0	0	.000	1	1	2	0	0	1	0	0	0	0	0.00
Phelps, Marion ... 9	3	0	0	2	2	1	.500	23	28	16	15	2	16	1	1	21	3	5.87
Potash, Marion* .. 2	0	0	0	0	0	0	.000	4	2	0	0	0	2	0	0	4	0	0.00
Pugh, Marion 12	8	1	1	2	4	0	.333	45	42	30	27	4	30	1	2	36	6	5.40
Reid, Kingsport* ..12	10	7	2	6	5	0	.545	85	69	41	28	7	30	0	2	87	5	2.96
Renfro, Bluefield . 1	0	0	0	0	0	0	.000	1	1	1	1	0	1	0	0	2	1	9.00

Pitcher—Club	G.	GS.	CG.	ShO.	W.	L.	Sv.	Pct.	IP.	H.	R.	ER.	HR.	BB.	Int. BB.	HB.	SO.	WP.	ERA.
Reynolds, Marion ..12	11	6	1	7	3	0		.700	80	67	29	23	5	13	0	3	74	5	2.59
Rivas, Marion 1	0	0	0	0	0	0		.000	1	1	0	0	0	0	0	0	0	0	0.00
Rizzardi, Bristol ..12	3	1	0	1	2	0		.333	37	32	19	16	3	12	0	2	35	4	3.89
Rooker, Kingsport . 9	8	0	0	1	6	0		.143	44	43	25	15	0	23	1	10	32	5	3.07
R. Salas, Kgpt* ...10	1	0	0	2	1		1.000	22	21	17	6	1	12	0	4	18	1	2.45
Shaw, Johnson C* . 6	0	0	0	1	0	1	1.000	8	8	7	1	7	0	0	4	5.73
Sheets, Johnson C* . 8	3	1	1	1	2	0		.333	28	24	10	8	0	7	0	1	25	1	2.57
Shook, Covington . 8	6	2	0	1	4	0		.200	42	37	27	17	1	25	0	1	42	1	3.64
Simendinger, Blu . 7	7	3	1	4	1	0		.800	43	31	16	9	2	22	1	1	51	2	1.88
Sosa, Covington ...10	10	1	0	2	5	0		.375	55	42	31	21	1	40	0	6	50	6	5.44
Sosa, Kingsport ... 6	0	0	0	0	1	0		.000	7	5	0	0	0	2	0	2	6	1	0.00
Stratton, Cov 12	12	8	0	7	5	0		.583	93	87	39	34	5	20	0	4	107	2	2.81
Streleski, Cov* ... 5	0	0	0	0	1	0		.000	11	16	22	17	1	20	0	2	12	2	13.91
F. Thomason, Pul*.11	9	4	1	6	2	1		.750	67	63	29	22	3	20	2	7	62	3	2.96
M. E. Thomason, P..14	12	4	1	4	5	1		.444	85	72	34	27	4	26	1	3	77	5	2.86
Underwood, Bir .17	4	1	0	6	2	2		.750	57	48	22	20	4	27	0	1	47	3	3.16
Urquiola, Cov ...11	0	0	0	3	2	3		.600	22	22	11	9	4	9	1	1	19	1	3.68
Utz, Pulaski 1	0	0	0	0	0	0		.000	1	5	5	5	0	2	0	0	0	0	45.00
Vargason, J C* 5	1	0	0	1	1	1		.500	11	16	14	10	0	9	0	0	9	1	8.18
Velander, Johnson C 2	0	0	0	0	0	0		.000	2	3	2	2	1	0	0	0	2	1	9.00
M. Villalobos, Cov.19	1	1	0	3	1	11		.750	33	15	4	3	0	14	0	1	35	2	0.82
Walker, Bristol ... 8	5	0	0	2	4	0		.333	32	39	22	16	7	12	0	1	19	2	4.50
Ward, Kingsport .14	0	0	0	1	2	3		.333	32	21	10	6	3	8	0	1	31	2	1.69
Whalin, Pulaski* .13	6	2	1	2	3	0		.400	35	38	27	19	2	11	0	4	40	5	4.89
R. Williams, Mar .12	2	0	0	2	3	1		.333	31	39	25	20	3	13	1	4	16	5	5.81
Witkowski, Bristol .10	2	0	0	2	3	1		.400	20	18	10	8	1	8	1	0	15	0	3.60

BALKS—Galasso, Griggs, Underwood, 2 each; Agosto, Behar, Buys, Denison, Hammond, House, Isom, Keister, Reynolds, Rizzardi, Rooker, Salas, Shaw, Sosa (Cov), F. Thomason, Whalin, 1 each.

COMBINATION SHUTOUTS—Galasso-Hutson, Hickey-Briddell-Hutson-Johnston-Agosto, Bluefield; Knowlton-Harris, Horn-Witkowski, Bristol; Midura-Urquiola, Stratton-Moore, Covington; Martin-Masteller, Pulaski.

NO-HIT GAMES—Rooker (five innings), Ward (three innings), and Sosa (one inning) Kingsport, lost to Bristol, 1-2, June 26; Pugh, Marion, defeated Kingsport, 12-0, August 11 (seven innings); Martin, Pulaski, defeated Kingsport, 4-1, August 26 (seven innings).

ALONG THE MINOR LEAGUE TRAIL . . . .

(Continued from page 574)

fore being shipped to Jacksonville (Southern), complained that what he needed was work-work-work-and-throw-throw-throw. So they started him against Charlotte and he threw 96 pitches in the first five innings. . . . And the Jax' general manager, Art Parrack, got around the Florida ban on "Lucky Number" nights by tossing $200 from the grandstand roof onto the fans seated below. However, he also mixed in "about a million dollars" in play money. A gust of wind carried some of the paper onto the field and scrambling fans delayed the game while they played bonus-bogus with the windfall. . . . Coos Bay-North Bend (Northwest), a new team in the league, was welcomed by the defending league champion, Medford, in its opening series. How? The title Dodgers flattened the newcomers three times before they had finished bowing. . . . Bob Guindon of Tulsa (American Association) must wonder what does it profit a man, etc. Against Des Moines, he drove in seven runs and pitched three innings of one-run relief, yet the game was lost by six runs. Des Moines had an 11-1 lead before Guindon exploded. . . . Tom Hannegan, Greenville, (Western Carolinas) third base-

(Continued on page 593)

Gulf Coast League

ROOKIE CLASSIFICATION

CHAMPIONSHIP WINNERS IN PREVIOUS YEARS

1964—Sarasota Braves ... .610 1968—Oakland .... .650
1965—Bradenton Astros .. .632 1968—Oakland .... .650
1967—Kansas City ...... .614 1969—Montreal .... .585
1966—New York AL ..... .667

(Note—Known as Sarasota Rookie League in 1964 and Florida Rookie League in 1965.)

STANDING OF CLUBS AT CLOSE OF SEASON, AUGUST 31

Club	Chi.	Mont.	Cleve.	Minn.	St.L.	Cinn.	Tour.	Pitt.	W.	L.	T.	Pct.	G.B.
Chicago AL	..	2	7	4	5	4	8	6	36	24	0	.600	....
Montreal	7	..	3	4	7	3	6	6	36	27	0	.571	1½
Cleveland	0	6	..	6	5	7	3	7	34	26	0	.567	2
Minnesota	5	5	3	..	4	4	7	6	34	29	0	.540	3½
St. Louis	3	2	4	4	..	6	5	7	32	28	0	.533	4
Cincinnati	5	6	1	5	1	..	5	2	25	35	0	.417	11
Tourists	3	3	6	2	4	4	..	4	26	37	0	.413	11½
Pittsburgh	1	3	2	3	2	7	5	..	23	40	0	.365	14½

NOTE—Chicago, Cleveland, Minnesota and St. Louis based at Sarasota, Florida; Cincinnati, Montreal and Pittsburgh based at Bradenton, Fla., Tourists club was visiting club at both cities. Club names indicate major league connections; Tourists roster filled by Pittsburgh.
Playoff—None.
Regular-Season Attendance—8,772. No playoff. All-star game—1,509.
Managers: Chicago—Joe Jones; Cincinnati—Ron Plaza; Cleveland—Joe Lutz; Minnesota—Fred Waters; Montreal—Ed Sadowski; Pittsburgh—Dick Cole; St. Louis—Tom Burgess; Tourists—Ed Napoleon.
All-Star Team: BRADENTON TEAMS: 1B—Russo, Cincinnati; Viefhaus, Montreal; 2B—Mullinax, Montreal; 3B—Johnson, Pittsburgh; Polanco, Tourists; SS—Baez, Montreal; Boyd, Cincinnati; OF—Kirkland, Cincinnati; Murray, Montreal; Gandy and Parker, Pittsburgh; Melvin, Tourists; C—Foote, Montreal; Say, Pittsburgh; Kotowski, Tourists; P—Andujar and Stan Kmet, Cincinnati; Dostaler and Lang, Montreal; Buckley and Currence, Pittsburgh; Hewlett and Swinchock, Tourists; Managers—Sadowski, Montreal; Napoleon, Tourists. SARASOTA TEAMS: 1B—Newman, Cleveland; Crigler, Minnesota; 2B—Hairston, Chicago; Bozich, Cleveland; 3B—Shinn, Minnesota; Wheeler, St. Louis; SS—Carlson, Minnesota; OF—Norton, Chicago; Flowers, Gloede and Tucker, Cleveland; Heenan, St. Louis; C—Reynolds, Chicago; Saylor, Minnesota; Hill, St. Louis; P—McClain, Chicago; Lowe, Cleveland; Meyers and Wagner, Minnesota; Denny and Shepard, St. Louis; Managers—Jones, Chicago; Waters, Minnesota.

(Compiled by Howe News Bureau, Chicago, Ill.)

CLUB BATTING

Club	G.	AB.	R.	OR.	H.	TB.	2B.	3B.	HR.	RBI.	SH.	SF.	BB.	Int. BB.	HP.	SO.	SB.	CS.	LOB.	Pct.
Montreal	63	2074	326	283	521	706	71	24	22	267	25	15	229	6	20	430	32	13	439	.251
Chicago AL ...	60	1949	304	287	480	598	58	21	6	259	25	27	331	9	20	462	49	20	499	.246
Minnesota	63	2060	267	273	507	611	57	9	9	209	20	20	255	9	25	371	39	9	514	.246
Cincinnati ...	60	1969	249	296	480	618	55	19	15	183	26	16	212	11	21	456	55	23	442	.244
Cleveland	60	1920	315	267	462	612	54	21	18	241	27	21	305	9	21	414	90	22	481	.241
Tourists	63	2180	268	264	522	671	70	26	9	206	25	17	183	8	22	405	69	23	491	.239
St. Louis	60	1926	272	255	458	608	55	25	15	217	21	17	193	9	20	435	67	26	391	.238
Pittsburgh ...	60	2019	271	347	473	612	57	11	20	210	17	18	284	12	30	499	39	23	516	.234

INDIVIDUAL BATTING

(Leading Qualifiers for Batting Championship—195 or More Plate Appearances)
*Bats lefthanded. †Switch-hitter

Player and Club	G.	AB.	R.	H.	TB.	2B.	3B.	HR.	RBI.	SH.	SF.	BB.	HP.	SO.	SB.	CS.	Pct.
Carlson, Mark, Minnesota ..	59	217	53	78	95	8	3	1	18	6	0	33	3	18	13	2	.359
Gloede, Gary, Cleveland† ..	60	200	49	70	107	11	7	4	43	1	2	58	4	37	25	4	.350
Basey, Lawrence, Cincinnati*	46	173	37	58	70	3	1	1	14	2	0	11	1	16	16	8	.335
Hairston, Jerry, Chicago† ..	56	183	37	61	76	8	2	1	36	5	4	51	2	24	5	5	.333
Parker, David, Pittsburgh* ..	61	239	34	75	107	8	3	6	41	1	2	12	4	54	6	5	.314
Newman, Jeffrey, Cleveland ..	55	195	27	61	88	9	0	6	53	2	4	17	0	35	4	0	.313
Melvin, Kenneth, Tourists ..	62	240	28	74	105	15	2	4	33	1	1	16	2	39	8	6	.308
Polanco, Ovidio, Tourists ..	45	182	37	56	68	5	2	1	20	9	1	13	2	26	19	4	.308
Murray, Robert, Montreal ..	54	202	39	62	82	10	2	2	36	4	4	25	2	37	4	1	.307
Wheeler, Charles, Minnesota*	55	222	46	68	71	3	0	0	8	0	0	26	4	6	14	2	.306

Departmental Leaders: G—T. Johnson, 63; AB—Melvin, 240; R—Flowers, 55; H—Carlson, 78; TB—Gloede, Parker, 107; 2B—Melvin, 15; 3B—Gloede, 7; HR—Gorinski, Newman, Parker, 6; RBI—Newman, 53; SH—Carlson, DeMaria, 6; SF—Beach, Dent, T. Johnson, 5; BB—Gloede, 58; HP—Gandy, 6; SO—T. Johnson, 67; SB—Flowers, 33; CS—Basey, 8.

(All Players—Listed Alphabetically)

Player and Club	G.	AB.	R.	H.	TB.	2B.	3B.	HR.	RBI.	SH.	SF.	BB.	HP.	SO.	SB.	CS.	Pct.
Abram, Gary, Tourists	8	21	1	2	2	0	0	0	3	0	4	0	10	0	0		.095
Albertson, Bradley, Tourists*	36	149	14	39	50	3	4	0	15	0	2	6	3	16	3	0	.262
Alcala, Santo, Cincinnati ...	11	22	0	1	1	0	0	0	0	2	0	2	0	18	1	0	.045
Aloway, Tommy, St. Louis*	43	131	21	34	47	7	3	0	22	1	3	16	1	30	3	0	.260
Anderson, A. Allen, St. Louis*	6	3	0	1	1	0	0	0	0	0	0	0	0	0	0	0	.333
Andujar, Joaquin, Cinn† ...	12	29	1	2	2	0	0	0	0	2	0	1	0	14	0	0	.069
Ash, Robert, Cleveland	12	6	0	0	0	0	0	0	0	3	0	0	0	2	0	0	.000
Auchmutey, Charles, Chicago	14	4	0	0	0	0	0	0	1	0	0	2	0	3	0	0	.000
Auger, Robert, St. Louis ...	10	16	1	1	3	0	1	0	2	0	0	0	0	4	0	0	.063
Baez, Rafael, Montreal	53	184	28	45	54	6	0	1	16	2	2	10	1	31	1	0	.245
Baker, Jeffrey, Cleveland ..	20	13	2	2	3	1	0	0	1	0	0	1	0	7	0	0	.154
Basey, Lawrence, Cincinnati*	46	173	37	58	70	3	3	1	14	2	0	20	1	16	16	8	.335
Beach, Randolph, Minnesota .	52	159	17	38	45	5	1	0	20	0	5	30	2	21	3	2	.239
Bedard, John, Pittsburgh ..	4	4	1	1	1	0	0	0	1	0	0	2	0	1	0	0	.250
Berdell, Michael, Chicago ..	11	12	1	1	1	0	0	0	0	1	0	1	0	7	0	0	.083
Berry, Richard, Pittsburgh*	40	120	13	23	33	0	2	2	13	0	2	15	2	35	0	0	.192
Beyersdorf, James, Cleveland	4	2	0	0	0	0	0	0	0	0	0	0	0	1	0	0	.000
Blake, Michael, Cleveland ...	16	21	2	1	1	0	0	0	1	2	1	0	0	6	0	0	.048
Bock, Lawrence, Montreal ..	22	72	7	15	22	1	0	2	13	0	2	3	0	13	0	1	.208
Boehning, Gregory, Chicago*.	10	21	3	3	3	0	0	0	2	2	0	2	1	11	0	0	.143
Bosley, Stephen, Tourists ...	11	13	2	2	2	0	0	0	0	0	0	0	0	5	1	0	.154
Bowman, Terry, Pittsburgh*	35	105	14	22	22	0	0	0	7	1	1	7	2	30	2	2	.210
Boyd, Eric, Cincinnati	47	134	14	31	38	4	0	1	13	1	0	25	1	8	2	2	.231
Bozich, Tom, Cleveland	56	171	17	33	34	1	0	0	20	3	1	21	0	19	1	2	.193
Branch, Stafford, St. Louis .	8	7	0	1	1	0	0	0	0	0	0	1	0	0	0	0	.143
Braun, John, Minnesota	13	9	0	1	1	0	0	0	0	1	0	1	0	5	0	0	.111
Bright, William, St. Louis* .	1	3	1	2	4	0	1	0	2	0	0	1	0	0	0	0	.667
Brooks, Kenneth, Cleveland .	13	15	3	5	5	0	0	0	1	1	0	3	0	4	0	0	.333
Brown, David, Pittsburgh ..	11	2	1	0	0	0	0	0	1	0	0	1	0	2	0	0	.000
Brown, Harold, Minnesota ..	18	40	3	8	9	1	0	0	3	0	1	1	0	8	0	0	.200
Brown, Michael, Chicago ...	1	1	0	1	1	0	0	0	0	0	0	0	0	0	0	0	1.000
Browning, James, St. Louis .	2	1	0	0	0	0	0	0	0	2	0	0	0	0	0	0	.000
Buckley, Anthony, Pittsburgh	13	16	3	5	7	2	0	0	2	0	0	2	1	4	0	0	.313
Burkert, Thomas, Cleveland*.	16	10	4	3	3	0	0	0	1	0	0	2	0	3	0	0	.300
Byers, David, St. Louis* ...	16	45	5	11	11	0	0	0	1	0	0	0	0	5	0	1	.244
Byrne, Michael, Chicago ...	23	13	2	4	4	0	0	0	1	0	1	1	0	1	0	0	.308
Cannon, Bruce, Cleveland ..	23	64	8	10	20	3	2	1	7	1	0	11	0	22	2	0	.156
Carlson, Mark, Minnesota .	59	217	53	78	95	8	3	1	18	6	0	33	3	18	13	2	.359
Cingle, Raymond, St. Louis*	13	31	0	9	9	0	0	0	3	0	1	0	9	3	0		.290
Clark, J. Randall, Tourists .	53	190	24	51	62	5	3	0	15	0	1	16	3	19	7	2	.268
Clemmons, Forrest, Cinn ..	12	14	1	3	3	0	0	0	3	0	3	2	3	1	1		.214
Clites, Robert, Tourists	8	20	1	4	4	0	0	0	1	1	0	0	0	3	0	0	.200
Collins, Lee, Montreal	1	2	0	0	0	0	0	0	0	0	0	2	0	1	0	0	.000
Collins, Thomas, Cincinnati .	17	8	0	1	1	0	0	0	0	0	0	0	0	4	0	0	.125
Coltin, Olin, Montreal	3	5	0	1	1	0	0	0	0	0	0	0	0	3	0	0	.200
Cooper, David, Chicago	10	6	0	0	0	0	0	0	1	0	0	1	0	2	0	0	.000
Cope, Edward, Cleveland ...	11	9	2	1	1	0	0	0	2	0	1	4	0	2	0	0	.111
Cordova, Angelo, Pittsburgh*	31	86	4	14	16	0	1	0	5	0	0	7	0	21	0	1	.163
Covert, Mark, St. Louis	10	9	3	3	3	0	0	0	1	2	0	2	0	2	0	0	.333
Crigler, Landon, Minnesota *.	59	217	21	55	63	8	0	0	30	0	1	28	3	35	0	1	.253
Cruz, Cirilo, St. Louis* ...	5	14	1	2	2	0	0	0	2	0	0	1	0	2	0	0	.143
Cruz, Hector, St. Louis	3	9	3	4	6	0	1	0	2	0	0	0	0	1	0	0	.444
Cuddy, Fred, St. Louis	4	8	1	2	2	0	0	0	2	0	0	0	0	3	0	0	.250
Cummins, Michael, Minnesota	13	3	0	0	0	0	0	0	0	0	0	0	0	0	0	0	.000
Cunningham, Richard, Chi ..	12	4	1	1	1	0	0	0	1	0	0	1	0	0	0	0	.250
Curlee, Barry, Chicago	31	59	9	13	17	4	0	0	6	0	0	10	1	15	2	0	.220
Currence, D. Lafayette, Pitt	12	28	4	5	6	1	0	0	1	1	0	3	0	4	0	0	.179
Damran, I. Paul, Cincinnati	39	113	9	31	40	3	3	0	11	0	2	7	0	23	2	1	.274
Darnell, Jack, Cleveland ...	16	18	2	2	2	0	0	0	1	1	0	1	0	10	0	0	.111
Davis, John, St. Louis	7	4	0	0	0	0	0	0	0	0	0	1	0	3	0	0	.000
Davison, Ronald, Minnesota .	18	42	3	7	9	0	1	0	2	0	1	5	0	11	0	0	.167
DeFreitas, Arturo, Cinn ...	36	119	13	25	27	2	0	0	5	1	1	0	2	31	2	1	.210
DeLuna, Michael, Minnesota*	5	4	0	1	1	0	0	0	0	0	0	0	0	0	0	0	.250
DeMaria, Richard, Tourists*	52	157	21	35	45	7	0	1	14	6	1	11	3	30	7	3	.223
DeMay, Richard, Chicago ..	11	25	4	3	3	0	0	0	0	0	0	3	0	13	0	1	.120
Denny, John, St. Louis	11	11	3	2	2	0	0	0	1	0	0	0	2	5	0	0	.182
Dent, Russell, Chicago	22	77	18	27	31	2	1	0	13	1	5	22	0	6	2	0	.351
DeZuba, Charles, Tourists ..	7	3	0	1	1	0	0	0	0	0	0	1	0	1	0	0	.333
Diaz, Victor, St. Louis	35	95	12	23	33	4	3	0	14	0	2	5	2	15	0	1	.242
Dirks, Rodney, Tourists* ...	11	25	1	5	5	0	0	0	3	1	0	1	0	4	0	0	.200
Dostaler, Michael, Montreal .	20	6	1	0	0	0	0	0	0	1	0	0	0	3	0	0	.000
Downing, Brian, Chicago ..	34	96	16	21	24	1	0	0	14	1	0	16	0	20	2	0	.219
Drewett, Michael, Chicago ..	27	72	9	12	19	4	0	1	13	0	2	9	2	25	2	1	.167
Duhon, Dennis, St. Louis ...	10	15	2	4	5	0	0	0	3	0	0	1	0	6	0	1	.267
Dunham, James, St. Louis ..	28	65	3	13	16	1	1	0	3	3	0	3	0	16	3	3	.200
Edwards, Jesse, Minnesota* .	19	5	1	2	2	0	0	0	1	0	0	3	0	2	0	0	.400
Erickson, Virgil, St. Louis ..	2	3	1	0	0	0	0	0	0	0	0	2	0	1	0	0	.000
Estrellas, Thomas, Pitt*	9	5	0	1	1	0	0	0	0	1	0	0	0	3	0	0	.200
Evans, Larry, Montreal	7	9	0	2	2	0	0	0	0	0	0	0	0	2	0	0	.222

Player and Club	G.	AB.	R.	H.	TB.	2B.	3B.	HR.	RBI.	SH.	SF.	BB.	HP.	SO.	SB.	CS.	Pct.
Faria, Kenneth, St. Louis*	19	41	3	11	13	2	0	0	4	1	0	6	1	12	1	0	.268
Farrow, Willie, St. Louis†	26	73	9	17	27	5	1	1	10	0	1	10	1	32	2	2	.233
Favreau, Richard, Montreal	3	1	0	0	0	0	0	0	0	0	0	0	0	1	0	0	.000
Fenton, Stanley, St. Louis	6	14	1	1	1	0	0	0	0	0	0	2	1	2	0	0	.071
Florez, Roy, St. Louis	24	69	11	9	15	0	0	2	9	0	2	12	1	18	3	1	.130
Flowers, Burnel, Cleveland*	60	227	55	61	77	5	4	1	22	1	2	41	5	49	33	7	.269
Foote, Barry, Montreal	46	143	26	38	54	7	0	3	29	0	0	24	2	22	0	0	.266
Fuller, Joseph, St. Louis	4	4	0	0	0	0	0	0	1	0	0	0	0	2	0	0	.000
Gandy, Gary, Pittsburgh	49	161	29	45	57	7	1	1	15	2	4	34	6	21	5	3	.280
Garver, Gregory, St. Louis*	31	88	16	21	23	0	1	0	8	1	0	9	0	20	4	2	.239
Gasperino, Mark, St. Louis*	31	82	11	20	31	3	1	3	14	1	2	10	0	22	1	0	.244
Gause, Robert, Minnesota	11	4	0	0	0	0	0	0	0	0	0	0	0	1	0	0	.000
Geitner, John, Minnesota	59	200	23	48	59	8	0	1	30	2	2	37	3	49	4	0	.240
Gentile, John, Montreal	4	7	0	0	0	0	0	0	0	0	0	0	0	1	0	0	.000
Gloede, Gary, Cleveland†	60	200	49	70	107	11	7	4	43	1	2	58	4	37	25	4	.350
Gomez, Jose, Montreal	13	8	0	1	1	0	0	0	0	0	0	2	0	5	0	0	.125
Gorinski, Robert, Minnesota	60	210	33	50	79	7	2	6	30	0	3	17	4	59	3	0	.238
Gossage, Richard, Chicago	3	6	1	1	1	0	0	0	0	0	0	0	0	2	0	0	.167
Gregory, Jimmy, St. Louis*	12	14	0	1	1	0	0	0	1	0	2	0	3	0	1		.071
Griggs, David, St. Louis	13	26	4	5	5	0	0	0	2	0	0	7	0	7	1	0	.192
Gunter, Chester, Pittsburgh	7	11	3	3	6	0	0	1	2	1	0	6	0	5	0	0	.273
Gustafson, Gregory, Minn	12	21	0	2	2	0	0	0	0	0	0	2	0	6	0	0	.095
Hagadorn, David, Cincinnati	2	1	0	0	0	0	0	0	0	0	0	0	0	1	0	0	.000
Hairston, Jerry, Chicago†	56	183	37	61	76	8	2	1	36	5	4	51	2	24	5	5	.333
Hale, Mark, St. Louis*	9	29	5	11	16	0	1	1	5	1	0	3	0	3	2	0	.379
Hanzlik, Joseph, Minnesota*	13	21	1	1	1	0	0	0	1	0	0	2	0	4	0	0	.048
Haugen, Paul, Minnesota	10	12	0	2	2	0	0	0	1	0	0	2	0	4	0	0	.167
Hayes, Cliff, Chicago	10	13	1	4	4	0	0	0	0	0	1	0	2	0	0		.308
Hays, Wilson, Pittsburgh	19	21	1	4	4	0	0	0	1	0	0	0	0	2	0	1	.190
Heenan, John, St. Louis	35	101	7	17	18	1	0	0	8	3	10	1	29	4	1		.168
Helton, Jesse, Cincinnati	46	147	17	35	39	2	1	0	8	1	0	18	4	54	7	0	.238
Hernandez, William, Cleve	26	69	5	14	17	1	1	0	7	1	0	8	3	19	3	0	.203
Hess, Samuel, Minnesota	26	66	3	10	12	0	1	0	5	1	1	4	0	13	0	0	.152
Hewlett, Carl, Tourists	12	16	2	2	3	1′	0	0	2	2	0	2	0	7	0	0	.125
Heykens, Douglas, Cincinnati	21	75	12	23	47	10	1	4	10	0	0	6	0	22	3	0	.307
Hill, Marc, St. Louis	28	78	6	15	18	3	0	0	6	2	0	8	0	27	0	1	.192
Hockett, Nicholas, Cleve*	2	3	0	1	1	0	0	0	0	0	0	1	0	0	0	0	.333
Hopkins, Donald, Montreal*	22	41	5	11	12	1	0	0	4	0	0	2	1	11	2	1	.268
Horsch, James, Montreal	13	22	3	1	1	0	0	0	0	5	0	7	0	14	0	0	.045
Hund, John, St. Louis	45	144	23	37	43	3	0	1	8	3	1	16	1	30	11	0	.257
Jackson, Charles, Montreal	8	16	0	3	3	0	0	0	8	2	0	0	1	0	0		.188
Jackson, Cleothus, Chicago	14	22	2	8	8	0	0	0	4	1	2	2	0	4	0	0	.364
Jacome, David, Cleveland	30	99	16	24	28	1	0	1	10	1	2	14	1	21	7	0	.242
James, Murray, Montreal	10	1	0	0	0	0	0	0	0	0	0	2	0	1	0	0	.000
Johnson, Kevin, Cincinnati	10	15	2	1	1	0	0	0	1	0	3	0	1	0	7	0	.067
Johnson, Steven, St. Louis	11	14	2	4	5	1	0	0	1	0	0	0	0	3	1	0	.286
Johnson, Theodia, Pitt*	63	237	34	59	78	9	2	2	31	1	5	22	2	67	10	1	.249
Johnson, Weldon, Cleveland	46	126	11	29	38	7	1	0	14	2	1	11	0	24	0	2	.230
Johnson, W. Scott, Tourists	4	13	2	1	1	0	0	0	0	0	0	0	0	4	0	0	.077
Kehoe, William, Minn	6	14	3	3	3	0	0	0	0	0	0	0	0	3	0	0	.214
Kelley, Gary, Pittsburgh	41	138	15	28	33	5	0	0	9	0	0	15	3	32	1	2	.203
Kelley, T. Michael, Cleve*	19	5	0	0	0	0	0	0	0	0	0	0	1	0	0	0	.000
Ker, Clifford, Montreal	8	22	0	3	3	0	0	0	4	2	0	2	0	6	1	0	.136
Kerr, Dewayne, Cincinnati*	5	4	2	1	1	1	0	0	0	0	0	2	0	1	0		.250
Kershaw, Kenneth, Montreal	5	6	1	1	1	0	0	0	1	0	0	1	0	2	0	0	.167
Key, Bobby, St. Louis	3	4	1	1	1	0	0	0	0	0	0	1	0	0	0	0	.250
Kimak, Thomas, St. Louis	1	2	0	0	0	0	0	0	0	0	0	0	0	2	0	0	.000
King, Gary, Cleveland	53	125	20	30	32	2	0	0	6	1	1	20	0	22	3	0	.240
Kinner, Ronald, St. Louis	27	105	26	26	31	2	0	1	11	0	5	4	27	7	0		.248
Kinney, Dennis, Cleveland*	14	4	0	1	1	0	0	0	0	0	0	3	0	0	0		.250
Kirkland, Ronald, Cincinnati	35	117	22	41	62	8	5	1	27	1	3	16	0	24	4	1	.350
Klinger, Stephen, Cinn*	17	8	1	3	3	0	0	0	1	1	0	0	0	1	0	0	.375
Kmet, Michael, Cincinnati†	10	13	2	3	3	6	0	0	1	1	0	3	0	4	1	0	.231
Kmet, Stanley, Cincinnati	12	9	2	2	2	0	0	0	0	0	3	0	4	1	0		.222
Knuth, Everett, Chicago	25	36	6	3	5	0	1	0	1	0	0	2	1	7	1	0	.115
Kooyman, Kevin, Cincinnati	11	31	3	7	7	0	0	0	2	0	0	2	1	6	1	0	.226
Kotowski, Mark, Tourists	46	156	21	30	35	5	0	0	14	1	2	20	1	22	5	1	.192
Lacour, Leon, Chicago	6	8	1	0	0	0	0	0	0	0	0	3	0	6	0	0	.000
Ladd, Michael, Minnesota	12	15	4	1	1	0	0	0	0	0	0	0	3	0	7	0	.067
Lang, Robert, Montreal	13	24	4	5	5	0	0	0	2	1	0	3	0	10	0	0	.208
Letsom, William, Minnesota*	12	21	0	3	3	0	0	0	0	1	0	2	0	9	0	0	.143
Lowe, David, Cleveland	19	18	3	2	2	0	0	0	0	0	0	10	0	8	0	0	.111
Machado, Omar, Cleveland	2	4	0	0	0	0	0	0	0	0	0	1	0	4	0	0	.000
Madison, Keith, Montreal	5	4	0	0	0	0	0	0	0	0	0	0	0	2	0	0	.000
Marcinik, Edward, Tourists*	36	99	8	15	20	1	2	0	7	0	0	13	1	19	0	0	.152
Marks, Gary, St. Louis†	3	5	1	1	1	0	0	0	0	0	0	0	0	1	0	0	.200
Marshall, Jerry, Minnesota	15	12	2	2	2	0	0	0	1	0	0	2	0	6	0	0	.167
Marshall, John, Tourists*	7	13	3	3	5	2	0	0	1	0	0	6	1	7	0	0	.231
Mathey, Gregory, Chicago	52	168	25	43	54	6	1	1	23	2	2	22	2	48	2	1	.256
McArthur, Joseph, Cleve	30	48	9	11	11	0	0	0	5	0	1	12	0	14	1	1	.229
McBride, Arnold, St. Louis*	17	71	15	30	46	2	4	2	13	0	0	8	1	9	5	2	.423
McCarthy, Daniel, Minnesota	5	6	0	0	0	0	0	0	0	0	0	0	0	3	0	0	.000

Player and Club	G.	AB.	R.	H.	TB.	2B.	3B.	HR.	RBI.	SH.	SF.	BB.	HP.	SO.	SB.	CS.	Pct.
McClain, Harold, Chicago* ..	15	33	7	5	7	0	1	0	1	3	0	6	0	8	0	0	.152
McCord, Donald, Montreal ..	6	2	0	0	0	0	0	0	0	0	0	0	0	0	0	0	.000
McDonald, Donzell, Tourists	31	109	14	26	41	5	5	0	8	0	0	10	1	28	2	0	.239
McDonough, Daniel, Chicago	16	43	5	10	14	2	1	0	7	0	1	13	0	11	3	1	.233
McGehee, Patrick, Cincinnati	28	77	10	14	19	2	0	1	3	1	1	6	0	34	1	3	.182
McSween, Denis, Montreal* ..	14	3	1	0	0	0	0	0	0	0	0	2	0	2	0	0	.000
Melvin, Kenneth, Tourists ..	62	240	28	74	105	15	2	4	33	1	1	16	2	39	8	6	.308
Mendoza, Mario, Tourists	47	167	21	44	53	5	2	0	21	2	3	12	1	29	3	3	.263
Mercedes, Domingo, St. Louis	16	36	5	4	4	0	0	0	2	0	0	4	1	8	3	0	.111
Mercedes, Manuel, Pittsburgh	45	139	12	32	38	6	0	0	9	0	1	23	0	37	2	4	.230
Metz, Nicholas, Minnesota ..	20	45	4	8	10	2	0	0	1	0	4	0	18	0	0	.178
Meyer, Gary, Tourists	3	9	1	2	2	0	0	0	1	0	0	1	0	1	0	0	.222
Meyers, Peter, Minnesota* ..	17	12	1	2	2	0	0	0	1	0	0	3	0	3	0	0	.167
Mitchell, Emery, Chicago ...	23	67	9	18	23	3	1	0	6	0	0	16	0	22	1	1	.269
Montilla, Victor, Cincinnati	45	141	17	34	34	0	0	0	10	1	0	23	3	37	2	2	.241
Moreno, Omar, Tourists* ...	51	219	32	51	69	7	4	1	19	0	2	11	1	44	9	1	.233
Morillo, Heriberto, Pitt	46	112	17	15	17	2	0	0	8	3	1	39	2	41	2	0	.134
Mugica, Rufino, Cleveland ..	1	1	0	0	0	0	0	0	0	0	0	0	0	1	0	0	.000
Mullinax, Allen, Montreal ...	51	178	22	52	76	5	5	3	29	1	0	19	1	33	3	0	.292
Murray, Robert, Montreal ...	54	202	39	62	82	10	2	2	36	0	4	25	4	37	4	1	.307
Newman, Jeffrey, Cleveland .	55	195	27	61	88	9	0	6	53	2	4	17	0	35	4	0	.313
Norton, Fred, Chicago	51	199	32	58	75	8	3	1	41	0	2	23	2	35	8	2	.291
Olson, Gerald, Pittsburgh ..	11	21	4	6	8	2	0	0	4	2	0	5	0	6	0	0	.286
Palas, Lee, Minnesota	4	3	0	1	1	0	0	0	0	0	0	0	0	0	0	0	.333
Parker, David, Pittsburgh* ..	61	239	34	75	107	8	3	6	41	1	2	12	4	54	6	5	.314
Pavlacka, Robert, Montreal .	5	19	3	5	6	1	0	0	3	0	0	2	0	4	0	1	.263
Peterson, Randy, Cleveland ..	11	16	0	2	2	0	0	0	4	2	1	1	0	5	0	0	.125
Pinkham, L. William, Cinn ..	33	100	7	18	24	4	1	0	6	0	0	10	1	20	2	0	.180
Plischke, Steven, Minnesota .	6	1	0	0	0	0	0	0	0	0	0	1	0	1	0	0	.000
Polanco, Ovidio, Tourists ...	45	182	37	56	68	5	2	1	20	3	1	13	2	26	19	4	.308
Pompili, Michael, Cleveland .	6	2	0	0	0	0	0	0	0	0	0	0	0	1	0	0	.000
Pope, Vincent, Cleveland* ..	26	36	2	5	6	1	0	0	1	0	0	3	1	12	1	0	.139
Queen, Dennis, Cleveland* ..	8	4	0	0	0	0	0	0	0	0	0	0	0	2	0	0	.000
Reed, Donald, St. Louis	11	7	0	0	0	0	0	0	0	0	0	1	0	5	0	0	.000
Regensberger, Michael, Tour .	7	4	0	0	0	0	0	0	0	0	0	3	0	1	0	0	.000
Reynolds, Michael, Chicago .	33	94	12	18	31	4	3	1	9	3	2	15	1	27	0	1	.191
Rivera, Jesus, Montreal	39	125	25	30	52	8	1	4	20	1	1	20	0	33	1	1	.240
Rivera, Luis, Montreal*	7	5	1	1	1	0	0	0	3	0	1	1	0	1	0	0	.200
Rodriguez, Anthony, Chi	39	139	19	28	31	1	1	0	10	3	2	8	2	18	3	1	.201
Rousseau, Arthur, Tourists ..	3	4	0	1	1	0	0	0	2	0	1	1	0	1	0	0	.250
Ruhe, David, Cleveland*	39	66	12	13	21	2	0	2	9	0	1	8	1	24	0	0	.197
Russo, Marion, Cincinnati* ..	34	121	21	36	50	2	3	2	20	1	0	12	5	21	4	0	.298
Sadowski, James, Pittsburgh	5	16	2	3	3	0	0	0	0	1	0	0	0	5	0	0	.188
St. George, John, St. Louis .	9	29	6	8	8	0	0	0	2	0	0	3	0	4	0	1	.276
Salaya, Simon, Chicago	25	86	13	20	22	2	0	0	5	1	0	8	2	13	0	1	.233
Salazar, William, Montreal ..	16	41	4	8	11	1	1	0	4	0	0	2	0	8	1	0	.195
Salyer, Ronald, Cleveland* ..	19	9	0	1	1	0	0	0	1	0	0	6	0	6	0	0	.111
Sanford, James, Pittsburgh .	3	4	0	1	1	0	0	0	2	1	0	0	0	0	0	0	.250
Sarna, Edward, Pittsburgh ..	9	12	2	2	2	0	0	0	1	0	0	2	0	6	0	0	.167
Sawatski, John, St. Louis* ..	23	67	7	13	17	4	0	0	5	0	0	7	1	5	1	1	.194
Say, Joseph, Pittsburgh	26	88	15	25	44	4	0	5	16	0	0	24	2	16	1	0	.284
Saylor, Bruce, St. Louis	5	12	1	6	10	0	2	0	3	0	0	0	0	3	2	0	.500
Saylor, David, Minnesota ...	43	84	11	20	21	1	0	0	6	0	2	18	1	13	0	0	.238
Scanlon, J. Patrick, Mont* ..	12	39	5	7	14	2	1	1	7	0	0	3	1	12	1	1	.179
Schade, Craig, Pittsburgh ..	12	7	1	0	0	0	0	0	0	0	0	4	0	7	0	0	.000
Schneider, Dean, Cleveland* .	7	12	4	5	11	1	1	1	5	0	0	4	0	4	0	0	.417
Sexton, James, Pittsburgh ..	33	113	17	32	34	2	0	0	7	0	0	23	0	19	8	3	.283
Shepard, Ricky, St. Louis* ..	13	17	3	3	4	1	0	0	1	0	0	1	0	8	0	0	.176
Shinn, James, Minnesota ...	51	175	21	48	53	5	0	0	20	0	0	23	0	17	0	0	.274
Shoup, Larry, Chicago	45	141	16	31	35	2	1	0	14	0	0	32	1	35	5	1	.220
Sievers, Robin, St. Louis* ..	6	18	3	6	7	1	0	0	3	0	1	2	0	1	0	2	.333
Simontacchi, John, Tourists*	9	20	1	6	6	0	0	0	2	0	0	0	0	5	5	0	.300
Slagle, Dennis, Pittsburgh ..	4	12	0	1	1	0	0	0	0	0	0	0	0	4	0	0	.083
Smith, Cannon, Montreal* ...	37	78	10	14	26	2	2	2	14	1	0	14	0	35	2	0	.179
Smith, Dennis, Chicago	55	155	28	44	56	10	1	0	26	0	1	36	1	37	2	1	.284
Smith, William, Cincinnati ..	36	106	10	27	37	2	1	2	14	1	1	6	2	14	0	0	.255
Steele, Ronald, Cincinnati ..	47	176	19	39	53	8	0	2	21	0	1	16	0	38	2	3	.222
Stephenson, Richard, Tour* ..	19	43	3	9	11	2	0	0	1	2	0	1	1	3	1	0	.209
Stewart, Robert, Pittsburgh .	41	149	24	38	44	4	1	0	12	1	2	19	1	14	2	1	.255
Stollmeyer, Kenneth, Tour ..	52	187	19	42	55	5	1	2	16	0	1	14	1	41	3	1	.225
Stuart, Richard, Tourists ...	31	83	8	12	14	2	0	0	6	1	1	13	0	30	0	1	.145
Suarez, Carlos, Cleveland* ..	10	1	0	0	0	0	0	0	0	0	0	0	1	0	0	.000
Sullivan, Thomas, Cleve	9	9	1	2	2	0	0	0	1	0	0	0	0	4	0	0	.222
Swaim, Ronald, Cincinnati* .	12	14	0	5	7	2	0	0	2	0	0	1	0	4	0	0	.357
Swinchock, Richard, Tourists	9	21	2	6	6	0	0	0	3	2	0	3	0	1	0	0	.286
Templeton, Stanley, St. L* ..	31	89	13	20	31	4	2	1	8	0	0	4	1	14	3	0	.225
Thompson, Robert, Cincinnati	7	1	0	0	0	0	0	0	0	0	0	1	0	0	0	0	.000
Tinsley, Keith, Montreal	36	115	17	27	38	3	4	0	12	2	1	9	2	19	4	2	.235
Todd, Stanley, Montreal	24	69	9	13	17	0	2	0	7	2	0	7	2	15	0	0	.188
Tominsian, Gregory, Cinn	6	8	1	1	1	0	0	0	1	0	0	0	0	3	0	0	.125
Trott, Terry, Cleveland‡	55	133	20	31	42	6	1	1	14	0	1	25	3	15	1	3	.233
Tucker, Gary, Cleveland* ...	56	190	43	46	59	2	4	1	17	4	1	26	2	30	9	4	.242

Player and Club	G.	AB.	R.	H.	TB.	2B.	3B.	HR.	RBI.	SH.	SF.	BB.	HP.	SO.	SB.	CS.	Pct.
Valdes, Juan, Cleveland	5	0	1	0	0	0	0	0	0	0	0	1	0	0	0	0	.000
Valenty, Jim, Cleveland ...	5	4	0	1	2	1	0	0	0	0	0	1	0	0	0	0	.250
Valenzuela, Ramon C., Mont	21	58	8	19	20	1	0	0	9	0	1	11	1	9	3	0	.328
Van Bogelen, Craig, Montreal	10	5	1	0	0	0	0	0	0	1	0	0	1	0	0	0	.000
Velez, Javier, Montreal ...	21	87	23	26	37	2	3	1	7	0	0	7	0	6	0	0	.299
Ventura, Ernesto, Tourists ..	13	17	1	3	5	0	1	0	1	1	0	2	0	9	0	1	.176
Vicente, Juan, St. Louis‡ ...	14	34	4	8	9	1	0	0	5	0	0	4	0	9	0	1	.235
Viefhaus, Randolph, Mont*	52	181	34	48	57	4	1	1	20	2	1	22	0	31	0	1	.265
Volkening, Larry, St. Louis .	2	5	0	1	1	0	0	0	2	0	0	0	0	3	0	0	.200
Wachutka, Bruce, Minnesota	51	193	17	42	58	9	2	1	28	0	2	6	4	39	2	2	.218
Wagner, Michael, Minnesota	13	27	0	6	6	0	0	0	2	1	0	2	0	7	0	0	.222
Waiss, Kenneth, Pittsburgh.	13	15	0	3	5	2	0	0	3	0	0	1	0	3	0	0	.200
Wargo, Edward, Cincinnati*.	34	123	22	29	31	2	0	0	7	2	0	17	0	19	3	0	.236
Weidman, Dennis, Chicago* .	49	160	24	37	47	1	3	1	22	0	3	23	2	51	10	3	.231
Whaley, Kennon, Pittsburgh.	13	13	0	0	0	0	0	0	0	0	0	2	0	7	0	0	.000
Wheeler, Charles, Minnesota	55	222	46	68	71	3	0	0	8	0	0	26	4	6	14	2	.306
Wheeler, Edward, St. Louis .	42	135	25	39	62	8	3	3	20	1	1	22	0	15	4	3	.289
White, Jerome, Montreal ...	55	201	32	58	75	10	2	1	16	1	0	18	4	34	8	4	.289
Whitman, Randolph, St. L...	15	16	2	5	5	0	0	0	4	1	0	3	0	3	0	1	.313
Williamson, Ronald, Cinn*..	20	55	4	7	10	1	1	0	3	0	0	3	0	26	1	0	.127
Wright, John, Minnesota ...	3	2	0	0	0	0	0	0	0	0	0	0	1	0	0	0	.000
Wright, Wallace, Montreal ..	27	93	17	25	35	7	0	1	7	2	1	8	2	24	1	0	.269
Yesenchak, Charles, Pitt ...	50	144	21	30	44	3	1	3	21	1	0	15	5	54	0	0	.208
Yetsko, Stephen, St. Louis ..	13	27	4	6	7	1	0	0	1	0	0	3	0	9	0	1	.222
Zachry, Patrick, Cincinnati .	9	17	1	2	2	0	0	0	0	0	0	2	0	8	0	1	.118

The following pitchers had no plate appearances (listed alphabetically by club, games in parentheses):

CLEVELAND—Crawford, Clifford (6).
MINNESOTA—Adams, Ronald (2); Tokash, Frank (1).
MONTREAL—Balne, Douglas* (1); Patin, Robert (6).
ST. LOUIS—Parent, Gerald (2).
GRAND-SLAM HOME RUNS—Bock, Florez, C. Smith.
AWARDED FIRST BASE ON INTERFERENCE: Ruhe (D. Saylor).

CLUB FIELDING

Club	G.	PO.	A.	E.	DP.	PB.	Pct.	Club	G.	PO.	A.	E.	DP.	PB.	Pct.
Minnesota	63	1620	638	120	45	12	.950	St. Louis	60	1535	631	142	41	11	.938
Cleveland	60	1521	619	115	32	14	.949	Montreal	63	1618	601	146	53	16	.938
Tourists	63	1570	631	133	41	16	.943	Pittsburgh	63	1569	620	154	35	30	.934
Chicago AL	60	1584	602	137	33	16	.941	Cincinnati	60	1540	517	153	35	26	.931

Triple Play—None.

INDIVIDUAL FIELDING
(Ten or More Games)

*Throws lefthanded.

FIRST BASEMEN

Player and Club	G.	PO.	A.	E.	DP.	Pct.	Player and Club	G.	PO.	A.	E.	DP.	Pct.
Gasperino, St. L*	25	167	11	1	14	.994	Cordova, Pittsburgh*	24	168	8	6	12	.967
Berry, Pittsburgh	17	125	8	1	6	.993	Mitchell, Chicago	21	155	11	6	7	.965
Ruhe, Cleveland	25	128	10	2	4	.986	Smith, Montreal*	18	117	3	5	16	.960
Clark, Tourists	11	62	2	1	1	.985	Aloway, St. Louis	13	87	6	4	6	.959
VIEFHAUS, Montreal	47	405	16	9	33	.979	Shoup, Chicago	45	351	8	17	23	.955
DeMaria, Tourists*	47	356	22	11	25	.972	Damran, Cincinnati	26	171	13	9	12	.953
Russo, Cincinnati*	32	216	21	7	15	.971	Boyd, Cincinnati	10	36	4	2		.952
Crigler, Minnesota	57	444	22	15	32	.969	Faria, St. Louis*	17	100	10	6	5	.948
Bowman, Pittsburgh*	26	198	10	7	12	.967	Cannon, Cleveland	15	100	7	7	4	.939
Newman, Cleveland	39	289	7	10	20	.967							

(Fewer Than Ten Games)

Player and Club	G.	PO.	A.	E.	DP.	Pct.	Player and Club	G.	PO.	A.	E.	DP.	Pct.
Schneider, Cleveland.	4	22	2	0	0	1.000	Pope, Cleveland	1	1	0	0	0	1.000
Say, Pittsburgh	3	15	0	0	0	1.000	Hale, St. Louis*	8	61	2	1	4	.984
Gandy, Pittsburgh .	1	9	2	0	1	1.000	Brown, Minnesota	9	54	0	1	5	.982
Simontacchi, Tour .	1	8	0	0	0	1.000	Cingle, St. Louis*	9	65	4	2	2	.972
Stephenson, Tour* ..	1	5	0	0	0	1.000	Moreno, Tourists* ..	6	50	1	3	4	.944
McGehee, Cincinnati.	2	5	0	0	0	1.000	McDonald, Tourists	7	40	2	4	1	.913
King, Cleveland ...	1	3	0	0	0	1.000	Kershaw, Montreal .	1	5	0	1	0	.833
Wachutka, Minnesota	1	2	1	0	0	1.000	Griggs, St. Louis ..	2	2	0	1	0	.667

SECOND BASEMEN

Player and Club	G.	PO.	A.	E.	DP.	Pct.	Player and Club	G.	PO.	A.	E.	DP.	Pct.
Wargo, Cincinnati ..	14	28	26	1	5	.982	Stewart, Pittsburgh	36	93	84	13	14	.932
WHEELER, Minn ..	54	170	153	11	26	.967	Diaz, St. Louis ...	52	57	68	10	15	.926
Marcinik, Tourists ..	27	46	54	4	10	.962	Trott, Cleveland ..	14	20	15	3	2	.921
King, Cleveland ...	40	60	74	6	9	.957	Florez, St. Louis ..	11	18	27	4	5	.918
Mullinax, Montreal .	50	119	111	12	32	.950	Albertson, Tourists .	10	14	18	3	2	.914
Bozich, Cleveland ..	23	30	56	5	8	.945	Clark, Tourists ...	22	42	38	8	13	.909
Berry, Pittsburgh ..	13	21	27	3	6	.941	Carlson, Minnesota .	10	28	17	5	9	.900
Montilla, Cincinnati.	17	32	31	4	4	.940	Helton, Cincinnati ..	20	39	37	17	9	.817
Hairston, Chicago ...	55	129	130	19	20	.932	Williamson, Cinn ...	17	29	31	14	4	.811

SECOND BASEMEN—Continued
(Fewer Than Ten Games)

Player and Club	G.	PO.	A.	E.	DP.	Pct.
Mendoza, Tourists	7	9	11	0	0	1.000
Gandy, Pittsburgh	3	11	4	0	0	1.000
McArthur, Cleveland	6	2	7	0	0	1.000
Pavlacka, Montreal	2	2	5	0	0	1.000
Wheeler, St. Louis	2	4	3	0	2	1.000
Cuddy, St. Louis	1	1	0	0	0	1.000
Morillo, Pittsburgh	6	11	18	1	3	.967
Dent, Chicago	3	10	12	1	3	.957
Griggs, St. Louis	9	15	22	2	2	.949
Hund, St. Louis	9	17	19	2	1	.947
Mercedes, St. Louis	3	9	6	1	1	.938
St. George, St. L	7	17	21	3	2	.927
Rodriguez, Chicago	4	6	6	1	1	.923
Bock, Montreal	3	4	5	1	1	.900
Polanco, Tourists	2	6	0	1	0	.857
Velez, Montreal	7	17	10	5	4	.844
Sexton, Pittsburgh	8	11	14	6	2	.806
Salazar, Montreal	4	7	6	4	1	.765

THIRD BASEMEN

Player and Club	G.	PO.	A.	E.	DP.	Pct.
Bock, Montreal	12	14	26	1	7	.976
Salazar, Montreal	11	8	18	2	2	.929
Clark, Tourists	20	16	41	5	2	.919
JOHNSON, Pitts	63	76	131	20	9	.912
Trott, Cleveland	36	18	54	7	5	.911
Boyd, Cincinnati	17	14	26	4	1	.909
Polanco, Tourists	29	28	60	10	4	.898
Newman, Cleveland	12	8	23	4	1	.886
Helton, Cincinnati	11	17	20	5	1	.881
McArthur, Cleveland	11	8	21	4	2	.879
Wheeler, St. Louis	24	29	36	9	5	.878
King, Cleveland	12	5	9	2	0	.875
Shinn, Minnesota	40	34	63	14	5	.874
Wright, Montreal	22	24	40	10	1	.865
Velez, Montreal	14	10	15	4	0	.862
Mathey, Chicago	39	27	75	18	3	.850
Wachutka, Minn	24	23	46	13	4	.841
Dent, Chicago	16	14	32	9	2	.836
Albertson, Tourists	17	17	26	9	4	.827
DeFreitas, Cincinnati	34	28	66	20	7	.825
Byers, St. Louis	11	5	16	5	1	.808

(Fewer Than Ten Games)

Player and Club	G.	PO.	A.	E.	DP.	Pct.
Gloede, Cleveland	8	10	15	0	0	1.000
Sievers, St. Louis	5	5	11	0	2	1.000
Cuddy, St. Louis	2	2	3	0	0	1.000
Cannon, Cleveland	3	2	3	0	0	1.000
Diaz, St. Louis	1	0	3	0	0	1.000
Sexton, Pittsburgh	1	1	0	0	0	1.000
Mercedes, St. Louis	2	2	0	0	0	1.000
Bozich, Cleveland	2	0	1	0	0	1.000
Melvin, Tourists	2	0	1	0	0	1.000
Florez, St. Louis	8	13	18	3	0	.912
Drewett, Chicago	7	2	11	2	1	.867
Scanlon, Montreal	9	12	14	5	2	.839
Kinner, St. Louis	9	8	14	8	1	.733
Kotowski, Tourists	1	0	2	1	1	.667
Marcinik, Tourists	1	1	1	1	0	.667
Yetsko, St. Louis	8	4	4	8	0	.500
Mullinax, Montreal	1	2	0	2	0	.500

SHORTSTOPS

Player and Club	G.	PO.	A.	E.	DP.	Pct.
Wargo, Cincinnati	20	19	40	3	5	.952
Polanco, Tourists	15	28	47	4	8	.949
Mendoza, Tourists	41	51	115	10	10	.943
Sexton, Pittsburgh	25	29	52	6	12	.931
CARLSON, Minn	46	68	129	15	16	.929
Jacome, Cleveland	30	39	76	9	11	.927
Knuth, Chicago	10	3	9	1	0	.923
Rodriguez, Chicago	35	51	88	12	9	.921
Mercedes, St. Louis	12	11	21	3	4	.914
Davison, Minnesota	13	19	28	5	8	.904
Albertson, Tourists	10	15	29	5	4	.898
Baez, Montreal	53	81	147	26	28	.898
Salaya, Chicago	21	30	48	9	9	.897
Montilla, Cincinnati	29	37	49	10	8	.896
Hund, St. Louis	37	53	93	18	12	.890
Bozich, Cleveland	31	43	84	18	6	.876
Helton, Cincinnati	15	28	43	12	7	.855
Wheeler, St. Louis	17	25	33	12	6	.829
Morillo, Pittsburgh	36	58	82	31	10	.819

(Fewer Than Ten Games)

Player and Club	G.	PO.	A.	E.	DP.	Pct.
Florez, St. Louis	5	10	9	0	2	1.000
McArthur, Cleveland	4	2	7	0	3	1.000
Wright, Montreal	2	4	4	0	1	1.000
Hays, Pittsburgh	1	2	1	0	0	1.000
Boyd, Cincinnati	1	1	0	0	0	1.000
Dent, Chicago	4	6	11	1	1	.944
Drewett, Chicago	3	3	7	1	1	.909
Bock, Montreal	7	14	15	3	2	.906
Shinn, Minnesota	7	7	21	3	3	.903
Stewart, Pittsburgh	6	7	8	3	0	.833
Pavlacka, Montreal	4	6	10	4	1	.800
Byers, St. Louis	2	1	6	5	1	.583
Berry, Pittsburgh	3	1	3	3	0	.571

OUTFIELDERS

Player and Club	G.	PO.	A.	E.	DP.	Pct.
McBride, St. Louis	17	27	1	0	0	1.000
McGehee, Cincinnati	20	21	1	0	0	1.000
Boyd, Cincinnati	11	21	1	0	1	1.000
GORINSKI, Minn	58	75	4	1	0	.988
Gloede, Cleveland	53	61	6	1	1	.985
Steele, Cincinnati	47	93	4	2	2	.980
Templeton, St. Louis	28	40	3	1	0	.977
Dunham, St. Louis	26	33	1	1	1	.971
Garver, St. Louis	25	31	2	1	0	.971
Valenzuela, Montreal	21	28	2	1	0	.968
Aloway, St. Louis	28	27	2	1	0	.967
Murray, Montreal	54	104	2	4	1	.964
Gandy, Pittsburgh	46	73	5	3	0	.963
Melvin, Tourists	62	113	14	5	3	.962
Stollmeyer, Tourists	49	81	6	4	1	.956
White, Montreal	52	102	5	5	2	.955
Geitner, Minnesota	59	77	7	4	3	.955
Smith, Cincinnati	11	18	3	1	1	.955
Farrow, St. Louis	21	19	2	1	0	.955
Yesenchak, Pittsburgh	45	52	7	3	1	.952
Tucker, Cleveland*	55	73	3	4	1	.950
Norton, Chicago	51	90	2	5	0	.948
Moreno, Tourists*	44	79	8	5	1	.946
Heenan, St. Louis	31	47	4	3	1	.944
Beach, Minnesota	46	75	6	5	1	.942
Heykens, Cincinnati	19	25	4	2	1	.935
Flowers, Cleveland	60	101	8	8	2	.932
Curlee, Chicago	22	26	0	2	0	.929
Parker, Pittsburgh	61	91	10	8	0	.927
Kirkland, Cincinnati	33	50	5	5	1	.917

OUTFIELDERS—Continued

Player and Club	G.	PO.	A.	E.	DP.	Pct.
Wachutka, Minnesota	25	32	1	3	0	.917
Smith, Chicago	55	80	7	8	1	.916
Kelley, Pittsburgh .	37	71	4	7	0	.915
Basey, Cincinnati* .	44	69	0	7	0	.908
Kinner, St. Louis ..	17	16	3	2	1	.905
McDonald, Tourists .	23	32	4	4	1	.897
Tinsley, Montreal ...	32	54	2	7	0	.889
Newman, Cleveland ..	10	5	3	1	0	.889
Weidman, Chicago ..	44	54	5	8	0	.881
J. Rivera, Montreal .	35	45	5	7	0	.877
Drewett, Chicago ...	13	11	1	2	0	.857

(Fewer Than Ten Games)

Player and Club	G.	PO.	A.	E.	DP.	Pct.
Downing, Chicago ..	6	13	2	0	1	1.000
Damran, Cincinnati .	6	11	1	0	0	1.000
Mathey, Chicago ...	7	9	2	0	0	1.000
Stephenson, Tour* ..	9	10	0	0	1	1.000
Simontacchi, Tour ..	4	7	0	0	0	1.000
Hopkins, Montreal ..	8	5	1	0	0	1.000
Carlson, Minnesota .	3	5	0	0	0	1.000
Cannon, Cleveland ..	4	4	0	0	0	1.000
DeMaria, Tourists* .	4	4	0	0	0	1.000
Hays, Pittsburgh ..	4	4	0	0	0	1.000
H. Cruz, St. Louis .	3	4	0	0	0	1.000
Morillo, Pittsburgh .	1	2	0	0	1	1.000
Saylor, St. Louis ...	3	3	0	0	0	1.000
Gasperino, St. Louis*	1	2	1	0	0	1.000
Bowman, Pittsburgh*	2	1	0	0	0	1.000
Brown, Minnesota ..	2	1	0	0	0	1.000
Bright, St. Louis ...	1	1	0	0	0	1.000
Buckley, Pittsburgh .	1	1	0	0	0	1.000
Sarna, Pittsburgh ..	2	1	0	0	0	1.000
McArthur, Cleveland.	4	6	0	1	0	.857
Ventura, Tourists ...	5	8	2	2	0	.833
Pope, Cleveland	9	3	1	1	0	.800
C. Cruz, St. Louis* .	3	3	0	1	0	.750
Trott, Cleveland	3	2	1	1	0	.750
Berry, Pittsburgh ..	2	0	0	1	0	.000

CATCHERS

Player and Club	G.	PO.	A.	E.	DP.	PB.	Pct.
Peterson, Cleve ...	11	57	7	0	0	3	1.000
Gustafson, Minn ..	10	26	2	0	0	1	1.000
Reynolds, Chicago.	29	236	25	1	0	8	.996
Sawatski, St. L ..	22	169	13	1	1	4	.995
Downing, Chicago.	21	154	9	1	0	2	.994
JOHNSON, Cleve.	43	259	32	2	2	6	.993
Smith, Cincinnati.	19	138	6	1	1	11	.993
Hill, St. Louis ..	27	176	24	2	5	0	.990
Say, Pittsburgh ..	24	155	22	2	1	12	.989
Kooyman, Cinn ..	10	71	3	1	1	4	.987
Hess, Minnesota .	25	126	14	2	0	3	.986
McDonough, Chi ..	14	99	8	2	0	6	.982
Foote, Montreal ..	42	268	21	7	1	16	.976
Saylor, Minn	20	99	12	6	0	3	.973
Metz, Minnesota .	20	123	11	4	1	3	.971
Kotowski, Tourists	43	269	32	9	2	12	.971
Todd, Montreal ..	22	114	15	4	0	0	.970
Mercedes, Pitt ..	43	258	29	10	0	18	.966
Pinkham, Cinn ..	31	206	10	8	2	9	.964
Vicente, St. Louis	11	68	7	3	0	4	.962
Hernandez, Cleve.	25	138	10	6	1	5	.961
Stuart, Tourists ..	22	144	19	9	3	4	.948

(Fewer Than Ten Games)

Player and Club	G.	PO.	A.	E.	DP.	PB.	Pct.
Gentile, Montreal.	3	17	2	0	0	0	1.000
Tominesian, Cin ..	6	13	1	0	0	0	1.000
Collins, Montreal.	1	8	0	0	0	0	1.000
Erickson, St. L...	1	8	0	0	0	0	1.000
Valenty, Cleve ...	1	4	0	0	0	0	1.000
Fenton, St. Louis.	5	31	1	1	0	2	.970
Boyd, Cincinnati.	6	49	1	2	0	2	.962
Ladd, Minnesota .	6	18	2	1	0	2	.952
Cope, Cleveland ..	4	14	0	1	0	0	.933
Kinner, St. Louis.	2	11	1	2	0	1	.857

PITCHERS

Player and Club	G.	PO.	A.	E.	DP.	Pct.
DeMAY, Chicago ..	11	9	10	0	1	1.000
Olson, Pittsburgh .	10	4	9	0	1	1.000
Gause, Minnesota .	11	4	8	0	0	1.000
Brooks, Chicago ...	13	2	10	0	1	1.000
Hewlett, Tourists .	11	5	6	0	0	1.000
Swaim, Cincinnati* .	12	3	8	0	0	1.000
Lowe, Cleveland ...	13	5	6	0	0	1.000
Boehning, Chicago* .	10	1	9	0	0	1.000
Byrne, Chicago* ...	13	2	8	0	1	1.000
Schade, Pittsburgh .	12	1	8	0	0	1.000
Baker, Cleveland ..	13	3	4	0	0	1.000
James, Montreal ...	11	1	5	0	0	1.000
Clemmons, Cinn ...	10	2	3	0	0	1.000
Ash, Cleveland	12	0	5	0	0	1.000
Letsom, Minnesota* .	12	1	4	0	0	1.000
Duhon, St. Louis ..	10	0	4	0	1	1.000
McSween, Montreal* .	14	1	3	0	0	1.000
Klinger, Cinn*	17	2	2	0	1	1.000
Dostaler, Montreal .	20	2	1	0	0	1.000
Edwards, Minnesota .	19	1	1	0	0	1.000
Salyer, Cleveland* .	19	1	1	0	0	1.000
Suarez, Cleveland* .	10	2	0	0	0	1.000
Auchmutey, Chicago.	14	0	1	0	0	1.000
McClain, Chicago* .	15	5	19	1	0	.960
Darnell, Cleveland .	16	4	18	1	0	.957
Wagner, Minnesota .	13	7	14	1	0	.955
Braun, Minnesota ..	13	2	12	1	1	.933
Covert, St. Louis ..	10	7	6	1	0	.929
Meyers, Minnesota*.	14	1	12	1	0	.929
Horsch, Montreal ..	13	4	21	2	1	.926
Van Bogelen, Mont .	10	2	9	1	0	.917
Hanzlik, Minnesota*.	13	1	9	1	1	.909
Johnson, Cincinnati .	10	5	4	1	0	.900
S. Kmet, Cincinnati .	12	3	6	1	0	.900
Waiss, Pittsburgh ..	12	0	9	1	0	.900
Gregory, St. Louis* .	12	0	8	1	0	.889
Marshall, Minnesota.	15	2	6	1	0	.889
Whitman, St. Louis .	15	2	12	2	0	.875
Burkert, Cleveland* .	10	2	5	1	0	.875
Bosley, Tourists ...	11	4	3	1	0	.875
Gomez, Montreal* ..	13	0	7	1	0	.875
Shepard, St. Louis* .	13	6	14	3	0	.870
Collins, Cincinnati .	17	3	9	2	0	.857
Cooper, Chicago ...	10	1	5	1	0	.857
Haugen, Minnesota .	10	1	5	1	0	.857
M. Kmet, Cinn	10	4	2	1	0	.857
Denny, St. Louis ...	11	1	5	1	0	.857
Kinney, Cleveland* .	14	2	4	1	0	.857
Jackson, Chicago* ..	14	1	16	3	0	.850
Johnson, St. Louis .	11	1	10	2	0	.846
Whaley, Pittsburgh .	13	5	11	3	0	.842
Buckley, Pittsburgh .	11	2	8	2	0	.833
Reed, St. Louis	11	1	4	1	0	.833
Kelley, Cleveland* .	19	0	5	1	0	.833
Dirks, Tourists* ...	11	4	15	4	0	.826
Alcala, Cincinnati .	11	4	14	4	0	.818
Hays, Pittsburgh ..	15	3	6	2	0	.818
Andujar, Cincinnati .	12	6	9	3	1	.813
Blake, Cleveland ...	12	0	16	4	1	.800
Cummins, Minnesota.	12	0	4	1	0	.800
Brown, Pittsburgh ..	11	2	1	1	0	.750
Cunningham, Chi* ..	12	1	4	2	0	.714
Berdell, Chicago ...	11	2	5	3	0	.700
Lang, Montreal	13	0	13	7	0	.650

PITCHERS—Continued
(Fewer Than Ten Games)

Player and Club	G.	PO.	A.	E.	DP.	Pct.	Player and Club	G.	PO.	A.	E.	DP.	Pct.
Jackson, Montreal ...	8	2	17	0	1	1.000	Hagadorn, Cincinnati	2	0	1	0	0	1.000
Abram, Tourists	8	0	9	0	1	1.000	Hockett, Cleveland* .	2	0	1	0	0	1.000
Auger, St. Louis	9	3	6	0	1	1.000	Machado, Cleveland .	2	1	0	0	0	1.000
Kehoe, Minnesota ..	6	1	7	0	0	1.000	Parent, St. Louis ...	2	1	0	0	0	1.000
Johnson, Tourists ...	4	0	7	0	0	1.000	Stuart, Tourists	1	0	1	0	0	1.000
Branch, St. Louis ...	8	1	5	0	1	1.000	Gunter, Pittsburgh ..	7	1	11	1	0	.923
Key, St. Louis	3	2	3	0	0	1.000	Clites, Tourists	7	5	10	2	0	.882
Meyer, Tourists	3	2	3	0	0	1.000	Sadowski, Pittsburgh.	4	3	4	1	0	.875
Valdes, Cleveland ..	5	1	4	0	1	1.000	Estrellas, Pitt*	9	1	6	1	0	.875
Stephenson, Tour* ..	9	0	4	0	0	1.000	Currence, Pitt*	8	1	12	2	1	.867
Marks, St. Louis* ..	3	1	3	0	0	1.000	Ker, Montreal	8	1	11	2	1	.857
Fuller, St. Louis ...	4	1	3	0	1	1.000	Ventura, Tourists ...	8	4	1	1	0	.833
Kershaw, Montreal ..	4	2	2	0	0	1.000	Regensberger, Tour ..	7	0	5	1	1	.833
Queen, Cleveland* ..	5	2	2	0	0	1.000	Zachry, Cincinnati ..	9	3	10	3	0	.813
Anderson, St. Louis ..	6	2	2	0	0	1.000	Sarna, Pittsburgh ...	7	1	7	2	0	.800
L. Rivera, Montreal*	7	1	3	0	1	1.000	Gossage, Chicago ...	3	0	4	1	1	.800
Brown, Chicago* ...	1	1	2	0	1	1.000	Marshall, Tourists* .	7	2	8	3	2	.769
Volkening, St. Louis.	2	1	2	0	0	1.000	Patin, Montreal	6	0	3	1	1	.750
Madison, Montreal ..	5	1	2	0	0	1.000	Swincheck, Tourists*	9	2	3	2	0	.714
McCord, Montreal ...	6	1	2	0	0	1.000	Slagle, Pittsburgh ..	3	1	3	2	0	.667
DeZuba, Tourists ...	7	1	2	0	0	1.000	Thompson, Cinn* ...	7	1	1	1	0	.667
Plischke, Minnesota .	6	0	2	0	0	1.000	Browning, St. Louis.	2	0	3	2	1	.600
Favreau, Montreal ..	3	1	1	0	0	1.000	Evans, Montreal	7	3	0	3	0	.500
Kimak, St. Louis ...	1	1	1	0	0	1.000	Sullivan, Cleveland .	9	0	3	3	0	.500
Parker, Pittsburgh ..	1	1	1	0	0	1.000	Crawford, Cleveland .	6	1	0	1	0	.500
Pompili, Cleveland ..	6	0	1	0	0	1.000	Davis, St. Louis	7	0	1	1	0	.500
Coltin, Montreal	3	0	1	0	1	1.000	McCarthy, Minnesota	5	0	3	3	1	.400
Rousseau, Tourists ..	3	0	1	0	0	1.000	Palas, Minnesota* ..	4	0	1	2	0	.333
Sanford, Pittsburgh .	3	0	1	0	0	1.000	Bedard, Pittsburgh .	4	0	0	4	0	.000
Wright, Minnesota* .	3	0	1	0	0	1.000							

The following players do not have any recorded accepted chances at the positions indicated; therefore, are not listed in the fielding averages for those particular positions: Adams, p; Balne, p; Beyersdorf, p; Bowman*, p; DeLuna, utility; Hayes, of; Kerr, p; Lacour, of; Mugica, ph; Ruhe, p; Simontacchi, p; Tokash, p; Williamson, p.

CLUB PITCHING

Club	G.	CG.	ShO.	Sv.	IP.	H.	R.	ER.	HR.	BB.	Int. BB.	HB.	SO.	WP.	Bk.	ERA.
Tourists	63	29	2	3	523	442	264	175	10	286	8	23	389	41	13	3.01
Cincinnati	60	13	5	10	513	498	296	174	17	258	20	19	445	14	11	3.05
St. Louis	60	10	2	20	512	426	255	177	12	241	2	22	441	56	7	3.11
Montreal	63	14	5	16	539	509	283	197	21	238	3	34	391	43	4	3.29
Minnesota	63	9	2	17	540	507	273	203	17	265	19	17	478	33	9	3.38
Cleveland	60	14	6	14	507	481	267	195	12	197	8	14	446	44	5	3.46
Chicago AL	60	20	9	11	528	506	287	215	14	251	7	29	471	29	8	3.66
Pittsburgh	63	25	2	4	523	534	347	244	11	256	6	21	411	55	8	4.20

PITCHERS' RECORDS
(Leading Qualifiers for Earned-Run Average Leadership—63 or More Innings)
*Throws lefthanded.

Pitcher—Club	G.	GS.	CG.	ShO.	W.	L.	Sv.	Pct.	IP.	H.	R.	ER.	HR.	BB.	Int. BB.	HB.	SO.	WP.	ERA.
McClain, Chicago* .15	12	6	3	10	2	0		.833	92	53	27	13	0	38	1	5	108	4	1.27
Ker, Montreal 8	8	3	0	6	1	0		.857	63	43	19	9	1	33	1	3	43	9	1.29
Blake, Cleveland ..15	7	4	1	6	1	2		.857	70	62	22	14	0	10	0	1	62	1	1.80
Currence, Pitt* 8	8	6	0	4	4	0		.500	66	56	34	18	1	32	0	2	70	8	2.45
Wagner, Minnesota .13	11	3	0	6	2	0		.750	77	72	33	24	0	32	0	1	80	2	2.81
Alcala, Cincinnati ..11	10	2	1	4	6	0		.400	72	74	34	24	2	40	2	1	54	3	3.00
Darnell, Cleveland .16	8	2	2	5	3	1		.625	63	58	31	21	0	20	1	1	51	2	3.00
Hanzlik, Minn* ...13	10	0	0	5	4	0		.556	67	64	32	23	3	19	0	1	55	0	3.09
Horsch, Montreal ..13	12	6	2	8	2	0		.800	86	72	39	30	2	16	0	2	47	0	3.14
Olson, Pittsburgh ..10	10	5	0	3	2	0		.333	66	66	37	23	0	24	2	6	39	4	3.14

Departmental Leaders: G—Dostaler, 20; GS—Lang, 13; CG—Abram, Currence, Horsch, McClain, 6; ShO—DeMay, McClain, 3; W—McClain, 10; L—Dirks, Lang, Whaley, 7; Sv—Dostaler, Edwards, 7; Pct.—Blake, Boehning, Ker, .857; IP—McClain, 92; H—Andujar, 86; R—Andujar, 58; ER—Andujar, 38; HR—Boehning, Salyer, 4; BB—Dirks 57; IBB—Braun, 6; HB—Byrne, Jackson (Montreal), Olson, 6; SO—McClain, 108; WP—Baker, 12.

(All Pitchers—Listed Alphabetically)

Pitcher—Club	G.	GS.	CG.	ShO.	W.	L.	Sv.	Pct.	IP.	H.	R.	ER.	HR.	BB.	Int. BB.	HB.	SO.	WP.	ERA.
Abram, Tourists 8	7	6	0	5	2	1	0	.714	60	55	32	22	1	29	0	2	50	2	3.30
Adams, Minnesota* .2	2	0	0	0	1	0	0	.000	5	11	11	11	2	6	0	0	1	2	19.80
Alcala, Cincinnati ..11	10	2	1	4	6	0	0	.400	72	74	34	24	2	40	2	1	54	3	3.00
Anderson, St. Louis .8	2	0	0	0	2	0	0	.000	12	24	23	19	0	18	0	0	6	0	14.25
Andujar, Cinn 12	12	4	1	3	5	0		.375	82	86	58	38	2	56	1	2	88	2	4.17
Ash, Cleveland 12	3	1	0	1	2	3		.333	30	32	18	17	1	6	1	2	31	2	5.10

Pitcher—Club	G	GS	CG	ShO	W	L	Sv.	Pct.	IP	H	R	ER	HR	BB	Int. BB	HB	SO	WP	ERA
Auchmutey, Chi ...14	14	1	0	0	2	1	3	.667	29	36	13	11	1	10	2	1	28	0	3.41
Auger, St. Louis ... 9	9	6	2	0	1	1	0	.500	43	36	15	11	2	11	0	0	45	1	2.30
Baker, Cleveland ..13	13	6	0	0	2	2	0	.500	38	30	27	22	1	28	0	1	30	12	5.21
Balne, Montreal* .. 1	1	0	0	0	0	0	0	.000	⅔	1	3	3	0	3	1	2	0	0	40.50
Bedard, Pittsburgh . 4	4	0	0	0	0	0	0	.000	13	15	8	8	0	10	0	1	5	3	5.54
Berdell, Chicago ..11	11	8	2	0	0	5	0	.000	50	50	35	24	3	27	0	2	33	0	4.32
Beyersdorf, Cleve .. 4	4	0	0	0	2	1	0	.667	6	8	8	8	0	4	0	0	4	2	12.00
Blake, Cleveland ..15	15	7	4	1	6	1	2	.857	70	62	22	14	0	10	0	1	62	1	1.80
Boehning, Chi* ...10	10	8	4	2	6	1	0	.857	60	56	23	17	4	24	0	0	48	1	2.55
Bosley, Tourists ..11	11	3	1	0	2	1	1	.667	46	36	14	9	2	14	2	1	16	1	1.76
Bowman, Pitt* 2	2	0	0	0	0	0	0	.000	2	1	4	2	0	6	0	0	2	1	9.00
Branch, St. Louis . 8	8	4	0	0	2	1	1	.667	21	20	16	13	1	24	0	4	13	6	5.57
Braun, Minnesota .13	13	4	0	0	0	3	0	.000	44	35	24	15	1	27	6	2	22	2	3.07
Brooks, Chicago ..13	13	0	0	0	2	3	1	.400	42	50	37	31	0	29	0	2	33	4	6.64
Brown, Chicago* .. 1	1	0	0	0	0	0	0	.000	4	6	4	2	0	3	0	0	3	0	4.50
Brown, Pittsburgh .11	11	0	0	0	0	1	0	.000	16	22	23	18	1	17	0	1	9	2	10.13
Browning, StL 2	2	2	0	0	1	0	0	1.000	9	2	0	0	0	3	0	0	11	0	0.00
Buckley, Pitt 11	11	4	1	1	3	4	0	.429	44	41	32	21	1	27	1	3	28	10	4.30
Burkett, Cleve* ...10	10	8	1	0	2	0	0	1.000	33	38	21	13	0	14	0	0	27	4	3.55
Byrne, Chicago* ...13	13	5	1	0	3	2	3	.600	47	44	24	22	0	14	0	6	56	1	4.21
Clemmons, Cinn ...10	10	9	3	1	4	4	0	.500	58	53	28	19	3	21	1	4	45	2	2.95
Clites, Tourists ... 7	7	3	0	0	2	2	0	.500	51	42	28	17	1	23	0	1	40	3	3.00
Collins, Cinn 17	17	0	0	0	2	2	4	.500	34	31	16	12	2	10	1	1	31	0	3.18
Coltin, Montreal .. 3	3	0	0	0	0	1	0	.000	16	11	5	4	0	14	0	2	10	2	2.25
Cooper, Chicago ..10	10	4	1	0	1	2	0	.333	26	34	23	18	1	13	0	2	12	2	6.22
Covert, St. Louis ..10	10	5	2	0	2	3	0	.400	37	35	24	17	2	31	0	2	29	10	4.14
Crawford, Cleve .. 6	6	0	0	0	0	1	0	.000	6	4	3	1	0	4	0	0	7	2	1.50
Cummins, Minn ...12	12	0	0	0	2	1	2	.667	17	14	9	7	2	9	2	3	8	1	3.71
Cunningham, Chi* .12	12	0	0	0	2	1	2	.333	20	26	18	14	1	17	1	1	17	5	6.30
Currence, Pitt* .. 8	8	6	0	0	4	4	0	.500	66	56	34	18	1	32	0	2	70	8	2.45
Darnell, Cleveland .16	16	8	2	2	5	3	1	.625	63	58	31	21	0	20	1	1	51	2	3.00
Davis, St. Louis .. 7	7	0	0	0	1	0	0	1.000	19	6	4	2	0	9	0	2	9	2	0.95
DeLuna, Minn* 1	1	0	0	0	0	0	0	.000	⅔	1	0	0	0	1	0	0	0	0	0.00
DeMay, Chicago ...11	11	8	4	3	7	2	0	.778	75	73	34	28	1	32	1	5	50	9	3.36
Denny, St. Louis ..11	11	5	1	0	2	2	2	.500	42	32	14	6	0	9	0	2	43	3	1.29
DeZuba, Tourists .. 7	7	1	1	0	1	1	2	.500	15	11	5	3	0	7	0	1	11	1	1.80
Dirks, Tourists* ..11	11	11	4	0	3	7	0	.300	69	54	44	32	0	57	3	5	55	11	4.17
Dostaler, Montreal .20	20	1	0	0	1	1	7	.500	32	24	14	9	1	11	0	1	41	3	2.53
Duhon, St. Louis ..10	10	4	0	0	3	1	0	.750	45	51	22	21	2	17	1	1	32	4	4.20
Edwards, Minn ...19	19	0	0	0	2	2	7	.500	24	23	14	13	1	16	4	2	28	7	4.88
Estrellas, Pitt* ... 9	9	2	0	0	0	2	0	.000	24	19	16	11	0	19	0	0	17	0	4.13
Evans, Montreal .. 7	7	0	0	0	4	0	0	.000	30	34	27	21	2	21	0	1	20	2	6.30
Favreau, Montreal . 3	3	0	0	0	0	0	0	.000	6	11	8	2	1	2	0	0	3	0	3.00
Fuller, St. Louis .. 4	4	2	0	0	0	0	0	.000	15	11	4	3	0	0	0	1	11	1	1.80
Gaines, Minnesota . 4	4	0	0	0	0	0	0	.000	5	5	1	1	0	1	0	0	2	0	1.80
Gomez, Montreal* .13	13	1	0	0	3	0	1	1.000	23	23	4	4	0	11	3	1	23	0	1.57
Gossage, Chicago .. 3	3	3	0	0	0	0	0	.000	16	11	6	5	1	4	0	3	21	1	2.81
Gregory, St. Louis* .12	12	8	1	0	3	4	2	.429	54	44	33	19	0	25	0	4	53	7	3.17
Gunter, Pitt 7	7	1	0	0	2	2	0	.500	39	34	25	18	1	25	0	3	48	7	4.15
Hagadorn, Cinn ... 2	2	0	0	0	0	1	0	.000	5	4	3	2	0	6	1	0	4	0	3.60
Hanzlik, Minn* ...13	13	10	0	0	5	6	4	.556	67	64	32	23	3	19	0	1	55	0	3.09
Haugen, Minnesota .10	10	3	1	1	2	1	2	.667	38	27	14	11	1	8	0	0	30	3	2.61
Hays, Pittsburgh ..15	15	1	0	0	2	2	0	.000	36	30	25	19	1	11	1	0	20	5	6.58
Hewlett, Tourists ..11	11	6	1	1	3	2	0	.500	42	38	17	13	2	16	1	1	38	1	2.79
Hockett, Cleve* ... 2	2	1	1	1	1	0	0	1.000	9	4	0	0	0	0	0	1	9	0	0.00
Horsch, Montreal ..13	13	12	6	2	8	2	0	.800	86	72	39	30	2	16	0	2	47	0	3.14
Jackson, Chicago* ..14	14	11	2	0	4	4	4	.500	67	67	43	30	2	40	2	2	62	2	4.03
Jackson, Montreal . 8	8	8	2	2	4	2	0	.667	48	36	19	12	2	22	0	6	33	2	2.25
James, Montreal ...10	10	1	0	0	3	0	0	1.000	23	28	11	7	1	2	0	1	8	0	2.74
Johnson, Cinn 10	10	8	0	0	2	3	0	.000	49	46	32	18	2	23	1	1	22	1	3.31
Johnson, St. Louis .11	11	2	0	0	3	3	1	.250	30	26	21	13	2	25	0	1	25	3	3.90
Johnson, Tourists .. 4	4	3	3	0	1	2	0	.333	33	22	14	9	0	21	0	1	26	4	2.45
Kehoe, Minnesota .. 6	6	2	0	0	2	1	0	.667	27	32	13	11	2	13	0	0	14	0	3.67
Kelley, Cleveland* .19	19	2	0	0	1	4	2	.200	33	36	21	16	0	15	1	3	33	6	4.36
Ker, Montreal 8	8	8	3	0	6	1	0	.857	63	43	19	9	1	33	1	3	43	9	1.29
Kerr, Cincinnati .. 2	2	0	0	0	0	0	0	.000	5	12	8	3	0	2	0	1	2	0	5.40
Kershaw, Montreal . 4	4	1	0	0	1	1	0	.500	19	17	10	7	0	8	0	0	18	2	3.32
Key, St. Louis ... 3	3	1	0	0	2	1	0	.667	10	9	3	2	0	2	0	1	9	0	1.80
Kimak, St. Louis .. 1	1	0	0	0	0	0	0	.000	1	1	0	0	0	0	0	0	1	0	0.00
Kinney, Cleveland* .14	14	2	0	0	3	2	0	.600	31	21	11	6	0	18	0	1	35	2	1.74
Klinger, Cinn* ...17	17	1	0	0	3	1	1	.750	28	15	11	7	0	12	0	1	25	1	2.93
M. Kmet, Cinn ...10	10	8	0	0	3	4	0	.429	35	29	24	12	2	17	4	0	31	0	3.09
S. Kmet, Cinn ...12	12	1	0	0	3	1	2	.750	28	15	14	10	1	22	1	2	35	1	2.93
Lang, Montreal ...13	13	13	2	0	2	7	0	.222	74	70	42	33	3	29	0	5	71	8	4.01
Letsom, Minnesota* 12	12	11	1	0	4	2	0	.667	57	46	24	15	1	41	0	3	59	6	3.00
Lowe, Cleveland ..13	13	9	3	1	5	3	0	.625	59	52	23	18	2	12	1	2	48	3	2.75
Machado, Cleve ... 2	2	1	1	1	1	0	0	1.000	11	8	0	0	0	1	0	0	11	0	0.00
Madison, Montreal . 5	5	0	0	0	2	0	0	1.000	14	7	2	2	1	7	0	1	9	2	1.29
Marks, St. Louis* .. 3	3	2	0	0	1	0	0	1.000	14	14	6	5	0	4	0	1	6	1	4.09
Marshall, Minn ...15	15	6	0	0	2	5	3	.286	48	53	27	21	3	18	1	2	41	2	3.94
Marshall, Tourists*. 7	7	7	0	0	1	1	0	.500	47	37	26	15	0	50	0	1	30	5	2.87

Pitcher—Club	G	GS	CG	ShO	W	L	Sv	Pct.	IP	H	R	ER	HR	BB	Int.BB	HB	SO	WP	ERA
McCarthy, Minn .. 5	2	2	0	2	0	1		1.000	22	22	10	7	0	9	2	0	31	0	2.86
McClain, Chicago* .15	12	6	3		10	2	0	.833	92	53	27	13	0	38	1	5	108	4	1.27
McCord, Montreal .. 6	1	0	0	0	1	0		1.000	13	14	8	4	2	5	0	1	6	1	2.77
McSween, Mont* ..14	5	0	0	2	3			.500	28	24	13	10	0	13	1	2	33	3	3.21
Meyer, Tourists 3	3	2	0	1	2	0		.333	20	21	12	12	0	9	0	0	15	2	5.40
Meyers, Minnesota*.14	7	0	0	3	5	1		.375	54	47	35	18	0	32	0	1	59	4	3.00
Olson, Pittsburgh .10	5	0		3	6	0		.333	66	66	37	23	0	24	2	6	39	4	3.14
Palas, Minnesota* . 4	1	0	0	1	0			1.000	13	16	9	6	0	9	1	0	8	3	4.15
Parent, St. Louis .. 2	0	0	0	0	0			.000	2	2	0	0	0	3	0	0	3	0	0.00
Parker, Pittsburgh . 1	0	0	0	0	0			.000	4	7	2	2	0	1	0	0	2	0	4.50
Patin, Montreal 6	0	0		1	0			1.000	12	13	12	9	0	14	0	2	10	3	6.75
Pischke, Minn 6	1	0	0	0	2	0		.000	14	11	8	7	0	9	0	1	11	1	4.50
Pompili, Cleve 6	2	0	0	0	0			.000	9	14	6	6	0	5	0	0	6	1	6.00
Queen, Cleveland* .. 5	2	0		1	1			.500	15	12	12	10	0	19	0	1	19	2	6.00
Reed, St. Louis ...11	2	0		1	1	5		.500	30	25	16	9	2	11	0	0	26	4	2.70
Regensberger, Tour 7	2	0	0	2	0			.000	19	17	13	10	0	11	1	2	13	3	4.74
L. Rivera, Montreal* 7	5	0	0	2	1			.667	22	27	17	15	1	15	0	2	13	2	6.14
Rousseau, Tourists . 3	1	1	0	1	0			1.000	13	7	3	2	1	6	0	0	8	2	1.38
Ruhe, Cleveland ... 1	0	0	0	0	0			.000	1	1	2	1	0	1	0	0	0	0	9.00
Sadowski, Pitt ... 4	4	0		3	1	0		.750	33	25	13	10	1	8	0	0	32	2	2.73
Salyer, Cleveland* .19	3	0	0	1	0			1.000	43	43	27	18	4	11	2	0	31	0	3.56
Sanford, Pitt 3	0	0	0	1	0			1.000	11	8	3	3	0	1	0	0	11	0	2.45
Sarna, Pittsburgh . 7	2	2		2	1			.667	26	32	20	12	2	9	0	0	13	1	4.15
Schade, Pitt 12	3	1	0	2	4	0		.333	35	42	30	27	1	8	0	1	24	1	6.94
Shepard, St. Louis*.13	7	2	0	3	5	1		.375	60	44	34	25	1	33	1	1	52	11	3.75
Simontacchi, Tour . 1	0	0	0	0				.000	3	5	5	1	0	4	0	1	0		3.00
Slagle, Pittsburgh . 3	3	2	1	1	2	0		.333	21	19	9	7	0	11	0	1	15	3	3.00
Stephenson, Tour*.. 9	2	1	0	1	4	0		.200	30	31	17	10	0	9	1	1	30	0	3.00
Stuart, Tourists ... 1	0	0	0	0	0			.000	2	0	0	0	0	2	0	1	0	0	0.00
Suarez, Cleveland* .10	1	0	0	1	2	1		.333	14	12	10	5	0	10	1	0	14	3	3.21
Sullivan, Cleve 9	5	1	0	2	4	1		.333	29	26	15	11	1	17	1	1	31	0	3.41
Swaim, Cincinnati*.12	3	1		3	4	1		.429	37	37	18	9	1	17	3	1	32	3	3.19
Swinchock, Tour* .. 9	3	1		3	4	1		.429	57	40	23	10	1	24	0	3	46	6	1.58
Thompson, Cinn* .. 7	0	0	0	0	1			.000	11	10	6	6	0	12	0	1	13	0	4.91
Tokash, Minn 1	0	0	0	0	0			.000	1	2	3	3	0	4	0	0	0	0	27.00
Valdes, Cleveland .. 5	0	0	0	0	0			.000	7	14	11	9	3	3	0	1	6	1	11.57
Van Bogelen, Mon 10	1	0		1	4	3		.200	24	35	19	12	1	13	0	1	12	1	4.50
Ventura, Tourists .. 8	0	0		1	5	0		.167	18	26	11	10	2	4	1	3	10	0	5.00
Volkening, StL 2	0	0		2	0			1.000	12	7	2	1	0	0	0	0	14	0	0.75
Wagner, Minnesota .13	3	0		6	2	0		.750	77	72	33	24	0	32	0	1	80	2	2.81
Waiss, Pittsburgh .12	11	0	0	0	4	1		.000	47	64	35	25	0	19	0	0	39	6	4.79
Whaley, Pitt 13	5	2	0	2	7	0		.222	51	53	31	20	2	28	2	3	37	2	3.53
Whitman, StL 15	6	2	0	4	2	5		.667	55	35	16	11	0	19	0	2	46	3	1.80
Williamson, Cinn .. 1	0	0	0	0	0			.000	1	0	0	0	0	1	0	0	1	0	0.00
Wright, Minnesota*. 3	1	0	0	0	0			.000	8	8	3	3	1	1	0	0	8	0	3.38
Zachry, Cinn 9	8	3	0	1	4	0		.200	54	53	29	15	3	24	4	4	55	1	2.50

BALKS—Alcala, Braun, 4 each; Brooks, Byrne, Clites, Dirks, Edwards, Gregory, Horsch, Jackson (Chi), Johnson (Cinn) Regensberger, Sadowski, Swaim, Whaley, 2 each; Abram, Anderson, Boehning, Browning, Buckley, Clemmons, Collins, Cunningham, Denny, DeZuba, Dostaler, Estrellas, Hanzlik, Kelley, Ker, Kerr, Kinney, Letsom, Marks, Meyer, Meyers, Parent, Queen, Salyer, Schade, Simontacchi, Stephenson, Sullivan, Swinchock, Ventura, Waiss, 1 each.

COMBINATION SHUTOUTS—Boehning-Auchmutey, Chicago; Alcala-Collins, Clemmons—S. Kmet, Cincinnati; Hanzlik-McCarthy, Minnesota; Ker-L. Rivera, Montreal; Browning-Gregory, St. Louis.

NO-HIT GAME—Horsch, Montreal, defeated Pittsburgh, 6-0, August 28 (7 innings).

ALONG THE MINOR LEAGUE TRAIL . . . .

(Continued from page 583)

man, didn't get clipped, but he got clipped. The team was told to get all long hair shortened or be fined by Manager Rac Slider. All but Tom did it —he didn't think he needed one. Next day, he tucked his hair under his cap and went through a heated warmup session. His wet locks fell down and covered his eyes. Slider clipped him $5. . . . When something big comes down the road, you get out of the way or get run over. Mobile

(Continued on page 601)

Pioneer League

ROOKIE CLASSIFICATION

CHAMPIONSHIP WINNERS IN PREVIOUS YEARS

1939—Twin Falls* .... .581
1940—Salt Lake City .... .608
     Ogden (4th)* .... .492
1941—Boise .... .623
     Ogden (2nd)* .... .598
1942—Pocatello† .... .690
     Boise .... .683
1943-44-45—Did not operate
1946—Twin Falls‡ .... .585
     Salt Lake City† ... .585
1947—Salt Lake City .... .618
     Twin Falls† .... .600
1948—Pocatello .... .611
     Twin Falls (2nd)* .595
1949—Twin Falls .... .624
     Pocatello (3rd)* ... .595

1950—Pocatello .... .635
     Billings (3rd)* .... .571
1951—Salt Lake City .... .618
     Great Falls (3rd)* . .559
1952—Pocatello .... .595
     Idaho Falls (2nd)* . .573
1953—Ogden .... .679
     Salt Lake C. (4th)* .527
1954—Salt Lake City .... .595
     Great Falls (4th)* . .530
1955—Boise .... .588
     Magic Valley (4th)* .489
1956—Boise .... .561
1957—Salt Lake City .... .650
     Billings† .... .582
1958—Great Falls .... .582
     Boise† .... .615

1959—Boise .... .633
     Billings (2nd)* .... .523
1960—Boise† .... .686
     Idaho Falls .... .650
1961—Boise .... .638
     Great Falls* .... .571
1962—Boise§ .... .565
     Billings† .... .706
1963—Idaho Falls .... .702
     Magic Valley† ...... .643
1964—Treasure Valley ... .615
1965—Treasure Valley ... .530
1966—Ogden .... .591
1967—Ogden .... .621
1968—Ogden .... .609
1969—Ogden .... .620

*Won four-club playoff. †Won split-season playoff. ‡Ended first half in tie with Salt Lake City and won one-game playoff. §Ended first-half in tie with Billings and Great Falls and won playoff.

STANDING OF CLUBS AT CLOSE OF SEASON, SEPTEMBER 2

Club	I.F.	Ogd.	M.V.	Bil.	Cald.	G.F.	W.	L.	T.	Pct.	G.B.
Idaho Falls (3*)	..	6	7	9	10	12	44	26	0	.629	...
Ogden (17)	8	..	8	6	10	11	43	27	0	.614	1
†Magic Valley (13)	7	6	..	9	10	9	41	29	0	.586	3
Billings (7*)	5	8	5	..	9	10	37	33	0	.529	7
Caldwell (14)	4	4	4	5	..	6	23	47	0	.386	21
Great Falls (24)	2	3	5	4	8	..	22	48	0	.314	22

†Magic Valley club represented Twins Falls, Idaho, and surrounding towns.
Key to major league farm teams (indicated by numbers after clubs in standing) shown on Page 384.
Playoff—None.
Regular-Season Attendance—Billings, 21,007; Caldwell, 15,670; Great Falls, 20,217; Idaho Falls, 39,361; Ogden, 33,669; Twin Falls, 17,657. Total, 147,581. No playoff. No all-star game.
Managers: Billings—Dave Pavlesic; Caldwell—Spencer (Sparky) Davis; Great Falls—Harvey Koepf; Idaho Falls—Bob Clear; Magic Valley—Paul Snyder; Ogden—Buddy Hollowell.
All-Star Team: 1B—Ortenzio, Billings; 2B—Mixon, Ogden; 3B—Mengo, Magic Valley; SS—Granville, Idaho Falls; OF—Nettles, Idaho Falls; Owens, Billings; Daniels, Ogden; C—Smith, Billings; Lombardo, Great Falls; P—Lange, Idaho Falls; Raible, Ogden; Manager—None named.

(Compiled by William J. Weiss, League Statistician, San Mateo, Calif.)

CLUB BATTING

Club	G.	AB.	R.	OR.	H.	TB.	2B.	3B.	HR.	RBI.	SH.	SF.	Int. BB.	BB.	HP.	SO.	SB.	CS.	LOB.	Pct.
Ogden	70	2363	432	311	624	874	118	30	24	352	18	20	335	9	27	520	128	31	543	.264
Billings	70	2337	384	354	606	844	80	25	36	299	26	26	292	2	23	530	147	37	505	.259
Idaho Falls ..	70	2358	398	356	602	848	85	28	35	325	18	11	300	4	28	719	91	26	537	.255
Magic Valley	70	2381	455	434	603	893	95	18	53	357	6	8	412	5	28	612	69	22	576	.253
Great Falls ..	70	2265	296	443	533	736	70	17	33	234	10	15	277	3	11	624	54	25	508	.235
Caldwell	70	2336	379	446	547	749	61	24	31	316	20	25	404	10	18	676	85	18	581	.234

INDIVIDUAL BATTING

(Leading Qualifiers for Batting Championship—217 or More Plate Appearances)
*Bats lefthanded. †Switch-hitter.

Player and Club	G.	AB.	R.	H.	TB.	2B.	3B.	HR.	RBI.	SH.	SF.	BB.	HP.	SO.	SB.	CS.	Pct.
Nettles, Morris, Idaho F* ..	52	203	43	75	106	10	6	3	29	0	0	35	2	54	23	1	.369
Daniels, Joe, Ogden*	56	181	40	65	88	6	4	3	43	0	2	31	3	50	12	3	.359
Granville, Gary, Idaho F ..	68	260	57	88	132	15	1	9	39	0	1	34	5	33	12	6	.338
Mixon, Elmer, Ogden	70	273	70	88	137	21	8	4	36	2	2	41	9	48	15	3	.322
Ortenzio, Frank, Billings ..	58	190	45	60	105	11	2	10	26	0	2	30	5	50	9	1	.316
Ruiz, Manuel, Magic Valley	63	225	47	71	101	12	3	4	24	0	0	33	3	33	10	1	.316
Prest, David, Great Falls ..	68	221	44	68	115	15	1	10	39	0	0	24	0	46	7	2	.308
Wohlford, James, Billings ..	62	221	42	68	88	7	2	3	37	0	2	25	2	17	32	7	.308
Briggs, Dan, Idaho Falls* ..	62	190	44	58	83	11	1	4	34	0	0	27	7	52	5	1	.305
Mengo, Marc, Magic Valley .	70	282	53	86	138	10	3	12	59	0	1	38	4	46	3	1	.305

Departmental Leaders: G—J. Hughes, Mengo, Mixon, Pierce, Schuldies, 70; AB—Schuldies, 297; R—Mixon, 70; H—Granville, Mixon, 88; TB—Mengo, 138; 2B—Mixon, 21; 3B—Mixon, 8; HR—Mengo, 12; RBI—Mengo, 59; SH—Davis, 5; SF—Odom, 8; BB—Cox, 59; HP—Mixon, 9; SO—Butts, 86; SB—Wohlford, 32; CS—Peters, 9.

(All Players—Listed Alphabetically)

Player and Club	G.	AB.	R.	H.	TB.	2B.	3B.	HR.	RBI.	SH.	SF.	BB.	HP.	SO.	SB.	CS.	Pct.
Acevedo, Rafael, Caldwell† ..	22	2	1	2	2	0	0	0	1	0	1	0	0	0	0	0	1.000
Alim, Eugene, Great Falls ..	9	22	4	4	6	2	0	0	2	0	0	2	0	9	0	0	.182
Amiama, Rafael, Great Falls	54	137	20	23	39	0	2	4	11	0	1	22	2	46	5	4	.168
Aschermann, Kurt, Caldwell	42	140	10	24	30	3	0	1	14	1	1	18	0	51	1	1	.171
Autry, Albert, Billings	7	17	1	1	1	0	0	0	0	0	0	0	0	11	0	0	.059
Babieracki, Stanley, MV* ..	15	26	3	7	9	2	0	0	5	0	0	4	0	5	0	0	.269
Balaz, John, Idaho Falls ...	21	86	12	22	27	2	0	1	4	0	0	4	1	34	1	0	.256
Ballantine, Michael, Bil ...	16	29	2	4	4	0	0	0	3	4	0	1	0	2	0	0	.138
Ballard, Daniel, Ogden	18	3	0	1	1	0	0	0	1	0	0	0	0	0	0	0	.333
Barletta, Anthony, Ogden* ..	23	63	10	16	26	5	1	1	9	0	0	13	2	21	0	0	.254
Barnes, Paul, Ogden	48	124	21	35	47	7	1	1	22	2	3	16	0	42	4	2	.282
Barneson, Dennis, Idaho F ..	3	2	0	0	0	0	0	0	0	0	0	0	1	0	0	0	.000
Bates, William, Great Falls.	17	6	0	1	1	0	0	0	0	0	0	0	0	4	0	0	.167
Beard, Clarence, Billings* ..	40	123	17	27	34	2	1	1	9	0	0	13	1	24	5	4	.220
Benedickt, Thomas, IF*	6	14	0	2	2	0	0	0	0	0	0	2	1	5	0	0	.143
Benjamin, Charles, Caldwell	46	132	15	31	48	6	1	3	17	1	1	18	1	44	1	0	.235
Berge, Glen, Great Falls ..	15	38	6	6	7	1	0	0	2	0	0	12	0	8	1	1	.158
Bogacki, David, Magic V* ..	14	18	2	2	2	0	0	0	2	1	0	2	0	7	0	0	.111
Borchetta, Albert, IF*	5	0	0	0	0	0	0	0	0	0	0	2	0	0	0	0	.000
Briggs, Dan, Idaho Falls* ..	62	190	44	58	83	11	1	4	34	0	0	27	7	52	5	1	.305
Brookins, Lendon, Magic V	40	68	17	19	27	3	1	1	8	0	0	20	1	14	1	0	.279
Browne, Michael, Idaho F* ..	10	22	1	3	3	0	0	0	1	0	0	0	0	5	0	0	.136
Bussie, Robert, Idaho Falls	17	35	9	10	18	1	0	2	8	0	1	10	0	6	4	0	.286
Butts, W. Timothy, Cald ...	60	202	45	46	70	4	1	6	26	0	1	50	1	86	13	3	.228
Byroade, David, Ogden	7	2	0	0	0	0	0	0	0	0	0	0	0	1	0	0	.000
Cabrera, Jose, Ogden	9	1	0	0	0	0	0	0	0	0	0	0	0	0	0	0	.000
Campbell, Donald, Billings* ..	18	9	0	0	0	0	0	0	0	0	0	0	0	5	0	0	.000
Campbell, Richard, GF	7	10	1	1	1	0	0	0	0	0	0	1	0	2	0	0	.100
Cana, Nelson, Magic Val ...	55	195	38	36	41	3	1	0	20	0	0	48	2	58	13	7	.185
Canepa, Gary, Caldwell	6	7	0	0	0	0	0	0	0	0	0	1	0	4	0	0	.000
Capilla, Douglas, Great F* ..	28	21	4	2	2	0	0	0	0	0	0	4	0	13	0	0	.095
Carden, Richard, Great F* ..	3	3	0	0	0	0	0	0	0	0	0	0	0	2	0	0	.000
Carpenter, Arthur, Great F*	30	0	1	0	0	0	0	0	1	0	1	0	0	0	0	0	.000
Case, Richard, Idaho Falls ..	13	6	0	0	0	0	0	0	0	0	0	2	0	1	0	0	.000
Caudle, Kenneth, Great Falls	37	82	8	21	30	3	0	2	9	0	0	9	0	24	1	0	.256
Chapple, C. Perry, Magic V†	17	18	3	3	3	0	0	0	1	0	1	0	0	5	0	0	.167
Childress, Edward, Magic V	15	10	1	0	0	0	0	0	0	0	0	1	0	5	0	0	.000
Clampitt, Michael, Caldwell	20	41	1	4	5	1	0	0	3	0	0	8	0	19	0	0	.098
Clark, Ronald R., Ogden ...	17	11	1	0	0	0	0	0	0	0	0	1	0	8	0	0	.000
Clear, Allen, Idaho Falls* ..	58	197	35	44	68	5	2	5	35	1	1	34	1	54	8	5	.223
Cooper, Arthur, Caldwell ...	6	1	0	0	0	0	0	0	0	0	0	0	1	0	0	0	.000
Corder, Thomas, Ogden	44	168	23	40	53	8	1	1	31	0	1	16	0	22	2	4	.238
Cowens, Alfred, Billings ...	62	237	45	67	107	9	5	7	47	0	2	18	0	37	25	5	.283
Cox, J. Thomas, Magic V ...	61	170	46	45	64	5	1	4	29	0	0	59	2	64	6	5	.265
D'Acquisto, John, Great F ..	14	20	2	1	4	0	0	1	1	0	0	1	0	15	0	0	.050
Dade, L. Paul, Idaho Falls ..	46	158	28	48	68	7	5	1	35	0	2	22	2	49	7	0	.304
Daniels, Joe, Ogden*	56	181	40	65	88	6	4	3	43	0	2	31	3	30	12	3	.359
Danielson, Kenneth, Great F*	18	52	8	13	22	1	1	2	9	1	1	6	0	10	3	0	.250
Darrow, Darrell, Idaho Falls	43	155	17	37	43	4	1	0	15	2	2	15	4	36	10	2	.239
Davis, Ralph, Ogden	14	29	3	5	5	0	0	0	2	5	0	0	0	13	0	0	.172
De Leon, Angel, Great F* ..	16	7	0	0	0	0	0	0	0	0	0	1	0	3	0	0	.000
Devine, Paul, Magic Valley .	14	21	1	2	2	0	0	0	0	0	0	0	0	0	0	0	.095
Dorothy, William, Caldwell	58	177	36	40	53	5	1	2	29	2	5	56	1	55	7	0	.226
Duckworth, Howard, Magic V	22	60	10	11	16	2	0	1	6	0	1	7	0	17	4	0	.183
Dumler, Freddie, Caldwell ..	26	74	12	13	16	1	1	0	8	0	1	11	1	18	1	0	.176
Eckert, Steven, Caldwell	15	36	9	9	9	0	0	0	7	1	0	1	0	5	0	1	.250
Eller, William, Caldwell	6	8	4	1	1	0	0	0	1	0	1	4	0	1	0	0	.125
Erickson, G. Charles, GF	67	204	19	58	81	13	2	2	26	0	0	17	0	32	4	3	.284
Faria, Stephen, Great F	43	65	3	10	12	2	0	0	5	1	0	16	2	19	0	1	.154
Ferri, John, Caldwell	20	40	5	7	10	1	1	0	4	1	0	7	0	9	0	0	.175
Fickert, Stephen, Idaho F ..	21	11	1	0	0	0	0	0	3	0	0	0	0	6	0	0	.000
Figueroa, Domingo, MV* ...	3	4	0	0	0	0	0	0	0	0	0	0	0	0	0	0	.000
Fink, Michael, Caldwell	47	127	19	32	36	4	0	0	8	2	1	13	6	42	3	1	.252
Fisher, Michael, Great Falls	19	46	7	11	11	0	0	0	3	0	1	6	1	21	1	2	.239
Flen, John, Great Falls	20	24	5	7	10	1	1	0	5	0	1	2	0	6	1	0	.292
Ford, Brian, Billings	24	9	1	0	0	0	0	0	0	2	0	0	0	3	0	0	.000
Ford, David, Magic Valley .	14	19	3	2	2	0	0	0	0	1	0	1	0	5	0	0	.105
Forry, Dewey, Ogden	53	151	30	39	54	4	1	3	24	0	2	21	3	42	9	1	.258
Franks, Ronny, Idaho F† ...	41	134	20	31	42	2	3	1	19	0	1	16	1	59	6	6	.231
Galindez, Luis, Magic V ...	53	188	33	42	64	7	3	3	23	0	0	20	0	41	7	2	.223
Gancasz, Sigmund, Magic V	5	7	1	1	1	0	0	0	0	0	0	0	0	3	0	0	.143
Gaylord, John, Billings* ...	14	20	2	7	9	2	0	0	6	4	2	1	1	4	0	0	.350
Gilbreath, Rodney, Magic V	56	198	37	55	91	7	1	9	35	0	0	22	2	50	4	2	.278
Gleason, Thomas, Ogden* ...	14	6	1	2	2	0	0	0	0	0	0	1	0	1	0	0	.333
Goldwire, Willie, Idaho F* ..	20	56	13	14	15	1	0	0	10	0	1	14	1	15	2	0	.250
Gordon, Richard, Great F ..	25	41	5	12	15	1	1	0	7	0	1	19	0	14	0	0	.293
Granville, Gary, Idaho F ...	68	260	57	88	132	15	1	9	39	0	1	34	5	33	12	6	.338
Gray, Lee, Caldwell*	11	8	2	3	4	0	0	0	0	0	0	4	0	3	1	0	.375
Groth, Robert, Idaho Falls* ..	17	66	12	24	28	4	0	0	6	0	0	4	0	3	5	1	.364
Hagen, Gary, Magic V*	13	14	1	1	2	1	0	0	3	1	1	5	0	9	0	0	.071
Haller, James, Ogden	14	31	5	6	9	0	0	1	2	1	0	1	0	10	0	0	.194

Player and Club	G.	AB.	R.	H.	TB.	2B.	3B.	HR.	RBI.	SH.	SF.	BB.	HP.	SO.	SB.	CS.	Pct.
Hammon, Randal, Billings ..	5	4	0	1	1	0	0	0	0	0	1	0	0	0	0	0	.250
Haren, Dennis, Ogden	50	164	22	41	68	10	1	5	29	1	2	25	1	41	2	0	.250
Harris, Kenneth, Idaho F* ..	29	98	14	17	34	4	2	3	18	0	0	5	0	40	0	0	.173
Hartline, Forrest, Magic V†	27	60	8	14	20	3	0	1	9	0	0	9	2	20	0	0	.233
Haynes, Michael, Great F* ..	51	134	19	33	41	4	2	0	7	0	0	16	0	49	8	3	.246
Heierle, Tommy, Magic V ..	39	136	29	38	60	13	0	3	22	0	1	18	2	23	3	0	.279
Henard, Gailand, Idaho F* .	9	12	0	2	2	0	0	0	1	3	0	1	0	4	0	0	.167
Henderson, Clinton, Cald	11	2	2	0	0	0	0	0	0	0	0	1	0	1	0	0	.000
Hiranuma, Kazuo, Great F† .	20	6	2	1	1	0	0	0	0	0	0	5	0	4	0	0	.167
Hirsch, Walter, Caldwell ..	10	12	3	1	1	0	0	0	1	0	0	5	0	4	0	0	.083
Hockenbery, Charles, Ida F†	18	20	0	3	3	0	0	0	2	0	0	3	0	10	0	0	.150
Hogan, Gary, Caldwell	19	8	0	1	1	0	0	0	1	0	0	0	0	3	0	0	.125
Holve, Jared, Idaho F*	11	24	1	3	4	1	0	0	3	0	0	2	0	8	0	0	.125
Houston, Gary, Billings	5	10	0	1	2	1	0	0	2	0	0	2	0	7	0	0	.100
Hubbs, Gary, Caldwell	6	8	1	1	1	0	0	0	1	0	0	1	0	0	0	0	.125
Hughes, John, Ogden*	70	281	52	76	105	18	1	3	46	2	1	34	2	43	16	3	.270
Hughes, Michael, Ogden ...	19	56	9	14	16	2	0	0	11	0	0	16	0	11	1	0	.250
Hypes, Kyle, Great Falls† ...	18	29	3	5	7	2	0	0	1	1	1	4	0	5	0	0	.172
Jacobson, William, Great F*	3	7	1	2	2	0	0	0	0	0	0	2	0	3	0	1	.286
Jenkins, Thomas, Ogden* ...	62	194	38	53	67	10	2	0	28	0	2	45	2	40	19	8	.273
John, William, Idaho Falls*.	21	64	9	11	20	2	2	1	9	0	0	6	0	25	0	0	.172
Johnson, Robert F., Idaho F .	7	16	1	2	3	1	0	0	0	1	0	1	0	3	0	0	.125
Joseph, John, Billings	64	209	34	45	66	11	2	2	20	0	2	25	2	68	10	2	.215
Kapano, Randolph, Great F ..	45	127	21	33	51	3	0	5	20	0	2	20	1	28	1	0	.260
Keller, George, Magic V	1	0	0	0	0	0	0	0	0	0	0	0	0	0	0	0	.000
Kelly, Calvin, Magic Valley .	7	31	5	9	10	1	0	0	5	0	1	0	0	5	3	0	.290
Kelly, Jimmy, Caldwell ...	7	2	0	0	0	0	0	0	0	0	0	0	1	0	0	0	.000
Kimbrell, Michael, Ogden ..	49	134	21	29	36	3	2	0	11	0	0	12	2	24	7	0	.216
Kinder, Gregory, Billings ...	12	7	1	1	1	0	0	0	0	1	0	1	0	4	0	0	.143
Knox, Michael, Magic V	14	17	0	1	1	0	0	0	1	1	0	1	0	7	0	0	.059
LaCock, R. Pierre, Cald*	69	231	43	65	96	13	2	4	49	0	3	54	1	40	19	5	.281
Landesberg, Glen, Magic V*.	15	22	2	2	4	0	1	0	2	0	0	3	0	9	0	0	.091
Laney, Duff, Billings*	25	54	7	9	18	1	1	2	7	0	2	15	0	14	2	0	.167
Lange, Richard, Idaho F	16	46	5	9	9	0	0	0	5	3	0	2	0	17	0	0	.196
Lashmet, Richard, Billings ..	22	60	8	12	15	1	1	0	3	0	0	7	0	19	6	1	.200
Lewis, Martin, Great Falls .	16	17	2	1	4	0	0	1	1	0	0	0	0	6	0	0	.059
Lipke, David, Billings	12	4	2	0	0	0	0	0	0	0	0	2	1	1	0	0	.000
Liscano, Tomas, Caldwell ...	22	7	0	0	0	0	0	0	0	0	0	0	0	3	0	0	.000
Little, Lanny, Idaho Falls ..	9	32	6	7	14	1	0	2	5	0	0	3	0	11	0	0	.219
Lombardo, Raymond, Great F	49	112	14	26	28	2	0	0	5	0	0	12	0	27	0	0	.232
Luna, Domingo, Ogden	10	2	0	0	0	0	0	0	0	0	0	1	0	2	0	0	.000
Lundgren, Thomas, Ida F* ..	8	4	0	0	0	0	0	0	0	0	0	1	0	4	0	0	.000
Maneely, Robert, Caldwell .	15	31	9	9	14	2	0	1	3	4	0	3	1	6	0	0	.290
Marikos, David, Idaho F	13	38	4	5	7	0	1	0	3	0	0	5	0	16	1	0	.132
Marquez, Ronald, Idaho F ..	21	60	11	14	14	0	0	0	5	0	0	7	0	23	3	0	.233
Matlock, Laron, Idaho Falls	36	100	25	35	37	4	1	2	16	0	1	28	1	35	3	1	.350
Mattison, Vandon, Ogden* ..	8	2	2	1	1	0	0	0	0	0	0	3	0	1	0	0	.500
McDaniel, Jerry, Billings* ..	6	0	0	0	0	0	0	0	0	0	0	0	0	0	0	0	.000
McKenzie, Nicholas, Caldwell	14	32	3	6	9	0	0	1	5	1	0	3	0	9	0	0	.188
McManis, Scott, Billings ...	13	22	5	5	5	0	0	0	1	0	1	1	9	0	0	0	.227
McNeil, Melvin, Great Falls	7	10	0	1	1	0	0	0	1	0	0	0	0	2	0	0	.100
Mengo, Marc, Magic Valley .	70	282	53	86	138	10	3	12	59	0	1	38	4	46	3	1	.305
Metzger, Clarence, Great F	16	27	1	4	4	0	0	0	1	0	0	1	0	10	0	0	.148
Milani, Glenn, Great Falls* .	30	57	7	17	20	3	0	0	13	0	2	13	1	7	1	0	.298
Minton, Gregory, Billings† .	27	29	2	7	11	0	2	0	3	1	0	4	0	11	0	0	.241
Mixon, Elmer, Ogden	70	273	70	88	137	21	3	4	36	2	2	41	9	48	15	3	.322
Monge, Isidro, Idaho Falls† .	17	23	1	0	0	0	0	0	0	1	0	1	0	18	0	0	.000
Mosley, A. C., Billings	29	56	12	8	15	2	1	1	4	0	0	17	2	25	4	0	.143
Murray, Leon, Great Falls ..	26	72	8	20	27	1	0	2	15	0	1	6	1	26	2	1	.278
Nageleisen, James, Magic V .	21	73	29	25	37	4	1	2	10	0	0	24	1	18	11	0	.342
Nelson, Terry, Great Falls ..	38	114	18	31	40	5	2	0	8	0	0	9	1	27	4	0	.272
Nettles, Morris, Idaho F* ..	52	203	43	75	106	10	6	3	29	0	0	35	2	54	23	1	.369
Nichols, Michael, Billings* .	17	34	4	15	17	2	0	0	7	1	0	1	0	6	0	0	.441
Nitz, Rick, Ogden	15	35	4	5	6	1	0	0	3	0	0	3	0	9	0	0	.143
O'Brien, Paul, Idaho F	9	20	3	3	3	0	0	0	1	0	0	6	0	12	0	0	.150
O'Brien, Thomas, Caldwell .	32	98	11	14	17	0	0	1	6	1	0	6	1	29	1	1	.143
Odom, Dennis, Caldwell	69	223	44	66	89	11	3	2	50	1	3	56	0	45	14	0	.296
Ogden, John, Great Falls ...	34	37	7	11	11	0	0	0	2	1	0	5	1	1	1	0	.297
Orozco, W. Bolivar,																	
10 Ogden-14 Ida F	24	58	10	11	14	3	0	0	5	0	0	4	1	21	1	1	.190
Ortenzio, Frank, Billings ...	58	190	45	60	105	11	2	10	26	0	2	30	5	50	9	1	.316
Ortiz, Humberto, Great Falls	2	1	2	1	2	1	0	0	1	0	0	0	0	0	0	0	1.000
Page, Paul, Caldwell†	3	4	0	0	0	0	0	0	0	0	0	2	0	4	0	0	.000
Partin, David, Ogden	9	8	0	0	0	0	0	0	0	0	0	0	0	3	0	0	.000
Patino, Victor, Caldwell* ...	24	13	1	2	2	0	0	0	0	0	0	0	0	4	0	0	.154
Patrick, Michael, Billings ..	4	2	0	0	0	0	0	0	0	0	0	0	0	1	0	0	.000
Paulson, Noel, Billings†	47	149	25	32	38	3	0	1	12	3	2	23	2	40	3	2	.215
Pavlesic, David, Billings† ...	3	11	1	7	8	1	0	0	4	0	0	0	0	0	0	0	.636
Pedersen, Ernie, Magic V*...	50	126	35	35	50	5	2	2	20	0	1	41	0	27	4	0	.278
Peters, Robert, Billings	53	175	40	51	78	4	4	5	29	1	1	33	1	47	10	9	.291
Pierce, L. Jack, Magic V* ..	70	281	44	79	124	16	1	9	58	0	2	24	6	69	1	2	.281
Pratt, Thomas, Billings*	7	6	0	1	1	0	0	0	0	0	0	0	0	1	0	0	.167

Player and Club	G.	AB.	R.	H.	TB.	2B.	3B.	HR.	RBI.	SH.	SF.	BB.	HP.	SO.	SB.	CS.	Pct.
Prest, David, Great Falls ...	68	221	44	68	115	15	1	10	39	0	0	24	0	46	7	2	.308
Raible, Bruce, Ogden* ...	15	43	6	10	10	0	0	0	1	2	0	4	0	8	0	0	.233
Rautzhan, Clarence, Ogden ..	14	38	2	4	4	0	0	0	2	1	0	1	0	14	0	1	.105
Reed, Lonnie, Billings	6	8	1	0	0	0	0	0	0	0	0	3	0	5	2	0	.000
Rich, James, Ogden	57	162	39	47	79	12	7	2	23	1	2	27	0	36	10	4	.290
Roakes, Barney, Great Falls†	1	0	1	0	0	0	0	0	0	0	0	1	0	0	0	0	.000
Rosen, Stephen, Idaho F	7	20	1	1	1	0	0	0	0	0	0	0	0	11	0	0	.050
Rothan, William, Idaho F ..	1	0	0	0	0	0	0	0	0	0	0	0	0	0	0	0	.000
Ruiz, Manuel, Magic Valley	63	225	47	71	101	12	3	4	24	0	0	33	3	33	10	1	.316
Russell, D. Michael, Cald ...	6	6	1	1	3	0	1	0	0	0	0	1	0	5	0	0	.167
Sanborn, Gilbert, Magic V ..	3	5	0	1	1	0	0	0	1	0	0	1	0	2	0	0	.200
Schell, Robert, Caldwell	28	105	21	24	30	0	3	0	7	1	0	19	0	24	5	1	.229
Schlagenhauf, Gary, Billings	58	191	29	53	75	7	3	3	24	1	1	30	1	55	7	3	.277
Schroeder, John W., Idaho F	8	19	0	2	3	1	0	0	1	0	0	1	1	7	0	0	.105
Schroeder, Richard, Great F*	3	13	2	4	7	1	1	0	3	0	0	2	0	3	1	0	.308
Schuldies, Donald, Cald*	70	297	47	82	114	6	7	4	35	3	0	20	3	70	16	4	.276
Schwear, Jerome, Ogden	5	0	0	0	0	0	0	0	0	0	0	0	0	0	0	0	.000
Selph, Scotty, Magic Valley .	21	61	7	12	20	2	0	2	10	0	0	8	1	32	0	2	.197
Sencion, Jose, Great Falls ..	58	125	15	25	31	2	2	0	7	2	0	12	0	41	3	1	.200
Serrano, Luis, Magic Val ...	13	4	1	0	0	0	0	0	0	1	0	0	1	2	0	0	.000
Shiffer, Eric, Idaho Falls ...	33	111	18	33	49	9	2	1	19	0	1	9	1	35	1	0	.297
Smith, James A., Billings ...	55	181	27	50	62	7	1	1	28	1	5	12	1	24	23	1	.276
Smith, Thomas J., Great F†	41	126	13	34	41	4	0	1	17	0	0	13	0	27	3	2	.270
Smith, William, E., Idaho F	8	6	0	0	0	0	0	0	0	0	0	0	0	3	0	0	.000
Smythe, Terry, Magic Valley	6	3	0	1	1	0	0	0	1	0	0	0	0	1	0	0	.333
Snider, John, Ogden†	55	181	30	41	52	9	1	0	22	1	3	20	3	30	8	1	.227
Stallworth, Wilson, Magic V .	5	3	0	0	0	0	0	0	0	0	0	0	2	0	0	0	.000
Steffany, Hector, Great F ...	2	0	0	0	0	0	0	0	0	0	0	0	0	0	0	0	.000
Stout, Jeffrey, Billings	63	228	31	66	74	8	0	0	21	1	4	19	1	31	8	1	.289
Suzuki, Hiroshi, Great F* ..	55	96	13	15	26	3	1	2	11	0	1	10	2	28	1	1	.156
Talley, Gary, Idaho Falls* ..	7	6	1	3	3	0	0	0	1	0	0	1	0	1	0	0	.500
Taylor, Albert, Ogden	11	2	0	1	1	0	0	0	0	0	0	1	0	1	0	0	.500
Tener, Steven, Great Falls ..	16	12	0	1	1	0	0	0	4	1	0	0	0	4	1	0	.083
Vary, Richard, Caldwell	13	36	7	8	8	0	0	0	4	0	0	4	0	12	0	0	.222
Vaughn, James, Great Falls .	2	1	0	1	1	0	0	0	0	0	0	0	0	0	0	0	1.000
Veloz, Guaroa, Great Falls .	51	140	9	28	33	0	1	1	6	0	0	10	0	41	3	1	.200
Waldal, Robert, Idaho Falls .	2	1	0	0	0	0	0	0	0	0	0	0	0	0	0	0	.000
Watson, Thomas, Magic V ..	17	33	2	3	3	0	0	0	2	0	0	5	1	16	1	0	.091
Weiss, Michael, Caldwell ...	15	22	2	4	4	0	0	0	1	0	0	1	0	7	0	0	.182
White, Calvin, Caldwell† ...	54	162	25	42	68	4	2	6	26	0	3	28	0	50	3	1	.259
Williams, Gary, Great Falls .	17	8	0	0	0	0	0	0	0	0	0	0	0	4	0	0	.000
Williams, John F., Cald	17	31	7	9	11	2	0	0	1	0	0	5	0	9	1	0	.290
Williams, Rodger, Billings ..	15	44	5	9	9	0	0	0	4	0	1	3	2	10	2	1	.205
Wilson, Steven, Ogden	7	1	0	0	0	0	0	0	0	0	0	0	0	0	0	0	.000
Winters, Van, Idaho Falls ..	11	4	1	0	0	0	0	0	0	0	0	0	0	3	0	0	.000
Wohlford, James, Billings ..	62	221	42	68	88	7	2	3	37	0	2	25	2	17	32	7	.308
Wolfe, James, Caldwell	10	9	1	1	1	0	0	0	1	0	0	3	0	5	0	0	.111
Woodward, Brian, Idaho Falls	5	1	0	0	0	0	0	0	0	0	0	0	1	0	0	0	.000
Young, Richmond, Magic V ..	7	3	0	0	0	0	0	0	0	0	0	0	0	1	0	0	.000

GRAND-SLAM HOME RUNS—Clear, Daniels, Gilbreath, Joseph, 1 each.

AWARDED FIRST BASE ON INTERFERENCE—Joseph 4 (Lombardo 2, Flen, M. Hughes); Dumler 2 (Goldwire, Marikos); Rich (Beard).

CLUB FIELDING

Club	G.	PO.	A.	E.	DP.	PB.	Pct.	Club	G.	PO.	A.	E.	DP.	PB.	Pct.
Magic Valley ...	70	1803	699	161	55	32	.940	Great Falls	70	1738	605	181	34	32	.928
Billings	70	1819	712	170	47	23	.937	Caldwell	70	1815	718	198	38	37	.927
Ogden	70	1812	740	174	58	21	.936	Idaho Falls	70	1821	737	207	63	35	.925

Triple Plays—None.

INDIVIDUAL FIELDING
(Ten or More Games)

*Throws lefthanded.

FIRST BASEMEN

Player and Club	G.	PO.	A.	E.	DP.	Pct.	Player and Club	G.	PO.	A.	E.	DP.	Pct.
Peters, Billings	26	196	9	3	16	.986	Ortenzio, Billings ..	42	298	23	15	18	.955
J. HUGHES, Ogden*	69	607	24	11	49	.983	Benjamin, Caldwell .	29	204	8	11	9	.951
John, Idaho Falls* ..	18	124	7	3	12	.978	Murray, Great Falls .	22	125	5	7	10	.949
Pierce, Magic Valley	67	497	30	20	34	.963	Briggs, Idaho Falls*.	50	388	24	23	37	.947
White, Caldwell	47	374	12	16	21	.960	Erickson, Great F ...	17	46	5	3	2	.944
Milani, Great Falls*.	26	115	3	5	8	.959	Suzuki, Great Falls*.	45	172	16	12	10	.940

(Fewer Than Ten Games)

Player and Club	G.	PO.	A.	E.	DP.	Pct.	Player and Club	G.	PO.	A.	E.	DP.	Pct.
Mengo, Magic Valley	5	29	5	0	2	1.000	Holve, Idaho Falls* .	7	44	3	1	7	.979
Gray, Caldwell	4	13	1	0	0	1.000	Mosley, Billings	8	56	0	2	6	.966
Pedersen, Magic V ..	3	10	0	0	3	1.000	Barnes, Ogden	4	17	1	1	1	.947
Page, Caldwell	1	5	0	0	1	1.000	Cox, Magic Valley* .	1	2	0	1	0	.667
Danielson, Great F*.	1	1	0	0	0	1.000	Prest, Great Falls ...	1	0	0	1	0	.000

SECOND BASEMEN

Player and Club	G.	PO.	A.	E.	DP.	Pct.	Player and Club	G.	PO.	A.	E.	DP.	Pct.
Peters, Billings	14	24	32	1	5	.982	Ruiz, Magic Valley	43	100	78	9	20	.952
Caudle, Great Falls	15	17	18	1	4	.972	Franks, Idaho Falls	12	31	19	3	9	.943
Nelson, Great Falls	14	16	16	1	0	.970	Schell, Caldwell	22	32	47	5	6	.940
Stout, Billings	36	87	96	6	19	.968	Mixon, Ogden	70	156	174	22	40	.938
Pedersen, Magic V	27	54	62	5	5	.959	Berge, Great Falls	11	15	14	2	2	.935
Groth, Idaho Falls	13	26	39	3	10	.956	Darrow, Idaho Falls	43	98	111	16	26	.929
DOROTHY, Cald	47	103	104	10	15	.954	Sencion, Great Falls	50	73	95	17	11	.908

(Fewer Than Ten Games)

Player and Club	G.	PO.	A.	E.	DP.	Pct.	Player and Club	G.	PO.	A.	E.	DP.	Pct
Williams, Caldwell	4	3	14	0	1	1.000	Alim, Great Falls	8	9	8	2	3	.895
Hartline, Magic V	2	3	6	0	1	1.000	Paulson, Billings	7	7	9	2	1	.889
Sanborn, Magic V	2	3	3	0	2	1.000	Wohlford, Billings	5	8	8	2	0	.889
Smith, Great Falls	1	1	0	0	1	1.000	Williams, Billings	8	20	17	6	3	.860
Schroeder, Great F	3	9	8	1	2	.944	Amiama, Great Falls	3	1	3	1	0	.800
Lashmet, Billings	7	18	11	2	1	.935	Marquez, Idaho F	4	2	6	3	1	.727
Kelly, Magic Valley	6	12	17	2	2	.935	Veloz, Great Falls	6	5	5	4	0	.714
Kimbrell, Ogden	4	4	6	1	1	.909	Fink, Caldwell	2	2	3	4	0	.556

THIRD BASEMEN

Player and Club	G.	PO.	A.	E.	DP.	Pct	Player and Club	G.	PO.	A.	E.	DP.	Pct.
Fink, Caldwell	25	26	39	8	1	.890	Stout, Billings	18	16	25	8	1	.837
Dade, Idaho Falls	43	44	84	16	10	.889	Franks, Idaho Falls	17	15	41	12	3	.824
MENGO, Magic V	67	64	123	25	13	.882	Veloz, Great Falls	48	40	44	19	2	.816
Snider, Ogden	29	22	52	10	2	.881	Kimbrell, Ogden	38	25	56	22	2	.786
Odom, Caldwell	24	22	51	10	4	.880	Paulson, Billings	36	21	51	20	2	.783
Gordon, Great F	19	7	10	3	3	.850	Erickson, Great Falls	25	8	28	11	2	.766
Haren, Ogden	12	8	18	5	0	.839	Peters, Billings	11	6	14	8	3	.714

(Fewer Than Ten Games)

Player and Club	G.	PO.	A.	E.	DP.	Pct	Player and Club	G.	PO.	A.	E.	DP.	Pct.
Daniels, Ogden	3	1	5	0	0	1.000	Smith, Billings	6	3	10	2	0	.867
Hartline, Magic Val.	3	2	3	0	0	1.000	Mosley, Billings	3	3	3	1	0	.857
Vary, Caldwell	4	1	2	0	0	1.000	Benjamin, Great F	8	9	13	4	0	.846
Williams, Billings	3	1	2	0	0	1.000	Schroeder, Idaho F	4	2	7	2	0	.818
Pedersen, Magic Val.	1	2	1	0	0	1.000	Marquez, Idaho Falls	3	2	12	1	0	.800
Mixon, Ogden	1	1	1	0	0	1.000	Caudle, Great Falls	8	5	8	4	1	.765
Aschermann, Cald	1	0	1	0	0	1.000	Granville, Magic F	9	3	18	7	1	.750
Dorothy, Caldwell	7	3	12	1	1	.938	Wohlford, Billings	2	1	1	1	1	.667
Schell, Caldwell	6	4	9	1	0	.929	Lashmet, Billings	1	0	1	1	0	.500
Clampitt, Caldwell	4	3	7	1	0	.909	Brookins, Magic Val	2	0	0	1	0	.000

SHORTSTOPS

Player and Club	G.	PO.	A.	E.	DP.	Pct.	Player and Club	G.	PO.	A.	E.	DP.	Pct.
Lashmet, Billings	12	6	22	2	2	.933	Snider, Ogden	29	39	72	17	10	.867
Clampitt, Caldwell	11	9	11	2	0	.909	Gilbreath, Magic Val	54	62	133	30	14	.867
Hartline, Magic Val	11	25	33	6	8	.906	Wohlford, Billings	55	63	149	33	24	.865
GRANVILLE, I F	58	89	166	30	37	.895	Smith, Great Falls	39	35	73	20	4	.844
Corder, Ogden	44	62	156	28	31	.886	Franks, Idaho Falls	10	12	32	10	4	.815
Odom, Caldwell	44	57	143	27	17	.881	Fink, Caldwell	14	12	24	9	3	.800
Nelson, Great Falls	23	26	49	11	7	.872							

(Fewer Than Ten Games)

Player and Club	G.	PO.	A.	E.	DP.	Pct	Player and Club	G.	PO.	A.	E.	DP.	Pct.
Stout, Billings	4	8	8	0	2	1.000	Vary, Caldwell	7	5	16	2	1	.913
Rich, Ogden	1	1	4	0	0	1.000	Sencion, Great Falls	9	9	8	2	0	.895
Schell, Caldwell	1	2	2	0	0	1.000	Marquez, Idaho Falls	5	5	12	3	0	.850
Alim, Great Falls	2	2	1	0	1	1.000	Hubbs, Caldwell	1	2	3	1	1	.833
Dorothy, Caldwell	1	1	0	0	0	1.000	Peters, Billings	1	2	3	1	1	.833
Ortiz, Great Falls	1	0	1	0	1	1.000	Cana, Magic Valley	7	8	18	6	2	.813
Cowens, Billings	5	9	12	1	3	.955	Amiama, Great Falls	8	4	12	4	0	.800
Berge, Great Falls	5	5	10	1	1	.938	Williams, Caldwell	4	7	7	5	0	.737

OUTFIELDERS

Player and Club	G.	PO.	A.	E.	DP.	Pct.	Player and Club	G.	PO.	A.	E.	DP.	Pct.
Harris, Idaho Falls*	23	25	1	0	0	1.000	Butts, Caldwell	54	91	5	5	0	.950
Fisher, Great Falls	17	18	0	0	0	1.000	Joseph, Billings	62	88	4	5	0	.948
Danielson, Great F*	13	15	0	0	0	1.000	Barnes, Ogden	37	33	3	2	2	.947
Nageleisen, Magic V	20	49	5	1	1	.982	Schuldies, Caldwell*	70	112	8	7	1	.945
PREST, Great Falls.	64	69	10	2	2	.975	Laney, Billings	16	16	1	1	0	.944
Amiama, Great Falls	43	48	6	2	1	.964	Orozco, Ogden–IF	16	16	0	1	0	.941
Jenkins, Ogden	57	72	5	3	0	.963	Ortenzio, Billings	13	12	2	1	0	.933
Daniels, Ogden	50	50	1	2	0	.962	Forry, Ogden	46	40	1	3	0	.932
Ruiz, Magic Valley	20	19	3	1	1	.957	Nettles, Idaho F*	52	110	6	9	0	.928
Kapano, Great Falls.	42	40	2	2	0	.955	Schlagenhauf, Bill	54	60	7	6	1	.918
Cowens, Billings	57	73	8	4	1	.953	Matlock, Idaho Falls	32	31	2	3	0	.917
Cana, Magic Valley	47	86	13	5	3	.952	Cox, Magic Valley*	55	55	12	7	2	.905

OUTFIELDERS—Continued

Player and Club	G.	PO.	A.	E.	DP.	Pct.
Galindez, Magic Val.	51	48	7	6	1	.902
O'Brien, Caldwell ..	23	29	5	4	0	.895
LaCock, Caldwell* ..	68	76	6	10	1	.891
Clear, Idaho Falls* ..	57	55	2	8	0	.877
Brookins, Magic Val.	14	12	2	2	0	.875
Rich, Ogden	46	53	8	9	1	.871
Haynes, Great Falls*	39	24	2	4	0	.867
Balaz, Idaho Falls ..	21	22	3	4	0	.862
Erickson, Great Falls	26	18	2	4	1	.833
Mosley, Billings	15	10	0	2	0	.833
Bussie, Idaho Falls .	15	12	2	3	0	.824
Watson, Magic Valley	10	4	1	3	0	.625

(Fewer Than Ten Games)

Player and Club	G.	PO.	A.	E.	DP.	Pct.
Pedersen, Magic Val.	8	15	0	0	0	1.000
Smith, Billings	9	13	1	0	0	1.000
Little, Idaho Falls ..	9	10	3	0	1	1.000
Hirsch, Caldwell ...	7	6	0	0	0	1.000
Groth, Idaho Falls ..	4	6	0	0	0	1.000
Jacobson, Great Falls	3	3	0	0	0	1.000
Hypes, Great Falls* .	1	2	0	0	0	1.000
Minton, Billings	2	1	0	0	0	1.000
Nelson, Great Falls .	2	1	0	0	0	1.000
McNeil, Great Falls .	3	0	1	0	0	1.000
Capilla, Great Falls*	5	8	1	1	0	.900
Ogden, Great Falls .	8	7	0	1	0	.875
Marquez, Idaho Falls	7	3	1	2	0	.667
Reed, Billings*	4	1	0	1	0	.500
Faria, Great Falls ..	1	0	0	1	0	.000

CATCHERS

Player and Club	G.	PO.	A.	E.	DP.	PB.	Pct.
Faria, Great Falls	32	207	11	1	0	9	.995
Goldwire, Idaho F	19	174	15	2	0	7	.990
Selph, Magic Val.	19	137	10	2	0	5	.987
Erickson, Great F.	10	65	1	1	0	5	.985
McKenzie, Cald ..	10	57	2	1	1	5	.983
ASCHERMANN, Caldwell	40	305	41	7	3	15	.980
Haren, Ogden ..	38	293	18	7	2	12	.978
Heierle, Magic Val	39	324	26	9	6	18	.975
Beard, Billings ..	38	307	31	9	0	5	.974
Smith, Billings ..	36	289	41	9	2	13	.973
Lombardo, Great F	48	327	30	10	3	11	.973
Flen, Great Falls.	11	35	0	1	0	1	.972
Marikos, Billings F.	13	92	12	3	0	3	.972
M. Hughes, Ogden	17	133	14	5	0	4	.967
Barletta, Ogden ..	19	150	14	7	1	4	.959
Caudle, Great F.	16	85	5	4	1	6	.957
Duckworth, MV ..	20	149	10	8	1	6	.952
Shiffer, Idaho F .	31	249	23	17	2	14	.941
Dumler, Caldwell	24	162	9	11	0	11	.940

(Fewer Than Ten Games)

Player and Club	G.	PO.	A.	E.	DP.	PB.	Pct.
Pavlesic, Billings .	3	38	4	0	1	2	1.000
Laney, Billings ...	5	28	1	0	0	3	1.000
Eller, Caldwell ...	4	25	1	0	1	2	1.000
Pierce, Magic Val	3	19	1	0	0	3	1.000
Lipke, Billings ...	1	9	0	0	0	1	1.000
Schroeder, IF ...	1	1	0	0	0	0	1.000
O'Brien, Idaho F.	7	62	4	2	0	8	.971
Rosen, Idaho F ...	6	47	4	2	0	3	.962
Benjamin, Cald ..	3	22	1	1	0	1	.958
Russell, Caldwell .	3	15	2	2	0	3	.895
Partin, Ogden ...	7	15	1	2	0	1	.889

PITCHERS

Player and Club	G.	PO.	A.	E.	DP.	Pct.
FORD, Magic Valley*	14	5	11	0	1	1.000
Nichols, Billings ...	15	0	14	0	1	1.000
Babieracki, Magic V*	13	2	11	0	0	1.000
Kinder, Billings	12	4	8	0	1	1.000
Liscano, Caldwell ..	22	3	8	0	0	1.000
Fickert, Idaho Falls.	21	2	9	0	1	1.000
Tener, Great Falls ..	15	3	6	0	0	1.000
Williams, Great F ..	17	1	8	0	0	1.000
Minton, Billings	16	1	6	0	0	1.000
Bates, Great Falls ..	17	0	7	0	0	1.000
Serrano, Magic Val .	13	1	4	0	0	1.000
Lipke, Billings	11	1	4	0	0	1.000
Winters, Idaho Falls	11	1	1	0	0	1.000
Case, Idaho Falls ...	13	1	1	0	0	1.000
Raible, Ogden	15	2	24	1	2	.963
Davis, Ogden	14	5	13	1	1	.947
Metzger, Great Falls	14	3	10	1	0	.929
Ferri, Caldwell	17	1	24	2	0	.926
Monge, Idaho Falls*	17	3	9	1	1	.923
Landesberg, Magic V*	15	2	10	1	0	.923
Haller, Ogden	14	9	13	2	2	.917
Hockenbery, Idaho F	18	3	8	1	0	.917
Campbell, Billings* .	18	0	11	1	2	.917
Chapple, Magic Val .	16	3	7	1	1	.909
Browne, Idaho Falls.	19	3	7	1	0	.909
McManis, Billings ..	13	2	8	1	0	.909
Ballantine, Billings .	16	6	12	2	0	.900
Devine, Magic Valley	14	1	17	2	1	.900
Nitz, Ogden	15	2	15	2	0	.895
Patino, Caldwell* ...	21	2	14	2	0	.889
Eckert, Caldwell ...	14	3	12	2	2	.882
Lange, Idaho Falls ..	14	6	16	3	0	.880
Rautzhan, Ogden* ..	14	2	19	3	2	.875
Hypes, Great Falls* .	11	1	13	2	1	.875
Lewis, Great Falls ..	16	2	11	2	1	.867
Gaylord, Billings* ..	14	1	11	2	0	.857
Ballard, Ogden	18	2	4	1	2	.857
Hogan, Caldwell	19	1	5	1	0	.857
Wolfe, Caldwell	10	1	5	1	0	.857
Knox, Magic Valley .	14	2	8	2	0	.833
Bogacki, Magic Val*	14	0	10	2	0	.833
Ogden, Great Falls .	23	2	3	1	0	.833
Maneely, Caldwell ..	15	2	20	5	0	.815
D'Acquisto, Great F.	12	3	9	3	0	.800
Carpenter, Great F .	29	1	7	2	0	.800
Childress, Magic V .	15	0	4	1	0	.800
Ford, Billings	22	5	6	4	0	.733
Acevedo, Caldwell ..	22	3	7	4	0	.714
Clark, Ogden	17	1	9	4	0	.714
Weiss, Caldwell	15	1	8	4	1	.692
De Leon, Great F*..	12	0	4	2	0	.667
Capilla, Great F* ...	17	1	7	5	1	.615
Gleason, Ogden*	14	0	3	2	0	.600
Hagen, Magic Valley	13	0	6	5	0	.545

(Fewer Than Ten Games)

Player and Club	G.	PO.	A.	E.	DP.	Pct.
Houston, Billings* ..	5	0	9	0	0	1.000
Talley, Idaho Falls* .	7	0	6	0	0	1.000
Wilson, Ogden	7	0	4	0	0	1.000
Hammon, Billings ..	5	0	4	0	0	1.000
Smythe, Magic Valley	6	2	1	0	0	1.000
Cabrera, Ogden	9	1	2	0	1	1.000
McDaniel, Billings* .	6	1	2	0	0	1.000
Young, Magic Valley.	7	1	0	0	0	1.000
Kelly, Caldwell*	7	0	1	0	0	1.000
Mattison, Ogden* ...	9	0	1	0	0	1.000
Woodward, Idaho F.	5	0	1	0	0	1.000
Barneson, Idaho F* .	3	0	1	0	0	1.000

PITCHERS—Continued
(Fewer Than Ten Games)

Player and Club	G.	PO.	A.	E.	DP.	Pct.
Carden, Great Falls*	2	0	1	0	0	1.000
Watson, Magic Valley	1	0	1	0	0	1.000
Johnson, Idaho Falls	6	3	7	1	0	.909
Campbell, Great F*	7	2	6	1	1	.889
Briggs, Idaho Falls*	7	1	7	1	0	.889
Henard, Idaho Falls	9	3	6	2	0	.818
Benedickt, Idaho F*	6	3	9	3	1	.800
Autry, Billings	7	1	7	2	1	.800
Cooper, Caldwell*	6	1	2	1	0	.750

Player and Club	G.	PO.	A.	E.	DP.	Pct.
Canepa, Caldwell	6	2	2	2	0	.667
Smith, Idaho Falls	8	1	1	1	1	.667
Henderson, Caldwell	9	0	2	1	0	.667
Pratt, Billings*	7	1	1	2	0	.500
Patrick, Billings	3	0	1	1	0	.500
Steffany, Great Falls	2	0	1	1	0	.500
Lundgren, Idaho F	8	0	0	1	0	.000
Stallworth, Magic V	5	0	0	1	0	.000
Waldal, Idaho Falls*	6	0	0	1	0	.000

The following players do not have any recorded accepted chances at the positions indicated; therefore, are not listed in the fielding averages for those particular positions: Amiama, 1b-3b; Benjamin, of; Borchetta*, p; Byroade, p; Figueroa*, p; Franks, p; Gancasz, p; Gordon, 1b; Granville, of; Hiranuma, 3b-p; Jenkins, ss; Kapano, 1b; Keller, p; C. Kelly, of; Luna, p; Prest, 2b; Rothan, p; Schwear, p; Sencion, 3b; Shiffer, p; Suzuki*, p; Taylor, p; Vaughn, p; R. Williams, ss.

PITCHERS' RECORDS
(Leading Qualifiers for Earned-Run Average Leadership—70 or More Innings)

*Throws lefthanded.

Pitcher—Club	G.	GS.	CG.	ShO.	W.	L.	Sv.	Pct.	IP.	H.	R.	ER.	HR.	BB.	Int. BB.	HB.	SO.	WP.	ERA.
Lange, Idaho F	.14	14	10	3	13	0	0	1.000	111	70	28	24	0	54	0	1	151	14	1.95
Ballantine, Billings	.16	10	6	1	4	6	0	.400	91	77	35	25	1	19	1	6	103	0	2.47
Rautzhan, Ogden*	.14	14	4	0	7	1	0	.875	85	73	43	25	3	36	0	1	84	8	2.65
Raible, Ogden	.15	14	7	1	9	4	0	.692	113	87	44	34	6	38	0	2	119	9	2.71
Nitz, Ogden	.15	12	4	0	6	5	0	.545	94	88	44	34	3	36	0	2	70	7	3.26
Davis, Ogden	.14	14	4	0	6	4	0	.600	86	78	39	32	2	30	0	2	81	5	3.35
Nichols, Bill*	.15	13	5	1	4	5	1	.444	81	76	39	31	2	34	2	2	86	3	3.44
Haller, Ogden	.14	13	2	1	5	4	0	.556	80	60	46	34	7	38	0	4	70	8	3.83
Ferri, Caldwell	.17	13	7	1	3	9	1	.250	117	115	62	50	8	37	0	0	124	6	3.85
Maneely, Caldwell	.15	15	5	1	5	7	0	.417	99	59	44	6	37	0	2	81	4	4.17

Departmental Leaders: G—Carpenter, 29; GS—Maneely, 15; CG—Lange, 10; ShO—Lange, 3; W—Lange, 13; L—Ferri, Metzger, 9; Sv—Fickert, 5; Pct.—Lange, 1.000; IP—Ferri, 117; H—Ferri, 115; R—Eckert, 72; ER—Ferri, 50; HR—Ferri; D. Ford, Hogan, 8; BB—D'Acquisto, 74; IBB—Johnson, 4; HB—Henderson, 7; SO—Lange, 151; WP—Lange, 14.

(All Pitchers—Listed Alphabetically)

Pitcher—Club	G.	GS.	CG.	ShO.	W.	L.	Sv.	Pct.	IP.	H.	R.	ER.	HR.	BB.	Int. BB.	HB.	SO.	WP.	ERA.
Acevedo, Caldwell	.22	0	0	0	1	0	1	.000	25	28	16	12	0	16	2	1	20	1	4.32
Autry, Billings	.7	7	2	1	2	5	0	.286	43	41	40	30	2	42	3	1	49	5	6.28
Babieracki, MV*	.13	7	3	1	8	0	1	1.000	64	64	30	27	7	17	0	2	53	1	3.80
Ballantine, Bill	.16	10	6	1	4	6	0	.400	91	77	35	25	1	19	1	6	103	0	2.47
Ballard, Ogden	.18	0	0	1	2	3	0	.333	27	18	13	9	0	14	0	0	38	2	3.00
Barneson, Idaho F*	3	1	0	0	0	1	0	.000	7	11	4	3	0	2	0	0	4	1	3.86
Bates, Great Falls	.17	1	0	0	2	2	0	.500	29	28	31	17	2	21	2	0	36	1	5.28
Benedickt, IF*	.6	6	2	1	3	2	0	.600	40	40	17	12	1	19	1	2	23	9	2.70
Bogacki, Magic V*	.14	11	0	0	4	3	0	.571	55	53	37	27	2	49	0	2	66	13	4.42
Borchetta, IF*	.5	0	0	0	0	1	0	.000	6	9	12	9	0	8	0	0	6	0	13.50
Briggs, Idaho F*	.7	3	0	0	2	1	1	1.000	28	20	8	4	2	19	0	0	33	5	1.29
Browne, Idaho F	.10	9	2	0	3	5	1	.375	56	55	33	22	6	26	2	4	42	4	3.54
Byroade, Ogden	.7	0	0	0	1	3	0	.000	10	13	8	6	1	4	0	0	10	0	5.40
Cabrera, Ogden	.9	0	0	0	1	0	1	.000	9	7	2	2	1	5	0	0	10	1	1.64
D. Campbell, Bill*	.18	1	0	0	3	0	1	1.000	37	37	18	11	2	14	1	1	52	4	2.68
R. Campbell, GF*	.7	5	0	0	0	3	0	.000	32	35	25	18	2	24	0	1	25	3	5.06
Canepa, Caldwell	.6	6	0	0	1	0	0	.000	27	24	18	10	0	15	0	3	24	2	3.33
Capilla, Great F*	.17	5	0	0	2	5	0	.286	38	24	37	28	0	57	0	4	69	12	6.63
Carden, Great F*	.2	1	0	0	0	1	0	.000	4	6	3	1	0	6	0	1	3	2	2.25
Carpenter, F*	.29	0	0	0	4	1	1	.800	36	29	16	8	3	17	1	2	49	4	2.00
Case, Idaho Falls	.13	0	0	0	0	0	0	.000	27	26	26	19	3	19	0	0	22	6	6.33
Chapple, Magic V	.16	2	0	0	2	1	3	.667	53	45	25	18	3	21	0	2	55	4	3.06
Childress, Magic V	.15	7	0	0	3	1	4	.750	40	38	27	17	1	20	0	5	42	1	3.83
Clark, Ogden	.17	2	1	0	5	4	4	.556	37	38	29	14	2	17	1	1	36	5	3.41
Cooper, Caldwell*	.6	0	0	0	0	1	0	.000	11	7	6	5	1	10	0	2	7	2	4.09
D'Acquisto, GF	.12	11	0	0	2	5	0	.286	55	53	46	32	3	74	0	5	84	13	5.24
Davis, Ogden	.14	14	4	0	6	4	0	.600	86	78	39	32	2	30	0	2	81	5	3.35
DeLeon, Great F*	.12	6	0	0	0	5	0	.000	36	36	36	23	2	37	1	4	32	8	6.09
Devine, Magic Val	.14	12	0	0	5	6	0	.455	66	80	45	28	3	25	0	3	51	5	5.18
Eckert, Caldwell	.14	13	3	0	4	7	0	.364	87	99	72	48	7	41	0	5	57	8	4.97
Ferri, Caldwell	.17	13	7	1	3	9	1	.250	117	115	62	50	8	37	0	0	124	6	3.85
Fickert, Idaho F	.21	1	2	1	6	2	8	.750	48	39	23	19	1	13	1	1	59	2	3.56
Figueroa, Magic V*	3	0	0	0	1	1	0	.500	13	11	7	6	1	8	0	0	20	1	4.15
B. Ford, Billings	.22	3	0	0	1	2	3	.333	41	47	25	21	2	14	2	3	53	4	4.61
D. Ford, Magic V*	.14	8	1	1	2	3	1	.400	56	62	47	38	8	48	0	1	49	8	6.11
Franks, Idaho F	.1	0	0	0	0	0	0	.000	2	0	0	0	0	2	0	0	1	0	0.00
Gancasz, Magic V	.5	2	0	0	1	0	0	.000	14	22	20	16	1	13	0	2	13	2	10.29
Gaylord, Billings*	.14	10	2	0	8	0	1	1.000	68	58	25	19	2	33	0	3	71	6	2.51
Gleason, Ogden*	.14	0	0	0	1	1	0	.500	20	9	8	7	1	15	0	1	20	3	3.15
Hagen, Magic Val	.13	7	1	0	3	5	2	.375	57	60	45	29	6	30	0	2	57	8	4.58

Pitcher—Club	G	GS	CG	ShO	W	L	Sv	Pct.	IP	H	R	ER	HR	BB	Int. BB	HB	SO	WP	ERA
Haller, Ogden 14	13	2	1	5	4	0	.556	80	60	46	34	7	38	0	4	70	8	3.83
Hammon, Billings .. 5	2	0	0	1	2	0	.333	17	15	11	8	1	6	0	1	14	0	4.24
Henard, Idaho F* . 9	4	0	0	2	1	1	.667	33	44	33	21	1	22	0	3	28	5	5.73
Henderson, Cald .. 9	0	0	0	0	2	0	.000	13	16	17	12	3	10	0	7	17	1	8.31
Hiranuma, GF 14	1	0	0	0	2	0	.000	21	25	19	14	0	11	0	0	33	3	6.00
Hockenbery, IF 18	10	2	1	5	4	2	.556	63	58	33	23	4	24	0	0	50	12	3.29
Hogan, Caldwell . 19	3	1	0	0	2	4	.000	41	47	35	24	8	17	0	0	37	0	5.27
Houston, Billings* . 5	3	0	0	1	3	0	.750	33	30	15	12	0	10	0	0	30	1	3.27
Hypes, Great F* ..11	8	3	0	3	5	1	.375	62	48	23	16	4	18	0	2	70	1	2.32
Johnson, Idaho F .. 6	6	2	1	2	3	0	.400	40	27	20	18	4	30	4	0	42	5	4.05
Keller, Magic V .. 1	0	0	0	0	0	0	.000	1	7	7	6	0	1	0	0	1	0	54.00
Kelly, Caldwell* .. 7	0	0	0	0	0	0	.000	7	20	25	21	2	18	0	1	9	6	27.00
Kinder, Billings ..12	3	0	0	1	1	0	.000	27	25	31	28	1	34	0	1	23	10	9.33
Knox, Magic Val ..14	8	0	0	3	3	3	.500	53	70	36	30	2	22	0	3	49	7	5.09
Landesberg, MV* ..15	8	0	0	5	4	1	.556	66	55	40	32	6	44	0	2	91	5	4.36
Lange, Idaho Falls .14	14	10	3	13	0	0	1.000	111	70	28	24	0	54	0	0	151	14	1.95
Lewis, Great Falls .16	7	0	0	1	2	2	.333	56	61	54	39	0	49	0	2	52	6	6.27
Lipke, Billings 11	1	0	0	1	1	2	.500	20	26	20	14	0	12	0	0	24	4	6.30
Liscano, Caldwell ..22	0	0	0	5	4	1	.556	33	33	18	12	2	15	1	0	40	0	3.27
Luna, Ogden 9	1	0	0	1	0	2	1.000	11	12	11	6	0	15	0	2	11	3	4.91
Lundgren, Ida F .. 8	0	0	0	3	1	0	.000	13	28	19	13	1	13	0	0	15	2	9.00
Maneely, Caldwell .15	15	5	1	5	7	0	.417	95	99	59	44	6	37	0	2	81	4	4.17
Mattison, Ogden* .. 7	0	0	0	2	0	0	.000	7	9	3	2	0	7	0	0	8	0	2.57
McDaniel, Billings* 6	0	0	0	1	0	0	.000	8	8	10	9	0	7	0	0	3	1	13.50
McManis, Billings .13	11	4	1	5	3	0	.625	75	70	44	35	2	50	1	1	73	4	4.20
Metzger, Great F ..14	13	1	0	2	9	0	.182	82	80	49	38	5	38	2	2	92	7	4.17
Minton, Billings ..16	3	1	0	1	4	2	.200	40	37	23	14	2	16	1	2	36	3	3.15
Monge, Idaho F* ..17	6	2	0	5	1	1	.833	62	60	35	29	5	42	0	0	54	4	4.21
Nichols, Billings* ..15	13	5	1	4	5	1	.444	81	76	39	31	2	34	2	2	86	3	3.44
Nitz, Ogden 15	12	4	0	6	5	0	.545	94	88	44	34	3	36	0	2	70	7	3.26
Ogden, Great Falls .23	0	0	0	2	1	2	.667	32	34	20	14	0	14	1	1	40	0	3.94
Patino, Caldwell* ..21	5	0	0	3	4	1	.429	51	56	49	36	2	48	1	2	52	10	6.35
Patrick, Billings .. 3	1	0	0	1	0	0	1.000	10	10	6	6	2	2	0	0	11	0	5.40
Pratt, Billings* .. 7	0	0	0	2	0	0	1.000	15	12	12	9	1	18	1	0	27	3	5.40
Raible, Ogden 15	14	7	1	9	4	0	.692	113	87	44	34	6	38	0	2	119	9	2.71
Rautzhan, Ogden* ..14	14	4	0	7	1	0	.875	85	73	43	25	3	38	0	1	84	8	2.65
Rothan, Idaho F .. 1	0	0	0	0	0	0	.000	2	1	1	1	0	0	0	0	1	0	0.00
Schwear, Ogden .. 4	0	0	0	0	0	0	.000	4	4	0	0	0	1	0	0	3	0	0.00
Serrano, Magic V ..13	0	0	0	4	0	1	1.000	23	28	14	11	2	6	0	2	17	1	4.30
Shiffer, Idaho F .. 1	0	0	0	0	0	0	.000	1	1	0	0	0	0	0	0	1	0	0.00
Smith, Idaho Falls . 8	1	1	0	1	0	1	1.000	15	9	6	3	0	17	0	1	16	3	1.80
Smythe, Magic Val . 6	3	0	0	0	1	0	.000	11	15	15	15	4	13	0	0	8	1	12.27
Stallworth, MV 5	0	0	0	1	0	0	1.000	12	26	25	23	6	6	0	0	8	2	17.25
Steffany, Great F .. 2	0	0	0	0	0	0	.000	2	2	2	0	0	1	0	0	2	0	0.00
Suzuki, Great F* .. 1	0	0	0	0	0	0	.000	1	0	0	0	0	0	0	0	1	0	0.00
Talley, Idaho F* .. 7	4	0	0	1	2	0	.333	23	29	25	21	1	22	0	1	19	1	8.22
Taylor, Ogden 11	0	0	0	1	1	0	.500	11	20	15	15	1	7	0	1	9	2	12.27
Tener, Great Falls .15	8	0	0	2	4	2	.333	40	49	36	33	4	29	0	1	51	8	7.43
Vaughn, Great F .. 2	0	0	0	1	0	0	.000	3	7	7	7	1	3	0	0	2	0	21.00
Waldal, Idaho F* .. 2	0	0	0	1	0	0	1.000	3	5	2	2	0	1	0	0	3	0	6.00
Watson, Magic V . 1	0	0	0	0	0	0	.000	2	2	0	0	0	2	0	0	2	0	0.00
Weiss, Caldwell ..15	9	1	1	2	5	0	.286	62	59	50	42	4	36	0	2	47	4	6.10
Williams, Great F .17	7	0	0	1	2	1	.500	49	62	36	22	3	17	0	0	53	3	4.04
Wilson, Ogden 7	0	0	0	1	0	1	1.000	9	7	5	5	0	7	0	0	11	0	5.00
Winters, Idaho F ..11	0	0	0	0	1	0	.000	20	24	14	11	3	10	0	0	12	0	4.95
Wolfe, Caldwell ...10	6	1	0	1	1	0	.500	33	35	19	15	3	13	0	1	35	2	4.09
Woodward, Idaho F 5	2	0	0	2	0	0	.000	8	8	17	9	0	17	1	0	13	5	10.13
Young, Magic V .. 7	1	0	0	0	0	0	.000	10	13	12	12	0	20	0	6	11	6	10.50

BALKS—Figueroa, 5; Devine, D. Ford, 3 each; Eckert, McManis, Nitz, 2 each; Bates, Bogacki, Borchetta, R. Campbell, Capilla, Carpenter, Chapple, D'Acquisto, Davis, De Leon, Fickert, Gancasz, Gleason, Haller, Hypes, Johnson, Kinder, Lipke, Maneely, Metzger, Patino, Tener, Winters, 1 each.

COMBINATION SHUTOUTS—None.

NO-HIT GAMES—None.

ALONG THE MINOR LEAGUE TRAIL . . . .

(Continued from page 593)

(Southern) tried to buck the telecast of the major league All-Star Game with a contest against Charlotte. The tilt drew 87 paid. . . . Frank Duffy of Indianapolis was low man on the totem pole on his American Association all-star squad. He made the team only because two other players

chosen ahead of him couldn't appear. What did he do? He drove in the game's only run and won the MVP award. . . . You know ball parks, with their peanuts, popcorn, hot dogs, etc. Well, Honolulu (Pacific Coast) is a bit different. The Islanders added saimin, manapua, crack seed and corn on the cob for their ethnic multi-lingual fans. . . . The bakers had a night at Reading (Eastern), but Bob Kelly ran home with the bread. He won $10 in prizes for getting the first hit and scoring the first run. . . . Manager Dave Pavlesic of Billings (Pioneer) directs the Mustangs on the field, but he did his best job of team directing when their bus driver slumped at the wheel and the vehicle veered in the path of an on-coming trailer-tractor unit. Pavlesic grabbed the wheel, steered it back to its proper lane on the highway and brought the bus to a safe halt. . . . Bob Kennedy, player personnel director of the parent St Louis Cardinals, touring the minors, stopped at St. Petersburg (Florida State), where he instituted an edict calling for fresh haircuts and short sideburns. Some on-the-ball ballplayers questioned him about the abundant hair styles of Cardinal stars Richie Allen, Joe Torre and Bob Gibson. Kennedy, caught short, stammered, "Well, er, eh, ah, that's up to the individual manager." The edict died aborning. . . . Pitcher Ed Sprague didn't profane the second base position, even though that's how he got there. Iowa shortstop Dwain Anderson cussed American Association umpire Ed Jansen and was banished. Sprague filled in at second, vacated by Ron Clark, who moved to the open shortstop post. Ed snagged a line drive and handled the only grounder that came his way. . . . Walter Mitty is spelled K-e-n G-i-l-l. Gill was hit on the back of his gloved hand in the fourth inning by a hard shot, felt severe pain, but shook it off. He pitched a 3-0 shutout for Charlotte (Southern) over Savannah August 5, and even beat out a bases-loaded bunt in the seventh. Next morning, X-rays showed a broken wrist. Move over, Walter.

MAJOR LEAGUE ATTENDANCE FOR 1970

AMERICAN LEAGUE	Home	Away
Baltimore	1,057,069	1,312,337
Boston	1,595,278	1,072,111
California	1,077,741	976,786
Chicago	495,355	967,903
Cleveland	729,752	865,587
Detroit	1,501,293	1,105,797
Kansas City	693,047	794,193
Milwaukee	933,690	745,027
Minnesota	1,261,887	1,220,644
New York	1,136,879	1,167,611
Oakland	778,355	971,568
Washington	824,789	885,571

A. L. 1970 Total—12,085,135.

NATIONAL LEAGUE	Home	Away
Atlanta	1,078,848	1,351,676
Chicago	1,642,705	1,484,057
Cincinnati	1,803,568	1,605,874
Houston	1,253,444	1,155,731
Los Angeles	1,697,142	1,337,513
Montreal	1,424,683	1,154,572
New York	2,697,479	1,673,050
Philadelphia	708,247	1,287,094
Pittsburgh	1,341,947	1,387,888
St. Louis	1,629,736	1,465,159
San Diego	643,679	1,202,071
San Francisco	740,720	1,557,513

N. L. 1970 Total—16,662,198.

AMERICAN LEAGUE ALL-TIME CLUB SEASON RECORD

Club	Home	Year	Finished	Road	Year	Finished
Baltimore	1,203,366	1966	First	1,312,337	1970	First (E)
Boston	1,940,788	1968	Fourth	1,779,936	1946	First
California	1,400,321	1966	Sixth	976,786	1970	Third (W)
Chicago	1,644,460	1960	Third	1,280,554	1955	Third
Cleveland	2,620,627	1948	First	1,762,564	1948	First
Detroit	2,031,847	1968	First	1,414,126	1950	Second
‡Kansas City	902,414	1969	Fourth (W)	854,225	1969	Fourth (W)
§Kansas City	1,393,054	1955	Sixth	938,214	1967	Tenth
Milwaukee	933,690	1970	Fourth (W)	745,027	1970	Fourth (W)
Minnesota	1,483,547	1967	Second	1,325,806	1967	Second
New York	2,373,901	1948	Third	2,216,159	1962	First
Oakland	837,466	1968	Sixth	992,124	1969	Second (W)
Philadelphia	945,076	1948	Fourth	1,562,360	1948	Fourth
St. Louis	712,918	1922	Second	1,170,349	1948	Sixth
Seattle	677,944	1969	Sixth (W)	889,578	1969	Sixth (W)
*Washington	1,027,216	1946	Fourth	1,055,171	1948	Seventh
†Washington	918,106	1969	Fourth (E)	1,042,638	1968	Tenth

American League Attendance, Season.....................11,150,099 in 1948 (8-club league)
11,336,923 in 1967 (10-club league)
12,134,745 in 1969 (12-club league)

*Former Washington club (now Minnesota).   †Present Washington club.   ‡Present Kansas City club.   §Former Kansas City club.

NATIONAL LEAGUE ALL-TIME CLUB SEASON RECORD

Club	Home	Year	Finished	Road	Year	Finished
Atlanta	1,539,801	1966	Fifth	1,398,368	1966	Fifth
Boston	1,455,439	1948	First	1,308,175	1947	Third
Brooklyn	1,807,526	1947	First	1,863,542	1947	First
Chicago	1,674,993	1969	Second (E)	1,484,057	1970	Second (E)
Cincinnati	1,803,568	1970	First (W)	1,605,874	1970	First (W)
Houston	2,151,470	1965	Ninth	1,155,731	1970	Fourth (W)
Los Angeles	2,755,184	1962	Second	2,141,212	1966	First
Milwaukee	2,215,404	1957	First	1,633,569	1959	Second
Montreal	1,424,683	1970	Sixth (E)	1,154,572	1970	Sixth (E)
*New York	1,600,793	1947	Fourth	1,228,330	1948	Fifth
†New York	2,697,479	1970	Third (E)	1,673,050	1970	Third (E)
Philadelphia	1,425,891	1964	§Second	1,459,482	1966	Fourth
Pittsburgh	1,705,828	1960	First	1,634,404	1966	Third
St. Louis	2,090,145	1967	First	1,532,595	1968	First
San Diego	643,679	1970	Sixth (W)	1,202,071	1970	Sixth (W)
San Francisco	1,795,356	1960	Fifth	2,207,530	1966	Second

National League Attendance, Season......................10,684,963 in 1960 (8-club league)
15,015,471 in 1966 (10-club league)
16,662,198 in 1970 (12-club league)

*Former New York club (now San Francisco).   †Present New York club.
§Tied for position.

OPENING DAY AT HOME

American League			National League		
Club	Attendance	Year	Club	Attendance	Year
Baltimore	46,354	1954	Atlanta	50,671	1966
Boston	35,343	1969	Boston	25,000	1935
California	*31,284	1966	Brooklyn	34,530	1949
Chicago	41,660	1960	Chicago	43,824	1929
Cleveland	73,163	1948	Cincinnati	35,747	1924
Detroit	53,572	1969	Houston	*42,652	1965
†Kansas City	31,895	1955	Los Angeles	78,672	1958
‡Kansas City	18,127	1970	Milwaukee	43,640	1955
Milwaukee	37,237	1970	Montreal	29,184	1969
Minnesota	24,606	1961	†New York	54,393	1936
New York	54,826	1946	‡New York	52,812	1966
Oakland	*47,233	1968	Philadelphia	*37,667	1957
Philadelphia	32,825	1927	Pittsburgh	35,546	1948
St. Louis	19,561	1923	San Diego	*25,215	1970
Seattle	14,993	1969	St. Louis	*47,568	1970
†Washington	31,728	1948	San Francisco	42,894	1964
‡Washington	45,125	1969			

* Night game.   †Former club.   ‡Present club.

NATIONAL LEAGUE SCHEDULE—EAST

Bold figures denote Sundays
Asterisks * denote night games

Major League All-Star Game at Detroit—July 13, 1971, 8:00 p. m.
Hall of Fame Game, Cooperstown, N. Y.—Aug. 9—Cleveland vs. Chicago (N. L.)

	AT CHICAGO	AT MONTREAL	AT NEW YORK	AT PHILADELPHIA	AT PITTSBURGH	AT ST. LOUIS
CHICAGO		May 7°, 8°, **9** July 26°, 27°, 28° Sept. 28°, 29°, 30°	May 3°, 4°, 5°, 6 July 30°, 31 Aug. **1** Sept. 15°, 16	May 10°, 11°, 12° July 23°, 24°, **25** Sept. 17°, 18, **19**	May 28°, 29, **30**, 31 Aug. 10°, 11° Sept. 6, 6, 8	May 25°, 26°, 27° June 25°, 26°, **27** Sept. 3°, 4, **5**
MONTREAL	April 27, 28, 29 July **18**, 19 Aug. 30, 31 Sept. 1, 2		April 6, 7, 8 July 5, 5, 6°, 7 Sept. 13°, 14	April 10, **11** July 8°, 9°, 10°, 10°, **11** Sept. 15°, 16°	May 17°, 18° June 18°, 19, **20**, 20 Sept. 3°, 4, **5**	April 30° May 1°, **2** July 15°, 16°, 17° Sept. 24°, 25, **26**
NEW YORK	April 23, 24, **25** July 20, 21, 22 Sept. 21, 22, 23	April 13, 14 June 24°, 25°, 26°, **27** Sept. 6°, 7°, 8°		May 19°, 20° June 28°, 29° Sept. 2°, 3°, 4°, 4°, **5**	May 14°, 15°, 16 June 21°, 22°, 23° Sept. 17°, 18, **19**	April 26°, 27°, 28°, 29 July **18**, 19° Aug. 30°, 31° Sept. 1°
PHILADELPHIA	Apr. 30 May 1, **2** July 15, 16, 17 Sept. 24, 25, **26**	April 20, 21° July 2°, 2°, 3°, **4** Sept. 20°, 21°, 22°	May 25°, 26° June 18°, 19, **20, 20** Sept. 10°, 11°, **12**		April 6, 8° Aug. 6°, 7, **8, 8**, 30°, 31° Sept. 1°	Apr. 22°, 23°, 24°, **25** July 20°, 21°, 22° Sept. 13°, 14°
PITTSBURGH	June 7, 8, 9 July 2, 3, **4**, 5 Sept. 13, 14	May 21°, 22°, **23** Aug. 3°, 4°, 5° Sept. 10°, 11, **12**	Apr. 16, 17, **18, 18** June 30° July 1 Sept. 24°, 25, **26**	Apr. 12°, 13°, 14° June 25°, 26, **27, 27** Sept. 28°, 30°		June 10°, 11°, 12°, **13**, 28° 29° Sept. 21°, 22°, 23°
ST. LOUIS	Apr. 6, 7 June 17, 18, 19, **20** Sept. 10, 11, **12**	May 10°, 11°, 12° July 23°, 24°, **25** Sept. 17°, 18, 19	May 7°, 8, **9** July 26°, 27°, 28 Sept. 27°, 28, 30°	May 3°, 4°, 5°, 6° July 30°, 31° Aug. **1** Sept. 6°, 7°	June 1°, 2°, 3° Aug. 12°, 13°, 14°, **15** Sept. 15°, 16°	
ATLANTA	June 14, 15, 16 Aug. 27, 28, 29	May 24, 25°, 26°, 27° June 30° July 1	May 21°, 22, **23** July 2°, 3, **4**	Apr. 16°, 17, 18 Aug. 2°, 3°, 4°	Apr. 20°, 21°, 22° July 9°, 10, **11**	May 28°, 29°, **30, 31**° Aug. 10°, 11°
CINCINNATI	June 11, 12, **13** Aug. 23, 24, 25	April 16, 17, **18**, 18 June 28°, 29°	April 10, **11** Aug. 2°, 3°, 3°, 4	May 21°, 22°, **23, 24**° June 30° July 1°	May 25°, 26°, 27° July 6°, 7°, 8°	June 14°, 15°, 16 Aug. 27°, 28°, **29**
HOUSTON	April 20, 21, 22 Aug. 20, 21, **22**	May 4°, 5°, 6° July 30°, 31° Aug. **1**	May 10°, 11°, 12 July 23°, 24, **25**	May 7°, 8, **9** July 26°, 27°, 28°	June 4°, 5°, **6** Aug. 16°, 17°, 18°	April 12°, 13 July 9°, 9°, 10°, **11**
LOS ANGELES	May 21, 22, **23** June 28, 29, 30	June 11°, 12°, **13** Aug. 23°, 24°, 25°	June 14°, 15°, 16 Aug. 27°, 28, **29**	June 8°, 9°, 10° Aug. 20°, 21°, **22**	April 27°, 28°, 29° July **18, 18,** 19°	May 18°, 19°, 20 Aug. 7°, **8,** 9°
SAN DIEGO	May 14, 15, **16**, 16 Aug. 4, 5	June 14°, 15°, 16° Aug. 27°, 28°, **29**	June 8°, 9°, 10 Aug. 20°, 21°, **22**	June 11°, 12°, **13** Aug. 23°, 24°, 25°	April 30° May 1, **2** July 15°, 16°, 17	May 21°, 22°, **23, 24**° Aug. 2°, 3°
SAN FRANCISCO	May 18, 19, 20 Aug. 7, **8, 8**	June 8°, 9°, 10° Aug. 20°, 21°, **22**	June 11°, 12, **13** Aug. 23°, 24°, 25	June 14°, 15°, 16° Aug. 27°, 28°, **29**	April 23°, 24, **25** July 20°, 21°, 22	April 10, **11, 11** Aug. 4°, 5°, 6°

NATIONAL LEAGUE SCHEDULE — WEST

Bold figures denote Sundays
Asterisks * denote night games

Major League All-Star Game at Detroit—July 13, 1971, 8:00 p. m.
Hall of Fame Game, Cooperstown, N. Y.—Aug. 9—Cleveland vs. Chicago (N. L.)

	AT ATLANTA	AT CINCINNATI	AT HOUSTON	AT LOS ANGELES	AT SAN DIEGO	AT SAN FRANCISCO
CHICAGO	June 4*, 5*, **6** Aug. 16*, 17*, 18*	June 2*, 2*, 3* Aug. 13*, 14*, 15	April 8*, 9*, 10*, **11** Aug. 2*, 3*	April 12*, 13* July 6*, 7*, 7*, 8*	April 14*, 15* July 9*, 10, **11**, 11	April 16*, 17, **18, 18** June 22*, 23
MONTREAL	May 19*, 20* June 21*, 21*, 22*, 23*	May 14*, 15*, 16 Aug. 6*, 7*, **8**	April 23*, 24*, 25 July 20*, 21*, 22*	May 31* June 1*, 2* Aug. 13*, 14*, 15	June 4*, 5, **6, 6** Aug. 17*, 18*	May 28*, 29, **30, 30** Aug. 10*, 11
NEW YORK	May 17*, 18* Aug. 5*, 6*, 7*, **8**	April 20*, 21* July 9*, 10*, **11**, 11	April 30* May 1*, **2** July 15*, 16*, 17*	June 4*, 5*, **6** Aug. 16*, 17*, 18*	May 28*, 29*, **30** Aug. 10*, 11*, 12*	May 31 June 1*, 2 Aug. 13*, 14, **15**
PHILADELPHIA	May 14*, 15*, **16** July 5*, 6*, 7*	May 17*, 18* June 21*, 22*, 23*, 24*	April 26*, 27*, 28* July 18, 18, 19*	May 28*, 29*, **30** Aug. 10*, 11*, 12*	May 31, 31 June 2* Aug. 13*, **15, 15**	June 4*, 5, **6, 6** Aug. 17*, 18
PITTSBURGH	April 9*, 10*, **11** Aug. 23*, 24*, 25*	May 19*, 20 Aug. 19*, 20*, 21, **22**	June 14*, 15*, 16* Aug. 27*, 28*, **29**	May 7*, 8*, **9** July 27*, 28*, 29*	May 11*, 12* July 23*, 24, **25**, 25	May 4*, 5 July 30*, 31 Aug. **1, 1**
ST. LOUIS	June 7*, 8*, 9* Aug. 20*, 21*, **22**	June 4*, 5, **6** Aug. 16*, 17*, 18*	May 14*, 15*, 16 Aug. 23*, 24*, 25*	April 14*, 15* June 21*, 22*, 23*, 24	April 16*, 17*, **18** July **4**, 5*, 7*	April 19, 20*, 21 July 1, 2*, 3
ATLANTA		April 5, 7* June 17*, 18*, 19*, **20, 20** Sept. 13*, 14*	June 10*, 11*, 12*, **13**, 28*, 28*, 29* Sept. 15*, 16*	May 11*, 12* July 23*, 24*, **25** Sept. 17*, 18, **19, 19**	May 4*, 5*, 5* July 30*, 31* Aug. **1** Sept. 3*, 4*, **5**	May 7*, 8, **9, 9** July 27*, 28, 29 Aug. 31* Sept. 1
CINCINNATI	April 12*, 13*, 14* June 25*, 25*, 26*, **27** Sept. 28*, 30*		June 8*, 9* July 2*, 3*, **4**, 5* Sept. 17*, 18, **19**	May 4*, 5*, 6* July 30*, 31* Aug. **1** Sept. 3*, 4*, **5**	May 7*, 8*, **9** July 27*, 28*, 29* Sept. 6*, 7*, 8*	May 10, 11*, 12 July 23*, 24, **25, 25** Sept. 15*, 16
HOUSTON	June 1*, 2*, 3* Aug. 12*, 13*, 14*, **15** Sept. 6*, 7*	May 28*, 29*, **30, 31** Aug. 10*, 11* Sept. 10*, 11*, **12**		April 16*, 17*, **18** June 18*, 19*, **20** Sept. 28*, 29*, 30*	May 25*, 26*, 26* June 22*, 23* Sept. 24*, 25*, **26**	April 14, 15 July 6*, 7, 8 Sept. 3*, 4, **5, 5**
LOS ANGELES	April 30* May 1*, **2** July 15*, 16*, 17 Sept. 24*, 25*, **26**	April 23*, 24, **25, 25** July 20*, 21*, 22* Sept. 21*, 22*	April 5*, 6*, 7* Aug. 4*, 5*, 30*, 31* Sept. 1*, 2*		April 19*, 20*, 21* July 1*, 2*, 3* Sept. 9*, 10*, **12**	May 14*, 15, **16** July **4**, 5 Aug. 2*, 3 Sept. 13*, 14*
SAN DIEGO	April 23*, 24*, **25, 25** July 20*, 21*, 22* Sept. 21*, 22*	April 27*, 28*, 29 July 18, 18, 19* Aug. 30*, 31* Sept. 1*	May 17*, 18*, 19*, 20* Aug. 6*, 7*, **8** Sept. 13*, 14*	April 9*, 10*, **11** June 25*, 26*, 26*, **27** Sept. 15*, 16*		April 12, 13* June 18*, 19, **20**, 20 Sept. 17*, 18, **19**
SAN FRANCISCO	April 27*, 28*, 29* July **18, 18, 19*** Sept. 10*, 11*, **12**	April 30* May 1*, **2** July 15*, 16*, 17* Sept. 24*, 25, **26**	May 21*, 22*, **23** June 25*, 26*, **27** Sept. 21*, 22*, 23*	May 25*, 26*, 27* July 9*, 10*, **11** Sept. 6*, 7*, 8*	April 6*, 7*, 8* June 28*, 29*, 30* Sept. 28*, 29*, 30*	

AMERICAN LEAGUE SCHEDULE—EAST

Bold figures denote Sundays   Brackets [ ] denote holidays   Major League All-Star Game at Detroit—July 13, 1971, 8:00 p. m.
Asterisks * denote night games   TN denotes twi-night doubleheader   Hall of Fame Game, Cooperstown, N. Y.—Aug. 9—Cleveland vs. Chicago (N. L.)

	AT DETROIT	AT CLEVELAND	AT BALTIMORE	AT WASHINGTON	AT NEW YORK	AT BOSTON
OAKLAND	May 4°, 5° July 23°, 24, **25-25**	May 11°, 12° July 30°, 31, Aug. **1-1**	May 7°, 8°, **9** July 27°, 28°, 29°	April 5 June 4°, 5°, **6** Aug. 17°, 18°	May [31-31], June 1° Aug. 13°, 14, **15**	May 28°, 29, **30** Aug. 10°, 11°, 12
CALIFORNIA	May 10°, 11°, 12° July 30°, 31, Aug. **1**	May 7°, 8, **9** July 27°, 28°, 29°	May 4°, 5°, 6° July 23°, 24°, **25**	May [31], June 1°, 2°, Aug. 13°, 14°, **15**	May 28°, 29, **30** Aug. 10°, 11, 12°	June 4°, 5, **6** Aug. 16°, 17°, 18
KANSAS CITY	May 7°, 8, **9** July 27°, 28°, 29°	May 4, 5 July 23°, 24, **25-25**	May 10°, 11°, 12° July 30°, 31°, Aug. **1**	May 28°, 29°, **30** Aug. 10°, 11°, 12°	June 4°, 5, **6** Aug. 17-17, 18°	May [31-31], June 1° Aug. 13°, 14, **15**
MINNESOTA	June 11°, 12, **13** Aug. 23°, 24°, 25°	June 14°, 15°, 16° Aug. 27°, 28, **29**	June 8°, 9°, 10° Aug. 20°, 21°, **22**	April 26°, 27°, 28° July 17°, **18,** 19°	April 23°, 24, **25** July 20°, 21, 22	April 29°, 30°, May 1, **2** July 15°, 16°
MILWAUKEE	June 8°, 9°, 10° Aug. 20°, 21, **22**	June 11°, 12, **13** Aug. 24°, 25°, 26°	June 14°, 15°, 16° Aug. 27°, 28°, **29**	April 23°, 24°, **25** July 20°, 21°, 22°	April 30°, May 1, **2-2** July 15, 16°	April 26°, 27°, 28 July 17, **18,** 19
CHICAGO	June 14°, 15°, 16° Aug. 27°, 28, **29**	June 8°, 9°, 10° Aug. 20°, 21, **22**	June 11°, 12°, **13** Aug. 24°, 25°, 26°	April 29°, 30°, May 1, **2** July 15°, 16°	April 27°, 28° July 11, **18-18,** 19°	April 23, 24, **25** July 20°, 21°, 22
DETROIT		May 19°, 20° June 17°, 18°, 19, **20-20** Sept. 28°, 29°	April 9°, 10, **11-11** June 28°, 29° Sept. 13 TN, 14°	May 14°, 15°, **16** July 9°, 10°, **11** Sept. [6], 7°, 8°	April 13, 14, 15 June 22-22, 23° Sept. 3°, 4, **5**	May 17°, 18° Aug. 5°, 6°, 7, **8,9** Sept. 21°, 22°
CLEVELAND	April 6 June 24°, 25°, 26°, **27** Aug. 31 TN, Sept. 1°, 2°		May 25°, 26°, 27° July 9°, 10 TN, **11** Sept. [6°], 7°	May 17°, 18° Aug. 5°, 6°, 7°, **8** Sept. 20°, 21°, 22°	May 14°, 15, **16-16** June 28°, 29 Sept. 17°, 18, **19**	April [19], 20, 21 June 21°, 22°, **23** Sept. 3°, 4, **5**
BALTIMORE	April 20°, 21° July 2°, 3, **4,** [5] Sept. 17°, 18, **19**	April 13, 14, 15 June 30 TN, July 1° Sept. 24°, 25, **26**		May 19°, 20° June 21°, 22°, 23°, 24° Sept. 3°, 4°, **5**	May 17°, 18° Aug. 5°, 6°, 7, **8** Sept. 20°, 21°, 22°	May 14°, 15, **16** June 25°, 26, **27** Aug. 31°, Sept. 1°, 2°
WASHINGTON	May 21°, 22, **23-23** Aug. 2°, 3°, 4° Sept. 15°, 16	April 17, **18-18** July 2°, 3, **4,** [5] Sept. 13°, 14	April 7 July 6 TN, 7°, 8° Sept. 9°, 10°, 11°, **12**		April 20, 21 June 25°, 26, **27-27** Aug. 31°, Sept. 1, 2°	May 24°, 25°, 26°, **27** June 28°, 29° Sept. 24°, 25, **26**
NEW YORK	May 25°, 26°, 27° July 6°, 7°, 8° Sept. 24°, 25, **26**	May 21°, 22, **23-23** Aug. 2°, 3°, 4° Sept.11, 12	April 16°, 17°, **18** June 17°, 18°, 19°, **20** Sept. 15°, 16°	April 9°, 10, **11-11** June 30°, July 1° Sept. 28°, 29°, 30°		April 6 May 19°, 20° July 2°, 3°, **4,** [5] Sept. 13°, 14°
BOSTON	April 16, 17, **18** June 30°, July 1° Sept. 9°, 10°, 11, **12**	April 8, 10, **11** July 6°, 7 TN, 8° Sept. 15°, 16°	May 21°, 22, **23-23** Aug. 2°, 3°, 4° Sept. 28°, 29°	April 12°, 13°, 14° June 18°, 19°, **20** Sept. 17°, 18°, **19**	June 2, 3° July 9°, 10, **11** Sept. [6-6], 7°, 8	

AMERICAN LEAGUE SCHEDULE — WEST

Bold figures denote Sundays   Brackets [ ] denote holidays   Major League All-Star Game at Detroit—July 13, 1971, 8:00 p. m.
Asterisks * denote night games   TN denotes twi-night doubleheader   Hall of Fame Game, Cooperstown, N. Y.—Aug. 9—Cleveland vs. Chicago (N. L.)

	AT OAKLAND	AT CALIFORNIA	AT KANSAS CITY	AT MINNESOTA	AT MILWAUKEE	AT CHICAGO
OAKLAND		April 20°, 21°, 22° July 2°, 3°, **4,** [5] Aug. 31°, Sept. 1°	May 13°, 14°, 15, **16-16** Aug. 2°, 3° Sept. 13°, 14°	April 14, 15 June 21°, 22°, 23°, 24 Sept. 3°, 4, **5**	April 12, 13 June 18°, 19, **20-20** Sept. 17°, 18°, **19**	April 16°, 17, **18-18** July 6°, 7°, 8 Sept. 15 TN
CALIFORNIA	May 25°, 26° July 9°, 10, **11-11** Sept. [6], 7°, 8°		April 14°, 15° June 17°, 18°, 19, **20-20** Sept. 15°, 16°	April 16, 17, 18 July 6°, 7°, 8 Sept. 28, 29, 30	April 10, **11** June 21°, 22°, 23°, 24 Sept. 3°, 4°, **5**	April 12, 13 June 25°, 26, **27-27** Sept. 17°, 18, **19**
KANSAS CITY	April 9°, 10, **11** June 25°, 26, **27-27** Sept. 28°, 29°	April 6°, 7°, 8° June 28°, 29°, 30°, July 1° Sept. 21°, 22°		April 19, 20, 21 July 9°, 10, **11** Sept. 17°, 18, **19**	April 17, **18-18** July 6°, 7°, 8° Aug. 31°, Sept. 1°, 2°	May 25°, 26° June 21°, 22°, 23 Sept. 3 TN, 4°, **5**
MINNESOTA	May 21°, 22, **23** June 28°, 29°, 30° Sept. 10°, 11, **12**	May 17°, 18°, 19°, 20° Aug. 6°, 7°, **8** Sept. 13 TN	April 12°, 13° Aug. 4 TN, 5° Sept. 24°, 25, **26-26**		May 25°, 26°, 27 July 2°, 3, **4,** [5] Sept. 15°, 16°	April 9, 10, **11** Aug. 2°, 3° Sept. [6-6], 7°, 8°
MILWAUKEE	May 18°, 19°, 20° Aug. 4°, 5° Sept. 23°, 24°, 25, **26**	May 14°, 15°, **16** Aug. 2°, 3° Sept. 9°, 10°, 11°, **12**	May 21°, 22, **23** Aug. 6°, 7°, **8** Sept. [6°], 7°, 8°	April 6, 7 June 25°, 26, **27-27** Sept. 20, 21, 22		April 14, 15 July 9°, 10, **11-11** Sept. 28°, 29°, 30
CHICAGO	April 7-7 Aug. 6°, 7, **8-8** Sept. 21 TN, 22°	May 21°, 22°, **23** Aug. 4°, 5° Sept. 23°, 24°, 25°, **26**	May 18°, 19° July 2°, 3°, **4,** [5] Sept. 10°, 11°, **12**	May 14°, 15, **16** June 17°, 18°, 19, **20** Aug. 31°, Sept. 1°	April 20, 21 June 28°, 29°, 30 TN, July 1° Sept. 13°, 14°	
DETROIT	April 23°, 24, **25** July 15°, 16°, 17	April 30°, May 1°, **2** July 20°, 21 TN	April 26°, 27°, 28° July **18-18,** 19°	May [31], June 1°, 2° Aug. 13°, 14, **15**	May 28°, 29, **30** Aug. 10°, 11°, 12	June 4°, 5, **6-6** Aug. 17°, 18°
CLEVELAND	April 30°, May 1, **2-2** July 20°, 21°	April 26°, 27°, 28°, 29° July **18,** 19°	April 23°, 24, **25** July 15°, 16°, 17	June 4°, 5, **6** Aug. 16°, 17°, 18°	May [31°], June 1°, 2° Aug. 13°, 14°, **15**	May 28°, 29°, **30** Aug. 10°, 11°, 12
BALTIMORE	April 26°, 27°, 28°, 29 July **18,** 19	April 23°, 24°, **25** July 15°, 16°, 17°	April 30°, May 1, **2** July 20°, 21°, 22°	May 28°, 29, **30** Aug. 10°, 11°, 12°	June 4°, 5°, **6** Aug. 16°, 17°, 18°	May [31-31], June 2° Aug. 13°, 14°, **15**
WASHINGTON	June 15°, 16° Aug. 27°, 28, **29-29**	June 11°, 12°, **13** Aug. 24°, 25°, 26°	June 8°, 9°, 10° Aug. 20°, 21°, **22**	May 7°, 8, **9** July 27°, 28°, 29°	May 4°, 5° July 30°, 31, Aug. **1-1**	May 11°, 12° July 23°, 24, **25-25**
NEW YORK	June 11°, 12, **13** Aug. 23°, 24°, 25°	June 8°, 9°, 10° Aug. 20°, 21°, **22**	June 14°, 15°, 16° Aug. 27°, 28°, **29**	May 4°, 5°, 6° July 30°, 31, Aug. **1**	May 11°, 12° July 23°, 24, **25-25**	May 7°, 8°, **9** July 27°, 28°, 29°
BOSTON	June 8°, 9° Aug. 20°, 21, **22-22**	June 14°, 15°, 16° Aug. 27°, 28°, **29**	June 11°, 12°, **13** Aug. 24°, 25°, 26°	May 11°, 12° July 23°, 24, **25,** 26°	May 7°, 8, **9** July 27°, 28°, 29	May 4°, 5° July 30°, 31, Aug. **1-1**

OFFICIAL AMERICAN ASSOCIATION SCHEDULE FOR 1971

AMERICAN ASSOCIATION 1971	AT TULSA	AT OKLA. CITY	AT WICHITA	AT DENVER	AT OMAHA	AT IOWA	AT EVANSVILLE	AT INDIANAPOLIS
TULSA	ANNUAL	May 22-23-24-25 June 11-12-13-14 July 23-24-25-26	May 6-7-8-9 July 18-19-20-21 Aug. 30-31 Sept. 1-2	April 16-17-18 July 15-16-17-18-18 Aug. 22-23-24-25	May 2-3-4-5 June 28-29-30 July 1	April 28-29-30 May 1 June 23-24-25-26-27	June 8-9-10 Aug. 5-6-7-7-8-9	June 3-4-5 Aug. 10-10-11-13
OKLAHOMA CITY	May 14-15-15-16 July 2-3-4-5 Aug. 26-27-28-29	AMERICAN	April 16-17-18-19 June 16-17-18 July 15-16-17-18 Aug. 22	July 18-19-20-21 July 29-30-31 Aug. 30-31-31 Sept. 1	April 28-29-30 May 1 June 23-25-26-27	May 2-3-4-5 June 28-29-30 July 1	June 3-4-5-6 Aug. 10-11-12-13	June 7-8-9-10 Aug. 5-6-7-8
WICHITA	June 19-20-21-22 July 20-20-21-22 Aug. 18-19-20-21	May 10-11-12-13 June 15 July 27-28-29-30 Aug. 23-24-25	ASSOCIATION	May 22-23 July 2-3 July 23-24-25-26 Aug. 26-27-28-29	June 7-8-9-10 Aug. 9-10-11-12-13	May 26-27-28-29 Aug. 14-15-16-17	April 24-25-26-27 July 10-11-12-13-14	April 20-21-23 June 23-25-25-26-27
DENVER	April 24-25-26-27 June 16-17-18 Aug. 14-15-16-17	April 20-21-22-23 June 19-20-21-22 Aug. 18-19-20-21	May 14-15-16-17 May 24-25 June 11-12-13-14 July 4-5	ALL-STAR	May 26-27-28-29 July 27-28-29-30	May 30-31 June 1-2 June 9-10-11-12-13	May 6-7-8-9 July 6-7-8-9	May 10-11-12-13 July 10-11-12-14
OMAHA	May 10-11-12-13 July 10-10-11-12-14	May 6-7-8-9 July 6-7-8-9	May 30-31 June 1-2 Aug. 1-2-3	June 3-4-5 Aug. 4-5-6-7-8	GAME	May 30-31 June 1-2 Aug. 18-19-20-21	May 6-7-8-9 July 6-7-8-9	May 18-19-20-21 June 19-20-21-22 July 23-24-25
IOWA	April 20-21-22-23 July 6-7-8-9	April 24-25-26-27 July 10-10-11-12-14	June 3-4-5-6 Aug. 4-5-6-7-8	June 8-9-10 July 31 Aug. 1-1-2-3	April 18 May 22-23-23-24-25 July 4-5 Aug. 26-27-28-29	MONDAY	May 10-11-12-13 June 19-20-22 July 23-24-24-25	May 6-7-8-9 July 20-20-21-22 Aug. 22-23-24-25
EVANSVILLE	May 30-31 June 1-2 July 27-28-29-30	May 26-28-29-29 July 31 Aug. 1-2-3-4	June 2-3-4-5 June 28-29-30 July 1	April 28-29-30 May 1 June 23-24-25-26-27	May 14-15-16-17 July 20-20-21-22 Aug. 14-15-16-17	May 18-19-20-21 July 15-16-17-18 Aug. 30-31 Sept. 1-2	JULY 19	April 18-19 June 11-12-13-14 July 2-3 Aug. 26-27-28-29
INDIANAPOLIS	May 26-27-28-29 July 31 Aug. 1-2-3-4	May 30-31 June 1-2 Aug. 14-15-16-17	April 28-29-30 May 1-1 July 6-6-7-8	May 2-2-4-5 June 28-29-30 July 1	April 24-25-26-27 July 15-16-17-18 Sept. 1-2	May 14-15-16-17 June 15-16-17-18 July 27-28-29-30	April 16-17 May 22-23-24-25 July 4-5 Aug. 18-19-20-21	1971

OFFICIAL INTERNATIONAL LEAGUE SCHEDULE FOR 1971

	AT CHARLESTON	AT LOUISVILLE	AT RICHMOND	AT ROCHESTER	AT SYRACUSE	AT TIDEWATER	AT TOLEDO	AT WINNIPEG
CHARLESTON	International	April 22, 23 June 14, 15, 16, 17 August 14, (15), 16, 17	May 18-18, 19, 20 July 9, 10, (11) August 4, 5, 6	June 4, 5, (6) June 28, 29, 30 July 1 August 18, 19, 20	May 31 June 2, 3 June 25, 26, (27) August 21, (22), 23	May 21, 22, (23) July 12-12, 14 August 7, (8), 9, 10	May 7, 8, (9) July 29, 30-30, 31 August 31 September 1, 2	April 26, 27, 28, 29 June 18, 19, (20) July 26, 27, 28
LOUISVILLE	April 24, (25) May 10, 11 August (1), 2, 3 August 11, 12, 13	League	May 21, 22, (23-23) June 22-22, 23 July 19, 20, 21	May 31 June 1, 1-2, 3 July 2, 3, (4) August 21, (22)	June 4, 5, (6) July 5, 6, 7, 8 August 18, 19, 20	May 18, 19, 20 June 18, 19, 20 July 15, 16, 17, (18)	April 26, 27, 28, 29 June 29, 30 July 1 August 28, (29), 30	April 30 July 1, (2) July 29, 30, 31 August 24, 25, 26, 27
RICHMOND	May 13, 14 June 10, 11, 12, (13) July 15, 16, 17, (18)	May 15, (16), 17 June 7, 8, 9-9 July 12, 13, 14	All-Stars	April 22, 24, (25) June 14, 15-15, 16 July 29, 30, 31	April 27, 28 June 17, 18, 19, (20-20) July 26, 27, 28	April 29, 30 May 10, 11 August (1), 2, 14, (15) September 1, 2	May 27, 28, 29, (30) July 2, 3, (4) August 18, 19, 20	May 24, 25, 26 July 5, 6, 7, 8 August 21, (22), 23
ROCHESTER	April 19, 27, 28, 29, (30) June 21, 22, 23	April 16, 17, (18) May 24, 25, 26 August 4, 5, 6, 7	May 1, (2-2) July 22, 23, 24, (25) August 27, 28, (29)	vs	April 29, 30 May 8, (9) August 14, (15), 16, 17 August 30, 31	May 4, 5, 6, 7 July 19, 20, 21 August 24, 25, 26	May 13, 14 June 10, 11, 12, (13) July 5, 6, 7, 8	May 15, (16-16), 17 June 7, 8, 9 July 6, 7, 9
SYRACUSE	April 16, 17, (18) May 25, 26 July 22, 23-23, 24, (25)	May 12, 13, 14 June 10, 11, 12, (13) July 9, 10, (11)	May 4, 5, 6, 7 June 29, 30 July 1 August 24, 25, 26	May 10, 11 August (1), 2, 3 August 11, 12, 13 September 1, 2	New York Yankees	May 1, (2-2), 3 July 2, 3, (4) August 27, 28, (29)	May 15, (16-16), 17 June 7, 8, 9 July 15, 16, 17	May 12, 13, 14 July 13, 14
TIDEWATER	May 15, (16), 17 June 7, 8, 9 July 5, 6, 7, 8	May 12, 13, 14 June 10, 11, 12, (13) July 9, 10, (11)	May 8, (9) August 3 August 11, 12, 13 August 16, 17 August 30, 31	April 26, 27, 28 June 25, 26, (27) July 26, 27, 28	April 23, 24, (25-25) June 21, 22, 23 July 29, 30, 31	In Rochester, New York	May 25, 26 July 22, 23-23, 24, (25) August 21, (22), 23	May 27, 28, 29-29, (30) June 14, 15, 16 August 18, 20
TOLEDO	April 30 May 1, (2) July 19, 20, 21 August 24, 25, 26, 27	May 3, 4, 5 June 25, 26, (27-27) July 26, 27, 28	April 16, 17, (18) June 4, 5, (6) August 7, (8), 9, 10	April 26, 27, 28 June 17, 18, 19, (20) July 12, 13, 14	May 21, 22, (23-23) June 14, 15, 16 July 9, 10, (11)	April 19, 20, 21 May 31 June 1, 2, 3 August 5, 6	June 24	May 10, 11 August (14-14), 15, 16 August 18, 20
WINNIPEG	May 3, 4, 5 July 2, 3, (4-4) August 28, (29), 30	May 7, 8, (9) July 22, 23, 24, (25) September 1, 2	April 20-20, 21 May 31 June 1, 2, 3 June 25, 26, (27)	May 21, 22, (23) July 15, 16, 17, (18) August (8), 9, 10	May 18, 19, 20 July 19, 20, 21 August 4, 5, 6, 7	April 16, 17, (18) August 4, 5, (6) June 28, 29, 30 July 1	April 23, 24, (25-25) June 21, 22, 23 August 11, 12, 13	1971

OFFICIAL PACIFIC COAST LEAGUE SCHEDULE FOR 1971

	AT HAWAII	AT SALT LAKE CITY	AT PHOENIX	AT TUCSON	AT EUGENE	AT PORTLAND	AT TACOMA	AT SPOKANE
HAWAII	1971	May 27-28-29 July 17-18-19-20 Aug. 29-30-31 Sept. 1	May 30-31 June 1 July 31 Aug. 1-1-2 Aug.21-22-23-24	June 2-3-4 Aug. 3-4-5-6 Aug. 25-26-27-28	May 22-23-24-25-26 July 27-28-28-29-30	May 17-18-19-20-21 July 21-22-23-24-25*	Apr. 28-29-30 May 1-2* June 24-25-26 June 27-27*	Apr. 23*-24*-25*-25* Apr. 27 June 19-20*-21-22-23
SALT LAKE	Apr. 20-21-22 June 29-30 July 1-2-3-4-5-6	IS	June 2-3-3 Aug. 3-4-5-6 Aug. 25-26-27-28	May 30-31 June 1 July 1 Aug. 1-1-2 Aug. 21-22-23-24	Apr. 28-29-30 May 1-2 June 19-20*-21-22-23	Apr. 23-24*-25* Apr. 26 June 24-25-26 June 27*-27*	May 17-18-19-20-21 July 26-27-28-29-30	May 22-23*-24 May 25-26 July 21-22-23-24-25
PHOENIX	June 5-6-7-8 Aug. 7-8-9-10 Aug. 11-12-13	May 13-14-15-16* Aug. 14-15-16-17 Aug. 18-19-20	THE	Apr. 20-21-22 June 29-30 July 3-4 July 17-18 Aug. 29-30	Apr. 23-24-25*-26-27 June 24-25-26*-26 June 27*	Apr. 28-29-30 May 1*-2* June 19-20*-20* June 22-23	May 22-23*-23* May 25-26 July 21-22-23-24-25*	May 17-18-19-20-21 July 26-27-28-29-30
TUCSON	May 13-14-15-16 Aug. 14-15-16-17 Aug. 18-19-20	June 5-6-7-8 Aug. 7-8-9-10-11 Aug. 12-13		PACIFIC	May 17-18-19-20-21 July 21-22-23-24-25	May 22-23*-23* May 25-26 July 26-27-28-29-30	Apr. 23-24-25*-25* Apr. 27 June 19-20*-20* June 22-23	Apr. 28-29-30 May 1*-2* June 24-25-26-26-27*
EUGENE	May 3-4-5-6-7 July 7-8-9-10-11	May 8-9*-10-11-12 July 12-14-14-15-16	Apr. 15-16-17 Apr. 18*-18* June 14-15-16-17-18	Apr. 10-11*-11* Apr. 13-14 June 9-10-11-12-13	COAST	June 5-6*-7-8 July 31 Aug. 1* Aug. 21-22-22* Aug. 23-24	Apr. 20-21-22 July 3-4*-5-6 Aug. 17-18-19-20	May 27-28-29* Aug. 7-8-8-9 Aug. 29-30-31 Sept. 1
PORTLAND	Apr. 15-16-17-18-19 June 14-15-16-17-18	Apr. 10-11*-12-13-14 June 9-10-11-12-13	May 8-9*-10-11-12 July 12-13-14-15-16	May 3-4-5-6-7 July 7-8-9-10-11	May 30-31 June 1 July 17*-18*-19-20 Aug. 10-11-12-13	LEAGUE'S	May 13-14-15-16* Aug. 7-8*-8* Aug. 14-15* Aug. 31 Sept. 1	June 5*-6*-7-8 July 31 Aug. 1-2 Aug. 21-22-23-24
TACOMA	Apr. 10-11-12-13-14 June 9-10-11-12-13	Apr. 15-16-17-18*-19 June 14-15-16-17-18	May 3-4-5-6-7 July 7-8-9-10-11	May 8-8*-9*-11-12 July 12-14-14-15-16	June 2-4 Aug. 3-4-5-6 Aug. 25-26-26-27-28	May 27-28-29 June 29-30 July 1-1-2 Aug. 29*-29*-30	69th	June 2-3-4 July 3-4-5-6 Aug. 17-18-19-20
SPOKANE	May 8-9-10-11-12 July 12-13-14-15-16	May 3-4-5-7 Aug. 8-9-9-10-11	Apr.10-11*-12-13-14 June 9-10-11-12-13	Apr. 15-16-17-18*-19 June 14-15-16-17-18	May 13-14-15-16* June 29-30 July 1-2 Aug. 14-15-16	Apr. 20-21-22 Aug. 3-4-5-6 Aug. 25-26-27-28	May 30-31* June 1 July 17-18*-19-20 Aug. 10-11-12-13	SEASON

Index to Minor League Clubs, Cities

Index to Contents

AMERICAN LEAGUE

NATIONAL LEAGUE

1970 Game Scores

1970 Game Scores

NATIONAL ASSOCIATION (MINOR LEAGUE) AVERAGES

(See Page 611 for Alphabetical Listing of Minor League Clubs)